TROUT

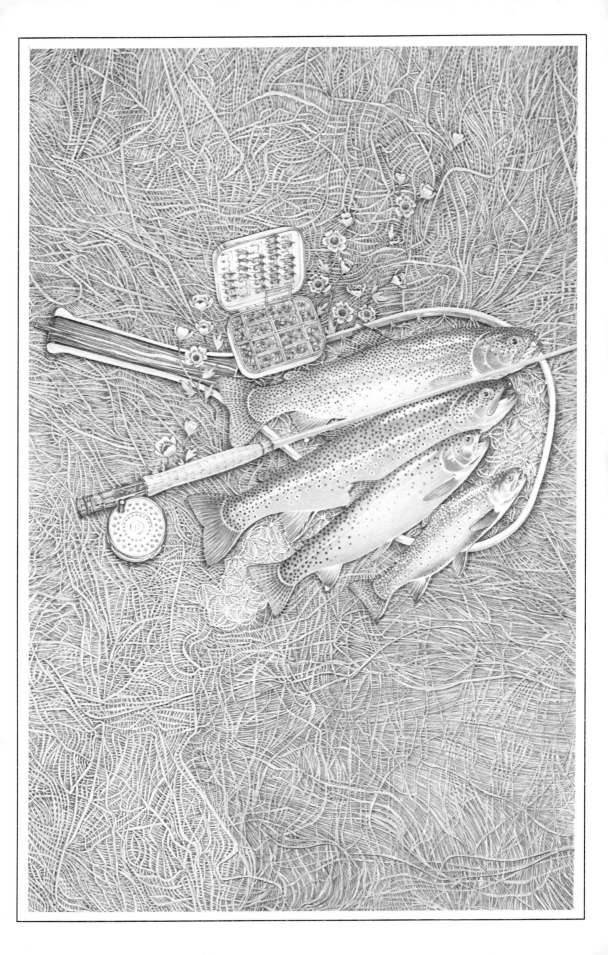

OTHER BOOKS BY ERNEST SCHWIEBERT

Death of a Riverkeeper (1980)
Nymphs (1973)
Remembrances of Rivers Past (1972)
Salmon of the World (1970)
Matching the Hatch (1955)

TROUT

BY

ERNEST SCHWIEBERT

Illustrated by the author

T·T

A Truman Talley Book
E. P. DUTTON, INC.   NEW YORK

Published in the United States by Truman Talley Books • E. P. Dutton, Inc., 2 Park Avenue, New York, N.Y. 10016

Library of Congress Cataloging in Publication Data

Schwiebert, Ernest George.
Trout.

"A Truman Talley book"

Bibliography: p.
Includes indexes.
1. Trout fishing. 2. Trout. I. Title.
SH687.S25   1984   799.1'755   84-8564

ISBN: 0-525-24269-4 (set)

Published simultaneously in Canada by Fitzhenry & Whiteside Limited, Toronto

Designed by Jacques Chazaud

10 9 8 7 6 5 4 3 2 1

First Edition   October 1978 • Two printings
Second Edition   September 1984

For all those fellow anglers throughout the world who have shared our sport, and particularly for my son Erik, still only ten years old, who remains free to choose or not to choose the pastime that has possessed his father since boyhood.

This past spring he took his first good trout with the fly, a strong eighteen-inch fish at the Ledge Pool in the Brodheads, and gently released it. Perhaps Erik will also come to understand that storied French angler of the eighteenth century, the almost legendary Duc de Choiseul, who wrote—

La pêche est ma folie!

CONTENTS

ix

BOOK SIX: TROUT STRATEGIES, TECHNIQUES AND TACTICS

NOTE ON THE
SECOND EDITION

This 1984 Second Edition of *Trout* contains completely revised material on carbon graphite tackle, and it carries a comprehensive new chapter on the modern boron-fiber rods, which includes new black-and-white illustrations. A number of chapters have been revised and updated. Former appendix material has been integrated into the text, and new appendix notes added. A new full-color painting appears as frontispiece and slip-case poster illustrating the four predominant North American trout species. And *Trout*'s new colored endpapers portray four scenic drawings of famous American rivers—the storied Beaverkill, the Au Sable in Northern Michigan, the Snake near the Grand Tetons, and the steelhead-rich Umpqua in Oregon.

INTRODUCTION

It has been almost forty years since the celebrated Ray Bergman first published his classic *Trout*, and thirty-two years have passed since I spent five dollars of hard-earned allowance money to purchase my first copy at Von Lengerke & Antoine in Chicago.

That first copy still occupies an honored place in my library, its margins filled with my notes and its key passages extensively underlined. Its worn bindings are shelved between the scarce first edition, which Bergman originally published with an obscure publishing firm in Philadelphia in 1938, and the second edition that Knopf published in 1952. Knopf had already exhausted a memorable thirteen printings of its original edition, which had first appeared in New York in 1939, firmly establishing *Trout* as the unchallenged best seller in fishing.

Generations of trout fishermen have been tutored through its pages, its gentle teachings couched in deceptively simple prose; *Trout* was a revelation that completely changed my life.

Reading Bergman's chapters long into the night, until I finally fell asleep at daylight listening to the melancholy wail of the four o'clock freight on the steep grade past Sager's Lake, was a sweet, forbidden pleasure. Many nights were spent immersed in Bergman, imagining: the night sounds fishing at Cranberry Lake on the Oswegatchie; working his bivisibles and spiders on the Ausable at Upper Jay; watching the local fishermen cover the Rondout and the Neversink with their skillful three-fly casts; stripping his bucktails on the Madison and the Encampment; night-fishing sessions among the Au Sable deadfalls in my Michigan boyhood country, experimenting with nymphs on the upper Brodheads, fishing bright-feathered brook-trout patterns in the Penobscot, and sharing the Callicoon with the venerable Sparse Grey Hackle.

His pages were filled with selective fish on the Appalachian limestone streams like Spring Creek at Bellefonte; working his deliberate hand-twist retrieves on the headwaters of the Hackensack; sinking his wet flies deep in the springholes of the Laurentides country; fighting immense rainbows in the rapids at Sault Sainte Marie; stalking skittish fish in the Arcularius meadows on the Owens in California; witnessing an incredible mayfly hatch at Bridgeville on the storied Neversink; casting to the cruising cutthroats at Trapper's Lake in Colorado; fishing his fan-wing Coachman during dog-days on the Willowemoc; weekends on the Flat Brook and Paulinskill in the shadow of Manhattan itself; hiking through the lodgepoles after grayling at Grebe Lake in the Yellowstone; daydreaming about the coin-bright summer steelheads on the Umpqua in Oregon; and while sorting through these pot-shard fragments of Bergman in my mind I have been fishing a hot-spring stretch below Biscuit Basin on his beloved Firehole—a reach of beautiful water described in his *Trout* with letter-perfect detail forty years ago.

Reading Bergman's *Trout* during the war years, when travelling north to my boyhood trout streams in Michigan and Wisconsin was impossible, became a workable substitute for fishing itself. During those summers, the book richly sustained my daydreams of trout fishing, although I never fathomed that I might fish the many rivers that tumbled through Bergman's world myself. Such daydreams have since proved true.

Twenty years after I first bought Bergman, my own little *Matching the Hatch* was accepted for publication at Macmillan, where the late John Gaylord Case predicted it would remain in print for more than twenty years. Although it seemed an impossible dream, the publication of my book *Trout* occurs more than twenty years after *Matching the Hatch* first appeared in 1955, giving his prediction the strange overtones of alchemy and clairvoyance.

Virtually everything has changed in trout fishing since Bergman first published his *Trout* in 1938. Fishing for native species like the richly spotted brook trout and cutthroat has tragically declined, their populations decimated by mining and timber cutting and agriculture until their survival lies in spring-fed tributaries and back country. Many classic rainbow streams have been eradicated thoughtlessly, and many are still threatened. European brown trout have inexorably filled the vacuum that followed the decimation of our native species, bringing problems of shyness and sophistication that have completely transformed both American trout fishing and the philosophical tenor of the American trout fisherman.

Knowledgeable anglers have demonstrated a growing fascination with the rich literature and history of fly-fishing, both in its European beginnings and our surprisingly fertile American heritage. Postwar studies in ichthyology have radically changed our understanding of the American species and their patterns of distribution, and have identified several wholly new species of trout. Fresh knowledge of the physiology, sensory perceptions, behavior, and ecosystemic requirements of both trout and grayling is transforming both techniques and tactics. Radical changes in fly-dressing have taken place since midcentury too, and in less than fifty years, our writers have restlessly catalogued the fly hatches of an entire continent. The studies that began with the late Preston Jennings and his classic *Book of Trout Flies* in 1935 have expanded and leapfrogged explosively in recent years—including my own books *Matching the Hatch* and *Nymphs*.

Anglers are unmistakably shaped by both the character of their rivers and their times and it should be remembered that Bergman did most of his fishing in our eastern mountains, from the gentle ridges along the Raritan and Paulinskill in northern New Jersey to the swift Oswegatchie and Ausable that drain the glacier-scarred Adirondacks. His journeys to our western mountains were accomplished on trains, and started in the cathedrallike waiting room at Grand Central Station in New York, where he boarded the famous Twentieth Century Limited.

Bergman changed trains in Chicago, crossing the cavernous spaces of Union Station behind a porter struggling with luggage and fishing gear. His trip farther west was via magnificent trains that I once rode in my boyhood summers, sleek streamliners like the Rocky Mountain Rocket and the City of Denver. The Yellowstone trains once arrived at the timber trusswork station in West Yellowstone, where the entire population turned out to greet them. Such trains are gone now, replaced with aircraft so swift that it is possible to leave Manhattan after breakfast and fish the Yellowstone before dinner.

The remarkable success of *Matching the Hatch* and *Remembrances of Rivers Past* and *Nymphs* has made it possible to fish more widely than Bergman ever dreamed possible, and it is often difficult to comprehend that my fly-fishing odyssey has reached from distant waters in Patagonia and Tierra del Fuego and the Antipodes, to the subarctic barrens of the Labrador and the Valley of Ten Thousand Smokes and Lapland. Technology has made it possible to fish a swift Yugoslavian river in the mountains of Dalmatia just weeks before it is time to work a summer steelhead riffle on the swift Deschutes in Oregon. The poetry of speed has made it possible to know the secrets of rivers that drain the Himalayas in Nepal as we understand the Nimpkish or the Namekagon, and fish the remote Serrano in Tierra del Fuego as often as the half-legendary Beaverkill—the Catskill river that played a major role in shaping both Bergman and his books.

Cacophonic change is perhaps the most obvious bench mark of the forty years since Bergman first published his *Trout,* and fishing tackle has changed explosively too. Modern synthetics have worked a revolution in rods and leader performance and lines. Reels are virtually unequalled in their precision and performance and the strength of their lightweight alloys. Split-cane rods of remarkably sophisticated tapers and craftsmanship remain available, while fiberglass and still more exotic fibers like boron and carbon graphite promise startling rod performance in the future. Such change has been accompanied by a parallel cornucopia of innovations in clothing and wading equipment and other tackle. Casting techniques and the compound line tapers to exploit such skills have been refined so much in the past twenty years that distance work once limited to the tournament platforms is now possible under fishing conditions. Such radical developments were still largely on the horizon when Bergman first published his *Trout* in 1938, and their evolution was still in its infancy when the second edition appeared fourteen years later.

Declining health severely restricted his fishing in the years after midcentury, and Bergman was forced to retire from his magazine work in 1959, after twenty-six years in the limelight, because his heart condition had finally made writing an ordeal.

Those were happy years, Bergman once explained, *but it was taking a month to write a piece that once took a couple of days.*

It is typical that Bergman chose to spend his entire life in Nyack, just a few miles above Manhattan on the Hudson. Bergman was born there in 1891, and spent the last decade of his life in that quiet river town. Several times I tried to meet him, succeeding only once, and he politely declined all offers of fishing.

Bergman had hoped to complete another book, and his personal copy of *Trout* was filled with handwritten notes in its margins. His father had lived to reach ninety-four, making daily walks across town to visit his son, but Bergman seemingly knew that he might not live long enough to complete another book. It was never finished, and there were no fresh magazine articles for his loyal readers. His health continued to fail, and he finally died in 1967.

The perspective of art history teaches that no painter ever works with a completely empty canvas. Any artist always finds his imagination filled with the kaleidoscopic images of other painters who have gone before. Bergman was a generous man who would have applauded the revolution that has transformed his sport in the past half century, although that revolution inevitably made his *Trout* obsolete. Its homespun style and rudimentary viewpoint on fishing no longer parallel mine, but perhaps the finest tribute to our boyhood heroes is to build on their foundations rather than to echo their work mindlessly.

My *Trout* is my homage to that tutor of my boyhood.

Yellowstone
Spring
1975

TROUT

Volume I

BOOK ONE

✦ ✦ ✦

THE
EVOLUTION
OF
FLY-FISHING

1. The Genesis of
a Fisherman

Whip-poor-will! The call came softly.

Memories of those early summers on the rivers of Michigan and Wisconsin are inextricably mixed with whippoorwills. Their melodic calling came from the timbered ridges, its melancholy muted in dense thickets of cedars and jack pines.

There is river music in those memories too. Sometimes we travelled north on the narrow concrete highways to fish them on the opening weekend. Leaving the springtime behind in the suburbs above Chicago, we often found snowbanks lying in the sheltered places along the rivers. April sun filtered weakly through the rattling branches, and winter died slowly in the north country. Bloodroot and skunk cabbage and violets grew first in the forest bottoms above the swift currents, and later the cardinal flowers and cowslips were blooming.

Opening weekends were always too brief.

Fishing was an obsession, and our opening weekends were always sandwiched into my school calendar and my father's lecture schedule at the university. Those brief weekends in April were always a prelude to the trout fishing we began with each summer vacation; and in those simpler times, our summers held a sweetness that is long past.

There were happy times when we both played hooky. Sometimes we took a long weekend of fishing in May, finding that spring had finally arrived farther north on the Manistee and Pere Marquette and Ontanagon. The trees were budding then. Geese were working northward in ragged phalanx that straggled across the morning skies. The river bottoms were dark with dense stands of cedars and hemlocks mixed with the pale counterpoint of birches, and seeing their milk-white trunks still awakens echoes of those happy north-country summers. Such rich memories of springtime rivers are always mixed with memories of their twilight sounds.

Whip-poor-will! It is the sound of summers past.

Finally, the pale willows and swamp maples transformed our rivers into leafy arboretums. The fishing changed its character too, and the days became more pleasant with each passing week, until the earth was washed clean of winter. The cowslips and dogwoods were gone, with the shadbush and dogtooth violets. Bright leaves shrouded the elms and poplars and beeches.

Whip-poor-will! echoes the memory.

Their calling still raises shivers of anticipation after more than thirty years, since hearing them in those boyhood summers always spelled trout country. It is difficult to pinpoint the precise genesis of my fascination with fly-fishing, but my first trout was taken with grasshoppers on a meadow creek in Michigan. Its secrets were my primer in those summers before the war, and I spent every waking hour on its willow-sheltered holes.

My first fly-caught trout was caught on a wet Cahill along the upper Pere Marquette. It fell to a technique that was perilously close to bait-fishing, with the wet fly hanging downstream in the current. It barely measured ten inches. Its spots were the color of cardinal flowers, its belly pale yellow and fat from a diet of mayflies. The fish was small, but I have taken twenty-pound salmon that are less pervasive in the mind and that gave me less pleasure. It was lying in the shadows of a willow-hung bend. where the river turned against a steep moraine.

It followed the teasing swing of the fly into the sunlight and hooked itself solidly. Such episodes are familiar in any fly-fishing life, but it ended countless hours of bait-fishing with worms and grasshoppers. The effusive praise of my father and his fishing friends was a heady reward.

Now you're an angler, they smiled.

We celebrated the capture at our campsite along the Little South that afternoon. Coming in with that ten-inch brown in my creel seemed to mean I had finally entered their world of fly rods working their bright ballet of silk lines across the currents, a world that politely ignored a trout killed on hardware or bait.

The symbols and images of that world in those years are still familiar, and the mind savors them again in daydreams. There is the fragrance of woodsmoke and the glow of cook-fire coals long after supper, with the music of the river in the darkness. The fishing coats were stained with paraffin fly oil and citronella, and there was the canvas smell of waders in the sun.

There were sounds like the gentle rhythm of rain starting on canvas and its drumhead thunder on a waterlogged tent long after midnight. Mixed with such percussion were the contrapuntal themes of kettles and saucepans under a leak; sometimes a tent snapped like a sail in the gusts, with a wild score of wind music in the trees.

Fly-fishing equipment itself is a cornucopia of memories. There were supple silkworm-gut leaders coiled and soaking between glycerin-saturated pads in delicate aluminum boxes. Our wicker baskets were lined with fiddleback ferns and fresh-picked mint from the river bottoms. Other things are remembered—like tackle vests bulging with English pipes and aromatic mixtures in soft leather pouches. They rattled with intricate Wheatley fly boxes, fly retrievers, thermometers, surgical forceps, dry-fly oil, mucin line dressing, scissors, sheepskin-lined fly books, scales, leader pads, and amadou for drying our flies.

There was the smell of moth crystals in sealed tins of gamecock necks and the faint tung-oil-varnish smell whenever a rod case was opened, revealing the elegant split-cane rods and their intricate silk wrappings, ferrules and reel fittings gleaming, their grips stained and velvet-smooth after many seasons astream.

Still other memories are mixed with fishing. Trout country and its tumbling rivers became the consuming passion of my boyhood. Each summer was entirely spent fishing, and the fall and winter were filled with daydreaming of north-country rivers, reading books, tinkering with fly tackle, and painfully teaching myself to dress flies from the books of Reuben Cross and William Bayard Sturgis.

Summer finally returned again, and we travelled north along the Michigan dunes into a pastoral landscape of orchards and small towns and cornfields. There were empty barns painted with the bright graffiti of tobacco advertising, and sometimes we played the alphabet game with road signs to pass the miles.

Pennzoil! Its signs always ended such games.

Sometimes we drove north from Winnetka to Milwaukee, where the car was loaded onto the night ferry to Ludington. It was eerily strange to watch the loading under floodlights, like the biblical ark ingesting a procession of machines, and the cool winds eddied off the lake in the darkness while the ferry maneuvered from its slip—cables straining and screws churning water against the pilings.

Several times we crossed the lake in moonlight, and driving up through the fruit orchards, we finally reached the timber. It was all second growth but, with more than a half century to heal after the rapacious lumbering, it was a primeval forest to a boy who knew only the cities and rolling farm country farther south.

Finally, all trace of that pastoral landscape dropped behind, and the highway penetrated a world of lakes and swamp-birch marshes and timber. Daydreams of that north country were enough to fill me with delicious shivers of anticipation in those early years. It was another world above Newaygo and Ludington and Big Rapids. The pavement ended, and the gravel and axle-deep sand stretched north into the jack pines. Mist shrouded the tamarack bogs and still stump-bordered lakes at daylight, and the swift trout streams were utterly unlike the sluggish silt-yellow rivers farther south.

My first dry-fly trout was caught one warm evening along the Little Manistee. It was a quiet reach of water, working deep in a sweeping bend against the grass. It eddied through a log tangle below the meadow and disappeared again into the trees. Deadfalls and jack pine sweepers interrupted the slow, sucking currents below the bridge where we left the Oldsmobile.

There was a picnic ground a half-mile downstream, with a single weathered table under the trees. The twin-rut track wound in through the hemlocks and swamp cedars, filled with roots and rain potholes and stumps. There were no trout rising at the bridge. We walked the last fifty yards of pavement where the sandy right-of-way reached north like a plumb line, and the picnic road turned downriver, ending in the single picnic-table clearing.

Just below the turnaround, there was a dark tea-colored tributary that drained the cedar swamps between the river and the springheads of Syers Lake. Its brook trout scattered when we crossed its icy flow, and I entered the Picnic Ground Pool in its tail shallows. During our half-mile hike from the M-37 bridge, the mood of the little river had changed. There were caddisflies hatching now, and the birds were catching them.

Cautiously, we slipped into the smooth current and stood watching the pool upstream. It was a stretch typical of the Little Manistee. The current flowed smooth and deceptively swift over a bright gravel bottom, shelving off into deeper water. Alders and willows enclosed the water. There was a dark chest-deep eddy filled with logs where a deadfall hung throbbing in the smooth flow of the river.

Whip-poor-will! Its calling came from the cedars.

The birds were wheeling and working over the river now, eagerly capturing the fluttering caddisflies as they escaped the current. The fish were working too. Their rises splashed eagerly at the hatching Trichoptera in the throat of the pool. They were not large fish. The best rises bulged and died against the deadfall. The trout were rising freely now, porpoising to the emerging pupae and splashing awkwardly at the adults. The small Adams spent-wing settled above the fish, cocked nicely, rode the current, and disappeared in an exciting rise.

The fish was hooked when I tightened. The slender Granger throbbed into a tight circle when the fish bored deep along the gravel. The gut tippet ticked and pinked among the snags, but it held and the fight continued into the open pool itself. It was a fat twelve-inch brown. Finally it surrendered to my waiting net—and somehow I was captured too. The trout was still threshing in the meshes, and I waded eagerly downstream to find my father in the darkness.

Got one on a dry fly! I yelled happily.

It is strange how such details remain imprinted in the mind, and I can still see that Picnic Ground Pool clearly in the twilight. It was the genesis of a fly-fishing odyssey spent seeking rivers of greatness across the world.

Like most beginners, in those early years of increasing skills, I measured success solely in terms of weight in the creel. My first limit came on the Pere Marquette during a late afternoon swarm of butter-colored

Ephemerella spinners. It seemed like an important milestone. Several times that summer I creeled the Michigan limit of fifteen trout, revelling in the envy and admiration of older fishermen along the river. My father seemed proud of my prowess too.

But there was an old fly-fisherman who had a cottage on a high bluff above the Little South, about three miles above its junction with the Pere Marquette. The old man chided me one afternoon about a fine morning catch that so filled my creel it was impossible to close its wicker lid.

Too many! He shook his head unhappily and mopped his face with his red handkerchief. *Too many!*

I stared in disbelief. *It's the limit!*

It's too many, he continued. *You're killing far too many fish this summer!* His quiet voice seemed sad.

Since he seldom returned to camp with fish, we were convinced that he was a luckless angler, yet the old man always carried a creel. His casting was flawlessly smooth and controlled. *Hell, I ain't never seen him with a limit,* scoffed a boyhood Michigan friend. *He ain't much!*

He's only jealous, I agreed sullenly.

But I watched him secretly from the alders a few weeks later. It was a still reach of the Little South, full of slow currents and tangled deadfalls and overhanging trees. Its brush-pile trout had frustrated us many times. Fishing the Little South was difficult, and we usually lost flies in the branches or broke off fish among the stumps and sweepers. Watching the old man fish this stretch was a revelation. His casting was lazily poetic. It worked in low under the trees, placing drag-free floats tight against the logs. The old man fished a brush-choked half mile of river without losing a fly or making a single clumsy cast. Fourteen trout came to his fly that morning, and he hooked and landed thirteen, releasing each fish gently.

It was obvious that he could creel a limit of fish any time he wished, and that his split-willow basket was empty because he chose to release his catch. Several days later I saw him on the river.

Why do you carry a creel? I blurted suddenly after some river small talk. *You don't kill any fish?*

The old fly-fisher smiled. *Carried one from the time I was big enough to wade these rivers,* he replied. *Sometimes I just like the feel of its harness and the fresh smell of the mint inside.*

It seemed a strange answer then.

The memory of his pale fly line working rhythmically in the morning sun, and its poetic *swish-swish* music at nightfall have endured for almost thirty years. His lessons have been digested slowly. It was difficult in the beginning to understand a skillful fisherman who regularly caught trout only to release them. It was several years before I began to understand fully, and I continued to kill every legal trout foolish enough to take my flies. There were many limit catches in bulging creels before I finally realized that we had decimated many favorite runs and pools ourselves, and that our secret places on the river were less special without trout.

Five summers passed, and I saw him many times on the river, although we only waved. The first weeks of that fifth summer were beautiful, their weather cool and days sunny with a wind that tasted like a fine Pouilly Fuissé. The river flowed smooth and clear, its surrounding jack pine forests carpeted with columbines and buttercups, and as the summer progressed there were gentians and pye-weed and swamp lilies in the marshy bottoms.

It was the summer I began releasing trout, killing only an occasional brace of good fish, and when the old fly-fisher saw me release a ten-inch brown in the pool below his cottage he came slowly down the path to the river.

Come up to the cabin, he waved cordially. *I've got some fresh iced tea and something I want to give you.*

It's hot, I agreed. *Thank you.*

We climbed the path and I stripped off my waders on the porch, and the old man came back with a tray of iced tea. There was a book on the tray and he handed it to me.

You're fishing well now, he began, *and I've seen you letting trout go these days—it's time you learned something about the history of this sport.*

History? I was surprised.

It's an ancient and honorable sport, the old man continued. *It's time you learned something about its traditions.*

With this book? I asked.

Yes, he said. *It's a simple little book written by a Michigan fisherman—you should enjoy it.*

Thank you, I said.

It was a slim volume titled *Fly Patterns and Their Origins,* its author a tournament caster named Harold Hinsdill Smedley. Its first page told the history of dressing the Adams spent-wing, a favorite pattern in those early boyhood summers. It had been born on the feather-littered workbench of Len Halliday, fifty miles north of the Pere Marquette country.

You celebrated a birthday in camp last week, the old man smiled. *You're getting old enough to appreciate things like history and tradition—how old are you now?*

Fourteen, I said awkwardly.

My own boys were never interested in fishing. The old man stared out across the river absently. *It's a birthday present.*

It's a great present, I said.

It has since proved one of the best presents I ever received, for it opened a whole world of the mind. Its pages were filled with references to a parade of great anglers and their books. Smedley was also filled with the stories of familiar fly patterns like the Cahill and Royal Coachman and Hendrickson. It was my initial passkey to the writings of Walton, La Branche, Harding, and Dunne. It was fascinating, and I spent the afternoon devouring its pages beside the Little South—particularly intrigued with its brief history of Theodore Gordon and the collection of dry flies Halford first sent to Gordon in 1890.

It also mentions Claudius Aelianus in its section on the origins of the hackle flies. Aelianus unmistakably described the beginnings of fly-fishing for trout on the swift rivers of Macedonia in the third century A.D. The search to learn more about Aelianus and his *Natura Animalium* led me inexorably to other treasures, like Radcliffe and his compendium of historical sources titled *Fishing from the Earliest Times*, and the elegant *Walton and Some Earlier Writers on Fish and Fishing*, which Marston published in 1894. It appeared at the apogee of dry-fly development on the British chalk-streams, four years after Gordon received the folio of dry-fly prototypes from Halford.

My growing interest in angling history soon led to the books of Major John Waller Hills: first his pastoral *Summer on the Test*, and finally his *A History of Fly-fishing for Trout*, which is filled with rich observations on the past. The discovery of such books was a milestone in my fly-fishing since their pages were a rich cornucopia of trout-fishing tradition and provided the beginning of a mature perspective about our sport.

Such books taught me that fly-fishing is the art of catching trout with a rod, line, and hook dressed with feathers and silk. It is an ancient and honorable sport, just as my old friend had observed along the Little South. Its roots lie deep in the past, and it has a long and pervasive tradition to govern its conduct. Its philosophy is codified in the words of Izaak Walton and Charles Cotton, who taught generations of anglers to learn stealth and deception and guile and to apply whatever wisdom and knowledge they have gathered over the years; for shyness and sophistication are the hallmark of the fish, and their river-armored strength makes them worthy adversaries.

Yet our tradition urges that the contest be fairly fought and that a fisherman respect the equilibrium of life in his lakes and streams. Fishing is obviously possible with other methods and other motives, although there is no doubt that fly-fishing in terms of its centuries-old tradition yields the most satisfaction and pleasure, and that its character is the most soothing to the spirit.

These truths lie at the root of our sport. It is perhaps the only field sport left in our time that provides the blood rhythms of the hunt and the stalk, including the ritual of the kill, without the actual death of our prey. The fisherman who aspires to polishing his skills will do well to pursue a traditional course. There is no question that we fish to catch fish, but a thorough education in the history of angling can teach us important things about catching them—particularly a respect for the poetic character of both the fish and their lives.

The fly-fisherman who has fully mastered his craft is truly a many-sided man. He has become an amateur ichthyologist who understands the life cycle, feeding habits, physical skills, and temperament of the trout. The best fishermen are also versed in entomology, the understanding of the annual cycle of fly hatches on their rivers. They must learn the lessons of the river, sensing its sheltering currents and holding lies, and understanding its hydrochemistry. Knowledge of meteorology will enable an angler to anticipate the weather, and the best will have an almost extrasensory feeling about a river when its moods are right.

Such fishermen must also become craftsmen thoroughly versed in their tools. They know what flies to use when they observe a hatch of naturals coming off the current and what tactics to employ when they study the feeding patterns of the fish. They can cast skillfully enough to place their flies over a rising trout at will, exactly where the current will carry it to its feeding station, and without frightening a skittish fish. The reflexes must respond crisply to a rise without breaking off the delicate tippet, and finally the skilled fisherman instinctively senses the capacities of his rod, line, and leader once that fish is hooked and fighting.

Beyond the mere considerations of tactics and technique lies a whole world of overtones and sensory perceptions. The polished fisherman senses the ever-changing moods along his rivers and the ecological spider web that ties their myriad creatures together in a delicate fabric of life.

His senses are finely tuned to the fish: the half-seen variation in a current tongue, the faint sound of a rise against the tumult of the river, and the imperceptible flash in a swift run that all spell a feeding trout.

There are other wild creatures too, like the fat summer deer melting soundlessly into the trees after fording the stream, raccoons crayfishing stealthily among the rocks, phoebes and swallows catching mayflies in flight, woodcock probing for night crawlers in the alder bottoms, and whippoorwills calling softly at twilight. The fly-fisherman cannot ignore his role in these rhythms of life and still become a skilled fisherman or truly call himself an angler.

Both the perspective of time and the literature of angling have improved and enriched my fishing. The genesis of fly-fishing is always twofold: it happens when we discover our passion for trout and the tumbling crystalline rivers of trout country, and when we ultimately discover that we are part of a contemplative sport that is rich with the overtones of centuries and deeply rooted in antiquity.

And poetry too.

2. The Ancient Origins of Angling

The roots of angling lie deep in world prehistory. Silk lines and thornwood rods are mentioned in manuscripts written before the Shang Dynasty. *What were the dates of such manuscripts?* I asked an expert in Chinese literature at Princeton.

What were the dates of Noah and his Flood? he laughed.

Although it was preceded by semilegendary Chinese kingdoms, the Shang Dynasty is the bench mark of Bronze Age civilization in China. Historians believe that modern archaeological evidence demonstrates that advanced techniques of bronze casting existed in central China as early as the second millennium before Christ, more than 4,000 years back into the timeless mists of the Asian cultures. Some scholars argue that our evidence points to the abrupt arrival of metalworking technology in central China. They conclude that the relatively sophisticated metallurgy of the Shang Dynasty must have arrived with tribal migrations from Asia Minor, since its culture remained surrounded by more primitive Neolithic peoples in other parts of China.

Such theories are founded in the apparent absence of archaeological evidence from more primitive Bronze Age cultures that could have evolved into the Shang civilization. Such transitional cultures are common in the better known Bronze Age sites of Europe. Their metalworkers used crude open moulds to cast their knives and axe heads and ornamental objects, but the earliest known bronze artifacts from Chinese sites attest to surprisingly advanced techniques.

Modern scholars largely agree that the extensive archaeological work of the past thirty years should not have missed the transitional Bronze Age sites, but most admit that the primitive state and sprawling expanse of

China make such omissions possible. It is also possible that bronze-working techniques evolved independently in Asia. Perhaps such metallurgy not only evolved without the influence of Europe and Asia Minor but also originated in the semilegendary Hsia civilization that preceded the Shang artisans, who perfected their skills in the ancient fortified city at Cheng Chou.

Such oriental craftsmen forged both hooks and gorges of bronze for fishing, and the remarkable Shih Ching *Book of Odes* tell us that fishing rods of bamboo and lines of silkworm gut were used before the first millennium. Fishermen of the Chou Dynasty, which endured almost a thousand years, commonly used tapered cane rods and silk lines on the Chi River in Hunan Province. Gold hooks were described in the Chuh Tzu manuscript, along with a dressing of ornamental kingfisher feathers. The passage is not entirely clear in its complete meaning, since the wording could mean that either the line or the hook could have displayed such plumage. Ornamentation of the line might have been intended as a form of homeopathic magic, since the kingfisher subsists on a diet of fish—but if the gold hooks were dressed with its turquoise feathers, we have our first description of fly-fishing four centuries before Aelianus.

Although there are trout and grayling and salmon in the north-flowing rivers of Mongolia and Manchuria, apparently there is no mention of these species in these early Chinese manuscripts. Chinese fishing was primarily focused on the carp and its sister Cyprinidae.

Late in the Chou Dynasty, the Chinese sage Chiang Tzu-Ya argued that angling was both contemplative and morally edifying, clearly anticipating the thesis found in the *Treatyse of Fysshynge wyth an Angle* more than 2,600 years later in medieval Britain. Chiang Yzu-Ya went so far in his philosophy of angling that he ultimately fished without a hook concealed in the bait. Such beliefs are certainly the genesis of fishing as sport.

Confucius was the principal philosopher of the Chou Period. Like Aristotle some two centuries later, his intellect ranged freely across the full spectrum of life, and his work dominated Chinese thought. Confucius himself was an ardent fisherman who believed in both using hooks inside his bait and catching fish, and while he opposed netting, he equated rod fishing with sportsmanship.

Chang Chih-Ho carried the philosophy of Chiang Tzu-Ya even farther in the eighth century, advocating neither hooks nor bait. His argument is archetypal of the singular ethical detachment in oriental philosophy, since Chang Chih-Ho did not want the contemplative mood of his fishing interrupted by fish.

During the same Tang Dynasty, which lasted almost until the close of the tenth century, the writer Lu Kuei-Meng completed the scrolls that established him as the Walton of the Orient. His writings cover the full range of fishing methods. The elegant ink-and-wash drawings found in the sixteenth century *Tu Shu Chi Cheng* encyclopedia illustrate these Lu Kuei-Meng techniques in poetic detail.

Both William Radcliffe, author of *Fishing from the Earliest Times*, and John Waller Hills, author of the classic *History of Fly Fishing for Trout*, believe the fishing reel was a European development of the seventeenth century. Their principal evidence lies in its literary debut in *The Art of Angling*, which Thomas Barker published in 1651. Unfortunately, both Radcliffe and Hills were unaware of recent evidence concerning the history of science and technology in China.

Six winters ago my good friend John Bonner called me in a state of excitement and enthusiasm. Bonner is the son of the late Paul Hyde Bonner, author of poetic sporting books like *The Glorious Mornings*, and is chairman of the Biology Department at Princeton. His summers are spent in isolation, writing on biology and fishing for salmon on the Margaree. His agitation stemmed from leafing through a newly published volume of *The History of Chinese Science*, the monumental work that Joseph Needham has been writing at Cambridge for more than thirty years.

Bonner had stumbled on a painting attributed to Ma Yuan, a famous artist of the Sung Dynasty in the twelfth century. The painting was titled *Angler on a Wintry Lake*, and its imagery unmistakably includes a fishing reel mounted on the top of the rod. Princeton has a fine circle of experts in oriental art, and they not only dated the painting to the middle of the twelfth century, but also traced the original to the Tokyo Museum. Their counsel also resulted in the discovery of another painting which clearly depicts a fishing reel, a work at the Freer Gallery in Washington painted by the Chinese master Wu Chen in the fourteenth century. Both paintings not only anticipate Barker and *The Art of Angling*, but were also executed two to three centuries before the *Treatyse of Fysshynge wyth an Angle* first appeared at Saint Albans.

Joseph Needham is not content to rest his case for Chinese invention of the reel on such recent evidence. His meticulous notes for *The History of Chinese Science* include earlier examples. Needham cites a book of Buddhist morals, the *Thien Chu Ling Chin* of the thirteenth century, which includes a woodcut with each of its parables. Two of its plates clearly illustrate fishing rods and reels. Still more evidence lies in a twelfth-century parchment gospel from Armenia. Its illuminations include both rod and reel in a pastoral fishing scene, and Needham explains its existence by referring to the major commerce that existed between Armenia and China during that time. Needham concludes his brief for the Chinese invention of the fishing reel with the legend of Tao Tzu Ming, who was allegedly fishing in the third century when a dragon rose from the lake and transported him to paradise in the sacred mists of the Linghang mountain. His transfiguration was subsequently investigated on the orders of a Taoist emperor, and inquiries were made about his tackle—unmistakably using the Chinese phrases for both fishing rod *and* reel.

The scholarship of *The History of Chinese Science* clearly demonstrates that the fishing reel was probably derived from the sophisticated technology of spinning bobbins and spools developed in China more than 1,500 years ago. Perhaps spaghetti and gunpowder were not the only Chinese inventions that Marco Polo brought back to Venice in 1295.

Fishing was also found in the Middle East. But, although their cultures were deeply involved with all kinds of sports and consumed large quantities of riverine fish, the ancient civilizations of the Tigris and Euphrates country have left no record of rod fishing for sport. The abundant reeds found in the tidal marshes of those rivers are still used in the primitive architectures of the marsh-dwelling tribes, and certainly could have served as fishing rods.

The Sumerian culture flowered in these coastal regions some 5,000 years ago, but left no record of its fishing practices except that fish played a considerable role in the diet of its people. Babylon reached its apogee in the third millennium, but depictions of angling were not found in its tablets and sculptured walls and other artifacts.

The Assyrians came later, with their storied Code of Hammurabi proclaimed during the second millennium. The reliefs of Nineveh clearly illustrate hand-line fishing in both fresh-water and estuarine zones, in elegant fired-ceramic reliefs of bold carving and composition. The absence of rod fishing in both Assyrian literature and art is puzzling, since there was considerable military and commercial intercourse with Egyptian civilization, where the fishing rod had finally appeared in wall paintings after the third millennium.

Assyrian wall relief—Nineveh, 1000 B.C.

Egyptian tomb mural at Beni Hasan, 2000 B.C.

Egyptians fished the Nile extensively, and were using the rod in sporting terms as early as the parallel Shang Dynasty in ancient China. However, neither the artificial fly nor the fishing reel apparently has its roots in Egyptian history. Rod fishing in Egypt was apparently practiced both by ordinary river folk and their ruling classes. The tomb paintings discovered at Beni Hasan, about halfway between Aswan and the Mediterranean, display several fishing scenes from the third millennium. The figures in the paintings employed a full palette of techniques including the spear, hand line, seine, and fishing rod. Among the murals of the Middle Kingdom, there is the second-millennium spindle reel used for the running line behind arrows and spears. It is a simple device, its spindle held in a semicircular handle. Such implements seem about a foot to fifteen inches in length judging from the tomb paintings, and it is surprising that the obvious transition from these spindles to a fishing reel did not occur.

Egyptian history is filled with references to fishing. Plutarch described the sport in his *Life of Antonius*, which included passages about Cleopatra and Antony fishing from the royal barge on the Nile. Fishing was clearly a part of their bacchanalian excursions on the river, and Plutarch tells us that the young Egyptian queen loved the sport:

> She hath used to take delight, with her fair hand
> To angle happily in the Nile, where its glad fishes
> As though they saw who 'twas sought to deceive them
> Contended eagerly to be taken.

Both Plutarch and Shakespeare relate the fishing legends of Cleopatra and Antony, and both include the ruse used by the Romans to insure that their commander caught the most fish. His military aides secretly swam under the royal barge and attached live fish to his hook. Cleopatra quickly discovered the subterfuge, interrupted the Roman aides, and had a diver of her own attach a salted fish to the line of their general.

Antony struck eagerly on the signal, fought his prize with false heroics, and wrestled it aboard to a chorus of ridicule and laughter. When the laughter died, Cleopatra observed that Antony seemed better suited to warfare and politics. He attempted to stem the ridicule with the observation that he had taken the oldest and wisest fish in the Nile. Cleopatra sealed her prank with the comment that Egyptians had invented the fishing rod, and that it seemed awkward in Roman hands.

Homer is probably our first European source on fishing, and both the *Iliad* and the *Odyssey* are filled with references and metaphorical comparisons based on the sport. Early scholarship on the Homeric period has argued that sport in abstract terms had not really become a part of Hellenic culture, since both hunting and fishing were not pastimes, and were entirely preoccupied with the gathering of food. Homeric sources clearly lend substantial impetus to that view, except for the passages in the *Odyssey* that describe Artemis and her enjoyment in hunting.

However, we have subsequent evidence concerning an evolving philosophy of sport in the excavations at Tiryns, a Peloponnesian city of considerable wealth and splendor in the Homeric Age. Heinrich Schliemann led the expeditions that excavated Tiryns in the late nineteenth century, and his discoveries were published in 1912. Among the treasures unearthed at Tiryns was a marvelous fresco from late in the first millennium that portrayed two noblewomen driving a chariot in a boar hunt, and arriving in time for the kill—their participation proves that hunting had evolved beyond mere food gathering, and the existence of rod fishing seems to indicate that fishing had become a sport too.

Sappho reinforces the Homeric view of fishing in her verses about two centuries later. Fisherfolk are equated with a hard life, and in her verses an epitaph of poverty and pain is their reward. Similar themes are found in the later poetry of Alcaeus and Theocritus, whose piscatory ecologues are surprisingly extensive. Sappho described the death of a young fisherman with these simple lines:

> Meniscus, mourning now his only son,
> The younger toil-worn fisher, Pelagon,
> Has placed upon his tomb a single net and oar,
> The badges of his painful life and poor.

Xenophon followed Sappho about two centuries later, a soldier and philosopher who was born into a prosperous family in Athens. His formative years were spent as a disciple of Socrates, but later Xenophon volunteered to serve with the force of Greek soldiers that fought under Cyrus the Younger. His army acquitted itself bravely in the disastrous battle fought at Cunaxa, and had literally to fight its way back from Persia to Greece. Its commanders were treacherously assassinated enroute, and Xenophon was elected one of the leaders of the retreat.

His military campaigns led him to admire the military discipline and cultural life of the Spartans, and he ultimately joined their army under Agesilaus at the battle of Coronea. The conflict finally ended with a Spartan victory over Athens, and its citizens subsequently banished him forever. Sparta granted him an estate at Scillus, where he ultimately retired to write and cultivate his land.

XENOPHON

His descriptions of the Persian campaigns were written with such immediacy and rich detail that Xenophon has been called the first war correspondent. His knowledge of military history and tactics led him to continue the work started by Thucydides in the *History of the Peloponnesian Wars*, but his other writings are charming and comprehensive essays on various subjects. Among these less well-known works are treatises on Socrates, the economics of farming and housekeeping, cavalry tactics, horsemanship, and the remarkable *Cynegeticus*—the first known essay to treat hunting in terms of sport.

Xenophon hunted behind hounds, much like modern coursing in Portugal or fox hunting in England. The *Cynegeticus* also described boar-hunting with knowledge and excitement, which is not surprising for such a vigorous and daring military leader, and history tells us that the exiled Xenophon engaged in the field sports throughout his life.

Yet his character was disciplined and meticulous too. His attention to detail was unequalled in other writings of his time, and his discourses on hunting included his thoughts on choosing, grooming, maintaining, breeding, and training hounds for his pack. Xenophon considered the field sports an optimal medium for training both the body and the mind, arguing that they provide an equilibrium between the primordial instincts and evolving intellect of men.

Herodotus of Halicarnassus is the father of history, his career beginning at about the middle of the first millennium. Modern historians speculate that he was banished from Halicarnassus after his participation in an abortive revolution. The loss to his native city proved the gain of the civilized world, for exile carried Herodotus throughout Asia Minor and the eastern Mediterranean. His accounts of the Persian wars are often compared with the history of Thucydides on the Peloponnesian campaigns. Thucydides is perhaps more rigidly accurate in purely historical terms, but his work lacks the rich tapestry of culture and experience found in Herodotus.

Herodotus gives us our first knowledge of the lake-dwelling cultures in northern Europe. His description treated a tribe on Lake Prasias, which he compared to tribes on the Volga. There are obvious parallels with the lake dwellers of Austria, Germany, Switzerland, and the British Isles, and Herodotus described them in the following observations:

> Platforms supported by tall pilings stand out in the lake, which are approached from the land by a narrow causeway. Earlier, these pilings were driven by each citizen, but since that time the prevailing custom for seating piles is this: each citizen drives in three for each of his wives. Now the men all have many wives each, and this is the manner in which they live. Each has his own dwelling house on one of the platforms, and each house has a trapdoor providing access to the lake beneath. These lake people secure their infant children with cords around one ankle, to save them from falling into the lake.
>
> They feed their horses and other beasts on fish, which abound in the lake to such a degree that one has only to lower a net through his trapdoor, wait a short time, and draw it up again with the rope quite filled with fish.

Although metal fishhooks originated in Asia, Asia Minor, and Egypt, these European lake-dwelling cultures also had fishhooks of bronze and gold at surprisingly early dates. Similar metal fishhooks existed among the aboriginal tribes of northern California, and have also been found in excavations of the Aztec, Maya, and Inca civilizations.

Lorthet antler carvings

Theocritus was born at Syracuse, almost three centuries before Christ, and this Alexandrian poet is the father of the pastoral verse form. Many literary historians believe that Theocritus was never surpassed at such poetry, with its mixture of polished language, bucolic characters, and reverence for nature. Theocritus has had many famous imitators over the centuries, Vergil and Spenser among them. Perhaps Theocritus composed his finest pastoral in *The Fisherman's Dream*, but it may only be my preoccupation with angling that causes me to favor it above his other works:

> 'Tis poverty alone, Diophantus, that awakens the arts; poverty is the very teacher of labor. Nay, not even sleep is permitted from weary cares to men that live by toil, and if, for but a little while, one should close his eyes, cares throng about him suddenly, and disquiet his slumber.

> Two fisherfolk, in times past, two old men lay down together and fell asleep. They had strewn dry sea-moss for their bed in their hut of wattle-and-daub, and there they dozed beside the leafy wall. Beside them lay the tools of their toil-roughened hands; the willow creels, delicate rods of reeds, hooks, sails bedraggled with seaspoil, lines, weirs, lobster pots woven of rushes, seines, two oars, and an old coble on its props. Beneath their heads was a thin matting, with their clothes and their sailor's caps.

> Here was all their toil and all their wealth. The threshold had never seen a door, nor a watch dog; things seemed to these men superfluous, for poverty was their sentinel. There was no neighbor near them, but the sea below their hut.

> The bright chariot of the moon had not yet reached the midpoint of her course. But the time of their familiar toil had come and awakened them; from their eyelids they cast off slumber, rousing their souls with speech.

Theocritus has the fisherman Asphalion complaining that even summer nights are much too long. His slumber has been filled with a kaleidoscope of dreams and daylight is still behind the dark horizon. Asphalion has experienced a strange dream, and he begged his comrade for interpretation:

> Sleeping late, amid the salty labors of the seas (and truly, not too well fed, for we had supped early, if thou remember, and did not overtax our bellies) I saw myself busy on a rock, and there I sat and watched the fish swimming about, and I kept spinning the baits.

> And finally, one of the fishes nibbled, a fat one, for when sleeping I dream of big fish and strong fights, just as a sleeping dog dreams of chasing bears. The fish was tightly hooked, and my blood was running well, and the rod was heavily bent with its struggling.

So with both hands I strained back, and had a difficult time with such a monster. It seemed impossible that such a fish could be subdued with such small hooks and tackle. Finally, just to remind him that he was hooked, I gently pulled, pricked him, and slackened; when the fish did not panic, I retrieved line.

My difficult toil ended with the sight of my prize. It was a golden fish, all richly plated with gold. Then a terrible fear possessed me, lest this monster prove some fish beloved of fierce Poseidon; perhaps even some treasured jewel of the sea-grey Amphitrite.

Gently, I unhooked this trophy, lest even my hooks should retain some of the riches of its mouth. Then I dragged him fully ashore with ropes, and swore that never again would I travel the seas, but remain on the land and jealously husband my wealth.

Theocritus responds to this dream through the other fisherman in the simple hut, who stares at his friend when the tale of the dream is finally finished. The fishermen then look out across the restless sea and the friend replies:

Nay, fear not, thou art no more sworn that thou hast found the golden fish of thy vision; dreams are only lies. But if thou will search these coastal seas, but awake and not sleeping, there is some hope lying in thy slumbers: seek the living fish of flesh, lest we perish of famine during all thy dreams of gold!

Plutarch followed about a century after Theocritus, and his descriptions of fishing along the Nile in his *Life of Antonius* are not his only concern for the sport. Plutarch was apparently a fisherman himself, since his essays contain references to the use of horsehair leaders. His advice concerns the selection of pale white or grayish hairs to deceive the fish, particularly the tails of stallions and geldings; he argues that the hairs from a mare's tail are too weakened with urine for fishing.

Pliny the Elder follows Plutarch in our catalogue of angling history, since fishing played a considerable role in his remarkable *Historia Naturalis*, which appeared in the first century. His masterpiece of natural history consists of thirty-seven books. Their contents include his observations on the universe, zoology, anthropology, botany, geography, medicinal uses derived from both animals and plants, mineralogy, pigments and dyes, and a history of the fine arts. Pliny is the first to mention trout and salmon in the mountains of Italy, Spain, Dalmatia and Macedonia. His description of salmon in the rivers of Aquitaine was introduced with the following words from the *Historia Naturalis*:

Indu Aquitania salmo fluvialis marinis omnibus piscibus preferatur.

Martial was a minor Roman poet whose birthplace was on the swift-flowing Salo in Spain, and in *Fishing from the Earliest Times*, Radcliffe argues that a boyhood on such a river probably had considerable influence on the fishing images in his verses. His descriptions of that pastoral youth were well known to fellow poets like Juvenal and Licinianus and Oppian. Later in life, Ovid was his neighbor in a simple country house along the Tiber. Martial also fished sometimes for sport, and his poetry includes a wry discussion of fishless days and of releasing fish smaller than about three pounds.

The writings of Martial also include the first mention of the jointed fishing rod, but perhaps his most striking claim for a place in the history of angling comes with the poetry that contains the first mention of an artificial fly in Western literature. These historic lines were written in the second century:

> Who has not seen the scarus rise,
> Decoyed and caught with fraudful flies.

However, all through history the references to fly-fishing and fishing as a sport are fragmentary, usually occurring in natural histories or descriptions of leisure among the nobility. The first unmistakably clear discourse on fly-fishing over trout in a mountain river is found in the third-century essays of Claudius Aelianus.

Aelianus was a Roman born late in the second century, but his education and subsequent travels across the Adriatic Sea left him with a remarkable facility in Greek. His classic *De Natura Animalium* appeared rather early in the third century and ultimately became the standard work on zoology. Its contents are mildly amusing to the modern reader, since Aelianus moves soberly from a factual discourse on elephants to a straight-faced discussion of dragons, but we can only applaud a writer who tells us that he prefers the observation of fish and other creatures, listening to nightingales, and watching the annual migrations of cranes to the acquisition of riches and wealth. The quality of his science and his apparent pillaging of earlier sources are not terribly important to modern fly-fishermen, but a dissertation titled *De peculari quadam piscato indu Macedonia* firmly places Aelianus on the threshold of fly-fishing literature. His account is charming and simple:

> I have learned about the Macedonian method of catching fish, and it is this: between the cities of Beroea and Thessalonica flows a river called the Astraeus, and in this river are fishes with spotted skins; what these fishes are called among the river people one must learn from the Macedonians themselves. These spotted fishes feed on insects peculiar to this countryside, which flutter over the river. The insect is not like flies found elsewhere, nor does it resemble the wasp in appearance, nor could one describe its configuration as like the midge or the bee, yet it has something of each of these. Its boldness is like a common fly, its size resembles

the midge, its coloring imitates the wasp, and its humming sounds like a bee. The river people call it the Hippouros.

These flies apparently seek food above the river, but do not escape the attention of the spotted fishes swimming below. When the fishes observe a fly on the surface, they swim up stealthily, careful not to disturb the currents, lest they should frighten their prey. Coming upward like a shadow, they open their mouths gently and seize the flies, like wolves carrying off sheep from the fold, or eagles take geese from a farmyard; having captured the flies, the fishes slip back into the rippling currents.

Although the fisherfolk understand this, they cannot use these insects as bait for the fishes; for when a man's hand touches them, they lose their natural coloring, their wings wither, and they become unfit food for deceiving fishes. For this reason, the fishes have nothing to do with such damaged flies, refusing them for their spoiled character.

But fishermen have planned another snare for these spotted fishes, and have deceived them with their craftiness. The fisherfolk wrap ruby-colored wool about their hooks, and wind about this wool two feathers, which grow under a cock's wattles and are the color of dark wax.

Their rods are about six feet, with a line of similar length attached. With this they cast their snare, and the fish, attracted and made foolish by the colors, come straight to take it, thinking from its pretty image to savor a dainty mouthful; when, however, it opens and closes its jaws on the feathers, it is caught by the concealed hook and enjoys only a bitter repast, and is captured.

There are other passages elsewhere in *De Natura Animalium* which deal with fishing. Aelianus states clearly that ancient fishing techniques remained limited to spears, nets, weirs, and hooks. Like Confucius more than 2,600 years earlier, Aelianus argued that fishing with hooks and rods represented the ultimate in angling sport. His observations include a discussion of horsehair leaders, and fly-dressing materials like feathers of several colors and crewel in red and blue.

Aelianus is the first writer to mention the European grayling in his works, describing the many-spotted species of Dalmatia and its delicate odor of thyme. His discussion of the grayling includes the observation that it is most easily deceived with tiny flies, a judgement readily confirmed by any modern fly-fisherman who has fished the species on European rivers. Aelianus also mentions the Atlantic salmon, in a brief anecdote about a wealthy angler who had so many flies that his companions ridiculed his collection on the stream. The fisherman replied that his flies might not deceive a salmon, but they would prove adequate for coarser species.

Ausonius composed his *Book of Idylls* in the fourth century. The tenth of these books was a long fishing poem that was a great favorite of Izaak

Walton more than a thousand years later. This tenth book was titled *Ad Mosellam*, and the history of literature tells us that it clearly proves Ausonius the last of the major Latin poets, as well as the father of French poetry. Ausonius was born in Bordeaux, and his tutoring of Gratian ultimately led to an appointment as a Roman consul and to the wide travels that resulted from those duties. His most famous writings include the *Ordo Nobilium Urbium*, which described the principal European cities of his time. The pastoral *Ad Mosellam* is perhaps his best poetry, describing a leisurely journey on the Moselle. It is the longest angling poem in classical Latin, and its passages include descriptions of both salmon and trout—certainly the first unmistakable reference to *Salmo fario* in literature.

> *Qui necdum Salmo, necdum salar, ambiguusque amborum medio, fario, intercepte sub aevo.*

Apollinaris Sidonius was born about the middle of the fifth century in Lyon, played a minor role in Roman politics, and ultimately became the Bishop of Clermont. His panegyric verses and letters are relatively minor, and their chief value lies in their rich tapestry of historical details. History tells us that Sidonius was perhaps more interested in hunting and angling than in clerical matters. His appointment as the Bishop of Clermont and his duties to both the region and the Vatican seriously interfered with his pursuit of salmon and trout in the tumbling rivers of Gascony and the Auvergne.

Sidonius lived in a cacophonic century that had already seen Alaric conquer and pillage Rome. About the time of his birth, history repeated itself when northern tribes took the city again. The last emperor was Romulus Augustulus, and with the collapse of his rule toward the close of the fifth century, historians place the bench mark that closes the Classical Period—describing the centuries that followed as the Dark Ages.

Carolingian and Merovingian culture are based upon the conscious rebirth of civilized thought, and the political unity forged across the European continent with the coronation of Charlemagne was clearly the prelude to the Medieval Period.

It is certain that neither fly-fishing nor hunting ceased during these times, in spite of their absence from literature, since both sports surfaced again in the following centuries. Their renaissance occurs in surprisingly sophisticated form, for by then angling literature had clearly evolved beyond the writings of Martial and Aelianus. The proof of this is the fifteenth-century *Treatyse of Fysshynge wyth an Angle*, which was written a half century before Columbus reached the New World. However, subsequent material will demonstrate that there was a remarkable literature of sport between Sidonius and Dame Juliana Berners. The rich parade of centuries in the history of angling had already spanned some 3,000 years by the time that Ausonius and Sidonius were writing. Its tradition reached from China before the Shang Dynasty to the subsequent collapse of the Roman Empire.

The discovery of fly-fishing in ancient Macedonia is clearly the threshold of our sport. Its beginnings belong to a strange and beautiful world with pale crags and mottled limestone escarpments and barren passes. Its rivers are often born full-blown in giant springheads that come welling up from the pressures of vast underground flowages. Such rivers occasionally vanish into fissures in the earth as suddenly as they appear, but where they meander across a valley floor, these rivers are as rich as any British chalkstream. The classic Gäcka is perhaps the best, its trout rising steadily to fine fly hatches in the trailing beds of ranunculus and fountain mosses. Such valleys, with their water meadows and white-washed villages with onion-topped churchtowers, are a marked contrast to the arid wind-seared highlands of Macedonia and Dalmatia. The fish are free-rising browns and grayling, mixed with big rainbows imported centuries after Aelianus. But in the afternoons, when the misting overcast darkens the rivers of Dalmatia, and the fish begin working to hatches of mayflies and fluttering caddis in the current, it is possible to imagine the fly-fishermen of antiquity working their hackle patterns over the deeper pools, in a simple prologue to the centuries that would follow.

3. Charlemagne, Berners, and the Medieval Period

The dark masonrywork of the millrace winds through the village from the cold little river, its swift currents slowed in undulating beds of fountain weed and stoneworts. Its channel is lined with algae. Its walls and gravel bottom are bright with *Spirogyna* moss. The millrace parallels the minor stone-paved streets of the town, swelling with the flow of a swift tributary that tumbles from the hills behind the houses. Its currents pass behind the town hall and the cobblestone marketplace, filling the lily-pond moat of the castle before spilling into the Regnitz.

The castle began as a simple thatched hunting manor, but its final evolution included the moat and steep roof slates rising above intricate half-timbered gables. The onion-topped stairtower is a solemn accent to the pond lilies below the drawbridge.

Forcheim is a postcard town on the ancient Bamberg post road that winds north from Nürnberg. Dark roof slates and red tiles crown the houses that line the slow-flowing river. White geese quarrel in the shallows, and storks nest on the chimney pots. The valley floor is rich with hay meadows and cabbage fields and grain, and in the distance lie the soft smoke-colored hills of the Franconian plateau. There are still deer and *wildschwein* and hares in the forests, although in our time there are few stags south of the Thuringian border. Trout fishing in the tributary river above Forcheim is still excellent, but the Atlantic salmon that ascended these rivers when Charlemagne used this simple castle for fishing and hunting are tragically extinct in the entire watershed of the Rhine.

Charlemagne is principally remembered for the military and cultural force his Holy Roman Empire slowly forged at the close of the eighth century. His campaigns against the Lombards, the Moors, the Saxon tribes

25

northeast of his Frankish kingdom, and the Slavic peoples as far east as Pomerania secured him vast territories across Europe. His intervention against Lombardy in its quarrels with Pope Adrian I provided Charlemagne with an important alliance in Rome. When he again aided the papacy by intervening in a rebellion against Pope Leo III, the reward was his formal coronation as emperor of the Holy Roman Empire in 808. His political influence was a major force in both restoring the prestige of Rome, and in reversing the tragic inertias of the Dark Ages.

Charlemagne was more than a soldier. Although his military skills established a relatively secure civilization that reached from Dalmatia to Spain and from the Slavic frontiers to the English Channel and Frisian Coast, his political abilities and cultural judgement have proved more important in the perspective of history.

Civil order and the codification of laws followed his armies. His network of communication and control in outlying provinces was a model of effective administration. His concern for the poor and his ethical conduct were widely documented and extended into his control of the church in his lands. Trade was stimulated with Britain and Asia Minor, and the imperial court at Aachen became a fulcrum for both commerce and culture.

The Carolingian School developed under Charlemagne became famous throughout the civilized world. Other academies were established for the instruction of children, and the intellectual circle at the focus of this Carolingian renaissance included scholars like Alcuin, Peter of Pisa, and Charlemagne himself.

Charlemagne was fascinated with knowledge and art, and worked tirelessly to improve his Latin. His architects built the remarkable Abbey at Lorsch, and his own court chapel was copied from the Byzantine church of San Vitale that he had earlier admired at Ravenna. The *Lindau Gospels* and magnificent manuscripts produced at Lorsch are examples of the powerful cultural revival that Charlemagne instigated, the keystone of which was the collection and copying of classical literature for his court library. His programs were intended both to preserve these sources, many of which had been lost in the sieges of Rome, and to make their influence available to the half-civilized subjects of his northern empire. Charlemagne himself took an active part in this ambitious attempt to restore classical civilization and suffuse his rule with its prestige; and since his ambitions and talents were equally remarkable, his revival succeeded so brilliantly that most of our oldest, surviving texts of classical literature are found in his Carolingian manuscripts. Modern civilization owes an incomparable debt to Charlemagne and his scholars; and without their foresight in preserving ancient sources, fly-fishermen would be completely ignorant of the classical roots of their sport in the writings of Martial and Aelianus.

Charlemagne died in 814, and his power waned under the ineffective rule of his descendants, but his influence almost single-handedly ended the Dark Ages that followed the collapse of Rome in the fifth century.

The literature of sport has its next milestone in tenth-century Britain,

Gold effigy on the reliquary
containing the bones of Charlemagne

in the several works of Aelfric the Abbott. Aelfric is considered the best writer to emerge from Britain during Saxon times. He received his education at Winchester, on the pastoral banks of the Itchen. He served as the abbot at Cernel in Dorsetshire, and later at Eynsham cloister near Oxford. His famous grammar, Latin glossary, and the celebrated *Colloquy on the Occupations* became standard texts for the study of Latin in the British monasteries. His lucid, richly textured prose was the model of its time. His *Colloquy* does not discuss the sports, since it is devoted to more serious daily work, but it does eloquently discuss fishing. Aelfric discusses the use of nets, fishhooks, spears, and baits by the professional fishermen of the tenth century. It was a time when the grayling were apparently imported to Britain from the European continent, and placed in streams near English abbeys and monasteries. Although the *Colloquy* tells us nothing of their capture, we can presume that not all of the clerics fished for them with merely utilitarian ends in mind. Although our first dissertation on fly-fishing in English was still five hundred years in the future, its author was the prioress of Sopewell Nunnery.

The medieval chronicles between Aelfric and Dame Juliana Berners did not discuss angling, but their manuscripts are much concerned with the field sports. The rebirth of hunting literature came in these centuries after Charlemagne, and it celebrated a pastime that had become an important privilege of the nobility. Balzac observed centuries later that the privileged classes of every age have always invented a life style that others could not share. Hunting occupied that role in medieval times, providing both the pleasures of the chase and the rich trappings of status. The nobility not only hunted but began to write about its sporting life, and from this marriage of chivalry and the hunt has come our entire fly-fishing tradition.

Many of these works are a mixture of the literature of sport and the natural sciences. Adelard of Bath wrote about falconry and the diseases of hawks, but his manuscript went farther to include observations on the sport of the hunt and its place in life. John McDonald made the observation in his book *The Origins of Angling* that the field sports were a marriage of learning and chivalry—learning in their detailed manuals of instruction and chivalry in the high-minded arguments for sport.

The medieval chroniclers sought to leaven the warlike ferocity of the medieval knights, and their manuscripts celebrated sacrifice, courage, heroism, honor, manners, justice, fidelity, and other qualities of mind and spirit. Chrétien de Troyes was perhaps the most celebrated poet of the twelfth century, and his manuscripts are perhaps the first to proclaim the Arthurian legends. The prologue to his *Cligès* is a perfect example of the rebirth of civilization after Charlemagne:

> Our manuscripts have extolled the chivalry and knowledge that once belonged to Greece. Chivalry then was passed to Rome, together with a level of learning that has ultimately come to France.

God grant that it might be cherished here, and that it may be made welcome, that the honor which has found refuge among us may never depart from our soil. God had once awarded it to others, but of Greece and Rome no more is heard; their fame is passed, and their glowing ash is now dead.

The rebirth of civilization was not limited to Britain and France, and our next milestone in the history of the field sports lies in the works of Frederick of Hohenstaufen at the middle of the thirteenth century. Frederick ruled as King of Sicily, King of Jerusalem, Emperor of the Holy Roman Empire, and was the last of the Hohenstaufen Dynasty. His monumental *De Arte Venandi cum Avibus* explored the techniques of falconry in almost six hundred pages of meticulously reasoned Latin, and was completed shortly before his death in 1250.

It was the labor of thirty years. Its pages covered the full theory of the practice of hunting with birds of prey, and also treated their care, training, feeding, diseases, breeding and character in such comprehensive fashion that *De Arte Venandi cum Avibus* is a prelude to modern ornithology.

Frederick of Hohenstaufen was the unique mixture of ruler, soldier, and scholar that Charlemagne had admired almost five centuries earlier. Charlemagne had excelled at politics and military science, while encouraging the arts through enlightened patronage; Frederick was relatively unimpressive as a soldier, but his scholarship was genuinely polished and his role in the thirteenth century was unique. He was a German emperor ruling from his Sicilian kingdom, and his court at Palermo was a cultural crossroads filled with courtiers from Asia Minor, Constantinople, Rome, and northern Europe. His familiarity with Jewish, Moslem, classical, Byzantine, and Germanic cultures gave him a uniquely cosmopolitan outlook for his time—and this background caused him to revive ancient learning as both scholar and patron.

The collection and reproduction of ancient manuscripts begun under the reign of Charlemagne was virtually completed under Frederick of Hohenstaufen. His court library at Palermo was filled with scholars who laboriously translated the original classical and Arabic texts into Latin. Frederick not only instigated this literary renaissance, but he also was familiar with its progress. His knowledge of Aristotle was comprehensive enough that he could both quote the Greek philosopher and challenge his observations on bird life:

We have learned through hard-won experience that the deductions of Aristotle, whom we followed when it appealed to our reason, were not entirely reliable, more particularly in his description of the character of certain species.

Frederick of Hohenstaufen loved falconry and believed it was widely misunderstood. His intellect and powers of observation were such that he ultimately rejected most of what had been written earlier about his sport.

His introduction to *De Arte Venandi cum Avibus* explains that its purpose is intended to clarify past misinformation about falconry and outlines how he conducted his original research and writing:

> We have investigated and studied with great solicitude, and in minute detail, all that relates to this art, exercising both mind and body so that we might eventually be qualified to describe and interpret the fruits of knowledge acquired from our own experiences or gleaned from others. For example, at great expense we summoned from the quarters of our world the masters in the practice of falconry. We entertained these experts in our own domains, meanwhile seeking their opinions, weighing the importance of their knowledge, and endeavoring to retain the memory of the more valuable of their words and deeds.

Anglers who love their sport would never question such intellectual effort and expense, and to understand such discipline and devotion is to understand what the field sports have meant to men for thousands of years. Their meaning lies beyond spectacle, beyond mere adventure, beyond mere relaxation and diversion—and close to the basic rhythms of life.

Falconry held each of these aspects in its character. Frederick of Hohenstaufen was challenged by the difficulty of training such bold, rapacious birds and controlling them in the hunt. His manuscript scorned hunting with nets, spears, bows and arrows, snares, and other instruments, even disdaining a hunt behind dogs or cheetahs. The monograph continues with the observation that these other methods were too easily mastered and relatively crude:

> It is true that these methods are more popular, because their technique is crude and simple to learn; falconry, on the other hand, is less familiar and does not commend itself to the majority, because skill in its pursuit is difficult to acquire, and because it is more refined.

Fly-fishermen can readily understand a passion for a sport that is difficult and beautiful, and identification with Frederick of Hohenstaufen is made easier when we realize that his patronage was partially responsible for our knowledge of the classical writers on angling, completing translation of the transcripts begun under Charlemagne.

Our expedition through the history of angling and sport now returns to thirteenth-century France, and the narrative poetry of Richard de Fournival. This author was chancellor of the cathedral at Amiens, which was built during much of the thirteenth century. It is not known whether Fournival lived to witness the completion of the cathedral's soaring nave, but his participation in its beginnings, when the powerful columns and flying buttresses and piers were started, is certain. His Latin poem was titled *Vetula*, and was at first falsely attributed to Ovid, but in the fourteenth century a subsequent translation in French appeared. Its later French title was *La Vielle*, and it had been translated into a series of rhyming couplets. *La Vielle* was filled with a jackstraw tangle of medieval observations on manners, diversions and amusements, and contemporary life. Its posture was often childish, and its pages were filled with a mixture of superstition and pornographic overtones, but it also offered superb glimpses of medieval life. Descriptions of music, games, chess, and sport are included, along with an extensive account of fishing. Fournival describes spears, nets, and eel traps—along with rods, lines, floats, plummets, and hooks. He also discusses fishing for pike, chub, roach, barbel, bream, carp, and trout, and his poem contains a reference to flies in these striking lines:

> *D'autres engins assez avoie,*
> *Par lesquelz decevoir povoie*
> *Autres poissons es épues douches,*
> *A morceaulx de vers ou de mouches.*

John Waller Hills, in his charming *History of Fly Fishing for Trout*, acknowledges his temptation to translate these final lines to mean artificial flies, but concludes that its precise meaning is unclear. In the context of later passages it could be merely metaphorical or it could mean using live insects as bait, but it could also refer to an artificial fly pattern fashioned of feathers and dubbing and silk.

Our focus remains in France with the fourteenth-century *Livre de Chasse*, which was written by Comte Gaston de Foix, ruler of Foix and Bearn on the northern slopes of the Pyrenees. Gaston was destined from birth for his life of wealth and accomplishment. His kinsmen included the Kings of Aragon, Navarre, and England, and his bloodline is filled with almost legendary warriors. While Frederick of Hohenstaufen loved the refinement and finesse of the hunt, Gaston de Foix gloried in its military aspects—the bloodletting and its physical perils. Although his feudal domain included superb trout and salmon rivers, the pastoral and contemplative moods of angling were apparently unsuited to his temperament. Yet his writing is a major milestone in the evolution of a modern sporting code.

His castle was a foothill stronghold, richly appointed to echo his feudal status as a prince of formidable wealth and standing among the royal houses of Europe. Its kennels held 1,600 hounds in several hunting packs, and according to his biographer Jean Froissart, when Gaston de Foix rode to Tarbes to meet the wedding party of his cousin Edward, the Black Prince of England, there were six hundred horsemen in his company.

Celebrations at his castle were legendary for their lavishness and display of wealth. His invitations were understandably coveted throughout the European nobility. But festivities were not the only life of the castle and its court, and in addition to having kings, princes, dukes, counts, and ambassadors as its regular guests, the castle also sheltered a surprising number of major artists, scholars, and poets over the years.

As Frederick of Hohenstaufen loved falconry, so Gaston de Foix loved the chase, for his military temperament was more suited to its methods than to the skilled refinement of hunting with swift birds of prey. Gaston coursed on horseback behind his hounds and insisted on making the kill himself, according to the code of chivalry governing the hunt. The medieval romance of *Sir Gawain and the Green Knight*, part of the Arthurian legend from an unknown author, describes the chivalry and the challenge implicit in the code of the chase:

> But then came the lord himself, spurring his horse forward, and discovered the boar at bay. He dismounted swiftly and left his horse standing to rein, and drew his bright sword, and charged forward with long strides, passing through the ford to where the grim beast was waiting. The boar watched him coming with his weapon in his hand, and his bristles rose and he snorted with such ferocity that many feared for the knight.
>
> The boar charged straight at him, and the man and beast fell locked together, and the water swirled about them. But the beast took the worst of the fray, for the man stood the first charge calmly, and drove the steel of his sword firmly into its throat, right to the hilt, and pierced the heart.
>
> The boar snarled angrily and gave up the fight, and retreated back across the stream, but the hounds fell upon him, biting furiously, and the beaters forced him farther to open ground where their faithful hounds finished the struggle.

It was a sporting climax that Gaston de Foix clearly lived many times, and his *Livre de Chasse* is unquestionably written from firsthand experience with both the hunt and its perilous codes of conduct. His writing is filled with the mixture of respect and dread that is the hallmark of the man who hunts dangerous game:

> The boar hears wonderfully well and clearly, and when he is hunted and comes out from the forest and brush, or when he is hunted and compelled to abandon his territory, he sorely dreads leaving his cover for open country; he, therefore, puts his head out from the bracken before he exposes his body. Then he remains awhile and watches silently, and samples the wind from every side.
>
> And if at that time, he sees anything that he thinks might hinder him in leaving his cover, he will turn back again into the woods. Then he cannot be forced from his cover, though all the hunting horns and shouting of beaters were there.
>
> But when he has undertaken the way out of the wood, he will spare nothing, but will hold his charge throughout. When he finally flees, he makes few turnings; but when he once turns at

bay, then he will turn upon the hounds and upon their masters; and for no stroke or wound that men inflict will he complain or cry, but when he runs upon the men he menaces, strongly snorting and squealing.

Gaston de Foix had considerable respect for his quarry, and his mixture of homage and fear reach us with a sense of ultimate knowledge and drama after more than five hundred years:

> The boar is the beast of our world that is most strongly armed, and can more quickly slay a man than any other. Neither is there any beast he could not slay, if they were alone, sooner than any other beast of prey might slay him, be they lion or leopard, unless they should leap on his shoulders, where he could not turn on them with his deadly tusks.
>
> And there is neither lion nor leopard that kills a man at a single stroke, as the boar does, for they usually kill with their claws and through biting through the neck, but the tusks of the boar can slay with one stroke like a dagger.
>
> It is a proud beast, fierce and perilous, for many times have men witnessed the harm he has done. For some have seen him slit a man from knee to breast, and slay him stark dead, without speaking a word. Many times I have been charged and thrown to the ground, and my courser with me, and once the gallant horse was himself killed.

Gaston de Foix began his *Livre de Chasse* in 1387, when his age had reached fifty-six years, and he was undoubtedly in a contemplative mood that compelled him to record his experience and skill. It proved a wise choice for our history of hunting, since only four years later he met his death while coursing for bear in the beech forests above Pamplona. Froissart tells us the day was exhaustingly hot, and that the hounds had pursued the bear from morning until late afternoon. Gaston participated aggressively at the kill and attended the ceremony that followed, finally retiring to the neighboring village to rest. His huntsmen brought cold water to wash his face and neck, and as the count extended his hands, he suffered a massive stroke and heart seizure and died.

The evolution of the sporting ethic after Gaston de Foix can ultimately be traced to Edward Plantagenet, Duke of York, early in fifteenth-century England. His sporting heritage clearly came from his father, Edmund of Langley, who put his profound love of hunting and falconry above his duties of state. Edward of York was a warrior knight who relished both combat and the intrigues of fifteenth-century British royalty. History estimates that he survived forty challenges to mortal combat at arms, and his intrigues also found him imprisoned by Henry IV at Pevensey. Whatever his character, there is no question that the young Duke of York was devoted to the chase no less fervently than Frederick of Hohenstaufen loved falconry and Gaston de Foix relished hunting wild boar.

His classic *Master of Game* was written in 1405, when Edward was only thirty-two, and some historians have argued that his monograph might not have been completed without his imprisonment at Pevensey. His motives for writing the *Master of Game* seem to have been political as well as sporting. His ultimate release from Pevensey depended upon his regaining royal favor, and Edward also needed a vehicle to express his gratitude on escaping the headsman's axe for his treason. His manuscript was dedicated to Henry IV in a flowery prologue that served its purpose—the young Duke of York was permitted to leave Pevensey, and was subsequently designated the Royal Master of Game, a title he held until his death at the Battle of Agincourt in 1415. Edward of York clearly states his preferences in hunting, like Frederick of Hohenstaufen and Gaston de Foix before him:

> For, although falconry with hawks for the heron and for waterfowl is noble and commendable, yet it seldom lasts, at the most, over half the year. And even if man found enough game to hawk at between May and August, no one could find hawks to hawk with. But for hunting, there is no season of the year that cannot right well be found in every good region, and hounds ready to chase it.

The *Master of Game* is largely structured on a meticulous translation of the work of Gaston de Foix, but Edward of York added his own rich observations on its practices in England. These original sections on British hunting are of considerable interest, since they are in large measure the literary genesis of the entire British sporting tradition. Almost three centuries had passed since William the Conqueror won his climactic battle at Hastings, bringing with him an entire medieval code of chivalry and sport from Europe. The impact of that culture on England was immense, and its echoes are still evident in both the concern for literary posterity and the refinements of sporting technique that are found throughout the *Master of Game*. The manuscript concludes with this epilogue of its purpose:

> And in my simple manner, as best I could, and as might be learned of old and many diverse, gentle hunters, I did this business in this rude manner to put the craft and the terms and the exercise of this said sport, more in remembrance, and openly to the knowledge of all lords, ladies, gentlemen and women, according to the customs and manners used in the High Noble Court of this Realm of England.

It was these noble princes who forged the traditional chivalry of the field sports in the fourteenth and fifteenth centuries, and defined a creed that exists almost unchanged among gentlemen hunters and fly-fishermen today. Their manuscripts are unmistakably committed to the argument that sport is a unique equilibrium of passion, intelligence, and art. The passion of the stalk lies at the root of both hunting and angling, and its blood rhythms are a fundamental driving energy, making these field sports an obsession to be loved in themselves—but their passion is also shaped and polished by tradition, and these overtones are as important as the sport itself.

Angling historians have long contended that it was angling, however, that first brought about our preoccupation with the contemplative side of sport. Most students of angling literature believe that the genesis of such attitudes came in 1653 when Walton published *The Compleat Angler* with its explicit subtitle *The Contemplative Man's Recreation*. However, there is a curious manuscript in the archives of Trinity College at Cambridge which seemingly disproves this common allegation. Titled *Piers Fulham* and written by a little-known author about 1420, it contains the earliest known reference in English to the sport of angling. Its author briefly refers to pike and bream and tench, and to his several known methods of fishing:

> But in rennying ryvers that bee commone,
> There will I fysshe and taake my fortune
> Wyth nettys, and wyth angle hookys,
> And laye weris and sprenteris in narrow brookys.

The prefatory lines written by Piers of Fulham for this tract on medieval fishing contain the first mention of angling as a contemplative sport:

> Loo, worshipful sirs, here after ffolle-weth a gentlymanly treatyse
> full convenyent for contemplatiffe lovers to rede and understond,
> made by a noble clerke, Piers of Ffulha, sum tyme Ussher of
> Venus Schole, which hath brieflye compyled many praty concen-
> tis in love under covert terms of ffysshynge and ffowlynge.

About the middle of that same century, some thirty years after Piers of Fulham and his primitive manuscript, the first comprehensive monograph on fishing was compiled in an English nunnery. It was a remarkable monograph on the sport, totally without precedent in English or any other language, and its title was *The Treatyse of Fysshynge wyth an Angle*. It clearly represents the birth of fly-fishing literature as such, and it was written by an angler with considerable experience on the rivers of England—it is richly unique in both character and scope.

It is attributed to the half-mythical Dame Juliana Berners, although her authorship and authenticity have been challenged several times over the centuries. There have been many authorities who doubted her existence, except among the several myth-heroines of the fifteenth century, but the *Biographia Britannica* describes the *Treatyse* at considerable length, and vouches for the character and authorship of the noblewoman who compiled its richly illuminated pages. It clearly identifies the author of *The Treatyse of Fysshynge wyth an Angle* as the prioress of Sopewell Nunnery at Saint Albans. It describes her as a gentlewoman of noble lineage, much celebrated in her time for her wisdom, scholarship, and charm; and she was apparently well versed in the field sports. In 1496 Wynkyn de Worde printed the edition of *The Boke of Saint Albans* that included the earlier

Berners monograph, to which the prioress added the following prefatory remarks:

> And for by cause that this present treatyse sholde not come to the hondys of eche ydle persone whyche wolde desire it yf it were enprynted allone by itself, and put in a lytyll playnflet, therefore I have compylyd it in a greter volume of dyverse bokys concernynge to gentyll and noble men, to the entent that the forsayd ydle persones, whyche sholde have but lytyll mesure in the sayd dysporte of fysshynge, sholde not by this meane utterly dystroye it.

The controversy over the authenticity and existence of Berners was largely fuelled in 1881, when William Blades attempted to demolish Dame Juliana and her claims to authorship of the *Treatyse* in the facsimile reprint of the work published in that year by Elliot Stock. Our chronological proximity to this edition, and our tragicomic predilection toward muckraking in this century have perhaps recruited an army of doubters. However, anglers interested in the history of their sport owe a singular debt to John McDonald, and his *Origins of Angling*, for a remarkable job of literary archaeology. McDonald discovered that the first identification of Dame Juliana Berners as a prioress of noble birth had been made by William Burton, an antiquary who lived about a century after the *Treatyse* appeared in *The Boke of Saint Albans*. Such testimony from a source relatively close in time to the printing of the *Treatyse* itself has considerable credence. The basic Burton documents are four handwritten annotations in authentic

Dialogus Creaturarum Moralisatus, 1460

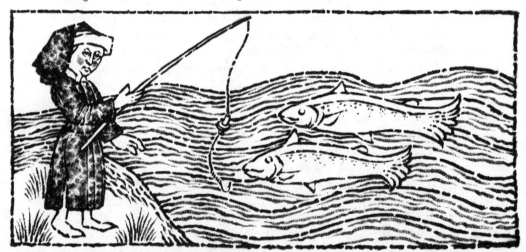

folios of the fifteenth and sixteenth centuries. These manuscripts are remarkable pieces of original evidence, but were apparently unknown to Blades when he prepared the Stock facsimile edition.

The *Origins of Angling* points out that these sources were widely known in the eighteenth century and were accepted at face value by antiquarians. John McDonald was apparently the first modern historian to subject these handwritten annotations to comparative paleography. The first piece of Berners evidence is in the collection of the University Library at Cambridge. It consists of handwritten notes made in a copy of *The Boke of Saint Albans* that was acquired from the library of a wealthy bishop, and is listed in the Cambridge library catalogue of fifteenth-century books belonging to its archives. The first brief annotation is unsigned and reads as follows:

> This Booke was made by the Lady Julian Berners, daughter of Sir James Berners, of Berners Roding, in Essex, Knight, & Sister to Richard Lord Berners. She was Lady Prioresse of Sopwell, a Nunnery neere Saint Albons, in which Abby of Saint Albons this was first printed 1486, 2 H.7. She was living 1460, 39 H.6. according to John Bale, Centur,[8] Fol. 611.

The second Burton annotation in the Cambridge copy of *The Boke of Saint Albans* is clearly in the same handwriting, except that it is written in sixteenth-century Latin.

> *Ex Lelando Et Baleo*
> *Juliana Barnes, Faemina illustris, corporis et animi dotibus abundans, et formae elegantia spectabilis, claruit author huius operit: 1460: J: E4:*

The third annotation lies still deeper in the text, and although in Latin, it unmistakably refers to William Burton himself:

> *Liber Willmi Burton Lindliaci Leicestrensis, morantis apud fold com staff: ex dono consanguinet mei charissimi Thomae Purefey de Barwell iuxto Lindley in com: Leicester: Arming: 1612:*

For comparative purposes, McDonald obtained photographic copies of an exhaustive folio that Burton made of the *Itinerary* assembled toward the middle of the sixteenth century by John Leyland, a distinguished scholar, chaplain, and librarian who served as court antiquarian to Henry VIII of England. Burton was fully aware of the valuable information in the Leyland *Itinerary*, and apparently prepared a rough folio of more than 250 pages. Proof that this handwritten folio was prepared by Burton clearly lies in the text itself:

> The itinerarye of John Leiland the famous Antiquarie. Begunne before or about anno dominie 1538, AN.30 H.8. The first part copied out from the originall, 1628, by me William Burton.

McDonald carefully subjected these handwriting samples to the yardsticks of modern paleography, comparing the notes regarding Juliana Berners with the folio known to bear Burton's handwriting. Superficially, the writing appears to have been made by a single person, although McDonald meticulously points out that there are obvious differences in both the chronology and the pens used in the various samples; such discrepancies are not unusual, given the fragile quill penpoints of the period, and rather wide variations in the time of their writing. However, critical parallels in forming key letters are unquestionably present between *The Boke of Saint Albans* from the Cambridge collection and the handwritten Burton notes on the Leyland *Itinerary* found in the Bodleian Library at Oxford.

The *Origins of Angling* fairly points out that a Cambridge antiquarian had advanced a similar conclusion concerning the authorship of these annotations in 1733. However, it remained for John McDonald to ferret out the several known handwriting samples, and to subject the notes in the Cambridge *Boke of Saint Albans* to rigorous comparison with the Oxford folio copied from Leyland. His comparison provides incontrovertible proof that they were both written by Burton, and that it is his authority—careful antiquarian that he was—that identified Dame Juliana Berners as the author of *A Treatyse of Fysshynge wyth an Angle*, and offered a few brief details of her life. Verification of the Burton handwriting evidence unmistakably points to the authenticity of Berners herself, and hopefully to the conclusion of the *Treatyse* controversies.

The history of *The Boke of Saint Albans* begins in 1486, with its first printing limited to the techniques of hunting and armor. It was structured in three separate monographs treating falconry, hunting, and weaponry. There is evidence that the *Treatyse of Fysshynge wyth an Angle* was actually written as early as 1450; but it was almost half a century later, in 1496, that Wynkyn de Worde published his second edition of *The Boke of Saint Albans*, and added the Berners manuscript to its contents.

It has been more than five centuries since Dame Juliana Berners assembled her unique manuscript on angling, and a modern reader of its pages is both surprised and charmed. The folio is a mixture of technique, descriptions of fishing equipment, and the philosophy of angling, all expressed in a remarkably Chaucerian mood.

Although the recommendations for tackle in the *Treatyse* are woefully outdated, given the headlong pace of our technology, so are the chapters on tackle in such recent authors as Hewitt and Bergman.

The *Treatyse* discusses well-seasoned, jointed rods of three sections. The hollow butts were made from well-seasoned hazel, willow, or aspen. The butt was joined to a middle section with a ferrule, and such middle sections were often constructed of hazelwood. The top joints were often shaped of blackthorn, meddler, crabtree, or juniper wood, and were usually connected with the spliced taper-connection still found on some British fly rods today.

Berners also suggested that the materials for a rod should be cut in

Salamon in his parablys sayth that a good spyryte makyth a flourynge aege that is a fayre aege & a longe. And syth it is soo: I aske this questyon. Whi che ben the meanes & the causes that endure a man in to a mery spyryte. Truly to my beste dyscrecōn it semeth good dysportes & honeſt gamys in whom a man Joy eth wythout ony repentaunce after. Thenne folowyth it ẏ go= de dysportes & honeſt games ben cauſe of mannys fayre aege & longe life. And therfore now woll I chose of foure good dyspor tes & honeſte gamys, that is to wyte: of huntynge: hawkynge: fyſſhynge: & foulynge. The beſte to my ſymple dyſcrecōn whẏ che is fyſſhynge: callyd Anglynge wyth a rodde: and a lyne

First-page facsimile of
Berners' *Treatyse of Fysshynge wyth an Angle*, 1496

winter between Candlemas and Michelmas. The wood should be straightened in a heated oven—not unlike modern heat-treating with split bamboo—and then allowed to cool and season for a month. After curing was complete, the butt material was seated firmly against a heavy timber template frame. Its pith core was hollowed out and tapered inside with a red-hot mandrel of iron. Its hollow center was enlarged with a series of tapered and progressively larger irons and then permitted to cool. Forty-eight hours of cooling were recommended before the butt section was unfastened from its template, and smoke-dried while hanging from the roof beams. The middle and top sections were seasoned and cured in similar fashion, and Berners described the tip piece as a slender shoot of blackthorn. It is obvious that the *Treatyse of Fysshynge wyth an Angle* was not recommending a stiff trolling rod:

> And thus shall ye make you a rodde so prevy that ye maye walke therewyth: and there shall noo man wyte where abowte ye goo: it woll be lyghte and full nymbyll to fysshe wyth at your luste and redynesse.

Dame Juliana Berners recommended that the line be attached to the rod at the spliced joint between the tip and middle sections, and then strung through a guide on its blackthorn tip. Such a system had a cushioning effect when the rod was stressed, and in case of a fracture, the line was still securely fastened.

The Berners folio also described recipes for dying horsehairs several colors useful for fishing purposes. Compounds for coloring the hair yellow, sepia, olive, reddish, dusky gray and straw-colored were given. These formulas in the *Treatyse* were copied almost word for word in *The Compleat Angler* more than 150 years later. The Berners monograph continued with instructions on weaving horsehairs into lines, with various specifications for different species of fish. Nine to twelve hairs were specified for trout and grayling, with a sixteen-hair line recommended for Atlantic salmon.

There were also primitive instructions for hookmaking. The relatively crude woodcuts failed to illustrate the delicacy and craftsmanship described in the *Treatyse*, but its text recommended that the hooks be fashioned of fine steel needles. The angler was told how such needles could be softened, cut to shape the barbs, formed into proper bends, and retempered for strength. Instructions on how to snell the line under silk windings below the eyeless shank of the hook were also included by Berners.

The flies described in the ultimate pages of the *Treatyse of Fysshynge wyth an Angle* were proof that a gradual evolution of fly dressing had unfolded between the dressings described in the writings of Claudius Aelianus and the imitative patterns listed in Berners. The flies were keyed to corresponding months and their fly hatches, and outlined in such an offhand manner that the fly dressings must have been quite generally known on the rivers of England. Berners introduced her patterns with this charming preface:

Berners' fly patterns, 1450

Twelyve flyes wyth whyche ye shall angle to ye trought and graylynge, and dubbe lyke as ye shall now here me tell.

Berners then systematically described fly dressings for each month of the season. There were two patterns recommended for March: the first dressed with partridge and brownish-gray crewel dubbing on a rather large hook, not unlike the modern March Brown; and the second a smaller fly, not unlike the Hare's Ear or Blue Dun pattern. April was the season for a relatively large stonefly imitation, and for May, the *Treatyse* prescribed two dun patterns with bodies of yellow or rust-colored dubbing. There was also a dark little palmer-tied pattern recommended for May that perhaps served to imitate the Grannom caddisflies. June was blessed with three patterns: the Maure, with its wings of brown mallard and body of rough grayish crewel; the Donne cutte, dressed with dark wool and wings of bustard sections; and the Tandy fly, with its wings of pale barred mallard and pinkish-gray body. July was the month for terrestrials, and the *Treatyse* specified a wasp fly, along with a pattern that may have imitated a hatching blue-winged olive. August concluded the twelve patterns for trout and grayling with a drake pattern of mallard wings and ribbed dubbing. The dressings are unfailingly rich with the patina of centuries:

> The Donne flye, the body of the Donne woll and the wyngs of the pertryche. Another Donne flye: the body of blacke woll: the wyngs of the blackyst drake, and tay under the wyng and under the tayle.

Dame Juliana Berners described the salmon as the most stately fish that men might angle to in fresh water, at once difficult to capture and gentle, and a fish that kept to the deep pools of major rivers. The prioress was also the first to observe that the salmon could be taken with a relatively small fly pattern, and that its rise was as subtle as a trout or grayling. The *Treatyse* described the grayling in almost reverent terms, with reference to its delicate taste and its willingness to rise to flies. Berners's admiration for the brown trout in British rivers bears repeating:

> The troughte for by cause he is a ryght deyntous fysshe, and also a ryght fervente byter, we shall speke nexte of hym. He is in season from Marche unto Mychelmas. He is on clene gravelly grounde and in a streme.

Berners continued with an outline of baits and tackle recommended for trout fishing in British rivers. She made the observation that such equipment was effective except in what she called the leaping times— obviously, a rise of fish to hatching flies—when fly-fishing was the method that must be employed.

> From April tyll Septembre ye trought lepyth. Thenne angle to hym wyth a dubbyd hoke accordynge to the moneth, which dubbyd hokys ye shall fynde in thende of this treatyse.

Reading her descriptions of a river and the places where it sheltered trout, one is invariably struck with the modernity of her observations. Berners advised that a skillful angler would keep out of the river as much as possible, and entirely out of sight of the trout, perhaps concealed behind a streamside willow. Her advice also cautioned against letting the shadow of an angler or his rod fall fleetingly over the fish, observing that shadows frighten them, and that once it has been frightened a trout or grayling will not rise. There were also opinions on the best weather for fishing, and suggestions for reading a river to understand its secrets and its holding places:

> But in a ryver ye shall angle in every place where it is depe and clere by the grounde: as gravell or claye without mudde or wedys. And in especyall yf that there be a manere whyrlynge of water or a covert. As an holow banke: or grete rotys of trees: or longe wedes fletyng above in the water where the fysshe maye covere and hyde theyself at certayn tymes whan they lyste. Also it is good

for to angle in depe styffe stremys and also in fallys of waters and weares: and in floode gatys and mylle pyttes. And it is good for to angle where as the water restyth by the banke: and where the streme rennyth nyghe there by: and is depe and clere by the grounde and in ony other placys where ye may se only fyssh hove or have only fedynge.

Reading these sentences more than five centuries after they were written is an intriguing experience, additional evidence that there is truth in the French proverb that the more anything changes, the more it remains the same. Certainly the *Treatyse* outlined the basic premises of trout-fishing tactics as clearly as they are spelled out in Bergman, in spite of the intervening centuries of technology and change. There is even a brief sermon advocating a reverence for the rivers and their fish, anticipating the ethical themes of modern ecology:

Also ye shall not be to ravenous in takyng of your sayd game as to mouche at one tyme, wyche ye maye lyghtly doo if ye doo in every poynt as this present treatyse shewyth you on every poyt, wyche shoude lyghtly be occasyon to dystroye your owne dysportes and other mennys also.

Also ye shall besye yourselfe to nourysshe the game in all that ye maye: and to dystroye all suche thynges as ben devourers of it. And all those that done after this rule shall have the blessynge of God and Saynt Petrus, wyche he theym graunte that wyth his precyous blood vs boughte.

Poets and anglers alike have always been shaped in part by the character of their landscapes and their rivers. Brief exposure to the British rivers is enough to explain the pastoral mood that occurs in *A Treatyse of Fysshynge wyth an Angle* and again in the lyric prose of Walton, who marked the beginning of our modern tradition in angling literature. The philosophy of fly-fishing that evolved in these British landscapes still shapes our attitudes today.

Much of the countryside that shaped the moods of the *Treatyse* is still visible in the rolling hills and river valleys northwest of London, and in country towns like Saint Albans and Broxbourne and Stanstead Abbots. There are thatched-roof villages and ancient marketplace crosses and medieval inns with names like The Feathers and The King's Head and The Fighting Cocks in Saint Albans where Dame Juliana Berners served as the prioress of Sopewell Nunnery. It is a gentle flint-hill country, drained by little rivers like the Lea and the Cherwell and the Ouse. There are moss-covered churchyards and medieval cathedrals like Ely and Peterborough and Saint Albans itself, their belltowers rising above the rooftops and chimney pots and trees. Twilight across this landscape has a softness, its quality mirrored in the rivers, rich with a sense of history and echoed in the tolling of bells.

Except in their cooler tributaries and headwaters, these rivers are often too warm for trout and grayling in modern times, but it is not difficult to imagine them five centuries ago. Their currents flowed smooth and clear in trailing beds of chara and ribbonweed, eddying deep along the alders and mossy banks, and tumbling through weirs and stone-arched bridges and timber hatches. Fish are working to a delicate hatch of pale little mayflies below a riffle of bright gravel, and in the Sopewell Cloister across the water meadows from the cathedral at Saint Albans, the prioress is beginning a parchment manuscript:

> And therefore now woll I chose of foure good dysportes and honest games, that is to wyte: of huntynge: hawkynge: fysshynge: and foulynge. The beste to my symple dyscrecion whyche is fysshynge: called anglynge with a rodde: and a lyne and an hoke.

For supplemental notes on Berners' *Treatyse*, see Afterword.

4. Walton, Nowell, and the Classic Age

I ts pages are richly filled with charming observations and moods, and like all great literature, *The Compleat Angler* creates a unique universe in itself. Its poetic images range from descriptions of swift-flowing riffles to the silken currents of deeper pools, eddying musically under the roots of beech trees that shelter the water. Walton writes about beech-leaf patterns flickering kaleidoscopically on his rivers and the April smells of rain in the awakening earth, with the first wildflowers in the water meadows.

London has enveloped much of its surrounding countryside in the explosive growth that followed the Second World War, but the pastoral landscapes of seventeenth-century England still live in *The Compleat Angler*. Its pages permit a modern angler to share that century along the Lea, passing the thatch-roofed cottage at Hoddesdon and the timber-vaulted market hall at the center of the village. We fish again in the long-vanished channel that once flowed past Tottenham High Cross, and stalk the trout that hide under the alders at Flander's Weir. The first day is spent walking the Lea valley from London to Hoddesdon, sometimes on the Amwell highroad and sometimes along the towpath of the canal. Our journey passes the slate roofs and chimney pots of Standon Hall, the family seat of Sir Ralf Sadler, and the crenellated belltowers of the parish churches at Tottenham and Chingford. Walton's itinerary crosses the weathered planking of the Cook's Ferry catwalk, winding through the water meadows at the Pickett lockhouse on the canal. There are weathered headstones in the churchyard beside the Edmonton almshouses, their inscriptions illegible with moss and time, and the Waltham Cross still stands.

Walton and his characters close the first day on the river at the

Thatched House in Hoddesdon, securing lodging for the night and making preparations for a hearty supper. The brushwork in the opening pages of *The Compleat Angler* paints a pastoral landscape of a river valley that inspired other poetic minds, like Gray in his familiar *Elegy in a Country Churchyard* a century later:

> The curfew tolls the knell of parting day,
>   The lowing herd winds slowly o'er the Lea,
> The ploughman homeward plods his weary way,
>   And leaves the world to darkness and to me.

However, there were a considerable number of fishing books written in the centuries between *A Treatyse of Fysshynge wyth an Angle* and Walton's first edition of *The Compleat Angler*, which appeared in 1653. Several of these books are merely later elaborations on the work of Berners, although one is a unique folio which was totally unknown until its yellowed pages and vellum binding were discovered in London in 1954. Its structural themes present a surprising prologue to Walton and his *Compleat Angler*, and its pages are a revelation to blind Waltonian disciples.

Although the title page of this unknown monograph is missing, its publication occurred in 1577, more than a century after Berners, and it was printed in the London shop of Henry Middleton. Its last page bears this information and adds that the book was sold at his shop in Saint Dunstan's Churchyard. Its title was *The Arte of Angling*, and it was discovered by the famous American collector Carl Otto von Kienbusch in the summer of 1954, during the cataloging of books from the storage attic of an old British country estate. It retained its original vellum covers and the handwritten inscriptions of three earlier owners, made between the seventeenth and nineteenth centuries. Since its original title page was missing, the bookseller who originally found the library had loaned the little folio to the British Museum, hoping that the antiquarians there might identify its origins and establish its worth. The museum experts reported that its existence was unknown, and noting obvious similarities in structure and content, raised the question about its relationship to *The Compleat Angler*, which made its appearance almost a century later in the Marriott edition of 1653.

Kienbusch had purchased an angling riddle, which he carried back to the United States and generously presented to the famous angling collection at Princeton University. There he pressed for the publication of a facsimile edition of *The Arte of Angling*, enlisting the aid of Henry Savage, archivist of the Carnegie Library at Princeton, and the critical skills of Professor Gerald Eades Bentley to establish the historical context of the book—perhaps even the identity of its author.

Kienbusch himself wrote a distinguished introduction to the facsimile edition, pointing out that the obvious parallels between both *A Treatyse of Fysshynge wyth an Angle* and *The Arte of Angling* and the subsequent writings of Walton should not be judged too harshly in modern terms. Such plagiarism was widely accepted practice in seventeenth-century Europe.

There were five other fishing books published between the *Treatyse of Fysshynge wyth an Angle* and Walton's *Compleat Angler*. Following *The Arte of Angling* in 1577, the first of these was the little volume titled *A Booke of Fishing with Hooke and Line*, which Leonard Mascall wrote thirteen years later in 1590. The second was a remarkable monograph on natural science called *Certaine Experiments Concerning Fish and Fruite*. It was written by John Taverner and printed in 1600, and it contains the following prophetic observation about the nymphs of aquatic insect life:

> I have seene a younge flie swimme in the water too and fro, and in the ende, come to the upper cruste of the river, and assay to flie up: howbeit, not being perfitly ripe or fledged, hain twice or thrice fallen downe againe into the bottome: howbeit, in the ende receiving perfection by the heate of the sunne, and the plesant fat water, hath in the ende within some halfe houre after taken her flyte, and flies quite aweaye into the ayre, and of such younge flies before they are able to flie aweaye, do fish feed exceedingly.

The third fishing book of the period was published in 1613, and was titled *The Secrets of Angling*. Its author was John Dennys, and it was a didactic poem filled with a reverence for nature and the joys of fishing. Gervase Markham was the author of *The Pleasures of Princes*, which included an extensive discourse on angling and its secrets, and was printed in 1614. It is of considerable historical interest, but its author was a notorious compiler of previous works on fishing, often openly paraphrasing Mascall in many passages. Thomas Barker wrote the fifth book between *The Arte of Angling* and the first edition of Walton; the Barker book first appeared in 1651, just two years before *The Compleat Angler*, and was coincidentally titled *The Art of Angling*.

Echoes of each preceding writer are found in Walton, and each is mentioned somewhere in his work. There are also obvious overtones of Berners in Walton, but it is not certain whether he knew the *Treatyse* in its original form, and he makes no references to it in his work. Although there are striking parallels between the Kienbusch manuscript and Walton, his classic also makes absolutely no mention of *The Arte of Angling*.

These several books are the foundations for the entire literature of angling as a contemplative sport, and each owes a considerable debt to the *Treatyse of Fysshynge wyth an Angle*, although that wellspring of information is seldom acknowledged. Perhaps a brief recounting of these interrelationships is worth our analysis, since they will help us understand both Walton and his *Compleat Angler*.

Although fly-fishing itself failed to make major conceptual advances in the 150 years after Dame Juliana Berners, the period that lies between the rash, undisciplined tyranny of Henry VIII and the tight-lipped dictatorship of Cromwell was not entirely barren in the arts. Paradoxically, its exciting tumult included the Elizabethan epoch of literature and drama, and its angling literature was no exception in its richness.

When Leonard Mascall wrote *A Booke of Fishing with Hooke and Line*, Edmund Spenser was seeking publication of the *Faerie Queen*, and William Shakespeare was witnessing the performance of his first work. Mascall was an original writer on various subjects, and his observations on dendrology, trapping pest species of rodents, poultry and animal husbandry, and hygiene are noteworthy. His *Booke of Fishing* is an almanac of information, apparently gathered from widely disparate sources. Its discussion of fisheries biology is strikingly original, and firmly establishes Mascall as a pioneer in pisciculture; but its observations on sport fishing are clearly pirated from the *Treatyse of Fysshynge wyth an Angle*. However, the fishing passages in Mascall are not entirely void of original contributions to fly-fishing theory and technique. There is good advice on both striking and playing fish, and a surprising prelude to the dry fly in his recommendation of cork-wrapped foundations for fly bodies—it is surprising to find that this allegedly modern concept in fly tying is almost four hundred years old.

It is clear that Walton had knowledge of Mascall and his *Booke of Fishing*, since the lists of fly patterns are identical in the work of both authors. Mascall correctly copied only eight of the dozen classic flies outlined in Berners, and incorrectly named the remaining four patterns. Walton echoed precisely the same mistakes, and his book subsequently cites the authority of Mascall to buttress one of his arguments.

Walton apparently did not read Taverner, since that author's surprising knowledge of aquatic fly hatches is missing from *The Compleat Angler*. Taverner also knew about nymphal forms of subaquatic insects—knowledge that is clearly evident as seen in the paragraph from his *Certaine Experiments Concerning Fish and Fruite* quoted earlier in this chapter—and that knowledge would have prevented the following mythology in *The Compleat Angler*:

You are to know that there are so many sorts of flies as there be fruits: I will name you but some of them; as the dun-fly, the stone-fly, the red-fly, the moor-fly, the tawny-fly, the shell-fly, the cloudy or blackish-fly, the flag-fly, the vine-fly; there be of flies, caterpillars, and canker-flies and bear-flies; and indeed too many either for me to name or for you to remember: and their breeding is so various and wonderful that I might easily amaze myself, and tire you in my relation of them.

And yet, I will exercise your promised patience by saying a little of the caterpillar, or the palmer-fly or worm; that by them you may guess what a work it were, in a discourse, but to run over those very many flies, worms, and little living creatures with which the sun and summer adorn and beautify the river-banks and meadows, both for the recreation and contemplation of us anglers; pleasures which, I think, I myself enjoy more than any other man that is not of my angling profession.

Pliny holds an opinion that many have their birth or being

from a dew that in the spring falls from the leaves of trees; and that some kinds of them are from a dew left upon herbs or flowers; and others, from a dew left on coveworts and cabbages: all which kinds of dews being thickened and condensed, are by the sun's generative heat most of them hatched, and in three days made living creatures.

John Dennys was mentioned twice in *The Compleat Angler*, and his *Secrets of Angling* contains some of the best poetry in the entire literature of sport. John Waller Hills, in his charming studies titled *A History of Fly-Fishing for Trout*, even argues that *The Secrets of Angling* may well be the finest didactic poem on any subject. Dennys certainly ranks with poets like Wotton, Marlowe, Doubleday, Stoddart, Drayton and Lang in his angling verse, and his poetry also outlined the whole spectrum of early seventeenth-century angling. The original edition of *The Secrets of Angling* is filled with methods, techniques, and tackle. Dennys describes his tackle meticulously, including the first descriptions of the bamboo rod and the landing net and the wicker creel.

The Secrets of Angling does not mention fly-fishing in the edition of 1613, but it was included in a second edition that appeared seven years later. Its editor was a north-country angler, perhaps one whose skills had evolved on the swift Yorkshire rivers, judging from his preferences in tackle and flies. Other than his writings on agriculture and gardening, nothing else is known about this William Lawson, but he has earned his primary position in the history of fly-fishing solely through the brilliantly original notes he added to the second edition of Dennys. These notes are so completely fresh and written in such an attractive prose that it is a tragedy for angling literature that Lawson failed to write his own book on fly-fishing—just as it is that we have no books from the creative minds of George Selwyn Marryat and Theodore Gordon.

Lawson recommended a smooth rod of supple action, without the top-heavy calibrations apparently fashionable in seventeenth-century England. His preferences in hooks were austere, and he rejected the shop-fabricated hooks that had become available in his time, shaping his own hooks from needles made in Italy and Spain. Lawson believed that trout afforded the summit of fly-fishing sport, and his notes provide our first exposition of both dapping and casting flies. There are descriptions of fly hatches, and his knowledge of tactics is thorough:

You must fish in, or hard by, the stream; and have a quick hand and a ready eye and a nimble rod, strike with him or you loose him. If the winde be rough and trouble the crust of the water, he will take it in the plaine deeps, and then, and there commonly the greatest will arise, when you have hookt him, give him leave, keeping your line straight, and hold him from rootes and he will tyre himselfe. This is the chiefe pleasure of angling.

Gervase Markham is also mentioned in *The Compleat Angler*, and he is archetypal of the gentleman fly-fisher. Markham was a professional soldier, having served as an officer in both Ireland and the Low Countries. Eventually he resigned his military career and turned to his writing, using his remarkable working knowledge of Latin, French, Italian, Spanish, and probably Dutch. His reputation for pirating the works of others is justly deserved, yet his prose is fluent and pleasing, and the books he copied were worth rewriting—posterity is deeply in his debt, since his plagiarism unquestionably preserved a great many books whose content would otherwise have been lost.

His *Book of the English Husbandman* fails to mention fishing, but it does not omit much else of interest in a British country house. There are observations on the care of horses and a hunting pack, fertilization of barren or acid soils, the costs of all aspects of rural husbandry in both time and money, livestock diseases and remedies, all types of crops suitable in the British climate, baking and brewing and other cookery, household medicines and remedies, archery and tennis, free ballooning, bee keeping, the diet of gamecocks, falcons and falconry, the catering of feasts and banquets, and a whole encyclopedic welter of other subjects.

It is pertinent to remember that Dennys' *Secrets of Angling* also appeared in 1613, the same year Markham's first *Book of the English Husbandman* was published. It is typical of Markham that its material was quickly translated into prose and inserted swiftly into the *Second Book of the English Husbandman*, which was published the following year. Markham titled his material *A Discourse of the Generall Art of Fishing with the Angle*, and it has ironically become better known than the original Dennys poem. William Lawson's observations on angling have also been reprinted many times under Markham's authorship, although a serious reader must agree with John Waller Hills that the style of Lawson is utterly different from the soberly structured prose of *The English Husbandman*. It is known that Markham and Lawson subsequently collaborated at times, their work sometimes published under a single title. Hills points out in *A History of Fly-Fishing for Trout* that the fly dressings in Markham were ultimately updated and revised by a superb fly-fisherman—angling notes in these later editions of *The English Husbandman* still carry echoes of both Mascall and Dennys, but much of their material is boldly original, and were probably written by Lawson.

In 1651, Thomas Barker's *The Art of Angling* was the last fishing book to appear between Dame Juliana Berners and Walton. Barker is a workmanlike author, writing simply from his own experience in such things as fishing tactics and cookery, and in his pages lie the first English reference to fishing reels. It was long believed to be the first discussion of the reel in the entire history of angling, and that such fishing reels were invented in medieval Britain, until our recent discovery of the unmistakable reels in Chinese paintings from the twelfth century.

Barker was a Cromwellian cook in charge of the state kitchens where food was prepared for foreign ambassadors. His book is disarmingly uncultivated, filled with apologies for his unscholarly prose, but it deserves an important place in the literature of angling. Some of Walton's observations on fly-fishing seem to have come from *The Art of Angling*, and Barker is full of amusing asides and solid information about his favorite pastime. His book is punctuated with brief verses on cookery, and he recommends the tackle sold by Oliver Fletcher, not far from Saint Paul's Cathedral at the Sign of the Three Trouts.

Henry Peacham and his book *The Compleat Gentleman* appeared in 1627, and although it was not a fishing book, it was also a minor prologue to both Walton and Cotton. Its title was probably not lost on Walton, just as the literary skeleton of Nowell's *Arte of Angling* ultimately found its way into *The Compleat Angler*. Most of the Peacham observations on fishing are shallow and insignificant, and yet there is suddenly this observation, as exciting as the discovery of a fine trout poised in a riffle of bright gravel:

> For the making of these flyes the best way is to take the naturall flye, and make one so like it that you may have sport: for you must observe what flyes haunt the water for seasons of the yeare, and to make their like with cottons, woole, silke, or feathers to resemble the like.

It is impossible to praise Walton and *The Compleat Angler* too highly, since it is perhaps the best-known single book on sport in the whole of English literature. Walton was sixty when his Marriott edition of *The Compleat Angler* was printed in London in 1653. It has endeared itself forever to the angling fraternity, for it contains not only a discourse on fish and fishing but also a pastoral philosophy of life. History tells us little of Walton's education, but the stature of angling friends like John Donne and Sir Henry Wotton in the intellectual climate of the seventeenth century indicates that Walton's education was undoubtedly adequate, regardless of its source or the extent of its formal nature.

Walton and his friends lived in troubled times. Charles I had been executed, and England was torn with bitter warfare between the Royalists and the Roundheads under Cromwell. Yet the tranquility in the prose of *The Compleat Angler* carries no hint of this strife, its gentle moods tempered in quiet British rivers from Staffordshire to the English Channel.

Although there is nothing particularly original on fly-fishing in Walton, his work cannot be judged in terms of mere tackle and techniques. *The Compleat Angler* is a little book of prose idylls and moral observations, steeped in a compelling reverence for nature. Its style is virtually unique, and it has proved of immense importance in both the literature of angling and English literature itself. Its role in angling lies in its technical precedents and its singular qualities of character.

The historical perspective of literature is complex and its viewpoint is always threefold: any book is measured in terms of its obvious contributions to the state of knowledge in its time, its sense of craftsmanship and literary skill, and its visible impact on subsequent writers in terms of both style and thematic content.

It is obvious that using this threefold yardstick to judge *The Compleat Angler* will yield mixed results. The literary quality of Walton is difficult to fault, and it was a compendium of the technical knowledge of its time. Judged by the standards of the seventeenth century, Walton seemingly had few peers as a writer. It is possible that his reputation would have been even higher were it not for a phalanx of outrageous disciples. John Waller Hills explored a similar viewpoint in his *History of Fly-Fishing for Trout*:

> He has suffered sadly at the hands of his disciples and admirers: his admirers have indulged in unbalanced and indeed intemperate panegyric, which has detracted from his real merit: whilst his disciples have either assiduously copied his weaknesses, or, if they have attempted his excellencies, have only succeeded in producing a caricature.
>
> His book has been an obsession to subsequent writers, which has lasted to the present day and has been an influence by no means entirely for good. For this he is not to blame: but no one who has waded through the many books in dialogue form which strew the two hundred years following him—books in which the dialogue, measured against that in *The Compleat Angler*, is as a dull and lifeless canal running between straight banks compared with the winding reaches of some shining river—but must have wished irreverently that the master had chosen to cast his thoughts in some other mould than the dialogue.
>
> For assuredly dialogue is at once the most difficult of all literary forms, and also the most dangerous, for its apparent simplicity lures the unskilled to his irretrievable disaster. Charles Lamb was right, as he usually is in literary judgements, when he said that Walton's book is the only treatise written in dialogue which is worth a halfpenny, for in him everything is alive, whereas in others the interlocutors are merely abstract arguments.

Walton himself lives in his prose, wise and watchful, always striking an equilibrium between tactics, technique, and sensory enjoyment. His prose explains his world perfectly and helps us in our search for an unconscious harmony in the cacophony of our century. His love of fishing is always interwoven with a love of books, the rhythms of the seasons, and the matchless English countryside. His chapters on fishing for trout include these remarkable passages:

> But turn out of the way a little, good Scholar, towards yonder high honeysuckle hedge; there we'll sit and sing, whilst this shower falls so gently upon the teeming earth, and gives yet a sweeter smell to the lovely flowers that adorn these verdant meadows.

Izaak Walton

Look! Under that broad beech tree I sat down when I was last this way a-fishing. And the birds in the adjoining grove seemed to have a friendly contention with an echo, whose dead voice seemed to live in a hollow tree, near to the brow of that primrose hill.

There I sat viewing the silver streams slide silently towards their centre, the tempestuous sea; yet sometimes opposed by rugged roots and pebblestones, which broke their waves and turned them into foam.

And sometimes I beguiled my time by viewing the harmless lambs; some leaping securely in the cool shade, whilst others sported themselves in the cheerful sun; and saw others craving comfort from the swollen udders of their bleating dams. As I thus sat, these and other sights had so fully possessed my soul with content, that I thought, as the poet hath happily expressed it:

> I was for that time lifted above earth,
> And possessed joys not promised in my birth.

We must remember that *The Compleat Angler* still stood alone when John Waller Hills was writing, since it would be another thirty-three years before Carl Otto von Kienbusch discovered an earlier treatise on angling in dialogue form. The slim little *Arte of Angling* preceded Walton by seventy-six years, and its parallels in both content and form are unmistakable.

The original edition of Walton consisted of thirteen chapters, which concealed their exposition in description, dialogue, and story line. Viator is a hunter who meets a fisherman, Piscator, by chance along the river path and remains for several days of fishing, wandering along the stream, and engaging in varied conversations. There is some fishing and much fishing talk—in about the same ratio that exists today among most anglers—and a description of charming inns along the river. Most of the conversation is dominated by Piscator and his discourses on fish and the techniques of angling and its antiquity. Some of these discourses are started spontaneously by the fisherman, but most are explanations in response to questions posed during his dialogues with the huntsman Viator. Subsequent editions of Walton changed the character Viator to the better-known Venator, the huntsman familiar to the generations unfamiliar with the first Marriott printing of 1653. The literary structure of these dialogues is varied with a counterpoint of minor characters such as the dairy woman and her milkmaid daughter, wandering hunters, the wife of the innkeeper, and other fishermen met along the river. Such contrapuntal interruptions are also varied with poems and rambling anecdotes and songs.

The basic structure of a two-character dialogue between Piscator and his companion Viator was believed uniquely the property of *The Compleat Angler* until the recent discovery of *The Arte of Angling* revealed an earlier work organized on the same skeletal armature. It is this structural form that had seemed unique, separating Walton from the earlier English fishing books. These known works, from the legendary Dame Juliana Berners to the workmanlike Thomas Barker, all virtually omitted any trace of dialogue. Therefore, it was believed by both literary historians and angling writers that Walton had completely abandoned the conventional literary devices of earlier authors, introducing both dialogue and impersonation as his structure, and adding the gradual conversion of Viator into an angler as his thematic plot. These elements give *The Compleat Angler* much of its singular flavor, but the discovery of the earlier *Arte of Angling* means that such devices were not solely the creation of Walton.

The title page of *The Arte of Angling* is missing. Therefore, it is impossible to determine if this running title on subsequent pages is the actual title of the unknown monograph, since *A Dialogue Betweene Viator and Piscator* was unquestionably its subtitle. The running title was also used in Markham for his angling section in the *Second Book of the English Husbandman*, published thirty-seven years after our unknown author's book was printed in the late sixteenth century; it was also repeated in the book that Thomas Barker published seventy-four years later. There is no doubt of the printer and bookseller, and its date and place of publication, since all of this information is found in the surviving colophon:

> Imprinted at London in Fleetstreate at the Signe of the Faulcon
> by Henrie Middleton and are to be sold at his Shoppe in Saint
> Dunstan's Churchyarde. Anno. 1577.

It seems strange that no other copies of this unknown book have survived into modern times, since its quality and authenticity are unmistakable, and the annotation of three owners over the centuries attest to its popularity. Whatever the fate of the other copies, there seems no question that Walton saw and used *The Arte of Angling* in writing *The Compleat Angler*. Gerald Eades Bentley has assembled impressive evidence of that fact in his prefatory essay to the American facsimile of *The Arte of Angling*, which was published at Princeton University Library in 1956. His first comparative study involved Walton's directions for securing larval baits:

> Take a piece of beasts liver and with a cross stick, hang it in some
> corner over a pot or barrel half full of dry clay, and as the gentles
> grow big, they will fall into the barrel, and scowre themselves, and
> be alwayes ready for use whensoever you incline to fish; and these
> gentles may be thus made til after Michelmas.

There are similar directions for collecting and keeping blowfly larvae in *The Arte of Angling*:

> Of a peece of a beastes liver, hanged in some corner over a pot, or
> a little barrel, with a crosse sticke and the vessel halfe full of red
> clay, and as they waxe big, they will fall into that troubled clay,
> and so scour them, that they will be readie at all times, these you
> may make untill Allhallowtide, fro time to time.

Walton included these instructions in his thirteenth chapter, which discussed fishing for roach and dace, and also is our first introduction to the caddisfly larvae. That same chapter of *The Compleat Angler* contains these instructions for a malt bait in fishing such coarse species:

> Get a handful of well made mault, and put it into a dish of water, and then wash and rub it betwixt your hands til you make it cleane, and as free from husks as you can; then put that water from it, and put a small quantitie of fresh water to it, and set it in something that is fit for that purpose, over the fire, where it is not to boil apace, but leisurely, and very softly, until it become somewhat soft, then put your water from it, then take a sharp knife, and turning the sprout end of the corn upward, with the pointe of your knife take the back part of the husk off from it, and yet leaving a kind of husk on the corn, or else it is marred; and then cut off that sprouted end (I mean a little of it) that the white may appear, and so pull off the husk on the cloven side (as I directed you), and then cutting off a very little of the other end, so that your hook may enter, and if your hook be small and good, you will find this to be a very choice bait either for winter or summer, you sometimes casting a little of it into the place where your floate swims.

Other than its candid recommendation of chumming a pool to attract its fish to the bait, these passages bear a striking resemblance to the advice the unknown author of *The Arte of Angling* gives for roach fishing:

> You must take a handful of well made malt, and rub it betweene your hands in a fair dish of water to make the as cleane as you may, then in a small vessel of water, seeth the simpering wise, until they be somewhat softe, whiche you shall discerne by feeling one of them between your finger and your thumbe, then take them off and dreane the water from them, then must you have a fine knife, turning up ye sproute ende of the corne upward, and with the point of your knife, take of the backe part or houske first, leaving another houske notwithstanding, or else all is marred, then cut off that sprouted end a little, that the white may appeare, and so pull off the houske, on the cloven side, as afore, and then cutte off a little of the nether end, so putting it on your hook, which must be very fine, made of card wyre, and cover the point of your hooke in the cleft of your malt corne, beard and all, then thrust out betwene your finger and thumbs end, the white of ye corn a little, that the fish may see it.

Walton often mentions the famous sixteenth-century Swiss writer, Konrad von Gesner, and Gesner was the author of a four-volume *Historia Animalium*, published at Zurich more than one hundred years before Walton. The author of *The Arte of Angling* also cites Gesner, relating the apocryphal story of a pike caught in Europe that was 267 years old. It is possible that Walton actually used Gesner as his original source but it is more likely that he used *The Arte of Angling* since his text includes the mistakes it makes in quoting Gesner. Walton displays the following version in his *Compleat Angler* chapter on pike:

> And yet Gesner mentions a pike taken in Swedeland, in the year 1449, with a ring about his neck, declaring he was put into that pond by Frederick the Second, more than two hundred years before he was last taken, as by the inscription in that ring (being Greek) was interpreted by the then Bishop of Worms.

And again—this time from *The Arte of Angling*:

> But or ever I speak any further of him, I must tell you a story of the age of a luce or pike, which Gesnerus doth make report of with a ring about his neck, of this fashion hereafter drawn.
>
> In the Year of our Lord 1497, a pike was taken in a lake about Haslepurn, the imperial city of Swethland, and a ring of copper found in his gills, under his skin; and a little part thereof seen shining, whose figure and inscription about the compass of it was such in Greek as we here exhibit, which John Dalburg, Bishop of Worms did expound it thus: "I am the first fish of all, put into this lake by the hands of Frederick the Second, Ruler of the World, the fifth day of October, in the Year of Our Lord 1230."

Other than giving an earlier date for the capture of this monster pike, Walton has identified its location as Sweden, making the same mistake as our unknown author. The passages in *The Arte of Angling* refer to a nonexistent capital city in Sweden, and Walton apparently fell into the same error unknowingly. Konrad von Gesner wrote in Latin, and his actual text from the *Historia Animalium*, which has been called the fountainhead of modern zoology, describes the capture of the giant pike outside Heilbronn, the former capital city of Swabia. Frederick of Hohenstaufen was made Holy Roman Emperor at the close of the twelfth century, and Johann von Dalberg became Bishop of Worms in 1482. The legend of the dinosaur-sized pike outside Heilbronn is consistent with the biographies of both Frederick and the Bishop of Worms, and the chronology of their lives fits the alleged age of the fish—even if its mythical age of more than 250 years is an obvious fabrication.

These several clues seem to establish unmistakably that Walton both knew and used *The Arte of Angling* in his own writings, yet he made no mention of its existence in *The Compleat Angler*. However, it is possible that he did mention the author without adding the title of his book. It is equally clear that other authors also made ample use of *The Arte of Angling*, since it outlined thirteen important attributes essential to the well-tempered angler that are not found in the much older *Treatyse of Fysshynge wyth an Angle*, which outlines six ethical commandments of its own. The classical thirteen are apparently original to *The Arte of Angling*, and both Dennys and Markham repeat twelve of the list in their subsequent books.

The several borrowed passages and mistakes that Walton reworked into his *Compleat Angler* are relatively minor. The important consideration is the full-blown organization and literary framework he found in *The Arte of Angling*, its structure a ping-pong of dialogue between the characters Piscator and Viator.

This parallel with Walton and his *Compleat Angler* is striking. The dialogues of *The Arte of Angling* between Piscator and Viator, who meet accidentally on the river, involve the instruction of a half-willing beginner in fishing. The lessons take place along the stream, and sometimes while eating their catch, prepared by the wife of Piscator, a strong-willed woman named Cisley who hates fishing—the prototype of a galaxy of fishing widows in angling literature.

His structural form was thought to identify Walton's most striking departure from earlier fishing books, but that contention is less viable when we discover that the literary framework of *The Arte of Angling* and *The Compleat Angler* is virtually identical. Even the companions Piscator and Viator are the principal characters in both books, although Walton modified this copybook similarity in subsequent editions of his classic, changing the name of his huntsman to Venator. It is apparently clear that Walton readily adapted the basic plan of *The Arte of Angling* to his own purposes, since his first edition adopts both of its primary characters, and there are such unusual similarities in the two texts that mere coincidence seems unlikely. However, Walton completely transformed the material he took from the earlier manuscript, and that transformation clearly has the touch of genius. Although his prose is highly skilled, the anonymous author of *The Arte of Angling* has virtually nothing of the pastoral charm present in Walton. His book has little trace of the richly idyllic moods found in *The Compleat Angler*, yet the writing is not the work of an amateur. Except for Walton himself, the literary quality of *The Arte of Angling* is unmistakably the best of the early angling books. Like the worldly Gervase Markham, Walton was clearly a fine judge of quality in other writers, and it is small wonder that he was drawn to the well-developed dialogue form he found in *The Arte of Angling*. It is obvious that our newly discovered classic will never displace *The Compleat Angler* from either its popular or literary position, for Walton shaped a lyric prose style that was unmatched in his time. However, Gerald Eades Bentley makes the following observations in his essay on *The Arte of Angling*, and his critical judgments are worth repeating:

> Its author, however, is no unlettered angler whose enthusiasm has led him to a halting exposition of his fishing lore; I think he understands dialogue better than Walton does, and his powers of characterization are more highly developed—at least in his secondary figures.

In contriving his situations to elicit the exposition, he shows great skill; he is easy in the handling of a dramatic problem at which Walton is sometimes awkward. His Piscator does not have the charm or the depth of Walton's, but his pupil seems more fully realized than Viator. His assurance in dialogue and characterization persuade me that he was not an inexperienced writer. His skill and his new prominence in the genealogy of English fishing books make his anonymity all the more challenging.

Bentley also argues that the author's identity is unquestionably concealed in his conceivable identification with the principal character, and in the clues of names and places found in his dialogues. Walton could certainly be identified from such personal and geographical clues scattered throughout *The Compleat Angler* if its authorship were also unknown. Walton is richer in such bench marks, but *The Arte of Angling* also has its singular fingerprints.

The author often mentions fishing the Ouse above its coastal marshes and describes netting its pools above Huntingdon Bridge and Saint Ives. Huntingdon Bridge still exists today, its six arches of masonry completed in 1332, and one passage in *The Arte of Angling* seems to suggest that the author had a country house about three miles from Saint Ives. Another clue is the reference in *The Arte of Angling* to living in Switzerland. The author mentions Lac Lemán at Lausanne, in the harbor channel at Geneva, and in the swift currents of the Rhône below the city. Other references to the Swiss countryside also suggest that our anonymous fisherman lived with a large colony of English expatriates in Geneva. Such a colony in that period points to the Marian Exiles, who left England for refuge in cities like Frankfurt and Geneva at the middle of the sixteenth century.

The Marian Exiles were prominent English Protestant leaders and their families, who fled the terror under Mary I of England—the infamous religious persecutions of Bloody Mary.

Protestant clergymen like Archbishop Cranmer and bishops like Latimer, Ridley, and Hooper were mercilessly imprisoned when they refused exile. But mere imprisonment was not enough to satisfy the brooding queen, and the bloody full-scale persecutions soon began. Cranmer and his colleagues were burned as heretics, and scenes of public execution at both the block and stake became common. More Protestants were executed in the last two years Bloody Mary occupied the throne than had been put to death under the heresy laws in the preceding century and a half. More than three hundred churchmen were apparently martyred, while thousands of Protestants languished in miserable dungeons and prisons throughout England. Protestants who escaped tried to flee Bloody Mary and her terror—and it is perhaps among these Marian Exiles that our anonymous author for *The Arte of Angling* is hiding, a highly educated clergyman who loved fishing and found political refuge in Europe.

These quarrels were quite old.

After the execution of Sir Thomas More in 1535, the position of many prominent Catholics had become perilously insecure in the England of Henry VIII. Feelings smouldered for several years until the Pilgrimage of Grace, in which Catholic nobles, wealthy gentry, and clergymen opposed the anticlerical tyranny, tragically ended with the execution of many of their number. The king followed the Pilgrimage of Grace with a climate of oppression that drove many Catholics into exile.

Henry VIII died in 1547, his early promise, unquestionable ability, and popularity long forgotten in a trail of wives and bloody executions, and England was swept with a sigh of thanksgiving and relief. His successor was his son, young Edward VI, who was crowned in early boyhood. With the death of Henry VIII, who had merely wished to retain the existing church under British sovereignty and control, the floodgates of a radical Protestant reformation were opened. With his designation as the Lord Protector of Edward VI, the Duke of Somerset virtually became ruler in 1547; and in concert with a group of radical reformers he soon established a totalitarian policy aimed at completely decimating the influence and wealth of the Catholic gentry.

The Duke of Northumberland became the Lord Protector of young Edward VI in 1550, without actually taking that title. Somerset was imprisoned and subsequently executed for his role in a plot against Northumberland. The radical policies that had existed under Somerset abated somewhat, but the old hatreds still smouldered against the Protestant excesses throughout England. When tuberculosis struck down young King Edward VI in 1553, a frightened Northumberland attempted both to prolong his power and prevent the coronation of Mary I, since she was a devout and militant Catholic.

However, the daughter of Henry VIII was not easily defeated in her legitimate aspirations to the throne.

Mary I began her reign in a happy climate of general rejoicing, and in the beginning she seemed to choose more moderate nobles and clergymen as her court advisers. Except for the execution of Northumberland, Mary I took a surprisingly lenient course in the first months of her rule, sparing most other participants in his plot and even allowing many members of her late brother's council to remain in office. However, the mood of her reign soon changed to create the Marian Exiles.

Gerald Eades Bentley points out another possible clue to the author of *The Arte of Angling*, in the dialogue about trout fishing that occurs between Piscator and Viator near its conclusion. It includes an aside about a colleague who jealously regarded his reputation as a trout fisherman and was apparently the warden of a church where both men served.

> I dare not well deale in ye angling of ye trout, for displeasing of
> one of our wardens, which either is counted the best trouter in
> England, or so thinketh, who would not (as I suppose) have the

taking of that fish common, but yet thus muche I may say, that he worketh with a flie in a boxe.

Bentley believes these several clues could point to several men, each having some qualification for having written *The Arte of Angling*. It seems certain that our mystery author was a Marian Exile who lived in Geneva, or visited the colony of English expatriates quartered there. There is an obvious familiarity with the rivers around London, particularly the Ouse in Huntingdonshire. Our anonymous author shared some duties with the trout-fishing warden of a church or some other institution, and that warden was a troublesome angler who was jealous of his knowledge and skills. Bentley is convinced that the quality of *The Arte of Angling* demonstrates an experienced writer, and that our anonymous author had unquestionably written other books. It is certain that he knew and loved angling.

Bentley offers us his candidate for authorship in his essay on *The Arte of Angling*, and his man was not only a distinguished clergyman, but also prepared the English catechism of the Protestant Reformation. His high clerical position forced him to join the Marian Exiles, our knowledge of his life definitely places him in Frankfurt-am-Main during the persecutions, and a visit to Switzerland is likely since he worked in liaison with several colonies of English expatriates. The rivers he fished after several years in exile were the Thames and the Ash, since the Bishop of London granted him special fishing rights in Hertfordshire, yet earlier experiences near Huntingdon Bridge and Saint Ives along the pastoral Ouse are easily

ALEXANDER NOWELL

possible. The troublesome warden could have served in the London parish where this candidate for authorship of *The Arte of Angling* was also an official. Bentley concludes that the author had written before, had wide education and experience, and was so well-known in terms of angling that his portrait at Brasenose College in Oxford includes his fishing tackle—his candidate for the authorship of the little *Arte of Angling* is no less than Alexander Nowell, Dean of Saint Paul's Cathedral in London.

Walton fails to mention *The Arte of Angling* in his *Compleat Angler*, although we have irrefutable evidence that he made extensive use of its text in his first edition, and unblushingly borrowed its dialogue structure between Piscator and Viator. However, Walton does mention Nowell himself, describing Nowell as the model of an outstanding figure who exemplifies the contemplative sport:

> The first is Doctor Nowel, sometime Dean of the Cathedral Church of Saint Paul's in London, where his monument stands yet undefaced: a man that in the reformation of Queen Elizabeth (not that of Henry VIII) was so noted for his meek spirit, deep learning, prudence, and piety, that the then Parliament and convocation both, chose, enjoined and trusted him to be the man to make a catechism for public use, such a one as should stand as a rule for faith and manners to their posterity.
>
> And the good old man (though he was very learned, yet knowing that God leads us not to heaven by many nor by hard questions), like an honest angler, made that good, plain, unperplexed catechism, which is printed with our good service-book.
>
> I say, this good old man was a dear lover and constant practicer of angling, as any age can produce: and his custom was to spend, besides his fixed hours of prayer (those hours which, by command of the church, were enjoined the clergy, and voluntarily dedicated to devotion by many primitive Christians), I say, beside those hours, this good man was observed to spend a tenth part of his time in angling; and also (for I have conversed with those who conversed with him) to bestow a tenth part of his revenue, and usually all his fish, amongst the poor that inhabited near to those rivers in which it was caught; saying often that charity gave life to religion; and that on return to his house, would praise God he had spent that day free from worldly trouble; both harmlessly, and in recreation that became a churchman.
>
> And this good man was well content, if not desirous, that posterity should know that he was an angler; as may appear by his picture, now to be seen freely, and carefully kept, in Brazen-Nose College (to which he was a liberal benefactor), in which picture he was drawn, leaning on a desk, with his Bible before him, and on one hand of him his lines, hooks and other tackling lying in a round; and on his other hand are his

angle-rods of several sorts: and by them this is written, "That he died 13 February 1601, being aged 95 years, 44 of which he had been Dean of Saint Paul's Church; and that his age had neither impaired his hearing, nor dimmed his eyes, nor weakened his memory, nor made any of the faculties of his mind weak and useless." 'Tis said that angling and temperance were great causes of this blessing, and I wish the like to all who imitate him, and love the memory of so good a man.

Another clergyman was proposed as the author of *The Arte of Angling* when Thomas Harrison discovered a reference to such a fishing book in *The History of Serpents*, which was published by Edward Topsell in 1608. Professor Harrison had stumbled upon a brief description of fly dressing in Topsell, and it seems curious that Walton mentions the same Topsell passage in his first edition of *The Compleat Angler*, almost a half-century later. The principal clue lies in *The History of Serpents*, buried in this passage:

> Such times use a caterpillared hook, which kinde of fishing fraude, if you should be better instructed in, I must refer you to a little book dedicated to Robert Dudley, the late Earl of Leicester, written by Master Samuel Vicar, of Godmanchester in Hunting-donshire.

Harrison soon explored the records of the Marian Exiles, and the public registry of Huntingdonshire, for the little-known Samuel Vicar mentioned in Topsell and his *History of Serpents*. His success was frustrated until he suddenly realized that his secret might also lie buried in the clerical parish records of Godmanchester.

With that sudden epiphany, Harrison discovered a surprising amount of information about William Samuel, who had served as the vicar at the Church of Saint Mary in Godmanchester for many years. His name was sometimes spelled Samwell and Samuell, and the vicar had lived among the Marian Exiles in Geneva. His parish house at Godmanchester still stands only a few miles from Saint Ives, just as passages in *The Arte of Angling* suggested, and the parish records demonstrate that Samuel fled to Switzerland in 1556. The second volume of *The Victoria History of the Counties of England* tells us that the vicarage of Godmanchester included land-holdings, vicarial tithing-rights, and two residences. William Samuel apparently served as the vicar at Saint Mary's in Godmanchester between 1550 and 1556, and joined the expatriate congregation that formed in Switzerland around John Knox.

Returning from Geneva in 1559, Samuel was both reinstated as vicar in Godmanchester and appointed to the rectory at Eynesbury. Samuel also received a royal appointment to the board of the Queen Elizabeth Free Grammar School in 1561, and it is quite likely that the vicar was presented to the monarch when she visited Huntingdonshire three years later.

Professor Harrison describes William Samuel as a well-known country clergyman, rather than a fully educated university-trained mind, but argues that his vicar was unmistakably able and widely read. Gerald Eades Bentley earlier suggested that the anonymous author who wrote *The Arte of Angling* displayed such skill that he must have written other books. Just as the distinguished Doctor Nowell prepared the well-known Protestant Catechism, William Samuel published several works on theological matters, including his *Abridgement of all the Canonical Books of the Olde Testament*, published in 1569. Samuel apparently died in 1580, just three years after *The Arte of Angling* was printed at the Fleetstreate shop of Henrie Middleton.

However, neither Gerald Eades Bentley nor Thomas Harrison has offered us incontrovertible proof for the authorship of *The Arte of Angling*, since Edward Topsell failed to identify the fishing book he attributed to the vicar of Godmanchester. Literary history is filled with such puzzles, and Arnold Gingrich discussed the disputed origins of *The Arte of Angling* with me a few months before his death.

Professor Harrison seems to have advanced the best case for authorship thus far, Gingrich observed wryly over lunch at the Theodore Gordon Flyfishers, *and it seems that fishing has its own Shakespeare-Bacon quarrel!*

It is also interesting that Alexander Nowell is mentioned at some length in *The Compleat Angler*, while no mention is made of his having written a book on fishing. The evidence that Walton knew and made extensive use of *The Arte of Angling* is unmistakable, and such evidence can be interpreted in two ways, depending on our degree of doubt and suspicion. Walton could have failed to mention *The Arte of Angling* in his brief history of Alexander Nowell because Nowell did not write it, but perhaps he omitted mentioning it because his debt to Nowell was painfully large.

Walton still remains a giant, and his disciples and admirers should not jettison their hero simply because he did not invent his *Compleat Angler* out of whole cloth. The perspective of history should teach us that none of our heroes ever forges his art using an entirely empty canvas.

The pastoral countryside of seventeenth-century England lives again in Walton and his *Compleat Angler*, with all the rich detail of landscape paintings by Constable, and nothing of that quality lies in Nowell or the other fishing books that came before. Walton's work is filled with soft breezes riffling the surface of his rivers, glittering silver in the summer mornings, and the busy marketplaces of the villages and towns. Through Walton's pages we meet fishermen like Sir Henry Wotton, the poet and provost of Eton College, and the almost legendary poet John Donne, who was both a fine angler and the Vicar of Saint Dunstan's Church near Walton's house in Fleet Street. Walton fishes with a worm and a minnow to secure a brace of trout for supper, and he asks us to watch a silver shower of rain falling softly through summer sunlight, and to smell the sweetness of the earth and its meadows. There is the coolness of spreading beeches beside

JOHN DONNE

the river, the peace of listening to bird music in the branches, and watching the spring lambs happily at play in the grass. Walton loved poetry and song almost as well as angling, and at one point Piscator and Viator search out a herdswoman and her milkmaid daughter to have them sing the familiar songs of Christopher Marlowe and Sir Walter Raleigh.

The historical stature of Walton does not lie in the fishing methods he outlined, or merely in the qualities of literary structure and form in *The Compleat Angler*, but in its pastoral mood and themes of contemplative sport. Walton was obviously a master fisherman in terms of tactics and equipment, but his true genius lies in his understanding that fishing is infinitely more than catching fish and his singular ability to express its gentle philosophy.

Walton was born late in the sixteenth century, at a village near Stafford where his father was the innkeeper. It was a gently rolling English countryside, with the wild moorlands lying in the north, and a lyric time to grow up and fish rivers like the Trent and the Sow. It was a world that would ultimately be sacrificed in the Industrial Revolution, its charming villages scarred with factories and collieries and kilns. Many of his boyhood rivers soon became running sewers.

Walton's early years were not entirely happy. His father died tragically when he was only four, his mother subsequently remarried, and Walton was seemingly apprenticed to a London ironmongery. His apprenticeship went well and he apparently prospered, since at about twenty-five, Walton married Rachel Floud in London. His wife was a descendant of Archbishop Cranmer, one of the principal churchmen under Henry VIII who was martyred in the bloody reign of Mary I. Marriage into such a distinguished family indicates that Walton had achieved both moderate wealth and status in London after a surprisingly brief time.

Rachel Floud bore him seven children, but none survived beyond its infancy, and she herself died in 1640. Seven years passed before Walton married Anne Ken, the half sister of the distinguished Thomas Ken who ultimately became Bishop of Bath and Wells, during the Restoration of Charles II. History records little about Anne Walton, but she produced three children and Walton often wrote warmly about her loving character. Two of their children survived, the son ultimately becoming the canon of Salisbury Cathedral, and the daughter marrying Doctor William Hawkins, who became canon of the somber cathedral at Winchester.

Their London house was a charming timber-framed structure with intricate leaded windows in Fleet Street, not far above the Chancery Lane in Saint Dunstan's Parish. John Donne was Vicar of Saint Dunstan's and already a famous poet, and it was perhaps through Donne that Walton became a member of a literary circle that included Sir Henry Wotton, John Hales of Eton College, the river poet Michael Drayton, and the famous playwright Ben Jonson.

The bitter climate of religious warfare and persecution still smouldered through England, but although Walton was a Royalist with Protestant leanings, the widespread strife did not touch his family directly. His character caused him to abhor the destruction of the monasteries and churches, like the burning of the Fountains Abbey in Yorkshire or the wanton smashing of magnificent stained-glass windows and statuary at Ely, in the Chapel of Our Lady, simply because they were Catholic. When bitter civil war exploded in 1642, Walton had already accumulated a modest fortune that enabled him to retire to Staffordshire. Walton was fifty years old, and he spent his remaining forty years fishing, writing and revising *The Compleat Angler*.

There was one adventurous moment of espionage in his life. It came during the writing of his masterpiece, after the Royalists were decisively beaten at Worcester in 1651. Robert Milward was a close friend of Walton, perhaps even a minor relative through his wife's family, and Milward received the clandestine assignment of protecting an especially valuable

Walton's Norington Farme in Hampshire

jeweled ring belonging to the royal family. The baggage of Charles II had fallen into Cromwellian hands after Worcester, but a daring Royalist officer had been able to save the ring, known as the Lesser George. The officer took refuge in the Blore Pipe House near Eccleshall, leaving the ring with its proprietor. The proprietor got the ring secretly to Robert Milward, who in turn passed it briefly to Walton for safekeeping in London.

Meanwhile, the Royalist officer who had originally recovered the Lesser George was imprisoned in the Tower of London. It was a perilous situation, since it was that officer who was ultimately intended to receive the Lesser George again from Walton. His escape was finally arranged, Walton contrived to get the ring into his hands, and it was smuggled out of the country to France, where Charles II had fled after his crushing defeat at Worcester. It was a brief episode that could have cost Walton his life, had the Royalist intrigues been exposed.

The closing years of his life were quieter. Walton moved to Norington

Farme at Hampshire in the south of England, living above Stockbridge near his only daughter and her husband. With his son, the canon at Salisbury Cathedral a few miles west in Wiltshire, Walton unquestionably fished the classic chalkstreams of the region—the Avon above Salisbury, the storied Test at Stockbridge, and the smooth-flowing Itchen farther east at Winchester.

Anne Walton had died in 1662, and was buried in the floor of Worcester Cathedral, with an epitaph lovingly composed by Walton and carved into the granite cover. It is very much like them both:

> Here lyeth buryed soe much as
> could dye, of ANNE the wife of
> IZAAK WALTON
> who was
> a woman of remarkable prudence
> and of the Primitive Piety: her great
> and general knowledge being adorned
> with such true humility and blest
> with soe much Christian meekness, as
> made her more worthy of a more memorable
> Monument
> She dyed (Alas that she is dead!)
> the 17th of Aprill 1662 aged 52
> Study to be like her

Walton had become extremely close to Doctor George Morley, who was the Bishop of Worcester, where Anne Walton was buried. Walton first knew Morley when he was canon of Christchurch at Oxford, but he was expelled from his canonry in the religious quarrels at the middle of the seventeenth century.

It is believed that Morley once took refuge with Walton at Staffordshire, remaining for about a year. Their lifelong friendship was apparently forged there, and with the Restoration of Charles II to the throne, Morley was made dean of Christchurch at Oxford. Shortly after that appointment, Dean Morley also became the Bishop of Worcester. It was apparently during a visit with Bishop Morley that Anne Walton became ill and died, and this is the reason for her interment in the cathedral there.

Morley was appointed the Bishop of Winchester not long after her death, and invited Walton to share his home there. Walton accepted and went to live at Winchester, with occasional trips back to London and Farnham Castle, the episcopal residence of Bishop Morley. The time that Walton spent at his own Norington Farme was mostly limited to fishing. His correspondence places Walton at Farnham Castle on Christmas of 1678, and his last journey from Winchester was also to Farnham. That journey came in the spring of 1683, and there is no record of another trip anywhere. There are passages in *The Compleat Angler* in which Walton captures his English springtime:

I could sit there quietly; and looking on the water, see some fishes sport themselves in the silver streams, others leaping at flies of several shapes and colours; looking on the hills I could behold them spotted with woods and groves; looking down the meadow I could see, here a boy gathering lilies and ladysmocks, and there a girl cropping culverkens and cowslips, all to make garlands suitable to this present month of May.

Later that summer Walton reached ninety years, and on his birthday he decided to make his will. It was to occupy a week of writing, and was executed in his own hand with a number of erasures. The will was signed, sealed and witnessed on October 24, 1683, with an extensive codicil listing his beneficiaries. Walton fell seriously ill in late autumn, and was taken to stay with his daughter and her husband, who still served as the canon of Winchester Cathedral. The illness grew steadily worse, and Walton finally died on December 15, 1683, having reached slightly more than ninety years, with a long and richly filled life.

His burial took place in Winchester Cathedral, in Prior Silkstead Chapel, a sheltered corner in that brooding richly carved church. Its enclosure lies behind an elegant Gothic screen, with a tomb of Corinthian columns and Gothic arches, encrusted with carvings of stone lions and the saints. Walton was buried beneath the smooth stone floor of the chapel, his narrow crypt covered with a heavy slab of granite. The master fishing writer of *The Compleat Angler* was dead, his epitaph carved into the polished timeworn stone—its final line in Latin telling us that his faithful disciples mourn with their modest prayers.

Here resteth the Body of
MR. ISAAC WALTON
Who dyed the 15th of December
1683
Alas he's gone before
Gone to returne no more!
Our panting Breasts aspire
After their aged Sire,
Whose well spent life did last,
Full ninety years and past
But now he hath begun
That which will ne're be done
Crown'd with eternall blysse:
We wish our souls with his.

Votis modestis sic flerunt liberi

For observations on sources influencing Walton, see Afterword.

5. Charles Cotton and the Roots of Modern Fly-Fishing

The Renaissance fishing house is still there. Its warm masonry walls, stone-arched door and sandstone quoins are richly weathered with time. The little house stands in a circle of trees planted in a geometric enclosure, echoing in a rudimentary way the fashionable landscape planning of the late seventeenth century. Its purpose is simple, yet its formal cruciform plan is nothing less than Palladian, clearly demonstrating that its builder was a gentleman of taste.

There are heavy rust-colored shutters. Through the leaded windows anglers have been observed on the Fishing House Pool for centuries. The slates are dark with moss on the steep, pyramid-shaped roof, its apex topped with a sphere and a trout-shaped weathervane.

The sandstone steps are worn with the fishing boots of almost three hundred seasons. The simple iron-grate fireplace is flanked with staghorn trophies. There are yellow cornflowers under the windows and buttercups in the grassy lawn that reaches less than one hundred feet to the river. It is a peaceful place that seems almost suspended in time. The lawn has a round, sandstone table set on a pillarlike base, where the fishermen could sit studying the river for rising trout, dressing flies and fussing absently with other tackle.

It was built by the celebrated Charles Cotton of Beresford Hall. It is not difficult in this setting to imagine Cotton tying a delicate fur-bodied dun at the stone table, working with wings of mallard and a dark dubbing on yellow silk. The little house was completed in the time when Walton regularly visited Cotton at Beresford, and they must have rested at the round table, sharing a springhouse-cold ale, while watching the smooth currents and talking of their sport. There were always fish working to sporadic hatches, lithe grayling and fine bright-spotted trout porpoising softly to the fluttering little mayflies. It is a gentle river here, and its pianissimo music is mixed with the calling of doves and meadowlarks. There were certainly scraps of laughter, since Cotton was renowned for his ribaldry, pornographic verses, and spontaneous wit. Although the pious Walton undoubtedly blushed at times, he must have laughed heartily too, since this fishing companion of poets and bishops was certainly no tight-lipped Puritan.

Considering our knowledge of their characters, the close friendship between Walton and the younger Cotton seems improbable. Some historians have expressed distaste for the Rabelaisian life attributed to Cotton, and have argued that angling was the only thing he could have held in common with the saintly Walton; but such historians have chosen to ignore Walton's parallel reputation for long evenings over food and drink with his literary friends. Some of them were clergymen, but others were legendary for their carousing, and even the celebrated John Donne was known for a life that mixed poetry and theology with a happily misspent youth. It was Donne who wrote these famous lines of verse:

> Come live with me and be my love,
> And we will some new pleasures prove
> Of golden sands and crystal brooks,
> With silken lines and silver hooks.

There is tangible evidence of the friendship between Walton and Cotton in the arched doorway of the fishing house on the river above

Charles Cotton's fishing house at Beresford Hall

Beresford Hall. Its keystone is incised with the initials of both men, in a handsome symmetry of letters interlocking in the sandstone. There was also a handsomely carved metope with *Piscatoribus sacrum 1674*, set on the ochre-colored lintel above the entrance. Both men loved the fishing house and the river, and the richly pastoral mood of its Derbyshire valley.

The river they shared was the jewellike Dove. Like the classic rivers of southern England, the Dove is born in the cretaceous, springhead fissures of the Derbyshire hills. It is a region of rolling foothill countryside, still covered with forests and scarred with high-walled gorges. Its rivers are fertile and productive, gathering the subterranean flowages of springs and limestone caverns. The source of the Dove is just such a bubbling spring, a few miles above Ashbourne Church, and is described in *The Compleat Angler* as little larger than a sweeping cavalier's hat. These headwaters are dark with bottom algae and mossy ledges, like most of the Derbyshire rivers, although the Dove runs gin-clear below its giant springs a few miles from Beresford Hall. Cotton loved its valley and described it with these lines:

> Oh! My beloved nymph! Fair Dove,
> Princess of sweet rivers, how I love
> Upon thy flowery banks to lie,
>   And view thy silver stream,
>   When gilded by the summer's beam,
> And in it all thy wanton fry
>   Playing at their liberty;
>   And with my artful, feathered fly
>   The all of subtle treachery
> I ever learn'd to practice and to try!

Charles Cotton enters the history of fly-fishing and its literature in 1676. When Walton published the sixth edition of his *Compleat Angler*, it included a second book titled *Being Instructions How to Angle for a Trout or Grayling in a Clear Stream*, and its author was Charles Cotton of Beresford. Legend tells us that his appendix was written in ten short days, yet its competence and thoroughness and its list of original fly patterns have unquestionably enshrined Cotton as the father of modern fly-fishing.

Cotton was a member of the landed gentry, his parents having come from the most respected families in both Derbyshire and Staffordshire. He was born at Beresford Hall along the Dove, and details of his youth are rather vague, just as little is known of the young Walton in Staffordshire. However, Cotton was of nobler birth, and we know something about his father from passages in the autobiography of Lord Clarendon. It is also known that the character and the chronology throughout the lives of both Cottons were similar. Charles Cotton was certainly a gentleman of considerable property and fortune, and was so well-educated and handsome that he was widely considered the finest landowner in Derbyshire.

His flowing wit and conversation were envied, and his knowledge of literature and the civilized world were apparently remarkable, although he

CHARLES COTTON

had actually failed to complete his studies at Cambridge. His contemporaries observed that his Cambridge years plus the company of truly-edu-
cated scholars and extensive travels in France gave considerable polish and
force to his discussions; yet this facility gave many the impression that his
knowledge of literature was greater than it actually was. Perhaps this
judgement was accurate, but it is equally possible that it was merely rooted
in provincial jealousies. Cotton was the sort of man who was always in the
center of things, and his character sometimes evoked strong feelings.
Companions who knew Cotton well loved him for his cultivation and wit,
his exceptional humor, and the delightful spectrum of his conversation.
Cotton was equally at home with the peasantry of Derbyshire, the
cloistered life at Cambridge, and the intellectual posturing found in both
London literary circles and the royal court. However, his youth also had its
ribald character, and Cotton was not unfamiliar with the earthier pleasures
available to a gentleman of his cleverness and wealth after the Restoration
of Charles II.

His adult character evolved a sharper side too, quarrelsome and quick
to anger, although his fearlessness and sense of fairness were unquestioned.
His temper and his courage often combined to cause trouble, and Cotton
was sometimes angry and impatient with men who failed to grasp what was
obvious to him. It has also been observed that his youth, especially in the
collaboration with Walton, went much better than his later years.

History tells us that Ralph Dawson tutored Cotton in his early years, a
fragment of his biography confirmed in Cotton's dedication to his *Poems on
Several Occasions* of 1689. Cotton was apparently accomplished in Latin and
Greek and also had an excellent working knowledge of French and Italian.
There is evidence that he had loved books and written poetry from
boyhood, although none of his work was published until after the
Restoration. Poetry apparently ran in his family, which boasted other
minor poets like Richard Lovelace and Sir Aston Cockayne.

Cotton married at twenty-six, taking his cousin Isabella Hutchinson as
his bride in 1656. His wife was the daughter of Sir Thomas Hutchinson,
and the marriage was apparently happy enough, although the death of his
father two years later had considerable impact on Cotton. His public career
started in 1660, with a prose panegyric celebrating Charles II on his
coronation. He had earlier written unpublished elegies on the death of Lord
Hastings and the tragic execution of the Earl of Derby. Cotton published
his popular *Scarronides*, a vigorous burlesque subtitled *The First Book of Virgil
Travestie*, in 1664. It was typical of the theatrical wit of his time, and its mild
pornography sold through fourteen editions. Its success led Cotton to devote
most of his time to writing, more to fill the boredom he often experienced in
the months when there was no fishing on his Derbyshire water rather than
for the profit in his work.

Isabella Cotton died in 1670, leaving three sons and five daughters at
Beresford. Cotton had recently published a translation of *The Moral
Philosophy of the Stoics*, and he buried his grief in a subsequent translation of

Gerard's *History of the Life of the Duke of Espervon*, which he dedicated to the Archbishop of Canterbury.

Cotton married again after five years, taking as his wife the daughter of Sir William Russell, the widow of the Earl of Ardglass. His critics have intimated that this marriage was made to bolster his assets, since both father and son had squandered the Cotton fortune, leaving the family land-rich and money-poor. Cotton was plagued with creditors all his life, and even spent a brief time in a debtors' prison.

Walton had grown up in nearby Staffordshire, and returned to purchase a country place there at Shallowford in 1642. Charles Cotton was then only twelve years old, but already a familiar figure on the trout beats of the Manifold and the Derwent and the Dove. There is evidence that their friendship had its roots in those early summers, and that Cotton's skills at fly-fishing were well known to the older Walton long before their collaboration in the sixth edition of *The Compleat Angler* in 1676. It was certainly an old friendship, and Cotton dedicated these lines of *Contentation* to the man he called Father Walton:

> 'Tis contentation that alone
> Can make us happy here below,
> And when this little life is gone,
> Will lift us up to heav'n too.
>
> Who from the busy world retires
> To be more useful to it still,
> And to no greater good aspires,
> But only the eschewing ill.
>
> Who with his angle and his books
> Can think the longest day well spent,
> And praises God when back he looks,
> And finds that all was innocent.
>
> Untrodden paths are then the best,
> Where the frequented seem unsure,
> And he comes soonest to his rest,
> Whose journey has been most secure.

Cotton continued his minor literary career at Beresford, while Mary Cotton managed the household. Their monetary problems continued, and twice Cotton was forced to petition Parliament for permission to sell portions of his estates. He had completed a translation of Corneille's *Les Horaces* in 1671, along with a less successful burlesque based upon an imaginary voyage to Ireland. During the next three years there were translations of the commentaries of Blaise de Montluc, Marshal of France, and a series of minor French novels. The book of amusements titled *The Compleat Gamester* has also been attributed to Charles Cotton, and it was published in 1673.

The superb volume on the cultivation of orchards titled *The Planter's Manual* was published by Cotton two years later. The little fishing house beside the Dove was started in 1674, and during preparation of his sixth edition of *The Compleat Angler*, Walton asked Cotton to contribute a treatise on fly-fishing for trout and grayling—the aspect of British fishing that Walton understood least.

Cotton himself tells us that he completed *Being Instructions How to Angle for a Trout or Grayling in a Clear Stream* in only ten days. The manuscript was hastily dispatched to Walton, and their joint edition of *The Compleat Angler* was published in London in 1676. The fishing house on the river above Beresford Hall had been completed two years earlier, and Cotton describes it in these dialogues:

Viator: 'Tis a delicate morning, indeed; and now I think this is a marvelous pretty place.

Piscator: Whether you think so or no, you cannot oblige me more than to say it; and those of my friends who know my humor, and are so kind as to comply with it, usually flatter me that way. But look you, sir, now you are at the brink of the hill, how do you like my little river, the vale it winds through like a snake, and the situation of my little fishing house.

Viator: Trust me, 'tis all very fine, and the house at this distance seems a neat building.

Piscator: Good enough for that purpose; and here is a bowling green too, close by it; so, though I am myself no very good bowler, I am not totally devoted to my own pleasure; but that I have also some regard to other men's. And now, sir, you are come to the door, pray walk in, and there we will sit and talk as long as you please.

Viator: Stay, what's here over the door? *Piscatoribus sacrum.* Why then, I perceive I have some title here; for I am one of them, though one of the worst; and here below it is the cypher too, you speak of, and 'tis prettily contrived. Has my Master Walton ever been here to see it, for it seems new built?

Piscator: Yes, he saw it cut in the stone before it was set up; but never in the posture it now stands; for the house was but building when he was last here, and not raised so high as the arch of the door. And I am afraid he will not see it yet; for he has lately writ me word that he doubts he is coming this summer; which, I do assure you, was the worst news he could possibly have sent me.

Viator: Men must sometimes mind their affairs to make more room for their pleasures; and 'tis odds he is as much displeased with the business that keeps him from you, as you are that he comes not. But I am most pleased with this little house of any thing I ever saw: it stands in a kind of peninsula too, with the delicate clear river flowing about it. I dare hardly go in, lest I should not like it so well within as without; but, by your leave, I'll try. Why, this is better and better, fine lights, fine wainscoted, and all exceeding neat, with a marble table and all in the middle.

These dialogues lack the disarmingly simple moods of Walton, although they are skillfully copied on his structure and style. They are jammed with information about the rivers of the district, tackle and tactics, strategies for trout and grayling in several reaches of the Dove, observations on the fishing inns and churchtowers and villages nearby, fly dressing and entomology and fly patterns, and everything from the strength of the horsehair tippets in Derbyshire to the quality of French wines available at the Peacock Inn in Rowsley, where the Dove flows into the larger Derwent. It is the first modern treatise on fly-fishing.

Richard Le Gallienne argues, in his superb edition of *The Compleat Angler*, that the mood and style affected by Cotton in his dialogues for *Being Instructions How to Angle for a Trout or Grayling in a Clear Stream* border on the impertinence of parody. Other angling historians have voiced similar viewpoints, but I doubt that Cotton would have indulged himself in any manner that might have damaged his older friend. Cotton conceived his dialogues with such facility and skill, especially considering that they were written in ten short days, that they come surprisingly close to Walton's style—but I am convinced that this was a gesture of friendship and respect, an attempt to accommodate his later appendix on fly-fishing to the mood and character of the earlier *Compleat Angler*.

The expository skill of condensing so much knowledge into a structural form of an earlier book is remarkable. Its comprehensive treatment of fly-fishing practice both codified everything on the subject since Aelianus, and added a surprising cornucopia of personal knowledge. Its passages are filled with observations about places on the river that still exist today, like the slender monolith of stone that rises from the still current at the storied Pike Pool and the mossy stepping stones that cross the river on the hotel water of the charming Izaak Walton, which still houses anglers on a gentle rise of ground above the water meadows where the Dove and the tumbling Manifold meet.

There is no question that Charles Cotton expertly imitated the style of the older Walton in his dialogues, and that he did it far better than countless other imitators who are best forgotten. But to condemn his dialogues as an impertinence or outright parody is perhaps too austere, and would undoubtedly have triggered hearty laughter and another river-chilled ale between Walton and Cotton along the river.

The dialogues of *Being Instructions How to Angle for a Trout or Grayling in a Clear Stream* are somewhat stiff and wooden, especially following the spontaneity and evocative charm of *The Compleat Angler*. It is particularly intriguing that the free-living Cavalier who squandered the wealth of his Beresford inheritance wrote in such a conservative purse-lipped style—a prose infinitely tighter and more self-conscious than the style of the more pious Walton.

Cotton uses the same characters and story line that Nowell seemingly invented in *The Arte of Angling* and that Walton reworked in the first edition of his masterpiece. Piscator is transformed into a skilled fly-fisher from Derbyshire, and meets Viator on horseback along the Brailesford Road. Their conversation opens with pleasantries about the bright spring weather and the surprising scale of the mountainous hills.

> Piscator: So, sir, now we have got to the top of the hill out of town, look about you, and tell me you like the country.
> Viator: Bless me, but what mountains are here! Are we not in Wales?

There is the amusing scene of stopping for ale, since the morning is unseasonably warm, and drinking it still on horseback outside the fishing inn at Talbot. Both men enjoy the company and the conversation, and the traveller agrees to stay with his new-found friend instead of in his room at the Black's Head hostelry. Like most enthusiastic anglers, the fisherman cannot resist talking and talking about his favorite sport, even though his captive audience is clearly an unbeliever.

Fly-fishing is filled with a number of basic truths, and Cotton was the first to articulate several of them. Although his knowledge of aquatic biology was rudimentary and totally mistaken in some instances of entomology, he was far better than most authorities of his time. Some years ago, it was widely believed that only Taverner, in his *Certaine Experiments Concerning Fish and Fruite*, was aware that aquatic insects hatched from nymphal forms in the river. It was a popular viewpoint that led me to observe in my recent book *Nymphs* that Cotton knew little about subaquatic entomology, and that most of his knowledge—like the belief that both mayflies and stoneflies hatch from caddis worms and creepers—was often mistaken at best.

Yet Cotton did realize that fly hatches came from the larval forms in the river bottom, and described them more accurately than anyone else had, from Aristotle to Walton. These passages from his *Wonders of the Peake* are some evidence of that awareness:

> The silver Dove! How pleasant is that name!
> Runs through a vale high-crested cliffs o'er shade
> By her fair progress much more pleasant made;

But with so swift a torrent in her course
As spurs the nymph, flies from her native source
To seek what's there deny'd, the sun's warm beams,
And to embrace Trent's prouder, swelling streams.

Cotton believed in matching the hatch, and outlined a list of sixty-five original fly patterns for the entire season on the Dove. He fished these wet flies across and downstream, often dapping them over a fish from the streamside alders, but he also advocated fishing upstream with the direction of a strong, surface-rippling wind. Cotton was obviously a skillful fly dresser—although he credits his Derbyshire neighbor, Captain Henry Jackson, with being best fly tier in the region—and his words about fly tying are surprisingly modern:

In making a fly hook then, you are first to hold your hook fast betwixt the fore-finger and thumb of your left hand, with the back of the shank upwards, and the point toward your finger's end; then take a strong small silk, of the colour of the fly you intend to make, wax it well with wax of the same colour too, and draw it betwixt your finger and thumb, to the head of the shank, and then whip it twice or thrice about the bare hook, which you must know is done, both to prevent slipping, and also that the shank of the hook may not cut the hairs of your towght, which sometimes it will otherwise do; which being done, take your line, and draw it likewise betwixt your finger and thumb, holding the hook so fast as only to suffer it to pass by, until you have the knot of your towght almost to the middle of the shank of your hook, on the inside of it; then whip your silk twice or thrice about both hook and line as hard as the strength of silk will permit; which being done, strip the feather for the wings proportionable to the bigness of your fly, placing that side downwards which grew uppermost before, upon the back of the hook, leaving so much only as to serve for the length of the wing of the point of the plume, lying reversed from the end of the shank upwards; then whip your silk twice or thrice about the root-end of the feather, hook, and towght; which being done, clip off the root-end of the feather close by the arming, and then whip the silk fast and firm about the hook and towght, until you come to the bend of the hook, but not further; which, being done, cut away the end of your towght, and fasten it, and then take your dubbing, which is to make the body of your fly, as much as you think convenient, and holding it lightly with your hook betwixt the finger and thumb of your left hand, take your silk with the right, and twisting it betwixt the finger and thumb of that hand, the dubbing will spin itself about the silk, which when it has done, whip it about the armed hook backward, 'til you come to the setting on of the wings, and then take the feather for the wings, and divide it equally into two parts, and turn them back towards the bend of the hook, the one on the one side and the other on the other of the shank, holding them fast in that posture betwixt the fore-finger and thumb of your left hand; which done, warp them down so as to stand and slope towards the bend of the hook; and having warped up to the end of the shank, hold the fly fast betwixt the finger and thumb of your left hand, and then take the silk betwixt the finger and thumb of your right hand, and where the warping ends, pinch or nip it with your thumb-nail against your finger, and strip away the remainder of your dubbing from the silk, and then with the bare silk whip it once or twice about, make the wings to stand in due order, fasten, and cut it off; after which, with the point of a needle, raise up the dubbing gently from the warp, twitch off the superfluous hairs of your dubbing; leave the wings of an equal length (your fly will never else swim true) and the work is done.

The meticulous detail, sound theory and outright wisdom of these words on fly dressing are striking, since they are almost three centuries old. His advice about fly dressing is virtually as modern as the opinions of writers as modern as Stewart and Leisenring and Skues, and his advice on stream tactics is timeless. He liked the rods made farther north in Yorkshire, fashioned of strip fir and lancewood sections, since they could handle the relatively delicate tackle needed for the shy fish of his beats. His lines were tapered of braided horsehair, with two strands at the fly and some six or seven strands at the rod tip. Cotton argues candidly that a man who cannot take a trout of twenty inches on a two-strand horsehair tippet does not deserve the name of angler. And with his dictum on fishing a fine horsehair with long casts—the classic axiom of fishing fine and far-off—Charles Cotton entered the pantheon of fly-fishing immortals with the principal rule of fishing trout and grayling.

Although Cotton is the primary bench mark of fly-fishing literature in the entire seventeenth century, there were other writers who worked in this period between Walton, Cotton and the Bowlkers more than half a century later. The books of Franck, Venables and Cox, as well as the French *Les Ruses Innocentes*, emerged between Walton and Cotton. Chetham is the final important voice of the seventeenth century, and his *Angler's Vade Mecum* was published in 1681.

The eighteenth century began with Howlett, included several French texts like the *Amusements de la Campagne* and the classic *Traitte de Toute Sorte de Chasse et de Pêche* of 1714, and proceeded through the subsequent books of Gay, Saunders, and Brookes before *The Arte of Angling* introduced Bowlker to fly-fishing readers at midcentury. Thomas Best and his *Concise Treatise on the Art of Angling*, and Shirley's *The Angler's Museum* conclude the eighteenth century.

Captain Richard Franck was a Cromwellian soldier like Thomas Barker, and although his *Northern Memoirs* was not published until 1694 it was written in 1658, barely five years after Walton had published his masterpiece. Franck was a less than distinguished writer, but was obviously a skilled and experienced fly-fisherman. His prose became the despair of Sir Walter Scott, who published a subsequent edition of Franck, and John Waller Hills, the author of *A History of Fly-Fishing for Trout*—both awarded him the all-time championship for turgidity.

Franck is chiefly remembered for his strange animosity toward Walton, which seems composed in equal parts of jealousy, politics, and the pious superiority of a fly-fishing snob toward a bait-and-hardware fisherman. Veiled in the tangled, unintelligible prose is considerable evidence that Franck might have been the father of fly-fishing for salmon, much as Cotton was the progenitor of fly-fishing for trout and grayling. Yet his description of the fishing from the storied Tweed to the swift-flowing Sutherland rivers high on the northeast coast is so muddled with moral asides and indecipherable observations on the politics of Scotland at the death of Cromwell that none of its content is clear on any subject. The whole odyssey is so badly written, Sir Walter Scott observed dryly, that angling literature would have been infinitely richer had Walton made this Scottish journey instead of Franck—and what we might have had from Walton, with his sense of place and his pastoral moods, and the innovative Cotton, with his superlative knowledge of fly-fishing, is an exciting literary speculation.

Francois Fortin published *Les Ruses Innocentes* in Paris in 1660. It is perhaps the first French work to mention rod fishing, and there were four editions before the end of the seventeenth century. Fortin was a cleric, skilled in both fishing and the several field sports. John Waller Hills argued that Fortin has echoes borrowed from either Mascall or *A Treatyse of Fysshynge wyth an Angle*. Such echoes are largely found in the discussion of rods, but *Les Ruses Innocentes* is still a work of strength and originality. It gives the first description of eyed hooks a full two centuries before Frederic Halford and Henry Hall perfected their metallurgy and manufacture. There are woodcuts of nets, traps, gigs, snares, rods, lines, and a crude spindle-stick reel, along with the triangular landing-net frame, which the good friar Fortin apparently invented centuries before the modern chalk-stream types popular in both England and France.

Colonel Robert Venables was another Cromwellian officer skilled both as a soldier and a fly-fisher. Venables' military career was long and distinguished, carrying him to Ireland in the command of a considerable expeditionary force, and later into a Caribbean campaign with a general's commission. Although his Spanish expeditions in the New World were largely a failure, Venables and his troops did finally secure Jamaica for the growing British Empire. Oliver Cromwell, however, could not accept failure of any kind, and Venables subsequently lost both his rank and his command. During the Restoration of Charles II in England, Venables found his Cromwellian background a serious liability—and his premature retirement from both military and public life resulted in a first-rate book on fly-fishing that Venables published in 1662, and his *Experienced Angler* rightfully takes its place on our shelf of classics.

Venables was first to notice, in his *Experienced Angler*, that trout take some time to adjust to a new fly hatch, that they take it best late in a hatching cycle, and that they will often reject other naturals on the water. He observed that the fish might concentrate on two or three different hatches in the course of a single day, and was the first writer to mention upstream presentation, discussing the tactical differences in fishing upstream or down in surprisingly modern terms. Venables also understood that the man working upstream could approach much closer to the fish and that in fishing down the fisherman risks being seen at surprising distances. The discussions in his *Experienced Angler* explore the difficulties of wading against the current and the fact that the extra work means covering less water. Venables also discusses the variables involved in having the fly approach the fish from above, reaching it before it sees the horsehair line, and the problems of casting the fly above a fish with the tippet falling near its holding lie. Venables concluded his discussions in favor of upstream fishing on small streams and downstream fishing to cover big water—and his wisdom precedes both Stewart and the rise of the upstream school by almost two hundred years.

Venables is the first fishing writer to mention silkworm-gut tippets. In his *Experienced Angler* he writes that he had first discovered the material in use on stringed musical instruments. He also observed that it must be used quickly, since silkworm gut is fragile and rots easily. Gut tippets must have become popular rapidly, since we have this parallel evidence from the diary of Samuel Pepys in the spring of 1667:

> This day Mr. Caesar told me a pretty experiment of his angling with a minikin, a gutt-string varnished over, which keeps it from swelling, and is beyond any hair for strength and smallness. The secret I like mightily.

Nicholas Cox assembled his *Gentlemen's Recreation* in 1674, but it is little more than a summary of contemporary fishing practices, and there are none of the original insights found in the work of contemporaries like Cotton and Venables. It is *The Angler's Vade Mecum*, published by James Chetham at Smedley in 1681, that stands as the final important contribution to the fishing literature of the seventeenth century in England. Chetham was a Lancastrian flymaker, and although much of his work was borrowed from earlier writers like Cotton, it is a sensible and practical manual. The prose style is calm and clear, and its tone is a welcome change from the tedious posturing and florid character of many books that preceded it.

Chetham unblushingly pirated most of the Cotton fly patterns that had earlier appeared in *Being Instructions How to Angle for a Trout or Grayling in a Clear Stream* only five years earlier, but included his own catalogue of original patterns too. The Chetham patterns are not only keyed to the seasonal cycle of hatches but are also an advance on the Cotton list and are described along with intelligent advice on materials for fly dressing. His original patterns include the March Brown, Grannom, and the classic little Blue Dun. *The Angler's Vade Mecum* is a curious mixture of plagiarism, shrewd wisdom and practicality, original and creative thought, and a credulous belief in witchcraft—his book also recommends ointments for his baits reduced from the fat of cadavers and powdered human skulls.

Eighteenth-century angling theory had its genesis in Robert Howlett and his book *The Angler's Sure Guide*, which was published in 1706. Howlett was a skilled wet-fly man who used multiple flies and the downstream method. Like many other writers of his time, Howlett borrowed freely from his colleagues, with enough original thought and content to give his work longevity. Howlett is filled with tactical observations that make his work worth reading still:

> If you cannot discern your flie upon the water, for more sureness, strike as soon as you perceive a fish rise within reach of your rod and line; and if you miss him, throw your flie immediately beyond him, and draw it gently over the place; if he like it, he will take it; and always carefully watch, that you may strike at the first rising of the fish, if you can; and lest you should not see when you have a rise, strike so soon as you see the line go from you; and sometime keep your flie always in a gentle motion, that a fish may hang himself though you strike not.

It was not until the early eighteenth century, late in the reign of Louis XIV, that fly-fishing unmistakably appeared in the sporting literature of France. Almost a half century had passed since Francois Fortin had written his *Les Ruses Innocentes*, when Louis Liger first published *Amusements de la Campagne* in 1709. This work was reprinted five years later in the better known *Traitte de Toute Sorte de Chasse et de Pêche*, which borrowed liberally from the earlier Fortin as well. The lovely engravings from *Les Ruses Innocentes* were also incorporated wholesale into the *Traitte*, but it included much completely new material too. There was a list of fly patterns that clearly related to fly hatches on the rivers of the continent. John Waller Hills observes in *A History of Fly-Fishing for Trout* that the secondhand character of the entire *Traitte* would indicate that these French fly dressings are also borrowed—they are definitely not English, yet we know nothing of their origins in French fishing literature.

John Gay later appeared across the English Channel with his *Rural Sports*, published at London in 1720. It was a two-volume work of pastoral verse, its best poetry devoted to fly-fishing. Gay was obviously skilled on his rivers, and although a classical style of verse seems poorly suited to the field sports, his sense of countryside and sport transcend the stilted character of eighteenth-century literature. Gay was unquestionably a fly-fisherman, judging from these lines in *Rural Sports*:

Around the steel, no tortured worm shall twine,
No blood of living insect stain my line,
Let me, less cruel, cast the feathered hook,
With pliant rod 'cross pebbled brook.

John Waller Hills is perhaps correct when he suggests that this poetry is better than the river verses of Michael Drayton, Charles Cotton and John Dennys in the seventeenth century, and although its contents are erratic in quality, John Gay and his *Poems on Several Occasions, Containing Rural Sports* is well worth our attention.

James Saunders follows in our lexicon of eighteenth-century authors with his book *The Compleat Fisherman* in 1724. His work describes fishing for trout in the alpine rivers of Switzerland and the Italian Dolomite country, also mentioning the use of silkworm-gut leaders on those waters. It is apparently the debut of tapered gut in British books on fishing. Within fifty-odd years it was readily available in the London tackle shops; and it had totally replaced horsehair leaders by the threshold of the following century.

Richard Brookes and his *Art of Angling* appeared next, having been published in London in 1740. His book was a minor prelude to the Bowlkers, whose work would soon follow before midcentury, but it was important enough to rank among the best half-dozen books of the period. The author was a downstream wet-fly man, and his book would perhaps have stood higher in the literature of angling if the Bowlker book, also titled *The Art of Angling*, had not appeared soon afterward.

Richard Bowlker was a celebrated fly-fisherman from Ludlow in Shropshire, and the first edition of his book was published at Worcester. The date of first printing of *The Art of Angling* is actually unknown, but the Bodleian Library at Oxford places its approximate publication in 1747. There was a second edition in 1774, and in the third edition published six years later, his son Charles Bowlker is given as the single author. Well before his death in 1779, Charles Bowlker was considered the finest fly-fisher of the entire eighteenth century. There were sixteen editions of his books, the last published in 1854. It is a history of publication surpassed only by *The Compleat Angler* and *A Treatyse of Fysshynge wyth an Angle*—and John Waller Hills describes it as his fishing bible throughout his beginning years astream.

The excellence of *The Art of Angling* is threefold: it discusses the upstream strategy in its directions on technique; its directions on fly making are excellent; and its knowledge of fly hatches is superior to the streamcraft of earlier books. Although Charles Cotton richly deserves his place as the father of fly-fishing, it is unmistakably the work of Richard and Charles Bowlker that introduced the age of modern fly dressing. There were numerous angling books published in the eighteenth century, and certainly none was distinguished in a literary sense. However, through their sixteen editions the Bowlkers, who came from the rivers draining the pastoral hills of Shropshire, dominated both their century and half of the century that followed.

Charles Bowlker equalled and surpassed the fishing skills of his father, and his stature as the finest fly-fisherman of his century has been amply confirmed by the perspective of history. Bowlker is simple and direct in his style. His importance lies in jettisoning the mythology and debris of earlier fly-dressing practice, and in his sizable contributions to trout-stream entomology. Bowlker had no compunctions about disposing of earlier fly-making theories from Dame Juliana Berners through Cotton and Chetham, candidly listing their flies as patterns of limited usefulness, and then outlining his own catalog of thirty-odd imitations. Bowlker includes surprisingly modern versions of now-standard patterns like the Blue Dun, which James Chetham first described in a no-hackle version, and the classic little Iron Blue. Other favorites that apparently originated with Bowlker were the Cowdung, Willow Fly, Grannom, Yellow Sally, both Green and Gray Drakes, Black Gnat, Whirling Blue Dun, and Welshman's Button. Authorship of so many flies that have survived almost two centuries is an impressive feat, and the following passages on fly dressing are surprisingly modern:

> When you make an artificial fly, you must, in the first place, make choice of a hook of a size proportionable to the fly you intend to copy, which must be whipped on to your gut or hair in the same manner you would whip on a worm-hook; only with this difference, that instead of fastening near the bend of the hook, you must fasten your silk near the top of your shank, and let your silk remain; then, taking as much feather as is necessary for the wings, lay it even as you can upon the upper side of the shank, with the butt of the feathers downward, towards the bend of the hook, and tye it fast three or four times with the silk, and fasten it; then, with a needle or pin, divide the wings as equal as you can; then, take your silk and cross it three or four times between the wings, bringing the silk still downwards, towards the bend of the hook; then taking your hackle feather, tye it fast at the bend with the point of the hackle upwards; next, your fur on dubbing being ready, which is to make the body of your fly, take a little bit of it and twist it gently round your silk, and work it upwards to the butt of the wings, and there fasten it; then take your hackle and rib it neatly over your dubbing, and fasten it; then, bending the wings and putting them in the form you desire, bring on the butt end of your hackle towards the head, and there fasten it firmly; then, taking a bit of dubbing or fur, as near to the colour of the head of the live fly as you can, whip it twice round your silk, and then fasten it just above the wings; so your fly is completed.

Bowlker still used the reverse-wing dressing evolved in earlier centuries. His flies were slender, sparsely tied, and graceful. Their configuration clearly anticipates the true north-country style of fly dressing, sometimes ribbed with a twist of silk or a hackle. His theories advocated the use of hackles to suggest legs, but such delicately palmered fur bodies are also excellent imitations of many nymphs with well-defined gill structures.

His twenty-nine patterns, and especially the comments for fishing them, indicate the remarkable knowledge of stream entomology that Bowlker possessed. His theories clearly embraced the observation of the natural fly hatches, in terms of color, form, shape, and size. Bowlker matched the size of his prototypical insects by specifying hook sizes.

Certainly there are still echoes of Bowlker found in fly-dressing practice throughout the United Kingdom, as well as in the fashionably sparse dressings of both James Leisenring and the Catskill school of Theodore Gordon. The singular influence of the Bowlker flies was widespread. Patterns dressed at Kilbreda in Ireland about 1789 are clearly tied in the Bowlker style, and similar patterns remained fashionable in Hampshire until about 1825. Yorkshire is still renowned for its slender-bodied flies, and equally sparse dressings were found on the Tweed and the Clyde, as well as the swift-flowing Usk not far from Shropshire.

Like Bowlker, Thomas Shirley argued for the upstream presentation in his book *The Angler's Museum* of 1784. It was published in London and lasted through several editions. Shirley largely copies Bowlker, but his confirmation of the upstream presentation is intriguing. Both men argued for stalking a rising trout from below, casting about three feet above its feeding stations rather than directly to its rise forms, and letting the fly drift back naturally with the current. Their theories are clearly a prelude to Stewart sixty-odd years later, and ultimately to the revolutionary dry-fly practice of Halford and Marryat after 1875.

Thomas Best continued eighteenth-century fly-fishing literature with his *Concise Treatise on the Art of Angling* in 1787. There were thirteen editions of this book, and although Best unmistakably reverts to the downstream school of wet-fly fishing, John Waller Hills argued that he was second only to Bowlker in his role among the angling writers of the eighteenth century. His work is the principal epilogue to the century. Although other writers appeared before 1800, Best unquestionably closes the period of conceptual evolution that reaches from Cotton to Scotcher, and the subsequent nineteenth-century rise of the scientific school. Cotton, Chetham, and Bowlker had laid the foundations of modern fly-fishing, and their philosophy of matching the hatch is clearly stated in these lines from the river poetry of John Gay:

> Oft' have I seen a skilful angler try
> The several colours of his treacherous flies;
> When he, with fruitless pain hath skimmed the brook,
> And coy fish reject his teasing hook,
> He shakes the boughs that on the streamside grow,
> Which o'er the stream, a waving forest throw;

When, if an insect fall (his certain guide),
He gently picks him from the whirling tide;
Examines well his form, with curious eyes,
His gaudy vest, his wings, his tails and size.
Then 'round his hook the chosen fur he winds.
And on its back, a speckled feather binds.
Upon the rippling surface, let it glide,
With natural motions from thy hand supplied;
Against the stream, now let its feathers gently play,
Now in a rapid eddy, drift away.

6. Alfred Ronalds and the Nineteenth-Century Renaissance

Beresford Hall lies in ruins now, overgrown with trees and wildflowers and vines. Its Walton chamber with the oak-panelled walls and leaded windows and fireplace is gone, along with the richly curtained bed where the author of *The Compleat Angler* once dreamed of fly hatches on the Dove. The few remaining walls and massive stone lintels are almost lost in the copse of vines and trees that shroud its broken masonwork. It was once a graceful manor house, lying above the water meadows along the Dove with the tower of the Alstonfield church standing in the trees two miles downstream. The parish church still stands, its square belltower rising above ranks of mossy headstones and a dense cloak of surrounding trees.

Its somber nave still holds physical evidence of the time that Charles Cotton lived and fished at Beresford, for there is a richly canopied pew where Cotton and his family attended services. Tissington Hall also remains today, with the stone Renaissance vault above the basin that encloses the swiftly flowing limestone spring that gives birth to the Dove.

The Beresford fishing house still stands too. It was built by Cotton across the river from Beresford Hall itself, about a half mile upstream from the manor house. The steep-roofed fishing house has been lovingly restored, the quiet patina of its seventeenth-century architecture completely attuned to the river and its moods. Downstream from the Beresford water, where the silken currents of the Dove meet the darker tea-colored water of the Derwent, the charming Peacock Inn at Rowsley shelters anglers in our century. Its intricate brickwork chimneys and slate-covered roofs have housed generations of travellers and anglers alike. The swiftly tumbling Manifold joins the Dove below the village at Thorpe Cloud, riffling down through its gentle valley floor of hedgerows and meadows.

It is strange how history sometimes chooses past settings to stage its fresh dramas, and the landscapes that shaped Charles Cotton are virtually the same river valleys that produced the genius of Alfred Ronalds two centuries later. It is equally strange that history chose to locate the most important contributors to the nineteenth-century renaissance in British angling literature on the north-country rivers instead of choosing the famous southern rivers that have become our fly-fishing shrines.

Derbyshire is another world, a hundred miles north of London. It is the background in which Ronalds, the first major angling writer of the nineteenth century, wrote his classic *Fly-Fisher's Entomology.* Two hundred miles farther north, in the border lowlands of Scotland, we find the landscapes and swift-flowing rivers that shaped W. C. Stewart and his book *The Practical Angler,* which both extolled and codified the upstream school. These central figures in the century that followed Bowlker set the stage for both the dry-fly method and the contemporary philosophy of matching the hatch. W. C. Stewart was fishing and writing about border-country rivers like the Whitadder in the Lammermuir hills at midcentury, and Ronalds completed his classic *Fly-Fisher's Entomology* in Derbyshire in 1836. However, there were several earlier writers of importance in the same half century, and the best were men like Scotcher, Bainbridge, Carroll, and Stoddart, whose books form a prelude to the fly-fishing renaissance that started at Chepstow in 1800.

George Scotcher published his little *Fly-Fisher's Legacy* at Chepstow on the very threshold of the century. It is memorable chiefly because it was the first book to depict aquatic fly hatches in color, and there is a single puzzling reference to fishing a floating fly. The slim *Legacy* is the prelude to perhaps the most remarkable century in the history of fly-fishing. Alexander Mackintosh was the first writer to devote a work entirely to the chalkstream style of fishing, and his little *Driffield Angler* appeared in 1806, including an impressive list of imitative fly patterns. Its river setting was the fertile Driffield in Yorkshire, the most northern chalkstream in the United Kingdom.

During these same early years of the nineteenth century, Thomas Doubleday was writing some of the finest fishing verse in the language. His sonnet on fishing luck was written in 1818, and is perhaps the best of his poetry:

> Go, take thine angle, and with practiced line,
>> Light as the gossamer, the silken current sweep;
>> And if thou failest in the calm still deep
> In this rough eddy, may a prize be thine.
> Say thou'rt unlucky where the sunbeams shine;
>> Beneath the shadow, where these flowing waters creep,
>> Perchance the monarch of the brook shall leap.
>
> For fate is ever better than design
> Still persevere: the giddiest breeze that blows

> For thee may blow with fame and fortune rife;
> Be prosperous, and what care if it arose
> > Out of some pebble with the stream at strife,
> > Or that the light wind dallied with the leafy boughs?
> > Thou art successful—such is human life!

Sixteen years later, George Bainbridge published his *Fly-Fisher's Guide* at Liverpool. It is a superb fishing book, thoroughly grounded in practical stream experience, and has five comparatively good color plates of the aquatic hatches in his west-country rivers. William Carroll assembled his *Angler's Vade Mecum* in the early years of the nineteenth century, and it was ultimately published at Edinburgh in 1818. It included many color plates of flies, but their draftsmanship was so poor in quality that the fly hatches are virtually impossible to identify. Except for its patina of time, the Carroll book is only of marginal value to a serious fisherman, although its charm makes it valuable in a well-stocked library. However, these books and their color plates of flies are merely bellwethers for the work of Alfred Ronalds and his *Fly-Fisher's Entomology* in 1836.

However, before Ronalds contributed his masterpiece to the literature of the sport, there was another border fisherman in Scotland who fished and loved both the Tweed and its many tributaries. Fly-fishing prose had a considerable revival in the nineteenth century, and no writer produced better work than Thomas Stoddart of Kelso-on-Tweed.

Although he was actually born in Edinburgh fifty miles north of the Tweed, Stoddart came from an old border-country family. His superb *Art of Angling as Practised in Scotland* was published at Edinburgh in 1835, and it was the first treatise of its scope and character written there. John Waller Hills believes that Stoddart might have been a superb poet except for his preoccupation with fly-fishing, but the rhythms of his native Tweed and the character of its sport were in his blood. Its physical beauty is remarkable, and Stoddart is not alone in his love for its river country. Its moods have captured other writers too, writers as distinguished as Sir Walter Scott. Although Stoddart wrote in a fine prose style, occasionally tarnished with small absurdity or excessive sentiments about the importance of fly-fishing, it is perhaps as a Scottish dialect poet that he is best remembered:

> And Gala too, an' Teviot bright,
> > An' mony a stream o' playful speed;
> Their kindred valleys a'unite
> > Amang the braes o' bonnie Tweed!

Alfred Ronalds appeared with his brilliant *Fly-Fisher's Entomology* in 1836, only a year after Stoddart published his Scottish book at Edinburgh. Ronalds published his book in London, more than three hundred miles south of Edinburgh and Kelso-on-Tweed, but in a technical and philosophical sense there is considerably more distance between them. Ronalds was an aquatic biologist of exceptional gifts: and with his precise watercolors of

the naturals and their imitations and his accurate taxonometric identification of fly hatches, the empirical literature of fly-fishing had finally entered
the scientific age.

Ronalds lived beside and fished the classic Derbyshire rivers that had
fascinated both Walton and Cotton two centuries earlier. His fishing and
his entomological studies had carried him to most of the famous beats,
including the Peacock Inn water on the Dove and Derwent at Rowsley, the
lovely Manifold valley above Thorpe Cloud, and the Beresford mileage
with the Renaissance fishing house that Cotton had built beside the river.
Ronalds owned a fishing beat on the gentle Blythe in Staffordshire too, not
far from Creswell Station, and there he had his river laboratory and
observation platform on a little bridge. It was octagonal in design, with
viewing windows on three sides, and hung less than five feet above the
current. Each window was fitted with a curtain having a fine peephole and
commanded a regular holding lie. The stream laboratory enabled Ronalds
to make a whole catalogue of original observations about trout and their
behavior. Ronalds discovered that his fish were extremely sensitive to noise
transmitted through the water, streambank, and bridge structure, but that
loud noises transmitted solely in the atmosphere did not disturb them. His
diagrams of stream character and its effect on both holding places and
taking lies were pioneering techniques in a fishing book. His diagrams on
the refraction of light entering the river and its effects on both fishing tactics
and the vision of a trout are utterly unique for their time. Similar diagrams
have appeared in countless fishing books since, but neither subsequent
authors nor their illustrations have surpassed Ronalds in either their
precision or their understanding of the complexity of stream refraction.
Hugh Sheringham observes in his notes to the twelfth edition of *The
Fly-Fisher's Entomology*, published in 1920, that Ronalds anticipated the
disciplined research conducted almost a century later by Francis Ward at
Ipswich. Ward confirmed the work of Ronalds on the vision of trout in his
remarkable book *Animal Life under Water,* which was not published until
1919.

Ronalds also explored the subjects of taste and smell in trout, along
with their selective feeding behavior, and included some remarkable studies
on the role of ants, leafhoppers, and beetles in the trout diet. With this
work, he anticipated some of the recent findings of Vincent Marinaro that
were published in *A Modern Dry-Fly Code* almost 150 years later. Sheringham
also observes that while the chalkstream studies of writers like Halford and
Moseley have increased our knowledge of the principal British hatches, no
modern work has surpassed Ronalds' disciplined identification of species or
his watercolors of the insects themselves. His book remains a standard work
in the United Kingdom, although the modern work of writers like Goddard
and Harris in *Trout-Fly Recognition* and *An Angler's Entomology* have largely
replaced Ronalds in recent years.

The Fly-Fisher's Entomology passed through twelve editions, its life span
lasting more than a century. It is a seminal book in both its roles, as the

concluding prologue of past centuries and its catalytic genesis of the entire scientific school that followed. Although the concept of matching the hatch has its true historical roots in Berners and her *Treatyse of Fysshynge wyth an Angle*, its philosophy did not fully crystallize until Ronalds and his pioneering entomological studies. The equilibrium between poetry and technical discipline in *The Fly-Fisher's Entomology* was perhaps the catalyst for a whole generation that would flower more than a half-century later, in modern fly-fishing giants like Marryat, Halford, Skues, Mottram, Dunne, and the brilliant Colonel Harding.

Ronalds is entirely original in his observations, owing little to the writers of earlier centuries, and there is virtually nothing in his *Entomology* that has been derived from contemporaries like Scotcher, Bainbridge, and Carroll. His work is both popularly written and scientifically accurate. Although many of his taxonometric identifications were made obsolete by subsequent changes in the entomological keys—particularly when Pictet completed his definitive *Histoire naturelle, general, et particuliere des insectes*

Ronalds' fly patterns, 1836

Neuropteres in Paris in 1843—we must remember that Ronalds was working on his *Entomology* before its definitive taxonomy was available.

The watercolor plates of *The Fly-Fisher's Entomology* are a poetic counterpoint for the scientific names, making a modern reader wish that Halford and Moseley had employed better illustrations for their later books. The precision of the Ronalds plates set the standards for subsequent writers on stream entomology; and the illustrations in the books of men like Wheatley, Theakston and Jackson soon attempted to match the yardstick established in *The Fly-Fisher's Entomology*—a yardstick that would measure all future work on fly hatches.

Hugh Sheringham concludes the introduction to his edition of *The Fly-Fisher's Entomology* with a similar observation, and adds a perceptive viewpoint which explains the singular importance of Ronalds to fly-fishermen throughout the United Kingdom:

> Ronalds might, perhaps, have given some geographical ascription to his book, for it is chiefly concerned with the Staffordshire and Derbyshire rivers. This is really a very important circumstance, for these rivers may be considered as midway between the mountain streams and the rivers of the chalk country in their character and fertility. While not quite so rich in fly-life as the chalkstreams, they are rich enough to give plenty of data, and they also have some of the mountain-stream flies, such as the March Brown and the Gravelbed. It would, therefore, be difficult to find waters more useful for a general survey of our trout-fishing entomology.

Alfred Ronalds is one of the principal milestones in the entire history of fly-fishing; with his *Entomology*, the rational basis of the scientific method had reached angling in full flower. The graphic work is beautifully executed, and the copper-plate lithography remains equal to most modern printing technology. Alfred Ronalds is the prototypical mixture of angler and aquatic biologist that would emerge again after midcentury, and continues to play a major role in fly-fishing theory.

John Younger came next in the parade of history, and his famous *On River Angling for Salmon and Trout* was published at Edinburgh in 1840, four years after Ronalds made his debut in London. Younger was one of the first to write convincingly of the role of nymphal forms in the trout diet. His techniques of fishing soft hackle patterns of partridge and grouse, which are superb imitations of a hatching caddis, are both simple and effective. Younger believed in casting his flies dead across a current, and even slightly upstream in slower places, allowing his flies to swim naturally on the tension of his line swing. John Younger did not develop conscious imitations of nymphs, although in his speculation on their importance, Younger is the first writer to consider them after Taverner and Cotton.

Edward Chitty published his *Fly-Fisher's Text Book* in London in 1841, and Edward Fitzgibbon followed six years later with his *Handbook of Angling*, adding his voice to the growing school of upstream fishermen. Both Hewitt Wheatley and John Beever published their books in 1849. Wheatley was a disciple of Ronalds in *The Rod and Line*; but his home countryside was farther south than the classic Derbyshire rivers fished by his master, and his entomological contributions were largely devoted to ants, grasshoppers, and beetles. Beever titled his book *Practical Fly Fishing*, and it also included an extensive list of flies. It is a modest though intriguing book with dyeing instructions for imitating the Green Drake with gray mallard flank feathers. There are also lesser-known writers like James Wallwork and Henry Wade, whose fly-dressing books appeared in this period.

The prelude to the imitative school of fly dressing concluded with *The Fly-Fisher's Entomology* in 1836, and the gradual evolution of upstream presentation laid the groundwork for the dry-fly method. Although the dry fly would not appear in the sense of a fully developed philosophy of fly-fishing until midcentury in the writings of Pulman and Halford, it had apparently evolved much earlier on the Itchen at Winchester. Popular legend ascribes the dry-fly method to the celebrated William of Wykeham, a famous fourteenth-century clergyman educated in that cathedral town. Wykeham was deeply involved in the political strife of his period, having entered the service of the royal court in 1347. His consecration as the bishop of Winchester occurred twenty years later, after a career of completing its cathedral and building major additions to Windsor Castle, service as the royal secretary, and subsequent appointment as the lord privy seal. His statesmanship as lord chancellor after 1367 was erratic and mediocre at best, and Wykeham is most remembered for the founding of New College at Oxford in 1379 and his own Winchester College beside the Itchen in 1394. Bishop Wykeham also completed the sprawling Gothic nave of the Winchester Cathedral, and he fished the weedy little river religiously.

However authentic the legend of Wykeham and his role in the evolution of the dry-fly method, the technique apparently did evolve along the Itchen at Winchester. Hugh Sheringham tells us that men who had attended Winchester College about 1845 were already familiar with fishing a floating imitation. Other graduates who had attended the school twenty years later fished the dry fly exclusively on the Itchen, according to letters published in *The Field* as recently as 1906. One such correspondent to *The Field* included the following lines about his youthful sport:

> I was at school at Winchester in 1862 and 1863, and fished both seasons nearly every day in the college water, in what was then called the Millpond and the Old Barge. In those days, I never saw anything used but the dry fly, and out of the many fish caught, I do not think more than a dozen were caught with a wet fly, and those only on very windy and rainy days, when it was impossible to use the floating imitation.

George Philip Rigney Pulman is the writer who first described the dry-fly method in his classic *Vade Mecum of Fly-Fishing for Trout*, which first

George Philip Rigney Pulman

was published in 1841. The second edition appeared five years later and a third edition was published at midcentury. Pulman had observed the fish on his favorite Devonshire beats carefully and had seen them taking mayflies from the surface. Logic compelled him to suggest in the *Vade Mecum* that flies designed to float on the current might prove the best solution for such rising trout on his beats of the Axe. Pulman clearly understood that such fish were watching the surface for naturals, and that a wet fly would ride below them, perhaps passing unnoticed—and then these remarkable lines from the first edition of his *Vade Mecum*:

> But if the heavy and wetted fly be exchanged for a dry and light one, and passed in artist-like style over the feeding fish, it will, partly from the simple circumstance of its buoyancy, be taken, in nine cases out of ten, as greedily as the living insect itself.

These words clearly describe a floating fly cast above a rising fish. Yet in this first edition they have a certain ambiguity. Pulman was apparently aware that his meaning had not fully been understood by his wet-fly colleagues, and in a reworking of these same lines a few years later, he not only clarified his intent but unmistakably mentioned drying the fly as well:

> Let a dry fly be substituted for the wet one, the line switched a few times through the air to throw off its superabundant moisture, a judicious cast made just above the rising fish, and the fly allowed to float towards and over them, and the chances are ten to one that it will be seized as readily as the living insect.

John Waller Hills points out in his *History of Fly-Fishing for Trout* that the surprising thing about the appearance of the dry-fly method in Pulman's writings is its theoretical completeness. Pulman further observes that not only is a good copy of the natural insect required but the behavior of the natural insect on the water must also be suggested. The dry-fly philosophy rises in the *Vade Mecum of Fly-Fishing for Trout* as a complete edifice from foundations to ridge beams. It recognizes that a specific dry-fly fish must be taking food from the surface; that a floating artificial must match its color, configuration, and size; that it must remain cocked on the surface film; that it must arrive above the fish softly without alarming feeding rhythms; and that it must come over the fish's feeding position naturally and without drag. Thus the dry-fly method made its literary debut in Pulman's work full-blown in both theory and practice. However, Hugh Sheringham has written that he cannot accept the popular premise that the dry-fly method germinated and evolved in the mind of a single fly-fisher:

> It is indeed within recent years that Pulman has been recognized as the first dry-fly writer. His little book attained two later editions, but it probably circulated chiefly in Devonshire, where Pulman himself lived, and it may be that its success was largely

owed to the celebrity of his bigger work *The Book of the Axe*, which is topographical rather than piscatorial. In any case it does not seem that his dry-fly teaching, somewhat rudimentary as it was, materially altered the course of fishing history.

I should be puzzled to say who was chiefly responsible for the alteration which undoubtedly took place. I suspect that we owe the dry-fly doctrine to the Itchen, and quite possibly to the ancient and honourable foundation of William of Wykeham. But so far I have not been able to convince myself that in such a year, the dry-fly method was not, while in the next year it was.

George Pulman was a well-known tacklemaker from the small Devonshire town of Axminster. He primarily fished rivers like the Barle and the Exe, but his home beats were really on the larger Axe, in the eastern hills of Devonshire. Pulman wrote a number of worthwhile fishing books, and John Waller Hills argues tentatively for Pulman's invention of the dry-fly method in these passages from *A History of Fly-Fishing for Trout*:

The fact that Pulman is the first to describe the floating fly is puzzling, and for this reason. It was practiced on the Itchen, probably in the forties, certainly in the fifties, of the last century. It has a continuous history on that river. On the other hand, I know no other reference to it on the Axe. Nor can I find any mention in Pulman's books of fishing on the Itchen. And yet Pulman must either have introduced it from the Itchen, or have discovered or invented it himself on the Axe. The last contingency is possible, but not likely, for it would mean its invention at approximately the same time on two rivers widely separated in distance and character.

And it is also unlikely, for the reason that does not appear to have survived on the Axe, where it has, however, since been reintroduced. On the whole, while admitting that it is guess work, I incline to think it more probable that his knowledge came from Hampshire, directly or indirectly. He does not actually claim to be its inventor, nor does he write as such.

Frederic Halford observes in his *Autobiography* that his introduction to the dry-fly method came at Carshalton on the Wandle; and an anonymous letter written to *The Field* in the winter of 1853 also mentioned that a dry-fly cast upstream was common at midcentury among the men who fished the Carshalton beats. Francis Francis had just been appointed angling editor of *The Field* when he published an article on fishing the Hampshire chalkstreams in 1857. Describing the wet-fly method on those waters when the surface is windless and smooth, Francis observed that a wet-fly swing or working line sometimes frightened the trout. Francis recommended the dry-fly method at such times, pointing out that it fished over a shy trout without any line motion or other disturbance. He also observed that the wings, body, legs, and tail whisks should match the size and coloring of the hatching duns, and that he and his colleagues had been experimenting with both matching the hatch and the dry fly for several years on the Hampshire streams.

John Waller Hills also tells us in *A History of Fly-Fishing for Trout* that Wilfred Foster of Ashbourne was dressing floating upright-wing flies as early as 1854. Stoddart did not describe the dry-fly method in his first edition of *The Angler's Companion* in 1847 but in the second edition, which appeared six years later, he discussed it on his home rivers north of the Tweed. Its philosophy had clearly travelled the length of England before midcentury.

Michael Theakston lived at Ripon, and his sport was primarily confined to the gentle, grayling-rich Ure in Yorkshire. Like other anglers of his period, Theakston was strongly influenced by Ronalds, and that admiration is obvious in his book *A List of Natural Flies*. It was published at Ripon in 1853, and in spite of its technical inaccuracies—Theakston persisted in calling caddisflies duns and in making other glaring errors in nomenclature—it is still one of the great books on angling.

John Jackson was another Yorkshire fly-fisherman who fished and lived on the little Ure at Tanfield Mill, and his book *The Practical Fly-Fisher* was published at Leeds in 1854. Jackson included a personal series of sixty-five flies in his book and firmly took his place among the writers of the north-country school.

William Blacker emerged with *The Art of Fly-Making* in 1855, when it was first published in London. Blacker provides another milestone in the evolution of modern fly dressing, with his innovation of forming the wings from matched feather sections, cut from precisely opposite wing quills. Blacker is also the first writer to explore the possibilities of detached or extended bodies in tying mayfly imitations. Like his colleagues—Beever, Pulman, Theakston and Jackson—before him, William Blacker included a list of forty-odd patterns in his *Art of Fly-Making*. It also contained valuable observations on fly materials, hooks, sizes, fly proportions, and many personal secrets of dyeing feathers and dubbing as well.

William Stewart with his *Practical Angler* is one of the bench marks of fly-fishing history, although the book strangely contained no mention of the dry-fly method evolving south of London on the Hampshire streams. *The Practical Angler* was published at Edinburgh in 1857, and the fact that it has remained in print well over a century is obvious evidence of its stature. Stewart was the acknowledged dean of a circle of skilled fly-fishers who lived in the watershed of the Tweed, especially on tributary rivers like the Whitadder and Teviot; and it is this lowland country that figures in his writings. It is easy to understand the character of both *The Practical Angler* and its author in a brief odyssey through this Scottish-border world of ruined abbeys, forests, and moors. It is a country drained by tumbling little rivers like the Gala, with its gracefully vaulted Packhorse Bridge, and marked by the hedgerow landscape of sheep meadows where the Lammer-

WILLIAM C. STEWART

muirs slope gracefully toward the sea at Cockburnspath. It is a countryside of old places steeped in history, villages like Selkirk, Peebles, Galashiels, Melrose Abbey, and Kelso-on-Tweed—where the present Duke of Roxburghe, perhaps the most widely experienced salmon fisherman alive today, continues to live quietly among the crenellated parapets of his Floors Castle.

Stewart skillfully fished a cast of upstream wet flies on his beloved Whitadder, the pastoral Teviot in the hills of Roxburghshire, the gentle little Gala and the bigger smooth-flowing Tweed itself—from its lower reaches at Ladykirk to its tumbling headwaters at Peebles. The Tweed drains a beautiful region, its valleys partially cleared into pale green meadows with hedgerows and stone-walled fences. Sheep meadows have been carved on the gentle shoulders of the hills, forming sharp man-made patterns in the pine forests. The winding country roads into the Lammermuir hills are lined with gnarled beech trees. There is brooding Melrose Abbey in its open watermeadows and the somber Romanesque skeleton of the church at Jedburgh. There are grain mills and whisky distilleries with conical tile roofs. It is a countryside of small whitewashed churches and weathered ruins like Whithorn Priory standing in its ancient churchyard of rain-streaked headstones.

There are row-cottage villages with white stonework walls and thatched roofs, while other villages are constructed in dour granite masonry with slate and red tile roofs and worn staircases winding between their houses. Some villages form an irregular semicircle of houses along inlets of steep-walled hills, with a slender jetty of granite blocks to break the seas. The winding roads are rich with the shadow patterns of hazelnut, catkin, and beech leaves, and the early summer thickets are bright with elder flowers. Cockburnspath once sheltered a hundred fishing boats, but less than a dozen packets moor along its jetties now. It rises from the sea, its marketplace with a fine stonework cross and church that survived the destructive barbarism that accompanied the Reformation in Scotland. There is an exceptional fifteenth-century collegiate church at Dunglass, not far from Cockburnspath. Its transept and massive slate roof and tower are well preserved, because the Reformation armies requisitioned it to stable their cavalry mounts, and it was not stripped or surgically purified of Catholic ornament and imagery. Haddington lies north toward Edinburgh. It has a fine Reformation church, some of the most charming streetscapes in Scotland, and a pair of superb medieval bridges—John Knox was born in its narrow streets, in one of its seventeenth-century stone houses.

Stewart was a distinguished attorney, but like Skues and other fly-fishermen who were barristers, Stewart spent an inordinate amount of time fishing and thinking about fishing. His linen-page fly book was filled with traditional patterns like the Grouse and Green, Woodcock and Brown, and Blue-winged Hare's Ear, but his own patterns like the Grouse Spider and Dotterel Spider and Starling Spider were apparently originals.

Stewart codified the philosophy of the upstream school of presentation,

Stewart's fly patterns, 1857

and his soft-hackled wets with their palette of mottled and subdued feathers had considerable impact on later writers like Pritt, Skues, Webster, and our own Leisenring. Perhaps these charming recollections of A. G. Bradley, which appeared as a review for a new edition of Stewart in *Macmillan's Magazine* in 1907, are the best epitaph for Stewart and the importance of *The Practical Angler*:

> For my own part, when the book fell open at some beautifully reproduced illustrations from Stewart's old patterns, of spiders black and red, grouse and woodcock: time and space were annihilated.
>
> I seemed to feel once more the waters of the Whitadder gurgling about my feet, and to hear the Cheviot sheep bleating on the hills around Saint Balthans, and the grouse and curlews calling in the solitudes of Cranshaws and Priestlaw. The Whitadder was one of Stewart's many rivers and he was a king among us—if two long seasons, from February to October, may entitle the writer of this modest tribute to account himself sealed of the tribe.
>
> For what an age is a year or two of youth when one lived and rejoiced in every day of them!
>
> My first impulse was to hunt for an old fly-book that has been with me for over thirty years untouched, and for twenty virtually lost. This is not surprising, for in library parlance it would be classified as a medium quarto. In the fishing circles of my youth, there was a robust abhorrence of anything finnikin or, as we called it, cockneyfied, and a prodigious veneration of home-made devices. Indeed, the prejudices of some localities in these trifles would be inconceivable to the modern mind.
>
> This particular angling relic is constructed from some parchment deeds relating to an Exmoor church, lawfully come by in an Exmoor rectory, and no doubt, therefore, intrinsically worthless. It is interleaved, of course, with generous breadths of flannel, and filled with compartments in the parchment of all shapes and sizes for the storing of flies, casts, silk, fur, feathers, loose hooks, scissors, tweezers, and so on; for most of us made part, at any rate, of our own flies.
>
> As a schoolboy I was passing proud of the design, which was thought out somewhat carefully, and above all of the result, contributed to by the deft needle and thread of some female relative. It was not, to be sure, altogether original, being inspired at least by one that an old gentleman (who taught me to tie flies of a kind) had carried about the rivers of North Wales, and from Waterloo to the Crimean War.
>
> Nothing but a full shooting-pocket would hold it, and generally it travelled in a special compartment of the creel, often,

in periods of excitement, actually among the fish themselves.

In these days of eyed flies and neat metallic boxes it presents a most uncouth appearance; even in those days it must have had a picturesque and antique flavour, since a weak youth and would-be fisherman from East Anglia, more concerned with the appearances than the realities of sport, used periodically to offer me considerable sums of money for it, honestly affirming that it would be the making of his reputation in his own county, where there were very few trout even thirty years ago.

It still contains some odds and ends of tackle, moth-eaten flies, rotten gut, the partial wing of an Exmoor snipe, the lug of an East Lothian hare, some feathers from a Peebleshire black-cock, and assorted hackles of barnyard fowls from anywhere.

But what I have been trying to arrive at, is the rediscovery in the depths of one of its myriad pockets of a bunch of wonderfully well preserved spiders, patterns and relics of the Stewart period (speaking piscatorially and not historically) and of the rivers he used to fish.

What memories this ancient fly-book invokes!

Although here we are only concerned with those relating to the reign of this angling Stewart, and near the end of it too, for this King of the Border Flyfishers died in the winter of 1872.

I was in East Lothian at the time, and remember hearing much obituary talk among angling friends, and reading long accounts in the Scottish papers concerning his funeral, which was attended by a goodly following of the craft. He must surely have been regarded as a great man; when I once found myself, on the sole occasion I can remember to have set eyes on him, I remember the sensations of swelling excitement and wonder.

Stewart's name was certainly one to conjure with, beside the banks of those eastern border streams, at any rate, while 'round the firesides of the homely little fishing-inns his prowess and his opinions were a frequent theme. How could you stand against a man who quietly proved his theories by always killing more fish than anybody else astream, and that too, in waters open to the public and frequented literally by hosts of practised and knowledgeable fishermen?

Stewart certainly did not invent the upstream presentation of his wet flies, since it had been used and written about earlier. Certainly, it dates back into the prior centuries dominated by fishermen like Berners, Nowell, and Walton. John Waller Hills argues that the controversy between the downstream and upstream methods was decided locally. Scotland and the southern counties of England, from Derbyshire to Cornwall, fished their wet flies downstream. Yorkshire and the Scottish border counties fished their flies upstream, at least when Stewart was writing at midcentury.

His exposition in *The Practical Angler* attempted to prove that the wet-fly method was more productive on small rivers when the upstream presentation was employed, because the wary fish are more easily approached from below. Wet-fly men have always experienced the most luck when their rivers were slightly discolored with rain, indicating that the fish responded more eagerly to them and their tackle when their vision was veiled with spate water. Upstream wet flies were a deadly clear water method too. The technique approaches the fish from behind, and a hooked fish is always played in currents that have already been fished; a downstream fisherman is clearly visible and inevitably finds the fight carrying below him into unfished places. The upstream method also has a higher percentage of hooked fish, since the strike draws the fly back into the fish's jaws instead of out of its mouth. It permits a skilled angler to suggest insects that ride the current without swimming or fluttering. There are such diet forms best imitated with a teasing, downstream swing of the flies, and a skilled angler who understands his stream entomology will use both methods, depending on fly-hatch behavior. With these advantages, the nineteenth-century angler could kill wary fish in low, clear water. It was obvious and simple, like all major innovations, but before Stewart no writer had proven its case clearly and finally.

Stewart did not conceive upstream fishing of whole cloth any more than Darwin completely created the natural selection of species, but Stewart was the first writer in two centuries to outline a thoroughly reasoned case, and *The Practical Angler* was the first to argue it convincingly. Stewart unquestionably exaggerates the novelty of his creed—though perhaps he did believe it was his invention—yet his book deserves much credit, since it converted the world just as surely as Darwin's *Origin of Species*.

Stewart had a good working knowledge of entomology, although he was not a proponent of exact imitation. His work clearly demonstrates that he fully understood the importance of mayfly and stonefly nymphs in the trout diet, along with the role of the hatching sedges. *The Practical Angler* codified the philosophy of the upstream school, and some angling historians have credited its invention to Stewart in its entirety. Others have pointed to his upstream technique as a prelude to the dry-fly method, but since the floating imitation was unquestionably at least twenty years old when Stewart was published, it seems wiser to underline his role as parallel to the evolution of dry-fly theory.

Other wet-fly fishermen wrote compellingly about their craft in the years that followed Stewart, and perhaps the most charming was the Canon Charles Kingsley, whose *Chalkstream Studies* were published in 1858. Kingsley wrote both essays and novels at midcentury while still a professor of church history at Cambridge, and is best known for fiction like *Alton Locke, Hypatia*, and *Westward Ho!* His famous children's poem *Water Babies* was published in 1863, and ten years later, Kingsley was appointed canon of Westminster Abbey. Canon Kingsley was a superb fisherman and amateur naturalist, the fly dresser who developed the Alder wet-fly pattern, and an angler who chose to ignore the floating-fly method that had begun to evolve on his rivers. His catches and his character, with its commitment to the wet-fly traditions of earlier centuries, both demonstrated convincingly that the sunk techniques remained viable on the chalkstreams in spite of dry-fly dogmatics.

H. C. Cutcliffe wrote *Trout Fishing in Rapid Streams* in 1863, a practical and cogent book based upon years along the west-country streams of Devonshire. His book offers a concise account of fly patterns and techniques on those west-country rivers with particular emphasis on the adjustments in fly-dressing and fishing that Cutcliffe had developed for swift currents. His tactics included stalking the fish carefully, and fishing upstream to conceal himself from his quarry. Cutcliffe thoroughly believed in fishing his upstream wet flies into the pocket water and understood the skittish behavior of trout in small fast-water streams. His theories clearly distinguished between quiet currents, where exact imitation is critical, and the swifter currents, where a fish must take quickly or remain hungry. Cutcliffe also grasped the life cycle of aquatic insects, understood their relative importance to the trout at different seasons, and made the following remarkable observation about nymphs:

> I find so much spoken about the natural fly and its imitation, but little about the insect before it has arrived at maturity. How seldom does one imitate the larva or pupa of the insects.

Four years after Cutcliffe, in 1867, Francis Francis published *A Book on Angling*, and its rational equilibrium was welcome. While Kingsley had refused to adopt the dry-fly method in his chalkstream fishing, Francis became thoroughly versed in both techniques. His book clearly demonstrates that Francis was undoubtedly the most open-minded fishing writer of his period, refusing to take sides in the harsh quarrels developing between the traditional wet-fly men and the austere dry-fly disciples forming around George Selwyn Marryat on the club beats of the Test. Francis argued convincingly that a skillful fisherman must master all methods, and the perspective of moderation in his *Book on Angling* served to dampen the bitter arguments that surrounded the dry-fly school in the half century that followed.

Both the wet-fly experts and the aggressive young exponents of the dry-fly method would continue in the coming century to explore their sport in major books. Although men like Pritt, Webster, and Cutcliffe were wet-fly fishermen who published their work in the fifty years after Stewart, it was a period that virtually belonged to George Selwyn Marryat and his dry-fly method. The nineteenth-century renaissance of fly-fishing had concluded its half-century prelude; and the entire tradition of the sport had combined with the entomology of Ronalds to forge the threshold of the scientific approach to trout fishing that followed. The perfection of the dry-fly method and its rational topologies of matching the hatch would ultimately lead to the nymph-fishing theories that also evolved in Hampshire at the close of the century.

George Edward MacKenzie Skues was the genius who would dovetail and fit the evolving science of trout-stream entomology to the centuries-old tradition of the wet fly. His nymph techniques were finally taking shape at the beginning of our century and were first published just before the First World War, so that both the theory and technique of nymph fishing have been largely perfected in our century. Skues was a solitary London bachelor who fished and loved the Itchen at Winchester for fifty-odd years, and his studies unquestionably made him the conscious forefather of modern nymph techniques.

It is strange that Winchester and its silken little Itchen were the catalyst for both the dry-fly method and the later subsurface technique of the nymph. The shy trout of this half-legendary chalkstream and its sister rivers in the rich south-country watersheds of Hampshire and Wiltshire were a challenge solved during the nineteenth-century renaissance in fly-fishing. Such chalkstream fish were the yardsticks of modern angling, yet earlier giants like Ronalds and Pulman and Stewart were the authors of the principal fly-fishing books written in the first seventy-five years of their century—and none of these giants was a chalkstream man.

7. Halford, Skues, and the Rise of the Scientific School

Hampshire is a richly pastoral landscape of villages and water meadows and country churchyards. Huge springs bubble from fissures in the chalkdown geology of the region, flowing over beds of watercress and pale gravel and rannunculus. It is a setting worthy of both fly-fishers and poets, its quiet beauty like the landscapes of such British painters as Turner and Constable, who both loved fishing the Hampshire chalkstreams.

There are weirs and millraces and fields of fat dairy cattle. Medieval inns with intricate half-timbered gables house both anglers and travellers. The countryside is filled with a sense of history. Salisbury Cathedral rises across its Wiltshire river bottoms, its single tower slender and archetypally Gothic above the spreading greens and the roofs of the town. Several miles farther east lies the somber cathedral at Winchester, the brooding echoes of centuries in its weathered Romanesque and Gothic stonework. Its chapels and chambers include the tomb of Izaak Walton; its Norman stonework vaults are clumsy and dark compared to the soaring chapter house and high stained-glass spaces of Salisbury. It is a tranquil world with a unique character.

The chalkstreams flow smooth and crystalline through their dense growths of chara, pondweed, watercress, river celery, ribbonweed, nitella, and starwort. There are dropwort and water buttercups rooting deep into the chalky silts, the source of the fly-rich fertility of these British rivers. The principal chalkstreams are found in Hampshire and Wiltshire on the south coast of England, with the Salisbury Avon, the Test, and the Itchen as perhaps the most notable river systems. Slightly less famous are the Dorsetshire Frome, the Kennet, and several tributary streams on the major flowages—gentle minor rivers like the Coln, Nadder, Lambourne, Wylye, and the lyric Bourne at Hurstbourne Priors. It is an unmatched corner of the world.

Master anglers are both shaped and polished by their rivers, and the demanding ecology of the chalkstreams has produced a legion of skilled fly-fishermen over the past two centuries. The shy fish of these difficult rivers were the supreme challenge that shaped fly-fishing giants like George Selwyn Marryat, Viscount Edward Grey of Fallodon, George Edward MacKenzie Skues, and the parade of brilliant chalkstream fishermen who followed—Mottram, Moseley, Hills, Dunne, Harding, Wilson, Sawyer, and Kite.

The chalkstream tradition is venerable and rich. Walton fished the gentle Itchen in his twilight years and is buried in the Winchester Cathedral not far from the river. William of Wykeham fished it during the fourteenth century and is considered the patron saint of its angling disciples. Perhaps the earliest account we have of fishing the chalkstreams is a diary compiled on the Test at Chilbolton before 1820.

It was the distinguished Richard Durnford who wrote *The Diary of a Test Fisherman*, and his little book reveals him to have been an ardent and skilled fly-fisherman. His powers of observation were quite remarkable, and he anticipated many insights found in the entomological studies published by Ronalds in 1836.

Richard Durnford was rector of the Chilbolton parish on the Test, and he fished its weedy alder-lined water meadows as often as possible each season. His diary was subsequently edited by Henry Nicoll and not published until 1911. The selections Nicoll made are limited to the period between 1809 and 1819, although Durnford described fishing the Test over a longer span. His pages describe the chalkstreams at the zenith of the wet-fly tradition, half a century before the dry-fly method utterly transformed the Test and its fishing practices. Skilled modern fishermen will find little of practical value, but the Durnford book is filled with the moods of Hampshire almost two centuries ago—a pastoral age important to the history of fly-fishing.

Pulman and Kingsley were chalkstream fishermen too, and *The Angler's Vade Mecum of Fly-Fishing for Trout* is partially based upon experiences along the Itchen and the Test. Canon Kingsley regularly fished the Test in these same years, but while Pulman provided the fanfare that introduced the dry-fly method, Kingsley resisted such innovations throughout his life, and his fishing is perhaps an epilogue to many centuries when the wet fly reigned supreme. Harold Cholmondeley-Pennell was part of the philosophical rear guard of wet-fly fishing, and he published his *Modern Practical Angler* in 1870. Dry-fly fishing was already in full flower on the Wandle, the Itchen, and the Dorsetshire Frome, but Cholmondeley-Pennell was still crossing swords with Stewart over fishing his wet flies upstream or down.

James Ogden of Cheltenham was perhaps the finest fly dresser of his time, and in his book *On Fly Tying*, he claims the structural innovations that fashioned the modern dry fly as his own creation. The book was published in 1879, and Ogden tells us that he had been dressing dry flies for forty-odd years. His case would indicate that the essential fly-dressing techniques implicit in the floating fly appeared a few years before Pulman and his first edition of *The Vade Mecum of Fly-Fishing for Trout* in 1841. Ogden also describes his introduction of a floating imitation of the Green Drake during a heavy hatch on the Derbyshire Wye in 1865. Anglers there usually fished with the live mayflies impaled on a hook and dapped over the rising trout. However, the new Ogden flies were so effective that the owner of the fishing rights closed his beats to further fishing with the live insects, and Ogden fled the anger of a virtual mob on the river. Ogden had seventy-odd years of flymaking experience when his book appeared, and his style was marked by its elegance.

The rare and remarkable folio that W. H. Aldam published in 1876 includes two dry-fly imitations of the *Ephemera* drake hatch on British waters. His work is the unique *Quaint Treatise on Flees and Artificial Flee-Making* that includes the actual flies and the palette of materials used in their patterns, elegantly set into shadow boxes. The Aldam *Treatise* is worth almost $400 a century after its publication, and its exquisite Ogden mayfly patterns and their extended bodies are perhaps the oldest examples extant of the dry-fly dresser's art.

In his introduction to *The Fly-Fisher's Entomology*, Hugh Sheringham made a striking observation that captures the birth of the dry fly in terms of its innovations in fly dressings:

> So the rough general principle of dry-fly fishing was easily grasped—the fly must float, and it must be accurately delivered. The recognition of this led to various developments, most important of them perhaps the modification of tackle. That a fly might float better, attention was paid to its configuration and materials. It was found that stiffness in the hackles was an aid to buoyancy, so cock's hackles were preferred to hen's hackles. It was found too, that a better balance was given to the fly by short upright wings set at an angle of forty-five degrees, and further that if these wings were a double thickness, they stood the wear and tear of casting and kept their shape better than if they were single. The typical dry fly that evolved had strong, perky wings and stiff, well-splayed hackles that are a considerable triumph of mechanics.

However, the wet-fly method was not dead. The emerging techniques of the dry fly held the limelight during the last twenty-five years of the nineteenth century, but some skillful fishermen continued to experiment with older methods on both the chalkstreams and the swift rivers farther north. David Webster published his book *The Angler and the Loop Rod* in 1885, just before Frederic Halford made his debut with the classic *Floating*

Flies and How to Dress Them a year later. Webster illustrates and describes a Scottish-border style of dressing wet flies with upright wings and extremely sparse materials—patterns that would influence Skues and the development of his hatching-nymph theories in revolutionary books a quarter century later.

T. E. Pritt was another brilliant wet-fly man, and his book of *Yorkshire Trout Flies* was published at Leeds in 1885. Pritt was part of the strong wet-fly tradition of Ronalds, and was angling editor of the *Yorkshire Post*. His book had eleven superbly hand-tinted plates with sixty-two patterns of wet flies. It preserved many of the best wet-fly patterns of his time, and most of the flies that had their roots in the steep-walled dales of Yorkshire. The color plates, although accurate and good, do not equal the superb copperplate watercolors found in *The Fly-Fisher's Entomology*. However, they do preserve the timeless character of the north-country wet-fly dressing. Like the Webster patterns, these elegant little flies listed in the work of Pritt—with their delicate proportions, precise size, use of subdued coloring, and sense of craftsmanship—had considerable influence on Skues.

Meanwhile, the dry-fly method was evolving rapidly on the south-country chalkstreams, among an exceptionally talented circle of anglers, fly makers and theoreticians. George Selwyn Marryat was perhaps its fulcrum, a man widely acclaimed as the finest fly-fisherman in England during the last half of the nineteenth century. Henry Hall was the brilliant engineer whose work with forged light-wire hooks was a remarkable advance on the eyed-hook design that originally appeared in the frontispiece of Brookes' *Art of Angling* in 1740. There were several professional fly dressers who unquestionably played a role in this dry-fly evolution—skilled artisans like James Ogden at Cheltenham, his daughter Mary Ogden-Smith, and the celebrated David Foster of Ashbourne—and there were others, less famous, who worked at feather-littered workbenches in south-country fishing towns like Salisbury, Stockbridge, and Winchester. However, the painstakingly disciplined genius who recorded and codified the history of the dry-fly method was the legendary Frederic Maurice Halford. Halford tells us in his *Autobiography of an Angler*, which he published in 1903, that his introduction to the dry-fly method came at Carsharlton on the Wandle in 1868. The book describes his subsequent evolution as the principal historian of the dry fly on rivers like the Itchen, Kennet, and Test.

Halford produced his first book *Floating Flies and How to Dress Them* in 1886, and its contents both outlined a philosophy and prescribed a revolution. It codified the dry-fly method after a half century of conscious refinement, and with his several later books, it established Halford as the principal writer on the chalkstreams and the emerging dry-fly method. He was a man of disciplined intelligence and strong opinions, and his influence led to the serious investigation of aquatic fly life on the trout streams of the United Kingdom, as well as a precise philosophy of fly dressing and matching the hatch. His precision shows in every phrase of *Floating Flies and How to Dress Them*, as seen in the following definition of the dry-fly method:

FREDERIC MAURICE HALFORD

To define dry-fly fishing, I should describe it as presenting to the rising fish the best possible imitation of the insect on which he is feeding in its natural position. To analyse this further, it is necessary, firstly, to find a fish feeding on the winged insect; secondly, to present him a good imitation of this insect, both as to size and color; thirdly, to present it to him in its natural position or floating on the surface of the water with its wings up, or what we technically term cocked; fourthly, to put the fly lightly on the water, so that it floats accurately over him without drag; and fifthly, to take care that all these conditions have been fulfilled before the fish has seen the angler, or the reflection of his rod.

There were no less than seven books written by the prolific Frederic Halford between *Floating Flies and How to Dress Them* and *The Dry-Fly Man's Handbook*, which appeared a year before his death in 1914. His fishing career with the dry fly began in 1868 on the Wandle, and a modern angler must remember that neither paraffin dressings nor silicone oils were available to dry his imitations. Halford pioneered the use of the amadou fungus for drying his flies, but the other chemical fly-dressing developments came much later, and silicone did not appear until almost a century after Halford had his baptism into fly-fishing.

It was as much a problem of fly-tying techniques as it was of ointments to keep the flies floating. Although Ogden claims the invention of the upright dry-fly configuration for himself in about 1840, the primitive floating patterns in use on the Itchen and Wandle almost thirty-odd years later were still relatively crude experiments. Such flies did not always float, seldom drifted upright, and rarely cocked properly on landing. Sometimes the flies rode on their sides, and sometimes they landed upside down or face down, with their tails in the air. Other fly dressings absorbed water and drowned quickly. Our modern flies are often predressed with a diluted silicone before they are used, and the protective silicone film sheds water readily. Such flies can be made buoyant again with a few brief false casts, and after a fish has mouthed them into sinking, a brisk washing and a patient series of false casts will usually get their hackles floating.

But Halford had to replace a water-logged fly after each fish. Obvious improvements like stiff cock's hackles, upright matching wings, and body materials that did not absorb water like sponges evolved slowly. The early experiments still employed silk and cotton flosses and crewel-wool bodies that soaked up water as quickly as a floundering sheep. Some fly dressers began spinning body dubbing from other animals associated with aquatic life like otters, muskrats, and beavers, and such furs were found to float readily. Peacock and ostrich herl and chenille also waterlogged rather quickly and were gradually abandoned. It was several years before the basic structural problems of the dry fly were fully worked out and the chalkstream philosophers had evolved a palette of naturally buoyant materials.

Various kinds of quill were used for bodies long before Frederic Halford, since the writings of earlier flymakers recommend various feather quills for many patterns of flies. Both the Blue Quill and Red Quill were in use on the Itchen and Kennet at midcentury, and Lord Grey of Fallodon tells us in his exquisite *Fly-Fishing* that he used a Red Quill to take his first dry-fly trout on the Itchen in 1877. Lord Grey meticulously described its dressing, pointing out that it lacked the elegant matched-and-divided wings that were developed in later years by fly dressers like Ogden, Hall, Marryat, and Halford. Halford describes his mixed feelings about substituting quill for dubbing rather early in his first book. He believed that in choosing quill over fur-dubbed bodies, his flies had gained less absorbent bodies but had sacrificed the marvelous translucency and juiciness of wet fur. Both fur dubbing and quill hold their coloring when wet, while silk discolors badly as it absorbs moisture. Our modern techniques use synthetic floss and fibrous dubbing materials that do not discolor radically when wet. Pale working nylons coupled with white-lacquered hook shanks that did not discolor light-colored materials emerged in the experiments of J. W. Dunne in 1924. But these refinements did not exist in Halford's kit bag of materials and skills, and both floss and dubbing are so summarily dismissed in his books that we can draw this single conclusion: Halford was quite satisfied with his dry raffia and horsehair and quill bodies. He tells us in his *Modern Development of the Dry Fly* that he was meticulous about his body colors, even indulging in such strange practices as immersing his imitations in the specimen bottles where he preserved the naturals. Halford then compared the coloring of his artificials with the preserved insects, a rather esoteric and illogical act that Halford fails to explain. Disparate materials are affected in different fashion by the same immersion process, and a preserved insect is usually so discolored from its enbalming that it is almost worthless as a color prototype in fly dressing.

Halford collaborated closely with George Selwyn Marryat and Henry Hall for several years, and these men played a considerable role in perfecting the symmetrical two-winged upright dressings that still dominate the practice of tying dry flies a century later. The modern dry-fly dressing was a singularly creative act.

Captain Marryat was clearly the finest fly-fisherman of nineteenth-century England, and Halford tells us that Marryat put a rich lifetime of notes, observations, and skills at his disposal. Halford was unquestionably more than a collaborator, since his books are filled with original insights made long after Marryat's death in 1896, but Marryat and his theories clearly live in Halford's books—and what a book on chalkstream fishing George Selwyn Marryat himself might have written.

Marryat was so skilled that chalkstream legend tells us he could drop his fly on a half crown at sixty feet once or twice in a half-dozen casts, and history records his introduction to the dry-fly method on the lovely Frome in Dorsetshire. Marryat lived at Winchester near the Itchen, although his fishing odysseys regularly carried him to the other chalkstreams.

Henry Hall was a perceptive engineer who worked out the sophisticated metallurgy, delicate forging techniques, and tapered eyes of the
modern fly-tying hook about 1879, although Aldam had experimented with
less refined eyed-hook designs in the preceding decade. In *Trout Fishing from
All Angles*, Eric Taverner makes the following observation concerning the
singular innovations of Hall and Marryat:

> Marryat and Henry Hall together evolved the modern dry fly
> which could easily be made to sit upright upon the water and
> cocked; this was a tremendous step forward. There are many
> details connected with the successful achievement of this enter-
> prise which cannot be discussed here, but it should be remem-
> bered that a share of the credit must be given to Hall whose
> invention of the eyed trout-fly hook made it easier, if it did not
> actually make possible the development of the floating fly.
>
> It would, perhaps, be fairer to say that he was responsible for
> one essential in its evolution. What this means anyone can
> demonstrate for himself. Let him take a fly hackled with a stiff
> feather, but dressed on gut and a heavy hook, and without oiling
> it try to make it float under normal fishing conditions.
>
> If anyone will study the articles written by Henry Hall in *The
> Field*, or included in the *Salmon and Trout* volume in the Badminton
> Series, he will be struck with similarities between his flies and the
> patterns in *Floating Flies and How to Dress Them*, and surprised how
> much the development of the dry-fly must be attributed to him.
> The great inventive genius of the dry-fly method was still George
> Selwyn Marryat, the inspirer of Halford and focal personality of
> the chalkstream experts.
>
> It is probably due to Marryat that Halford included a new
> method of fly winging in his *Floating Flies and How to Dress Them*.
> Instead of the two slips being taken from the web of the same
> wing, they were taken or cut from the web of quills from a pair of
> wings, and where possible from quills occupying the same position
> on opposite wings. There was no longer that former tendency of
> the fly to be spun by the wind acting on slips of feather, the tips of
> which have a definite pitch, which makes them function as a
> propellor.

Taverner is incorrect in his belief that this method of fly winging was
original with Marryat and Halford. It first appeared in Blacker's *Art of
Fly-Making* in 1855, although it was limited to down-wing wet flies.

Halford discussed the evolution of the forged light-wire eyed hooks in
Floating Flies and How to Dress Them and its implications in the design of the
modern dry-fly style. He argued that body weight was considerably reduced
by eliminating the silk wrappings and gut snell of the traditional wet-fly
construction. Flies did not have to be discarded when a tippet frayed,
although a snelled wet fly was ruined when its gut was worn. Tippets of

various thickness could be used to meet varied conditions, and the disturbance made by the snell loops was eliminated entirely, a considerable advance in fooling shy chalkstream trout. These observations on tackle all seem obvious to the modern reader, but they were a revelation to British fishermen in 1885.

It was a neighbor of Captain Marryat who contributed a superb leader knot for the new Halford dry flies and their elegant eyed hooks. Major W. G. Turle fished the weedy currents of the Itchen at Winchester, living quietly at the village of Newton Stacey. His original little Turle knot both perfectly suited a fine drawn-gut tippet and imparted a relatively rigid connection for the fly; it held a settling dry fly in the cocked position as it floated down toward the surface, and it remains a superb knot today. Turle had retired from the British Army after serving in the Indian Mutiny of 1857 and suffering grave wounds at the Siege of Delhi. Since he was retired and living in Hampshire, he fished the chalkstreams almost daily, and died at Newton Stacey in 1909.

Halford played a principal role in the development of the modern fly line too, even though the woven oiled-silk line had already been introduced when he and Marryat joined conceptual forces on the Test. The woven horsehair lines had long been supplanted by the hard enamel-finish lines of the late eighteenth century. The supple lines of oil-finished silk were a revolution in themselves, but Halford and Marryat were still not satisfied. Working with various manufacturers, they developed even better oil-finished lines and the prototypes of the modern double-taper design. The method used in weaving and dressing the new lines was carefully described in Halford's *Dry-Fly Fishing in Theory and Practice* of 1889—a book that was another major bench mark in both matching the hatch and the codification of the dry-fly method.

The dry-fly revolution was fully launched. Halford had successfully overturned the order and tradition of centuries with *Floating Flies and How to Dress Them* in 1886, and *Dry-Fly Fishing in Theory and Practice* enriched and embellished the flowering of the dry-fly philosophy. These are probably his best books. Halford is still less than dogmatic in their pages, and we find them filled with original observations expressed in a pleasant and simple style. He was already studying the fly hatches on the chalkstreams and arguing for better dry-fly imitations. But in those first two books, Halford continued to list fly patterns that did not imitate specific naturals. However, there were already many fly patterns designed to suggest the color and configuration of fly hatches that Halford had collected on the chalkstreams, although no plates and descriptions of these insects were published.

Most of the theory and exposition of *Dry-Fly Fishing in Theory and Practice* remain as true today—particularly on still currents and overskittish trout—as they were a century ago on the Hampshire chalkstreams. It is not so much that the lessons of Halford have weakened in intervening years, but more that he conceived a fabric of thought that has supported a century of subsequent discoveries. Halford described and explained the method with both a discipline and a relaxed charm almost totally absent from his later books. It was a large book for its time—more than three hundred pages—and it was remarkable for its scope and general standard of quality. It is difficult to select particular passages, but the chapters on dry-fly theory and technique are a superb achievement. His gratitude to his mentor Marryat is both generous and is handsomely expressed, but much of the book clearly belongs to Halford himself.

Dry-Fly Entomology appeared next in 1897, and it suffers from many serious flaws. Halford was a great fly-fisherman, but it was a book that almost demanded formal training in aquatic biology. It treats a curiously limited spectrum of fly hatches, and surprisingly omits color plates of the natural flies. It is a failing that cannot be easily explained, since the literature of angling was already filled with remarkable lithography and color work of trout-stream insects. Ronalds' *Fly-Fisher's Entomology* had clearly established a standard sixty-odd years before that the Halford *Entomology* simply did not meet.

Modern Development of the Dry Fly was published thirteen years later in 1910 and was also a relative disappointment. It might have become Halford's masterpiece had it only included plates that equalled the copper lithography in Ronalds' watercolors of 1836. However, in spite of the obvious omission of color illustrations, Halford did collect data on the chalkstream fly hatches with impressive discipline and detail. The natural flies are described and imitated with almost too-meticulous precision, and we are still refining many of these Halford imitations, using modern synthetics like cellulite and polypropylene and other synthetic dubbings with pale working nylon and exploring a direction Halford had abandoned in 1885.

His final manuscript was *The Dry-Fly Man's Handbook*, published at London in 1913, and it too was a surprising disappointment. It fell short of his earlier books, and his reputation was perhaps considerably reduced after its publication because its character is deeply flawed with dogmatism and *ex cathedra* arguments. Throughout his fly-fishing life, Halford had found the traditional wet-fly method unsuited to his personality, and even in his early years on the Wandle he did not find himself attuned to fishing it. Toward his closing years, the high priest of the dry-fly method did not just dislike wet-fly fishing—he bitterly adopted a posture of outright hostility toward it. Halford wanted the traditional wet-fly fishermen banned from the chalk-streams, particularly those who used sunk-fly techniques that only covered the water blindly and did not present the fly to a specific trout.

Halford also rejected out of hand the upstream wet-fly method that did fish to rising trout, and he was particularly hostile at the end of his life to the nymph-fishing theories that Skues practiced on the Itchen, a few miles farther east at Winchester. Skues had published his tentative *Minor Tactics of the Chalk Stream* in 1910, three years before Halford released his last book. Nymph fishing progressively enraged Halford, since he had become so invested with dry-fly purism that he had come to regard all chalkstreams as exclusively dry-fly waters—and his influence today still restricts some club waters on both sides of the Atlantic to dry-fly fishing, with its rather arrogant posture of moral and esthetic superiority.

Yet we must never let the sad pomposity of his final books, with their mixture of narrow-minded and faulty logic, obscure the fact that Halford produced a monumental shelf of books. His works proved epoch-making in their impact; he played a primary role in the evolution of the modern dry-fly construction, and he taught his colleagues to collect aquatic insects and imitate them carefully. His personal checklist of fly hatches and their imitations formed a comprehensive code of dry-fly practice on the south-country British rivers. Halford died in the late winter of 1914, before the tragic events of the following summer plunged his pastoral world into a bitter war, an ordeal that would strip England of an entire generation in Flanders poppy fields and along the bloody Somme.

In spite of his monumental flaws, Halford remains the prophet of a company of superb fly-fishermen, and he was clearly the outstanding fishing writer of his time. John Waller Hills includes an excellent summary of Halford and his position in angling literature in *A History of Fly-Fishing for Trout*. Hills was perfectly aware of Halford's character with its puzzling mixture of genius and prejudice, and in his chapter on the evolution of the dry-fly method Hills makes these observations:

> Halford is the historian of the dry fly. He did for the dry-fly method what Stewart did for upstream fishing. Neither were pioneers, for both described what they did not invent; but both, by practice and writing, made an unanswerable case for the system they advocated.
>
> With Halford was associated a band of enthusiasts who devoted themselves to perfecting the art and spreading their creed. Among them, they systematised the practice; they dealt with and solved technical difficulties; they developed rods, lines, hooks and flies to their present excellence; and all that they acquired or invented was told to the world in sober and convincing English. Never was a reformation worked out with greater ability or presented to the world with lucidity.
>
> Halford's first book, *Floating Flies and How to Dress Them*, was published in 1886, followed three years later by *Dry-Fly Fishing in Theory and Practice*. He wrote five others, the last published in 1913, shortly before his death. Two of the seven deal with special subjects, fishery management and entomology, and of the five that deal generally with fishing and fly dressing, the first two are by far the best. His later books are considerably less good.
>
> Halford's place in the history of angling is clearly marked. He is the historian of a far-reaching change, and as such, it is probable that he always will be read. Halford was well fitted for the task. He possessed a balanced temperament and a reasonable

mind. He took nothing for granted, and proceeded only by observation and experiment. He is also the master of a style suited to his theme, for while he never rises to great heights, he commands in his earlier books a prose which is apt and direct and essentially his own.

Halford established the dry fly as we know it, and there have not been many changes since he first wrote. Tackle has been refined still further; rods, reels and lines are, if possible, even more excellent, flies are more closely copied, and, in particular, the modern nymph and spent mayfly spinner are novelties.

But the method of fishing is unchanged. You still have to find your trout rising or willing to rise, and to cast accurately and delicately. Halford's directions on stream tactics are as good and as useful as on the day they were written.

If he is to be criticised, it is because like most strong reformers he overstated his case. He considered that the dry fly had superseded for all time, and in all places, all other methods of fly-fishing, and believed that those who thought otherwise were either ignorant or incompetent. He did not realize, and perhaps it is impossible that he should have realized, that the coming of the floating fly did not mean that previous experience and previous knowledge were as worthless as though they had never been; but that it did mean that from then onwards, fly-fishing was divided into two streams. These streams are separate, but they also run parallel, and there are many cross channels between them.

Other writers and fishing books soon joined the dry-fly theology, and one of the finest was an unpublished manuscript titled *Dry-Fly Fishing on the Exe and Other North Devon Streams*. It contains a remarkable list of fly-patterns that are still standards in our modern fly boxes. Its author was R. S. Austin and it was written about 1890. Its fly list included the Blue Upright, Half Stone, Dark Blue Quill, Dark Blue Dun, Dark Olive Dun, Light Olive Dun, Black Gnat, Yellow Quill, Pale Evening Dun, Claret Spinner, Jenny Spinner, Dark Silverhorns, Pale Summer Dun, and many other fly patterns not found among the Halford imitations.

Perhaps the most charming early work on the dry-fly method was *The Book of the Dry Fly*, which George Dewar published in 1897. Its first edition was illustrated with color plates of naturals and their imitations, while the second added a number of pastoral watercolors painted along the storied Test, Itchen, Whitewater, Loddon, Darenth, Wye, and the pastoral Avon at Salisbury. George Dewar was a quiet voice in the bitter quarrels of dry-fly dogmatics, and like Francis thirty years before, his *Book of the Dry Fly* called for tolerance and moderation:

> It is only the prig who sneers at the sight of the laborious wet-fly angler fishing the whole stream from morn 'til eve; only the man too stiff or self-conscious to learn, who scoffs at what he regards as

the affectation of the dry-fly angler assailing a single feeding trout, sometimes for over an hour at a stretch. Though there are bores and faddists who handle the rod, one is pleased to think that the ranks of true anglers do not contain a large number of aggressive and intolerant folk. Those that do exist are at a discount among most anglers by the streamside in the day-time, and at night in the smoking-room of the angling inn, lord it over their peers with difficulty, and do not lord it long. The extremists thus disposed of, there is no reason why anglers, dry and wet, should not in this freemasonry forget their little differences, or if they must argue, then argue gently, as Father Walton advised his pupil to place the worm upon the hook.

Dewar was certainly no Walton, but compared with the dour Halford and his endless philosophy of tactics and technique, the *Book of the Dry Fly* exhibits a touch of the poet. The book also explores nymph feeding, and these paragraphs from its introductory chapter are typical:

Both rejoice in the rise of fly, in promising angling weather, and in the long delicious day by the ever-companionable river, and in the beauty of the scenery—for what stream where the trout and grayling thrive has not, throughout its angling season, great beauty?

The scenery which the dry-fly angler enjoys is not to be compared to that which so constantly opens out before the salmon fisherman amid the hills of Scotland, or in the rugged landscape of fjord and field. Yet it has a quiet beauty and a sweetness of its own. It takes us, this pursuit of trout in the bright, low-murmuring streams of the Home Counties, by secluded woodland glades and dells, where the sun strikes through a dense overgrowth of oak and ruddy beechtree leaves; where the slender wood-warbler trills its song through the lengthening days of spring; to the edge and fringe of many little coppices, where, if you lie low and affect a cunning unconcern, you will see much bird and animal life; will see the gorgeous pheasant strut forth and pick up a fat meal in the grasslands; the noisy jay and the intensely nervous wood cushat flutter down from the hazel boughs, and eye you for a space with profound suspicion; the rabbit pop out from its retreat, and for a moment alarm, and be alarmed by, its feathered friends.

This pursuit of trout will take us, too, through the luxuriant meadows, where the chalk stream seems to flow clearer than the clean air itself, where many a step crushes some scented water-flower, and where the corncrake never tires of confusing us as to its real hiding spot in the tall grass; to dim groves of planted trees, where the mossy path is strewn with fir-cones, and the squirrels chase each other in glad security; to stately parklands, where the gnarled oak tree stretches forth its vast limbs in such fantastic forms, and where the hare will almost suffer you to tread upon it rather than stir from its form; and often, in sleepy south-country shires, to the remote thatched homes of humble country-folk, where bunches of herbs hang above the great red-bricked hearth, and where you are almost always kindly welcome.

To those who have no soul for scenery, and to whom there never comes that intense longing to be steeped in the odours, colours, and delicious sensations of spendthrift summer, which has always seemed to me inseparable from this pastime, dry-fly fishing cannot sincerely be recommended.

Before the nineteenth century ended, angling history produced one of the best fishing books ever written, the classic *Fly Fishing* written by Sir Edward Grey of Fallodon in 1899. His little masterpiece has many devoted admirers, including a few who believe that *Fly Fishing* is the finest work in all of angling literature. His prose is beautifully written and polished, and the book sometimes surpasses Walton in its ability to transport the reader to streamside. Its pages are filled with the perfume of wild flowers and water meadows, the sounds of thicket melodies and the harsh cries of rookeries and the river music itself, and the sight of mayflies hatching among the undulating strands of weed:

> What the angler thinks about in the evening will not be only of angling, but of the scenes in which he has spent the day. I am often ashamed to think how much passes unnoticed in the excitement of angling, but the general impressions of light and colour, and of his surroundings, are never lost. Some is noted at the time, and some sinks into one's mind unconsciously and is found there at the end of the day, like a blessing given in great bounty to one who was too careless at the time to deserve it.

Lord Grey loved his chalkstreams, particularly in their lush weeks of late spring and early summer, and believed that the chalk downs and water meadows of Hampshire were the loveliest part of England in the spring:

> May is the time of blossom and promise, the month of fresh leaves and bright shrubs, but June is the month in which the water meadows themselves are the brightest. The yellow iris, ragged robin and forget-me-not make the damp places gay with colour, and the clear water in the little runnels amongst the grass sparkle in the sun. Of the wild shrubs which flower in June, there are two so common that they seem to possess the month and meet the eye everywhere. One is the wild rose, and the other is the elder, and great is the contrast between them. The common wild rose is surely the most delicate of shrubs in spite of its thorns. It is exquisite and delicate in its scent, colour, character, and form, and there is nothing more graceful in nature than the way in which a long spray of wild rose in full blossom offers its beauty.

It is possible to fish the chalkstreams through the medium of Lord Grey's senses, in close harmony with the rhythms of the river, working flawless casts and floats over each rising fish. It is possible to locate a good trout sipping at the fluttering hatch of Medium Olives, dry the hackles of the fly gracefully with an effortless series of false casts, deliver it softly above the trout, and share the several heart-stopping moments while it floats toward the rises of our prey. There are three fine chapters on chalkstream fishing, with charming autobiographical passages about his college seasons at Winchester on the Itchen:

> It would not be suitable for me to attempt to tell here the full tale of my gratitude to Winchester, for to do this would lead me into many reminiscences which have nothing to do with angling. It will be enough to say that the memory of those days is altogether happy, and that the Itchen and its trout played a part in the happiness.

It is obvious from these lines that Grey understood that a fine trout stream and a fine college can provide a similar kind of pleasure, particularly in the memory of later years. Lord Grey wrote *Fly Fishing* when the evolving dry-fly philosophy had reached its peak, before the fresh revolution of Skues and his nymph-fishing theories, and its gentle lessons are as valuable today as they were more than seventy years ago.

The wet-fly method was never fully eclipsed by Halford and his new religion. E. M. Tod published his slender *Wet-Fly Fishing* in 1903, and his sparsely-tied patterns with their delicate wings and dubbed bodies are a prologue for Skues and his chalkstream nymphs. It is fascinating that history also turned to the south-country chalkstreams for the development of nymph fishing. Their fly hatches were rich, and their fish were challenging and difficult. It was this setting that deeply influenced both the dry-fly method and the nymph technique, a setting remarkably pastoral and contemplative in its moods.

George Edward MacKenzie Skues was a famous attorney who divided his life between a law practice in London and his beloved fly-fishing on the Itchen. Skues was a fly-fishing bachelor, like his American colleague Leisenring on the Brodheads in Pennsylvania, and it gave him ample time for his sport. Although the dry-fly method was at its zenith on the British rivers, Skues was blessed with an intelligence that would not accept dogmatics or discard past truths. He refused to jettison the skills and rich knowledge of the entire wet-fly tradition simply because the new dry-fly techniques had become fashionable. Although he remained primarily a chalkstream fisherman all his life, Skues continued to explore fresh alternatives to the dry-fly method on those waters.

His investigations were first published in the remarkable *Minor Tactics of the Chalk Stream*, which Skues assembled in 1910. The book and its conclusions were based upon a penetrating logic, a deeply rooted distrust of dogmatics, a comprehensive knowledge of the literature, a sense of the tradition of fly-fishing, and a whole spectrum of highly original thought. It made an eloquent case for employing wet-fly tactics on the chalkstreams, and although it aroused a chorus of vocal opposition among the Test disciples, its arguments were so convincingly articulated that the premises of *Minor Tactics* have never been successfully refuted. The book remains a classic of fly-fishing literature, its structure a subtle and elegantly argued brief for fishing the wet-fly method on the chalkstreams. It triggered an inexorable swing back from the fashionable dry-fly pendulum of the Halford school to the more broadly based philosophy of present-day tactics—and it is *Minor Tactics* that began the modern philosophy of nymph fishing. Skues faced strong and surprisingly bitter opposition in this high-noon period of the dry-fly method. Other chalkstream regulars had already become rigid disciples of Halford and Marryat, and Skues had voiced a philosophy that challenged their unbending *ex cathedra* theology that the dry-fly method was the only method worthy of their Hampshire and Wiltshire waters. It was a foolish argument that *Minor Tactics* easily parried.

Even a free-rising chalkstream trout takes eighty-five to ninety percent of its diet in nymphal and pupal forms. Skues rejected the notion that he should feel guilty for fishing his delicate nymphs on waters that Halford and his disciples had consecrated to the dry-fly method. The publication of *Minor Tactics* precipitated years of argument in London and along the famous south-country rivers. The feud between the nymph and the dry fly reached its climax in a famous encounter at the Flyfisher's Club in London, when the aging Halford challenged Skues.

Young man! Halford began testily. *You cannot fish the Itchen in the manner you describe in your book!*

But I've done it! Skues replied softly.

Skues died at the ripe age of ninety in 1949, almost forty-odd years after this encounter with Halford at the Flyfisher's. Since the Halford books published in this century tended to diminish his reputation, most angling authorities concur that Skues was clearly the finest modern writer on fly-fishing. Certainly, longevity played a role in his reputation, since he fished for trout over eighty-three years of his life, and the last seventy seasons were spent fly-fishing. Skues possessed superb powers of observation, and a mind sharpened by the disciplines of jurisprudence. His passion for angling was perfectly married with both that remarkable intelligence and a facility for lucid well-wrought prose. Skues' writing was both prolific and intensely personal with a pleasant humor in virtually everything he wrote; and his books taught gently, with deductions made from his own carefully observed experience on the river. His experience was exceptionally varied, and his turn of mind is so stamped with originality that Skues often explored concepts that had never appeared in the work of other writers. His books freely display this experience and wisdom, and are completely empty of the dogmatic and the didactic.

GEORGE EDWARD MacKENZIE SKUES

The principal laboratory for his experiments was the lovely Abbots Barton water on the Itchen above Winchester. Although *Minor Tactics of the Chalk Stream* did not appear until 1910, Skues had fished his Abbots Barton water for almost thirty years when it was published. He had also spent considerable time on the European continent, particularly along the gentle limestone rivers of Franconia in northern Bavaria. His passionate interest in both fishing and imitating nymphal forms had been growing steadily across those thirty-odd seasons, and there is evidence that his development of nymph fishing closely parallels the chronology of the dry-fly method after 1880.

Unlike the speculation in the books of Younger and Cutcliffe, who merely observed that nymphs and larvae deserved more attention from anglers, the work of Skues in *Minor Tactics* was a patient and disciplined search for precise imitations of nymphal life. Skues began the book in a posture of complementing the dry-fly method, but his writings in various British journals attracted such wrath from the dry-fly purists that he found himself outside the pale of accepted doctrine. It was a climate similar to the political animosity that engulfed the religious reformers of the sixteenth century. Historians have already begun to speculate on the single-minded dedication of Skues' later work on nymphs, and whether its intensity was a reaction to the angry criticism of Halford and his disciples. Without their bitterness Skues might have pursued his nymph fishing at a more leisurely pace, mixing the nymph technique with dry-fly fishing—and perhaps the wet-fly too—during periods of surface feeding. His exceptional success on chalkstream fish made Skues a legend in his own time, and his pragmatic willingness to adapt himself to both the moods and rhythms of the fish made him consistently successful. His principal transgression perhaps lay in easily outfishing his dry-fly rivals, and that fact was utterly unforgivable on the Itchen and the Test.

The nymph-fishing work first published in *Minor Tactics of the Chalk Stream* was subsequently expanded in 1921, with the introduction of the Skues classic *The Way of a Trout with a Fly*. It was a masterpiece in which Skues' fertile mind hopscotched freely over the entire spectrum of chalk-stream fishing with the full palette of traditional wet flies and dry flies and nymphs. It included a polished doctrine of imitating and fishing his nymphal imitations.

Sufficient time has elapsed to allow us a workable perspective on both Skues and his books. His writing is thoroughly grounded in fly-dressing theory and technique from Berners through Halford, with particular awareness of such north-country writers as Cutcliffe, Blacker, Webster, and Pritt. Skues' books are among the finest in the entire literature of angling, ranking him firmly with Berners, Walton, Cotton, Bowlker, Ronalds, Stewart, and Halford in his own historical importance. However, neither *Minor Tactics* nor *The Way of a Trout with a Fly* was actually conceived and written in book form. Most of his books were assembled from pieces that Skues had contributed to *The Field*, and the more insular *Journal of the*

Flyfisher's Club of London, and the only one of the six volumes conceived and written as a book was *Nymph Fishing for Chalk Stream Trout*, which was not published until 1939. *Side-lines, Side-lights, and Reflections* is perhaps his weakest book, although it is filled with useful observations, but it must be remembered that it was published against his better judgement in 1932. Two other Skues books were published posthumously: *Itchen Memories*, assembled by a younger brother from articles and notes on angling, and finally *The Angling Letters of George Edward MacKenzie Skues*, which Commander C. F. Walker selected and edited in 1956. Unfortunately, *Itchen Memories* is extensively flawed with mistakes, most stemming from the difficulties encountered in deciphering the handwriting of Skues' later years, but many of his *Angling Letters* cast considerable light on Skues' thinking about problems not fully discussed in the earlier books. Skues' several books are absolutely necessary to the modern angler.

When his experiments with the sunk fly were ultimately codified in *Nymph Fishing for Chalk Stream Trout*, which appeared on the eve of the Second World War, Skues was already in his eighties, rich with the fullness of his chalkstream years. However, *Nymph Fishing* is sadly flawed with a detailed and almost bitter critique of the obvious fallacies in Halford. It is unfortunate that Skues found it necessary to sustain an argument won thirty years before with a theoretical adversary already twenty-five years in his grave. *Nymph Fishing* includes a lifetime of experiences and observations on the behavior of both nymphs and trout, fishing the nymph, and the methods and materials best suited for imitating the natural subaquatic flies. It attempted to reform the tackle shops of the time and stop the continued sale of the mindless confections they incorrectly called nymphs. Skues failed in the attempt, although his nymph list of fifteen chalkstream patterns is most valuable.

My favorite Skues book is the earlier *Way of a Trout with a Fly*, and it is filled with strikingly original speculation on many aspects of fly-fishing. There are studies in the sensory perceptions of the trout, with special emphasis on its visual powers. It explores the details of rise forms and their character. There are little essays on fly dressing, and the art and theory of the craft, as well as many anecdotal parables from his field experiences. The book discusses special problems in fly hatches, tactics in playing fish on light tackle, glycerine and amadou, the origins of the dry-fly method, the excommunication of wet-fly fishermen by Halford and his circle of acolytes, and observations on all types of flies. *The Way of a Trout with a Fly* is filled with intelligent debate, like the following discussion of hackles in fly dressing:

> Recent books on trout-fly dressing are to blame for the prevalent opinion that the purpose of a hackle is to represent legs of a fly. It would be wrong to say that it is never the purpose of a hackle, but it is wrong—the wrongest kind of wrong—to represent it as the sole purpose or as invariably one purpose of a hackle.

In some of the old books, one finds instructions for the dressing of winged flies with no hackle, but anyone who tried such a pattern in medium sizes nowadays with moderately shy trout would find them apt to be frightened by the violence of the fall of the fly on the water.

The first function, then, of the hackle is to break the fly's fall, to let it down lightly on the water. And that is equally true whether it be a cock's hackle or a hen's, or a soft hackle from one of the smaller birds.

When the fly reaches the water, another function or other functions of the hackle, comes or come into play. If the fly be a floater, winged and hackled at the shoulder only, then the functions are, first, floatation and secondly (and often in a very secondary degree) imitation of the legs of the fly. Many good fly-dressers hold that the body is the really attractive part of a trout fly, and that in a floater, a hackle which is sufficient to ensure adequate floatation, and is otherwise colourless and inconspicuous, serves its purpose best. Good cock's hackle, such as is required for floating flies, is extremely sharp and bright when held up to the light, and even in the ruddy shades lets but little colour through. There can, however, be no harm and it is probably safer if the hackle, as held to the light, bears a fairly close resemblance in colour to the legs of the fly which its pattern represents.

The winged floater, hackled all down the body with cock's hackle to represent a sedge—or even a similar pattern without wings—is probably taken for a fluttering sedge by reason of the buzz effect.

A floater hackled with a sharp cock's hackle at the shoulder only, and without wings, is probably the best method of suggesting a spinner, spent or still living. The wings of the natural spinner have an iridescent glitter which is well suggested by the extended fibers of a first-rate rusty or honey or blue dun cock's hackle. Such a hackle thus serves (beyond the purpose of breaking the fly's fall) the double purpose of floatation and wings.

There are preludes to many modern fly-dressing theories in these brief paragraphs and an unspoken postlude to the Halford theories of dry-fly mechanics. Skues could not foresee the no-hackle revival of our time, which is partially based on the buoyancy of synthetic dubbing materials, but his attitudes would raise some doubts about the floating qualities and parachute behavior of any no-hackle dry flies in larger sizes. Skues does not support the Halford equation between hackles and legs, although he does not make the quantum leap of Marinaro in *Modern Dry-Fly Code* and suggest that hackles should primarily reinforce wing color and imitate legs only in their light-pattern indentations in the surface film. Skues' observations about a sedge imitation with a fully palmered hackle along its body anticipate both the long-standing caddis tradition on the Brodheads in Pennsylvania and the more recent theories of Leonard Wright and his *Fishing the Dry Fly as a Living Insect.* The shoulder-hackle spinner is another prologue to the fly-dressing theories of later writers like Dunne, Harding and Marinaro, and its conceptual thinking is not far from the hen-wing spinners of Swisher and Richards.

Skues' *Way of a Trout with a Fly* is also filled with penetrating observations on nymphs and nymph fishing, as well as detailed descriptions of tying the Skues patterns. The two basic methods are illustrated with exquisite watercolors from the paint trays of Captain Sainte Barbe-Goldsmith, and it is interesting to compare the following exposition with similar descriptions in Cotton or Bowlker:

> Placing your hook in your vise, begin whipping near the eye, and whip halfway down the shank. Tie in there, with the point towards the head of the hook, a bunch of six or eight fibers of heather of suitable colour, regulating the length so that when the fiber is bent over to the eye of the hook and tied down, there will be enough of the points left to be pressed out on either side to represent legs.
>
> Then pass the silk under the ends of the fibres of feather on the side of the bend of the hook, and whip on the bare hook to the tail; tie in two short, stout, soft whisks of suitable colour, tie in gold or silver wire, twirl on dubbing thinly, and wind to the place where the fiber is tied in; wind on the wire in regular spacing to the same point, and secure on the head side of the place where the fiber is tied in; thicken the dubbing, and wind over roots of feather fibre to head.
>
> Then divide the points equally, and press backward from the eye; bring over the feather fiber to the head, and tie it down with two turns, including a half-hitch, cut off the waste ends, and finish with a whip finish on the eye. Thus the legs are forced to stand out at right angles, or rather more backward, from the eye, and below the level of the hook shank, and the effect of wing cases is produced.

Such mechanics of fly dressing sound drab when removed from the mainstream of the book and its prose, and without the elegant watercolors of Sainte Barbe-Goldsmith, much of the mood of Skues is lost. Skues had that uncommon mixture of craftsmanship and technical creativity, and his books will be read as long as there is fly-fishing. He also had the clarity of a legal mind; his intelligence was fully trained to reason and define; and he possessed the ability of the scholar to sift and weigh both the evidence of the past and his own powers of observation. Such impressive gifts enabled him to succeed where lesser minds might have failed, yet there is a leavening of charm and humor in his books. These brief verses from his best book, *The Way of a Trout with a Fly*, are typical of his wry turn of mind:

> Oh, thrilling the rise to the lure that is dry
> When the shy fish comes up to his slaughter
> Yet rather would I have
> The turn to my fly,
> With a cunning brown wink under water.
> The bright little wink under water!
> Mysterious wink under water!
> Delightful to ply
> The subaqueous fly,
> And watch for the wink under water!

It should be understood that Skues had thoroughly digested the angling literature that preceded him, and that his powers of observation and intellect inevitably led him toward unbroken ground. He fully grasped the limitations of fishing theories evolved on the chalkstreams, including his own, and his writings bear evidence of that awareness. The catalog of fly hatches on these south-country British rivers is clearly limited, just as the heavy hatches on the limestone rivers of our eastern states and western spring creeks are restricted to relatively few species. Most stillwater insects are swimming flies, and move about in the current, both during their normal subaquatic lives and the brief period of hatching. There are many more varieties of aquatic insects found in riverine biosystems of mixed character, such as the swifter rivers of Shropshire and the northern border counties of both England and Scotland, while our American rivers are a lexicon of water types sprawling across an entire continent. Such exceptions to the Skues philosophy would be no surprise to Skues himself, and in no way weaken his importance in the history of angling. The conditions endemic to the chalkstreams are also found on slow-flowing alkaline rivers in geothermal or limestone regions, the occasional stillwater reaches of most watersheds, and lakes and impoundments everywhere. Skues is still unquestionably the father of nymph fishing, as surely as Cotton and Bowlker were the fathers of modern fly-fishing techniques. Skues and his chalkstream studies are the touchstone of our subsequent investigations, even though our increasing knowledge of fly hatches and their nymphal behavior make it clear that Skues' theories cover something less than the full scope of American nymph tactics.

Other fine British writers were also working during the Skues years on the British south-country streams. Their books covered both the chalkstreams and some of the swift-flowing rivers of the English Midlands and the Scottish border country. These other writers fully recognized the limitations of both dry-fly and nymph-fishing theories that were predicated on chalkstream fishing alone. They were aware that chalkstream biology restricted fly hatches to the slow-water mayflies and sedges, and that species attuned to high alkalinity were obviously more abundant. Stomach autopsies on trout from waters everywhere clearly confirm that the nymphs, larvae, and pupal forms of the aquatic flies are the primary components of the daily trout diet—in overwhelming percentages. Small crustaceans are especially important in weedy, alkaline environments and crayfish are important in the diet of larger fish. Terrestrial insects such as ants and leafhoppers and beetles are more important summer foods than we suspected in the past, particularly in combinations of hot and windy weather. Adult mayflies, caddisflies, and stoneflies remain important in their symbiotic relationship to the dry-fly method, although the stoneflies are important dry-fly hatches only on the swift rivers of our western mountains.

Doctor Francis Ward published his unique *Marvels of Fish Life* in 1911, almost a year after Skues made his debut with *Minor Tactics*. His work provided scientific confirmation of the refraction physics and trout-vision theories first postulated in Ronalds' *Fly-Fisher's Entomology* in 1836. Ward had considerable impact on fishing writers working on both sides of the Atlantic. He is mentioned in virtually every British book that ventures into the sensory perceptions of trout, and we find him being discussed in the books of fine American writers like Hewitt, Jennings, Grove, Fox, and Marinaro. Ward published a second book titled *Animal Life under Water* in 1919, and its observations on the visual images of trout flies from the trout's point of view are remarkable. The influence of Ward's experiments on subsequent books from superb British anglers like Mottram, Dunne, and Harding is obvious to the most casual reader.

Leonard West published a growing catalog of trout foods in his *Natural Trout Fly and its Imitation*, a year after which appeared *Marvels of Fish Life*. It was privately published in 1912 and copiously illustrated to depict more than a hundred insects, including the materials required to dress their imitations. His checklist surprisingly included a great many terrestrials, such as ants and leafhoppers and beetles. Unfortunately, West chose to use only the popular nomenclature for his naturals—as Carroll had in his *Angler's Vade Mecum* a century before—and it is not possible to identify them with certainty. It is a charming book in spite of this sizable flaw, particularly in its extensive color sketches of British trout-stream insects, artificials, and various fly-dressing materials.

J. C. Mottram was a skillful and famous English surgeon who focused his dexterity and his intelligence on fly-fishing, with a rich palette of impressive insights and creativity. His fishing studies were assembled in the interesting little volume titled *Fly-Fishing: Some New Arts and Mysteries*, which appeared in 1916. Mottram explored a number of original ideas on fly dressing and the vision of the fish and a fly in the surface film. There is also interesting speculation on nymph fishing and some no-hackle nymph patterns. The genesis of many concepts that reached more extensive development in the later work of important writers like Dunne and Harding in the United Kingdom can be traced to Mottram.

Martin Moseley was a first-rate entomologist whose interest in fly-fishing derived from his uncle, the half-legendary Frederick Halford. Moseley produced the definitive taxonomy for the British caddisflies in his purely entomological research, but he also published a handbook designed for fishermen to carry on the stream. It was written with the encouragement of Halford, who died before the Moseley handbook came to fruition, and the First World War delayed the publication of *The Dry-Fly Fisherman's Entomology* until 1921. Moseley was one of the few fishing writers formally trained in aquatic biology. His handbook was principally intended to provide the color illustrations omitted in the Halford *Dry-Fly Entomology* published almost twenty-five years before. Unfortunately, the amateurish hand-tinted watercolors provided in the Moseley handbook are poor in quality, and their flawed character is the key to the entire Moseley text. Mosely was desperately unhappy with the quality of the lithography and handcoloring work in his little *Entomology*, and it is tragic that his publishers were so misguided that they did not grasp the primary importance to the handbook of these illustrated fly hatches. Without adequate plates the Moseley book is virtually useless, although it contains an impressive quantity of basic information on British stream insects.

Major John Waller Hills wrote *A Summer on the Test* in 1921, the first of his superb books on fishing. Hills is among the first rank of fly-fishing authors, and his books on chalkstream fishing are an impressive display of knowledge and experience, written in a prose that is both lucid and filled with charm. His *History of Fly-Fishing for Trout* belongs in the library of any serious angler, and his excellent *Riverkeeper* is a biography of the legendary William Lunn, who served as keeper on the Houghton water for a half century. The structure of *A Summer on the Test* is the cycle of an entire season on that famous Hampshire chalkstream, and although its chronology has the surface texture of autobiography, it is filled with a series of teaching parables. Its prose makes delightful reading, and its pages include a number of beautiful dry points executed along the Test by the British painter Norman Wilkinson.

J. W. Dunne published his fine book titled *Sunshine and the Dry Fly* in 1924. It is an intriguing and challenging work. Dunne has some striking observations on fly structure, silhouette, light pattern in the surface film, translucency, and color mixes in his fly dressings. His book is fascinating to explore, with its notes on chalkstream hatches and a series of thirty-nine imitative patterns. His interior monologues are both absorbing and amusing to a modern reader, and his thoughts are lively with the counterpoint of original ideas:

> Many years ago I bought, in preparation for my first visit to a real chalk-stream, a complete set (one dozen each of twenty-seven patterns) of the smaller Halford trout flies. And for many years after, it used to afford me considerable satisfaction to inspect the contents of twenty-two nicely labelled compartments—appor-

tioned between two fly boxes—and speculate upon the day when I should discover the prototype of one or another of these beautiful little things actually hatching out upon the water.

The remaining five patterns had already justified, in some measure, their purchase. I had scooped from the water a female Welshman's Button, which was simply the Number 30 come alive; a fly which looked like the Female Olive Spinner took the air each evening; and once, in the late dusk, I had glimpsed, drifting past the bank a spinner remarkably like the Female Olive. The little red-headed Black Gnat had proved remarkably deadly. And there had been a morning when, finding a small blue-winged fly hatching in great numbers, I had put up, after some hesitation (for the body seemed entirely different) a Male Iron-Blue, and had annexed, therewith, three hefty Test fish. So I had no reason to doubt that the remaining patterns would, in due course, prove their worth.

But to tell the truth, I was more than a little puzzled at the number of Test flies which were *not* in the Halford series. Every day, all day long, these neglected insects were hatching out in hosts. They were all duns, sober looking little duns with almost colorless legs and *setae*, with wings varying from crinkled pewter to the tint of Sheffield plate worn thin, and with plain, monochromatic bodies varying from palest honey to darkest amber.

I could only conclude that these flies were peculiar to the Longparish part of the Test, and that for beautiful barred olives, and for cream-striped pale wateries, one must journey downstream toward Stockbridge.

Since, however, these latter *Ephemeridae* were not to be found where I was fishing, I had to make the best of a bad job, and, with the assistance of the Little Marryat and the Whitchurch Dun, did well enough on the whole.

It is interesting to travel with Dunne through his period of transition from Halford discipledom toward the developing maturity of his own concepts in fly tying and imitative patterns. Dunne recounts his sense of awe over the exquisite Halford dressings, his collection of delicate little mayflies that resembled nothing in the Halford descriptions, and his subsequent search for translucency:

Hunting through materials for body dressing, I turned up a skein of one of those artificial silks which have come into prominence of late years. They possess certain advantages over the ordinary floss silk. They are far more brilliant, and they look more translucent. They are more pleasant to work with, for the fibres are fat and glossy, and do not catch in every little roughness of one's fingers in the maddening fashion peculiar to floss silk.

It is in fact the easiest stuff to wind on a fly that I have so far come across. The slipperiness of the fibres is so great that they are able to slide longitudinally upon one another, and the stuff, consequently, packs more evenly in winding, and gives a smoother less wooly result when wound than real silk. Finally, owing to this slipperiness, the fibres comb out and separate at a stroke; and this peculiarity enables one to blend together strands of different colors as easily as one mixes paints.

But it is, of course, a commonplace of fly-dressing tradition that all silk darkens hopelessly when oiled; and I had no reason to anticipate anything else in the case of this artificial material. Nevertheless, the beautiful sheen of the stuff tempted me to such an extent that, more in idleness than with any serious purpose, I tied a mayfly body therewith. Then I oiled it.

The body promptly turned black.

So unexpectedly black, indeed, that it occurred to me to unwind the still-oily silk and examine it. To my immense surprise, I found it had not noticeably darkened at all! The solution to the mystery was obvious. What looks like darkening in such cases is merely the *black hook* showing through its sheath of transparent covering.

Eric Taverner published his comprehensive *Trout Fishing from All Angles* in 1925, and it remains today a virtual dictionary of trout theory and technique in the United Kingdom. Except for its discussions of trout and their several rise forms, it is not an unusually original book, although it does codify most of the best fly-fishing theory from Bowlker to Halford and Skues. Taverner is also quite useful to American fishermen, since his *Trout Fishing from All Angles* is a wide-ranging cornucopia of fishing literature, the biology of trout, tackle and fly-casting techniques, aquatic entomology, flies and fly dressing, knots and lines and leader design, field problems and experiences, rise forms, lake fishing, grayling, the biology of scale counting, legal aspects of fishing rights—and even a primer on the ecology of trout water and its management as a fishery biosystem.

Harold Plunkett-Greene published his remarkable book *Where the Bright Waters Meet* in 1929, and the literature of angling was enriched with perhaps the first truly poetic book since Walton or the exquisite *Fly Fishing* that Lord Grey of Fallodon published in 1899. It is a delightful book that should be in every library on angling, along with the warmly written *Golden Days* by Romilly Fedden—the fishing diary of a painter living on the Brittany trout streams. Plunkett-Greene was a famous tenor who lived for several years along the lyric Bourne in Hampshire in the decade before the First World War. The book describes his experiments with dry flies and nymphs, and his prose perfectly captures the character and mood of his favorite river. *Where the Bright Waters Meet* is a log of both fishing and English village life in those unspoiled years before the cataclysmic summer of 1914. There is still excellent fishing on the Bourne, especially the reach of water at the Hurstbourne Priors, and the country churchyard where Plunkett-Greene lies buried among the moss-covered headstones.

Colonel E. W. Harding published his little-known book *The Fly-Fisher and the Trout's Point of View* in 1931. It is a particularly noteworthy study, singular in its considerations of the sensory perceptions of trout and their relationship to turbidity, light transmission and subaquatic refraction, optics, light patterns of various insects in the surface film, and a labyrinth of factors affecting the response of the trout to both their natural foods and our artificial flies. Harding was a friend and regular correspondent of Skues in his later years, and his book is a sophisticated extension of the ideas in Skues, Mottram, and Dunne. Harding has had considerable influence on American fly-fishing, and important books like *A Modern Dry-Fly Code* and *Selective Trout* plus my own *Matching the Hatch* and *Nymphs* owe a remarkable debt to this contemplative officer who exercised an almost military discipline in his fishing. It is unfortunate that Harding's untimely death robbed us of a sequel to *The Fly-Fisher and the Trout's Point of View*. Its introductory chapter contains a passage much admired in *A Modern Dry-Fly Code*, and it has become the creed of a thinking fly-fisher on any river:

> To some all this may seem like taking a recreation far too seriously. If these objectors can take lightly the sense of baffled disappointment following on failure by the waterside; if they are content to enjoy success as though it were some caprice of chance; if, in short, they are content to be the slaves and not the masters of their fishing fate, then perhaps they are right: but to me the sense of bafflement robs me of half my pleasure, and casual unexplained success is but Dead Sea fruit to the palate of enjoyment.

Colonel E. W. Harding was an important convert to nymph fishing, along with other superb fishermen like Mottram and Hills and Taverner. Roger Wooley added his prestige to the nymph technique in his book *Modern Trout-Fly Dressing* in 1932. It included both patterns and contemporary techniques, with some four hundred dressings and illustrations of many natural fly hatches.

Doctor E. A. Barton published his book *Chalk Streams and Water Meadows* in 1932. Barton died just after midcentury, at the age of eighty-nine, after many seasons on the English south-country rivers. The riverkeeper on the Leckford water of the Test considered Doctor Barton the best angler on the river in those days, and he often fished on the Itchen with his friend Skues.

John Waller Hills completed his book *Riverkeeper* in 1934, and although it is his biography of the famous William Lunn, riverkeeper of the Stockbridge water of the Houghton Club, it is also a superb book on flies and fly-fishing. William Lunn was the Houghton keeper from 1887 until 1931, starting a hereditary line of keepers that exists today at the Houghton Club. Some of the most intriguing experiments in river management, artificial stocking of natural fly hatches, and fish planting are described in

WILLIAM JAMES LUNN

the book—along with a handful of innovative fly patterns like the active little Caperer, which anticipates the caddisfly theories of Leonard Wright and his *Fishing the Dry Fly as a Living Insect* by almost a full half century.

C. E. Pain also published his autobiographical *Fifty Years on the Test* in 1934, and although it is not a creative book in the sense of new tackle or tactics, it is a remarkable personal account of the Test during the half century that witnessed the development of both the dry fly and the nymph. Pain also includes prose and dry-point portraits of the major figures who fished the river after 1880 and played a part in both the river and its role as the historic challenge for great anglers like Hall, Marryat, Halford, Mottram, Barton, and Skues.

While aquatic entomology had steadily been progressing on British rivers, from Cornwall to the Scottish border counties, little work had actually been done on the lakes of northern England or the Scottish lochs. Skues had rather obliquely referred to this omission in his articles for *The Field*, and a similar observation is found in *Loch Fishing in Theory and Practice*, which R. C. Bridgett published in 1924. Many British anglers still consider it the best book written on the subject, in spite of its obvious omissions in entomological matters. Although Bridgett was not a skilled biologist, in the sense that he had collected and studied the principal fly hatches of his home waters, he clearly understood the principal insect orders and methods of imitating them. Except for a disciplined catalog of stillwater entomology, Bridgett covered every conceivable aspect of lake fishing. It is obvious from *Loch Fishing* that he was fully aware of his omission:

> It is somewhat difficult to decide to what extent the angler should be versed in the entomology of the loch, but I think that most will agree that a little knowledge at least of the subject is essential. My own opinion is that the slow advance in the art and science of loch-fishing is largely accounted for by the lack of interest displayed in the food of the loch-trout.

Similar arguments were advanced in 1934, when Sidney Spencer published his *Art of Lake Fishing with the Sunk Fly*, and his slim book is filled with fresh insights. Its arguments are important for fishermen who have believed, perhaps in unthinking obedience to the dry-fly theology of Halford and Marryat, that selective feeding does not occur with wet flies and nymphs. Spencer argued correctly that matching the hatch was equally important in both dry flies, and with imitations fished below the surface. Our expanding knowledge of lake and reservoir entomology unquestionably confirms his judgements.

H. P. Henzell followed the work of Spencer with *The Art and Craft of Loch Fishing* in 1937. It is a short, delightful book that perfectly captures the character of the lochs and the problems of fishing them. Henzell clearly rejected the notion that lake or reservoir fish lack sophistication and argued that a knowledge of entomology is the keystone to predictable success in stillwater fishing. His book further argues that our fishless days on lakes and streams alike are less indicative of inactivity among the fish than our ignorance about their diet. This excerpt from *The Art and Craft of Loch Fishing* clearly demonstrates that Henzell understood our lack of knowledge:

> It is a reasonable assumption that trout, like other fish and animals, feed sometime during each day, and the fact that no fish are breaking the surface is much more likely to mean that they are feeding on subaqueous forms of life, than that they are not feeding at all. The face of the loch may remain as undisturbed as a mirror, and all our wiles fail to induce one solitary trout to take

the fly. We can imitate very well, by the use of nymphs and wet
flies, the various larvae of flies and freshwater shrimps, and that if
we study the entomology and learn to fish these imitations
properly, there will be few blank days on the loch, and interest in
our fishing will tremendously increase.

Skues was also fully aware of the problems in loch entomology. His
writings in the *Journal of the Flyfisher's Club* of London, which regularly
appeared just after the First World War, argued that fast rivers, lakes and
impoundments required a patient group of creative investigators like Hall,
Marryat, Halford, and Moseley to ferret out their entomological secrets in
the future. Skues deplored the empirical trial-and-error approach of most

CHARLES RITZ

FRANK SAWYER

fly-fishermen, because he found it undisciplined and lazy-minded, and, like Harding, condemned haphazard fishing—unhappily adding that the majority of anglers deserved such censure.

Skues died at midcentury, and since his death there has been a growing number of his disciples among the roster of important British fishing writers, Perhaps the most widely known is the legendary Frank Sawyer, his fame undoubtedly coming from the effusive praise of Charles Ritz in his *Fly Fisher's Life*, a charming book that has been read around the world. Sawyer is a well-known riverkeeper on the pastoral Avon above Salisbury, and his skills with the small nymph are so remarkable that he has become famous throughout Europe and the United Kingdom.

It was Wilson Stephens, the former editor of *The Field* in the United Kingdom, who assembled and edited the writings of Sawyer into two superb books. The first was the idyllic *Keeper of the Stream*, which Stephens gleaned and polished from Sawyer's rough notebooks and published in 1952. It covers the cycle of an entire year and its effects on the rhythms of the river, and it reveals this Wiltshire keeper to have both a striking knowledge of river ecology and a considerable touch of the poet. Sawyer published his second book with Stephens six years later, the definitive *Nymphs and the Trout*, which codifies the style of minute-fly nymphing Sawyer worked out on the Netheravon beats above Salisbury. Skues argued that casting nymphs to rising fish is rather like dry-fly fishing, but Sawyer disagrees, believing that it is completely different, somewhat more difficult in many ways, and in no way inferior to the dry-fly method. Sawyer has had more than fifty 'years of experience as the riverkeeper on the smooth-flowing Avon near Stonehenge. It is a landscape worthy of both anglers and poets, and his books reveal that Sawyer is able to see deeply into the river, not just into its physical secrets of fish and fly hatches, but almost into the soul of its gentle weed-trailing currents.

Brigadier General H. E. Carey also published his charming book *One River* in 1952. Both Sawyer and Carey were writing about the little Avon above the cathedral town of Salisbury and about the same fishing beats, the Officers' Association water at Netheravon. Its members are largely retired army officers, since the famous British School of Infantry is located on the Salisbury Plain, and generations of British soldiers have trained there. During their training and service, many British officers fished the Avon watershed and its tributary streams like the Wylye, Nadder, Ebble, and the classic little Bourne. Such soldier-anglers often returned to fish these rivers upon retirement from the British Army, and skillful fishermen like Marryat, Turle, Harding, Heywood-Lonsdale, Carey, Walker, Coke, Hills, and Kite were all military men.

J. R. Harris also published *An Angler's Entomology* in 1952, adding much new information to the cumulative knowledge of fly hatches found in the books of Ronalds, Pulman, Halford, Dewar, Moseley, Skues, and West. Harris' *Angler's Entomology* has assembled a compendium of original research on fly hatches and other trout foods in the British Isles. His book covers the principal river and loch insects throughout Ireland and the United Kingdom, observations on their morphology and imitative fly patterns, and maps pinpointing their distribution and range. Harris and his *Angler's Entomology* not only treat the principal mayflies, sedges and stoneflies, but also cover the damselflies, dragonflies, midges, crustaceans, craneflies, ants, and tiny reed smuts. It is a major book which has richly expanded the catalog of fly hatches indigenous to the British Isles.

Colonel Jocelyn Lane was the first fishing writer to work with the *Angler's Entomology* at his elbow, and his *Lake and Loch Fishing for Trout* was published two years later in 1954. The influence of Harris is readily apparent, although it is obvious that Lane has not merely relied on Harris.

His *Loch Fishing* is constantly enriched by his own observations on the fly life of quiet waters. Lane made extensive use of aquarium studies to observe the diet forms eaten by the trout of the lochs. Two chapters of his *Loch Fishing* are devoted to fly hatches and other foods common to such waters, and Lane holds the conviction that imitative flies are critical to success on the lochs—admitting that the usefulness of the fancy loch patterns he had once recommended was on the wane.

Commander C. F. Walker published his book of fly hatches titled *Chalk Stream Flies* during this same period. Apart from the work of Frederic Halford, this is the only book on aquatic entomology to focus entirely upon the fly life of the chalkstreams. It includes four color plates of naturals and their imitations, and augments some of the entomological studies conducted by earlier authorities. Walker completed his second book on aquatic entomology a decade later, the original *Lake Flies and Their Imitations*, and it is still perhaps the best book on the entomology of lakes and impoundments in the United Kingdom. Its contents include a relatively thorough coverage of mayflies, caddis, midges, beetles, dragonflies and damselflies, alderflies, stoneflies and crustaceans. Walker is strongly in favor of imitation and clearly understands the importance of nymphs in lake fishing. The knowledgeable modern angler must know *Lake Flies and Their Imitations* whether he fishes the United Kingdom or the United States.

The most recent work of British aquatic entomology is *Trout Fly Recognition* by John Goddard. It includes detailed descriptions of virtually all the natural fly hatches common on British trout waters, but its most impressive feature consists of excellent color photography of 125 natural flies. It is rapidly becoming the standard work on the subject of the British aquatic diet forms.

Major Oliver Kite is the most recent British author to explore nymph-fishing techniques in his book *Nymph Fishing in Practice*, first published in 1963. Major Kite includes a number of valuable observations on south-country nymphs, their life cycles, habits and behavior. His chapters correlate the imitative flies developed for the chalkstreams with practical manipulation intended to suggest their subaquatic movements. Studies in the natural species, artificial fly patterns, basic solutions for nymph-fishing problems, and nymphing tackle are combined with portraits of fishing days on such varied south-country rivers as the Avon, Torridge, Bourne, Test, and the Wylye on its charming beats at Heytesbury and Fisherton-de-la-Mare.

Oliver Kite completes the circle of nymph development that began with George Edward MacKenzie Skues almost a century before. The relative simplicity of his fly books and presentation is testimony to the limited variety of fly hatches found on the chalkstreams below the Salisbury Plain. Kite clearly acknowledges his intellectual debt to Skues and his prolific writings, and in his preface, he also offers his gratitude to Frank Sawyer—his mentor in that landscape of water meadows, thatched-roof cottages and parish churchyards along the pastoral Avon.

It should be understood that across that same century preceding the writings of contemporary British anglers like Walker, Sawyer and Kite, American fishermen were exploring the character of their new world. Our fly-fishing heritage reaches back well before the Civil War, and its evolution is a history of adapting British theory to singularly American conditions. Its beginnings are preoccupied with fishermen like Thaddeus Norris and the frail, tubercular Theodore Gordon jealously husbanding both his health and his knowledge of fly dressing beside a potbellied stove in the old Anson Knight farmhouse on the Neversink. Theodore Gordon was the Catskill genius who adapted the dry-fly theories of Halford to our more varied fly hatches and conditions. His work and that of later giants like Edward Ringwood Hewitt and George La Branche, whose books soon followed, formed the basis of our American tradition.

American nymph fishing also evolved its own directions through the famous correspondence between Skues and Leisenring in Pennsylvania. It was the threshold in the mastery of an entire continent and its fishing problems, and its genesis is found on the classic rivers of our eastern mountains—from the tumbling little Brodheads in Pennsylvania to soon-legendary Catskill rivers like the Beaverkill and the Willowemoc.

8. The Evolution of American Fly-Fishing

Our history and tradition have roots in the mountains of Pennsylvania. It is a region of timbered plateaus and shallow forest-rimmed ponds, rising almost 2,000 feet above the Delaware Water Gap at Stroudsburg. Eagles and ospreys soar on the midsummer thermals, and the woods are alive with the shrill chatter of chipmunks and squirrels. Deer are still numerous in the region, foraging in the overgrown colonial farms and orchards on the high ridges. Woodcock covers and grouse thickets are common, and bears are killed by the deer hunters each winter. Lynx and bobcats and foxes thrive in its hemlock swamps.

The wind-swept ridges are punctuated with rolling summits like High Knob and Mount Pocono and Big Hickory. Century-old clubs like Forest Lake and Blooming Grove and the Brodheads Forest and Stream are fishing and bird-shooting enclaves long-rooted in their timber acreages. These are coupled with storied grand hotel resorts like Skytop and Buck Hill Falls, their own roots deep in the gilded age of a parlor-car society escaping the heat of midsummer in Philadelphia and New York. The immense numbers of brightly speckled native trout are gone now from the bigger rivers since the original forests of pines and hemlocks were lumbered and the springheads began to run warmer throughout the region.

Wild brook trout still spawn in the coldest tributary creeks. Such fish are brightly jeweled little trout of the icy headwaters, deep in the surviving hemlock and rhododendron thickets, high on the tumbling sources of the Tunkhannock, Sawkill, Tobyhanna, Lackawaxen, Blooming Grove, Bushkill, Swiftwater, Shohola, and the storied Brodheads itself.

These rivers, except for the crystalline Brodheads, run tea-colored from their swampy origins, rushing along the slate-colored ridges and sandstone outcroppings until they drop from the Pocono escarpment toward the sea in a series of charming lacework waterfalls.

Pocono rivers have a long history and tradition, since they were accessible to weekend Philadelphia and New York fishermen almost half a century earlier than their sister Catskill rivers farther north. The Pocono flowages feed the larger Delaware, from Mast Hope where the legendary Dan Cahill lived to the mouth of the Lehigh at Easton. Zane Grey lived and worked for many years in a farmhouse that still stands half-concealed among the trees above the Lackawaxen, and Hewitt described his encounters with rattlesnakes along the Shohola in his *Trout and Salmon Fisherman for Seventy-five Years*. The Lehigh drains the western slopes of the Poconos, its watercourse gathering the currents of smaller rivers like the Tobyhanna, Tunkhannock, Pohoqualine, and the Little Lehigh—the easternmost of the famous limestone spring creeks of Pennsylvania.

Gifford Pinchot lived at Milford and regularly fished at his own estate on the forest-cloaked Sawkill, and also along the charming little Bushkill farther south. The beautiful Brodheads is perhaps the largest of these east-flowing rivers that drain the Pocono escarpment, and since its currents are the most fertile of the Pocono streams, its fishing has been famous since 1836. The principal drainage course winds down its gentle valley from Canadensis toward the Delaware at Stroudsburg, and its tributaries are famous too—tumbling little rivers like the Swiftwater and Buck Hill, and the famous branch at the half-legendary Henryville House.

The story of the Brodheads is recounted in considerable detail in my book *Remembrances of Rivers Past*, which observed that the muses often proved fickle, and their treatment of angling history is no exception. American fly-fishing tradition has long considered the Beaverkill and its Catskill sisters the cradle of our fishing literature, but in recent years considerable evidence has emerged to indicate that the Brodheads is perhaps the true wellspring of the American angling heritage. There is also evidence that the Henryville House on its laurel-sheltered headwaters is the oldest trout-fishing hotel in America. Its rambling clapboard structure sheltered a phalanx of celebrities and fly-fishing presidents and every major American angling writer, from its beginnings in 1836 until the Great Depression.

Tradition along the Brodheads is old and rich. Its watershed was already well known for fishing when the Delaware tribe camped on its banks to fish and hunt through the pleasant Pocono summers. The Indian encampments never killed more fish than they could eat or cure for the winter or plant with their corn, and brook trout were still plentiful in colonial times. Both Delaware hunting parties and brook trout were plentiful when the Brodheads was still called the Analomink, but its poetic Indian name was forgotten once the tribal lands were settled.

Captain Daniel Brodhead negotiated for Pennsylvania acreages in 1734, dealing with the half-larcenous sons of William Penn. Brodhead emigrated into the Analomink Valley three years later, not long after the infamous Walking Purchase had fraudulently taken vast tracts of the region from the Indian tribes. Brodhead and his family in wagons lumbered through the primeval forests between New York and the Delaware Water Gap, ferried across the river there, carved fifteen hundred acres from the wilderness, sowed their crops, and prospered. Their original timber-framed cabins were soon replaced with a beautiful fieldstone house. The swift little Analomink flowed through Brodhead's Manor and emptied into an eddying side channel of the Delaware. Its waters teemed with trout, while the river also held salmon and walleyed pike and bass, and millions of coin-bright shad entered it to spawn each spring. The Analomink was a beautiful river, but it was not long before it became known simply as Brodhead's Creek.

The Delaware tribes remained hostile in those early years. Old hatreds still smouldered after the Walking Purchase, which had defrauded the Delawares and Minisinks of some twelve hundred square miles. The vast Walking Purchase acreages included both the entire Analomink watershed and Brodhead's Manor at its mouth. The tribal hatreds festered and journeyed westward into Pennsylvania with the displaced Indians, until the wounds erupted in the bitter Indian Wars of 1755. Painted war parties ambushed and ravaged isolated wagon trains, settlements and farmsteads. The savage fighting raged above the Kittatinny Mountains, and settled the old scores of the Walking Purchase in a series of massacres that drove the settlers south in terror.

Captain Brodhead and his five sons, who refused to join the refugees, barricaded themselves into their fortlike manor and successfully defended their family and servants. Soldiering was an old tradition with the clan, rooted in the experience of the ancestor who had served as an officer with the British Grenadiers that took New Amsterdam from the Dutch garrison in 1664. The five sons of the Brodhead family were well tempered in frontier skirmishes with the Indians, and later they all served as officers under Washington.

There was little fly-fishing in America during these years, except for occasional British officers who enjoyed the sport and had carried their tackle with them to the American colonies. American fishing remained primarily a matter of seeking food rather than sport, and our eastern fly-fishing shrines did not really become focal centers of angling until more than a century after the Walking Purchase. The Brodheads' angling tradition really begins with Halfway House, built by Arthur Henry on the freight wagon trace between Easton and Scranton in 1836. His primitive log-framed inn prospered with its clientele of mule skinners and stagecoach passengers. There were a few grouse hunters and fishermen too, and the little timber hotel was subsequently enlarged into Henryville House in 1848.

George Washington Bethune served as editor for the first American edition of *The Compleat Angler* in 1847. Its appendices included fly patterns and tackle recommendations for the Brodheads and its sister rivers. Bethune undoubtedly visited the Halfway House in his pilgrimages, and

GEORGE WASHINGTON BETHUNE

was probably the first major writer to pay his homage to Henryville. Its first fly-fishing celebrity was unquestionably Joseph Jefferson, famous both as a travelling actor and a frequent fishing companion of Grover Cleveland. Jefferson stayed with his entire family at Henryville House during the summer of 1848, and his autobiography describes fishing the Brodheads in those years, when it tumbled through a forest cathedral-dark with pines and hemlocks.

Frank Forester omitted specific mention of the Brodheads in his *Fish and Fishing* of 1849, the first completely original American book on angling, but like Bethune he discussed the remarkable brook-trout fishing available in the Pocono country. Forester was probably the second fly-fishing writer to explore the Brodheads and its sport, while Robert Barnwell Roosevelt was unquestionably the third in its changing cast of pilgrims. Brodheads fishing was well known in Philadelphia and New York by the time his famous *Game Fish of the Northern States and British Provinces* called it a great stream in 1862. The freight wagons and canal boats were already waning, and when the railroad pushed upstream toward the developing coal fields farther west, the little Brodheads witnessed a fly-fishing boom.

Thaddeus Norris is perhaps the most famous of these early fishermen along the Brodheads, and to grasp his stature in American fly-fishing literature we must understand that Norris was both our Walton and our Cotton combined in a single angler. The elegant calligraphy of his signature is found in the old register at Henryville House as early as 1851. Brodheads fishing played a major role in Norris' life, and its character permeates *The American Angler's Book*, which he published in 1864. It was the first American book with a sweep that reached from the smallmouth rivers of the Atlantic Coast to the wilderness salmon rivers in the north country, and Norris had also fished the grayling rivers of Michigan before their primeval forests were destroyed. James Henry was the proprietor of Henryville House in those midcentury years, and his son Luther often accompanied Norris along the stream. The prose of his *American Angler's Book* has a curious music in our ears. It is patterned on the fishing dialogues fashionable after Walton, and in one passage he exclaims to his young disciple Luther Henry:

> What pretty bright trout there are in this bold rock creek! It would full be called a river in England, and so it is!

Thaddeus Norris experimented with primitive floating flies, and his exploratory tactics are described in detail in *The American Angler's Book* of 1864. Norris used two flies that settled softly on the current and were taken by the trout before they sank. It seems unlikely that his floating flies were more than heavily hackled wet flies with fat well-dubbed bodies, but such primitive dry-fly methods were apparently practiced on the Brodheads almost twenty-five years before the tactical innovations of Theodore Gordon in the Golden Age of the Catskills.

Norris also played an important role in the evolution of the modern split bamboo rod. His frequent companion astream on the Brodheads was Samuel Phillippe, the famous gunsmith and violinmaker from Easton. It was Phillippe who invented our modern four- and six-strip methods of bamboo construction, with the power fibers of the cane on the outside. Although British rodmakers had long experimented with various three-strip bamboo rods, as Edward Fitzgibbon tells us in his *Handbook of Angling* in 1847, the surface fibers of their cane were placed along the glue faces inside the rod. Hugh Sheringham finds a later reference to such rods in *Fishes and Fishing*, which Doctor William Wright published in 1858. Wright was the court surgeon to Queen Charlotte of England, and his book described a Welsh rodmaker who built him a three-strip bamboo rod in 1805. Apparently the split bamboo rod has its three-strip origins at the threshold of the nineteenth century, sometime between the work of writers like Bowlker and Ronalds.

Samuel Phillippe worked out the first modern six-strip design in his shop at Easton. His finished sections were hexagonal and turned round, glued with their power fibers on the outside, and Phillippe apparently evolved the concept with Calcutta cane about 1845. British rodmakers were still making three-strip rods as late as about 1860, according to Sheringham in his introduction to the *Fly-Fisher's Entomology*, although some had begun to place the bamboo power fibers on the outside as well. However, it was apparently the skilled hands and inventive mind of Phillippe that developed modern four- and six-strip bamboo construction. Phillippe passed on his knowledge and techniques to Thaddeus Norris, who became one of the great rodmakers of the nineteenth century, and their buckboard fishing expeditions along the Brodheads played a considerable role in the history of split cane.

Norris and Phillippe shared their river in those halcyon years with other famous anglers. Perhaps the most famous was the wealthy Chancellor Levison, whose first trip to Henryville occurred more than ten years before the Civil War. Levison would become a founding member of two Olympian organizations in the history of American fly-fishing: the storied Brooklyn Flyfishers' and the prestigious Anglers' Club of New York. During the Civil War years, Chancellor Levison apparently limited his trips to the Nissequogue and Suffolk Club waters on Long Island, but the surrender at Appomattox saw his return to the Brodheads with his friends Charles Bryan and Henry Wells. Both Bryan and Wells were also destined to become famous American anglers. Levison was a well-known tournament caster, who later drew huge crowds to witness his skills at Prospect Park in Brooklyn and the Haarlem Mere casting platform in Central Park. Levison also served as the impeccable bowler-hatted fisherman for the casting plates in *Fly Rods and Fly Tackle*, which Henry Wells published in 1885. Levison and Bryan joined two other founders of the Anglers' Club of New York for opening weekend in 1885, their names clearly visible in the fading register of Henryville House on the Brodheads: Chancellor Levison, Charles Bryan, Edward Baldwin, and Edward Rice. The following season they were joined by two British guests and two years later, in 1887, their first trip was cheered with six inches of spring snow. Bryan and Rice stayed on and fished, while their less hardy companions returned to New York. The river was coffee-colored with snowmelt, and both men confessed in the Henryville register that their forty trout were taken on worms.

These pioneers were joined by another early member of the Anglers' Club of New York—Henry Ingraham, who first fished the Henryville water in 1887. Ingraham later served as president of the Anglers' and published his classic *American Trout Streams* in 1926. It now commands a price well over a hundred dollars in the American collector's market, having been published in a limited edition of 350 copies. William Cowper Prime was another major figure who fished the Brodheads after the Civil War. His disparate worlds included an extensive legal practice in Manhattan, lectures in art history at Princeton, and authorship of popular angling books like the famous *I Go A-Fishing* of 1873. Prime was the bellwether for a considerable parade of Princeton-educated anglers that included men on the Brodheads like Henry Van Dyke, Edward Ringwood Hewitt, Otto von Kienbusch, Victor Coty, Eugene Connett, Manning Barr, Henry Davis, Dudley Mills, Russell MacGregor, Philip Nash, Frederic Barbour, Bradley Heald, Sidney Stone, and the celebrated fishing writer Dana Lamb. Prime

THADDEUS NORRIS

was quite famous in his time, and books like *I Go A-Fishing* provided fireside reading for an entire generation of gentleman anglers.

There were a number of important American books that appeared before the nineteenth century ended. Doctor W. N. Fry began the science of American fish culture in 1854, with a book titled *Artificial Fish Breeding*, and the celebrated Genio Scott published his famous *Fishing in American Waters* in 1875. The remarkable folio of paintings by S. A. Kilbourne, titled *Game Fishes of the United States*, was first published in 1878 with a superlative text by Brown Goode of the Smithsonian Institution. Pisciculture was explored further in books like *Fish Hatching and Fish Catching*, which Seth Green and Robert Barnwell Roosevelt published together in 1879. *Artificial Propagation of Fish* was published by Doctor Theodatus Garlick the following year, and Henry Wells appeared with his pioneering *Fly Rods and Fly Tackle* in 1885. Brown Goode followed two years later with his commentaries on the Kilbourne paintings and his excellent book *American Fishes*. His charmingly literary style and knowledge of ichthyology make Goode a pleasure to read almost ninety years later.

The Brodheads' tradition provided the prologue. Henryville House was not the only shrine in those years, and other inns, boarding houses, and hotels appeared and prospered in the closing years of the nineteenth century. Other anglers made regular pilgrimages from Philadelphia and New York, and their fly-fishing retreats in those tranquil Pocono summers are famous too—the Ledge Pools on the Haase Farm, the productive dry-fly flats on the La Bar stretch, the austere little hotel operated by Charlie Rethoret on the lower river at Analomink, the Lighthouse Tavern, and the ill-fated Spruce Cabin Inn have all passed into Brodheads history and legend. These landmarks from the past have either fallen victim to tragic fires and floods or evolved into private fly-fishing clubs. Henryville House alone remains as a living symbol of the past—an historic inn as old as American fly-fishing itself—although its fishing mileage has also passed under the control of a private club called the Henryville Flyfishers.

James Henry died at the close of fishing in 1888, and the primeval brook-trout years died with him. The hotel register at Henryville is filled with yellowing records of the phenomenal catches in the twenty years following the Civil War, but then the little river declined. The impressive forty-fish baskets of large speckled trout had taken their toll, along with the rapacious lumbering that ravaged the magnificent virgin pine forests to provide railroad ties and framing lumber and mine timbers. It was a carnal waste that felled the hemlocks, stripping their bitter bark for the acid required in the tanneries, their naked trunks left rotting in the woods. The forests were culled for their hemlocks to process the flood of buffalo skins and cowhides coming east from frontier railroad towns like Abilene and Wichita and Dodge City. The uncontrolled lumbering and the clearing of land for orchards and farms had changed the eastern trout streams forever. The fantastic brook-trout fishing of the colonial period had been wantonly eradicated, and the Brodheads soon became too warm for *Salvelinus*

HENRY VAN DYKE

fontinalis—the last big brookie recorded in the century-old hotel register at Henryville was a two-pounder taken in the spring of 1893.

During the years before its decline, the Brodheads had hosted a procession of fly-fishing celebrities. John Sullivan and Lily Langtry and Jake Kilrain added the brash and raffish glamour of the prizefight world and the music hall to Henryville House; Grover Cleveland and Benjamin Harrison had fished there too. But in spite of such celebrated outsiders, fishing and fishing writers were still the nucleus of life along the Brodheads, and the Henryville register includes these lines from Henry Van Dyke:

> Over the hill to Henryville
> 'Tis oft' the fisherman's cry,
> For I'll catch a fourteen-incher
> With an artificial fly!

The celebrated scholar Henry Van Dyke achieved equal fame as a professor of religion and English literature at Princeton, and as a trout-fishing writer of eloquence and skill. Van Dyke was a familiar sight along the Brodheads during the last twenty years of the century. His books are considered classics now, particularly *Fisherman's Luck* and *Little Rivers*, which he published just before 1900. His writings tell us that he loved the Brodheads, and the tumbling little Swiftwater tributary above Henryville. Van Dyke described his encounter on the Swiftwater with Joseph Jefferson, when the old thespian had made a sentimental journey back to Henryville in his twilight years. Jefferson had spent an idyllic summer there with his family almost a half century before, but let these words from *Fisherman's Luck* describe their meeting on the river:

> One May evening, a couple of years since, when I was angling in the Swiftwater, and came upon Joseph Jefferson stretched out on a large rock in midstream, and casting his fly down a long pool. He had passed the three-score years and ten, but he was eager and happy as a boy in his fishing.
>
> "You here," I cried, "what good fortune brought you to these waters?"
>
> "Ah," he answered, "I fished this brook forty-five years ago. It was here in the Paradise Valley that I first thought of Rip Van Winkle. I wanted to come back again for the sake of old times."

Paradise Valley is a local name for the Henryville branch of the Brodheads. Local historians claim it was given that name by the celebrated northern cavalry officer, General Philip Sheridan, who spent a recuperative summer there after the Civil War. Joseph Jefferson owed his fame to the drama *Rip Van Winkle*, which he performed in hundreds of theatres across the country, and that fame ultimately led to fishing trips with Grover Cleveland.

Opening day in 1895 was historic at Henryville. It marked the beginning of the Brooklyn Flyfishers, and the event is recorded in the time-stained pages of the hotel register. The founding document is a full page of intricate nineteenth-century penmanship, listing fifteen names as charter members. These founders were wealthy brewers and merchants from Brooklyn, and their club is immortalized in the classic *Fishless Days* from the pen of Sparse Grey Hackle. Their annual ritual of the scroll was repeated each season until 1897, when the names of James Walker and William Oxford were added to the roster. Charles Bryan was in Britain that spring, and the Brooklyn Flyfishers registered Bryan in absentia, wishing him good fishing on the Itchen and Test.

The Brooklyn Flyfishers left the Brodheads after a disappointing season in 1897 and sadly observed in the log that its once great fishing for brook trout seemed finished. History tells us that the clan migrated north into the Catskills, establishing themselves in a log cabin above the Hardenburgh farm on the Little Beaverkill. These Brooklyn Flyfishers played a major role in the Brodheads tradition, and their aura travelled with them into the Catskills, where Theodore Gordon was already at work evolving an American dry-fly code. The fame of the Catskills had been steadily growing, especially with the completion of the Ontario & Western Railroad into the Willowemoc and Beaverkill, and the departure of the Brooklyn Flyfishers from the Brodheads marked the end of our Pennsylvania beginnings.

Although the Brodheads' tradition is older, it is the several Catskill rivers that are considered the shrines of American fly-fishing. Club water has closed most of the prime fishing on the Brodheads in our time, but there is still much public mileage on the Catskill streams. Their source lies in a surprisingly small cluster of high ridges lying west of the Hudson. It is still a wild and beautiful region behind its tragic facade of roadside diners and elaborate summer colonies and borscht-circuit resorts. Drive-in theatres and harness-racing tracks and village dumps scar the highway approaches, but the high Catskills still rise unscarred between the Hudson and the Delaware, their rolling summits covered with forests, their massive shapes smoke-colored in the distance.

These high ridges are a series of somber outcroppings, polished and wounded with the grinding force of the primordial glaciers that shaped them millennia ago. Red-tailed hawks and solitary eagles soar on the winds that sigh across these barren heights. Bears and bobcats are killed each winter. Hunters on snowshoes tramp the hemlock thickets in search of winter hares, and sometimes there is still the report of a cougar. There are thousands of deer in the second-growth forests, whitetails that have waxed fat with the apples of colonial orchards long overgrown and abandoned. Wild turkeys are coming back above the Schoharie. Ruffed grouse and woodcock are still plentiful enough for birdhunters who know the covers. Great blue herons feed in the mist-shrouded Catskill ponds at daylight and horned owls flush from the hemlock thickets. There are kingfishers along the streams, and the phoebes and barn swallows dart and wheel among the hatching aquatic flies. Sometimes an angler can glimpse a rare pileated woodpecker in the Catskills.

The Catskill rivers are still beautiful. Some of their character and solitude has been lost to the cacophonic landscape of roadside diners and automobile graveyards and developers. The wilderness frontier that existed when the Dutch farmers settled the Hudson Valley has gradually disappeared or retreated to the highest ridges. These Dutch settlers often lost livestock to the cougars and bobcats in the valleys that drained toward the Hudson, and they named one little river for these predatory mountain cats. *Kaaterskill*, the Dutch settlers named the river that tumbles down from Blackhead Mountain.

The surrounding region is a mother of rivers. Catskill Creek is no longer an important trout stream, but its sister river across the ridges of Blackhead Mountain is the famous Schoharie, winding toward its junction with the Mohawk Valley. The east branch of the Delaware has its beginnings on Bearpen Mountain, which turns the currents of the Schoharie toward the north. Two minor Catskill rivers rise in the southern ridges of Sullivan County. The swift Callicoon joins the big water of the middle Delaware between Port Jervis and Long Eddy, and the tea-colored Mongaup joins the Delaware farther downstream. These are the peripheral Catskill rivers.

The principal rivers of the Catskills are born on the forest-covered shoulders of only two mountains. Doubletop Mountain rises 3,868 feet in the western ridges, and its maternal springheads are the source of three well-known rivers—Dry Brook at Margaretville, the smooth Willowemoc above Livingston Manor, and the legendary Beaverkill itself, perhaps the most famous trout river in America. Slide Mountain reaches 4,207 feet from the Hudson west of Kingston. It is an impressive forest-covered ridge, sprawling above the lesser mountains and rolling foothills. Its ravines are the genesis of the Rondout, the swift-flowing currents of the Esopus, and both branches of another famous Catskill river—the Neversink of Theodore Gordon and Edward Ringwood Hewitt.

This round handful of classic Catskill rivers is the second wellspring of American fly-fishing literature. Many of the famous anglers who began their fishing careers on the Brodheads in Pennsylvania were later found on the rivers of the Catskills, and the Beaverkill and its sister river the Neversink quickly became the home waters of figures like Theodore Gordon, Herman Christian, Roy Steenrod, Edward Ringwood Hewitt, Albert Hendrickson, Leslie Petrie, George La Branche, Reuben Cross, Emlyn Gill, and the controversial Louis Rhead. It is the Valhalla of American fly-fishing.

Fishing pressure, the construction of reservoirs, and pollution have decimated the character of several Catskill rivers. The Rondout figured prominently in the Bergman books like *Just Fishing* and *Trout*, but it is no longer a major trout fishery because of its reservoir. The rainbows on the Callicoon are only a minor echo of the dry-fly fishing enjoyed by George La Branche before the First World War, and the Mongaup still surrenders a few monster browns although it is marginally warm in places. Major impoundments on the Schoharie, Esopus, Delaware, Rondout, and Neversink have drowned some first-rate fishing mileage. However, in some cases they have created new trout fishing in the reservoirs themselves, and impressive upstream migrations of big spawning browns. The icy deepwater tailings of some impoundments have also improved and extended some trout habitat downstream, while others too often release insufficient flow to purge their watersheds of silt and sustain both fly hatches and spawning.

These are the rolling tree-covered Catskills and their sister Pocono Mountains that lie across the Delaware in northern Pennsylvania. It is a beautiful region steeped in the history of fly-fishing. Its role in our tradition is so pervasive that of seventy-odd books with a major role in the evolution of American fly-fishing, almost fifty volumes have had their primary inspiration in the gentle rivers of these eastern mountains.

The threshold of our century saw the publication of a minor classic, *The Brook Trout and the Determined Angler*, in which Charles Bradford described his adventures on these Catskill and Pocono watersheds. It is a charming book that has recently been reprinted. David Starr Jordan and Barton Evermann published their monumental book *American Food and Game Fishes* in 1902. It is lavishly illustrated and runs almost six hundred pages. Some of its nomenclature of species and subspecies has changed, with the variable winds of modern taxonomy, but it has remained the definitive work in the field for almost seventy-five years.

Theodore Gordon had already fished the Catskills for some twenty-odd years before the Brooklyn Flyfishers moved north to the Hardenburgh farm on the Beaverkill. Old-time regulars on the Catskill rivers like Herman Christian and Roy Steenrod knew Gordon better than anyone else during the closing years of his life. Such men cannot remember when Gordon first arrived in the Catskills, but they all agree that he was a summer fixture along the Neversink as early as 1895.

Gordon was born at Pittsburgh in 1854, although his parents were both from New York. His mother came from a family of considerable means in the Mohawk Valley, and his father was from an old Manhattan family. They were married in 1850, while both were living in the South. The elder Gordon had travelled to Alabama for his health, and Fanny Jones Gordon had gone there to live with relatives after her parents died. The young couple journeyed briefly back to the North, for Theodore Gordon was born in Pennsylvania, only four months before his father died tragically of malaria at thirty in the Gulf Coast city of Mobile.

Antebellum sentiments against Northern visitors were already rising in those years, and Fanny Jones Gordon soon took her young son back to Pittsburgh. They arrived in 1860, and lived there with relatives. Theodore Gordon was six years old that summer, and his relatives owned a farm in central Pennsylvania near Carlisle. The rich cornfields, limestone spring creeks and millponds of the Cumberland Valley were a paradise for a small boy who had come to love the countryside. It was the fertile region of Big

Spring and the Yellow Breeches and the Letort Spring Run, superb little brook-trout streams born in the upwellings of huge limestone springs. The hills above the rich valley floor were filled with deer and woodcock and grouse, and there were egrets and herons in the bottoms. It was a world teeming with life, from the egg-filled chicken houses and dairy herds to the wild things in the incomparably rich watersheds and mountains. It unquestionably affected Gordon deeply, and perhaps ultimately caused him to abandon both the cities and the comfortable life-style of his birth.

The winters that he spent in Pittsburgh after the Civil War were another matter. The cold winds buffeted the steep-walled streets of the city, raw and unchecked in their passage across the Ohio farmlands farther west. The city winds were foul, grimy with the belching smelters, potbellied stoves and furnaces that shrouded rooftops in a man-made overcast and acrid yellowish sulphur, dioxides. Theodore Gordon suffered during the bitter seasons for he was never really strong. His frail body thrived in the hot country summers at Carlisle, but winters back in Pittsburgh were desperate. Gordon was a boy who was always sick, and a series of heavy colds, flu, sinus problems, earaches, bronchitis, and frequent bouts of pneumonia plagued him throughout his childhood. Fanny Gordon became overly protective and distraught, and young Gordon missed so much school that he soon fell behind his classmates. His disposition became moody, ill tempered, and withdrawn.

Soon after the surrender at Appomattox, Fanny Gordon decided to take her frail son back south, into a more gentle climate. The young widow and her son lived briefly in a number of cities, finally settling in Savannah about 1879. There are virtually no details of these years, yet it was the period in which Gordon acquired the manner and education commensurate with his birth. During the postwar years in Savannah, Gordon apparently worked as a bookkeeper, bank teller, or securities agent. Perhaps he worked at all three, and it is unfortunate that we know nothing of his formal education.

Theodore Gordon remains something of a mystery, and his history is particularly mixed after 1880. Some historians believe that he went north to New York after a relatively brief time in Savannah, staying occasionally with relatives at Haverstraw. There is evidence that he fished the small brook-trout tributaries that tumble down into the upper Hackensack near Haverstraw. Gordon certainly was not solely a trout fisherman in those years, and there is evidence that he sometimes fished the ponds at Congers for pickerel and bass. We know that he returned briefly to selling securities in New York, since his letters tell us as much; but when his cash reserves seemed marginally adequate, Gordon soon disappeared into the Catskills with his fishing duffel.

During this period, Gordon apparently developed his fanatic passion for trout fishing and began learning to dress flies. It is still not certain where he learned this skill. Roy Steenrod received most of Gordon's books after his death at Bradley in 1914, and among the volumes was a dog-eared copy of

THEODORE GORDON

The Fly-Fisher's Entomology. It contained a superb color plate that illustrated each step in dressing a wet fly, and Gordon perhaps taught himself to dress his elegant wet flies from these copper lithographs and the accompanying instructions. Gordon himself tells us in his notes and letters that he learned about dry flies from Halford's *Floating Flies and How to Dress Them* and from subsequent correspondence with Halford himself. Gordon wrote the following passages on the dry-fly method about twenty-five years later:

> My attention was first seriously engaged soon after the publica-
> tion of Frederic M. Halford's fine work in England, I think in
> 1886, but the dry fly had been used at least a quarter of a century
> earlier. In Thaddeus Norris' *American Angler's Book* published in
> 1864, there is a description of dry-fly fishing on the Willowemoc.
> Norris, using two flies tied expressly for the occasion and a leader
> of the finest gut, was able to lay them so lightly upon the glossy
> surface that the trout rose and were hooked before the flies sank.

Gordon often observed that he had contracted the dry-fly bacillus about 1889, apparently from reading Halford's books, and that he soon imported the necessary tackle from England to tie them himself. Frederic Halford sent a complete set of his imitative, chalkstream dry flies to Gordon in 1890. These flies were subsequently willed to Gordon's close friend and fly-dressing protégé, Roy Steenrod, and the historic collection is now housed at the Anglers' Club of New York.

Gordon's health failed badly about 1900, forcing him to move from Manhattan to live with his relatives at Haverstraw, with his fly-dressing and living quarters in a carriage-house flat. Gordon moved permanently to the Catskills about 1905, both because of his advancing lung disorders and his continual poverty. During the summers, Fanny Gordon sometimes travelled to Liberty not far from the Neversink that Gordon fished and loved for so many seasons. Sometimes Gordon joined his mother during her vacations there, and people who knew him remember both his baskets of trout and his skill in preparing them for supper. Fanny Gordon was ultimately too frail to visit her son and remained with her relatives in New Jersey at South Orange. She died just before Christmas in 1915, having lived eighty-six years, and was totally unaware that her son had died of tuberculosis at Bradley near the Neversink earlier that same year. The Gordons were a tragic pair.

Herman Christian was another half-legendary Catskill fisherman who lived along the Neversink. Christian was one of the few men who truly knew Theodore Gordon well, having been permitted behind the public façade of his surprisingly brusque and suspicious character. In the closing years of Gordon's life, Christian lived approximately a quarter mile from him and fished more with the master than anyone else in the entire Neversink valley.

Christian ultimately owned the lovely Neversink Farm on the Big Bend Pool at Hall's Mills, in a region that still retains a surprising sense of wildness. Much of its solitude stems from the narrow mountain roads above Curry and Claryville, winding macadam and gravel without guardrails that discourage traffic. Christian worked his mountain farm for its honey, timber, firewood, and maple syrup. He trapped along the river and its feeder brooks, raised vegetables in his garden, hunted woodcock and ruffed grouse and hares, and spent as much time fishing as possible.

It's a good living—Christian always leavened his hawklike features with a fleeting smile—*but my best crop is trout flies!*

Theodore Gordon often expressed a grudging admiration for Christian's knowledge of the Neversink and his ability to read the river and catch big fish. Christian had been born in 1882 on the famous Rondout. His father died two years later, and Christian was working in the Neversink Valley as a hired farmhand in 1896. Like many Catskill farmboys, Christian lied about his age and joined the United States Army after the Spanish-American War, serving with the Tenth Infantry in Cuba and the Philippines. Christian began fishing the Neversink around Hall's Mills as early as 1891, when he was only nine years old. During the summer of that year he camped with two older men above the Big Bend, on a timbered hillside he would own half a century later.

Caught my first brown trout with an eel set in 1896, Christian explained at his farm. *Weighed two-and-a-half pounds and sold him in Liberty for fifty cents.*

Christian could never remember exactly when he began fishing with flies, but he was sure he was fly-fishing the Neversink as early as 1897. Gordon was already a fixture in the Catskill country, and Christian wanted some of his elegant flies. Gordon had an almost impenetrable reserve, but Christian knew he sometimes gave flies to his friends in the valley. In *Fishless Days and Angling Nights*, Sparse Grey Hackle quotes Christian on their first real meeting at Hall's Mills:

> Around 1906, I wanted to get Theodore Gordon to tie some flies for me—in those days, he was generous in giving his flies to people he knew. I asked Bruce Leroy about it, and he said that Gordon did not give flies to everybody, and suggested that I get some good feathers for him. I got some blue duns and pale gingers, and took them to Mister Gordon, and we became acquainted.

Bruce Leroy was also quite close to Gordon, having inherited a prosperous mountain farm at Leroy's Corners about three miles from Bradley, where Gordon spent the last years of his life. Like Gordon's friends Christian and Steenrod, Leroy was a Catskill man who preferred hunting and fishing to work; and he became close enough to Gordon that his family named a son after the famous fisherman, but unfortunately Leroy died before his impressions of Gordon could be recorded.

Christian remembered those early years quite clearly and recalled that when Gordon moved from the boardinghouse at Neversink, he went to live with the Anson Knight family. Their farm was near the Neversink Bridge, and the post office would not deliver Gordon's mail there. Christian began to bring it across the bridge every afternoon, and they would sit talking afterwards for hours. Sometimes Gordon offered his visitors a glass of cognac or whisky, but he seldom drank himself. Christian obviously held Gordon in great esteem:

> Whenever I located a nice, big fish, the next day I'd take Mister Gordon down to fish for it. I wouldn't take a rod myself. I'd ten times rather see him catch it. But almost always he insisted on my fishing a little with his rod. He would not fish at all, no matter how many fish rose, until the fish he wanted began to feed. When he got him, he usually would stop fishing. He never kept more than three or four fish, but always good ones. He liked to give a brace of fish, or a brace of partridge or woodcock, to the summer people he liked.

Gordon was a tiny man, weighing only about ninety to a hundred pounds, and stood only slightly more than five feet. He was considered a superb wingshot and liked upland bird hunting, although he lacked the stamina for a long day in the Catskill grouse and woodcock covers. Gordon often took walks along the country roads, carrying the bamboo tip case of his Payne rod as a combination cane and swagger stick. His cigarettes were a fierce chain-smoking habit, and Gordon rolled his own, using only one hand like a cowboy, working the paper between his thumb and fingers. Almost everyone who knew Gordon well remembers his skill with home-rolled cigarettes and the fact that he never licked them but secured the tobacco with an expert twist of the paper. Gordon always took only a few puffs, threw the cigarette away restlessly, and immediately rolled another—his death from tuberculosis might well have included overtones of emphysema and lung cancer.

Sometimes Gordon stayed briefly at the simple little York Hotel in Claryville and at several inexpensive boardinghouses along the Neversink. During the last three years of his life, Gordon principally lived at the old Anson Knight farmhouse near Bradley. Before his health failed him completely, he fished widely on all the famous Catskill rivers, but in those final years he seldom ventured more than an easy walk along his beloved Neversink from his quarters in the Knight farmhouse.

Theodore Gordon was obsessively secretive, and jealously guarded his fly-dressing skills in those Catskill years. They were skills that were largely self-taught, presumably from the writings and diagrams in the books of Ronalds and Halford and through later correspondence and samples sent from Halford himself. Christian describes Gordon's mysterious attitude toward his skills in these quotes recorded in *Fishless Days and Angling Nights*:

> As a fly-maker, there was one outstanding fact about Theodore Gordon. He never taught anybody to tie, never showed anybody anything, even me. When I went to his room, if he had a fly in the vise half-finished, he would take it out and lay it on the table. I

used to show him flies that I made, and sometimes he would say, "That one ought to take fish," but he would never say anything about the way they were tied. He liked me, and he would make me flies, but he would never let me see him make a fly.

Herman Christian remained an extremely close friend, and Gordon gave him a treasured rod a year or two before his death. It was a superb three-piece Payne that Gordon had ordered from Highland's Mills in 1895. Gordon was typically short of cash and finally paid for the rod with thirty-nine dozen flies in barter—about fifty dollars' worth of elegant woodduck-winged dry flies in the elegant style of the Catskill school. The Payne was a three-piece rod measuring nine and one-half feet, and with the slow action fashionable in those years. Gordon gave the rod to Christian in 1912, and it is now in the collection of the Anglers' Club of New York.

Roy Steenrod was another famous Catskill fisherman who knew Theodore Gordon intimately over the years. Steenrod subsequently became a great fly dresser in his own right and originated the Hendrickson pattern along the Beaverkill two years after Gordon's death. Steenrod shared

ROY STEENROD

Gordon's fly-tying materials with Christian after Gordon finally died in 1915. Steenrod was born at Liberty in 1882, a few miles from the Neversink, and caught his first trout in one of its tributaries when he was only five years old. He became a postmaster at Liberty in 1904, when Gordon was staying there at the Liberty House with his mother. Steenrod often wrote postal money orders for the materials, Hall-type dry-fly hooks, and other fly-dressing equipment that Gordon regularly imported from England. Although Herman Christian believed that Gordon absolutely refused to share his knowledge of making flies, it was Steenrod that he trusted enough to share at least some of that knowledge. Gordon insisted that Steenrod be bound to secrecy and suggested that he first learn to dress flies without using a vise, in order to match the hatch along the stream. Steenrod learned his lessons well.

The postmaster also received Gordon's collection of fishing books after his death at Bradley. It was not an extensive library, but it was a well-chosen selection. It included the handbook *Amateur Rodmaking* that Perry Frazer had published in 1906 and there was a copy of *The Dry Fly and Fast Water* that Gordon had treasured, generously and elegantly inscribed by its author George La Branche. Emlyn Gill was also represented, through his *Practical Dry-Fly Fishing*, although Gordon had once told Steenrod he did not think much of the book. The copy of Ronald's *Fly-Fisher's Entomology* that probably taught Gordon the rudimentary techniques of dressing the wet fly was in the collection. There was also a heavily thumbed copy of Francis' *Book on Angling*; and it is surprising that Gordon also owned a copy of Kelson's *The Salmon Fly*, although its inscription tells us that it was a gift from the famous R. B. Marston in England. Since Gordon was allegedly disinterested in the exact imitation theories of the Halford school, it is equally surprising to find *The Natural Trout Fly and Its Imitation*, which Leonard West published privately in England only a few years before Gordon died.

Finally, there was the cherished shelf of Halford books themselves. There was the famous *Floating Flies and How to Dress Them* of 1886, his masterpiece *Dry-Fly Fishing in Theory and Practice* of 1889, the handbook *Dry-Fly Entomology* of 1897, and the later *Modern Development of the Dry Fly*, which Halford published in 1910. Gordon had also acquired *The Dry-Fly Man's Handbook*, which had been published less than a year before his death. From his fly-fishing library, it is not difficult to understand how completely Gordon had mastered the techniques of the first half century of the dry-fly method—and how the Catskill expert achieved his stature as the father of dry-fly fishing in America.

Although he obviously treasured his friendship with Theodore Gordon, Steenrod shared the opinion of his other Catskill neighbors that Gordon was often moody, brusque and withdrawn. Gordon received ten or twelve letters every day, mostly from his fly-tying customers and other fishermen, although there was some mail from his relatives in New York, New Jersey, and Georgia. Steenrod remembers that Gordon kept his natural blue dun hackles in envelopes bearing his name and an address in Savannah. Gordon seldom mixed with his neighbors, except for Bruce Leroy, Herman Christian, Steenrod, and a few families of summer people from New York. Sparse Grey Hackle included this quotation from Steenrod in his *Fishless Days and Angling Nights*:

> If Gordon liked you, it was all right, but if not, you had better keep out of his way; he was kind of a cranky old cuss. When I was working in the Post Office, I had Wednesday and Saturday afternoons off, and I seldom missed walking over to Bradley to spend the afternoon with him.

Sparse Grey Hackle makes the observation that conversations with Steenrod about those days were always somewhat veiled, perhaps to protect the memory of Gordon from some of the unhappy history of his life. There are two photographs of Gordon fishing with a mysterious lady along the Neversink, a few hundred feet above the old Neversink Bridge at Hall's Mills. Both were photographer's proofs fixed with a sepia tint, and were found among the pages of Gordon's books after his death. The picture of the two reclining at a streamside picnic remains unpublished, and the other photograph of the pair actually fishing later became the frontispiece for *The Complete Fly Fisherman*, for which John McDonald carefully edited the copious notes and letters of Theodore Gordon. Steenrod acknowledged the existence of these puzzling photographs, and identified their setting as the river at Hall's Mills, but would reveal little else about the matter. Herman Christian was almost as tight-lipped on the subject of the woman in Gordon's life, but he did reveal the following scraps of information to Sparse Grey Hackle:

> Gordon was disappointed in love, and the girl in the picture is the one. She was definitely not a local girl—and I just don't know who she was.

Steenrod tells us that, judged by modern standards, Gordon used relatively clumsy tackle but that he cast effortlessly with a light silk line and fine leader in spite of his frail body. His placement of the fly was delicate and precise. Gordon read water flawlessly and stalked his fish like an otter. His early tactics employed the traditional wet fly fished downstream, although ultimately he fished nymphlike wets upstream just under the surface. Steenrod was not given to false illusions about the past—as are many fishermen who reach their eighties—and he argued candidly that Gordon was probably not equal to the best modern anglers and fly makers, but in his time he stood virtually alone.

Theodore Gordon died in 1915, during the week when the first dry-fly hatches would start coming on the Neversink, but a late spring snow had blanketed the valley. It reached the windows at the old Anson Knight farmhouse where he lay and drifted through the weathered headstones in the Claryville churchyard. The gravelly earth was still too deeply frozen from the bitter Neversink winter for the gravediggers, and only memorial services were held for Gordon in the Catskills. Gordon's death came as a surprise in spite of his poor health. Steenrod and four relatives attended the memorial service in the simple Claryville church that has a carved wooden trout for a weathervane. Bruce Leroy and Herman Christian had failed to learn about either the death or the church services, and Gordon's body had already been shipped south on the Ontario & Western before they heard the unhappy news. Both men were heartbroken all the rest of their lives.

SPARSE GREY HACKLE

Gordon was not interred at Claryville, and the site of his grave remained a mystery until Sparse Grey Hackle helped to ferret out its location in 1957. Official records were ambiguous on the subject of his actual burial, and his friends and relatives widely disagreed about its possible site. The rather vague records of the town clerk at Neversink simply list New York as the place of burial. The files of McGibbon and Curry, the morticians from Liberty who handled the funeral arrangements for Steenrod and Gordon's relatives, revealed that his simple casket had been shipped on the Ontario & Western a day after the memorial services. It had been consigned to a nephew in New Jersey, and the records indicate that it was received at the Weehawken railroad terminal.

Beyond that brief skeleton of fact was silence. Some friends and neighbors had mistakenly believed that burial had taken place at Claryville, but the rumor was promptly refuted. Steenrod believed that Gordon had been buried by his family in New Jersey, although one relative remembered that Gordon had been interred in an old city cemetery in Manhattan. Others argued for a burial site at Haverstraw, where Gordon had lived with his relatives at times. Cemetery records in these places were checked without results. Finally, the riddle began unravelling with the hypothesis that Gordon's mother had died only nine months after his death, raising the possibility that they had been buried together. Gordon's mother had been living with relatives in New Jersey; and in the municipal archives of South Orange, the following record was found:

> Fanny Jones Gordon, aged 86 years and one month, residing at 444 Hillside Place, South Orange, died of cerebral hemorrhage and arteriosclerosis, December 23, 1915, and was interred in the New York Marble Cemetery.

There are two similarly named cemeteries in Manhattan, and the records of both were quickly checked. Gordons were numerous in the records of both cemeteries, but no record of Theodore Gordon or his mother was found. There were no headstones in either cemetery; like several old-time cemeteries in New York, these burial grounds consisted of stone vaults containing the last remains of several people. Only the name of the vault owner was found on the identifying markers, and the only complete record of the bodies interred is often in the books of the cemetery corporation. This was the case with Theodore Gordon and his mother, and the following was finally discovered in the records of the Board of Directors:

> At the first meeting of the Directors in 1916, it was reported that among those interred in the New York Marble Cemetery during 1915 were Fanny Jones Gordon and Theodore Gordon, both in the vault of George Gordon, No. 26.

New York Marble Cemetery is the cul-de-sac interior of a block of shops, drab tenement buildings, shabby townhouses, and flophouses that shelter the detritus of city life. It lies not far above the financial district, between Second and Third Avenues in downtown Manhattan. Its only visible clue from the street is a locked wrought-iron gate in a narrow sidewalk passageway between two buildings. Its lacework arch is crowned with a tiny cast-iron angel. There is a second wrought-iron gate exactly like the entrance grillwork at the street and beyond this second gate is the bare-grass courtyard of the cemetery. Through these gates on the wintry April morning that I visited the place, only the high rubble masonwork of the walls and a thin patch of grass were visible in the pale sunlight beyond the wrought-iron grilles. The entire cemetery is less than an acre, its barren floor carpeted simply with grass and silence, and it is sad to think that a man who lived his final years on the sun-bright riffles of the Catskill rivers lies imprisoned in the abrasive cacophony of lower Manhattan.

The late Guy Jenkins knew Gordon on those Catskill rivers in the early years of this century, and like his distinguished father before him, Jenkins bought flies from the old master. Gordon and Jenkins carried on an extensive correspondence over the years, and many of those letters were included by John McDonald in *The Complete Fly Fisherman*. Gordon's letters are filled with happy images of fly hatches on summer rivers mixed with the loneliness of the bitter Catskill winters. It is possible to share the hush of snow on windows glazed with frost and shiver with the wind whistling along the roof slates of that little farmhouse on the Neversink. Sometimes it is possible to imagine the frail Theodore Gordon on such nights, his coughing almost sepulchral after midnight, dressing exquisite flies in the Skues-type vise he later willed to Roy Steenrod. It was a tragic and difficult life, and although it was spent doing something he truly loved, the image of a frail Dickens-like Gordon at work near his potbellied stove is disturbingly melancholy.

Jenkins included a brief series of recollections about Gordon in *The Gordon Garland*, a limited edition published by the Theodore Gordon Flyfishers in 1965. It concludes with a letter received from the old master at the Anson Knight farm, unhappily written only a month before he died. Gordon lists the twelve dozen flies he is shipping and renders a bill for fifteen dollars, plus twenty cents charge for registering the package.

My bank account is pinched, the brief letter ends in a wistful note. *Hope yours is fuller.*

Although Gordon did not live to finish his book—and family stories tell us that its partially finished manuscript was foolishly burned after his death in fear of tuberculosis—his mastery still lives in *The Complete Fly Fisherman*. It was lovingly assembled by John McDonald in 1947 from the notes and letters of Gordon. Its brilliance and perception are undeniable, and no angling library is complete without a copy.

The death of Theodore Gordon lowers the curtain on the genesis of American fly-fishing. More than any other angler, Gordon was the philosophical architect whose work successfully spanned the distance between the historic European tradition and our American beginnings. His mind and experiences reached across the landscape of centuries from Dame

Juliana Berners and Izaak Walton to the classic *Dry Fly and Fast Water*, which George La Branche published less than a year before Gordon died on the Neversink. Theodore Gordon provided the bridge between the chalk-stream philosophy and the problems of our burgeoning continent. His experimental work along the Catskill rivers was soon followed by the books of other anglers like Gill, Southard, La Branche, Hewitt, and Camp. The twenty-five years between the death of Gordon and the Second World War became a rich period in the history of American fly-fishing.

Emlyn Gill published his *Practical Dry-Fly Fishing* in 1912. It was an introductory work that openly advocated fishing the water and dropping a floating pattern in likely looking places in the current. It discussed fishing an open riffle or pool with a checkerboard pattern of casts, making sure its trout would see the fly. It was a philosophy totally unlike the British method, with its emphasis on casting to each rising trout, and its haphazard methodology still dominates most American dry-fly tactics.

George Michel Lucien La Branche was an elegantly groomed and tailored young stockbroker who published *The Dry Fly and Fast Water* two years later. His book helped to codify the American dry-fly philosophy of fishing the water, rather than casting to individual rising trout, and its lucid prose became the bible for an emerging generation of American anglers. It also triggered a bitter rivalry between Gill and the younger La Branche, since Gill believed that *The Dry Fly and Fast Water* had merely copied his earlier book, and that its widespread critical acclaim should have justly been his. History is sometimes fickle, but in the case of *Practical Dry-Fly Fishing* and *The Dry Fly and Fast Water* its judgements seem just. La Branche owes little to the work of Gill in his theory and practice, and virtually nothing to *Practical Dry-Fly Fishing* in terms of character and style.

La Branche fully deserves his acclaim as the writer who consciously modified British chalkstream theory to the swift rivers of the Catskills and the Appalachians. *The Dry Fly and Fast Water* was shaped primarily on the Bordheads, Beaverkill, and Willowemoc. Although his reputation among fly-fishermen is focused on his studies in the dry-fly method, La Branche was also skilled in other techniques of fly-rod work. He was expert with bucktails, wet flies, and nymphs, and he was never narrowly committed to the dry fly. His conjectures in *The Dry Fly and Fast Water* suggest fishing a sparsely-tied wet imitation to a nymphing trout, choosing a color and configuration and size suggestive of the natural insects, and working it past a rising fish to simulate a hatching nymph. La Branche cut quite a dashing figure with his graceful casting, striped silk tie, soft-brimmed British fishing hat, and Burberry shooting coat with its Norfolk tailoring. The lovely etching executed by Gordon Stevenson along the Neversink has captured his elegance forever, from the custom waders and three-ounce Leonard rod to the perfectly trimmed regimental moustache. But it is his effortless casting on a stream with myriad pitfalls of overhanging branches and alders that is remembered best on the Willowemoc. Sparse Grey Hackle mentions these half-legendary skills in *Fishless Days*:

GEORGE MICHEL LUCIEN LA BRANCHE

But if distance is not necessary to the angler's cast, control—the ability to cast accurately and delicately—is. Accuracy is a prime necessity when obstacles make it difficult to reach the fish. When deep water, overhanging trees, or the lack of room for a backcast forbid the use of that best of all fish-getters, the short straight cast, the angler must resort to high art flavored with black magic—the skillful manipulation of rod and line which so defies analysis and classification that it is called, simply, tip work. George La Branche likely may have been the greatest of them all at this, his forte. His preference was for smallish water, and the limitations imposed by so restricted an environment required him to perform blackest magic.

The first American to attempt the Halford-like correlation between artificial flies and the fly hatches of our American waters was Louis Rhead, whose *American Trout-Stream Insects* was published in 1916. His fly collections were made largely on the Beaverkill, where the solitary Rhead was a familiar figure after the First World War. Like several British writers early in the nineteenth century, Rhead unfortunately used popular insect names of his own invention rather than accept scientific nomenclature, and his entomological drawings were far from clear. It is virtually impossible to identify the species he so carefully collected, and his work now has little more than historical interest.

Edward Ringwood Hewitt made his debut with the book *Telling on the Trout* in 1926, the same year that Henry Ingraham published his notable *American Trout Streams*. Hewitt ultimately wrote several important books about fly-fishing, and truly deserves his reputation as a technician and creative thinker. The famous Hewitt Big Bend stretch of the Neversink, with its home camp and hatchery and laboratory, was the scene of a lifetime spent experimenting with the problems of fish culture, trout-fishing techniques, and methods of fishery management. Such research ultimately led to the 1931 book *Better Trout Streams* that outlined his theories for stream management and improvement. His river property is now largely buried under the depths of the Neversink Reservoir, except for a few log-cribbing pools that survive at the Big Bend Club. It was a reach of river famous for its tree-hung flats, the waist-deep impoundments above its cribwork dams, and the foam-covered spillway pools downstream. Big fish loved the highly oxygenated flows under the dams. The Neversink is still a surprisingly cold habitat for its latitude and size, with sweeping riffles and strong chutes and incredibly limpid ledgerock pools, all holding good fast-water hatches of mayflies and Plecoptera and sedges. Its slightly acid chemistry and temperatures favor insects that are more common on trout streams much farther north, like the clinging flat-bodied *Rhithrogena* nymphs and the strikingly triangular *Baetisca* mayflies. Hewitt's tireless experiments on the river led to dry-fly spiders and bivisibles and Hewitt skaters, with their unusually long stiff-fibered hackles. There were also unusual experiments with leader color and taper design. Hewitt compiled his slim *Handbook of Fly Fishing* in 1933, and the following year he published the famous pamphlet titled *Nymph Fly Fishing*. The Neversink held unusual populations of flat-bodied and triangular nymphs that led to the development, in concert with John Alden Knight in the Hewitt farmhouse on the Neversink, of shaping lacquered bodies with a pair of notched needle-nose pliers. Although these early experiments were relatively crude, Hewitt clearly recognized that his fast-water nymphs included ecotypes not found among the round-bodied species described by Skues. The slender *Nymph Fly Fishing*, more pamphlet than book, proved itself a pioneering work in spite of its omissions and faults.

Hewitt concluded his long career with *A Trout and Salmon Fisherman for Seventy-five Years* in 1948, and its pages were largely based upon the earlier *Telling on the Trout* and *Secrets of the Salmon*. Hewitt lived a long and important fly-fishing life. Both Hewitt and his fishing camp on the Neversink are gone now, along with his ancient Buick with the rod holes cut in its roof. The lower river and its rhododendron ledges are drowned in the waters behind the dam. Change continues to erode the pastoral beauty of the region, although its sense of the past still survives in a few fishing camps and the white clapboard church at Claryville with its wooden trout weathervane.

Charles Zebulon Southard first published his encyclopedic *Trout Fly-Fishing in America* in 1914, and it was a remarkable success, with its surveys of American rivers and its twenty color plates of flies. Its success resulted in a second Southard volume, the monumental *Evolution of Trout and Trout Fishing in America*, which appeared in 1928. It contained an added eight color plates of American trout species and has become a fine collector's item on the rare book lists.

The thirties provided a surprisingly rich series of angling books, considering the widespread depression that gripped America. Hewitt published three works in this period, and the decade began with the charming *Taking Trout with the Dry Fly* by Samuel Camp. It was a book that followed in the footsteps of Gill and La Branche, and presented a summary of American dry-fly practice in the thirty-odd years after Gordon.

Eugene Connett published his superb tactical text, *Fishing a Trout Stream*, on reading the character of a river in 1934. Preston Jennings wrote his marvelous *Book of Trout Flies* in these same years, and the Derrydale edition published by Connett was released in 1935. It included exquisite line drawings and hand-tinted watercolors. It was the genesis of the disciplined studies in American stream entomology that Theodore Gordon had proposed in his notes and letters fifty-odd years earlier. Its precise taxonometric identification of fly hatches and the color plates of the insects themselves equalled the fine British books of Ronalds, Halford, and Moseley. Jennings fished widely along our eastern rivers, collecting important hatches from the Raritan and the Brodheads to the south, through all the major Catskill rivers, and as far north as the Chazy and

EUGENE CONNETT

PRESTON JENNINGS

Ausable and Battenkill in northern New York. His fly patterns were
elegantly tied in the style of the Catskill school, and they remain workable
imitations of our principal eastern hatches. Jennings was a frequent visitor
to the charming West Kill Tavern, while he fished the swift West Kill and
the pastoral Schoharie at the bottom of its valley. The proprietor of the
tavern was the equally famous Arthur Flick, who learned to dress flies from
men like Jennings and Leslie Thompson and Chip Stauffer, and had his
own role to play in American fly-fishing before midcentury.

John Alden Knight was fishing and writing in these same years, and his memorable book *The Modern Angler* was published in 1936. It was a fine introductory work covering trout-fishing practice in the thirties with many useful tips on tackle and tactics, plus an exposition of the solunar theory in fishing. Its color plates of contemporary fly-dressing practice were expanded in the later *Theory and Technique of Fresh Water Angling*, which Knight published on the threshold of the Second World War. The *Field Book of Freshwater Fishing* came four years later in 1944, but it was repetitive and did not match the earlier books, which form the core of his best work. The last book to come from John Alden Knight was written in concert with his son, the late Richard Alden Knight, whose charming boyhood portrait had first appeared as the frontispiece of *The Modern Angler*. Their collaborative volume is the excellent *Complete Book of Fly Casting* and, excepting Knight's strange preference for the side-thumb grip of the casting hand, it remains the best comprehensive modern text on the subject.

Reuben Cross wrote his attractive *Tying American Trout Lures* in 1936, and followed it four years later with the poetically titled *Fur, Feathers and Steel*. These two companion volumes on fly dressing formed the written doctrine of the Catskill School of tying, and have since been combined in the reprinted *The Complete Fly-Tier*. Cross was perhaps the best professional flymaker to follow immediately in the footsteps of Theodore Gordon, and the impressive gifts of both men still live in the skillful dexterity of tiers like Harry Darbee, Walter Dette, Ray Smith, and Art Flick.

JOHN ALDEN KNIGHT

RAY BERGMAN

Two years later, the legendary Ray Bergman published his immensely successful *Trout*, a major textbook on the sport that would remain in print for almost forty years. It has been the best comprehensive book on American trout fishing since its first publication at Philadelphia in 1938. The impact of its offhand vernacular was phenomenal, awakening familiar echoes in each of its readers; and its deceptively casual anecdotes were a subtle method of teaching without didactive overtones. Bergman led his readers through his early experiences with the wet-fly method and bait, the emerging techniques of nymph fishing, bucktails and streamers, dry-fly tackle and experiences with various patterns under different conditions on widespread rivers, exercises in reading and fishing various types of water, and a disarmingly unsophisticated exposition of the trout in terms of its senses and behavior. There were also chapters on fishing ponds, some experiences with steelheads on the Pacific Coast, grayling in the Yellowstone, and landlocked salmon and grilse in Canada. The stature of *Trout* fulfilled the promise of Bergman's earlier *Just Fishing*, which also contained several superb chapters on trout techniques. *Trout* has a warmly personal narrative quality that has enabled it to dominate the field long after its technical recommendations and tackle were rendered obsolete by new methods and materials. *Trout* also included fifteen color plates of its relatively full dictionary of fly patterns. Done from oil paintings by the late Edgar Burke, they made the book an important reference work as well as a comprehensive study of tackle and tactics.

James Leisenring emerged with his little-known book *The Art of Tying the Wet Fly* in 1941. Its publication was lost in relative obscurity, since our sudden entry into the Second World War ended all thought of angling, and these important American studies in fishing wet flies and nymphs went virtually unnoticed. Leisenring was an unsophisticated Pennsylvania toolmaker whose heavy accent betrayed his family origins in the German Palatinate, but his mind was as precise as the finely machined objects that took shape in his hands. Leisenring was not really a polished writer, and his protégé Pete Hidy assisted him extensively in assembling *The Art of Tying the Wet Fly*. As Gordon had corresponded with Halford fifty years earlier, Leisenring exchanged many letters with Skues in England. Our myopic American preoccupation with the dry-fly method mixed with a curiously blind devotion to the trinity of Gordon, La Branche, and Hewitt led most anglers to neglect Leisenring and his sunk-fly theories for the more glamorous myth-heroes of American fly-fishing. Yet it was Leisenring who quietly adapted the wet-fly methods of Cutcliffe, Stewart, and Skues to the character and fly life of American rivers, just as Theodore Gordon and George La Branche modified the British dry-fly theories for the swift-flowing rivers of the Catskills.

Leisenring fished primarily on the Brodheads, and its difficult fishing had considerable influence on both his fly patterns and his methodology. It was the favorite river of Edward Ringwood Hewitt and George La Branche in the early years of this century, and La Branche even owned a farmhouse near Canadensis at one time. The Brodheads also played a primary role in his *The Dry Fly and Fast Water*, and it was home water for Leisenring and his disciples—wryly called the Twelve Apostles whenever they gathered for supper at the Hotel Rapids in Analomink.

Charles Wetzel published his *Practical Fly-Fishing* in 1943, at the height of the Second World War. Wetzel is the dean emeritus on the Weikert stretch of the Penns Creek in Pennsylvania. Although the book added to our knowledge of eastern fly hatches, the illustrations in *Practical Fly-Fishing* were inaccurate pen sketches that did not attempt to depict the color of the natural insects.

The years immediately following the Second World War were also richly productive in fishing books. Arthur Flick published his slender *Streamside Guide to Naturals and Their Imitations* in 1947, compiling years of research along his beloved Schoharie on the northern face of the Catskills. Flick ultimately came to know its fly hatches and to dress imitative patterns as exquisitely as the best of his tutors, masters like Preston Jennings and Leslie Thompson and Chip Stauffer, and his research on the Schoharie is unique. It was Leslie Thompson and the late Raymond Camp, fishing editor for *The New York Times*, who badgered Flick into completing his collection of fly hatches and ultimately into writing his *Streamside Guide*. The fly-fishing world is in their debt. It has become the definitive portrait of a typical Catskill river and its fly hatches and an essential volume in any working library on American trout fishing. Flick still ties his precise

JAMES LEISENRING

PRINCIPAL SPECIES OF TROUT AND CHAR

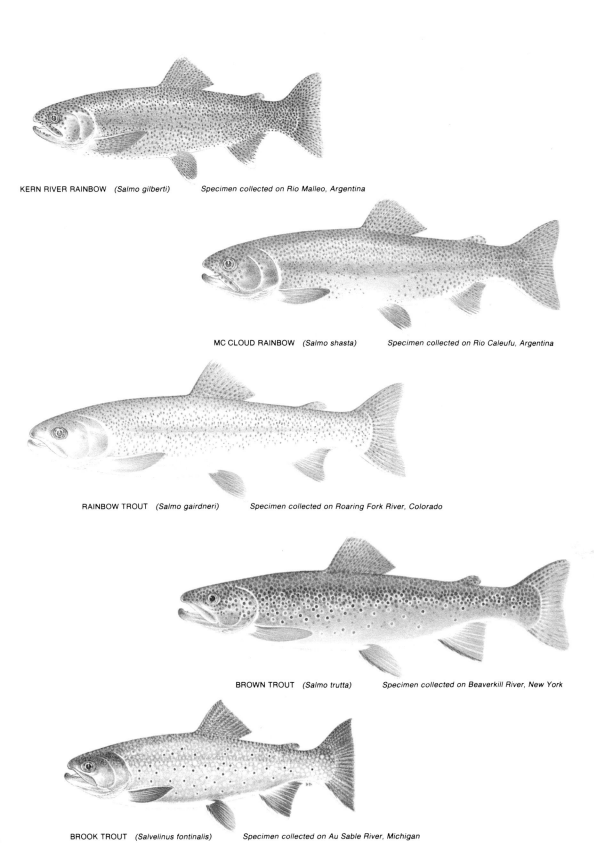

KERN RIVER RAINBOW *(Salmo gilberti)*   *Specimen collected on Rio Malleo, Argentina*

MC CLOUD RAINBOW   *(Salmo shasta)*   *Specimen collected on Rio Caleufu, Argentina*

RAINBOW TROUT   *(Salmo gairdneri)*   *Specimen collected on Roaring Fork River, Colorado*

BROWN TROUT   *(Salmo trutta)*   *Specimen collected on Beaverkill River, New York*

BROOK TROUT   *(Salvelinus fontinalis)*   *Specimen collected on Au Sable River, Michigan*

WESTERN BLACK-SPOTTED SPECIES OF TROUT

JACKSON HOLE CUTTHROAT *(Salmo carmichaeli)* — Specimen collected on Blacktail Spring Creek, Wyoming

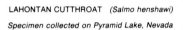

LAHONTAN CUTTHROAT *(Salmo henshawi)*
Specimen collected on Pyramid Lake, Nevada

YELLOWSTONE CUTTHROAT *(Salmo lewisi)*
Specimen collected on Hellroaring Creek, Yellowstone

COLORADO CUTTHROAT *(Salmo pleuriticus)*
Specimen collected on South Fork of the White, Colorado

COMMON CUTTHROAT *(Salmo clarki)*
Specimen collected on Clark's Fork River, Montana

RIO GRANDE CUTTHROAT *(Salmo virginalis)*
Specimen collected on Rio Chiquito, New Mexico

BONNEVILLE CUTTHROAT *(Salmo utah)*
Specimen collected on Virgin River, Utah

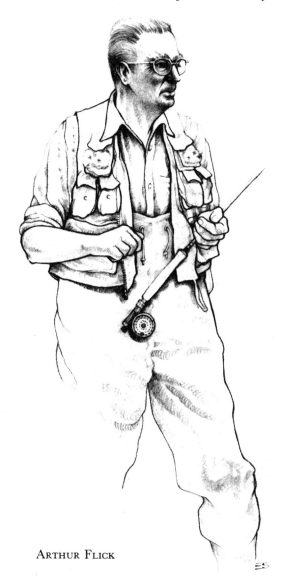

ARTHUR FLICK

sparsely dressed flies and fishes the Schoharie regularly, but his charming old West Kill Tavern is gone. It was lost in a winter fire that engulfed its rambling clapboard structure several years ago, licking at its priceless tiger-maple chairs, antimacassar couches, and faded oriental runners, and melting the Victorian glass cases of woodcock and grouse.

In 1950 Vincent Marinaro published his strikingly original *Modern Dry-Fly Code*. Its pages are filled with fresh insights into the behavior of hard-fished trout as well as advanced concepts of fly dressing. British writers like Mottram, Dunne, and Harding had speculated about such theories in fishing the brown trout of their chalkstreams. But Marinaro found concrete

applications of those theories for the equally selective trout of the Letort Spring Run and its neighboring limestone streams in Pennsylvania. His brilliant jassid-style imitations of the leafhoppers, beetles, and thorax-style dry flies make *A Modern Dry-Fly Code* one of the most important books in the history of American fly-fishing. Marinaro also worked out fine imitations of the elegant *Ephemerella* spinners that fill the twilight with their mating swarms in the limestone country, their butter-colored egg sacs bright in the evening sun. His chalky porcupine-quill imitations of the coffin fly are also brilliant in their simplicity. Marinaro is the creative mind behind a veritable galaxy of innovative ideas, from his photographs of rising fish to his theories of light pattern and silhouette in the surface film.

John Atherton wrote the treatise titled *The Fly and the Fish* at midcentury; it was a rich mixture of technical skills, creative speculation, and poetic insights into fishing. Atherton is filled with lyric overtones, not unlike the classic book *A River Never Sleeps* that Roderick Haig-Brown had published five years earlier. His fly patterns and nymphs and streamcraft are excellent, and his book is perfectly attuned to the tumbling music of the Battenkill and the Neversink.

Alvin Grove published his *Lure and Lore of Trout Fishing* in that same vintage year, and it has been acclaimed in the essays of Arnold Gingrich as one of the finest books in American fly-fishing literature. It is a book firmly rooted in the tradition of the limestone spring creeks and tumbling Appalachian streams of the Pennsylvania mountains, particularly the classic Spruce Run and Spring Creek at Bellefonte.

Another excellent book appeared, just after midcentury, and its original studies in nymph fishing are singularly appropriate in the year that witnessed the death of Leisenring. Edward Sens was its author, another expert fly dresser who closely studied the nymph life of our Catskill rivers. The result of his work was a carefully detailed series of imitative flies, keyed

JOSEPH BROOKS

to produce nymphal dressings for our better known dry-fly patterns. It was the origin of perhaps the most popular nymphs on our eastern trout streams, artificial nymphs that have an ancestry traceable directly to Skues in England. However, Sens added two completely original pupal imitations of caddisflies and both proved themselves deadly. Edward Sens did not write about his nymph-fishing theories himself, leaving that work to Ray Ovington in *How to Catch Trout on Wet Flies and Nymphs*. Written in 1951, it was a book that largely codified the philosophy of Sens, and its literary importance is rooted almost solely in its exposition of his work. Many of the Sens patterns have evolved into Catskill standards.

William Blades published his comprehensive *Fishing Flies and Fly Tying* the following spring, and it quickly became the standard American work on fly tying. It holds a special significance for me, because Blades was the master fly dresser who taught me the art of tying flies more than twenty-five years ago.

A. J. McClane published his *Practical Fly Fisherman* in 1953 and followed it with *The American Angler* a year later. These two books are well written and solidly based on wide experience on American trout streams. Their knowledge is so unmistakable that the singular *McClane's Standard Fishing Encyclopaedia* should have come as no surprise, yet this remarkably inclusive reference work has virtually no equal in the history of angling.

Joseph Brooks added his *Complete Book of Fly Fishing* to the growing shelf of American fly-fishing literature in 1956, and it was structured on fly-fishing for all types of fish, although its treatment of trout-fishing theory and practice is thorough. Brooks would wait another sixteen years before his book *Trout Fishing* was published, and his tragic death the following September in Montana robbed us of both his good fellowship on the Yellowstone and his vast knowledge of the sport.

Charles Fox wrote his book *This Wonderful World of Trout* more than a decade ago, triggering a major new cycle of original American angling books. Fox collaborated with Marinaro in their now-legendary experiments on the Letort Spring Run, and his *Wonderful World of Trout* and the subsequent *Rising Trout* are filled with both wisdom and anecdotes about fishing the limestone spring creeks, fly-dressing theory, experiments with wild trout genetics, and transplanting fly hatches in Pennsylvania. It is intriguing to have this record of a modern collaboration of great anglers along the Letort that seems destined to stand with the Halford-Marryat legend a century ago on the British chalkstreams.

E. H. Rosborough wrote his fine *Tying and Fishing the Fuzzy Nymphs* in 1969, outlining his fly patterns and personal tying methods that have evolved over the past thirty-odd years on Oregon waters. His flies include not only the common types of mayfly, caddisfly, and stonefly imitations, but also crustaceans, damselfly and dragonfly nymphs, pupal flies, and midge patterns. Although his full catalog of imitations is based upon insects and crustaceans found on the rivers of the Pacific Northwest, both his nymphs and his fishing methods are effective on trout waters everywhere. Rosbor-

CHARLES FOX

ough and Sens have been perhaps the first original thinkers in the evolving genesis of American nymph fishing, and their work is based solidly on the pioneering studies of Skues and Leisenring earlier in this century.

Fly-fishing books of quality are still being published, and Douglas Swisher and Carl Richards have made a remarkable contribution to American angling with the comparatively recent appearance of their book *Selective Trout.* It is a sizable volume unusual in the scope of its original studies in American entomology, its experiments in fly design and construction, its studies of light pattern and silhouette, its fresh studies in nymph behavior, and its particular emphasis on emerging nymph imitations.

Their work obviously builds on the conceptual thinking that can be traced directly from writers like Halford, Skues, Mottram, Dunne, Harding, and Marinaro. Most fishermen have been fascinated with their no-hackle and parachute-style flies, believing that these demonstrate a completely new development in the art of fly dressing. Such critical judgements could come only from anglers who are not fly tiers themselves, or from men unfamiliar with the history of fly construction, because no-hackle flies have existed since Berners and have been consciously fished in the surface film since the days of Cotton and Bowlker and Pritt.

Although its theories are not invented of whole cloth, that fact in no way diminishes the achievement of *Selective Trout*, and the book is filled with original contributions to American fly-fishing theory and technique.

The principal innovations of *Selective Trout* lie in the areas of identifying a whole new phalanx of aquatic fly hatches, observations about their singular behavior before and during emergence, insights into the flight patterns of egg laying, the attempt to devise a whole series of flies for the precise imitation of the various stages of a hatch, experiments with hatching mayflies and sedges in the surface film, and a whole galaxy of ideas for

EDWARD RINGWOOD HEWITT

simulating nymphs and pupae. Perhaps their most unusual innovation is a modified version of the extended-body nymphs explored by others, a hinged body extension that wriggles and flutters freely in the current, suggesting the writhing body movements of a nymph enroute from stream bed to surface film. The major importance of these concepts has sometimes been missed in the preoccupation with the dry-fly innovations and color photographs of living insects found in *Selective Trout*, and its cataloguing of new fly hatches alone makes it valuable.

Our fly-fishing theory and fly hatches still need much fresh thinking and field work. Fishing pressure increases steadily each season, and our stream-bred trout on heavily fished waters seem smarter every year. Bold innovation in tackle and fly dressing will continue to evolve, and these steps will trigger future changes in tactics and strategy. American fly-fishing has travelled an immense distance in the past century. Its almost explosive maturity is perhaps most obvious in our books on fly hatches and their imitations, a field that was in its infancy on American waters when Bergman wrote *Trout* forty-odd years ago.'

The evolution of fly-fishing entomology has progressed at a more measured pace in the British Isles. It has taken more than a century and a half to complete work that reaches from Ronalds' *Fly-Fisher's Entomology* in 1836 to the recent books of British writers like John Goddard with his *Trout Fly Recognition* and Richard Harris with *An Angler's Entomology* in Ireland. Harris has fished and collected fly hatches widely throughout the British Isles. During the fishing months, Harris continues his research almost daily on the Rye and the headwaters of the Liffey outside Dublin—where he is sometimes found in the off-season, supervising his fly dressers or offering his expert counsel behind the fly counters at Garnett's and Keegan's.

British fly-fishing entomology has been a remarkable achievement, yet our subsequent American work is perhaps even more remarkable. American fishing writers have collected and imitated a veritable galaxy of fly hatches in less than forty years, and their work has been forced to consider the species of an entire continent. The cumulative work of fishermen like Jennings, Flick, Wetzel, Grove, Marinaro, Swisher, Richards, and others has already created a surprising literary legacy. Our fly-hatch studies will unquestionably continue in the future, since American stream entomology is still incomplete. Fresh innovations in tackle are always on the horizon too. Other writers will emerge and add to our knowledge of fishing, just as *Hatches* and *Selective Trout* and my recent book *Nymphs* have attempted to expand our catalog of fly hatches since my slender *Matching the Hatch* appeared almost twenty-five years ago.

There will always be fresh riddles to solve and missing pieces in the rich puzzle of our fly hatches. The past forty-odd years of American fly-fishing literature clearly demonstrate that young writers will continue to arrive, eager to solve fresh problems—and some will enrich the literature of our sport with language as lithe and richly colored as the trout themselves, working softly to a fluttering hatch of flies over sun-washed gravel.

BOOK TWO

✣ ✣ ✣

AMERICAN SPECIES OF TROUT AND GRAYLING

1. The Prehistory of Trout and Grayling

The trout and its related fish species have origins deep in the primordial history of the earth, perhaps as long ago as 300 million years, when our/continents were first sculptured under the impact of almost incomprehensible forces. Fetal volcanoes spewed rivers of lava into restless primeval seas. Seismic wrenchings and upheavals raised entire mountain escarpments from their seething depths. Fresh volcanoes were born in violent explosions of sulphurous ash and steam. Thousand-year storms shrouded our evolving planet, eroding its emerging topography with fierce winds and torrential rains, spreading unfathomable layers of alluvial sediments into the shallow seas. Our world and its myriad fish species were born across interminable cycles of geomorphic activity and precipitation and time, cycles of change that took hundreds of millions of years.

The early ancestors of our modern trout and grayling probably first appeared about one hundred million years ago in the Late Mesozoic period. Such primitive fishes were unquestionably marine ecotypes that ultimately evolved into both anadromous and landlocked species. Our present evidence indicates that these ancestral species first thrived in the icy seas of the northern latitudes, providing the prototypical life forms to spawn several evolutionary lineages that ultimately produced the several Salmoniform fishes.

The Salmoniformes group encompasses the primary stocks in the mainstream of bony-fish evolution. Our modern taxonomy defining the group is largely based upon the combined work of several British and American ichthyologists in recent years using both new evidence and methods of interpretation to redefine our past theories of classification. Those past taxonomic systems evolved from the studies earlier in this century of British ichthyologist Tate Regan and the distinguished Russian biologist Lev Berg.

Our modern perspective no longer groups the Salmoniformes in a clear taxonomic category, but rather considers them an assemblage of diverse marine and freshwater fishes that share several primitive structural and physiological similarities. These common anatomical features are clearly

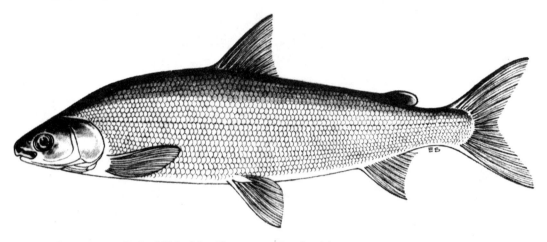

Common or Lake Whitefish *(Coregonus culpeaformis)*

representative of relatively early stages in the evolution of our contemporary bony-fish genotypes. Modern taxonomy has separated the Salmoniformes into a system of eight suborders and thirty-seven families, creating more an evolutionary yardstick in the phylogeny of the bony-fish families than a well-defined taxonomic structure. No single anatomical character or combination of characters can distinguish all of the Salmoniformes. The order includes trout, salmon, char, whitefish, smelt, grayling and other parallel fishes in the suborder Salmonoidei, which totals approximately one hundred species. These species are among the most familiar and widely studied fishes, famous for both their economic importance and their sporting qualities. Yet there are also Salmoniformes known only to surprisingly few ichthyologists, since their habitat is restricted to the intermediate and lower depths of the open seas, and our knowledge of these unusual species is largely based upon fragmentary information.

The largest of the Salmoniform fishes are paradoxically anadromous or landlocked species, rather than the totally salt-loving marine ecotypes. The Chinook salmon of the Pacific Northwest, the predatory Siberian huchen, and the Caspian salmon all attain weights well over one hundred pounds. The largest Salmoniformes found in salt water are the slender lancet fishes of the Alepisauridae, which measure more than six feet at maturity but weigh less than fifty pounds. However, most marine species in the Salmoniformes order measure less than six inches when fully developed, although these tiny fish are just as predatory as their larger relatives. Such small Salmoniformes have evolved some remarkable anatomical variations that enable them to attack and ingest diet forms larger than themselves. Many of the marine Salmoniformes have evolved beyond obvious structural similarities with the Salmonoidei, although many species share the adipose fin found between the dorsal and caudal fins in trout and salmon, which has clearly been inherited from a common marine ancestor in the Late Mesozoic.

Comparative studies of the anatomy and skeletal system are the basis of Salmoniform classification. These fishes are grouped in terms of parallel morphology, held in common with many other bony-fish species. Both the evaluation of evolutionary relationships and the interpretation between primitive and highly developed states of evolution in a single anatomical feature are now largely based upon the premise that such features cannot reappear in their most primitive forms once they are lost or substantially modified through evolution. Such anatomical features as the adipose fin, the mesocoracoid bone of the pectorals, and teeth on the maxillary structure of the mouth are all primitive Salmoniform characters. The absence of these basic structural elements in the Salmoniformes is clear evidence that a specimen under consideration has evolved well beyond its primitive origins and cannot have played an ancestral role to the modern ecotypes that still display these features. None of the Salmoniformes possesses all of these primitive evolutionary characters, although the Salmonidae and Osmeridae families clearly inherited most of them in their modern species.

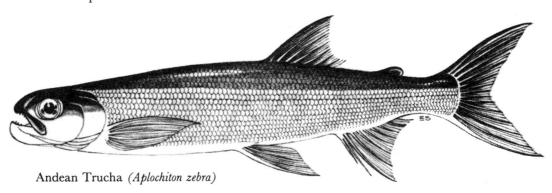

Andean Trucha (*Aplochiton zebra*)

The primitive denticular structure of the ancestral Salmoniformes displays teeth on both the maxilla and premaxilla of the upper jaw and on the dentary structure of the lower mouth. Primitive dentition inside the mouth includes teeth on the median vomerine structure, as well as on the pterygoid and palatine bones on either side, and in the lower mouth there are teeth on the tongue and the basibranchial plate. Many separate strains of the Salmoniformes exhibit the loss of denticular character on the maxillary bone and the dominance of the premaxilla over the maxilla, forming the primary configuration of the jaws. The primitive morphology of the pectoral girdle is distinguished in the ventral position of its fins, and

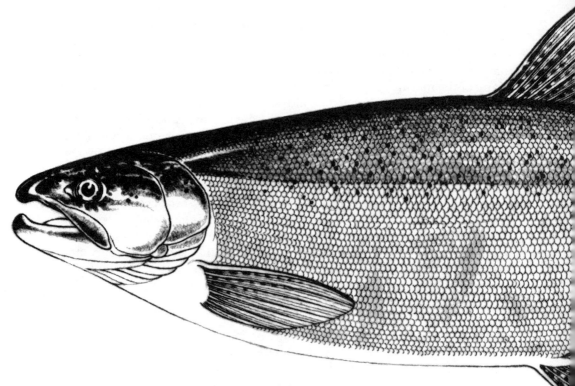

Chinook Salmon *(Oncorhynchus tshawytscha)*

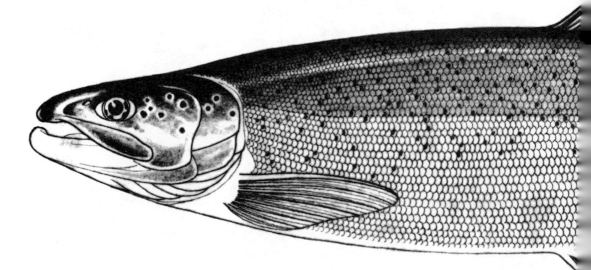

Huchen *(Hucho hucho)*

African Tigerfish *(Hydrocyon lineatus)*

Dorado *(Salminus maxillosus)*

the presence of a supporting mesocoracoid bone. Higher evolutionary states of development have more laterally positioned pectorals and the gradual loss of the mesocoracoid structure.

Primitive anatomical features of the caudal skeleton in the Salmoniformes include three separate vertebrae and minor bony components supporting the hypural plates, which form the root of the tail structure. Such skeletal systems are probably vestigial echoes of more ancient evolutionary states. Other primitive morphological fingerprints are found in minute abdominal ducts from the body cavity to the ventral orifice, vestigial evidence of the spiral-valve intestines found in the most primitive Salmoniformes, and the absence of female oviducts. Swim bladders are invariably connected with the esophagus in the more primitive strains, while the more highly developed Salmoniformes either lack the connecting duct or have lost the swim bladder altogether. Pyloric caeca are found on the intestinal systems of the ancestral Salmoniformes, but are not invariably present on each of the modern species.

Earlier taxonomic classification was based on grouping most of the primitive fishes with soft fin structures and fusilliform scales among the Clupeiformes, although some ichthyologists argued for structural relationships with the Cypriniform fishes. The arguments which favored Clupeiform origins for the Salmoniformes were based upon ethmoidal parallels in their cranial structures and otolithic similarities in the ear cavities. Ichthyologists who argued for Cypriniform origins did so largely because of structural relationships between the auditory systems and the swim bladders of the Cypriniform and Salmoniform fishes. However, these earlier theories on the primitive origins of the modern Salmoniformes have largely been abandoned.

Payara *(Hydrolicus scomberoides)*

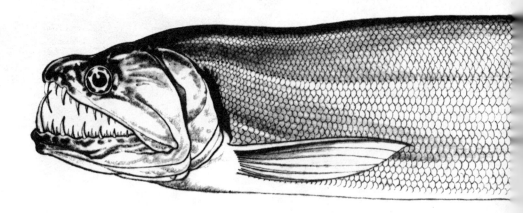

The Salmoniformes order has been recently created to distinguish and separate many diverse groups of fishes having only tenuous relationships with the Clupeiformes. The Myctophoidei suborder was established to group almost five hundred marine species in the Salmoniformes order, although the proponents of such taxonomic changes agree that their revisions have added little fresh knowledge concerning the evolutionary relationships between the several Salmoniform suborders, and no fully coherent picture of their origins has emerged.

The Myctophoidei have evolved a considerable distance from their common origins with the Salmoniformes, and some British researchers have proposed their grouping in a totally separate Myctophiformes order. Since fossil evidence of several Myctophoid families is known since the Cretaceous period of the Late Mesozoic period, it now seems clear that these fishes have experienced an evolution widely separated from the other Salmoniformes in the last one hundred million years, and ultimate acceptance of the separate Myctophiformes order seems likely among many ichthyologists.

Perhaps future research will provide fresh evidence of the evolutionary cycles that occurred between fifty and one hundred million years ago, and their effects on the many suborders and families now grouped in the Salmoniformes. Modern researchers agree that the traditional methods of taxonomy based upon mere parallels in anatomy and bone structure cannot clarify the missing pieces remaining in the Salmoniform puzzles. Such clarification must wait until additional fossil evidence is discovered, or the newer techniques of comparative chromosome studies and investigations in molecular biology can establish evolutionary relationships beyond conventional taxonomy.

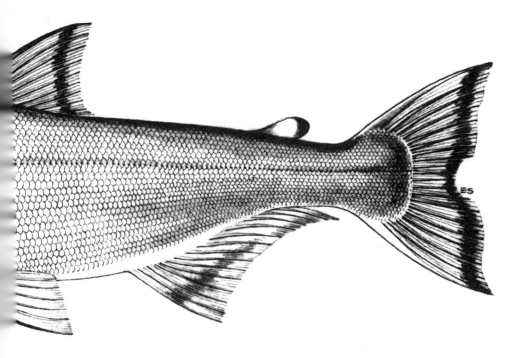

Salmoniform fishes are native to all continents and throughout the oceans of the world. Many of the suborders and families are widely distributed across the cool freshwater habitats of the Northern Hemisphere. The populations of the Salmonidae family are circumpolar in distribution, ranging from tributary watersheds of the Arctic Ocean to river systems draining into the Gulf of California in Mexico. Native populations are also distributed in the mountains of Lebanon and Morocco, the north-flowing rivers in the Kirghiz and Hindu Kush, and the mountains of Turkey and Iran. The Salmonidae in Asia are widely found from the north-flowing rivers of Siberia to the highlands of Kyushu and Taiwan.

The development of an anadromous life cycle, in which spawning occurs in freshwater environments and maturity is achieved in the sea, has played a considerable role in the relatively wide distribution of the Salmonidae. Migratory behavior during periods of marine growth permitted the Salmonidae to extend their distribution easily, both by exploring the expanding perimeters of the primordial oceans and by entering the river systems of recently glaciated terrain. Such migratory capabilities allowed the Salmonidae to expand their populations far beyond their original habitats, particularly into regions inaccessible to species that are limited to freshwater environments alone, and their migrations are the reason that the Salmonidae include the principal species found in the recently glaciated waters of the Northern Hemisphere.

The Esocidae family, which includes the pikes and their related species, have a similar pattern of distribution throughout the temperate latitudes of the Northern Hemisphere, although their native populations are not found in the extreme northern and southern latitudes typical of the Salmonidae. The distribution of the pikes across Europe, Asia, and North America is perhaps the most extensive range found in any single species. Pikes are typically freshwater fishes throughout their modern range, except for the curious brackish-water populations commonly found in the coastal regions of Denmark. Their distribution has largely been achieved through interconnecting freshwater systems, although the Danish estuarine pikes indicate that marine migrations were once part of their behavior.

The Osmeridae family includes the various marine and freshwater smelts found throughout the Northern Hemisphere. Their freshwater populations have marine origins and have been isolated in relatively recent geological times. Most smelts are wholly marine or anadromous, and no species has penetrated deeply enough into inland waters to match the wide distribution of the Salmonidae.

The Plecoglossidae family includes the troutlike ayu fishes distributed in Asian waters, and the Salangidae consist of the remarkable ice fishes found in both the Arctic and Antarctic seas.

Salmoniform fishes physically similar to trout, whitefish, and smelt are also found in the freshwater habitats throughout the Southern Hemisphere. Populations in brackish waters are also recorded in South America, and freshwater populations are found in Africa, Australia, Tasmania, and New

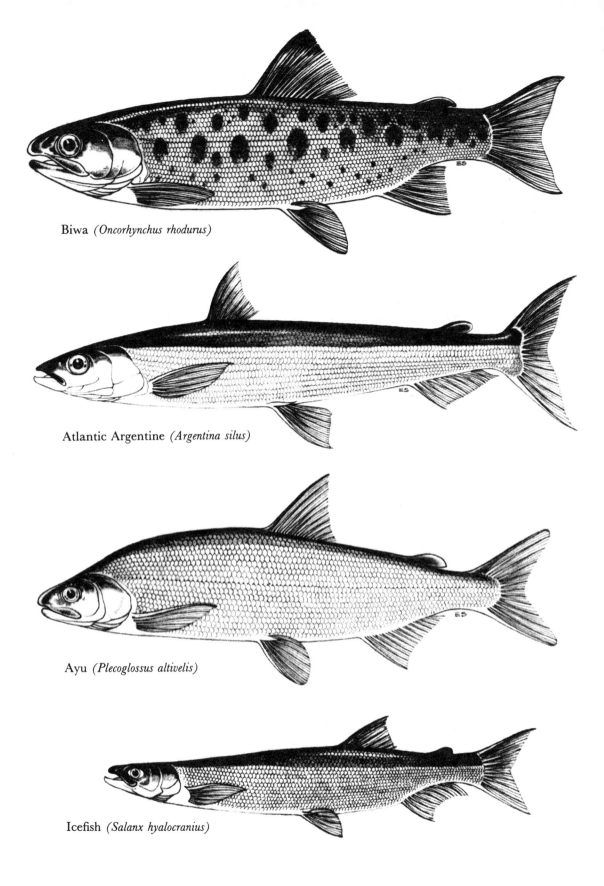

Biwa *(Oncorhynchus rhodurus)*

Atlantic Argentine *(Argentina silus)*

Ayu *(Plecoglossus altivelis)*

Icefish *(Salanx hyalocranius)*

Zealand. These southern Salmoniformes are classified in the Galaxiodei suborder and include families like the Prototrocidae, Aplochitonidae, Retropinnidae and Galaxidae. The Prototrocidae include two troutlike species found in Australia and New Zealand. The Aplochitonidae family consists of three species native to South American waters, and a single tiny species from Tasmania. The Retropinnidae include approximately six species distributed in Australia, Tasmania and New Zealand. The Galaxidae are more widely distributed, and their forty-odd species are recorded in southern Africa, Australia, Tasmania, New Zealand and South America. These tiny Salmoniformes often provide baitfish forage for the introduced populations of salmon and trout found in suitable habitats throughout the Southern Hemisphere.

The remaining suborders of the Salmoniformes are wholly oceanic in distribution and include the Argentinoidei, Stomiatoidei, Alepocephaloidei and Myctopoidei fishes. There are approximately thirty-odd families and some eight hundred species among these marine suborders, and they are typically found in open seas at depths ranging from six hundred to 6,000 feet. Many species and their surprising abundance were almost totally unknown before the development of modern sonar and oceanographic research vehicles.

The Salmonidae are unquestionably the most important family among the Salmoniformes order, since they include both trout and grayling species, as well as the commercially valuable whitefish and smelts. There is fossil evidence that primitive populations of these species emerged in Eocene times, with examples of the extinct Thaumaturidae fishes recorded from the Lower Tertiary watersheds in Western Europe. It is quite probable that both trout and grayling evolved from common marine ancestors that thrived in the Arctic seas, and during later glacial epochs these prehistoric Salmonidae migrated into the cooling waters of more southern latitudes. The warming climates that followed each period of glaciation unquestionably decimated these southern species, leaving relict populations in the headwaters of mountain streams, and forcing the oceanic survivors into cold pelagic depths or toward the polar latitudes again. Such relict populations are still found in southern Italy, Portugal, Lebanon, Morocco, Spain, Turkey, and other mountainous regions of the Middle East. These fish have survived in such latitudes since the prehistoric glaciers covered most of Europe and North America, and the tropic seas off Africa and Central America were surprisingly cold.

Similar relict populations of brook trout survive in the mountain headwaters of many southern rivers in the United States, and there are several unique residual strains of trout in the Baja California and the Sierra Madre mountains of Mexico. Other ancestral populations of troutlike fishes apparently failed to survive the warming climates of postglacial times, and neither the Mediterranean nor the Gulf of California can sustain marine populations of anadromous trout today, although such colonies clearly existed in the past. These primitive troutlike fishes retreated north with the melting glaciers, and when the shrinking ice fields fed evolving river

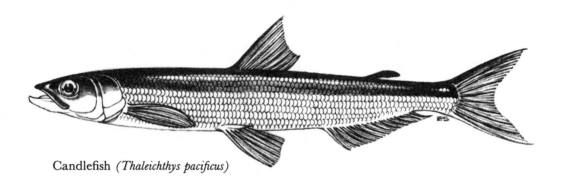

Candlefish *(Thaleichthys pacificus)*

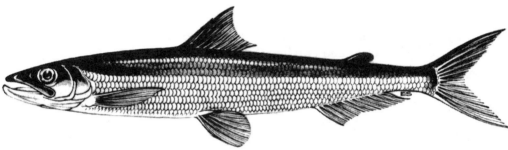

American Smelt *(Osmerus mordax)*

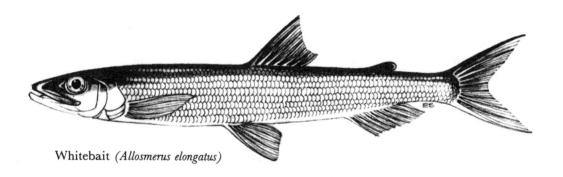

Whitebait *(Allosmerus elongatus)*

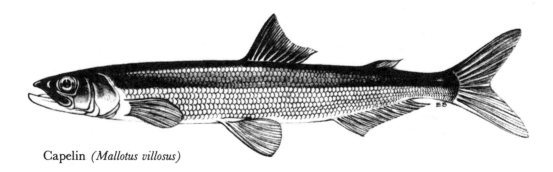

Capelin *(Mallotus villosus)*

systems, the migrating schools sometimes ascended them. Many thousands of years later, some of these riverine migrants subsequently found themselves trapped in freshwater habitats. Other migrant populations found such rich inland feeding grounds that they chose to remain, and still others were isolated by warming seas. These strains evolved the ability to reproduce in fresh water, and two distinct behavioral patterns developed: stationary or landlocked populations, and the anadromous strains that migrated between their parent rivers and the sea.

Geological evolution and its related impact on climate and water temperatures had considerable effect on the ultimate distribution of the Salmonidae. Their range was largely determined through seismic and volcanic transformations, the less obvious effects of weather in its millions of years of wind and precipitation and erosion, and the glaciers that gouged and polished our planet in their cycles of imperceptible ebbing and flowing. The impact of geological change has been so pervasive in the evolution and distribution of trout and grayling that a brief discussion of geological cycles would prove helpful in our understanding of their modern distribution.

Perhaps the most ancient exposed formations found on our planet are outcroppings from Archeozoic times, although most igneous rock from such primordial volcanic activity is commonly hidden under more recent geomorphic layers. Some geologists believe that the earliest Archeocene formations were born in volcanic eruptions and lava seepages that occurred as much as six hundred million years ago, and the water quality of our northern rivers is closely related to their origins. Canada possesses some of the largest of these Archeocene outcroppings in the sprawling bedrock shield that reaches from the Great Lakes into the coastal mountains of Labrador. The Canadian formations are extremely ancient, and their geology is a rich palette of limestone, marble, granite, schist, gneiss and quartzite. Although the char populations found in Canadian habitats are found in all types of water, including the acid-water chemistry typically associated with igneous geology, the fish are far more abundant in those regions composed of sedimentary deposits like limestone. Keewatin, Coutchiching and Laurentian geology is based upon igneous formations rooted in volcanic activity, although the geology of the Grenville formations is composed of limestone, quartzite, marble and other metamorphosed sediments. Geologists believe that the granite and gneiss found in the Laurentians are much younger than other Archeozoic outcroppings, perhaps having been extruded through fissures in earlier deposits in igneous forms. The Laurentian and Grenville formations were followed with still later deposits of the Sudburian sediments, and the igneous layers that form the Algoman outcroppings farther north. The chronology of these formations is quite ancient, although we have fossil evidence of extensive fish life in both the Algoman and Sudburian sediments, which were deposited on the threshold of the Proterocene period.

These following Proterozoic millenniums witnessed much larger cycles of sedimentation than had occurred in the earlier Archeocene times, and these deposits still have a primary impact on both water quality and fish populations. Volcanic eruptions and deposits of igneous materials were less widespread during these times, although metamorphism and seismic warping produced considerable topographic change. Perhaps our largest Proterocene deposits are found enclosing Lake Superior, although their sediments are layered over extensive Archeocene foundations that had been heavily weathered and eroded for thousands of years. During these cycles of weathering, entire mountain ranges that had formed in earlier volcanic eruptions and cycles of seismic warping were completely eroded into rolling plains and surprisingly gentle hills. The evolving earth was covered with shallow seas in many regions, and extensive glaciation also appeared in these Proterocene times. The sedimentary deposits of the Huronian sandstones, slates and quartzites are richly structured with fossil evidence of their origins in marine epochs and consolidated glacial drift. Such geological forces played a major role in the shaping of the Great Lakes, as well as the primodial sediments and seas that once covered the Lahontan and Bonneville basins farther west. These sediments would provide remarkably fertile trout habitats in our time, and prehistoric trout populations freely ranged these saline inland seas. Vast reaches of our continent were covered with such marine shallows and the icemelt of receding glaciers, and these Proterocene cycles prevailed another 500 million years.

The Proterozoic millenniums also witnessed the birth of vast carbonaceous deposits, the sprawling coal seams, petroleum fields, and iron lodes that reach from the Mesabi country in Minnesota to the rich subarctic deposits of the Labrador. Our continent experienced several subsequent millenniums of weathering, sedimentation, and metamorphism before its surface formations were fissured and torn during another cycle of volcanic eruptions and earthquakes. The seismic violence was followed with an epoch of warping and upthrusting that formed whole new escarpments and mountain ranges, particularly in our western states. These eruptions and barriers unquestionably eradicated some prehistoric trout populations and isolated others, providing the zoogeographic stocks that subsequently evolved our modern strains.

Although fossil evidence of fish life from the Proterocene outcroppings and sediments is surprisingly limited, the variety and complexity of fossils from the preceding Cambrian millenniums clearly demonstrate that the evolution of both flora and animal life was well advanced during the five hundred million years of the Proterozoic cycles.

During the Paleocene epoch that followed, the continents began evolving toward their relatively modern configurations, and extensive sedimentary layers of shales, sandstones and cretaceous deposits were laid down throughout the sprawling region that would become the Rocky Mountains and Great Plains. Although most of the continent was elevated in these times, the entire Atlantic and Gulf Coast topography was submerged in prehistoric seas that reached inland along the Mississippi to its junction with the Ohio. Primitive populations of trout and grayling travelled these inland seas in vast migrating schools. Geologists also believe that the Great Valley of California was submerged in coastal waters filled with prehistoric Salmonidae thousands of years before the birth of the fertile San Joaquin and Sacramento drainage systems, and the wave action of the primordial storms washed against the upthrusting escarpments of the Sierra Nevada and Rocky mountains.

Paleocene times were followed by the Eocene millenniums, and their unfathomable cycles of erosion, weathering and vast sedimentary deposits have played a major part in creating our most productive lakes and rivers. Eocene formations along the Caribbean and Atlantic coastlines are principally composed of clays, sandstones, and marl deposits mixed with lignites and fertile limestone outcroppings. Pacific formations that were shaped in the Eocene millenniums are largely shales and sandstones, and similar Eocene deposits of sandstone, volcanic ash, and shale are equally common in the Rocky Mountains. The dramatic river gorges found in the drainage systems of the Colorado and Arkansas watersheds are largely carved into these Eocene formations, which also include the sprawling oil-shale deposits found in the arid mountains of western Colorado and Wyoming.

Europe was largely free of marine inundation through the early millenniums of the Paleocene Age, although its intricate coastal topography was later flooded from northern France and the Frisian lowlands along the southern Baltic to the Karelian forests of Finland and Russia. It was during such marine cycles that the fossil ancestors of trout and grayling were trapped in the gathering sediments, and late in the Eocene period there was apparently an incredible flood that raised the Mediterranean and adjacent Eurasian seas until most of southern Europe, Asia Minor and North Africa was drowned. Vast sedimentary formations of limestone were deposited across Europe from the Carpathians to the British Isles during this Eocene flooding, and similar cretaceous deposits are also found throughout the Mediterranean—it is these rich sedimentary deposits that created the legendary European rivers, from the chalkstreams of southern England and Normandy to the limestone waters of the Traun in Austria or the weed-rich Gäcka in Yugoslavia.

Eocene flooding and sedimentation apparently lasted 100 million years and witnessed an explosion of the mammalian species, until their populations became the principal forms of life. The primary species in the preceding Paleocene millenniums were the strange insectivores, lemuroids, marsupials and other primordial ecotypes. Early Eocene species included both hoofed and flesh-eating prototypes of relatively modern animal life. These populations were well enough developed that their evolution had largely taken place in other latitudes, and they had probably migrated northward when the glacial climatology of the Paleocene millenniums gradually changed in the steady warming that accompanied the Eocene period. The plant life of these millenniums was also remarkably well advanced, and similar fossil evidence from the Eocene sediments in Europe unmistakably demonstrates that trout and grayling existed in primitive ancestral species. Literally thousands of years were still ahead in their evolutionary cycles, millenniums of seismic wrenchings and glacial periods and primordial oceans that would ultimately isolate, distribute, and define their populations throughout the entire Northern Hemisphere.

Oligocene times were a fresh cycle of change that followed millenniums of Eocene flooding and sedimentation. During this period, the American continent was largely free of the prehistoric marine shallows that had covered its interior. Formerly-marine populations of the Salmonidae found themselves isolated in fresh water. Our southern coastal plains were submerged in subtropical seas, but most of the Atlantic coastline was elevated almost to the periphery of its continental shelf. Pacific topography was also elevated in these Oligocene millenniums, while incredible precipitation and storms eroded the coastal escarpments born in the volcanic and seismic forces of the Proterocene Age. Oligocene weathering multiplied the sedimentary layers that had been distributed in the Eocene seas, and the Proterocene mountains were metamorphosed into coastal hills, providing the water quality in many of our most fertile sport fisheries. Similar forces were at work everywhere. Vicksburg limestones are a well-known example of these phenomena, eroded during thousands of years from southern mountains and creating fly-rich rivers like the Ozark drainages. Similar western formations of shales, sandstones, clays, fine aggregates, and conglomerates are typical Oligocene deposits from the Great Plains to the Sierra Nevada. Such formations are found in vast layers, although some still form gargantuan alluvial fans that are the remaining echoes of prehistoric alpine escarpments in earlier millenniums, and late in the Oligocene Age there were fresh earthquakes and eruptions. The violence of these seismic upheavals and late Oligocene eruptions is almost incomprehensible. Volcanic ash and pumice smothered entire continents, and extensive fossilization took place in the prison of their abrasive shroud. Fish populations were isolated in seismic refuges and surviving habitats or totally destroyed when entire lakes and river systems were buried.

Oligocene times were only a minor prelude to the cataclysmic cycles of change that shaped our planet in the Miocene times that followed. North America was more extensively submerged and repopulated with marine Salmonidae during its Miocene Age than before, and although prehistoric seas washed across much of our evolving continent, their stillness was often shattered with the birth of fresh volcanic eruptions and seismic tidal waves. Atlantic coastal regions were again completely flooded, and the sedimentary layers of cretaceous marls, clays, fine aggregates, and diatomaceous materials enriched our world in fertile Miocene formations that reach from Massachusetts to Florida. The rich limestones that produced the famous spring-fed streams in our eastern mountains, particularly limestone waters like Big Spring and Falling Spring Run and the classic Letort in Pennsylvania, were sedimentary deposits distributed in Miocene times.

These same millenniums found the Great Valley in California submerged in restless Miocene seas, imperceptibly collecting sediments of sandstones, clays, conglomerates, shales and diatomaceous precipitates. These sprawling fjordlike seas reached deep into California from the present site of Palm Springs to the existing coastline of the Gulf of California in Mexico. River silts eroded during the formation of the Grand Canyon ultimately divided the Miocene waters of the Gulf of California below Mexicali and Yuma, isolating its upper reaches into the primordial saltwater lake that covered the desert floor from Mexicali to Palm Springs. The present-day Salton Sea is the tiny echo of the saline Lake Cahuilla that covered the entire region during Miocene times. The prehistoric silts that filled the Gulf of California and closed the mouth of the Colorado probably trapped and isolated vast marine populations of trout. These stocks undoubtedly evolved into our modern cutthroat subspecies found in Utah, Nevada and western Colorado, and were also the ancestral forms for the unique trout species of Arizona and New Mexico.

It is probable that these prehistoric coastal seas were also connected with marine shallows that covered the Mojave Desert, reaching still farther inland to include the salt-water lakes that covered central Nevada and Utah. Some geologists argue that these seas were once connected to the Pacific, and that their waters were isolated in the violent upthrustings and volcanic activity that pushed the Sierra Nevada escarpment to higher and higher elevations. These seismic changes also isolated the parent strains of coastal rainbows and cutthroat populations from Los Angeles to the mouth of the Columbia. It is also possible that the Great Valley itself, reaching from Bakersfield to Redding for almost four hundred miles behind the coastal ranges, was isolated and shaped when earthquake warpings pushed these coastal mountains to elevations unmatched since the Proterocene Age. Prehistoric seas that covered Death Valley and the Mojave Desert were perhaps once joined with the fjordlike waters that filled the Great Valley, before the wrenching stresses raised the San Bernardino and Tehachapi mountains from the ocean floor. Separate subspecies can also be traced to these geological events. Such cycles of seismic activity and volcanic eruptions continued throughout our western mountains and were followed with fresh cycles of weathering and erosion and marine inundation. The echoes of these sprawling inland seas that once covered Nevada and Utah are still visible in their desert lakes, and in the wind-riffled expanses of the Great Salt Lake. And from our contemporary knowledge of their present zoogeographic distribution, it is obvious that prehistoric forms of our modern trout and grayling existed there in Miocene times.

The climatological forces that accompanied these Miocene millenniums included an imperceptible process of cooling from the junglelike conditions of the Oligocene Age, eradicating the tropical and subtropical forests that once thrived across our continent and enlarging its savannahs and grasslands. During the Pliocene period that followed, the grazing mammals prospered and the flesh-eating predators found good hunting.

Fish life also evolved toward the threshold of its modern ecology and its ultimate patterns of distribution, and during these Pliocene millenniums the topography and drainage systems of our continent began taking shape. The coastlines during these Pliocene times displayed a surprisingly contemporary look, and the seas continued to recede from their earlier Miocene configurations. Smaller coastal regions remained submerged but the Miocene waters that had once covered central California and the Atlantic coastlines from Texas to New England had largely retreated, leaving vestigial echoes like Chesapeake Bay, the Gulf of California, and the beautiful San Francisco region, where the gentle coastal mountains enclose the estuary of the San Joaquin and Sacramento.

Violent changes in topography and drainage systems resulted in radical Pliocene transformations of the world, elevating and tilting and upthrusting virtually all of its existing mountain ranges. The Cascades in the Pacific Northwest, the spinal ramparts of the Rocky Mountains, and the weathered summits of the Appalachians were all raised higher in a massive process of warping forces, and these gargantuan stresses in the surface of the planet radically tilted the Sierra Nevada escarpment toward the Pacific and forced it higher and higher. Volcanic and seismic activity continued in the western mountains throughout the Pliocene Age, particularly in the alpine systems that reach along the coast from California to Alaska. The climatology of their high escarpments still provides suitable cold-water habitats in arid western basins and surprising latitudes as far south as Mexico and the Great Smokies.

The Pleistocene millenniums experienced the most celebrated glaciation in the entire history of the world, and their glaciers were perhaps the most important single evolutionary factor in the final development of the Salmonidae and their ultimate distribution. Sprawling ice fields covered most of the northern latitudes, eradicating the remaining subtropical flora and animal species in their bone-chilling embrace. Glaciation during the Pleistocene era radiated southward from the polar regions, although huge secondary glaciers took shape on the principal mountain ranges throughout the Northern Hemisphere. Immense glacial networks reached south from the alpine structures of Asia, their icemelt draining into the Indian Ocean, and other glaciers gathered and drained into the landlocked Eurasian seas north of the Hindu Kush. During these millenniums, the glaciermelt formed the legendary river systems of the Indus and Ganges and milk-colored Brahmaputra.

North America also witnessed vast cycles of early Pleistocene glaciation, its northern latitudes sheathed in ice fields. The southern perimeters of the glaciers reached deep into the United States, creeping inexorably down the Atlantic coastline into the northern foothills of New Jersey and eastern Pennsylvania. Other glaciers penetrated into West Virginia and the drainage system of the Ohio Basin, tracing the outlines of the Great Lakes with their patterns of gargantuan ice scour. Other glaciation worked into the headwaters of the Missouri and Mississippi, covering the northern plains and filling the foothill valleys of the Rocky Mountains. Alpine glaciers took shape along the high summits of the Colorado mountains, spreading and growing in the Tetons and the back-country topography of northern Idaho. Separate glacial structures also formed along the serrated ramparts of the Sierra Nevada, and some regional glaciation even occurred in the Great Smokies.

Pleistocene glaciation covered extensive regions of northern Europe too. Scandinavia, Finland and the north-country regions of the Soviet Union were all buried under incalculable masses of ice. The northern coastlines of Central Europe were also covered with glaciers and separate glacial structures buried the British Isles and Iceland. Secondary glaciers took shape along the higher elevation of the Pyrenees and the Alps. Minor glaciers evolved at the apogee of Pleistocene geology in the mountainous regions of Yugoslavia and Italy and Albania, and still farther south in northern Greece and Lebanon and Morocco. It is interesting that Lake Ohrid in the highlands of Macedonia is perhaps the oldest geological lake in Europe. It experienced little glacial impact and has sustained a remarkable continuity in its aquatic life, including several relict species of Salmonidae that predate Pleistocene times.

The headwaters of the Tigris and Euphrates drainage basins and several minor riverine habitats in southern Turkey clearly demonstrate that glaciation affected the distribution of ancestral Salmonidae in southern latitudes well beyond the northern seas where their primordial marine ancestors evolved. Salmonidae native to Outer Mongolia, Manchuria, and the cold headwaters of the Yangtze network in China also seem to demonstrate the effect of such glaciers on the Asian zoogeography of trout and grayling. Glaciation was also found in the mountains of Japan and Korea, perhaps explaining the distribution of several Salmonidae in those regions, although only marine migratory populations in the cooling postglacial seas explain the char and landlocked masu on Taiwan.

Subsequent cycles of glaciation occurred throughout North America during these same Pleistocene millenniums, and the primary ice fields radiated southwards in two sprawling glacial tongues. The so-called Keewatin Shield gradually took shape and inched toward the south from the tundra barrens west of the Hudson Bay region, and the smaller Ungava Shield evolved in the subarctic latitudes of Labrador. Hudson Bay and its adjoining James Bay were both scoured and sculptured under these glacial shields. The western drift of the Keewatin Shield eroded the eastern escarpment of the Rocky Mountains into a series of smooth foothills, leaving their soils distributed southward across the Great Plains. Similar glaciation spread across the Appalachians, slowly rounding and smoothing their original summits into the gentle tree-covered mountains of modern times, and it was the Keewatin Shield that shaped the Great Lakes. Each of these glacial systems and drainage networks evolved singular populations of trout, grayling and char, displaying clear zoological evidence of the impact of these ice fields.

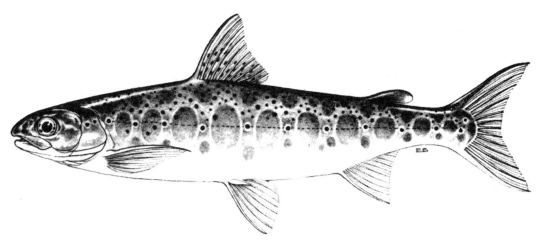

Dalmatian Salmon *(Salmothymus obtusirostris)*

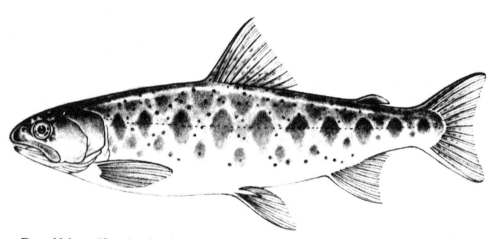

Dwarf Masu *(Oncorhynchus formosanus)*

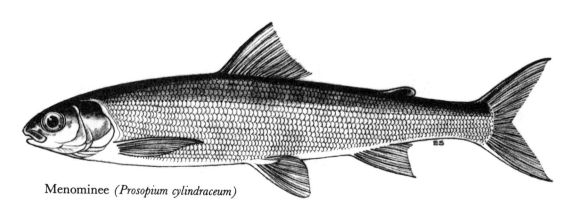

Menominee *(Prosopium cylindraceum)*

Pleistocene glaciation was not continuous over these thousands of years, but consisted of several glacial cycles that ebbed and flowed. Sometimes vast glaciers retreated northward with the melting ice of warming climates. Cold lakes and rivers formed behind these shrinking ice fields and ichthyologists are relatively certain that the marine ancestors of our modern Salmonidae entered many freshwater drainage systems when the cold glaciermelt was mixed with the salinity of our northern seas. Such ancestral populations probably retreated south during cold climatological periods, when the ice fields grew more rapidly again. The early millenniums of the Pleistocene Age were an epoch rich with extensive evolutionary forces and zoogeographic change.

There were a series of major glacial periods in both Europe and North America. Our cycles of glaciation exhibited remarkable variations between the scope of advancing ice fields and warming periods of interglacial centuries. The primary Aftonian interglacial period, which had large-scale impacts on the distribution of trout and grayling, was followed with the vast Kansan glaciers that reached deep into our continent. These glaciers gradually receded during the warming centuries of the Yarmouth cycle, until their relatively mild climatology abruptly ended in the Illinois glacial period, which was in turn followed with its own warming cycle. The Iowa glaciation that followed soon receded with the relatively brief thawing cycle of the Peorian centuries, and the subsequent Wisconsin ice fields were the ultimate period of Pleistocene glaciation in North America.

Central Europe experienced four similar cycles of glaciation and warming during Pleistocene times. The periods of major glaciation in Europe have been designated the Günz, Mindel, Riis and Würm glacial cycles. Their ice fields imperceptibly travelled southward, polishing and weathering the geological formations underneath their creeping masses, and distributing vast deposits of glacial drift across the European continent. The subsequent erosion of this glacial drift resulted in richly fertile soils, as well as dense beds of peat and loess. Such soil types were widely distributed across the coastal lowlands and river valleys of an evolving European continent.

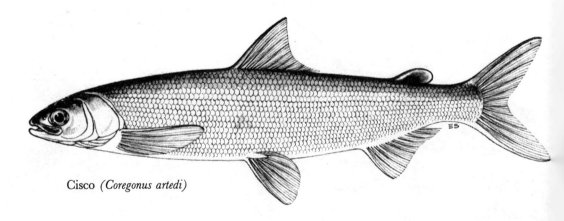

Cisco (*Coregonus artedi*)

NORTHERN SPECIES OF GRAYLING AND CHAR

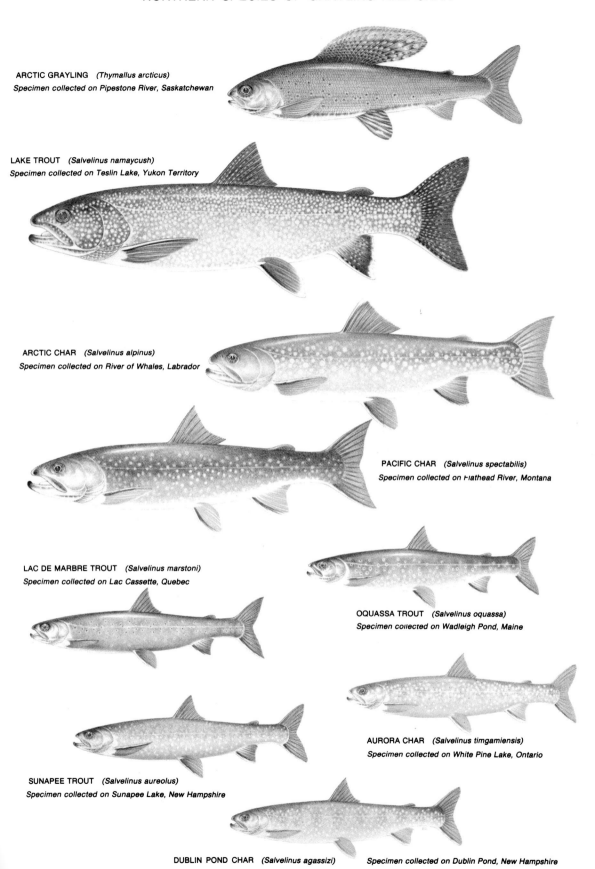

ARCTIC GRAYLING *(Thymallus arcticus)*
Specimen collected on Pipestone River, Saskatchewan

LAKE TROUT *(Salvelinus namaycush)*
Specimen collected on Teslin Lake, Yukon Territory

ARCTIC CHAR *(Salvelinus alpinus)*
Specimen collected on River of Whales, Labrador

PACIFIC CHAR *(Salvelinus spectabilis)*
Specimen collected on Flathead River, Montana

LAC DE MARBRE TROUT *(Salvelinus marstoni)*
Specimen collected on Lac Cassette, Quebec

OQUASSA TROUT *(Salvelinus oquassa)*
Specimen collected on Wadleigh Pond, Maine

AURORA CHAR *(Salvelinus timgamiensis)*
Specimen collected on White Pine Lake, Ontario

SUNAPEE TROUT *(Salvelinus aureolus)*
Specimen collected on Sunapee Lake, New Hampshire

DUBLIN POND CHAR *(Salvelinus agassizi)*   *Specimen collected on Dublin Pond, New Hampshire*

RARE ALPINE SPECIES OF TROUT AND GRAYLING

SOUTH FORK GOLDEN *(Salmo agua-bonita)*

Specimen collected on South Fork of the Kern, California

SODA CREEK GOLDEN *(Salmo whitei)*

Specimen collected on Soda Creek, California

VOLCANO CREEK GOLDEN *(Salmo roosevelti)*

Specimen collected on Volcano Creek, California

PAIUTE TROUT *(Salmo seleniris)*

Specimen collected on Silver King Creek, California

MEXICAN GOLDEN *(Salmo chrysogaster)*

Specimen collected on Rio Culiacan, Mexico

ALPINE CUTTHROAT *(Salmo alpestris)*

Specimen collected on Chilliwack Creek, British Columbia

SELKIRK TROUT *(Salmo whitehousei)*

Specimen collected on Six-Mile Lake, British Columbia

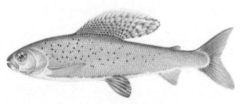

MONTANA GRAYLING *(Thymallus montanus)*

Specimen collected on Big Hole River, Montana

Pleistocene glaciation was primarily responsible for shaping the modern geography of the world, including much of its topography, its patterns of weather and climate, its lakes and drainage systems and the relative salinity of coastal seas, and some of their offshore bathography. The brooding power of these ice fields transformed the physiography of our continent, grinding dramatic alpine escarpments into gentle ranges like the Appalachians, and polishing lesser mountains into the pastoral foothills of the Piedmont regions. Rolling topographies were smoothed into plains, and the loose drift of earlier glaciation was typically displaced and carried farther south. Glacial depressions were often gouged and eroded still deeper by the grinding ice. Such depressions became shallow lakes during the warming interglacial periods and were excavated deeper with each succeeding period of increasing glaciation. Major riverine drainage systems were radically changed when their primitive channels were completely erased or filled in with glacial overburdens. The glaciers also left their fingerprints in the drumlin, the smoothly polished mounds of earlier glacial aggregates, and the linear patterns of glacial moraines, which are composed of relatively loose remains of glacial drift and conglomerates. Such moraines often define the configuration of modern lakes or the directions of ancient glacial flowages, and through their boundaries define the distribution of trout and grayling.

The vast prehistoric lakes that formed behind the receding ice fields of the Pleistocene period have largely vanished in modern times, although the Great Lakes and the large freshwater lakes found from Manitoba into the subarctic barrens of the Northwest Territories are substantial echoes of Pleistocene glaciation. Millions of smaller freshwater lakes formed during these glacial millenniums are still found throughout the northern United States and the Canadian Provinces, and the zoogeographic distribution of the Salmonidae family is closely tied with Pleistocene geology and climate. The melting glaciers that followed the Wisconsin glacial era soon filled the prehistoric lakes and drainages with a flooding spate that raised the coastal seas, lowering their temperatures and again flooding our coastlines throughout the eastern United States and the Maritimes.

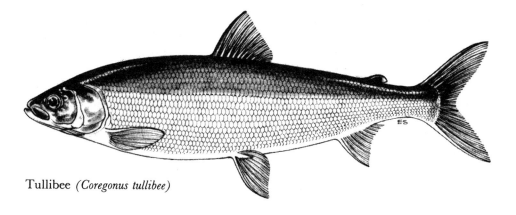

Tullibee *(Coregonus tullibee)*

There is evidence that both Lake Ontario and its outlet drainage basin, the Lake Champlain watershed farther south, and the coastal plains bordering the Gulf of Saint Lawrence were all drowned under shallow brackish seas. There is also evidence that the entire Hudsonian region was a marine channel connecting these inland seas with the Atlantic farther south. Seismic elevation subsequently altered the postglacial drainages of the Hudson, changing the Pleistocene character of both the eastern United States and Canada, but the existence of landlocked and anadromous populations of Atlantic salmon in these river systems during colonial times would add strong ichthyological evidence in support of such theories of postglacial evolution on the Atlantic Coast.

Pleistocene glaciation also had surprising impact on the latitudes that remained totally free of its ice fields. The flooding icemelt that followed the glaciers resulted in extensive erosion throughout North America. Gargantuan alluvial fans of silts, fine aggregates, clays, limestones, phosphates and other sedimentary materials were freshly carried into the coastal shallows of the entire continental perimeter. The spates of glaciermelt at higher altitudes in our western mountains and the heavy rainfall that accompanied the postglacial warming cycles were responsible for incomprehensible erosion—centuries of flooding that now seem almost impossible in the arid sagebrush country between the Rocky Mountains and Sierra Nevadas.

Glaciermelt transformed the remaining inland seas that covered these prehistoric landscapes, diluting their salinity with a gathering flood of fresh water that pushed their boundaries over vast regions. Sedimentary deposits greatly multiplied their fertility. Lake Bonneville covered thousands of square miles in western Utah, and Lake Lahontan sprawled across vast reaches of Nevada along the Sierra foothills. Other saline lakes unquestionably existed, particularly in the desiccating basins of central Nevada and southeastern Oregon. The brackish waters of the Pyramid and Walker lakes are the fingerprints of the ancient Lahontan shallows. Lake Malheur and its connecting drainage systems are all that remains of the brackish seas that once covered southeastern Oregon in postglacial times, and the Great Salt Lake is all that remains of prehistoric Lake Bonneville. Each of these inland seas has echoes in its singular species and subspecies of cutthroats and cutthroatlike trout.

These residual inland seas are evidence of both the melting ice fields that followed Pleistocene glaciation and the heavy almost-tropical rainfall that accompanied the many cycles of interglacial warming. The impact of such postglacial flooding is dramatically visible. The Black Canyon of the Gunnison, the Royal Gorge of the Arkansas, the towering river-scoured walls at Dinosaur National Monument on the lower Green, and Glenwood Canyon of the Upper Colorado are well-known examples. Farther north lie the bright-walled Grand Canyon of the Yellowstone and the ominous Hells Canyon of the Snake that separates Oregon and Idaho. All are evidence of the incredible erosion that accompanied the melting of the Pleistocene glaciers, but the most remarkable example of those millenniums of precipitation and glaciermelt flooding is found in the Grand Canyon of the lower Colorado.

These dramatic examples of geological change that followed the Pleistocene epoch often had demonstrable impact on regional populations of the Salmonidae family. Unique subspecies of cutthroat trout evolved in the separate drainage systems of the Arkansas, Rio Grande, Colorado, Snake and Yellowstone. Lake Lahontan completely escaped Pleistocene glaciation, and a remarkable strain of lacustrine cutthroat once survived in its receding waters, fish that regularly reached weights of forty-odd pounds in Pyramid Lake. Lake Bonneville was apparently a brackish inland sea in these postglacial times, since its waters evolved another unique strain of cutthroat that could not have survived the present toxic salinity of the Great Salt Lake. Other unique trout are found in southeastern Oregon and northern California, surviving in the drying basins of ancient lakes that once filled the Great Basin topography there—particularly the rare Paiute and Oregon red-banded trout.

Salmonidae found in high-country drainage systems that once reached the Gulf of California, when its colder postglacial shallows supported anadromous populations of ancestral rainbow and cutthroat ecotypes, are additional evidence of the impact of both Pleistocene glaciation and postglacial flooding on the zoogeographic distribution of species. The unique species that occupy the cold headwaters of streams once tributary to the Gulf of California are found in both Mexico and the United States. The remarkable Mexican populations include trout native to the Baja Peninsula, and several other species found in the coastal rivers draining the Sierra Madre on the mainland, from Mazatlan on the Tropic of Cancer to Guaymas and Hermosillo five hundred miles farther north. Other rare species with their prehistoric origins in the Gulf of California are the populations in the San Gorgonio Mountains, the remarkable cutthroatlike species found only in the back-country headwaters of the Salt and Gila rivers in New Mexico and Arizona, and the extinct species of trout once found in the Verde drainage north of Phoenix.

The evolutionary geology of the past several hundred million years is closely tied to the evolution and distribution of our American species of trout and grayling. Recent fossil evidence of unmistakable Salmonidae fishes in the Miocene strata of Nevada indicate that the North American species were well established before glaciation finally reshaped the continent, and that the individual divergences of our modern genetic strains from their common Salmoniform ancestors are surprisingly ancient even when measured in geological time.

The Salmonidae family includes ten acknowledged genera in terms of accepted modern taxonomy. Pacific salmon are classified in the genus *Oncorhynchus* and are distributed throughout marine habitats and suitable coastal rivers along the Asian and North American boundaries of the northern Pacific. North American populations are found from Alaskan rivers tributary to the Bering Sea southward to the drainage system of the

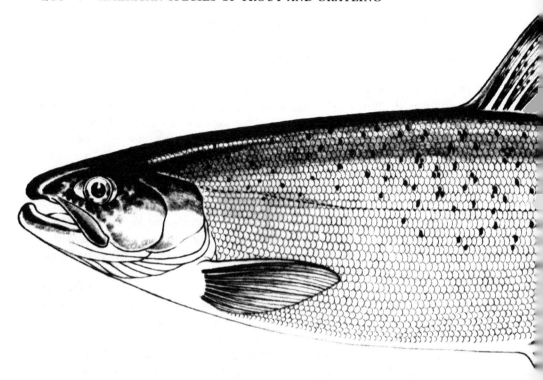

Coho Salmon *(Oncorhynchus kisutch)*

Sacramento in California. Atlantic salmon and the so-called true trouts are both grouped in the genus *Salmo*, and trout species are found in both Atlantic and Pacific drainage systems, as well as waters tributary to the Baltic, Mediterranean, Black and Caspian Seas. Postglacial relict populations are known from Italy, Yugoslavia, Greece, Turkey, Iran, Syria, Lebanon, Morocco, and northern Spain, clearly demonstrating that the Mediterranean once supported ancestral Salmonidae. Populations in the headwaters of the Tigris and Euphrates and in suitable south-flowing streams that lose themselves in the desiccating basins of northern Iran are unquestionably the echoes of migratory populations that reached these regions during the cycles of Pleistocene glaciation. Salmonidae in the genus *Salmo* also include several minor Asian trout, as well as the familiar rainbows and cutthroats indigenous to North American waters. Less familiar are several rare species also included in the genus *Salmo* like the Paiute trout, Oregon red-banded trout, Apache trout, Gila trout, California golden trout, and several closely allied species found in several Mexican coastal rivers.

Salvelinus is the generic description of numerous species and subspecies

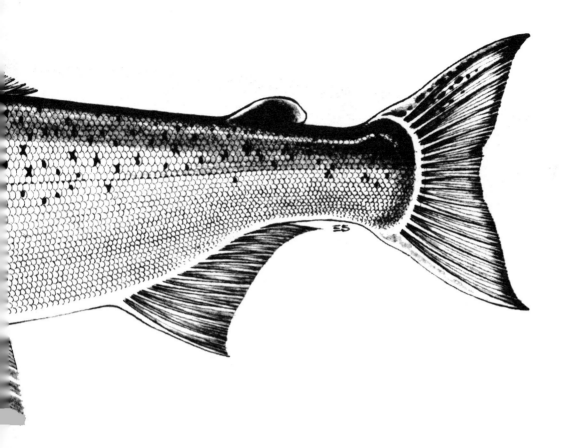

of char found throughout northern Europe, Asia and North America. The genus includes the brook trout originally found from northern Georgia to the Ungava waters of the Labrador, and farther west in the drainage systems of the Great Lakes and Hudson Bay. It also includes the larger lake trout of the United States and Canada. Both species are widely distributed in lakes and streams, particularly in the northern latitudes of their range. *Salvelinus* also includes the Dolly Varden char of the Pacific watersheds, and the several sea-going Arctic chars that have a more northern distribution. Minor subspecies closely related to these Arctic char were originally found in several deepwater, lacustrine habitats in Maine, New Hampshire and eastern Canada, where ancestral populations were apparently landlocked during Pleistocene times. Similar relict populations from glacial times are recorded from several deepwater lakes in Europe and the British Isles, and widespread populations are known across northern Europe and the Soviet Union. Glacial relict populations of char are also found in the mountain lakes of France, Switzerland, Germany, Austria, Italy, and Yugoslavia, and curious relict populations are found in deepwater lakes in the Japanese mountains.

Sheefish *(Stenodus leucichthys)*

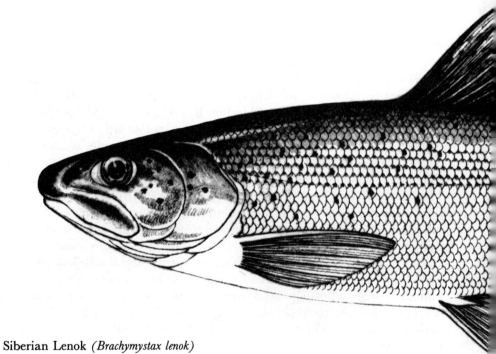

Siberian Lenok *(Brachymystax lenok)*

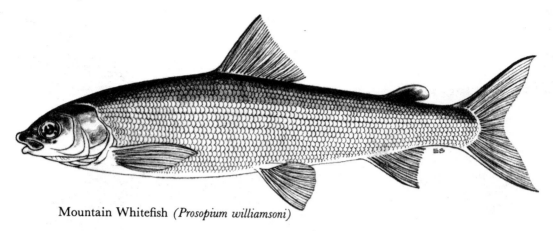

Mountain Whitefish *(Prosopium williamsoni)*

The graceful genus *Thymallus* includes the common European grayling and the several subarctic and arctic graylings found across northern Europe, Asia and North America. There are also intriguing relict grayling populations of unique species in Yugoslavia and Outer Mongolia. Similar isolated populations which echo the influence of Pleistocene geology are found in the headwaters of the Missouri in Montana, and of course there is the tragically extinct Michigan grayling.

Coregonus is the taxonomic classification for several whitefish species and subspecies found across Europe, Asia and North America, including both lake and riverine populations. Sometimes these whitefish, ciscoes and mooneyes are grouped in the fully separate Coregoninae subfamily, along with the current-loving *Prosopium* whitefish found in the rivers of North America, and the large sheefish of the *Stenodus* genus, which are found in subpolar watersheds from the Canadian Northwest Territories to the White Sea tributaries of the Soviet Union.

The remarkable genus *Hucho* is limited to riverine populations from the headwaters of the Danube throughout the Eurasian continent to the coastal seas off Manchuria, Korea and the Kurile Islands. The best-known species is perhaps the huchen found in the Danube and other tributaries of the Black Sea. But the most widely distributed species is the taimen, which is found throughout much of the Soviet Union. Perhaps the least-known species is the Chinese huchen recorded from the headwaters of the Yangtze, on the mountain threshold of Tibet. Huchen are almost wholly river fishes, although anadromous species are known in Korean, Manchurian, and Japanese waters. These seagoing Asian species are sometimes classified in the genus *Parahucho*, although not all taxonomists accept this classification. Since there are several recorded instances of natural hybrids between populations of the *Hucho* genus and the unique *Brachymystax* species found mixed with huchen populations in Asian and Siberian tributaries of the Sea of Okhotsk, some ichthyologists believe that the *Brachymystax* fishes have a subgeneric relationship to the more widely distributed huchen and taimen populations.

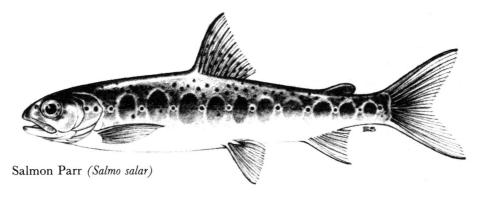

Salmon Parr *(Salmo salar)*

Salmothymus is the generic classification given to several species of primitive Salmonidae described from Lake Ohrid and several adjacent drainage systems in Yugoslavia. *Platysalmo* is a relatively new generic description developed to identify a previously unknown member of the Salmonidae family—the strangely unspotted Taurus trout native to several south-flowing rivers draining into the Mediterranean in southern Turkey.

Several modern ichthyologists believe that these Eurasian genera, particularly the *Brachymystax* fishes, are relict forms of ancestral Salmonidae. The full distribution of the Salmonidae family is a cornucopia of puzzles, demonstrating that both their evolution and their endemic habitats are quite closely tied to past geological and climatological factors, working across literally millions of years. Recent research unmistakably demonstrates that ichthyologists have perhaps exhausted the classic system of taxonomy, which is based on structural and anatomical character in identifying species. Further clarification of the Salmonidae and their evolutionary interrelationships must depend on methods more sophisticated than mere morphological factors—particularly comparative studies of chromosomes and other biochemical characters—and make use of the computer and its role in sorting through the taxonomy of thousands and thousands of specimens.

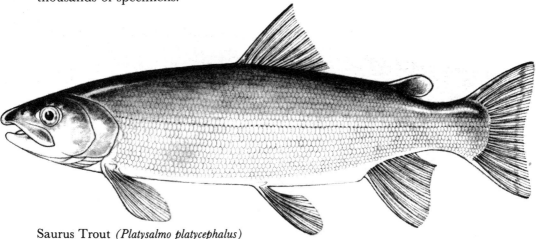

Saurus Trout *(Platysalmo platycephalus)*

Both salmon and trout populations are remarkable examples of the evolutionary forces at work during the cycles of Pleistocene glaciation. Salmon are perhaps the most striking members of the Salmonidae family, and their oceanic migrations probably remain closer to their prehistoric ancestors in the behavioral sense. Both Atlantic and Pacific species of salmon demonstrate a remarkable relationship between their natural range and the glacial character of Pleistocene times. Atlantic salmon and brown trout unquestionably share a common ancestral species from comparatively recent geological times. Natural hybrids between Atlantic salmon and sea-run browns have occurred on many European rivers. Atlantic salmon are known in the Pechora drainage system in the northern Soviet Union and the southern limits of their natural range were once the Douro and Tagus in Portugal. Salmon no longer inhabit these Portuguese rivers, although limited populations still enter the Asturian and Galician rivers along the northwest coast of Spain. Some trace populations are also still found in French watersheds that rise in the Pyrenees, although the Atlantic salmon is virtually extinct in all the coastal river systems between Portugal and Poland. There are a few salmon in the rivers of Brittany and Denmark, but the great spawning migrations that once entered the Seine and Loire are gone, and few anglers realize that the entire watershed of the Rhine once brought vast runs of Atlantic salmon as far upstream as Liechtenstein. Atlantic salmon are still moderately abundant in the Baltic, spawning in rivers from southern Sweden to the Gulf of Bothnia, and south again from the Gulf of Finland to several rivers that rise in the Polish mountains. Salmon are common too in the famous Norwegian rivers from Oslo to Kirkenes, high above the Arctic Circle on the Russian border, and in the famous salmon fisheries of the British Isles. Perhaps the finest sustaining populations of Atlantic salmon anywhere are found in the surprisingly fertile rivers of Iceland.

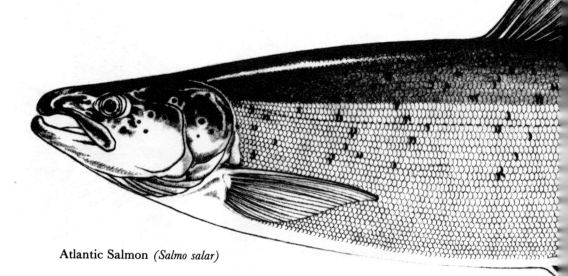

Atlantic Salmon *(Salmo salar)*

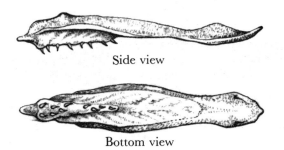

Side view

Bottom view

Atlantic Salmon Vomerine Bone

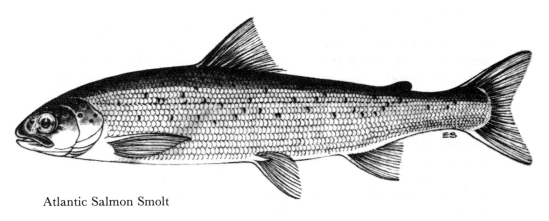

Atlantic Salmon Smolt

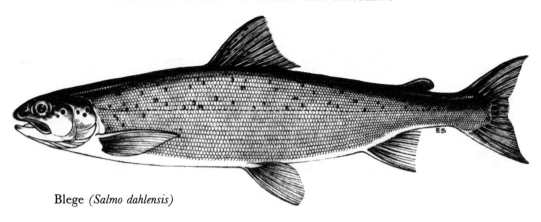

Blege *(Salmo dahlensis)*

There are several dwarf landlocked strains of Atlantic salmon in Scandinavia, where seismic and glacial changes have occurred in relatively recent geological times. Such dwarf subspecies inhabit several recently glaciated lakes in Norway and Sweden and are also recorded from the Karelian lakes in the Soviet Union. Other landlocked strains which rival our landlocked salmon from eastern North America exist in several lakes in Sweden and the Soviet Union. Dwarf salmon called blege are found landlocked in three Norwegian rivers where waterfalls have blocked their ancestral migrations, and there is a curious subspecies found in the Namsen near Trondheim—it has access to saltwater along with the larger anadromous salmon in the river, but it seldom leaves fresh water.

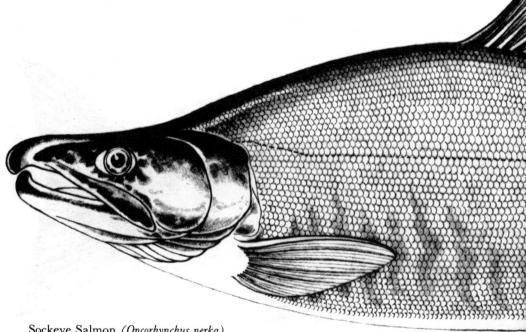

Sockeye Salmon *(Oncorhynchus nerka)*

There is wide disagreement about the relationships between the Atlantic salmon and several other Salmonidae that are found from Yugoslavia to the Caspian Sea. Some experts have held that the riverine *Salmothymus* in Yugoslavia and Macedonia are perhaps dwarf salmon descended from primitive salmonlike fishes that once inhabited the Mediterranean and Adriatic. Others believe that both the huchen and taimen are related to the Atlantic salmon through a common prehistoric species isolated in the Black Sea, perhaps in postglacial times, and that the large salmonlike fish which spawn in the rivers draining the Caucasus suggest that similar ancestral species were isolated in the receding waters that formed the Caspian Sea. However, recent studies based on chromosomes and biochemical tissue factors seem to indicate that fishes of the genera *Salmothymus* and *Hucho* are more closely allied to the brown trout—although like the recently identified *Platysalmo* fishes in southern Turkey, such genera are the echoes of extremely ancient species. Both genetic evidence and conventional taxonomic factors suggest that a common ancestral species once ranged the ancient sea that connected the Mediterranean with the Caspian drainage basin. Geological evidence verifies the existence of such marine shallows reaching across these latitudes and supporting both ancestral trout and salmon.

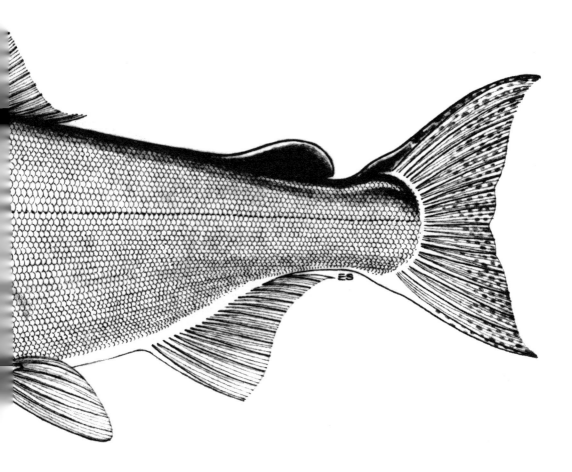

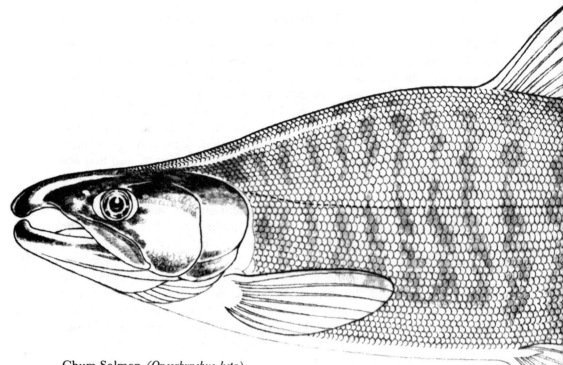

Chum Salmon *(Oncorhynchus keta)*

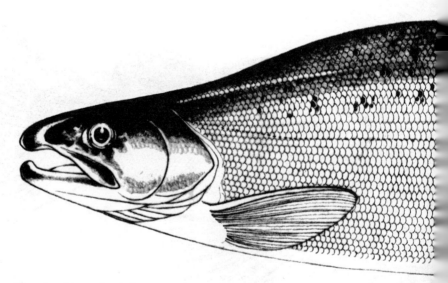

Pink Salmon *(Oncorhynchus gorbuscha)*

Pacific salmon are grouped in the genus *Oncorhynchus,* and include six fully anadromous species. Chum salmon are distributed along the waters off Korea and northern Japan, northward into the Sea of Okhotsk and Kamchatka, and along our Pacific coasts from the Bering Straits to San Francisco. Pink salmon are native throughout the northern Pacific from Hokkaido to the Bering Sea, and southward from the Colville watershed on the northern coasts of Alaska to the estuary of the San Lorenzo in California. Coho salmon were originally found from the coastal waters off northern Japan to the Anadyr watershed in the Koryak mountains of the Soviet Union, although heavy populations are seldom encountered as far south as the Sea of Okhotsk. Coho populations are much heavier along the coastline of North America from the Aleutians to northern California, and introduced populations are presently thriving in the Great Lakes. Chinook salmon are also primarily concentrated in North American waters from the Sacramento drainage system in California to Bristol Bay in Alaska, although these fish are also found in several rivers draining the Kamchatka Peninsula. The Japanese masu is the only *Oncorhynchus* species limited to Asian waters, and its range carries it into much warmer latitudes than the other Pacific salmon. Masu are found in the waters of Taiwan and Kyushu in surprising numbers, and these small Asian salmon are particularly abundant off Sakhalin and the Kuriles. Sockeye salmon are more common in North American waters than their populations in Asian watersheds and coastal seas, and although large schools of sockeyes are seldom taken south of Kamchatka, there are landlocked subspecies in the deepwater lakes of Siberia and northern Japan. Perhaps the most abundant sockeye populations in Asian waters are found entering the Anadyr, and other adjacent rivers tributary to the Bering Sea. Sockeye salmon are remarkably abundant in North American waters from the Bristol Bay drainages of Alaska to the rivers of northern California, and sizable spawning migrations occur in several major river systems that rise in the interior of British Columbia. Landlocked strains of sockeyes were originally found in a number of Canadian lakes, and like their Asian cousins, these Kokanee salmon are a dwarf subspecies that seldom reach two pounds. It is interesting that only the Japanese masu and the sockeye salmon have landlocked dwarf strains, among the several prolific *Oncorhynchus* species that inhabit the Pacific. Such dwarf populations in northern Japan, Siberia and British Columbia clearly indicate prehistoric isolation when seismic changes and volcanic eruptions and glaciation radically affected their distribution, and the shrinking seas of postglacial times trapped their ancestors in the headwaters of their parent river systems.

Since the brown trout is not native to the waters of North America, and the closely related Atlantic salmon was once abundant from the Delaware to the waters of Ungava Bay, it is clear that our salmon stocks first reached this continent through long-range Atlantic migrations. Rivers like the Hudson and Connecticut and Merrimack once teemed with immense runs of salmon. However, their modern range is limited in the

United States to eight rivers in Maine, where they were reintroduced to American waters in a salmon restoration program started in 1948. Farther north, the Atlantic salmon is still found in most Canadian rivers between New Brunswick and the Hudson Straits. Perhaps the finest salmon fisheries are found in the drainage systems of the Bay de Chaleur, the glittering Gulf of Saint Lawrence and Ungava Bay. Populations of Atlantic salmon were unknown beyond the coastal mountains of Cape Chidley until surprisingly recent times, when their presence was discovered during the iron-ore explorations of the past twenty-five years.

Seismic disruptions and receding coastal seas explain the isolation of several landlocked strains of Atlantic salmon, including the cartwheeling ouananiche found in several watersheds of subarctic Quebec and the Labrador, as well as the celebrated landlocked salmon of Maine.

Similar echoes of prehistoric glaciation and seismic isolation are found among grayling populations. Arctic grayling are almost circumpolar in distribution, although the Thymallidae are apparently not found in the watersheds entering Hudson Bay, or the rivers farther east into the Canadian Provinces. The absence of grayling in the drainage systems of Baffin and Hudson Bay and Greenland is a puzzling fragment of biological evidence that points to geological connections between Europe, Asia and North America millions of years ago. Europe and North America were apparently already separated by ancient seas when the genus *Thymallus* evolved in most arctic watersheds. Grayling are also absent from the rivers of Iceland, and history tells us the species was originally introduced into the British Isles when the first French monks established their monasteries after the Battle of Hastings.

European grayling are found distributed from southern Scotland into the central provinces of the Soviet Union, and from subarctic Scandinavia southward to northern Italy and Yugoslavia. Dalmatian rivers have a species of richly spotted grayling that some ichthyologists once believed were a phylogenetic bridge between grayling and brown trout, although modern techniques of chromosome and biochemical analysis have largely discredited such opinions. Other species of the Thymallidae are found in the waters of southern Siberia and Outer Mongolia, particularly rivers entering Lake Baikal.

Relict populations from Pleistocene glaciation are the only grayling indigenous to American waters, and these Thymallidae are still relatively common in some headwater lakes and rivers of the Missouri drainage system. Montana grayling are still surprisingly plentiful in the Beaverhead, high in the Bitteroots of the Bannock Pass country, and in the Big Hole headwaters between Wise River and Wisdom. The Michigan grayling that once thrived in the fertile forest-sheltered rivers of both the Upper and Lower Peninsulas are extinct. Perhaps the largest grayling populations were found in major Lower Peninsula rivers like the Manistee and Pere Marquette and Au Sable, which drain extensive layers of glacial aggregates and drift that lie over outcroppings of limestone bedrock. Since no other

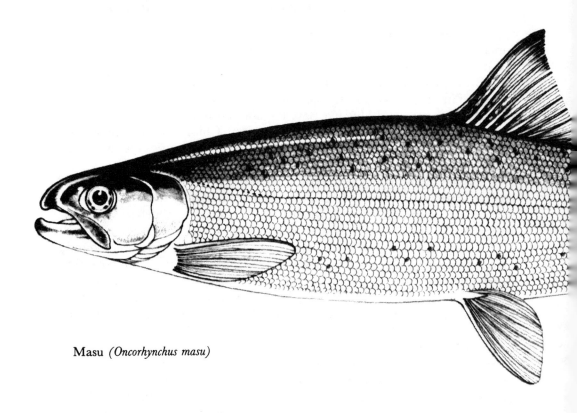

Masu *(Oncorhynchus masu)*

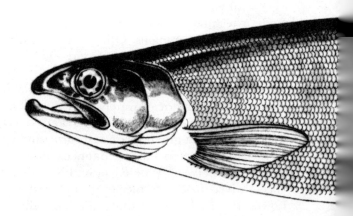

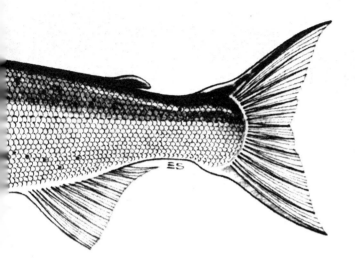

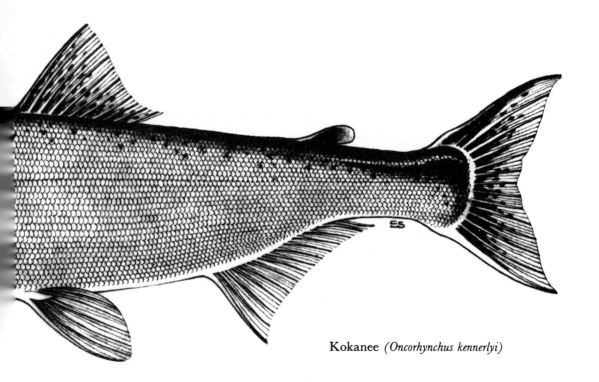

Kokanee *(Oncorhynchus kennerlyi)*

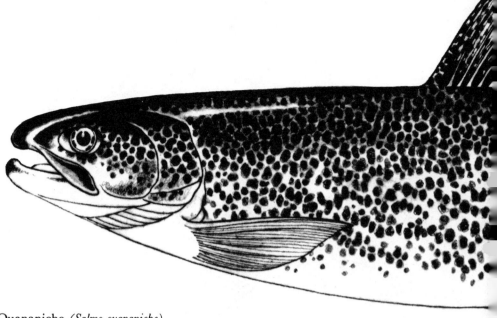

Ouananiche *(Salmo ouananiche)*

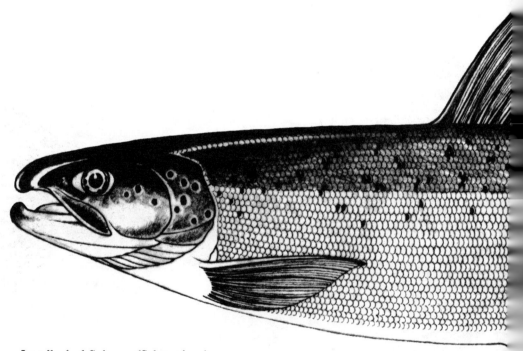

Landlocked Salmon *(Salmo sebago)*

Thymallidae are found within hundreds of miles of these grayling habitats in Michigan and Montana and these drainage systems are found in regions that experienced widespread Pleistocene glaciation, glacial transport and subsequent geographic isolation might account for such fisheries much farther south than any other North American populations of the Thymallidae. Some grayling are reported from estuarine habitats in the Canadian and Siberian arctic, although fully anadromous behavior outside these brackish shallows is not recorded among either Asian or North American graylings. Such sea-run behavior could have extended their range throughout arctic waters, making the Thymallidae circumpolar in distribution—like the restless saltwater migrations of the Arctic char.

Unlike the closely related Atlantic salmon, which engages in saltwater migrations lasting thousands of miles, the natural range of the modern brown trout originally reached no farther west than the rivers of Scotland and Iceland. Both species have common marine ancestors, and although the brown trout failed to arrive naturally in North American waters, the prehistoric cycles of marine flooding and glaciation distributed them extensively through Europe, North Africa and Asia—from the Atlas Mountains in Algeria and Morocco northward to the Finnmarksvidda in arctic Norway, and eastward from the subarctic wastes of Iceland to Lebanon, the Turkish headwaters of the Tigris and Euphrates and the rivers draining from the Hindu Kush into the brackish Sea of Aral. Such wide distribution suggests that much colder seas once washed the Mediterranean shores, and these ancestral browns travelled them freely to reach glacial streams in North Africa and Lebanon and the Middle East, moving along the brackish coastal shallows that reached from Gibraltar through Asia Minor to the threshold of China and Tibet.

The brown trout populations in the headwaters of the Tigris and Euphrates watershed and in adjacent south-flowing rivers in the northern mountains of Iran are puzzling in zoogeographic terms. Such populations perhaps formed as glacial refuges in Pleistocene times, although some ichthyologists have suggested that these populations in rivers tributary to the Persian Gulf might be attributed to the widespread inundation of ancient seas or even the penetration of ancestral prototypes through the Red Sea into the northern coastal shallows of the Indian Ocean.

Similar cycles of glaciation and marine inundation offer explanations for natural brown-trout populations in the principal islands of the eastern Atlantic, their remarkable abundance throughout Scandinavia, extensive stocks in suitable habitat between the Mediterranean and the Baltic, and their presence in the eastern Soviet Union from its arctic coastlines to the Black and Caspian seas—and surprisingly beyond the Ural Mountains into the forests of western Siberia.

Since the widespread populations of the *Salvelinus* chars require extremely cold, pollution-free waters, their distribution is unmistakably related to Pleistocene glaciation and their ability to travel the brackish coasts. The circumpolar abundance of its sea-run species are indicative of their hardiness and the migratory habits developed since Pleistocene times. However, it is the relict subspecies of char isolated in many deeply glaciated lakes around the world that exhibit the most intriguing relationships to Pleistocene geology. The abundance of these landlocked subspecies, populations trapped behind shrinking glaciers or receding seas, is not surprising to fishermen familiar with the *Salvelinus* fishes and their prehistory. Several beautiful subspecies are known from North America, like the Sunapee and Dublin Pond and Oquassa chars native to Maine and New Hampshire, and the Aurora and Lac de Marbre chars from Quebec. Other chars are found scattered across Scandinavia and the Soviet Union, and similar landlocked *Salvelinus* populations are found in a few deepwater lakes of Iceland and the British Isles. Landlocked chars are common in the cold alpine lakes of central Europe, from the foothills below Geneva to the Salzkammergut in Austria.

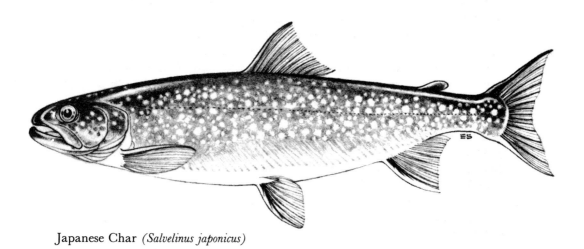

Japanese Char *(Salvelinus japonicus)*

There are also some curious landlocked *Salvelinus* populations found in Japanese waters, like the Oshima char from Lake Shikaribetsu, the small river chars found on both Hokkaido and Honshu, and the brightly colored little Kiso char found in the headwater streams in the mountains behind Tokyo. The landlocked char found in the depths of Lake Biwa are indigenous to approximately the same latitudes as the brook-trout populations in northern Georgia and South Carolina, making them the southern-most natural stocks of these ecotypes. The Biwa subspecies are in a remarkable setting—the peaceful lake outside ancient Kyoto, with its beautiful bark-roofed palaces and temples and pagodas.

The distribution of the common brook trout is equally intriguing, although perhaps the recent geology of its range is less dramatic than the seismic and volcanic origins of the Japanese archipelago. The natural range of the brook trout sprawls across some of the most ancient geological formations in North America, the igneous outcroppings that spewed to the surface in Archeozoic times. These volcanic shields reach from the Great Lakes to the coastal highlands of the Labrador.

Our eastern mountains provided the principal longitudinal armature extending the range of the brook trout into southern latitudes, and these mountains reached their most dramatic configurations during the Pliocene millenniums. Fossil evidence clearly dating to the Pliocene epoch has been identified as *Salvelinus* in its ancestral state of development, but it was the extensive glaciation of the Pleistocene weather cycles that eroded the Appalachians toward their gentle configuration in modern times, flooded our Atlantic coastlines from Florida to Newfoundland and the Labrador, and submerged the Great Plains in brackish shallows. It was a period of cataclysmic change, and its violence suggests that ancestral brook trout must have retreated into several refuges that remained relatively ice free during glacial times. Such glacial refuges perhaps sheltered many separately evolving brook-trout populations. Coastal seas from Cape Chidley in the Labrador to Cape Hatteras were unquestionably marine refuges, and the existence of natural brook-trout populations in the foothill mountains of Georgia and South Carolina suggests that ancestral *Salvelinus* might have ranged even farther south along the Atlantic Coast. The modern boundaries of the brook trout also suggest that the wetlands of the Chesapeake, Delaware and Hudson might have served as primary glacial sanctuaries for extensive concentrations of many anadromous species. Similar coastal refuges during periods of extreme glaciation probably existed in Long Island Sound and the Bay of Fundy, along with the fertile Bay de Chaleur and Gulf of Saint Lawrence farther north. Glacial retreats also existed in Hudson Bay, the coastal seas of the Ungava drainage basins, and the inland seas surrounding the Great Lakes region.

Brook trout were originally limited to Atlantic drainage systems from the Eskimo settlement at Sugluk on the subarctic Hudson Straits to the mountains of Georgia and South Carolina. Good populations were found in all the suitably cold habitats in between. Native populations were also found in the Appalachian headwaters of the Ohio and the Tennessee, suggesting that their ancestral strains weathered Pleistocene glaciation in shallow inland seas. Still other brook trout inhabited tributaries flowing into the Great Lakes from both the United States and Canada. The original western limits of their range were the rivers draining from Manitoba and the Northwest Territories into Hudson Bay, in the barrens above York Factory and Churchill.

Although the record brook trout was caught sixty-odd years ago in the Nipigon, which connects Lake Nipigon with Lake Superior, the finest brook-trout habitat lies elsewhere in modern times. Perhaps the best is found in northeastern Manitoba rivers like the Nelson and Limestone and Gods watersheds, the wild Albany that drains into James Bay in northern Ontario, the almost matchless Broadback and Mistassini watersheds in Quebec, and in the Ashuanipi and Minipi country farther east on the threshold of the Labrador. Floatplane fishermen have taken several brook trout better than ten pounds from these waters in recent years, although the Nipigon record remains intact.

Both brook trout and migratory Arctic chars share their northern habitats with the lake trout, the primitive *Salvelinus* populations that are perhaps the most widely distributed species among the Salmonidae of North America. Their range also displays remarkable interrelationships with Pleistocene glaciation, and these prolific char are unmatched in both the scope of their principal distribution and in the extensive relict populations that survived the postglacial warming at the southern limits of their range. Although there is some evidence of minor sea-run behavior in the extreme northern latitudes of its range, no fully ocean-going populations are known—and the geography of the lake trout seems entirely linked with the cycles of glaciation and interglacial melting.

The brook trout and lake trout are believed to have evolved from common primitive ancestors in eastern North America. Brook trout evolved into a somewhat more highly developed species, tolerating a relatively wide range of environmental considerations, while the lake trout has remained primitive and developed into a predator feeding largely on the baitfish indigenous to widespread North American lakes and rivers. Obvious physical differences indicate that the evolutionary development separating the brook trout from its lake-trout cousins is quite ancient, occurring no later than Pliocene times. There are some who argue that the lake trout is the most primitive member of the *Salvelinus* fishes, and it is unquestionably a strikingly stable ecotype, particularly in comparison with the rich variety of species and subspecies found among other members of its genus.

Lake trout are the only species that ranges far into the arctic latitudes of Alaska and the Northwest Territories and yet is not also established across the Bering Straits in the Soviet Union, as are the common sea-run chars. Such extensive marine migrations have clearly proved beyond their capability, yet some lake trout are found in barren lakes in the remote arctic archipelagos above Hudson Bay. Such populations unquestionably point to marine emigration in relatively recent millenniums, since many of these barren Northwest Territories have emerged from the sea as recently as the last Ice Age. The widespread natural geography of the lake trout from Nova Scotia to the northern drainage systems of Alaska, and from the Great Lakes to Baffin Land, is virtually unmatched among our Salmonidae. Such wide distribution seems to indicate several glacial refuges, since no other species has achieved such extensive postglacial voyaging from a single Pleistocene source. However, such migratory dispersal is believed possible from a relatively limited number of glacial refuges, since the hardy lake trout is perfectly equipped to travel the interconnecting networks of swelling rivers and short-lived lakes that formed behind the melting ice fields in the warming centuries.

Fossil evidence demonstrates the existence of ancestral lake-trout strains in Wisconsin during Pleistocene times, and natural populations are native to several deepwater lakes in Wisconsin and Minnesota, particularly in the headwaters of the Mississippi. However, there are other natural populations in surprising isolation, since the species is also found in several Montana lakes at the headwaters of the Missouri. Since the topographic separations between the Great Lakes and the headwaters of the Mississippi are relatively minor, the ancestral lake-trout populations might well have traversed these regions during periods of interglacial or postglacial flooding. Similar migrations might have occurred between the populations in the headwaters of the Missouri and the extensive lake-trout domains farther north in the Saskatchewan. The proximity of lake-trout populations in these adjacent watersheds is intriguing, since these fisheries lie in a linear tongue of atypical lake-trout habitats, reaching far below other lake-trout colonies in western Canada.

The Montana populations may have migrated south into the United States, travelling the floodwaters of melting glaciers, and some researchers have theorized that the Saskatchewan lake-trout populations might have migrated from the headwaters of the Yukon. Such fish perhaps finally reached the Missouri headwaters along the many-channelled courses of the glaciermelt. There are some mysteries in the lake-trout populations of the Yukon country too, missing pieces in the vast puzzle of their zoogeography. Lake trout are curiously absent from the lower reaches of the Yukon watershed, although adjacent populations in mountain ranges both north and south of its drainage basin are well established. Such paradoxical gaps in their distribution seem to indicate that the Lower Yukon may have been a shallow Pleistocene sea, inhospitable to the freshwater requirements of ancestral lake trout.

Natural populations of lake trout farther east in the Finger Lakes country of New York and many suitable lacustrine habitats throughout New England and the Adirondacks suggest still other Pleistocene holding zones. Their original geography in Pleistocene times was apparently much more extensive, reaching well below their modern range, and the warming lakes and drainage networks that followed the melting ice fields perhaps became too warm—eradicating the ancestral species from southern latitudes well below the limits of Wisconsin glaciation.

It is curious that lake trout have been successfully introduced into suitable waters lying between the limits of natural populations and the southern perimeters reached during the centuries of Wisconsin glaciation. There are many such lakes where the species has been successfully introduced and has thrived, yet natural stocks of lake trout were absent. There are other curious voids in the natural distribution of the lake trout in Canada and the United States. Original populations were lacking on both Newfoundland and Vancouver Island, although the species has subsequently been introduced with success. Such puzzling gaps in its distribution are apparent evidence that lake trout are strangely reluctant to enter saltwater habitats. Since oceanic temperatures and levels of salinity were unquestionably quite low during the long millenniums when the Wisconsin ice shields were melting and shrinking, it is curious that lake trout failed to cross the relatively narrow straits separating both Newfoundland and Vancouver Island from the mainland. Perhaps these ancestral populations simply failed to reach or find shelter in these adjacent habitats when the coastal seas provided an acceptable environmental bridge, and their thwarted migrations were subsequently ended when the postglacial warming cycles triggered higher levels of marine temperatures and salinity.

Although both their modern distribution and fossil evidence point toward several primitive populations of lake trout in southern latitudes during Pleistocene times, the species is puzzlingly absent from our Pacific drainage systems below the glacial perimeters. The potential ecological niche of such lake-trout populations in these Pacific waters is aggressively occupied by the western char popularly known as the Dolly Varden. Lake trout thrive in the Pacific drainages north of the Fraser watershed in British Columbia, perhaps after ancient migrations from habitats in Alberta and the Yukon Territories. The topography in northeastern British Columbia suggests that such migrations might easily have been accomplished in the sprawling Peace and Athabasca river systems, particularly during cycles of glacial melting.

Alaskan populations of the lake trout include several relict populations dating from Pleistocene times, populations too widely separated and remote for postglacial migrations. Lake trout are found in the tributaries draining into Bristol Bay, in the foothill lakes of the Kilbuck Mountains, and on both watersheds of the Brooks Range lying north of the Yukon. The species is remarkably well suited and abundant in the Canadian headwaters of the Yukon, while the seemingly optimal lacustrine habitats farther downstream apparently lack the depths usually associated with glaciation. There are surprisingly no lake-trout colonies in the waters of the Seward Peninsula, in spite of its large numbers of lakes that apparently provide suitable conditions for such populations. Lake trout are abundant in the Kobuk country above Kotzebue, some four hundred miles inland from the Bering Straits, and there are no known populations closer to Siberia.

Although the lake trout is less important to fly-fishermen than our other North American species, except perhaps in subarctic watersheds where it reponds readily to bucktails and streamers throughout the season, its remarkably widespread distribution and its relationships to geological prehistory help us understand the zoogeography of our Salmonidae.

Similar fingerprints of these same geological and glacial forces are visible in the evolutionary prehistory of the celebrated rainbow and cutthroat trouts, and their several related species and subspecies. There is disagreement on the precise taxonomy of these rainbow and cutthroat populations. Although most groupings place them in the *Salmo* genus originally described in European waters, there are enough minor physical differences that the separate *Parasalmo* genus has been proposed to describe the North American populations. Our rainbow and cutthroat stocks are closely related fishes that readily interbreed in nature, often resulting in unfortunate hybrid strains after thoughtless introductions of hatchery rainbows into optimal cutthroat habitats. Primitive ancestral species of both rainbows and cutthroats have developed unusual offshoots in isolation, including the golden trout populations in the Sierra Nevada of California and the Sierra Madre of Mexico.

The original distribution of the rainbow trout lies along the Pacific Coast from the drainages of the Kuskokwim country in the Bering Sea to both the Baja Peninsula and the coastal rivers of Mexico on the Tropic of Cancer. The behavior of most rainbow stocks is closely tied to its primitive oceanic ancestors, and its sea-run tendencies are largely dominant, except for isolated subspecies that have been geologically isolated since Pleistocene times. Research has confirmed that the seagoing tendencies are primary behavior among rainbows, and that the nonmigratory qualities of the several landlocked subspecies become quickly lost in hatchery hybridization. Such hybridization occurred rather early in the history of American pisciculture. Our fascination with the discovery that trout could be reared in artificial hatcheries permitted our separate and special genetic strains of rainbows to interbreed and lose their singular nonmigratory behavior.

Rainbows have such a compelling affinity for the Pacific that their anadromous behavior seems clearly to point to glacial refuges in its sanctuary, and to their landlocked subspecies as having been trapped in the alpine headwaters of several California and British Columbia rivers in times of shrinking seas and geological change. No natural populations of rainbow trout were found in the east-flowing rivers of the Sierra Nevada, where thriving cutthroat populations evolved, or in any other drainage system not connected with the Pacific in relatively recent geological times. Perhaps the ancient relationships of the rainbow and its pelagic beginnings are best expressed in these observations from *A Leaf from French Eddy*, the posthumous collection gleaned from the work of Ben Hur Lampman:

> There were thin pearl-colored films of sunlight slanting through the pool, and these revealed, as the multitudinous mists are seen that lesser life that eludes the eye—the microcosmic water world as dense and tenanted as any jungle, yet impalpable as vapor. The sun, the life-giver, and the river that is his mate, these are miracles.
>
> Hasten if it please you, to the sea, swiftness of whispering currents, to the sea and forgetting, as it was in the ancient times, ever returning—go swiftly in haste and river laughter.
>
> Here in the embrace of the meadow, bent greenly to shield its flowing, rests the refuge of quiet and drowsy water, and thimbleberry blossoms are mirrored in the shallows. There is no haste in the alder pool.
>
> Do not the trout parr have leisure and wisdom, that move through the golden water and rise for midges as are not seen to the eye? There is peace for a long, great while in these drowsy waters,

peace and pretending to greatness, and play in the shallows—and after, but only after, there will come the compelling swirl of the river running in spate.

But long after, and long, time enough for unreckoned tomorrows. Time enough yet for the sea. This is a drowsy, meditative and useful water, golden with peace.

Strange sun-tinted water here, wearing tall sedges of comely verdure, in a green and amber quietude drawn apart from the urgent stream, that life may increase and learn prudence here—prudence and courage—before it commits all to the venturesome seas. Dunes and headlands, seas that fail not to call and claim them, you must call for a season. Listen. She calls to the trout parr that one day shall hear her music. Yet now there is nothing of such urgency in this drowsy pool.

A drowsy sun-drenched loitering of chill mountain water whereon the whirligig beetles, each gleaming dervish of them all, dance tirelessly and strong in their joyousness. And there the water striders dance and dart, their footfalls shadowed on the vital ooze.

Strange life, persistent and recurrent, fecund beyond all imaginings and brave to dare, upward and upward, the microcosm of the pool, its golden scarcely-stirred placidity—upward and outward, into the hastening flow, and to the sea's self waiting yonder.

Listen now. She is calling to the trout parr, the sea is calling faintly. But they rise softly for midges in the golden water, where dragonflies are born. They poise and hover over the drowsy pool. Listen. The sea is calling. But where the thimbleberry blossoms are mirrored, in the place of the pool that rests in the arms of the meadow, there is nothing of haste.

Let it come in a time of spate, in a wildness of pewter-colored rain, on some distant tomorrow. Listen. The primordial sea calls restlessly. But there is no haste in a time of drowsy water.

There are several relict populations of rainbow subspecies in surprisingly southern latitudes. Perhaps the most puzzling is the rainbow subspecies found in the San Gorgonio Mountains of southern California, in small watercourses draining into the desiccating basin that once held the Gulf of California. The relict population found in the mountains of Baja California is a similar echo of postglacial times, and there are also isolated rainbowlike stocks in the Sierra Madre Mountains of Mexico.

Cutthroat trout clearly share a common ancestry with their rainbow cousins, although their primitive distribution suggests that their genetic separation from the rainbows is quite ancient. The original range of the cutthroats is extensive, reaching from the east-flowing Rocky Mountain tributaries of the Mississippi to the numberless Pacific watersheds from the

Eel in northern California to the Alaskan rivers of Prince William Sound. The principal distribution of the cutthroat species and subspecies lies on both sides of the Continental Divide, in the headwaters of the Columbia and Missouri, and in the headwaters of the Colorado, Arkansas, Platte and Rio Grande farther south. The cutthroat populations in the Great Basin that lies between the Rocky Mountains and the eastern escarpment of the Sierra Nevadas evolved several subspecies in waters flowing both toward the Columbia and the Gulf of California.

Other riverine and landlocked populations were originally found from British Columbia to the mountains of northern Mexico. Such widespread distribution of the cutthroat across several independent drainage basins, including topography that escaped primary glaciation, has evolved a highly variable family of cutthroat species and subspecies. Migratory, estuarine, fluvial, and landlocked lacustrine populations are all known throughout their original range, although their sea-run habits are less adventurous than the marine behavior of the rainbow. Unique lacustrine species once existed in the Twin Lakes, high in the headwaters of the Arkansas, and in the faintly saline habitat of Pyramid Lake in western Nevada—large cutthroat subspecies that are presently extinct because of manmade water storage systems and irrigation. Pyramid Lake is a curious echo of the inland seas that once covered Nevada, and the Great Salt Lake is all that remains of similar marine shallows that once covered the Bonneville Basin of Utah. Other seas once covered southeastern Oregon and the Columbia Basin farther north. Lesser inland seas covered the Bridger and Big Horn and Shoshone Basins in Wyoming, and each of these primordial waters played an evolutionary role in the cutthroat species and subspecies still found between the Sierra escarpment and the Great Plains.

Marine shallows also covered the Gila Basin in southern Arizona, and three species closely allied to the cutthroat evolved in the isolation of separate headwater streams. Cutthroatlike species also evolved in northern California and southeastern Oregon. Several other lacustrine subspecies were originally described in field studies made late in the nineteenth century, although several have apparently been eradicated in the past fifty-odd years. The volcanoes and seismic warping and upthrusting that created the Rocky Mountains apparently trapped and isolated parent colonies of cutthroats in newly formed lakes and drainage systems.

Our contemporary distribution of cutthroats along the Continental Divide echoes these dramatic geological forces, and their subsequent isolation triggered a number of fully identifiable strains. The Arkansas and South Platte drainage basins evolved a common subspecies, suggesting that its taxonomy had fully developed before the geological events that elevated the Mosquito Range—separating the headwaters of the Arkansas from the South Platte drainage in the marine bottoms of the South Park.

The evidence of a clearly separate cutthroat subspecies in the western-slope rivers of the Colorado Mountains, particularly the waters of the Elk, Yampa, White, Eagle, Roaring Fork, Crystal, Gunnison, Lake

Fork, Taylor, Frying Pan, and the Colorado itself, seems to demonstrate that the Continental Divide must have been born in some cataclysmic upthrusting before cutthroat evolution was complete. The western-slope populations unmistakably diverge from the classic greenbacked cutthroats that were originally indigenous to the watersheds of the Arkansas and the Platte. The Continental Divide must have played a major role in that subsequent evolutionary path along with the Cochetopa and San Juan mountains farther south, which separated the Gunnison drainage system from that of the Rio Grande. Its cutthroat subspecies perhaps had its origins in the primordial seas which covered the rich San Luis Valley, once the volcanic birth and seismic wrenchings of the Sangre de Cristo Mountains had isolated its table-smooth bottoms from the high plains farther east.

Three fully separate cutthroat strains were produced in Colorado and New Mexico. The so-called Colorado cutthroat is distributed from the headwaters of the Green in Wyoming, throughout the Colorado drainage basin to the Gunnison and Uncompahgre waters farther south. The rare little greenbacked cutthroat was once abundant in all the east-slope rivers draining the Rockies, in both the Platte and Arkansas systems, from the pastoral Sweetwater in Wyoming to the tumbling Purgatoire and Cucharas in southern Colorado. There was a cutthroat subspecies in the Rio Grande watershed as well, found from the headwaters of the Pecos above Santa Fe to the Conejos and the Puerco and the Chama—as well as a series of smaller rivers that rise in the Gallinas and San Mateo and Mimbres mountains of southwestern New Mexico.

It is possible that these mountains began forming in both Eocene and Miocene times, separating the ancient marine shallows into isolated seas that formed on the eastern plains of Colorado, in the extensive basin of the North Platte in Wyoming, the Gila drainage basin in Arizona, alpine enclaves like the San Luis Valley south of Saguache, and the South Park high in the mountains behind Colorado Springs. Other marine shallows probably existed in the Colorado Basin, perhaps near Gunnison or Grand Junction, and each of these separate Pleistocene seas could have provided distinct parent strains for the postglacial distribution of the cutthroats in Colorado, New Mexico and southern Wyoming—as well as the mountains of Utah and Arizona.

Inland seas also covered southern Idaho, Nevada, Utah, the several high-plains basins in western Wyoming, and the eastern foothill grasslands in Montana, all serving as Pleistocene sanctuaries that evolved distinct cutthroat species and subspecies. Mountain lakes also inundated lesser basins like the Big Hole country in Montana, Jackson Hole in Wyoming, the Flathead Lake bottoms at Kalispell, and the high-country basin of Yellowstone Lake. Separate populations of cutthroats evolved in these isolated habitats, including the exquisite subspecies found in Jackson Hole and the richly colored cutthroats in the headwaters of the Yellowstone.

There is disagreement on the parent-strain origins of the golden trout subspecies found in British Columbia, Oregon, California and Mexico.

Some taxonomists believe golden trout evolved from ancestral cutthroat strains, while others argue that the several golden subspecies are descended from ancient rainbow populations. Recent phylogenetic studies seem to indicate that both viewpoints are correct, based upon unmistakable chromosome and biochemical data run through computer programs. Although the results are still inconclusive, ichthyologists have begun to find a better phylogenetic structure of the several golden trouts and their ties to the cutthroat and rainbow than was possible with traditional taxonomic methods—most golden trouts appear genetically closer to the cutthroats, except for the Mexican golden, which is widely separated from both parent strains.

The native distribution of our western Salmonidae has been radically altered in the past century, both through our development of former frontier regions and through our fish-management programs. Shrinking habitats, careless intermixing of genetic strains in hatcheries, and indiscriminate introduction of hatchery strains capable of dominating or assimilating native populations have decimated or completely eradicated many original stocks. Such ecological and genetic rape has unquestionably blurred the natural zoogeography of the cutthroat and rainbow as each evolved in postglacial times.

Our discussion of the Salmonidae family and its prehistory on the North American continent has focused on its apparent evolutionary relationships, and the geological and climatological forces that contributed to the genetic character of its several genera and species. Their evolution occurred over millions and millions of years, and in modern times it is almost incomprehensible to fathom the violence, imperceptible weathering and erosion that accompanied these primeval cycles of change.

The awesome geological forces that shaped the Sierra Nevada escarpment and our other western ranges are almost beyond our ability to envision. However, like the Yellowstone earthquake that dammed the Madison and entombed a campground filled with tents and trailers in recent years, there was a frightening Sierra quake that killed twenty-five people in 1872. Its shocks and shuddering tremors were a tiny footnote in the shaping of the mountains themselves, yet the entire village of Lone Pine was annihilated. Huge river bottoms were elevated or collapsed, lakes were formed and swallowed up, and a fifty-foot earthquake fault was torn open along a sagebrush bench. The swift-flowing Owens reversed its flow for several hours, until its bottom dried up and its trout lay stranded and gasping among the stones. Many people fled their farmhouses and summer cabins in terror, but others stood transfixed, watching the fearsome avalanches in the high country. The remarkable John Muir witnessed the Lone Pine quake, rushing from his simple cottage in the Yosemite, and revelling in the tremors a hundred miles from its epicenter:

> The shocks were so violent and varied, and succeeded one another
> so closely, that I had to balance myself carefully in walking, as if

on the deck of a ship among waves. Suddenly there came a tremendous roar. Eagle Rock on the south wall, about a half mile up the valley, gave way and I watched it falling in thousands of great boulders, pouring to the valley floor in a free curve, luminous from friction, making a sublime spectacle of glowing, passionate fire. The sound was so tremendously deep and broad and earnest, the whole earth like a living creature seemed at last to have found its voice, and was calling to its sister planets. In trying to tell something of the size of this awful sound it seems to me that if all the thunder of all the storms I have ever heard were condensed into a single sound, it could still not equal the thunder of this rock-roar.

Such incredible violence is only a minor postlude to the mind-boggling earthquakes and volcanic eruptions that actually shaped both our continent and the distribution of its fish life, and these western escarpments are still imperceptibly elevating and evolving after five hundred million years.

The evolving zoogeography of our many Salmonidae remains an intricate puzzle of half-understood clues, each closely tied to climatological changes and geological traumas lying deep in the prehistory of the planet. Countless centuries of evolution have given us a singularly rich palette of streams and lakes and rivers, populated with many unique species and subspecies. Millions of tiny brooks abound like capillaries across the continent, from the tea-colored tamarack bogans of Maine to the tumbling high-country creeks of California. Their currents are either crystalline over bedrock or sombre with the beaver-stick leachings of the headwater marshes. They cut deep under the wildflower banks of trailing grasses in some Wyoming meadow or plunge down faces of stream-polished granite in a rhododendron thicket in the Appalachians. There are other rivers too, like the smooth-flowing Michigan streams with their pale gravel beds and willow-hung bends and cedar deadfalls throbbing in the current—and the classic spring creeks from Pennsylvania to northern California, their smooth weed-trailing currents rich with fly hatches and watercress.

Our continent is equally rich with trout and grayling lakes, from the glacial networks in the Labrador to the high-country lakes of our western mountains, clinging precariously to their treeless escarpments and snow-field barrens. There are still forest-rimmed ponds from Oregon to Massachusetts, where the morning mists echo to the startling melancholy of a loon in their bulrush shallows. There are the wild deadfall rivers in Maine, tumbling through outcroppings of granite between their pewter-colored ponds, where the dimpling patterns of the rain shatter the mirror reflections of the conifers. There are the trout streams of the Catskills, where American fly-fishing had its beginnings, their still pools and swift riffles in a gentle landscape of covered bridges and mountain farms and villages with white church steeples rising above the trees. There are southern rivers too, surprisingly swift rivers draining the forest-covered foothills of the Great Smokies, in a region of hardscrabble farms and fruit-jar whiskey and mountain people. There are the tailwater fisheries we have created with the icy discharges of reservoirs, restoring the trout fisheries in the Delaware and transforming a round handful of smallmouth rivers from Georgia to the Ozarks into first-rate trout habitats. Our western rivers are richly varied watersheds, ranging from the strange hot-spring upwellings in the Yellowstone country to the rivers that drain the serrated ridges of the Sierra Nevadas in California. The large mountain rivers are varied too, from the wild Roaring Fork in Colorado to the cacophonies of the Umpqua and the Rogue.

Our continent has evolved a rich tapestry of trout waters through millenniums of prehistory. Their populations of trout and grayling echo cycles of geology and climatic change reaching back thousands of years. The beauty of these American species conceals a character that has survived numberless centuries of profound change. Their parent colonies thrived through almost timeless cycles of plenty in their ancient seas, endured terrible threats of eradication in later volcanic and seismic upheavals, and somehow survived during periods of glaciation. It was perhaps the glaciation and the icemelt drainages following each glacial cycle that ultimately had the most subtle and profound effects on our American trout and grayling. The ultimate cartography of their distribution is deeply rooted in these prehistoric millenniums. When grinding forces polished the topographic face of the continent and during the rainfall and icemelt of interglacial warming cycles, erosion softened the mountains and cut gorges in seismic crevasses and faults. The glaciers grew imperceptibly across vast reaches of time, their melting spread across the Pleistocene world in intricate lacework patterns of lakes and streams, and in these networks ancestral populations of trout and grayling evolved. It is fitting that the lyric trout and the graceful grayling were finally shaped during these cold millenniums. And it is equally fitting that John Muir understood the forces that shaped their world and ours.

> In the development of these alpine formations, nature chose for its tool not the earthquake or the volcano, but tender snow-flowers falling noiselessly through the unnumbered centuries.

2. The Aphrodite of the Hemlocks

I t was a cool morning of early summer in Michigan, with a wood thrush deep in the thickets across the brook, and a ruffed grouse drumming somewhere in the abandoned orchard behind the farm. There were deer still browsing for apples in the orchard just at daylight, and they melted into the trees when the sun began burning off the last layers of ground fog. The deer were already fat with summer, sleek and fox-colored when they finally disappeared in the jack pines, and the morning sky was clearing after the rain.

Several blue-winged teal settled into the marsh below the barn. Farmers were wrestling their steel milk cans on the platforms beside the Baldwin road when we started. The warm milk sloshed inside the cans, its froth trickling down and dripping into the grass. We drove slowly north along the sandy twin-rut road toward the brook-trout river we were fishing that morning.

Its iron bridge was ahead now. Its trusswork spanned the swift current, where the river came down through a sweeping bend in the trees. Raindrops still glittered in the grass. The bridge planking rattled when it took the weight of the Oldsmobile, scattering sand and fine gravel between the boards into the current. The morning sunlight sparkled in the tiny jewels of moisture that hung in a cobweb across the path, and the cool summer wind tasted sweet.

It's beautiful, I thought happily.

The swift-flowing Pine is a lovely river in the forests of lower Michigan, and below its trusswork bridge, its flow winds through a wide hook-shaped series of bends. Cedar sweepers and jackstraw tangles of fallen trees break and slow its current tongues. The logs are bleached with time, their underwater labyrinths bright with pale green growths of *Dichelyma* moss and algae. There are deep eddies where the current circles slowly, dark and emerald-green among the throbbing deadfalls, and downstream are shallows of bright gravel.

Its fish were mostly brookies in those boyhood summers, bright-spotted little trout with darkly mottled backs and bright white-edged orange fins. We could see them holding restlessly among the cedar sweepers and dead-falls, especially when the sun was high and penetrated deep into the swimming-pool green currents. Sometimes I lay on my stomach in the warm summer grass, watching the brook trout and feeding them an occasional grasshopper.

They're like jewels, said the retired classics professor who fished the river with us that summer.

The brook trout is not a wild, cartwheeling fighter like the rainbow, and it is foolish and naïve compared with the brown. Brook trout, being comparatively short-lived, do not reach the huge sizes common for the other Salmonidae. The fight of the brook trout is stubborn and strong rather than dramatic and spectacular. It is a species for the cold waters of northern latitudes or high country, and it seems to thrive better in slightly acid environments than its cousins. The world-record fish is only fourteen pounds eight ounces and was taken on the famous Nipigon above Lake Superior by Doctor William Cook in 1916.

American fly-fishers love the brook trout because of its history, sense of tradition and beauty. Its size and sporting qualities and wariness are certainly not the reasons it is loved, since these facets of its character do not begin to measure its true worth. It is its rarity in a time of warming habitat and its jewellike beauty that attract us still—the same qualities that tempted a painter like Winslow Homer to capture the brook trout in his exquisite watercolors at Mink Pond in the Adirondacks.

The original range of the brook trout was surprisingly large. It was found from the mountain headwaters of Georgia and South Carolina to the Eskimo settlement of Sugluk at the mouth of Hudson Bay. Its anadromous range of migration into its saltwater estuaries once included almost all coastal watersheds from Long Island and the Hudson drainage system to Cape Chidley in the Labrador, and west to major rivers like the Seal and Knife systems that reach Hudson Bay above Churchill and York Factory. Such migratory brook trout still thrive from Maine throughout the Maritime Provinces and Newfoundland. The western limits of the species in the United States were originally the headwaters of the Mississippi above northern Iowa and Illinois, and the rivers draining into Lake Superior— including the storied Nipigon in Ontario and the equally famous Brule in Wisconsin.

The best brook-trout regions lie farther north in our time, since we have forever changed the ecology of our American waters. The Nipigon is no longer a great brook-trout river, and American brook-trout fisheries like the Brule and Au Sable and Allagash are no longer as productive as they were a century ago. It is ironic that the decline of the brook trout in America is closely linked to the Texas trail herds and the death of the buffalo. The slaughter of the buffalo herds took place for the profit in meat and hides, and was encouraged in order to reduce the military effectiveness of the hostile Plains tribes. Trainloads of buffalo pelts and cowhides went east to the tanneries, and forests from Minnesota to South Carolina were stripped of their hemlocks to provide enough acid bark for the leather-making. Coniferous pines and hemlocks contain and keep cool more eventual spring water in their root structures than other trees. Once the great pine forests were lumbered off, every river and springhead in the brook-trout range flowed warmer. The great rivers in the indigenous zoogeography of brook trout today lie farther north. Their roster includes the rivers draining into Hudson Bay—the magnificent subarctic systems like the Nelson and Gods rivers in Manitoba, the swift-flowing Albany in northern Ontario, and the Broadback and Mistassini watersheds in the scrub-pine forests of Quebec.

Brook trout have been introduced outside their original habitats and in many other parts of the world. The species has been transplanted throughout the United States, and in some of our western mountains it dominates the high-altitude streams and lakes where it has been stocked. Limited stocking of brook trout has occurred in several European countries, but the most success with introduced populations of *Salvelinus fontinalis* has been experienced in South America and the Antipodes.

There are fine populations of big brook trout in some of these adopted countries of the Southern Hemisphere. O. S. Hintz describes one fishery in his charming *Trout at Taupo*, with its stories of six-pound brookies in the cold Taupo tributary called Hatepe. The remote Andean lakes of Argentina also have superb fishing for brook trout, with a quick growth rate in volcanic lacustrine waters that never freeze in winter. Such low winterkill influences and a rapid growth mean that a certified world-record brook trout from Argentina will one day break the Nipigon record that has stood for almost sixty years. Lago Fontana and Lago Generale Paz are among the finest brook-trout waters of the world, having surrendered several fish above the world record that were never submitted for certification, since they seemed small to Argentine fishermen accustomed to seeing rainbows and browns over fifteen to twenty pounds. These lakes are drained and fed by swift glacier-cold rivers like the Pico, Corcovado, Engano and Carrenleufu, and lie deep in Patagonia almost two hundred fifty miles below San Carlos de Bariloche.

The travelling fly-fisher in search of trophy-size brook trout can find them closer to San Carlos de Bariloche too, particularly in the first autumn weather of April, when the fish are schooling at the cold-flowing inlet *bocas* to spawn. Such inlets are found under the Tronador volcano at Lago Mascardi, and the Pireco and Millaqueo and Totoral are all superb brook-trout places in the headwaters of the vast Lago Nahuel-Huapi. The inlet flowages of the Pichi Traful, Lolog, Hermoso, and the storied five *bocas* of the Meliquina are equally fine brook-trout spots. Knowledgeable anglers fully expect the future world record to come from these Argentine lakes in April, when its brook trout are gathering in the bone-chilling inlet of some Andean river.

Such a trophy fish is certainly a prize, since the eastern brook trout is one of the most beautiful fish in the world. It has been virtually worshipped since British officers stationed in America first explored our forest rivers with flies in the eighteenth century. Its beauty and grace have always been treasured by anglers who refuse to measure their sport in terms of mere muscle, pole-vaulting acrobatics and size. Austin Hogan is perhaps our most knowledgeable historian of the roots of American fly-fishing. Hogan serves as curator of the Museum of American Fly-Fishing, located at Manchester in the rolling tree-covered mountains of Vermont. His archives clearly demonstrate that our brook-trout rivers were being fished by Englishmen as early as 1775, since there is considerable written evidence verifying that date. Sir William Johnson apparently fished even earlier, since he was the Royal Superintendent of Indian Affairs in the American Colonies. His duties became less pressing with the end of the bitter French and Indian Wars, and Johnson sought both fly-fishing and solitude in the tumbling waters of the Kenyetto, in the foothills of the wild Adirondacks. It was still an uncharted wilderness before the American Revolution.

Sir William Johnson was of a breed of anglers virtually unknown on the frontier American rivers. His birthright was a place among the sporting gentry of Ireland, at a sprawling manor with fishing rights and stables for hunters and foxhound kennels. There were woodcock dogs and retrievers for bird-shooting, and there was stalking for red stag in the hills. The streams held both salmon and trout, with riverkeepers to patrol them against poaching and gillies to help with the fishing. His tackle was still in the tradition of Walton and Cotton, with slender rods and tiny reels and lines of woven horsehair. His fly books were filled with favorite European patterns, dressed on snelled hooks with bright silks and glittering tinsel and feathers. Sir William Johnson was a transplanted fly-fisherman, and on the swift little Kenyetto only his riverkeeper and gillies were missing. The river flowed through primeval forests that stood cathedral-dark with hemlocks and conifers, and pileated woodpeckers drummed in the trees.

Fishing was excellent, although the brook trout on the Kenyetto were small. Johnson loved them for their bright colors, and found them extremely eager to take his flies. Sport was so good on the Kenyetto that he soon acquired property and built a lodge at Sacandaga. It was burned during the frontier wars of 1781, and Johnson subsequently built a second fishing house on the headwaters of the Kenyetto near Northampton. It survived its builder and was eventually bought by Major Nicholas Fish. It subsequently became known among Adirondack brook-trout fishermen as the Fish House.

The brook trout is inextricable in our angling history and tradition. The famous Delmonico's restaurant in New York, where legendary figures like Diamond Jim Brady, Gentleman Jim Corbett and Lily Langtry dined, was renowned for its brook trout stuffed with crabmeat in 1840. Charles Lanman described his sport with the brook trout in his *Adventures of an Angler in Canada* in 1848, and the celebrated Thaddeus Norris filled his classic *American Angler's Book* with brook-trout episodes fifteen years later. The first American book entirely devoted to the species appeared in 1869, when R. G. Allerton published his *Brook Trout Fishing*. It was a fine little volume filled with the current music of eastern rivers and tea-colored trout ponds rimmed with conifers and birches.

Many early figures like Cotton Mather, Joseph Secombe, Daniel Webster, and Henry Ward Beecher were often found on trout water. Brook trout from the slow-flowing Nissequogue and weedy little Carman's River on Long Island were favorites of Daniel Webster, and the region still abounds in anecdotes about his brook-trout fishing. There are two versions of the story of Daniel Webster and his record brook trout on Long Island. One has the site of its capture as the millpond of the old Wyandanche Club on the Nissequogue. The other version places the capture of the giant fish outside the graceful colonial church at Brookhaven, where Webster and his friends often fished at the Suffolk Club.

Brookhaven is still a quiet village among the beach-grass dunes and sheltered harbors of the South Shore. Its snug colonial saltboxes and elm-shaded streets have a special character, dominated by the slender belltower of its Presbyterian church, built by local shipwrights in 1745. Such a patina of time is often enough to give a church some measure of fame, but this church is also part of the Webster legend. One hundred forty years ago its congregation apparently witnessed his legendary exploit with the giant brook trout. Evidence supporting the story is relatively meagre: it consists of a carved cherrywood facsimile of the fish, obscure records and diaries, the brass plate of the Suffolk Club in one of the church pews, and the famous Currier & Ives lithograph of Webster catching the trout—a colorful lithograph that ultimately became part of the Congressional Record in 1854.

Webster himself is part of American folk legend, and his fame lies in several directions: orator, statesman, lawyer, congressman, and fly-fisherman. Webster was born at Franklin in the White Mountains of New Hampshire in 1782 and graduated from Dartmouth College. During both his boyhood and his college years Webster spent much time fishing the mountain brooks and brook-trout ponds of New Hampshire. He was elected to the Congress in 1813, and soon moved his residence to Boston. The legendary Dartmouth College case first gave him great fame as an attorney in 1819, and his defense of the United States Treasury in *McCullough vs. Maryland* cemented his reputation in the circles of power. His growing fame soon brought him into contact with men like Martin Van Buren, who would become president of the United States in 1837; Philip Hone, the mayor of the city of New York; and John Stevens, pioneer developer of steamboats, boilers, and locomotives. These men were all dedicated fly-fishers, and they subsequently invited Daniel Webster to join their Suffolk Fishing Club on Long Island.

Webster became a senator from Massachusetts in 1827, having established flourishing law offices in both Boston and New York. History tells us that he loved the brook-trout rivers found on eastern Long Island, and that his circle of fishing friends spent many weekends in the Fireplace Tavern operated by Sam Carman. It was a hard-fishing crew, fond of free-flowing rum and conversation, that regularly gathered in front of his hearth, although each Sunday morning found them across the road in the Presbyterian church, nursing their headaches in the pew reserved for the Suffolk Club.

It was a bright spring morning in 1823 when Philip Hone first discovered the huge brook trout in the little river below Carman's Tavern. Hone quickly found Webster, and both men tried their luck for several hours without interesting the fish. Webster became obsessed with the huge brook trout, but it was four years later before he saw it again. Webster and Hone had left on the last Friday stagecoach from Brooklyn, and arrived at the Fireplace Tavern long after dark. They found the dining room alive with stories of the giant fish. Downstream from the tavern Sam Carman also operated a general store and grist mill, and that afternoon his employees had been working on its water wheel. When the work—dismantling the big cypress-framed wheel—had started, the huge brook trout had darted out from the millrace into the weedy channel upstream.

Webster and Hone fished the millpond through the following day without locating the big trout again. Saturday night found them commiserating their poor luck in Jamaican rum, with liberal tankards of Carman's hard cider for variety, and both men were ultimately carried to bed by Carman's black servants. It proved a difficult and restless night. The following Sunday morning both men were faithfully seated in the pew across the road, perhaps groaning inwardly that the Presbyterian sense of austerity forbade such ornamental amenities as stained-glass windows that might reduce the glare and mollify their headaches. Carman accompanied them to services that morning, but left instructions that his servant Lige should stand watch at the millpond for the giant trout. It was a beautiful spring morning and every man in the church stared longingly at the little river, with its pale willows and shadbush blooming and the ruby-colored buds of the swamp maples in the bend above the grist mill. Parson Jedediah King was also a fly-fisherman, but his long-winded sermons typically lasted all morning, and that morning was no exception. King droned endlessly about temptation, the eternal faults of mankind, wickedness, hellfire and brimstone, gluttony, carnality—and fixing his fierce blue-gray eyes on the Suffolk Club pew, debated the evils of cider and Jamaican rum.

The sermon lasted an eternity itself. *Shall we gather at the river*, the congregation finally chorused, *the beautiful, beautiful river?* The hymn finally ended, but the service still had thirty-odd minutes left.

There was a soft scraping at the churchyard door just as the congregation was settling for a second harangue from Parson King. Carman knew instantly what it was, and turned to see his servant Lige tiptoeing along the side aisle. Lige had located the big brook trout in the millpond, and only his orders to report sighting the fish could have forced Lige to interrupt Parson King and his morning services.

Lige slipped into the pew, and whispered to his employer briefly.

Senator, Carman whispered to Webster, *Lige has seen the big trout—it's lying in the throat of the millrace, and it's rising!*

There is no subterfuge for leaving the front pew inconspicuously in the middle of a church service. Webster and Hone looked at each other briefly, averted their eyes and stood awkwardly, and quietly filed out of the church. The minister stopped and the congregation watched the four men leave. Every eye in the church watched them slip out the panelled door, quietly closing its polished-brass latch, and everyone in the pews knew about the big fish.

Some of the men soon followed, nodding shamedfacedly toward the pulpit and their wives, and soon only the pious women and children were left. Finally the minister himself succumbed, giving a hasty benediction as he moved down the aisle, and the remaining congregation followed. It gathered by the river to watch, as Lige rowed Senator Webster and Mayor Hone into position above the millrace where the fish was lying.

Webster caught a small brookie, and the millpond congregation groaned, thinking the big trout had been frightened. Thirty minutes passed and most of the congregation began walking home, when Webster made a long cast toward the grist mill and the fish was hooked. Like all brook trout, this fish fought stubbornly under the trailing weeds and along the masonry foundations of the mill, and finally Webster forced it into the open, gravel-bottomed channel in the elodea and pickerel-weed. The struggle lasted almost as long as the church service and sermon, with cheers and groans from the congregation, and finally the huge trout came grudgingly toward the skiff.

It was almost black from living in the dark masonwork shadows under the mill wheel, its mottled gill covers and white-edged orange fins moving weakly. The faithful Lige reached expertly with the long-handled boat net. His words when he slipped the trout into its meshes are included on the Currier & Ives print that recorded the event, and were later placed in the Congressional Record.

We hab you now, sar! Lige laughed.

The congregation stood cheering along the millpond, and Parson King threw his prayer book into the air. Sam Carman and Lige wrestled the fish ashore, and carried it to the general store. Legend holds that the fish weighed as much as the current world record of fourteen pounds eight ounces, but it seems unlikely at best. Carman and Hone traced its outline on linen, and their tracing was later transferred to a cherrywood plank. The carpenter made another wooden facsimile of the fish, enlarging it a third to give it a proportion equal to its lofty place on the weathervane of the church steeple. Reducing its size one-third would make the trophy about twenty-five inches, and its weight even for a thick-bodied brook trout was perhaps only nine or ten pounds—but the Webster fish probably did stand as the record until the Nipigon fish was caught in 1916.

The fish was authenticated by the euphoric Parson King and his congregation, and its capture was entered in the records of the church. The catch was also witnessed by Philip Hone and Martin Van Buren, and they immediately set out with Webster for Manhattan with the trout. The trophy was served at Delmonico's the following night in a rich sauce of sour cream and sliced almonds and white wine.

The little river is still named for Carman, although his Fireplace Tavern and house were razed forty-odd years ago. The millpond pool still yielded trout less than twenty years ago, when both the gristmill and its dam were demolished for a parkway crossing. It is doubtful that even the legal skills of Daniel Webster could have changed the mindless alignment of its right-of-way, although he did successfully protect the fishing from an ill-designed railroad bridge in 1845.

The weathered Presbyterian church was moved two miles from the original site beside the river a few years ago, but both its cherrywood weathervane and the pew reserved for the Suffolk Club survive. It is possible to sit in its time-polished seats and wonder about the morning that Daniel Webster sat there, wrestling with the interminable sermon, his wavering conscience and the temptation of the giant trout. It was unquestionably one time that Webster lost to Mephistopheles, and the legend intertwines the brook trout with the folklore of both fishing and politics in America.

It is typical of the species. The literature concerning the brook trout continued to expand in the half century after Daniel Webster. Charles Farrar published his *Guide Book to the Androscoggin Lakes* in 1888, with its remarkable descriptions of brook-trout fishing in that region of Maine. Henry David Thoreau is obviously worth reading whether one searches his prose for fishing stories or not, and his charming *Week on the Concord and Merrimack* appeared in 1889, but brook-trout pilgrims always happily discover his brief passages on fishing the Katahdin trout in Maine:

> While yet alive, before their tints had faded, they glistened like the fairest flowers, the product of primitive rivers; and he could hardly trust his senses, as he stood over them, that these jewels should have swam away in that Aboljacnagesic water for so long, so many Dark Ages—these bright fluviatile flowers, seen of aborigines only, made beautiful, the Lord only knows why to swim there!
>
> I could understand better for this, the truth of mythology, the fables of Proteus, and all those beautiful sea-monsters—how all history, indeed, put to a terrestrial use, is mere history; but put to celestial use, is always Mythology.

Thoreau was fascinated with the jewellike beauty of the brook trout, like many others who followed in his thoughtful footsteps. Charles Bradford sought their beauty in the gentle Pocono Mountains of Pennsylvania, and his recently reprinted *The Brook Trout and the Determined Angler* is the record of those pilgrimages. It appeared originally in 1900, just two years before the celebrated Louis Rhead published *The Speckled Brook Trout*, which has become a collector's classic. Dillon Wallace followed with *Lure of the Labrador Wild* in 1905, and K. B. Alexander added to our knowledge of the brook trout and its range in *The Log of the North Shore Club*, which recorded the sport on a hundred swift rivers draining into Lake Superior. Alexander published his logs in 1911, and three years later, W. C. Kendall published the first volume of his monumental *Fishes of the Northeast*, which included extensive information on the brook trout and its related char species. Doctor John Quackenbos was the author of the first limited edition published by the prestigious Anglers' Club of New York, and his slender *Geological Ancestors of the Brook Trout* remains a rare and fascinating volume in the collections of only three hundred bibliophiles. It appeared in 1916, the same year that William Cook took his world-record brook trout on the Nipigon in Ontario, and a year later, E. E. Millard wrote his charming *Days on the Nepigon.*

The celebrated Edward Ringwood Hewitt visited the Nipigon twice in the late nineteenth century, and in his classic *Telling on the Trout* he devoted a chapter to its character and sport. His notebooks reveal that the Nipigon brook trout then averaged almost four pounds, and Hewitt took sixty-three over six pounds, along with twenty-four that scaled better than seven. Hewitt took one brute on a fly-and-spinner rig that measured twenty-six inches in length, and twenty inches in girth. Using the standard formula for estimating the weight of a trout or salmon from its girth and length, his best brook trout on the Nipigon scaled about thirteen pounds. Such huge trout were apparently common on the Nipigon before 1900, when they used both the Nipigon Lake and Lake Superior to fatten like salmon on the smelt and alewives and ciscoes and entered the river to spawn in the fall. The mill dam that was built later undoubtedly ended the free movement of the fish between the lakes, and the brook-trout fishing soon declined. Before it was spoiled, the Nipigon was unquestionably the finest brook-trout fishery in the world, but let Hewitt describe it in these words from *Telling on the Trout* in 1926:

> At the Hudson Bay station at the head of Lake Nepigon, Mr. Anderson, the Company Factor, told us that they took a large number of big trout in nets near the spawning beds every autumn, which were used as their winter supply of fish, and were shipped by sleds to the other Hudson Bay stations within reach. They packed them in ice and kept them the year round.
>
> I asked him what size the fish averaged. He replied he did not know exactly, but could get some. We went out to the

ice-house, dug out four or five fish, and brought them into the store and weighed them on the store scales.

They were cleaned with the heads left in place. They weighed from ten to twelve pounds apiece after being on the ice eleven months. He said the whole catch of many tons ran about this size. There were still about a thousand pounds of these fish in the ice-house.

Many of these fish were undoubtedly larger than the certified world-record brook trout, and Hewitt relates a Nipigon tale of a nineteen-pound fish caught by an early survey party. There are also uncertified brook trout bigger than fifteen pounds caught regularly from the *bocas* of bone-chilling Argentine rivers like the Corcovado and Totoral and Pichi Traful. It is likely that any new record will come from either the Assinica country of Quebec, with its unique subspecies of long-lived brook trout, or from these remote river inlets deep in the Patagonian lakes.

Fisheries biologists have classified the brook trout *Salvelinus fontinalis,* its taxonomic name meaning a little salmon of the cold springs. Technically speaking, these fish are actually a species of char rather than a true member of the trout family. Char can be recognized by their coloring in most cases, but anatomical evidence in the roof of the mouth is unequivocal evidence. The boat-shaped structure of the tooth-bearing vomerine bone is the primary bench mark. Char have teeth on only the head of this vomerine bone, while its inner surfaces are smooth and toothless. The lake trout is an exception among the char family; it has a clearly raised vomerine ridge covered with strong teeth. Trout classified in the *Salmo* genus have one or more rows of teeth on the flat vomerine shaft, and these clearly distinguish the brook trout from the true trout family.

Salvelinus fontinalis is a species of beauty and grace, perhaps equalled only in its spawning colors by the spectacular golden trout of the high country in California. Its dorsal surfaces are bluish gray to olive with strong vermiculated patterns. Its sides are a little paler, and covered with spots like yellowish opals and rubies in delicate bluish aureoles of color. Baby brook trout have eight to ten parr markings. During most of the season their whitish bellies are faintly tinged with ochre in the females and a pale yellowish orange in the males. Spawning colors vary considerably, with lower flanks of bright yellowish orange in the henfish, and a gaudy reddish orange in the mature hookbills. The dorsal fins are heavily spotted and vermiculated, like the adjacent dorsal surfaces. Caudal surfaces are often reddish with darker vermiculations, and the dorsal edges resemble the strongly mottled back markings. The ventral edges of the caudal fin are chalky white in mature specimens, with a blackish coloring on the inner ventral rays of the tail. The pectoral, ventral, and anal fins are perhaps the most easily distinguished brook-trout coloring. These spectacular lower fins are yellowish orange to scarlet, depending upon the cycle of the season, with black and chalk-colored lower edges. Such coloring varies widely in

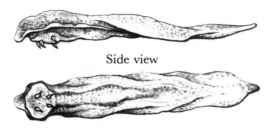

Side view

Bottom view

Brook Trout Vomerine Bone

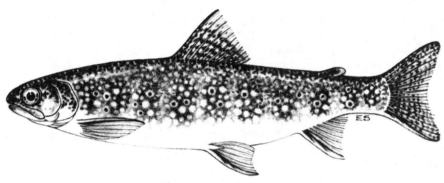

Brook Trout Parr *(Salvelinus fontinalis)*

different habitats, along with average size and configuration. Fish from alkaline waters with pale bottom gravel are often less brightly colored than specimens from tea-colored acid streams, or spring-fed ponds with bottoms of blackish muck. Such acid-water fish are often highly colored trout.

The typical configuration of the brook trout is more heavily set than its sister species. The body of a fully matured fish is only about five times its depth, although small specimens under a pound more nearly resemble other trout forms. The caudal fins of brook trout are only slightly forked, especially in larger fish, and this configuration has given them the colloquial name of squaretails. The fish are also known as native or speckled trout in some regions. Like the other trout, its fins are soft-rayed in structure. The dorsal fins have 10 rays, while there are 9 rays in their anal fins. The char family is rather delicately scaled when compared with the true trout species. They usually display between 150 to 200 diagonal rows of scales at the lateral line, and a diagonal scale count of 15 to 20 between the lateral line and the adipose fin. There are 50 to 75 pyloric caeca attached to the alimentary tract.

Brook trout are typically autumn spawners. Populations in the Northern Hemisphere spawn from late September until early December, depending upon latitude. Argentine populations are found spawning in May and June. Since brook trout are often sexually mature at relatively small size, fecundity can vary quite widely. Six-inch females may oviposit only one hundred eggs, while a pound fish may lay as many as 1,200. More mature henfish of the Assinica or Broadback strains in Quebec are nearly as fecund as rainbows or browns, with a six-pound female typically carrying as many as 6,000 eggs. Incubation varies with latitude and water temperature, and research indicates that eighty-five days are required to hatch brook-trout eggs at forty degrees. Two hundred and ten days are required at thirty-three degrees.

Like other species of the Salmonidae, the brook trout constructs a spawning redd in suitable gravel and small stones. Its spawning beds are somewhat smaller in area and greater in depth than those of the other species. Such nesting characteristics perhaps result from the hydrodynamics of a thick-set brook trout working its body to shape its redds. Its habitat requirements for streams are quite rigid, and it seeks out the extremely cold currents of the smallest tributaries. Brook trout also spawn successfully in lakes with good inlet or outlet flowages, and in some shallow areas with sufficient wave action to oxygenate the fertile ova.

Brook trout are sufficiently fertile, and become sexually mature at such relatively small size, that they thrive too well in remote waters. Overpopulation with six- to eight-inch fish is common in such places. Canada and New England are filled with such ecosystemic problems, and introduced populations of brook trout in the high lakes and beaver-pond habitats of our western mountains are often in similar trouble. It is difficult to overfish such waters. There are high lakes in Oregon where a daily limit of thirty fish has been allowed for fifteen years. This is done in the hope of reducing the overpopulation without demonstrable change in the numbers of dwarf brookies, which seldom reach ten inches in length.

Like those few storied rivers that have always produced large Atlantic salmon of high average weight, rivers like the Restigouche and Cascapedia and Moisie in Canada, and the Alta and Vossa and Årøy in Norway, the rivers that regularly produce big brook trout have apparently evolved and sustained such populations for millenniums. Brook trout are far less adaptable than either the rainbow or the ubiquitous European brown. Good brookie water has rather narrowly defined limits of chemistry and physical character. Its food chain and associated species and physiography must meet certain ecological criteria—and because the brook trout is gullible it must also be remote.

There are few waters in the United States that still meet these demanding standards. Maine has some relatively inaccessible brook-trout fishing on rivers like the Upper Kennebec, Moose, Kennebago, and the famous Allagash along its northern borders. Seventy-five years ago there were many squaretails from Maine lakes like Rangeley and Mooselookmeguntic and Moosehead, fish of nine to ten pounds that often approached world-record class. But such waters are too accessible for these trophies now. Three-pound brook trout are unusual, and a five-pounder is relatively rare. Elsewhere in its American range, from Minnesota to Georgia and South

Carolina, the brookie has been driven higher and higher into the eastern mountains, and ever deeper into the cedar swamps and cold little tributaries and springholes. A two-pound speckled trout in the upper Middle West would be a rare trophy these days, except for the coasters that school and cruise the river inlets of Lake Superior. The species has retreated high into the plunging tributaries of the eastern mountains, cold little headwater streams deep in the thickets of rhododendron and hemlock. But in these waters, a twelve-inch brook trout is rare, and most of the fish are only seven or eight inches, brightly jeweled little ornaments of the Appalachian headwaters.

There are a few first-rate fisheries holding good stocks of *Salvelinus fontinalis* in our western mountains, in the headwaters of Montana rivers like the Beaverhead and the Big Hole. The late and cantankerous Bob Carmichael, who reigned for years as the fishing sage of Jackson Hole from his fly shop at Moose Crossing, always knew a few spring-fed bogans and beaver ponds that held six- to eight-pound brook trout. Big brookies are regularly caught at Henry's Lake in Idaho too, by working a weighted shrimp imitation deep over the bottom moss in its spring-fed tributary channels. Colorado, Wyoming, Idaho, and Montana all produce the occasional six- to eight-pound brook trout, but for every fish of this size taken in the Rocky Mountains, perhaps a hundred are caught in the drainage systems of Manitoba and Quebec.

Many factors limit the widespread success of brook-trout populations around the world. *Salvelinus fontinalis* is absolutely true to its taxonomic description and demands icy-cold rivers and lakes with sufficient depth or springholes to provide a respite from drought and hot weather. Its temperature ceiling is seventy-five degrees maximum, considerably less than its species of sister trout and salmon. However, brook trout never quite achieve abundance in a habitat that fails to provide some year-round refuge where water temperatures do not exceed sixty-five degrees. Cold tributary brooks and the bone-chilling seepages of springholes usually provide such temperatures in most optimal habitats, and lakes lacking pronounced cold-water inlets or seepages can sometimes have sufficient depth to produce an optimal layer of forty-five to sixty-five degree temperatures above the thermocline.

Brook trout are gullible and sometimes easy to catch, and I have had them milling greedily in frantic clouds around my bucktails in remote rivers of the Labrador. Such gullibility and naïveté have unquestionably played a role in their decline in the past seventy-five years, although rapacious lumbering, mindless land development, agricultural and grazing clearage, fertilizers and pesticides, endless road building, septic tanks and poorly treated sewage, and industrial wastes have all played important roles in the fate of *Salvelinus fontinalis*.

The decline in sport about the time of the Civil War led pioneer fisheries biologists like Seth Green and Fred Mather to construct hatcheries for the artificial propagation of brook-trout populations. Seth Green

FRED MATHER

experimented with an artificial strain of book trout that matured quite early, becoming sexually fecund at eight to ten inches. Green and his colleagues mistakenly believed that such early spawning might help repopulate our declining brook-trout fisheries, and all of the hatchery strains we have stocked over the century since their Caledonia hatchery opened have carried this artificially created genetic flaw. Their small fish bred small fish. Their work has spread a short-lived strain of brook trout that has weakened the genetic stocks of the fish in our once-famous fisheries from Minnesota to Maine and North Carolina.

Dwight Webster and colleagues in pisciculture like William Flick have been experimenting in recent years with wild brook-trout strains from Quebec in an attempt to correct this mistake of the fisheries biologists in the nineteenth century. Existing brook-trout strains have about a four-year life span. Disease, predators, lack of adequate food supplies, and the winterkill factors associated with their northern latitudes all contribute to rather high brook-trout mortality within this relatively short four-year span. Our coddled hatchery strains have so weakened our domestic stocks that for every 10,000 eggs that hatch, approximately five hundred fish survive a year. Three hundred of these fish will last another twelve months, and about half of these fingerlings will live three seasons. Only twenty-five hardy specimens will attain the average life span of four years, and less than five will live a year longer—only a solitary brook trout of the original 10,000 will live six years. It is this relatively high factor of mortality that has allowed the brook-trout record of fourteen pounds eight ounces to last so many years, and bigger fish must come from the few undiluted strains that survive. Dwight Webster has been experimenting with the remarkable Assinica strain of wild fish from Quebec, and his Cornell studies indicate that its specimens have an atypical life span of approximately ten years. Brook trout of the genetically isolated Assinica type seem to offer great promise for upgrading the declining stocks that have been available to fisheries biologists in recent years.

Roderick Haig-Brown tells us, in his classic *Fisherman's Winter*, that the many three- to four-pound brook trout he caught at Meliquina in the Argentine were only three years old. His observations parallel the fish-scale studies I have made these past several years at Pireco, Totoral, Auquinco, Gutierrez, and Pichi Traful in the same Argentine watersheds. Laddie Buchanan has become interested in bringing some brook trout of the Assinica strain to his Patagonian rivers, and we are attempting to get a stock of eyed ova to the federal hatchery at San Carlos de Bariloche. These Argentine lakes are already producing eight- and nine-pound brook trout in a biological strain with an average life span of only four years—the men who have come to love the cold little rivers that drain the Argentine threshold of Chile can hardly wait to discover how large such Assinica fish might grow after ten years in these rich volcanic habitats.

Dwight Webster has discovered other intriguing data in his work with the Assinica strain. These wild fish were stocked in a controlled environment with a hatchery strain that had almost a century of domestication in its history. The two stocks were raised in adjacent troughs for twelve months. The domestic strain had reached slightly more than five inches, while the wild fish were an inch and a half smaller and the wild fish were more active and clearly exhibited more stamina. The domestic fish were obviously attracted to the biologists, displaying no fear and expecting food, while the wild fish continued to flee and seek concealment under the protective screens. Both strains were subsequently planted in a small test stream in the Finger Lakes country of New York.

About two months later, eighty percent of the larger hatchery fish were dead, but only sixty-seven percent of the wild fish had perished. The domestic strain had grown only one-third of an inch in the wild state, but the Assinica trout had grown almost a half inch. Similar growth and survival rates prevailed in the following months, clearly demonstrating that trout eggs stripped from Assinica wild fish are superior to hatchery brood stock. There is virtually no comparison between the fecundity and survival rate for the offspring of such wild fish compared to those few domestic trout that survive until spawning time. Male brook trout are the first to arrive in the spawning areas, migrating upstream in late summer. The females arrive later and immediately begin constructing their redds in the gravel. Brook trout select pea gravel in bottom areas of both riffles and pools that have upwelling flow through the river bed. Optimal spawning flow is about five to ten inches per second. Such conditions assure the fertile ova a rich supply of well-oxygenated water at relatively stable temperatures.

Nest building is facilitated by the flowing current, which buoys up the gravel and fine stones displaced by the ripe females. The females construct the nest, usually without much help from the males. The typical redd is approximately forty to fifty square inches. It is roughly circular and from two to eight inches deep. The females build their redds with vigorous rolling motions of head and tail, displacing coarse bottom materials with the hydrodynamic forces of the current, distributing the aggregates alongside and downstream from the depression shaped to receive the eggs.

During construction of the nest, the male brook trout prowls the adjacent shallows, driving off both potential suitors and predators. The quarrels can become spirited and aggressive. The male brook trout look almost like dark little sockeye salmon, with their flanks fiercely reddish orange at spawning time. The spawning redds are typically surrounded with smaller brook-trout males seeking stray eggs to eat, and in the case of some dwarf cockfish, a hope of actual participation in the spawning. Between such quarrels with intruders, the male brook trout attempts to excite the female with his body and his hook-jawed kype. Some males slide into the nest alongside the females and vibrate their bodies quite rapidly, and as the spawning act advances, the males may force the females on their sides deep into the bottom of the redd. The actual egg-laying soon follows, but it is usually lost in the clouds of milky sperm and displaced silt that comes with oviposition and the considerable postcoital shuddering. The female immediately slides above the nest and starts covering its eggs. The specific gravity of the ova is slightly heavier than water, making them sink deep into the gravelly bed, and their gelatinous covering adheres to the stones. The sticky covering quickly hardens in the icy currents, holding the ova firmly in place until they are covered with bottom aggregates.

The fertile eggs are covered by the building of a second redd immediately upstream from the last. The pebbles, gravel, and small stones displaced during this second nest building soon carry across the eggs and cover them. The freshly built mound covering the eggs fills the nest as high as the undisturbed bottom or slightly higher. The time required to construct the nest and fill it with eggs varies from a few hours to half a day, and once spawning has begun, it commonly proceeds both day and night. Males do not assist in covering the freshly deposited ova, but station themselves nearby and engage predators attempting to gobble the fertilized eggs.

The late Paul Needham conducted a number of stomach autopsies on specimens of *Salvelinus fontinalis* over the years, and his data revealed a number of significant facts about their feeding behavior. The research showed that his specimens had ingested a diet of almost thirty-four percent terrestrial insects. The remainder of their diet consisted of aquatic insects, crustaceans, and other common waterbred forms.

Two-winged Diptera forms were slightly more than twenty-two percent of the terrestrial foods consumed. These were various midges, two-winged flies, bluebottles, craneflies, and other staple insects readily available to the fish throughout the season. Other important terrestrial foods taken included leafhoppers, which formed almost nineteen percent of the diet, and a little more than fifteen percent were beetles. Ants, bees, and wasps were about nine percent, grasshoppers comprised approximately six percent, and four percent were common earthworms. Such land organisms were primarily forms which inadvertently fell into the water. Many such terrestrial insects will float readily in moderate currents and are taken as surface foods. Others sink and are swept downstream to be taken underwater by the trout. The data clearly show that such drowned foods may be both terrestrial or aquatic forms.

Aquatic foods comprised slightly more than sixty-six percent of the diet in the two hundred fifty brook trout that Needham autopsied. Caddis larvae and pupae were more than forty-three percent of the total aquatic insect diet. More than seventy-five percent of the stomach samples contained these Trichoptera in immature stages. Mayfly nymphs were almost twenty percent of the total aquatic food, and two-winged larval and pupal forms were the third most important diet type, totalling slightly less than seventeen percent. Miscellaneous ecotypes like snails, subaquatic beetles, water boatmen and backswimmers, stonefly nymphs, dragon and damselfly nymphs, and small crustaceans formed the remainder of the brook-trout diet.

Needham also made comparative studies of the importance of adult fly hatches with the percentage of nymphal and larval forms in the diet of brook trout. His data is strikingly important in understanding the feeding behavior of *Salvelinus fontinalis*, as well as the fishing tactics designed to suggest that diet. Needham found that only fifty-seven adult caddis were found in his specimen stomach counts, while almost 1,200 larval and pupal Trichoptera had been ingested by the same fish. Similar differences were found between the immature and adult stages of other aquatic insects in the typical brook-trout diet, which tends to suggest that the species is highly oriented toward subsurface foods. Perhaps ninety percent of the brook-trout diet is taken below the surface, even in the summer months when winged insects are readily available.

Paul Needham assembled the following table from his two hundred fifty test specimens. The fish studied ranged from three to nine inches, and were collected over a twelve-month period which started early in 1929. The field-study figures unquestionably demonstrate that these brook trout preferred caddisflies, two-winged flies, and mayflies in that order of importance. Stoneflies and crustaceans each accounted for less than two percent, although their importance would have undoubtedly increased in environments having large populations of such diet forms. Only nineteen fish had taken salamanders or baitfish, and most of the small minnows were tiny brook sculpins. Eleven percent of the stomach specimens contained crayfish. It should be remembered that these figures give considerable insight into the organisms that are staples of the small-trout diet, and fish of larger average size would undoubtedly have taken a greater percentage of foods like the crayfish, sculpins, and other baitfish species.

The stomach-contents data compiled by Paul Needham in his classic book *Trout Streams* are as follows, and no serious angler can ignore the implications of its high percentage of caddisflies:

TYPE	TOTALS	PERCENT
Caddisflies	1,223	30.0
Two-winged flies	755	18.5
Mayflies	716	17.6
Beetles	268	6.6
Springtails	264	6.5
Leafhoppers	260	6.4
Ants, bees, and wasps	123	3.0
Crustaceans	69	1.7
Grasshoppers	66	1.6
Stoneflies	61	1.5
True bugs	48	1.2
Earthworms	47	1.1
Snails and slugs	35	.8
Salamanders and baitfish	21	.5
Miscellaneous	122	3.0
Totals	4,078	100.0

During the years of research for my book *Matching the Hatch*, more than two hundred stomach samples were checked. This work was conducted eighteen to twenty years later than the Needham studies tabulated above, and its sample brook trout averaged about ten inches. The studies were made in several parts of the country, including the Adirondacks and the Rocky Mountains, so exact comparisons with the Needham data are impossible. However, the data offer some intriguing insights for fly-fishermen:

TYPE	TOTALS	PERCENT
Caddisflies	2,173	29.1
Two-winged flies	1,207	16.2
Mayflies	961	12.9
Beetles	613	8.2
Stoneflies	611	8.2
Leafhoppers	423	5.7
Ants, bees, and wasps	397	5.3
Salamanders and baitfish	296	3.9
Crustaceans	290	3.9

TYPE	TOTALS	PERCENT
Grasshoppers	103	1.4
Earthworms	61	.8
True bugs	49	.7
Springtails	47	.6
Snails and slugs	41	.6
Miscellaneous	184	2.5
Totals	7,456	100.0

These figures certainly reflect the feeding behavior of a larger average test specimen, both in terms of the quantity of food ingested per fish, and in the increased percentages of diet forms like sculpins and sticklebacks and dace. Since *Matching the Hatch* was published in 1955, much of my brook-trout fishing has occurred on the limestone spring creeks of our eastern states. The special character of those habitats is unquestionably reflected in the following table:

TYPE	TOTALS	PERCENT
Caddisflies	2,321	23.4
Two-winged flies	1,413	14.1
Mayflies	987	9.9
Beetles	913	9.2
Crustaceans	907	9.1
Leafhoppers	879	8.9
Ants, bees, and wasps	726	7.3
Grasshoppers	702	7.1
Stoneflies	415	4.2
Salamanders and baitfish	279	2.8
Earthworms	87	.9
True bugs	43	.4
Springtails	41	.4
Snails and slugs	39	.4
Miscellaneous	187	1.9
Totals	9,939	100.0

The slight increase in total foods ingested across these experimental seasons is perhaps the result of the relatively even water temperatures in the limestone spring creeks. Such temperatures would generate a fairly steady level of feeding throughout the year, in both winter and summer, when thermal extremes tend to depress feeding and digestion in more typical habitats. Therefore, stomach counts in the hot-weather months on streams like Big Spring and Falling Spring Run and the Letort would be somewhat higher than the volumes of food ingested on warmer freestone waters, with their sunfishlike temperatures in the late weeks of July and August.

The somewhat higher percentages of beetles, crustaceans, leafhoppers, ants, and grasshoppers also reflect the character of the eastern limestone streams, with their pastoral farm-country meadows. Beetle percentages echo the transitory importance of the Japanese beetles on streams like Letort Spring Run. Since the beetle population has been checked and virtually eradicated, any new investigation of stomach contents would undoubtedly reflect a parallel reduction in the number of Coleoptera taken by the fish across the summer. The crustaceans are also extremely abundant in the elodea and watercress of the limestone streams, and these populations of scuds and sowbugs are reflected in the data above. Disproportionately high numbers of leafhoppers, ants, and grasshoppers also parallel the populations of such insects in the water meadows that border little limestone creeks like the Letort Spring Run. These figures should not be compared uncritically with either the Needham data or the research compiled for *Matching the Hatch*, since they were not collected in the same test-base environments. However, they afford us pertinent information for both understanding and fishing the brook trout.

The distinguished ichthyologist Albert Hazzard conducted some comparative studies several years ago on the behavior of brook trout under fishing pressure at the Pigeon River Research Station in Michigan. The test water was a controlled mile of state-owned water, between weirs that enclosed the experimental-fish population. Hazzard confirms the gullibility of *Salvelinus fontinalis* in his Pigeon River studies, and the naïveté of these Pigeon River brookies is typical.

His data demonstrate that forty percent of the brook trout stocked in the Pigeon Research Station were caught within forty-eight hours. Subsequent electrical-shock studies revealed that only five percent of these planted brookies remained at the close of the fishing season. Fifty-five percent of the hatchery-propagated specimens were no longer found in the test mile between the weirs. They had apparently succumbed to their genetic foolishness and frailty, their inability to adjust to natural diet patterns, and their vulnerability to natural predators and fishing pressure. These results would indicate that brook trout are a poor long-term investment for stocking, except in the few superb brook-trout waters that still exist. Paradoxically, the lack of sophistication typical of *Salvelinus fontinalis* might prove an asset in our time of put-and-take pressure. Perhaps it is the species that should be planted in concentrated numbers for the opening-day crowds, since its gullibility means a comparatively high ratio of fish-per-hour recovery after stocking. Fifty to sixty percent of the brook trout stocked in our marginal eastern waters are recovered within a few days, before such streams become too warm in late spring, making them a far better short-term investment than other hatchery-bred species.

Like the acrobatic rainbow, however, the full character of the brook trout cannot be explained in mere terms of its biology, the components of its diet, and statistics of its behavior under fishing pressure. Brook trout are rare and elusive enough so that their true nature lies outside the world of measurable facts, just as the full worth of jewels cannot be accurately described in terms of their size or price alone.

There are many memories of *Salvelinus fontinalis* over the years, including my first trout on the small meadow creek in Michigan. My first big brook trout was a fat twenty-inch male from a Colorado beaver pond, taken more than twenty-five years ago in the Frying Pan country, and there have been others that size in later seasons from Maine to the Labrador. There were many five-pound squaretails in the Minipi country, and several big brook trout on the sprawling George fifty miles below Indian House Lake. Prospecting for salmon with a floatplane along Ungava Bay once produced an unexpected prize when an eight-pound brook trout fresh from salt water took my streamer on the River of the Martens. Perhaps some future journey into the Gods River country of Manitoba, or the famous Broadback and Assinica watersheds in Quebec, will bring more personal memories of *Salvelinus fontinalis* in the best of his native waters.

There are also brook-trout memories of the Argentine rain-forest rivers. My first Argentine brook trout was caught at the Boca Auquinco more than a dozen years ago, and it weighed about six pounds. Some years later during a purple twilight at the Boca Totoral, I took six brook trout between five and nine pounds, and this past season a brace of fat five-pounders were netted just at nightfall on the Pichi Traful. There is still time to daydream about trophy brook trout in the remote mountains below the Andean frontier outpost at Esquel, and some autumn morning in April, we may still make a *campamento* for fishing the Pico and the Corcovado, hoping for that fifteen-pound world record.

Such fish are not impossible in those waters, and my daydreams always return to a still morning in the bone-chilling shallows of the little Boca Auquinco. My deep-nymph retrieve stopped in the shelving depths where the current eddied into the lake. It was a slow-pulling weight that meant a big brook trout, holding sullenly beyond the shelf. Fifteen minutes of head shaking and threshing deep along the dropoff followed, and finally it grudgingly surrendered line and slipped into the gravel shallows.

It looked like a four-pound brookie—smaller than average for the Auquinco—and I started to force it unceremoniously toward the beach. Suddenly a huge submarine-dark fish followed the struggling trout into the shallows, circling curiously with a bow-wave ahead of its powerful body. Its mottled back and gaudy scarlet belly and white-edged orange fins clearly identified its species against the pale bottom. It passed ten feet out, its dorsal fin cutting the surface like a shark, and I stared in awe.

My God! I thought wildly, *It's an absolute monster—that fish is better than thirty inches!* Since the world-record fish from the Nipigon was about that size, memories of that giant Auquinco brookie always give me shivers.

There are still such trophies in the depths of several Argentine lakes, but the secret of brook-trout fishing lies outside the world of wilderness lakes and rivers, outside considerations of mere trophies and records. Thirty-inch brook trout are so rare that I would probably release such a prize if it actually took my fly and were finally caught. *Salvelinus fontinalis* are like priceless little pearls. Their worth is not measured in terms of size and strength, and in the world of fly-fishing, brook trout are like chamber music in an age filled with a deafening cacophony of amplified sound. Their worth has little muscle in a world preoccupied with pike and cartwheeling tarpon and muskellunge. But such comparisons are foolish, just as the blare of symphonic trumpets cannot be compared with the delicate *pianissimo* melodies of a flute. Brook trout are the minor trophies of our rivers, and their character has a lyric quality. Its melodies are still found among the hemlocks and cedar thickets and rhododendron-sheltered brooks from Minnesota to Georgia, and in the cold lakes and spring-fed ponds and bogans of Maine.

Such happy poetry filled those boyhood mornings on the swift-flowing Pine in Michigan, when deer browsed warily in the overgrown orchards, and dew glittered on the cobwebs in the grass. Birches were chalk-colored against the tamaracks across the quiet pools. The river music was pastoral, its riffle currents tumbling through our legs as we fished the tangled deadfalls. Kingfishers and ospreys worked the shallows downstream, and in a quiet bend I startled a heron into the rising mist. Later that morning, with the sun penetrating deep into the current beside a pulsing logjam, I hooked a bright-spotted fish of fifteen inches.

It's a beauty! I exclaimed.

The old classics professor tilted his bifocals awkwardly, and studied its brightly jeweled sides deep in the shining meshes of the net. *It's a beautiful fish*, the old man nodded happily. *It's the Aphrodite of the Hemlocks!*

3. The Trout on the Flying Trapeze

The pastoral philosophy and tradition of trout fishing has its roots in Walton and his *Compleat Angler*, and in the poetic descriptions of fly-fishing on the Dove that Charles Cotton added to Walton's masterpiece in 1676. Their sport was fishing for brown trout and grayling in rich water meadows filled with the ruins of fourteenth-century abbeys, and Walton lived out his final seasons on the Test and the Itchen, its currents reflecting the Romanesque cathedral at Winchester.

Our eastern brook trout lie in this tradition. Brook trout are beautiful fish in the cold tea-colored springholes of our north country, and the brown trout is the same sophisticated fish of fly-rich rivers from the Yellowstone to the watercress rivers of Yugoslavia. Rainbows are a different breed, and wherever they have been introduced, there is something primordial about rainbows.

Anglers have journeyed the world in search of rainbows, and fly-fishermen who found themselves emigrating to remote parts of the earth—the alpine threshold of Kashmir and Zululand and Tasmania—have transported the hardy, cartwheeling rainbow to exotic mountain rivers that had everything but trout. The rainbow has been transplanted to virtually every suitable habitat around the world, and no one is neutral about the species and its sporting qualities. Rainbows are favorites from Alaska to the swift rivers of Tierra del Fuego, and from New Zealand to the beehive villages of Zululand. The species thrives everywhere there are cold, tumbling rivers equal to its character.

Twenty years ago in his classic *Fisherman's Spring*, Roderick Haig-Brown spent a full chapter exploring that character and its full spectrum of moods. Haig-Brown acknowledged in his essay that famous subspecies like the Kern and McCloud and Kamloops strains are actually local variations of the rainbow trout. Ichthyologists once separated seagoing rainbows into the classification *Salmo gairdneri*, and their smaller stay-at-home cousins were placed in a fully separate species called *Salmo irideus*. Such taxonomic distinctions are no longer accepted among modern fisheries experts and rainbows are all classified *Salmo gairdneri* in contemporary taxonomy. Haig-Brown sifted through this genetic puzzle of rainbow subspecies, and finally concluded that the special qualities of the rainbow trout cannot be explained in mere biological terms. Their rough-and-tumble character is unique.

Roderick Haig-Brown is the fly-fishing poet of British Columbia, and has fished and savored its rivers for fifty-odd years. Fishermen around the world know his books. Through words as brilliant as the rivers he has fished, readers who will never travel to British Columbia have known his home water on the Campbell, wading the swift Cowichan during the autumn runs and working the bone-chilling Nimpkish in winter.

The conclusion about rainbows reached in *Fisherman's Spring* is typical of Haig-Brown. *When to call a fish a rainbow?* Haig-Brown writes admiringly. *When he seems like a rainbow!*

RODERICK HAIG-BROWN

Rainbows are so easily raised in hatcheries, and their biology and behavior are so pliable, that they are great favorites with most fish culturists and hatchery men. Fertile rainbow ova are transported readily, and this hardiness has helped in transplanting the species everywhere. It has thrived, in almost all cases, even in the snow-fed equatorial rivers of places as surprising as northern Panama, Colombia, Costa Rica and Ceylon. There is excellent rainbow fishing on many adopted rivers in North America, Europe, Asia, South America, Australia, Africa, and the fertile waters of the Antipodes.

The footloose species was originally found only in Pacific-flowing watersheds from the Kuskokwim country of Alaska to coastal Mexican rivers on the Tropic of Cancer. Contrary to popular fly-fishing mythology, rainbows are not indigenous to the rivers of eastern Siberia and Japan. There are closely related species like *Salmo peshinensis*, the small, relatively scarce ecotype found in rivers entering the Sea of Okhotsk; and the more widely distributed relative *Salmo mykiss,* which is recorded from the Amur in Manchuria to the Kalakhtyka on the Bering Sea. British Columbia and Alaska still have some of the finest rainbow fisheries, but their sport is rivalled now by the fly-fishing found in some of its adopted countries.

There is superb rainbow fishing in the icemelt headwaters of the Jhelum, which drains the Hindu Kush and the mountains of Kashmir. Argentine rivers like the Limay and Collón Curá and Chimehuin are justly famous, along with swift Chilean rivers like the Trancura and Calcurrupe, and there are near-legendary rivers like the Tongariro and Waitahauii in New Zealand.

Hemingway wrote about still another adopted rainbow river where the species has been introduced and thrived. Finally home from his journalism in Paris, and his harsh baptism of artillery fire along the Piave fifty miles above Venice, the budding writer filed a story called "The Best Rainbow Trout Fishing in the World" for *The Toronto Star* in the late summer of 1920. Ray Bergman also described fly-fishing in the same Soo Rapids between Lake Superior and Lake Huron in his *Trout.* Their unbridled enthusiasm for this fishing undoubtedly came from their lack of knowledge about the rainbow fisheries of British Columbia and Alaska. Both men probably knew little about the rapid growth of rainbows in South America and the Antipodes, but Hemingway did understand the character of the species.

Rainbow-trout fishing is as different from brook-trout fishing, Hemingway wrote with laconic perception, *as prize fighting is from boxing.*

Fish culture had begun with Seth Green and Fred Mather in 1864, and in only ten years these men had worked out primitive techniques of shipping fertile trout eggs in moss-lined trays. The travels of the highly prized California trout began with the genesis of this fish-handling technology. Seth Green was the first professional fish culturist who worked for the State of New York, and he later served on its pioneer Fish Commission. Green operated the Caledonia hatchery for many years, and its first shipment of rainbow trout arrived in 1874. Although rail con-

ERNEST HEMINGWAY

nections were completed across the United States in 1869, service was too unreliable for shipping fertile trout eggs across the hot prairies. Such travels demanded shipment during summer months through the wintry seas around South America. Like the superb European brown trout, which would arrive in New York on the German steamship *Werra* nine years later, the California rainbows arrived in New York harbor after a journey down the long coasts of Chile and Peru. Their improbable odyssey had carried them through the Straits of Magellan, past the treeless coastal pampas of Patagonia and the tropical seaports of Brazil. The ice-chilled trays in which the eggs were transported finally arrived at the hatcheries at Cold Spring Harbor and Caledonia.

The rainbow trout had completed the first of its many epic voyages. It seems almost ironic a century later that the exotic California species was planted in the swift piedmont rivers of New Jersey, Pennsylvania, and New York several years before they were introduced to the brook-trout rivers of the Middle West and the tumbling cutthroat rivers of the Rocky Mountains.

Seth Green and Fred Mather exchanged several thousand fertile ova stripped from their brood rainbows at Caledonia and Cold Spring Harbor for the brown-trout eggs that arrived from Germany in 1883. Other shipments of Caledonia rainbow eggs had established the species in some Michigan rivers before 1895. It was also Green who shipped fertile eggs from Wisconsin to Wyoming and Colorado, and the famous hatchery at Caledonia was the source of rainbow eggs for the rivers of Patagonia. It was Seth Green who actually christened the exotic fish rainbows.

The stockings of these California trout were not all planned by the politicians and fish culturists. Edward Ringwood Hewitt is famous for a whole shelf of books, ending with his *Trout and Salmon Fisherman for Seventy-Five Years*, and he often fished the rivers that feed the Delaware from the Poconos and Catskills. Hewitt sometimes fished with the little-known Daniel Cahill. He was a simple man who fished and worked as a brakeman on the Erie & Lackawanna, and who invented the famous Cahill fly pattern. Hewitt was fond of telling Cahill stories, and perhaps the best was the stocking of rainbow trout at Callicoon Creek in 1884. It was a searingly hot summer in the Catskills, and Cahill was working a Lackawanna freight above Port Jervis. There were several cans of big brood-stock rainbows aboard, and when his freight was stalled behind a derailed work train, Cahill knew the shipment of big rainbows was doomed in the midsummer heat. Irish charm talked the nonfishermen in his train crew into carrying the heavy fish cans more than a mile back to the Callicoon, and this unplanned Catskill stocking resulted in half a century of fine rainbow fishing—sport so good that it often attracted both Hewitt and the legendary George La Branche.

Other fine rainbow fisheries were developed on eastern rivers in the closing years of the last century. California trout were soon firmly established on rivers like the Esopus, where they still thrive today, and on larger streams like the Willowemoc and the Beaverkill. Hotel records at Henryville House mention a twenty-inch rainbow from the Brodheads in Pennsylvania as early as 1897. There were other fragments of evidence fifty-odd years ago. William Schaldach describes large rainbows in the Catskills in *Currents and Eddies,* and Ray Bergman included the portrait of a fine hen rainbow from the Willowemoc in *Just Fishing.* Big fish descended from these early stockings are still found in the Delaware, and still ascend some lesser Catskill rivers to spawn in the late winter.

However, our best fishing for eastern rainbows is found in big swift-flowing rivers that feed major lakes or impoundments. There are fine spring runs of spawning fish that enter the Esopus from the Ashokan Reservoir, and several creeks that are tributaries to the Finger Lakes have similar migratory rainbows. Catherine Creek is particularly famous for its late-winter runs, and fishermen travel for miles to gather in crowds when the fish are migrating out of the lakes to spawn. Other famous rivers like the Ausable and Great Chazy and Lamoille once had superb runs from Lake Champlain, and there is still first-rate spring fishing for rainbows in the Willoughby above Lake Memphremagog in Vermont. Good fly-fishermen have always travelled to the headwaters of the Connecticut above Colebrooke for its big rainbows, and probably our most unusual eastern fishing of *Salmo gairdneri* is for the steelhead-type fish that migrate from saltwater into the Manasquan in New Jersey. Perhaps the most difficult rainbows in the east are found in Falling Spring Run, surprisingly selective fish in the chalkstreamlike currents of that Pennsylvania limestone stream.

Few anglers in the Rocky Mountain states realize that rainbow trout are not indigenous to their waters. The great rainbow trout habitats like the Gunnison in Colorado, the willow-lined Green above Flaming Gorge in Wyoming, and the serpentine Silver in Sun Valley are all the result of transplanted trout.

During the glacial Pleistocene epoch, the western mountains were not directly subjected to the eroding forces of the polar ice shields but the thermal patterns of our climatology were so lowered that the Rocky Mountains and Sierra Nevada escarpments themselves generated substantial ice fields and glaciation. The geology of our western mountains bears unmistakable evidence of these primordial ice fields, and relict strains of cutthroat and rainbow subspecies in the southern United States, Mexico and Baja California are ichthyological evidence of a colder climate in past millenniums.

The subspecies of black-spotted trout described as *Salmo gilae* and *Salmo apache* found in small high-country streams just north of the Mexican border and such relict subspecies of rainbows as *Salmo nelsoni* and *Salmo chrysogaster* in the mountains of Baja California and Mexico are probably biological echoes of the glacial past. Warming seas and rivers and the erosion that accompanied the shrinking Pleistocene glaciers ultimately eradicated all but such isolated subspecies from the watersheds draining toward the Gulf of California.

JUDGE DANIEL FITZHUGH

It was the rivers of southern Michigan that received the first transfusion of California rainbows from Seth Green in 1876. Judge Daniel
Fitzhugh of Bay City, who was also instrumental in stocking brook trout to
replace the decimated Michigan grayling, planted the first rainbows in the
Au Sable. Two years later, another major shipment of adult rainbow brood
stock reached Francis Clark at his Northville Hatchery, and fry grown from
their spawn were stocked in the Au Sable and the Au Gres. Another
shipment of *Salmo shasta*, the superb rainbow subspecies from the McCloud
watershed in California, arrived in Michigan in 1880. Its parr-mottled fry
were planted in the swift-flowing Sturgeon.

The famous attorney Carter Harrison is perhaps better remembered
by most historians for his several terms as mayor of Chicago, but his
fly-fishing skills are half legendary from Idaho to New Brunswick. Many of

his early summers were spent on the trout streams of Michigan and Wisconsin, and his memoirs are filled with days on the Wolf and the Sturgeon and the Maple, which was still a grayling river in his time. Harrison confirms the success of the freshly planted rainbows on the Sturgeon, since a favorite anecdote of this fly-fishing Chicago politician involved taking a strong twenty-three-inch California trout on a slender four-ounce Leonard.

The trout hatchery at Big Rapids received a shipment of rainbows in 1885, and these fish were ultimately stocked in the Pere Marquette. Fish culturists monitored their progress in its fertile headwaters after twelve months, and found the new arrivals had grown seven inches. It is a river saturated with the rich marl-bog seepages of its headwaters. During the next five years, Michigan stocked the Muskegon and the Hersey from its fish hatchery at Big Rapids.

Ten thousand rainbow fingerlings were planted in the Platte above Frankfort in 1893, and Seth Green again supplied fish that were later stocked in the Big Manistee. Several rivers above the Straits were planted with California trout before 1895, and these fish were the genesis of the rainbow waters in Lake Superior and the Soo Rapids. Such stockings also introduced big rainbows into the Two-Hearted country made famous by the Hemingway story.

Early fish culturists had proved too eager in their gathering of rainbow brood stocks for their hatcheries. Landlocked subspecies like *Salmo shasta* and the *Salmo gilberti* strain from the headwaters of the swift-flowing Kern had been indiscriminately mixed with migratory sea-run steelheads. The precious nonmigratory traits of the McCloud and Kern river strains were tragically diluted and lost in the subsequent genetic mixture. The eggs coming east had become hopelessly hybridized, and the process was continued in our eastern hatchery stocks. Some fish in rivers like the Au Sable and Sturgeon seemed to remain where they were planted. Others appeared to migrate downstream almost as quickly as they were released. Michigan biologists were soon convinced that the California trout were worthless in small streams, and that the only sport they offered on the rivers occurred during their smoltlike migration downstream toward the Great Lakes. Some big fish remained in the lower reaches of the larger rivers, but most were seldom caught unless they returned from the Great Lakes to mate and spawn in the spring. Such steelheadlike fishing is justly famous in big rivers like the Manistee, Pere Marquette, Au Gres, Muskegon, Au Sable, and the Platte—and in the swift Sturgeon above Cheboygan, although most Michigan fish are caught on lures and bait.

However, opposition to the California species sprouted in various parts of Michigan. Like the immigrant brown trout from Europe, the rainbows were arousing considerable antagonism. Angry brook-trout fishermen argued that no more rainbows should be planted in streams that still supported the native species. Their vigilance is still visible today in fine brook-trout streams like the Black and the Pine.

Jack-pine people change their opinions and ways grudgingly, and opposition to the California trout persisted. There was a river character on the Little Manistee during my boyhood years who lived in a tar-paper shack above Peacock. *Sorriest day in my life,* Jim Seeley always muttered about the immigrant trout from California, *when they put them goddamn rainbows in my river!* There were many angry voices in Michigan.

Fred Clark began experimenting with undiluted steelheads at Northville in 1904, and his pure sea-run strains were placed in several rivers in the following years. Ten years of subsequent studies convinced Clark that most of the sea-bright migratory rainbows appearing in Michigan rivers were his fish, returning from the Great Lakes like their Pacific ancestors, and some of these lake-run rainbows were large. The celebrated river guide from Sault Sainte Marie, Pete Vigeant, took a magnificent sixteen-pound rainbow on a big streamer at the Soo Rapids in 1908.

The tragic extinction of the Michigan grayling was virtually complete when the introduced rainbows took hold, although a few isolated catches were reported from the Au Sable and Manistee and Maple early in this century. Brook trout had been introduced in some declining grayling rivers, but the old-timers feared that the rainbow would endanger this new species too, in competition for food and spawning riffles. The biologists completed their studies of these alleged conflicts in 1916, proving little or no spawning competition between the spring-spawning California trout and the autumn-spawning brook trout. Since the newly arrived brown trout seldom entered the extremely cold tributaries favored by the brook trout, often choosing to mate in the open riffles of the river itself, there was little competition between these species either. Yet these immigrant rainbows and browns became solidly established while the brook-trout population gradually dwindled.

The timber barons were the real culprits. Both the grayling and the brook trout had lost their optimal habitat with the rapacious clear-cutting that followed the Civil War. Stream temperatures rose as the watersheds were stripped of their sheltering pines and hemlocks, and the springheads ran warmer too. Cold clear springs and feeder brooks were inextricably tied to the coniferous forests that had covered Michigan, and when they were gone the Michigan grayling was annihilated and the brook trout were forced back into the cedar swamps and headwaters.

Western anglers like the California trout. There have always been good resident stocks of big nonmigratory fish in rivers like the McCloud and the Kern, the wild MacKenzie and Deschutes in Oregon, and Colorado rivers like the Gunnison and the tumbling Roaring Fork below Aspen. No odyssey in search of big river rainbows should miss the Pit and the Feather in California, the fabled Babine in British Columbia, and the giant spring-fed Henry's Fork of the Snake in northeastern Idaho.

There are also superb western spring creeks, not unlike the British chalkstreams or the limestone streams of Pennsylvania. Many of the famous British fishing clubs in Hampshire and Wiltshire are stocking rainbows these days, and Falling Spring Run in the Chambersburg valley of southern Pennsylvania is a famous rainbow fishery too. Perhaps the most famous spring creeks in our western mountains are in Montana, on the Armstrong and Nelson ranches above Livingston. Montana has another large spring creek at Lewiston and a galaxy of other small watercress-bordered flowages on the Madison, Gallatin, and Big Hole. Jackson Hole has some fine rainbows in its spring creeks, and I once took several between three and five pounds one summer in an icy tributary of the Snake above Moose Crossing. Hot Creek in the eastern Sierra foothills of California is justly famous, like the Firehole in the Yellowstone, but many rainbow addicts cast their ballots for perhaps the finest spring creek anywhere in the entire west—the serpentine reed-bordered Silver Creek near Sun Valley.

History tells us that the first rainbow eggs that were shipped from California were probably the subspecies *Salmo shasta* from the McCloud watershed along the Oregon border, and the elegant fine-spotted *Salmo gilberti* from the tumbling Kern in the high Sierras. Both subspecies were probably landlocked through volcanic and seismic changes in the geology of their drainage systems and eventually lost the migratory urge common to their red-striped cousins in other waters. Hatchery stocks of these species were indiscriminately mixed with more common riverine strains of rainbow, creating hybrid strains of river fish that were originally classified as *Salmo irideus* by ichthyologists. Most stocking used these hybrids, while others were planted with sea-run *Salmo gairdneri* steelheads.

There are many other rainbow subspecies. The dwarf subspecies of rainbows once found in the San Gorgionio Mountains below Los Angeles and the rare *Salmo nelsoni* found in a single river of the Baja Peninsula are perhaps the southernmost coastal examples. Both are probably extinct or hopelessly mixed with introduced rainbow and cutthroat stocks. There are also several rainbow subspecies in Mexican rivers tributary to the Gulf of California between Guaymas and Mazatlan, particularly the fish of the Rio del Presidio and the Rio Truchas. The most famous subspecies of rainbows are perhaps found in the lake country of British Columbia. There are two primary strains: the high-altitude subspecies classified as *Salmo whitehousei* and the better known *Salmo kamloops* originally found in famous fly-fishing lakes like Babine and Peterhope and Shuswap.

Although contemporary biologists are convinced that the taxonometric differences in these subspecies are primarily environmental in origin rather than being genetic aspects of their morphology, structural variations unquestionably exist. *Salmo shasta* specimens of the McCloud and Shasta rainbows average 145 to 150 scales along the lateral line, and their diagonal scale counts from the lateral line to the adipose fin average 12 to 14 rows. Kern River rainbows display almost identical scale counts, but their colors and markings are strikingly different. Perhaps the only regions where these remarkable California subspecies are presently found in undiluted populations are several small rivers where they were introduced in Argentina and Chile a half century ago.

The *Salmo whitehousei,* the high-altitude subspecies found landlocked in British Columbia, average 150 to 160 scales along the lateral line. The nonmigratory strain identified as *Salmo kamloops* is a subspecies with occasional access to salt water, and its scale counts along the lateral line average 130 to 153 rows, depending on the altitude of their habitat. Like the nonmigratory subspecies from California, these British Columbia rainbow stocks are valuable for establishing riverine fisheries.

Migratory steelheads typically exhibit linear scale counts of 130 to 140 rows, although in some rivers as many as 145 scales have been recorded. Like most other rainbow strains, steelheads average from 10 to 12 rays in both their dorsal and anal fins, 11 to 12 branchiostegals, and 35 to 70 pyloric caeca. Their marine growth rate is explosive.

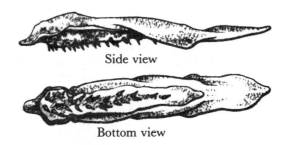

Side view

Bottom view

Rainbow Trout Vomerine Bone

Steelheads demonstrate the full-growth spectrum of rainbow-trout coloring in their life cycles. Their fingerlings and parr have olive-gray dorsal surfaces, and are heavily marked with fine spotting on their bodies, as well as their dorsal and caudal fins. Small steelheads have seven to thirteen parr markings, like the other riverine rainbow populations. Some specimens display spotting at the anterior of the pectoral and anal fins. Fine spotting also occurs well down the flanks and belly surfaces, but not on all rainbow ecotypes. Whitish tip coloring is sometimes found on the dorsal apex, and there are often chalk-colored tips on the anal and ventral fins. Both gill covers and sides are flushed with pinkish lavender, which becomes silvery with a faint rose cast at eight to ten inches, when the steelhead smolts begin their migration downriver toward the sea.

Mature steelheads return from salt water with no trace of their spotting and pinkish gill covers and striped sides. Their dorsal surfaces are steel-colored, like the gleaming finish of a new rifle, and there is sometimes an elusive, roseate cast over their coin-bright sides. Such fish are strong and sea-armored like salmon.

Some volcanic lakes in the Southern Hemisphere provide such rich ecosystems that their rainbows resemble steelheads fresh from a marine diet of shrimps and candlefish and herring. Titicaca in Peru is such a domain, and another is the magnificent Laguna Maule in the Chilean Andes. The rich lacustrine habitat of Taupo and its several rivers in New Zealand are filled with steelheadlike rainbows, and Argentina has storm-tossed lakes like Huechulafquen and sprawling Nahuel-Haupi at Bariloche, where the local fishermen call rainbows *plateadas* in celebration of their sleek polished-silver bodies.

Rainbow trout are spring spawners. Variations in altitude, however, can result in a spread of several months across the full range of the species. Fish culturists report that due to wide variations in altitude across California, rainbows are spawning somewhere virtually all year in its waters. Unlike these exceptions, most specimens of *Salmo gairdneri* spawn in late winter and early spring.

Such behavioral tendencies toward spring spawning makes the rainbow a fine prospect for high-lake stockings. The fish can utilize the snowmelt in the swelling tributaries and outlets of such lakes to oxygenate their eggs. Some eggs are lost when these thawing spates end, leaving the freshly-made redds without oxygenation, but many survive to hatch. The temperatures of high-altitude waters are often much too cold for brown trout, and like the autumn-spawning brook trout, such fish often find insufficient inlet and outlet flowages without fall rains to facilitate successful egg laying. Cutthroat trout were once indigenous to most high-altitude lakes in our western mountains, and their spring spawning behavior, which clearly parallels the closely-related rainbows, is ideally suited for survival in such wilderness habitats.

Spawning steelheads face similar problems related to rainfall and water level. Fish returning to their parent coastal rivers in the fall are blocked from entering fresh water by late-summer sand bars. Such fish must wait until the autumn rains swell the rivers, breaching these sand barriers and cutting fresh outlet channels across their estuaries. Marine biologists believe such fish often wait outside these brackish sand bars for several weeks, feeding on baitfish and crustaceans until a fall spate clears the mouth of their rivers.

Biologists have speculated widely on the methods these fish use to return to their parent rivers. Most anadromous fish discern the olfactory tastes or smells of their home river even when faintly mingled with the coastal seas, but a river mouth closed by sand bars cannot distribute such odors in anything more than imperceptible traces. Paul Needham tells us in *Trout Streams* that such minuscule dilutions are apparently sufficient for such coastal migrants to find their parent rivers in spite of the late-summer sand bars that completely close their estuaries. River fingerprints filtered through the sand and river-polished pebbles are measured only in infinitesimal parts per billion—yet the returning steelheads readily sense such minute olfactory clues in the offshore seas.

Like their cousins the salmon, steelheads are apparently encoded with the unique fingerprints of their parent rivers while still fingerlings and smolts. Such memory coding is sufficient for coastal and estuarine feeding, but little is understood about the outbound pelagic migrations and homing instincts of the few that embark on extensive migrations in open seas. Most steelheads range farther afield in salt water than sea-run browns, harvest cutthroats, and anadromous brook-trout populations. Such other anadromous species are primarily estuarine in behavior, and remain relatively close to the outlets of their rivers. Steelheads and coho salmon range more freely along the coastal shelves, but seldom migrate into full-blown mesopelagic journeys. Exceptions to such coastal behavior are found among the steelhead strains from the Columbia, King Island and Skeena watersheds. Some of these atypically large steelheads have been captured by commercial trawlers as much as 2,500 miles into the open Pacific.

Big steelheads similar to those that spawn in rivers like the Sustut and Kispiox and Skeena are an unusual strain of fish, spending two and three years in their salmonlike migrations, and such big rainbows tend to breed big rainbows. Their heredity is not just a matter of two- to three-year feeding cycles in the sea but is also a factor of the big river-polished stones and coarse gravel in their prime spawning grounds. Such bottom conditions and heavy currents make poor egg-laying conditions for smaller fish, weeding out the two-pound summer fish and average steelheads from the population. Such natural selection is a little like the half-legendary Atlantic salmon rivers of Norway, rivers like the Alta and Vossa and Årøy, where powerful currents and rocky bottoms favor the survival of extremely big fish. These British Columbia rivers offer perhaps the finest steelhead fishing in the world.

Coastal steelhead are usually smaller, ranging from six to twelve pounds, and there are also yearling steelhead that return to their parent rivers after only a few months in salt water. Such small steelheads resemble the yearling grilse in Atlantic salmon rivers. Summer fly fishermen on rivers like the Eel and Umpqua and Rogue call these smaller fish half-pounders, and fishing the greased line on these two- to four-pound steelheads is intriguing light-tackle sport.

Riverine pigmentation begins to return after a relatively few hours in the brackish tidal zones, and steelheads taken in the lower river soon begin to display traces of their freshwater coloring. Unlike salmon, steelhead trout apparently continue feeding once they have completed the transition from their tidal estuaries to fresh water. Bright steelheads caught just above the tidal reaches often contain undigested marine diet forms. However, such fish quickly turn to riverine foods like the stonefly nymphs and freshly spawned salmon eggs and baitfish. This river diet is limited for a run of relatively large fish, but it does sustain them through the full spawning cycle. Pacific salmon die once their egg laying is finished, but many steelheads apparently winter successfully and survive.

Most big-fish migrations occur in deep fall and early winter, and in his superb essay on steelheads in the anthology *Fisherman's Bounty*, Paul O'Neil describes the puzzling behavior of true steelhead-fishing addicts. Such men are a peculiar breed who love the rattle of fall rains on their slickers, and huddle around gravel-bar fires thawing frostbitten hands and feet. Winter fishing for these sea-armored rainbows is bittersweet sport, and O'Neil captures its aberrations with perfect pitch:

> The rest of the world's trout are taken in summer, to the sound of birds and the pleasant hum of insects, but the steelhead—the big seagoing rainbow of the northwest coasts—is winter's child.
>
> To know him you must gird for war and wade the rivers when they are bitter cold—in sleet-filled gloom or in freezing blue weather when the leafless alders gleam in pale sunlight along the streams, and ice forms in the guides of your rod.
>
> To understand and know the steelhead, you should hurt with cold and nurse a little fear of the numbing current which pushes against your waders. It can pull you down and make you gasp with cold and drown you, as steelhead rivers methodically drown a few of your fellow fishermen each passing year.
>
> The steelhead may be pursued in fairer weather and in easier ways. It runs as far south as the Sacramento River in California. Some of its number run in the early spring, and in such rivers as the Snake and Oregon's famed Rogue, it runs in the summer too. But it is a northern fish. When it leaves the sea to spawn, it comes mostly to the rivers of Oregon, Washington, British Columbia, and Alaska, and it migrates chiefly during December, January and February. The fisherman who has not met the steelhead in the cold has not been properly introduced. Winter sets the stage for the steelhead and makes him unique.
>
> There is an ominous drama in the very look of a chill, green river on a dark and stormy afternoon, and a man fighting cold and snow to wade it is being properly conditioned for his moment of revelation. For the steelhead is a fish which makes an impact upon the adrenalin-producing glands rather than the intellect. The steelhead is invariably large (six to thirty pounds) and it burns with the savage energy from the limitless feed of the ocean it has left behind. It can hurtle into the air a split second after it is hooked, and flash hugely out of the murk, like the sword Excalibur thrust up from the depths—at once a gleaming prize and a symbol of battle.

O'Neill invokes a world of winter fires and thermos bottles filled with black coffee and a raw wind across the somber lead-colored currents. Fish in the mood for fly-fishing are few in a river swollen with December rains. Such winter sport on the steelhead rivers is a happy madness that parallels the suffering of foul-weather duck hunters in ice-skim blinds from Barnegat Light to the frozen marshes of Merrymeeting Bay.

Most rainbows typically spawn in the late winter currents of the small tributary streams. Some steelheads deposit their eggs in surprisingly small riffles, so long as they provide current speeds of ten to twenty inches per second. Like the hardier brown trout, some rainbows choose spawning gravel in open river and complete their egg laying successfully. Fisheries biologists have also recorded viable egg-laying in the downwind shallows of western lakes, where relatively constant winds generate sufficient wave action to oxygenate the redds.

Ripe females carry between two hundred and 10,000 eggs depending upon age, size, and physical condition. Mature henfish of five to six pounds will produce approximately 4,000 to 7,000 fertile ova. The depth of flow over a spawning site is about six to thirty inches, and most rainbows prefer bottom aggregates ranging from pea gravel to small stones. The henfish shape the nests with their bodies, rolling and gyrating powerfully in the current. Their undulations displace the bottom materials and gradually develop a shallow depression. The displaced gravel and stones drift downstream with the smooth current. Work continues until a saucerlike depression of four to six inches in depth is completed. The fully developed redd measures twelve to fifteen inches in diameter, and its gravel tailings form a mound immediately below. During the nest making, the males protect the females and the spawning territory.

Female rainbows are most particular about the depth and configuration of their redds. Fisheries biologists have observed them settling deep into their gravel spawning beds, apparently employing their anal and ventral fins to measure proper structure and configuration. During this redd-shaping process, the cockfish watch their mates closely, stimulating the females with the shuddering contact of their bodies. Their conjugal working and writhing displaces even more gravel, but the primary activity of the males is guarding the nest-building henfish.

Other males are often lurking on the periphery of the mating pair. Considerable quarrelling can occur between the principal cockfish and these secondary males. The smaller rainbows both hope to participate in the spawning, and perhaps consume some of the surplus eggs. The primary male typically chases these interlopers viciously, often pursuing them through the riffles and adjacent pools.

Completing the spawning redds, the females drop well back into their saucer-shaped depressions and are joined by the males. Both fish work and writhe together, and the male sometimes strokes its mate along the caudal peduncle with the distended spawning kype of its jaws. Both males and females work their jaws in a gasping rhythm, and the writhing female often breaks the surface current with her snout. While the two fish gasp and shudder together, both eggs and milt are extruded simultaneously into the nest. There is usually so much milky sperm that the spilling ova are virtually invisible as they settle into the redd, and the mixture subsides quickly. Surprisingly few eggs are lost to tumble with the current, where they are quickly gobbled by the secondary males and coarse-fish predators. The primary cockfish continues to writhe with the female throughout the two- to three-second orgasm—the cloud of eggs and milt settling thickly into the streambed.

There is little trace of the fertilized eggs only seconds after oviposition is finished. The females quickly move upstream above the redd, writhing again to displace the gravel for a second nest. Her movements tumble fresh stones and streambed aggregates into the current, which quickly cover the earlier eggs and nest. The fertile nest is safely covered in only minutes, and a second redd has been started.

The female rainbows work vigorously on the new spawning site, but the attending cockfish seldom displays much interest until several minutes have passed. Approximately two hours are required to prepare the second redd. Its completion is a signal for the male rainbow to rejoin his mate and the entire egg-laying ritual is repeated. The second orgasm floods the nesting site with its milky mixture of eggs and sperm, and the henfish immediately starts a third redd. Such spawning rites can continue for twelve hours to an entire week, depending on the weather, river temperature, and the fecundity of the mating pair.

Large rainbows can cluster a number of redds across as much as sixty square feet of streambed. The current flows both above and beneath the bottom gravel, oxygenating six to ten separate nesting sites. Each nest can hold from five hundred to 1,000 fertile eggs, depending upon the size and ripeness of the female.

Both females and cockfish are almost fully spent after spawning. These kelts drift downstream slowly, facing the current until they reach deeper water and gradually recover their strength in some quiet pool. Steelheads begin dropping back toward salt water, stopping to winter in connecting lakes and deep pools, looking thin and dull like tarnished pewter. Their emaciated bodies are darkly spotted again, their red gill covers and stripes like a faded flag. It will take weeks of feeding on smelt and oil-rich candlefish and crustaceans before their strength returns, and their bodies gleam with the richness of the seas.

Lake-run rainbows from fertile waters are similar, from the Great Lakes to the fjordlike fisheries of the Andes. The spawned-out kelts drifting back in the Pere Marquette and the Manistee will recover quickly on a diet of perch and alewives and smelt, and their cousins in the rivers of Argentina and Chile quickly regain strength with a riverine diet of *puyen* baitfish and *cangrejo* crabs. Fishing them on small Patagonian rivers like the Ñirihuau and Pichi Traful and Quilquihue, or the swift little Riñinahue and Cumilahue in southern Chile is exceptional sport—last October I experienced a scrambling two-hundred-yard fight with a big rainbow kelt on the Cumilahue, and its strength amply demonstrated the recuperative powers of such a diet.

Egg incubation of fertile rainbow ova varies widely with altitude, latitude, and water temperature. Four to six weeks are required for hatching under average conditions, and in extremely cold habitats three months can pass before the tiny rainbow alevins finally wriggle out through the gravel. Several days of energy are stored in the tiny yolk sacs attached to their bodies. Once these yolk sacs are expended, the half-inch fingerlings are forced to utilize the river foods. Like all baby trout and salmon, these

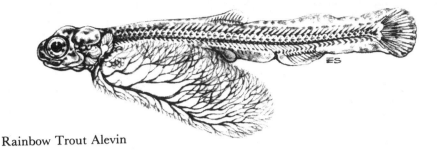

Rainbow Trout Alevin

tiny rainbows first concentrate on zooplankton and other minute aquatic organisms. The mottled fingerlings grow rather quickly on their diet of water fleas and diatomaceous life. Growth is relatively rapid, and the hungry parr soon turn to the diet forms common to larger fish. Subaquatic nymphs and crustaceans and tiny baitfish are staple components of the small rainbow diet.

However, rainbows are virtually unique among the Salmonidae in the sense that they never fully lose their liking for minute algal forms and zooplankton. Some fisheries are so rich in such minutae that even adult cutthroats and rainbows consume as much as thirty percent of their diet by weight, mixed with the larger food types associated with other fish. Paul Needham found that rainbows of surprisingly large size continue to subsist on relatively minuscule life forms, and his research is extensively recorded in *Trout Streams*. Edward Ringwood Hewitt confirmed those findings in his own research with rainbows. Hewitt believed that their unusual adult emphasis on tiny water fleas and zooplankton and midges was perhaps a primary clue to the migratory urge unique to the species—and that its liking for rich salt water feeding grounds of zooplankton had a major role in the rainbow's mysterious desire to reach the sea.

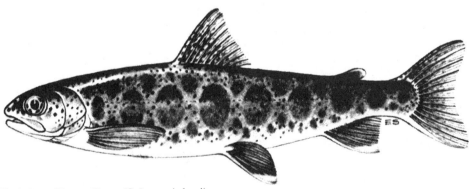

Rainbow Trout Parr *(Salmo gairdneri)*

The rainbow growth rate is relatively rapid. It slightly surpasses the growth of brown trout, and most baby rainbows have reached three to five inches in their first season. More rapid growth is possible in alkaline waters. Volcanic lakes like Titicaca and Huechlafquen and Nahuel Huapi in southern Argentina, and famous Lake Taupo in the geothermal basin of New Zealand, are typical of such fertile habitats. Particularly rich rivers in those latitudes like the Tongariro in New Zealand, the Quilquihue in Argentina, and the silken fly-rich Cumilahue in Chile have unusual growth patterns in their rainbows. Most rainbow trout will reach seven to nine inches in their first two seasons, in habitats of average fertility, but these exceptional exotic habitats can produce fifteen-inch fish in only two years. American streams like the spring creeks of Montana and Silver Creek in Idaho are rainbow waters that can sustain equally spectacular rates of trout growth.

Although there are stories of fifty-pounders, the world-record rainbow taken on sporting tackle is a forty-two-pound-two-ounce fish caught at Bell Island in the Alaskan tidal waters near Ketchikan. It was caught by David White on June 22, 1970, and measured forty-three inches in length. The new record supplants a thirty-seven-pound rainbow taken on trolling gear at Lake Pend Oreille in Idaho. It was caught on a wobbling spoon in 1947, and the world fly-record for *Salmo gairdneri* is still the thirty-three-pound steelhead that Karl Mausser took on the Kispiox in British Columbia in 1967. Several nonmigratory rainbows better than twenty pounds have been taken on flies in both South American and the Antipodes—fish that grew to such size in freshwater lakes and were caught in their *boca* tributaries.

Rainbow trout are less wary than their European cousins, the brown trout, but they are seldom as gullible as the other American species except in remote wilderness habitats. Cutthroats and brook trout are more easily caught, and their fatal curiosity has been a major factor in their decline under the fishing pressures of the past half century. Michigan studies indicate that about forty-five percent of stocked rainbows are caught during the same season that planting takes place. Twenty-five percent survived their first season when constrained by the weirs of the Pigeon River Research Station, while almost thirty percent were lost to annual mortality. Obviously, the twenty-five percent of stocked rainbows that remained after a year in the Pigeon test mileage were unable to migrate downstream because of the weirs, but without such barriers, rainbows are such a restless species that they promptly travel downstream.

Their migratory tendencies make rainbows a poor long-term stocking investment, in spite of their high ratios of recovery, unless a lake or manmade impoundment contains their desire to reach salt water. The ability of the rainbow to thrive in wide variations of temperature and water chemistry makes it the most widely distributed member of the Salmonidae family. Rainbows are surprisingly found thriving in habitats that are both quite acid and alkaline, and at temperatures varying between forty and eighty-odd degrees. Rainbows survive at temperatures as high as eighty-three degrees on the Firehole in the Yellowstone, with its currents strangely warmed by hot springs and geysers. Their survival at such high temperatures in Hot Creek and the Firehole is only possible because the water is highly oxygenated, both from its tumbling riffles and the photosynthesis of its abundant weeds. Such an ability to tolerate a wide spectrum of environmental conditions, and their adaptability to hatchery rearing, make the *Salmo gairdneri* species a great favorite of fish culturists.

Biologists have also discovered that sustaining an excellent anadromous steelhead fishery is possible. The method involves rearing the baby steelheads until they reach the migratory smolt size by holding them in riverside ponds. These fish are grown from eggs stripped in a wild-fish trapping program, insuring both genetic coding of their migratory behavior and the high survival ratios that go with their wildness. High percentages of these smolts are returning from salt water, providing greatly improved steelheading on the rivers being stocked. However, the returning runs of fish are highly seasonal, like most natural fisheries based upon anadromous trout behavior, and during much of the year such rivers rarely produce rainbows of much size.

Stomach autopsies conducted in the Needham studies at Cornell some thirty years ago suggest a number of facts about rainbows. The Needham test specimens were taken on eastern, freestone streams of the slightly acid character typical of the Appalachian watersheds. Such algal phytoplankton as *Cladophora* were found in a number of these fish. Although the sample population consisted of only eighty rainbows, ranging from three to twelve inches in length, the data gathered in these studies form an important step in understanding the feeding character of the rainbow:

TYPE	TOTALS	PERCENT
Mayflies	490	37.1
Caddisflies	247	18.1
Two-winged flies	234	17.8
Beetles	105	7.9
Ants, bees, and wasps	88	6.6
Stoneflies	44	3.3
Moth larvae	17	1.2
Snails and slugs	14	1.1
Leafhoppers	13	1.0
Crustaceans	13	1.0
Sialidae larvae	11	.8
Grasshoppers	7	.5
Salamanders and baitfish	6	.5
Miscellaneous	34	2.5
Totals	1,323	100.0

Several intriguing patterns are found in these data. Almost five hundred mayflies were consumed, although more than eighty percent of these Ephemeroptera were nymphal forms. Less than two percent of the caddisflies ingested were taken in the adult stages, and most were in their larval and pupal stages. Virtually all of the two-winged flies were taken in their immature subaquatic stages in the surface film, and the relatively few baitfish are indicative of the small average size of the test-sample rainbows studied. Fully eighty-five percent of the rainbow diet consists of these subsurface foods.

Similar autopsies were recorded on fifty bigger rainbows during my own diet studies for *Matching the Hatch*, and most of these fish were taken on Rocky Mountain rivers. Perhaps the most obvious differences are the percentages of stoneflies, midge pupae and sculpins found in the digestive tracts of these bigger fish:

TYPE	TOTALS	PERCENT
Caddisflies	781	26.4
Mayflies	439	14.9
Two-winged flies	412	14.0
Stoneflies	396	13.4
Beetles	313	10.7
Crustaceans	207	7.0
Ants, bees, and wasps	161	5.4
Hemiptera	87	3.0
Moth larvae	43	1.4
Leafhoppers	17	.6
Snails and slugs	15	.5
Grasshoppers	13	.4
Salamanders and baitfish	13	.4
Miscellaneous	51	1.9
Totals	2,948	100.0

Fifty more stomach samples of rainbows averaging twelve inches have been taken since *Matching the Hatch*, primarily on large western rivers with exceptional populations of big stonefly nymphs. Sculpins are also found in good numbers on these rivers, and both sculpins and the predatory stonefly nymphs tend to decimate and suppress mayfly populations. The sharp increase in two-winged pupal forms reflects a number of test fish caught on western impoundments, as well as slow-flowing streams like Silver Creek and the upper Frying Pan and the Henry's Fork of the Snake, with their concentrations of tiny insects in the film. These remarkable western rivers hold populations of surprisingly selective rainbows, fish that free-rise regularly to almost continuous hatches of tiny flies in smooth currents. Rainbows on these difficult rivers can match wits with the supercilious brown trout on classic English chalkstreams like the Itchen and Test:

TYPE	TOTALS	PERCENT
Caddisflies	813	20.8
Stoneflies	799	20.4
Two-winged flies	761	19.4
Mayflies	394	10.1
Beetles	317	8.1
Crustaceans	219	5.6
Ants, bees, and wasps	190	4.8
Salamanders and baitfish	115	2.9
Leafhoppers	71	1.8
Moth larvae	63	1.6
Hemiptera	61	1.6
Grasshoppers	29	.7
Snails and slugs	21	.5
Miscellaneous	65	1.7
Totals	3,918	100.0

The surprising incidence of beetles in these stomach counts is explained by a spring of unusually high water levels at Eleven Mile Reservoir in Colorado. The rising waters flooded considerable acreages along the south shoreline, large numbers of terrestrial *Poecilus* beetles found themselves emerging in shallow water rather than in their accustomed sagebrush and bunchgrass flats, and the fish came after them into surprisingly shallow water. The rainbows inspected that evening had gorged themselves on these beetles until they literally crunched when handled, as if their alimentary tracts were filled with gravel or tiny beans. Once cruising fish were located, hooking them on a 6x tippet and a small beetle imitation proved relatively easy—but containing their wild cartwheeling runs in the flooded sagebrush was another matter altogether.

Rainbows also display a surprising interest in ants. Perhaps their lifelong interest in minute diet forms is easily translated to ants and leafhoppers and tiny bark beetles when such insects are available. Several times I have taken rather large fish that have literally stuffed themselves with ants on rivers from Patagonia to Montana. There was a fat six-pound rainbow in a shallow run on the Cumilahue that had consumed literally hundreds of minute ants, and I once took a huge rainbow of better than eight pounds on a small spring creek in Jackson Hole that had been sipping big carpenter ants from a blizzardlike mating swarm.

Although rainbow trout are usually a prime wet-fly fish, unlike the brown trout with their demonstrable interest in surface foods, rainbows will rise eagerly to a hatch. Browns are somewhat more selective on most waters too, but on the weedy flats at the Armstrong Ranch in Montana, Falling Spring Run in southern Pennsylvania, or the Henry's Fork of the Snake in Idaho, the surface feeding rainbow can be a remarkably selective dry-fly challenge.

Salmo gairdneri will continue to play a major role in future trout fisheries management around the world, although our past ignorance in the hatchery mixing of genetic strains has caused some problems. Haphazard mixing and crossbreeding has resulted in a hopeless spaghetti tangle of blood lines, and some experiments in breeding have been myopically concerned with little more than maximum growth at minimal cost and time. Some hatcheries have achieved new strains of rainbows that exhibit remarkable rates of growth and a high ratio of pounds-per-dollar produced in the hatcheries. Yet the unique qualities of character that make all trout both beautiful and difficult to catch have too often been sacrificed to increased rates of growth. Most hatchery strains of rainbows no longer resemble their wild brood stocks, have lost all traces of the precious nonmigratory tendencies of the landlocked California subspecies, and behave somewhat like patients after a frontal lobotomy. Our federal fisheries experts might consider a program of restoring the lost traits of our original landlocked California rainbows in future genetic experiments. Several small rivers in South America have relatively pure strains of *Salmo shasta* and *Salmo gilberti,* and superb fisheries like the swift Malleo in Argentina could prove the source of beautifully configured and colored brood stock for such a program.

Some Argentine fish culturists fail to realize what superlative strains of trout have evolved in the isolation of Patagonia, since the pure California species were introduced early in the century, and are always talking about more rainbows and coarse species from various parts of the world. Such imports would inescapably consist of hatchery stocks vastly inferior to the steelheadlike strains of rainbows found at Nahuel-Huapi, and the land-locked California subspecies in the Malleo headwaters. Argentina definitely needs no bass or walleyes or northern pike in its unique waters, but some fish managers in the government have raised that frightening possibility for the future. Importing new hatchery strains also raises the spectre of disease, but sound heads will hopefully prevail in these matters, permitting Argentine hatcheries to raise fish with eggs stripped from their virtually matchless wild strains of rainbow trout and landlocked salmon. In preserving the genetic integrity of those species, Argentina could possibly replenish the world with superb brood stocks of both lake-run and land-locked rainbows.

Future rearing and stocking programs for rainbows might consciously segregate the optimal anadromous, lake, and riverine stocks for both their genetic behavioral coding and their unique physical character. Excellent migratory, lacustrine, and nonmigratory populations would result—with perhaps optimal equilibrium for each subspecies in each type of environment—while improving the explosive, cartwheeling fight that has made the rainbow trout fishing favorite around the world.

Perhaps my most pervasive memory of a rainbow was a strong, fourteen-pound female at the Boca Ñirihuau below San Carlos de Bariloche. It was an unusually still morning, with the autumn color starting in the April poplars along Nahuel-Huapi, and I was sleeping after a late dinner at the Vizcacha.

Douglas Reid and Laddie Buchanan are perhaps the best outfitters now working the rivers of Patagonia and both have been good friends for more than a dozen seasons. They were noisily pounding my hotel door at daylight.

No wind, Buchanan explained.

Schwiebert likes to sleep late, Reid laughed. *We'll never get him out of the sack at five o'clock!*

I'm awake! I growled from the blankets.

Wind is the principal factor in fly-fishing the Boca Ñirihuau and the larger Boca Limay at the *pampas* outlet of the Nahuel-Huapi lake. It sprawls almost one hundred miles across the Andes, with its headwaters on the threshold of Chile. The lake is famous for the *pampero* winds that howl its full length from Chile into the Argentine foothills, winds that raise a fierce surf and impossible casting conditions at its outlet. April mornings without wind are so rare and the fishing is so superb that no serious angler could conceivably sleep late.

We started down the corniche along the lake under cloudless skies, and gentle little swells washed in against the rocky beaches where Laddie turned the pickup into the river bottoms that surround the Boca Ñirihuau. Its quiet currents riffled down the steep gravelly shingle of the beach into the lake, its tongues working and eddying out one hundred yards into the deeper water. It was strangely still, yet most autumn mornings have an April *pampero* that howls straight down the lake toward the Ñirihuau, driving the best double-haul casts back into your teeth. Big bucktails can become as dangerous as shrapnel in such weather.

It's perfect! Laddie sighed happily.

The smooth expanse of Nahuel-Huapi reached west toward Cerro Catedral and the Tronador volcano, with the tile-roofed houses of San Carlos de Bariloche bright across the water. Laddie gestured like a deerstalker and we worked stealthily along the open beach, studying the little river where it winds through the bottoms and spends itself in the lake. It was a wine-dark sky reflected in the waters, and I saw a good fish porpoise eighty yards out.

They can lie in close too, Laddie whispered.

Sometimes right at the mouth, Douglas added, *and they can really be spooky this time of year.*

Big rainbows move well up into the Ñirihuau shallows at night, feeding in the swift river currents where they work out into the lake. We slipped into the smooth shallows about eighty feet from the riffling river mouth itself.

What should I try? I asked.

They've been trolled and spooned to death! Laddie shook his head thoughtfully. *Plenty of bucktails too!*

One of your big nymphs, Douglas suggested.

Buchanan rummaged through my fly books and selected a big muskrat-bodied stonefly nymph. It dropped across the riffling current tongues, and I worked it teasingly through the swing, taking a step deeper after every cast. It took only five casts before the fly swing stopped with a gentle, plucking hit and the line tightened almost lazily.

The rainbow hung sullenly in the gathering currents for several moments. Suddenly it exploded into the lake in a run that stripped two hundred yards off the shrieking reel. Its cartwheeling jump ended clumsily in a huge splash, far out across the still surface of the lake. The Hardy was screaming again, almost before the spray of its first jump had settled, and the big rainbow pirouetted into the sun sixty yards farther out.

Some fish! Douglas yelled from the beach.

He floats through the air, Laddie laughed and sang happily off-key above the protesting ratchet-whine of the reel, *with the greatest of ease!*

The line was slack now and the reel had suddenly stopped, and I worked frantically to recover backing. The big rainbow jumped again, this time only fifty yards down the beach, almost drydocking itself on the gravel.

That's my fish? I yelled.

Si como no! Laddie cackled puckishly. *But it's not your fish just yet!*

It bolted back into deep water, raising rooster tails of spray in the shallows. Six times the big henfish stripped the reel into the backing before it jumped again, pole-vaulting across the smooth water, and each time its gleaming length was a quicksilver flash in the sun. It slowly surrendered one hundred yards of line, and then came grudgingly back along the *boca* currents. Finally, it was rolling in the shallows off the beach, circling weakly just beyond our reach. It was another fifteen minutes before I worked my fingers across its gill covers, and carried the gleaming rainbow ashore.

Douglas waved the scale and applauded. *Good fish!* Douglas studied the calibrations carefully. *Fourteen pounds!*

My wrist ached. *That was some fight!*

Rainbows are always like that! Laddie laughed. *They're the Trout on the Flying Trapeze!*

4. The Black-Spotted Trout of the American Frontier

Bob Carmichael was a unique Wyoming character, holding court in his cluttered tackle shop at Moose Crossing on the Snake. His shop was a simple place not far from the tiny log-framed Chapel of the Transfiguration, and it became the meeting place for good fishing talk in western Wyoming in the old days. Carmichael was one of the principal protagonists in a whole cast of fishing characters that populated the Jackson Hole country thirty-odd years ago.

His reputation was fierce, in part stemming from irascible but good-natured dialogues so formidable that I never really dared to engage him in conversation until after my college years. But I was often in his shop, eavesdropping on its stream of gossip about killing fly patterns and good stretches of cutthroat river and secret spring creeks. It was many years later that I learned how Carmichael had taught old friends to fish, like the famous *Life* photographer George Silk, who retreated from covering combat in the Second World War to the solitude of the Teton country. It was a time of happy summers, fishing sometimes with Carmichael and using nothing but his three favorite patterns: the two long-hackle variants tied for his shop by the skilled Roy Donnelly, and the mixed-hackle Carmichael's Indispensable.

Those were unforgettable summers and Carmichael was a memorable character. Weeks were spent in nomadic odysseys, sleeping outside in goose-down bags in good weather, and jackknifed uncomfortably into car seats when it rained or sometimes snowed even in midsummer, or when park bears attracted to the cooking smells coming from my twilight fire sent me scuttling back into the Oldsmobile. That seems comically foolish now, since its convertible canvas top would have offered minimal protection.

Those were summers without problems or responsibilities, when I travelled and fished like a river gypsy. They took me from the Cucharas and Conejos in southern Colorado to the brawling Madison and Big Hole and Yellowstone in Montana, with countless mountain streams, rivers and lakes in between.

There were pastoral little rivers too, like the willow-lined creeks on our family cattle ranch west of Leadville, and the now-famous Frying Pan and Crystal near Aspen. It was a time of transition in skills, when the easy boyhood years were ending and we had the rivers almost to ourselves like private preserves. It was the time of my baptism on the difficult spring creeks, with extremely shy brown trout on the Gibbon and the Firehole in the Yellowstone. Cutthroat trout had already retreated into the cold headwaters of our western rivers before my boyhood years—and into high lakes and back-country beaver ponds. Their once countless numbers had been reduced by the mining booms, by timber cut to manufacture charcoal for the smelters, by lumbering for railroad ties and tunnel beams and pithead frames, and by professional market fishing for frontier hotels like the Brown Palace in Denver and the Antlers in Colorado Springs.

We had sometimes sought cutthroats in the tributary creeks and beaver ponds in Colorado. I remember those back-packing boyhood climbs into lakes like Horseshoe and Snowmass and Treasure Vault, when our legs and lungs ached searingly and our mouths tasted like bitter pennies. The cutthroats were brightly colored little fish of the high altitudes, their sides pale yellowish below olive-green backs. Their fins were yellowish too, and they all carried the bright little slashes of scarlet in the membranes of the lower jaw, markings which distinguish the several cutthroat subspecies and give these black-spotted trout their name. There were subtle differences in the cutthroats we caught in those boyhood years, although we did not understand that we were seeing the living echoes of a number of subspecies. The pale delicately spotted cutthroats we took at Wagon Wheel Gap on the headwaters of the Rio Grande were quite different from the smaller green-backed cutthroats we found in the high-altitude lakes and mountain streams of the Arkansas watershed. These little fish were heavily spotted toward their tails, and had fewer spottings on their sides and shoulders. The fish we caught in the Gunnison and Frying Pan and Eagle watersheds were more heavily spotted over their entire bodies, and I can remember catching them in high lakes like Water Dog off Monarch Pass, and in the wilderness South Fork plateau north of the Colorado itself.

It is impossible to forget seeing them on that first trip to Hot Sulphur Springs, but it would be many years before I realized that they comprised a subspecies once found throughout the Colorado River country, from its headwaters in Rocky Mountain National Park to the forest-covered plateaus of northern Arizona and New Mexico. These boyhood cutthroats were small fish of the high country, seldom approaching a pound in weight, and I had always held a lukewarm opinion about the species.

Bob Carmichael taught me about cutthroats in Jackson Hole. It was not fishing for the brightly colored little natives of those first Colorado summers, but the big current-loving cutthroats in the Gros Ventre and the swift many-channeled Snake. It took me several years to work up enough courage to start a real conversation with Carmichael, who always sat like some magnificent bulldog near his mahogany chest of beautifully tied flies, glaring balefully at the summer people who came into the shop for snelled hooks and salmon eggs. When I finally expressed my disappointment over the lack of brown trout in the Teton country, and ventured a faintly negative opinion about cutthroat fishing, the old man glowered fiercely and cleared his throat.

Young man! he rumbled with failing patience. *When you know enough about this part of the country to have an opinion about the fishing—you'll know there's cutthroats and there's cutthroats!*

Carmichael was undeniably right. His strategy for my education sent me to the Gros Ventre first, describing two lower pools along the county road to Kelly, carefully diagramming their chalky ledges and emerald-colored holding places on the back of an envelope. Carmichael warned me that I would see many rises in the smooth middle currents of both pools, and in their spreading tail shallows, but that I should ignore them.

Whitefish! Carmichael snorted disdainfully. *You'll find the Gros Ventre cutthroats in the strongest currents, lying right in the throats of the pools!*

The cutthroats I've caught never behaved like that, I said. *Are these Wyoming fish a different species?*

Carmichael exploded in a rich gravelly laugh. *Bet your sweet ass!* he growled and shook his head testily. *These fish ain't no pantywaists—they're Jackson Hole cutthroats!*

They sure sound different, I said sheepishly.

Bet your sweet ass! he growled.

His description of the pools along the county road was accurate, even to the huge sandwich-bite notch in the ledges. The evening sun penetrated deep into the pools, highlighting their jade-green throats, and there was a hatch of dark little mayflies coming when I reached the tail shallows. The smooth currents were covered with rises, just as Carmichael had predicted, and I foolishly made the mistake of wasting time on them.

The fish worked steadily all along the current tongues, and when I finally hooked one it was a whitefish. *Forget your matching the hatch!* Carmichael always ragged me unmercifully. *Fish these big variants right in the rips—and you'll learn something about real cutthroat fishing!*

The swift riffles upstream shelved off deep and strong against the chalky bluffs and ledges across the river. Swallows worked among the hatching flies, and in the gathering twilight I thought I saw the splash of a feeding trout in the heaviest currents. It was impossible to get a dry-fly float over the trough where the fish seemed to be working, because the main current tongues would catch the line and drag the fly downstream. The only possible float was a cast directly upstream, with line and leader and fly all lying in the same current, and I crossed the tail of the pool to fish the ledge from below. The current was deceptively strong, and I crossed it warily, leaning heavily into its flow.

There was a quiet little run in the swift water, ebbing and then swelling up again, silky smooth in the rips. *There he is again!* I thought. *Rising with a quick little splash when the current comes smooth.*

The river worked and tumbled around my knees, and I shot a short cast into the twilight upstream. The dark little Donnelly Variant had scarcely reached the water when it disappeared in a porpoise roll.

He's on! I thought. *He's hooked!*

The cutthroat was surprisingly strong, boring straight up the throat of the main current. It gave a stubborn fight, hard and muscular in the heavy water, until finally the trout surrendered and circled weakly in the tail shallows. It slipped into the net, threshing heavily in the meshes until I released its sleek eighteen inches.

Two pounds! I thought aloud. *That's the biggest cutthroat you've ever caught—and they're really strong!*

Six casts later with a fresh variant, I soon hooked another big cutthroat, but this fight was different in character. I was crouched on the ledge itself now, since the pool was too deep for wading, and the fish bored past me, bulldogging so angrily along the bottom that it took me by surprise and actually wrenched the rod tip into the current as it passed.

It was a fish that I never saw in its entire five-minute fight. The cutthroat took the ninety feet of fly line in seconds, hung momentarily in the tail shallows, and then accelerated past me again into the heaviest currents in the throat of the pool. The bellying line ripped harshly upstream until its dragging weight sheared the tippet, and the cutthroat settled back into his sheltering currents with my fly.

Broke me like nothing, I explained the next day.

Thought you said cutthroats were pantywaists! Carmichael laughed raucously. *Weak sisters!*

You were right about these cutthroats! I admitted.

Bet your sweet ass, he cackled deep in his throat. *What size tippet you use last night on the Gros Ventre?*

Three-pound platyl. I shook my head.

Cobwebs! he scoffed. *You got to have more muscle for a big variant—and for these cutthroats of ours!*

You're right! I said ruefully.

It was my baptism on the big cutthroats still found in the watersheds of the Snake and the Yellowstone and the Salmon, the only large cutthroat fisheries that remain in a frontier that once teemed with the species. Colorful accounts of that period have come down to us from the frontier explorers, including a drawing of a cutthroat in the journals of George Meriwether Lewis.

Others also described the cutthroat trout they found in the mountains of our western frontier. John Colter first discovered and explored the Yellowstone country, which the frontiersmen soon called Colter's Hell, and the legendary Jim Bridger spun fantastic tales of its strange sights and the abundance of fish and game. Zebulon Pike and Captain Gunnison found other subspecies of cutthroats in their military expeditions into the Colorado mountains, and the ill-fated Reverend Meeker found them in the rivers and lakes above his frontier mission, before its citizens were all killed in a tragic massacre. Major Wesley Powell found native cutthroats in the cold little streams that tumble into the Grand Canyon from its Arizona rim, and Edward Ringwood Hewitt describes the frontier fishing in *Telling on the Trout*, with an account of his pack trip to the headwaters of the Yellowstone at the turn of the century.

Cutthroats are closely related to rainbows, and undoubtedly evolved from a common ancestral species. The original cutthroats were very likely isolated in their mountain refugia by receding primordial seas, melting glaciers and cataclysmic geological upthrustings. Further isolation within the mountain drainages themselves then produced the many subspecies that are in turn classified under *Salmo clarki*, the taxonomic umbrella used to define the entire cutthroat group today. However, the rainbow and the cutthroat remain so closely related that they often successfully mate in the wild state, producing a handsome hybrid trout that has plagued fisheries managers hoping to protect the undiluted native strains. Such hybrids are common in the Jackson Hole and Wind River country of western Wyoming and at Pyramid Lake in Nevada.

There are a surprising number of cutthroat subspecies. The primary cutthroat ecotype was first encountered and described by George Meriwether Lewis and William Clark during their famous expedition into the wilderness of the Louisiana Purchase in 1804. It was graphically depicted in their journals, drawn roughly but unmistakably on the diagonal, across two full pages. Its taxonomic classification is *Salmo clarki*, describing the classic species among the several cutthroat forms. It is found primarily in the Yellowstone country, and the east-flowing drainage systems of Montana, where Lewis and Clark first described it during their trek into the headwaters of the Missouri. The expedition crossed the Continental Divide in the Beaverhead country, where Sacajawea outfitted them with horses before they travelled high across Lost Trail Pass. The Bitterroot River was a natural highway north, since Sacajawea advised against trying the tumbling rapids of the Salmon, which led more directly west to the lower Snake canyon. Her tribe called it the River of No Return, and it remains a great cutthroat river in its swift wilderness reaches. Sacajawea led Lewis and Clark over the Bitterroot Range at Lolo Pass, using the ancient river trail broken by the Pacific tribes along the Clearwater, toward its junction with the mighty Snake below Hell's Canyon. Although Lewis and Clark failed to record the fact, the native cutthroats they encountered in the Columbia watershed below the Clearwater were the silvery subspecies later classified as *Salmo gibbsi*. It is still the principal cutthroat trout species found in the remote mountains of the wild-flowing Salmon.

Salmo clarki is a graceful trout with the small scales typically found in

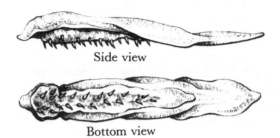

Side view

Bottom view

Cutthroat Vomerine Bone

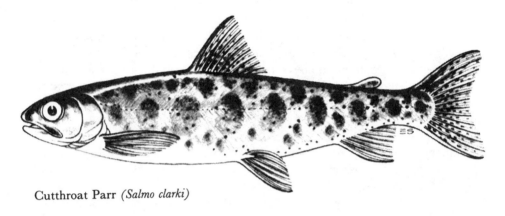

Cutthroat Parr *(Salmo clarki)*

cold-water species. Common scale counts among these cutthroats are from 140 to 270 in lateral series. There are 30 to 50 pyloric caeca. The bodies of these typical cutthroats are elongate and compressed, with relatively short and elegantly shaped heads. The maxillary does not reach far behind the eye. Teeth on the vomerine bone are set in an irregular zigzag series, and are also present on the hyoid bone, except in old specimens. Dorsal fins are relatively small, and the caudal fin is only slightly forked. There are ten dorsal rays and ten rays in the anal fin. Coloring is olivaceous and rather silvery, with the dorsal surfaces, sides and caudal peduncle heavily speckled with round spots. Some specimens exhibit spots on the heads, lateral surfaces, and even the belly. Heavy spotting on the dorsal, adipose, and caudal fins is prototypical. The lateral surfaces often display a diffuse roseate cast and this rose-colored flush is also common on the head and gill covers. The overall lateral coloring is pale yellowish, with silvery white undersurfaces. The inner edge of the mandible has a deep reddish blotch under the dentary bone, definitive of the entire cutthroat-related group of species and subspecies.

The principal cutthroat subspecies are widespread. Perhaps the best-known subspecies in the Snake and Columbia system is the unique cutthroat named *Salmo lewisi*, for George Meriwether Lewis. It is a subspecies isolated in these systems above the limits of natural rainbow habitats, a prime example of an ecotype created by some profound seismic event in prehistory. It was these Snake River cutthroats that Bob Carmichael fished and respected more than twenty years ago, when he taught me their secrets at Jackson Hole. Structurally, it is virtually identical to the Montana black-spotted trout found in the headwaters of the Missouri and the lower tributaries of the Yellowstone, although in its coloration it is delicately speckled over its body and caudal surfaces. The populations found in Yellowstone Lake are also *Salmo clarki*, along with riverine populations above its waterfall barriers downstream. Such taxonomic parallels may be the result of a common ancestor in comparatively recent times. Isolation of lakes like Flathead and Pend Oreille created major populations of the *Salmo alpestris* subspecies. Other populations are isolated in the Snake drainage basin above Idaho Falls. Its fins are orangey yellow, and the dorsal, adipose, and caudal appendages are olivaceous with heavy mottlings of fine speckles. These fine spottings are most dense on the caudal peduncle and tail. The gill covers are quite often rose-colored. The bodies are golden ochre with a silvery aquamarine cast, except during the mating season when the lower lateral surfaces are strongly flushed with orangey red. *Salmo lewisi* is a superb game fish that thrives on storied rivers like the Hoback, Grays, Teton, Bechler, Gros Ventre, Buffalo, and the huge many-channeled Snake itself.

There is another superb subspecies of cutthroat once native to the Rio Grande headwaters, although only trace populations survive in modern times. Its designation was *Salmo virginalis*, and its original range was the Rio Grande drainage system, including high-country rivers draining the Sierra de Madera Mountains in Sonora and Chihuahua. Typical scale counts number about 145 to 185 along the lateral line. The head configuration of this subspecies is distinctively its own. It is relatively short, its upper surfaces arched, and its shape perhaps more curved or rounded than any other species. The mouth is large, its maxillary reaching back well past the eye, and the vomerine teeth are found in two distinct series. There are 18 to 21 gillrakers and 25 to 50 pyloric caeca. The frontal posture of the dorsal fin is rather low, although relatively high in its last dorsal ray, which is often a full two-thirds of its anterior ray. The subspecies is remarkably square-tailed, its caudal rays virtually equal in length. The dorsal, lateral, and caudal surfaces are heavily spotted. Such markings are more heavily distributed on the caudal peduncle, as well as the adipose and caudal fins. Pale parrlike blotches distinguish the lateral surfaces, and the overall coloration is yellowish, with olive dorsal areas. Good populations still exist in Trinchera Creek in Colorado, the Rio Chiquito near Taos, and in Indian Creek on the Mescalero Apache Reservation near Alamogordo. Perhaps the best fishing for *Salmo virginalis* once existed in the swift headwaters of the Rio Grande, high in the San Juan Mountains at the mining camps of Creede and Wagon Wheel Gap.

Salmo gilae is another cutthroat-related species found in the 7,000-foot headwaters of the Gila in New Mexico. Its lateral scale-counts are 134 to 168, and there are typically 23 to 42 pyloric caeca. Some biologists argue that the Gila trout is a fully separate species, and its separation from the closely-related Rio Grande forms into the west-flowing Gila may be relatively recent in geological terms. Gila trout are small red-striped fish of the cold high-altitude streams in the Elk and Mongollon mountains of southern New Mexico, less than one hundred miles above the Mexican border. It has been a protected species in recent years.

Salmo apache is a similar but fully separate cutthroatlike trout isolated in the headwaters of the Salt in Arizona. It displays lateral scales totalling 140 to 175, and there are 22 to 40 pyloric caeca. Fine populations exist in the White River Apache Reservation, but these unique trout are threatened by lumbering operations.

The sprawling basin of the Colorado River also evolved its own subspecies of cutthroat, the strongly spotted *Salmo pleuriticus*, originally found from the western slope streams of Rocky Mountain National Park to the native cutthroats of the San Juan in Colorado, northern Arizona, and northwestern New Mexico. These fish are quite similar in morphological terms to the typical *Salmo clarki* specimens, although their body scales are relatively small. Scale counts in specimens taken from high-altitude lakes range from 175 to more than 200 along the lateral line, and there are 30 to 40 pyloric caeca. Although the spots are relatively large, they are gathered primarily along the posterior lateral and dorsal surfaces, with the cranial zone almost free of such markings. The pectoral, ventral, and anal fins are typically bright reddish orange, although environmental isolation can vary coloring extensively. General coloring of the lateral surfaces is often strongly golden or ochreous, sometimes with a faint reddish lateral band and gill opercle. The jaw markings of scarlet are present. These handsome fish were once the indigenous species of Colorado rivers like the Fraser, White, Yampa, Gunnison, Roaring Fork, Crystal, Frying Pan, Eagle, Lake Fork, Taylor, and the swift-flowing Colorado itself. The species was also found in many east-flowing tributaries of the Green from the Uinta Mountains to the Dirty Devil watershed in Utah. Trapper's Lake in Colorado and its White River drainage system once held remarkable lacustrine populations of *Salmo pleuriticus*. They have disappeared from all but the headwaters and the high-country lakes that gather and hold the snowmelt in their watersheds. Perhaps the best riverine populations survive in the Rocky Mountain sources of the Colorado itself, the Frying Pan headwaters in Colorado, and the tumbling South Fork of the White, which drops down from the wilderness Colorado plateau above Meeker.

Colorado and Wyoming share another principal subspecies of cutthroat trout. It is the little green-backed cutthroat classified as *Salmo stomias*, and was originally described from specimens taken in the headwaters of the Arkansas above Leadville, high in the Colorado mountains. It was also found in the upper reaches of the Platte, both in its South Park country around Fairplay and in its North Park headwaters in Wyoming and Colorado. The distribution of *Salmo stomias* in both the North and South Platte watersheds may have been the result of common marine ancestors found east of the present Rocky Mountain system, perhaps as early as Miocene times. *Salmo stomias* is no longer abundant, since mining, irrigation programs, and lumbering have irreparably damaged its original range. The subspecies was already virtually extinct in the Leadville country during my boyhood years, although we caught them occasionally in the high-country streams and lakes on Mount Massive, and the best specimens rarely exceeded a pound. Their mouth structure is relatively small, scale counts range from 185 to 215, and there are 59 to 62 pyloric caeca. Its scales are much finer than the other cutthroat types. Its dark spots are typically larger than those found on related subspecies, and are heavily concentrated on the caudal peduncle. The sole remaining fisheries of *Salmo stomias* are probably the few unstocked high-altitude lakes remaining in the Collegiate and Mosquito ranges in Colorado, or perhaps in the back country west of the Encampment in Wyoming. The thermal pollution resulting from irrigation, lumbering, and the mine-tailing wastes have forever ended the reign of these elegant little green-backed cutthroats over most of their original riverine systems, although federal biologists have located some relatively pure populations in the headwaters of the Big Thompson and the Cache la Poudre in northeastern Colorado.

Salmo macdonaldi was a unique lake-bred subspecies of cutthroat known as the Colorado yellow-finned trout, and was endemic only to the Twin Lakes in Colorado. It was a unique lacustrine cutthroat, and spawned in the principal tributary of the two lakes, the swift little Clear Creek that tumbles down from Mount Harvard and Independence Pass. *Salmo macdonaldi* apparently coexisted with the green-backed cutthroat *Salmo stomias* in the Twin Lakes, but grew to much larger average sizes. Its taxonomic description included the twelve dorsal-fin rays, and eleven rays in the anal fin. Typical scale counts averaged about 185. The cranial structure was long and moderately snoutlike and pointed. Its mouth was relatively large, with a maxillary projecting well behind the eye. Hyoid teeth were unmistakably present. The general coloring was a pale olive, with a somewhat lemon cast on the lower lateral surfaces. The pectoral, anal, and ventral fins were golden yellow. No reddish highlights were present, except for the typical cutthroat slashes on the jaw membranes. The head, as well as the anterior dorsal and lateral surfaces, was virtually free of spotting. Fine dark spots covered the posterior body areas, especially concentrated at the caudal peduncle, and the dorsal, adipose, and caudal fins were profusely spotted as well. David Starr Jordan and Barton Evermann first described the subspecies in 1896, including it in their monumental four-volume *Fishes of North and Middle America*. The following quotation in their popular *American Food and Game Fishes*, is eloquent testimony to a departed species:

> This interesting and beautiful trout is known only from Twin Lakes, Colorado, where it occurs in company with the green-back trout. The two are entirely distinct, their size, coloration and habits being notably different.

The yellow-fin reaches a weight of eight or nine pounds while the other rarely exceeds a pound. The former lives on a gravel bottom in water of some depth, while the latter is a shallow-water trout running into small brooks. As a game-fish the yellow-fin trout has attracted much attention from local anglers by whom it is highly regarded. It is taken chiefly by trolling, though it rises promptly to the fly and is a splendid fighter.

Two brief paragraphs are virtually all that remains of this apparently superb cutthroat subspecies. Lumbering for the mines and the charcoal kilns that fired the Leadville smelters, clearing the forests on Mount Harvard, Mount Elbert, and Independence Pass began the damage to its thermal environment. Twin Lakes were deepened and their ecology further altered when the natural outlet was dammed and elevated with earthworks and a spillway. The diversion tunnel through the Continental Divide transferred Roaring Fork water to the eastern-slope tributary of the Twin Lakes, and changed both the temperatures and seasonal flow in Clear Creek, making spawning virtually impossible. Finally, fisheries biologists eager to experiment with exotic species introduced brook trout into the Clear Creek headwaters, and the predatory *Salvelinus* lake trout into Twin Lakes themselves. The result of these manmade factors over the past century has been the extinction of *Salmo macdonaldi*.

Utah has its own cutthroat subspecies found in the relict populations that date back into the prehistory of western Utah, when shrinking seas became the vast Lake Bonneville. The remaining Great Salt Lake is the modern echo of those Pleistocene times, along with the little *Salmo utah*, which originally was found in all suitable streams draining into the ancient Bonneville Basin. There were also large lacustrine strains once indigenous to Lake Utah at Provo. *Salmo utah* is a profusely and finely spotted cutthroat, its speckled markings distributed rather evenly across its dorsal and lateral surfaces. Its 145 to 180 scales along the lateral line attest to a slightly warmer biosystem at somewhat lower altitudes, and there are 35 to 55 pyloric caeca. The dorsal fin has ten rays, while there are eleven in the anal. Its coloring is olivaceous, with orangey yellow pectoral, ventral, and anal fins. Richly alkaline waters, like Utah Lake, from which it was originally described, produce relatively pale color variations of this subspecies. Such specimens have only a few tiny spots on their dorsal surfaces. In such food-rich environments, specimens of *Salmo utah* often attained weights of eight to ten pounds. Fish biologists have unfortunately contaminated the native cutthroats in the Bonneville Basin with hatchery stocks from the Strawberry River in eastern Utah, which were *Salmo pleuriticus* mixed with introduced rainbows, and it is doubtful if undiluted populations of *Salmo utah* still exist. Perhaps future research parties will discover relict habitats in remote, desiccating watersheds once draining into Lake Bonneville.

The vast Columbia and Snake River drainage system originally sheltered several subspecies of cutthroat. The first is *Salmo lewisi*, which is isolated in several watersheds between Shoshone Falls and the Idaho and Wyoming headwaters of the Snake. The second, the subspecies *Salmo alpestris*, is found in the Columbia and its principal cold-water tributaries like the Clark Fork and the Clearwater. In the wild canyon of the Salmon and in the Columbia above the Cascades, there is the third important subspecies, classified as *Salmo gibbsi*. It was once also common in the Deschutes and Payette watercourses in Oregon and Idaho. The fourth subspecies was indigenous only to Waha Lake in Idaho, the delicate little cutthroat *Salmo bouvieri* that is now tragically extinct, like the unique *Salmo eremogenes* once found on Crab Creek in Washington.

The handsome Snake River cutthroat classified as *Salmo lewisi* is one of the best game-fish species anywhere. It seeks the swiftest current tongues in the cold, remarkably clear headwaters and tributaries of the Snake. It has 140 to 200 lateral scales and 30 to 50 pyloric caeca. Its range was once limited to the Snake watershed above Shoshone Falls in southern Idaho, but it has been even further reduced by the construction of several large reservoirs between Twin Falls and the Palisades Dam on the Wyoming line. It has fallen back from the impact of civilization until its most important refuges are in Jackson Hole and major tributaries of the Henry's Fork of the Snake. Populations on the remote Darwin Ranch headwaters of the Gros Ventre, the chalkstreamlike Teton, Flat Creek and Spring Creek in Jackson Hole, Henry's Lake, the remote Bechler in the southwest corner of the Yellowstone, and the swift-running Snake itself still offer exceptional sport, and are among the best cutthroat fisheries left.

Salmo gibbsi is a similar cutthroat subspecies originally found below the impassable Shoshone Falls on the Snake. It is somewhat silvery when compared with the Snake River strains upstream. It has average scale counts of 140 to 150 along the lateral line. The ten-rayed dorsal fin and eleven anal rays are typical of the entire cutthroat group. The specimens average forty-odd pyloric caeca. The fish are olive gray on their dorsal surfaces and silvery, with a faint roseate cast, on their lateral areas. Some specimens display a thin wash of lemon yellow on the upper belly between the pectoral and caudal fins. The spots are moderately large and irregularly shaped. Spotting patterns are most dense at the caudal peduncle, and relatively few spots appear below the lateral line between the gill covers and the ventral fins. The dorsal, adipose, and caudal fins are dark olive gray and rather densely spotted. Pectoral, ventral, and anal fins are grayish orange. The gill covers sometimes display a roseate cast, and the two typical cutthroat slashes under the jaw are reddish orange. It is no longer found in the Deschutes, Snake, Payette, Clearwater, or the mighty Columbia itself in any significant numbers, although the wilderness reaches of the Salmon— the ominous River of No Return that Sacajawea avoided in leading the Lewis and Clark expedition westward—have thriving populations of *Salmo gibbsi* and still offer some of the best cutthroat fishing in the entire Pacific drainage.

Waha trout were found only in the glacier-cold waters of Waha Lake in northern Idaho, and have been designated *Salmo bouvieri* in the taxonomic tables. This diminutive subspecies had ten dorsal rays and eleven rays in its anal fin, like the more common cutthroats. Its cold high-altitude environment is evident in its scale counts of between 170 and 180 along the lateral line. Coloring was darkly olivaceous on the dorsal areas, washed with golden yellowish on the lateral surfaces. Fine dark spots are found on the dorsal, adipose, and caudal fins, while relatively large spots on the lateral surfaces are typically confined to the upper caudal peduncle. The red throat markings are conspicuous. The head is shorter and more blunt than in other cutthroats, with a round snout and maxillary extending only a short distance behind the surprisingly large eyes. The caudal fin is relatively forked, and specimens average some six to seven inches in length.

The California mountains evolved several other cutthroat subspecies. These species are the Tahoe cutthroat designated *Salmo tahoensis*, the rare and endangered little Paiute trout found in a single watershed of the eastern Sierra Nevada, and the more widely distributed *Salmo henshawi* found in the several watersheds draining into the primordial basin of the vast Lahontan Lake, the remnant of inland seas dating back into Pleistocene times.

Salmo tahoensis is endemic to beautiful Lake Tahoe on the eastern slopes of the Sierra Nevada Mountains in California. Its environment is uniquely clear and cold, lying more than 6,000 feet above the arid valleys that were once the immense reaches of Lake Lahontan. Both Tahoe and its cutthroat subspecies were first encountered by John Charles Fremont and a party that included the frontiersman Kit Carson in 1844. The dorsal fin of *Salmo tahoensis* has nine rays and its anal fin has twelve, according to Jordan and Evermann. Scale counts above two hundred are typical and reflect the cold temperatures of its biosystem. Larger specimens are muscular and robust. The mouth structure is large, its maxillary extending well beyond the eyes. The caudal fins are rather lunate and semicircular, almost fully truncated when spread. The dorsal surfaces are dark and olive-colored. The lower lateral areas are silvery, with a faint yellowish cast, and both the flanks and gill covers are coppery orange in color. The membranes of the lower jaw are yellowish. The orangey jaw markings are not as conspicuous as with other cutthroat subspecies. The dorsal surfaces are heavily mottled with large spots, from the head to the caudal fin. Spotting is heavier and rather variegated toward the caudal peduncle and adipose fin. The bellies of typical specimens are heavily speckled with fine spottings, and some display even more delicate spotting on the lower jaw. The dorsal, adipose, and caudal fins are heavily mottled, with fine oblong markings. Pectoral and ventral fins are spotted too, with a few delicate markings at the root of the first rays. The anal fin is mottled with rather numerous round spots. *Salmo tahoensis* was considered a superb game fish for a century, but it is doubtful if any genetically pure strains still exist.

Salmo seleniris is the taxonomic designation for the rare little Paiute trout, considered by some fisheries biologists as a singular subspecies lying somewhere between the golden trout of the Kern River country farther south, the Oregon red-banded trout of desiccating basins farther north, and the cutthroat subspecies indigenous to the ancient Lahontan Basin. *Salmo seleniris* is native only in the headwaters of the Silver King Valley on the eastern slopes of the Sierra Nevada. Some specimens have been transplanted to streams closer to Lake Tahoe, although it is doubtful if their genetic integrity has survived. Paiute trout seldom reach more than a half pound in weight. Their dorsal fins have the ten-ray structure typical of cutthroats, and eleven rays in their anal fins. Body configuration is relatively slender, with delicate fins and a strongly forked tail structure. Their heads are less rounded than most cutthroat ecotypes, and the slender caudal peduncle and fin are somewhat like those of a small salmon. The heads are surprisingly snoutlike for such small fish, with relatively large mouth parts and a delicate maxillary extending well behind the eyes. Coloring is striking, almost as brilliant as the better-known golden trout originally found in the Pacific watersheds of the Sierras. Dorsal surfaces are brownish olive with some spotting, although more noticeable are the blurred parrlike markings on the upper lateral areas. The dorsal, adipose, and caudal fins are only faintly spotted. The upper edge of the tail structure is marked with five to seven oblong spots, lying parallel to its rays. Two large round spots lie on either side of the lateral line at the root of the tail, although the dorsal surfaces and sides completely lack spotting. Ten dark brownish parr markings lie along the lateral, which is strongly flushed with rosy orange. The lower lateral surfaces are bright yellow, and the pectoral, ventral, and anal fins are orangey. The gill covers are marked with rosy orange, and the jaw membranes are flushed with scarlet orange. Like the Apache and Gila trout of Arizona and New Mexico, the brightly colored little Paiute trout is a distinct species, and deserves our care and protection throughout its limited range in the future.

Salmo henshawi is the remarkable cutthroat subspecies prototypical of the rivers and lakes in the ancient Lahontan Basin, a vast marine environment whose saline waters once spread over thousands of square miles along the eastern slope of the Sierra Nevada escarpment in California, Oregon and Nevada. The subspecies is indigenous to a large number of lakes and streams that remain from the Pleistocene watersheds, and it originally included both the riverine Lahontan and lacustrine Pyramid strains. The lacustrine populations are remarkably piscivorous, feeding heavily on coarse baitfish species in preference to insect life. Such behavior is perhaps closely tied to their marine origins. The dorsal fin of *Salmo henshawi* has eleven rays, with twelve in the anal fin. Scale counts along the lateral line vary from 160 to 185, with Tahoe specimens running about 170 scales in longitudinal series. Pyloric caeca typically average 43 and mature specimens exhibit four to six more gillrakers than other cutthroat types. The maxillary reaches about halfway behind the eye, and the vomerine teeth are set in a zigzag pattern. Teeth typical of cutthroats are present on the hyoid bone. The caudal peduncle is relatively slender and the caudal fin is strongly forked. The inner edge of the mandible exhibits the roseate slash typical of the cutthroat group. Colors vary somewhat through the range of *Salmo henshawi*, from the dark silvery olive of specimens from mountainous Lake Tahoe to the pale green cutthroats from the saline waters of Pyramid Lake in the arid Nevada foothills. The lateral surfaces of these Lahontan trout from Pyramid are rather silvery, with a pronounced coppery overtone. The dorsal zone is rather evenly spotted from head to tail. Lateral spotting is relatively sparse. Fine round speckling is sometimes found on the belly. Spots on the head are generally large and dark, with some spotting evident on the snout and lower jaw. Both dorsal and caudal fins are spotted, and the adipose fin is small and dark olive. The anal fin typically displays a few large spots. *Salmo henshawi* is an interesting subspecies, and its original range included such major rivers as the Truckee, Carson, Walker and Humboldt in Nevada, and Lahontan Basin lakes such as Tahoe, Pyramid, Walker, Heenan and Independence.

The lacustrine populations once found at Pyramid Lake were unique, since their habitat was apparently an unglaciated sanctuary in Pleistocene times. Their spawning runs entered the Truckee watershed, the only available tributary for reproduction, and irrigation systems closed this river and reduced its flow about thirty-five years ago. The original Pyramid strains of *Salmo henshawi* have been lost forever, and although reasonably pure Lahontan trout have been reintroduced from Heenan Lake in California, their maximum growth is about half that of the remarkable Pyramid cutthroats that existed in frontier times. The average weight of two hundred specimens collected during the last spawning run in 1938 was more than twenty pounds, and these fish were probably the largest of our freshwater trouts of the *Salmo* genus. Since ichthyologists believe that Independence Lake in California holds our finest surviving population of purely lacustrine cutthroats, we must ban all future introductions of other put-and-take hatchery fish. The world-record cutthroat was a fish of this subspecies taken from Pyramid Lake by John Skimmerhorn in 1925. It weighed forty-one pounds.

Modern taxonomists seem certain that several cutthroat ecotypes found in the desiccating lacustrine basins of Utah, Oregon and Nevada will ultimately be designated as fully separate species. The Moriah cutthroat is indigenous to a few small high-country streams in Utah and eastern Nevada and is apparently a relict subspecies of the Bonneville type. The Oregon red-banded trout is also cutthroatlike, although its morphology bears surprising relationships to both rainbow and golden trout taxonomy. It is found in several headwater streams draining into the desiccating basin between Goose Lake in northern California and the Silvies watershed in the Malheur Basin of southern Oregon. The Alvord cutthroat is found in two small tributaries of the Owyhee in the Alvord Desert basin of Oregon, and its survival is precarious, both because of marginal water temperatures and overgrazing. The Humboldt cutthroat is a riverine species closely related to other Lahontan populations, although it has fewer scales and gillrakers. These remarkable cutthroatlike trouts were rare and endangered, like the Gila and Apache trouts farther south, almost before their identity as separate species was known to ichthyologists—it would be tragic if they were eradicated and lost before taxonomists could award the fish their Latin names.

Like their closely related rainbow cousins, cutthroat trout are spring spawners. Since they are primarily a species from the icy biosystems of high altitudes, the precise spawning time can vary widely over their full range of distribution.

Spawning typically occurs in the snowmelt currents of late winter and early spring. Egg laying can occur in surprisingly shallow water, and can sometimes occur as late as May and June. Once I spent several hours watching late-spawning *Salmo lewisi* cutthroats on Blacktail Spring Creek in the river bottoms of Jackson Hole. Two spawning fish had constructed their redds in unusually shallow water, in a musical little run only inches deep. Both trout were twenty-odd inches, and their dorsal fins were frequently out of the water. Their mating dance was beautiful in its erratic rhythms, with the female rolling to shape her nest, while the cockfish drifted close or dropped back into slightly deeper water. Two twelve-inch males hovered nearby, but every time either attempted to approach the nest, the bigger cockfish quickly routed them.

Optimal cutthroat spawning currents are similar to the preferences of the rainbow, and measure ten to twenty inches per second. Cutthroats typically prefer small tributaries for their spawning, although some subspecies chose surprisingly large rivers for their mating grounds. The spawning outlet of Yellowstone Lake is an example of such riverine spawning behavior in a unique biosystem, and hundreds of thousands of cutthroats oviposit their eggs in its pale gravel each spring. Riverine spawning also characterized the original Pyramid Lake species. Fisheries researchers have also observed viable egg laying in the downwind gravelly shallows of high-altitude cutthroat lakes, where the constant winds cause sufficient wave action to oxygenate the fertile eggs. The outlet flowages and swift inlet shallows of such high cutthroat lakes are alive with cutthroats in spawning time, their currents flashing reddish gold with the fish.

Between skirmishes with lesser cutthroat males, the cockfish excites his mate with body pressures and his hook-jawed spawning kypes. Such body movements involve sliding alongside the female and making shuddering vibrations as spawning approaches its climax. Cutthroat males sometimes force the females deep into the redds. Oviposition itself soon follows, but the eggs are shrouded in a milky flood of sperm.

Like their rainbow cousins, the cutthroat henfish immediately slide upstream over the rim of the nest, and begin writhing their bodies to displace more gravel. The specific gravity of the ova is heavier than water, sinking them deep into the gravelly bed of the redds. Their gelatinous covering adheres to the polished stones. Its stickiness quickly congeals in the cold water, seating the eggs firmly against the bottom until the writhing female successfully covers them with fresh gravel. These stones are displaced from the beginnings of a second redd. The currents carry a tumbling little stream of stones and pea-size gravel and pebbles, completely covering the first eggs with a gentle mound. Several more hours are typically required for the smaller cutthroats to construct a nest and complete oviposition, and like the closely related rainbows, cutthroats spawn both day and night once mating has started. Cutthroat males are like other trout in the sense that they do not participate in covering the eggs, but ward off predators eager to gorge themselves on the freshly expelled ova.

Unfortunately, the late Paul Needham failed to include stomach autopsies of *Salmo clarki* and its related subspecies in his studies, and there are no data to compare with my own later work on cutthroat diet forms. The sixty-two specimens I used ranged from half-pounders of the *Salmo pleuriticus* type caught high in the headwaters and tributaries of the Frying Pan in Colorado to the trophy-size cutthroats of the Snake and the Yellowstone and the Middle Fork of the Salmon. There were many from such rich waters as Slough Creek in the Yellowstone, the weedy channels of Henry's Lake in Idaho, and the several spring creeks and sloughs found in Jackson Hole. These are food systems rich in tiny crustaceans, and their contribution to these cutthroat-feeding data is obvious:

TYPE	TOTALS	PERCENT
Caddisflies	2,101	27.0
Two-winged flies	1,172	10.5
Crustaceans	1,037	10.0
Beetles	983	9.5
Mayflies	977	9.4
Leafhoppers	865	7.2
Ants, bees, and wasps	849	7.2
Grasshoppers	748	6.2
Stoneflies	742	6.0
Salamanders and baitfish	311	3.2
Snails and slugs	178	1.3
True bugs	83	0.7
Earthworms	81	0.7
Springtails	46	0.3
Miscellaneous	101	0.8
Totals	10,274	100.0

These are interesting figures, considering their preoccupation with caddis forms, two-winged larvae and pupae, crustaceans, and beetle larvae.

These are typical of most high-altitude lakes, and the alkaline spring creeks and runs that support major cutthroat populations. Mayflies and stoneflies are scarcely more important in these data than terrestrial insects like ants and grasshoppers and jassids. These figures are perhaps explained by the grassy bottoms along Flat Creek, Slough Creek, Fish Creek, and the several Teton country spring creeks where many of these fish were caught, and it would be interesting to compare their diet with the more piscivorous Lahontan strains.

There is a considerable range in size and distribution among the many subspecies of cutthroats. Average fish at high altitude may run only five or six inches, from the mountains of northern Mexico to the alpine tributaries of Alaskan rivers. Cutthroats are extremely popular trout in Alaska, British Columbia, and the Pacific Northwest, and in those waters they can commonly attain four to six pounds. There are also sea-run cutthroats distributed along the Pacific Coast from northern California to Prince William Sound in Alaska and these are typically the school fish of one to four pounds that are popularly called harvest trout.

Cutthroats are gaining in favor now that the prejudices of the postfrontier days have died out, and a fresh concern for this rare frontier species has emerged. The fighting qualities of the species are worthy, although its strategies are stubborn and strong, usually fought deep along the bottom. Sometimes a hooked cutthroat jumps, particularly a fish sea-armored with estuarine feeding, but it is true that most lack the wild, cartwheeling acrobatics of the rainbow.

Cutthroats are similar to the brook trout in their need for cold waters almost completely free of pollution, and in their preference for solitude. Originally they were native everywhere in our western mountains from huge rivers like the Columbia and the Snake to remote glacial lakes and beaver ponds between ten and twelve thousand feet high.

Although they once filled our rivers and thrived in unnumbered populations, cutthroats have proven relatively fragile under artificial breeding. The strains were difficult to handle in the hatcheries until more durable hybrids were developed by fisheries experts. However, such hybrids unfortunately lost many qualities endemic to the original subspecies and genotypes. Stocking cutthroats takes place from both federal and state rearing stations, particularly in Teton National Park, although handling them in hatcheries is more difficult than handling rainbows.

Except for the cutthroats in brawling rivers like the Snake and Gros Ventre and Salmon, and in the wilderness rapids deep in the Yellowstone Canyon, most specimens of *Salmo clarki* and its related subspecies have a quiet disposition. Typical cutthroats display behavior rather more like the brook trout than their cousins the rainbows. Cutthroats are commonly found in holding lies similar to those chosen by *Salvelinus fontinalis*—under deadfalls and snags and undercut banks in relatively quiet current tongues. Their fatal curiosity about spinners and wobblers and spoons is also found in the brook trout. Like brook trout, cutthroats will also respond readily to the dry-fly method, but most are probably taken on wet flies and nymphs. Cutthroats are often easily fooled into taking gaudy patterns that no self-respecting rainbow or brown trout would favor. *Salvelinus fontinalis* is also fond of bright colors and tinsel, and these traits have combined with that susceptibility to polished and flashing lures to decimate both species. Perhaps the most singular parallel with the brook trout is a love of brackish estuaries. Cutthroat trout with access to salty coastal waters use these shallow feeding grounds extensively. Brook trout still exhibit similar behavior from Long Island to the subarctic latitudes of the Labrador.

Throughout its entire range of distribution, the cutthroat drops down from its parent rivers into coastal and estuarine waters, returning later to these rivers to spawn. Like the steelheads of most rivers, sea-run cutthroats remain in coastal waters, but unlike their ocean-going rainbow cousins, cutthroats seldom venture outside the brackish tidal zones of their own rivers. Sea-run cutthroats grow quickly in the salt water, but they seldom remain there long. Steelheads are not commonly caught at sea, but these estuarine cutthroats are often caught along the rivermouth beaches in the spring, and the best times match the shifting tides. These particular cutthroats are superb fish, silvery and sea-tempered like the salt-water rainbows, powerful with the rich diet of their feeding grounds.

Sea-run cutthroats begin gathering in the tidal reaches of their parent rivers in midsummer, often mingling with the first coho salmon. Cutthroats keep returning in ever-increasing numbers as the summer wanes, and anglers on the Pacific coastal rivers call these later runs harvest trout—the harvest season is followed by the autumn rains and the arrival of these fish in silvery phalanx.

J. R. Dymond has written perhaps the best monograph on these harvest cutthroats in *The Trout and Other Game Fishes of British Columbia*, which appeared in 1932. Roderick Haig-Brown has written extensively about these harvest cutthroats too, like these lines from his poetic book *A River Never Sleeps*, which describe a December afternoon along his home river:

> I fish the Campbell with a sense of ownership fully as strong as that of any legitimate owner of fishing rights in the world, not because I do own any part of the river, nor even because I should like to, or should like to keep other people away from it; I should not care to do either of these things. The sense of ownership comes with knowing the river.
>
> I know the easiest ways along its banks and the best ways down to the pools. I know where to start in at a pool, where to look for the fish in it, how and where I can wade, what point I can reach with an easy cast, what lie I can barely cover with my strongest effort.
>
> This is comfortable and pleasant, and might well begin to seem monotonous sooner or later, were it not something of an

illusion. I have a fair idea of what to expect from the river, and usually, because I fish it that way, the river gives me approximately what I expect of it.

But sooner or later, something always comes up to change the set of my ways. Perhaps one day, waiting for a friend to fish down a pool, I start in a little farther up than usual and immediately hook a fish where I had never been able to hook one before. A little more of the river becomes mine, alive and productive to me. Or perhaps I notice in some unusual slant of light what looks to be a glide of water along the edge of a rapid; I go down to it and work my fly through, and whether or not a fish comes to it, more of the river has become known and is mine.

For years I have promised myself to fish through the sort of half pool below the Sandy Pool. It starts almost opposite my own Line Fence and is little more than a smoothing off of the long rapid that runs right down to the highway bridge; but there are many big rocks in it and—I can say this now—some obvious holding-water. I fished it twice this spring. On the first evening, I caught two or three fair-sized cutthroats and once a really good fish broke water at the fly. I went down earlier the second evening. A three-pound cutthroat came to my first cast. There was a slow silver gleam as the fly came around on the second cast, a solid heavy pull and the 2x gut was broken. I hooked two others along the pool that evening, and the pool is the Line Fence Pool now, something so close to home and so obvious that I took ten years to learn it.

Since *Matching the Hatch* and those boyhood cutthroat years on the high-country waters of Colorado, there have been many opportunities to correct my early ignorance of *Salmo clarki* and its phalanx of subspecies. There have been big cutthroats on the weedy chalkstream currents of the Tetons and the shrimp-rich shallows of Henry's Lake in Idaho, along with the gullible wilderness cutthroats in the wild rips of the Salmon and the Grand Canyon of the Yellowstone. Big cutthroats cruise in schools along the serpentine meadow bends of the Slough Creek headwaters, and the wild little Bechler in Yellowstone Park, and in the tule-lined bottoms of Flat Creek in Jackson Hole. There are many big cutthroats in several watercress spring creeks in Jackson Hole, and in the jade-green pools of the Gros Ventre, and there have been many good fish along the many-channelled Snake itself.

My best cutthroat for many years has been an eight-pound Jackson Hole fish I took on a fat Carpenter ant imitation during the early mating swarms along Blacktail Spring Creek. Jim Rikhoff and John Dear were fishing its marshy flats with me, and we marvelled at its sleek heavily spotted length in the gathering twilight, with the Tetons silhouetted against a dying sun.

Sometimes our most pervasive memories are not of the biggest fish or the most spectacular landscapes. My most persistent recollection of cutthroat fishing had the Yellowstone as its setting, and perhaps there is a fitting poetry in that fact. The finest cutthroat fishing in the world is still probably in the Yellowstone in its protected headwaters. The Yellowstone has its origins in the immense clear-water lake that lies near the center of Yellowstone Park, its amphitheatre of forests and mountains pale and smoke-colored across the water. Boiling springs bubble and steam along its rocky shoreline. Thick growths of bulrushes line its weedy bays and inlets. Dense forests of spruce and lodgepole pine and ponderosa surround its shoreline, their pewter-colored deadfalls bleached and slowly rotting in huge jackstraw tangles along its gravelly shallows. Gulls and gregarious pelicans and fish eagles work the outlet of the lake, where its flow gathers and slides into the huge cutthroat flats that lie for miles downstream.

It is a carefully protected reach of water, since both the *Salmo clarki* cutthroats and a colony of rare trumpeter swans use it for their nesting grounds. It is closed to fishing in spring and early summer. It is virtually impossible fishing during the summer vacation months. The famous timber trusswork bridge spans the outlet of the lake, and it is thronged with tourists like a party boat chartered off Galveston or Perth Amboy or Sausalito. The cutthroats have always been there, some dutifully surrendering to the flailing lures and salmon eggs and cheese, but most have reached the final stages of sophistication described a half century ago by George Edward MacKenzie Skues—trout that are at first frightened by awkward fishermen, coming ultimately to ignore their clumsiness, and then feeding as though such alien creatures did not exist.

It is like that on the headwaters of the Yellowstone. There are huge flats below the communal regiments that line the Fishing Bridge. These silken flats look more like extensions of the lake instead of the genesis of a major river. Giant layers of weeds undulate in the still currents. Swans and pale egrets and herons frequent the river, and the fisherman must compete with the odd, solitary buffalo or cantankerous moose rooting out milfoil and spatterdock in the shallows.

Fly hatches are almost constant there. Millions of midge pupae drift on its gathering currents and flats, born in the inexhaustible volcanic-marl fertility of Yellowstone Lake. There are stillwater Trichoptera riding the upstream wind at twilight, and thousands of tiny mayflies emerge in vast regattas of delicate little duns. Scuds and shrimps inhabit the dense beds of weeds, along with the slender damselflies and predatory *Odonata* and aquatic beetle larvae. But the most dramatic rises of fish are perhaps triggered by the big swimming mayflies that emerge in late summer, with a crescendo of big, fluttering *Siphlonurus* drakes in September.

Fly life on the river is so incalculably rich that fish are almost always rising in those great flats below Fishing Bridge, and it is probably the most prolific cutthroat fishery left since the decimation that has followed frontier times. Its character survives because of its calm meadow currents and the selective feeding they cause, and because of the strict regulations and careful husbandry of Yellowstone Park.

It has been twenty years since I took the cutthroat there, during a hatch of big *Siphlonurus* drakes, and I have never forgotten the look of the current carpeted with fluttering mayflies or the greedy rise forms of the feeding fish. It was a cold mist-shrouded morning in September. The preceding night I had argued with a hungry bear, its ulcers protesting the sudden absence of schoolchildren and their cornucopias of popcorn and candy bars. It had been attracted to the cooking smells of my cutthroat chowder at the Tower Falls campground, and I spent an uncomfortable night in the car, listening to it fumbling and rooting around in my aluminum pots. It was a nerve-wracking and sleepless night, particularly since the car was a canvas-topped convertible.

It was misting rain at daylight, and I was exhausted. I was so tired that I finally stopped a few miles upstream above the Buffalo Ford for a late-morning nap. Although it was raining harder, sleep came quickly without bears beating out percussive rhythms on my kettles. Sometimes we can sleep through thunderstorms and fire engines, but sometimes we waken to surprisingly delicate sounds. Rain squalls drummed intermittently on the canvas top and the windshield, half wakening me when they started, and each time I had sleepily dozed off again, but now there was another sound.

Fish! I thought groggily. *It's rising fish!*

There were a dozen big fish working just below the car. They were cutthroats of three to five pounds, porpoising and rolling to the hatch, and I waded into position carefully. Several big grayish nymphs were in my fly books, and I selected one that matched the size of the hatching flies. The third cast hooked a heavy cutthroat that bored angrily past me, slicing the leader audibly across the deepening current. It sullenly stripped yards of line from the reel, threatening to eat deep into the backing, and I turned awkwardly to follow.

It was a slow-footed mistake. There are lava outcroppings in the deceptively smooth Yellowstone bottom that are icy-slick with algae in the coarse gravel, and as I turned to follow the angry cutthroat, my left brogue slipped sickeningly.

One desperate moment hung suspended while I almost recovered my balance, and then the current caught me and I was down. It was bone-chillingly cold and strong. The river forced me into deeper water, and I was carried ponderously downstream. It was too deep to wade and there is no point in fighting a river since it holds all the cards. Its currents are too strong for swimming and I simply rode the current, touching bottom now and then to keep balance and my head above water.

Stay with it, I thought. *Just stay with it!*

Finally my wading brogues touched bottom again and held, and I wrestled my way clumsily ashore. My sodden clothing hung heavily on my body, and my muscles felt limp and tired. The shivering started when I checked my wading vest. There was a fly box missing and my dignity had evaporated, and then I discovered the fish was still hooked.

This is some cutthroat! I thought as it still took line from the dripping fly reel. My waders were full and I stripped off my drenched wading vest and heavy sweater, and both fell soddenly to the beach. The fish started another run and this time I turned it. Finally the big cutthroat came stubbornly into the shallows, wrestling along the bottom like a brook trout to reach the deeper current tongues. It tried again and again, but finally it came head first into the net.

Six pounds, read the scale.

The car heater was not working. It had stopped raining, but the wind was raw. There were some large boulders along the river, and the snowmelt freshets had left a tangle of driftwood in the rocks. Stripping off my remaining wet clothes and waders, I wrapped myself in a raincoat to break the wind, and huddled there until the fire finally caught and grew.

Thank God, I shivered.

Its heat was welcome. The waders and wading vest and sweater were draped across the rocks, drying in the wind. My skin was covered with goose pimples, and I briskly rubbed my icy hands and feet. Life and feeling slowly ebbed back, and suddenly there was a human voice.

No fires here, the park ranger said.

Yes, I admitted. *I'm outside the campfire areas—but the car heater's not working, and I'm freezing!*

Take a spill in the river? he smiled.

Yes, I said. *Hooked a big cutthroat and slipped on one of those slick ledges out there!*

Get the fish? he asked sympathetically.

Yes, I laughed. *It went six pounds!*

Well, that's something anyway, the park ranger laughed. *Put it out when you're warmed up again!*

My teeth chattered. *Thanks,* I said.

5. The Golden Trout of Mexico and California

It was early summer in the high Sierra escarpment, and the back-country lakes were finally open. Rotting snowdrifts filled the ravines and hung in sculptured cornices from the rock slides. There would still be some ice crust in the shallows, particularly in the chill sunless places under sheltering cliffs. It had been cold at daylight and we shivered.

The trail horses were sweating now and their breath plumed high in the morning light. The cool morning wind smelled of the live oaks and sycamore meadows and digger pines at lower altitudes. The narrow trail wound over a glacier-scarred outcropping, and dropped gently into a meadow basin where the creek looped like a careless willow-lined necklace through the wildflowers. The sun was already high and bright in a cloudless sky. The meadow trail was easier and the pack train settled into a steady gait. Their hooves clattered on the stones and ledgerock, and thudded wetly in the seepage places where the grass was bright with alpine poppies and owl clover.

The sweating horses were shiny in the sunlight. The odor of their saddle blankets was stronger with the heat of their sweating flanks, and their bridles and reins were becoming soaked. The horses were breathing easier in the meadow bottoms, and they began trotting a little now. There was a loose kettle or frying pan hanging on one of the mule strings, and it alternately thumped and clanged against the pack frame. Our climb into the high country was only two hours old, but its impact was already profound on my aching thigh muscles where they worked to grip the creaking saddle.

There were trees ahead, where the little stream tumbled in a series of lacy channels down the rocks. The stands were dark with fir and ponderosa, and the morning was filled with the wind music in their needles. Such Sierra species can grow as tall as two hundred feet, their trunks deeply textured in irregular bark plates. Their groves were shadowy and dense above the trail, completely unlike the open live-oak stands in the valley below. It was a new world above 5,000 feet, and in the middle meadows on this pack trail, even the flowers were different. The stream banks below were rich with lupine and shooting star and larkspur, and the flats were purple with more larkspur and the pale blossoms of mustang clover. There were the white-blossomed cranesbill and mountain misery, and in some places the grass became bright with yellow clumps of mule ears.

The horses were sweating again, clambering and working up the steep-walled trail into the higher basins ahead, and the elegant forests were red fir and slender lodgepole pine. The firs rose as much as one hundred fifty feet above the carpet of pine needles; their trunks were a rich reddish brown and their branches swept gracefully like the eaves on some improbable pagoda. Their long purplish cones were clustered at the tips. The smaller lodgepole pine were more numerous, and sometimes reached a height of eighty feet. But most were smaller at these altitudes, and they looked like courtiers with their slender trunks beside the taller firs.

The meadows were rich with rainfall here. There were corn lilies and camas and snowflowers. Tiger lilies and yellow monkey flowers would come later, when the summer was almost finished, and the scarlet snow plants were always the first to blossom. These bright red shoots are unique to these meadows; they bear no leaves and cannot utilize the photosynthetic process of other plants, living instead on the decayed matter surrounding their singular tonguelike root structure.

Both horses and riders were breathing hungrily now, lungs heaving in the thin high-altitude atmosphere. There had been a hard frost the night before. It was growing warmer, but in the marshy seepage meadows along the creek, the mud was puckered with frost boils. There were still frost crystals on the sedges and pine needles in the shadow of the mountains. Mule deer had heard the pack train coming and, scenting both men and horses on the rising wind, had melted into a copse of trees.

Two marmots watched us pass, sitting restlessly halfway up a sprawling rockfall of granite. High above the trail, a mountain coyote hunting deer mice and ground squirrels stood motionless until the pack train had disappeared into the lodgepole pines. The beaver ponds were ahead, and we stopped to watch a plump, slate-colored ouzel dive deep into the gravelly shallows to forage along the bottom. The rock slide above the ponds sheltered a half-comic pika that scurried among the shattered granite, with grass carried crosswise in its bulging jaws.

It was high country now, with thin stands of whitebark pine among the rocky outcroppings. The timberline lay just above the final switchbacks in the trail. The morning was almost hot except for the faint knife edge in the wind; but nights are always raw at these altitudes, and plant life has an ephemeral three months of growth, the bitter alpine frosts killing it at any season. Both plants and animals survive in a delicate equilibrium of life, and summer is a brief season limited to a few sunny mornings of the year. Mark Twain loved the high country of the Sierra Nevada, both during his Cavaleras mining-camp years and on later trips, and he wryly observed that its seasons consisted of a spring thaw and the following winter.

The Cottonwood Lakes were ahead now. The wind sighed down from the highest summits of the Old Army Pass, less than 1,000 feet above the water. It lightly riffled their ice-blue surface. Snow drifts had eroded into miniature mountain ranges above our heads. Yellow cinquefoil grew in the lichen-covered crevices in the cliffs, and there were beds of blue flax in the saddle of the pass itself.

There are few plants and little life at such altitudes. The wind is raw and almost constant above 10,000 feet. It seldom rains and the dry snow is stripped from the barren rocks in billowing wind plumes. The gritty soil is granite dust, and it sheds the meager rainfall much too quickly. Although it is always cool in high country, the low humidity and the intense solar radiation that penetrates the thin atmosphere dehydrate both plants and animals. Life survives precariously, and the flora hug the rocky earth and hide in sheltered places to avoid the searing winds. Their anatomy retains their photosynthetic heat with dense foliage, and many have evolved a morphology not unlike the desert plants. Thick root stalks store both moisture and food. The diminutive leaf systems are leathery and tough and have tiny glands and hairs also designed to hold moisture. Such formidably armored alpine plants produce surprisingly elegant little flowers, like fireweed and yellow columbine and phlox, and along the snowfields there are avalanche lilies.

It is a world balanced on the precipice of existence itself. Its Lilliputian flowers are pale and lovely, fragile and almost foolish in this barren landscape of naked granite and glacier-polished basalt. It is a world fixed in a fierce and frozen light, its minuscule blossoms and wind-shaped trees a poignant footnote to the tenacity of life. The scarred emptiness is also broken with high-country lakes, bright little blue-green emeralds in the craters and glaciermelt basins. Such tiny reservoirs of life are precious above 10,000 feet, and they are justly famous among American trout fishermen.

Such lakes shelter the legendary California golden trout. Popular legend tells us that these lakes were originally barren of fish life, and that prospectors and other mountain men carried the golden trout in coffeepots to the Old Army Pass high country from their original habitat in the headwaters of the Kern River system.

David Starr Jordan and Barton Evermann record several subspecies of golden trout in their definitive *Fishes of North and Middle America*, and in a later edition of their popular *Game Fish of America* there are fine color plates of three of these exquisite species. Their coloring is matchless among the Salmonidae, and virtually every fisherman that has caught one of the golden trouts has marvelled at its beauty. Although the golden trout have been transplanted widely in adjacent waters of the high California mountains and viable populations have been established at several alpine lakes in Wyoming and Montana, no future stockings outside its native Sierra country will be permitted by state and federal authorities. Minor transplanted populations also exist in Idaho, Colorado, Washington, and Oregon, where the various subspecies have been introduced into high lakes—and have unfortunately mixed with their existing cutthroats and rainbows into sterile hybrids.

Jordan and Evermann held the theory that the golden trout are evolved from *Salmo gilberti*, the landlocked strain of rainbow originally found only in the headwaters of the Kern River. Its distinguishing anatomy and palette of colors were perhaps evolved in tributaries of the Kern, where the fish lay at high altitude in the headwaters and were isolated from their ancestors by cataclysmic geological changes. It is interesting that recent phylogenetic studies tend to demonstrate that *Salmo gilberti*, the so-called Kern subspecies of rainbow, has chromosome characters identical to some golden trout. Chromosome and other biochemical studies also confirm strong genetic ties between *Salmo gilberti*, the California goldens, the newly discovered Oregon red-banded trout, and the Gila and Apache trout in New Mexico and Arizona. Since these fish are also related to cutthroats, they raise the possibility of a genetic bridge between *Salmo clarki* and *Salmo gairdneri*—or the possibility of a third group relatively independent of both cutthroats and rainbows.

There were originally four distinct subspecies of golden trouts in the Kern River country of the Sierra Nevada. Coyote Creek was perhaps the original habitat of *Salmo whitei*, the golden trout named for the biologist Stuart Edward White, although stocking records suggest it may have come from the Little Kern. It is genotypical of the strains originally inhabiting the western tributaries of the Kern, particularly Coyote Creek and the Little Kern. Both dorsal and anal fins have eleven rays. There are approximately 26 to 48 pyloric caeca. Scale counts along the lateral line range from 140 to more than 190. The lower lateral surfaces of the Coyote Creek strain are yellowish, like all subspecies of golden trout, although not so intense in chroma as the ecotypes originally found in other tributary headwaters of the Kern. Their bellies are pale cadmium, less intense than the specimens found in Volcano Creek, and their lateral lines are flushed with bright rose over eleven parr markings. The dorsal surfaces are olivaceous, delicately spotted with darker speckles and faint mottlings like smaller, irregular parr markings. The operculate gill covers are touched with rose, like the belly and flank coloring. The flanks of the Coyote Creel goldens are lightly flecked below the parr markings, with slightly denser speckling on the caudal peduncle. The dorsal, adipose, and caudal fins are darkly spotted, and the dorsal fin is tipped with black and orangey white. The head is lightly spotted. Pectoral, ventral, and anal fins are pale orangey, and both ventral and anal fins are tipped with white. The subspecies is typically a small trout in its native habitat, seldom exceeding eight inches. Although *Salmo whitei* was originally limited to the western tributaries of the Upper Kern, especially the Coyote and the Little Kern, it was later introduced into Soda Springs Creek, the Little Kern above its falls, and the South Fork of the Kaweah.

Salmo roosevelti is the taxonomic name given to the golden trout subspecies endemic to Volcano Creek, which lies on the eastern drainage basin of the Upper Kern. It was the best-known original golden trout species, perhaps because it was named in honor of Theodore Roosevelt by the distinguished ichthyologist Barton Evermann. It is characterized by the extreme smallness of its scales, which can range between 150 and 200, its intense coloration, and the absence of black spotting on its head and body. Such fine scales are typical of high-altitude habitats. Its dorsal, adipose, and caudal fins are heavily mottled, with a few spots on the caudal peduncle. The dorsal fin is edged in black and tipped with pale orange. There are eleven dark olive parr markings. The dorsal surfaces are a rich olive green, and the lateral surfaces are pale yellow. The belly is a bright cadmium. The gill covers and lower jaw membranes are similarly colored, and the lateral line is flushed with a roseate stripe. The pectoral, anal, and ventral fins are a bright orange, while the anal and ventral fins are tipped with black and white markings.

According to Jordan and Evermann, whose *American Food and Game Fishes* appeared in 1904, these Volcano Creek goldens had already been transplanted to adjacent streams like Rock Creek and Whitney Creek, on the east side of the Kern. *Salmo roosevelti* attained approximately twelve inches and about a pound in weight in its original habitat, although larger specimens were sometimes found in Rock Creek. The ecotype found in the exquisite watercolor lithograph of the Volcano Creek golden in *American Food and Game Fishes* was painted from a specimen taken on Volcano Creek by Barton Evermann in the summer of 1904.

Ezra Bowen has described his first encounter with these golden trout, which occurred along his campsite in the Rock Creek meadows of the Upper Kern, in his book *The High Sierra*:

> I never felt badly about killing a fish until I caught my first golden trout. Up to that point, I had the conventional American attitude toward fish as fair game to anyone with hunger pangs or an impulse for a low-risk sport.
>
> My first encounter with a golden came on one of those superb frost-cold Sierra mornings along Rock Creek near the headwaters of the Kern River. The sun was too bright and, by the time I was fully organized, already too high for good fishing. But we had time to burn. A planned trail ride was delayed by the nocturnal departure of two mules and one horse, whose tracks indicated they had wandered toward their home corral.
>
> The packer grumpily started after them at dawn, muttering through mouthfuls of canned peaches about the ancestry, morals,

and intelligence of all livestock. I decided to use the hour or two of his travail by taking a walk alongside the creek with my rod, and a handful of splendid little flies tied to order by a Connecticut neighbor's son, after he had done much research into the particular entomology of these mountains.

The walk itself was delightful. At each bend and riffle the creek subtly changed the low, chuckling tone of its voice. I moved downstream to a place where a waterfall had carved a perfect pool—deep water with a rock in the middle where a trout could lie still, out of the current, then flicker off to strike at whatever food might float into sight.

I fished the pool carefully, staying in the shade as much as possible, squatting down on my heels to cast, so as not to throw a disturbing shadow over the fish. After perhaps an hour I managed to drop a caddisfly right at the bottom of the falls, so that it swirled in a natural manner just past the rock, and perhaps six inches under the water. A shadow darted out and I felt a delicate, almost subliminal touch on the line. By happy chance I was raising the rod tip for another cast, so the hook was set.

In perhaps three minutes I had the fish ashore. It was perhaps ten inches long, its back and tail a glistening olive green, the body shading from yellow to rich gold along the sides, to vermillion down the center of the belly. The gill covers gleamed bright red, as did the lower fins, with an added touch of white along the edges. The tail fin, dorsal and back were speckled with black dots, while oval patches of gray punctuated the golden side strips. The trout was as striking in color as many tropical fish, far too handsome to be yanked out of the water as someone's breakfast, and I immediately wished that the creature were back swimming free beneath the falls.

The *salmo aquabonita* subspecies of golden trout was originally isolated in the headwaters of the South Fork of the Kern. It has been classified in the original taxonomic description of David Starr Jordan in 1892, and it is more richly colored than both the Coyote Creek and Volcano Creek strains. It is quite likely the most beautiful trout in the world, and for that reason it has been widely transplanted. It has from 150 to 210 scales along its lateral line, 17 to 21 gillrakers, and 25 to 40 pyloric caeca. *Salmo aquabonita* was also the first golden subspecies to travel outside the headwaters of the South Fork of the Kern, when a prospector carried them from Mulkey Creek across Old Army Pass in a coffeepot in 1876.

The old prospector planted these colorful coffeepot fingerlings in Cottonwood Creek and the several high-country lakes in its headwaters. It was a propitious accident, since the transplanted South Fork goldens survived handsomely, thriving and spreading downstream along this icy little tributary of the Owens. Their progeny have supplied most of the subsequent brood stocks planted in other states and watersheds from California to Wyoming and the wild Beartooth country in Montana.

The high Cottonwood Valley is part of the Owens drainage system on the eastern escarpment of the Sierra Nevada, and the Cottonwood Lakes are presently a golden trout breeding ground maintained by the California Department of Fish and Game. Each spring its fish culturists strip some 750,000 eggs from its spawning goldens, replenishing the populations in other waters of the High Sierras.

Salmo rosei is a possible subspecies of golden trout from the Culver Lakes originally described by Jordan in 1924. These lakes lie on Arroyo Creek, which drains into the Upper Kern about six to eight miles above Coyote Creek and Volcano Creek. Native rainbows were once found in the Arroyo, and it is known that it was stocked with *Salmo roosevelti* in 1894. Some ichthyologists believe that *Salmo rosei* is a hybrid between these introduced goldens and the indigenous strains, although others argue that it is a genuine subspecies, perhaps isolated in the Culver network of lakes in the icemelt of postglacial times. Specimens display 150 to 180 lateral scales, above the scale counts of adjacent rainbow stocks, and 31 to 43 pyloric caeca.

These remarkable golden trout are as colorful and unusual as the swift, tumbling mountain streams where they were originally discovered. These little Sierra tributary rivers all lie at about 10,000 feet, and each provides a unique biosystem, with a colorful stream bed of reddish granite. Ichthyologists believe that the several species of goldens evolved sometime after the Pleistocene Age, when seismic forces and volcanic eruptions abruptly isolated local populations of trout in the Upper Kern Basin—it is particularly interesting that the Wisconsin glaciation stopped at the Coyote Creek and Volcano Creek, covered the Culver Lake drainages, and left the South Fork of the Kern relatively ice-free.

Ichthyologists are divided on the parent strain for the California goldens, some arguing for cutthroats because of the hyoid and basibranchial teeth, pelvic fin rays, and their fine scale counts, and others pointing to the beautiful *Salmo gilberti* rainbows indigenous to the primary Kern River system. Such rainbows display finer scale counts when hatched and raised in high-altitude lakes, and isolations in such cold biosystems could have evolved the golden from such a parent rainbow strain. Yet the similar little Paiute trout and Oregon red-banded strains are clearly cutthroat derivatives, having been isolated in their native waters from the related Lahontan strains by ancient geological events. The Gila and Apache trout are parallel relict forms isolated by changing climates and shrinking glaciers in the headwaters of desiccating drainages in New Mexico and Arizona.

The little-known golden trout of Mexico were classified as *Salmo chrysogaster* by the late Paul Needham in 1964. The Mexican goldens are found in the swift Fuerte, Sinaloa and Culiacan, tributaries of the Gulf of California below Guaymas. Basibranchial and hyoid teeth typical of the cutthroats are lacking in these Mexican goldens. Scale counts range from

135 to 165, and there are 10 to 30 pyloric caeca. *Salmo chrysogaster* is a highly divergent species in the golden trout group, with unique otolithic bones for the Salmonidae family, and its phylogenetic relationships are unclear. It is perhaps closest to the Apache trout in its biomorphology, but its relationships to the cutthroat and rainbow are fairly distant, although the rainbow is somewhat closer.

There is perhaps more supporting evidence for the parent rainbow theory farther north in British Columbia. Fish biologist J. D. Dymond has described a high-altitude subspecies of rainbow in his excellent book *The Trout and Other Game Fishes of British Columbia*. Its coloring and scale counts are remarkably like *Salmo aquabonita*. Dymond has described his variation of the Kamloops rainbow as *Salmo whitehousei*, and observed that specimens reared at lower altitudes lose both their characteristic coloring and fine scale counts. Golden trout grown at lower altitudes also display similar changes in their morphology, suffering a surprising loss of color.

Some biologists have cited the natural hybrids that often occur between rainbows and goldens as evidence of their origins in a parent strain of rainbow, although similar hybrids are also found in the wild state between rainbows and cutthroats. Such hybrids are a considerable problem in fine cutthroat fisheries like the headwaters of the Snake—where the government fish culturists of Teton National Park have continuously struggled to maintain the purity of its unique *Salmo lewisi* cutthroat.

The Kern headwaters still comprise a surprisingly isolated region, and it is not difficult to understand how these brightly colored fish evolved in its tributaries, with their river bottoms of yellowish sand and reddish granite. It is a remarkable world, beautifully described by Charles McDermand in *Waters of the Golden Trout Country*, particularly in these passages about his first backpack into the Kern:

> So this was the Kern!
> Clearer by far than the hazy Indian summer air, shaded by giant pines, it was a broad and friendly stream where riffles and pools and deep stretches formed a crystal chain. From its sparkling currents, I looked up at gigantic mountain walls bulging against a steel-blue sky. Thanks to its grim loneliness and the high altitude of its surrounding timberline passes, the Upper Kern is relatively untouched by man. Northward, its headwaters spring from the formidable barrier of the Kings Canyon divide, the 14,000-foot peaks of the main Sierra guard it from the east. Impassable gorges forbid access from the south. And the upthrust of the great western divide bars the teeming highways coming from the west. Only on foot or by pack-train can you visit the Upper Kern, but well-marked trails enter the canyon from all directions except the south.
> When I reached the edge of the canyon, I forgot all about the long foot-sore miles from the giant forest. The smashing view from

the shoulder of the cliff dwarfs a dozen Yosemites laid end to end. Straight as an arrow, the two-thousand-foot gash of the canyon stretches south for thirty miles. The timbered bottom of the great cleft was threaded with the silver ribbon of the Kern.

It is the *Salmo aquabonita* strain that has been transplanted into the beautiful Wind River wilderness in Wyoming, where it has developed some remarkable high-lake fisheries. It is a richly colored subspecies. Its dorsal surfaces are a rich olive green, its lateral surfaces a soft pale yellow. The lateral line is striped in bright scarlet. The belly, the gill covers and the membranes of the lower jaw are cadmium. The dorsal, adipose and caudal fins are darkly spotted. The dorsal surfaces are less heavily spotted, although the spots are somewhat more closely spaced on the caudal peduncle. There are nine parr markings along the lateral line in the genotypical specimens described by Jordan and Evermann. The dorsal fin is edged in black with an orangish-white tip, and the pectoral, anal, and ventral fins are bright cadmium orange. The lower tip of the caudal fin is flushed with orangish coloring, while both the anal and ventral fins are dramatically edged in black and strongly tipped with white.

Salmo aquabonita is an unforgettable species of trout. Although it seldom reaches three pounds in its adopted High Sierra domains and rarely exceeds a foot in its native streams, it does grow larger in some lakes having introduced populations. Perhaps the largest goldens are now found in the Beartooths in Montana, and in the Wind River region of western Wyoming, where Cook Lake surrendered the world-record golden in the late summer of 1948, when Charles Reed caught a *Salmo aquabonita* trophy that weighed a remarkable eleven pounds.

However, few golden trout of such size exist in either the native or adopted range of the species. The several strains are essentially fish of remote high-country glacial basins above 10,000 feet. Such opalescent lakes in their native Sierras bear names like Emigrant, Sapphire, and Timberline—all appropriate to these trout with their ecotypical roots near the roof of the world. It seems particularly fitting that *Salmo aquabonita* inhabit the highest lake in America, the dark jewellike Tulainayo that lies 12,863 feet above the Pacific in the Sierra Nevada. Tulainayo lies well above Wales Lake on a barren shelf in the bitter wind-chilled granite, its remote setting unblemished by any trail. Its world is truly the realm of *Salmo aquabonita* and its bright-colored cousins. Its waters are sweet and pure, much like the atmosphere itself at such dazzling altitudes. The sunlight is piercing in its razor-sharp intensity, highlighting each outcropping and cornice of the mountains reflected in the blue-green depths. Each stone and trail pebble and flower is caught in a fiercely bright focus, the light virtually undiminished in the thin atmosphere. Mark Twain was fascinated with the quality of the atmosphere in his beloved Sierra back country, finding it cool and deliciously bracing and pure.

And why shouldn't it be? he wrote. *It is the same air the angels breathe!*

6. The Chars of Our North-Country Waters

The wild subarctic mountains were scarred and polished with the grinding force of the ancient Pleistocene glaciers that shaped them. There was almost no vegetation clinging to their barren plateau outcroppings, except the scrub pines and pale caribou moss in the sheltered places. The tiny Labrador lakes in their saddles and shelflike basins were as black as Chinese drawing ink, and their depths looked forbidding and seemingly lifeless, far beneath the aluminum floats of the Cessna.

The scattered stands of scrub pines and firs grew along the sheltered moraines beside the George, but the subarctic treeline ended these forlorn-looking conifers less than one hundred feet above the river, except in a few sheltered places facing toward the sun.

Fort Chimo and its trading post lay more than one hundred miles west of our position on the chart, where the shadow of our floatplane crossed the George at Helen Falls. There was a sizable shallow lake ahead, together with a series of smaller lakes strung like beads on the necklacelike river that forms its headwaters. Ungava Bay loomed on the horizon now, its vast pewter-colored expanse shrouded in impenetrable sea fog. There was a short mile of river, winding through the bracken and scrub-growth pines at its outlet, that connected the lake with the sprawling tidal flats of the Ungava. We circled warily on a reduced throttle setting, studying the lake for shoals and shallow-water outcroppings under its light wind riffle. Fierce tides and the offshore fog were worrisome, so we rejected landing on the estuary itself.

The fog could move in and cover the beach, Bob Bryan yelled over the engine and propeller wash, *and the tides could strand us on mud flats!*

There's no beach on the lake, I said.

But we'll have enough water there to land and take off, no matter what the tides do in an hour or two, Bryan added.

Maybe we can moor the plane in that rocky cove and face it back into the wind, I suggested. *We can lash its lines to the rocks and bracken.*

Bryan nodded. *It's the best solution.*

We pulled the plane into a tight turn and flew the pale lake carefully again, measuring it for a later takeoff run, and studying its surface for shoals and outcroppings and floating debris.

We're well under gross weight, Bryan yelled. *We should get her off easily when we're through fishing.*

Okay, I said. *Let's try it!*

The light wind was coming from the south, gently riffling the shallow oval of the lake and holding the ominous sea fog a mile or two offshore. We made a slow, downwind pass to study the lake for landing hazards again, and turned above the outlet into our final approach. Bryan unreeled some radio aerial.

Six-nine-easy calling Chimo, Bryan called.

Hello six-nine-easy! Fort Chimo answered almost immediately. *What is your present position?*

Static crackled in the cockpit. *We are setting down on the first river west of the George,* Bryan answered. *It has no name on the charts—we'll fish about two hours and return to our base camp on the George before nightfall.*

Roger, six-nine-easy, said Chimo. *Good luck!*

Roger, Bryan concluded his transmission. *Contact you again when we're airborne to base camp.*

Roger easy, Chimo signed off.

Our final turn aligned us with the wind, low over the glittering surface of the lake, and we throttled back on full flaps. The floatplane crabbed slightly on the gentle crosswind and Bryan eased it back with the rudder bar. The rocky Ungava beach and the scrub bracken along the lower river flashed under our floats, and our shadow darted across the deep outlet of the lake. Bryan steadied the plane gently as its stall horn sounded, and when the pontoons touched and skimmed the lake, we quickly lost flying speed and settled in the water. Spray flew from the floats and the propeller wash.

Water rudders! Bryan ordered.

The ring chain was unhooked and dropped. *Water rudders down!* I yelled happily. *We're here!*

Bryan kicked the rudders and wheeled the plane around sharply, and he advanced the throttle to cross the lake with spray showering behind our streaming wake. We cut the throttle offshore and I stepped down on the starboard float, and when we drifted into the shallows I dropped off into the water to swing the Cessna around with its struts. We moored the little yellow plane facing out into the nameless lake, running its anchor lines back into the bracken. It rocked amiably in the gentle swells.

Bryan wrestled our gear from the plane, and passed the fly rods to the beach from the aluminum canister attached to its starboard float strut. *Well,* he laughed, *let's find out about the fish!*

Unless they are too shallow to prevent winterkill, Labrador lakes are seldom barren, but they vary widely in their fertility. The rust-colored lakes are usually too acid for good fishing; the richer waters are deep blue. It is possible to tell something about their probable sporting qualities from a floatplane by their bathography and color. The best are only faintly acid, and have sufficient shallows to sustain the food chain, and sufficient depth to provide cool summer temperatures and oxygen during the long ice-locked winters.

We rigged our equipment and clambered along the rocky cove toward the outlet. Its deep green water shelved off among the boulders, and the outlet currents gathered into the first pool of the river. The pool and its swift tail shallows were a quarter mile below the plane, and we began fishing halfway down. Our big bucktails and streamers rolled out into the current, and we stripped them back swiftly.

Fish! Bryan shouted. *Fish!*

It was an acrobatic twelve-pound lake trout, the white salt-water streamer firmly seated in its jaw, and it threshed wildly across the surface. Before Bryan wrestled it ashore, my attention was snapped back to my own retrieve by a sullen strike. The rod doubled over into a tight semicircle. The big fish bulldogged angrily past me with the red-and-yellow bucktail in its mouth, and I saw that it had company.

My God! I shouted in disbelief. *This fish is being followed by twenty or thirty others—it's like a hatchery!*

Mine too! Bryan laughed happily.

For more than an hour, we hooked a ten- or twelve-pound lake trout on every retrieve until we were surfeited with the lack of challenge and began prospecting downstream for other species. The gathering currents above the first pool flowed strong and smooth, dark and olive green among the algae-covered boulders of the lake.

My bucktail worked out in a double haul and dropped along the rocky shelf across the current. It had scarcely started its swing, when there was a slashing strike as a big fish turned suddenly from its lie, and took the bellying fly.

It's no laker, I yelled. *It's stronger!*

The slender almost reddish lake trout had taken our flies eagerly, but their fight was more stubborn and sluggish than exciting. This trout was different. Its spadelike tail threw water as it turned over after its first angry run deep into the lake, and it hung across the gathering current, shaking its head sullenly. Its muscled sides flashed silver in the sun, but it was definitely not a salmon, judging from its strong square-cut tail and bulldogging fight. Its fierce runs and head-shaking were still powerful, and it came past me in a stubborn semicircle, working its head deep.

It's a sea trout, I thought.

Bryan waved when the fish continued to fight. *What is it?* he yelled downstream. *Arctic char?*

It's a sea-run brookie, I answered. *Big one!*

Such anadromous brook trout are found from Long Island and Connecticut to Hudson Bay and the Labrador, and most of them run about fifteen inches, although five-pounders are common on some rivers. This fish looked bigger, and it fought me to a standstill. Finally it surrendered, and I carried it ashore with my fingers seated over its gill covers. It was silvery with its salt-water feeding, almost without any trace of its red spots and dorsal vermiculations, and only its pale mottling remained. It was a beautiful fish, fully twenty-eight inches and about eight pounds, and I released its lovely sea-bright length carefully in the shallows. It held near me for a few moments, its gill covers working slowly as it recovered its strength, and then it was suddenly gone.

The swift depths of the pool were filled with two- and three-pound river brookies, and we caught them on virtually every cast, with a hatcherylike cloud of trout following every retrieve.

You ever see so many? I yelled. *They're like the bottom coming to life and rising to meet the sinking fly!*

It's a terrible problem, Bryan laughed.

The brook trout continued taking eagerly for an hour, and then they stopped and only followed the bucktails, unlike the gullible lake trout in the last quiet water of the outlet. We continued to take brookies steadily on weighted nymphs, fishing deep along the bottom where the green moss worked in the current.

We've got to get started back soon! Bryan shouted.

The dense sea fog was closer to the shore, and it looked ominous as its swirling mists shrouded the tidal flats. *Just let me fish out the tail of the pool?* I shouted. *Just a few more casts?*

Okay, he answered. *But hurry it along!*

The principal current leaving the pool flowed deep and emerald green in a shelving channel along the rocks. Its gathering run looked like it might hold a salmon, and on the first fly swing a strong fish took the working bucktail in a savage strike. It immediately burned line off the reel like a bonefish, its run carrying a hundred yards downstream, and I stumbled over the slippery rocks trying to follow.

Just like a salmon, I thought, *but it hasn't jumped.*

There were no jumps during the stubborn fight, although it made three reel-searing runs that forced me farther downstream. It was still fighting when I finally beached it on the pea gravel in the shallows. It was a strange species to me then, silvery gray with a faint olive cast and a dark olive back. Its dorsal, adipose, and caudal fins were reddish with a distinct olivaceous cast. Its sides were heavily mottled with faint yellowish spots. Its lower fins were a dull orange-yellow, and its lower belly already carried the first bright reddish cast of its autumn spawning rites.

What is it? Bryan yelled from the plane.

Arctic char! I answered. *It's the first char I've ever caught and it gave me some fight!* It was a hard-muscled fish of only six pounds, but its raw strength had surpassed a fresh-run salmon's, although it had failed to jump during its fierce struggle.

They're delicious, Bryan shouted. *Bring that one!*

The char was the only fish we killed, and when we grilled it that night at our base camp on the George below Helen Falls, we discovered it was excellent eating. They are a superb game fish, although Arctic char take hardware more readily than flies after they reach a pound or two. It had been a remarkable fishing day on that uncharted and unfished lake outlet in the Labrador, almost too easy for really good sport, yet its waters had generously surrendered three distinct species of north-country chars.

The celebrated *Salvelinus fontinalis,* our familiar eastern brook trout, was discussed in its own earlier chapter, but there are several other important chars of the genus *Salvelinus* found in North American waters. Relict char populations found in several deep New Hampshire ponds and in White Pine and Wilderness Lakes in Ontario are remarkably close in morphological terms to both brook trout and Arctic chars. The lake trout and Arctic char are the Salmonidae most widely distributed across our continent, along with the Pacific chars found from California north to Alaska, and inland in the Columbia watershed to Idaho and Montana. The Pacific char is the bull trout or Dolly Varden. There are also a number of relict species of Arctic char that have been classified, and others may exist in remote subarctic lakes. Taxonomic subspecies related to the Arctic chars have been discovered in the Matamek drainage and Lac de Marbre in Quebec, and in several deep lakes and ponds in Maine and New Hampshire. These geographically stranded species remain from periods of Pleistocene glaciation, and the anadromous populations of other chars are only found hundreds of miles farther north.

There are also isolated subspecies of Arctic char found in the barren Northwest Territories and the remote arctic islands above the Hudson Straits. These subspecies include strains found in landlocked populations in the Boothia Felix Peninsula, the barren Discovery Bay region in Baffin Land, and in Lake Victoria in Queen Elizabeth Land—at more than eighty-two-degrees latitude, and are the most northerly landlocked species of Salmonidae known.

The chars differ from the true trout in a number of uniquely distinguishing taxonomic features. Chars are characterized particularly by the peculiar boat-shaped structure of the tooth-bearing vomerine bone, which is located in the center of the upper mouth. The vomerine bone displays a relatively small growth of teeth on its head or crest, while its rearward extension is depressed and lacking teeth in most char species.

Lake trout are the only char that vary from this taxonomy, and their vomerine morphology is different from other species in the *Salvelinus* group. The vomerine is clearly raised in the lake trout, unlike the other char, and exhibits several teeth. The structure of the vomerine ridge once caused the lake trout to be classified in *Cristivomer,* a fully separate genus with its name

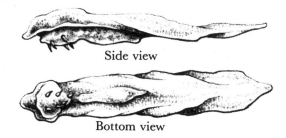

Side view

Bottom view

Lake Trout Vomerine Bone

derived from its crestlike vomerine bone. True trouts differ from the several char species, having teeth distributed well down the vomerine ridge along the entire roof of the mouth.

The *Salvelinus* char group is distinguished by its fine scale counts, with numerous minuscule scales typical of cold-water species. Such counts along the lateral line commonly exhibit more than two hundred rows of scales. Lake trout have slightly larger scales, and typical specimens exhibit from 180 to slightly more than 200 scales along the lateral line. Most other chars have extremely high lateral scale counts, from 230 to 250. The highest counts are perhaps found among Arctic char in the most northern latitudes of their range, and in the relict subspecies of those char in several recently-glaciated lakes of Canada and the United States.

Savelinus namaycush is the current taxonomic designation given to the lake trout, since the older *Cristivomer* designation has been dropped. It is not usually a fly-fishing species, although it can readily be caught on baitfish imitations in the spring when it forages in shallows and shoals. Warming surface temperatures force the lake trout into the chilly mesopelagic depths in midsummer, and it once again migrates into shallow waters in anticipation of its fall spawning. Warm summer temperatures seldom occur in the northern latitudes of its range, and in such north-country regions, the lake trout is found throughout the summer in both shallow lakes and their connecting rivers. Such populations are commonly taken on bucktails and streamers throughout the season. Lake trout in substantial riverine populations are found in the subarctic barrens of the Yukon, Quebec and the Labrador, as well as the labyrinthine watercourses of its Canadian and Alaskan zoogeography.

The original range of *Salvelinus namaycush* closely parallels the southern threshold of Pleistocene glaciation. Its zoogeography is extremely interesting, and is outlined in the chapter on the prehistory of the Salmonidae. South of the drainage systems of Hudson Bay, the Saint Lawrence, and the sprawling network of the Great Lakes, sustaining populations of lake trout occur historically in New Brunswick and Nova Scotia, the headwater lakes having sufficient depth in Maine and New Hampshire and Vermont, the Finger Lakes of western and the Adirondack lakes of upstate New York, both Upper and Lower Michigan, and in certain cold recently glaciated lakes in Wisconsin and Minnesota. Farther west, there were natural populations in British Columbia from Shuswap north, in virtually all the interior lakes draining into the Pacific. Relict populations also occur in the headwaters of the Missouri and in the mountains of northwestern Montana. Alaskan populations are found in coastal streams above the Fraser watershed and northward to the Cook Inlet. Lake trout are also found in the foothill lakes and riverine systems draining into Bristol Bay. The species is widely distributed in the headwaters and tributary lakes of the Yukon, but colonies are apparently absent from the unglaciated basin of the lower river. Isolated populations also exist in the foothill lakes and higher waters on both drainage slopes of the Brooks Range in northern Alaska. The species was not originally found in lower British Columbia and Vancouver Island, although it has apparently entered and crossed other salt-water zones to found natural populations on Prince William Island, Baffin Land, and other islands of the Northwest Territories. Extensive populations also exist in the Ungava watersheds of northern Quebec and in the labyrinth of the riverine systems of the Labrador, but lake trout were curiously absent from Newfoundland as a native species.

South of its natural range, *Salvelinus namaycush* has been successfully transplanted to form sustaining populations in certain cold lakes and reservoirs of New England, the upper Middle West, and throughout our western mountains. Artificial lake-trout fisheries exist in suitable waters as far south as northern New Mexico.

Most lake trout spawn in the wave-washed shallows of rocky shorelines and shoals, but stream spawning is reported in widespread Alaskan and Canadian waters, and some northerly rivers draining into Lake Superior. Riverine spawning grounds are rather typical of *Salvelinus namaycush* in most watersheds in the subarctic. The survival of the species in relatively southern latitudes depends upon lakes exhibiting adequate thermal stratification, as well as those that hold sufficient dissolved oxygen in their depths.

Lake trout are typically large and relatively coarse chars when compared with the Arctic char and the brook trout. Its vomerine bone exhibits a raised crest, fully separate from its shaft, and this cartilagenous ridge is covered with teeth. The hyoid teeth also form a strong cardiform band. There are 11 rays in the dorsal and anal fins, and there are 11 to 12 branchiostegals. Scale counts along the lateral line run from 185 to more than 200. The body of the species is typically long, with a relatively elongated head structure, while its mouth is large and has a well-developed maxillary extending behind the eye. The heads and jaws are rather pointed when compared with other trout and char. The dorsal fin is fairly large, and the caudal fin is proportionately small. Coloration varies widely with water character and quality, as well as with its primary food-chain communities, and ranges from pale gray to dark reddish brown. Spawning fish are quite reddish in late summer and early fall, and on the redds their caudal, pectoral, ventral, and anal fins are tipped a deep rust color and edged in white. During other seasons the lake trout are heavily spotted over their heads, gill covers, dorsal surfaces, sides and belly, and the caudal peduncle. The dorsal, caudal, and anal fins of the lake trout are also spotted with dense, pale, watery mottlings in a boldly dramatic pattern.

Lake trout are fall spawners. Subarctic populations gather over the spawning redds as early as September, and those in Lake Superior have commonly gathered over their egg-laying reefs and shallows before October. Populations in Lake Michigan and Lake Huron reach their spawning peaks in early November, with their oviposition lasting almost until Christmas.

Typical spawning grounds are reefs and shoals, usually well offshore in many large lakes, and in waters from six to almost one hundred feet in depth. Lake trout are not known for their fecundity. Twenty-five-pound henfish can produce as many as 15,000 fertile ova, although an average female of five to ten pounds may generate only 5,000 to 6,000 eggs. Breeding occurs on rocky ledges, coarse gravel, or honeycomb-weathered shoals. Unlike the other species of trout and char, the spawning lake trout do not construct an actual redd. The chosen nesting site is merely swept clean of silt and detritus. The spawning itself is attended by a female and several males, and the resulting eggs are scattered rather freely over the bottom. These ova are about one-fifth of an inch in diameter, and their specific gravity causes them to settle and adhere to the rocky bottom. Predation is fierce, and large numbers of eggs are lost to waiting trout, suckers, bullheads, sculpins, eels, perch, and other coarse fish. Incubation occupies more than 160 days at a temperature of thirty-seven degrees, and fifty degrees will hatch the eggs in about the same number of days. The new alevins and fingerlings remain at surprising depths. Light, temperature, and water pressure are apparently critical factors in their development, since hatchery-reared fingerlings raised in bright sunlight develop cataracts and other physiological problems. Young lake trout feed on deep nymphs, tiny baitfish and crustaceans. Adult specimens of *Salvelinus namaycush* thrive on a relatively piscivorous diet, although their ravenous appetites lead them to ingest virtually anything. Fully grown lakers greedily devour crustaceans and baitfish like ciscos, whitefish, smelt, alewives, mooneyes, sculpin, yellow perch, and other small species. Mature lake trout are formidable predators, exceeded in size throughout their range only by the sturgeon, and these large fish have no serious natural enemies except for the lamprey eel.

Lampreys have proven highly destructive to the lake-trout populations in the Great Lakes, since their accidental introduction to those waters through the construction of the Welland Canal between Lake Ontario and Lake Erie. Jordan and Evermann, in their definitive *American Food and Game Fishes*, included the following historical information on the Great Lakes populations before the lampreys arrived:

> The lake trout fisheries of the Great Lakes are exceeded in commercial importance only by those of the whitefish. At one time, the lake trout was so abundant that it did not command a

price at all commensurate with its edible qualities, but as the catches decreased, the price went up, until in 1886 it equalled the value of its more delicate rival.

In that year, the artificial propagation of the lake trout was begun by the federal and certain state governments. The output of the hatcheries increased gradually until, in 1895, that of the government hatchery at Northville alone amounted to more than 11,000,000 eggs; and the species had become so abundant in the lakes in 1896 that the fishing boats ceased operations, the market being glutted, and the obtainable price not justifying the labor involved.

The method of capturing these lake trout is by gillnets, pound-nets, hook and line, and in the winter, by spearing through the ice. The majority, however, are taken by means of gillnets operated by steam tugs. Some of these tugs carry five or six miles of nets and catch in a single lift from 1,000 to 10,000 pounds of trout. Fishing is done from the time the lake ice breaks up in the spring, until late in the fall.

As gamefish, the lake trout are held in different degrees of esteem by different anglers. There are those who regard it with slight favor, while with others it is rated as a fish which can give the angler a great deal of sport. It is usually taken by trolling either with the spoon or live minnow, and, as it is a most powerful fish, strong tackle is required. Thaddeus Norris, most delightful writer among American anglers, mentions hooking several trout on stout Kirby hooks baited with a white rag and a piece of red flannel, and the hooks, in every instance but one [a small eight-pound fish] were straightened or broken and the fish lost.

The lake trout is known by several local names in various parts of its range. It is called a togue in Maine and New Hampshire, and a longe in neighboring Vermont. Gray trout is its common name in Canadian waters, and among the north-country Indian tribes it is known as a namaycush or masamacush. It is the largest of all the freshwater trout and chars excepting *Salmo caspius* of the Caspian Sea, which reaches a length of several feet and weights to 125 pounds. The world-record lake trout on sporting tackle was taken on Lake Superior in the spring of 1952. It measured more than fifty-one inches and weighed slightly over sixty-three pounds. Larger fish will undoubtedly be caught in the future, now that subarctic waters like Great Slave Lake and Lake Athabaska are being fished extensively. Monsters still exist in such distant little-fished regions.

Although *Salvelinus namaycush* is the lake-trout genotype, the subspecies *Salvelinus siscowet* has been identified primarily from Lake Superior, and other large mesopelagic lakes at northern latitudes. This subspecies is often taken at depths of three hundred to six hundred feet. No geographically consistent variation on the morphology of the species has been identified in ichthyological circles. However, there are countless local populations that display strong differences in color, configuration, average growth, and mature weight that are undoubtedly based upon water quality and diet. These seemingly distinct local variations are random in distribution, and ichthyologists still lack sufficient evidence of actual genetic divergences arising from separate glacial effects. However, comprehensive phylogenetic investigation over the full range of *Salvelinus namaycush* will likely reveal a number of new subspecies. Arthur Leith Adams contributed these observations about lake trout in his famous studies of our north-country aboriginal peoples:

> The Indian indulges his love of the marvelous in talking about togue; even in the absence of written history, one may detect figments of their wild legends and mythology, strangely mingled even with the traditions of their earliest Christian instructors, of monster togues and sturgeons that appeared on the surface of the lakes at night, striking such terror in the tribe that they were forced to abandon their fishing grounds; indeed such, with the pygmy fairies, giants and other offspring of their ever-fruitful imaginations, rendered famous whatever localities these apparitions were said to frequent.

Arctic chars are genotypical of the several species and subspecies found in the waters of North America. These species include relict chars like those found in New Hampshire, Maine, and Quebec, as well as the Pacific species and four subspecies of Arctic char found in arctic Canada.

Salvelinus alpinus is the taxonomic description of the principal arctic species that is circumpolar in its distribution. There are at least ten American species and subspecies, and even more are found in the zoogeography of Europe and Asia. Arctic chars exist in both anadromous and landlocked forms. Their ecotypes are numerous in the arctic marine environments throughout the North American and Eurasian coastal areas. Extensive marine populations exist in the brackish waters around arctic islands from the Northwest Territories and Greenland, to subarctic Iceland and the archipelagoes of Spitzbergen and the Russian arctic territories. Landlocked char are found in the alpine lakes of Central Europe, Scandinavia and Siberia, and as far south as southern Japan.

Most of these European and Asian chars are subspecies of *Salvelinus alpinus*, the same Arctic chars found in Alaskan and Canadian coastal waters. The chars typically found in the alpine lakes of Switzerland, France, Austria and southern Germany are the common *Salvelinus salvelinus*, and the deep-water char *Salvelinus profundus*, which often shares the same lakes at mesopelagic depths. The landlocked Scandinavian chars found in arctic and subarctic lakes from Iceland to the Karelian Steppes of northern Russia are usually the *Salvelinus lepechini* subspecies.

There are several lacustrine populations of chars in the British Isles. Cole's char is the most common form in Ireland, and is the small *Salvelinus coli,* although Lake Coomarsaharn boasts *Salvelinus fimbriatus,* with an atypically high number of gillrakers. *Salvelinus willoughbi* is the Windemere char of northern England, and similar subspecies are found in many Scottish lakes.

The Siberian lake chars are numerous, and closely related to adjacent anadromous populations. *Salvelinus melanostomus* is the dwarf shallow-water char found in the Kola Peninsula, and the larger *Salvelinus segosericus* is a sympatric fish-eating char found in the same waters. *Salvelinus erythrinus* is the Baikal char, a relict subspecies echoing a widespread population the prehistory of southern Siberia.

Lake Taimyr was once an arm of the Laptev Sea, and is geological evidence of the postglacial isolation of the parent-char strains. The region is particularly rich in subspecies. *Salvelinus drjagini* is found in a lake in the Pyasina drainage. The Khatanga Basin has populations of *Salvelinus boganidae* and *Salvelinus tolmachoffi.* Lake Taimyr itself has two sympatric chars, the relatively small subspecies *Salvelinus taimyricus* and the piscivorous *Salvelinus taimyri,* which is a larger deep-water form. There are other relict species in the Soviet Union, including *Salvelinus jacuticus* and *Salvelinus andriashevi,* and the *Salvelinus neiva* from Okhota in the Gydan.

The anadromous and landlocked chars of Kamchatka, and the Bering Straits are a taxonomic nightmare, and the overlapping populations in Alaskan waters are equally mixed. *Salvelinus alpinus* is apparently seldom found in the seas below the Gulf of Anadyr, although a landlocked population is known from Lake Dalyne on the Kamchatka Peninsula. *Salvelinus malma* is the coastal char found farther south, its range overlapping both the Arctic chars and the anadromous *Salvelinus leucomaenis* known from Japanese and Korean seas. It is interesting that chars were not found in the Aral, Caspian and Black seas.

Japanese waters include *Salvelinus saghalensis,* which is primarily an anadromous subspecies frequenting coastal seas, and the related riverine strain *Salvelinus japonicus,* which is found in headwater streams from Tokyo to Kyoto. Resident river populations of Honshu chars are *Salvelinus pluvius,* and the remarkable little *Salvelinus miyabei* found in Lake Shikaribetsu on Hokkaido has scale counts as high as 260. Much research is still needed in *Salvelinus* taxonomy in Asia.

Arctic char share common ancestors with both the brook trout and *Salvelinus spectabilis,* the Pacific char popularly known as the Dolly Varden. Our Arctic char lacks the rich vermiculations found on the dorsal surfaces of *Salvelinus fontinalis,* and its dorsal surfaces are usually olive green or grayish blue, with pale silvery sides on specimens fresh from tidal waters. The dorsal, adipose, and caudal fins often have a dull orange cast. The lower lateral surfaces are often silvery when the char are fresh-run, becoming pale yellow to orange with each day spent in a riverine environment. Fresh-run fish are not heavily spotted like the trout and other chars and display relatively large pale markings. These mottlings are sometimes white, cream-colored, pale orange and even a light watery pink. The pectoral, anal, ventral, and caudal fins are orangey and edged in white. The char are completely silver while they remain in salt water and are often mistaken for salmon in Greenland and other arctic regions.

Arctic chars have distinctly forked caudal fins, and their bodies are more rounded in cross section than the relatively ovoid configuration of their brook-trout cousins. Typical specimens have eleven rays in their dorsal fins, and ten rays in their anal structures. Lateral scales range from 160 to 215. There are eleven branchiostegals, and from 30 to 45 pyloric caeca. The maxillary does not extend far behind the eye. The teeth are relatively small, and include a band of hyoid teeth. The general configuration of our Arctic chars is elongate in character, and the cranial structure and snout of the male are rather long and pointed. The preopercule is rather short, and its preopercular structure is conspicuously and deeply striated. Fin structure is relatively large and well developed, with pectorals reaching more than half-way to the adjacent ventral structure, and the ventral fins themselves are rather long and pointed.

Most Arctic char weigh about two to eight pounds, although there are dwarf species in some lakes and landlocked river populations, as well as large anadromous specimens. Trophy-size fish of twenty to twenty-five pounds have been recorded from a number of arctic and subarctic rivers in North America. Certification of record fish has not been properly handled in the past, and the current records from Europe, Asia, and North America are being reviewed. However, several large specimens from the Tree River in the Northwest Territories have been claimed as world-record char in recent years.

Spawning colors of *Salvelinus alpinus* are remarkable. Their belly surfaces and pale spots become a bright orangey scarlet, with a curiously intense chroma. The pectoral, ventral, and anal fins take on a similar, slightly darker coloring. The dorsal, adipose and caudal fins become a dark reddish olive, ranging to steely bluish black in some specimens. The pectoral, ventral, anal, and the lower edge of the caudal fin are all boldly edged in black and white. The caudal fin is sometimes posteriorly edged in reddish coloring, along with the dorsal. Reddish coloring is also sometimes found on the jaw membranes.

These fish are unforgettable, and their coloring becomes even more striking as they advance into their spawning time. The males develop exaggeratedly undershot jaw structures and a strong salmonlike kype. Their steely blue dorsal surfaces become a strange reddish olive, almost like a spawning sockeye, but without a distended humplike distortion of its back. Both lateral surfaces and the lower fins become the same intense scarlet, while the carmine spotting now lies in a pale reddish or olivaceous background. The dorsal fin and tail are tinged with orangey red.

Migratory Arctic char conform to general cyclical patterns throughout their north-country range. Populations in major watersheds drop seaward in their riverine environments, descending into salt water when the ice breaks up in early summer. Downstream char migration occurs under the ice in some rivers, particularly in the Siberian range of the species. Such behavior is apparently common in the rivers of Novaya Zemlya, deep in the Arctic Ocean off the north coasts of the Soviet Union. These char summer together in considerable schools, feeding in coastal and estuarine waters. Their diet consists primarily of baitfish and crustaceans, although Russian studies find codfish larvae an important staple in some waters.

Sea-run char return to their parent rivers in late August and September, and the bellwether populations are those fish ready to spawn in the coming autumn. Research indicates that these char spawn in the interconnecting lakes and quiet reaches of their parent watersheds. The egg laying itself occurs in late fall and early winter. The nomadic existence of Arctic char begins after two to three years in some Siberian rivers, but most populations enter the marine environment after five to six seasons in their parent rivers, and life spans of more than twenty years have been recorded.

The range of *Salvelinus alpinus* in North American coastal waters lies from the mouth of the Kuskowim on the Bering Sea, eastward throughout the offshore archipelagoes of the Northwest Territories, into the upper latitudes of Hudson Bay and the Ungava country, and down the Labrador coasts to Nain and Goose Bay.

Freshwater growth is limited by the food available in the relatively acid ecosystems of the arctic and the brief season of optimal feeding temperatures. The fry, fingerlings, and smolts of the anadromous char all drift toward the sea in surprisingly early years of their life span. Food consists primarily of the Trichoptera and Chironomidae, which abound in the subarctic rivers, as well as other aquatic insects and freshwater crustaceans. Principal foods in Canadian coastal waters are capelin, sand eels, and crustacean larvae. Arctic char along the northern coasts of Iceland feed extensively on small herring and capelin, but in the rivers their diet consists largely of the two-winged *Anisomera* midges in their larval and pupal forms. Some dry-fly fishing is possible when such gravel-loving midges are hatching in July and August. Paradoxically, these char are most active in cold weather, and a series of sunny days in subarctic Iceland will make them sluggish and reluctant to feed. They are surprisingly strong fighters and are superb table fare.

Sexual maturity and fecundity vary widely among these chars. Most specimens make a spawning migration one year after reaching sexual adulthood. Males are often slightly larger than females. The Novaya Zemlya strain of sea char averages 3,500 eggs. Landlocked strains of *Salvelinus erythrinus* lay from 500 to 1,500 eggs. The common dwarf chars of Iceland, Norway, Sweden, Finland, and Karelia are the landlocked *Salvelinus lepechini*, and their fecundity ranges from 2,500 to 6,000 eggs. Other strains of dwarf char in Lake Onega in northern Russia develop only 800 to 2,500 ova.

Spawning beds are usually found at depths of eighteen inches to thirty feet, and like the lake trout, these char do not actually construct a complete redd to shelter their fertile ova. Spawning can occur on both gravel and coarse sand. Incubation in the Soviet subarctic typically requires 150 to 165 days, and similar periods are undoubtedly required by parallel species in the American and Canadian arctic. Since these Arctic chars have considerable importance as a commercial species in both northern Russia and Siberia, fisheries research on the species and its several subspecies has been more extensive in the Soviet Union than in other parts of their range.

Although growth and feeding are more rapid in the sea, the chars apparently never remain there. Commercial fishermen in arctic Norway and the Eskimoes on the subarctic coasts of Canada universally believe that the species always returns to its riverine beginnings. *Salvelinus alpinus* is at its peak as a sporting game fish when it is newly arrived from salt water.

Like fresh-run salmon, Arctic char show themselves by jumping and porpoising and rolling in the tidal currents, tasting the half-remembered odors of their rivers. Their schooling behavior is not limited to salt water. Riverine chars also migrate upstream in huge sea-bright shoals of fish, and a mile of current can be teeming with fish, while pools above and below are empty. The angler must hopscotch along the river prospecting for a school of migrating char. Such schools are usually fish of the same approximate size, and when you catch a two-pound char, the others in the pool will be harness mates.

Arctic char are hardware fish once they return from the sea, reflecting their piscivorous behavior in the coastal seas, and they are not a superb fly-fishing species in the usual sense. Fresh from a rich diet of silvery little baitfish, char are gullible for the whirling blades of a spinner, or the flashing rhythms of a wobbling spoon.

They usually collect off the mouths of tributary streams, and cruise the rocky shallows in adjacent bays. Most schools choose depths of two to four feet of water. Chars are not known for wariness. Fishing a fresh-run swarm can be too easy for a truly skilled angler to hold his interest, and like the closely related Dolly Varden, these fish have a singular pattern in taking a retrieved wet fly. Both species follow the retrieve almost lazily, and only take after a prolonged inspection. Sometimes they postpone their strike until a fisherman is almost ready to lift the line for a fresh cast, and their following stalk can last forty or fifty feet.

Arctic char are sometimes disappointing. Their migrations upriver can last as much as two hundred miles in some watersheds, and the long odyssey can weaken their temperament and strength. Other rivers are relatively short. There the fish are strong and fresh-run even when they reach their spawning grounds. Fresh-run and covered with sea lice, Arctic char are stronger than grilse and can make initial runs on light tackle that rival bonefish. The six-pound char will move one hundred yards with reel-searing speed, but he seldom leaps. Fish on the lower George in New Quebec will run well into the backing several times before they become exhausted.

The secret of taking these Arctic char lies in bright wet flies like the Scottish sea-trout patterns, fished deliberately and deep along the bottom. Char take close to the bottom even in surprisingly shallow water. Steelhead flies and mylar marabous are exceptionally good on fresh-run char, and the bright-topped polar-bear patterns with the Schwab brass- and copper-wire bodies have proven particularly effective on *Salvelinus alpinus*.

Salvelinus spectabilis is the scientific designation of the Pacific char known popularly as the Dolly Varden trout. Ichthyologists are still divided about its taxonomy, with some choosing the classification *Salvelinus malma*, the designation of a parallel species found in Kamchatka and the rivers draining into the Sea of Okhotsk. The controversy has existed for years, and in *American Food and Game Fishes*, Jordan and Evermann classified our species *Salvelinus parkei*.

Salvelinus spectabilis is a related subspecies of the more widespread Arctic char, and it exhibits similar color variations in its migratory and landlocked strains. It is sea-bright and silver in its marine and estuarine forms, while miles from the sea in the headwaters the species is a richly spotted and brightly colored char. Landlocked specimens often display a pale ochre-colored spotting, primarily on the dorsal surfaces. Faint vermiculations are also found on the dorsal surfaces in the northern latitudes of its zoogeographic range.

The species has eleven dorsal rays, and its anal fin has only nine. The vomerine bone is relatively short, with teeth only at its head structure. There are 240 to 250 scales along its lateral line. The pyloric caeca are relatively large, numbering between 45 and 50. Body structure is relatively slender. However, lake-dwelling specimens with good parallel populations of Kokanee dwarf salmon are fat, deep-bellied char. The head is large, with a broad and somewhat flattened snout. The mouth is relatively large, with its maxillary extending well behind the eye. Fin structure is rather short for a derivative species of Arctic char, with the caudal fin slightly forked. The general coloring is bluish or olivaceous in cast. There are pale reddish or orange-yellow spots, rather widely spaced, and about the size of the eye. The dorsal surfaces are more heavily marked with somewhat finer spotting. Faint vermiculations may occur on the dorsal surfaces in the northern zones of its range. Like the other char, the dusky orange fins are edged in black and white. Migratory specimens of *Salvelinus spectabilis* are silvery, with the pale spots faintly showing or totally absent.

The parallel species in Asia is found from the Bering Sea to the coastal drainages of Japan, and *Salvelinus spectabilis* is found originally in Pacific slope streams from the headwaters of the Sacramento Basin in California northward to the Aleutians. Estuarine migrations into salt water occur principally in its northern latitudes. The species is indigenous to some rivers and headwater lakes in Montana, Idaho, Washington, Oregon, California, British Columbia, and Alaska. Dwarf landlocked forms are also found in the Aleutians. Several isolated populations of *Salvelinus spectabilis* are known from lakes on both drainage slopes of the Brooks Range in Alaska, and other relict populations survive in surprising isolation in rivers in Nevada and Idaho. The world record weighed thirty-two pounds, and was caught in 1949 by N. L. Higgins at Lake Pend Oreille in Idaho.

Salvelinus spectabilis has any number of local names, like Oregon char, coastal char, bull trout, salmon trout and Dolly Varden, as well as some unprintable ones resulting from its carnivorous habits. Pacific char is perhaps a better nomenclature. The Pacific char spawns in stream currents, actually building an egg-laying redd in most cases. Where the coastal estuaries are part of its life cycle, seaward migrations occur in the spring and fall spawning runs follow later. Its young feed on insect forms and small crustaceans, but later these char develop voracious appetites for small salmon, fingerling trout and baitfish. Typical stomach checks will reveal a half dozen to a dozen trout and salmon fingerlings mixed with other species, and preying on the eggs of spring-spawning fish is a staple in their diet cycle. Their predatory reputation has occasionally led to the payment of bounties for catching and killing them in major salmon fisheries in the Pacific, and fishermen continue to have mixed feelings about them, although *Salvelinus spectabilis* is a welcome species in cold headwaters and tributaries. Lake fishermen find them sluggish fighters, but are impressed with their size. Pacific char are a better hardware fish than a fly-fishing species, like the related Arctic char, but when caught at the mouths of Pacific rivers in the tidal flowages of late summer, these Pacific char are exceptional game fish of excellent table quality. The following observations of David Starr Jordan and Barton Evermann in their *American Food and Game Fishes* are valuable:

This interesting trout is one of the best known species in the west. It reaches a length of two to three feet, and a weight of five to twelve pounds. An example 26 inches long weighed five pounds, one ounce. Like its eastern relative, it is a highly voracious fish, feeding freely on whatever offers, and is especially fond of minnows. At Lake Pend d'Oreille, where the bull trout is an abundant and popular gamefish, we have commonly found two species of minnows and the miller's thumb literally stuffing the stomachs of the fish.

It has been our pleasure to fish for the Dolly Varden trout in many different waters, among which we recall with particular satisfaction the Pend d'Oreille River from the Great Northern Railway to the international boundary, Lake Pend d'Oreille itself at Hope and Sand Point, the Redfish Lakes and Upper Salmon River, high among the Sawtooth Mountains of Idaho, and in a little stream near Unalaska, in which dwells a dwarfed Dolly Varden of unusual beauty.

During July and August, as well as in early spring, it may be caught in any of these waters. In the smaller lakes it is most abundant about the mouths of the inlets, but the best fishing is usually in the streams, as the fish there will rise to the fly more readily, and are usually more gamey. Anything will serve as a lure—artificial fly, grasshopper or any other insect of fair size,

small minnow, pieces of fish or other meat, salmon eggs, trolling
spoon, frog, salamander, and even the bright colored leaves of the
Painted Cup or other flowers.

The gameness of the Dolly Varden trout varies greatly with
the character of the water and the season, just as with any other
gamefish. Those taken in lakes are apt to be sluggish, but when
taken in cold streams, with a good strong current, or in the rapids
where the water tumbles and boils, then the Dolly Varden
displays the superior game qualities which show its kinship to its
eastern and better known congener, the Brook Trout.

There are four subspecies of Arctic char recorded from North American waters at extreme northern latitudes, and these basic types are
closely related to the Pacific char as well. There are probably more
subspecies yet unclassified in remote arctic waters and much ichthyological
work remains before the taxonomy of these chars is clear. However, the four
known subspecies are found in several lakes near Discovery Bay in Baffin
Land, in the lakes of Boothia Felix near the Prince Regent Straits, the
rather common Greenland char also found well-distributed in our arctic
archipelagoes, and the Lake Victoria char of remote Queen Elizabeth
Land.

Biologists have classified the Baffin char as *Salvelinus naresi*, and it is
apparently a relict species closely related to the better-known Oquassa
trout of Maine. It seldom reaches more than a pound in weight. Its habits
are similar to those of parallel relict dwarf char in Iceland and Scandinavia. Its coloring is a rich grayish olive, with a reddish cast to both its body
and its fins in late summer. It is sprinkled with fine scarlet spotting. The
lower fins are deep orange-red with ochreous margins. *Salvelinus naresi* is a
delicious little fish, although with its relatively small average size, little
attention has been given it among anglers in the arctic.

Salvelinus alipes is the long-finned char found in the lakes of Boothia
Felix peninsula near the Prince Regent Straits. According to Jordan and
Evermann, the long-finned char is also reported from several landlocked
biosystems in Greenland, and it is closely related to several subspecies of
saibling found in the mountain lakes of Europe. Its morphology is closely
parallel to other arctic ecotypes, although there are several important
variations. Like other char, the body is relatively elongate with a flattened
and somewhat pointed snout. The lower jaw clearly projects beyond the
upper jaw structure. The maxillary is long and rather slender, projecting
well behind the center of the eye. Preopercular structure is relatively short,
with a truncate lower morphology. Both opercle and preopercle are
conspicuously and deeply striated. The fins are large and relatively
exaggerated in size. The dorsal structure is rather pointed, its proportions
higher than its width. The pectorals are slender and rather sharply
terminated, reaching more than halfway to the ventrals. The ventral fins
are also long and rather pointed, and the anal fin is also rather sharply

tipped. The tail is strongly forked, and these char seldom exceed two to three pounds in weight.

Salvelinus stagnalis is the well-known char found in Greenland and it is also common in both fresh- and salt-water habitat throughout the islands of the Northwest Territories, deep in the Canadian arctic archipelagoes. It is quite closely related to the genotypical *Salvelinus alpinus*, which is widely distributed throughout the arctic regions in North America, Europe and Asia. Their configuration is typically slender and elongate. The pectoral fins are rather short and relatively rounded when compared with other subspecies, and reach less than halfway to the adjacent ventral structure. Its gillraker count is unusually high compared with other related subspecies of Arctic char, and its dorsal is less sharp and exaggerated than its long-finned cousins. It commonly reaches eight to fifteen pounds. Its coloring is an elegant dark greenish olive on the dorsal surfaces, with occasional dark barring and mottling. The lateral surfaces and belly are silvery, with pale yellow spots. Its spots are slightly smaller than the eye. The dorsal, adipose and caudal fins are olive green. The pectoral, ventral and anal fins are pinkish yellow. Sea-run specimens entering the rivers in late summer are so silvery and strong they are commonly mistaken for salmon, although the Atlantic salmon rarely enter the rivers of Greenland.

Salvelinus arcturus is the intriguing subspecies of small char found only in Lake Victoria, deep in the Canadian arctic in Queen Elizabeth Land. Its habitat lies more than eighty-two degrees north, making it the most northern member of the Salmonidae family. It is therefore the arctic equivalent of the relict rainbow population from the coastal mountains of Mexico at Mazatlan. *Salvelinus arcturus* is somewhat slender, its head is small, and it has a moderate mouth structure with a rather obtuse snout. The teeth are small and include a hyoid band. The caudal fin is only moderately forked, the dorsal fin has eleven rays, and there are ten rays in the anal fin. Thirty to 45 pyloric caeca are recorded. Coloring is a dull greenish gray, with silvery flanks and yellowish lower fins. Spotting is pale yellowish white, often faint and virtually absent, and no reddish spots are present although a reddish cast is common at spawning time.

There are five elegant relict char described from lakes in New England, Quebec and Ontario, subspecies that have survived in isolation since the Pleistocene glaciation. These are the marvellous red trout originally discovered at Lac de Marbre in Quebec, the small silver-colored Dublin Pond char from southern New Hampshire, the almost extinct Oquassa trout once plentiful in the Rangeley Lakes of northwestern Maine, the aurora char recently found in the White Pine and Wilderness Lake country of Ontario, and the remarkably beautiful golden char of Sunapee Lake in New Hampshire.

Salvelinus marstoni is the ichthyological designation for the rare red trout found in southern Quebec. It is a remarkable relict species of small char, and was originally described by Professor Samuel Garman from specimens taken at Lac de Marbre in 1893. It is found in deep postglacial lakes over much of its Canadian range, which lies in the rivers north of the Saint Lawrence. Other specimens are recorded from several lakes of the famous Laurentides Club, and the subspecies is also known from the Lac Cassette and the Matamek drainage. Red trout are also numerous in the Red Lakes flowage in the Maskinonge country of Quebec.

The red trout of Lac de Marbre have thirteen rays in their fourteen dorsal fins, and thirteen in the anal fin structure as well. There are fourteen rays in the pectoral fins, and nine rays in the ventrals. The scales are extremely small, and there are 230 to 250 scales along the lateral line. The configuration is relatively subfusiform, slender at the caudal peduncle and somewhat pointed in the snout. Mouth structure is large, with a straight maxillary extending almost to the posterior margin of the eye. The maxillary structure is tooth-bearing along virtually its entire length, with even stronger dental forms on the mandible and intermaxillary, and four hooked teeth are present on either side of the tongue. The opercle is thin with a few faint striations. The dorsal and anal fins are slightly immarginate, while the pectoral and ventral fins are relatively small. The caudal lobes are noticeably pointed, and the entire caudal fin is strongly notched. The dorsal surfaces are unspotted and colored a dark olive brown, with an iridescent bluish cast. The dorsal and adipose fins are almost black. The pectoral, ventral and anal fins are orangey with pale yellow margins, and the lateral surfaces are somewhat paler than the back, shading to a reddish cast toward the whitish belly. The ventral surfaces are scarlet in spawning season. The gill covers are silvery bluish, fading to white under the jaw. There are fine scarlet spots rather widely scattered along the lateral line. These Lac de Marbre fish are elegant and slender. Their maximum size extends to about sixteen inches and slightly more than a pound.

Salvelinus oquassa is the elegant, almost tiny blueback char endemic to the Rangeley Lakes district of Maine. It is both a small and singularly handsome subspecies. It almost never exceeds ten inches in length. It is clearly a relict species from Pleistocene glaciation, and although *Salvelinus oquassa* is visibly different in its configuration, these char exhibit no major taxonomic differences separating them from the small European saibling found in alpine lakes from Austria to France.

There are ten dorsal rays, and nine in the anal fin structure. The lateral line exhibits 230 to 240 scales. The pyloric caeca number 30 to 45. The general configuration is compressed and elongate. The dorsal profile is flatter and considerably less arched than the other char species and subspecies. The head is smaller than any other trout form, its dorsal surfaces relatively flat. The mouth is quite small, and its maxillary is short and rather broad, scarcely reaching the posterior margin of the eye. The jaws are approximately equal in length. The pectoral and ventral fins are not elongate. The caudal peduncle is quite slender and the caudal fin is strongly forked. There are no concentric striations on the opercular structure. General coloring is a steely iridescent bluish-black, with a scattering of bright reddish spots. These tiny spots are smaller than the eye, and there are traces of bold parrlike mottlings on some specimens. The pectoral, ventral and anal fins are orangey, boldly edged in black and white. They strongly resemble the coloration of other char subspecies from the Discovery Bay region of Baffin Land, and the red trout of Lac de Marbre.

Salvelinus oquassa was once abundant in the pelagic lakes of the Rangeley district, but became virtually extinct in its original range in the closing years of the nineteenth century. Its early populations were so extensive that a commercial fishery was possible, but the fragile ecological web found in their habitat was shattered when fish culturists introduced landlocked salmon about 1890. Although their decline is popularly attributed to the predatory feeding of the salmon, its correct cause was probably the introduction of smelt as salmon forage, since the smelt competed directly with the Oquassa char for available food. The species is protected today, although it survives in less than a dozen smaller Maine lakes—perhaps the best fishery is Wadleigh Pond.

Salvelinus agassizi is the silvery Dublin Pond char originally found in a few Connecticut-drainage ponds of southern New Hampshire, all lying within sight of Mount Monadnock. It is the smallest of these several char, and it is on the edge of extinction. Its general coloration is pale grayish, with so few red spots that its pale mottlings are dominant, like the coloring of a lake trout. Its coloring resembles the darker brook trout, with its striking white-edged fins, except that it is much more slender. There are 11 to 13 branchiostegals and 40 to 60 pyloric caeca. The caudal lobes are more sharply pointed, and the caudal fin itself is more deeply notched in the Dublin Pond char. The lateral surfaces are somewhat iridescent and silvery, although the fingerlings are considerably darker. Its maximum size is seven to eight inches, and strong measures are required to save any remaining populations.

The similar little aurora char was first mentioned in 1925, in studies of the sympatric population of brook trout found in White Pine Lake in Ontario. It was accepted as a fully separate species in the past ten years, and classified as *Salvelinus timgamiensis*. Its coloring is quite similar to the Dublin Pond char, except for the roseate faintly ochreous cast that led to its name. Aurora char hybridize readily with introduced brook trout, and cautious management is needed to protect the species. Similar char populations are found in the Matamek watershed in Quebec.

Salvelinus aureolus is the unique and handsome golden char of Sunapee Lake in New Hampshire. Taxonomists presently hold that the Oquassa and Lac de Marbre strains are virtually inseparable in their morphology, while the Sunapee trout is a clearly distinct species. This hypothesis is unresolved and its taxonomic position is relatively unclear. It was totally unknown to ichthyologists until after the Civil War, nor was it named and biologically classified until subsequent research at Sunapee Lake in 1888.

It has ten dorsal rays and nine rays in the anal fin. Its cold-water mesopelagic habitat results in 230 to 250 lateral scales. There are 30 to 45 pyloric caeca. These fish are slender and strongly muscled, with a scarcely arched dorsal profile. The pectoral fins are sharply pointed, but the ventral and anal fins are less elongate. The caudal fin has rather sharply pointed lobes, but is not so deeply forked as the blueback char of Maine or the Lac de Marbre subspecies. The lower jaw clearly protrudes beyond the upper mouth structure, and the mouth itself is somewhat larger than *Salvelinus oquassa*. The maxillary extends only to the posterior margin of the eye. The caudal peduncle is somewhat less slender than in the other relict subspecies of lacustrine chars.

It is surprising that such a boldly colored and unique species could be unknown for more than a century in its easily accessible habitat at Lake Sunapee. Certainly its aboriginal waters were not unknown to both anglers and market fishermen, as well as trained ichthyologists. Its habit of remaining almost entirely at mesopelagic depths, and its spawning on reefs in the open lake in late autumn are perhaps the major factors in its strange obscurity. The primary spawning reefs at Sunapee are also dangerously exposed to fall storms which render the major New England lakes unsafe for relatively small boats.

Salvelinus aureolus was originally described from Sunapee Lake, but it was also indigenous to three other postglacial lakes in New England. Aboriginal populations of golden char were discovered at Big Dan Hole Pond in New Hampshire, Averill Lake in Vermont, and the icy depths of Flood Pond in Maine.

It has been widely introduced to other waters in New Hampshire, but with relatively limited success. Sunapee trout were briefly established in the Third Connecticut Lake, but the subsequent introduction of lake trout soon led to the golden char's disappearance. Occasional fish are still taken from Corner Pond at Ossipee, where an introduced population exists in ecological competition with the related *Salvelinus fontinalis*. Biologists are uncertain if natural spawning occurred among these introduced populations, although there is evidence of a marginally sustaining population of Sunapee char in the Tewksbury Pond, which has recently been poisoned and then reclaimed by biologists in New Hampshire.

During the hot midsummer months at Sunapee Lake, its unique char remain at depths of sixty to one hundred feet, where the temperature is less than fifty degrees. The habitat of all three original environments sheltering aboriginal populations of Sunapee char is exceptionally pure and cold. Bottom temperatures range from thirty-eight to fifty-two degrees, depending upon depth, and the maximum depths of all three lakes are in excess of one hundred feet. Their bottoms are typically composed of bedrock, white sand and fine pea gravel, providing both propitious spawning conditions and rich populations of baitfish and crustaceans. Following ice-out in springtime, these Sunapee char are found in comparatively shallow water along the shorelines. Little is known of their winter behavior, except that specimens are sometimes taken through the ice.

The golden char gather to spawn on a deep reef off Sunapee harbor in early October. Actual spawning rites occur from late October until the end of November. The species is more prolific than its related chars. Average female fecundity can range from 1,200 to almost 12,000 eggs, with a ratio of approximately 1,200 ova per pound of henfish weight. With access to heavy populations of smelt, growth rates of the Sunapee char are rapid. There are historical accounts of fish from twelve to twenty pounds, although the certified world record is a fish of eleven and a half pounds, caught by Ernest Theoharis in the late summer of 1954.

Fish culturists report that *Salvelinus aureolus* is hardy and susceptible to artificial propagation, and its fertile ova are readily transportable. Its fingerlings display a singular quality of wariness, hiding almost constantly and avoiding both open water and high levels of subaquatic illumination. Their thermal resistance is remarkable, and hatchery biologists confirm their ability to thrive in water much too cold for brook trout. Fishery management policy for many years has consisted of netting the Sunapee char from their spawning reefs, stripping their eggs and milt, and hatching these fertilized ova under controlled conditions. The fingerlings are raised to yearling size before restocking in the lake, obtaining a higher rate of survival than is possible in the natural state. Such hatchery procedures have been considered more effective than permitting the fish to propagate themselves, although such tray-raised fingerlings do not always adapt quickly to their microscopic natural foods. The species is protected with a twelve-inch minimum size and a two-fish bag limit, but it remains in serious danger of extinction, perhaps because of subtle ecological changes in its habitat and our overmanipulation of its parent stocks.

These remarkable golden char must be protected and preserved in self-sustaining populations. Perhaps the most intriguing work on *Salvelinus aureolus* and its closely related subspecies is *The Geological Ancestors of the Brook Trout* written by John Quackenbos in 1916. This little book was published as a limited edition of only three hundred copies, the first undertaken by the Anglers' Club of New York, and it contains the following passages typical of his ornamental prose:

> These char are distinguished by the presence of a broad row of teeth on the hyoid bone, between the lower extremities of the first two gill-arches; the absence of mottling on the dark sea-green back, and the excessively developed fins; inconscpicuous yellow spots without aureola: a square or slightly emarginate tail; a small and delicately shaped head; diminutive, aristocratic mouth; liquid planetary eyes, and a generally graceful build; a phenomenally brilliant nuptial colouration, recalling the common foreign appellations of blood-red charr, gilt charr, and golden saibling. As the October pairing time approaches, the Sunapee fish becomes richly illuminated with its maturing passion.

The steel-green mantle of the back and shoulders now seems

to dissolve into a veil of amethyst, through which the daffodils of midsummer gleam out in points of flame, while below the lateral line, all is dazzling orange. The fins catch the hues of adjacent parts, and the pectoral, ventral, anal and lower lobe of the caudal are marked in lustrous white.

It is a unique experience to watch this American saibling spawning on the Sunapee shallows. Here in all the magnificence of their nuptial decoration flash schools of painted beauties, circling in proud sweeps about the submerged boulders they would select as the scenes of their loves—the poetry of an epithalamium in every motion—in one direction, uncovering to the sunbeams in amorous leaps their golden-tinctured sides, gemmed with the fire of rubies; in another, darting in little companies, the pencilled margins of their fins seeming to trail behind them like white ribbons under the ripples. There are conspicuous differences in the intensity of general colouration, and the gaudy dyes of the milter are tempered in the spawner to a dead-lustre cadmium with opal spots.

The wedding garment nature has given to this char is unparagoned. Those who have seen the bridal march of the glistening hordes, in all the glory of colour and majesty of action, pronounce it a spectacle never to be forgotten.

7. The Grayling of North America

The river is low and clear in September, winding through the bare ochre-colored prairies above Twin Bridges, and the aspens are already pale in the high country. The willows are a rich yellow after the first hard-frost nights, and finally the cottonwoods begin to turn, scattering the bright confetti of their leaves into the pools. The sagebrush country of the river bottoms is brown-trout water, with its flats and half-mile pools and sweeping riffles. There are dark tea-colored runs under the willows, and deep holes filled with tangled cottonwood deadfalls. The big trout lie there, hiding among the fallen trees. The first cold autumn nights start them moving upriver to spawn, and it is pleasant fishing during the shirt-sleeve days that follow in October.

It is sprawling, open country in the basin. There are several ranches along the lower river, their red corrugated roofs bright among poplar windbreaks. The haying is finished and the stacked bales are piled high in the meadows along the water. September mornings are clear and still, except for the distant music of the river and a bawling steer separated from its herd in the willow bottoms.

Our camp was in the tall cottonwoods along the river at Biltmore Hot Springs. Its simple cabins and main building were sheltered under the wind-smooth bluffs a quarter of a mile from the stream. Below the tension tents ran a long, two-hundred-yard pool, its current swelling deep and smooth under the sheltering willows.

The river winds upstream from Twin Bridges, working against the low series of hills that separate the river's flow from the valley of the Beaverhead. There are rocky bluffs south of the river now and this is rattlesnake country. The shattered ledges and outcroppings cast deep shadows in

341

the afternoons, and the river banks are still lined with cottonwoods at Melrose and Divide, with the Beaverhead Range beyond its currents in the west. Here the river flows south, and its sweeping riffles and deep olive green pools shelter some enormous rainbows and brown trout. September finds serious brown-trout fishermen from all over the United States gathering in these towns along the lower river, and comparing notes in log-framed bars filled with the antlers of mule deer and elk, and the melancholy sounds of country music. Sometimes there is a billiard table, its lights gleaming from the racked balls and soft on the worn felt, and there are always garish pinball machines.

The mountains rise in the west, behind the first foothills with their stands of scrub oak and ponderosa, their summits reaching more than 11,000 feet into the pale September skies. The river forces its flow through these first ranges in the steep-walled canyon above Divide, and its crescendos batter among the truck-sized boulders. It is water that has surrendered some trophy rainbows over the years, and it tumbles through its fierce rapids into deep ledgerock pools.

It is a fertile river, leaching its rich nutrients from the phosphate and limestone hills, and its character changes above the Watercress Spring at Jerry Creek Bridge. Its valley opens here in the sheltered Wise River country. Its altitude has changed the trees to ponderosa and lodgepole pine, although there are still cottonwoods around the ranches. The Wise adds its icy flow to the river meadows here, and with the several spring creeks in the bottoms, the river is much colder above Jimmy New Creek and the Jerry Creek Bridge. Whiteface cattle graze across the water meadows, and the stacked hay is fenced to protect it from the elk that drift down from the Anaconda range to winter at Wise River.

It is a simple town, with more than its quota of unforgettable characters. There is the flamboyant irrigation contractor, with a waxed regimental mustache, who keeps a covey of gleaming vintage cars, including a gull-wing Mercedes, an elegant pewter-colored Aston Martin, and a stately Rolls-Royce, in his weathered hay barn. There is the gruff Scottish rancher whose family settled at Wise River after the boomtown years in the mines at Virginia City and were already working cattle before General Custer and his cavalry troop were annihilated on the Little Big Horn. The general store is the switchboard for a unique mixture of gossip and ribald wit and information about the surrounding country. It boasts a genial proprietor improbably named Walter Gnose, and both the town and the valley would not be the same without the Gnose Mercantile Company store.

Snow gets tired out here, Gnose explains deadpan to strangers, with a furtive wink at his local audience. *Blows back and forth all winter from Twin Bridges to Wisdom—and it gets plumb wore out!*

It is difficult country in the winter.

The snow works in eave-deep against the houses, and the outbuildings are often totally lost in its drifts. Firewood supplies are critical. The livestock is shaggy with winter hair and huddles in sheltered places out of the wind, its collective breath pluming high like the steam from the hot springs. The watercress creeks at Wise River keep the winter-locked river partially open below the town, but there is so much snow farther west that its winding course is completely erased under the winter drifts. The river is colder here, with fewer and fewer brown trout above the town. The big *Pteronarcys* stoneflies, the ones that are famous for the salmon-fly hatches in early summer, virtually disappear in the riffles above the Glaus Ranch at Wise River.

Farther west lie the towering wilderness mountains of the Anaconda Range, and the sprawling high-altitude basin that the frontier trappers called the Big Hole. It is the country where Chief Joseph and his gallant Nez Percé warriors lost the decisive battle that led to their surrender. It has given its name to the river too, and the Big Hole is still one of the finest trout streams in America.

Lewis and Clark came through this region, exploring a route west across the Louisiana Purchase, and the mountain men and fur trappers soon followed. They found a sprawling world of high plains, smooth grass-covered foothills, huge rivers and tumbling cutthroat streams, and towering mountains. Montana is a sprawling country in itself, much larger than Germany or Japan, and its people have always loved its immense scale. Its mountains are the source of the Missouri, which drains 500,000 square miles and journeys almost 2,500 miles before it finally reaches the Mississippi. The fur trappers followed the beaver into the headwaters of the Missouri, providing their thick pelts for the fashionable top hats and bowlers worn in Philadelphia and New York and London.

There were other riches in these headwaters, in addition to the minerals and wild game and cattle, since the high-altitude sources of the Missouri also shelter a unique and incomparable game fish, the Montana grayling. These beautiful fish are found in the snowmelt headwaters of the Beaverhead and the Madison and the Big Hole. Although they are all but extinct in the headwaters of the Madison in Yellowstone Park, there are still substantial populations in the Beaverhead and the Big Hole country— in high-altitude streams cold enough to shelter a relict subspecies isolated from its parent strains of Arctic grayling in Pleistocene times, and the only surviving species of American grayling.

Our waters once held two unique species. The Montana grayling and the Michigan grayling were similar relict species dating back to ancient glaciation, but the rapacity of lumbering in Michigan after the Civil War totally eradicated the Michigan species. It is one of the singular tragedies in the history of American angling.

Fortunately, the Montana grayling is still thriving in much of its original habitat in the headwaters of the Missouri. Like the other species of grayling in Europe and Asia, it is remarkably similar to the trout and char in both external character and behavior. The primary taxonomic differences lie in the structure of the skull, and the presence of epipleural spines found on the anterior ribs. The parietal bones meet at the center, separating the frontals from the supraoccipital bone. Although there is some truth to the conventional wisdom that the grayling is a species intermediate between the whitefish and the trout, the argument cannot be supported by its skeletal evidence.

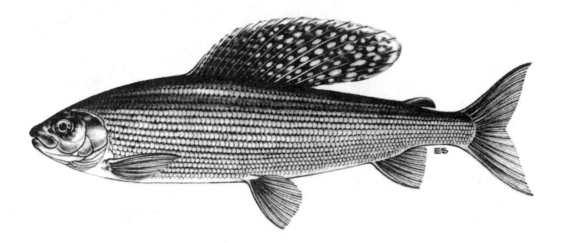

European Grayling (*Thymallus thymallus*)

Although there are about a dozen species of grayling found in Europe and Asia, only three were originally found in North America. Singular in each of the species and subspecies of the *Thymallus* genus is a large sail-shaped dorsal fin that carries more than seventeen rays. The grayling have relatively large and coarse scales, particularly when compared with the char, and there are typically only ninety to a hundred scales along the lateral line. Coloration varies radically, both within a single region and sometimes in a single river system. Specimens can seem bluish, gray, brown, bronze or silvery. Both the dorsal and lateral surfaces of the body can display spotting, in rather irregularly shaped markings, primarily behind the opercular structure. Color varies considerably with the hourly quality of light, until their slender bodies reflect silvery lilac and gold, and the entire grayling can have a brassy metallic sheen of great beauty. Saint Ambrose of Milan called them the Flower of Fishes, and French clerics recorded the speculation that their diet consisted of gold, but it was *The Compleat Angler* in which these observations were made by Walton:

> And some think he feeds on water-thyme, for he smells of it when first taken out of the water; and they may think so with as good reason, as we do, that the smelts smell like violets at their first being caught, which I think is also a truth.

The grayling is a delicate and elegant fish, worthy of the praise it has received over the centuries. Its physical character is defined in its oblong, relatively compressed body and its limited elevation. The mouth is delicate and small. The maxillary is short, extending past the center of the eye, but not fully to its rear margin. The teeth are sparse on the maxillaries, premaxillaries, and lower jaw structures. The vomerine bone is short and displays a small patch of teeth. There are also teeth present on the palatines. The tongue is almost toothless or virtually without teeth. The scales are relatively loose. The dorsal fin can have as many as 24 rays and is quite exaggerated in the males. The air bladder is proportionately large, and there are only 15 to 18 pyloric caeca. The adipose structure is rather slender and small, and the delicate tail of the grayling is strongly forked.

Thymallus montanus is the subspecies that survives and still thrives in our western mountains. Late in the nineteenth century it was still widely distributed throughout the headwaters of the Missouri above Great Falls. It was first reported from these native waters in 1860, by a frontier cavalry surgeon named J. E. Head. According to Jordan and Evermann in *American Food and Game Fishes*, the Montana grayling was particularly abundant in rivers like the Jefferson, Gallatin, Beaverhead, and Madison. Its lowest habitat in the Missouri watershed was perhaps the Smith River, draining the Big Belt Mountains and joining the Missouri itself only a few miles above Great Falls. Jordan and Evermann also mention the Red Rock River, its headwater lakes and the glacier-cold Elk Creek tributary above the lake. The federal hatcheries at Bozeman were already collecting grayling eggs from specimens taken at Elk Creek during their spring spawning runs in 1902.

Thymallus montanus reaches optimal spawning in April and May, depending on weather and temperature. With the approach of spawning, the grayling once migrated up the Jefferson, and into its tributaries, the Beaverhead and Red Rock. The fish then passed through the fourteen-mile length of the Red Rock Lake, high on the threshold of the Continental Divide, and into the inlets of the upper lake. The primary spawning grounds lie in Elk Creek, and Jordan and Evermann describe its grayling in the following passage:

> At spawning time Elk Creek is fairly alive with grayling on the gravelly shallows, where their large and beautiful dorsal fins are seen waving clear of the water, in the manner of shark's fins on a flood tide.

Doctor James Henshall was the fish culturist who began the artificial propagation of these Montana grayling at Bozeman in 1898. These fish exhibit a fecundity of 2,000 to 4,000 eggs per fish, and their average size was ten to twelve inches in the past. They are not much smaller now, and the grayling in the Big Hole will run about nine to ten inches. Henshall regularly harvested five million eggs and hatched some four million fry for

James Henshall

stocking. His work has preserved sustaining populations in the Big Hole, Red Rock and Gibbon, as well as a number of high lakes in Montana and the Yellowstone.

Thymallus montanus is a selective and superb little game fish, and I have caught many of them in the smooth flats of the Big Hole, several miles above Wise River. Their diet on that stretch of river primarily consisted of relatively small Trichoptera and two-winged flies, with tiny mayflies important as well. The most impressive rises of grayling in my experience have been focused upon midge pupae, and tiny dark-hackled wet flies and nymphs were most effective. The flesh of the Montana grayling is firm and sweet, and broiled *meunière* with lemon and melted butter, the delicate Montana grayling is perhaps better than trout.

Ray Bergman fished these grayling with wet flies at Grebe Lake in the Yellowstone country, describing his experiences in *Trout*. He too had a high opinion of their sporting and table qualities. Bergman had earlier fished for whitefish, which the local anglers had erroneously called grayling, on the Elk in northern Colorado and was disappointed in their drab coloring and indifferent fight. Bergman expressed his poor opinion of what he thought were grayling in a subsequent article and triggered an avalanche of angry letters from experienced grayling fishermen in Wyoming and Montana. Bergman relates the incident in his grayling chapter, and its pages are filled with his admiration for the species:

> All this made me more determined than ever to catch some grayling. About this time I received a letter from Vint Johnson of West Yellowstone. He spoke of grayling and said we should come there for them, so we speedily made arrangements to do so.

It was the 19th of September when we arrived at West Yellowstone, and by this time some grayling waters were already closed. I had thought we'd find some in the Madison, but was told this was exceedingly uncertain. But Scotty Chapman, Park Ranger, came to the rescue. He had a pet pond where he said we'd be sure to catch all we wanted.

This was Grebe Lake, deep in the forest. After a two-mile drive on a lumber road you still had a long two miles and a bit more to walk to get to the fishing.

All that Scotty said about the pond was true. The location was beautiful and wild, and there were plenty of grayling in it. When I saw the first one I wondered how I ever could confuse them with whitefish. They were graceful, racy and colorful. When you looked at them in the water preparatory to landing them, they looked like fish-shaped, animated purple flowers.

Bergman found that his most effective fishing was a deliberate hand-twist retrieve, started once the flies had sunk deep enough to almost touch the weeds. Our modern sinking lines did not exist in those years, and Bergman had his best results with an old waterlogged fly line of silk. Most takes were so subtle that one was almost unaware of the fish. Bergman found that these grayling were not shy, and that stopping his retrieve when a rise was missed invariably brought a second plucking hit. Sometimes a grayling would follow his retrieve, taking it several times, until the fly was lifted from the water for a fresh cast.

His experience confirmed the fact that grayling often take a fly when it touches the water, and that they are difficult to hook when they take so quickly. The fish also took frequently while the fly was sinking toward the weeds, although the take was often so imperceptible it could not be felt. Bergman watched carefully to see if the faint twitching of his leader might betray a grayling that had taken his fly.

Bergman also observed that certain places would produce a number of fish, and then suddenly go dead and unproductive. When such changes of mood occurred, another area nearby would often become productive, and he concluded that the grayling primarily moved in schools. My own experience has been almost entirely with small flies fished just in or under the surface film rather than a deep hand-twist retrieve in high lakes, but the grayling in the big smooth-water flats of the Big Hole otherwise behaved much like his delicate little fish of Grebe Lake.

Bergman obviously loved fishing the grayling in the tree-bordered little pond in the Yellowstone, its fish cruising in nervous schools above the mossy bottom. His warm regard for *Thymallus montanus* is found in *Trout* and these closing passages in his chapter about grayling:

As a morsel of food the grayling is most appetizing, by far the best freshwater fish I've ever eaten. The flesh is firm and sweet and has a really distinctive flavor. In this respect the Rocky Mountain whitefish is a close rival, being in my opinion much better eating than trout.

The wild aspect of Grebe Lake and the forest walk leading to it makes a visit there something to be cherished in the memory. One trip there we had snow, and the evergreen forest was trimmed with a mantle of pure fluffy white. On the lake the wind blew strong and cold. Our lines froze to the guides as we retrieved and finally we had to quit because we could not use our hands. We left in a small blizzard. As far as our feelings went, we might have been trekking the frozen northland hundreds of miles from the nearest habitation, instead of being only a few miles from our car, with its heater and other modern conveniences.

And besides this aspect of the Yellowstone, one is always encountering wild life. Never a day went by in our stay there that we didn't see something to make us stop and marvel. Bear, deer, elk, and other wild life makes each day an adventure. Even as I write this my wife and I are reserving a little cabin in West Yellowstone.

Arctic grayling are the genotypical North American species that formed the parent strain of both the Montana and Michigan subspecies. It has been classified *Thymallus arcticus* by fisheries biologists, and is highly prized for its sporting qualities and beauty. Although it is extremely abundant and easily caught throughout its range, its remote subarctic habitat makes it a comparatively rare species for most fly-fishermen.

The grayling is found in both Europe and Asia, as well as the western subarctic of British Columbia, Alberta, Saskatchewan, Yukon and the Northwest Territories. It is an extremely abundant species in many Alaskan waters. Virtually all of the major oligotrophic lakes in the Canadian northwest, particularly the Athabasca, Bear, Reindeer, and Great Slave lakes, contain major lacustrine populations of Arctic grayling. Their average weight is slightly over a pound, and a two-pound specimen is a fine grayling even in the arctic, though three-pounders are not uncommon. The present world-record North American grayling is a five-and-a-half-pound male taken by Jeanne Pranson from the Northwest Territories in 1967.

Europe and Asia also hold a number of subspecies. *Thymallus thymallus* is the handsome grayling of Europe, found commonly from the ruined abbeys of medieval Britain to the classic Traun in Austria, and south to the rivers of Dalmatia and Montenegro. It exists in sustaining populations throughout the continent except for southern France, Spain, Portugal, Ireland, and southern Italy. Its full range reaches east to the Urals in the Soviet Union, and it is abundant in the cold headwaters of the Volga.

Several subspecies of Arctic grayling are found in Scandinavia, Russia, and Siberia. Perhaps the best known is the red-finned strain found in the northern latitudes of Norway, Sweden, and Finland. There are also the distinct strains from western Siberia, Kamchatka, Amur, and in Lake

Baikal, where the black Angara grayling and white Baikal grayling exist in distinct sympatric populations. There is also a unique red-spotted Dalmatian grayling in Yugoslavia. Other singular species include the dark little *Thymallus nigriscens* grayling of Lake Kosogol in Russia, and *Thymallus brevirostris*, the river grayling of northern Outer Mongolia.

Specimens of our *Thymallus arcticus* studied by Jordan and Evermann displayed 17 to 24 dorsal rays, and 11 rays in the anal fin. There were 90 to 100 scales along the lateral line, and 18 pyloric caeca. The configuration was elongate, the head relatively short, subconic, and slightly depressed. The dorsal profile was contiguous with the anterior curve of the back. The mouth is moderate and proportionately small, and its jaws were approximately equal in length. The scales were moderate and rather typically fragile in their attachment to the fish. The maxillary extended below the middle of the eye. The lateral line was nearly straight, and there was a tiny bare space behind the isthmus. The dorsal fins of the males were flamboyantly exaggerated, the adipose fin was slender and relatively small, while the caudal structure was deeply forked.

Coloration is spectacular in these Arctic grayling. The caudal, pectoral, and anal fins are typically a dusky yellow-olive. However, the ventral fins display longitudinal striations of dark gray and a surprising pinkish-violet. The dorsal fin is the unique feature of the species. It is large in both male and female grayling, and its configuration is particularly exaggerated in the males. It is reversed in shape, starting low and sweeping high toward its posterior margins. The dorsal has irregular and distinct rows of dark spots, and is tinged with pink and white and a greenish iridescence when freshly caught. The dorsal surfaces are purplish olive, with a similar sheen, and there is sometimes a pale roseate cast on its gill covers. Like the polychromatic dolphin caught in salt water, the grayling is one of those fish whose delicately rich palette of colors quickly disappears at death.

Thymallus arcticus spawns from late March until early summer, depending on latitude and seasonal fluctuations. It can be remarkably fecund in the larger females, ovipositing from 1,000 to 15,000 eggs. It reaches sexual maturity at three years, and its spawning occurs in small swift-flowing streams. Arctic grayling seldom construct a full-fledged redd like many trout and char. The females merely sweep the pea gravel or coarse bottom aggregates free of silt, while the males hover nearby protecting the nest. Their exaggerated dorsal fins are part of a ritual territoriality, and are raised like the hackles on a gamecock when another male approaches a female.

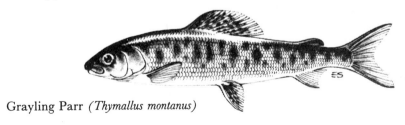

Grayling Parr *(Thymallus montanus)*

Izaak Walton may be partially responsible for the myth that grayling have a tender mouth and are easily lost during the fight. His opinion in *The Compleat Angler* about the soft-mouthed grayling has been allowed to continue unchallenged in fishing books for more than three centuries.

The grayling mouth is actually rather leathery and tough, and once a fish is firmly hooked, it is surprisingly difficult to lose. However, like the whitefish its mouth is proportionately quite small, and unless the fly is small it is difficult for the hook to lodge. There is also a natural reflex on the part of the angler not to strike firmly enough, because the grayling often takes the fly in a salmonlike roll, and does not actually have the fly in its mouth until relatively late in its rise-pattern. As with the salmon, the experienced angler learns to pause while the grayling fully takes the fly. Lost grayling are usually the result of a premature strike, rather than a soft mouth structure. Charles Ritz is perhaps the most analytical grayling fisherman in Europe, and his regard for the species is obvious from the discussions in his *Fly Fisher's Life.* Ritz advocates the delayed strike and recommends delicate black patterns on size eighteen and twenty double hooks for the *Thymallus* rivers of Scandinavia, Britain and France, as well as the legendary grayling fisheries of southern Germany and Austria.

Grayling like tiny flies! Ritz outlines his theories with the dramatic punctuation of agitated hands and expressive Gaullic eyebrows. *Particularly little black patterns, and the tiny little doubles hook and hold beautifully!*

Arctic grayling also travel in schools, like the gregarious subspecies Bergman fished over at Grebe Lake in the Yellowstone forty years ago. Catching one grayling is sure to signal the presence of others. Lacustrine populations are often found cruising the shallows, particularly in the morning and evening when their lakes lie still. Most experienced fly-fishers will either wade and fish a suitable shoreline or work a canoe parallel to it watching for their telltale rise forms. The presence of a school might be revealed through its spectral movements above a pale bottom, bulging to nymphs or pupae, or a galaxy of dimpling rises to surface insects.

Stream populations can inhabit virtually any part of a watershed, but knowledgeable grayling fishermen are convinced that *Thymallus arcticus* usually selects particular types of habitat. Sometimes the fish choose deep, slow-flowing channels. Other schools may select a deep eddy, or the smooth basin-shaped lies that form around a major deadfall or boulder. It is not unusual to find many grayling lying deep in such crystalline currents on our large arctic rivers in Alaska and the Yukon.

Grayling also have the strange habit of lying deep on the stream or lake bottom even when rising to surface fly hatches. They tend to rise swiftly and almost vertically from a holding lie, taking the fly with a splashy roll. Arctic grayling often leap over a dry fly and take it on the return trip down. The rise typically occurs behind the holding position of the fish, and grayling seem to prefer taking a fly several feet behind their actual lies, rather than drifting right or left, or intercepting it by moving upstream in anticipation like a trout. Charles Ritz observes in his *Fly Fisher's Life* that grayling are more demanding of an angler's skills in the sense that they will not move to right or left from their rather precise and narrow line of drift. However, such critical demands on presentation are not often coupled with wariness, and the grayling resembles the brook trout in its gullibility and curiosity. Grayling are often tippet shy, but will rise again and again to virtually all the patterns in the fly box. However, selectivity can often make matching the hatch advisable on hard-fished waters in both Montana, and on the venerable grayling rivers of Europe. A. J. McClane has some sage advice for grayling fishermen in his *Standard Fishing Encyclopedia:*

> The main difference between trout and grayling fly-fishing is that, for the latter, downstream casting is usually more effective than fishing upstream.
>
> Because the fish can be extremely leader-shy in rivers which get any amount of angling pressure, the grayling expert tries to wade into a position where he can drift the fly over the fish, showing the fly first. This is accomplished with a slack line cast by aiming the fly a yard or so short of the target. When the maneuver is done correctly, the fly falls lightly as thistledown on the surface, and drifts down into the grayling's feeding lane without drag. The knack of downstream casting with a slack line is easily learned with a little practice. Of course, you can work across-stream too, if the fish is in an awkward position.
>
> Leader shyness is probably not the only reason for the higher scores made fishing downstream. When working with the current, the angler can cover more water with less effort.
>
> This combination of factors is important when you realize that grayling usually take their stations on the bottom and require a bit more time to get to the top than a trout. They also have a common tendency to follow a fly before taking it; there is a brief time-lag involved, and the upstream fly which floats back so quickly often moves, but does not earn a fish.
>
> Of course, the same can be said of a wet fly or nymph. Ordinarily, it's best to fish them across and downstream, minimizing drag as much as possible so that the fly sweeps around below. However, be ready for a strike at the moment the line has straightened out directly downstream. The grayling, as noted, has a habit of pursuing the fly for a distance, and many strikes occur just as you pick up for a new cast.

The elegant Michigan grayling is tragically extinct. It was once the principal species of Lower Michigan, before the greed of clear-and-slash lumbering eradicated its habitat. Large populations existed in Michigan rivers like the Pere Marquette, Manistee, Cedar, Sturgeon, Jordan, and the several tributaries of the Au Sable. It was also native to cold little Otter Creek in the Upper Peninsula, where the last sustaining population existed before the Michigan grayling disappeared. Fish culturists collected specimens from the Otter for stripping as late as 1932, in a doomed attempt to preserve the unique Michigan species.

Thymallus tricolor was so numerous in the nineteenth century that anglers who made the arduous journey north on the Jackson, Lansing and Saginaw or the Grand Rapids and Indiana could easily catch three grayling on every three-fly cast. Such ingenuousness combined with the destruction of the surrounding forests to destroy the Michigan grayling in less than a half century. Fred Mather tried desperately to propagate the Michigan grayling in hatcheries, in a vain effort to prevent its extinction, and his book *My Angling Friends* contains a memorable description of the subspecies:

> There is no species sought by anglers that surpasses the grayling in beauty. They are more elegantly formed and more graceful than the trout, and their great dorsal fin is a mark of loveliness.
>
> When the well-lids were lifted, and the sun's rays admitted, lighting up the delicate olive-brown tints of the back and sides, the bluish-white of the abdomen, and the mingling tints of rose, pale blue, and purplish-pink on the fins, they displayed a combination of colours equalled by no fish outside the tropics.
>
> The pectorals are olive-brown, with a bluish tint at the ends; the ventrals are striped with alternate streaks of brown and pink; the anal fin is plain brown; the caudal is very forked and plain, while the crowning glory is the immense dorsal, which is dotted with large, brilliant-red or purplish blue spots, surrounded with a splendid emerald green which fades after death—the strangely changeable shade of green found in the peacock's tail.

The existence of a unique grayling subspecies in Lower Michigan was a great surprise to American ichthyologists, and it was virtually unrecognized before 1850. Minor scientific papers were published in the decade that followed, based on specimens taken from the watershed of the Muskegon, but the first disciplined taxonomy of the Michigan grayling was not published until 1865.

It described specimens displaying 93 to 98 scales along the lateral line. The dorsal structure was less dramatic than the arctic genotypes, being both lower in profile and smaller, and having only a maximum of 21 to 22 rays. Otherwise its taxonomy was virtually identical to the Arctic grayling, and it was a curious glacial relict subspecies, isolated and surviving more than 1,000 miles from its adjacent related populations.

James Milner was the Deputy United States Commissioner of Fisheries in the years following the Civil War, and Milner played a major role in the development of fisheries science in America. Judge Daniel Fitzhugh of Bay City was one of the notable fly-fishermen in nineteenth-century Michigan, and it was Fitzhugh who organized an expedition to the swift little Jordan in northern Michigan for Milner. Their expedition provided both the experience and the specimens for an elaborate scientific essay on the

Michigan grayling, which Milner published in the Second Fish Commission Report. Their field work was conducted in 1871 and 1873, and Milner compiled what may be the most precise description of *Thymallus tricolor* and its primeval habitat:

> In the centre of the Lower Peninsula of Michigan is a wide elevated plateau, a sandy region with a soil containing a very small percent of organic matter, and covered with a dense forest of pines, generally the Norway pine, *Pinus resinosa*, growing in grand dimensions, the long limb-free shafts making wide boards free from knots, yet but little utilized, while immense forests of the favorite lumber material, white pine, *Pinus strobus*, are as yet uncut. From this plateau arise several large streams and rivers flowing each way into Lakes Huron and Michigan. Among these are three rivers of note, the Muskegon and Manistee emptying into Lake Michigan, and the swift Au Sable, entering into Lake Huron.
>
> Among the minor streams are the Cheyboygan, Thunder Bay, and Rifle, all tributary to Lake Huron, and the Jordan, emptying through Pine Lake into the Traverse Bays of Lake Michigan. A few branches and springfed streams are formed, in which the water has a uniform degree of coldness throughout the summer, seldom rising above fifty-two degrees.
>
> The rivers Rifle, Au Sable, Jordan, Hersey Branch of the Muskegon, and the headwaters of the Manistee all have this character, and in all of these, and only in this limited locality, short of the Yellowstone region, is found the already famous Michigan grayling.

Artificial propagation of the Michigan grayling was attempted as soon as its existence became known. Fred Mather and Seth Green, the near-legendary biologists at the Cold Spring Harbor and Caledona hatcheries in New York, were the earliest experimenters with its artificial breeding.

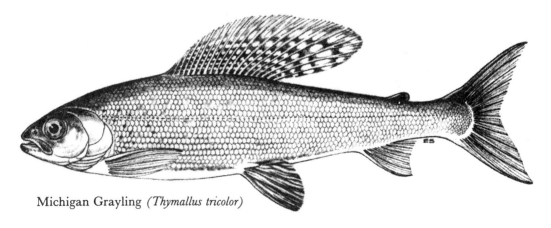

Michigan Grayling *(Thymallus tricolor)*

Mather was the first, travelling to the Au Sable in the late winter of 1874. His trip proved too early, since the fish were not yet ready for spawning. Seth Green arrived in late April, when the grayling had already left their spawning beds, but his party were able to recover a few fertilized eggs from the gravel. Although more than one hundred ova were gathered, the Green expedition was also a failure.

Fred Mather journeyed to Michigan again in 1875, arriving on the Au Sable in early April, and obtained some 8,000 ova. These were successfully brought back and hatched at Cold Spring Harbor, and the young grayling were introduced into various streams in Michigan and western New York. Perhaps the most interesting fact observed in the course of these experiments conducted by Mather and Green was the striking fecundity of the Michigan grayling. Its average yield of fertile eggs easily surpassed brook trout of comparable size, with a typical 3,000 to 4,000 ova, yet their last-ditch efforts failed. The enthusiasm that greeted the discovery of the Michigan grayling in the nineteenth century was unable to prevent its extinction.

It is true that grayling are mildly disappointing in their fighting qualities when compared with the trout. Once hooked, grayling usually make a darting run with several threshing leaps in the surface against the tension of the rod tip, and then work deep in a series of head-shaking circles. The fight seldom lasts, and it usually ends as suddenly as it begins, with the fish surrendering meekly. Yet the worth of the grayling cannot be measured in muscular terms alone, and far too many yardsticks for fishing sport are based solely on mere strength and acrobatics. These words of Mather capture a subtle poetry we have forever lost:

> As we embarked in our light boats in the early morning, and our bows broke the trailing mist which covered the river, it was as if we were brushing the fresh bloom from newly plucked fruit, so untouched by man did everything seem in this untraversed wild.
>
> Quietly the guides poled the boats down the rapid current, while we adjusted rods, lines and leaders, using a lead-colored and brown and black hackle.
>
> Several favourite spots were tried before a fish was struck, but before we reached the site of our chosen encampment, seven of the graceful creatures were swimming in the well of one boat and four in the other. The campstores were put on shore, and we began the work of the day in earnest, dropping our flies at just the spots where trout would be sought for.
>
> They rise rapidly from the bottom or middle of the water, darting upwards, and having seized the fly, return to their stations. Hooking a large one, we had good evidence of their plucky qualities; the pliant rod bent as he struggled against the line, curling his body around columns of water that failed to sustain his grasp, and setting his great dorsal fin like an oar

backing water, while we cautiously worked him in, his tender mouth requiring rather more careful handling than would be required for a trout; making a spurt upstream, he requires a yielding line, but after a time he submits to be brought in, rallying for a dart under the boat or beneath a log, as an attempt is made to place a landing-net under him. Finally, brought on board exhausted, he is easily removed from the hook and slipped through the hole in the cover of the well.

Nine were taken from a deep hole under projecting willow bushes. Several times two were taken at once, and Judge Fitzhugh, by skillful management, landed three on one fortunate cast. They are strong, free biters and cannot be considered very shy, as they will rise repeatedly to a fly if a failure is made in hooking them. The first day's efforts resulted in the capture of seventy-two, and the second day brought up the score to one hundred and forty-three, from those measuring five inches in length to those larger specimens weighing a pound and a half.

The Au Sable was unquestionably the queen of the Michigan grayling rivers in those days of Mather and Fitzhugh and Green. It is a beautiful river system of many secrets, its several branches born in the cedar swamps and marl-bog springs of northern Michigan. The Middle Branch rises in a series of springholes east of Otsego Lake, while the East Branch has its origins in other marl swamps. The two tributaries merge at Grayling. The Au Sable is a full-blown river now, winding through the sandy moraines and second-growth forests below the town. Its bottom is pale amber-colored sand and gravel, and its smooth currents sliding past deadfalls of downed cedar and pine. It is these tangled cedar sweepers that are part of its secret, since they shelter a surprisingly large population of trout. Its secret is also an icy flow that seldom rose above sixty degrees before the lumbering, and its final secret is its rich alkalinity—its origins in the lime-marl bogs and subterranean limestone and plentiful springheads of the Michigan sand-country forests.

The old grayling days on the Au Sable are dead. Arnold Gingrich is fond of telling how his father and uncles fished for grayling on the Au Sable and other rivers, and how he failed to discover his passion for fly-fishing until long after leaving his Michigan home for the literary life. My father never fished for grayling either, but he did fish the Michigan rivers in their golden brown-trout years.

Fish them sweepers, Earl Madsen used to chide my father. *Get your fly in closer to them sweepers!* Madsen held the slender Au Sable riverboat steady in the current.

Madsen knew that fishing tight against the deadfalls is critical on the Au Sable. *Fish them sweepers,* he repeated firmly.

It's not so easy! my father laughed.

The main river gathers its strength slowly, flowing past the old fishing camp at Wash-Ka-Da, its broad riffles spreading below the canoe landing just downstream from Stephan's Bridge. The bridge is named for Henri Stephan, who emigrated with his family from the ancient cathedral city of Rouen in France, where Joan of Arc was burned. His sons later became well-known guides on the Au Sable.

The river receives the outpourings of major springs below the Black Bend water, and cold little Barker Creek comes in from the north above the famous Rainbow Camp. It is a full-blown river at the Wakeley Bridge, where the leisurely half-day floats down from Stephan's leave the stream, its smooth currents flowing deep and strong in the twilight.

The famous South Branch did not hold grayling in the old days, perhaps because its water from Lake Saint Helen was too warm for *Thymallus tricolor*. Judge Daniel Fitzhugh tells us that a few grayling were found in the bottom stretch of the South Branch, where large springs merge their flow with the river and drop its temperatures. The origins of the river lie in a surprisingly wild region near Roscommon, and Beaver Creek joins it below the town. The South Branch flows east from Beaver Creek into the famous stretch once owned by the late George Mason. His mileage reached almost to the main Au Sable below Smith Bridge and the Oxbow Club. It was intended that the fourteen-mile reach of water remain virtually unchanged, although Michigan and its population have not entirely honored the stipulations of the Mason Estate, which willed the mileage to the fly-fishermen of the state in 1954, providing no physical access roads or improvements were built to intrude on its almost primeval character.

During the Mason years on the South Branch, its fourteen miles of virtual wilderness were unblemished by man except for the Mason Camp itself. George Mason was a superb fly-fisherman who sought to protect his South Branch reserve through his bequest, restricting access to backpacking and float trips and fly-fishing in perpetuity without killing the fish. Unfortunately these conditions of his generosity in making fourteen miles of the river public have not always been fulfilled.

The North Branch joins the main river downstream from the South Branch and Oxbow. It rises in a series of springs north of Lovells, the logging camp named for a timber company surveyor, gathering the outflows of Turtle and Opal Lakes. It is already a sizable river when it reaches the site of Dam Two, about ten miles upstream from Lovells. The dam was constructed by logging engineers in 1869, opening the vast timber reserves of the North Branch. Dam Three was not far above Lovells, and the site of Dam Four was four miles downstream. Their impoundments were used to collect and float huge flotillas of logs, carrying them downstream in the spring high water. The North Branch lumbering operations were in full swing when the Jackson, Lansing and Saginaw lengthened its trackage from Grayling across the pine flats to Lovells. Its huge sawmill was completed along with the right of way. The railroad brought lumberjacks and a rough brand of civilization and fishermen to the North Branch.

There were a number of fishing camps and hotels constructed on the river at the turn of the century. The little Douglas Hotel was the social fulcrum of a booming timber-and-railroad town, with a peak population of more than 1,000, and Tom Douglas was its leader. Edward Kellogg built his homestead cabin downstream at Kellogg's Bridge, and later built log cabins and fishing camps throughout the Au Sable country.

WILLIAM MERSHON

William Mershon located and developed his famous place below Lovells too, and in books like *The Passenger Pigeon* and *Recollections of My Fifty Years Hunting and Fishing*, Mershon recorded his apprehension and sorrow for the extinction of the Michigan wilderness he loved. His worst fears for its wild places have been fulfilled.

There were other places on the river, like the Kantagree Club and Halfway House and the old Morley Place. Big Creek is a principal feeder of the North Branch, and its Big Creek Lodge has long been a private reserve of some eight hundred acres. Big Creek merges its cold waters with the North Branch below the Kellogg Bridge. Between its forest-sheltered mouth, and the winding stretch where the North Branch joins the main Au Sable below McMasters Bridge, there are a number of famous camps. Scott's Lodge is a cluster of pleasant cabins below the junction with Big Creek. The old Pierce-Breakey Camp lies at Flashlight Bend. Arnold Copeland was once poet-in-residence on the North Branch of the Au Sable, fishing the river from his charming Brush 'n Rod not far below the

Pierce-Breakey water. Doctor Hazen Miller is the author of *The Old Au Sable*, a superb collection of historical anecdotes and stories about the Au Sable and its cast of characters over the years. Miller himself has a lovely fishing camp on the North Branch, with this well-chosen fragment of Shakespeare above its door:

> And this our life, exempt from public haunt
> Finds tongues in trees, and books in running brooks,
> Sermons in stones, and good in everything.
>   I would not change it.

The Au Sable itself is already a powerful river in the famous Stillwater below the South Branch, and it is almost too much water for serious fly-fishing. Downstream from the McMaster's Bridge and the mouth of the North Branch, its current is a compelling force too deep for wading.

The Au Sable was totally a grayling river in its aboriginal times. It has a surprisingly long history that reaches back into a primeval and tribal past. It was an ancient right-of-way across Michigan, its currents well travelled when the Ojibwa and Chippewa and Ottawa tribes fished and hunted its forests. French influence in Michigan is quite old, starting with the famous wilderness expedition of Etienne Brulé in 1618. These explorers were followed by a generation of fur trappers and traders who traversed its lakes and forests and rivers, and it was these French *voyageurs* who named it the Au Sable.

Both the aboriginal tribes and the fur trappers used the river to cross the Lower Peninsula of Michigan. Leaving the wind-swept expanse of Lake Huron above Saginaw Bay, they travelled upriver more than two hundred miles on its winding riffle-bright currents until they reached the looping riverbend site of modern Grayling, which was a major Indian settlement.

The river winds north here, and the hardy *voyageurs* trekked a few miles west to the reedy shallows of Portage Lake. According to George Brown Goode, in his text accompanying the portfolio of S. A. Kilbourne's *Game Fishes of the United States*, there were also grayling in Portage Lake when the Kilbourne folio was published in 1879. Like the tribes who travelled the Au Sable before them, the French traders made their encampments on the sheltered north shore, and from there it was a simple morning portage to the headwaters of the Manistee. It was also a grayling fishery, and it carried them the swift three hundred miles to Lake Michigan, a journey now repeated every summer by eager campers travelling in brightly painted canoes.

Saginaw was well established as a frontier garrison and trading post when Alexis de Tocqueville arrived there in 1831. He found a virtually unknown and impenetrable wilderness farther north. Henry Schoolcraft negotiated his treaty of Saginaw with the Indians in 1836, opening the vast timber acreages of the Michigan territories to the railroads and lumber barons and settlement. It was both the beginning of modern Michigan, and the end of the Michigan grayling and its wilderness.

Development came slowly in the marginal forest soils and sandy moraines of Lower Michigan, until the eastern mines and the building of the railroads and the coming of the Civil War created an insatiable market for Michigan lumber. Its timber camps expanded so rapidly that lumbering was in full swing long before Appomattox. Spring log drives used the thawing spates of late winter to carry the cut timber to Lake Huron, and in the thirty years that followed the Civil War more than five billion board feet of pine were cut from the watershed of the Au Sable. There were a third of a billion board feet cut in 1890, and the Michigan wilderness was filled with the contrapuntal sounds of axes, the thunder of falling trees, and the screaming whine of sawmills.

The miracle of the Au Sable lies in its ability to survive that rapacity even though the fragile *Thymallus tricolor* could not—and five billion board feet in uncontrolled cut-and-slash lumbering over only thirty years is an almost unthinkable rape. The cutting and clearing of the deadfalls and sweepers from the river came first, opening its channel to the log drives that followed and erasing its fish cover. The timber sluice dams followed, using their impounded waters to collect the logs on the ice, snaking the fallen trees out through the winter woods. The logging dams blocked the spawning runs. The lumberjacks did their work well, taking the big pines for lumber and stripping the hemlocks of their acid-rich bark for the tanneries. The hemlock logs themselves were simply left rotting in the forest. The rivers were consequently stripped of shade, and the soil eroded quickly from the barren banks and moraines, collecting in the sluice-dam impoundments. The roots of the coniferous trees were lost too, and with them, their unequalled ability to entrain the rainfall in the earth. With these forests gone from the Au Sable, every springhead in the region ran several degrees warmer.

The logging ponds raised the temperatures as well, and their stillwaters reduced the habitat of the fast-water hatches. Silt collected behind the dam cribbings and settled in the quiet reaches of river. Sawdust from the mills was added, its subaquatic rotting a source of acidity that counteracted the rich water quality of the marl bogs and limestone springs. The sawdust combined with the silt to smother both the riffle hatches and the spawning beds downstream.

The manmade floods released for the logging drives did flush the accumulated silts, but those silts would not have collected in the first place except for the lumbering. These spates from the logging dams cleared the silts, but they also scoured out fertile spawning redds, erased algal growth and zooplankton, killed both adult and fingerling fish life, and decimated the remaining fly life. The grinding log drives themselves scarred the shallows, smashed deadfall cover, and uprooted the cedar sweepers and willows along the banks. Between the logging drives, armies of anglers and market fishermen killed the grayling in astronomical numbers. Dozens of ice wagons took fish daily to the railheads in Grayling and Lovells for shipment to the fish markets and red velvet Victorian dining rooms in

Detroit and Grand Rapids. Like the buffalo and the passenger pigeon, it seemed that such a prolific species could never be endangered.

It was another illusion of plenty, and the gentle Michigan grayling was doomed. The rapacity of the lumber barons stripped the great forest cover from the thin soils until they lay naked and exposed. Warming springheads had altered their biosystem irrevocably. The side effects of the logging dams, accumulated beds of sawdust and silt, manmade spates and impoundments that drowned the river every few miles, warming surface waters behind their cribbings, the blocked spawning runs, and the log drives were perhaps a fatal blow in themselves, but the Michigan grayling was already doomed.

There were guides and river folk who understood the danger, but these men were recluses and outcasts who worked only when it suited them, and even then such river people lived by guiding sportsmen or timber surveyors and jacklighting a deer in the river bottoms when they needed meat. Such men carried no weight in the corridors of power. Their names are largely forgotten now, except among anglers who have fished the Au Sable since boyhood. The most colorful was probably Chief Shoppenagons, the Saginaw tribal leader who lived out his final years guiding hunters and fishermen along the river. Some of the others on the main Au Sable were Ike Stillwagon, Arthur Wakeley, Charles Shellenbarger, Henri Stephan, Len Jewell, and the celebrated Rube Babbitt. Tom Douglas, Vinegar Bill Christenson, and Ed Kellogg were early guides along the North Branch. It was the colorful Len Jewell, a battle-scarred veteran of the Fourteenth Michigan Light Infantry in the Civil War, who guided famous fly-fishermen like Fred Mather, Grover Cleveland, Seth Green, Joseph Jefferson, and the famed Thaddeus Norris on the Au Sable.

REUBEN BABBITT

However, it is perhaps Rube Babbitt who deserves our gratitude for his role in the history of the river. His father had first come to the Au Sable in 1873 with a surveying party for the Jackson, Lansing and Saginaw Railroad. The older Babbitt liked the Grayling country and stayed on, settling in a frontier farmstead along the river. His sons grew to manhood with the rhythms of the Au Sable and its grayling in their blood. Rube Babbitt was the favorite guide of Judge Daniel Fitzhugh of Bay City, and the two men often fished the river together. It was entirely a grayling river then, and in the beginning, no one seemed to realize that it was a unique species native only to Michigan. Judge Fitzhugh sent the first specimens to Washington, where the government biologists were surprised to discover his collection was a totally unclassified species.

The efforts of both Judge Fitzhugh and William Mershon could not save the Michigan grayling, and both anglers clearly foresaw its extinction. They started searching for a replacement species even before the grayling's demise was complete, and decided such a species should be able to survive the warming temperatures that followed the cutting and the logging. There were brook trout in the dark tea-colored rivers farther north, and great streams like the Pigeon and Thunder Bay and Black are still famous for their populations of *Salvelinus fontinalis*. Both men soon became intrigued with the idea of stocking brook trout in the grayling rivers.

It seems strange to reflect, a hundred years later, that transplanting Michigan brook trout south to the freshly lumbered rivers was impossible because of poor transportation, and that it was easier to ship fingerlings from the hatchery at Caledonia in New York. However, the first Caledonia shipment arrived in 1870, when old A. H. Mershon received a consignment of brook trout from Seth Green. These fish were successfully introduced in the Tobacco watershed near Clare, and Judge Fitzhugh later transferred some of these brook trout from the Tobacco to other rivers like the Hersey, the headwaters of the Muskegon, and the swift little Rifle. The grayling were nearly gone now, but the brook trout were the beginning of a revival for several Michigan rivers. It was a renaissance that continued with the planting of rainbows from California, and the European brown trout from Germany and the United Kingdom.

It was Rube Babbitt who first carried the brook trout on a train in milk cans from the Rifle to the Au Sable. Babbitt fully understood the ecological tragedy that had changed his world forever, and that the days of his beloved Michigan grayling were numbered. His sadness is obvious in some observations recorded not long before his death.

> The loggers were responsible for the death of the grayling. When the pines went, the streams became impure through erosion. Soil was washed into them by the rains, and the grayling could not live in the dirty water. No longer sheltered by the trees, the rivers rose in temperature, and the grayling needed cold water, almost as cold as ice.

When the logs came down the river they raked the spawning beds, destroying the eggs and young fish. The others were too easy to catch. In the big jams, the bark was ground off the pines, filling the water with fine particles that sifted into the grayling's gills. I found innumerable dead fish with festered gills, and in every case, fine particles of bark were the cause.

The grayling can never return, because the character of the streams has changed. They have tried to plant Montana grayling below the Straits in recent years, but they always died. The grayling is gone forever—gone with the pines and the passenger pigeons and the Michigan that used to be.

8. Salmo Trutta *Is* *a Gentleman*

Summer ends in the first storms of September. Its soft winds turn raw in the river twilight, and its pale skies darken behind the mountains in the north. It is a prelude to winter on brown-trout rivers from the swift Ausable in the Adirondacks to the tumbling Nantahala in North Carolina, and its opening passages are harsh in our western mountains. The bitter wind scatters the ashes of summer campfires from the Frying Pan in Colorado, to the Yellowstone and Big Hole country. Sometimes there is fresh snow in the high range at daylight, and grizzled sheepherders huddle around their breakfast fires.

Sometimes these first storms are blizzards, and the brown-trout fishermen can find their sleeping bags covered with snow in the morning. The snow is usually gone before lunch, and there are soft shirt-sleeve afternoons and hard-frost nights that last well into late October.

The morning sun is warm in the foothills, and the cottonwoods and willows along the river turn yellow. The fall storms have already stripped the aspens in high country. The wind stirs and rises in late morning, scattering the bright ochre-colored leaves into the rivers, and at twilight the mountains are dark silhouettes against the pale windless skies. The cold nights start the greenhead mallards migrating downriver toward the Missouri, and the big brown trout begin moving upstream to spawn.

It is the best time to fish our western rivers. Their waters are low and clear, and almost empty of other anglers, and their brown trout are in the mood. The species offers the most difficult fly-fishing around the world, so wary and selective in its feeding that knowledgeable anglers everywhere regard its rivers as the ultimate challenge.

Douglas Reid is a fine outfitter and guide on the remote rivers of

Patagonia, where the trout see fewer fishermen in the entire season than hatchery fish avoid the first hour of opening day, but his attitude toward the wariness of the brown trout is typical.

Clients are always crazy for rainbows! he observed this past April on the Chimehuin, which has twice produced world-record browns on flies. *But I like the brown trout better—they're out there, but they're never easy, and when you get one you're doing something right!*

Skilled fishermen everywhere have this respect for the brown trout, from Argentina and Tasmania where it was introduced, to its indigenous watersheds from Lapland to Morocco and the Caspian Sea. The famous brown-trout fisheries of Europe are almost legendary shrines of the fly-fishing world—rivers like the pastoral Gäcka in Yugoslavia, the gentle Traun with its watermills and timber walkways in Austria, and the historic chalkstreams in the rolling hills and water meadows of Normandy and Hampshire.

Our western mountains have the best brown-trout fishing in America, and each September there is a migration of skillful anglers that coincides with the spawning run of big browns. There are trophy-size fish moving up into the headwaters above the reservoirs on Montana rivers like the Ruby and Missouri and Madison. Similar fish are found from the Gunnison and South Platte in Colorado to the Wind and Sweetwater and Green in Wyoming. Browns in the weedy channels of the Firehole shake their summer lethargy and begin gathering at the spawning tributaries in Biscutt Basin and the Nez Percé bottoms and Ojo Caliente. Others migrate slowly in the channels of the Big Hole and Beaverhead and Gallatin, and many expert fishermen gather each season to fish the tumbling Yellowstone.

The odyssey of the brown trout does not begin with these mountain rivers, even for the relatively brief history of the species in American waters. Like most Americans, the brown trout is an immigrant from Europe. W. L. Gilbert of Plymouth, Massachusetts, received 4,000 brown-trout eggs in 1882. Most of these ova died in transit, but Gilbert succeeded in hatching about twenty-five fry. Three fish lived to spawning size, but their progeny did not play a significant role in the distribution of *Salmo trutta* into American waters, since they remained in his personal collection. The historic shipment of brown trout arrived in the February chill of the New York waterfront of 1883. It had come on the German steamship *Werra*, and virtually unnoticed in its unloading of passengers and their baggage were 80,000 trout eggs, gleaming like pearls in their chilled moss-lined trays.

The shipment of these fertile ova was consigned to Fred Mather at his Cold Spring Harbor hatchery on Long Island. It was a story that began in the tumbling streams of the Black Forest, swift little rivers that drop down toward the Rhine through villages of steep-roofed *Schwarzwald* houses. Hemingway fished those rivers, high in the forests above Freiburg-im-Breisgau, in the years after 1918, but Mather fished them much earlier.

Fred Mather had travelled to Berlin in 1880, serving as a delegate to the International Fisheries Exposition held there that summer. He met

Baron Friedrich von Behr, the minor German nobleman who was president of the German Fisheries Society, and was invited to fish the Baron's private water above Baden-Baden in the Black Forest.

Mather was impressed with the shyness of the red-spotted trout he found there, and its obvious ability to thrive in warmer streams than the native brook trout of our eastern mountains. They proved harder to catch than the speckled trout he caught on the Nissequogue, where Mather often fished on Long Island, and Mather became convinced that these European fish could withstand the fishing pressure already building from cities like New York and Philadelphia. Their ability to thrive in temperatures above seventy-five degrees seemed also to offer hope for eastern watersheds being stripped of their white-pine forests and hemlocks to furnish lumber and acid bark for the tanneries.

Mather hatched the newly arrived brown-trout eggs without fanfare. The fish were planted in several eastern rivers, but their introduction went almost unnoticed. The Commonwealth of Pennsylvania did not even bother with official records of such stockings. Two other shipments of

SETH GREEN

brown-trout eggs arrived the following year. The first came from Sir Ramsey Gibson Maitland and his famous Scottish hatchery at Loch Leven; the second arrived from the silken chalkstreams of Hampshire and was hatched in Michigan at Northville.

Few records of the early stockings from these shipments of brown-trout eggs have survived. Yet there is evidence that the Contequot and the gentle Nissequogue on Long Island provided the genesis of brown-trout fishing in America. The storied Beaverkill in the Catskills, the weedy Musconetcong in New Jersey, and the swift little Brodheads in Pennsylvania soon followed. The Michigan shipment of eggs was hatched at Northville, and subsequently planted in the Pere Marquette.

The rest of the odyssey is a classic American folk tale, with its misunderstood hero, and years of controversy and struggle before the final curtain. The story of the brown trout is still unfinished, and in many parts of the country the polls remain unclosed. Some old-timers still fervently dislike the browns.

The species quickly established itself, and good brown trout were caught on the Brodheads as early as 1889. Big fish were soon recorded from the sandy, weed-rich rivers of Long Island, the classic waters of the Catskills, and the limestone meadows of the lower Musconetcong. But the wind music in the hemlock ridges and whippoorwill bottoms along our rivers was completely drowned out by the bitter cacophony of crackerbarrel opinion.

Brook-trout fishermen were angry. Their arguments contended that the brown trout was ugly; that it was dull and colorless; it lacked fighting and sporting qualities; its flesh was coarse and unpalatable; it did not respond well to flies; it drove out the native species; it was a cannibal that preyed on other fingerling trout; and during the strident sentiments of 1914, it was actively disliked because it was German.

They just ain't worth a damn! the old-time brook-trout fishermen used to argue along the Pine in Michigan. *Them browns just lie there looking at you—but they don't never take!*

None of these arguments about brown trout is true. The species clearly lacks the gaudy coloring of the brook trout, and it disdains the purplish sides and gillcovers of the rainbow, but there is nothing plain about its richly spotted dorsal surfaces and its tiny accents of ruby-colored spots. Wild brown trout often have a deep, reddish tinge in their dorsal, caudal and adipose fins, and their anal and ventral fins are edged in white; in spawning time, their bellies are a bright yellowish orange. Placed in a creel lined with fiddleback ferns, or laid on a background of snow buttercups on a meadow bank, brown trout have a subtle beauty entirely their own.

It is true that a brown trout does not usually fight with the wild, cartwheeling acrobatics of a rainbow or the stubborn bulldogging deep along the bottom so typical of the cutthroat or the brookie. But their fight is shrewd and strong, trying to reach a deadfall or work back under a boulder to shear the nylon, and wild browns often jump when hooked.

The old-time brook-trout boys were dead right when they argued that browns ignored their flies. But the problem lay with their fly patterns, not with the newly arrived fish. Brown trout have been fished with flies since before Aelianus recorded the sport in Macedonia in the third century. Their foolish ancestors have simply not survived the centuries of fishing. But fly-fishing for brook trout is only two hundred years old at best, and our native species are more easily caught. Self-respecting brown trout ignore a heavy three-snell leader that trails gaudy and implausible brook-trout patterns like the Paramachene Belle and Belgrade and Tomah-jo. No wonder the venerable brook-trout fishermen were frustrated!

Their one-time argument that the brown trout was forcing out more desirable native species is clearly false. It was commercial rapacity that timbered off the Appalachians, and stripped hemlock bark for the tanneries. The eastern coniferous forests were decimated too, and when they were gone, the springheads dried up or ran warmer, and the ecology of the eastern rivers was changed. Their currents were too warm for the brook trout, and the European immigrant readily moved into the vacuum created by our growth and greed.

They're nothing but cannibals! the charge is still heard often in fishing inns and watering places in trout country. *They go through baby trout like a damned meat grinder!*

Big brown trout are undeniably meat eaters, but they are no more fond of baitfish than any other species once they have grown to better than sixteen to twenty inches. Old-time brook-trout fishermen seldom saw such fish except perhaps in Maine, and men who have fished the Labrador know there is no worse meat eater than *Salvelinus fontinalis* once it grows large enough. Brown trout have come by their reputation for cannibalism simply because many more of them survive to the larger meat-eating sizes.

Old-timers who argued that browns were poor eating compared with their native fish had a debatable point, since the wild brook trout is a rare culinary treat. However, anyone who has tasted a brown trout broiled in butter and lemon juice at a chalkstream inn in Wiltshire, or simmered with sour cream and white wine and sliced almonds in Normandy, or prepared *truite au bleu* at a small country hotel in Provence would laugh at the argument that the brown trout fails to grace a proper table.

Sauerkraut trout! sneered the Michigan fishermen on my boyhood rivers thirty years ago. *Sauerkraut trout!*

The old-time brook-trout fishermen thought these newcomers were German fish, and many minds were still poisoned with anti-German sentiments that had their roots in the First World War. Even this foolish charge was rooted in ignorance. Our first major shipment of brown-trout eggs came from Germany, but the full range of the brown-trout species reaches from the rivers of Iceland to Afghanistan—and from Lapland in arctic Norway to the Atlas Mountains of Morocco.

Modern taxonomy classifies the brown trout under the name *Salmo trutta,* since research has determined that the numerous European strains are largely subspecies of local origin. Brown trout have been introduced to every continent except Antarctica, and excellent fisheries have evolved in Tasmania, New Zealand, Australia, Ceylon, Pakistan, India, Africa, Chile, Argentina, and Tierra del Fuego.

There are dozens of subspecies found from the remote lakes of Iceland to the subarctic forests of Siberia. Some ichthyologists still use the taxonomic name *Salmo fario* to designate the stay-at-home strains of brown trout that do not migrate from freshwater lakes and rivers, using *Salmo trutta* to define their sea-run cousins.

The morphology of the brown trout is unique. It has heavy chocolate-colored spotting, with contrapuntal accents of bright orange to ruby-colored spots in various watersheds. Some subspecies are virtually lacking in these reddish markings. Particularly rich streams and lakes can result in dorsal, caudal, and adipose fins heavily tinged with red. The pectoral and pelvic fins are often richly orange. The lower sides are yellowish orange, with their orange cast pronounced in spawning season. Brown-trout parr usually exhibit nine to ten parr markings, which typically disappear after their first or second year. The caudal fins are shallowly forked. Horizontal scale counts above the lateral line average 125 to 140, and a diagonal count between the lateral line and the adipose fin will average between 13 and 16 scales, with 14 a common reading. Dorsal and anal fins typically display 10 to 12 rays, and there are 30 to 60 pyloric caeca.

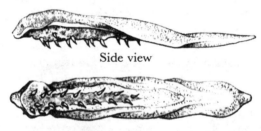

Side view

Bottom view

Brown Trout Vomerine Bone

Some subspecies are relatively famous. Brown trout are found in eastern Europe from the north-flowing rivers that drain the Ural Mountains to the basin of the Black Sea. The species is also well distributed in Iceland and the British Isles. Its migratory forms do not inhabit the Mediterranean region, although riverine populations are found in Spain, southern France, Turkey, Italy, Morocco, Lebanon, Yugoslavia, Albania and Greece. The basin of the Black Sea is represented with brown-trout populations in Rumania, Bulgaria, Turkey, Russia, Georgia and Armenia. These Black Sea strains are classified as *Salmo labrax*, and are a relatively rare subspecies that lives in estuarine zones and spawns in the rivers. The Caspian trout are found in the tumbling rivers draining Armenia and the Caucasus, and the best populations of *Salmo caspius* are found in the Terek and Kura watersheds. Native browns are also found in Iran, as well as the Turkish headwaters of the Tigris and Euphrates. Aral trout are found farther east, and have been designated *Salmo aralensis,* with anadromous behavior similar to the Caspian and Black seas strains. The river systems draining into the Aral Sea have their origins in the Afghanistan mountains and the Kirghiz above Tashkent, and are the Eurasian limits of the endemic brown-trout range. The subspecies called *Salmo ischchan* is found at Lake Sevan in Armenia, and it consists of several polymorphous forms.

Yugoslavia also shelters several distinct strains like the marble trout, the powerful *Salmo marmoratus* of Montenegran rivers, and the *Salmo letnica* found at Lake Ohrid in Macedonia. Dalmatia also has the unique trout-like fishes classified as *Salmothymus ohridanus* and *Salmothymus obtusirostris,* the rather strange soft-mouthed trout found in some watersheds. Other Yugoslavian subspecies include *Salmothymus zetensis,* found in the rivers of Macedonia, and *Salmothymus montenigrius* from Montenegro. *Salmo dentex* and *Salmo visovacensis* are other subspecies from Adriatic and Aegean tributaries, while *Salmo taleri* and *Salmo farioides* are found in Macedonia.

Similar relict subspecies are also found in Italy, especially the famous *Salmo carpio* indigenous to Lake Garda. Distinct subspecies of brown trout are also found in several alpine lakes from Geneva to the Traunsee in Austria. *Salmo macrostigma* is the brown-trout subspecies found isolated in the mountains of Lebanon, *Salmo pallaryi* is a relict alpine form from Morocco, and the recently discovered *Platysalmo platycephalus* is a related species from southern Turkey.

Several lake strains are also found in the British Isles, especially in Ireland and Scotland. Perhaps the best-known subspecies are *Salmo stomachichus,* the snail-eating Gillaroo trout from Ireland, and the legendary *Salmo levenensis* from Loch Leven. These Scottish browns are darkly spotted, living in the bog-stained acid waters on its rainy eastern coast. Their heavy body markings are unrelieved by the reddish orange spots typical of more familiar brown trout. The unique coloring is quickly lost when the subspecies is mixed with the dominant *Salmo trutta* stocks, and the federal stockings made thirty-five years ago in our western mountains have largely lost their identity, although there are American rivers where these Loch Leven trout have been so isolated that their genetic integrity survives.

The history and tradition of fly-fishing itself is closely related to the brown trout and its subspecies. It was the brown trout that Aelianus found in the rivers of Macedonia, and it was the brown trout that generated the *Treatyse of Fysshynge wyth an Angle* and its classic twelve fly patterns. Walton and Cotton also fished them in the seventeenth century. Brown trout were perhaps always difficult, and the shyness and selectivity of the species on rivers from the Moráca in Montenegro to the silken Metolius in Oregon have led to constant cycles of fishing refinement over the years.

It has paradoxically been the brown trout that also played a major role in American trout fishing. It was their choosiness that led to the fresh perceptions of men like Theodore Gordon, Edward Ringwood Hewitt, and the elegant George La Branche. Gordon adapted the imitative theories of dry-fly fishing from the British chalkstreams to the Catskills. Hewitt catalogued his innovations in *Telling on the Trout*, and *The Dry Fly and Fast Water* that La Branche published on the eve of the First World War is a milestone in the literature of American angling.

Selective-feeding behavior is common among trout, but it is even more deeply ingrained in the brown trout, and matching the hatch becomes the hallmark of consistent success with the species. Selectivity consists of a fish concentrating on a particular insect form during its brief hatching season, rising only to that insect species. Such trout cannot be fooled without artificial fly patterns designed to imitate the natural insects they are taking. The whole science of aquatic entomology and its relationship to fly dressing is based upon such selective-feeding behavior.

It was such behavior that ultimately led to *The Fly-fisher's Entomology* that Alfred Ronalds published in 1834. Although it had several ancestors in the first years of the nineteenth century, Ronalds was the first disciplined book on trout-stream insects. It included color plates of the principal British fly hatches, along with recommended imitations. Ronalds was followed by Frederic Halford in the next half century, and classics like his *Dry-Fly Entomology* were filled with elegant watercolors of both flies and aquatic hatches.

American fly-fishermen were almost totally unaware of this tradition and literature of technique when the brown trout was introduced in 1883, and their methods were too primitive for the new species. Twelve years after the first brown trout were stocked in the Pere Marquette, Michigan fisheries experts had decided that the species was completely inferior to both the brook trout and the rainbow. Their resources were soon focused entirely on the two native species.

No more spotted suckers! the hot-stove league roared its approval and congratulated itself smugly.

But these crackerbarrel experts were largely unaware of the environmental changes inflicted on Michigan during the timber boomtowns and tenderloins. Their rivers were growing too warm for the native brookie, and although the brown trout was no longer bred and stocked, *Salmo trutta* was no limp-wristed Fauntleroy in the rough-and-tumble of the river.

The brown had survived since its fossil origins in the Miocene period, and apparently evolved from marine ancestors. Before the glacial periods, those ancestors were apparently migratory prototypes travelling the Arctic seas. When primordial glaciers pushed south, these prototrout ancestors travelled with them into Mediterranean latitudes. Later the ice fields receded, and with the gradual warming of these southern seas, the primitive trout migrated back into northern waters. The warming seas trapped isolated colonies of fish in the colder rivers they had entered, and when these rivers became warmer too, the fish moved up into mountainous headwaters—like the trout populations in southern Italy and Morocco and Spain.

It was a struggle to survive such forces in the evolution of the species and compared with the hostile environment of millenniums past its adopted American habitats were perfect. Although the Michigan fisheries biologists stopped raising and stocking browns, the species did not wither away like the Montana grayling and cutthroat trout that had also been planted in Michigan rivers. The brown trout survived the fishing, distributed themselves in search of spawning gravel, and wintered in the lower reaches of their adopted watersheds. The species also spread itself into river mileage already too warm for the native brook trout. The brown trout not only survived its new-found habitats, but also resisted every subsequent attempt to eradicate it from American rivers.

Similar situations exist today, particularly in the Rocky Mountains, where year after year the hatcheries produce and plant mostly rainbows. It is unmistakably true of the heavily fished Deckers water on the South Platte in Colorado. The river is sardine-packed with hatchery trout every spring and summer, and fishermen catch them in astonishing numbers. Yet when each season ends in late October, most of the fish that remain are brown trout, survivors of the wild fish descended from the last federal stockings thirty-odd years ago.

Their hardiness is important for our waters. The ability of the brown trout to tolerate moderate levels of pollution and relatively high water temperatures make them a species of the future. There are recorded temperature ceilings of eighty-one degrees in typical brown-trout habitat, and even higher readings are found at both Hot Creek in California, and the Firehole in the Yellowstone.

The ecosystemic character of the Firehole is unusual. Its alpine headwaters are as cold as any mountain stream, but its currents are quickly mixed with the seepages and eruptions of hundreds of hot springs and geysers. Its brown-trout population survives temperatures in excess of eighty-one degrees, perhaps because the oxygen concentrations typically exceed twelve parts per million. The source of such high oxygenation is found in its tumbling riffles and its heavy growth of weeds—but *Salmo trutta* has also thrived in the Firehole simply because it is hardier than its American cousins.

Like the native brook trout, the brown trout is an autumn-spawning fish. Its spawning occurs when the rivers are low and clear. Bright males and females gather over pea gravel and stones of suitable size from late September into February, depending on climate and latitude. Their spawning beds vary considerably in shape, but will average about sixty square inches. Unlike the native American species, brown trout will spawn in both small tributary creeks and the open river itself. Toleration of such varied spawning conditions is another key factor in their hardiness and their ultimate survival.

Spawning behavior among brown trout is similar to its related genera and species. Paired fish select a smooth-flowing current running five to fifteen inches per second over beds of clean well-oxygenated gravel. Males protect the selected egg-laying sites while the females shape the nests, rolling and working their bodies in the current to displace the stones. The finished redds are saucer-shaped and about four inches deep, with a small mound of gravel tailing off downstream.

The female settles into its nest, gasping and working its body until the male joins its mating dance. During the actual egg laying, both fish work and writhe together until the eggs and milt settle into the gravel. Both fish rest momentarily, before the male moves aside to defend the nest from predators, and the female slides immediately upstream. It works its body in the upstream currents, slowly displacing enough fine stones and gravel to cover the fertile eggs. Fecundity is similar to that of the rainbow, varying between two hundred and 8,000 eggs, depending on the size and condition of the henfish.

Spawning lasts about a week, until both fish lie spent and exhausted nearby. Finally they drift back slowly to the lower pools of the river to await the ordeal of winter. Both male and female kelts are easily recognized the following spring, thin and emaciated from their spawning rites and the sparse diet of winter.

The period of incubation varies widely from river to river. Average conditions require about a month to produce eyed ova, and in about eighty days the tiny alevins wriggle up through the gravel to escape the nest. Their first nourishment is stored in delicate yolk sacs attached to their tiny bodies, and when their yolk is expended, the tiny half-inch fingerlings are forced to survive by themselves in the stream or brook currents. Their early diet consists of zooplankton and other minute aquatic organisms; after twelve months when they have grown three to five inches, they turn to aquatic fly hatches for food.

Growth is relatively predictable. Males mature at approximately nine inches, and females reach fertility at twelve inches, about one year later. Five-year brown trout measure from sixteen to twenty inches. However, more rapid growth is possible. Famous alkaline streams like Hot Creek in the Sierra foothills, the Firehole and Madison in the Yellowstone, the myriad spring creeks in Montana and Wyoming, and the famous limestone streams of Pennsylvania all support more rapid growth rates. The British chalkstreams display similar fertility, along with the rivers of Normandy, immediately across the English Channel. European limestone streams like the Liffey and Maigue in Ireland, the silken little Pegnitz in Bavaria, and the Gäcka in Yugoslavia are similarly rich habitats. Both Argentina and Chile have such rich water quality from the volcanic origins of their rivers, like the watersheds of Iceland and New Zealand.

The growth rate of the famous Letort Spring Run in Pennsylvania is typical of such fertile water. Several years ago, we conducted an experiment on the Letort, stocking fin-clipped brown trout of three to five inches in the shallow headwaters below its springs. The stockings were made in March, and at the close of the season in early September many of these fish had reached twelve to thirteen inches.

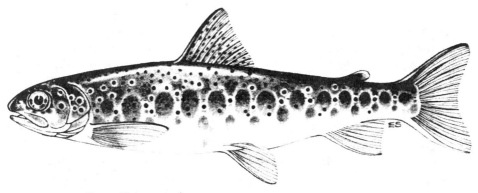

Brown Trout Parr *(Salmo trutta)*

Fisheries biologists long believed that brown-trout growth stopped after about eight years. But several known specimens have lived from fifteen to thirty years, although a ten-year fish is a patriarch. One huge trout at the Bellefonte hatchery in Pennsylvania lived fifteen years; in the last four years of its life, it grew from thirty-two to thirty-five inches in length. The fish had added a full inch of girth, and went from twenty-three to twenty-seven pounds. Its growth proves that a trout continues to grow throughout its life span, the changes recorded in its scales, like tree rings.

The world-record brown weighed thirty-nine-and-a-half pounds, and was taken by William Muir in 1866, at Loch Awe in western Scotland. The biggest brown ever recorded was perhaps the fifty-three-pound monster taken in a commercial trap from the sprawling lake at Lillehammer in eastern Norway. For many years the world fly-record brown trout was a twenty-four-pound hookbill taken by my good friend, Bébé Anchorena, at the Boca Chimehuin in Argentina. It has since been displaced by a twenty-six-pound brute, taken seventy-five miles farther south at Boca Correntoso.

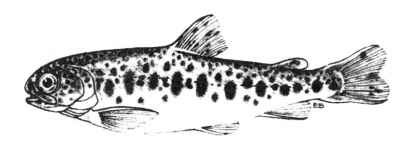

Brown Trout Fry

Such brown trout are not easily caught. Fisheries research indicates that while twenty percent of brown-trout stockings are recovered in the first season, about thirty-five percent survive both fishermen and their natural enemies. Approximately forty-five percent succumb between plantings and the winterkill cycle in their initial year, and about fifteen percent survive into the following spring. Their mortality is relatively low, and the species clings most tenaciously to life.

Such ability to survive is a remarkable quality. It makes the brown trout poor as a species for put-and-take stocking, since such fisheries policy is designed for high short-term harvests. Planting brown trout is a long-term investment, because of their shyness and high rate of survival; it is foolish to stock browns in marginal streams simply because they are able to survive the lower threshold of sunfishlike temperatures. The species is not suited to immediate catch-ratio gratification and should not be wasted on marginal watersheds that cannot support spawning.

The wariness of the species is no myth. Letort fish are perhaps typical in their sophisticated brown-trout behavior. Their catalogue of rise forms was outlined by the celebrated Vincent Marinaro in his *Modern Dry-Fly Code* in 1950. Marinaro wrote with a mixture of humor and chagrin: the simple rise which has the trout coming to take the fly quietly; the compound rise that follows several moments of cocked-under-the-fly inspection; and the complex rise, which passes through both simple and compound stages and ends in a rapier-quick rise after several feet of vacillating inspection and hesitating refusal.

Such selectivity is not unusual on hard-fished water. The three-rise catalogue outlined in *A Modern Dry-Fly Code* is a standard part of theory and practice on the Letort. My own experience with its selective fish has led me to add another exasperating rise type to the list—the compound-complex rise that proceeds through the whole sequence and still ends in complete rejection!

Stream-spawned browns are especially wary, but even hatchery specimens can become difficult a few days after stocking. Fishing on the public streams of northern New Jersey is typical; friends who regularly fish the South Raritan and Musconetcong and Paulinskill have worked out an unusual strategy for catching brown trout in such waters.

We unmatch the hatch! they tell me jokingly.

Their system is amusingly simple. For example, during a hatch of slate-colored mayflies they fish a straw-colored Cahill. Fish that will take the pale dry fly are usually chubs or rock bass or bluegills. Fish that refuse the straw-colored patterns are invariably brown trout, rising selectively to the dark-winged hatch.

When we locate a choosy fish, my friends explain, *we snip off the Cahills and start fishing an imitation!*

It's called unmatching the hatch! they laugh.

My own experiences on the Henryville beats of the Brodheads give another example of brown-trout behavior. Most of the Henryville Flyfishers are skillful fishermen who understand brown trout and their unpredictable moods. The club members typically fish on a no-kill basis through most of the season. Their fish are caught and released so much that their jaws are sometimes riddled with small hook scars. Such catch-and-release exposure during the first sixty days of the season makes the Henryville fish extremely selective.

Their response to subtle variations in fly color is remarkable. Two closely related hatches emerge on the Brodheads in late April, sometimes coming together on the water. *Ephemerella subvaria* and *Ephemerella rotunda* provide some exceptional dry-fly sport, perhaps the high point of the year when their hatches are heavy.

The nymphal forms of *Ephemerella subvaria* are found in various current speeds, but *Ephemerella rotunda* nymphs need more oxygen, and are found in the riffles and pocket water. Such requirements of habitat mean that a fish in a quiet pool or waist-deep flat are probably seeing mostly *Ephemerella subvaria* during a hatch, while a fast-water trout in the primary current tongues is seeing more of *Ephemerella rotunda*. The pool fish will take a well-dressed Hendrickson during such a hatch, but the fast-water trout will refuse that pattern, eagerly accepting the similar Red Quill tied to imitate *Ephemerella rotunda*—yet the sole difference in these mayflies and their imitations is a minor variation in their body color.

Brown trout are also quite moody. Brodheads fish are annually exposed to superb hatches of small green-bodied caddisflies. Fine catches are common when these little *Rhyacophila* sedges are on the water. Once I took thirty-seven fish from a single pool during a particularly fine hatch. The trout measured from ten to eighteen inches and were all carefully released. Two days later I fished that same pool again. The weather was almost identical, except for a cool wind blowing steadily upstream; there was another fine hatch of caddisflies, but the fish simply refused to take them. There is almost nothing as lifeless as a brown-trout river when its moody fish are strangely off their feed.

Ed Schlecter is an old fly-fishing friend, whose portly figure is fuelled with the rich diet of his Pennsylvania German ancestry. Schlecter knew the old-time Pocono experts like John Wise and James Leisenring, and after almost seventy years on the Brodheads and Tobyhanna, he has become philosophical about brown trout.

It's simple enough, Schlecter grumbles good-naturedly. *They're just cantankerous, stubborn, smart German trout!*

Stomach autopsies taken over the years have suggested many significant facts about brown trout. The late Paul Needham discovered in his research that the browns in his field-laboratory streams consumed a diet of almost eighty percent mayfly forms. His experiments were published in his *Trout Streams* in 1938; he found that seventy-five percent of these mayflies were ingested in the nymphal state.

His results also indicated that brown trout tended more toward surface foods, making them more susceptible to dry flies. Needham found that only forty-six specimen brown trout ingested five times as many winged insects on the surface as a test-group of more than two hundred fifty brook trout. Although these statistics are more than thirty years old, and were taken on slightly acid eastern streams before modern pesticides decimated certain types of aquatic insects, they remain significant to modern anglers:

TYPE	TOTALS	PERCENT
Mayflies	1,907	79.3
Caddisflies	230	9.5
Two-winged flies	61	2.5
Earthworms	51	2.1
Slugs and snails	30	1.3
Beetles	28	1.2
Ants, bees, and wasps	22	1.0
Stoneflies	17	.7
Leafhoppers	17	.7
Crustaceans	16	.7
Salamanders and baitfish	9	.3
Grasshoppers	8	.3
Other	10	.4
Totals	2,404	100.0

These figures were compiled across a full season on test streams of average character. Freshets in the early season were unusual during the test year, and resulted in a disproportionate worm count in the overall diet sample. Meadow trout would have perhaps taken more nonaquatic terrestrial insects. Since the fish sampled were largely under a pound in weight, the total number of baitfish is unquestionably low for normal brown-trout behavior. The relative absence of terrestrial insects in the table would also indicate that brown trout have somewhat altered their feeding habits over the past thirty-odd years.

Pesticides and warming rivers and pollution are perhaps the cause of this evolution. The mayflies are a relatively fragile family of aquatic insects, and are highly susceptible to decimation of their habitat. During the research for *Matching the Hatch*, similar diet studies were made. Fifty brown trout were caught and checked for stomach contents, and comparison with the earlier Needham research is particularly interesting:

TYPE	TOTALS	PERCENT
Mayflies	1,861	71.8
Caddisflies	365	15.2
Two-winged flies	67	2.9
Beetles	61	2.6

TYPE	TOTALS	PERCENT
Ants, bees, and wasps	47	1.6
Leafhoppers	32	1.5
Stoneflies	23	.9
Slugs and snails	20	.8
Crustaceans	19	.8
Grasshoppers	15	.7
Earthworms	11	.5
Salamanders and baitfish	9	.4
Other	7	.3
Totals	2,537	100.0

There are some surprising differences between these figures and the Needham studies of fifteen years earlier. The mayflies have diminished in importance, while caddisflies increased almost six percent in the stomach samples taken at midcentury. But the most significant change is perhaps in the terrestrial forms, like ants and leafhoppers and beetles. Another series of stomach autopsies performed in the past twelve years for my recent *Nymphs* indicates that these trends have continued, particularly with the caddisflies and terrestrials.

TYPE	TOTALS	PERCENT
Mayflies	1,372	52.3
Caddisflies	501	19.4
Two-winged flies	183	7.1
Beetles	107	5.1
Leafhoppers	91	4.0
Ants, bees, and wasps	77	3.8
Stoneflies	69	2.8
Crustaceans	39	1.5
Grasshoppers	37	1.4
Salamanders and baitfish	21	.7
Earthworms	13	.4
Slugs and snails	13	.4
Other	29	1.1
Totals	2,483	100.0

These are rather startling figures. The trend in the trout diet away from mayflies to caddis forms is apparently continuing, and terrestrials are growing more important. Mayflies have declined from almost eighty percent of the brown-trout diet to slightly better than half of its foods. Caddisflies have increased from less than ten percent of the diet to just under twenty percent, virtually a doubling of their earlier importance as a primary trout food.

The relatively abrupt rise in the percentage of terrestrial insects is perhaps indicative of their hardiness, while the extensive use of pesticides in our eastern forests has damaged our famous aquatic hatches. Two-winged insects experienced a sharp increase in importance in these figures, and the explanation lies in atypically heavy swarms of red-legged *Bibio* flies in one particular season. Peak populations of green inchworms also resulted in a surprising increase of the miscellaneous category. It should perhaps be recognized that brown-trout samples on western rivers would find larger percentages of stoneflies, owing to the vast numbers of big *Perla* and *Acroneuria* and *Pteronarcys* nymphs in such watersheds.

Like our eastern brook trout with its need for extremely cold water, our traditional eastern fly hatches have suffered major damage to their habitat. Our rivers are suffering from a creeping thermal gain, as well as visible forms of pollution from agricultural, community, and industrial wastes. Pesticides used to control the gypsy moth in our eastern forests and similar parasites in our western mountains have also damaged our aquatic hatches. Soil erosion from lumbering and poor farming practices has caused pollution through turbidity and gill-wearing particulate matter. Fertilizers leaching into our rivers and phosphates in our detergents continue to wreak havoc by spurring the weed growth of our rivers and the resultant eutrophication of our trout ponds. Recent years have witnessed natural problems too. Eastern brown-trout rivers have suffered grinding floods, hard winters with anchor ice and collapsing snowbanks, and searing summer droughts that have forced even the brown trout into springholes and bridge weeps, frying the fly hatches in the shallows. The mindless process of environmental erosion continues; and with the decline of once-classic hatches, the adaptable brown trout has scavenged and foraged his rivers in search of other foods.

Conditions are still changing, and the challenge of recent days on brown-trout water remains fresh in the mind. There are marked contrasts between my early experiences with the species and the incidents of recent years. Two episodes will demonstrate that striking evolution.

My first really big fish was caught one summer twilight at the mirrorlike tail of Seven Castles on the Frying Pan. Its high blood-colored escarpments were reflected in the current, and a soft wind blew upstream from the foothills of the Roaring Fork. The spates of snowmelt had passed, and there were good hatches of big *Ephemerella* flies on those July evenings in Colorado.

The big trout was working just below the roots of a slender lodgepole that leaned precariously over the pool. The smooth current eddied past the twisted roots, and the fish held tight against the stones. The light wind riffled the surface occasionally, and the trout rose in a steady, frustrating rhythm. It had foiled me for a week. The smooth current was deceptively strong and had imperceptible problems of drag where the fish was lying. It was difficult chest-deep wading and trying to cast a long line to reach its feeding station. The fish also proved unusually selective. It refused my flies on several evenings. Finally I dressed a workable imitation and delivered it with a perfect hook cast. It cocked perfectly on the smooth current. It reached the fish and disappeared in a smooth porpoise roll that showed the trout's head and dorsal fin and tail lazily; it was hooked.

He took it! I yelled explosively.

The fish shook itself almost in surprise, disturbing the silken flow below the roots. Suddenly it bolted upstream, stripping line from the reel with ratchety arpeggios as it bored deep along the gravelly bottom. It felt stronger than any fish I had hooked before, and it forced the rod tip perilously close to the surface during its first angry run. Finally it stopped sullenly, deep in the current.

The stalemate lasted several minutes. Suddenly the fish jumped clumsily across the pool and turned downstream, the nylon slicing audibly through the current. The reel was really losing fly line now. Its pale backing blurred into the guides, and the big fish shook itself angrily, wallowing in the swift-water cribbing along the road. It jumped again in the heavy currents, and I was forced to follow, picking my route clumsily down the rocky shallows. The fight slowed in the deep stillwater downstream, and then the fish bolted past another angler.

Coming through! I shouted. *Sorry!*

Finally the struggle quieted and I recovered line gratefully. The fish came grudgingly out from the strongest currents. My knee ached where I had banged it on the rocks. There was one last run, when the fish tried feebly to reach the tail shallows and the ledgerock chutes downstream. I turned it patiently and coaxed it back up the pool, and the fight was over.

It measured twenty-three inches.

That was more than twenty years ago on the Frying Pan, but the last big dry-fly trout I hooked lives deep in a slate-ledge pool on the Brodheads. It does not feed often, but it takes minute insects in the surface film surprisingly well for a fish of its size. Its rises are tiny bulges, tight against the mossy wall.

Several times it had refused my flies, and once I hooked it momentarily on a tiny nymph. It was hot the morning I last found it working softly in the shadows. It inspected and refused several patterns, and I added a fragile 7x tippet to my leader. It looked again, but refused to take until I tried a tiny black ant. The tiny imitation dropped softly and flirted with the ledge, drifting through leafy patterns of sunlight and shadow, and disappeared in a sucking dimple.

Like its cousin years ago on the Frying Pan, the big brown threshed in its sullen surprise. It bolted deep along the ledge and held sulking along the bottom. Steady pressure gently worked it off balance, and triggered a second angry run that stripped my little Hardy deep into the backing. It jumped in the chute at the head of the pool.

Five pounds! I thought wildly.

The fish held there briefly in the swift shallows, before drifting back on the current. It turned lazily downstream, gathering speed until it bull-dogged deep along the ledge. The leader pinked against an outcropping or root, and caught again rakingly under the overhanging slate. It worked itself deep under an unseen boulder, and easily sheared the delicate tippet. Heavier nylon might have held the fish, but it was too wise to take a fly on such coarse tippet material.

These two big brown trout clearly illustrate the changes of the past twenty-five years on American waters. The Colorado trout had taken the dry fly on a 4x tippet scaling .007, which was considered fine tackle on the nine-foot rods typical in those days. The fly pattern was a Red Quill dressed on a size-ten hook. Rodmaking had not yet fully evolved actions and tapers capable of fishing lighter tippets, and the modern limp nylons from .005 to the cobweb-fine .003 did not exist. Our fishing today has floating and sinking lines, delicate rods under three ounces that offer both precision and power, and fragile leader tippets delicate enough for minute flies from sizes twenty down to twenty-eight—selective brown trout are the sole catalyst for such change.

Both our tackle and the species are still evolving. Brown trout seem more difficult each season, and some of our old patterns and tactics no longer work as well. Our policy of public fishing and the explosive growth of our population have combined to produce fishing pressure beyond our worst nightmares. Some eastern rivers like the Croton and the Musconet-cong have fishing crowds on opening day that rival the ticket lines of a pop-music concert.

Although I have taken larger sea-run fish in Norway and Tierra del Fuego, and from the tumbling lava rips of the Boca Chimehuin in Argentina, my largest river brown was caught on a small river in Chile.

The Ñilahue is a swiftly flowing tributary of Lago Ranco that rises in a volcanic basin under the Sierra Negra. Its volcanic history is quite recent in geological terms, since only thirty-five years ago an eruption destroyed the Araucan farmsteads in its middle drainages, and buried the fields under a shroud of abrasive silts. The lower river still flows milky with these sediments between its volcanic barrens and its spreading boca-shallows at the lake. The lower reaches of the river lie enclosed in a dramatic postpile gorge, its boulder-strewn floor a hundred feet below the cane thickets that conceal its rim.

There is a beautiful waterfall where the Ñilahue suddenly spilis into its postpile gorge, and the afternoon that we took the big fish actually began as a trip to photograph the Falls Pool.

Adrian Dufflocq and Riccardo Vargas, two skilled Chilean fishing companions who love the Calcurrupe country at Llifen, were along that spring afternoon in late November. Mel Krieger had also travelled south from San Francisco to join us in the foothills beyond Lago Ranco.

It was a relatively dry spring that year, and the Calcurrupe flowed surprisingly low and clear where the raftkeeper waited to ferry our jeeps across the river. The narrow dirt road climbs high above the lake, crosses a saddle in the *colihue* foothills, and switchbacks down toward the bridge at the Furaleufu. We left the vehicles beside a stand of bamboo.

Where's the river? I asked.

Ernesto! Riccardo Vargas laughed. *You must trust us!*

We rigged our equipment and followed Dufflocq into the bamboo, crawling on our hands and knees through a leafy tunnel in the cane. It was surprisingly dark in the thicket, and after thirty yards the hidden trail ended in a fifty-foot cliff. There was a forked limb of tough *rauli* wood hooked through the lower trunks of a copper beech thicket, its slender branches reaching down toward a tree placed like a ladder against the cliff. The fallen tree had been notched with footholds.

We climb down that? I whispered in disbelief.

Dufflocq and Vargas laughed and lowered themselves on the forked *rauli* branch to the footholds on the fallen tree. They reached the rockfall below and stood grinning while I followed them cautiously down their primitive ladder. Krieger sat waiting in the bamboo thickets above, and clambered down with surprising agility.

Coming throught the rockfall from the huge elephant-ear plants into the valley was a revelation. Feather waterfalls spilled from the cane-thicket rim of the gorge to the river-polished stones, their pale spray drifting in the trailing vines. The little river itself roared over its broken precipices in a series of conflicting falls, and finally plunged fifty feet in a single cascade to the surging currents below.

The Falls Pool was still in sunlight. Its thundering falls were half-shrouded in a series of overlapping rainbows and mist. Downstream from the falls, where the churning currents finally escaped the pool, the river dropped swiftly in the shadow of the cliffs. Birds whistled and warbled and cried shrilly in the vines. Bamboo and flowering trees and gunnera grew in the postpile niches. We walked upstream to fish the Falls Pool while the photographic light remained good, and when the sun finally left the river, the little steep-walled valley was suddenly plunged into twilight.

Although I had not planned to fish, the deep swift-flowing stretch between the waterfall and the first pool under the cliffs looked inviting. Mel Krieger offered me a beautiful Howells and opened the aluminum case, drawing its elegant split-cane craftsmanship from its poplin bag. It was eight and a half feet, and I quickly rigged it with a six-weight sinking line to fish a big nymph in the deeper runs. It was a relatively delicate rod and perhaps a little light for fishing a river like the Ñilahue.

Casting upstream to sink the nymph deep into its drift, I let the line belly lazily into its swing with a series of mends, and teased it gently with the rod as it began to fish. There were no rises in the first few yards, and I had worked halfway down the run, taking a step and repeating each cast as I covered the water. There was suddenly an immense swirl where the numph was drifting, and I felt a strong pull. The fish shook itself and its entire length caught the dwindling light, flashing dully in the milky flow, and I felt its strength and weight.

My God! I shouted. *It's like a salmon!*

The trout simply held in the heaviest currents, telegraphing its sullen strength back into the straining rod. Suddenly it changed its stubborn tactics. It wheeled in a shower of spray, forced itself easily into the strongest flow, and I followed it awkwardly down the rocky shallows. I backed out of the river and hopscotched among the rocks and boulders. The fish ended its strong run in the deep postpile pool under the cliffs.

It held there stubbornly in the swift currents. When I finally reached the pool, pumping and reeling wildly to recover the backing, the big fish changed its tactics again. It bolted across the pool, working deep along the unseen outcroppings, and then it jumped.

It's a big brown! Dufflocq yelled.

But it's jumping like a rainbow! Krieger shouted as the fish cartwheeled and fell clumsily. *Browns aren't supposed to jump!*

He doesn't know it! Vargas observed wryly.

It was a stubborn fight, and the fish jumped full length and fell back six times. Each time it collapsed clumsily on its spade-sized tail, a huge splash echoing along the cliffs, and each time it bolted downstream into the backing again. Several times I forced the big fish close, only to have it turn and bulldog back into deeper water. It was remarkably strong and persistent on the slender six-weight rod, and the fight lasted almost an hour before I worked it close and tailed it like a salmon.

Bravo! Vargas came running. *Bravo, Ernesto!*

It was a huge male with a thickly muscled body and a mammoth hook-jawed head and gill-covers. We measured it slightly more than thirty-two inches in length and almost eighteen inches in girth. The brown was so thick across the shoulders that I could not close my fingers over its gill-plates, so I simply cradled it in my hands, facing its head into the flow. Brown trout of such length and girth can weigh as much as fifteen pounds, and my hands were shaking with excitement as we photographed it.

The fish recovered slowly, working its gills steadily in the flow. It grew stronger and stronger, until finally I could no longer hold it, and it fought free in a wild eruption of spray. The trout drifted out across the chalky gravel, held there briefly like a pewter-gray ghost, and then it disappeared into the depths of the pool.

It was a beautiful fight! Krieger said.

Perfect fight! I agreed happily. *It was a beautiful fish!*

It's still a beautiful fish, Dufflocq smiled.

Chile lies several thousand miles southwest of the British rivers where fly-fishing was perfected some five centuries ago, although its brown-trout drainages are among the finest in the world, and my fight with the Ñilahue fish had a poetry worthy of those British beginnings.

The fish on classic chalkstream beats of Europe remain as shy and sophisticated as their ancestors in the Halford years, but on hard-fished public streams in the United States the fish see a veritable picket line of fishermen in a supermarket competition for hatchery-bred trout. With such exposure to hordes of fishermen, the brown trout on our public waters have often become a greater challenge than their fabled cousins of the British chalkstreams. The species continues to survive and multiply on our rivers from Maine to California. Its emigration is virtually complete, and the brown trout is established in forty-odd states. Its wary sophistication is the primary yardstick in most American tackle and tactics. The ability of the species to withstand fishing pressure, and to survive warming and less-than-pure rivers has clearly made it our fish of the future.

Although brown trout are a species for the future, we should not forget their origins in the past. Brown trout are inextricably involved with our tradition, and that sense of chivalry and the past is a major part of modern fly-fishing.

Its tradition was taught me one afternoon many years ago on the famous Lauterach above Regensburg. The afternoon sun was warm on the valley floor when we reached Schmidsmühlen, with its steep-roofed houses and churchtower. It was the season of the biggest mayfly hatches of the year, and I had spent the past few evenings dressing imitations of the fat *Ephemera* drakes, using the exquisite watercolors in a book on European fly hatches.

Petri heil! we greeted the riverkeeper.

The old man shook hands and completed the ancient Bavarian greeting among fly-fishers. *Petri dank!*

The mayflies were gathering in their annual mating swarms over the swift millrace, and we stopped for a late lunch in the half-timbered inn. The old riverkeeper agreed to meet us in another hour. We went inside the *Gästhaus* and sat down to a huge tureen of rich potato soup, fresh sausages and cabbage. The beer was dark and strong, and after wild strawberries and coffee we were ready to fish the Lauterach.

Our lines were stretched and oiled with mucilin, and we stood in the cobblestone street rigging our gear. The elegant rods were slipped from their cases and poplin sacks, and the English fly reels clicked smoothly as the freshly dressed lines were carefully retrieved. Children gathered in the street and watched. There were storks nesting on the mill. Finally we pulled on our waders, laced our brogues and shouldered into our fishing coats. The old riverkeeper arrived and studied us gravely.

We cannot fish, he said.

The millrace slipped past the inn, and the street was filled with mating mayflies. *Why not?* we stammered.

You are not wearing ties, said the old man.

Ties? We were puzzled.

The riverkeeper studied his intricately carved pipe. *The brown trout is a gentleman,* he explained patiently, *and when you fish my river—you must dress yourselves as gentlemen!*

BOOK THREE

✸ ✸ ✸

PHYSIOLOGY, HABITAT AND BEHAVIOR

1. The Physiology of
Trout and Grayling

There was a simple tractor bridge in the haymeadows of a boyhood stream in Michigan, and I spent many hours there, peering down through its timber planking at the trout lying over the pale bottom gravel. The fish were like diminutive ghosts, shadows that darted and held in the swift currents that eddied through the cribbing, searching out the patterns of flow that brought them food. Small fish sometimes drifted back from the planking shadows, hovering on wavering fins above the fence line, but the big trout never left their sanctuary. The big fish held in the swelling currents along the cribbing, restlessly changing position and gliding back to their original lies in the dancing shadows.

The trout had a singular litheness and poetry in the rhythms of their lives, something between the darting swarms of flycatchers during a morning hatch of sedges and the rapier-swift attack of an osprey after its lazy circles of reconnaissance. The fish were endlessly fascinating and I watched them often that summer. People ask what it was about trout fishing that first intrigued me, before the sport became an odyssey in later years. It is not a simple question, but it was clearly the trout themselves that first captured my imagination.

Like the young protagonist in Hemingway's *Big Two-Hearted River* who crossed a railroad trestle high above a smooth-flowing pool, my heart has always tightened and increased its rhythms when I looked into a river and saw its trout. It is a feeling that has never dimmed.

Trout clearly have the quality of magic for many people, even people who will never be anglers. Schubert was certainly no fisherman, but the lyric beauty of the fish and their rivers lies in the score of his *Forelle*, the lyric trout quintet composed in 1819. William Butler Yeats also loved their

387

beauty, weaving fly-fishing passages into several of his poems, and in the "Song of the Wandering Aengus" he used these images:

> I went out to a hazel wood
> Because a fire was in my head,
> And cut and peeled a hazel wand
> And hooked a berry to a thread;
> And when white moths were on the wing
> And moth-like stars were flickering out,
> I dropped the berry in a stream
> And caught a little silver trout.

It is curious that many fishermen feel the poetry of trout and trout water, yet miss the lyricism in the fish and their singular physiology. The biology of the trout is equally as beautiful as the fish themselves. There is a similar reluctance to study stream entomology, even among fly-fishermen who might find almost infinite rewards in its discipline. Yet few things in our world have the magic of a hatching nymph, or the balletlike grace of a mating dance of mayflies.

The biosphere is filled with such lyric topologies, and the world of trout water is a rich universe in itself. Its many organisms are woven into an intricate fabric of life. Its trout and grayling have a unique beauty, and in our knowledge of their anatomy and physiology lies a host of important lessons for thoughtful fly-fishermen.

Most life forms have evolved in the atmosphere, and since fishermen share this environment with myriad air-breathing plants and animals, we readily understand our world. Aquatic species are cold-blooded organisms deriving their metabolic temperatures from the water that envelops them. Their aquatic world is completely different from our atmosphere, and our understanding of trout and grayling hinges upon a knowledge of their habitat. Both the fish and their subaquatic world display a remarkable harmony.

Our atmosphere and theirs share several qualities. Both are fluids in one sense, although we are seldom aware of the density of our atmosphere until a strong wind reminds us, and water is almost eight hundred times the density of air. Both media have currents and eddies, and like the flowage along the bottom of a stream, wind also loses velocity in its friction against the terrain. The density of water makes its currents quite powerful, and even trout and grayling have difficulty moving in their subaquatic world. Swimming can teach us much about the density of their environment, and swimming under the surface quickly demonstrates that we are ill equipped to propel ourselves in water.

Water density also bothers the fish. However, that density has its compensations in its ability to displace the weight of the fish, counteracting the negative effects of gravity. Fish are virtually weightless in the water. Their weight is only a factor when they are cartwheeling during a fight, or when we force them into the shallows, where they are not fully covered. It is no accident that most leaders are broken when fish are jumping, or struggling in the shallow water, and it is their weightlessness in the water that makes ultralight tackle workable.

Water density has also evolved and shaped the remarkable fusilliform structure of many species. Their configurations reflect a remarkable plasticity in their accommodation to both aquatic density and currents. Current-loving fish like trout and grayling are slender and highly streamlined in hydrodynamic terms; each part of their anatomy is adapted perfectly to minimize hydraulic drag.

Even fish scales play a role in reducing such drag, and the relatively fine scales of trout and grayling increase swimming ability through minimizing friction. Most fish swim with a serpentine or so-called anguilliform motion, undulating their bodies against the water pressure. These rhythmic undulations ripple along the body muscles, ending with a final punctuating stroke of the caudal fin. The entire musculature of a fish is utilized in swimming, from its bony head to its cartilaginous tail, and its flesh is a series of tightly muscled layers. Each layer of flesh can be flexed separately, in a controlled sequence that ripples along the fish, and each layer is coordinated with its opposite layer on the other side. The contracting muscle is matched with a simultaneously relaxed opposite muscle. Such muscle coordination is truly remarkable, considering the speed and dexterity of a swimming trout or grayling.

The muscle rhythms end with alternate thrusts of the tail, its structure a membrane stretched over a thin, fanlike structure of cartilage and bony rays. It is rooted to the spine with a combination of skeletal plates, ligaments, and connecting muscles. It is a morphology that is both supple ˌand strong. The tail proportions of a trout or grayling are approximately fifteen percent of its body length, and twice the depth of its caudal peduncle when normally extended. The tail is beautifully shaped, but its configuration is also an optimal structure of delicacy and suppleness and strength. Its trailing margins are thin to achieve minimal drag, yet their membranes are strong enough to withstand the abrasive wear of nest building in the spawning gravel. Trout generate enough swimming power for approximately five-miles-per-hour cruising speed in heavy water, and twice that speed in moderate currents. Considerably more speed is available when a trout darts for cover or scatters baitfish through the shallows, and trout are capable of fifteen to twenty miles per hour in brief accelerations. One useful rule of thumb for swift fish like trout and grayling is about ten times body length per second. It should be understood that trout swim primarily with anguilliform undulations, alternately flexing and relaxing their muscles in a rippling sequence along their entire bodies, literally using the hydraulic pressures of their habitat to propel them. The tail stroke is only the final thrust in their movements, not unlike the sculling oar in a duck shooter's sneak boat, and it is also used to alter direction.

The body configuration, fin structure, and rhythms of propulsion in the trout lie somewhere between the strength and agile maneuverability of the bass and the acceleration and speed of a pickerel or pike. Bass are structured to root and forage among rocks, deadfalls, and dense subaquatic vegetation. Pike are more reptilian in their behavior, using stealth and the camouflage of their coloring to lie absolutely still in the weeds. Their primary fins are located well back along their bodies, perfect for a snakelike strike at their prey, but virtually useless for holding in strong currents. Trout are not as perfectly shaped for speed as the powerful tuna or the shy bonefish, which has survived as a species on its ability to flee predators, since its feeding grounds are both shallow and greatly exposed. But trout are still an elegant, highly streamlined species well adapted to acceleration and speed. Their fin structure gives them both the maneuverability of the bass and the quickness of the pike, and although a trout may lack the rough-and-tumble stamina of a smallmouth, it has considerably more agility and grace.

Its structure also enables the trout to thrive in both still ponds and swift rivers. Its configuration and fin structure make its feeding habits quite versatile, from its sipping rises to midge pupae and other minutae, to its slashing attack on a school of stickleback or dace. It has an unusual equilibrium of speed and striking power and strength, mixed with the supple poetry of a ballerina.

Curiously, big fish can swim faster than their smaller relatives, and biologists estimate that trout and salmon are capable of about seven to ten miles per hour for each foot of body length. There are exceptions to this rule, because such sustained cruising speeds are a function of health and other variables. Big migratory trout like steelheads or sea-run browns are capable of ten miles per hour for considerable periods of time, and much faster speeds for negotiating waterfalls and rapids. Many times I have taken sea-run fish with sea lice still attached as much as two hundred miles from the tidal estuary of the river. Since the sea lice atrophy and fall off a fish in less than forty-eight hours, it is obvious that such fish can sustain high speeds for long migratory distances.

Although the primary function of the gills is respiratory—the extraction of life-giving oxygen from both fresh- and salt-water habitats—the gill structure plays a surprising twofold role in swimming as well. Fish force water through their gill systems, creating a small amount of hydraulic propulsion, but this minuscule flow also passes smoothly along the scales and lessens drag. It is a familiar principle in aircraft called laminar flow. Without its buffering layers along the skin, tiny little back-eddies of flow might develop considerable turbulence and drag, and with its effects a fish can swim much faster for the energy expended. Gill-cover position is important too. Trout are like many fast-swimming species, in the sense that the position of the gill covers is set at the optimal angle and opening for maximum laminar flow. Biology is filled with such examples.

The dermal covering of fish is quite unlike the more familiar skin of mammals, and is structured from living cells to its outermost layers. It is coated with a slimelike secretion which considerably reduces hydraulic friction, insulates the skin from most parasites and diseases, and even plays a role in the breathing and excretory functions. The slime also serves as a colloidal barrier between the water and the body fluids of the fish itself, and without its water-sealing properties, these fluids could pass freely through the skin. It is a remarkably strong and supple covering, and in trout and grayling its slimy secretions are used as a kind of ablative coating that is worn off in the turbulence of swimming. It is continually replaced with fresh secretions from under the scales, and this slime actually reduces drag as much as sixty percent in a swimming trout and grayling.

Some relatively sedentary fish types use their fins for swimming, but swift species like the higher Salmoniformes use their fins for changing direction, stabilization, maneuvering, and other special functions. The most subtle warping or fluttering of a single fin can affect a trout's position, since the fish is weightless in the water. Trout and grayling actually fold their fins, except for the caudal and anal structures, when they accelerate to maximum speeds. It is a little like the variable wing geometry found in modern attack aircraft. The dorsal, pectoral, and ventral fins in a trout can be folded completely, the anal fin has a variable position between its swimming position and its position at rest, and the tail is alternately contracted and spread in rhythms of glide and stroke. Watching trout move in a fluvarium, with a tempered glass window looking out into the flow of an actual pool, is endlessly fascinating.

The pectoral fins can be warped and extended, helping a fish to rise or descend at will, and by exaggerating the attitude of one pectoral a fish can control its turns. The ventral fins play a similar, although secondary, role and help stabilize a fish in the water. Sometimes a resting trout will use its pelvic fins like a bicycle kick stand, literally spreading them tactilely against the bottom.

The single dorsal and anal fins are used as vertical stabilizers, not unlike the rudder on the tail empennage of aircraft, or the keel under a sailboat. Their hydraulic function is to maintain the stability of the fish while it is swimming, inhibiting its tendency to roll or wobble, particularly at rest or at relatively low speeds. These fins are folded or partially compressed when a fish is swimming at higher speeds, since less fin surface is needed for control.

The paired fins are also used for braking, like the spoilers and dive brakes on a high-performance aircraft, and can be thrust out suddenly to slow a fish or stop it. Since the fish are in virtually a weightless state, the abrupt use of a single fin or the sudden extension of the pectorals will throw the fish off balance. It compensates with its other fins, even warping its dorsal, anal, and caudal surfaces to reverse these unstable forces. These fins are also used to stabilize a fish when it jumps, either in migrating upstream against waterfalls and rapids or in capturing flies, and the fish that jump best are usually the fast-swimming species. Jumping a high waterfall is a remarkable act, and I have watched both steelheads and salmon migrating upstream past falls as high as ten to twelve feet. The pool at the bottom of

392 / PHYSIOLOGY, HABITAT AND BEHAVIOR

the falls must have sufficient depth for an adequate running start, angling upward against the flow. The trout I have watched seem to undulate their bodies with an extremely rapid fluttering of their muscles, knife into the air with their bodies held absolutely still, and instantly start their swimming motions again the moment their bodies strike the falls. Sometimes a waterfall slides swiftly along a water-smoothed face of bedrock scarcely deep enough to immerse an average-sized trout, and yet a jumping fish too large to lie in such shallow water can literally swim up such a shallow falls. Fish also jump to capture fluttering insects, and sometimes when they are pursuing a hatching nymph or pupa, their velocity takes them clear of the surface. Many fishermen believe that a hooked fish will tire itself while jumping, but this is a mistake. The density and drag of the water are so much greater than the resistance of the atmosphere that when a fish breaks through its surface film its writhing acrobatics are suddenly freed. Except for its sudden exposure to gravity, such a fish is infinitely less encumbered when airborne. It is a little like an astronaut finding himself weightless or able to move easily in the minimal gravity of the moon, and a cartwheeling fish can complete gyrations impossible below the surface. It is more the anxiety and panic of being hooked, rather than its physical fatigue, that finally defeats a struggling trout or salmon.

The skin of a fish consists of membranes, mucous glands, and thousands of scales. Only the scales themselves are not living tissue, although like fingernails they can replace themselves and grow. The number of scales is relatively constant throughout the life of a fish, although in the higher Salmoniformes they record its growth like the sapwood rings in a tree. Although the number of scales is sometimes a result of habitat and water chemistry, scale counts play an important role in the taxonomic classification of species. The small-scaled trout and grayling are typical of species living in swift currents, and their cycloidal scales are smooth and semicircular.

The scales and skin also consist of chromatophores, the cells which control the chroma, hue, value, and patterning of coloration in a fish. These chromatophores include red, yellow, blue, black, and white cells working a little like color lithography to achieve various shading and color intensity. Color is also affected by iridocytes, derived from excretory substances, which produce both the silvery coloring of a sea-run fish and the iridescent sheen of some specimens. Color patterns and coloring have several functions. Many species use them for protective coloring, helping to conceal them in the bottom colors of their habitat, and the mottling of a trout is no exception. The parr-markings on a small fish are a natural adaptation, breaking up their outlines while baby trout are particularly vulnerable. It is intriguing that fish of the same species have different coloring, and fish lying over an open bottom of wheat-colored pea gravel are much paler than fish that hide under a root-tangled bank, or over a black bottom of volcanic sand or muck.

Countershading is a camouflage function typical of many species of fish. It consists of the gradual coloring changes from the relatively dark dorsal surfaces to the silvery whiteness of the belly. Aquatic habitat invariably looks dark, regardless of water clarity, and from the bottom the surface and sky beyond look pale. Countershading tends to make a fish's coloring blend with both the bottom and the sky, but it has another function too.

It tends to erase configuration and dimension, compensating for a complex pattern of light sources. The many species of trout and salmon all exhibit variations of countershading. Their parr markings are examples of combined blotches and barring and are superb camouflage. The vermiculations and mottlings of adult fish are also effective patterns of concealment, and a trout in salt water is like many marine species, with its gun-metal back and silvery flanks. Even the most spectacularly colored trout species are virtually invisible against the bottom in their parent streams.

However, many biologists argue that color pigmentation originally evolved for other physiological reasons, so that protective coloring may have only been a welcome side effect of functions that are infinitely more complex. Some chemical pigments are critical in terms of light energy, reflecting intensity and wave lengths that could damage tissue. Other pigments apparently serve to absorb wave lengths supplying extra warmth in marginal temperatures. Vivid color patterns also have a function in spawning and territoriality among the Salmonidae, allowing males and females to recognize each other in the pairing and forming of redds, and in enforcing territorial control of the spawning zone. Vivid coloring is clearly not solely ornamental.

Anadromous trout that have entered coastal and estuarine waters are perfect examples of reflective coloring. Their dark dorsal surfaces are obviously viable protection from predators stalking them from above, but the sea-bright flanks seem a poorly adapted defensive color. The silvery pigment cells result from iridocytes and the guanine concentrations they form in the scales. Thyroid is apparently a factor in developing these cells, but experiments with antithyroid depressants indicate that the silvering process continues with thyroidal activity suppressed. We still lack the keys to the puzzle of silvery marine coloring. The guanine that silvers a sea-run fish with its iridocytes is apparently an excretory substance, symptomatic of the physiological changes that permit a fish to function in salt water. Reflective coloring is nakedly obvious on a freshly-caught fish, but in its own environment, a silvery fish reflects its surroundings. Its mirrorlike scales are perhaps the best camouflage among the fish species, since they reflect the character of the habitat itself.

Color changes in fresh water are complex and are accomplished in two ways. Biochemical transformation is a process with roots in cardiovascular flow, responding gradually to the stimulus of a changed habitat character. However, trout have an emergency chromatic response too, and the abrupt triggering of adrenalin can alter the color of frightened or excited specimens.

Both water density and the dynamic stresses of swimming demand that the skeletal structure of fish must be quite strong. Yet it must be supple and yielding, combining unusual strength without constricting weight or rigidity. Fish are strikingly unusual organisms.

Fish share with all other vertebrate ecotypes the need to ingest food to generate energy and growth. Oxygen entrained in the watery habitat must be extracted for the metabolic generation of that energy. Fish must be capable of ready movement in their dense environment, both for survival and for capturing food. Their reproductive systems must function to replenish the species, and individual specimens must be capable of controlling their bodily functions. All organisms share a structural skeleton or form, along with a mouth and digestive tract and alimentary canal. Respiratory and circulatory networks are also required, along with the glands and organs that monitor and expedite their functioning. The skin and its covering of scales enclose and protect this complex anatomy of musculature, skeleton, and life-sustaining systems.

The trout is streamlined and fusilliform in shape, its structure a conventional skeleton. The bony case of the skull and mouth system shield the fragile brain, gill structure, nostrils, glands, and eyes. The skeleton itself is both flexible and remarkably strong. The spine is the principal member of this framework, attached to the skull and the caudal structure at its opposite ends. It is connected to both its own vertebrate pieces and its flaring rib cage with cartilage, and its hollow longitudinal cavity holds the delicate spinal cord.

The skull itself consists of the neurocranium, which encases the brain, and the branchiocranium protecting the jaws and gill covers and other structures. These elements are formed of bony plates and a membranous covering stiffened with cartilage. Three sensory organs are paired and enclosed in cartilaginous hollows, and all of these many parts comprise the skull, along with the gill arches and tongue. Skull structure in the bony fishes is much more rigid in its cartilaginous joinings, and is combined with bony plates into an intricate assemblage of surprising toughness.

The vertebrae and connecting tissue of the spine form it into a supple framework, enclosing the dorsal neural cord. It is called the notochord. The spine also contains and protects the hemal blood-carrying canal in the ventral and caudal region. Fibrous ring-shaped connectors, cartilaginous tissue, and membranes join the vertebrae together.

Vertical spines project upward from the dorsal side of each vertebral segment and downward from the vertebrae beyond the stomach cavity. Surrounding the internal organs and alimentary tract, these sternal spines project in pairs to form the rib cage. Bony projecting spines extend from the dorsal rays, interlocking with the spinal structure along the back. This framework supports the muscles and provides a foundation for their attachment. The rib cage forms a structure that resists hydraulic pressure, thereby giving strength and alignment to the anguilliform swimming muscles and sheltering the viscera and organs.

Trout and grayling have a so-called emarginate tail structure, and such homocercal caudal fins begin in a platelike fusion of cartilage and bones, from which the fins radiate. The pectoral and pelvic fins are supported on bony girdles of closely parallel rays. The anal and dorsal fins are supported by cartilage and bony projections, and the spiny rays of the pectorals are attached to the semicircular cartilage behind the gills. The cartilaginous primary and secondary jawbones are both flexible and strong, and able to open and close swiftly. Opercular covering plates form a compound structure to protect the fragile gills and gill arches.

Like other vertebrate organisms, trout and grayling have three types of primary muscular tissue. There is the smooth muscle enclosing the visceral cavity, the major skeletal muscles used to swim and move, and the involuntary cardial and respiratory muscles. The entire muscle system from the base of the skull to the caudal root is used in swimming. Each mytomic layer of muscles is divided into upper and lower sections. Other muscles and tendons have special functions, like moving the eyeballs and working the gills, or manipulating the jaws and fins.

The digestive tract consists of the stomach, intestines, pancreas, and liver, all connected directly or indirectly to the mouth by the gullet. The configuration of the mouth is dependent on the diet of fishes; and trout are primarily insect feeders and carnivores, although there is some indication of minor herbivorous feeding among rainbows, cutthroats, and grayling. Generally, the stomach in carnivores like trout is relatively short, while true plant-eating fish have long, slender digestive pouches. The intestines are also relatively short in trout and grayling, while fully herbivorous species have long, intricately convoluted intestinal tracts. Digestion occurs all along the stomach tract from gullet to intestines, and a series of pale, wormlike pouches called pyloric caeca are attached to the anterior structure of the stomach itself. The pyloric caeca participate in the digestion of fats and the production of enzymes, and are important in identifying species. The gastric juices of a trout or grayling are extremely acid, quickly dissolving foreign objects like aluminum tabs from canned beverages, and even highly tempered hooks that have been ingested. The liver stores both fats and sugars, while participating in both digestion and other metabolic functions. The gall bladder is a bile-green organ that stores liver secretions, and the pancreas also serves in digesting foods through the production of enzymes. The spleen is attached to the lower stomach and is a relatively large, vascular organ that plays a role in the structure and chemistry of the blood.

Digestion typically requires ten to twelve hours at optimum temperatures, although the temperature of the water directly controls its rate. It is easy for us to forget that we regulate our own body temperature and metabolic process, while the metabolism and digestive abilities of a trout depend on the temperature of its habitat, since it has no body temperature of its own.

The effects of temperature on digestion have obvious importance for fishermen. Digestion is quite slow with the water temperature under about forty-six degrees, and the fish retard their feeding at about seventy to seventy-five degrees in hot weather. Fishermen should remember that fish feed seldom in winter or in high-country streams and lakes that do not often get warm, because they digest their food so slowly at such temperatures. Fish that find themselves in such icy waters usually concentrate their feeding activity in midday and early afternoon, when air temperature and sun penetration are both effective in warming them slightly. Digestion can take as much as five days at such times. However, when the water temperature has reached sixty to sixty-five degrees, a healthy trout will digest its food in about ten hours. It is interesting that a bass will require a day or more to digest its food at such temperatures, since it is both more lethargic and more adapted to warmer habitat than a trout or a grayling. Trout fishermen know that most early-season feeding, with a river at forty-five to fifty-five degrees, takes place in late morning and early afternoon. Later in the year the fish will feed at any time during the course of the day, depending on the hatches. Warming temperatures will find the trout feeding early before the sun is on the water, and again in the evening when the river finally flows cool again. Low water and really hot weather may find the river cool enough for good feeding and digestion only in early morning, after the nighttime hours have dropped its temperatures. Evening feeding can be sparse in such hot weather, since the effect of the midday heat is not fully dissipated until well after nightfall.

Fish assimilate the nutrients in their diet with a wide range of effectiveness, both in different types of habitat and among the many Salmoniform species. Protein utilization is typical. Young parr-size trout assimilate a surprising forty percent of the protein ingested, while a six-year-old specimen group utilized only twenty-five percent. Clearly an older trout has a declining potential for growth, which is the increase of new tissue and skeletal structure and not the mere accumulation of fats. Protein utilization is critical for growth.

Adult trout have similar trouble assimilating fats and carbohydrates too, utilizing only fifteen percent of these diet forms. Young trout can assimilate three times that percentage. Such ratios of efficiency are the reason for rapid early growth among trout, and the slow rate of growth among larger fish. Fish culturists estimate that fingerlings in a hatchery pen grow approximately five to six percent of their body weight, and only two percent or less in ten-inch specimens.

Hungry fish also assimilate their food better than specimens that have fed heavily. Biologists believe that optimal assimilation of food occurs when fish have ingested less than their full capacity, although radical deprivation of food apparently decreases the digestive capabilities of trout.

Research indicates that trout convert the foods ingested at a ratio of ten to twenty percent. Such ratios mean that from one to two pounds of nutrients are focused upon growth for every ten pounds of food ingested. The calories that remain are burned off in catching more food, swimming, migration, spawning, and the metabolic processes of assimilating the food itself. Therefore, growth is quite slow in most trout waters, and as a trout grows larger, its rate of growth declines progressively. The growth-rate in fish of our wilderness lakes is incredibly slow, given their temperatures and brief summers and relative acidity, and a trophy-size trout is quite old. Knowledge of the time it takes to produce a really large fish should also give us some measure of its worth—such trout should not only be shared with other fishermen, but they also deserve to survive and spawn and perpetuate their big-fish qualities.

Respiration is the basic function of life itself. The body cells of a trout require a continuous supply of oxygen to function and replenish themselves. Each of its vital processes is based upon acquiring and burning oxygen. The carbon dioxide that remains from the metabolic cycle must be eliminated continually, just as mammals exhale such wastes, except that a fish must utilize its gills. Both oxygen and carbon dioxide are exchanged in the gill system. The blood conveys oxygen from the gill filaments to the tissue cells and completes its circuit to the gills, saturated with carbon dioxide wastes. Because the oxygen is extracted from a liquid rather than our atmosphere, the exchange between the water and the blood is a little more complex than our respiratory cycle. However, as our lung tissues utilize the atmosphere, the gill structure of a trout is designed to bring oxygenated water and blood into close proximity.

Trout have four pairs of gills. These paired gills are covered by operculate gill covers. Each gill arch is supported on a cartilaginous segment, fringed with its feathery blood-colored filaments. These gill filaments are densely structured with a network of microscopic capillaries that extract oxygen from the water and discharge the waste carbon dioxides. The gill arches also have a series of comblike projections called gillrakers that are often a factor in the taxonomy of species.

The physical act of a fish's breathing is fascinating. The cycle is started by closing the gills with the operculate gill covers as water fills the mouth. The mouth cavity is then sealed, the gill arches contracted, and the operculum is opened slightly. The action forces the water out through the gill structures, accelerating its flow through the Venturi effect, and out of the gill chamber entirely. The volume of flow can be controlled with the jaw muscles and oral membranes, while the speed of its flow can be manipulated by contracting the oral lining and setting the gill openings at various angles.

The quantities of oxygen required vary with species, water chemistry, metabolic functions, and subaquatic temperatures. Trout are particularly adapted to cold water highly saturated with oxygen, although there is a paradox in their metabolic needs. Their demand for oxygen is increased when their rivers grow warmer, yet those warming currents contain less and less oxygen in their chemistry. The knowledgeable fisherman knows the fish move into swift runs and broken pockets in hot weather, where the river entrains additional oxygen from the atmosphere.

The gills have peripheral functions too. Through its gills, the trout expels excretory wastes of nitrogen and regulates the salinity of its own tissues and fluids. Respiration in fish also occurs through the membranes lining the mouth cavity and throat, and directly through the dermal surfaces as well. There is also a false gill or so-called pseudobranchial arch inside each of the gill covers. It has the remarkable function of supplying oxygen to the eyes, and it also apparently serves as a glandular source of enzymes.

Trout fishermen seldom realize that the ability of many Salmoniformes to migrate back and forth between fresh water and marine seas is unusual, yet these anadromous species are capable of a metabolic transformation that is virtually unique. It is one of the unsolved mysteries in biology.

Earlier we discussed the remarkable color changes that occur before a trout actually enters salt water, when thyroidal activity triggers the iridocytic cells to produce a silvery guanine, clothing them in the protective coloring of the seas long before they reach its tidal estuaries. Their feeding rhythms are radically increased during the migrations downstream, anticipating the voracious feeding that finally occurs in the sea, yet the fish actually lose water content from their tissues and suffer a weight loss when they leave the river. The weight loss stops after several days, and the fish begin a period of explosive growth. Since their new habitat is saline, and its saltiness can penetrate through their dermal covering, the fish could easily accumulate fatal concentrations of chlorides without some means of controlling salt content. The freshwater chemistry of the gill filaments is radically transformed, using two chemical mechanisms to expel saltiness. Special cells in the gills quickly adapt to the new biosystem, and pass both sodium and chloride ions back into the sea, helping the fish to acclimatize themselves.

The swim bladder lies under the kidneys. It is found in relatively primitive fish ecotypes as well as highly advanced species like trout and grayling. It actually produces noises that some trout biologists believe may form a means of communication, and it also serves as a resonator, picking up simple noises transmitted through the water. It also has a hydrostatic function that helps a trout adjust its ability to float easily at varying depths of water.

Few anglers understand that a trout is heavier than water, and would sink without the buoyancy of its swim bladder. The bladder consists of a transparent airtight sac that helps control flotation, and its functions are variable. The fish can expand or contract its swim bladder at will, adjusting its buoyancy to compensate for changes in barometric and water pressures. The air bladder is also affected by the tidal variations in gravity outlined in the solunar cycles. With its swim bladder properly adjusted, a trout can hold either just under the surface or deep in a high-country lake, expending minimal muscular effort.

The centroid of the swim bladder, both in its expanded and contracted dimensions, is also the fish's center of gravity. Its location is another example of optimal adaptation in nature, as an off-center swim bladder would unbalance a fish and force it to expend corrective energies. Since the passage of water through the gills creates a small amount of hydraulic thrust, a trout must continually counteract this force with its fin action, and the swim bladder also achieves a balance between these energy displacements.

Trout have their swim bladders slightly below their center of gravity. Such a slightly offset center of buoyancy tends to create a slight disadvantage in hovering or lying dormant in the water, but helps a fish to maneuver or pursue an agile baitfish. Since many diet forms are taken near the surface, and a skittish trout feels dangerously exposed there, the swim bladder helps it rise and return quickly to a safer lie. Its skeletal and muscular structure permit a trout to flex better laterally than vertically. Its rise consists of a vertical approach, maintaining the depth perception of binocular vision as long as possible, and a quick roll on its side as it reaches its prey. Such a maneuver is called flexed rotation, instantly converting the thrust of its rise to the reverse direction. Its momentum forces it back toward the bottom instantly, in a single graceful turn.

The swim bladder is typically larger in freshwater species than in their saltwater cousins, since their habitat lacks the buoyant salinity of the seas. Freshwater species have a swim bladder capable of compensating from about six to twelve percent of body mass, while marine ecotypes require only four to six percent. Since trout are anadromous species capable of survival in either biosystem, they must have swim bladders capable of adjusting to this full range of variables.

The air bladder also has its disadvantages for a fish. Trout that change depth too quickly experience considerable discomfort when the air in their bladders expands. When the fish rises voluntarily, it expands the sac to expedite its change in depth. The laws of physics tell us that the pressure in the swim bladder must be reduced fifty percent for each change in depth of thirty feet. Theoretically, it would quadruple in size in a journey to the surface from sixty-odd feet. The remarkable ability to vary pressure without changing the size of the bladder radically makes it possible to avoid expansion quadrupling its size. However, its rapid expansion is sufficient to cause a fish considerable discomfort, making it difficult to return quickly to its original depths.

Fish lying at great depths, like lake trout or other char during hot weather, are often fatally injured when they are hooked and quickly forced to the surface. Their air bladders can rupture or expand so radically that the esophagus is almost forced into the mouth cavity. Such fish can bob helplessly to the surface, totally out of control, and awkwardly flounder there. Unless the pressure change has damaged vital organs or ruptured the air bladder itself, such fish may recover. However, excess air must be dissipated through the bloodstream, and a fish cannot manage it quickly. Similar discomfort is unquestionably experienced by a fish removed from the water, since its air bladder is suddenly expanded in contact with the atmosphere—its density is almost eight hundred times less than water, and its effect on the air pressure inside the bladder is clearly traumatic.

Returning such a fish as quickly as possible to the water is important in reducing the stress of bladder expansion, and is most critical for fish that were hooked in deep water. Changing pressure also affects their fighting qualities. Trout hooked deep in a lake will fight to stay at the depths where they were lying, both for the cooler temperatures and because their air sacs are adjusted to the pressures there. Both diving and surrendering to shallower depths will force a fish out of control, and the fighting qualities of a fish that has been forced out of deep water cannot readily be judged. It has been carried upward faster than its air bladder could dissipate the pressure, and the fish experiences such distress that it literally seems to give up suddenly.

The circulatory system in fish is much less complicated than the cardiovascular network in mammals. Fish have a single circulation of the blood, unlike the double circulation system in higher forms of life, and it is pumped through a rudimentary two-part heart. The cycle starts with the blood being pumped toward the gills, where the exchange of carbon dioxide and oxygen occurs with the water. The freshly oxygenated blood travels back along the primary arterial canal, into the secondary arteries and capillaries of the body tissues and organs. The blood makes a similar exchange there, suffusing the tissue with life-giving oxygen and absorbing wastes and carbon dioxide. The blood then returns in the veins, through the cleansing action of the liver, to the heart.

The circulation of the blood carries metabolic wastes, oxygen, carbon dioxide, minerals, and nutrients both to and from the tissues. The principal bodily fluids of trout consist of these same materials along with enzymes and hemoglobin. The blood itself begins in the bone marrow, lymphatic network, and functioning of the spleen. The heart is located quite close to the gills, just ahead of the pectoral fins.

Like the mammals, fish use their kidneys to rid themselves of excretory wastes. The kidneys in both trout and grayling lie immediately under the spinal column, and consist of a slender reddish agglomeration that resembles coagulated blood. Their actual structure is made up of numerous tubules filled with intricate networks of capillaries that function in the removal of metabolic wastes and poisons from the blood and digestive tract. Such wastes are collected into two excretory ducts that lie along the full length of the visceral cavity and are connected to the urinary bladder and duct.

Blood chemistry in all organisms has an optimal level of relative alkalinity, and the blood of a trout is very slightly alkaline. Death results if its blood acidity radically increases. Since the blood of a fish is exposed to water chemistry as it pulses through the capillaries of the gills, it has long been puzzling how trout protect the slight alkalinity of their blood from an acid habitat.

Recent studies indicate that the freshly oxygenated blood is made acid in its proximity to an acid environment, and that blood is quickly dispatched into the kidney system along the spine. The kidney system modifies the proteins in the fish's diet into compounds that neutralize the acidity of the blood, and it is clear that its kidneys control that chemistry. Trout studiously avoid highly acid waters, which indicates that their ability to protect the alkalinity of their blood is limited. It is also a biomechanism that cannot instantly adjust to radical changes in acidity. Fish can easily be transported from acid waters to alkaline habitat, but trout from an alkaline chemistry cannot easily survive stocking in an acid stream.

Similar problems exist with salinity. Osmotic action tends to diffuse salts from high concentrations to lower chloride volumes. Such osmosis poses some interesting physiological problems for anadromous fish like trout and salmon. When they are in freshwater, they steadily lose body salts to the surrounding habitat. Water is absorbed into the body tissues through the lining of the mouth cavity and gullet, the membranes enclosing the alimentary canal, the gills and the body covering itself. Freshwater trout produce a concentrated urine in their kidneys, and their kidneys are enlarged to expel water and retain the chlorides. The endocrinal system and the brain are also involved in the control of optimal salt concentrations, and the gills also possess salt-retaining cells.

However, trout that migrate into the tidal and marine environments outside their parent rivers must reverse these functions. Their bodies continually lose water and absorb chlorides from the saltier habitat, and must regain water content through the mouth cavity, gill structures, and throat. Potentially lethal concentrations of chlorides are alleviated through the gill filaments, the visceral walls and cavity, and the excretory process. The chloride cells in the gills stop retaining salinity and expel the excessive sodium and calcium chloride ions. Endocrinal activity monitors and controls these changes.

Endocrinal organs are found in the lowest forms of fish, and are quite advanced in the higher Salmoniformes. More sophisticated vertebrates have endocrine systems permitting them to adapt their coloration to their habitat, like the proverbial chameleon. Endocrinal activity also participates in growth, adaptation to salinity and other water chemistry, pancreatic secretions, perceptual sensitivity, migratory behavior and navigation, adjustments to temperature and light, and the processes of metabolism itself.

The pituitary gland is responsible for growth, color adaptation, reproduction, and the critical metabolic functions of the gills. The thyroidal functions control metabolic rates, and various other glands affect calcium and sodium concentrations, heart action and cardiovascular pressure, digestion and assimilation of food, sexual fecundity, and the process of reproduction.

Spawning and reproduction are closely associated with the excretory function in the urinogenital system. The reproductive organs of the female trout and grayling consist of two ovaries suspended along the spine in the upper part of the visceral cavity. The eggs or ripe ova are formed there. Fully developed ovaries may occupy as much as twenty-five percent of female weight at spawning. These ovaries are like flexible sausages, circular and saclike in cross-section, and covered with a smooth, semitransparent tissue. The ovipository duct through which the eggs are ultimately extruded is clearly visible in the developed ovaries. Unripe eggs of a partially developed size are also visible. The Salmonidae strangely lack the separate oviducts that convey the ripe eggs to the anal orifice at spawning times and pass their eggs directly into the body cavity, ovipositing them from there. Male testes occupy the same linear position directly above the visceral mass. Fully developed, the testes are a pair of slender chalk-colored sacs filled with spermatozoa. Somewhat smaller than the ovaries in a female of equal weight, the testes are about twelve percent of body mass. The sperm are dispersed from each of the testes through a series of delicate ducts, ultimately connecting with a larger sperm duct that discharges its fertilizing secretions into the anal vent.

Trout and grayling are bisexual, requiring a female to produce the eggs and male sperm to fertilize them. Small trout and grayling are often sexually identifiable only through examination of their gonadal systems, but mature males are clearly different from females. Skull structure is quite different between male and female trout, and in the grayling, there are clearly discernible differences in the shape of the dorsal fin. Fully mature males also develop physiological distortions of the skull and dorsal musculature at spawning time, particularly the extended upper jaw and the hooklike lower jaw or kype. Male trout and grayling typically display exaggerated coloring as egg-laying approaches, and in these species spawning occurs only once a year.

Like higher forms of life, fertilization of trout and grayling occurs when the ripe egg is suffused with the milty sperm. The successfully fertilized embryo divides in half, and the subsequent cellular growths divide again to form the prelarva and its primary organs. During its prelarval period in the ova, the embryo absorbs nutrients from both its yolk and its habitat.

Following its emergence from the egg, the larval trout or grayling wriggles up through the bottom gravel, capable of only feeble swimming motions and still partially dependent on the yolk sac attached to its thoracic structure. Its survival is dependent upon the variables of winds, currents, and tides. Freshwater species like trout do not experience a radical metamorphosis from larva to adult—unlike tarpon or flounder or bonefish—and resemble their adults at a relatively early stage of growth. The final transformation from parr to adult is typically combined with changes in pigmentation, color pattern, and reproductive organs.

Theoretically, trout are capable of infinite growth, although their rate of growth clearly decreases with age. Both growth and age are measurable by maintaining specimens in captivity or studying the growth markings on scales and skeletal structures. Skeletal bench marks and growth rings on the

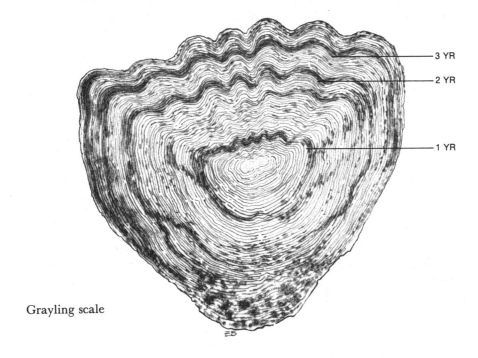

3 YR

2 YR

1 YR

Grayling scale

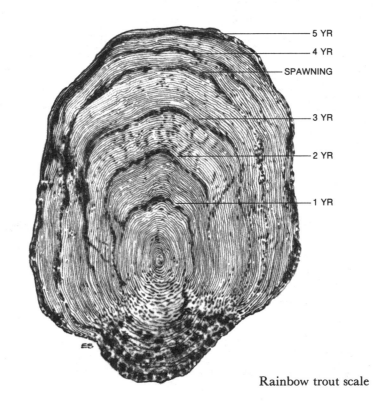

5 YR

4 YR

SPAWNING

3 YR

2 YR

1 YR

Rainbow trout scale

scales are deposited as a fish experiences growth, and these markings can be studied to calibrate growth. Scales grow at approximately the same rate as the skeleton and body, and the number of scales remains constant throughout the life of the fish. The growth of each scale is recorded in the several circuli or growth rings deposited each year. During periods of optimal feeding and water conditions, growth is relatively rapid and the circuli are closely spaced. During the spawning time, when the fish stop ingesting food and take some time to recover from spawning itself, growth is quite slow. Scale growth ebbs too, and the circuli are so close together that they form a dark little band. Winter fasting and the conditions of drought can cause these darkening circuli, and only the winter rings delineate each year.

Annulus is the name given to these winter rings, and in recording each winter cycle, the scales record the passing of the year. Skilled ichthyologists can determine both the age and spawning history of a fish from its scales. Since the growth rate of anadromous fish is radically increased during their periods of salt-water feeding, it is also possible to determine the amount of time a fish has spent in the sea. Some lakes are rich enough in water chemistry so that time spent in them is clearly visible in the annuli of the scales, their food supplies triggering surprising rates of growth that rival that of the sea.

It is also possible to estimate the length of a fish at various stages in its growth, since the ratio between the size of its scales and its known length is measurable. That ratio also existed at earlier scale sizes. Applying it to the measurements of the scales at any winter annulus stage, the length of the fish at that time can be projected. Such techniques are valuable in fisheries research.

Other methods of determining age are also used. The bony plates of the gill operculum reveal stages of growth, and like the vertebrae of the spine, display the fingerprints of winter rings. The otolithic bone found in the ear is composed of calcium, and its concentric growth records time much like the scales.

Growth among a single species of trout or grayling is not a constant factor. Variations exist among individual fish. Different populations and strains of fish are probably the product of particular environments. Abundant food can produce a population of relatively young fish of high average weight, like the trout in the lakes of South America and New Zealand. Poor water chemistry produces much less food, and fish of the same species are stunted or small. Variations in temperature also affect growth. Fish grow slowly in winter and more quickly at warmer temperatures. High-country lakes have a brief six-week summer and stunted populations are common, while limestone streams and spring creeks have similar temperatures all year. Their trout feed at a relatively constant rate, both winter and summer, and experience remarkable growth. Waters receiving substantial geothermal flowages, like famous Hot Creek in California and the Firehole in Yellowstone Park, stay ice-free all winter

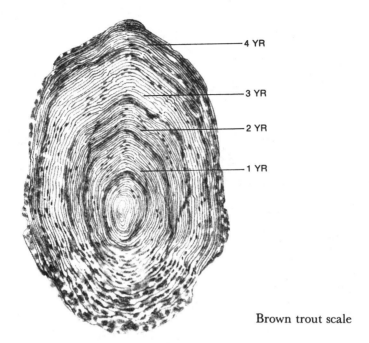

4 YR

3 YR

2 YR

1 YR

Brown trout scale

and have excellent winter hatches. Specimens from such habitat do not display such marked patterns in their annuli, except from their obvious cycles of spawning.

Since alkalinity results in higher rates of growth, water chemistry has a role in fish growth too. Other factors like climate, altitude, changes in water level, fluctuations in reservoir depth, types of available food, coarse species competing for available habitat, population densities, and predators all affect fish populations as well as their growth and physical condition. Hard knowledge about such populations, including average age and rates of growth, are valuable tools in fisheries management. Stunted populations of small average size could benefit from regulations that encourage overfishing and harvest. Short-lived populations should also be caught within reasonable bag limits, while fish with a greater longevity should perhaps be protected. Sometimes the trout populations in remote northern lakes exhibit a large average size and excellent condition, but the fish are also of high average age. Such waters can be fished out in surprisingly short periods of time, and bag limits should be severely restricted. Trout fisheries that are in optimal equilibrium, with fine populations of good average age and condition, should be protected carefully too, because they are quite rare in our time.

The brain coordinates a complex sensory network consisting of the spinal cord, neural organs, and a nervous system which monitors the perceptual responses and motor actions of the fish. Although the network is similar to the higher life forms', it is far less sophisticated in its circuitry.

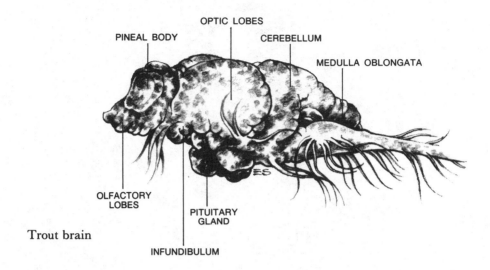

OPTIC LOBES

PINEAL BODY

CEREBELLUM

MEDULLA OBLONGATA

OLFACTORY
LOBES

PITUITARY
GLAND

Trout brain

INFUNDIBULUM

However, its sensitivity is sufficiently developed to produce some remarkably cerebral behavior under fishing pressure. Trout have a three-part brain which is a focal enlargement of the spinal cord. Its anterior, middle, and posterior segments are all housed in the cranial cavity of the skull. The spinal cord runs from its bony cranium along the full length of the fish, the vertebrae threaded along it like the beads on a bony necklace. The anterior segment of the brain is principally responsible for smell and taste. Its olfactory sensitivity is highly developed, particularly among the trout and salmon ecotypes. The middle of the organ is designed to monitor light through its pineal nerve, as well as the remaining sensory stimuli. It is also involved in endocrinal functions, controlling the entire matrix of glandular activity. Visual perception is concentrated in the primary core of this middle brain, in its pair of sophisticated optic lobes. The posterior part of the brain consists of the cerebellum and medulla oblongata. The cerebellum controls orientation, balance, and simple motor activities like swimming. The medulla monitors all sensory networks except the olfactory and visual functions. It is the primary switchboard between the spinal cord and the brain, the neural fulcrum for such basic physiological problems as saline equilibrium in the body tissue, and the intricate web controlling respiratory cycles.

Trout have only a rudimentary neural cord. It has both spinal and cranial nerves connected directly to the medulla oblongata. All of the sensory perceptions received by the fish are transmitted along its delicate circuitry. The primitive neural system of fish is sophisticated enough to implement both conditioned responses to familiar stimuli and a surprising display of instinct and intelligence. Behavioral research unquestionably demonstrates that fish can distinguish color and quickly learn to associate certain sounds, odors, or visual stimuli with either trouble or gratification.

Anadromous trout clearly retain the olfactory fingerprints of their parent rivers in some primitive form of memory, since like the salmon, they eventually return to their freshwater origins. Most seagoing trout exhibit only coastal or estuarine behavior, but unique strains like the big steelheads in some larger British Columbia rivers actually travel into open seas. Their memory imprints obviously include mesopelagic bench marks for long migrations far beyond the coastal trace chemistry of their river origins.

Conditioned response and learning facility varies widely among various ecotypes, and obviously within each species as well. Wild trout are superbly attuned to danger from predators, but surprisingly vulnerable to fishing pressure. Hatchery fish are completely ill equipped to cope with both solitude and freedom once they are stocked. Their lives have been hermetically sealed off from both their natural predators and the diet forms found in open habitat, and men have coddled and fed them since their emergence from the oxygenated eggs. Certainly freshly-stocked hatchery trout do not recognize fishermen as potential enemies, and their pen-raised lives have consciously bred out many of the qualities that make trout unique in the world of fish life.

It is the trout and grayling populations that have been exposed to fishing pressure that most clearly demonstrate the ability of the Salmonidae species to learn. Wilderness fish and hatchery trout can learn too, but they are seldom permitted to survive past their first mistakes. It is the wary public-water trout that sometimes become canny enough to avoid capture consistently, feeding in spite of the parade of fishermen they encounter daily. Their ranks include both hatchery fish that have miraculously survived the fishing pressure, in a curious kind of instant Darwinian selection, and fish that have been spawned naturally in hard-fished waters. It is these skittish and selective fish that are truly wild, in the sense that their wariness makes them worthy of our best skills.

The eyes of trout and grayling are similar to those of other vertebrate organisms, except for their structural adaptations to subaquatic life. Trout eyes consist of a transparent cornea, the lens and iris, the retina, and the eyeball itself, plus the entire sclerotic capsule and the oculatory muscles controlling its movements.

Only the more sophisticated types of fish life, like trout and grayling, are capable of regulating iris diameter. The eyes are not fitted with eyelids, and are smoothly streamlined to match the fusilliform contours of the skull. The lenses are spherical, totally unlike the elliptical cross section of mammalian lenses. Focal resolution is accomplished by adjusting the position of the spherical lenses rather than by altering its shape. Although fish are often nearsighted, trout and grayling are capable of good vision across a surprising range of focal lengths. The position of their eyes gives them a wide field, with exceptional binocular vision both forward and above, perfectly adapted to their unique feeding problems. Good lateral vision is also possible, along with the ability to observe the bottom well, although these fields of view are largely monocular. Such visual fields are quite variable, because the fish are able to adjust the position of each eyeball slightly, both separately and in coordination. The retina is structured with cones that function in intense levels of illumination and rods designed for relatively limited light. Although some fish species have evolved eyes equipped primarily with cones, since their feeding is largely concentrated in daylight periods, other fish adapted to extremely deep marine habitat have eyes with a high percentage of rods. Trout and grayling are surprisingly well suited to both conditions and are able to feed on minute insects long after nightfall.

Color perception is highly developed only in those species which inhabit relatively shallow waters, in both freshwater and marine habitat, since color is a function of light and its penetration into the depths that sustain pelagic species. Trout can clearly distinguish hue, chroma and value. Their color sense is unquestionably capable of measuring subtle differences in color, its relative intensity, and its range of shadings from light to dark. Some research indicates that both trout and grayling are capable of detecting colors in the violet range of the spectrum that are completely beyond most higher organisms, including trout fishermen themselves.

The pathology of trout and grayling includes several common forms of disease, and many of their problems with diseases and parasites are shared with migrating salmon. Some are endemic to salt water and others are found inland, while still others are a problem in both biosystems.

Perhaps the best known parasitic forms are the so-called ectoparasites which infest the external structure of the fish. There are both vertebrate and invertebrate forms. Vertebrate parasites are the marine lampreys, which have been inadvertently introduced to the Great Lakes through the construction of the Welland Canal. The Atlantic lamprey is the familiar *Petromyzon marinus,* and its infestation virtually eradicated the thriving lake trout population in the Great Lakes before fisheries biologists discovered toxic substances that killed the lampreys selectively when they entered the rivers to spawn in early summer. Both the Lampricide TFM (3 trifluo-romethyl-4 nitrophenol) with granular Bayer 73 and a program of electrical trap weirs have checked the lamprey population, although the lake-trout populations had become almost extinct by 1962. The result was a second infestation of their habitat. Without the predatory lake trout, alewives, which reached the Great Lakes along with the lamprey eels, experienced an unchecked population explosion. There are also some instances of lamprey predation on trout and landlocked salmon in Canada and New England. Unfortunately, little is known of lamprey infestation on both trout and salmon in estuarine and marine habitats and there is accumulating evidence that the lampricides are also toxic to the silt-burrowing *Hexagenia* mayfly nymphs that play such a major role in the food chain of the Great Lakes rivers.

Similar problems exist on the Pacific Coast watersheds, and research has discovered extensive predation by the *Entosphenus tridentatus* lampreys on both salmon and sea-run trout. Sockeye salmon and pink salmon apparently suffer worse infestation than other Pacific Coast species. Recent studies found sixty-seven percent of the sockeyes in one river system had been attacked by lampreys, and six percent had serious wounds. Twenty percent of the pink salmon had suffered from *Entosphenus tridentatus* predation, and two percent sustained moderate or severe tissue damage. Since both fish species exhibit large-scale schooling behavior, the availability of fish normally attacked by lampreys would be roughly equal, with perhaps even larger numbers of the smaller pink salmon. Size might be a possible answer. Sockeye salmon are much larger fish, and that might explain why sixty-seven percent of their migrating population were infested. Sea-run cutthroats are relatively small, and seem to suffer rarely from lampreys. Steelheads can run much larger, rivalling the salmon in average size on some British Columbia rivers, although they display less schooling behavior. There is some evidence of lamprey predation on larger sea-run rainbows, but it is not as serious as their impact on salmon stocks, although more research on this problem is needed.

Perhaps the best known invertebrate parasite is the tiny *Lepeophteirus salmonis*, the prolific sea lice familiar to many trout and salmon fishermen. Sea lice cannot live more than about forty-eight hours in fresh water, and their presence on a sea-run fish is clear evidence of its recent entry into the river. However, some biologists have evidence of longer periods of survival in fresh water when river temperatures are under forty-five degrees. Although sea lice are not often a serious problem, there are instances of extremely heavy infestations. Both salmon grilse and steelheads have been captured with so many sea lice on their dorsal surfaces that their natural coloring was obscured. Severe infestation can result in such extensive damage that loosening skin and a form of dermal necrosis occur, and skin cells are unquestionably part of the diet ingested by sea lice. Fish suffering from such damage, which is apparently worst in low and relatively warm water, have a so-called white-spot necrosis first described by W. L. Calderwood in 1906.

The most common freshwater parasite is *Salminicola salmonea*, the ubiquitous little gill maggot. Like the sea lice, gill maggots are a small parasitic copepod, although they bear little physical resemblance. Both salmon and trout become infested in fresh water. The free-swimming larvae attach themselves to the gills, and moult twice before adulthood. Before breeding, both male and female gill maggots move about freely, and after copulation the males die. The fertilized females then become rooted immovably to the gill filaments, and their eggs are fully mature in six months. The females moult again and oviposit their eggs. Other egg laying can occur, depending on the time spent in fresh water, and if infected fish return to the sea, the maggots can remain attached to the gills. Reproduction is inhibited in the sea, but reproduction resumes if the fish returns to freshwater. However, gill maggots drop off at this stage, leaving ugly wounds in the respiratory filaments, and such fish are highly susceptible to either reinfection or other diseases. Although gill maggots are seldom a serious threat, infestation can cause extensive damage to the fragile lamellae of the gills. Sea-run trout are sometimes infested with *Discocotyle* trematodes, which also attack the gills.

Freshwater lice of the *Argulus foliaceus* species are also a parasitic problem in some waters. Like the marine types, the freshwater *Argulus* lice are flat and disc shaped. They attach themselves to both gills and dermal surfaces, perforating the skin covering to extract the blood. Its feeding proboscis is too slender to accept the blood cells themselves, but it does drink the plasma. The proboscis can cause local infections, but its slow denigration of the blood supply is more serious, weakening a large fish against other dangers. According to some studies, the *Argulus* lice also secrete enough toxicity that immature trout and salmon can be killed by only two or three parasites.

Some instances of leeches infesting both trout and salmon are recorded, particularly during the winter months when the water temperatures radically lower the metabolism rate and the activity of the fish. Such infestations of *Piscicola geometra* are reported from a number of European rivers. There is some incidence of American brook leeches, like the ovoid little *Glossiphonia complanata*, infesting smaller trout. The larger species of the *Macrobdella* are known to attach themselves to fish, although their principal targets are perhaps turtles, salamanders, and wintering frogs. Worm leeches like *Herpobdella punctata* are common in northern lakes and ponds, and although their feeding is concentrated on worms, insect larvae, and decaying matter, they are sometimes attached to wintering trout. Severe leech attacks can result in erosion of the gills, serious skin lesions, and virtually complete destruction of the fins.

There are also a number of internal parasites like flukes, tapeworms, spiny-headed worms, and nematodes. Perhaps the best known are the *Eubothrium* tapeworms, which can grow much longer than the fish they infest and are lodged in the pyloric caeca. Tapeworms are often ingested along with baitfish. Urinary parasites like the *Phyllodistomum* are also common, and the *Dacnitis* and *Crepidostomum* worms infest the pyloric caeca. The alimentary tract behind the pyloric caeca is subject to infestations of *Crepidostomum* and *Neoechinorhynchus* parasites. Blindness is sometimes caused by the larval flukes of the *Diplostomum* genus, which typically form cysts in the eyes of both trout and salmon, although trout are more commonly affected. Opacity of the lens and bulging eyes are the most obvious symptoms, and sometimes the blind fish turns almost black. Larval tapeworms also spend part of their metamorphosis in trout, and epidemics of *Diphylobothrium* larvae are known in Canada, the United States, and throughout the British Isles. The intensity of parasitic infestation is often greater in larger trout, and infected fish often appear perfectly normal in configuration and coloring. However, as these tapeworm flukes multiply, the host fish becomes emaciated and sluggish. Its encysted stomach and pyloric caeca can often be felt in handling an infected trout, and sometimes there is ventral bleeding. Cysts sometimes also occur on the liver, swim bladder, spleen and genitalia, but are curiously rare in the intestines. Obstructions of the intestinal tract can be caused by tapeworms and the spiny-headed worms of the *Echinohynchus* type. Nematode larvae form disc-like cysts quite unlike the spherical growths of the tapeworm larvae. The parasitic nematodes of the *Eustrongylides* genus are tiny roundworms, usually bright scarlet in color. European research has found that the *Terranova* nematodes are common in fish captured in both fresh riverine environments and in marine and estuarine habitats.

It is a tiny myxosporidian called *Myxosoma cerebralis* that is parasitic in the organs and cartilage, causing the familiar whirling disease in trout. The brain and other balancing organs are affected, along with obvious deformation of the cartilage. Symptoms usually include a darkening of color pigmentation in the caudal region, spinal curvature at the dorsal and adipose fins, and endless cycles of whirling tail-chasing behavior. Infected fish are known to carry the *Myxosoma* spores from as little as four months to as long as three years before death occurs. The spores are released into the habitat on the death of the host fish, and are ingested by small fish or organisms in their food chain. The ingested spores develop polar filaments in the intestinal tract and the sporoplasm emerges, invading both the intestinal wall and the cartilage of the skull. Multinucleate sporoplasm is typically found through the cartilaginous tissue from forty days to three months after infection. Second generation spores are lodged in the bone and granulomas about four months after infection and are released into the habitat when death occurs. Whirling disease is a familiar problem in hatchery populations, but it has also been observed in the wild state in recent years.

Recent studies suggest that whirling disease is transmitted through tubifex worms, an aquatic organism that thrives in waters of declining quality. Tubifex worms thrive in habitats so rich in decomposing pollutants that their oxygen is threatened. Such tubifex colonies are common in the effluents discharged by both hatcheries and sewage systems.

Furunculosis is a common disease resulting from *Aeromonas salmonicida* infections. Its bacteria are short, nonmitile organisms and do not form spores. Fish suffering from furunculosis have a variety of symptoms, including deterioration of the fins, furuncular lesions, and ventral discharges of blood. However, some infected trout may only display fin congestion, lacking other external symptoms. Furunculosis is most common in low-water conditions, with water temperatures above fifty-five degrees. Some of the worst infestations occur when extreme drought congregates too many fish in dwindling pools, although there are also records of winter epidemics among spawned-out fish. It is curious that these infected kelts are less likely to develop external symptoms than fish not yet spawned, and males are particularly susceptible. Fish that die are possible sources of fresh infection, and the bacteria remain viable in the decaying fish as much as three to six months. These dead fish can infect other uncontaminated trout as they are carried downstream, or as the healthy trout migrate through the places they have lodged. *Aeromonas salmonicida* bacteria are known to survive exposure to salt water, migrating downstream with a juvenile fish and remaining in its tissues until its return to the parent river. It is suspected that many returning adults are already carrying the disease before they reach fresh water.

There is a necrosis of trout kidneys and spleens that has been reported from both Europe and North America, although it was first described from the Dee in Aberdeenshire, in studies conducted in 1933. The host fish in this instance were salmon, and specimens were found to have minute necrotic lesions of the spleen. Symptoms are not useful in diagnosis, because the ventral bleeding and fin congestion and muscle hemorrhaging are typical of other infections. The internal symptoms are more significant, with widespread petechial hemorrhage of the muscles lining the intestinal cavity. The kidneys are also affected in many cases. Healthy kidney tissue is a dark reddish brown, but infected kidneys develop grayish blotching that can evolve cystlike encrustations. Infected spleens are also relatively common, and their tissue is covered with chalk-colored lesions, ranging from the size of a pinprick to approximately one-eighth of an inch in diameter. The number of these whitish lesions varies widely. Some fish may have only a few, while others are covered with lesions in dense poxlike patterns. The liver may also become infected. However, its lesions are never quite as numerous and its pathology is less chronic. The swim bladder may also suffer with petechial hemorrhaging.

The disease can evolve more virulent forms, usually found in the cold early-season water temperatures. Infected fish display a whitish membrane covering their internal organs, genitalia, and peritoneal muscles. Such membranes are loosely attached to the infected tissues, and peel free easily, leaving the muscles and organs looking relatively healthy. Seriously infected trout often have the pericardial sac filled with a milky fluid, its chemistry rich in tissue cells and bacilli. Some fish are affected with both these membranes and necrotic lesions, and studies indicate that the virulence of the disease is related to water temperatures. Fish with a pathology indicating the most advanced infections are usually found in surprisingly cold water, with temperatures below fifty degrees, while the least virulent specimens are typically found at temperatures as high as sixty-three degrees. The organism responsible for the disease was identified as a *Corynebacteria* type in 1964, when a summary of the pathology and symptoms of its infections were finally recorded in Great Britain.

Dermal necrosis has widely manifested itself among both trout and salmon populations in the past century, and its precise causes are still not fully understood. It was first recorded from both salmon and trout in the Scottish border rivers in 1877, and in only five years it had spread well across Scotland and farther south into Ireland and Wales.

The first symptoms of the dermal necrosis are ash-gray discolorations of the skin, usually occurring on those dorsal surfaces that are devoid of scales, such as the skull or surrounding the adipose fin. Sometimes the dermal covering at the roots of the other fins is affected, and once a patch of diseased skin has developed, it quickly spreads and merges with adjacent lesions. The original infected area soon changes into large, relatively soggy pieces that flake off easily. The skin in these zones is completely atrophied and gone, and the vascular tissues exposed. The diseased areas may grow so extensive that the papyraceous coating can cover a relatively large fish from its head to its caudal extremities. However, infection is not limited to the dermal covering. The exposed vascular tissues soon become deeply ulcerated, forming a bleeding wound, and the necrosis soon eats into the flesh deeply enough to reveal the skeletal structure of the fish below. Studies commissioned to investigate the outbreak of this dermal necrosis determined that the bacillus could be transmitted from dead fish to other dead remains lying in a river, that clean fish could be infected through proximity to such dead specimens, and that the disease thrives in cold water temperatures. Although there was considerable disagreement about the cause of the dermal necrosis, the distinguished Thomas Huxley believed the *Saprolegnia* fungus was the primary agent in the infection.

Similar pathology in trout and salmon has appeared again in recent years, reaching epidemic proportions in several rivers on the southwest coast of Ireland in 1964. The new outbreak of ulcerative dermal necrosis followed parallel patterns in the spread of the disease, the external symptomology is undeniably similar, and a direct relationship between the virulence of the infection and cold water temperatures has been established. Several biologists studying the disease have even argued that *Saprolegnia ferax* is perhaps the causative bacillus in this modern epidemic.

The infection spread quickly along the Irish coast, although it took irrational patterns like those recorded almost a century before. Some rivers were ravaged, while others remained surprisingly clean. It is believed that sea-run trout contributed more to the spread of the disease than the salmon, because they range freely from estuary to estuary along the coast. Biologists in Scotland discovered that sea-run browns in some rivers became infected several weeks before diseased salmon were observed. Writing in the *Scottish Fisheries Bulletin,* Pyefinch and Elson described the symptoms of the new outbreak of dermal necrosis, and the parallels with similar descriptions from the nineteenth century are intriguing:

> The first signs of the disease are the appearance of small bleached areas of the skin, on the head, back, and near the dorsal fin and on the tail. As the disease progresses areas of a bluish-grey, slimy growth develop over these bleached areas, making the fish very conspicuous in the water. The appearance of the fish at this stage has been likened to that of a fish heavily infected with fungus but, if the fish is taken out of the water, the affected patches show none of the woolly or fuzzy appearance which characterizes a fungal infection, instead they resemble masses of sodden blue-grey blotting paper. Further these slimy masses can be readily pulled away, exposing inflammation or ulceration of the skin.

As the disease progresses, more patches appear and the others spread, so that considerable areas over the head, back and the wrist of the tail are affected and, at this stage, the head may be so badly affected that it seems largely covered by raw, reddish areas. As often happens when the skin of a fish is damaged, fungus may infect these exposed areas but it is important to recognize that this fungus growth is a secondary effect, consequent upon primary infection, and not a primary symptom. Once established, however, the fungus spreads and, in the most advanced stages of the disease, the head and tail regions of the fish may be largely covered with fungus.

Modern pathologists have discovered associated involvement of the gall bladder, and in fish displaying early stages of infection, the gall bladder is frequently empty and distended. Many infected fish are observed aquaplaning futilely or weakly jumping with agitated rhythms, the floundering of a fish in obvious distress. It has clearly been demonstrated that adult fish are more susceptible than immature trout or salmon, since relatively few parr or smolts have been noted. Pathologists have also learned that diseased specimens exhibit a clear deficiency in serum proteins. Disagreement still persists concerning the pathogenic source of the infections. Both *Aeromonas* and *Pseudomonas* bacilli have been isolated in studies of ulcerative dermal necrosis, but pathologists are convinced that these genera were only secondary agents. *Saprolegnia* fungus was also discovered and some infectivity studies were performed. Both direct injection and habitat contaminated with the disease were tried. Although this work demonstrated the pathogenicity of several suspected organisms, actual necrotic lesions were never fully duplicated.

Extensive studies were also made to survey the dermal bacteria present on healthy fish, and it is interesting that various skin flora associated with infectious conditions were present on almost forty percent of both salmon and trout examined from marine, estuarine, and freshwater habitats alike. Apparently fish carry the bacilli of the disease constantly, and serious outbreaks only occur when a strain of fish gradually loses its resistance to infection.

It was also discovered that many fish were already infected before reaching their parent rivers. However, these specimens had ulcerated areas on their heads but lacked the accompanying fungus in the infected zones. These specimens were captured in both coastal and estuarine environments. Some pathologists found that the bacteria collected from their ulcerations were not culturable, but tissue from both the kidneys and liver revealed the presence of viral contamination. It was also demonstrated that the aetiological agent was apparently unaffected by antibiotics, and that the lesions associated with ulcerative dermal necrosis are microscopically small in the beginning.

Some rivers took twelve to fifteen years to purge themselves of the salmon disease in the nineteenth century, and in the spring of 1973, several Irish rivers that had become infected about a dozen years earlier were finally free of infection. That spring I took a number of salmon and fine sea-run brown trout from Lough Currane at Waterville, and was told that none of the fish taken earlier or observed in the famous Butler's Pool was diseased. Perhaps the salmon disease will again run its course.

During these recent epidemics, some pathologists also isolated cultures of columnaris bacteria from infected specimens. *Chondrococcus columnaris* is a well-known pathogenic bacillus, and although it was present in the fungus-covered ulcerations, it too was apparently a secondary infection. Columnaris remains a serious skin disease of trout and salmon in its own right, particularly in hatchery management.

Vibriosis is a marine bacillus that is known to attack many species in salt water. It is highly pathogenic to salmon and sea-run trout, and is also recorded from eels and plaice. Its cause is *Vibrio anguillarum*, named for its common incidence in eels, and its symptoms are serious hemorrhagic lesions on the lateral and belly surfaces. The internal organs also show necrotic symptoms, and the disease is found persisting long after an infected trout or salmon has entered fresh water. Vibriosis is often mistaken for furunculosis, since they share some common symptoms, and a bacteriological investigation is necessary for a proper diagnosis between them.

The pathology of trout and salmon is a discipline that will require much study in the future, both for artificial cultivation in hatcheries and in understanding the relationships between pathogenic infestations and water quality.

Since no-kill regulations have begun to receive more widespread acceptance on our waters in recent years—perhaps because their undeniable success has produced fine trout populations on hard-fished waters—understanding the physiological stress involved in playing and releasing trout is important to fishermen. Most anglers know that trout which bleed seriously from the gill structure are unlikely to survive, but many seemingly unhurt fish also die after being released. Such fatalities are apparently the result of a complex ping-pong between physiological and other stress factors, not unlike the puzzling deaths of seemingly uninjured people who have experienced traumatic psychological stress in accidents or disasters.

Some fishing writers have blamed such deaths simply on concentrations of lactic acid in the muscle tissues after periods of stress. It is too simple an explanation, although severe physiological problems do result from such accumulations of lactic acid, and from the parallel drop in blood alkalinity. Excessive fatigue during migration and after being hooked results in the build-up of lactic acid in the muscles, and such acid dissipates again during periods of rest. Well-oxygenated blood rinses the excessive acidity from the tissues, just as sufficient rest will eventually restore the aching muscles of a tired athlete.

But it is far more complicated than that, and fish that have been hooked and released are also suffering from serious metabolic stress. Lactic-acid accumulation in the muscle tissue is not causal, but merely symptomatic in character. Such fish have far more serious physiological problems in both their metabolic anoxia and acidotic imbalance of their blood chemistry.

Trout blood is slightly more acid than human blood, and it is protected from the external acidity of their habitat by the normal functions of the kidneys. Metabolic rates are commonly described as aerobic, because their processes occur when their systemic oxygenation is in relative equilibrium. However, severe physical stress and anxiety result in anaerobic metabolic problems, not unlike the muscular distress and gasping respiration of any organism. Normal metabolic action converts oxygen, food, and water into carbon dioxide and gastrourinary wastes. The anaerobic metabolism associated with syndromes of stress results in serious oxygen deficiencies and creates large quantities of lactic and pyruvic acids. Their concentration in the body tissue, along with an accelerating oxygen deficiency, results in increasing vasodilatation of the blood vessels. Blood begins pooling in the primary organs, further depriving the muscles, or secondary tissues, of oxygen. Adrenalin is triggered into the system, but its principal effect is to raise blood pressure by constricting the circulatory network and increasing the heart rate. It is a stimulus that works briefly, when a fish is swimming to escape a predatory otter or kingfisher or osprey, but during the stress of a prolonged fight it is counterproductive. Its effects on the cardiovascular system are the opposite of the fish's needs, and constriction of blood circulation can lead to failure of the kidneys.

Renal failure is obviously fatal, but even minor impairment of kidney action is serious. Blood acidity is controlled by the kidneys, and even minimal loss of kidney action can impair the ability of the fish to neutralize the effects of an acid habitat. Therefore, stress problems may prove more severe to the trout's metabolism in acid than in alkaline waters. Both the liver and the muscles also accumulate glycogens, and these starchlike substances are transformed into blood sugar as the fish needs it. However, such glycogenesis is a relatively slow process. The stress of struggling with an angler expends the surplus glycogens recklessly, and they are often completely gone when the blood most needs them. Sometimes the glycogens are so completely used that a fish has started to metabolize its body fats too, particularly after a long fight in heavy water, and accumulations of fatty acids are the result. Each of these processes combines to produce acidotic blood chemistry, and a downward spiral of anoxia, constriction of the vascular network, diminishing blood pressure, and ultimately renal failure. It is the physiological equivalent of the domino theory, in which each metabolic problem triggers more serious pathogenic results.

The problem is still more complicated because of several other factors. The metabolism of the trout is controlled by the temperature of the water, and its swim bladder is adjusted to the density of its environment. Serious effects on the swim bladder can distort the balancing abilities of a fish when it is released. Trout also have relatively little blood, and even minor bleeding can seriously deplete both vascular pressure and the ability to help a tired and frightened fish recover. The air pressure is almost eight hundred times less than the water pressure in which the fish was struggling, and its removal from that pressure triggers instant internal stress on its swim bladder and other organs. Since its body temperature is always much colder than ours, contact with our hands is still another metabolic shock. Atmospheric temperature is often much higher than the temperature of the fish's habitat, so both our body heat and the air temperature can multiply its anaerobic distress.

Oxygen deficiency, acidotic blood and muscle tissue, and failure of the kidneys to process wastes and control the increasing acidosis are the principal reasons for the death of released fish that were otherwise seemingly undamaged:

Obviously, virtually all trout will survive capture and release if they are handled properly. The success of catch-and-release management programs clearly proves the point, and private management of some experimental water on the Brodheads provides corroborative evidence on a known fish population. Our discussion of metabolic shock and its relationship to releasing trout is intended to help you handle your catch with better understanding. It is clear that you should play your fish as quickly as possible, use a landing net to minimize playing time and handling time, and keep the fish in its own habitat as much as possible. Each of these will help a trout suffering from potential metabolic shock, and together they can greatly multiply its chances for survival.

Feeding and the subsequent assimilation of food are an equally intriguing process. Such a minuscule number of trout and grayling survive into adulthood that each big fish is remarkable in itself. Survival and attrition begin at the moment the eggs are extruded by the spawning females. Some of these ova are never successfully fertilized by the milt of the cockfish. Others are eaten by predators or damaged in the current, and still others are lost when the spawning beds are smothered in bottom silts and sands. Some lose oxygen when the bottom gravel freezes or the stream level drops, and too many fish using a limited spawning zone can damage the earlier redds. Diseases also exact their toll of eggs.

The hatching alevins and fry are highly vulnerable once they have wriggled up through the bottom gravel. Their lives are a frightening obstacle course of hazards, and less than one percent survive to adulthood. Both survival and growth are dependent on a fish's methods and strategies of feeding, as well as its sensory defenses and wariness.

Growth depends on the ability of a fish to capture, ingest, and assimilate its food efficiently. Its metabolic processes must digest and distribute sufficient nutrients into the oxygenated blood. Food is utilized in several ways. Most is instantly employed to supply energy for internal processes and muscular action. With sufficient food supply, any additional nutrients are used to construct new bone, muscle, and body tissue in the process called growth. Excess food secured beyond the needs of metabolism, muscle activity, replacement of cellular tissues, and growth is stored in the form of glycogens and fats. Fat is developed and stored only when the other primary physiological needs are satisfied.

Life is difficult for a trout, poised continually between calories ingested and calories expended in survival, and this ratio of efficiency governs the growth, daily behavior and survival of every fish in the stream.

Perhaps the largest amounts of energy are expended in capturing food, although a current-loving trout or grayling uses considerable energy in simply maintaining its position. Other energy is required for survival and the ordinary rhythms of daily existence. Specimens that cannot maintain their nutritional minimums become stunted, perish from starvation, succumb to disease, or are killed by predators. Ichthyologists conclude that a trout or grayling must capture and assimilate a minimum of one percent of its weight daily. Such amounts of food are mandatory for mere survival. Using this rule of thumb, a three-pound trout must have approximately an ounce of food per day just to survive—and more than twelve pounds a year. Such a fish would be poorly conditioned, its energy totally consumed in the capture and assimilation of such marginal amounts of aquatic food.

Such a fish might easily take twice as much food in a richly alkaline habitat, yet extra energy is expended to capture and utilize that food, and it may grow only a half pound in the year. Fish usually conserve their energy well, often taking only diet forms carried to them in the current and expending calories actively only when large amounts of food are available. Heavy fly hatches can trigger such vigorous feeding periods.

Fish are incapable of swimming continually or stalking and pursuing food whenever it is available. Fish populations practice regular cycles of feeding and rest, expending energy briskly while capturing food and resting for long periods, and digesting it and recovering from their exertion. Such rest periods are necessary to purge tissue and blood acidity, and restore the critical glycogenic reserves. Survival is also predicated on sufficient energy reserves to flee the ever-present predators. Studies performed on the Pacific Coast indicate that migrating fish expend vast energy reserves, and that both salmon and sea-run rainbows frequently stop to rest on their journeys. Both steelheads and sockeye salmon require from three to six hours to recover from periods of moderate upstream migration, and recovery from fatigue is progressive.

Trout migrating upstream to spawn expend remarkable amounts of energy, ascending rapids and fish ladders and waterfalls in their journey to egg-laying gravel. Their travels often leave them exhausted, and the fish stop frequently to rest. Such resting fish are often found in holding pools immediately above and below obstacles of difficult water. Like salmon, migrating trout seem to hold deep in resting lies or choose shallows with currents approximating optimal rates of flow for the spawning cycle to come. Unlike salmon that have returned to their parent rivers, trout migrating upstream to spawn usually continue their feeding periods.

Recent studies with fresh-run steelheads indicate that they are capable of swimming twelve to fifteen miles per hour for brief periods, but that these fish quickly reduced their speed to three or four miles per hour after a few minutes. The fish in the studies were permitted to rest briefly and were startled again. Their reaction was agitated flight, but they were incapable of reaching ten miles per hour and quickly slowed their speed. After fifteen minutes of recovery time, these same fish did not attempt to escape by swimming but sought cover in shadows and among the boulders.

The instant reserves of energy for escape, as we discussed earlier in this chapter, come from the glycogenic sugars stored in the muscles. Stress triggers the release of epinephrenal catalysts, increasing the sugar concentrations of the blood. These compounds are quickly exhausted, and an average-size trout can use up half its sugar reserves in only two to five minutes of strong exertion. Once all of the glycogens are wasted, it can take a healthy fish as much as eighteen to twenty-four hours of rest to recover from its hypoglycemia and restore its energy reserves.

Feeding trout also expend energy in their foraging. Since a fish that is lazily hunting its food along the bottom is virtually weightless and is grubbing for caddis cases or nymphs in the bottom trash and detritus, it expends very little energy compared to a fish vigorously pursuing minnows and dace. Capturing a diet of baitfish can only occupy brief periods of feeding activity, since a fish can easily waste more energy reserves than it acquires from its freshly ingested food. Trout that are calmly taking emerging nymphs or feeding on freshly hatched mayflies on the surface are expending surprisingly small amounts of their energy.

Trout and grayling both select feeding lies that enable them to waste minimal energy while waiting for a primary current tongue to bring them food. The fish do not swim against the flow to take the nymphs and hatching flies. Holding steadily in the current or along the bottom, they simply adjust their fins and body position to drift upward with its flow, timing themselves to intercept their prey. It is a performance that never loses its fascination, as precise as a falcon capturing a partridge in midflight, but infinitely more subtle. When the fish reaches the insect, it opens its mouth and its gill covers, allowing both the current and its quarry to flow through. Merely opening its mouth would not work. The insect would simply float around, just as it slides past the palm of your hand when you try to dip it from the water. It is the slightly opened gills that complete the process and make it possible. The gillrakers keep the insects from floating through the opened gills, and the trout closes its gill arches and opercles in imperceptible succession. Its prey is now safely inside the throat and is drawn into the gullet, and the trout darts back to the bottom, using the current force again. Its flow is greatly reduced along the stones or bank, and the trout quietly returns to its original lie.

Although the basic mechanics of the rise are the same for both groups, the feeding behavior of trout and grayling are not entirely alike. Trout are often demonstrably more selective in their feeding, but they are also more willing to forage outside their precise line of drift. Charles Ritz makes the point in his *Fly Fisher's Life* that trout are quixotic and temperamental fish, willing to break their normal rhythms, while grayling are disciplined and consistent.

Trout will come to the fly in literally any direction from their position if they are in a feeding mood, particularly if the fly suggests common diet forms. Surface foods can trigger a rise anywhere in a 360-degree circle around its holding lie, although an insect coming down a feeding lane is most frequently taken. Trout may be lying at the bottom, hovering just under the surface, or holding at any intermediate depth. There is usually some entomological explanation for the choice of depth, but sometimes their behavior lacks any apparent cause other than some inexplicable mood. Its unpredictability is seldom shared by grayling, which always lie near the bottom. Their rises invariably occur behind their holding lies and almost always in the exact plane of their bodies.

Grayling fishing in the Canadian subarctic and Alaska is generally so easy that anglers fish lazily for its simple pleasures, seldom observing such fine points in the behavior of the fish. There are so many fish in the grayling lies that almost any line of float will move one. But this does not mean that our grayling behave differently from their European cousins on famous rivers like the Ammer or Pegnitz or Traun.

Trout are variable in their response to our flies, and sometimes they even refuse naturals. During a hatch of fluttering sedges or mayflies skittering along the current with the wind, trout will rise quite excitedly. Sometimes their rise forms are bold swirls, and sometimes only a tiny dimple betrays a feeding fish. Confidence, boredom, timidity, apprehension, anger, and an almost fatal curiosity are all moods that color their feeding activity.

Grayling sometimes lie on the bottom gravel, ignoring both natural and artificial flies, but during periods of active feeding their behavior is surprisingly consistent. Since they prefer relatively small insects, their rises are quiet and subtle, and they inspect almost everything that floats down their lines of drift with an intriguing catlike curiosity.

Trout are much more skittish and unpredictable in temperament, triggering in panic at the sight of a fisherman or his clumsy casts or the shadow of a predatory kingfisher. Grayling are more sophisticated and are seldom frightened by either an angler or his techniques.

Although trout are more selective in terms of color and imitative silhouette and size, their tastes are quite catholic and their feeding is aggressive. Grayling are particular about the size and configuration of the flies they will accept, since they prefer a diet of minute mayflies and terrestrials and midge forms, and flies smaller than sixteen are most productive. Arctic grayling are seldom this particular, in either our northern subarctic latitudes or the arctic waters of northern Europe. But my experience with difficult grayling in Montana confirms the wisdom of dark fly patterns dressed on tiny hooks and fished on delicate tippets, much as experienced grayling fishermen recommend from the pastoral Unica in Yugoslavia to the Wharfe and Ure in Yorkshire.

The mouth structures of trout and grayling are quite different. Trout have a relatively large mouth, formed of both cartilage and bone, and their bite is strong. Grayling have a smaller mouth of a largely cartilaginous structure and a more delicate bite. Their mouth is located more under the head, while a trout has its jaws more forward. The morphology of a grayling's mouth is both relatively fragile and small, making them easiest to hook with small flies, and they should be played with a gentle hand.

Because of these many behavioral differences, presentation of the fly to trout and grayling varies. The zone of presentation for a trout is roughly circular and relatively large, completely surrounding its position. Sometimes trout will rise to meet a fly, and sometimes they drop back like a grayling. They will also move laterally to take drifting food, sometimes moving as much as several feet to capture a grasshopper or inchworm that has fallen heavily on the water. Repeated casts can make a trout nervous, and the first two or three presentations that float drag-free into its optimal taking circle are most likely to succeed.

Grayling demand a precise line of drift and a relatively long drag-free float. Considerable slack is necessary to prevent drag. The taking zone is a rather narrow ellipse, lying behind the grayling and exactly in the plane of its body. Successive casts and floats seldom alarm a grayling, and patient repetition of drag-free presentations can pay off. Sometimes the percentages of taking a grayling after a dozen or more casts are better than with the first few tries so critical in catching trout. With average depths of approximately one to three feet over clean beds of fine gravel, the grayling tends to rise rather lazily and take only slightly behind its observation lie. The depth of the current means that the fly is relatively close to the fish before it enters its cone of vision.

Grayling will also rise through as much as six to eight feet of water from their holding lies along the bottom. Their rises come more quickly from such depths. Their cone of vision becomes progressively larger as their depth increases; it means that a grayling can see an approaching fly sooner and start its drift toward the surface. The speed of the rise is directly proportional to current speed, and the placing of the fly depends on that speed and depth. Sedge hatches can entice grayling to lie near the surface like trout. Precise imitation is probably less important than a perfect float with grayling, since their feeding zones are so small. Sometimes selectivity can also play a role in grayling fishing, and the following lines from *A Fly Fisher's Life* are worth repeating:

> Hatches normally succeed each other throughout the day with very different effects. Those toward the end of the afternoon are the most difficult and only the very smallest flies will produce results. Between hatches, the fish are practically untakeable. I shall never forget two places on the Traun where the current is

fairly rapid, one below the dam at Marienbrücke and the other at Danzermühle; on days when the water was normal, and there were big hatches with continuous feeding that often lasted for nearly two hours, I never succeeded in persuading a grayling to rise boldly. Most of the flies in my boxes were tried, presented by Hans and myself. Hans admits that he has never been able to discover the explanation for these repeated failures. It may be that during these hatches, only live flies with moving wings were taken.

Since my old friend Charles Ritz does not really believe in the serious application of stream entomology and writes flatly in the most recent edition of *A Fly Fisher's Life* that he does not believe in the philosophy of matching the hatch, this paragraph is both surprising and revealing.

It is particularly surprising that a mind with a tireless reputation for the minutiae of tackle balance and design refuses the disciplines of studying the diet of his fish. Certainly, the collection of those puzzling hatches on the Traun would have revealed details of color or configuration or size that might explain the failure of his fly patterns.

Ritz clearly prefers grayling since their usual behavior and rise-form mechanics are perfectly suited to his remarkable casting skills. Trout are a little less demanding in terms of a precise line of float and more demanding in the range of their selective feeding behavior. Obviously, the author of books like my *Matching the Hatch* and *Nymphs* is fascinated with selectivity and its problems in fly dressing, and I much prefer the trout of hard-fished streams to grayling. It is interesting that Ritz includes these observations in *A Fly Fisher's Life*, with their grudging praise of trout:

> If one is prepared to admit that fish possess a certain degree of intelligence, the trout is in a higher class than the grayling. But the latter compensates for this inferiority by a more precise and detailed inspection before selecting a fly. It is a tireless worker and always subject to the most rigorous self-discipline. It fights less intelligently, always plays itself out, has no tricks and is always taken completely exhausted. It does not know, as does the trout, how to use the obstacles on the bottom, so dangerous to the leader. It does not react to the landing net. Its nervous system must be of considerable delicacy. Once in hand, a light flip on the nose often renders it motionless and facilitates the difficult removal of the hook. If placed in a retaining pool made of large stones, it makes no attempt to jump out as does the trout.
>
> The sight of the fisherman and his tackle often makes no difference to its continuing to rise. This is not the case with the trout which, more often than not, retreats with full speed at the merest false cast, even if it is behind it. On the other hand, grayling can be easily disturbed at the sight of other fish coming from downstream or by a fisherman in waders, just like a trout.

Perhaps the most basic things about the mechanics of the rise—for both grayling and trout—are the two facts that the fish are usually lying above the actual zone of their rises and that they may drift back a surprising distance with a fly before either taking or rejecting it. Sometimes we can see a rising fish, but more often we can only observe their rises. Fishermen must remember to place their flies slightly above the rises of a trout—and considerably above a grayling. Placing the fly close to the rise forms can mean it might be dropped right over a fish, spooking it badly and triggering it upstream, or behind a fish so far that it fails to see its float. The distance that a fish rises behind its observation post depends on its species and the speed and depth of the current. Experience with a specific river and its fish will teach an angler where to place his flies.

The line of drift of the naturals is important to presentation too, and the fly must be placed to duplicate its route. Fish also establish rhythms in their feeding, tilting into the current and rising toward the surface and drifting back to inspect the flies. Tilting back down after a rise, a fish uses the current to descend back to the bottom, moving upstream again in the slower bottom currents to its original lie. The skilled fisherman observes the lapsed time of the rise behavior, delaying his presentation until the fish has returned to its station.

Obviously, the fish expends energy in both its rise-form behavior and holding its position in the flow, just as a cruising fish surrenders energy in quiet water. Energy is also expended protecting the integrity of their feeding zones. Stream fish select a feeding station during a hatch, while stillwater fish stake out a cruising zone. It is interesting to watch their behavior in a lake or reservoir, picking up minute *Callibaetis* flies or *Tricorythodes* spinners, since they often retrace their foraging routes in a patient series of ragged, racetracklike circuits.

Territoriality plays a role too. Trout are more solitary in their habits than grayling, which often exhibit a degree of schooling behavior, and spend a lot of time protecting their feeding zones. Many times coarse species infringe upon a trout's foraging territory, and a trout also expends both time and energy rooting out its own kind.

Similar displays of territoriality occur during periods of spawning activity, when the cockfish sometimes exhaust themselves driving other fish away from their mates. Later during the actual egg laying, predators come near the open redds, hoping to scavenge some of the fresh ova. The quarrelling can become quite violent at such times, with huge boils and angry splashing in the shallows. Large gouts of water are thrown high into the air, and the fish often rush each other like wild pigs, writhing with their bodies out of the water. Several weeks ago I witnessed such spawning quarrels in the egg-laying riffles of a small river in northern California, and the threshing fights in the shallows far across the current were surprisingly loud—like an angler wading noisily upstream along a gravel bar or a pack-horse string fording its tumbling flow.

Some kinds of feeding behavior are almost this active, when big trout are concentrating on baitfish There are many examples of such feeding among large trout, particularly in British Columbia, when the Babine rainbows gorge on salmon fry migrating downstream. Similar aggressive tactics are reported in studies of Kamloops rainbows feeding on spring schools of shiners, attacking them in the shallows almost like striped bass or bluefish, and scattering them in terror.

Although the predatory feeding behavior seems random and out of control, the big rainbows are actually heartlessly efficient, like an experienced bird shooter who has disciplined himself to take a single bird from the exploding covey. The rainbows stalk a school of baitfish, choosing their prey from the foolish shiners that wander away from the others. Such behavior is basic in understanding the feeding tactics of trout in their predatory moods—they stalk only one victim at a time, they choose individual baitfish that are separated from the baitfish school, and they can seldom resist a crippled minnow.

However, it is not this kind of feeding that most fishermen have observed and remember: it is the quiet rises to hatching insects in a swift river, fish capturing fluttering sedges in a quiet pool, and dimpling for midge pupae on a still evening lake. For an angler, the entire physiology and behavior of the fish are both focused in the moment of the rise, in some strange kind of alchemy, and it is this poetic moment that lingers pervasively in the mind.

It has an imagery of spring seepages trickling into the river through mossy ledges and fiddlebacks, and a current dark with hemlock shadows. Sometimes the bottom is virtually black with winter algae and leaf drift in the backwater eddies. Skunk cabbage and violets are in the bottoms along the river, and the weak April sun filters down through the branches. The current is cold, and it has been a bitter winter, its faint echoes still lingering in the rawness of the wind. Fishermen cover the water with their flies, not really expecting a hatch or rising fish but more in a ritual that has endured for centuries.

The wind drops at midday and the sun seems almost warm, and after lunch there are a few mayflies hatching. Sometimes a phoebe sits nervously in the bare branches along the pool, darting out to catch a fluttering dun over the current. It is almost warm in the sheltered places along the stream, where the sun reaches the bright clumps of coltsfoot, and its heat penetrates the tail shallows.

The current tongues slide past a large boulder, eddying down a dark algae-covered ledge and flowing smooth over a pale mossy bottom. There are more hatching flies on the water now, and finally in the smooth bulge of current upstream there is a soft porpoiselike rise.

2. The Fish and Their Senses

Like most beginning fishermen, at least those who are introduced to trout fishing in boyhood, my knowledge of the trout and their sensory behavior started with frightening them in the shallows of a meadow creek in Michigan. My first glimpses of fish were always fleeting, brief encounters with darting shadows that scuttled upstream and disappeared. They were gone, hiding under logjams and grassy banks, almost before I saw them. It was a frustrating and humbling lesson that I have never forgotten.

The fish were spotted ghosts that eluded me for weeks. The Culvert Hole had a tree to hide behind. There was tall grass above the Crayfish Hole, and the milkweed lined a swift run under the willows. These places offered me some concealment, and I soon learned to hide myself before I fished them.

My first trout came from the Culvert Hole, and I was lying belly-flat behind the tree. The other places were finally productive too, and I found that I could crawl close to the water there and see the fish before they spotted me. But in the open meadows below the tractor-bridge planking, it was more difficult to approach them. There was no cover and the banks were soft. Sometimes their trembling grass transmitted vibrations that frightened the trout long before I was close enough to fish. Sometimes my shadow scattered them like quail, and they milled frantically, crisscrossing the pale bottom in terror. Once I frightened a water snake from its sleeping perch on a deadfall, and its lazy undulations frightened the trout as far as thirty yards downstream.

Such frustrating lessons were dutifully noted and remembered, and several summers passed before I finally mastered the patience and stealth

425

required to stalk the trout effectively. It was knowledge that was painstakingly slow in coming.

There were other lessons too.

It was some time before I realized that a dragging grasshopper made the fish suspicious, even when it was still alive and kicking. Too large a hook was also less productive. Too heavy a leader frightened the trout, yet when I fished too delicate a tippet, I often broke them off clumsily. Sometimes the trout were alerted even though they had not seen me or sensed my approach through vibrations in the bank. The sight of my rod tip and line projecting through the grass triggered them too. My respect for their sensory perceptions is still growing, and their senses have a primary role in our strategy and tactics.

The sensory network of trout and grayling consists of the brain, spinal column, nerves, and sensory organs. It monitors perception, motor actions, and sensory stimuli, although its subtleties cannot be compared with the senses of more advanced vertebrates.

The brain and its functional parts are discussed at length in the preceding chapter, along with the spinal cord that is closely associated with the brain itself. These primary components control the senses of vision, olfactory discrimination, hearing and balance, respiration, cardiovascular rhythms, taste, touch, memory, temperature perception, and all primary motor responses. Such sensory responses are so basic to the fly-fisherman that we have decided to isolate them from our discussions of physiology and anatomy.

Hearing and balance are closely interrelated in our sensory networks, and trout are no exception. Since their hearing apparatus is rudimentary, and structured to monitor relatively low-frequency sound, trout and grayling may not detect sound in the higher frequencies. The detection of auditory stimuli occurs through the body itself, in the case of high-energy sounds transmitted through the water, the reception and detection of pressure changes on the swim bladder, the cartilaginous structure of the inner ear, and the lateral line along the body. The lateral line is a delicate little cord stitched through the skin from the opercular gill covers to the root of the caudal fin. It is sensitive and highly tuned, with neural branches distributed under the dermal covering, and it can detect surprisingly faint sounds and vibrations. The lateral line can also monitor temperature, and variations in currents and depths, and there is some evidence that it has a sonarlike function in detecting both vibrations from other organisms moving in the water and vibrations of a fish's own movements echoing off underwater obstacles. It is also important in maintaining balance, and its function in equilibrium is continuous.

The lateral line contains a sensory core in its canal, with a series of filamentous nerves, branching up along the dorsal surfaces and down along the flanks and belly. It is protected with a delicate single-cell covering having multiple pores. Each pore in turn houses a neural filament in direct contact with the water. Sensory organs lie immediately beneath the porous covering, amplifying stimuli of delicate changes in water pressure and temperature. Branchial nerves carry these stimuli to the lateral cord itself. The lateral line is joined to the supraorbital nerve canal between the eye sockets and the brain. The infraorbital canal is connected to these other primary neural circuits at the same junction. It is a continuous pulsing of tiny electrical charges along the neural network that makes the system function. These tiny pulses of energy travel back and forth between the brain and the delicate little neuromasts that collect stimuli transmitted through the water.

The neuromasts consist of tiny sensory pods called cupolas, and each cupola is filled with microscopic hairlike filaments. When any delicate variations in water pressure reach these minute sensory pods, their filaments respond like weeds in a current, and the direction of their movements increases or decreases the neural energies transmitted back through the lateral canal toward the brain itself.

Fish also have ears. The ears are not external like ours, but are surprisingly sophisticated, sensitive enough that they can detect the wriggling vibrations of a swimming nymph or the struggles of a crippled baitfish several feet away. Fish have an inner ear network, buried in twin cavities of the skull that lie quite close together on each side. These ears consist of membranous sacs filled with fluid, and sensory organs receive both vibrations and other stimuli for hearing and balance. These stimuli are transmitted directly through the water into the dermal covering, cartilage, bone, and tissue of the head to the inner hearing chambers, without the eardrum typical of higher vertebrates. The canals within the inner ears contain otolithic stones that control and monitor the body movements and equilibrium of the fish.

Trout and grayling have extremely sensitive hearing, and its delicacy is multiplied in a connection between the swim bladder and the inner ear. The connection is effected through a series of modified vertebrae that intensify sound stimuli before they reach the elastic air-filled swim bladder. Its membrane is held in delicate tension, facilitating its function as a subaquatic microphone, sound amplification device, and tiny resonating drum. It also responds to subaquatic vibrations, transmitting sound so effectively that the fish can perceive surprisingly low decibel levels, and those fish whose anatomy includes this Weberian hearing structure can detect sounds of thirty decibels less than other species.

Both the hearing and balance mechanisms have obvious effects on the behavior of trout and grayling, and are perhaps the most versatile of their sensory systems. Their auditory acuity is so precise that they hear many sound frequencies outside our hearing range.

Sounds play a constant role in the lives of fish, particularly when the water is discolored or at night. Fish can actually hear the movements of their prey, as well as the presence of predators. Sounds, travelling five times faster in water than through the atmosphere, can both attract or frighten fish. Fish also respond to a wide spectrum of frequencies, and their reaction to the sound of a grasshopper falling into the water is completely different from their response to the rattle of an oarlock or the sharp clatter of a bait can on a pier. Fish cannot hear our voices, and loud noises in the atmosphere are not transmitted into the water except in the impact of their vibrations against its surface film. However, fish quickly respond to the vibrations of someone walking clumsily along the bank. Trout and grayling lying together in a pool or smooth-flowing flat display interesting school behavior when frightened by a sudden underwater sound—the panic of a single fish is instantly transmitted to the others.

The other fish in the pool can both see and literally feel the vibrations of that fear, transmitted through the water at a velocity of almost a mile per second. Evolution has made the hearing of fish more acute than their visual senses, since water transmits sound far better than it does light. Most fish species hear well in the range of 200 to 800 cycles per second, although highly developed fish like trout and grayling can hear auditory stimuli ranging between fifteen and 10,000 cycles per second. Our human hearing threshold varies from approximately twenty to 20,000 cycles per second.

The hearing acuity of trout and grayling varies widely in different types of water. Swift-flowing riffles and tumbling rapids mute the transmission of sounds and mask them with background noise of the water itself. Wind creates surf and light surface ripples and whitecaps. Each of these conditions creates its own unique fingerprints of sound. It is possible that the masking effects of such water sounds, both in a swift current and a wind-riffled lake, are part of the reason why trout are more easily caught under such conditions—the water sounds dampen the vibrations caused by

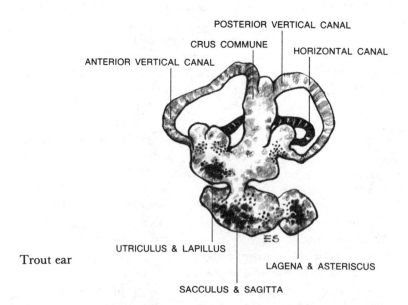

POSTERIOR VERTICAL CANAL

CRUS COMMUNE

HORIZONTAL CANAL

ANTERIOR VERTICAL CANAL

ES

UTRICULUS & LAPILLUS

Trout ear

LAGENA & ASTERISCUS

SACCULUS & SAGITTA

our angling mistakes, from a clumsy cast to noisy wading on a stony bottom.

There are two zones of hearing important in understanding the auditory senses of trout and grayling. Low-frequency sound carries only limited distances in the water, reaching less than forty to fifty feet. Such frequencies are detected by the highly sensitive sensory filaments of the lateral cord. Relatively high-energy sounds vibrate through the molecular structure of the water at considerable distances. Such sounds operate at frequencies between 250 and 10,000 cycles, frequencies best detected by the Weberian system of the swim bladder and the inner ear. The lateral line is used to measure the intensity and source of sounds between fifteen and 250 cycles per second, lying below the human threshold of hearing.

It is intriguing that a small fish has the advantage in the low-frequency range of sound, since it will always sense a larger predator first. The larger predator triggers vibrations of greater intensity and is easily detected by the lateral line. Tumbling pocket water and the wind-roughened shallows of a high-country lake are ideal protection for baitfish, since the water energies conceal their weaker vibrations, and the swimming movements of the predators are audible. However, baitfish schools create sound frequencies multiplied by their numbers, in a kind of cumulative low-frequency effect, and are more easily detected by a predatory fish.

The detection of sound, using both the lateral line and the inner-ear system, is absolutely vital in feeding and survival. It is surprising how many people still believe the old wives' tale about not talking when fishing, because the sounds of conversation will frighten the trout. It is completely untrue, since human conversation ranges from about forty to sixty decibels, too little energy to affect the fish's environment. Water is so dense that it will reflect virtually any sound triggered and transmitted through the atmosphere. In *The Fly-Fisher's Entomology,* Alfred Ronalds made the following observations:

> In order that we might be enabled to ascertain the truth of a common assertion, that fish can hear voices in conversation on the banks of a stream, my friend, the Reverend Brown of Grawich, and myself selected for close observation a trout poised about six inches deep in the water, while a third gentleman, who was situated behind the fishing house, diametrically opposite to the side where the fish was, fired off one barrel of his gun. The possibility of the flash being seen by the fish was thus wholly prevented, and the report produced not the slightest apparent effect upon him.
>
> The second barrel was then fired. Still he remained immovable, evincing not the slightest symptom of having heard the report. This experiment was often repeated, and precisely similar results were invariably obtained. Neither could we ever awaken symptoms of alarm in fishes near the hut by shouting to them in the loudest tones, although our distance from them sometimes did

not exceed six feet. The experiments were not repeated so often that they could become habituated to the sound.

It is possible that fishes may be in some manner affected by vibrations communicated into their element, either directly, or by the intervention of aerial pulsations; although it does not seem to be clearly proved that they possess any organ appropriated exclusively to the purpose of hearing. At all events, it appears that neither the above-mentioned explosions, nor the loud voices, had power to produce vibrations or undulations in the water which could so affect them.

However, vibrations that frighten a fish are transmitted through objects in direct contact with the water. The heavy-footed fishermen who walk along the stream, or kick stones together in a swift current, or grind the soft-iron caulks of their heels on a ledge are all triggering sounds into the water. Similar vibrations are caused by a paddle laid carelessly across the thwarts of a canoe, the metallic scrape of a bailing can, or the rattle of the anchor chain. Experienced fishermen walk carefully along a stream, circle well away from still pools, wade as stealthily as possible, and handle boats and canoes with equal care.

Since the lateral line is a kind of neural sonar, fish can use it to measure both the intensity and source of a sound. The direction of a swimming minnow or a working bucktail can be sensed with the lateral sensors as far away as fifteen to twenty feet. Vibrations of a big grasshopper or caterpillar falling into the water can be detected too, and within two or three feet a trout can pinpoint the exact position of a swimming baitfish or grasshopper without its eyes.

Beyond fifteen to twenty feet, the ability to detect the precise source of a sound is sharply diminished. The lateral line is less important than the swim bladder and inner-ear structure at such distances. The fish can probably recognize the source of a sound, instantly determining its potential as a possible threat, and might also detect an increasing or decreasing intensity. The fish would know if that threat were moving away or coming ominously closer. Such a fish could locate the source of a sound quickly, triangulate its vibrations, and precisely measure its origins.

Many fishing writers have explored the blood scent and struggles of a crippled baitfish and the obvious excitement it generates in a predatory trout, but few have seemed aware that an injured minnow creates unique subaquatic vibrations. Those helpless sounds are totally unlike the swimming sounds generated by a healthy form of prey. Most fishermen have had the experience of having a hooked fish attract a larger fish into striking. Many times I have had a small chub or shiner take my fly, and had its splashing struggles trigger a large brown into forgetting its lethargy and attacking. Such big fish were probably not feeding, but the distress of the baitfish was transmitted through the frantic, hapless quality of its swimming and proved impossible to resist.

Fish make sounds as well as detect them. Biologists have actually made recordings of trout and grayling under water, and apparently both biological and mechanical sounds are involved. The biological sounds could include actual communication between trout, as well as echo-ranging to navigate or pinpoint a predator. Such intentional sounds seemingly include contractions of the swim bladder and gullet, and perhaps the gill structure. Mechanical sounds can include spawning, nest building, rooting out crustaceans and caddis larvae on the bottom, chasing baitfish or swimming nymphs, and chewing the captured prey.

Fish sounds have numerous functions. Many species actually have mating calls which attract spawning partners. Some use auditory bench marks in their schooling behavior. Others make sounds to maintain their territoriality. The swim bladder is used to make such noises by contracting the abdominal muscles against its taut membrane, emitting low-frequency noises that other fish can detect at relatively close range. Some species of baitfish also generate unique sounds, both swimming and at rest, and their noises awaken the predatory urge in gamefish. It has been demonstrated that trout respond to the feeding noises made by other trout. Fish are a little like hens in a chicken yard, and such feeding activity can prove contagious. Since sound is transmitted five times faster under water than in the atmosphere, it is possible to estimate the intensity of the splashy rise that just attracted our attention with its noise. Its subaquatic noise level is detectable at considerable distances, and the vibrations of predatory swimming or rise forms could trigger the feeding urge in other trout.

Considerable research into the noises generated by trout and grayling, as well as their systems of sound detection and balance, still remains in the future. However, our present knowledge is sufficient to translate into practical fishing wisdom. Sounds both attract and frighten fish, and understanding the difference will pay dividends in your sport.

Taste, touch, and smell are also important sensory perceptions in trout and grayling. Taste and touch are cutaneous perceptions, based upon actual contact with external objects, while smell is an olfactory sense that works at a distance. Smell also plays an obvious role in taste, just as it does in higher vertebrate species like man.

The taste sense permits a fish to detect food, chemicals dissolved into its habitat, relative acidity, alkalinity, and the salinity of marine or estuarine habitat. Highly sensitive taste sensors are present over the entire dermal covering of the mouth, jaws, tongue, vomerine surfaces, gullet and throat. Trout and grayling also display some taste sensitivity in their olfactory nostrils and, to a diminishing degree, in the external mouth surfaces. Taste and smell are based upon sensory perception of chemical compounds in extremely faint concentrations. Smell is a prologue to the tactile quality of taste. Smell is a primary factor in locating food, while taste delicately tests and samples it. Touch also has a role in sampling the viability of food.

Trout that are stalking baitfish in the shallows probably find their prey by sensing their faint underwater vibrations, smelling their subaquatic odors, and then targeting them visually. Sometimes the vibrations and the baitfish themselves excite a trout enough that it falls back on its visual skills, pursuing its prey on sight alone. Another fish that takes a tiny darkly hackled dry fly is also relying primarily on its visual apparatus, but once both trout and grayling have actually captured their prey, taste and touch are involved. The hapless shiner or stickleback or dace is a real baitfish, with the odors and configuration and weight that the fish has learned to associate with food, and the trout greedily turns it crosswise in its mouth like a bulldog with a bone. The dry fly taken by the second fish is another matter. It looks like a fluttering mayfly until the fish actually takes it, but its bristly texture is totally unlike the richly filled chitinous feel of a live aquatic insect, and it is tasteless. The fish swiftly rejects it after a millisecond of tactile inspection.

The result of these behavioral episodes is a big trout lying back in its sheltering run, happily swallowing its wriggling minnow headfirst, and a puzzled surface-feeding fish that has instantly ejected the artificial fly. Its taste and texture were both wrong, although it had looked like the other hatching duns coming down the current.

The taste organs in both trout and grayling are much like those in higher vertebrates. Although our taste organs are found on the tongue and palate and are combined with our olfactory senses in measuring the quality and character of our food, the taste sensors of fish are more widely distributed. Taste buds are found outside the mouth, along the snout and jaw covering, as well as in the throat and mouth itself. They are a series of microscopic organs connected to the medulla oblongata with the suborbital, infraorbital and supraorbital canals. The nasal organs and their neural connectors are located among the delicate branchial fans joining the upper taste organs with the brain. It is a complex system of taste and smell, and this ability of a trout to taste something without actually taking it in its mouth poses a problem to trout fishermen.

The fish can actually test their food simply by touching it with the taste buds on their snouts and jaws. The odors of prospective food are sometimes detectable in close proximity, so a suspicious trout can inspect it without actually touching it. This means that the sensory impressions of taste begin before a trout actually reaches its food, increase as the food first touches the snout and jaw covering, intensify inside the mouth, and continue until the food is swallowed.

We have all watched fish approach a sunk fly, follow it until they are quite close, and turn away without touching it. We have also watched both trout and grayling come to the fly and touch or bunt it gently without opening their jaws. It is a particularly maddening type of behavior with a floating fly pattern, since the fish disturbs the surface with its false rise and is never fairly hooked. There can be many reasons for such last-second refusals, but the ability to investigate and taste a fly without actually taking it clearly stacks the cards in favor of the fish.

Trout and grayling, and particularly their relative the salmon, have highly developed olfactory senses. It is their olfactory ability that enables them to sort through a complex fabric of odors in the sea, and unerringly locate the unique fingerprint of smells that pinpoints their parent streams. The unique odors and water chemistry of such rivers is quickly diluted into tiny traces in the sea, measurable only in parts per million, and beyond their immediate estuaries these delicate clues are faintly diluted into parts per billion. More work has been done in measuring the olfactory skills of salmon than with trout and grayling, and salmon are clearly able to detect trace odors in parts per billion.

Some remarkable experiments with salmon have been performed, and perhaps the most unusual were conducted with coho salmon at the entry of a fish ladder. Such substances as fish oil, shark repellent, human odors, bear scent, sealskin, and sea lion—fifty-four odors in all—were introduced to the fish ladder. Few of these affected the ascending fish, but they did react strongly to human, bear, dog, seal, and sea-lion scents; these odors actually caused the salmon to retreat back down the ladder. Sea lion and seal made fish waiting to enter the ladder move back out into the river, although they were fully one hundred yards downstream from the testing point.

Some fishermen believe that a salmon can detect the odors and tastes of man's skin on a fly, and there was an old riverkeeper on the Stryn in Norway who used to touch his flies with cod-liver oil to mask the odors of his fingers. This past winter I fished with a group of remarkably skilled fly-fishermen for steelheads and chinooks in the headwaters of the Sacramento, and their lexicon of tricks included a paste of sardines to dress their flies and kill the odor of their hands. It is not fully known if trout and grayling are as sensitive to odor as salmon, but the old ghillie who taught me nymph fishing on the Lauterach in Bavaria believed that a particularly selective fish could probably smell his fingers on his flies. His secret was a leader soak box—its thick felt pads saturated in trout slime—for his nymphs.

Such tactics may seem foolish to many anglers, but they should realize that the olfactory senses of fish are more highly developed than ours. The largest segment of the trout's brain is concerned with the perception of odors, and that piece of knowledge is essential in our fishing. The example of the migrating coho salmon unquestionably demonstrates that fish detect a far greater range of odors dissolved in their habitat than we can detect in ours. It logically follows that such olfactory acuity is based on a highly developed physiology. Fish have two olfactory nostrils. Their nostrils are located between the snout and the eyes. Each nostril has a tiny canal leading to a separate olfactory organ, although these canals do not join with the throat as they do in many air-breathing species. The nasal canals end in a chamber lined with an epithelial surface so sensitive that it has more than 400,000 odor-sensing cells per nostril.

Olfactory perception depends on continual water change over these epithelial cells. Water circulation is accomplished with the rhythmic pulsing of tiny hairlike cilia that endlessly inhale and expel it from the nasal chambers. Trout have a multiple system of nostrils, alternately inhaling and exhaling water in sequence, insuring an unbroken flow of clean water past the delicate olfactory cells.

The odor signals are telegraphed to the paleocortical or telencephalic zone of the brain, which consists of both right and left cerebral lobes. Large neural canals join each lobe to an intricate odor-sensing organ between the nostril and brain. Each bulblike sensing organ is connected to the epithelial chamber with a primary neural canal. The species of Salmonidae having relatively large forelobes and olfactory bulbs have highly developed senses of smell.

However, in spite of our knowledge about the olfactory systems in trout and grayling, we still do not know exactly how they perceive odors and discriminate between them. The fish clearly display more sensitivity when they are initially exposed to olfactory stimuli, and when they are hungry, than after a prolonged exposure to a single stimulus. But still we are baffled by the extreme olfactory sensitivity of the Salmonidae, since they unquestionably react to chemical traces so faint that our instruments often cannot detect them.

Touch is a twofold perception, involving the ability to discern both tactile contact and variations in temperature. The tactile senses of trout and grayling begin with microscopic touch organs concentrated throughout their dermal covering. The sense of touch is especially acute in the pectoral and pelvic fins, and both inside and outside the mouth. Most fish biologists believe that the tactile sensitivity in fish is less highly developed than in humans, but little definitive research has been done. Certainly, most fishermen have taken fish with body wounds that would have disabled a higher vertebrate species, and this would suggest a relatively simple neural system with a high threshold of debilitating pain. Several times I have caught sea-run trout and salmon with seal bites so deep that the skeletal structure of the fish was partially exposed, yet these fish were obviously still feeding and fought well once they were hooked.

Still we know surprisingly little about the role of a fish's tactile sensitivity in its feeding or territorial behavior. Touch is clearly used for navigation in discolored water, and it is used extensively in courtship and spawning. Paul Needham observed in his book *Trout Streams* that spawning fish use their pelvic fins to measure the diameter and proper concavity and depth of their spawning redds. Courtship includes extensive tactile activity between the males and the females. Their bodily contact includes rubbing, wriggling and writhing, and light touching movements. Many observers have described a shuddering contact between the males and females at the precise moment of oviposition, when the cockfish extrudes its milt.

Schooling behavior also involves touch at its most sensitive levels, coupled with the delicate measuring skills of the lateral neural cord, permitting many fish to swim together rapidly without collisions. It is intriguing to observe a dense school of fish, threading and weaving through itself as it moves, turning and changing speed with great precision. Panic in a single member of the school is instantly communicated to the others. Yet even in their panic it is possible to find a strangely dynamic order, each fish holding its position in an intricate phalanx of flight.

Temperature perception is another facet of the tactile sensory organs, and it is highly developed in the cold-water species like trout and grayling, since their habitat has a surprisingly limited range of acceptable temperatures. Behavioral experts have found that the Salmonidae are capable of sensing temperature changes that are less than five percent of a single degree, exhibiting a thermal sensitivity infinitely beyond our human temperature perceptions.

The effects of temperature on habitat are well known among knowledgeable anglers, but fish also use thermal bench marks in less familiar ways. Salmon and sea-run trout often navigate using minuscule signposts of temperature and salinity in the sea, and without such thermal sensitivity their ability to duplicate the migrations of their ancestors would be impaired. Obviously, some thermal stresses can kill trout and grayling under natural conditions. Thermally sensitive species are more quickly affected by a sudden rise in temperature, and although a gradual increase can acclimatize a trout or grayling population to some degree, even these fish have a thermal ceiling. Death from thermal stress is both metabolic and environmental, since sudden changes can result in a form of thermal shock, and temperature increases also have some inexorable side effects on habitat. Toxicity of many compounds is multiplied at higher temperature levels. Rising temperatures diminish the dissolved oxygen levels entrained in the water, while simultaneously increasing the critical minimums of oxygen necessary for survival of the fish.

Perhaps the most unusual example of thermal variations in natural trout habitat is the Firehole in the Yellowstone country. The little river has conventional origins in the snowmelt and cold springheads of the Continental Divide, but once it reaches Lone Star Geyser and Old Faithful, its ecology changes radically. Hundreds of geothermal springs add their flow in the next few miles, both warming the river and making it surprisingly alkaline. It is a unique ecosystem, and in places its cool flow receives steaming chutes of water. It is the only river I know where the trout feed greedily, lying literally inches from a current that could cook them alive in seconds.

It should be remembered that the fish have no body temperature of their own, except at times of extreme exertion or fear, and their bodies are at the temperature of the surrounding water. Temperature is directly exchanged between the fish and its habitat by simple osmotic transfer. The water either dampens or accelerates the metabolism of the fish by its temperatures, passing through the cellular structure of the skin and gills. The temperature of the blood is adjusted in the delicate capillaries of the gill filaments, where it constantly exchanges carbon dioxide for oxygen.

Such thermal equilibrium is not an instantaneous process, and abrupt temperature changes can result in fish kills. Although small fish have proportionately larger gill systems for their weight, and can generally adjust better to thermal changes than adults, Derek Mills has demonstrated in his book *Salmon and Trout* that brown-trout fry are far more fragile in terms of temperature than adults. Separate studies in Europe, Canada, and the United States established different thermal death ceilings for brown trout in different habitats. The research in the United Kingdom pinpointed seventy-eight degrees as the death point, while Canadian studies with acclimatized brown-trout populations established a lethal temperature just under eighty degrees. Other acclimatized populations in the Yellowstone are thriving at temperature ceilings of eighty-two degrees. However, Danish studies with brown-trout fry indicate that their thermal ceiling was seventy-four degrees, proving that the ability to compensate for thermal change is not solely based on ratios of gill size to weight.

Muscular stress and anxiety also have thermal echoes. The rapid muscle flexing in a hard struggle with an angler or predator generates heat. Such heat is quickly dissipated in small fish, but a trophy-size trout can sometimes suffer thermal gain of as much as five degrees. Such thermal gain is another subtle factor contributing to metabolic shock in a fish we intend to release.

Although each of these sensory networks is important to the angler, in terms of our sport, vision is perhaps the most critical faculty of the trout. It has been discussed since the earliest times, and trout vision received a surprisingly scientific analysis in *The Fly-Fisher's Entomology* in 1836, indicating that Ronalds knew more of aquatic science than mere entomology. Ronalds' diagrams explaining refraction of light passing into the water have never been surpassed, both for their optical validity and their graphic clarity.

Sight is extremely important to both trout and grayling, and the ability to pinpoint and intercept minute insects in relatively swift water demonstrates striking visual acuity. Fish eyes are similar in morphology to those of the higher vertebrates, except that they are adapted to function in the density of the water instead of in the atmosphere. Their eyes consist of the eyeball, corneal structure, iris and lens, retinal surfaces, sclerotic capsule, and muscles for both movement and focus. Trout and grayling are among the highly developed fish species capable of making minor adjustments in the iris diameter, and their eyes are smoothly fitted to the streamlined surfaces of the head.

The basic structure of our eye is remarkably like the eye of a trout or grayling, in spite of the obvious differences between the density of their habitat and our atmosphere. Like our eyeball, the eye of a fish is basically a camera. Light impulses enter the eye. The impulses are modified and focused in its lens, which is transparent and spherical. The lens is the fulcrum of the visual process. It is the lens that distributes the radiation of light impulses deep into the eye, focusing their images on the ultrasensitive cells of the retina.

The iris of the visual mechanism is like the lens opening in a camera, excluding light rays and images outside its field of vision. Our eyes have an iris which adjusts itself to varying levels and intensities of light. Its diaphragm dilates or shrinks in diameter, depending on the available light impulses. The capability exists only in highly developed fish species like the Salmonidae, although their ability to adjust the iris opening is far less adaptable than in many higher vertebrates. Minor adjustments to variations in brightness occur in the retinal cells themselves.

The sensory lining of the retina consists of two basic types of receptor cells: the rods and the cones. Their cellular character and distribution play a major role in the physiology of sight. Both rods and cones telegraph the images received by the retina to the brain. The rods are superb light sensors that function in extremely low levels of illumination. Rod cells are used when less than a single footcandle of light is available, although they do not

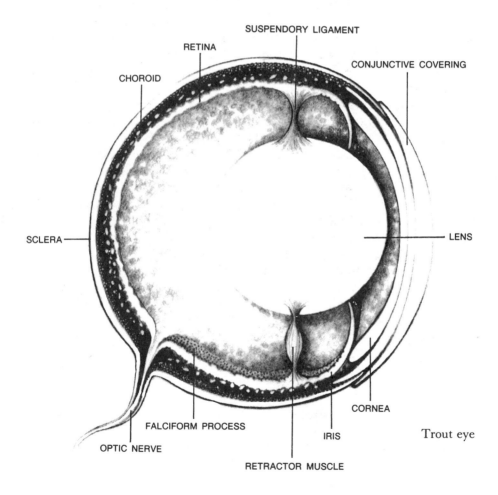

Trout eye

detect and transmit color. In trout and grayling the rods are approximately fifty times as sensitive as the cone cells. These cones are the color-sensitive cells and are used in the daytime levels of light. Both rods and cones are retractable, and in periods of low illumination, the cones are retracted into the retinal covering. During bright weather, the cones are pressed forward into the retinal surfaces, while the rod cells are steadily withdrawn to protect them from light damage.

Fish do not change from daytime vision to the nighttime rod cells abruptly. It is a gradual transformation that takes about five hours. The changes include an anticipatory phase, in which the trout or grayling begins to prepare for diminishing or increasing levels of light. Optical experiments indicate that a fish starts to utilize its rod cells in late afternoon. The rods are almost fully extended at sundown and completely extended by nightfall. The fish sees quite well in the dark, primarily in terms of silhouette and size, although the cones remain active enough to transmit minimal color information too. The light-sensitive rods remain fully extended about five to six hours before the process begins to reverse itself. The rods start to retract imperceptibly, and the cones start extending in anticipation of daylight. It is a much slower process preparing for dawn, but the fish's eyes are fully adjusted and ready. These daily cycles in the retinal covering are filled with endless variations, since the cycles of daylight and darkness are continually changing with the seasons. It is one of the most unusual examples of circadian rhythms in the entire world of zoology.

Understanding these daily cycles is important. Many fishermen talk about matching a specific hatch well during the daylight hours, only to have the killing fly pattern perform badly in late afternoon and evening. It is during these hours that a trout changes from its cones to its rod cells in the retinal surfaces. Color gradually becomes less important than size and light pattern in the film and silhouette, and the pattern that deceived the fish in the daylight hours is suddenly refused in the gathering darkness. Sunlight also plays strange tricks with some colors both in terms of hue and chroma. My early book *Matching the Hatch* talked about the problems of dry-fly hackles dyed pale olive for several western hatches, and quoted my old Colorado fishing companion Frank Klune:

> During these pale olive hatches the trout become extremely choosy, especially in beaver ponds and still pools. Very slight differences in the color of the artificial may mean the difference between catching a large number of big trout or none at all. The fish seem to be fooled more easily on dark days than on bright ones with these olive flies. My theory is this: sunlight affects these olive hackles in some unusual way, making the artificial appear quite unlike the dull-colored pale olive naturals.

It is an interesting observation, and it is possible that both cone vision and the sheen of the hackles in the sunlight played a role in his experience with the olive hatches. The late John Alden Knight liked to talk about his experiences with an olive-bodied imitation he dressed for the little green sedges that hatch on the Loyalsock, and in his book *The Modern Angler* are the following lines:

> It is not at all unlikely that the trout's eye is equipped to pick up colors in the spectrum of sunlight which lie outside the color range of the human eye. Consequently, the two flies, when subjected to light rays that have been diffused and divided into their component parts, will in all probability reflect these rays differently.
>
> Viewed thus, how may we tell just what color vibrations are set up by rays reflected from natural colors, and what from unnatural or synthetic colors, and what effect these resulting reflections may have on the eye of a trout? Frankly, I am content in the knowledge that there is a difference, and that the preference of the trout seems to lean toward the natural colors.
>
> With the dry fly, which is not subjected to the same light conditions as the wet fly, due to the fact that it floats slightly above the surface and is therefore in the unchanging light of the sun, this preference for the natural over the artificial colors is not so noticeable. Also the dry fly is seen against the light. Viewed in this way, color is much less easy to distinguish by the fish.
>
> Some years ago I began tying a dry fly which, for convenience, was called an Olive Badger. This fly had an olive silk body and was palmer-tied with its tail, hackle and palmer-rib of black-and-white badger hackle. It had no wings. Many times I found this fly to be quite effective when fished in the open stream during the day. As time went on I noticed that there were some occasions when not a trout could be taken on it. Then one day I made a discovery.
>
> The trout were rising freely both near the bank and out in the open water. I had no difficulty in taking the trout in the open water with an Olive Badger, but the fish along the bank refused to have anything to do with it—in fact, once it drifted over them they went down and stayed down. Not until I had put down several good fish did I learn the answer: as soon as the fly drifted out of the sunlight, and into the shadow of the bank, not a fish would look at it. Its appearance to the trout must have been entirely different under the two light conditions, as in the sunlight I could take fish on it just as readily as I could put them down with it in the shadow. It is not known as the Olive Badger any longer—we call it the Sunshine fly.

The skilled angler should remember that the effectiveness of his flies will depend on many things, including the effects of both sunlight and shadow, and the intricate physics of rod-and-cone vision. Consistent results depend on our understanding and mastery of such refinements.

Since fish adjust quite slowly to changes in light, sudden illumination with artificial light can temporarily injure the delicate rod cells used for night vision. It is a retinal shock not unlike the snow blindness that can come after prolonged exposure to arctic sunlight. The extent of such retinal shock depends on the degree of night adaptation that has occurred, and the relative exposure of the rod cells. Sudden exposure to intense light levels typically results in disoriented swimming or a kind of anxious immobility and helplessness. The duration of retinal shock is a result of both light intensity and the extent of a fish's night adaptation and rod-cell exposure. Fish that are fully adapted to darkness may suffer retinal shock for ten to fifteen minutes, but a partially adapted fish just before nightfall or daylight will recover rather quickly.

Trout on hard-fished streams are particularly wary of any artificial light along the water, since they have learned to associate such lights with fishermen. Never play your headlights over a pool you intend to fish. Avoid the sudden flare of a cigarette lighter or match, and leave the water to use a boat torch or flashlight, or use it sparingly inside a fishing coat or your waders.

Primitive fishing cultures often used fires to mesmerize their quarry with retinal shock, spearing the fish before their eyes could readjust. Burning the water survived into the nineteenth century on the Scottish salmon rivers, and is beautifully described by William Scrope, in 1843, in his classic *Days and Nights of Salmon Fishing on the Tweed*. But a technique based on temporary blindness is ill suited to the tactics of fly-fishing. Use lights sparingly while fishing.

Trout and grayling are among the most successful species in their ability to adapt their vision to changing levels of light. Their visual acuity in marginal light is perhaps better than the eyesight of many baitfish species. Few predators see as well as trout and grayling in such marginal levels of light, making them feel relatively secure and encouraging their feeding at daylight and dark. Both are primary feeding times.

Metabolism also plays a role in this cycle of morning and evening feeding. Since digestion requires about six to twelve hours, and the fish often stop feeding heavily after midnight, morning finds them growing hungry again. Food ingested in a feeding period just at daylight is well digested by early evening, and the fish are ready to feed again. It is a circadian cycle that is seldom interrupted under normal conditions—except perhaps when fine fly hatches occur during the day—and it is a major factor in fishing success.

Feeding is also easier at those times. The trout are less worried about predators, and feel free to concentrate on their prey. Their superior vision in marginal light and their highly developed sensory systems give them a tactical advantage in low levels of illumination. Weather can also play a role, since fish feel more secure on overcast days, and are likely to feed if the barometer is steady and good fly hatches are coming. Bottom feeding in lakes and deep pools will begin earlier on clear mornings, since adequate levels of light will penetrate the depths sooner. Water clarity and turbidity are also factors. Penetration of light is controlled by clarity, and even in extremely transparent water most illumination is gone within thirty feet of the surface. Turbid water can also filter out most of the available light in the first ten feet of depth. Its discoloration can come from spates and siltation, but there are also waters that are tea-colored with the plant-decay leachings of their swampy origins. Murky water can be a problem, although in bright weather there is often still enough light for feeding at moderate depths.

Water conducts sound far better than it transmits light. Lateral visibility under water seldom reaches one hundred feet, even under conditions of extreme clarity, and fifty feet is a better average for most trout lakes. Few streams are large enough to permit such unfettered lateral vision, although they are sufficiently clear.

Most turbidity is caused by detritus and silt particles and minute organisms, and can reduce lateral visibility to as little as five to fifteen feet. The turbidity diffuses the light energy and disrupts its transmission, just as dust and smoke and fog sometimes obscure our vision. Feeding fish must rely on their acute sense of smell and their ability to detect the faint vibrations of their prey when poor water clarity impairs their obvious visual skills.

Many fishermen recommend brightly colored flies at such times, particularly patterns dressed with glittering tinsel or mylar, since they catch and reflect the marginal light. Milky water or brown coffee-colored spates are often perfectly suited to dark flies like the Montana nymph or a big black marabou. Perhaps because of their color contrast, it is a tactic often found on slightly milky limestone streams like Spring Creek and Penn's Creek in Pennsylvania.

Trout and grayling are among the unique group of game fish having an exceptionally broad range of visual acuity. Their sight adjusts to many levels of light, with far more sensitivity than ours. They are species whose diet includes a large number of minute organisms, the obtaining of which depends on their visual skills. With the light fading quickly in late evening, registering less than a footcandle of illumination at the surface, the fish are largely adapted to rod vision. Their feeding behavior starts to emphasize silhouette and light pattern in the film and size, although any experienced angler on hard-fished streams will argue that a fish's color sense is not entirely lost at nightfall. This color sense would tend to prove that cone cells are not entirely retracted by trout and grayling at night.

From the viewpoint of contrasting color, it would make sense to use a dark fly pattern against a bright sky and something pale with a touch of tinsel in overcast weather. Similar logic will work under conditions of poor water clarity. Windy conditions or heavy boulder-broken water also demand fly patterns that are perhaps bigger and more readily visible. The fish are quite myopic. The lenses of their eyes are spherical, perhaps to function under the greater stresses of water density. The shape of these lenses cannot be adjusted, and focus is achieved literally by changing their relationship to the retina. Unlike our eyes, the rods and cones can be exposed or retracted. Our neural structure has a single filament connecting each rod and cone with the visual switchboard of the brain, while the trout collects light impulses through several sensors for each nerve. It is a system that trades strong neural impressions, at relatively minimal levels of illumination, for a reduction in clarity and precision.

Such light sensitivity is a liability in extremely bright weather, since the fish has no iris or eyelids to protect the retinal surfaces from too much energy. Trout not only seek out the shelter of boulders and deadfalls and shadowy places because bright weather makes them feel vulnerable and exposed but also to shield their eyes from the glare.

Myopia is not a serious liability in trout or grayling since they have little need for far-sighed skills. Most of their enemies and their feeding lie at close range. Fish cannot adjust the lenses of their eyes to focus on distant objects, although their muscles do retract the spherical lenses into the eyeball, shortening the focal length between the retina and the lens. Since the unadjusted focal length is perfect for close-range work, the lens is only designed to retract. Among all the game fish, trout and grayling have perhaps the optimal ability to adjust and refine their focal acuity. The character of their lenses and retinal surfaces enable them to focus on objects virtually touching their eyeballs, while simultaneously achieving a work-able focus on an angler fifty feet away. Such simultaneity is a crude type of bifocal vision. It is possible because their eyeballs are not perfectly spherical but are egg-shaped, with the apical end reaching toward the retina.

Fish do not have our total binocular vision. Their eyes are placed on opposite sides of their heads, giving them monocular vision since they can use only one eye at a time. However, there are overlapping fields of vision above and ahead where a trout or grayling has binocular eyesight that uses both eyes. The total parameters of their vision exceed ours, and they have almost complete peripheral coverage, in separate fields of 180 degrees. The placement of the eyes and their inability to move them very much mean that trout and grayling have a blind zone directly behind and below their bodies.

The binocular field of vision is relatively narrow, measuring less than forty-five degrees, varying with the size and configuration of each fish. In this limited zone the fish have effective stereoscopic vision and can accurately measure distances and perceive depth. It is this binocular field of vision that is employed in the final milliseconds of a rise, yet it is less sharp than a fish's peripheral eyesight, because the images are focused on the retinal perimeters. The sharpest focal surfaces lie toward the retinal centers, giving a fish its best vision along the lateral axis of each eye. Some field research tends to demonstrate that trout and grayling show a preference for using either their right or left eyes again and again.

Since a grayling has its eyes placed slightly more forward than the trout, it has a slightly larger field of binocular vision. Its forward eye placement also means that insects in the stereoscopic zone are more sharply focused, since their images are received farther toward the center of the retina. Such minor differences in visual morphology may partially explain the differences between trout and grayling in their rise-form behavior. Sometimes a trout can be seen weaving back and forth across its line of feeding drift, perhaps to focus on approaching objects more clearly by using both monocular and binocular vision in a series of overlapping sensory images.

Fish use the relative movement of their prey as another visual clue in their feeding behavior. Mayflies coming down the current, motionless and drying their freshly hatched wings, can make a fish suspicious of an imitation that moves or drags. Fluttering sedges are another problem which Leonard Wright explores in his *Fishing the Dry Fly as a Living Insect*, and twitching them can prove more successful than a drag-free float.

Most wild things are alarmed at a sudden movement. It is possible to approach a deer with almost imperceptible steps, freezing still when the deer stops browsing to watch the surrounding woods. But any sudden movement will trigger it into flight, its white tail raised like a warning flag as it bounds off into the trees. It is the same with trout and grayling. It is possible to approach a pool, intentionally frighten its fish, and then sit watching quietly until they forget and resume feeding. Eventually you become part of the landscape to the fish, and they will come surprisingly close as long as you make no movement. But if you move suddenly, the fish will panic and scatter everywhere.

It is clear that movement can signal both food and danger at times. Fish are extremely curious if nothing has alarmed them. Optical experiments have unmistakably demonstrated that any motion is instantly sensed in the retina. The fisherman has the problem of suggesting the precise movement of the diet form he is imitating, from the dead-drift float of a hatching mayfly to the erratic convulsions of an injured baitfish. Curiosity must be coaxed into the feeding reflex. Sometimes a fly can be worked to suggest that the prey might escape. Sometimes its crippled swimming movements will trigger the predatory instincts of a fish, and sometimes a varied fly speed will entice a following fish to take. Sometimes accelerating a retrieve and stopping it suddenly will force such a following trout into breaking off its pursuit or striking.

Another aspect of a trout's vision is the undulating mirror on the surface of its world. Its habitat has constantly changing levels of light, in the daily cycles of daylight and darkness, and from the surface to the bottom. Light energy is rather subtly dispersed under water, but its change in intensity is abrupt at the surface. Light penetrates the water there, its impulses sharply distorted by refraction, shattered by the kaleidoscopic effects of broken water, diffused with millions of bubbles, and is sometimes reflected back into the atmosphere.

When the surface meniscus is relatively smooth, unbroken by project-ing rocks and deadfalls, or not riffled with wind, its ceiling is like a highly polished mirror to the fish. Trout and grayling cannot only see around themselves laterally, but can also see the entire bottom reflected on the surface. Any movement is seen twice: directly through the water itself and echoed again in its surface reflections. It is useful in both hunting food and detecting a stalking predator. Alert fish can see a crayfish beyond a log, using its reflection to locate the prey, though the fish obviously cannot see it through the deadfall. Predators using subaquatic boulders or other obstacles to mask their intentions often fail, not because the trout or grayling sees them directly, but because their reflections betray them.

Perhaps the most important aspect of light refraction at the surface film was first described by Alfred Ronalds in his *Fly-Fisher's Entomology* almost 150 years ago. Although Ronalds did not call his discovery the cone of vision as many later angling books did, he was clearly the first fishing writer to understand this optical phenomena.

The cone of vision is intriguing. It is based upon precisely measurable laws affecting the penetration of light from the atmosphere into the water. When a light ray enters the water at any angle of incidence other than a perfectly vertical passage, it is sharply refracted or bent. Its angle of refraction is constant and predictable according to the laws of physics.

The simple circular diagram explains such optical laws. Imagine a circle with its center B lying in the surface film AC, and its geometry in a plane ninety degrees from the meniscus. Imagine further a theoretical ray of light lying in the surface of the water at BC, and penetrating it at the center of the circle. Divide the surface line BC into three equal segments. Plot a horizontal line equaling two of these segments, intersecting the vertical axis of the diagram and the circumference of the circle at D. The resulting line DB describes the angle of the theoretical light ray BC, once it has penetrated the surface film.

The ratio between the horizontal line BC and the plot line intersecting the circle at D is precisely three to two, the optical index of refraction between water and the atmosphere. The angle ABD will measure forty-eight and a half degrees, which is the constant angle of incidence.

Another light ray BF intersects the surface at B, and is refracted in the water. Construct a horizontal line from F to the vertical axis and trisect it into three equal parts. Describe another plot line below the surface, using two of those parts and intersecting the circle at E. The resulting line EB defines the subaquatic angle of the light ray BF once it has actually entered the water.

Light penetrating from the atmosphere is always refracted at forty-eight and a half degrees, and light passing back into the air is bent at the same angle. Simple geometry will demonstrate that this angle of refraction defines a cone of vision. Beyond its limits the surface of relatively still water is an undulating mirrorlike ceiling, but inside its circumference a fish can see out into our world.

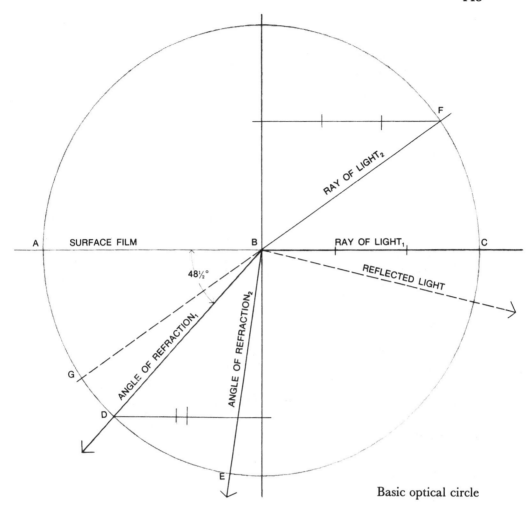

Basic optical circle

Energy attempting to penetrate back into the atmosphere along the vector GB, or any other angle less than forty-eight and a half degrees, cannot penetrate the mirrorlike meniscus. It is simply reflected back toward the bottom. It is this optical phenomenon that explains the cone of vision, and the diagram constructed from two refraction-angle circles defines its profiles. The lines AB and EF lie in the surface film, and the angles CBD and DEC both measure forty-eight and a half degrees. With a fish looking toward the surface at D, the refractive behavior of light entering or escaping its environment controls exactly what it can see. Any image lying inside the angle BDE, which is the profile of the fish's cone of vision, can be seen both under water or beyond. Images lying outside this profile are not visible if they lie above the surface film, and these sight lines are simply reflected back toward the bottom.

The scale of this cone of vision is a result of depth in the water, and as the depth CD increases and the angle BDE remains constant, the diameter BE is proportionally increased. Simply put, it means that the deeper a fish is lying in its world, the more it can see out into ours.

The cone of vision is rather like looking upward from the throat of an imaginary funnel. Any image lying inside the inverted cone of that funnel is completely visible to the fish, whether it lies below the surface film or in the atmosphere beyond. It can see into our world at any angle of forty-eight and a half degrees or more. Outside that angle it can see only reflections of the bottom and other subaquatic objects. The complete cone of vision is fully defined by the angle BDE, which totals eighty-three degrees.

The angle of incidence into the water is a factor in the percentages of light energy that will penetrate, and the percentages which are reflected off the surface. Light entering the water at ninety degrees transmits ninety-nine percent of its energy through the meniscus, and twenty-five percent still penetrates at a shallow angle of less than one degree. More than seventy percent penetrates at ten degrees, and almost ninety percent passes through the meniscus at a twenty-degree angle. More than ninety-five percent is transmitted at forty-five degrees.

These physical phenomena translate into a number of important considerations for fishermen. Light refraction can mean that a fish has often seen an angler long before he has spotted its position, and the higher the fisherman is above the fish, the more likely that he has been detected. Objects that are low on the trout's horizon, where less than seventy-five percent of light energy penetrates the meniscus film, are not as well illuminated or defined for the fish. Refraction of the light also means that the fish's image of objects beyond the film is flattened and distorted.

Edward Ringwood Hewitt conducted some interesting experiments that photographically demonstrated these phenomena. Working with James Clark, who built some remarkable camera equipment for the distinguished naturalist Carl Akeley, Hewitt designed a special photographic tank to study the distortion of light when it passes through the surface film. Hewitt included photographs both of the apparatus and his experiments in his book *A Trout and Salmon Fisherman for Seventy-five Years*, and they form a remarkable proof of these optical theories.

The photographs of Hewitt himself clearly demonstrate the principles of image distortion and illumination. Taken through both still and moving water, his head ebbs and flows in a series of distorted amusement-park images, ranging from the unrecognizable to the comic. The single portrait shot through a perfectly still surface film is distorted into a round dwarflike head, and beyond the cone of vision objects on the bottom of the tank are unmistakably reflected on the gently undulating ceiling formed by the meniscus.

It is also important to remember that the circle described on the surface by the cone of vision varies in size. It is quite small in shallow water, and grows larger as the depth increases. The fish's window is less than a foot in diameter at six inches depth, but in six feet of water its circular view

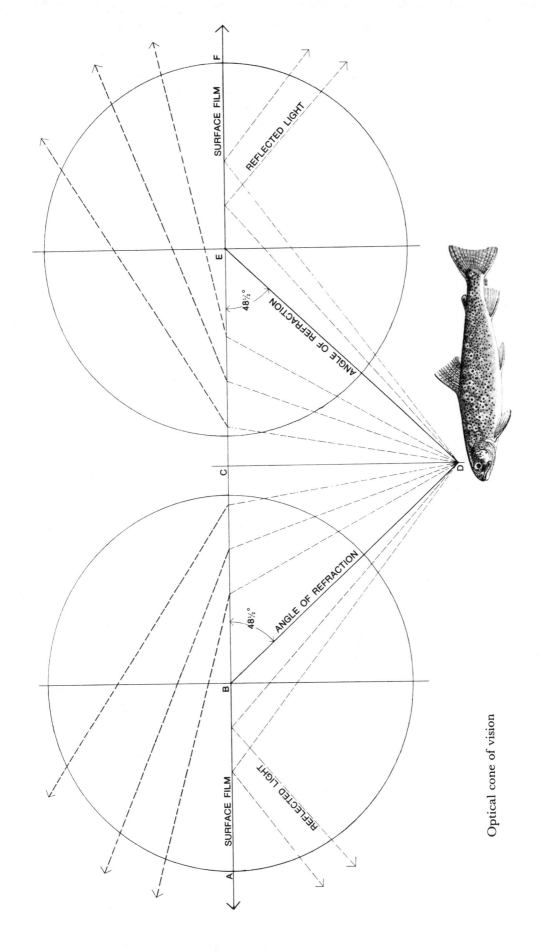

Optical cone of vision

beyond the surface film increases to more than ten feet. This means a dry fly must be placed quite close to a trout rising in a shallow flat, in order to enter its visual window, yet such a presentation is quite likely to frighten it. The trout lying deep in a six-foot pool can see a dry fly or floating insect a full five feet in any direction from its eyes.

It should be remembered also that a fish can detect an insect or dry fly floating outside its actual window. Such images are limited to the so-called light pattern formed where the artificial or natural lies in the surface film, its indentations clearly visible as intense little images of light. It is only those parts of both naturals and artificials that touch or puncture the film that are visible when a fly is floating outside the fish's window. With an imitation this can include tail fibers, hackles, and the hook itself. Sometimes a wing is pinioned in the meniscus too, and water tension creates a miniature light-catching globule surrounding each contact point. Air bubbles are entrained in fur and hackle fibers. Although a fish cannot see the fly beyond the surface film, when it lies outside the circular window, these tiny points of glittering intensity are visible well beyond its cone of vision.

Fluttering flies and naturals must seem like a kinetic fireworks of tiny hopscotching lights to a trout. The soft impact of a fly on the surface film is a similar explosion of microscopic light sources, unquestionably visible at considerable distances, and certainly exciting to a hungry fish. It is these tiny clues that alert the fish to its food, and these dancing light patterns in the film are most obvious with floating naturals and artificials.

Wet flies are less obvious, although their feathers and dubbing also entrain glittering air bubbles in their fibers. There is more movement and light pattern and life than one might expect, and wet flies are surprisingly visible against the tumbling, bubbling spume of a swift-flowing surface. Wet flies are also readily visible against the glittering surface film and its broken mirror effect. Still surface currents provide a unique double image for wet flies and nymphs, since a fly riding near the surface is perfectly reflected in the underside of the meniscus. It is an intriguing piece of knowledge, for it means a trout can see both sides of a sunk fly under certain conditions—the structure it can see directly and the materials on the opposite side, reflected as they are in the surface film.

It is possible that one of the reasons a fish sometimes misses a swinging wet fly or bucktail or nymph is its double image. Sometimes a trout may pursue the reflection instead of the fly, taking the wrong reflected image at the critical point of the fly swing. Water clarity and illumination and surface smoothness all play a role in such dual images, along with the distance of the fly from the meniscus. The reflection becomes more precise as the fly comes closer to the surface, and the images gradually tend to coincide, until they double in size as the two images first touch.

Similar effects occur with leaders lying in or immediately under the surface film. Some synthetics are quite shiny, and being semitransparent they collect and condense light energy. The places where they touch or penetrate the surface can create glittering linear light patterns and points of light. Coiled leader floating largely beyond the surface film is less visible, except when its coils actually touch the film or cross the cone of vision. It is surprising how many fishermen believe a leader is relatively invisible once it is sinking, forgetting that it may be reflected in the surface film if it lies close enough. Lying there under a smooth surface, the leader may look like two leaders lying together. Fortunately, the undulating rhythms of the surface distort these effects enough that our tactics work, and a fine tippet makes more sense than a larger diameter dressed to sink.

Generally speaking, the ambient surface distortions in the water cast more obvious shadow patterns than the leader, and they also shatter the reflective mirrorlike effect on the underside of the meniscus. The bold shadows cast on the bottom by a floating leader are less important then, and a sunk leader is not clearly reflected in the tumbling surface. Flat water is another problem in bright weather. The tippet at the fly should sink to minimize its shadows, and a skilled angler will often wait until a passing cloud diffuses and mutes the sunlight before making his presentation.

It was Alfred Ronalds who first made the basic optical observations on streamside tactics in 1836, with the diagrams he prepared for *The Fly-Fisher's Entomology*, and his arguments remain valid for fishermen today. Ronalds surprised an entire generation of anglers with the thesis that light refraction made it possible under certain conditions for a fish to see them even though it remained totally invisible to their eyes. His diagrams thoroughly proved the point, although they were relatively complex and much too small for easy deciphering, and the diagrams in these pages are adapted from his earlier work.

Ronalds proposed that we consider a pair of fishermen approaching a moderately deep pool, although still some distance away from the water, and on a slight rise of ground. The pool was approximately as deep as the men were tall, and the theoretical day was windless and still. The actual height of the men AB could not be seen by the trout at D, near the bottom of the pool, if the fish were forced to work with direct line-of-sight perceptions between AB and its position. Direct perception of the fish from eye level is also obscured by the profile of the river bank at C. Most fishermen would assume that any trout lying near the bottom, well below their line of sight, could not see their approach if they could not see its position.

Ronalds clearly proved them wrong. The laws of optical refraction demonstrate that the fish lying above the bottom at D does not see out of its pool on a direct line of sight. Such perception is only possible in its habitat or our atmosphere, but light energy transmitted from the fish toward the men and back is refracted and bent at E. The angle of refraction is such that the height of the men AB is transmitted above the outcropping at C, and the angle of incidence in their image is deflected downward approximately at E, reaching the trout's eyes at D just above the bottom. However, refraction distorts the perception of the fish, shrinking the apparent height of the anglers and making them seem high above the water, walking along the slope of its visual window from the optical position FG.

It is perhaps instructive to note that these relationships would no longer hold true in low-water conditions. With the water reduced to a midsummer level barely covering the fish at D, refraction would still occur under the same optical laws, but the high banks at C would conceal the approaching anglers. It is also clear that an infantry-style approach, keeping their silhouette low along the intervening ground, might bring the approaching fishermen within casting range before the fish had detected their presence.

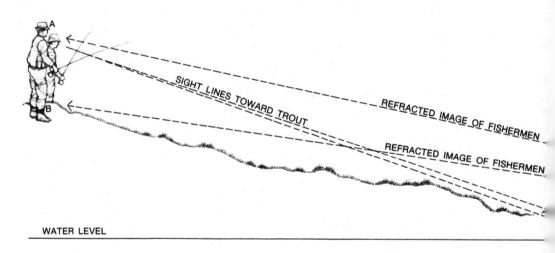

Ronalds' walking anglers

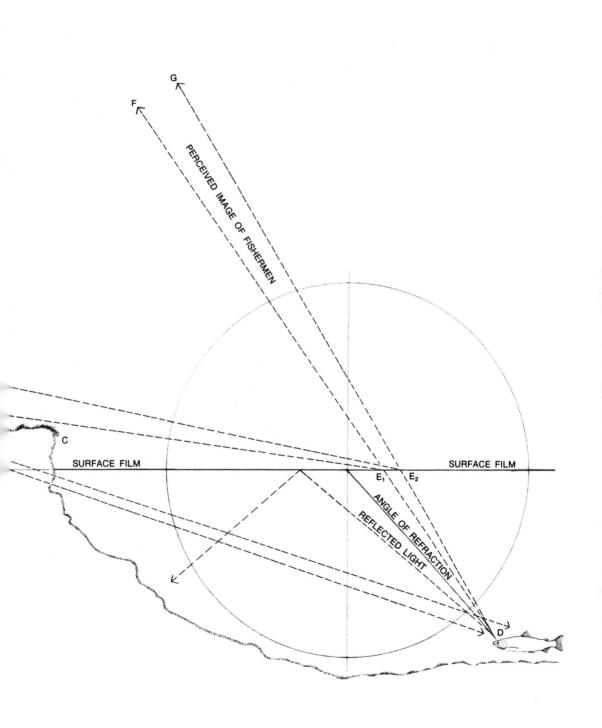

G

F

PERCEIVED IMAGE OF FISHERMEN

C

SURFACE FILM   SURFACE FILM

E₁   E₂

ANGLE OF REFRACTION

REFLECTED LIGHT

D

Ronalds makes a similar point in his *Fly-Fisher's Entomology*, using a wading angler in his example. The images perceived by the fish lying at F are now totally transformed by the position of the angler in the water itself. Surprisingly enough, the trout cannot see the entire height of the fisherman, even though he has entered the water. The legs CD are seen clearly and directly, and when the surface is still, they are seen twice. The trout sees the legs themselves, simultaneously seeing their reflected image, upside down on the surface film and radically shortened. Light refraction at E bends the image of the fisherman downward toward the trout lying at F near the bottom. However, the fish cannot see the entire height of the angler above the water. The optical laws refract only his partial height AB, making it appear to lie at the position GH, high above the water. The middle of his body BC is probably obscured totally, or is so faintly defined that the fish cannot identify its character. It is even possible that the trout may not even connect the legs it sees dimly at CD, because of their lateral distance and the water's clarity, and the distorted head and shoulders it sees at GH. It is an intriguing exercise in the relationships between the optical laws of physics and everyday stream tactics.

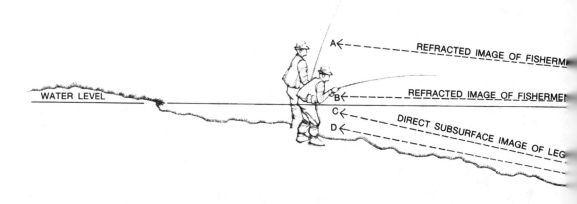

Ronalds' wading anglers

However, it is possible to extend these lessons to still another step in fishing over selective fish that see too many people. Suppose the fisherman has still chosen to fish from his position at D, and the fish is still lying above the bottom at F, but now he is crouching low, placing little more than his head in the trout's field of vision, greatly reducing the height AB perceived by the fish. Virtually nothing is left of the diminished image it seems to see at GH, high above the water, and the advantages are obvious.

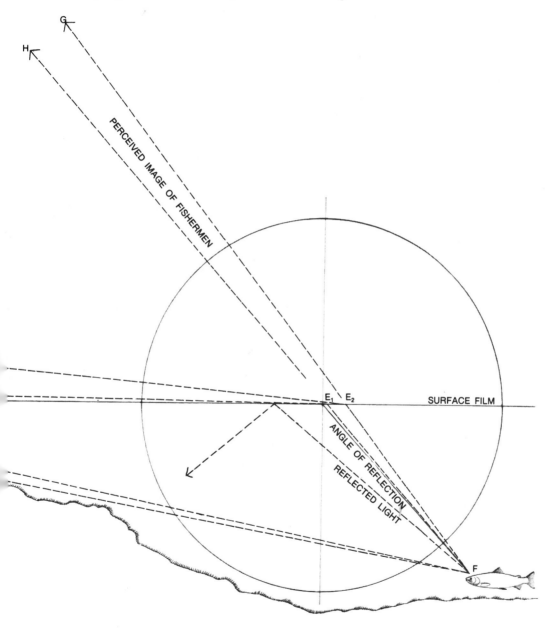

There have been many times over the years when friends have found me crouched low, standing in a quiet flat or sun-dappled pool, and their comments are predictable.

Back problems? they laughed.

Streamside humor is pretty transparent, but if your back can stand the muscle strain of a long day's fishing, such crouching positions will pay surprising dividends on difficult trout. Understanding the relationships between optics, the trout's field of vision, and stalking tactics is a primary factor in successful fishing.

During the nineteenth century, German studies in the color perception of fish seemed to prove that they were completely color-blind and responded only to brightness. The early experiments were not conducted on trout or grayling, and illuminated the test aquarium with the colors of the spectrum. The test specimens always gravitated to the yellow zone, causing the preliminary conclusion that fish were rather like color-blind people, able to sense only that yellow was palest in terms of its hue. Later studies were made, intensifying the other colors in controlled succession. The fish invariably moved to the palest color, whatever its hue or chroma. It was an ill-planned experiment that has since been widely discredited, but its conclusions that fish responded to brightness instead of color itself received widespread attention, and it is surprising how many fishermen still believe, a century later, that fish are color-blind.

Old mythology dies hard, but subsequent research has totally refuted the color-blind theory. Not only are fish highly responsive to the spectrum and to many shades of color, they are extremely sensitive to ultraviolet energy. Contemporary studies conclusively prove that trout and grayling, as well as other high orders of fish life, can discriminate colors at the red and blue ends of the spectrum far better than people.

The basic experiments were brilliantly conceived by several German experts, and although they were conceptually sophisticated, the apparatus was both simple and ingenious. Crystalline rods were assembled in a test-system that held them at the surface film of the fish tank. Each rod could be illuminated with any color of the spectrum, without changing either the rod or its position. The test fish were subsequently conditioned to accept food from a single color, whatever its position in the tank when illuminated. The rods were finally lowered into the tank and the fish unfailingly sought the color that had signalled available food. Both brightness and chroma were quite brilliant in these preliminary tests, although they tended to prove color discrimination.

However, the research team wished to refute the brightness hypothesis completely, and embarked on a second series of tests designed to test its assumptions. The intensity of light was then varied across the full spectrum of colors in an attempt to observe if the fish would continue to seek the color they associated with food in spite of the brightness of the other hues. The trout used in these experiments unmistakably came to the lighted crystalline rods, even when their energy was reduced to such minimal intensity that the observers were not able to discern the presence of any color. It was these studies that proved the ability of trout to distinguish both red and violet wavelengths well below the thresholds of our senses.

The experiments were expanded to determine if the trout could also distinguish form. It was quickly determined that they were able to separate circles from squares, accepting a shape that signalled food and rejecting the other. The results were interesting but subsequent tests were more surprising. The fish quickly were taught to recognize both circles and oval forms, and ultimately between ovoids of varying ellipticity. Objects of various sizes were also tested, and it was found that the test fish were again able to measure subtle differences in several shapes.

Modern color technology has demonstrated that color is the result of wavelengths of light energy. Such energy is described as light when its wavelengths are recorded in the retinal cells of the eyeball. Our sensory networks detect light waves between .00033 and .00067 in length, and energy in this range defines the spectrum we see. Both ultraviolet and infrared light lie outside our visible spectrum, but they both exist, even though our eyes cannot detect their presence. Infrared light waves are beyond .00067 in length, and our senses detect them primarily in terms of their heat. Ultraviolet light is found in solar radiation. Most of its energy is absorbed in the atmosphere, and its wavelengths are shorter than .00033, lying between the visible spectrum and the wavelengths used in radio-therapy and radiographs. Ultraviolet radiation is strongest in clear weather, and at certain intensities it can make some materials fluoresce visibly.

Hewitt firmly believed that the colors in our fly hatches often took on a slight fluorescence in strong light, and in his book *Telling on the Trout* he argued that only natural gamecock hackles and undyed dubbing could fully match this quality in the naturals. John Alden Knight echoed that speculation in his book *The Modern Angler*, and Preston Jennings also experimented with the color spectrum and the effects of ultraviolet light. All three men insisted that undyed dun-colored hackles were unquestionably superior to dyed shades, because of their qualities in ultraviolet radiation. Their theories might well be true, although natural dun necks are usually limited to the rusty and iron-blue shades.

Since our fly hatches have many other colors of blue dun across the full spectrum of our American species, the natural shades are not enough to match many of our trout-stream insects, and some dyed or phototreated duns are also needed. Many skilled fly dressers are no longer convinced that natural blue-dun shades are invariably better than dyed hackles of the same color, and the dry-fly quality of dyed necks is generally better than the webby dun of naturals.

Color varies across the full spectrum in delicate shadings, starting with the blue light waves. These are the shortest visible pulsations of energy, and are followed by sequential bands of green, yellow, orange, and red. The red wavelengths are the longest pulsations of light energy visible to our sensory system. The laws of optics prove that black is indicative of the total absence of color, while white is paradoxically composed of every hue in the entire spectrum.

Optical experiments can quickly demonstrate that color does not really exist in an object itself, but consists of its ability to reflect only the mixture of the full chromatic spectrum we perceive. The remaining wavelengths of color are absorbed. Color is therefore completely dependent on the presence of light energy, although we should remember that some light exists even in the darkest nights.

Our senses are conditioned to defining color transmitted in the atmosphere. It is changed when its energies penetrate and refract in a fluid as dense as water. The radiant energy of light is absorbed into the water as heat, and its spectrum is rapidly changed as it passes downward below the surface. The water filters out different wavelengths as they reach specific depths, altering both the spectrum and its perceived colors.

The absorption of color intensity occurs both as the light penetrates through the water to objects under water, and again as it is reflected back toward our eyes. Our flies can lose much of their effective color because of the loss in light energy. The fish do not suffer the double loss of color intensity, because it is only the first penetration of light that affects the color of objects at their depths. The deeper the light penetrates, the more its energy is dissipated and the light rays are absorbed. Some light energy is always radiated back toward the surface in the relatively shallow depths frequented by trout and grayling.

Water absorbs the red wavelengths first, and the yellow radiation follows, leaving the blue wavelengths of the spectrum reaching deepest into the water. These optical phenomena mean that little of the red wavelength energy remains at depths of thirty to fifty feet, even in exceptionally clear water, and at greater depths only the blue and green wavelengths remain. It is interesting that orange and yellow light penetrate deeper than red, because their wavelengths are shorter. Green penetrates still deeper, but not as deep as the blue radiation of the spectrum. The following table has been calculated for extremely clear trout and grayling habitat, and demonstrates the energy penetration for different wavelengths of light:

PERCENTAGES OF LIGHT PENETRATION

	10 FEET	20 FEET	30 FEET
Red	10	0.9	0.1
Orange	55	35	15
Yellow	75	60	45
Green	90	80	70
Blue	98	95	90

Water chemistry, turbidity, and the reflective character of the bottom can all affect light transmission in the fish's habitat, and these estimated depths of penetration can vary widely in different waters. Projected depths of penetration are also different between fresh water, brackish habitat, and the extreme salinity of a marine environment.

The factors of chromatic penetration in water have a number of practical effects on our fishing. Each color of the spectrum is changed in hue, chromatic intensity, and value as it sinks deeper. The red in our flies is the first color to darken and lose its chroma in relatively moderate depths. Orange holds its color integrity at somewhat greater depths of water, although it darkens and becomes reddish, and the yellow wavelengths are the first to remain yellow at depths beyond twenty-odd feet. Yellow loses some chroma there, but is still clearly recognizable in character. The green wavelengths experience little significant change at depths of thirty-odd feet, and blue displays virtually no reduction of its chromatic integrity at twice such depths. However, since the habitat itself has a similar background coloration, flies dressed with materials toward the blue wavelengths of the spectrum are not readily visible at the blue-green depths of water.

Marginal intensity of light at daylight and dusk multiply these chromatic effects. Red is quickly lost at such times, and although yellow is surprisingly persistent, it is soon lost too. Blue and green hold their hues longer. When the measurable light is calibrated below a single footcandle of energy, trout and grayling are almost entirely committed to their rod-cell light perception, and their ability to distinguish between colors is greatly reduced.

Early morning poses similar problems as the fish switch from rods to cones in the retinal system. However, the sequence of their color perception is reversed. The blue and green wavelengths are the first colors to reach full chromatic resolution, although yellow soon follows. Finally there are sufficient footcandles to illuminate red objects under water. It should be remembered that both early-morning and evening light are marginal at best, although they are accompanied by a surprisingly illuminated sky. It is against this pale background that objects are observed, and many fly-fishermen like dark patterns in such light. Years ago, in his book *Currents and Eddies*, William Schaldach described night fishing on the Beaverkill just after the First World War. Richard Robbins was the dean of the Beaverkill in those years, and he fished the river at night with a pattern he jokingly called the Higgins Special. It was simply a big wet fly soaked in a well-known brand of draftsman's ink, and Robbins clearly understood the worth of completely black fly patterns after nightfall.

The theory that fish were color-blind would have been clearly laughable had we understood better the light-sensing cells of the retina. Virtually all fish species have retinal cones, with the physiological function of color perception. However, their color perception varies with habitat and biological adaptation, and the shallow-water species apparently have the most advanced chromatic sensitivity.

Many studies tend to confirm that their color senses are fully equal to ours, and experiments with trout prove their ability to distinguish more than twenty shades of color between the visible ends of the spectrum. The Salmonidae also possess color perception in the infrared and ultraviolet wavelengths that lie beyond our sensory apparatus, indicating that their discriminatory powers exceed ours in terms of color.

Several years ago, a research study conducted in the United States seemed to prove trout had a color sense that was inferior to that of bass, muskellunge, and northern pike. The conclusions received widespread attention, but there were obvious flaws in the methodology of the experiments. The studies were conducted with aquarium specimens, instead of being done *in situ* in the natural habitat of each species. Artificial illumination was also used, virtually eliminating the ultraviolet overtones present at streamside, but perhaps the most serious flaw in the studies lay in the test fish themselves.

The specimens of bass, muskellunge, pike, and panfish were all the progeny of wild parentage, since these species are not adaptable to the techniques common in trout pisciculture. Unfortunately, the trout used in the experiments were not wild fish, but typical hatchery stocks bred only for optimal growth. Experts in the genetic characteristics of trout culture have long been aware that hatchery fish are often inferior strains, since hatchery operations for the nonmigratory species of trout are based on the egg production of tame brood fish. Few anglers equally familiar with trout and the other test species doubt the color senses of the Salmonidae, but more research would prove welcome. Certainly, the greater densities of color-sensing cells in the retinal tissues of trout and grayling point to superior chromatic perception.

Fly-fishermen have been concerned with the visual acuity and sensory perceptions of trout for many centuries. Matching the precise colors of important fly hatches has its roots in the third century. The precise colors involved in fly dressing were also a primary concern in the fishing manuscripts of the fifteenth and sixteenth centuries, reaching a peak in the writings of Charles Cotton. His *Being Instructions How to Angle for Trout and Grayling in a Clear Stream* was written in 1676, and is filled with observations on fish behavior, and the importance of color in fly dressing.

The book firmly established Cotton as the father of fly-fishing. Its pages are filled with charming descriptions of his Derbyshire trout country, and some remarkably advanced techniques of fly tying. The dialogues include a description of Cotton's dubbing bag, and its cornucopia of fly-dressing materials. The fish in his water on the Dove were working selectively, and Cotton artfully dressed a fly to match the hatch. His pupil is quickly taught to respect the wariness of the Derbyshire trout, for he frightens two good fish that come short to the freshly tied imitation.

Cotton's preoccupation with the importance of subtle variations in color is obvious in his Waltonian dialogues. When his pupil observes that the fresh dubbing seems too black, Cotton agrees it is darker, but adds these observations on the skittish behavior of the fish in bright weather,. and its effects on materials and fly color:

It appears black in the hand; but step to the door and hold it up betwixt your eye and the sun, and it will also appear a shining red. Let me tell you, never a man in all England can discern the true color of a dubbing in any way but that, and therefore, choose always to make your flies on such days as this, which also you may all the better do, because they are worth nothing to fish in.

It is interesting that Cotton believed in dressing his flies in the natural light of streamside, like James Leisenring three centuries later on the Brodheads in Pennsylvania. His book *The Art of Tying the Wet Fly* insisted on dubbing his bodies in the same light where they were fished. Our

Cotton's fly patterns, 1676

perception of a given color depends on the colors that surround it, one of the first lessons learned in architecture and painting. Both Cotton and Leisenring clearly understood color, and the truth that subtle color perception is ultimately conditioned and changed by the quality of the light at streamside. It is a lesson worth remembering in our fly dressing.

The senses of both trout and grayling are becoming more important each season, since the hordes of fishermen on crowded waters are making our fish increasingly selective and shy. Our knowledge of their senses is critical to success on such waters in the future. Our understanding of the sensory perceptions of the trout is still growing, yet its scientific and technical intricacies should not diminish our love for the quicksilver poetry of the fish themselves.

3. The Ecosystems of Trout Streams

Roderick Haig-Brown concludes his poetic book *A River Never Sleeps* with the observation that his love of fly-fishing is only an excuse to experience the moods and rhythms of his favorite rivers. His words carry us to steelhead riffles and pools on the Campbell and Nimpkish in British Columbia, and although we may never fish them, his knowledge makes them as familiar as our own rivers.

Yet each man possesses the rivers he knows best, understanding their rhythms and their moods, and finally reaching a stage of experience and wisdom which tells him a river can never be possessed or fully understood. It is perhaps enough to know that loving and fishing a river can slowly unlock its secrets, but no matter how many secrets we discover down the years of a fly-fishing life, there are always fresh puzzles. Each river has its own fingerprint, its character and chemistry, its unique mixture of the physical and the metaphysical. The history of fly-fishing is filled with stories of anglers who chose burial beside a favorite pool, or whose wills asked that their ashes be scattered into a river they had fished for many years. Such feelings are difficult to explain to men who have never fished, and though often an unspoken bond among anglers, they are widely shared along trout streams.

Our memories of fishing are widely shared too, yet they are also unique. It is certain that we fish for many years, preoccupied with catching trout, before we realize how much their rivers mean to our sport. Our memories teach us in later years, since the fish and fishing often fade with time, leaving us with the images of rivers we have loved.

Yet our memories and experiences alone are not enough to sharpen our fishing skills. Study and knowledge of the rivers themselves are also

461

critical in a time of hard-fished water and increasing population. Under-standing the chemistry and biology of a trout stream is becoming indispensable for a modern angler, and in the knowledge of its ecology lie many secrets we could never learn from the fishing itself.

Freshwater ecology is the study of the intricate interrelationships between aquatic organisms and the chemistry of their habitat, as well as the subtle fabric of their relationships to each other. It is a uniquely rich tapestry of life. Limnology is focused on the entire spectrum of fresh water, its character and water chemistry, geology, biology, entomology, and temperature. Lakes are often the principal concern of limnology, while potamology is the study of the biosystemics in a flowing stream.

As a life-supporting habitat, water is a totally different medium from our atmosphere. It displays some unusual properties. It condenses and contracts slightly as it cools, like many familiar metals and gases, but it curiously starts expanding again slightly below forty degrees. It becomes slightly less dense and lighter until it finally reaches the freezing point, where its volume suddenly increases ten to eleven percent.

These physical properties have some obvious practical echoes in terms of fish life. Before water reaches its freezing point, its coldest molecules rise toward the surface layers, and ice itself floats once it has formed. Consequently, shallow streams and lakes seldom freeze completely to the bottom in all but the most hostile altitudes or arctic latitudes. Such total freezing, where even the anchor ice freezes solid in the riffles, is invariably fatal to higher forms of fish life.

Water is also a highly effective heat-sink, accepting thermal gain rather slowly, and surrendering more thermal energy than an equal mass of almost any other medium when it cools. It requires surprising amounts of heat, beyond its ambient temperatures, to start it warming. Its high latent heat of evaporation makes it a perfect medium for cooling systems.

Even at its boiling point, water still will not become vapor without surprising amounts of additional heat. It requires more than five hundred times the heat to vaporize water at the boiling point than it takes to increase its temperature a single degree before it reaches that state. However, water sometimes may vaporize without boiling, and at high altitudes it will boil at temperatures so low that it cannot cook an egg. When water freezes in an almost metaphysical change at thirty-two degrees, it surrenders almost sixty times as much heat as it would release in lowering its temperature a single degree at higher temperatures.

Such cooling properties have remarkable effects on both the biosystem and our biosphere itself. Evaporation releases surprising amounts of heat, cooling the water's surface and the surrounding atmosphere. Water evaporates from life forms, lakes, rivers, and oceans in exactly the same manner, gradually saturating the atmosphere until precipitation returns it to the biosystem again. It is this poetic cycle that sustains all forms of life, described in Ecclesiastes with these famous passages:

The sun also ariseth, and the sun goeth down, and hasteth to the place where he arose. The wind goeth toward the south, and turneth about into the north; it whirleth about continually, and the wind returneth again according to his circuits. All the rivers run into the sea; yet the sea is not full; unto the place from whence the rivers come, thither they return again.

Water has a remarkable capacity to entrain and store heat and can either surrender or absorb large amounts with surprisingly small changes in its own temperatures. Such thermal stability is the reason for the vast climatological effects of our oceans and the surprising regional impact of major lakes on microclimate.

Water is a relatively dense medium to the organisms living in its habitat, exerting tremendous external pressures on their bodies and impeding their movements. Its viscosity is protective too, since it both impedes predators and transmits sound exceptionally well, warning potential prey. The viscosity of the water also changes with temperature and is twice as thick at the threshold of its freezing point as at the upper thermal limits of trout and grayling.

It weighs more than sixty-two pounds per cubic foot at approximately thirty-nine degrees, its bench mark of maximum density. Its weight is cumulative with depth, and the fish are subjected to steadily increasing pressures as they move toward the bottom. Trout habitat can sustain pressures as high as seventy-five pounds per square inch at extreme depths. Both density and viscosity are echoed in the surface film or meniscus, where air pressure also plays a role, and its tensile strength is surprising. The fish penetrate the meniscus easily, but it is a formidable barrier to fly life and other tiny organisms. It can support surprisingly heavy objects, and midge-sized insects literally slide across it like figure skaters. Its tension on a relatively heavy insect-form is distorted downward, while it buoys upward along the perimeter of lighter objects. Small organisms that sink below the surface film are usually trapped and drowned, while subaquatic creatures that penetrate upward too quickly are equally trapped in a hostile environment. Insects like aquatic spiders and water boatmen and back-swimmers are well known for their ability to maneuver with great agility on the surface film. Hatching aquatic insects must also penetrate the tensile character of the meniscus, many using its unique properties literally to peel themselves from their nymphal and pupal skins. It is a barrier as dangerous to aquatic forms of life as the hostility of space is to astronauts.

Light also penetrates the meniscus and the water itself with difficulty, losing surprising amounts of energy in the process. Virtually all light is dissipated in the clearest freshwater lakes between depths of six hundred to seven hundred feet. Light penetration in turbid water is abruptly limited by the silt particles. During spates when the current is highly discolored, or when a lake is blooming with algal growth, there is very little light only three feet down. Water clarity and light penetration are critical to the oxygenation of the habitat, since light is necessary for photosynthesis.

Virtually all aquatic life begins with basic organisms in the food chain, and their viability depends on primary chemicals in solution. Water is a surprisingly universal solvent. It has some effect on virtually anything immersed in it, and it does not radically change the substances dissolved. Their properties are easily utilized by aquatic organisms, leaving the solvent itself unchanged.

Chemicals in solution tend to ionize, dissolving into microscopic particles carrying an electrical charge. These ions form and reform in almost infinite combinations, so almost any life-sustaining compound is available to the minute forms of aquatic life. The water is a catalyst for many chemical changes that could not occur without its properties. Basic water chemistry is neither acid nor alkaline, but when carbon dioxide is expelled by subaquatic species or entrained from physical contact with the atmosphere, the water and carbon dioxide join into a dilute compound of carbonic acid. Its mild acidity then reacts with other trace chemicals.

Water begins with evaporation and the saturation of the atmosphere with its vapor. Its distribution is the result of ascending patterns of flow in the atmosphere, temperature cycles, the effects of moisture-bearing winds, marine temperatures and currents, geographical relationships, and topography. Rising air is cooled as it expands, changing its vapor into visible cloud formations, and finally triggering new condensation of moisture. Raindrops form and grow, coalescing with other droplets and adding condensation on their cool surfaces. Finally they become so heavy that gravity forces them to start falling. Evaporation continues from the moment a raindrop responds to gravity, and under some conditions of temperature and humidity it may evaporate completely before it reaches the earth. Atmospheric saturation results in rainfall, and under some temperatures, such precipitation is further transformed into hail, snow, or freezing rain.

Rain and snow are the principal sources of our lakes and streams. Both forms of precipitation entrain some oxygen from the atmosphere as they fall, trickle, erode the surface geology, are absorbed into mosses and dead leaves and pine needles, fall directly on plant life, and are imperceptibly leached into the water table. Some precipitation runs off into lakes and streams directly. It acquires trace chemicals from the atmosphere, dissolves other substances on the surface, and entrains still more in its subsurface hydrology. Some precipitation falls directly into existing fish habitat, but most is gathered in intricate labyrinths of seepages and springheads.

Surface water is typically filled with foreign matter it has eroded, and it causes extensive turbidity in both lakes and streams. Spring seepages are often crystalline. Although some major springheads can run murky after unusual periods of rainfall, they are usually charged with dissolved chemicals from their subsurface flowages. Their chemistry is varied, depending upon the soils and underground geology through which the water has been leached. Its percolation may have taken weeks, months, or even years. It may have travelled surprising distances, particularly in regions rich in formations of sedimentary geology like limestone. Water chemistry is intricately mixed with geology and soils and is infinitely varied. Leached through igneous formations like granite or gneiss, spring water is sometimes soft and slightly acid. Water that has been percolated through limestone or sandstone geology, like the rich valleys of eastern Pennsylvania or Virginia, is hard and quite alkaline.

Such basic water chemistry has an immense impact on the quality of a fishery. Except for the character and profusion of aquatic plants, the relative acidity or alkalinity of trout water is invisible, yet the richness of our lakes and rivers depends directly on their lime content. With accurate calibration of the alkalinity of the habitat it is possible to predict the species, growth rate, population, and average size of the fish it supports.

Fish culturists typically classify trout habitat in five categories of basic water chemistry. Very soft water is acid and rather poor in its ability to support fish life in significant numbers. It entrains less than five parts per million of carbon dioxide, indicating virtually no lime content. Soft waters have more alkalinity, testing between five and ten parts per million of bound carbon dioxide, and supporting twice as much aquatic life.

Medium waters are almost neutral, and will support good populations of fish and their food chain, measuring between ten and twenty parts per million. Trout inhabiting such waters are not forced to cleanse their blood of acidity resulting from their respiratory processes, and the water chemistry sustains four times the aquatic diet forms of a very soft habitat. The food supply means four times the trout population too. Some famous rivers like the Rogue and Yellowstone and Umpqua are classic examples of medium water.

Medium hard waters are richer still. Generally speaking, their fish-supporting qualities are good to excellent, since they hold twenty to thirty parts per million of bound carbon dioxide. Such alkalinity spells six times the fish life and food supply found at only five parts per million. The medium hard waters in the United States include such famous trout streams as the Brule and the Deschutes and the South Platte and the Snake in the Rocky Mountains.

Hard trout water is rare and precious, and must be carefully regulated and preserved. Such habitat will calibrate from thirty to one hundred parts per million carbon dioxide, supporting as much as twenty times the food supply and trout population of acid waters. There is a long roster of famous rivers having a lime content between thirty and sixty parts per million, including famous western rivers like the Eel and Gunnison and North Platte. Michigan has a lexicon of excellent streams like the Manistee and Pere Marquette and Au Sable in its Lower Peninsula and the Whitefish and Ontanagon in its forest-covered Upper Peninsula. Wisconsin has rich watersheds like the Namekagon and Wolf, but none of the famous Catskill and New England rivers are of comparable water quality. Such alkalinity is extremely valuable.

There are a few trout streams in the United States that are even richer, rivalling the cretaceous chalkstreams of England and Normandy. Such rivers have bound carbon dioxide ratings well beyond sixty parts per million. Their rich alkalinity usually comes from the generous subsurface hydrology found in limestone country, but it can also stem from deposits of marl, phosphates, and extensive geothermal activity.

Marl swamps are often the cause of high carbon dioxide counts in Michigan and Wisconsin. Phosphate deposits explain much of the alkalinity that has made the Big Hole in Montana famous. Hot springs are the source of the richness found in Yellowstone rivers like the Gibbon and Madison and Firehole. The volcanic geology of the Lassen country in northern California is the explanation for the superb fisheries that rise there, and the geothermal springs at Hot Creek on the eastern slope of the Sierras are responsible for alkaline flowages at a year-round temperature of sixty-three degrees. Rainbow trout raised in the hatchery there displayed the remarkable growth rate of almost an inch per month, starting with fingerlings of four to five inches. But the streams with the richest water chemistry in the United States are the limestone waters of Pennsylvania, like Big Spring and Falling Spring Run and Spring Creek—and the half-legendary Letort Spring Run at Carlisle that boasts an incredible ninety-five parts per million of bound carbon dioxide.

It should be understood, however, that the estimates of productivity from waters of such chemical richness is tied to adequate photosynthesis and light penetration. Without such penetration of solar radiation, oxygenation and food production are seriously truncated, in spite of their alkalinity ratings. Tea-colored water will inhibit fertility as much as thirty percent, discolored water can result in a forty percent drop, and really turbid conditions can cost a lake or stream as much as sixty percent of its full potential.

Assuming that a specific trout habitat is relatively clear, admitting light energy to penetrate to thirty-odd feet, there are some interesting rules of thumb for productivity. The following table provides a workable yardstick for fishermen, in pounds per acre of both trout and populations of other aquatic life:

BASIC WATER QUALITY AND PRODUCTIVITY

WATER TYPE	CO_2 PPM	TROUT LBS/ACRE	COARSE FISH LBS/ACRE	FOOD LBS/ACRE
1	0–5	5	45	100
2	5–10	10	90	200
3	10–20	20	180	400
4	20–30	30	270	750
5	30–60	40	360	1,500
6	60–95	60	540	3,500

These bench marks of water quality are also obviously conditioned by temperature cycles, and the physiography of the water systems themselves. The bathographic character of a lake or reservoir and the physical character and rates of flow of lotic waters are modifying factors too.

Subsurface hydrology and springheads are unusual influences on surface water. The thermal character of spring flowages is relatively constant in both winter and summer. Their volumes are too large to suffer much modification in contact with atmospheric temperatures. Minor variations in the heat of the earth occur seasonally, but such changes are infinitely less than the climatological cycles of the seasons. The result is a tempering effect on surface waters that warms them in winter and cools them in summer. The temperatures of springs flowing from relatively shallow strata will demonstrate more seasonal variations than springheads from major underground rivers and caverns. Hot springs occur primarily on our western streams and lakes, and their flowages can encourage good winter rates of feeding and growth; and in keeping some parts of the habitat ice free, they help suppress winterkill.

However, the water chemistry of springheads is somewhat different from surface hydrology. Along with their obvious temperature benefits, springs also pose some chemical problems. Their waters emerge from depths where both temperatures and pressures are unlike conditions at the surface. Springs entrain only minuscule amounts of oxygen, usually combined with excessive amounts of carbon dioxide. High carbon dioxide concentrations can result in fish kills when coupled with oxygen deficiencies. Spring flowages quickly entrain oxygen after relatively brief exposure to the atmosphere, and potentially lethal counts of carbon dioxide are purged, particularly in broken water. Volcanic and geothermal springs sometimes contain concentrations of various free acids. Nitrogen is also found issuing from some springheads in concentrations that are clearly toxic to trout and grayling.

Streams are formed in many ways. Precipitation is absorbed into the surface geology, and evaporates unless there is sufficient rainfall or gradual snowmelt to saturate the ground. Soils that retain water effectively sometimes release it steadily across the year in permanent springs, forming the headwaters of streams. Other springs are only intermittent, depending on snowmelt or continuing precipitation, and in regions having extensive rainfall there are streams entirely dependent on surface runoff.

Topography sometimes collects the surface water in shallow depressions, forming marshes and intermittent ponds. Some large swamps are ancient lakes that have experienced eutrophication and are slowly becoming new land. Other swamps result from radically altered topography, particularly in earthquake country. Seismic activity is also responsible for the formation of many lakes. The volume of precipitation and the porosity of the surface geology both affect the character of our watersheds, and as lakes, marshes, and ponds overflow larger streams are formed. Their outlets may flow lazily, filling other depressions at lower elevations, or tumble and plunge down dramatic escarpments. Permanent flowages ultimately form larger streams, becoming rivers that eventually reach the sea, although there are exceptions to this truism. Several of our rivers disappear into subterranean caverns, and in several arid western states, trout streams are totally absorbed at lower altitudes in the desertlike soils of ancient dry lakes and dessicating basins.

Wind and water erosion continues, cutting deeper watercourses and forming new depressions in higher elevations. These basins collect moisture, saturate, and eventually overflow toward existing water systems downstream. Glaciers continue to shrink at high altitudes, exposing eroded basins under their ice fields, and forming new lakes. These forces are still evolving, and headwaters are working deeper into our mountains.

Our streams result from this mixed hydrology. Melting snow fields and glaciers combine with high altitude rainfall to drain the mountains, flowing into the rolling foothills and piedmont, and finally into the bottomlands and plains. Obvious runoff is combined with the outfall of lakes and ponds, the slower drainage of marshland, and the surface outlets of underground hydrology. These aquatic networks are treelike, their delicate branches reaching into the high country, their waters literally sustaining life throughout their valleys.

Alpine streams have steep profiles, falling rapidly down the valleys and slopes. The gradient or rate of fall is measured in feet per linear mile of flow. Mountain streams can drop hundreds of feet per mile. Foothill gradients are less dramatic, ranging from ten to thirty feet per mile, and such profiles flatten once the flow reaches the eroded topography downstream. Obviously, the profile of a typical watershed is progressively less and less, except for seismic faults and geological barriers, as the water journeys toward the sea. Its coastal reaches may ultimately measure less than a half foot per mile, until finally the sluggish river merges imperceptibly with the reversing current tongues of its tidewaters. It is a richly varied biosystem.

Velocity of flow is obviously related to topography. Steep profiles trigger plunging rates of flow, foothills and piedmont zones range from broken chutes to deep pools and glassy flats, and in the bottoms, streams can become sluggish and still. Velocity of flow is calibrated in linear feet per second. Currents can vary widely in a single cross section, a variation caused by the effects of lateral profiles and the character of a stream's banks and bottom. It is hydraulic friction that slows the flow rates, creating both vertical and lateral layers of flow. These layers flow at diminishing rates as they approach the banks and bottom. The surface layer is relatively fast, since it lies farthest from the bottom friction, just as the current tongues at midstream flow more quickly than the currents against the bank. The primary currents lie just under the surface, in the second layer of flow. The surprisingly slow third layer of flow lies along the bottom, its reduced current speeds resulting from the smooth hydraulics of a sandy bottom to the surprisingly effective friction of grapefruit-size stones.

Typical trout-stream rates of flow can be measured with a current meter, and the calibrations would surprise most experienced anglers. Flow against the bank and along the bottom will average about one-third of a foot per second. Surface flow is a little over one foot per second, three or four feet from the bank, and the velocity is about fifteen percent faster a foot deeper. These current-meter readings mean that the primary layer just below the surface is two hundred percent faster than the bottom flow. Approximately five feet from the bank, where the rate of flow was measured at one-third of a foot per second, the surface layer was clocked at a foot and one-half per second. The difference in surface speed of three hundred percent is striking.

The volume of flow is measured in cubic feet per second. It steadily increases as tributaries and springheads join the flow, varying with rainfall and subsurface hydrology and the cycle of the seasons. Such flowages are capable of transporting surprisingly large volumes of organic matter and minerals. The larger the volume and velocity of flow, the larger its capacity to carry eroded materials. Since stream flow is downstream, except in the reversing patterns of the tidal reaches, eroded matter is permanently carried down the current. It is sometimes replaced by fresh materials eroded farther upstream, but this material is loosely deposited, carried away again with the next rise of water. Such cycles of erosion, transportation, and the deposition of silt materials are primary factors in the ecology of rivers and streams. Turbulence and character are also important factors in the biosystem of any river or stream, affecting everything from its silt burden to the fish themselves.

Current is also a potential threat to the equilibrium of a flowing biosystem. It can smother a food-sheltering bottom or spawning redds with lethal deposits of silt. Fresh spates can scour out such bottoms or recently deposited beds of silt and detritus, destroying trout eggs and food organisms alike. Sometimes high water is beneficial, cleaning silt and bottom trash from primary beds of gravel, stones, and sheltering structures of small boulders.

Various species are adapted to such habitat. Algal forms cling to the stones with various physical systems, often covering the bottom with black and olive-colored and chocolate carpets of living organisms. Many Diptera larvae cling to the bottom stones too, along with other immature larval and pupal forms. Some mayflies and stoneflies cling to the rocks in swift-flowing currents, and there are also swift-water Ephemeroptera that swim and hopscotch among the stones like acrobats. Caddis larvae build delicate little net systems to shelter themselves and collect their food from the current. Other organisms find naturally sheltered places along the bottom, in crevices behind and between stones that break the flow. Such microhabitat can even provide tiny deposits of silt and trash, sustaining both clambering and burrowing nymphs of many species. These current-loving organisms are typical of rapid streams.

Other organisms are adapted to moderate currents and quiet reaches of any stream. Clambering bottom species of many orders live in these microhabitats, ranging from tiny mayflies to predatory dragonfly and aquatic beetle nymphs. Other quiet-water insects are agile swimmers, like the damselflies and *Siphlonurus* and *Callibaetis* nymphs, while still others burrow into the silt and trash on the bottom. Such organisms complete the full spectrum of a riverine food community.

Such aquatic communities are not static, but are subject to continual cycles of change. Streams carve deeper into both channels and banks, eroding fresh drainage courses and filling in old pools. Deep runs become shallow riffles. Headwater rivulets and streams erode deeper into foothills and mountains, continually extending the length of any riverine system from its mouth. During these cycles, there is a remarkable spectrum of physicochemical change. The sources are usually found in relatively steep topographic zones, tumbling or brawling downstream. These tributaries and headwaters erode their channels inexorably, transforming their character. Once-steep watercourses become slower and deeper, widening and changing their channels. Gradients, rates of flow, and volumes are gradually transformed, until the lower reaches have become mature riverine environments and some zones are almost pondlike in character. The current-loving organisms retreat upstream as a watercourse slowly matures, and the aquatic communities better suited to moderate and comparatively still flowages increase their range. Such cycles of change, in which aquatic communities merge imperceptibly into each other, are called biotic successions in stream ecology.

Water temperature is perhaps the single most important factor in the zoogeography of trout and grayling. The thermal boundaries of any biosystem affect both its food chain and the fish. Aquatic organisms derive their metabolic body temperatures directly from their habitat. Any abrupt changes in water temperatures result in severe physiological stress. Such thermal stress can kill both the fish and their food chain, and both excessive cold and warmth can be traumatic. Brook trout and grayling experience discomfort in water warmer than seventy degrees, and seventy-five degrees is about their thermal ceiling, although there are instances of brook trout populations surviving temperatures one or two degrees higher. Cutthroats display similar thermal preferences. Brown trout have a thermal ceiling of approximately eighty-one degrees in American rivers, although death will sometimes result at slightly lower temperature readings. Rainbow trout are commonly believed to have low temperature thresholds, but there are many instances of their survival between eighty and eighty-three degrees.

Generally speaking, the fish require four times as much oxygen at seventy-five degrees as they need at only forty-odd degrees. Optimal average temperatures typical of spring-fed streams can trigger fine rates of growth, while low average temperatures and brief growing seasons can seriously impair fish populations. Extremely cold temperatures can completely negate the latent fertility of alkaline waters. Temperature and water chemistry are the keys to fishing quality.

It is typically the headwaters and tributaries of trout streams that are coldest and support cold-loving fish like char, cutthroats, golden trout, and grayling. Downstream the water is warmer, supporting rainbows and browns, with the cold-water species in thinning numbers. Cultivated land offers less shade from solar radiation than forest country, and such lower reaches become entirely brown and rainbow water. Since the rainbow often has migratory tendencies, it is usually the brown trout that dominates our lower river systems, replacing native species that once thrived there—before lumbering, agriculture, and pollution completely changed the habitat.

Maximum summer temperatures generally affect our fisheries for only brief periods, lasting at worst several days. Such thermal problems can also display daily cycles. Temperature ceilings are commonly reached in late afternoons under drought conditions, although evaporative cooling starts to lower temperatures as soon as the sun is off the water. Atmospheric temperatures are also a result of altitude and topography. High altitude streams experience lower temperatures and relatively few hot days. Cooler temperatures mean cooler streams. The trout habitat found in many arid regions of our western states and the relict streams that disappear in several dessicating basins from Arizona to southeastern Oregon are possible because of altitude.

It is interesting that thermal variations occur in a trout stream at various depths in both winter and summer. Winter poses some interesting thermal problems. Swift-flowing streams with little springfed volume experience an unusual phenomenon called anchor ice. Since the currents are slowest along the bottom, ice surprisingly forms there first, followed by ice crust along the banks. The ice on the bottom is structured in smooth, current-polished formations that root deep into the stones and gravel. The anchor ice grows steadily as the stream temperatures drop below the freezing point. Finally, the buoyancy of the ice is sufficient to uproot it from the bottom, ripping free food-sheltering layers that become imbedded in the cakes. Sometimes there is enough current to sweep the ice downstream, terribly grinding and damaging the river bed. Such ice floes cause great damage to both the food chain and the fish, freezing or uprooting their spawning redds, and anchor ice can often explain some relatively barren streams.

It has also been found that some thermal stratification occurs in the deeper parts of streams. Trout will seek the bottom zones in search of warmer temperature strata, and an opposite effect is evident in hot weather. It is similar to the temperature layers experienced in lakes and ponds. There is evidence that a really deep pool may have as much as two degrees difference in its surface and bottom temperatures in hot weather. The bottom zone of thermal stratification might have as much as a part per million less oxygenation, but since the fish require less oxygen at lower temperature readings, the cooler bottom flow is often preferable.

Snow is a mixed problem on trout streams. Heavy snowfall can form in floating masses on the surface, impairing rates of flow and accelerating the formation of ice. Thick drifts that have formed over a frozen stream can totally block out sunlight and virtually end photosynthesis. Oxygen deficiency and fish mortality can result. Some organisms are also killed by collapsing snowbanks and bridges, although partial snow coverage can insulate a stream against extremely cold weather, helping its aquatic communities survive the winter.

Water transparency is also a factor in the ecology of a trout stream. Many anglers understand the role of light penetration in lakes and impoundments, but few realize that solar radiation is equally important in lotic environments. Yet research unquestionably demonstrates the presence of more food-chain organisms in open riffles than in shaded zones, even though the latter have constant water temperatures and chemistry. Light penetration, thermal gain and photosynthesis are a partial explanation.

Diatomaceous life, dissolved minerals, silt and detritus, algae, decomposed plants and animals, and other materials all limit the penetration of light into the stream. Such suspended matter cause visible turbidity. Water coloring usually comes from mud, silt, microscopic plants, and tiny organic organisms suspended in its currents. Streams draining densely forested regions or marshes, or having extensive beaver colonies in their headwaters, often carry organic materials from submerged and decomposing plant materials. Newly filled reservoirs also create such water chemistry, forming a surprisingly fertile habitat when their waters are first impounded. Later these leached-out plant materials create tannic acids, and the reservoirs become dark and tea-colored, losing their fertility.

Stream flowages, because of their dynamic character, transport far more matter in suspension than lakes. Lakes and ponds do receive surface runoffs, and wave action can erode shorelines, but erosion is a much greater factor in the rate and volume of flow. The heavy runoffs resulting from precipitation and melting ice and snow often trigger considerable erosion. At such times water transparency suffers badly from the suspended soils. Construction and surface mining also discharge large quantities of silt and gravel into a stream, completely ending the transmission of light energy and ruining its fishery.

Sometimes turbidity results from excessive amounts of algae and other zooplankton suspended in the currents. Streams having rich lakes and impoundments in their headwaters are often filled and discolored with vast populations of algal life floating downriver. Such organisms sustain a rich food chain of life, and in spite of their effects on water transparency, they are often beneficial.

Dissolved gases are equally important in the habitat of trout and grayling, since they are the basis of life itself. Oxygen and carbon dioxide are the primary life-sustaining components of our atmosphere, and dissolved in the water, they play a comparable role in aquatic habitats. Oxygen is absorbed through the gill systems of fish and tracheal tissues of the entire food chain, while they expel the carbon dioxide generated in their metabolic processes. The algae and other plants use the carbon dioxide wastes of the higher organisms in photosynthesis, incorporating solar energy to transform the carbon dioxide into oxygen. Bubbles of oxygen can often be observed rising from plant growth in bright weather, and chemical analysis will demonstrate relatively high levels of oxygenation at such times. Darkness reverses the process, and stream organisms must utilize daytime oxygen after nightfall. The lowest oxygen counts of the daily cycle are typically recorded just before daylight.

The sources of both oxygen and carbon dioxide in a stream are varied. Our atmosphere holds a mixture of these critical gases, along with other matter in gaseous form, but the diffusion of oxygen and carbon dioxide from the air into the water is quite slow. Most of the dissolved oxygen and carbon dioxide in any aquatic habitat is the result of metabolic processes among its plant and animal communities. Other oxygen is entrained through the aerating effects of rapids and waterfalls and riffles. Carbon dioxide is also absorbed in small quantities from the atmosphere. However, most dissolved carbon dioxide is generated in the subaquatic decomposition of organic matter, and the respiration of its biotic populations.

Water temperatures have a direct impact on the oxygenation of aquatic habitat. Cold water holds more oxygen than warm water. Studies have shown that water under constant atmospheric pressure can entrain almost twice the oxygen at thirty-two degrees that it can hold at eighty-six degrees. Such measurements in parts per million are based upon an atmosphere holding 20.9 percent oxygen and a sea-level air pressure of 760 millimeters. The following oxygen readings indicate the maximum solubility of oxygen under the temperatures and conditions described, but it should be understood that much lower counts are likely under actual conditions:

SOLUBILITY OF OXYGEN
AT VARIOUS TEMPERATURES

THERMAL READING	OXYGEN PPM	THERMAL READING	OXYGEN PPM
32°	14.6	68°	9.2
41°	12.8	77°	8.4
50°	11.3	83°	7.9
59°	10.2	86°	7.6

Atmospheric pressure changes also affect the solubility of oxygen in the stream. Less oxygenation will occur in high-country streams and lakes at the same temperatures, since the density of the atmosphere is far less than at sea level. It is interesting that a simultaneous increase in air pressure and decrease in atmospheric temperatures will dramatically increase oxygenation. These are precisely the conditions that prevail when a cold front purges a period of hot weather and increased oxygen triggers the feeding urge of the fish. The reverse is also true. Low-pressure fronts are accompanied by decreasing temperatures and atmospheric pressure and a sharp drop in both dissolved oxygen and the fishing.

Rainfall and snowmelt also have interesting effects on oxygenation of trout habitat. Hewitt observed many years ago in *Telling on the Trout* that snowmelt consistently put the fish down and stopped their taking moods. His conclusions were based on the positive electrical charge of raindrops and the negative charge of snowflakes and that such ionization affected his trout. Hewitt offered no explanation for their behavior on the Neversink, but some years ago I experienced some unusual fishing in northern Europe that offered possible insights into the problem.

Norwegian brown trout are like most fish in marine climates, thriving on continual rainfall. Unless the precipitation is unusual their rivers remain normal and flow clear, but bright weather is another problem. Sunshine and clear skies are unusual in Norway, and it makes the rivers rise and run a little milky. The bright weather melts the glaciers and snow fields in the mountains, and the fishing soon deteriorates. The curious cycle is predictable and can be explained in terms of differences in dissolved oxygen.

Falling rain increases oxygenation and carbon dioxide, both in its passage through the atmosphere and its agitation of the surface film. The rise in dissolved oxygen triggers increased activity in the fish and their feeding rhythms. However, a heavy downpour can result in too rapid an increase in oxygen and a kind of hyperventilation. Snowmelt is completely different in its effects. It increases the volume and rate of flow, but does not provide a proportional increase in the level of dissolved oxygen. The result is a rapid drop in oxygen, and the fish experience enough discomfort to stop their activity. Rain and snowmelt have different thermal effects too. Rainfall usually passes through air much warmer than the river, at least in early and late season, and its temperature tends to warm the water slightly. Midsummer rains fall through cool upper air and can temper the effects of river temperatures that are marginal and too warm. But snowmelt is usually much colder than the river itself, and large amounts of melting snow entering a stream can result in a form of thermal shock.

Dissolved oxygen is obviously the result of many factors. Temperature and atmospheric pressure are basic, along with physicochemical aeration in contact with the atmosphere. The photosynthetic effects of aquatic plants are important too, and are balanced by oxygen-burning organisms. Weather, solar illumination, and time of day all affect oxygenation in continuing patterns of change, along with irregular periods of turbidity. Finally, the effects of precipitation and snowmelt are important in determining dissolved oxygen.

Various studies demonstrate that trout and grayling can survive marginally low oxygen levels for brief periods without expiring. Brook-trout habitat will cause asphyxiation if its dissolved oxygen falls under four parts per million. Brown trout have similar oxygen limits, although they can withstand higher temperatures. Rainbows have the highest thermal limits among the principal species, although they cannot tolerate such warm temperatures unless the oxygenation is approximately eight parts per million. Studies in dissolved oxygen indicate that four parts per million is a safe rule-of-thumb minimum for trout habitat, certainly preventing asphyxiation, but higher levels are critical for optimal feeding and growth. However, at any thermal reading within the limits of tolerance for trout and grayling the precise minimums of dissolved oxygen needed to prevent death are not fully understood.

Some intriguing research has been performed with brown-trout fingerlings in eastern waters, demonstrating that oxygen stagnation can occur well within thermal tolerances. Oxygen and carbon dioxide readings were taken regularly, along with observations of water temperature and the respiratory rhythms. This experiment confirms a study performed at the Hackettstown hatchery in New Jersey forty-odd years ago.

OXYGEN DEFICIENCY
IN BROWN-TROUT FINGERLINGS

OXYGEN PPM	CO_2 PPM	WATER TEMPERATURE	GILL RATE
7.0	9.2	54°	120
5.7	12.1	57°	132
4.6	13.9	60°	139
3.0	17.8	64°	161
2.7	20.1	65°	170
2.5	21.0	66°	170
2.3	21.7	67°	170

Although they differ somewhat from those obtained in the earlier work, these results are intriguing. The fish were agile and actively feeding with an oxygen level of seven parts per million and a temperature of fifty-four degrees. Water temperatures steadily increased into the afternoon, exhibiting a rise of thirteen degrees over an eight-hour period. Both the activity and condition of the trout seemed excellent with the water temperature at fifty-seven degrees and the oxygen at just under six parts per million, although their respiration had increased to 132 gill pulses per minute.

The fish displayed considerable distress and darted restlessly in their aquarium when the dissolved oxygen had dropped below approximately four parts per million. The first fingerling died at three parts per million dissolved oxygen and slightly more than seventeen parts per million carbon dioxide, although the water was still an optimal sixty-four degrees. The pulse rate of the gill system was a fluttery 161 per minute.

The fish were floundering and gasping in the surface film when the soluble oxygen dropped well below three parts per million, with a carbon dioxide level seven times that concentration, and the temperature only sixty-six degrees. Beyond this point, virtually all the fish were dead or dying, and the respiration had reached 170 gill pulses per minute. It is interesting that the pulse rate remained constant once the oxygen count dropped under three parts per million, indicating that it may define some physiological ceiling.

Trout streams are particularly rich in dissolved oxygen, and such viable habitat does not reach the minimal concentrations needed by the fish to survive. Most trout and grayling waters seldom reach seventy degrees over the yearly cycle, and at these relatively low temperatures, the ambient levels of dissolved oxygen are well above the lethal threshold. Oxygen depletion seldom occurs in unpolluted streams having either a rapid flow rate or adequate weed growth.

Most trout streams test between five and ten parts per million of dissolved oxygen. Since both natural and manmade forms of pollution cannot decompose without consuming oxygen, thereby making contamination a threat to viable oxygen concentrations, slow-flowing streams too acid to support much oxygen-producing plant life, low water and prolonged hot weather, and pollution can all combine to produce dangerously low levels of oxygenation.

The effect of carbon dioxide on a trout stream is not fully understood. Its reciprocal relationship with oxygen consumption and photosynthesis is obvious enough, and the role of bound carbon dioxide in indicating alkalinity is relatively well known among anglers, but its character also has a darker side in trout and grayling habitat. High concentrations of carbon dioxide are seldom injurious to a fishery unless they are matched with minimal levels of dissolved oxygen. Carbon dioxide has little effect in waters having good oxygenation, but some springheads are known for extremely high levels of both carbon dioxide and nitrogen. There are many examples of subsurface hydrology having high carbon dioxide levels. Such springs become toxic to the fish when drought conditions reduce normal surface flow to dangerously low volumes. These so-called soda springs of carbonated water are found throughout the west. Little is known about a proper equilibrium between oxygen and carbon dioxide under these conditions, but studies indicate that trout ova simply do not develop at carbon dioxide levels of twenty-two parts per million, with oxygen concentrations of under five parts per million. The same ova developed normally and hatched with fifteen parts per million of carbon dioxide, and an oxygen concentration of five to six parts per million.

Lime salts are combined with carbon dioxide to form calcium carbonate concentrations, and sometimes ambient magnesia exist to form magnesium carbonates. These simple carbonates are virtually insoluble in habitats deficient in carbon dioxide, but with it in ample concentrations, they become soluble bicarbonates. Marls and limestones are ancient calcium and magnesium carbonates, formed about the skeletons of numberless crustaceans, snails, shellfish, and lime-encrusted plants. Since carbon dioxide is critical to dissolving these alkaline riches in trout waters, its concentrations are also a valuable bench mark of their fertility. Marl deposits are often surprisingly thick, and ancient lakes that have eutrophied into swamps often provide alkalinity to adjacent streams. Waters displaying rich alkalinity derived from carbonates, bicarbonates, and various allied salts provide exceptional fish habitats. Limestone regions often generate unusually large springs, with their remarkable subsurface hydrology, and flowages rich in calcium oxides. Watersheds leaching through phosphate deposits also produce rich fisheries. Perhaps the best known river of this type is the Big Hole, which is cold and less fertile above the Glaus Ranch. It receives alkalinity from a small spring creek on the Mallon property downstream and several larger spring creeks on the old McGinley Ranch. The Wise River is partially alkaline, receiving the leachings of several creeks draining phosphate basins, and joins the Big Hole across from Jimmy New Creek. Jerry Creek lies downstream, its drainage basin partially structured of phosphate deposits, and the watercress springs below the Jerry Creek Bridge are also a rich source of alkalinity. Although many fishermen are familiar with the Big Hole much farther downstream, between its canyon and the arid cottonwood country below Melrose and Divide, few of them realize that much of its rich alkalinity begins in the Wise River basin.

There are many other factors in water chemistry, and some of them are not entirely beneficial. Others which are usually harmful can help under certain conditions. Dissolved carbonic acid is a typical example. Many springs are leached through ancient igneous formations and reach the surface virtually devoid of lime salts and oxygen, with free acids included in their flow. The famous spring at the Hewitt Camp on the Neversink, which Sparse Gray Hackle describes so movingly in *Fishless Days*, was actually fatal to trout in spite of its sweet-tasting water. Its dissolved oxygen was slightly more than five parts per million, in concert with fifteen parts per million of carbon dioxide. Its calcium oxide measured nineteen parts per million. None of these readings is necessarily indicative of problems, but without more alkalinity and bound carbon dioxide, the fourteen parts per million of carbonic acid are invariably fatal to trout. However, Edward Hewitt found that ample dissolved lime salts simply combine with carbonic acid to form bicarbonate compounds, even when the acid concentrations reached thirty-five parts per million.

Nitrogen is another problem. Our atmosphere usually consists of seventy-nine parts nitrogen to only twenty-one parts oxygen, along with other components. Some biologists believe that the fish often stop feeding after a hard rain due to nitrogen being entrained in the raindrops in their passage through the atmosphere. Free nitrogen is sometimes found in water samples from springheads, deep impoundments and lakes, and in many wells. Nitrogen is probably mixed in surface waters from nitrogen-producing bacteria or physicochemical contact with the atmosphere. Few waters have excessive concentrations of nitrogen, since the natural aeration of a tumbling current quickly releases it from a stream. Nitrogen has been isolated as the principal cause of the so-called gas disease in trout. Its primary symptoms are gas bubbles in the fins, internal organs, gill system, under the dermal covering, and behind the eye sockets—causing the eyeballs to protrude grotesquely.

Fish holding in springholes and flowing sinks in limestone country are often the victims of this popeye disease. Such trout have chosen the worst possible habitat, since they are lying directly in the spring as it wells up from the bottom. The water has no chance to expel its nitrogen, and under some conditions acute distress and mortality can result. Toxic concentrations of nitrogen have also recently been recorded below several large western reservoirs. Apparently it was formed in their extremely deep impoundments and released through penstocks, directly from the nitrogen-saturated strata, and extensive fishkills have occurred in recent years. Such toxic concentrations of nitrogen were obviously never considered in the performance specifications and design of modern reservoirs, and a successful fish ladder is relatively meaningless unless such biosystemic problems are solved to facilitate downstream migrations.

There is a fine little spring creek in Jackson Hole that has spring seepages visibly bubbling up from the bottom in one waist-deep flat. It was always empty of fish, although the creek was filled with big cutthroats and the odd rainbow, and it was another hundred yards before we found trout. It always puzzled me until I took some water samples of the cold spring water and found they held almost toxic levels of nitrogen.

Methane is common swamp gas. It is generated by the decomposition of bottom materials at extremely low concentrations of dissolved oxygen. It is not encountered in streams having steep gradients and strong rates of flow. It is primarily found in backwaters and beaver ponds and marshy sections of streams, where the soft bottoms are composed of silt and rotting plant materials and diatomaceous organisms. Considerable volumes of methane are formed in summer, and its fetid bubbles are often released from the muck by a wading fisherman. The marshy backwaters of the Nissequogue are rich in methane concentrations. Methane is inflammable, and its spontaneous combustion occurs in marshes on hot summer nights. There was often swamp fire in the bogs along my first boyhood creek in Michigan, and sometimes its eerie flashes danced on the headstones in a cemetery above a favorite meadow.

Hydrogen sulphides are also generated in some slow-flowing streams, and quite low concentrations are often toxic to trout and grayling when they occur. Ambient stream conditions typically include trace concentrations far less than one part per million. Research with brook trout indicates that these fish die at approximately .85 parts per million of hydrogen sulphide, while browns and rainbows seem able to withstand concentrations of about .88 parts per million. Hydrogen sulphides are often found in trout hatcheries, generated by the decomposition of surplus food pellets and excretory wastes from the fish. Similar problems can exist below the effluents of food-processing plants or cattle feedlots or trout farms.

Through the process of photosynthesis weeds play a major role in generating oxygen for both the fish and their food chain, as well as purging biodegradable wastes from their habitat. Compared with the lexicon of plant forms which exist on land, relatively few species are truly aquatic, and even their reproductory pollens are transmitted through the atmosphere. They blossom above the water, although their respiration and root structures are subaquatic, and they are usually members of larger terrestrial orders. Their ecology is like the mayflies', since most of their lives are spent in the underwater cycle, yet they enter our world to reproduce.

Most aquatic plants are found in ponds and reservoirs and lakes, although there are some which are endemic to swift-flowing habitats suited to trout and grayling. Aquatic liverworts and mosses are plant forms loving shade and moisture, absorbing water eagerly and losing it again rapidly, so their cells must constantly replace it. Most liverworts and mosses are found in moist places on land, and a few are found in quiet waters, but many more are found in flowing streams. Liverworts are similar to algae in some traits that indicate they may have wholly aquatic origins, but their present morphology more closely parallels the mosses. The liverworts are members of the class Hepaticae, and their metabolic processes occur in a leaflike thallus. Its function echoes the role of roots and leaves in higher plants.

Aquatic mosses are quite similar to liverworts and lichens. Unlike the liverworts, true mosses have flat leaves. The most common water mosses are slender plants which undulate gracefully in the current, their roots often attached to rubble and stones. The pale green *Dichelyma* is perhaps the best known genus, and our most common species is yellowish toward its leafy tips and chocolate colored toward the roots. Its aquamarine stems are densely matted, and the reproductive spores mature in the summer months. Fountain mosses are most numerous in swift streams, densely rooted on the bottom deadfalls and stones, and are less common in quiet waters. Their stems average about three inches, branching their spreading leaf systems on irregular stems. Fountain mosses are members of the *Fontinalis* genus and are quite common in our waters. The giant fountain moss is readily distinguished by its densely armored leaves. Its spores mature in summer, but the capsules are concealed by the leaves. The hypnums are pale green and medium green mosses of the *Hygrohypnum* genus, and have delicate branches averaging two to four inches in length. Its growths are also rooted on the rocks in swift currents.

The aquatic seed-type plants are similar to terrestrial species in their biology. Many species thrive quite well in marshy places and on damp shorelines. Most have a typical plant morphology of roots, stem, leaves and blossoms, and these components function like the parallel parts in terrestrial plants. Like such terrestrial species, the aquatic plants have a petiole or stem, and leaf blade and midrib structure. Their flowers have a pedicel or stalk, the male pollen-producing stamen, and the pistils, which receive the pollen cells and transmit them to the ovaries. The sepals shape these several parts and protect them, while the blossoms themselves are designed to attract pollen-carrying insects to their sexual parts. The pistil is rooted in the core of the flower. Its enlarged bulbous root is the ovary and ovular system. Its stigmatic tip supports the pollen cells. The stamens enclose and encircle the pistil. Each stamen consists of a stemlike filament and its anther tip, which holds the pollen grains. The pollen is transported by the wind or carried by insects, and pollination is achieved when it reaches the stigma of the pistil. Finally the core of the pollen cell fuses with the egg, which evolves into a seed inside its protective covering.

The *Potamogetons* are leaf-type plants found in American trout waters, although none is known to thrive in fully lotic habitats. The long-stem types are the floating-leaf pondweed, bass weed, ruffle-leaf pondweed, muskie weed, and oval-leaf pondweed. The ribbon-leaf pondweeds include a floating-leaf species, the narrow-leaf pondweed, the flat-stemmed eel grass, and the familiar sago pondweed. These several pondweeds are first-rate oxygenators and are extremely common in alkaline environments. Only the sago pondweed is found extensively in streams, even thriving in brackish tidal zones. It is classified as *Potamogeton pectinatus* and sprouts from its tubers in the spring, one of the earliest plants to emerge each season. It thrives in water from one to six feet deep, its stems reaching lengths of six to eight feet. There are approximately forty species of this group, and they are perhaps our most important angiospermic aquatic growths. Their roots are firmly seated in the bottom, and in still waters their drifting leaf structures are wholly submerged, except for their flowers. Some species have floating leaves. Their luxuriant growths provide sustenance and shelter for the entire biosystem.

The filamentous and thread-leaf plants include some species ideally suited to trout streams. However, these genera also include hornwort and the bothersome *Elodea*, which plagues many of our eastern limestone streams. Coontail and hornwort usually grow in ponds or slow-flowing waters throughout our temperate latitudes, and its extensive growths are usually submerged. The common hornwort is *Ceratophyllum demersum*, and its delicately formed leaves are gathered in circular whorls around the stems. Drifting stems measure from one to three feet in length, and are not rooted into the bottom. The coontail and hornwort beds are often so dense that they eradicate competitive species, and these dense, aquatic fernlike growths shelter and feed rich food-chain communities. Although these beds are troublesome in most trout streams, they are present in some fine natural fisheries like Silver Creek in central Idaho, and on productive little Putah Creek near San Francisco.

The common water weed *Elodea canadensis* should never be introduced into a trout stream, since it is a vigorous plant that threatens to choke any habitat. Perhaps its worst trait is the tendency to collect silt around its root systems, smothering formerly clean areas of pea gravel. It is remarkably adaptable and truly aquatic. It thrives both loosely-rooted and floating free of the bottom, drifting downstream in its trout-stream communities. It thrives so well that it often literally forces a small stream from its banks. Its fat stems are densely textured with delicate whorls of darkly translucent leaves. Each has a single vein and its fibers are paper thin. Its stems are fragile, breaking off frequently and drifting in the currents. These fragments can thrive and grow separately, quickly rooting new plants and filling its channels. *Elodea canadensis* is a beautiful species with its delicate flowers on slender stems that reach the surface, but it spreads with amazing rapacity and chokes out more desirable plants. It shelters exceptional populations of scuds and mayfly nymphs and sowbugs in richly alkaline habitat, although its growth usually eradicates any fishable channels. It is widespread in our northeastern states, reaching south to Virginia and Tennessee, and westward as far as Colorado and Wyoming. It thrives best in alkaline waters, and its lush growth is a difficult problem on limestone streams like Big Spring and Spring Creek and Letort Spring Run in Pennsylvania.

There are several milfoils found in slow-flowing American trout streams. The common mare's tail *Hippurus vulgaris* is a perennial aquatic plant, rooting itself in the shallows. It is easily recognized by its cactuslike appearance, and its whorls of six to twelve spiny leaves. The leaves are stiff and thornlike above the water, but below the meniscus they are flaccid and drooping. Its minute blossoms encircle the stem at the base of the leaves. It is not especially valuable as either an oxygenator or shelter for food-chain populations. The foxtail milfoil is *Myriophyllum spicatum* and is rooted with rich fernlike beds in slow-flowing American streams. It is a superb oxygenating species. Its roots reach deep into the silt and detritus, and its graceful stems and filaments reach toward the surface. Its richly colored little flowers project into the atmosphere where pollination occurs, and it has some importance in slow-flowing streams. Its range is from Labrador into the Great Lakes system and south along the Atlantic seaboard to the Carolinas. There are several American species.

Watercress is a familiar aquatic plant, since it is often a part of our diet. It is a fine oxygenator, thriving best in cold spring-fed streams of rich alkalinity. Its branching stems work in vinelike runners along the bottom, forming new roots and greatly expanding the cress beds. Most of their growth is submerged through much of the year, although in the summer particularly lush beds of cress project as much as a foot above the water. There are tiny white flowers, their petals in a delicate cruciform shape which typically identifies the Cruciferae family of plants. During the winter on the spring-fed limestone creeks of Pennsylvania the green watercress along the banks contrasts sharply with the barren stream bottom and snowbanks. Particularly dense beds of watercress are often surprisingly buoyant, even supporting the weight of an angler who moves about carefully on his knees. Many times I have used them in getting my fly over a difficult trout on the Pennsylvania limestone streams.

There are two filamentous aquatic plants that are particularly recommended in trout streams. The chara or stonewort is a fine oxygenator that thrives in cold-water biosystems, and the bushy pondweed *Najas flexilis* is another. Bushy pondweed grows best in alkaline water, but chara will thrive in waters as acid as five parts per million of carbon dioxide. The pondweed grows in an intricately matted carpet, its soft grainlike leaves measuring about one-half inch, and in summer it can cover the bottom of the quiet backwaters. Both species are excellent sources of food and shelter for nymphs and tiny crustaceans and larvae, and introducing them to any suitable habitat is advisable.

The pad and strip-leaf weeds are not usually found in trout streams, but there are fine stream environments that include food lilies and spatterdock and water lilies in their quiet eddies and shallows. The yellow pond lily *Nymphaea variegata* and the spatterdock lily *Nymphaea advena* are perhaps the best known species. The common water lily *Castalia odorata* is perhaps less important in trout streams than its smaller cousins. These plants are not particularly good oxygenators, and since they grow best out of the principal currents, they are not exceptional cover for trout.

Eel grass is somewhat better, providing excellent oxygenation and food-chain shelter. Our most familiar species is perhaps *Vallisneria spiralis*, always seen with its slender leaves streaming in the current. It is a bottom-rooting plant, with leaves as long as two to three feet, although seldom more than three-eighths of an inch in width. Its tiny green flowers are found on such delicately supple stems that they remain at the surface in spite of the current or the wind. The male blossoms develop from the root system, separating from their stems upon reaching sexual maturity and buoying toward the surface. Once there, the male flowers either float or drift with the current until they contact the female blossoms. After pollination is complete, the female stems contract and draw the maturing seeds back toward the bottom. Although eel grass is unquestionably more important in lakes and ponds, it can also play a useful role in trout-stream ecology.

Although commonly found in slow-flowing habitat, plants like arrowhead and pickerel weed are only fair oxygenators, and lie well away from fish-holding currents. Dragonfly and damselfly nymphs often creep through the surface film on their stalks, shedding their skins and hatching in the atmosphere. Cattails and bulrushes and tules are only fair oxygen-generating plants, along with duckweed and stargrass and smartweed. There are many stretches of fine spring-fed streams, like famous Silver Creek in Idaho, that are densely bordered with tules as high as your head. Our waters have many other small stiff-leafed aquatic plants like water grass and creeping buttercups and quillwort, but they are rarely found in trout streams.

It is these primary species of plant life that sustain and shelter the principal foods of the trout. It is advisable to cut and maintain viable channels in dense growths of weed, but permanent beds should also be preserved. Their role in oxygenation and fly life is critical. Desirable species of aquatic plants can be transplanted by weighting root cuttings down on the silt and gravel bottoms, allowing them to take hold and spread naturally. Sometimes an undesirable species of weed is able to displace plants better suited to trout streams. Such pest species can often be cut or uprooted, and once these troublesome weeds are cleared, it is worth trying to recultivate the original ecotypes. However, except for chara weed, virtually all of the plant forms grow best in neutral or alkaline water. It is impractical to transplant them into acid streams having little existing vegetation. Lush growths of aquatic plants are symptomatic of stream fertility, although some fishing writers have mistakenly believed they were its primary cause, rather than merely another result of a lime-rich water chemistry.

Stream fertility is also the result of the character and size of its watercourse. Trout and grayling occupy the head of the aquatic food chain, and productivity of these species varies widely. Poor waters deficient in lime salts can grow as little as five pounds of fish life per acre annually, while extremely rich waters produce as much as sixty pounds. It is interesting that relatively narrow streams grow many more fish per acre than larger waters, because the banks and shallows shelter proportionately more food. Edward Ringwood Hewitt estimated in *A Trout and Salmon Fisherman for Seventy-five Years* that the average American trout stream produced and sustained about fifteen pounds of fish per acre. However, Hewitt was largely unfamiliar with the water chemistry of the richly alkaline rivers from Michigan to the Pacific Coast, particularly the fly-rich streams of northern California in the headwaters of the Sacramento Basin. Twenty-five pounds per acre is perhaps a better annual average of stream productivity, although Hewitt is unquestionably correct about our eastern mountain streams. Using the twenty-five pound average, harvesting these fish at minimum legal size would mean one hundred quarter-pound trout. Catching them at half-pound size would mean fifty fish available per acre of stream, but the same acreage would produce and sustain only twenty-five trout weighing a pound. The following table is workable in estimating trout populations for different widths of stream:

FACTORS OF STREAM SIZE
AND BOTTOM ACREAGE

STREAM WIDTH	FEET PER ACRE	MILES PER ACRE
10 feet	4,400 feet	.83 mile
25 feet	1,760 feet	.33 mile
50 feet	880 feet	.16 mile
100 feet	440 feet	.08 mile
150 feet	330 feet	.06 mile
200 feet	220 feet	.04 mile
250 feet	165 feet	.03 mile
300 feet	110 feet	.02 mile

These yardsticks mean that five miles of stream averaging fifty feet in width totals slightly more than thirty acres of water. Such acreage will produce and support approximately 750 pounds of trout and grayling, meaning 1,500 half-pound fish or 750 averaging a pound. Such fish populations are surprisingly small, and the fishing pressure near our major cities could quickly decimate them.

However, the estimate of twenty-five pounds per acre is based on streams of slight to moderate alkalinity. The bound carbon-dioxide rating of such waters would average between twenty to twenty-five parts per million. Famous Catskill rivers like the Beaverkill, Willowemoc and Neversink are far less productive, since their water chemistry averages about five parts per million or less of bound carbon dioxide. This slight acidity means five miles of water approximately fifty feet wide will produce only 150 pounds of fish. Such a yield factors out into only 300 trout of the half-pound size and 150 of the desirable one-pound average.

It is interesting to compare these estimates of productivity with the Firehole in Yellowstone Park, Hat Creek in northern California, and Letort Spring Run in Pennsylvania—three of the richest streams in the United States. The Firehole averages from sixty to eighty parts per million of bound carbon dioxide, and can produce as much as sixty-odd pounds of trout per acre of bottom. Our theoretical five-mile stretch of its waters would produce 1,800 pounds of brown and rainbow trout or some 3,600 half-pound fish. Hat Creek has a similar water chemistry, capable of sustaining almost 3,200 half-pound trout in only five miles of water. Letort Spring Run is almost twice as rich as the Firehole, with between ninety and one hundred parts per million. It can produce and sustain a remarkable eighty pounds of fish per acre, and that means our theoretical river could hold 2,400 pounds of trout. Such a population could mean 4,800 half-pounders, or 2,400 twelve-inch fish in only five miles of water. However, the Letort is actually much smaller. Its four miles of water above Carlisle averages more nearly ten to fifteen feet in width and totals about seven to eight acres of bottom. Such an acreage could still mean 500 to 700 pounds of fish in a relatively small stream. Since its lower mileage is polluted by the town of Carlisle and its complex of industrial and military facilities, its incredible potential as a fishery is lost below the town. Its reclamation could add perhaps 10,000 wild catchable fish to one of the finest trout streams anywhere.

Such streams are highly atypical in their fertility, and rivers having between 300 and 1,000 catchable fish in five miles of water are a better yardstick of water quality. It is obvious why many streams are quickly fished out, if their natural productivity is the only source of their fish population. Of course, few streams rely on static populations in any given mileage. Fish are added from the smaller nursery-size waters upstream and from spawning redds in the tributaries. Other larger trout migrate upstream from wintering holes in the lower reaches of river, or to escape its midsummer temperatures. Such upstream migrants often make a given stretch of trout stream seem more productive than its basic fertility.

Where substantial fishing pressure exists, obviously 300 to 1,000 catchable trout in five miles of water cannot provide continuing sport. Such a fishable population cannot sustain very many limit catches before a stream is emptied of its trout. Our traditional solution, deeply rooted in hierarchical organizations of hatcheries and the local politics of stocking programs, lies in planting enough fish to keep providing dead trout in the creel. It is a solution that has never worked anywhere, yet its failure is still not apparent to many politicians and fishery commissions. Surprisingly small percentages of the trout planted in our streams are ever recovered by fishermen. Sometimes as few as forty percent are actually caught. It is interesting to speculate how many other state and federal spending programs would be permitted to continue, particularly in support of leisure recreation, if research clearly proved half the money was wasted.

Stocking catchable trout in concentrated numbers and placing them in easily accessible pools along roads and highways and bridges can improve the percentages of recovery. But fresh concentrations of foolish truck fish also attract crowds of meat fishermen, eager to recoup their license fees in dead hatchery trout. Eighty percent of these fish can be harvested, but the method makes a hollow mockery of our sport, with its history of skill and tradition and solitude.

Statistics also underscore another fact. The fifty percent of stocked trout that escape angling pressure are ill equipped to survive. Knowing nothing of predators or natural diet and expecting food when they see a fisherman, they are pale imitations of the stream-bred trout. Hatchery fish are also poorly suited to competing with existing fish populations. Recent studies indicate that stocked fish are accustomed to the population densities of hatcheries and tend toward a form of schooling behavior that unnerves the resident trout, which prefer solitary lies and exhibit strong instincts of territoriality. Quarrels often erupt between the new truck-fish arrivals and the established residents, with the old fish pursuing the pen-raised immigrants in wild gyrations through the shallows. It is a symptom of too many hatchery trout superimposed on a pool with an adequate existing population.

It is interesting that hatchery fish are recovered soon after stocking on public water or not recovered at all, and that they play a minimal role in catches later in the season. Studies of catch figures across the full season will reveal, particularly on our western streams, that most of the fish taken during a full season were spawned naturally. Since hatchery trout are unaccustomed to wild forage, those that do survive the fishing season and the following winter are invariably in rather poor condition. Our experience in recent years indicates that many one-pound stocked fish will attempt spawning their first autumn or spring in the stream, some actually building successful redds that contribute young fish in future seasons. However, these hatchery fish seldom recover well from the weight loss and protein deficiency that follows their spawning, and their poor condition provides only marginal sport the following spring.

Stocking programs should perhaps be limited to replacing estimated winterkills, with long-range management efforts focused on so-called Vibert stockings of fertile eggs and low bag-limit regulations. The Vibert box has better than ninety-percent survival of the eggs to the alevin size, while less than five percent reach that stage of growth from the actual spawning redds. Unlike stocked fingerlings, which have been raised on artificial foods and fail to recognize the microscopic diet forms of baby wild trout, the fry emerging from the Vibert box are conditioned to a stream diet from the start. The Vibert fry also see predators from the beginning of their lives and are not placed directly from their incubatorlike isolation into the hostility of river life, where their first mistake is their last.

But the best solution to better fishing lies in reducing the considerable fishkill that results from heavy angling pressure. Fly-caught trout suffer quite small mortality rates when properly handled and can offer good sport again and again, unless they are creeled the first time they are caught. Reducing existing limits fifty percent means that fishing is twice as good without any other change in fisheries management or costs. No-kill regulations can make the sport ten times as good in states having ten-fish limits now. There is no other workable solution. Such management strategies have little relationship to the poetry of our trout streams, except that a trout stream tragically emptied of its trout is rather like a jewel box without its jewels.

Trout streams are richly interwoven with the regions through which they flow, shaded in dense forests or providing a fragile thread of life in the arid foothills of our western mountains. Streams trade the life force of their water for the elements eroded from their beds and bank soils and the nutrients of plant and animal life that decompose in their currents. Such interrelationships are less intimate as a stream grows larger, until finally a river is virtually a biosystem in itself, depending less and less on interaction with its banks. The bottom silts of such rivers are both a product of their own erosion and transport and of their ancient origins in primordial lakes and glaciers. Their water is the cumulative ecology of countless spring-heads and tributary streams, each leaching through different geology and soils and each having its unique chemical fingerprints. Such rivers are hybrids in that sense, their character so pervasively independent of their surroundings that they sometimes dominate an entire valley. Each river evolves its own singular community of life, increasing its biota in size and diversity as its volume grows. Its lower mileages even develop their own spectrum of plankton and zooplankton, until its currents finally mingle with tidewater, and the river begins losing its identity in the sea.

Rivers are the ancient routes used by marine forms of life to evolve toward terrestrial life, and their tidal estuaries are modern echoes of those primordial millenniums. It is here that freshwater organisms adaptable to marine life are carried into a brackish habitat, and salt-water species capable of tolerating less salinity are carried upriver on the tidal cycles. Sometimes we forget that our rivers are constantly changing, and that the natural forces which originally shaped them have not stopped. We must remember that any river system is transitory in geological terms, its morphology and physiology changing before our eyes, in spite of our intentions for its future. Its geomorphology and water chemistry harbor infinitely more pervasive forces than any reservoir or source of pollution, since they are part of the imperceptible changes we seldom observe and cannot really change radically. It is a valuable perspective to understand that our effects, for better and for worse, are minor beside the effects of climatological changes, shifting channels, seismic uplifts and landslides, violent storms, and volcanic eruptions and lava flows. Yet even these natural forces are minor compared with changes measured in terms of changing climates or geological time, and in attempting to preserve the character of our rivers, it is important to understand exactly what it is possible to save.

It is equally important that we accept our ignorance of their topologies, no matter how much we know of riverine life. The full mystery of their rhythms remains clearly beyond our knowledge, and if we truly understood a river, we could also measure the parameters of life. But the ultimate poetry and biology of a trout stream remain as puzzling as the full spectrum of fly-fishing itself.

4. The Biosystems of
Lakes and Impoundments

It was dark with willows and conifers above the meadows. In some places the little stream flowed through quivering bogs of sand and calcareous marl, and finally its cedar-swamp springs reached the sunlight in a logging pond. The shallows there were filled with stumps and deadfalls. There was a huge beaver house below the inlet shallows, where the tea-colored eutrophic riches of the headwater swamps were thick with pondweed and bladderworts.

The brook trout held deep over the emerald-colored beds of *Dichelyma* moss, cruising in nervous ghostlike schools. The fish were bright with color in these swampy waters, and they cruised beyond the range and skills of my boyhood casting.

Although I regularly caught trout in the serpentine meadows downstream, the fish in the pond eluded me. Sometimes I frightened them into terror-stricken flight up the channel into the bottom moss and bladderwort. Bright sunlight illuminated every strand of weeds and waterlogged sticks with remarkable clarity. Each pebble was visible on the bottom near the inlet, where the faint current eddied through the fountain mosses. The trout completely vanished each time I startled them.

Finally I learned to stalk the fish, creeping low along the cribbing of the dam, but even on the mornings when the impoundment was lightly riffled by the wind, my luck was invariably poor. My casting was both clumsy and weak in those early summers, and I took most of my fish merely dapping the fly along the creek itself. Still mornings were completely hopeless. The trout scattered like quail at the first presentation of my flies, and it was a summer of frustration. Sometimes I sat in the grass after the fish had disappeared into the weeds, watching the damselfly nymphs on the cribbing that reached down into the still water. It was a world I failed to understand, and its trout escaped me easily.

Lakes and impoundments seem less complicated than streams, but in many ways their ecology is more complex. Fishing them with a wind-riffle on the water is relatively easy, but a still lake in bright sunlight is a really demanding yardstick of our skills. There is neither a current nor a wind riffle to mask our mistakes.

Lakes are literally the prisoners of their topography, since to exist they must occupy a natural basin. The zoography of the trout and grayling and char is circumpolar, their original range limited to the northern hemisphere. The millions of lakes lying in these temperate and subarctic latitudes are largely the product of ancient glaciers. Their grinding forces are clearly visible above the tree line, where the linear fingerprints of the ice fields are deeply scarred into bedrock. The lakes themselves are linear, lying parallel and radiating from the arctic source of the glaciers that carved them. Some lakes were deeply scoured when the ice fields encountered the relatively loose aggregates of ancient streambeds. Others were formed when huge deposits of ice were imbedded in giant moraines of glacial drift and subsequently melted. Still others were shaped by the impounding topography of their terminal moraines, or trapped by ancient earthquakes and eruptions.

Such forces still exist in modern times. Less than a dozen years ago, an earthquake with its epicenter in the northwest section of the Yellowstone triggered a massive landslide in Montana. The collapsing mountain permanently blocked the Madison River, forming a surprisingly large new lake. It was a tragic echo of the seismic violence that has given birth to many such lakes. Earthquakes in Chile have radically changed the gradients of many streams, slowing their rates of flow, warming their temperatures, and changing the thermal character of many Chilean lakes. Abrasive silts stirred from the bottom in violent earthquake shocks and volcanic ash transported across the Andes on the winds have caused extensive fishkills in some Argentine lakes and watersheds.

Some lakes are the relict geology of ancient lakes that sprawled over vast regions, while others are actually echoes of primordial seas. Great Salt Lake and the Bonneville salt flats are the remains of such marine epochs, and the salinity of residual seas is still evident at Pyramid Lake in Nevada, one of the best cutthroat fisheries in North America. Oxbow lakes are shaped when old river channels are abandoned and isolated from their parent streams. The volcanic origins of crater lakes are obvious, and seepage waters sometimes expose caverns and sinkholes through erosion.

The basic geomorphology of lakes clearly affects their productivity. Deeply-scoured lakes or sinkholes having extremely limited shallows support a marginal food-chain community and relatively few fish. Lakes that are too shallow may become too warm for trout or grayling, lacking the depth for adequate thermal stratification; and some shallow lakes lack sufficient volume to prevent asphyxiation and winterkill in heavy snow

490 / PHYSIOLOGY, HABITAT AND BEHAVIOR

country. Moderately deep lakes with small food shelves are relatively productive, but the best trout lakes combine several primary factors—fertile water chemistry, good light penetration, extensive food-shelf shallows, and a deep-water bowl extensive enough to accommodate thermal stratification in summer and to provide enough oxygen to prevent winterkill.

Water transparency is basic, since the richest water cannot produce oxygen or food without the penetration of solar energy and photosynthesis. Since lakes are usually deeper than streams, their turbidity and transparency are more critical. Light penetration is usually measured in terms of a standard index of water color, It is calibrated with a device called a Secchi disk, measuring about fourteen inches in diameter. Its faces are divided into four equal parts, its diagonally opposite quadrants painted black and white respectively. The Secchi meter is attached to a light nylon cord at the point where the four quarters meet and is lowered into a lake until it is no longer visible. It is then raised until its color pattern is barely visible, and the average of these two depths is established as the Secchi rating.

Sometimes turbidity can be measured in parts per million. Its standard index unit is the suspended matter and water color produced by a single part per million of silica in distilled water. However, the Secchi reading is easy and perfectly workable, and the optimal time for such ratings is obviously midday, when maximum sunlight penetration occurs. Some lakes have very clear waters, while others are surprisingly turbid and brown. Wide variations in the Secchi readings occur, although it is reasonable to assume the fish can see almost as far in their world as we can see into it. Trout lakes are somewhat less turbid than warmer biosystems, and the following Secchi table can tell us something about both subsurface visibility and the effects of turbidity on light penetration and oxygen levels. The comfort depths are probably the deepest levels the fish will range, and the oxygen threshold is the maximum depth they can tolerate.

SECCHI FACTORS IN WATER TRANSPARENCY

WATER TYPE	SECCHI RATING	FISHABLE DEPTH	MAXIMUM DEPTH
1	1–2 feet	6 feet	8 feet
2	3–5 feet	10 feet	12 feet
3	5–10 feet	15 feet	18 feet
4	10–15 feet	20 feet	25 feet
5	15–20 feet	25 feet	30 feet
6	20–25 feet	30 feet	35 feet
7	25–30 feet	35 feet	40 feet
8	30–35 feet	40 feet	45 feet
9	35–40 feet	45 feet	50 feet
10	40–45 feet	50 feet	55 feet
11	45–50 feet	55 feet	60 feet
12	50–55 feet	60 feet	65 feet

These are the probable limits of light penetration and visibility in very clear water, although thermal stratification in midsummer can provide optimal temperatures and viable concentrations of oxygen between seventy-five and 150 feet. It is doubtful that trout lying at such depths feed visually, although success with bait would indicate that food is found through smell and taste.

The Secchi factors also have some interesting lessons for fly-fishing our lakes and reservoirs. With a visibility reading of one or two feet, only twenty percent of the available light is penetrating to the trout. Such readings are typical of excessive turbidity or periods of dense algal bloom. Rich water chemistry and sunlight combine to trigger a remarkable plankton explosion that can reach densities as high as thirty million of these microscopic organisms in a single gallon of water. During such periods of algal overpopulation, the fish can see only one or two feet, but the photosynthesis triggered by the phytoplankton counts can enrich the water with oxygen well below eight to twelve feet down. Such dark brown or pea-colored water is roughly as turbid as undiluted coffee. It should be fished at depths of three to six feet, and casts should be not more than three or four feet apart to make sure they are seen by the fish.

Similar fishing tactics can be derived from the Secchi table for each water clarity. Our flies should be worked between the surface and the maximum fishable depths, and our casts should be spaced closely together in turbid water, or farther apart in clear-water habitats. Lakes of optimal clarity will permit casts as much as ten to twenty feet apart, since a Secchi rating of ten feet means a fish can see its prey that far in all directions. Casts spaced ten to twenty feet apart are certain to drop within their vision range. Such tactics also make sense in terms of skittish fish, since turbidity masks the frequent, closely spaced casts advisable in dark waters. Too much casting will only alarm the fish in clear-water lakes and ponds, and because they can be made farther apart, fewer casts are needed.

Temperature is also a primary factor in the comfort depths chosen by the fish, and in the growth of all aquatic organisms. It can easily be measured in shallow water with an ordinary thermometer, although other instruments designed to record deep-water temperatures are also available. Such reversing and thermal-lag thermometers are extremely useful in both fish management and fishing.

There are intriguing cycles of temperature that occur annually in temperate-zone lakes and impoundments, cycles that are closely tied to the relationships between water temperature and density. Freshwater lakes are at maximum density with a temperature of slightly more than thirty-nine degrees, and it is less dense and lighter both above and below this thermal reading. The fact is that water grows less dense as it approaches its freezing point since lakes freeze from the surface down, instead of from the bottom up like streams. Such thermal behavior has great ecosystemic impact. Lakes that froze from the bottom, like streams, would freeze completely solid in our northern latitudes, melting only slightly in summer. Obviously no life could exist in such a habitat, but since a lake begins freezing at its surface, its thermal cycle is remarkable.

Spring thaws melt the snow and ice cover that shroud our trout lakes, and the surface layer is quickly warmed. Since the variation in water density between its freezing point and its thermal point of maximum weight is extremely small, the spring winds quickly mix the warming surface zone with both the ice-chilled water and the warmer depths below. Since the water of maximum density is slightly more than thirty-nine degrees, this temperature layer lies at the bottom. The combination of thawing winds and simultaneous warming raises the temperature of the entire volume of the lake to its maximum density. When this homogeneity of temperature is achieved, wave action can easily circulate the entire aquatic mass. Such mixing and circulation at the point of homothermal equilibrium ends the winter oxygen depletion in the deeper reaches of a lake, while chemical nutrients like calcium and phosphorus and nitrogen are transported from the bottom to the warmer food-producing levels nearer the surface. It is a singular period of change.

The thawing winds ultimately increase the water temperatures and decrease its density. The biological impact of this gradual transition is not apparent in the early weeks of spring and summer. The variables of water densities are not enough to prevent the mixing of thermal layers.

However, summer begins a cycle of warming sufficient to produce wide temperature variations between the surface and the depths below. When these temperature differences are large enough to induce great differences in density, the water cannot mix readily and a heterothermal imbalance occurs. This imbalance evolves almost imperceptibly, until strong differences in thermal stratification develop. Such strata may prove only temporary, existing only in brief periods of unseasonably warm weather and dispersing in colder weather or high winds. During these periods of change, vertical temperatures decrease rapidly from the surface readings to the colder water below.

Actual summer stratification evolves three distinct layers of water that persist throughout the summer months, sometimes lasting into the early autumn. Biologists identify these strata as the epilimnion, thermocline, and hypolimnion. The epilimnion is a moderately deep stratum of comparatively warm water, circulating freely with both wind and wave action. Its temperatures respond quickly to changes in weather and thermal conditions in the atmosphere. The depths of the epilimnion and the other layers characteristic of thermal stratification are the result of several factors. Seasonal temperatures, solar penetration, wind, latitude, microclimatic influences, and the geomorphology of a particular lake all play a role in each thermal layer. The epilimnion zone of circulating water ends rather suddenly, when it reaches a shallow layer of cooler water called the thermocline or mesolimnion.

The thermocline is a zone of surprisingly rapid temperature drop. Its waters decrease slightly more than half a degree per foot. It is often no more than five or six feet in depth. Because the colder water below is often poorly oxygenated, fish seek the thermocline and hold just above it during hot weather. Knowledge of the thermocline and its role in the biology of lakes and reservoirs is important to anglers.

The thermocline ends rapidly in the relatively deep zone called the hypolimnion. Its temperatures drop rather slowly to the minimum readings of any given day, and the average minimums are constant for most lakes and reservoirs deep enough to stratify. Bottom readings can lie at maximum water density, but in most lakes they will probably fall in the forty to forty-five degree range. Extremely deep lakes, and particularly deep reservoirs, will regularly reach maximum density at slightly more than thirty-nine degrees because of the immense water pressures from above. There is very little oxygen in the hypolimnion of most lakes, and little fish life is found there.

Sometimes thermal stratification is dissipated with the accumulated heat gain of the summer months. The depth of the surface epilimnion steadily increases, and the thermocline stratum becomes surprisingly thin. The epilimnion layer in a really large lake or reservoir can measure thirty feet in late spring, reaching as deep as sixty to seventy feet in late summer. Small lakes and ponds develop a superficial thermal layer no deeper than ten or fifteen feet, and in darkly turbid lakes it might reach a depth of only five feet, because solar radiation is quickly absorbed in their reddish-brown waters. It is interesting that such boggy lakes can experience higher surface temperatures on a given day. Their epilimnion layer might reach seventy-five to eighty-five degrees in hot weather, while a clear lake of virtually identical geomorphology could seldom reach seventy-five degrees at the surface.

There are really large freshwater lakes having such exceptional volumes of cold water and such continuous winds that summer stratification never really occurs. Subarctic and arctic lakes may receive so little solar energy that their surface layers seldom rise above fifty degrees. Such epilimnial temperatures are colder than the temperature reading of the thermocline in more temperate lakes. Prevailing summer winds can also trigger surprising variations in the thermal stratification of large lakes. Multiple thermocline zones can occur, but their duration is always brief. Strong prevailing-wind action tends to accumulate a perceptible water drift in the windward direction, piling up water along a downwind shoreline. Such piling effects cause a depression in the thermocline, forcing it slightly deeper to windward, and elevating it slightly on the leeward shore. The wind effect increases the depth of the relatively warm epilimnion in some places and reduces it in others. When the thermal layers return to equilibrium, the entire lake oscillates like a huge imperceptible seesaw. Subaquatic patterns of flow develop, running under the surface wind currents in the opposite direction. Such oscillations also result from changes in atmospheric pressures, as well as from tributaries.

The thermal stratification of most temperate-zone lakes may find the thermocline only eight or ten feet down in late spring, dropping to twenty or twenty-five feet as the water warms. It may be found as deep as forty feet in extremely clear lakes. The thermocline is cold, but it is always oxygen-poor, and the hypolimnion is virtually without dissolved oxygen. The implications of these facts for anglers are simple: the epilimnion layer has most of the oxygen and fish; the thermocline has few fish because its oxygen is limited; and the hypolimnion is virtually devoid of both oxygen and fish.

Trout fishermen should remember that cool temperatures are important too, and their quarry will seek trade-offs between oxygen concentrations and thermal conditions. The diagram demonstrates the depths, oxygen concentrations, and temperatures of typical northern lakes having clear water and depths beyond fifty feet. Such temperatures in a trout lake mean the fish will probably seek the coldest waters they can find, as well as adequate concentrations of dissolved oxygen. That is, the seventy-one-degree layer twenty-seven feet below the surface where the fish can find almost eight parts per million of dissolved oxygen.

OXYGEN ppm	DEPTH feet	TEMPERATURE degrees	
8.5	0	72	
8.4	16	72	
8.3	20	72	EPILIMNION
8.2	23	72	
7.8	27	71	
6.7	30	70	THERMOCLINE
1.7	32	63	METALIMNION
1.1	37	59	CHEMOCLINE
0.1	38	58	
0.0	39	57	
0.0	40	56	
0.0	50	54	
0.0	60	52	HYPOLIMNION
0.0	70	49	
0.0	80	45	
0.0	90	42	
0.0	100	40	

Typical summer thermal stratification

Virtually all the trout-supporting lakes of the United States and Canada are subject to thermal stratification. It usually occurs in late May and early June. High-altitude lakes are not warmed quickly, and their thermal behavior is less dramatic. Some high-country lakes remain cold enough at the surface all summer that such thermal changes have only minimal effect on fish behavior.

Autumn triggers a surprising thermal change of its own. It is called a thermal overturn. The cooler weather that arrives in the first weeks of fall soon lowers the temperature of the epilimnion layer. The density of the water increases as it cools. It sinks lower and lower into the lake, until its density and temperature match the cold hypolimnion at the bottom. When that homogeneity is finally achieved, the lower depths of the lake rise and literally turn over, circulating fresh surface oxygen into its depths and bottom nutrients into the shallows. The entire lake becomes fertilized and supersaturated with dissolved oxygen at levels as high as twelve parts per million, enriched and waiting for winter. Such oxygen concentrations start the fish feeding greedily, almost as if they sense the need to store body fats and glycogens and proteins to survive the hostile season ahead.

Winter brings an inverse thermal stratification, with the coldest and least dense layers at the surface. Once these upper strata reach approximately thirty-nine degrees they freeze rather quickly, because the water below is denser and holds it in close proximity to the atmosphere. Once the ice cover has congealed, it traps the thirty-two-degree water just under its crystalline ceiling, and except for a narrow layer on the threshold of freezing, the body of the lake hovers near its maximum density just above thirty-nine degrees. Some large lakes freeze much later than others because of a thermal-storage effect in which they grudgingly surrender the heat entrained during the summer. Lakes that do not freeze continue to circulate with the winter winds, and remain the same temperature from surface to bottom. Their temperatures continue to drop through the winter, and finally constant thermal levels of thirty-four to thirty-seven degrees can be recorded. It is a strange phenomenon that a frozen lake stays much warmer in its depths, and as long as the light can penetrate the ice, it will remain well oxygenated. Its frozen surface cuts off the effects of the wind or any other outside factor, so the inverse stratification is a form of winter stagnation.

Deeply drifted snow on the ice presents a completely different spectrum of problems. It can prevent any solar penetration, virtually ending all photosynthesis. The fish will range well down in a frozen lake, although its autumn saturation of oxygen is cut in half before midwinter, dropping from twelve to six parts per million. The steady depletion of oxygen forces the trout steadily toward the colder water just under the ice, where photosynthesis slowly replenishes it even in winter. Dense snow cover can virtually end that process until the fish are driven gasping to the frozen surface layer itself, where they sometimes are trapped in the ice or asphyxiated.

Such winterkill leaves the shallows filled with rotting fish when the ice breaks up in the spring. Oxygen has been depleted both by the fish and the decomposition of organisms on the bottom. Such decomposition and respiration also saturate the water with high levels of carbon dioxide. Depth is a factor in this process, since the ratio between the total volume of a lake and its biological oxygen demand, from both living and decomposing organisms, is critical in a frozen lake. Winterkill is most common in shallow-water lakes and ponds rich in organic detritus and bottom trash. Methane and hydrogen sulphite are also involved, generated steadily under the ice and trapped there.

Western mountain lakes in the high country sometimes lack inlet streams, and are often totally locked under ice and snow from October until July. Their entombment is so complete that absolutely no photosynthesis occurs. Oxygen-consuming matter on their bottoms is scarce, and their extremely cold temperatures suppress both the metabolic activity of the fish and the decomposition of dead matter. Over the years, I have encountered some tragic fishkills in the high lakes of Colorado and Wyoming, and heavy snows were usually the catalyst.

ICE COVER	OXYGEN ppm	DEPTH feet	TEMPERATURE degrees	
	7.0	0	32	
	6.5	16	34	
	6.0	20	36	
	5.6	23	38	EPILIMNION
	2.2	27	39	
	1.1	30	39	
	0.1	32	39	
	0.0	37	39	
	0.0	38	39	
	0.0	39	39	
	0.0	40	39	
	0.0	50	39	
	0.0		39	HYPOLIMNION
	0.0	60	39	
	0.0	70	39	
	0.0	80	39	
	0.0	90	39	
		100		

Typical winter thermal stratification

The water chemistry of lakes and impoundments is different from that of streams in many ways. Atmospheric chemistry and water vapors are exchanged at the surface film, mixing them through both solution and evaporation. The water naturally entrains the mixture of gases found in the atmosphere, and the amount dissolved into a lake or reservoir is inversely proportional to its temperature. It also depends on atmospheric pressure, temperature, and density at the water surface. Sometimes gases at high levels of saturation are lost back into the atmosphere. Gas bubbles can literally be seen rising from weed growth during periods of optimal photosynthesis, and there are also springs that bubble with incredible concentrations of carbonic acid and carbon dioxide. Wind action on lakes and reservoirs often performs the same function as tumbling falls and broken currents in a stream. Its whitecaps and a crashing surf both serve to entrain additional oxygen and other gases from the atmosphere. Under such conditions, dissolved gases can also escape solution more rapidly than when the lake lies still.

But photosynthesis is still the principal key. It involves plant life taking in carbon dioxide from the water, and in the production of glucose the

SNOW COVER	OXYGEN ppm	DEPTH feet	TEMPERATURE degrees	
	2.0	0	32	
	1.0	16	34	
				CHEMOCLINE
	0.0	20	39	
	0.0	23	39	
	0.0	27	39	
	0.0	30	39	
	0.0	32	39	
	0.0	37	39	
	0.0	38	39	
	0.0	39	39	
	0.0	40	39	
	0.0	50	39	
	0.0	60	39	HYPOLIMNION
	0.0	70	39	
	0.0	80	39	
	0.0	90	39	
	0.0	100	39	

Winter oxygen starvation

plant life gives off oxygen. Since solar energy is the catalyst, such oxygen production is limited to the photic, illuminated shallows along the shores and the euphotic zone in open water, where algal life also engages in photosynthesis. The scope of the euphotic zone is limited by the degree of turbidity, and its effect on light penetration. Therefore, oxygen generation in a lake itself is the combined result of photosynthesis in plants, plantlike phytoplankton, and zooplankton. Dissolved oxygen is the key to the fertility of lakes and reservoirs.

Carbon dioxide is important too, since it unlocks the alkalinity of a fishery. It is dissolved in the habitat through rainfall that has passed through the atmosphere, the decomposition of organic matter in the lake, surface runoff and springhead flowages, the respiration of oxygen-using species, and the deterioration of chemical compounds already extant in the water. Carbon dioxide is also a primary factor in plant metabolism and is therefore essential in photosynthesis. It is also present in other forms. Some carbon dioxide reacts naturally with the aquatic environment to produce carbonic acid. It can also combine with calcium or magnesium to form calcium carbonate or magnesium carbonate. Carbonic acid can also react with carbonates to form various bicarbonates, particularly calcium bicarbonate. Several other bicarbonate compounds are possible.

When carbon dioxide escapes solution in the water, some carbonic acid decomposes again into its components of water and carbon dioxide to replace it. This change triggers the separation of bicarbonates into carbonic acid and insoluble bicarbonates. When plants and phytoplankton extract still more carbon dioxide from the habitat, calcium and magnesium carbonates can escape solution and filter to the bottom. Sometimes these carbonates are actually visible on weeds and stones. Particularly rich lakes and reservoirs can precipitate out these carbonates in the form of lime-marl deposits. So-called hard water is the result of bicarbonate compounds with carbon dioxide. Since the true carbonates are insoluble, such water contains disproportionate levels of bound carbon dioxide. It is these various forms of carbon dioxide or its several related compounds which determine the acidity or alkalinity of a lake or impoundment.

Since potential hydrogen-ion concentrations are not valid for calibrating alkalinity in the normal fishing months, because their results are distorted by atypical plankton growth, bound carbon-dioxide testing that uses hydrochloric acid is more workable in lakes since it cuts through such microscopic algal concentrations. This is the reason that fish culturists often prefer using bound carbon dioxide in assessing alkalinity—although potential hydrogen-ion counts are also common—and the reason that alkalinity is expressed in terms of fixed carbon dioxide in these chapters.

While thermal circulation and wave action are freely mixing the waters of lakes and reservoirs, their concentrations of carbon dioxide are relatively constant. Surplus saturations are easily surrendered into the atmosphere, while deficiencies are corrected by surface turbulence and precipitation mixing with the air. Summer thermal stratification and winter ice can inhibit interchanges with the atmosphere, leading to both oxygen depletion and seriously toxic levels of free carbon dioxide and other gases.

Water is such an exceptional solute that virtually all of the geological compounds are ultimately dissolved and drained into lakes and impoundments. Such concentrations are sometimes almost imperceptible, even with modern instrumentation, yet they can prove critical even in such dilute forms. Some dissolved elements are organic and biodegradable, although such substances are primarily metabolic wastes or the result of decomposing plant and animal life. These dilute substances are typically colloidal glucose, proteins, and amino acids. It is not fully understood how the microscopic aquatic organisms utilize these substances as food, but research clearly indicates that the life forms at the bottom of the food chain use them directly as nutrients.

The inorganic substances appear as salts in surprising concentrations, reaching an aggregate of one hundred to two hundred parts per million in most lakes. Calcium is utilized directly in skeletal structures and shells and is typically found as calcium bicarbonate. Nitrogen is a primary building block of proteins that commonly appear as nitrites, ammonia, and nitrate salts. Phosphorus is also essential in the chemistry of many proteins; it plays a critical role in the energy functions of both plant and animal cells and is usually present as phosphate. Boron, manganese, and copper are also present as salts, along with more common elements like sodium, potassium, and iron. Silicates are critical to the shells of diatomaceous life. Other elements essential to the creation of hemoglobin and to optimal cell chemistry are present in extremely faint traces. The absence of any single element will invariably mean the biological community in that lake or impoundment will be limited. Such missing pieces in the food-chain puzzle mean fewer fish per acre of water.

The geomorphology of lakes is complex. It includes three basic zones common to all lakes and impoundments: the littoral shallows and shoreline, the limnetic or offshore acreages, and the mesopelagic or profundal depths where solar energy no longer penetrates. The littoral shallows can be both large or small in proportion to the acreage and volume of a lake, depending on its geology and configuration. Its littoral is the zone in which aquatic vegetation thrives, depending on the composition of the bottom. Extensive littoral acreages are often indicative of relatively high organic production. Rooted plants cannot exist in the limnetic, offshore zone of a lake or reservoir, and its flora consist primarily of phytoplankton.

However, the classification of lakes is usually based upon such yardsticks as water chemistry, relative acidity or alkalinity, turbidity, bottom fauna, productivity factors, geological enclosures, and the presence of thermal stratification. These criteria are so variable that they have largely been replaced with considerations of primary biological productivity. Such factors of productivity are based on the rate at which photosynthesis creates energy in forms that can directly be utilized as food.

Oligotrophic lakes are relatively barren and poor. Such waters are typically found in glacially eroded bedrock or mountain country. These lakes are relatively deep, with a hypolimnion zone much larger than the surface epilimnion. Littoral acreages are comparatively small. Aquatic plants and phytoplankton densities are quite low. Since basic nutrients are scarce, the cyclical explosion of phytoplankton and zooplankton populations that bloom and discolor the water are rare. Oxygen depletion in the hypolimnion depths of most lakes is primarily based upon the cumulative precipitation of organic matter from their surface and shallows. Since oligotrophic lakes are less fertile, their profundal zone is not subject to this collection of decomposing matter, and their depths are not subject to severe oxygen depletion. Deep lakes with a well aerated hypolimnion are almost invariably oligotrophic in character and support cold-loving species like whitefish and char in surprisingly deep water. Relict populations of char are almost entirely restricted to the hypolimnion zone of many lakes in England, Scotland, Ireland, and North America. Although they can actually be thousands of years old, oligotrophic lakes are relatively young in geological terms, and have changed little since they were formed. Ultimately, they will slowly fill with erosion, their dissolved nutrients and water chemistry will change, and their fertility will increase.

Eutrophic lakes are both shallower and richer. Their hypolimnion zones are relatively small and their productivity is exceptionally good. Such lakes are usually found in older geological regions in which erosion is quite well developed. Aquatic plants are typically abundant, and the dense populations of phytoplankton and zooplankton trigger characteristic periods of bloom. Relatively large amounts of organic matter now filter down into the small hypolimnion typical of eutrophic lakes. Their slow decomposition can deplete their deep-water oxygen, eliminating the mesopelagic stocks of whitefish and char. Both erosion and the decomposition of organic matter are slowly filling such lakes, and the aquatic growth feeding on such deposits of nutrients on the bottom accelerates the cycle.

Many marshes and bogs are former lakes in relatively advanced states of eutrophication, and some ancient lakes have so completely atrophied over the past 10,000 to 15,000 years that they are covered with high-canopy forests. It is important to remember that all lakes are relatively ephemeral, speaking in terms of geological time, and they are all becoming more and more eutrophic. Our impact on the pace of eutrophication in the past two centuries has been frightening. It begins with the simple erosion triggered by poor agricultural technology, in both developed and undeveloped countries; and the fertilizers used excessively in both Europe and the United States have accelerated eutrophication. The organic wastes of modern feed-lot ranching, horse and dairy farming, and marginal sewage treatment are eutrophic factors too—and few fishermen seem to understand that a lake can become so fertile that it literally dies.

Dystrophic lakes are quite rich in organic matter; their composition is largely undecomposed plant materials, like the dense layers of peat in the

Irish bogs. The retarded decomposition is the result of calcium deficiency in the water chemistry of dystrophic lakes. Bottom deposits are often extensive, but the dissolved nutrients are too scarce to support new aquatic vegetation. The water is typically dark brown and acid, supporting little phytoplankton because of acidity and limited light penetration.

There are other types of lakes. Salt lakes in our western regions are either leached from the highly saline beds of ancient seas or are actual remnants of their waters. Desert lakes can be seasonal or result from flash floods and cloudburst, and can have highly toxic concentrations of alkali, arsenic, and other poisons. Some lakes are the result of seismic faults, landslides, lava flows, and volcanic craters.

Fishermen should remember that the littoral shallows are not limited to shoreline areas. Outcroppings and shoals well out in a lake may provide food-rich littoral zones, where light penetrates to the bottom and plants grow readily. Such littoral acreages may occupy the entire area of particularly shallow lakes. Extremely turbid lakes may have shallows that fail to develop the characteristics of true littoral zones, since light cannot penetrate them well. On the other hand, aquatic root systems seldom grow well on sandy bottoms even though they are considered part of the more fertile littoral areas because solar energy does reach the bottom.

The food-producing zones of a typical lake are measured in terms of both acreage and depth. The obvious food-chain communities in the shallows, and the phytoplankton and zooplankton contributions found in the limnetic depths offshore, are included in the trophogenic zone of a lake. The deeper waters of the hypolimnion are classified as tropholytic, since organisms in these depths consume food more quickly than it is grown.

It is extremely important for anglers to understand the basic differences between drainage and seepage lakes. Drainage lakes are obviously bodies of water having an outlet or inlet or both. The inlet is a stream or tributary brook entering a lake, and an outlet is its downstream exit. But seepage lakes are landlocked, being without visible inlets or outlets. Their waters are accumulated from springheads along the shore or the bottom, underground seepage, and seasonal precipitation. Whenever a small dam backs up several acres it creates a flowage, and lumberjacks called a stretch of river held back by natural obstructions a widewater. Both situations create drainage lakes with exaggerated inlets and outlets.

The fish in drainage lakes are often migratory, coming through them or abandoning them in search of cooler temperatures or good spawning areas. Drainage lakes are filled with surprises. Fish can survive thirty or forty feet down in quite turbid water, where little or no oxygen exists in a static lake. The subsurface currents that connect the inlets and outlets diffuse adequate saturations of oxygen at depths where light cannot reach and photosynthesis cannot exist. Such invisible rivers in the depths of a flowage carry nutrients and ample food-chain organisms to the fish holding there. Oxygen and food mean fish, and searching a flowage lake for its primary current-tongues is the secret to fishing it effectively.

Seepage lakes are an equal challenge, although they receive no outside sources of food, oxygenation or other fish life. Their dissolved oxygen, fertility-producing elements, and fish life are completely self-contained, and adjacent seepage lakes are often completely different.

Both drainage and seepage lakes can exhibit a full range of acidity and alkalinity. The water chemistry of drainage lakes is dependent on the character of their inlet systems. Seepage lakes are quite often more acid, but limestone geology or phosphate deposits of marl can make them alkaline. Since their ecology is contained, seepage lakes are more easily managed and understood. Coarse species can be poisoned and replaced. Since there is no current flow to oxygenate their eggs, seepage lakes inhibit the spawning of trout and grayling, except where relatively constant winds and wave action break across gravelly shorelines and shoals. Seepage lakes also display interesting population behavior. Trout must usually be stocked continually in such waters and can be fished out rapidly in an acid habitat. Overstocking can result in stunted, poorly conditioned fish in acid lakes, and in acid drainage lakes where spawning is successful, stunted populations often keep mating and increasing their numbers of big-headed trout. Perhaps such waters should have special regulations, thinning out the small fish with generous kill-limits, but leaving the few large trout to balance the remaining food supply and population.

Seepage lakes tend toward better water transparency, particularly with sand or gravel shallows. Their chemistry is usually alkaline. The fish can see quite well in such habitat and are relatively skittish and shy. Territoriality is primary in the fish behavior of seepage lakes, and the best holding lies are more easily understood. The fish of drainage lakes and flowages are more footloose, but in seepage waters you should stalk the obvious big-fish places as carefully as you fish a stream. Once a good fish has been taken there, another will likely replace it. If we fail to take fish in the obvious holding lies of a clear seepage lake, we can only blame our tactics and technique.

Our seepage lakes are steadily shrinking. Without the steady flow of inlet waters, they suffer from evaporation and careless tampering with their surrounding water table. Marsh drainage, land-fill, and deep wells all harm the ecology of adjacent seepage lakes. Seepage lakes were often drainage lakes in the last century, but changing patterns of rainfall and subsurface hydrology have dried up both their inlets and outlets. Dwindling water levels make them dangerously vulnerable to winterkill and the phenomenon known as an ice push. Ice push is a barn-size accumulation of surface ice that can build natural barriers of silt and gravel across an outlet or divide a lake by isolating its shallow inlets and bays, building subaquatic moraines like a miniature glacier. Although most seepage lakes are slowly dying, the process is usually occurring in the measured beat of geological time, and there will still be ample time for fishing them.

Large reservoirs are completely different, since they are sometimes too large to qualify as either drainage lakes or flowages, and are still dynamic biosystems with inlets and outlets in spite of their static acreages. Like natural lakes, there are several types of impoundments. Major reservoirs can total thousands of acres, receiving the flow of relatively large river systems. Impoundments in their headwaters are also sometimes large, and sometimes they can have considerable depth. Their biology is based on the character of a much more limited watershed. Small earthen dams are sometimes used to collect the waters of spring-fed ponds, forming another type of habitat. The functions of such impoundments are even more varied. Reservoirs are designed for flood control, correcting erosion problems, navigation systems, irrigation waters, potable water storage, industrial and mining operations, electrical power, and recreation. Most impoundments are conceived for some primary function, with a policy of multiple use. However, few reservoirs provide first-rate fishing after many years.

Impounded waters differ from natural lakes. Reservoirs designed for irrigation, flood control, and hydroelectric power are subject to radical variations in water levels. Draw-down discharges can drop the surface of a reservoir thirty to fifty feet, completely eradicating aquatic plant systems and the biological communities usually associated with the littoral zone along their shorelines. Thermal stratification is completely changed, spawning areas are left exposed to the atmosphere, the oxygen-rich surface waters are released, fish are forced into the oxygen-depleted volumes remaining, rooted plant life is damaged or killed, both phytoplankton and zooplankton are surrendered past the dam, and the entire food chain is decimated. Pump-storage reservoirs are the worst example of such impoundments, since their draw-down cycle is so frequent there is no time to develop and sustain a viable biosystem.

Turbidity and siltation are problems too. Both constant inflow and release from reservoirs either carry silt or stir up bottom detritus with their turbulence. Incoming water may be much warmer or colder than the impounded water. It can stratify in a new layer above or below the existing patterns of stratification. Its density can also form a moving-current layer. The depth is determined by the existing thermal structure in the reservoir, its flow seeking the point at which it is lighter than the chilled water below, and cooler and less dense than the surface layers. Therefore, reservoir trout can hold at variable depths in hot weather.

Since topography and soil mechanics are basic factors in the selection of reservoir sites, these impoundments also give us some interesting ratios of volume to the cost and magnitude of construction. Planners attempt to contain maximum acreages and depths at the lowest capital commitments. Narrow sites along a watercourse, with maximum impoundment potential upstream, are typical dam sites. Canyon sites form extremely deep reservoirs with hypolimnion zones so cold they are virtually thermal deserts. Such depths can also generate toxic concentrations of nitrogen, rivalling the chemistry of underground lakes and rivers. Topographic considerations also result in lakes having a relatively large perimeter compared with their surface acreages.

However, reservoirs are not entirely negative in their impact on trout fishing. Some have created good fisheries in arid regions and provided cold-water habitat in desiccating basins where the remaining trout streams quickly became too warm or simply vanished in the desert. Such reservoirs can improve the fishing in the relict streams by providing a kind of manmade inland sea where fish can grow large and return to their headwaters to spawn. Some impoundments enrich the flowages downstream by releasing plankton and other nutrients, and can cool the water of streams having marginal trout-stream temperatures. Their cold tailings can also create trout fishing where it never existed before or restore a river that no longer supports cold-water species because of past lumbering or land clearing for agriculture. The changing stream levels that come from cycles of storage and release cause some unique problems in fishing tactics, but that seems a small price for the creation of new fisheries or the restoration of old rivers. Where irrigation is involved, particularly on our Rocky Mountain watersheds, the construction of a storage reservoir can cause less long-range damage than present methods. The jerry-built networks of ditches and sluice gates that have evolved since frontier days are often fed by temporary coffer dams. The ranchers build these dams each season, excavating their materials with power equipment from the bottom gravel and stones. The dams divert considerable water from the river, and hundreds of acres of bottom are uprooted to build them, destroying millions of insects and crustaceans and microscopic organisms. The water is borrowed from the river in the summer months after snowmelt, when its ecology can least afford to lose it. Both fish and fly life tragically follow the borrowed water into the irrigation ditches, along with countless millions of zooplankton, only to perish when the system is drained for hay cutting in late summer. It is doubtful that a storage reservoir and irrigation network could do as much damage to a river, even though it might erase several miles of its course. It would end the practice of excavating coffer dams from the river bottom, and since it would store water from snowmelt, more water could be released to the river than it now receives in irrigation season. Too often we are opposed to all impoundments, not realizing that a carefully selected site combined with a well designed dam can immeasurably restore a fishery.

Rooted plants and plankton are not only more numerous in lakes and impoundments, but since the oxygenation of current action is largely absent, they are also more important to stillwater ecology. Both forms convert carbon dioxide into dissolved oxygen. The aquatic mosses are also more numerous in lakes. The seed-producing plants are found in great profusion in quiet waters, and there are many more species there than in streams. The blue-green algae are common, often producing a scum on the surface of lakes and reservoirs in the spring and fall. The tiny single-cell flagellates also contribute to such cycles of bloom. Some of these microscopic organisms ingest nutrients like animals, often eating the tiny plantlike phytoplankton, yet also producing oxygen like plants.

Both botanists and zoologists claim these intriguing forms of life. Many believe they are primordial organisms, perhaps even ancestral to modern plant and animal species, although taxonomic relationships are no longer obvious. Some of these microscopic species must be magnified 500 to 1,000 times before they are visible, and some are even smaller. The species that are plantlike in metabolism are called phytoplankton, and those more clearly resembling animal life are zooplankton. The tiniest species are the nannoplankton, so small that thousands can filter through the meshes of a fine linen handkerchief. Twenty to thirty million are found in a single quart of water. Using a microscope, it is possible to find zooplankton feeding on phytoplankton like cattle around a bale of fodder.

Both types of plankton are found in the littoral and limnetic zones of lakes, drifting at the mercy of winds and temperature changes and currents in the trophogenic depths. The plankton also sometimes grow attached to the bottom and submerged debris. Lakes are rich in plankton, since heavy populations are largely a function of quiet waters and often enrich their outlet flowages for miles downstream.

Streams that flow into a lake or reservoir virtually barren can leave almost saturated with lake-grown plankton. However, it is quickly dissipated in a swift-running river after only a few miles, unless there are many slow-flowing pools and quiet backwaters. Flowages and widewaters can sustain rich populations of plankton too, since their ecosystems are more closely related to lakes than rivers. It is possible for sizable population densities of plankton to develop in large, slow-moving rivers, although these densities never rival the concentrations found in lakes. It is intriguing how many of the great fisheries are rivers enriched with lake-bred plankton. Several of the superb salmon fisheries of Europe, like the Altá and Vossa in Norway, are rivers with rich sources of lake-bred plankton in their headwaters. The famed Klamath in California carries the plankton generated at Klamath Lake in Oregon, and farther north in British Columbia, the half-legendary runs of giant steelheads in the Babine are found in a riverine system rich with the plankton of huge lakes in its headwaters. ·

It is also the large alpine lakes in the Andes, their incredible fjordlike depths rich in microscopic life, that are the secret of the superb trout fishing in South America. The storied Chimehuin in Argentina has its origins in the Lago Huechulafquen, the larger many-channeled Limay is born in the hundred-mile inland seas of Lago Nahuel-Huapi, and the fine little Malleo and Quilquihue also have their beginnings in lakes. The Chilean river Calcurrupe is remarkable too, with ten miles of sweeping current that connects Lago Maihue with sprawling Lago Ranco. The river has its beginnings in reed-lined plankton shallows that feed its currents with nutrients, and its outlet at Llifen receives runs of huge browns and rainbows that have fattened in the plankton-rich depths of the bigger lake.

The biology of the plankton is filled with puzzles. Many species are transparent, microscopic crustaceans that are almost always females.

Reproduction is consistently through parthenogenesis, without the fertilization by males, and the young are always females too. Males are only hatched when the entire population is threatened, perhaps in cycles of drought and the desiccation of the habitat. The eggs fertilized by the males survive both winter and drought, and hatch when their habitat is restored by spring rains. But the freshly hatched plankton are all females again.

There are thousands and thousands of phytoplankton and zooplankton species. Sometimes the individual species are so uniquely endemic to certain regions that an expert in the taxonomy of plankton can identify the water quality and specific sources of a specimen collection. Other species are so prolific in such habitat that they are found almost everywhere.

It is useful in fishing a lake or reservoir to understand how plankton population varies, since it is seldom uniformly distributed. Drift species are carried on wind and wave action and are concentrated along the downwind shores in regions having strong prevailing winds. Coves and inlets and bays offer sheltered microhabitats where plankton can thrive. Swimming forms are often migratory. Some spend the daylight hours in the surface layers, returning to the thermocline as darkness falls, while others surface at night and retreat from the daylight.

Plankton populations also ebb and flow through the year, increasing and decreasing in radical cycles. Common peaks occur in both spring and fall. Large volumes of bottom nutrients are transported toward the surface in the thermal upwelling that occurs then, and temperatures are optimal. Solar radiation and photosynthesis are optimal between spring and fall too, triggering high rates of reproduction. Dissolved oxygen concentrations also rise in direct ratio to phytoplankton growth, and the following graph draws some interesting conclusions: both plankton population and oxygen cycles peak after simultaneous rises in water temperature, nutrients, and solar radiation.

Both plants and animals that live among the bottom detritus and other materials of a lake or impoundment exist in what biologists call a benthic community. Rooted aquatic vegetation is not included in the benthos, although many other plant forms and some types of phytoplankton are part of its living organisms. The bottom of such habitat is divided into two zones: the littoral zone where light washes its depths, and the hypolimnion, where the bottom is called the profundal zone, and very little illumination and oxygen are found.

Obviously, the biotic transition between these two zones is gradual rather than abrupt, with considerable overlapping. Seasonal changes also occur as the intensity of solar radiation varies. During these cycles, the concentrations of oxygen and carbon dioxide are inversely proportional, depending on light and photosynthesis. The overlapping zone is extensive enough in some benthic environments to have a separate sublittoral status, and extremely deep lakes are sometimes found with an abyssal zone lying beyond its profundal bathography. Lakes subject to almost continuous wave action often display a unique community of organisms.

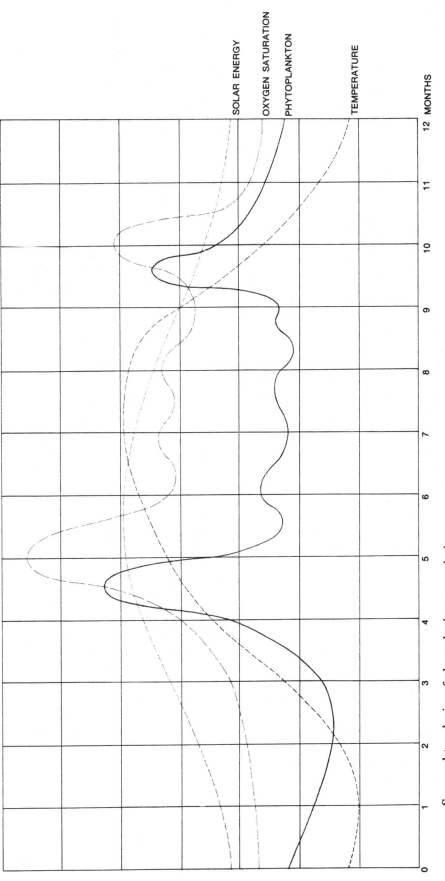

SOLAR ENERGY

OXYGEN SATURATION

PHYTOPLANKTON

TEMPERATURE

12 MONTHS

Seasonal topologies of phytoplankton populations

The effects of physicochemical factors like temperature, dissolved oxygen, light, and fixed carbon dioxide are modified by the physiographic character of the bottom itself. Detritus, bottom trash, sand, gravel, small stones, boulders, mud, ledges, outcroppings of bedrock, and decomposing plants all directly affect the nature of their benthic communities.

Silt particles and other eroded materials are washed into lakes and impoundments, or carried on inlet flowages, and settle out slowly toward the bottom. Dead aquatic plants and animal life contribute to the character of the benthos too, along with terrestrial organisms and vegetation that have either drowned or have been washed in from the shoreline. Where sufficient photosynthesis and oxygen are present, decomposition proceeds normally and the bottom absorbs the inorganic remains of organic compounds that were once alive. Such inorganic components of the bottom often contribute to the nutrients that fuel the benthic communities and are recycled into aquatic plant and animal life. Clear oligotrophic lakes have enough deep-water photosynthesis and dissolved oxygen concentrations in their hypolimnion zones that decomposition of organic matter there is relatively complete. Such lakes are less densely populated in their shallows than the eutrophic kind, and there is substantially less precipitation of organic materials from their epilimnion. Particularly rich eutrophic lakes create organic bottom sediments faster than they can be degraded and broken down, particularly in the profundal and abyssal zones.

The bottom is rich in nutrients for the benthic organisms. However, oxygen content is critical there. Even though dissolved oxygen levels may remain viable at the bottom itself, only a few inches into the silt and detritus and mud there is no oxygen left. Some anaerobic decomposition that uses no oxygen is possible, but more often dense layers of partially decomposed matter are accumulated over a period of time.

Little life exists in the turbid profundal of eutrophic lakes, and the benthic population in clear lakes is not much better. Oligotrophic lakes with good oxygenation and minimal carbon dioxide can support as many as three hundred to five hundred species, but most are bacteria and other microscopic forms, and the aggregate population of any single organism is usually rather slight. Bottoms composed of pea gravel and small stones are usually the most prolific. Few species are found in the benthic zones of highly eutrophic waters, except for microscopic organisms and the *Oligochaeta* bristleworms, which thrive on marginal levels of oxygen. There is abundant food in the profundal and abyssal depths of any lake or reservoir, but without oxygen only sparse benthic communities can develop.

The benthos of the littoral is affected by the character of the bottom, just as bottom materials affect the life forms in the deeper parts of a lake or reservoir. Subsurface currents in drainage lakes and impoundments, wave action and surf, light energy levels, and the sheltering qualities of the bathography, plant growth and other cover, aquatic plant forests, deadfalls, large boulders and bedrock outcroppings, tree roots, rock pilings, and other upright structures also form a habitat for benthic organisms. Other benthic species can swim for extended periods, and can travel into both the littoral and limnetic zones.

Wave-swept beaches are relatively barren ground. Sand is a continually shifting world, abrasive and unstable, sometimes saturated with water and sometimes barren. Shellfish are perfectly designed to cope with such environmental problems, but it is hostile and harsh to most other organisms. There is a richer spectrum of life when a sandy shoreline is mixed with eroded soil materials. The higher the percentages of soils combined with the sand, the more organisms are found per square yard of bottom.

Wave action can also provide much higher levels of aeration than are normally found in lakes, and some ecotypes associated with the tumbling currents of streams are sheltered along rocky shores, where continuous winds provide oxygenating surf.

Sometimes I have caught trout in high-altitude lakes, and on checking the contents of their stomachs, have found current-loving nymphs of aquatic insects. Once at Hermit Lake, high in the Sangre de Cristo range of Colorado, I recovered a half dozen large stonefly nymphs in a stomach autopsy. Both inlet and outlet were barely flowing that August, with too little oxygen to sustain such fast-water *Acroneurias.* Yet the fish had clearly found them, and only the aeration of the waves along the rockfall of the south shore could provide the proper habitat.

Habitat selection is also a readily identifiable form of behavior among benthic organisms. The pyramidal structure of life forms found on gravel and boulders and stones—algal and diatomaceous life, and aquatic insects—is a population that develops slowly. Leaf systems in the forests of aquatic plants are a less permanent habitat. Their organisms are the short-lived algae and *Porifera* and mosses, and the transient nymphs of the damselflies and swimming mayfly nymphs and dragonflies.

The rooted aquatic plants have a richly important role in the ecology of lakes and impoundments. Their function as oxygen producers is primary, but they also provide both food and shelter for a galaxy of benthic plants and animals, including fingerling trout and grayling. Aquatic vegetation also multiplies the effective littoral acreage of the lake since its biota are supported in its plant structures as well as on the bottom. Thus, the importance of these aquatic plants cannot be exaggerated.

Their role is surprisingly recent in terms of evolution. The bacteria and phytoplankton and fungi are much more primordial forms of plant life, having existed for perhaps millions of years. The rooted plant species lie between the purely aquatic forms and the terrestrial genera that evolved from ancient lakes and seas. The seed-bearing aquatic plants have adapted to remaining rooted in the benthos, while their reproduction occurs through the atmosphere. Some leaf structures stand in the atmosphere, some remain submerged, and still others lie suspended in the surface film—halfway between the aquatic world and ours.

The upright aquatic plants—the rushes and cattails and tules—stand rooted in rich deposits of silt as much as two or three feet below the waterline. The next plant group—pondweeds like lilies and bass weed and spatterdock—lies deeper in the water, their leaves floating on the surface connected to flexible stems. These floating-leaf species are only semiaquatic, in the sense that respiration is accomplished through the snorkellike stomata in the upper surfaces of their leaves. Oxygen, carbon dioxide, and water vapor all pass through these stomata. Such floating-leaf species are found as far out into the littoral shallows as eight to twelve feet, depending on water clarity. Greater depths make it difficult for the plants to breathe through their slender stems. Other species like duckweeds have solved that ecological dilemma by adaptation, floating on the surface with tiny unrooted tendrils in place of fixed root structures. Still others have evolved into totally aquatic ecotypes. Their metabolic process no longer extracts carbon dioxide from the atmosphere and expels oxygen in return, for they have adapted to drawing their respiratory needs directly from their subaquatic habitat. Typical genera in this group include the *Potamogetons* and candelabra weed, as well as common hornwort and milfoil. Some of these weeds are better oxygenators than others, but they all are important in enriching the habitat of our trout and grayling lakes.

Lakes and impoundments include vast numbers of algal forms among their plantlike types of phytoplankton. These include rudimentary plants whose physiology varies to include slender and multi-branched filaments, crescent forms, stars, chains, hourglass shapes, microscopic doughnuts, circles, arrowheads, bell-shaped flowers, minute rods, and tiny richly woven ribbons. The filamentous algae grow in slender necklacelike threads, their narrow cells attached in tandem. Other filament types are branchial, attached like tiny rooted plants to dead trees and stones. Many microscopic algal forms are single celled, like the diatoms and desmids. Diatomaceous cells often cling together in circular colonies or slender ribbons that undulate in the water.

Freshwater algae are yellowish, bluish green, or bright olive, because their chlorophyll components are clearly visible in their transparent cell systems. Diatoms are yellowish to yellowish brown, their chlorophyll rich with diatomin. Desmids are intensely green with chroma. The red or purplish algae are virtually all marine species. The blue-green algae are perhaps the most common in our lakes and impoundments. Under certain types of illumination they are turquoise or aquamarine, although at other times they are a rich purplish blue. The necklace-shaped *Anabena* are perhaps the best known of the species that float and drift freely in the water. The dark bluish-black *Oscillatoria* are dense little root-tangles on underwater ledges and boulders and the riprap facing of reservoirs. These microscopic algal forms writhe and oscillate and coil surprisingly with every movement of the water.

It is the even tinier *Rivularia* species that are attached in dense clusters of minute, gelatinous fingers to the stems and leaves of cattails and candelabra weeds. There are other filamentous algae too, like the embroidery of the *Spirogyra* chains, interlaced with the more delicate *Zygnema* species. These algae can literally blanket a trout or grayling pond in the spring, providing food for the tiny insect nymphs and larvae that, in turn, nourish both more predatory nymphs and the fish themselves. The spherical *Volvox* algae are like bright green pinheads to our naked eyes, and hundreds of thousands can saturate a single collecting flask. Each sphere is constructed of hundreds of cells, each fitted with a delicate filament designed to propel the algal structure with its swimming motions. Later in the season, the smaller *Euglena* algae can cover a small lake or impoundment with a velvetlike scum of intense bluish green. These tiny arrowhead-like organisms are propelled with a microscopic flagellum. Such algae are basic to the food chain.

Diatoms and desmids are also important building blocks in any benthic community. The diatoms are microscopic single-celled algae which drift free or attach themselves to the leaves and stems of the larger rooted plants. There are many patterns and configurations. Some species have solitary habits, while others gather in incredible accumulations. Diatoms are the most abundant microscopic organisms in our waters, densely coating the stems of aquatic plants and deadfalls, and even the respiratory filaments of nymphs and larvae. Reproduction occurs primarily in the spring, with astronomical numbers of diatomaceous forms covering the stones and boulders on the bottom. Diatoms are sheathed in tiny shells of silica, transparent and delicately patterned with cells. Some species are formed of minute wedge-shaped cells, arranged in a circular ring. The common *Tabellaria* look like tiny shredded-wheat biscuits. The desmids are single-celled algae like the diatoms. Many are hourglass-shaped, slightly constricted or merely colored at the waist, and live desmids are an almost glowing green of considerable intensity. The *Closterium* type are shaped like tiny boomerangs, while the circular *Micrasterias* are a little like bright green sand dollars. The narrow-waisted type are the *Tetmemorus*, and it is impossible to exaggerate their importance to our aquatic biosystems.

These phytoplankton are both food and oxygen producing and occupy a position at the genesis of plant life in our lakes and reservoirs. The intriguing aquatic plants called stoneworts are an intermediate form of development between algae and phytoplankton and the higher plant types. Structurally, the stoneworts are quite similar to algae, but their intricate candelabralike forms are more like higher types of plant life. Stoneworts are rooted plants, usually growing about one or two feet high in extensive, submerged meadows. The stoneworts secrete lime salts, and it is these shell-like layers on their spiny whorls of branches that give them their name. Our common American genera are *Chara* and *Nitella*, which are among the few plants that are valuable in both lakes and streams. Subaquatic gardens of our most common candelabra *Chara fragilis* are typically found in richly alkaline waters offering excellent cover and oxygenation. Its brittle stems are nodal, and each node supports a whorl of spiny little branches. Single linear cells connect the nodes in the main stems. The branchial cores also consist of single cells, although their cellular cores are covered with a membranous layer of smaller cells. Reproduction is accomplished by pear-shaped ovaries and a bright orange spermary, each carried at the roots of the branches. Thousands of sperm cells are generated, and the fertilized eggs detach themselves from the ovaries, settling to the bottom to start a new plant. *Chara fragilis* is most dense in midsummer, when its oxygenation is critically needed to sustain the trout, and its rich branchial populations of diatoms and desmids are a primary habitat of food-chain species. Muskgrass is more delicate structurally than candelabra weed, but its physical appearance is quite similar. *Nitella* branches grow in whorls from nodal points in the stem. Both the branches and stems are virtually naked linear cells, fragile and translucent in character, and their delicacy easily identifies the genus. Its reproduction closely resembles the *Chara* plants', and it is widely distributed in American waters, although subaquatic *Nitella* gardens are much less common.

Tiny, bell-shaped growths of *Vorticella* and *Epistylis* are the pale whitish blotches found on deadfalls and stones, and often in parasitic colonies on many of the larger aquatic nymphs. Sometimes these little flowerlike clusters grow in incredible densities, their bell-shaped heads as much as one-eighth inch high. Although they look a little like aquatic moss, they are really tiny protozoans.

The liverworts and mosses are closely related to the algae, loving both moisture and shade. Most of these *Bryophyta* are terrestrial, growing in dense carpets wherever suitable habitat is found. Liverworts have a slender leaf-shaped thallus which houses the entire metabolic processes found in the leaves and root structure of flowering plants. Chlorophyll suffuses the cells with bright green color in the more delicate liverworts, and some have rootlike outgrowths. The crystalworts are different, drifting free in the water or only rooting loosely in the silt. The common species *Riccia natans* has a lobed thallus, and has adapted to drift loosely like duckweed, while the intricate *Riccia fluitans* is a bright green plant with a network of branches that resemble some species of marine coral. The liverworts are so hardy they often thrive when their habitat dries up.

Many plants can be used as indicators of acidity or alkalinity and the fertility of trout waters. The muskgrasses and candelabra weeds are sure signs of fertile lime salts wherever they thrive, while liverworts, crystalworts, creeping buttercups, needle rushes, waterworts, quillworts, and pipeworts are all acid-loving species.

The mosses are next in our hierarchy of lake plants. The *Musci* can thrive on the surfaces of stones and deadfalls where food is scarce, and where other plants cannot survive. Like the liverworts and lichens that are their close relatives, mosses grow in densely matted colonies, but their flat microscopic leaves identify them unmistakably. Common terrestrial lichens like caribou moss are leafless, just as the liverworts and crystalworts are leafless. True mosses are slender stemmed and delicate with flat needle-shaped leaves layered like scales above a tiny rhizoid root system. During reproduction, spore capsules develop at the tip of delicate tendrils. Several genera are semiaquatic, and a few are completely water species. Reproduction is accomplished through the spores, which travel with both wind and water currents until they root and germinate new mosses. Some mosses are male and others are female. The spore capsules are always found on the female plants. Fertile spores develop into plants without needing other cells. Aquatic mosses are mostly slender dark green species with delicate, streaming branches. They root in among the stones and silty places and deadfalls, their slender filaments undulating with wave action, and the faint currents of some drainage lakes. The familiar species *Dichelyma capillaceum* is abundant in springfed lakes and ponds. Its slender branches are usually three to five inches long, reaching from primary stems two or three feet in length, and are yellowish green. The fountain mosses are more widely distributed, although they are more prolific in streams than lakes. The *Fontinalis gigantea* is the giant fountain moss, with delicate branching leaves. The water mosses are similar in configuration, although they have more delicate leaves and spore stalks. Common American species like *Hygrohypnum ochraceum* are found in many northern streams, although they are also found in the inlets and outlets of lakes, where there are adequate currents to sustain them.

The seed-bearing aquatic plants begin with the long-stemmed leaf-bearing species. The important *Potamogetons* include both broad-leaf and ribbon-leaf types, are superb oxygenators, and are important in most lakes and reservoirs. Several broad-leaf *Potamogetons* are extremely important in trout and grayling habitat. These plants are most commonly found in alkaline water chemistry, and none really do well under acid conditions. Some botanists feel that these pondweeds are perhaps the most important group in our freshwater biosystems. Fifty-odd American species are known. Their roots are sturdy, and their luxuriant leafy growths occupy acres of fertile lakes and reservoirs. Except for their flowers at pollination time, most grow fully submerged, although a few species float some of their leaves in the surface meniscus. The petiole pondweed *Potamogeton natans* is quite common in relatively shallow water. Its floating leaves are slender and spear-shaped, and only the threadlike petioles are developed on the submerged vegetation. The ruffle-leaf pondweed *Potamogeton crispus* is quite different in its anatomy. Its broad, translucent leaves have wavy edges and often grow in pairs at regular intervals along the primary stems. Its flower stalks carry as many as ten small blossoms. Each flower has both stamens and a pistil, although they do not reach maturity simultaneously, and pollination can occur only from one blossom to another. *Potamogeton crispus* thrives in both lakes and slow-flowing streams, particularly along shorelines with good wave action. It commonly roots in three to five feet of water, but in relatively clear lakes its stalks can reach as much as seven to ten feet. Although it was originally introduced from Europe, it is already widely distributed in our eastern waters. The common bassweed *Potamogeton amplifolius* is our largest submerged plant, with its youngest leaves floating just under or in the surface. It is a species that particularly thrives on alkalinity, its thick leaves as much as six inches in length. The leaves sprout from the stem on alternate sides, like a giant fiddleback fern growing under water. *Potamogeton richardsoni* is the lesser bassweed, slightly smaller and found only in highly alkaline lakes. Another giant pondweed found in waters having bound carbon-dioxide concentrations of more than twenty parts per million is *Potamogeton praelongus*, which is called muskie weed in the marl-bottom lakes of Wisconsin. Muskie weed is a fine oxygenator. It has crinkled boat-shaped leaves, less densely clustered than the leaves of the giant bassweed. The leaves of the muskie weed grow widely spaced and the main stem is almost comically bent to meet the base of each leaf. Both species of bassweed and the muskie weed are commonly found in three to twelve feet of water.

The ribbon-leaf *Potamogeton* pondweeds are found in less alkaline waters too. These are more delicate fringe-leafed and grassy species that thrive in relatively shallow places. The familiar ribbon-leaf pondweed *Potamogeton epihydrous* grows best in alkaline lakes, but with a richly silted bottom it can flourish in surprisingly acid habitats. The delicate flat-stemmed *Potamogeton zosterifolius* is primarily an alkaline-water plant commonly called eelgrass. *Potamogeton pusillus* is the narrow-leaf pondweed. The familiar sago pondweed is *Potamogeton pectinatus*, a particularly lush species found in lime-rich shallows throughout the United States. It is perhaps the first to emerge each spring. It thrives in one to six feet of water, although its tubers can root themselves in a fertile bottom as much as eight feet down. Its fragile hairlike leaves grow in dense fringes, and two or three separate stalks may sprout from a single root structure. These delicate leaf systems wave restlessly in the water, and their metabolism is adapted to a totally submerged existence.

The compound and thread-leaf plants include the hornworts, milfoil, bushy pondweed, and *Elodea* waterweed. The common coontail hornwort is the species *Ceratophyllum demersum,* which grows fully submerged in relatively deep water. Its beds are remarkably dense in suitably alkaline environments, often thick enough to make wading difficult. The leaves are three-forked filaments, growing in whorls at regular nodal intervals. The floating branches are two to three feet long, and actual root structure is absent. The seeds germinate in the bottom silts, but the young plants do not develop roots and drift up toward the surface film. The minute male and female blossoms grow in fruitlike clusters along the stem. These reproductive organs never reach the surface, but their male stamens are buoyed upward to the meniscus, precipitating their pollen back down to the female flowers. *Centrophyllum demersum* is entirely tied to an aquatic existence, since its pollination is even dependent on the water. Its branches often break into small pieces in late summer and early fall, drifting with drainage-lake currents and winds until they sink to the bottom as winter comes. They lie virtually dormant until spring, when they seek the light of the epilimnion and develop into fully grown beds of hornwort. Coontail hornworts are poor in streams, since they can choke out all other plant life, but in lakes and impoundments they provide vast populations of food-chain organisms and superb oxygenation.

Water milfoil is another important plant, both the mare's tail and fernlike foxtail species. The mare's tail, *Hippuris vulgaris,* is a strange perennial, adapted to both moist shoreline soils and shallows. It prefers alkaline waters rich in lime salts. It is a strange plant form, its spine protruding from the water above a firm root system. Beyond the surface, its leaves are stiff and sharp-looking, but underneath they are slender and drooping like the hair of a horse's tail. Its reproductive blossoms cluster around the stem nodes at the root of each whorl of leaves. It is widely distributed. Water milfoil is a common plant, and its dense, fernlike growth is typical of slow streams and relatively shallow lakes. The common American species *Myriophyllum spicatum* is a fine oxygenating plant. Its roots grow firmly in the bottom, with graceful branches that reach almost to the surface. However, their coarsely clustered flowers project above the water, and pollination occurs in the atmosphere. The primary stem is relatively thick, with approximately four delicate leaves like fiddlebacks projecting from each node. The bushy pondweed *Najas flexilis* grows like a darkly colored carpet on the bottom, its stems densely tangled together in spiralling layers. Its qualities of food and shelter for bottom-hugging nymphs and larvae are excellent, it provides good oxygenation, and it is one of the few stillwater species that are also well adapted to streams.

The ubiquitous Canadian waterweed *Elodea canadensis* is a disaster in streams, and can cause serious problems in alkaline lakes. *Elodea* is a truly aquatic plant, existing in both a free-floating and a rooted state. It thrives so successfully in trout water that it can literally choke a small lake, or force a small stream from its banks. Its stems are thickly clustered in three-leaf whorls spaced a half-inch apart. Each leaf has a single longitudinal vein and is as transparent as fine parchment. The stems are quite fragile. Their broken fragments drift free and develop into wholly new plants. This ability quickly multiplies its thickets of growth, and creates frustrating problems in weed management. Cutting these weeds is useful, except that the cut pieces and fragments will continue to flourish, and the dismembered stems cannot be left in the water. The flowers of the *Elodea* plant are tiny and inconspicuous. It is the female blooms that grow on the stems which actually reach the surface. The male flowers are subaquatic until they are ready for pollination. Ripe male flowers break free from their short stems and buoy up to the surface, where pollination ultimately occurs. *Elodea* is so dense in alkaline streams that a single handful can shelter hundreds of snails and tiny crustaceans, but it so chokes out available open water that it is a serious problem in most waters.

The common water celery *Vallisneria spiralis* is another plant that often chokes out optimal habitat. The shallows of alkaline lakes and ponds are often clogged with its slender leaves, undulating with the slightest wind riffle on the surface. It is a conventionally rooted plant, and its streaming underwater leaves can be three to four feet in length. Water celery has tiny greenish yellow female flowers which bloom at the surface, attached to long spiralling stems. Its male flowers develop in spear-shaped clusters near the bottom. Each separate flower generates enough oxygen when it reaches fecundity to buoy itself up to the surface. The *Vallisneria* pollen is quite sticky, and the male flowers finally adhere to the females. Once pollination is accomplished, the female stems contract the fertilized blossoms to the bottom silt. The species is extremely well distributed in our trout-water latitudes and is a fine oxygenator.

Water smartweed is a species found in calcium-rich ponds and many lakes in our northeastern states. *Polygonum amphibium* has pink and rose-colored flowers that sometimes grow in great abundance. The smart-weed is a shallow water plant, and its smooth elliptical leaves float on the surface. Several species are found in the United States, varying between three to six inches in height.

The round-leaf sundew *Drosera rotundifolia* has a series of lollipop-shaped leaves, growing in a rosette from the base of its single stem. The leaves are covered with glandular filaments. Each filament secretes a sticky fluid designed to trap small insects, and the leaves are often covered with flies, their juices slowly draining into the plant tissues. The five-petaled whitish flowers blossom with several tiny buds on the stem below. Other American species have spear-shaped and threadlike leaves that all secrete a similar fluid. The sundews are plants of springfed ponds and bogs.

Utricularia vulgaris is a graceful plant that seems less ominous than the predatory sundews, but that is an illusion. The bladderwort is deadly. Its stems are clustered with tiny sacs that capture and digest minute water organisms and nymphs. The bladderworts all have slender stems, and delicate branchial filaments. Each leaf system carries small utricles or traps. The *Utricularia* plants lack true roots. The root functions are performed by dense dark green rhizoids at one end of a drifting bladderwort stem. *Utricularia vulgaris* has pale yellow flowers on stems that reach three or four inches past the surface. Each bladderlike sac has a labial opening filled with bristling filaments, and inside there are more delicate hairs. Digestive secretions are produced from these glandular filaments and tissues. The labial filaments are sensitive to the presence of prey and stimulate the sac to open. The opening bladder draws in water and prey together, and the predatory bladderwort is so deadly that a large plant can simultaneously trap and digest as many as 100,000 living organisms. *Utricularias* are found in our trout-producing latitudes, particularly in richly eutrophic habitat, and when the alkalinity-loving plants are absent from a lake or impound-ment, the presence of bladderwort is certain evidence of their acid water chemistry.

The duckweed plants are similar to the pond lilies and spatterdock in appearance, although they are much more primitive in character. They also include the diminutive *Wolffias,* the smallest of all flowering plants.

These several genera have no true leaf structure or stems and use a leaflike thallus to perform both functions. Almost microscopic flowers grow from their upper surfaces, the male blooms consisting only of a single stamen. The female blossoms are only a delicate pistil. However, most duckweeds reproduce by a budding process in which the thallus separates into two distinct plants. *Spirodela polyrhiza* is a common duckweed in our waters, forming chlorophyllic coverings on still ponds. Thousands of single plants make up such duckweed masses, each with four to fifteen tendrils hanging below its circular thallus. *Lemna triscula* is the widely distributed ivy-leaf duckweed. Its wrinkled daggerlike leaves form puzzling zigzag chains which float like subaquatic lattices in the water, with both leaves and stems interlocking. The lesser duckweed *Lemna minor* is tiny, but in spite of its size it can literally cover the surface of a springfed pond. The thallus of these tiny duckweeds is oval shaped and less than a quarter of an inch in length, and a single tendril is from two to three inches long. *Wolffia columbiana* is typical of the smallest flowering species in our aquatic habitat. These microscopic plants drift just under the meniscus, looking like minute greenish flecks of dust floating among the tendrils of the larger duckweeds. The thallus of these tiny plants is less than a thirty-second of an inch in diameter, and has no tendrils or roots. Their role in the oxygenation of fish habitat is intriguing, and at the beginning of autumn, their cells are so saturated with starch that they drift to the bottom and winter there.

Water lilies are familiar plants in quiet lakes and impoundments with both white and yellow species living together in large communities. The yellow ecotypes are more common, and thrive in many lakes and ponds where the white-flowered varieties are not found. The common spatterdock lily *Nymphaea advena* has coarsely ovoid leaves. Its flower is a yellow or pale yellowish-green bowl composed of overlapping petals. The cylindrical pistil and pale stamens are tightly clustered inside. During pollinization, the six petals open to admit insects carrying pollen from other flowers. Later the flower opens wider, and its pollen is collected by other insects. They carry it to the ripe stigmata of other lilies, thereby preventing self-fertilization. The stems are extremely strong, rooting deep in the detritus and bottom silts. *Nymphaea variegata* is a yellow spatterdock having flowers touched with purplish mottlings. It is found in the more northerly latitudes. There are other species, and *Nymphaea microphylla* is a smaller version of the larger yellow pond lilies. The common sweet water lily *Castalia odorata* is quite familiar on American lakes and impoundments. The lily pads are thick and leathery, and are rooted on stalks so hardy they are quite difficult to break or cut. The upper surfaces are waterproof, and the undersides are sometimes richly flushed and veined with bright crimson. Heavy winds and rain cannot damage the beds of lilies. The flowers are brilliantly white or the palest pink, and their exceptional fragrance when they are blooming is carried some distance from the water on the wind. Like the common spatterdock, these lilies expose their stamens and pistils at different times to inhibit self-pollinization. The blossoms remain closed until the morning sun warms their petals, and they close again in early afternoon. Lilies are poor oxygenators but provide good fish cover.

Like the mangrove colonies in salt water, pickerel weed is continually invading aquatic habitat. Our common species *Pontederia cordata* is common in drainage lakes and flowages, often crowding into the inlet zones where the currents settle out dense concentrations of silt and nutrients and detritus. Pickerel weed grows one to three feet high, with thick trowel-shaped leaves. Its violet flowers grow in bottle-brush clusters about three inches long. It is common along slow-flowing streams and lake shallows, blooming from June until October. Pickerel weed is only fair as an oxygenator.

The broad-leaved arrowhead *Sagittaria latifolia* is another aquatic plant that is highly adaptable to different levels of water, like the pickerel weed. Arrowheads grow in the shallows of silty shorelines or shoals, reaching from six inches to two feet in height. Their leaves are like the pointed blades of a one-way cultivator, rising stiffly above the water. The flowers are rosettes of three petals, growing from the nodes of the stalk in groups of three. The female blossoms are typically the lowest on the stalk. Wave action and water depth are known to affect the configuration of the leaves, and alkalinity clearly affects their size. Arrowheads found in the deeper areas of the littoral usually have narrower leaves, and plants that are often submerged or subject to strong wave action develop relatively slender leaves. It is interesting that an arrowhead colony that has lost its usual water levels soon sheds its narrow leaves, and exchanges them for larger leaves better suited to function in the atmosphere. Arrowheads are poor oxygenators.

Our common water plantain *Alisma plantago-aquatica* has delicate, blade-shaped leaves. It grows both on moist shores and in quiet shallows. Water plantain readily adapts to semiterrestrial life. It grows from one to three feet high. The leaves are strongly veined, with petioles that grow directly from the roots. Given optimal depths of water, the plants develop both leaves that project through the surface and slender ribbonlike leaves that undulate below the surface like water celery. Its tiny flowers are both pinkish and white, almost microscopic on its delicate candelabralike branches. Plantain is a poor oxygenator, unless it has well-developed subaquatic leaves in permanent shallows.

The immersed upright types of water plants include the bur reeds, cattails, and bulrushes. Like the other semiaquatic plants, these slender species thrive in the shallow water and moist soils of bogs and impoundments and lakes. They are also found growing at the borders of slow-flowing streams, and although they are primarily a stillwater plant and we seldom associate them with trout fishing, there are a surprising number of streams where they do thrive.

Bur reeds are a type of aquatic vegetation which combine slender, swordlike leaves and green burs formed of densely packed seeds. The giant bur reed *Sparganium eurycarpum* is often found in company with water plantain, arrowheads, pickerel weeds, and cattails. It grows from three to six feet in height. There are very slender leaves about three-quarters of an inch in width. The spherical flowers sprout above the larger pistillate burs. The branching bur reed *Sparganium americanum* is similar, although it is more slender and has a clearly defined stem. It grows only one to two feet in height. Bur reeds are poor oxygenators.

Cattails are familiar plants of our lakes and impoundments and marshes. Typical growths range from four to eight feet in height. The plants are extremely prolific, with creeping root-systems that grow in all directions. These creeping roots sprout new plants each spring, until each parent cattail is the focus of an entire colony. Their leaves are slender, rising well above their flower stems, blowing and shining in the wind. Both broad-leaved and narrow-leaved species are common.

The broad-leaf cattail *Typha latifolia* has a two-part flower spike. Its upper section contains the male staminate functions, while its lower pistillates are female. Pollen is carried between plants on the wind. The male stamens atrophy soon after fertilization is accomplished, leaving the female pistillates to develop into the chocolate-colored cattail head. Its growth reaches about an inch in diameter and lasts through the entire winter. Its structure contains as many as 250,000 seeds, and in the spring it loses its smooth cylindrical form, as the seeds loosen and scatter into the water. *Typha latifolia* is widely distributed throughout North America and blooms in midsummer. Its structure shelters an extensive insect community throughout the year. Plant lice and leaf-mining moths are found on the leaves. Other moths lay their eggs in the cattail pistillates. Snout beetles feed on both the roots and the core of the stalks. The roots themselves shelter marchfly and cranefly larvae, and hatching *Odonata* often clamber up their leaves to hatch. *Typha angustifolia* is the narrow-leafed cattail; both its leaves and its flowering spikes are more slender than the more common species. Its range is largely eastern, from the Labrador to the Gulf of Mexico, and it blooms in late June or early July. Fishermen seldom think of cattails along trout water, but my memories include bankside cattails from the springfed trout lakes on Long Island to beaver ponds in Colorado and Wyoming.

The hard-stemmed bulrush *Scirpus acutis* is a poor oxygenator, like the similar cattails and reeds, and it thrives in the shallows of many wind-riffled lakes. Although it grows in much thinner colonies than the cattails, readily admitting the wave action of the open lake, the hard-stemmed bulrush has an intricately interwoven lacework of roots. Such root systems grow in concert with other plant species until their fabric is strong enough to support a wading fisherman if he moves with care. The hard-stemmed rush is a hardy plant of surprisingly tough fibers and a needle-sharp point. *Scirpus validus* is the slender soft-stemmed tule, and it is also found in the silty shallows of fertile lakes. These rushes lined the shallows of the first trout lake I ever fished, a small eutrophic pond just below the timberline on Mount Massive in Colorado. Although we seldom think of them as trout-stream plants, they also thrive along streams like Silver Creek in Idaho, and I have often stalked shy rainbows there, moving through rushes higher than my head—literally dividing them with my left hand to create a narrow corridor wide enough for a casting stroke.

Aquatic vegetation can tell us much about the fishing potential of a lake or reservoir, and about tactics of fishing it. Some plants are clear indicators of alkalinity, good fly hatches, and fine populations of trout or grayling. Others suggest acid water chemistry, sparse hatches, and a small colony of poorly conditioned fish. Alkaline waters are usually rich with freshwater shrimps and sowbugs, and weeds provide both food and shelter for many organisms in the fish's diet. Weeds also delineate the channels and dropoffs, where fishing is often best. Since still waters lack the oxygenation of flowing streams, their weeds are both more numerous and more important.

Although our explorations into the ecology of lakes and impoundments have touched on many secrets of their underwater world, the skilled biologist is still humbled by the puzzling cornucopia of mysteries that remain beyond his knowledge. Life in a lake or reservoir is still a microscopic incident in the fabric of the entire biosphere. Its water is held in a minuscule depression in the lithosphere, literally cupped in the structure of the earth. Its meniscus undulates gently against the pressure of the atmosphere, and the liquid underneath the surface is a tiny facet of the aquatic world.

The water on the surface of our planet is a vast circulatory rhythm, with the seas functioning as its primary reservoir, and the energy of solar radiation fueling the entire system. The flow of energy triggered through a high-country pond or spring-fed drainage lake is a complex series of interrelationships, and only in recent years have we begun to grasp their intricate clocklike topologies. Solar insolation performs two functions—its obvious thermal impact upon both habitat and the metabolic processes, and its subtle triggering of the photosynthetic process and its subcycles of life-giving energy.

The boundary between the hydrosphere and the atmosphere is obvious, while their interrelationship is more subtle and complex. Both hydrosphere and atmosphere function in concert, with the continuous evaporation of moisture into the air, and the life-giving gases in the atmosphere passing into solution: all life in our biosphere is hinged on this interlocking cycle, yet the biology of a lake is still unfathomable, as the late zoologist Marston Bates observed in his book *The Forest and the Sea:*

> While the life of a pond may not be as spectacular as the life of a reef, its marvels are of the same kind. I have spent many hours of my life sitting quietly by ponds or looking into the water as my canoe drifted over the shallows of a lake, trying to understand what was going on in that unique world shut off by the surface of the water.

A pond, especially, has the fascination of the miniature. It is a world clearly limited by the shores and bottom and surface; a sufficiently self-contained world, a small enough world so that you should be able to figure out everything going on there, describe it, analyze it, perhaps fit the relations among the living things there into neat equations—and solving the equations, solve all mysteries. Understanding the pond, one would fully understand the biosphere.

But the pond still eludes me.

5. The Biology of
Pollution and Dams

It has been more than twenty-five years since those summers in the forests above Rottenbuch, where its Augustinian monastery lies in the gentle pine-covered hills of the Pfaffenwinkel. It is an ancient valley once travelled by Roman soldiers and trade caravans moving through the mountains from the marketplace of Augsburg to the rich warehouses of Venice.

The river winds north into the foothills of Bavaria. It flows swiftly past charming villages and steep-roofed farms, and in the country above Unterammergau and Bad Kohlgrub it has carved itself an impressive limestone gorge. Above its deeply cut bedrock cliffs, its tumbling character is changed. Its valley is a rich patchwork of meadows and grainfields and mountain farms. The villages are clustered about their churches, and on the slopes above their onion-topped towers, the foothills are darkly forested.

Oberammergau is the famous village in the meadows where the little river winds north from its alpine headwaters in the lovely Graswang valley. It is a beautiful village of richly decorated houses, their walls covered with biblical frescos and carved timbers. Most of their gables shelter carved crucifixes, and woodcarving is the primary source of income for the population. The Kofelberg and the other mountains of the Ammergau shelter it from the northern winter storms. Its gentle valley is enclosed by other mountains like the Kolbenalm and Sonnenbergspitze and Pürschlingberg, well laced with hiking paths and small huts and shrines.

Beyond these peaceful mountains the towering Wetterstein escarpment rises above Garmisch-Partenkirchen, on the threshold of the Tyrolean Alps. The silent forests cover these mountains, with high meadows far above the valley floor. The tinkling bells of the summer herds are mixed with the shrill calls of the marmots, and there are chamois herds in the barren peaks. The forests have long been royal hunting preserves for the Bavarian monarchs, with such fine herds of red stag that the valley was chosen for the remarkable little Linderhof Castle—a jewel box of exquisite Baroque architecture in a setting of magnificent grottos and gardens, its reflecting pool crowned with a fountain of gold sculpture.

Oberammergau has a unique history. Swedish armies were finally driven from the region in 1632, only to give way to the greater terror of outbreaks of bubonic plague in nearby villages like Eschenlohe and Garmisch-Partenkirchen and Mittenwald. The harvest of death was unthinkable. Oberammergau posted guards outside the village and forbade all commerce with the region. The quarantine failed when a farmhand from Eschenlohe became so worried about his family that he evaded the cordon of guards and crossed the mountains at night. It was a foolish errand. The poor workman collapsed and died when he returned, and the plague returned with him.

Hundreds died in both the village and the valley, until the town elders made a vow to perform a religious pageant based on the life of Christ every ten years, if the remaining population of the village were spared. It was a desperate pledge, but the terrible blight suddenly ended as quickly as it had begun. The villagers performed the first *Passionspiel* in 1633, and the succeeding generations have kept the vow made by their ancestors, repeating the performance every decade for almost 350 years.

It is tragic that Oberammergau has worried less about the river than its religious traditions. Although the Graswang valley above the village is carefully protected and preserved, and the little Ammer flows swift and cold in its alpine meadows, the village discharges a surprising amount of pollution downstream.

It was a river I fished and loved in those years spent in Germany after the war, staying in a charming *Gasthäus* with carved doorframes and lintels and delicate frescos on its masonry walls. My room was high under the sheltering, timber-framed eaves and was filled with heavy traditional furniture. The bed was covered with a huge feather-stuffed quilt, and there was a small scrollwork balcony that looked down into the street that led toward the river. Sometimes I dressed nymphs there in bright weather, drinking coffee and eating fresh *Brötchen* still hot from the kitchen, but on overcast days and evenings I was usually on the stream.

There are many happy memories, like the April when there were so many trout in the willow-lined stretch just above the town, and they rose greedily to the dark little *Baetis* hatches. There was a fine meadow run about three miles above Oberammergau, and sometimes I walked along the river in good weather and fished back toward the town. There was a sheltered bend in the river away from the road, and I often left a bottle of Piesporter or Gewürztraminer chilling there in the watercress. The wine was deliciously cold when I came back downstream and stopped for a lunch of ham and fresh sausages and hard rolls along the stream. There was a cold, spring-fed beat above the town that lay along the Ettalkloster road where the trout rose softly among the ranunculus and trailing mosses. There were mallards nesting there one summer, and I often fed the greenhead male a few pieces of fresh *Brötchen* when it came downstream to defend its mate. There was a big rainbow on the edge of the village, just above a millpond weir, but it usually ignored my flies.

Finally I caught it one morning when a fine hatch of purple-bodied *Paraleptophlebia* duns was coming off the millpond. It was a good fish of twenty-odd inches, and while I was fighting it in the shallows, the innkeeper came walking along the stream.

Guten morgen! he waved. *Good fish?*

Jawohl! The rainbow made a strong run into the deep moss-lined channel and jumped spectacularly.

Regenbogenforelle? he asked.

Ja! I yelled back. *It's a fine rainbow!*

Bravo! he applauded.

It was almost an anticlimax after weeks of trying for the millpond rainbow, and although I released it carefully, it was curiously gone the next time I fished that water.

Sometimes I fished below the town, hiking along the Füssen road to the limestone gorge downstream, where the path led down past the woodcutter's cottage to the lower river. It was there that I took a three-pound grayling, fishing a dry fly along a mossy ledge. It was a beautiful fish, and when I left it with the woodcutter's wife, she invited me inside for coffee mixed with the raw potato *Schnaps* the farmers distill in the region.

However, the time that persists in the memory was the afternoon below the slaughterhouse. There was a good hatch of sedges coming off in the swift run below the footbridge. The fish were rising eagerly, but they refused all the flies I tried for almost an hour. It was a dark little Welshman's Button that finally worked, and I took a dozen fish quickly. There were two large fish working along the timber pilings that supported the center of the footbridge, their rises showy and strong. Several times I had watched the fish lying in the shadow of the pilings, and there was one that looked almost black which was at least four or five pounds.

It could be the big fish! I thought excitedly.

My sedge fly was carefully dried and preened after taking a small fish, and I was false casting to reach the big trout when a pipe below the slaughterhouse suddenly discharged a torrent of brightly colored effluents and offal. The river smelled of the waste scraps and torn viscera and clotted blood from the livestock that had been slaughtered that morning; its currents were totally discolored with the ugly flood. The fetid water lasted several minutes, and when the river cleared again, the hatch was finished and the smell clung to my waders. Small pieces of flesh and clotted blood had lodged between the stones, and a length of entrails had tangled around a drowned limb. It was a nauseating shock, and I never fished happily below the village again.

It was like a fatal sickness in the family.

Such forms of organic pollution are both obvious and ugly, but contamination of our lakes and streams takes many less obvious forms. It is critical for fishermen to understand that the more subtle kinds of pollution are perhaps the most damaging to our fisheries. It is equally important to grasp the fact that not all pollution is manmade, and that nature itself can destroy a stream as inexorably as a factory.

The physicochemical and biological impacts of pollution typically occur in several ways. Such impacts can damage trout habitat in themselves, or work in a combination of eroding factors. Urban sewage is one type of pollution covering the full spectrum of negative effects. The toxicity of poisonous compounds and acid drainages is an obvious danger. Organic wastes from population centers, animal husbandry, and food processing can reach such densities that the available dissolved oxygen is depleted in decomposing them, leaving too little oxygen for the fish and their food chain. Suspended solids can totally choke the bottom zones where spawning takes place and can smother food-chain organisms. When such particulates are highly abrasive, like pumice and volcanic ash, their grinding effects on the gill filaments can prove fatal to trout and grayling. Excessive fertilization from industrial and agricultural land use is a troublesome factor in many regions, smothering habitat with aquatic vegetation and the turbidity of algal bloom. Nontoxic salts are less damaging to anadromous species like trout and salmon, which migrate freely between their parent rivers and the sea, but they can pose a serious problem in heavily populated areas.

Temperature changes that raise a habitat toward the maximum thermal tolerances of the fish or lower its temperatures below workable metabolic levels are perhaps the most deadly form of pollution. Such thermal pollution can result from the obvious cooling effluents of energy plants and industrial processes. It can trigger dramatic fishkills or the rapid loss of habitat, but it can also come imperceptibly and without fanfare—as in two mindless American centuries of building dams for sawmills and gristmills, clearing millions of square miles for agriculture, cutting numberless trees to build our cities and railroads and to string wires for power and communications, stripping the hemlock forests to provide acid bark for the tanneries, and finally producing the explosive midcentury growth of power generation and suburban development.

Poisons can occur in solution from many sources. Industrial poisons can include many free acids and alkalies, chromium salts from tanneries and metallurgy, zinc from galvanization, toxic dyes, cyanides and phenols from mining and chemical production, and various pesticide compounds. Perhaps the most common toxic substances of the inorganic type are free hydrogen sulphide, ammonia, chlorine, copper, zinc, lead, silver, chromium, and the deadly mercury. Surprisingly small concentrations of such compounds can eradicate both the fish and their diet forms. Dissolved zinc or copper can denigrate the gill systems and impair respiration. Phosphorus invariably results in fatal haemolysis. Fluorine is lethal to fish life in concentrations of more than five parts per million. Acidity itself creates fatal metabolic problems for both trout and grayling. Some poisons are relatively degradable, but others stubbornly resist precipitation. Ammonia is rather quickly assimilated, although it is still quite deadly. Phenolic compounds and cyanides will also oxidize, but their absorption in trout habitat is painfully slow.

Heavy-metals pollution from copper, cadmium, nickel, cobalt, lead, and zinc can virtually eradicate life from lakes and streams having only faint concentrations of these minerals. Copper and zinc are lethal at 0.5 parts per million, and lead will kill fish at only 0.3 parts per million. The toxicity of metals like mercury, cadmium, and cobalt is evident at approximately 0.3 parts per million. Cyanides prove fatal in minuscule solutions of 0.05 parts per million. Streams gradually dilute such poisons as more and more tributaries and springheads add their flow but such poisons are deadly.

Many poisons are precipitated through normal chemical processes, while organic types are often oxidized and made nontoxic. Natural textile dyes were originally obtained from plant materials and minerals, but they have been almost entirely replaced with synthetic compounds. Most of these artificial dyes are made with a coal-tar base, particularly hydrocarbons like benzene or anthracene, and analine dyes which combine carbon, hydrogen, and nitrogen are perhaps the most important. Acids are the catalytic media for many dye processes, along with the work of the tanneries. Such industrial effluents have severely damaged many watersheds in the past.

Other poisons are used extensively in forestry, animal husbandry, and agriculture. Most pesticides are highly toxic to aquatic life. Endrin is so deadly that less than a quarter of a pound in a million gallons of water is fatal to trout and grayling. Some toxic compounds accumulate in the bottom silts and minute aquatic organisms until they are passed along the food chain, their concentrations multiplying in the flesh and fat content of each succeeding predator, until dangerous concentrations are finally lodged in the anatomy of the fish themselves. Others so thoroughly eradicate the food chain and the aquatic insects critical in fly-fishing that the fishing is ended. Pesticides have been used in recent years to control insect populations, suppress undesirable vegetation, eliminate crop fungus and contamination, eradicate predators, and destroy undesirable species like rats and pocket gophers.

Poisons used in pesticides are usually grouped into two primary categories: toxic substances used against the digestive tract; and substances which attack the neural or respiratory systems. The application of most insecticides is done through dusting, spraying, fumigation in a sealed-off space, and with aerosol sprays which release the toxic compounds in a fine mist of deadly impact.

Arsenics are perhaps the most widely known of the poisons which work in the digestive tract. Other gastric poisons include many fluorine compounds, lead and other metallic salts, and organic substances. Contact poisons that enter through the integument and respiratory systems include sulphur compounds, nicotine, petroleum, and coal-tar derivatives, rotenone, pyrethrum, chlorinated hydrocarbons, and the organo-phosphorus compounds. Rotenone is well known for its toxicity to fish, since it paralyzes their gill systems, and it has long been used to gather food in primitive cultures. The chlorinated hydrocarbons are also highly toxic to fish. It is a group of toxic compounds that includes benzene hexachloride, aldrin, dieldrin, toxaphene, endrin, lindane, heptachlor, and dichloro-diphenyl-trichlorothane—the now infamous DDT developed in World War II, which has had tragically widespread ecological echoes everywhere in the past thirty years.

Some of these compounds are especially deadly, since they are not readily dissipated in the environment, and are also not broken down in the digestive processes of fish and other wildlife. Concentrations persist in the organisms of the food chain, and in digesting these diet forms, the poisonous residues of insecticides like dieldrin and heptachlor and dichloro-diphenyl-trichlorothane accumulate steadily in the fat and body tissues of the trout. DDT is particularly guilty of such residual concentrations. Fish that safely metabolize a trace quantity of pesticide from one spraying can find their bodies unable to survive accumulations in their tissues from subsequent applications.

There are many examples of such residual poisons. Serious concentrations of dieldrin are known in the brown trout population of Loch Leven in Scotland, and persist several years after the source of the contamination has been eliminated. Fishkills and serious damage to fly life have occurred on many eastern trout streams in recent years as a result of controlling infestations of spruce budworm and gypsy moth larvae. Large-scale spraying of commercial forests in both Canada and the United States has caused numerous instances of high fish mortality. Spruce budworm operations in Maine resulted in extensive fishkills, and high concentrations of dichloro-diphenyl-trichlorothane were later found in the tissues of surviving trout and salmon. Its lethal properties on fish populations are evident with concentrations of only a half pound per acre, and only fifteen to twenty percent of that mixture will eradicate as much as ninety percent of the plankton.

Similar spraying along the Miramichi in New Brunswick was conducted over a twenty-year period, until nearly ten million acres were poisoned by 1969. Extensive fishkills among brook trout and baby salmon occurred in these years, and in 1954 test fish were caged in a river during spraying. Sixty to ninety percent died within three weeks, while there was only a two percent mortality in the cages on an adjacent stream that remained unsprayed. The studies were an intriguing introduction to the pathology of insecticide poisoning. The primary symptoms were extreme agitation, followed by severe respiratory ataxia and paralysis, and the initial symptoms were tremors in the skeletal muscles.

Perhaps the most interesting example of biological magnification is the Michigan experience using dichloro-diphenyl-trichlorothane in spraying both the forests and the orchards farther south in the Lower Peninsula. Its poisons leached and drained through the riverine networks into the Great Lakes. High mortality among small fish in the rivers occurred, and concentrations persisted in both the small trout and their diet forms. Research indicates that seventy-five percent of newly hatched fish were dying from pesticide concentrations in their larval yolk sacs. The pesticide also gravitated into the plankton and other tiny organisms in the lakes, where they were eaten by alewives and smelt. Through the puzzling phenomenon called biological magnification, the concentration in parts per million of pesticide increased with each organism in the food chain. Finally, the trout and salmon that had migrated downstream into the lakes gorged themselves on the alewives and smelt, and more than fifty parts per million of dichloro-diphenyl-trichlorothane were ultimately found in their body fats, concentrations that made them unfit for human consumption—a tragic escalation of the original poisons.

The organo-phosphorus compounds are more numerous than the hydrocarbon types, but are less commonly used. Production volumes are relatively small. These pesticides include malathion, phosphamidon, parathion, and menazon. The group is generally less toxic to fish life than the chlorinated hydrocarbons, although our experience with their long-term effects is brief.

Organo-mercury fungicides have also proved themselves highly toxic to aquatic life. Several extensive fishkills have resulted from concentrations of alkyl mercury compounds like methyl mercury dicyandiamide; these are common agricultural fungicides used in the preparation of seeds. Phenyl mercury compounds commonly escape into lakes and streams from paper-pulp operations and industrial processes that employ chlorine-alkaline compounds. Phenyl mercury is a particularly deadly poison.

Other poisons commonly used in agriculture are herbicides, disinfectants used on livestock, and pesticides used to control rodent populations. The primary herbicides include compounds like 2-4-D, Mecoprop, and 2-4-5-T. Recent tragedies have taught us that such petrochemistry is literally riddled with toxic compounds, particularly the lethal threat of dioxins. The phenolic disinfectants often contain toxic compounds like dieldrin and benzene hexachloride, which are highly toxic to fish life. Both sodium and potassium cyanide are commonly used to suppress and control rodent populations, but there are instances of use in illegal fishing.

Toxic effluents display some interesting impacts on both the species found in a biosystem and its population dynamics. Mortality is often complete at the source of the poisons, and their effect in a seepage lake is concentrated and contained. Drainage lakes, reservoirs, and flowages also purge themselves slowly, but a flowing stream has surprising resilience if no fresh sources of toxicity are encountered. High mortality occurs for some distance below the initial source of pollution, but then a gradual increase in the types and numbers of aquatic species occurs. It is interesting that the types of aquatic life increase more rapidly than the total population, depending on the variables of distance, volume and velocity of flow in a particular drainage system.

Toxic pesticides are sometimes used in managing a fishery in both lake and riverine systems. Mosquito suppression has long been a standard procedure, starting with the use of petroleum to smother the pupae attempting to breathe through the surface film and using DDT in recent years. Other insecticides are now in use in controlling malaria, equine encephalitis, and other mosquito-carried diseases. Herbicides and pesticides have been used to suppress explosive algal growth and zooplankton populations. Similar population controls are sometimes used where Diptera larvae and other minute organisms have multiplied to unacceptable densities in potable water supplies, or where such biting and nonbiting midges threaten summer colonies and waterside recreation. There are also lakes where the populations of burrowing mayflies, particularly the *Ephemera* and *Hexagenia* nymphs, are so large that their spent adults lie rotting like a heavy snowfall on the beaches or darken the porch screens of summer cottages along the Great Lakes.

Pesticides are also commonly used to control predators, coarse-fish species, and baitfish populations that have been accidentally introduced into trout habitat, thrived, and damaged the equilibrium of an optimal biosystem. Such lakes are sometimes poisoned to remove all fish species, and restocked with game fish once the toxicity has dissipated. Special lampricidal poisons have been developed to eradicate spawning lamprey eels in the Great Lakes drainage system. The toxicity of these lampricides apparently has no effect on higher forms of fish life, although evidence is growing that the toxic compounds slowly accumulate in bottom silts, and are affecting the burrowing mayfly nymphs so important in the food chain of the Michigan and Wisconsin rivers.

It should be remembered that the toxicity of pesticides will vary widely in different biosystemic situations. Variation is also observed in the susceptibility of different organisms within a single biotic community. Other variables exist too, in terms of the solvents, wetting agents, and other media used in aquatic application of pesticides. Associated bird life, terrestrial species, and amphibians can result in unexpected hazards, possibly carrying toxic concentrations to other waters. Seasonal influences can also play a considerable role. Migratory species can transport toxic compounds surprising distances, and aquatic organisms that hibernate can be exposed to toxic compounds that have precipitated into bottom silts and detritus in lakes that have otherwise purged themselves. The return of such lesser species to the food chain can result in fresh contamination or biological magnification. Therefore, the dissipation of toxicity and the recovery of a particular fishery habitat depends on more factors than the mere toxic concentration and character of its subaquatic community.

The thermal pollution resulting from temperature changes has only been studied in recent years. Its impact on a fishery can prove as serious as the effluents of sewage wastes or toxic substances, even though the habitat remains uncontaminated when its temperature range is changed. Minor increases in temperature can prove a major problem in trout and grayling habitat, although such changes might not be considered thermal pollution in coarse-fish waters. Cold water biosystems are infinitely more fragile. Temperature has a direct effect on the solubility and concentration of oxygen. Fresh water at sea level under a constant atmospheric pressure can entrain as much as fifteen parts per million oxygen at the threshold of freezing, approximately ten parts per million at sixty-eight degrees, and only seven parts per million at eighty-five degrees. Therefore, thermal changes alone can deplete oxygen.

The discharge of heated effluents from industrial plants and the cooling effluents from power stations can result in a temperature increase of several degrees. Such a temperature rise in a stream or lake already seriously polluted with organic wastes can create a high biochemical oxygen demand. That demand can further deplete the available oxygen to the threshold of asphyxiation for fish and other aquatic organisms. The depletion of oxygen is not only tied to its reduced solubility at the higher temperatures but also to the acceleration of both the metabolic rate of aquatic species and the decomposition of the pollution itself. These factors account for the curious availability of oxygen in polluted waters during the winter months and the virtual absence of both oxygen and aquatic life in midsummer.

It is interesting that the toxicity of some poisons is also influenced by temperature. Rotenone is a poison which affects the respiratory system of the fish, and since the pulse rate of their gills increases with temperature, its toxicity increases with thermal pollution. Such effects are not universally true, however, since the toxicity of potassium dichromate, sodium cyanide, ammonia, and phenyl mercury compounds remains almost constant at a wide range of water temperatures.

The comprehensive impacts of thermal stress on trout are not fully understood, although some workable data are known. The fish can acclimatize themselves to rising temperatures, while the rates of increase remain gradual, but death occurs once their absolute thermal ceiling is reached. Sudden temperature changes resulting from the discharge of warm effluents, or cold water from the hypolimnion of a deep reservoir, can kill trout quickly. It is interesting that the warm effluents of a power plant can concentrate wintering fish populations, and that thermal shock can cause a cold-water fish mortality if operations are halted for maintenance or repairs. Hydraulic friction in the penstocks of a hydroelectric plant or a pump-storage facility also increases the temperature of the water downstream. Such increases are not so dramatic as the heated discharges of nuclear or fossil-fuel power plants, but in habitat already marginal for trout, comparatively small rises in temperature can prove critical. Field investigation of many thermal discharges finds they are often difficult to relate to effects on specific organisms. Such heat pollution can have unpredictably adverse effects on aquatic communities. It can eradicate or suppress many desirable species, while triggering population explosions in such nuisance organisms as bristleworms or scum-forming algae.

Although our recent awareness of thermal pollution has largely been focused on increased temperatures, little attention has been paid to decreased temperatures. Extremely cold discharges in midsummer can also kill. Such discharges can occur in the tailwaters of extremely deep impoundments, which are sometimes almost devoid of oxygen and can hold lethal concentrations of nitrogen. The regular discharge of tailings at forty-odd degrees into a trout stream at approximately sixty-five or seventy degrees can create a thermal desert at the cold end of the spectrum.

Heated effluents are potentially lethal to trout and grayling, although such discharges do not always trigger fishkills. The fish quickly learn to avoid them, just as they avoid natural hot springs and geyser discharges in our western rivers, and the heated water tends to stratify at the surface, leaving a bottom layer at almost normal temperatures. However, when the ambient river temperatures are marginally high, the discharge of heated effluents can cause extensive mortality. Much research is still needed in these problems, and trout habitat is particularly vulnerable to pollution from thermal discharges. Our current knowledge makes it impossible to predict the precise impacts of heated effluents on all riverine biota, but no thermal discharges raising the normal temperatures of a trout stream are advisable.

Turbidity and suspended solids are also critical forms of pollution in trout and grayling fisheries. The impact of such inert dissolved solids lies in both their effects on photosynthesis and oxygen and in their smothering of spawning gravel and the entire benthic community of organisms that sustain the fish themselves. Turbidity is the optical character of water which causes light energy to become diffused and absorbed rather than transmitted to the bottom. It can result from such inorganic materials as talcum-fine particles, the abrasive emissions of volcanic eruptions, or such calcareous materials as marl deposits. The effluents of coal washing and pottery manufacturing and mine slurries all contribute to fine-particle turbidity. Such tiny particles do not settle rapidly to the bottom and remain suspended in the water for considerable time.

Much coarser kinds of turbidity are produced in surface mining, gravel and stone quarries, sand-pit operations, rock crushing and concrete batch-plants, sawmills and woodworking plants and millwork shops, steel and aluminum mills, tanneries, pulp mills and paper manufacturing, dairy products, slaughterhouses, textile weaving and dyeing, and petroleum wastes. Turbidity can also result from soil erosion, overfertilization from agricultural wastes or sewage, siltation collected in the root systems of excessive weeds, bacterial growth, sewage, rotting plant materials, and the population explosions of microscopic phytoplankton and zooplankton.

The opacity of the water prevents the penetration of sunlight, limiting plant growth and photosynthesis. When there are heavy concentrations of particulates, their deposits smother all plant life and mosses and cover the clean gravel bottom. Large deposits of fine silts destroy vegetation, and even the small amounts coming from minor soil erosion or washing farm machinery regularly can alter the flora and benthic organisms. Current-loving plants found in silt-free conditions are gradually replaced by silt-loving species like *Elodea canadensis*, which rapidly collects more silt around its roots and chokes the open current-flow. Coarse particles from gravel-washing operations or surface mining can scour the bottom, destroying both algal growth and the food chain of the fish themselves. Coarse particles can also sift between stones and bottom rubble, greatly reducing the habitat of fly life in a given acreage of stream. Spawning fish will also avoid turbidity, searching out clear water to lay their eggs, and as the available spawning zones shrink the survival rate of those eggs shrinks too. Sometimes silt pollution occurs after spawning has been accomplished, its fine particulates saturating the loose gravel of the redds until water circulation through the gravel stops and the eggs are suffocated. Sometimes the particulate accumulations are literally so heavy that the eggs are crushed. Fine silts and abrasive sediments quickly kill the freshly hatched alevins, and can cause considerable distress among adult fish.

Seasonal spates and short-term turbidity associated with storms seldom damage bottom flora and fauna, except when the streambed is already densely layered with silt. Anywhere the bottom stones and gravel are free of sediments the entire benthic community usually survives, although the total population is obviously limited.

Such inert particles gradually diminish with their distribution downstream, since their volume is diluted and precipitated out. The rate of settling depends on several variables. The density and character of the particles are factors, along with stream gradients and volumes of flow. Silt often accumulates when a stream drops swiftly to a valley floor, where its sediments quickly settle in the quiet currents and eddies. Quiet reaches of river are obvious places for silt accumulations on the bottom. Sediments also gather in pools, backwaters, quiet eddies, and above weirs and other structures. The bottom wastes of sand pits, gravel washing operations, clay products, and pottery manufactures will slowly accumulate farther and farther downstream over several years. Subsequent floods are the transporting media, disturbing existing beds and distributing their particulates over and over again.

The impact of siltation on aquatic life displays some interesting relationships. Abrupt declines in both total population and the number of species occur immediately downstream from the source of such particulate pollution. Without fresh sources of silts, the populations and types of subaquatic organisms begin gradually to recover, eventually returning to the levels that existed above the pollution.

Bottom-choking accumulations of organic solids, like the sewage wastes of housing developments, can have completely different effects on aquatic

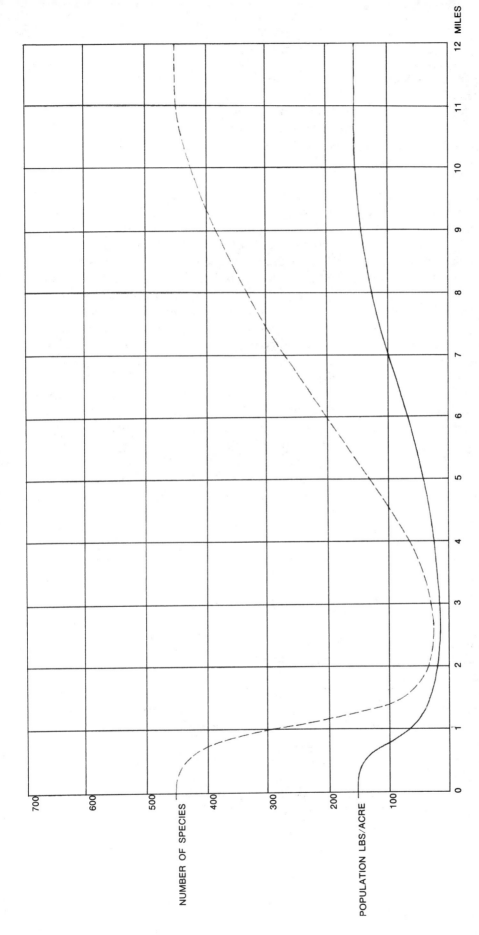

Typical impact of sedimentary pollution on stream biota

life. Where dissolved oxygen concentrations remain high and the organic solids display a minimal toxicity, stream biota will not be totally eradicated. Such solids will radically change the character of the aquatic populations, however, and the desirable gravel-loving species are quickly replaced by several undesirable organisms that seemingly thrive in decomposing sludges.

The physicochemical changes triggered by high concentrations of organic sludge in varying sections of stream result in different biological communities in those zones. Upstream from the source of the effluents the normally rich spectrum of trout-stream life exists. Bottom acreages that are recently polluted are biosystems in transition. Emulsified and floating organic solids interfere with the penetration of light. Sludge deposits start to accumulate in eddies and backwaters, and turbidity levels are high. Ambient populations of aquatic organisms are gradually forced out, and species of plants and phytoplankton and other organisms adapted to survival in decomposing sludge experience a rapid population increase. Since predators are among the species eliminated, population of these species accelerates rather quickly. While the total population is radically increased, the types of surviving species suffer an abrupt decline. Such new species include *Tubifex* and bristleworms, sowbugs, some kinds of snails, flatworms, and leeches. Fish life rapidly becomes scarce or virtually nonexistent. Flowering weeds soon disappear, preferring gravelly bottoms or normal silts for their root systems. Beneficial species of algae are soon replaced by aquamarine ecotypes that form directly on the sewage wastes, in gelatinous coverings of blue-green slime. Such growths occur primarily in shallows along the banks. Turbidity is increased with each discharge of organic wastes until ultimately the sludge accumulations are virtually deserts of decomposing sewage. Concentrations of sludge can finally result in such high biochemical oxygen demand that virtually all oxygen is utilized in its decomposition, leaving little more than ugly growths of *Sphaerotilus* fungus and *Tubifex* larvae alive in the overripe deserts of the bottom.

Similar biological deserts result from extensive deposits of inorganic particulates. Perhaps the worst examples are the result of glass silicate mining, talc extraction operations, or the crushing of sandstones to obtain silica fine enough for glass manufacturing. Long-term residues of such operations can have a worse impact on biological communities than organic wastes. Field data from streams in the United States indicate that such fine particulates can eradicate life below their source, until only a sparse population of drifting phytoplankton, filamentous algae, and a few species of snails exist over a chalk-colored bottom. Slimy blue-green algae become the single most important organisms, its gelatinous growth primarily concentrated along the banks. The bottom materials are completely smothered under six inches to two feet of microscopic silica residues, and aquatic deserts persist as much as six to twelve miles downstream from their source.

Fine agricultural silts have also been found to create similar biological vacuums. Poor farming technology can result in talcum-fine deposits of silt from six inches to six feet in depth, reaching as much as fifty miles downstream. Valuable aquatic organisms are seldom found in such linear wastelands, except on boulders or bridge structures kept relatively clean by the current.

Petroleum wastes both emulsify and cover the meniscus film. The emulsified sludge deposits are so deadly that even the indestructible algal species and *Tubifex* worms are often killed. Turbidity from oil emulsions and surface slicks is so dense that almost all solar energy is blotted out, ending both oxygen and photosynthetic replacement of oxygen concentrations. Heavy oil slicks can prevent oxygenation from the atmosphere, and similar biological penalties are caused by industrial and detergent foam. Gill filaments of both nymphs and fish life become fouled, impairing respiration even where oxygen concentrations remain adequate, and fatal ulcerative conditions can occur in the digestive tracts of the fish. Petroleum on the surface film itself can also terminate the respiration of fly life which breathes through the film, and it can make hatching impossible, since flies emerging through the meniscus are hopelessly imprisoned in oil.

Oxygen depletion caused by the decomposition of organic wastes is well known, but it can result from other factors too. Exploration of organic wastes has identified such varied sources as feedlots, cattle pens, compost and ensilage storage, trout hatcheries, livestock barns, dairy-products operations, canneries, slaughterhouses, textile mills and dyeing processes, laundries, food-processing and fish-meal plants, pulp mills, paper manufacturing, tanneries, sugar mills, breweries, overworked sanitation plants and untreated human wastes.

The effluents of these sources include highly complex compounds in both solution and suspension. Such wastes typically include various salts and toxic substances. Effective decomposition of these effluents uses vast quantities of dissolved oxygen. Such denigration of oxygen concentrations is critical to the survival of game fish populations. Oxygen depletion is extremely serious when organic wastes are discharged directly into sewerage networks, multiplying the concentrations of biodegradable sludge. Waste concentrations can attain such densities in the lower reaches of rivers that anadromous fish cannot penetrate to the sea.

The inorganic pollution which also increases biochemical oxygen demand can occur in several kinds of manufacturing effluents. Sulphides and sulphites are common types. These compounds deplete the oxygen, along with the ambient ferrous salts found in many springheads. Mine tailings often contribute even larger volumes of ferrous salts from subsurface hydrology. The acidity of these salts is a serious problem in the metabolism of trout and grayling. However, their natural biochemical neutralization is filled with more subtle effects on the habitat. Carbon dioxide is lost to the atmosphere, the ferrous materials are decomposed by bacterial catalysts, and ferric hydroxide is distributed over the bottom—its familiar rust-colored slime choking out the bottom-loving organisms of the food chain.

Recent experiments have met with some success in reclaiming trout streams that have been ruined by the ferric hydroxide seepages of abandoned mines. Revolving drums filled with soft limestone and powered by the currents of tributary streams have been surprisingly workable. However, such grinding means of creating alkalinity are ugly and the source of excessive noise, and lime treatment stations are perhaps a better long-term strategy in reclaiming acid waters. Such treatment stations have been demonstrated to be workable. Pennsylvania has a pilot installation in operation on its Slippery Rock Creek.

Its network of trout streams has surrendered hundreds of miles of viable habitat to mine-acid drainages in the past two centuries, and the history of the Slippery Rock is typical. It drains more than four hundred square miles in five western Pennsylvania counties. Its watershed is honeycombed with coal shafts and scarred with strip mines. Many of its deep-shaft mines are a century old and have been abandoned for thirty years. However, mining permits were granted at more than five hundred sites in the past twenty years. Illegal coal mining probably took place at another hundred mineheads and pits. Water regulations were seldom enforced under the formal permits, let alone at the bootleg operations, and the ferrous drainage from all the mines in the watershed totalled as much as 4,000 pounds per day.

Abandoned mines were also still draining into the creek, and high acid concentrations had accumulated in strip-mine cuts and swampy tributaries and bogs over many years. Some of these bogs were ferric hydroxide deserts covering hundreds of acres, their rust-colored slime totally devoid of life. Their seepages into the main stream combined with the drainage of the active mines and strip pits to produce as much as 16,000 pounds per day of ferrous poisons that reached the creek. Although many anglers protested, state officials continued to issue coal-mining permits.

Fishing declined rapidly, but the trout stubbornly tried to maintain themselves. Their survival was possible because of several alkaline tributary streams and the effluents of a limestone crushing quarry that fought the acidity. The limestone mill shut down its operations in 1957, changing the chemistry of the stream overnight. Its fishing was in desperate trouble, but it was nature herself that delivered the *coup de grâce* that same year. Torrential rains delivered almost three inches of precipitation in a single day. The centuries of accumulated acids throughout the watershed, in the abandoned mines and rust-colored swamps and strip pits, were flushed into the hapless Slippery Rock. More than 50,000 pounds of acid skyrocketed its waters to extreme toxicity, killing more than two million fish, including literally every trout in its entire five-county length.

Legislation which had traditionally exempted mine-acid drainages from industrial waste codes was superseded, although the coal interests fought the proposals bitterly. Future mining permits could not be granted until the coal companies filed detailed strategies for protecting adjacent waters, and liability for acid discharges was clearly made their responsibil-

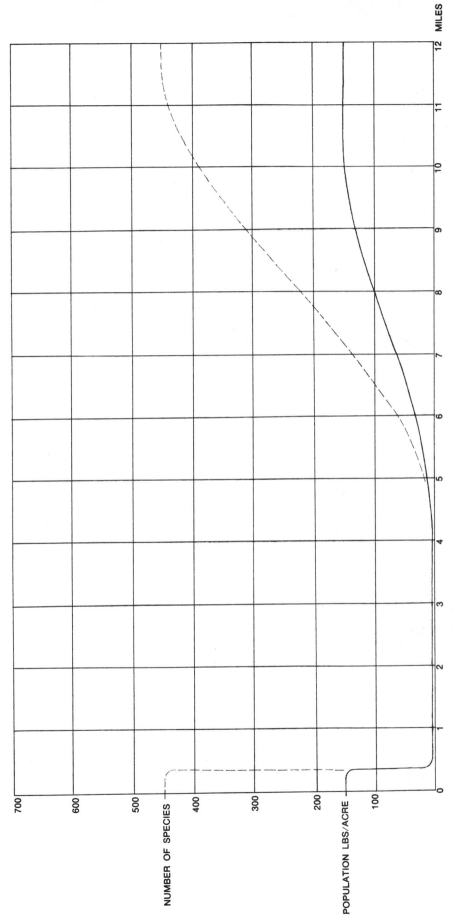

Typical impact of toxic pollution on stream biota

ity. Other active mines were forced to comply with these standards too. But the new legislation covered only working mines, offering no solution to the acid discharges of abandoned sites. Tributaries collecting these discharges required lime-salt treatment or the mines themselves had to be sealed off. Potential hydrogen-ion tests revealed one tributary creek as a primary source of mine-seepage acidity. Its volume of flow totalled more than five million gallons per day, and planning was started for a lime-treatment facility there in 1967. It was completed two years later, its cost reaching more than $800,000.

The facility diverted the tributary creek into a stilling lagoon, and its waters were then drawn into the plant itself. Approximately 1,200 pounds of hydrated lime is mixed into the flow chamber, changing the potential hydrogen-ion concentration from an average acidity rating of four to a variable alkalinity of seven to nine. The result is five million gallons per day that have been changed from toxic concentrations to rich alkalinity rivalling some of the limestone streams of central Pennsylvania.

But the benefits of the lime-treatment process reach farther afield than the Slippery Rock itself. The mixing chambers flush a rich calcium sulphate effluent into two settling basins where it precipitates out as alkaline sludge. The sludge is removed from one basin while the other is in active use, loaded on trucks, and used as alkaline spoil in abandoned mines and strip pits.

The impact of the project on both water quality and fishing was so remarkable that work extended into other reaches of the watershed. Abandoned mines that contributed more than six hundred pounds of daily acid drainage were sealed along another tributary, and its flowages soon became alkaline. Although many strip pits and deep-shaft mines remain in the four hundred square miles of the watershed, it is believed that filling them with the calcium sulphate spoil of the treatment plant and sealing their entrances will eventually terminate most of the mine-acid drainage.

The obvious success on the Slippery Rock has led to other lime-treatment facilities along other streams, and research into several methods of controlling mine-acid problems is under way. The practicality of reclaiming acid-polluted trout streams has been demonstrated in Pennsylvania, and the restoration of literally thousands of miles of water across Canada and the United States is clearly possible in the future.

Similar problems with acid oxygen-depleted waters can also occur in less obvious situations. Bottom trash and detritus can concentrate in secondary spate channels along natural watercourses. Their chemistry is acceptable at times of high water and adequate flow, since their acidity and lack of oxygen are neutralized and diluted then. Low-water conditions are trouble, since the large volumes of organic matter are concentrated in limited amounts of water and the toxicity of the stagnant side-channel pools is quickly accelerated. Sometimes our sewage treatment plants are incapable of handling storm runoff, and surprisingly high percentages of untreated organic wastes are flushed away in the spate. Such discharges have little effect at times of high water and maximum dilution, but rapid putrefaction occurs when the rivers return to normal levels of flow and the untreated wastes collect in the dwindling side channels.

Stagnation results in minimal recharging of oxygen from the atmosphere, since turbulence and flow are absent, and turbid shallows have little photosynthesis. Ferric hydroxides and blue-green algal slime appear. Anaerobic bacteria dominate the resulting ecosystem, reducing its nitrate constituents to ammonia and its sulphates to harsh sulphides. The remaining sludge and water has a high oxygen debt and concentration of poisons, and a sudden summer thunderstorm can transport this lethal accumulation into the mainstream.

Sometimes a spate that flushes such side-channel wastes can trigger dramatic fishkills, particularly in hot weather and low water. The secondary channels remain valuable as safety valves, absorbing sudden spates and abnormal snowmelt and protecting the primary benthos and its community of life from the damage of a scouring flood. Yet the fishkills which come from the sudden flushing of side-channel wastes are often blamed on industrial spills or the malfunctioning of a waste-treatment facility, when the root causes are often a natural function of stream ecology—slightly compounded by our manmade wastes and agricultural fertilizers and the erosion that accompanies our land-use technology.

The effluents of organic human wastes are well-known sources of pollution, but it comes as a surprise to many fishermen that agriculture and livestock can trigger even more serious problems of organic sludge and eutrophication. It is the respiratory demand of micro-organisms involved in the decomposition of waste effluents that plays a major role in organic types of pollution. Such oxidization burns off large quantities of dissolved oxygen. The biochemistry of the habitat develops the foul-smelling symptoms of an anaerobic state in which all forms of plant and animal life perish.

The intensity of such organic and inorganic pollution is typically calibrated in terms of the oxygen depletion in a liter of the contaminated effluent at sixty-eight degrees after five days. The oxygen depletion in parts per million is the resulting biochemical oxygen demand. The range of biochemical oxygen demand in familiar kinds of effluents is surprising to most fly-fishermen, since serious pollution is usually associated only with human and industrial wastes. Animal husbandry and agriculture can also produce some shocking oxygen demands. Untreated domestic sewage can have a biochemical oxygen demand of 300 to 500 parts per million. Dairy wastes can range from 500 to 5,000 parts per million in some effluent concentrations. Between 5,000 and 15,000 parts per million are found in the drainage effluents of riding stables and cattle-feed-lot operations. Ensilage is perhaps the worst form of organic pollution encountered in modern agriculture, its effluents having a biochemical oxygen demand ranging from 15,000 to 60,000 parts per million. Since ensilage can produce as much as forty gallons of effluents per ton of fodder, this means the wastes of only 400 tons can equal the domestic pollution of 75,000 people.

Oxygen-consuming wastes from industrial processes are also a factor in our fisheries, and their biochemical impacts can prove surprising too. Paper manufacturing is an example of industrial wastes requiring surprisingly high biochemical oxygen-demand to decompose their effluents. Pulp-mill wastes consist of sulphites, pulp, bleach-plant effluents, and paper-machine products, all having high oxygen-depleting properties. Based upon comparative factors of effective population, the biochemical oxygen-demand triggered in the production of five hundred daily tons of sulphite can equal the sewage effluents of two million people.

Other paper-making wastes from pulping and nonchemical wood processing are harmful to fish habitat because of their dense particulate saturations. Relatively low oxygen demand is involved in the decomposition of organic matter leached from the wood. The fine wastes from woodworking and sawmills pose similar problems, since their constituents are poor bacterial foods and decompose slowly. The biochemical oxygen demand is relatively low, but since it persists for considerable time, its long-term impact on water quality is sizable. Perhaps the best-known example of such pollution in recent years was the Battenkill, where the broom factory wastes literally choked the bottom in its quiet pools and backwaters. The sawdust and wood chips were a deadly blanket that smothered the bottom organisms, created both methane and acids in their rotting, and imposed a damaging biochemical oxygen-demand over many seasons.

The rate of oxygen depletion triggered by various effluents depends on their particular chemistry. Some industrial wastes contain chemical-reducing agents, such as ferrous salts or sulphides, that consume oxygen chemically. Such depletion occurs quite rapidly in a river.

Organic wastes are oxidized bacterially. The rate of their decomposition depends on both the proximity of suitable bacteria and their suitability as food for such microscopic organisms. Sterile wastes like phenols seldom have suitable populations of bacterial flora. Their composition may include too few nutrients for bacterial growth, even after they are diluted in the natural habitat. Raw sewage is saturated with bacteria, its spectrum rich with varied compounds, and its decomposition proceeds rapidly with sufficient concentrations of dissolved oxygen.

Eutrophication is another form of pollution that has increased with the growth of industry and cities. Wastes having large concentrations of nitrogen and phosphates cause serious pollution and result in choking growth rates of many organisms. Agricultural fertilizers and domestic detergents are common sources of such pollution. The aquatic species which respond to overfertilization are algae and phytoplankton and rooted plants. Such overfertilization is a growing problem. Streams, reservoirs, and natural lakes have experienced equally rapid acceleration in their rates of eutrophication because of the wastes from communities, industry, and agriculture.

Both organic and inorganic compounds containing nitrogen and phosphorus are the fulcrum of this manmade eutrophication, which chokes

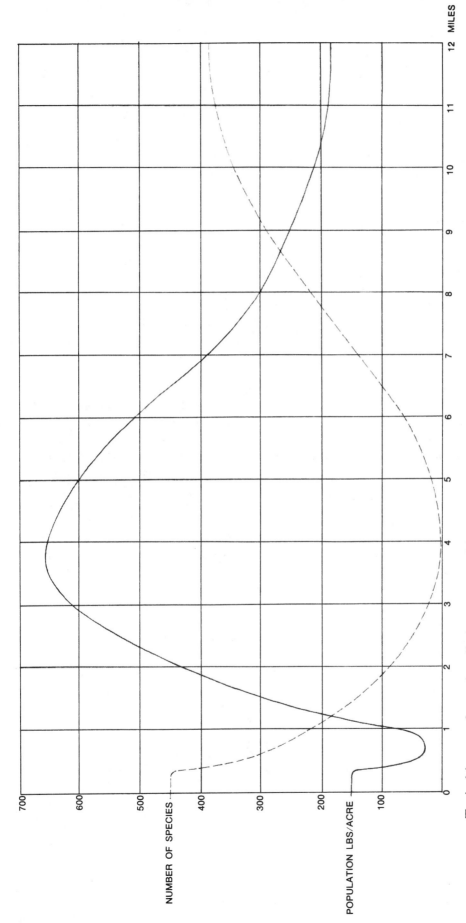

Typical impact of organic pollution on stream biota

habitat with weeds and triggers serious algal populations. Modern waste-treatment technology commonly removes the dissolved inorganic and mineral components of municipal and industrial wastes through oxidization and the precipitation of their sediments. Some organic compounds are treated to separate their inorganic nitrogen and phosphorus, multiplying their effects on eutrophication when final effluents are discharged. Waste-treatment effluents can release more nutrients than untreated sewage. Therefore both sewage and nontoxic industrial wastes pose serious problems of overfertilization in our trout waters, and effluents overripe with nitrogen and phosphorus should not be discharged directly into most game fish habitat.

However, even waste-treatment plants designed to extract and with-hold such chemical nutrients from adjacent fisheries cannot always prevent eutrophication. Agricultural drainages which leach residual nitrogens and phosphates from fertilizers into trout waters can trigger explosive growth in nuisance species. At the close of winter in many lakes, such residual concentrations have often achieved densities in sufficient parts per million that excessive algal blooms are certain to follow. Some detergents also contain sufficient fertilizing compounds that their waste waters have radically accelerated the growth of weeds and algae in adjacent fisheries, and have entered the subsurface hydrology in dangerous concentrations through septic tanks and leaching fields and cesspools. Lawn fertilization has been found to have leached into storm drains at extremely high concentrations of both nitrogen and phosphorus, and most storm-drainage outfalls flow directly into adjacent streams and lakes. Irrigation systems also transport large concentrations of nitrogen and phosphorus back into the parent streams once irrigation of the fields has been accomplished. Such irrigation technology can annually collect as much as twenty-four pounds of nitrogen and four pounds of phosphorus per acre, distributing it into waters downstream, and conventional cultivation can lose as much as forty pounds of nitrogen and seven pounds of phosphorus per acre through erosion and surface drainage. Cultivated fields can also lose six hundred to seven hundred pounds of organic erosion per year. The cumulative effect of such fertilization can literally choke adjacent waters.

Using existing waste-treatment demand, average annual per capita contribution of treated sewage wastes is sufficient to fertilize five acres of water with nitrogen and thirty-five acres with inorganic phosphorus. Although such waters have received only highly treated waste effluents, and are no longer polluted in conventional terms, their overfertilization is a new kind of pollution with ominous implications for the future.

Although such large-scale problems were seldom fully anticipated, the problems of local algal blooms have long been familiar in many municipal water systems. Such densities of algae cause unacceptable tastes and odors in potable supplies, result in unattractive turbidity, clog the filtration systems in public water-treatment plants, and leave an unsightly rotting scum throughout a potable water network. However, these problems are not limited to the obvious concerns of filtration technology and palatability and odor. The esthetic and recreation problems are well known. Many studies have been done on overfertilization from surface drainage and waste treatment and the accelerated eutrophication that follows, but too little is known about its long-term ecological problems.

Recurring cycles of algal bloom could become a serious physico-chemical problem as well as a seasonal nuisance. Some algal blooms have contributed directly to fishkills, since the nighttime respiration of the growing biomass depletes the oxygen in their habitat. Disproportionate numbers of that biomass include bacteria at work decomposing the organic wastes in such highly eutrophied waters. Algae and weeds create oxygen through photosynthesis during the daylight hours, but photosynthesis obviously stops at night. Turbidity also inhibits light penetration and photosynthesis except for the surface layers of water, and algal bloom can become so dense that even cloudy weather, with its reductions in light intensity, can seriously deplete dissolved oxygen concentrations. Trout streams choked with weeds and algal bloom from overfertilization can range from fifteen parts per million oxygen on sunny afternoons to only three or four parts per million just before daylight. Fishkills are inevitable with such radical variations in dissolved oxygen, but perhaps even more important is the mortality rate of the smaller food-chain organisms.

Weed growth and normal algal bloom were long considered seasonal bench marks of fertility in a lake or stream, but that fertility is now threatening to choke on its own riches and could become a plague in future years. It is possible that algal bloom could eradicate the major organisms and species now found in our freshwater systems. The signs and portents of such tragedies are obvious. Agricultural practices have their primary adverse effects on lakes and streams through surface drainage, and the increased erosion that began with the initial clearing and cultivation of the land. Our record of clearing acreages that should better have been left in timber, and plowing frontier grasslands that should never have been cultivated, is a sorry chapter in our history.

Drainage systems are often a problem. Although they do accomplish the drainage of farmlands until cultivation with machinery is possible, they also collect and flush precipitation more quickly. Surface and bank erosion is increased too. Particularly acid soils are leached directly into the river, threatening its fertility and water chemistry, and silts increase its turbidity. Photosynthesis steadily drops and increased silt loads are transported downstream, slowly accumulating from the headwater drainages until the spawning gravel and nursery shallows of fingerling trout and fly life are gradually smothered.

Drainage networks also radically diminish surface water over many years of development. British drainage practices cut herringbone channels approximately a foot deep, and twenty years of erosion can open them into large, ragged gullies as much as twelve feet in width and four feet in depth. This often results in relatively dry fields between periods of heavy rainfall, but studies on the Ribble and Lune in Lancashire found that as much as 1,500 to 2,000 pounds of suspended particulates were transported downstream in only 250,000 gallons of flow during spate conditions.

Such drainage practices actually cause more flash flooding than intended, since their efficient collection and channelization of surface waters result in increased volumes of surge. Panic resulting from hurricane-triggered spates in 1955 led to radical surgery on the lower Brodheads, with straight channels below Analomink and high flood embankments paralleling the stream. During periods of heavy rainfall the river rises and falls rapidly in spate, because its lower drainage is quite efficient. It is also a tragic echo of the fishery that once existed downstream from Analomink, and many thoughtful people in the valley wonder if extensive reforestry and rebuilding of the original channels and pools would not have been both cheaper and better.

Large acreages of both Europe and the United States have been drained in past centuries, opening farm and grazing lands with both good and poor soil chemistry. Perhaps the most dramatic example is the Kävlinge drainage basin in Sweden. Kävlinge farming practices in the past 150 years have led to such ditching, channelization, and cultivation that only five sizable lakes and three streams remain where literally thousands once existed in a network that almost covered the region. Cultivation ultimately became so intense that every parcel of land was ditched, drained, and plowed. Drainage and erosion were slow in the original network of forest-rimmed lakes and ponds and birchwood swamps. Swedish studies found that topsoil losses in the region radically increased with the acreages drained and cultivated. The concentrations of humus in a cubic yard of drainage effluent averaged slightly less than two ounces, and almost four ounces of minerals in solution. Transposing these concentrations to adjacent drainages, more than sixty cubic yards of water per second is discharged along the Kävlinge during flooding rates of flow. It is transporting seven to eight pounds of humus, and between fifteen and sixteen pounds of minerals in solution. Therefore average erosion every twenty-four hours throughout the Kävlinge watershed averaged more than 1,500,000 pounds of humus and dissolved minerals.

Eroded minerals and soils can also come from cultivation on steep topography, overgrazing by both cattle and sheep, and the practice of burning off ground cover in primitive livestock and farming practices. Sheep are particularly hard on both ground cover and soils. Their grazing habits crop the vegetation so closely that it often dies out or can no longer prevent erosion. Like other kinds of livestock, sheep cut tracks in steep hillsides which further contribute to the loss of soils and minerals. Some biologists are convinced that the remarkable success of the fisheries in the Yellowstone is directly related to the absence of extensive grazing. Burning off winterkilled vegetation is common, and in Scotland such practices are used to prevent the regeneration of trees on the heather moors. It is also found among the Araucan Indians, who clear briars and brushy shrubs with fire from their steep farmlands above the Rio Calcurrupe in the Chilean lake country.

Peat bogs can also have interesting effects on acidity and accelerated eutrophication, since they are actually the remains of primordial swamps and lakes that were finally eutrophied themselves. Their peat is organic matter that never fully decomposed before it became isolated from aerobic functions. Concentrations of peat silt in a watershed clearly limit its fertility and its food-chain populations. Irish studies point to parallels between peat acids, the mortality of trout eggs, and the growth of the baby fish themselves. Larger fish are not usually affected by peat-bog drainages, unless the concentrations are high enough to threaten their metabolic ability to neutralize acid habitat.

In *A Trout and Salmon Fisherman for Seventy-five Years*, Edward Hewitt records an intriguing experience with peat-bog acids that occurred on the Blackwater in southern Ireland. His fishing was on the famous Carysville beats, and although the river was filled with fish, the sport proved disappointing. The water was slightly tea-colored and a little high for the season. Its color led Hewitt to suspect peat-acid drainage. The river traverses limestone country through its lower mileage, with a dark sandstone geology starting about thirty miles above Carysville. The headwaters flow from extensive peat bogs, and because of the postwar coal shortages, peat cutting had doubled its production.

Hewitt took water samples from the peat-bog effluents and at other points along the Blackwater. His tests provided some interesting insights into the effects of a watershed that varied from acid to alkaline and back again. The metabolic processes of fish are designed to function when the potential hydrogen-ion concentrations of the blood are 7.2, slightly alkaline in its chemistry. When there had been normal rainfall, the Carysville beats on the Blackwater normally flowed at 7.4 to 7.6, and the effects of the limestone geology dominated its water chemistry. But the peat-bog drainage had a hydrogen-ion concentration of 5.6, a level of acidity unfavorable to the metabolism of the fish, and the river itself tested between 6.7 and 6.8 downstream toward Carysville. Hewitt found that normal river chemistry ranged between 7.0 and 7.6, but that peat cutting and rainfall could change its alkalinity quickly. When the rains in the headwaters stopped for a few days, the river became alkaline again.

Acid water chemistry quickly makes the blood chemistry of the fish acid too, as the acidity of the water is transmitted and circulated through the gills. Serious acidosis can result in mortality unless the trout quickly neutralize its acidity in their kidneys, which manufacture countering ammonia compounds from proteins. The process must begin the moment that a spate of peat-bog drainage changes the river chemistry from alkalinity to acidity.

These oscillations in water chemistry apparently caused rapid cycles of distress in the fish population, as their metabolism was forced to compensate back and forth with the ebb and flow of peat-bog drainage. It is like our being forced to oscillate between breathing oxygen or some other gas, in a ping-pong process causing such metabolic stress that normal feeding behavior is postponed. Similar problems exist in the waters of the United States and Canada, where highly eutrophic lakes and bogs can trigger acid drainages during periods of heavy rainfall. Mines and beaver ponds and strip pits can cause similar problems.

Forestry and lumbering have also had major ecological impacts on our trout and grayling fisheries. Although fish are found in high-country lakes beyond the timberline and in latitudes where only caribou moss survives, most of our American trout and grayling habitat is found in heavily forested regions of the country.

Dense high-canopy forest provides shade and a sense of shelter and maintains cool water temperatures. Comparative studies of meadow and forest watersheds, all other factors being relatively equal, have demonstrated that the unsheltered habitat ranges ten to twenty degrees warmer across a typical season. Streamside plant physiography also provides a supplemental food supply of terrestrial organisms for the fish. Its leaf-drift provides fertilization in most waters where eutrophication is not a problem, and its detritus feeds the food-chain organisms. Vegetation serves to stabilize soils and stream banks against erosion, although high-canopy forests are less effective in combating erosion than second-growth plant cover. Mature trees crowd out second-growth and shrubs, and it is these smaller plant hierarchies that prevent erosion. Streams easily erode the larger root systems, exposing them to the current and felling the trees into the river. The hydrology of forest regions is generally good, with highly permeable soils and relatively slow runoff and erosion. Forest regions usually demonstrate high storage capacity. The physical structure of a forest also multiplies the effective surface acreage of a region to intercept and store precipitation, as well as multiplying the evaporative surfaces and photosynthesis. Forest cover also tends to benefit mayfly populations, providing shelter for the molting duns after they have hatched from the river.

Forest watersheds are clearly less vulnerable to serious flooding and drought conditions. Clear-cut lumbering or clearing timber for agriculture quickly terminates leaf litter and reduces both soil percolation and water storage.

Higher percentages of rainfall and snowmelt are lost in surface drainage. Peak flooding discharges are immediately increased, while drought minimums are even farther reduced. Accelerated surface drainage means increased erosion. Higher flood levels mean damaged banks. Turbidity and sedimentation are radically increased. Reduction of mid-summer flowages seriously reduces spawning areas and habitat for fly life, as well as raising temperatures to potentially lethal ceilings. It is an irreparable loss to stream ecology, since no program of reforestation can ever equal the original high-canopy cover, in spite of the rhetoric that flows ceaselessly from the timber lobby.

Postlogging studies indicate radical changes in both temperature and dissolved oxygen, and there is considerable evidence of upstream migration by the fish. During actual logging operations felled trees often interfere with normal currents, diverting both water and oxygen from spawning areas. Tangled logjams sometimes block spawning runs and seasonal migrations. Logging trash and sawdust choke the food-rich riffles and lie decomposing in the backwaters. The obstructions caused by deadfalls and brush can also cause accumulations of bottom-smothering silt, which becomes a plague with no trees to mute the impact of erosion. The tragic effects of logging operations in both Canada and the United States are well known, and in earlier chapters we discussed the relationships between lumbering off the Appalachians and the loss of brook-trout habitat in untold thousands of miles of streams. It is unfathomably tragic that cattle drives, the slaughter of the buffalo, and the decimation of the hemlocks to get tannic acid to process astronomical numbers of hides have played a major role in the decline of both the rivers and their brook trout from New England to North Carolina. Similar lumbering still continues on classic salmon and steelhead rivers in British Columbia, where the economic value of salmon spawning on each watershed in a single year can equal the total market value of its timber resources. Such economic myopia is frightening.

But our sorry history of lumbering is also responsible for the extinction of the Michigan grayling, the species uniquely endemic to Michigan a century ago. It was lost forever in the rapacious lumbering that followed the Civil War, and it seems likely that another unique species will be lost in the next five years. The remarkable Apache trout, found only in a few isolated streams on the Apache reservation in Arizona, is scheduled to lose its original habitat as this is being written. The Bureau of Indian Affairs is supporting clear-cutting of the vast forests in the high country of the reservation, dooming the Apache trout and its original habitat in a single guillotinelike stroke. While the encouragement of enterprise controlled by the Apaches is a desirable goal, the extinction of a unique species and the loss of a remaining wilderness in their tribal heritage is a terrible and shortsighted price to pay for it. Neither the forests nor the fish can ever be replaced, in spite of the removal of brood stock to hatcheries. And restocking them in other places can never equal the primeval streams where they evolved—streams we propose to ravage for all eternity.

Extracting water from our rivers and lakes for agriculture and industry and potable uses also has considerable effect on the ecology and the quality of fishing. Such borrowing or water abstraction is both long term, in the sense of its removal into municipal water supplies, and short term, for industrial uses. The water is all returned eventually into the biosphere, but industrial volumes are discharged back into the same biosystem.

Water borrowing has several effects on the character of a fishery. Part of its flow is diverted into new drainage systems, its ecology changed to a flowage-type impoundment. The volume of flow is reduced, and its temperature regime is changed. Water chemistry is also changed, and some original streambed is lost under the impoundment, altering the food chain and drowning spawning areas. The physical barrier of spillways, diversion weirs, and dams also blocks spawning and seasonal migrations.

Municipal water systems usually employ reservoirs in the headwaters of a river and its tributaries. While small cities and towns may have a single impoundment, a sprawling megalopolis like New York has built a whole galaxy of reservoirs and interconnecting aqueducts and flowages, and Los Angeles and Denver obtain their potable supplies from hundreds of miles into the mountains. Sometimes the aqueduct systems use natural water-courses that transport the water to the municipal treatment and distribution networks. These natural aqueducts often provide good fishing, like the Eleven Mile and Deckers Canyon stretches of the South Platte in Colorado, or the surprisingly productive Croton and Amawalk outlet streams an hour from Times Square.

Sometimes the cold-water discharges of large reservoirs, like the Ozark and Tennessee tailwaters, can create wholly new trout fisheries down-stream. The Peapacton Dam on the east branch of the Delaware has transformed a marginal trout river, perhaps better known for its small-mouths, into the best major trout stream in our eastern mountains. Reservoir construction on the San Juan in New Mexico has changed a coarse-fish habitat into a superb rainbow fishery. The creation of such new habitat and the potential for regenerating old habitat lost through clear-cut lumbering and agriculture must be weighed against the loss of drowned riverine mileage under impounded waters. It is a choice that will prove critical in future years.

Water storage obviously reduces the flow of a river below such dams and impoundments, although tributaries farther downstream help to restore its currents. Permissible volumes of discharge are decisive to the survival of fisheries below a dam, since cutting off the water completely can destroy their habitat, and even minimum compensatory flow can prove damaging as well. Such fixed volumes of compensatory discharges are typically much less than the normal riverine flowages at any given season. Water temperatures are a problem in summer weather. The surface acreages, average depths of pools and riffles, and widths of the streams are all reduced. Food-chain organisms are also reduced. There is much less habitat, sense of shelter, nursery and spawning acreages, and the fish are much more exposed to predators. Reduction of flow also increases the likelihood of disease, although the compensatory discharge policy at many reservoirs seems totally to overlook the environmental problems involved in large reductions of flow.

Population growth clearly points to the need for more and more reservoirs in the future, particularly since we can already see the ultimate exhaustion of our petroleum reserves, and our need for pollution-free energy will lead to more hydroelectric plants. Our choices cannot oppose reservoirs thoughtlessly, but our energies must still be unswervingly focused on selection of their sites, bathography, design configuration, fish ladders, volumes of compensatory discharge, and the thermal stratification in the depths of their impoundments—carefully selecting designs and discharge systems to influence temperatures below the dam.

The water required in industrial production is no less important than the acre-footages needed for hydroelectric plants and municipal water supplies. Industrial volumes are so large that the necessity for future impoundments is obvious, both for cooling purposes and manufacturing itself. Perhaps the largest industrial water consumers are industries like chemicals, steel, oil refineries, tanneries, textile mills and dyeing plants, wood pulp processing, paper manufacturing, nuclear reactors, and fossil-fuel power generation. The water is employed for power, cooling, transporting materials, washing, tempering, and as an ingredient in the production of goods. Few anglers realize how much water is used in normal industrial functions.

Industry has multiplied tenfold since the beginning of this century, and its water needs have grown even more rapidly, until our average existing rates of growth indicate that American industry will unquestionably require 500 million gallons per day at the close of the century. The following table outlines the quantities of water required in various industries, and demonstrates the roots of our industrial demand.

Aluminum	320,000 gallons/ton
Steel	50,000 gallons/ton
Wood Pulp	50,000 gallons/ton
Paper	32,000 gallons/ton
Tanneries	16,000 gallons/ton
Wool Washing	2,000 gallons/ton
Coal	100 gallons/ton

Most anglers are also surprised to learn that a dairy uses almost 5,000 gallons of water to process 1,000 gallons of milk, the local brewery needs 10,000 gallons of water for 1,000 gallons of beer, and a distillery must have a surprising 70,000 gallons for each 1,000 gallons of whiskey.

Potable water demand in the United States is approximately ten billion gallons per day, and demographers expect our needs to reach fifteen billion gallons per day in less than thirty more years. Agricultural demand has spiralled radically since the beginning of the century, when slightly more than twenty billion gallons per day were needed. Present water demand for agricultural uses is approximately 150 billion gallons per day, with an average daily demand of 300 billion gallons anticipated before the close of this century. Such projections mean that our existing water demand of 360 billion gallons per day is likely to reach the mind-boggling total of more than 800 billion gallons in thirty-odd years.

Obviously, facing such needs for potable water in the future, we no longer have the luxury of watching our winter snowmelt and summer spates and fall rains flow toward the seas unused. It means we must select some watersheds for their unique biosystems or scenic value now, and establish strategies for preserving them as widely and totally as possible. This must be accomplished not only a mile on either side of their flowages but also to the topographical limits of their drainage basins, since their ecology is a fabric reaching to the snowmelt fields of avalanche lilies and the fiddleback springheads of their forest beginnings.

It also means that rivers not selected for total preservation must be impounded at optimal points, their dams treated as a problem in systems planning, and ecological and scenic considerations given equal weight in the decision-making process. Mere technical and cost criteria are no longer enough, since the damage caused by ill-planned dams and impoundments built at the lowest possible cost are an expensive short-term saving we can no longer afford.

It is important to understand the obvious environmental problems associated with the design and construction of large-scale impoundments, since there will be many in the future and both our opposition and our influence must be rational and informed. There are four primary types of dams and impoundment systems. The most basic is perhaps the simple barrage which diverts water into an adjoining water system or another impoundment. The dam that is integrated with a generating plant is also a familiar type; its flow surges from the reservoir, through the turbine chambers and penstocks, and back into the river immediately downstream. The third type places its power station some distance below its impoundment, using the difference in elevation to generate more energy with the same volume of water. The pump-storage reservoir is designed to produce peak energy on demand, or to provide cooling capacity on a river that experiences minimal summer flowages, with volumes too unreliable without the additional pump-storage capacity.

Each of these types has its particular effects on the ambient ecology of its watershed, both above and below the dam site. The volume and the method of water abstraction used will affect the biology of both the impoundment and the river downstream. The diverted flowages during storage can obviously affect the surface acreage, width, and average depths of the river. Reductions in flow will invariably increase temperatures, while discharges from the colder strata in the depths of the impoundment will lower them. Warmer temperatures and reductions in flow combine to increase susceptibility to disease. The drowned river acreages under the impoundment mean a loss in current-loving stream organisms, lotic habitat, and potential spawning gravel. Impounded waters mean the river downstream will receive discharges of reservoir-grown plankton, along with huge populations of midge larvae and pupae. The feeding behavior of the fish below a dam is changed by its physical and thermal effects on the food chain, just as the diet forms in a lake or impoundment are largely unfamiliar to a river-bred trout or grayling.

Each primary type of reservoir, except for the pump-storage system, also has the problem of determining compensatory volumes of flow to protect the fishery and food-chain community downstream. Some large or particularly deep reservoirs also develop occasional concentrations of nitrogen that prove fatal to fish downstream. Such concentrations of dissolved nitrogen are sometimes found in large springs and underground rivers, but their presence in impounded waters is not fully understood.

Pump-storage systems are a special problem. Their basic concept lies in building a reservoir separate from the river itself, and water is pumped up to their higher elevation during the night, or at other times when energy demand is relatively low. The water is discharged down through penstocks to the power plant during periods of peak energy demand. The generators are usually at river or reservoir level, while the pump-storage impoundment lies in a natural or modified depression several hundred feet above. The pump-storage concept is unthinkable except in relatively affluent societies, since virtually the same energy is expended in pumping the water uphill as the system extracts in discharging it. The only advantage of a pump-storage system lies in its ability to supply its impounded energy on demand, or the capability of holding cooling effluents in reserve against midsummer drought conditions, which is under study above several nuclear sites. Although a pump-storage system does not construct a permanent structural barrier across the river in all cases, and does not create thermal discharges that compare with either nuclear or fossil-fuel plants, it is still a potential environmental problem.

Its powerful intake pumps ingest vast quantities of plankton and baby fish and other organisms, with extensive impact on the benthic population, and its generating discharges create instant spates and changes in dissolved gases and turbidity. Such daily fluctuations in volume and rates of flow have a serious impact on the river, but the changes are even more radical in the pump-storage impoundment itself. It is filled and emptied daily, permitting no food chain or benthic community to develop, since most of its waters are changed every few hours. The shallows of the impoundment never have any chance to develop a community of life before they are drained. The system collects water from the river at night when energy demand is the lowest, thereby removing it at its lowest temperatures and concentrations of dissolved oxygen. Having lost so much cold water before daylight, the river has reduced ability to resist daytime warming, and the water filling the storage basin is oxygen deficient. Although the water is not used to cool fossil-fuel generators and its discharge is not a form of thermal pollution in the usual sense, it is heated slightly through hydraulic friction in its plunge through the generators and penstocks. Since the pump-storage discharge is both warm and lacking in oxygen and is returned when the river itself is warm and oxygen-poor in late afternoon, its impact on marginal trout habitat can be serious.

Although pump-storage reservoirs designed to furnish cooling effluents during occasional drought cycles have time to develop a viable food chain, their pyramidal structure of organisms is a house of cards that collapses when cooling effluents are needed downstream. Its rates of draw-down are too abrupt for the benthic community to adjust, and a pump-storage reservoir is an unlikely habitat for long-term management. The concept is marginally suited to any kind of sport fishery, since its benthic communities can be eradicated as quickly as they become established, and it is poorly suited to populations of trout or grayling.

Freshly impounded lakes usually experience a rapid increase in biological productivity. New reservoirs, filling an existing impoundment, and the flooding of former shorelines during unusual periods of water storage all trigger such fertility. The cause is the leaching of organic and mineral nutrients into the impounded waters from the freshly inundated soils. Terrestrial life like insect larvae, earthworms, and insects are added to the food chain. It is a familiar phenomenon on western reservoirs, and over the years I have had some remarkably good fishing during the drowning of flat meadows beside impoundments like Eleven Mile and Antero in Colorado, when fat prairie root-beetles were emerging in the newly flooded sagebrush and buffalo grass.

Forage acreages are greatly increased, and the shallows that support a rich food-chain population are also multiplied. With a sudden increase in water, the existing population densities of the fish are reduced and their food supply is increased. Growth rates often increase dramatically. However, such improved rates of growth only last for two or three years, depending on the ratio of shallows to deep water after flooding. Where subsequent water levels remain stable and really large photic zones are created, the fertility experienced when the impoundment was originally filled might stabilize and sustain itself.

Although fluctuations of water level and draw-down in conventional reservoirs are not as serious as pump-storage cycles of filling and discharge, such changes in water volumes damage fisheries too. Weed growth and food organisms associated with the fertile shallows of the littoral are greatly diminished and even eradicated. The primary fly hatches are usually the first to suffer, although an increase in the tiny Diptera species is often found. However, the net effects are a general reduction in available food and fish population.

Perhaps the most obvious effects of such dams and barrage structures lie in their barriers against fish migration. During periods of relatively limited discharge, both migratory populations waiting in the estuarine reaches of a river and fish seeking cooler temperatures upstream are blocked. Little is known about how long sea-run populations can postpone entering a river or moving farther upstream without losing their effective spawning times. Water chemistry, increased temperatures, and the effects of ambient pollution are all subject to magnification and change by dams. Thermal stratification in the depths of particularly large impoundments can discharge oxygen-poor water or excessively nitrogen-charged water downstream. Long periods of water storage or turbine shutdown, coupled with minimal compensatory flow through the dam, seem to multiply the effects of temperature stratification and rates of bottom decomposition usually associated with self-contained lakes. When the ratio of a tiny compensatory discharge to a relatively large volume of impounded water is maintained for a substantial period, poor water quality is inevitable.

Obviously, the upstream migration of the fish is obstructed by the presence of dams. Most dams on rivers having important migratory populations are designed with fish ladders, but these structures are not universally effective. The principal trouble with these fish passes lies in the ability of the fish to locate their entrances easily. Volumes of flow in the fish ladders also affect the ability of the ascending fish to find and use them. The structure and gradient of the fish passes are also critical, as is the placement of their discharges in the downstream currents to make their rights of way clear to the fish.

Migrating fish that fail to locate the fish ladder entrance easily may struggle futilely against the spill under the dam, fatally tiring or injuring themselves trying to ascend; others are lost when they enter badly screened turbine discharge systems. Even when fish ladders are effective, they impair migration. The delays they cause are not part of the biosystem that evolved the spawning cycles in the genetic memory of any river's fish population, and their interference with a spawning migration unquestionably affects both fecundity and egg-laying behavior.

Diversion of water from one riverine system to another has obvious effects on water chemistry, sometimes reversing the original acidity or alkalinity. Such changes clearly affect the fertility of a watershed, but there are also profound changes in its fingerprints of odor. The trout that migrate back and forth between coastal seas and their parent rivers find their way home largely with olfactory clues. Water diversion from one river to another can cause fish to stray, entering the wrong river because their memory imprints are confused by varying relationships of natural currents and compensatory flowages and discharges. Such straying results from the singular odors of their parent rivers being diverted and discharged along an adjacent watershed. These strays may find incompatible spawning conditions in the secondary river, or find their homing instincts hopelessly scrambled when they fail to ascend past the source of water diverted from their original parent stream. Such stray fish may spawn effectively in a strange river, or ascend an unfamiliar river system, only to reach an impassable source of their parent-river odors—a power station, a barrier without a workable fish pass, or the outlet flume of a diversion tunnel or irrigation canal.

Sometimes discharges from a generating plant are erratic, because of energy demand or the performance specifications of the turbines. Fluctuations might commonly rise to turbulent spate levels of flow, and return to droughtlike minimums as many as three times in a single day. Such erratic discharges can confuse migratory species, attracting them upstream on artificial spates, and trapping them in hostile shallows when the current drops. Water chemistry and dissolved gases and turbidity all change radically with these cycles, and temperatures also suffer erratic fluctuations. Radical variations in flow also cause the fish to suffer surprising levels of metabolic stress, affecting natural cycles of spawning, fish growth and feeding, and interfering with the safety and quality of our sport.

Dams affect downstream migrations too. Adult fish drifting into the lower reaches of a river system to winter may choose the impoundment instead, but others may find their migrations blocked. Spawned-out fish are also frustrated by dams and barrages, and migrating steelhead kelts are often observed prowling the lower shorelines and upstream faces of dams in search of an exit back toward the sea. Fish ladders work reasonably well in downstream migrations, and spillways can work well if their volumes of flow are proper for adult trout to use them safely. Such kelts have difficulty traversing a turbine system, although surprising numbers of small fish negotiate them safely.

Such young fish include both riverine species and smolts in migration toward salt water. Their normal itineraries are frequently interrupted by dams, until the migrating shoals of immature fish locate the fish ladders or enter the turbine intakes. Although most intake throats are screened, blocking small migratory fish, many succeed in entering the turbine systems. Others are killed on the screens themselves, caught in the meshes or pinioned against the wires by the force of the intake currents.

Small fish that actually enter the turbines experience twenty to sixty percent mortality. Their deaths are attributed to such factors as rate of flow, turbulence, water pressure, cavitation, and actual impacts with the turbine structures or vanes themselves. Migrating fish are subjected to swift flowages, turbulence, water pressure, and cavitation for only brief periods of time, and these factors are apparently seldom fatal. Field investigations indicate that such fish are not injured by water pressures equivalent to a hundred feet of depth. Some mortality is caused by extreme penstock turbulence inside the turbine housings, but most fishkills in a power-generating system result from injury by the free-wheeling turbine machinery itself or severe nitrogen poisoning.

The earliest types of fish ladders were the pool type, in which a series of small basins are connected with small spillways that migrating species can negotiate easily. Smaller pools soon evolved, like stairsteps linked together with a series of narrow chutes. Other designs eliminate the need to jump from one stage to another, using an opening that simply connects the pools underwater. There are also designs which stairstep up the steep terrain beside a dam, in a series of switchbacks that sometimes wind away from the river. Perhaps the most original fish pass design is a tower system, with the climbing stairstep pools arranged in a spiral layout inside.

Pool fish ladders are often expensive, and sometimes the terrain adjacent to a dam makes them impractical or prohibitive in cost. The Borland fish-lift concept was designed to reduce construction costs in such situations. It works like a canal lock, with one chamber at the impoundment level and the other at river level below the dam. Both pools are completely enclosed inside the dam. They are connected by a sloping ferroconcrete shaft that is also inside the structure of the dam.

The tailwater discharge from the lower chamber attracts the fish into the sluice, and its gate is periodically closed. Reservoir water quickly fills the connecting shaft until the entire system is full. The fish rise with the accumulating water, attracted by the light-filled upper chamber, until finally they reach reservoir level and enter it. Such Borland fish passes are often automatic, operating regularly on two-hour and four-hour cycles, although many Borland installations are worked manually. The water level in reservoirs often rises and falls dramatically, depending on the season and energy demand. It is necessary to construct several Borland fish ladders to allow the fish to traverse the dam at several levels of water. Borland passes in pairs are common, and the Orrin Reservoir in Scotland has four, each designed to function at a different level of water.

Perhaps the main failing of fish ladders is the lack of an entry throat the fish can find easily. The discharge of a fish ladder must be carefully placed, and its rate of flow must be metered precisely so that its exiting currents are unmistakable. The spillways and turbine discharges and fish passes all combine in a tumbling confusion of current tongues, totally unlike the flow of the parent river before the dam was built. The outfall of any fish ladder is a typically small part of the total discharge below its impoundment. Sometimes extra volumes of flow are introduced at the throat of a fish ladder to entice migrating fish to enter against its currents. The method used to augment fish ladder discharges is usually a small turbine tube, closely paralleling the fish ladder itself, and screened to prevent entry by immature fish. These supplemental discharges are released through the floor of the bottom chamber in a stairstep installation, and are adjacent to the outflow of a Borland-type lower chamber.

Sometimes fish will enter and ascend a fish ladder more readily when deepened holding zones are also provided below its entry. Fish seem to migrate upstream in cycles, moving readily at some times and resting at others. Migrating behavior is often tied to sudden rises in water, although fish seemingly choose to ascend a river for reasons totally unrelated to river conditions.

Curiously, the fish tend to utilize a fish ladder more and more after its initial seasons of operation. Some observers have suggested that the odors of earlier fish migrations induce subsequent fish to enter them more freely. It is more likely that three other factors are more important. The first is the riverine character of a new fish ladder, since a season or two is perhaps necessary for minute aquatic organisms and zooplankton to establish themselves in its system, reinforcing the olfactory flow. New fish ladders unquestionably contribute a kind of antiseptic overtone to the river scents coming past the dam, and such migratory signposts are also changed by its impoundment. The second factor is perhaps the color of the fish ladder. New construction often exposes any fish ascending the system, highlighting them against the pale bottom, and it takes time for water mosses and algae to give a new fish ladder a sensitivity of sheltering colors. The third factor is the fish themselves, since the descending steelhead smolts on their way to the sea are imprinted with a memory of the fish pass. Yearling fish that have spent only a few months in estuarine waters will use the ladder without hesitation when they return upstream, perhaps inducing older fish to follow. Once a few generations of descending smolts have used a fish ladder, its existence is part of their memory code for the river and its physiography.

Encouraging fish migrating downstream to use fish ladders is also a problem for both spawned-out kelts and small fish migrating toward salt water. Like ascending fish, downstream migrants sometimes have difficulty finding the intake throats of ladders. Thoughtful placement of their outlets and adequate spillway flow are necessary to make them obvious exits. Descending smolts may postpone their downstream migrations, depending on how easily they find the fish-way entrances.

Field observations indicate that spawned-out adults migrating downstream avoid obstructions in the water, while small fish are persistent in trying to wriggle past barricades and screens. Ascending adults have to be excluded from turbine discharge currents, while migrating smolts and spawned-out kelts are both problems in their downstream odysseys.

Ascending fish are blocked with mechanical screens or electrical fields that repel them with intermittent shock pulses. It is obvious from many studies that the alignment and position of these barriers are a factor in herding fish to both upstream and downstream intakes of the bypass ladders. Turbine penstocks that discharge directly into the river channels or have a relatively short tailrace seldom need screens in actual practice. However, unless the turbines are operated at velocities which discourage the fish, many will attempt to enter these discharge throats.

The spacing between the meshes in properly designed smolt screens must be fine to prevent the fish from entering, and the screens must be tightly fitted or the tiny fish will easily wriggle past. Dirty screens that are covered with detritus and debris are a twofold problem: dead organisms and current trash pinned against the meshes can diffuse considerable pollution into a river, and small fish can be trapped and killed against a dirty intake screen, since the discharge currents from the turbines increase in velocity through the meshes that remain unclogged.

Electrical fish screens for the discharge tailings below the dam require only minimal energy to discourage penetration against the flow. Alternating or rectified currents are adequate at such discharge points, since fish that are stunned are simply carried back downstream to recover safely. Most fish easily avoid electrical screens located downstream from an impoundment.

Upstream intake screens are more complicated. Small fish that enter the electrical field and are only slightly incapacitated are carried farther toward the charged meshes by the gathering currents before they can fully recover. Such harmful effects are mitigated through a pulsing current with electrical lapses that permit a fish to recover its senses in time, and an alignment of the charged screen that diverts a stunned smolt toward the desired spillway or fish ladder.

Sometimes the configuration of a particular dam and its surrounding topography make workable fish ladders impractical, and traps below the dam are used to capture upstream migrants. Bag nets and traps are set for fish travelling downstream. Sometimes these fish are simply lifted or lowered past the dam, and sometimes they are carried some distance from the dam in oxygen-equipped fish trucks. Transporting spawned-out kelts is generally less successful than the fish-truck transfer of smolts.

Dams and impoundments present perhaps the most traumatic impact that manmade structures can have on a trout river, and there will be more of them in the future. Our population exploded from only 76,000,000 at the beginning of this century to twice that number at midcentury, and twenty-five years later it had accelerated to more than 200,000,000. Demographers believe that almost 300,000,000 Americans are likely before the end of the century, so our knowledge of both the pitfalls and the potential virtues of reservoirs is vital if we wish to see future dams cause minimal damage to our fisheries.

Similar vigilance must accompany any construction that has a major impact on trout habitat. Bridges, sewage-treatment plants, solid-waste facilities, sanitary landfills, and highways are obvious examples of such structures. The organic forms of pollution associated with municipal wastes are a familiar problem, but the type of processing chosen is also critical, since eutrophication of our waters can result from some treatment systems. Many kinds of contamination can drain from solid-waste and sanitary landfill areas.

Bridges and highways also have many effects. Concrete aggregates are too often excavated directly from the river, or from borrow pits nearby that continue to erode and drain into the biosystem of the river. Cut-and-fill operations during construction often leave similar barren areas that remain like open wounds afterward. Tributary streams are damaged. Steep slopes are stripped of vegetation, and rights of way are cleared of tree and plant cover that prevent erosion and augment the subsurface hydrology. The roadbed earthwork and riprapping often encroach on the streambed, just as bridge abutments and piers require heavy construction operations in the river itself. Construction is frequently more damaging to a watershed than the finished highway, since earthwork and raw topography create vast amounts of turbidity and sedimentation. Recent data suggest that highway surfaces entrain solar energy and create a linear halo of microclimate. Siltation and construction obviously damage fly-life. But the microclimate over pavement can trigger more subtle tragedies, seducing egg-laying insects to oviposit most of their ova on the highway surfaces.

Yet construction is not intrinsically bad. Several years ago fishermen were alarmed over the new highway proposals in the watersheds of the Beaverkill and Willowemoc. Dire predictions that their legendary waters would be eradicated were heard everywhere in the Catskills, yet several years after completion of the highway, the fishery remains excellent. The old highway along the river is virtually empty now, its winding right of way no longer echoing with the gearbox whine and rumble of huge trucks, and many Beaverkill regulars agree their solitude and sport have actually improved. It is true that more fishermen can reach the watershed in less time, but it was the thoughtful wit of writer Ed Zern that focused on the mixed blessings in any major highway project.

When I heard about the highway and all those bridges, Zern observed wryly over lunch in New York, *it made me absolutely furious—and then I remembered that every big Catskill fish I'd ever caught lived under a bridge!*

The full spectrum of problems caused by pollution and water abstraction and dams is only partially understood, although most of the impacts are obvious. The loss of volume to irrigation, municipal water systems, or cooling systems has an unmistakable effect on trout habitat. Organic sludge and petroleum and silt all asphyxiate the bottom-loving organisms of the food chain and smother both fertile eggs and newly hatched fish. Poisons and other toxic substances eradicate both the trout and their diet forms. Turbidity and decomposing wastes deplete life-giving oxygen in the water. Organic wastes, agricultural chemicals, and some municipal effluents can literally choke a trout stream or destroy a lake through eutrophication and algal population explosions. The physical barriers caused by dams, barrage structures, and weirs have unquestionable effects on fish migration and the downstream distribution of nutrients and spawning. Changes in acidity and alkalinity can be critical too. Pollution and reductions in water level or flow can increase fish diseases or cause tainted flesh. Radical chilling of trout habitat or surprisingly small increases in its temperature both cause thermal pollution as deadly as the most toxic pesticides or chemical compounds.

However, it is also important for fishermen to understand that natural forces are neither totally free of pollution nor entirely benign. Natural history is filled with examples of ecological disasters completely unrelated to human populations. Forest fires are started by electrical storms, and parasites and drought and disease all combine to strip tree cover from the biosystems surrounding trout habitat. High winds sometimes result in extensive deforestation. Swamps are natural collecting basins for natural acidity and oxygen-poor water, and atypical rainfall can flush these effluents into adjacent lakes and streams. Muskrats can erode and damage banks, while beaver ponds ultimately become sources of acids leached from the rotting vegetation and organic detritus that collect in their depths. Spates sometimes breach their dams and release their acidity and accumulated sedimentation into the waters downstream. Peat-bog drainage can result in fish kills during periods of heavy rainfall. Many cold springheads are saturated with carbonic acid or nitrogen in lethal concentrations. Alkali, arsenic, and other toxic materials are often naturally leached into lakes and streams. Fish diseases occur in natural cycles. Geysers and hot springs sometimes poison fish or destroy habitat with unusual volumes of discharge, particularly after earthquakes have changed their underground passages and geological strata.

Such seismic activity can also trigger landslides, create waterfalls, change stream gradients and rates of flow, drain lakes or deepen them, flood entire forests or transform swift-flowing rivers into sluggish canals, reverse directions of flow, and even swallow an entire stream in new faults and crevasses. Volcanic activity can have equally dramatic impact on the biosphere. Vast quantities of carbon dioxide and other gases are released into the atmosphere. Lava flows can divert rivers and smother lakes and utterly transform their drainage systems. Eruptions expel incredible tonnages of volcanic ash into the atmosphere. Sometimes enough of its abrasive particles are transported over adjacent drainage systems that turbidity and fishkills can result. The precipitation of volcanic ash is sometimes dense enough to kill vegetation, accelerate erosion, poison and smother soils, and drain gradually into the lakes and streams with every storm. However, astonishing clouds of volcanic ash remain aloft in the atmosphere, and it is surprising to learn that more stratospheric pollution still remains today from the terrible eruptions that shook volcanoes like Hekla and Krakatau more than a century ago than has accumulated from all our cities and technology and factories since the beginnings of the Industrial Revolution.

It is necessary to understand the ambivalence and hostility in nature itself before we can begin to jettison some of the mythology in the environmental movement. Technology in itself is neither evil nor good. Its rhythms and miracles are morally inert, and its thoughtless social and ecological side effects are the result of our technical myopia.

Science and technology have obviously been too preoccupied with mere technical and economic factors. Their sins have been the evils of omission. Their failures commonly result from our inability or unwillingness to consider their side effects, and the social and environmental prices we pay for them. It is these external costs we must learn to anticipate and avoid; and the performance criteria in future technology must include a wider perspective, panoramic enough to consider all the costs—and all the benefits. Blind opposition to all technology is no solution, since only an enlightened technology can solve our existing problems of pollution and urban growth, and fuel much-needed social change.

Water and energy are inseparable; and unpolluted water is critical to industry, potable supply, and agriculture. Our society's future needs for water are far more important than its role in fishing. However, we can play a major role in the development of our water resources. Our focus should be the preservation of cold, unpolluted watersheds, however they are used or controlled—and if we succeed in that goal, we will perhaps have more trout fishing than we have now.

Such results depend on new technical yardsticks and attitudes. Optimal technical performance in the future is impossible unless it is achieved at minimal social and environmental costs—and unless mankind begins to understand where the echoes of technology die.

6. Studies in
Fly-Fishing Entomology

It was late afternoon on a sweeping bend of the Boardman, where the river came down through the trees to the Mayfield Bridge. It is a beautiful river that begins in the cedar swamps and second-growth forests above Kalkaska, the old lumber camp that holds an annual trout festival, and it is still one of the finest streams in Michigan.

It is a swift-flowing river with currents almost as vigorous as the Sturgeon, farther north at Wolverine. It is already a tumbling stream above Fife Lake, its gravelly shallows rich with fly life and lined with deadfalls bleached and polished after years of throbbing in its icy currents. The stones in these upper reaches are sometimes chocolate-colored with algal growth, with bright green patches of *Dichelyma* moss in the currents. These reaches above the power company dam are knee-deep and surprisingly swift, tumbling musically through the legs of a wading fisherman, and the conifers are rich with the counterpoint of chalk-colored birches.

Below the power company dam, where the old iron trusswork bridge once crossed the river, its moods are changed. It is a swift little forest stream between Fife Lake and Kalkaska, where I often startled woodcock in the thickets along the banks, but its character changes at Mayfield.

It is waist-deep and strong there, its leg-wearying power more obvious at the end of the day, and the lower Boardman is a river you like better in your middle years. It is big water below Arbutus Lake, where we once rented a cedar-roofed cottage in the trees, and I never really liked it in my boyhood years. It was one of the final redoubts of the ill-fated Michigan grayling, and when the old-time professional fly makers like Art Winnie and Len Halliday started fishing the Boardman about 1885, it still held brook trout and grayling in equal proportions.

560

Len Halliday is the tier who developed the Adams, naming it for an Ohio attorney who had a summer place on Arbutus Lake, and it was christened on the Boardman in 1922. Its birth alone has given the river a place in fly-fishing history.

During those early summers I struggled against the swift currents of the Sturgeon and the Boardman and the Black, fishing local flies like the Madsen and Michigan Mosquito and Blue-winged Adams. Sometimes we used a Michigan Hopper, which Art Winnie had developed along the Boardman too, and sometimes it was a Woodchuck or Cabin Coachman or Corey Calftail. There was a circle of anglers that fished the Boardman and Manistee from their camp on Fife Lake who liked the hairwing Royal Coachman and another white hairwing with a gold tinsel body and ginger-colored hackle sold at Von Lengerke & Antoine in Chicago. Another group of friends who liked fishing the Pentwater bought their flies from the late Art Kade in Sheboygan, using his version of the Michigan Hopper and the hairwing Kade Coachman.

It was a simple boyhood time. The fish were much less skittish and selective in those days, and our fly boxes held a relatively basic lexicon of patterns. The men who fished the Michigan streams in those years knew little or nothing of matching the hatch, because it was unnecessary to fish imitative flies.

There was an early summer evening in a shallow deadfall-lined bend of the Boardman when the river taught me about selectivity and mating swarms and fly hatches of aquatic insects. The ragged shadows of the pines reached out across the pale gravel riffles, and the waning sunlight was bright in the bend downstream. The river flowed swiftly through my waders, and there were no fish showing anywhere. It seemed like a fine evening, but there were no flies on the water, and the river was strangely lifeless. Almost an hour passed, and except for a small hatchery trout that came splashily to my little Adams, the current seemed empty. The change was almost imperceptible when it finally came, and the working swallows were the first clue.

The swallows gathered high above the river in the twilight, wheeling and darting in intricate aerial patterns. *That's strange,* I thought. *Wonder what they're doing?*

The first birds were soon joined by others, threading a rich dancelike fabric in the twilight. Their hungry ballet came lower and lower, and then I saw the mayflies the birds were capturing. The flies were rising and falling in their graceful mating dance, rising high into the fading light above the trees and fluttering back toward the river.

Soon the males joined the dancing females just above the water, clasping them with their forelegs and the tiny calipers at the tips of their bodies. Mating occurred in flight, with the males hanging under the larger females until the eggs were fertilized. The males then flew off in search of another mate, while the females dropped toward the current. These were pale little *Ephemerella* flies, and the females partially extruded their eggs in bright butter-colored sacs. Their eggs were oviposited into the river when the females dipped low along the current, dropping them into the surface film, and as the flies began touching the water the fish began to rise.

The rhythms of the mating swarms increased quickly, and as more and more mayfly spinners were laying their eggs, the trout were working greedily on the surface. It was a frustrating night, since they refused every fly pattern in my vest.

Such selectivity was a revelation. It ultimately led to my study of stream insects, and I quickly began to collect both nymphs and adults, as well as the stomach contents of the fish we caught. The trout were sometimes surprisingly catholic in their diet, ingesting a wide spectrum of insects and crustaceans, but often their stomachs contained only the nymphs and freshly hatched adults of a single species.

It was not long before I understood that it was selective feeding and not some inexplicable whim of the fish that explained their single-minded preference for one fly pattern or another. Strangely, Ray Bergman was never interested in the relationships between stream entomology and effective fly patterns, and in books like *Just Fishing* and *Trout*, his recommendations on flies are largely based on widely assorted colors and sizes. Such flies were simply presented on a trial-and-error basis until he found a pattern the fish wanted.

It was obvious that many of the flies we used bore little or no resemblance to the fly hatches I collected along the streams and from my stomach autopsies of the trout. It was a nagging fact that bothered me, although we could always catch a few fish on almost anything we used in those days. Yet there were other times when the trout were rising steadily and nothing worked. It was those failures that lay naggingly in the memory, failures that echoed through my mind in those last moments before sleep, and my work with fly hatches soon started.

Success with selective trout gradually followed, although there were still many times when the fish ignored my attempts at matching the hatch in those boyhood summers. Over the years there have been many days when rising trout proved an impenetrable puzzle, but stream entomology has helped make them rarities.

It is obvious that casting skills and a mastery of tackle and a sense of tactics are paramount. But it is equally obvious that once these skills of streamcraft and presentation have been polished, the problems of selectivity remain even for the most accomplished fisherman. Solving those problems invariably means matching the hatch, observing the naturals carefully, and dressing flies to imitate them. Succesful imitation of the naturals also means suggesting their movements and behavior, particularly the swimming rhythms of many nymphs, and the fluttering hopscotch of some adult insects. Both fly patterns that match the hatch and imitative techniques of fly manipulation are impossible without a thorough knowledge of fly-fishing entomology.

Such detailed knowledge is available in books like the *Streamside Guide to Naturals and Their Imitations* and *A Modern Dry-Fly Code* and *Selective Trout*, and in my earlier books *Matching the Hatch* and *Nymphs*. These books are essential in the working library of any fly-fisherman, since they pinpoint the principal diet forms of our lakes and streams.

Yet our hard-fished waters mean no general work on trout fishing is complete without a basic primer on the important fly life, terrestrials, and crustaceans. The principal aquatic insects are the mayflies, sedges, stoneflies, and the two-winged species like craneflies and midges and gnats. Less important aquatic species include the fishflies and dobsonflies and alder flies, along with water beetles and backswimmers and the restless *Corixa* bugs. Dragonflies and damselflies are important on slow-flowing streams and ponds, and on some waters aquatic moths are important too. The principal crustaceans include scuds and freshwater shrimps and sowbugs. The terrestrial insects can also prove important in fly-fishing, particularly in the midsummer months. Ants and grasshoppers and beetles are perhaps the most familiar terrestrials, although inchworms and caterpillars are sometimes important too, along with the two-winged flies that are land-bred species. Sometimes wasps and sawflies and bees are also taken in good numbers on our trout waters, along with robberflies and gauzewings. But perhaps the most important terrestrials are the agile little leafhoppers and ants—species that are discussed in considerable detail in the writings of skilled Pennsylvania fishermen like Vincent Marinaro and Charles Fox.

Mayflies are perhaps the best-known hatches. Like most aquatic insects, the mayflies spend all but a few days of their lives in their parent lakes and streams. Although they are relatively small, like most organisms of interest to the fly-fisherman, the mayflies are extremely important in the trout diet. Their importance lies in the surprisingly rich milligram-for-milligram food value of aquatic insects, compared with baitfish and other common diet forms. Few anglers are aware that the insect population living in our better lakes and streams is sufficient to sustain even the largest trout.

The fact that aquatic insects spend most of their life cycles in their immature stages of growth means the fish concentrate most of their feeding below the surface. Fly hatches of adult insects occupy only a brief period of the season, while in the subaquatic stages these same insects are available to hungry fish throughout the year. It is surprising how many fly-fishermen believe that more food is available to the trout between spring and early fall. Yet the knowledgeable entomologist knows that it is the winter months—when the river is rich in nymphs and pupal forms and larvae—that will provide the entire cycle of fly hatches in the coming year and offer the richest supply of food-chain organisms.

Like other aquatic forms of life, the insects are structured of living cells. Their anatomy and physiology are composed of cellular systems, nutrients absorbed through their metabolic -processes, and the wastes expelled in those functions. Most cells are microscopic, containing a tiny nucleus suspended in a translucent fluid-filled sac. It is the nucleus that controls the cell itself. The fluidlike material is called cytoplasm. This collects and stores nutrients until they are passed into the bloodstream through the cellular membranes. Cells are replaced through multiplication, in which a healthy cell divides into two new cells and each divides again in turn. The cells of our common fly hatches perform many functions. Some form the skeletal materials, while others are structured into less rigid tissues. Still others are responsible for the secretion of digestive, reproductive, and moulting substances.

Insect metabolism requires a continuous flow of oxygen to the cells to extract the energy from their diet, and that process expels carbon dioxide in the same cycle found in higher organisms. Respiration is not affected through either lungs or gills as in mammals or fish life. Adult insects breathe through a network of delicate tracheae that feed a system of still more delicate tubes called the tracheoles, which branch out like capillaries through the entire anatomy. The mayflies have a pair of spiracular openings in most of their abdominal segments. Oxygen enters these spiracles and is diffused through the intricate network of microscopic tracheae and tracheoles, and the exhalation of waste carbon dioxide is accomplished through the same network.

Mayfly nymphs and many other subaquatic insect forms absorb some oxygen from the water directly through their body integument. However, the mayfly nymphs have gill covers which protect their tracheal networks, and the gill filaments underneath collect most of the oxygen they need. It is interesting that many swift-water species have relatively exposed gill filaments, while others that love bottom detritus and silts are protected from abrasion by opercular gill covers. Some burrowing nymphs have remarkably feathery gills. Most important aquatic insects are as vulnerable to pollution and oxygen deficiencies as the trout and grayling themselves.

Unlike the skeletal structures of higher organisms, the aquatic insects have skeletons composed of their external secretions or cuticle. Such external structures are called exoskeletons. They are composed of a series of flexible plates connected by softer cells. Such abdominal and thoracic segments are obvious in the anatomy of most aquatic insects, and are particularly obvious in the anatomical structure of the mayflies.

The body integument of the several aquatic flies is constructed of both cuticle and skin. Its cells secrete the chitinous and sclerotinous materials which provide both the elasticity and the strength of the exoskeleton.

The cuticle has three distinct layers. The epicuticle is relatively rigid and inelastic, and is composed largely of sclerotin. The exocuticle is the middle layer, formed of both sclerotin and chitinous tissue. The endocuticle is soft and elastic, containing only chitinous cells, and it lies inside the other two layers. Insect cuticle is distributed throughout the anatomy, including the thorax, eyes, abdominal structure, wings, legs, and tail. The membranes covering the wings and eyes are thin and translucent, while the thorax and body are formed of heavier integument.

The semirigid plates of the thorax and abdomen are called sclerites, and are joined together with flexible tissues to form an exoskeleton that will twist and flex gracefully. It is also capable of limited expansion and contraction. Each segment of both the thorax and abdomen is formed of four sclerites, covering the dorsal and belly surfaces as well as their sides. The dorsal plates are called tergites, the ventral surfaces are the sternites, and the connecting lateral segments are pleurites. The thoracic structure is somewhat more complicated than the abdominal segments, since it supports both wings and legs.

Adult mayflies have a basic anatomical structure consisting of the head, thorax, and abdomen. The head is relatively small and complex. It supports a pair of antennae, light-sensitive organs called ocelli, large compound eyes called oculli, and atrophied labial parts and jaws. The thorax or chest structure has three parts. The protothorax lies behind the head and supports the anterior legs, while the larger mesothorax supports both the middle legs and primary forewings. The metathorax carries the atrophied rear wings and posterior or hind legs. The abdomen consists of ten segments. The upper leg is called the femur and the lower leg is the tibia. The tails grow from the final segment of the body. The male mayflies have a pair of forceps or styli attached to the ventral surfaces of the body in the ninth segment, and extending well under the last segment in fully developed specimens. The females extrude their eggs from a tiny orifice between the ninth and tenth segments of the body. The tails are more properly described as caudal filaments and are called cerci in the two-tailed species. The center tail in the three-tailed species is called the telofilum, or median caudal filament. Past fishing writers like Alfred Ronalds and Frederic Halford often referred to the tails as setae, but this word is now used to describe the hairlike filaments on the tails themselves.

Freshly hatched mayfly nymphs are virtually microscopic not long after eclosion from their eggs. Their configuration is a miniature prelude to the mature nymphs they will become, although they lack gill systems and wing cases and fully developed eyes. Respiration is accomplished directly through the integument until the tracheal networks are mature. The thoracic segments more closely resemble the remaining abdominal structure than their ultimate wing-case development, and several instars or moults occur before a nymph achieves its mature form.

Moulting consists of shedding the outer skin. The dorsal surfaces of the thorax and head are split, and the nymph wriggles free from its epicuticle. The color of a freshly moulted nymph is always much paler for a number of hours, until its normal coloration is regained. Many species are pale whitish-cream when they first escape a discarded nymphal skin. The fresh epicuticle is soft and flexible for a brief period, but contact with the cold water quickly hardens its exoskeletal shell. The growth of the nymphal form is constant inside that exoskeleton, but its epicuticular development proceeds through a series of stages. Each stage is called an instar, and the total number of instars in the growth of any nymph varies from species to species, and the number of instars for each ecotype is unknown.

However, some studies of instar development in the mayflies have been made in recent years. Specimens of the *Baetis* flies were found to progress through twenty-seven stages of nymphal growth. The thread-gill *Stenonema* nymphs have approximately thirty-six instars, while the similar *Heptagenia* and *Epeorus* genera seem to pass from thirty to thirty-three stages.

It is important to remember that a cycle of instar growth in a particular species affects the possible range of hook sizes in a single imitation. Most fishing books suggest nymph sizes based on their mature growth just before emergence, but the instar cycle means that smaller sizes are also workable.

Duration of nymphal life is affected by temperature and water chemistry. Favorable conditions mean a nymph will reach maturity in less time, and the nymphal life span varies widely from species to species. Mayflies of the big *Hexagenia* genus have a life cycle of three years, while the *Ephemera* flies apparently have a life span of two. *Baetis* and *Callibaetis* mayflies occupy the opposite end of the spectrum, with three broods hatching across each season. The spring broods mature in only six months, hatching out in the following October. The August broods hatch the following May, and the October broods reach maturity again in late summer. The broods which must pass a winter and its water temperatures require three to four months longer to hatch. The Caenidae have a year-long nymphal cycle like most mayflies, but their adulthood lasts a brief twenty to thirty minutes.

Nymphs feed principally on phytoplankton, vegetation, and zooplankton. Diatoms and desmids are particularly important, and some larger nymphs are fiercely carnivorous, even devouring less developed nymphs of their own species. Many swift-water species literally capture the diatomaceous and algal life carried along in the currents, like an infielder picking up ground balls. The plant-loving genera indigenous to slower currents and ponds literally graze like tiny cattle along the stems of subaquatic plants, cropping the microscopic algae from their stalks and leaves. Such nymphs feed methodically, pausing sometimes to lift their heads and masticate their food before taking more.

As in most predominantly herbivorous species, the jaw structure of the mayfly nymph is virtually useless in defense against predators. Agility and concealment are its principal defenses. Some swimming nymphs are as swift as baitfish, and others burrow like moles in the soft bottom. Protective coloration is particularly well developed among many nymphal forms, and often a swimming nymph will flee swiftly, stopping just as quickly to lose itself against the background of its habitat.

Configuration of the mayfly nymphs depends on their behavior and the character of their environment. Slender specimens are usually swimming or burrowing types, while the clambering nymphs are fat and clumsy, living among the stones and bottom detritus. Free-ranging nymphs found in swift currents are agile and fusilliform species, while the clinging types fasten their flat bodies, gill systems, and legs like barnacles to the undersides of stones and deadfalls.

All mayfly nymphs are typically found in riverine habitats, since a trout stream often has such a varied ecology that all types of water are available. Slow-flowing pools and flats and weedy stillwaters provide habitat more like lakes and ponds than the remainder of the stream. Tumbling chutes and rapids offer the opposite extreme, yet even such reaches may have quiet shallows and backwater eddies where slow-water nymphs can live. Other pockets of relatively quiet microhabitat can also exist behind boulders and other obstructions.

Finally the nymphs are fully grown, having escaped the epicuticle of their last growth instar, and they cease to grow and feed. Their mandibles and mouth parts atrophy. The nymphs darken slightly, and their wing cases become almost black in some species. Feeding stops and the alimentary tract is empty and translucent. Emerging nymphs reach the atmosphere in several ways. Some escape the nymphal shuck at the bottom, or within a few inches of the surface, and wrapped in their embryonic wings and a sheath of gaseous bubbles, continue toward the surface to hatch. Others generate such bubbles inside their nymphal skins, using their buoyancy to carry them toward the atmosphere and the brief adulthood typical of the mayflies. Still others migrate into the shallows to hatch, or like the *Isonychia* genus, cling to rocks at the waterline to escape their epicuticle and emerge. Some flies escape their nymphal skins clumsily and slowly, while others pop fully developed through the surface meniscus and are almost immediately capable of flight.

Our principal dry-fly hatches are often those insects which are relatively clumsy in escaping their nymphal skins and often ride the current for prolonged periods of time. It is these insects that trigger good periods of surface feeding. The species that emerge in the surface film literally attach themselves to the tensile undersurface of its meniscus, their thoracic bulk swollen and pressing upwards. Wriggling and pinioned in the film, the nymphs split their skins across the thorax and head, withdrawing their wings and bodies from the exuvial skins in a single shuddering movement. It is a remarkable transformation from the ugliness of the nymphal forms to the sailboatlike elegance of the mayflies.

The freshly hatched mayfly is called a subimago or dun, and is the catalyst in much of our dry-fly sport. Although trout take infinitely more nymphal forms across the full spectrum of the year, their surface feeding to freshly hatched flies is both obvious and considerably more dramatic. The fish respond eagerly to both nymphs and hatching duns.

Fishermen who know little or nothing of the rhythms of life in a river often think it is lifeless and empty, and many fail to understand that fly hatches are literally born in its depths. The surface of a river can flow undisturbed by either insects or rising fish. Finally a fly appears suddenly on the surface, where nothing was visible a millisecond before, and flies unsteadily toward the alders after floating briefly with the flow. Others quickly follow, until there are many on the water and in flight, and many more are preparing to hatch below the surface. Chimney swifts and barn swallows and phoebes are darting and wheeling to catch the hatching flies and suddenly the trout have started rising for them too.

As it leaves the surface currents, the flight of a subimago is largely controlled by the wind. Few are able to fight even the slightest breeze. Their flight is jumbled and erratic on truly windy days; they struggle into the air only to be blown back, hopscotching and fluttering on the water. Their flight is clumsy and weak. Mayflies have a singular attitude in flight, wings spread wide above the trailing pendulum of their bodies, and a skilled angler has no trouble identifying them.

Still days and hot weather will find them ascending higher and higher above the water until they are virtually lost from sight. But such optimal conditions are rare, and the freshly hatched duns usually find refuge in the trees and streamside foliage. Particularly windy days are difficult, driving the flies horizontally along the water into the bankside limbs and grass. Strong winds can carry them through the outer layers of foliage, deep into the inner branches and sheltered foliage. During heavy fly hatches, the vegetation along a fertile lake or stream is literally rich with insect life.

The newly hatched subimago hides on the undersides of leaves and plant stalks and limbs. Like a nymph concealing itself among the stones and bottom trash, a moulting dun seeks a sheltered place where it can rest, out of the wind and rain and direct sunlight. It will remain there unless a predator disturbs its trancelike state, darkening as its epicuticle begins to atrophy and loosen. The final moulting consists of splitting away the entire integument covering the wings, head, thorax, abdomen, legs, and tails of the insect. The exuvia that is finally shed is a chalk-colored skin not unlike the nymphal shuck the fly first escaped when it emerged.

When a subimago is moulting it spreads its wings horizontally, splitting its skin across the dorsal surfaces of the thorax. It patiently wriggles its head, wings, thorax, and legs free, using this tiny opening to escape its shuck. The particularly delicate epicuticle covering the wings is also shed, collapsing into dark little appendages not unlike the wing cases of a nymphal form. The cast skins of mayflies are remarkably like the flies themselves, perfectly echoing their full morphology, even to the tails and genitalia. The cast exuvia is frequently left on streamside vegetation, pale and delicately transparent.

The time required for moulting varies widely. The large *Hexagenia* and *Ephemera* flies require as much as two or three days, while the tiny Caenidae take only a few minutes. It is not uncommon to have these diminutive mayflies moulting on your waders and fishing jacket and hat during particularly heavy periods of emergence, leaving them covered with the brittle little skins. Weather and temperature and humidity all affect the moulting period. Cold rainy days can inhibit moulting, while fair weather accelerates it, and when conditions are right huge mating swarms soon follow the hatch.

The freshly moulted mayfly is called an imago or spinner, and it has now reached the sexually mature stage. Like the hatching nymphs and duns, the spinners do not ingest any food during the remaining hours of mating and egg laying before their death. Large flights of imago mayflies are most commonly found in calm, relatively mild weather, while many duns hatch best on rainy, overcast days.

Spinner swarms are quite common along rivers and above sheltered bays and shallows of lakes. The male flies often gather into swarms high above the water, and are finally joined by more and more females. The swarm itself maintains a generally fixed location above the water. Particularly ripe males and females engage in the graceful, hovering flight typical of the mayflies, rising and falling in their unique balletlike mating rites. It is one of the beautiful riddles of aquatic life.

The mayfly swarms choose their mating sites carefully, using the proximity of the water as well as terrain and plant physiography. Weather and wind direction can also play a role. Some mating behavior is typical of all mayflies, yet each species may demonstrate singular patterns of flight in its egg-laying swarms. These unique characteristics can also affect the feeding responses of the fish, just as the trout adapt their feeding to the hatching behavior of different insects.

The mating flight of the mayflies varies with each species. Flies of the *Callibaetis* genus rise and fall delicately, their wings beating rapidly as they fly upward, forelegs and tails extended to balance them. Rising briefly with the rest of the swarm, and then setting their wings to flutter down again, falling down to the lowest levels of the other flies, their rising and falling continues in endless repetition, zigzagging and drifting on the wind, occurring most often on warm days in bright weather. The small *Heptagenia* flies exhibit similar behavior, and are commonly found in twilight swarms. They rise upward slowly, facing into the wind as they gain altitude, and then dancing vigorously up and down as the apogee of the nuptial dance is reached. *Paraleptophlebia* spinners dance up and down in compact little swarms during the late mornings and afternoons. The delicate *Baetis* spinners seem to prefer the morning hours for their mating and egg laying, while the larger *Siphlonurus* flies dance in large swarms along the shores of lakes and streams in late afternoon and evening. The big spinners of genera like *Potamanthus* and *Hexagenia* and *Ephemera* are famous for spectacular twilight mating swarms that can last until well after dark. During my boyhood summers in Michigan and Wisconsin, we often found our porch screens literally covered with fat *Hexagenia* spinners, and the fish often took the naturals until one and two o'clock in the morning after particularly heavy swarms. Many of the numerous *Ephemerellas* typically mate in graceful, undulating flights in late afternoon and early evening. The relatively large *Isonychias* are most active at twilight, and continue their egg laying after dark, like the stream-loving *Epeorus* and *Heptagenia* flies. The intriguing white-winged *Tricorythodes* duns hatch early in the morning, moult almost immediately, and join in remarkably dense nuptial swarms before breakfast.

James Needham described the nuptial flight of summer spinners in his classic *Biology of Mayflies* with these observations of a mating swarm at Walnut Lake in Michigan:

> After sundown, the beautiful mayfly, *Ephemera simulans*, appears in companies of males over the edge of the water. The flight of one of these companies is a most delightful performance to witness, it is so light and graceful, and appears, withal, so exhilarating. Yet it is all up and down in vertical patterns. With its upturned head each individual flies rapidly upward, mounting to a height of perhaps ten or fifteen meters; then, spreading its wings out horizontally, it falls upon them, with long forelegs extended forward and longer tails extended backward full length, rudderlike, keeping it always facing into the wind. Thus it descends, floating on the air, yet not drifting, until at the lower levels of the swarm (four or five meters above the water), it lifts its head and rises rapidly again in flight. And the whole company flying and falling thus, weaving up and down vertically, and passing and repassing each other creates a scene of graceful animation.

Mating itself occurs during flight. Copulation is both agile and acrobatic, its positions probably impossible except in midair. The males climb vertically, synchronizing their rising flight with the females, until their exaggeratedly long forelegs reach up and grasp the thoracic structure of the females. The female spinners bend their bodies down, carrying them both with their larger wing-surfaces and musculature, until the males can arch their bodies up enough to seat their forceps around the ninth segment of the females. The mating attitude is surprisingly graceful, considering the contortions involved and the fact that the female supports both insects in flight as they leave the swarm. Once fertilization is completed, the male rejoins the nuptial swarm and mates again, while the female begins her egg-laying dance.

The egg laying occurs in three basic ways: some species drop down to ride the current several times, washing off a few eggs each time; some develop tiny egg sacs under their bodies, extruding them all in one or two sacs by dropping them or brushing them off in the water; and some actually fold their wings around their bodies, migrating through the surface film to lay their eggs on the deadfalls and stones along the bottom.

Spinners of the *Epeorus* and *Heptagenia* genera are of the types that indulge in rapid rising and falling flight, drop down to extrude a few eggs by riding the current, and climb back into the air again. *Siphlonurus* and *Ephemerella* and *Isonychia* are among the genera that form spherical egg sacs, and flutter down either to drop them into the current from a few inches away, or touch them off in its surface tension before flying back to rejoin the dancing females. The big *Ephemera* and *Hexagenia* drakes form little cucumber-shaped egg sacs that hang pendulously from their bodies. Sometimes these ova are dropped from the air in flight, and sometimes they are extruded while the big females lie spent and shuddering in the surface film. It is the *Baetis* and *Callibaetis* flies that clamber down boulders and deadfalls and weedy stems, ovipositing their eggs in a ribbon or patch in the sheltered places.

Obviously, the fish cannot feed on these mating mayflies until they flutter close to the water, ride the current while ovipositing, or fall spent in the surface. Many anglers are puzzled when the twilight is filled with dancing spinners, yet the river flows unmarred by rising trout. It was my old friend Art Flick who pointed out in his *Streamside Guide* that mating spinners are in the air and not yet on the water, and that lack of availability is the reason the fish are not working. Many years ago, on my boyhood water of the Pere Marquette in Michigan, I stood baffled in a twilight that was literally a blizzard of mating drakes.

Why aren't the fish rising? I asked.

It's a brush hatch, one old-timer answered in the darkness. *Them flies come outta the brush to lay their eggs.*

You mean the fish are just waiting? I puzzled.

That's right, he laughed.

Mayfly eggs are remarkable examples of natural adaptation. Some have buoyant little flotation appendages, while others are equipped with intricate, threadlike coils. These are meant to permit the eggs to drift to

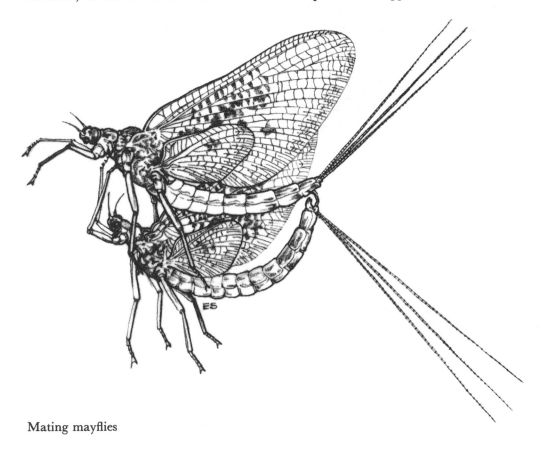

Mating mayflies

safety in the weedy shallows, or catch and hold on the bottom detritus or vegetation. Still others are covered with a gelatinous coating that adheres the eggs to the bottom stones, but not to each other. Some eggs are equipped with an adhesive cap, and some have microscopic adhesive nodules at the tips of their threadlike tendrils. The adhesive properties of these nodules are striking. The minute ova of *Tricorythodes* are like acorns with six tendrils, while *Brachycercus* eggs are shaped like microscopic peanuts. *Caenis* eggs range from acornlike forms with coiled filaments to other ovoid shapes with a limpetlike parasol at one terminal surface. It is remarkable that each of our six hundred to seven hundred mayfly species has its own singular eggs—distinctive in both their morphology and their function.

Once their oviposition is completed, the female spinners weaken and fall on the water or the shoreline nearby. Windy days can tumble the spinners into the current long before they are fully exhausted and spent, and many imago flies are trapped in the film before they have extruded their eggs. Others manage to complete their egg laying, but still hold their wings upright when they fall or are blown into the water. Such flies are best imitated with conventional imitations, with symmetrical wings that are dressed upright and divided.

Spent imago flies are another problem altogether. Some species have mating swarms of such concentration that their spinner falls attract genuine

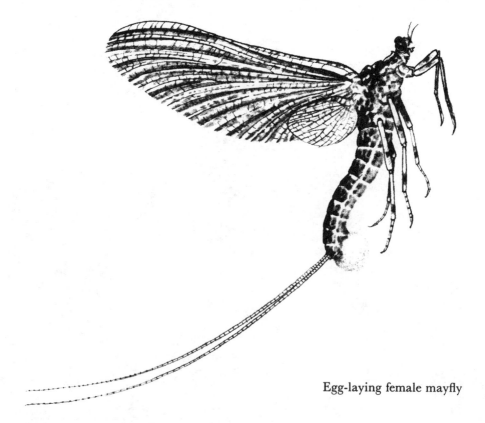

Egg-laying female mayfly

rises of fish. Several American hatches of *Isonychia* and *Hexagenia* and *Ephemera* drakes have particularly thick mating swarms, like the famous Michigan mayfly flights and the coffin flies on our eastern rivers, from the Adirondacks to the Great Smokies in North Carolina. There are many *Ephemerella* hatches from Maine to California that have particularly fine spinner falls of medium-size flies. Our western spring creeks and lakes have dense spinner falls of speckle-winged *Callibaetis* flies, and the tiny morning falls of white-winged *Tricorythodes* are important from the Battenkill in Vermont to weedy Putah Creek a few miles above San Francisco.

The transparent wings of most spent mayflies, some perfectly clear and others delicately mottled, lie pinioned with the legs in the surface film. The combination of flush wings and clumsily spraddled legs creates a unique translucency and light pattern in the meniscus. Some species have translucent bodies as well, ranging from a pale chalkiness to the deep claret color of a spent Hendrickson imago. Some even have pink, yellowish, sherry-colored, or orangey bodies of surprising chromatic intensity.

Fully spent and exhausted spinners are virtually impossible to see on the water. Many seemingly unexplained rises of fish, particularly in late afternoon and evening, are triggered by large numbers of dead or dying spinners lying flush in the surface film. Often the only method of identifying such a spinner fall lies in identifying the mating swarm that precedes it, or observing the dwindling flight of male spinners that remain over the water. Really skilled fishermen can actually anticipate good spinner-fall rises of fish from the hatching duns that precede them, knowing approximately how long their moulting in the streamside vegetation will last. Since heavy feeding on spent flies often occurs in late evening, when it is impossible to identify anything on the water, understanding the relationships between hatching duns and male spinners and spent females is the secret of spinner-fall fishing.

It is equally important to understand something of the singular habits and habitat of each mayfly genus that plays a major role in the diet of trout and grayling. Perhaps the best-known American mayflies are the relatively large drakes of the *Ephemera* genus. There are three famous species on the rivers of Europe, from the richly alkaline waters of the British Isles to the limestone streams of Yugoslavia. American waters have six important species, ranging from the classic Green Drake of the Catskills to the brownish mottle-winged *Ephemeras* found in Rocky Mountain waters from Montana to New Mexico.

The nymphs of these *Ephemera* drakes reach optimal populations in alkaline habitat, like the limestone rivers of Pennsylvania or the marl-rich waters of Michigan and Wisconsin. Bottoms having extensive beds of fine gravel and sand or fine silty mixtures of marl and micro-aggregates provide exceptional environments. Some of the best hatches are found in lakes.

Unlike the burrowing nymphs of the similar *Hexagenia* flies, these slightly smaller nymphal forms are found in both flowing, lotic-type environments and quiet lenitic habitats. They are relatively slender and

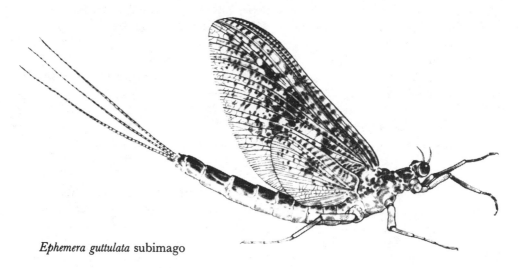

Ephemera guttulata subimago

somewhat flat bodied, with delicately plumose gills along their upper abdomens. The *Ephemera* nymphs are also equipped with tapering heads and the sharp mandibles typical of the burrowing ecotypes. Their forelegs are not as powerfully shaped as those found in the *Hexagenia* nymphs. The legs are folded back under the thorax while they are swimming. These burrowing nymphs are quite shy, scrambling like moles to escape the light if dislodged. Their diet is largely diatomaceous material and decaying leaf drift. Although pollution and residual concentrations of pesticides and the bottom scouring of heavy spates have combined to decimate the *Ephemera* hatches on many waters, there are still heavy riverine populations across the United States.

The subimago stages of these hatches are relatively large and handsome insects with richly mottled wings and three slender tails. Both their dorsal and ventral surfaces are covered with intricate markings, although these fade in the spinner stage of *Ephemera guttulata* to an almost unblemished chalkiness. Their thoracic surfaces are richly mottled too, and the femora of the legs are subtly varied in color.

These subimago flies typically emerge sporadically throughout the day, escaping from the water almost immediately unless a misting rain or

Ephemera guttulata nymph

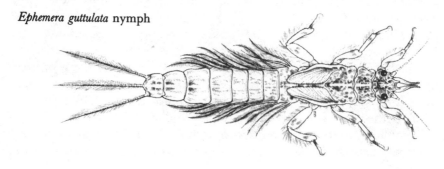

strong breeze keeps them on the water. The rhythm of a hatch seems to increase toward evening, with more and more flies coming down until their hatching is lost in darkness. Good hatches are remarkably heavy, and once the emerging duns reach the trees, literally thousands can be found in the foliage. The shallow bays and backwater eddies are often covered with a delicate scum of empty nymphal shucks, their gills and translucent skins pale echoes of the wriggling nymphs they once housed.

Many American fishing writers have spoken of their troublesome experiences with *Ephemera* nymphs. Preston Jennings found them so difficult to imitate that his *Book of Trout Flies* omits them completely. It was Art Flick who first speculated that the nymphs were perhaps darker than the adult flies, and that they swam so quickly toward the surface that he could not capture them. Sometimes the trout feed heavily on these nymphs when they are dislodged by high water, but they are more readily available during emergence periods. During such hatches, the nymphs dart rather swiftly to the surface and rises are decisive and strong. Often the largest fish gorge themselves along the bottom, taking the nymphs greedily as they abandon their burrows and start toward the surface. Weighted nymphs fished deep are also effective during spates, while light-wire imitations should be fished with a minnowlike retrieve during periods of emergence.

Sometimes fish that are feeding heavily on these migrating nymphs will change readily to their hatching duns as the rhythms of the hatch steadily progress. Periods of emergence are relatively brief, lasting a week to ten days at most. Hatching builds slowly to an explosive crescendo of two or three days, and the fish often refuse the adult flies in the first stages of emergence. Once the peak has passed, the flies quickly dwindle in numbers. Hatching typically starts in late morning and lasts until early evening, although fishing writers in both Europe and the United States have recorded unusual delays in a hatch until four or five o'clock in the afternoon.

The *Ephemera* spinners are remarkable insects. After two or three days of moulting, they reappear from the foliage along the water to commence their mating swarms. Typical nuptial flight occurs from ten to twenty feet above the surface film, but where extensive forest cover is found, the mating swarms can gather high above the trees. The spinners are so large that most anglers know them, and their nuptial dance is familiar. The flies climb upward three or four feet on rapidly beating wings, descending again on outstretched wings and widely spread caudal filaments. The tempo and animation of a mating swarm increases roughly in proportion to the number of flies present, and they begin gathering in the afternoon. The swarms are fully populated about three hours before sunset, although extremely bright or hot weather may delay them. Overcast days may find them present earlier in the afternoon, and they usually seek shelter in the trees at nightfall.

Spent females and males are present in such numbers that they are important to both fishermen and fish. Many egg-laying spinners ride the surface while extruding their eggs, and are eagerly taken by the trout. These flies are drifting spent in great numbers on the water once oviposition is completed, and finally the spent males are also available to the trout.

Many writers have observed that these mating swarms and spinner falls often stimulate better rises of fish than the hatching duns, since the duns appear sporadically and the spinners are found in exceptional concentrations. It is often possible to predict a good mating swarm by seeking out the first small nuptial flights of the males, which gather along the bankside foliage in late evening. The foliage is usually filled with ripening females. When such swarms are absent, or only sparsely populated by early evening, it is unlikely that any real rise of fish will occur later.

The big *Hexagenia* mayflies found on many American waters are similar in their habitat and behavior, but are generally much larger than

Hexagenia limbata nymph

any of the *Ephemera* drakes found in either Europe or the United States. Their succulent nymphs prefer somewhat more lenitic habitat than the *Ephemera* species, burrowing into the bottom silts and detritus and marl of many lakes and slow-flowing rivers and ponds. Many are also found in the backwaters and quiet eddies of swifter water types. The *Hexagenia* nymphs are less slender and their bodies are relatively flat. The gill systems are plumose and flamboyant, undulating rhythmically during respiration. The nymphs are equipped with narrow, tapering heads and tusked mandibles. Their powerful forelegs are ideally suited for burrowing into bottom sediments, and they are virtually as shy as the trout themselves, reacting in panic when dislodged from their burrows.

The nymphs subsist on a diet of rich diatomaceous ooze and decomposing vegetable matter in the silt beds that shelter their burrows. Their beds are most commonly found in the shallow littoral zones of lakes and streams, and they sometimes actually burrow into the banks in marshy places. The genus has a nymphal cycle lasting three years, so specimens are available to the fish in a wide range of sizes. Populations are unusually

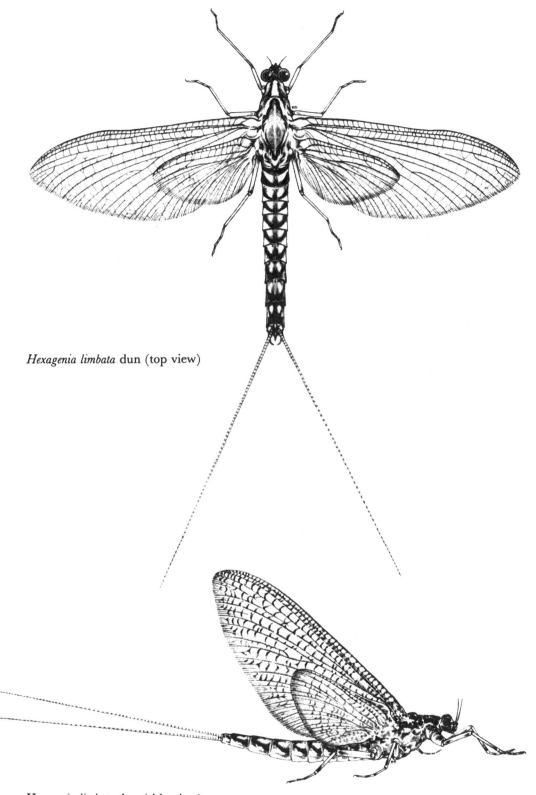

Hexagenia limbata dun (top view)

Hexagenia limbata dun (side view)

heavy in optimal habitat, producing unquestionably the most impressive fly hatches found on our waters. The *Hexagenia* group also includes the largest of our many mayfly species, its succulent insects reaching body lengths of more than an inch.

Both hatching times and behavior are quite similar to those of the burrowing *Ephemera* nymphs, their duns emerging sporadically through the day and reaching a peak toward nightfall. The duns are quite large and are easily recognized by their two tail filaments. Coloring ranges from pale sulphur and cream in some species to dark olive-grey and slate-colored wings and bodies in others. The dorsal surfaces of their bodies are often rather boldly patterned with darker coloring, and less dramatic markings are found on their sternites.

Perhaps the best-known species is *Hexagenia limbata*, the big drake that appears in early summer in exceptional numbers on the waters of Michigan and Wisconsin. Its heaviest populations occur in habitats having relatively firm bottom silts. The nymphs form unusual U-shaped burrows that are structurally unsound except in silt beds and marl deposits firm enough to support such delicate tunneling. Their tunnels penetrate as much as six inches into the bottom, and marl swamps provide such habitat in almost unlimited acreages. The fully grown nymph is quite large, and during emergence it is available in incredible numbers.

Although hatching of this species has been recorded from early June until September, the principal hatches typically occur before July. Like all of the burrowing mayflies, the nymphs are available during spate conditions, but the largest numbers are eaten during a hatch. Stomach autopsies performed over the years in Michigan indicate that these nymphs are a primary trout food all year—and research clearly points to their presence in the fish diet in surprising numbers throughout the fall and winter months.

The peak hatches occur about twilight, and dry-fly fishing can prove excellent at such times. There are evenings when only the smaller fish work on the surface and nymphs take the trophy-size trout. Strong hatching activity can last until nine or ten o'clock, and the fisherman who has never witnessed a hatch of *Hexagenia limbata* has missed one of the most explosive orgies of rising fish imaginable. Since optimal water chemistry and habitat can produce as many as five hundred nymphs per square yard of bottom marl, the resulting hatches of big mayflies are remarkable.

The mating swarms and spinner falls are often even heavier, filling the night like a blizzard. It is difficult to imagine the night alive with fluttering spinners, their crystalline wings measuring as much as two inches across, and their pale bodies rich with butter-colored eggs. These mating flights are usually fully developed at nightfall and can last until well past midnight, when the spinner fall coaxes the largest fish to feed until two and three o'clock in the morning. During such a spinner fall, there can literally be thousands and thousands of spent *Hexagenia* flies on the water, and even the biggest trout go wild.

The *Potamanthus* mayflies are similar in appearance to the burrowing species, but their fringe-gilled nymphs are sprawling and swimming ecotypes. Their relatively large, plumose gill systems clearly demonstrate a relatively high oxygen requirement for a genus that prefers a slow-moving lenitic habitat. The nymphs are slender and relatively round in shape. Their bodies, tails, and legs are richly mottled, and their round-shaped bodies are obviously not adapted for burrowing into bottom silts. The tails are fringed and delicately marked, and the fragile tibiae of the legs are less powerfully developed than those of the true burrowing nymphs. There are eight American species, although not all of them are found in cold-water habitats associated with trout. The nymphs inhabit sediments and bottom trash without actually burrowing into them. They prefer quiet currents, living out of the primary current tongues, and some are also found in fast water.

Louis Rhead wrote about these flies in his *American Trout Stream Insects*, describing the hatches of more than forty years ago and calling them golden drakes. Fifteen years later, Preston Jennings described these hatches in his *Book of Trout Flies*, but observed that he had seldom witnessed good hatches when the rivers were still at optimal temperatures for fishing.

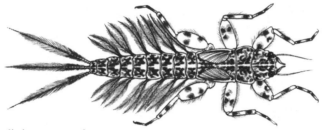

Potamanthus distinctus nymph

The bright-yellow-winged *Potamanthus* drakes hatch in midsummer on most rivers. Their wings are relatively broad, and their bodies are fat and succulent. Many species have orangey forelegs, and many have orangey dorsal and pleural markings on their bodies. There are three pale-colored tail filaments. Overcast days can trigger good hatches in late afternoon, and such afternoon behavior is relatively common on well-shaded streams that

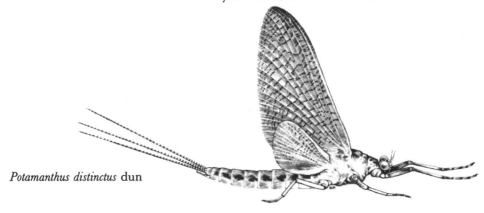

Potamanthus distinctus dun

wind through acreages of high-canopy forest. However, the best hatches are usually found in late evening, with good activity lasting well beyond nightfall. The spinners have glittering, transparent wings faintly touched with yellow and orange, their veins sharply etched in their integument. Their mating swarms are largely nocturnal, and spent imago flies are found drifting in the beam of a flashlight long after midnight.

The mayflies of the *Siphlonurus* and *Siphloplecton* genera are superficially similar to these nocturnal *Potamanthus* flies, but their behavior and habitat are quite different. Both the *Siphlonurus* and *Siphloplecton* nymphs are large

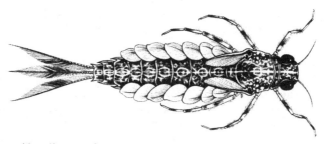

Siphlonurus occidentalis nymph

enough that big trout will take them readily in lakes and streams where they are abundant. Their thoracic structures and slender bodies are distinguished by their smooth hydrodynamic shapes and a series of gill plates capable of extremely rapid movements. The legs are delicately shaped, but agile and strong. The wing cases and thorax are rather strongly humped, being somewhat higher than their width. Their heads are relatively small and round. There are dense lateral fringes on both edges of the median caudal filament and along the inside edges of the other two tails. Such caudal filaments combine both lateral and vertical stabilization, with the added capability of a sculling-oar propulsion.

These nymphs are widely distributed in both lakes and slow-flowing rivers. The most species are found in richly alkaline waters like the Yellowstone headwaters, the bigger limestone creeks of Pennsylvania, the

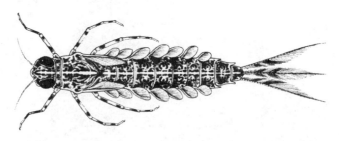

Siphloplecton basale nymph

Henry's Fork and Silver Creek in Idaho, and rich watersheds on the Pacific Coast like the north-flowing streams born in the country of the Lassen escarpment—superb little rivers like the Hat and the Rising and the Fall River, rich with weeds and slow-water mayfly hatches. Many western reservoirs also provide optimal biosystems for these *Siphlonurus* and *Siphloplecton* nymphs, along with many half-legendary lakes like Henry's in Idaho, fertile Wade and Hebgen in Montana, and the sprawling geothermal basin of Yellowstone Lake.

These swimming nymphs are extremely agile, capable of rapid movements both to hatch and to escape predatory species. Imitative nymphs should be fished to suggest their swift baitfishlike swimming. Such motion is achieved by swift, vertical undulations of the abdominal structure, the respiratory rhythms of the gill plates, and the sculling flutter of the tails. The pattern of their swimming is highly erratic, with swift little

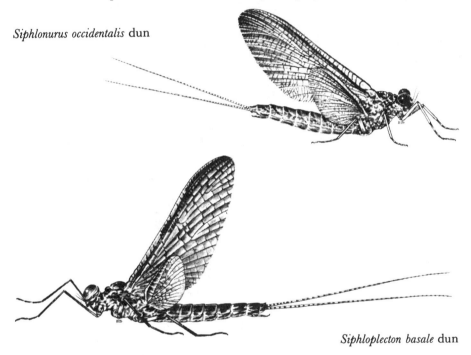

Siphlonurus occidentalis dun

Siphloplecton basale dun

pulsing movements and abrupt pauses. Both the legs and gill systems are used in starting and stopping their irregular, subaquatic migrations. However, respiration is the primary function of the gills, as they fan in the current to filter oxygen from the water. When the nymphs are resting in the weeds or hanging stationary near the surface film their gills are still moving. The respiratory sequence starts with the gill plates near the tails, fluttering them in pairs along the body toward the wing cases.

Both *Siphlonurus* and *Siphloplecton* are primarily species of relatively open water and are readily available to the trout. Their nymphs seldom venture deeply into the weeds. Hatching can occur in both shallow bays, where they use the surface tension to help split their nymphal skins, and in the weeds, where stems and deadfalls help them hatch at the waterline. Some species also migrate toward the shores, escaping their nymphal shucks on the boulders and gravelly beaches.

The freshly hatched duns are graceful mayflies with slender wings and bodies, their dorsal surfaces and sternites strongly marked and stippled with darker coloring. Their wings are duns and soot-colored greys, held well back over the bodies at a sharp angle. The legs are delicate, the forelegs dark and projecting from the exaggeratedly upturned thorax, and the two tails are quite long. The abdomen is typically held in the graceful curve found in all mayflies, dipping back slightly toward the caudal filaments. Hatching is sporadic on dark, overcast days and is often heavy in periods of misting rain. Some of the best hatches I have seen occurred on quiet reaches of the Au Sable in early July and on the Yellowstone in September; and this past season with Jack Hemingway and Pete Van Gytenbeek on the famous Silver Creek in Idaho, there was a rainy afternoon when a heavy *Siphlonurus* hatch came off the weedy reed-lined channels in huge regattas of fluttering drakes.

The *Siphlonurus* spinners hover over quiet runs or shallow bays within a few yards of shore. Their mating swarms range from about six feet above the water to as much as thirty or forty feet. They do not dance up and down quickly but hover motionless on rapidly beating wings, and then ascend a few feet before slowly gliding down again. Their rising and falling rhythms are graceful and deliberate. The forelegs and tails are exaggeratedly long. The mating swarms occur in late afternoon and evening and seem most numerous about sunset. The ripe spinners typically extrude bright-olive egg sacs under their bodies and are eagerly taken by the fish on windy evenings. The spent flies are obviously large enough to create eager rises of fish where they are abundant.

The diminutive *Baetis* mayflies are important to fly-fishermen in spite of their tiny size because they are available in such vast numbers in good waters. There are more than forty American species, and new species are still being described and classified. Their nymphs are remarkably abundant in swift, relatively shallow streams, preferring a bottom of coarse gravel and stones with sparse beds of fountain moss and algae. Although a few *Baetis* nymphs are found at the edges of streams, in weeds and leaf-drift and detritus, these tiny swimming nymphs are largely agile, current-loving organisms.

These *Baetis* nymphs are small, ranging from an eighth of an inch to naturals measuring three times that length when both species are at their full prehatching maturity. The nymphs are sleek and streamlined, moving in a swift current with surprising agility. The smooth heads and thoracic structures are ideally suited to lotic habitats and are held in a slightly downward-looking posture. Their legs are relatively long and slender. The gills are fusilliform and small. *Baetis* nymphs have three delicately fringed tails, with the median filament shorter than the outer pair.

Baetis hiemalis nymph

Preston Jennings wrote in his *Book of Trout Flies* that these little mayflies were a group of early season species having only minimal importance on our waters. It is one of the few questionable observations in his writings. Our streams sustain these *Baetis* flies in incredible numbers, and their availability lies across the full spectrum of the fishing year. The *Baetis* mayflies are a many-brooded species, with three separate hatches in a single year.

The hatching duns are sometimes the first mayflies of the season and can be watched on cold, rainy mornings drifting forty or fifty yards before their wings are ready to sustain flight. The hatches are widely distributed, and although alkaline waters obviously have the best ones, there are also good populations on relatively acid waters. Some species are found in weedy habitat, while others seem to prefer small, swift-running streams with stony bottoms.

The wings of these little flies are relatively slender and are held in an upright position. They are varied in coloring from pale bluish-dun to a dark iron-blue. Their delicate little bodies are pale rusty-brown to a dirty olive-grey, with some being a deep sooty olive. There are two tails, and sometimes the hatching *Baetis* duns are like a miniature regatta on the current.

Hatches are highly irregular and sporadic, and emergence often occurs in surprisingly inclement weather. Blustery winds, dull overcast skies, and bitter rain are often compatible with good hatches of *Baetis* flies. Emergence typically begins in late morning, and the flies gradually increase in volume

Baetis vagans dun

as midday approaches. It is interesting that these little subimago mayflies are often mixed with other hatches of larger species, yet the fish concentrate on them greedily. It is not unusual to find the summer fly hatches of the genus starting before noon, with a sporadic trickle of duns coming off all day until late afternoon, and a rise in the hatching tempo toward twilight. Some observers have noted that the early season hatches are slightly larger and darker than the broods of summer and fall.

Baetis spinners are delicate little two-tailed flies. Large colonies are often found in sheltered foliage along the stream or hovering over weed beds and rushes. Gusts of wind can cause them to seek shelter, and they reappear once the wind drops down again. During calm weather they fly at considerable heights, almost too high to identify the species in a mating swarm. Their nuptial dance is erratic and agitated. Their ascent is quite rapid, coupled with a deliberate, slow, fluttering glide toward the water, facing into the wind. Their descent is brief, to avoid being blown too far laterally when their wing beats slow. The mating swarms delight in bright weather, dancing in both morning and afternoon in pale-winged little groups, rising and falling over the water. Sometimes the swarms hover along the banks, and sometimes they mate over the meadows, as much as fifty yards from the water. Spinners can often be seen weaving in and out between each other, with erratic dancing flight, and sometimes they hover almost steadily with hummingbird-quick wing beats. Since their oviposition occurs under water, these little *Baetis* spinners seem to disappear in late afternoon and evening. Actually they have crawled along stones and plant stems and deadfalls, wrapping their bodies in their wings and slipping through the surface film to lay their eggs in places sheltered from the current. Sometimes on western spring creeks and eastern limestone streams, I have experienced exceptional sport during their egg laying—fishing tiny wet flies suggestive of these spinners.

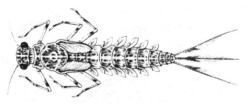

Callibaetis americanus nymph

The *Callibaetis* mayflies display similar patterns of hatching and egg-laying behavior, although they are slightly larger and prefer the lenitic habitats of slow-flowing ponds and streams. The genus is most important on western waters, particularly shallow lakes and reservoirs and spring-creek sloughs. There are good nymphal populations in virtually all suitable habitat, clambering through subaquatic vegetation and swimming with great agility in the sheltered bays and channels. These slender little nymphs are also many-brooded, producing three separate hatches in a single season. Mottled little *Callibaetis* nymphs are among the most elegant inhabitants of our lakes and slow-moving streams and ponds, particularly in fairly alkaline water chemistry with rich growths of nymph-sheltering weeds. Their abundance makes them a favorite diet form of the fish and many carnivorous nymphs and larvae. Full grown nymphs range from one-quarter to five-sixteenths of an inch in length.

Callibaetis americanus dun

The delicate speckle-wing duns have two tails and typically hatch in late morning, continuing to come off sporadically through the day. Emergence sometimes lasts until nightfall. The nymphs often hatch by creeping along the weedy growths and stalks of aquatic vegetation to wait for their thoracic skins to split. Some nymphs hatch normally, seeking out the surface film in quiet bays and pockets in the weeds. Several times I have watched *Callibaetis* nymphs by the thousands, lying on the parget walls of cattle tanks and irrigation-system weirs and farm-pond dams, waiting patiently to hatch in the late morning. The wings of these freshly hatched duns are uniquely marked and mottled, ranging from the pale grayish eastern hatches to the dark, heavily speckled western species like *Callibaetis coloradensis* and *Callibaetis nigritus*. Perhaps the most unusual species is also a Rocky Mountain hatch, the pale yellowish olive *Callibaetis* mayflies that I have often collected on beaver ponds and shallow lakes in Colorado.

These speckle-wings are extremely important fly hatches on weedy reservoirs in our western mountains, occupying a position quite similar to the lake and pond olives found on the alkaline lakes and impoundments in the British Isles. Sometimes they hatch in cold, rainy weather and are sailboated downwind, gathering in a delicate scum of tiny mayflies along the shorelines of a beaver pond or reservoir, and the trout follow them there.

The speckle-winged spinners are quite common in bright weather, mating in small swarms and drifting spent on the surface, until they gather in large numbers in the downwind shallows. Mating swarms are seldom concentrated, but are dispersed over adjacent shorelines and meadows.

Callibaetis coloradensis spinner

Callibaetis spinners are easily identified from the unique mottling on their wings, which have strikingly barred markings along the leading edge of their otherwise crystalline wings. Mixed flotillas of freshly hatched speckle-wings and their spinners can trigger some impressive rises of fish on western reservoirs, and on slow-flowing streams like Putah Creek in California, or the reedy flats of Silver Creek below Sun Valley.

The *Isonychia* mayflies are a handsome fast-water species of remarkable strength and agility, and they form some of the most important fly hatches on our American rivers. Their behavior is unique among our lotic, current-loving mayfly nymphs, since they do not cling or clamber on the bottom stones and bedrock outcroppings. *Isonychia* nymphs swim boldly in the swiftest currents. They love the crevices between large rocks and boulders, holding in the rubble of the riverbed, in spite of the flow. Others choose even more exposed places, seeking out the swiftest, thin-flowing currents over ledges and bedrock bottoms. The nymphs demand sliding currents rich with oxygen and food, feeding on the outcroppings and half-submerged stones.

Their agility and precision are striking as they dart from foothold to foothold in the current. Once a fresh feeding station is reached, the nymphs anchor themselves by their middle and rear legs, with the oxygen-bringing currents flowing past their pulsing gill plates. The nymphs wait motionless, poised like aquatic mantises, their heads erect and forelegs extended. Their fringed caudal plumes trail flat against the bottom. These tails are fringed

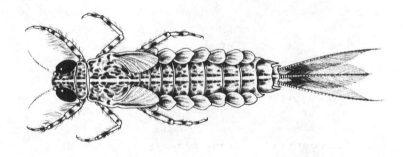

Isonychia bicolor nymph

on both edges of the center filament, while the outer pair are fringed only on the inside edges. These *Isonychia* nymphs wait motionless in the current, like predatory herons waiting for a hapless quarry to venture too close.

Their food-gathering system is unique. The forelegs are fringed with two rows of stiff little hairs on their anterior edges. These bristles are sharply angled, extended upstream, and open into the current. Held closely together they form a collecting basket, gathering microscopic foods from the current. The head and its mouth parts lie at the base of this food system.

Emergence involves migration from the swift-water habitat into the shallows and quiet eddies. Hatches usually occur in late afternoon and evening, but in overcast weather the *Isonychias* can hatch sporadically throughout the day. Their great agility, the fact that their emergence occurs away from the primary fish-sheltering currents, and the fact that most of the duns crawl from the water to hatch on rocks and outcroppings and deadfalls all combine to protect them from the hungry trout.

Like the stoneflies, these nymphs strangely favor certain stones and deadfalls to hatch. The puzzle may have its explanation in the surface textures or current tongues of such favored hatching sites. It is common to find several nymphs using the same stones, emerging at precisely the same water level. Yet adjacent stones may bear no trace of nymphs. It is another of the manifold enigmas of nature. The trout are completely aware of such nymphal behavior, since they predictably follow the migrating nymphs into the shallows.

Isonychia duns are big and juicy looking, providing a mouthful for even the largest fish, and they have produced some remarkable fishing over the years. Charles Wetzel described marvelous hatches and mating swarms in the old days on Kettle Creek in Pennsylvania, when he fished from the little Trout Run Hotel. Preston Jennings and Art Flick both wrote of the virtues of the *Isonychias* on swift rivers from the Ausable in the Adirondacks to the

Isonychia albomanicata dun

Brodheads below New York; and in my recent book *Remembrances of Rivers Past*, I described some exceptional hatches on the swift-flowing Namekagon in northern Wisconsin.

The wings of the *Isonychias* are usually slate colored, and their middle and rear legs are relatively pale. There are two slender tails, and when a subimago is resting on its rear legs, its forelegs are almost held in an attitude of prayer. Various species of *Isonychias* are found hatching from late spring until early fall, and on rivers where October fishing is legal, these drakes can offer surprisingly good dry-fly sport. Hatching is normally limited to late afternoon and evening, with twilight often the peak emergence period.

However, rainy days with good cloud cover can produce fine hatches from late morning throughout the day, and one of the finest periods of fishing I ever experienced on the Brodheads in Pennsylvania occurred when two days of misting rain coincided with the heavy late-spring hatches of *Isonychia bicolor*—it produced several dry-fly fish between sixteen and nineteen inches on both afternoons.

Sometimes the big *Isonychia* spinners can trigger periods of exceptional fishing. Their wings are glittering and crystalline with strong vein patterns and highlights. Their bodies vary in color, mostly from a rich shiny chocolate to a bright rusty color, and their two tails become gracefully slender. The eyes of the male spinners are a deep reddish brown. The rear and median legs are typically chalk-colored or yellowish cream, while the forelegs are chocolate or reddish. The females extrude fat little sacs of greenish eggs and are a succulent feast for any trout. The medium-size imago of *Isonychia albomanicata* is distinguished by its pale little forelegs, which are held out in the attitude of handshaking when the flies are resting in the foliage, and have given these handsome little spinners the popular name of White Gloved Howdy.

Charles Wetzel described a remarkable spinner flight he encountered one boyhood summer, in his *Practical Fly-Fishing* in a chapter on the early days in the Kettle Creek country. The Kettle was once one of the finest brook-trout fisheries in America, flowing through some of the finest coniferous forests in the world. But even in those years after the First World War, the rapacious lumbering of the nineteenth century had already taken its toll, and the brook trout had gathered in the Trout Run tributary by early June. It is a fascinating piece of history, telling us about mating *Isonychia* swarms, as well as the state of American fly-fishing:

> Very few men actually knew how to tie a fly, and the few that did know kept the operation a jealously guarded secret. Yet it was in this vicinity that I first learned to tie a fly.
>
> I had been fishing Kettle Creek all day with very poor success, having caught nothing but a few smallmouth bass. It was quite warm, and apparently the trout had already moved up into the feeder streams, so rather disconsolately, I wandered up along Trout Run.

Near the Forks, I encountered a fisherman drowsily puffing away on his pipe, and evidently he had also found the fishing poor, for judging from his indolent position he had not moved in the last few hours.

His gear looked quite expensive, that of a city fisherman, I mentally noted, and I had decided to pass by him when he hailed me from the opposite bank.

"Come over and rest," he invited. "The trout are not rising yet." There was truth in what he said, so we sat in the shade and talked about fishing while waiting for the evening rise.

"The trout are not in the main creek any more," he said. "Did you notice them lying in all the pools as you came walking up the run?"

"Yes," I answered, "right over there by that leaning beech tree, there are hundreds lying in the pool. Big ones too!"

"You and I are going to catch plenty of them before the evening's over," he went on confidently. "See if we don't. In the meantime, I'll tie a few flies like those that were found over the water last night."

Here was a real fisherman, one who did not care if his secrets were discovered, and you may be sure that I made the most of the situation!

Dexterously, he whipped the gut to the hook and continued out to the bend, where he fastened a few fibers from a grey feather. Then from his old brown sweater he unravelled a piece of yarn and wound it on the hook, forming the body of the fly.

"It would be best probably with a red quill body," he said, "but since we have none this will do. The trout took it fine last evening."

"I think I know what it's going to be," I broke in. "It's that brown spinner that has been on the water for three days already. No one seems to know what its name is. Its front feet are white, as well as its middle and hind legs, and it has long whitish tails."

"Correct," he answered with a twinkle. "Now I'm going to put on his wings."

With the same feather from which the tail was formed, he cut a section and folded it and bound it fast to the hook. "Now for his legs," he said, smiling at the interest I displayed.

One envelope of his fly-book was filled with chicken feathers, and from it, he selected one white and one brown hackle. These were fastened to the hook near the eye; then both were given two turns around the hook, and the waste ends clipped off.

"A good fly should never have more than two turns of hackle wound on, for it will not sink readily," he explained. "Now watch this closely, for I'm going to fasten it off with the whip finish."

Then followed such a swift, intricate manipulation of thread, hands and fingers, as to leave me spellbound. "Do you mean to say that it's fastened and will not unravel?" I gasped in astonishment, as he finished and tore off the thread.

Wetzel continued with a description of his first halting attempts at dressing a second fly pattern, and his hopeless frustration with the whip finish. The old man gave him a piece of twine to practice the technique, and while Wetzel fumbled with it, tied several more imitations. When the trout started rising fitfully, the old man quickly finished his last fly and put his field kit away.

"We had better hurry now," he warned. "The trout are just starting to jump."

Hastily, we scrambled down toward the pool by the leaning beech tree. Each of us had two of the recently tied wet flies on our leaders. Here and there, the white-legged brown spinners, later identified as the White Gloved Howdy, had already started their erratic flight over the water.

Upstream near the head of the pool, my new-found friend was already leading a nice fish toward the shore.

"We are going to have fine sport this evening," he called downstream. "The flies are getting thicker every minute."

And indeed they were!

Everywhere one looked they were rising and falling over the water. Mosquitoes, gnats and other pests which make life miserable joined the assembly, and mixed with an easy familiarity among the spinners. The still twilight air hummed with the somnolent drone of myriads of winged insects.

The trout were rising furiously, and the pool resembled a boiling cauldron. Then I made a double, both trout being hooked on the new flies. Every time I glanced upstream my friend was either knocking a trout on the head or leading one into the net. Verily, I believe we could have cleaned out the entire pool, for the water was low, the fish were hungry, and the mayflies kept riding the water in ever increasing numbers, but my new friend was a sportsman, and after a time he called a halt.

"Let's quit," he called downstream. "How many fish did you catch?"

"Eight," I answered. "How many did you get?"

"Twelve," he said, "and all nice fish. I'll have to hurry, for a friend has arranged to meet me, and I'm overdue already."

Hastily I started removing his flies from my leader, but he shook his head laughingly. "No," he said. "You keep them—tomorrow night you might have the same luck."

Happily I trudged back to the hotel, and then with a shock I remembered that I had never inquired his name.

The thick-gilled *Leptophlebia* nymphs are often the first large mayflies to hatch on many eastern and midwestern waters. The genus prefers slow-flowing habitats. The gentle Nissequogue on Long Island is one of the best. Good hatches are also found on the Schoharie, particularly in the long flats below Lexington, and the still headwaters on the west branch of the Ausable are also known for their heavy populations of this genus. The lower mileage of the Beaverkill, particularly the big pools at Baxter's and Cook's Falls, and the South Raritan are also fine habitat. Otter Creek and the Battenkill are both famous for good hatches. Wetzel also describes them in *Practical Fly-Fishing*, remembering his sport on Penns Creek and Big Fishing Creek in Pennsylvania. There are also fine hatches in Michigan, particularly on the Big South Pere Marquette and the Little South, and the still waters of the Big Manistee and the Au Sable are excellent.

Many mayflies now classified in the *Leptophlebia* genus were formerly grouped among the *Blasturus* hatches, in the definitive taxonomy found in the Needham *Biology of Mayflies*, and *Blasturus* is no longer used. The result for knowledgeable fly-fishers is a number of past books which discuss these hatches in terms of a taxonomic system no longer recognized in aquatic entomology. Jennings, Wetzel, and Flick have all used the earlier generic keys in their work, in discussing the familiar *Blasturus cupidus* hatches found on eastern streams, and these familiar flies are now grouped together in the *Leptophlebia* genus.

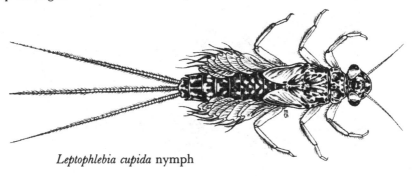

Leptophlebia cupida nymph

The genus has no parallel among the famous European fly hatches. Its nymphs are distinguished by their exaggerated lamellate gill plates and the slender emargination at their tips. The gills are double and lamelliform, spreading like tiny leaves with apical stems, and are found clustered on the first seven abdominal segments.

Jay Traver made extensive studies of these mayflies, particularly in the monograph titled "Observations on the Ecology of the Mayfly *Blasturus cupidus*," which she published in 1925. Her studies concluded that the nymphs and freshly hatched duns are rather sluggish in character. After their eggs have been laid in the swifter reaches of water, the nymphs migrate into the quiet currents and survive more from protective coloration than swiftness of movement. Their sluggishness even extends to feigning death when they are disturbed.

The nymphs have relatively long antennae and tails. Their antennae are longer than the head and thorax together, and their caudal filaments are longer than their bodies. The three tails in the nymphal stage are of equal length, while the median filament is rather short in the adult duns and spinners.

These nymphs are quite common in March and April, mottled with pale markings against their overall chestnut coloring and exaggerated gill systems. Their stillwater habitat consists of eddies and backwaters and bogs, with their silt and detritus-covered bottoms. The nymphs clamber and scuttle about in the bottom trash and swim laboriously from place to place. They seem relatively unafraid of the light and forage boldly.

Leptophlebia nymphs are uniquely gregarious, and congregate together in sizable colonies. Migration can also occur just before emergence. The nymphs school together like tiny baitfish, swimming slowly upstream in the quiet shallows and backwaters along the banks. Such colonies can number as many as a hundred nymphs and travel as much as a mile. During their actual emergence, the nymphs are very restless, sometimes making as many as ten to fifteen trips between the bottom and the surface film. The slow rhythms of their swimming make them easy prey for the trout, and they are easily imitated by a slow hand-twist retrieve.

Leptophlebia cupida dun

Freshly hatched *Leptophlebia* duns are somber and sluggish flies, fluttering along the cold early-season currents from the Namekagon in Wisconsin to the Nantahala in North Carolina. They are dark slate-colored flies, the wings of some larger species washed with a distinct brownish cast. The legs and tails are dark grayish brown. Their thoracic and abdominal coloring is slate gray to dark brownish gray, although some species are distinctly rust-colored in both tergites and sternites. Hatching usually occurs in late morning, and the flies usually come fluttering clumsily down the current in the weak April sunlight. Midday emergence is typical of these *Leptophlebia* flies, and in the early spring they ride the current for long distances. Since the duns often hatch from large colonies of nymphs, emergence can be heavily concentrated in some parts of the stream, and sparsely distributed or almost absent in others. Many times I have floated the Au Sable in the spring, paddling through the stretches where no fish were showing, and have stopped to fish carefully in those reaches where good hatches were coming off.

The *Leptophlebia* mating swarms are distinguished by their hyaline wings, faintly stained with brown near their tips. The thorax is dark blackish brown. The dorsal surfaces of the body are a rich reddish brown on many species, paling slightly on the sternites underneath. The three caudal filaments are ringed with dark brownish markings, and the genus is distinguished by a median caudal filament that is quite noticeably shorter than the outer pair. The darkly stained wing tips are most obvious in the species *Leptophlebia nebulosa*, which is the largest of the genus and hatches in late April and early May on many eastern and midwestern streams. Later species are somewhat smaller, and emerge well into early summer, with sporadic hatches coming as late as autumn.

Mating swarms begin gathering at midday, but the actual nuptial dance does not take place until late afternoon and evening. Swarming may occur along the surface, as close as two to four feet above the current, and on calm evenings the spinners can be seen mating as high as the bankside treetops. The female imago extrudes its egg masses slowly, repeatedly washing them from the tip of its abdomen by leapfrogging along the water. Such mating and oviposition will continue until dark on temperate evenings, and the spinner fall can prove quite productive.

The *Paraleptophlebia* genus is extremely important to fly-fishermen in spite of its small insects, and its tiny fork-gilled nymphs are a staple in the trout diet. These little fork-gilled nymphs are crawling ecotypes, with slender bodies and delicate lamelliform gills. They are regularly found in lakes, streams, and ponds, and are relatively poor swimmers compared with the agile little *Baetis* and *Centroptilum* nymphs. European species typically love soft-bottom habitats like silt, detritus, gravel, sand, and moss-covered stones. Perhaps the most active of the European species is *Paraleptophlebia cincta*, with its streamlined little nymphs. Its tails are slender, and it has delicate ribbonlike gills. This species more closely parallels our American *Paraleptophlebias*, which are perhaps more current-loving than their European counterparts.

Paraleptophlebia adoptiva dun

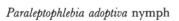

Paraleptophlebia adoptiva nymph

American species prefer smooth-flowing reaches of river with weeds and trailing water mosses, requiring slightly more oxygenation than the slow-water species of nymphs. Like the somewhat larger *Leptophlebias,* these little nymphs have relatively long antennae and caudal filaments. The antennae are longer than the head and thorax combined, and the tails are longer than the body. The gills on abdominal segments two through seven are the double-forked type, with paired apical extensions of the medial trachea. These diminutive little nymphs are like their larger cousins in their habit of schooling like tiny baitfish. Their schools also migrate in the shallows before their emergence time, sometimes concentrating in eddies and backwaters in surprising numbers. Gravelly shallows with currents from six inches to two feet in depth are optimal habitat, and heavy hatches can come from the concentrated nymphal schools.

The handsome little duns of the *Paraleptophlebia* species commonly start hatching in late morning, and continue to emerge sporadically all day. Some species emerge as early as April on eastern streams, and I have found other species hatching as late as September and October in the Rocky Mountains. Their wings vary in color from light grayish dun to a dark iron-blue dun. There are three tiny tails on the freshly hatched subimago. The legs are usually somewhat paler than the thorax. The best hatches of my experience have been found on overcast days mixed with a light misting rain. My notebooks are filled with episodes on rivers like the Beaverkill and South Raritan and Brodheads, and one late April afternoon on the Au Sable above the Wakeley Bridge is vivid in the memory. There are western memories too, like the afternoon on the South Platte below its junction with the Tarryall, or the exceptional hatches of *Paraleptophlebia heteronea* that used to hatch on rainy afternoons along the Frying Pan below Ruedi—before its marvelous stillwater stretch was drowned forever in the icy depths of the Ruedi Reservoir, several miles above Basalt.

Since these subimago flies hatch from densely schooled nymphs, their moulting swarms are also concentrated in the foliage along certain stretches of optimal habitat. The result is thick mating swarms of elegant little *Paraleptophlebia* spinners. Their swarms are composed of extremely agile rising and falling flight, and they gather over swift-flowing shallows. The dainty little flies are sunshine-loving spinners and gather over the riffles and water meadows in late morning to dance in its gathering warmth. Mating flights usually begin seriously in the afternoon, continuing on into the twilight hours. Their three delicate tails become quite long, as do the pale forelegs of the males. The bodies are darkly banded with brown in some species, ranging to bright reddish brown in others. Since they gather in dense swarms, these little flies can result in good rises of fish on a still evening when their spinner fall drifts down a quiet current tongue.

The Caenidae are a group of tiny mayflies which are surprisingly important to fishermen, despite the fact that many of their species measure less than one-eighth of an inch in length. American fly hatches in this group include genera like *Brachycercus, Tricorythodes,* and the diminutive *Caenis* flies.

These tiny mayflies have given me some exceptional sport over the years. My memory is filled with happy episodes on the Ausable and Battenkill, and all the smooth-flowing flats of the Catskill rivers. There are memories of Michigan too, fishing a still current just at daylight on the Au Sable and Pere Marquette and Manistee, with the trout dimpling everywhere to the tiny *Tricorythodes* flies in the film. Canoe fishermen who travel the Upper Delaware in late summer have witnessed such incredible hatches on its smooth half-mile flats that autopsies on a three-to-four-pound rainbow can reveal as many as three or four thousand of these tiny flies.

Their nymphal forms are lenitic ecotypes. They are primarily found in silt-bottomed ponds and impoundments and quiet streams. They are stiff-legged nymphs covered with delicate hairlike filaments. They have fat little bodies and little fringed tails. Their tiny size, the protective coloring they achieve when their bodies are covered with fine sediment, and their sluggish clambering along the bottom all combine to protect them from the fish. Their safety largely depends on camouflage rather than agility of movement. When collected along with their bottom silts, these tiny nymphs are invisible in the screening until they betray themselves with motion, starting to clamber about sluggishly.

The nymphs love their habitat of silt and bottom trash and weeds. Such quiet habitat requires gill structures that filter out turbidity, cleansing the abrasive silts that could damage their gill systems and interfere with respiration. Therefore, their gills are somewhat unique.

The anterior pair of gills is relatively broad, with an operculate cover over their delicate tracheal tissues. These gill covers overlap the gill systems themselves, protecting them from abrasion and clogging. These opercles are alternately opened and closed in respiration, and interlacing fringes at the gill margins serve to filter the turbid water. This respiratory system permits these tiny nymphs to survive silt concentrations that would smother less hardy ecotypes. The filtration systems in the *Caenis* nymphs are even more effective than those in the related *Brachycercus* and *Tricorythodes* genera.

The little nymphs of the *Brachycercus* mayflies prefer still waters and relatively warm temperatures, and are found in both lakes and quiet streams. Like their silt-loving sister nymphs, these immature mayflies are well camouflaged with detritus and sediments. The nymphs travel laboriously over the bottom, and migrate so sluggishly toward the surface on

Brachycerus prudens dun

Brachycerus lacustris nymph

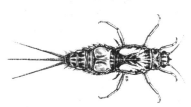

hatching that a dead-drift presentation is necessary to imitate them. The nymphs emerge in the early-morning hours, and most species hatch in late summer. Such hatches can be extremely heavy on alkaline waters. The freshly emerged duns have unusually well developed thoracic structures, with relatively broad chalk-colored wings. The thorax and body coloring is usually brownish, and there are three pale-colored tails. The duns shed their skins only a few minutes after hatching, their chalky wings becoming relatively hyaline in color. Although these little mayflies are not as numerous as the other Caenidae, their hatches and spinner falls can precipitate some fine rises of highly selective fish.

Tricorythodes stygiatus dun

Tricorythodes stygiatus nymph

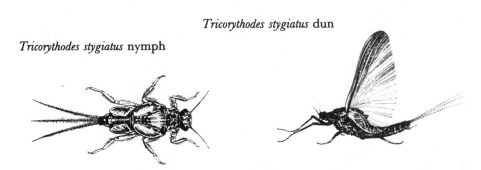

The *Tricorythodes* mayflies are more numerous and are also an early-morning genus. The nymphs are quite small, never exceeding three-sixteenths of an inch in body length. The gills are covered with triangular lamelliform opercles, protecting them from the turbidity. The nymphs prefer bottoms of sediment, mixed with sand and fine gravel. Sometimes they gather in weeds and algal mosses, and their anatomy is so covered with delicate hairs that they collect microscopic silt and debris from the current, slowly hiding in their habitat itself. The tiny early-morning duns are blackish brown, with pale cream-colored wings and tails. Emergence occurs just at daylight, sometimes lasting as long as two or three hours, and the duns moult almost immediately. Many are shedding their skins almost before their freshly hatched wings are fully dried. The tiny imago flies closely resemble the duns, except that their wings are brightly transparent and their tails and forelegs are longer. Mating swarms and spinner falls come virtually within a half hour of emergence, and can last until late morning, providing fishing almost until noon on overcast days. Despite their tiny size, these mayflies are extremely important to fly-fishermen. Their emergence typically occurs from midsummer to early fall, when most fly hatches have passed, particularly on eastern trout waters. These little flies occur in such numbers that the fish take them greedily.

The tiny *Caenis* mayflies are similar in both size and abundance, but are primarily twilight-loving hatches. Their distinctive taxonomy is descriptive of the entire Caenidae subfamily. Like their sister Caenidae, the nymphs are found in both streams and shallow lakes and are fond of sluggish currents. Silty bottoms mixed with sand, bottom detritus, and fine gravel are preferred, although populations also thrive in algal growth among the stones, and in silt-collecting species of aquatic weeds.

Like the other members of the subfamily, *Caenis* nymphs are covered with microscopic filaments that camouflage them with layers of silt and decomposing plant materials. Sometimes they even lie half-buried in the silt and bottom trash, their gill systems perfectly adapted to such conditions. *Caenis* nymphs are therefore common in both cold- and warm-water environments, their gill systems capable of withstanding even the agricultural silts of many sluggish streams and turbid lakes in cultivated regions of the country. *Tricorythodes* is perhaps more commonly found in cold trout-stream habitats.

Caenis mayflies are typically found hatching from late June until September and October. Emergence is not found in early morning, like the other Caenidae genera, although many fishermen believe the spinner falls they find at daylight are a *Caenis* hatch. The duns actually hatch at twilight, and continue coming off after nightfall. Moulting occurs almost immediately, and they begin their nuptial dancing and mating. Their mating dance is impatient and irregular. The spinners may hover motionless, drifting steadily forward and sideways, and then drop rapidly before rising again. Sometimes they simply rise and fall rhythmically, and at other times their dance is choppily erratic. Oviposition typically occurs after dark, and spent spinners are still present at daylight. The tiny broad-winged duns and spinners range from sizes twenty-two to twenty-eight hooks, and their small size makes them difficult to imitate—so difficult that the British have long called them angler's curses, hating the twilight rises to these little white-winged flies.

Caenis simulans dun

Caenis simulans nymph

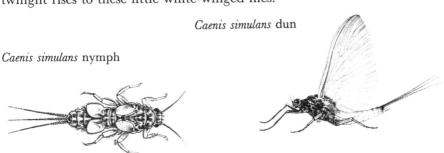

Western fishermen have come to appreciate these tiny *Caenis* and *Tricorythodes* flies in recent years, particularly since increased fishing pressure is making their trout more and more selective. The men who know about matching these tiny hatches can have some excellent sport in our western trout country, once they have evolved beyond the fish-the-water simplicities of big flies and bucktails common between the Rocky Mountains and the Pacific. There is excellent early-morning sport on reservoirs like Hebgen at West Yellowstone. There are western rivers too, big rivers like the Snake and the Yellowstone and Henry's Fork in Idaho, where tiny mayflies cover the silken flats every morning for weeks. There are superb hatches and spinner falls on our western spring creeks too, particularly the famous streams at Livingston and Lewiston in Montana. Other superb spring creeks are in Jackson Hole and, farther south in Wyoming, the silken little New Fork of the Green. There are also excellent hatches of the Caenidae on the Silver at Sun Valley and farther west on several rich tributaries of the Sacramento, their weedy flats and sloughs perfectly suited to these tiny silt-loving flies.

Yet it is still our classic eastern limestone streams, from the Musconetcong in New Jersey to the exquisite Falling Spring Run, that first taught me about the importance of these minute mayflies. It is these fertile little rivers in the farm country of New Jersey and Pennsylvania that invariably come to mind with thoughts of fishing the Caenidae.

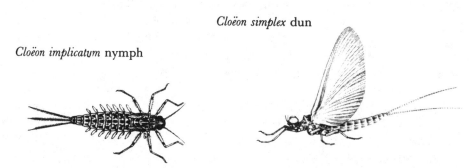

Cloëon simplex dun

Cloëon implicatum nymph

Over the past few seasons a number of other minute mayflies have proved important on widespread American streams. Specimens have been identified as *Cloëon, Neocloëon,* and the tiny *Pseudocloëon* genera. Their populations are quite dense in alkaline habitat, like spring creeks and limestone streams and marl-bog creeks. Optimal habitat is always such weedy lime-rich water. Like the other minute mayflies, their diminutive size is no indication of their importance to fishermen, and their activity can generate impressive rises of fish.

Cloëon nymphs are tiny swimming species, slender and delicately fringed with gills. There are three fringed tails, and the legs are typical of such ecotypes. The tails are fringed on their outer margins, and are free of such caudal setae on the lower third of their tail filaments. These nymphs are among the types that ascend to the surface film in open water, splitting their nymphal skins across the thoracic surfaces, and shedding it in the surface tension of the meniscus film. Various nymphal ecotypes accomplish this journey to the surface both through voluntary swimming and through the generation of buoyant gases inside the nymphal shucks. It has been suggested that those which migrate voluntarily are attracted to the light, while the buoyant gases inside the nymphal integument cause the nymphs to rise involuntarily once the hatching process has started. The *Cloëon* nymphs are among the latter.

Most emergence occurs in relatively shallow water, ranging from six inches to approximately three feet. Before hatching occurs, the darkening wing cases of the nymphs are quite evident, and they cling to the bottom stones and vegetation. When they are dislodged from their footholds, they are buoyed directly to the surface, instead of merely swimming to a new station. Once they reach the meniscus film, they emerge in a relatively few seconds. Before the nymphs begin generating their nymphal gases, they lose their typical caution and are found openly in the weeds or on the upper surfaces of the bottom stones. They are quite restless then, swimming or crawling from one place to another, and some even make preliminary half-wriggling ascents to the surface.

The adults are tiny mayflies ranging from pale ochre to dark olive brown, their wings pale grayish to medium grayish dun. The adults have only two tails. The ventral surfaces of the male spinners are chalky yellow

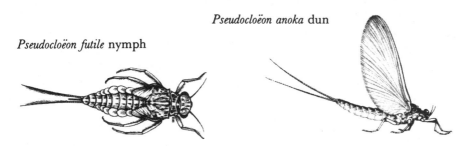

Pseudocloëon anoka dun

Pseudocloëon futile nymph

to rusty brown, while their dorsal surfaces are usually darker. The female spinners are somewhat paler in coloring. The unique taxonomic character of these *Cloëon* flies lies in the absence of the tiny rear pair of wings found in most mayfly species. The genus *Neocloëon* is closely allied to these little two-winged mayflies, although it is limited to a single American species. Needham offers the conjecture in his *Biology of Mayflies* that these differences in taxonomy may yet be resolved, establishing the genus as merely a single aberrant species of the *Cloëon* group, even though its nymphs more closely resemble those of the *Centroptilum* flies.

The tiny two-winged mayflies of the related *Pseudocloëon* genus are surprisingly important for fly-fishing, since they often hatch in great numbers. Like the *Cloëon* and *Neocloëon* genera, the *Pseudocloëon* flies are many-brooded, and several cycles of egg laying and hatching can occur in a single summer. However, there are usually two peak periods of fly hatches. The first is usually in late spring, while the second comes in autumn.

The nymphal forms are streamlined, almost as fusilliform as the slender *Baetis* nymphs. However, their morphology is somewhat more robust. Their thoracic proportions are wider than the abdominal segments, and their bodies are slightly swollen before tapering toward the tails. The gill systems vary somewhat from related nymphal forms. There are only two fringed tails, totally lacking filaments on their basal thirds, and a vestigial medial tail that is barely visible. When emergence is approaching, the ripening nymphs can be observed crawling restlessly on the bottom gravel and trailing fountain mosses.

Dark overcast days can find these tiny flies hatching in late morning, with sporadic flurries coming until dark. More typical summer weather finds them starting to emerge about an hour before sundown and hatching steadily until nightfall. The adults have only two wings, the anterior pair being totally absent. Their bodies range from pale chalky yellow to pale brownish olive, and perhaps the best-known species has a body of surprisingly pale olive green. The spinner stage has pale translucent-looking bodies and two slender chalk-colored tails.

The tiny, swimming nymphs of the *Centroptilum* flies are similar to many larger species, in both their configuration and their behavior. Their bodies are slender and streamlined. The thoracic structures are slightly humpbacked, while the heads are small and rounded. The genus is not widely distributed on either American or European waters, although the books of fishing writers like Skues, Dunne, Sawyer, Goddard, and Harris have made them more important to British and Irish anglers in recent years. They were a genus of mayflies virtually ignored in the writings of Ronalds, Halford, and Moseley, although on many rivers of the British Isles they provide some excellent fishing.

Centroptilum convexum dun

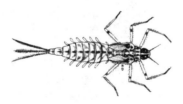

Centroptilum elsa nymph

Our American species are found in both lakes and streams, and the riverine populations are indigenous to a surprisingly full spectrum of current speeds. The tiny swimming nymphs are fond of sheltering aquatic weeds that border the swifter flow, although in the quiet backwaters they forage openly.

It is interesting that the European species are found in both acid and alkaline waters, but form significant hatches only in the limestone and chalkstream watersheds. It is equally curious that the *Centroptilum* flies have gone virtually unnoticed on our major rivers, first becoming obvious only on the lime-rich spring creeks of Montana and Idaho. The relationship between their importance and alkalinity is worth exploring.

Centroptilum nymphs are quite small even at full growth, and although they travel boldly, their swimming lacks the agility of other small swimming-type mayfly genera. Their gills are slender and blade-shaped.

Their caudal filaments are only lightly fringed, but they still function as efficient sculling-oars. Imitations should be fished with either a deliberate retrieve, or a dead-drift current swing during an actual hatch of flies.

The hatching duns are many-brooded, peaking in late spring and early fall. Autumn hatches are usually quite heavy, perhaps because the summer-grown nymphs reach maturity under less harsh conditions than their sister broods, which must endure the winter. Similar hatching behavior has been observed in the *Centroptilum* flies in Europe. The subimago flies are rather pale-winged species with bodies ranging from chalky yellow to olive and rusty brown. There are two tails, and the legs are pale olive or grayish brown, while the rear wings have a single marginal intercalary vein and are spur-shaped. It is the shape of these tiny hind wings that have given these flies the popular name of spurwings among British fishermen. The duns often sit holding their thoracic structures and heads quite high off the water when at rest. The early broods that appear in the spring are usually found hatching throughout the entire day. Later broods emerge in late afternoon and early evening, and the hatching peaks vary on different waters. The fish seem to demonstrate a marked preference for these little duns, even when they are available in only moderate numbers, particularly on the spring creeks in Jackson Hole and the Yellowstone country.

The *Centroptilum* spinners are equally important, and when they are on the water in good numbers, the trout seem to relish them. Their thoracic structures and bodies are usually pale yellowish or amber. Spurwing spinner flights begin in late afternoon, when the males gather over the water meadows and gravelly flows. Sometimes these male swarms are blown into the water, and the fish take them greedily. The actual mating dance comes in early evening, with the subsequent spinner fall at twilight. The female spinners are also eagerly accepted by the trout, and they often feed on the spent males the following morning.

The two-tailed *Epeorus* flies are among the most important fly hatches on American streams. They are flat current-loving flies, and on our classic eastern rivers their hatches are the harbingers of springtime. Their oxygen requirements are quite high, causing them to live and hatch in the swiftest currents and pockets, clinging to the undersides and crevices of the stones. Such high oxygen demand means these flies have a fragile threshold of pollution, and their need for cold, uncontaminated habitat virtually rivals that of the brook trout.

Epeorus humeralis nymph

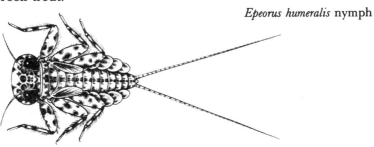

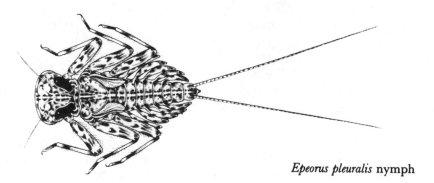

Epeorus pleuralis nymph

Their nymphs can easily be identified from their two tails, when all other immature mayflies have three, except for the tiny little *Pseudocloëon* species. The bodies of these *Epeorus* nymphs are quite flattened ventrally, and convex across their dorsal segments. There are two basic subgroups among these nymphs. The principal type has slender bodies and slender lance-shaped gills, while the others are fatter, with oval-shaped respiratory systems that are overlapping and lamellate. Knowledge of their behavior is important to fishing imitations properly. Nymphs that are about to hatch cling to the bottom, and do not migrate to the surface when it is time to split their nymphal skins. They escape their epicuticles on or near the bottom, where the hydraulic friction slows the currents. Wrapped in its bubble-filled hydrofuge, the half-developed adult is buoyed toward the surface by its emerging wings and partially shed skin. The fish capture many of these nymphs at intermediate depths, just after they leave the bottom, and before they arrive at the surface to hatch and fly off.

These partially hatched nymphs have embryonic wings and cannot swim. They are buoyed to the surface by their hydrofuge effect, and the self-generated gases that helped them escape their nymphal skins. Since they are carried helplessly toward the surface, imitations should be fished dead-drift. Such half-winged nymph imitations are often effective when fished to rising trout, and the fly should be cast upstream almost like a dry-fly presentation. The nymphs that are not hatching are seldom available to the fish, since they cling to the undersides of the stones. Sometimes they are dislodged in high water, or lose their footing while out foraging for diatomaceous nutrients along the bottom. Both of these instances are best imitated with a weighted nymph fished dead-drift and upstream along the bottom in their fast-water habitat. There are several hatching nymph dressings that are effective when the *Epeorus* flies are emerging on the bottom. Fly tiers with a sense of tradition prefer a nymph tied with slightly undersized wings of mallard or starling. Other tiers like E. H. Rosborough, who wrote *Tying and Fishing the Fuzzy Nymphs*, dress their hatching nymphs with ragged marabou-down wings, and Ted Rogowski and I have long experimented with rolled hatching wings of nylon-mesh stocking materials. Such hatching nymphs have proved highly effective for

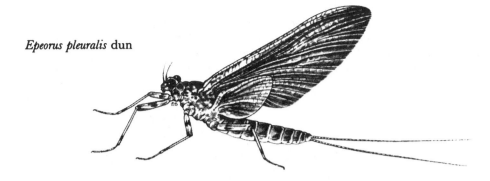

Epeorus pleuralis dun

me during emergence periods on widespread rivers, from the Battenkill in Vermont to the Big Wood in western Idaho—particularly on hatches like *Epeorus fraudator* and *Epeorus humeralis* in the east, and the similar *Epeorus longimanus* and *Epeorus albertae* flies on our western rivers.

The subimago stage of these mayflies includes some of the best-known hatches found on American waters. There are several species of eastern mayflies, including the familiar *Epeorus pleuralis* and *Epeorus fraudator* fly hatches found in a number of American books on fly-fishing entomology. These are the hatches commonly imitated on our famous eastern trout streams with a delicate Gordon Quill, perhaps the best-known dressing of the Catskill school. Although the notes and letters of Theodore Gordon, the patron saint of dry-fly fishing in America, make no mention of his dressing the Gordon Quill to match these specific hatches, his best-loved fly is deadly when these *Epeorus* duns are on the water.

These duns are handsome subimago flies, their bodies somewhat more slender than the other early-season hatches. Their wings are pale grayish blue in the straw-colored species, reaching a deep slate-colored dun in the larger flies. The pale *Epeorus* include hatches with yellowish gray bodies and species that have a faint cast of pink or olive. The darker hatches are distinctly ringed with brown or gray in slender bodies that suggest bleached peacock or condor quill. The legs are slender too, their femora often banded with darker coloring, and there are two delicate tails. It is interesting that the darker species are usually found hatching in the daytime. The famous Gordon Quill hatches are typically found coming off in the afternoons, and on many eastern streams they often hatch precisely at half-past one o'clock, so regularly a fisherman can almost set his watch by them. However, there are some exceptions to this rule of thumb, and in his little *Streamside Guide*, Art Flick describes such an afternoon on the lower reaches of his beloved Schoharie in the Catskills:

> With normal water conditions, they emerge at about one-thirty, the main hatch coming at that time. As mentioned previously, there may be a small hatch in the morning, but the one in the afternoon is of most importance to fishermen.

Higher than normal water temperatures have an adverse effect on this fly, as with all mayflies. I recall one season when the streams were much lower than normal in the spring, as there had been very little snow in the mountains and the spring rains failed to materialize. Because the weather had been unusually mild, the streams were as low as they would generally be in June.

Quill Gordons started to emerge on April 22, nearly two weeks before the average date, and came at about their regular hour for two days.

On the third day it was extremely warm, and the water temperature was quite a bit higher than normal for the time of the year. A companion and I were on the stream at about twelve forty-five, each on a different part of the stream, and we had agreed to get together again at five.

There being no flies on the water when I reached the stream, and no sign of fish working, I put on a wet Quill Gordon. I took a few small fish, but as the anticipated hour arrived and no flies showed up, it had me puzzled. I knew that the part of the stream that I was fishing was good water for *Iron fraudator*, and there were also some good trout there, but try as I might with wet, dry, and bucktail, all that I could interest were small fish.

The weather was ideal, one of those spring days when we expect all nature to be on the move, certainly the kind of day to expect good fly fishing, and as the water temperature was only sixty, I could not understand why the flies did not come.

I was not sorry when the hour came for our meeting. My friend had no better luck than I, and if anything he was a bit more disgusted. We had about all the fishing we wanted for a while, and returned home for a bite to eat, and no doubt for one or two of those things we drink to pick up our spirits. After stowing away some groceries I suggested that we go back to the stream, but my partner had sufficient fishing for one day.

Although I could not coax him to get into his waders again, he did agree to drive to one of our pet pools to see what, if anything, was doing. I had a hunch that the unseasonable heat had put the flies back and they would come in the evening, although I had never seen this happen with the Quill Gordons except for a few stragglers.

We sat on a ledge, legs dangling down toward the pool, and had been there only a few minutes when a few fish started dimpling right in front of us. I moved along the ledge to an eddy, and sure enough, my hunch was right, for there were some Quill Gordons hatching.

It was plain dumb luck that we had all of our equipment in the car, with the exception of our waders and shoes, but as you can well imagine that slight detail did not worry us, and in just a few minutes we were in action. We had some of the nicest fishing one could wish, and my friend wound up by tying into one the size of which you read about but seldom see.

Many important western hatches like *Epeorus longimanus* occur in the late morning above 7,500 feet, but are late afternoon flies at lower elevations, and come off in early evening at 5,000 to 6,000 feet. The trout respond eagerly to these current-loving little mayflies everywhere good populations are found.

The *Epeorus* spinners are delicate and elegant, dancing gracefully over the swift riffles. Like the duns, the imago flies exhibit both morning and evening behavior, depending on the altitude and species. The early-season spinners on eastern waters and the morning hatches found at higher elevations in our western mountains are usually found in midday mating swarms. They are mayflies with reddish darkly-ringed bodies, two long tail filaments, and extended forelegs. Their glassy wings glitter in the bright sunlight, when the males gather in acrobatic little swarms in the late morning and are joined by the ripening females about noon. Over the years I have had some fine sport with these spinner flights on April afternoons, and there was an entire week on the Frying Pan almost thirty years ago when we had marvelous mating swarms of *Epeorus longimanus* every day—and the fish rose greedily in the swift pools above the Ruedi stillwater, splashing as the females dipped down to lay their eggs.

The pale little *Epeorus* spinners are usually swarms that gather in late afternoon, and oviposition occurs at twilight. These little flies are found on widespread rivers, their straw-colored swarms in a delicate ballet over the riffling currents. They are usually smaller than the darker species, but the fish still love them when they are available. There have been many experiences with these pale imago swarms on many rivers. The memory returns to an evening on the swift Pine in Michigan, and a happy afternoon on the East Fork of the Iron in Wisconsin, with the late Arthur Besse. My father and I had a fine evening on the upper Ausable in New York, when the fluttering little spinners filled the twilight—and there have been some fine evenings over the years with spinner flights like *Epeorus albertae*, when the western rainbows and browns hungrily took the pink-bodied little females in the swift riffles.

The clinging, plate-gilled *Rhithrogena* mayflies are also an important swift-water genus, particularly in our western mountains and the northern latitudes. Many of the riverine mayfly hatches on the acid tea-colored Canadian watersheds are fast-water species of this unusual genus. The nymphs are unique. Their heads are remarkably flattened, with both antennae and eyes on the dorsal surfaces. They have broad, rather muscular femora, slender forelegs, and widespread, stabilizing tail filaments. They cling with their flat-legged posture, holding their bellies and tails flat in the algal growth on the bottom, almost sliding rather than crawling as they move. These nymphs move laboriously, working a single

Rhithrogena impersonata nymph

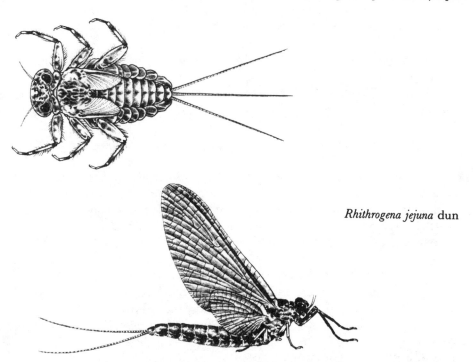

Rhithrogena jejuna dun

step at a time, loosening one leg at a time. Much of the clinging ability stems from the unique gill structure of the *Rhithrogena* nymphs. The tracheal plates are larger than those of the other fast-water ecotypes, with each gill overlapping the next in an irislike lamellate system that can be focused to increase its suction. The gills spread laterally, extending the ventral surfaces of the sternites. These lamellate gills press tightly against the stones. The first and last gill plates literally interlock underneath the abdomen, forming an unbroken circle of suction. Its force is so strong that the nymphs achieve a limpetlike grip on smoothly polished bottom stones and outcroppings, maintaining their position when other nymphs would be washed away. The surprising strength of their suction is apparent when one tries to break their leechlike tenacity. The *Rhithrogena* nymphs cling so efficiently they seem almost incised into the stones, and are often so firmly attached that they are virtually impossible to see until an angler turns their stones bottom-up into the light and waits for the nymphs to move in their algal hiding places.

Rhithrogena duns are robust mayflies of varied coloring and are important fly hatches in habitats where they are abundant. Hatching is usually brief but prolific. Sometimes the swift currents are empty of flies, and then suddenly the freshly hatched duns are literally everywhere. Since the clinging nymphs are found only in the swiftest broken-water reaches, the hatches are most abundant immediately downstream from the fastest shallows. The fish seem to like the hatching nymphs, and a subsurface presentation is quite often more effective than a dry-fly imitation. There are dark slate-colored species with darkly ringed bodies and other species of mottled olive and brown. The wings are quite boldly shaped, with upright rear wings, and there are two tails. Emergence usually comes during the day, beginning about noon and peaking in the late afternoon and early evening, although there are some instances of these mayflies continuing to hatch well after nightfall.

The mating swarms start gathering in late afternoon. These *Rhithrogena* spinners ascend almost vertically, holding their bodies in an upright position, and then flutter back toward the riffles. The swarms assemble about twenty feet above the water, climbing higher as actual fertilization takes place. Oviposition rarely takes place before dark, and the fish rarely get a chance to feed on the spinner fall of the females. Sometimes there is some fishing to the male spinners the following morning, but the swift character of the typical *Rhithrogena* river makes for poor spinner fishing, since the spent naturals are rather quickly drowned.

There are several other genera of clinging mayflies on our American rivers, and over the years I have experienced some good fishing with the *Cinygmula* and *Heptagenia* flies. Both groups of nymphs are fast-water clinging types, with strongly flattened heads and bodies. Their heads are proportionately somewhat larger than other mayfly nymphs'. The mouth parts are entirely on the ventral surfaces, while the eyes are wholly dorsal. Gills are found on the first seven body segments, and there are three tails. The gills are both lamellate and fibrillar in structure, and the gills on the

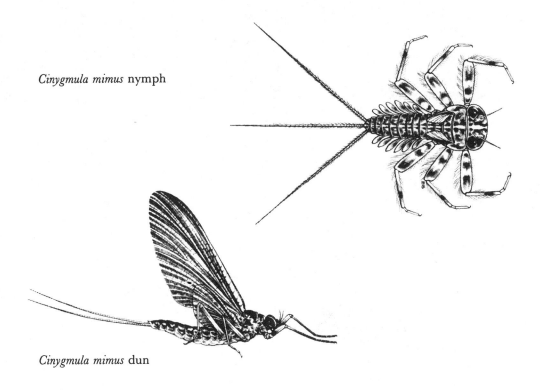

Cinygmula mimus nymph

Cinygmula mimus dun

seventh body segment do not resemble the threadlike seventh gills found in the related *Stenonema* nymphs. Sometimes these nymphs develop a pale median stripe, and the general dorsal coloring is a heavily mottled, blackish brown or brownish olive.

The *Cinygmula* and *Heptagenia* duns are an intriguing group of fly hatches and are particularly important on our western rivers. The adults are two-tailed, with lightly speckled wings and a wide range of colors. The better known *Cinygmula* and *Heptagenia* hatches are western species ranging from the pale chalk-colored flies of late summer on rivers like the Taylor and Lake Fork and Gunnison to the early hatches with rust-colored bodies and dark bluish wings. The largest is perhaps *Cinygmula mimus*, which is found throughout our western states from the Rocky Mountains to the Pacific Coast, and resembles our eastern Gray Fox hatch. *Heptagenia pulla* is distributed throughout our northeastern states and hatches throughout the summer sporadically. Its wings are a dark smoky gray with a dull olive body, and except for the two tails, it is quite similar to the Blue-winged Olive hatches—superb hatches found on both American and European trout rivers.

Some of the pale yellowish *Heptagenias* are widely distributed and are heavily concentrated in some watersheds. They are relatively small mayflies, but their coloring makes them easily seen, and they look larger in flight than they actually are. Hatching is highly sporadic, and many fishermen actually believe the fish dislike them. Perhaps the thoughtful explanation offered by the British writer John Goddard in his recent *Trout Fly Recognition* is worth considering here:

> They hatch out in twos and threes during the day, and are thought to be disliked by the fish. Whether or not this is due to the fact that they are unpalatable is not definitely known, but certainly I rarely see a fish take one. I think that a more likely explanation is that their typical emergence is more spasmodic than collective.

My own experience with the *Heptagenia* flies in this country tends to confirm these observations on British streams, although other factors are

Heptagenia hebe dun

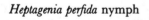

Heptagenia perfida nymph

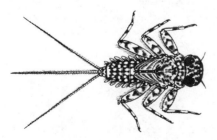

apparently involved on our hard-fished streams. Many times I have seen selective, crowd-shy trout inspect and refuse a pale mayfly simply because it seemed suspicious of its coloring, after a steady diet of darker hatches. However, since the nymphs are darkly mottled, it can usually be demonstrated that the fish are taking them greedily under the surface— even though the freshly hatched duns are observed floating unmolested on the current, and it may seem that the fish dislike them.

It has also been observed that many of these *Cinygmula* and *Heptagenia* flies are often more common on small streams, with their swift, clear-water riffles and lack of pollution. Some species are apparently more common in the colder habitats found at higher elevations, and in the tumbling back-country streams of our western mountains.

The *Cinygmula* and *Heptagenia* spinners typically hover over the swiftest shallows. Their mating dance is deliberate and steady, although its primary rhythms are often broken with the counterpoint of erratic variations. Sometimes a hovering spinner will drift forward, backward or laterally, in abrupt changes of direction, and then gracefully resume its slowly executed up-and-down rhythms. During periods of sultry weather, particularly before a breaking rainstorm, these spinners often gather in large swarms during the late afternoon and evening. Mating and oviposition usually continue until after dark, with the primary imago swarms dancing slowly about twenty feet above the water.

Few fishermen have had much experience with the *Baetisca* mayflies, since they are found primarily in swift mountain trout streams of slightly acid water chemistry and in the tea-colored rivers draining our northern latitudes. Six species have been classified from our American waters. Both the nymphs and muscular adults are unique. The *Baetisca* nymphs are a stout-bodied form with a bony, shell-like carapace covering the thorax, legs, and first five abdominal segments. The dorsal surfaces of the body display a conspicuous protuberance, which anchors the posterior margins of the carapace. The final body segments taper rather quickly to the three caudal filaments. These tails are relatively short. The legs are also relatively short and delicate, considering the muscular thorax. Both the head and the thorax are covered with bony, hornlike projections. Such an exaggerated

Baetisca laurentina nymph (top view)

Baetisca obesa dun

Baetisca carolina nymph (side view)

thoracic carapace is found elsewhere only in the relatively rare *Prosopistoma* mayflies found in some rivers of northern Europe.

The subimago *Baetisca* flies usually hatch in late spring and early summer and are muscular little two-tailed duns. The bodies are broad and taper abruptly from segments six to ten. Hatches are steady and sporadic rather than concentrated in real periods of emergence. The smoky wings are often heavily mottled with brown, and the bodies are a dark brownish olive. Some hyaline areas are also found, particularly around the cross veins, and some reddish brown abdominal segments are almost purplish in several species. The imago flies have typically crystalline wings, lightly flushed with pink toward their thoracic roots in two species. The thorax itself is dark purplish or brown, the bodies become somewhat paler, and the eyes of the males are exaggeratedly small. While the nymphs are often taken by bottom-foraging trout in rivers with good populations, the duns and spinners are seldom available in hatchlike numbers on most streams. However, my friend Leonard Wright, whose book *Fishing the Dry Fly as a Living Insect* makes no mention of mayflies, tells me that the headwaters of the Catskill streams he fishes often trigger good *Baetisca* hatches.

Wright believed these hatches were the more common *Stenonema* mayflies when he first observed them on the upper Neversink, but his hastily collected specimens were obviously not the familiar March Browns of the Catskills. However, the fish took them greedily.

The *Stenonema* mayflies are not identified from drainage systems west of the Great Lakes, but they include some of the most prolific fly hatches in American trout fishing. The genus includes the largest and most important mayflies of the entire Heptagenidae family. The nymphs have relatively high oxygen requirements, and are therefore concentrated in fast-water habitat. Each species clearly demonstrates the flattened configuration of the family and genus, with large heads and lamellate gills and three tails. The caudal filaments are of approximately equal length, and are proportionately rather long. It is in the nymphal state that the *Stenonema* mayflies exhibit the unique respiratory anatomy that gives them their taxonomic name—the filamentous threadlike gill that follows the lamellate gill plates found on the first six body segments, and unmistakably identifies the *Stenonema* nymphs.

These nymphs have three distinct types, within the confines of the *Stenonema* genus, each unique in its anatomy and proportions. Each has the combination of lamellate gills and the final threadlike tracheae, yet each is structurally identifiable in its own right.

The *Tripunctatum* nymphs are clearly identified through their lamellate gill plates and the rounded apical margins on their slender bodies. The posterolateral segments typically have spinules. The final threadlike gills are fringed with delicate hairlike filaments on a forked tracheal structure. It is perhaps the least important subgenus.

The *Pulchellum* group of nymphs is much more important, and is distinguished by the truncated apical margins of the gill plates on the first six body segments. Their threadlike gills lack a true tracheal spine. The subgenus includes more than a dozen common species, including several of our best-known hatches, like the mottle-winged *Stenonema fuscum* and the larger *Stenonema vicarium*—the exciting Gray Fox and March Brown fly hatches that fill our American fly-fishing literature.

The *Interpunctatum* nymphs are identified by the absence of pectination on their claws. The apical margins of their gill plates are distinctly pointed. The tracheal structure is not forked and is distinctly fringed on its margins. There are only a few species in this subgroup, but they include *Stenonema canadense*—the famous Light Cahill hatch found in the books of Jennings and Bergman and Flick.

Stenonema tripunctatum nymph

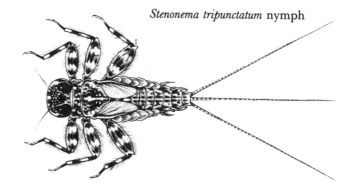

Stenonema pulchellum nymph

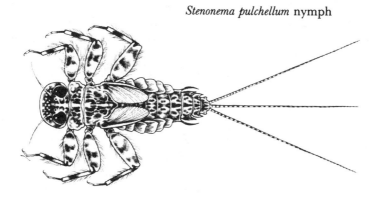

Stenonema interpunctatum nymph

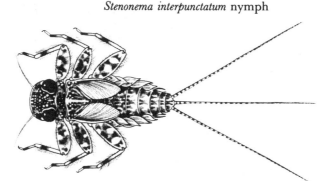

Art Flick describes an unusual behavior pattern among these nymphal forms in his *Streamside Guide*, which outlines their tendency to migrate from their swift riffles toward the shallows to hatch. It is not always found during these fly hatches, but this migratory behavior has occurred during some March Brown hatches I have observed over the years. It is almost like the emergence of the big fast-water stoneflies, when the trout follow the nymphs from their normal habitat into the rocky shallows, and an artificial fished there is often quite deadly. It is a secret about the *Stenonema* nymphs worth remembering in the future.

Freshly hatched *Stenonema* duns are handsome mayflies with delicately mottled wings and two slender tails. There are usually dark bands on the femora too. Distinct ringing delineates the body segments on most species; it is darkly colored on the tergites of species like *Stenonema vicarium* and only faintly colored on the dorsal surfaces of hatches like *Stenonema integrum*. Emergence of the several species in this genus can last from early May until as late as October, although the principal hatches are typically found in late spring and summer. The darker subimago flies like the Gray Fox and March Brown hatches often hatch sporadically, particularly in the overcast weather of late spring, although the heaviest emergence is usually found in the afternoon. The paler *Stenonema* flies are more common in the late afternoon and twilight hours, and experienced fishermen are familiar with their fluttering emergence in the last hour before nightfall. These hatching duns are often quite clumsy. The period of time taken by a wriggling nymph to escape its nymphal epicuticle can last twenty to forty seconds. Such laborious hatching behavior can mean that a hatching nymph can drift sixty to eighty feet on the current before it is fully emerged and floating on the surface, where it can still float a considerable distance, hopscotching and fluttering in its attempts to fly. The rise forms to such hatching flies can be spectacular.

Stenonema spinners are also important flies. Mating swarms of the large dark-bodied species are often found gathering in the afternoon on dark days, although oviposition seldom occurs before twilight. The large imago swarms of *Stenonema vicarium* are found mating as much as twenty to fifty feet above the water, while the *Stenonema fuscum* flies gather at much lower

Stenonema fuscum dun

heights. Nuptial flights and oviposition occurs later in the pale-bodied species, with the actual egg-laying coming after dark. The egg masses are usually bright yellowish and are extruded in midflight or laid while the females actually ride the current. Both their size and their behavior are attractive to the fish, particularly the egg-rich females, and there is often a spinner fall the following morning that can entice the trout to rise again. I have occasionally found some big fish picking up these spent early-morning flies from the Catskill flats and the smooth-flowing bends of Michigan rivers like the Au Sable and Pere Marquette.

Perhaps the most important mayfly genus is composed of the ubiquitous *Ephemerella* hatches, which produce superb fly-fishing from the spring-fed rivers of Long Island, in the shadow of Manhattan, to the superbly alkaline rivers of the Pacific Coast—from the Owens meadows in California to the weedy reaches of the Upper Deschutes and Metolious.

There are more than seventy known species of *Ephemerella* mayflies identified from American waters, making them the largest and most important genus among our Ephemeroptera. These seventy-odd species are grouped together in eight distinct groups and subgenera, starting with their nymphal taxonomy. The habits of the *Ephemerella* nymphs seem almost perfectly designed to make them available to the fish. Large numbers are found regularly in the alimentary tracts of the trout, and their behavior during actual emergence is also optimal for availability to both the fish and birds. The maturing nymphs first expose themselves restlessly on the bottom a few hours before hatching. Generating gases inside their nymphal skins, the nymphs are finally buoyed toward the surface, riding the eddying underwater currents. Such stages in the hatching cycle are typical of mayflies that emerge in open river, except that instead of escaping their nymphal skins at the surface, the *Ephemerella* nymphs typically shed their epicuticles and unfold their wings while still five to ten inches below the meniscus film.

Struggling free from their hatching shucks, their bubble-filled envelopes prevent drowning in the few seconds required to reach the atmosphere. Sometimes the hatching flies are still partially tangled in their nymphal skins when they reach the surface. Once they reach the film, the duns often ride their shedding skins like tiny life rafts, expending several seconds in unfolding and drying their wings. Studies also indicate that the freshly hatched flies are often incapable of flight until their thoracic muscles reach a higher body temperature than they maintained during their subaquatic stages.

The newly emerged subimago often tries its wings in a few tentative beats, fluttering into the air before skip-roping back to the surface. The entire process of hatching and wing drying can easily last more than thirty to sixty seconds, as the duns drift as much as thirty to fifty feet in the half-winged nymphal state and spend another forty-odd feet in surface float. Cold weather or misting rain can inhibit the entire cycle; the wings remain unformed and the musculature of the thorax is stiff and unworkable, keeping the hatching flies on the water. During the entire process of hatching, the *Ephemerella* mayflies are remarkably vulnerable to the fish, almost as if nature had provided them for the fly-fisher.

The happy results are obvious in my fishing notes over many years, and from hundreds of stomach autopsies. The trout clearly relish these mayflies and take them eagerly at all stages of their hatching cycle: the nymphs along the bottom an hour before a hatch, and again migrating toward the surface at intermediate depths; the winged half-hatched nymphs about a half foot below the surface; the relatively clumsy partially winged adult just below the film; and the freshly hatched duns are all taken freely by the trout.

This means both weighted and unweighted nymphal patterns are important in our fly books, dressed on hooks of different weights to fish at varying depths and suggest different stages of a hatch. Since the *Ephemerella* nymphs are so numerous and play an almost daily role in the trout's diet, fishing a weighted imitation dead-drift near the bottom is effective for covering the water when no fly hatches are apparent. Hatching versions are important when such flies are actually coming off. Unweighted nymphs with rolled nylon-stocking wings on fairly heavy hooks are useful for imitating the hatching nymphs a foot below the surface, and the experiments of Doug Swisher and Carl Richards, described in their book *Selective Trout*, demonstrate the need for nymphs dressed with duck or starling wing-quill sections on light-wire hooks. Such fully winged hatching nymphs are dressed with wings about forty percent of their normal length, and should be fished half-floating and awash in the surface film. Swisher and Richards continue to experiment with hatching flies, particularly their so-called stillborn duns which have failed to escape their nymphal skins. Such emerging fly patterns are extremely important in imitating a mayfly genus that emerges into a partially winged state before it reaches the surface.

The widespread distribution of the *Ephemerella* mayflies can also be attributed to their ability to cope with a broad spectrum of water types. Some species live on the edges of the primary current tongues and in the back eddies and bottom pockets of the swiftest rapids and runs. Other *Ephemerella* nymphs prefer moderate currents, and still others choose the quiet backwaters, where they clamber in the bottom trash and detritus. Their ability to tolerate such wide variations in habitat results in heavy populations, and optimal habitats can produce as many as 1,200 of these nymphs in a single square foot of riffle gravel.

Such adaptability has evolved a number of variations in nymphal configurations in the *Ephemerella* genus. Several basic types have evolved through millenniums of natural selection and biosystemic evolution. Some display slender highly streamlined bodies for living in moderate flows, while others exhibit flattened legs and ventral surfaces for faster currents. Many have developed prominent dorsal tubercles and spinules on the lateral surfaces of the body. Several species are more smooth, and others are covered with delicate filamentous hairs. Gill plates are found on body segments three to seven in some species and on segments four to seven in others. Some species have operculate or semioperculate gills on their fourth body segments, covering all or part of the remaining gill pairs. All *Ephemerella* nymphs have wholly dorsal gill systems. There are always three tails of equal size and of the same length or slightly shorter than the body length of the nymph, depending on individual species.

There are ten species in the *Bicolor* group of flies. The nymphs of this subgenus bear a rudimentary gill system on the first body segment, no gill pair on the third segment, and an operculate gill on the fourth. Prominent dorsal spines are often evident on the tergites. The lateral margins of the body segments are flattened and expanded into posterolateral spinules. Such nymphs typically inhabit quiet eddies, concealing their spiny anatomy in the bottom trash.

The *Simplex* subgenus is quite small, numbering less than five species. Its nymphs have gills on segments four through seven, with the fourth gill semioperculate. Distribution is predominantly northeastern, but the subgenus includes *Ephemerella attenuata*—the handsome little Blue-winged Olive first described in my book *Matching the Hatch*, one of the superb hatches encountered in my boyhood on the Pere Marquette.

There are more than a dozen species in the *Serrata* subgenus, and their nymphs have gill plates on abdominal segments three through seven. None of the gills is fully operculate in structure. The species are largely eastern hatches.

The *Needhami* subgenus have nymphal gills on segments three through seven, and nine species are known from our American rivers. The femora have only minor spinules on their margins, and none are present on their upper surfaces. However, spinules are common on the dorsal margins of the body segments. These species include the tiny blue-winged Red Quills that hatched on my boyhood rivers in June—the handsome *Ephemerella needhami*

Ephemerella bicolor nymph

Ephemerella simplex nymph

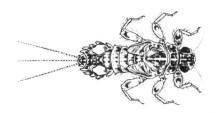

Ephemerella serrata nymph

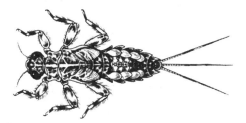

Ephemerella needhami nymph

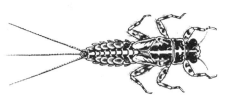

duns that produced some fine sport in those early summers, fishing on storied Michigan rivers like the Au Sable and Little South.

The *Hecuba* subgenus consists of a single species. The spinules of the freshly hatched duns are like atrophied gills, and the nymphal head is exaggeratedly wide along its frontal margins. Gills are found only on body segments four through seven, with an operculate gill pair on the fourth body segment. There are dorsal spinules on segments two through eight, and lateral toothlike spines on the margins of segments two through nine. Sharp spines are found on the apical margins of the femora. *Ephemerella hecuba* is a large species, its nymphs camouflaged with the bottom trash and detritus of its local habitat. Its freshly hatched duns are big mayflies, measuring a full ten in the hook size of its imitations, with dark smoky dun wings and juicy bodies darkly ringed with a rich purplish brown on both dorsal and ventral surfaces. It has produced some superb fishing over the years, and is big enough to attract even the largest fish to the surface.

The slow-water subgenus of *Fuscata* nymphs is perhaps the largest among the entire genus, with more than twenty individual species. These nymphs are thick-bodied and corpulent. Many of these species bear spines or tubercles on the anterior margins of their femora. Gills are found on body segments three through seven, with three tails that are relatively short. The subgenus includes well-known eastern hatches like *Ephemerella fuscata* itself and other olive-bodied flies like *Ephemerella walkeri* and *Ephemerella lata*. It also contains such fine western species as the olive-bodied *Ephemerella flavilinea* and the red-bodied *Ephemerella doddsi*—and the green-bodied *Ephemerella grandis*, which is the largest mayfly in the entire genus.

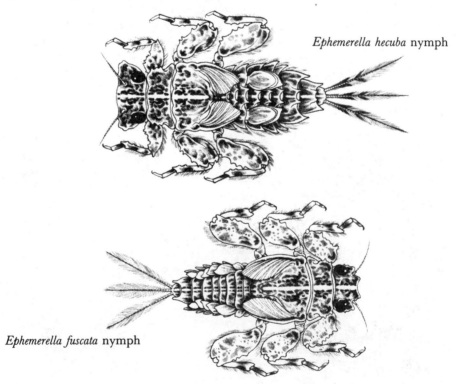

Ephemerella hecuba nymph

Ephemerella fuscata nymph

Although it is not as large as the preceding subgenus, the *Invaria* group includes most of the best-known hatches found among the seventy-odd *Ephemerella* flies. These nymphs are generally characterized by the relatively slender spines along the posterior margins of the femora. There are also spinules on the upper margins of the forelegs, often in irregular transverse bands near the apical ends, and whorls of delicate setae are absent from the tails. Both eastern and western hatches are included. The famous eastern species are the Red Quills and Hendricksons and Pale Sulphurs, and the less famous western fly hatches like the Pale Morning Dun and the yellowish Pale Morning Olive result in some equally fine dry-fly fishing when the naturals are on the water.

Like the nymphs and duns, the behavior of the *Ephemerella* spinners often triggers a fine rise of trout. Since populations of these flies are typically heavy, their mating swarms are exceptionally thick. Except at altitudes above 7,000 feet, where I have observed their nuptial flights at midday, these imago flies usually gather in late afternoon and evening. Vast swarms are often observed high in the late afternoon sunlight, with the males gathering first at treetop heights. Their mating dance is quite varied. It sometimes hovers quite low over the water, but can also take place sixty feet over a streamside meadow. Sometimes it rises up and down slowly in patient, almost somnolent rhythms—and at other times it is more staccato in character, climbing and fluttering back in erratic rhythms.

Watching a single imago is intriguing, since it often almost hovers steadily in a light wind, and sometimes rises and falls again slowly with only two- to three-foot changes in height. Sometimes it will shift sideways, or

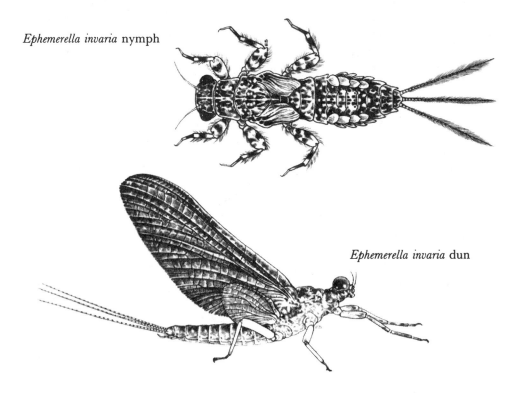

Ephemerella invaria nymph

Ephemerella invaria dun

move forward or back. The entire swarm behaves in similar rhythms, in such vast numbers that their individual behavior is difficult to sort from the intricate airborne traceries of the full choreography.

When such a nuptial swarm is seen against dark foliage, their wings are clearly held in an oblique attitude. The bodies of the females are held dangling below the fluttering wings, their angle changing with the rising and falling flight. During mating swarms that have gathered high above the current, their descending flight occurs in a series of steplike stages. The fluttering imago interrupts its downward journey with several momentary pauses, almost as if the wing beats were used as dive brakes to check its rate of descent. The swarms also vary in their choice of a mating ground, sometimes choosing swift shallows that will provide optimal habitat for their progeny, and sometimes gathering as much as forty or fifty yards inland over the water meadows. The mating occurs in several loosely organized dances that form in early afternoon, and these smaller swarms consolidate in larger and larger nuptial rites as the twilight gathers.

The female *Ephemerellas* carry their freshly extruded eggs cupped under their tails. When the egg masses collect from the tiny vent between the ultimate and penultimate segments of the body, they are apparently held in place between the caudal filaments and a pair of grasping lobes formed by the lateral body segments. These egg masses are typically olive or yellowish or bright green, depending on the species. The females press the egg sacs so tightly under their bodies that a permanent cavity is formed.

Egg laying occurs just above or actually on the surface, and the fertilized spinners usually fly upstream. During this part of *Ephemerella* mating flight, more and more eggs squeeze toothpastelike from their abdominal vents. Some spinners fly surprising distances along the river before they release their eggs, and on evenings of particularly heavy swarms, these egg-sac females pass in a remarkable aerial procession. Their flight is steady and consistent at such times, with small dipping and undulatory patterns and a quick return to the original behavior. Finally, the ripe females approach the water individually, usually selecting a swift gravelly shallow to release their ova in midflight or gracefully dip them off in the current.

Following their egg laying, some spinners immediately fall spent on the water, but most are strong enough to reach the streamside vegetation. The males remain swarming above the current, mixed with males that have participated in the mating dance of the night before. Toward nightfall, these old males fall spent on the water in large numbers, while the others return to the foliage. The following morning many of the spent females, mixed with a few exhausted males, come down the stream pinioned in the surface film. It is interesting that these *Ephemerella* spinners are found spent in such large numbers, and that they are so relished by the fish that their feeding on the female spinner falls sometimes rivals their reaction to the hatching duns—and their feeding on the spent males is virtually unique, since the trout also respond to them quite greedily.

Nothing beats them egg-sac flies! the old-timers used to laugh along the Baldwin and Pere Marquette and Pine. *Nothing all year beats them yellow egg-sac flies for stirring up the trout—except maybe the caddis hatches!*

Those Michigan old-timers understood their rivers and the trout, their experience layered like mossy wildflower ledges above a pool dripping with fiddleback springs. Since our mayflies have declined on many American rivers because of pollution and water abstraction and temperature problems, the caddisflies of the Trichoptera order seem more important each season. Our American caddisflies are prolific and varied, numbering hundreds and hundreds of individual species, ranging from the big nocturnal *Stenophylax* and *Platyphylax* sedges to the diminutive microcaddis flies of the Hydroptilidae.

Caddisflies resemble many moths and are actually related to some moth families, although there are anatomical differences in their wings. The behavior of sedges in flight also resembles the moths, but their wings lack the powdery wing covering typical of our common Lepidoptera. The wings of caddisflies are covered with surprisingly dense layers of microscopic hairs, their profusion varying from species to species. Sedges are less muscular in their thoracic structures, are somewhat more slender, and hold their wings more tightly along their bodies when at rest. Such resting caddisflies form a tent-shaped covering with their wings, obscuring both the dorsum and the dorsal surfaces of the body.

The caddisflies are grouped in the Trichoptera, and while their basic anatomy superficially parallels that of the better-known mayflies, there is little resemblance in their actual configuration. The head carries a pair of moderate-sized compound eyes, with as many as three ocelli. The antennae are often quite long, measuring as much as three times the body length of the adult flies. The mouth parts are on the ventral face of the head. The thoracic structure consists of the pronotum, mesonotum, and metanotum. Each of its segments carries a pair of legs. The primary wings are rooted in the mesonotum, while the broad secondary wings are controlled through the musculature of the metanotum. The abdomen consists of nine segments, with the ultimate segment held between the sexual claspers, and there are no cerci or tails.

These sedges have a complete metamorphosis, unlike the mayflies, which do not pass through a pupal stage. The Trichoptera have a full life cycle consisting of egg, larva, pupa, and adult stages. Caddisflies are small to medium-sized insects, generally somber or darkly mottled in coloring, and are secretive and shy in their behavior. Flying sedges are difficult to capture, and resting sedges hide among the stems and foliage of bankside vegetation, scuttling restlessly in the grass and leaves when threatened by birds or other streamside predators.

The fertilized ova of the caddisflies are deposited in both the water or the moist soil along the shorelines. These eggs are laid in stringlike masses or tiny sphere-shaped sacs. The females of some species actually enter the water, like the *Baetis* mayflies, and lay their eggs on stones and ledgerock along the bottom. Other species fly upstream in large mating swarms, dipping to the surface to extrude their ova, while still others oviposit their egg masses above the water on plants and limbs that overhang the current. Once eclosion occurs, the freshly hatched caddisfly larvae fall into the water and quickly work their way toward hiding places on the bottom.

Preoccupation with mayflies extends far beyond the work of fishing writers; therefore, compared with the voluminous technical literature on the Ephemeroptera, surprisingly little entomological work has been done on the caddisflies. Our lack of knowledge is perhaps most evident among the larval forms of caddis, since less than fifteen percent of our known adult species have been correlated with their respective larvae.

Caddis larvae are generally rather juicy, grublike organisms with six legs and relatively dark heads. The thoracic structure consists of a pronotum, mesonotum, and metanotum, with each supporting a pair of legs. Most larvae exhibit an enlarged body segment behind the metanotum called the lateral hump. The gills are rather hairy, multiformed filaments on the ventral surfaces of the abdominal segments. Delicate filaments often are found on both dorsal and lateral surfaces of the body, and there are ten body segments. The ultimate segment is densely covered with filamentous projections and a pair of protuberances called anal legs. Typical coloring consists of chocolate head and thoracic structures, with paler body segments ranging from chalky white to a chromatic green.

Such larval forms are divided into two distinct groups: the case-building and caseless caddis worms. The best known are the case-building genera, which build themselves protective shelters of tiny pebbles, grains of sand, microscopic fragments of leaves and shells, and various other plant materials. Since they work with a palette of materials from their own habitat, the protective coloration of their cases is remarkable. These case-building larvae attach themselves to the bottom stones, bedrock outcroppings, deadfalls, and aquatic vegetation. Many of the case builders clamber along the bottom, or forage on deadfalls and weed stalks, but they are seldom found ranging about freely in the water.

Many innovative fly tiers have experimented over the years with imitations of these various larval cases, and some use the actual cases themselves. Various foundations are constructed of crewel or floss, using pliobond or epoxy cement to seat the cases once they are hollowed out and cleaned. Leaving enough hook shank either along the bend or the eye, the head and thorax and legs are then imitated conventionally. It is an effective technique in making cased caddis patterns.

Less familiar to most fishermen are the Trichoptera larvae that do not build delicate protective cases, and hide themselves or range rather freely among the bottom stones in search of food. These so-called campodeiform caddis larvae are extremely important to fly-fishermen, since their relatively freewheeling behavior along the bottom makes them both readily available to the fish and easily imitated with fly-fishing tactics.

However, before exploring the campodeiform genera, we should perhaps discuss the case-building types. There are a number of primary ecotypes that a knowledgeable fisherman should recognize. His ability to recognize such species can provide him with important tactical insights in his fishing.

The *Arctoecia* larvae build cases shaped from leaf fragments and are common in cold-temperature biosystems on both eastern and western waters. These cases average about an inch in length. They are triangular in cross section, constructed of vegetable matter and tiny pieces of leaves, tightly cemented together with silken secretions. It is a genus that hatches in midsummer.

Larvae of the *Brachycentrus* sedges are most common in the cold headwaters of our trout streams and in larger watersheds that remain relatively pollution-free and have not been warmed by lumbering or agriculture. The case is formed of tiny fragments of sticks and bark in a square cross section, tapering from its upstream opening to the smaller posterior dimension. While these larvae are young and in their early stages of development, they do not build cases and are solitary feeders living in the shallows. Later they move toward the primary currents, encrusting the bottom with gregarious colonies of tapered cases.

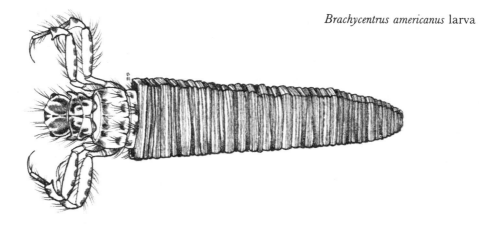

Brachycentrus americanus larva

Glossosoma califica larva

Chilostigma caddisflies build heterogeneous, cylindrical case-shelters of tiny pebbles and sand mixed with a few plant fibers. Their cases are ovoid in cross section, with a gently cornucopia-shaped length. The genus consists of species that gather in clusters among the deadfalls and stones.

The relatively small *Goera* sedges are quite common. Their larval forms cleverly attach themselves to the rocks in the swiftest riffles, using larger pebbles to anchor their sand-grain cases. The larvae are often found in biosystems ideally suited to the *Psilotreta* and *Glossosoma* caddisflies, where they fasten themselves to the bottom in mixed colonies. The larvae close both ends of their cases with tiny pebbles. Most adults emerge during late spring and early summer, and their larval shelters are quite common throughout the year. The genus is widely distributed.

Glossosoma larvae construct cases of minute pebbles and tiny grains of sand. The larvae move about freely in search of food, carrying their cases with them, and fasten them tightly to the stones during the pupal stages. Literally thousands of these cases cover the bottoms of most American streams. Hatching is found throughout the entire summer and early fall, and the three stages of larva, pupa, and adult are readily taken by the trout. The genus is a staple in their diet.

The unique spiral-shaped *Helicopsyche* larvae are snaillike in their cases. Their configuration so resembles tiny snails that our early taxonomy actually included these sedge larvae with the *Planorbis* and *Trivolvis* genera, believing they were an unusual fast-water species of tiny snails. These helical caddis cases are found in surprisingly swift water and range freely in the heavy bottom flow in search of food. During the pupal stages their cases are closed with a delicate silken webbing. The fish literally pry the larval and pupal cases from the stones, not only the *Helicopsyche* cases, but also those of the other Trichoptera.

During such periods of extensive bottom feeding, the trout actually rub their noses raw, and their digestive tracts become filled with sand and vegetable matter and tiny pebbles. Such roughages in their alimentary canals are seldom accidental, but are the remains of caddis cases.

Leptocellia larvae build true cornucopia-shaped cases of fine stream-washed sand. They are relatively communal species and gather together in large numbers on the bottom. The larvae forage boldly, clambering and searching among the crevices between the stones.

The sheltering larval cases of the *Limnephilus* flies are constructed of various materials. Some species build their relatively rough cases of sand, tiny pebbles, and microscopic bits of shell. Other species have extremely heterogeneous cases made from shredded bark, seeds, toothpick-sized sticks, tiny stones, and pine needles. Most larvae of this genus are quiet-water forms, with heavy populations in lakes and ponds and good populations in slow-moving streams. Some pond-loving species are like tiny hedgehogs, all prickly with minute plant stems and sticks. The popular Strawman nymph developed by the late Paul Young is an imitation of these larvae. Some *Limnephilus* larvae build such jackstraw cases in their early, shallow-water

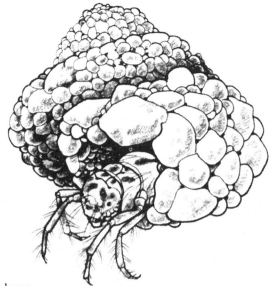

Helicopsyche borealis larva

Leptocellia albida larva

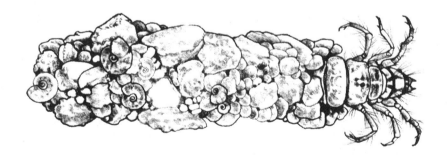

Limnephilus assimilus larva

stages of growth, later making cigarlike shelters out of plant wrappings.

Ganonema larvae construct their cases of actual stick fragments, hollowing out the fibrous cores. Such larvae are slow-water insects that feed in the pond-weed shallows, where their stick cases are concealed in the bottom trash.

Mystacides larvae build slender sand-vault cases anchored along their sides with scraps of shell and tiny stones. The *Leuctotrichia* flies also build larval cases of fine sand, shaped like tiny hotwater bottles with delicate openings placed at either end, and one flat surface adhering firmly to the stones.

Hesperophylax and *Ochrotrichia* both build cases of coarse, stream-washed sand and tiny pebbles. Their cases are roughly tubular, slightly tapered and curving, and the larvae themselves anchor them to the bottom. The *Neophylax* larvae build their cases of rougher materials, constructing a rude little vault buttressed with larger chips of stone. Flat little cases of sand are also made by the small *Molanna* larvae. They then place them on sandy bottoms in quiet currents, where they are virtually invisible. These cases are slightly hooded to shelter the heads of the larvae and conceal them from predators. The superb sand-bottomed rivers of our upper Middle West, rivers like the Brule and Namekagon in Wisconsin and the Pere Marquette and Au Sable in Michigan, are biosystems ideally suited to colonies of case-building caddis larvae of these genera.

The *Neuronia* larval forms build their slender cases of leaf fragments, tightly wrapped into slightly curving tubes. Such cases measure approximately an inch in length, and clamber actively among the pondweeds and slow-flowing streams. The larvae of the *Phryganea* sedges have similar habits, rarely venturing from their aquatic vegetation to forage on the bottom. Their adults are summer-hatching flies.

The *Platyphylax* caddisflies include some of the largest American species. The genus is found in very cold streams and spring holes, particularly in flowages that seldom freeze in winter. Their cases are cylindrical in cross section, sometimes tapering slightly toward the rear. Large species like *Platyphylax designatus* can measure as much as two inches at full larval growth. Their cases are constructed of sand, minute fragments of shell, tiny slivers of wood, bark, leaves, and small pebbles. The adults are largely nocturnal in both their habits and hatching.

The pebble cases of the *Psilotreta* genus are surprisingly elegant. Their larvae are quite common in our trout rivers, from the northern latitudes of Maine and Minnesota to the high-mountain streams of Georgia and North Carolina. Their larval cases are little curving tubes, tapering delicately toward the rear. They are fashioned of tiny pebbles and current-polished sand. During the first weeks following their eclosion from the egg, the tiny *Psilotreta* larvae forage openly over the bottom. But once their cases are fully built, and the pupal cycle is about to start, the larvae gather in colonies among the stones. Before pupation, each larva seals its case with a tiny pebble at each end, and then spins a watertight silken cocoon.

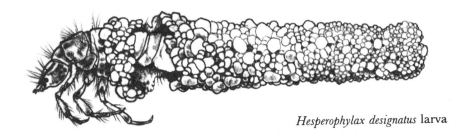

Hesperophylax designatus larva

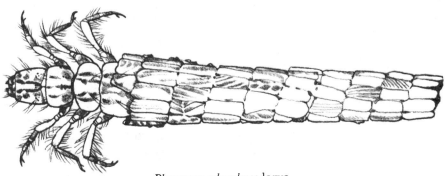

Phryganea coloradense larva

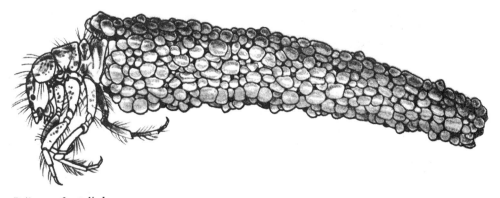

Psilotreta frontalis larva

Sericostoma larvae are also well distributed in the swift mountain streams. The famous Welshman's Button sedges that Halford described from the British chalkstreams are of this fast-water genus. Although they seemingly abound in swift-flowing habitat, with its relatively high concentrations of oxygen, their larvae seek out eddies and pockets in the current. During periods of high water, large numbers of these larval cases are washed downstream with the spates. Fully developed cases measure as much as one inch in length. The cases are shaped of fine-grained sand held in a delicate and surprisingly strong matrix of silk.

The cinnamon-colored nocturnal sedges of the *Stenophylax* genus are common on American streams. Their larvae often reach slightly more than an inch in length, and are distinguished by the linear stick-layers of their cases. The tiny fragments of wood are assembled in a rough cylinder, aligned lengthwise to form the barklike cases. They are numerous in acid headwater streams, and on the Pinchot water of the Sawkill in Pennsylvania I once collected a dozen *Stenophylax* cases from a single log wedged across the stream, its bark covered with hundreds of larvae.

Triaenodes larvae prefer slow-flowing streams and quiet ponds. Their larval cases are between three-quarters of an inch and an inch in length, shaped from leaf-drift cut, and lapped in a spiral tube of remarkable tightness and precision. The genus is unique in the sense that its larval cases are not fixed to the bottom, or clambering among the water plants and stones. Its larvae swim freely, moving with surprising agility generated by their delicately fringed legs. The coloring of the cases varies, depending on the plant materials available. Since they are free-swimming larvae, they are useful as prototypes for artificial flies.

The so-called campodeiform caddis larvae do not construct sheltering cases, and are readily available to the trout as they forage among the bottom stones. It is these caseless genera which are most easily imitated in fly-fishing.

There are six primary genera numbering literally hundreds of species among these campodeiform types. Since the natural larvae seldom range free of the bottom, their imitations are best fished weighted and deep. Dead-drift presentations are excellent. The large number of species make the imitation of specific sedge hatches impractical, but important caddis-flies are useful as imitative prototypes for our fly books. It is important to match the range of larval sizes and colors.

The little *Chimarrha* sedges are tiny net-spinning species with pale yellow and dull orangish larvae, measuring only slightly more than a quarter of an inch in length. Their nets are usually a parallel series of delicate tube-shaped tunnels, firmly cemented to the stones. The mesh-woven tubes both shelter and collect food for the larvae. The tiny *Wormaldia* and *Dolophilodes* genera are similar net-spinning sedges, principally western in distribution.

The small *Polycentropus* and *Phylocentropus* sedges are also net-spinning genera and are locally quite abundant in a wide variety of water types.

These insects construct delicate paraboloidal tubes of microscopic silken filaments, hanging them in the crevices in a remarkably intricate tensile system. These tensile structures also collect food for the larvae.

Stenophylax scabripennis larva

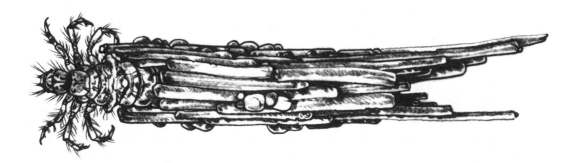

Triaenodes tarda larva

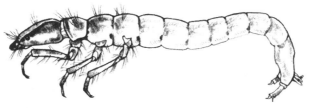

Chimarrha atterima larva

Perhaps the most numerous of our American sedges are the *Hydropsyche* flies. It is a remarkable net-spinning genus that inhabits our riffles by the thousands. Good populations are also found in lakes having sufficient wave action to oxygenate the shallows and transport food into their collecting webs. These nets are funnel-shaped and look like miniature bag nets, and are suspended between crevices in the stones. The larvae construct a tiny, semicircular enclosure at the apex of their nets, feeding on minute organisms and plant materials trapped by their meshes. When the larvae are frightened or resting, they retreat deep into the tiny pebble shelter at the bottom of the net. Such net shelters measure about three-quarters of an inch at their outer margins, but they are so numerous that they are easily located by an observant angler. The sites for such net shelters are typically found in the swift places between stones, the depressions and faults in stream-polished ledges, and the gathering tail-shallows of a pool.

These *Hydropsyche* larvae have a delicate fringe of ventral gills along their belly segments. The several species measure from one-quarter inch to a full inch in length. The trout are extremely fond of these larvae, and can often be found rooting them out of the crevices between the stones, their sides catching the light as they turn and their tails disturb the current. The color of these little larvae is typically chalky white to pale yellowish cream, with darker heads and thoracic segments and legs. There are other closely related net-spinning genera, particularly the *Cheumatopsyche* and *Arctopsyche* sedges, which are important on American streams.

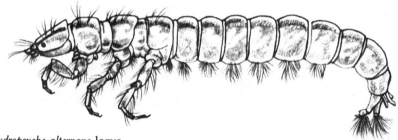

Hydropsyche alternans larva

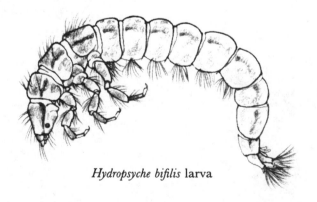

Hydropsyche bifilis larva

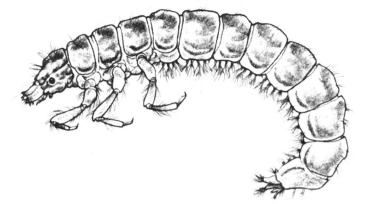

Macronema zebatum larva

Cheumatopsyche gracilus in flight

Since their larvae neither build food-gathering nets nor construct sheltering larval cases but forage openly among the stones and bottom trash, the *Rhyacophila* caddisflies are among the most important to fly-fishermen. Their larvae are extremely abundant in American waters. Their palette of color varies from a pale olive to a bright green, rich with chromatic intensity. The genus is widely distributed on our swift-flowing rivers and streams, ultimately hatching into the green-bodied sedges that produce such fine dry-fly fishing on so many waters—from the tumbling little Brodheads in Pennsylvania to swift Pacific rivers like the Pit and the Feather in northern California.

The Hydroptilidae family includes a number of minute caddisflies which average less than three-sixteenths of an inch in length. There are twelve genera, and thirty-odd species are known from American waters. Their habitat is varied, including both lotic and lenitic biosystems, and abundant populations are known. The larval cases of these microcaddisflies are flat little parchmentlike shelters, shaped like little coin purses and firmly attached to the bottom. They are dark grayish and dirty-yellow larvae, and sometimes the trout strip them from the stones.

Caddisfly larvae are virtually omnivorous, feeding on plant materials and animal organisms and the eggs of other aquatic insects. The smaller ecotypes tend more toward herbivorous diets, while the larger larvae display carnivorous behavior, although both will feed heavily on decomposing fish and other animals. Caddis larvae in waters having heavy populations so greedily consume the eggs of other insects, particularly those of the mayflies, that the other insect orders are decimated and suppressed. John Waller Hills tells us in his book *Riverkeeper* that the legendary William Lunn, who managed the Houghton Club water on the Test for fifty-odd years, found that both insect and trout eggs were extremely vulnerable to caddis larvae—and that incubating ova had to be protected from both egg-laying sedges and their larval forms.

It is interesting that the case shelters built by many larval forms of caddisflies are multipurpose. Camouflage is an obvious function, and cases that provide it are so effective that many larvae are virtually invisible unless they move. The cases also protect the larvae from predators and the abrasive effects of turbidity. Their specific gravity is designed to help the larvae in their chosen habitat. The cases of fast-water species are heavy, helping them hold their positions in the current. Slow-water larvae build buoyant cases. Martin Moseley tells us in his *British Caddis Flies*, the definitive monograph on the Trichoptera of Ireland and the United Kingdom, that his research confirms these observations:

> Speaking generally, we find that species inhabiting the fast-running water attach heavy stones to their cases to avoid being swept away in the strong current. Others, living in ditches, ponds or slow-running rivers, employ bits of wood which no doubt render their cases more buoyant and enable them to move more easily to fresh feeding grounds.

Finally the caddis larvae are fully grown, and it is time for pupation. It begins with the spinning of a silken cocoon from the salivary glands in the mouth of the larva. The case-building genera simply seal the anterior and posterior openings of their shelters. Although the pupal sac protects the larvae once they begin pupation, it is porous enough to admit oxygen-rich water. The campodeiform species spin an ovoid pupal cocoon, anchoring its perimeter with a circle of minute pebbles.

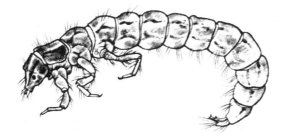

Rhyacophila lobifera larva

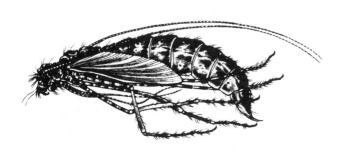

Stenophylax scabripennis pupa

Rhyacophila basalis adult

The transformation from larva into pupa is not unlike the metamorphosis from caterpillar to chrysalis in butterflies. The pupal process includes moulting, when the larvae shed their epicuticle and expose the pupae underneath. These pupae are quite different from their larval forms; they stop eating completely and engage in something like hibernation. The pupal cycle can take from a few weeks to an entire winter.

When the pupation is complete and the hatching time approaches, the emerging caddis perforates its cocoon with its sharp mandibles. The anatomy of the pupa bears a considerable resemblance to its adult development. Its thoracic structure and abdomen are distinctly formed. The evolving wings are readily visible inside their pupal sacs, with the legs and antennae held closely parallel to the bodies, projecting well beyond the ultimate segments. The legs are heavily fringed at this stage of growth, helping the pupae swim to the surface and hatch.

Caddis pupae ultimately hatch in two ways. Many simply migrate to the surface and emerge there, using the tensile character of the meniscus to split their pupal skins. Others creep from the water on plant stalks or deadfalls or boulders to shed their epicuticular shucks and fly off.

The Trichoptera are clearly available to the trout in the hatching pupal stages, perhaps more easily captured than at any other moment in their metamorphosis. Some swim readily toward the surface and hatch quickly, while other species drift some distance with the current. Those which migrate into the shallows, creeping out on rocks and plant stems and logs, are also captured readily as they travel from their pupal hiding places to their hatching sites.

Therefore, most feeding on the Trichoptera occurs during the cycle of pupal emergence, when the insects are both vulnerable and available. The logic behind the behavior of the fish is clear. It is much easier for them to capture the swimming pupae enroute to the surface or the pupal sedges helplessly pinioned or emerging in the film, than it is to slash and leap at the fluttering adults once they have hatched.

Stream-bred trout are never illogical. Their lives are a delicate equilibrium between the calories ingested and energy expended. Since the pupal stages of the caddisflies are vulnerable, readily available, and easily imitated by fly-fishing tactics, it is easy to understand their importance to anglers. And it is an importance that is increasing, since the caddisflies are perhaps better equipped to survive the impacts of pesticides and warming streams and oxygen-burning pollution than the delicate mayflies and oxygen-loving stoneflies.

The selection of a particular diet form over other available food types and the consistent concentration on such foods by a feeding trout or grayling are explained in a relatively simple pattern of relationships. The relationships lie between the availability of a food type, its weight and caloric content, and the difficulty of capturing it. Assuming optimal feeding and digestive conditions are present in the fish's habitat, these topologies play a remarkably important role in their preference for taking the caddisflies in their hatching pupal forms. My book *Nymphs* expressed these relationships in this simple formula:

$$\frac{\text{Energy expended per}}{\text{calorie ingested}} = \frac{\text{Availability of ecotype} \times \text{its caloric content}}{\text{Factors of capture}}$$

Caddisflies are widely distributed in American trout waters, and are found in brooks, reservoirs, flowages, lakes, beaver ponds, rivers, and small tributary streams. Their physiology can accept wide variations in water chemistry, from the relative acidity of an Adirondack beaver pond to the remarkable alkalinity of a California hot-spring creek. Their tolerance of pollution, wide ranges of temperature, turbidity, and pesticides is hardier than the better-known mayflies. Like the brown trout, their ability to survive in our decimated ecosystems makes the caddisflies more and more important in our trout-fishing future. Fly-fishermen have too often ignored the caddisflies, and my own book *Matching the Hatch* was relatively guilty of this omission. Although there are many American species, most are remarkably similar, and a few basic imitations of their adults, larval forms and hatching pupae will cover most important Trichoptera.

Stoneflies have been similarly neglected, except perhaps for the big *Pteronarcys* and *Acroneuria* nymphs on our western rivers, and our American Plecoptera deserve better treatment. More than four hundred species of stoneflies are known from American trout waters, about half as many species as our mayfly hatches, and their relatively high oxygen demand limits their habitat to swift streams and lakes having sufficient wave action to oxygenate their shallows. Nymphal stoneflies are divided into two behavioral groups, the plant-eating Filiopalpia genera and the Setipalpia nymphs, which are both herbivorous and prey on other aquatic insects. Their life cycle is incomplete, consisting only of the egg, nymphal, and adult stages of development.

Stonefly nymphs reared in captivity have displayed between twenty-two instars in the smaller species to thirty-five stages of growth in the larger ecotypes. The smaller species which feed principally on plant tissues have a life cycle of only one year. The larger carnivores can spend two to three years in their nymphal stages and are therefore available to the trout in a wide range of sizes at any single time. Unlike the mayfly nymphs, immature stoneflies do not have gill systems on their abdominal segments. Their respiratory filaments are found between their legs and their supporting thoracic segments, and in anal gill filaments at the root of their tails. Vestigial gill filaments sometimes persist in the adults after hatching, and are important in classifying several stonefly species.

Mature stonefly nymphs have two rather exaggeratedly long antennae, which clearly separate them from most mayflies. Their jaws consist of a broad labial structure and strong maxillary palps. The heads display relatively bold eye structures and are broad and flattened in most types, tapering back into the protothorax, which supports the first pair of legs and gill filaments. The mesothorax and metathorax support legs and wing cases and their own respiratory systems. There are ten abdominal segments, and the two cerci or tails also display filamentaceous gills at their roots. The paired tails also distinguish the Plecoptera nymphs from all of the similar looking mayfly nymphs, except for two-tailed genera like *Epeorus* and the tiny *Pseudocloëon*.

Several of the plant-eating genera are important to fly-fishermen in their nymphal stages. Some twenty-five species of the small *Nemoura* nymphs are found in our streams, and the somewhat larger nymphs of the *Capnia* and *Taeniopteryx* stoneflies hatch into the dark little flies of late winter and early spring. The tiny rolled-winged stoneflies hatch from the *Leuctra* nymphs, which are slender little subaquatic forms. These plant-feeding nymphs are generally quite dull in coloring, ranging from pale grayish to dark reddish brown, with several gun-metal-colored species. Some of the most strikingly beautiful nymphs found in our American trout streams are the pale, richly patterned stages of many smaller stoneflies.

There are several stonefly genera of medium size, and their nymphal forms are generally included with the flesh-eating ecotypes, although they are omnivorous in their feeding habits. These nymphs include the tiny pale green *Chloroperla* genus and the pale yellowish *Isoperla*, *Alloperla* and *Paraperla* flies. *Arcynopteryx* and *Oroperla* are similar western genera, and these nymphal forms are all pale yellowish to medium brown.

The larger Plecoptera nymphs are primarily carnivorous, and many western rivers that boast unusually large populations of these genera find the stonefly nymphs subsisting at the expense of sympatric populations of mayflies in their subaquatic stages. Because of their size, these Plecoptera are obviously important factors in the diet of the fish on many rivers. The big *Perla* nymphs are perhaps the best known, since they were written about thirty-five years ago by Preston Jennings and Charles Wetzel, although the much larger western *Pteronarcys* nymphs have become increasingly well known in recent years. Our western rivers have large *Acroneuria* populations too, although the *Perlinella* and *Perlesta* genera are also important in local habitats, and the eastern *Perla* nymphs have a closely related western genus in the similar *Claassenia* types.

Mating stoneflies lay their eggs in the swift riffles. Incubation lasts from a relatively few hours in some tiny genera to more than three and four months for the larger species at cold temperatures. The most rapid incubation apparently occurs in the *Capnia* and *Isocapnia* flies, which emerge in late winter and spring. Three to five weeks is about average incubation for most stoneflies.

The tiny nymphs which finally eclode from the eggs are insects that

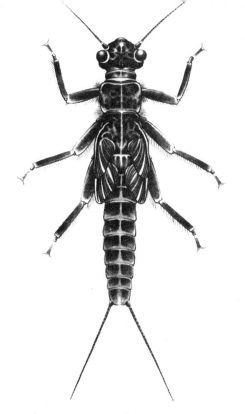

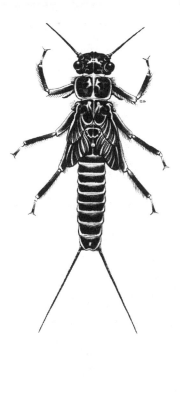

Capnia vernalis nymph

Taeniopteryx fasciata nymph

Isoperla bilineata nymph

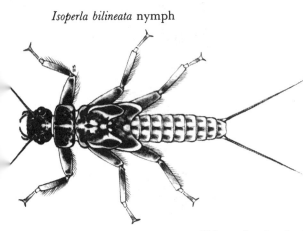

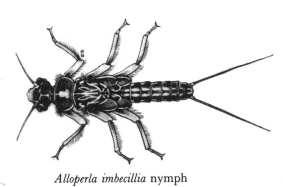

Alloperla imbecillia nymph

Chloroperla coloradensis nymph

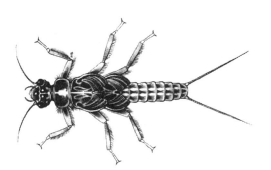

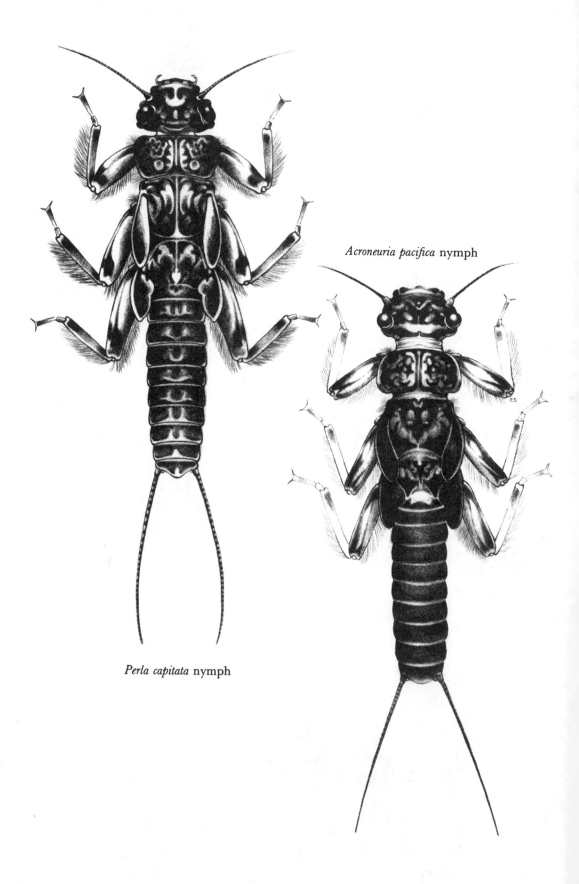

Acroneuria pacifica nymph

Perla capitata nymph

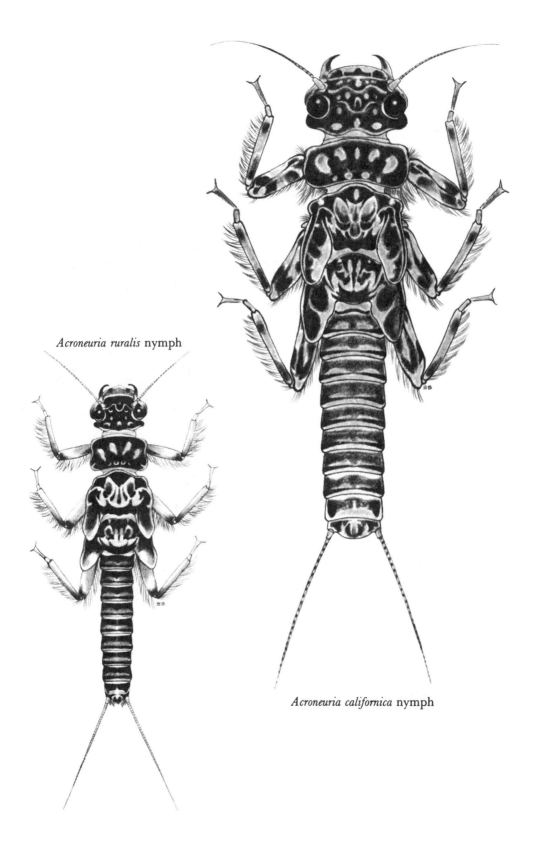

Acroneuria ruralis nymph

Acroneuria californica nymph

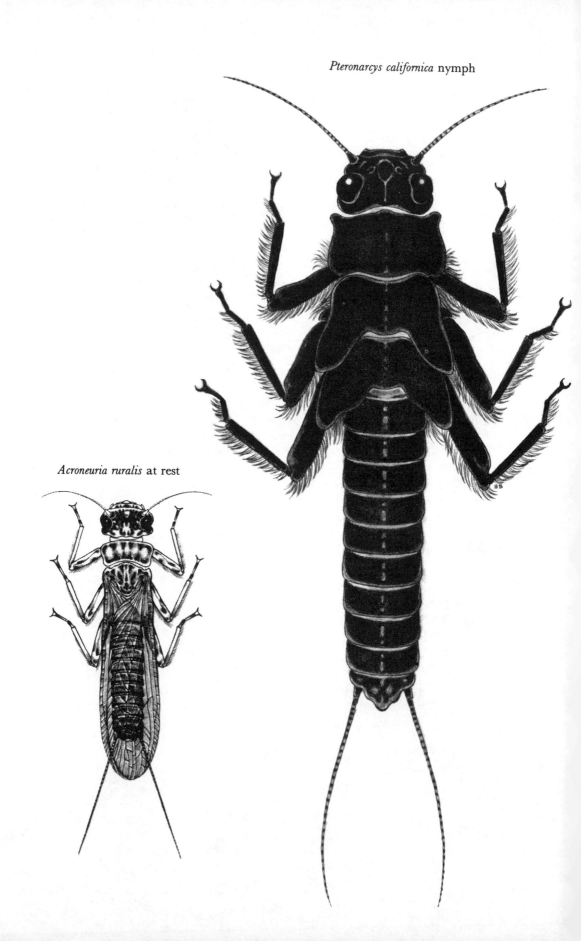

Pteronarcys californica nymph

Acroneuria ruralis at rest

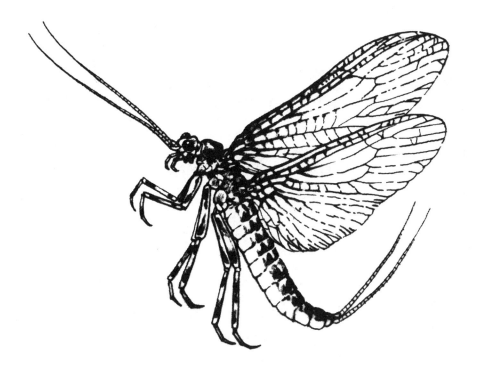

Perla capitata in flight

crawl rather than swim, although they effect a relatively clumsy swimming motion with leg action and undulation of their bodies. Therefore, stonefly nymphs are best imitated with a studied mixture of upstream dead-drift presentation and working across and downstream with a teasing rhythm of the rod. The nymphs are extremely agile in the bed of the river, moving in all directions with remarkable dexterity.

The larger stonefly nymphs are well known to most fishermen, who call them water crickets on eastern rivers. Western fishermen incorrectly call them helgrammites, since the true helgrammite is really a member of the completely different *Corydalis* genus, which is not a stonefly at all. Catching these giant stonefly nymphs to sell for bait has been a thriving business on many western rivers over the years. It is a particularly unfortunate practice, since imitations of these big nymphs fish superbly, and such systematic harvests of the principal diet form in many of our major western rivers should probably be banned.

The smaller stonefly nymphs are similar in their morphological character, although their proportions are slender and more delicate. These herbivorous stoneflies typically eat mosses, tiny phytoplankton, higher plant-form tissues, and some zooplankton species of algal life. All of the Plecoptera nymphs occasionally eat herbivorous materials, but flesh-eating behavior is more typical of maturing nymphs like the giant *Pteronarcys* stoneflies. These subaquatic carnivores eat large quantities of minute zooplankton, but other animal organisms in their diets are typically the smaller nymphs and larvae of other orders. There is even widespread cannibalism, particularly in the genera having two- and three-year life cycles, when fully mature nymphs prey on the smaller generations. The heavy populations of such predatory *Acroneuria* and *Pteronarcys* nymphs on many western rivers is a mixed blessing, since the relatively sparse mayfly hatches on such streams often come from the decimation of their nymphs by the fierce predation of the Plecoptera. The big stoneflies provide dry-fly sport during an orgy of hatching in early summer, when the salmon flies and giant golden stoneflies and willow flies typically hatch on many famous western rivers. However, the penalty for such stonefly blizzards is a reduction of dry-fly sport during later mayfly hatches, since their populations have been heavily cropped in the nymphal stages.

The big stoneflies are virtually unique in the sense that an imitation of the adult Plecoptera is perhaps the oldest fly pattern to reach us almost unchanged in both dressing and name. Dame Juliana Berners included a stonefly imitation in her legendary series of twelve patterns, when the *Treatyse on Fysshynge wyth an Angle* appeared almost five centuries ago. Stoneflies are still important in modern fishing.

Flights of adult stoneflies are rather sporadic on our eastern rivers although the smaller, early-season *Taeniopteryx* and later *Isoperla* flies can sometimes emerge in sufficient numbers to trigger a surprisingly good rise of fish. The large eastern stoneflies like *Perla* and *Pteronarcys* sometimes emerge in sufficient numbers, usually in the first hour or two after daylight, that good fish will often prowl the shallows in search of their hatching nymphs. Such hatching activity rarely produces dry-fly sport like the early-summer orgies on western rivers.

Adult stoneflies differ from mayflies and sedges in a number of obvious anatomical features. Their wings are relatively glassy and brittle, resembling the texture and character of the dragonflies in the larger species. When stoneflies are not in flight, their wings are folded flat and are held rather tightly sheathed above the abdominal segments. Their folded wings protrude well beyond their bodies. There are two long antennae at the head and two conspicuous tails reaching slightly past the tips of their folded wings. Larger Plecoptera look relatively flat with their wings folded, while the little *Leuctra* genus wraps itself so tightly in its wings that its adults are called needle flies. Stoneflies are relatively subdued when at rest and are easily collected from the streamside foliage immediately after they have hatched. Later they scuttle with surprising agility to avoid capture.

The same flies look surprisingly large in flight, since their wings are relatively large for their bodies, which hang somewhat vertically under their spreading wings. Their flight is somewhat clumsy and lumbering, like an aircraft at the edge of stalling speed. Adult Plecoptera consist of head, protothorax, mesothorax, metathorax and abdominal segments. There are prominent antennae and tails. The head and thoracic sections together are approximately equal in length to the body. The protothorax supports the forelegs, while the two rear body segments support both legs and paired wings. The legs are powerful and well developed, having rather stout femurs and claws. The first two joints of each leg, the coxa and trochanter respectively, are knucklelike and small. There are three segments in the tarsal feet. The primary structure of each leg consists of the femur, which is rather like the upper arm in human morphology, and the tibia or forearm. The forewings are relatively slender like a narrow leaf, while the rear wings are larger and wider. The buzzardlike hatches of the big *Acroneuria* and *Pteronarcys* flies on western rivers like the Gunnison and Big Hole and Henry's Fork of the Snake are an experience that makes the bacchanalia of mayfly hatches on the chalkstreams or limestone loughs in Ireland seem tame—and even the early-summer hatching of our eastern *Pteronarcys* stoneflies can produce remarkably fine big-trout fishing for a skilled nymph man just after daylight.

It was the late Bill Blades, who also taught the masterful Poul Jorgenson to dress flies, who first told me about trout feeding on the Hemiptera. Blades had encountered feeding on the larval forms in the brook-trout lakes of Ontario, and his book *Fishing Flies and Fly Tying* included two imitations. It was not until fifteen years later, on a shallow reservoir in Colorado, that I first found the fish taking Hemiptera in large numbers.

Most of the subfamilies and genera in the trout diet dive and swim with great agility, always returning to hang and breathe in the surface film.

Their behavior is a rather erratic rhythm between hunting their prey and resting to breathe and such patterns should be suggested in fishing an imitation. These water bugs are only partially committed to an aquatic existence, since tracheal gill systems are absent. The nymphal forms closely resemble the adults, except for their half-developed wings, and no visually significant change occurs between the nymph and adult stages. While there are not many subfamilies or species important to the trout fisherman, individual populations of Hemiptera are often extensive. There are sixteen families or subfamilies occurring in or along trout waters, although only three play any significant role in the diet of the fish. The Pleidae include the creeping pygmy bugs, the Corixidae are the ubiquitous water boatmen, and the Notonectidae are the backswimmers.

The Hemiptera all have biting and sucking mouth parts, usually in the form of a slender beak. Their wings are rather simply veined, and there are scent glands in the thoracic structure. Corixidae and Notonectidae are extremely numerous and widely distributed, occupying a wide range of habitat types. Populations are found in high lakes, reservoirs, swamps, beaver ponds, streams, rivers, and even geothermal springs. Their ecological role is apparently that of predators and scavengers at the intermediate level of the food chain. The Hemiptera all winter as adults in the sedimentary bottom materials, mate and lay eggs in the spring, hatch and develop through the summer, and repeat the cycle in the coming fall. Five nymphal instars are typical of most species. The eggs are oviposited in a variety of egg-laying sites. Eggs are typically attached to various objects like deadfalls or plant stems or the backs of the males. Respiration is unique in

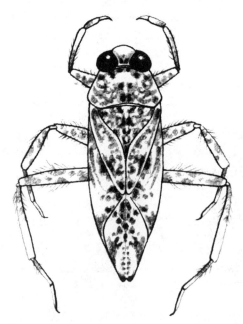

Notonecta unifasciata adult

each of the subfamilies. Hemiptera are almost totally dependent on surface oxygen inhaled through the anterior tip of the abdomen for the *Plea* and *Notonecta* bugs and through the pronotum of the Corixidae. However, hydrofuge filaments on the belly surfaces also collect supplemental oxygen. Stridulation is also found among the *Plea* bugs, backswimmers, and water boatmen, although their cricketlike calling is extremely rare.

Few anglers realize that the aquatic Hemiptera are capable of flight, and that their ability to migrate has permitted them to survive drought conditions and recolonize desiccated habitats. Corixidae are sometimes found attracted to lights along the river and gather and swarm around them, although such nocturnal flights are apparently not a factor in either mating or oviposition.

Water boatmen are the most populous of all the aquatic Hemiptera and are found from sea level to as high as fifteen thousand feet, as well as in a remarkable range of water temperatures. The Corixidae play a major role in the entire aquatic community because they convert plant tissues into animal materials ingested by higher predators. Water boatmen also prey on zooplankton and algal life, and there is evidence that they feed extensively on mosquito and midge pupae. Fish stomachs often reveal Corixidae in good numbers, particularly their partially grown nymphs in early spring. However, feeding on the adults often appears to be an acquired taste, with one fish taking them regularly and others having none. Perhaps the Corixidae are unpalatable because of their texture, or perhaps because their scent glands affect their taste.

The morphology of the Corixidae is rather typical of other Hemiptera found in the trout diet. Their anatomy is rather fat and boat-shaped. The heads are broad, meeting a shoulderlike pronotal disc, and the propisternum, mesopisternum and metapisternum. There are eight body segments tapering back gracefully toward the anal surfaces. The forelegs are quite powerful and short, and are strongly bristled to assist their swimming. The middle legs are longer, and the muscular rear legs are the primary swimmers, with extensive fringes. The bladelike forewings and triangular rear wings are concealed under wing covers called the ebolia, much like the terrestrial beetles.

Backswimmers have a strikingly similar anatomy although their bodies are slender and more streamlined. These Notonectidae are common in our trout ponds and are fiercely predatory, attacking prey much larger than themselves. Their name is derived from their curious habit of swimming upside down, with their ventral or belly surfaces toward the surface. The antennae are short and partially concealed, and there are no ocelli. The forelegs and middle pair are adapted for capturing prey or grasping stems and water grasses, while the rear legs are heavily fringed and used for swimming. The nymphal forms lack scent glands and are therefore more attractive to the trout. The *Plea* bugs are much less slender and were once grouped with the backswimmers, but they are now tentatively grouped in their own subfamily.

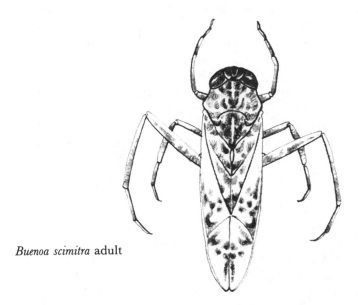

Buenoa scimitra adult

These insects return to the surface film at fairly regular intervals to replenish their oxygen. Their breathing filaments penetrate the meniscus, while the insects are suspended head down with the rear extended and motionless. Oxygen is gathered through the abdominal troughs, diffusing through the ventral spiracles to the thorax filaments. Their eggs are laid in plant tissues, and on fallen logs or stones. Some species inject their eggs into the stalks of aquatic vegetation, and incubation varies widely. Five instars or stages of growth are typical. Their diet is virtually omnivorous, consisting of small crustaceans, insect nymphs and larvae, the pupal forms of many insects, fish fingerlings and alevins, tadpoles, and literally anything they can capture and devour.

Their distribution is somewhat puzzling. The backswimmers are almost universally found throughout the world, although their *Buenoa* genus is limited to North and South America. The *Plea* pygmy bugs are largely tropical insects, although many are found in our eastern coastal drainage systems.

These Hemiptera frequent sheltered waters where there are thickly grown aquatic plants and dead vegetation, although some are found in quiet streams and backwaters. There they forage widely for other organisms and plant materials, and many scavenge among dead aquatic and drowned terrestrial animals. The Hemiptera often end their hibernation before the ice has melted off their lakes and ponds, and become quite active after ice-out. Mating and oviposition occur in early spring. Their intense metabolism requires a vigorous regimen that lasts well into winter, when many other aquatic forms are hibernating. Hemiptera winter themselves in sluggish little colonies hiding in the pickerel weed and spatterdock and moss. Most Hemiptera live longer than a year.

Beetles are grouped in the Coleoptera order. There are approximately 300,000 species, in some eighty-odd families and subfamilies. Only a few of these, however, are aquatic forms, numbering about 5,000 species in American waters. The mature larvae of virtually all beetle forms spend their pupal lives in moist burrows near the water, although a few spin pupal cocoons. The methods of larval respiration are remarkably varied. Some have tracheal gills which permit breathing under the surface, like the Gyrinidae and a few of the Hydrophilidae. The widely distributed Dytiscidae breathe through respiratory spiracles at the rear of their bodies. The tiny *Berosus* and *Peltodytes* larvae breathe through bristling body filaments, while the grublike *Tropisternus* must return to the surface film to breathe. Some larval types, like *Haliplus* and *Brychius*, accomplish cutaneous respiration directly through their skins. The larvae of the *Donacia* and *Noterus* beetles frequent the root structures of aquatic plants, and since they lack abdominal spiracles for breathing, they accomplish respiration by piercing the plant stalks and extracting intercellular oxygen. These larvae can also breathe in the surface meniscus. Hydraenidae typically acquire their oxygen through respiratory spiracles distributed over their bodies. Most Hydrophilidae must breathe with their posterior spiracles in the surface film, like the tiny little larval forms of the Helodidae. The riffle beetles of the Elmidae subfamily breathe through gills in a caudal chamber.

The habitat of these beetle larvae is varied. The Gyrinidae larvae of the well-known whirligig beetles are largely found in ponds, backwaters, and lakes, in company with the Dytiscidae and Hydrophilidae. Small forest

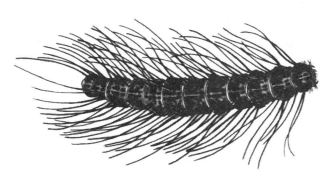

Peltodytes edentulus larva

Gyrinus punctellus larva

Tropisternus americanus larva

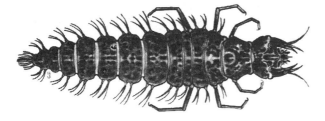

ponds contain few species, except for the Helodidae. Rocky shorelines with good wave action and swift boulder-strewn currents support the fast-water populations of riffle beetle and water penny larvae, the turtlelike Psephenidae. Streams also have their quiet backwaters and bottom eddies, and in such sanctuaries are the beetle larvae that love quiet currents but still require relatively high oxygen levels. These fast-water sanctuaries shelter the larvae of the Dryopidae, Elmidae, Psephenidae, and Ptilodactylidae. Detritus and bottom silts attract the Hydraenidae, Hydrophilidae, and Helodidae. Shoreline silts and small stones and gravel sustain populations of the Hydrophilidae, Hydraenidae, and Gyrinidae. Stream-loving algal growths are rich with the larvae of Haliplidae and Hydraenidae beetles. Deep pools and backwaters often have fine populations of Dytiscidae and Gyrinidae in their shallows. Cold springholes often support surprisingly good populations of Dytiscidae, Gyrinidae and Helodidae. Geothermal flowages on our western streams sustain larval forms of the Hydrophilidae, Hydraenidae, and Elmidae riffle beetles in remarkable numbers.

The flesh-eating beetle larvae are remarkably predatory but they are not without their enemies. Dragonfly larvae are fiercely predacious too, and feed extensively on aquatic beetle larvae. Turtles and waterfowl and birds also consume large quantities of Coleoptera larvae, and these predatory beetle larvae are also among the hunted. Beetle larvae also decimate themselves, since they are fierce cannibals from their eclosion, feeding on each other almost immediately after hatching.

Although the Coleoptera larvae are predacious and agile in capturing their prey, their swimming and clambering in the aquatic growths are quite deliberate and clumsy. Fishing imitative patterns of these larvae should work a slow bottom retrieve suggestive of this behavior. These larvae are both wormlike and heavily gilled, and their antatomy is a revelation to anglers who are unfamiliar with the aquatic beetle larvae.

The heavily fringed gill systems are the answer to an old fly-dressing puzzle. There are many grublike wet flies with thickly dubbed bodies and palmer-tied hackles that are consistently successful without apparent prototypes in aquatic entomology.

Well, many friends have chided me over the years, *you believe in matching the hatch, and the concept that a really deadly pattern can always be traced to some insect prototype—what about palmer grubs and woolly worms?*

It is a question I once found difficult to answer, although I was convinced that the consistent success of such flies had an explanation in nature. Subsequent experience with the thickly gilled larvae of the subaquatic Coleoptera has supplied the missing pieces of that puzzle.

There are a few genera of the order Megaloptera that are often important to trout fishermen. There are two families, the Sialidae and the Corydalidae, and there are twenty-odd genera. The alderflies are found in the Sialidae, while the Corydalidae include the larger *Chauliodes* hatches and the dobsonflies.

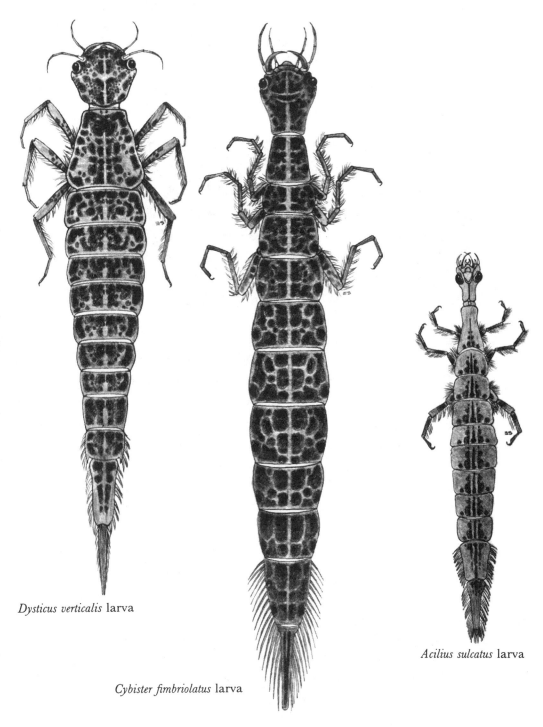

Dysticus verticalis larva

Cybister fimbriolatus larva

Acilius sulcatus larva

Dineutes vitatus larva

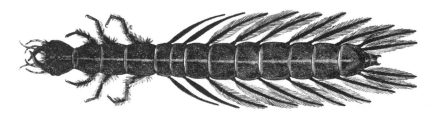

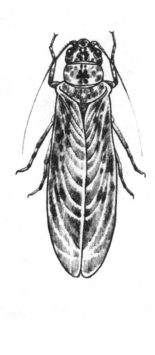

Sialis mohri adult

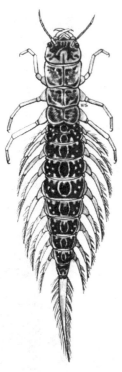

Sialis infumata larva

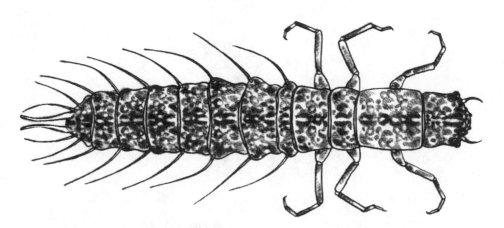

Chauliodes pectinicornis larva

The alderfly larvae are typically found in streams with good current-flow, and in still reaches of rivers that are highly oxygenated. These *Sialis* larvae are not actually riffle insects, but occupy the bottom eddies and backwaters in the accumulated bottom trash and detritus. Swift-water *Sialis* larvae are sometimes under the stones in swifter currents, and they are found throughout North America, although the principal populations are eastern. The adults are diurnal flies that hatch and swarm during the daylight hours. They are awkward and clumsy and are small- to medium-size insects that resemble sedges. Their flight is labored and usually confined to the vicinity of the streamside foliage. Alderflies will often scuttle away along a branch rather than resort to flight. Larvae are easily recognized by their prominent lateral gills and their single taillike trachea. Their abdominal segments are pale brown to chalky yellow. The lateral gills are five-jointed tracheal structures, while the terminal trachea contains respiratory filaments but is not segmented. Judging from their soft half-atrophied mouth parts, adult *Sialis* flies are probably rather short-lived. The flies are extremely active in bright weather, often mating and laying their eggs at midday. Their fertile ova are oviposited in flat little pancake-shaped masses of two hundred to five hundred eggs. Egg laying usually occurs on a leaf, bridge timber, deadfall, or highway abutment above the current. The hatching larvae fall into the current and reach about an inch in length before entering the pupal stage. Pupation occurs in the moist roots along the bank and has little interest for anglers. The adults are counterparts of the British *Sialis lutaria*, the dark little alderfly that has enriched the literature of angling since Charles Kingsley lovingly described it in his *Chalkstream Studies* in 1858. It was his favorite fly pattern, and his writings made the alderfly popular on British waters. British anglers christened them alderflies because large midday swarms were often found in the streamside foliage.

The Corydalidae include both fishflies and dobsonflies, and some of the largest aquatic insects. Their immature stages range from the *Chauliodes* larvae to the predatory three-inch helgrammites. The fishflies of the *Chauliodes* genus are perhaps the best known, although there are five closely related genera. The larvae of both the fishflies and the dobsonflies prefer coarse aggregates and rubble bottoms where they can stalk their foods among the crevices and find shelter from the current. Some colonies are found in silt-bottom backwaters. The *Nigronia* fishflies are of these slow-water types, and the larvae are hardy enough to thrive in intermittent watercourses in our arid western regions. The sizeable populations of fishfly larvae seem to indicate much larger numbers of adults than are commonly observed, suggesting that the adults are largely nocturnal. Dobsonflies exhibit similar populations and behavior. The larval forms all display relatively long lateral projections along their abdominal segments, and these serve as respiratory tracheae. The fishfly larvae have two slender projections at the abdominal terminus, except for the immature stages of *Nigronia* flies, which have delicate breathing filaments added to these gill systems. The dobson larvae have elaborately tufted spiracles on their lateral abdominal pleurae and are surprisingly agile among the bottom stones, moving both forward and backward with a mixture of crawling and snakelike undulations. These larvae are fiercely predatory, particularly the *Corydalis* species, and they forage aggressively during the night. Dobson larvae devour anything they can corner and subdue, including each other when subaquatic populations are sparse. Larval duration varies from two years among most fishflies to three years in the dobsonflies. Maturing larvae leave the streambed, seek the moist banks, and burrow into the soil to fashion their pupal cells. Pupation lasts approximately ten days to two weeks, and most adults emerge in late afternoon and evening. Entomologists believe the Corydalidae are quite primitive insects, surviving almost intact from prehistoric times, and their voracity makes the helgrammites the flesh-eating dinosaurs among subaquatic insects.

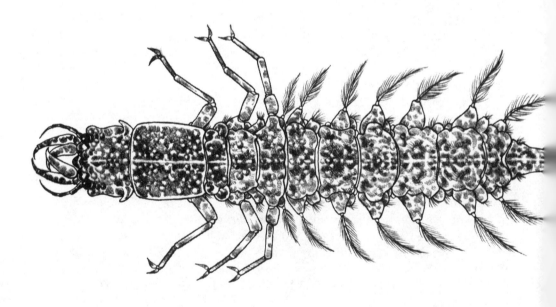

Corydalis cognata larva

The corpulent dragonfly nymphs of the Anisoptera suborder are highly predatory too, and share the Odonata order with the more delicate damselflies. Adult dragonflies are the swift-flying snake doctors, devil's darning needles, and horse stingers popular in folklore across the United States and Canada.

Dragonflies are wholly aquatic until they hatch into the winged stages and their nymphal forms are utterly different from the adults. Dragonflies, like many other aquatic insects, have an incomplete metamorphosis consisting of eggs, nymphs, and adults. Most of the nymphal populations develop in permanent streams and bodies of fresh water, although some are found in intermittent bogs and brackish habitats. Although the nymphs are largely confined to aquatic environments, adult dragonflies sometimes range several miles from their parent waters.

Dragonfly nymphs are highly predacious. They capture their food in a completely different fashion from the airborne adults, lying in wait like a muskellunge in the weeds. Although they are capable of agile movements and surprising acceleration, these Anisoptera nymphs usually trap their victims with a lower labial jaw structure that snaps out like the tongue of a frog. Its extensive dexterity is remarkable, and it is powerful enough to capture a baby trout. The nymphs have a unique swimming method. The lower intestine is thin-walled and functions as a respiratory organ, absorbing oxygen from water drawn in and expelled through the anal orifice. Some respiration is also accomplished through the tracheal spinules. The dragonfly nymphs are stout and muscular when compared to the damselfly nymphs of the related Zygoptera suborder. Nymphal life lasts from two to three years, depending on the individual species, and when they are fully developed they crawl from the water on a deadfall, boulder, or reed—climbing slightly above the water to split their nymphal skins and hatch. Adult dragonflies are the strongest fliers in the world of insects, and they retain the predatory behavior of their nymphs. Mating occurs at rest on bulrushes and streamside branches and reeds, and oviposition is varied. Some dragonflies drop their eggs into the water, others fasten their ova to the leaves of aquatic plants, and still others inject their eggs into the stems with a stingerlike ovipositor.

Adult dragonflies capture millions of mosquitoes and biting gnats and other insects in midflight, darting back and forth in swift, perfectly controlled movements, and snaring their prey in a basketlike trap between the forelegs and the thorax. Their aerial patrolling and pursuit of insect foods is remarkably graceful and swift. However, this beneficial aerial diet is a mixed blessing, since considerable predation on alevins and fingerling trout, as well as on important organisms in the trout diet, occurs in the nymphal period of growth. Most nymphal movements are relatively sluggish, except when the dragonfly nymphs are trying to escape a foraging trout or wading bird. Imitations should usually be fished with a deliberate retrieve along the bottom, although a staccato rhythm is often effective in the middle depths of water, particularly along dense beds of weeds, for this

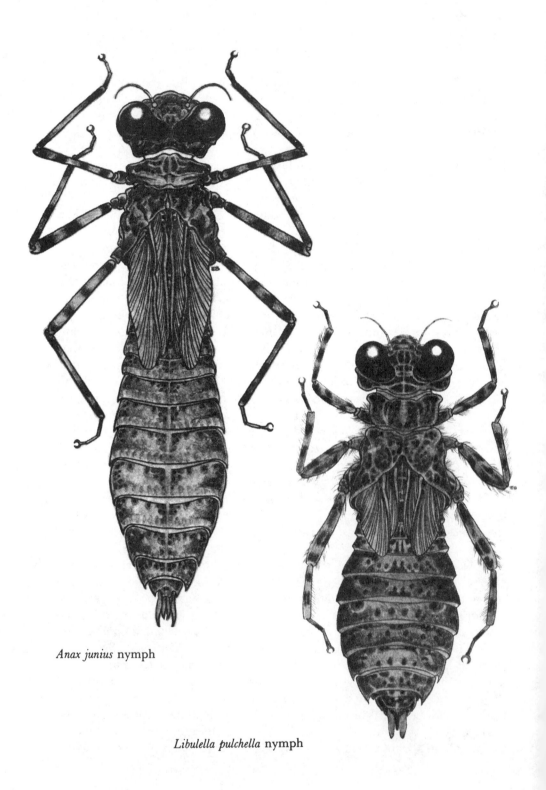

Anax junius nymph

Libulella pulchella nymph

action suggests the rapid acceleration possible when a dragonfly nymph expels its respiratory water with a sudden contraction of its elaborate lacework gills.

The slender-bodied nymphs of the damselflies are totally different and are classified in the Zygoptera suborder. Although they are closely related to the dragonflies, both their nymphs and their adults are totally different. The slender Zygoptera are a sizable clan.

Damselfly nymphs are agile and restless swimmers, using their bladelike posterior gills as sculling oars. Some species produce several broods each season. Both dragonfly and damselfly nymphs pass the winter in semihibernation, hiding in the silts and bottom detritus. Like their dragonfly cousins, the damselfly nymphs are predatory and voracious, devouring each other and many lesser organisms. Although both dragonfly and damselfly nymphs are capable of rapid movement, they usually stalk their prey with cunning and stealth, reserving their agility and acceleration to escape predation themselves. Their appetites are fierce. The nymphs are slender and are equipped with three lamella-shaped gills at the posterior of their abdomens. Their flattened heads and widely spaced eyes are quite different from their delicate bodies. Their legs are relatively long and thin, and are used for swimming and clambering swiftly in the weeds. Most species are abundant in silt-bottomed lakes and ponds with rich aquatic vegetation, although some species thrive in slow-flowing streams like the limestone spring creeks—from the lower Musconetcong in New Jersey to weedy little Putah Creek north of San Francisco, or the rich currents of Hat Creek farther north in California.

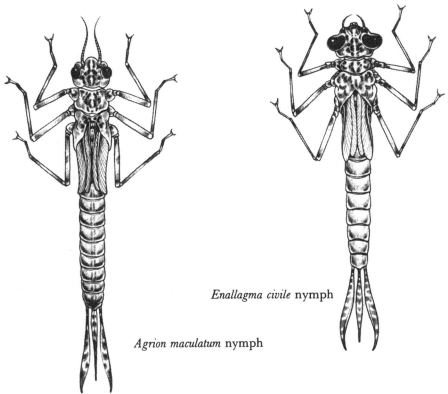

Enallagma civile nymph

Agrion maculatum nymph

Emergence begins in late spring, and the nymphs usually migrate into quiet shallows along the banks. Damselfly nymphs clamber just above the water to hatch, and after they have escaped their nymphal skins, it is possible to find these shucks clinging to deadfalls and sticks and bulrushes along the shorelines.

The adult damselflies differ strongly from the larger dragonflies in their wing anatomy. Resting dragonflies hold their wings horizontally, while adult Zygoptera hold their hyaline blade-shaped wings trailing back behind their thoracic structures. Damselflies have slender bodies capable of remarkable contortions during mating and oviposition. Males fertilize the females by grasping the female thorax with their calipers, while the female grasps her own abdomen, bending it back sharply to contact the male organs under the thorax of the males. Both males and females often fly together, while the male is still clasping the female above the thorax, and I have seen trout take a mating pair that were blown into the current. The thoracic structure of the damselflies is slender but muscular, while their eyes are quite proportionately large. Oviposition usually finds both insects alighting on a plant stem, with the female arching her abdomen high enough to lay her eggs in its tissues. Favorite sites for oviposition are tender young branches of willows and alders. Hunting adults typically rest on the foliage in the sunny exposures of streamside vegetation, darting out ten to fifteen feet to capture their prey, and often returning to the same resting place. Egg-laying females deposit about six to ten ova in each puncture of the bark, and may girdle a branch or stem with enough penetration to shelter seventy-five to two hundred eggs. The incubation typically lasts through the winter, and the eggs eclode the following spring. This past summer on Silver Creek in Idaho there was an evening when the biggest rainbows ignored the steadily hatching *Callibaetis* mayflies, and waited in the weedy channels for a mating damselfly to fall clumsily into the currents—and they took the fluttering damselflies with greedy, explosive rises that shattered the smooth twilight.

Although the small freshwater crustaceans are not really aquatic insects, imitative fly patterns matching these scuds and shrimps and sowbugs are important in any fly box used on American waters. The freshwater crustaceans are widely distributed in American waters, particularly those with high alkalinity and good oxygenation. Many of our most famous trout streams and mountain lakes are rich with diminutive amphipods and fairy shrimps and sowbugs. The checklist of famous lakes would have to include remote brook-trout fisheries like Ashuanipi and Assinica, sprawling Yellowstone and Henry's Lake in the northern Rockies, superb fly-fishing lakes like Davis and Hosmer in the Pacific Northwest, the small galaxy of forest-rimmed ponds in the Kamloops country of British Columbia, and thousands of lesser-known fisheries rich in weeds and crustaceans and lime salts. Streams famous for their populations of scuds and sowbugs and shrimps certainly begin with several Pennsylvania limestone streams, particularly the little Lehigh and Big Spring and the storied Letort Spring Run. The tailwater rivers of the Ozarks are unusually rich in such species, and sowbugs are the principal diet form of the North Fork and the Little Red below the Greer's Ferry Dam. Western chalk-streams like the South Platte in Colorado, the several spring creeks in Jackson Hole, the Gibbon and Firehole and Madison in the Yellowstone, the many watercress spring creeks in Montana, the Teton and Henry's Fork and Silver in Idaho, and the weedy little rivers of northern California—like the Putah lagoons near San Francisco, Hot Creek in the eastern foothills of the Sierras, and fertile little Hat Creek and Rising River in the Sacramento headwaters—these are all habitats remarkably rich in crustaceans.

Freshwater crustaceans form a somewhat more limited spectrum of organisms than their salt-water cousins. Marine forms include a galaxy of lobsters, crayfish, crabs, shrimps, and prawns. Freshwater ecotypes include the true *Palaemonetes* prawns, the common crayfish, fairy shrimps, scuds, and sowbugs. There are also a multitude of tiny crustaceans like water fleas, copepods, and ostracods in freshwater lakes and ponds, forms so minute that they are virtually impossible to imitate. The *Daphnia* water fleas are typical of these microscopic organisms.

Superficially, the crustaceans resemble insects in their jointed append-ages, although in crustacea there are many more of these joints. Unlike the aquatic insects, these little shrimplike organisms have heads that are broadly jointed, and a definite neck structure seems lacking. They breathe with a system of abdominal gills. Their bodies are covered with a rigid exoskeleton, secreted through a layer of cells just under its surfaces. The shell can be firm and surprisingly hard, which accounts for the abundance of crustaceans in relatively alkaline waters, and the shell can also be virtually transparent as it is in the microscopic *Daphnia* fleas. Lime and calcium entrained in the water form the primary building blocks of these exoskeletal shells, and during their several stages of growth, the crustaceans must discard their outgrown exoskeletons just as aquatic insects molt between instars.

Freshwater crustaceans have intricately jointed bodies, antennae, legs, and even multiple mouth parts. Larger forms like crayfish visibly demon-strate their multi-jointed anatomy. Such jointed appendages are both the most diverse and the most characteristic quality of all crustaceans. Their structure clearly expresses the functions of breathing, swimming, eating, and egg laying.

Nearly all crustaceans breathe through tracheal gill systems. Crayfish have their gill systems on each side of the thorax, protected by the shell-like carapace that covers the thoracic structure and head. Water continually flows through these gills. Sowbugs and fairy shrimps and scuds have ventrally located respiratory filaments.

Crustaceans are separated into two principal groups. Larger ecotypes are classified among the Malacostraca, while smaller forms are grouped under the Entomostraca. Crayfish, freshwater shrimps, sowbugs, scuds, and other similar types are included in the taxonomy of the former group, while the fairy shrimps, copepods, ostracods, and flealike organisms are placed in the latter. Since the microscopic crustaceans are too tiny and transparent for practical imitation, the only member of the Entomostraca of importance to the fly-fisher is the ubiquitous fairy shrimp.

These fairy shrimps are classified in the suborder Branchiopoda, and measure between five-eighths of an inch and an inch in length. Common colors are amber, olive, and pale bronzish yellow. These little *Eubranchipus* shrimps are the largest members of the Entomostraca order, and are easily recognized by the leaflike appendages of their feet. These tarsal appendages are really both feet and respiratory gills combined, rooted in the body segments underneath their bodies. Fairy shrimps always swim on their backs, waving the gill plumes of their feet above them, and their imitations should be weighted so the hook shanks ride down like a keel. These delicate little crustaceans are often so transparent that it is possible to observe the pulsing rhythms of their cardiovascular networks through their slender bodies. Female fairy shrimps are infinitely more abundant than males, which accounts for the remarkable fecundity of their populations. Mating occurs when the males and females swim together, the males grasping the females to their ventral surfaces. Just behind their gill systems, located on segment eleven of their bodies, are the tubelike penes which fertilize the females. The females carry their fertilized eggs in conspicuous brood pouches until they actually hatch. Fairy shrimps live in small cold-water habitats, and are widely distributed. They cavort actively on their backs, darting and swimming and hovering in tiny baitfishlike schools. While they are most active in late winter and early spring, many oviposit their young into the silt and bottom trash. Their food consists of microscopic organisms like zooplankton and other diatomaceous life, and they feed voraciously in their shallow spring-fed ponds. Fairy shrimp imitations are most effective in the early seasons, when their populations explode after a bitter winter of dark hibernation.

Malacostraca are perhaps best known because they include the common crayfish, which is classified in the genus *Cambarus* and is typically found in quiet backwaters or hiding in the bottom rubble of swifter currents. Crayfish also thrive in the hard-water chemistry of alkaline habitats, scuttling along to scavenge their food from decaying organisms and tiny aquatic animals. Crayfish are virtually omnivorous, eating decaying matter and plant materials and insects with equal relish. Their eggs and young are often both carried among their short swimmers, along the ventral surfaces of the abdomen. The gill filaments are along their sides, lying between the roots of the legs and the overhanging carapace of the thoracic shell. Crayfish have five pairs of legs, the first armed with lobsterlike claws. Some species mate in the autumn and spawn the following spring, while others mate and lay eggs all year. The eggs typically hatch in seven to eight weeks. Crayfish larvae conceal themselves and ride among the legs and swimmers of their mothers for as much as a week.

Crayfish are three to five inches at full maturity, too large to serve as workable prototypes for fly patterns, although the smaller Malacostraca are important both as trout foods and species worth imitating. These smaller species include the true shrimps of the *Palaemonetes* genus, the scuds, and the many-legged sowbugs. Scuds are a rather large and widely distributed group, classified under the suborder Amphipoda. Sowbugs are flat little crustaceans designated in the Isopoda suborder and are found in remarkable profusion in many American waters.

Freshwater scuds are much smaller than the crayfish and have quite a different configuration. These scuds are excitingly agile acrobats, jumping and climbing and darting rhythmically through the water. Their anatomy is relatively flealike, with a highly arched dorsal shell over their bodies. There are climbing legs tightly grouped under the thorax, and the longer swimming legs are found farther back along the abdominal segments. Their coloring is typically yellowish gray, olive, tan, grayish, or pale brown. Scuds love the weedy growth of quiet, spring-fed ponds and slow-flowing streams, clambering and darting among the forest of interlocking stems. They are voracious scavengers, the tiny vulturelike swarms that clean their subaquatic world of dead fish and drowned animals and other carrion.

Scuds of the *Gammarus* genus are the largest of the American species, and fully developed specimens measure three-quarters of an inch to an inch in length. Populations are extensive in both streams and ponds. Their fertility lasts from April through November, and fecundity is so high that a single female can produce more than twenty eggs every two weeks. Such fertility can produce a pyramidal family tree of 20,000 progeny from a single pair of parent scuds each year. The *Gammarus* genus is not particularly fond of soft water, demonstrated by its relative absence from habitats lacking as much as seventy-five parts per million calcium. It loves streams lined with thick beds of watercress and candelabra weeds, and in western spring creeks having particularly rich alkalinity, more than 5,000 scuds are commonly found in a single cubic foot of coontail or elodea. Scuds are widely distributed in American waters, although they clearly prefer cold spring-fed habitats of constant temperature and flow. The ability to thrive is apparently tied to relatively low water temperatures, alkalinity, and the food and shelter provided in the undulating, thickly grown weeds. The *Gammarus* scuds are clearly identified through their primary antennae, which are longer than the secondary pair, and the presence of secondary flagella. There are filaments on the dorsal surfaces of the last three abdominal segments, and tiny posterior appendages on the abdomen.

The freshwater scuds of the *Eucrangonyx* genus are widely distributed in marshy, spring-fed waters, often including habitats of limited alkalinity. Their taxonomy is remarkably parallel to the closely related *Gammarus* scuds, although they can easily be recognized through their lack of hairy filaments on the dorsal posterior segments. The relatively small posterior appendages on the abdomen are rudimentary.

Scuds of the *Hyalella* genus are the smallest of these prolific crustaceans, and they are extremely common in our waters. During the first weeks of spring, these tiny scuds are thick in the undulating fountain mosses, feeding on decaying plant materials. Older scuds are omnivorous, eating dead organisms like snails and tadpoles and fish. Some biologists have observed these tiny crustaceans swarming like piranhas on drowned animals and avifauna, and they are equally fond of decaying elodea and stoneworts and pondweeds—and once I found several hundred *Hyalella* scuds foraging hungrily on a drowned heron carcass.

During their mating cycles the male *Hyalella* clasps the female with its forelegs and swims in animated fashion, sometimes holding his mate for several days. The females carry their freshly hatched young in their thoracic legs for several weeks, sometimes still sheltering a prior brood during a new mating period. Fecundity can produce a clutch of fifteen to twenty eggs every week over a period as long as five months. Although they are smaller than either *Gammarus* or *Eucrangonyx,* their populations are both heavier and more widespread. They are far more tolerant of varied water chemistry, thriving in both acid and alkaline habitats. Silt bottoms and weed beds are equally acceptable, as well as both lakes and streams. *Hyalella* is distinguished by its two projecting spinules on the dorsal surfaces of its posterior body segments. The primary antennae are typically shorter than the second pair, and *Hyalella* also lacks the dorsal filaments typical of the larger *Gammarus* scuds. Such tiny scuds are found in most western lakes between five and ten thousand feet, and I have collected *Hyalella* specimens from spring-fed bogs at almost 12,000 feet in Colorado.

Sowbugs are small crustaceans grouped in the Isopoda suborder. Optimal habitat is found in the quiet currents of watercress and decaying leaf drift and pondweed. Sowbugs are remarkable fourteen-legged crustaceans, with their legs held projecting along the sides. They are omnivorous bottom scavengers, but decaying aquatic vegetation is their primary staple. Sowbugs are readily taken by the trout, and the fish are often seen rooting them from the weeds. Mating among these *Asellus* bugs begins in early spring and continues through the summer. Fresh broods are commonly produced every five to six weeks, and female sowbugs are often still sheltering fifteen to twenty freshly hatched offspring while the mating cycle begins again. Some limnologists have described them as minute armadillo-like crustaceans, and sowbugs are so numerous in alkaline waters that several thousand are not uncommon in a cubic foot of watercress or elodea. Ozark rivers support them in remarkable numbers.

The fat-bodied little Sisyridae are the only completely aquatic family in the Neuroptera order. Their larval forms occur in parasitic colonies on freshwater sponges, deriving both shelter and food from their hosts. When fully grown these *Spongilla* larvae leave the water and pupate in the moist soils along the banks. The adults are called *Spongilla* flies, and are small sedgelike insects with curving antennae and rather mottled darkly-veined wings folded tentlike over their bodies. The fat little larvae superficially resemble the sowbugs. There are six genera and thirty-odd species,

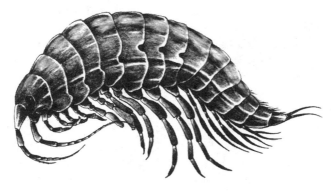

Gammarus fasciata scud

Hyalella americanus scud

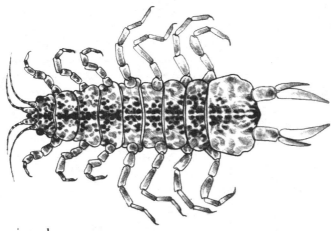

Asellus communis sowbug

although only two are unquestionably found in American trout waters. Larval respiration is accomplished with tracheal filaments on the abdominal segments, and the larvae vibrate them rapidly to create an oxygenating flow of water. *Spongilla* eggs are commonly laid in a crevice or shallow depression on a branch or bridge abutment overhanging the water. Small clusters of eggs are concealed under a silken cover. Eclosion occurs in eight to ten days. Larval coloring varies from green to yellowish brown. *Spongilla* larvae migrate to a pupal shoreline when they are fully grown and spin a curious, geodesic pupal cocoon. Emergence occurs just at nightfall, and the adults live approximately two weeks. Mating flights take place between sunset and midnight, and each female lays about fifty eggs. Two or three broods are possible each season. Most studies have been made with the *Spongilla* genus, which is widely distributed in both trout habitat and in warmer, coarse-fish environments. *Climacia* flies are common in cold, spring-fed ponds, while *Sisyra* larvae are generally found only in warmer biosystems. *Spongilla* flies are found in both lakes and slow-flowing streams, and good hatches have been observed in both Adirondack lakes and large western rivers like the Eel and Williamson and Deschutes. Sisyridae are important on some waters.

Aquatic Lepidoptera are also frequently mistaken for caddisflies, even by knowledgeable fly-fishermen. Most of the more than 100,000 known species of moths are terrestrial insects, and few of the aquatic forms spend both larval and pupal stages in the water. However, the subfamily Nymphulinae is wholly aquatic, and plays a significant role in the trout diet in many regions. There are apparently ten aquatic genera found in American waters, although almost a hundred are known from tropical and subtropical habitats. The Nymphulinae are separated into plant-feeding species and rock dwellers that subsist on algal life.

The larval stages of many herbivorous aquatic moths are relatively well known in our waters, while a considerable void exists in our knowledge of the rock-dwelling larvae that feed on algal organisms. Ecological relationships between several aquatic moths and specific aquatic plants have been established, particularly with pond lilies and *Potamogeton* beds. Eggs are typically laid on the undersides of floating hydrophytic vegetation, and the larvae often cut protective cases from its leaves. Larvae meet their oxygen requirements with periodic vibration of their abdominal breathing filaments and direct absorption through the cutaneous covering of their bodies, although some species have fully developed tracheal gills. The pupal period occurs in a silken little cocoon inside the pondweed larval case. The *Nymphula* and *Synclita* genera are typical of the pond-dwelling American species, while the prolific little *Paragyractis* moths are typical of the swift-water forms. The current-loving larvae build delicate little tentlike shelters, foraging along the bottom for diatoms and other algal foods. Pupation occurs in dome-shaped cocoons that are fitted with both upstream and downstream perforations, and the pupa itself is wrapped in a watertight silken lining. Although the adults are remarkably caddislike, there are strong morphological differences, particularly in the powdery wing coverings that collect on the dense hairlike filaments of their flight organs. Aquatic moths are somewhat more muscular in their thoracic structures, and their rear wings are held at a distinct downward angle below the abdomen while at rest. Adult females leave their mating swarms and enter the water, using their strong hind legs like oars, and lay their eggs in clusters several feet under the water. Such behavior is effective as a wet-fly prototype, and I have observed huge swarms at Cottonwood Lake in Colorado—as well as swift-water mating on the Ausable in the Adirondacks, the Namekagon in Wisconsin, and the Truckee in western Nevada.

The two-winged flies of the Diptera order are precisely named insect suborders and families and genera having only two wings, and have a complete metamorphosis consisting of the ova, larva, pupa, and mature adult. Unlike the mayflies, sedges, and stoneflies, which have two pairs of wings, the aquatic Diptera have a completely atrophied second pair of wings called halteres. There are microscopic scales called calypteres above these knoblike halteres, and some species display a tiny lobe-shaped alula at the root of the wings. There are more than 10,000 American species, although few are wholly aquatic, and their larval and pupal forms are important in the trout diet.

The Tipulidae include the aquatic and terrestrial species of two-winged craneflies. Most craneflies are only semiaquatic, living in wet forests and most streamside soils and decaying tree trunks. Bogs and marshes are prime habitat. There are probably more than 3,000 species. The Tipulidae also include a large number of species found in our trout waters. Pupation has only marginal importance for American fly-fishermen, since it commonly takes place outside the water in moist soils and decaying vegetation. The larvae vary from one-eighth of an inch to almost three inches in length. Such larval forms are abundant in the silt and bottom trash of quiet-flowing streams and ponds. Cranefly larvae forage in decaying aquatic plants and leaf-drift for their food. Their bodies are relatively translucent, their coiled respiratory tracts clearly visible from the outside. Such larvae are perfectly suited for imitation with weighted flies dressed with roughly dubbed bodies. *Tipula* larvae are variously colored and wormlike, ranging from one-half of an inch to two inches in the length of the largest species. Springhole craneflies have more slender larvae and are classified in the *Pedicia* genus, while the much smaller *Helius* larvae are found in the backwaters of spatterdock and slender bulrushes. Riffle craneflies include the *Epiphragma* and *Antocha* larvae, while the *Limnophila* larvae burrow in the bottom silts. The larvae of the *Holorusia* craneflies are the largest, with abdominal structures almost three inches long, while the tiny *Dasymolophilus* larvae are one-eighth of an inch in length. The tiny little snowflies that bring such puzzling midwinter rises of fish in many western rivers are the minute *Chionea* craneflies. The *Phalacrocera* larvae are heavily fringed with respiratory filaments, while the *Limonia* worms are almost as slender as a midge larva. The larval stages of the Tanyderidae are quite strange, particularly genera like the six-tailed *Protoplasa* and the strangely graceful *Bittacomorpha* larvae of the rat-tailed flies. The tiny swift-water larvae of the *Antocha* flies are completely aquatic in their larval state, like the slightly larger *Hexatoma* worms. Many of the larger cranefly larvae are collected by bait dealers in our trout country, along with minnows and nightcrawlers. The larvae are captured by mucking through bogs and backwaters, sluicing the silt and bottom trash through a screen to filter out the worms for sale. The fat Tipulidae larvae are relished by both fishermen and fish.

Fish-wigglers! the old-timers always called them along the South Platte during my boyhood summers in Colorado. *Forget them flies and work with fish-wigglers above Deckers!*

Adult craneflies look like giant mosquitoes, with their slender delicately-veined wings and exaggerated legs. Skilled ghillies on the storied fly-fishing lakes of Ireland, like Lough Sheelin and Lough Corrib and Lough Mask, call the craneflies a hatch of Daddy Longlegs. Their fluttering and hopscotching behavior can trigger some explosive rises of fish. Craneflies are also prototypical of the twitched and skated variant or spider perfected by Edward Ringwood Hewitt. The males are easily recognized by their slender bodies, while the abdominal structures of the females are slightly fatter and more curvilinear. Mating usually occurs under leaves or bridge structures or limbs, with the males and females touching at their abdominal tips. The eggs are deposited both in the water and along the shore, depending on genus and species, and in marshy places nearby. During major periods of hatching and mating, the craneflies can provide excellent dry-fly sport—their hopscotching along the grassy meadow banks of my boyhood rivers in Colorado made the Red Variant dressed in England one of our favorite patterns, and they came in the elegant little Hardy boxes we all remember fondly.

The Psychodidae are the hairy little mothflies that thrive in the moist places along the water, sometimes swarming in remarkable numbers. The wormlike larvae are cigar-shaped and darkly colored at both ends. Their habitat is only semiaquatic in both the larval and pupal stages, making the swarming adults part of the trout diet.

The *Ceuterophlebia* flies are found primarily at high altitudes, which has given them the popular name of Alpine midges. These strange little broad-winged smuts are placed in a single genus, and their immature forms are common in cold little alpine streams, clinging to the stones in the swiftest currents and broken riffles. Populations are seldom important except in our western mountains, where they become significant in the diet of high-country cutthroats and goldens.

The net-veined midges are found in the Blepharoceridae family, and these slender little flies with the tiny exaggeratedly long legs are quite prolific. Their wings have microscopic creases from being folded tightly

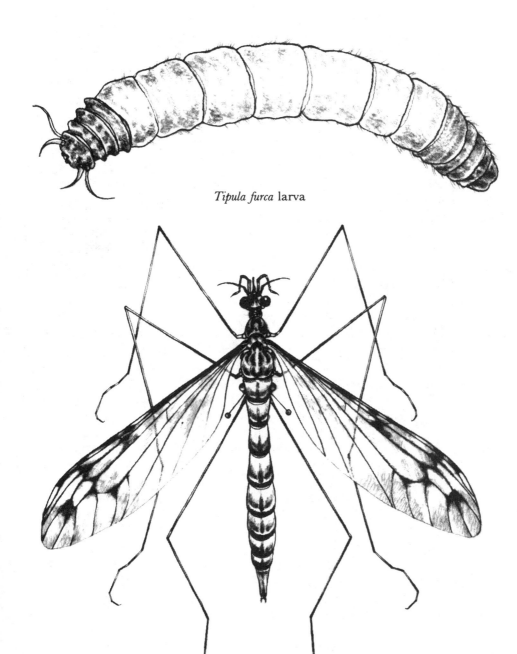

Tipula furca larva

Tipula trivittata adult

inside their pupal cases. The adults are commonly found resting on streamside boulders or swarming under streamside foliage. Larvae are found clinging to the bottom stones in rapid currents, often choosing the tumbling currents and spray below waterfalls. Their diet is algal slime on the bottom. The larvae have rather broad, flattened heads and strongly segmented bodies with five segments. There are six tiny suction organs under the head and each of the body segments. The lateral appendages of each body segment bear respiratory filaments and gills, and there are tiny antennae. The *Blepharocera* midges have pale little larvae, as well as darkly mottled species, while the *Agathon* genus is composed of delicate net-veined flies. The larval forms of the *Bibiocephala* are fat and almost grublike, their body segments less strongly articulated. Mating swarms are familiar to most anglers, and the females migrate into the current to lay their eggs.

The Chaoborinae subfamily consists of three basic genera, each having strange little larvae with gill filaments on the ventral surfaces of the final body segments. These spotted little midges are quite similar to the closely related mosquitoes, although they are nonbiting insects. The males have slender bodies, while the females are surprisingly corpulent insects, and the wings are extended laterally from their thoracic structures both during flight and at rest. Larval wigglers and pupae are quite populous in suitable aquatic habitats, and the *Corethra, Chaoborus,* and *Ecorethra* genera are sometimes important in the trout diet. These tiny spotted-winged midges are familiar to back-country fishermen.

The Dixidae are remarkably delicate flies with transparent wings and extremely attenuated legs. These *Dixa* flies are also sometimes mistaken for mosquitoes, although their legs are more exaggerated in length. Their larvae and pupae also differ slightly, particularly in their caudal appendages. *Dixa* larvae resemble the larval forms of some mosquitoes, except that their thoracic structures are not fused into an exaggeratedly swollen thorax, and one or two pairs of prolegs are found on the ventral surfaces. Adult Dixidae are usually found resting on the shaded side of stones not far above the water. *Dixa* swarms engage in relatively little diurnal activity, although small mating swarms gather over the river at twilight. Mating occurs both in flight and on the stones and bridge abutments along the stream. Eggs are laid in a gelatinous mass just above the current. Larval colonies are concentrated in the backwaters behind stones and deadfalls. Dixidae are separated into two groups in terms of their larval behavior. Larvae of the subgenus *Meringodixa* lie under the surface film, hanging head-down with their caudal gills in the meniscus. *Dixa* and *Paradixa* larvae cling to stones and fallen trees just at the waterline, holding their bodies in a curious U-shaped position, with their heads and caudal filaments just in the surface film. Some actually live above the water, sliding about on the stones and fallen trees in a film of water spread by the tumbling currents. *Dixa* larvae all subsist on microscopic organisms in the surface film. Pupation occurs with the tiny mosquitolike pupa clinging to the stones about two inches above the water, although the *Meringodixa* sometimes remain in the

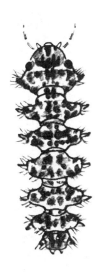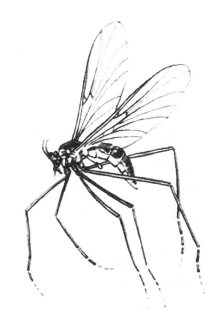

Blepharocera cinerea larva and adult

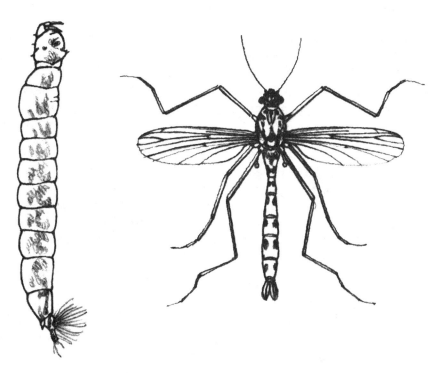

Chaoborus astictopis larva and adult

meniscus tension. The swarming adults are often taken by the trout when they are readily available.

The Simulidae are the familiar riffle smuts and include the infamous black flies that plague our northern rivers in late spring and early summer. The family includes the buffalo and turkey gnats. The adult Simulidae are small broad-winged flies with fat bee-shaped bodies. Many have strongly speckled legs. The females of most species are biting flies that feed on blood, although most prefer animals to man. Feeding occurs during daylight hours, and sometimes their feeding lasts into the nocturnal hours. Adult swarms often range considerable distances from their parent streams. Riffle smut larvae are dirty grayish to black in color, measuring about one-quarter to three-eighths of an inch at larval maturity. There are often so many of these little larvae clinging to the riffle bottoms that the stones appear black with their bodies undulating like fountain mosses in the flow. The larvae cling to the stones with tiny suction-cup appendages at their abdominal posteriors, their mouth parts free to ingest the diatomaceous organisms collected on adjacent fan-shaped filaments. The larvae maneuver from one suction point to another, duck-walking clumsily along the bottom. When they lose their footing, the Simulidae remain attached to a silken thread that is attached to their former footholds. Such salivary filaments are not only anchor lines but also a means of lowering the larvae downstream to a fresh feeding zone, like a rock climber rappelling down a precipice. Respiration is accomplished with retractile blood gills located between the clinging feet, and a preference for the swiftest currents seems to indicate a need for relatively high levels of oxygenation. Both large and small streams have sizable colonies. The larval bodies are soft and saclike, swelling noticeably in their lower third, and at maturity their respiratory networks are visible inside. Simulidae larvae spin a pouchlike cocoon for pupation, with its primary opening facing downstream. The respiratory filaments of the pupae hang downstream from the pupal sac, waving partially in the currents. The adults migrate toward the surface enclosed in a glittering hydrofuge of air bubbles, and the adults fly off immediately on reaching the surface film. Riffle smuts are more important in our streams than many anglers realize, and this past season their imitations were the secret on several glassy flats along the Brodheads just at twilight—tiny imitations dressed with pale hackle wings and fat little bodies of black polypropolene on size twenty-six and twenty-eight hooks.

Pelopinae larvae are fiercely predatory, feeding extensively on other midge forms and occupying the pupal sacs of their victims. They are widely distributed in all types of habitat. Larvae are distinguished by their retractile antennae and prominent prophoracic legs. Caudal gill filaments are also quite prominent, particularly in the *Pentaneura* and *Pelopia* genera. The pupae are quite similar to the pupal forms of the better known mosquitoes. The larval forms are quite similar to those of the Dixidae, while the *Clinotanypus* and *Trichotanypus* and *Coelotanypus* adults are robust, humpbacked little gnats.

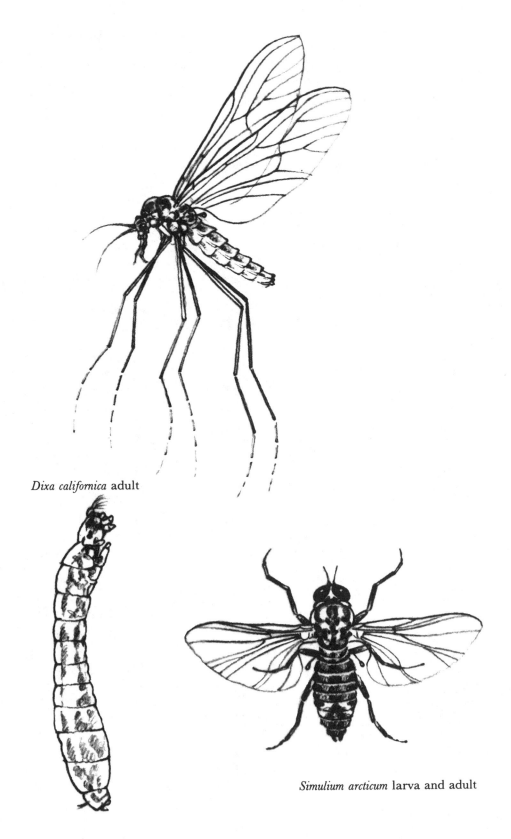

Dixa californica adult

Simulium arcticum larva and adult

The Phoridae are tiny humpbacked gnats that live in the decaying bottom trash and leaf drift, their fat little larvae like grubs in the plant materials. Pupation often takes place in the moist soils of the banks. The *Diploneura* adults are muscular little midges, with broad wings and strong tightly-bunched legs. The Empididae are the slender little dance flies, and their nymphs are highly predatory, living in the moist margins of lakes and streams. The tiny *Hilara* flies are common on eastern waters, and the *Hemerodromia* dance flies are found distributed across the continent. The larval forms are surprisingly similar to the *Atherix* snipe fly larvae. Such flies are considerably more important in the trout diet, particularly along trout lakes and quiet flowages, than most fishermen have believed in the past. The larval forms inhabit the silty roots of elodea and other aquatic weeds, with dense populations in the eddying shallows. During peak cycles of emergence, which occur cyclically through the season, the fish lie waiting to intercept the evolving pupae migrating from their weed-bed cocoons toward the surface. The final prehatching moments are sometimes spent with their respiratory filaments in the surface film, and the pupae are available by the thousands and thousands. Although they are minuscule, the pupae are so numerous that even large trout can fill their stomachs while expending minimal energy.

The Ceratopogonidae are tiny, biting midges, and include such tiny sand gnats and punkies as the *Palpomyia* and *Culicoides* midges. The *Palpomyia* gnats feed on other insects, while the fierce little *Culicoides* sand midges are bloodsuckers that seldom hesitate to feed on man. The immature larvae are mostly aquatic, including both fresh and brackish coastal habitats. The larvae are slender and eellike, completely legless along their serpentine lengths, and have a few short respiratory filaments at the tip of their bodies. Larval populations are found in all types of water, from silty backwaters to weedy currents and the boulder eddies in swift streams.

Although some entomologists include the Tabanidae and the larval forms of the *Syrphus* flies among the common trout foods, these insects usually inhabit stagnant stream margins and marshy backwaters along lakes and impoundments, and trout seldom inhabit or forage in such marginal waters. However, the similar Stratiomyidae are worth imitating. The soldier flies have only a few aquatic species. They are not exceptionally abundant, but the trout seem to take them with relish. The larvae of the *Stratiomyia* and *Odontomyia* soldier flies are spindle-shaped, with a fine series of plumelike bristles that protect the breathing spiracles. Soldier-fly larvae are largely carnivorous, and scavenge with surprising agility. Pupation occurs in the moist soils along the banks. Snipe flies are found in swifter habitats, loving the coarse gravel and bottom stones of many trout streams. Their larvae creep cautiously among the bottom currents, using their leglike protuberances to travel. The heads of these *Atherix* larvae are chisel-shaped to enable them to face into the current, and their bodies terminate in a pair of fringed gills. These Rhagionidae are more available to the trout, and the ability to withstand radical variations in habitat makes

Metriocnemus edwardsi larva and adult

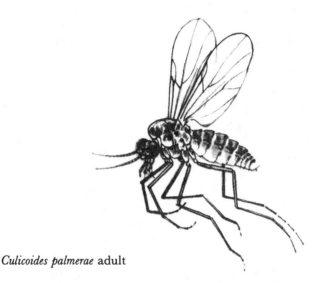

Culicoides palmerae adult

them intriguing—specimens are even recorded from geothermal springs in both Lassen National Park and the Yellowstone.

The Tendipedinae subfamily includes a number of aquatic midge genera, and these tiny flies are so prolific and widely distributed that they are extremely important in the trout diet. These midges vary from the minute *Microtendipes* flies, which average less than one-eighth of an inch in length, to the half-inch adults of the larger *Chironomus* midges. With the exception of the *Calopsectra* genus, most of these Tendipedinae live in quiet waters. Some exist at surprising depths in lakes and impoundments, although most are found in beds of aquatic vegetation and silt in water less than ten feet deep. Only a few species inhabit the mesopelagic depths. Fishermen largely know these delicate midges in terms of their *Chironomus* species, which have been written about widely, although there are actually more than a dozen closely related genera.

These two-winged midges are so prolific that particularly fertile lakes can harbor as many as 2,000 pupae in a single cubic yard of water. There is some confusion in our knowledge of the Tendipedinae, since various scholars have classified both larvae and adults separately, without much correlation between stages. The midges hatch sporadically from early spring to late autumn, and on many rivers and lakes that remain relatively ice-free there are sizable winter swarms. Although the most impressive populations are unquestionably found in lakes and reservoirs, the midges are also found in profusion on major rivers. Over the past thirty years I have observed many impressive rises of fish to these midges, from the flats of the Delaware and Connecticut and Beaverkill to the extensive pupal feeding on famous western rivers like the Henry's Fork and Yellowstone and Frying Pan.

There are 10,000 possible species. The adults are relatively long-legged flies with bodies slightly longer than their wings. Their thoracic shoulders are slightly humpbacked. Size ranges from one-eighth of an inch to one-half of an inch in length. The wings are grayish blue to pale chalky hyaline. Male bodies are slender and semitransparent, while the female midges are more corpulent. Since these prolific midges are undeniably the most important trout foods in the entire Diptera order, it is impossible to place too much importance on their relatively unnoticed role in fly-fishing. Our myopic neglect of the midges is understandable, given our preoccupation with the larger and better known aquatic hatches.

Some British writers have called these insects short-winged gnats, but it was Alfred Ronalds in his *Fly-Fisher's Entomology* who first called them midges. Most modern anglers use his terminology. However, several popular names have evolved on waters in Ireland and the United Kingdom. Scottish anglers have long talked about their midges with names like the Blae and Black, while on the fertile limestone lakes of Ireland they are often called buzzers and duck flies. British anglers call them midges and gnats.

During their transformation from the larval stage of development to the point of pupal emergence, the Tendipedinae are available to the trout in almost astronomical numbers. Emergence occurs when vast quantities of these minuscule insects migrate toward the surface, where they drift suspended with their gill filaments breathing in the meniscus film. During the pupal time, the insect reaches its prehatching maturity and then splits its pupal sac to hatch. When these pupae are readily available, schools of fish sometimes cruise the lake-size flats of our larger western rivers, and reservoirs from Eleven Mile in Colorado to the weedy shallows of Crane Prairie and Wickiup in Oregon, taking midge larvae and pupae by the millions in gentle porpoising rises.

Chironomus riparius larva

Chironomus riparius pupa

Adult midges have tiny heads which virtually merge with their thoracic shoulders. The dorsal surface of the thorax is clearly humped. The mesothorax is exaggerated and supports a single pair of wings. These wings are relatively small when compared with the legs and length of the abdomen. Some species hold their wings back along their bodies, and the delicate *Anisomera* midges are typical of such flies, hatching in profusion on many swift-flowing European rivers. Other midges hold their wings at right angles to the thorax, almost like tiny spent-wing mayflies without tails, and there are nine body segments. The midges are completely devoid of even atrophied cerci. Males are distinguished from females in several points. They have conspicuous plumelike gills that are absent in the females, and the male abdomen is quite slender. The final body segment has tiny microscopic forceps. The females are slightly fatter and delicately tapered, and are somewhat larger in size. Midges have a complete metamorphosis, consisting of the egg, larva, pupa, and adult form. There is little change between emergence and egg laying, except for a slight darkening.

Larval forms are surprisingly active, swimming in open waters and ranging the mesopelagic depths of many lakes. There are almost numberless colonies in the shallows too, reaching optimal populations in alkaline waters. Distribution of the pupae is somewhat dependent on weather, wind conditions, direction of current flows, and water temperatures. Weather and water temperatures affect the length of time spent escaping the pupal skin, and both currents and winds affect their lines of drift.

Midges thrive in all types of water. Specimens are commonly found in ditches, ponds, marshes and bogs, lakes, reservoirs, canals, rivers, streams, and tiny brooks. Emergence in their diurnal hatching cycles varies both with species and time of year. During the early weeks of the season the dark little midges come off at midday and into the afternoon. Females return to join the mating swarms and lay their eggs in the evenings. Most midday flights are composed of males, and the male swarms are usually found well inland from their parent lakes and streams. Later in the year, emergence occurs later and later in the afternoon, until the late summer midges hatch at nightfall. Some species are apparently nocturnal. Other summer species hatch just at daylight, and I once witnessed an immense rise of fish to emerging midge pupae just after daylight at Ferdon's Pool on the Beaverkill. Winter hatches are also common, and a few years ago I fished over a fine February rise of trout at the Slaughterhouse Bridge on the Roaring Fork—when the population of Aspen was preoccupied with the peak of the Colorado skiing and the lodgepole thickets were dark against the snow.

Midge imitations are always in my fly boxes these days. The imitative patterns have worked many times in recent years, from the still twilight flats in the Catskills to the sloughlike bends of the California spring creeks. Such flies have also worked miracles from the grayling lagoons of Alaska and still cutthroat flats of Montana to the still weed-trailing bends of the Malleo in Argentina or the smooth boat-pools of the Calcurrupe in the foothill forests of Chile.

Our observations on aquatic entomology have been intended as an introduction to the basic insect forms in our trout waters, without any details of specific species and fly hatches. Such details are found in a number of fine books, such as *The Streamside Guide* and the more recent *Hatches* and *Selective Trout*, or my earlier books on fly-fishing entomology, *Nymphs* and *Matching the Hatch*. These pages are merely a primer on our aquatic insects, with some insights into both their habits and the response they trigger from the trout. More detailed knowledge of our specific fly hatches on a particular reach of water is the final piece in our fly-fishing puzzle, once the other techniques of angling are mastered.

Such knowledge is perhaps our ultimate skill.

7. Observations on Feeding and Rise Forms

Dunraven Castle is a forbidding pile of crenellated ramparts and terraces that reach down toward the castle-beat meadows on the Maigue. Peacocks and pheasants wander its lawns. Its Victorian tower dominates a series of formal views at various points on the estate, its roof slates glisten with rain. The river is perhaps the best of the Irish limestone streams, winding across its water meadows through the fox-hunting village of Adare.

The village street is lined with whitewashed thatch-roofed houses, and it was filled with fox hounds and riders in scarlet coats waiting for the master of hounds to start the hunt. It was raining softly and the hounds shook themselves restlessly. The horsemen sat their sleekly groomed hunters in the rain, watching the pewter-colored clouds with dismay.

It's a soft morning, said the riverkeeper. *Better fishing than fox hunting in this weather.* The rain fell steadily in the street.

Much more softness and we'll drown! I replied wryly.

Like all limestone streams, the Maigue has a remarkably rich water chemistry and abundant fly hatches. There are such heavy hatches in late spring that an angler can gather specimens like berries from the foliage along the river meadows.

The problem is not just matching the hatch. Since there are several flies hatching almost every day, and more of some species are found in some water types than others, individual fish can be seeing more of one particular insect than another. Fish below one of the swift-water weirs may be concentrating on the Trichoptera that hatch from their oxygenated currents. The trout in a smooth run of the meadows above the castle are frequently taking small Iron Blue Duns, particularly on rainy spring

673

mornings, while the fish in still reaches of the Maigue are often feeding on the big *Ephemera* drakes that hatch from their silt beds. Typical mornings find the current covered with rises, and it is the character of the rises that forms a principal clue in what attracts each fish.

Roger Foster is the riverkeeper on the Dunraven Castle beats of the Maigue. Foster is knowledgeable about its fly hatches, and is a skilled fly dresser in his own right. His ability to determine what any single fish is taking is remarkable.

There is a fine reach of water below the castle where the ruins of a twelfth-century abbey lie half-concealed in ivy and mosses across the meadows. Its alders and water grasses and reeds were filled with slate-colored caddisflies, and in the quiet reach of river upstream, cinnamon-colored sedges were fluttering off the water. The fish were already working steadily when we crossed the ancient three-arch bridge and left the car at the fence stile below the monastery.

Look at the Iron Blues coming down! I pointed. *The fish must be taking them!* The rises were splashy and bold above the stone weir.

Perhaps! Foster studied the water.

There were several good trout working in the smooth, gathering currents above the weir. Tiny Iron Blues were emerging, along with the odd hatching sedge that fluttered downstream. Some big green-winged mayflies were hatching too. My first cast worked out and dropped an Iron Blue over a fish against the weeds.

He refused it! I muttered.

Several more floats were rejected, although they came over the trout drag-free and riding perfectly on the current. The fish did not even bother to acknowledge the fly.

It's not the Iron Blue, I sighed. *What're they taking?*

The rises are either strong swirls, Roger Foster observed thoughtfully, *or rather splashy.* The fish continued to work steadily.

Maybe it's hatching sedges?

Perhaps you're right, Foster agreed. *I don't think they're feeding on the surface.*

Let's watch them, I said.

Downstream from the stonework bridge there was a splashy swirl and a caddisfly lifted above the rise. The trout took a second splash at the natural and missed again.

That trout tried for a hatching sedge pupa, I said eagerly, *and it missed its adult too!* Another fish showed splashily against the grass.

Exactly. Foster nodded.

Roger Foster is British, from the border rivers of Yorkshire, and his fly books are filled with soft partridge-hackled wet flies. *You have a Partridge and Orange?* I asked. *Or maybe a Woodcock Spider with a hare's mask dubbing?*

I've got both, Foster replied.

That fish was chasing a cinnamon-colored fly, I said. *Can you let me have a Partridge and Orange?*

It's yours! He searched his sheepskin case.

My fly line darted out into the misting rain and dropped the little partridge-hackled pattern above the fish. It settled and sank and started its current swing. Following the swing with the rod tip, I felt the wet fly coming around just above the trout and I teased it once. There was an eager swirl, and I tightened just as the tug of a good fifteen-inch fish telegraphed back through the rod. The fish fought stubbornly along the thick beds of ranunculus weed.

That's it! I thought happily.

It was the secret for the trout rising on that particular stretch, but as the morning progressed, the misting rain soon dropped the temperature several degrees. The tiny slate-colored *Baetis* flies began coming down the current and the rise forms changed in the smooth run above the castle weir. These were small suction rises now, slow and full of confidence, as the trout picked off the hatching Iron Blues like berries.

They've switched, I yelled.

Perhaps, Foster agreed. *Watch for the bubbles—they tell you if they're surface feeding now.* The trout porpoised lazily now.

Let's try Iron Blues, I suggested.

The darkly hackled little dry flies were the answer, and we took good fish steadily for more than an hour, until the hatch reached its peak and began to ebb. Some fish continued to take the little upwinged dun, but now there were many refusals. Finally every fish kept working steadily without taking our flies.

What's wrong? I asked.

I'm not sure, Foster replied. *Let's watch them a while and try to find out what they're doing now.*

The rises were coming frequently again, although there were few hatching duns left on the current. There were far too many rises for the insects visible on the water, and the fish had adopted a steady feeding rhythm to something we could not see. The rise forms were clearly surface types, large rings filled with tiny bubbles in the smooth current.

Spent spinners?

It's possible, Foster agreed thoughtfully. *There've been some pretty good mating swarms of mayflies.*

It would explain the steady feeding, I said.

You're right, Foster nodded, *and the size of the rise forms rules out smuts or gnats.* The soft rises continued.

Iron Blue spinner tied spent?

Try one, Foster said.

It was the solution, and we took fish steadily again until it was time for me to start south to Lough Currane on the Ring of Kerry. We started down through the meadows toward the planted grove of sequoias where we had left the cars. Descending from the upper weirs in the meadows above the castle beats, Foster spotted a big brown working boldly along the alders. It was a seventy-five-foot cast away, and its strong rise forms were utterly unlike the gentle spinner feeding upstream.

What the hell's he doing? I asked.

He's not taking spent spinners, Foster laughed. *Not with big, showy swirls like those!* The big fish rose again.

There was an occasional Green Drake hatching too, and the sporadic intervals between rises suggested that the fish might be taking these big *Ephemera* mayflies. The size of the rise forms also suggested such large insects might be the answer, and we stood watching the trout's feeding station.

Maybe he's taking the big drakes, I said.

Very likely, Foster agreed. *There are good marl beds above that fish—he could be seeing a lot of them coming down.*

Two big mayflies came fluttering and hopscotching down the current, directly over the trout, and passed its position untouched. The flies had scarcely passed before there was a flash deep in the current, and its force worked to the surface in a strong boil.

He's nymphing! I thought aloud.

Yes. Foster started searching his fly-books. *And the rises are too strong for anything but the nymphs of those big flies.*

That must be it! I said.

It was unquestionably the solution, since I dropped an imitation *Ephemera* nymph above the trout and teased it along in the manner of a swimming natural about to hatch. The fish took hard, and I left the nymph in its jaws when the 5X tippet parted deep among the alder roots.

That fish was at least four pounds, Foster said.

Owe you a nymph, I said sheepishly.

And that was the end of a typical late-spring morning on one of the best limestone streams in Europe, a few hours filled with a sequence of important lessons in reading rise forms and behavior.

Such behavior offers an extremely important series of clues concerning fly selection and presentation, for both subsurface rises and surface feeding. The study of rise forms is not entirely new. Skues first explored the subject brilliantly in his *Way of a Trout with a Fly* in 1921, and Colonel E. W. Harding enlarged our knowledge in his perceptive book *The Fly-Fisher and the Trout's Point of View* exactly a decade later. Taverner also discussed the rise form in his *Trout Fishing from All Angles* during this same period, while Bergman made several fresh observations on rise forms and behavior in *Trout* just before the Second World War. Vincent Marinaro also contributed a series of original concepts to our theory of rise forms in his book *A Modern Dry-Fly Code,* and added several striking photographs of rising fish in his subsequent book *In the Ring of the Rise.*

There are a surprising number of subsurface and surface rise forms in the catalogue of trout behavior, and each is important in the process of matching the hatch. We all know that a rise form is the visible disturbance of the current when a fish is feeding on something. The character of these rises is affected by the size and movements of the natural, its depth or position near the surface film, the sucking action required to ingest the insect, the speed of the current, and the density of the water. Large flies tend to provoke relatively large, showy rises. Insects that flutter across the surface or dance above it laying their eggs cause the trout to rise quickly to prevent their escape. Flies poised on the surface film, lying imprisoned in its meniscus tension, or drifting just under the surface elicit specific and recognizable types of feeding. Both flying insects and hatching caddis pupae can cause a fish to jump clear of the surface, as it tries to capture the first in midair and pursues the second toward the surface and as it leaves the water. Wild fish and stocked trout also make distinctive rise forms while feeding. Native specimens are confident of their feeding skills, and capture their foods as quietly as possible, with the expenditure of minimal energy. Since their existence consists of a delicate equilibrium between calories expended and food ingested, such behavior is understandable. Hatchery fish are ill-mannered and less skillful in their feeding. Like chickens in a yard, they have been forced to compete for their food, snatching it from their fellow cellmates greedily. They are unaccustomed to feeding in a current, and often clumsily miss their prey. Both their lack of table manners and their clumsiness result in splashy rises bearing little relationship to the size and habits of the fly hatches.

Much speculation has taken place among anglers concerning a trout's motivation for the rise. Some observers have identified ten different drives, each with close parallels in human behavior, and it certainly does not seem illogical to ascribe rises to hunger and curiosity. Sometimes territoriality and defensive anger seem to become a factor. Hunger is relatively constant at optimal feeding temperatures, so mere availability may trigger a rise of fish. Repetitive casting or an enticing retrieve can sometimes coax or tease a trout into taking the fly. Such discussions can never reach any concrete conclusions, but they offer interesting hypotheses in clubrooms and fishing camps everywhere.

The starting point lies in the truth that trout do indeed rise. Why they rise is an endlessly intriguing puzzle, but their tendency to rise is the blessing upon which much of our sport is constructed.

Subaquatic rises are less varied than those caused by surface feeding. Big nymphal forms in shallow water or swimming types of subaquatic insects often trigger swirls or splashy rises not unlike surface-feeding activity. Some swirls are a delayed echo of a fish turning deep in the current, its displacement of water strong enough to bulge the surface. The flash of a trout turning on its side along the bottom, the sun catching its pale flanks, is a viable rise-form. Sometimes a swirl echoes to the surface from a flash rise, demonstrating clearly the sequence of a delayed swirl. These are common underwater rise forms.

Nymphal activity is often focused in terms of bulge and hump rises. Such fish typically lie in shallows below a rich lodge of nymphs or in the currents underneath a trailing reach of weeds, ranging back and forth to seize the hatching nymphs and pupae. Such subaquatic forms are also simply foraging or migrating, and the fish instinctively select an effective position of effortless feeding. When such a fish discovers a nymph swimming just beyond its normal line of drift, it sometimes turns and follows hastily, takes its prey with a bold subsurface rise, and drifts back to its feeding station. The hasty turn often results in a bulging displacement of the surface, punctuated with the swirling rise itself. The surface meniscus is not actually broken, although its disturbance is often strong.

Such fish are quite commonly found over weedbeds from our western spring creeks to the classic limestone streams of our eastern mountains. Bulging rises are typical in such rich waters. Their feeding is often distinguished by a torpedolike wake and bow-wave bulging ahead of the fish. Such diagonal wakes in the water are often made by a frightened trout bolting for cover, but a bulging fish that is feeding quickly returns to its original station.

Similar distortion and stretching of the surface film occurs in the humping rise. This maneuver involves an underwater porpoise roll in a vertical plane rather than the typical subsurface swirl that terminates a bulge-rise sequence. Such a humping roll usually results when a fish intercepts a hatching nymph just before it reaches the surface. Hatching mayflies and sedge pupae both spark these rise forms. Flat little ripples often emanate from a humping rise, but these are quickly dampened and lost in the current. Both bulging and humping are sometimes accompanied by a kind of rooting activity, in which the fish moves into the weeds to dislodge nymphs, and then turns to take them downstream.

Tailing itself is the result of foraging head-down in relatively shallow water, until such efforts are betrayed by the disturbance of the caudal fin in the surface. Such feeding is typical in streams particularly rich in shrimps and sowbugs, although snails and cased sedge larvae are also disloged from the bottom by tailing. Such head-down feeding along the bottom also occurs in relatively deep water, and I have taken fish on big western rivers that literally have rubbed their noses raw among the stones. Many fishermen believe that a visible tail disturbing the surface invariably indicates tailing activity, but a large fish lying horizontally in the current can also break the film with its tail during its rise forms. Such rises are not true tailing, which occurs only when a feeding trout is rooting head-down on the bottom.

The subsurface wedge rise is one nymphing activity in which the tail of the fish does disturb the surface. It consists of a trout lying in wait just under the meniscus film, intercepting the nymphs with lazy confidence and skill. Its head does not disturb the current when the hatching nymph is taken, but its dorsal surfaces and tail do distort or penetrate the film. The rise form is wedge-shaped and strong, its apex into the current upstream. The speed of the current has an effect on the size and configuration of this rise form. Slow current tongues mean more elapsed time between the displacement of the back, and the visible disturbance of the surface by the tail. Fast water compresses these effects into a tighter wedge-shaped rise that is quickly lost in the current.

The lexicon of surface rises is more varied. The common suction rise is typical of a good fish in relatively quiet water. It is strongly circular and lazily confident in character. There is usually an audible sucking sound, leaving one or two bubbles riding the film. The true suction rise occurs to an insect riding *on* the current, and the bubbles confirm its surface feeding. The presence of such bubbles after a rise is interesting. It is possible to understand them if you try to pick an insect from the current. It is virtually impossible unless you catch it by the wings. Letting an insect float into your palm sounds easy, but it never works. Your hand divides the current and diverts the fly to one side or the other.

The fish is confronted with a similar problem. Its jaws could easily divide the current and divert an insect past its mouth. Yet a fish does not rise for an insect in this fashion. It simply opens its gill covers and its gills, lets the current flow through, and the hapless insect is trapped in its gills or throat. It swallows as it settles back into positon, releasing the air bubbles through its gills. Of course, some fish pick a fly from the surface with a rapier-quick thrust or a vertical sipping rise, but these rise forms are more common with small insects or spent flies.

However, the bubbles that follow a rise are often the echoes of air ingested with the prey, and clearly indicate that the fly was riding *on* the surface. Sometimes bubbles result solely from the rich oxygenation of the water or the vigor of the rise itself, but in a quiet rise form such telltale signs usually point to unmistakable surface feeding.

The smutting or dimple rise is typical of fish feeding on small diet forms in quiet currents or flats. It consists of a subtle little ring in the water, and is commonly associated with feeding on terrestrials or small spent mayflies. Dimple rises are calm and unhurried and can sometimes conceal a surprisingly good fish, particularly on waters rich with small flies and nymphs and midges.

The common swirl is sometimes rather showy and is frequently audible. The swirl is caused by a fish taking something from the meniscus with a sidewise turn under the surface and is usually the result of moving to take an insect coming down outside the fish's direct line of drift. Its eagerness is often a clue to the size of the insect taken and perhaps an indication of its hopscotching and fluttering action on the water.

The head-and-tail rise is a surface version of the wedge rise to a hatching nymphal form. It is perhaps the most common of surface rises to insects pinioned *in* the film, and consists of the snout and dorsal fin and tail breaking the surface in swift succession. Trout taking food with a head-and-tail rise are quite commonly taking spent mayfly spinners, but other small insects hopelessly caught in the film are also taken in this manner. Sometimes hatching flies are imprisoned in the film in rainy or windy weather, or their wings are trapped in the meniscus in broken currents. Then head-and-tail rises often result. Sometimes a good fish concludes its head-and-tail sequence with an almost joyous wriggle of its tail once the insect has been captured. Such tail wriggling was aptly labelled a satisfaction rise by the late Ray Bergman in *Trout*, and it precedes the return of a successful fish to its station.

The sipping rise is a particularly subtle variation on the sucking rise form, usually focused on smuts and terrestrials and other tiny insects in the film. It signals a fish that is feeding both lazily, and with irritating confidence and calm. Such trout often hang almost vertically under the surface in executing a sipping rise, drifting back with the same smooth current-speed of its prey. Francis Francis made a remarkable observation in his *Book of Angling* in 1867, with these lines on the sipping rise:

> Always pay particular attention to the fish which you see sipping under the banks; and don't be deluded into the notion that because you see a fish make no more break on the water than a minnow would, that he is a minnow, for he is quite likely to be a three-pounder. It is strange how quietly a big fish will often take fly after fly, close to a bank, with only just his upper lip pushed into the surface to suck in the victim.

Francis makes an important point about rise forms. Many experienced fly-fishermen too often assume that only a determined or showy rise indicates a trout, and that tiny rises are made by baitfish or other coarse species. It is a frequent mistake. Eric Taverner also discusses the sipping rise form in his *Trout Fishing from All Angles*:

> Duns which are carried out of their course along the main stream into little bays and eddies close to the bank sail around on the reverse current, and it is exceptional for one of them to make any effort to fly away into the air, either because they are defective in some way, and have been unable to dry their wings, or have become partly waterlogged.
> Their handicap is at once appreciated by the trout, which cruise calmly under them, break the surface very gently with the nose and take them with a sip, making a tiny ring within the smooth area of which there is rarely a bubble. The rise as far as one can see does not really seem to break the surface. Perhaps the intake of water with the sipping generates a gentle vortex which causes the rise-form.

The slash rise points to the capture of a fluttering sedge, the egg laying of mayflies, and any large insect skittering across the current on the wind. The fish are forced to strike quickly at such times, and one may often find the slash rise in relatively swift currents when a good hatch excites the trout into feeding.

The jump rise frequently occurs when a fish is holding underneath a swarm of sedges or gnats. It is especially common on rivers that hold heavy populations of Trichoptera, and can result both from pursuing an emerging pupa or trying to capture a hopscotching adult caddis. Sometimes a jump rise is focused upon other flying insects, like mayflies dancing in their mating flights, or laying their eggs on the surface. Trout working in this manner are difficult to catch, since the naturals are typically in flight, but sometimes it is possible by quickly delivering an imitation to the last position of a rise. It must be done instantly before the trout leaves the spot, and such tactics are important on some waters. The famous Lauterach in Bavaria is such a river, and in late spring it has heavy hatches of *Ephemera vulgata* drakes. They emerge and mate in clouds of naturals, and the brief season when they are present is called the *Sprungzeit*—the leaping time.

The pyramid rise is a particularly vigorous activity between the slash rise and an outright jump. It is a vertical rise form that rather violently displaces the surface. It can be both an extreme example of the hump rise, or a jump rise that fails to clear the water. Sometimes it seems like a slash rise exaggerated by the gusting wind, and it is perhaps most commonly found with big sedge pupae about to hatch. However, I have also observed the trout working with pyramid rise forms to other species, particularly the larger *Stenonema* and *Isonychia* drakes in windy weather. Salmon fly and willow fly hatches can trigger such behavior on our western rivers. Bergman mentions a similar experience with the pyramid rise during a hatch of Green Drakes in windy weather, and in *Trout* he described an incredible fishing day on the Neversink at Bridgeville.

The double-whorl rise is a kidney-shaped disturbance of the surface film, consisting of two interlocking rings. The center of the rise form is disturbed and sometimes punctuated with the telltale bubble. The rise is quite vigorous in its character. The faster the current, the more tightly the two rings are interlocked, and tend to condense into a single circle. However, the two rings seldom coincide except in a very swift current-tongue. Eric Taverner makes the observation in *Trout Fishing from All Angles* that as the two kidney-shaped rings converge, their center is often covered with a sprinkling of tiny bubbles. It is a rise form most commonly found with relatively large insects that hatch in great numbers, like the Hendricksons on our eastern rivers and the Pale Morning Duns in the Rocky Mountain country. Taverner describes similar behavior with the fine hatches of Blue-winged Olives on the British rivers, and as this is being written at the Fellows cottage on the North Branch of the Au Sable, we have been seeing these rise forms during heavy *Ephemerella* hatches.

The double whorl is similar to the head-and-tail rise, coupled with a sucking rise that leaves a bubble. It does not seem to result from penetration of the surface by either the head or the tail, but from a bulging pressure of both below the film. Sometimes the snout and the dorsal generate the interlocking circles. The rise is quick and eager, and these two subsurface impressions come in rapid succession, forming the interlocking rings. Although it is not often observed, the head sometimes breaks the surface, and the air taken along with the floating prey is expelled through the gills. The bubble always lies in the upstream ring. The double-whorl is constant in shape in quiet currents, but in faster water its typical configurations are condensed and considerably distorted.

The bubble ring is a subtle rise form filled with little bubbles. It is very typical of still-water rises to spent mayflies or other insects trapped in the surface film, and is mostly observed in quiet flats and pools and eddies. It is perhaps related to a head-and-tail rise that barely breaks the meniscus.

The porpoise roll is another rise form most commonly found in connection with insects imprisoned in the film. It clearly resembles a porpoise following a ship's hull, and some writers have compared it to a hunting horse taking a hedgerow. It is perhaps a relatively vigorous head-and-tail rise that exposes the entire dorsal surface of the fish from snout to caudal fin. Although it is usually found with big spinners riding flush within the surface film, it does occur with other insect forms.

The inspection rise is the first of a series of refusal rises. It consists of rising to a drifting natural or artificial and riding the current downstream while the morsel is studied and inspected by the fish. It often indicates that the fly is rather close in color and size to the naturals. Sometimes an inspection rise is executed by a fish locked under the fly, and sometimes a fish hangs almost vertically beneath it, in a kind of incomplete vertical sip rise. The inspection rise is typical of good trout in relatively quiet currents. The angler who has not experienced a big fish drifting back cautiously under his fly cannot imagine how unsettling it can be, particularly on a smooth-flowing flat. Two things can happen after an inspection rise: the wary trout may simply return to its orginal station—the usual result—or it may start back to its feeding position, turn with a sudden change of heart, and take the fly hard.

The investigation rise is less nerve wracking. It involves pulling a fish off its station to examine an approaching fly, although not as closely as in a true inspection rise. Such movements by the fish can be both vertical and lateral, including a minimal rise in the water toward the fly and a slight shift toward the left or right. It indicates that the fly pattern is interesting enough to attract the attention of the trout, but not a close enough imitation to trigger a better inspection of its details.

The flash rise typically occurs under a floating fly, or behind a wet artificial in the act of being retrieved. It indicates a definite interest in the fly, although something in its character or presentation is unquestionably off or wrong. There is little or no disturbance on the surface, only the flash of a turning fish. Often after such a fish has been rested, it will take a smaller fly of the same pattern on a slower, teasing retrieve. The flash rise is common to both spiders and variants, and has earned these flies the name of fish-finders. One can frequently discover the holding lies of large trout with such lures, returning another time during a hatch to take them with more conventional hatch-matching tactics.

Splash rises to spiders and variants are equally common, and are sometimes mistaken for actual rises by inexperienced anglers. Such rises usually consist of a splashy, half-hearted strike, and usually result in a missed or lightly hooked fish. Such missed rises indicate the fish are not really interested, and even a novice does not often miss a trout when it really wants the fly. Splash rises are usually indicative of more interest in the fly than a mere flash of a turning fish beneath its drift. Nymphing fish will sometimes respond splashily to a floating imitation, and can sometimes be taken with an appropriate nymphal pattern.

Skues has described the *fausse montée* in his writings, and the false rise can be confusing in certain light conditions. It consists of a rise toward the fly that comes in relatively close to the fish's line of drift or current swing, and then a rapid, alarmed retreat back to the original feeding lie. This sudden reversal often causes a swirl to reach the surface slightly downstream from the actual turning of the fish. It can be mistaken for a rise if the light makes it impossible to see either the bottom or the fish. Of course, the actual position of the fish is above both the subsurface turning of the trout, and the transmitted swirl that reaches the surface still farther downstream. Depending upon current speed, the fish can lie as much as two or three feet above the position of its false rise, or virtually anywhere along the full current-swing of a wet fly if it has followed it around. With a good fish leaving the swirl of a *fausse montée* in the surface currents, it pays to rest the trout briefly and try it again, either with another drag-free float or a somewhat slower, teasing subsurface swing of the fly.

The rejection rise is the despair of any angler who frequents hard-fished water with highly selective trout. It consists of a fish coming all the way from the holding lie to the peak of the rise and touching or almost touching the fly without actually taking. It is extremely frustrating, since it is often the result of moodiness rather than anything to do with the angler or his artificial. It almost seems as if the fish touches the fly to examine its viability. Perhaps the best example of consistent rejection-rise behavior in my experience was the difficult fish in the Barnyard stretch of Letort Spring Run that Ross Trimmer angrily christened one August evening when it had come a dozen times to touch his fly without actually getting hooked.

Trout-without-a-Mouth! Ross grumbled.

It would free rise steadily in its channel in the *Elodea*, coming steadily to a perfect float with a leafhopper or beetle imitation, but it touched the fly without actually taking it. That trout became legendary all that summer. Visitors were led there to fish for it unwittingly, and found its steady rise forms and refusals a terrible initiation to the Letort and its selective trout. The fish was finally taken with a tippet size slightly finer than average, even for that light-tackle shrine, and a beetle imitation dressed a little smaller than the naturals.

Vincent Marinaro outlined a number of important observations on rise-forms and behavior in both editions of his *Modern Dry-Fly Code*. He points out that in moderate currents, the sequence of the rise is often structured on three separate points in the stream. The first is the threshold of vision, at which a fish first senses the approach of either the natural or its imitation. The second is its observation post or holding lie, the station chosen by the trout to watch for food coming down its line of drift. The third point is the zone, lying slightly downstream from its observation post, where a fish actually intercepts and takes its prey. The distance between these three points varies widely with the speed and character of the current.

It is either compressed in slow water or diffused in faster rates of flow. It is extremely important to remember these three positions when you cannot see the fish or its holding lie, since many fishermen waste time casting to the position of the rise form they can see, rather than to the threshold of vision above the actual observation post used by the fish. It is a critical facet of tactical knowledge.

It was along the Letort that Ross Trimmer and I watched another footnote to rise-form behavior. There was a good fish beside a brushpile in Otto's Meadow, and it was inspecting each float of my beetle with the intensity of a microbiologist using an electron microscope. It was frustrating to watch the trout study my fly thoughtfully.

What's wrong? I asked unhappily.

Nothing! Ross Trimmer ejected a stream of tobacco into the grass. *Fish can't see your 7X tippet and likes your fly—he's just waiting for the legs to kick!*

8. Streamside Studies in Selectivity

Thirty-five years have passed since that summer evening on the Little South Pere Marquette in Michigan. Its smooth currents eddied through the deadfalls below our camp, their dancing flow reflecting green and gold from the dying sunlight in the treetops. Smoke from the cookfire of our campsite upstream drifted down on the imperceptible stirrings of the wind, and there were no rises anywhere as I walked down the logging trace beside the river and slipped into the Forks Pool.

Fishing was more simple in those summers past.

We usually fished only two or three fly patterns, and they were enough in those days. Our fly boxes held hairwing Royal Coachmen and the Adams spentwing in several hook sizes. There were other patterns too, like the Corey Calftails so popular in Michigan during those years, and elegant Female Beaverkills dressed spent with pale ginger hackles to imitate the *Ephemerella* mating swarms of spring and early summer. There were a few wet flies and streamers as well, but most of our fish were caught on the Royal Coachman or the dark mixed hackle patterns like the Woodchuck or the Adams spentwing, tied just as it was born on the feather-littered workbench of old Len Halliday at Mayfield. It was usually unnecessary to fish anything else.

Fish the hairwing Royal or the Corey, the Michigan regulars always said, *and when they won't work on a rising fish you should switch to the Adams.*

It was a basic formula that worked.

Such rudimentary theorems were common before our exploding population filled the Michigan rivers with fishermen, and an angler experienced at fishing in the shadow of our eastern cities can only smile at his own remembered naiveté. The fish came greedily to our flies and the world seemed to revolve with simpler rhythms in boyhood years.

685

But that evening long ago on the Little South was a prelude to the future and its hard-fished streams. The songbirds fell quiet, and the whippoorwill began calling softly from the jack-pine thickets when I saw the first slate-colored caddisfly hatch and flutter into the alders. There was another sedge hopscotching down the current, and then two more emerged beside a cedar sweeper. Others started hatching from the swift currents along the cedar roots upstream, and it was there that the first trout rose splashily.

The rhythms of the hatch increased. Fluttering *Psilotreta* flies were coming faster and faster, until the twilight was literally filled with slate-colored sedges, and the trout went absolutely crazy in the gathering darkness.

Two were feeding steadily along the tree roots, and several more were rising under the alders. It was the miracle of a heavy hatch of flies, and the trout were soon taking them greedily.

Look at them, I thought happily. *Feeding like crazy should make them easy—it's going to be a night to remember!*

It was a memorable night, but not the way I imagined.

The white-winged Corey Calftail floated perfectly over trout after trout, but they ignored it. There were even more rises now. Fish were working everywhere under the trees, and my white-winged flies covered them perfectly. The fly floated through faultlessly, riding drag-free on the smooth currents, but they were utterly ignored.

They won't take my Calftails, I yelled upstream.

They're picky tonight, my father answered. *Why don't you try the Blue-winged Adams.* Rising trout were everywhere.

It was our usual answer to the problem of selective feeding, but that night it failed miserably. The little Adams was rejected as completely as the gaudy-colored hairwings, although the fish rolled and porpoised and slashed at continually hatching flies. The trout fed greedily until it was dark, and an occasional rise could still be heard when I waded from the almost invisible river in defeat.

It was a sobering experience.

It was an early exposure to total selectivity, and I have never forgotten its lessons. Selectivity remains the principal obstacle to consistent angling success, since its requirements influence our fishing long after we have refined our tackle and presentation and casting. It consists of the preoccupation of feeding trout with a particular diet form to the exclusion of all others, and the persistent refusal of all artificial flies that do not imitate the particular insect or crustacean on which the fish are concentrating. It is perhaps the single saving reason why trout on hard-fished waters are not extinct, and it is the cardinal challenge in all of angling. Selectivity requires a workmanlike knowledge of stream entomology, which had only reached its infancy on American waters when Ray Bergman published *Trout* forty years ago. Selective trout are the chesslike essence of our sport. Faced with selective feeding, the trout fisherman must diagnose two

RARE DESERT TROUT SPECIES

HUMBOLDT TROUT   *(Salmo humboldtensis)*   *Specimen collected on Magpie Creek, Nevada*

GREENBACKED TROUT   *(Salmo stomias)*   *Specimen collected on Como Creek, Colorado*

GILA TROUT   *(Salmo gilae)*

Specimen collected on Diamond Creek, New Mexico

APACHE TROUT   *(Salmo apache)*

Specimen collected on Bonito Creek, Arizona

OREGON RED-BANDED TROUT   *(Salmo oregonensis)*

Specimen collected on Swamp Creek, Oregon

MORIAH TROUT   *(Salmo behnkei)*

Specimen collected on Goshute Creek, Nevada

ALVORD TROUT   *(Salmo alvordensis)*   *Specimen collected on Whitehorse Creek, Oregon*

ANATOMY OF A BROWN TROUT

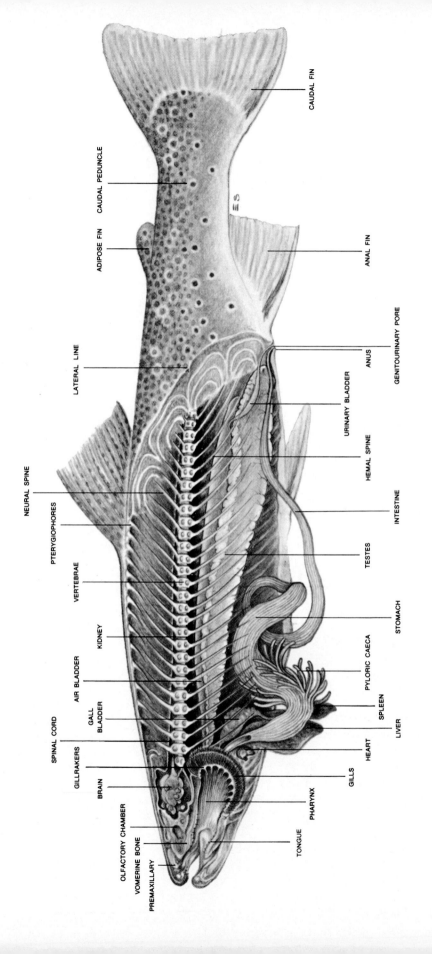

CAUDAL FIN

CAUDAL PEDUNCLE

ADIPOSE FIN

ANAL FIN

GENITOURINARY PORE

LATERAL LINE

ANUS

URINARY BLADDER

HEMAL SPINE

INTESTINE

NEURAL SPINE

PTERYGIOPHORES

TESTES

VERTEBRAE

STOMACH

KIDNEY

PYLORIC CAECA

AIR BLADDER

SPLEEN

GALL BLADDER

LIVER

SPINAL CORD

HEART

GILLRAKERS

BRAIN

GILLS

PHARYNX

OLFACTORY CHAMBER

TONGUE

VOMERINE BONE

PREMAXILLARY

basic facts: what natural the trout is taking, and what artificial fly pattern they will accept in its place.

It is true that there are days when the trout rise with abandon, and it seems they will take virtually anything. Such eager cooperation is often typical of high lakes and back-country beaver ponds and the wilderness of Canada and the Labrador. Fishing such wilderness trout, with a fish on almost every cast, is the dream of many anglers. It fuels many tales and reveries, particularly when an angler suspects in his secret heart of hearts that he may never fish such waters. But a cornucopia of unsophisticated fish would become quickly boring to the experienced angler, since he knows that little skill is required on truly wild trout that have seldom if ever been tested. The freshly stocked trout of many private clubs are equally foolish. Consistent success on hard-fished water is the more rewarding yardstick.

The days when fish on well-travelled water will take almost anything are increasingly rare. Selectivity is infinitely more common. Since selectivity becomes the angler's primary dilemma, once the other skills of presentation have been mastered, it seems logical for the modern angler to prepare for it.

Selectivity has been attributed to many faculties of the trout. Many angling writers have speculated on its psychology, believing that a fish becomes accustomed to seeing a particular insect form, tries one or two in a venturesome mood, finds them both palatable and safe, and settles into a pattern of response that stimulates his feeding reflex only when that particular insect reaches his feeding station. Trout on hard-fished streams are suspicious not only of fly patterns that fail to match the hatch, but also display suspicion toward the natural flies that come next in the hatching calendar. It is quite common on my home water, the hard-fished Brodheads of Pennsylvania, to see trout taking the dun and slate-colored hatches of early season readily and refusing the pale straw-colored *Epeorus* and *Ephemerella* flies that soon follow. We have often watched them inspecting these at-first-unfamiliar insects suspiciously, drifting downstream under a fluttering mayfly and refusing it. Several days often pass before the fish seem to understand that these yellowish insects are actually food and begin taking them without suspicion. Such behavior is also typical of the legendary Green Drake hatches on both our own rivers and the famous European beats. The big *Ephemera* mayflies are so much larger than the hatches that precede them each spring, riding the currents and eddies like olive-colored sailboats, that the fish eye them warily when they first begin to emerge. It is a behavioral pattern I have observed on widely separated rivers: the Beaverkill and the Ausable in New York, the British Test and Itchen, the weedy Maigue below Limerick in Ireland, and Bavarian limestone streams like the Lauterach and the Pegnitz.

Sometimes selectivity varies with the changing ecology of a particular stretch of river. Certain hatches require specific environments, both in and out of the water. Some insects frequent slow currents, while others with higher oxygen requirements are found in swift riffles and tumbling pocket water. Some terrestrial insects favor meadows, while others thrive in willows or tree-sheltered reaches of river. Hatching and feeding to a single diet form is found only with those insects whose ecosystemic requirements are so general that they emerge from virtually all types of water.

It is possible on my home river at Henryville to find many trout selective to hatching *Epeorus* flies. Such fish are usually lying below a fast flow of water ideally suited to these swift-water insects. Sometimes other fish lying in quieter pools are selective to other flies at the same times. The habitat of the early *Ephemerella* hatches is less restricted, and some fish see more of them than the fast-water *Epeorus* species. It is even possible on certain April afternoons to find simultaneous selectivity to two *Ephemerella* species, depending on the feeding lie of a specific fish. The biosystemic needs of *Ephemerella subvaria* are less demanding, and these handsome little mayflies are found emerging from all types of water. The oxygen requirements of *Ephemerella rotunda*, with its rust-colored sternites, are somewhat higher. It is found primarily in swifter currents, and a trout holding below a tumbling riffle or white-water pocket would see a higher percentage of these flies. During these same days of the early season, there are late morning hatches of *Taeniopteryx* stoneflies from the swifter currents, as well as sporadic hatches of slow-water *Paraleptophlebia* duns from the quiet pools. It is a complex spectrum of early fly hatches.

The response of the fish is intriguing. Some trout lying below a fast reach of river are seeing a plethora of *Epeorus* flies and will accept only a well-tied Gordon Quill. These insects hatch in early afternoon. The red-bodied little *Ephemerella* duns emerge about an hour later, and then the fish are often selective to the handsome little Red Quill developed by Art Flick on the Schoharie. Earlier that morning, these same fish would have been selective to the *Taeniopteryx* stoneflies coming off the riffles, while trout in the pools would concentrate on the slow-water *Paraleptophlebias* hatching sporadically all day, turning to the bigger *Ephemerella subvaria* flies when they hatch in midafternoon. Such an intricate pattern of selective feeding based on micro-habitat is not uncommon, and a knowledgeable fly-fisherman will observe and follow its rhythms throughout the day. Similar secrets can be unravelled on your home river too.

There are other feeding patterns based on habitat. Perhaps the most interesting example lies in the response of the trout to the apple-green inchworms of early summer. These pale little larvae seem to prefer buttonwoods and oaks on our eastern rivers, and there have been many afternoons of inchworm-feeding when I have walked the river, fishing an imitation under these trees with great success. My earlier book, *Matching the Hatch*, describes a day on the Ausable in New York, when my good friend Jeff Norton took a nice brown that was literally sausage-tight with caterpillars. It had been taken under a huge oak and was stuffed with these hairy worms. None of the other fish taken by our party contained a single caterpillar, although these juicy morsels were numerous. It seems that a psychological focus on these larvae, plus their availability under one of the trees preferred by the worms, had coupled to produce a striking example of total selectivity: a single fish feeding in a specific locale.

We have all experienced days when the fish were rising to a specific insect not available in large numbers, paying little or no attention to other species on the water in much larger quantities. It is behavior that is difficult to explain, yet it is surprisingly common. Trout often concentrate on tiny *Paraleptophlebia* flies when the juicy Green Drakes are also riding the current. Similar examples occur on all rivers. The fish quite commonly take a minute diet form, ignoring much larger naturals available in good numbers. Perhaps it is a question of numbers and mere availability, but the reasons are often more obscure. It is doubtful that we can ever fully understand such selectivity, or the preferences that cause the trout to take a hatching mayfly one afternoon and focus on its nymph the following day, and I wonder if knowledge of such secrets might not dull our sport. Such mysteries surely contribute a sense of the ancient rhythms, beyond man's beginnings, that still rule the instincts of the natural world.

It is selective feeding that evolved the theory of imitative fly-dressing. Its exponents argue that a choosy fish can be caught only with a fly that exactly simulates its food of the moment. We know that trout are selective. Any fisherman who frequents hard-fished waters is familiar with such behavior, and it becomes more common with each passing season.

It has long been proven that trout see variations in color quite clearly. It is unimportant to know if the fish distinguish hue, value, and chroma as humans perceive them, since *how* they see color is less important than the fact that they *can* unquestionably sort through its variables. Research has also proven that their abilities in distinguishing shades of color at the outer limits of the spectrum are far better developed than those of humans, just as many animals hear and see better at night than we do. It is intriguing, and well worth remembering, that the fish distinguish subtle color variations in precisely those calibrations of the color scale that define most of their common diet forms.

William James Lunn was one of the finest imitative fly dressers in the history of angling, and he practiced his craft in more than half a century as keeper of the Houghton Club on the Test. Lunn believed that eyesight and disciplined observation were the primary skills of an angler confronted with selective trout.

John Waller Hills was the biographer who recorded Lunn's life on the chalkstreams in the charming book *River Keeper*, which was first published in 1934. It recounted Lunn's belief that a perceptive angler is able to distinguish the colors of several fly species coming down. Such powers of observation are not easy on the European chalkstreams, since a hatch may include two or three Olives mixed with the darker Iron Blues. The fish often will be taking only one of these flies. Sometimes a heavy hatch is mixed with midge pupae, and the fish are smutting to the exclusion of the mayflies. Other times the hatching duns are mixed with a procession of spent spinners. Most will concentrate on the duns, but some in quiet flats and eddies will be taking the spent-winged imagoes and nothing else. It is difficult to detect spent mayflies in the surface film, and even harder to isolate a fish that is clearly taking them.

Hills describes an April morning on the Lower Park beat with the old riverkeeper. It was his first day on the Test after his election to the Houghton Club. The current was covered with *Baetis* Olives, and using an imitation, Hills quickly captured two good fish without a refusal. Suddenly, the two men found a large brown working steadily that ignored Hills's Dark Olive imitation. It did not even bother to inspect his fly. Lunn watched it continue taking something while Hills's fly drifted down flawlessly, and then he shook his head.

That fish is taking spent, Lunn said quietly.

Hills tells us that the old riverkeeper selected a spent-winged Lunn's Particular, dropped it perfectly above the fish, and it was taken instantly. It was a singular example of observation. There was a brisk wind disturbing the water, the hatching flies were thick, and every fish seemed to be taking them. Yet Lunn saw a subtle clue that led to his solution.

The moral which I drew is that, besides being able to see, Hills writes, *you must know what to look for!*

Lunn often argued that success was invariably measured by the proper fly pattern, properly presented to the fish in the proper season of its hatching, but Hills argues that his incredible color perception was also a factor in Lunn's superb bag of skills. Apparently Lunn saw more subtle variations in color than the members of the Houghton Club who fished his beats. Hills tells us that Lunn once showed him two virtually identical pinches of mixed fur dubbing at the fly-dressing table in the Houghton keeper's cottage.

What? Lunn said. *Can't you see the difference?*

Lunn was not an exponent of exact imitation in the mold of Frederic Halford, although his fly patterns are the work of a craftsman who unmistakably believes in imitation. Yet the most casual observer is aware that even the artfully-dressed flies of such tiers as the late William Blades, and his young disciple Poul Jorgenson, are far from exact replicas of the delicate naturals.

This obvious fact is frequently pounced on by opponents of the imitation theory. But the abstract concept of exact imitation is patently impossible in precise terms, and our flies obviously need not be exact replicas of the naturals to take selective fish.

It is clear from experience on a wide variety of streams that trout are selective to specific fly hatches year after year, and that only certain fly patterns work at such times. Such repetitive behavior cannot be explained outside the theory of imitation. The word *imitation* itself seems the fulcrum of our arguments. The opponents of imitative theories of fly dressing argue that our so-called imitations do not duplicate the natural flies. Yet it is hardly important that our fly patterns look like exact imitations to our senses, when the fish take them readily while feeding selectively to specific hatches, and it is the *selective* trout that are the ultimate yardstick of our fly-dressing skills.

The controversy surrounding the theory of imitation is primarily semantic. Flies that consistently take selective fish during specific fly hatches are unquestionably *practical* imitations, and the fact that *we* do not consider them exact replicas is relatively unimportant.

John Atherton discusses these questions in *The Fly and the Fish*, and he advances the proposition that our techniques of so-called imitation are more accurately a theory of *impressionism*, not unlike the painterly school of impressionism that evolved in Paris during the nineteenth century. It did not create images of photographic reality, but captured an illusion of reality through consciously obscure and imprecise brushwork. Atherton was an

JOHN ATHERTON

artist and fully understood the parallels between his fly dressing and the nineteenth-century Paris school of painting. His book argued that fly patterns that consistently take selective fish are truly imitations in any pragmatic sense of the word. Such flies give the fish a workable *impression* of its food, and even the most selective brown is often duped into rising. Such patterns of cause-and-effect are the essence of imitation in actual fishing practice.

Selectivity and imitation are the biggest factors in trout-fishing success on hard-fished waters. They are the dual reasons behind my books *Matching the Hatch* and *Nymphs*, for a disciplined study of aquatic entomology would be pointless if selectivity and imitation did not exist. The factors of trout-water insects and crustaceans would prove of little interest to anglers, as would the hundreds of accepted fly patterns.

Fortunately, our sport is not that simple. Our fish are wary and selective, particularly on any water that receives some fishing pressure. Hard-fished trout are frequently so wary that anglers have trouble fooling them consistently. Figures compiled in Michigan at the Pigeon River Research Station show that half of its fishermen caught little or nothing. Two percent of the anglers who fished the experimental stretch were considered expert by the field biologists, and these men accounted for seventeen percent of the annual catch. Such figures clearly argue that trout-fishing luck consists primarily of finding the trout in a feeding mood. Skill and knowledge and patience are the several keys to consistent fishing success beyond such luck.

Such selectivity varies widely. Neither hatchery trout nor wilderness fish are any real measure of selective feeding. Sometimes wild-country trout are selective too, and I have experienced such behavior in improbable locations like the unfished pampas of the Collón Curá in Patagonia, when the fish became partial to a hatch of green-bodied caddis. Club-water fish in both Europe and the United States have seldom been demanding, since club policy in earlier times often encouraged killing a limit of fish. Public-water trout are usually hatchery fish infrequently permitted a second mistake, since they are creeled when caught, and caught in many instances with treble hooks or bait. It is catch-and-release trout, or fish on the restricted-method or low-limit waters, that are the most selective feeders and the most likely to survive. Since they are the most experienced and demanding, it seems logical to prepare for them, and their degree of selectivity is a direct function of exposure to fishing pressure. The angler who can consistently take selective fish can also catch the easy ones, but the man who prepares only for the fancy-pattern fishing is going to have a lot of fishless days on difficult water.

It is a problem that will grow worse. Present demographic trends point to a future American population of 300 million within the lifetime of many living Americans. Such densities, fifty percent larger than today, can only result in more and more fishing pressure. The velocity of growth and change is already such that more people now live on the eastern seaboard from Boston to Washington than occupied the entire country when my father was born. Therefore, it is wise and sensible to prepare for increasingly selective trout, rising everywhere to specific hatching flies and ignoring everything but a proper imitation.

The factors that distinguish the right fly from the wrong fly are among the most complex in all of angling. The problems of color and size are obvious, but they are not the only factors. Silhouette and configuration are important as well. Some insects are translucent, while others are relatively opaque, and opacity is a factor in selectivity. The light pattern that a dry fly creates in the surface film is also critical, along with full or sparse dressing. Even the relative weight of a fly pattern has an effect on its image in the film. Leader diameter, color, relative opacity, and shininess are also important. Other factors such as drag-free floats, poor casting or presentation, the relative speed of a wet-fly swing, or the rhythm of the retrieve are all critical in fishing selective trout. My own experience over such fish confirms the theory advanced by Doug Swisher and Carl Richards in *Selective Trout* that tippet size is somewhat less critical than fly pattern. Swisher and Richards also make another observation on fly size that challenges conventional wisdom: that fly-size is more critical below size twenty than above, since the difference between a twenty-eight hook and a twenty-two is more than forty percent. Most writers believe that trout are less selective to color and size in such tiny flies, but my experience unmistakably contradicts that premise.

Having the right fly pattern is not only the most effective solution to the problem of selectivity, but it is also the most satisfying facet of our sport. The angler who can take a selective fish is not satisfied to cover extensive water in order to catch an occasional trout. His yardstick is the ability to move every fish rising in the pool or run. Each fish need not be hooked, but each must come to his flies and be missed or pricked. Such anglers will spend an hour working on a single rising trout, while a less demanding fisherman would rapidly move on.

Such skills are the result of discipline and ability and patience. Before one can reach such levels of proficiency, he must expend the time and effort required. It is impossible to learn everything there is to know about trout fishing, but each fragment of information and experience can be stored away for future reference in both mind and stream diary.

Solving our problems of selectivity is rather like the process of medical diagnosis, in which a rich matrix of experience and technical knowledge and intuition is focused upon a natural phenomenon. It is a rational method in which past experience and knowledge are used to identify possibilities, which are then tested on the trout.

Selectivity unquestionably proves that trout are shy and discriminating. Their wariness demands our attention. But the most considerable advantage of the fish lies in the riddle of selectivity, and we can only solve that ever-changing maze with a thorough knowledge of their seasonal and daily diet forms.

We have seen in this chapter that trout are wary and sophisticated beyond measure. It is this facet of their character, coupled with their tradition and their lithe beauty, that makes them so highly prized. To overcome this shyness and sophistication, we must observe and study their habits carefully. Our casting and tactics are physical skills that become refined with many years of practice and a growing knowledge of our rivers. However, understanding the selectivity of trout is a function of the angler's mind and attitudes; it must be approached with a knowledge of aquatic entomology and the ability to apply that knowledge along the stream. Selectivity is the sole reason for studying trout-stream entomology, and it is frequently the weak link in many fine anglers' skills. Our other skills—getting the fly over a fish not yet aware of our presence and having it reach that fish naturally—are rendered virtually useless when an artfully presented fly fails to match the hatch and is refused. Stream tactics and casting are solely the products of fishing experience, but stream entomology demands serious study.

Few anglers make the effort.

Several times each year, anglers challenge me with a similar question about stream entomology. Such queries often make wry references to early failures with Latin, either in classrooms or during brief careers as choirboys.

Why do you confuse us with those Latin names? they ask. *Why not use the popular names for our hatches?*

Such people seem to think that our important hatches are limited to relatively few species, that those insects are widely found throughout the United States, and that all major hatches *have* widely accepted popular names.

None of these concepts is true.

There are probably several thousand species of mayflies, stoneflies, and caddis on our waters. Many still remain unclassified. Fewer than a hundred have popular names. Several species have several popular names, on rivers only several hundred miles apart. The famous Green Drake is typical. It is a burrowing mayfly designated *Ephemera guttulata* by taxonomists. The species is closely related to similar insects, *Ephemera danica* and *Ephemera vulgata,* in Europe. Since these European flies have been imitated with the barred flank feather of mallard drakes for centuries, the adults of these burrowing mayflies are popularly called drakes.

Our American flies are quite similar. British writers thought they were the identical species and called them Green Drakes when they fished them here.

But even that refused to remain simple. *Ephemera guttulata* is called a Green Drake on the Beaverkill, and its egg-laying spinner is called a Coffin Fly. But on other eastern rivers, these insects are called Shadflies, and their egg-laying spinners are Gray Drakes. Shadflies on the Beaverkill are not even mayflies, but a prolific caddis species of the *Brachycentrus* genus. The so-called Green Drake on western rivers is a mayfly species, but it does not have mottled wings imitated by barred drake feathers, and it does not hatch from burrowing nymphs. It is not remotely related to the true drake hatches of western Europe and the Appalachians. It is related to the Blue-Winged Olives of both Europe and the United States, and should probably be called the Great Lead-Winged Olive.

Why do they call them Green Drakes? I asked.

It's pretty simple, André Puyans responded wryly. *They don't know any better!*

Biology faced the chaos of popular names centuries ago when it began its systemic discipline of Latin taxonomy. It precisely defines and separates the species through their unique physical details.

Several recent books on fly-fishing entomology have added fresh species to our important fly hatches. Genus identifies a group of species which share a common set of physical characters. The Latin adjective which follows the generic designation defines a single species within each generic group.

Some recent books have been lavishly illustrated and produced, and have received lavish praise in the fishing press. These books identify only genus. Identifying a fly hatch to its generic status is virtually useless in a fishing situation. Most genera have similar patterns of behavior, but a genus like *Ephemerella* has species that vary from size eight to eighteen, and from slate gray to pale yellow. Helping a baffled fisherman identify the freshly hatched *Ephemerella* in his fingers to its genus is so little help that it borders on a bad joke.

Forget about learning all those Latin names. It is familiar advice from an entire school of fishing writers. *All you need to know is pretty simple—are they little brown flies or little gray ones?*

Selectivity is not that simple.

Observing that a particular fly on the water is either brown or gray is seldom enough. The fish are not always working on the fly itself. Sometimes they are taking the migrating nymphs as they drift toward the surface, or travel into the shallows to hatch. Sometimes the fish focus on nymphs still pinioned in the surface film, and under some weather conditions, more nymphs are stillborn and trapped in the meniscus than actually hatch.

And the nymphs are seldom the same color or configuration as the adult flies. Brown or gray is not enough, just as genus stops short of hatch-matching.

Identification of species is critical.

And it is impossible to identify a particular species without knowing its proper Latin name. Before you tell me that is more than you want to know, let me suggest that you may not understand its full spectrum of benefits. Having correctly identified a species along the stream, you have solved a complex riddle.

It is like winning at chess.

The delicate insect in your fingers is suddenly more than merely brown or gray. It is a catalyst that tells you a cornucopia of secrets.

Armed with such knowledge, you know what the fish are doing, but you also know much about yesterday and tomorrow. Yesterday fills a startling list: where the nymph has spent its year of growth and moulting in the river, what its color and configuration are, how it ranges about the current or holds fiercely to the stones, how it migrates to reach the surface and hatch, how far it drifts while hatching, how long it spends in the surface film, how much time the freshly hatched fly rides the current, and how gracefully it flies when its wings are drying.

Merely observing that a freshly captured insect is brown or gray tells us nothing more.

But identification of its species tells us many things about tomorrow too: it tells us where a freshly hatched fly will moult, how long it will spend moulting, about its egg-laying stage in both color and shape, what it looks like when ripe with fertile eggs, where and when the mating swarms will gather, the type of water where the ova will be laid, when such oviposition occurs, precisely how (dropping the eggs from above the current or touching its surface to lay them) the females complete the mating cycle, when and where a spinner fall of spent females will take place, and approximately how long the particular species might remain a major factor on your stream.

And you have broken the code.

BOOK FOUR
↯↯↯

THE
TOOLS
OF
THE TRADE

1. The Theory and Practice of Modern Fly Dressing

The flies were exquisitely tied on fine British hooks with gleaming hackles and woodduck wings, and in other drawers there were north-country patterns that glittered with tinsel and junglecock eyes and exotic brightly colored feathers like kingfisher and blue chatterer and macaw. The flies filled their trays by the thousands, and I stood looking at them, pattern by pattern, on that boyhood afternoon, with a sense of awe.

Finely tied flies have always held a fascination for trout fishermen, since their patterns have an elegance and delicate quality and tradition found in no other sport.

The polished mahogany fly chests at Von Lengerke & Antoine in Chicago were a revelation, with drawer after drawer of meticulous dressings smelling faintly of moth crystals. My excitement was so great that my father bought me several dozen patterns, and I examined them for days under my study-table lamp, marvelling at their precision, sense of proportion, and the quality of their materials. It was then that I really determined to learn to tie flies. Fly-tying catalogues began arriving in the mails, and I soon decided to meet some really skilled fly dressers. My first exposure to professional tiers came the following summer, when we travelled north to fish the Michigan rivers.

Our fly-fishing in those early years was often concentrated on the famous trout streams around Baldwin. It was my father who discovered that Harry Duffing tied flies professionally in his barber shop on the dusty main street. Sometimes we stopped to ask him about fly hatches on nearby streams, particularly when the big *Hexagenia* drakes were emerging at twilight in early summer. Sometimes we even went in for unnecessary haircuts to get to know him better—the price was only thirty-five cents in the years after the Depression—and finally Duffing let me see his tying table and equipment and the materials he used in his famous Michigan night-fishing patterns.

There were other famous fly tiers in the years that followed, like Arthur Kade in Sheboygan, where we always stopped on our way north to fish the Brule and Namekagon and Wolf in Wisconsin. Art Winnie tied his caddis patterns and Michigan hoppers at Traverse City, and there were many hours spent with Len Halliday at his cluttered workbench where the spent-wing Adams was born a full fifteen years before I first fished the Boardman. Those were sunlit years in spite of the Great Depression, and few men could smell the growing winds of war.

It was not until after the Second World War that I met William Blades, one of the finest fly dressers who ever lived. It was a complete accident that came about after attending a competition of the North Shore Casting Club in Chicago. There was a young girl casting in the dry-fly accuracy event, and her final score placed second.

That's strange, my father said suddenly. *I believe that girl is in one of my classes at the university!*

Let's try to meet her, I suggested.

The girl caster was the daughter of the famous Frank Steel, the first man ever to make a perfect score in dry-fly accuracy in actual tournament competition. Steel was one of the pioneers who developed our modern arm-casting techniques, not only for distance work but also for working with precision at distances under sixty-five feet. It was a controlled style of casting with a closed wrist. His daughter introduced us to Steel that evening, and when he found we lived in Winnetka, we were invited to the weekly casting sessions held during the winter in the gymnasium at New Trier High School.

It was a distinguished group of casters, with roots dating back to the years when Fred Peet and Call McCarthy dominated the American tournament casting circuit. Fred Peet first became National Casting Champion in 1909, and had won fourteen casting titles before the First World War. Call McCarthy came from Ireland, from a family of Irish river keepers and fly dressers. His titles included three American national championships between 1914 and his tragic death in 1921, not long after he had successfully defended his title. At the time we met him, shortly after the Second World War, Frank Steel was a worthy heir to that tradition of great Chicago tournament casters, and William Blades was the unchallenged court wizard with a fly vise.

Blades did not publish his remarkable *Fishing Flies and Fly Tying* until many years later, but he was already a legend in the trout country of Michigan and Wisconsin. For some reason, he adopted me through two winters while he cajoled and criticized and coaxed me into tying better flies. Blades was a difficult and demanding teacher. His lectures about proportions and tapered fur bodies and the proper winding of hackles were all delivered with bulging eyes and a reedy intensity of voice; the echoes and admonitions still ring naggingly in my mind more than twenty-five years later. Blades accepted nothing short of perfection, and although I never really became such a complete disciple that I tied only his extended-body mayfly dressings and nymphs with moose-mane legs, his uncompromising proportions and standards are still part of my yardstick when I look at flies today.

Fly dressing has a long tradition reaching deep into the history of fishing itself. The hook is certainly among the oldest tools, and probably evolved from the gorge shortly before primitive metallurgy emerged some 7,000 years ago. The gorge was a piece of stone, antler, shell, or bone. It was sharpened at both ends and attached to the line at its middle. The bait was used to hold a gorge parallel to the line, so that a fish might swallow it easily and unsuspectingly. Once the bait had been ingested by the fish, tightening the line turned the gorge crosswise in its gullet. Primitive hooks of fish bone appeared in Neolithic times, probably in the cultures evolving between Egypt and Turkey, just on the threshold of later metalworking civilizations.

Artifacts of stone were still being polished and ground, but some primitive smiths were already working with copper and iron. Archaeology clearly reveals that the first metal fishhooks were made of copper, and more than ten centuries would pass before the combination of copper and tin produced an alloy that proved strong and easy to work. Bronze marked the beginnings of new civilizations, particularly on Crete and throughout the Mediterranean. Bronze hooks with barbed points and needlelike eyes in their flattened shanks are known to have come from Crete more than 5,000 years ago. Fishhooks fashioned of bronze are also known to have appeared in China about a thousand years later, and gold hooks are recorded together with lines of silk and bamboo rods in *The Book of Odes* written about 3,000 years ago. The first artificial flies apparently evolved before the *Chuh Tzu* manuscripts, slightly more than 2,000 years back into the prehistory of China. Such flies were dressed with pheasant and kingfisher feathers on delicate hooks of gold.

Ironworking probably emerged in Egypt about 4,000 years ago, and had already spread into southern Europe centuries before the Christian epoch. The precise origins of steel remain unclear, although such metallurgy already existed from Damascus to Toledo when fly-fishing first developed in Macedonia during the third century.

Modern hooks probably evolved in Europe approximately seven centuries ago, although the industrial production of hooks can be traced to London in the seventeenth century. Its evolution coincides with the rise of needlemaking there, and perhaps the most famous early manufacturer of hooks and needles was the celebrated Charles Kirby. His firm was already well known for its fishhooks when Walton published *The Compleat Angler* in 1653. Kirby greatly improved the tempering and hardening of his steel. His Kirby hook pattern is still copied across the world, and his methods of hookmaking provide the basis for hook manufacturing in our time.

The plague that decimated the population of London was followed by terrible fires in 1666, and the hookmaking industry was scattered across England. Almost a century passed before it had gathered again at Redditch in Worcestershire, where both needles and clothing hooks were made. Another century found all of the world's hookmaking centered in Worcestershire, and the quality of the hooks made by manufacturers like Allcock, Farlow, Bartlett, and Sealey has never been surpassed. Their absolute dominance of the industry would last almost 150 years, although the subsequent growth of Mustad in Oslo, after its founding in 1832, was a prelude to the decline of British dominance in hookmaking. Today Viellard-Migeon also makes a fine line of fly-dressing hooks in France—both wet-fly and dry-fly designs in a full range of sizes.

Fishhooks were not high among the industrial priorities of the British Government during the Second World War, and the Attlee Government placed no importance on reviving the industry. The British hookmakers were ordered to concentrate on needles, and British hooks were no longer available in good numbers. Mustad rapidly filled the vacuum in the postwar fishing world, and now thoroughly dominates the trade, in spite of hook manufacturing in Japan, France, and the United States.

Although fishhooks were made almost entirely by hand until surprisingly recent times, modern hooks are made completely by factory methods. Only the most expensive fly-tying hooks are still partially made with hand methods, particularly in the small trout sizes. Our hooks are formed of eighty to eight-five percent fine carbon steel. It is cut into precise lengths of the proper diameter for each hook size. Both ends are ground to fine points and the wire is cut in the middle, forming two separate hooks in a single operation. Machines taper the wire slightly and shape the eye, and form the point into the proper bend. The barbs are sometimes cut by hand and the points on the best hooks are often hand-sharpened slightly. The eyes are left ringed, and turned up or down according to their type. The hook bends are then forged slightly flat. Although the hook is fully shaped, its wire is still untempered enough for fishing. Heat treatments are applied to harden and temper the unfinished ones. Such heating leaves them covered with a coarse scale that is ultimately removed by tumbling them in abrasives. Scouring is followed with a bronzed finish. Counting, inspection, and packaging complete the typical hookmaking process.

The character and quality of hooks are absolutely critical to making flies that will fish well and imitate natural prototypes. Beautifully tied flies on poor hooks are virtually worthless. Hook character and quality start with wire diameters and sizes, and each hook size requires a different wire. The wire diameter of hooks is designated in terms of its X-rating and the terms Stout or Fine. Hooks that are labelled 1X Fine are formed of wire usually found in hooks a size smaller, and 2X Fine hooks have the wire diameter of hooks two sizes smaller. Hooks are seldom manufactured in wire sizes smaller than 3X Fine, like the Mustad 94833, although Orvis is marketing an excellent 4X Fine hook manufactured in England to its own

Mustad 94840

light-wire specifications. Such fine-wire hooks are intended primarily for fine leaders under three-pound test and dry flies, although emerging nymphs fished in the film also demand light-wire types. Heavy-wire types are labelled in a reverse progression. Hooks marked 1X Stout have been shaped with wire normally used in the next larger size, and a 2X Stout hook is twice as heavy as normal hooks of that size. Wire diameters heavier than 4X Stout are rarely made, and are usually found in salt-water and steelhead hooks.

Orvis Premium 4X Fine

Wire temper and hardness are important too. Heavy hooks are strongly made and hook well, but are obviously unsuited for imitations intended to float or fish awash in the film. Light-wire hooks that bend and spring sometimes work themselves free, although their sharpness tends to penetrate the jaw membranes easily and hook well. Some light-wire hooks are too brittle and break with the slightest strain, while others have too soft a temper and spread open when a fish is hooked. It is important to fish a delicate tippet with extremely light-wire hooks. Obviously the perfect hook is not so brittle that it breaks easily, and not so soft that its gap opens under bending strain.

Mustad 3906

Although it is often alleged on trout water, few hooks are actually broken in fish. They are usually broken on the stones or ledges behind a fisherman when his backcast drops too low or when a working cast ticks the fly into the flexing rod. Any fish that subsequently takes is quickly lost, and when inspection reveals a broken hook, the fault probably lies in sloppy casting. If you often find broken hooks, the remedy undoubtedly lies in your backcast and not in the quality of your hooks.

Mustad 94720

Hook shanks are also rated in terms of X-numbers, with the supplemental description of Short or Long. Such coding means a hook labelled 1X Long is made with a shank length normally found in hooks one size larger. Hooks 2X Long and 3X Long have shanks twice and three times as long as standard lengths in their size. Such extra long hooks are seldom found with shank lengths exceeding the Mustad 94720, with its 8X Long specifications. Moderately long hooks are commonly used for nymphs requiring a slender silhouette, and the extra long types are used for streamers. Fly-tying hooks are also manufactured in short-shank designs. Spiders and variants are often dressed on 4X Short hooks like the Mustad 94825 or 5X Short types like the Mustad 95235. Such hooks have reduced shank lengths, four and five sizes shorter than normal. Hook shanks less than 9X Short are seldom made.

Mustad 94825

Hook eyes found in typical trout flies are either turned up or turned down, and are finished in three basic ways. The ball eye is formed without any deviation from the wire diameter of the hook shank. It is usually found in rather inexpensive hooks for nymphs, wet flies, and streamers. The tapered eye is shaped with a gradually reduced wire diameter slightly behind its ring and in the eye itself, and is commonly used for dry flies and the more expensive grades of sunk patterns. Loop-eye hooks are most typically found in salmon flies, for both their strength and the smoothness of their eyes. The loop eye is formed with a finely tapered eye looped back and laid along the shank. It is used extensively in trout fishing for big nymphs and streamers on designs like the Mustad 9575, a superb Limerick style hook with a 6X Long shank.

Mustad 9575

Hook sizes are not measured in terms of their overall configuration, but by the dimension of their gaps. Hook gap is measured from the point to the shank in a vertical line, while the throat of the hook is measured from its point to the inside of its bend. The shank is the relatively straight shaft between the bend and the eye. Hook points are measured from the barb slice to the apex itself.

Hook points in trout fishing are commonly found in four basic styles. Spear points are relatively inexpensive to manufacture, lack the quality of quick penetration, and are not often used for first-grade flies. Needle points are hand polished, have excellent hooking qualities, and are relatively expensive. Most well-tied flies are dressed upon hollow-point-style hooks. Such points are designed for excellent penetration and hooking, and are called hollow because they are sharpened into a convex curve between the tip of the barb and the apex of the point. Barbless hooks are made both without barbs or kinked points which do not tear the jaw membranes when they are worked out, and since the Mustad 94845 has been made in sizes twelve through twenty-two, it has become quite popular. However, hollow points are the most popular.

Mustad 94845

Hook styles are the Bartlett-type sneck bend, the Limerick-type bend, the sproat-style bend, and the round or Model Perfect design. Few flies tied on American waters still employ the sneck-type hooks, although the other three types are relatively common. Sproat- and Limerick-style hooks are used primarily for wet flies, bucktails, and streamers. Most dry flies are tied on round or Model Perfect bends, since they offer optimal strength in the light-wire hooks designed for high-floating performance. Turned-up and turned-down eyes are also a factor in both function and style. It is doubtful that any measurable difference in hooking qualities exists between turned-up and turned-down eyes in normal sizes, but in sizes below eighteen or twenty, the turned-up eyes offer a completely open hook gap that is free of the eye itself. Some flies are more easily constructed on down-eye hooks and are usually dressed on them in spite of their small sizes. Since my boyhood years and the elegant Hardy flies my father sometimes bought, such patterns dressed on turned-up eyes have always been my yardstick for esthetic perfection—particularly in the imitations of mayflies and sedges.

The scale of hook sizes is rather unusual. Trout and salmon flies are tied on the sizes above and below number one at the middle of the scale. The smaller sizes are manufactured in standard numbers from two to twenty-eight, with hook size decreasing as the numerical designation increases. Larger sizes work upward from 1/0 to 9/0 irons, and flies as large as 3/0 are sometimes used on big trout in heavy-water tactics.

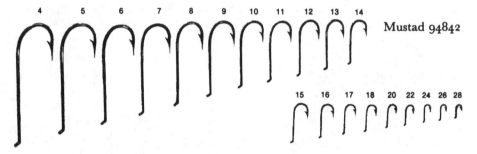

Mustad 94842

Modern flies can be traced back along a conscious line of evolution and lineage since the *Treatyse of Fysshynge wyth an Angle* in the middle of the fifteenth century. The primitive dressings prescribed in Berners included a hackleless version of the British March Brown, and several soft-hackled patterns of partridge and grouse. Simple down-winged wet flies had their literary genesis in the *Treatyse*, although it was Charles Cotton who elevated such dressings to the level of art in *Being Instructions on How to Angle for a Trout or Grayling in a Clear Stream*, which was published as an appendix to the edition of *The Compleat Angler* that appeared in 1676. Superb fly dressers and

Stewart Wet Fly

fishermen like Bowlker and Chetham rallied the faithful during the century that followed, and the modern wet fly was fully evolved a full quarter century before Alfred Ronalds published his *Fly-Fisher's Entomology* in 1836. Stewart revived the soft-hackled border patterns on the Whitadder in Scotland at midcentury, and except for the hairwings that first evolved in Canada and the United States before 1900, the wet-fly method was complete.

Hampshire Wet Fly

However, there were surprising regional variations in style throughout the British Isles. The relatively sparse flies described in the *Treatyse* had dominated English fly dressing for two centuries by the time Charles Cotton mentions the differences in styles found on the streams near London and his own Derbyshire flies. Typical Hampshire wet flies were dressed with slender tails imitative of mayfly spinners, roughly dubbed bodies, rather full hackles, and generous wings of duck quill sections set at about forty-five degrees. The basic wet-fly wing is fashioned with both conventional- and reversed-wing styles, setting the paired wing-quill sections both on top of the hook and at its sides. These variations result in four distinct configurations of wet-fly winging techniques. Such flies still dominate the American wet-fly school.

Cotton fished flies of totally different proportions and style. Their tails were less dramatic in length, suggestive of freshly hatched mayflies. Although their bodies were rather fully dubbed, they were relatively short, and the hackles were quite sparse. Their slender wings were shaped from duck quill sections and set quite high, at an angle of eighty to eighty-five degrees. Such flies would sink readily, breathing with both their hackles and wings when retrieved, offering a completely different silhouette and

Derbyshire Wet Fly

behavior in the water. Wingless flies are still popular fished wet on the rivers of Yorkshire and Devonshire. The Yorkshire style has slender bodies that utilize only sixty percent of the hook, extremely long hackle fibers sparsely dressed, and no tail filaments. Devonshire hackle wets are more fully dressed, with tail fibers, fully dubbed bodies, and heavily tied hackling. Fly dressers on the Teme evolved rather long-tailed patterns with fat bodies, relatively full wings laid back at about thirty degrees, and sparse hackles. Kilbreda dressings from Ireland in the eighteenth century were often tied with a sparse rolled wing, no throat hackles, rather elegantly dubbed bodies mixed with a few guard hairs at the wing, and delicate tails. Such Irish flies had their wings laid back at a thirty-degree angle over their bodies. Similar flies evolved on the Tweed in Scotland, except that their bodies used only half of the shank length, and their wings were virtually upright and divided like the dry-fly wings that evolved in Hampshire before the middle of the nineteenth century. Wet flies dressed on the Usk had slender bodies, divided wings with their concave sides set together and low over the hook, and sparse hen hackles. Usk patterns were tied without tails. Remarkably sparse wet flies also evolved on the Tummel and Clyde, their slender wings set slightly forward of the vertical. Tummel dressings displayed delicate dubbed fur bodies that commonly occupied less than half

Usk Wet Fly

of the hook shank, and hackles proportioned slightly smaller than conventional hook sizes would dictate. Clyde-style patterns had proportionately longer bodies and hackles.

Such variations in style are interesting when they are studied for parallels in stream entomology. These patterns are all dressed with slate-colored wings and dun hackles and bodies dubbed from a hare's mask, except for the Yorkshire and Devonshire types that omit the wings. Each is a regional version of the classic Blue Dun.

However, wet flies in a larger sense are dressed to imitate drowned aquatic insects and terrestrials, as well as some species that emerge or lay their eggs under water. Strictly speaking, the Blue Dun is tied to suggest

Tweed Wet Fly

any number of small mouse-colored mayflies in many sizes from twelve to twenty-eight. Yet these patterns are tied both with and without wings, and several omit the tail fibers. Clearly the winged and tailed flies popular on rivers like the Itchen and the Teme are mayfly imitations, and the exaggerated length of their tails suggests that, when they are dressed on small hooks, they are intended to simulate drowned spinners or *Baetis* flies that lay their eggs under water. The Derbyshire pattern, with its sparse wings and hackles and short tail, is obviously intended as a hatching mayfly dun. So is the heavily hackled Devonshire style, but the Yorkshire hackle

Clyde Wet Fly

Tummel Wet Fly

version is tied without wings or tails, and is perhaps better suited to imitating a hatching caddis pupa. The down-wing patterns typical on the Usk water are also dressed without tails, and from their proportions are superb imitations of either a drowned sedge or caddis that goes beneath the surface to lay its eggs. Although they are also dressed without tails, the upright wings on the wet flies of the Tweed, Clyde, and Tummel suggest that they are intended as mayfly patterns. Perhaps they were dressed to imitate a hatching dun, its wings working free of the epicuticle, while its legs and tail are still tangled in the membrane, its silhouette lost in the splitting nymphal skin.

However, the standard wet-fly dressing is perhaps too much an imitation of the mayflies, both drowned specimens and those genera that lay their eggs under water. Several rolled-wing patterns with tails are excellent stonefly imitations, and there are many sedge-type flies that have been fished wet for centuries. Paul Stroud used to monitor fly production at Von Lengerke & Antoine in my early years in Chicago, and he insisted that wet flies were caddis imitations. For that reason, his fly drawers were filled with wet patterns that were not just conventional down-wing styles, but literally placed the wing sections along both sides of the body, like an adult sedge. Modern vinyl-type feather lacquers have made it feasible to dress really durable stonefly imitations in a flat-wing style. Some version of the palmer-tied wet fly without wings has been tied since the time of Berners' *Treatyse*, and is found in the fly lists of every major writer of the four centuries that followed. Ronalds included several caterpillar imitations in

Idaho Hairwing

his *Fly-Fisher's Entomology*, and palmer-tied wets that imitate beetle larvae are popular on many waters. Hair-wing wet flies evolved almost a century ago on the Henry's Fork of the Snake in Idaho, and are found tied in both down-wing and flat-wing styles. Typical flat-wing wet flies tied with hair are the several big stonefly imitations popular on many western rivers, and there are also a number of down-wing caddis-style flies that have evolved in recent years on the Pacific Coast. Hair-hackle wet flies also evolved in the fly vises of western anglers, particularly Franz Potts and the incredibly creative George Grant in Montana.

There are a number of wet-fly dressings designed to imitate terrestrials, dating back to the fifteenth century patterns, in both the *Treatyse* and the fly lists of Charles Cotton. Patterns like the Cowdung, Sawfly, Hawthorn fly, Marchfly, Oak fly, Soldier fly, Bottle fly, and Marlow Buzz were common in 1800. There are even wet-fly imitations of leafhoppers in the Ronalds *Entomology*, and patterns tied to suggest wasps, bees, beetles, and ants are centuries old. The modern lacquer-body ants, both with and without wings,

McCafferty Ant

undoubtedly evolved in the fly vises of many anglers—although history credits the late Bob McCafferty with their invention on the famous limestone streams of Pennsylvania more than a half century ago.

Wet flies reigned alone through the first two millenniums of fly-fishing history, although a number of angling writers discussed dapping and fishing their wet flies in the surface film. The precise origins of the dry-fly style are unknown, except that its genesis clearly lies on the smooth, fly-rich currents of the Wiltshire and Hampshire chalkstreams. It is logical that the beginnings were found on such waters. Wet flies would float on relatively windless days, and the rich palette of fly hatches on these rivers led naturally to large numbers of surface-feeding trout.

History tells us that legendary fly dressers like James Ogden of Cheltenham were making dry flies as early as 1840, about the time that George Pulman published his first edition of *The Vade Mecum of Fly-Fishing for Trout*, the book that introduced the dry-fly method in print. Such flies

Ogden Upright

were already well known in England at midcentury to have Wilfred Foster of Ashbourne supplying upright-wing dry flies for the trade as early as 1854, which proves that the theory and technique had reached the Dove, Derwent, and Manifold in Derbyshire. Stoddart also describes using the dry fly on Scottish rivers as early as 1853, in his second edition of *The Angler's Companion*, unquestionably demonstrating that dry-fly theory had journeyed completely northward throughout Britain.

History also demonstrates that the divided-wing upright and fan-wing styles of dressing evolved quite early. James Ogden credits himself with both types in his book titled *On Fly Tying*, which was published in 1879. No evidence to discredit his claims is found anywhere in the literature of angling. His elegant divided-wing uprights were tied with double thicknesses of duck-wing-quill sections laid back-to-back, imitating the upright wings of a floating mayfly dun. Their two hackles were wound on both sides of these gracefully cocked wings, holding them securely in their upright position. Slender bodies and tails completed the mayfly imagery. Palmer-tied uprights also evolved before 1850, and although many patterns were dressed with tails, such flies are most effective as imitations of fluttering sedges. The sheen and density of their hackles, the dark silhouette of their duck-quill wings, and their performance during Trichoptera hatches and egg-laying swarms all point to their role as caddisfly patterns. Local styles involving reverse-wing and forward-wing dressings also evolved on many rivers, for both mayfly and sedge imitations.

Ogden also developed the fan-wing dressing to imitate the large *Ephemera* drakes that hatch on the lakes and slow-flowing rivers of the British Isles in early summer. His elegant patterns can still be studied if you have access to a copy of Aldam's *Quaint Treatyse on Flees and Artificial Flee*

Ogden Fanwing

Making, which includes both the actual fan-wing drakes tied by Ogden and their materials. Fan wings are designed to suggest the large, delicately mottled wings of big mayfly duns and spinners, and their lineage is more than a century old since their genesis on the Derbyshire Wye.

Sedge-type dry-fly dressings with their down-wings also evolved in the eighteenth century. Such flies have their roots in palmer-tied down-wing wet flies, like those painted in the several books on fly hatches and their imitations that were published shortly after 1800. Ronalds included such caddis patterns as the Sand fly, Grannom, Cinnamon Sedge, and Red

Cinnamon Sedge

Sedge in his *Fly-Fisher's Entomology*, and the transition to similar palmer-tied flies dressed with dry-fly quality hackles is logical. Before the close of the century similar down-wing caddis imitations like the Giant Red Sedge, Cinnamon Sedge, Black Silverhorns, Caperer, and Welshman's Button all evolved on British trout streams.

Extended- or detached-body imitations of large mayflies were also common before 1900, and Frederic Halford included such flies in his fly lists. These early detached bodies were tied on stiff cores of silkworm gut, and the late William Blades, who was a primary American advocate of such fly patterns, regularly used foundations of hard nylon. Detached bodies of cork and buoyant hair are also found on some rivers, and extended bodies of hair are popular in the West for imitating larger mayflies. Soft adhesive rubber was briefly popular for translucent mayfly-type bodies, but it was a short-lived material that soon became tacky and discolored, and is seldom used today. I first learned the nylon-core extension system from Blades himself, not long after the Second World War, and later stumbled on a surprisingly easy method of tying detached bodies in 1956.

It was during the years when I was part of the government agency established to design and build the United States Air Force Academy. One morning when I stopped to visit a contractor on the Cadet Quarters Complex, I found a spool of delicate .008 stainless music wire on his desk and asked him about it. Stainless music wire is available in a number of finer sizes down to .0025, and I was immediately intrigued with its potential as the core for detached fly bodies. My first experiments worked in the standard Blades method, tying the wire to the hook shank with heavily waxed silk, cutting it to proper length, fastening in the tail fibers, and constructing the body conventionally. Such flies were the best detached-body flies I had ever seen, but they were still extremely difficult to tie. It was easier when I began leaving the wire foundation long enough to hold it

Schwiebert Drake

taut with my left hand, and not trimming it off at the base of the tails until the fly was completed.

One afternoon in the winter months I happened to glance at two fly vises lying on my work table, and suddenly thought about a surprisingly simple method of making a detached-type body on a delicate wire core. Quickly I mounted both vises on the table, jaws facing each other, and stretched six inches of wire between them. The wire was quickly wound with working thread at the proper length, the tails were tied in, and a dubbed body was wrapped over the waxed base. Both body and tails were prefabricated on the tautly stretched wire, and suddenly I realized that there was room to tie three or four more sets of bodies and tails on the same core. The wire was released from the vise and the prefabricated fly bodies lay in a circular coil. It was easy to cut them free from the coil, trimming the wire precisely at the tails and leaving some seating length at the opposite end. The seating length was then wrapped firmly to the hook shank, its free end projecting beyond the hook eye, and then bent back and tightly wrapped with working silk. The wire remains flexible and springy underneath the fully dressed body, and such music wire cores are a superb method for making a detached body. The wings and hackles are then dressed conventionally, concealing the hook perfectly.

In recent years I have been experimenting with a remarkable British hook that has just appeared on the American market, and it achieves the same balance and silhouette as the mayfly imitations I developed with music wire cores almost twenty-odd years ago. The new Yorkshire

Fly-body Hook

extended-body hooks are much easier to use in dressing such flies; they can be seated with the extended shank projecting out for the bodies and tails and reversed with the hook eye projecting in the conventional manner to complete the pattern. The hooks are like all creative ideas—deceptively simple once someone conceives them—and consist of a single wire forming both the body core and a short shank hook which lies in the finished hackles. The structure and silhouette of these new flies is remarkably lifelike, and I have found them singularly effective on difficult and selective fish throughout the United States.

During the heavy *Ephemerella* hatches on the Au Sable in Michigan this past spring, we were dressing flies long after midnight at the Averill place on the Whippoorwill water downstream from Stephan's Bridge. The fish are picky there, having been caught and released regularly during the first week of the season, and we turned to the Yorkshire-style hooks in desperation. Walter Averill was also dressing flies, while Don Phillips and Arthur Neumann offered a stream of criticism and sardonic advice. The Yorkshire-style hooks were unknown to them, and they were greeted with excitement.

They're really something! Walter Averill marvelled. *Now why didn't we think of them first?*

We dressed our imitations with full hackles in the thorax style and parachute style for the swifter currents below Black Bend and the Recreation Club water, and there were also a few no-hackle versions tied for the Whippoorwill Stretch. The flies were a remarkable success, particularly on fish that refused conventionally tied imitations.

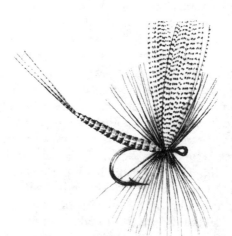

Fly-body Drake

In *Modern Dry-Fly Code* Vincent Marinaro describes another type of detached-body mayfly imitation using natural and dyed porcupine quills to suggest the almost translucent bodies of spent Ephemeroptera once their eggs are laid. Marinaro dresses his porcupine-quill imitations without wings, simply trimming their hackles out above and below the hook to create the illusion of spent wings, in a structure suggested earlier in the

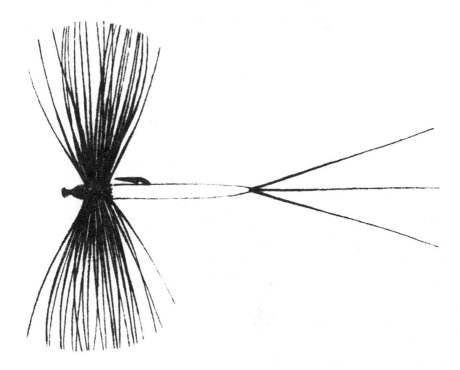

Marinaro Porcupine Spinner

works of British thinkers like Mottram, Dunne, and Colonel Harding. Such Marinaro spinners are elegant and original patterns.

Another interesting method of imitating the translucent bodies of mayflies is the Darbee extended-feather technique, which was developed by Catskill tier Harry Darbee and has grown popular with a number of fine American fly dressers. It is used widely on the difficult western spring creeks, with considerable success on their selective rainbows and browns. The feather-body dressings are the essence of simplicity itself, shaping the

Darbee Feather-body Drake

detached silhouette from a soft breast or flank feather of the proper color. These bodies have color and translucency, but completely lack thickness and are virtually without weight. Typical dressings include rolled wings and hackle-point wings, along with conventional hackles trimmed out under the thorax for subimago imitations, and flat for spinners. Tails are merely cemented with vinyl lacquer to the extended body, and such flies are remarkably translucent and delicate. Poul Jorgenson ties a hybrid version, combining the thorax or parachute configuration with a shaped feather body extending beyond the hook.

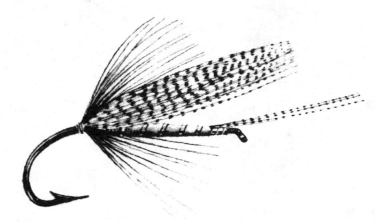

Holberton Reverse-style Wet Fly

Wakeman Holberton was granted a patent for a reverse-tie wet fly in 1886, in the normal down-wing style. It was believed that such a dressing would cast with less atmospheric friction and that its wings and hackles would flutter when retrieved. Reverse-tied floating flies are also found on some American streams, with the theory that full dry-fly hackling conceals the hook. Such dry flies are currently popular on the Nantahala in the mountains of North Carolina.

Spent-wing spinner imitations evolved on British rivers late in the nineteenth century, possibly in the talented hands of innovators like William Lunn, the famous riverkeeper of the Houghton Club on the Test. Lunn worked out a number of excellent spent-wing imitations, particularly the Sherry Spinner, Houghton Ruby, and the Lunn's Particular. Large spinner patterns, like the spent stages of big *Ephemera* drakes on the British chalkstreams and Irish limestone lakes, are often imitated with four hackle points tied spent to suggest their large wings. Perhaps the most popular American spent-wing pattern is the Adams, which is typically successful during caddis hatches and mating swarms in spite of its tails. Its hackle

DOWN-WING WET FLIES

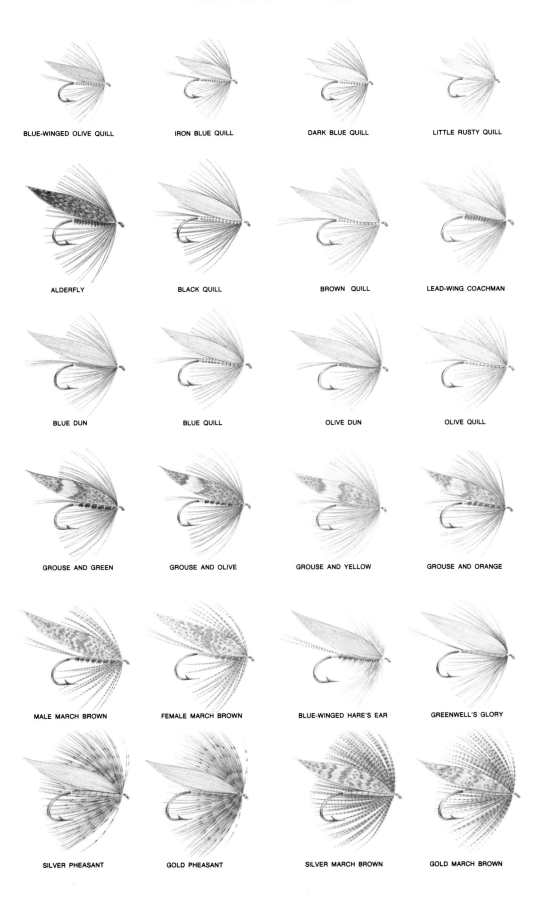

BLUE-WINGED OLIVE QUILL	IRON BLUE QUILL	DARK BLUE QUILL	LITTLE RUSTY QUILL
ALDERFLY	BLACK QUILL	BROWN QUILL	LEAD-WING COACHMAN
BLUE DUN	BLUE QUILL	OLIVE DUN	OLIVE QUILL
GROUSE AND GREEN	GROUSE AND OLIVE	GROUSE AND YELLOW	GROUSE AND ORANGE
MALE MARCH BROWN	FEMALE MARCH BROWN	BLUE-WINGED HARE'S EAR	GREENWELL'S GLORY
SILVER PHEASANT	GOLD PHEASANT	SILVER MARCH BROWN	GOLD MARCH BROWN

ROLLED-WING WET FLIES

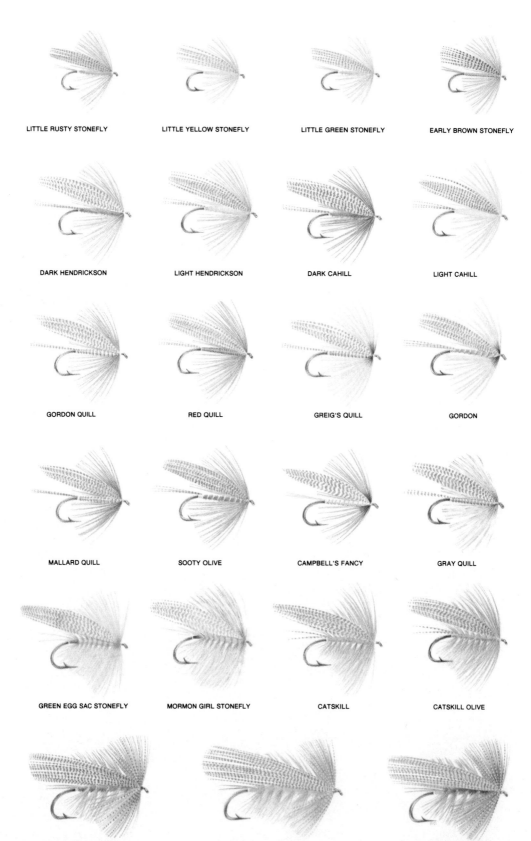

LITTLE RUSTY STONEFLY   LITTLE YELLOW STONEFLY   LITTLE GREEN STONEFLY   EARLY BROWN STONEFLY

DARK HENDRICKSON   LIGHT HENDRICKSON   DARK CAHILL   LIGHT CAHILL

GORDON QUILL   RED QUILL   GREIG'S QUILL   GORDON

MALLARD QUILL   SOOTY OLIVE   CAMPBELL'S FANCY   GRAY QUILL

GREEN EGG SAC STONEFLY   MORMON GIRL STONEFLY   CATSKILL   CATSKILL OLIVE

BROWN WILLOW FLY   GREAT SUMMER STONEFLY   EARLY SUMMER STONEFLY

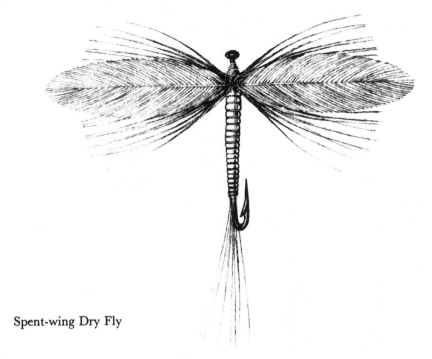

Spent-wing Dry Fly

color-mix and silhouette suggest a fluttering sedge. Several regional patterns like the Woodruff and Whitcraft are similar American spent-wing flies, but most spent dressings are intended to imitate mayflies.

Split-wing flies tied with hackle points tied flat and trailing at thirty to forty-five degrees were developed to suggest such insects as flying ants, saw-flies, midges, soldier flies, oak flies, gnats, marchflies, and several kinds of winged beetles. Some fly tiers have also tied small stonefly imitations with split-wing dressings to imitate the fluttering split-winged Plecoptera of early spring. Sail-wing dressings are not common in modern trout flies, although sail-wing flies were typical in the early history of fly-fishing. The locally famous Madsen pattern is a palmer-tied sail-wing popular on the Au Sable in Michigan, and was first tied by the late Earl Madsen, who guided fishermen below Grayling.

Sail-wing Dry Fly

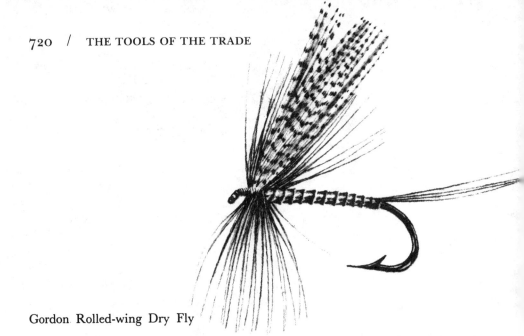

Gordon Rolled-wing Dry Fly

The rolled-wing dry flies achieved their popularity in the Catskills late in the nineteenth century, and the technique perhaps originated with Theodore Gordon on the Neversink. Gordon dressed several early Catskill patterns with single rolled-wings of woodduck, tied upright in a single bunch like the wings of a mayfly held closely together. Both the yellow-bodied Gordon and the classic Gordon Quill had such wide influence that Gordon himself became the lone wellspring of the Catskill school. It subsequently included such famous tiers as Roy Steenrod, Herman Christian, Reuben Cross, and William Chandler in the generation that followed Gordon, and their skilled fingers were responsible for rolled-wing patterns like the Hendrickson and Light Cahill. Living members of the Catskill school include Walter Dette and Harry Darbee, who live along the Willowemoc above its junction with the Beaverkill, and Art Flick on the Schoharie. Preston Jennings and John Atherton are both dead now but their works, *A Book of Trout Flies* and *The Fly and the Fish*, are still with us, helping to codify the theory and practice of the Catskill school. Fly patterns like the March Brown and Gray Fox are original with Jennings, and the Red Quill was developed by his protégé Art Flick. Both the Light and Dark Cahills, as well as the Light and Dark Hendricksons, are typical Catskill dressings too.

Such rolled-wing flies of woodduck and mallard flank have evolved into divided-wing dressings since Gordon and Steenrod, who was Gordon's principal disciple. Bergman described such a divided rolled-wing dressing in *Trout*, with a series of step-by-step photographs in the making of a Cahill pattern. Rolled spent-wings of woodduck and mallard are also found on some watersheds. Such divided-wing flies are typical of the modern Catskill school, and are a significant American contribution to the history of fly dressing.

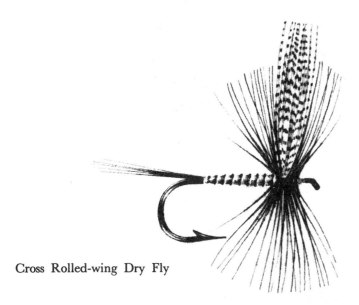

Cross Rolled-wing Dry Fly

Variant-type flies originated on the rivers of Yorkshire in 1875, where sparse wet flies had always been tied, and it is logical that dry flies with exaggeratedly long hackle fibers should evolve there. Doctor William Baigent originated the variant-style dry fly, and evolved a series of twelve patterns that became known commercially as Refracta flies. Baigent believed that the shiny fibers of his long gamecock hackles created the illusion of fluttering life, as well as floating his flies easily on relatively swift currents. The Refracta series mixed hackle colors, or used badger and furnace hackles. The dark colors were intended to suggest the legs, and the longer fibers created both the illusion of fluttering and a distorted refraction in the surface film that could deceive a selective fish. Baigent's flies included four spinner imitations and eight variants of different subimago patterns. His flies included the basic insect colors found on British rivers, and I can remember the baskets of heavy trout we took in my Colorado boyhood summers after the Second World War, using exquisite Baigent Red Variants that arrived in elegant little Hardy boxes.

Baigent variants were conventional flies with upright divided wings, bodies, tails, and hackles of exaggerated-length fibers. Bergman advocated multicolor variants, long-hackled patterns dressed of radically different hackle colors that originated with Albert Barrell on the Housatonic at Pittsfield. Bergman defined the variant-type fly as having long hackle fibers, tails, foreshortened bodies, and slightly undersized wings. His definition has not survived past midcentury, however, since Flick patterns like the Gray Fox and Dun Variants completely omit wings, and famous western dressings like the Donnelly Dark and Donnelly Light Variants have rather long hackle-point wings. These western flies are the work of Roy Donnelly, who lives on the Pacific Coast and developed his Variants in the Jackson Hole country of Wyoming. The late Bob Carmichael, who

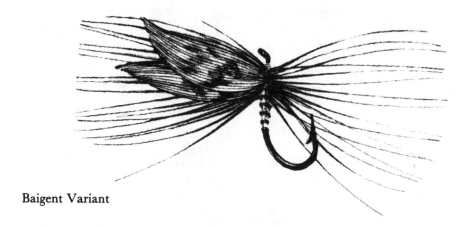

Baigent Variant

operated a famous tackle shop at Moose Crossing in the halcyon Wyoming days after the Second World War, used to rate the two Donnelly Variants essential flies for any western dry-fly man.

Donnelly developed his Variants in Jackson Hole fishing with us, Carmichael explained the summer before his death. *But the credit for them is entirely his—they're a little like the Dark and Light Cahills for you boys back east.*

They're that good? I asked.

Bet your sweet ass! Carmichael grumbled happily. *Wouldn't step into the Snake or Gros Ventre without them!*

Carmichael was right about his Donnelly variants.

Such flies have superb floating qualities for their hook sizes, and it is understandable that they would prove popular on strong swift-flowing rivers. They are most effective during hatches of big fluttering insects, and are often deadly on meadow streams having good numbers of clumsy, long-legged craneflies. The success of the Flick patterns on large eastern

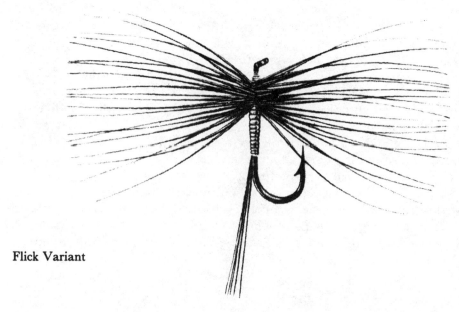

Flick Variant

waters like the Upper Connecticut, Esopus, Delaware, West Canada, Neversink, Lower Beaverkill, and the West Branch of the Ausable are ample proof of the theory. The Donnelly variants are equally popular on heavy western rivers like the Yellowstone, Big Hole, Madison, Snake, Beaverhead, Gros Ventre, and Salmon, and such long-hackled flies are superb big-water patterns.

Bivisible flies were developed to provide optimal floating qualities as well as dressings visible to both fishermen and fish alike. Bivisibles were invented by the incomparable Edward Ringwood Hewitt, who tells us in *A Trout and Salmon Fisherman for Seventy-five Years* that he was experimenting with them well before 1900. Bergman recommends them highly in both *Just Fishing* and *Trout*, particularly the brown, black, and grizzly patterns developed by Hewitt, and the badger-hackle pattern first tied by Charles Merrill of Detroit. Bivisibles are also favorites of Charles Ritz on European streams. The flies consist of hackle-fiber tails, primary hackle colors tied in tip-first and tightly palmered the length of the shank, and finally several turns of white hackle at the head. The palmer-style dressing floats high and its white face hackling is readily visible in marginal light.

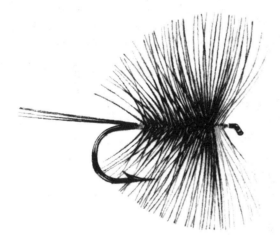

Bivisible

Many fishermen who dislike the theory of matching the hatch point happily to the bivisible, believing its success is a complete rebuttal to concepts of fly imitation. However, over the years I have attempted to correlate success with bivisibles to fly hatches coming off the water. Their floating qualities alone ensure a consistent level of success in swift-flowing pocket water, but their success on selective fish in flat water was puzzling until I discovered a curious parallel between sedge hatches and bivisibles. Many times a soggy bivisible fished awash in the film was deadly when caddisflies were hatching clumsily, drifting along tangled in their pupal skins. Other times a high-floating bivisible worked well during mating swarms of Trichoptera and hatching sedges, although a bivisible does not seem to resemble such flies. It was a puzzle that worried me for several months, until I sat studying a box of bivisibles one morning.

That's it! I thought suddenly. *Maybe bivisibles are just caddis imitations tied in reverse—sedges tied backwards!*

It was a simple explanation.

The problem had been my inability to reconcile the tails on the bivisible, since sedges and caddisflies lack tails completely. The naturals also have dark forewings and pale rear wings, while the relationship of dark and light hackles are exactly the opposite on a bivisible. But I had been fallaciously comparing bivisibles and caddisflies, assuming the hook eye of the artificial equalled the head of the naturals.

The reverse is true, but you must ignore the position of the hook to see the parallels between sedges and bivisibles. The antennae of a caddisfly can suggest the tails of a bivisible. Its dark palmer-tied hackles imitate the dark forewings, while its pale face hackles suggest the milky or hyaline rear wings of the naturals. Such juxtaposition of color and silhouette and form seem to explain the marked success of bivisibles during sedge flights.

Edward Ringwood Hewitt also developed spiders and skaters on his famous Neversink pools and flats. These long-hackled flies are much simpler than the variants that originated in Yorkshire, and it is believed that Hewitt began experimenting with such dressings shortly before the First World War. His spiders were dressed with tail fibers, stiff hackles palmered tightly on a short-shank hook, and a facing of white gamecock. Bergman was a strong advocate of such Hewitt spiders, and both *Just Fishing* and *Trout* are filled with anecdotes about using them from the Owens in California to the Ausable in the Adirondacks, where Bergman often fished from the late Byron Blanchard's famous little country hotel at Upper Jay.

Neversink skaters were a refinement of the earlier Hewitt spiders and were dressed completely without tails or white facing hackles. Hewitt tied his skaters to dance and hopscotch across the current, using only two

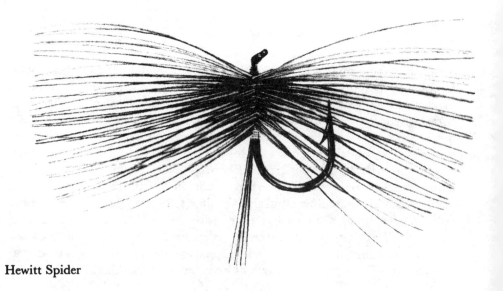

Hewitt Spider

hackles of a single color. Honey, badger, furnace, brown, ginger, black, and natural dun are all popular skater colors. Structurally, the skater was not possible until the development of nylon shortly before the Second World War. Nylon working thread left slippery and unwaxed is the secret. The unwaxed nylon is used to form a smooth thread foundation, and the rear hackle is wound tightly and tied off, with its shiny face toward the bend of the hook. Then it is pinched between the forefingers and thumbnails of both hands, and compressed as tightly as possible. The second hackle follows, its shiny face toward the hook eye, and is pinched tightly against the initially tied hackle. Once the entire fly is hackled, it is compressed together as much as possible at mid-shank, until the tips of both hackles come together at the perimeter. The slippery elasticity of the nylon made this possible, and the stiff rim of hackle fibers form a springy circle that will hop, skip, and jump on cue from the rod tip. Such skaters were designed to fish dead drift and cocked high, or skittered across the film like a fluttering cranefly, and Hewitt often fished a combination of both techniques on a single cast.

Hewitt is also credited by some angling historians with development of flat-winged dry flies designed to imitate the Plecoptera, particularly the small stoneflies that emerge in April on the Catskill streams. His little patterns used a pair of duck-quill sections laid with their convex surfaces together, stroked as straight as possible, and set in clear feather lacquer. Such wings imitated the wings of a stonefly folded absolutely flat over its dorsal abdomen. Since these early Hewitt flat-wings, many other fly dressers have tied stonefly imitations in this style. Most are using flat-wings of hair to suggest the big Plecoptera that hatch on our western rivers in early summer, but some use a wing layered of three or four hackles tied flat over the body, and Dan Bailey has long dressed a stonefly imitation with a body of woven nylon under a wing of veined synthetic material.

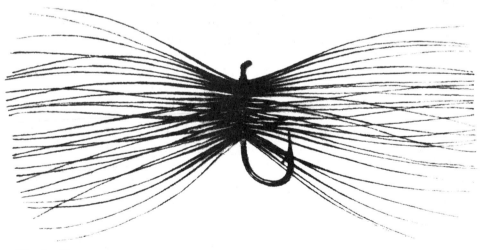

Hewitt Skater

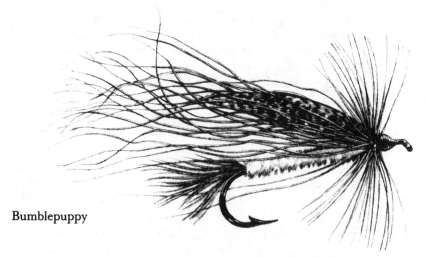

Bumblepuppy

Bucktails have their roots in the Bumblepuppy patterns that Theodore Gordon developed on the Neversink in 1880, and William Scripture was dressing hair baitfish imitations before the close of the century. Herbert Welch constructed feather-winged imitations of smelt on his Maine lakes and rivers as early as 1902, and the true feather-winged streamer is probably the work of Alonzo Stickney Bacon.

Baitfish imitations fall generally into three basic categories: bucktails with wings made entirely of hair, streamers with wings fashioned completely of feathers, and patterns which mix their wings in combinations of both feathers and hair, like the famous Muddler Minnow.

Hair-wing minnow imitations are dressed in several styles. The old Scripture-type bucktails have a down-wing laid tight along the hook, and the Reuben Cross method tied in dark bucktail above the shank, with light-colored hair underneath the hook. Paul Young tied a type of split-winged bucktail on the Michigan rivers as early as 1925, with hair slightly flared on either side of its body. Salt-water bucktails are sometimes used on big trout water, and the best-known type has two hair wings—the first is tied in like an oversized tail, and the second is laid down over the entire body and tail like a conventional bucktail.

Scripture Bucktail

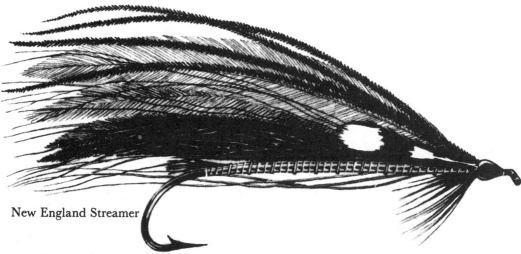

New England Streamer

Feather-wing streamers incorporate wings of both hackles, and softer fibers like ostrich and marabou. Streamers dressed with wings of neck and saddle hackles have their origins in New England, along with dressings that mixed such feathers with sparsely tied hair. Alonzo Stickney Bacon, Carrie Stevens, Herbert Welch, and Herbert Sanborn are responsible for several of the better known patterns. The original marabous were dressed by the late A. M. Ballou of Dighton, Massachusetts. Mylar is a shiny, reflective plastic originally developed for inflated communications satellites, and it has found its way into a number of fine baitfish imitations. Adhesive sheet-mylar is used extensively as shiny overwings along the flanks of marabou streamers. Fine tinsel mylar is sometimes mixed into the marabou like glittering synthetic hair, and it is also woven into mylar tubing, which is slipped over

Ballou Marabou

a body foundation of tapered white curon. Western fly tiers also favor bodies wound from Christmas rope-tinsel and trimmed to a pencillike diameter under both saddle hackle and mixed marabou wings. Such rope-tinsel and mylar flies move through the water with an enticing flash-and-glitter, catching the light like a crippled shiner tumbling weakly in the sunlight. Their light-catching qualities often cause them to dramatically outfish conventionally tied bucktails and streamers.

Muddler minnows were born in 1948, when a Cree Indian was guiding Don Gapen on the famous Nipigon in Ontario. The guide caught a sculpin among the bottom stones, telling Gapen it was the principal diet form of the large brook trout in the river. It was the late Joe Brooks who probably carried the Muddler west to Montana, where its success led Dan Bailey to dress it commercially in vast numbers. Muddlers were tied and fished from big sizes like 1/0 to small hooks like size twelve. Its big sizes were probably taken for sculpins, while the middle sizes are taken both for baitfish and big nymphs. Some fishermen report that small Muddlers are effective during hatches of big *Hexagenia* and *Ephemera* flies, and I have taken fish on a Muddler fished slow and deep when they were feeding on big dragonfly nymphs. Others have caught fish when they were taking big grasshoppers and stoneflies. It was the remarkable Dan Bailey who first combined marabou with the Muddler concept, adding a body of Christmas rope-tinsel. Bailey tied several patterns, using thick marabou wings of white, brown, yellow, gray, and black fibers. Gordon Dean, who once operated the fishing department at Abercrombie & Fitch in New York, developed the yellow-winged variation of the standard pattern. His Yellow Muddler was based on the conventional turkey wing mixed with hair and the clipped deerhair collar and head. The Spuddler is another variation on the sculpin-type fly which uses wings mixed of hair and darkly mottled saddle hackles. It is also a pattern developed by Dan Bailey on the Yellowstone in Montana. Perhaps the best Muddlers yet tied are the multicolored dressings developed by Dave Whitlock, using flattened heads and bodies of woven mylar tubing. However, these Whitlock patterns are imitations of silvery baitfish rather than the sculpins that were prototypes for the original.

Hair-wing flies had their beginnings on the Henry's Fork of the Snake before the First World War, when Benjamin Winchell and Carter Harrison first concocted them in honor of Alfred Trude, their host at a large ranch in Idaho. The first hair wings subsequently travelled with one of the party, Colonel Lewis Thompson, to the salmon rivers of the Maritime Provinces. These primitive flies were dressed down-wing over the body, and it was not until shortly before the Depression years that hair-wing dry flies evolved. Ralph Corey lived on the Muskegon in Lower Michigan, and his Corey Calftails were down-wing dries that became widely popular after the First World War. Wings tied upright and divided of hair appeared almost simultaneously on the Beaverkill and the Ausable of New York in about 1929.

Corey Calftail

The hair-wing Royal Coachman dry fly was the creation of L. Q. Quackenbush, one of the early stalwarts of the Beaverkill Trout Club a few miles above Lew Beach. Quackenbush liked the fan-wing Royal Coachman, except that it was fragile and floated badly, and in 1929 he suggested to Reuben Cross that white hair wings might work better. Cross tied some using upright wings of calftail and tail fibers of natural brown bucktail. It worked perfectly, and Catskill fishermen soon labelled it the Quack Coachman in honor of its peripatetic inventor.

Lee Wulff also worked out his famous Gray Wulff and White Wulff patterns in the Adirondacks in 1929, in a successful effort to find imitations of the big *Isonychia* duns and *Ephemera* spinners that would float well on the tumbling Ausable at Wilmington. These Wulffs have proven themselves superb flies, from Maine to California and British Columbia, and have spawned a large family of patterns using different bodies and hackles.

Wulff Dry Fly

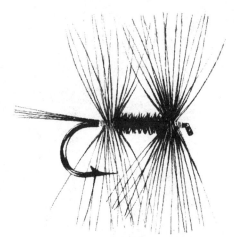

Fore-and-Aft Fly

Wulffs have so completely dominated the upright hair wings that L. Q. Quackenbush and his hair-wing Coachman are almost forgotten, and his innovation is now commonly called the Royal Wulff.

The heavy early-summer hatches of large *Pteronarcys* on our western rivers have led to a number of dry-fly patterns intended to imitate these big stoneflies. Don Harger developed an early hair-wing salmon fly with a raffia body over a kapok core. Bird's stonefly and the sofa pillow pattern soon followed, and a number of other imitations with hair wings have evolved in the fly vises of professionals like Granny Granstrom, André Puyans, Polly Rosborough, Bob Jacklin, and Phil Wright. Similar down-wing caddis patterns are found on many western rivers, and hair wings are a staple on heavy currents.

Fore-and-aft flies are not terribly new, and Ray Bergman was tying commercial fore-and-aft grasshoppers about the time that *Trout* was published some forty years ago. Such winged flies with hackles at both the head and the tail were popular on the limestone streams of Pennsylvania for many years, and Charles Fox was still using these Bergman grasshoppers on the Letort as late as 1956. Fore-and-aft dry flies have become quite popular on western rivers since the Second World War, and the Renegade is probably the best known of these patterns. Harry Darbee ties a pale little fore-and-aft pattern to imitate the delicate yellow and honey-colored Plecoptera that hatch on Catskill streams, and I have long believed that the hackle silhouette of the wingless fore-and-aft dressing is a workable imitation of a fluttering stonefly or sedge.

Parachute dressings had their beginnings in the inventive mind of William Brush, the distinguished automotive engineer from Detroit who once fished from the Pere Marquette Rod and Gun Club. Brush developed

Brush Patent Hook

a special loop-eye hook for tying parachute dry flies, about the same time that Quackenbush and Wulff were experimenting with hair-wing patterns, and he applied for a patent in 1931, which was granted three years later. Parachute flies are tied in the normal manner, except for the hackles, which are wrapped horizontally around the hackling spindle on the Brush-patent hook. Such hackling provides an aerodynamic effect which settles the fly softly and hook-down on the surface. It also provides a unique light pattern of hackle fibers—flush and full in the surface film—not found in a conventional hackle structure. Since they were developed there originally, parachute flies were around during my Michigan boyhood years, but I had never used them until an afternoon on the Little South Pere Marquette, fishing with the late Gerry Queen of Detroit.

It was a warm afternoon, with sunlight bright on the pale bottom gravel and casting deep shadows under the trees. The morning had been productive. Small sedges with mottled wings had hatched sporadically, and we had taken fish steadily with a conventional spent-wing Adams. We stopped for lunch on a cedar deadfall, shared our sandwiches and two chocolate bars, and drank gratefully from the river itself.

Two fish started rising along a brush pile upstream where the willows shaded the current. Their rise forms did not come often, but they were showy and made strong dimples that travelled downstream and disturbed the quiet currents. The rises concealed a brace of fine trout.

You try them, Gerry Queen suggested.

The earlier success of the small Adams made it a logical choice, and I waded carefully into position. The second fish was lying in the eddying currents below a willow stick that hung throbbing in the flow. It came up several times before I was sure of its position, and when I had marked it down, I finally made the cast. The little Adams settled perfectly, flirted briefly with the willow stick, and floated over the fish without drag. It was refused without inspection.

He doesn't want the Adams, I said.

Three or four good floats confirmed that diagnosis, and I waded back toward Queen. *Try one of these*, he said.

It was a parachute-tied Adams.

But they've already rejected an Adams, I frowned. *What makes you think a parachute will work?*

Try it! Queen smiled.

It was a conventional Adams with mottled spent wings, except that its brown and grizzly hackles were wound flat in the plane of the surface film. It settled like a pancake in the meniscus, riding so low that it was difficult to see on the water. It reached the fish and disappeared in a quiet rise.

He took your parachute! I yelled happily.

It was a fat thirteen-inch brown, it surrendered after a brief struggle, and I carefully dried the bedraggled parachute fly. The first fish looked a little bigger and it was still working. The parachute Adams worked out and dropped softly, and it was also taken without hesitation.

They both took it! I said with satisfaction. *I've got to check their stomachs and find out why.*

The gullets of both fish were crammed with caddisflies, except for about two dozen *Asilus* flies, their mottled wings and slender bodies in a tangled mass.

What were they taking? Queen asked.

Robber flies, I replied.

It was a striking case of selectivity to light pattern in the film. Color, size, and silhouette were virtually identical, and only the indentations of the parachute hackles in the surface film were different. It was simply a problem of giving the fish the spraddle-legged light pattern they were looking for that warm afternoon in early summer.

Clipped-hair bodies were added to upright and divided wings of hair when fly makers like Harry Darbee in New York and Joseph Messinger in West Virginia developed flies with bodies shaped of deer and elk hair. Such flies became popular on eastern streams shortly before the Second World War. History tells us that Darbee experimented with them first, although Messinger was highly skilled in dressing clipped-hair bass bugs and frogs, and boasts a number of partisans who argue that his Irresistible was the first trout pattern with a clipped deer-hair body. It had deer-hair wings and tails, and with its dark bronze-blue hackles, the Messinger Irresistible closely resembled the earlier Gray Wulff. It floated like a cork and is quite popular on rivers that are notorious for their angry currents.

Percy Jennings exploited the early clipped-hair experiments of Harry Darbee with a Catskill pattern his family named the Rat-faced McDougal. It is tied both with upright wings of natural hair, and with spent wings of grizzly hackle points. Since those beginnings a whole family of clipped-hair patterns has evolved for big water fishing, and other hair-body dressings like the Humpy and the Goofus Bug have been developed on our western rivers. The original hair-body flies had imitated big mayflies, but these patterns were juicy-bodied patterns suggestive of beetles and other terrestrials. There are also several clipped-body grasshoppers and stoneflies, like the salmon fly imitation developed by Philip Wright on the Big Hole in Montana.

Since midcentury several other remarkably creative fly dressers have been experimenting with basic fly-tying theory and practice. Dry-fly theory began with imitations of the Ephemeroptera, and although these recent studies include mayfly patterns, other common aquatic insects have also been studied. Such American flies owe some debt to the theories of Skues, Mottram, Harding, and Dunne. Their books were interested in the relationships between fly configuration, light, translucence, refraction factors in both atmosphere and water, surface-film effects, silhouette, and the visual perceptions of the fish. Their speculations have caused a profound impact on fly tying in the past twenty-five years, and that impact has triggered some remarkable echoes in the United States.

Perhaps the best known of these men is Vincent Marinaro, whose

Modern Dry-Fly Code was published in 1950, and quickly became the focus of an underground cult. It was not fully recognized as a book of major stature and its original sales were disappointing. Its reputation grew steadily over the years, until it commanded prices on the collector's market that rivalled and surpassed the books of Halford and Skues. It was singled out as the most literate fishing book published in America since George La Branche's *Dry Fly and Fast Water* made its debut in 1914, and that critical judgement came from Professor James Babb, Curator of the Wagstaff Collection of Angling Literature at Yale. Its lyric style and technical originality richly deserve such praise.

Marinaro and his studies with the equally famous Charles Fox are the subject of an entire chapter in my book *Remembrances of Rivers Past*, which describes both these men and their fishing on Letort Spring Run in Pennsylvania. It points out that difficult fish have been the principal catalyst for most innovations in fly-fishing theory and practice. Anglers are always shaped by the character of their rivers, and the shy fish of the Itchen and Test that originally produced British dry-fly theory have equally shy counterparts in the work of Fox and Marinaro.

The brown trout of the Letort are fished only with flies and are seldom killed. Their wariness and selectivity are honed to a fine edge, and each successive capture and release makes them even more shy and skittish. Certain fish become old friends and worthy adversaries, and their holding and feeding lies are well known to the Letort regulars.

Marinaro was a Halford disciple in the beginning, completely committed to the dry-fly code worked out on the British chalkstreams a century ago. *It was the fish that spoiled my religion,* Marinaro admits unhappily. *Our limestone trout simply rejected imitations based on the Halford formulas!*

It was a nagging revelation for a disciple.

Halford argued for exact imitation in terms of size, color, and silhouette, yet his flies often fell short of those criteria. The bodies were opaque and their wings were almost totally obscured by the color of their hackles. J. W. Dunne also recounts his difficulties using the Halford patterns in his book *Sunshine and the Dry Fly*, when the selective browns on the Longparish beats of the Test began refusing them. The naturals on the Longparish water were ethereal insects, with hyaline wings and pale bodies the color of fresh honey and amber and wine in a crystal goblet. Some duns had wings the color of woodsmoke, and others had dark slate gray wings or wings of a remarkable purplish dun. The first Blue-winged Olives that Dunne collected were such a revelation that he believed the hatches at Longparish were a different species. Their richly olive bodies had no echoes in the dark thinly dressed bodies of the Halford imitations, and the Halford patterns performed miserably on difficult fish.

Dunne tells us that he composed imaginary letters to angling periodicals, pointing out that his collections indicated a whole spectrum of natural flies apparently not included in the Halford series of imitations. The truth was painful when he finally realized that the naturals he was collecting were the living prototypes of the dour Halford dressings. Marinaro experienced a similar pattern of self-education on Letort Spring Run when he found its selective brown trout less than enthusiastic about imitations of its hatches that were based on the Halford formulas.

The conventional dry fly largely evolved from the work of thinkers like Ogden, Marryat, and Halford in England. It was carried to fruition during the last half of the nineteenth century, and was modified slightly with the rolled woodduck wings of Theodore Gordon and the Catskill school.

Such dry flies have both wings and hackles just behind the hook eye, body materials occupying most of the hook shank, and tails that were rather exaggerated in length. Wings were upright and divided, shaped of fragile wing-quill sections or duck breast feathers. The stiff gamecock hackles and tail fibers were designed to support and float the imitation on the surface film. Stiff hackles and tails were combined to float the flies as high as possible, and a whole liturgy of high-floating flies evolved. It was argued that the physical presence of the hook made exact imitation virtually impossible, and that fine hackles and long tails could obscure the hook by holding it above the surface meniscus. Ray Bergman echoes these theories in *Trout*, complete with diagrams showing the floating characteristics of Cahills tied on light- and standard-weight hooks, and adds the following observations:

> To begin with I doubt that close imitations are essential for success. As a matter of fact I believe that it is impossible to create an artificial duplicate of a natural insect. No matter how cleverly we tie our flies we can never attain that ethereal lightness, delicacy and definite lusciousness which is so apparent in the real thing.

Few modern fly dressers who fish our really difficult waters, like the western spring creeks or the limestone streams of the Appalachians, or any river within two hours of a major city, would agree that imitation is unimportant to their success. The regulars on Letort Spring Run have mercifully refused to collect innumerable wagers from strangers who insist that their favorite patterns will work anywhere. Letort trout are simply not interested in conventional Cahills and Hendricksons and Royal Wulffs, unlike their cousins in less demanding freestone streams.

However, the most creative tiers will agree that an exact duplicate of the naturals is impossible. Their elegance, ephemeral coloring, and hyaline character are beyond our reach in absolute terms. We are after an effective duplicate that creates the illusion of a natural insect and deludes a selective fish. Such difficult trout are the final yardstick of our skills.

Bergman was clearly unconvinced by the whole history of imitation, reaching from the *Treatyse of Fysshynge wyth an Angle* through Cotton and Ronalds to Halford and his *Dry-Fly Entomology*. Fishing was easier in the Bergman years, even on the Catskill streams and the rivers of northern New Jersey that he fished regularly and wrote about, and it is easy to understand that fly patterns seemed less important forty years ago. Fishing writers are a little bewildered by the recent changes in our sport, but demographers understand what has happened. There are now more people living within five hours of the Catskills than the total population of the entire United States when Theodore Gordon began to fish their storied rivers.

Bergman knew that the hook was obviously essential to fishing and believed that its necessity formed an insurmountable handicap to exact imitation. It is unquestionably true that no natural possesses a hooklike appendage hanging from its body. However, Bergman also believed that a dry fly floating high on its hackles and tail fibers concealed the hook and cancelled out its existence:

> There are some qualities which tend to make our manufactured flies more lifelike and so more productive. One is the lightness of wire of which the hook is made. There isn't any doubt that a fly tied on a light wire hook is more advantageous to the angler than one tied on a heavy wire hook. For one thing, the light wire hook enables the flytier to use less hackle and yet have a fly which will float. Besides, if on a light wire hook you use the amount of hackle needed to properly float a heavier hook, you would have a fly that would float higher and so prevent the hook from penetrating as far under the surface, surely an advantage; that is working along the idea that we should imitate a natural as nearly as possible. After all the hook is the one thing we can't do without and also it is the most glaring discrepancy between an artificial and a natural. Therefore, if it can be kept above the surface of the water, that part of the artificial fly which touches the water should appear more like a natural than it would if the entire hook could be seen under the surface.

Light-wire hooks are undoubtedly important in floating a dry fly with the least dubbing and hackle necessary to float it properly on a given piece of water. No modern fly tier would challenge that premise, but the rest of the argument is no longer valid, although an entire generation came to manhood religiously accepting such orthodoxy.

It is still possible to overhear similar dogma on the porches of venerable fishing camps on rivers across the United States. Halford informed the world that mayflies rode the water on their toes, and surprisingly few men challenged him despite the obvious evidence of their own eyes. Mayflies do not ride the current on their toes, despite the drawings in Halford's *Dry-Fly Entomology* or the mayflies depicted in Jennings' *Book of Trout Flies* half a century later. Mayflies ride the current dumpily, their thoracic segments and belly sternites riding flush in the surface film, and their legs straddled clumsily at the sides. Sometimes they ride the current well, wings together and balanced like Halford's perfectly cocked dry flies, but sometimes their float is less than perfect. Their wings flutter and ride asymmetrically, sometimes getting trapped in the surface film, and a hatching dun is often skated and blown off balance until one wing is awash and the other rides upright. Sometimes the entire body and its tails are pinioned in the surface too, and *none* of these conditions, including the normal belly-flat posture of both body and thorax, is imitated by a dry fly floating high on its hackles and tail fibers—with both hook and body held above the surface film.

There is a whole generation of innovative fly dressers who discovered these fallacies for themselves. J. W. Dunne went so far in *Sunshine and the Dry Fly* as to argue that body color and translucency were the principal factors in selectivity, and Colonel E. W. Harding guardedly supports that theory in *The Fly-Fisher and the Trout's Point of View*. The first American fishing writer to challenge orthodox dry-fly philosophy was Vincent Marinaro. In his *Modern Dry-Fly Code* Marinaro not only rejected the Halford formulas but also proposed a wholly new theory of dry-fly structure.

Halford chose his palette of materials for dry flies in the following system: hackles were correlated to leg color; wings imitated the wing color and configuration of the naturals; bodies were interpreted in terms of the sternite or belly-segment colors; and the caudal filaments were imitated by the color of the delicate tail fibers.

Marinaro tied his early imitations of the Pennsylvania fly hatches using the Halford formulas faithfully. His prototypes worked reasonably well, but the hyperselective fish of Letort Spring Run rejected them consistently. Something else was obviously needed. His Letort experience convinced Marinaro that two conceptual errors flawed the Halford theory of fly dressing. Choosing leg color for the hackles obscured the more important color and silhouette of the wings, distorting the principal color mix of his flies. Halford also failed in his interpretation of wing position as well as thorax and body length. Mayflies typically ride the current with slightly upturned bodies, foreshortening body length in both the surface film and the vision of the fish. Halford interpreted body length literally in his imitations, and ignored thorax length entirely. Wing mass in the naturals slants backward toward the center of thorax and body length. The most cursory observation of mayfly anatomy will prove that a sizeable percentage of overall body length lies in the head, plus those thoracic segments lying ahead of the wings. That percentage of total body silhouette is completely ignored in conventional dry-fly theory, and hackle color based on leg color is unworkable when its fibers completely obscure both wing color and silhouette.

Experiments along the Letort confirmed the Marinaro theory that hackles should ignore leg color on most dry flies and should be chosen to reinforce wing color. His wings were designed to suggest wing color and silhouette, and should be seated farther back along the hook, both to echo their real position in fly silhouette and to make room for the thorax. Doctor Edgar Burke anticipated these thorax-style dry flies in his writings, but his dressings merely omitted the thorax and constructed the wings and hackles with a bare shank well behind the hook eye.

The Marinaro fly structure is revolutionary. It places trimmed hackle-point wings toward the center of the hook shank, working the hackles around them at exaggerated crossing angles. The trimmed wings were worked out by William Bennett, who collaborated with Marinaro in much of his work.

Similar cut-wing theories are advocated by J. W. Dunne in his *Sunshine and the Dry Fly*. The Marinaro body material is tapered in a slender cigar shape, both behind the hackles in a conventional body and ahead of the hackles to imitate the thorax. Body length behind the hackles is shortened proportionally, since the curving, upward posture of a mayfly body tends to foreshorten its apparent length when viewed from below. Marinaro

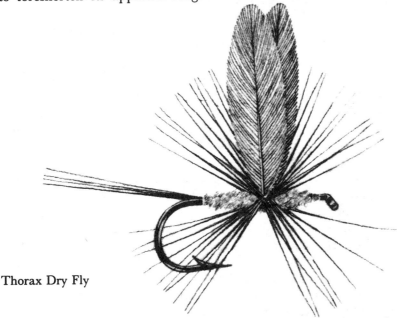

Thorax Dry Fly

sometimes trimmed out his hackles under the thorax, in the style of J. W. Dunne, and sometimes cross-wound them to expose the thorax. Such flies were designed to float the fly solely on the hackle and body structure, ignoring the presence of the hook, and laying a light pattern of thorax, body, and hackles in the surface film. Its imagery echoes the thoracic structure, sternites, and legs lying in the meniscus. Marinaro cocked his tails high, just as mayflies hold their setae high and free of the water in many cases, although this subtlety is probably unnecessary. The thorax style of dressing has since proven itself thoroughly on the selective fish of Letort Spring Run, and my own slight modifications of the concept have regularly proven themselves in my daily fishing.

Marinaro did not stop with his thorax-fly theories.

His work also focused on the unique problems found in imitating terrestrial insects like ants, beetles, and leafhoppers. Other fishermen had developed ant imitations for subsurface fishing, and flying-ant patterns already existed in the seventeenth century, but it was Marinaro who first worked out minute ants designed to float in the surface film. His patterns included seal-fur dressings with delicate little hackles between their thorax and gaster segments, and the intriguing horsehair ants were tied without working silk. The hair both formed bodies and secured their hackles.

But there had been ants before, even if they were not tiny imitations dressed to float awash in the film, and perhaps the most remarkable Marinaro contribution lies in imitating the leafhoppers. Although Ronalds surprisingly mentions these tiny terrestrials in his nineteenth-century *Fly-Fisher's Entomology*, his imitations are ineffective as leafhopper patterns. It was Marinaro who discovered both the contemporary importance of these insects and an approach to fly dressing that could imitate them with precision.

The ultimate day of discovery is eloquently recorded in his *Modern Dry-Fly Code*, which describes fishing the Letort with Charles Fox near their little fishing hut. No insects were visible on the water, but the fish were working busily in its glassy channels. Conventional flies had failed consistently in the past and proved no better that frustrating afternoon. The rise forms were the familiar bulge rings so familiar on Letort Spring Run. Fox and Marinaro tried fish after fish in the meadows, resting first one and then another, and exchanged helpless gestures as they moved along the stream.

Marinaro writes that his increasing frustration finally proved too much for him, and he stopped fishing to study the current. Lying prone in the warm grass, Marinaro watched the silken current slide hypnotically past. Considerable time elapsed in pleasant daydreaming before he suddenly became aware of almost-invisible insects on the water. Marinaro rubbed his eyes in disbelief, but there they were: tiny mayflies struggling in their diaphanous nymphal skins, beetles so small they looked like bubbles in the meniscus, minute ants awash in the surface film, and countless other minutae pinioned helplessly in the tension of the smooth current.

His mind stirred with excitement.

Marinaro hurried to the fishing hut and fashioned a fine-mesh seine with sticks and mosquito netting. Its meshes quickly collected a delicate residue of insects at its water line. There were tiny mayflies with wings less than one-eighth of an inch in length, beetles less than three-thirty-seconds of an inch in diameter, tiny black and rusty pink ants, and minute leafhoppers in astonishing numbers.

It was the moment Marinaro discovered the jassid.

Modified conventional patterns consistently failed to take fish feeding on leafhoppers in the days that followed. New fly-dressing theories were clearly needed. The basic concepts of the jassid-style tie were painfully slow in coming, and early attempts were less than fruitful.

It was not a problem of really imitating a jassid, Charles Fox explained thoughtfully at his bench on the stream one evening. *It was more a problem of suggesting silhouette and light pattern in the film.*

The actual shape and thickness of the leafhoppers was ultimately forgotten, and a silhouette theory of terrestrial imitation evolved. Since many of the tiny *Cicadellidae* or leafhoppers have banded multicolored wings, Marinaro chose a down-wing dressing with a similarly colored junglecock feather. The first patterns were tied with conventional hackling, and although they caught some fish, the jassid imitations were not really effective until Marinaro trimmed the hackle fibers to lie flat in the surface film. Their success was striking, and it was clearly the result of his fresh theory: that fish cannot really sense the thickness of small insects drifting over them, and that opacity and silhouette and light-pattern distortion in the film are the secret of the jassid-type fly and its success.

Since the prototypes were dressed with junglecock feathers, many anglers assume that such leafhopper imitations are impossible without wings that use these rare little eyed feathers. Nothing could be farther from the truth, since leafhoppers come in virtually the entire range of colors, from milky white and pale green to richly mottled purples and dark blackish browns.

Jassid

Leafhoppers can be imitated with any number of small feather types set in clear vinyl lacquer, in various colors and hackle combinations, depending on the naturals you observe in the grass. The jassid-type imitation did not die out when the Asian junglecock was declared rare and endangered, and the importation of their capes was forbidden.

Marinaro also developed a silhouette-style imitation of the Japanese beetle in those years. The selective trout of the limestone streams were quick to discover that these destructive little Coleoptera from the Orient were both abundant and food-rich. Some fish clearly disliked them, and we laughed at the occasional trout that shook its head disdainfully after taking a beetle, disturbed at the wriggling and crawling in its gullet. Others took them readily, and a dedicated beetle-feeder was often so stuffed with them that they literally crunched and rattled when we handled it in the net. It was a totally new problem in imitation.

Beetle imitations soon proved surprisingly difficult. Small coffee beans were first tried; and they were filed and mounted on the hook with cement in the manner of tiny bass bugs. These imitations floated too low and landed too hard, and the fish apparently wanted none of them. Cork and balsa wood beetles were not much better. Clipped and folded deer-hair patterns worked, but they also absorbed too much water and were not ovoid enough to simulate the Japanese species. Black sponge rubber was tried; although it worked surprisingly well, it tended to twist on the hook, making it difficult to hook a rising fish. All of these flies took fish on most limestone streams, but the wary Letort trout remained skeptical.

Like the jassid-style dressings, the full configuration and thickness of the beetles were ultimately forgotten, and the Marinaro principles of opacity and silhouette were applied. Marinaro used large junglecock eyes in his first patterns. Their opacity was quite good, and they took fish rather well, although such flat-tied wings tended to be fragile. The silhouettes were too linear for the oval-shaped beetles, and the tendency of the feathers to split led me to abandon them quickly. Obviously, other fly-dressing options were needed, although Marinaro had already worked out the basic structural principles involved.

Ross Trimmer and I were cooling out in the Turnaround Meadow on the Letort one afternoon late in August. I was lazily dressing flies and accidentally noticed several pheasant-skin pieces in a hackle canister. One fragment had a few dark little throat feathers from a ringneck cock-bird.

Look, I said, *they're the exact color of the beetles!*

You're right, Trimmer agreed.

It was not long before I had palmered three black gamecock hackles on a sixteen hook and trimmed them flat along the top of the shank. Two ringneck feathers were laid with their concave sides together and saturated with vinyl lacquer. Once fully dried, these feathers were trimmed into an oval beetlelike shape, pressed flat over the hook, and tied into cement. Finally, a single untreated neck feather with a greenish bronze sheen was laid over the underwing and trimmed to shape. When the hackling under the hook was trimmed out, the little feather-wing beetle would ride flat and opaque in the surface film.

Looks pretty good, Trimmer said eagerly.

What should we call it? I said.

Well, Trimmer cut himself some fresh chewing tobacco, *what about the Schwiebert beetle?*

I've never liked naming flies that way. I shook my head.

Letort beetle? he suggested.

Better, I said.

Our success with the new beetle was instantaneous. We tried them over the beetle-feeding trout in the Barnyard and Otto's Meadow. The first fish was working under the big willow in the Barnyard, and it took without hesitation. We worked upstream slowly, stopping well above the trestle, and took twenty-one fish between us. Such a score on the difficult beetle-feeders was unbelievable.

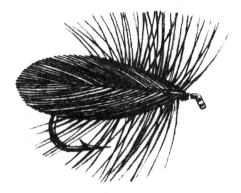

Letort Beetle

The small Marinaro ants also proved themselves in my first few seasons on the Letort, and I soon began experimenting with ant imitations dressed with dubbing. Crewel wool picked apart and spun on the tying silk made excellent wet flies, using the dubbing to shape the configuration of head, thorax, and gaster that suggests the silhouette of an ant. Soft webby hackling completed the sunk patterns. Various types of natural fur and synthetic dubbing was tried on my ants dressed to float awash in the surface film. Seal's fur and dyed kapok proved themselves, and now we have nylon wools and the more exotic polypropylene fibers to pick apart and dub on the tying thread. Their specific gravity is so much lighter than water that their floating properties are good, they shape into elegant little ants, and a few turns of stiff gamecock hackle completes the pattern. However, Gary Borger has developed a series of parachute-hackle ants on the limestone streams of southern Wisconsin. These ant patterns lie superbly in the surface film, providing a better light pattern than my conventional dressings, and I have started using these tiny ants extensively.

Crowe Beetle

Grasshoppers are another staple in the midsummer trout diet, particularly on meadow streams like Letort Spring Run. Marinaro and his collaborator, William Bennett, developed a so-called pontoon hopper made of feather quills. Such patterns are difficult to tie and they cast rather clumsily. I have not used them much, although they have produced some Olympian fish for Marinaro and his friends.

Art Winnie was an old-time tier in the Boardman country of Lower Michigan, and once reigned as King of the Kalkaska Trout Festival. Many traditional Michigan patterns originated in his prolific fly vise, including his Michigan Caddis and Michigan Mosquito dressings. Perhaps his best-known pattern is the Michigan Hopper, which has fathered a number of offspring like the widely sold Joe's Hopper, the elegant Kade dressings in Wisconsin, and the modern variations born in the skilled fingers of Dave Whitlock in Oklahoma

The conventional grasshopper pattern is found in the color plates of Bergman's *Trout*, and Bergman himself tied a fore-and-aft variation of these typical turkey-wing dressings. Such flies were found in the fly boxes of most fishermen on the Pennsylvania limestone country, but the selective Letort browns seem more difficult every year, and they started refusing these old-time imitations with an irritating frequency.

New patterns seemed necessary. Like the 'neck-feather beetle imitations, our first attempts were tied in the Turnaround Meadow on Letort Spring Run. My western experiments with hair wings and clipped-hair bodies had worked well on big cutthroats in the Jackson Hole country, on the picky rainbows of Silver Creek in Idaho, and the fat brown trout lying under the grassy banks of the Madison in Yellowstone Park.

Many good fishermen were reporting success with a Muddler Minnow soaked in silicone paste during late summer orgies of grasshopper feeding. *It worked beautifully on Flat Creek,* the late Wayne Buszek once explained. *It floated like a cork, and when we plopped them down hard—those big cutthroats came after them like crocodiles!*

His experience provided our catalyst.

It was still early summer, and the grasshoppers in the Letort meadows were relatively small. Size sixteen hooks seemed about right, and my first attempts were relatively simple flies. The bodies were nylon wool picked apart and dubbed; the nylon wool was chosen both for its ability to hold color when wet and for its specific gravity. Since the naturals were small, we tried a wingless imitation consisting only of a three-quarter collar of deer body hair. Its strands trailed back in a tight hopperlike silhouette, and its flaring butts were trimmed into a blocky grasshopper-shaped head. These prototypes seemed to work better than our conventional patterns, but not many early summer fish were actively looking for them that week.

The grasshoppers in the meadows grew larger as the summer progressed. Subsequent refusals and successes finally caused us to restore the familiar turkey-section wings and alter the deer-hair dressing slightly. The silhouette of the wings folded over trailing underwings of deer hair, with a

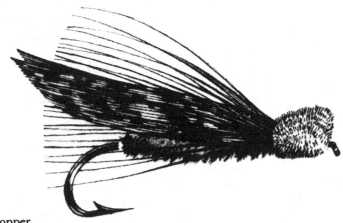

Letort Hopper

trimmed collar and trailing outer layer of hair, proved itself on the stream. The absence of conventional hackling permitted the full bulk of the fly and its yellow-dubbed body to float flush in the surface film. We floated it over a small mirror in a shallow pan with a live grasshopper, and its light pattern looked hopperlike and promising.

Looks pretty good, Ross Trimmer observed. *Maybe we'll name it the Letort Hopper.* Trimmer cut some chewing tobacco.

It's christened, I agreed.

The selective fish liked it fine. We devised additional refinements as the summer reached the end of the season, modifying body color and exaggerating the trimmed hair into grasshopper-shaped heads. Sometimes we added trailing legs of knotted condor quill, dying their tips to suggest the red-legged hoppers that were everywhere along the stream. It was important to remember that the flaring deer hair had to be carefully trimmed out underneath to insure that the dubbed body laid flat on the surface. Our modern polypropylene dubbings have a lighter specific gravity than nylon, and provide several hopperlike body colors with exceptional floating properties.

It was not long before Edward Shenk and his collaborator Edward Koch developed their Letort Cricket. It was an entirely black pattern using the same principles of silhouette, floating properties, and light pattern as our Letort Hopper. The grasshopper took several three- and four-pound fish in its first few seasons, and I had an even larger brown break off in the moss on a slough near the Beaverhead.

But the cricket imitation had a more impressive launching ceremony when Ed Koch took a nine-pounder with it from Otto's Meadow on the Upper Letort. It was taken early in the morning, well into the 1962 season, and it has been verified as the largest dry-fly trout ever caught in Pennsylvania.

Succeeding summers found our tree-sheltered mountain rivers infested with pale green inchworms. These larvae vary from three-eighths of an inch in length when the fish begin taking them, to slightly more than an inch when they are fully grown and about to build their cocoons. Such larvae have no leg structure, so no hackles can be used to float an imitation, and only the body material itself serves this function. It was the late Paul Young who tied the first green inchworms that I ever used, and these were fashioned of apple-green deer hair tightly bound along the hook shank with strong nylon working thread. The flaring tips and butts were trimmed off close. Some versions were tied with extended bodies and others are dressed on long-shank hooks. It was a deadly pattern in inchworm season, and it took some muscular deep-bellied browns on the foliage-dark rivers of my Michigan summers—particularly the South Branch of the Au Sable.

Edward Ringwood Hewitt also tied some primitive inchworm imitations that had apple-green bodies dubbed on slender hooks with a sparse collar of olive hackles. His pattern was sold by William Mills & Son in New York as late as a dozen years ago. Ray Bergman also recommends this pattern in his first book *Just Fishing*, and similar patterns are still fished both wet and dry on many eastern streams.

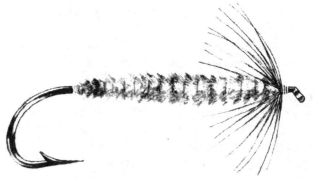

Hewitt Inchworm

Such flies work well enough on broken water, but the fish on our glassy Brodheads flats were another matter, and we clearly needed better dressings. The behavior of the inchworm larvae was the secret. The delicate green worms performed their midday acrobatics up and down their silken cords over the current, and they often worked so far from the foliage that they actually trailed in the water. It was usually their almost imperceptible wakes that attracted attention and started the fish working on them, and a delicately dragging fly was needed.

The solution had to float with nothing more than its dubbing materials, and that meant a relatively delicate hook. Structurally the imitation should also skim like an aquaplane in the current, and its color should have the intense green chroma of the live inchworms. Wet imitations sometimes worked, tied with pale greenish synthetic yarn on long-shank hooks with a fine wire ribbing, but such patterns refused to float except on relatively still currents. It was a stubborn problem until I thought of tying dubbed bodies on cores of fine stainless wire.

The stainless core material was stretched taut between two fly vises, and a bright green synthetic wool was picked apart and dubbed on waxed silk. Five or six bodies were quickly prefabricated on the .005 wire, and I sealed their ends with vinyl lacquer. When the wire-core bodies were snipped from the wire, they were virtually weightless, and I selected tiny little lightweight hooks to secure under them. The hooks were wrapped with waxed pale green working nylon and then lashed at either end of the shank, with their eyes about a quarter of the body length back from the head. Soaked with silicone paste, these flies proved reasonably buoyant, and the position of the hook eye caused them to skim perfectly on a light nylon tippet.

The principle of buoyant synthetic dubbing, shaped in a linear silhouette without other distortions of the light pattern, proved itself again with the gypsy moth larvae. These insects are sombre slate-colored worms before they become fully grown caterpillars. Wet-fly imitations were tied of black wool dubbing and palmered with a grayish saddle hackle, its fibers trimmed to about one-sixteenth of an inch in length.

Black polypropylene or seal's fur dubbing on a fine stainless core also worked well, before the gypsy moth larvae were an inch long, and they regularly took selective fish. These imitations were also fitted with tiny hooks hanging underneath their bodies, and sometimes they hang suspended on their silken cords, trailing in the current like inchworms. Gypsy moths have not been important for many seasons on our eastern streams, but the eager response of our trout this past summer to imitations of proper color and silhouette and size indicates that this tree-killing pest is an important new trout food.

It's like the Japanese beetles all over again, Alvin Grove observed recently on the Battenkill. *Mixed blessings.*

Many innovative fly tiers are still working with experimental patterns and fly structure, and knowledgeable anglers are aware that we are

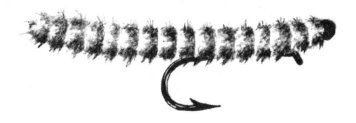

Wire-body Inchworm

experiencing a period of considerable creativity and innovation. Most dry-fly types are focused on the Ephemeroptera, but there are also some remarkably creative imitations of stoneflies, caddis, and damselflies on widespread waters.

Perhaps the first fly dresser to experiment with structural hybrids, combining extended bodies with parachute-style hackles and both fan wings and rolled wings, was the late John Gaylord Case. His elegant little upright-wing drakes were dressed with woodduck tails and extended bodies spun from natural and dyed kapok. His wings were either slender fan wings or conventional rolled wings of mallard, woodduck, and teal, depending on the wing color of the hatches. Although he was an eastern fly-fisherman from New York—and my first editor on *Matching the Hatch*—Case did a lot of fishing on our Rocky Mountain spring creeks. His experimental patterns reflected a knowledge of the mottled-wing naturals on many American rivers—particularly the *Stenonema* flies on our eastern waters, and the several *Callibaetis* speckle-wing hatches found in profusion on slow-flowing western streams.

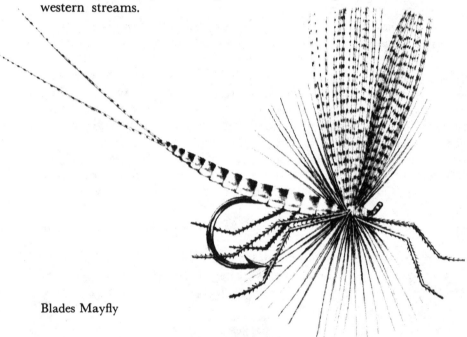

Blades Mayfly

The wing image and extended-body silhouette of these dressings is superb. The parachute hackling at the root of the wings creates a light-image illusion of spreading legs, and floats the body and thorax right in the film. Case achieved a synthesis of several centuries of fly dressing theory with his mayfly work, although he never wrote a book about his studies. His fragile imitations were superbly conceived for eastern fishing and the western spring creeks he loved over many summers, and it was not long before other tiers were working with the same structural theories and more buoyant synthetic materials.

Paradun

In *Selective Trout* Douglas Swisher and Carl Richards describe extensive experiments with parachute-style imitations using various types of rolled wings and fan-wing type dressings. These so-called paradun dressings are quite effective, and a number of hair-wing parachute ties have evolved in recent seasons using both calftail and elk in rolled upright sail-wings. Swisher and Richards also detail the techniques of making an elk-wing mayfly imitation with a detached body of deer hair. Such adaptations of the detached-body parachute dressings provide rough-water floating qualities that the delicate Case-type imitations lacked. Perhaps the best of this elk-wing school are tied by Andre Puyans of San Francisco, and I have several samples of his *Ephemerella grandis* drakes on my table as I write. They are dressed for the heavy early-summer hatches of big Lead-winged Olives on the Henry's Fork of the Snake, perhaps the best trout stream in America.

Swisher and Richards are certainly better known for their no-hackle dun and spinner imitations. It is these patterns that have made *Selective Trout* extremely successful since its publication in 1971—although it is perhaps more important for its original studies in entomology and previously unknown fly hatches, its work on fly and nymph behavior, and its emphasis on hatching nymphs. Most fishermen are fascinated with the no-hackle and parachute dry flies, believing them a totally new contribution to fly dressing. Such opinions could come only from fishermen who do not tie themselves, or from fly tiers who are not knowledgeable students of the history of their art.

No-hackle flies have unquestionably been fished in the film since Cotton and Bowlker and Pritt, and the original dozen patterns described in the *Treatyse of Fysshynge wyth an Angle* were similar no-hackle dressings from

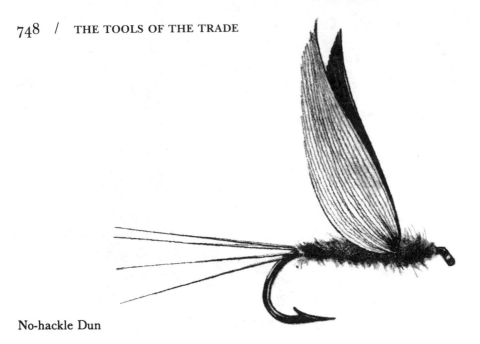

No-hackle Dun

the fifteenth century. Skues mentions the remarkable performance of the Hare's Ear on the heavy *Baetis* hatches that literally cover the Itchen late in April. It is a relatively ancient pattern with roots several centuries deep in the history of fly-fishing. It has no-hackle dressing, like many of the north-country patterns of Yorkshire and Roxburgheshire. It also has a roughly dubbed body of hare's mask ribbed with fine gold tinsel, completely unlike the olive green sternites of the hatching Medium Olives. Skues devotes a brief chapter of *The Way of a Trout with a Fly* to the puzzle of matching these Olives, wondering both about its lack of conventional hackling and its coloring. His observations clearly indicate that the Itchen trout do not take the Hare's Ear as a lure, but take it when specific insects are hatching. Skues' experience with this no-hackle pattern more than a half century ago is intriguing, both because it is clearly a problem of imitating a hatching dun only half-free of its nymphal skin and because it underlines an almost continuous history of no-hackle dressings in the United Kingdom.

Selective Trout is unique not so much in its discussion of the structure of the no-hackle pattern as in its authors' recognition that a no-hackle dressing offers some unique elements of light pattern and silhouette, particularly in the smaller sizes. Detached bodies, parachute-style hackling, and spent parachute-hackle spinners have also been tied and fished for many years in both Europe and the United States.

Such criticism is not aimed at the remarkably original content of *Selective Trout*, but for those who believed these theories were completely new, and without antecedents in the history of fly-dressing. Their contribution can be traced directly from the fifteenth-century flies listed in Berners to the contemporary observations of Skues, Mottram, Harding, and

Marinaro. The no-hackle duns and hen-wing spinners are also a result of modern synthetic dubbings like polypropylene, as well as the structural proportions and refinements worked out by Swisher and Richards. Such original concepts would justify *Selective Trout* in themselves, but the book offers many other fresh theories in its cornucopia of ideas.

These past two weeks I have been fishing with Carl Richards and Doug Swisher on the Au Sable, in Michigan. The difficult trout on the fly-water of the North Branch, and the river itself between Stephan's and the Wakeley Bridge, were the critics that helped shape their no-hackle theories. Heavy fly hatches and smooth currents characterize both stretches. Most of the fish can be taken on conventional flies during a good hatch, but there were a number of selective browns that made a believer of me—when they inspected and refused conventional flies before accepting a carefully dressed no-hackle imitation.

Other innovators are working in these years too, and their fly vises have produced several unusual imitative mayfly patterns. Some use completely new synthetic materials, and others employ old fly-tying materials in fresh ways. It was Chauncey Lively of Pittsburgh who originally developed the intriguing wonder-wing style of tying, using small body feathers tied in by their tips, drawn upward into their final slender configuration, and trimmed off. His flies can be tied in surprisingly small sizes, and their wings are both lifelike and durable. Another strikingly original use of conventional materials is the work of André Puyans of San Francisco. His little loop-wing duns and spinners are tied in both upright and spent-wing versions, using goose quill and other feather fibers to suggest only the outlines of the wings. It is a remarkably simple method of suggesting the crystalline wings of mayfly spinners, and Puyans even mottles the leading edge of some loop-wing patterns with lacquer to

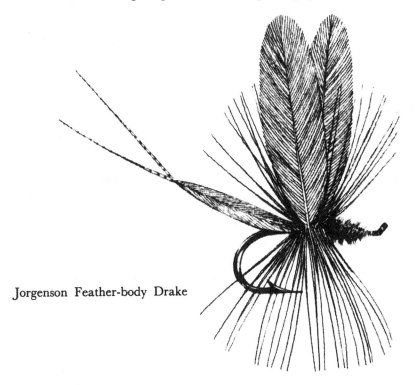

Jorgenson Feather-body Drake

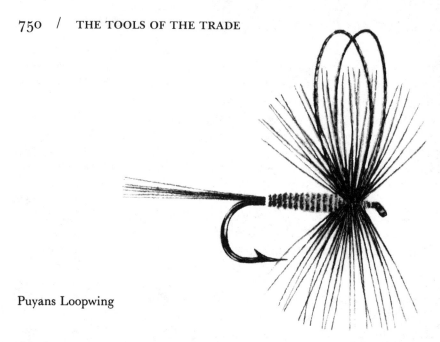

Puyans Loopwing

simulate such speckle-wing mayflies as *Callibaetis nigritus*. It is also possible to dress these Puyans loop-wings with thin nylon monofilament, and their performance during a fine spinner fall of *Callibaetis* on Silver Creek proved their worth—its selective Idaho rainbows are the acid test of any imitation, and we took fish after fish on a windless evening.

Mayflies are not the only fly hatches on our trout streams, and on many American rivers their importance is waning. Pollution, warming rivers, and water drawn off in reservoirs and irrigation networks have decimated the Ephemeroptera and made other insects more important. During recent years, experimental flies dressed to imitate stoneflies, marchflies, damselflies, and caddisflies have displayed considerable originality. Edward Ringwood Hewitt also liked to dress flat-wing stoneflies for his Neversink hatches. During recent years we have experienced serious flooding from rains triggered by late-summer hurricanes. The scouring damage of these floods both decimated and eradicated many aquatic species; until the stoneflies and the sedges have become increasingly important on our eastern streams.

Almost twenty years ago, we experienced some heavy hatches of small brown-mottled caddisflies, and once our fish had gorged themselves they became extremely selective. The usual dry-fly imitations failed consistently, and one afternoon I stopped fishing and caught a few of the naturals. The fly vise was attached to the table in my corner room above the porch at Henryville House, and I was rooting around in my material canisters when I knocked the little box of live caddisflies to the floor. The insects fluttered around the room, and several quickly settled on the window screen. Their dark silhouettes suddenly caught my attention.

They're like a big jassid, I thought excitedly, *except for the notch-shaped silhouette of the wings!*

It proved a workable solution. Brown partridge hackles were saturated with vinyl lacquer, and stroked into a thin caddislike shape before they dried. Once they were fully dried, I trimmed them with the V-shaped notches to suggest the silhouettes of caddisflies with their wings folded. Brown and grizzly hackles were palmered the length of a sixteen hook, and trimmed out along the belly and the back, so the imitation would lie flat in the film. The notched partridge hackle was laid jassid-style in two drops of cement, and pressed flat along the shank of the hook. It was both simple and effective.

It was so successful with the selective fish on our Brodheads flats that I tried it with small Plecoptera imitations the following spring. These fluttering little stoneflies were taken more readily by the trout that season than usual, perhaps because our mayfly hatches had not yet recovered from the flood damage in 1955. Since stoneflies often lie awash in the current with their wings folded flat along the body, imitations in the jassid-style seemed promising. Pale rusty pink and black and dark brown bodies were dubbed along the entire hook, with short tail fibers and a single dun hackle delicately palmered behind the hook eye. The hackles were trimmed out along both the back and bottom of the shank, and either gray or dun-colored hen hackles shaped like stoneflies and set in vinyl lacquer were tied flat over the dubbed bodies. The patterns worked extremely well.

The following season we experienced unusually heavy hatches of dark little *Bibio* flies, and the fish in our eastern streams fed on them eagerly. It was the same pattern of feeding behavior that had occurred with the caddis two years earlier. The trout took so many marchflies that they became stuffed and stopped taking them, but in the succeeding days there were sporadic hatches that the fish took well. These *Bibio* hatches came in the middle hours of the day, and the fish became typically selective in their feeding. These red-legged marchflies were not easily imitated, and we tried several patterns before finding a workable dressing. The naturals are rather

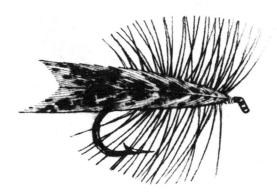

Flat-wing Sedge

antlike, with their black bodies and reddish-tinged legs, except that their pale grayish wings are folded flat over their bodies. The basic jassid-type theories of silhouette, light pattern, and color worked again. We dressed a body and thorax of black seal's fur with a dark reddish furnace hackle tied parachute between the segments. Pale grayish hen hackles were shaped and set in vinyl lacquer and laid flat across the back once the upper fibers were trimmed flat. The dressing took many selective fish during the times the *Bibio* flies were hatching in good numbers.

Our western spring creeks exhibit the unusual characteristic of sporadic and predictable feeding on adult damselflies. The large numbers of these slender-bodied Zygoptera on such streams clearly demonstrate the fact that their weedy alkalinity provides an optimal habitat for damselflies. Particularly on famous Silver Creek in Idaho, the local fishermen have begun tying extended-body damselflies with flat monofilament dyed bright blue, bright green, and several shades of brown. Both conventional hackling and parachute ties are seen. Such flies are surprisingly deadly in late summer when the damselflies are mating.

Several tiers have been experimenting with other caddisfly imitations on widespread waters in recent years since sedge hatches have become more important on streams depleted of their mayfly populations. Hair-wing patterns like the Woodchuck were sedge imitations in wide use on my Michigan boyhood streams, and their simplicity was striking. Woodchuck dressings were tied without bodies, simply using down wings of mottled body hair and a conventional hackling of mixed brown and grizzly. Although the Michigan Mosquito has slender pheasant-fiber tails, it also has duck-quill sections tied down over its quill body. The pheasant tails were fragile and broke off quickly, leaving an effective sedge imitation.

Damselfly Nymph

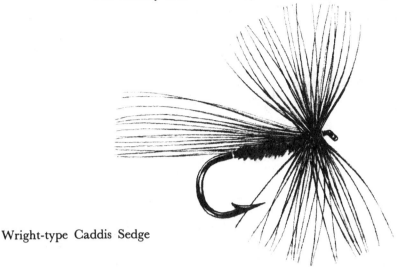

Wright-type Caddis Sedge

Similar dressings are found in *Fishing the Dry Fly as a Living Insect*, a recent book by Leonard Wright, in which both the sedges and their fluttering behavior receive attention. Larry Solomon is a first-rate tier from New York who is tying a flat-wing sedge using two flaring hackle points over the body. Such dressings are not totally new, since they have a prelude in the work of chalkstream thinkers like Skues and Lunn, but the revival of the Trichoptera found in the work of both Solomon and Wright is long overdue on our waters.

Perhaps the most unusual caddis imitation in recent years is the work of two British anglers. John Goddard is the author of *Trout-Fly Recognition*, which has been called the definitive book on fly hatches in the United Kingdom. Clifford Henry is a remarkably innovative fly dresser who illustrated Goddard's book with sketches and diagrams, and their collaboration has produced a strikingly original clipped-hair caddisfly. Goddard has two small photographs of their clipped-hair sedge in his recent book, and its ingenious character is not fully apparent.

Like many innovative solutions, the concept is both simple and obvious. It consists of a heavy strand of darning cotton that matches the body color of the natural being imitated tied in under the hook, trailing off toward the rear. Two antenna fibers are tied in lying forward from the eye. The beginning is not unusual, but the next step is remarkable: the entire hook shank is filled with bunched body hair of deer, caribou, elk, or antelope, depending on the wing color of the hatch. The hair is densely flared along the hook like a bass bug, and then trimmed into the tent-shaped bulk of a sedge. The fly body is formed simply by dubbing fur or polypropylene on the darning cotton rather roughly, and stretching this cotton core taut along the underside of the shank. The fly is conventionally hackled, and the upper fibers are clipped off at the thorax. The concept has been widely adopted on the white-water rivers of our Pacific Coast, and André Puyans dresses large versions of these clipped-wing sedges for the

Goddard Clipped-wing Sedge

rivers north of San Francisco. His variation also razor-trims a tapering notch at the center of the flaring wing mass to simulate the V-shaped space between the wings. These clipped-wing sedges are a remarkable mixture of sophisticated British silhouette theory and the floatability of clipped deer hair, which developed on the rough-and-tumble American rivers.

Except for hatching imitations like the Hare's Ear, and the soft-hackled border patterns that suggest emerging sedge pupae, our imitations of aquatic nymphs, larvae and pupal forms are largely a product of this century. Skues is the father of both the mayfly nymph imitation and its chalkstream fishing techniques. His nymphs were already fully developed when *The Way of a Trout with a Fly* was published in 1921, and the exquisite watercolors of Captain Sainte Barbe Goldsmith illustrate the Skues-style nymph in a pair of color plates. Skues tied his nymphs with short soft-fiber legs and tails, bodies roughly and delicately dubbed on colored silk, and a thickly dubbed thorax. This slightly exaggerated thorax was covered with a

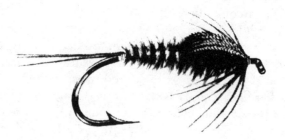

Skues Nymph

wing case formed of pheasant-tail fibers. The proportions of these flies are elegant and studied, and the remarkable Skues-style nymph is still the principal influence in our thinking today.

Both Mottram and Harding dressed similar nymphs, and our own Preston Jennings advocated conventional wet flies with their wings clipped or tied short in his *Book of Trout Flies*, which created a silhouette in the Skues tradition. Edward Hewitt tied flat-bodied nymphs of similar proportions, but his hard lacquer bodies were only lifeless echoes of the elegant Skues prototypes.

Both James Leisenring and Art Flick tied patterns closely matched to American nymphal forms, but their proportions and style are not unlike their English antecedents. It was Charles Wetzel who started a nymph-tying school of precise imitation, complete with individual wing pads and legs of knotted moosemane. However, Wetzel was not a highly skilled tier in the sense that his patterns were beautifully wrought works of art, and it was William Blades who developed the tying of precise nymphal patterns to the point of excellence. Blades was my fly-dressing mentor for several years, and although his exacting patterns have a strange, lifeless quality to them, no one has excelled their craftsmanship. Blades was an artisan of exceptional talents, and disciples like Poul Jorgenson and Ted Niemeyer are superb fly dressers in the Blades tradition.

Edward Sens is another American nymph fisherman, and although he never wrote about his entomological studies, his fly patterns were outlined by Ray Ovington in his *How to Take Trout on Wet Flies and Nymphs*. The Sens dressings were also keyed to familiar dry-fly hatches, with wing cases of cut feathers rather than the Skues-type feather sections tied down over the thorax. The basic proportions of the Sens nymphs are still obvious echoes of the Skues prototypes, but his little caddis pupae are completely original. These imitations of hatching sedges consisted of little more than rough dubbing along the body, two half-developed wings along the sides, and a thorax of darker dubbing mixed with rough guard-hairs. These emerging caddis were the prelude to a whole philosophy of hatching nymphs and pupae found in the work of writers like Hidy, Swisher, Richards, Rogowski,

Sens Pupa

Rosborough, and in my own book *Matching the Hatch*. Such a philosophy is a modern American innovation of considerable importance.

Frank Sawyer wrote his book *Nymphs and the Trout* in 1958, and his two favorite patterns for the Avon above Salisbury are unquestionably derivative of the half-century Skues tradition. His small Pheasant Tail, Grey Goose, Pale Watery Nymph, Spur-wing Nymph, and tiny pinkish cream shrimps are pure simplicity. The three mayfly patterns are very much in the Skues style, except that they dispense entirely with leg fibers. The late Major Oliver Kite was a dedicated Sawyer disciple, and Kite also fished the chalkstreams near the cathedral town of Salisbury. Kite was so convinced that the Sawyer pheasant-tail dressing was sufficient for his home waters that his *Nymph Fishing in Practice* recommends carrying only that pattern in a number of hook sizes.

Ted Rogowski is an eastern fly-fisherman transplanted to Seattle to work as a federal attorney for the Environmental Protection Agency. During his years in Manhattan with a distinguished Wall Street law office, he was an active member of the Anglers' Club of New York and one of the founding officers of the Theodore Gordon Flyfishers. Rogowski is a tier of nymphs that are consciously descended from Skues, but his dressings are

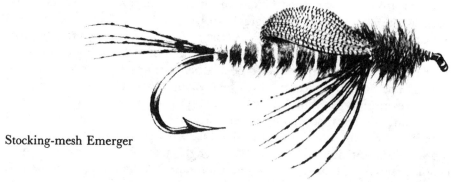

Stocking-mesh Emerger

also thorax-style configurations adapted from the dry-fly theories of Marinaro. His work is described in *American Fly-Fishing* in a long, discursive chapter dealing with experimental fly dressing; about fifteen years ago his studies included emerging wings shaped from sections of women's nylon stockings. The air held in the stocking meshes tends to buoy these fur-bodied nymphs, holding them just within the meniscus like a hatching fly. Such emerging patterns are a major step after the beginnings found in the work of Sens.

George Grant is a skilled fly dresser from Butte, with a lifetime of fishing on Montana rivers like the Ruby and Beaverhead and Big Hole. His work is described in a paperbound folio entitled *The Art of Weaving Hair Hackles for Trout Flies*. His woven-body nymphs with hair and plastic hackle fibers are his most famous innovations, but it is the hybrid nymphs that are perhaps his most important work. These patterns combine both traditional

Swisher-Richards Emerger

soft hackles like grouse, ringneck pheasant, and woodcock and bodies of flat nylon monofilament wound smoothly over cores of synthetic wool and floss. These underbodies are mottled, edged with indelible felt pens, and marked to suggest the body coloring of the naturals. Flat nylon monofilament is an unusually effective material for simulating naturals that have bodies glowing with inner chroma, like the bright greens muted inside the loosening pupal skin of a hatching sedge.

Polly Rosborough is a professional tier from Chiloquin in the mountains of Oregon, and his fur-bodied nymphs are widely known on American rivers. His roughly tied patterns are practical, easily tied, and effective on difficult fish. Some are frankly impressionistic in concept, capable of suggesting a number of subaquatic diet forms. Others are clearly imitative nymphs focused on a particular hatch. Rosborough has assembled his fly patterns and philosophy of nymph technique into a slim book titled *Tying and Fishing the Fuzzy Nymphs*, and its tying concepts are an intriguing synthesis. His exaggerated heads are painted dark on their dorsal surfaces, obviously intended to suggest the thoracic structure of the naturals. Some smaller mayfly and stonefly forms are dressed without leg fibers, while his larger nymphs have sparsely tied legs. Rosborough ties his wing cases with various fibers like mallard, lemon woodduck, and marabou, sometimes leaving a few sparse fibers trailing to suggest emerging wings. Other Rosborough dressings clearly suggest hatching nymphs with soft, feather-wing cases reaching back more than half the body length. The full series of patterns includes several important western mayflies and stonefly species, along with caddis larvae and the pupal imitations of hatching sedges. Midge pupae and freshwater shrimps are also found in the Rosborough fly books, and his patterns are an important facet of American nymph tactics.

Dave Whitlock and Ron Kusse are two nymph experts whose patterns are not focused on specific hatches. They tie general imitations that suggest groups of major species. Both men like soft body-hackle fibers in their nymphs. Their skilled use of fur dubbing for imitating the abdomen and thoracic structure of their nymphs, and the delicate light-catching qualities of tinsel ribbing to suggest both body segments and a loosening nymphal skin, is clearly in the Skues tradition. Their feather wing cases of peacock and dark quill sections of turkey are tied in the same manner found in the watercolors of *The Way of a Trout with a Fly*, and their tying style is quite similar to my own. Whitlock also experiments with new materials, and his vinyl-backed freshwater shrimps are typical of his inventive mind. His shrimp imitations also work with bent hook shanks to suggest the body posture and swimming motions of the naturals. Ron Kusse also works with distorted hook shanks, particularly in his slender imitations of big Ephemeroptera and damselflies, because he believes that a living nymph does not hold its abdomen ramrod straight in life—and that slender nymphs tied on long-shank hooks look lifeless unless they are kinked to suggest restlessness and movement.

Steenrod Rolled-wing Dry Fly

Although their no-hackle dry flies have perhaps attracted the most attention, Douglas Swisher and Carl Richards have included a number of important observations on nymphs, larvae, and pupal forms in their book *Selective Trout*, as well as their emphasis on emerging subaquatic insects. Their work in these areas closely parallels my own, although our basic studies are concentrated in different geographic regions.

Swisher and Richards have explored the all-fur nymphal imitations first worked out by W. H. Lawrie in his *All-Fur Flies and How to Dress Them*, which covered conditions in the United Kingdom, and other patterns in *Selective Trout* were entirely constructed of fur dubbing except for their throat hackles and tails. Some patterns are dressed in precisely the Skues style, while others have wing cases of bunched peacock and ostrich herl. Although the first detached-body nymphs were described in my writings over fifteen years ago, *Selective Trout* has expanded on my work, which was devoted only to damselfly nymphs. Swisher and Richards have worked out delicate detached-body mayflies, using both feather section and breast feathers set in vinyl lacquer. Their hatching mayfly nymphs have been dressed with wings of hackle points, hen hackles, and rolled wings of soft hackles and duck flank feathers. Similar tying methods are used in their emerging sedge pupae, with soft, roughly tied materials that trap tiny air bubbles and glisten with moisture, working almost imperceptibly in the current. My recent book *Nymphs* catalogues most of the important American subaquatic species and their imitations, using all of these fly-dressing techniques.

Although Charles Wetzel outlined the first midge pupal imitations in his *Practical Fly-Fishing* more than thirty years ago, and my own *Matching the Hatch* included both larval and pupal imitations of these tiny insects, many young tiers are adding to our knowledge of selective patterns for these minutae. Some of the most knowledgeable midge-fishing experts are tiers like Edward Koch and Sidney Neff in Pennsylvania, Eric Peper and Robert Linsenman in the Catskills, John Alevras and Len Codella in northern New Jersey, and Swisher and Richards in Michigan.

But perhaps the most unusual innovation in *Selective Trout* is the concept of a nymph tied with an articulated body, designed to wriggle and flutter in the water. These so-called wriggling nymphs are a remarkable concept for imitating the many swimming species as well as those ecotypes which struggle clumsily in hatching. Frank Sawyer discusses his inability to imitate the Blue-winged Olive nymphs in his *Nymphs and the Trout*, and his

Wriggle Nymph

British experience has parallels for the many related fly hatches found on our own rivers. Such nymphal forms are poor swimmers. These nymphs are clambering types that crawl awkwardly along the bottom, and the fish often take them most readily when they are struggling clumsily just under the surface to hatch.

The Blue-winged Olive nymph is a wriggler, Sawyer writes to explain his lack of success, *and it is necessary to imitate the wriggle as well as the nymph.*

Sawyer is absolutely correct. Our rivers support many species closely related to the Blue-winged Olives of the United Kingdom, and our fish relish them as much as their chalkstream cousins. Their hatching behavior is a series of erratic, undulating motions as they struggle toward the surface. The trout take them with showy rise forms, obviously excited by their writhing bodies and half-emerging wings and working legs. Such helpless movements invariably attract the fish into seizing its prey. The wriggle nymphs are the kind of creative fly dressing that continues to evolve in these latter years of our century.

The generation of innovative anglers that has emerged in the past dozen years is continuing to expand our horizons. Synthetic materials are playing a surprising role, particularly for their reflective qualities, translucency, and sparkle. Synthetic dubbing is creating fly-bodies that seem almost iridescent and alive. The floating properties of polypropylene and other exotic fibers have been used to tie hatching nymphs fished in the film, and for translucent wings to imitate spent mayflies.

Other tiers are experimenting with upright polywing flies in both parachute and conventional patterns. Some are dressing downwing sedges with polypropylene too.

Still other young tiers are exploring cutwing patterns with synthetic fabrics and films, like wedding veils and mailing envelopes. Such materials create surprisingly lifelike imitations of freshly hatched mayflies and spentwing spinners.

It is nothing less than a fly-tying renaissance.

2. Some Notes on
the Modern Fly Line

It was a birthday gift of fly tackle that firmly launched me on the odyssey that has carried me throughout the trout-fishing world. The fly line was a braided level type with a hard enamel finish and it lay coiled and stiff in its box. Stretched and finally broken in along the river, it would work and shoot as well as my boyhood skills could fish it. However, when its brittle finish began to crack and wear, my enamel line refused to float and cut ragged grooves in the guides.

Line like that's impossible, one old-timer on the Pere Marquette observed. *Cut the guides right off the rod!*

It was a bright morning in early summer on the willow-lined Baldwin when another fisherman watched me fishing and gave me my first silk line. The trout were working eagerly to the hatching *Ephemerella* flies, and I had already taken several when a friendly voice startled me.

You're fishing beautifully. The strange fisherman stepped into the stream. *How old are you?*

Ten, I replied shyly.

The man nodded and smiled. *May I see your equipment?* he asked. *It's fishing well for you already.*

He took the rod gently, flexing out a series of elegant false casts, and dropped my fly along a deadfall. *It's well balanced,* he smiled, *but this linoleum line you've got is too stiff and clumsy for real dry-fly work.*

Linoleum line? I echoed.

We call them linoleum lines, the man laughed, *but they're not really made of linoleum—they're not so bad!*

What should I have? I asked.

British silk, he replied. *British double tapers woven of silk are the best fly lines in the world.*

What does one cost?

They're pretty expensive, he smiled, *but you walk up to my car and I'll show you.* We waded across the current, and his trunk was a cornucopia of beautiful split-cane rods and reels and mahogany tackle boxes filled with flies and assorted fishing gear.

The man rummaged down in a leather duffel and came up with a half dozen Hardy leaders of exquisite silkworm gut, tapered down to .007 at the tippet. The leaders were shiny and hard, and their delicate calibrations were a revelation, with a breaking strain of a pound listed on the elegant rice-paper envelopes.

They're beautiful! I exclaimed.

Yes, the man agreed, *but an English silk line is even more beautiful, and together with a fine silkworm-gut leader, it can be nothing less than poetry!*

The man searched deeper into his gear and held out an elegant Halford fly line, its darkly gleaming coils lying in its rice-paper wrappers. It was in my hands now and it was supple and smooth, its solid woven core flexing easily in my fingers, and its oil finish felt rich to the touch. Its oily, faintly waxen odor is unforgettable almost thirty-five years later.

It's yours, the fisherman said in a voice that would take no back talk, *along with the silkworm-gut leaders.*

You're serious? It was incredibly generous.

Yes. We shook hands.

The silk fly line and the half-dozen leaders were worth thirty-odd dollars during the Depression years, but it was some time before I fully understood his generosity. The man waded off downstream while I was still soaking a coiled leader in the shallows, and I never thought to ask his name. The synergy between my new silk line and its matching gut leaders was poetic, and although our modern polyvinyl fly lines and nylon leader materials are a technical revolution in trout fishing, the superb handling qualities of silk have never been equalled.

The evolution of the fly line has occupied the span of many centuries, with the first recorded use of a braided silk line dating to the Chou Dynasty, and Chinese fishermen on the Chi River in Hunan Province. Unlike the fishing reel, the braided silk line apparently did not migrate to Europe with the trading caravans, since Claudius Aelianus described a horsehair line in use by the ancient fly-fishermen of Macedonia almost five centuries later. Dame Juliana Berners still recommended a horsehair line in *Treatyse of Fysshynge wyth an Angle,* and even described preparing lines of different colors for different seasons and types of water. It was Charles Cotton, in his *Being Instructions How to Angle for a Trout or Grayling in a Clear Stream,* who first described a finely tapered line in 1676:

> Now to have your whole line as it ought to be, two of the first lengths nearest the hook should be of two hairs apiece; the next three lengths above them of three; the next three above them of four; and so of five, and six, and seven, to the very top; by which

means your rod and tackle will, in a manner, be tapered from your very hand to your hook; your line will fall much better and straighter, and cast your fly to any certain place, to which the hand and eye shall direct it, with less weight and violence than would otherwise circle the water, and fright away the fish.

Such lines were common on the trout streams of Europe and North America until the close of the nineteenth century, and some tradition-minded anglers were still using braided horsehair forty years later. Cotton-braided lines enjoyed a brief vogue on British waters in the latter half of the nineteenth century, and enamel-finished lines were first developed shortly after 1860.

Compound braided lines of horsehair and silk preceded the pure silk lines that emerged in these same years. Level lines of oiled and raw braided silk were available in the United States from Dame, Stoddard & Kendall of Boston as early as 1875. These primitive oil-finished lines were apparently an American development, although the first tapered fly lines woven of silk and cotton clearly originated in England. The Manchester Cotton Twine Spinning Company and Eaton & Deller of London were simultaneously responsible for perfecting these tapered designs. The Manchester product was fashioned of both cotton and silk, and was twisted rather than actually woven, while Eaton & Deller developed the first truly woven fly line tapered in silk and oil-dressed. These technical innovations were perfected about 1880, and the Eaton & Deller lines were clearly the prologue to our modern tackle.

Orvis still advertised silk-tapered fly lines with enamel finishes in 1884, when Frederic Halford was already working with a surgical instrument manufacturer to develop a solid woven-silk line with a fast-taper construction. Other makers experimented with hollow fly lines because of their obvious floating potential, but hollow lines proved extremely fragile. Walter Durfee Coggeshall, who was a good fishing friend of Skues on the Itchen, carried Halford's research even further with his excellent tapered silk lines. Coggeshall finished his delicate lines with several thin coats of linseed oil and varnish, each coat being allowed to dry thoroughly and hand-rubbed before the next coat was applied. When the silk braid was completely covered and sealed under these oil-finish layers, the entire line was hand-polished to a hard gloss. Some companies introduced an evaporating agent to their finish formulas, to accelerate the critical drying process. American tackle companies were quick to copy these innovations, but they were slow to catch on with our fishermen. Abercrombie & Fitch, the famous sporting goods store in New York, apparently did not carry them in stock until after 1910.

Silk fly lines tapered to the Halford calibrations and finished according to the final Halford patents were the bench mark of quality for the first fifty years of this century. Their character and workmanship were superb. The soft oil finish was a revelation to generations of Americans accustomed to the brittle enamel-finished lines that often chipped and cracked and coiled tightly on the reel, and the new lines seemed to sweeten and become more supple with time. Tackle catalogues early in this century described a so-called secret process in the manufacture of these lines, but this was a fabrication. The lines were braided solidly of silk and immersed in a pressure tank containing a mixture of refined linseed oil and Kauri-gum varnish. Atmospheric pressure in the finishing tank was then sharply reduced, drawing the air entrained in the braiding from the line and permitting a controlled quantity of the oil-finish formula to saturate the silk. The foundation created in the pressure tank formed the base for a series of oil-and-varnish coats, each carefully rubbed down with rottenstone and pumice before the next layer was applied. Talcum powder was finally used to polish the finished product.

Silk lines had a lithe and supple poetry about them, partially because of their inherent properties, and partially because they are heavier than nylon lines of the same diameter. This means a four-weight silk line is thinner than a four-weight nylon taper, and its reduced wind resistance played a considerable role in its casting qualities.

However, these beautiful lines of oil-finished silk had problems as well. The finishes were relatively soft and wore away quickly, and the lines readily absorbed water when fishing. It was necessary to dress them daily to repel the water and keep the lines floating, and it was wise to strip them from your reel each night onto the skeleton frame of a line drier. Many anglers bought two lines, which enabled them to fish one and dry the other simultaneously. Oil finishes also oxidized and became quite tacky. Although immersion in a highly alkaline solution neutralized their tackiness, it also removed much of the finish, and it was necessary to refinish the braided core with successive coats of linseed oil and varnish. The silk was also highly susceptible to fungus and rot. Such problems were easily avoided by purchasing a new line, although it was painful to discard an expensive Halford fly line in any condition.

These double-taper lines were the peak of fly-fishing theory and practice until midcentury, although weight-forward line theories had been advanced for salmon fishing in Ireland as early as 1885. Hardy Brothers had developed primitive forward tapers for trout in concert with Philip Trench of Dublin twenty-five years later, although another quarter century would pass before the superb distance casters of our western American steelhead rivers would adapt and refine weight-forward tapers and shooting-head designs into our modern tools for long-range work. Such line theories evolved to perfection on our Pacific rivers and tournament-casting platforms, along with the double-haul technique capable of exploiting their distance qualities, particularly in the hands of pioneers like Dick Miller, Marvin Hedge, and Peter Schwab.

Nylon fly lines were first developed during the Depression years, but were not available in commercial quantities until after the Second World War. The potential of nylon was obvious, since it was stronger than silk and did not rot with protracted exposure to fishing. It was also considerably more elastic than silk. The traditional oil finishes simply could not cope with this exaggerated elasticity; and finding a synthetic finish with a compatible modulus of elasticity proved difficult. The elasticity of the nylon core literally stretched and shattered its outer finish, and the line was quickly ruined. All fishermen remember how short-lived these early nylon lines were, and what damage their cracked finishes did to rod guides. Nylon fly lines were held in low esteem in those years, and their longevity was the butt of many streamside jokes.

The first true sinking lines had been manufactured and sold just before the end of the nineteenth century by Foster Brothers, whose shop is still near the British Dove in Ashburton. It was a silk line braided over a brass core, and similar lead-core lines are currently popular on our Pacific coastal rivers for deep-water tactics.

However, laboratory technicians were busily working to solve the problem of a synthetic finish with an elasticity equal to the braided nylon cores. The solution finally came in 1949, when practical methods of using polyvinyl chloride in fly-line finishes were perfected. It was first used with a hollow-woven line of nylon, but such lines had the same defects as earlier hollow lines of silk and cotton and other fibers. Such lines were much too fragile, their hollow cores eventually shipped water and sank the lines, and their tapers were achieved by varying the thread counts at various points in the line. Such hollow cores were difficult to fabricate and control with precision, and they were expensive.

Three years later, another milestone was reached in the development of the modern fly line. It became possible to control the design taper in the polyvinyl chloride finish rather than taper the woven core itself.

It was a remarkable technical breakthrough, and it had an immediate impact on the cost of manufacturing tapered fly lines, placing them within the economic reach of the average fisherman. It also permitted linemakers to produce tapers with unbelievable precision, virtually identical in their finish calibrations and with tolerances of less than .001 inch. Manufacturers suddenly found themselves capable of producing lines of uniformly consistent density and weight.

The first polyvinyl chloride finishes were conceived with minuscule bubbles and low specific gravity, and were designed to float faultlessly. Chemists soon perfected synthetic finishes capable of producing compound sinking-tip lines, as well as sinking lines of varied specific gravity and sinking ability. The short-lived sinking lines braided entirely of dacron were soon rendered obsolete. The sinking polyvinyl lines offered anglers a whole new spectrum in their sport, permitting them to fish nymphs and wet flies and streamers with more precise control of depth than had ever been possible in the past.

The series of remarkable technical developments since midcentury had a revolutionary impact on fly-line construction and manufacture. Our lines differ considerably from the wonderfully sophisticated innovations of

Halford and Coggeshall and Marryat in the nineteenth century. Polyvinyl chlorides make it possible to braid a level core of simple construction with a precisely tapered coating, instead of the intricately woven solid or hollow tapers of the past. The synthetic vinyl finishes are heat-cured and can be applied to control density and, through their specific gravity, the sinking and floating qualities of the lines themselves.

Such heat-cured plastic finishes made mass production of fly lines possible for the first time in history. Manufacturers can fabricate them continuously in long skeins, duplicating a controlling taper formula in virtually exact copies. Diameters are controlled within .001 of an inch and total line weight is monitored to within 1/500 of an ounce. Such precision is achieved through variable dies having a controlled orifice that can modify both line diameter and weight at any point along the core.

Production becomes relatively simple. It begins with a core of braided nylon, fiberglass or monofilament in the floating lines. Dacron is usually used in the sinking tapers because of its high specific gravity. The core is treated with bonding agents to implement adhesion of the polyvinyl finishes. The treated core is then passed through its first plastic bath and is forced through the operable die system. Its controllable aperture shapes the polyvinyl chloride into its final calibrations and tapers. Heat curing hardens the plastic and fuses it to the core material. The ends of each double- or forward-taper line are marked when its die sequence is complete, and a run of several lines is wound on a storage reel. The completed fly lines are finally cut apart for coiling and inspection, and are ultimately wrapped and packaged for shipment.

Precise control of diameter and the wide variation of weight within a single diameter soon made a new designation system necessary for our modern fly lines. It has been a century since the manufacturers evolved a scale of measurements based upon line calibrations, and a system of designated letter equivalents. The American and European calibrations in the old system are as follows, with the metric measurements in rounded figures:

EUROPEAN AND AMERICAN LINE CALIBRATIONS

SIZE	1/10 MM	1/100 MM	1/1000 INCH
A	15.0	150	.060
B	14.0	140	.055
C	13.0	130	.050
D	11.5	115	.045
E	10.0	100	.040
F	9.0	90	.035
G	8.0	80	.030
H	7.5	75	.025
I	6.0	60	.022

Obviously, the earlier nomenclature for fly lines based solely on diameter became unworkable with the perfection of polyvinyl chloride finishes, since two lines of identical diameter and taper systems could vary radically in weight. Most knowledgeable trout fishermen in my boyhood years were using rods that called for HDH and HCH double-tapered lines. Some big-water anglers in our western mountains could even be found wielding GBG tapers on heavy currents, and there were already skilled light-tackle men fishing rods with calibrations delicate enough to balance elegantly with an HEH line in oil-finished English silk. Some variation in the specific gravity and weight of these lines was possible too, because of weaving technology and the specifications for the oil finishes, and HDH lines from one manufacturer were not always identical to HDH tapers from another maker in terms of casting with a specific rod. Balancing rods and lines was a difficult kind of alchemy.

Originally, silk fly lines were designed in three basic types. The level line had a constant diameter over its entire length and was relatively easy to manufacture. It was inexpensive, and therefore the type purchased first by many beginners, but in the larger diameters, it delivered the leader clumsily on the water under difficult conditions and has largely disappeared from the market. Single-taper silk lines were also popular because of their lower price, and consisted of a relatively fine level head of about three feet, ten to twelve feet of front taper, and the remainder of their ninety feet in the heavier belly diameter. Since few anglers could cast more than fifty to sixty feet, and fewer still ever experienced actual fishing problems that required such casting, fishermen soon discovered that when a single-taper line was worn out, almost half of its level belly remained brand new and gleamingly intact in the inner windings of the reel. The silk double-taper design was therefore conceived in terms of its long-range economy, even though it was more expensive to make. It was literally two single-taper designs joined back-to-back in a single line. Double-taper specifications resulted in a perfectly symmetrical design that could be reversed when one end was worn out, doubling the fishing life of the average silk line.

Multiple tapers remained in their infancy in the years before the Second World War, and the knowledgeable men who really knew something about their theory and design were a relatively small group of tournament casters and steelhead fishermen who were as closed-mouthed about their secrets as a medieval guild.

These men spliced varying lengths of level fly line together in hundreds of experimental homemade tapers for distance casting. Tackle cranks like Dick Miller, Peter Schwab, and Marvin Hedge badgered Pacific Coast rodmakers and line manufacturers into producing precisely what they needed, even though many of their more radical concepts were unworkable for less skilled casters and were virtually unmarketable. Peter Schwab had a favorite weight-forward design that consisted of a five-foot steep taper from .025 to .045 with no level head, ten feet of level .045 working into ten more feet of .050, followed by ten feet of homemade back taper between .045 and

.037. The shooting line consisted of fifty-five feet of .037 lovingly polished with graphite, and with the entire multiple head weighing only 140 grains, a fisherman skilled with a fine eight-and-a-half-foot rod could deliver the whole fly line while waist-deep in a heavy steelhead riffle.

The empirical work taking place on our Pacific Coast exploded into the world of international tournament casting in 1938, when Marvin Hedge demonstrated the double-haul techniques he had worked out to exploit these new multiple tapers to their full distance potential. It was a method conceived to instantly exaggerate line velocity, a velocity perfectly matched to shooting long lengths of the level running line behind the weight-forward head. Tournament distances in the trout-fly class quickly cartwheeled beyond 150 feet, and when Dick Miller reached 179 feet in registered competition, the weight-forward line and the double haul utterly ruled the world of distance fly casting.

Early weight-forward theory was so esoteric that tackle men like Marvin Hedge actually made and sold compound Hedge tapers designed for specific distances. Hedge had specifications for casts of 75, 100, and 150 feet. The tournament casters and steelhead crowd all wanted the extreme distance model, but few had the tackle, physical strength, and timing to lift it cleanly from the water.

Our modern weight-forward lines evolved rapidly from these hand-made prototypes. Typical early specifications for factory-produced lines offered approximately two to three feet of level head, nine to ten feet of relatively steep taper, twenty-odd feet of weight-forward belly, two to three feet of exaggerated back taper, and the remaining lengths a fine running or shooting line of constant diameter. Such lines radically lengthened the casting distances of most fishermen, even before they fully mastered the double-haul methods that could take them beyond seventy-five or eighty feet.

However, mere distance without delicacy is limited to broken water and big rivers, since the velocity of a double-haul tends to drop the weight-forward belly rather harshly on the surface. Fishermen quickly discovered that it was difficult to straighten an uncoiling front taper without gently snubbing its shoot late in the cast, and that even this refinement dropped their terminal tackle too crudely for a selective fish in relatively smooth currents. Obviously, future developments were needed to wed the distance capabilities of the new multiple tapers with the reasonable subtlety of a double-taper fly presentation. Such hybrids are never fully successful, but the modified long-belly designs that have evolved in the past five years are certainly a step in that direction. Their specifications call for lengthening the belly of the weight-forward head from twenty to twenty-five and thirty feet, which helps dampen the clumsy velocity of the longer shots and turns the line over smoothly with a properly timed checking of the shoot. It is doubtful whether a hybrid taper capable of both fishing fine and fishing at distances that Charles Cotton never dreamed possible is fully workable.

These early fly-line concepts all involved floating lines, and their tapers were described in terms of the letter designations familiar to almost all fly-fishermen. Level lines were labelled with a single letter equivalent to their constant diameters. Most fishermen on trout water worked with level lines from E to B designation or calibrated between .040 and .055 inches. Single-taper lines were typically HE lines for fishing fine, HD and HC tapers for all-around work, and an occasional GB design was seen on big water. These designations translated into a taper from .025 to .040 on difficult fish, lines that ran from .025 to either .045 or .050 to balance the average trout rod, and big-water lines that varied from .030 to .055. Double-taper lines are still the most popular, and under the old system of sizing them, their trout-fishing types commonly ranged from HEH to a relatively muscular GBG. The HEH specified a taper that progressed from .025 through .040 and back to .025 in a perfectly symmetrical design. HDH and HCH lines were perhaps the most popular models in America at midcentury. Their tapers were also symmetrical, running from .025 through bellies of .045 and .050 back to .025 at the opposite head. Few anglers wanted to work hard enough to muscle a GBG double taper all day, with its taper of .030 to .055 and back to .030, but a surprising number were sold and used on western rivers.

Multiple-taper distance lines were also described with the letter nomenclature when they were first developed. Big-water and bassbug tapers were the most common early designs, and the HCF, GBF, and GAF weight-forward lines were popular from the beginning. These were the so-called three-diameter types. The HCF had a compound taper ranging from .025 to its belly of .050, and its running line measured .035. The popular GBF size ran from its head of .030 to a shooting belly of .055 and tapering back to its .035 running diameter. Fishing a rod that could handle a GAF silk forward taper in split cane was not easy, and hauling a line that varied from .030 to .060 in its belly and head, dropping back to a shooting diameter of .035 produced some Herculean fatigue.

The perspective of time indicates that both the double-taper and weight-forward lines were manufactured with level heads that were much too long until recent years. Level heads of six to ten feet were common and typically failed to deliver a complete cast and turn over the leader under fishing conditions. It was often necessary to cut back a series of trial-and-error lengths from these level heads to find the proper behavior with a specific rod. It was a little like shortening the legs of a table, cutting and cutting until the sorry moment when you realize that you have sawed off too much and the table is ruined. Thousands of fly lines were damaged just like that, snipping and trimming the level heads to balance a particular rod. Our lack of knowledge was certainly a factor, but erratic standards of manufacturing and consistent diameter-to-weight ratios were perhaps the worst problem in balancing lines, leaders, and fly rods.

The basic tapers were all woven of silk and finished in linseed oil and Kauri-gum varnish, made by different manufacturers, and varied somewhat in weight-per-foot. Nylon core lines were somewhat lighter when fabricated in the same tapers and diameters. The nominal length of casting line worked in the air without double-hauling was a maximum of forty to fifty feet in the double tapers, and about fifty to sixty feet in the forward-taper designs. Behind that nominal casting length lies a so-called holding length of level running line that is constantly chafed back and forth while casting.

The length of line which defines the maximum loading weight that a fly rod can accommodate before it is overstressed is its lift capacity. It is the maximum free length of line that can be held in motion during false casting, using only a single left-hand casting haul. The maximum free-line loading with double tapers consists of the forward taper plus about sixty percent of the belly, depending on casting skills and rod action. Maximum loading with weight-forward type lines equals the level head, forward taper and belly and back taper, the holding line, and as much as the caster can handle of the shooting length to about seventy-five feet.

Basic comparative considerations between double-taper and weight-forward lines in actual fishing have not changed since the development of our modern polyvinyl chloride finishes, except that sinking lines are thinner than floating lines of equal weight, and will work better in both the atmosphere and a wind because of less wind resistance.

Double-tapered lines are superb fishing tools at ranges of fifteen to seventy-five feet, delivering and turning over smoothly without frightening a hard-fished trout. Since their belly length is heavier, casting rhythms are relatively slow, and line velocity on delivery is quickly dampened by the inertia of the level belly diameters. Long casts are slowly developed by false casting to build line velocity, while velocity is quickly achieved with a weight-forward taper. Such forward-taper lines are demonstrably more effective in a wind, regardless of their specific gravity. Since windy weather invariably riffles a smooth current holding selective fish, a weight-forward line is sometimes a good choice on a stream where it would normally be too clumsy when sufficient wind is present to mute mistakes. Casting rhythms and line velocity are relatively fast with a forward taper, which means presentation to a cruising fish is quicker. Speed of presentation is important under some conditions, and the most important quality of the weight-forward line is unquestionably its distance capability.

It is interesting to compare typical weight-forward specifications for lines having .050 belly diameters from several major manufacturers when *Matching the Hatch* was published twenty-odd years ago. Some makers varied their three-diameter designs radically, even changing belly length as much as eight to ten feet in their own lines with diameters from .050 to .060. The short level heads, short front tapers, and relatively constant belly lengths were already standard among the Pacific Coast linemakers even then, and the influence of thinkers like Schwab and Hedge is obvious. It is also apparent from these specifications that some eastern manufacturers were already aware of the optimal criteria for a weight-forward design.

Both manufacturers and fishermen soon became aware that the new polyvinyl chloride finishes, with their nylon and dacron cores under plastic tapers of widely varying specific gravity, were rapidly making the old letter designations obsolete. Lines could no longer be compared in terms of diameter alone, and the traditional HDH and GBF labels were utterly unworkable. Weight became the basic criterion in sizing lines, yet radical variations in weight were possible in the same diameter with finishes of air-impregnated plastic or high-density polyvinyl. The traditional alphabetical designations were now meaningless, yet no standard system of classification had emerged to replace them.

New standards were finally worked out by the fishing-tackle industry in concert with casting clubs in both Europe and America, and these standards were based primarily on weight. Since thirty feet was a reasonable average of maximum line loading before line velocity was built with the double haul, it was adopted as the bench mark by which weight could be measured and compared. The weight of the front thirty feet, regardless of taper specifications, was determined in grains. The unit of measure is derived from the average weight of wheat, with approximately 7,000 grains per pound. It was a complicated system of comparative measurement, but it translates into a simple formula for the modern angler. The system was defined in a code based on weight in grains for the terminal thirty feet of any taper, and the maximum allowable variation in that weight ranged from six to twelve grains. The standard code was resolved in the following terms:

STANDARD MANUFACTURING LINE-WEIGHT CODE

LINE CODE	WEIGHT IN GRAINS	MINIMUM TOLERANCES	MAXIMUM TOLERANCES
1	60	54	66
2	80	74	86
3	100	94	106
4	120	114	126
5	140	134	146
6	160	152	168
7	185	177	193
8	210	202	218
9	240	230	280
10	280	270	290
11	330	318	342
12	380	368	392

These new designations based upon line weight for the first thirty feet in grains correspond approximately to several of the past alphabetical designations familiar to most fly-fishermen. It might prove helpful in this period of transition from the old system to the new code to study the following table:

COMPARATIVE TABLE OF FLY-LINE SIZES

CODE	WEIGHT IN GRAINS	DOUBLE-TAPER	FORWARD-TAPER
3	100	IFI	IFG
4	120	HFH	HFG
5	140	HEH	HEG
6	160	HDH	HDG
7	185	HCH	HCF
8	210	GBG	GBF
9	240	GAG	GAF
10	280	G2AG	G2AF
11	330	G3AG	G3AF
12	380	G4AG	G4AF

The tackle industry also outlined an alphabetical code to identify taper specifications and relative specific gravity in each line, since a cornucopia of performance specifications had quickly evolved after the introduction of synthetic cores and polyvinyl chloride finishes in fly lines. Level lines were identified with an L-designation, and ST-type lines indicated a single-taper design. Double tapers were coded with the letters DT, an obvious choice, and WF was the code selected for weight-forward lines. Specific gravity finishes designed to sink were identified with an S-coding, and air-impregnated plastic coating designed to float was given an F-designation. Sinking-tip lines received a coding FS to note their hybrid floating and sinking capability, in which the initial ten feet of their tapers sink readily, and the remaining line is designed to float. Such lines permit a skilled fisherman to fish with precision at intermediate depths, and a running line that floats will pick up from the water and shoot readily. The new alphabetical code, with its identification of taper specifications and floating or sinking qualities, was combined with the numerical weight code. The combination defines a modern fly line with a precise and workable standard description.

It is a relatively simple system. The designation L6F means a level fly line weighing 160 grains in its first thirty feet and having an air-impregnated finish that floats. Lines labelled ST5S are single tapers weighing 140 grains in the terminal thirty feet and finished with a high-density plastic that sinks. The package marked DT5F contains a familiar double-taper line that weighs 140 grains and floats like a bobber, and a WF8S label identifies a weight-forward taper weighing 210 grains that sinks like an anchor. The relatively new sinking-tip lines are usually forward tapers, and a WF7FS designation points to a line weighing 185 grains that is built to sink its forward taper, with its remaining eighty feet designed to float. The new line code is simple, concise, and defines the full specifications and character of a modern fly line.

The design tapers of the contemporary Aircel floating and Wetcel sinking lines contain much valuable data, and are produced by the firm that pioneered the polyvinyl chloride lines. The Aircel lines in both double-taper and weight-forward specifications clearly demonstrate the comparisons between the new coding method and the past alphabetical system. The Aircel weight-forward models found in the chart on pages 774–775 provide an interesting comparison with the earlier tapers described in this chapter, the pioneer forward-taper lines produced by several manufacturers twenty-odd years ago.

Sinking lines have a higher density than plastic floating lines of equal weight, and therefore have a much smaller diameter. Both their specific gravity and their reduced atmospheric friction make a polyvinyl sinking line seem much heavier than its actual weight in casting. Such sinking-line effects are well known to manufacturers and anglers alike, and linemakers have compensated by actually reducing the weight of their sinking lines within the same line-weight coding. For example, rods matched perfectly with a DT6F floating double taper are handling a line that weighs approximately 165 grains in its first thirty feet. Those same fly rods cannot handle a high-density sinking line of 165 grains, and to avoid overstressing its line capacity a comparable DT6S line should be reduced to only 155 grains. Such reductions are obvious in the diagrams on pages 776–777 of the Wetcel double tapers and weight-forward lines.

These modern fly lines with their synthetic cores of nylon and dacron are remarkable technical innovations, and they offer our generation a rich spectrum of fishing methods never available before. Our fathers fought constantly to keep their double-taper lines dressed and floating, and tournament-distance casts of seventy-five to eighty-five feet were exceptional. The distances on modern competition platforms are easily twice that, and we owe them both to better technique and our sophisticated weight-forward lines.

High-density lines were totally unknown thirty years ago, and the modern angler is fishing his flies at depths unthinkable in the past. These innovations are perhaps only a prelude, since manufacturers are now experimenting with plastic finishes on fiberglass cores and clear polyvinyl chloride tapers formed over a translucent monofilament core. Cortland has just perfected a line finish of a synthetic foamlike material, and its microscopic air chambers are formed over a delicate dacron core. Pacific Coast fishermen have been experimenting widely in recent years with shooting heads of lead-core trolling lines spliced to special running lines or monofilament. Such rigs can reach distances of 150 feet under actual fishing conditions, and can fish a big nymph or bucktail right on the bottom in the heaviest currents. Technical breakthroughs in line construction are evolv-

Double-taper Floating Lines

DT-4-F HEH DOUBLE TAPER FLOATING LINE

2 FEET — 2 FEET 4.9 GRAINS — 8 FEET 26 GRAINS — 30 FEET 120 GRAINS — 22 FEET 94 GRAINS — 48 FEET 4.2 GRAINS PER FOOT — 58 FEET — 8 FEET — 2 FEET

.030 .030 .042 .042 .030 .030

DT-5-F HDH DOUBLE TAPER FLOATING LINE

2 FEET — 2 FEET 5.1 GRAINS — 8 FEET 29 GRAINS — 30 FEET 146 GRAINS — 22 FEET 117 GRAINS — 48 FEET 5.3 GRAINS PER FOOT — 58 FEET — 8 FEET — 2 FEET

.033 .033 .047 .047 .033 .033

DT-6-HCH DOUBLE TAPER FLOATING LINE

2 FEET — 2 FEET 5.2 GRAINS — 10 FEET 45 GRAINS — 30 FEET 170 GRAINS — 20 FEET 125 GRAINS — 48 FEET 6.1 GRAINS PER FOOT — 58 FEET — 10 FEET — 2 FEET

.035 .035 .052 .052 .035 .035

2 FEET — 2 FEET 5.3 GRAINS — 11 FEET 58 GRAINS — 30 FEET 195 GRAINS — 19 FEET 137 GRAINS — 48 FEET 7.2 GRAINS PER FOOT — 58 FEET — 11 FEET — 2 FEET

.036 .036 .056 .056 .036 .036

Weight-forward Floating Lines

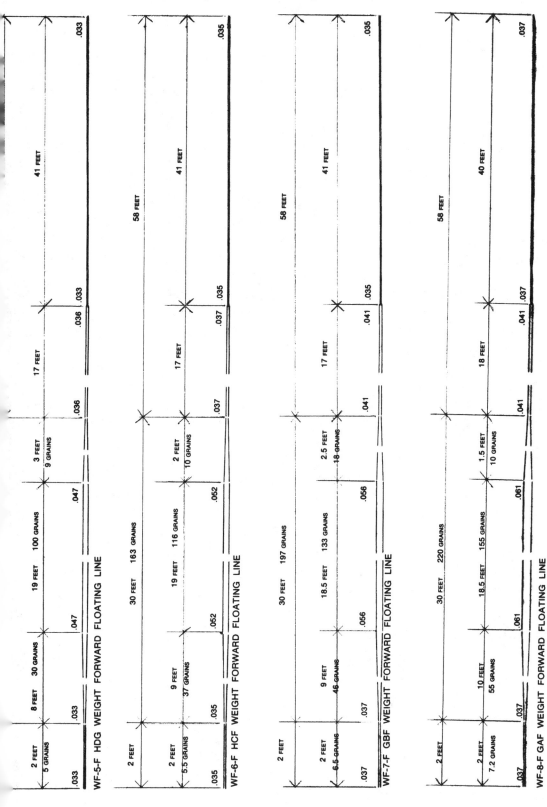

WF-5-F HDG WEIGHT FORWARD FLOATING LINE

WF-6-F HCF WEIGHT FORWARD FLOATING LINE

WF-7-F GBF WEIGHT FORWARD FLOATING LINE

WF-8-F GAF WEIGHT FORWARD FLOATING LINE

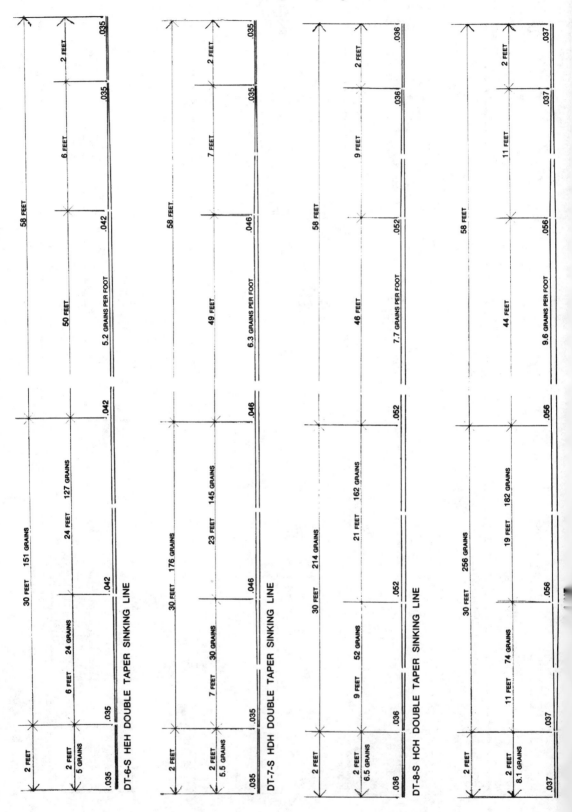

DT-6-S HEH DOUBLE TAPER SINKING LINE

DT-7-S HDH DOUBLE TAPER SINKING LINE

DT-8-S HCH DOUBLE TAPER SINKING LINE

Weight-forward Sinking Lines

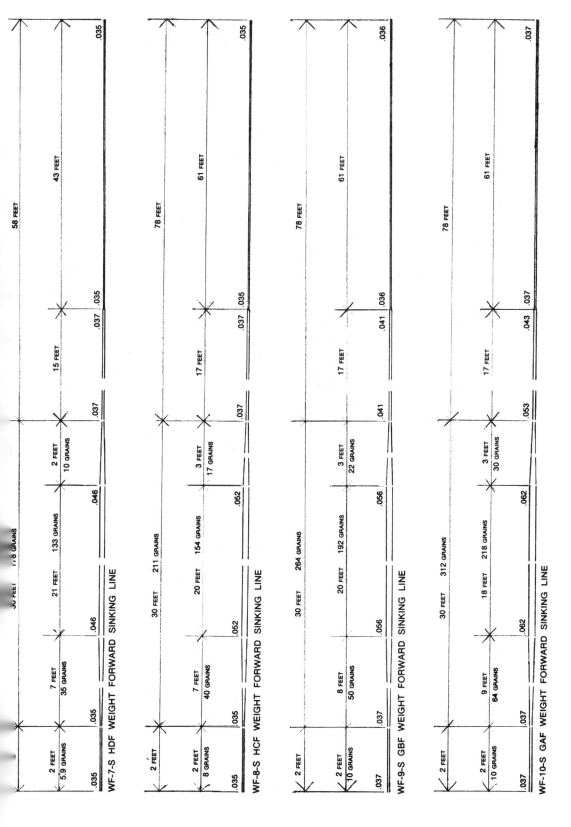

WF-7-S HDF WEIGHT FORWARD SINKING LINE

WF-8-S HCF WEIGHT FORWARD SINKING LINE

WF-9-S GBF WEIGHT FORWARD SINKING LINE

WF-10-S GAF WEIGHT FORWARD SINKING LINE

ing at a remarkable pace, and our modern lines are providing more effective fishing time with less maintenance, reaching fish at unthinkable distances, and catching bottom-feeding trout that our predecessors could never have taken.

Controlled sink rate is another refinement created to provide lines of varying specific gravity, taper, and weight that will fish at several depths of water. Slow-sinking types are available that fish about three to five feet below the surface of a lake or reservoir, and are perfectly suited to fishing a nymph along the bottom of smaller streams. Medium-sinking lines have also been developed to fish at intermediate depths; they provide an excellent choice for a fisherman whose budget is limited to a single sinking-type line. High-density lines were originally conceived for fly-fishing in salt water, since its buoyancy and tidal currents demanded a polyvinyl chloride line of extreme specific gravity. However, fishermen quickly discovered that the exaggerated sink rate of these salt-water lines made them ideal for fishing as deep as fifteen to thirty feet in lakes, and at feeding depths in the heavy currents of big trout streams and steelhead rivers. Controlled sink rate is also available in lines with sinking tips, providing a floating line with a ten-foot head designed to drown a stubborn leader quickly, and a full shooting-head that sinks quickly ahead of its air-impregnated running line. The latter design will offer most of the tactical advantages found in a fast-sinking taper, yet its floating back taper and shooting line can be readily mended to get the current-swing deep and dampen fly speed effectively. It is also possible to shoot the buoyant running line from the surface more easily.

Thirty-foot shooting tapers are also available in these controlled sink-rate finishes, and they provide an average fisherman with a remarkable distance tool. Shooting heads consist of thirty-foot sections from standard weight-forward tapers, minus the back taper and normal running line, and were originally worked out in steelhead country. The front tapers and shooting bellies were attached to light running lines of twenty to twenty-five pound monofilament in the early years, and later shooting-head experts spliced light polyvinyl running lines to their weight-forward tapers. One hundred feet of running line was usually spliced to the thirty-foot shooting head, and regular dacron backing filled out the reel. Such tackle will generate remarkably long casts with minimal effort and skill, and the new oval-shaped monofilaments are proving themselves as running lines ideally suited to shooting-head tactics. Shooting heads will seldom deliver a fly with dry-fly accuracy. Delicate presentation is also impossible with shooting heads, and they are not recommended for fishing shy trout under most conditions, since the forward tapers land too hard and the limp running line makes it difficult to control fly speed with precision. Yet lake or big-water conditions in which distance outweighs all other considerations are so perfect for the shooting-head technique that it should become a part of every fisherman's repertoire of tactics.

British line manufacturers Philip Tallants and Terrence Colling-bourne have recently developed a new concept in polyvinyl designs. Their

Masterline series employs new plastics technology, making their finishes vulnerable to other line cleaners, and a fresh concept in shaping both tapers and finishes. Taper specifications vary with changing line weights, and the tips are designed to float just under the film, casting a smaller shadow. The weight-forward tapers utilize a series of long-belly designs to improve their fishing qualities, but the finish of the Masterline is perhaps its most surprising feature. The finish is made intentionally irregular, rather than die-smooth like the other plastic lines. Contrary to popular mythology, which holds that the smoothest lines cast more effortlessly, these irregular finishes hopscotch through the guides with considerably less casting friction. Masterlines come in the relatively expensive Chancellor grade, the medium-priced Oxbridge series, and the moderately priced Graduate grade. Although the design concepts in these lines are quite new, their exceptional performance has led several American manufacturers to experiment with similar line specifications.

Most modern fly lines are packaged on vinyl spools designed to help in transferring them to the reel, once an adequate length of twenty- to thirty-pound dacron backing is in place and spliced to the running-line tip. The backing provides a filler that occupies enough space on the reel spool that the line itself is stored in the largest possible coils. It also enables a fisherman to play a fish with more efficiency, since a single turn of the reel recovers more line when the spool is nearly filled than when it is empty and nearing the spindle. Backing is also insurance against the strong fish that strips the entire fly line from the reel in a ratchet-screaming run, for without its extra one hundred to two hundred yards behind the line, such trophy fish might easily be lost. Many anglers use nylon braided line or cheap monofilament as backing, but the elasticity of such materials is dangerous. It can stretch so much under the strain of a really big fish that it can warp or damage a fine-alloy reel during the fight, and salt-water fishermen have had reels literally self-destruct under the elastic stress of a backing line stretched by a big tarpon. The backing line should be twenty- to thirty-pound test, not because its full breaking strain is needed, but because its diameter is thick enough to prevent a big fish from wedging it deeply into the remaining coils, when a strong run is suddenly triggered.

You seldom need backing, is a common observation heard on big-trout rivers from Tierra del Fuego to the Valley of Ten Thousand Smokes. *But when you need backing—you really need it!*

Transferring a new line to the reel begins with turning its packaging spool upside down, twisting it apart, and removing the coil wrappings without disturbing the line itself on its plastic arbor. Unwind about twenty inches of the running tip that is attached to the backing and close the shipping spool, taking care not to pinch the new line. The reassembled plastic spool is then centered on a pencil or small wooden dowel, and with the line under tension from your fingers, wind it clockwise on the reel. Lines are usually supplied with small, pressure-sensitive markers provided to adhere to the reel and identify the line stored on its spool. These markers should not be fastened to the reel spool or frame, but should be trimmed and placed inside the reel-seat foot, making them invisible when the reel itself is mounted on its matching rod.

Maintenance of these modern polyvinyl fly lines is infinitely simpler than taking care of the oil-finished silks of the past. The new lines are a remarkable equilibrium between durability and soft, supple handling. The plastics are unusually capable of withstanding abrasion and water chemistry and wear that would have shredded the finish of a traditional British oil-finished silk in the past.

However, these modern lines are not indestructible. Avoid wedging your line under stones, and when they become fouled there, exercise the patience to free them properly. Pinching a line between the reel spool and flange can bruise its finish, and you should obviously avoid stepping on your line, particularly on ledges and stones, and with hobnailed boots or wading chains. Poor backcast timing can crack-the-whip, developing forces in the terminal length of the line that no material or bonding process can withstand, and it is a common cause of line damage in fishing.

Like a fresh nylon leader, your line should be stretched slightly to eliminate any twisting or coiling when it is new or has been stored on the reel. Anglers who grew up with the fussy intricacies of pampering silk fly lines and their interminable cycles of cleaning and daily dressing and drying are invariably baffled with a line that can simply be left on the reel. It not only can be left there overnight and between fishing trips, but it can also be stored there over the winter. Storage coils that develop on a reel will straighten quickly with a simple stretching. There are fishermen who derive much pleasure from coddling and fussing over their equipment, and who actually enjoyed the daily rituals of cleaning their silk lines, lovingly dressing them with British mucilin—in spite of the containers that could seldom be opened—and stripping the line each night for drying on a wooden frame. The younger members of the angling fraternity will never miss this daily ritual and will welcome the trouble-free character of the polyvinyl chloride lines.

However, there are some problems with vinyl finishes. Solvents found in many suntan creams and lotions, line dressings, dry-fly ointments, fuels, lacquer thinners, and insect repellents are chemically incompatible with their plastic finishes. Modern fly lines should never be stored in hot places or subjected to prolonged exposure to sunlight, particularly inside a locked automobile. Solar radiation is damaging to many synthetic materials and bonding agents after long periods of exposure, which results in a surprising molecular denigration. Ordinary fishing time is no problem in this regard, since solar atrophy of your line will have less demonstrable effect on its lifespan than the abrasion of normal usage and wear.

Polyvinyl lines should be cleaned when they float poorly or begin to shoot grudgingly on long casts. Fishing waters swarm with microscopic organisms that collect on the line and dry after a few days of fishing, accumulating in sufficient numbers to affect its floating and casting qualities. Both these tiny organisms and the residues they attract to the finish absorb minuscule amounts of water than can sink a floating line or make it ride too low in the surface film for an easy line-lift on pickup. Cleaning and polishing these lines will quickly restore their unique qualities. Weekly attention is probably enough, except in exceptionally alkaline waters with their atypically rich concentrations of microorganisms. The line manufacturers all provide excellent fly-line cleaning compounds for their particular products.

Minor repairs on these lines are possible when their synthetic finishes do crack or fray slightly. The best method is to keep a small bottle of fresh synthetic-base varnish in your gear. It should be heated in a saucepan of moderately hot water to thin its viscosity and applied with the index finger in extremely thin coats. Forty-eight hours drying time is about right, and the varnish should finally be polished smooth with talcum powder and a fine wool cloth. Varnish can be applied with a needle to repair a small hinge or chipped place in the line. Fraying and wear typically appear in the few inches of line that ride back and forth in the tip guide during the normal range of casting. The length of this casting wear will vary with individual casting habits and the average length of casts on a particular stream, and such line wear is understandably exaggerated by habitual double hauling.

Line color is perhaps the single failure of the modern polyvinyl chloride fly line. My reservations about the palette of colors now available undoubtedly come from the sensory impressions of boyhood, and my first exposure to the rich, waxy odors of the Halford and King Eider silks, with their gleaming mahogany and pale amber coils wrapped in rice paper. Sensory impressions and esthetics play a surprising role in fly tackle, although many anglers are unwilling to admit it. Given a choice between the olive and richly glistening brown or pale amber fly lines, and the garish pinks and sickly pale greens and blues displayed on our modern tackle counters, my preferences are obvious. Multicolored camouflage finishes and two-color lines are also bothersome, and a simple color spot or indentation in the finish would be enough to tell the eye or fingers where a compound line changes from sinking to floating. The white lines becoming so popular were originally developed for photographic purposes, and I first used them in making a salmon film in the Labrador. The hot orange line had similar origins, since its chroma is remarkably visible in poor levels of light.

These past few seasons, experience on widespread streams would indicate that in floating lines used for dry-fly tactics and nymph fishing just under the surface the white and hot orange photographic lines do not frighten the fish. Berkeley recently introduced a series of beautiful straw-colored floating lines that remind me of the silk lines of my boyhood years, and they performed beautifully in a week of field testing with Doug Swisher on the Au Sable in Michigan. The visibility of these pale lines to the fisherman is useful too, particularly in following a dry-fly float or wet-fly swing at long distances in poor light.

Yet I still use a dark mahogany-colored line for the difficult, hyperselective fish on my home waters in our eastern mountains, and I feel it has been more effective on the shy fish of our famous western spring creeks. Fishing deep I prefer darker colors, like the rich greens of the Wetcel lines or the medium brown finish on the Cortland sinking line over pale sand and gravel bottoms. Pale colors are unwise in a sinking line that works deep among the fish, and is viewed laterally against the adjacent colors of the bottom. It can also be argued that a wooded stream poses identical problems in a floating line, and although a pale line is not readily visible against the sky, it is shockingly visible against a leafy canopy of trees and sheltering alders. Perhaps the line manufacturers should produce sinking lines that echo typical streambed environments, like the deep greens of a big river flowing over a bottom encrusted with fountain moss and algae, the pewter-colored boulders of a western sagebrush stream, and the rust-colored ledges of a foothill river like the Frying Pan in Colorado. Dame Juliana Berners prophetically wrote about keying line-color to stream bottom more than five centuries ago in her *Treatyse of Fysshynge wyth an Angle*, and perhaps it is not too late to listen to her wisdom.

Past books on fly-fishing often provided tables matching fly rods of typical lengths and weights to recommended line weights and tapers. Such tables always seemed a doubtful help, since they said little about the calibrations in two rods of otherwise equal length and weight. Wall thickness in the split bamboo also produced radical differences in the tip speed and power of superficially similar rods and demanded a heavier fly line. Polyvinyl chloride finishes and synthetic cores scrambled these equations even more, and the introduction of modern fiberglass rods produced chaos in past recommendations concerning balanced rod-to-line ratios. Graphite and boron fly rods promise to cause even more confusion in matching lines to rod lengths and weights. These technical changes have largely been introduced since midcentury, and did not intrude upon the relatively simple discussions on matching rods and fly lines in the earlier writings of men like Hewitt and Bergman and Knight.

However, such tables recommending basic rod specifications to fly-line weights are perhaps useful to novice fishermen, provided their assumptions and data are updated to include the world of synthetic rods and lines. Most manufacturers still recommend lines for their production rods, although this traditional convenience is proving difficult in the experimental carbon graphite and boron rods undergoing field research. Carbon graphite has an amazing capability of molding its stress behavior to line weight and loading, and a good caster has virtually no timing adjustments to compensate for using lines from four-weight through eight-weight on the same graphite rod. The perfection of these sophisticated synthetics in rod manufacture will further complicate our theories of tackle balancing. Although I am fully aware of its obvious pitfalls, the following table catalogues the work of several manufacturers who produce first-rate rods in fiberglass, and it may provide some useful comparative data:

FIBERGLASS FLY RODS AND LINE WEIGHTS

LENGTH	WEIGHT	FLOATING	SINKING	OLD CODE
6	1¼	DT4F	DT4S	HEH
6½	1¾	DT4F	DT4S	HEH
6½	2½	DT5F	DT5S	HDH
7	3	DT5F	DT5S	HDH
7½	3¼	WF5F	WF5S	HDG
7½	3¾	WF6F	WF6S	HCF
8	3½	WF6F	WF6S	HCF
8	3¾	WF7F	WF7S	GBF
8½	3¾	WF7F	WF7S	GBF
8½	4	WF7F	WF7S	GBF
9	4½	WF8F	WF8S	GAF
9	5	WF9F	WF9S	G2AF
9	5¼	WF10F	WF10S	G3AF
9½	5½	WF10F	WF10S	G3AF
9½	5⅞	WF11F	WF11S	G4AF

Perhaps the most obvious surprise in this table, particularly for fishermen who are more familiar with split-cane construction, lies in the relatively light rod weight and heavy line-weight capacity of these fiberglass rods for their length. These qualities are most striking in the big-water rods, where the distance capability with a relatively heavy line on fly rods as light as three-and-a-half to five-and-a-half ounces can mean a big difference in fatigue at the day's end. Building a bamboo rod capable of double hauling a forward taper WF10S with only nine feet and less than five ounces of cane is clearly impossible.

The carbon graphite and boron rods that I have seen and fished are most unusual, and they include prototypes from Berkeley and Orvis and Fenwick, as well as privately built boron fiber designs. Their performance makes conventional wisdom about rods and matching fly-line tapers a shambles. The rods are light for their lengths and line weights, but even a two- or three-ounce graphite rod cannot be considered delicate. The most delicate synthetic I have fished was a solid wire-core boron prototype that weighed slightly more than a half ounce, and took a four-weight line, like a three-ounce split bamboo. The following table lists several boron and carbon graphite rods with their recommended lines:

BORON AND CARBON GRAPHITE ROD AND LINE RECOMMENDATIONS

TYPE	LENGTH	WEIGHT	FLOATING	SINKING
Boron	6	½	DT3F	DT3S
Boron	6½	⅝	DT4F	DT4S
Graphite*	6½	¾	DT5F	DT5S

BORON AND CARBON GRAPHITE ROD AND LINE RECOMMENDATIONS (continued)

TYPE	LENGTH	WEIGHT	FLOATING	SINKING
Boron	7	1	DT6F	DT6S
Graphite*	7	1	DT6F	DT6S
Graphite	7	$1\frac{1}{2}$	DT6F	WF6S
Boron	$7\frac{1}{2}$	$1\frac{3}{4}$	DT6F	WF6S
Graphite*	$7\frac{1}{2}$	$1\frac{7}{8}$	DT6F	WF6S
Graphite	$7\frac{1}{2}$	2	DT7F	WF7S
Graphite	8	$1\frac{7}{8}$	DT6F	WF6S
Boron	8	$2\frac{1}{4}$	DT4F	WF4S
Graphite	8	$2\frac{3}{8}$	DT7F	WF7S
Graphite	$8\frac{1}{2}$	$2\frac{7}{8}$	DT7F	WF7S
Graphite	$8\frac{1}{2}$	$3\frac{1}{4}$	WF8F	WF8S
Graphite	9	$3\frac{3}{4}$	WF9F	WF9S
Graphite	9	4	WF10F	WF10S

* Solid graphite rods on a wire core

Experienced trout fishermen will recognize the improbability of a three-ounce rod taking an eight-weight line, or double hauling a hundred feet of nine-weight taper on a rod weighing less than four ounces. Boron and graphite will undoubtedly work a revolution in our thinking about balanced rods and fly lines.

The following table of modern split-bamboo rods offers an interesting comparison between fiberglass and the other synthetics and cane, at least in their power-to-weight ratio, and relative casting power. It should be understood that in delicate work with tiny flies, split bamboo still has a clear superiority in skilled hands, and the ultra-light line tapers used with the small cane rods have no workable counterparts in glass construction. Many manufacturers are included in this chart:

SPLIT-BAMBOO RODS AND LINE SPECIFICATIONS

LENGTH	WEIGHT	FLOATING	SINKING	OLD CODE
6	1	DT3F	DT3S	IFI
6	$1\frac{1}{2}$	DT3F	DT3S	IFI
6	2	DT4F	DT4S	HEH
6	$2\frac{1}{2}$	DT4F	DT4S	HEH
$6\frac{1}{2}$	$1\frac{3}{4}$	DT4F	DT4S	HEH
$6\frac{1}{2}$	$2\frac{1}{8}$	DT4F	DT4S	HEH
$6\frac{1}{2}$	$2\frac{5}{8}$	DT4F	DT4S	HEH
7	$2\frac{3}{8}$	DT3F	DT3S	IFI
7	$2\frac{1}{2}$	DT4F	DT4S	HEH

SPLIT-BAMBOO RODS AND LINE
SPECIFICATIONS (continued)

LENGTH	WEIGHT	FLOATING	SINKING	OLD CODE
7	$2\frac{3}{4}$	DT4F	DT4S	HEH
7	$2\frac{7}{8}$	DT4F	DT4S	HEH
7	3	DT5F	DT4S	HEH
7	$3\frac{1}{4}$	DT5F	DT5S	HDH
7	$3\frac{3}{4}$	DT5F	DT5S	HDH
$7\frac{1}{2}$	$2\frac{1}{2}$	DT4F	DT4S	HEH
$7\frac{1}{2}$	$2\frac{3}{4}$	DT4F	DT4S	HEH
$7\frac{1}{2}$	3	DT4F	DT4S	HEH
$7\frac{1}{2}$	$3\frac{1}{8}$	DT4F	DT4S	HEH
$7\frac{1}{2}$	$3\frac{3}{8}$	DT5F	DT5S	HDH
$7\frac{1}{2}$	$3\frac{1}{2}$	DT5F	DT5S	HDH
$7\frac{1}{2}$	$3\frac{5}{8}$	DT5F	DT5S	HDH
$7\frac{1}{2}$	$3\frac{7}{8}$	DT6F	DT6S	HCH
$7\frac{1}{2}$	4	DT6F	DT6S	HCH
$7\frac{1}{2}$	$4\frac{1}{4}$	DT6F	DT6S	HCH
8	$3\frac{3}{4}$	DT6F	DT6S	HCH
8	4	DT6F	DT6S	HCH
8	$4\frac{1}{8}$	DT6F	DT6S	HCH
8	$4\frac{1}{2}$	DT6F	DT6S	HCH
8	$4\frac{1}{2}$	WF7F	WF7S	GBF
8	$4\frac{3}{4}$	WF7F	WF7S	GBF
8	5	WF7F	WF7S	GBF
$8\frac{1}{2}$	$4\frac{1}{4}$	DT5F	DT5S	HDH
$8\frac{1}{2}$	$4\frac{1}{2}$	DT6F	DT6S	HCH
$8\frac{1}{2}$	$4\frac{3}{4}$	WF7F	WF7F	GBF
$8\frac{1}{2}$	$4\frac{7}{8}$	WF8F	WF8S	GAF
$8\frac{1}{2}$	5	WF8F	WF8S	GAF
$8\frac{1}{2}$	$5\frac{1}{8}$	WF8F	WF8S	GAF
$8\frac{1}{2}$	$5\frac{1}{2}$	WF8F	WF8S	GAF
$8\frac{1}{2}$	$5\frac{7}{8}$	WF9F	WF9S	62AF
$8\frac{1}{2}$	6	WF9F	WF9S	G2AF
9	$4\frac{3}{4}$	WF7F	WF7S	GBF
9	5	WF7F	WF7S	GBF
9	$5\frac{1}{8}$	WF8F	WF8S	GAF
9	$5\frac{1}{4}$	WF8F	WF8S	GAF
9	$5\frac{1}{2}$	WF8F	WF8S	GAF
9	$5\frac{3}{4}$	WF8F	WF8F	GAF
9	6	WF8F	WF8S	GAF
9	$6\frac{1}{8}$	WF9F	WF9S	G2AF
9	$6\frac{1}{2}$	WF9F	WF9S	G2AF
$9\frac{1}{2}$	$5\frac{1}{2}$	WF8F	WF8S	GAF

SPLIT-BAMBOO RODS AND LINE
SPECIFICATIONS (continued)

LENGTH	WEIGHT	FLOATING	SINKING	OLD CODE
9½	5¾	WF8F	WF8S	GAF
9½	6	WF8F	WF8S	GAF
9½	6¼	WF9F	WF9S	G2AF
9½	6½	WF10F	WF10S	63AF
9½	6¾	WF10F	WF10S	63AF
9½	6⅞	WF10F	WF10S	G3AF

The obvious comparison between typical nine-foot glass rods taking a nine-weight G2AF line with a total weight of slightly more than five ounces and nine-foot bamboo rods that must be fifteen to twenty percent heavier to throw the same line is remarkable. The nine-foot graphite rod weighing three and three-quarter ounces and taking the same 250-grain taper is even more remarkable. The variables in cane density and design calibrations that affect the performance of bamboo fly rods are evident in these comparative tables, along with the weight differences of their reel seats. Glass and graphite are obviously excellent materials for average fishing and distance problems, while bamboo is still the optimal solution to problems of delicacy and precision.

However, our discussions of fly-line development and the technical revolution in lines that has taken place since midcentury are only partially helpful in matching lines to specific rods and fishing conditions. There are such variables in rod performance that only empirical casting can really balance a fly rod and its matching line, and such casting is the only viable test, because there are also critical variables in casting style.

Rod length and weight are an important clue to line weight, but they give us only a general impression of actual rod dynamics under the stress of casting. Rod taper can produce soft tip action with a stiff butt, relatively stiff action that carries from the tip guide well into the butt section, and the progressive taper which flexes with a slow, smooth power into the grip itself. Each action is possible within surprisingly similar rod length and weight, and each will take lines of different specifications.

It is important in line selection to remember the basic physics of rod-and-line dynamics. It is the weight of the fly line that is cast, not the fly we are presenting to the fish. It is the weight of the line working beyond the rod tip that causes it to flex and cast. Short-range tactics with a typical double taper find too little line extended, so false casts are often used to build enough line velocity to compensate, working them in a rapid flick-flick rhythm.

Such false casting often lacks sufficient line weight to stress the rod properly, and the line travels in an exaggeratedly narrow loop. It often fails to unroll properly, taking the leader with it, and the fly often catches the leader or the line. Average casting ranges provide enough line weight to accommodate the character of the rod, the casting rhythms slow as line is lengthened, and the fly works out in a graceful loop that unrolls and turns over cleanly. However, the double-taper line quickly reaches its performance ceiling, since a distance cast soon dies when the velocity of its shoot is equalled and dampened by the belly weight it is pulling behind.

Each fly rod has a definite ceiling on the length of line it can strip cleanly from the water, and another limit to the line weight and length it can load and carry in the air when false casting. Such limits are quickly reached with double-taper lines. Weight-forward lines are designed to exploit and overcome these limiting factors, placing most of their weight beyond the tip guide where it is instantly available for the left-hand shoot. Its thin shooting line lies immediately behind, and its weight imposes infinitely less drag on the velocity of the cast. It is the weight of the shooting front taper and belly that pulls the cast and the length of its shoot. The back taper is like the tail of a kite, helping to keep the shooting head riding true. Beyond such obvious factors, it is line velocity that generates distance, and that velocity is entirely a function of tip speed.

Such tip-speed effects mean that an eight-foot rod throwing its proper line weight at a high enough velocity will equal the distances achieved with a nine-foot stick delivering a heavier line at slower speeds.

Tip speed is limited by casting skills and timing, the character of the rod action, wind velocity, and atmospheric friction that varies with temperature. The principal resistance a caster must slice through is atmosphere and wind, the drag factors that dampen the velocity of both rod and line. Basic physics describes inertia in terms of both static objects and objects in motion. Rod flexure is a result of the dynamic inertia imparted by the caster, plus its bending to overcome the static inertia of the atmosphere. The dynamic inertia of the wind contributes still more bending under stress. Casting simply overcomes atmospheric inertia and wind, and its rhythms are quickly converted to the dynamics of inertial acceleration. When peak acceleration is reached, the rod is loading at optimum tip speed. Skilled casters are able to deliver their shots at that maximum tip speed, and stressing the rod with a double haul just before that velocity is reached works to exaggerate both the tip acceleration and the distance the rod tip travels in unloading the cast.

The cast should always be delivered when line velocity and tip speed are identical. The catapulting spring of the rod adds virtually nothing to distance, and during the millisecond the flexing rod begins to straighten, it is no longer participating in line velocity. Its straightening is a form of rapid deceleration, and when tip speed drops behind, the line shoots out over the water fully separate from the rod. It flexes well past the horizontal direction of the cast, and its only effect on its velocity and distance at this point is negative, consisting of guide friction and line slap along the rod itself. Rod loading under the stress of casting is expressed in its resistance to bending and atmospheric drag, and it continues to resist flexure until its ability to fight these loads has reached equilibrium with its casting speed.

Translated in terms of your casting skills, you should not attempt to fish with rod weights and actions that you cannot bring to maximum tip speed. The lines you select should match your rods. The rods should pick up approximately forty feet of line and shoot fifteen or twenty for average fishing, and for distance work, should lift fifty-odd feet and shoot enough line to reach eighty. Any fly rod you can stress to its peak tip speed will also fit your physical skills at slower velocities. It will generate optimal distance in your fishing and result in less fatigue.

Properly designed line tapers matched to such rods will neither flutter nor sag in casting, and will float through the cushioning effect of the atmosphere smoothly. Such tapers will turn over gracefully, taking the balanced leader and fly along. The full weight will not drop to the surface until the cast has fully straightened, and it is that taper weight and its distribution that are the basic factors in line choice.

Raw line weight is the primary factor in a cast, once the rod has carried it to optimum speed. Weight is obviously effective when it is concentrated in a lead-head jig, but its efficiency and inertia decrease as its casting length increases in the form of a fly line. Its entire weight distributed along a seventy-five-foot cast is exposed to high ratios of skin friction in the atmosphere. Double tapers are designed for delicate presentation, fine leaders and tiny flies, roll casting, and casting distances of less than seventy-five feet. Weight-forward lines have been worked out to fish at ranges between fifty and one hundred feet, with accurate delivery of the fly and a subtle dry-fly presentation considerably diminished. Shooting heads were developed for the extreme ranges between seventy-five feet and as far past one hundred feet as individual casting skills permit, although neither accuracy nor fine presentation are possible with them, and even the precise control of fly speed is sacrificed.

Line length ahead of the front taper is critical in both double-taper and weight-forward types. When this level section connected to the leader is too long, the fly turns over completely out of control. It can fall at the mercy of the slightest wind or casting fault, dropping both right and left of its own leader butt and sometimes on the line itself. When the level head is too short, the fly and leader will roll over too hard, their inertia will carry over well past the horizontal, and strike the surface too hard. Several manufacturers now precut these level heads at the proper length, and you should not modify them without first checking their specifications.

Specific gravity is also a factor in line selection. The fisherman who fishes relatively shallow waters will need a floating line, designed to handle dry flies on the surface, and wet flies and nymphs immediately under its film. Fishing intermediate depths of water call for a slow-sinking line, and a medium-sinking line is suited to slightly deeper places. High-density lines are needed for deep lakes, sinking as much as thirty feet with patience, to reach down toward bottom-feeding fish in heavy currents. Compound sinking-tip lines have been designed to fish at moderate depths, with a running line that floats and strips from the surface smoothly in shooting. The fishing conditions of your favorite waters should dictate your selection of lines. Generally speaking, your equipment should begin with a floating double taper, and you should add a basic weight-forward sinking line to your gear as soon as possible. More specialized lines are optional for most conditions.

Charles Ritz has described a simple field test for checking rod action against optimal line loading. It is outlined in his book *A Fly Fisher's Life,* and begins by lengthening the line without false casting. Each successive length of line should be delivered easily, without particular effort, until the rod is finally loaded with too much line weight. Such overload is clearly evident when the backcast falls too low, the casting loop flutters and pauses, and the rod seems to collapse when pushed toward maximum bending stress. The forward casts also tend to belly low and drop too quickly toward the water. Approximately forty to forty-five feet should not overload a fly rod, if the line weight is proper for its action.

Ritz has also developed a good method of trying out a fly line in actual casting dynamics. It is best if a knowledgeable friend is observing from the side to study the motions of the line. His observations should provide a lateral appraisal of your casting, while you can evaluate the longitudinal behavior of the working line yourself.

The first series of trial casts should reach out approximately thirty to forty-five feet. Such lengths are sufficient to give the observer a viable picture of line behavior and extension, the casting oscillations in the line, any ragged casting flow and loss of speed, if the water is being struck on either backcasts or forward casts, and the relative smoothness of leader rollover and delivery.

Vertical casting oscillations in the backward and forward extensions of the line can have several causes. Such oscillations usually result from poor hand movements and timing, and mean the smooth rhythm between backcasts and forward extensions is being broken. The resulting drop in line speed causes the cast to oscillate and waver in midflight. Sometimes these erratic line waves indicate a rod taper too soft for the line weight and specifications.

Sloppy hand movements that vary from open- to closed-loop rotation can also affect the smoothness of line flow. Casting oscillations can also result from a line too heavy for the tip calibrations of the rod, although it may seem to match its general bamboo weight and length. Tip calibrations that are too heavy for the line and for the lower rod tapers result in so much line speed for the rod weight that casting flow is rough and jerky. Both backcasts and forward extensions that are completely free of oscillations and flutter are quite rare, even among highly skilled casters, and are the hallmark of perfect timing and technique.

Oscillation and flutter can also result from a level head in front of the forward taper that is either too short or too long. Both conditions can affect the smoothness of your casting as well as leader turnover.

Line flutter is also caused by shooting heads that are too thick for your rod, and running lines that are too light in diameter to stabilize the fly line in flight. Trial casts of sixty to seventy feet with a moderate left-hand haul and an observer watching the line flow are quite useful. Running lines that are too light will usually flutter badly and lose their equilibrium in the shoot, and in extreme cases such lines can even tangle in themselves under the accelerating cast. Forward tapers too thick for a specific rod can be pinpointed with a series of slow false casts that work the fly rather close to the water, since thick line belly and front tapers that are too long will fold and wobble clumsily at such line speeds. It should be remembered that some rods may have performance envelopes that lie precisely between standard line tapers and weights, and in such cases a skilled fisherman will invariably choose the lighter line. Its weight can be magnified with left-hand work, stressing the rod perfectly with line speed instead of weight, and a lighter fly line will fish with greater subtlety.

Many anglers seem quite unaware that our evolving line technology was perhaps the most remarkable development in tackle since the six-strip bamboo rod. Fly lines were a relatively simple problem only thirty years ago, when all types were oil-finished nylon and silk, but the introduction of polyvinyl chlorides has permitted us to control specific gravity. Precise manipulation of line density and weight has created a complex spectrum of tapers designed to float and sink at varying speeds. Proper choice of fly lines and the techniques of fishing them have become infinitely more complicated since midcentury. Detailed knowledge of these lines and their varied performance specifications is sometimes critical to success on our hard-fished waters.

But technology is merely a tool of fishing, and we should not lose sight of that fact in our preoccupation with fly lines, entomology, and tactics. Our technical skills must ultimately be focused on the selective fish of some difficult stream, and those rare days when the myriad pieces of the puzzle fall into place are worth all the discipline and study.

Perhaps the best stretch of fly water left in the United States is the classic Henry's Fork of the Snake in eastern Idaho. It is formed in a series of mammoth springs, rich in alkalinity and remarkably clear water and incredible fly hatches.

It was a warm September twilight on the huge flats of the Railroad Ranch. The evening sky was rich with color behind the gentle mountains across the river, and although the bright sun had made the trout shy through the midday hours, they were starting to work greedily now. No flies were visible on the smooth currents, and the gentle porpoise rolls of the nymphing fish seemed to promise a coming hatch.

The subtle rise forms were coming regularly along a bed of undulating weeds, and I searched my fly book for a delicate little pheasant tail or olive-bodied nymph. There was a rough olive dressed with a filmy wing case of nylon stocking, and I briefly held it soaking in my mouth while I studied the fish that seemed the largest. It was working in a small indentation in the weeds, and I quickly realized that a dry-fly float was virtually impossible in spite of the 6X tippet.

The Henry's Fork is demanding water in the sense that its fish are tippet-shy and sometimes lie at considerable distances from the angler. It calls for a difficult mix of requirements in both tackle and fishing skills. Eighty-foot casts are not unusual in themselves, but working at such distances with tiny flies and tippets as fine as .005 is rare, and the casts must be made with both softness and accuracy. Anticipating this set of problems, my baggage roll of rods included a superb eight-and-a-half-foot Leonard packed just for the Henry's Fork on its windless evenings. It is lighter than most eight-and-a-half-foot Leonards, weighing only four and a quarter ounces with tip calibrations so delicate that it takes only a five-weight line. Since relatively long casts seemed likely, I had selected a reel with a weight-forward WF5F and a long-belly taper to mute the hard delivery typical of multiple-diameter lines. It is an unusual outfit, but the Henry's Fork is an unusual river.

Let's try them, I whispered to myself.

The Leonard worked smoothly, false casting the little hatching-nymph imitation with the lengthening line, and my fly settled above the rising fish. It entered the current imperceptibly and I teased the nymph as its swing passed across the trout; it porpoised eagerly and I tightened even before the darting leader signalled that it had taken. The fish wallowed in surprise, and then it bolted downstream and jumped.

Good fish! I thought. *Two or three pounds!*

The Hardy Princess was whining again as the rainbow stripped another twenty feet of line. It jumped again in the twilight, and when it finally surrendered I admired its richly colored sides and gill covers in the meshes. It rested next to my waders when it was released, and finally it melted into the weedy currents.

It was a night when everything worked.

There were several good fish from twelve to sixteen inches in the hour that followed, and then the little nymph strangely stopped working. The trout were feeding more heavily, but the fly was refused consistently by fish after fish.

Maybe they've started feeding on top, I muttered.

There was little light remaining, but I studied the smooth current carefully for hatching flies. It was virtually covered with tiny pale-olive duns and spent-wing spinners, and while it was still possible to see, I selected a Blue-winged Olive and was surprised when the tippet threaded easily through its eye. It was lightly sprayed with silicone, and I dried it with a series of impatient false casts.

Downstream in the twilight there was a huge rise in the reflections on the current. It was not a rise form that threw spray or seemed spectacular, except that its deep sucking sound caught my attention, and the undulating disturbance that followed the rise was impressive.

Pretty far! I thought. *Maybe ninety feet.*

It was getting dark now and I was not familiar with the bottom, so it was unwise to wade out closer. It was more than eighty feet across the smooth current. The Leonard quickly lengthened the cast, and only a few turns of line remained on the spool when it settled across the river. The tiny dry fly cocked perfectly in the afterglow, and the fish came up again still farther out. It looked large.

The second cast was almost ninety feet, and I was happy to have the full eight-and-a-half-foot rod and the long-belly taper to reach that distance. It fell right, and it was impossible to see the fly on the water, but I tightened anyway when the fish rose softly. It threshed angrily and the reel protested in the gathering darkness as the fish ran upstream and jumped. It looked huge in the dying light, and its threshing cartwheels were too much for the fragile tippet. Suddenly the fish was gone.

It's a good ending, I smiled happily.

It was not really a failure, since reaching that big rainbow with such fine terminal tackle and hooking it with a tiny dry fly was a minor triumph at almost ninety feet. It was an example of the right tackle married to the right fly pattern, and it would have been impossible before the development of the modern polyvinyl line and the new long-belly tapers.

For even more recent developments, see Appendix: Notes on New Equipment.

3. Problems in Leaders, Knots, and Backing

The morning star glittered brightly, and just after daylight the air was cold and still. The station wagon was silver with its crystalline coating of frost, and I shivered a little outside the cabin. The sun already looked warm on the mountains, but it was still almost dark on the valley floor, and there was a faint dust of snow on the high peaks lying west of the river. It would be gone after breakfast. The cold air tasted sweet in my lungs. Mist still rose steaming from the currents, and a heron flew ponderously downstream, its wing beats working slowly in the morning light. My breath plumed in surprising clouds on the first stirrings of the wind, and I shivered again as I walked down to the Yellowstone below the outbuildings.

The trees across the river were shedding their leaves. The dark currents of the river worked and whispered through the log-cribbing foundations of the bridge. Except for a milk truck and two railroad workers from the switchyard, and a drunk cowboy just sober enough to find his way back to the boarding house beyond the tracks, the streets of the town were silent. The morning wind stirred again in the cottonwoods and poplars. The neon signs of the saloons were no longer pulsing their blatant promises, and the jukeboxes and pinball machines inside stood quiet.

October mornings are like that in Montana, and after breakfast we drove upstream toward Armstrong's Creek. It was still chill and clear, and the somnolent music of the cattle across the river carried crisply in the slowly warming air.

The station wagon rattled across the kingpost hay-wagon bridge, and several pintails exploded from the shallows as I walked lazily downstream. The sprig ducks climbed north and wheeled back along the Yellowstone

793

bottoms and were gone. No flies were hatching yet. The smooth current was riffled with the wind that blew steadily now. It ebbed and sighed in the willows and cottonwoods above the watercress sloughs, stripping them of the last of their bright yellow leaves, and sail-boated them almost playfully across the current.

The sun grew steadily warmer and it started a few flies hatching. The tiny duns that had the temerity to emerge were quickly scuttled or foundered against the weeds. Finally a few good rainbows began to feed.

They're finding something, I thought.

The trout in these Yellowstone spring creeks are justly famous for their shyness and selectivity. Daily hatches of minute flies have made them diffident about their feeding activity, and suspicious of large imitations and naturals alike. These rise forms were only soft porpoise rolls that barely disturbed the wind-riffled currents. My little dry-fly imitations, patterns that usually worked on these late-season hatches of small mayfly species, were all refused without any sign of interest or inspection.

Several good fish were working steadily now, lying mostly along a thick bed of elodea about eighty feet across the current. The rises there were quiet swirls and lazy porpoise rolls, punctuated with an occasional showy splash that looked like a fish after a swimming natural about to hatch.

They're nymphing, I concluded.

The smaller fish working in the open currents at midstream quickly took my dark little olive nymph, but the fish along the elodea were another matter. The best position for fishing my nymph over them placed me opposite a break in the cottonwoods, and facing almost directly into the wind. It took an eighty-foot cast with a delicate tippet, and the leader balked at turning over into the wind at that range.

I was using a standard knotless leader of limp nylon, because hooked fish are often lost when a series of blood-knots collect pieces of floating weed in such spring creeks, but it simply refused to deliver the fly properly. Several times the leader butt collapsed and fell clumsily back on itself when I punched it out hard, and when I tried to force it with a left-hand haul, it simply tangled around the nail knot on the line. Slowing my casting rhythms and letting the line develop less velocity unfolded the leader and fly properly, but it lacked the line speed to reach out the eighty feet necessary to cover the fish along the weeds.

Stiffer butt diameters, I thought aloud.

There were several spools of stiff nylon in my duffel, and I walked back to the station wagon. The commercial leader I was using had a butt diameter of .017 inches, too much drop from the .033 polyvinyl tip of the fly line for the wind I was facing, and it was too limp to transfer casting power smoothly from line to leader. The tippet was the .005 that I use for most work on selective fish these days, dropping finer on the stream as needed. The stock knotless taper was nine feet, and I added a foot of .017 hard nylon to make the transition from the limper German material. Another foot of .019 was followed with .021, and I nail-knotted a short length of .023

to the line. It worked rather well, although a little more than four feet of hard nylon might have gone better, with a little less limp material than the nine feet of the original knotless taper.

The modified leader punched the cast cleanly into the wind, and I finally got my little nymph over the larger fish working at the bottom of the weeds. It settled into its swing, and the riffling current humped almost imperceptibly. The water exploded when I raised the rod and tightened, and the two-pound rainbow tail-walked downstream from its friends. It jumped several more times, spending its energy in the open water downstream, and when it tried to regain its weedy sanctuary it was too late. My gentle side-pressure stopped it short, and I turned the rod low along the water, forcing the fish toward me. Finally it circled weakly in the shallows and came to my net.

The little nymph took five more rainbows between fifteen and eighteen inches, deep-bellied fish completely unlike the smaller rainbows feeding in the open shallows, and I admired their bright markings while they recovered in my hands. It was fast sport, and the last fish was a rainbow of about four pounds that quickly submarined and broke me in the moss.

My fly worked well, until the wind dropped in the early afternoon, and the fish stopped taking. The little spring creek eddied again in its weedy growth, its currents silken and difficult in character.

Maybe it's too stiff, I thought. *Maybe it's coming down too hard, and it's not fishing limp enough.*

I removed most of the hard-nylon butt and replaced it with limp .0186 and .0239 German nylon. The results were better in terms of presentation, rolling out smoothly and settling softly enough for the more difficult conditions, but the fish still refused the nymph. Checking the current briefly, I found the hatch had not changed and continued with the nymph. It still failed and I stopped to watch the fish. The rise forms were clearly different, but I had become overconfident with several hours of success and had missed the obvious clues.

They're feeding on top, I thought sheepishly.

The lack of wind had changed everything, and now the tiny mayflies were drifting normally down the current tongues, riding the feeding lanes that regularly carried them over the trout. It was obviously dry-fly time.

But the dry flies failed too.

There was a good rainbow lying in plain sight just twenty feet above my position, and a few feet farther out over the weeds. It studied each tiny imitation with enough interest to cock under the fly for a brief moment, but then drifted back to its feeding station. The hatching flies had still not changed, so I decided to reduce the tippet diameter to .005 and keep fishing my tiny *Pseudocloeon* imitation. The first good float produced a positive reaction. The rainbow drifted back with the fly, coming closer and closer, and darted back so late that its movements created a spreading false rise behind its drift.

Fausse montée, I smiled.

The 6X tippet was clipped back to only twelve inches, and I added a sixteen-inch length of .004 limp nylon. The tiny Blue-winged Olive settled above the fish and was taken without hesitation. It is impossible to know if the rainbow was fooled because the thinner nylon made a better float possible, or because the fish could not see it. However, it is an episode that clearly demonstrates many of the problems and solutions in modern leader design and performance.

Curiously, the concept of the leader is relatively new in the history of angling. The separate leader connecting the line with the fly did not exist in the Chinese beginnings of our sport, in which only a delicate line of woven silk was used, and a horsehair line connected fly with rod in third century Macedonia. Similar tackle is described in the *Treatyse of Fysshynge wyth an Angle*, although Dame Juliana Berners did discuss dying the horsehair to camouflage it in streams of different background color and character. Charles Cotton did not advocate the separate leader in *Being Instructions How to Angle for Trout and Grayling in a Clear Stream*, but his philosophy did understand the relationship between light tackle and selective trout, and the need for playing fish skillfully:

> But he that cannot kill a trout of twenty inches long with only two
> hairs, in a river clear of wood and weeds, as this and some others
> of ours are, deserves not the name of angler.

Samuel Pepys records in his *Diary* that a varnished filament of gut string made a superb tippet at the fly, much stronger and smaller than horsehair. Pepys was fishing in the same years that found Walton and Cotton fishing together on the Dove in Derbyshire, and yet Cotton strangely made no mention of gut in his writings. Cotton was remarkably innovative, and its use cannot have been widely known in the seventeenth century if Cotton was ignorant of its properties.

The secret of silkworm filaments was obviously out a century later, and leaders tapered of Spanish silkworm gut were common long before the American Revolution. Such tapered designs are always better than the level leaders that persisted on some American waters as late as the threshold of the Second World War. Tapered leaders are necessary to transmit the energy of casting, delicately and progressively, from the fly line to the fly. Such leaders were relatively expensive, and during the Great Depression, level leaders of Japanese synthetic gut enjoyed a brief vogue. Such leader material was the first synthetic fiber available.

Many fishermen are so fascinated with learning to cast a fly past seventy-five feet that they forget most fish are taken at thirty feet or less. The cast that splashes down at thirty yards will catch far less trout than a good presentation at thirty feet, and many men who can cast ninety feet often forget that truth, preferring the exhilaration of their skills to the taking of fish. Such casting skills are eagerly sought by every fisherman, but much closer work should not be forgotten.

Leader specifications and performance are often more important than casting ability, and poor leader behavior is often a problem in butt diameter, taper, or tippet size. The leader is not only used to suggest an invisible connection between the fly and its caster, but its tapers also should deliver that fly as delicately as possible. Such performance means correct diameters and design. The weight and wind resistance and taper of the leader are critical in both good presentation and fishing technique.

The two principal components of a properly tapered leader are its tippet, the terminal section connected to the fly, and its butt section connected to the line.

Most polyvinyl fly lines found on American trout waters are from .030 to .037 in their tip calibrations, and to transmit their power smoothly we need leader butts from .023 to .028 diameter. Micrometers are invaluable in determining actual thickness of both lines and leader materials. Breaking-strain ratings are inadequate information for designing and tapering your own leaders since the difference in diameter between two leader strands is critical in knot strength and can override any other factors. Many commercial leader spools are carelessly labelled, and most experienced anglers are familiar with the tapering mistakes that are possible with unverified diameters.

Two common errors in commercial leader design prevail: most are too thin in their butt diameters, and many are too short in their heavier butt tapers. Commercially tapered leaders are often incorrectly made, because it is easier to construct them of strands having an equal length. It is still possible to purchase stock tapered leaders with butt tapers that begin as fine as .014, which is an unthinking echo of silkworm gut behavior and the .025 tip diameters of oil-finished silk lines. Gut strands were costly and trimming them was wasteful. The typical 3X or 4X trout point diameter was not possible in a length of nine-foot leader, since fifteen-inch strands stepping only .001 at each barrel knot soon reached .014 calibrations, unless the butt stopped there. The silkworm-gut tapered leader was typically a prisoner of its material, and its variables of length and breaking strain and diameter. Such leaders were filled with knots, but the limitations of silkworm gut are no longer a factor in leader design. Its fragile breaking strains were perhaps its most serious flaw, and even its finest expensive grades were relatively impractical in the diameters finer than .006, as the following table demonstrates:

SPECIFICATIONS OF SILKWORM GUT MATERIAL

TYPE	GAUGE	METRIC	ENGLISH	TEST
Drawn	7X	.10	.004	.3
Drawn	6X	.125	.005	.5
Drawn	5X	.15	.006	.8
Drawn	4X	.175	.007	1.2
Drawn	3X	.20	.008	1.6
Drawn	2X	.225	.009	1.8

SPECIFICATIONS OF SILKWORM GUT MATERIAL
(continued)

TYPE	GAUGE	METRIC	ENGLISH	TEST
Refina	1X	.25	.010	2.2
Refina	0X	.275	.011	2.8
Fina	10/5	.30	.012	3.2
Fina	9/5	.325	.013	3.5
Regular	8/5	.35	.014	4.5
Regular	7/5	.375	.015	7.0
Padron	6/5	.40	.016	8.7
Padron	5/5	.425	.017	10.2
Marana	4/5	.45	.018	12.5
Marana	3/5	.475	.019	15.2
Imperial	2/5	.40	.020	19.0
Hebra	1/5	.525	.021	23.5

It is clear from these specifications that a fisherman working our modern tippet-shy trout would be in trouble with silkworm gut in spite of its poetic synergies when matched with a line of oil-finished silk. The breaking strain of .010 gut is virtually identical to the strength of .005 tippets in the modern nylons exactly half the diameter. Many hard-fished streams cannot be fished successfully with tippets heavier than .007, and still finer tippets of .006 and .005 are better. My own fishing over selective trout is concentrated in these sizes, with an occasional .004 tippet under particularly difficult conditions. None of these diameters tested much over three-quarters of a pound in the finest Murcia silkworm gut, hardly workable for the average fishing we enjoy with such diameters.

Silkworm gut was commonly called catgut in my boyhood years, but this was a colloquial mistake heard everywhere on trout water. It actually consists of the silk that a mature silkworm has not yet extruded from its glandular sacs. The silkworm itself is the larva of the Asiatic moth classified *Bombyx mori*, and its domestic cultivation began in China many centuries ago. The species has been transplanted virtually everywhere that mulberry trees are found thriving, and perhaps their most successful introduction occurred in the southern Spanish province of Murcia. British tackle manufacturers purchased vast quantities of the most select silkworm gut from the Murcia growers for more than a century.

The life cycle of the silkworm begins in late winter, and it takes six weeks to reach maturity. It then starts a curious series of brief hibernations, in which it lies dormant for two or three days, after which it suddenly returns to its ravenous diet of mulberry leaves. Cultivation of the larvae occurs in small buildings, where they are kept on fragile feeding racks. Mulberry leaves are distributed across each rack several times each day, and they are quickly consumed by the larvae. The silk glands of these larvae consist of two long thin-walled sacs lying inside the abdominal structure, and feeding a single spinning orifice. When the silkworm reaches maturity its sacs are gorged with a clear fluid of considerable viscosity. The fluid quickly congeals and hardens on contact with the atmosphere, and the fully mature larva spins itself a pupal cocoon of raw silk.

Larvae destined for silkworm gut must be killed just before they spin their pupal enclosures. Six weeks of heavy feeding on mulberry leaves are ended in killing tubs filled with water and acetic acid. The silkworms remain for several hours in this brine, which congeals their glandular sacs into a consistency that may be stretched into gut strands. Their quality, thickness, and length vary radically with the chemistry of the brine, temperature, humidity, the size and health of the worms, and the skill of the hand strippers. The freshly drawn strands are dried in the sun, and their surface film dissolved and rubbed off.

The most difficult phase in the process is sizing and sorting for quality. Skilled hands discriminate endlessly between lengths, diameters, relative straightness, and general filament quality. Proper sorting requires exceptional skill and experience. Silkworm-gut quality was always critical and elusive. Its selection was possible only through experts, since even a highly skilled fisherman found that most top grades of raw gut looked pretty much alike. His criteria were usually resolved on the stream, since a Select tippet of .007 diameter held his fish, and a poorer grade simply broke. Competition for the finest silkworm gut was fierce in the early years of this century, and the prices spiralled after the First World War.

Earlier prices were high enough, and well over a century ago there was a large-scale effort to develop an American silk-growing industry in South Carolina. Huge mulberry groves were planted, and organized cultivation of the *Cecropia* moth was started. The *Cecropia* moth is closely related to the Asiatic silkworm species. These American insects have unusually large glandular sacs in their larval stages, sacs capable of stretching into strands of more than six feet. The economic collapse that followed the Civil War abruptly ended the American experiments.

Strength and quality were the grail in silkworm gut leaders, and there was both competition for supplies and marketing subterfuge. Hardy took pride in its dominance over other European firms as importers of the finest Murcia gut. Their drawn gut was made only from the best quality, and extruded through precise jeweled dies. It had a high reputation for its strength, but that reputation was the result of a clever stratagem—Hardy 4X tippets calibrated a full .008 inches, while their competitors commonly used the standard .007 diameters.

Japanese gut was the first synthetic fiber available to American fishermen, and its performance was so marginal that the subsequent response of American anglers to the introduction of nylon was lukewarm. The synthetic Japanese gut was really twisted silk saturated with a hard waterproofing gum, and when the gum binder washed out, the leaders often unwrapped and quickly frayed. It was a poor substitute.

Nylon was a totally synthetic material developed in the United States shortly before the Second World War. It is primarily derived from coal, water, and atmospheric components. It can be readily shaped into filaments, and it is characterized by its singular qualities of strength, elasticity, chemical and abrasive resistance, and its limited absorbency of moisture. It can be permanently formed with thermal setting, and it was first introduced in bristles and hosiery. Its chemistry consists of a series of linear polymeric amides with repetitive amide groups and is produced by the controlled polymerization of dibasic acids, diamines, and amino compounds. Literally thousands of such potential polymer structures exist, and the radical improvement of nylon leader materials in recent years is an example of these variables.

Primitive nylon leader material became available just after the Second World War, and since the production of Spanish gut had been seriously truncated during the conflict, many fishermen were forced to use nylon before it was really perfected. Du Pont nylon leader material was manufactured with the following specifications until well after midcentury.

DU PONT STANDARD NYLON LEADER MATERIAL

GAUGE	METRIC	ENGLISH	TEST
5X	.15	.006	1.00
4X	.175	.007	1.25
3X	.20	.008	1.75
2X	.225	.009	2.25
1X	.25	.010	3.00
0X	.275	.011	3.50
10/5	.30	.012	4.50
9/5	.325	.013	5.00
8/5	.35	.014	6.00
7/5	.375	.015	8.00
6/5	.40	.016	9.00
5/5	.425	.017	10.00
4/5	.45	.018	11.50
3/5	.475	.019	12.00
2/5	.50	.020	13.00
1/5	.525	.021	15.80

Knowledgeable anglers will quickly see that these calibrations and breaking strains are quite inferior to the nylon leaders we now have twenty-odd years later, but it is obvious that their strength then was slightly superior to the finest silkworm gut. It was about the time that *Matching the Hatch* was being written that the modern German nylons first appeared on the American market, and they were a remarkable advance over the nylon leader materials I had first used on European rivers earlier.

Advanced polymeric combinations have evolved several excellent types of these European nylons. Their limpness and elasticity and knotting qualities are striking, and their capabilities are a fly-fishing revolution fully equal to the development of the polyvinyl fly lines a few years later. Some comparative specifications are interesting:

GERMAN PLATYL NYLON MATERIAL SPECIFICATIONS

GAUGE	METRIC	ENGLISH	TEST
7X	.10	.0041	1.2
6X	.123	.0047	2.1
5X	.15	.0061	3.3
4X	.175	.0071	4.3
3X	.20	.0081	5.2
2X	.225	.0091	6.3
1X	.25	.0098	7.2
0X	.275	.0111	9.1
8/5	.325	.0129	12.6
7/5	.35	.0145	15.2
5/5	.40	.0159	17.8
3/5	.45	.0177	21.5
2/5	.475	.0186	25.7
0/5	.60	.0239	34.8

These German filaments were a revelation when they first became available to American fly-fishermen, particularly on eastern streams where the tippet-shy fish were getting wary enough to reject the 4X material we had used for years.

It was John Crowe, the author of *The Book of Trout Lore*, who gave me the first spools of German nylon more than twenty years ago on Spring Creek in Pennsylvania. Crowe had watched me fishing over several particularly selective trout without much success. The fish were lying in plain sight, and it was frustrating to watch them come to my dry flies, inspect them for a few inches of drift, and turn away without taking. These were all brown trout that had been caught and released before, and had obviously learned from the experience. Crowe became interested in the stalemate and stopped to watch.

It was embarrassing to have an audience.

The fish rejected my carefully tied imitations of the hatch for almost an hour before Crowe introduced himself, and I waded out of the water to talk. *These fish are picky,* I said sheepishly.

Yes, Crowe said. *They've seen flies many times.*

My fly pattern should be right. I showed him the specimens of the hatch I had collected. *It usually works on these insects.*

It looks fine, Crowe agreed.

The fish still dimpled and sipped the hatching duns in the swift run along the bank. The fluttering mayflies were still the same species. *Something's wrong,* I said unhappily.

Maybe they're tippet-shy, he said.

Tippet-shy? I asked. *I'm fishing 4X now.*

4X? Crowe chuckled softly. *Tippets that heavy look like ropes to these selective limestone trout.*

It's the finest material I've got, I said.

Try this nylon, he offered.

Crowe had two spools of German nylon and I studied them closely. The plastic .0061 spool was marked with a breaking strain of more than three pounds, and the still finer .0047 spool was surprisingly listed at slightly over two-pound test.

It's fantastically thin and strong! I gasped.

Crowe smiled. *Give it a try.*

The delicate .0061 material was twice as strong as my conventional nylon tippet, and Crowe gave me enough strands to build a taper from .0081 to .0047. It was a quick taper in twelve-inch lengths with a twenty-inch tippet, and I finally blood-knotted it to my regular leader.

The selective fish became surprisingly easy, and I took a fourteen-inch brown on the first cast. The delicate little nylon fooled every trout that had been feeding under the trees, the same fish that had humiliated me consistently for an hour.

That's pretty convincing, I admitted. *Those fish really are tippet-shy, and this stuff really works!*

It works well, Crowe nodded.

Since those early years, such remarkable European leader material has been widely imported into the United States, and its unique specifications have proved a revolution fully equal to the introduction of polyvinyl fly lines. Their calibrations and strengths have been a fishing breakthrough, and it is doubtful that we could fish many of our hard-pressed rivers successfully without these new nylons. Certainly the eastern streams and western spring creeks would prove difficult with silkworm-gut tippets no finer than .007, and the brittle postwar nylon that calibrated .006. Such leaders would test at a pound or less, while it would take a tippet of .009 gut to match the breaking strain of our modern 6X leaders. Our selective trout would collapse in hysterical laughter at such 1X tippets these days, although such clumsy point diameters were common thirty years ago.

Bergman made a number of recommendations concerning leaders in *Trout,* although in his chapters fishing a fine tippet meant carrying leaders tapered to .008. His book also suggested carrying a few coiled gut tippets of .007, adding these to his leaders under difficult low-water conditions or bright weather. Many fishermen fail to realize the magnitude of our recent revolution in leader materials, which make practical tippets as fine as .004 and .003 readily available.

Perhaps the comparative specifications and breaking strains of several other modern European nylons are worth studying; types commonly available are manufactured as follows:

GERMAN MAXIMA CHAMELEON SPECIFICATIONS

GAUGE	METRIC	ENGLISH	TEST
7X	.10	.004	1
6X	.125	.005	2
5X	.15	.006	3
4X	.175	.007	4
3X	.20	.008	5
2X	.225	.009	6
1X	.25	.010	8
0X	.275	.011	9
10/5	.30	.012	10
9/5	.325	.013	12
7/5	.375	.015	15
5/5	.425	.017	20
2/5	.50	.020	25
1/5	.55	.022	30
0/5	.60	.024	40

Maxima is a superb nylon leader material of the limp type, and although it has not been available as long as other German and French materials, it has a chorus of vocal advocates on widespread rivers. It has superb fishing and knot-making capabilities, qualities that also distinguish the Luxor nylon produced in France by Pezon & Michel:

PEZON & MICHEL LUXOR NYLON SPECIFICATIONS

GAUGE	METRIC	ENGLISH	TEST
7X	.10	.004	1.1
6X	.125	.005	1.4
5X	.15	.006	2.4
4X	.175	.007	3.2
3X	.20	.008	3.8
2X	.225	.009	4.5
1X	.25	.010	5.5
0X	.275	.011	6.4
10/5	.30	.012	7.5
9/5	.325	.013	8.6
7/5	.375	.015	11.6
3/5	.475	.019	19.2
1/5	.525	.021	23.7

Luxor is not quite as strong in its breaking strains as some of the more recent polymer variations, but it is a material that combines the elasticity and knot-making behavior of the finest limp nylons with slightly more stiffness. Tortue is another French nylon that is made in still finer diameters of fishable strength. Its .0039 diameter has a breaking strain of one pound, and its .0031 tests a remarkable three-quarter pound. Knowledgeable anglers add both diameters to their 7X tippets, not because there is much difference in breaking strain between .004 or .0041 and the .0039 Tortue but because of the critical character of knots between different diameters in such delicate nylons. However, only the most delicate rod calibrations designed for three- and four-weight lines are fully capable of fishing such fragile leaders in practical terms.

American manufacturers have recently been working to produce similar leader material. Gladding, Cortland, Berkeley, and Mason are making exceptionally fine nylon for fly-fishing, although the Mason product is a hard polymer for anglers who prefer a relatively stiff leader. It is also excellent for making compound leaders of hard-nylon butts with limp-nylon tippets and tapers. The Mason leader materials are available in the following diameters, and Leonard is fabricating knotless leaders of this hard nylon in a full range of sizes and tapers:

MASON HARD-TYPE NYLON SPECIFICATIONS

GAUGE	METRIC	ENGLISH	TEST
8X	.075	.003	0.5
7X	.10	.004	1.0
6X	.125	.005	2.0
5X	.15	.006	3.0
4X	.175	.007	4.0
3X	.20	.008	5.0
2X	.225	.009	6.0
1X	.25	.010	7.0
0X	.275	.011	8.0
10/5	.30	.012	10.0
9/5	.325	.013	12.0
7/5	.375	.015	14.0
5/5	.425	.017	18.0
3/5	.475	.019	20.0
1/5	.525	.021	22.0
0/5	.575	.023	25.0

Cortland is packaging its knotless tapers with two tippet strands of limp nylon for attachment to a seven-and-a-half-foot leader of stiffer material. It is convenient and workable and is proving popular with many fishermen. The specifications for the Cortland nylon leader materials are found in the following table:

CORTLAND CROWN NYLON SPECIFICATIONS

GAUGE	METRIC	ENGLISH	TEST
6X	.125	.005	1.5
5X	.15	.006	2.0
4X	.175	.007	3.5
3X	.20	.008	4.5
2X	.225	.009	6.0
1X	.25	.010	7.0
0X	.275	.011	9.0
9/5	.325	.013	12.0
7/5	.375	.015	15.0
5/5	.425	.017	18.0
3/5	.475	.019	21.0
1/5	.525	.021	23.0
0/5	.575	.023	25.0

It is interesting that these diameters are not quite as strong in the extremely fine sizes, yet are demonstrably strong in several intermediate sizes suited to average fishing. Cortland knotless tapers are also available in butt weights from .025 to .029, and are therefore extremely useful as prefabricated foundations for compound tapers based on your particular streamside needs. Their standard butt diameter of .029 is the heaviest now available in a machinemade knotless taper. Cortland is making a flat monofilament material originally intended as running line for shooting heads, but many fishermen have also been using it in the twenty-five-pound calibration for distance leader-butt nylon. Since it is a relatively flat oval in cross section, it unfolds and rolls out in a self-enforcing plane of delivery, and must be mounted carefully on the fly line to insure that its flat axis lies horizontal in normal casting. Like a good split-cane rod, which flexes only through its flat axis and fights poor casting habits, the Cobra flat monofilament will deliver cleanly in a vertical plane. It is an intriguing development that can provide a little better accuracy in making very long casts and is worth trying on your waters.

Berkeley is also making a so-called Magnum butt leader of modern nylon with a quick-taper design and .028 butt diameter similar to the Cortland .029 in performance. However, Cortland provides its .029 butt diameter in only a nine-foot leader tapered to fifteen-pound test, while the Berkeley tapers are available from ten-pound to 4X diameters. Berkeley is also treating its nylon with a special nontoxic compound to lubricate and increase the wetting qualities of its leader material. This wetting agent lasts as long as you would normally fish the leader without risk of casting-knot damage or molecular fatigue, and it seems far superior to the etch-tipped experiments tried by several manufacturers in recent years. However, it is probably not desirable to have your entire leader sink unless you are fishing wet flies, nymphs, or streamers. Specifications for these Berkeley leaders are from the following nylon diameters:

BERKELEY SINKING NYLON SPECIFICATIONS

GAUGE	METRIC	ENGLISH	TEST
6X	.125	.005	1.75
5X	.15	.006	2.0
4X	.175	.007	2.5
3X	.20	.008	3.0
2X	.225	.009	4.0
1X	.25	.010	5.0
0X	.275	.011	6.0
9/5	.325	.013	8.0
7/5	.375	.015	10.0
5/5	.425	.017	12.0
3/5	.475	.019	14.0
1/5	.525	.021	17.0
0/5	.575	.123	20.0

Berkeley is also introducing a line of unusual knotless leaders, which are a flattened oval in cross section and become round when they reach the tippet diameters. Field experiments indicate that these developments have a remarkable future, and Berkeley is testing some new nylons that could provide greater strength-to-diameter ratios than our best modern filaments, perhaps making tippets finer than .003 possible.

Gladding was perhaps the pioneer in importing the European nylon to the United States, and it obtained the exclusive rights to the German Platyl material twenty-odd years ago. The company still manufactures and sells nylon leader material made with the specifications outlined earlier in this chapter. It is packaged on color-coded plastic spools, and it is now treated with a modern process designed to stabilize its elasticity. Standard knotless tapers are available in heavier butt diameters than were manufactured in the past, and the nine-foot types tapered from butts of .0239 and .0275 are excellent foundations for building an all-limp leader tapered as fine as .004. Such ready-made leaders should be quick tapers starting with their tips of .009 and .013, using short, ten-inch strands to the final diameter. The ultimate leader tippet should be about twenty inches in length, until you are working below .005, and then it should be progressively shortened because its fine diameter simply will not extend properly when cast.

Tippet diameter is not only a function of delivering the fly softly and providing the illusion of an unattached insect, but also related to fly weight and wind resistance. Many fishermen still use the traditional rule of thumb which multiplies the tippet ratings below 0X times four to determine average fly size for each diameter. The Rule of Four holds that a 3X tippet is perfectly suited for a size twelve fly, since three times four equals twelve.

Many European fishermen recommend tippets as heavy as 2X for size twelve flies, and suggest a relatively coarse oX for size ten. Such diameters are indicative of the private trout fishing found on most European rivers, where there are fish that see only a few anglers, compared with the large numbers found on public waters within a few hours of most American cities. There is no question that a 2X or 3X tippet will cast a size twelve fly perfectly, but it is equally clear that it will frequently put down the leader-shy fish on most eastern and many western streams. The following table is designed for such hard-fished waters, although the tippets might be shortened to insure proper turnover, perhaps to as little as twelve inches if necessary in a wind:

LEADER DIAMETERS AND HOOK SIZES

GAUGE	HOOK SIZE	GAUGE	HOOK SIZE	GAUGE	HOOK SIZE
8X	24–26–28	5X	14–16–18	2X	6–8–10
7X	20–22–24	4X	10–12–14	1X	4–6–8
6X	16–18–20	3X	8–10–12	oX	2–4–6

These ratios are valid for conventionally dressed flies on average-weight hooks. Windy conditions or particularly bushy hackles mean heavier tippet diameters, and really big nymphs or streamers need point sizes heavier than .011 nylon. Heavy-duty hooks commonly used on big western nymphs and steelhead patterns also demand leaders with more muscle, and fishing a long-hackled skater without the stiffness of a 1X or 2X point is futile. Conditions and your casting will tell you when your tippet is too light for the fly you are punching out, and when it refuses to deliver cleanly, you should try heavier diameters.

Leader shyness is also related to observation time. Trout have more time to inspect a fly floating or swinging in relatively slow currents and are much less tippet-shy in fast runs and pockets. Flies that are fished fast, like streamers and long-hackled skaters, move too quickly to give the fish a careful look. Such conditions and tactics will permit the successful use of heavier tippets.

Therefore, leader selection and design vary widely with the condition of the river, the character of its fish population, and the techniques employed. Dry-fly leaders are generally longer to insure both a delicate delivery and drag-free float, and similar leader performance is needed to fish wet flies and nymphs just under the surface or in the film itself. Leaders fished with a sink-tip or full sinking lines should be relatively short, since their buoyant character will tend to cancel out the sinking qualities of the polyvinyl high-density lines. Butt diameters should still have sufficient thickness to match the tip diameter of the lines.

Standard ready-made leaders were once seldom available in lengths over seven-and-a-half feet, although nine-foot designs are common now, and several manufacturers are also making twelve-foot tapers in both knotted and knotless types. Many experts regularly use leaders much longer than twelve feet, although iconoclasts like Charles Ritz and Polly Rosborough disdain such refinements, arguing that any fish can be taken with tapers of six-and-a-half to ten feet. Rosborough and Ritz are probably correct, except that their fishing seldom calls for the extreme cobweb-size tippets in common use on many particularly difficult or hard-fished American streams. It is not so much the length that the long-leader fanatics are after, but a leader working in relatively sophisticated compound tapers from butt diameters above .023 to ultrafine tippets under .005. It is difficult to make a workable leader under twelve feet that will meet these specifications, and fifteen feet is easier.

However, breaking strains are less important than diameter in fishing selective trout, both because of reduced visibility and the flexibility of a fine tippet. The average trout on most eastern streams will weigh something under a pound. Our famous western rivers hold a higher percentage of big fish, but their average is perhaps only a pound or slightly better.

Such fish are easily handled on .005 and .006 tippets, and with proper rods, even the finer .004 and .003 nylons are workable. Much heavier trout can be handled with gentle striking and playing skills. Such fine diameters are a problem with really big trout, especially in moss-filled spring creeks, but they are often the only tippet sizes that will coax them into taking the fly. There are few rivers where three- and four-pound trout are found in good numbers, except perhaps in Chile, Argentina, and the Antipodes. Such fishing calls for leaders from 4X to 0X, although dropping back to 5X and 6X may prove necessary at times. Skilled anglers can successfully take big trout, fish weighing eight and ten pounds, with leaders testing only two or three pounds of breaking strain. However, it is wise to select leaders that match your skills rather than fish too fine and lose the fish of a lifetime.

Edward Ringwood Hewitt insisted that silkworm gut stained with silver nitrate in a patented Hewitt process was the only effective color for a leader. His patent covered the gut with a crystalline structure of microscopic metal, which undoubtedly helped it sink readily. It also muted its natural glitter and flash in certain kinds of light, which was probably its chief virtue. Certainly the shine of a tippet can cancel out the benefits of its otherwise cobweblike diameter. Preston Jennings insisted that trout could not see a leader dyed his special shade of purple. Leader color has been the subject of countless arguments in trout-fishing camps everywhere, although my own experience would indicate that color makes little difference in actual fishing. A. J. McClane makes a similar observation in his book *The Practical Fly Fisherman*, in the following paragraph:

> The color of leaders, and whether they should sink or float, are both debatable points. I have made dozens of leaders dyed with methylene blue, potassium hydroxide, malachite green, tea, coffee, iodine and Bismarck brown. Aside from messing up the sink, they left no other mark on fishing history.

McClane is probably right in arguing that a dull, mist-colored leader is least visible to the trout, and anyone who has spent any time under the surface of a swift-flowing stream is aware that it has more kaleidoscopic reflections than a carnival hall of mirrors. Leader glitter is often lost in this world of bubbles and refraction and dancing light, but it undoubtedly ranks with a stiff coiled-spring leader lying in the surface film as a warning to a skittish fish.

However, I still believe that a dull mist color is best for dry-fly work, and that a leader for fishing deeper should be dyed to match the background colors of the river bottom. Dull green would match a weedy river, dark gray for a river with a bed of slate-colored stones, brown for a still current of tea-colored detritus and algae, and rust color for a river of reddish ledges of lava and basalt.

Conventional wisdom also argues that a leader should sink in order to fool a difficult trout, but a fully sunk leader is also difficult to tighten with sufficient speed when a fish takes the fly. It can also be argued that the fish usually see the leader no matter what subterfuge we use to disguise its presence. The dry-fly leader should probably be dressed except for its final tippet, and even half the leader should probably be oiled with silicone to fish a nymph or wet fly near the surface. Sink-tip and full sinking lines demand a leader that sinks and sinks readily.

Charles Ritz makes the point in his *Fly Fisher's Life* that a well-tapered leader should deliver its final taper and the fly with precision on the first cast, and that its specifications should provide that kind of performance in both wind and weather. It should provide such complete harmony with the fly line and the rod that it faithfully transmits the caster's art through its tapers to the fly. Such synergy comes largely from casting skill, but it is impossible without perfectly balanced tackle.

It was undoubtedly Charles Ritz who first developed the basic concepts for our modern nylon tapers, since his indefatigable tenacity became focused on the potential of nylon leader material virtually from its introduction in 1939. It took only six months of experimenting with the first samples from Rhodiaceta to convince Ritz that silkworm gut was ultimately finished as a leader material. It took other fly-fishing experts another dozen years to accept nylon, and there are still diehards who argue for silkworm gut and its Golden Age.

The conventional silkworm-gut leaders had always been made in a uniform taper using strands of approximately equal length working from .014 to a tippet of .007 to .006. Such tapers took five or six strands, and worked well enough with oiled-silk lines that had tip diameters of only .025. Limp nylon and polyvinyl chloride lines with tip diameters of .033 to .035 soon changed such conventional wisdom. Ritz soon realized that nylon was not constrained by the average length of its strands, and that the length of any single diameter in his progressive tapers should be determined by performance alone. It was a radical concept well ahead of its time.

Ritz also worked out the basic principle that a nylon leader should be tapered with sixty percent in its heavier diameters, twenty percent in its forward taper, and about twenty percent in its terminal diameters. It is a formula that works quite well, although the considerations of manufacturing caused the original knotless tapers of nylon to resemble earlier designs in silkworm gut and their uniform tapers from butt to tippet. The result was a series of leaders based upon this relatively heavy butt diameter and quick-taper formula which Ritz called his Rafale Storm specification.

However, the basic leaders in the Ritz series of Parabolic Normale, Super-Precision, and Short P.P.P. tapers is based on tippets no finer than .010 to .007 nylon. His formulas also included a nymphing design with an exaggeratedly supple front taper designed to sink and fish the fly with a free and unencumbered drift. Ritz recommended nymph-fishing tippets of .007 and .006, and under many conditions his tapers are excellent.

Yet such specifications fail to meet either the high-wind conditions of our western mountains, or the ultralight tippet requirements of our hard-fished eastern rivers. The following tapers are better adapted to American problems, both for momentum into a wind and for delivering a fine tippet with precision.

These leaders have proved themselves under many conditions in many parts of the country, and their balance and performance are exceptional. Their feel and the behavior of the fly are telegraphed exquisitely to the fisherman through his tackle, giving him remarkable control of both casting and presentation. Casting rhythms have considerable effect on leader dynamics, and leader tapers of these specifications work equally well when a cast is lengthening and has reached optimal line load for the rod. This means the leader must accommodate both the rapid flick-flick timing of the cast at close ranges, the more deliberate rhythms between thirty and forty-odd feet, and the slow rhythms beyond sixty feet. It must also transmit the varied patterns of delivery and line speed for the several basic casts.

Backing material is important too, far more critical than many writers have indicated in past books. Few trout fishermen have much experience in playing really strong fish that carry them regularly into the backing, and such lessons are truly learned on steelhead water, shallow bonefish and tarpon flats, and salmon rivers. Many anglers believe that backing strength and diameter are relatively unimportant, that the principal function of backing is merely in filling out the reel, and that its role in providing extra line for the rare fish strong enough to take the entire fly line is only a secondary factor.

Such truisms can cost you trophy-size fish, and it would be tragic to lose one of the few really big trout you will hook in a lifetime of fishing. Your tackle should be rigged to handle the solitary six-pound rainbow lurking in your home river, not the foot-long fish you usually take.

Modern fly reels are often machined from ultralight aluminum alloys, and the silk and nylon backing line we once used is no longer practical. Silk line like the old bait-casting type was too vulnerable to mildew and rot, and its weight tended to spin a light-alloy spool with too much inertia when a fish started running. Its weight also caused enough static inertia that a bolting fish could sheer a 6X or 7X tippet before the reel spool could respond. Nylon backing has too much stretch for backing performance. During a strong fight with a good fish, as much as a hundred yards of backing can be stripped from the reel. The strength of the fish added to the pull of a heavy current can stretch nylon enough that it can damage the spool. It is recovered grudgingly in its stretched condition, and is layered tightly as it is recovered on the reel. The elasticity of the nylon can literally distort a light-alloy spool, causing it to warp and bind. Its freezing means a lost fish when things go well, and such a reel malfunction could result in a shattered rod if your luck goes badly.

Dacron has solved these problems of elasticity in the backing line, and it has become quite popular in recent years. However, many fishermen are using it in diameters that are too thin for good backing performance, perhaps because they have no need for fifteen- and twenty-pound breaking strain in their fishing. Such misguided sportsmanship has cost many a well-meaning fisherman the best trout of his career. It is not the breaking strain of their backing that matters, but an equilibrium between its maximum reel capacity and its elastic behavior in coming off the spool under stress.

Obviously, the smaller diameters of backing provide optimum footage on any size reel. Such fine diameters can also bite deeply into themselves when a strong fish bolts suddenly, jamming tightly into its underlying layers. It is a bitter lesson I first learned on big rainbows in Patagonia. Although careful rewinding during a fight can reduce the possibility of such a backing jam, it requires a fisherman to pay too much attention to his reel while fishing, and too little to the fish and their fighting behavior. It is better to use backing of heavier diameters, since even the heavier synthetic lines are lighter than the older lines of linen or silk.

My preference is fifteen-pound dacron for light trout fishing, twenty-pound test for average work, and thirty-pound breaking strain for big-fish water. It is not strength that matters in selecting such lines, but their diameters and behavior under stress.

Several manufacturers produce dacron backing line of excellent quality. It is braided with a smooth finish, has only minimal elasticity, and is dimensionally stable either wet or dry. It is available in connected spools of as much as 300 yards, as well as bulk spools of 1,000 yards. Ashaway makes dacron lines in twenty- and thirty-pound test. Gudebrod has an excellent fifteen- and twenty-pound type, and Cortland Micron includes a superb thirty-pound line. Orvis also offers dacron backing line in the optimum twenty- and thirty-pound breaking strains. Such lines are all workable as backing.

Proper knots for modern leaders, lines, and backing are as critical as these pieces of tackle themselves, since knots are often the weak link in our equipment. It is not possible to become a really skilled fly-fisherman without a proficiency in knotmaking. Many of the finest trout fishermen are

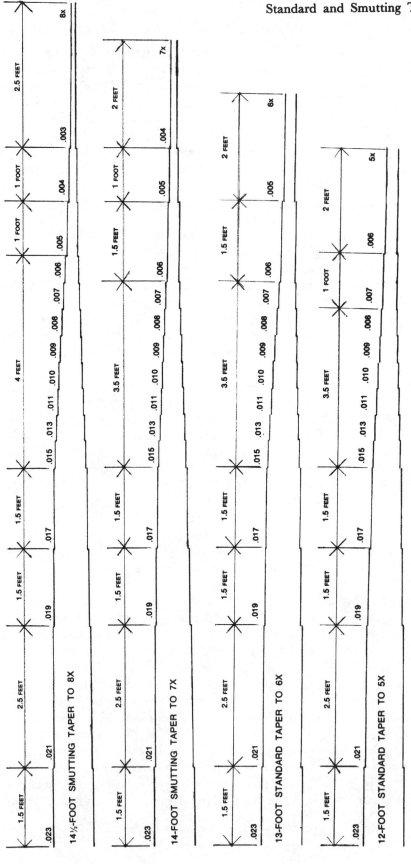

14½-FOOT SMUTTING TAPER TO 8X

14-FOOT SMUTTING TAPER TO 7X

13-FOOT STANDARD TAPER TO 6X

12-FOOT STANDARD TAPER TO 5X

Nymph Leader Tapers

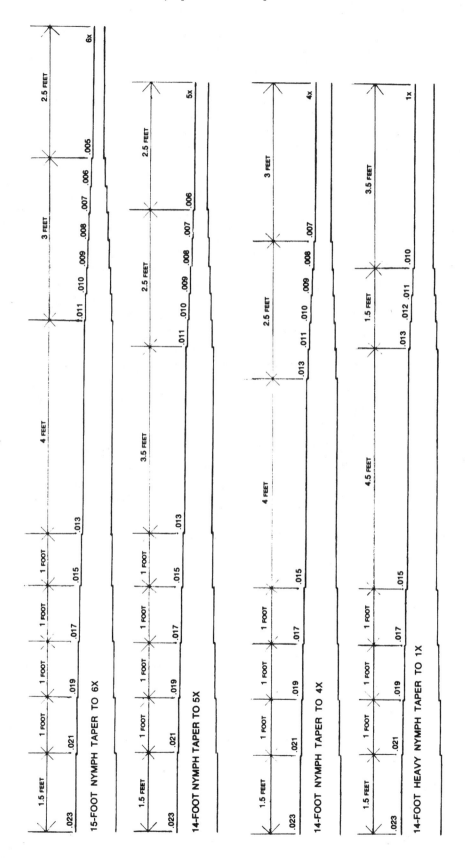

so aware that faulty knots are the primary cause of lost fish that they insist on tying their own knots and making up their own equipment. Such men are not austere or overly fussy. Experience has taught them that knots are more than mere connections, and that bad knots are an abomination. There are no universal fishing knots that will serve every possible need. Modern synthetic lines and leader materials have made all the fishing knots of my boyhood years obsolete, or relegated them to an extremely minor role, since silk lines and silkworm gut are largely gone. We no longer use the thread-wrapped loops at both ends of our lines, or the perfection loops in our leader butts and backing, and the Turle-type knot is now used only for attaching big flies and skaters. Modern fishermen are confronted with a galaxy of knots based on modern synthetic leaders and lines. Knowledgeable fishermen make it their business to know what knot to use and when that knot is needed.

Poor fishing knots are usually configurations that weaken the ambient breaking strain of the material used, filaments damaged by the thermal effects of tightening too quickly, and knots that are tightened too carelessly or have been incorrectly and sloppily trimmed. Bulky knots that will not travel freely through the rod guides will cost you fish. Your knots are poorly tied if you habitually must add an overhand knot in the end of your material, or touch the free monofilament tip with a cigarette, to prevent its slipping through and coming free under the strain of a fish.

Good knots will not slip when freshly tied. All knots in modern nylons slip just before they fail, but a knowledgeable angler will either discard or reseat his knots before that happens. Good knots must be equal to the breaking strain required in the situation for which they have been chosen. Such knots are neat, correctly trimmed, and have adequate strength. The best knots are those that deliver most of the unknotted breaking strain of their materials, since a poor knot can reduce that original strength more than fifty percent.

Good knots will part far below the rated breaking strain of the nylon, and it is best to use the knots described in this chapter for trout fishing. There are still stronger knots that have been developed for taking marlin and sailfish and tarpon with fly tackle, but such knots are relatively complex and their strength is unnecessary in our sport. It is foolish to employ complicated knots simply because they exist, when a less elaborate knot will perform adequately.

Knots should be learned and tied when you are not actually fishing, since expert knot tying requires both patience and practice. Some knots are more difficult than others. Concentrate on a few basic knots and attempt the more difficult types when you have mastered the primary types. Relatively few knots are actually needed, and your skill in executing them is infinitely more important in your fishing than the number of fishing knots in your full lexicon of skills. Practice will permit you to tie fresh knots in a fishing situation without problems and anxiety. Complex knots should never be attempted on the stream until you can execute them easily. It is infinitely better to execute a marginally acceptable knot expertly, than tie the best knot badly.

Popular knowledge clings happily to the myth that modern synthetic leaders, fly lines, and backing last virtually forever. It is simply not true. Humidity and temperature and light all play a role in their gradual denigration. Tippets listed at two-pound test might actually have weakened to fifty percent of their original breaking strain. Frayed leaders and lines are seriously damaged, will cost you fish, and should always be changed. Such fraying can result from badly worn and abrasive guides, tangling in the canoe or under stones, being stepped on, and raking over sharp ledges and boulders during the fight. Badly frayed lines should be discarded, and a leader should be jettisoned at any sign of deterioration.

Leader nylon should always be inspected for any brittle or stiff character, since it loses its lubricants and wetting agents with time. Such nylon has a wiry, springlike behavior. Comparison with fresh nylon of the same type will quickly dispel any doubts in your mind. Expert fly-fishermen will change lines regularly, and new leader material is inexpensive insurance against tackle failures. Most will change leaders after a single prolonged fight with a heavy fish if they think it may have touched a sharp ledge or stone or has been stretched too much during the struggle. Losing good fish is more costly than changing leaders.

Knots should be replaced as well. Freshly tied knots will lose about ten percent of their breaking strength in the first twenty-four hours. Some of this loss results from drying, since the knots were at their tightest while fighting your fish, and some results from nylon memory behavior. Such memory behavior means the nylon tries to find the earlier configuration of its storage spool, and its homing instinct causes its knots to stretch and open slightly. Slippage and weakening are often the result. Experienced fishermen will retighten their knots regularly to offset this tendency, and any knot that tightens too much should also be replaced. Big fish can also subject the fly knot to exceptional stress, and I always replace the fly after fighting a particularly large trout, making sure its knot is fresh and sound. The fly should be freshly attached after a few average-size fish are taken. It is perhaps wise to change all knots several times a season, and on major trips in big-fish country, knots should be replaced regularly.

The strength of nylon leader material is also affected by humidity and temperature and light, even when it has never been fished. High temperatures exceeding about 120 degrees for extended periods of time are trouble, although temperatures of as much as 200 degrees occur with a fly line sawing back and forth over the tip guide during a double haul. Nylons melt at about 500 degrees, but they lose much strength at considerably lower thermal readings. Storage in a hot automobile trunk is unwise, and leaving a reel lying in the sun inside a locked car can easily damage both leaders and lines. Many synthetics are weakened by exposure to both infrared and ultraviolet radiation in sunlight, and modern line and leader synthetics are no exception.

Nylon Wind Tapers

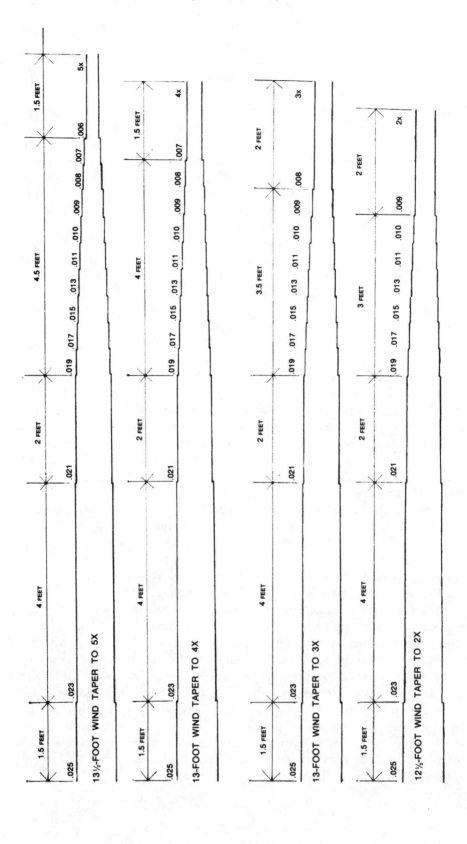

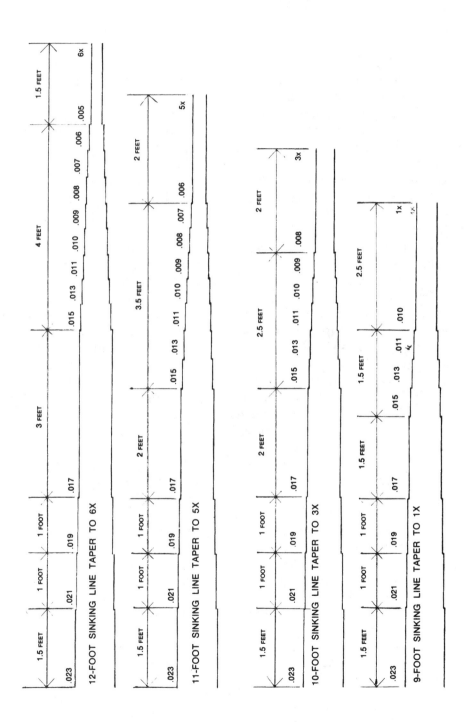

12-FOOT SINKING LINE TAPER TO 6X

11-FOOT SINKING LINE TAPER TO 5X

10-FOOT SINKING LINE TAPER TO 3X

9-FOOT SINKING LINE TAPER TO 1X

Such radiation exists in smaller amounts in normal levels of light, as well as some artificial sources of illumination. Nylon leader material should never be exposed to fluorescent lighting. Such factors in the shelf life of leader material mean a loss of strength before it is sold to the fisherman, and it is doubtful that you should keep using leaders and tippet spools more than a year old.

Reel oils, suntan lotions, and insect repellents often contain chemicals that are damaging to synthetic leaders and lines. Such chemicals must be kept away from nylon and polyvinyl line finishes. Their chemistry can either directly attack the molecular structure of the synthetics themselves, or quarrel chemically with their lubricants and moisture-entraining agents, making them quite wiry and brittle.

Humidity and moisture content are also critical to the working life of nylon leader materials. During actual fishing, leader nylon can absorb as much as nine percent moisture content, and it becomes quite limp. Evaporation after fishing can make a line stiffer, and in storage its stiffness accelerates until only one percent moisture remains. Nylon is rather brittle at this point, although you should immerse it and test its breaking strain before discarding it altogether.

There are two diametrically opposed schools of thought on the subject of limp nylon versus the stiffer types. Eastern fishermen who frequent difficult rivers from the Brule in Wisconsin to the Beaverkill in the Catskills are disciples of the limp-nylon school, since its flexibility gives them a relatively drag-free float. Western anglers who must cope with high winds and distance casting are often partisans of the hard-nylon school. There is no question that a stiffer leader will cast better in a wind and at relatively long ranges, and that a limp leader fishes better because the fly is relatively free of the leader and its influences in the current. The best leaders are probably compound types that use hard nylon through eighty percent of their length, and limp nylon for the remaining taper and tippet.

It is surprising how few fishermen realize that knots reduce the breaking strain of leader material. The raw tensile strength of the nylon is its listed rating. Manufacturers are constantly trying to find polymeric structures that will increase unknotted breaking strain and simultaneously reduce diameter. Such improvements mean less wind friction for a leader unrolling behind the line, and less visibility to the fish. All knots diminish the unknotted breaking strain of the leader material, and the best knots diminish it the least.

Bad knots are points of stress concentration under loading, but good knots tend to distribute the same stress over their entire coiled structure. Cycles of stress and unloading, such as wide variations in the pressure on a heavy trout if you play it clumsily, seriously weaken a tippet already stressed at the threshold of its breaking strain.

Knot strength is the percentage of rated breaking strain that remains after a specific knot has been tied. There are several knots that achieve something between ninety-five and one hundred percent of rated breaking strain, provided they are tightened slowly and moistened to minimize friction and prevent thermal damage.

Exceptionally limp nylon often has poor knotting qualities. It deforms under knotting pressures, creating a weak minimal diameter where stress is concentrated. The simple overhand knot that forms itself while you are casting is perhaps the worst for leader nylon, since each loop in the knot is deforming the other. Such casting knots can weaken a leader to less than forty percent of its rated breaking strain. Extremely stiff nylon can pose other knotting problems. Its wiry qualities can refuse to coil and seat tightly enough to provide a sound knot, and later failure can result.

Impact loading is another common problem. Watching a delicate-looking saleslady break strong wrapping twine during a Christmas rush, snapping it with a sharp application of strength, is a way to understand the difference between a simple breaking strain under steady pressure and the instantaneous effect of impact loads. The breaking strain of a line is based on static testing, and has little relationship to the physical deformation and molecular displacement of an impact-type stress. Such stress dynamics are related to material length and the duration of loading. Such performance under impact-type stress has important lessons for our fishing techniques. Heavy-handed striking subjects our tippets to similar dynamic loads, and too much reel palming or rod pressure during the fight can focus similar stresses to the failure point.

The elasticity of modern synthetics and the calibrations of the rod are our safety valves against such impact loads. Few anglers are aware of the full elasticity of their lines and leaders until they try to break off a fouled fly. Generally speaking, there is more elasticity in limp nylon than hard nylon. Too much elasticity means poor hooking qualities and erratic variations in tension while you are fighting a fish. Too little stretch in a stiff-nylon leader makes it difficult to shield a tippet against impact loads. Elastic behavior is clearly a two-sided coin.

The ability of lines and leaders to resist the normal abrasion of fishing is important too. Nylon leader material is remarkably resistant to abrasion, and its limpness or stiffness has surprisingly little influence on these qualities. Limp nylon is slightly better in its ability to resist cuts and scuffing, since its elasticity recoils slightly from objects that are hard and sharp. Some abrasion of lines and leaders comes from contact with ledges and stones in the river, but most occurs from worn guides and rough places on the reel itself.

Nylons are also surprisingly responsive to atmospheric variations in moisture. High humidity can result in wide variations of moisture content and breaking strain. Fully saturated leaders containing nine percent entrained moisture are about fifteen percent weaker than the same nylon when dry. Saturation is a function of diameter and duration of immersion in the water, but it takes from twenty-four to forty-eight hours to achieve full absorption of water. Such water absorption can vary with the reel you are using. Older closed-frame and spool designs like the Hardy Perfect

DOUBLE NAIL KNOT

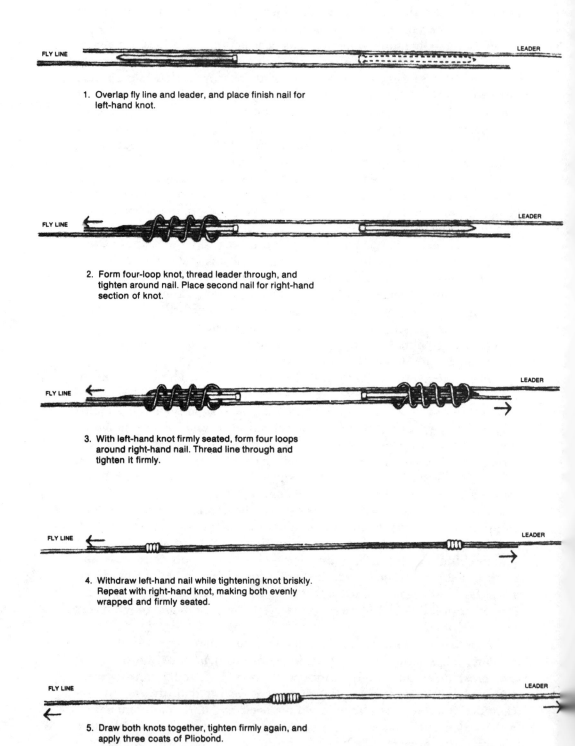

1. Overlap fly line and leader, and place finish nail for left-hand knot.

2. Form four-loop knot, thread leader through, and tighten around nail. Place second nail for right-hand section of knot.

3. With left-hand knot firmly seated, form four loops around right-hand nail. Thread line through and tighten it firmly.

4. Withdraw left-hand nail while tightening knot briskly. Repeat with right-hand knot, making both evenly wrapped and firmly seated.

5. Draw both knots together, tighten firmly again, and apply three coats of Pliobond.

OFFSET NAIL KNOT

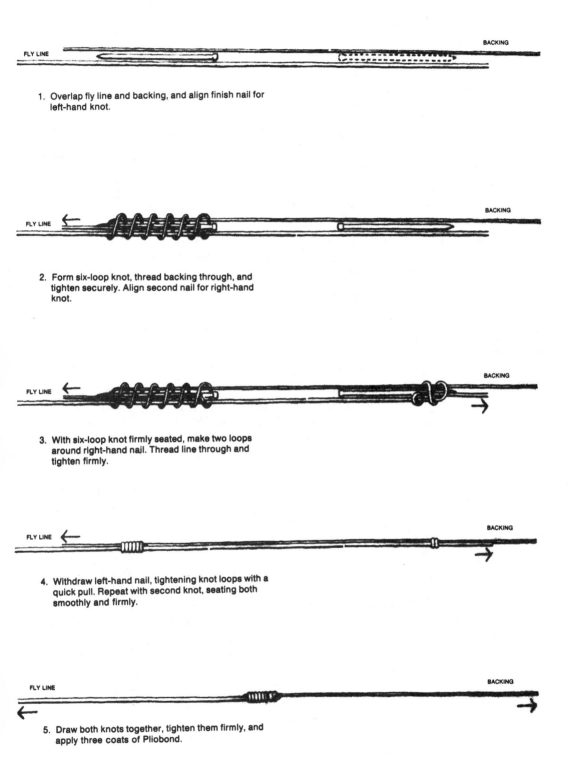

1. Overlap fly line and backing, and align finish nail for left-hand knot.

2. Form six-loop knot, thread backing through, and tighten securely. Align second nail for right-hand knot.

3. With six-loop knot firmly seated, make two loops around right-hand nail. Thread line through and tighten firmly.

4. Withdraw left-hand nail, tightening knot loops with a quick pull. Repeat with second knot, seating both smoothly and firmly.

5. Draw both knots together, tighten them firmly, and apply three coats of Pliobond.

permit less drying than a new reel like the Orvis C.F.O. with its fully perforated spool and back-plate design. The loss of breaking strength from water saturation can mean a serious loss of performance in the very fine leader diameters, and such delicate nylon strands should be replaced regularly throughout a day's fishing.

Perhaps the most common failure in making knots occurs when the strands of a properly started knot is drawn and seated together. Particularly in nylon leader material, tightly seating your knots is absolutely critical to success. Slippage is always the prelude to knot failure. However, a knot drawn and seated too quickly can generate enough thermal friction to damage the nylon itself. Knots should always be lubricated and cooled with saliva before tightening them, and then they should be drawn together with a firm and uninterrupted application of pressure. When a knot is tightly seated, test it with a series of strong pulls. It is far better to experience knot failure before you start fishing.

Properly tied knots can be trimmed quite close. Such trimming can be done with scissors, fishing clippers, or scissor pliers. It should never be done with a cigarette or other application of heat since temperature transfer can damage both knots and leaders. However, knots should be trimmed as close to their main coiled structures as possible. The tag ends of a poorly trimmed knot are continually picking up floating debris and weed in many streams, generate unwanted friction in running through the guides, and can even cause a leader to tangle more frequently.

Extralong leaders mean that at some point in the fight the connecting knot between the leader and line must pass smoothly into the guides. Strong fish can bolt from the net and strip the knot between the line and its backing out through the guides at surprising velocities, and that knot must also come back along the rod before the trout can be netted. Such knots should be laminated and smoothed with a series of thin applications of Pliobond cement or fly-head lacquer. It will harden without losing its elastic properties, permitting the knots to slip freely through the guides, and it will protect them from minor cuts and abrasions and brief impact loads when they catch along the rod.

The following knots are the kinds I use in fishing for trout, and they are fully adequate for anything short of taking billfish or tarpon on fly tackle. With the exception of the Turle knot developed on the Hampshire chalkstreams when Henry Hall introduced the first eyed hooks, these knots have all evolved in the last twenty-five years. Many would have been meaningless in silkworm gut, and their configurations are designed for the character and behavior of modern nylon. It is unnecessary to use the more exotic knots developed for salt-water tactics on our trout waters.

Perhaps the most basic knot is designed to attach the backing line to the reel spool, since its failure means not only the loss of a trophy fish but also the loss of the entire leader, line, and the dacron backing itself. Some reels have special fittings for attaching the backing line, but others have completely smooth spindles. Such reels demand a special backing knot. My favorite consists of looping the dacron around the spool, feeding it both in and out through the proper opening in the reel frame or its line guard. The backing is then secured with a simple overhand knot around itself, with a secondary overhand knot seated in its end. Seat the terminal knot and tighten the primary knot around the line. Pull both knots slowly until they tighten down flush with the reel spool and do not trim the excess line. Both knots and excess line should then be seated under a thin strip of electrician's tape. It will secure the knots and provide a mildly adhesive foundation under the first layer of backing.

Both modern nylon and polyvinyl chloride lines have resulted in a number of knots that would have proved worthless twenty-odd years ago. Our familiar nail and tube knots would have been ineffective with gut leaders and oil-finished silk lines, since the gut was not supple enough and nylon would have simply cut through the silk. Yet the knots are perfect for our more modern mix of synthetic lines and finishes, and the more tension applied, the tighter these nylon knots become. Our old clinch or jam knots, which joined our knotted leader loops to silk fly lines, are totally obsolete. It is not simply a question of their catching in the guides when a fish came in close and you were fishing a leader longer than your rod; with the development of ultralight nylon tippet materials smaller than .005, connecting knots between leaders and lines became a critical problem, and the nail knots were perfected. Properly tied, they will seat smoothly and pass through the guides without trouble, since even the lightest impact can shear a .003 tippet. Nail knots were originally tied using a finish nail as the armature for forming them, so the name is still used even though a small tube or pair of scissors is perhaps a better tool.

Two basic knots are useful for joining your backing to a fly line, depending on your tackle, and the character of the river and its fish. Small rivers with moderate-size trout mean light backing lines and relatively light fly lines, and in recent seasons I have been using the double nail knot with such tackle. Since big fish and strong currents mean distance casting and somewhat heavier gear, joining your backing to a fly line of much greater diameter is the problem. The offset nail knot is the solution that I prefer. Both knots result in relatively small splices that do not deteriorate like the old silk-whip type and offer much less bulk than the rolling splice popular on salt water.

The double nail knot is formed in separate operations. It consists of lapping the materials being spliced with the backing material and reel on the left and the fly line at the right. The backing is knotted first, holding both lines together along a small ten-gauge aluminum or brass tube with the left hand. The backing is started into a right-hand nail knot by looping it back over itself, around the fly line and tubing, in a series of three turns. These turns should be held firmly in place with the index finger of the left hand, and the free end of the dacron is then inserted into the left end of the tubing and pushed through it with the right hand. Make sure the three loops around the tubing and lines are not permitted to slip, and draw both

SPEED NEEDLE KNOT

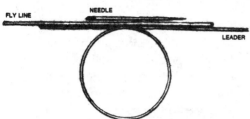

1. Lay needle along fly line and form loop of leader material, holding loop open with thumb and index finger.

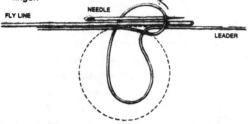

2. Warp loop upward, wrapping it over fly line and needle in a clockwise motion, and secure under the fingers.

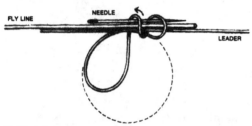

3. Wrap loop over again, tightening each succeeding loop against the last, until six turns are complete.

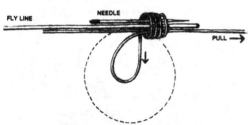

4. Holding the coiled loops in alignment, draw the leader itself to the right until the knot is seated tightly.

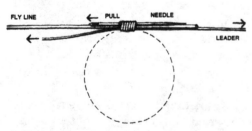

5. Tighten both ends of leader and withdraw needle.

6. Trim line and leader ends, and coat with three applications of Pliobond.

TUBE KNOT

1. Lap fly line and leader, leaving a foot of leader material to form knot. Lay tube in position shown.

2. Hold line, starting loop and tube firmly in left hand. Make six complete wraps of leader, working from left to right.

3. Hold all six wraps securely and insert leader material back through the forming tube.

4. Seat coils carefully, still holding them in the left fingers, by pulling at the leader material.

5. Pull both tube and leader material through briskly, simultaneously tightening leader to right.

6. Pull slowly and firmly at both ends of leader to tighten and seat knot into finish of fly line.

FLY LINE ———————————————————— LEADER

7. Tighten with leader and line pressure, finishing with three coats of Pliobond.

NEEDLE KNOT

Use fresh razor blade to shape leader butt into hair-fine point and insert into small needle. Force needle into lower quarter-inch of fly line, and work out through side.

Hold fly line and needle in left hand. Grip needle point with pliers, and pull both needle and leader through line completely.

Trim delicate leader point off and draw enough nylon through to shape a four-loop nail knot.

Form four nail-knot loops around finish nail and tighten.

Withdraw nail, seat and trim knot, and coat with Pliobond.

SIMPLE NAIL KNOT

1. Lap fly line and leader, and align forming nail.

2. Wrap five loops and thread leader through along nail.

3. Withdraw forming nail and seat knot firmly with tension at ends of leader material.

4. Test knot and apply three coats of Pliobond.

REEL SPOOL KNOTS

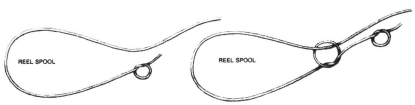

1. Loop backing around reel spool and form overhand knot in end.

2. Form second overhand knot around backing, close tip knot, and tighten on spool.

the tubing and backing carefully from the core of the knot. Before releasing the fingers still holding the partially seated coils, tighten these coils carefully, pulling gently on both the backing and its free end. When you are certain the knot is formed perfectly, with its coils seated in perfect alignment but not fully tightened, it should be slipped along the fly line to make room for the left-hand nail knot in the line itself that completes the operation. With ultrafine tackle, joining twenty-pound backing to lines finer than a DT5F, some fishermen are content to seat this right-hand nail knot tightly into the line finish, and coat it with Pliobond. It is sufficient for small fish and fine tippets. Other anglers like to remove the polyvinyl chloride finish from the line and complete the rest of their double nail knots using only its dacron or nylon braided core. It is usually possible to form the knot between the fingers without the tubing when you are using only the core of the line. Otherwise the left-hand nail knot formed around the backing with the core of the line is simple enough. It is started with the line, backing, and tubing (or without the tubing if your dexterity is good) held in the right hand. Four turns of the line are worked back toward the right, the free end is inserted in the right end of the tubing, and pushed through toward the left. The knot should be seated slowly until it is completely formed but not fully tightened. The double nail knot is then two-thirds finished, with two knots formed around the opposite material. Pull the four ends of the knot tight. It is complete when a careful tightening on both line and backing draws the two knots together, seats them firmly against each other, and tightens them securely with a steady pressure of about twenty pounds. The knot ends should be trimmed at forty-five degree angles with a razor blade. Coat with Pliobond and allow to dry.

The offset nail knot is better for joining a heavier fly line to dacron backing of about thirty-pound test. It is shaped exactly like the double nail knot, except that the heavier material is started first and is tied with only two turns before it is worked back through the knotting tube. Then it is partially tightened around the backing. The backing is then formed around the fly line by shaping eight turns and holding them in place with the fingers. It is then threaded through the tubing from right to left. Slip the tubing out carefully and close the knot. Completing the full offset knot involves pulling the untrimmed ends tight, and then tightening the lines with a strong tension until the knot is fully secure.

Similar knots are used to join shooting-head lines to backing and their running lines. The special running lines of the Aircel-type measure about .029 in diameter and join easily with a double nail knot to thirty-pound dacron backing material. The offset nail knot is fine for joining this running line to the back taper of the shooting head too, and I also use it with flat monofilament running lines, both for splices to the backing and the fly line. Many anglers prefer a flat monofilament running line, because it resists tangles and coils in the water and it tends to unroll in the plane of the cast.

Several variations of the basic nail knot are also becoming popular for joining leaders to lines, since leaders longer than the rod are necessary on many hard-fished rivers. Nail knots must be particularly tight and neatly formed and must pass effortlessly through the guides if a fish suddenly bolts with the leader inside the tip guide. Salt-water nail knots involve seating a loop of fly line inside the coiled leader material, and provide a relatively symmetrical exit for the leader from the centerline of the knot. The simple nail knot relies on its tightening and friction alone, omitting the internal loop altogether, and projects asymmetrically from the end of the line. The speed nail knot is similar in its configuration, but has been worked out for execution at streamside. Each of these knots is excellent, although they all display the tendency to crack through the adjacent polyvinyl finish, creating a hinge action in the line.

The needle knot was developed to provide a system of joining the leader butt to the line, with both leader and line on the same longitudinal axis. It also is a superb knot that resists hinging and provides a smooth continuity of casting power. The development of the needle knot on the salt-water flats off Florida soon led to experimenting with a simpler version of its construction that secured the leader inside the fly line with epoxy. George Keough worked out the pioneering epoxy knots on steelheads along the beautiful North Fork of the Stillaguamish, and they are unquestionably the best type for running freely through the rod guides, and providing a hinge-free transition of casting power. Dave Whitlock has worked out a similar knot which adds a short length of bright-colored plastic or fly line over the leader, both for visibility in nymph fishing and to prevent hinging and provide smooth power transfer in casting. Such knots both involve threading through the core of the line, and its diameter obviously limits the diameter of the leader worked inside. Elasticity and diameter in the line are the controlling factors in the calibrations of your leader butt, making some of the magnum-butt tapers impractical. However, for fishing relatively light tackle the Keough and Whitlock knots are superb.

The original nail knots evolved on salt water where fishermen were desperately searching for methods of using the full strength of the remarkable modern nylons. Their knotting behavior did not resemble silkworm gut or even the more primitive nylons, and knots worked out for these older materials failed miserably on tarpon. Big salt-water fish were so explosive with their infighting near the boat that knot performance in the guides became critical. Poor knots or tangles that jammed when a strong fish bolted could strip guides from a rod like popcorn, and the salt-water nail knot was the result. It is also useful on really large trout in heavy currents, like steelheads or the big rainbows in Argentina and Chile.

Tying the salt-water nail knot involves holding the line, leader, and knotting tube in the left hand, with the leader material lying on the right. The fly line should be turned back in a loop and held between the fingertips. The leader material is passed inside the loop, rolled back outside, and coiled three to five times around the entire system. Its free end is then inserted from the left and threaded back through the tube toward the right. Draw the tube free carefully, tightening the free end of the leader at the

BLOOD KNOT

1. Overlap leader material to be joined.

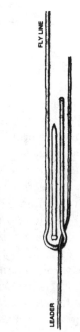

2. Twist left-hand tippet five turns and fold back carefully.

3. Thread tippet through and hold firmly in place.

4. Twist right-hand tippet five wraps, fold back smoothly, and insert through center loop.

5. Moisten knot, seat with gradual tension, and trim.

SALTWATER NAIL KNOT

1. Lap finish nail with fly line.

2. Loop fly line back along nail and thread leader through.

3. Wrap leader six times around nail and folded line.

4. Withdraw nail and thread leader through entire knot.

5. Tighten knot and coat with Pliobond.

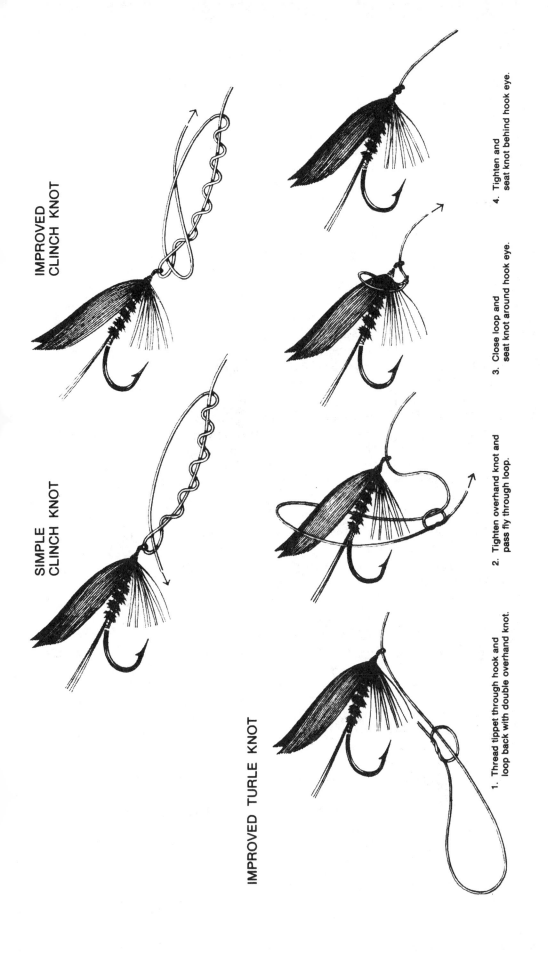

SIMPLE
CLINCH KNOT

IMPROVED
CLINCH KNOT

IMPROVED TURLE KNOT

1. Thread tippet through hook and loop back with double overhand knot.

2. Tighten overhand knot and pass fly through loop.

3. Close loop and seat knot around hook eye.

4. Tighten and seat knot behind hook eye.

same time. Tighten both lines and free ends until the coils are properly aligned and seated, and finally tighten with a steady pressure. Trim the ends and saturate the knot with Pliobond.

The simple nail knot omits the interior loop of fly line and is a rudimentary friction type. Such knots are much less difficult to execute than the diagrams suggest and they are surprisingly strong. The fly line should lie with its free end toward the right and the nylon leader with its end lying toward the left. The knotting tube is placed between them, and all three are held in the left hand. The tube should lie with its right end aligned with the tip of the line. The leader is lying on top of the knotting tube, with about ten to twelve inches of knotting length lying past its left end. The free end is started back toward the right in a series of four clockwise loops. Thread the free end of the leader back toward the left, and tighten the coils against each other, just like the other nail knots. These coils must be held tightly in sequence while the knotting tube is slowly withdrawn, and the coils must still remain between the fingers while the free end of the leader is pulled deliberately. Once the coils are seated together in a smooth sequence, tighten firmly by pulling both the leader and its free end. The tightened knot should then be secured permanently with firm tension on both the leader and the fly line.

The speed nail knot was developed for the legions of tangle-fingered anglers who have trouble with conventional nail-knotting techniques and find a nail knot too difficult at streamside. It is also called the thirty-second nail knot on some rivers. It requires a small sewing needle instead of the small knotting tube. The fly line is extended with its tip toward the right and the leader toward the left. The needle is laid on top of the line with its point lying toward the right. Form a loop of leader material about ten inches in diameter by holding it between the left thumb and index finger so it hangs below the needle. The free end of the leader should project to the left, about one inch past the eye of the needle. The loop and its free end total about thirty inches, and will form the belly coils of the knot. The free end is the leader butt, and its tip projects no more than one-half inch past the line and the point of the needle. The butt end of the leader is then started clockwise over the core of the knot, working five or six coils back toward the left. Hold the coils tightly between the fingers and pull the tip of the leader on through toward the right. The nylon should be firmly seated together by pulling on both ends, and the needle is slowly withdrawn, eye first. Tighten the knot again by pulling hard on both nylon ends, and then test the fully seated security of its friction coils by strong tensile pressure on the line and leader. It should not slip, and after its excess ends have been trimmed, it should be secured with Pliobond.

There are two versions of the needle knot. It is designed to provide the strength of a nail knot, the power transition of the epoxy-type knots, and a leader butt lying at the longitudinal axis of the line itself. The conventional needle knot involves shaving the leader butt with a fresh razor blade or model-building knife until it is shaped into a delicate tapering filament.

The tapered filament is threaded through the eye of a small sewing needle, and the needle is worked into the core of the line from its tip. Penetration should last about one-half inch before the needle is angled out through the side. Grasp the half-inch section of line penetrated by the needle with the left thumb and forefinger, with the shaved nylon threaded tightly into its eye. Grip the needle firmly with a pair of point-nosed pliers and draw both needle and leader nylon smoothly through the core of the fly line. Continue pulling the nylon through until enough length is strung beyond its exit from the line. Complete with a conventional four-coil nail knot, and coat smoothly with Pliobond.

The Bates needle knot involves pliers and moderate heat. The needle is carefully forced into the tip of the line along its core, and out the side, skewering about one-half inch of line on its steel shaft. The needle is held with the pliers and heated briefly with a match until the polyvinyl finish of the line begins smoking faintly at its tip. Push the line toward the heated eye-end of the needle. Now you strike a second match and heat the point of the needle until its exiting point from the line smokes slightly too. Overheating the polyvinyl chloride finish can seriously weaken the fly line, so heat must be applied with caution. The heat cauterizes the rim of the needle's entry and exit points in the plastic finish, keeping them open when the needle is withdrawn. The open core is then threaded with a knotless tapered leader, inserted tippet first into the side of the line, and drawn out through its tip until about twelve inches of its butt diameters remain. This length is then worked into a conventional nail knot of four coils, tightly seated and trimmed and coated with Pliobond.

The Keough epoxy knot is similar to the standard needle knot in its beginnings. The leader butt is carefully shaved to a slender filamentlike point, and the line is penetrated about one-half inch with a needle, entering at its tip. The needle point is allowed to exit at the side of the fly line. The shaved nylon is threaded through the needle's eye, along with a two-inch length of cotton darning thread saturated in epoxy. Both the nylon leader material and the epoxy-soaked thread are then drawn through the fly line with pliers until the leader is inside the line along with the epoxy-saturated darning cotton. The shaved nylon is carefully trimmed, along with the excess lengths of epoxy thread. Finally, the side exit-point is coated with epoxy, and epoxy is also applied to the leader and line tip. Such epoxy knots are exceptionally strong when properly executed and cured, but since their strength depends solely on the thin internal coating of the adhesive, the Keough-type knots should be tested vigorously before fishing them.

The Whitlock epoxy knot is essentially the same in its execution, except for the addition of a sleevelike length of line on the leader before the knot is started. The sleeve is usually one-half inch of fire-orange fly line or fine plastic tubing provided by the line manufacturer. It is hollowed out with a needle, and the shaved nylon butt is drawn through its full length. The sleeve is then slipped down the leader several inches. The entire sequence of the Keough-type knot is followed through, and once it is completed, approximately one-half inch of the leader below the line is coated with additional epoxy. The sleeve is slipped back up the leader and seated tightly against the line. Epoxy is also used to seal the point between the leader and the free end of the sleeve. It is my experience that the Whitlock knot is slightly more secure than the Keough type, and better transmits the dynamics of a cast from the line into the leader. Both epoxy knots limit the butt diameter of the leader material, but otherwise these knots are superb for trout fishing.

The blood knot is the only configuration that passes unchanged from the silkworm-gut years into our era of modern polymeric nylons. It is used to attach a fresh leader to the butt strand that has been permanently attached to the line. It is also used to join leader strands together in building specially tapered leaders, or adding fresh tippets. The blood knot is the strongest possible method of joining two leader strands together, delivering ninety-five percent of rated breaking strain when the diameter change between strands is only .001 inch. It is started with the two strands overlapping and held between the thumb and index finger of both hands. Approximately four to six inches of overlapping ends are needed in forming blood knots of trout-size leader materials. Holding the right-hand strands firmly, twist the left end around the main tippet with a rolling motion of the fingertips for five to six turns. Bend the free end back, lay it in the slot between the leader and right end, and hold its position firmly in the left hand. The right strand is then twisted about the main leader an equal number of turns. Its free end is then bent back and inserted through the same loop holding the first tippet. Holding both free ends to keep them from slipping, tighten the knot carefully with a steady pressure. Then trim the knot carefully. Less pressure is obviously required to seat blood knots in the fine diameters below .009 inches. The blood knot is perhaps the most basic knot in fly-fishing.

The extension blood knot is used to provide dropper tippets for fishing wet flies and nymphs. It is executed in exactly the same manner as the standard blood knot, except that its heavier strand is exaggeratedly long and remains untrimmed once the knot is fully seated. The knotting angle of the extended strand and its thickness tend to hold the attached fly away from the leader in both casting and fishing.

Turle knots were developed on the British chalkstreams in the late nineteenth century, and although the development of modern nylon has made them virtually obsolete, a modified version is useful. Our nylons slip too easily for use in the conventional Turle knot. However, it is useful when you wish to have a relatively rigid connection between the leader and the fly for such tactics as skittering a variant or skater. It must be seated carefully to prevent its slipping. The original Turle works on hook sizes below fourteen, but larger sizes demand an improved Turle knot, with its better friction and control. The Turle knots deliver about seventy-five percent of rated breaking strain.

The original Turle knot is formed by threading the tippet through the hook eye, looping it back on itself behind the eye, and closing it with a simple overhand knot. This loop is shaped below the hook with the down-eye type, and above it with a turned-up eye. The loop is opened and slipped over the hook, wings, and hackles until it can be tightened and seated behind the eye. It should be pulled firmly to make sure all slipping is stopped. Such knots insure enough rigidity to hold a skater or variant high on its hackles, and are still extremely useful in such tactics when carefully and firmly executed.

The double Turle knot is a modification based on the character of our modern synthetic leaders. Both their limpness and their smooth finish cause traditional knots to creep and work and slip free. Many fishermen have completely abandoned the original Turle knot to use the double type, except in very small tippets and hooks. The double Turle knot is formed exactly like the single Turle, except that the simple overhand knot is replaced with a two-twist slip knot. Three twists are sometimes used with heavier tippets and large flies.

The simple clinch knot is perhaps the best fly knot developed for attaching flies in trout sizes. The tippet is simply threaded through the hook eye, looped back along the leader, twisted four or five times, and inserted back into the loop at the hook eye again. Hold the leader tip and fly with your left hand, and then tighten and seat the coils with a steady tension. Properly tied, this knot delivers almost one hundred percent breaking strain, and is my favorite for trout flies smaller than size twelve.

The improved clinch was developed for larger hook sizes, and it is rated at ninety-five percent of breaking strain. The tippet is inserted through the hook eye, turned back along the leader itself, and twisted four to five turns. Its free end is inserted through the loop at the hook eye, as the fly is held with the left hand and the knot is worked toward its conclusion with the right. The final step is threading the free end back through the large loop remaining, and holding the half-finished knot firmly while it is tightened. There are endless arguments along trout water about the clinch knot versus the improved clinch, and except in cases of slippage with relatively light leaders and large hook eyes, my own preference lies with the ordinary clinch knot. Its fishability seems stronger to me in the ultrafine tippet diameters, and I use it regularly.

These are the several knots used in rigging my tackle, from seating the backing on the reel to attaching my flies. Although many readers may consider discussions of leader calibrations and breaking strains and knots excessively dull, these details are too often our Achilles' heel. It is impossible to give too much emphasis to the problems of terminal tackle.

The truth of this observation brings to mind the loss of a big fish on the Gunnison in Colorado. It was a heavy brown of seven or eight pounds that lay under a logjam in a side channel of the river. It had been hooked any number of times that summer, and it had smashed several leaders and rods. It was a fish that was becoming legendary.

Geronimo, my old friend Herb Salzbrenner shook his head and grinned. *He's getting some reputation!*

Geronimo was not taken that summer, and when I returned to the Gunnison that next year it seemed the big fish was still there downstream from the Cooper ranch. Several fishermen had broken off in a heavy brown.

You think it's still Geronimo? I asked.

It's possible, the ranch foreman nodded. *He's lying right under the logs where Geronimo always stayed.*

They think he's a big fish? I pressed.

Big enough! he said.

The first evening I fished the hole carefully, working so deep under the dead trees that I fouled and lost several big wet flies and nymphs. The only fish that took were several small rainbows and a brown of about two pounds. The cabin beside mine was occupied with a new party that had just arrived, and it included a surgeon from Denver who had been fishing only two or three seasons. The man was absolutely a fanatic on fly-fishing, building his own split-cane rods and tying flies and making his own tapered leaders. The table on the screen porch of his cabin was covered with English hook boxes and gamecock necks and fly-tying tools, and he was busily at work on a fresh twelve-foot leader tapered to a .006 tippet.

Like some coffee? he waved from the porch.

Yes, I said gratefully.

Making up some leaders! he explained and poured two mugs of black coffee, and pushed the sugar bowl across the table. *River looks a little low now.*

They're a little shy, I agreed.

Heard some talk in Gunnison, the doctor began. *Boys in the tackle shop were talking about a big fish below here.*

That crowd in the tackle shop? I asked.

Yes, he nodded. *Know anything about it?*

What did they say? I parried.

Something about a fish called Geronimo, he continued. *They said he's here on the Cooper stretch, just below the corrals.*

It's possible, I smiled. *We had a big brown called Geronimo last summer.*

But they talked about this year! the doctor said.

There's another big fish in the same pool, I said. *It might be Geronimo—and then again it might not.*

Where is he? the doctor asked eagerly.

Just below the corrals, I replied. *You'll see the logs jammed in along the willows.*

And he's under the logs? he asked.

Yes, I said. *He's there.*

The doctor finished his leader and tightened the final blood knot skillfully, but he tightened the knots almost too facilely, and failed to test them with a steady pull. It was obvious he was a good fisherman and had mastered an impressive catalogue of skills in a remarkably short time. But watching him swiftly rig leaders told me that his experience with big fish was lacking.

What flies should I use? he asked.

Big flies worked deep under the logs, I laughed. *Biggest you can find!*

The doctor nodded and got the coffee pot from the coal stove inside the cabin. *Like some more coffee?* he asked.

Please, I said.

We fished the Gunnison for more than a week, and there were good fly hatches each morning. The fish came readily when the flies were on the water. Fishing was excellent, and several two- to three-pound rainbows and browns were brought in almost every day. Several fishermen tried the big trout under the deadfalls below the ranch without luck.

Hey! the doctor waved from his cabin. *I've got something I'm going to try on Geronimo!* His fly-tying tools were out and he had gone into Gunnison that morning. He poured us both fresh mugs of coffee and handed me a box of big bait-fishing hooks.

They're 3/0 trolling hooks, he said.

Think they're big enough? I laughed. *Where'd you find hooks this size?*

Had them in the tackle store, he explained eagerly. *Found them in the back of a drawer.* He adjusted his vise to hold the hooks.

They're three inches long! I said.

They're perfect! The doctor was excited now. *I'm going to make the biggest bucktails you've ever seen!*

They're big all right, I smiled.

The next morning I took a fine brace of two-pound rainbows a mile below the ranch, and I was wading back slowly when I met a local character who was a living legend along the river. The old man offered me a pinch or two of his Copenhagen as we compared the morning's results.

Chew? The old man held out the can.

It was an old ritual between us. *No,* I shook my head. *Don't think I'm ready for your brand just yet.*

No? the old man cackled raucously.

Thanks anyway, I said.

We waded upstream through the shallows, following the side channel downstream from the corrals. Someone was fishing the deadfalls where the big fish stayed, and suddenly we heard him shout excitedly above the river sounds. It was the doctor and he was into a heavy fish at the throat of the pool. The old fisherman looked at me and I stared back.

Well, he spat a dark stream of tobacco. *I'll be damned!*

Geronimo! I said in disbelief.

We waded quickly upstream along the gravelly riffles and found the surgeon fearfully holding his straining rod. The man glanced at us in alarm as the great fish stripped thirty feet of line from the reel. It threatened to penetrate the logs, but finally it turned and the doctor forced it back. It fought deep for another ten minutes before it came to the surface.

That there's some brown trout! The old fisherman released another stream of tobacco for punctuation. *Biggest I seen this summer!*

How big? the doctor asked excitedly.

It's big enough, I said quietly.

The huge brown was a strong, hook-jawed male of six or seven pounds, and I did not want to excite him with an estimate of its size. The surgeon seemed nervous enough. The big fish threshed heavily on the surface, but its strength was ebbing now, and the doctor increased his rod pressure.

Suddenly the leader parted, and the doctor stared in shock. *He broke me!* he wailed. *He broke me!*

Geronimo's broke a lotta folks, the old man said softly.

What did I do wrong? the surgeon asked.

His freshly tied leader had broken in its heavier middle tapers where the strands were better than twelve-pound test, and its broken end had the little pigtail curl that spelled a poorly made knot that had slipped.

You didn't do anything wrong now. I showed the curled pigtail of nylon to the old man and shook my head.

What do you mean now? the doctor protested.

You played that fish jest fine. The old man tucked a fresh wad of tobacco high inside his cheek. *It's them leader knots you tied at breakfast.*

Dammit! the doctor shook his head angrily. *Surgeons tie knots every day that people's lives depend on.*

Doctor, the old man replied, *the patient jest died.*

For recent developments in tackle, see Appendix: Notes on New Equipment.

4. Random Thoughts on Waders, Clothing, and Other Equipment

Boyhood memories are a strange mixture of people and places and occurrences worth remembering. No odyssey of growing up is without its measure of pain and frustration, and thoughts of happy times are always mixed with less happy times. It is curious that many youthful memories are a scrapbook of sensory echoes, and such memories often become more intense as we grow older.

It is possible to remember the tastes and smells and sounds of boyhood with a sharpness that erases the intervening years, and I remember the house with its high ceilings and the huge porch across the entire front with its newelled railings and trellis of roses. The big house creaked and groaned during a storm, and sometimes its millwork and flooring cracked in hot weather. The bay window looked out from the library, and I often sat there on summer afternoons, reading in the leaf-flickering shade of a giant maple whose branches also sheltered my room upstairs. Robins nested regularly outside my window, and I watched them carrying worms to their babies in early summer. Their birdsongs had a lilting note heard only after a rain. Sometimes late at night, I can almost hear the freight trains whistling balefully on the long grade past Sager's Lake. There was an ineffable poetry in those steam-driven trains, and their melancholy music still echoes clearly in my mind.

The white-carbon street lamps of boyhood were always swarming with moths, each circling dizzily in its own mindless orbit, and katydids and crickets filled the night with their rich orchestrations. Other sounds and smells are remembered too. There was a fierce crackle of lightning that once shattered an oak across the street, and its terrible thunderclap rattled the windows and shook the entire house. Locusts filled the August doldrums with their droning chorus, and that was the summer I attended my first funeral. It was unbearably hot and the wind eddied through the cornfields. The locusts made it impossible to hear the services or the parched soil clattering across the coffin. Walking back from bluegill fishing the following summer, I took a shortcut through the country cemetery, and I will never forget the scent of the shrivelled roses that surrounded the tombstone of that boyhood playmate.

There are happier memories too.

There were ice wagons rattling through the streets on hot summer afternoons. We ran after them noisily, begging the iceman to chip off small pieces that we could suck like lollipops. The corner store had lollipops and licorice and jawbreakers in huge apothecary jars, and I can remember the rattle of the penny gumball machines.

My mother often stopped in another store where fresh coffee was ground, and I listened as the hard chocolate-colored beans spilled into the hopper, anticipating the rich smells that would soon fill the shop. The butcher shop was a different world, with the faint pine fragrance of fresh sawdust on its floor. Blue pike and whitefish and smoked shrimps lay in the freshly-cracked ice of the trays. Beef and sausages and lamb hung in the cooling chests behind the butcher-block counter. Freshly baked bread had its unforgettable fragrance too, and I remember the summer I first delivered the Chicago paper on my bicycle. The paper boys always stopped for fresh doughnuts that were almost too hot for our fingers when we sat on the bakery steps to eat them.

There was fishing tackle at the hardware store, along with a few small-calibre rifles and shotguns off in a corner, with red and green boxes of ammunition locked behind the glass-doored cabinets. The guns gleamed with oil and we were forbidden to touch them, and they stood neatly in the racks with a strange totemic power. There were several split-cane rods racked on a circular display stand, although these were factory rods without any particular pedigree. Bass plugs and a few flies shared a simple glass case with fly lines and leaders and small bottles of citronella.

There are similar memories of the huge sporting goods store in downtown Chicago, and I was totally unprepared for its riches the first time my father took me there. Its handsome interior was overwhelming.

What's this store called? I whispered softly.

It's Von Lengerke and Antoine. He smiled. *It's the best sporting goods store between New York and San Francisco.*

It's beautiful! I stood awestruck.

There were big-game trophies and beautifully mounted fish above the walnut cabinets, and rich wall-to-wall carpeting covered the aisles and fitting rooms. The gun room was lined with glass cases enclosing racks of gleaming rifles and finely engraved European shotguns. Its subtle odors were a delicate mixture of gun oil and Spanish leather cases and handsomely grained and tooled stocks, but they were nothing like the leathery smells of boots and fine English saddles and luggage in the other departments. The camping department was a trove of similar treasures, such as wicker baskets bursting with stainless plates and cups and tableware, costly down-filled sleeping bags, and the delicate paraffin smell of tenting. The racks of gleaming fly rods, with their bright varnish and beautifully machined ferrules and fittings, were intoxicating for a small boy, and several cases smelling faintly of moth crystals held tray-on-tray of exquisitely tied trout and salmon flies.

It's fantastic! I whispered reverently.

It was that afternoon that my father bought several dozen dry flies, and I used most of my allowance money to buy a copy of *Trout*, and on the trip home in the Oldsmobile it was impossible not to sneak a glance at the color plates in Bergman. There was also a copy of the Von Lengerke & Antoine catalogue, and poring over its pages of tackle and equipment and gadgets soon became a boyhood vice.

The celebrated Sparse Grey Hackle, in his commentary for *Great Fishing Tackle Catalogs of the Golden Age*, tells us that such fascination with tackle catalogues is not a particularly rare disease. Catalogues are unquestionably an addiction. My room was quickly filled with them, and sometimes I sat reading them with a flashlight under my blankets until late at night, wondering about these stores in distant cities I had never seen. The catalogues of Abercrombie & Fitch and the celebrated William Mills & Son, where the legendary Bergman once worked as a tackle salesman, were familiar to me many years before I first travelled to New York. The Orvis catalogues were old friends long before I had seen the forest-covered mountains above Manchester or fished the Battenkill River below the Orvis factory and store. Twenty years would pass before my rod collection included either an Orvis or a Leonard, but with their catalogues I was like the hungry boy outside a candy store, and I read them hopefully hundreds of times in those boyhood winters.

Fishing-tackle catalogues are still favorite reading matter when they arrive in the mail, and for most serious American anglers they are a primary source of equipment. Their pages are filled with a galaxy of temptations, although relatively few items included are absolutely essential. Perhaps the best frame of reference for discussing waders, clothing and other equipment might be to explore my own choices and preferences in everyday fishing gear.

Wading equipment is absolutely critical. Generally speaking, waterproof footgear is classified in two primary categories: boots or hip-length waders and the full chest-length waders. Most waders are constructed with rubber or rubberized feet, while the stocking or full-trouser parts are usually made from a rubberized cloth of various natural or synthetic fibers. The waterproof cloth is intended to reduce the weight and cumbersome effect found in all-rubber equipment.

Hip-length waders or hip boots are often adequate for brooks and small trout streams and the shallows of larger rivers. Their lightness and shorter length function perfectly and provide better comfort in extremely hot weather. Most hip boots are fitted only with cleated rubber soles that are best suited to marshy streams and open gravel-bottomed riffles, but always remember that such soles are dangerous on larger stones and ledges slippery with algal growth. Well-made boots will be equipped with cushioned insoles, reinforced arches, and strongly serrated cleats. Reinforced toes and sides are found in the better quality footgear, and some hip boots are also available with felt soles, which are vital when wading among ledges and slippery rocks. Hip-length waders are rather dangerous when a fisherman becomes preoccupied with his sport and works into swift currents too deep for his boot length. Such boots fill quickly and completely, and can have a dangerous sea-anchor effect in a heavy current.

Chest-high waders obviously permit wading in much deeper water. These waders are absolutely essential on big streams, and they also provide surprising tactical mobility on average water. Full-length waders are obviously warmer and drier in cold or rainy weather. They come in two styles: waders fabricated with regular cleat-soled boot feet, and waders with stocking-type feet intended for wear with separate wading shoes called brogues. Both styles have their partisans. Boot-foot waders are more commonly stocked in most sporting-goods stores and are much easier to pull on and strip off, but most expert anglers still use brogues with stocking-foot wader construction. One distinct advantage lies in their better protection for the feet and their tighter fit at the ankle and along the lower legs. Stocking-foot waders can more easily be turned inside out for drying after a day's condensation. Although the stocking-foot waders are comparatively light in themselves, and pack compactly in a duffel bag, their brogues are bulky and cumbersome. Since the brogues are separate from the waders, they may be packed at the ends of such travel bags, forming a durable shield for the more fragile items lying in between.

Boot-foot waders are more clumsy for travelling but have their advantages too. They are clearly preferable on marshy bottoms and for silt-type wading, since the tangle of mud weeds that gathers in wading socks is an unpleasant mess. Their wading shoes need not be removed for drying after each day's fishing. Many boot-foot waders are fitted with a heavy ankle material that reaches halfway up the lower leg, protecting it from deadfalls and stones. It is more snag-proof too. Some fishermen find it difficult to dry the condensation inside a pair of boot-foot waders, but it is possible to turn them down as far as their ankles, drying them in the sun or in the heat rising from a radiator or fireplace. The small hair driers popular in recent years are perfect for drying boots too, and one manufacturer actually makes an electric boot drier.

Both from a sense of tradition and because I thoroughly believe in the foot protection and traction possible only with British wading brogues, I have used nothing but stocking-foot waders for years. There are many fishermen who still use hip-length boots for their fishing, particularly on shallow streams in hot weather, but I prefer full waders even under those conditions. It is important on all types of water to have the capability of wading and crossing the current as freely as possible. Such freedom of movement is useful both in terms of convenience and in searching out effective casting angles and positions for fishing difficult currents. Hot weather usually means relatively low water, and waders also permit crawling infantry-style to stalk the fish and cast from your knees. Such mobility is important on low or hard-fished water.

The quality of waders has sadly declined in recent years, and many plastic finishes and synthetic fabrics simply have not worked out. Like some fly lines woven of synthetic fibers that proved incompatible with their finishes and cracked badly after relatively minor use, many synthetic wader fabrics stretched too readily for their waterproofing. Tiny checks and layered cracking occurred along primary seams and stretch-points. Poor workmanship has become unacceptably common with even the well-known manufacturers at the same time that prices have spiralled higher and higher. It is only prudent to purchase your waders today from a major sporting-goods house or a well-known tackle shop, since these stores are more likely to replace defective waders as a matter of course.

Some fishermen have been turning to industrial types of waders in the hope that their heavy-duty materials might last. It is an understandable choice. However, industrial wading equipment is not designed for the movement and agility involved in fishing a trout stream, its workmanship and materials being specified for wear rather than mobility. In spite of these obvious problems, heavy-duty waders have developed loyal fans.

Why, one argued enthusiastically in a group of fly-fishermen not long ago, *they'll even withstand hydrochloric acid!*

That's pretty strong, I admitted.

Hydrochloric acid! somebody repeated waggishly. *How long's it been since you saw a good hatch of mayflies on a riffle of hydrochloric acid?*

You're right, the man said sheepishly.

The perfect fishing waders must have several qualities. Their fabric and waterproofing must be strong enough to resist a lot of hard wear, including the abrasive effects of bottom sand and volcanic materials in some waters. The seams must be strong enough to withstand the twisting involved in climbing a steep bank and the constant stretching caused by pulling waders on and off. Both the fabric and its waterproofing must be tough enough to resist snagging on briars and brambles and to retard penetration by sharp beaver sticks in the shallows. The waders must also be heavy enough to provide a degree of thermal insulation in extremely cold water. However, with all of these qualities the waders must still provide enough mobility to permit easy movement along the stream and be light enough that on a hot midsummer afternoon fishing in them is cooler than a Finnish sauna.

Modern wader construction employs basic materials far better than the British waterproof fabrics that evolved in the nineteenth century. Rubberized cotton and linen were common when I began trout fishing just before the Second World War. My father rented waders at a tackle shop in

Baldwin, near the famous Pere Marquette of Lower Michigan, and I can remember how even the smallest pair in the rental rack accordioned comically down my legs. Such waders were a rubberized cotton with rubber-boot feet. The wader-rental business subjected those waders to unbelievable amounts of relatively steady wear, although the sand- and gravel-bottomed trout streams of Michigan cannot equal the rocky streams farther east or western volcanic rivers, with their abrasive sands and razor-sharp ledges of fractured lava, in wear-and-tear on waders. Yet the workmanship in the seams was far better than anything we seem able to produce today, since the crotch seam and the seam between the upper waders and their feet are obviously the Achilles' heel in most modern wading products.

The best waders I have worn in recent years were fashioned of synthetic materials. Orvis is using a new three-layer fabric of rubber pancaked between layers of nylon. Marathon is sandwiching industrial nylon cloth between an outer layer of natural rubber and an inner layer of neoprene. These fabrics have proven themselves both light and strong in recent years, resisting as many as 30,000 machine abrasion tests without showing unacceptable wear.

Both fabrics are light enough to provide boot-foot waders across the full range of men's sizes weighing between five and eight pounds. Synthetic fibers are highly resistant to rot and mildew, unlike the waders of English manufacture we used in our boyhood years. Their outer finishes will readily accept temporary patching with either Pliobond or the new heat-stick adhesives designed for temporary repairs. Orvis is using excellent soft-rubber soles of the Vibram cleated type, and Marathon specifies gum-rubber cleats of a deep-lug design. Both makers reinforce their arches with steel shanks. The felt soles provided by both companies are relatively good. Orvis is using a new woven felt highly praised for its durability, while Marathon is using the dense, hard felt popular with fishermen over the years. It should be remembered that wading felt wears well in the river, and poorly when you are walking along the streamside roads and paths. Four belt loops are provided for cinching the waders securely around the waist, and I prefer a sturdy, perforated leather belt with a strong two- or three-tongue buckle. The perforations allow it to dry quickly after deep wading. Inner chest pockets and drawstrings are also important; drawstring cords around your wader tops that are too long should always be trimmed to prevent their tangling in the reel while you are playing a fish.

There should be at least eight suspender buttons on your waders to distribute the strain of twisting, stooping, and climbing. Mills-type wading suspenders of solid nylon webbing reinforced with leather are preferable. Such suspenders have an H-shaped yoke across the back which prevents the tangling, rolling, and slipping common with the cheaper criss-cross pattern. Like the older British-design suspenders, the Mills type are mounted with two-loop elastic cords or button straps at either end. Hip boots are usually supported by belt-loop straps, although a shoulder harness is preferable.

Experienced fishermen trim off the extra length of the boot-harness straps, since they often loop and tangle the fly line in a casting shoot or the slack accumulated in fighting a hooked trout. All good waders provide such thoughtful details.

Some fishermen have been using the less expensive stocking-foot waders of pure gum rubber in recent years. They are relatively light and quite elastic, easily permitting you to stoop, climb steep paths, bend and refasten the laces of your brogues, or sit and kneel in the current. Their cost is about sixty percent less than the price of regular waders. The feet are seamless and fit well without wrinkling, and the gum rubber is easily patched. Chest-length, waist-, and hip-type waders are available in a full range of sizes. But the still cheaper vinyl waders found on the market cannot really be recommended. They are manufactured in both waist- and chest-high types, using both lightweight and heavy-duty vinyls. The seams often tear out, particularly when extremely cold water has made the plastic much too brittle. It also punctures and tears easily, its thickness offering little thermal protection against a bone-chilling current, yet it is so airtight that it is extremely hot and uncomfortable in warm weather. Such waders might prove acceptable as a backup in emergencies, but their durability is so limited that they are expensive in the long run, in spite of their undeniably low first costs.

Canvas wading shoes with felt soles are marginally acceptable, but only the true British brogues really offer the advantages of such footgear. British-made wading shoes are typically shaped from expensive chrome-tanned leather throughout. The box-type reinforced toes and rigid soles provide the superior foot protection that only a wading brogue can give your feet. Drainage grommets are found along both sides of the instep, and strong grommets hold the laces. The best models provide a back-strap pull and reinforced heel, and perhaps the most important advantage lies in the shoe bottoms themselves. Soles and heels of the finest hard felt are one option. The combination a felt sole with a leather heel, its wearing surface studded with eight soft-iron hobs, is highly practical and popular. It provides both the ability of felt to hold on very smooth surfaces and the bite of iron hobnails through thick layers of algae and moss. Rivers where these latter conditions prevail and slippery patches of marl or clay are perhaps negotiated best with brogues having an all-leather sole and heel, both studded with soft iron caulks. It should be understood that hobnails do make sharp sounds on the rocks, which are readily transmitted underwater, but are not as noisy as other metal studs.

The American wading shoes manufactured with combination uppers of leather and canvas are usually more easily purchased in the United States, and they have performed equally well in the past few seasons, although they are available only in a felt sole and heel. These Russell brogues have strong canvas uppers and a full bellows tongue. The lacing eyelets and sides are reinforced with dark brown shoe leather, and four weep grommets drain the shoe. The reinforced box toes and heels are covered in extremely heavy leather, and the soles are made of the finest hard white felt. Hopefully, American manufacturers will also provide the option of caulked leather heels in the future.

Wading underwear and socks are important too. Some fishermen like goosedown and nylon-fleece undergarments for cold weather, while others use waders manufactured with insulated feet and thick fabric uppers. Both solutions to cold water wading are bulky, and the insulation of down is clearly diminished when the water pressure forces it tight against the legs. Pure silk underwear is possibly the finest cold-weather solution for warmth without bulk or weight, and experienced skiers have long used silk for their basic next-to-skin layer of clothing. Silk undershirts and socks are also highly recommended. Really cold conditions find me wearing Norwegian mesh longjohns under a layer of silk, and when the water pressure forces my pants tight around my legs, the mesh traps a layer of body heat between the silk and my skin. Such string-type underwear is extremely elastic, but you should buy a size larger than your normal measurements since mesh underwear that is too tight can bind you like a suit of armor—and its patterns can wrinkle your skin like a waffle.

Brogue socks worn under a stocking-foot or boot-foot wader cushion the foot and give it some warmth. Some fishermen have come to like the German slipperlike wading socks in recent years, and they have a fleece layer quilted between nylon stretch cloth. Such construction permits condensation to pass through the fleece and form on the outer lining. Norwegian boot socks are readily available, and are a fine combination of eighty percent wool and twenty percent nylon and Spandex. Silk underneath will multiply their warmth and protect those who are allergic to wool. Wading brogues also require a sock between the stocking-foot wader and the brogues themselves. These socks are used to prevent chafing, and the abrasive effects of volcanic sands and ash in many rivers. They are most effective in a thickly woven wool or wool mixed with nylon and a similar synthetic. Because I believe a dark-colored wading sock is less visible to the fish, and I like a bright spot of color too, I have been using the fine Thermo socks woven entirely from virgin wool. These socks have a three-dimensional stitch across both the instep and the full twelve-inch ankle, with bright red trim at the ankles. Since fish are more startled by value in colors, their relative lightness or darkness, rather than the hue itself when lateral visibility underwater is involved, the red border around the ankles does not disturb the trout and I like the color accent of its happy chroma.

Brogue and wader sizes are figured by the combination of your shoe size plus your sock requirements. Brogue sizes are controlled by water temperature, as well as the sock layers inside the stocking-foot waders. The brogue must fit around a silk sock and a thick wool-and-nylon sock on your foot, the wader foot itself, and another wading sock that goes on between the brogue and the wader material. Proper cold-weather footgear thus includes a brogue approximately two or even three sizes larger than normal shoe size. Its fit must accommodate the three layers of sock, plus the wader thickness. It should also be remembered that water pressure and the factors involved in downstream wading subject the toes to wedging problems not unlike those found when backpacking down a mountain trail. Wading shoes should fit firmly without pressure while dry, since the softening in the river will probably be neutralized by water pressure. The fit must not cramp the toes; it must allow enough room for the feet to flex and move properly. Fishermen who seldom work a really cold river can omit heavy socks inside their waders, and can perhaps use brogues only one or two sizes larger than normal shoe size.

Stocking-foot waders must be identical with shoe size when only light socks are worn underneath, and a size larger with a heavy wading sock inside. Boot-foot waders should match shoe size for a summer trout fisherman, and should be a size larger with cold-water socks layered underneath. Some manufacturers make only full-size shoes on their waders, and if you take a half size, you should perhaps go a size larger. However, foot size is not the only factor in wader fit. Chest measurement is important too, and should be taken under the armpits with the lungs relaxed. The inseam measurement is taken between the floor and crotch and should be made wearing shoes. The outseam is also taken with shoes on and runs from the floor to the wader tops. The seat dimensions should be made at the widest measurement around the hips. Standard wader size-tolerances are approximately as follows, and if your measurements lie within the chart, you should not require custom-made waders to achieve a proper fit:

CHEST-LENGTH WADER MEASUREMENTS

SIZE	CHEST	INSEAM	OUTSEAM	SEAT
5	36–40	29–30	50	40–44
6	37–41	29–30	51	41–45
7	38–42	30–31	51	42–46
8	39–43	30–31	51	43–47
9	40–44	30–31	52	44–48
10	41–45	31–32	53	45–49
11	42–46	31–32	54	46–50
12	43–47	32–33	55	47–51
13	44–48	33–34	56	48–52

The principal wader manufacturers all provide wader repair kits with adhesives and patching fabrics compatible with their own products. Pliobond cement can also be used as a temporary patching compound for seepage holes and seams that have started to leak slightly. It must be applied each night for the next day's fishing. Punctures, snags, and small tears can be temporarily repaired with the flexible patches made with a thermal repair stick. It can be used along the stream while you are still in your damaged waders; it requires roughing the surface with the sandpaper on the repair stick itself, and melting the adhesive with a match. It softens and spreads like old-fashioned ferrule cement, seals the leak, and remains as flexible as the rubber itself when it dries.

Fishermen who prefer ordinary boot-foot waders with cleated soles, or who cannot afford the more expensive stocking-foot waders and felt-sole brogues, can still improve the gripping qualities of their equipment with several types of wading sandals. Leonard provides a superb wading-chain sandal that can make a dangerous rubber sole as secure as wading with hobnails. Leather sides secure the four chains below the ball of the foot and lace across the instep, and a buckle-strap sling loops back around the heel. Felt wading sandals with half-inch woven-felt soles are also available, and the Mills-type with two instep straps and a heel strap is excellent. Umpqua-type sandals are popular on western steelhead rivers, and there is no better test of wading gear. These sandals have felt soles that fit under both the foot and the heel, with leather side panels reaching over the toes and in front of the ankle. These side panels lace with four grommets across the instep and two at the ankle, and the felt soles are studded with twenty-eight carboloy studs under the foot, plus eleven steel caulks under the heel. Steelhead fishermen also developed the aluminum-grid wading sandals popular on some rivers, and they are extremely good. Flexible aluminum plates form an interlocking grid under the ball of the foot, as they are strapped over the toes and around the ankles securely. There are expert big-river fishermen who swear by grid-type wading sandals.

After the expense of a first-rate rod and reel, proper wading equipment is the most important part of our gear, and a fisherman should spend that money carefully. His wading jacket is perhaps the next item in terms of its importance.

Lee Wulff is certainly the man who conceived the first tackle vest for deep wading, and his design has since been the prototype for a veritable blizzard of copies and mutations. Since its development, the Wulff wading vest has become a kind of uniform for fly-fishermen, rivalling the pin-stripe suit for bankers and corporate lawyers. The original tackle pack had two sheepskin fly patches high on the shoulder blades, with two small pockets just below. Three small pockets were next, lying like cartridge loops on either side of the chest. Two zipper pockets on either side of the belt buckle parallel the bottom of the vest, with matching zipper pockets inside. Two small pockets were located under each armpit, and a huge zipper pocket reached across the back, large enough for an extra reel, rain jacket, and lunch. Wulff also added a net ring behind the neck, and a loop and snap holder to secure the rod when you need both arms. There was also a small nylon-mesh creel that zippered along the left side of the vest, although most fishermen soon left it behind.

Orvis has modified the original Wulff design since it appeared more than twenty-five years ago, and there are now two basic models. One is designed for normal fishing and waist-deep work, and the other is for really deep wading.

LEE WULFF

Both are still made from the tan cotton poplin with the water-repellent sizing that Wulff specified years ago. The fabric is now machine washable, and the pocket flaps have abandoned the old-fashioned snap closers for Velcro fasteners. The sheepskin fly patches are now removable, and I firmly believe they should be left off. Flies allowed to dry there are flattened and hopelessly bent out of shape, and some fall off and are lost. Others are blown off in high winds, or frequently stripped off in casting when the hooks snag on a sleeve or catch in the shooting line.

The regular Orvis waist-length fishing vest is practically identical otherwise. It has abandoned the small pockets under the armpits, since it was virtually impossible to use them without taking the vest off completely. There are more small changes inside the new jackets. The sunglasses pocket now has a zipper closure, which prevents a costly pair of prescription Polaroids or tempered shooting glasses from wedging upward due to casting rhythms until they are lost. Opposite the glasses pocket is a square Velcro-flap pocket for packaged leaders, and each bellows pocket inside has a flap pocket designed for eight tippet spools. The material is impregnated with silicone to waterproof the lower pockets and protect your costly flies. There are also permanent loops for clippers and scissor pliers. It is a superbly designed piece of clothing, and it performs its function perfectly, simultaneously carrying and organizing tackle on the stream.

The Orvis modification for deep-wading tactics is virtually the same except it is made about six inches shorter, and it omits the middle row of small pockets to make the bottom that much higher. The vests can now be purchased in a fabric of sixty-five percent Dacron and thirty-five percent cotton. Older fishermen and men with physical problems affecting their wading skills will welcome the flotation vest available from Orvis now. It is made in a handsome dark tan material, and has almost as many pockets as the standard vests. It has a surprising lack of bulkiness, and will float almost as well as an inflated life jacket. All three Orvis jackets are fitted with a detachable creel that clips onto the bottom hemline.

There is a Japanese copy of this Wulff fishing vest in a dark tan cotton poplin that has been waterproofed. It has an incredible fourteen small pockets with Velcro flaps. Four large horizontal zipper pockets are provided in front, with eight smaller pockets mounted on them in turn. It has all of the other features too, along with chrome-plated rings inside for connecting scissor pliers or clippers. The rod-holder flap is matched with a ring system below, and front closure is accomplished with a nylon zipper. These Japanese vests are available from a number of small fly-fishing shops, and the imitation has some worthwhile features the more expensive originals might copy.

Western steelhead fishermen have also evolved some valuable muta- tions of the Wulff-type vest. The North Umpqua design is fashioned of fifty percent nylon and fifty percent rayon in a deep moss green. The fly-box pockets are zippered inside and out, with big bellows pockets both places, and smaller zip pockets on the larger outside faces. Two rings are provided under each small chest pocket, and the entire back is a roomy rucksack-sized pocket that zippers horizontally just below the net ring at the neckline. The Kalama deep-wading style is similar, but about eight inches shorter, barely covering the wader tops. The inner pockets are zipper-closed at a steep angle, with the zipper secure in the high position. Steelhead fishermen carry much less equipment and flies, like most Atlantic salmon anglers, and this fact has some influence on the relatively simple design of these vests. Both have some original features.

Perhaps the best fishing jacket I have used is the new wading vest designed by my good friend André Puyans and manufactured for his California tackle shop in Hong Kong. It is also featured by Dan Bailey in Montana. It is made of fifty-two percent polyester and forty-eight percent cotton poplin in antelope tan, with a strong fabric reinforcement along its edges. The regular length model is my current wading vest. It has two small Velcro pockets high on the chest that are fitted with metal rings for attaching clippers or surgical forceps or scissor pliers. Two larger pockets are located against the ribcage, and are sized to accept the Wheatley-type fly boxes, like the zippered bellows pockets at the waist. The left-hand bellows pocket has another Wheatley-size pouch fitted on its face, with two generous leader-size pockets on the face of the right-hand bellows. There are two Wheatley snap pockets inside the vest at waist level, plus two zippered pockets inside the upper vest, with a large bellows pouch across the back for extra reels and a rain jacket. The deep wading variation on this Puyans design is five inches shorter and lacks the two Wheatley-size pockets in front, raising the two larger zippered pockets against the ribcage. Both vest designs include a rod-holding snap loop and butt attachment. Interestingly, they both omit an attached creel and sheepskin fly-holder patches—André Puyans obviously shares some of my prejudices about killing trout and manhandling fine flies.

All fishing vests are worn over bulky clothing and are usually filled with fly boxes and other equipment. Experienced fishermen always choose a vest one or two sizes too large in order to have a roomy fit for easy casting. There are three unique pieces of equipment designed for fishing deep water safely. The small life preservers that firmly clip to your vest and inflate when pressed hard with the fingers are good insurance. Although I have never triggered one in actual fishing, sailboating friends tell me they work beautifully when you get too tired in difficult situations. Although I own a handsome split-cane wading staff, which Orvis salvaged and converted from a surplus of their impregnated ski poles manufactured during the Second World War, it is seldom used. Several times when I was using my staff on a difficult salmon river, it became tangled in my legs or the loose loops of fly line that hung downstream in the current. Other times the sense of security the staff provided led me to wade too deeply into currents I might otherwise have shunned, and I almost never carry it these days. Perhaps it will come out of my tackle closet in my geriatric years, if my health survives a life of too much fishing. The third piece of equipment is a floating tube, and although I have never used one, such tubes are becoming popular on high lakes and back-country ponds and marshy spring-fed streams like Silver Creek in Idaho. The method has become so common there that it has led to strange-sounding conversations in the restaurants and bars at nearby Sun Valley.

Hey! It was a young man sitting at the bar in the Ore House. *You guys finally finished with my tubes?*

Yeah, came the reply. *They worked fine.*

That's good. The young man took a long pull at his beer mug. *Where'd you leave my tubes?*

They're in your jeep, they answered. *Thanks.*

Okay, the young man nodded.

The fishing tubes are similar to the inner tubes we played with at the beach as children, except that they are fitted with a strong canvas seat and a heavy webbing strap. The tube itself is a standard truck-tire inner tube capable of supporting two hundred fifty pounds. Its canvas cover is silicone treated, providing both a seat system and a pair of zippered equipment pouches. The webbing crotch strap has a simple release buckle that readily allows an angler to mount and disengage himself from the tube. It is worn with full-length waders, of course, and a pair of ingenious aluminum fins. The fins strap around the heels firmly, and are designed to flip out on the swimming stroke, folding cleverly to reduce water friction on the back stroke. Having seen them used expertly during the *Tricorythodes* hatches in the Yellowstone country, and on the sloughs of Silver Creek at Sun Valley, I can testify to their practicality and worth. The tubes are useful both for safety in potentially dangerous wading, and to reach fish in still currents too deep to wade. Yet they are not infallible, and one tube fisherman was drowned on Silver Creek this past season.

Foul-weather gear is also important. My own rain jacket folds virtually to handkerchief size and stows perfectly in the bellows pocket across the back of my fishing vest. It both sheds the rain and breaks the wind. It is an ultralight Austrian product designed for mountain climbers and alpine hunters, and is made of forest green featherweight nylon. It has a light nylon zipper and a hood with a drawstring. It also has a clever back vent with a nylon mesh closure; its covering flap is designed to ventilate with a bellows action as you move. It has served me faithfully for more than ten seasons, and until the past year its equal was not available here.

However, both Orvis and Marathon are marketing a product that is perhaps better suited to fishing. The Orvis jacket is made in both parka and wading lengths, with matching foul-weather pants. It is fabricated of soft, high-count nylon so light that even the ankle-length raincoat will fold compactly enough to slip into the back pocket of a wading vest. It has a drawstring hood, lightweight zipper, and nylon-mesh venting under the armpits and across the back. It is also a deep forest green. The hood is cut to keep the rain off your fishing glasses. There are tape closures at the wrists, and generous raglan-cut shoulders. Orvis has added two front pockets with

Velcro-flap closers, a feature missing in my Austrian cape. The Marathon wading-length rain jacket is quite similar in its detailing, except for its elastic wrists and zipper pockets. These rain jackets are both relatively expensive, but their comfort, lightness, and performance over years of fishing are well worth their additional cost.

These past few years I have fished extensively in some climates notorious for their cold weather and wind. Norway, Iceland, and the subarctic latitudes of the Labrador are legendary for their foul weather, as are Patagonia and Tierra del Fuego. Norwegian sweaters and the soft knitted sweaters from Iceland, with their rain-shedding unwashed wools, are superb cold-weather garments. The traditional folk patterns are worked in intricate mixtures of black and gray and white in Norway, and in interlocking patterns of black and brown and gray and white in Iceland. Over the years I have acquired matching pullovers and button-front cardigans that I wear in raw winds and subarctic temperatures. The outer cardigan is easily removed if the weather improves, and it is a system that has worked for me. These sweaters are beautiful and practical.

Extremely cold weather demands other measures. Silk undershirts and mesh underwear are useful, and a lightweight goosedown shirt has no equal for such conditions. The best I have used is made from a tightly woven waterproof nylon, with its insulation quilting more than an inch thick. The fabric is a pale sand color that matches the poplin fishing pants and shirts I commonly use. The front zippers shut and there are two muff-style pockets for warming the fingers from the chill of evaporation and wind. Such down vests and shirts are compact and weigh less than two pounds.

My preference in fabric for fishing shirts and trousers is the cotton poplin material commonly found in safari-type clothing. The well-known Abercrombie & Fitch poplin trousers and front-pocket shirts are excellent, providing durability, warmth without the thickness that can prevent hot-weather ventilation, and absorption of perspiration or condensation inside your waders. Orvis makes a similar cloth in a safari-tan color and tailors it into trousers and shirts specially designed for fishing. Their cut is generous to facilitate wading and casting. The shirts have four button-pockets in front, sized to take the smallest Wheatley boxes, and another button-pocket on the left sleeve. The sleeves are cut full for the motions of casting and the left-hand haul, and there is even a butt loop and snap loop for a rod in shirtsleeve weather, when you might fish without a wading vest. Woolrich makes matching tan poplin trousers and military-type shirts that are fine summer gear. Leonard has designed a finely crafted leather belt box for really hot weather when even a wading vest feels like an overcoat. It has two large compartments for fly boxes and two small pockets out front, and is perfect in hot weather with a multipocketed shirt. Some fishing pants are also fitted with snap-fastening tabs that hold them tightly rolled at the ankles, and keep them from riding up inside your waders. Such clothing is practical and well designed.

Foul-weather protection for the head and hands is important in fishing too. Headgear has several primary functions. It protects us from both heat and cold, from precipitation, and from too much sun. It must be shaped to keep the rain off your fishing glasses and outside your collar. It must be waterproof or water-resistant enough to keep your head dry. Its brim should shade both glasses and eyes. It should also have enough weight to stay on in high winds, and enough thickness to protect your head from a misguided double-haul cast with a really big bucktail. Light poplin hats meet all these criteria, except stay-put performance in strong winds and protection from a fly travelling at considerable speed. The years spent in Germany after the Second World War fishing the mountain rivers and hunting the forests with the *Jaegermeisters* and their beaters taught me respect for their loden hats and shooting capes. Loden is a material originally made for the damp cold encountered in the mountains while stalking red stag and chamois at considerable altitudes. Hats made from loden are excellent for fishing, virtually waterproof, heavy enough to stay put in a wind, warm, and enough like a helmet to protect your head from a fly that comes screaming off the tip speed that shoots a hundred feet of line. Some fishermen have adopted the Scottish tweed deerstalker, since its front and rear brims protect your glasses and neck from rain in a traditional foul-weather design. The traditional Irish tweed hats from Donegal and Connemara are excellent fishing hats too, meeting each of the criteria well, since they were designed for fishing rain-swept mountains and moors. The ordinary sailor hat of cotton poplin or denim is good in hot weather with little or no wind, although it offers minimal protection from casting. However, fishing in the fierce midsummer winds of Patagonia is impractical in normal hats, and there we soon bought the head-clinging Basque berets worn by the sheepherders in the hills around Junin de los Andes. Their berets were not waterproof, and they were too soft to offer much protection from a clumsy cast, until we discovered that an application of silicone dry-fly spray added some of these qualities.

Cold hands are a serious problem in marginal weather. Raw temperatures are trouble in themselves, and handling a wet line or fish simply adds evaporation to the problem. Some fishermen like full gloves of the supple shooting-type, and often wear tight silk gloves under them. The leather can also be treated with silicone spray. Other fishermen find that actual gloves are too confining and hamper their dexterity. British fishermen have solved the problem with wool-knit mittens treated with silicone, the fingertips left uncovered and free.

Raw winds are also a problem for the throat as well as the head itself. The past few seasons I have learned to use silicone-treated turtlenecks of stretch nylon or Merino wool. Their high collars keep the neck warm and protect it from the wind, although there are still times when only a wool scarf is warm enough. Traditional red bandanna handkerchiefs are also useful around the neck in hot weather or insect country.

No discussion of fishing clothes would be complete without some comment on the effect of color on fish. It is perhaps safe to argue that the ability of a color to reflect or intensify light, like the proverbial white shirt or shocking yellow rain slicker, makes it the most obvious to the fish. Color technicians call this quality value, describing a color hue totally in terms of its relative darkness or lightness. Hue itself is simply a color in abstract terms, without any consideration for its paleness or darkness, let alone its chromatic intensity. Schiaparelli coined the term shocking pink to describe the intensity of the Bangkok silks used in her superb couture, and many of the modern synthetic fibers also glow with an inner fire that is the very soul of a technical color word like chroma.

Fishing talk is often trapped in some alarming axioms, typically based on local experience. There are fishermen who argue for camouflage fabrics, which were originally developed for jungle tactics and work well in forests, yet a figure in jungle camouflage is comically visible in the pale straw-colored grass along a western river like the Firehole or Silver Creek. Forest green wading vests and shirts are popular among many steelhead addicts, whose rivers tumble toward the sea in dense rain forests, sliding past slate-colored boulders made leaden with autumn rains. The color makes sense on those rivers. But a dark green figure makes little sense in the bright ochre canyon of the Yellowstone, or silhouetted against the October cottonwoods and pale sagebrush hills along the Big Wood in Idaho. Bright red shirts and the soft chamoislike yellow shirts have been popular in recent years. Such colors certainly provide a chromatic focal point to photographs, and that is why you see so many of them in fishing magazines, but they are too visible to the fish. Bright red is probably better than bright yellow, since it is darker in a light-to-dark scale and bounces far less reflective light. Weather and the variables in light on a given day provide almost infinite patterns of change even against a background of dense foliage, and trying to imitate such a spectrum of colors with a piece of clothing is futile.

Which brings our ruminations full circle, to the conclusion that good fishing clothes are neither too pale and light-reflecting nor too dark against a pale background. In fact, they should never present too much of a contrast against any background or too much chromatic intensity. The grayish tan of our traditional poplin meets each of these criteria.

Before we leave talk of fishing clothes for a discussion of the equipment we carry on the stream within or attached to our fishing vests, perhaps we should discuss the problems of packing our gear for travel. Fishing pressure on the rivers near our cities, the technical revolution in air travel that has occurred since midcentury, and our relative affluence have all combined to allow us to travel more widely than our ancestors dreamed. It is possible to fish the rivers in Argentina and Chile, six thousand miles on the other side of the earth, in less time than our grandfathers took to reach the rivers of Maine or the Adirondacks from New York, or the forest-dark rivers of Michigan and Wisconsin from Chicago or Detroit. It is a climate of remarkable change.

Travelling with fly rods and reels has some special considerations, and fishing travel is a happy by-product of writing about the sport. Some years I have totalled as much as 50,000 miles in search of trout and salmon, and that much travel teaches a footloose angler something about packing his gear. The lessons are useful, since much of our fishing equipment is relatively fragile.

Shipping expensive rods in the baggage holds of aircraft frightens me even when they are fully protected by aluminum tubing. Years of airline travel have convinced me that the mechanical engineers who design baggage-handling equipment have a standard performance specification: their equipment automatically damages one suitcase in every twenty-five pieces of luggage. Skis tagged for Switzerland arrive uncannily in San Juan each winter, and I once wandered in shock in New York when a canvas roll containing six expensive split-cane rods failed to arrive from Denver. The airline located them only hours later in Detroit, and they were happily returned undamaged the following day. It might have been worse.

When I travel with one or two rods, their aluminum cases are not really enough protection either separately or taped together. For such trips I have come to like the fine saddle leather rod cases available from makers like Orvis and Leonard, although some airlines will not permit them as cabin baggage. These cases are made with a high-strength aluminum tube inside the stitched leather cover. The cases have leather caps and adjustable carrying straps that make them convenient to carry on your flight as a handsome piece of hand luggage.

Sometimes an extended trip can mean several rods to match varied fishing conditions, as well as provide a spare rod or two in case of breakage. My favorite method of packing several rods is the lightweight canvas rod roll that combines the strength of three or four cases. Three aluminum tubes pack into a triangular shape of considerable strength, and four are even stronger. Orvis has made a superb canvas carrying roll for some twenty years, and I have worn out three of them with air travel. It is made of heavy-duty tan canvas. It is designed to hold a standard aluminum rod case in a deep bellows pocket at the butt, with two wide canvas loops at its third points, and a generous flap that folds down over the caps. When the entire case is rolled up, the top flap is firmly wrapped inside, and three leather straps tightly bind the roll together. There is a leather strap for carrying the roll when it is packed and secure. The roll will carry four aluminum cases two inches in diameter and is long enough for a two-piece rod measuring nine-and-a-half feet. The loop beside the rolling spline will accept only one two-inch case, but each of the others will take two rod cases of the normal diameter. Packed this way, the roll will hold seven rods. However, I have purchased four two-inch diameter cases especially for packing in the canvas roll. It is possible to pack eight trout-size rods in them, with the butt of one in the bottom of each case and the other slipped in carefully with its butt under the machined cap. The second rod should be worked in cautiously to prevent damage to both tip sections and guides that might catch together. Leonard is now making a beautiful leather rod carrier in lengths of forty, forty-eight, and fifty-six inches. It has a zipper closure and carries as many as eight standard diameter cases.

Fly reels are expensive and fragile too, and should not be packed loose in a suitcase or duffel bag. Several times I have watched men unpack their equipment thousands of miles from home to find a reel has unhappily travelled as well, working its way through layers of clothing to rest against the outside of a suitcase. Sometimes in the rough-and-tumble of baggage handling such a reel can receive a blow that shatters its frame or bends its spool. Such tragedies can ruin a costly trip, and can easily be avoided. Good packing can prevent some damage, but a good reel case is also important. Hardy once made excellent saddle-leather cases lined with chamois skin, and later used exquisite plum-colored velvet linings. The early reel cases were buckled, and later versions used a spring-loaded catch. These cases were superb protection for an expensive reel, providing an equilibrium between rigidity and softness, and someone should resurrect them. They pack well either lid-down in a suitcase or with the reel-shaped bottoms down in the center of a duffel. Some fishermen pack them lid-to-lid in their luggage for greater stability. Two weeks ago I was examining several century-old Hardy reel cases that once belonged to the famous Arthur H. E. Wood, who developed low-water fishing for salmon on the Dee. Like most well-made things, these leather cases grow more beautiful with time.

Modern reelmakers are using vinyl zipper-cases with white foam linings that cushion the reels perfectly, and hold them in place with a hole cut into the plastic foam for the handle. Such cases would be better if the manufacturers exercised the taste and restraint to stop disfiguring them with gaudy trademarks and colors. Many fishermen like the suede and vinyl cases that zipper around the perimeter and are lined with sheepskin. These cases are inexpensive and adequately protect a reel from abrasion, but it is doubtful that they could protect it from a damaging impact in the baggage hold of an aircraft. Buckskin reel bags are also handsome, but provide little protection from sustained weight or an impact load. Cowhide backs offer a little more protection, but not enough for a really sharp blow. The handsome vinyl cases also available from two or three reel manufacturers have the same failing, but they do omit the sheepskin lining, which has the nasty habit of shedding and working deep into the finely machined entrails of an expensive reel it is supposed to protect—ask the men who make and repair reels how they feel about sheepskin cases.

Fishing tackle luggage is another problem. Tackle boxes are useful filing cabinets for the myriad small items and gadgets we all collect and use, but most tackle boxes have been designed for bait casting. Some open to reveal an astonishing number of aluminum trays, levering out from the depths of the box to improbable, cantilevered displays of glittering spoons and frog-colored baits and traditional red and white plugs, with treble hooks hanging like tinsel on a Christmas pine. The soft-rubber nightcrawlers and preserved pork rinds that really catch modern bass are concealed at the bottom, like the secret entrance to a bootlegger's cellar.

Both Orvis and Abercrombie & Fitch sold beautifully made tackle boxes of mahogany, with fitted wooden trays and mirror-bright finishes of clear lacquer. Canvas coverings are also made to slip over these cases to protect their finishes, but such cases are unable to withstand the rigors of shipment on airlines, with or without their covers. They are superb for filing and storing tackle, and for automobile travel to and from the stream. Mills once sold a saddle-leather tackle box that enclosed aluminum trays, and a full metal interior that came out for cleaning. It had heavy suitcase-type latches and a strong lock, with a generous leather handle and fittings. Such cases were superbly adapted to travelling, like the saddle-leather trunks especially fitted for tackle that British anglers once took to Scotland and Norway for salmon fishing, and some firm should make them again in a medium tackle-box size. Such boxes are perfect, both for organizing the sundry small items of tackle that wander around loose through a duffel bag, and for providing a rigid shell around a collection of expensive reels and fly boxes in transit.

However, the duffel bag is a superb piece of luggage for packing bulky rough-tackle items like waders, wading brogues, foul-weather gear, fishing vests, thermal underwear, and bulky sweaters. My trips have thoroughly proved the practicality and wearing qualities of the standard flat-bottom station-wagon bag. It is made of strong thirteen-ounce sailcloth that has been treated to shed water and resist mildew. There is an outside two-snap pouch which I seldom use, and a full-length zipper, modified with a grommet ring in its leather tab for a small combination padlock. Such bags come in three sizes, and the smallest twenty-four-inch type comfortably holds my brogues, waders, rain gear, fishing vest, two or three sweaters, and miscellaneous smaller equipment. It is usually packed sausage-tight on a trip, and I have two that have served me faithfully for more than a dozen years, although they are getting a little dog-eared. The end-loading duffel bags of the military type are not recommended, since they must be unpacked completely to find anything, and even the full-zipper round duffels are too limp for convenient handling when partially opened. The station-wagon type is easier to use in camp. Some fishermen like the lighter tote bags and duffels made of extremely light parachute nylon that are watertight and mildewproof. The round bag weighs an incredible six ounces, and measures twelve inches in diameter and a full thirty inches in length. The bag is reinforced with heavy nylon webbing and has two carrying straps. The full-length steel zipper provides convenient access and packing capability. Two brass buckle straps secure the opening and reduce strain on the zipper, and the entire bag is encircled with nylon webbing. There is a larger nylon tote made by the same manufacturer, except that it is fifteen inches square and thirty inches long. It has generous bellows pockets at either end and along one side, each closed with nylon zippers. Its capacity is unequalled for its surprising eight-ounce weight, and its zippers can be modified to take small combination padlocks. Both nylon bags are also available in sailcloth duck, but it is their incredibly light weight that makes them valuable on air trips, since excess baggage charges are prohibitive outside the country.

Leonard is making a round duffel bag of top grain cowhide as elegant as its fly rods. It is secured with two leather straps that work around the entire bag, which measures ten inches in diameter and twenty inches in length. The leather duffel easily fits under a plane seat and is designed for packing reels, cameras, clothing, and other small gear. Many anglers carry their film in their hand baggage to protect it from fogging, overexposure and other curious effects associated with electronic inspection of baggage. Leonard also makes a larger cowhide duffel with two leather handles and a shoulder strap, designed as a matching piece of tackle luggage. It is closed with a full leather flap and two buckle straps of leather wrapped completely around the bag. There is also a carrying handle at one end, and both bags have full-length zippers. These bags are a little heavy, but there is something beautiful about fine leather, and both are readily accessible without unpacking their entire contents.

Some thought should also be given to what the late John Alden Knight called his falling-in bag. It carried dry underwear and socks, clean shirt and trousers, sneakers, and an extra sweater in case you take a pratfall in some bucolic riffle. It should even provide a towel or two.

Several manufacturers recommend strapping rod cases under the handles or along the sides of their duffels, but my unhappy experience with air travel makes me wary, and I will not expose my fly rods to such risks. There are also combination duffels that pack normally through full-length zippers, and then hold three aluminum rod cases under a second flap on the outside. Unlike the canvas rod rolls, these canvas loops do not combine the three cases in a self-reinforcing triangle, and the rods are relatively vulnerable to loading impacts. Their safety is also threatened when the duffel itself is not tightly packed. Two years ago I witnessed the fracture of two split-cane rods on a trip to Buenos Aires, and the villain was a loosely packed bag. Apparently, the contents shifted in flight and formed a fulcrum across a hard lump of equipment. The trip was a little rough coming into Ezeiza Airport, with towering thunderheads over the pampas, and the weight of other baggage simply deformed both aluminum cases across the gear inside the duffel itself.

Creels are unfashionable these days, not because the classic wicker baskets of the past are at all ugly, but because killing a creelful of trout is in disfavor. Although the wicker creels are bulky and cumbersome when you are wading deep, their ventilation keeps fish fresh even in hot weather. The nylon-mesh creels attached to most fishing vests are also quite practical, in spite of their short length, which was obviously designed for catchable-size hatchery trout. The British-type flat bass of woven straw were much preferred by Edward Ringwood Hewitt, and he advocated them so persistently that the old Mills catalogues even called them Hewitt creels. Flat bags measure about twelve by fifteen inches, have a webbing-reinforced opening, and are carried on a simple clip harness. Filled with freshly picked mint or ferns, the straw bass keeps fish beautifully, and can be quickly cleaned with a hose. Ray Bergman recommended the Hewitt creel in *Trout*, and used nothing else in his fishing, although he recognized that they seldom lasted more than one or two seasons.

Stripping baskets are a creellike piece of equipment that evolved on our steelhead rivers to take full advantage of weight-forward lines, the technique of the left-hand haul, and the more recent shooting-head equipment. The baskets are canvas trays on a stainless wire frame, with several holes in the bottom to drain moisture carried on the fly line. Some are worn across the stomach, with an adjustable strap across the back. The basket is semicircular in shape, and about fifteen inches along its straight side. It functions a little like a spinning reel, since you retrieve your running line into the basket in precisely layered coils after a long shot with a sinking line or shooting head. The entire fly line or monofilament running line behind the sinking head can be coiled in the basket, and when a long cast powers out across the current, the running line leaps cleanly from the stripping basket and scurries after the heavier weight-forward belly and head. Hundred-foot casts are relatively easy with a stripping basket, since the line is freed of the water friction involved in shooting it free of the surface. Left-hand coils also tend to knot and tangle with the line velocity of a strong double-haul, sometimes jamming hard against the butt guide. Distance casting is easier with a stripping basket, although it is clumsy looking and a bother to wear. Some fishermen who are expert with a stripping basket have fabricated their own designs, wearing them along their left sides, and making them large enough to hold still more shooting line in generous loops.

Landing nets have become almost as unfashionable as creels in recent years, although it is paradoxical that releasing fish is the cause. Some anglers subscribe to a code that believes landing a trout without a net is more difficult, and therefore gives the fish an advantage that is more sporting. It may also make that fish more frightened and tired. It is harder to hold a trout to work the hook free without the friction of the net meshes, and you can easily press too hard into the gills or around the belly. Internal injuries, exhaustion, and shock kill more released fish than hook damage or fungus, and fishing without a landing net both extends the struggle and makes releasing a fish more difficult. Forget the arguments for fishing without a net, land your trout as mercifully and quickly as possible, and take advantage of a landing net to handle them gently. It is unfair to tire a fish unnecessarily and risk injuring it as it struggles in your hand when you ultimately intend to release it.

For most stream fishing I prefer the old-fashioned wood frame landing nets I have used since boyhood. Such nets are usually hung from a frame of laminated birch or hickory, with an ornamental walnut spacer in the handle. The net bag itself should be fashioned of a synthetic fiber like Dacron or nylon, since it is extremely strong and resists rot, although superb bags of heavy waterproofed cotton have long been used in Europe.

Some nets are made with double strands in their loops along the frame, and the mesh size should diminish progressively from the throat to the bottom of the bag. Such details provide both strength and sufficient current drag to blossom the meshes instantly. The dimensions of the net frames are often much larger than necessary in standard designs. Frame width of ten to twelve inches, and a throat length of fifteen to eighteen inches are common. Such nets are usually fitted with a bag about twenty inches deep, and in skilled hands, nets of these dimensions can easily handle fish of twelve to fifteen pounds. Some makers have added ornamental corded grips and leather trim to their nets, but I find them unattractive and unnecessary. Except for the tightly wound linen reinforcing where the laminated frame bows out from the walnut spacer in the handle, I believe a net should be free of embellishments. Its beauty lies simply in the character of its wood and its craftsmanship, like a fine fly rod or delicate violin.

These past years I have been using a little net built with great skill and simplicity by Joseph Swaluk, who later made similar landing nets for Leonard. Its frame is top-grade hickory with a handle of burled American walnut, and its gleaming lacquer finish is applied in the Leonard rod factory. It meets each of my specifications for landing-net design, and its frame is relatively small, measuring only eight inches across the throat. It has handled fish as large as ten pounds easily, and like all beautifully designed equipment, it is a pleasure to own and use. Guyrich is manufacturing similar nets made entirely of walnut with grip spacers of exotic hardwoods like Macassar ebony. Their design and craftsmanship are remarkable.

Some fishermen like the collapsible nets popular in Europe, and I have used both the Pezon & Michel model from France and the slightly more expensive British design. The French product is made in two handle lengths of a fixed type, while the British net has a handle that extends from seventeen to thirty-two inches. The extra length is clearly necessary on the chalkstreams of Normandy and Hampshire, where an angler is often on a high bank above the water, with a current too deep to wade. Last season I fished the Maigue in Ireland, a small limestone river below Limerick, where I soon learned the advantages of a borrowed net with an extension-type handle. This spring on the Abbots Worthy water of the Itchen, and the Kimbridge beats of the Test, it was obvious that such long-handled nets are valuable. The less expensive collapsible nets manufactured in Europe are made with oxidized brass handles and aluminum frames, while the better models are entirely aluminum alloy. Both types extend to a total length of forty-three inches, and the triangular frame has a fourteen-inch throat. These collapsible nets are snapped open and extended with a sharp flick of the wrist, and although I have never seen one fail, the collapsible net that refuses to open is one of my nightmares.

Anything that can go wrong, runs the now-familiar theorem of fallibility called Murphy's Law, *will!* And usually at a crucial moment.

Landing nets can be attached to the fisherman in several ways, and a swivel-clip lanyard of elastic was common on my boyhood rivers. It was simply looped over one shoulder and slung under the opposite arm, which worked perfectly well out in the river, but walking a brushy path could transfrom it into a lethal weapon. Its meshes would invariably catch in the branches, stretch the lanyard like a bowstring, and catapult the frame back into your kidneys. Eastern fishermen soon jettisoned the lanyard with its swivel connection, and replaced it with a French-type clip. The clip was connected to the net with a small split ring, and consists of a spring-actuated clamp. The clamp closes itself until finger pressure across the middle of the device opens its jaws. These clips were attached to the small ring that hangs down the back of most wading vests, although many fishermen found it difficult to unhook it there. Such understandable clumsiness soon led to the pin ring, a leather loop connecting a stainless ring with a strong industrial safety pin. It could be fastened anywhere on a fishing vest, depending on the preferences and dexterity of its user. However, many fishermen lost nets when they tried to disengage them while fighting a fish, and watched them tumble downstream into heavy water. Others who were more agile succeeded in bringing their nets into play, netted their fish and then released them. Having learned to fish in a time when nets were hung from the shoulder with a lanyard, they sometimes forgot and lost a net when they simply let it go.

It once happened to me in the excitement of a big fish on the Gunnison in Colorado years ago, and it soon led to the hybrid system I have now used for many seasons. My net eye is connected to the old-fashioned lanyard clip with a stainless split ring, and the elastic is looped to the jacket ring hanging behind my neck. The French clip is then permanently fastened to my fishing vest slightly behind my left armpit, and clamps around the split-ring connection. It can be located anywhere. The system has the advantages of a net that is secured with an elastic lanyard, and can be dropped when the fish gets a second wind that requires both hands. Yet its French-clip connection prevents the catapult effect when the net snags in the brush, and it is still easily reached and freed.

Fishing glasses are often overlooked, but they are quite important in several ways. Obviously, dark glasses reduce eye strain and glare in bright weather, and prescription lenses are a modern blessing. Polaroid filters allow us to see more readily into the water, and are invaluable in both observing and playing a fish, yet few fishermen have learned to use the yellow shooting glasses to magnify light. Such lenses are a surprising help on dark days and in evening fishing, although an angler who carries a camera will quickly discover that they distort his judgment for good filming light. Optometrists tell us that therapeutic use of dark glasses in bright sun will insure improved night-fishing vision later in the day. Clear glasses with tempered lenses are good eye protection in night fishing. Fishing glasses should always have tempered shatterproof lenses, since they also have the function of protecting the eyes from a poor double haul.

There are other optical devices a fisherman can find useful along the stream. Hardy manufactures the Wardle magnifier, which is designed to help a man with failing sight tie knots in delicate nylon, and to thread tippets of such nylon through the minuscule eye of a twenty-eight hook. It is a precision lens mounted in a sturdy black-oxidized frame which clips firmly to your clothing, leaving both hands free. There is a light cross brace that prevents twisting or rolling while you are using the lens, and the device folds flat when not in use. It stows easily in a small poplin shirt or fishing-vest pocket.

The British magnifying spectacles called the Bishop Harman glasses are a remarkable fishing tool. They are perfect for threading small flies on fine tippets. Since their lenses are not corrective, supplying only a remarkable magnification, no prescription is needed. The glasses are worn at the tip of the nose, in front of your prescription glasses. The Bishop Harman spectacles are expensive, but are invaluable at streamside.

Space technology has also perfected a remarkable monocular less than three inches long, weighing only two ounces, yet it has full eight-power magnification. It is useful for watching a rising fish. Fishermen who are dedicated to collecting and imitating the hatches and other diet forms on their rivers will find two other optical gadgets useful. The first is a kind of mini-microscope called a linen tester, and it consists of a folding anodized frame with a calibrated bottom, a half-inch lens of 9X power, and a focal length of slightly less than an inch. The second is a small hand magnifying glass two inches in diameter which does not require a flat surface like the linen tester, and swivels into its own attached leather case. The pocket magnifier can also be used to concentrate solar energy and start an emergency fire if both you and your matches are soaked. Both gadgets are quite compact when folded and are easily carried astream.

Other useful gadgets are available for the streamside study of trout foods. Common round-throat kitchen strainers or square aquarium nets can be stripped of their short handles and equipped with a twelve-inch basswood dowel handle. Such strainers make picking an insect from the water remarkably easy, and with a small stainless screw eye attached to the dowel, a hatch collector can easily be fastened to a belt loop on your waders with a small chain button. Catching a fluttering caddis or an egg-laying mayfly spinner in flight can prove frustratingly difficult, and biologists have long used a small butterfly net with a slender bamboo handle. Handles as long as twenty feet may be required for spinners that swarm high above the current. Such equipment is impossible to carry while fishing, although any serious student of fly hatches should fabricate one for his research. It is also possible to make a wire frame that will fit in the back bellows pocket of a wading vest, and attach to your rod to make a collecting net. Hardy made such gadgets just before the First World War, when the streamside entomology of Halford and Moseley was in vogue on British streams. Their collecting net had a bag of mosquito netting fastened to a circular rim of aluminum wire. Fine nylon mesh seems to damage flying specimens less than cotton material. The wire frame had two loops and a waterproof cotton cord attached to the center of the wire. After the two loops were slipped onto the rod, the cord was threaded through the tip guide. Then it was threaded between both wire loops, extended down the length of the rod, and held taut with the hand. It was both ingenious and effective, since mating aquatic insects are typically shy and difficult to capture, and I once saw a friend fall and almost smash a favorite rod trying to catch a dancing *Isonychia* spinner with his fishing hat.

Several manufacturers are selling a small nymph-collecting net these days. It consists of a fine nylon mesh seine measuring ten by twelve inches, and it rolls into a ten-inch package the thickness of two pencils. The free edges are reinforced, and the whole net is easily carried along the stream. It also has a white nylon center panel intended to make it easy to examine a captured nymph, but this white fabric is a well-intentioned mistake. Clambering and clinging nymphs are easily captured in spite of the white panel, but many swimming nymph species see it too easily and deftly avoid the net. You can make a fine pocket seine yourself, omitting the white panel and adjusting its length to your needs. One fisherman I know carries his rolled and secured with a rubber band, and hung from his belt loop with a screw eye and chain button. It can easily be disengaged for use. However, for serious nymph collecting you should construct a larger hand seine from fourteen-mesh metal or nylon window-screen material, and attach two three-quarter-inch dowels about thirty inches long to either end. The dowels should project about two inches below the seine. The seine area itself should measure about two by three feet. Small split-shot can be attached along the bottom of the seine to hold it along the river bed. The nymphs are then dislodged by disturbing the detritus and bottom trash and stones upstream from its meshes.

Burrowing nymphs that live in the bottom silts are most easily captured with a steel-frame scap net used in fish hatcheries. It consists of a relatively strong quarter-inch steel-wire frame that is virtually rigid and attached to a sturdy wooden handle. Its mesh bag should be strong enough to excavate and lift several pounds of bottom silts, and you will need a large white enamel hospital pan for sorting through the silts and organic detritus for your specimens.

Many swimming nymphs that inhabit open currents are as shy and quick-witted as baby trout, and are seldom captured with seines or scap nets. For them, fine nylon screening can be used on a heavy wire frame about twelve inches in diameter, attached to a sturdy wooden handle about six feet long, and used in the manner of a landing net to capture specimens. Eight-inch strainers attached to similar wooden handles are sometimes used to collect burrowing nymphs in deeper water, and can deftly capture specimens from surprisingly deep water when skillfully used.

Collecting freshly hatched and molting duns from the streamside foliage with the fingers is relatively easy for the larger species. Specimens of the tiny genera are more difficult, and such collecting must be done carefully to avoid damaging the insects. Mayflies are particularly fragile, and the slightest damage to their wings can make subsequent molting impossible. Some anglers have modified surgical tweezers for this purpose by rounding their points and fastening a thin surface of felt inside the jaws with modern adhesives. Others have constructed cube-shaped collecting traps of white bobbinet, leaving one flap open and illuminating them all night with electric torches from the inside. Many species are attracted to the light and gather on the netting. Specimens that land outside can be placed inside by hand. The collecting traps should be small enough to fit in a station wagon, since they can be used to transplant insects from one river to another while they are molting. The traps can be sited in a shady place where the newly hatched duns will feel secure and molt successfully to their imago stage. Sometimes you will find several species hatching together, and a number of outdoor molting cages may prove necessary to separate the specimens, making sure you will know which spinners hatched from which immature subimagoes. Such work is fascinating and rewarding.

Rearing live nymphs into their adult stages is difficult, but it is the only way we can be certain that a specific nymph hatches into a particular dun. Nymphs and duns are often more important to both fishermen and fish than the spinners, yet it is only the male spinners that are consistently described in the taxonomic tables that identify each species. Hatching nymphs evolve into duns in captivity, clearly establishing the identity of both stages, and when the subimagoes molt, the resulting spinner can be easily identified from the taxonomic keys.

Most nymphal forms can be reared and hatched in aquariums and photographed and observed through the glass walls. Constant water temperatures accelerate nymphal maturity, making a species hatch earlier than in its wild habitat. Some fast-water species adapt poorly to aquariums, needing both more oxygenation and current to thrive, although some success is possible with a striated board placed to receive a strong flow of cold water. Such species can also be raised and hatched in cylindrical wire cages, hung from a styrofoam raft that has been anchored in their natural habitat, using actual river stones laid on the bottom mesh. Portable vibrator aerators are required to furnish sufficient oxygen for many species in aquariums, and large beakers of the type used to incubate trout eggs are ideal mini-aquariums for isolating many carnivorous ecotypes. Water temperatures of sixty to sixty-five degrees are needed, and a few stones or plants from their original waters are advisable. Both tank aquariums and the beaker-size containers should be fitted with screened tops to trap the adult insects when they hatch, and a cylindrical cage fitted upside down is perfect for the beaker-type chamber. Fast-water nymphs are extremely interesting in aquarium conditions, and are often found clustered on the air hoses and beakers, holding tenaciously in the streaming bubbles.

Specimens can be preserved in glass lip-vials of the standard laboratory size. Ordinary corks are adequate stoppers for freshly collected material still under study, but rubber stoppers are mandatory for permanent storage. Strips of good paper should be carefully labelled with India ink from a fine-point pen like a ooo Rapidograph. Date, location, water character and other data are important. With nymphs reared in captivity, it is good practice to place the cast nymphal skins along with the hatched insects. Four parts ethyl alcohol to one part distilled water is a fine permanent preservative for the adult insects, with three parts alcohol to one part water for nymphs. Some technicians add a few drops of acetic acid to set the original color as much as possible, although it is difficult to preserve such color. Storage bottles must be full at all times or the specimens will incur breakage. Final storage should be cool and dark.

Collecting bottles carried on the stream are another problem, involving both easy handling and a relatively open throat that makes removing a specimen fairly simple. The killing-jar solution should be about ten parts distilled water, five parts ethyl alcohol, and one part acetic acid. This mixture is less expensive than the formulas outlined above, and much killing-jar fluid is lost in stream collection while fishing. The best collecting bottle I have found is the small Alka-Seltzer type, with its wide throat and smooth lip-free design. It is also important to carry one or two deep plastic boxes that fit into your wading-vest pockets, perhaps drilled with a few tiny ventilating holes. These are used to keep freshly hatched insects alive until they can be transferred to the molting cages.

Final identification of species is often based on wing venation in many aquatic insects. Experts mount the actual wings in microscope slides, but a wide-field binocular microscope would be much too costly for a fly-fishing entomologist. The wing venation can just as readily be studied by mounting the actual wings in a glass color-projector slide, projecting its image on a large sheet of paper, and tracing its outlines and venation for large-scale comparison. Other factors in identification of specific insect forms will be found in their physical structure, since the taxonomic keys are also based on abdominal morphology.

There are gadgets that can extract the contents of a trout's stomach without injuring the fish. Skues and others pioneered the use of a stainless marrow scoop for recovering stomach contents through the fish's throat. It took more than a little skill, both to penetrate the throat without hurting the fish and to withdraw the scoop without damaging the insects. Orvis is now offering a plastic suction device manufactured in England that is much safer and easier, and fishermen interested in what their fish have been eating can find out without killing them first by using the Aymidge extractor. It is a worthwhile development, I suppose, though it is also a somewhat insensitive violation of something as beautiful as a trout.

Stream thermometers are an important piece of equipment for a skilled angler. Hardy makes an excellent stream thermometer that resembles a fountain pen, its glass scale calibrated in both fahrenheit and centigrade. It is encased in a bright, temperature-sensitive metal shell. The thermometer and its casing are designed with a five-minute temperature lag to provide accurate water readings. Its top is fitted with both a keeper ring and fountain-pen clip, and I have used one for a number of years. Orvis is marketing a similar clip thermometer encased in a light metal case, with water perforations at its bulb. Its scale is not calibrated in centigrade readings. Both thermometers are quality products and easy to carry on the river, measuring only about six inches in length.

Vexilar manufactures a special thermometer designed for taking temperature readings in lakes and impoundments. It is lowered on a measuring line, allowed to remain for a few minutes, and quickly retrieved again. It has a built-in depth and thermal lag to provide accurate readings. Its information will pinpoint the thermocline temperature layers in a lake and help locate trout in hot weather.

Orvis is selling a field kit for testing water quality and chemistry. It will provide readings of dissolved oxygen, alkalinity and phosphates, carbon dioxide, nitrogen, hydrogen sulphide, and coliform counts. Such information will provide exceptional insights into the cycle of the season on your favorite waters, as well as monitor any denigration under the effects of pollution in the watershed. Armed with such information, you can actually trace the concentrations as well as the sources of that pollution, and function as a watchdog on your home waters. The kit has sufficient chemicals for approximately twenty-five tests, and each component is easily replaced. This pollution monitoring ability will unquestionably grow in importance in the years ahead.

My fishing friends Jim Ong and Roy Reinhardt originally designed the popular angler's log for William Mills & Son, but now this special diary is widely available from Leonard and other first-rate tackle shops. It is a thoughtfully designed item that can definitely catch you more fish in the future. It provides a two-page checklist for each day's fishing, and comes with twenty-five of these two-page fillers in a six-ring vinyl booklet. It is handsome and remarkably easy to use. Its checklist organizes all the necessary daily data in a series of brief entries that take most of the drudgery out of keeping an effective stream diary. Most entries merely involve checking a box or simply circling a number. The printed entries include fishing time, air and water temperatures, weather, barometer, wind, water conditions, and a galaxy of other relevant information. Refill pages are available. Having such a log before writing *Matching the Hatch* twenty years ago would have simplified my life.

Other gadgets are equally important. Fishing knives have always fascinated me since I first discovered a ring knife made just for dressing trout in a Von Lengerke & Antoine catalogue thirty years ago. The first really good basic fishing knife I owned was a Puma made in Solingen of beautiful German steel. It had a three-quarter-inch chromium steel priest opposite a razor-sharp blade and disgorger. The priest was heavy enough to dispatch a tarpon with authority. Its handles were handsomely grained Brazilian rosewood. The Puma knife was later stolen in Argentina, and since it had been a birthday gift, I have tried in vain to discover another place where it was sold.

There are two good fly-fishing knives available. One has a thirty-eight-inch tape in its handle, and it conceals a knife, file, small screwdriver, and a superbly machined pair of small scissors. Its entire length is slightly more than three inches, and it is made of fine nickel-alloy steel. Unfortunately, it does not have a clevis that can fasten it to a chain pin. Case made the ring-type trout knife years ago, and I have one of their stainless steel fly-fishing knives. Its handle is engraved with a three-inch rule. Its tools include a knife blade, stiletto, screwdriver, disgorger, and a small scissors precise enough to trim the wings and hackles of an overdressed fly. It has a clevis for clipping to a fishing vest, and totals four inches in length. Some fishermen like the occasional cold beer, though my preference leans toward a dry river-chilled Riesling or a fine bottle of Pouilly Fuissé. Such raffish tastes demand bottle openers and corkscrews, and I carry one of the incredible Swiss military knives that includes so many blades and attachments that it is literally a three-inch toolbox. Widely available, it is all stainless steel with a bright red handle. It has two sizes of knife blades, and two screwdrivers. It provides a can opener and a bottle-cap lever. One blade is both a nail file and a metal saw, and another is a combination of punch and reaming blade. The combination bottle opener and large screwdriver also has a wire-stripping slot, wire bender, and wire scraper. The disgorger has a fish-scaling edge, and a fine pair of scissors folds into the handle. The knife even has a toothpick and tweezers, a shackle is provided to attach it to your jacket, and its final triumph is a gleaming little corkscrew.

Most fly-fishermen use the standard angler's clipper that provides a stiletto, small blade, and disgorger on a strong woven lanyard. It is a fine little tool, useful for trimming off excess nylon protruding from a freshly tied knot. Hardy has a similar device in its small stainless scissor pliers, with finger holes thin enough to take the clip ring attached to a chain button inside your jacket. The jaws are useful for removing stubborn hooks from the fish—so long as they are not imbedded too deeply in the throat—and for seating lead shot on a leader. Both the scissors and the clipper must be closed when not in use, since any fly-line slack tangles easily in such gadgets in casting or playing fish.

Surgical forceps and hemostats are an essential component in the fishing vest of any skilled angler. Six inches long and exquisitely made with slender curving jaws, their ability to reach deep inside the throat of a fish, clamp a tiny fly with precision, and work its hook free with a simple push is unequalled. Forceps are also excellent for removing hooks from fishermen, breaking off hook shanks, and flattening barbs with precision. Their stainless steel workmanship is superb, and the locking device across the handles makes it possible to hang the forceps from the jaws outside your jacket—or use a pair as a streamside fly vise in emergencies.

It is surprising how long the fly retriever has been around. William Mills & Son illustrate an excellent version of this handy gadget in their catalogue of 1899. It was an even better design than the present type, with a rounded top for ready penetration into the foliage, and its cord pulled straight down from its cutting notch. It was seated on the fly rod with a rubber sleeve and raised over the twig where the flies were tangled. The rod was then slipped free and held away from danger, leaving the angler to pull hard on the cord and cut the offending foliage. Even when the branch was too thick to cut, you could often pull it within reach with the cord and free your leader. The Mills fly retriever came in a leather case. The modern version is a skeletal shape with a pin that slips into the tip guide, while the ten-foot cord held taut along the rod keeps it there until it is hooked over the intended branch. It is packed in a three-inch vinyl case.

Sharp hooks are far more important than many fishermen realize. Hook hones are not a recent fishing tool, but there are two types available today that are excellent. For streamside hook sharpening I use the miniature nickel-silver files with gem surfaces that have been developed in recent years. They are packaged in a thin vinyl case with a punched hole that can be attached to your vest. One is coarse-grained for big hooks, while the other is finely abrasive for tiny midge-sized flies. Orvis has recently introduced a new metal hone with a gem-surfaced groove, and a punched hole for attaching a lanyard. It comes highly recommended by skilled fishermen I respect. Pezon & Michel also make a fine French-designed carborundum hone that I keep in my fly-tying box. It is about two inches long, square in cross section, and tapered into a thin wedge. Hones should not be ignored in precise fishing.

Scales are something I seldom carried in the early years, when a two-pound brown looked like a broadbill swordfish, but on the rivers of Patagonia and our western mountains a lucky fisherman can often catch a fish worth weighing. Quality spring-loaded scales are usually built of nickel-plated brass. My equipment includes three scales. The smallest is an eight-pound balance manufactured by Hardy, and I carry it on most trips in the United States. The middle size is a thirty-pound scale that I bought the first time I went salmon fishing, and the largest is a fifty-pound scale purchased in Oslo after I had seen a forty-four pound salmon weighed in at Jøraholmen on the Alta. The following season it was a breathtaking thrill when that fifty-pound scale touched bottom with a Norwegian salmon of mine.

No tackle box is complete without a finely machined pair of needle-nose pliers. My pair is dual-chromium-plated to prevent corrosion, has lightly serrated jaws at the tips, and measures about eight inches in length. It includes a tempered wire cutter and is superb for removing hooks from people and fish.

Considerations of first aid and survival are also important in your tackle, particularly for fishing in frontier regions and back country. Cutter makes fishing first-aid kits and insect repellents. Their first-aid kit measures only five by eight inches, and contains medication for everything from a headache or minor hook prick in your finger to bleeding that must have a tourniquet or a rattlesnake bite. It is perfect for your tackle box, and Cutter also makes a letter-size pocket kit for a fishing vest. I also have no qualms about carrying prescription antihistamines, medication for diarrhea and dysentery, hyperacidity, muscle inflammation, and bursitis from too much casting. Fishing in our western mountains often means sun, very low humidity, and incessant wind. It can dry your skin until lips and fingers crack and split painfully. Your medicine kit should include healing cream for your hands and fingertips, chapsticks for your lips, and antisolar ointments if the sun broils your nose. Cutter also makes excellent insect repellents in both lotion and spray foam. Both types come in containers small enough to fit in a fishing-vest pocket easily. Western fishermen who fish in snake country, like the Big Wood Canyon below Magic Reservoir in Idaho or the Lower Deschutes in Oregon, commonly carry a separate Cutter snakebite kit on the stream. It includes a suction device, a surgical blade, antiseptic, and a one-hand lymph constrictor.

Survival presents some other equipment requirements. Waterproof matches are available, and in the back country I also carry a package of windproof matches wrapped and taped inside a vinyl sandwich bag. The two-ring cable saw consists of an eighteen-inch toothed wire, and when coiled it is smaller in diameter than a fly reel. The two rings can be used to stretch the saw taut like a bowstring by anchoring a bent limb between them. Since my trout fishing started in Michigan, I have carried a stainless two-piece drinking cup, purchased from the late Paul Young when I was only sixteen. It is a unique gadget made of two ovoid pieces of steel connected by a fixed pin that rides in a curved slot. The cup lies flat in your fly-box pocket, but warps and catches in a conical shape under pressure from the fingers. It has held everything from the icy water of snowmelt lakes in the Sangre de Cristo mountains of Colorado to exquisitely chilled Dom Perignon champagne, celebrating my first salmon in Norway. The so-called space blanket developed in recent years folds to pocket size, and is worth carrying in the back of your wading vest whenever you are in back country. It weighs only eleven ounces. It uses the principle of reflective insulation with its mylar lining, stays pliable at all temperatures, will not mildew or rot, and is completely windproof and watertight. Unfolded it measures fifty-six by eighty-four inches and, wrapped around your body, it functions as a temporary sleeping bag and tent combined. Wilderness fishermen should carry a compass like the fine little Silva Huntsman which folds flat in your pocket or the watch-size little German compass I carry. Military survival kits have given us another useful tool in the tiny one-ounce distress flares available in a three-flare vinyl pack. Each flare is about four inches long, and fires with a simple pull-chain. It will function in high winds and driving rain, shooting hundreds of feet above the water. The flare will burn with sufficient intensity to attract attention from miles around, in both darkness and daylight. Its casing is rustproof and floats. Like the pocket snakebite kit, this three-ounce watertight pack of flares could mean your survival in a crisis.

Many types of flashlights are used in fishing. Some anglers keep pencil-size lights in their pockets, and I have carried small conventional flashlights in my wader pocket. The flex-light type is designed for fishing, and will concentrate its beam exactly where it is needed, leaving both hands free to work. It is less than ten inches long. It consists of a barrel for the batteries, with a strong locking clip to anchor it firmly in the long inside pockets of a standard fishing vest. Its light is separate, attached to the battery case with a flexible gooseneck that will hold any position you choose. However, light should be used sparingly on the stream, since it can frighten the fish. Any time-consuming work should be done away from their principal holding lies, with your back turned to the trout.

Head nets are clumsy and annoying, but they are less annoying than the swarms of mosquitoes and biting blackflies along our north-country waters, particularly on a still evening in early summer. Orvis makes a head net attached to a cotton poplin hat with two layers of material, and a light ring at its brim. The net is a soft nylon mesh fitting with a second ring that hangs at about chin height, and enough length to fit down around the shoulders like a wrap-around muffler. Wearing such gear is far less troublesome than the insects—once I had both eyes almost swollen shut by blackflies on a river in the Labrador.

Your tackle box should also include a small tool kit with some reel lubricants. It ought to carry a small screwdriver and several assorted bits, a miniature adjustable wrench, small pliers, and oil in a handy pressure-needle applicator.

Reuben Cross used to like the story of the meticulous Wall Street investment banker who was a steady customer for the exquisite dry flies that made Cross a legend in the Catskills. The man had a battery of expensive fly rods that were sent back to their makers each winter for refinishing, his reels were impeccably cleaned and lubricated, the lines were British oiled silk which the man dressed and dried religiously, and he always wore a button-down shirt and silk challis tie when he was fishing.

But with my carefully tied flies, Cross paused and shook his head, *the man was a bloody barbarian!*

Cross would wince as he described the way the man clamped them tightly in his fist, and stuffed them into fly boxes already jammed with flies. It is tragic what such treatment can do to fine dry-fly hackles and tail fibers and perfectly cocked wings. Only putting flies away wet is worse.

Reuben Cross was certainly the robust Tintoretto of the Catskill school, and the perfect dry flies that came from his powerful hands were miraculous. Cross looked more like a rugged stevedore or lumberjack than an artist who worked in fur, feathers, and steel, but like all artists, there was something he gave of himself in everything he made. It was possible to buy his flies, but impossible to own them completely, and to treat such works of art with anything less than reverence is unacceptable. Only the trout should ultimately destroy them, since that fate is both their purpose and their destiny.

Dry flies should not be allowed to dry by themselves after fishing, and should never be hooked into those sheepskin pads that are ritually fastened on fishing vests. Such pads dry them beautifully, but flies become hopelessly bent out of shape against the wool. Knowledgeable fishermen carefully dry their flies before replacing them, both to prevent hook corrosion and its discoloration of a fly, and the matting of its delicate hackles. It can be done easily by carrying a piece of amadou, a dark European fungus once used by primitive surgeons for its remarkably absorbent qualities. Amadou quickly dries the fly and its hook, and a stubbornly matted hackle can sometimes be fully restored in the steam from a tea kettle. Silicote fly dressing can be applied to your dry flies before you fish with them, limiting the amount of water they will absorb. Some fishermen prefer to treat their flies in advance with a spray silicone rather than fully immerse them in silicote.

Deep wading often soaks into fly boxes and sheepskin hooks, and a fisherman should remove his flies to dry both their feathers and their containers. Cleaning and drying a fly on the stream when I was a boy usually consisted of washing it briefly in the current, drying it with a handkerchief, and dressing it with a homemade mixture of shaved paraffin and carbon tetrachloride. Bergman's *Trout* recommends a similar formula. Other anglers with more money and better sources of supply used the exotic amadou, which sounded like a palace in some Arabian fairytale in my boyhood years, and the liquid mucilin made by Aspinall in England. Its base is a mineral grease and its evaporative agent did not discolor the most delicately colored flies. Some fishermen preferred the paste mucilin, brushing the hackles of their flies lightly with a thin film of the dressing on their fingertips, and some purists like the late John Alden Knight, advocated using both liquid and paste mucilin on their flies.

Our modern silicone fly dressings are infinitely better than the traditional mineral- or paraffin-base ointments and oils. Their only fault is their cost. Silicote was the first of these modern fly dressings that became widely available after the Second World War, and it is still popular. Donald Du Bois is the author of the *Fly-Fisherman's Dictionary of Trout Flies*, and an old friend from past summers on the Letort Spring Run in Pennsylvania. Du Bois developed the fine dry-fly flotative called Up, which was the first pure silicone liquid for fishing. Unlike the earlier silicone oils, the Du Bois formula needs no drying immediately after application, and its restorative powers on the stream were a revelation. It is now available in a spray can for fishermen who prefer that method of application. Cortland and Orvis are both manufacturing a similar dry-fly oil in a small spray can, and I have used both with satisfaction. Charles Ritz is rapidly becoming the most famous tackle tinkerer in the history of the sport, and his contribution to dry-fly dressings is a remarkable silicone paste packaged in small plastic capsules. It is applied to the hackles in a fine film by the fingertips, and is a perfect solution for the fisherman who liked mucilin paste better than anything else. Pezon & Michel also makes a Siliflot dry-fly dressing packaged in a spray can, and a fly treated in their silicone-base spray plus a light application of paste on its hackles is virtually unsinkable. These new fly-floating products are superb.

Du Bois also developed a granular product for cleaning and drying the blood and fish slime from a fly. It is simply spilled into the palm, and the fly is rolled in it briefly. It dries such sinking dry flies, cleans their slimed and matted hackles almost instantly, and conditions their fibers like new. Du Bois called his formula Fly-Dry, and it solves a problem dry-fly fishermen have had since Pulman first described floating flies in 1841. Cortland is making a similar new compound that performs well, and Orvis is now selling a product which consists of a fine white powder. These fly-cleaning mixtures are not only useful at streamside, but also in maintaining a fine stock of flies.

Each line manufacturer makes a fly-line cleaner and conditioner for its products. Modern polyvinyl chloride lines are virtually indestructible in normal fishing, but they must be periodically cleaned of the microscopic aquatic residues that collect on their finishes. Plastic finishes must occasionally be conditioned and fed with a paste solvent to prevent hinging and cracking. Charles Ritz has developed a new Parabolic cleaner with Pezon & Michel that is among the finest available, and I use it regularly in my fishing. The best polyvinyl floating lines also need occasional dressing on the stream to function properly and float high. Mucilin and the red stag fat once sold by Hardy Brothers were long the finest line dressings available, but the appearance of the silicone pastes has ended their supremacy. Silicote is perhaps still the finest, and it should be lightly kneaded into the finish with the fingers along its final thirty feet only. Although there are handsome leather line dressers with felt linings, a line should probably be cleaned with a conditioner and handkerchief. It should be rubbed along its full length with your fingers twice, and then the excess paste should be removed with a clean handkerchief or felt pad. Such dressing is needed about once a week.

Modern nylon leaders also require much less maintenance than the silkworm-gut leaders of the past. Their relative specific gravity is higher than gut, and leader-sinking compounds became more important as the surprisingly tough, limp nylons began to make gut leaders obsolete. Various leader-sink formulas are available, and are usually detergents and other wetting agents. Such dressings are important in getting a wet-fly presentation on a high-density line to sink readily, for the buoyancy of the nylon can ride back toward the surface and neutralize the depth of swing achieved by the line. Many old-time fishermen used ordinary soap on their leaders, and it was the cantankerous Bob Carmichael who predictably discovered the most unusual leader sink.

Hang on! He growled and hobbled to a garbage can behind his fly counter. *You need some leader sink.*

I've already got some, I said.

Not like my secret compound! he wheezed theatrically. *It's the best damn leader sink in the world.*

What is it? I asked him innocently.

Carmichael's mud! he said.

Bob Carmichael loved his private jokes, and he laughed to himself as he filled two little boxes with a dark slate-colored clay. His leader-sink compound was excellent, but he never would tell me what it was. Carmichael always shrugged like some wry bulldog and called it Carmichael's mud. Twenty-five years later I discovered it was really bentonite, an unusual clay soil common in Wyoming that readily absorbs water and expands radically when wet.

Leader-sink compounds are widely used as a quick wetting agent for flies and nymphs, and bentonite is superb for that purpose too. However, saliva is also useful and the spectacle of an old-time fisherman with three snelled flies in his mouth was familiar on my boyhood rivers.

One minor problem with nylon is its memory, particularly in the hard, relatively stiff types. It twists and kinks badly, often spiralling off a fly reel like a coiled spring. Stretching it carefully will straighten a nylon leader in a few seconds, and many fishing writers have recommended carrying a piece of inner tubing to fold over the leader and draw firmly along its full length. This straightens a leader partially by stretching it and partially with heat generated by friction. Like bamboo in a fine rod, the molecular structure of nylon is essentially linear and parallel to the leader itself. Stretching a coiled or twisted leader with a little heat forces the molecules back into their linear alignment, pulling it straight again, but too much heat scrambles its molecules and seriously weakens its breaking strain. Thermal strain and its resulting molecular dislocation is the reason why a perfectly formed nylon knot sometimes breaks when it is too hastily drawn tight. Knots that are too quickly tightened can generate enough heat to destroy the tensile strength of their nylon. Donald Du Bois worked out a superb leather-backed rubber pad for stretching leader material, which he christened the Curl-A-Way, and a similar leader straightener is since available at Orvis.

Leader materials are often incorrectly marked, perhaps through careless sorting and spooling at the factory, and in making your own leaders or splicing fresh tippets the nylon strands should not drop more than .001 inch in the small diameters. New tippet spools should always be checked, and only a precision micrometer can provide accurate data. Such micrometers are also useful for checking line diameters and taper specifications. Orvis offers one that gives convenient dial readings, with a table of line and leader diameters on its back, although it is less precise than the small micrometers used in industrial work.

Many nymph fishermen have learned that a little split shot on the leader will get their flies on the bottom, and take fish that are seldom taken with conventional gear. Scissor pliers are needed to seat them on the leader, and there is a fine six-compartment rotary pack of assorted shot sizes made by Pezon & Michel. Some of these tiny shot seem virtually impossible to make, and are difficult to attach to anything but the finest tippets. Their delicacy makes it possible to cast with something approaching normal rhythms, because their smallness creates little atmospheric drag or eccentricity of concentrated weight. The reusable split shot are also effective under many conditions, and can be carried in several sizes.

There are a number of gadgets for forming blood knots for making tapered leaders, but I have always found it harder to master such knot-making devices than simply forming the knot with my fingers. The best blood-knot former is only an inch square, and there are fishermen who use it religiously. However, there is one important knot that cannot be shaped without a proper tool. Bud Lilly sells a nail-knot tool for attaching leaders and backing to line. It is a simple steel eye pin with a flattened and perforated tip and a lanyard for hanging it from a fishing vest. However, some weeks ago I was asked to demonstrate a simple nail knot in a friend's shop, and in searching for an adequate mandrel for shaping the knot, we discovered that a small Phillips-head screwdriver was perfect. The leader butt could be threaded effortlessly under the primary coils of the knot, and it seated cleanly when I pulled it from the bit with a gentle tug. Perhaps a nail-knot tool with a slotted tip would prove more effective.

Leader cases are another problem. Mine are fifteen years old, the elegant British type made years ago by Wheatley. The covers are light brown pigskin about five inches square and close with an intriguing German silver expansion hinge. The insides consist of six interlocking bellows pockets made of parchment. These leader books were expensive fifteen years ago, and it is unfortunate that they are no longer made. Many seasons ago, my father gave me a round leader box of aluminum. It was designed to store silkworm-gut leaders between felt pads moistened with glycerine and distilled water. When nylon became better, I continued to use the case out of mere habit, but eventually I came to dislike its rolling around in my inside bellows pockets. It invariably jammed awkwardly among my fly boxes or got hidden in a far corner. There are a number of snap-closure leader cases available in both leather and vinyl, with transparent envelopes sewn inside. Wheatley still makes a fine aluminum fly and leader box with separate compartments for leaders and flies. Its fly compartment provides seventy-five spring clips for several sizes of wet flies and nymphs. Its leader compartment has a snap cover with felt pads and a protecting flange to hold them in place.

Fly books have long been a weakness of mine, ever since I sat in the grass along the Platte in Michigan twenty-five years ago admiring the pigskin fly books of my father and his friends. Their books were literally bulging with huge numbers of English wet flies and streamer patterns from Maine, rich with feathers of junglecock and bright accents of kingfisher and blue chatterer and macaw.

Since that time I have preferred fly books for carrying streamers as well as wet flies or nymphs too small for the English clip boxes. Leather books lined with fine sheepskin are perfect for holding and carrying big streamers and bucktails so long as they are not so crammed with flies that the feathers are bent and crushed. The sheepskin dries the moisture and prevents hook corrosion, although wading too deep can play havoc with a leather fly book when it really gets soaked. Bucktails and streamers should be stroked into shape with the fingers while they are still damp, and then folded carefully between the covers of a fly book. Wet flies and nymphs smaller than about size fourteen are dressed on hooks of wire so fine that they will not clip firmly in a wet-fly box. Such small flies are perfectly suited to fly books, and there is an excellent leather-covered Reed fly book with a number of soft pressed-felt leaves. It is fine for carrying tiny wets and midge-size nymphs in large numbers.

Fly boxes have been another serious weakness of mine since that long-ago afternoon at Von Lengerke & Antoine in Chicago, when I first saw the English Wheatleys with their transparent spring-clip lids over each compartment. Such boxes are only three-quarters of an inch deep and should not be used for dry flies larger than about ten or twelve, since they will hold too few of each pattern without crushing their hackles. For larger patterns I still use the standard plastic boxes with twelve or sixteen compartments, depending on fly size. These transparent boxes are surprisingly strong and fitted with stainless hinges. Standard plastic boxes measure eight and one-quarter by four and one-quarter by one and one-quarter inches in the depths suited to large dry flies. Orvis is making a similar eighteen-compartment box with a white opaque bottom and clear plastic lid. They are also making a pair of slim plastic boxes measuring seven and a half by three and one-quarter by seven-eighths inches, with the same white bottoms and transparent lids. The eighteen-compartment design is excellent for small dry flies, and the six-compartment box has three-and-one-quarter-inch trays for bucktails and streamers.

The Richard Wheatley boxes offer something more than mere fly storage to a serious fisherman. They are like a fine split-cane rod or an exquisitely machined reel in the sense that their design and functional qualities and workmanship are combined into a character that can only be described as esthetic. That fine equilibrium between function and beauty has a primary role in the ethic of fly-fishing. Wheatley boxes are made of a heavy gauge aluminum alloy in a smooth satin finish. The fly clips are stainless steel. The transparent plastic covers for each dry-fly compartment are held in place with delicate stainless springs and clip latches. It is easy to understand how anglers have been enchanted with these Wheatley boxes since the Halford era on the chalkstreams.

Wheatley boxes come in a large number of designs. Some have a foam pad in the lid for drying flies, while others provide a numbered index table to identify their contents. Such tables are fine for those lazy-minded fishermen who never seem to remember the names of their fly patterns, let alone the insects they imitate. Their forgetfulness means that the contents file occupies lid space that could hold more wet-fly clips.

The Silver Seal models that I prefer and carry are the clip-style that carry wets and nymphs in both bottoms and covers. For dry flies I use the compartment-type boxes with wet-fly clips in their lids. The following designs are my favorites in the exquisite Wheatley line:

F224–6   The most simple wet-fly box, measuring five-eighths by three and a half by six inches, holding 140 flies in its bottom and lid.

F231–6   The slightly larger swing-leaf wet-fly box is an inch thick and adds a thin middle leaf of aluminum. Its capacity is 280 wet flies and nymphs.

F234–6   This one-inch-thick fly box has a swing-leaf and stainless clips for 140 larger wet flies and nymphs.

F251–6   This one-and-a-half-inch-thick box has spring-lid compartments in both lids, totaling thirty-two sections. It is the premium trout-fly model.

F251C–6   This model comes in either ten or sixteen snap-lid compartments, and measures one by three and a half by six inches, with fifty-eight wet-fly clips in the cover. The sixteen-compartment box is designed for smaller flies, and the ten-compartment version comes with six compartments of one and three-eighths by one and five-eighths inches, for larger dry flies.

F251C–4¾   This model also comes in two types, both having forty-one wet-fly clips in the lid. One provides twelve spring-lid compartments, and the other has only eight, since four are of the larger dry-fly size. These designs are perfectly suited to the intermediate size pockets found on many of the new wading vests.

F251C–3½   The tiny compartment box measures only three-quarters by two and three-eighths by three and a half inches, and has six spring-lid compartments with clips for twenty-one wet flies and nymphs. It is small enough for a shirt pocket and ideally suited for minute dry flies or hot weather.

F299A   This fly box measures only one-half by two and three-quarters by three and a half inches with tiny clips for fifty-one wet flies and nymphs.

F298   Also designed for wet flies and nymphs in a shirt-pocket size, and fitted with a swing leaf. It is a one by two and three-quarters by three-and-a-half-inch design holding 102 fly patterns.

Wheatley has also introduced some new Black Seal fly-box designs that hold the flies in stainless coil springs. The F273–1 has ten springs mounted across the width of both the bottom and lid. It will hold any type of fly, of course, but it will hold delicate no-hackle and trimmed spent-wing spinners and long-tailed drakes better than anything else. Such flies are tied with delicate tail fibers, and their wings and hackles should lie absolutely flat in the surface film. The coil-spring clips should hold such flies by their hook bends and protect their delicate dressings. Some nymphs are tied with flat bodies that will not lie properly in a standard clip box, or have legs tied to project laterally from the thorax. Such nymphs should perhaps also be stored in the coil-spring boxes.

The Wheatley fly boxes complete my observations on fly-fishing tackle and clothing, except for a precision device recently perfected in Switzerland for Orvis. It is a remarkable new wristwatch that Orvis has appropriately called the solunagraph.

The watch naturally records standard solar time and has a sweep second hand, but it has a number of other unusual features. The stop-watch chronograph dials record duration time of a trip, given compass heading in poor visibility, and elapsed time for fuel capacity or scuba-tank oxygen. The bezel indicates the hour in the time zone of your departure while the watch itself displays the time at your destination. The watch can tolerate diving operations well below three hundred feet, so it is clearly waterproof enough for a fly-fisherman. But the unique feature of the Solunagraph is a lunar dial that records the phases of the moon, tidal actions, and the solunar feeding periods of the fish.

It was the late Samuel Jennings who first argued for combining the hatching calendars in *Matching the Hatch* with the solunar theory. Jennings had also worked out his own Catskill version of Howitt's *Book of the Seasons*, combining it with charts on the entomology of his favorite rivers and the solunar tables. His chronography equated the early stoneflies and Gordon Quills with the first budding leaves, Red Quills and Hendricksons with flowering shadbush, and the first hatching of the fluttering olive-bodied sedges with the dogwoods.

My time in life means old tweeds fit my character, Jennings explained wryly before his death. *Complicated theories give me comfort, and I like intellectual crutches in difficult currents and difficult times. Hardy makes a bamboo wading staff for a fisherman like me, and just any old stick won't do!*

Samuel Jennings is gone now, part of those eternal cycles he observed and loved on the storied Catskill streams, but I have never forgotten that fly-dressing night years ago at the Fraunces Tavern quarters of the Anglers' Club of New York.

Howitt understood the clues in the seasons, Jennings ended his soliloquy. *He called them the silent language of the Deity.*

Jennings intrigued me with his observations, and I started to study the relationships between the solunar cycles and the fly hatches that started the fish working. Local weather conditions sometimes cancelled them out, along with factors like excessive water temperatures and turbidity, but it was surprising how often the fly hatches and heavy rises of trout coincided rather well with the solunar theories.

There was an unusual example this last year on my home mileage of the Brodheads in Pennsylvania. It was a cold April morning with a raw wind when we reached the stream, and I did not feel much like fishing. My father had not yet fished that spring, and he was eager to get started in spite of the slightly milky current. It started to rain when I opened the trunk of the Mercedes, hard and straight down into the river, and it erased the last of my own urge to fish that morning.

You going to try it? my father asked.

No. I shook my head. *It's too wet and cold, and look at the river—it's like strong coffee and getting worse!*

What'll you do? he asked.

Don't know, I said. *Maybe I'll tie flies in the car.*

Think I'll try fishing, he said.

The rain settled into a steady rhythm on the roof of the car, and I sat in the feather-littered seat with the vise attached to the glove compartment. There was a row of dark little Blue Quills sitting beside the vise, and I suddenly realized I was hungry. The picnic basket was still in the trunk, and the rain had stopped when I carried it toward the weathered table two hundred yards below the bridge. The river looked less milky.

Strange, I thought, *with all the rain.*

The sandwiches tasted good with the hot coffee from the thermos, and I sipped it slowly, studying the river beyond the trees. It looked different in some unexplained change of mood, and a warm wind eddied downstream. Fly hatches usually come between noon and three o'clock that week in April, and I glanced at my solunagraph. It was now almost four, but the moon clock predicted a major period of activity. The river flowed smooth and silent under the buttonwood trees, and suddenly, tight along the willows upstream I saw the first trout rise.

The fish came up again several seconds later, and then I saw a tiny *Paraleptophlebia* mayfly coming off the current. Two others flew downstream, working toward the wet foliage, and several fish were rising steadily now. It was clearly a hatch, and I quickly shouldered into my fishing gear.

The little Blue Quills lying on the glove compartment door were a perfect imitation, and I coaxed them into a fly box carefully. I clinch-knotted one to the leader and sprayed it lightly with silicone. The fish were working greedily in the run along the willows upstream, and when I dropped my little fly above the fish that had been the first to rise, it took quickly. It was the best hatch I saw the entire spring and I took twenty-odd fish in the next two hours. It was simply a matter of getting a decent float over a fish, landing and releasing it quickly, and getting the fly in shape to float again. Slowly the rhythms of the hatch ebbed and died, and I waded happily back to the car.

My father was already breaking down his tackle, and he was smiling broadly. *You tried it after all. How'd you do on this pool?*

Pretty well the last two hours, I said.

Fish started coming about four-thirty at the Slide Pool. My father capped his rod case. *Took a small Blue Quill for an hour.*

That's right, I said.

What were those little flies? he asked.

Paraleptophlebia adoptiva, I replied. *They usually hatch in late morning and early afternoon this time of year.*

How do you explain their hatching so late?

My solunagraph said it was a major period, I laughed.

Your solunagraph was right! he said.

Orvis has recently developed an unusual fishing tool. Its accuracy is remarkable, and that episode on the Brodheads has been repeated many times on trout and salmon rivers in several countries. My solunagraph is a regular companion these days.

Several years ago Ed Zern observed that my book *Matching the Hatch* was outrageously expensive when its cost-per-pound was considered. Zern has since decided, fixing me with a level eye, that somebody like Orvis should design a tiny chest-pack computer with the data of both *Nymphs* and *Matching the Hatch* in its memory bank. The fisherman could then take temperature readings of both the water and the atmosphere, determine the barometric conditions, check the current for alkalinity and dissolved oxygen, describe the fly hatches of the preceding days from insects trapped in the cobwebs between bridge struts, record pertinent data about cloudiness and precipitation and water clarity, and feed in the solunar data. Zern concluded his poker-face dissertation with the observation that a fisherman could finally press the read-out button on his computer and it would tell him exactly what tippet and fly to use.

But they had to abandon it, he mused sadly.

Why? Somebody delivered the straight line like a hatchery brookie taking a Mickey Finn. *Why give it up?*

Cybernetic science has its limits, Zern continued. *They don't build those old trusswork bridges any more, so the spiders can't spin cobwebs that catch yesterday's fly hatches, and we had trouble with the computer prototypes.*

What kind of trouble? I asked.

Maybe it lacked enough circuits or transistors or something. Zern added more sour mash whiskey to his glass and sat philosophically admiring its slowly mingling colors. *But even with its memory bank stuffed with entomology and solunar theory, it always came up with the same answer.*

What was that? I laughed guardedly.

Worms, he smiled.

For recent developments in streamside equipment, see Appendix: Notes on New Equipment.

5. Observations on the Modern Fly Reel

It was surprisingly warm that evening on the Alta, almost a dozen years ago, when I had been invited to fish the river in a party that included the Duke of Roxburghe. It is a legendary river among fly-fishermen, lying deep in the forest barrens of arctic Norway. The writings of Charles Ritz had first introduced me to the Alta legend in his charming *Fly Fisher's Life*, and the anticipation of fishing it made me restless. After dinner in the charming old Jøraholmen farmstead, I wandered out to the ghillies hut while the other anglers gathered their tackle for the night's fishing.

It never really gets dark during midsummer on the Alta, almost a thousand miles north of Oslo, and the sun was still warm on the rough-sawed walls of the ghillies' hut. The boards were brightly painted with a primitive mixture of iron oxides and milk, the ancestor of thousands of red outbuildings and barns from arctic Lapland westward to Oregon and British Columbia.

Carved larchwood hooks held a dozen fly rods under the protective eaves of the moss-grown roof. Most of the rods were the two-handed type, of English and Scottish manufacture, with a single Castle Connell Greenheart from Ireland, and there were two or three American rods only slightly smaller—exquisite Paynes with their richly perfect finish, Leonards with their pale bamboo, and a newer two-handed Orvis.

The reels were primarily English, like the four- and five-inch Hardy Perfects with the patina of a fine double shotgun. The Paynes and Leonards carried elegant Vom Hofe and Walker reels, and the solitary Orvis was fitted with a finely machined Bogdan.

It was a rich display of beautiful salmon tackle, but three of the rods were mounted with unfamiliar aluminum reels that I had never seen before. These huge reels were almost eight inches in diameter, elegantly machined and perforated, with the look of highly skilled hand labor. The aluminum already had the gleaming quality of time, the character usually found in antique rifles or pistols from the American frontier, and they were engraved with the name Roxburghe. Finally, the Duke of Roxburghe came down to the ghillies' hut to check his equipment.

Those are remarkable reels, I said. *I've never seen anything like them.*

The Duke smiled faintly. *They're quite old,* he explained. *Hardy built them for my grandfather almost a century ago.* He took his rods down and passed them carefully to his boatmen.

But they look like aluminum! I said.

They are. Roxburghe nodded.

But modern aluminum processing didn't start until 1886, I said, *and the famous Conroy aluminum reels first appeared in 1878—that makes these even older!*

Yes, Roxburghe shook his head. *Hardy made each reel specially by hand to my grandfather's specifications—he was fascinated with aluminum and he wanted reels with enough diameter that each turn retrieved considerably more line.*

Reels? I asked. *How many were there?*

Twelve, Roxburghe replied. *Each was engraved with his name and its identifying number.*

And these are numbers six and nine, I said.

Yes, Roxburghe nodded.

It's remarkable that you're still fishing them almost a century later. I shook my head in disbelief. *They're probably the first examples of aluminum reels.*

Perhaps they are, Roxburghe agreed.

Although our early chapters demonstrate that fishing reels first evolved in China before the twelfth century and that Thomas Barker apparently introduced reels to British literature in his *Art of Angling* five hundred years later, the modern fly reel is surprisingly recent.

Primitive reels were probably fashioned of wood. Black walnut reels were still manufactured and popular as late as 1930, and British makers like Foster and Hardy regularly featured them in their catalogues. But reels of brass and German silver and aluminum had begun to dominate fly-fishing toward the close of the nineteenth century. Since few trout fishermen had much experience with fish large enough to make reel-wearing runs deep into the backing, and our fine modern nylons were not introduced until after midcentury, most fishing writers paid surprisingly little attention to reels.

Bergman is a good example. His classic book *Trout* devotes surprisingly little space to fly reels, except to comment on line capacity for steelhead fishing and his preference for left-hand reeling. Other well-known writers seem to concur in the observation that reels are meant merely to store line and backing, and are both the least expensive and least important item in one's tackle boxes.

It is time to terminate such mythology. Our lack of concern for the importance of the fly reel and its performance undoubtedly results from two factors. Our major fishing writers were British or American experts with little experience with big fish and really big water. When *Trout* was written, Bergman had had only a brief exposure to steelhead and salmon, and to the grinding stresses such fish can place on our tackle. Our trout were far less crowd-shy in those years, and a .008 silkworm-gut tippet was considered fishing really fine. Modern limp nylons with their delicate .003 to .005 diameters were not available then, so the smooth-running qualities of a precision reel in surrendering line to a bolting fish were much less critical. The lessons of our big western rivers, with their sea-armored steelheads and cartwheeling rainbows, have taught us that line capacity, fine machining, and firm drag systems are extremely important. Twenty years of experience at the opposite end of the spectrum, with fragile tippets on highly selective trout, have also demonstrated the unmistakable importance of delicate click-and-drag mechanisms that will not shear .003 nylon on a running fish. Fine reels must contend with both kinds of problems.

Webster is correct in defining a reel as a diminutive windlass fitted to the butt of the rod, its principal function to surrender and retrieve line in fishing—but a truly modern fly reel is much more. It should provide sufficient weight to balance the rod and complement its casting dynamics, it must provide sufficient capacity for both fly line and backing, its precision and drag system must be smooth enough to fish relatively fine leader tippets without shearing them, and its ability to surrender line grudgingly and retrieve it swiftly are also important qualities in playing a fish once it is hooked and fighting.

Past ratios of rod-and-reel balance recommended that a reel should weigh approximately fifty percent more than the rod. Application of such ratios means that a four-ounce rod would call for a fly reel weighing six ounces. However, these ratios evolved during the years when split-bamboo rods ruled the fishing world, and reels were principally made of aluminum and German silver.

Modern materials have upset such traditional thinking, in both the construction of rods and fly reels. The conventional ratio dictating a reel weighing fifty percent more than the rod should not be applied too literally. Reels are being made of remarkable new alloys of surprising weight reductions and strength. English fly reels of conventional aluminum weighed about three and a half ounces in a three-inch diameter model, but aerospace metallurgy has made it possible to fabricate reels of that size weighing only three ounces. In converting from German silver to modern aluminum alloys, the superbly crafted Walker trout reels have become a full three ounces lighter in the three-inch model. Similar reductions in weight first came with the hollow-built Winston and Powell rods on the Pacific Coast, which reduced the weight of eight- to nine-foot rods as much as ten to fifteen percent. Such developments in cane construction made the usual line- and reel-weight recommendations obsolete. Fiberglass rods caused even more radical changes. Rods balanced with eight-weight lines weighed about four and three-quarter ounces in bamboo to only three and three-quarter ounces in the new synthetic materials. Such changes mean that a weight ratio of two-to-one for reel and rod is possible—and a three-ounce fiberglass rod is perfect with a six-ounce reel.

Recent field experience on the Pacific Coast steelhead rivers with an experimental tubular rod of carbon graphite clearly proves that our formulas for matching our rod-and-reel weights are totally outmoded. Both high-modulus graphite and boron fiber fly rods are so light, relative to their stiffness and power, that a rod designed for an eight-weight line in these synthetic materials can weigh much less than three ounces. Such graphite and boron construction will undoubtedly make a six-ounce reel a viable match for rods weighing as little as two and one half ounces.

Capacity can also dictate similar rod-and-reel weight ratios, particularly when we are fishing tackle somewhat lighter than usual for the water. Perhaps fishing big rainbows with light gear yet needing the capacity for more than one hundred yards of backing to handle their tail-walking runs is typical of situations where the reel might be twice the weight of the fly rod. Steelhead fishing offers even more exaggerated examples: a field-testing session in California once found me fishing a graphite rod weighing just over three ounces with a ten-weight forward taper line and two hundred yards of backing on a British reel weighing eight ounces.

Such fishing also means relatively long casting, and with average line lengths beyond sixty feet, the old ratios of rod-and-reel balance no longer matter. The length of line load brings an extra heavy reel into perfect equilibrium. Obviously there are no immutable rules-of-thumb for balancing fly rods and reels. It should be decided by your strength, your casting skills, and what feels right in covering the kind of water you usually fish; adding lead weights or lengths of solder inside your reel frame to meet theoretical ratios of weight is merely an inertial preoccupation with obsolete theories of balance.

Reel specifications and design are important too.

Obviously, basic reel design lies between the polarities of the most line capacity at the lightest weight. The larger the line capacity the greater the stresses on reel frame and spool and parts, yet maximum reduction in weight pares away at the thickness of each component. Big fish can actually rack the reel frame of a lightweight design, and the dynamic loading of thin backing can even distort a delicate reel-spool alloy, causing it to bind and freeze. Reel frames that are cast or brazed into a single piece are superior to reels assembled with set screws, since the screws both add weight and tend to work loose. Some anglers modify such reels by setting the screws in a locking compound, but this makes dismantling for repairs difficult.

Precisely machined tolerances in the gears and ratchets are important too, along with the fit of the drag springs and pawls. Poor springs are a serious problem. Sometimes fishermen forget to release their drag settings between fishing sessions, seriously fatiguing the temper of the springs. Metal fatigue can cause a drag spring to snap under the run of a heavy fish, and its metallic death rattle is a harsh and frightening sound.

Breaking a drag spring means the reel is free-spooling dangerously out of control, and it can easily overrun and snarl the line. Such a tangle can break off the running fish, and if the rod is held high to counter a really long run, its fragile tip is in danger too.

Line-guide design is also important. Early fly reels were not fitted with special line guides, and this resulted in excessive wear on the frames at the pillars. Some manufacturers responded with a primitive version of the rolling pillars now found on expensively made modern reels. The classic round line guide had its debut on the exquisitely made Hardy Perfect, its hand-polished agate guides fitted into a delicate German silver fitting seated into the frame with four tiny set screws. It was a beautifully designed reel of classic simplicity, and it still sells for as much as fifty to eighty dollars when a well-kept Perfect is available. But experience with round line guides on big fish points up a serious conceptual flaw in their performance, however beautiful their appearance. The round line guide inescapably concentrates the line in the center of the spool, reducing its capacity before the line accumulates and binds against the pillars. Line can also slip off the mounding layers in the center of the spool, tangling and jamming when a good fish starts to run and strip out line. Such reels are not recommended in the larger big-fish sizes. Reels fitted with semicircular line guides of heavy gauge steel wire are also troublesome, and the best designs are the simple U-shaped line guides of German silver, stainless steel, and specially hardened alloys fitted to the reel frame. Such guides allow the fisherman to distribute the line evenly and smoothly on the spool as he retrieves it from a good fish, and they effectively reduce wear when line is stripped off while casting. Rough places and nicks should be polished down with a fine file or abrasive cloth, should they form in a reel frame, and a damaged line guide should be replaced.

Performance in capacity and drag systems is easily attained in reels not required to have a click mechanism precise enough and smooth enough to fish .003 to .005 tippets, but only the finest reels are capable of both qualities. Such reels are not inexpensive, and a serious angler should not buy cheap copies. Such economy can cost you the biggest fish of your career if it makes a run strong enough to test a reel, and good fish hooked on light tippets will probably shear them by simply bolting against the click system. Even some light reels ostensibly designed for delicate rods have click mechanisms too balky and coarse for nylon finer than .005, and their intermediate price is money wasted on hard-fished trout.

Line capacity is also important. Obviously, sufficient backing is needed to handle big fish in heavy water, but the backing has another function. It has a silent role in playing every fish you hook, even if many are not large enough to take out much line. Such backing forms an arbor, magnifying spool diameter and the length of line recovered with each turn of the reel. Quick recovery of line is a major factor in playing a fish effectively, and the backing multiplies the rate at which line is returned to the spool.

Few trout will make runs that strip an entire fly line from the reel, except for big rainbows or steelheads fresh from salt water. However, a good reel should have the muscle to stand up under such pressure. Since there are trout large enough to make runs of more than 150 feet in many average-size streams—including the gentle brown-trout rivers of our eastern mountains—reels that cannot hold thirty yards of fly line with another fifty yards of backing are not workable tools. Some of the tiny reels designed for ultralight rods under two ounces provide only twenty yards of backing behind a three- or four-weight line. Although these reels are exquisitely machined, their limited line capacity rules them out on water holding really large trout with sufficient room to make a sustained run. It is wise to choose your tackle on the basis of the biggest fish that might be hooked on your favorite waters, not by the prevailing fashions in lighter and lighter equipment. Too little line could cost you the fish of a lifetime.

The quality of the drag system is critical in a reel intended for fishing big water. Few conditions call for leader tippets of more than twelve-pound breaking strain, except perhaps huge bucktails or marabous in high winds, and a drag system capable of exerting eight to ten pounds is more than adequate for the most demanding sea-run fish. Such systems vary widely in quality and design, and few trout reels are capable of drag settings much over three or four pounds. Few rivers will require heavier drag systems, and most small reels have drags designed primarily to prevent inertial overruns that can free-spool and tangle the line.

Drag systems are designed to operate only when the line is running out with a fish. Retrieving line is not wound against the drag setting, only the click mechanism is engaged. It should be remembered that drag systems are usually set when the reel is relatively full. Therefore, the effective moment arm forcing line from the spool equals the distance from the center of its spindle to the outermost layers of fly line. When line is stripped from the reel, this radius becomes shorter and shorter. With half of the line capacity expended, the distance is also reduced by fifty percent, and the force required to turn the spool must be doubled. The laws of physics mean that a three-pound drag set when the reel was filled will resist a six-pound pull when it is almost empty, and this strain is added to line friction in both the rod guides and the water. Drag settings must be used judiciously, because of the strain exerted by an emptying reel on the tippet diameter.

Cheap drag systems pose a more serious problem. The tension required to start the spool is heavier than the drag exerted once the reel is spinning. Such performance spells trouble. The starting tension might be set at three or four pounds, but while a fish is running, only one or two pounds are working. Such a run might last fifty yards into the backing, increasing the inertial drag steadily as the dwindling line decreases the moment arm between the axis of the spool and its pulling point. Such radical variations in drag are troublesome, but a fish that suddenly stops and bolts again is a disaster. The two- or three-pound drag of the turning reel drum ends abruptly, and a fresh run that starts the spool with most of the line gone can exert as much as six or seven pounds of drag. These radical changes in pressure can both break a leader or literally work the fly free. Such oscillating drag systems are unacceptable. Since the best drag mechanisms exert considerably more tension as the reel spool is emptied, the drag should never be set at more than forty percent of rated breaking strain for the leader. It is a lesson that must be learned.

Reel-spool design is also important. The workmanship must be precise, with a strongly made spindle and side plates. The drum should be as light as possible without distorting under the tension of a heavy fish. The drum plates should be smoothly tapered or slightly convex, so the width at the spindle is approximately forty to fifty percent less than the outer width of the spool. Such refinements mean the line layers more quickly near the spindle, where the mechanical advantage is least, and most of the line is concentrated near the circumference of the spool. Line can be controlled and recovered better there, and the reel will spin less rapidly while line is being surrendered to a running fish. Fine reels like the Hardy Lightweight series carry this convex spool feature one step farther, placing more exaggerated convexity on the ratchet face of the spool and the midpoint of its spindle off center, locating it approximately halfway between the weight of the gear system and backplate and the position of your fingers on the handle of the reel. It is such refinements, as well as exquisite workmanship, that make an expensive reel easily worth its price.

Automatic reels are designed with a tightly coiled spring system surrounding the spindle. The spring is tightened by turning the face cover of the reel or by stripping out line, and its tension recovers line with a slight finger pressure on their triggers. Although automatic reels are made of aluminum, and their manufacturers were among the pioneers in using that material, the working springs are steel and relatively heavy. Automatic reels lack the capacity to hold more line than the fly line itself, and their inability to provide backing is a serious fault. Automatic reels also weigh from eight to twelve ounces, without the extra weight of the fly line, an unacceptable weight-to-capacity ratio. The inadvertent triggering of the reel can shear a light tippet, and the spring is wound tighter and tighter as a fish takes line. Such tension can break a fine leader, and although some automatic reels can release their tension with a half-turn of the casing that encloses the spring, it is such a crude system that it can also shear a tippet or tear the fly free from a running fish. These shortcomings make automatic reels unsuitable for serious trout fishing, and the loss of a big rainbow on the Gunnison in my boyhood years convinced me that single-action reels were infinitely better.

The modern reel has an interesting history. Its evolution can certainly be traced to the simple brass and nickel-plated reels common before the Civil War, and the elegantly made German silver variations imported from British tackle makers. Thomas Conroy was selling fine fly reels with black rubber faceplates and spools, plate trim, and other fittings of German silver as early as 1873. Many of the best early reels were sold under the trademark of Dame, Stoddard & Kendall, the fine old tackle company in

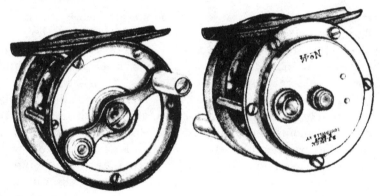

B. F. Meek Trout Reel
from the collection of G. H. Howells

Boston. Conroy also provided trout reels for the old Charles F. Orvis Company in Vermont, and featured two elegantly detailed designs. The inexpensive model was machined from nickel-plated brass and had a spool enclosed in hard-rubber end plates. It sold for less than two dollars in 1875, and its more expensive version ranged from four to five dollars and was fashioned from German silver with hard-rubber plates and German silver fittings. Thomas Conroy was one of the early giants of American tackle design and was selling his first reels about 1873. His craftsmen were working with hard-rubber end plates and aluminum only five years later, and his elegant raised-pillar designs ultimately evolved into the classic Leonard trout reels, which remained in production until only a few years ago at William Mills & Sons.

Orvis patented its unique perforated end plate and spool reel in 1874, and although it was machined from nickel-plated brass, it was a prelude to similar modern designs. The perforations were intended to reduce weight,

Dame, Stoddard & Kendall Reel   Orvis 1874 Patent Reel

facilitate drying the fly line and backing, and help free the reel of dirt and sand. It was machined of fine brass alloys and heavily plated with nickel, so carefully finished that the examples I have examined have a beautiful patina and luster in their pewter-colored plating. The click system is simple and effective. The reel is exaggeratedly narrow, placing its center of gravity as far from the rod as possible. Such configuration also supplies a remarkable mechanical advantage for so small a reel, recovering an optimal amount of line on each turn of the spool. The reel was made in two sizes, with capacities of twenty and seventy yards of fly line, and is about the diameter of the original Hardy Lightweight. The handle was made detachable and fitted into a black walnut case beside the reel, with the unconscious elegance of the best nineteenth-century design.

Julius Vom Hofe also began building his own remarkable fly reels in these same years, and began experimenting with hard-rubber end plates in 1874, the year the Orvis reel was patented. Vom Hofe is a half-legendary name in the history of the fly reel. History is unclear on the genesis of the German silver and black rubber designs, since both Vom Hofe and Conroy were experimenting at about the same time. Some historians believe that Vom Hofe built the Conroy reels as well as his own. It is clear that Vom

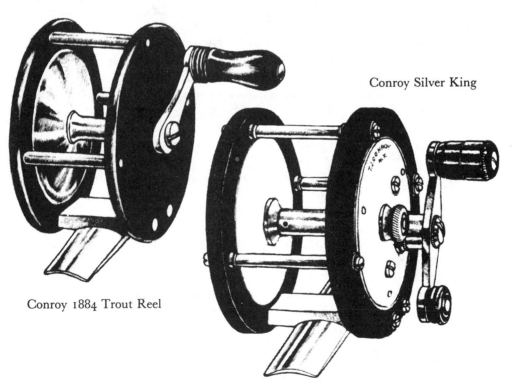

Conroy Silver King

Conroy 1884 Trout Reel

Vom Hofe Reel

Hofe built nothing but reels with black rubber end plates after 1881, while Conroy liked his reels primarily of German silver, except for the contract models his workmen produced for Orvis, Wilkinson, and William Mills & Son. Conroy's work for Wilkinson included a fine little reel with hard-rubber end plates, and Conroy also produced an aluminum reel for Wilkinson patterned after the Leonard raised-pillar design.

Vom Hofe also produced a few reels for other tackle sellers like the fine Abbey & Imbrie shop in New York, both under their trademark in a raised-pillar model and under his own name. Vom Hofe reels are still highly prized in the used tackle market, like the beautifully machined reels later built by Otto Zwarg, whose fly reels are among the finest ever designed. Otto Zwarg, who had his workshop in Brooklyn, never made trout reels, concentrating on models with specifications designed for tarpon and Atlantic salmon. Conroy and Vom Hofe both designed smaller reels for trout fishing. With the death of Edward Vom Hofe, the halcyon years of American reel building came to an end. Salmon reels were later produced under the Vom Hofe name in Philadelphia, but this shop never machined trout-size models.

Although his reels were never in a class with the workmanship in a Conroy or Vom Hofe, August Meisselbach produced large numbers of serviceable, inexpensive reels early in this century. His plant was originally located in New Jersey, although later some Meisselbach reels were also made in Ohio. The Meisselbach Expert models were perhaps the earliest examples, although the skeletal Featherlight designs soon followed. The Rainbow series was closely patterned after the Hardy Uniqua reels, with their crescent-shaped spool catches. The Symploreel was a similar design fabricated in Bakelite. Meisselbach was absorbed by the Bronson Reel Company in about 1932.

Leonard 1877 Patent Reel

The lovely Leonard fly reel is no longer made, although it also commands an excellent price in the used tackle market. It was a classic design of simple elegance. Its back and face plates are hard rubber, with raised pillars and frames of brightly polished duraluminum alloy. The raised-pillar design originally developed by Conroy slightly increased its line capacity. Its click system was both smooth and firm enough to prevent an overrun of its spinning drum. The reels were made in three sizes, from two and a half inches to three inches in diameter. Like all such reels, these Leonard types are relatively heavy, ranging from three and three-quarters to four and three-quarters ounces, for their line capacity. However, such reels are living artifacts of another time, like the Burberry fishing coats worn by Edward Ringwood Hewitt and George La Branche in old photographs taken on the Brodheads and Willowemoc and Neversink— their intricately wrapped rods fitted with elegant Leonard reels.

Hardy ultimately began building its prototypical aluminum trout reels late in the nineteenth century, although the custom-made Roxburghe designs had come almost twenty-five years earlier. Apparently the perforated-spool concepts in the Roxburghe were only used to reduce the weight in such large spools, and were not considered important in the smaller trout models. Some of the early types were the simple closed-drum Uniqua reels popular before the First World War, and subsequently recommended by writers like Eugene Connett and John Alden Knight.

The Hardy Perfect series also featured a closed spool and back plate, machined from three pieces of solid alloy, and it combined aluminum frame-and-drum specifications with ball bearings and the classic revolving line guide of agate. It also offered a superb compensating drag-and-click system. Earlier British reels had displayed a disturbing tendency to freeze at certain drag settings, and the Hardy Perfect solved this problem. The reel

Hardy Uniqua

pawl that engaged the spool gear was fastened under a steel bridge, secured to the back plate with four screws. The slotted pawl allowed its contact point to work freely among the gear teeth, as well as rising back against the drag spring in case of any malfunction. The drag-spring design is still used in the modern Hardy Lightweights, although the tension and pawl system is much simpler now. The regulator screw was fitted with a knurled head, and forced the tension arm to compress the spring. Elements of this system

Hardy Perfect

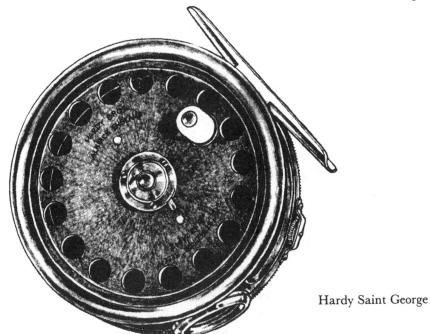

Hardy Saint George

are found in most British-made reels more than fifty years later, although the perforated spools found in the Eureka and Silex coarse-fishing reels still had not influenced the trout-size models. However, the elegant Hardy Saint George was not long in coming, with its partially drilled drum and fitted agate line guide. The modifications cut a full ounce from the weight of the Hardy Perfect, dropping the three-and-three-eighths-inch model to only six and a half ounces. The Hardy Saint John reels also had a partially drilled spool, but did not offer the circular line guide, and were made only in a heavy-trout diameter and weight. The tiny Hardy Saint George of less than three inches, with its perfectly fitted line guide and fine machining, is one of my most prized possessions.

These reels are no longer manufactured in our time, although Hardy is considering reintroduction of the Perfect and the Saint John. The developments worked out in these reels fifty-odd years ago are still found in the modern Hardy Lightweight series, as well as in similar reels produced for Orvis and Scientific Anglers. Such reels are clearly the best large-production reels available to fishermen who want acceptable quality, line capacity at surprisingly light weight, and not too much cost.

The lightweight aluminum alloys available at midcentury led to the Hardy Lightweight series of reels. Their introduction fifteen-odd years ago resulted in unparalleled popularity, and the line was expanded to six models. The first design was three and three-sixteenths inches in diameter and weighed a surprisingly little three and three-quarters ounces, almost half the weight of a comparable Hardy Saint George, and a full four ounces lighter than the three-and-three-eighths-inch Hardy Perfect. It was named in honor of Laurence Robert Hardy.

Hardy Saint John

The startling potential of the new alloys and designs was soon apparent, and Hardy quickly introduced its Featherweight and Princess reels to the Lightweight line. The lovely little Featherweight measures slightly under three inches and weighs only three ounces, a fine design for four-weight lines and rods. The Princess was a larger model. Its diameter was three and three-sixteenths inches, slightly smaller than the largest Saint George, and it weighed only three and a half ounces. The Princess is a superb reel for a six-weight line, its assembly capable of handling tippets lighter than .005, as well as medium-size salmon and steelhead.

The dainty little Hardy Flyweight is virtually a toy, although it is still a practical fishing tool designed for rods weighing between one and two ounces. Its capacity is sufficient for a three-weight line and a limited amount of relatively light backing. The Flyweight is two inches in diameter and weighs two and one-eighth ounces, and is not fitted with an adjustable drag system. It is a handsome, jewellike object.

The success of these four lightweight models led Hardy to add two larger designs a half-dozen years after the first design was introduced. The Saint Aidan was intended as a heavy-trout and light-salmon type, measuring a full three and three-quarters inches and weighing only six ounces. It was designed for seven- and eight-weight lines, with capacity for as much as two hundred yards of backing. The Saint Aidan will strip smoothly enough for a .006 tippet with only one of its pawls engaged. The Saint Aidan is also workable for nine-weight lines, but Hardy also developed the still larger Saint Andrew model, which was rarely sold in the United States and has now been discontinued. While the reel frame of the Princess had been only an inch, the Saint Aidan frame was widened to one and three-sixteenths inches, and the Saint Andrew was a full one and five-eighths inches. The Saint Andrew was a generous four and one-eighth inches in diameter, and weighed seven ounces, but it carried a full eleven-weight line with 250 yards of thirty-pound backing. However, the Saint Aidan was about the limit of the lightweight design, and its springs often failed. The bigger Saint Andrew proved less workable. Although its drag bridge and screw were bigger, the larger springs were rather brittle, and the weight of the frame often worked it slightly loose from the reel-seat flange. It was not entirely successful, although it did carry an incredible amount of fly line and backing for its weight—the four-and-a-half-inch Hardy Perfect weighed almost a pound, more than twice the weight of the similar Saint Andrew.

Less than a half-dozen years ago Scientific Anglers convinced Hardy to build a similar reel for their series of lines and fiberglass rods, and the Lightweight series was discontinued. It was a major footnote to the law of qualitative obsolescence that fishing writer Ted Trueblood expressed unhappily some years ago.

When you find a piece of equipment you like, Trueblood argues wryly, *buy five or six—they'll soon stop making it if it's really good!*

However, this time Trueblood was wrong, and Hardy has happily started making its Lightweight series again. The reels are again available in all sizes from the Flyweight to the Saint Aidan. Their workmanship is still enviable, with a precision and hand-detailing that belies their production volumes. The fit between spool and frame is so finely machined that even a leader cannot easily slip between and tangle. Fine aluminum alloy is used for both spool and frame, and the German silver line guard is reversible. It can be turned around and the pawl reversed, to permit left-hand operation. The handles are smooth and nonfouling, and the reels come apart easily for maintenance or repairs, using the small spring-loaded latch that secures the spool to its spindle.

Scientific Anglers retained all of these features, and added several modifications of their own design. The most obvious is a rolled spool rim that laps the outside of the reel frame, and is intended as a manual brake

Hardy Lightweight Series

Flyweight Featherweight Lightweight   Princess   Saint Aidan

that can be palmed when a fish is stripping line. It is a feature better suited to salt-water species and hard-mouthed fish like steelhead and Pacific salmon. However, the rolled, external drum-flange can bind against waders or clothing in a salt-water lock position, with the butt of the rod in the stomach. Also, reel palming should seldom be tried with fine leaders and strong fish, and these reels employ an unusual drag system. Instead of the conventional Hardy spring mechanism, these reels use a circular spring encased in neoprene. There is a single, slotted pawl mounted on the back plate near the flange, and opposite its position is a twelve-notch eccentric that activates the drag tension. It is set with a nylon button on the back plate of the reel, and an extremely strong drag-setting is possible if the spool is removed, forcing the eccentric past its final notch. However, the spring should not be left at this heavy setting. It is a drag system that cannot be fouled with dirt or sand, although it does not exert a really firm pressure and has a tendency to fade on a really strong fish.

The spool is released from its spindle with a simple push-spring latch and is fitted with a line notch in its back flange to help keep the line clear of the reel frame when it is being reseated. The nylon housing over the spindle on the back plate seems less desirable than the aluminum fitting on the Hardy Lightweights, and the line guard is a much lighter nickel-plated fitting than the genuine German silver line guard on the original British prototypes. However, the larger models are fitted with corrosion-resistant components for fishing salt-water and sea-run trout.

These reels are also somewhat heavier than comparable models in the earlier Lightweight series. The two-and-three-quarters-inch System Four Reel weighs a full half-ounce more than the Hardy Featherweight, while the System Eight model weighs about the same as the similar three-and-three-quarters-inch Saint Aidan. The Lightweight and Princess reels are significantly lighter than the System Six and System Seven designs, so the difference in weight could be important in the smaller trout-size reels. The Scientific Anglers' specifications also provide the easy conversion to left-hand wind found in all Hardy-built reels, and even the smallest System Four provides the rolled flange for applying manual drag.

Hardy has also started making a Viscount Series of fly reels using somewhat less expensive components, but derived directly from the Scientific Anglers' designs. The frames and spools are pressure die-cast of high strength aluminum alloy, but unlike the more expensive systems, the reel foot and rim are cast integrally with the frame. The spool-handle pivot and cup are cast with the drum itself. The line guards are identical, but there is no rolled rim for manual braking with the palm. The drag systems are adequate and precise, with a full range of settings. The Hardy Viscount reels are made in three sizes, designed to accommodate four-weight, five-weight, and six-weight lines, the basic sizes for most trout fishing. Their price is moderate, about half the cost of the more expensive reels in the Hardy line.

Cheaper still are the several Japanese copies of the Hardy Lightweight

System 4

System 5

System 6

System 7

System 8

System 9

series being marketed by companies like Berkeley and Heddon. The Berkeley models are available in three sizes. The 530 is a size approximately equivalent to the Hardy Featherweight, with its two-and-a-half-inch spool diameter, but it weighs more than the Lightweight. The Berkeley 540 is virtually identical to the Hardy Lightweight in size and appearance, but it weighs almost as much as the larger Hardy Princess. The 550 reel is the largest of the Berkeley series, its diameter roughly equal to the Hardy Princess, yet it weighs almost as much as the bigger Saint Aidan. The metals are slightly heavier and less costly throughout than the English prototypes, but they do provide a single-piece frame, an easily removable spool, a heavily plated brass line guard, an acceptable drag with a slightly coarse click mechanism, and ready conversion to left-hand use. The Berkeley reels are about one-third the price of an original Hardy, and the Heddon copies of the Lightweights are even less expensive.

The Heddon imports are such accurate copies of the Hardy prototypes that the spools are interchangeable with the Featherweight and Light-weight models. Their appearance is virtually identical, although a knowl-edgeable eye can easily detect the differences in workmanship. The adjustable drag is smooth and positive, the frames are solid and well built, and the reels are reversible to left-hand operation. Skilled anglers who have fished them agree that for average fishing problems such Japanese copies are probably satisfactory, but that such facsimiles are not equal to the more costly British products for really difficult fishing conditions—big steeple-chasing rainbows in heavy water or a reel that must surrender line smoothly enough to cushion a 7X tippet against a bolting fish.

Pflueger has built a single-action reel for many years that is widely used on American trout waters, and the company is more than a century old. The Medalist series has been undeniably popular. It includes six reel designs. The Pflueger 1492 is about the diameter of a Hardy Featherweight, and its thirteen-sixteenths of an inch spool will hold more line, but it weighs a full ounce more. It is without an adjustable drag, and its click mechanism

Pflueger Medalist

is a little too harsh for tippets finer than .005 nylon. The 1494 Medalist is slightly smaller than a Hardy Princess, although it weighs much more, and the next larger model is a little larger than the three-and-a-half-inch Hardy. However, it weighs a full six ounces, as much as the Hardy Saint Aidan. The 1498 reel has a four-inch diameter and is roughly equivalent to the Saint Aidan, although almost three ounces heavier. It is fitted with a reinforced back plate and spool, and a stronger drag system than the other Medalist reels.

These American-built reels are workhorse designs that will take more abuse than their more elegant British cousins. They are constructed of strong aluminum alloys with a machined-steel spindle. Although the spool cover for the spindle head is plastic, it houses a practical push lever securing the spool in the frame. The pillars, cross plates, and line guard are all finely tooled brass with a heavy nickel plating. The drag system is the oscillating type that can vary radically between stopped drag tension and the pressure on a spinning drum, but it is adequate for most fishing, and only fishermen skilled enough to fish the delicate tippets from .003 to .005 will find its click system harsh. Perhaps the two-part frame assembled with set screws seated in the pillars is the worst fault of the Medalist, since vibrations of fishing and travel and casting seem to work them slowly loose. Lost screws can cause the frame to rack and bind the spool, and I have had Medalist reels freeze with big rainbows in South America. However, the fisherman who prefers a serviceable fly reel manufactured in the United States will find the Pflueger practical and moderately priced.

Perhaps the most remarkable fly reel to evolve from the Hardy Lightweight series is the recently developed Orvis CFO. Although it was conceived and designed in the United States, it is machined and assembled by the British craftsmen at Hardy Brothers. Its development came in part from some experiments by the famous Stanley Bogdan, using highly sophisticated new alloys and some of the old Hardy Lightweight components. One of his experiments with a drilled inside spool and back plate that considerably reduced the weight of the standard Hardy-type reel is displayed at the Museum of American Fly Fishing in Vermont. But working with still more sophisticated alloys led to the exciting discovery that the outer rim of the reel frame could be jettisoned entirely, along with two of the three pillars, leaving only a single T-head pillar at the bottom of the reel. Its curved head was matched with a machined rail on the reel-seat flange mount, and a precisely tooled rim on the reel spool itself provided the circumferential track for the T-head pillar and flange mount.

The click-and-drag mechanism is a symmetrically loading echo of the tongue-activated, drag-spring system originally introduced before the First World War on the Hardy Perfect, but it incorporates more sophisticated metals. Instead of the screw-tightened yoke used in the Hardy Lightweights, paired springs are symmetrically placed inside the back plate and tightened with a pair of curving metal tongues. The tongues are adjusted with a smooth cam and turning button. The drilled back plate and spool are complemented with three additional perforations in the reel-seat flange, the center hole penetrating both the flange and its mounting bar. These drill patterns achieve a marked reduction in weight, as well as providing ventilation for a wet fly line and backing. The minimal frame results in a slight increase in line capacity, and the spool can be removed and reseated without pinching the line in the reel cage.

But these functional considerations, important as they are, seem less important than the esthetic and historical qualities of these reels. It should be remembered that although the Roxburghe aluminum reels built by Hardy for salmon fishing about 1875 were a remarkable design break-through using a sophisticated new metal, the fully perforated trout reel patented by Charles F. Orvis in 1874 was equally important. It did not employ advanced metallurgy, but it did introduce the fully drilled spool and back plate to fly-fishing. After a full century has passed, the new Orvis CFO reels have updated the concept with modern aerospace alloys and superb craftsmanship.

Orvis is also a firm with a sense of history. The conceptual debt these new reels owe to old Charles F. Orvis has been acknowledged by christening them in his memory, and the Orvis CFO series of reels promises to take its place in a long and honorable tradition. These CFO reels are elegantly designed and made, and fly-fishermen everywhere have come to appreciate their character and quality.

There are presently four models in the CFO series. Its smallest size is the CFO II, indicating that Orvis may have a smaller design in mind. At a jewel-tiny two and a half inches and two ounces, this diminutive reel is the same weight as the Hardy Flyweight, although it is a half inch bigger. The CFO III is a particular favorite of mine after seven seasons of light-tackle work. It is three inches in diameter and weighs three ounces. The CFO IV weighs three and one-quarter ounces with a diameter of three and one-quarter inches, much lighter than the comparable Hardy Lightweight. The largest model in the series, the four-inch CFO V, has sufficient capacity to hold a WF10F fly line and a full 150 yards of backing. It weighs only four ounces, two full ounces under the smaller Hardy Saint Aidan. Such weight reductions result in remarkable capacity-to-weight ratios, although the larger CFO reels have demonstrated some problems in racking and binding under the strain of recovering line from a particularly strong fish. Extreme pressure can distort the ultralight alloys enough to bind the rim groove of the spool on its contact points, and both must be kept well lubricated and absolutely clean. Such care has resulted in faultless performance from the CFO reels in my collection.

There is a three-inch CFO prototype that I particularly prize, since it is one of the first produced. Leigh Perkins of Orvis sent it to me for field testing before its back plate was engraved, and it is utterly without markings. However, its workmanship and design are so striking that it needs no trademark nor identification, like any classic piece of equipment that is instantly identifiable.

Orvis CFO Series

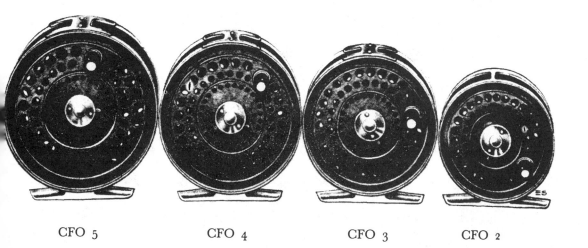

CFO 5   CFO 4   CFO 3   CFO 2

Orvis CFO 3

The best thing about that reel is its functional simplicity, I told Leigh Perkins after fishing it a few weeks. *It's exquisitely made and can speak for itself—and I hope it will not be marred with trademarks.*

The first reels are already engraved, he said.

Well, I said, *I hope the future reels are perfectly plain, like the prototype.*

Perhaps they will be, Perkins smiled.

Orvis also markets the Battenkill Ultralight reel manufactured for them by the J. S. Sharpe Company in Scotland. These little fly reels are not made from the fine aluminum found in the Hardy Lightweight series, or the ultralight alloys of the CFO reels designed at Orvis, but are still workable tools capable of yeomanlike performance. While their click systems are not quite as smooth as the Hardy mechanism, and can prove troublesome on leaders finer than a .005 calibration, their price is considerably less than the Hardy-built reels. There are three models in the Battenkill series. The Flyweight measures two and three-quarters inches and weighs slightly more than three and a half ounces. The Featherweight is a half-ounce heavier, with a diameter of three inches. The Lightweight model is three and one-quarter inches and weighs almost four and a half ounces, making it slightly less than an ounce heavier than the comparable Hardy Lightweight. The spool is perforated on both drum plates, and its inner rim is notched to hold the line during reassembly. The drag spring is activated with a cam and curved-tongue lever. Although the design and workmanship of these Battenkill Ultralight reels are not equal to the expensive British types, they are only slightly more than half their cost and offer the fisherman an alternative cost range between Pflueger and Hardy.

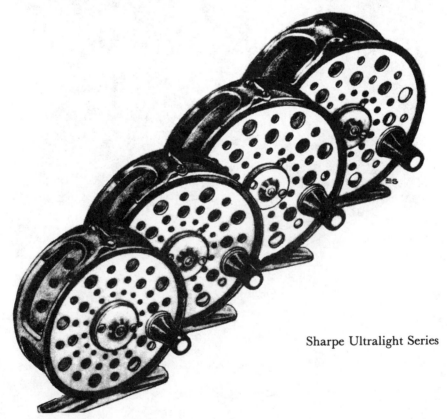

Sharpe Ultralight Series

The Morritt reels are also made in England and are quite popular there because of their reputation for durability at a moderate price. The Intrepid Rimfly series includes the Lightweight at three and three-eighths inches and four and three-eighths ounces, the Regular at three and a half inches and five and one-quarter ounces, and the King that measures three and five-eighths inches and weighs a full six ounces. Both cage and drum are made from aluminum alloys, with an exposed flange for exerting drag with the palm. There is no adjustable drag system. Morritt reels are sold through the Gladding Corporation in the United States.

The Sharpe's reels include the Cobra series, with models of three and one-quarter inches and six ounces, and three and a half inches and six and three-quarters ounces. The famous J. W. Young reels include the Beaulite model, which is made of ultralight magnesium alloys in a three-and-a-half-inch trout reel. It features an exposed rim for manual drag, a plated line guard, and adjustable tension. The Speedex is similarly fitted, but provides a geared multiplying system with an approximate two-to-one ratio. It is three and a half inches in diameter and weighs only five and a half ounces. Both are narrow frame trout reels with moderate capacity.

However, there are other reel builders who produce work of such quality that price is virtually no object. Their work is almost totally hand crafted, and in a time when there are few surviving artisans, there is still a small circle of dedicated fly-reel men.

The late Joe Brooks used to like the smaller Fin-Nor reels for fishing trout where a strong drag system was needed, although these reels were originally developed for fishing bonefish and tarpon on the salt-water flats

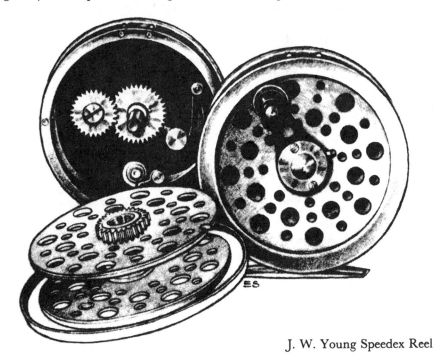

J. W. Young Speedex Reel

Tycoon Fin-Nor Reels

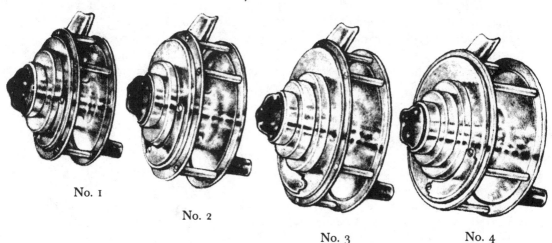

No. 1

No. 2

No. 3

No. 4

off Florida. The spool and back plate are machined from a solid dowel of costly high-density aluminum alloy and anodized to reduce corrosion. The drag system is set with a strong tightening knob and will deliver fourteen pounds of nonoscillating tension. The Fin-Nor One will hold a six-weight line with more than one hundred yards of twenty-pound backing, and it weighs about ten ounces. The Fin-Nor Two will carry a full WF9F fly line with almost two hundred yards of twenty-pound backing, and although it weighs slightly more than twelve ounces, it sometimes is found on big trout streams. The Fin-Nor Three is almost too much reel for trout. It has sufficient capacity for a ten-weight salt-water taper with almost 250 yards of twenty-pound backing filling out the spool. It weighs a full sixteen ounces, and like the Fin-Nor Two, it is available with an antireverse mechanism that protects a fisherman from a spinning handle when a trophy fish makes a wild run. Each of these reels has a full-circle-disc drag system that adjusts quickly from a delicate setting to tension stern enough to handle a sailfish or marlin. It is firm and will not fade. However, the Fin-Nor reels have a relatively delicate center spindle, anchored deep in the back-plate structure, and rough treatment can jar it out of alignment. When the spindle is not perfectly centered, the drum can bind against the frame of the reel cage. Although the Fin-Nor reels are expensive, their quality is exceptional, and an angler will have no problems with fading or erratic drag nor a spinning reel spool that will seize or bind.

Stanley Bogdan is justly famous for the quality of his trout and salmon reels, and their workmanship and design are excellent. Like the Fin-Nor, the Bogdan is machined from solid high-density aluminum stock. Both the reel frame and the spool are perfectly fitted, with no cross-frame pillars to work loose. Although I prefer more traditional German silver or aluminum fittings, the gold-anodized finish of the Bogdan reel is extremely effective against corrosion. Unlike the other fly reels, the Bogdan design has a multiplying gear system that delivers a two-to-one ratio. The drag employs a double brake-shoe system with seven settings, ranging from a tension barely stronger than the click mechanism to a full fifteen pounds. The click can be either audible or silent. Both left- and right-hand models are available. The end plates are hard rubber, returning to the traditional configuration that started with the flawless nineteenth-century work of Conroy and Vom Hofe.

The Bogdan reels are made in three sizes. The trout reel measures three and one-quarter inches in diameter and weighs eleven ounces, since lightweight design was not a requirement. It will hold a full eight-weight line with 250 yards of twenty-pound backing. The salmon model is three and three-quarters inches in diameter and weighs thirteen ounces, with a capacity of 250 yards behind a nine-weight forward taper. The salt-water reel is even larger. It has a slightly wider spool in the same three-and-three-quarters-inch diameter and weighs fourteen ounces. Its drum can accommodate a ten-weight salt-water taper with almost 300 yards of twenty-pound Dacron filling out the spool. Although these reels have a relatively heavy weight-to-capacity ratio, their flawless performance on really big fish and big water make them useful for heavy work. Cost was also no object when Stanley Bogdan worked out his reel designs, and the Bogdan series is even more expensive than the Fin-Nors. His experiments with sophisticated new alloys, which played a role in the evolution of the CFO reels for Orvis, have led Bogdan to add fully perforated side plates and spools to his trout-size reels—materially reducing weight and improving their performance for trout fishing.

Bogdan Reels

Although the Bogdan reel is clearly derived from the traditional Conroy, Vom Hofe, and Zwarg designs, with their solid frames and hard rubber end plates and counterweighted handles, the character and workmanship of those early masterpieces still lives virtually without modification in the matchless Walker series.

The Walker firm has been making exquisite reels on the Vom Hofe patterns since 1942, although modern materials have led to many internal modifications and refinements. The prototype reels designed by Conroy and Vom Hofe almost a century ago had simple click systems, employing a two-way dog, tension spring, and ratchet. Walker manufactured its reels with these same components until about 1959, when they began exploring other directions, hoping to evolve a fresh design that might trigger a renaissance in high-performance trout reels—reels of a quality they believe died with Edward Vom Hofe and the nineteenth-century patents worked out in his shop.

These old Vom Hofe trout reels were marvelous, Arch Walker gestures and rolls his eyes for emphasis. *They still function well in spite of the hairline cracks in their rubber end plates—like aristocratic ladies just starting to look their age!*

Their experiments in the past fifteen years have led the Walkers to conclude that a major problem with the old Vom Hofe patents lay in our modern trends toward light tackle on large, free-wheeling fish. Handling a six-pound rainbow in heavy water placed demands for high-speed running on reels that were originally designed for eastern brook-trout fishing. Such problems soon led to highly sophisticated alloys and steels in the drag system, spool, and frame and to a unique compound ratchet that separates the functions of running and retrieving.

The most recent Walker reels are based upon completely fresh patents granted in 1972 and employ the high-speed compound ratchet. The trout reels are supplied without an adjustable brake system, having a click only firm enough to prevent overrun and subtle enough to cushion a .005 nylon tippet. Current experiments are playing with a system delicate enough to surrender line with only a .003 point smoothly, for extreme light-tackle work with a reel as solidly built as the Walker. Such performance is beyond the fine leader capabilities of the Bogdan and Fin-Nor reels, and the Conroy and Vom Hofe prototypes as well. Medium-size Walker reels, lying between the trout and heavy-duty sizes, are fitted with a superb self-lubricating drag. It is adjustable and will not fade. These trout- and medium-size reels have performed well in my fishing, handling trout and Atlantic salmon and bonefish much larger than their performance specifications intended. Sturdily made, these reels could easily handle these larger fish, except for the obvious ceiling imposed by their line capacity. Two considerations were paramount in the modern Walker trout reels: optimal performance in high-speed running and longevity in reels that are literally intended to outlive their owners.

The heavy-duty Walker reels are like the classic Rolls Royce and look exactly like the old Vom Hofe patterns, although their internal specifications and components have been radically improved. The new waterproof drag can be adjusted to handle anything that swims, and it can be set so tightly that a sudden lunge from a big billfish could strip the guides from a rod like popcorn. Weight is not one of the performance criteria, and these big Walkers are not exactly lightweights.

How solid are they? Arnold Gingrich posed a rhetorical question over lunch in Manhattan. *Would you believe a silver-plated bulldozer?*

These reels are too heavy for trout fishing. Both single- and multiplying-action models are available. There are six types holding from 200 to 1,200 yards of thirty-pound Dacron backing, to satisfy anything from a bonefish flat in the Bahamas to the gargantuan billfish that come to the surface and feed on the calm mornings off the coast of Ecuador and Baja California and Panama. The salmon modifications have spools turned from solid barstock of high-density aluminum alloys, but the salt-water models feature spools of gleaming stainless steel, capable of backing-line pressures of 45,000 to 56,000 pounds per square inch. The edges of the hard rubber end plates on the salmon and salt-water models are encased in rings of delicate German silver, in exacting homage to the traditions started by Julius Vom Hofe in 1875.

The new series of exquisite Walker trout reels also continues firmly in the Vom Hofe traditions, although it has abandoned German silver for brightwork and spools of sophisticated new aluminum alloys. The result of these changes is a remarkable reduction in weight.

These reels are fully machined from solid high-density stock, completely without stamping or casting or synthetic components. Such attention to quality makes the Walker trout reel unique. The spindle is fashioned of corrosion-resistant steel, revolving in bronze bearings machined to tolerances as fine as .0002 inch. The reels are sold with a five-year warranty, and their appearance honors their Vom Hofe ancestry right down to the counterweighted, balance-type handle. Experience in servicing reels built by Conroy and Vom Hofe and Zwarg has led the Walkers to continue using their classic end plates of hard rubber.

Their hard-rubber fittings are still perfect after fifty years of fishing, Arthur Walker explains, his eyes twinkling behind his silver-rimmed glasses, *and we like them. Need a better reason?*

The Walker series of trout reels begins with the exquisite TR-1, which is the Midge at two and a half inches in diameter and weighing only three and three-quarters ounces. Such light weight is unusual in such a solidly made reel, and is possible only because of high-performance aluminum. It is intended for matching with superb fly rods under two ounces, and will hold 100 yards of ten-pound dacron behind a three-weight double taper. Like the other three trout-size reels, the Midge has a spool diameter of fifteen-sixteenths of an inch, and is adjusted to fish .005 tippets. Walker will modify its internal design to accommodate tippets as fine as .003 nylon, and unlike most fishing equipment, the smallest reel is the most expensive.

The TR-2 is the light trout model in the Walker series. It measures two and three-quarters inches in diameter and weighs slightly more than four and three-quarters ounces, and is intended for two- to three-ounce rods. Its capacity is a four-weight double taper ahead of 150 yards of ten-pound Dacron, although if large fish are a possibility, backing of heavier diameter is more practical to prevent biting and binding with a strong run.

The Walker TR-3 is the standard trout reel in the line. It has a full three-inch diameter and weighs just over five ounces. It is intended for fly rods of three to three and three-quarters ounces, and will hold almost 200 yards of ten-pound backing behind a four- or five-weight line. My own TR-3 reels are fitted with twenty-pound backing, although the Walker specifications are for light-tackle trout. The heavier backing was used to fish big rainbows on the Caleufu and Malleo in Argentina, where a good day can total twenty or thirty cartwheeling fish over twenty inches. Field-testing one of the first TR-3 prototypes on these strong rainbows caused some modifications of the click system, although it is unthinkable that normal trout fishing could give a reel that kind of beating. However, the Walker family is utterly dedicated to excellence, and they insisted on improving the unimprovable. The modified TR-3 was given the acid test on the Grimsá in Iceland, fishing it on fresh-run Atlantic salmon in spite of the limited backing possible with a twenty-pound test. It has since taken almost one hundred salmon between six and twenty-eight pounds, including eleven fish between six and eighteen pounds in a single morning, although its performance criteria were clearly never intended to accommodate the stresses of such fishing.

Well, Arch Walker beamed with pleasure, *you can kill an elephant with a little rifle—but a little muscle is wiser!*

The Walker TR-4 is the heavy-trout model. It has the identical precision click system with a setting designed to fish a .005 tippet, and finer settings can be specified. The TR-4 measures three and one-quarter inches in diameter and weighs just a fraction under six ounces. It works beautifully with rods weighing four to five ounces, and holds a five- or six-weight line

Walker Trout Reels

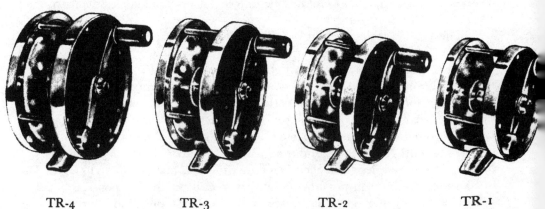

TR-4   TR-3   TR-2   TR-1

with almost 250 yards of ten-pound Dacron backing. Its capacity of twenty-pound backing makes it a workable reel for most trout fishing, although it still has a smooth click system set fine enough for 6X points. Its proportions are also visually attuned to the proportions of trout-rod grips and reel seats, while the smaller Walker reels look a little undersized with most fly rods.

The medium-size Walker reels with their adjustable brake systems and larger diameters have just become available. Several experimental ratchet and drag mechanisms are still being field-tested at this writing. These reels still feature a click system fine enough to fish .005 nylon with the drag disengaged, and are available in three models from three and one-eighth inches to three and five-eighths inches in diameter. They are designed to balance rods from four to six ounces, and lines from six- to eight-weight tapers, with enough backing for big sea-run rainbows on the Pacific Coast.

Walker fly reels are superbly conceived and made, worthy heirs to a virtually unbroken tradition in American craftsmanship and angling. It is often argued that lighter reels are more attuned to contemporary fishing, with its growing emphasis on light tippets and selective fish, and that a reel like the Walker is too well made for trout-fishing performance. The Walker family would probably agree with these arguments, except that they are artisans rather than mere craftsmen, passionately opposed to the slightest compromise in workmanship or quality. Their reels are dedicated to the proposition that precision and costly materials are essential in the full achievement of their art, and that price is secondary once the goal of absolute quality has been established. The firm continues to experiment with new patents and materials and models. It was Arnold Gingrich who described the Walker firm perfectly, and his recent book *The Joys of Trout* contains the following observations:

> The Walkers are clearly to reels as the late Jim Payne was to rods—sworn enemies of any least semblance of compromise, and passionate adherents to a standard of craftsmanship that in the old Vom Hofe days might have been taken for granted, but in this slapdash age seems downright eccentric, not to say fanatical.

It was also Arnold Gingrich, in his pleasurable book *The Well-Tempered Angler*, who observed that reels with a silent click system were certainly no improvement, and that only a poacher could find virtue in a reel that made no sound. Gingrich also noted that a temperament that could appreciate the matchless finish of fine violins or the whine of a superbly tuned Alfa Romeo would also find beauty in the shrilly protesting music of a fine fly reel. But that music has a practical side, too, which only experience in playing big fish can reveal: its tonality is another tool in knowing just what a strong fish is doing, and how quickly it is doing it. Such complex sensory clues are critical in trout fishing, but ultimately it is the complete poetry of a fine fly reel that really matters.

Several years ago I was fishing the Brodheads in Pennsylvania with Colin Pittendrigh. It was an April morning with a cool west wind, and weak sunlight between minor showers. The fish were surprisingly selective quite early in the season, and a good hatch of tiny *Paraleptophlebia* duns was coming down the current. There were some excellent fish working quietly, and when we coaxed them into taking, they often bolted and ran well down the shallow flat.

Our tippets were delicate, and we allowed the better fish to take line freely, enjoying the fragile melody of our reels. Pittendrigh was working over a particularly selective fish, and I waded out to give him a special little blue-winged dry fly dressed with a slender body of rust-colored quill. It worked on the second float along the alders, and the fish bolted along the shallows, stripping line melodically from the delicate reel.

Lovely! Pittendrigh sighed happily. *Isn't that reel making one of the sweetest sounds in the world?*

You're right, I replied.

For recent developments in fly reels, see Appendix: Notes on New Equipment.

TROUT

Volume II

Published in the United States by Truman Talley Books • E. P. Dutton,
Inc., 2 Park Avenue, New York, N.Y. 10016

Library of Congress Cataloging in Publication Data

Schwiebert, Ernest George.
Trout.

"A Truman Talley book"

Bibliography: p.
Includes indexes.
1. Trout fishing. 2. Trout. I. Title.
SH687.S25   1984   799.1'755   84-8564

ISBN: 0-525-24269-4 (set)

Published simultaneously in Canada by Fitzhenry & Whiteside Limited,
Toronto

Designed by Jacques Chazaud

10 9 8 7 6 5 4 3 2 1

First Edition   October 1978 • Two printings
Second Edition   September 1984

6. The Iconography of the Split-Cane Rod

The first really fine fly rod that I ever saw was an eight-foot Payne owned by a physician in Chicago. It had been built by Edward Payne, one of the original apprentice disciples of Hiram Leonard in Bangor, and had been refinished by James Payne many years later. Their names meant nothing to an eight-year-old who was still more interested in catching fish than in the subtle rituals and liturgies of fishing. However, the craftsmanship and beauty of the rod were obvious, although I found it strange that the doctor loved his gleaming four-ounce Payne so much that he utterly refused to fish with it. The old man laid it reverently on his red felt desktop in the lamplight and looked at the exquisite rod for hours. It obviously had the overtones of some religious relic.

It would be many years later before I fully understood that a skilled fisherman did have almost religious feelings about his tackle. It had great beauty and fished with elegance, and had the votive powers to reawaken memories of rivers past. It was my first exposure to the iconography of the split-cane rod.

The Payne was kept in a saddle-leather case, its heavy stitching frayed and pale against the tube and cap. There was a leather strap attached to the case that slipped through two loops on the cap and fastened with a small leather-covered buckle. Both the case and its cap were scuffed and worn, smelling faintly like a fine saddle or a favorite pair of English riding boots, but their patina was only a prelude to the sensory riches they contained.

The first impression was the faintly musty smell of the original poplin bag that held the rod, plus the rich perfume of the tung-oil varnish, its gleaming mirror flawlessly smooth and perfect. The delicate silk wrappings were a pale brown that almost matched the color of the bamboo itself, and they were embellished with ornamental wraps of yellow. It was a three-piece rod with a classic medium Payne action. The German silver ferrules were beautiful, and each female socket was protected with a perfectly fitted German silver plug. There were no silk wrappings except at the guides, ferrules, grip check, and tip tops. The guides were exquisite English tungsten steel in a bronzed finish, while the stripping guide and tip tops were entirely tungsten. The grip was beautifully shaped of handcut specie cork, remarkably solid and free of checks and markings. It was the classic Payne-style grip, slightly flared at the butt to conceal a reel cap inside the cork. The reel-seat filler was darkly grained American walnut, and its reversed fittings gleamed like fine jewelry. The locking threads were perfectly machined and specially designed to inhibit binding or jamming. Although the heavy locking hood was made of high-quality aluminum alloy, its weight and elegant knurling and richness seemed more like fine sterling—as beautifully conceived and executed as a silver piece displayed on velvet in the windows at Cartier or Tiffany.

The doctor assembled the rod in his library, hovering protectively while I flexed it hesitantly. Its action was delicate and smooth, with a sweetness and elusive poetry impossible to describe, like the subtle quality of a fine Burgundy or a seasoned full-bodied Bordeaux.

Such perfection is rare, and it is easy to understand the half-religious feelings of a fisherman for his trout rods. Although salmon tackle has similar overtones, it is unquestionably the light split-bamboo instruments designed for trout that evoke the most reverence. Fly rods from the skilled hands of artisans like Garrison, Payne, Halstead, Gillum, Orvis, Leonard, Winston, Young, Edwards, Thomas, or Howells are probably more cherished than the equipment used in any other sport.

Fine guns are perhaps their only rival. Certainly an elegantly stocked big-game rifle, with its raised comb and cheekpiece and gleaming engine-turned bolt, is beautifully designed and made. The simple beauty of a fine double shotgun is probably a better comparison, particularly the traditional English-style with its slender stock and sleekly tapered forepiece, elegant and totally devoid of decorations or embellishments. Such guns were first conceived in the shop of Joseph Manton, who set the classic imagery that has governed double shotguns ever since, just as Hiram Leonard first worked out the technology and esthetics that evolved into the modern fly rod more than a century ago.

Shotguns and split-cane rods have much in common. Both achieve their functional purpose afield, perfectly attuned to the grouse covers and bright gravel riffles of the Catskills. Both are almost living extensions of the body and the senses when they are skillfully used. Yet the split-cane rod is alive, flexing gracefully in its response to the touch and will of its owner. It has its own singular character, yet it fully accommodates itself to the character and moods of anyone who fishes it. The favorite trout rod is a constant friend. Trout seasons are longer than bird seasons, and a woodcock

DANIEL BREMAN ROD IN THE COLLECTION OF THE ANGLERS' CLUB OF NEW YORK

FARLOW 1845 FIVE-PIECE GREENHEART

JAMES HENSHALL ROD IN THE COLLECTION OF THE ANGLERS' CLUB OF NEW YORK

SAMUEL PHILLIPPE 1847 FOUR-PIECE BAMBOO

hunter will fire his precious Fox or Greener or Purdey only a few times compared with the thousands of casts delivered each day astream. Perhaps only an exquisite violin is equally alive, its fragile wood vibrating in concert with its strings. The violin is beautiful too, particularly the flawless instruments conceived by craftsmen like Antonio Stradivari and Giuseppe Guarnieri, who were the apogee of the legendary School of Cremona. Like a fine split-bamboo rod, their work probably represents the ultimate equilibrium of utility and craftsmanship and esthetic qualities.

Leonard Wright caught something of this subtle mixture between poetry and function in his essay on bamboo rods for the *American Sportsman Treasury*, adding his observations on the stream itself as a fitting place to fish a particularly beautiful rod:

> The trout stream is set apart from the other scenes of sport with its hemlock and rhododendron, willow and warbler, the play of sunlight on a riffle. Many fine authors have tried to capture this magic, but it simply beggars description. One great naturalist described a trout stream as the artery of the forest. It is that and more. It is also the life blood of the trout fisherman.
>
> In this setting and in this spirit, a rod becomes far more than just a tool for casting. And fortunately, this bond between rod and man is an especially happy one. The experienced angler seldom blames his rod. In fact, he is liable to consider it perfection.
>
> This happiness with things as they are can be observed in almost any fine tackle store. There are seldom requests for unconventional rod actions or special embellishments. If you examine a sampling of rods by the finest makers, you will see that they are almost uniformly modest in appearance. The cane glows warmly through the clear varnish. The reel seat is harmonious butternut or walnut. Windings will usually be some neutral hue. This is the quiet beauty of the partridge, not the gaudy beauty of the cock pheasant.

Yet a knowledgeable fisherman knows the fingerprints with which each maker signs his work. Silk wrappings are signatures in both color and character, and in their absence or embellishments. The windings on a Powell are typical, since those with semihollow construction were always identified by a distinguishing mark in the silk: narrow wraps of white and black just ahead of the cork grip, while the solid rods had a single color at the keeper ring. The grips are another hallmark. Even when the fittings and silk wrappings are identical, an expert can separate a rod built by old Edward Payne from the work of his son, since James Payne preferred a slightly more slender grip. Cane construction is often a clue, particularly in the placement of the nodes. The nodes of an artist like Everett Garrison is unique, since the graining of the same node in the same face of each tip clearly reveals its origins in adjacent strips of the original cane.

The color of the cane is another fingerprint of its original maker.

ROBERT WHITMAN ROD IN THE COLLECTION OF THE MUSEUM OF AMERICAN FLY FISHING

FARLOW   1851   THREE-PIECE BETHABARA

DOROTHY TEMPLE FULLER ROD IN THE COLLECTION OF THE ANGLERS' CLUB OF NEW YORK

THADDEUS NORRIS   1853   THREE-PIECE SNAKEWOOD

DOROTHY TEMPLE FULLER ROD IN THE COLLECTION OF THE ANGLERS' CLUB OF NEW YORK

THADDEUS NORRIS   1859   THREE-PIECE LANCEWOOD

Garrison and Leonard and Winston pride themselves on the pale natural color of their bamboo. Gillum cane is darker, a rich medium brown, like the work of Payne and Howells. Gillum and Garrison both used dark modern adhesives which make their glue lines clearly visible. Orvis and Halstead rods are often darker still, while Thomas chose to work in both natural cane and a rich chocolate color. Paul Young was a fanatic about flame-tempering his bamboo, and his rods reveal that penchant in the contrast between their pale nodes and almost carbonized surfaces.

The number of split-cane strips is also revealing, since most split-cane rods employ the conventional six-strip hexagonal construction. Most other systems varied from three to twelve strips and were soon abandoned since they either failed to improve performance or radically multiplied the work involved in building rods. However, William Edwards continued to make his four-strip quadrate rods until his recent death, and a five-strip rod is usually the work of Robert Crompton, Nathaniel Uslan, or Frank Wire. These three remain the leading partisans of five-strip theory.

The perspective of history tells us that split-bamboo rods evolved slowly over thousands of years. Chinese fishermen used rods of thornwood and natural bamboo centuries before Christ, and *The Treatyse of Fysshynge wyth an Angle* tells us that Dame Juliana Berners preferred a rod with butt section of hazel, willow or aspen and a tip section fashioned of blackthorn, crabtree, medlar or juniper. Almost two centuries later, Charles Cotton recommended a Yorkshire rod between fifteen and eighteen feet. Cotton favored a butt section of fir with a tip section of thornwood, juniper, or yew. Across the next 150 years, English rodmakers dominated the art, and their Empire provided them with an astonishing spectrum of exotic woods for rod building.

Craftsmen experimented tirelessly with ash, basswood, hornbeam, barberry, cedar, blue mahoe, osage orange, degma, lancewood, bethabara, greenheart, lemonwood, yew and American bamboo. Hickory had briefly dominated the trade after its introduction into American rod building in 1660, although the nineteenth-century craftsmen in the United States soon experimented widely.

Thaddeus Norris published his *American Angler's Book* in 1864, and included both a discussion of contemporary rod building and a happy recommendation for carrying a wicker creel generous enough to hold his clothing, catch, and a bottle of fine claret. His favorite rod consisted of a white-ash butt section, a middle joint of ironwood, and tip section of four-strip bamboo derived from the inventive mind of Samuel Phillippe. Norris later manufactured Phillippe-type bamboo rods in Philadelphia, and his firm was one of the pioneers in American rodmaking.

Genio Scott added his *Fishing in American Waters* to the literature of the sport in 1873, providing his observations on the evolving technology of the fly rod. It is clear that split-cane construction had not yet triumphed. Scott recommends a rod butt of ash, lancewood for the middle joint, and a split-bamboo tip section. Other anglers of that period advocated rods of maple, ash, and lancewood. Spliced lancewood and bamboo hybrids were also popular, and Henry Wells strongly recommended rods of ash and lancewood for trout fishing. His book *Fly Rods and Fly Tackle* was published in 1885, and it was quickly acclaimed as the definitive work of its day. Wells argued that greenheart was still the premier wood for fly rods in his time, although he also liked bethabara, snakewood, Cuban mahoe, ironwood, hickory, beefwood, paddlewood, and shadblow. Other acceptable materials listed in *Fly Rods and Fly Tackle* were exotic woods like pyengadu, chow, pingow, ironbark, kranji, purpleheart, dagame, and jucaro prieto. It is interesting to observe that several American builders like Phillippe, Green, Norris, Murphy, and the celebrated Hiram Leonard had all been making split-cane rods for years when Wells published his book, and superb Murphy and Leonard designs were available to American fishermen as early as 1873.

However, the triumph of split bamboo came gradually. Spliced-cane rods had a minor place in the price lists of John Krider that were published at Philadelphia in 1878. Dame, Stoddard & Kendall of Boston still listed only lancewood and greenheart rods in their catalogue of the same period. Thomas Chubb was a major manufacturer of fishing tackle in 1882 with a surprisingly large plant in Vermont. Although his catalogue advertised bamboo fly rods, its principal emphasis still lay with ash and lancewood. The Orvis catalogue published in 1884 included rods of ash, lancewood, hornbeam, and split bamboo alike. Chubb published another catalogue in 1890. It still included rods of ash, lancewood, and greenheart, but it gave a place of growing prominence to bamboo construction.

William Mills & Son was clearly the watershed in American triumph of split cane. Mills had become sole agents for Hiram Leonard in 1877, three years after Leonard had perfected his six-strip rods, and he soon purchased an interest in the rod company. Mills took controlling interest in the Leonard concern a few years later and in 1881, moved its rodmaking subsidiary and Leonard himself to Central Valley, a few miles up the Hudson from New York. The Mills catalogue published in 1894 still offered rods of greenheart and lancewood, but its emphasis clearly lay with cane. There were four-piece cane rods with independent handles and three-piece models with cane-wound grips. The famous Catskill series of Leonard rods had already evolved, with nine-and-a-half-foot models weighing four and five-eighths to three and one-eighth ounces. These rods were awarded a special gold medal at London in 1883, leading Thomas Bate Mills to propose the still lighter Catskill Fairy. It was a slender three-piece rod of eight and a half feet, and it weighed a remarkable two ounces. The catalogue also illustrated the Leonard ferrule patents of 1875 and 1878. These introduced a waterproof cup inside the female socket and the split ferrule that eased the transfer of stress between the metal and the cane in casting. It is obvious that fishermen were first wary of split-cane construction on esthetic grounds, simply because they had learned to like the appearance of round fly rods, and found the hexagonal bamboo ugly. The Mills catalogue included these comments on such arguments:

> It had become evident to us that many parties, in considering this question of round rods, have in many cases quite overlooked the maker in considering the principle.
>
> It should be borne in mind that the great bulk of round rods [we think we can safely say nine-tenths] were made by Mr. Leonard, and it was on the merits of the rods made by him that the excellence of split bamboo was first established. But Mr. Leonard was the first to make a six-strip rod and leave the outside hexagonal; in his increased experience on this work, and after severely testing the hexagonal rod, he has been manufacturing them almost exclusively for the past twelve years, and recommends his hexagonal rod as being far superior to any round rod, which we most heartily endorse.

The Leonard waterproof ferrule was an important development in a time when split cane was assembled with fish or animal adhesives, because it protected the integrity of its laminations. The screw-locking reel seat was also a Leonard innovation, as was the split-type ferrule that permitted the smooth transfer of casting stress across the rim of the metal. But perhaps more important was the growing awareness that it was the power fibers in the outer layers of bamboo that provide its primary resiliency and strength. With rods of more than six strips, these power fibers are considerably reduced, while the glue surfaces and the deadening effects of the adhesive itself is greatly multiplied. Leonard was also aware that in delicate rod calibrations, the cane strips in the tip sections are reduced to fragile shavings. There was often more glue than cane. Once the importance of the power fibers was understood, making his hexagonal rods round in a lathe was also foolish, since it completely sacrificed them at the corners and left only a fraction of the original enamel in each face of the finished rod. His understanding of rod dynamics, his innovative fittings, and his understanding of the attributes of bamboo clearly establish Hiram Leonard as the true father of the modern split-cane rod.

However, its origins lie almost a half century earlier when rod building was dominated by lemonwood, lancewood, and greenheart. Lemonwood, the lovely *Pittosporum eugenioides* plant, is found in New Zealand, and has relatively light weight, good resiliency, fine resistance to moisture, and a straight, densely formed graining. Lancewood was largely harvested in British Guiana, coming from the graceful *Oxanda lanceolata* tree, and it boasts similar qualities. Short of split cane in its modern square, pentagonal and hexagonal construction, greenheart was probably the premier wood for rod building in the nineteenth century. Greenheart is finely textured, surprisingly heavy, and is remarkably resilient and strong, having about twice the bending strength of select white oak. It is classified as *Nectandra rodioei* and is also predominantly harvested in British Guiana. Greenheart

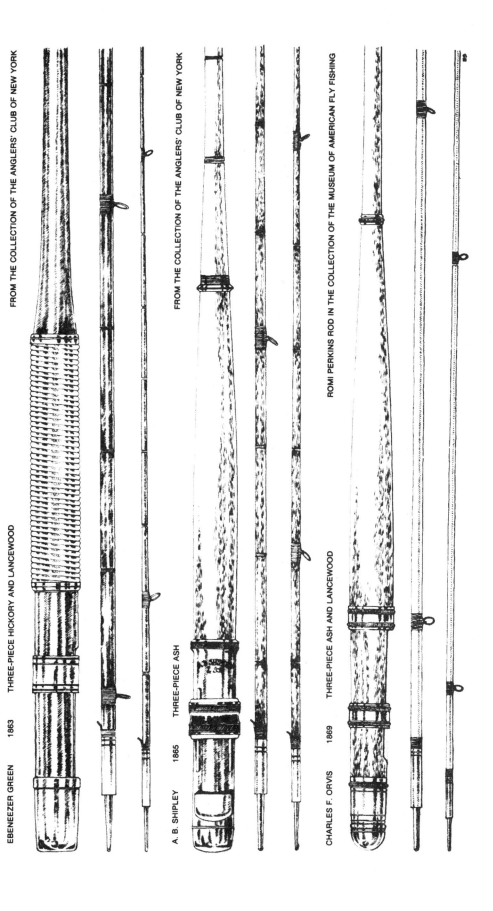

FROM THE COLLECTION OF THE ANGLERS' CLUB OF NEW YORK

EBENEEZER GREEN   1863   THREE-PIECE HICKORY AND LANCEWOOD

FROM THE COLLECTION OF THE ANGLERS' CLUB OF NEW YORK

A. B. SHIPLEY   1865   THREE-PIECE ASH

ROMI PERKINS ROD IN THE COLLECTION OF THE MUSEUM OF AMERICAN FLY FISHING

CHARLES F. ORVIS   1869   THREE-PIECE ASH AND LANCEWOOD

works easily under a semicircular rodmaking plane, but cross-grain work with a lathe is difficult. It can be dried to twelve percent moisture content, and weighs between sixty-five and sixty-eight pounds per cubic foot. It is dense and strongly resistant to water rot and fungus. The color of its heartwood varies from olive to almost black with pale, veinlike patterns. Although these dark heartwoods were once considered the best material for rods, the pale olive greenheart is equally suited. Rodmakers also used *Piptodena africana*, the golden brown African greenheart, in many antique rods. Jamaican greenheart was also popular, and the heartwood of *Ceanothus chlorozylon* is a strong yellowish green material.

Greenheart was popular with nineteenth-century rodmakers, particularly in the United Kingdom. It makes up into a heavy, relatively slow rod ideally suited to wet-fly work for both salmon and trout. Its rhythms are ponderous, making false casting relatively difficult, but its character is perfectly adapted to the classic Spey and switch-cast techniques. Some of the old greenhearts were truly fine wet-fly rods, but with the rise of the dry-fly method on the Hampshire chalkstreams, their popularity rapidly declined among skilled trout fishermen.

However, greenheart has not suffered total oblivion in modern times. Last year there were many slender greenhearts in evidence during the Irish mayfly season on Lough Derg, twenty miles above Galway, dapping live *Ephemera* flies downwind on delicate blow lines of silk. Some boats in the sheltered bays at Oughterard bristled with archaic greenheart and lancewood rods as long as seventeen and eighteen feet.

It's almost funny, Clare De Bergh laughed. *Some of the larger boats will look remarkably like hedgehogs!*

This year on the classic Balmoral water of the Dee, my friends Jock Ropner and Angela Farrar still fished beautiful spliced greenhearts made in the workrooms of Sharpe's at Aberdeen, partly from a sense of tradition and partly because of their Spey-casting qualities on several beats. Their rods would clearly perform feats impossible with cane, on famous pools like Punt and Laundry near Balmoral Castle, and on the famous Cairnton water downstream at Banchory.

Snakewood was also used in many American rods well into the nineteenth century, and there was a famous Samuel Phillippe rod built as late as 1876 which combined eight milled strips, four of snakewood and four of Calcutta in a handsome pattern of alternating woods. Snakewood is the *Moraceae piratinera* widely distributed along the northeast coast of South America. It can be air-dried to approximately twelve percent moisture content and is dense enough to weigh as much as eighty to ninety pounds per cubic foot. Its sapwood is pale and unsuitable for rods. The heartwood is a rich brown marked with darker graining, with a dense, relatively straight grain that works easily.

These materials were all available in lengths between four and six feet, that naturally evolved into rods between twelve and eighteen feet and weighed more than a pound. Such woods were hand-ripped into long

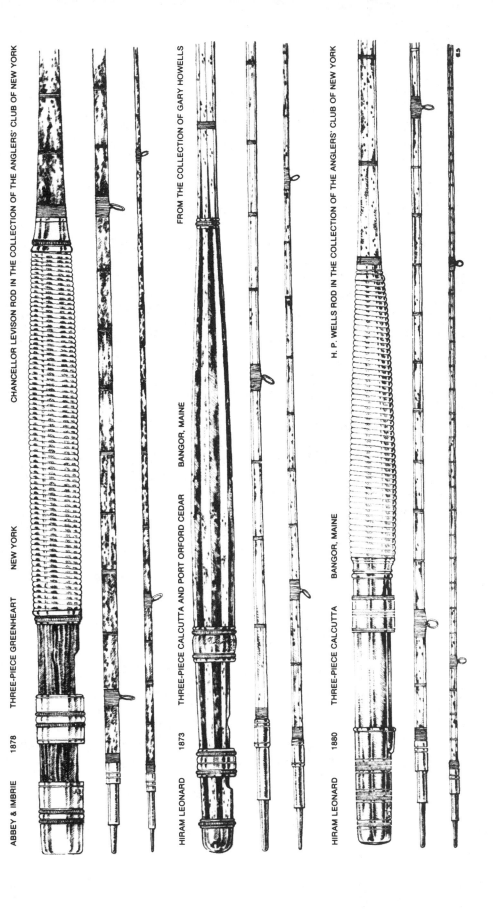

ABBEY & IMBRIE   1878   THREE-PIECE GREENHEART   NEW YORK

CHANCELLOR LEVISON ROD IN THE COLLECTION OF THE ANGLERS' CLUB OF NEW YORK

FROM THE COLLECTION OF GARY HOWELLS

HIRAM LEONARD   1873   THREE-PIECE CALCUTTA AND PORT ORFORD CEDAR   BANGOR, MAINE

H. P. WELLS ROD IN THE COLLECTION OF THE ANGLERS' CLUB OF NEW YORK

HIRAM LEONARD   1880   THREE-PIECE CALCUTTA   BANGOR, MAINE

splines ranging from one-quarter inch to one inch square. These roughcut sections were seldom straight and were hung either in a drying kiln or a warm, relatively dry place for several months.

The calibrations specified by Thaddeus Norris in his *American Angler's Book* are typical of American rod design in the period before the Civil War. His favorite rod measured an inch along its first eight inches, tapering to fifteen thirty-seconds of an inch eighteen inches above the butt. Two feet from the butt it calibrated twelve thirty-seconds of an inch, and eleven thirty-seconds at the first ferrule, forty-eight inches above the grip. The taper had dropped to nine thirty-seconds at the six-foot point, and at the second ferrule it measured seven thirty-seconds of an inch, eight feet above its butt. Ten feet out the rod had reached four thirty-seconds and tapered to a surprisingly delicate one-sixteenth of an inch at its tip guide. Such delicate tip calibrations made these solid wood rods extremely fragile, far more susceptible to breakage than laminated bamboo.

Henry Wells described the details of fabricating such rods in his *Fly Rods and Fly Tackle*, recommending a series of thin brass templates for monitoring rod diameters at each foot of its length. Each template was a semicircle cut in one-thirty-second-of-an-inch plate, placed over the partially tapered section and slipped carefully toward the butt. When a template failed to reach its checkpoint, more wood needed planing to hold a relatively straight taper between calibrations.

The semicircular planes were relatively simple to make. Cutters of the proper diameter were fashioned from steel of blade quality, and were fitted into planing blocks as a ninety-degree angle. These planing blocks, which fitted comfortably into the hands, were rectilinear and milled with a precise, semicircular groove on their working faces.

Greenheart, snakewood, lemonwood, and lancewood all worked easily once they were properly cured and straightened. The planing blocks readily achieved the proper tapers and were useful in making minor corrections. The splines were first planed to a rough approximation of their final tapers. Properly aged woods planed with surprising precision and ease, and amateurs flourished throughout the greenheart era, its techniques being better suited to handwork than machine tools. Yet however difficult it may have been to cast beyond thirty or forty feet with these rods, they clearly performed as superb tools for manipulating a three-fly cast.

Modern fishermen who attempt to fish a trout rod of greenheart or lancewood are invariably disappointed and surprised. Typical trout rods measured ten to twelve feet and weighed between ten and thirteen ounces. Such rods were so heavy that William Mills & Sons neglected to mention their weight in the catalogue of 1894 because their split-cane Leonards were so much lighter. Surprisingly, when such a rod is assembled and strung with a matching line of silk it can be bent into a perfect semicircle. Its tip will flex down smoothly until it reaches the level of the handle, although it will not bend back to touch the handle without fracture. It is almost impossible to flex the butt sections of ash or hickory or maple unless they are assembled into a whole rod. Yet with a relatively light casting load, these butt joints bend freely, accepting the loads from the middle and tip joints like a living part of the entire rod. Although they are rather heavy, and badly balanced by modern standards, these antique wood rods produce a casting action that is surprisingly whippy and soft.

Although casts longer than fifty feet were virtually beyond reach and popping off flies was a continual hazard, it was possible to propel remarkable roll casts with such rods. Controlling fly swing and mending line—both primary techniques of wet-fly tactics—were accomplished far more easily with these supple rods longer than ten feet. And the Spey cast, which lifts the flies from the bottom of its downstream swing to a fresh entry directly across the current in a single rolling twist, is completely impossible with our fashionably shorter modern tackle.

These antique rods of exotic woods were unquestionably more than the primitive tools of a handicraft culture. It is foolish to assume that their owners were merely marking time until the appearance and development of split bamboo. They fished the wet fly both downwind and downstream with virtually no false casting, and their rods performed beautifully.

The origins of split-cane construction are clouded in controversy, with British partisans arguing for its invention in the United Kingdom and Americans fiercely claiming credit for the United States. History tells us that both positions are based on considerable fact. The case clearly hinges on what is meant by the origins of the split-cane methods. Mere rending of the raw bamboo, without regard for the placement and role of the bamboo power fibers under stress, unquestionably evolved among the bowmakers of England. Both four-strip and six-strip construction, using Calcutta cane worked into round cross sections, and the later hexagonal sections that preserved the power fibers intact are clearly American inventions.

James Chetham mentions building rods by sawing and planing wood in *The Angler's Vade Mecum*, first published in London in 1681. Chetham actually recommends using a bowmaker for building laminated rods, although bamboo was clearly not the material being split and assembled into fishing rods, since tip sections of natural, unsplit bamboo were still in use early in the nineteenth century. Alfred Ronalds describes using a bamboo tip in his *Fly-Fisher's Entomology*, which appeared in 1836, but there is strong evidence that his tip sections were still unsplit cane. History also tells us that similar rods of raw bamboo were used in Chinese fishing thousands of years ago, during the Chou Dynasty.

R. B. Marston pointed to *Blaine's Encyclopaedia Of Rural Sports*, which mentioned split-bamboo construction in its section on fishing rods in 1840. That historical footnote seems to prove that the basic concept of rending and laminating cane first appeared in England. No details concerning the techniques of such split-bamboo work were included. Edward Fitzgibbon clarified this puzzle in his *Handbook of Angling*, written seven years later, when he described a three-strip rod fashioned of bamboo. Charles Bowness of Temple Bar in London was its maker, and Fitzgibbon clearly states that his rod had been made several years before his book was written. William Little was another London tacklemaker mentioned in the *Handbook of Angling*, and it described his similar techniques of handling bamboo. The butt sections of both the Bowness and Little rods were both made of kiln-dried ash, while their middle joints and tip sections were three-strip cane. Bowness placed the power fibers inside his rods, filling the core with fish glue, and turned the pith surfaces into a round rod joint. Little worked the slender Calcutta cane into three strips, cutting its pith core into 120-degree glue faces and placing the dense power fibers outside. The evidence clearly places the origins of split-bamboo rods, with their power fibers placed both inside and out, in the United Kingdom.

Samuel Phillippe was also building two-strip and three-strip bamboo rods in Pennsylvania as early as 1844. Phillippe was a famous gunsmith and violinmaker from Easton, a small canalboat town on the Delaware, and had received a silver medal for one of his stringed instruments at the Franklin Institute in Philadelphia. Phillippe was also a skilled trout fisherman who often travelled to the Brodheads with American angling notables like Thaddeus Norris, and local experts like Thomas Heckman, William Green, Colonel T. R. Sitgreaves, Judge James Madison Porter, and Phineus Kinsey. It is logical that a skilled craftsman like Phillippe should turn to rodmaking, and his parallel knowledge of metallurgy was soon applied to manufacturing the Kinsey hook pattern.

Since Phillippe was born in 1801, and his family history tells us that he was apprenticed as a gunsmith at sixteen in the shop of Peter Young, his skills were probably well developed before 1830. His shop unquestionably produced rods of ash, hickory, greenheart, snakewood, lancewood, and lemonwood before 1845. His close friendship with Thaddeus Norris indicates that rod specifications meticulously described in *The American Angler's Book* probably originated with Phillippe, and other sources tell us that his first cane rods appeared in 1846.

Dr. James Henshall is the angling historian who documented the developments attributed to Phillippe before the old rodmaker died in 1877, corresponding with many of Phillippe's disciples and fishing companions and customers before he published his *Book of the Black Bass* in 1881. Henshall knew Phillippe's family well, particularly young Solon Phillippe, who had joined his father in gunsmithing and rod building in 1849. Although many other rodmakers attempted to claim the invention of modern four-strip and six-strip construction for themselves and sought to discredit Phillippe and his work, the evidence of Henshall and his exchange of letters with many of Phillippe's contemporaries clearly vindicate the Pennsylvania craftsman and his claim to fame.

Phillippe first tried two-strip and three-strip rods, with their power fibers outside, and fitted with butts of ash and unsplit bamboo. Obviously, these experiments loaded eccentrically and refused to deliver a cast properly. Phillippe soon turned to four-strip construction with the power fibers outside, and found they cast much better, although such quadrate rods are still demanding under casting stress. Four-strip rods are slightly stronger and more resilient than other cane construction of equal weight, because they place more power fibers in the bending plane, slightly farther from the longitudinal axis of the section. However, four-strip rods are also unforgiving taskmasters, refusing to cast clearly if a fisherman has poor casting habits and works outside the casting plane. Such demanding temperament soon led Phillippe to experiment with other theories of split-cane construction, although he built many four-strip rods completely split from bamboo as early as 1846. His six-strip rods entirely built of cane were also perfected before he sold his first bamboo rod in 1848, although Phillippe earlier made a four-strip rod with an ash butt section for Colonel Sitgreaves.

Phillippe's account books clearly show that the first all-bamboo rod sold in 1848 was a four-strip design, featuring a cane tip, middle joint, and swelled butt section. Solon Phillippe was making his own six-strip rods as early as 1859, using twelve laminated strips of hardwood and bamboo in the grip. Similar rods were later made by famous makers like Ebenezer Green, Charles Murphy, and Hiram Leonard. Solon Phillippe and his father made both six-strip and eight-strip rods between 1865 and 1870, when ill health ultimately forced the retirement of the elder Phillippe, who died in 1877.

Doctor Henshall interviewed a number of Phillippe contemporaries to confirm the elder Phillippe's role in bamboo rod theory and construction. Thomas Heckman knew Phillippe across sixty-odd years, and fished with him often, sometimes camping for a week along the Bushkill or Brodheads. Heckman watched Phillippe building bamboo rods in 1846, and machining his own ferrules, reel fittings, and ring-and-keeper guides. Phillippe built two rods for Heckman, and another was built for Edward Innes, who often visited his rodmaking shop after 1840. Innes confirmed watching Phillippe make a bamboo fly rod in the winter of 1847, and George Stout reported seeing a Phillippe rod when he arrived at Easton in 1851. Stout later became an amateur rodmaker, building about a dozen in the Phillippe style, starting in 1860. Charles Imbrie also corresponded with Henshall concerning Phillippe and his rods. Abbey and Imbrie was a fine Manhattan tackle house that evolved from the older Andrew Clerk & Company in 1875, two years before Phillippe died at Easton. Andrew Clerk & Company had been founded in 1820, and Clerk had sold Phillippe rods well before the Civil War. The letter from Charles Imbrie to Henshall contains this revealing paragraph:

> Your account of the origin of the split-bamboo rod is perfectly correct. Our Mister Abbey was the active member of Andrew Clerk & Company at the time of the origination, by Mister Phillippe, of the split bamboo rod, and is therefore well acquainted with its history to the present time.

Doctor W. W. Bowlby of Manhattan also exchanged letters with

Henshall concerning Phillippe and his bamboo rods. Bowlby lived in New Jersey, just across the Delaware from Easton, and often saw Phillippe on rivers like the Musconetcong and Pequest. According to Bowlby, Phillippe was already fishing with a split-cane rod in 1852, and it was the first time he had seen such tackle.

Perhaps the most revealing evidence confirming the role that Phillippe played in development of the bamboo rod is a little-known letter from Charles Murphy to Doctor Henshall. Many angling historians argue that Phillippe did not originate the prototypes of modern split-cane construction, preferring to believe other rodmakers and angling writers. Some jealous contemporaries admitted that Phillippe had invented four-strip and six-strip construction, but attempted to downgrade his workmanship—yet the three Phillippe rods that I have examined demonstrate a technical skill superior to the first work of Hiram Leonard.

The Phillippe rod in the collection of the Anglers' Club of New York, and particularly the Phillippe in the Oldenwalder collection, unmistakably confirm his rodmaking skills. The Oldenwalder rod was calibrated by Vincent Marinaro, himself a skilled rodmaker and author of *A Modern Dry-Fly Code*, when it was exactly a century old. It measured eleven feet in three joints of six-strip bamboo. The rod featured a swelled handle of cane that calibrated an inch, tapering to seventeen thirty-seconds of an inch just above the grip. It tapered to twelve thirty-seconds at the midpoint of its butt joint, and eleven thirty-seconds at the first ferrule. The ferrule was rolled and soldered from German silver, measuring nineteen sixty-fourths of an inch. The middle section calibrated ten thirty-seconds at the first ferrule, tapering to nine thirty-seconds at its center and seven thirty-seconds at the upper ferrule. The second ferrule measured twelve sixty-fourths of an inch, while the tip section tapered from six thirty-seconds to a delicate three thirty-seconds at its tip ring. It is interesting to compare these tapers with the specifications recommended by Thaddeus Norris in lancewood, lemonwood, or greenheart. The swelled grip was finished with the precise checkering typical of a highly skilled gunsmith.

Several other critics of Phillippe argued that his butt joints were always shaped from ash, and that his rods were never fully made of bamboo. William Mitchell was a skilled British rodmaker who emigrated to the United States, and Mitchell was apparently the first rodmaker to appreciate the unique properties of Tonkin cane, and he used business contacts in London to acquire his supply of culms from China. His articles in *The American Angler* promoted the role of Ebenezer Green and Charles Murphy in the creation of the first bamboo rods, downgrading the earlier pioneer work of Phillippe. Later articles echoed the Mitchell story, including a piece that was printed in *The New York Times* in 1881. It granted that Phillippe had discovered the utility of split bamboo, but that Green and Murphy had built the first completely bamboo rods after 1860, erroneously crediting Murphy with the creation of the first all-cane trout

FROM THE COLLECTION OF HARRY DARBEE

JOHN KAY   1870   SIX-PIECE ASH AND JACARANDA

J. M. KAUFMANN ROD IN THE COLLECTION OF THE MUSEUM OF AMERICAN FLY FISHING

C. F. MURPHY   1875   FOUR-PIECE CALCUTTA

rod in 1863. Murphy apparently did build his first cane trout rod in that year, although both Samuel and Solon Phillippe preceded him. The following observations were made by Charles Murphy in his letter to James Henshall, and contain some striking facts:

> Mr. Charles Luke, of this city, formerly of Easton, Pennsylvania, used to fish and hunt with Mr. Phillippe, and frequented his workshop, where he saw him use split bamboo for fly rods certainly as far back as 1848.
>
> Luke moved from Easton to Newark in 1850. I am very certain you can give Phillippe credit for the discovery of split bamboo for fly rods without fear of being contradicted. While he was making rods for Andrew Clerk & Company, Mr. Abbey, of that firm, showed Mr. Green and myself a rod made by Mr. Phillippe, the top and second joint made of split bamboo, with the butt joint made from white ash.

Murphy was clearly a major figure in the history of the bamboo fly rod, and there is evidence that he believed the first complete bass, trout, and salmon rods were his. Perhaps Murphy himself was the source of the contention that Phillippe never built rods entirely made of cane, since his letter to Doctor Henshall is careful to mention a butt section of white ash on the first split-bamboo rod he had seen. It is interesting that Murphy places Ebenezer Green with him that day at Andrew Clerk & Company, when they both examined the Phillippe rod.

Thaddeus Norris and Ebenezer Green were both making split-cane rods for their own fishing in 1860, after earlier contact with Phillippe and his work. Charles Murphy started selling split-cane trout rods in considerable numbers in 1863, marketing many of them through Andrew Clerk. Two years later, Murphy made the first bamboo salmon rod, using the four-strip method. This rod was carried to Scotland by Andrew Clerk, where it was quickly admired and copied. Murphy also used four-strip construction for the first cane bass rod in 1865. Until it was dissolved in 1875, Andrew Clerk & Company exported surprising numbers of American six-strip, eight-strip, and twelve-strip rods to the United Kingdom.

Ebenezer Green was a fine cabinetmaker in Newark, and many of his practical skills undoubtedly influenced Murphy in the period just before the Civil War. Green built excellent rods, but largely for himself and his fishing friends, and few apparently survive today.

Charles Murphy is not the most celebrated rodmaker in the evolution of American fly-fishing, since that position clearly belongs to the younger Hiram Leonard, who followed in 1870. Murphy did not build the first trout rods made entirely of split bamboo, since both Samuel Phillippe and his son have that honor. However, the design and casting qualities and calibrations of his rods unquestionably influenced later craftsmen, including the younger Leonard himself. Murphy also was thoroughly versed in the theory and technology of rod construction.

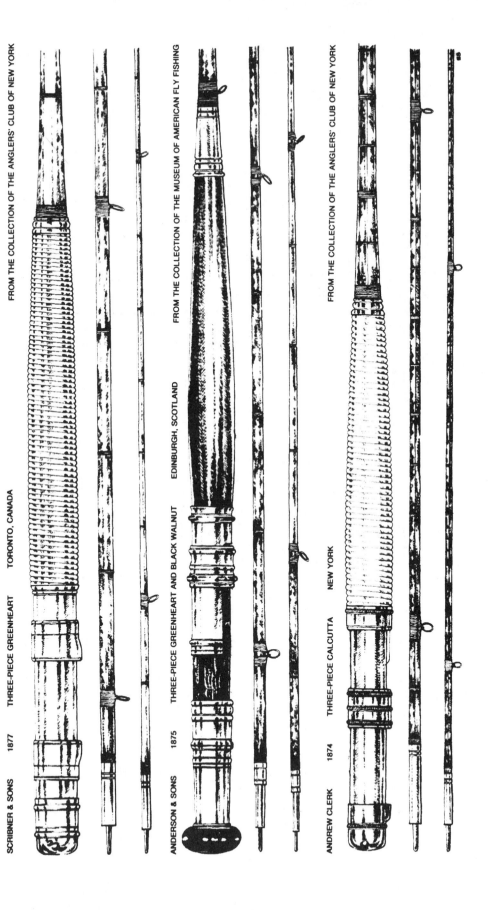

SCRIBNER & SONS   1877   THREE-PIECE GREENHEART   TORONTO, CANADA

FROM THE COLLECTION OF THE ANGLERS' CLUB OF NEW YORK

ANDERSON & SONS   1875   THREE-PIECE GREENHEART AND BLACK WALNUT   EDINBURGH, SCOTLAND

FROM THE COLLECTION OF THE MUSEUM OF AMERICAN FLY FISHING

ANDREW CLERK   1874   THREE-PIECE CALCUTTA   NEW YORK

FROM THE COLLECTION OF THE ANGLERS' CLUB OF NEW YORK

Fred Mather was the distinguished fisherman and pioneer ichthyologist who later imported the brown trout to the United States, and his book *My Angling Friends* describes meeting the talkative Murphy at the Manhattan tackle shop of J. C. Conroy in 1865:

> I listened with wonder to the talk of angles, tapers, gluing, and other details, until I thought that the building up of a split-bamboo rod required more careful attention than the grinding of a lens for a great telescope.

Murphy was posturing and voluble in his encounter with Mather, claiming full credit for the development of the bamboo rod, and adding that he was experimenting with six-strip construction. Genio Scott fished the four-strip Murphy salmon rod with Andrew Clerk in Canada, and praised its casting qualities in *Fishing in American Waters*.

Later in his life, Murphy became increasingly insular and cantankerous, perhaps echoing his combative Irish heritage. It was commonly said that Murphy would rather quarrel than eat, although he was a relatively small man. His sullen moodiness led to increasing claims that he alone had invented split-cane construction, contradicting his earlier letter to Doctor Henshall. His combativeness and ego eventually annoyed Charles Imbrie so completely that their long-standing business relationship was ended. Imbrie believed that Murphy might have been a splendid rodmaker, perhaps the equal of Hiram Leonard, had he exercised more self-discipline—adding in his letter to Henshall that Murphy failed to grow after 1870, in terms of both his craftsmanship and his character.

Murphy failed to compete in the mercantile atmosphere that followed the Civil War, the split-cane production coming from the shops of rodmakers like Orvis, Leonard, and Chubb. Other craftsmen were able to organize and direct the work in their shops, while Murphy trusted only himself, and was still working alone in his home in 1881. Such solitary craftsmen seem romantic now, but Murphy's disposition and pride both cost him a chance at greatness, and his historical position unquestionably suffered from a limited output during the years when his skills should have matured and flowered.

The famous Murphy trout rod from the Kauffmann collection that is displayed at the Museum of American Fly-Fishing shows that Murphy was a superb craftsman. The Kauffmann rod was made about 1867 for Samuel Kauffmann of Washington, and was apparently used primarily at the Oquossoc Club in Maine, which was formed in 1869. Its workmanship equals the best of the early Leonard rods and clearly displays the promise that Charles Imbrie encouraged before he subsequently quarrelled with Murphy at Abbey & Imbrie in New York.

The Kauffmann rod is made in three sections and measures a full twelve feet. Despite its length it surprisingly weighs only seven and a half ounces. The Murphy is a delicate two thirty-seconds of an inch at its tip ring, four thirty-seconds of an inch at the midpoint of the tip joint, and measures a slender six thirty-seconds at its upper ferrule. Unlike the Norris and Phillippe patterns, the Murphy tapers apparently held constant across a ferrule, at least in the Kauffmann rod, indicating that Murphy better understood the dynamics of the casting stress between rod sections than either Norris or Phillippe. The middle joint tapered from six thirty-seconds to ten thirty-seconds at the lower ferrule. The butt section calibrated ten thirty-seconds at the ferrule, tapering to fourteen thirty-seconds approximately four inches above the German-silver grip check, and swelling to twenty-four thirty-seconds at the check itself. Such swelled grips had originated with the Phillippes before 1860, and a swelled bamboo grip checkered like a gunstock had been a striking detail of the Oldenwalder rod. Such swelled grips were quite difficult to make, since each bamboo strip was sharply widened so the handle swelled gracefully over a cedar core. Anyone who has ever worked with split-cane construction respects the high degree of skill needed to finish a swelled grip, instead of the modern method of concealing the butt inside its reel seat and cork. The Murphy rod was distinguished by the elegance and surprisingly modern proportions of its grip design. Its butt cap was gracefully shaped and engraved, measuring about an inch, and showing a brief length of swelled bamboo between its upper edge and the handsome welt of the check that secured the sliding reel band. The reel band itself measured about three-quarters of an inch and was engraved with six ornamental rings. The grip itself was wound with rattan, split and laid with great precision in a shallow spiral, its ends concealed under a pair of half-inch rings.

The Murphy rod made for Kauffmaun is in exquisite condition and could easily be fished today. Its silk windings have grown a little brittle in the past century, and its guides are ring-and-keeper fittings of brass. The German-silver ferrules are probably frail, enclosing their dowelled slides in a tube formed of a rolled and soldered plate of thin alloy. The sections are round, their hexagonal corners planed off until only the delicate glue lines reveal the number of split-cane strips. It is curious that the butt and middle sections are six-strip work, while the delicate tip uses four-strip construction. Murphy probably chose this hybrid design because such tips were much easier to make, but the Oldenwalder Phillippe rod had used six-strip construction throughout its length fifteen years earlier, clearly demonstrating that the controversial Murphy was not the only wellspring of craftsmanship in bamboo. The famous 1873 Leonard, in the Howells collection at San Francisco, also incorporates the more difficult six-strip construction throughout its length.

The Kauffmann rod is a superb example of Murphy's work, and its great value extends beyond its actual worth, since it teaches us much about the history of American fly rods. It closely resembles the vintage Leonards that appeared a decade later, with their grip fittings and rattan handles, their bayonet ferrules, and their bamboo culm cases with caps of elegantly machined brass. The Murphy rod is surprisingly modern, and although Leonard is better known because several of his apprentices later became fine rodmakers in their own right, Murphy unmistakably influenced the future.

No roster of early American rodmakers would be complete without Charles F. Orvis, who founded the present tackle company in 1856. Orvis was born at Manchester in 1831, along the Battenkill in central Vermont. It is a lovely New England village sheltered in a beautiful valley, and fishing between Manchester and Arlington occupied most of his boyhood summers, mixed with woodcock and grouse shooting in the fall. Orvis was a precocious craftsman, tirelessly repairing clocks and toys in his youth, and turning to fly rods and reels in later years. His first rods were made in about 1854, using butts of white ash and upper sections of lancewood, much like the early work of Norris and Phillippe. Orvis enjoyed a superb reputation with his contemporaries, leading James Henshall to comment in his *Book of the Black Bass* that Orvis was among the finest and most honest tacklemakers of his time.

CHARLES F. ORVIS

Orvis was fully aware of the developments in the workshops of Phillippe, Green, Murphy, and Leonard, and his company was producing split-bamboo rods as early as 1874, the same year that Orvis patented the first perforated-spool reel for fly-fishing. Orvis produced sixteen catalogues before 1884, the probable date of the remarkable Orvis publication reproduced in *Great Fishing Catalogs of the Golden Age*. That 1884 catalogue was a Victorian classic, with its embossed and gilded cover secured by a silk binding cord and tassel. It offered fly rods of hornbeam, lancewood, and lancewood with a white-ash butt, as well as hexagonal split-cane designs of the Leonard type. The common grips were wound rattan, walnut with longitudinal flutings, and lightweight sumac that had a florid grain pattern clearly appealing to the Victorian eye. Orvis also offered cork grips on its so-called ladies' rods of lancewood and hexagonal cane, when they were introduced in the United States in 1880. Cork proved popular with fishermen too, and the specie-cork handle was king after only a decade. It still reigns today, although first-quality cork is increasingly difficult to import for rodmaking.

The style of the most expensive Orvis rods was still unmistakably derived from the bamboo prototypes of Murphy and Leonard, with their swelled cane handles wound in rattan, and their German-silver fittings. These premium Orvis rods included a patented internal spring which secured the sliding reel band. The walnut, cork and sumac grips were fitted along the rod shaft itself, an easier task than tapering a swelled handle of split bamboo, and their designs were a prelude to the modern Orvis rods. The 1884 catalogue also includes the Orvis patent reel, with its fully perforated drum, as well as two elegant Vom Hofe reels of the period.

Orvis was building relatively modern fly rods of hexagonal split bamboo in 1900, concentrating on three-piece designs as light as four ounces. The entire Orvis stock now featured cork grips exclusively. There were bargain models selling at less than five dollars, with nickel-plated ferrules and metal reel seats. These rods were still fitted with ring-and-keeper guides, varied between ten and ten and a half feet, and weighed from six and a half to seven and a half ounces. The Orvis five-dollar grade had similar fittings, but offered more delicate tapers. Its rods were nine to ten and a half feet in length, and weighed between five and six and three-quarters ounces. The ten-dollar series ranged from nine to eleven feet, and offered weights from five to seven and one-quarter ounces. The most expensive fly rod offered English snake guides, which first appeared on American rods late in the nineteenth century. Its ferrules, reel bands, grip check, and butt cap were all machined of German silver. It sold for only fifteen dollars, measured eight feet three inches, and weighed only four ounces. Except for its relatively soft action, its length and weight compare favorably with a modern Orvis Battenkill, which sells at twelve times the price. It is interesting to note that the Orvis catalogue found it necessary to comment that a rod weighing only four ounces was not a toy.

The reputation of Orvis bamboo rods was already excellent in 1881, beginning a tradition for quality that endures today. Ned Buntline was famous in the late nineteenth century for popular novels extolling figures like Wyatt Earp and Buffalo Bill Cody on the American frontier. His 1881 article in *Turf, Field and Farm*, a major periodical in those years, described a day along the Beaverkill with his favorite Orvis. Buntline died in 1886, and from his final sickroom he wrote these lines for opening day:

> Tomorrow a hundred rods will bend over bright waters in my happy Catskills, yet I can only stare at my Orvis in the corner, and let its bamboo rest.

Hiram Lewis Leonard is the father of the modern fly rod, both in the remarkable technical knowledge and craftsmanship his work displayed and in the great rodmakers he trained in his shop. Leonard was born in Maine in 1833, on the estuary of the Penobscot at Bangor. His early apprenticeships taught him metalworking and cabinetmaking skills, and Leonard had subsequent training as an engineer.

His rodmaking career started at Bangor in 1871, with his first efforts constructed of white ash and lancewood. Since Leonard loved fishing and made the rod for himself, his career almost remained a hobby but a friend suggested that the rod should be shown to Bradford & Anthony, the famous sporting goods house in Boston. Its partners were so impressed that Bradford & Anthony agreed to market his entire production and encouraged Leonard to experiment with cane. Leonard also built many lancewood rods in these early years, although Bradford & Anthony soon talked him into building rods in four-strip bamboo. The early Leonard in the Howells collection is exquisite proof that Hiram Leonard was building six-strip rods as early as 1873.

The Howells Leonard was built in Bangor in 1873; its fixed-reel band is inscribed from H. L. Leonard to H. H. Howells and the date is unmistakably engraved underneath. It is the oldest known Leonard in any collection, and H. H. Howells was an attorney in Maine when the rod was built. Since it is obviously a presentation rod from its maker, Howells apparently performed the legal services in securing the first ferrule patents for Leonard. Howells went west about 1875, practicing law in Wyoming for many years before finally travelling to San Francisco, where he was ultimately appointed to the bench. Judge Howells was the grandfather of Gary Howells, one of our finest American rodmakers.

The Howells rod itself is remarkable. Its calibrations are surprisingly modern considering its age. It measures ten feet and was made in three sections, weighing approximately nine ounces. The reel seat is cut into the laminated handle and measures two and seven-eighths inches, and the slender grip is nine and seven-eighths inches in length. The shaft itself is only two thirty-seconds of an inch at its tip guide, reaches three thirty-seconds of an inch at the middle of the tip section, and five thirty-seconds at the ferrule. The middle joint is six thirty-seconds at its upper ferrule, eight thirty-seconds at its midpoint, and nine thirty-seconds

HIRAM LEWIS LEONARD

at its lower ferrule. The butt calibrates ten thirty-seconds at the ferrule, twelve thirty-seconds halfway to the handle, and fourteen thirty-seconds at the grip check. The swelled handle tapers from fourteen thirty-seconds of an inch at the check to twenty-eight thirty-seconds of an inch at its thickest point, tapering back to twenty-five thirty-seconds at the fixed band of the reel seat. The handle is only eighteen thirty-seconds of an inch at the butt cap. These calibrations would probably produce a ten-foot rod weighing only four to five ounces, except for the weight of its swelled, laminated grip.

The ferrules were originally the slender dowel-type patented for Leonard two years later. The tubing was rolled and soldered from a thin sheet of German silver and reinforced at the throat with a simple welt. There were two ornamental rings engraved at the base, the ferrules were pinned with brass, and there were still no serrations. Ring-and-keeper guides were used throughout. The reel seat is fitted with a small hole, perhaps to receive a particular reel. Elegantly machined fittings of German silver form the grip check, the fixed-reel band, and the sliding reel-seat ring. The butt cap is also shaped from nickel silver into an elegant ornamental cup, and the fixed bands are so tightly fitted into the handle that a rattan covering seems unlikely. The exquisite laminated handle with its six strips of cane swelling with alternating splines of Port Orford cedar is quite ornamental and unique. This 1873 Leonard in the Howells collection is one of the rare bench marks in our angling history.

Hiram Leonard loved the hunting and fishing in those early years in Maine and was such a skilled angler that he fully understood the dynamics of fly casting. It is obvious that Leonard also possessed the rare ability to communicate his skills and knowledge and love of rodmaking to others. Several young Bangor craftsmen joined his shop crew as apprentices, and a surprising number ultimately became famous rod builders—men like Edward Payne, Fred Divine, Eustis Edwards, Thomas Chubb, Fred Thomas, and the Hawes brothers all made rods in later years.

During their Bangor years, the Leonard staff was a happy family that fished and hunted together across Maine. Hiram Leonard also loved music, and his shop repaired and made musical instruments. The staff had its own musical group and played together often.

It was pretty well known, Arthur Mills explained many years ago, at William Mills & Son in downtown New York, *that you had to play some instrument to work for Leonard.*

Unfortunately, their idyllic life together began to sour. The principal markets for their work lay in New York and Philadelphia, and a business relationship for selling Leonard rods was forged with Thomas Bate Mills of William Mills & Son. Leonard suffered money problems in 1878 and grudgingly surrendered a controlling interest to the Mills family. Thomas Bate Mills moved Leonard south to a new rod plant in Central Valley, fifty-odd miles above Manhattan, in the summer of 1881. Leonard and his staff moved reluctantly, in spite of their new proximity to famous Catskill rivers like the Beaverkill and Willowemoc, and the mood of their workrooms never matched the bucolic years in Maine. However, the Catskill trout ultimately did become the yardstick for Leonard's achievements, and their rivers became the perfect proving grounds for the evolving Leonard rods.

Thomas Chubb decided against the move to southern New York, and chose to establish his own tackle company in Vermont. His boldness paid off, and Chubb had established a thriving plant at Post Mills in 1886. Fred Thomas and Eustis Edwards agreed to leave Bangor. Thomas became the foreman, and soon enticed Edward Payne to join them with his glowing descriptions of the trout streams and bird shooting. Payne soon found himself homesick for Maine and went back, but his wife had been born near Central Valley, and loved its milder winters. Her arguments finally persuaded Payne to rejoin Leonard. But the camaraderie they had found together in Maine was never rekindled, and their growing skills made several members of the Leonard staff restless. Thomas, Edwards, and Payne soon left and formed their own partnership. The following year they sold their budding firm to the United States Net and Twine Company, in concert with several other wealthy backers, and their rodmaking operations were moved to Brooklyn. It seems their new facilities were the property of their backers, and the Wilkinson Company was chosen as the primary sales outlet, but the new ownership had misjudged its new employees. Fred Thomas soon resigned and started making his own rods with his son Leon in Bangor. Eustis Edwards followed Thomas to Maine, and moved later to Connecticut, where he built rods with his sons William and Eugene Edwards.

Edward Payne had finally adjusted to leaving his native Maine for the Hudson Valley, but commuting each day to Brooklyn was the final straw. Payne finally exploded under the abrasive pressures of Brooklyn and bought back his remaining interest in the new rod company. Payne joined the Leonard foreman Frank Oram in a fresh partnership under his own name. The fledgling Payne rod company was located at Highland Mills, a few miles north from Central Valley. His son James and other apprentices joined the Payne operation, and the younger Payne continued in the family business after his father's death. It was James Payne who ultimately became the principal heir of Hiram Leonard, and perhaps the finest rodmaking craftsman who ever split a culm and worked a planing block—although many fine fishermen would argue that perhaps Everett Garrison also deserves that title, without diminishing the exquisite work of Payne and his incredible skills.

Loman and Hiram Hawes were Leonard's nephews, and remained loyal associates until Hiram Leonard died in 1907. Thomas Bate Mills acquired the last outstanding shares of Leonard after its founder's death, and most of the employees skilled enough to make an entire rod themselves soon left. Loman Hawes was the mechanical genius who had conceived the Leonard bevel cutter that still remains one of the finest ever designed, and a partnership with his brother Hiram was soon established. It was a marriage of creativity and skills that held great promise, but Loman Hawes died suddenly, before that promise was tested or fulfilled. Hiram Hawes was a fine tournament caster and craftsman who had married one of Leonard's daughters, and he ultimately produced a number of excellent rods under his family trademark. The most successful years for the Hawes rods probably occurred after the First World War, when Abercrombie & Fitch sold them in good numbers.

Fred Divine was perhaps the only former employee who failed to follow in the Leonard tradition, although he clearly had the skills to equal the work of his colleagues. Divine held a unique patent on a spiral-laminated bamboo rod, which had been granted in 1892, but it never became popular. Such rods were tapered, glued, and pressure-wrapped like conventional cane sections. The freshly wrapped bamboo was then twisted and held in tension until it dried. The result was an extremely stiff rod section of great strength, and many are still fishable today. However, the Divine patent is rather difficult to implement, and many finished sections must be rejected. His only disciple was probably Letcher Lambuth, the famous amateur rodmaker and fishing companion of Roderick Haig-Brown in the Pacific Northwest. Lambuth rods fabricated with the Divine spiral patent are rare, but owners like Steven Raymond are sold on their performance on brawling steelhead rivers from northern California to British Columbia.

Divine had pliable standards of workmanship and design, and his rods varied radically in quality over the years. Divine made large numbers of lancewood and lemonwood rods after his departure from Leonard, using proportions and fittings of surprising elegance. Their workmanship and performance were good. Divine probably knew bamboo was better, but he eagerly supplied what his buyers wanted. His catholic tastes included four-strip and eight-strip cane, although as a former Leonard employee, Divine unquestionably knew six-strip rods were better. He also worked his rods from Calcutta and Tonkin cane with equal relish.

Tonkin cane was first imported through New York in 1895, and few knowledgeable craftsmen used anything else after 1910. Divine made six-strip and eight-strip rods in large numbers for Abercrombie & Fitch in 1911, charging more for the eight-strip rods, and telling his customers that octagonal sections cast better because they were round. His eight-strip rods varied from eight to ten feet, and between four and a half and eight ounces. The six-strip series weighed from a delicate three and a half ounces to eight and one-quarter ounces, and measured between eight and ten and a half feet. The most expensive rods that Divine made for Abercrombie & Fitch weighed three and three-quarters ounces to six and one-quarter ounces, and varied from eight to nine and a half feet. Their cost stemmed from being completely wrapped in white silk from grip check to tip guide. The silk virtually disappeared when the rod was varnished, revealing the nodes and graining in the bamboo, and its varnish-soaked weight was enough to deaden the spirit of the finest cane.

SOLON PHILLIPPE · 1881 · THREE-PIECE CALCUTTA AND BLACK WALNUT · EASTON, PENNSYLVANIA

JOHN FARQUAR ROD IN THE COLLECTION OF THE ANGLERS' CLUB OF NEW YORK

WILLIAM MITCHELL · 1885 · THREE-PIECE GREENHEART AND ROSEWOOD · NEW YORK

JEREMIAH RICHARDS ROD IN THE COLLECTION OF THE ANGLERS' CLUB OF NEW YORK

HIRAM LEONARD · 1896 · THREE-PIECE TONKIN BAMBOO · CENTRAL VALLEY, NEW YORK

FROM THE COLLECTION OF THE ADIRONDACK MUSEUM

African steel-vine rods appeared shortly before the First World War and were an utter and laughable fraud. Catalogue copy touted African steel vine as the strongest rod material in the world. Steel vine simply did not exist. It was actually Calcutta bamboo formed into a six-strip taper and planed round into its pith core. Theodore Gordon was the first to observe that African steel vine looked like the internal fibers of Calcutta bamboo, but except for Gordon, the steel-vine hoax went undetected for twenty-odd years. It is typical of Divine that he willingly made African steel-vine rods in large numbers after his rod company was absorbed by Horrocks-Ibbotson in New York.

The eighty years between Samuel Phillippe and the accomplishments of Hiram Leonard and his disciples are the Golden Age of American rod building. Leonard died before his company had started working in Tonkin cane, although his younger colleagues and their sons would ultimately build rods of the new Chinese bamboo that easily surpassed the performance of the earlier Leonards.

The vintage years had passed, and their fingerprints are found in the specifications and fittings of the vintage rods. The history of fly-fishing is written in such tackle. The principal clues indicating the age and historical importance of a particular fly rod are found in its tip guide, running guides, ferrules, shaft materials, grip and reel-seat design, and ornamental wrappings. These bench marks identifying both the maker and birth of any rod are only found in the physical character of the rod and its fittings.

Tip guides have varied surprisingly over the years. Several curious designs evolved in the beginning, particularly the Chubb-patent type, which looked a little like a golf tee. Its top was cupped and its sides were perforated to receive the line. The three-ring top was a skeletal version of the same concept. Two German-silver rings were set on edge and flared out like a yoke, receiving a third ring set flat on top. Another version set a ring of agate or agatine on top, seating it in a band of nickel silver. The early Phillippe, Green, Murphy, Leonard, and Chubb rods all used a simple ring guide with its delicate ring set in the plane of the rod and not turned down like a modern tip guide. Later Leonards used a ring of agate soldered at a ninety-degree angle to its tubing. Early Hardy rods used a similar agate guide, but reinforced it with a pair of slender German-silver supports. Other braced types were also common, and have surfaced again in the modern graphite rods. It was Fred Thomas who developed an intriguing tip guide designed to be secured to the cane even when the glue deteriorated. To the regular tubing it added a slender tongue of German silver that lay along the top face of the rod concealed under the usually ornamental silk wraps. Modern rodmakers have almost universally accepted the so-called perfection tops, which consist of a slender tube with a pear-shaped guide bending down to align with the snake guides—limiting their creative energies merely to optional finishes in silver, oxidized silver and black.

The running guides have experienced a similar evolution. Before fly reels were widely used, only a flat-ring top was needed. Early rods largely

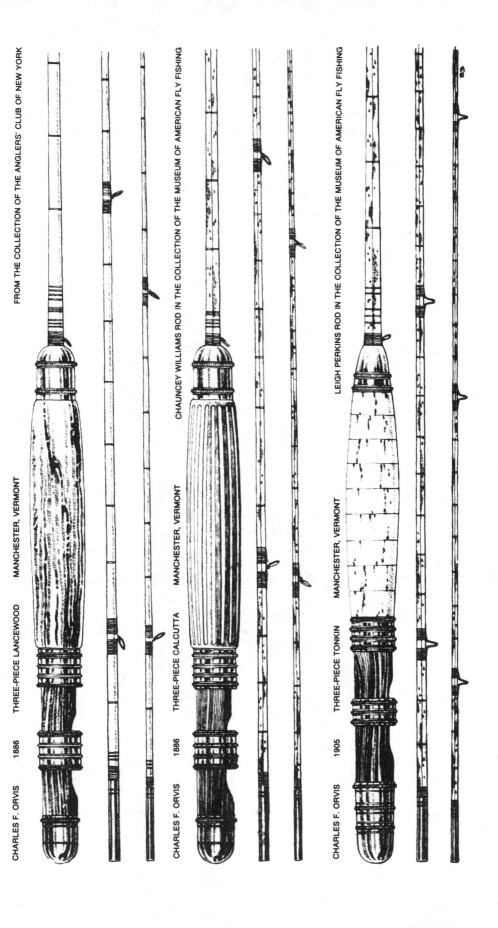

FROM THE COLLECTION OF THE ANGLERS' CLUB OF NEW YORK

CHARLES F. ORVIS   1886   THREE-PIECE LANCEWOOD   MANCHESTER, VERMONT

CHAUNCEY WILLIAMS ROD IN THE COLLECTION OF THE MUSEUM OF AMERICAN FLY FISHING

CHARLES F. ORVIS   1886   THREE-PIECE CALCUTTA   MANCHESTER, VERMONT

LEIGH PERKINS ROD IN THE COLLECTION OF THE MUSEUM OF AMERICAN FLY FISHING

CHARLES F. ORVIS   1905   THREE-PIECE TONKIN   MANCHESTER, VERMONT

employed ring-and-keeper guides of various metals, although they often collapsed and pinched a shooting line, quickly killing the velocity and distance of the cast. Such guides were typical between 1800 and 1900. Tunnel guides soon followed, although their openings were too small for good casting performance. The double twist guide was a curiously intricate ancestor of the English snake guide that first appeared about 1900, and the simpler single-wire snake guides quickly doomed the double twist design. English snake guides are formed with their openings toward the right, while a modern American type opens to the left. Double ring guides achieved a brief popularity between 1890 and 1900. American snake guides were used almost exclusively in this country after 1915, when the First World War interrupted trade in such items—except for the independent Fred Thomas, who stubbornly continued to use the English snakes until he died, perhaps because he knew it would identify his work in the future.

Ferrules are another clue to the origins of an antique rod. Their quality is often indicative of the quality of the rod itself. German silver has been the hallmark of rod quality since the Civil War, although brass and copper alloys sometimes were used earlier. Some modern builders like Paul Young have used first-grade aluminum ferrules in their passion for reducing weight, and western artisans like Lew Stoner, Doug Merrick and Gary Howells prefer duronze alloy. Nickel-plated and lacquered brass clearly indicate poor rod quality or poor judgment on the part of its maker.

Dowel-type ferrules were popular throughout the nineteenth century. Sometimes they were also called spike, bayonet, and dowel-and-pin ferrules. The names came from a tapered pin projecting axially from the end of the male ferrule. Before the Civil War, most of these ferrules were merely straight tubing rolled from a thin sheet of German silver. Their solder lines were clearly visible. No welts or raised shoulders were used. Sometimes delicate rings were engraved to embellish these primitive ferrules, and nothing prevented water from reaching inside the female socket to penetrate and damage the cane. Simple ferrules without dowels were also used on many rods, exposing the bamboo to moisture and fungus both inside the female ferrule and at the bottom of the male. More sophisticated ferrules began to evolve about 1860. The open ends of the female ferrules were reinforced with soldered welts, both strengthening them and improving their appearance. The two-piece male ferrule soon followed; it was shaped from two nickel-silver tubes of different sizes, fixing the smaller inside the larger with solder. The smaller tube was polished to fit inside the female ferrule, while the larger formed a shoulder to control the depth of its penetration.

Hiram Leonard introduced his ferrule patents in 1875, which seated the dowel pin in a waterproof socket. The water stop was conceived to protect the cane. The split-shoulder ferrule was also introduced by Leonard three years later. Its sliced edges were designed to permit the smooth transition of bending stress through the entire rod, eliminating the cutting wear of a rigid ferrule. These concepts were revolutionary in their time, and

Leonard engraved his two patent markings on every female ferrule manufactured between 1878 and 1925.

Many variations soon emerged from other rod shops, as the several Leonard competitors scrambled to work out similar designs. W. H. Reed introduced a ferrule in 1885 which tapered its tubing to a paper-thin edge under its silk wrappings and was swaged or die-formed to create a shouldered ferrule from a single piece of tubing. In 1890, George Varney patented a fully serrated ferrule in which long triangular slots were filed into the thin wall of the ferrule. Fully serrated ferrules are excellent, but demand a lot of handwork and are expensive. Varney was a relatively obscure member of the Leonard team after the move to Central Valley, but his later independent career ultimately led to managing rod production at Montague. Eustis Edwards was awarded his patent for the curiously named Kosmic ferrule in 1890, and it was briefly machined by Edward Payne at the old self-winding-clock factory in Brooklyn. It was used on the Wilkinson Kosmic rods, which were made in limited numbers there after 1895. The Kosmic ferrule abandoned the dowel pins altogether, added an intriguing water stop and gluing joint inside the female ferrule, and flared the edge of the ferrule away from the rod over a tapered collar of celluloid.

British rods are often fitted with the so-called lock-fast ferrules that appeared just after the turn of the century and added a locking hook to the male ferrule designed to engage a raised spiral thread at the mouth of the female ferrule. It still retained a dowel center pin on the male. It was the ancestor of dozens of ingenious screw-thread, latching, and snap-catch ferrules that later flooded the market, particularly in the United Kingdom. Such ferrules were an abomination, unnecessarily heavy, and prone to oxidize and stick after surprisingly little use. The lock-fast type was seated by twisting it into place, placing dangerous twisting forces on the cane and wearing the ferrules spirally. However, it did embrace the watertight cup principle invented by Leonard, and it improved the split corners fitted to the cane. That Hardy feature still dominates modern ferrule work seventy-odd years later.

The stolid British refusal to trust the simple friction ferrule persists even today. It led Halford to design a special trout ferrule for Hardy in 1913 that was a masterpiece of overcomplication. It still retained the dowel pin, adding a split female mouth that was machined inside to close over a raised ring formed on the male ferrule. There was a sliding lock ring outside the female ferrule which was slipped toward the male when the two were seated, tightening the mouth of the female until it engaged the locking ring on the male. It was elaborate, secure, and completely unnecessary in the design of a foolproof ferrule since the modern friction-type was already well known—and being used by Hiram Leonard and most of his skilled protégés in the United States.

The modern ferrules we take for granted evolved quite slowly across the past 150 years, and all fine rods incorporate the waterproof plugs and serrations first introduced by Hiram Leonard. Rodmakers that were technically trained in dynamic stress theory fully understood the advantages of these principles, and European craftsmen made another important contribution to ferrule theory after the First World War. The reverse-stepped ferrule that has no shoulder on its male plug is believed to have developed in Bavaria or Austria, but it has firmly become entrenched in American rod theory as the Swiss-type ferrule. Its design is intended to create a ferrule in which minimal cutting of the bamboo, for both the male and female fittings, is required. The male ferrule is simply a straight German-silver tube with six serrated cuts. It fits into a female socket larger than the male diameter or the bamboo itself, which necks down to a serrated diameter designed to fit the rod. The Swiss-type ferrule is clearly best in terms of a rod's stress performance and life span, but it is clumsy-looking and expensive to make. It failed to achieve popularity for those reasons, but is still·used on the rods built by Walton Powell.

Louis Feierabend is the rodmaker who designed the famous Super Z ferrules, attempting to adapt the principles of the Swiss-type into a fitting that was more conventional in appearance. Feierabend was so successful that a cavalcade of fine rod builders, including the late Paul Young and Everett Garrison, quickly relied on his ferrules. The design was simple. It consisted of a male ferrule with six serrations and no shoulder, either swaged or stepped of separate tubing. The female ferrule was formed of separate German-silver tubes, the larger forming the socket and housing the waterproof plug. The outside tube was gradually tapered until its final edge was thin enough to form a winding stop. The Feierabend ferrule company was finally bought by the larger Garcia Corporation, which soon found its minuscule profits unacceptable and discontinued the production of these remarkable ferrules.

Perhaps the most unusual modern ferrule was developed by William Edwards for his four-strip quadrate rods. Hexagonal rods are virtually round and readily accept a conventional ferrule, but a square section is a problem. Virtually all the power fibers would be lost in turning down a four-strip rod to receive a tubular ferrule, and the transition between its round configuration and the rectangular rod was clumsy at best. Edwards ultimately designed a beautiful ferrule, utterly unique in its appearance, with a square neck receiving the cane and tapering smoothly into its round socket and plug. The water stop was fitted in the round female socket, and a handsome welt reinforced its throat. The quadrate ferrules were slotted at the corners. The male ferrules were embellished with an engraved ring, and both males and females were oxidized German silver. These quadrate ferrules are still being used on the exceptionally handsome four-strip rods made by Samuel Carlson in Connecticut, who now owns the Edwards patents and equipment.

The bamboo work and its coloring are often important clues to the origins of a fine fly rod. The species of cane is critical, since the transition from lath-turned Calcutta to Tonkin bamboo was clear-cut, except for the fraudulent African steel-vine rods. Configuration and node placement are

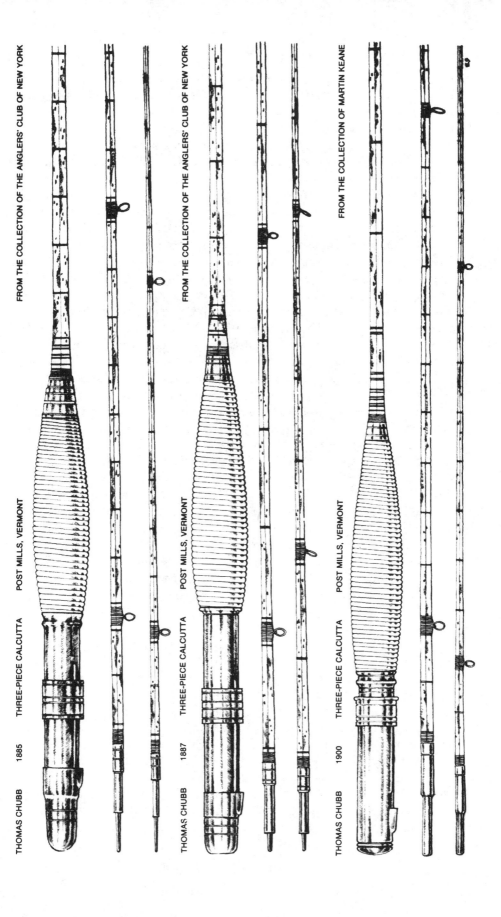

THOMAS CHUBB   1885   THREE-PIECE CALCUTTA   POST MILLS, VERMONT   FROM THE COLLECTION OF THE ANGLERS' CLUB OF NEW YORK

THOMAS CHUBB   1887   THREE-PIECE CALCUTTA   POST MILLS, VERMONT   FROM THE COLLECTION OF THE ANGLERS' CLUB OF NEW YORK

THOMAS CHUBB   1900   THREE-PIECE CALCUTTA   POST MILLS, VERMONT   FROM THE COLLECTION OF MARTIN KEANE

important too. Until the middle of the nineteenth century, rod tapers were more like billiard cues, working straight from tip to handle. Hickory and ash were common in both butts and midsections, with tips of lemonwood and lancewood; greenheart made up entire rods. There were also some bamboo rods of three-strip and four-strip construction, but these were limited to a handful of makers in England and the United States. Such rods were surprisingly clumsy.

After the Civil War, rod shafts became more slender and sophisticated in their tapers. Such sections flexed much farther toward the grip. Complete six-strip rods were produced in the Phillippe shop, particularly by Solon Phillippe, as early as 1857. However, six-strip construction first appeared in the butts and middle sections while the tips were still made of four strips. It was not until almost 1870, that rodmaking skills had evolved that could produce a really delicate six-strip tip. Specimens of these early bamboo rods are rare collectors' items today, particularly the rods of Phillippe, Green, Murphy, and Leonard.

However, these rods were Calcutta cane with their corners rounded off, and the advantages of rods constructed fully of hexagonal sections were not widely understood until 1880. Leonard was the first to discover such concepts, perhaps learning them first from his own six-strip tips, since the classic Howells Leonard has an hexagonal cane tip above its lower joints of rounded bamboo. It was built in 1873. After 1878, when Leonard became convinced that hexagonal sections were better, he built round rods on special order only. Other makers continued to work with hickory, ash, bethabara, greenheart, snakewood, lemonwood, and lancewood and had a stolid following of anglers slow to accept the advantages of split bamboo. Such exotic woods were used until well after the First World War and were found in the catalogues of first-rate tackle firms like Thomas Chubb, Von Lengerke & Detmold, and the celebrated William Mills & Son.

Tonkin cane was first imported in 1895, and was not received with any particular enthusiasm. Fishermen adapt slowly and stubbornly, and insisted on Calcutta bamboo with its darkly mottled sections, instead of Tonkin cane and its pale node patterns. Tonkin cane took about twenty years to displace its rivals, and after the First World War, Calcutta was finally relegated with lemonwood, greenheart and lancewood to the back pages of the catalogues—except for its resurrection in the African steel-vine rods.

Grip proportions and design are certainly the most obvious signature of a particular craftsman. Each rod handle holds myriad clues concerning its origins and the craftsmanship and sense of design possessed by its maker. Before 1850, rods had changed surprisingly little from the weapons described by Berners in her *Treatyse of Fysshynge wyth an Angle*. Such rods measured from ten to twenty feet in length. Tightly grained and elegantly finished, these javelins lacked grips or handles in modern terms. The wood itself was simply tapered into a butt thick enough to serve as a handle. The reel was typically seated in the upper or middle part of the grip—not unlike a two-handled salmon rod—so a fisherman could wield his weapon.

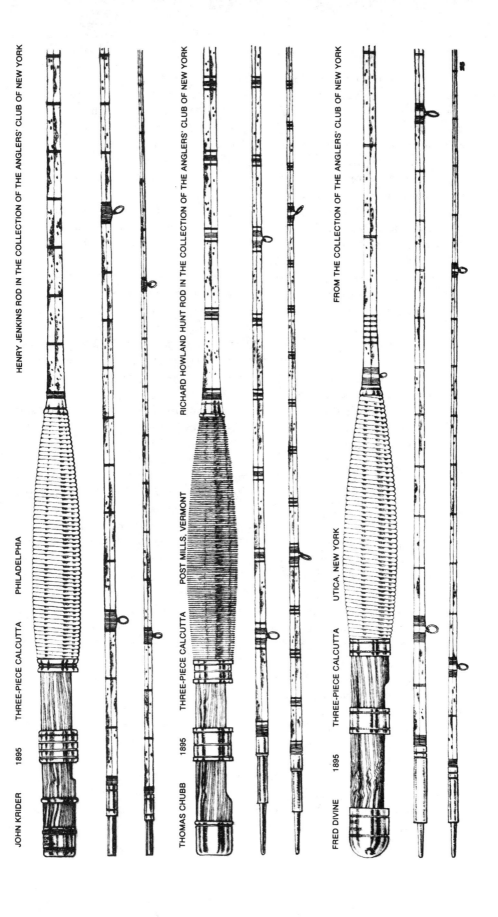

HENRY JENKINS ROD IN THE COLLECTION OF THE ANGLERS' CLUB OF NEW YORK

JOHN KRIDER   1895   THREE-PIECE CALCUTTA   PHILADELPHIA

RICHARD HOWLAND HUNT ROD IN THE COLLECTION OF THE ANGLERS' CLUB OF NEW YORK

THOMAS CHUBB   1895   THREE-PIECE CALCUTTA   POST MILLS, VERMONT

FROM THE COLLECTION OF THE ANGLERS' CLUB OF NEW YORK

FRED DIVINE   1895   THREE-PIECE CALCUTTA   UTICA, NEW YORK

Later rods became slender and more graceful. Although many manufacturers continued to place the reel above the grip as late as 1875, the more creative makers started seating it below the handle like our modern rods. Phillippe, Green, Murphy, and Leonard are all typical of this climate of change. The character of the bigger, traditional rods still echoed in the work of these men, although their grips were smaller and their specifications were designed for one-hand casting. The new grips were sometimes left bare, alternating the split cane with snakewood or cedar or walnut, and sometimes they were wrapped with a spiral of dark celluloid or pale rattan. Other makers soon adopted grips completely covered with tightly wound celluloid or lacquer-finished twine or rattan, and the evolution of the modern grip had started.

Fine craftsmanship and elegant proportions became the watchword of rodmakers. The German-silver grip check appeared after 1860, and some workmen soon discovered that rare grip materials like tiger maple, cherry, fruitwood, butternut, walnut, and Brazilian rosewood greatly enhanced their work. Sterling silver fittings and rich engraving enjoyed a vogue in the Victorian period, and some almost baroque presentation rods were made for royalty and captains of industry and politicians, heavy with expensive brightwork and other embellishments.

The period after 1875 witnessed a cornucopia of changes in grip and reel seat design. Hollow butt sections were devised for storing an extra tip. Cork grips were introduced at Orvis in 1880, and seamless German-silver reel seats appeared about that time. Detachable handles also enjoyed a brief period of popularity. Grips of fluted or checkered wood, celluloid or rattan winding, rubber, and cork veneer were common. Cork rings followed in about 1886, usually cut from sheets less than half an inch thick. Mills patented a locking reel seat that appeared on salmon rods in 1893. Screw-locking reel seats apparently developed on trout rods in England well before the First World War, since there are Hardy DeLuxe rods in this country with serial numbers old enough to place their origins slightly before 1900. Handsome screw-locking seats had evolved for trout rods on both sides of the Atlantic before 1925, with exposed fillers of hard rubber and elegant woods replacing the heavier full metal seats of German silver—except on the work of isolated craftsmen like Cross in the Middle West and Goodwin Granger in Colorado.

Hiram Leonard refined the earlier work of Phillippe, Green, and Murphy into a polished art and contributed pivotal concepts in the design of ferrules and six-strip sections, yet Leonard did not live to witness the fruition of his work in Tonkin cane. Leonard worked largely in Calcutta, which is slender porch-furniture bamboo, incapable of being made into a modern split-cane rod.

Calcutta bamboo is the slender *Dendrocalamus strictus* and is principally found in the rain forests of southern India, as well as other coastal regions in Burma, Thailand, and Malaysia. It grows to surprising heights, as much as thirty to sixty feet in optimal habitat, and its culms can measure two to four inches in diameter. The culms are almost solid, but they lack the strength of the so-called Tonkin canes. Calcutta is no longer used in fly rods, except in a few cheap Asian imports.

Tonkin bamboo is not actually found in the Tonkin Province of North Vietnam, but is cultivated in a surprisingly small area in the Kwangtung and Kwangsi provinces of southern China. Calcutta became available in Europe and the United States much earlier because of the British trade in India, and the Chinese cane later reached the Western world through Macao and Canton. Portuguese influence in Macao is extremely old, and had Portugal played a role in the history of rodmaking, we might have used Tonkin cane earlier than the first British commerce in Calcutta from India. Most Tonkin now reaches Europe and the United States through the British colony at Hong Kong and is known as Tsing Li bamboo there. Its scientific name is *Arundaria amabilis*, and the taxonomist who first classified it was perhaps an angler since its Latin name describes it as the lovely reed, and it is fitting that such a poetic material should find its ultimate purpose in an elegant split-cane rod.

The monsoon winds howl fiercely off the South China seas, driving the storm tides into the coastal lowlands behind Macao, and the yearly rainfall can reach several hundred inches. Fishing mythology holds that the finest bamboo for rodmaking grows on the hilltops, where its culms are wildly bent and tempered by the wind. Whether it is the climate that tests the canebrakes above Canton, or whether the resilient bamboo itself has evolved to test the violent winds and rain, we cannot be certain. Many anglers would prefer the obvious poetry of the latter. Whatever the cause, it is clear that some happy alchemy is wrought in this remote corner of the world. The vigorous shoots of bamboo that grow there, reaching toward the rainswept monsoon skies, have drawn the best from their climate and soil. And the artisans who have lovingly cured and shaped such bamboo into fly rods have learned to draw the best from its qualities.

The peculiar climate and other conditions that apparently limit *Arundaria amabilis* to its tiny corner of the world are not fully understood. The provinces where it thrives are hot and semitropical during most of the year, although the winters are dry and surprisingly cold. Its growers call it tea-stick bamboo. Too much summer heat and humidity are apparently poor for the cultivation of rod-quality cane, and the excessive heat and humidity found in the Tonkin Province of North Vietnam make it unsuitable for the tea-stick species.

The soils of Kwangtung and Kwangsi are varied. The river bottoms are richly fertile, although the foothills are rugged and barren. *Arundaria amabilis* is a plant species that grows best in the uplands, and fertile soils are not critical to its cultivation. Botanists believe that climate and drainage properties are more critical than soil quality. The molecular structure of the cane and the remarkable definition of its tension and compression fibers indicate that the strong prevailing winds of the rainy season do play a role in its rodmaking qualities.

The principal expert in the botany and cultivation of the Tsing Li bamboo was probably Doctor F. A. McClure, who served in the Biology Department of Lingnan University at Canton. It was McClure who worked out the taxonomy of *Arundaria amabilis* and published the definitive technical papers on this species of bamboo. McClure concluded that his new species was perhaps limited in its distribution because it was cultivated largely in its original habitat, and that its growers lacked the technology and resources to search for other equally suited growing regions—let alone the time necessary for experimental plantings.

Such new groves were established in its original range, however, to meet the demand of Western rodmakers. New sites for planting were usually chosen on southern or southeasterly slopes of steep hillsides or mountains, to provide good solar orientation and exposure to the monsoon winds. Southwest sites provided too much sun and less direct exposure to the seasonal storms tracking off the Pacific from the southeast. The jungle and scrub are cleared and burned to prepare a new grove. Clusters of travelling rhizome roots containing one or two upright culms are planted in a geometric grid, six to ten feet on centers. The freshly tilled earth is firmly tamped with the feet. Subsequent growth is monopodial, covering the open spaces with its travelling root systems. Bamboo roots travel just below the surface, parallel with the ground level, and send up new stems at fairly regular intervals. The stems are surprisingly larger than the roots themselves, and they quickly grow straight and uncrowded into the air. The rhizomes spread and sprout fresh shoots aggressively. The new grove expands quickly, bearing larger culms until optimal growth is reached. However, development of a mature grove is relatively slow. Ten years are required to reach the point of first harvest. Such a grove is productive for about fifty years, except when the bamboo is flowering.

Flowering occurs at irregular intervals, unpredictable even to the growers themselves, and during these periods a grove ceases to produce. Folklore once held that a grove lost its commercial value once it had flowered, but Professor McClure proved that a mature stand of cane will recover from flowering and resume production much sooner than a freshly planted grove. However, extensive periods of flowering triggered a great financial loss to the growers.

Freshly planted groves require no irrigation and remarkably little attention between harvests. The stands grow straight and tapering slightly to heights of forty to fifty feet, with maximum diameters of two and one-quarter inches. Most culms reach about half that height. Green culms are often marked to identify them for cutting three to four years later. Bamboo culms grow dense and hard with maturity. Their deep olive color gradually becomes a pale primrose yellow. Harvesting is done all year, although the best growers confine their cutting to autumn. The growth and health following the monsoons is optimal, but such culms must be thoroughly dried. The cane is cut with a heavy sharp-bladed machete that slices the culms with a steeply angled blow at the base.

Harvested culms are tied into bundles of convenient size for transportation by hand to the nearby rivers. Sometimes the bundles are assembled into rafts, although the most knowledgeable growers carry them overland to keep their moisture content low. The bundles are taken to sandbars along the rivers, where they are scoured to remove the fungus and lichens and stains. Some growers scrub the cane in the shallows, while others use only dry sand to keep the culms dry. Fresh bundles are assembled after scouring into equal numbers, loosely bound around the middle, and spread in an hourglass-shaped fan to dry and bleach. The bundles are placed under shelter at night and in rainy weather. Such first curing takes about a week in good weather, after which the cane is ready to start its journey.

The bundles are carefully sized and cut to lengths specified by the export agents in Canton and Hong Kong. These bundles are shipped by sampan down the Bambus and Sui Kong rivers to Fatshan. The culms are heat treated and straightened over earthen fire pots in the warehouses of the exporters. The Chinese workmen sort the culms into bales, wrapping each bale in tea mats for shipment down the Pearl River in junks to Canton and Macao. Ultimately these bundles reach exporters in Hong Kong, where they are sold to importers in Europe and the United States. Before the Second World War, when bamboo-rod production was at its zenith, more than $1,000,000 in tea-stick cane was exported annually for split-cane work. Consular records indicate that in 1937 almost $700,000 worth of *Arundaria amabilis* was exported to the United States alone.

It is probable that vintage bamboo rods had adventures long before they reached the shops of their makers in Europe and the United States or throbbed in response to a cartwheeling rainbow. The sampans and junks that carried the bundled culms to Canton were often stopped by river pirates demanding tribute, and similar extortion was frequent in the coastal seas between Canton and Hong Kong.

The Sino-Japanese War found both Canton and Fatshan under Japanese occupation in 1940. Japanese control of the Pearl River estuary was so complete in the autumn of 1938 and their gunboats patrolled so mercilessly that no cane reached Hong Kong for months. However, the enterprising Chinese soon found overland routes, wrapped the cane in smaller bundles, and transported them on the backs of coolies to several remote inlets along the coast between Canton and Hong Kong. Sampans transported the bamboo from those secret beaches to junks offshore, which carried it through the Japanese blockade. It was tortuously slow and expensive. It was hazardous too, since Chinese hill bandits demanded tribute and there were frequent patrols of Japanese soldiers. History tells us that more than one caravan was ambushed by the Japanese, and many of the coolies were killed. The flow of bamboo to Europe and the United States had dwindled to less than half of the normal trade by 1940, and with the Japanese attack on Pearl Harbor the following year, the cane trade virtually ended altogether.

Some bamboo trade resumed with the Japanese surrender in 1945, but the war in China had so disrupted the cultivation of rod-quality cane that shipments were unpredictable. Much of the cane imported in those years was virtually useless, although a trickle of first-rate bamboo continued to arrive in Europe and the United States through the Panama Canal. This rebirth of the cane market was brief, at least for American importers and tacklemakers. The wartime truce between Chiang Kai-shek and the powerful forces of Mao Tse-tung dissolved into open warfare in 1946, and China was wracked by civil war until 1949, when the defeated Chiang Kai-shek was driven into exile. The United States proclaimed an embargo against the government of Mao Tse-tung, ending all American trade with mainland China.

Practically all of the tea-stick cane imported into the United States after 1895 was handled by the late Charles Demarest, who began his career in the bamboo trade as a clerk with the D. A. Shaw & Company. Demarest subsequently acquired that firm and played a major role in the rise of Tonkin cane in American rod manufacturing. Harold Demarest served for many years in his father's business and was in Hong Kong early in 1950, when he acquired the last shipment of *Arundaria amabilis* that legally entered the United States.

It was just a matter of luck, Demarest later described his good fortune. *I happened on a bamboo shipment in a Hong Kong godown in April, and it was our last shipment out of China.*

The United Kingdom had recognized Mao Tse-tung earlier in 1950, and the American embargo was imposed in December, so limited amounts of bamboo continued to arrive via England. It was second-rate cane, however, because British rodmakers like Hardy and Millward and Sharpe understandably kept the best culms for themselves. Fortunately, there were large supplies of aging Tonkin on hand in many shops, and major tackle manufacturers often bought supplemental cane from smaller rod builders. Some stocks of bamboo were lost when large companies abandoned cane for fiberglass, and priceless inventories of aged Tonkin were tragically destroyed. Because of its embargo of Chinese goods, no first-quality culms of bamboo entered the United States until Leigh Perkins of the Charles Orvis Company succeeded in receiving a waiver on tea-stick bamboo—demonstrating with the technical assistance of David Ledlie, a knowledgeable biology professor at Middlebury College, that Orvis could not function without Chinese cane.

However, the bamboo shipments that have arrived thus far are erratic in quality, and it is apparent that skilled cultivation and preparation of the tea-stick bamboo has been a casualty of the traumatic events in recent Chinese history. Hopefully, the Chinese growers will recultivate the horticultural and handling skills their countrymen possessed before the Second World War.

Much experimenting with cultivation of *Arundaria amabilis* in the United States has been done, starting in about 1933 with the successful shipment of living shoots and rhizomes. Propagation was disappointingly

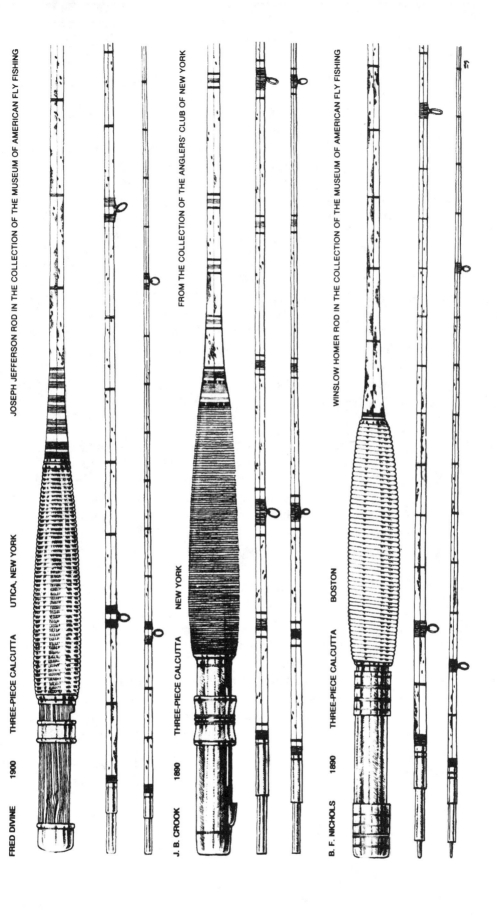

FRED DIVINE   1900   THREE-PIECE CALCUTTA   UTICA, NEW YORK   JOSEPH JEFFERSON ROD IN THE COLLECTION OF THE MUSEUM OF AMERICAN FLY FISHING

J. B. CROOK   1890   THREE-PIECE CALCUTTA   NEW YORK   FROM THE COLLECTION OF THE ANGLERS' CLUB OF NEW YORK

B. F. NICHOLS   1890   THREE-PIECE CALCUTTA   BOSTON   WINSLOW HOMER ROD IN THE COLLECTION OF THE MUSEUM OF AMERICAN FLY FISHING

slow, and groves being cultivated by the Department of Agriculture flowered only a half-dozen years after planting. The second planting in Louisiana did not flower, but bamboo of first-rate quality in commercial quantities was not obtained. These experiments in the American cultivation of tea-stick bamboo lost their impetus when fiberglass replaced cane in volume rod production, but our increasing interest in bamboo might reawaken the interest once shown in growing rod-quality Tsing Li in our southern states. Prices continue to rise sharply, the quality of Chinese cane remains unpredictable, and more bamboo rods are being made and sold each year.

The yardsticks of quality for raw Tsing Li are that the culms are ripe and yellow. Their graining and shafts must be relatively straight and should rend cleanly in linear splits and checks. The cane must be clean and free of worms or decay. The culms should average six feet in length and exceed one and one-quarter inches in diameter. The manufacturers must hold sufficient stocks of cane to insure that they are working with seasoned culms averaging three to five years in age. The finest culms are hard and resilient, relatively uniform in size, and densely grained. Good bamboo tends to split straight down the length of the culm. Seasoned culms are a perfect straw color, free of stains and bad water marks. The enamel and its underlying power fibers are hard and abrasion resistant, and a fine stick will ring with a clear bell-like tone when struck.

Skilled rodmakers have an eye for a fine culm of tea-stick cane. Such judgment is perhaps their finest skill since even the best bamboo varies widely in quality. Each stick is carefully examined for irregularities in graining, dents, scratches, mold, dry rot, insect damage, sand cuts, and variations in wall thickness and density. There is also a sixth sense.

You can tell a good culm by its heft, Wes Jordan of Orvis explains, holding a length of tea stick reverently. *It has a certain feel and strength you can unmistakably sense with your fingers.*

Fully half the culms in a bundle of fifty are rejected in their first shoring at the factory, and others are rejected later, when cutting and milling reveal other imperfections. The best culm has a hard enamel underneath its waxiness. The density of these longitudinal fibers gradually decreases toward the inner wall of the culm, although the inner fibers are pithy and less resilient. The nodes of the cane, which are the leaf rings of the living plant, occur at regular intervals along its length. These nodes form weak points in the culm, once they are worked flat and their inner bulkheads are removed. These nodes give the exterior of the raw culm the characteristic jointed look of bamboo, like the fishing poles on the sunfish ponds of our youth.

It's painstaking work, the late Jim Payne gestured toward his stock of aging bamboo. *It takes a hundred and forty-five separate operations and two months from the raw cane to a finished fly rod.*

These basic operations of rod building are common to virtually each of the makers, although each also has personal variations on these basic

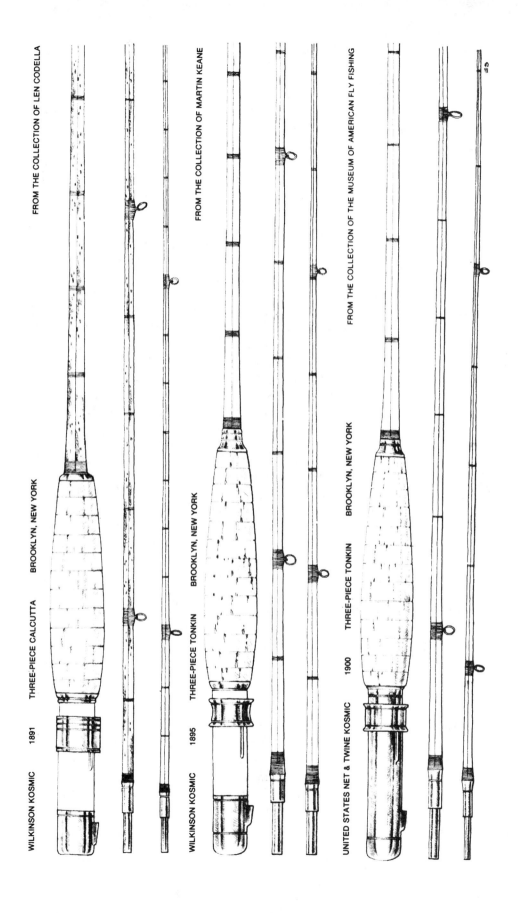

WILKINSON KOSMIC   1891   THREE-PIECE CALCUTTA   BROOKLYN, NEW YORK

FROM THE COLLECTION OF LEN CODELLA

WILKINSON KOSMIC   1895   THREE-PIECE TONKIN   BROOKLYN, NEW YORK

FROM THE COLLECTION OF MARTIN KEANE

UNITED STATES NET & TWINE KOSMIC   1900   THREE-PIECE TONKIN   BROOKLYN, NEW YORK

FROM THE COLLECTION OF THE MUSEUM OF AMERICAN FLY FISHING

themes. Choice culms are chosen for seasoning, and are split along one wall full length. The prepared culms are cured under precisely controlled temperature and humidity. Several famous makers age their cane as much as twenty years, and some allow the cane to season another full year after it is split into rough splines.

Once his seasoning period is complete, the rodmaker culls through his stocks for culms of the proper wall thickness for the size rod being made. Straight culms with widely spaced nodes, free of blemishes and water stains and checks, are selected for splitting. The strips or splines are split longitudinally from the culms with a knife or cane wedge in the best shops, and sawn into rough cuts in factory operations. Either method is workable, although a serious connoisseur of bamboo work will argue that hand-splitting will work along the natural grain of the culm, while a machine-cut is likely to cut across the grain at a shallow angle in a slightly twisted culm. Good bamboo will invariably split straight along its grain.

Skilled hands and eyes play a primary role in inspecting each roughly split strip of cane. The splines are closely examined for irregular graining and serious flaws. Each is carefully flexed to observe its resilience and rate of recovery from stress. Sluggish or soft strips are discarded, along with any spline that fails to bend in a constant curve.

The select strips are finally filed carefully to remove the nodes without damaging the adjacent power fibers. The inner nodal walls are removed with a gouge. The edges are planed smooth, and preliminary cuts are made to remove the excess pith before final cutting of the tapers. Some rough splines display slight twists and warping at this stage of work. These strips are perfectly workable, and are delicately heated and straightened while still warm. Final planing and bevelling follows when they have cooled.

Heat tempering can occur at various stages of work. Orvis tempers its cane in the raw culms once they are properly seasoned in controlled storage. Its rich brown color comes from this delicate heat tempering. Craftsmen like the late Lew Stoner and Everett Garrison temper their cane much less, Gary Howells oven tempers his cane slightly more, and the late Paul Young actually flame-tempered his culms in a ring-shaped gas jet. Pezon & Michel use a sensitive electric kiln of French design. Other makers oven temper the rough-cut splines before the final tapers are made.

Some heat tempering is absolutely necessary, but it must be carefully executed. Too much heat and the cane is literally robbed of its moisture and strength, and excessive tempering can make a rod short-lived and brittle. Controlled application of heat increases bamboo strength and stiffness. Moisture content is reduced and the tendency to set is reduced. The cane fibers are partially sealed against the later penetration of moisture by polymerization of their natural resins. The precise formulas for heat tempering are often closely guarded secrets.

Hand tapering is usually accomplished by placing the rough splines in a steel or hardwood planing form. Sharp planes are used to shape them into triangular strips. The grooves in the planing forms are tapered along their length, deep enough to accommodate the butt tapers of the largest salt-water calibrations, and delicate enough at their shallow ends to shape the minuscule strips that make up into tip sections of three sixty-fourths and four sixty-fourths of an inch. The planing is done on the two pith faces of the splines. Each pass of the plane cuts away the coarse, relatively weak inner fibers of the cane. The dense exterior fibers are carefully preserved, and the rough strips are staggered to mismatch the nodes before final bevelling. Some makers offset their splines to place the brittle nodes in alternating faces of the finished cane, since aligning nodes in adjacent faces results in a fatally weak spot in the rod. Other makers spiral their nodal patterns before final tapering in their planing forms, and Everett Garrison is perhaps the last craftsman to rely entirely on handwork.

It's both difficult and simple, Garrison smiles faintly and his eyes twinkle with years of knowledge. *You work the rod into the planing grooves at the right design tapers and keep planing until the blade fails to touch the bamboo.*

Other rodmakers use machines to cut their tapers. Milling is usually accomplished in two operations. The first machine cuts an approximate taper and strips off the excess pith fiber. The finish milling machine usually employs a cutting wheel formed with a series of precise cutting teeth. Some machines place the tungsten carbide cutter vertically above the spline being tapered, while the Orvis cutter passes each strip horizontally past its cutting head. Extremely fine tolerances are possible with such milling machines, although the cutting heads are quite costly and difficult to sharpen. Cheap cane rods were often made with cutting heads designed to mill each strip at an angle of slightly more than sixty-one degrees. Poor workmanship and ill-fitting tolerances could easily be concealed in the exaggerated glue joints between such strips, while the glue faces of splines cut to exactly sixty degrees must fit with remarkable precision. No reputable manufacturer uses exaggerated glue joints today.

It was Loman Hawes who designed and built the famous milling machine still used at Leonard. It survived the disastrous fire that almost ended the company after a century of production, and is still mounted on its fluted cast-iron bases. Instead of placing a rough spline on its back and milling its pithy fibers into an equilateral triangle, thereby processing it through a single cutting head, the Hawes milling machine places the rough strip with its power fibers up. Two interlocking cutters then form the finished spline, shaping the cane with its pithy apex down. William Edwards designed and built his milling machine on similar principles, although the exact specifications of such machinery are usually trade secrets, and the finish milling rooms are often forbidden territory.

Please, an embarrassed Arthur Mills often stopped casual visitors to the Leonard shop, *we don't permit anyone to see our Leonard milling machines—we're awfully sorry, but it's been off limits for seventy-five years!*

Other methods of tapering are also used. The Randle bevelling system used adjustable, interlocking boards of hard mahogany on a base of seasoned long-leaf yellow pine. Four-sided measuring blocks were common thirty years ago, with different increment of a design taper cut into each face. The Moss forming block also enjoyed a brief vogue after the Second World War. It was a triangular block slightly longer than each section, with its apex slightly fluted to receive a rough-cut spline of bamboo with its power fibers down. The enamel surface is glued to the forming block, its tapers are carefully shaped to match the bevelled surfaces of the Moss template, the temporary glue joint is worked free, and the strip is ready. Adjustable steel planing blocks are very expensive to make, and few machinists have the necessary skills. Track-type planing blocks are designed to control the shaping strokes with precision.

Whatever the method used in tapering a spline, it must frequently be checked closely with a micrometer to insure that each strip has the same taper. The tungsten carbide cutting heads or planing blades must constantly be sharpened, since fine bamboo quickly dulls even the finest steels. Precision of the highest order is needed, particularly to avoid pocking or shearing the glue faces. Cautious grinding removes any rough corners, and at their final assembly and gluing, these strips will calibrate within an incredible .001 inch. The differences in workmanship between a fine split-cane rod and its cheaper competitors are minuscule, but are absolutely critical to its performance.

Once careful checking of the splines with a micrometer has established that they meet the .001 tolerances demanded by a fine rod, they are glued together and tightly wrapped. The early adhesives used were hot fish or animal glues, particularly the fine glue made from the air bladders of the Caspian sturgeon. However, such hot glues are greatly affected by weather changes, and rods assembled in rainy weather are softer than rods made up with hot glues during dry weather. Hot adhesives keep for long periods in a glue tank and are heated when a rod is ready for gluing. The finished splines are assembled and taped lightly at the heavy end. The assembled splines are dipped in the glue tank, the surplus glue is quickly wiped off, and the stick is slowly run through a pressure-wrapping machine.

The basic process is similar with most contemporary rods, except for their use of modern adhesives. Fish and animal glues remain water soluble after they have set, and without their protective varnish, rods assembled with the hot glues could come apart in rainy weather. Synthetic adhesives have solved that problem although they are considerably more difficult to use. Their fully cured strength is incredible. The glue faces in a modern rod are much stronger than in the rod itself. Synthetics are also costly and each batch must be mixed immediately before gluing. The rod splines are assembled with tapes, the tapes are slit through one corner, and the splines are laid flat still adhering to the tapes. The synthetic resins must then be brushed on the strips by hand. Orvis, Young, Sharpe's, and many other firms are using Bakelite resins to glue their rods, while Everett Garrison and the late Pinky Gillum preferred compounds. Most reputable builders are using synthetic adhesives now.

Pressure wrapping is a standard procedure in all split-cane rod shops, although pressure-wrapping equipment varies widely from builder to builder. Small bench wrappers are still used by several rodmakers. Cotton cord is used since the stronger linen and nylon can fray and break under pressure, or actually mar the cane at its corners. The bench wrapper lays uniform windings from end to end, always working from the larger calibrations to the smaller. Working both clockwise and counterclockwise, the finish wrappings are a spiral cross wind. The larger firms use heavy pressure wrapping benches in assembling and gluing their rods, and the late Paul Young built his wrapper with the components of a war surplus B-29 bomb hoist. Some variations in the angle of wrapping, the tensile forces applied, and the uniformity of pressure occur from shop to shop, but the basic principles are always the same.

Freshly wrapped sections sometimes are warped or display a slight twist. Such deformation is not unusual. There are several ways of correcting these problems before the glues have set. Middle and butt sections are often struck gently across a flat workbench to realign the strips inside the pressure windings. Minor twists or warps can often be hand-straightened by simply bending the section carefully. Such corrections must be made in the first five minutes after wrapping, before the adhesives can start curing. Some of the modern adhesives set so quickly that corrections are impossible once the splines are wrapped. Some makers hang weights from their suspended sections, insuring that these postwrapping corrections remain in the stick.

The pressure wrappings are not removed from a stick for about a week, and after they are stripped the section is stored in a dry temperature-controlled room for three to six months. Such final curing allows the stresses in the fibers to equalize, and the moisture of the glue is finally dried out. The excess moisture both softens the action of a finished rod and slightly expands its calibrations, making a permanent ferrule fit difficult. Final straightening of a bamboo section can be accomplished by hand over a small steam jet or bunsen burner after the pressure wraps are stripped, and careful application of heat can also straighten a finished rod.

Once a wrapped section is stripped of its windings, it must be carefully scraped by hand to remove the excess glue. Cheap rods were often cleaned with power equipment, both to remove the glue and to sand off the bamboo enamel layers. These enamel layers contribute nothing to the performance or appearance of the finished rod. However, the use of power tools always risks damaging the thin layer of power fibers lying just under the enamel, seriously injuring the bamboo itself. The glues and enamels are always scraped, filed, and carefully hand-sanded from a fine rod section to protect its power cells. The section is finally polished with the finest steel wool, and a first-rate piece of cane will have no glue lines visible along the entire length of the rod—except in rods using the dark synthetic glues.

The cleaned sections are checked with a micrometer to verify their calibrations and straightened again with heat. Orvis, Phillipson, and Sharpe's immerse their finished sections in pressure-impregnation tanks at this point in their manufacture, sealing the cellular structure of the cane with Bakelite resin. Impregnation takes about a week. It makes the rod so impervious to heat, moisture and fungus that no varnish is needed to protect it once the rod is finished.

Impregnation will stand most anything, Wes Jordan insists with obvious pride in his Orvis rods. *It will stand up to ice, boiling water, rain, sun, blizzards, bug dope—even a spilled nine-to-one martini!* Such rods are not ultimately varnished, but are simply buffed to a deep polish, since the Bakelite finish lies in the cells of the cane itself.

Other builders subject their finished rod sticks to another drying cycle of several months, although some shorten this final curing with thermostatically controlled ovens. Properly seasoned cane will shrink much less than .001 inch in this final drying period. Most rodmakers stockpile their most popular rods in the form of glued and fully seasoned sticks, selecting them from the curing racks as needed for assembly.

Seating the ferrules comes next. The cane is checked to insure that no bamboo enamel remains, and the section is measured to verify its length. Since the female ferrule is hollow, its socket length must be calculated into the finished length of each piece. Final cutting of sticks to length should always occur at their butt calibrations. Fitting the ferrule to the bamboo properly is a difficult operation, as anyone attempting to fit a ferrule himself soon discovers.

Female ferrules are mounted simply by shaping a distance along the rod shaft equal to the depth of the tubing to the water plug inside the throat. Many craftsmen employ a small metal lathe, using its hole gauge and tool-post fitting and carriage, turning the ferrule seat to a diameter .002 above the ferrule itself, and feathering the corners of the cane in transition between the ferrule and its five- or six-strip section. Four-strip ferrules of the Edwards type require almost no feathering. Male ferrules of the Swiss-type or Feierabend design lack the internal stepped shoulders typical of other quality ferrules and are seated just like a female type.

Stepped male ferrules require an additional cutting operation. Using a medium-fine metal file, the cane is shaped in a lathe to fit the ferrule tubing below the step. The fit should be precise and tight prior to final gluing and seating on the finished sections.

Modern rodmakers are using synthetic ferrule cements like Pliobond and Silhower, which remain slightly elastic after setting and flex in harmony with the rod. Some maintain that their ferrules are heated and driven home with a dry fit so precise that no cement is required. Others still use the stick-type cement that was common in my boyhood years, melting it with a controlled flame and coating the cane quickly to seat the ferrule before the adhesive cools. The synthetic cements take from two to four weeks to dry.

Several methods for seating ferrules are used. Some builders simply start the ferrule over its carefully worked seat and press it home firmly against a workbench. Ferrule-driving plugs are also common. Properly

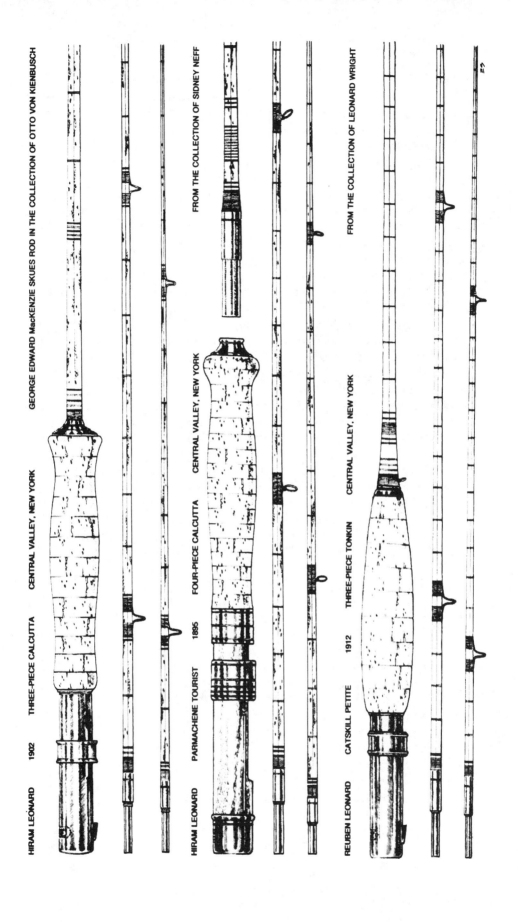

HIRAM LEONARD 1902 THREE-PIECE CALCUTTA CENTRAL VALLEY, NEW YORK GEORGE EDWARD MacKENZIE SKUES ROD IN THE COLLECTION OF OTTO VON KIENBUSCH

HIRAM LEONARD PARMACHENE TOURIST 1895 FOUR-PIECE CALCUTTA CENTRAL VALLEY, NEW YORK FROM THE COLLECTION OF SIDNEY NEFF

REUBEN LEONARD CATSKILL PETITE 1912 THREE-PIECE TONKIN CENTRAL VALLEY, NEW YORK FROM THE COLLECTION OF LEONARD WRIGHT

machined driving plugs fit inside a female ferrule and enclose a male fitting, supporting and protecting the fitting as it is driven home. Separate driving plugs are required for each diameter ferrule. The ferrule is started by hand, then fitted with a driving plug that matches its size, and the plug is tapped home with a soft mallet. Most large firms use driving plugs in concert with a small metalworking lathe that starts the ferrule and fits it with a driving plug. The ferrule is seated with a hardwood block placed between its plug and the lathe. It is forced home by turning the tailstock.

The cork grip follows the ferrules. Some makers prefabricate their handles by gluing the rings with a tension bolt and end washers. The best rodmakers make their grips by seating only a single ring of specie cork at a time. Each ring is tightly set in glue against the last. Many factory rod grips were often shaped with a grinding wheel designed to produce the desired shape. Twenty-four hours are needed for the glue to dry. Prefabricated handles are forced over the ferrule end of the butt section, and the cane is coated with glue at its final grip position. The grip is then pressed steadily and firmly into place, using a template block to reserve enough space for the reel seat filler. Grips assembled and glued on the rod shaft are usually shaped with a file and sandpaper on a small metal lathe, using fine garnet paper to finish the cork by hand.

There are many grip configurations, and most originated with famous anglers and rodmakers. The classic full Wells style is named for Henry Wells, the nineteenth-century author of *Fly Rods and Fly Tackle.* It has been used by many craftsmen over the years, and variations on the standard Wells are found on Winston, Powell, Young, Uslan, Montague, Phillipson, and some rods built in the shops of makers like Hardy, Sharpe's, and Howells. Half-Wells grips are found on many rods built by Hardy, Sharpe's, Young, Montague, Dickerson, Heddon, South Bend, and several others. Reverse Wells are popular with makers who like to conceal their hooded caps in the cork itself. These grip designs are found on the rods built by Edwards, Carlson, Thomas, Heddon, Payne, Montague, Granger, Gillum, Leonard, Hardy, and Howells.

The classic cigar-type handle is attributed to Samuel Phillippe, although the historical ties are tenuous at best. Modern craftsmen sometimes using the Phillippe cigar grip or minor modifications clearly based on its original design are Leonard, Payne, Hardy, Sharpe's, Divine, Edwards, Uslan, Orvis, Dunton, Jenkins, Cross, Jordan, Thomas, Montague, Heddon, Young, and Thomas & Thomas.

Hardy is probably responsible for both the classic Hardy fishtail grip, which combines a reverse Wells silhouette at the reel seat and tapers to a slender taper at the grip check. It was found on a galaxy of Hardy rods like the Houghton, Halford, Tournament, Perfection, Pope, Viscount Grey, J. J. Hardy, L. R. Hardy, Crown Houghton, and the classic Fairy model—the favorite rod used by Ernest Hemingway on rivers from Silver Creek in Idaho to the Black Forest in southern Germany.

Some historians also credit Hardy with the slender reverse cigar grips that appeared after the First World War, particularly on models like the

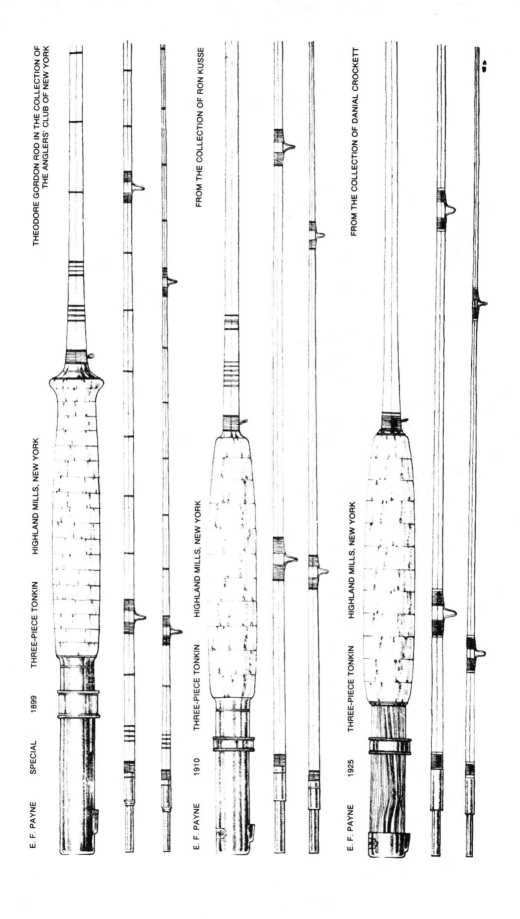

THEODORE GORDON ROD IN THE COLLECTION OF
THE ANGLERS' CLUB OF NEW YORK

FROM THE COLLECTION OF RON KUSSE

FROM THE COLLECTION OF DANIAL CROCKETT

E. F. PAYNE   SPECIAL   1899   THREE-PIECE TONKIN   HIGHLAND MILLS, NEW YORK

E. F. PAYNE   1910   THREE-PIECE TONKIN   HIGHLAND MILLS, NEW YORK

E. F. PAYNE   1925   THREE-PIECE TONKIN   HIGHLAND MILLS, NEW YORK

Casting Club de France, Mainwaring Sussex, Fairchild, Marvel, and the contemporary Palakona line. These grips are still found on the modern Hardy Lightweights, and are also found on rods like the Orvis Flea or the Thomas & Thomas Paradigm and Individualist.

Other variations of these designs are found on the rods of other great craftsmen. Charles Ritz prefers a simplified Phillippe taper grip which increases in diameter from the reel seat to the grip check. Such handles provide a working taper for the thumb and hand to generate the high-speed, high-line stroke in the Ritz style of casting. Everett Garrison has evolved from his original cigar grips to a similar increasing grip taper, although its diameter increases only one thirty-second of an inch in its full length. Halstead and Summers rods use a slender grip similar to the Garrison design. Hiram Hawes was a tournament caster and developed a strangely tapering grip with a swelled thumb stop as a fulcrum for his powerful casting style.

It was the late Paul Young who first developed a specially shaped thumb depression in his grips. The idea was later adapted by Wes Jordan in the postwar rods developed for South Bend and is still found on his special series of autographed rods for Orvis. Young continually experimented with variations in grip design, from his graceful Perfectionist and half-Wells designs to the flat bull-nose grips often found on his Parabolic 15 and Parabolic 17 tapers. Paul Young clearly favored utility over esthetics, although most rodmakers lean toward traditionally slender elegance in their rod-grip design.

Reel seats precede cork grips on many rods, depending on their size and design. Trout rods are generally fitted with reel seats measuring three-quarters and five-eighths of an inch, although some midge rods can be smaller, with their cork fillers and delicate aluminum reel bands. Solid metal reel seats are usually fitted with a wood core; birch, sumac, cedar, and basswood are commonly used. The filler plug is seated first, its cement allowed to dry thoroughly, and the reel seat barrel follows. Some tubular reel seats were fixed and pinned with German-silver wire. Fine rodmakers like Goodwin Granger, Hiram Leonard, Wes Jordan, Heddon, and Cross all used solid metal reel seats, although such full-metal seats are seldom used today.

Skeletal screw-locking seats with functional specie-cork fillers are common, along with ornamental fillers of various hardwoods like butternut and American walnut. Other exotic woods are often used: fine burled walnut and Macassar ebony are found on the exquisite Heddon rods, rosewood fillers are used on some of the finest Wes Jordan rods made at Orvis, and the talented Gary Howells likes zebrawood for his exquisite, darkly grained reel seats. Some reel seats require fixing the hooded butt cap with a pin or screw set into the cane on its longitudinal axis, and the rodmakers sometimes reinforce the butt of the section with a small collar of thin aluminum tubing. The skillful young rod builders at Thomas &

Thomas are making unusually functional reel seats which cut away the barrel of a locking seat until only the threads remain, and the threaded sleeve is morticed into the walnut seats. The skeletal sliding-ring seats built at Thomas & Thomas do not use a butt plate to protect the flared seat, preferring the look of the cane itself exposed inside the cork.

Richard Held is a private rodmaker who mortices cork into the hardwood of his sliding-band seats, using its resilience to hold the reel tightly in place, in a uniquely handsome design. For twenty years I have been experimenting with a reversed sliding-ring seat which conceals a hooded cap inside the cork handle, and uses a single ring that is tightened from below. It is a system that is unusually secure, since the weight of the reel is self-tightening. My own rods include a fine Leonard ACM 38 and an exquisite seven-and-a-half-foot Young Princess that are fitted with my skeletal grips, and Robert Summers is building excellent bamboo rods with a similar handle design on both his cork and hardwood seats.

Several makers finish the entire rod with a thin first coat of tung-oil varnish, polyurethane, or tung oil itself at this final stage of assembly, achieving a remarkably smooth finish base before the guides are seated and wrapped. Others buff their impregnated sections before winding.

The grip check is slipped down the butt section of the rod and seated against the cork handle. Neither the reel seat nor the guides can be aligned and placed until the stiffest bending profile of the rod has been tested. Some makers check the stiffness of each section on a deflection board, while others use less sophisticated methods. It is possible to hold a rod section at a forty-five-degree angle with its butt on a table and its upper end in the left hand. The section is then rolled with the right hand, making it possible to feel the stiffest bending face. The reel seat and guides are aligned opposite that stiffest side in a fly rod, so the strongest bending fibers are subjected to maximum stress during the pickup and the forward casting stroke. These fibers in the top face of the rod are placed in tension during the high-lift stroke and are radically compressed in delivering a cast.

Guides are made from several materials, and a number of designs have evolved since the ring-and-keeper fittings of the nineteenth century. Tungsten, monel, stainless steel, chrome-plated beryllium copper, and chromium-plated brass have all been used. Tungsten and chromium-plated tungsten are probably best, since they are remarkably hard and resist line wear. English snake guides, which are formed in a configuration opposite to that of American guides, and the side-supported ring guides are all popular. Side-supported guides are most commonly found on rods intended for big-water and long casts. Butt guides are usually metal ring-mounted guides of stainless steel, carboloy, chrome-plated beryllium copper, and tungsten. Such guides are common on virtually all fly rods, although the late R. W. Crompton used an ordinary snake guide in place of a heavier stripping guide. Older rods often used butt guides lined with agate or agatine, and some of the new English and Scottish rods are using synthetics like aqualite and sintox. The new carbon graphite rods are using butt- and tip-guide rings lined with a black aerospace ceramic originally developed for missile nose cones and rocket nozzles.

Tip guides of the American type with a simple pear-shaped configuration are probably best. The finest are made from tungsten, chromium, or stainless steel. Tip guides should be large enough to permit the leader knot to enter the guides readily when a fish is worked close. All of the guides should be large enough to facilitate long casts, and the butt guide should not be too close to the grip. It should be easily reached with the left hand, yet far enough up the butt section to take the exaggerated line shoot of the left-hand haul. Many butt guides are too close to the grip. The feet of the guides are usually filed or ground down to a razor-fine edge, making the silk wrappings absolutely smooth when they are wound. Most rodmakers include a fly-keeper ring or guide or bent wire loop in the windings at the grip check.

Several methods of placing guides are used. R. W. Crompton liked the same number of guides as there were feet in the rod so that nine guides were required for a three-piece rod of nine feet. However, Crompton spaced his guides with one important difference. The butt guide on the butt joint was completely omitted. Four guides were used on the middle section, and five were placed on the tip. The American standard technique uses a stripping guide on the butt section, five snake guides on the middle section, and five on the tip. Using one more snake guide than the rod length is a fine rule of thumb. Samuel Phillippe developed a method used by many American manufacturers. One stripping guide was placed on the butt, four were placed on the middle joint, and five guides were seated on the tip. Many European makers use guide spacings identical to the Phillippe method, although some British and Scottish manufacturers use only three guides on the middle joint and four on the tip. Seven or eight guides are clearly too few on a nine-foot rod. Such rods should be fitted with a nine thirty-seconds of an inch stripping guide, number two snake guides on the middle section, and number one guides on the tip. Snake guides smaller than size 2/0 should not be used, and stripping guides under five thirty-seconds of an inch do not shoot a cast readily.

Guides are wound by hand on the best-quality rods. The guide is placed in its proper position and temporarily held with masking tape. The winding silk is started about one-sixteenth of an inch in front of the first foot of the guide. The thread is wound over itself. The silk is wound carefully up the sloping foot of the guide, each winding being laid tightly against the last, until the wrapping lies about one thirty-second of an inch past the shoe. Then a loop of winding thread is wound under the last few turns, the free end of the silk is threaded into the loop, and the loop is used to pull the thread back under itself. The remaining silk is trimmed carefully with a razor blade. The tape is stripped from the other foot, and it is secured with winding silk. Rodmakers like Winston and Howells double-wrap their guides, working back along the wire toward the feet. The ferrule serrations or splits are firmly wound too, with small ornamental wraps at the tip guide and above the grip check. In the days when fish and animal glues were common, regularly spaced wrappings of silk were necessary to hold the bamboo splines together. The only relatively modern rodmaker who used intermediate wraps was Edwin Powell, and his wraps were actually needed to reinforce his patented method of hollow construction. Rod windings vary widely from maker to maker, from the simplicity of Garrison transparent wrappings at the guides to the intricate silk embellishments on the butt sections of Thomas and Edwards.

The windings are set with a color preservative in most shops, and then coated with tung varnish, epoxy, or polyurethane. Once the guides are dried, it is time for the final finish of tung oil, polyurethane, epoxy, or rod varnish. Four hand-rubbed coats of hot varnish are still perhaps the finest protective finish, although a modern dipped finish is better looking. Everett Garrison finishes his rods in an ingenious tubular dipping tank about two inches in diameter, and a timing mechanism designed to remove a rod section slowly—its rate of withdrawal synchronized with the drying rate of the finish, producing a gleaming surface as perfect as a mirror.

Hand-applied coats of varnish are usually rubbed with lava stone and felt, making them smooth and hard. The final coat is left bright by some makers, who like its brilliant glitter, and rubbed to a dull matte finish by others. Ten days to two weeks are required for a fine tung-oil varnish to dry completely, particularly before rubbing down between coats. Once the final coat is dry, the rod is ready for fishing in all types of weather, and its beauty is remarkably enhanced, particularly in the work of builders like Payne and Carlson and Howells, who are famous for the quality of their finishes.

The late Lew Stoner believed that varnishing was far more important than many anglers believe. Stoner argued that too much varnish can deaden a rod and increase its tendency to set, and that too little varnish can leave the cane without adequate protection from mildew and rot.

Found out the hard way years ago, Stoner always explained. *Unless the finish is as elastic and hard as the cane itself, it soft-sleeves the rod and deadens its action—it gets bent and stays bent beyond the power of the cane to force it back into shape after a hard day of fishing.*

The basic operations are similar with all rodmakers, but in matters of casting action and the structure of the rod, there is considerable difference in rod theory and construction. Some builders prefer a fast, crisp action in their rods, others like the traditional delicate tip and stiff butt tapers, and still others lean toward a compound taper that flexes more in the butt than in the upper calibrations. Modern rods are still built in four-strip and five-strip sections, although most are still the common six-strip construction, and each of these types displays its own distinctive character under casting stress. Preferences in rod action are highly personal. Some fishermen prefer an extremely fast action, like many of the rods built by Pinky Gillum and Lyle Dickerson. Others like a slower rod, the exquisite compound tapers found in the work of men like Garrison and Young.

It's a question of personality, insists Art Neumann of the Wanigas Rod

Company. *The ulcer type is a driver, and needs a fast rod to keep up with his choppy casting strokes—the more relaxed fisherman is the one who likes the Parabolics, and their deliberate casting rhythms.*

Minor variations in rod tapers result in these major differences in casting performance. Each of the manufacturers tapers its rods to carefully engineered calibrations that vary surprisingly from maker to maker. Such tapers are a highly competitive aspect of the rod-building business, and some manufacturers are endlessly experimenting with new theories and rod actions. Many craftsmen will make special tapers to suit a knowledgeable fisherman's specifications, providing he is willing to pay the price.

It is surprising how few anglers realize that rod tapers are milled at extremely fine tolerances, and that differences of only .005 inch can make the difference between a fast and slow butt action. Differences of less than .002 can make a radical change in the casting and hooking delicacy of a tip section. Two rods of identical calibrations from the workbench of a single craftsman can also vary radically. Bamboo is a variable wood, quite heterogeneous in its molecular structure and varying widely in its wall thickness from culm to culm. Heat treatment of the cane can also produce variables in its casting performance. It is this combination of variables that can make a rod great—its sweetness a poetry impossible to describe—or merely another fine casting tool. There are two excellent Young Parabolic 15s in my collection that demonstrate this fact perfectly. One is a surprisingly fast Parabolic action, while the same compound taper in the other produces a slow casting rhythm that works well into the butt. Such subtle differences are impossible to predict—just as the tonality in a particularly fine Stradivarius never quite duplicates the richness or brilliance found in another made by the same master.

There are also surprising variations in rod behavior between four-strip, five-strip and six-strip rods of identical weight. Both cross section and taper profile are factors in rod performance. The quality of its cane will determine how a rod might perform, but it is taper and construction that largely determine the character of that performance. Fly rods are forced to bend in almost every plane while casting, since few anglers cast without bad habits and torque, so any rod must perform both across its flats and its corners. Many anglers believe their cane rods will not bend in the diagonal planes of their corners. Early rod builders thought so too, and rounded their bamboo rods to eliminate the corners. It took many years before they discovered that turning their rods down ruined the power fibers of their cane. Four-strip rods were easily milled, and involved much less work than six-strip, eight-strip, ten-strip, or twelve-strip sections. Six-strip rods soon eliminated the more complicated designs, and their casting strokes were less demanding than four-strip tapers. Three-strip rods were tried and abandoned before 1850, but the five-strip theory did not evolve until the late R. W. Crompton proposed its superiority forty-odd years ago.

Crompton planed his first five-strip rod in a specially made tapering block that required two grooves for each section, milling the splines at

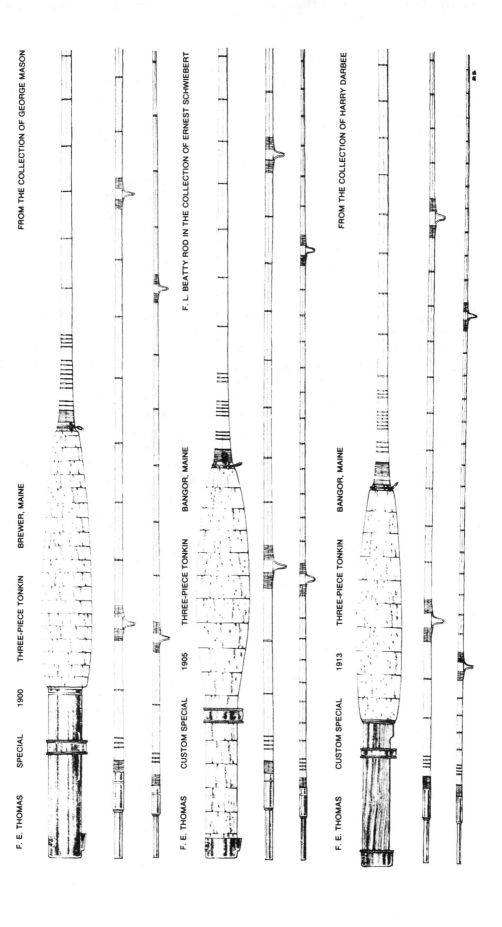

FROM THE COLLECTION OF GEORGE MASON

F. E. THOMAS   SPECIAL   1900   THREE-PIECE TONKIN   BREWER, MAINE

F. L. BEATTY ROD IN THE COLLECTION OF ERNEST SCHWIEBERT

F. E. THOMAS   CUSTOM SPECIAL   1905   THREE-PIECE TONKIN   BANGOR, MAINE

FROM THE COLLECTION OF HARRY DARBEE

F. E. THOMAS   CUSTOM SPECIAL   1913   THREE-PIECE TONKIN   BANGOR, MAINE

precisely fifty-four degrees. Each spline is an isosceles triangle in cross section, measuring fifty-four degrees at its outer corners and seventy-two degrees at its apex inside the rod. A five-strip section has a corner opposite its bending plane, stiffening and reinforcing its character. Such rods are much stiffer than four- or six-strip rods of equal weight and similar tapers. However, five-strip rods often respond with considerable eccentricity under casting loads, and sometimes fracture in the hands of anglers with erratic casting habits. The bending behavior of these five-strip rods is difficult for an average fisherman, and they have never achieved wide popularity. Nathaniel Uslan, who once worked in the Payne shop, is the best-known disciple of R. W. Crompton and his five-strip tapers—although the late Frank Wire on the Pacific Coast was also an advocate of the Crompton five-strip theory.

Four-strip rods are also demanding in their casting behavior, and never achieved much popularity, although they require much less work than either five- or six-strip tapers. The principal arguments for four-strip fabrication lie in easier construction, the fact that it has more power fibers per diameter than the other cross sections, and that its power fibers are concentrated slightly farther from the neutral bending plane of the rod. However, a four-strip taper is slightly heavier per diameter than a similar five- or six-strip taper, and the extra power fibers are often fully occupied in compensating for the additional weight. The principal advocate of four-strip design was the late William Edwards—although his father Eustis Edwards and his brother Gene Edwards were both six-strip partisans—and his famous Edwards Quadrate rods are beautiful. Samuel Carlson is presently building equally fine four-strip rods in his Connecticut shop, using the superb Edwards tapers.

Six-strip rods are more difficult to make, having twelve gluing faces that must be precisely milled, instead of the ten faces in a five-strip taper and only eight in a four-strip design. However, their bending character makes them easier to cast in the hands of an average fisherman, and they dominate modern rod building. Six-strip rods are more nearly round, and flex almost as readily across the corners as the bending planes. The flexing stresses are also more uniformly distributed in a six-strip rod, and the principal manufacturers in both Europe and the United States all use six-strip construction.

However, the arguments between the adherents of four-strip, five-strip, and six-strip construction still continue. Their prelude came in the first exchanges between R. W. Crompton and authors on split-cane construction like Perry Frazer and George Parker Holden. Crompton argued that his five-strip method was theoretically superior, although it took him almost fifty years to work out practical tapers. His theories held that there was no continuous glue line across the median bending plane as there was in a six-strip rod. There was approximately fifteen percent less glue, and the extra glue in rods built with six to twelve strips was a liability contributing nothing to their action. A. J. McClane added his experience to the

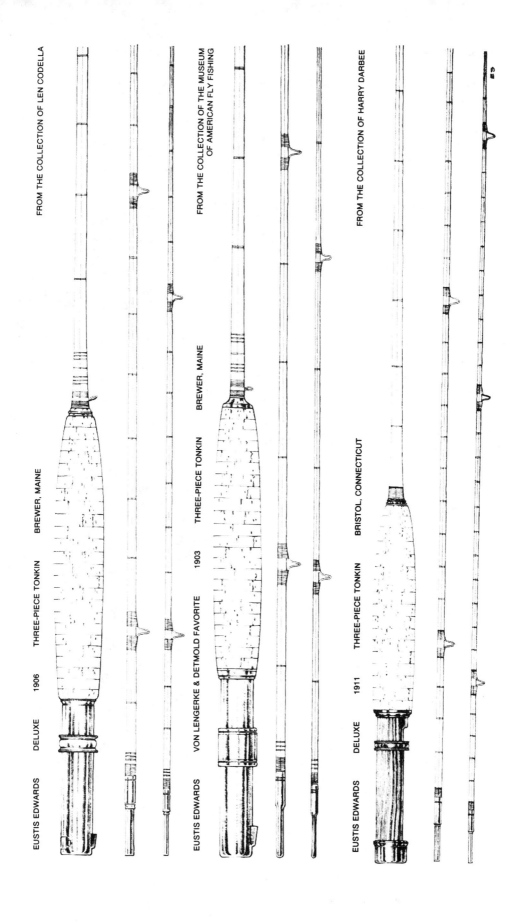

EUSTIS EDWARDS   DELUXE   1906   THREE-PIECE TONKIN   BREWER, MAINE

FROM THE COLLECTION OF LEN CODELLA

EUSTIS EDWARDS   VON LENGERKE & DETMOLD FAVORITE   1903   THREE-PIECE TONKIN   BREWER, MAINE

FROM THE COLLECTION OF THE MUSEUM OF AMERICAN FLY FISHING

EUSTIS EDWARDS   DELUXE   1911   THREE-PIECE TONKIN   BRISTOL, CONNECTICUT

FROM THE COLLECTION OF HARRY DARBEE

controversy in *The Practical Fly Fisherman,* and his observations are interesting:

> The corners in a five-strip rod act as backbones extending the length of the rod, but in four- and six-strip rods they are in the same plane, directly opposite each other. Since there are three pairs of flats, it follows that the action, or bending, will occur in one or more of these planes.
>
> In theory, if the fisherman forces a corner to take some of the load, it simply shrugs the load over to one of the adjacent flat sides, with the result that the cast doesn't go exactly where he directs it. This is an inherent characteristic of all rods having an even number of sides according to the pentagonal theorists.
>
> A five-strip rod doesn't respond in such a manner. In this case each weak flat has a reinforcing backbone on the opposite side. Naturally, the strengthening is greatest right at the five corners. At points slightly to one side or the other of these corners the effect diminishes slightly, only to increase again to full value as the center of the bordering flat side (remember that there is a corner opposite this flat) is reached. A four-sided rod prefers to bend up-and-down and sideways. To use shooter's parlance, it wants to swing directly from twelve to six o'clock or from three to nine, but it resists bending slightly more in any other combination of bending stress.
>
> By the same reasoning a rod of six-strip construction will flex evenly from twelve to six, from two to eight, and from four to ten. It is reluctant to bend in any other direction. The five-strip rod is no exception to this tendency to bend in any other direction.
>
> But where are these paths and how many of them are there? According to Nat Uslan they're not at the corners because these regions are strongest; nor are they at the flats because, as pointed out before, there is always a corner opposite a flat. Since there are ten such combinations of corners and flats, we can assume that a five-strip rod doesn't care which way you shoot your cast.

Stream experience with all three types of rod cross sections tends to verify some of these theoretical arguments and to discount others unmistakably. Four-strip rods are poetry in motion, sweet and smooth in their casting planes, but any deviation from those planes and the poetry is broken. The rod reacts almost roughly, forcing the casting loads back toward the bending faces, and it is unforgiving in the hands of a careless fisherman. Five-strip rods are undeniably stiff for their weight, since they increase the moment of inertia in cross sections of equal area. The moment of inertia in a circle is a function of its diameter to the fourth power. The circular perimeter in a five-strip rod is slightly larger than the circumference of a six-strip cross section having an equal area, which means that if its diameter is only one-tenth larger, its moment of inertia and stiffness are increased almost fifty percent. These mathematical relationships are expressed in the following equations for the three types of construction:

$$D_1^4 = 1.0 \ \times 1.0 \ \times 1.0 \ \times 1.0 \ = 1.0 \ \text{(six-strip)}$$

$$D_2^4 = 1.1 \ \times 1.1 \ \times 1.1 \ \times 1.1 \ = 1.46 \ \text{(five-strip)}$$

$$D_3^4 = 1.12 \times 1.12 \times 1.12 \times 1.12 = 1.57 \ \text{(four-strip)}$$

The moment of inertia and theoretical stiffness of the three cross sections seem to point toward optimal stiffness in the four-strip sections, although the placement of the glue lines, the relativity of corners and flats, and the heterogeneity of bamboo are equally critical in rod action. Actual rod behavior under casting loads involves other factors too. The alignment of the reel seat and the guides stresses a rod with eccentric loads in a clearly preferred bending plane. The guides themselves displace a rod's center of gravity from its longitudinal axis and affect bending dynamics.

Stiffness and performance under stress are not just functions of moment of inertia, since the modulus of elasticity implicit in a rod's material is equally important. Its dynamics are not like those of a spring or cantilever beam, as early mathematical analysis usually sought to prove.

Rods stress according to wave linear equations, Everett Garrison explains, *like the progressive uncoiling of a bullwhip.*

The loads of casting are complex. When the line is being picked up off the water, the primary forces are its hydraulic friction, line weight and atmospheric drag, air resistance against the rod, and the casting energy imparted by the caster. Line weight and its mixture of hydraulic and atmospheric drag are distributed through the guides to the rod in a series of concentrated loads. Secondary forces are the impact load of the pickup haul on the stripping guide, the inertial forces of rod and reel weight, and the choppy torque that comes from poor casting habits.

The loads of the forward stroke are slightly different. Line weight remains the same, but line drag is entirely atmospheric unless a careless backcast hits the water. Rod inertia and atmospheric drag on its length remain the same, unless the variables of wind direction and velocity intrude. The combined line forces are more uniformly distributed along the rod, since during the forward cast, the line rides back against the cane itself. The impact load of a strong left-hand haul begins parallel to the rod, but quickly exerts force vectors on the butt guide as the stroke starts forward. The inertial forces of the reel remain the same, except that they may take the form of counterclockwise torque on the forward cast. Many skilled distance casters allow the reel to ride out sideways during the backcast, while the line is extending, and its twisting loads are clockwise. Poor casting habits can also exert a minor counterclockwise load on the butt section. Arm force is usually equally distributed on both the backcast and the forward stroke, although the final left-hand haul in the forward cast exerts an accelerating impact load on the rod and its butt guide.

The arm stroke is not a constantly accelerating load either. The pickup starts gently to break the hydraulic friction of the surface film and finishes with a sharply accelerating stroke once the line is skimming lightly across the surface. The forward cast accelerates powerfully and ends with a sharp wrist snap in the follow-through. The cumulative force in both strokes is roughly equal, although that force is not delivered in the same way.

Many anglers may find such stress analysis disturbing and dislike any attempt to explain the poetry of a fly rod with mathematical equations. The pleasure transmitted through a fine rod to our senses defies mathematical explanations, but many rodmakers do argue about their work in scientific terms. Our brief discussion will at least make the reader aware of their conflicting theories and the performance variables of their rods. However, didactic sermons about moment of inertia, bamboo and its modulus of elasticity, and the number of strips in a rod are infinitely less important than its taper; and rod tapers are seldom openly discussed. There are surprising differences in rod calibrations and tapers from one manufacturer to another—ranging from the soft actions found in the classical Leonards to the extremely stiff tapers typical of Lyle Dickerson or the exaggerated tip actions built by Sewell Dunton.

Several engineers have worked out methods of comparing rod actions in past years. Systems of measuring the vibrations of a rod have not proven significant since they often fail to describe the variables in radically different tapers. Perhaps the best known of these systems was the Montague Free Deflection Method, which sought to evaluate rods in terms of their oscillations per minute. The tensile stress a rod exerts against a scale is meaningless in terms of casting qualities, although it was widely used for many years. The British system, which loaded a rod in deflection until fracture occurred, was also quite meaningless in evaluating its fishing qualities. The Crompton Deflection Board was perhaps the best method used in judging the character of fly rods. It placed a test rod on a graphic grid, fixing its grip and reel seat on the base line and attaching a four-ounce weight to its tip. The curvature of the various rods could then be photographed or plotted for ready comparison, and their stiffness profile was clearly pinpointed.

In recent years, Don Phillips has developed another method of comparing fly rods. The Phillips Stiffness Profile is clearly the most knowledgeable and scientific approach to the comparison of rod behavior under stress. Few of our past rod builders were technically trained in the modern sense of understanding stress analysis, and since the essential mathematics governing a fly rod in casting lie in both aerodynamics and static structures, it should not be surprising that an aerospace engineer like Don Phillips has married these disciplines in analyzing rods. Most of our famous rodmakers, including formally trained engineers like Hiram Leonard, were incapable of real stress analysis. Their finest tapers were largely empirical designs, painstakingly evolved over the years by trial and error. Even famous Payne tapers like the eight-and-a-half-foot dry-fly rod that virtually became the company's trademark were largely accidental.

ALBERT EVERETT HENDRICKSON

Jim Payne was forever building salmon rods for Albert Everett Hendrickson, the man for whom the Hendrickson fly patterns are named, and once built forty-eight ten-foot tapers before Hendrickson was satisfied. Hendrickson also had a twelve-foot salmon rod that Roy Steenrod, who developed the Hendricksons, and Jim Payne were trying out at Four Maples on the Esopus. When they had finished, and Steenrod was taking it apart, he happened to flex the tip and middle section in a casting stroke.

That's it, Jim! he exclaimed to Payne. *You add a handle to that and you've got the perfect dry-fly taper!*

The tapers of other famous rods were often accidents too. The superb Ritz design called the Fario Club evolved from a traumatic encounter with a bicycle. Charles Ritz was planning a trip to the Lech in Bavaria and had sent a favorite rod to the shop of Pezon & Michel for some minor repairs. It was a conventional nine-foot rod, fairly stiff in the butt tapers at the grip and too soft in its tip calibrations. It was also a travel rod, built with a detachable grip that received a male ferrule fitted to the bottom of its butt section. There was no extra tip and the rod was protected with only a simple poplin rod sack. When it was ready, Pezon & Michel sent it over to the Hotel Ritz with a messenger on a bicycle.

It was a mistake. During the trip from the shop to the Place Vendôme, the messenger boy allowed the cloth rod sack to catch in the spokes of his bicycle. Its front wheel was damaged, and the boy hurt his elbow and knee in the resulting tumble.

But the rascal said nothing about catching the rod in the spokes, Ritz laughs today. *He simply delivered the cloth sack to the hotel concierge, and left the Place Vendôme as quickly as possible!*

Ritz failed to examine the rod and simply packed it in his little Lancia when he left for Germany. When his party arrived on the Lech, Ritz was dismayed to find that both the tip section and butt joint of his rod were completely sheared off. The tip had lost about three inches at its top guide and another three inches were gone at the butt ferrule just above the grip.

It was a disaster! Ritz shrugs eloquently.

Ritz had no extra rod along, and no one else had thought to bring a spare. There was no alternative to making temporary repairs on the damaged rod, and Ritz quickly stripped off a snake guide and fitted the tip top in its place. The ferrule was heated and removed from the broken butt section, and refitted on the remaining cane. The resurrected rod measured about eight and a half feet, and Ritz half-heartedly walked down to the Lech to test it. Ritz is one of the finest casting stylists who ever lived, and the rod behaved strangely after its surgery in the field, but he soon adjusted to its unusual rhythms. Its stroke was slow and exotic, with most of the bending in its butt section, and the tip a little stiff and top heavy.

Fantastic! Ritz explains excitedly.

The modified rod could carry a remarkable line load in its false casting and lift a surprising length from the water. It did both of these things better than before. Its timing was exotic and slow, but the reduction of tip flexing made the butt function in bending and the tip perform like a lever. The upper two-thirds of the rod delivered full casting power to the line at the point of release with almost no oscillation or follow-through.

The rod was a revelation then, Ritz continues. *It would deliver an absolutely straight line at eighty feet!*

It was a happy accident, and although its action was a little clumsy and difficult to master in its timing, the half-crippled Pezon & Michel was one ancestor of the modern semiparabolic tapers found in the work of master craftsmen like Everett Garrison, Lew Stoner, Jim Payne, Paul Young, Edwin Powell, Doug Merrick, and Gary Howells.

Don Phillips has been working out a more disciplined approach to the design and analysis of rod tapers. His stiffness profile is a static method of analysis which merely treats a rod like a deflecting cantilever beam. Although such analogies are too simple, since they exclude the radical dynamics of casting, they do offer some preliminary bench marks for evaluating and comparing rods. Phillips even grants some credibility to a rudimentary deflection board analysis, although he has a number of reservations about its usefulness. Perhaps the most obvious flaw in deflection analysis is the fact that a rod has a constantly varying cross section throughout its length. The grip and lower butt section are not fixed during a casting stroke, like the rod butt is fixed on a deflection board, but are constantly moving and subject to wrist torque. The inertial forces imposed by the weight of the rod itself vary along its entire length, and local variables in acceleration also occur.

Atmospheric drag varies with rod diameter, and wind direction can produce intriguing variables in the atmospheric loads imposed on a rod. Lateral winds can cause eccentric loads and compensating torque well into the delicate calibrations of a rod, and buffetting and gusts in variable winds are another complexity affecting the stress analysis of actual casting performance. The static load of a lead weight in simple deflection analysis is not a viable simulation of the accelerating dynamics and momentary impact loads of either line work or a hooked and fighting fish. These loads are also erratic, being transmitted back into the rod through its guides. The direction of these loads is dependent on the constantly changing position of each guide, and the angles of the line entering and leaving it. Phillips also argues that the relatively minor deflection caused by a four-ounce weight on the tip is a faint echo of the radical deflections that occur in long-range casting or playing a strong fish.

There are two basic equations in analyzing such static deflection, and both are derived from common structural design. The first defines total tip deflection, and is expressed in the following terms:

$$\text{Deflection in inches} = \frac{0.25 \text{ pounds} \times \text{rod length in inches}^3}{3 \times \text{modulus of elasticity} \times \text{moment of inertia}}$$

The modulus of elasticity is expressed in pounds per square inch, while the moment of inertia for a given cross section is defined in inches to the fourth power. Moment of inertia is critical to all structural analysis and is often derived as follows:

$$\text{Moment of inertia} = \frac{3.1416 \times \text{rod diameter in inches}^4}{64}$$

Don Phillips is quick to point out that these classical equations of stress analysis are useful in describing fly-rod behavior only when the deflection is minor. Their relationships apply to a cantilever with a load concentrated ninety degrees to its axis. It is obvious that in exaggerated deflection, when the tip bends down to align with the direction of the load, it is entirely subjected to tensile loads rather than the mixture of tension and compression found in less radical bending behavior. Since a four-ounce weight will easily cause exaggerated deflection in most light rods, Phillips pinpoints this as the principal limitation of using a deflection board in analyzing rod actions. However, modulus of elasticity and moment of inertia are the only forces affecting a rod's deflection and resistance to deformation.

Other factors are external, Phillips insists, *and lie outside the parameters of static deflection analysis.*

Phillips believes that a well-designed rod taper behaves in a series of wave-linear deflections, permitting its tip to oscillate back and forth in a crisply defined path. When the casting rhythms are broken and that path is not relatively straight, wavy loops will form in the line that kill both accuracy and distance. High concentrations of bending stress can occur in distance casting, with the bending moment in rod deformation as follows:

$$\text{Bending moment in inch/pounds} = \frac{\text{Stiffness factor in pounds/inch}^2}{\text{Radius of curvature in inches}}$$

The stiffness factor is a constant in this equation, and the maximum stresses occur in the tensile forces along the outside curvature of the power fibers, and in the compressive forces concentrated in the inside curvature of the rod. Standard stress analysis tells us that these stresses occur at the extremities of the cane, while the bending stresses along its axis remain neutral. Years ago I had an engineering professor who described such bending phenomena with his hand extended palm down, with his fingers together and straight. Bending his fingers up, he demonstrated the tensile stresses in a deflecting beam with the tightly stretched skin across his palm and compressive stresses with the wrinkled skin that formed across the back of his hand. Bending his fingers down wrinkled the skin in his palm and tightened the skin across the tendons in his hand, and I never forgot that simple lesson in the dynamics of bending stresses. Maximum tension and compression in bending is determined with this equation:

$$\text{Bending stress in pounds/inch}^2 = \frac{\text{Bending moment} \times \text{radius of rod}}{\text{Moment of inertia}}$$

Don Phillips argues that these mathematical expressions of bending moment and bending stress can be combined in a new equation that better defines the maximum stress at the maximum distance from the neutral axis of the rod. His new equation shows that in any radius of rod curvature, stress can be reduced by using materials with a lower modulus of elasticity or designing rods of smaller diameter. Phillips' equation is as follows:

$$\text{Bending stress in pounds/inch}^2 = \frac{\text{Modulus of elasticity} \times \text{radius of rod}}{\text{Radius of curvature}}$$

Radius and modulus of elasticity have obvious limits in split-cane construction, but engineers like Don Phillips are working beyond bamboo and fiberglass to exotic materials like carbon graphite, boron, PRD-49, and various hybrid structures using these synthetic fibers with glass.

Phillips is correct in insisting that both stress and stiffness must be considered in terms of simultaneous interaction, and an integral part of the design process. Stress should be permitted to reach relatively high levels, as long as the material has a sufficient safety factor between maximum stress and its fracture point. Phillips points out that the maximum rod curvature in fiberglass is much greater than the allowable curvature in bamboo, a material with a much higher modulus of elasticity. The fracture behavior of cane suggests that future synthetic rod materials demand close attention to these relationships between maximum bending stresses and their structural limits, since they have a modulus of elasticity that lies well beyond the finest Chinese bamboo.

Phillips' theories clearly recognize the complex relationships involved in casting stresses, and that a rod is not subject to static loads but performs in a series of dynamic wave-linear vibrations. The tensile stresses affecting the tip during the pickup, false casting, and the forward casting stroke are filled with variables that virtually define numerical analysis. Cyclical variations occur throughout these casting oscillations as the line loops accelerate and form and extend in both directions. Phillips has evolved this equation to describe for the frequency of these oscillations:

$$\text{Casting frequency } F_n = \frac{1}{2\pi} \sqrt{\frac{3EIg}{PL^3}}$$

Don Phillips defines EI as the stiffness factor in pounds per square inch, and multiplies it with a constant gravitational factor of 386 inches per second squared. The value of π is 3.1416, and the combination of 0.25 pounds P multiplied by the rod length in inches to the third power has its origins in our first equation for tip deflection.

The Phillips frequency equation establishes the oscillatory behavior of any rod in cycles per second, and is a workable simulation of its character, provided the distributed loads are negligible and dampening action is not a major factor. However, it should be understood that the Phillips concept of natural frequency is limited to a rod's recovery from bending stresses, consciously excluding its inertial factors and atmospheric loads. It can be argued that rod stiffness and length, as well as the distribution of that stiffness through taper calibrations, are the basic factors in fly-rod design. The other primary factors are external forces imposed on the rod by the dynamics of the working line, the atmosphere and hydraulic friction, and casting skills.

However, these external forces cannot be ignored. Fly casting involves muscular energy that either accelerates or decelerates the rod in its normal casting cycles. Its velocity varies constantly throughout its length. The basic laws of Newtonian physics state that an accelerating force in one direction always occurs in concert with an equal inertial force in the opposite direction. During the early moments of a forward casting stroke, the rod accelerates at increasing speeds toward the tip because of its proportionately increasing moment-arm distances above the grip. Rod length and simple rotation are the forces involved. Comparable inertial forces occur at each point along a rod taper, matching each increasing vector of acceleration. Phillips uses a surprisingly simple equation to describe the total force concentrated at such points along the rod in question. It divides the weight of the rod segment, multiplied with its acceleration in inches per square second, by the gravitational constant of 386 inches per square second. The equation is as follows:

$$\text{Total force in pounds} = \frac{\text{Weight in pounds} \times \text{acceleration}}{\text{Gravitational constant}}$$

It is important to understand that inertial forces occur only when the rod is accelerating or decelerating, and its composite velocities are changing. No inertial loads are generated by a rod oscillating at a constant rate of speed. Weight and diameter are therefore the factors that affect bending performance through inertial loads, while acceleration depends directly on the angler.

Atmospheric drag imposed by air density, wind velocity and direction, and the hydraulic drag that occurs when the line is lifted from the water are other external forces with a primary influence on casting performance. These factors of drag are exerted on the line and transmitted to the rod, as well as exerted directly in terms of atmospheric resistance on the rod itself. Aircraft designers and naval architects are perhaps best acquainted with

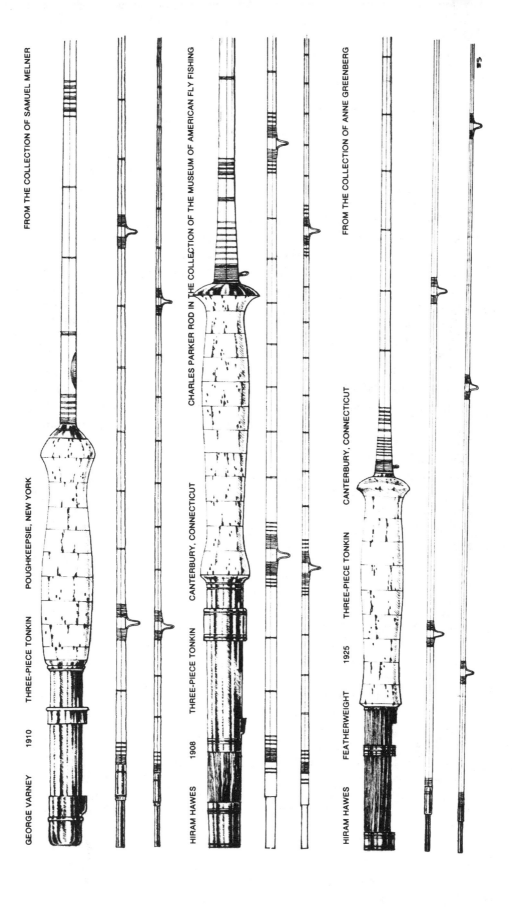

FROM THE COLLECTION OF SAMUEL MELNER

GEORGE VARNEY   1910   THREE-PIECE TONKIN   POUGHKEEPSIE, NEW YORK

CHARLES PARKER ROD IN THE COLLECTION OF THE MUSEUM OF AMERICAN FLY FISHING

HIRAM HAWES   1908   THREE-PIECE TONKIN   CANTERBURY, CONNECTICUT

FROM THE COLLECTION OF ANNE GREENBERG

HIRAM HAWES   FEATHERWEIGHT   1925   THREE-PIECE TONKIN   CANTERBURY, CONNECTICUT

such drag analysis, and their accepted formula for computing drag is the following:

$$\text{Drag in pounds} = C_d V^2 L_d \frac{W}{2g}$$

This equation predicts drag forces in terms of an empirically determined coefficient of drag, the velocity of the rod itself in feet per second, the diameter and length of the rod, and a factor consisting of atmospheric or hydraulic density in pounds per cubic foot divided by the gravitational constant times two. Effective rod length is less than the full length of the rod at rest, and is measured between the hand and tip when it is subjected to bending stresses. Since velocity is not equal at any two points along a rod in flexure, drag is also distributed unevenly along its length. Unlike inertial forces, which both resist acceleration in a rod at rest and multiply once the casting stroke is fully started, drag always acts in direct opposition to rod casting-stroke velocity.

Because of its negative influences on rod dynamics, drag is still fighting the casting stroke near the completion of its forward extension, while its inertial forces have joined in its velocity. Phillips is quick to call our attention to an intriguing facet of drag and its effect on casting. The drag equation makes it clear that atmospheric drag is directly proportional to the square of the rod's casting velocity. Practically speaking, atmospheric drag is radically multiplied when a skilled caster really powers his stroke. It means that mere casting strength has an unmistakable point of marginal return, and that manipulating line speed with a delicately timed double haul is more important in distance work than muscle. The factors of drag imposed on a rod are clearly related to its diameter and length—and the velocity of its working rhythms is a function of the fly caster.

Although each of these equations describes an important facet of rod performance, Don Phillips agrees that understanding them is not critical to your fishing skills. Stress analysis and casting dynamics are really the territory of skilled engineers. However, Phillips is correct in his contention that the length of a rod, its stiffness profile, the factors of diameter and weight implicit in its tapers, its capacity for deflection without fracture, and its inherent recovery from stress are the principal components of fly-rod behavior while casting.

Rod length affects casting performance in several ways. Longer rods keep the line higher above the water, free of the atmospheric turbulence there, although their diameter and length make them subject to greater drag. Their frequency of oscillation is slower. Short rods are fast because of their higher frequency, less atmospheric resistance, and less deflection. The optimum profile of stiffness is more elusive. Most anglers agree that a limp taper without backbone is just as abominable as a rod that is too stiff. *But there are a multitude of stiffness profiles in between,* Don Phillips observes,

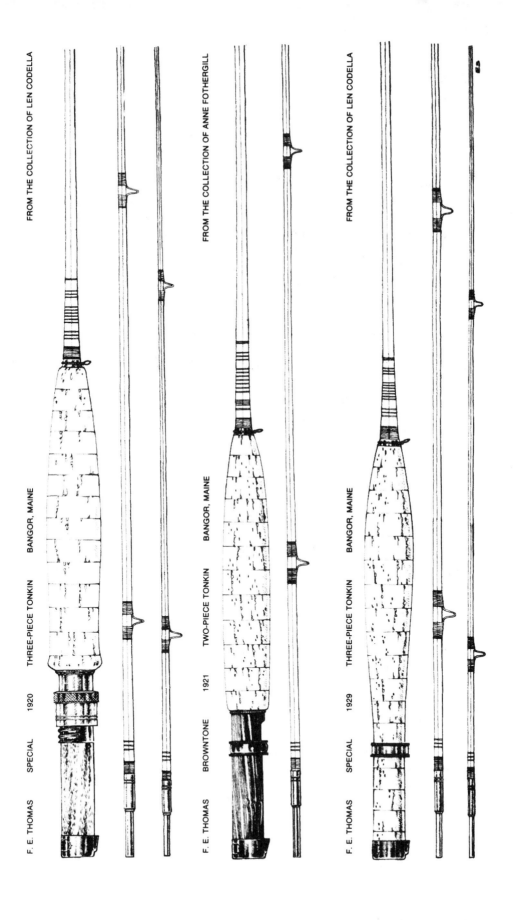

FROM THE COLLECTION OF LEN CODELLA

FROM THE COLLECTION OF ANNE FOTHERGILL

FROM THE COLLECTION OF LEN CODELLA

F. E. THOMAS   SPECIAL   1920   THREE-PIECE TONKIN   BANGOR, MAINE

F. E. THOMAS   BROWNTONE   1921   TWO-PIECE TONKIN   BANGOR, MAINE

F. E. THOMAS   SPECIAL   1929   THREE-PIECE TONKIN   BANGOR, MAINE *and they all have their fans—the principal variables in such choices are the character of the water being fished, the shyness and selectivity of the fish, and the personality and character of the fisherman himself—expressed in his casting style.*

Stiffness is a result of two independent variables, as we have discussed earlier: the modulus of elasticity implicit in a material and the moment of inertia of its cross section. The modulus of elasticity in bamboo varies with the density of its power fibers and wall thickness, and the moment of inertia varies in four-strip, five-strip, and six-strip rods of equal weight. More dramatic variables occur in synthetic materials like carbon graphite, boron, fiberglass, and PRD-49. It is possible to obtain similar stiffness profiles using a high modulus fiber like boron in a small-diameter section or with a low modulus material like fiberglass in a much larger diameter.

The distribution of rod weight involves the volume and density of its material, and in the calibrations of its tapers. The physical volume of any rod varies with its tapers and the geometry of its structure. Rod density obviously varies with the quality of its bamboo and with the density of the several synthetic fibers. Both volume and density play a role in moment of inertia, and therefore in the relative stiffness of any rod. The laws of physics demonstrate that any increase in rod weight, particularly in the middle and tip calibrations, will slow its casting rhythms because of increased inertial loads. Parabolic tapers and the hollow-cane construction used by California rod builders like Stoner, Powell, Merrick, and Howells are typical examples of such stress behavior.

Moment of inertia is also closely related to the variables of rod diameter, both in the number of strips and their geometry and in the particular design tapers involved. Atmospheric drag is also directly proportional to the size and distribution of rod diameter. Both Don Phillips and the late Peter Schwab, who was one of the finest steelhead fishermen and distance casters on the Pacific Coast, agreed that atmospheric drag is the primary factor affecting the power stroke in distance casting. Schwab played a major role in the evolution of both the weight-forward line and the early Stoner patents for the fluted hollow construction.

Wind resistance and drag are almost the whole thing in casting, Schwab always argued persistently, *and they are murder on achieving high tip speed—that's why the same casting stroke will sometimes get more distance with a lighter rod!*

Deflection is actually a series of overlapping stress curvatures, and optimal flexure in any rod is achieved through cane tapers that resolve the problems of equilibrium between its diameter, its varied modulus of elasticity, and the bending capacity of its shaft material in pounds per square inch. Maximum rod deflection without fracture is also closely related to its stiffness profile and the relationships between its diameters and its distribution of stress.

Dampening is also an important factor in any structure designed to vibrate with a regular frequency. It is the tendency of any material to recover from oscillatory stresses, as its molecular structure and flexural properties tend to inhibit and control vibration. The rate of recovery from stress through dampening is important in fly rods, because a taper that continues to vibrate after a cast has been delivered is trouble. Its oscillations transmit waves into the line that kill velocity, and the slap of the line inside the guides and against the rod also affect the shoot.

Several factors affect dampening action in rods during the dynamics of casting. Atmospheric drag on tip speed is primary. Some casting forces are absorbed in the physiology of the caster himself, as well as the handle, reel seat, and inertial counterweight of the reel. Some dampening occurs in the glue joints of the cane, which is one of the reasons why eight- to twelve-strip rods were finally abandoned. Normal line friction in the guides also dampens rod vibrations. There is also considerable dampening through cellular friction implicit in bamboo itself, including the molecular behavior called hysteresis. Some dampening also occurs in the friction surfaces of the male and female ferrules. Don Phillips has performed a number of experiments in rod dampening which indicate that internal dampening forces are relatively minor, compared with the external stresses.

Phillips summarizes his work with the observation that length, stiffness, weight, diameter, and bending properties are the five basic parameters of fly-rod action. Stiffness is largely a function of moment of inertia and the modulus of elasticity implicit in a rod material. Weight is defined in terms of density and volume. Bending properties are derived from diameter, the modulus of elasticity, and the maximum acceptable stress of the material in question. It is interesting to observe that rod length, moment of inertia, volume of structure, diameter and calibrations are variables of design and fabrication, while the modulus of elasticity, strength and density of a rod's structure are properties implicit in the material itself.

Focusing on these properties of density, strength, and elasticity, Don Phillips has worked out a simple system for measuring stiffness profile in fly-rod design. Theoretical analysis is clearly beyond most fishermen, particularly considering the variable properties in any two culms of bamboo. It is much easier to calibrate a rod's stiffness profile directly, using a series of rudimentary deflection tests made at regular intervals along its length. The rod is firmly clamped on a test frame, and the test gauge is secured at the first calibration point. The test weight is suspended from each testing point, and deflection is measured on the gauge. Average stiffness between the bench clamp and the test point can be calculated with this formula for stiffness:

$$\text{Rod stiffness} = \frac{\text{Test weight} \times \text{section length}^3}{3 \times \text{observed deflection}}$$

The equation is derived from the classic structural equation describing static deflection in a fixed-end cantilever with a concentrated load. The deflection tests are then repeated at twelve-inch intervals along the full length of the rod, and the average stiffness of each foot-long section is plotted in units of pound-inches squared on a logarithmic scale so the stiffness behavior of any rod is graphically delineated. The stiffness profiles of several rods can be plotted on the same graph, making comparisons remarkably easy.

Many craftsmen have explored a remarkable number of ways to multiply the stiffness profile of their rods beyond their usual casting properties. Double-built and triple-built sections were tried to create a rod composed entirely of bamboo power fibers, completely eliminating the pithy layers, and increasing both density and strength. Cross is best known for his double-built rods, which planed away the pith of two splines, glued them together with their power fibers toward the outside, and milled the resulting laminated strip into a final taper. Eugene Edwards patented another method of double-built construction in 1885. It laminated two splines back to back, concentrating the dense power fibers at the surface and the core. It did not prove popular with either anglers or rodmakers. Fred Divine patented his spiral construction in 1892, and although it unmistakably stiffened a rod by concentrating more power fibers in a slightly reduced length, it involved too much extra work. British manufacturers experimented extensively with wrapping or centering rods with steel. Their wrapped designs included both cross-wrapping and rods covered with a continuous spiral, like the bamboo and lancewood rods completely wrapped in varnished silk. Foster rods were perhaps the best known of the steel-ribbed types, and although the Foster patent clearly improved the loading capacity of a rod, breaking strength has little relationship to casting performance. Hardy was briefly fascinated with steel-core construction, and milled the bamboo strips to house a steel center; but even though such sections were quite strong, the added weight also greatly multiplied their inertial forces and deadened their actions.

Two other surprising innovations were introduced in 1933, and both were based on the same principles. Making a tubular split-cane rod could theoretically eliminate the pithy fibers and their unnecessary weight, retain all of the power fibers in the outer surfaces, and increase the effective moment of inertia by permitting larger rod diameter at the same weight. Various methods of hollow construction were tried, but planing away the core layers of pithy fibers also reduced the effective gluing surfaces between the bamboo splines, and such rods were fragile.

It was the incomparable Lew Stoner who first solved the problem successfully, with the patent he developed for his superb Winston rod. Stoner developed a technique which milled a small U-shaped groove from the apex of each spline removing considerable pith and reducing weight while leaving relatively large glue faces between adjacent strips. These fluted hollow-built rods were an immense success, setting a new distance record of 147 feet in the hands of Marvin Hedge in 1934. Two years later, G. L. McLeod extended that record two feet, and Dick Miller used his Winston to reach an amazing 183 feet during tournament competition in 1938. Winston rods and their fluted construction have dominated tournament casting ever since their baptism in competition at Saint Louis forty years ago, particularly in the skilled hands of men like Steven Rajeff, Myron Gregory, and the late Jon Tarentino of San Francisco.

Edwin Powell instantly recognized the unique potential of the Stoner patents, and patented his own method of building a semihollow bamboo rod later that same year. The Powell system did not attempt a continuously hollow core, but cut away the pith in a series of semicircular arcs. Between these semicircular cuts, the splines remained intact. The rods were relatively fragile, and their hollow sections were always reinforced with wrappings of silk, but a fine Powell rod is an exquisite fishing tool.

These hollow-built rods were a revelation, explains Doug Merrick of Winston, *in both distance and accuracy competition.*

Edward Hewitt played a major role in the evolution of American rods after 1900, often working closely with Hiram and Reuben Leonard. Early fast-action tapers for dry-fly work were the legacy of writers like Halford and Marston, and in the beginning Hewitt unquestioningly echoed their opinions on rod action. His legacy is still found in the fast action rods of craftsmen like Dunton, Dickerson, and Gillum.

Hewitt advocated the rapier flick-flick rhythms of a steep-taper design for false casting the moisture from a dry fly, although he apparently abandoned his fast-action theories in the last years of his life. The old master had reached his eighties when *A Trout and Salmon Fisherman for Seventy-five Years* was published in 1948, and it tells us that he no longer preferred the stiff butt tapers and soft tip actions he recommended half a century earlier.

Hewitt and many other experts of his generation preferred three-piece rods because the shorter sections were more easily transported, although most knowledgeable casters agreed that the single ferrule in a two-piece design weighed less and placed only one dead point in the flow of its bending action. Hewitt argued that a single ferrule at the midpoint also occurred at a critical nodal point in its flexing under stress. Since his books have become less influential in the years past midcentury, modern rodmakers and fishermen have turned increasingly to two-piece construction. The trend represents both a desire to reduce weight and a search for optimal power flow.

Most fishermen believe that two-piece designs are superior. It is certainly true that a single ferrule reduces the weight of a delicate rod, and it means slightly more power in ratio to that weight. Such concepts are clearly more significant in rods under eight feet, and for most rods they are more theoretical than practical considerations. Contemporary rodmakers are almost universally committed to two-piece rods under nine feet, except perhaps for the young tradition-conscious artisans working at Leonard. However, the practical superiority of two-piece rods over the older three-piece designs is probably more critical in the minds of modern anglers than it is demonstrable in actual fly-rod dynamics or performance.

Hewitt and George La Branche pioneered a number of modern concepts in rod fitting too. Their sense of craftsmanship and elegance is obvious in the beautifully-machined reel fittings on the rods built by Reuben Leonard and Edward Payne in later years. Larger snake guides with a much closer spacing were another Hewitt suggestion, along with an oversized stripping guide, placed well out from the grip to facilitate shooting the line. Such placement of the butt guide also helps with the line work in the double-haul. Closely spaced guides distribute both casting and fish-playing stress more evenly along a delicate rod. Their spacing must achieve an equilibrium between the effects of cumulative guide friction on a cast and its line slap against the rod.

Early in this chapter, the influence of Hiram Leonard on American rodmaking was discussed at length, tracing the subsequent careers of his early Bangor disciples. Most of those early apprentices left the Leonard shop before 1900, except for the Hawes brothers, who were related to Leonard and remained until his death in 1907. However, the loss of exceptional craftsmen like Fred Thomas, Eustis Edwards, and Edward Payne did not end the production of fine rods at Leonard. Reuben Leonard ably continued his father's tradition of excellence after 1907. His principal assistant in the period just before the First World War was George Reynolds, and when Reuben Leonard finally died, Reynolds took the helm. His son Harold Reynolds ultimately followed in his footsteps at the Leonard shop in Central Valley, producing superb rods from before the Second World War until his retirement in 1965. Reynolds himself retired after a disastrous fire swept the Leonard plant, and it seemed the Bangor tradition had died. Arthur Mills greeted me in the store his family had operated since 1826, and his eyes glistened with tears.

It's terrible! Mills shook his head sadly. *The factory at Central Valley burned down last week—the Hawes milling machine was almost destroyed too, and Leonard may be finished completely!*

His predictions were happily premature, for knowledge and craftsmanship had always been passed on in the Leonard shop like the secrets of a medieval guild, and another generation of artisans was waiting in the wings. Hap Mills had cast his lot with rodmaking in 1957, choosing the Leonard shop instead of the family store, the famous William Mills & Son in lower Manhattan. Mills was determined that Leonard should not die after a century of rodmaking, and soon embarked on a process of resurrection. The Leonard shop was rebuilt, including the vintage bevel originally designed by Loman Hawes, and Tom Bailey was persuaded to return to making his elegant German-silver fittings. Mills was soon joined by Ted Simroe, a former professor of literature at West Point, and a superb bamboo craftsman in his own right. Several other fine young craftsmen have joined them, new bevels and other equipment have been added, and Mills and Simroe are plunging into the reams of back orders that have always plagued Leonard—building exquisite fly rods in the tradition that started in a little workshop at Bangor more than a century ago.

Hiram Leonard had already established the basic character of the modern Leonard rod by 1894. The William Mills & Son catalogue issued in

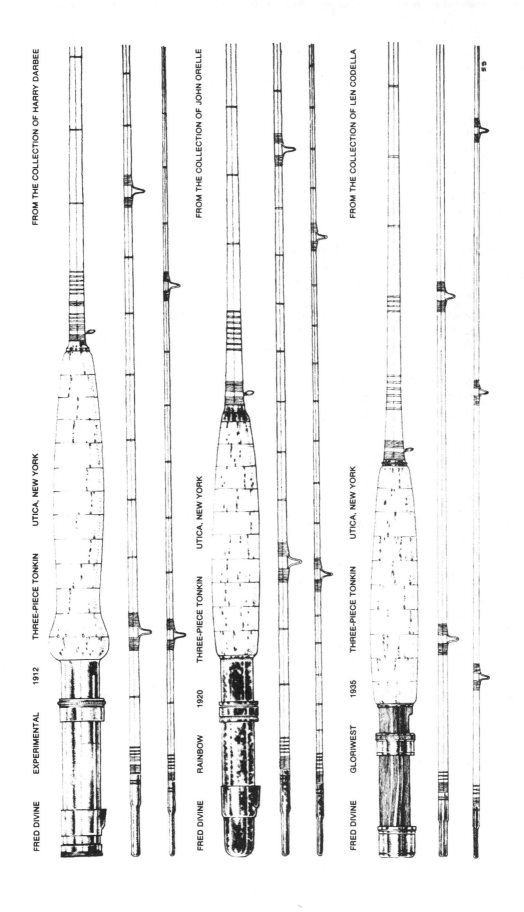

FROM THE COLLECTION OF HARRY DARBEE

FROM THE COLLECTION OF JOHN ORELLE

FROM THE COLLECTION OF LEN CODELLA

FRED DIVINE   EXPERIMENTAL   1912   THREE-PIECE TONKIN   UTICA, NEW YORK

FRED DIVINE   RAINBOW   1920   THREE-PIECE TONKIN   UTICA, NEW YORK

FRED DIVINE   GLORIWEST   1935   THREE-PIECE TONKIN   UTICA, NEW YORK

that year included skeletal reel seats with hardwood fillers, butt caps, and sliding bands. There were luggage rods made with full Wells-type detachable handles, trout rods with slender cigar grips and reel seats of German-silver tubing, and the Catskill Fairy had already made its debut in a three-piece design weighing only two ounces.

It was under Reuben Leonard that the modern cigar grip typical of the modern Leonards first appeared, with full metal reel seats of German silver, sliding bands, and a reel hood soldered to its barrel. These rods were embellished with intermediate wraps and intricate silk windings above the grip check. Like the earlier Leonards, they were provided with tip cases of Calcutta with machined butt fittings and screw caps of brass. Most rods of this period were three-piece designs, ranging from eight to nine and a half feet, although I recently examined a beautiful, two-ounce Catskill Fairy of seven and a half feet that was built in 1914. Except for its intricate silk windings and heavier reel-seat fittings with their richly ornamental machining, the rod looks surprisingly like a modern Leonard.

The Leonard tournament rods built in this same period featured slightly longer cigar grips and full metal reel seats with soldered caps and sliding bands. The examples I have seen were usually nine feet and weighed between five and one-quarter and six ounces, although I recently examined a special tournament Leonard of nine and a half feet that weighed six ounces. These special tournament rods introduced the bright scarlet silk and black trim found on the contemporary Leonards, although their intermediate wraps reveal their true vintage.

The classic screw-locking seat found on the modern Leonards apparently evolved after Reuben Leonard died, and its design is attributed to George Reynolds. It has embellished a generation of rods like the three-piece 50DF, which weighed four ounces and measured eight feet, or the famous Hunt pattern that was also an eight-footer. It had a slightly faster action at four and five-eighths ounces, and had oxidized ferrules and reel fittings. It was designed by the late Richard Hunt, author of the classic *Salmon in Low Water* and a familiar figure on the Brodheads before the Second World War. The Hewitt pattern built by Leonard was also an eight-footer, with a cane taper that weighed four and a half ounces. Hewitt originally liked rods with fairly stiff butts and fast tips when he first made the transition to dry-fly fishing, which his book *A Trout and Salmon Fisherman for Seventy-Five Years* tells us also took place on the Brodheads. His Hewitt-pattern rods flex most in the butt and the lower third of the middle section, with fairly level tapers halfway through the tip. Such calibrations make the middle and tip less flexible and a little tip-heavy in feeling, adding a steep taper to a relatively delicate hooking tip that permitted Hewitt to use his patented nitrate-stained tippets of 5X gut.

Before the Leonard fire in 1964, both the Hewitt- and Hunt-pattern rods were still made, and the Leonard 50DF was unquestionably the most popular model in the entire line. Some of the 50DF rods made after the Second World War were fitted with graceful reverse cigar grips that

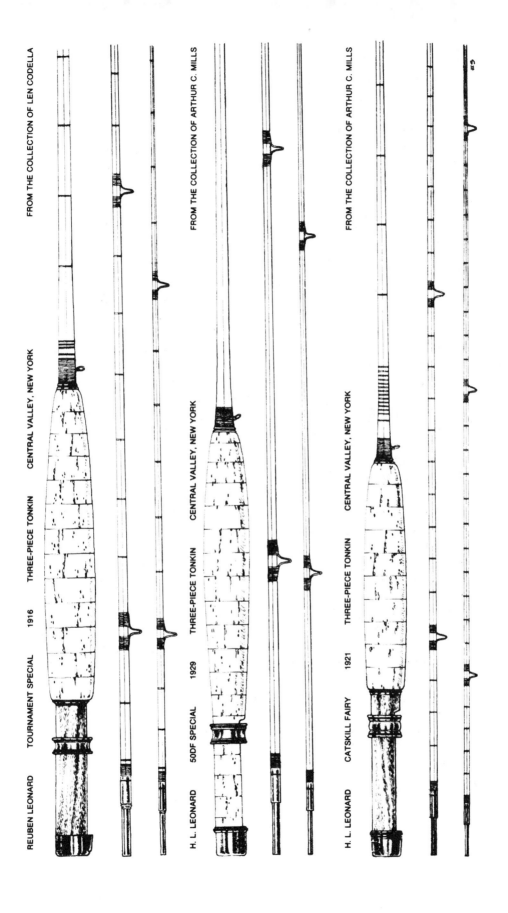

REUBEN LEONARD   TOURNAMENT SPECIAL   1916   THREE-PIECE TONKIN   CENTRAL VALLEY, NEW YORK   FROM THE COLLECTION OF LEN CODELLA

H. L. LEONARD   50DF SPECIAL   1929   THREE-PIECE TONKIN   CENTRAL VALLEY, NEW YORK   FROM THE COLLECTION OF ARTHUR C. MILLS

H. L. LEONARD   CATSKILL FAIRY   1921   THREE-PIECE TONKIN   CENTRAL VALLEY, NEW YORK   FROM THE COLLECTION OF ARTHUR C. MILLS

tapered directly to the hooded butt cap, with a sliding ring on the continuous cork handle. It was the favorite dry-fly rod of Arthur Mills after its introduction in 1915, although two-piece rods of lighter construction were gradually becoming popular at midcentury, and Leonard Catskill models like the elegant ACM 38 dominated sales by the time the original Leonard shop perished in the fire. Arthur Mills was responsible for the ACM 38, just as his father Thomas Bate Mills had suggested that Hiram Leonard should design the original Catskill Fairy in 1890. The Leonard ACM 38 was a seven-footer weighing two and one-quarter ounces, and was the jewel in a series of fine two-piece designs.

The Baby Catskill line ranged from the 37L at six feet and a single ounce to the 38H, which measured seven feet and weighed two and three-quarters ounces. It also included the Arthur Mills ACM 37, which took a three-weight line and weighed one and a half ounces. These rods were usually fitted with the standard cigar grip and skeletal butternut reel seat, although after 1960, many were made with the reversed cigar handles shaped entirely of cork and fitted with extralight reel bands. Recently I fished an exquisite 38L of this type which weighed only one and three-quarters ounces. It took a three-weight silk and had oxidized fittings. One of my favorite rods is an experimental version of the lovely ACM 38, measuring seven feet and weighing only two and one-quarter ounces. It has calibrations one ferrule size larger than comparable Catskill Fairy tapers, but eliminates the swelled butt and holds a surprisingly flat taper into the grip. The tip guide is a delicate four sixty-fourths of an inch and takes a DT4F—it was originally intended to fish terrestrials on cobweb-fine tippets of .003 and .004, and it has performed that function perfectly on many streams.

Before the fire, Leonard also made a series of three-piece rods with a delicate three-piece action suited to traditional wet-fly work. These designs ranged from the 35 model at seven feet and two and three-quarters ounces to the Leonard 46, which weighed five and a half ounces and reached a full nine and a half feet. The Leonard 36 was a seven-and-a-half-footer that weighed three and one-eighth ounces, and the 40 design was a fine eight-foot rod at only three and a half ounces. Both were extremely popular rods in their day, although modern fishermen now find them a little too soft. Yet these rods had some important partisans in the past half century.

It's hard to believe, Arthur Mills once told me with a note of quiet pride, *but George La Branche once had forty Leonards in the shop for refitting and refinishing at the same time!*

Leonard was also making two-piece rods larger than the Catskill series after midcentury. These rods were available in eight sizes, from the 65 model at seven and a half feet and three and a half ounces to the powerful Leonard 67H at six ounces and nine feet. These rods were usually fitted with the standard screw-locking seat, and they are superb fishing tools. Charles De Feo always liked the Leonard 51W rods, which weighed only six ounces at a full nine and a half feet, even with the oversized grips originally found on the special tournament rods built before the First World War. But the apogee of the Leonard tradition was perhaps found in the one-piece bamboo rods they built over the years. Other builders have made six-foot rods without ferrules, but not like the Leonards, weighing less than an ounce—let alone one-piece rods of seven, eight, and eight and a half feet.

It's unthinkable that we once had culms long enough to make rods like that, Hap Mills shakes his head unhappily, *and we lost most of them in the fire.*

Since the fire and the subsequent resurrection, Leonard has completely revised many of its rod designs and tapers, although attention to quality and craftsmanship remain unchanged. Four groups of fly rods are included. The Letort series is named for Letort Spring Run in Pennsylvania, the temple of light-tackle fishing, while the Ausable series is named for that famous Adirondack stream. Heavier trout rods ideally suited to big water are found in the Miramichi tapers, and the Leonard Duracane series is intended to provide a full range of weights and tapers with first-quality Leonard fittings at a moderate price.

The ancestry of the Letort series is unmistakable. Their grips and butternut reel seats have obvious roots in the rods that Reuben Leonard started building before the First World War. The butt caps and sliding bands are a little simpler in their machining, but the grip checks are virtually unchanged. The silk wrappings are rich scarlet tipped with black. The Letort rods are all two-piece designs. The remarkable Letort 36L is six feet long and weighs only one ounce, taking a level L2F line. The 40L taper is the heaviest at eight feet and three and three-quarters ounces, taking a four-weight line perfectly. Two years ago, Leonard built a special three-piece rod of eight feet that weighed three and three-quarters ounces and was designed to fish a four-weight line because of its delicate tip calibrations. It lies between the delicacy of the eight-foot 40L in the Letort series and the 50 series rods designed for six-weight lines.

The first time I saw the rod it was merely culms of dense-walled Tonkin bamboo, and on my second trip to the Leonard shop it had become four split-cane sections newly mounted with ferrules and tip guides. Hap Mills and Ted Simroe fitted it together, and Tom Bailey came over from his lathe where a delicate German-silver ferrule was being finished. Simroe happily waggled the unfinished sticks and handed it to me.

It's really sweet, Simroe grinned. *It's so lovely I wish I could own it myself.* Hap Mills nodded in agreement.

It's beautiful, I sighed happily.

It was ultimately finished with a butternut reel seat and a silver butt cap and sliding ring. Although it was a new Leonard, its guides and ferrules and keeper were wound in traditional lime green silk with yellow trim. Its action was poetic, fishing perfectly in close and handling distances of eighty to ninety feet with ease; and its baptism came on a late summer evening near Sun Valley in Idaho.

André Puyans and David Inks had taken me to try the difficult rainbows of Silver Creek, and I had planned to use a smaller rod designed for fishing a 6X tippet, because there was no wind and the current was mirror-smooth.

You going to try the new Leonard? Puyans asked.

Why not? I laughed.

Since the big rainbows were selective and shy, it seemed like too much rod—until I tried it. We had to fish .005 tippets and some of the fish were lying sixty to eighty feet away. There were also tall reeds along one reach of water, and I found its full eight feet valuable in keeping the backcasts high. The trout were porpoising steadily to a parade of tiny *Callibaetis* flies, and we took fish after fish that evening. The special 50L performed perfectly, taking a fine three-pound rainbow sixty feet out on a size 20 nymph imitation. There was a smaller fish that broke off when it took as I started to lift for another cast, but otherwise it fished the fine nylon tippet without problems.

The Ausable series is also typical of fine Leonard rods since the First World War. The sizes under seven feet are normally fitted with skeletal sliding-band seats, while the models between seven and a half and nine feet are made with Leonard screw-locking hardware. It is possible to have the seven-and-a-half- and eight-foot rods made with skeletal seats on special order, although the Leonard craftsmen believe the larger reels balancing their eight-and-a-half- and nine-foot tapers require the security of a locking seat.

Two-piece rods in the Ausable series range from the Leonard 36 model at six feet and less than two ounces, to the Ausable 41H weighing five and a quarter ounces and measuring eight and a half feet. The six-footer takes a DT3F and the eight-and-a-half-foot taper takes an eight-weight line. There are two models for different line weights in each length, offering a total of twelve rod choices in the two-piece Ausable weights. Seven other three-piece rods complete the Ausable series. The 48H model is a seven-foot taper taking a four-weight line and weighing three and one-quarter ounces, and is the smallest three-piece rod in the present Leonard weight line. The larger seven-and-a-half- and eight-foot designs take five- and six-weight lines. There are also three rods taking seven- to nine-weight forward tapers perfectly, the largest a nine-foot rod weighing five and seven-eighths ounces. My favorite rods in the Ausable series are probably the model 39, which is a seven-and-a-half-footer for a five-weight line, and the 40 and 50 designs, which are eight-foot rods for six-weight tapers in both two- and three-piece constructions. These are extremely versatile rods for all-around trout fishing.

The Miramichi series was developed by Ted Simroe. Although it is intended for salmon fishing, its rods are superbly adapted to big western rivers like the Snake and Yellowstone and Big Hole. Simroe designed the reversed half-Wells grips and reel-seat hardware, adding a two-inch fixed-cork extension. The eight-foot rod for a weight-forward seven weighs four and three-quarters ounces, and the eight-and-a-half-foot 61 model weighs five and a half ounces with a taper intended for eight-weight lines. Both the Miramichi 60 and 61 are two-piece rods. The 71 model is a three-piece design of eight and a half feet, weighing five and five-eighths ounces and taking a weight-forward eight. These are excellent big-water outfits.

The Duracane series of rods represents a departure for Leonard, since they replace the moderately priced Mills rods once sold through William Mills & Sons with a line of fine impregnated fly rods. These Duracanes are heat-treated bamboo with a rich brown tone produced for Leonard in Europe, fitted with the excellent screw-locking hardware typical of the more expensive Leonards, and finished with emerald silk windings. The lightest rod in the Duracane group is the seven-foot 700 model, which weighs two and seven-eighths ounces and takes a four-weight line. The seven-and-a-half-foot rod for a four-weight and the eight-foot model designed for five-weight are both particularly fine rods. The eight-foot Duracane 800 at four and one-eighth ounces takes an eight-weight taper and is an excellent all-around rod. There are also Duracane models comparable to the more expensive Miramichi rods, with their reverse screw-lock seats and extension butts, taking seven- to nine-weight forward tapers.

Appalachian pack rods are available in the Duracane grade, made in four pieces for easy backpacking and with full-cork reel seats and grips of the reverse cigar style. The Appalachian 700P is a seven-footer for a four-weight line, and the 800P is a versatile eight-foot rod that takes a six-weight taper. Like the other Duracane rods, the Appalachian trail rods are normally furnished with a single tip.

The Leonard tradition reaches both sides of the Atlantic, since the famous Skues used them extensively during most of his fishing career. Skues acquired his first Leonard through an American friend Walter Durfee Coggeshall in 1903. It was a ten-footer weighing six ounces, and it whetted his appetite for a smaller version.

Edward Hewitt and young Edward Bate Mills journeyed to the Crystal Palace at London in 1904, participating in the international casting tournament. Hewitt demonstrated a classic nine-foot Leonard weighing five and a half ounces to Skues during the tournament. Mills was part of William Mills & Sons, the principal agents for the Leonard rods, and showed Skues his catalogues. The following winter Skues completed a particularly successful case for his clients, and in gratitude for his legal expertise, Skues was offered the finest rod that British sterling could purchase. His clients and fishing colleagues were shocked when Skues immediately chose a fine nine-foot Leonard.

Skues observed that his new Leonard possessed a smooth, fluid action that was a marked contrast to the relatively stiff dry-fly tapers made fashionable by men like Halford and Marryat. Such rods were conceived to switch-cast the moisture from a floating fly before it is cast again. Skues observed that Hardy rods like the Halford and Houghton Club and Marston patterns seemed like weaver's beams once he had fished his first nine-foot Leonard. Its smooth rhythms permitted him to false cast without drying his delicate nymphs. Skues tells us in his book *Nymph Fishing for Chalk*

Stream Trout that its poetry and precise character were a major factor in the Itchen experiments that originated nymph fishing, and the old master fished his Leonard happily for half a century.

It caused a lot of talk, Dermot Wilson explained at his fishing hut on the Itchen, where Skues once walked the banks, *but Skues was convinced that Leonard made the best rods.*

Must have made your rodmakers unhappy, I said.

It did! he agreed. *It did!*

This past spring I have been fishing with Dermot Wilson on both the Itchen and its sister Hampshire river, the legendary Test at Stockbridge. When the young artisans at Leonard heard that I would be fishing the Itchen at Abbots Worthy, where Skues himself had often fished his nymphs, they insisted that we collaborate on a modern version of Skues' favorite Leonard rods.

What should it do? they asked.

Well, I began thoughtfully, *the fish are shy enough to make a 6X or 7X tippet necessary and the hatches are tiny.*

How tiny is tiny? Hap Mills interjected.

Twenty or twenty-two, I said, *because the fish will be on the little Iron Blues and Pale Waterys and Olives—and the rod has to be long enough to keep the backcast out of the bankgrass and weeds.*

And how long do you cast? Simroe asked.

Twenty to thirty feet on most beats, I replied, *but at Testcombe House on the Chilbolton beats, there's a reach of water where the big fish dimple steadily at least eighty to ninety feet away—lying right against the reeds.*

It's a tough prescription, Simroe sighed.

Their solution is a unique fly rod, even considering the rod quality that distinguishes the Leonard shop. The rod is a full eight-and-a-half-footer, long enough to hold a backcast above the fences and bullock herds and weeds that plague the backcasts of the chalkstream angler. Its tapers are slender enough, particularly at the delicate four sixty-fourths tip, to fish leaders testing under a pound. Yet it also has the power to punch out ninety-foot casts with accuracy and hook a good fish on 7X nylon without breaking off. It is finished with the Reynolds screw-locking seat and butternut filler traditional at Leonard for more than fifty years.

I know it's light enough for a four-weight, Simroe argues, *but an eight-and-a-half-foot Leonard looks better with a locking seat.*

Three weeks later, where the manicured lawns sweep down to the Chilbolton water from the richly timbered Elizabethan gables of the Testcombe, the rod had its baptism on the storied Test. Its trout were working steadily against the reeds, sipping nymphs in the smooth pondlike currents. Several times that day, casts were necessary that left the backing knot hanging just below the butt guide or left just a few turns of line on the reel. Many fish refused my tiny nymphs until I added a 7X tippet, yet the rod did not break off a beautiful three-pound brown that took more than eighty feet out. The Itchen fish at Chilland and Abbots Worthy are smaller,

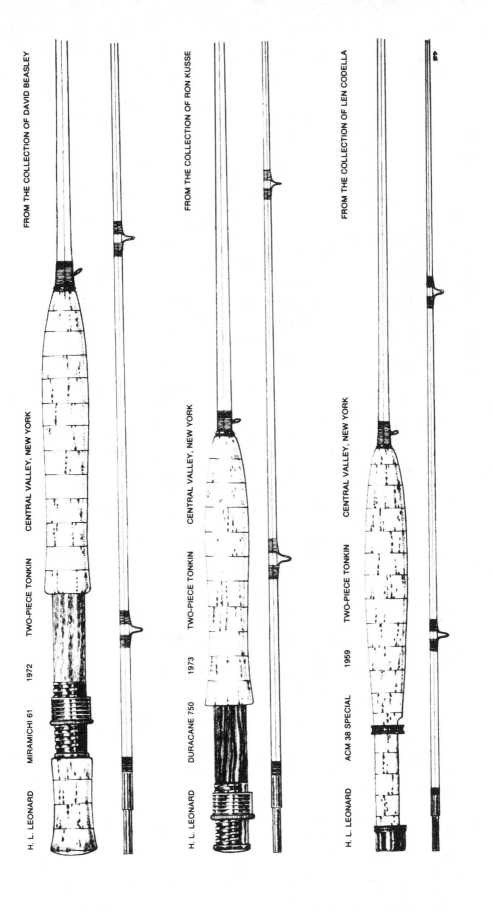

FROM THE COLLECTION OF DAVID BEASLEY

H. L. LEONARD   MIRAMICHI 61   1972   TWO-PIECE TONKIN   CENTRAL VALLEY, NEW YORK

FROM THE COLLECTION OF RON KUSSE

H. L. LEONARD   DURACANE 750   1973   TWO-PIECE TONKIN   CENTRAL VALLEY, NEW YORK

FROM THE COLLECTION OF LEN CODELLA

H. L. LEONARD   ACM 38 SPECIAL   1959   TWO-PIECE TONKIN   CENTRAL VALLEY, NEW YORK

since there is no supplemental stocking on that mileage, but I took several sixteen-inch fish on both beats, fishing at similar ranges with light tippets. The delicacy and distance were an unusual mixture of qualities, but the special Leonard admirably followed in the footsteps of the rods that Skues first used on the Itchen.

It's a remarkable rod, Dermot Wilson agreed. *It's delicacy and length are ideally suited to our chalkstreams–maybe Leonard should think about making more of them for your spring creeks, but trade on tradition and name it after Skues.*

Charles F. Orvis started his rodmaking company much earlier than Hiram Leonard, having founded Orvis more than twenty years before. The workshop where he produced the first Orvis rods is still standing in Manchester; less than a half mile from the Vermont headwaters of the Battenkill. However, Orvis had declined over the years until it was rescued from oblivion under the ownership of E. C. Corkran just before the Second World War, and it is the peripatetic Leigh Perkins who has pumped new life into Orvis in recent years—since the demise of William Mills & Sons, which had flourished in New York since 1822, Orvis has rapidly become the finest fishing tackle house in the United States.

Their early reputation was based as much on the quality of their flies as well as their first lancewood and lemonwood rods. The Orvis flies were the work of Mary Orvis Marbury, who had first learned the secrets of fly dressing at the insistence of her father. It must be remembered that skilled fly making was an occult art as late as the First World War—and how closely tiers like Theodore Gordon shielded their secrets.

When Mary Orvis Marbury learned to dress flies, it had all the trappings of a medieval guild. But she obviously had great talent, and Orvis flies were soon competing with the imported patterns sold at William Mills & Sons. Marbury published her encyclopedic *Favorite Flies and Their Histories* in 1892. Its exquisite lithography was a revelation, and its plates are still the classic reference for the garish flies fashionable on American rivers after the Civil War. Before her influence most American tackle dealers gave their patterns numbers rather than names, like the Mills No. 1, famous among the brook-trout fishermen on the Nissequogue at the Wyandanche Club. Orvis insisted on making standard patterns and giving them names rather than numbers, and we owe that institution to Mary Orvis Marbury.

The familiar Royal Coachman was one of those patterns, and it is perhaps the best known of the American flies. It was first dressed in 1878 in the New York shop of John Haily, who tied trout flies to order, and was the first American supplier of fly-tying materials. It was John Haily who journeyed to Vermont to teach Mary Orvis Marbury the secrets of his profession. Fred Mather received the following information from her father in a letter written in 1885:

> I had for many years made fishing rods and reels, and in filling orders for the same, had frequent requests for other tackle to be sent in the same package.

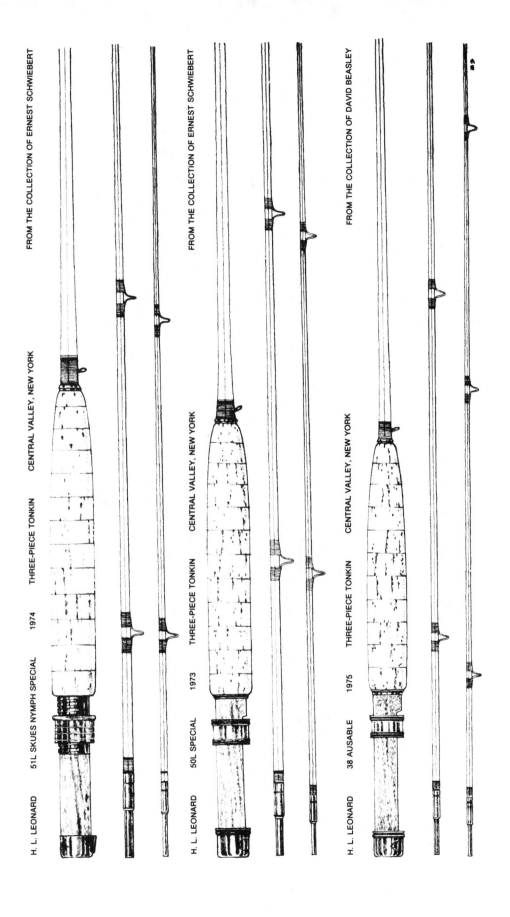

FROM THE COLLECTION OF ERNEST SCHWIEBERT

H. L. LEONARD   51L SKUES NYMPH SPECIAL   1974   THREE-PIECE TONKIN   CENTRAL VALLEY, NEW YORK

FROM THE COLLECTION OF ERNEST SCHWIEBERT

H. L. LEONARD   50L SPECIAL   1973   THREE-PIECE TONKIN   CENTRAL VALLEY, NEW YORK

FROM THE COLLECTION OF DAVID BEASLEY

H. L. LEONARD   38 AUSABLE   1975   THREE-PIECE TONKIN   CENTRAL VALLEY, NEW YORK

I then ordered, to supply these demands, small quantities of flies from dealers—first ordering a complete line of samples with the names attached.

These I received, but soon found it utterly impossible to duplicate my orders. I was continually disappointed by the substituting of other flies or sizes than the ones I had ordered, and in turn, I was forced to disappoint and apologize to my customers. I then thought that if there was any way out of this dilemma, caused by a confusion in names and a carelessness in copying exactly the pattern fly, I should seek it out.

In time, one of my family viewed with favor the idea of learning to tie flies. To this end, I employed one of the best fly tiers in the city to come to my house and stay until he had imparted his knowledge and skill, and when I felt that we were competent I advertised to fill orders exactly in accordance with a customer's wishes.

The Royal Coachman was first offered to purchasers by me. It did not, however, originate with me. The fly tier I mentioned long ago sent me a sample of the same, saying, "I have just been tying some flies to order for a gentleman. He says he likes the Coachman better than any other fly, but finds it very frail, and wants me to tie some with red silk in the middle, to make them stronger, and he also wants a little sprig of wood duck for a jib. I send you a fly to see, and I think it quite handsome."

The fly enclosed had a white wing, brown hackle, peacock body, bound in the center with red silk, and a tail of woodduck feather with the black and white bars.

One evening a number of us were gathered around a table looking at flies. My family, Mr. Horace Dunn of San Francisco, and Mr. L. C. Orvis of Hartford, were present discussing the propriety of every fly having a name, numbers giving them little or no individuality. I said, "But what is one to do? I do not propose to name flies. We have too many names already."

"Why not," said they, "if you make a new combination name it, else it will never become popular. No one can remember to distinguish flies by numbers. They get confused, but a name fixes a fly in your mind."

"Well," I answered, "that may be true. But look, here is this fly: it is similar to the Coachman, but it is not a Coachman. There is but one Coachman: that is the fly we all know, with a white wing, peacock body and brown hackle."

"I will tell you," exclaimed Mr. L. C. Orvis, "that is an extra-fine Coachman; all that scarlet makes it quite magnificent, indeed—call it—call it the Royal Coachman!"

It is obvious that the Orvis tradition is old and rich, although the modern Orvis rod bears little resemblance to its ancestors in the 1894 catalog. D. C. Corkran was a wealthy Philadelphian whose family had long occupied a summer home at Manchester, and after Corkran acquired Orvis in 1938, he persuaded Wesley Jordan to join him as his master rodmaker in the little shop on Union Street.

For thirty-five years, Orvis bamboo work has been synonymous with Wes Jordan, despite the fact that the company has produced as many as 15,000 rods a year. Jordan was born in 1894, and briefly served in the Royal Flying Corps late in the First World War, training at Hendon in the summer of 1918. Shortly after his discharge from the British Army, Jordan met an American rodmaker named William Forsythe, who introduced him to the mysteries of split bamboo. Jordan had found his metier, and he joined the Cross Rod Company late in 1919, having found his life's work except for a brief period just before the Second World War when he worked with automobiles.

His skills quickly blossomed working with Cross, building famous double-built designs like the Cross Tournament and the delicate seven-foot Sylph. Jordan forged a considerable reputation during his years with Cross, and when Cross died and his company was absorbed by South Bend in northern Indiana, Jordan went along to supervise the bamboo work. The fortunes of the tackle industry slipped badly during the Depression years, and Jordan was working with an automobile agency when Corkran rescued him to supervise rod building at Orvis in 1940.

Wes Jordan has been there ever since, inspecting every rod to come from the two-story clapboard workshop in Manchester. Rods that he built during his early years with Cross show strong influences of the Cross rods in action and reel fittings, but the grips are unmistakably the ancestors of his modern work at Orvis. Corkran introduced the pioneering techniques of impregnating the finished sections of split bamboo, eventually obtaining a patent on the process. It was Jordan who designed the screw-locking reel seat that has distinguished the Orvis rods since 1941 and added the exquisite reel-seat fillers of rich American walnut. His Orvis reel seats were originally designed with a single locking sleeve, like the Leonard and Payne type, but the present Orvis assembly no longer has a hooded butt cap made of a single piece—and the locking sleeve consists of two parts, which are less likely to oxidize and freeze tight on the threads.

The Battenkill series of rods has been justifiably famous since the Second World War and were once made in a large number of lengths, weights, and tapers. However, in recent years Orvis has limited its Battenkills to rods designed for six- to nine-weight lines. The more delicate end of the spectrum has been confined to a fresh palette of highly specialized actions and tapers. The modern Battenkills start with a crisp six-and-a-half-footer for a six-weight line that weighs only two and seven-eighths ounces. The heaviest stick in the series is an eight-and-a-half-foot, five-and-one-eighth-ounce rod designed for a nine-weight forward taper. Most of these rods have a fairly fast action, particularly suited to the fisherman who casts restlessly and likes to cover a lot of water. However, my own preference lies with the slower tapers that flex down into the butt, like the seven-and-a-half-foot, three-and-seven-eighths-ounce Battenkill, which many fishermen call the best overall trout model in the Orvis line. Some western anglers who fish slightly larger streams find the eight-foot, four-and-three-eighths-ounce Battenkill a better all-around rod for their purposes, and both have a smooth medium action.

My favorite Battenkills are slower still. The eight-foot version at four and one-eighth ounces is a fine rod for a six-weight line, and I fish it close with 6X tippets and double tapers, but it seems equally happy fishing the full length of a weight-forward line with a small streamer. It even took a number of salmon on the Nordurá and Grimsá in Iceland, including a fish of twenty-three pounds, and I fish it there often. The late Joseph Brooks liked the eight-and-a-half-foot Battenkill that weighs four and three-quarters ounces and takes a WF8S line perfectly, and he fished it from the Big Hole in Montana to the Boca Chimehuin in Patagonia. It is a rod I have also fished—its slow action working in lazy casting rhythms—from New Zealand to the Labrador.

Orvis still makes three Battenkill rods in three-piece construction for travel convenience. These designs include a seven-and-a-half-foot, four-and-one-quarter-ounce model for a seven-weight line, a popular eight-footer for the same line that weighs four and a half ounces, and a superb eight-and-a-half-foot rod weighing four and five-eighths ounces that is also milled to fish a WF7S or WF7F taper. The extra ferrule in these rods makes them slightly heavier than comparable two-piece designs, but the differences in action are virtually indistinguishable.

Orvis also makes a number of special rods in the Battenkill grade, and several of them fish beautifully under rather difficult conditions. The first of these rods is the Orvis Midge, measuring seven and a half feet and taking a five-weight line at only three and five-eighths ounces. It was designed in response to the difficult fishing on our eastern streams in low water, like the headwaters of the Battenkill in August, and it has become one of the most popular rods in the entire Orvis line. Its smooth semiparabolic action makes it a favorite with skilled anglers on our eastern spring creeks, although many experts who fish often with tippets of .003 and .004 nylon wish that Orvis would make its Midge with a more delicate tip.

The Orvis Flea soon followed the Midge pattern. It fishes with a four-weight line, and is a sensitive little six-and-a-half-foot rod of only two ounces. Its tip calibrations are also a bit too heavy for working 7X and 8X leaders, although its slow action makes 7X tippets possible in skilled hands. However, it is a rod I like in hot weather on small streams, particularly in brushy water where its six-and-a-half-foot length is perfect.

The Orvis Nymph is intended for fishing tiny nymphs and pupal imitations in the surface film, with an emphasis on delicacy instead of distance. It is an extremely slow eight-foot rod weighing three and three-quarters ounces and designed for a four-weight line. Unlike the four-ounce Battenkill at eight feet, it will fish nymphal and pupal patterns on .003 and .004 nylon points. Such refinements can be important for trout that are gorging on minute *Tricorythodes* nymphs on the Battenkill just after daylight or dimpling to the millions of midge pupae in the surface film of a western spring creek. Its tapers are clearly unsuited for windy days, and they lack the muscle to fish a sinking line with real control, but it is capable of exquisite work on smutting fish. It is best with a DT4F, and some anglers even fish it with a DT3F line. Nymphing with tiny imitations is its forte, and anglers having chalkstream conditions on their home waters should consider its unique properties: the eight-foot length permits ready manipulation of a nymph in quiet currents, while the four-weight lines drop softly enough for the most selective trout.

Leigh Perkins designed the Limestone Special after exposure to the difficult fishing on the Maigue near Limerick, which rises in the limestone hills above Killarney. His impressions were later confirmed on chalkstreams like the Itchen and the Test in England. These are smooth-flowing rivers that demand a subtle presentation with four- or five-weight tapers, and a six-weight has the guide angle of a stone when it comes to wild brown trout on the Itchen in bright weather. These rivers also mean relatively long casts, so the ideal rod must have some muscle too, and length is valuable for keeping the backcast out of the foliage.

It's not just for chalkstreams, Perkins explains enthusiastically about his Limestone Special. *We've got a lot of water like the Irish and English fishing, streams like the Pennsylvania limestoners and western spring creeks from California to Montana—and particularly the Henry's Fork of the Snake!*

The Limestone Special is eight and a half feet and weighs four and a half ounces, taking a six-weight long belly to fish delicately as well as long. Its backcast is crisp and high, and it will handle distance work with ease. Its character is smooth and slow, flexing progressively into the grip, and its length and delicacy are ideally suited to fishing the nymph.

We're pleased with the Limestone Special, Leigh Perkins adds, *and we're proud to have it featured in the Nether Wallop shop of Dermot Wilson—he's probably the best of the chalkstream fishermen, and lives in the middle of the chalkstream country only an hour below London.*

Like getting a good Broadway review, I laughed.

Exactly, he said.

The most delicate rod in the Orvis collection is another new design called the Orvis Seven-Three, its name coming from its specifications for a three-weight line and seven-foot length. Its tip calibrations take a four sixty-fourths tip top, much smaller than any other Orvis taper, and it is the only rod in the entire line that will fish .003 and .004 with security. It has been available only three seasons, but true fine-tippet addicts have already hailed the Seven-Three and its performance on difficult fish. The rod is balanced perfectly with a DT3F, and it weighs only two and one-quarter ounces. It has served me well on rivers where long casts were not needed, but 8X tippets were a regular prescription on smutting fish in ankle-deep flats. Its relatively short length is also valuable in tree-sheltered water like the Little Manistee and Little South Pere Marquette in Michigan, or eastern rivers like the Brodheads and Bushkill.

Orvis also makes a line of moderately priced split-cane rods made with impregnated bamboo. The sole difference between the Battenkill and Madison grades is esthetic, with subtle variations in graining or color of bamboo, since any structural seconds are destroyed. The Madison rods are sold with a single tip, although extra tips are available. The same first-quality fittings and walnut fillers are used in both the Battenkill and the Madison, and watermarked cane is often the only reason these rods have been finished in the Madison grade.

Three of the special Orvis tapers—the Flea, the Midge, and the delicate little Seven-Three—are also available in the less expensive grade. Two seven-and-a-half-foot rods for six-weight lines are also included, along with the fine eight-foot taper for a six-weight. The eight-and-a-half-foot Limestone Special taper is also furnished in the Madison price range, as well as the Brooks eight-and-a-half-footer taking an eight-weight line at four and three-quarter ounces. The eight-and-a-half-footer for nine-weight lines is also made in the Madison line.

It is probably fitting that the most expensive rods in the Orvis stable are named for Wes Jordan, the master craftsman who breathed new life into Orvis on the eve of the Second World War. Jordan liked his own rods with a bit more tip-muscle than most and a smoothly powerful action. His tapers are clearly in the American tradition, with oxidized German-silver ferrules and special jewel-finished reel fittings of fine aluminum alloy. The name of the owner is engraved in the butt cap. The cork grip is fitted with a thumb seat, a touch first introduced by the late Paul Young and placed into volume production by Jordan before he left South Bend. However, some Wes Jordan rods are also fitted with a depression shape for the heel of the palm, a feature original with Jordan. Some anglers dislike both designs, since casting fatigue can be partially relieved by changing the placement of the casting hand, and such a shift is impossible with a fully sculptured grip. The Wes Jordan rods are protected by an elegant saddle-leather case, with an aluminum tube lining the inside, plus a buckle top and carrying strap. Perhaps the most elegant touch found in the Wes Jordan lies in the hardwood reel-seat fillers that use exotic materials like rosewood, Circassian walnut, and darkly grained Macassar ebony.

The Wes Jordan series includes a seven-and-a-half-foot rod that takes a six-weight line and weighs three and seven-eighths ounces, and an eight-and-a-half-footer weighing five and one-eighth ounces for a nine-weight. The eight-foot rod has long been the most popular in the three-taper series, patterned after the original fly rod that Jordan designed for himself many years ago. It weighs four and three-eighths ounces and takes an eight-weight line, and its partisans argue that it is the most versatile fly rod ever built.

Orvis is perhaps the only rodmaker making split-cane rods in numbers

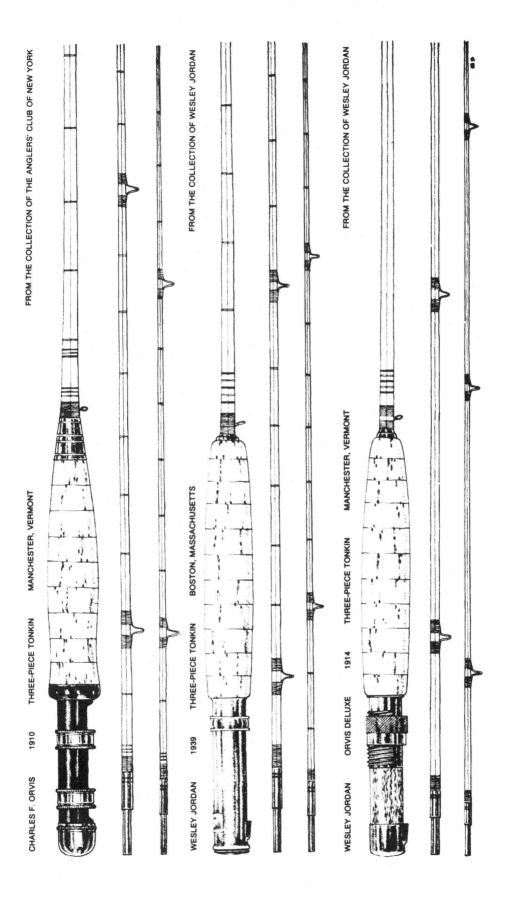

FROM THE COLLECTION OF THE ANGLERS' CLUB OF NEW YORK

CHARLES F. ORVIS   1910   THREE-PIECE TONKIN   MANCHESTER, VERMONT

FROM THE COLLECTION OF WESLEY JORDAN

WESLEY JORDAN   1939   THREE-PIECE TONKIN   BOSTON, MASSACHUSETTS

FROM THE COLLECTION OF WESLEY JORDAN

WESLEY JORDAN   ORVIS DELUXE   1914   THREE-PIECE TONKIN   MANCHESTER, VERMONT

that approach the demand, and much of its production capability comes
from the transfusions of fresh energy, ideas, and new equipment provided
by the indefatigable Leigh Perkins. His experience at the helm of Orvis
clearly belies the pessimism fashionable among many fishermen, particularly about the death of craftsmanship. Perkins writes with eloquence on
this argument:

> There are still young men in this day, as in any day, who take a
> deep abiding pride in fine workmanship. In fact, today, when
> mass production threatens to make pushbutton automatons out of
> workers, the best men often gravitate to those relatively few jobs
> where individual skills and a sense of pride and responsibility are
> still important.

Earlier in this chapter, we recounted the historic breakup that
occurred between Hiram Leonard and his original circle of disciples and
apprentices. Many of these men have historic roles in American fly-fishing
and became half-legendary craftsmen in their own right. Eustis Edwards,
Edward Payne, and the brothers Loman and Hiram Hawes were all superb
rodmakers, and Fred Thomas was unquestionably one of the best who ever
split a culm.

Fred Thomas returned to Bangor and started making rods under his
own name, first in partnership with Edwards, and then with his son Leon
helping prepare the sticks for bevelling. Although his Maine customers
were often heavy-handed, and fished huge streamers on leaders that could
hand-line a six-pound squaretail, Thomas also built a lot of poetic rods that
a blank check could not buy from their present owners.

His rods were made in two colors of bamboo, using both the flawless
straw-colored cane typical of his earlier experience with Leonard and
brown-tone rods the rich color of chocolate. The pale bamboo sticks were
fitted with matching reel-seat fillers of butternut, while the darker rods used
select black walnut. Most Thomas rods fitted with screw-locking seats used
a grip that echoed the Leonard tournament style, although some flared at
the reel-seat into a distinctive Thomas fishtail handle. Thomas also made
some grips and reel seats entirely of cork, their style offering homage to the
Leonard grips that characterized many of the early 50DF designs. Thomas
butt caps, which were more delicate than the Leonard type, used bright
aluminum on the pale-cane rods and oxidized finishes on the browntones.
Thomas used a Leonard-type grip check on his designs, but the grip check
at the silk windings was uniquely his. It was more generously proportioned
than the comparable Leonard grip check, and its engraved welt included
the keeper ring. The silk windings also distinctively bore the Thomas
fingerprint. The larger functional wraps that were brown with olive silk
trim were typical of his work. Above the grip, Thomas devised an intricate
signature of delicate brown windings, grouping the wraps in a series of
three, seven, and three, and finishing with a wider ornamental wrap of
brown silk. The ferrule wraps were brown tipped with olive, and there were

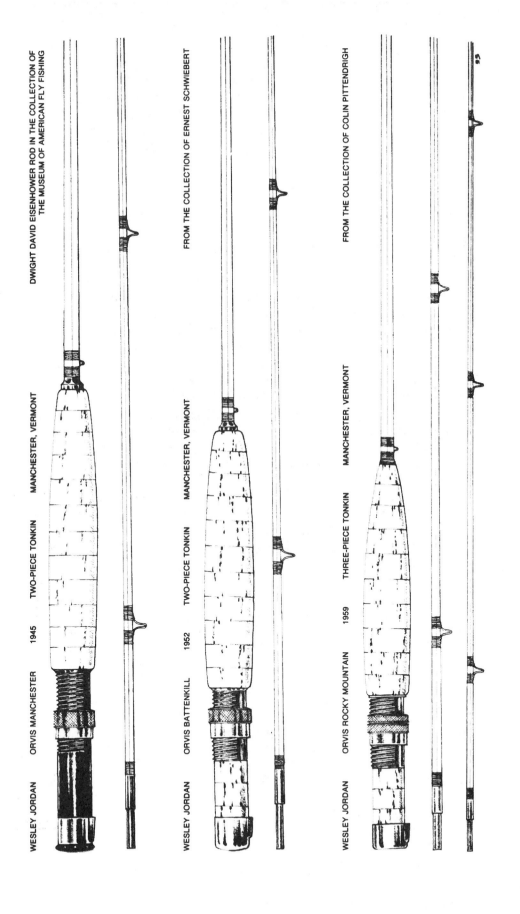

WESLEY JORDAN   ORVIS MANCHESTER   1945   TWO-PIECE TONKIN   MANCHESTER, VERMONT   DWIGHT DAVID EISENHOWER ROD IN THE COLLECTION OF THE MUSEUM OF AMERICAN FLY FISHING

WESLEY JORDAN   ORVIS BATTENKILL   1952   TWO-PIECE TONKIN   MANCHESTER, VERMONT   FROM THE COLLECTION OF ERNEST SCHWIEBERT

WESLEY JORDAN   ORVIS ROCKY MOUNTAIN   1959   THREE-PIECE TONKIN   MANCHESTER, VERMONT   FROM THE COLLECTION OF COLIN PITTENDRIGH

three fine ornamental windings too, spaced apart from the functional silk. Similar wrappings were used at the top guide, which had a unique little German-silver tongue under the silk. The early Thomas rods used agate tip and stripping guides, while his later products used a bronzed tungsten. Many of the first Thomas designs used a full metal seat, like the early Leonards and Montague rods, but his later work was dominated by skeletal locking and sliding-band designs. The Thomas rods were all supplied with an aluminum case, fitted with brass end caps and screw-locking tops like the cases still used at Leonard. However, Thomas also knurled his caps handsomely. The early reel-seat locks were cut with ornamental rings, while later rods built by Leon Thomas had locking rings that were plain except for the knurling. The Thomas ferrules had a handsome machined welt, and used a split ferrule typical of the Leonard patent issued in 1878. Although Thomas built rods that fully equalled the work of both Hiram and Reuben Leonard, his personal tapers still carried the unmistakable marks of his apprenticeship in Bangor, including the swelled-butt tapers above their cork handles.

The oldest Thomas that I have seen already used the English reverse-loop snake guides that marked his rods until the threshold of the Second World War. It had a full metal seat and was a three-piece eight-and-a-half-footer weighing five and one-quarter ounces, with the relatively strong semiparabolic action typical of Thomas' rod tapers. Similar eight-and-a-half-footers with locking reel seats and butternut fillers weighed about four and three-quarters ounces and are widely coveted among collectors today. Perhaps my favorite Thomas was an eight-foot, three-piece taper of only four and one-eighth ounces, with a skeletal cork reel seat and handle. It was an exquisite piece of split-cane artistry, but it would be difficult to choose between its character and a superb little Thomas browntone of seven feet that I once saw—it was a two-piece rod of only two and a half ounces and a surprising poetry.

Fred Thomas and his son Leon built rods under the Thomas mark for more than forty years, but after the elder Thomas died, the company foundered and passed into receivership. Its cane and cutting blocks and design tapers were subsequently divided between Walter Carpenter, who presently works in the Leonard shop, and Samuel Carlson—who also acquired the equipment of William Edwards, including the specifications and tools for his unique four-strip rods.

Eustis Edwards also made fine fly rods under his own name for a number of years, but it was his sons, William and Eugene, who fully flowered as rodmakers. Eustis Edwards was a cane workman of great skill, and performed the bamboo functions in his brief partnership with Fred Thomas and Edward Payne. Thomas had been the Leonard foreman, while Payne began as a ferrule maker and machinist. The early Edwards rods bear a strong family resemblance to the work of his colleague, the better-known Edward Payne, and the later rods designed and built by his son Eugene Edwards.

The first Eustis Edwards rods were relatively large three-piece tapers in six-strip construction, and I have seen several of nine feet weighing six to six and a half ounces. Edwards was actually more interested in photography than rodmaking, and he often made volume lots of bamboo rods for large companies or sporting goods stores, hoping to start another photographic studio. Such rods were often made for stores like Abbey & Imbrie, Abercrombie & Fitch, and Von Lengerke & Detmold. However, later in his career Edwards built some superbly modern fly rods that had considerable influence. Sparse Grey Hackle tells us in his *Great Fishing Tackle Catalogs of the Golden Age* that Edwards made a run of seven-and-a-half-foot trout rods for the Winchester Repeating Arms Company that were so exceptional that they created a sensation on the Catskill rivers—and the popularity of the seven-and-a-half-foot rod on American rivers has been largely attributed to Eustis Edwards.

His Edwards Special rods were dark, richly colored bamboo with purple wraps tipped in yellow, and most had a poetic medium action that worked down into the grip. Both screw-locking and skeletal seats were common on his later work, and the early rods used full-metal seats. The largest of these early designs was a ten-footer weighing seven and three-quarters ounces, and taking a full ten-weight line. There were also nine-and-a-half-foot tapers weighing five and three-quarters ounces and a particularly delicate eight-and-a-half-foot taper weighing four ounces and taking a DT6F. The collector Martin Keane owns an exceptional Edwards Special built about 1925, that measures eight feet and weighs a mere three and one-eighth ounces. It is a full ounce under a comparable Orvis Battenkill and takes a delicate four-weight floating line.

Its personality is a little exotic and slow, Keane waxes poetic about his Edwards. *But it's my pride and joy!*

It was William Edwards who broke the mold and boldly developed a unique line of four-strip rods. His unusual ferrules and grip checks and reel-seat fittings were singularly his trademark, and his actions were superb. There were a surprising number of these four-strip tapers. Like his father, William Edwards made a lot of fly rods between eight and nine and a half feet with surprisingly delicate tip calibrations. These rods encompassed a wide spectrum of actions, at least in terms of their relative delicacy.

One of the finest eight-foot rods I have ever fished was an Edwards of two-piece construction that weighed only three and one-eighth ounces and took a four-weight silk line perfectly. Edwards also made a three-piece rod of eight and a half feet and four and one-eighth ounces that required a five-weight. His nine- and nine-and-a-half-foot designs in three-piece construction, weighing five and one-quarter and five and three-quarters ounces, are also remarkably smooth rods for seven-weight lines. William Edwards also made a relatively powerful nine-and-a-half-foot three-piece rod, weighing a full seven ounces with the power to punch out a nine-weight forward taper. The late Leroy Whitney had a fine seven-and-a-half-foot Edwards Quadrate that weighed only three ounces and balanced a four-weight Kingfisher silk—one of the finest semiparabolic tapers I have ever been privileged to cast.

It is perhaps in these delicate quadrate tapers that William Edwards most excelled. His seven-foot rod weighing two and five-eighths ounces was a fine action for the four-weight line, and the six-and-a-half-foot Quadrate weighing two and one-eighth ounces was calibrated to handle a three-weight. The most delicate Quadrate was the little six-foot Model 40 that weighed only one and three-quarter ounces and took a DT3F silk. Its ability to handle .003 and .004 nylon make it one of the first true Midge-type rods—and the ability to work with leaders under 6X is the only real measure of such tapers, in spite of the popular definition which includes anything under two ounces.

History often takes curious pathways, surprising knowledgeable observers with its unpredictable patterns of evolution. Since Edward Payne was only the ferrule machinist in the original Leonard shop at Bangor, it is remarkable that it was his E. F. Payne Rod Company that ultimately equalled the bamboo work of his master, and there are vocal Payne disciples who believe that Payne rods became the ultimate in the rod builder's art.

Edward Payne joined forces with Frank Oram, who was a Leonard foreman, after his brief association with the United States Net and Twine Company in Brooklyn. Their new Payne company was started at Highland Mills, a few miles up the highway from Leonard. Their early work was fine enough that a sample Payne won the gold medal at the 1893 World Columbian Exposition in Chicago.

The rods designed and built by Edward Payne at the turn of the century were little different from the rods his company was making fifty years later. Some of the reel fittings were a little more ornate, and the proportions of his early cork grips were less slender and graceful, but there was surprisingly little change in the appearance of the Payne rod in the eighty-year life of the company. When Edward Payne died after the First World War, his interest in the company passed to his son, James Payne, who had worked in the shop since boyhood. The younger Payne had been involved in rodmaking since early childhood, since his father had sternly disciplined his son with an unfinished buff section of split bamboo. The Oram half interest passed to his wife, who had wrapped and finished the Payne rods from the beginning. Except for the Second World War, when James Payne worked for Curtiss-Wright Aircraft, his life was completely consumed with building rods. The design and workmanship of these rods were so remarkable that they command huge prices on the secondhand lists. When James Payne died in 1970, there was a run on the remaining inventory of Payne rods at Abercrombie & Fitch that drove their prices to six times the price of a Payne in 1929, and that had been less than the price of a moderately expensive fiberglass fly rod today.

The early rods built by Edward Payne featured reel seats of solid German silver with a soldered hood and sliding band, although many skeletal seats on black walnut or butternut were assembled before his death. The elder Payne featured both straw-colored cane and brown-finished bamboo. His stripping guides and tip tops were agate, and the balance were bronzed-steel snake guides. The choice of models was limited. The lightest Payne was an eight-footer of three-piece construction that weighed three and one-quarter ounces and took a four-weight line. There was a second

JAMES PAYNE

eight-foot taper of three and three-quarters ounces for five-weight silk and a relatively light eight-and-a-half-footer for a six-weight that weighed four and one-quarter ounces.

There were also several larger tapers. The nine-foot rod weighing only four and one-quarter ounces took a DT6F silk, and a second nine-foot model weighing four and three-quarters ounces was only slightly heavier. There were nine-and-a-half-foot rods weighing five and one-quarter and five and three-quarters ounces, plus a ten-foot model that took a nine-weight line and totaled only six and a half ounces. These rods were the Payne line, and smaller rods did not appear until the Great Depression.

James Payne finally dropped the rods of natural bamboo in favor of the dark finishes that ultimately became his hallmark. The fittings were the same, featuring reel seats of both German silver and oxidized skeletal seats with black walnut fillers. The butternut seats were dropped with the straw-colored cane. The younger Payne also added smaller rods.

The three-piece Paynes then included two seven-foot rods weighing two and seven-eighths ounces and three and one-eighth ounces, and a pair of seven-and-a-half-foot tapers of three and three and one-quarter ounces. The ten-footer had disappeared, but six two-piece rods had replaced them. There was a six-foot wand of only one and a half ounces, and a seven-foot model of two and one-quarter ounces. The seven-and-a-half-foot Payne weighed two and five-eighths ounces, while the eight-footer was three and seven-eighths ounces. The new eight-and-a-half-foot Payne was four and one-quarter ounces, while the nine-foot design went five and one-quarter ounces. The famous screw-locking seat had not yet appeared, even on the Payne salmon rods.

It was the famous little green catalogue that appeared just before the Second World War that introduced both the Payne screw-locking reel seat and a parabolic taper. These changes reflect the influence of famous anglers like George La Branche, Edward Ringwood Hewitt, and John Alden Knight. Payne had stopped building three-piece rods under seven and a half feet, but there were often fifteen rods between seven and a half and nine and a half feet, including five nine-foot models. The two-piece line had expanded. The six-foot taper now weighed one and five-eighths ounces, and the seven-foot design weighed two and three-quarters ounces. The seven-and-a-half-foot Payne weighed three ounces, with a three-and-a-quarter-ounce model available in the same length. Three eight-foot rods dominated the two-piece line, ranging from three and a half to four and one-eighth ounces. The nine-footer went five and a half ounces, and the famous eight-and-a-half-foot Payne that originally evolved from the Hendrickson salmon experiments weighed four and five-eighths ounces.

The Payne parabolics had also appeared. These radical tapers had been developed empirically by Charles Ritz in Europe, and it was John Alden Knight who worked with James Payne to produce American versions. The Payne two-piece parabolics were mounted with full cork reel seats to reduce weight and eliminate inertial damping of an action that flexed right into the handle. The specifications of these new tapers were a little strange. The smallest measured an inch over seven feet and weighed two and seven-eighths ounces, while the seven-and-a-half-footer weighed three and three-eighths ounces. There were two rods of seven feet nine inches that weighed three and three-quarters and four and one-eighth ounces. It was John Alden Knight himself who contributed these paragraphs to a later, more elaborate Payne catalogue:

> When Charles Ritz came to this country in 1936, we compared notes and rods. Then we went to the E. F. Payne Rod Company plant at Highland Mills, and had a talk with Jim Payne. He set up the first American rod in the true parabolic action. This rod, like Ritz's rods, demanded perfect timing but it was a surprising tool for angling. Soon, however, Mr. Payne modified the original patterns and produced a rod more acceptable for general use, and for which, I understand, there is an ever-increasing demand.
>
> Parabolic action means literally this: the working portion of the rod is the lower one-third, next to the grip. The middle one-third acts as a lever, to deliver the power created by the lower rod, while the top one-third imparts the power to the line. The upper third and lower third do most of the bending during the cast. The middle third of the rod bends very little, since it functions as a lever.
>
> True parabolic action is not satisfactory for the average angler. It demands too much in the way of timing and is not a pleasant rod to use. The parabolic rods that are being turned out today are, in effect, semiparabolic in that they are not top-heavy, and permit a certain laxity in timing. They are delightful rods to use in that they handle both short and long casts equally well, in addition to having a high ratio of power to weight.

A. E. Hendrickson was the principal benefactor of the Payne company during the Depression years, although his support was usually concealed in his role as Payne's best customer. Hendrickson was also an occasional financial life preserver, and actually owned four percent of the stock in the company. It was one of his special salmon tapers that led to the eight-and-a-half-foot trout rod—the rod that became the Payne trademark when Roy Steenrod tried casting with its middle and tip section.

Hendrickson also had a role in the ten-foot salmon rod designed for casting single-handed with dry flies. It also became a Payne trademark, and it too was an accident. Hendrickson had commissioned the rod for fishing tarpon at the Gatun Locks in the Panama Canal, but it proved immensely popular for light-tackle salmon work. After Hendrickson died, his small holdings of stock in the E. F. Payne Company were sold to Abercrombie & Fitch. Its management always hoped that holding Payne stock might get them the exclusive selling rights for the Payne rods, but James Payne had always refused. Some years after the Second World War, the Abercrombie

& Fitch holding was acquired by a wealthy manufacturer who subsequently bought the Oram half interest, giving him fifty-two percent of the stock. His dream was to control the production of the best fly rods, reels, and shotguns in the world, but James Payne stubbornly refused to sell—knowing that fifty-two percent of the stock meant nothing when the primary assets of the company were his knowledge and the finest hands that ever held a plane.

His intransigence defeated the dream, although later he sold his remaining stock to the late W. L. Collins, himself a superb fisherman and judge of rods. Collins established a new company with James Payne as its president and himself as vice-president and treasurer, but both Payne and Collins died before they could realize their dream of making the Payne rods a top-quality line with a wide national distribution. James Payne died in the late spring of 1970, having maintained and surpassed the austere standards of his father, himself a craftsman so fine that the legendary Theodore Gordon once bartered thirty-nine dozen of his dry flies to acquire one of the early Payne rods.

Sparse Grey Hackle provides a fitting epitaph for both Paynes in his commentary for *Great Fishing Tackle Catalogs of the Golden Age*, with these observations on their work:

> All the old Leonard workmen who set up their own shops were notable for their rigid adherence to the highest standards of workmanship in spite of small incomes and, often, outright poverty. But I think Jim surpassed them all in his fanatical adherence to his own incredibly high standards of craftsmanship, and his rigid determination to uphold the status of the Payne name as a tribute to his father. Jim was a king of craftsmen, a true friend, and a real gentleman.

The final Payne catalogue is a collector's item, particularly noteworthy if it contains Payne's autograph. It is bound with an uncut rag-paper cover with an exquisite bookplate engraving that adapts a scene from the famous Currier & Ives print of brook-trout fishing in America. It includes brief pieces by such notables as Edward Ringwood Hewitt, George La Branche, Mead Schaeffer, Frederick Barbour, Charles Phair, and Otto von Kienbusch. Their collection of essays alone makes the catalogue a priceless fragment of angling memorabilia.

Its fly-rod lists are the high-water mark in the evolution of the Payne rods, offering a choice of four reel-seat designs. The full-locking hardware added only a half ounce to the listed weight, in spite of its heavy jewel-finished alloys. Both the conventional seat with a hooded butt cap and ornamental end piece and the reverse-locking system with the hooded cap concealed in the grip were still available. The full metal seats of German silver had been dropped, keeping only the skeletal butt cap and band fittings with a select black walnut or cork filler. The three-piece Paynes listed in that final catalogue were the following models:

197	7½ feet	Dry-Fly	3½ to 3⅝ ounces
198	7½ feet	Fast Dry-Fly	3¾ to 3⅞ ounces
200	8 feet	Light Dry-Fly	3⅝ to 3¾ ounces
201	8 feet	Dry-Fly	3⅞ to 4 ounces
202	8 feet	Fast Dry-Fly	4⅛ to 4¼ ounces
204	8½ feet	Light Dry-Fly	4⅛ to 4¼ ounces
205	8½ feet	Medium or Fast	4½ to 4⅝ ounces
206	8½ feet	Medium or Fast	5 to 5¼ ounces
207	9 feet	Slow	4¾ to 4⅞ ounces
208	9 feet	Light Dry-Fly	4¾ to 5 ounces
209	9 feet	Dry-Fly	5¼ to 5¾ ounces
210	9 feet	Medium or Fast	5½ to 5⅝ ounces
212	9½ feet	Medium	5⅝ to 5¾ ounces
214	9½ feet	Fast	6 to 6⅛ ounces

The two-piece list included a six-and-a-half-footer that was missing from the earlier Payne catalogues. These rods are particularly prized among fishermen, and they include the incomparable tapers between six and seven and a half feet not found in the three-piece series:

95	6 feet	Dry-Fly	1⅝ to 1⅞ ounces
96	6½ feet	Dry-Fly	2¼ to 2⅜ ounces
97	7 feet	Dry-Fly	2⅝ to 2¾ ounces
98	7 feet	Fast Dry-Fly	2⅞ to 3 ounces
100	7½ feet	Dry-Fly	3¼ to 3⅜ ounces
101	7½ feet	Fast Dry-Fly	3½ to 3¾ ounces
102	8 feet	Light Dry-Fly	3⅝ to 3⅞ ounces
103	8 feet	Fast Dry-Fly	4 to 4⅛ ounces
104	8½ feet	Light Dry-Fly	4⅛ to 4⅜ ounces
105	8½ feet	Slow	4⅝ to 4¾ ounces
106	8½ feet	Medium or Fast Dry-Fly	4⅝ to 4¾ ounces
108	9 feet	Light Dry-Fly	5 to 5¼ ounces
110	9 feet	Dry-Fly	5⅜ to 5½ ounces

The Parabolics had been reduced to only two models, perhaps in response to the growing fashion of the little rod, although it is in the lengths beyond seven and a half feet that such tapers really excel. These rods had skeletal seats with cork fillers. The seven-foot one-inch model weighed two and seven-eighths ounces, and the seven-foot nine-inch taper weighed three and three-quarters ounces. These rods are similar to the Super Parabolic-PPP tapers that Charles Ritz calls the Featherlight and Colorado, manufactured in France by the firm of Pezon & Michel.

When James Payne left his shop for the last time in the winter of 1969, his customers and disciples were fearful, since Payne was not a man who would quit rodmaking easily. *I'm tired and I don't feel right,* he told Tom Bailey. *Don't really know when I'll be back.*

His company had been acquired by Gladding, primarily to assemble an expensive grade of fiberglass rods using the Payne name and hardware. Payne said little about those rods, although his silence itself was eloquent. Payne hated glass and its contribution to the death of craftsmanship, and it was almost funny to watch him flex one with a silent headshake and grimace that eloquently betrayed his opinion. But like everything else he touched, the glass blanks he fitted with Payne hardware were the finest fiberglass he could find.

There are countless anecdotes about Payne, each recounting his stubborn honesty and integrity or his restless odyssey in search of ultimate perfection. W. L. Collins liked to tell the story about how difficult it became to meet Payne's exacting specifications for German silver after the Second World War.

Big nickel suppliers don't exactly declare a dividend over the size of a rodmaker's order, Collins explained, *and we searched until we found a nickel company with a president who fished–when his rods were held up in delivery we got action!*

Payne himself admitted his fussiness about craftsmanship and detailing, and his solution for finishing the bamboo nodes is typical. The nodes are often marred with minuscule pits and checks that cannot be worked smooth without weakening the section, and they also mar the final varnish work. Payne finishes are legendary for their perfection, and part of their secret lies in his node work.

Getting them down flush with the rest of the stick can make a weak point in the rod when you use a file or sanding block, Payne revealed in his shop a few months before his death. *We worked out a heat-pressure technique that presses the nodes into the rod, and we don't have to risk cutting into the power fibers.*

When Payne finally died, Gladding permitted his apprentice David Decker to continue making rods under the Payne trademark, along with the fittings maker Tom Bailey, who had worked with both Payne and Leonard over the years. Their work used the same cane, milling machines and other equipment, ferrules, reel fittings, and proprietary techniques worked out by the Paynes over the years. Operations are still based in the original shop at Highland Mills. Briefly, the rods were produced under the Decker name, but the fledgling company soon wisely returned to calling itself the E. F. Payne Rod Company. David Decker is an exceptionally talented young craftsman, but it is difficult to honor a legend.

Payne was a tough act to follow, Decker admits grudgingly.

During those gilded years of American rodmaking, several large tackle manufacturers also produced rods of split-bamboo construction, and their premier grades sometimes approached the work of the fine custom builders. Montague was perhaps the first company to trigger this competition in the factory production of cane rods, and other fine equipment was made by Heddon and South Bend.

It is interesting that even this activity often stemmed from the Leonard tradition. George Varney was its primary catalyst at Montague and had served his apprenticeship at Central Valley while Hiram Leonard was still

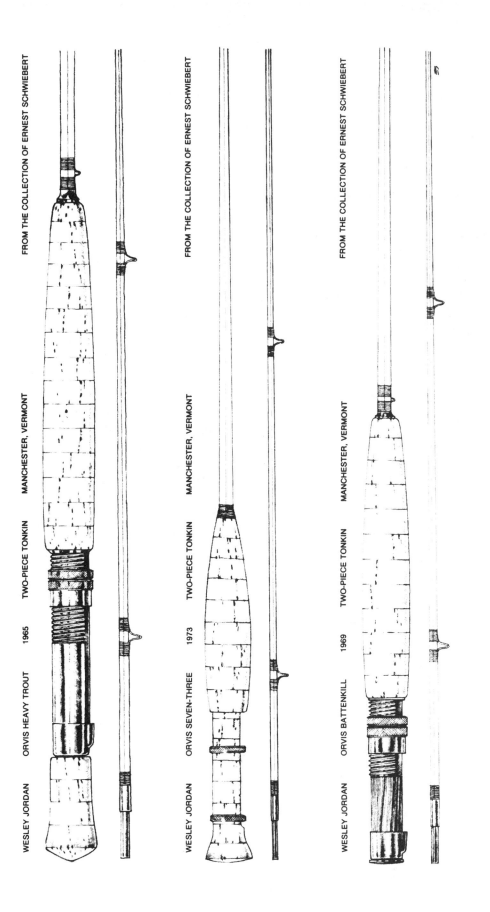

WESLEY JORDAN   ORVIS HEAVY TROUT   1965   TWO-PIECE TONKIN   MANCHESTER, VERMONT   FROM THE COLLECTION OF ERNEST SCHWIEBERT

WESLEY JORDAN   ORVIS SEVEN-THREE   1973   TWO-PIECE TONKIN   MANCHESTER, VERMONT   FROM THE COLLECTION OF ERNEST SCHWIEBERT

WESLEY JORDAN   ORVIS BATTENKILL   1969   TWO-PIECE TONKIN   MANCHESTER, VERMONT   FROM THE COLLECTION OF ERNEST SCHWIEBERT

alive. Montague made a lot of contract rods for major mail-order houses, but its own top-grade Varney rods were special. The oldest I have seen was a nine-foot three-piece rod weighing about six ounces. It featured a full nickel-silver seat with a hooded cap and sliding band as long as the grip itself, which was an exaggerated half-Wells design. Montague rods rivalled the work of Divine for their intricate, polychromatic windings above the grip, and the Varney rods also displayed intermediate wraps, with ornamental silk windings in the middle of the butt section. Later Montague rods included the Redwing, which had a simple Payne-style grip and full metal seat of German silver. The nine-foot Redwing was a three-piece rod weighing five and three-quarters ounces. Its swelled-butt tapers also echo Varney's work with Leonard, and it is typical of cane rods produced before the First World War. Redwing models were also produced which had full locking seats of German silver, combined with garish brass threads and lock-nuts. These were three-piece rods made in eight-and-a-half- and nine-foot lengths. Perhaps the best Montague rods that I have seen are the Fishkill series made just before the Second World War under the direction of Sewell Dunton. These rods had a half-Wells grip with a black locking seat and walnut filler, and were a prelude to the rods that Dunton made in western Massachusetts after he left Montague.

Sewell Dunton produced a series of moderately priced rods in western Massachusetts, both under his own premium trademark and as the Zwirz Favorite that Robert Zwirz sold through his tackle shop in midtown New York. The Dunton tapers were rather fast, featuring a stiff butt and soft tip-action performance. Although the fittings often varied in quality and several grip and reel-seat designs are common, Dunton rods display a number of basic features. The ferrules were drawn instead of machined, and like the reel fittings, they were anodized black. Most grips were a relatively fat Payne-type cigar design. The larger rods, between eight and a half and nine and a half feet, often had full-metal seats anodized black, while the seven and a half to eight and a half foot rods also had skeletal locking hardware with cork or walnut fillers. Dunton used skeletal seats consisting of a hooded butt cap and ring over both walnut and cork on his smaller rods. Black tungsten guides were used, and the silk wrappings were tastefully simple, with a dark brown intended to match the cane and black ornamental tips.

Dunton has since retired and sold his Greenfield shop to the young craftsmen who founded Thomas & Thomas. The company has no relationship to old Fred Thomas and his son Leon, but derives its name from its owners, Thomas Dorsey and Thomas Maxwell. Both are relatively young men who learned rodmaking in boyhood from the grandfather of Thomas Maxwell, and both continued making rods into their college years. They were teaching philosophy at the University of Maryland and building rods as a part-time profession until 1973, when they decided to abandon lecturing for craftsmanship and bought out Dunton.

Thomas & Thomas have now moved their operation from Mary-

FROM THE COLLECTION OF HARRY DARBEE

JAMES PAYNE   HEAVY TROUT   1947   THREE-PIECE TONKIN   HIGHLAND MILLS, NEW YORK

FROM THE COLLECTION OF FRANK MELE

JAMES PAYNE   LIGHT TROUT   1939   THREE-PIECE TONKIN   HIGHLAND MILLS, NEW YORK

FROM THE COLLECTION OF FRANK MELE

JAMES PAYNE   STANDARD TROUT   1931   THREE-PIECE TONKIN   HIGHLAND MILLS, NEW YORK

land to Dunton's old Greenfield plant and are building rods full time.

We're so awash in back orders, Dorsey explained this past spring, *that we're not really sure what full time means any more!*

Both men are dedicated artisans, determined to pursue their craft with militant fervor, and believe they have been fated to preserve the split-cane tradition. Some of that fanaticism has already been implanted in a growing circle of customers. Armed with the equipment acquired from Sewell Dunton, who still wanders into the shop from time to time, and one of the largest supplies of aged culms in the United States, the future of their fledgling partnership looks bright.

Originally, the Thomas & Thomas rods were impregnated with a polymer resin in a light brown finish, but varnished rods in the natural color bamboo are also available in each model today. The ferrules are handcrafted of nickel silver in a shouldered, hand-lapped design. The reel fittings are machined from first-quality aluminum with a gleaming jewel finish, and full-locking and skeletal seats are available. Oxidized ferrules and reel seats are also furnished. Chromed stainless snake guides and tip tops are used, with carboloy stripping guides. Morticed walnut fillers are supplied with both locking and skeletal seats, along with paired rings on either walnut or cork. The fully skeletal grip of aluminum rings is finished with a butt of delicately sculptured cork. It is typical of their work that the butt of the cane is not covered with a plate in these rods, but is sanded smooth and left exposed in a candid piece of functional design.

Thomas & Thomas have worked in a wide range of grip styles, since they are willing to produce virtually any shape to order, but a number of grips seem to echo the design sense of the makers. Both reverse and standard cigar grips are common in the work of Thomas & Thomas, along with cigar designs having exaggeratedly pointed front tapers ideally suited to the index-finger casting grip.

Thomas & Thomas are building their rods in three price ranges, with the Caenis and Paradigm series the most expensive. The Individualist grade is divided into three groups called the Midge series, the Hendrickson series, and the Montana series. The Thomas & Thomas Classic rods are the least expensive, and include the Gnat series, the Classic Paralights, the Limestoners, the Cahill models, and the Coachman series. These rods are designed to fulfill a remarkable range of fishing problems.

The Caenis series is a unique line of delicate rods designed for fishing terrestrial and minute mayflies on our eastern limestone streams, western spring creeks, and on any river under the fine-tippet conditions of late summer. Caenis tapers for two-weight lines include three models between six and seven feet, weighing from one ounce to one and seven-eighths ounces. There are five rods in the Caenis series for three-weight lines, ranging from the six-footer at one and a half ounces to a surprising eight-foot rod weighing only three and one-quarter ounces. According to Thomas & Thomas, the new Paradigm series is a response to my discussions of parabolic tapers and their particular capabilities with nymphs and delicate tippets. The action is slow and truly parabolic, with the ability to handle a surprisingly long line once its timing is mastered. Paradigm rods are made in lengths between seven and eight feet to provide enough rod to manipulate fly swing in fishing a nymph. There are two designs for four-weight lines, a seven-footer of two and three-eighths ounces and a seven-and-a-half-footer weighing three and one-quarter ounces. Two rods are built for five-weights, one seven-and-a-half-foot taper at three and five-eighths ounces and an eight-foot design at three and three-quarters ounces. The eight-foot Paradigm for a six-weight line weighs only four ounces, and is a superb all-around rod capable of fishing a 6X tippet and punching out a weighted nymph with authority. These Paradigm compound tapers are exquisitely conceived and constructed, and a welcome addition to our sport.

The Individualist Midge series was part of the original Thomas & Thomas line. It is characterized by its extremely fine tip calibrations in each of its several tapers. There are four designs taking four-weight lines. The lightest is six and a half feet long and weighs three and a half ounces. Two of the Midge series are balanced with five-weight tapers, the seven-and-a-half-footer weighing three and one-quarter ounces and the eight-footer weighing three and three-quarters ounces.

The Thomas & Thomas Hendrickson series is designed to serve a versatile spectrum of needs, using three- to six-weight lines. There is a seven-foot Hendrickson at two and one-quarter ounces for DT3F. The three designs for four-weight lines include a six-foot rod at one and three-quarters ounces, the six-and-a-half-foot Hendrickson of two and one-eighth ounces, and a seven-footer weighing two and three-eighths ounces. The five-weight tapers are a seven-foot rod of two and a half ounces, and a seven-and-a-half-footer that weighs three and one-quarter ounces. There are two six-weight designs, the seven-and-a-half-foot model of three and three-quarters ounces and the eight-foot taper of three and seven-eighths ounces.

The Montana series incorporates the larger full-loading tapers with a much slower casting cycle. The calibrations combine a capability for distance, as well as the delicacy to fish 5X and 6X tippets with a deliberate strike and reasonable care. Thomas & Thomas have worked out tapers for two four-weight designs, the six-and-a-half-foot rod at two and one-eighth ounces and a seven-footer of two and three-eighths ounces. The five-weight Montanas include a seven-foot design weighing two and a half ounces, and a seven-and-a-half-foot version of three and one-quarter ounces. The six-weight rod measures eight feet and weighs three and seven-eighths ounces, and a second eight-footer weighing four and one-eighth ounces takes a seven-weight taper. The biggest rod in the Montana series weighs four and three-quarters ounces and requires a weight-forward eight to function best.

The Thomas & Thomas Classic line of rods includes the Gnat series, the Classic Paralights, and the Limestoners. The Gnats include three rods for a DT4F fly line, the smallest a six-footer weighing one and a half ounces and the largest a six-and-a-half-foot taper of two and one-eighth ounces. There is also a six-and-a-half-foot Gnat weighing two and one-quarter ounces that takes a DT5F line. These are short rods with a crisp, accurate delivery on brushy, overgrown waters, but unlike similar rods made by other firms, their actions flex deep into the butt and fish a relatively fine leader point.

The craftsmen at Thomas & Thomas are particularly proud of their Limestoner rods. These tapers supply a crisp control, with a tight loop and superb accuracy, plus the length to keep a backcast high above the weedy meadows of our limestone streams. There are six Limestoners made by Thomas & Thomas, three for DT4F lines and three for five-weights. The four-weights are seven feet and two and three-eighths ounces, seven and a half feet and three and one-eighth ounces, and a full eight feet weighing three and five-eighths ounces. The tapers calibrated for five-weight lines include a seven-footer of two and three-quarters ounces, a seven-and-a-half-foot design at three and a half ounces, and a basic eight-foot rod weighing three and seven-eighths ounces. These are excellent rods where both length and relative delicacy are important.

The Cahill series consists of five models, beginning with a seven-foot, two-and-one-quarter-ounce taper for a three-weight line. Two other seven-foot rods of two and three-eighths and two and three-quarters ounces are designed for four- and five-weight lines. The seven-and-a-half-footer in the Cahill series weighs three and three-quarters ounces and takes a six-weight taper, like the eight-foot, four-ounce model. Thomas & Thomas also build a fine group of big nymph and streamer rods called the Coachman series. These rods range from a seven-foot, two-and-three-quar-ters-ounce rod for a five-weight line, to the nine-footer that weighs five and a half ounces and powers an eight-weight with authority.

The birth of Thomas & Thomas in recent years is a blessing, since only a decade ago conventional wisdom was predicting the death of the cane rodmaker's art. *Those two young men are a miracle,* my old friend Lawrence Banks insists. *Just when Jim Payne is on his deathbed, these two appear without warning—and with a good thirty or forty years ahead of them!*

The craftsmanship of Thomas & Thomas is perhaps a fitting conclusion for the equipment and bamboo stocks that Sewell Dunton acquired when Montague finally decided to abandon the production of split-bamboo rods.

However, the finest factory rods of split cane were probably made over the years at James Heddon & Sons in Michigan. Heddon is a name perhaps more closely identified with bass fishing, since the founder James Heddon shares the honor of inventing the surface bass plug with Anson Decker of New Jersey.

Heddon also made bamboo rods in a surprising number of models and grades, and since the plant was in Dowagiac, there were a great many Heddon rods in use on my boyhood Michigan rivers. The Heddon DeLuxe and the less expensive Black Beauty were highly prized in those days. Both were remarkably beautiful rods, particularly in the vintages manufactured before the First World War, and their traditional swelled butt tapers betrayed a possible connection between the Heddon craftsmen and the prototypes of earlier makers like Murphy and Leonard.

There were many Heddon rods made over the years, and the models priced at the top of the line were often of surprising quality. Such rods are still highly regarded by their owners. The Heddon Model 10 was moderately priced, with oxidized ferrules and skeletal reel-seat fittings over a cork filler. It was usually finished with scarlet silk windings, and the seven-and-a-half-footer at three and a half ounces was perhaps the favorite model. The Heddon Folsom was a superbly finished two-piece rod with a delicately slow action. It had oxidized ferrules and reel-seat fittings over a black walnut filler. The brown silk wrappings were tipped with yellow, and except for the swelled butt tapers typical of Heddon, the Folsom is remarkably like a Payne in appearance. The seven-and-a-half-foot Folsom was a classic rod, taking a four-weight line and weighing only three and one-eighth ounces. The Heddon Black Beauty was long a popular rod on the rivers of the Middle West. It had black silk wraps and fittings with a Bakelite screw-locking filler and a graceful half-Wells cork grip. The eight-foot Black Beauty was a three-piece rod weighing only four ounces, and with an action perfectly attuned to a four-weight line. It was highly prized among the men who fished the Michigan rivers during my boyhood summers there. The Heddon DeLuxe was an exquisitely made fly rod with black fittings over a richly burled-walnut reel filler. Its grip was a reversed half-Wells like the Granger type, and it was wrapped with brown winds tipped in black silk. The Heddon DeLuxe was made in eight-foot, eight-and-a-half-foot, and nine-foot models ranging from three and a half to five and a half ounces and was one of the finest factory rods.

But the vintage Heddon rods made before the First World War are my favorites. These rods were the prototypes of the Black Beauty and the DeLuxe models that followed, and their fittings were designed with unsurpassed sense of elegance and design. The Black Beauty already had its characteristic black silk wrappings and Bakelite reel-seat filler, although the hooded reel sleeve and slender discs of German silver at the grip checks were abandoned in the modern versions. It was the DeLuxe of this period that was perhaps the vintage Heddon, and the apogee of rodmaking in the shop of Dowagiac.

Its ties to Hiram Leonard are visible in the fully swelled butt and the relatively fat cigar-type grip, although the ornamental character of the reel seats and grip checks are unmistakably Heddon. The cork grip is rather short, and the reel-seat assembly is almost as long as the grip itself. Bakelite grip checks with German-silver spacers complete the grip, along with a Bakelite winding check that tapers into the swelled cane. The lock fittings consist of a German-silver hood and screw-nut, threaded on a Bakelite filler. The butt plate is Bakelite, with a relatively slender hooded sleeve of silver. The seat filler is burled American walnut, and the slim cork rings unquestionably date these rods to the early years of this century. During my boyhood years along the Pere Marquette, there was an old fisherman who used one of these vintage Heddons with enviable skill, and for many years I believed they were the finest rods in the world.

The South Bend Bait Company acquired the famous Cross Rod Company after the First World War, and for more than a decade the Cross-South Bend rods were excellent production work. These rods closely resemble the Leonard Tournament designs that were popular after the First World War, with their full German-silver seats and slender cigar-type grips. The rods were executed in double-built construction and pale honey-colored cane. The silk windings were English tan, and the action was a smooth semiparabolic that worked into the grip. The eight-and-a-half-foot, three-piece rod at five and one-quarter ounces took a surprisingly light five-weight line. Cross used agate butt guides and split ferrules with four spiral cuts, placed counterclockwise for a right-handed caster and clockwise for a left-handed owner. The full silver reel seats were engraved with a handsome Cross medallion. The famous Cross Sylph was a seven-foot, two-piece rod weighing only three ounces in spite of its double-built construction. Its grip and reel-seat assembly were much shorter than the conventional Cross designs. Following the Second World War, with Cross himself long dead and his protégé, the exceptionally talented Wes Jordan, at Orvis, South Bend continued to make good split-cane rods both under its own trademark and for Shakespeare. These rods used burgundy-colored reel-seat fillers with a locking butt-cap nut matching their anodized automatic fly reels. The similar Shakespeare reels were a deep forest green, and the rods built by South Bend for Shakespeare used matching anodized reel seats. Some later South Bend rods used burgundy and amber-colored reel seats of plastic, and even the fine 346 series ultimately featured plastic fittings, although the bamboo remained surprisingly good.

European rodmaking was dominated by the famous House of Hardy, after it was founded by William Hardy and his tournament-casting brother, John James Hardy, in 1872. Their influence was so great that the Hardy shop on Paikes Street soon lifted Alnwick, a small town in Northumberland, to international prominence in the fishing world. Donald Overfield made these observations in his article on the Hardy operation for *Trout and Salmon* in the spring of 1973:

> From the outset, it was their aim to produce the very best in rods, and so in some respects these two men were akin to Rolls and Royce, their philosophy being to design and produce the finest possible product. Price had a secondary nature. To succeed in business on this basis, one must be correct in the assumption that one's product is unquestionably the best.

John James Hardy and William Hardy were apparently correct in that confidence, because history tells us they were soon deluged with orders. Their success precipitated a move to larger quarters on Fenkle Street, but their reputation continued to grow, and to accommodate a landslide of orders they ultimately moved to new production facilities in Bondgate. Hardy Brothers remained at Bondgate until 1967, when they moved to a still larger plant at Willowburn. Donald Overfield again captures the spirit of Hardy in his short article for *Trout and Salmon* in England:

> Just what is it that has always linked the name of Hardy with quality? Three things: meticulous craftsmanship, inventiveness, and the exquisite finish details. These things, coupled with a family tradition of angling businessmen, reaches to the present.

Early in the history of Hardy Brothers, John James Hardy became intensely interested in tournament casting. His passion was largely rooted in the conviction that only tournament competition could improve and market their work, and the family tradition of tournament competition prevailed. John James Hardy often held the European championship in salmon- and trout-fly distance, as well as the dry-fly accuracy events. Laurence Reuben Hardy and Harold Hardy also followed that tradition and became British champions in salmon-fly distance and dry-fly accuracy. The dedication of the Hardy family to the performance of their tackle on the tournament circuit continues today.

The Alnwick shops have also been responsible for many design innovations over the years, including the spiral-lock ferrule patented in 1882, and the reverse-locking reel seat in 1911. The Casting Club de France rods were introduced that same year and are still treasured by many owners as the finest light trout models ever built. Using a slender Casting Club de France, which measured only seven feet and weighed only two and three-eighths ounces, John James Hardy set a French distance record on the French competition ponds in the Bois de Boulogne. There is still an old photograph in the Hardy offices that records that triumph with John James Hardy resplendent in Cheviot tweeds, surrounded by French casters wearing bowlers and top hats in the meadows at Tir aux Pigeons.

Hardy split-cane rods were largely produced by hand, using the planing blocks developed before Victorian times, until the introduction of a milling machine in 1925. Ten years later, Hardy began building split-cane sections with the pithy core of the bamboo removed and the inner glue faces replaced with a lighter apex of select American pine. It was a system similar to the method of construction developed about twelve years earlier by Edwin Powell in California. Hollow split-bamboo rods originated in 1933, with the separate patents granted to Edwin Powell and Lew Stoner on the Pacific Coast. But Hardy introduced a remarkably different hollow rod using modern high-stress adhesives twenty-five years later—and James Hardy quickly used the new Hollolight and Hollokona designs to break the European distance records in 1959.

The influence of the Hardy designs is obvious in many classic American rods, from the work of Payne in New York to the reverse-locking Bakelite reel seats used by Powell in California. The Hardy DeLuxe with

its sliding lock-nut reel seat first appeared in 1911, and the Hardy R. B. Marston with its reverse-locking seat, concealed band blade, and full Wells grip was introduced before the First World War. The Viscount Grey at ten and a half feet and eight and one-quarter ounces was introduced in these same years, with its heavy reverse-locking seat and rubber button. The famous Houghton Club and F. M. Halford rods ranging from nine and a half feet to ten and a half feet also appeared before the Treaty of Versailles. The Houghton Club came in three models, fitted with the locking nut and bank blade, and weighed as much as nine ounces. The Halford Special was a more modern reverse-lock seat, and its design had a wide influence in the United States. The famous J. J. Hardy model had a reverse-locking seat of the Granger type, its hood sliding over a Bakelite filler, and it was introduced in 1921. The delicate Hardy Marvel was introduced the following year, and weighed only two and three-quarters ounces at seven and a half feet. It featured a skeletal seat with a butt cap and two aluminum rings, one fixed and the other sliding. Herbert Hoover owned a later Marvel with the free screw-mounted hood still used on the modern Palakona series. There were also a few exquisite Hardy Marvels built at eight feet and three and one-quarter ounces, one of the finest tapers in Hardy history. The elegant Hardy Fairchild was introduced about 1925, and included a finely detailed butt cap and hooded sleeve, with a sliding jewel-finished reel band. It was developed before the First World War for Tappan Fairchild, using the basic tapers of the Casting Club de France and adding a nine-and-a-half-foot model weighing five ounces. Fairchild fished the classic water on the Neversink headwaters, and was one of the finest American trout fishermen of his time.

Later Hardy rods continued in the classic Hardy mold, particularly with the introduction of the Itchen and Fairy models on the threshold of the Great Depression. There was also a new version of the Hardy DeLuxe, with a lighter Halford-type locking seat and reversed half-Wells grip. It was made in models ranging from eight feet, four and three-quarters ounces to a muscular ten-footer at six and three-quarters ounces. The Hardy Itchen was an attempt to match the Leonards that Skues fished and wrote about with such enthusiasm on his Abbotts Barton water, much to the chagrin of the Hardy brothers and other British makers. The Hardy Itchen is a fine rod in its own right, with a light reverse-locking seat and full Wells-style grip. Like the famous Leonards owned by Skues, the Hardy Itchen was made in nine-and-a-half- and ten-foot lengths weighing six and a half and six and three-quarters ounces.

The Hardy Fairy is perhaps the most famous model in the minds of many American fishermen, for it is this rod that was selected by the late Ernest Hemingway in the Hardy shop at Pall Mall in London. Hemingway bought his rod after the remarkable success of *A Farewell to Arms*, and it was the eight-and-a-half-foot, five-ounce Fairy that he fished later in Wyoming and Idaho, particularly on Silver Creek near Sun Valley. The rod was purchased from the Hemingway estate by my good friend,

Prescott Tolman, and presented to the Museum of American Fly Fishing.

The familiar Hardy Phantom rods were introduced following the Second World War, with a slim cigar grip and skeletal seat of butt cap and sliding ring on a cork filler. Phantoms were made in many sizes from the four-and-a-half-footer of one and a half ounces to the nine-footer that weighed four and three-quarters ounces and took a surprisingly light DT6F line. The eight-foot Phantom at four and one-quarter ounces was probably the most popular Hardy in the United States. It balanced a five-weight line. It was in the larger Phantoms, rods between eight and nine and a half feet, that Hardy introduced the Hollolight and Hollokona construction. It is these rods that represented the Hardy line until recent years, when Harrington & Richardson acquired the exclusive rights to market the Hardy products sold throughout the United States. Several months ago I was invited by Edward Rowe, the young president of Harrington & Richardson, to meet with James Hardy over dinner in Boston.

We'd like you to see our new line of Palakona bamboo rods, Rowe explained. *You already know our Hardy reels.*

The modern Hardy line starts with the Palakona bamboo long famous in the finest British rods. The tapers are designed to produce a crisp and slightly fast dry-fly action, using six-strip construction in a two-piece design. Both grip and reel seat in the six- to seven-and-a-half-foot Palakona rods are cork, with the traditional capped butt, screw-fitted hood, and sliding band first used on the Casting Club de France in 1911. The ferrules are fine nickel silver with jewel-polished aluminum plugs; and the silk wrappings at the ferrules, grip checks, and guides are a traditional black with bright green tips. In the smaller lengths and weights, the grips are the graceful cigar type first used on the Casting Club de France and Hardy Marvel, and the Hardy fishtail grip is used with a Halford reverse-locking seat in the eight- and eight-and-a-half-foot models.

The Palakona Superlight of six feet and two ounces is designed for a five-weight line, while the seven-foot Superlight weighs three ounces and takes the same size taper. The seven-and-a-half-foot Palakona weighs three and five-eighths ounces and uses a six-weight line perfectly.

The Palakona medium action rods of eight and eight and a half feet are fine all-around tapers weighing four and five-eighths ounces and five and three-eighths ounces. The eight-foot model is designed for a seven-weight line, while the longer rod is balanced with an eight-weight. The larger sizes are now made of fiberglass, with a traditional black rubber button attached to the reverse-locking seat. The Hardy Fibatube operation began in 1968, and with the fabrication of its own glass sections, the history of Hardy began a fresh chapter. Donald Overfield concluded his essay in *Trout and Salmon* with these observations on the famous rods that came from Alnwick:

> The Jet fly rods produced from these blanks have rapidly become
> a firm favourite with countless anglers. While the name Jet is in

keeping with these modern times, it is also, in fact, a tribute to the great American tournament caster who helped develop their original design and action, J. E. Tarantino.

And so the story of the Hardy rod is brought up to date. Whenever flyfishers discuss quality rods, such famous names as the J.J.H. Triumph, L.R.H. Dry Fly, Halford Knockabout, Crown Houghton, Koh-i-Noor, and Perfection will emerge, to ensure a place in the history of flyfishing for that remote little town of Alnwick, in Northumberland, and for the two men who made it all possible, John James and William Hardy.

Although the history of British rods has unquestionably been dominated by the House of Hardy, there have been many fine rodmakers in England over the past century. Knowledgeable angling historians have admired the rods built by makers like John Forrest of Kelso-on-Tweed, Bampton of Alnwick, Westley Richards of Birmingham, Allcock and Walker Falcon of Redditch, Ingram of Glasgow, Joseph Braddell of Belfast, Farlow of London, Sharpe's of Aberdeen, Sealey's, Rogan of Donegal, and the famous British firm of Millward's. Few of these firms survive, except for the merged rodmaking efforts of Charles Farlow & Company and J. S. Sharpe of Aberdeen, Davenport and Fordham at Poole, and the relatively new workshop of Clifford Constable in Bromley.

The Farlow Featherweights are two-piece construction in four models. These rods are fitted with a hooded butt cap and sliding band over a cork filler. The seven-footer weighs three and one-quarter ounces and takes a five-weight line taper, like the seven-and-a-half-foot Featherweight of four ounces. The eight-foot designed for a six-weight line weighs four and one-quarter ounces, and the eight-and-a-half-footer of four and three-quarters ounces takes the same fly-line tapers. There are four rods of the Ritz staggered-ferrule type. The Farlow Eighty-eight measures eight feet eight inches in length, weighs five ounces, and takes a six-weight. The Eighty-three is five inches shorter, takes a five-weight line, and weighs four and a half ounces. The staggered ferrule places the German-silver joints well below the nodal point in the rod tapers. Farlow also manufactures a version of the famous Ritz Fario Club, named for the small circle of internationally known anglers that meets each fall at the Hotel Ritz in Paris. The Fario Club measures eight feet five inches and takes a five-weight line. These three rods have locking reel seats on a cork filler.

Dermot Wilson collaborated with Alan Sharpe to produce the Wilson-Sharpe, which uses a hooded butt cap and sliding reel band on a cork filler, with a tapered Ritz-style grip. It measures eight feet three inches, weighs four and one-quarter ounces, and takes a five-weight taper. It is a fine British version of the Ritz Parabolic theories.

It's a rod with an international pedigree, Dermot Wilson explains enthusiastically at Nether Wallop. *It's tapers combine the result of testing among friends from Normandy to New Zealand.*

The Farlow Elf is a small two-piece rod designed for small streams and relatively light tackle. It measures six feet ten inches and weighs three and three-quarters ounces, taking a five-weight line. The Wulff-Farlow Midge and Ultimate are familiar rods to Americans who know the similar rods that Lee Wulff designed for Orvis after the Second World War. The Ultimate is a five-foot ten-inch rod built as a single stick without a ferrule. It weighs only one and a half ounces but takes a six-weight line, like the six-foot Midge, which adds a ferrule and weighs two ounces.

The fine J. S. Sharpe rods include the three-piece Aberdeen and two-piece Scottie series. The Aberdeen trout rods include a nine-footer of six and one-quarter ounces designed for a six-weight line and a nine-and-a-half-foot, six-and-three-quarters-ounce taper for a seven-weight. The Scottie series of rods is justly popular in both Europe and the United States, and like the Aberdeen group, it is fitted with full metal reel seats. The eight-and-a-half-foot Scottie weighs five and a half ounces and takes a six-weight. The nine-footer weighs six ounces, and like the nine-and-a-half-foot model of six ounces, it also takes a surprisingly light six-weight line. Both the Farlow and the Sharpe's rods are milled from impregnated bamboo, which was originally developed at Orvis in the United States, and which the Sharpe's technicians call their armor-cane process.

Two rods designed and built by Davenport and Fordham are quite popular in England, although they are virtually unknown in America. The eight-foot Fordham Exclusive features a hooded butt cap and sliding reel band on a half-Wells grip. It weighs four and one-eighth ounces and takes a five-weight taper. The eight-and-a-half-foot Exclusive weighs four and three-quarters ounces and is designed for a six-weight line.

Clifford Constable of Bromley is building a moderately priced series of fine split-cane rods. The Constable R. H. Woods rods are perhaps best known in this country, with a semiparabolic action and staggered ferrules. The six-foot nine-inch model weighs two and seven-eighths ounces and matches a WF4F perfectly, while the seven-and-a-half-footer of three and a half ounces is designed for a five-weight. Dermot Wilson has also worked with Constable to produce a six-foot nine-inch model called the Wallop Brook. It weighs two and three-quarters ounces and takes a four-weight line. The seven-and-a-half-foot Wallop Brook weighs three and seven-eighths ounces and is designed for five-weight tapers. The third Wallop Brook rod measures eight feet two inches, weighs four and five-eighths ounces, and its tapers are calibrated to take a six-weight line. Clifford Constable also builds a surprisingly delicate nine-footer called the C. C. Lightweight. It weighs four and seven-eighths ounces because of its hooded cap and reel band fitted over a cork filler, and takes a six-weight perfectly. These Constable rods are enormously popular in England, since they are hand-planed bamboo, yet cost a little more than half the price of the comparable Hardy Palakona line. This past spring I had the privilege of fishing a Constable rod with Dermot Wilson on his Kimbridge beat of the lower Test. It was late during the hatches of big *Ephemera* drakes, and the

DERMOT WILSON

fish were working on both emerging sedges and the odd mayfly spinner drifting spent on the smooth currents. The seven-and-a-half-foot Wallop Brook punched out eighty-foot casts with precision, hooked two- and three-pound trout at that range without breaking off .005 tippets, and played the fish in the weedy channels with a mixture of delicacy and control. Their qualities were surprisingly good considering their cost.

We're quite proud of Cliff Constable, Dermot Wilson explained happily at his Kimbridge fishing hut. *His handwork continues in the best traditions of British rodmaking.*

The only serious rival to these British rodmakers on the European continent is the famous French shop of Pezon & Michel located at Amboise. Although Pezon & Michel were a fine tackle firm before their association with the celebrated Charles Ritz, there was nothing in their earlier work that suggests the innovative thought and creative *élan* that Ritz brought to their rods.

His family long ago gave its name to the English language as a superlative and as a synonym for quality, through their operation of a hotel in Paris that many believe the finest in the world. The Hotel Ritz in the Place Vendôme offers a quality of comfort and service that has made it a legend among travellers. The Ritz was founded by Cesar Ritz in 1898—just seven years after his son Charles was born in Molshiem—and King Edward VII of England told Cesar Ritz that his hotel held a more accurate embodiment of what European royalty would appreciate than did the character of their own households. Ernest Hemingway expressed his admiration for the Ritz in another way in 1944, when he pushed through its revolving door during the liberation of Paris.

I have taken the Ritz, he proclaimed to the war-weary concierge, *because it is the finest hotel in Paris!* Hemingway then whispered, *Germans around?*

The Hotel Ritz is historically the creation of Cesar Ritz, although Charles Ritz can clearly take credit for its modern reputation and character. The hotel has a worldwide fame, yet Charles Ritz is equally famous because of his parabolic rods and his writings about fly-fishing among anglers who know nothing of his connection with the half-legendary family hostelry.

Ritz came to the United States in 1916, working briefly at a small hotel in Connecticut while his father completed negotiations for the Ritz Carlton in New York. It was to this distinguished New York hotel that young Charles Ritz was ultimately dispatched, and his obscure office in its cellars had an anteroom that was soon filled with fly rods in varying states of repair. His daily walks after lunch took him to Abercrombie & Fitch, where he lovingly examined the racks filled with the gleaming rods of artisans like Cross, Thomas, Edwards, Hawes, and Payne.

But these treasures were only for dreaming, Ritz explains with twinkling eyes and an expressive shrug. *My father was a careful man with the purse strings—and I was always kept quite penniless.*

Ritz found his rods in the secondhand stores and pawnshops along

Third Avenue, bundling the results of his foraging back to the office in the basement of the Ritz Carlton. He simply refinished the better rods, keeping the best for himself and selling the others. But some were altered experimentally, by cutting back their tip sections and modifying their actions. Ritz soon concluded that tip calibrations should be relatively stiff in the last few inches in any rod meant for distance casting, giving the casting stroke an instantaneous start and building great line speed. His convictions on tip calibrations have not changed over the past half century, and it was a visit to the workshop of Jim Payne that provided Ritz with the lifelong inspiration for his experiments.

Ritz stayed in the United States more than a decade, and it was finally his mother who persuaded him to return to Paris, making a special trip to bring him back in 1928. However, Cesar Ritz had filled the management posts at the Hotel Ritz, and his sense of loyalty to his staff was so pervasive that no place was made for his son. Charles Ritz patiently waited for a vacancy, working in the Paris offices of an American securities broker. During this period, a client suffering from financial problems asked Ritz to assume the ownership of a shoe store he operated. Ritz eventually bought the shop, and it finally became profitable again, although its back room was soon a clandestine meeting place for the knowledgeable fishermen of Paris—its stockroom space gradually dwindling under a growing accumulation of fly rods and tackle-repair benches and fly-tying tables.

Ritz became both president and chairman of the board for the storied Hotel Ritz in 1953, when the members of the London-based syndicate that actually owns the hotel elected him to those posts. Ritz owns only one percent of its stock, according to the corporate structure assembled by Cesar Ritz and his original backers in 1896. The board chairman of the Ritz Hotel in London, Sir Guy Bracewell Smith, is the largest single shareholder at five percent. The remaining shares are held by anonymous investors in both England and Europe, their identities cloaked in a mist of family trusts, inheritances, and the Byzantine overtones of Swiss-bank secrecy.

However, during these same years of his Paris apprenticeship, Charles Ritz was building a formidable reputation for his skills in fishing and fly-rod design. It was the late Roger Pujo who first suggested that Ritz meet with the technicians of Pezon & Michel, and they travelled together into the Loire Valley toward Amboise. It was an historic journey for the fly-fishing world.

Edouard Plantet was the production expert at Pezon & Michel, and Plantet quickly sensed that Ritz had acquired incredible insights into the philosophy of fly-rod actions and tapers during his years in the United States. After a series of exploratory meetings, Pezon & Michel invited Ritz to serve as their full-time technical consultant. Ritz clearly had almost intuitive perceptions into the calibrations of first-rate rods, in perhaps the same way that Cesar Ritz intuitively grasped the details of creating the world's finest hotel, or the instinct that Bugatti had for building his remarkable racing machines.

Like Laurence Robert Hardy, who converted his Alnwick shops from handcraftsmanship to modern milling machines, Ritz and Plantet soon decided that the artisans in their workrooms at Amboise could not produce identical rod actions in the demanding compound tapers proposed by Ritz. It was Edouard Plantet that finally designed the high-precision milling tables and pressure-wrapping machines, equipment so beautifully conceived that they were virtually free of vibration. It was a fruitful collaboration.

The third member of the Ritz triumverate was Pierre Creusevaut, who was at one time world fly-casting champion. These men built hundreds of experimental rods, with Ritz suggesting modifications in their tapers, Edouard Plantet executing them faithfully in split bamboo, and Creusevaut and Ritz both appraising the finished rods on the testing platforms at Amboise and at the casting ponds of Tir aux Pigeons in the Bois de Boulogne.

Plantet, Ritz, and Creusevaut performed countless shop tests too, observing bench vibrations, stress curves, stiffness profiles, and other precise measurements. Preliminary casting trials were ruthless. Any rod that would not cast twenty-five meters and extend its backcast easily was discarded. Slow-casting rhythms were also tried to check for line wave and loop collapse. Punching casts into a strong headwind was another test, driving out line with a vigorous double-haul, and accuracy casting completed the work. Finally, each prototype was given to a select circle of expert fishermen and fished through a complete season. This full spectrum of results was assembled and compared before any set of rod specifications was placed into production.

Each taper followed the credo of the parabolic action, Ritz explains with animation. *It must flex progressively from tip to butt, with its most obvious working concentrated toward the grip.*

Ritz developed his first parabolic taper in 1937, and in the next decade he concentrated on designs that might improve the supple flexing of the rod without reducing its power.

We found the Parabolique P.P.P. action in 1949, Ritz continues. *Its abbreviation stands for progressive pendulate power.*

His basic specifications for the two-piece staggered ferrule fly rod were first worked out in 1943, using a short butt and longer tip. This basic structural change drops the ferrule from a critical nodal zone, lengthening the flexing arm of the tip section and allowing a given rod to handle a line one size heavier. The heavier line weights lead to increased line speeds in the hands of the average fly-fisherman.

Better wind capability and distance, Ritz explains.

Like other first-rate manufacturers, Pezon & Michel uses select Tonkin cane from China, milling only those culms with dense fiber structures, straight graining, the distance between nodes, relatively small nodal segments, and good recovery from high bending stresses.

Eduoard Plantet is a firm disciple of heat treatment and developed

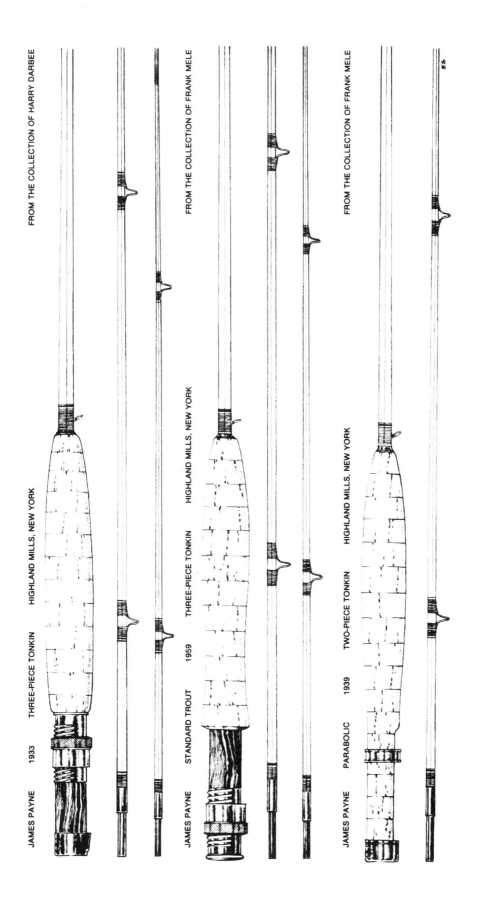

FROM THE COLLECTION OF HARRY DARBEE

JAMES PAYNE   1933   THREE-PIECE TONKIN   HIGHLAND MILLS, NEW YORK

FROM THE COLLECTION OF FRANK MELE

JAMES PAYNE   STANDARD TROUT   1959   THREE-PIECE TONKIN   HIGHLAND MILLS, NEW YORK

FROM THE COLLECTION OF FRANK MELE

JAMES PAYNE   PARABOLIC   1939   TWO-PIECE TONKIN   HIGHLAND MILLS, NEW YORK

special electrical kilns for drying and tempering the culms at Pezon & Michel. Both Plantet and Ritz argue that their kilns increase strength and stiffness, retard permanent distortion and sets in the finished cane sections, improve resistance to moisture absorption, and reduce moisture content.

Pezon & Michel makes three grades of parabolic rods. The Parabolic Speciale is the bottom of the line, the Parabolic Supreme rods are built of selected cane, and the Super Parabolic P.P.P. is the most expensive grade, using only the finest available bamboo. The Speciale and Supreme are made in two-piece construction with butt and tip sections of equal length. These grades are made in the *Normale* or medium action and relatively fast competition tapers. The Super Parabolic P.P.P. grade is made with a staggered ferrule design and the unique Ritz action except for the Midget, which has a lighter action taking a four-weight line. The ferrules are German silver, machined, and fitted by hand, with ground and split-end construction to ease the transfer of stress from metal to cane. Bronzed-steel snake guides and stripping guides are used on all three Pezon & Michel grades. Aluminum screw-locking reel seats with hooded butt caps and cork fillers are found on all Pezon & Michel rods except for the Midget and Featherlight, which use a butt cap and sliding reel band.

There are four models in the Parabolic Speciale grade, two in the Normale tapers, and two in the faster competition action. The seven-footers weigh three and a half ounces in the Normale calibrations and three and three-quarters ounces in the competition type. These rods take five- and six-weight lines. The eight-foot Speciale rods weigh four and one-eighth and five ounces in the two grades and are designed for six- and seven-weight tapers. The silk windings on the Speciale line are bright red, while the Supreme grade is wrapped in green. There are also four tapers in the Parabolic Supreme group. The seven-footers weigh four and four and three-eighths ounces, taking six- and seven-weight lines. The two eight-foot rods are four and three-quarters and five and one-eighth ounces, and are balanced by seven- and eight-weight tapers. The Super Parabolic P.P.P. series includes five models. The Midget is a six-footer weighing two and one-quarter ounces and was designed for DT4F lines. The Featherlight is a taper balanced with five-weight lines and weighs three ounces at six and a half feet. The seven-foot Supermarvel is a muscular four-ounce rod for six-weight tapers. The Ritz Colorado measures seven and a half feet and weighs four and one-quarter ounces, perfectly accommodating six weights. The Fario Club is a full eight and a half feet and weighs five ounces in the Pezon & Michel version. It also takes six-weight lines and is considered by many knowledgeable anglers to be the finest of the Ritz tapers.

Although Pezon & Michel had discontinued it, Dermot Wilson and other knowledgeable chalkstream fishermen in the south of England have insisted on the resurrection of the Sawyer Nymph. It is a superb eight-foot ten-inch rod specially designed by Charles Ritz after a session with Frank Sawyer on the Wiltshire Avon above Salisbury. Sawyer is the finest nymph fisherman in England, and his five-ounce rod is built to his specifications for

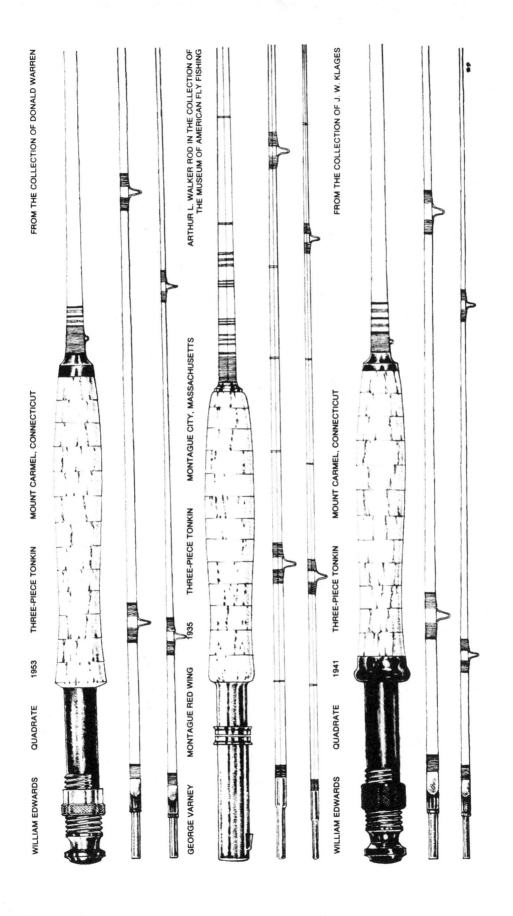

FROM THE COLLECTION OF DONALD WARREN

ARTHUR L. WALKER ROD IN THE COLLECTION OF
THE MUSEUM OF AMERICAN FLY FISHING

FROM THE COLLECTION OF J. W. KLAGES

WILLIAM EDWARDS   QUADRATE   1953   THREE-PIECE TONKIN   MOUNT CARMEL, CONNECTICUT

GEORGE VARNEY   MONTAGUE RED WING   1935   THREE-PIECE TONKIN   MONTAGUE CITY, MASSACHUSETTS

WILLIAM EDWARDS   QUADRATE   1941   THREE-PIECE TONKIN   MOUNT CARMEL, CONNECTICUT

a four-weight line and his tiny Pheasant Tail nymphs. Francois Michel is now making these exceptional nymph rods for British customers, and they are imported through Dermot Wilson at Stockbridge. It is made with a ten-inch detachable handle, its ferrule concealed in the grip. Its two-pieces are made in four-foot lengths, and its cork-filled reel seat is fitted with a butt cap and screw-locking assembly. The Sawyer Nymph is perhaps the finest slow-working action in the entire series of Ritz tapers, and it is one of the favorite rods in the collection of John Hemingway in Sun Valley.

American importers have attempted to modify the original Ritz designs for our market, changing his reverse-taper grips to the popular cigar shape and his reel seats to the locking type found on the Battenkill rods made by Orvis. It is hoped that Pezon & Michel will resist these pressures in the future, except perhaps for eliminating their purplish anodized reel fittings in favor of a simple jewel-finished aluminum. But the unique Ritz features found in the Pezon & Michel rods provide their singular Gaullic flavors, particularly in the three bright wraps above the grip check. Their delicate ornamental touch happily echoes the colors in the French flag.

Mais oui! Ritz exclaims. *It's the Tricolor!*

There are several other bamboo rodmakers in Europe, but the British and French firms unquestionably dominate the continental market. Perhaps the best known of these firms are Brunner of Austria, whose fine custom-made rods are favorites along the Traun, and the Horgård and Vangen shops in Norway.

American rodmaking has also continued to evolve, and its history is filled with some intriguing patterns. Although the influence of early artisans like Phillippe, Green, Murphy, Orvis, and Leonard is easily traced through the subsequent work of their employees and apprentices, there are also many famous American builders who developed in isolation—unique talents like Stoner, Powell, Granger, Dickerson, and Young.

The remarkable school of Pacific Coast rodmakers is perhaps the best example of this phenomenon and includes several of the finest rodmakers who ever lived. The first of these craftsmen was Edwin C. Powell, who fished the headwaters of the Sacramento, and began making fine fly rods in his shop at Marysville after the First World War. His first rod had been completed in 1912, using cane cut from the backyard of a local Chinese laundryman. Powell was thirty-six years old when he decided to build his rods full time, and the Marysville shop was already famous in 1922, when his son Walton became an apprentice. The Powell rods were all six-strip solid construction until 1933, when their patent for semihollow construction was granted.

The first Powell rods featured a relatively fat cigar-type handle, not unlike the Leonard rods made before the First World War, and a full metal German-silver reel seat with a sliding band and butt cap. Later designs clearly show the influence of the post war Hardy rods, with their Bakelite fillers and reverse-locking reel seat. Powell finally settled on a full-Wells grip about 1927, and his grips never varied until his death at midcentury.

Powell construction was always unusual, even in his solid six-strip rods. Borrowing again from Hardy, with its laminated cane and American pine sections of the period, Powell developed a similar method entirely his own. First he milled away the bamboo pith until only about an eighth of an inch of power fibers remained, and then he laminated a strip of Port Orford cedar on its inner face. Once the glue was fully set, the laminated spline was milled into a finished strip on a unique machine designed and built by the elder Powell—a remarkable technical feat considering that his education had stopped in grammar school.

Earlier in this chapter we have outlined the details of Powell's semihollow construction, which scalloped out six-inch hollows, leaving small solid sections for gluing. Powell designed and built a small saw specifically for this work, and the result was an extremely light rod with a delicate action for its length.

It was one hell of a lot of work, rodmaker Gary Howells explained one evening over dinner in San Francisco, *and I admire Powell for his exceptional talent and obvious self-discipline.*

Powell heat-tempered his culms by hand over a gas flame, and he remained loyal to the early water-soluble glues throughout his lifetime.

EDWIN POWELL

This made his hollow-built rods a little fragile, and the intermediate silk windings spaced about two inches apart were more than mere ornamentation. These wraps were actually structural, and helped to hold the splines of the semihollow butt section together. The wrappings at the grips and ferrules and guides were either brown or antique gold, and were double wrapped at the guides and ferrules. The tip guides were unusual. Their tubes were split with a fine saw, set in glue, and wrapped tightly to compress their serrated throats against the cane. The final wraps were applied in three layers, stepped like a delicate little Egyptian burial pyramid. The solid-built Powells simply held the keeper ring in a solid wrapping of silk, while the semihollow rods were always signed with delicate windings of white and black at the keeper silk. It is a maker's mark that identifies his finest work.

Powell also made his own ferrules and reel seats. His ferrules were drawn of German silver, with a swaged step on the male plugs and a hand-machined welt. Such Powell ferrules were a little brittle, and many split and broken examples have found their way into the repair shops at Winston and Leonard over the years. The reel seats were as elegant as the Hardy assemblies that Powell admired and copied, with Bakelite fillers and a reverse-locking design. The hooded cap was concealed in the cork, and Powell engraved his name and the location of his shop in a graceful ellipse on the lock nut. His name was also inked on the light brown cane ahead of the cork and protected with varnish. The grips and reel seats of the original Powell rods are so functional and classic in their beauty that many knowledgeable anglers wish that Walton Powell would resurrect them for the rods he is presently building under the original Powell patents.

Most vintage three-piece Powells are built of solid six-strip construction, and most two-piece designs use the semihollow technique that Powell patented in 1933. Powell concentrated on the longer fly rods suited to the northern California rivers. His Powell steelhead models measured nine and a half feet and weighed five and a half to six ounces, and his eight-and-a-half-foot trout tapers weighed four and a half to five ounces. The nine-footers varied from four and three-quarters to five and a half ounces, working smoothly into the butt section like most Powell actions, and taking six- and seven-weight lines. Powell built a few eight-foot rods weighing between four and four and a half ounces, and a seven-and-à-half-foot Powell is very rare. The craftsmen at Winston have refinished only two seven-and-a-half-foot, three-and-a-half-ounce Powells over the past twenty-five years.

Perhaps the finest Powell I have seen belongs to Douglas Merrick, the famous master rod builder at Winston. It was won by Merrick in a casting competition at San Francisco, and Merrick travelled north to Marysville to select the sticks personally in the Powell shop. The rod is on my work table as this is being written; its action is smooth and a little slow in true semiparabolic flexing, although Powell would have called it a regressive taper instead of a parabolic. It measures eight and a half feet and weighs four and a half ounces and is designed for a five-weight line. It is an exquisitely conceived rod, equalling any in the world.

Powell's place in the history of the art? Martin Keane observed thoughtfully at the Museum of American Fly-Fishing. *His cedar lamination and semihollow construction were not as structurally sound as the Stoner patents at Winston, but like the machinery in his Marysville shop they were entirely original—Powell was another step in the evolution of rodmaking, and a perfect example of the self-taught genius flowering in relative isolation.*

Edwin Powell died twenty-odd years ago, having lived well past eighty, and he worked with rods virtually until his death. His son Walton started working in his father's shop just after the First World War, at the fledgling age of seven years. Walton Powell is less than sixty, but already has almost a half century of experience on rodmaking, and with Tonkin cane available again Powell is building fine bamboo rods in the tradition of his father.

Walton Powell is using his father's patents and tapers, but has changed many details. His reel seats are full metal, machined from aerospace aluminum alloys, with a reverse-lock design and exposed grip slot. The handles are still the full-Wells shape, although less dramatically sculptured than the best work of his father. His wrappings are dark green on the Signature grade, and black silk on the Golden Signature series, based on the two-butt, two-tip section combination rods pioneered by Edwin Powell forty-odd years ago. Walton Powell has also adopted Swiss-type ferrules on his rods and is using an oxidized oil-and-gum finish found only on the Walton Powell product. Powell has strong ideas about rodmaking, as well as fly-fishing itself, and his combative character rises to argue over them at the slightest excuse. His temperament translated into cane has produced some excellent work, and Walton Powell already has a following of vocal partisans who insist that his rods are among the finest examples of the rodmaker's art. His father is a difficult act to follow.

I intend to carry on where my father left off, Powell insists vehemently. *His dreams and ideals shall not die, and the greatness of the Powell rod will continue to live and grow in my hands!*

It is Lewis Stoner who reigns as the acknowledged genius of the Pacific Coast rodmakers, and Stoner was the primal force behind the growth and reputation of the famed R. L. Winston Rod Company. Stoner was born in a small mining town near Walker Lake in Nevada in 1881. His father had travelled west from Kentucky during the Gold Rush, and ultimately settled at Hawthorne, where he worked as a millwright. History tells us that the elder Stoner had an exceptional reputation for making any kind of machinery, replacement part, or pithead frame needed in the Sierra Nevada mines.

The Stoner family moved briefly to California in 1893, returning to work in the mines at Reno nine years later. There was a complete woodworking shop, including a fine lathe and other machines, in a backyard garage during those Reno years. Lew Stoner continually puttered about there while his father worked, and he was a skilled woodworker before he was fifteen. Stoner tried college briefly and lasted only one half-hearted semester.

The world was too full of interesting things to do, Stoner explained to his friends, *and I finally left.*

He worked a few years in a shop that sold and maintained the Walker steam-driven automobiles and obtained one of the first chauffeur's licenses issued in California. Popular legend holds that Stoner started building rods to salvage his shares in a rod factory located in Oakland, across the bay from San Francisco, and that he began working full time in 1922.

His financial backer died a year later. Stoner returned to the tobacco business in San Francisco and spent several later years working in various machine shops. However, the bacilli of split-cane rod making had infected him, and he completed his design specifications for a power cutter that could mill the splines for bamboo rods in 1926. It was the same time that Hardy abandoned hand-milling for the accuracy of a mechanical cutter. Stoner returned to rodmaking in 1927, but the new company also dissolved in bankruptcy four years later. It seemed like the end of Stoner's dreams, but that same year Robert Winther provided a transfusion of fresh capital. With a contraction of Winther and Stoner, the famous R. L. Winston Rod Company was formed. Winston prospered in spite of the Depression, and when Robert Winther liquidated his interest in 1933, Stoner decided to leave the company name unchanged.

W. W. Loskot became a partner at the Winston shop the following year, and the partnership arrangement offers a revealing insight into the character of Lewis Stoner. Loskot was a young friend without capital and little knowledge of bamboo rodmaking and only limited experience in other business or manufacturing. However, Loskot did have a wife and children, and Stoner refused his suggestion of a half interest, although Stoner himself was Winston's primary asset.

We'll both draw a small salary to live on, Stoner insisted firmly to his fledgling partner. *Beyond that you've got a family to think about—you need extra money more than I do!*

Their partnership lasted twenty-odd years, until Loskot finally left Winston in 1953. Douglas Merrick had come into the Winston shop in 1945, shortly after his separation from the Air Corps, to purchase a new rod. Merrick had been a superb fisherman and tournament caster before the war. When the day ended, Merrick had left a better job to work at Winston, and he remains there today. Loskot sold his interest to Merrick in 1953, and the unique collaboration between Stoner and Merrick was probably the Golden Age at Winston.

These men were two of the finest artisans who ever split a culm, and with such giant talents in the shop, the fly rods that came out of the workrooms on Harrison Street in San Francisco were masterpieces. When Stoner died suddenly in 1957, Merrick became the future of the Winston Company, and that future was clearly in good hands. Winston advocates mourned the passing of Stoner, but they had come to understand that Merrick was virtually his equal in craftsmanship.

Doug was a better fly caster, Gary Howells explained, *and he has the finest instincts for selecting cane and modifying rod tapers that I have ever seen.*

That is high praise considering the fact that Howells himself has a rapidly growing reputation as a rodmaker of incomparable skills. Gary Howells started making rods in 1947, working in his cellar with a hand plane, micrometer, and planing block. His first rod took him more than a month to make and completely exhausted his supply of seasoned bamboo. Howells went to Winston for more culms and found both Stoner and Merrick unusually eager to help a beginner. With their encouragement, Howells began building a lot of rods, and the day finally came when Stoner told his young protégé that his latest effort was a rod that could stand with theirs in the Winston salesroom.

It was the proudest day in my life, Howells said.

Howells came into the Winston workshop the morning after Stoner died in 1957 and sat talking with Merrick for hours, reminiscing about Stoner over the years. The memory of the man filled the shop, and both remembered the slightly stooped figure bending over his lathes and cutters. His eyes had been bright and clear in spite of his age, and his hands were steady almost until the last. Except for his hearing aid, his skills and faculties remained almost unimpaired, and his honesty was as blunt as a granite headstone.

LEWIS STONER

Lew was one of a kind, Merrick finally said. *Why don't you come work with me now that Lew's gone?*

Howell started working the next day, performing the raw bamboo work like grading culms, splitting, sanding, node matching, gluing, and pressure wrapping. Merrick and Howells got along well together, and the younger man stayed at Winston thirteen years, finally graduating to perform the milling and fluting work itself. Many connoisseurs of fine rodmaking believe the rods they produced together after 1965 represent a second Golden Age in the exceptional workmanship at Winston.

It was a fine apprenticeship, Gary Howells remembers wistfully, *but at only forty dollars a week.*

Merrick recently sold his controlling interest in Winston to Sidney Eliason and Thomas Morgan, two well-known young western fishermen. However, Merrick remains firmly in charge of the rodmaking operations at Winston, and the quality of the workmanship remains unchanged. The quality of the Winston product begins with its supply of perfectly seasoned cane, and the Stoner patents for fluted hollow-built construction. That tradition of quality begins with Stoner himself, an artist who cared more for perfection than profit. Perhaps the best example is the unique Winston ferrules. Most manufacturers make ferrules of German silver, or even subcontract such machine work, but it was Stoner who discovered a silicon-copper and aluminum alloy called duronze. It is lighter, stronger than most steel, and highly corrosion-resistant. Winston ferrules are cut from bar-stock duronze, in spite of the fact that they are more expensive than nickel silver.

Winston rods are made from larger culms than most, giving them a denser layer of power fibers. The culms are split with a unique many-bladed wedge, its blades radiating like spokes from its striking hub. The eight-foot culms are first saw-cut to receive the multiple wedge, and then it is driven along each culm with a mallet. Eight to sixteen rough splines are formed with these Stoner wedges, depending on whether they are to be used in butts or tip sections. The raw splines are rough-milled first to approximate tapers, and then milled in the superb finish-cutter that Stoner first designed in 1926. Its maximum cutting tolerance is only .0075 of an inch, less than the thickness of the page on which this is printed. It is this Stoner milling machine that controls the taper, unique flexing behavior, action, and fine quality of every Winston split-cane rod.

After each spline is tapered properly, it is drawn through another special milling machine designed by Stoner to make the delicate U-shaped cut that removes the apex of the finished strip. Since the tips are completely structured of dense power fibers and are smaller than an average pencil lead in diameter, it is both foolish and impractical to flute them throughout their full length.

Such refinements represent an amazing evolution from the first bamboo section Stoner made to replace the middle joint of his broken Leonard in 1906, Gary Howells observes with admiration.

Each Winston ferrule is individually centered, bored, drilled, reamed, and hand-lapped for a perfect and permanent fit. It is tapered to rice-paper thinness at the transition point to the cane, and the cane itself is turned to match the exact internal dimension of the ferrule. It is driven home over a coat of special cement and pinned to secure it completely.

Winston reel seats are unique, and although many fishermen mistakenly believe they are merely a plastic unworthy of Winston rods, they are really quite expensive. The fillers are turned from a costly high-strength Bakelite that is almost totally free of expansion or corrosion. The reel fittings consist of a locking ring and hooded cap of jewel-polished aluminum. The smaller Winston rods are fitted with a slotted cork filler, lightweight butt cap, and sliding reel band. The cork grips are seated in cement, a single specie ring at each time, and lathe-turned to the Winston pattern of the popular half-Wells style.

DOUGLAS MERRICK

The ferrules, guides, and keeper rings are securely wrapped with special thread. The ferrules are completely wound in light beige silk with double wrappings at the transition to the rod. The guides are double-wrapped at the centers, and the tip guide is triple-wrapped. The silk is beige, to match the pale brown of the bamboo, and the tip windings are bright scarlet. Each wrap is coated with clear epoxy to set its color and secure it permanently before the final coats of varnish.

It was the cantankerous Peter Schwab who first badgered Winston into making its series of ultralight fly rods in 1931. *Leetle fellers,* Schwab cackled when he tried the first prototypes. *That's what these little bamboo beauties really are—they're leetle fellers!*

Lew Stoner found his term so descriptive that it is still used in the Winston catalogue today. These rods are intended only for the most skillful fishermen, and Stoner often refused to sell one to a customer whom he believed was unqualified to fish it properly. The tapers are designed for relatively short, accurate casts with great delicacy, demanding double-taper lines in three- and four-weight. There are four designs for a DT3F line: the five-and-a-half-foot Winston of one and three-quarters ounces, the six-footer of two ounces, the six-and-a-half-foot rod of two and one-eighth ounces, and the seven-foot taper weighing only two and a half ounces. The seven-foot Leetle Feller of two and five-eighths ounces and the seven-and-a-half-foot model of three and one-eighth ounces are both designed to handle a modern DT4F taper line.

Winston also makes a series of light trout rods designed for four- and five-weight lines. These rods are also remarkably delicate, but have slightly more muscle than the Schwab midge-sized tapers. Like the smaller rods, these models are assembled with a skeletal seat consisting of a butt cap and sliding ring, but the Winston screw-locking seat is available on order. It adds approximately half an ounce to the finished weight.

The light trout series includes two models designed for a four-weight taper, the five-and-a-half-footer of two ounces, and a six-foot rod weighing a quarter ounce more. The five-weight types include seven different lengths, weights, and actions: the six-foot model of two and a half ounces, the two six-and-a-half-footers of two and a half and two and three-quarters ounces, two seven-foot rods weighing two and seven-eighths and three ounces, and a brace of seven-and-a-half-foot tapers of three and one-quarter and three and a half ounces.

The Winston standard trout rods are perhaps the lightest for their length and power of any rods made, except for the similar tapers built by Gary Howells, since they use the hollow construction protected by the Stoner patent. They will fish with delicacy at relatively short ranges, yet handle surprisingly long casts with ease. These eight- to nine-foot rods are fitted with the locking Winston reel seats of black Bakelite and jewel-finished aluminum.

There is a single eight-foot Winston designed for a four-weight line, weighing three and five-eighths ounces. Three models are designed to take five-weight tapers, the eight-footers at three and three-quarters and four ounces, and an eight-and-a-half-foot rod of four and one-eighth ounces. There are two eight-and-a-half-foot Winstons for six-weight lines weighing four and one-quarter and four and a half ounces, and a third eight-and-a-half-foot, four-and-three-quarters-ounce taper for a seven-weight. The two eight-foot nine-inch rods weigh four and five-eighths and four and three-quarters ounces, and take seven- and eight-weight lines. The nine-footer is surprisingly delicate, weighing only four and seven-eighths ounces and taking a six- or seven-weight. Although they are rated as steelhead rods, the nine-foot Winstons of five, five and one-quarter, and five and a half ounces take eight- and nine-weight lines, and there are many expert anglers who like fishing them at maximum distances on big western trout rivers and reservoirs.

Winston rods are justly famous, and some remarkable visitors have come to their unpretentious little workshop in San Francisco. The late Crown Prince Axel of Denmark once appeared without previous fanfare, because he wanted to meet the people who had built his favorite sea-trout rod for fishing the Laerdal in Norway. But perhaps the best Winston story was told me last fall by a British fly-fisherman who has lived in San Francisco for many years. The displaced Englishman had always dreamed of owning a Hardy rod, savoring that dream since his boyhood in England. When he finally returned to London, he quickly travelled to the Hardy shop in Pall Mall.

What sort of fishing did you have in mind? the clerk asked.

Well, the transplanted British fisherman replied, *living in San Francisco, I've been fishing primarily for steelheads.*

And you want a steelhead rod from Hardy?

Yes, the fisherman said.

The finest steelhead rods in the world are made in San Francisco, the Hardy salesman smiled. *Winston makes them!*

Like other artists, the stature of a great rod builder is sometimes measured by the quality of his apprentices and the reputation they later achieve in their own workshops. Hiram Leonard is unquestionably the principal wellspring of such early influence on American split-cane rods, but the late Lew Stoner is also beginning to achieve some measure of fame in the work of his disciples. Douglas Merrick is one of the finest rodmakers alive, and the younger Gary Howells was strongly influenced by both men over the years. Howells left Winston to start his own small rod company in 1969, and his work has been highly successful.

Obviously, Howells explained last winter, *I wanted to build rods under my own name, but I also wanted to build rods with the lightness and power of a Winston or Powell—yet with the elegance and grace of a Payne.*

There is a rapidly growing circle of Howells' partisans willing to prove with their fly rods that he has succeeded in achieving his dream. Howells builds only two-piece rods. No better rods have ever been made, and their detailing is exquisite. His cane is tempered more than the Winston culms, giving his finished rods a slightly darker look. Since Howells is more fascinated with fishing minute flies on western spring creeks than with distance work on the steelhead rivers of Oregon and California, his delicate tapers are not carbon copies of the Winston specifications. His hollow-built butts flex smoothly and powerfully into the grips like the finest Winstons or Powells, but his tip calibrations are finer and better attuned to fishing tippets between .003 and .005. The ferrules use the same silicon-copper-aluminum alloy that Lew Stoner first used at Winston, machined by Howells himself from solid bar-stock. The males are hand-polished to tolerances of .0001, until they separate smoothly yet still pop like a bottle of fine California champagne.

Howells uses three grip styles on his rods. The tapers designed for three- and four-weight lines in the lengths under seven feet are fitted with a Payne-type fishtail grip, butt cap, and sliding reel band over a cork filler. The heavier seven- to eight-foot sizes feature the same elegant Payne-style grip with a reverse-locking reel seat. The reel cap is concealed in the grip, and although the screw-lock fittings resemble the Orvis Battenkill hardware, they are machined from slightly heavier aluminum stock and carefully jewel-polished. The hardwood fillers are turned from African zebrawood, which is richly colored and displays a darker graining than conventional walnuts. On the larger eight-and-a-half- to nine-and-a-half-foot Howells rods, the cork grips are a classic full-Wells style that echo the cork handles on the finest Powell rods.

The wrappings are exquisite, their medium brown silk and pale yellow tips a quiet homage to the work of Payne. The ferrules are completely covered in brown silk, each trimmed with a delicate wrap of yellow. Each guide is also secured with brown and yellow wraps, double-wrapped at the feet in the Winston style. The grip check consists of two delicate rings, a slim duronze band set inside an aluminum sleeve. The fly keeper is wrapped in brown, with red and yellow tips to identify its fluted hollow-butt construction. The trim wraps enclosing the Howells name, rod length, weight, and serial number echo the Winston silk windings, but the Winston wraps at the midpoint of the butt section are omitted in the Howells rods. The windings are set in clear epoxy before varnishing. Howells' finish is the equal of the Payne varnish work that most knowledgeable collectors agree is the finest rodmaking.

There's no secret about my finishes, Howells insists quietly. *Just four coats of the best varnish and a lot of work.*

Howells builds forty standard rod tapers, and because Howells insists on performing every operation himself, his production is limited to only one hundred rods a year.

The response has been beautiful, Howells continues, *and I'm always behind in my orders—like most rodmakers!*

There are three six-foot Howells rods. The one-and-three-quarters-ounce model and two-ounce tapers are designed for three-weight lines, and the two-and-a-quarter-ounce Howells takes a four-weight. There is a

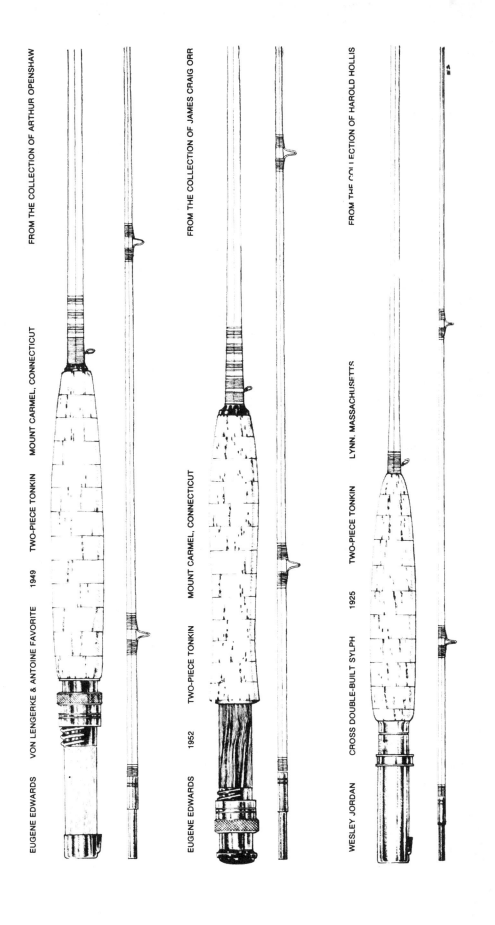

EUGENE EDWARDS   VON LENGERKE & ANTOINE FAVORITE   1949   TWO-PIECE TONKIN   MOUNT CARMEL, CONNECTICUT   FROM THE COLLECTION OF ARTHUR OPENSHAW

EUGENE EDWARDS   1952   TWO-PIECE TONKIN   MOUNT CARMEL, CONNECTICUT   FROM THE COLLECTION OF JAMES CRAIG ORR

WESLEY JORDAN   CROSS DOUBLE-BUILT SYLPH   1925   TWO-PIECE TONKIN   LYNN, MASSACHUSETTS   FROM THE COLLECTION OF HAROLD HOLLIS

delicate six-foot three-inch design, like the famous Young Midge, but the Howells version at two ounces is designed for a three-weight line. The six-and-a-half-foot rods weigh two and one-eighth and two and three-eighths ounces and are balanced by three- and four-weight tapers. There are five seven-foot models. The two-and-one-quarter-ounce taper takes a three-weight, while the two-and-a-half-ounce rod is a four-weight model of surprising versatility. The seven-footer at two and five-eighths ounces is designed for five-weight lines, like the slightly more powerful two-and-three-quarters-ounce Howells. The seven-foot, three-ounce taper takes a full six-weight line and has an action totally unlike the seven-foot three-inch, two-and-three-eighths-ounce rod for a DT3F. Howells makes six seven-and-a-half-foot models. The two-and-a-half-ounce version takes a three-weight too, and the three-ounce taper is a remarkable little fly rod designed for a DT4F. There are two versions for five-weight lines, excellent rods of three and one-eighth and three and one-quarter ounces, and the two seven-and-a-half-foot rods for six-weight lines are surprisingly powerful sticks of three and three-eighths and three and five-eighths ounces.

The eight-foot Howells rods are masterpieces of delicacy and versatility, starting with the three-and-a-half-ounce model for three-weight lines. The three-and-five-eighths-ounce rod is a delicate rod designed for a four-weight. There are two designed for five-weight lines, weighing three and three-quarters and three and seven-eighths ounces. There are also two eight-footers for six-weight lines, fine all-around tapers weighing four and one-eighth and four and one-quarter ounces. There is also an eight-foot three-inch model of three and three-quarters ounces for a four-weight line.

Howells makes seven eight-and-a-half-foot rods. The four-ounce model takes a four-weight line, while the four-and-one-quarter-ounce taper takes a five-weight. There is a second eight-and-a-half-foot rod of four and one-quarter ounces for a six-weight line, and the four-and-three-eighths-ounce rod takes the same line size. Both the eight-and-a-half-foot, four-and-a-half-ounce Howells and the four-and-five-eighths-ounce model take seven-weight lines. Howells adds an eight-and-a-half-foot, four-and-three-quarters-ounce rod designed for WF8F and WF8S fly lines, completing his eight-and-a-half-foot series of trout rods.

His big-water models include three rods of eight feet nine inches, weighing four and five-eighths to five ounces and designed for seven- to nine-weight lines. There are four nine-footers weighing from four and three-quarters to five and a half ounces which are balanced by seven- to ten-weight tapers. Howells also makes a powerful nine-foot three-inch rod weighing five and five-eighths ounces, designed for heavy-duty work.

Last year, Gary Howells built me a superb seven-and-a-half-foot, three-ounce rod with unique calibrations that is a joy in both fishing and casting. It is fitted with an exquisite African zebrawood filler and reverse-locking reel seat, and a slender Payne-style grip. It fishes beautifully, handling small streamers or sinking lines, as well as tiny flies on fragile .003 nylon. It has a supple poetry, and I have fished it happily from

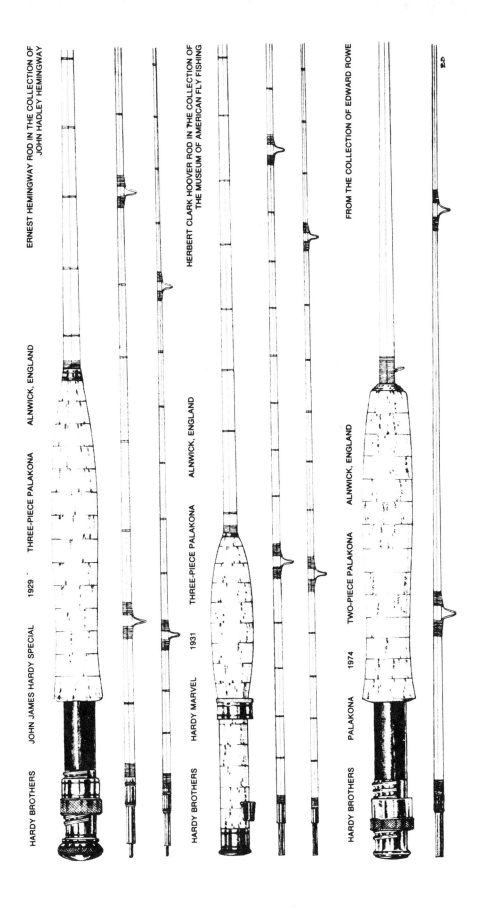

HARDY BROTHERS   JOHN JAMES HARDY SPECIAL   1929   THREE-PIECE PALAKONA   ALNWICK, ENGLAND

ERNEST HEMINGWAY ROD IN THE COLLECTION OF
JOHN HADLEY HEMINGWAY

HARDY BROTHERS   HARDY MARVEL   1931   THREE-PIECE PALAKONA   ALNWICK, ENGLAND

HERBERT CLARK HOOVER ROD IN THE COLLECTION OF
THE MUSEUM OF AMERICAN FLY FISHING

HARDY BROTHERS   PALAKONA   1974   TWO-PIECE PALAKONA   ALNWICK, ENGLAND

FROM THE COLLECTION OF EDWARD ROWE

the flats of Silver Creek in Idaho to the Longparish beats of the British Test, where it subdued a nymphing fish of almost five pounds.

It fished so beautifully that I called Howells after a particularly successful afternoon on the Brodheads, when our selective browns forced us to fish .003 and tiny flies.

It's incredibly lovely, I said. *It's so fine I've got to have the others.*

Well, Howells laughed, *we can make forty types.*

Yes! I groaned. *That's expensive!*

Like Powell and Stoner developing in isolation on the Pacific Coast, Goodwin Granger was a superb craftsman who designed and produced a series of fine split-cane rods in Denver. Granger began making his rods after the First World War, and these swelled-butt three-piece rod designs are still highly prized among both fishermen and collectors.

The first Goodwin Granger models were usually made with full-metal reel seats of German silver, with a reel hood soldered to the barrel and a sliding band. The Granger Champion had red silk wrappings tipped in black, and I have seen eight-footers weighing four and one-quarter ounces, eight-and-a-half-foot rods of four and three-quarters ounces, and powerful nine-foot rods of five and a half ounces. Granger probably also made a fine nine-and-a-half-foot Champion of six and a half ounces during these early years of his career. The Goodwin was a similar Granger assembled with a sliding-band seat of nickel silver, and jasper winds tipped in yellow silk, and was made in similar eight- to nine-and-a-half-foot tapers.

The Goodwin Granger Special had yellow silk windings, and introduced the German-silver screw-in locking seat typical of later Granger workmanship. It also introduced seven-and-a-half-foot calibrations weighing three and three-quarters ounces, and the early Granger Aristocrat with tan silk wrappings tipped in chocolate introduced an even lighter model of seven feet weighing only three and a half ounces. Later Aristocrats were simply wrapped in brown silk and changed the seven-foot model to a delicate two and three-quarters ounce design for four-weight lines. The early Granger De Luxe rods featured jasper windings tipped in yellow and embraced the full spectrum of Granger tapers from the seven-foot, two-and-three-quarters-ounce model to the nine-and-a-half-footer of six and a half ounces. These vintage Grangers have a smooth action typical of the later rods produced in his Denver workshop, and are exceptionally fine split-cane rods. Their character echoes both the Colorado climate with its low humidity perfectly suited to seasoning cane and building rods, and the exceptional craftsmanship of Goodwin Granger.

Granger was acquired by the Wright & McGill Company of Denver after the Second World War, and like the production work of Heddon and South Bend, their volume of split-bamboo rods continued to flow with surprising average quality. These Wright & McGill Grangers are clearly among the finest factory rods ever made. The production Grangers included six models at midcentury; and in these years the shop foreman was already William Phillipson.

The least expensive was the Granger Victory, with its orange and black variegated wraps tipped in black. It sold for only twenty-five dollars when I visited the Denver shop of Granger after the Second World War, and such rods are now worth four times that price on the secondhand market. The Granger Special was slightly more expensive, and was finished with wrappings of lime-colored silk. The Granger Aristocrat was next, its wrappings of tan silk tipped in chocolate. The Favorite was more expensive and had jasper winds tipped with pale yellow, plus yellow ornamental windings. The Granger De Luxe was still higher in price, and featured black and silver variegated windings tipped in bright yellow. It was the Granger Premier with its intricate yellow wrappings that held the top of the line, its price an astronomical seventy-five dollars in my boyhood years. These little Grangers were remarkable rods.

The first really good rod I owned was a fine eight-foot Granger Special with handsome lime green wrappings and a locking German-silver reel seat. It was the birthday rod my father gave me when I was seven years old. My recent book *Nymphs* includes these observations on that treasured boyhood companion:

> Granger built three-piece rods in those years, precisely wrapped in olive silk under a perfect finish of hand-rubbed varnish. The ferrules were exquisitely machined with elegant angular welts, and it had the hooded German-silver reel seat that ultimately became the Granger trademark. Its action was slow and smooth, perfectly matched with an HDH King Eider. It was years later that I came to appreciate fully its ability to fish a nymph, on the Grundbach in southern Germany.
>
> It is a pastoral reach of water. Mists shroud the mountains of the Allgäu in the mornings, and there are fine hatches. The little Grundbach is man-made, gathering several Alpine brooks into a half-mile millpond at Fischen-im-Allgäu. Its entire length measures about two miles from those duckpond beginnings to the bigger glacier-melt river below Oberstdorf.
>
> We fished it regularly after the war, finding good hatches of dark claret-bodied *Leptophlebias* almost every morning. Overcast mornings were best, with a light misting rain that hung in the valley. The trout rose steadily to these little mayflies, but one rainy weekend in September the fly hatches were unusually abundant.
>
> Good browns porpoised softly in the rain, working steadily in the weedy channels. The current was covered with mayflies, but we fished dry-fly imitations for several hours without results. Finally I tried a small nymph imitation, and took a fish promptly on the first cast.
>
> *They're nymphing!* I called to my father.
>
> Like most fly-fishermen these past few years, we were

intrigued with ultrasmall tackle, and I was fishing a two-ounce rod of six feet. It worked reasonably well on the trout working close along the bank, and those swirling to emerging nymphs along the weeds from forty to sixty feet out.

We took fish after fish that morning on nymphs, until I located a really large brown working in midchannel below the town. It was a cast of almost ninety feet, virtually beyond the little rod when I was waist-deep in the trailing weeds. There were conflicting currents between us that required mending the fly swing both up and down. It was a difficult problem.

Cast after cast worked out into the rain, and either fell short or dragged slightly just under the surface. The fish ignored me, porpoising every few seconds.

Finally I walked back to the car and put up the eight-foot Granger, stringing its undressed silk and selecting a ten-foot leader tapered to about .005. The worn little nymph that had taken fish steadily that morning was added to the tippet, and I waded back toward the trout.

The fish was still working. *Let it soak,* I thought, pressing the coiled leader into a layered bed of silt.

Finally, I was ready and the leader sank readily in the current. The nymph worked out and settled above the trout. The rod delivered the cast smoothly, without drying the fly, and it sank cleanly into a swing across the slow current above the fish. Raising the tip, I mended line and held the rod high as the fly reached its feeding station.

It porpoised lazily and I tightened. *He took it!* I shouted, *He took it and he's on!*

The trout finally surrendered, weighing almost five pounds and measuring twenty-four inches. The rod was perfect for reaching the bigger fish, and I continued to fish it when they were nymphing. Its length worked the fly swing perfectly in the cross currents among the weeds, its smooth action kept my nymphs wet and sinking, and its power was sufficient to reach fish beyond eighty feet easily.

The little Granger was a superb rod, and although it was stolen a year after our return from Europe, there are times when I still fish it happily in my mind.

It is interesting that a number of fine fly rods bearing the Granger De Luxe trademark were made after Wright & McGill decided to abandon split-cane rods for fiberglass. These rods use the standard Granger tapers and fittings, with some singular modifications to the reel seats, and adding the elliptical full-Wells grips that would later become the signature of a Phillipson rod.

The light seven- and seven-and-a-half-foot models were made with a skeletal cork grip, flaring slightly at the butt plate and holding the reel with a knurled sliding band and a fixed hood soldered to the grip check. These modifications reduced the seven-foot models to only three ounces and the seven-and-a-half-footers to three and one-quarter ounces. The larger De Luxe tapers were fitted with a skeletal locking seat, using the fixed and locking hoods with a walnut filler. These fittings also reduce the weight of the original Grangers. The eight-foot rod weighed three and three-quarters ounces, the eight-and-a-half-footer became four and a half ounces, and the nine-foot De Luxe weighed five and a half ounces. These rods were finished with bright scarlet windings, and in spite of their Granger markings, they are unmistakably early Phillipson products.

The most common is perhaps the Phillipson Peerless series, made with walnut screw-locking seats. Several lengths and weights were produced, starting with the seven-and-a-half-foot, four-ounce taper. The eight-foot Peerless weighed four and one-quarter ounces, the eight-and-a-half-foot model at five and one-quarter ounces was in great demand on my boyhood rivers in Colorado, and the nine-foot rod went a full six ounces. These rods were later made with full metal seats, in slightly heavier assembled weights. The functional and ornamental windings were black silk tipped with white. There were also a few rods made that paralleled the standard Peerless tapers. These models were called Peerless Specials, and their calibrations were designed to take a heavier line size in each corresponding weight and length in the Phillipson line.

The Phillipson Pacemakers were moderately priced bamboo rods incorporating these same tapers, ranging from seven and a half feet and four ounces to nine-foot, six-ounce models. These rods were fitted with brown and black anodized reel and lime winds tipped in yellow.

Perhaps the finest split-cane work was found in the Phillipson Paramount 51 series. These rods were made with both walnut and full-metal reel seat fittings and featured slightly more delicate tapers than the less expensive Phillipson grades. The seven-and-a-half-foot model weighed only three and a half ounces, the popular eight-footer weighed four ounces, the eight-and-a-half-foot Paramount was four and three-quarters ounces, and the nine-foot tapers weighed only five and a half ounces. These rods featured jasper winds tipped with yellow and black and had exquisitely smooth actions.

Phillipson also made several special models. The Phillipson Grand Teton was an eight-and-a-half-footer of five and a half ounces, designed to handle a seven-weight forward taper according to the specifications of the late Bob Carmichael. It had red silk windings and was made of impregnated cane. The Phillipson E. M. Hunter was named for the famous outdoor writer featured in the *Denver Post* during my boyhood years. His special Phillipson was a delicate eight-and-a-half-footer of only five and one-eighth ounces; it was designed for a six-weight double taper and had austere black-silk windings. Hunter once wrote a column about the fine sport that Frank Klune and I enjoyed on the Frying Pan in Colorado.

Phillipson also made a few two-piece rods. The best-known was probably the Phillipson Preferred; it was made in a seven-foot, three-and-one-quarter-ounce taper for four-weight lines and in a seven-and-a-half-foot version of three and three-quarters ounces for the same double taper in a four-weight. The Phillipson Preferred had functional wraps of chocolate silk and was a fine production fly rod of first quality bamboo.

It is intriguing that two exceptionally talented rodmakers also developed in Michigan before the Second World War. These men were Lyle Dickerson and the late Paul Young, two of the finest craftsmen ever to mill a strip of delicate Chinese cane.

Lyle Dickerson was born in Michigan in 1892, and grew up in his birthplace of Bellaire. He graduated from the local high school in 1909, and completed his degree from Hillsdale College on the eve of the First World War. During his high school years, Dickerson built a few bait rods from materials like ironwood and white cedar, but his fishing and rodmaking were interrupted by service with the fledgling Air Corps in France.

After the Treaty of Versailles, Dickerson returned to Detroit and started selling trucks and real estate. His interest in trout fishing was ultimately rekindled, and he spent a lot of time on the Au Sable, Pere Marquette, and Manistee. His work went fairly well until the Great Depression when everything collapsed and, like many others, Dickerson found himself without work. His frugal background had caused him to save enough cash to survive, and although there was almost too much time for fishing, Dickerson lacked decent tackle.

During the next few years, Dickerson found several months of work in Grand Rapids, and his association with the highly skilled furniture makers there ultimately led him into rod building. These artisans often spoke little English, having carried their guildlike skills from Europe, and Dickerson himself believes that it was their passion for quality that influenced his later craftsmanship. His Grand Rapids years also placed Dickerson in contact with furniture manufacturers like the late Ralph Widdicomb, who had a fishing cottage on the Pere Marquette. Combined with the automobile manufacturers and timber-cutting families from Bay City and Saginaw, these furniture makers formed the elite of the trout-fishing fraternity in Michigan. Dickerson did not know it, but these men would later become his principal customers.

When I finally decided to build bamboo rods, Dickerson explains, *I started searching the libraries for books that would tell me how they were made—and found absolutely nothing of help!*

Such books on rod building existed, but not in the jack-pine towns of northern Michigan, and the secrets of split-bamboo craftsmanship were closely guarded. The few men in Michigan who knew those mysteries worked for companies like Heddon, and their workshops were closed to outsiders. Rodmaking equipment was also unknown, although Dickerson did purchase a few culms of bamboo from Heddon, and he dismantled a few unserviceable rods to study their construction. Since they were

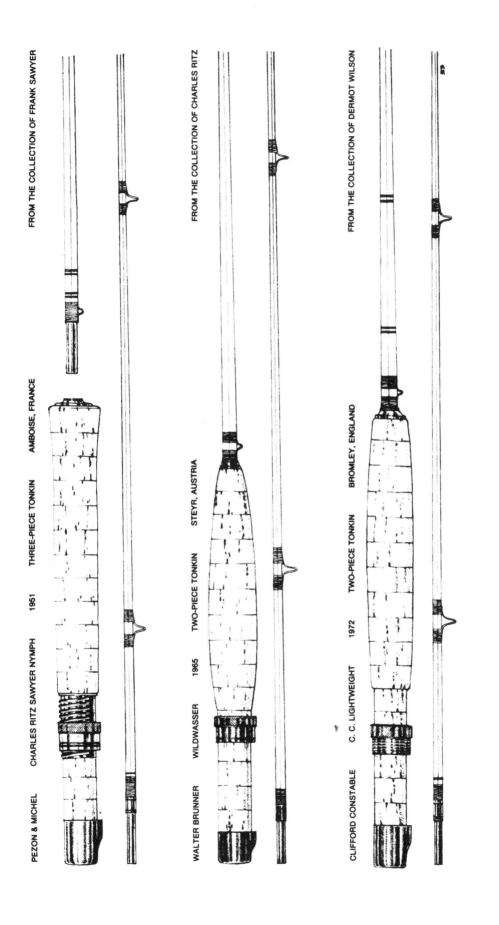

FROM THE COLLECTION OF FRANK SAWYER

FROM THE COLLECTION OF CHARLES RITZ

FROM THE COLLECTION OF DERMOT WILSON

PEZON & MICHEL   CHARLES RITZ SAWYER NYMPH   1951   THREE-PIECE TONKIN   AMBOISE, FRANCE

WALTER BRUNNER   WILDWASSER   1965   TWO-PIECE TONKIN   STEYR, AUSTRIA

CLIFFORD CONSTABLE   C. C. LIGHTWEIGHT   1972   TWO-PIECE TONKIN   BROMLEY, ENGLAND

laminated with fish-bladder glue, the strips could be separated by soaking them in water. Dickerson then borrowed some fine split-cane rods and took their calibrations, attempting to duplicate their tapers with homemade planing blocks and tools. Subsequent fishing on the Michigan rivers around Bellaire resulted in extensive modification of his tapers, and ultimately led to the unique performance associated with Dickerson rods.

Dickerson finally moved back to Detroit, and started building rods there in 1933. It was difficult work and there were few buyers of rods from a relatively unknown craftsman, even at the modest price of thirty-five dollars. It is surprising how few anglers could afford that cost, although the quality of the Dickerson rods rapidly became known in Michigan.

However, it was the late Ray Bergman who really launched Dickerson and his reputation for quality. Bergman travelled to Michigan to fish the Au Sable with his old friend Charles Merrill, and met Dickerson in Detroit. Before the success of *Trout,* Bergman had once been a tackle salesman for William Mills & Sons, and his favorite rod was a seven-and-a-half-foot Leonard of a relatively fast tournament-type action. Dickerson offered to match its action for Bergman, and took notes on its calibrations before the author travelled north.

Fast tapers were my meat, Dickerson explains.

Bergman was immensely pleased with his new Dickerson and expressed that pleasure in print, giving its maker his first taste of a national reputation. Dickerson rods later accounted for national dry-fly accuracy championships on two successive years; then the Second World War ended the shipments of bamboo. Dickerson soon exhausted his inventory of seasoned cane, and he stopped making rods until 1946.

Although solid fiberglass rods had just been introduced at Shakespeare, Dickerson was quickly swamped with back orders far beyond the capacity of a one-man shop, and his prices had climbed to sixty-five dollars. The Dickerson line included seven three-piece rods. His seven-and-a-half-foot, three-and-three-quarters-ounce and eight-foot, four-and-one-quarter-ounce rods were immensely popular, and his eight-and-a-half-footer of four and three-quarters ounces is one of the best all-around rods ever made. There were two nine-footers, weighing five and a half and six ounces, as well as a pair of nine-and-a-half-foot models of six and six and a half ounces. Two-piece Dickersons were made in five tapers. The beautiful seven-and-a-half-footer weighed three and a half ounces, and there were eight rod models of four and four and one-quarter ounces. The eight-and-a-half-foot rod weighed four and a half ounces and the nine-foot Dickerson in two-piece construction was a five-and-a-half-ounce rod for a seven-weight line. Dickerson used extremely large culms with extra heavy wall density, and his tapers magnified the quality of the cane into remarkably fast actions. The rods were fitted with the gun-blued ferrules typical of all Dickerson work and screw-locking seats with select American walnut fillers. His silk windings were chocolate with black ornamental tips.

Dickerson rods were unusually stiff and fast, with blue ferrules and a glass-perfect

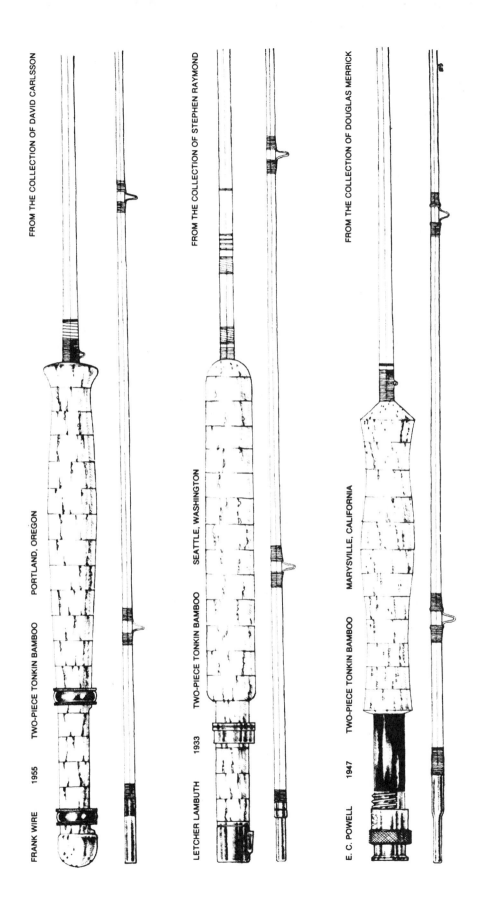

FRANK WIRE   1955   TWO-PIECE TONKIN BAMBOO   PORTLAND, OREGON

FROM THE COLLECTION OF DAVID CARLSSON

LETCHER LAMBUTH   1933   TWO-PIECE TONKIN BAMBOO   SEATTLE, WASHINGTON

FROM THE COLLECTION OF STEPHEN RAYMOND

E. C. POWELL   1947   TWO-PIECE TONKIN BAMBOO   MARYSVILLE, CALIFORNIA

FROM THE COLLECTION OF DOUGLAS MERRICK

finish, Martin Keane observed at his home in Connecticut, *and old masters like Lyle Dickerson never built anything that wasn't perfect inside or out!*

Dickerson tried to retire about fifteen years ago, but his customers continually badgered him into making repairs or replacing a broken tip section. Many loyal customers insisted that another Dickerson rod was absolutely critical to their future happiness, and Lyle Dickerson found old friends difficult to refuse. Finally he left Detroit, returning to his birthplace at Bellaire to escape his customers, and in his eighties, Dickerson is no longer working with bamboo. His lifetime production was slightly more than 2,000 rods and the three-piece specifications follow:

7½	761510	3¾ ounces	3 piece	HEH
8	801510	4¼ ounces	3 piece	HDH
8	801611	4½ ounces	3 piece	HDH
8½	861711	4¾ ounces	3 piece	HDH
8½	861812	5 ounces	3 piece	HCH
9	901711	5¼ ounces	3 piece	HDH
9	901812	5½ ounces	3 piece	HCH
9½	961812	5¾ ounces	3 piece	HDH
9½	961913	6 ounces	3 piece	HCH
10	102013	6¾ ounces	3 piece	HCH

Dickerson made the following two-piece rods:

7	7011	3¼ ounces	2 piece	HEH
7½	7312	3¾ ounces	2 piece	HDH
8	8013	4 ounces	2 piece	HDH
8	8014	4¼ ounces	2 piece	HCH
8½	8614	4½ ounces	2 piece	HDH
9	9015	5 ounces	2 piece	HCH

However, his knowledge and philosophy of rod building are still being translated into fine split-cane work. Dickerson has two disciples who have recently started building rods under their own trademarks. Perhaps the best known is Thomas Bedford, who was production manager for Kaiser automobiles and an ardent Dickerson fan almost thirty years ago. When Kaiser abandoned Detroit, moving its automotive operations to Argentina, Bedford was transferred to California in the Kaiser construction organization. Bedford himself finally retired near San Francisco and convinced Dickerson that his rodmaking equipment should continue making rods. Dickerson finally agreed, sold his tools and machinery and remaining stocks of bamboo to Bedford, and spent a month in California setting up a new rod-building shop there. The Bedford rods are painstakingly faithful to the

Dickerson specifications and quality, except that his work has added richly-patterned reel seat fillers of exotic hardwoods. His other disciple is Robert Summers, who learned his rodmaking skills from Paul Young, and now lives only forty miles from Dickerson at Traverse City. Summers has always admired both Dickerson and Young, and since Young died in 1960, his mentor these past years has increasingly become Lyle Dickerson.

Although I have never owned one of his rods, I once fished one of a matched pair of Dickersons that belonged to the late Gerry Queen of Detroit. It was fitted with a beautiful little Hardy St. George and a King Eider double taper, and I will never forget its ability to punch out big dry flies into a brisk headwind along a poetic reach of the Little South Pere Marquette in Michigan.

Arnold Gingrich has observed that Lyle Dickerson was the Guarnieri of the crisp dry-fly action, and if that analogy is accurate, it should be added that Paul Young was the self-taught Stradivari of the semiparabolic rod tapers—since like the legendary Italian violinmakers, both craftsmen lived and worked in the same city.

Paul Young was born in Arkansas in 1890, just forty miles west of Memphis. It was a curious beginning for one of the finest craftsmen in the history of American fly-fishing. Young was fishing at an early age, working set-lines for catfish in the Mississippi and fishing crayfish and minnows for smallmouth bass in the winding limestone valley of the White. Young hunted ducks in the bottoms too and was a skilled taxidermist long before he entered the University of Arkansas in 1908.

Following his graduation at Fayetteville in 1912, Young decided to travel extensively through Canada and the United States, sampling the fishing and shooting. His interest in taxidermy ultimately led to fly tying, and Young settled briefly in Minnesota in 1914, where he sold fishing tackle at Duluth and fished the nearby Brule and Namekagon in Wisconsin. After his marriage in 1921 to Martha Young, whose name graces one of his most popular rods, the couple moved to Detroit. His first job there was working as the principal taxidermist in the famous sporting goods store operated by Louis Eppinger.

Young opened his own tackle store on Grand River Avenue in Detroit only three years later, and his knowledge of trout fishing in both Michigan and Wisconsin soon made his shop a mecca for serious fly-fishermen throughout the Middle West.

Fishermen were always coming into the store, Martha Young explained last spring at her cottage on the Au Sable, *asking his opinion on their fly rods and other tackle problems.*

Young demonstrated his intuitive knowledge of actions and rod tapers quite early, and he soon began experimenting with eight and eight-and-a-half-foot lengths, modifying the fashionable wet-fly actions that still dominated American trout-fishing practice. Young built his first rods about 1923, using bamboo culms purchased from Cross in South Bend, and his experimental compound tapers first appeared in 1927.

Paul didn't know what to call those rods until John Alden Knight wrote about parabolic actions a dozen years later, Art Neumann told me along the North Branch last spring. *He called his first parabolics experimental actions—but he was playing with parabolic-type actions years before the famous bicycle accident in Paris that led to the Ritz Parabolics.*

The first rods made for sale were the Young Special series in both two- and three-piece designs. These were usually fast and medium-fast tapers. Four Young Specials existed as early as 1933, when Young himself published *Making and Using the Fly and Leader.* They ranged from a seven-and-a-half-foot, three-and-three-eighths-ounce dry-fly rod to an eight-and-a-half-foot, four-and-three-quarters-ounce model for a seven-weight line. There were two eight-foot Specials, weighing four and four and one-quarter ounces, and later Young added nine-foot tapers of five and one-quarter and six and a half ounces. The nine-foot Special 17 weighing five and one-quarter ounces was surprisingly delicate, taking a seven-weight double taper. The Special 18 weighing six and a half ounces was a three-piece powerhouse capable of handling big flies on a nine-weight line.

Later Young rods were all special designs, with each model made in a single length and taper. His little handbook lists seven experimental models, and it is possible to see future Young tapers in their prototypical specifications. One can anticipate the seven-foot, two-inch Driggs Special in the experimental seven-foot, two-and-three-quarters-ounce design listed in *Making and Using the Fly and Leader.* The popular Martha Marie of seven and a half feet, three ounces had its prelude in the experimental seven-and-a-half-foot, three-and-one-eight-ounce taper also listed in 1933. The versatile Parabolic 15 measuring eight feet and weighing three and three-quarters ounces has its unmistakable ancestry in an experimental design of eight feet, three and seven-eighths ounces that took a six-weight line. Its larger cousin, the powerful Parabolic 17 of eight and a half feet and five and a half ounces is clearly anticipated by the experimental nine-foot, five-and-a-half-ounce slow-action rod Young developed just before the Second World War. Most of his final tapers were fully worked out just after midcentury, along with his fittings and singular grip designs.

Young was a bit of a crank, Arnold Gingrich observes affectionately. *He was never interested in how his rods looked—only in the weight and taper and performance of their cane.*

Young was obviously a fanatic about weight. His specifications searched continually for new fittings and grips designed to shave mere fractions of ounces from their assembled weight, yet he always listed the weight of their bamboo separately. His fittings included a pair of free-sliding reel bands long before the Orvis Superfine made them popular, and he also developed a series of remarkable black-anodized aluminum ferrules. Although aluminum alloys lack the durability of German-silver fittings, these Young ferrules were surprisingly long-lived. Both the sliding-band and screw-locking reel seats on all Young rods are assembled with cork fillers. Young even experimented with unique skeletal grips in which a small gap existed between each cork ring to reduce weight beyond normal limits.

Young built few three-piece rods after 1952, and his midcentury bamboo work echoed the spiral-node construction pioneered by James Payne, a master craftsman Young greatly admired. His culms were flame-treated in a gas-jet ring devised by Young himself, tempering them to the threshold of brittleness to achieve exceptional power-to-weight ratios. The fingerprint of his aggressive flame tempering lies in the dark half-carbonized surfaces of the bamboo. His self-designed milling machine surpassed the tolerances that Young originally achieved with a hand plane and a skillfully worked Vixen file.

Young also developed a unique method of laminating and water-proofing the joints of his cane, using immersion in a secret process that involved synthetic resins. The exact resin formulas are still a closely guarded secret in the Young workshop at Traverse City. The bamboo sections laminated with this process are virtually as impervious to casting stress and water absorption as the fully impregnated rods made in the workrooms of Orvis and Sharpe's.

The Young pressure-wrap machine that laminated the freshly milled splines of bamboo was a surplus aircraft bomb hoist capable of achieving remarkable tensile forces. Young rods were so well bonded that their butt sections defied boiling, freezing in a block of ice, and multiple twisting without failure in their laminations. It is typical of Young rods that the heat-tempered cane itself fractures long before the glue faces fail.

Young is perhaps most famous for his Midge, an ultralight rod that has never been surpassed in its performance. It measures six-feet three-inches, weighs one and three-quarters ounces, takes a four-weight line, and its compound tapers make it radically different from any other rod of similar length and weight. Its calibrations are so unusual that its butt diameters are smaller, its ferrule is a size or two larger, and its tip guides are two or three sizes smaller than the specifications of comparable bamboo rods. The resulting performance is remarkable. The other so-called Midge rods are little power plants, capable of handling casts of eighty to ninety feet in highly skilled hands, but the Young Midge is utterly different. Most ultralight rods cannot handle fine tippets and often take surprisingly heavy lines in weight-forward tapers, but the Young version was designed for an honest DT4F combined with .005 and .006 tippets. Paul Young liked fishing tiny dry flies on the Au Sable in late summer, and his Midge was designed both for that delicate work and the highly specialized problems of the sophisticated fishermen on the limestone streams of Pennsylvania. The Midge made its debut as the lightest model in the Young line of a dozen different rods, and Young was greatly surprised to find his Midge commonly used for all-around trout-fishing problems. There were even light-tackle cranks like Arnold Gingrich who fished the Midge on salmon, and in his recent book *The Joys of Trout* he includes the following observations on Young and his remarkable Midge:

He rather grudgingly acknowledged its best-seller status in his line of rods, although for his own use he greatly preferred the Parabolic 15, an all-purpose rod of eight feet and three-and-three-quarters ounces weight, and regarded the use of a toothpick like his Midge for long casts and large fish as something of a perversion of its natural purpose. He testily refused either to claim, or even acknowledge, that he had pioneered the small rod craze, pointing out that the Leonard line had featured a Baby Catskill rod, at six feet and fifteen-sixteenths of an ounce, several years before he made his first Midge, and that William Mills & Son had even advertised it as the world's smallest fly rod.

Admitting that his Midge was clearly out of the baby rod class, which he considered about as practical as a wet noodle, he still contended that it was being put to uses for which he neither intended it nor considered it suitable, and he was both amused and puzzled when he saw the term "Midge Rod" come into generic use, categorizing all split-cane rods with light mountings, measuring under seven feet and weighing two ounces or less, and thus outgrow its original application to a specific model in his line of rods.

The Driggs Special is a seven-foot, two-inch rod weighing two and seven-eighths ounces and designed as a powerful little compound taper for fishing the brushy little river in northern Michigan for which it was named. Paul Young conceived it as a relatively short rod, with both the delicacy to fish 5X tippets and the power to turn a heavy fish away from logjams and brushpiles. It was a beautiful little Driggs that I found Martha Young using on the Au Sable above Stephan's Bridge this past season in Michigan, casting a long and skillful line in the April sunshine.

The Perfectionist is a superb seven-and-a-half-foot, two-and-five-eighths-ounce rod Young designed for general fishing with relatively fine tippets, its slender tip calibrations taking a four sixty-fourths of an inch tip guide. It has become the favorite rod of the celebrated Charles Fox in recent years, ever since he spent an evening with a Perfectionist of mine along Letort Spring Run. It is difficult to find a rod that will reach out ninety feet and fish a .004 tippet, but a man like Charles Fox can utilize its full spectrum of qualities, and its status as his favorite rod is a fine vote of confidence. The Perfectionist takes a DT4F in perfect equilibrium, and is one of the finest fly-rod tapers ever designed in bamboo.

Paul Young was a restless artisan, and his lifetime production of rods was relatively small. His work was never entirely limited to his standard tapers, so unusual variations on his basic themes are relatively common. Perhaps the finest of these special tapers was a variation of the Perfectionist called the Princess. It was a Perfectionist with a radically regressive taper, working in almost flat calibrations from the stripping guide into the grip assembly. Six of these Princess rods were built, measuring seven feet,

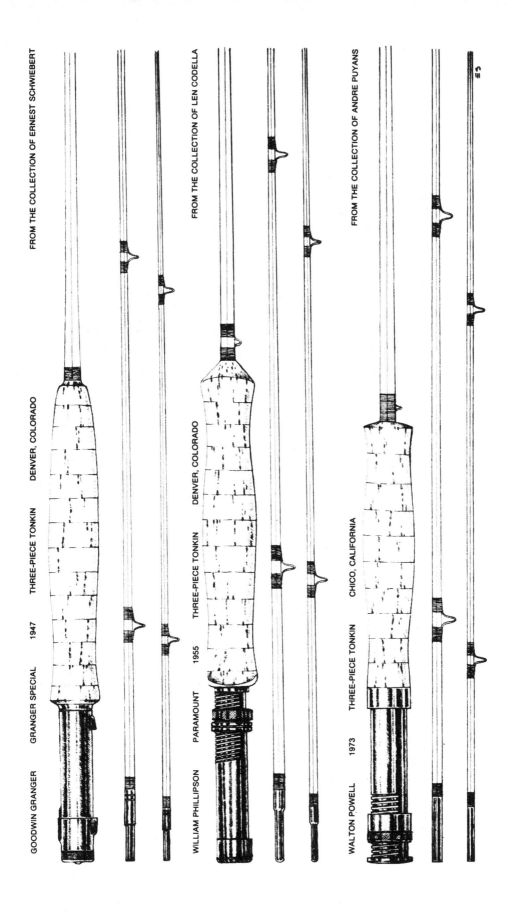

FROM THE COLLECTION OF ERNEST SCHWIEBERT

GOODWIN GRANGER   GRANGER SPECIAL   1947   THREE-PIECE TONKIN   DENVER, COLORADO

FROM THE COLLECTION OF LEN CODELLA

WILLIAM PHILLIPSON   PARAMOUNT   1955   THREE-PIECE TONKIN   DENVER, COLORADO

FROM THE COLLECTION OF ANDRE PUYANS

WALTON POWELL   1973   THREE-PIECE TONKIN   CHICO, CALIFORNIA

weighing two and three-quarters ounces, and taking a four-weight line. The rods were fitted with skeletal reel seats and wrapped in black silk, and were milled and assembled in 1958. These six rods have become highly prized collectors' items.

During the same production run, there was a single set of exceptional sticks that Young assembled into a unique seven-and-a-half-foot Princess for his own battery of rods. It was assembled with different tips, a standard feature with the larger Parabolic 15. The delicate tip had a four sixty-fourths of an inch top, making the rod weigh two and a half ounces, and the four and a half sixty-fourths of an inch tip added an eighth ounce to that assembled weight. Fitted with the light tip, it will readily handle .003 tippets and tiny flies. The heavier tip will easily punch a small streamer eighty feet if that kind of power is necessary. With its slow butt tapers and different tip sections, it is an extremely versatile rod for small streams and shy trout. This unique seven-and-a-half-foot Princess found its way into my hands after Young's death, and it is a treasure fitted with a reverse sliding-band reel seat assembly of my own design, along with a slender cigar-type handle. John Waller Hills observed that once in his life each fly-fisher encounters a rod so perfectly suited to his personality and temperament and physical skills that it becomes a part of him. Thus far in my fishing odyssey, the seven-and-a-half-foot Princess passed on to me from the collection of its maker is that rod—it is that exquisitely poetic balance of delicacy and power that comes alive in the hands.

Young designed another seven-and-a-half-foot standard model called the Martha Marie, named for the girl he married in 1921. It is a brisk three-ounce rod designed for dry-fly work on relatively large rivers, its butt power capable of handling bucktails while its tip calibrations are subtle enough to accommodate .005 and .006 tippets.

Paul Young himself loved the Parabolic 15. It is a remarkable eight-foot design, made with separate dry-fly and distance tips. The fine tip is fitted with a four and a half sixty-fourths of an inch top, while the heavier tip takes a five sixty-fourths top guide. The Parabolic 15 weighs three and three-quarters ounces with its dry-fly tip and a full four ounces with the distance taper. Most of the production models were made with a parabolic taper of surprising power, although many were also assembled with a slow-action butt in a rod called the K. T. Keller, honoring a past board chairman of the Chrysler Corporation. My own collection includes rods of both specifications, and I prefer the radical tapers of the Keller variation. It is probably the finest all-around trout rod in my collection, fishing both 6X tippets and handling big 1/0 Muddlers on western rivers at ranges beyond ninety feet. It has fished such large flies at such distances on rivers like the Big Hole and Yellowstone and Snake. It also once took a magnificent eight-and-a-half-pound rainbow on a small spring creek in Jackson Hole, fishing an ant imitation in the surface film with a tippet of .005. It is a superb fly-fishing tool.

Many partisans of the Young split-cane rods believe that the Parabolic

PAUL YOUNG

17 is the finest big-water trout rod ever built, and like the smaller Parabolic 15, it was made in two radically different variations. The standard model is eight and a half feet and five and a half ounces, taking an eight-weight line, and I have another experimental parabolic of this type that once belonged to Young himself. It has three separate tip sections. The dry-fly tip has calibrations taking a five sixty-fourths of an inch top, the delicate wet-fly tip has a four and a half sixty-fourths top, and the powerful distance tip takes a six sixty-fourths tip fitting. This rod also has an extra-slow butt taper, with little difference between the calibrations at the stripping guide and the grip. Its compound tapers are quite radical, displaying rather complex rhythms under stress. Its timing combines an ability to handle long casts easily, as well as sufficient tip delicacy to protect a 5X tippet. The distance tip will load and deliver a WF9S forward taper more than a hundred feet.

Most customers found this experimental Parabolic 17 too radical in its timing, but Paul Young loved its difficult character. It had been fished with commitment and care since its birth in 1952, and he had planned to use it during our meeting on the South Branch of the Au Sable the week he suffered his final heart seizure. His widow subsequently sent this unique Parabolic 17 to me on the eve of my first odyssey to Argentina.

Paul always wanted to fish Patagonia, Martha Young explained in the brief note that accompanied the rod. *You should fish it for him on those rivers down there—like he always dreamed!*

Young also made a number of bigger parabolics, remarkable rods almost too powerful for trout fishing. The Texan was an eight-and-a-half-foot, five-and-seven-eighths-ounce rod primarily designed for big poppers and hair frogs. The Bobby Doerr was a nine-foot, six-ounce parabolic named for the famous Boston second baseman at midcentury, who was a highly skilled fisherman on both steelhead rivers and bonefish flats. The Parabolic 18 was a similar rod of nine-feet, six and a half ounces designed for a nine-weight line. Young also made a number of Parabolic 19 models, nine-footers of six and a half ounces designed for ten-weight lines. The Powerhouse was a nine-and-a-half-foot, six-and-three-quarters-ounce rod balanced by eleven-weight tapers and was originally designed for tarpon, and I have used mine on the heavy salmon rivers of arctic Norway.

Paul Young was perhaps the most experimental craftsman in the history of the split-cane rod, and his tapers were much more radical than the compound tapers of Garrison or Ritz. Arnold Gingrich—who perhaps owns more Young rods than anyone—observed in his *Joys of Trout* that Paul Young was venerated in the last ten years of his life as the ultimate master of the Midge-size rod, and that he was a near-legendary cult figure at his death. After Young died in 1960, his rods were made by his son John Young and Robert Summers, who had worked closely with Young during the last four years of his life. John Young had displayed exceptional talent for split-cane work at an early age.

Jack will carry on, Paul Young always said thoughtfully in his workshop. *Jack is the one who was born with bamboo in his blood.*

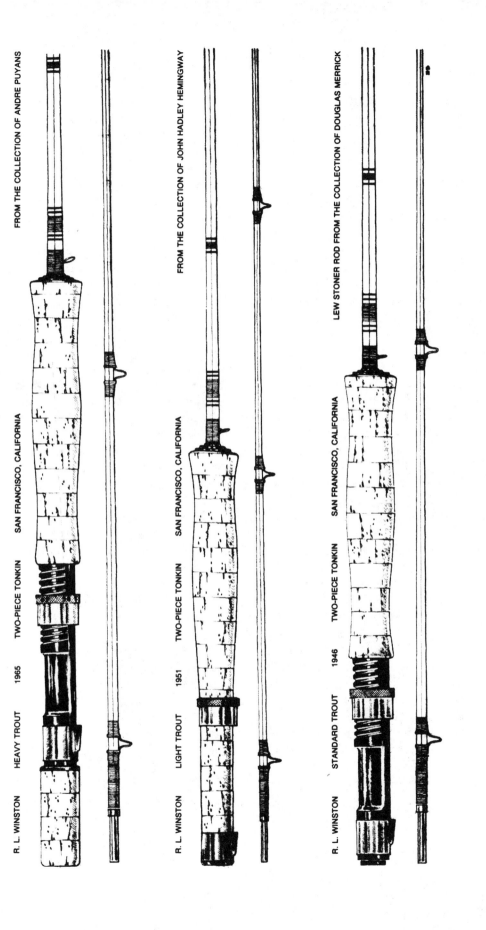

R. L. WINSTON   HEAVY TROUT   1965   TWO-PIECE TONKIN   SAN FRANCISCO, CALIFORNIA   FROM THE COLLECTION OF ANDRE PUYANS

R. L. WINSTON   LIGHT TROUT   1951   TWO-PIECE TONKIN   SAN FRANCISCO, CALIFORNIA   FROM THE COLLECTION OF JOHN HADLEY HEMINGWAY

R. L. WINSTON   STANDARD TROUT   1946   TWO-PIECE TONKIN   SAN FRANCISCO, CALIFORNIA   LEW STONER ROD FROM THE COLLECTION OF DOUGLAS MERRICK

Martha Young retired from active participation in the Young Company in 1969, and when the Southfield store was sold for the right-of-way new turnpike, John Young and Robert Summers moved the firm north to Traverse City. Young rods are still made there under the supervision of John Young, Robert Summers having since left to build bamboo rods under his own name. Just as Hiram Leonard and Lewis Stoner can be judged in terms of the craftsmen they groomed, Paul Young has left his legacy in the skilled hands of John Young and Robert Summers. Michigan has not had such a pair of artisans since both Paul Young and Lyle Dickerson were actively building rods at midcentury.

Summers started his apprenticeship with Paul Young in 1956, filing nodes and stripping the pressure wraps from freshly glued rod sections. Later he graduated to hand-scraping and filing the sticks under Young's watchful eye. It was routine work, but it was exacting and important. His work passed muster, since Summers received a pay raise after a few weeks.

Those years with Paul Young were happy, Summers told me at the Priest cottage on the Au Sable. *There were always fish stories and I was learning something I already loved, and sometimes a famous fisherman visited the shop.*

Summers left the Young workrooms briefly to work in a toolmaking shop in Detroit, attracted by the higher wages available there. It was interesting work, but Summers was already hopelessly infected with bamboo fever, and he soon rejoined Young in his rodmaking shop.

People love rods! he explains. *Not machine parts!*

When the Young rod-building shop moved north to Traverse City, Summers moved with it, and he soon became friends with Lyle Dickerson in Bellaire. Summers travelled regularly to visit Dickerson, talking about split-cane construction and examining his rods. Summers decided to start his own company in 1972, when he acquired the rodmaking machinery that had belonged to the late Morris Kushner, one of the finest amateur rod builders in the United States. Kushner was a retired mechanical engineer who had founded his own tool company and later built bamboo rods as a hobby. His stock of seasoned cane was sizable, and after adding new carbide cutters to the Kushner milling equipment, Summers started building bamboo rods of his own.

His first rods looked predictably like the Young designs, but in recent months the Summers rods have begun to evolve a character and quality of their own. His tapers are compound formulas that echo the work of his patron and principal tutor, but Summers has come to prefer the delicate tips and deliberate casting rhythms of the slower actions. His fittings still have echoes of Young, but his rods now use the reverse-locking seats found in the work of builders like Powell, Gillum, and Payne. His skeletal seats echo my own designs with a single reel band exposed and a second band concealed in the grip. It is simple and functional in its conception. The sliding band is below the reel. The system is self-tightening with the weight of the reel working down into the sliding ring, much as the head of an axe is seated with its own inertia.

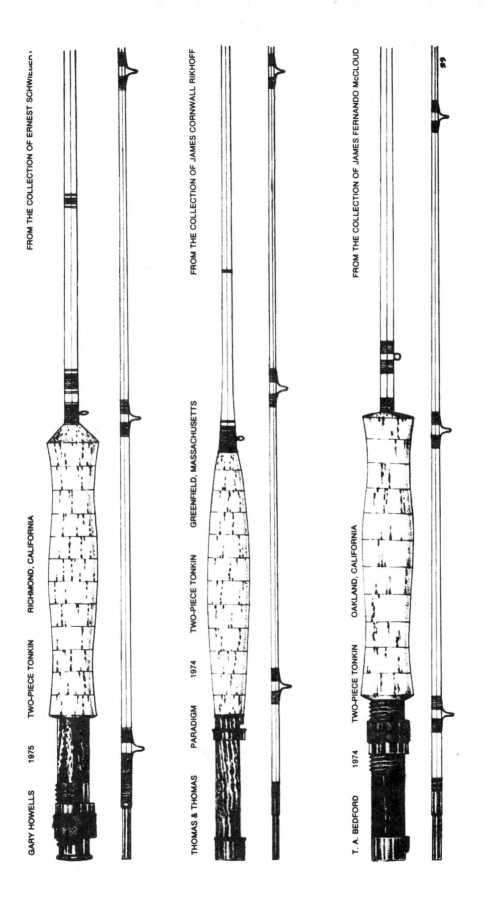

GARY HOWELLS   1975   TWO-PIECE TONKIN   RICHMOND, CALIFORNIA

FROM THE COLLECTION OF ERNEST SCHWIEBERT

THOMAS & THOMAS   PARADIGM   1974   TWO-PIECE TONKIN   GREENFIELD, MASSACHUSETTS

FROM THE COLLECTION OF JAMES CORNWALL RIKHOFF

T. A. BEDFORD   1974   TWO-PIECE TONKIN   OAKLAND, CALIFORNIA

FROM THE COLLECTION OF JAMES FERNANDO McCLOUD

The Little Manistee rods measure six and six and a half feet and weigh one and three-quarters and two ounces. They are assembled with cork reel seats and tiny grips and are slightly less powerful than the Young Midge or Driggs Special, ideally suited to small rivers and fine tippets. The Ontanagon series includes two seven-foot rods of two and one-quarter and two and five-eighths ounces, and seven-and-a-half-footers of two and a half and two and three-quarters ounces. The Pere Marquette series is fitted with a reel-seat filler of rosewood or Macassar ebony, using a single reel band of jewel-finished aluminum. It includes rods of seven and a half feet, two and three-quarters ounces and three and one-eighth ounces, eight-foot rods of four and four and one-quarter ounces, and an eight-and-a-half-foot design weighing four and three-quarters ounces. The Au Sable series is fitted with reverse-locking seats in brightly polished aluminum over fillers of exotic hardwoods. It includes a seven-foot rod of three ounces, two seven-and-a-half-foot models of three and one-quarter and three and five-eighths ounces, plus two eight-foot designs of four and one-quarter and four and a half ounces, and an eight-and-a-half-footer of five and one-quarter ounces. The Summers Big Manistee rods include an eight-and-a-half-foot, five-and-three-quarters-ounce model and a smooth nine-foot, six-ounce rod of surprising delicacy and power. The grip designs are modeled after the functional handles developed by Everett Garrison, and although there are traditional echoes in his work, the Summers rods have unmistakably evolved a unique character of their own.

Although most anglers are familiar with the work of famous eastern craftsmen like Gillum and Garrison, there are a number of other artisans who have built superb rods over the years. The roster includes familiar names like Uslan and Halstead, as well as much younger men like Baird Foster, Charles Jenkins, Walter Carpenter, Samuel Carlsson, and Minert Hull. These less famous craftsmen are artisans of remarkable skills and exceptional promise.

Nathaniel Uslan remains the principal disciple of Robert Crompton and his theories of five-strip construction, although Uslan no longer has his shop just outside New York at Spring Valley. Uslan was one of the first craftsmen to suffer from the shortages of first-quality Chinese cane that began in 1939. Uslan stopped making rods altogether in 1958, and moved to the outskirts of Miami, where he has been assembling fiberglass rods for salt-water fishing and machining German-silver ferrules and fittings for other makers. With the improving supplies of Tonkin cane, Uslan has resumed building his unusual five-strip bamboo rods in two-piece designs of seven to eight and a half feet.

The careers of Halstead and Gillum were curiously intertwined after Halstead left Leonard, where he had worked making reel seats and ferrules. George Halstead had little or no experience at milling cane, while Gillum was a genius at carpentry and precision metalworking and cabinetmaking, who had learned to build split-cane rods through a friendship with Eustis Edwards, one of the original Leonard apprentices at Bangor.

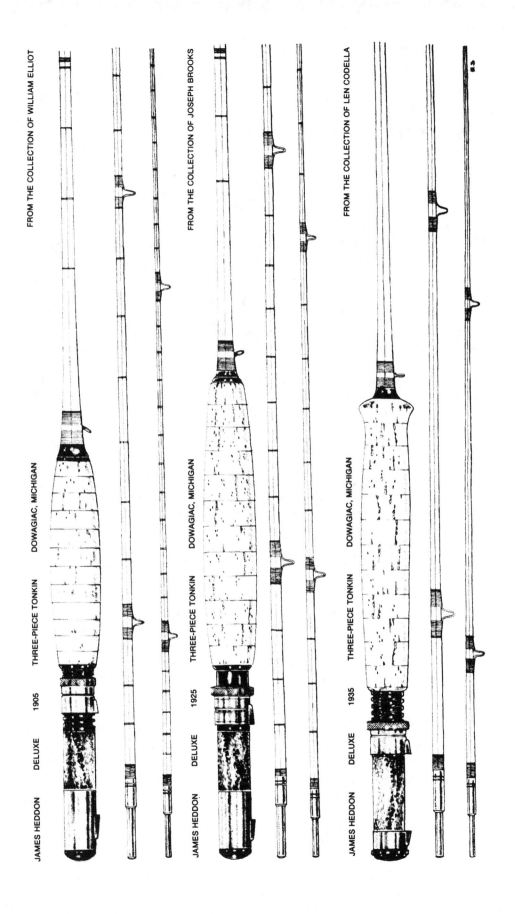

FROM THE COLLECTION OF WILLIAM ELLIOT

JAMES HEDDON   DELUXE   1905   THREE-PIECE TONKIN   DOWAGIAC, MICHIGAN

FROM THE COLLECTION OF JOSEPH BROOKS

JAMES HEDDON   DELUXE   1925   THREE-PIECE TONKIN   DOWAGIAC, MICHIGAN

FROM THE COLLECTION OF LEN CODELLA

JAMES HEDDON   DELUXE   1935   THREE-PIECE TONKIN   DOWAGIAC, MICHIGAN

Halstead once entertained the hope of a rodmaking partnership with Gillum, machining the ferrules and fittings, while Gillum made the rod sections. The partnership actually started at one point, but Halstead was late in delivering the ferrules, and when they finally arrived, Gillum was furious to find the ferrules were not completed. The welts, water stops and plugs were shipped loose, mixed in with the nickel-silver tubing for the male and female ferrules.

Gillum never forgave George, Harry Darbee told me one night along the Willowemoc. *It was the end of the partnership!*

George Halstead lived at Brewster, almost fifty miles above New York, with Gillum working nearby in Connecticut. Halstead made a few rods of surprisingly good parabolic action in his own shop, with his own ferrules and fittings. The bamboo workmanship was good, and the Halstead actions were similar to several Leonard tapers, although Halstead failed to assemble his rods with first-rate adhesives. Many of his rods separated along their glue faces, both in fishing and exposure to excessive moisture, and few survive today. Halstead died at a relatively young age, and his skills and rod specifications never reached their full potential.

Harold Steele Gillum had learned the rudiments of split-cane construction from Eustis Edwards, but his relatively close friendship with James Payne had a considerable influence on his later work. Some of his fly rods even include modified Payne ferrules and other fittings, and the character of a typical Gillum betrays an unmistakable admiration for the example of Payne.

Gillum was born at Ridgefield, just across the Connecticut line from Halstead's workshop in New York, at the turn of the century. His interest in fly-fishing came from his friendship with the older Edwards, but his later rods came closer to the dry-fly tapers developed in the Highland Mills shop of James Payne. Although the design and fittings of the Gillum rods varied extensively with his moods, his total production approached a thousand rods, with about eighty to ninety milled and assembled in his best years. Gillum began laminating his cane strips with an adhesive formula supplied by George Halstead, and when several of his first rods failed, he took a sample of the Halstead glue for precise analysis to a friend who was a chemical engineer.

It turned out to be pretty cheap stuff, Harry Darbee laughs about their glue-formula quarrels. *It was a hide glue without all of the animal fats taken out, and Pinky was furious—Pinky admitted there were a lot of things you could use for gluing rods, but never forgave Halstead for a glue that was part lard.*

Gillum never quite standardized his tapers or fittings, although the heavy locking nut that was engraved with his name and simply identified him as the maker, was pretty much a trademark. His early rods were often fitted with ferrules made by George Halstead, and after Halstead died he made a large number of rods using the old Super-Z ferrules. Some Gillum rods even have Payne ferrules, and finally Gillum turned to making his ferrules himself. Two-piece Gillums of seven feet, three ounces are the

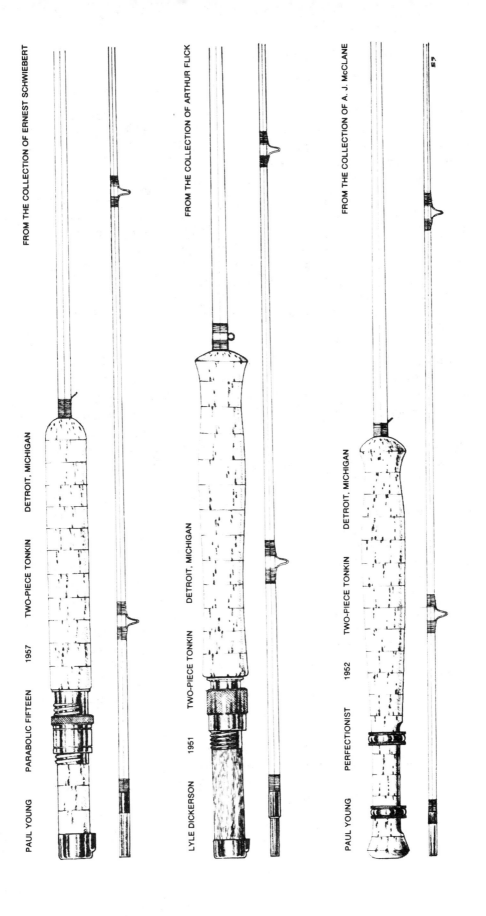

FROM THE COLLECTION OF ERNEST SCHWIEBERT

PAUL YOUNG PARABOLIC FIFTEEN 1957 TWO-PIECE TONKIN DETROIT, MICHIGAN

FROM THE COLLECTION OF ARTHUR FLICK

LYLE DICKERSON 1951 TWO-PIECE TONKIN DETROIT, MICHIGAN

FROM THE COLLECTION OF A. J. McCLANE

PAUL YOUNG PERFECTIONIST 1952 TWO-PIECE TONKIN DETROIT, MICHIGAN

smallest examples I have seen, except for two ōr three exhibition rods made for Ellis Newman, and there are many two-piece Gillums of seven and a half, eight, and eight and a half feet in the collections of men like Harry Darbee and Arthur Walker. These are probably the vintage lengths for the two-piece Gillums, although there are also nine- and nine-and-a-half-foot tapers as heavy as seven and a half ounces. Gillum also made a few rods that were sold under the trademark of the Daly Shotgun Company, although these were largely big two-piece rods designed for salt-water work. There were also a number of three-piece Gillums made, mostly rods of eight and a half, nine, and nine and a half feet. Most Gillum rods were assembled with the reverse-locking seats of the style perfected by James Payne, although Gillum made his wood fillers of both walnut and mahogany, arguing that his mahogany fillers were lighter than cork. Gillum also made a few rods with a conventional butt cap and locking-seat hardware.

Gillum refused to heat-temper his bamboo except to straighten the culms or milled sections, giving the cane a slightly slower action that he compensated for in his unusual tapers. His rod actions tended toward a relatively stiff butt, its flexing node a few inches above the grip check, and a fast tip that combined delicacy with surprising power. The late John Atherton, whose slim book *The Fly and the Fish* is an American classic, had two exceptionally fine Gillums that he loved on his Battenkill between Shushan and Arlington. The first was a seven-footer of only two and three-quarters ounces that Gillum had designed for a DT4F and late summer work. Atherton's favorite Gillum was an eight-footer, weighing three and seven-eighths ounces and balancing five-weights.

After his sorry experience with natural adhesives, Gillum turned to his friend Everett Garrison for advice. Garrison had the technical background to understand that a rod heats slightly in casting, as its molecular structure is flexed, and that during very hot weather the conventional fish and hide adhesives could reach temperatures that softened their laminations and reached the threshold of failure. Such adhesives are heated approximately 130 to 150 degrees during rod-assembly, and in casting during 100-degree weather, a rod can gradually become soupy and suffer permanent damage. Synthetic adhesives can withstand more than 300 degrees without structural denigration, a temperature range well beyond any thermal problems encountered in fishing. Garrison was the first to employ the modern synthetics for bonding his rods, preferring a black adhesive that is clearly visible as a razor-slim line in the finished sections, and Gillum quickly became a convert to his theories. Although his bamboo was darker, approaching the rich patina of a Payne, Gillum rods display the same cobweb-fine seam of black glue found in the pale sections of a Garrison. These synthetic glues are slightly less flexible than the conventional fish and hide adhesives, but they retain their exceptional strength and resilience for many years, and they are virtually impervious to moisture or heat.

Although the Gillum rod was not the equal of the comparable Paynes in their overall quality of fittings and workmanship, and his cork grips are

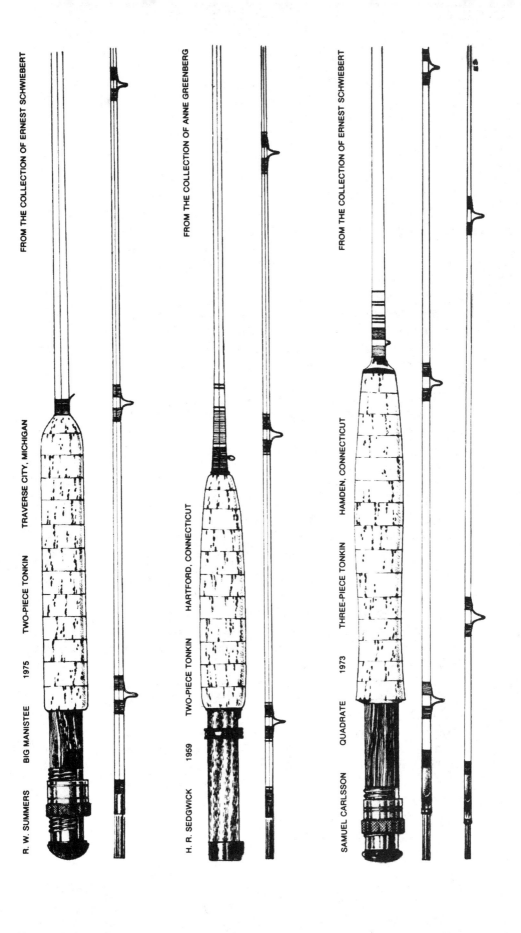

R. W. SUMMERS   BIG MANISTEE   1975   TWO-PIECE TONKIN   TRAVERSE CITY, MICHIGAN   FROM THE COLLECTION OF ERNEST SCHWIEBERT

H. R. SEDGWICK   1959   TWO-PIECE TONKIN   HARTFORD, CONNECTICUT   FROM THE COLLECTION OF ANNE GREENBERG

SAMUEL CARLSSON   QUADRATE   1973   THREE-PIECE TONKIN   HAMDEN, CONNECTICUT   FROM THE COLLECTION OF ERNEST SCHWIEBERT

often somewhat poorly finished, Gillum was probably more willing to experiment with his tapers than many of his contemporaries. Gillum partisans as well known as Harry Darbee, Arthur Walker, and John Atherton form an impressive jury of men who believe their Gillum rods are matchless weapons. Atherton praised Gillum highly in *The Fly and the Fish*:

> Every angler has his own favorites and he will undoubtedly find, at some time in his career, which is best for him. Whether or not we agree with the English anglers in their choice of rods, we must admit that with their fishing, the winds so constantly present on their streams, and the necessity of casting from the bank rather than from the water, an entirely different type of weapon is clearly called for.
>
> Rather than condemn it all as useless in America, we should profit by some of their discoveries. There are occasions here when the longer, softer rods might be an advantage. Wherever the delivery should be very delicate, or where a long, light cast is essential, our short powerful rods are sometimes unable to give us what we want. And particularly if one fishes where wind is a governing factor, it can be very discouraging to try to achieve the proper results with a rod inadequate for the job.
>
> Of course, for the man who can afford a large battery of rods of every length, weight and description, it is not difficult to find something to take care of the unusual condition. But for the one- or two-rod man, it is something else again. If I could only have a single rod for trout, it would be either eight feet, three inches or eight and one-half feet, of medium rather than stiff action, to handle a line not over size D in silk or nylon. This would enable one to fish delicately if desired, cover large water and handle a wind, or fish a short line. And I would ask my friend Pinky Gillum to make it for me.

Harold Steele Gillum was a moody, insular craftsman who did not marry until he was almost fifty, and his character had a cantankerous side that triggered quarrels with everyone, including close friends like Harry Darbee. Yet when Gillum died in 1969, men like Darbee mourned him deeply, and one of our finest craftsmen had passed into history.

Since the deaths of Lewis Stoner, Paul Young, and James Payne, Everett Garrison is unquestionably the Dean Emeritus of American rodmaking. His skills are so unique and his craftsmanship is so exacting that his stature on the threshold of eighty is richly deserved, and those skills have happily been passed on to protégés like Baird Foster and Charles Jenkins. Edmund Everett Garrison was born in Yonkers, a sprawling suburb of New York that lies along the Hudson, in the winter of 1893. He attended school in Yonkers, and later received a degree in electrical engineering at Union College in 1916.

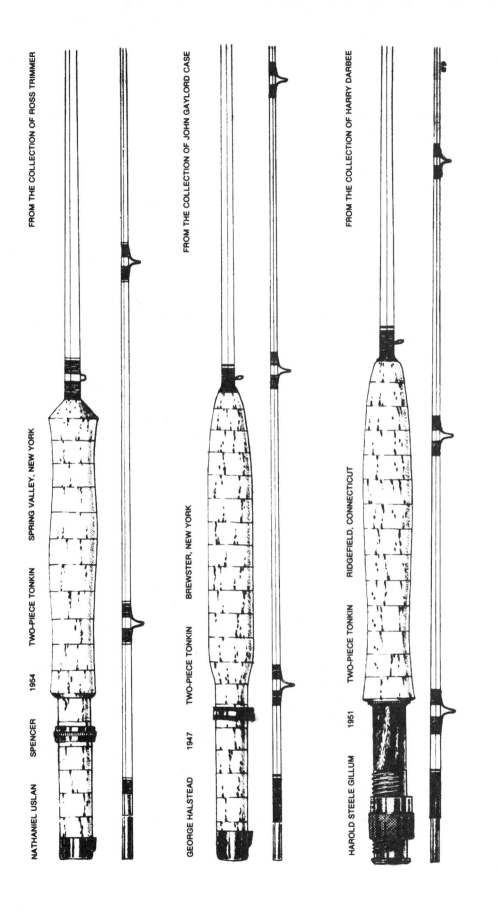

NATHANIEL USLAN   SPENCER   1954   TWO-PIECE TONKIN   SPRING VALLEY, NEW YORK

FROM THE COLLECTION OF ROSS TRIMMER

GEORGE HALSTEAD   1947   TWO-PIECE TONKIN   BREWSTER, NEW YORK

FROM THE COLLECTION OF JOHN GAYLORD CASE

HAROLD STEELE GILLUM   1951   TWO-PIECE TONKIN   RIDGEFIELD, CONNECTICUT

FROM THE COLLECTION OF HARRY DARBEE

His first work was with Curtiss-Wright, testing the metallurgical quality of the steels intended for their aircraft engines. Technology was obviously in his blood, since his father held two degrees in engineering from Columbia University. With the outbreak of American involvement in the First World War, Garrison tried to enlist in the Signal Corps, for flight training in its observation planes. There were continuous postponements of his enlistment that puzzled Garrison, until he discovered that officials at Curtiss-Wright had been quietly interfering in his plans to keep him in their plant. Garrison quit in anger and entered flight school in the summer of 1918, although his dreams of aerial combat ended six months later with the Armistice in France.

After the war, Garrison became involved in the design and construction of railroad trackage and structures, and he spent an increasing amount of time on Catskill rivers like the Neversink and the Rondout. The Rondout was his favorite, and when it was ruined with the construction of a reservoir for the New York water system in 1930, Garrison felt as though a member of his family had died.

Hiram Leonard had many apprentices who later made rods professionally, but there were also amateurs who regularly flocked to his shop at Central Valley. The most famous was perhaps George Parker Holden, who also made bamboo rods as a hobby at his house in Yonkers. Holden published his book *The Idyll of the Split-Bamboo* in 1920, and a mutual friend introduced him to Garrison two years later. Garrison was also a skilled amateur golfer who was building shafts of ash and hickory for his own clubs, and he was intrigued with the idea of club shafts made of split bamboo. Both men soon shared their love for trout fishing, and Garrison became fascinated with both the bamboo rods and the culms of seasoned cane in Holden's garage.

Garrison built his first rods using Holden's stock of cane, borrowing his first tapers from a two-piece Payne that belonged to a fishing friend. The results were unsatisfactory, according to Garrison himself, but he continued to build more rods with increasing success. It was a prelude to the most disciplined, painstaking approach to rodmaking in the entire history of split bamboo.

Other rodmakers were intuitive craftsmen who worked out their actions and tapers empirically, but it was Garrison who actually focused his background in stress analysis on the dynamics of casting behavior. His test rod in this analysis was a two-piece Payne of eight feet, four and a half ounces. Garrison calculated the working stresses at five-inch intervals under maximum deflection in bending. His studies indicated that bending stresses often reach 15,000 pounds per square inch and that maximum loading in the Payne occurred five inches from the tip. His search for a theoretical basis in predicting and designing rod actions evolved into a rich tapestry of mathematics, using a mixture of conventional calculus and moment-force diagrams and the progressive stresses found in the complexities of wave-linear dynamics. Although his rods are both hand-split and hand-planed,

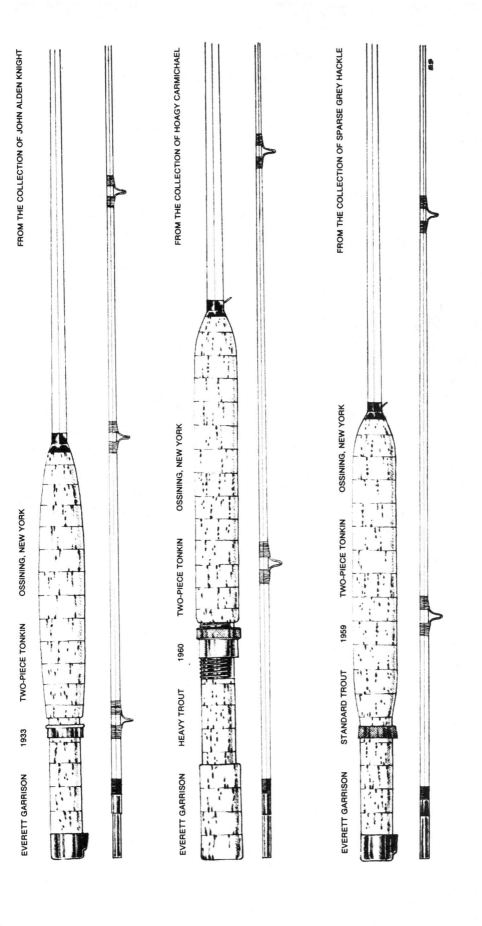

EVERETT GARRISON   1933   TWO-PIECE TONKIN   OSSINING, NEW YORK   FROM THE COLLECTION OF JOHN ALDEN KNIGHT

EVERETT GARRISON   HEAVY TROUT   1960   TWO-PIECE TONKIN   OSSINING, NEW YORK   FROM THE COLLECTION OF HOAGY CARMICHAEL

EVERETT GARRISON   STANDARD TROUT   1959   TWO-PIECE TONKIN   OSSINING, NEW YORK   FROM THE COLLECTION OF SPARSE GREY HACKLE

there is nothing empirical about his approach to rod tapers and actions. Garrison also designed his own planing blocks and tools and other equipment.

Tolerances are everything, Garrison explained one evening at the Anglers' Club of New York, *and I soon realized that Holden's hardwood planing forms were not precise enough.*

Garrison conceived an adjustable planing form of cold-rolled steel, and had it built by William Mallott at his machine shop on Seventy-second Street in Manhattan. Unlike the Holden blocks, which could only hold tolerances of between one thirty-second and one sixty-fourth of an inch, these Garrison forms used differential setscrews to control the tapers with exceptional precision.

They're quite good. Garrison adjusts his forms with quiet pride. *Each full turn of the screws opens or closes the planing forms exactly .008 inch—just what I needed in my work.*

The pressure-winding machine, used after the dark synthetic adhesive is applied to the splines, is typical of most rodmakers, although Garrison's design is capable of achieving a section almost uniquely free of torque or twisting stresses.

Garrison also developed other unique features in the assembly of his sections. Inspection of two Garrison tips laid side by side will reveal that the same nodes in each section were adjacent splines in the original culm, a Garrison refinement designed to make both rod tips as identical as possible. Perhaps more remarkable is the Garrison method of staggering his node patterns. Payne and Young employed a famous spiral-type pattern, while Leonard pioneered an alternating method in placing his bamboo nodes. Garrison took these principles another step, restlessly searching for absolute perfection, and has worked out a unique nodal system. It is so perfect that each bamboo node exists in complete isolation. Not only are there no other nodes in the adjacent strips of cane, one can also spin a Garrison section in vain, searching for other nodes anywhere at that point in the tapers. The result is split-cane sections so perfect that one rolls them in vain to find the bamboo face that bends the most, the low side of the section that usually receives the guides.

But without a high side, I once asked Garrison at a meeting of the Theodore Gordon Flyfishers in Manhattan, *it's impossible to pick a face for the guides—how do you select it?*

There's still room for intuition, he smiled.

Garrison even winds his guides in opposite directions to equalize the twisting forces in his sections. His restlessly inventive mind developed a highly sophisticated method of finishing his rods, using tall cylindrical tanks filled with warm polyurethane of carefully controlled viscosity. His rod sections are dipped with the ferrules plugged and wrapped with tape, and are withdrawn by a motor-driven system that exposes a freshly dipped rod at a speed synchronized with the exact drying rate of the finish.

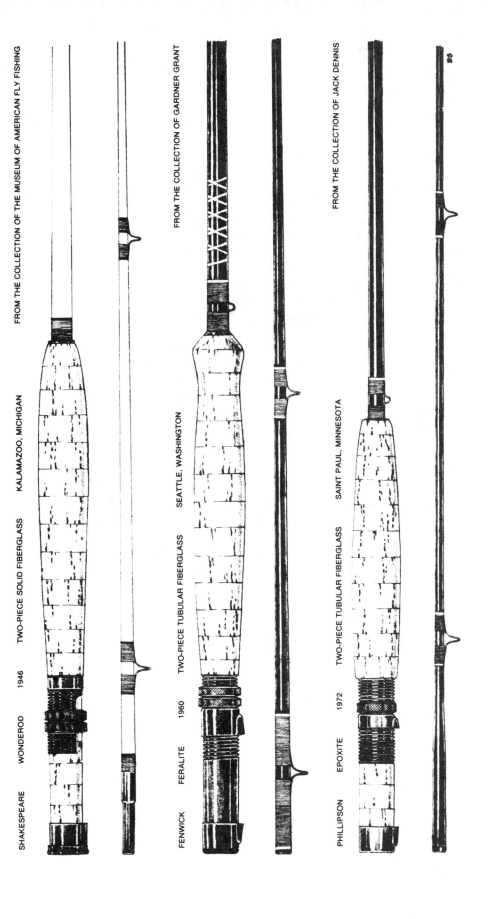

SHAKESPEARE   WONDEROD   1946   TWO-PIECE SOLID FIBERGLASS   KALAMAZOO, MICHIGAN   FROM THE COLLECTION OF THE MUSEUM OF AMERICAN FLY FISHING

FENWICK   FERALITE   1960   TWO-PIECE TUBULAR FIBERGLASS   SEATTLE, WASHINGTON   FROM THE COLLECTION OF GARDNER GRANT

PHILLIPSON   EPOXITE   1972   TWO-PIECE TUBULAR FIBERGLASS   SAINT PAUL, MINNESOTA   FROM THE COLLECTION OF JACK DENNIS

The tolerances in his rods are measured in terms of .001 or less, tolerances that give Garrison considerable pride.

Sparse Grey Hackle refused to believe that I could hold such tolerances with a hand planing-block, Garrison laughed with pleasure, *until he checked several sticks with a micrometer!*

The first rod that Garrison felt satisfied with was given to the late John Alden Knight, and it appears in his book *The Modern Angler* in a plate that demonstrates the open grip that Knight preferred in casting. It was fitted with the butt cap that Garrison still used, and a simple sliding ring machined with a knurled welt. His modern rods use a tapering band of knurled aluminum, a refinement that Garrison worked out so the ring would seat firmly on the reel and remain ninety degrees to the cork filler. It is typical of his concern for detail. The chocolate wrappings that replace the conventional grip check found on most rods are still found on Garrison rods forty years later, along with a circular fly keeper of unique design. Chocolate winding also secures the ferrules. The guides are wound in functional wraps of white silk that seem to vanish when the rod is finished. The Garrison grip is smoothly tapered to meet the bamboo, and its shape has changed from the cigar type of his first rods to a seemingly straight handle. The grips actually taper about one thirty-second of an inch from the reel seat to the thumb position, echoing the theories of Charles Ritz about grip design.

John Alden Knight did not mention Garrison specifically in *The Modern Angler*, but his chapter on rods contains these paragraphs about Garrison and his work in 1936:

Until a few years ago, I was under the impression that rods vary in their personalities just as the men who use them and, for that reason, to copy the action of one rod when building another was not possible. Today I do not believe this is entirely true. A skilled workman, who knows bamboo and who has the mechanical ability to work accurately and consistently in thousandths of an inch, can so nearly duplicate rod action that the most sensitive hand could not possibly tell the difference between the original and the copy. I fully realize that this is heresy—a stone hurled at one of the ancient and accepted beliefs of angling.

A rod has always been regarded by its owner as non-replaceable and therefore to be guarded with life itself. And then I saw the impossible accomplished. This particular rodmaker, an amateur who has recently turned professional, duplicated a rod perfectly for me.

I sat in his workshop and watched him make it, noting the meticulous care with which he set his steel forms. His micrometer readings and measurements where made with the aid of a powerful magnifying glass, and checked and rechecked before the final cutting of the strips.

When he had finished I tried both rods under actual fishing conditions and could not, I am positive, have been sure which was mine had not the silk wrappings on one differed from those on the original.

An accident, you say? Not at all. This man does not depend on accidents in doing his work. Before starting work on a new rod, he takes the old one and calibrates it at short intervals throughout its entire length, taking three readings at each interval so as to include variations in all six sides of each section in his measurements. Next, using a method best known to himself, he charts the stresses in the rod and shows them graphically in a stress-curve or power-curve. Seeing such a stress-curve of your pet rod is much like looking at an x-ray picture of your interior workings—and, to the layman, such a stress-curve means about as much.

However, with this record to check against as he does his work, there is little chance for error. Variations in bamboo strength are allowed for in the cutting and corrected later. In some cases, it is necessary to rebuild some sections. But the main point is that the job can be done—not just once in a while but as often as desired.

Garrison gave his second rod to his friend Vernon Heiney, who had lost his job during the Depression, and was planning to spend the summer on the Beaverkill. Heiney was a skilled caster and fisherman who used Payne rods of more conventional tapers, and he was critical of the casting rhythms in his first Garrison. But later Heiney learned to appreciate his Garrison so much that he revised his entire philosophy of casting to suit its singular rhythms.

Perhaps the most unusual Garrison is a rod with all of its nodes removed horizontally with almost surgical precision, completely eliminating the weak points in its cane.

It took forever, Garrison admitted. *I wanted to see if I could really do it!*

But the ordinary Garrison rods are instruments of such beauty and perfection that any angler who appreciates fine workmanship cannot help but revere them. Most anglers are looking for his seven- and seven-and-a-half-foot rods today, avoiding the eight- and eight-and-a-half-foot designs that were popular when he began building rods professionally in 1933. It is unusual that Garrison even makes his own rod cases of aluminum tubing, machining their end caps of hard yellow brass, and sewing the poplin rod sacks himself. His lifetime production of less than a thousand rods might have been larger had he not insisted on making everything himself, from the reel fittings to those poplin bags. Perhaps the final touch on the typical Garrison rod is the accent of bright silk on one tip section, an identifying mark of his work. The winding is intended to permit the disciplined rotation of each tip.

Every time a man fishes a rod he should alternate its tips, Garrison believed. *That way each tip section ages and deforms equally over the years—and a rod will have the same feel with either tip.*

Garrison rods are based on the same compound-taper theory, although the tip calibrations of rods intended for sinking lines and big-water tactics are proportionately heavier. Some use heavy-wall cane and are stiffer. His long three-piece designs are unusually slow but powerful. Garrison actions work deeply into their butt tapers, bend less in their middle and upper calibrations, and conclude with a delicate tip.

Garrison has fierce partisans, and each has favorite Garrison designs. The most popular rods in his series included the following models:

MODEL	LENGTH (FEET)	WEIGHT (OUNCES)	LINE WEIGHT
193	$6^{3}/_{4}$	2	4
201	7	$2^{1}/_{8}$	4
201E	7	$2^{1}/_{4}$	4
202E	7	$2^{1}/_{2}$	5
204E	$7^{1}/_{4}$	$2^{5}/_{8}$	5
206	$7^{1}/_{2}$	$2^{3}/_{4}$	5
209	$7^{1}/_{2}$	3	6
209E	$7^{3}/_{4}$	$3^{1}/_{8}$	6
212	8	$3^{1}/_{2}$	5
212E	8	$3^{3}/_{4}$	6
212	$8^{1}/_{2}$	4	6
212E	$8^{1}/_{2}$	$4^{1}/_{4}$	7
215	$8^{1}/_{2}$	$4^{3}/_{4}$	8

Many fishermen dream of owning the delicate seven-foot, two-and-one-quarter-ounce design for a four-weight. Other disciples prefer the stiffer seven-foot taper designed for a DT5F. Garrison particularly liked the seven-foot three-inch rod weighing two and five eighths ounces. It cast beautifully with a DT5F the afternoon he let me fish his 204E at Henryville.

The seven-and-a-half-foot Garrisons usually weigh between two and three-quarters and three ounces, and like the odd seven-foot nine-inch design, they take DT5F and DT6F tapers. The eight-foot Garrisons weighing four ounces, and fishing six-weight lines, are the original 212E rods that essentially made Garrison's reputation shortly before the Second World War.

Before I acquired one of these smaller Garrisons, I had cast and fished several, including a handful of his own rods.

Others included the 212E that Philip Nash let me fish at the old Haase farm water on the Brodheads, on a pretty April afternoon with barn swallows taking *Ephemerella* flies under the footbridge. Other exquisite examples included the 212 that Martin Bovey let me fish on the headwaters of the Ruby in Montana, and the 206 he offered on the Firehole a few months before his death. Such rods are worth twenty-five and thirty times their original cost today, and I salute those anglers who possess such masterpieces.

My collection of Garrison's work has grown since *Trout* was first published in 1978.

The smallest is a Garrison 201E, measuring seven and a half feet. It weighs two and a half ounces and takes a DT4E. The lovely 206 is a seven-and-a-half-footer that also takes a four-weight line, although it probably took a DT5F when it was new. The 212 in my collection is a poetic eight-foot rod. It weighs three and a half ounces and takes a DT5F, and was perhaps the most popular Garrison in his later years. The smooth 212E at eight and a half feet was my first Garrison trout rod. It weighs four and one-eighth ounces and has the quality of a fine violin. It was originally rated for a DT7F, but it is one of the early Garrisons, and casts better with a six-weight today. These four Garrisons are virtually a matched set between seven and eight and a half feet, and they are a source of great pleasure.

With the approach of eighty, Garrison was still building a dozen rods each year. His clients included a circle of anglers like Otto von Kienbusch and the late Sparse Grey Hackle.

During recent months, I have seen mint Garrisons sold and auctioned at startling prices. Some have gone for thousands of dollars. Such prices are a tribute to the quality of Garrison's work, and the relatively small number of rods he made during his life. Garrison produced his rods at a trickle after 1973, lacking the vigor and intensity of his early years. His time was spent puttering, modifying, and perfecting his equipment and tools, perhaps reluctant to leave artifacts behind that did not meet his yardstick of absolute perfection. Our sporadic conversations suggested that he lamented a growing scarcity of proper fittings, first-quality specie cork, and select culms of the Chinese bamboo.

Garrison drove himself unsparingly, unwilling to accept anything less than his dream. His standards were so austere that he refused to work with bamboo during the humid summers along the Hudson. His loyal partisans are grateful for each rod that met his standards and left his basement workshop.

Everett Garrison died on February 8, 1975.

He was a genius, a rare mixture of technician and poet who made six-strip rods of yellow cane so perfectly that his sticks lacked a high side. The most experienced hands have rolled them in vain to determine their stiff and soft planes of bending. His skeletal reel seats and cork grips are almost ascetic, utterly lacking affectation or artifice. The dark chocolate silk at the ferrules and cork are a functional counterpoint for the transparent silk that secures the guides. The tapered reel band, its outer surfaces tightly knurled and finished, is a simple accent on a fly rod whose visual character is eloquent testimony to its simple craftsmanship.

Like other great artisans, Garrison insisted on almost monastic under-statement in his work, refusing extra weight or the embellishment of bright silk wrappings. It is simple and sure-handed. His rods speak eloquently through their functional perfection and performance, archetypes of their craft, and a Garrison has become the ultimate iconography.

Other makers are in his footsteps.

Hoagy Carmichael made a documentary film about Garrison and his work, and unwittingly became a disciple and apprentice. Garrison and Carmichael were collaborating on a book when the master craftsman died. The apprentice lovingly pulled together a half-completed manuscript and a tangle of notebooks, cassette recordings, and photographs. Carmichael plunged into completing the book, forgetting his filmmaking business entirely. It finally became *A Master's Guide to Building a Bamboo Fly Rod,* which Carmichael published in 1977.

The Garrison story does not end there.

Like many disciples, Carmichael had become so completely involved with his patron that he has started building the Garrison tapers himself. The perfectly seasoned bamboo culms and technical data and Garrison's tools are all in Carmichael's shop today.

The first rods are superbly executed, and Carmichael is still building the full Garrison list. It is exciting to think that the classic Garrison tapers still live, and that the following designs are still split and hand milled on his original planing blocks:

MODEL	LENGTH (FEET)	WEIGHT (OUNCES)	LINE WEIGHT
193	$6^3/4$	2	4
201	7	$2^1/8$	4
201E	7	$2^1/4$	4
202E	7	$2^1/2$	5
204E	$7^1/4$	$2^5/8$	5
206	$7^1/2$	$2^3/4$	5
209	$7^1/2$	3	6
209E	$7^3/4$	$3^1/8$	6
212	8	$3^1/2$	5
212E	8	$3^3/4$	6
212	$8^1/2$	4	6
212E	$8^1/2$	$4^1/4$	7
215	$8^1/2$	$4^3/4$	8

The Carmichael rods are excellent, and the Garrison book has created a full circle of other disciples. Leon Hansen is building Garrison tapers full time at his Plymouth shop in Michigan. His rods are entirely hand tempered, lovingly split and planed, and use Garrison-style fittings. Hansen rods are made in the following models with walnut seats:

MODEL	LENGTH (FEET)	WEIGHT (OUNCES)	LINE WEIGHT
91-3	6½	2	3
91-4	6½	2¼	4
92-4	7	2½	4
93-4	7½	2¾	4
93-5	7½	3	5
93½-4	7¾	3⅛	4
93½-5	7¾	3¼	5
94-5	8	3½	5
94-6	8	3⅝	6
94½-4	8¼	3½	4
94½-7	8¼	4¼	7
95-8	8½	4¾	8

Gary Souffker is another Garrison disciple, and I first cast samples of his rods at an exposition in Seattle. His early work echoed classic tapers like the 212 and 212E, in eight and eight and a half feet. Souffker lacked the old dense-wall cane in the Garrison stocks, so those first prototypes were a little slower than the original Garrison designs. His rods are now being split and planed at Klamath Falls, in southern Oregon.

Edwin Hartzell builds his Garrison tapers farther north at Portland, and I have seen a number at meetings of the Flyfishers of Oregon. His workmanship is excellent, befitting the discipline of a retired teacher who drives a beautifully restored MG roadster and wears rumpled Cheviot herringbones.

I'm obviously entranced by old things of solid worth, Hartzell confesses. *Helplessly!*

Hartzell first introduced himself at the Kaufman store in Tigard, on the southern periphery of Portland, and we talked almost an hour before he showed me his work. It was a raw winter day, mixing cold rain and wet snow, and when it softened slightly we walked outside to cast the rods. His craftsmanship was obvious, and his variations on the Garrison 212 and 212E tapers easily cast an entire double-taper line. Later I was asked about his work. *Anybody who loves antique cars and herringbone tweeds,* I laughed, *can't be all bad!*

Several rod builders have recently started to mill split-cane tapers in New England and the Catskills, where our American tradition flowered.

Maine has disciples of its pioneers, craftsmen like Leonard and Thomas and Crocker. William Taylor is both artist and rodmaker, with old roots in the brook-trout tradition.

Connecticut has E. F. Roberts, whose little shop at East Granby carries on in the tradition of Gillum and Sedgwick and the entire Edwards family. Marc Aroner is working in fine Tonkin cane at Conway, farther north in the mountains of New Hampshire.

Ron Kusse once operated the Leonard fishing store at Central Valley, an hour north from Times Square, at the threshold of the Catskills. Kusse started the Leonard shop when the company was still owned by the family of the old William Mills & Sons store in lower Manhattan. Ted Simroe was its foreman, and old Tom Bailey still crouched over his lathe, turning German-silver tubing and billets into ferrules and reel-seat fittings. Central Valley has been the home for H. L. Leonard & Company for more than a century, and famous rodmakers like Payne, Edwards, Thomas, Hawes, and Varney all passed their apprenticeships in that little Catskill town. Payne returned to build his own shop in nearby Highland Mills, and when Leonard closed its tackle store in 1979, Kusse started his own rodmaking in Washingtonville.

Kusse had long been moonlighting at the Leonard shop, building and restoring rods for himself. His apprenticeship was obviously both diligent and attentive, for his split-cane work is excellent. The following models are currently available:

MODEL	LENGTH (FEET)	WEIGHT (OUNCES)	LINE WEIGHT
KSC-260	6	$1\,^1/_8$	2
KSC-360	6	$1\,^1/_4$	3
KSC-366	$6^1/_2$	$1\,^1/_2$	3
KSC-466	$6^1/_2$	$1\,^3/_4$	4
KSC-370	7	$2\,^1/_4$	3
KSC-470	7	$2\,^1/_2$	4
KSC-570	7	$2\,^3/_4$	5
KSC-476	$7^1/_2$	3	4
KSC-576	$7^1/_2$	$3\,^1/_4$	5
KSC-676	$7^1/_2$	$3\,^1/_2$	6
KSC-580	8	$3\,^3/_4$	5
KSC-680	8	4	6

His own collecting of antique Leonards and Paynes has led Kusse to ferrules and fittings machined from German silver. Ferrule plugs are included too. The rod cases have brass caps that are polished and knurled, like the Thomas cases from Bangor fifty years ago. Kusse offers butter-yellow bamboo, brownstone finishes like the old Hunt pattern at Leonard, and a strongly flame-toned cane that echoes the work of Paul Young. Special grips are available, including smooth and gunstock-checkered hardwoods, along with special rod tapers. The reel-seat fillers are elegantly finished, with richly grained walnut and cherry and tiger maple.

It's the little things, Kusse insists, *that made the old makers memorable.*

John Weir leads a family rodmaking firm with a history reaching back across the continent, from Los Gatos in northern California to our gentle

Appalachians. Its craftsmen still produce hand-planed tapers, although most of its rods are milled on a unique machine that can mill six strips simultaneously. Weir rods echo the early Leonards, exquisitely crafted and pale, and the following models are available:

MODEL	LENGTH (FEET)	WEIGHT (OUNCES)	LINE WEIGHT
LM603	6	$1\frac{1}{4}$	2
D603	6	$1\frac{3}{4}$	3
D661	$6\frac{1}{2}$	$2\frac{3}{8}$	3
D701	7	3	4
HW701	7	$3\frac{3}{4}$	5
LM763	$7\frac{1}{2}$	$2\frac{1}{2}$	4
M601	$7\frac{1}{2}$	$3\frac{3}{4}$	5
D761	$7\frac{1}{2}$	$3\frac{7}{8}$	5
HM761	$7\frac{1}{2}$	$4\frac{1}{8}$	6
LM803	8	$3\frac{3}{4}$	4
M801	8	4	5
D801	8	$4\frac{1}{8}$	6
D861	$8\frac{1}{2}$	$4\frac{1}{2}$	7

Gus Nevros is a rare artisan who still works in both five- and six-strip cane. His honey-colored sticks are slightly tempered. Both skeletal and down-locking hardware are available, with beautifully grained rosewood fillers. Nevros makes these five-strip rods:

MODEL	LENGTH (FEET)	WEIGHT (OUNCES)	LINE WEIGHT
N714-5	$7\frac{1}{4}$	3	3
N823-5	$8\frac{3}{4}$	4	4

The following six-strip bamboo designs are also available from Nevros:

MODEL	LENGTH (FEET)	WEIGHT (OUNCES)	LINE WEIGHT
N612-6	$6\frac{1}{2}$	$2\frac{1}{4}$	4
N712-6	$7\frac{1}{2}$	$3\frac{1}{4}$	5
N800-6	8	$3\frac{3}{4}$	6
N814-6	$8\frac{1}{4}$	$3\frac{3}{4}$	5
N823-6	$8\frac{2}{3}$	5	8

Michael Montagne is another young rodmaker with a sense of probity and great skill. His work has obvious roots in the four-strip theories of construction found in the Quadrate rods built by William Edwards in eastern Connecticut. His cork is a mixture of the Ritz and Garrison theories of grip design, but his silk wrappings are utterly transparent, in obvious homage to Garrison alone. The dark chocolate wraps at the ferrules and cork are echoes of Garrison too.

But Montagne is a craftsman of startling originality, and not all of his creativity is obvious. Edwards built symmetrical four-strip rods. Montagne builds his sticks at irregular angles to create their widest flats, and the primary power fibers, perpendicular to the planes of casting.

His four-strip design offers twice the density of cane power fibers found in six-strip construction of the same section thickness.

Such four-strip sections offer more than mere power fibers. Montagne rods resist bending across the corners, concentrating deflection in the casting plane. Such performance tends to correct casting faults that twist other rods. Better distance and accuracy are also improved. Wave-linear behavior is crisp and clean. The ratio of power fibers to inert cane along the neutral bending axis is multiplied, even slightly higher than power fibers in the earlier Edwards Quadrates.

Montagne oven-tempers his Tonkin culms and splits them by hand. The nodes are hand dressed and polished with pressure and heat. The lateral strips are triangular, and the strips in the bending plane are trapezoids. Both rind and waste pith are removed by meticulous hand-work, using files and perfectly sharpened planes. The asymmetrical strips are unusual, but the ascetic dedication is typical of our most meticulous craftsmen in rodmakers like Howells and Dorsey.

The Montagne rods part sharply with tradition in their reel-seat designs. The rod shaft is neither cut nor modified in any way. Its structural integrity is not affected. The seat fittings are a reverse-locking type, but they are utterly unlike other reverse-locking designs. Montagne's concept is almost defiantly creative, and still more monastic than the work of Garrison. There is no reel-seat filler, and the locking device is a truncated cone that places the reel foot in flexure, levering it firmly in position. It is lighter than conventional designs, both original and austere.

This past September I was fishing with Kirk Gay at Six-Mile Lake in Alaska. Although I had seen a few Montagne rods, I had never cast or fished one until another angler offered me his nine-foot steelhead model for a weight-forward eight line. Its smooth power and control in the Tularik winds were surprising, and its elegance was obvious. Its visual character was startling to other anglers, but its creativity and probity were unmistakable.

Montagne is building fourteen models. His series includes the following designs:

MODEL	LENGTH (FEET)	WEIGHT (OUNCES)	LINE WEIGHT
MM-763	7½	2¼	3
MM-764	7½	2½	4
MM-765	7½	2¾	5
MM-804	8	3	4
MM-805	8	3¼	5
MM-806	8	3½	6
MM-866	8½	3¾	6
MM-867	8½	4¼	7
MM-868	8½	4¾	8
MM-869	8½	5½	9
MM-906	9	5	6
MM-907	9	5¾	7
MM-908	9	6	8
MM-909	9	6¼	9

Orvis continues its innovations too, and its new bamboo models include the C. F. Orvis 125 series. It is intended to celebrate Charles Orvis and the tackle company he founded 125 years earlier.

Orvis 125 rods are exquisitely crafted and finished. Standard cigar, full Wells, reversed half Wells, and tapered cigar grips are available. All fittings are machined from German silver. Silver ferrule plugs are included. Reel seats available include a butt cap and sliding-ring design, reverse-locking type, and a down-locking design with a butt cap. The reel-seat fillers are beautiful bird's-eye maple. The C. F. Orvis 125 series includes the following rods, in cases intended for engraving and presentation:

MODEL	LENGTH (FEET)	WEIGHT (OUNCES)	LINE WEIGHT
JM9657-62	6½	2⅛	4
JM9353-62	7	2½	3
JM9705-62	7	2¾	4
JM9701-62	7	3½	6
JM9759-62	7½	3¾	5
JM9751-62	7½	4⅛	6
JM9809-62	8	4	6
JM9808-62	8	4½	6
JM9801-62	8	4½	7

MICHAEL MONTAGNE   TROUT   1983   TWO-PIECE TONKIN   OLEMA, CALIFORNIA   FROM THE COLLECTION OF BARRY MOORE

HOWARD STEERE   C. F. ORVIS 125   1983   TWO-PIECE TONKIN   MANCHESTER, VERMONT   FROM THE COLLECTION OF LEIGH PERKINS

THOMAS DORSEY   PARADIGM   1983   TWO-PIECE TONKIN   TURNER'S FALLS, MASSACHUSETTS   FROM THE COLLECTION OF ERNEST SCHWIEBERT

Twenty-five years ago, the angling world was filled with omens and gloomy predictions of the death of bamboo rods. Such predictions were a little premature. American artisans are not only building rods that match the best work of history, but there are also more first-rate rodmakers than ever before.

Like our decoy carvers, the most celebrated American rodmakers are finally receiving just recognition for the eloquence of their skills.

Thomas & Thomas was recently honored by the White House when a specially fitted Sans Pareil was selected as a gift of state for Prime Minister John Malcolm Fraser of Australia. The White House also chose my two-volume *Trout* as a gift of state, with a hand-tipped frontispiece and presentation vellum page. Both gifts were given to the prime minister in a brief protocol ceremony at the White House.

The rod posed some interesting problems. Protocol officials at the White House had become aware that the Australian leader was an avid trout fisherman. It was determined after a series of telephone calls that only his government could help us specify a correct rod for his sport, and a comedy of errors resulted.

Thomas Dorsey told me the story. *We asked the Australians to tell us where the prime minister liked to fish,* he said. *It could tell us exactly what to build.*

The Australian diplomatic service supplied our protocol officers with a list of favorite rivers, and it was ultimately decided to build a nine-footer for eight-weights. Dorsey had started to work when something curious happened.

My telephone rang early.

It was a young protocol officer attached to the White House, and the call had a comic desperation. The teletypes at the Australian embassy had received a strange message over the weekend, and it had puzzled the duty officers. It was obviously concerned with the gift of state intended for the prime minister.

It was in some kind of code, the young official explained. *But the cryptographers didn't have a clue about its meaning—their people or ours.*

What was the message? I asked.

Pretty strange stuff, the protocol officer continued. *Something about DT6F or WF8F.*

I started to laugh and stopped.

What's funny? she asked.

Line sizes! I was chuckling now. *Those are line-weight and taper codes!*

Line weights and tapers?

That's right, I said. *The prime minister knows about your little project—and he's telling us exactly what rod he wants—the WF8F line will fit the rod you've already got in the works.*

No wonder it wasn't in the code books!

The Sans Pareil was elegantly conceived and finished. It was flawlessly milled with a satin finish and a swelled butt taper. Both its ferrules and its reel-seat hardware were German silver, and the reverse-locking system is a precisely mortised design. It is quite simply the most beautiful locking hardware in rodmaking today, and its fillers are a richly polished pigeon-grade walnut. It had both a butt plug and a beautifully made extension butt. There were chocolate wraps at the ferrules, with clear silk at its other fittings. Silver ferrule plugs were included. The rod case was of highly polished ebony, and capped at both ends with brass. The smaller chamber housed the fighting butt in its own poplin sack. The polished caps were delicately knurled, but the crowning touch was a gold seal from Tiffany's, like a freshly minted coin: the blue-and-gold seal of the president of the United States.

It was a great success! The White House reported. *The prime minister loved it—and the book was perfect too!*

EVERETT GARRISON

My collection now includes a matching nine-foot rod for eight-weight tapers. It lacks the delicate inscription from the president to the prime minister and the gold seal from Tiffany's.

Thomas Dorsey is building remarkable artifacts at his little shop in northern Massachusetts. His work combines the grace of a concert violin, with the utility and beauty of a fine British double gun. There is an exquisite two-piece Paradigm in my collection too, a slender eight-footer for a DT4F. Its poetry rivals the delicate Young Princess that I have treasured for many years. It is a richly beautiful thing.

But his skills refused to accept its perfection, and my most recent prize is a three-piece Sans Pareil that Dorsey built me for fishing the Henry's Fork.

It is eight and a half feet and weighs four and a half ounces. Its delicacy is poetry itself. It is fitted like the White House rod, although its calibrations are designed for a DT5F line. Its reverse-locking hardware is German silver, mortised into beautifully grained walnut. Its brass-capped case is slipped into a sailcloth sack, along with a tip case that is also fitted with brass hardware. It carries a delicate surprise: two matching tip sections for a DT4F, giving the Sans Pareil remarkable versatility.

The torch has clearly passed. Other generations of craftsmen are telling us unmistakably that our skills have not atrophied. Our best modern work has never been surpassed, in spite of our stories and sentimentality.

The iconography of the split-cane rod still has the magic to capture our hearts, with its unique mixture of poetry and power.

It is the spirit of bamboo.

7. The Evolution of
the Fiberglass Rod

Histtory tells us that it was the restless mind of Edward Ringwood Hewitt that started the evolution of the modern synthetic rod. His role is not surprising to anyone who remembers his tenacity and his constant experiments with the problems of trout fishing. Hewitt was cantankerous and aggressively unwilling to stop puttering in the workshop of his mind, and he always displayed a Menckenlike suspicion of past dogma. His habitual inconoclasm inexorably led Hewitt toward new developments and fresh ground, and the technology evolving on the threshold of the century soon flooded the world with a cornucopia of synthetic materials.

It was the Belgian chemist Hendrik Baekkelund who opened the floodgates with the first synthetic resin in 1909. His Bakelite was quickly utilized in a number of industrial products, including the fittings of rods and reels, and it is still found in the impregnating process used to temper and moisture-proof bamboo at both Orvis and Sharpe's.

More synthetics evolved in the decade following the First World War, including many resins, polyesters, and a remarkable new fiber called nylon. It was nylon that fascinated Hewitt, and he experimented in several ways with its elasticity and tensile strength. Since the molecular structure of bamboo is linear, Hewitt soon tried to utilize nylon strands in a fly rod. Hundreds of fine nylon strands were stretched around a tapered wooden core to simulate the linear anatomy of split cane. Hewitt bonded the fibers together with a plastic resin, wrapping its entire length with a continuous nylon filament. Hewitt apparently built several prototypes just before the Second World War, using a uniformly tapered mandrel.

Hewitt soon abandoned his theories. The nylon proved far too elastic under the wave-linear stresses of fly casting; its fibers stretched too readily and failed to recover from major dynamic loads, and its flexing tended to fight with the resin bonds. The resins fractured and the rods failed quickly. However, Hewitt remained convinced that the remarkable new synthetic fibers and resins would ultimately provide fishermen with several exotic new rod materials.

History is still proving him right.

Fiberglass was the first synthetic fiber to provide the casting performance Hewitt had predicted. It was woven into a fabric of glass with remarkable properties, and many corporations and small manufacturers were soon experimenting with its potential.

It was Doctor Arthur Howald who built the first fiberglass fly rod in 1944. Howald was engaged in fiberglass research, and when he smashed the tip section of a favorite cane rod on a Michigan trout stream it was logical to attempt a replacement in glass. Split bamboo was virtually impossible to obtain during the war years. Howald was thoroughly versed in both plastics and fiberglass manufacturing processes, and he constructed a mold matching the size and taper of his broken tip. Howald shaped a wooden core and layered it with fiberglass, bonding both the fibers and the mandrel core together. Although his tip did not match the performance of his split-cane rod, and it looked milk-colored and strange in its casting oscillations, Howald happily fished it during the war years.

Shakespeare became interested in fiberglass rod construction the following year, and started a series of experiments with the new material. The first rods were introduced at the Chicago Coliseum in 1946, and the white Shakespeare Wonder rods were a sensation in a country that had wet-nursed its aging bamboo rods through the entire Second World War. The fiberglass butts were too stiff and the tips were mushy, although glass unmistakably offered some unique properties and the manufacturer was eager to exploit them. The material was both light and remarkably strong. It was capable of absorbing abuse and neglect that would ruin a bamboo rod, and fiberglass rods required virtually no maintenance. Fiberglass rods seldom take a twist or set, and moisture and temperature that could irreparably damage cane have almost no effect on the new rods. Oxidation and mildew were no longer a problem. Stress fatigue and denigration from exposure to light will gradually take its toll of fiberglass construction, but structural fatigue is more serious in both metal and bamboo. Glass is both more resilient and stronger than cane, measured ounce for ounce, but it can also fracture under a sharp blow or extreme casting load. Once I saw one smashed when an angler lost a big rainbow, struck the water in a mixture of anger and despair, and broke the tip section of his fiberglass rod.

Shakespeare soon abandoned the Howald wooden-core construction, and its first production rods were solid fiberglass designs. Shakespeare still controls many basic patents on fiberglass construction methods, for both tubular and solid blanks. Although modern fiberglass rods cost far less than fine split-cane rods even in the custom-modified designs made by superb fiberglass artisans like Neumann and Cummings and Peak, it should be remembered that the first Shakespeare fly rods were just as expensive as a vintage Leonard or Payne when they were introduced.

Conolon first developed the tubular fiberglass designs that now dominate modern rod production, forming the fiberglass cloth around a steel mandrel that is removed after curing. Shakespeare and Heddon soon adopted tubular construction. The fiberglass revolution quickly gathered momentum, and as the manufacturers worked out the details of production, their costs plummeted until glass dominated the tackle market. Workable glass rods are available at less than ten percent of the price a handmade Garrison commands, and even the most expensive fiberglass makers charge half the price of the Orvis Battenkill. More than three million rods are sold annually in the United States, employing more than half a million pounds of fiberglass, and less than two percent of total sales are bamboo.

The physical properties and character of any rod section are rooted in the fishing for which it is intended, the size of both the fish and the flies required, the character of the water, and the personal skills and philosophy of the fisherman. All blanks must provide an equilibrium between strength and resilience under the stresses of bending. Such performance must also spring from a relatively light tubular blank, with elastic properties that provide a rapid recovery from dynamic loads. The material should also have a pleasing visual character. Fiberglass offers these several properties to a remarkable degree, and provides them at relatively low cost.

Fiberglass construction aligns the fibers in optimal relationship to the longitudinal axis of the blank. Such alignment provides the performance under flexing stress. Blank diameters and wall densities provide recovery from bending, while the lateral fibers resist deformation of the tubular cross section. Fiberglass cloth and the plastic resins used to form it into finished rod blanks can provide relatively light weight, durability and strength, controlled calibrations and action, and reasonable esthetic character.

Solid fiberglass blanks were the first type that became available after the Second World War. Such blanks are drawn through a resin bath and then formed in a die and curing tube. The solid blanks are trimmed to length and ground to the required tapers. All the fiberglass strands lie parallel to the axis of the rod, providing good bending behavior, crush resistance, and strength. However, the most rudimentary knowledge of materials under bending stresses tells us that the core fibers add little or nothing to casting performance. Such production techniques are surprisingly simple, the materials and equipment are relatively inexpensive, and low-priced rods are possible. Performance is generally sluggish and poor, and such rods are seldom suitable for fly-rod-casting dynamics.

The Howell process is a technique in which fiberglass yarn is saturated with a polyester resin. The saturated fibers are then formed over a removable mandrel, with a spiral of cellophane tape to shape and control the wall thickness. The tape is stripped free once the resins have hardened and cured. The optimal performance of such blanks depends on the use of

DOWN-WING DRY FLIES

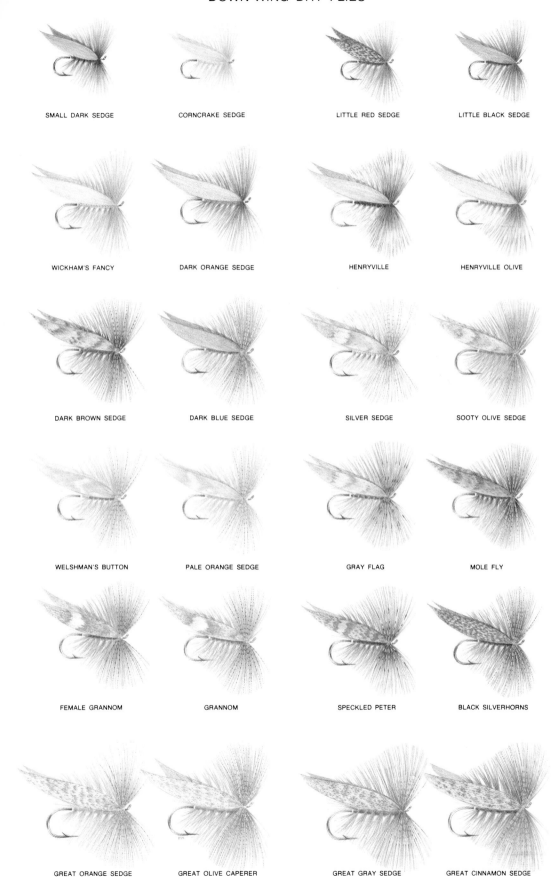

SMALL DARK SEDGE   CORNCRAKE SEDGE   LITTLE RED SEDGE   LITTLE BLACK SEDGE

WICKHAM'S FANCY   DARK ORANGE SEDGE   HENRYVILLE   HENRYVILLE OLIVE

DARK BROWN SEDGE   DARK BLUE SEDGE   SILVER SEDGE   SOOTY OLIVE SEDGE

WELSHMAN'S BUTTON   PALE ORANGE SEDGE   GRAY FLAG   MOLE FLY

FEMALE GRANNOM   GRANNOM   SPECKLED PETER   BLACK SILVERHORNS

GREAT ORANGE SEDGE   GREAT OLIVE CAPERER   GREAT GRAY SEDGE   GREAT CINNAMON SEDGE

ROLLED-WING DRY FLIES

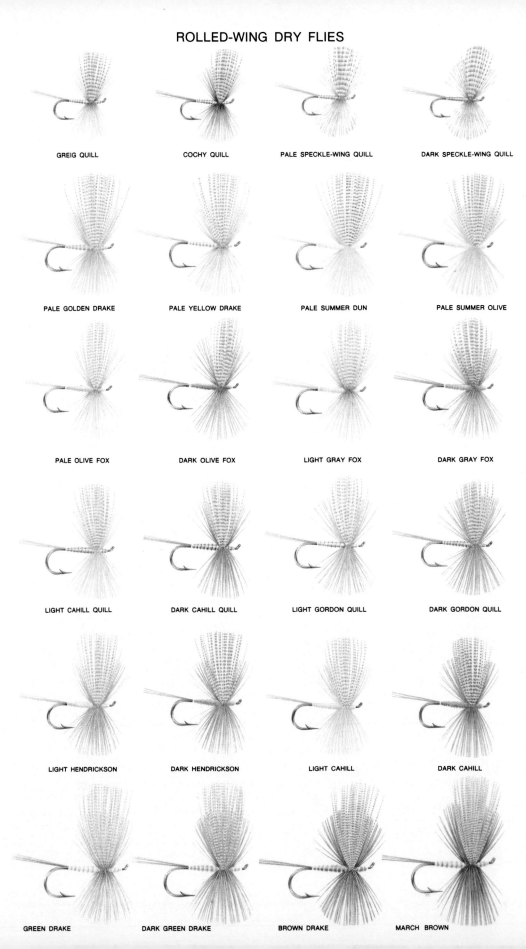

GREIG QUILL   COCHY QUILL   PALE SPECKLE-WING QUILL   DARK SPECKLE-WING QUILL

PALE GOLDEN DRAKE   PALE YELLOW DRAKE   PALE SUMMER DUN   PALE SUMMER OLIVE

PALE OLIVE FOX   DARK OLIVE FOX   LIGHT GRAY FOX   DARK GRAY FOX

LIGHT CAHILL QUILL   DARK CAHILL QUILL   LIGHT GORDON QUILL   DARK GORDON QUILL

LIGHT HENDRICKSON   DARK HENDRICKSON   LIGHT CAHILL   DARK CAHILL

GREEN DRAKE   DARK GREEN DRAKE   BROWN DRAKE   MARCH BROWN

polyester resins that have been specially developed for rods. Color is mixed into the resin, too. The core fibers are wrapped in a controlled spiral, providing tubular resistance to deformation under bending stresses. The surface cloth is applied to align its fibers longitudinally where optimal flexing performance is needed. Fine tip sections are not possible with tubular construction, since the inside diameters are too small for the mandrel method of construction. Such tips are usually of compound design, with solid tip calibrations and tubular construction in the middle and butt diameters. Rod sections fabricated with the Howell patent method are relatively durable and perform well in most fishing situations. Although considerably lighter than comparable solid blanks, tubular rods of this type are heavier than the tubular designs used in most fiberglass fly rods. However, since production of blanks with the Howell patent utilizes relatively inexpensive fiberglass and resins, and mass production techniques with little handwork are possible, such construction results in relatively inexpensive rods.

The best fiberglass rods are built using a specially woven cloth designed for fishing-rod performance. The rod fabric is a crow-foot weave with semi-unidirectional glass fibers. Such a weave is intended to maintain a large proportion of fiberglass filaments in the axial alignment, and these longitudinal fibers are positioned and held relatively straight along the axis of the rod section, with widely spaced cross weaves. Two cloth weights are commonly employed. The heavier type has ten axial fibers for each cross weave, and the lighter fabric is woven with a six-to-one ratio. These cloth layers are cut in trapezoidal patterns precisely worked out to control wall thickness and provide the desired casting performance.

When the fabric is patterned and cut for a rod section, the fiber direction is laid parallel to its axis, providing the longitudinal alignment of the fiberglass. The cross weaves lie circumferentially around the mandrel, aligning the axial fibers properly and providing lateral tube strength, and resisting the elliptical deformation of the glass under heavy casting loads. The stabilizing effects of these cross fibers are critical to the proper strength and casting power and action of any rod taper.

Several techniques of thermal curing have evolved. Primitive fiberglass rods were made with plasticized nylon phenolic resins. Its performance was excellent, but its coloring caused problems. Such phenolics darken with age, and these problems have been solved with newer epoxy and polyester resins that have replaced the phenolics. Some rods are finished with other colors, and still use the older phenolics. However, most modern fiberglass blanks have their color pigments mixed into their resins. Both polyester and epoxy resins are remarkably durable, and their coloring is relatively stable. The fabric method of tubular rod construction will permit an unlimited spectrum of rod tapers, depending on the cloth patterns and wall densities used, and their ultimate costs are a function of design complexity and metal fittings.

The early glass rods were relatively poor, since the manufacturers had not learned to handle the new material and shape it into workable fibers. Most early tapers were also the prisoners of the Hewitt influence that had advocated rather fast actions that could handle the rapier flick-flick rhythms Hewitt insisted were necessary to dry the hackles of the dry fly. Hewitt himself abandoned such fast-action tapers in his middle years, but his influence had a persuasive inertia. Basic fiberglass rod actions have evolved in terms of four primary designs, although the rigidity of a thin-walled tube of relatively large diameter is ideally suited to the Hewitt fast-butt theology. Extra-fast rods display their most dramatic curvature in the upper quarter of the rod tapers. Their quick rhythms are suited to a series of brisk false casts and are easily mastered by fishermen with marginal casting skills, which made them popular with both rodmakers and a large percentage of their customers. However, they will not fish ultrafine tippets well or accommodate extremely long casts except in the hands of a skilled power caster, and they are tiring to use. Fast-action rods do most of their bending in the upper third, and with maximum curvature confined to the upper two-thirds of the taper, a fly rod has a moderate fiberglass action. Slow-action rods that bend progressively from the tip into the handle are most desirable for trout fishing, since delicacy is more important than the raw butt power needed to break a tarpon. Such actions have long been the hallmark of the finest modern split-cane rods, particularly in the radical tapers of American builders like Garrison and Young—and in the Pezon & Michel parabolics worked out by the remarkable Charles Ritz.

Such refinements have been slow in coming in most fiberglass production rods, although considerable improvement has occurred in the past dozen years. The compound tapers found in the best modern bamboo, with their extremely fine tips and steep calibrations to a relatively muscular midsection and a flat taper flexing well into the handle from the butt guide, were first explored by craftsmen like Young and Garrison. Perhaps the most radical experiments came from the cane-littered workshop of Young, although some of the finest unquestionably were split and hand-planed by Garrison. Such compound tapers will fish a finer tippet and cast longer with greater delicacy and less effort, ounce for ounce, than any other fly rods ever built. Fiberglass production rods are much lighter than comparable bamboo tapers, but ultralight tippets and distance with both delicacy and precision are still a little beyond their technology. Perhaps the fiberglass rods of artisans like Neumann, Cummings, and Peak, who modify the wall thicknesses by hand after culling through first-grade blanks carefully, are the best examples of glass construction approaching the unique qualities present in a really fine bamboo rod. Most knowledgeable fiberglass partisans admit that glass has yet to equal the violinlike excellence of superb split-cane rods, and some major fiberglass manufacturers even admit they are still trying.

Bamboo is a pretty remarkable material, Jim Green of Fenwick observed at Sun Valley last summer, *and trying to match its unique qualities in glass can only increase your respect for cane.*

Fly-rod tapers are largely determined in the problems associated with the stresses and considerations of casting. Trout-fishing considerations seldom equal the fish-playing loads encountered in salt water, where the raw strength of billfish and tarpon becomes as important as the dynamics of fly casting. Few fiberglass rods are now manufactured with anything but medium actions, and the clublike tapers that were common in the early years have mercifully disappeared. The better fiberglass rods are approaching the smooth, progressive tapers that work well down the butt sections and into the grip itself. Such semiparabolic actions have some demanding rhythms, and the choice between them and more conventional tapers really depends on the skills and preferences of each fisherman.

The full spectrum of these factors is involved in the calibrations and design tapers of modern fiberglass rods. The skilled rod designer who knows fiberglass understands that the amount of filaments at any particular calibration in a blank will determine the casting performance and character of the finished rod. The density of glass fibers is controlled by varying the cloth pattern that is cut from a roll of fiberglass at the genesis of each fly rod. The fabric pattern itself is tapered, although it does not resemble a finished rod. Typical patterns are trapezoidal in shape, looking more like a classic leg-of-mutton gun case. The butt dimension of the cloth pattern is typically much wider than the tip fabric, and the diagonal between the two varies widely. Variations in casting performance are achieved by increasing or decreasing the width of the cloth taper along its diagonal chord.

Since increasing the fiber count at any point will stiffen the rod action there, and decreasing the number of glass fibers results in increased flexibility under stress, an almost infinite number of rod actions are possible with minor changes in the cloth pattern.

Hollow blanks are fabricated by rolling the cloth pattern around a tapered mandrel. Design of the mandrel is important, and when a slender mandrel is used the wall thickness of the blank is relatively heavy. Using the same cloth pattern and a larger mandrel will obviously produce a larger diameter blank with slightly thinner wall thicknesses. However, when identical patterns are used, both blanks will have identical weights, but the thinner wall rod will have much greater power. The reason is the increased distance from the axis of the blank to its outer walls. Therefore both mandrel and cloth pattern are primary factors in the action of a fiberglass fly rod, and an equilibrium between mandrel diameter and pattern design is necessary to produce an optimal fiberglass rod.

Such thin-walled blanks are superior to a thick-walled section of equal weight and a smaller diameter, although there are limits to their advantages. Too much butt diameter is clumsy-looking and offers unacceptable wind resistance in casting. Large thin-walled blanks are also difficult and expensive to manufacture.

Once a new taper has been successfully field-tested, it is placed in production. Its woven fiberglass fabric is impregnated with resin and passed through rollers to remove the excess. The glass cloth is then oven-dried to evaporate the solvents and dry the resins until they are slightly tacky. The impregnated fabric is then rolled again with a sheet of polyethylene to separate the layers. Most manufacturers unroll the impregnated cloth later, cut sections slightly larger than the patterns, and stack them in layers on a pattern-cutting table with the longitudinal fibers aligned with the axis of the blank. The size of the stack is determined by the number required in an economical production run. Heavy metal templates are laid on the stacked sheets and a single pattern-cut prepares a number of rods simultaneously. Metal templates are necessary both because scoring the cloth along their contours is easier and because their weight holds the several layers firmly, duplicating the pattern with precision.

Heat attaches the straight edge of the prepared pattern to its tapered mandrel, and it is tightly rolled into a tapered tube. Many industrial methods are used, but perhaps the best is rolling the prepared mandrel between two heated platens under controlled pressures. The precision of this process is absolutely critical in the production of a high-quality glass rod. The machinery must be quite precise to maintain uniform pressure and control along the entire length of the mandrel while the pattern is being rolled. The laminating material is important, too, and its wall density is the key to a quality glass blank. Really dense glass walls are almost totally free of porosity, and such integrity of lamination is critical in both lightness and strength. Making a dense laminate is impossible without inside and outside molding pressures. Obviously, the internal mold is provided by the mandrel, while the external molding pressures are accomplished by several methods. Cellophane film wrapped under tension is commonly used, but a tightly wrapped polyester or fleuroplastic film is also employed by some manufacturers. Silicone rubber tubing molded around the freshly wrapped fiberglass cloth is a third method. Whatever the method, the external pressures working on the laminates must be applied with a precisely controlled uniform tension. The quality of the laminate depends on the uniformity of the tensile wrapping, and its pressures accomplish two things: its primary effect is compression of the laminates during its original spiralling application, and its secondary effect is the increased pressure applied when it shrinks in the curing cycle.

Once the laminate is pressure-wrapped in cellophane or some other synthetic film, it is ready for the final curing of its resins. Final curing of the wrapped mandrel occurs when it is hung in a vertical oven and subjected to from 300 to 350 degrees, depending on the specific resin used, for thirty minutes to an hour. The thermal stresses force the resins to flow with a lowered viscosity, while the cellophane film simultaneously shrinks and applies great pressure to the laminate of fiberglass cloth and resins. During the proper curing period the gelatinous resin hardens and cures.

When curing is complete, the mandrel core is extracted from the freshly hardened fiberglass blank. Extraction is usually accomplished with a power ram and metal-plate die. The die consists of a hole precisely drilled

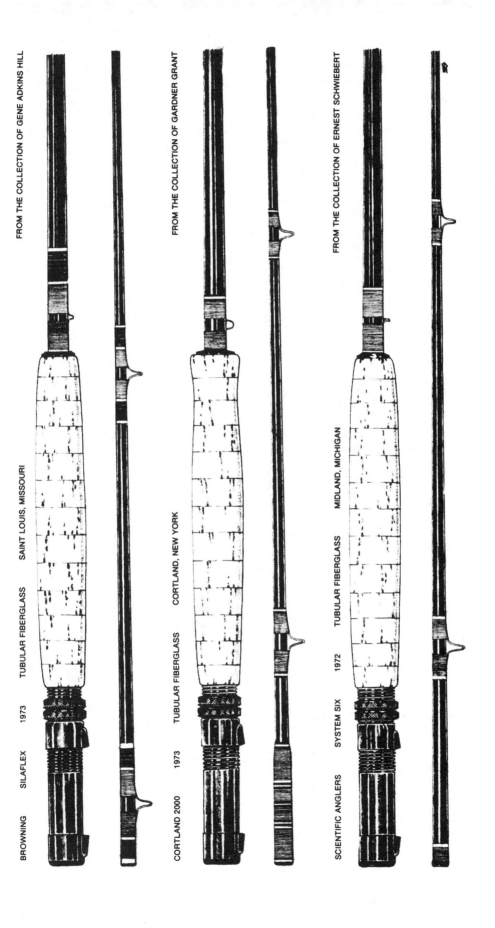

FROM THE COLLECTION OF GENE ADKINS HILL

BROWNING   SILAFLEX   1973   TUBULAR FIBERGLASS   SAINT LOUIS, MISSOURI

FROM THE COLLECTION OF GARDNER GRANT

CORTLAND 2000   1973   TUBULAR FIBERGLASS   CORTLAND, NEW YORK

FROM THE COLLECTION OF ERNEST SCHWIEBERT

SCIENTIFIC ANGLERS   SYSTEM SIX   1972   TUBULAR FIBERGLASS   MIDLAND, MICHIGAN to receive the mandrel butt, but not large enough to accept the freshly cured blank. The power ram strips the mandrel from the tubular blank, and it is cleaned and prepared to receive another cloth pattern.

The freshly cured blank is complete at this stage of fabrication, except for stripping the cellophane and finishing. The cellophane wrappings are removed with abrasive brushes, tumbling, conventional cutting and stripping, and high-pressure steam. With the film stripped and removed, the resin still carries the fingerprints of its spiral wraps. Some rodmakers leave these spiral wrapping patterns in the resin surfaces of the blank, perhaps liking their appearance, although they play no role in the performance of the finished rod. Other manufacturers polish their blanks to a satin finish, and a final finish will be applied later. Custom builders often polish the blanks at this point, not only to remove the resin spirals, but also to modify wall thickness and action.

The finish coating applied when the blank is completed is intended to protect the rod. It is usually a modern synthetic finish that improves both the durability and appearance of the fiberglass. Tough synthetics like epoxy, acrylics, and polyurethanes protect the glass from moisture, scratches, mars, solvents, and structural denigration from the ultraviolet components of sunlight. Such finishes also protect the material from temperature extremes, and must be applied in a series of thin coatings that will not dampen the rod's action and make it feel sluggish. The several coats are separately applied and buffed until the finish is hard and glasslike. The fiberglass blank is then finished and ready for assembly.

Mounting the ferrules that join the rod sections together is usually the first step of assembly, and most fiberglass rods were originally fitted with conventional metal ferrules. Chrome-plated brass is common because it is easily worked and relatively inexpensive. Anodized aluminum ferrules are also used extensively, because they are also easily fabricated and much lighter than the conventional chrome-plated brass. However, both aluminum and brass wear easily and their factory fit is short-lived. Some manufacturers have added a rubber or nylon gasket to their male ferrules to extend the life span of brass and aluminum stock. The custom builders use nickel-silver ferrules, like the traditional makers of fine split-cane rods, because they work and machine beautifully. The material is relatively expensive, but it holds its tolerances for many years, popping melodically like a bottle of fine wine.

However, several manufacturers have introduced variations of fiberglass ferrules in recent years. These ferrules have the advantage of a more flexible transfer of power than a metal ferrule can supply. The sleeve-type ferrule is fabricated by seating a larger sleeve of fiberglass over the rod tip and fitting the butt section inside that sleeve. Browning has added the wrinkle of a sleeve-type ferrule designed to wear continually into a deeper fit across the life of the rod. The spigot-type glass ferrule involves a solid fiberglass plug permanently seated into the butt section, and the hollow tip section is fitted tightly down over the plug. It provides the most secure fit of any fiberglass ferrule type, and it is more flexible than any metal design, although it is a little heavier than the sleeve-type joint. Perhaps the most unusual fiberglass ferrule is the Feralite design patented by Fenwick in 1962, in which the hollow tip section slides down over the butt. The female tubular fit is reinforced with a guide position directly over its stress zone, and the Feralite design is unquestionably the lightest joint available on modern glass production rods.

Assembly begins with mounting the ferrules. Mass production work usually supplies the blanks with an extra tab of fiberglass at the point where the ferrule will be seated. The blank is trimmed empirically in the shop and the glass is polished slightly to the proper fit. Most builders use a hot-melt cement to mount the ferrules on the blanks, permitting minor adjustments to achieve a straight fit that perfectly aligns the rod sections.

Once the ferrules are properly mounted, the reel fittings and grips follow. Some makers use preshaped cork grips, although the best fiberglass rods use the same specie-cork rings that fine bamboo craftsmen have used since the years that Halford reigned on the Houghton water of the Test and Gordon lived like a hermit on the Neversink. These rings are seated and glued separately and are shaped on a lathe after they are mounted on the butt section.

Cheap guides too widely spaced were too often a commonplace flaw in the early fiberglass rods. The same fine carboloy and stainless guides used on first-rate cane rods are used on the better fiberglass models these days. Too many guides create shooting friction in casting, while too few guides permit the line to slap the rod and generate even greater friction. First-rate cane rods have at least one snake guide per overall foot of length, plus the butt guide, to distribute casting loads properly. Since glass is less fragile, fewer guides are needed. The guides are mounted with thread wrappings in essentially the same fashion on both bamboo and fiberglass rods, although some fiberglass rodmakers have regrettably started to use garish wrappings of gold or silver mylar tapes—and even some of the best fiberglass rods are still guilty of tastelessly excessive ornamentation of their products.

The windings are usually fixed with a color preservative and finished with a protective coat of lacquer, varnish, or synthetic material. Cummings covers only the windings of his rods, leaving the rest in the matte finish of his hand-rubbed blanks. Lacquers are commonly used because they are cheap and provide a high lustre. However, most custom fiberglass rods are fully protected with a fine spar varnish. Modern rodmakers also have many other finishes available, including epoxies, polyurethanes, and various acrylics. These materials are infinitely more waterproof and wear-resistant than the finest varnish. Polyurethanes are readily available and are remarkably durable, although they are relatively difficult to apply and dry quite slowly. Modern epoxies are also durable when mixed with components that absorb ultraviolet light. Acrylics are usually available in colors, and are not readily available in clear solutions, since their primary market lies in automobile finishes.

Many anglers are still a little uncertain about the immutable differences between split bamboo and fiberglass.

Cane is just a rich man's affectation, is a common observation on our trout water these days. *Glass is just as good for anybody!*

There is some truth in their arguments. Certainly the fiberglass revolution has virtually eliminated the cheap and moderately priced cane rods that once flooded the market, particularly the imports of poor Japanese bamboo. Such rods deserved the extinction they suffered with the perfection of fiberglass designs, and only the moderately expensive and expensive bamboo makers have survived. The best fiberglass rods are lighter, more durable, and considerably less expensive than our modern split-cane rods.

The finest glass rods are better than many moderately expensive bamboo models, although they have yet to match the poetry of the best split-cane craftsmen. There has never been a question of making a glass rod that could equal the performance of first-rate cane since fiberglass is a medium with utterly different properties. Our best fiberglass craftsmen have finally begun to forget trying for a bamboo facsimile and have started to search for topologies of wall thickness and rod tapers true to the unique character of glass itself.

My experience with fiberglass rods over the past thirty-odd years has pinpointed an intriguing mixture of virtues and faults in the casting performance of glass. Bending stresses result in virtually no dimensional distortions in split-cane rods, except for the obvious rhythms of tension and compression that occur in its cellular structure. The more casting stress imposed on a bamboo section, the more power it generates toward recovery from that stress. Bamboo will continue to accept increasing loads and gather power progressively until it reaches its stress limits and shatters. Tubular glass behaves quite differently. Bending action in any tube tends to make its cross section elliptical, and when the bending-plane axis of the oval is exaggerated enough, the tube cannot accept the load. Bending an ordinary drinking straw will demonstrate the deformation of a tube under such stress. Tubular glass starts to accumulate power as quickly as its loading begins, but when the casting loads deform it too radically, it fails to gather power and accommodate those loads. Any caster skilled enough to handle a line longer than the loading capacity of his glass rod has felt it refuse such casting stresses, although its resiliency and strength keep it from fracturing—and it will handle such distances better with slightly reduced line velocity and loading. Such variables are the behavior differences between tubular and solid construction in any material, but their differences in recovery from stress are related to the physical properties of bamboo and fiberglass themselves.

Recovery from stress is simply the speed and manner in which a bent material recovers its original shape. It is relatively easy to demonstrate with a fly rod. The rod should be held out horizontally with a rigid wrist and stressed downward with a sharp stroke. Its tip section will snap toward the floor and recover swiftly, rising slightly above the horizontal before it returns to rest. The recovery rates of bamboo and glass are different. The finest cane rods recover a little more slowly, but their recovery is precise, and their oscillations end more quickly. Their behavior stems from their longer cell fibers, while glass rods have much shorter fibers and recover from flexure more quickly.

Strangely, the resilience and recovery of fiberglass under the loads of casting is so good that it becomes a disadvantage. The problems are readily apparent with the same stress-recovery demonstration: holding the rod horizontally and stressing it sharply downward. The tip section will recover rapidly, snapping back above its original plane, and it will continue to oscillate above and below the horizontal before it stops. Such behavior under stress is simply implicit in the character of fiberglass.

Skilled casters can partially compensate for this weakness, but it unquestionably affects their performance. Casting really well is difficult with fiberglass, and it is no accident that the finest fly casters invariably prefer bamboo. This preference lies partially in the willingness of split cane to accept the loading limits of the caster's full strength and timing and skills. Some of the ability of bamboo rods to accommodate stress and deliver power lies in their sharp recovery from stress, with less vertical oscillation in the tip section. Such oscillation results in line slap against the guides and the rod itself, causing friction that can kill the precision and velocity of a really long cast. Oscillation also tends to pull the line back, short of its full distance. Accuracy and distance both suffer, and delicacy is almost impossible in the lightest glass tapers.

Although their impacts are perhaps less obvious, ordinary fishermen are clearly affected by these problems; and because of his limited fishing time and practice a less skilled caster finds it difficult to compensate for them. Timing and accuracy are just a little more difficult to master. The methods of fiberglass fabrication also result in slightly thicker tip calibrations, which mean more power is required to drive the tip through the atmospheric resistance to the completion of the cast. Such extra power does not readily lend itself to subtle delivery of either line or fly, although it will throw a stylishly tight casting loop, and heavier tip diameters in a fiberglass taper are ill-suited to cobweb-fine tippets. The radical compound tapers found in the parabolic designs of craftsmen like Young and Garrison and Payne, with their steep final calibrations to a delicate hooking tip, are almost impossible in the fabrication of glass.

Fiberglass has three disadvantages for casting and fishing in modern terms: its tubular rod sections deform and become oval-shaped under ultimate casting loads; it tends to oscillate too much in its recovery from casting stress; and its fabrication techniques are not suited to really fine-tip diameters. Obviously, there are excellent fiberglass rods of superb performance and cheap products that fish poorly. The best quality blanks and tapers minimize the marginal properties of tubular glass construction, but these inherent physical problems exist.

However, this does not mean that a modern fisherman must confine himself to split-cane rods. Their cost alone places them beyond the reach of most anglers, while the price of a fine fiberglass rod is moderate. Glass requires less pampering and care, and is ideally suited to the beginner or occasional fisherman. It can also survive excessive moisture and temperature extremes, making it a good choice in some climates. It is much lighter than a comparable bamboo rod. Its weight makes a long rod less tiring to use, which can be important to children or women, since rod length is advantageous in learning to cast. Glass rods can combine both lightness and length. Such properties are also important where distance and continual casting are important—and even an expert fisherman can appreciate a fiberglass rod after a long day, simply because it fatigues him less.

It is virtually impossible to purchase a bamboo rod of poor quality cane if it has been produced in the United States, since our best rodmakers never exhausted their seasoned stocks, although the end was in sight for some companies. However, it is possible to purchase an inferior fiberglass rod. Tubular blanks come from many manufacturers and vary surprisingly in quality. There are many factors involved. Quality of fabrication, diameter, wall thickness, fiber alignment and calibration, type of weave, and the character of the taper are equally important. Perhaps the best advice lies in purchasing a glass rod from the best manufacturers.

The angler who fishes often and fishes difficult or demanding water should probably choose bamboo. Its performance will improve both his pleasure and his sport. It will give him great pride of ownership. Since it will last many years with reasonable care, it is not really expensive. But the man who fishes seldom and merely wants a rod available from time to time does not need a really first-rate piece of equipment. Spare rods and camp rods for guests fall into this category. It is doubtful that the best fiberglass rods are really necessary for such purposes. The cost and choice of a fly rod, in either fiberglass or cane, should be based on the skills that a fisherman already has or hopes to acquire. If his aspirations include selective trout on hard-fished waters, he must find a way to afford the finest possible rod.

There are several fine manufacturers who produce good factory-built rods of fiberglass, and there are also several artisans who modify factory blanks and add more expensive reel seats and fittings than are commonly found with glass. Several manufacturers of bamboo rods also assemble first-rate glass blanks with the fittings normally found on their more expensive split-cane products.

Fenwick was founded at Seattle in 1954, and its leadership in the fiberglass field dates to the arrival of Jim Green as its technical director six year later. Green is one of the finest fly casters in the world, and his work has led to several technical innovations. Fenwick pioneered the first fiberglass ferrules in 1962, and Green kept on experimenting with the fiberglass tapers and construction methods. He has continued to refine his Feralite ferrules, until their present design is an unusual combination of lightness and strength. Most ferrule connections consist of a single rod shaft

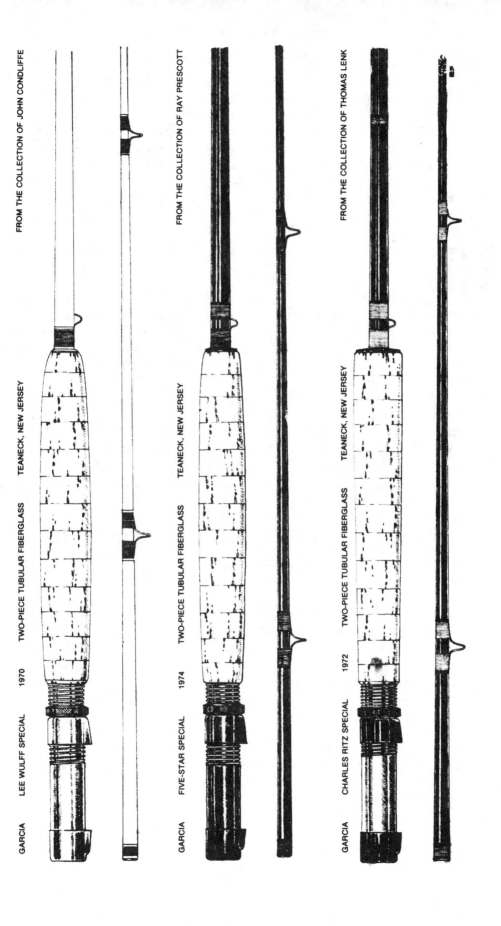

GARCIA   LEE WULFF SPECIAL   1970   TWO-PIECE TUBULAR FIBERGLASS   TEANECK, NEW JERSEY   FROM THE COLLECTION OF JOHN CONDLIFFE

GARCIA   FIVE-STAR SPECIAL   1974   TWO-PIECE TUBULAR FIBERGLASS   TEANECK, NEW JERSEY   FROM THE COLLECTION OF RAY PRESCOTT

GARCIA   CHARLES RITZ SPECIAL   1972   TWO-PIECE TUBULAR FIBERGLASS   TEANECK, NEW JERSEY   FROM THE COLLECTION OF THOMAS LENK

cut in two or three sections and joined together, but the Fenwick patent involves two separate rod blanks. The tip section has a hollow butt reinforced with a firmly seated guide, and the butt section has a tip reinforced with a solid glass plug. The design had some early problems, since it involved discontinuous rod tapers, and many expert casters felt it had some stress problems of power transfer. Fenwick clearly recognized the problem and acquired one of the major fiberglass blank manufacturers in 1969, hoping to control the discontinuous tapers by making the glass rod blanks themselves in Seattle.

High-pressure lamination and experimental mandrels have since produced fly rods that have successfully married the large hollow tip sections to the solid small-diameter butt. Although their tubular diameters are radically different, their performance under casting loads has now achieved good continuity of stress transfer. High-quality fiberglass and control of wall thicknesses have achieved this breakthrough. Fenwick achieves such high-density lamination that the glass fibers become almost homogeneous, leaving a smoothly lustrous finish that almost glows in bright sunlight and requires no opaque finish to conceal the blemishes and flaws so often found in fiberglass.

The fittings are typical of the best production glass rods. Anodized reel seats with a fixed butt cap, movable hood, and tightening rings are made of workable aluminum alloys. The guides are chromium-plated steel, and the nylon wrappings are a rich chocolate that closely matches the reddish brown translucency of the rod itself. Trim accents of black and white nylon finish the wrappings, and the rods and wrappings are protected with three hand-applied coats of clear epoxy. The understated appearance of the Fenwicks is perhaps marred slightly by the coarse nylon cross-wrappings on the lower butt and a trademark that is too large, but their performance is excellent. Their prices are in the medium range for good fiberglass production rods, and Fenwick rods have many partisans, particularly among the skilled fly casters along the Pacific Coast. There are several fine trout-size models.

Fenwick makes six fly rods for relatively delicate presentation and five-weight lines. The FF535 and FF605 weigh less than two ounces, are fitted with skeleton reel seats and sliding bands, and are five and a half and six feet, respectively. The FF705 is a delicate seven-foot taper weighing just under three ounces and is ideally suited to fishing fine with small flies on relatively small streams. It is fitted with the standard locking reel seat, like all the Fenwick rods above seven feet. The FF755 model is seven and a half feet, weighing three and one-eighth ounces, and taking a five-weight line. It is a fine all-round rod for delicate presentation on medium-size waters. The FF805 is eight feet, weighs three and three-eighths ounces, and is designed for relatively small-fly work on the larger rivers of our western mountains. The FF855 is a surprisingly delicate eight and a half feet and only three and five-eighths ounces, matched with a five-weight line, and is one of the best models in the Fenwick line. These six rods designed for five-weight lines are intended for normal casting ranges of ten to fifty feet, except for the two smallest models, which are intended for distances of ten to thirty feet in normal fishing. These small rods are capable of handling sixty-odd feet in the hands of skilled casters, while the others will punch out the entire fly line, although they are not primarily intended for distance work on big water.

There are four Fenwick rods designed for six-weight lines and more general trout-fishing problems, ranging from small dry flies to medium-size streamers, except for the FF706 model. It is seven feet long, weighs only three and one-eighth ounces, and is intended for general fishing with relatively small flies and light tippets. The FF756 is seven and a half feet, weighs three and one-quarter ounces, and is perhaps the best all-around rod of its size from Fenwick, although many knowledgeable anglers like the FF806. It measures eight feet and weighs three and a half ounces, and is also quite versatile, with the muscle to handle relatively large trout flies and streamers. FF856 is a superb long rod delicate enough for a six-weight line and weighs only three and seven-eighths ounces at a full eight and a half feet. It is a fine nymphing rod, with sufficient length to mend line and control fly speed, and it is also ideally suited to fishing the big western spring creeks, where a fisherman must false-cast in shoulder-high reeds or crawl infantry-style along the banks, with sufficient rod length to hold his backcasts high.

Fenwick makes two fly rods for the seven-weight line, which Jim Green believes is the best all-around line size for all kinds of trout fishing. The FF807 rod is his favorite design. It measures eight feet and weighs three and three-quarters ounces. Green believes his FF857 model at eight and a half feet and three and seven-eighths ounces is an ideal fly rod for general fishing on big-trout water. These rods are both designed for a normal casting range of fifteen to sixty feet, although eighty-foot casts are not beyond a good fisherman, and in the hands of a real distance man one-hundred-foot casts are possible.

The Fenwick rods designed for eight-weight lines are probably all the muscle any trout fisherman needs, except perhaps for really big steelheads. The FF858 is an eight-and-a-half-foot rod weighing four and one-eighth ounces, and will handle all the line you can throw. The FF908 is a similar taper measuring nine feet and weighing only four and a half ounces, giving the big-water fisherman the delicacy of an eight-weight with the extra length for deep wading. There are several larger fiberglass rods in the Fenwick line, but except for the FF909 for a nine-weight line, they offer more power than a trout fisherman needs—unless he fishes big water often with large bucktails and streamers.

Scientific Anglers have developed a series of fine fiberglass rods of excellent quality and design, matching them with fly lines of their own manufacture and reels of their own design that are built by Hardy in England. These matching rod systems have become quite popular in recent years, and the rods themselves are beautiful in their simplicity.

The high-density blanks are designed in a continuous slow-action taper joined together with a spigot-type glass ferrule, with a male plug in the butt section that fits into the hollow female tubing of the tip section. The tubular blanks are densely laminated out of high-quality fiberglass cloth, using phenolic resins under controlled pressures, and with a reasonably delicate tip calibration for each design. The actions are slow and work deep into the butt section under progressively longer casting loads. The ferrule system is a little heavier and less flexible than the Feralite type, but it is a little more secure, and some connoisseurs of fiberglass argue that it is better looking. The blanks are beautifully finished with multiple sandings, coatings, and bakings that result in a rich mahogany finish. Stainless snake guides and a carboloy butt guide are found with dark brown wrappings and paler trim. The reel seats are anodized a chocolate color to match the rods, although I have often thought some consideration might have been made to relating their fittings to the brightwork of their matching reels—thereby making them a visual system of fly tackle, as well as a system based upon the weight of the lines and reels alone.

Scientific Anglers offer a light rod of seven feet two inches, weighing three ounces, for a matching four-weight line. The System Four reel measures two and three-quarters inches in diameter and weighs three and a half ounces, making this the lightest fiberglass production rod from any manufacturer in terms of its matching line weight.

The System Five and System Six rods are medium-light to medium actions ideally suited to most trout-fishing problems. The Five is seven feet, seven inches long, weighs three and one-quarter ounces, and takes the matching five-weight lines. It is recommended for small- to medium-size water, while the six-weight rod is suited to slightly larger streams and fly sizes. It measures eight feet one inch and weighs three and a half ounces. The matching System Five reel is three inches in diameter and weighs three and three-quarters ounces, while the slightly larger System Six measures three and one-quarter inches and weighs four and one-quarter ounces. These are both excellent basic rods designed for knowledgeable trout fishermen, although their manufacturer does not recommend them for bucktails.

Their System Seven and System Eight tapers have the power for bucktails and bigger water. The Seven rod is eight feet five inches in length and weighs four ounces; its matching reel is three and seven-sixteenths inches in diameter and weighs four and a half ounces. The System Eight rod is eight feet eight inches and weighs four and five-eighths ounces, and its reel is three and five-eighths inches in diameter and weighs five and three-quarters ounces. These two fly rods have enough power to cast long lines and handle large fish easily, and I have taken many twenty-pound salmon on the System Eight—as well as several big bonefish on the Bahamas marl flats.

The System Nine measures eight feet eleven inches and it weighs a full five ounces. Its reel is three and three-quarters inches in diameter and weighs six and one-quarter ounces, taking a nine-weight forward taper with ample Dacron backing. Although the System Nine seems a little too powerful for most trout fishing, it has a surprising number of supporters on big western rivers like the Snake and lower Yellowstone and the swift-flowing Deschutes.

Some anglers have questioned the irregular lengths of the Scientific Anglers series of fly rods, arguing that varied wall thicknesses and tapers could have achieved the same equilibrium with line and reel weights. The quiet visual character of the rods is perhaps the best of the major manufacturers, and the four-weight model is unique among large-scale production tapers. Although their price range is among the most expensive of fiberglass rods, even from the bamboo makers who also market glass, these are superb fishing tools with first-rate workmanship and design specifications.

Although Phillipson does not make fiberglass rods for smaller lines than a five-weight taper, their products are among the finest available today. Phillipson uses the finest fiberglass cloth, cross-reinforced and having extremely high linear counts of glass fibers, and laminates it over a special inner mandrel with epoxy and unusually high pressures to achieve extremely dense tubular walls. Such epoxy laminates are demonstrably stronger than conventional tubular blanks, making smaller diameters possible throughout the length of the tapers, as well as lighter total weights. The finish is a delicate salmon-tinted brown, fashioned of smooth, durable epoxy, and concealing the seams in the sleeve-type ferrules. The ferrule sleeves are reinforced with a delicate metal band that has become a Phillipson trademark, and the guides are carboloy and stainless steel. The nylon wrappings have the simplicity found only in the work of first-rate bamboo craftsmen, as Bill Phillipson is part of the split-cane tradition, going back to his years of building bamboo at Granger. The anodized aluminum reel seats are nicely machined, and like many fine cane rods, the fillers are shaped of first-quality specie cork. Phillipson manufactures three grades of fly rods, although his Epoxite series is his finest achievement in fiberglass thus far.

There are nine tapers in the Epoxite series. Although they have not been available for long, many fishermen are extolling the virtues of the high-density laminates and their performance. The EF60 measures six feet and weighs only one and three-quarters ounces, taking either a four- or five-weight line. It is certainly one of the best midge-size rods in glass. The FF66 is a six-and-a-half-footer of two and one-eighth ounces, also rated for either four- or five-weight tapers, and it also is a fine midge-type rod. The Phillipson EF70 is a seven-footer weighing only two and a half ounces, taking the five-weight lines, and the EF76 is seven-and-a-half, weighing two and seven-eighths ounces. It also takes the five-weight tapers. The EF80 is a fine, all-around design at eight feet and three and one-quarter ounces, its six-weight tapers well suited to most American fishing with medium-size waters and flies. The EF86 is eight and a half feet and three and five-eighths ounces, taking a seven-weight taper and supplying a relatively delicate rod with a distance capability. The EF90 is a surprising rod for an eight-weight line at nine feet and only four ounces and is a superb tool for big-water problems at unusually light weight, but the most surprising design in the Epoxite series is unquestionably the EF96. It is nine and a half feet in length, but it weighs only four and one-eighth ounces and takes only a five-weight line—certainly an optimal tool for fishing fine on a big western river where distance is also needed; its delicacy and length make it a fine nymphing rod.

These Phillipson Epoxites are priced competitively with the Scientific Anglers' rods, and while I prefer the coloring of the Scientific blanks, the functional wrappings and skeletal-locking reel seat with cork fillers found on the Phillipsons should be commended for a simplicity and esthetic restraint seldom found on factory rods. It is almost impossible to convince the corporate mentality that our fishermen recognize and pay for performance and quality, and that the baroque ornamentation of mylar and variegated threads found on too many fiberglass production rods are really not important in fly-fishing sales.

Phillipson makes a second series of fiberglass rods at about half the price of his Epoxite models. These Royal Wand rods have a less expensive fiberglass ferrule of the sleeve type, and are made with less expensive glass blanks laminated with epoxy. Their finish is also epoxy, and the snake guides are still stainless steel. The stripping guide is carboloy, and there is an anodized full-locking reel seat. The smaller models in the Royal Wand line have cork reel-seat fillers, making them quite light although their matching lines are not as light as those in the expensive Epoxite.

The RWF60 is six feet and one and seven-eighths ounces, but its calibrations and action demand a six-weight line, like the RWF66, which is six and a half feet and weighs two and three-eighths ounces. The RWF70 is seven feet and two and five-eighths ounces, and like the RWF76 at seven and a half feet and three ounces, it also takes a six-weight line. The RWF80 at eight feet and three and three-eighths ounces is also designed for six-weight tapers. The RWF86 measures eight and a half feet and weighs three and five-eighths ounces, taking a relatively light seven-weight, and the RWF90 is a full nine feet. It weighs only four ounces, and its action is superbly accommodated with an eight-weight taper. Although the lighter models are a little muscular for fishing really fine tippets, taking six-weight lines in spite of their midge-size weights and dimensions, these Royal Wand rods in the lengths beyond eight feet are quite delicate. Their price lies in the Fenwick range.

Phillipson also manufactures its Master series of fiberglass fly rods, which cost about half the price of their Royal Wand line, yet many fiberglass partisans rate them the best of the inexpensive glass products. These are light brown blanks of quality glass fabric laminated in conventional phenolic resins and are—surprisingly, considering their low price—fitted with nickel-silver ferrules.

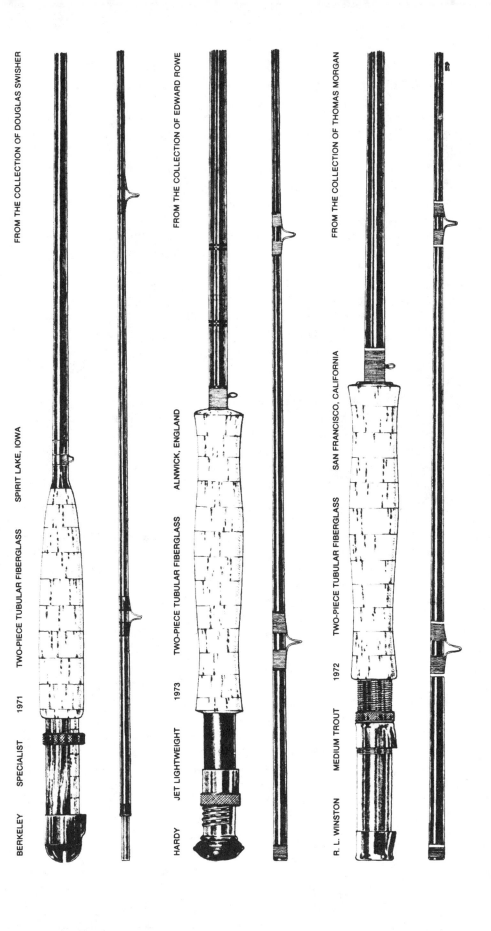

FROM THE COLLECTION OF DOUGLAS SWISHER

BERKELEY   SPECIALIST   1971   TWO-PIECE TUBULAR FIBERGLASS   SPIRIT LAKE, IOWA

FROM THE COLLECTION OF EDWARD ROWE

HARDY   JET LIGHTWEIGHT   1973   TWO-PIECE TUBULAR FIBERGLASS   ALNWICK, ENGLAND

FROM THE COLLECTION OF THOMAS MORGAN

R. L. WINSTON   MEDIUM TROUT   1972   TWO-PIECE TUBULAR FIBERGLASS   SAN FRANCISCO, CALIFORNIA

The MF60 has a cork reel-seat filler, measures six feet and weighs one and seven-eighths ounces. It takes a six-weight line like the MF66, which is six and a half feet and two and seven-eighths ounces with its full locking reel seat. The MF70 is a seven-foot rod weighing three and one-eighth ounces for a six-weight line. There are two seven-and-a-half-foot rods in the Phillipson Master series. The MF76L weighs only three and one-eighth ounces, taking a five-weight double taper perfectly, and the MF76 matches a six-weight line at three and a half ounces. The MF80L is also unusually light for its length of eight feet and weight of three and three-quarters ounces, and it is also rated for a five-weight taper. The straight MF80 is eight feet in length and weighs four ounces, taking a six-weight line. The MF86 weighs four and one-quarter ounces and is a full eight and a half feet. Its seven-weight line makes a fine big-water tool, and the MF90 takes an eight-weight line at nine feet and four and a half ounces. But the most intriguing rods in this series are the seven-and-a-half foot and eight-foot tapers for five-weight lines, particularly at their moderate cost.

Cortland is producing a similarly priced series of fiberglass rods it calls the FR2000 models, and many knowledgeable anglers endorse them without regard for their bargain prices. The Cortland rods are relatively light and their tapers are well designed considering their modest prices. These rods use a strong fiberglass ferrule with a firm spigot-type plug. Stainless steel snake guides and a carboloy butt guide complete the fittings, secured with chocolate wrappings and pale brown trim. The anodized double-locking-ring reel seat has a rubber butt plate like the more expensive Fenwick and Scientific Anglers rods. The fiberglass blanks and guide wrappings are protected by epoxy finishes. The six-and-a-half-foot model weighs two and three-quarters ounces and takes a five-weight double taper line. The seven-foot Cortland weighs a full three ounces and matches a six-weight taper, like the seven-and-a-half-footer at three and a half ounces. The eight-foot design weighs four and one-quarter ounces and takes a seven-weight, while the eight-and-a-half-foot Cortland requires a full eight-weight taper at four and three-quarters ounces. There are some big-water anglers who swear by these Cortland rods, particularly considering their relatively low cost, and I know several good fishermen who like the four-and-three-quarters-ounce rod for surprisingly heavy work.

Browning manufactures five fiberglass rods of fine, high-density phenolic laminates. The rods are a rich chocolate brown and are fitted with a glass-to-glass ferrule designed to wear into a deeper fit over the years. The anodized screw-locking reel seat matches the rod color, and the price range of the Browning rods is moderate. The seven-footer weighs two and a half ounces and takes a five-weight line, while the seven-and-a-half-foot model at two and three-quarters ounces is balanced with a six-weight. The eight-foot Browning weighs three and a half ounces for a seven-weight taper. The eight-and-a-half-foot model is a full five ounces and matches weight-forward taper in eight-weight. The nine-foot Browning weighs five and one-quarter ounces and will handle a nine-weight line.

Garcia controls the Conolon manufacturing operation that first developed the tubular fiberglass construction methods that still dominate the rod industry, and in recent years Garcia has worked with celebrated anglers like Lee Wulff and Charles Ritz to design new fiberglass tapers. Conolon also pioneered the longitudinal weaves, high-density laminates, and difficult phenolic bonding methods that have made our modern fiberglass actions possible. The Wulff tapers include the familiar six-foot design for ultralight salmon fishing, which has too much tip muscle for really light trout work, but the larger models include some tapers that work well down into the butt section under casting stresses. The Wulff series is surprisingly moderate in price. The Ritz tapers are somewhat more radical, coming from perhaps the chief proponent of the compound calibrations that Ritz christened the parabolic action thirty-odd years ago. Duplicating and improving the Pezon & Michel performance that Ritz developed over the years proved so difficult that Conolon retained Russ Peak, perhaps the most celebrated of the fiberglass craftsmen, to work out the Ritz templates for preparing the glass cloth in the Ritz series. Peak also added the aluminum ferrule covering that fits inside the glass tip like a conventional spigot-type joint.

The Wulff series for Garcia is finished in a dull blue epoxy with blue anodized locking reel seats and the spigot-type ferrules. The seven-foot model weighs three ounces and takes a seven-weight line; and the seven-and-a-half-foot, for seven-weight, weighs three and a half ounces. The eight-foot Garcia Wulff weighs four ounces and also is designed for seven-weight lines. The eight-and-a-half-foot rod at four and a half ounces takes an an eight-weight Wulff long belly beautifully, and many knowledgeable western trout fishermen find it the best in the Garcia Wulff series. The nine-foot model is designed for a ten-weight forward taper, weighs five ounces and has the muscle to cast big flies in high winds.

The Wulff series also has two one-piece rods fitted with skeletal sliding-band seats. The five-and-a-half-footer weighs one and a half ounces and takes a six-weight double taper. The six-footer weighs one and three-quarters ounces and is balanced with a seven-weight—the classic Wulff prescription for salmon fishing.

Charles Ritz has been fascinated with the potential of fiberglass for fly rods these past twenty years, ever since the first Harnell blanks became available in Europe. His bamboo rods were much more responsive and recovered better from stress, but even these first fiberglass sections demonstrated remarkable power-to-weight possibilities. Ritz experimented first with the tip section of a nine-foot Harnell married to the butt section of an eight-foot Pezon & Michel parabolic. It produced a remarkably powerful rod capable of handling three line tapers from eight- to ten-weight, something no split-cane rod could ever manage.

It could even cast a spoon, Ritz admits ruefully.

That's interesting, the late Cornelius Ryan replied puckishly over lunch in Manhattan, *but who would want to?*

Ritz found his first hybrids unsatisfactory. The tip section recovered too swiftly and sloppily from stress, and the butt was too stiff, but Ritz lacquered the entire rod black and embellished it with a skull and crossbones before sending it to Pezon & Michel at Amboise.

The death of cane is coming! Ritz added.

It is surprising that Ritz would not have tried a split-bamboo tip on a fiberglass butt section, since his cane parabolics were always compound tapers that felt a little top-heavy, and the brisk recovery from stress implicit in bamboo would solve the problems of most fiberglass rods. Such hybrid designs were not long in coming. The indefatigable Ritz soon married the delicacy and sharp-stress recovery of a fine bamboo tip with the lightness and power of a tubular glass butt. The production tapers of these hybrid rods were called the Variopower series, and they were manufactured at Pezon & Michel.

Variopower rods were certainly distance tools. The compound tapers and weight of their bamboo tips were magnified in combination with a tubular fiberglass butt. The glass had sufficient power to handle these tips without deforming badly under stress, and it made the Variopowers lighter than rods of comparable strength. The elasticity of the glass quickly multiplied the line velocity and casting loads of the double-haul technique, extending line length rapidly, while the bamboo presented the final cast with precision. Many steelhead fishermen still use these Variopower rods religiously, and the late Albert Godart used one to reach 150 feet in trout-fly distance competition. Ritz and Pierre Creusevaut, the former world fly-casting champion who had worked with Ritz since 1932, were elated as fiberglass improved in its loading and casting qualities. Both men became convinced that a fiberglass rod would soon be possible that flexed deeply into the butt, with the same decreasing flexure in the tip section, and almost no bending in the final twelve inches at the top guide. Ritz and Creusevaut reasoned that such a glass taper would match the superb line-lifting and high-speed-line work of their Fario Club in split cane.

But manufacturers were still closely tied to the American tradition of stiff-butt rods with free-flexing tip action. It is a tradition well suited to average casting skills, since its timing places minimal demands on the angler who fishes only a few days each season, and its casting rhythms are comparable to the driving restlessness of many American fishermen. Rod tapers that match their temperaments will never cast as long or fish as fine as the so-called parabolic tapers, but they do complement the character of their owners at leisure. Creusevaut and Ritz were both convinced that stiff-tip-action rods were the principal obstacle to really superb fiberglass rods, and that tip-action dogma made it virtually impossible to convince the glass rodmakers to change. However, both men continued to experiment with hand-modified glass blanks.

Their chance arrived in 1967, when Cornelius Ryan came to Paris and stopped a few days at the Hotel Ritz in the Place Vendôme. Ryan was the author of *The Longest Day,* the story of the Normandy invasion that was the beginning of the end in the Second World War. He was in Europe looking for film locations as well as trout and salmon, including two expeditions to arctic Norway, and Ritz engaged him in some fishing talk.

But enough talk! Ritz soon exploded.

His swift little Lancia was soon on its way toward the Bois de Boulogne, and the casting ponds of the Casting Club de France at Tir aux Pigeons. The back was filled with fly rods. Ritz bombarded Ryan with a drumfire of gestures and dialogue, punctuated with brief demonstrations of flawless high-speed, high-line casting techniques. Ritz continued his restless monologues while the Lancia careened back along the boulevards, its Michelin radials protesting shrilly in the turns. The session ended in the Ritz bar over several glasses of Chivas Regal.

Charles, Ryan finally interjected into the voluble spate of rod theory, *you are wasting your time in Europe!*

Ritz argued that his theories had already been rejected by American fiberglass rod builders with their stubborn commitment to tip-action rod tapers, and he doubted that they would be receptive. Cornelius Ryan was a close fishing companion of Thomas Lenk, who controls the Garcia Corporation and its Conolon fiberglass subsidiary, and he promised to discuss the Ritz theories with Lenk in the United States.

The following summer, Ritz was fishing salmon on the Nausta in western Norway when both Ryan and Lenk arrived to fish the Laerdal from the charming farmstead at Moldebø. Ryan arranged a meeting and Ritz travelled south into the Sognefjord to discuss building glass rods on the Ritz parabolic tapers. He subsequently arrived at the Conolon factory late in 1968, and in spite of the tip-action dogmatics among the technicians there, several prototype rods were soon produced for Pierre Creusevaut and the testing ponds. Two superb rods were among these first experimental tapers, and Thomas Lenk was surprised when they soon lengthened his casting distances as much as ten to fifteen feet.

The Ritz Garcia fly rods soon followed. Their performance specifications are not designed for delicacy and fine tippets, but their casting dynamics are superb. Conolon high-density blanks are laminated with phenolic resins, and their long-flex behavior in the Ritz tapers ensures a surprising capability to lift line from the water. Their flexing under casting loads keeps the rod in touch with the working line both behind and ahead of the angler. Such smooth control and transmission of power mean that excessive glass vibration during recovery from stress is largely a thing of the past, and line oscillation and flutter are easily mastered. Modern high-density fiberglass has overcome most of the casting faults found in earlier production rods and is increasingly able to accept casting stress without deformation. The increased flexing power, strength and weight ratios, and recovery from stress without excessive vibration of these rods are readily apparent. Casting distances are easily increased. High-speed performance under casting loads keeps the backcast amazingly high and reduces line drop and flutter. The ability to lift fifteen percent more line off the water reduces false-casting efforts, keeping the fly on the water where it belongs, and the rods throw a surprisingly tight loop.

The smallest rod in the Ritz Garcia series is six and a half feet in length, weighs three and a half ounces, and takes a six-weight line. The second rod is slightly longer than seven feet, and takes a six-weight line at only three and three-quarters ounces. The third model is slightly under eight feet, weights four ounces, and balances a seven-weight line. The taper that measures just over eight feet weighs four and one-quarter ounces and is designed for an eight-weight. It will lift and load more than fifty feet in the hands of a skilled fly caster. The eight-and-a-half-foot Ritz Garcia weighs four and three-quarters ounces and requires a nine-weight line. Its loading capacity is a surprising sixty to sixty-five feet of lift and casting stress. The largest model is just under nine feet, weighs five and a half ounces, and perfectly casts an eleven-weight forward taper. Its line ceiling is almost seventy feet, lifting it cleanly from the water and carrying it while false casting. Such performance is not found in other fiberglass rod tapers. Ritz tapers are designed for optimal distance-to-weight ratios, rather than for fishing cobweb-size tippets, and his seven-weight and nine-weight designs have proved the most popular.

Ritz is experimenting with synthetics like boron and carbon graphite fibers and has abandoned his earlier passion for split bamboo. His new infatuation with high-density phenolic glass is obvious in these lines from *A Fly Fisher's Life*:

> Given blanks of high quality and tapers of the correct design, glass is not only ideal, it is also the only material from which fly rods should now be made. This does not mean that other materials, lighter and with still more flex-power, will not be used eventually for rods. I am already experimenting with such materials, and have reason to hope that I shall be one of the first to perfect a fly rod of this type. But that is looking to the future: for the present there can be no question that glass reigns supreme.

Garcia makes a series of surprisingly inexpensive glass rods, starting with its seven-footer weighing three and a half ounces. There are also a fine seven-and-a-half-footer of three and a half ounces and an eight-foot model weighing four ounces. The eight-and-a-half-foot rod in the Garcia 5-Star line weighs four and a half ounces, and the nine-footer of five ounces has the muscle to handle ten-weight.

Berkeley is another large tackle manufacturer that is now experimenting with parabolic fiberglass actions, and although their Parametric series has the flaw of overembellishment so typical of production rods, their new Specialist designs promise both fine casting performance and great esthetic character. Their fittings and visual qualities and unique touches are the work of Douglas Swisher, the author of *Selective Trout* and the new technical director at Berkeley. His new Specialist series of rods are an optimal combination of casting power, delicacy, and appearance.

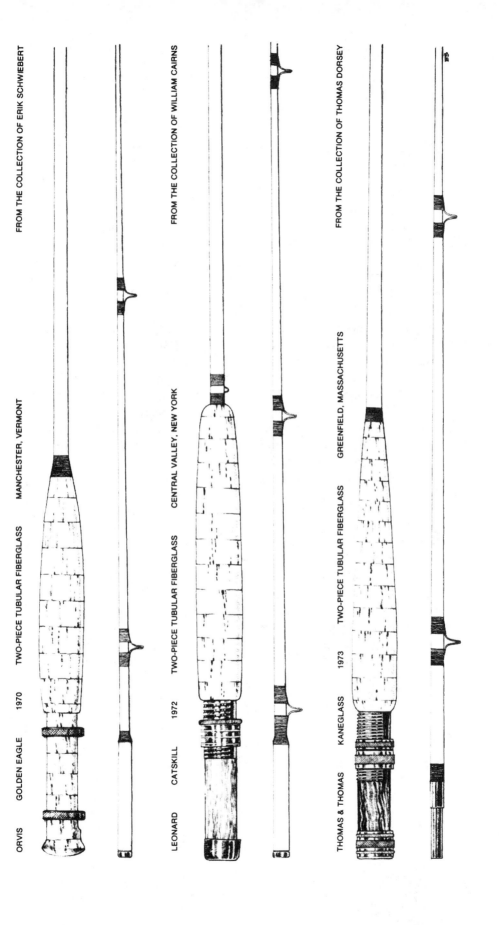

ORVIS   GOLDEN EAGLE   1970   TWO-PIECE TUBULAR FIBERGLASS   MANCHESTER, VERMONT   FROM THE COLLECTION OF ERIK SCHWIEBERT

LEONARD   CATSKILL   1972   TWO-PIECE TUBULAR FIBERGLASS   CENTRAL VALLEY, NEW YORK   FROM THE COLLECTION OF WILLIAM CAIRNS

THOMAS & THOMAS   KANEGLASS   1973   TWO-PIECE TUBULAR FIBERGLASS   GREENFIELD, MASSACHUSETTS   FROM THE COLLECTION OF THOMAS DORSEY

These Berkeley rods are built with hand-culled fiberglass blanks using high-density phenolic laminates, and are finished in a rich chocolate-colored epoxy. The functional wrappings are black and the carboloy butt guides are complemented with snake guides of stainless steel. The ferrules in these Berkeley rods are the glass-spigot type and are aligned with positioning dots. The specie-cork grip is a modified cigar shape, and the reel seat has two unusual features: its solid walnut filler has a hand-sanded cork inlay to seat the reel firmly, and is fitted with black anodized ring and butt cap. The butt is fitted with a slotted hard-rubber cushion, designed to protect the rod from abrasion and impacts and to prevent leader crimping when a nylon taper longer than the rod is necessary.

The six-and-a-half-foot Specialist weighs only one and three-quarters ounces and takes a four-weight line. The seven-foot model weighs two and a half ounces and is balanced with a five-weight taper, while the seven-and-a-half-foot taper weighs three ounces and uses a recommended six-weight line. These three fiberglass rods are excellent fishing tools, flexing well into the grip and fishing relatively light tippets. The seven-foot Specialist is a remarkably subtle rod, and these rods are the most impressive of the production fiberglass types. This past season, Doug Swisher and I fished the seven-footers extensively on the Au Sable in Michigan, and I found them a first-rate product in both appearance and performance.

Hardy Brothers have long been a bastion of split-bamboo tradition, but in recent years Hardy has turned to fiberglass, too. The Hardy glass series has been named its Jet line, which is perhaps appropriate to our age of turbines and sophisticated technology, although it lacks the romantic overtones of its traditional Palakona trademark.

The Hardy fiberglass rods are assembled from quality high-density blanks of a continuous slow-action taper. The ferrules are the solid plug-spigot type, which give fine glass-to-glass transfer of power in casting. High-quality fiberglass cloth is made into densely laminated blanks with phenolic resins, and like the Scientific Anglers line, the Hardy Jet series offers relatively fine tip performance for production fiberglass work. The blanks have a rich brown color, and their behavior under casting stress works deep into the butt calibrations under increasing line loads. The fittings are excellent and the polyurethane finishes are tough and mirror-bright. The reel seats are the typical Hardy hardware. The screw-locking seats are the aluminum reverse type, with a hooded ring concealed in the cork grip and a butt cap and filler of hard rubber. The lighter models have skeletal butt caps and sliding rings on a specie-cork filler, and except for the unfortunate trademark decal, the Hardy fiberglass rods are perhaps the most handsome production rods anywhere, with an elegance of fittings and understated wrappings worthy of split cane and beautifully matched to their handsome reels.

The seven-foot Hardy weighs two and three-quarters ounces and takes a four-weight line, while the seven-and-a-half-foot model at three ounces is designed for five-weight tapers. The eight-foot Jet matched with a six-weight line weighs three and a half ounces. The eight-and-a-half-footer at three and three-quarters ounces also takes six-weight line tapers, while a second design of the same length and four and one-quarter ounces works beautifully with an eight-weight line. Hardy offers three nine-foot models. The lightest weighs four and a half ounces and takes a seven-weight line, and the medium design is for eight-weight lines at four and three-quarters ounces. The largest of the three Hardy nine-footers weighs five and one-quarter ounces and takes a nine-weight, making it as muscular a stick as any trout fisherman needs. These Hardy rods are essentially American high-density blanks and cost a little more in this country because of import duties, but their fittings may satisfy a fisherman who cares about the visual character of his rods.

Dermot Wilson is the designer of the famous Silver Creek series of fiberglass rods, along with Jack Hemingway in Sun Valley. Hemingway took Wilson fishing on the famous Idaho spring creek in the bottoms at Picabo, and he soon discovered that Silver Creek had much in common with the chalkstreams at home in Hampshire. Its selective rainbows demanded fine tippets, delicate casting, lightness, and the ability to handle a long line in the wind.

It took a special type of glass taper, Wilson explains, *and we both felt the Hardy blanks might work best on Silver Creek.*

Hardy agreed to provide the blanks, and Wilson worked closely with Tony Fordham to perfect the final tapers. The production versions are handsome rods of typical British design and moderate price. The blanks are medium brown and joined with spigot-type ferrules.

The eight-foot Silver Creek weighs three and a half ounces and takes a five-weight line, while the eight-and-a-half-footer is a four-ounce rod designed for six-weight tapers. The nine-foot Silver Creek weighs only four and one-quarter ounces and also takes a six-weight forward-taper line, and there is a surprisingly delicate nine-and-a-half-foot model of five and three-quarters ounces designed for a seven-weight. All of these rods have reverse-locking reel hardware except for the butt cap and sliding band on the eight-foot design. These rods are wound with tan wraps tipped in pale orange, and the guides are all stainless steel. Their popularity in both Europe and the United States is well known, and testimony to the skills of their several designers.

Several of the famous American split-cane manufacturers have also added high-density fiberglass rods to their lines, using the same fittings found on their bamboo work. Such firms as Powell, Winston, Leonard, and Orvis all make fine fiberglass fly rods.

Walton Powell is carrying on the tradition started by his father E. C. Powell on the rivers of northern California just after the First World War. Powell was one of the great innovative pioneers of hollow split-cane construction, along with the late Lew Stoner of San Francisco, and his son Walton is equally skilled in both cane and fiberglass construction. His fiberglass rods are fashioned of high-quality glass fabric laminated with maximum linear fiber-counts and phenolic resins, with a lovely pale brown color protected with a clear epoxy finish. The guides are fine tungsten steel with simple olive wrappings. The ferrules are the Swiss-type machined by Walton Powell from fine nickel silver, giving a precise and long-wearing fit, and the reel seats are the same heavy aluminum locking type designed and machined for the Walton Powell bamboo rods. Powell fiberglass rods range from seven-and-a-half- to eight-and-a-half-foot two-piece designs, taking five- to seven-weight lines, and three-piece glass rods from eight to nine feet. The three-piece designs are perfectly matched for six- to nine-weight tapers. Since the Powell reel seats are designed for strength and security, total rod weights are heavier than most glass rods of comparable length, and Powell argues that assembled weights are rather meaningless. The Powell actions are smooth and relatively slow, working well down into the butt section, and they have many ardent admirers among skilled distance casters on the Pacific Coast.

Winston is perhaps the best-known American rod company on the Pacific Coast, long famous for their Stoner patent hollow-butt bamboo work, and now producing first-rate glass rods, too. The introduction of fiberglass rods with the Winston fittings and name did not happen overnight, just as Hardy waited in England before it adopted glass. The artisans at Winston began experimenting with fiberglass blanks twenty-five years ago, but they quickly concluded that the tapers were bad. The rods were too stiff and unresponsive in their butt calibrations and too soft toward their tips, and Lew Stoner and Douglas Merrick soon decided that glass would have to wait until better fabrics and laminating resins were available, and they could work out their own mandrel tapers.

Fiberglass technology had evolved to that point about ten years ago, and Winston started working out its own rod designs and forming mandrels. It is interesting that like the technicians at both Scientific Anglers and Hardy, Stoner and Merrick chose phenolic resins instead of epoxies or polyesters in laminating fiberglass cloth specially woven for fly rods. Finally, Winston had worked out tapers and forming cores and curing techniques that provided them with a fiberglass blank that approached the superb slow-butt tapers in their bamboo work. The blanks are finished with an oven-baked polyurethane applied in five separate coats that results in a rich color not unlike flame-darkened cane. The guides are first-quality stainless steel and the butt guides are carboloy. Winston has also developed its version of the spigot-type fiberglass ferrule, giving its rods a superb load-transfer in casting. The wrappings are maroon nylon with white trim, and secured in a clear epoxy coating. The grips are select specie-cut cork, and either a full-locking aluminum reel seat or a skeletal cork seat with a butt cap and sliding ring is available on the trout rods. The Winston glass rods are unquestionably among the finest.

Winston makes six ultralight models in its fiberglass series, each with a skeletal sliding ring and butt cap. The five-and-a-half-foot rod weighs only one and five-eighths ounces and takes a four-weight line. The six-footer weighs barely one and three-quarters ounces and is also designed for four-weight tapers, like the six-and-a-half-foot model that weighs two ounces. Both the seven-foot rod at two and one-eighth ounces and the seven-and-a-half-foot design at two and one-quarter ounces are designed to function with five-weight fly lines. These are perhaps the finest lightweight fiberglass rods made anywhere. Doug Merrick is adamant about the unfishability of short, lightweight rods that take relatively heavy lines and cannot accommodate really fine tippet diameters.

Any little rod that needs a six- or seven-weight line to make it cast decently is an abomination, he grumbles testily. *It's certainly no trout rod!*

The ultralight fiberglass rods are also available with a full-locking aluminum reel seat, and many anglers prefer them on the seven- and seven-and-a-half-foot models. However, they increase the weight of these exquisite lightweight glass rods approximately three-eighths of an ounce, which seems a little like forcing a fine gaited mare to pull a plow. Fishermen who want the security of a fully locking reel seat should probably fish the larger fiberglass rods from Winston.

Like their fine split-cane rods, these fiberglass Winstons are hand-culled from blanks that have already been inspected at the factory and are rigorously checked again before assembly. Only the finest workmanship and fittings are used. The wrappings are deep maroon with clear white trim, protected with a fine epoxy finish, and the specie-cork grip is shaped with the Winston half-Wells style. The guides are the same stainless and carboloy quality found on the Winston split-cane rods, and these beautiful fiberglass rods are also available with a butt cap and sliding ring over a cork filler. This skeletal reel seat reduces the finished weights three-eighths of an ounce.

The seven-and-a-half-foot rod weighs two and three-quarters ounces, with its locking reel seat, and takes a six-weight line. There are two eight-foot models in the standard glass series. The first is a surprisingly delicate three-and-one-eighth-ounce design that weighs only two and three-quarters ounces with a sliding-band seat and is matched with a five-weight taper. The second eight-foot rod weighs three and a half ounces and takes a six-weight. The three-and-a-half-ounce, eight-and-a-half-footer is an amazingly delicate rod that takes only five-weight lines, and the six-weight taper in the same length weighs only three and seven-eighths ounces. Both of these rods are quite smooth and subtle, considering their length and potential power. The eight-and-a-half-foot rods at four ounces take a seven-weight line and are more typical of most production fiberglass tackle. The nine-foot rods weigh four and one-quarter ounces and take seven-weight tapers, and it is interesting that the Winston rod builders think a heavier stick is not suited to fishing river trout—their fiberglass designs for eight- and nine-weight lines are recommended as steelhead tackle, and are fitted with a detachable three-inch butt.

The first nine-foot Winston weighs four and one-quarter ounces and takes an eight-weight forward-taper line, and the second nine-footer takes a nine-weight and weighs four and a half ounces. There are also nine-foot rods for ten- and eleven-weight lines and still larger designs for tarpon and king salmon and billfish on flies, but these rods have more muscle than any trout fisherman needs. The larger Winston fiberglass rods have radical compound tapers derived from the unusual tapers of their famous hollow-butt bamboo rods and are superb tools for effortless distance work. These superb Winston rods are more expensive than the comparable Fenwick models and slightly less expensive than the series of rods from Scientific Anglers and Phillipson.

Leonard is the oldest rodmaker in the history of American fishing tackle and still builds its split-cane jewels, but it has also made some first-rate fiberglass rods. The Leonard Spring Creek and Catskill series are fitted with the same elegant Leonard hardware found on their superb bamboo fly rods. The smaller rods are available with the standard skeleton seat, with the sliding ring and butternut filler and elegantly engraved butt cap typical of Leonard for a century. The two-piece rods are joined with the Leonard patent ferrules, hand-machined, and welted of German silver. The fiberglass models beyond seven and a half feet are fitted with the hand-machined Leonard reel seats and butternut fillers associated with the classic Leonard rods—like the beautiful 50L in my collection, which takes a five-weight line at eight feet, or the 50DF taper originally designed by Edward Ringwood Hewitt.

The six-and-a-half-foot Spring Creek rod weighs two ounces and takes a four-weight line, and the seven-foot Leonard weighs two and one-quarter ounces, taking a five-weight taper. These rods have either locking or skeletal seats with either cork or butternut fillers. The six-foot Catskill rod weighs two and seven-eighths ounces with its locking reel seat and takes a six-weight line. The seven-and-a-half-foot, two-and-three-quarters-ounce model also takes a six-weight taper, while the eight-foot, three-and-one-quarter-ounce rod takes a seven-weight. The eight-and-a-half-foot rods are designed for eight-weight lines and weigh three and a half ounces. Like the Winston series, these Leonard fiberglass rods are more expensive than the Fenwicks, being roughly competitive with the Scientific Anglers and Phillipson Epoxite rods.

Leonard is not the only tradition-minded eastern firm to enter the fiberglass lists, since the Orvis Company is making two separate grades of glass fly rods. The Orvis blanks are a gleaming pale olive fiberglass, rolled under extreme pressures and laminated with epoxy, like the Phillipson rods. Orvis builds its trout-size glass rods with two reel seats typical of their older bamboo designs. The guides are stainless steel with a carboloy stripping guide and are seated with functional wraps in variegated olive. The nylon wrappings are wisely limited to the ferrules, guides, grip, and tip winds, with admirable esthetic restraint. No garish trademark flaws the appearance of these rods, which are simply identified with ink script under a clear epoxy finish. The Orvis Golden Eagle rods employ a sleeve-type glass ferrule reinforced with an aluminum welt, and a solid glass plug reinforcing

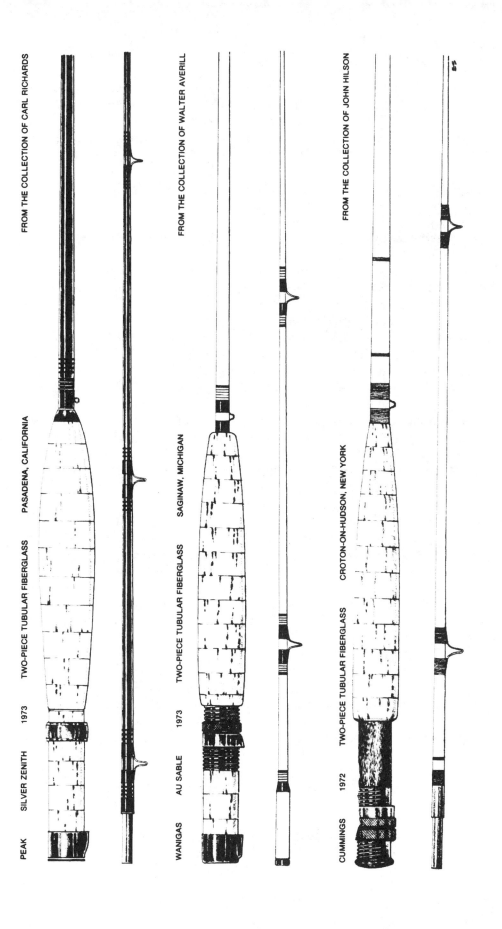

PEAK   SILVER ZENITH   1973   TWO-PIECE TUBULAR FIBERGLASS   PASADENA, CALIFORNIA   FROM THE COLLECTION OF CARL RICHARDS

WANIGAS   AU SABLE   1973   TWO-PIECE TUBULAR FIBERGLASS   SAGINAW, MICHIGAN   FROM THE COLLECTION OF WALTER AVERILL

CUMMINGS   1972   TWO-PIECE TUBULAR FIBERGLASS   CROTON-ON-HUDSON, NEW YORK   FROM THE COLLECTION OF JOHN HILSON

the ferrule end of the butt. These fiberglass rods have relatively fine tip calibrations and slow actions that work well into the grip zone, with the quick canelike dampening action typical of fine epoxy laminates. Orvis Golden Eagle rods are among the most expensive glass designs from a major manufacturer, but their fine recovery from stress and delicate tip tapers make them worth the price.

Orvis has found its most popular rod in the Golden Eagle line has been the six-and-a-half-footer at one and seven-eighths ounces, designed for delicate work with a four-weight line. It is a fine fiberglass taper, honestly designed to fish a 6X tippet with finesse, and one of the few glass rods in my collection. The seven-foot Golden Eagle weighs only two ounces and takes a five-weight taper, while the seven-and-a-half-foot rod weighs two and three-eighths ounces and is designed to fish a six-weight line. These three Golden Eagles are fitted with the slim two-ring Phillipe-style grip introduced years ago on the Orvis Superfine rods, and classic in its simplicity.

The larger Golden Eagles are fitted with the traditional Jordan cigar grip and walnut-filler reel seat used for many years on the Orvis Battenkills. The eight-foot model weighs three and five-eighths ounces and takes a seven-weight line. The eight-and-a-half-foot Golden Eagle weighs four and one-eighth ounces and is designed for an eight-weight taper, and is an excellent big-water instrument. There is also an eight-and-a-half-footer weighing four and three-eighths ounces and taking a nine-weight line, perhaps more rod than is needed for most work.

Orvis also offers its Fullflex series of fiberglass rods at about the same price as the Fenwick rods. These rods are a natural cane-yellow color, and although they are not quite as delicate as the more expensive Golden Eagle rods, their actions are the desirable slow type that flex deep into the butt section. The stainless steel snake and stripping guides are attached with bright scarlet wrappings, and the rods use the glass sleeve-type ferrules. The Jordan-type cigar grips and walnut screw-locking reel seats found on the Battenkills are also fitted on the Fullflex fiberglass series.

The seven-and-a-half-foot Fullflex, designed for a five-weight line and weighing three and one-quarter ounces, is perhaps the most delicate and popular rod in the series. The other tapers are a bit more heavy-handed, tending more toward all-around fishing than midge-type delicacy. The seven-foot rod weighs three and one-eighth ounces and takes a six-weight line, and there is a second seven-and-a-half-foot taper that weighs three and three-quarters ounces and is rated for eight-weight lines. The eight-and-a-half-foot model is also an eight-weight taper at four ounces, and is a first-rate big-water trout rod.

Thomas and Thomas are also building a line of fine fiberglass fly rods which they call their Kaneglass series. These fiberglass rods are fitted with the same fine grips, ferrules, and reel seats found on their Classic bamboo rods. Since their firm is deeply committed to craftsmanship in split bamboo, it is interesting that the modern high-density glass blanks have begun to approach their exacting standards in rod performance. Thomas Dorsey writes of their experience with earlier fiberglass rods with these candid observations:

> Glass has come closer to duplicating the qualities of cane than any material thus far encountered, but even it has fallen far short of matching cane. The nature of glass fiber, however, has offered nearly unlimited potential, as it is in many ways similar to the power fibers of bamboo. The problem has been to control the glass technologically, and to bind the fibers longitudinally after the fashion of natural cane. Modern techniques and bonding agents have been good, but not fully acceptable, for glass rod construction with these resins has had to retain a great amount of resin in the rod, and to incorporate into the structure a large percentage of fibers traversing the circumference of the rod. This has made glass rods relatively cumbersome, with as many as fifty percent of the fibers in the average glass rod wasted, contributing nothing to its performance in casting.
>
> We have a vested interest in the development of new rod materials at Thomas and Thomas, and we have observed as carefully as possible each new attempt to reproduce the properties of cane with synthetics.
>
> Nothing met our approval until the development of the new high-density glass blanks. These new blanks are truly remarkable. They overcome most of the problems in earlier glass rods which most manufacturers have attempted to avoid, or conceal by emphasizing the indestructibility of glass or substituting eye appeal for action. Epoxy and pressure are the secrets. This modern bonding agent and pressures as extreme as 2,000 pounds per square inch has led to greatly reduced resin content in the finished blanks. Less resin is required and excess resin is squeezed out during high-pressure lamination. The result is also much greater control of wall structure and internal tapers, permitting extremely fine tolerances and more flexibility in design tapers than were possible in earlier glass rods. Longitudinal alignment of virtually one hundred percent of the glass fibers is also possible with high-pressure epoxy.
>
> The result of this new technology is a line of fishing rods that actually approach the qualities of cane, and deserve assembly with first-rate fittings.

Thomas and Thomas make two tapers for relatively light fly lines, the seven-and-a-half-foot model that takes a four-weight and the eight-footer for a five-weight. There are also several designs for medium-weight lines. The six-footer of two ounces takes a six-weight line, like the six-and-a-half-footer that weighs two and a half ounces. The seven-foot, three-ounce Kaneglass also requires six-weight lines, along with the seven-and-a-half-foot model of three and one-eighth ounces and the eight-footer that weighs three and a half ounces. The eight-and-a-half-foot Kaneglass of three and three-quarters ounces is balanced with a seven-weight taper.

There are also three Thomas and Thomas Kaneglass models designed for heavier work. The eight-footer of three and three-quarters ounces has been conceived for eight-weight performance, like its companion rods of eight and a half feet and four ounces, or the nine-foot Kaneglass that weighs five ounces. These fiberglass rods are among the finest manufactured in the United States.

There are also a number of custom rodmakers who work only with hand-culled fiberglass blanks, their own grip and reel seat designs, and who modify the wall thickness of the densely laminated sections in their shops to get remarkable compound tapers of subtle delicacy and power. Perhaps the best of these craftsmen are Arthur Neumann from Michigan, Russ Peak on the Pacific Coast, and the master builder of the most delicate fiberglass rods, Vincent Cummings of New York.

Each of these makers has the standard glass-cloth templates modified to his specifications in production, and then hand-modifies their wall thicknesses after fabrication. Arthur Neumann prefers a chocolate-colored epoxy blank of high-density fiberglass and carefully manipulates the wall thickness of his tubular blanks to approximate his classic Wanigas bamboo designs. The fittings and wrappings are typical of his work. The lighter rods can be fitted with a skeletal reel seat of black anodized butt cap and sliding ring over a cork filler. The bigger rods are fitted with black locking seats and butt caps over cork. The Au Sable grade is fitted with a carboloy stripping guide and black tungsten snake guides, and there is a sleeve-type fiberglass ferrule. Neumann also makes a less expensive Pere Marquette grade and an economy grade called the Two-Hearted—after the famous Michigan river celebrated in the Hemingway story.

The six-foot Wanigas Au Sable weighs two and one-eighth ounces and is truly made for a four-weight line and reasonably delicate work. The six-and-a-half-foot model weighs two and a half ounces and is designed for a five-weight, like the seven-footer at two and three-quarters ounces. The seven-and-a-half-foot Wanigas weighs three and one-quarter ounces and takes a six-weight double taper perfectly. The eight-foot model weighs three and three-quarters ounces and takes a seven-weight, while the eight-and-a-half-foot rod takes an eight-weight at four ounces. There is also a Wanigas for a nine-weight line at nine feet and five ounces. Although Neumann modifies his blanks far less than builders like Peak and Cummings, his Wanigas rods have excellent light-tackle properties.

Russ Peak is probably the high priest of the fiberglass cult, and his rods are the equal of the finest split bamboo in their sense of craftsmanship and attention to detail. Peak has accumulated a growing circle of fierce partisans who argue that his rods equal the finest split-cane work, and his clan includes some impressive names like Charles Kerlee, Dan Holland, Carl Richards, and the celebrated Arnold Gingrich. It was Gingrich who

HACKLE-WING DRY FLIES

PALE WATERY DUN   PALE WATERY OLIVE   WHITE-WINGED BLACK   WHITE-WINGED CURSE

PALE SULPHUR DUN   PALE GRAY-WINGED OLIVE   MEDIUM GRAY-WINGED OLIVE   DARK GRAY-WINGED OLIVE

BLUE-WINGED WHITCRAFT   BLUE-WINGED ADAMS   DARK BLUE QUILL   LIGHT BLUE QUILL

DARK RUSTY DUN   MEDIUM RUSTY DUN   LIGHT RUSTY DUN   BLUE-WINGED HENDRICKSON

DARK BLUE DUN   IRON BLUE DUN   DARK BLUE-WINGED OLIVE   MEDIUM SLATE-WINGED OLIVE

GREAT LEAD-WINGED OLIVE   GREAT LEAD-WINGED DRAKE   GREAT SUMMER DRAKE   GREAT RED QUILL

MISCELLANEOUS DRY FLIES

LITTLE BLACK ANT

LITTLE RUSTY ANT

LITTLE CINNAMON ANT

LITTLE REDLEGGED ANT

BROWN JASSID

BADGER GNAT

FURNACE GNAT

BLACK JASSID

BLACK LETORT BEETLE

PARTRIDGE SEDGE

CINNAMON BEETLE

REDLEGGED CARPENTER ANT

BLACK CARPENTER ANT

BROWN CARPENTER ANT

YELLOW LETORT HOPPER

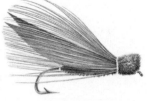

LETORT CRICKET

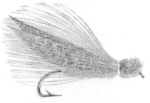

GREEN LETORT HOPPER

GIANT DARK STONEFLY

GIANT GOLDEN STONEFLY

first observed that when it came to delicate midge-size rods, Peak was the ultimate craftsman of fiberglass construction. The following observations from *The Joys of Trout* are vintage Gingrich and also tell us a lot about the workmanship of the Peak fly rods:

> With something over thirty cane fly rods in my upstairs storeroom at the time, I had thought the day would never come when I heard myself asking for a glass one, but after a day with it on the Firehole, I knew I couldn't live without a Zenith. So I took the one I'd been using, and some months later he came through with the one-piece job I'd been asking him about, that first day, finishing it in time to inscribe it with the annotation that it was a Christmas present to me from my wife Janie.
>
> Of course, nothing involving that much hard work can be cheap, in this day and age, and there's a lot of bamboo around for less than Russ Peak has to get for one of his glass rods. But this is one case where the medium is far from constituting the whole message, and the fact that Russ Peak happens to embody his ideas in fiberglass is as coincidental, say, as the circumstance that Benvenuto Cellini chose to work his artistry in a cup of gold. It would have been no less a marvel in silver or pewter or brass, or even in dull-colored lead.

Gingrich goes on to explain that he selects his fiberglass Peaks when he wants extra distance, longer casts than he can get from cane with the same expenditure of energy. Conversely, Gingrich chooses bamboo when he wants more tip delicacy than even fine artisans like Cummings and Peak can deliver.

There are no standard rods in the Peak series, although there are three basic grades. The Golden Zenith rods are the top of the line, with the most modification of wall thickness and remarkable compound tapers that flex well into the butt section. Peak Golden Zeniths are easily recognized by the delicate gold wrappings laid over the underwrap of mahogany silk. The Silver Zeniths have bright silver embellishments over the undersilk, and the Peak Zenith lacks these delicate ornamental wraps. There are white aligning dots at the ferrules, which in themselves are unique. Peak fits a delicate aluminum sleeve with a machined welt over the tip section, and the epoxy finish which conceals the ferrule is so strong that it actually becomes part of the rod structure itself. The male ferrule is a brightly polished aluminum plug which is finished with a silver ring at its fully seated position. The reel seats are all of the skeletal type, fitted with accents of copper on the Zenith series and delicate little wafer-thin stops of gold or silver on the more expensive Golden and Silver Zeniths. The reel-seat fittings are anodized a coppery color, with a butt cap and sliding ring in the ultralight models and a screw-locking assembly on the heavier rods. The grips are the relatively fat Peak cigar-style on both locking and skeletal types, although a full-Wells grip is common on his big-water rods. The fly-keeper ring is a spiral of fine copper, gold, or silver wire unique with the Peak designs, its color depending on its grade within the Zenith line. Like all custom builders, Peak supplies more guides on his rods than most, with two guides more than the rod length typical of his work.

There are no standard models in his Zenith line, since each rod is custom-made to order, although like all superb craftsmen Peak really builds each rod to suit his own standards of performance and design. The specifications listed are those of particular rods belonging to fishing companions across the entire United States and are typical of the Peak rods. There are one-piece Peaks available from five to six feet in length, weighing from one to one and a half ounces, and taking three- and four-weight double tapers. Two-piece rods in five, five and a half, and six feet are also available. The five-and-a-half-footers weigh about one and one-quarter ounces and take a four-weight taper. Arnold Gingrich owns several of these mini-Peaks, and describes the acquisition of his first in *The Joys of Trout*:

> I wondered, for instance, whether he could make me a six-foot one-piece rod like the Orvis Superfine, but a little more limber in the tip, because while I thoroughly enjoyed the Superfine for grilse I found its upper extremity a bit thick-ankled for trout.

The fact that these delicate Peaks truly balance three- and four-weight lines is eloquent testimony to their qualities. The six-and-a-half-foot two-piece Peak, weighing one and three-quarters ounces and taking a four-weight line is a joy in itself, like the four-weight rod at seven feet and a slender two ounces. There is also a seven-footer at two and one-quarter ounces for a five-weight taper. The screw-locking reel seats usually begin at seven and a half feet, weighing two and three-quarters ounces and matching a five-weight. There are several eight-foot Peaks with screw-locking seats, weighing from three and a half to four and one-quarter ounces, and taking lines ranging from a four-weight to a seven-weight forward taper. The eight-and-a-half-foot Peaks I have seen vary between three and three-quarters and four and three-quarters ounces, taking five- to eight-weight lines. Typical nine-footers weigh from four and a half to five and a half ounces and will take lines ranging from eight- to ten-weights. Generally speaking, the Peak rods represent fine craftsmanship mixed with superb power-to-weight performance ratios, and although they are relatively expensive, they are truly the zenith of fiberglass rods.

Vincent Cummings is an equally skilled custom rodmaker who chooses to work with modern high-density glass. Like Russ Peak, whose philosophy of fly-rod action is grounded in the distance casting needed on our western rivers, Cummings has his philosophical roots in the delicacy and refinement of the Catskill tradition above Manhattan. Cummings has created a superb fishing tool utterly without the embellishments of fittings or wrappings found in the work of Neumann or Peak—rods as ascetic in their simplicity as the work of Everett Garrison in split bamboo.

ARNOLD GINGRICH

His trout-size rods are fitted with skeletal reel seats using both sliding aluminum bands and full-locking designs. The locking seats are reversed in the Payne style, fitting the reel into a hooded cap concealed in the grip. Elegant walnut fillers are used in the screw-locking rods and walnut caps with the sliding-band seats. The grips are a gracefully tapered cigar shape, and the blanks are hand-rubbed to remove excess phenolic resins accumulated during lamination. Like the Orvis impregnated rods, the Cummings fiberglass receives no finish except for hand-waxing and polishing. Spar varnishing protects the functional wraps at the cork grip, guides, and ferrules. Cummings believes that the glass sleeve- and spigot-type ferrules can never provide the fit and lifespan of fine German-silver machining, and that the flexing of a sleeve-type glass connection is only a marginal benefit. There is minimal flexing in the solid fiberglass plugs used in spigot-type ferrules, and Cummings insists on using more costly German silver instead.

The Cummings rods are radically modified by handwork once the custom-designed blanks are received from the factory. Wall thickness of the densely laminated fiberglass is reduced empirically in the Cummings shop until the compound-taper feel is achieved. The typical Cummings action has a delicate hooking tip that rivals all but the finest bamboo, and the thin-walled butt section flexes dramatically into the cork grip itself, like the best of the Ritz and Garrison and Young parabolics. Cummings stubbornly resists questions about his special techniques for reducing wall thickness, and his secret heat process for straightening the tubular blanks.

Macy's doesn't tell Gimbels, Cummings concludes wryly, betraying his Manhattan beginnings. *Right?*

Like the one-piece designs of Russ Peak, Cummings makes a lovely six-foot trout rod in a single blank that weighs one and three-eighths ounces and has the delicacy to fish a four-weight line and a 6X tippet. There are two models just over six and a half feet. The lighter of these tapers weighs only one and three-quarters ounces and takes a four-weight line, while the heavier rod weighs two and a half ounces and is balanced perfectly with a five-weight. The heavier rod has a screw-locking reel seat. The seven-and-a-half-foot Cummings weighs three and a half ounces and takes a six-weight double taper. The eight-foot model is designed for a seven-weight line and weighs only three and three-quarters ounces. The eight-and-a-half-foot rod scales a full four ounces and fishes superbly with an eight-weight forward taper. The muscular nine-foot Cummings for a nine-weight line weighs four and a half ounces and is fitted with an extension butt for heavy work. My favorites in the Cummings series are the one-and-three-quarters-ounce model for a five-weight double taper, which is a superb tool for ultralight tippets and selective fish, and the eight-footer at three and three-quarters ounces is a fine all-purpose trout rod.

Cummings firmly believes that his phenolic high-density laminates demonstrate that modern fiberglass is now better than cane, and he abandoned split-bamboo construction eighteen years ago. Certainly the entire field of fiberglass rodmaking is rapidly coming to maturity in the work of craftsmen like Peak and Cummings. Even the most die-hard partisans of the bamboo tradition admit that their rods are remarkable, equalling all but the rare split-cane rods that have the qualities of an exquisite violin. The bamboo fanatics are increasingly limited to quibbling about esthetics, rod diameters, hardware, wrappings—and the fact that fiberglass rods are round.

Remember, Russ Peak chides gently in conversation, *the first split bamboo rods looked ugly to a generation raised on hickory and greenheart—and the early rodmakers had to make them round!*

Our discussion of fiberglass manufacturers would not be complete without adding three rodmakers from the Pacific Coast who have become important since the fiberglass chapter was written: the seasoned Harry Wilson at the Scott Powr-Ply Company, the energetic Ferdinand Claudio in San Francisco, and the computer-minded young technicians at Lamiglas in southern Washington.

Harry Wilson is the skilled artisan at the Scott factory who worked out the concept of using internal sleeves rather than modified wall thickness to achieve his compound actions and tapers. His blanks are a handsome medium brown, with dark brown wraps at the guides and ferrules, and simple grip and reel-seat designs. Both skeletal fittings and reverse-locking seats are available, along with fixed-extension butts of one- and two-cork designs. Like the late Paul Young, Wilson is primarily interested in the functional aspects of his rods, rather than preoccupied with problems of visual design. Scott presently builds the following trout rods in fiberglass:

MODEL	LENGTH (FEET)	WEIGHT (OUNCES)	LINE WEIGHT
F-60	6	$1^5/_8$	3
F-65	$6^1/_2$	$1^7/_8$	3
F-70	7	$2^1/_4$	3
F-71	7	$2^3/_8$	4
F-74	$7^1/_2$	$2^1/_2$	4
F-75	$7^1/_2$	$2^3/_4$	5
F-79	8	3	4
F-80	8	$3^1/_8$	5
F-81	8	$3^7/_8$	6
F-82	8	4	7
F-84	$8^1/_3$	$3^3/_8$	5
F-86	$8^1/_2$	$4^3/_8$	7
F-87B	$8^1/_2$	$4^7/_8$	8

Lamiglas has been building rod blanks of E-type fiberglass for other manufacturers for many years; it was not until development of the remarkable S-type glass that they assembled rods themselves. The surprising high-modulus performance of the new type of glass led the

Lamiglas craftsmen to become rodmakers too. S-glass rods are more sensitive, responsive to bending stresses, and twenty percent lighter than comparable equipment of conventional glass. Lamiglas has made full use of the computer technology available in the Seattle aircraft industry to design and perfect its tapers. The excitement of S-glass performance has led Lamiglas to introduce these models:

MODEL	LENGTH (FEET)	WEIGHT (OUNCES)	LINE WEIGHT
8175	$7\frac{1}{2}$	$3\frac{5}{8}$	5
8180	8	4	6
8185	$8\frac{1}{2}$	$4\frac{1}{4}$	7
8190	9	$4\frac{5}{8}$	8

Like his close friend Gary Howells, rodmaker Ferdinand Claudio is an advocate of both new technology and traditional esthetics. Howells works in split bamboo, while Claudio is a fervent admirer of modern fiberglass. Both craftsmen were also disciples of the late James Payne, perhaps the finest artisan to ever split a Tonkin culm, and their rods clearly owe their imagery to the Payne tradition.

Claudio spent his boyhood years within a half mile of the celebrated Golden Gate Casting Club in San Francisco. Its members have largely dominated tournament casting over the past fifty years, and its own tradition had its beginnings in 1893. Young fishermen all have particular heroes, and Claudio found his in skilled casters like Jack Horner and Ted Halvorsen. His apprenticeship ended long before Claudio himself became the president of the Golden Gate Casting Club.

His glass tapers are modified to produce the precise character and action that Claudio came to admire in years of competitive casting, yet his esthetic values are obvious too. Medium brown glass is combined with richly machined fittings, elegant cork-grip designs, beautiful hardwood fillers, precise golden windings and eggshell ornamental wraps, and a reverse-locking reel seat and handle clearly in the character of earlier Payne designs.

Claudio has succeeded in combining modern fiberglass tapers with the esthetic sense of the split-cane tradition, and the following models are among the most beautiful glass fly-rods made:

MODEL	LENGTH (FEET)	WEIGHT (OUNCES)	LINE WEIGHT
7o5B	7	$2\frac{3}{4}$	5
755B	$7\frac{1}{2}$	3	5
8o5B	8	$3\frac{3}{4}$	5
8o6B	8	4	6
855A	$8\frac{1}{2}$	$4\frac{1}{2}$	5
856A	$8\frac{1}{2}$	5	6
898A	$8\frac{3}{4}$	$5\frac{1}{2}$	8

Sage has introduced a series of fiberglass trout rods in recent years, using the finest high-modulus glass and templates. The fittings are stamped aluminum, with a pair of locking rings and cork and dark mahogany fillers. Like the Sage graphites, the glass rods are finished in a rich chocolate urethane. The fittings are serviceable, with brown wrappings and amber trim. The Sage high-modulus glass designs include the following:

MODEL	LENGTH (FEET)	WEIGHT (OUNCES)	LINE WEIGHT
SFL476	$7\frac{1}{2}$	$3\frac{1}{8}$	4
SFL580	8	$3\frac{1}{2}$	5
SFL686	$8\frac{1}{2}$	$3\frac{5}{8}$	6
SFL789	$8\frac{3}{4}$	$3\frac{7}{8}$	7
SFL990	9	$4\frac{1}{8}$	8

The Sage rods are handsomely designed and fitted, like the Claudio series, echoing the character of old Thomas and Payne bamboo. The select-cork grips, fillers, urethane finishes, wrappings, and hardware make them among the most handsome production rods in the entire fiberglass tackle industry.

Fiberglass is getting better and better.

Traditional values still die slowly in some circles, and while the fiberglass has yet to equal the finest split-cane work of artisans like Garrison, Payne and Howells, it is approaching such levels of perfection. However, there are bastions of tradition that stubbornly resist the revolution, and perhaps the most famous is the Anglers' Club of New York.

Sparse Grey Hackle was its unchallenged Dean Emeritus, a survivor of the Golden Age on the Catskill rivers and an angler so thoroughly steeped in tradition that he testily refused to fish anything but the exquisite butter-colored cane of his slender Garrisons and Leonards.

Sparse, one fellow member joked recently at the Anglers' Club, *when are you going to fish fiberglass?*

The old man took a thoughtful swallow of straight Laphroaig, a special pot-still whisky so strong it numbs the tongue.

I'll fish fiberglass, Sparse muttered behind his steel-rimmed spectacles, *the morning after some concertmaster plays a concerto at Carnegie Hall on a plastic violin!*

8. The Synthetic Fly Rods of the Future

When do the steelhead start coming? I asked.

The first ones usually come up from the lake in October, Dave Borgeson replied. *Usually the biggest cockfish come in the fall.*

Big October run? I continued.

No, Borgeson shook his head. *The runs start coming in late winter and early spring—starting in February and March.*

How many runs come then?

The first big run enters the river in late February and in March, Borgeson explained. *The biggest spring run usually comes toward the end of March, and a third run arrives in April.*

Just about now, I said.

That's right, Borgeson nodded. *The biologists have still been netting some in the estuary at Ludington, and there should be some bright fish in the river.*

Dave Borgeson is the director of the trout and salmon programs for the state of Michigan, having played a major technical role in a highly successful introduction of steelhead and salmon. However, his first love is probably the big steelhead that enter the Pere Marquette each winter to spawn in its headwaters. Borgeson was convinced that these rainbows could be taken consistently with flies, in spite of the salmon-egg tradition that argued against fly-fishing for Michigan steelhead, and he finally worked out the basic tactics. His steady parade of big fly-caught Michigan steelhead was irrefutable evidence and finally led to legal winter fishing on the beautiful flies-only water of the upper Pere Marquette.

Look familiar? Borgeson grinned.

Sure does. I shivered in the early light. *I used to fish it regularly from Waddell's Riffle to the Forks.*

It's probably better now than it was then, he said.

How's that? I asked.

It's fly-only from Danaher Creek to the M-37 Bridge, he explained, *and it has a fantastic population of wild fish.*

And no more put-and-take stocking, I said.

That's right, Borgeson nodded again.

It was cold on the Clay Banks above the Deer Lick Riffle, and an April snow filtered down through the jack pines and cedars. It was just after daylight, but there already was a camper parked in the Clay Banks clearing. The sandy trail leads down the ridge through the trees, and we could see the serpentine loops of the river far below, dark through the falling snowflakes. The Whirlpool was upstream, hidden in the wintry trees beyond the swift reach of the river the steelheaders call Shapton's Run.

You sure we had to get up this early? I laughed.

Feel like you're after pickerel? Borgeson stopped on the path where it started down to the Deer Lick. *The steelhead lie in the deep holes at midday, particularly in bright weather, and they move out on the spawning riffles just before dark. They work the gravel during the night, and early morning is a good time to fish them, since they haven't been bothered for several hours.*

You mean we fish spawning steelhead? I speculated.

They seldom take the fly, although a cockfish may attack a bright streamer defending his territory, Borgeson explained, *but it's usually other fish that take a dead-drift nymph.*

Stray males and females? I added.

Exactly, Borgeson said.

It was a stretch of swift-flowing river that I had not fished since boyhood, and twenty-five years had passed since my flies had covered the Whirlpool and Green Cottage and Deer Lick stretch of the beautiful Pere Marquette in Michigan.

Boyhood seasons had been summer fishing in the whippoorwill twilight, with sulphur-colored hatches coming off in the gathering darkness and spinner flights with their bright egg-sac females in the swarm. There were morning fly hatches too, like the small *Ephemerella* and *Paraleptophlebia* flies that emerged just after breakfast, but the fish were only eight to fifteen inches and our season was closed when the steelhead were running.

It had all started in 1885, when the hatchery at Big Rapids received a shipment of steelhead fry from the Caledonia Hatchery in New York. The baby steelhead were introduced into the Pere Marquette the following spring, and many were caught that summer, but the next year the silvery California trout had vanished. Crackerbarrel opinion pronounced them worthless, and many fisheries experts agreed, not realizing the fish had migrated to Lake Michigan. Since the big lake-fattened rainbows did not return to the Pere Marquette until October, long after the regular trout season was closed, and finished spawning before it opened again, it was many years before Michigan fishermen realized they had created a superb steelhead fishery.

It was Fred Clark, the distinguished biologist who operated the Northville Hatchery in Michigan, who first became convinced that the big rainbows turning up in the meshes of the commercial netters were the result of the river stockings between 1876 and 1895. Clark began experimenting with pure steelhead strains in 1904, and the modern Michigan fisherman can thank his efforts for the big lake-run rainbows in rivers like the Au Gres, Platte, Betsie, Pere Marquette, Muskegon, Manistee, Little Manistee, and the lower Au Sable.

Steelhead fishing in Michigan improved steadily as these stockings took hold, until several of its rivers were quite famous for their lake-run rainbows. Fishermen travelled great distances to fish the steelhead runs in rivers like the Platte, Muskegon, Manistee, and Au Gres, but most of the trout were taken by fishing bait. Popular wisdom argued that nothing but spawn sacs and night crawlers and hardware would work, and most of the fish caught were probably snagged.

Many skilled fly-fishermen tried and tried to take them with little or no success. With the completion of the Welland Canal, both the alewives and the lamprey eels entered the Great Lakes, and their ecology was irrevocably changed. When the lampreys attacked and swiftly eradicated the lake trout, the invading alewives and native smelts were virtually free of predators, and their populations skyrocketed. The bright rainbows also thrived on these exploding baitfish populations, and steelhead fishing in Michigan exploded too, until the merciless lampreys turned to them. The predatory eels soon decimated the steelhead population, and fishing them seemed tragically ended until chemical control of the lampreys checked their reign of terror, and the big rainbows stubbornly replenished themselves. Each winter more and more steelhead were found ascending the Michigan rivers, spawning there in March and April.

Skilled Michigan steelheaders all rig their terminal tackle to work their flies on the bottom. Perhaps the most effective method uses a tiny triangle swivel. The nine-foot leader to about twelve-pound test is clinch-knotted to the first swivel-ring, with a twenty-five inch tippet fastened to the opposite swivel. About six inches of ten-pound nylon is knotted to the bottom swivel with a knot in its lower end. The split shot are added to this dropper nylon, adjusting the number of shot to the depth and speed of the current. When the weight is right, it is possible to walk the lead right along the bottom gravel, feeling it tick against the stones. The fly rides slightly higher, buoyed on the specific gravity of the nylon, but working right in front of the fish. The most effective quality of the lead-shot dropper is that when it fouls the bottom, the lead strips free or the dropper nylon breaks, while the tippet and fly are recovered.

It isn't the most graceful fishing, Dave Borgeson admitted while we rigged our leaders, *but it works.*

How big do these steelhead run? I asked.

Twenty to twenty-five pounds, Borgeson replied. *Simmy Nolphe took one last fall on a fly that weighed seventeen.*

You sure you want to use that derrick? I pointed to his powerful fiberglass rod. *Looks too muscular.*

Safer than your three-ounce graphite, he said.

We'll see! I laughed.

The snow was still falling when we reached the Deer Lick, and I was looking forward to field-testing one of the Fenwick graphite rods on Michigan steelhead. Muscling such fish in the brushy runs and cedar deadfalls of the Pere Marquette would test a rod to its breaking point.

We waded across the river above the Deer Lick riffle, its swift currents strong and slightly tea-colored, sucking fiercely through our waders. *Somebody's fishing the Deer Lick already,* Borgeson pointed upstream. *Looks like it might be Ron Spring.*

Did he invent the Spring's Wiggler? I asked.

That's right, Borgeson nodded.

We walked downstream through the willows, past a ten-pound steelhead hanging from a cedar deadfall, where the fisherman was working his nymph in a dark run under the trees.

Hello! Spring waded ashore and shook hands.

Looks like you scored, Borgeson said.

Took that one right after we got here, Spring explained. *My partner got another one downstream under the cedars.*

Seen a lot of fish? Borgeson asked.

Some, Spring admitted, *but this riffle is full of good fish this morning—just look at the bottom out there!*

What do you mean? I asked.

The bottom is covered with winter algae, Borgeson explained, *but out there where the steelhead are working their redds, the yellow gravel is showing.*

So you look for a riffle with pale gravel areas like those, I pointed to the shallows, *where the bottom has measles?*

Exactly, Spring laughed.

Spring explained that he had fished the run above the overhanging cedars earlier, but without any luck, although he had seen three fish before it started snowing.

I've had enough, Spring said. *You fish them.*

It's all yours. Borgeson pointed upstream.

Spring climbed a sapling above the riffle to locate the fish.

There are three out there, he pointed, *and another pair against the deadfall.*

They're big fish, Borgeson added.

It was snowing harder now, and I shivered a little wading into position, but not from the cold. The current worked swiftly against the clay banks upstream, gathering under the trees above the Deer Lick. It was smooth and silky over the pale gravel redds where earlier fish had spawned, and the steelhead were there, dark pewter-colored shadows just off the sheltering cedars.

You see them? Borgeson asked.

I nodded and rolled a cast upstream, its three-shot dropper looping high and falling clumsily into the swift current, and raised the rod to tick the lead along the bottom. It took a little practice to fish it right, feeling the lead grab slightly in a crevice, and raising the tip gently to free the dead-drift swing of the nymph.

The first two or three casts worked deep along the bottom, and I took a shuffling half step downstream between fly swings, covering the current in a series of concentric quarter circles. The two biggest fish expressed no interest in the drifting nymph.

There may be more fish in that dark run along the bank. Ron Spring pointed downstream. *Try a swing through there.*

The cast rolled out and dropped just above the cedar deadfall, and I stripped a little slack until I felt the lead start ticking along the gravel. The nymph worked deep and started into a teasing swing through the dark tea-colored water under the overhanging trees.

There was a heavy pull. *Fish!* I yelled.

The big steelhead threshed angrily, throwing spray with its spade-sized tail, and the Orvis reel screamed as it turned into the swiftest current-tongues of the Deer Lick. It held stubbornly for several seconds, keeping its head tight against the bottom, and then it cartwheeled under the cedars and was running again.

How deep is the Deer Lick Bend? I yelled. *The way he's taking line I may have to follow him through there!*

You can wade diagonally down along the bar, they said.

It could come to that! I laughed.

The steelhead threw rooster tails of spray down the shallows, about twenty yards into the backing, and I picked my way carefully down along the alders in pursuit. Deer Lick Bend is a deep reach of water above the Anderson cottage, and there is a logjam tangled with brush on the far bank, just where the riffle shelves off into the pool. There is deep water under the deadfalls there, and even deeper water in the bend itself, on my side of the river. It is a tightrope act wading diagonally downstream between these holes, particularly with the April currents tea-colored and full.

He's stopped! Borgeson yelled.

I fought to recover line, and regained all of my Dacron backing. *But he might try for the brush pile.*

You think that little rod can hold him? Spring asked.

The fish had its second wind now, and it bulldogged stubbornly along the bottom toward the tangled logjam. *Damn!* I groaned and applied butt pressure. *He's trying to get under there!*

That's some bend in that lead-pencil rod! Borgeson said.

What kind of rod? Spring asked.

Graphite, I laughed.

The slender graphite butt throbbed and held, turning the fish short of the logs, and the fight was over. There were several short half-sullen runs that were easily parried, and some panicky threshing to avoid the net, but finally Spring netted the tired steelhead and waded happily ashore.

What'll he weigh? I yelled.

He'll go nine or ten pounds easy, Spring answered. *He's a lot of fish in heavy water on a light rod like that!*

Graphite is light, I nodded, *but it's pretty strong.*

What's that rod weigh? Borgeson asked.

Three ounces. I grinned.

You can't fish three split-shot and steelheads on a three-ounce rod, Borgeson admitted. *Not bamboo or fiberglass anyway!*

It's an amazing material, I added.

Carbon graphite is one of several new synthetic fibers that have emerged from aerospace research in recent years, and its remarkable properties threaten to displace fiberglass from its supremacy in fishing rods once production costs become competitive.

Many expert fly-fishermen have never really liked fiberglass rods, except for wrestling with big chinooks or salt-water species, and it is the moderate price rather than optimal performance that causes glass to dominate the marketplace. American fishermen purchase approximately 3,000,000 rods annually, and almost ninety-seven percent of those rods are glass, fabricated from more than 500,000 pounds of specially woven fiberglass cloth. Glass rods have completely dominated the fishing tackle field since the first crude fiberglass rod section was built by Arthur Howald in 1944.

Factory-made glass rods, however, have failed to solve some of the problems in highly skilled trout fishing. Glass is unquestionably stronger and more resilient than bamboo, but its superior elasticity is strangely a disadvantage in fly-rod performance. Its resilience under casting loads is almost too lively to provide delicate tip calibrations capable of fishing modern nylons from .005 to .003 in diameter. Such 6X to 8X leader tippets are critical for success on our hard-fished modern trout streams, particularly on eastern waters.

Although fiberglass cloth is both lighter and stronger than bamboo, it is formed over a steel mandrel into tubular form. Fine split-cane rods are made in four-strip, five-strip, and six-strip sections, although ninety-nine percent are made in the hexagonal six-strip tapers. Even the partially hollow bamboo rods manufactured on the Pacific Coast do not deform under casting stresses, accepting the loads evenly and progressively, until those stresses reach the fracture point.

Fiberglass blanks become slightly oval under bending loads, since a tube deforms into an ovoid cross section in flexure, regardless of its construction. Glass tubes will accept casting stress until their cross sections deform into exaggerated ovals, and abruptly refuse to gather and release more power. It is possible to overload them far short of their breaking strength, because of their elasticity and tubular resilience, although they seldom actually break or shatter.

Fiberglass has another quality related to its mixed virtues of elasticity and strength that affects your fishing. Its modulus of elasticity is comparable to fine structural steels. It involves the ability of a flexing material to spring back from any deflection under stress to its original alignment. Engineers call this its rate of recovery, and since fiberglass has a shorter fibrous structure than bamboo, it springs back more quickly than a split-cane section. Its normal rate of recovery is exceptionally fast, but paradoxically it recovers too quickly for optimal casting performance. Its recovery is so rapid that too much inertia develops in the opposite direction, and the tip oscillates beyond its original alignment before it comes to rest again. Such sloppy dampening behavior slaps the shooting line back and forth against the rod and its guides, killing both distance and control in a really long cast. The recovery of fine split cane is sharper.

However, a really fine fiberglass rod is still a third the price of the best bamboo work, in spite of its problems. Skilled fishermen soon learn to compensate for its faults, adjusting their timing and power stroke to minimize its heavy-handed behavior with delicate tippets, its tendency to deform and saturate under casting stress, and its oscillations after final delivery.

Since fiberglass has great advantages in its price range, it quickly cornered the fishing tackle industry. Sufficient time has passed that an entire generation has grown up fishing with fiberglass only, and it seems perfectly happy with its performance. During these same years, the artisans famous for bamboo fly rods began dying off, and it looked like their art might die with them. Many expert trout fishermen gloomily looked ahead to a future without split-cane rods. It seemed virtually certain that fiberglass would triumph.

Its ultimate triumph is less certain today. Aerospace technology has developed several completely new synthetic materials for fishing rods in recent years, each with its own unique properties and character. Several tackle manufacturers have been experimenting with synthetic fly-rod prototypes of such materials as boron fibers, alumina, advanced types of high-modulus fiberglass, silicon carbide, boron carbide, high-modulus carbon graphite, and a new fiber called PRD-49, being kept secret by its developer, Du Pont. PRD-49 has slightly less stiffness and strength than these other exotic materials, and has problems with compressive bending stresses, but it costs and weighs much less than promising materials like boron and graphite.

These materials have some exotic properties. Boron is a semimetallic compound, deposited in vapor form on extremely fine tungsten wire. Its vapors take shape in a filament varying from .003 to .004 in diameter. It has twice the strength and stiffness of the finest steels, yet it weighs seventy percent less. It has produced rods closely approximating the performance of split cane, including its delicacy and feel in some exaggeratedly slender prototypes built by Don Phillips in Connecticut. These experimental boron rods achieved a twenty-percent reduction in diameter and a forty-percent reduction in weight, compared with similar rods in bamboo.

However, boron has some problems in terms of its fabrication into fly rods. Its fibers are not woven into a synthetic fabric, like carbon graphite or

CORTLAND   1975   TWO-PIECE TUBULAR CARBON GRAPHITE   CORTLAND, NEW YORK   FROM THE COLLECTION OF LEON CHANDLER

FENWICK   H.M.G.   1973   TWO-PIECE TUBULAR CARBON GRAPHITE   SEATTLE, WASHINGTON   FROM THE COLLECTION OF ERNEST SCHWIEBERT

ORVIS   LIMESTONE SPECIAL   1975   TWO-PIECE TUBULAR CARBON GRAPHITE   MANCHESTER, VERMONT   FROM THE COLLECTION OF ERNEST SCHWIEBERT

glass, and are arranged in a longitudinal alignment in a boron epoxy tape. Such tape is tightly wound and cured around a wire-forming core instead of a tubing mandrel, and early boron epoxy rods were of solid rather than tubular construction. Since there are no lateral fibers, like the spacing filaments in both fiberglass and carbon graphite fabric, to provide hoop strength, some potential structural problems exist in boron-fiber construction. However, there is also remarkable potential in the material, and some of the finest synthetic-fiber rods that I have tried in tapers for ultralight tippets have been boron epoxy prototypes. Like carbon graphite fibers, boron is still costly enough that its use is largely restricted to aerospace systems, where its strength and lightness are worth the price.

Boron and carbon fiber are perhaps the most promising synthetic fabrics for building rods in the immediate future. The basic costs and problems of fabrication involved in the other exotic fibers suggest that their full-scale introduction to the tackle industry lies well in the future. But my first field experience with the Fenwick and Orvis tubular graphite tapers, more than two years before they reached the public, clearly indicated that we were on the threshold of a fly-rod revolution—perhaps more extensive than the recent impact of fiberglass on bamboo, or the earlier impact of bamboo on hickory and greenheart more than a century ago.

Don Phillips has performed some intriguing comparative studies with the new exotic fibers. His work suggests that the modern S-type fiberglass has a clear performance advantage over earlier glass cloth. Low-modulus graphite was not yet available for his studies. High-modulus graphite and exotics like PRD-49 fibers were less adaptable to bending loads than boron filaments, although they are remarkably strong.

His calculations were based upon a theoretical rod section of tubular fabrication measuring one foot in length, with a constant stiffness factor of 500 pound-inches squared. Constant diameter was also assumed, with the structural fibers laminated parallel to the longitudinal axis and distributed equally in a wall thickness of thirty percent fiber densities. Such densities are possible without die-molding techniques under high pressures, and Phillips points out that his test section suggested the properties typical of an eight-foot synthetic-fiber rod for a seven-weight line at its midpoint, which he proposed as average.

Phillips found that modern fiberglass weighs .056 pound per cubic inch when fabricated into his theoretical section. Boron fibers weigh .055 pound and graphite only .053 pound per cubic inch. The boron section was clearly superior in bending, sustaining loads as high as 125,000 pounds per square inch, more than 100,000 pounds stronger than structural steel. Carbon fibers can accommodate bending stresses of 115,000 pounds per square inch, while the advanced S-type fiberglass can sustain loading of approximately 112,000 pounds. Such performance is a remarkable calibration of these exotic fibers.

Working with his stress formulas, which are outlined in the chapter on split-cane construction, Phillips continued to explore the properties of such materials. He quickly discovered that bending modulus (resistance to deformation) is clearly the factor in which the exotic fibers easily excel even the finest fiberglass. The S-type glass has a modulus of elasticity of almost 4,000,000 pounds per square inch when laminated into Phillips' theoretical section. Carbon fiber in the same blank would display a modulus of more than 9,000,000 pounds per square inch—more than twice that of the finest-quality glass. Boron fibers can deliver a modulus of elasticity exceeding 19,000,000 pounds per square inch, which is approximately twice the performance of graphite in Phillips' comparative studies. Such remarkable properties are eloquent testimony to our technology.

Fully assembled into hypothetical rods, Phillips concludes, a boron-fiber prototype would be half the weight of a comparable fiberglass design. Carbon-fiber construction would be about forty percent heavier than the boron prototype.

Rod-diameter studies offer other interesting factors. Fiberglass required a section diameter of .228 inch at the midpoint of its seven-weight taper. Boron fibers in a comparable rod design measured a remarkably slender .152 inch. Carbon graphite fibers laminated into a similar rod were .183 inch in diameter, requiring a slightly larger tubular design. Boron displayed a moment of inertia roughly twice that of S-type fiberglass, while the moment of inertia in the comparable graphite section was almost twice that of boron. Both moment of inertia and rod diameter play a role in fly-rod performance and tip speed, which translate into casting.

Although several manufacturers were field-testing equipment laminated from exotic fibers, Fenwick was the first to exhibit its experimental rods in 1973. Their debut came at the annual summer conclave of the Federation of Fly Fishermen, which gathered in Sun Valley.

André Puyans, a highly skilled professional fly-dresser with a fine fishing shop near San Francisco, was out of breath when he found me having lunch at the Ore House.

You've got to try those new rods! he said excitedly.

What new rods? I asked.

Carbon graphite fibers! Puyans gestured with typical animation. *You've got to try those graphites!*

Can't I finish my lunch first? I teased.

No! Puyans insisted.

We walked back toward the casting pond after lunch to talk with Jim Green of Fenwick about his new high-modulus rods. Green is unmistakably one of the finest casters who ever lived, with a poetic stroke and great economy of style, and I was eager to have his opinion on the new carbon-fiber tapers. There were four prototypes in the rack. The smallest was seven-and-a-half feet and only two ounces.

Two ounces! I shook my head in disbelief. *Only two ounces and it's rated for a five-weight line?*

Green put the rod back in his rack. *Carbon graphite has some remarkable properties.* He smiled at my excitement. *Our eight-foot model weighs a half ounce more and takes a six line.*

Two and a half ounces! I flexed it.

It would probably weigh four ounces in glass, Puyans said, *and still more in bamboo.*

Look at the others too, Green suggested.

The slender eight-and-a-half-foot rod was rated for an eight line, and weighed only three and one-quarter ounces. Fiberglass rods taking an eight-weight forward taper usually weigh about an ounce more, and comparable cane rods can reach five ounces. The nine-foot graphite was as slender as a delicate bamboo, was rated for a ten-weight line, and weighed only four ounces.

It will even throw an eleven-weight, Green said.

You're joking! I protested.

He's serious, Puyans interrupted. *Try one!*

We took all four rods to the casting pond, and Green strung the eight-and-a-half-foot model with a floating forward-taper line. The line looked too delicate for an eight-weight.

That really an eight-weight floater? I asked.

No. Green smiled. *It's a six.*

But you said the rod was rated for an eight, I protested. *What weight line does it really take?*

Puyans laughed. *Just stop talking and cast!*

Okay, I agreed.

There was a light wind coming straight in toward our casting platform, riffling the pond. The graphite rod felt stiff until it had a line loading at about forty feet, and then its character became slower and more poetic. It possessed surprising quickness, and it was so light for its relative power that it seemed ridiculously easy to slice a tight loop into the wind.

Since casting beyond sixty-odd feet is a problem in overcoming atmospheric effects on both the rod and its working line, and in achieving optimal tip speed at the moment of delivery, both the relatively thin diameter of the rod and its incredible lightness were obvious advantages in making long casts with amazingly little effort. It was surprisingly easy to pick sixty to seventy feet of line off the water, something I had never seen done with comparable cane or glass, and the backcasts were tight and high. The tip speed effortlessly held a narrow loop, and although distance casting had not been a particular skill of mine, these casts rolled out and turned over some surprising lengths of fly line.

The little rod was so fast and light that I was stunned. *You're right!* I said. *It will really handle line!*

Green and Puyans smiled broadly. *You haven't seen anything!* they said. *That's a six-weight you're throwing.*

But it's rated for an eight! I said.

Green stripped the line from the guides and rigged it with another reel. *Try it with a ten-weight,* he suggested.

Ten-weight! I protested. *It won't throw it!*

Just try it! Puyans growled.

The little rod worked the line out with surprising ease, loading more and more distance in a tight loop. It picked seventy-five feet off the water cleanly, accepted still more in my reverse shoot into a high backcast, and laid the entire line out with a single left-hand pump. Perhaps the most remarkable aspect of its performance was the sensation that I had made only minor adjustments in my timing to accommodate a fly line two sizes larger than its rated weight. The narrow loop accelerated with a lazy double-haul, shooting the entire line and a dozen feet of pale backing.

Better than a hundred feet! I was stunned.

Wrong! Puyans laughed and took the rod. *That's thirty-five yards of tournament taper, plus some backing hanging out and your leader—and that's more like a hundred and twenty!*

But I can't cast a hundred and twenty! I said.

Puyans smiled. *You just did!*

Carbon graphite fiber is a remarkable development. It is produced in a series of heat treatments which expose polyacrylonitrile to increasing temperatures and decreasing densities of oxygen. The polyacrylonitrile fibers are first oxidized at 200 to 300 degrees centigrade. Carbonization is achieved in a second stage at 1200 to 1500 degrees C., and they literally become graphite at kiln temperatures of 2000 to 3000 degrees.

During these final kiln settings, which occur completely without oxygenation, microscopic crystals are gathered as carbon graphite fibers. These somber-looking little fibers become delicate filaments approximately .0003 inch in diameter, with ratios of stiffness and weight that closely parallel those of boron, although carbon graphite is less expensive.

Appreciating synthetic-fiber equipment involves an understanding of not only the bending stresses of a material in flexure, when a material is exposed to strong oscillations between tension and compression, but also the concepts governing modulus of elasticity. Tensile forces, found in a taut violin string, are also present in the upper fibers of a rod while playing a fish. Compressive forces, such as are exerted on a load-bearing building wall, are also found in the lower fibers of the rod under the strain of the struggling trout. During the rhythmic stresses of casting, any rod is constantly changing its power-fiber stresses from tension to compression and back again.

Modulus of elasticity is a theoretical measure of a material in terms of its resistance to deformation. Applied to rod action, modulus of elasticity calibrates an exotic-fiber tube in terms of its intrinsic stiffness and its rate of recovery from stress. The Phillips studies demonstrate that the modulus of elasticity in boron- and carbon-fiber rods displays a remarkably dramatic change over that of past materials, including S-type fiberglass. Our grasp of modulus of elasticity and its role in fly-rod action is critical in understanding exotic fibers.

Carbon graphite has rapidly become the principal synthetic fiber in modern rod construction. Raw carbon fibers have a remarkable modulus of elasticity, reaching as much as 50,000,000 pounds per square inch. Such fibers are easily woven into clothlike fabrics that can be formed around a mandrel into rod sections. The basic process is quite similar to the manufacture of most fiberglass blanks. But the astounding rigidity of carbon-fiber tubular sections makes it virtually impossible to deform them under casting loads, or exceed their capacity to accept more bending stresses, unlike earlier fiberglass tapers. Carbon-fiber rods will stress cleanly and return crisply to their original alignment, with swift rates of recovery that shame the finest bamboo.

Fenwick discovered in its first high-modulus prototypes that carbon graphite rods had half the butt diameter of glass rods of comparable performance, and were twenty-five percent lighter. Comparisons with split cane are even more striking. Fenwick found that its early graphite tapers were about thirty percent smaller than the typical butt calibrations of bamboo designs, and their weight demonstrated a surprising fifty percent reduction over split-cane construction.

When these early Fenwick prototypes were finally available, they cost almost as much as many split-cane rods. Such prices were surprising to a generation conditioned by glass, but perhaps we should remember that when the first Shakespeare fiberglass rods were introduced, after the Second World War, they cost as much as an exquisite Payne or butter-colored Leonard.

The early Fenwick prototypes had black-anodized reel fittings of both skeletal and locking designs. Chromium snake guides, and stripping guides and tops of ceramic aluminum oxide, were also standard equipment. These tapers were based upon a hybrid construction which combined both graphite power fibers and fiberglass for tubular strength in conditions of lateral stress. Both wall thickness and tip diameters were relatively overdesigned in these early models, and their relatively stiff actions were received with mixed reviews from the advocates of both glass and split bamboo, whose casting habits often failed to extract the full potential of these carbon-fiber tapers because they were used to softer actions in glass and bamboo. The following rods, built by Fenwick, were the first carbon-fiber designs in production:

MODEL	LENGTH (FEET)	WEIGHT (OUNCES)	LINE WEIGHT
GFF755	$7^1/_2$	$2^1/_2$	5
GFF806	8	$2^5/_8$	6
GFF856	$8^1/_2$	$2^7/_8$	7
GFF858	$8^1/_2$	$3^1/_4$	8
GFF901	9	4	9

My first experience with carbon graphite was with field-testing the eight-and-a-half-foot design for an eight-weight line, using a taper designed for trout fishing to fish giant chinooks in northern California. Its capacity to handle big salmon in strong currents was surprising, and its ability to make long casts with ten- and twelve-weight shooting heads was nothing less than remarkable. It was even able to accommodate experimental shooting heads fabricated of lead-core trolling line, easily throwing distances beyond a hundred and twenty-five feet, and subdued chinooks of forty to fifty pounds. However, Fenwick soon abandoned these early designs, both because they were too stiff for the average caster and because its planners had begun to understand that graphite possessed an unusual potential for rods of greater length and delicacy. The second generation of Fenwick carbon-fiber rods includes the following trout-fishing tapers:

MODEL	LENGTH (FEET)	WEIGHT (OUNCES)	LINE WEIGHT
GFF634	$6^1/_2$	$1^7/_8$	4
GFF7o5	7	$2^1/_4$	4
GFF755	$7^1/_2$	$2^1/_2$	5
GFF756	$7^1/_2$	$2^5/_8$	6
GFF8o5	8	$2^5/_8$	5
GFF8o6	8	$2^3/_4$	6
GFF856	$8^1/_2$	3	6
GFF857	$8^1/_2$	$3^1/_4$	7
GFF858	$8^1/_2$	$3^1/_2$	8
GFF9o5	9	$3^1/_8$	5
GFF9o8	9	$3^3/_4$	8

These later designs were fitted with sliding ring and butt cap reel fittings in the models lighter than the GFF755, and with a black-anodized reverse-locking reel seat in the bigger rods. Fenwick has steadily worked to improve its graphite rod-tapers, and these current designs include several exceptional models. My experience with the Fenwicks leads me to admire the eight-foot GFF8o5 for a five-weight, and the eight-and-a-half-foot GFF856 tapered for a six-weight line. My introduction to the unique nine-footer designed for a five-weight occurred in the Paulina country of Oregon, when tournament caster Steve Rajeff let me fish the GFF9o5 Fenwick prototype he was field-testing.

The third generation of Fenwick graphites has dropped the delicate four-weight GFF634 and GFF7o5 designs. It has added the GFF756 and GFF9o6, which are six-weight tapers. Other new models are the GFF9o7, which takes a seven-weight line, and the nine-and-a-half-footer for a nine-weight. The current Fenwick HMG series includes these models:

MODEL	LENGTH (FEET)	WEIGHT (OUNCES)	LINE WEIGHT
GFF755	$7^1/2$	$2^1/2$	5
GFF8o5	8	$2^3/4$	5
GFF9o5	9	$3^1/8$	5
GFF756	$7^1/2$	$2^5/8$	6

MODEL	LENGTH (FEET)	WEIGHT (OUNCES)	LINE WEIGHT
GFF806	8	$2^{3}/_{4}$	6
GFF856	$8^{1}/_{2}$	3	6
GFF906	9	$3^{1}/_{4}$	6
GFF857	$8^{1}/_{2}$	3	7
GFF907	9	$3^{1}/_{8}$	7
GFF858	$8^{1}/_{2}$	$3^{1}/_{8}$	8
GFF908	9	$3^{1}/_{4}$	8
GFF959	$9^{1}/_{2}$	$3^{5}/_{8}$	9

Orvis started its line of carbon-fiber rods shortly after Fenwick introduced its high-modulus designs. Leigh Perkins sent me an early experimental model completely without Orvis markings, although its Superfine grip style and delicate reel bands clearly revealed its origins. The prototype was an eight-foot trout rod weighing less than two ounces and designed for a six-weight line. Other models quickly followed the success of the first Orvis graphites, which were trout rods designed for six- and eight-weight tapers, and the initial catalog included these types:

MODEL	LENGTH (FEET)	WEIGHT (OUNCES)	LINE WEIGHT
M9270	7	$1^{5}/_{8}$	5
M9276	$7^{1}/_{2}$	$1^{3}/_{4}$	6
M9280	8	$1^{7}/_{8}$	6
M9286	$8^{1}/_{2}$	$2^{7}/_{8}$	8
M9290	9	$3^{1}/_{8}$	9

Perkins was so excited by the performance of these early graphite rods that he soon decided Orvis would build its own graphite rod plant, making it possible to control both design and quality. Each of these early prototypes remains in the Orvis line, although some modifications in taper patterns and lamination quality have occurred. Orvis fabricates its rods with the same excellent fittings originally machined for its justly famous Battenkill split-cane rods. Its carbon-fiber rod blanks are left with the curing wraps exposed, like the original Howald windings on the first fiberglass rods from Shakespeare. Leaving their graphite rods with the wraps exposed echoes the Orvis tradition of finishing the impregnated Battenkill line without varnish, and the technicians at Orvis' Vermont factory firmly believe that stripping the spiral wraps can damage the carbon fibers that will sustain maximum bending stress. Such stripping and polishing did not affect fiberglass performance, and some custom glass rodmakers often modify their actions by polishing down wall thickness intentionally, but it could prove fatal in graphite. Perkins is restlessly improving and changing his line of carbon-fiber rods; the following trout rods are in the second Orvis line:

MODEL	LENGTH (FEET)	WEIGHT (OUNCES)	LINE WEIGHT
M9250	5	$1\frac{1}{8}$	5
M9266	$6\frac{1}{2}$	$1\frac{3}{8}$	4
M9270	7	$1\frac{5}{8}$	5
M9276	$7\frac{1}{2}$	$1\frac{3}{4}$	6
M9276-2	$7\frac{1}{2}$	$2\frac{1}{8}$	6
M9280	8	$1\frac{7}{8}$	6
M9280-2	8	$2\frac{1}{4}$	6
M9287	$8\frac{1}{2}$	$2\frac{5}{8}$	6
M9286	$8\frac{1}{2}$	$2\frac{7}{8}$	7
M9286-2	$8\frac{1}{2}$	4	8
M9290	9	$3\frac{1}{8}$	9
M9297	$9\frac{1}{2}$	$3\frac{5}{8}$	8

These rods include some remarkable tapers that I have greatly enjoyed fishing in recent months. The first few hours of field-testing taught me that the more delicate Orvis designs were striving to provide actions capable of fishing nylon tippet diameters of .005 inch, and the responsive stroke and tip speed of tapers like the M9280 made roll casts as long as eighty feet possible. The more delicate M9287 design, at eight-and-a-half feet and well under three ounces, was specially conceived for fishing fine tippets and difficult spring-creek conditions. It is perhaps my favorite Orvis graphite, although steelhead and sea-bright coho salmon in Alaska have led me to appreciate the fine qualities of the nine-and-a-half-footer designed for an eight-weight forward taper. Orvis is continuing to refine and augment its carbon-fiber line, and I fully expect longer rods of surprising delicacy and performance.

Orvis is still experimenting widely, discarding some of its earlier graphite prototypes, refitting others, and adding fresh surprises. Its current catalogues include these trout-fishing models:

MODEL	LENGTH (FEET)	WEIGHT (OUNCES)	LINE WEIGHT
JM9272-1	$7\frac{3}{4}$	$1\frac{1}{2}$	2
JM9274-1	$7\frac{1}{2}$	$1\frac{1}{2}$	3
JM9277-1	$7\frac{1}{2}$	$1\frac{5}{8}$	4
JM9262-1	8	$2\frac{1}{2}$	4
JM9262-21	8	$2\frac{1}{2}$	4
JM9288-1	9	$2\frac{7}{8}$	4
JM9270-11	$7\frac{1}{2}$	$1\frac{5}{8}$	5
JM9279-1	$7\frac{3}{4}$	$2\frac{1}{8}$	5
JM9242-21	$8\frac{1}{2}$	$2\frac{1}{2}$	5

MODEL	LENGTH (FEET)	WEIGHT (OUNCES)	LINE WEIGHT
JM9293-1	$9^{1/4}$	$2^{3/4}$	5
JM9298-1	9	$3^{1/8}$	6
JM9278-21	$7^{1/4}$	3	6
JM9278-1	7	$2^{5/8}$	6
JM9276-1	$7^{1/2}$	$1^{3/4}$	6
JM9276-11	$7^{1/2}$	$2^{1/8}$	6
JM9280-1	8	$1^{7/8}$	6
JM9287-1	$8^{1/2}$	$2^{5/8}$	6
JM9292-1	$9^{1/4}$	3	6
JM9291-11	$9^{1/2}$	$3^{1/2}$	6
JM9283-1	$8^{1/4}$	$2^{1/2}$	7
JM9284-1	8	3	7
JM9294-1	9	3	7
JM9294-21	$9^{1/4}$	$3^{1/4}$	7
JM9286-1	$8^{1/2}$	$2^{7/8}$	8
JM9297-1	$9^{1/2}$	$3^{5/8}$	8
JM9290-1	9	$3^{1/8}$	9

The JM9280-1 model is still similar to the first prototype that Leigh Perkins sent me for testing in 1974, and the JM9287-1 is a current match for the earlier Limestone Special. The new JM9262-1 is an eight-and-a-half-foot rod, weighing only two and a half ounces, and is matched with a DT4F line. The JM9242-21 is designed for the Henry's Fork and its problems, and is a superb fly rod for taking large fish on light tackle. The Spring Creek design is currently listed as the JM9293-1 model, and is a favorite tool in the collection of Jack Hemingway. Although I have fished it with pleasure, with both Hemingway and Bill Mason, it is missing from my collection because its length makes travel difficult. The JM9297-1 is similar to the older M9297, which was originally christened the Presentation Special. The so-called Tippet is a delicate three-weight JM9274-1 model, which I have enjoyed on small trout streams. The most recent Orvis in my collection is the JM9272-1, which weighs $1^{1/2}$ ounces and is designed for a unique DT2F line. Its delicate casting stroke is a little startling, and I cannot wait to fish it in the spring.

Leonard quickly followed with its own series of pale-gray graphite rods, but its first production runs were rather ill-fated, using carbon-fiber blanks from a manufacturer with little tacklemaking experience. The early Graftek models were fitted with standard, fully machined Leonard fittings combined with black reel-seat fillers. Bright orange wrappings were a sharp contrast to the pale-gray epoxy finish. The following prototypes were the first Leonard graphite designs:

MODEL	LENGTH (FEET)	WEIGHT (OUNCES)	LINE WEIGHT
1310	7	$1^7/_8$	4
1312	$7^1/_2$	$2^1/_4$	5
1322	8	$2^3/_4$	6
1316	$8^1/_2$	3	7
1318	$8^1/_2$	$3^1/_2$	8

The rod-blank manufacturer unquestionably had problems with quality control in these early Leonard designs, just as several other tacklemakers experienced trouble in their first production runs. Considerable breakage occurred, both at the ferrules and in the graphite blanks themselves. Leonard obviously acquired some painful experience with its first carbon-fiber rods, and its lessons were not entirely technical. Their new production line consists of some of the most beautiful graphite rods yet made, and my experience with their character and performance is a testimony to their quality. The blanks are a rich golden brown, with a braided layer of carbon fibers to provide lateral tube strength to the longitudinal filaments that accept the bending stresses of casting. Black reel-seat fittings of typical Leonard excellence are mounted on cork or hardwood fillers in the skeletal and reverse-locking designs. The dark finish makes this series perhaps the most handsome of the current carbon-fiber rods, and it has been widely praised for its elegance. The following graphite models are found in the Leonard line:

MODEL	LENGTH (FEET)	WEIGHT (OUNCES)	LINE WEIGHT
504G	5	I	4
703G	7	$1^3/_8$	3
704G	7	$1^1/_2$	4
754G	$7^1/_2$	2	4
755G	$7^1/_2$	$2^1/_4$	5
756G	$7^1/_2$	$2^3/_8$	6
804G	8	$2^1/_4$	4
805G	8	$2^3/_8$	5
806G	8	$2^1/_2$	6
807G	8	$2^5/_8$	7
855G	$8^1/_2$	$2^1/_2$	5
856G	$8^1/_2$	$2^5/_8$	6
857G	$8^1/_2$	$2^3/_4$	7
858G	$8^1/_2$	$3^1/_8$	8
906G	9	$2^7/_8$	6
908G	9	$3^1/_4$	8

Carbon fibers were first developed in Britain. Leonard has christened these new rods its Golden Shadow models, and its blanks are fabricated entirely of graphite fibers in the United Kingdom. Since experiencing such troubles with its earlier sleeve-type ferrules, Leonard has changed to a boron-reinforced ferrule incorporating a spigot-type design. The strength of the boron fibers makes it possible to grind the spigot plugs to a precise ferrule fit. The reel-seat fittings used on these Golden Shadow rods are the same elegantly tooled fittings originally specified for the split-cane Leonards. The tapers designed for three- and four-weight lines are fitted with continuous cork handles and reel-seat fillers, mounted with butt caps and sliding rings. The carbon-fiber rods for five- to seven-weight lines feature elegant reverse-locking seats and hardwood fillers, with graceful Hardy-type handles. Golden Shadow rods designed for eight-weight tapers are fitted with standard down-locking Leonard hardware and cork grips.

There are several exciting graphite rods in the Leonard line. The seven-foot model for a three-weight is unique, and the 754G is a delicate graphite designed for a four-line that displays great promise. I have fished the eight-footer of just over two ounces that is rated for the four-weight tapers, and have found it perfectly suited to delicate spring-creek tactics. The eight-and-a-half-foot design weighing only two and a half ounces and taking a five-weight line is quite unusual too, and fishes well where the difficult mixture of long casts and fine tippets is required. The nine-footer for a six-weight is also intriguing.

Scientific Anglers has followed the success of its excellent fiberglass fly rods with a line of all-graphite models. Ceramic stripping guides are standard, and the running guides and tops are chrome stainless. The carbon-fiber blanks are built entirely of graphite, and the slender ferrules are exclusive with Scientific Anglers, combining high-performance alloys with spigot-type designs. Six models are available in tapers and line weights intended for trout fishing:

MODEL	LENGTH (FEET)	WEIGHT (OUNCES)	LINE WEIGHT
System G4	8	$2^3/_4$	4
System G5	$8^1/_4$	3	5
System G6	$8^2/_3$	$3^3/_4$	6
System G7	$8^5/_8$	4	7
System G8	$8^3/_4$	$4^1/_8$	8
System G9	$9^1/_3$	$4^1/_2$	9

Cortland has joined in the competition for the carbon-fiber tackle market, and recently introduced its line of uniquely built rods. Its Diamondback series takes its trademark from a combination of axial fibers and cross-braided graphite to provide an outer layer of power laminations. These diagonal hoop-strength fibers are visible, and inspired the Diamondback name. Cortland rods also combine tubular construction with solid tip-design for unique performance and durability. Aluminum oxide stripping guides are combined with hard chromium tops and guides. Cortland has also incorporated a solid exotic-fiber spigot ferrule. Several of its Diamondback series are trout-size equipment:

MODEL	LENGTH (FEET)	WEIGHT (OUNCES)	LINE WEIGHT
7034	7	$1^7/_8$	4
7056	7	$2^1/_8$	5
7645	$7^1/_2$	$2^1/_8$	5
7667	$7^1/_2$	$2^5/_8$	6
8056	8	3	6
8078	8	$3^3/_8$	7
8656	$8^1/_2$	3	6
8689	$8^1/_2$	4	8
9056	9	$3^1/_4$	6
9910	9	$4^1/_2$	9

Harry Wilson is the alchemist at the Scott factory, and after several months of empirical work, the company has selected its basic line of carbon-fiber rods. The following models are available:

MODEL	LENGTH (FEET)	WEIGHT (OUNCES)	LINE WEIGHT
G85-4	$8^1/_2$	2	4
G85-5	$8^1/_2$	$2^1/_8$	5
G90-3	9	$2^1/_8$	3
G90-4	9	$2^1/_4$	4
G90-5	9	$2^3/_8$	5
G90-6	9	$2^1/_2$	6
G90-7	9	$3^1/_4$	7
G95-8	$9^1/_2$	$3^1/_2$	8
G95-9	$9^1/_2$	$3^7/_8$	9

Lamiglas has totally accepted computer-design methodology to leap-frog the first-generation rods of other companies. Computer work has enabled the Lamiglas technicians to develop a surprising number of first-rate rod designs in the past two years. The company is also willing to build custom tapers and actions, and it offers a number of eight- to nine-foot rods of suppleness and remarkable delicacy. The present series of graphite tapers is available from Lamiglas:

MODEL	LENGTH (FEET)	WEIGHT (OUNCES)	LINE WEIGHT
F704	7	$1^7/_8$	4
F764	$7^1/_2$	$2^1/_{16}$	4
F765	$7^1/_2$	$2^1/_8$	5

MODEL	LENGTH (FEET)	WEIGHT (OUNCES)	LINE WEIGHT
F803	8	$1^{7}/_{8}$	3
F804	8	$2^{11}/_{16}$	4
F805	8	$2^{13}/_{16}$	5
F806	8	$2^{15}/_{16}$	6
F865	$8^{1}/_{2}$	$2^{15}/_{16}$	5
F866	$8^{1}/_{2}$	$3^{1}/_{16}$	6
F867	$8^{1}/_{2}$	$3^{3}/_{8}$	7
F904	9	$2^{7}/_{8}$	4
F905	9	$3^{1}/_{16}$	5
F906	9	$3^{3}/_{16}$	6
F907	9	$3^{5}/_{16}$	7
F908	9	$3^{15}/_{16}$	8
F909	9	$4^{1}/_{16}$	9
F964	$9^{1}/_{2}$	$3^{5}/_{16}$	4
F965	$9^{1}/_{2}$	$3^{1}/_{2}$	5
F966	$9^{1}/_{2}$	$3^{7}/_{16}$	6

Winston is another famous maker of split-bamboo rods that has accepted carbon-fiber technology. Based upon its testing of rods built by other manufacturers, Winston concluded that carbon fibers were best suited to fast- and medium-action tapers, that their exotic properties were perfectly suited to making powerful rods of surprisingly little weight, and that they held the promise of delicate fly rods of unusual length and lightness.

Winston turned to the same manufacturer that built its superb fiberglass sections, Kennedy Fisher of Los Angeles, and started a program of research and development. Taper patterns and delicate mandrels were required if Winston intended to translate its famous hollow-built bamboo performance into graphite. It took considerable empirical work to develop and perfect the right combinations of taper patterns and lamination mandrels, and to select the proper carbon-fiber cloth to fabricate rods of graphite and fiberglass for lateral reinforcing. The method resulted in rods composed almost entirely of graphite, and offered the Winston designers considerable versatility in their tip calibrations and performance. Sleeve-type ferrules are mounted on the tip sections, and are fashioned of fiberglass reinforced with carbon-fiber cloth. Winston fittings are of the same quality found on their split-cane designs. The light rods offer skeletal reel seats with sliding rings and butt caps on specie-cork fillers. Their medium trout models have elegant down-locking hardware and hooded butt-cap assemblies. The hardwood fillers are available in teak, black walnut, and richly grained rosewood. The classic Winston assembly of down-locking hardware on a Bakelite filler is still available on special order. Perhaps the most surprising feature of the Winston graphite line is its rich forest-green finish, combined with matching green wrappings, and offering the typical Winston craftsmanship. The following models will be available:

LENGTH (FEET)	WEIGHT (OUNCES)	LINE WEIGHT
$7^1/_2$	$1^7/_8$	4
$7^1/_2$	$1^7/_8$	5
8	2	4
8	$2^1/_8$	5
8	$2^1/_2$	6
$8^1/_2$	$2^1/_8$	4
$8^1/_2$	$2^1/_2$	5
$8^1/_2$	$2^5/_8$	6
$8^1/_2$	3	7
9	$2^3/_4$	5
9	$2^7/_8$	6
9	$3^1/_4$	7
9	$3^1/_2$	8
9	$3^5/_8$	9

Winston has several unique combinations of rod length and delicacy and line weight in its list, and its designers obviously do not believe in rod lengths under seven and a half feet for an exotic material with the high-modulus stiffness of graphite. The series includes an eight-foot rod and an eight-and-a-half-footer designed for the light four-weight lines, and nine-footers for both five- and six-weight tapers.

Ron Kusse has started building carbon-fiber rods of excellent design, using the same elegant fittings of German silver found on his split-bamboo work. His smoothly polished graphite shafts are available with either spigot or German-silver ferrules. Walnut, cherrywood, cork, and tiger maple reel-seat fillers are available on the following rods:

MODEL	LENGTH (FEET)	WEIGHT (OUNCES)	LINE WEIGHT
KCF-603	6	1	3
KCF-664	$6^1/_2$	$1^1/_8$	4
KCF-704	7	$1^1/_4$	4
KCF-705	7	$1^1/_2$	5
KCF-763	$7^1/_2$	$1^1/_4$	3
KCF-764	$7^1/_2$	$1^5/_8$	4
KCF-765	$7^1/_2$	2	5
KCF-804	8	$2^1/_8$	4
KCF-805	8	$2^1/_4$	5
KCF-806	8	$2^1/_2$	6

MODEL	LENGTH (FEET)	WEIGHT (OUNCES)	LINE WEIGHT
KCF-865	8½	2¾	5
KCF-866	8½	3¼	6
KCF-867	8½	3½	7
KCF-868	8½	3¾	8
KCF-906	9	3½	6
KCF-908	9	4	8

Jerry Fleming is a friend building fine graphite rods in British Columbia, and I first cast with them at a boat show in Oregon. The rods are beautifully fitted and finished, and their aesthetic character had an impact on the rods built by bigger manufacturers. My experience with the Fleming rods suggests that his five- and six-weight models are excellent, particularly in the nine-foot lengths. The small Fleming designs under eight feet are fitted with cigar grips and a sliding-band seat, and the longer rods offer reverse-locking seats and full-Wells grips. The Fleming series is the following:

MODEL	LENGTH (FEET)	WEIGHT (OUNCES)	LINE WEIGHT
JFG-763	7½	1½	3
JFG-764	7½	1⅝	4
JFG-805	8	2½	5
JFG-806	8	2¾	6
JFG-865	8½	2½	5
JFG-866	8½	2¾	6
JFG-867	8½	2⅞	7
JFG-905	9	3	5
JFG-906	9	3¼	6
JFG-907	9	3½	7
JFG-908	9	3¾	8
JFG-968	9½	4	8

Sage carbon-fiber rods are relatively new, but their quality has quickly established them in the marketplace. The quality and design of the Sage blanks are no accident. The technical excellence and quality of the Sage line comes from a cadre of old Fenwick staff members, including Les Eichorn and Don Green, who played major roles in the creation of the first carbon-fiber rods.

Fittings and finishes were a major part of our thinking, Eichorn explained on the Kulik in Alaska. *We wanted graphites that looked like the finest old bamboos—the old Leonards and Paynes.*

Sage manufactures and finishes its own blanks, and their tapers, cloth

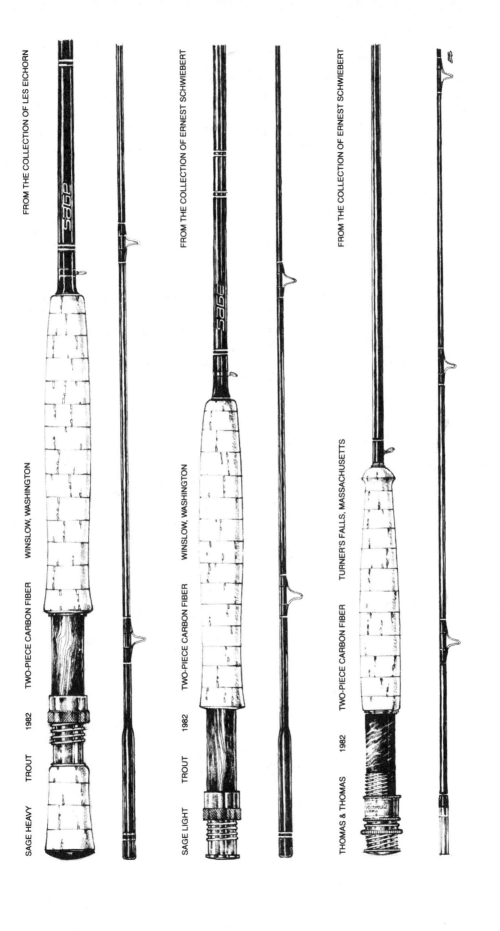

FROM THE COLLECTION OF LES EICHORN

SAGE HEAVY   TROUT   1982   TWO-PIECE CARBON FIBER   WINSLOW, WASHINGTON

FROM THE COLLECTION OF ERNEST SCHWIEBERT

SAGE LIGHT   TROUT   1982   TWO-PIECE CARBON FIBER   WINSLOW, WASHINGTON

FROM THE COLLECTION OF ERNEST SCHWIEBERT

THOMAS & THOMAS   1982   TWO-PIECE CARBON FIBER   TURNER'S FALLS, MASSACHUSETTS

patterns, and curing are exceptionally fine. Its fabrication equipment and techniques have explored fresh ground. Sage tapers have a distinct casting stroke, perhaps a little slower than some designs, but with the butt power to lift cleanly and control a tight casting loop. The Sage graphite rods are ninety-seven percent carbon fiber. The sleeve-type ferrules offer a taper-fit design, without boron or fiberglass or carbon fibers.

The rich brown finish is flawlessly cured and polished. The final epoxy coating is mirror-bright, compounded to resist abrasion, solvents, and the damaging effects of sunlight.

Sage specifications include quality most typically associated with traditional bamboo makers. The grips are select specie-cork rings cut from Spanish cork-oak trees. Shotgun-grade walnut fillers are used in Sage reel seats. Jewel-polished aluminum fittings are used in both standard and reverse-locking designs. Guides and fly-keepers are first quality. The hand wrappings are subtly keyed to the chocolate finishes of the rods: rich brown with a few ornamental turns of dull amber. The visual character of Sage rods is unique, although like most bigger manufacturers, its trademark is perhaps too large and garish. Sage produces a relatively large volume of rods, and its line is justly admired. The trout-fishing models in the Sage line include the following:

MODEL	LENGTH (FEET)	WEIGHT (OUNCES)	LINE WEIGHT
GFL470	7	$2^{1}/_{4}$	3
GFL476	$7^{1}/_{2}$	$2^{3}/_{8}$	4
GFL576	$7^{1}/_{2}$	$2^{1}/_{2}$	5
GFL676	$7^{1}/_{2}$	$2^{5}/_{8}$	6
GFL580	8	$2^{5}/_{8}$	5
GFL680	8	$2^{3}/_{4}$	6
GFL586	$8^{1}/_{2}$	3	5
GFL686	$8^{1}/_{2}$	$3^{1}/_{8}$	6
GFL786	$8^{1}/_{2}$	$3^{1}/_{4}$	7
GFL490	9	$3^{1}/_{8}$	4
GFL590	9	$3^{1}/_{4}$	5
GFL690	9	$3^{3}/_{8}$	6
GFL790	9	$3^{1}/_{2}$	7
GFL890	9	$3^{5}/_{8}$	8
GFL696	$9^{1}/_{2}$	$3^{5}/_{8}$	6
GFL896	$9^{1}/_{2}$	4	8
GFL996	$9^{1}/_{2}$	$4^{3}/_{4}$	9

My own collection includes three Sage rods, although I have either cast or fished most of its line. It is important to understand, as it was also true of Winston and Powell rods in their early years, that Sage rods almost unconsciously echo the unwritten criteria of western fishing. Most of these rods are keyed to fishing big water, wading deep, and distance work. Except for the shorter designs, which are fashionable eastern lengths and line-weight tapers, even the four- and five-weight designs offer enough length to mitigate the problems of selectivity and big fish on a daily basis. Few eastern anglers face more than selective feeding and small waters. Big fish are a rarity. Sage equipment manages a fine equilibrium between performance and aesthetics, and its line offers some unique designs. The GFL490 is nine feet and takes a four-weight. It is a favorite in both New Zealand and Alaska, on big trout in relatively small waters, and it is excellent on western spring creeks on days with little wind. The GFL690 is a nine-foot rod for a six-weight taper, and is better under windy conditions on such streams. The GFL896 is a longer eight-weight rod that easily casts an entire line under windy conditions, and has proved itself on difficult rivers from Alaska to the Antipodes.

Thomas & Thomas started working in carbon fibers about six years ago, and its first prototypes quickly rivaled the excellence of its craftsmanship in cane. Both fittings and performance were enviable.

With a growing tradition of delicate split-cane designs, Thomas Dorsey sought to transpose the best of his bamboo tapers into graphite patterns. The first models were entirely two-piece designs, with gracefully faired graphite-to-graphite ferrules, and a machined band of German silver to reinforce each ferrule throat. The rod blanks are entirely fabricated from carbon-fiber cloth. Carbide stripping guides were combined with stainless guides, tops, and flykeepers. The grips are first-grade Spanish specie cork. The early Thomas & Thomas graphites were fitted with the same elegantly machined butt caps and sliding-band hardware found on its cane rods, with shotgun-grade hardwood fillers. Models intended for fishing seven- to nine-weight lines have a Hardy-style grip and reverse-locking hardware, with both polished aluminum and wood fillers. The following rods were in the first Thomas & Thomas line:

MODEL	LENGTH (FEET)	WEIGHT (OUNCES)	LINE WEIGHT
TTGF-407	7	$1^{3/4}$	4
TTGF-467	$7^{1/2}$	2	4
TTGF-567	$7^{1/2}$	$2^{1/4}$	5
TTGF-408	8	$2^{3/8}$	4
TTGF-608	8	$2^{1/2}$	6
TTGF-668	$8^{1/2}$	$2^{5/8}$	6
TTGF-768	$8^{1/2}$	$2^{7/8}$	7
TTGF-868	$8^{1/2}$	$3^{1/8}$	8
TTGF-509	9	$2^{3/4}$	5
TTGF-809	9	$3^{7/8}$	8
TTGF-669	$9^{1/2}$	3	6
TTGF-969	$9^{1/2}$	4	9

These early Thomas & Thomas graphites were excellent rods, and I particularly enjoyed fishing the eight-foot model for a DT6F. The TTGF-509 of nine feet, and fitted with a five-weight line, was another early design of great promise.

Current Thomas & Thomas graphites have both fully machined German-silver ferrules and exquisite reverse-locking reel seats. Both pigeon-grade hardwood and polished aluminum fillers are available. Guide wrappings are ebony with silver ivory trim. The following Thomas & Thomas graphites have been added:

MODEL	LENGTH (FEET)	WEIGHT (OUNCES)	LINE WEIGHT
TTGF-568	8½	2½	5
TTGF-569	9½	3	5
TTGF-909	9	3⅞	9

Thomas Dorsey also introduced a series of unusually elegant carbon-fiber rods in his Special Dry Fly series. His modern template-patterns have been married to his sense of tradition in these designs. The Spanish specie-cork grips have been shaped into modified Hawes-style handles, both slightly old-fashioned and unique. The Special Dry Fly rods have quickly become best-sellers at Thomas & Thomas.

The tapers combine a slightly faster action with unusually sensitive tip calibrations. The first rod in the series was an eight-foot design intended for a DT4F or DT4½F taper. Thomas & Thomas owners soon asked for a slightly bigger dry-fly rod, intended for five- and six-weight performance. My experience with the SDF-408 suggests that it is a remarkably conceived piece of equipment, and I have fished mine widely. It has proved itself on difficult trout waters and even in bug-fishing on big bluegills, with Bob Buckmaster in Wisconsin. It has been such a pleasure that I bought a matching SDF-408 for my son, when he finished preparatory school in 1982. The Special Dry Fly series includes two superb trout rods:

MODEL	LENGTH (FEET)	WEIGHT (OUNCES)	LINE WEIGHT
SDF-408	8	2⅜	4
SDF-538	8¼	2½	5

Several other manufacturers are studying the potential of carbon-fiber technology, along with the justly famous custom builders who have worked extensively in glass. There are seemingly an infinite number of cloth patterns and mandrel tapers and hybrid laminations of fiberglass and graphite to explore.

Carbon-fiber rods have perhaps generated more short-term excitement among serious anglers than any other single bench mark in the history of fly-fishing equipment.

Some advocates have hailed the exotic new fiber as the ultimate material for rod construction, while others have expressed some nagging doubts. Considered solely in terms of its casting properties, graphite construction is quite remarkable. Its physical properties of stiffness and recovery from stress offer singular power-to-weight ratios, as well as tight casting loops combined with high line speed. Such qualities mean less fatigue, better casting performance on windy days, and more distance with less casting effort.

There is also a lot of crackerbarrel talk about greater tip sensitivity, which seems misplaced. Sensitivity seems to imply delicacy in fishing, and the delicacy of fine split-cane craftsmanship is relatively absent in most graphite rods. There is a relatively swift transmission of vibrations through a carbon-fiber structure, but that quality stems from its quickness rather than its sensitivity. Carbon graphite has remarkable speed in its recovery from stress, and that quality is rooted in its modulus of elasticity, yet its sharp response to stress and its brisk recovery from that stress cannot be considered sensitivity. Such properties are superb in casting, but in fishing they can also shear a fine tippet or tear the fly out of a head-shaking fish, particularly when the rod dances harshly.

Too many fishermen have interpreted the tensile strength and high modulus of elasticity found in carbon fibers as raw strength in rods. It has been a painfully expensive myth. Graphite rods are much more fragile than fiberglass, although less brittle than bamboo. Fabricated into tubular blanks, graphite is amazingly strong in its casting properties, but it will fracture easily under a careless lateral impact. It is important to understand that graphite rods are easily broken, even though the exotic fibers in their tubular structures are twice as strong as fiberglass, six times as strong as steel. Modulus of elasticity is the secret of both weakness and strength in graphite: while fiberglass will display as much as four percent deformation without failure, carbon graphite can accept less than one percent before fracturing. Graphite must be given the respect offered to bamboo.

Since fiberglass will deform without breaking, its followers have often developed some bad habits. Glass will often accept excessive casting loads before fracture, while graphite will continue to absorb stress until it literally explodes. I have broken two graphites in field-testing. The first sustained a spiral fracture while I was attempting to pick up exaggerated lengths of line from the casting pond. The second literally exploded in my hand. It was an eight-and-a-half-footer designed for a six-weight line, and we were double-hauling unusual distance casts. I had just picked up more than sixty feet, accelerating it high into the backcast, and was allowing line to shoot in to my forward false-cast. When I closed my fingers to check the forward shoot and started back into the second left-hand haul, the graphite exploded like a pistol shot under my casting hand and completely shattered the grip. Like any other fine piece of equipment, graphite rods must not be carelessly abused.

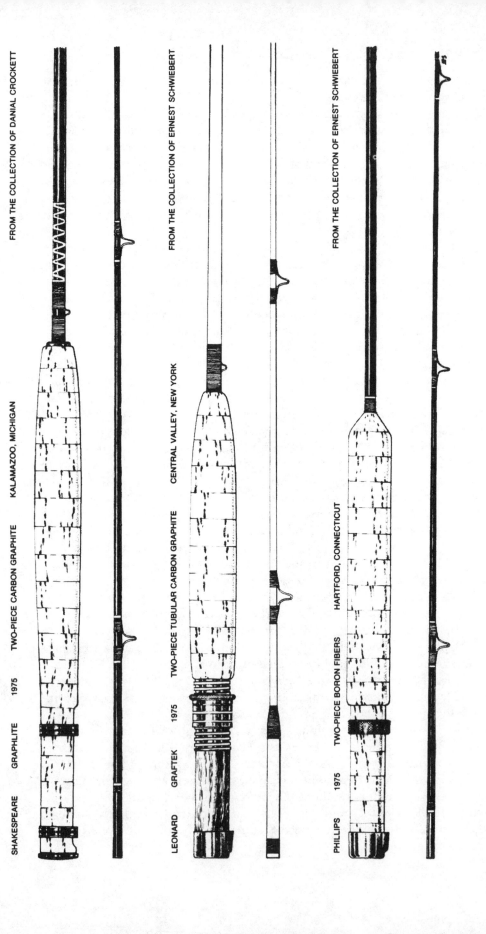

SHAKESPEARE   GRAPHLITE   1975   TWO-PIECE CARBON GRAPHITE   KALAMAZOO, MICHIGAN   FROM THE COLLECTION OF DANIAL CROCKETT

LEONARD   GRAFTEK   1975   TWO-PIECE TUBULAR CARBON GRAPHITE   CENTRAL VALLEY, NEW YORK   FROM THE COLLECTION OF ERNEST SCHWIEBERT

PHILLIPS   1975   TWO-PIECE BORON FIBERS   HARTFORD, CONNECTICUT   FROM THE COLLECTION OF ERNEST SCHWIEBERT

Fishermen have responded quite emotionally to graphite. The advocates of split-cane tend to dislike its somber appearance, its roots in a technology that utterly abandons the violin-building aspects of rodmaking, and a lack of delicate poetry in its action.

The fiberglass generation has embraced these exotic fibers as enthusiastically as their parents accepted the first Howald-patent glass rods after the Second World War. In those years the pot-belly stoves of trout-country bars and tackle shops across the country witnessed many sermons predicting the swift demise of bamboo. Similar talk is alive again, with a new generation, infatuated with exotic fibers, expecting the extinction of both fiberglass and cane.

It is important to understand that graphite rods have already experienced a surprisingly swift evolution in their brief history. The present carbon-fiber products vary widely, and are not as alike as many knowledgeable anglers seem to believe. There are striking variations in actions and specifications and tapers. Such differences reflect the understandable preoccupation of each rodmaker with either particular fishing problems or the preferences of its customers.

Since graphite tackle in several price ranges is starting to appear in the marketplace, there is some confusion among fishermen about carbon-fiber quality and costs. The quality of carbon-fiber cloth is relatively constant. Variables obviously exist in the technology of taper patterns, mandrel specifications, lamination, adhesives, and curing techniques. Price variables also relate to the percentage of graphite cloth used in a particular rod blank. Fiberglass-and-graphite laminates are common. Delicate layers of glass fabric are used both to reinforce the lateral strength of the tubular rod blanks and to soften a harsh graphite action. Some rods are fabricated with pure graphite fibers, while others are more than ninety percent carbon-fiber construction. Still others are sold as graphite equipment when in reality they are fiberglass blanks with a veneer of graphite cloth so thin it scarcely affects the action. It is wise to purchase these exotic-fiber rods from well-known manufacturers with a fine reputation to protect—and to expect to pay their prices.

Graphite and its sister synthetic fibers have both triggered a revolution in rodmaking and created a storm of controversy. The new rods have proved themselves quite popular, yet many experienced fishermen still seem a little baffled by their properties and character. Many anglers have sampled graphite rods only in the confines of tackle shops, and most carbon-fiber rods seem stiff without a line working.

Forget everything you think you know about rods when you wiggle a graphite without actually casting it, Jim Green observes wryly, having watched such meaningless rituals for many years. *You can't tell anything about graphite without a line in the air—because graphites are the first rods with insufficient density to flex themselves!*

Working with these fibers gives you a fresh respect for cane, Leigh Perkins argues. *They're more like bamboo than bamboo.*

9. *The Story of*
Borontrichloride

The day was cold and raw.

It was a strange time to test an exotic new fishing rod. The hotel doorman was busily hailing taxis from the traffic that filled Fifty-ninth Street, and a brittle winter sun tried to warm the bare trees in Central Park.

The Theodore Gordon Flyfishers were having their annual March banquet in Manhattan. The membership was gathering before lunch to explore the tackle manufacturers' booths and to attend the films and lectures scheduled in the ballroom of the Essex House.

Later I was sitting in the bar with Charles De Feo and Everett Garrison, enjoying a mixture of whisky and winter twilight among the leather and mahogany millwork and mirrors. It was early in 1973.

Can you spend fifteen minutes? It was Don Phillips, an aeronautical engineer from Hartford. Phillips held a slim six-foot tube in his hands. *I've got something here that might surprise you.*

Fly rod? I asked.

Heard you express some doubts about building really delicate rods with aerospace fibers, Phillips explained. *So I built you a surprise.*

Graphite, I asked, *or something else?*

Boron, Phillips said quietly.

We walked to the main ballroom, which stood empty after the last fishing program. We moved along the center aisle below glittering chandeliers, and through acres of folding chairs that had witnessed years of weddings, bar mitzvahs, and cotillions.

Phillips drew a frail-looking rod from its six-foot case. Its calibrations were startling, the butt was scarcely the diameter of a soda straw, and its tip section was as delicate as a pencil lead. Such diameters were a revelation after years of fishing the fat fiberglass tapers that evolved just after the Second World War.

Even the first tubular carbon-fiber prototypes, which I had field-tested before Fenwick introduced them, seemed fat in comparison.

It's pretty delicate, I said.

It's an exaggeration to make my point, Phillips admitted. *But I decided to copy the Leonard one-piece Baby Catskill in boron—because you thought it was impossible.*

Can we try casting it?

That's why I brought you in here, he said.

Phillips produced a Hardy Flyweight fitted with a two-weight British silk. It seemed strange in the empty ballroom, casting a half-ounce rod and its antique line, and watching it deliver casts on the faded carpets.

Well, I said sheepishly after a dozen casts, *I've been wrong before.*

Graphite and boron are hardly new.

As a young air force officer, I had first seen both materials in the aircraft testing laboratories at Wright Field, just after the Korean War.

Ten years later, working in test facilities planning, I saw these exotic filaments used in experiments with propellers and helicopter rotors and engines. It was startling to find such exotic technology being used in fishing rods.

Carbon graphite was the first aerospace material to emerge in the tackle industry. It was woven into a strong fabric like webbing that could be cut easily into patterns, and adapted to the tubular fabrication methods of fiberglass production at acceptable costs.

Although graphite and boron have similar properties, it is impossible to weave boron into a cloth, Phillips explained. *Boron is more difficult to make, and building it into rods takes some handiwork—so boron rods are more expensive.*

Boron is surprisingly common.

The element is widely distributed in nature. Its character includes a unique mix of strength, hardness exceeding the carbides, low density, a remarkable capacity to withstand distortion under both compression and tensile stress, and the ability to perform under extreme temperatures. Such properties have obvious attractions for aircraft technology.

Boron is most commonly found in borax. Armchair television historians will remember it was mined and transported by twenty-mule teams in early California.

Commercial deposits of borax are typically found in the sedimentary beds of desiccated seas. Its original commercial uses included antiseptic solutions, preservatives, soldering and welding fluxes, Pyrex glassware, shellacs, enamel finishes, ceramic colors and glazes, and cleaning compounds before detergents were widely introduced. Other remarkable uses have evolved in recent years. The ability of boron to resist abrasion and thermal stress, and its poor conductivity and inert chemistry, have led to sophisticated applications ranging from fuel additives to control rods in nuclear reactors.

It is curious that Sir Humphrey Davy, who is better known to fishing bibliophiles for his charming book *Salmonia*, discovered boron in his laboratory in 1808.

Davy would be fascinated by the sophistication of our boron technology today. Its fabrication at the Avco Laboratories near Boston has obvious overtones of science fiction. It has the tight security associated with other secret projects. Guards and security badges and checkpoints control access to its commonplace buildings, but its boron chambers themselves are firmly rooted in the future. Boron filaments are made in partially darkened chambers filled with glowing tubes. The corridorlike rooms are bathed in their eerie orange light resembling settings in books by Fleming or Deighton or LeCarré.

The boron-making process takes place in these glowing tubes. The tubes are filled with a secret mixture of gases that includes borontrichloride.

The entire process is monitored in each tube by its own fluttering meters and gauges. There is a thin tungsten wire at the axis of each tube, and it is fed through its chamber at a precisely controlled rate. The mixture of gases is held at exact temperature. The tungsten wire and gases are given opposite electrical charges, extracting boron crystals from the borontrichloride gas, and precipitating them on the slowly moving wire. Each boron filament is a crystalline structure on a tungsten core, and measures .004-inch in diameter. Avco scientists believe a similar process might be developed to precipitate boron crystals on a spiderweb filament of graphite, making still lighter and stronger boron fibers possible.

Each tungsten-core filament is collimated in quarter-inch Mylar tapes. Boron crystals are so abrasive that such parallel filaments cannot be permitted to cross or touch, since they would quickly cut or abrade one another. After quality-control testing, Avco uses a complex stagger-frame system that feeds the individual boron filaments into their final tape alignment through a fifty-three die plate. The fifty-three fibers are fixed to the Mylar tape with epoxy resins, and the quarter-inch tapes are assembled on fiberglass backing in twelve-tape increments, to a maximum width of forty-eight inches. Fully collimated and cured sheets are rolled between polyethylene to protect the boron filaments from themselves, and are shipped in Styrofoam containers.

The abrasive properties of boron crystals suggest that weaving their filaments into clothlike fabrics is unlikely, and that sandwiching them into fishing rods will remain a costly process.

Don Phillips was the first to understand the potential of boron filaments in fly-rod design.

It was a series of happy accidents, Phillips explains. *We were working on propeller and rotor applications of carbon fibers and boron at Hamilton Standard in 1966—and the stress analysis in propellers and helicopter rotors is surprisingly close to describing the oscillations of working stress in fishing rods.*

What about the bad rumors? I asked.

What rumors?

The stories about boron's being dangerous in a thunderstorm, I explained, *or that it can explode into needles when it fractures.*

Both things are myths, he said.

What happens?

Boron is such a poor conductor that it is used in lightning arresters and insulators, Phillips replied. *It fractures pretty much like bamboo—shattering across its linear fibers when it goes.*

Phillips built his first boron prototypes late in 1971, and took his first trout with one that following spring on the Battenkill. His first rods were adaptations of the early Howald patents in fiberglass construction, and their boron tapes were shaped around a balsawood armature. Phillips was excited about his first experiments, but admits they were relatively fragile. Other concepts were tried later, and he finally settled on a solid boron design formed around a .03-inch diameter tungsten core held in tension. It is a hundred percent boron construction, with its permanent tungsten armature. Phillips has filled more than 350 orders since 1972, and owns the pioneering patents on solid-boron fabrication and several boron-hybrid composite designs.

I took an eight-foot Phillips boron to the Yellowstone country in 1973, and its baptism took place on free-rising cutthroats at Buffalo Ford.

It was fitted with conventional guides and a sliding-band reel seat. Its solid construction on a tungsten core made both sleeve- and spigot-ferrule designs unworkable. Phillips decided on German-silver ferrules, like those still used on expensive cane rods, and his boron rods are still fitted with them today.

The action of the eight-foot Phillips was slow and smooth, designed for a DT4F line. Its slightly top-heavy feel demanded precise timing and patience. Its stroke could not be forced, or fished with a left-hand haul. Hard casts simply caused it to flutter, throwing a wavy line or unwanted hooks, but it cast cleanly with a slower casting rhythm. It was perhaps a bit too spaghettilike in its middle calibrations. Refusing the line loads of casts beyond seventy-five feet, it also had a tendency to bounce out-of-plane under the impact stresses of big head-shaking fish. Other synthetic rods have displayed similar problems. Erratic oscillation while playing large trout or forcing long casts has been troublesome in many light rods, in virtually all light, tubular fiberglass and carbon-fiber and boron designs. Yet the Phillips eight-foot rod offered exciting promise, fishing 6X tippets on big trout.

It was late September on the Yellowstone at Buffalo Ford, and on the winding flats at Slough Creek. The fish were taking minute *Tricorythodes* spinners in the late mornings, and hung just under the surface after lunch, sipping tiny midge pupae in the film. It took imitations of these insects, dressed on size twenty hooks and fished on fragile .005 nylon, to take the steadily rising trout. The rod fished the delicate tippets and tiny hooks flawlessly, its subtlety unmatched by the other synthetic rods of its time.

Although such prototypes were still flawed, the Phillips design was a revelation. It was completely unlike the stiff power-tapers of the first carbon prototypes I had tested on big chinooks in 1971. Boron was an exciting prospect.

The first graphites were casting cannons. I reported to Phillips when I returned from the Yellowstone. *Perfect for shooting heads and distance casting—but your boron rod has a lovely stroke, soft and a little like bamboo.*

We're still trying things, he said.

Five years ago, another Phillips prototype arrived for testing. It was a second eight-foot model that specified a three-weight line, and it had corrected the earlier problems. Three-weight rods are not designed for long casts, but the new rod delivered forty to sixty feet with both delicacy and crisp control. It was a delight to fish when I first tried it on the Brodheads.

Later that season, I fished the rod in northern Colorado, on a pretty river called the Little Snake. It winds lazily along the Wyoming border, its course circling under limestone bluffs and cottonwoods. It lies well off the paved roads, across a low pass between Saddle Pocket and Steamboat Springs. It is not a large river, even below its junction with Battle Creek, but it offers pleasant fishing and a surprising sense of history.

Its battle involved a party of fur trappers, including famous frontiersmen like Bridger and Meek, and a large force of Indians. The trappers were surrounded on a brushy island, but their weapons included Sharps buffalo guns mixed with a few Hawken and Creedmore rifles. Although they were surrounded, it was hardly a fair fight, given the marksmanship of the fur trappers.

Indian warriors were shot at extremely long ranges, and when their chief was literally exploded by a heavy-caliber buffalo round at several hundred yards, the war party stopped fighting.

Jeremiah Johnson wintered with his Indian wife along the Little Snake, building a comfortable dugout that looked south toward the river and its junction with Battle Creek. There is a still pool above its mouth today, at Saddle Pocket Ranch, where the fish rise greedily on late summer mornings to the swarms of *Tricorythodes* flies.

There is colorful outlaw history too. Butch Cassidy and his Wild Bunch often wintered at Brown's Hole on the Green. Their wanderings took them through most of these valleys in western Colorado and Wyoming; and across the Wyoming line, the explosive party held by the Wild Bunch in its old hotel was the high-water mark in the history of Baggs.

The first times I fished the Little Snake, I was on the Saddle Pocket water with Frank Meek, who operates a fishing shop at Steamboat Springs. Meek teaches courses on things as esoteric as *Finnegan's Wake* and *Ulysses* during the winters, although his family tree includes Joe Meek, the celebrated frontier trapper.

The river winds through the ranch in a series of small flats and pools. We never fished it together in the spring, with more water and better hatches. It was always difficult sport in late summer, with a hot sun on its arid September hills, and tiny flies hatching. But it still held a lot of fish, and a few good ones. The morning *Tricorythodes* swarms were dependable, but seldom produced large trout. Cloudy weather often triggered good hatches of little *Baetis* flies, and in the big flats above the ranch itself I took several sixteen- to eighteen-inch fish. The Big Bend downstream, its currents circling past large boulders and reflecting its high limestone bluffs, held such fish too. These trout were all selective, and it took tiny polywing spinners and duns and terrestrials to fool them, fishing 6 X and 7 X polyamide tippets. The experimental Phillips boron performed well, cushioning the fine tippets against setting the book and playing the fish. The boron performed better than the graphites I had fished at that point, in striking and playing trout on light gear, although the crisp stroke of the carbon-fiber rods makes them superb casting tools. The Phillips rod was a happy surprise.

I really like it, I told Phillips later. *It fishes like bamboo—I really like it.*

Congressman Pete McCloskey was in our party the third time I fished the Little Snake. We flew over from Steamboat Springs and landed at the Lidstone ranch, upstream from Saddle Pocket. It was pocket water, colder and with a steeper profile than the cottonwood pools downstream. It held few brown trout, mixing rainbows with some surprisingly large cutthroats. The day was hot and windy. The fish came greedily to a big Carpenter Ant fished wet, casting upstream into the pockets. The trees cast longer shadows across the river when I finally reached a bigger pocket under a fallen cottonwood.

It looked promising and I stopped fishing to study its problems. The best slick eddied tight against the roots. It was slipping into a late afternoon shadow, and I watched it several minutes.

There was a soft rise. *Looks like a good fish,* I thought. *Mark him down.* It rose again.

Several dark caddisflies were hopscotching over the water, mating and laying eggs. I changed the Ant to a dark sedge pattern, the slate-colored Hemingway Special. The fish sipped again, tight against the roots, and then porpoised almost lazily.

Good fish! I was getting excited.

The trout settled into steady feeding, and I made a tentative cast. Its line of drift circled too far from the roots. The second cast flirted with the shadows, bobbing under the roots, and the fly vanished. I tightened into a trout that bolted upstream and jumped.

Twenty inches! I guessed.

My guess was right, and the big cutthroat tested the three-weight Phillips to its limits. It bolted wildly again, probing stubbornly under the roots, and ran into the pockets downstream. The rod cushioned the delicate nylon, and it controlled the fish surprisingly well for a three-weight. Finally I netted the fish and released it, regretting that I carried no camera. It was a handsome native.

Pete McCloskey was sitting upstream, under a big cottonwood tree. The long flat there was completely in shadow, and a good fish rose steadily.

I'm dogging it, McCloskey explained. *Saved that rising fish for you.*

You try him, I suggested.

Already tried him, McCloskey laughed ruefully from the shade. *Show me what he'll take.*

I'll try, I said.

The trout was not as large as the fish I had just released downstream, but it was close. Its rises came steadily, too soft to suggest caddis activity unless it was on spent egg-laying sedges. Drowned *Baetis* spinners travel under the water to lay their eggs, creating a subsurface drift instead of a spinner fall, and were possible too.

The fish refused the sedge imitation that had worked before. Its rises were tiny bulges that came steadily. I tried a spent sedge pattern and the fish tipped up, inspecting it carefully. The fly drifted past its position untouched, and I retrieved it to try another.

Gary Borger sent me some small olive-bodied flies dressed with dun hen hackles several years ago, telling me they worked on such smutting fish. The pattern had worked for me during *Baetis* activity on many western streams, and I decided to try one. It was lightly dressed with dry-fly ointment, touching its hackles to get it to float slightly awash. The delicate tippet was free of casting knots, and finally I was ready again.

What're you trying now? McCloskey asked.

Junk pitches, I said.

The little nondescript fly fell gently into the right line of drift, and I lost it momentarily in the reflected light. The fish dimpled quietly, where I thought the fly might be, and I tightened.

The quiet pool erupted as the two-pound cutthroat threshed angrily, and bolted swiftly upstream. It had taken the Borger pattern.

Nice work! McCloskey called.

The delicate tactics that broke the code that September afternoon were methods that I had usually associated with expensive cane tapers specifically designed for such work. The Phillips three-weight boron had proved itself, and it is currently found in a fourteen-rod series:

MODEL	LENGTH (FEET)	WEIGHT (OUNCES)	LINE WEIGHT
SBP-160	6	3/4	2
SBP-260	6	1	4
SBP-370	7	1 1/4	3
SBP-470	7	1 1/2	4
SBP-575	7 1/2	1 3/4	3
SBP-675	7 1/2	2	4
SBP-775	7 1/2	2 1/4	5
SBP-875	7 1/2	2 1/2	6
SBP-980	8	2 3/4	3
SBP-1080	8	3	4

MODEL	LENGTH (FEET)	WEIGHT (OUNCES)	LINE WEIGHT
SBP-1180	8	3¼	5
SBP-1280	8	3½	6
SBP-1390	9	3¼	4
SBP-1490	9	3½	5

The Phillips rods are not tubular designs, but solid boron fabricated over a wire mandrel, which makes them much thinner than other manufacturers' rods, but also heavier, due to their density. The method has its obvious advantages; it also makes big rods for seven- and eight-weight lines impractical. Don Phillips understands his medium perfectly, and his excellent designs concentrate on slender rods for relatively light fly-lines.

Boron filaments are still costly and exotic.

The fabrication of such materials occurs at only two factories in the United States. Avco manufactures more than seventy percent of the total of American boron filament at its Lowell plant near Boston. Composite Technology Corporation produces virtually all of our other boron fibers at its Broad Brook facilities outside Hartford.

Few anglers understand the technology of materials behavior, and talk of such things as modulus of elasticity is familiar in strength-of-materials engineering but it baffles the fishing world.

The confusion has led many fishermen to assume that boron is substantially lighter than graphite, and that it is stronger and more sensitive. Boron is neither significantly stronger nor lighter than carbon fibers. Its alleged sensitivity is highly subjective. It is seemingly the result of connotations, rather than technical facts. Reams of copy have been written about the so-called sensitivity of both graphite and boron rods, but sensitivity is a term used to describe their quick response to stress. Both materials respond swiftly to stress, and their recovery is equally swift. But such character cannot be described in terms of sensitivity.

Poisson's ratio is familiar to all students who survive to reach the courses in mechanics, subjects usually taught in the sophomore year of any engineering curriculum. Statics, dynamics, and strength of materials are the subjects, and they teach a fledgling architect or engineer to employ mathematics in simulating the structural performance of their designs.

Modulus of elasticity lies at the root of Poisson's ratio. The stress performance of both graphite and boron are based on their singular modulus of elasticity. The modulus of any material is a measure of its ability to resist deformation, and its rate of recovery once deformed.

Modulus of elasticity in fishing rods has been slightly distorted in its meanings. It has come to describe their stiffness-to-weight ratios, their quickness, and their rate of recovery from stress.

Carbon fibers display a remarkable modulus of elasticity, offering as much as 50,000,000 pounds per square inch. Such performance is approximately seventeen times the modulus of fiberglass. Boron filaments offer a modulus of elasticity that is thirty percent higher still. But it is critical to understand that modulus of elasticity is relatively meaningless in fishing tackle until a material is translated into specific calibrations.

The important thing to know about boron filaments, explains Paul Goffman of the Avco Corporation, *is that they deliver more strength than our finest aircraft alloys at considerably less weight—and boron can take temperatures that could melt aluminum right off the air frame of high-performance aircraft.*

What about the boron stories? I asked.

You mean the horror stories?

That's right, I said.

The stories about exploding into microscopic particles? Goffman laughed and stared out across the old factories of Lowell. *And particles so toxic that we are forced to include a six-page warning pamphlet in every shipment we make?*

You've heard them too, I smiled.

It's difficult to know how such stories get started, Goffman said, *but it's just not true.*

What is true?

The myth of exploding comes from stories of its stiffness, he explained, *but boron is only thirty percent less elastic than graphite—and you've seen that we manufacture both at Lowell.*

What about toxicity?

Boron is mildly toxic, Goffman continued. *That's why it's used in some antiseptics, eyewashes, and astringents—but its toxicity is displayed only in large doses, extremely large doses.*

Boron fibers are not toxic?

Their chemistry is virtually inert, he said, *and the resins used in all tubular fishing rods—fiberglass and carbon fiber and boron alike—are more toxic than the rod materials themselves.*

Rodon Corporation uses the boron-filament tapes and fibers produced at Avco, and it introduced a hybrid design that combined boron fibers over a carbon-fiber armature. Its designs include a surprising range of tapers, from smutting trout to muscular salt-water rods. There have been many opportunities to fish their rods in recent months, and the full inventory of two-piece trout models is the following:

MODEL	LENGTH (FEET)	WEIGHT (OUNCES)	LINE WEIGHT
T-2704	7	$1^{3}/_{4}$	3
T-2753	$7^{1}/_{2}$	$1^{7}/_{8}$	3
T-2804	8	2	4
T-2755	$7^{1}/_{2}$	$2^{5}/_{8}$	5
T-2806	8	$2^{7}/_{8}$	5
T-2855	$8^{1}/_{2}$	3	6

MODEL	LENGTH (FEET)	WEIGHT (OUNCES)	LINE WEIGHT
T-2906	9	$3^{1/4}$	6
T-2807	8	$3^{1/8}$	7
T-2857	$8^{1/2}$	$3^{1/2}$	6
T-2908	9	$3^{5/8}$	8
T-2957	$9^{1/2}$	$3^{3/4}$	8

Rodon has also introduced a series of three-piece trout models, which are intended to pack and travel conveniently:

MODEL	LENGTH (FEET)	WEIGHT (OUNCES)	LINE WEIGHT
T-3856	$8^{1/2}$	$3^{1/8}$	6
T-3906	9	$3^{1/2}$	7
T-3857	$8^{1/2}$	$3^{1/8}$	7
T-3908	9	$3^{3/4}$	8
T-3957	$9^{1/2}$	$3^{7/8}$	8

Travel also dictated the introduction of four-piece trout rods at Rodon:

MODEL	LENGTH (FEET)	WEIGHT (OUNCES)	LINE WEIGHT
T-4806	8	3	6
T-4857	$8^{1/2}$	$3^{3/4}$	7
T-4908	9	$4^{1/8}$	8

The first Rodon model that I field-tested was a prototype of their T-2804, with a cork-filler reverse-locking seat. It was eight feet long and weighed $1^{7/8}$ ounces, and I fished it with a four-weight double taper. It was relatively soft and slow, and it shocked easily when I forced a cast, sending a fluttering oscillation along the line. But it was not intended for tight-loop work. It was designed to work close and fine, and it performed its function perfectly.

Its baptism came on the upper Firehole, where it took several decent fish on small nymphs and dry flies, but it really proved its worth when I was fishing with Mike Lawson at Last Chance, on the Henry's Fork of the Snake.

You want to test a four-weight boron? Lawson asked. *You're in the right place tonight.*

We drove to the river and waited, studying the banks for particularly good fish. Clouds of egg-laying caddisflies gathered along the grassy

FROM THE COLLECTION OF ERNEST SCHWIEBERT

TED SIMROE   1980   RODON   TWO-PIECE BORON   NEWARK, NEW JERSEY

FROM THE COLLECTION OF LEIGH PERKINS

HOWARD STEERE   1983   ORVIS   TWO-PIECE BORON   MANCHESTER, VERMONT

FROM THE COLLECTION OF ERNEST SCHWIEBERT

TED SIMROE   1980   RODON   TWO-PIECE BORON   NEWARK, NEW JERSEY

margins of the stream, and the small fish were already working as we arrived. We leaned against the truck and waited.

There! Lawson breathed.

He pointed to a smooth current that flowed tight against the grass. Seconds passed before the big rainbow came softly again. Its rise was only a sucking bulge, but its disturbance sent small waves undulating downstream.

Good fish! I nodded.

Let's wait, Lawson suggested. *We should let him settle into a steady rhythm. And others might start working.*

Like that one?

Lawson chuckled when a bigger trout rose softly, fifteen feet upstream. Its rises were subtle. It rose in a lazy steeplechase roll, showing its dorsal fin and tail. It was a big trout, and it was soon rising steadily.

He's really a good fish! Lawson said excitedly. *But you'll have to try the little one first.*

Little one! I laughed.

He'll go four pounds, Lawson admitted, *but the other one's bigger—and you'll have to fish the lower guy first.*

It won't be easy, I said.

Try it.

I circled well below both fish and slipped carefully into the water. Sometimes careless wading can spook a fish at surprising distances. I worked very slowly upstream until I was about fifteen feet behind the lower fish. Both trout were rising steadily. The rises were so quiet that most fishermen would assume they were small fish. Getting close was critical. The undulating weeds and grassy banks spawn a nightmare of half-seen currents, and too much line will quickly drag the fly. The first cast fell short. The tiny spent sedge pattern dropped perfectly a few false casts later, and the big rainbow inhaled it softly.

He took it? I was surprised.

The big fish shook itself momentarily, and bolted past me into open water. *Would I give you the wrong fly?* Lawson chuckled. *And the other guy's still working.*

The little four-weight boron parried its stubborn fight until it finally surrendered. It went twenty-one inches. I unhooked the tiny sedge from its jaw and slipped it back into the current. The fragile 7X tippet was a tangle, its elasticity all spent from the fight, and I replaced it. Lawson had given me a half-dozen spent sedges with partridge wings, and I knotted a fresh fly to the tippet.

The other fish was still rising. *He won't be so easy,* Lawson observed quietly. *He's moving around a lot between rises—settling and moving again.*

Rainbows are like that.

The fish was obviously bigger. It was working a beat, rising steadily in a feeding zone about the size of a bathtub. It was covering several lines of drift. *You'll just have to keep casting until he sees it,* Lawson chuckled, *but don't line him!*

Casting as softly as possible, I kept dropping the tiny fly in the feeding zone. The fish was still working quietly. Once it brushed the drifting leader, and there was a sudden, nervous swirl.

Scared him, I thought unhappily.

But the big trout settled back quickly into its feeding rhythm. It was a piece of luck. I lost count of the casts it took, with hundreds of spent caddis in the film and the fish working back and forth. It was a matter of timing. The trout had a steady rhythm, and I kept trying to introduce the fly just ahead of its rise patterns.

And finally it took.

Its dark head pushed above the film and intercepted the tiny fly, and I tightened. The shallows erupted. The big rainbow bolted and wallowed up the narrow channel between the bank and the weeds. It circled back into open water and jumped, running my shrill Princess deep into its backing.

Bigger than we thought, Lawson said.

It fought hard, forcing us to follow it downstream. It measured twenty-three inches, and the boron rod cushioned its struggles perfectly, protecting the fragile leader. Lawson got his camera while I unhooked the fly to hold the fish high, head down in my net.

He's pretty fat, Lawson said excitedly. *Could go six pounds on the Henry's Fork—he's a lot bigger than his rises looked.*

But I hooked a bigger fish at nightfall. It was holding in a silken current downstream that still reflected the failing light. It was a short check-cast into the bright water, but it was impossible to see the fly. It was too small and floating away. It was guesswork, and I tightened gently each time the fish rose.

We were both surprised when I hooked it, feeling its weight. Its response was unsettling. It simply drifted downstream and sulked in the shallows, until I followed it and applied a steady pressure, with the twilight gathering swiftly. I was fishing a 5X tippet and felt more secure. It rolled lazily, and catching the sunset sky it showed a dorsal and tail that made us both gasp.

That's some fish! Lawson laughed wryly, *but unless he feels some pressure, he might lie there all night—he might even swim back upstream and start feeding again!*

He's pretty big, I agreed.

It was getting darker, and the big rainbow just held there until some drifting weed collected on the leader. It seemed to annoy the fish. More weed touched the leader and caught. The trout started slowly downstream.

He's the biggest fish I've seen hooked on this river, Lawson was almost giggling.

The fish swam lazily with the river. My light reel was steadily emptied, just a step or two faster than we could follow in the waist-deep current.

You're in trouble, Lawson said.

We stumbled along for three hundred yards, with the boron rod straining and my backing nearly gone. The fish threshed on the surface far downstream. We crossed the main flow to follow. Lawson made it without trouble, but I stumbled and shipped a little water. The big fish circled back across the river. The entire line bellied and throbbed. The strain was finally too much, and the tippet parted. We stood laughing quietly in the darkness.

He was bored, I said.

Rodon first became involved in fishing tackle with its quality rod fittings. The company subsequently hired Ted Simroe, the master rodmaker at Leonard, to help expand its activities. Simroe has obviously made the transition from subtle split-bamboo construction to carbon fibers and boron-composite rods.

Working with Composite Development Corporation in California, which already had extensive experience with boron-composite shafts for golf clubs, Simroe experimented with rod specifications and construction. His solution was a composite design that placed longitudinal boron fibers on the surface of a light carbon-fiber armature.

We knew bamboo worked like that. Simroe recalls, *with its dense power fibers outside, and the pithy inside fibers only providing its gluing surfaces. We thought we might have something once we solved the problems of bonding the carbon fibers to the boron.*

The theory anticipated that moderate casting loads could be accommodated by the graphite core. Gradually increasing stresses would involve both the core and its boron shell. Maximum casting loads would be absorbed by the high-performance boron filaments.

Boron filaments have too much stiffness and memory to provide hoop strength in a tubular blank, Simroe explains, *and hoop-strength problems gave us trouble.*

What did you try? I asked.

The solution was both sophisticated and simple. Boron could not provide lateral hoop strength. Its fibers were too stiff to form around rod diameters, and could not cross or touch without damaging each other. Spiral boron wraps developed too much torque and twisting stress. Simroe ultimately decided to try forty-five-degree helical wraps of half-inch graphite tape around a mandrel in both directions. Boron filaments were laid longitudinally over the helical armature, and sandwiched in place with a longitudinal layer of carbon-fiber cloth and epoxy resins. Like other manufacturers, Rodon finally wrapped the freshly rolled blanks in a spirally wound shrink tape, and cured them in its ovens. The mandrel is later stripped free. The rod blanks are trimmed, the shrink tape is cut away, and the surface is polished. The Rodon composites use only ten to twenty percent boron in its sections, depending on the size of specific patterns and blanks.

Since tip diameters are too slender for the boron-fiber tapes, Simroe found that single boron filaments could be added by hand. However, their alignment must be symmetrical and precise, since the slightest error can result in eccentric bending and casting. Simroe also worked out a slim spigot-type ferrule, using a boron filament plug, and it has echoed Orvis in committing itself to high-quality machined fittings.

The finishes and aesthetic character of the Simroe rods are excellent, perhaps the most handsome of the boron designs yet made, owing a debt to the reverse-locking Hardy rods built just after the First World War. Such factors are more important to fly fishermen than many manufacturers seem to understand.

The Rodon T-3906 is a nine-foot rod designed for a six-weight line, and I have fished it extensively on both trout and salmon.

My first experience with a T-3906 came at a fishing exposition in New York. It seemed so smooth that I was eager to fish it later that year. Its first tests came in floats on the Madison and Yellowstone, throwing big salmon fly patterns in hours of lifting and casting. It is demanding work, more demanding than many wading anglers know, with its quick pickups and shots at passing targets. The T-3906 worked perfectly.

But what about delicate six-weight work? I thought after a float below Varney Bridge.

Bud Lilly first introduced me to the difficult fishing at Slow Bend, perhaps the finest dry-fly water on the Madison above West Yellowstone. It was a perfect challenge.

It has excellent early summer hatches each afternoon, particularly in cloudy weather, and its browns are quite selective. The fish see a lot of anglers. The flies come steadily, but on heavily fished stretches like the Slow Bend, the good fish rise only when the sun is off the water. Few trout work in sunny weather, but even a passing cumulus cloud can trigger a brief rise of fish. Such trout are a useful yardstick. Sometimes ninety-foot casts are needed, the fly hatches are small *Ephemerella* and *Baetis* duns, and twelve-foot leaders tapered to 6X are critical too.

The Simroe T-3906 performed well, taking fish to eighteen inches at such casting ranges, and with such terminal tackle. It offered a unique mix of delicacy and power, but its full capability was tested on salmon a month later in Iceland.

The summer had been unusually dry. The salmon were running well, but the low water had shrunk the number of fishable pools on the Grimsá to a handful. The salmon were so concentrated that fishing pressure had made them as skittish as hard-fished trout. The usual methods worked fitfully, and it was time to rethink our tactics. The conventional wet-fly techniques took a few salmon, and the greased-line method was fair, but we had still not broken the code. The riffling hitch actually seemed to frighten more fish than it teased into rising, although some fish actually took it well. Tube flies produced nothing, although they rolled a few curious salmon. It was time to try a six-weight rod and tiny flies, and trout-type leaders tapered to 4X.

Bob Buckmaster was fishing with me at the place called Oddstadarfljot when I tested my new theory, fishing a tiny Emerald Silk dressed on a size-ten double. Crawling along the gravel, like a late-summer fisherman stalking trout, I cast softly across a smooth holding-lie. The fly worked into its swing and stopped almost softly.

Fish! I called upstream.

I coaxed the salmon away from its holding water, keeping low while it came grudgingly downstream. Small flies and delicate equipment were the secret that week. The Simroe T-3906 hooked the salmon without breaking off, yet had the authority to play fish between five and twenty pounds. The tactics took four other fish from Oddstadarfljot, and I found Buckmaster behind me.

I don't know what you're doing, he laughed. *But you're not going anyplace until you tell me the secret!* We had broken the code, and Buckmaster bought two nine-foot boron rods that summer.

The past winter in New Zealand, I fished the rod on more than a dozen rivers on both islands, from Te Anau to Taupo. It performed well, stalking big trout in startlingly clear waters, mostly with dry flies and nymphs. It took a six-pound rainbow in the headwaters of the Greenstone, and a bigger dry-fly fish on the Worsley. The largest rainbow was a twelve-pound henfish that took a size-ten nymph at Rangeitiki, and cartwheeled in a swift fight that almost emptied the reel. It was as brightly polished as a summer steelhead, and its fight was explosive. But the ultimate test came at the Cliff Pool on the Wilkin, with five dry-fly rainbows between four and eight pounds. The best fish was a hundred feet out, rising steadily in the still current. The Simroe T-3906 delivered a soft cast at that range, and did not break off the 6X tippet when a pale eight-pound fish took my Royal Wulff.

When I got back, I called Ted Simroe to tell him about his T-3906 and the fishing. *That's some rod,* I teased drily. *Guess your computer got lucky.*

Fenwick introduced the first carbon-fiber rods in 1973, and its principal designer is still Jim Green, who is among the finest casters alive. Its line of graphite tackle has been highly successful, and has expanded to twelve excellent trout rods, but Fenwick quickly embraced boron. Its first prototypes were unveiled four years ago, at a fishing conclave in Spokane.

Jim Green stopped me in the exhibition hall. *We're playing with boron,* he said. *Tell me what you think.*

Green had experimental prototypes of his nine-footers, designed for five- and six-weight lines. The distinctive boron action was obvious. Both rods were a little slower than comparable graphite designs, but with a patient stroke they delivered effortless casts. The final Boron-X designs were added to the Fenwick trout rods:

MODEL	LENGTH (FEET)	WEIGHT (OUNCES)	LINE WEIGHT
XF-755	$7\frac{1}{2}$	$2\frac{3}{4}$	5
XF-806	8	3	6
XF-856	$8\frac{1}{2}$	$3\frac{1}{8}$	6

MODEL	LENGTH (FEET)	WEIGHT (OUNCES)	LINE WEIGHT
XF-857	$8\frac{1}{2}$	$3\frac{1}{8}$	7
XF-858	$8\frac{1}{2}$	$3\frac{1}{4}$	8
XF-905	9	$3\frac{1}{8}$	5
XF-906	9	$3\frac{1}{4}$	6
XF-908	9	$3\frac{1}{2}$	8

Orvis has also added a series of excellent boron rods to its lists. The trout models in its Powerflex series are composite designs, employing sixty percent boron filaments and forty percent carbon-fiber cloth. Its structure offers a higher percentage of boron filaments, giving its Powerflex designs surprising smoothness and power, although the concept is best suited to the heavier line-weight specifications. Orvis quality is obvious in these new boron rods, and these trout-fishing models are in the Powerflex line:

MODEL	LENGTH (FEET)	WEIGHT (OUNCES)	LINE WEIGHT
JM9483-1	$8\frac{1}{4}$	$3\frac{1}{4}$	7
JM9485-1	$8\frac{1}{2}$	$3\frac{3}{8}$	6
JM9486-1	$8\frac{1}{2}$	$3\frac{5}{8}$	8
JM9486-31	$8\frac{1}{2}$	4	8
JM9489-1	$8\frac{3}{4}$	$3\frac{3}{4}$	8
JM9490-1	9	4	9
JM9490-31	9	$4\frac{5}{8}$	9

Browning also started its development program with hybrid concepts using both boron and carbon-fiber composites. Its early rods were eighty percent boron and twenty percent graphite, like the Orvis rods for tarpon fishing. The first prototypes had problems, and were never placed in production. Browning retooled to try a one hundred percent boron structure over a thin fiberglass backing that provides lateral hoop strength. The blanks are formed on a conventional mandrel, but the Browning method of curing is unique.

Its freshly wrapped blanks are sheathed in a tightly fitted rubber sleeve, without a spiral shrink-tape covering, and pressure cured in a steam-heated autoclave. The freshly cured blanks are stripped from the rubber sleeves, polished, and finished in a handsome brown urethane. Browning builds only three rods. Its seven-and-a-half-foot model weighs two-and-a-half ounces, and is rated for a five-weight line. The eight-footer weighs three ounces and is rated for a six-weight. The Browning rods are less expensive, like the Lake King and Shakespeare series, but some fishermen have faulted their workmanship and fittings. Grip finishes are roughly worked on many rods, and their shapes vary surprisingly. The ferrules are big and clumsy and, like the anodized reel-seat fittings, seem better suited to cheaper materials. But Browning has pioneered a bold technique for fabricating blanks almost entirely of boron, and its methods offer great promise.

Ron Kusse is producing an elegantly fitted and finished line of boron-fiber rods. German-silver fittings are standard. Fully machined ferrules or spigot-type ferrules are available options, and shotgun-quality hardwood fillers are specified in reel seats. The Kusse boron rods are produced in the following models:

MODEL	LENGTH (FEET)	WEIGHT (OUNCES)	LINE WEIGHT
KBG-603	6	1	3
KBG-664	6 1/2	1 1/8	4
KBG-704	7	1 1/4	4
KBG-705	7	1 1/2	5
KBG-763	7 1/2	1 1/4	3
KBG-764	7 1/2	1 3/8	4
KBG-765	7 1/2	2	5
KBG-804	8	2 1/8	4
KBG-805	8	2 1/4	5
KBG-806	8	2 1/2	6
KBG-865	8 1/2	2 3/4	5
KBG-866	8 1/2	3 1/4	6
KBG-867	8 1/2	3 1/2	7
KBG-868	8 1/2	3 3/4	8
BKG-906	9	3 1/2	6
KBG-908	9	4	8

Boron is not best for everything. Ted Simroe admits readily. *Fly-rod action is a pretty personal thing—but all things considered, we're really excited about the character of boron rods.*

Temperament and personality traits in fishermen are important factors in rod performance. Some anglers display the same restless and aggressive character they bring to their work, are probably most suited to slower tapers, and can master the more difficult timing involved in a slower casting stroke.

It's not just the material, Simroe adds. *It's tapers and calibrations and wall thickness too—it's not just the boron itself.*

Stiff rods with a fast casting stroke are perfectly designed for the tight-loop work needed in distance casting and wind. Such character is also suited to shooting-taper technique, and a sharply executed left-hand haul can flutter a softer rod. The carbon-fiber rods, and the stiff boron designs made by Orvis and Fenwick and Rodon, are outstanding in such techniques. The stiffer tapers will not flutter in tight-loop casts, with a strong double haul, and are capable of fishing distances beyond our past daydreams. Wind is less troublesome too. Such rods will increase tip-speed for all of us, no matter how skillfully we cast, and distance will improve. But neither graphite nor boron will cure our poor casting habits.

These rods won't solve our problems, Lefty Kreh wryly pinpoints the trouble with most casters. *They just make our mistakes happen faster—and farther away!*

Slow-action boron tapers have a more demanding casting stroke, in terms of their deliberate casting rhythms, but they are ideally suited to the open-loop techniques associated with long fine-tippet leaders and tiny flies. Many of the boron and boron-composite tapers I have field-tested in the past several years have been excellent examples of such slow-action boron designs.

Some of the fast-action graphites I have fished are first-rate casting tapers, but have proved a little harsh in striking and playing fish. Their fast-stroke tapers respond almost too quickly to stress. Such performance is designed for casting loads, but it can break off fine tippets in striking, particularly in average hands. Similar problems can occur with big head-shaking fish, tearing out hooks and shearing a leader.

Earlier tapers of fiberglass and bamboo tend to dampen such impact loads. Considerable fishing time with the trout-size Phillips, Fenwick, and Rodon models suggests that boron responds to impact stresses with a subtle dampening effect that rivals the finest bamboo.

Since considerable casting energy is expended in merely slicing through the atmosphere, with both a working line and the rod itself, graphite and boron offer obvious advantages.

The diameters of rods made of these fibers are much thinner than comparable actions in fiberglass and cane. The boron systems of the Browning rods are thinner than other tubular blanks, and the Phillips construction techniques produce the thinnest rods made. Less atmospheric drag is unmistakably less effort. Our casting goes better on hot days and at higher altitudes, because the atmosphere there is less dense. Since a thinner rod means less casting effort is expended in penetrating atmospheric density, higher line speeds and distance are possible with less muscle.

Sometimes we get too caught up in casting, Simroe wisely points out. *Distance casting is always more dramatic—and we forget that delicate presentation, striking fish without breaking off, and controlling the struggles of a strong fish— these things are just as important as casting.*

Boron is not cheap. Its crystalline fibers are more than eight times the price of graphite, and forty times the cost of fiberglass. The prices of finished rods vary widely, depending on the quantity of boron fibers used in their construction, and the quality of their fittings. Boron is expensive, and it deserves fittings, grip quality, designs, and finishes normally associated with the tradition of split bamboo.

Testing boron rods included a late run of bright Chinook salmon on the Pere Marquette in Michigan, where I fished a nine-and-a-half-foot Simroe fitted with a ten-weight line and a Hardy Perfect.

It was a challenge.

October squalls had stripped the hardwoods of their color, and the summer cottages on the river were boarded up for the winter. The small Michigan towns were crowded with hunters, and there was an occasional shot from the clay-bank benches above the Pere Marquette.

The river was relatively low in the fly-only water above Bowman's Bridge, with bright leaves drifting through its shoals of salmon.

It seemed like I had the river to myself. There were so many fish in the shallows at Deer Lick and Whinnery's that I hunted them visually, fishing bright-bodied Comets on a floating line. It was possible to cast to specific fish, mending the fly into their faces. Several hook-ups stripped the Perfect deep into the backing, and I stumbled downstream in pursuit. Strong fish literally burned my fingers on the line. There was a stubborn twenty-pound henfish that took me almost to Waddell's before I beached it in the shallows.

Walking back upstream, I spotted several Chinooks in a gravelly pocket along the logs. Three were dark cockfish, already purplish with spawning color, but a brace of silvery hens lay slightly upstream. Their backs were spotted and pale olive. The henfish looked fresh run, and I stripped line and cast. The yellow-hackled Comet drifted toward both fish, ticking gently against the gravel, and I was astonished when the bigger hen yawned.

It took my fly softly.

My tongue still tasted like old pennies from chasing the last salmon downstream. And my feet ached from hours of October wading. The big fish held quietly a few moments, and suddenly ran a hundred yards downstream.

I'm not sure I need another one just yet, I thought, *and this one's bigger.*

It looked thirty pounds. It bolted past me through the shallows, its back showing above the water, throwing rooster tails of spray.

It turned back and wallowed through the riffles, reaching the stronger currents under the trees. The big hen jumped twice, forty yards downstream, writhing into the sun and falling back clumsily. It thrashed wildly and stopped, and I fought to recover backing.

Finally it seemed beaten.

Circling me stubbornly with great strength, the nail knot well into the guides, it refused to surrender. It looked strong and huge. Its thick, spotted back was mostly above water, and I failed to force it on its side. There was no beach and I had to tail the big henfish in open water. Each time I forced its head upstream and circled behind it, it bolted again and stripped out line. Each time I forced it back patiently, until my arms ached into my back muscles. Its final explosion almost broke it free.

The Chinook bolted past my legs, the leader deep into the guides again, and nearly brought me to my knees. It showered me with water. Its strength literally raked the tip guide through the stones.

She's still not beaten, I thought.

But the fish was almost spent, and I tailed it and wrestled its gleaming length ashore. Its gill covers were working as I laid it along a mossy log, and pushed the brightly hackled fly free.

The tip guide was flattened and bent back at an acute angle along the rod, but the boron tip had not shattered. The stress the big Chinook had placed on the rod was fierce, particularly in the butt section, when I was pumping and reeling. The fish was still alive.

The wintry chill was settling along the river when I carried it back gently. Its gills were working strongly as I held its graceful head into the flow. The October river was alive with salmon and brightly colored leaves. Cockfish were quarreling in the shallows, churning the swift currents, and I watched the big henfish drift back into the shadows with a sense of awe.

BOOK FIVE
↓↓↓

CASTING, WADING AND OTHER PRIMARY SKILLS

1. A Primer of Modern Fly Casting

I t was a simple cedar-shingled cottage that stood among the trees beside a lake that shimmered in the August heat. Lily pads crowded its silty shallows, turning over lazily and drifting slightly with a hot wind that smelled of orchards and cornfields farther south. The lilies were like the battered rowboats moored beside the jerry-built dock, shifting and swinging with the imperceptible wind until their stems stretched and pulled them back like anchor lines. The hot wind promised no relief.

The two rowboats were poorly maintained, with peeling paint and rusting oarlocks. Their seams desperately needed caulking. Moss-green water surrounded a bailing can in the boat that went with the cottage. The other boat was filled with water and rested on the bottom in the planking shadows of the pier. It held a colony of tadpoles hiding beside its sash-weight anchor cord.

The hot August wind dropped and died in late morning. Locusts started their strident humming in the trees. The little lake was a tepid mirror at midday, its still surface marred only by the restless hunting of its dragonflies.

My mother was sleeping upstairs. We had rented the little lakefront cottage for a month, and my father had planned to finish his history textbook, but the excellent bass fishing had interrupted his priorities. The clatter of his typewriter on the screened porch filled the midday silence with its erratic rhythms, and I lay in the summer grass thinking about the ice cream the farmer's wife made for sale across the lake.

One morning when my mother went for milk I watched the farmer's wife wrestling with her wooden tubs and cracked ice and salt. While she rested and wiped her face with her apron, she allowed me to turn the crank of the ice-cream maker. It was a summer of sweet corn and watermelon and redwing blackbirds.

But it was a difficult summer of poverty and poor crops, and in the following winter, college teachers like my father were approaching bankruptcy; and the mills stood silent and people lost their farms, but that boyhood summer on a lily-pad lake in lower Michigan was filled with riches, in spite of the Great Depression.

Bass fishing was part of our daily ritual.

My father usually rose just before daylight while my mother still lay sleeping. He went downstairs to the kitchen. The smells of eggs and fried bass and bacon drifted through the cottage, and in spite of his precautions to let us sleep there were always the grating sounds of the skillet on the stove, mixed with the muffled clatter of china. The rich aroma of the coffee was unsettling, too.

Sometimes the lake was still shrouded in fog, and I watched my father collect the oars from the porch, and walk down toward the rowboat with his tackle. It was delicious to doze, half-awake under the quilts, listening to the familiar sounds of his embarkation. The porch door scraped on the pine flooring; the lures rattled in the tackle box when he placed it in the boat; the metallic grating of the padlock chain and the lazy oarlock rhythms when he rowed out into the mists floated back to me.

It was a liturgy I was still too young to share, although one morning he took me with him into its mysteries, and I sat through breakfast with exquisite shivers of anticipation and excitement. We caught nothing that day, but I can still remember the spinning handles of his gleaming Meek casting reel as his casts arched out toward sheltering pockets in the reeds and bassweed and lily pads, and once there was a wild splash that engulfed his bobbing red and white plug. The bass was not hooked and it was the only strike. It was already getting hot when we rowed back down the lake, and I sat in the bow listening to the somnolent rhythms of his oars.

His manuscript occupied most of the midday hours, and the clatter of his typewriter travelled out across the lake. But late in the afternoon his interest in academia waned. It was time to oil and clean his prized little reel, polish his silver spoons and the blades on his bucktail spinners, cut fresh pork-rind strips, and sharpen the trebles on his plugs.

Supper always came early, and when the shadows lengthened across the shallows of the lake, it was time for bass fishing again. My father rowed slowly along the weeds, casting and working his lure with a steady rhythm, and working carefully along the shore. It was a ritual that seldom concluded until well after nightfall, and I usually met him in the darkness, standing in the shadows while he padlocked the boat chain.

It was always exciting when he reached down to lift his dripping stringer of fish. There were usually two or three bass, and once he walked proudly along the path toward the cottage with his flashlight bobbing on a six-pound largemouth.

It was a special summer, rich with memories of swimming and bass fishing and the cottage, but these experiences were eclipsed by a brief episode that occurred on a grocery trip into town. It was an important event in the structure of my life.

Our route into the general store crossed a trout stream, and my mother stopped the Oldsmobile beside the bridge when a fisherman caught my eye. The river flowed clear and icy cold through the timbers of the bridge, dancing and eddying over its ocher-colored gravel. Cedar sweepers and deadfalls lined its crystalline shallows, and downstream it gurgled and riffled among the stones until its lyric water music filled the morning air. The river emerged briefly from the forest, its gravelly riches lying in the sunlight until it disappeared again behind the sheltering cedars and hemlocks. Its bright currents seemed alive below the bridge, collecting the colors of the foliage and reflecting sunlight back into the trees. Its song was filled with half-understood messages and mysteries, and in spite of my remembrances of bass fishing, the most pervasive memory of that summer remains that solitary fly-fisherman—stalking upstream in those idyllic shallows, the current tumbling between his legs and the pale rhythms of his fly line working in the sun.

His poetic skills in handling its amber loops were a revelation that morning, drying his fly lazily and casting so that it settled with breathtaking delicacy on the water. The fisherman caught nothing while I watched him from the bridge, but I stood transfixed at the railing, and I have never forgotten the exquisite beauty of his fishing.

Although it is not absolutely necessary to become an expert fly caster to become a reasonably skilled trout fisherman, there is no question that advanced casting skills will pay dividends on difficult waters. Both the delicacy required on highly selective fish and the distance needed on a steelhead river are well beyond the capabilities of average casting. Such skills demand practice and careful training and experience.

Writing about fly casting is difficult, and anything written on the subject cannot teach you much about actual casting techniques. It can make you aware of casting methods, refinements and tactics beyond your present skills, and make you think about your own problems and idiosyncrasies. But there is no substitute for the observation and instruction possible under the tutelage of a first-rate instructor or a formal fly-fishing school. Casting instructors largely agree that about eighty-five percent of their pupils can achieve a surprising degree of proficiency in a relatively short time. Such coachability is particularly apparent among young beginners who have no bad habits to overcome, but experienced fly-fisher-men who want to polish their casting skills or learn the double-haul for distance work are often the most difficult students. Such students easily lapse into their earlier casting errors.

Perfect fly casting is a combination of finger pressure, wrist action, forearm work, and upper arm movements. Conventional casting does not require the exaggerated arm motions and body coordination found in

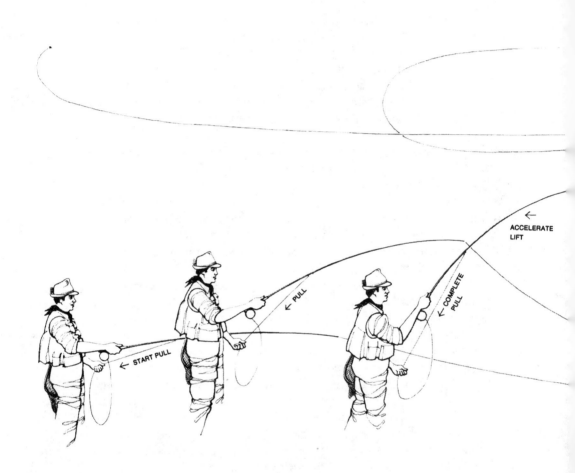

2. Accelerate lifting rod and start single haul

1. Start cast with lifting rod and line tension

3. Continue accelerating and finish left-hand haul

SIMPLE SINGLE-HAUL BACKCAST STROKE

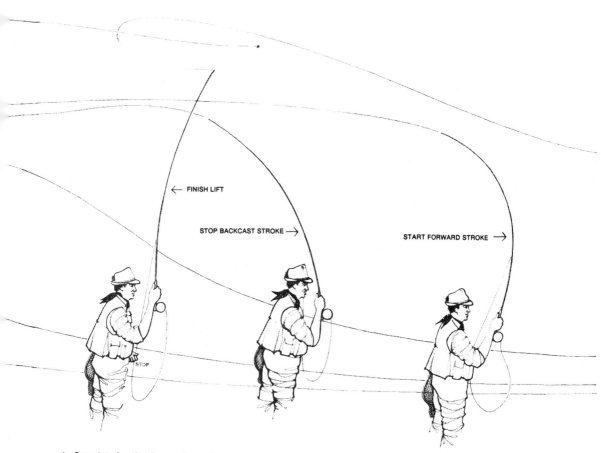

← FINISH LIFT

STOP BACKCAST STROKE →

START FORWARD STROKE →

STOP

4. Complete forming loop with wrist snap

5. Let rod drift with extending backcast and pause

6. Start forward stroke as backcast loop uncoils

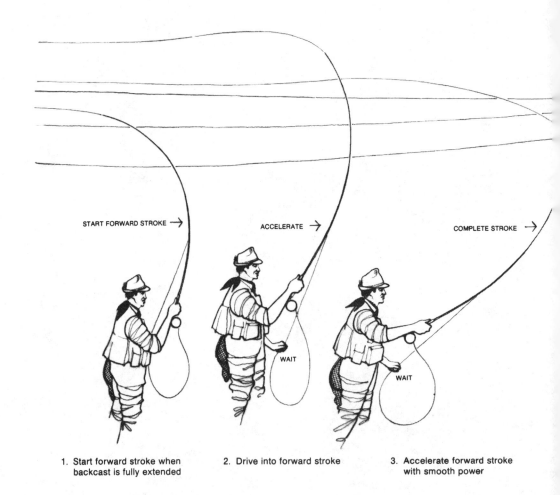

START FORWARD STROKE →   ACCELERATE →   COMPLETE STROKE →

WAIT   WAIT

1. Start forward stroke when backcast is fully extended

2. Drive into forward stroke

3. Accelerate forward stroke with smooth power

SIMPLE SINGLE-HAUL FORWARD STROKE

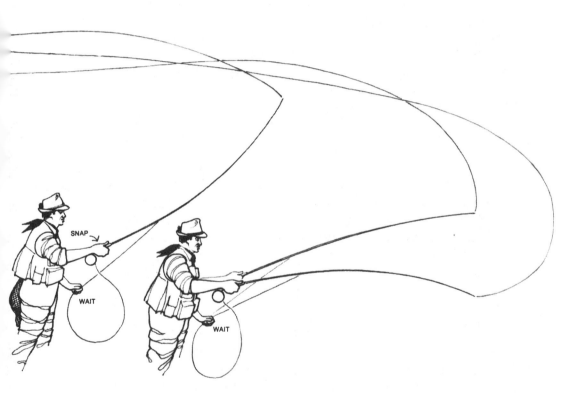

4. Apply final wrist-snap to cast

5. Permit power stroke to drive through and release left-hand slack into cast

distance work, since average distances under fifty feet are possible with minimal effort. Timing is infinitely more important than strength at all casting ranges, but average ranges are possible with almost imperceptible arm work. However, the timing involved in casting rhythms must change to accommodate any variations in the length of line; and few anglers seem to realize that casting requires varied application of accelerating or decelerating strength at different stages of each cast.

Each casting motion is a progressive application of power, and the timing must provide a perfect equilibrium between strength and its point of application. The precise application of strength is required to pick up the line from the water, flex the rod under the backcast loads, and deliver the forward cast. It is advisable to learn each movement in a separate and exaggerated fashion, and once each has been mastered, it is time to blend them into a complete casting cycle. It is important to remember that the only way to experience the *feel* of good fly casting is by working with an instructor who holds your rod hand and works it through the proper rhythms and studies your stroke.

Perhaps the most effective teaching would forbid actual fishing until the techniques of fly casting are a subconscious reflex. It is impossible to fish well or fully enjoy the sport until the basic rhythms of casting are accomplished without thinking about them. It is difficult to analyze the mechanics of fly casting into simple relationships of cause and effect, and it is also important to understand that the theoretical patterns of perfect casting must be adapted to the physical skills and timing instincts of each caster. Balanced tackle is important, too. The beginner should perhaps start with an eight-foot rod weighing about four ounces, using a suitable six- or seven-weight line. Expert casters can adjust their timing to compensate for poorly balanced equipment, but a novice would find such tackle hopelessly frustrating. The casting techniques and timing involved in smaller rods are also beyond a beginner, since such rods demand exaggerated casting motions in which the arm and shoulder of the fisherman literally become the butt section of the rod. All anglers know other fishermen who have used poorly matched equipment for years and seem utterly incapable of separating their own poor casting habits from their inadequate tackle. Similar problems exist with fishermen who attempt to fish the so-called midge rods before they have mastered the basic techniques of casting.

Our streams are lined with such fishermen. It is obvious that they lack the basic skills of accuracy and control, and cannot throw a consistently straight line. Their forward casts land splashily, scattering the fish in panic. Their backcasts continually get fouled in the foliage and grass behind them. They pop off their flies with a whiplike crack. They become tangled in the line or the rod itself and often break hooks on the gravel bars and stones with low backcasts.

These familiar problems can result from poorly balanced tackle. The line might be too heavy or light for the rod. The rod tip might be too soft. But in virtually all cases the principal fault lies with the caster himself and his timing. Sometimes body effort unnecessarily forces him off balance and distorts his rhythms, and sometimes his casting is all free wrist and no arm action. Instead of drawing the line off the water with a swiftly accelerating pull, many casters snatch it from the water with an abrupt lift that distorts both the backcast loop and its timing. Sloppy backcasts and weak forward delivery can also result from too much wrist work, allowing the rod to reach well past the vertical. This is something a skilled caster does habitually because he can keep his backcast high with faster line speed, but it is a fatal mistake for the novice.

Average casting between twenty and fifty feet should be accomplished with very little effort, letting the fly rod perform most of the work. Any fatigue from casting at such ranges is symptomatic of poor muscle tone or bad casting habits.

Working at such moderate distances, the flexing behavior of the rod itself is capable of accomplishing most of the work. The fisherman merely supplies the impetus, and monitors the rhythm and speed of his casting. Unfortunately, most beginners are more anxious to fish than to practice their rod work, and that anxiety is transmitted into their casting. Their efforts involve too much body work and too much wrist. The wrist becomes a floppy pivot, forcing the rod tip into an exaggerated circular path. Elbows are held out in awkward positions. Optimal control requires that the backcast tipwork be upward and slightly ovoid, while the forward cast starts circular and finishes straight. The wrist should stay relatively locked throughout the power cycles of the casting stroke, although many expert casters relax their wrists and allow them to float briefly while the backcast uncoils and straightens.

Windy weather or fish lying beyond an angler's normal casting range exaggerate his poor habits. In this case the inexperienced caster usually allows his wrist full play, letting the rod drop farther and farther toward the horizontal in the backcast. His hesitant line speed lets the backcast fall too low. The forward cast also lacks sufficient line velocity and the narrow loop that spells distance, and the backcast commonly strikes the foliage or water, breaking the symmetry of a perfect cast. Too many fishermen blame their equipment for such troubles, and embark on an eternal search for better line balance or fly-rod action.

Proper arm action and a locked wrist are the solution to these familiar problems. It is virtually impossible to make a poor backcast if your wrist remains almost rigid, and your casting rhythms pivot off a circular, upward stroke of the elbow. The path of the elbow is a surprisingly tight circle at moderate casting ranges, while shorter casts are easily accomplished using a forearm stroke alone, with a relatively fixed elbow and wrist. Distance casting with the free arm and locked wrist results in a narrow, clockwise oval in the path of the elbow—and these basic motions encompass the whole of modern distance-casting practice with the single-handed rod.

Relaxation is important in fine casting. Skilled fishermen hold their rods with surprisingly little pressure in short- to moderate-range casting,

START WRIST LOCK

START FORWARD CAST →

5

4

← CHECK BACKCAST

3

GODART CASTING STYLE

1. Start pickup stroke

2. Execute sidearm backcast

3. Let backcast extend and roll wrist sideways

4. Start overhead stroke

5. Close wrist and drive forward

6. Punch cast hard

7. Shoot left-hand slack

Tight loop work is best for distance and windy conditions

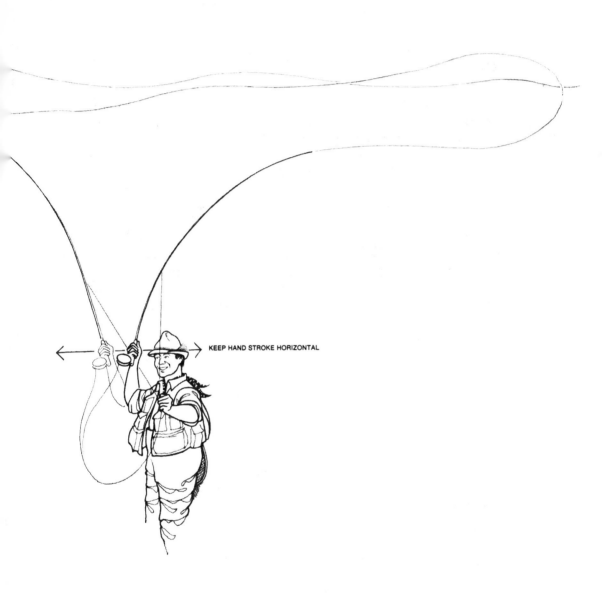

KEEP HAND STROKE HORIZONTAL

TIGHT OR CANDY-CANE LOOP TECHNIQUE

and a relaxed grip is perhaps half the secret of fine fly casting. Too many casters freeze both their muscles and their sense of timing when they start to cast, like a self-conscious boy in a dancing class; and this mixture of uncertainty and tension is directly transmitted into their casting. Bending the wrist becomes natural for such casters, lowers the backcast and magnifies their already jerky casting rhythms.

Muscle tone and condition are important too, and even a highly skilled caster experiences some casting discomfort after long periods of inactivity. Charles Ritz has developed a system of armchair calisthenics for winter that are useful for maintaining his casting muscles. He outlines these exercises in *A Fly Fisher's Life*, and it is typical that his calisthenic methods involve a wine bottle and a tennis ball to develop the proper condition of his arm and wrist.

Charles recommends the slender hock-type bottle that holds a fine Moselle or Alsatian wine, Cornelius Ryan observed wryly over dinner in Oslo. *How like him to recommend starting with an empty bottle—a prescription permitting us to select a fine vintage and empty it judiciously!*

Perfect for fishermen like us, I agreed.

The bottle method is started with the arm fully extended and rotated in the plane of the shoulders while swinging the wine bottle in both directions. The second exercise involves holding your elbow tightly at your side while the bottle is raised and lowered from the knee to a horizontal position at the waist. In the third exercise the elbow is locked and the bottle lifted from the knee to a horizontal shoulder height. The fourth exercise is a circular clockwise and counterclockwise rotation pivoted at the elbow. The fifth exercise involves a similar circular motion focused upon the casting wrist as it rotates freely to promote both strength and flexibility. Ritz advises gradually adding sand to the bottle to increase its weight.

You should not use a full wine bottle for my calisthenics, the hotelier of the Ritz concludes wryly, *unless you choose a vintage that travels well.*

Ritz also uses a tennis ball to strengthen his thumb, holding the ball in the palm and pressing it rhythmically.

You should start with an old ball, Ritz advises, *and exercise until your thumb has the strength for a fresh one.*

Charles Ritz and most other experienced casting teachers advise starting with a simple wet-fly cast for beginners, since it involves no false casting or sophisticated delivery. However, the basic wet-fly delivery requires casting a perfectly straight line, which often proves more difficult than the more complicated dry-fly techniques since it requires a relatively pure casting rhythm.

Grip and back-cast skills are critical. There are three basic casting grips. My preference is the primary grip, in which the thumb is placed on top of the rod handle, since this position best focuses the required muscles. The free-wrist grip is less workable, and its only influential partisan was the late John Alden Knight, who advocated it in a number of books. It restricts the wrist action in the backcast slightly more than the thumb grip, but

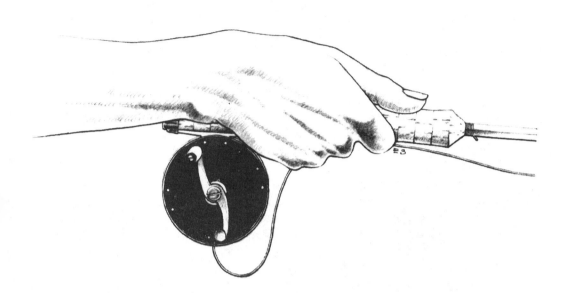

PRIMARY THUMB GRIP

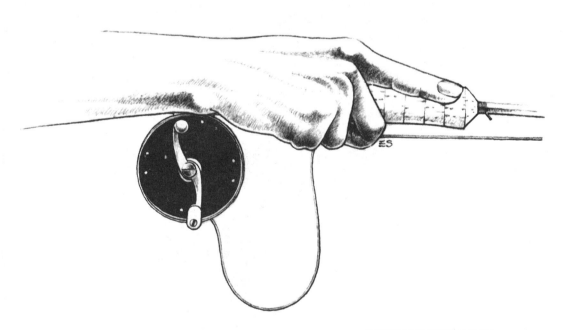

SECONDARY INDEX GRIP

Knight did not recommend his free-wrist grip for distance or salt-water fly-rod problems. In the index grip the index finger is placed forward, resting it on top of the cork. Fishermen who prefer the index grip argue that it gives them an added sense of delicacy and control, and although it has little application beyond fifty or sixty feet, there are often times when I use it to rest my casting hand while fishing.

Charles Ritz has perhaps done more than any other theoretician of fly casting to analyze and catalogue its physical components, having systematically observed the casting styles of world champions like Jon Tarantino and Pierre Creusevaut. His conclusions are meticulously outlined in *A Fly Fisher's Life*, and include several facets of casting technique that surprise even skilled casters.

The casting-hand action is typical of the subtle casting mechanics first described in the writings of Ritz, and such dynamics are unconscious components of technique, even among thoughtful and experienced anglers. During the casting pickup, the thumb is relaxed while the lower three fingers tighten around the rod grip. Both thumb and lower-finger pressure stop the backcast, and the index finger is so relaxed that it need not contact the grip. But during the forward cast, the thumb and all of the fingers apply a momentary pressure when delivery begins. The thumb drives into the follow-through, and finger pressure squeezes the grip to check the rod at the conclusion of the cast. Few fishermen are aware of the subtle role that changing hand pressure plays in their casting rhythms.

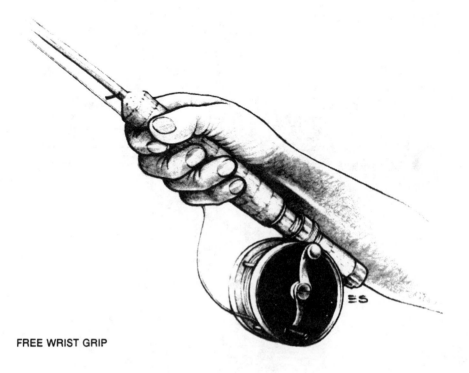

FREE WRIST GRIP

Even the rudimentary wet-fly cast consists of several fully separate motions blended into a single casting stroke. It should be practiced with the primary overhead delivery, since casting in the vertical plane is critical in fly-fishing, and absolute casting accuracy is difficult outside the basic overhead casting plane. It combines both the pickup stroke into the backcast, and the subsequent forward cast after a proper interval of backcast extension. The beginner should literally watch his backcast until he masters its problems, since the backcast is critical to his final presentation, and a proper backcast extension will automatically deliver a perfect forward cast. The optimal backcast should extend smoothly and lift high behind the angler, rising as steeply as thirty degrees.

The simple overhead cast begins with the rod held at a shallow angle of approximately fifteen degrees, its tip guide at eye level and at least fifteen feet of line stripped from the reel. The rod will feel awkward until that much fly line is flexing its action, since the fly is propelled by the weight of the line, and the only workable length lies beyond the rod tip.

The casting stance is relatively simple. Right-hand casters should place most of their weight on the ball of the right foot, slightly extending the left foot. Left-handed fishermen shift their weight and extend the right foot forward. The beginner should forget the left-hand manipulation of the line and simply concentrate on his casting motions. The line should be firmly held under the fingers, so that at first only a fixed length is cast.

With the tip guide held at eye level, the forearm should be extended parallel with the rod. The fingers are relaxed but the wrist is relatively stiff and locked. It should make your forearm feel like an extension of the rod butt, from the thumb to the elbow. Casting theory has changed radically in the past century, and modern instructors no longer advise a novice to cast holding a book between the elbow and his ribs. The elbow should hang free in a basic casting stroke, about two to three inches from the rib cage. The upper arm should be held in line with the shoulder itself, inclining in slightly from the elbow.

The late Frank Steel was my casting teacher just after the Second World War, and in winning several American dry-fly accuracy championships, Steel used the locked wrist and a pumping motion of his forearm. Steel also advocated a free elbow held slightly across the body until the casting hand works directly between the eyes. Obviously, the Steel fixed-wrist method was designed to implement dry-fly accuracy and is a technique that slightly distorts normal casting motions, but his record of the first perfect round in the history of dry-fly competition clearly speaks for itself. In this position it is impossible to relax the wrist and carry the backcast too low without hitting the forehead, and the alignment of the casting plane between the eyes is helpful in a beginner's accuracy work.

With the line extended on the water, the cast begins with lifting the line from the water in the pickup stroke. It is surprising how many relatively experienced fishermen fail to understand that the line is *not* lifted abruptly from the water in a single motion. The pickup is begun by gently

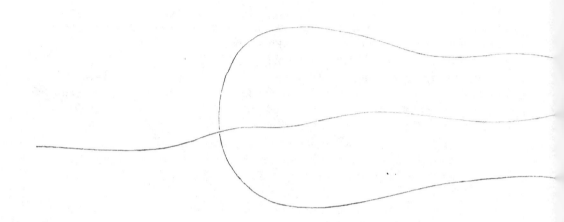

Open loop work is best for delicate medium- and short-range presentation
with long light-tippet leaders

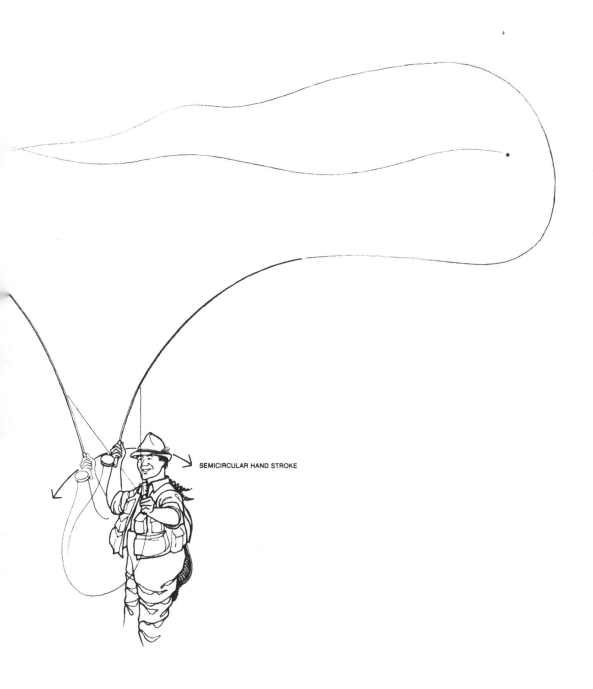

SEMICIRCULAR HAND STROKE

OPEN OR ROLLING-LOOP STROKE

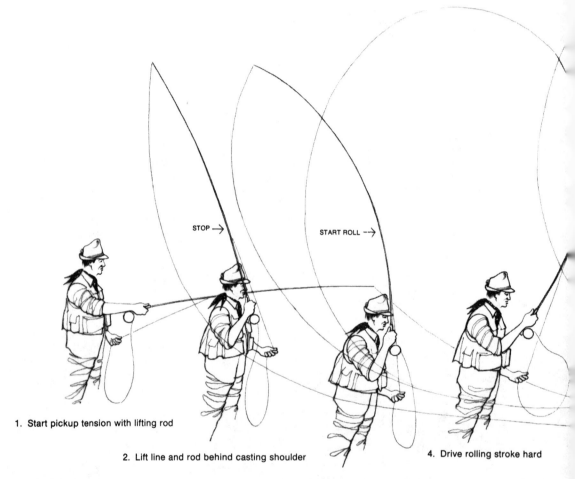

STOP →

START ROLL →

1. Start pickup tension with lifting rod

2. Lift line and rod behind casting shoulder

3. Start rolling forward stroke

4. Drive rolling stroke hard

COMMON ROLL CAST

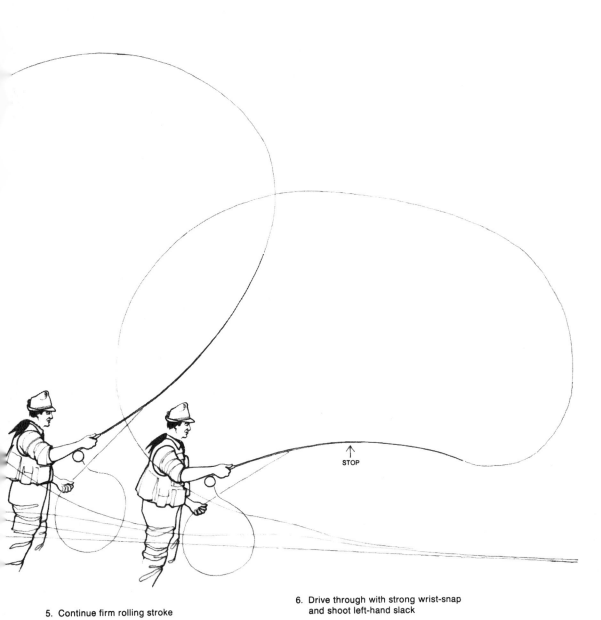

5. Continue firm rolling stroke

6. Drive through with strong wrist-snap
   and shoot left-hand slack

STOP

raising the rod tip to eye level to increase the tension on the line, teasing it imperceptibly along the surface of the water to diminish its hydraulic friction, and accelerating it gracefully into the final stroke of the wrist that actually lifts the line into the backcast. The wrist snap that shoots the backcast is surprisingly strong, although the wrist and forearm relax and float once the backcast starts to extend, relaxing until it is time for the forward stroke. The elbow is always the focal pivot of the cast, moving in a small circle at normal casting ranges, and providing the fulcrum for the pumping action of the forearm.

The initial wrist action ends with the pickup, and the wrist is progressively stiffened as the rod hand approaches eye level. Both wrist and arm are frozen as the rod reaches the vertical twelve o'clock position, its inertia carrying it slightly farther under the extending load of the backcast. With the backcast unrolling and extending, there is a definite pause and float in the casting sequence until the backcast is complete.

This pause is absolutely critical in fly casting. Starting the forward cast before the backcast is fully extended will snap a fly from the leader, and starting it too late will dampen its velocity and lose casting power. The forward cast must be started precisely at the moment when the backcast is fully uncoiled and extended, actually flexing the rod under its optimal inertia, just before that inertia drops below proper line speed and the backcast sags toward the water.

When the backcast is both smooth and high, with a clean tightly formed loop, the forward cast is merely a symmetrical, follow-through stroke that lays the line straight across the current. It is wise to practice your backcast with a fairly short line, perhaps twenty-five to thirty feet, without the leader at first. Pick up and lift the line into a high back-cast stroke, turning your head to watch its progress. Observing your own backcast is important. It will help you lift it high enough with sufficient velocity to extend its loop properly, and it will help you feel the timing necessary for it to uncoil and straighten behind you. Without proper timing and height in your backcast it is utterly impossible to become a polished caster.

Optimal forward casts are impossible without the prefatory foundation of perfect backcasts. We are too often preoccupied with the final casting stroke, forgetting that backcasts and forward casts are perfectly symmetrical in both effort and configuration. It requires the same expenditure of casting power to extend a forty-foot backcast, and keep it extending above the water, as it takes to deliver a forty-foot cast itself.

The forward cast is always simple if the backcast has been lifted and timed properly. Like the pickup and the backcast, the forward cast is a progressively accelerating stroke. There should be no choppy start that stresses the rod abruptly. Both the thumb and the fingers exert pressure on the grip. The forward stroke is concluded with a definite downward wrist-snap and thumb follow-through. It should feel as if you are snapping the tip into the cast, driving the line and leader to uncoil and extend. The proper forward cast should be aimed slightly high, and delivered toward an imaginary water surface two to three feet above the actual surface you are fishing. Using the imaginary water plane takes advantage of gravity and atmospheric resistance to mute your casting velocity and settle the fly and leader softly on the actual water.

Pick up the fly and lift it into another backcast, practicing the entire casting sequence. When you have begun to master both phases of the basic overhead cast, you are finally ready to combine them into a continuous casting motion. Work with a fixed length of line until both backcasts and forward casts are smooth and a matter of reflex action. Once the reflexes have been patterned at the basic line length, shorten or extend the line and experiment with the changes in the casting stroke and timing. Ultimately you will learn to adjust the timing of your casting rhythms without thinking, instinctively lifting the fly softly from the surface into a high backcast that loads the rod perfectly, and to place the fly lightly on target without giving thought to the problems of casting. Until your casting skills are an unconscious facet of your sport, and your conscious skills are entirely focused on observing the fish and matching the hatch, you are still not an accomplished trout fisherman.

Delivering a straightforward cast is the core of basic wet-fly technique, and perhaps a few observations on achieving it would prove worthwhile. The final thumb drive of the forward cast occurs at the critical instant of releasing the final stroke.

Most rod tapers lack the power in their tip calibrations to deliver the full energy required in casting. When the line is started forward, these upper calibrations merely ride along with its velocity, its power rooted in the middle of the action. With the forward cast free and moving on its own energy, the rod tip follows past its straight position and oscillates well beyond the horizontal. Its oscillation transmits an erratic downward wave in the line, causing a loss of the velocity and control required to deliver a really straight cast.

The final thumb drive that powers the tip section must be moderated and controlled to throw a straight line cleanly. It is a subtlety of the casting hand. Too little power in the concluding moments of the cast results in a poor delivery that fails to straighten across the current. Too much thumb drive results in a wavy forward extension of the line that dampens its shoot and control. Proper thumb drive varies between rods, and it cannot be achieved without experience—particularly since no two fly rods load and cast exactly alike, and the variable of wind is also a factor.

Wind plays a role in the plane of casting too. The late Paul Young fished with a classical flattened oval, which he outlined in his handbook *Making and Using the Fly and Leader*, and his rod travelled in a slender ellipse. Casting into a brisk headwind, Young worked his backcast on the outside and drove his forward stroke on the inside of the ellipse. Young used a similar elliptical motion with a crosswind coming from the side opposite his casting arm. Crosswind casting in a wind that comes from the casting side

SIDEARM CASTING STROKE

reversed that delivery. Young made his backcasts on the inner face of the ellipse and delivered his power stroke on the outside, forcing it against the wind pressure. Similar results are obtained with the figure-eight casts advocated by A. J. McClane in his book *The Practical Fly Fisherman*. In this cast the rod actually travels a narrow figure-eight pattern with the forward stroke outward in a right crosswind and inward with a crosswind coming from the left. Such subtle variations in tactics are important.

The Belgian school of casting evolved a similar exaggerated ellipse in its casting plane. Its methods were best exemplified in the brilliant technique of the late Albert Godart, who was world champion in the years before the Second World War. Under normal casting conditions with a left-hand crosswind, the Belgian method works with a rather wide ellipse. The backcast is brought back slightly sidearm, with the rod held at about seventy degrees, while the forward cast is delivered in the overhead plane. With a right-hand wind, the backcast is executed in a vertical plane and the forward cast is delivered in a sidearm plane, about seventy degrees off the water's surface.

Godart also evolved a superb fishing cast at normal casting ranges, although at distances beyond sixty feet it was necessary to add a slight left-hand haul to maintain line speed and keep the rolling backcast high. The Godart style is not easily mastered. Tournament galleries are usually a bored and knowledgeable crowd who quickly lose interest in the casting, visiting among themselves while the scores are posted and time passes.

Little crowd interest evolves until individual competitions take place to eliminate casters with equal scores or the past champions perform. But Albert Godart was an exception, and when he took the platform the social gossip in the galleries stopped. Huge crowds collected to watch him work, trying to analyze and define his casting secrets. His technique was always puzzling, and is similar to the style of Lee Wulff.

Godart never looked like he had full control of his swiftly moving line, particularly on his open-loop backcasts, but his results were undeniably superb. The backcast travelled so low that it appeared to lose viable casting speed, and then it climbed surprisingly and sharply upward, until it floated high overhead. People not only watched Godart work, but also began copying him widely in Belgium and France, since his technique had obvious advantages on their open wind-swept streams.

Godart was a small rather corpulent man with exceptionally burly forearms and strong hands. His sense of timing was utterly perfect. His casting style involved an exaggerated wrist action, with the rod tip describing a lazy semicircular path when viewed from above. The fly line drops gradually during the first part of the backcast, causing its rolling loop to form in a nearly horizontal plane, but in the last seconds the line will rise as the rod starts forward. Conventional backcasts have a tendency to falter and drop at full extension, while the Belgian-style backcasts rise and accelerate surprisingly. Gravity is only a minor factor in casting, while atmospheric resistance is the major casting problem. Godart had developed

BACKHAND STROKE

Execute common sidearm cast and underpower loop
to fall incomplete, just above the rise form

POSITIVE OR RIGHT-HOOK CAST

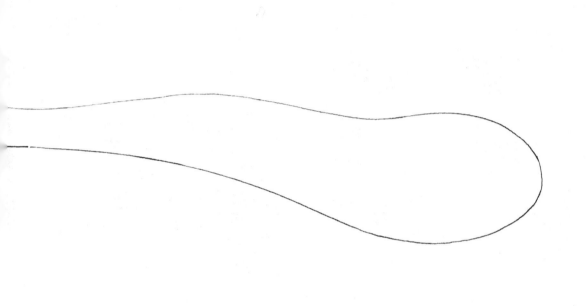

NEGATIVE OR LEFT-HOOK CAST

Execute common sidearm stroke and deliver cast with a strong
wrist-snap that overpowers the loop to fall above the rise form

a looping high-speed delivery which was finally checked just above the water, settling the fly as gently as a living insect. Godart was primarily a fisherman, and he had unconsciously evolved a casting style perfectly adapted to the open wind-blown meadows of Belgium and France—a style that has obvious implications on western spring creeks and rivers in the United States.

Narrow casting loops are ideally suited to combating wind and reaching out for distance, although wider loops are delivered with more delicacy of presentation. Narrow trajectories look better, their rhythms rapier-quick and controlled, but many experienced fishermen believe the open loop is a better fishing cast. Hand motion is the secret of loop configuration in casting, when working at equal line velocity. Flat loops are achieved with a tight horizontal hand motion. Open casting loops involve a small counterclockwise rotation of the casting hand, and a skilled fly caster will use both techniques to meet varying problems.

Difficult winds can also cause problems requiring more radical casting solutions. The ability to cope with a strong wind is a decided advantage, particularly on our western streams and reservoirs. In spite of opinions held by many anglers, headwinds are perhaps the easiest since they simply involve an exaggerated forward stroke. Holding the elbow slightly separated from the body and the forearm relatively stiff, the backcast is executed almost lazily since the wind will augment its speed to casting velocity. The secret of casting into a headwind is keeping the backcast high and the forward stroke low. High backcasts are basic to good casting, but even normal backcast height should become exaggerated in a headwind. The casting hand must be raised sharply, like a steeple cast thrown almost vertically behind the angler. The wind will temper its rising angle, forcing it lower and magnifying its flexing loads on the rod. The forward stroke must be a sharply progressive application of power, rather than a single hard delivery. With the rod hand high at the conclusion of the backcast, the forward stroke is started gradually before actually applying full casting power. Both forearm and wrist are locked as the cast is delivered, pivoting the cast from the elbow and driving through hard with wrist and thumb pressure. The rod should punch well below its usual stopping angle to slice the cast against a wind, reaching a full horizontal position before the left-hand slack is released. Since atmospheric friction is greatest against the water, lessening the velocity of the wind, a forward cast will travel best there. The final stroke should obviously occur where the wind velocity is lightest. The wrist follow-through should thrust the rod low, with the caster reaching forward like a rapier thrust, leaning forward a little with bent knees. The fly line will extend at optimal velocity, right along the surface of the water, particularly when a sharp left-hand pull is added in the final moment before the forward stroke. The so-called storm cast is a matter of simple aerodynamics: when the line velocity exceeds the velocity of the wind, the line will unroll and extend in spite of its atmospheric friction and gusting problems.

Tailwinds pose totally different problems. The basic rule of successful casting with a strong tailwind is obviously the opposite of working into a headwind. The backcast is driven hard and low, while the forward cast is unrolled high to ride the wind. Since a conventional overhead cast will not permit a low backcast extension, the backcast into a tailwind must be executed parallel to the water where wind velocity is minimal. The forward stroke is returned to a nearly vertical plane. Properly executed, the technique will reach out surprising distances without losing control, and with a skilled left-hand haul the line will extend at remarkable velocity. The winds in Tierra del Fuego are so strong that this method proved unworkable, since a backcast was virtually impossible. We soon worked out a technique that involved about forty feet of line stripped out beyond the tip guide and held in a series of slack loops in the left hand. Our running line lay coiled in the grass. The cast itself simply involved throwing the coiled loops high into the wind, letting its shrieking velocity catch and extend the cast, and pull the running line through the guides. It worked surprisingly well.

We've invented something! Laddie Buchanan yelled.

It's something new! I agreed and threw the slack loops of another cast above my head. *What do we call it?*

What about the tennis-serve cast? Buchanan grinned.

Perfect! I laughed.

The simple backhand cast is another method of coping with crosswind problems. Sometimes a crosswind blowing from the casting-arm side is brisk

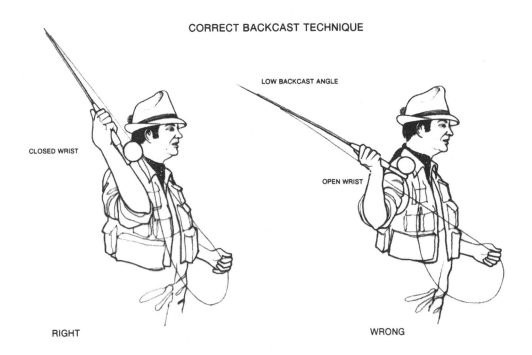

CORRECT BACKCAST TECHNIQUE

LOW BACKCAST ANGLE

CLOSED WRIST

OPEN WRIST

RIGHT

WRONG

FEED LINE

REACH WITH ROD

Check normal forward cast before it settles, pulling back to create a slack-line presentation, and feed line while reaching downstream to extend the drift

CHECK CAST

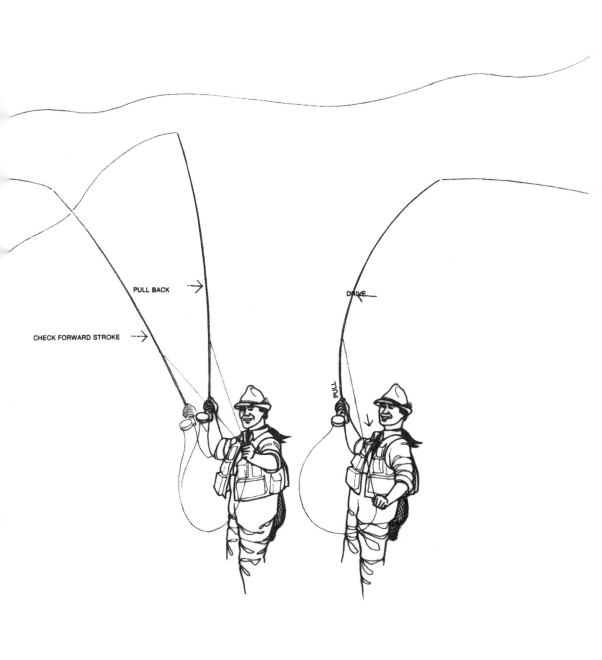

SERPENTINE OR S-CAST TECHNIQUE

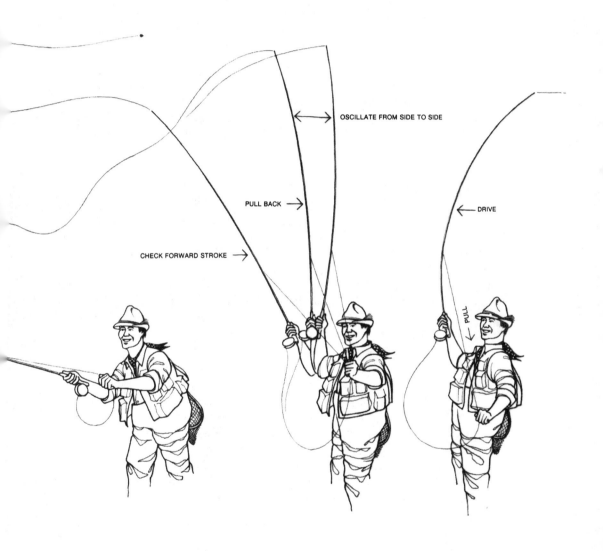

OSCILLATE FROM SIDE TO SIDE

PULL BACK →

← DRIVE

CHECK FORWARD STROKE →

PULL

Check forward cast as it starts to settle, pulling back
and oscillating the rod tip from side to side,
throwing a series of slack loops into the line

enough that the figure-eight method, or even the Belgian style of wind casting, are not sufficient to protect the caster from his working line and fly. The backhand cast is the solution to such problems, and a skilled caster can work backhand at any angle from his head to a fully horizontal stroke executed across his body. The backhand cast is simple to execute. The palm is held facing down with the thumb on top of the grip, and the rod is normally held at about forty-five degrees across and quartering away from the body. Line pickup is accomplished with the full forearm, pivoting on the fulcrum of the elbow and thrusting the casting shoulder forward. The rod is stopped about forty-five degrees, quartering away behind the shoulder. The forward cast swings back toward the vertical plane, but the wrist remains relatively locked. The forearm is lowered into the casting stroke, pivoting at the elbow and using a final wrist snap that adds velocity to the line. Adding a slight left-hand pull will magnify line speed and extend the cast perfectly.

Both the backhand cast and the horizontal cast are useful in normal fishing, since the backhand is useful when casting with a willow-lined bank on your rod side, and a horizontal stroke is sometimes needed under branches—particularly on our tree-sheltered eastern streams.

The techniques of the horizontal cast are obvious. Such casting planes are critical where overhanging branches make conventional tactics impossible. Horizontal casts are executed both forehand and backhand, with the rod worked almost parallel to the water. The pickup is executed in conventional fashion, while the backcast is thrown slightly above the horizontal to compensate for gravity. The casting elbow drifts out and slightly behind the body, cocking to wait for the forward delivery. The forward stroke is also aimed slightly above horizontal, keeping the line airborne long enough for full extension and leader turnover. It is best to execute a horizontal cast without too much thumb drive and arm follow-through, since unwanted hook casts will result.

Roll casting is obviously an ancient technique with its roots in the wet-fly tradition, and in my boyhood summers I watched in awe when the old-timers worked brushy rivers like the Pine and Little Manistee and Baldwin. Wading downstream stealthily, they rolled out thirty to fifty feet in a steady rhythm, gearing each cast to their progress downstream. There was both poetry and precision in their technique as they covered the willow-lined runs with a series of concentric quarter-circles. The roll cast was first developed for fishing without any backcast room, and its fundamentals are simple. Twenty-five to thirty feet of line should lie extended on the water before starting the cast. The rod is raised slightly behind the head until it inclines backward to the one o'clock position. The line should hang in a delicate curve from the tip guide toward the water. It is started with a decisive forearm and wrist-snap motion, whipping the rod down sharply in the direction of the cast. The line will strip itself from the water cleanly, unfolding and extending in a rolling loop until the cast is completed. Once you have mastered the timing needed to roll cast twenty-five to thirty feet cleanly, you should practice with longer lines and experiment with shooting five to ten feet of running slack. Such slack can be released into the forward cast, multiplying its distance as it shoots through the guides. With practice it is possible to throw both wide and narrow loops in your roll casting, depending on the tip speed imparted to the rod. Similar techniques of controlling line are found in conventional fly-fishing tactics. Wide loops are generated with less casting force and wrist-snap follow-through and by checking the rod at a relatively high angle. Such loops are useful with a following wind, sailing out with its velocity and shooting as much as twenty feet of slack. Narrow loops are thrown with a sharp downward stroke and wrist snap that carries close to the water, providing both accuracy and control.

The flowering of the dry-fly method a century ago on the British chalkstreams led to fresh casting problems. The dry fly is usually fished upstream, and it drifts back toward the angler the moment it touches the current. Left-hand slack accumulates rapidly, and a skilled dry-fly man controls it expertly, always ready to strike any fish that rises. Since a dry fly floats badly as it becomes saturated with water, in spite of its dressing and stiff hackles, it must be continually dried while casting. Such problems soon led to the evolution of the false cast, designed to evaporate excess water from hackles and dubbing.

The false cast consists of making a fresh backcast before the forward cast can settle to the water. Correctly executed, a series of false casts involve a much different technique than simple wet-fly work. Too many fishermen employ the same casting stroke and timing in the false cast as they use in conventional methods. Such false casting is too slow to dry excess moisture from the fly and leader.

The pickup is conventional, and the line is accelerated into a normal backcast, but any similarity to normal technique ends there. The backcast is not thrown high in false casting but is aimed almost straight back, letting the rod tip drift with it into an exaggerated follow-through. The rod actually reaches as low as the two o'clock attitude. The forward cast is accelerated gently before the backcast has fully extended itself, and is aimed four to five feet above the water. The rod follows through to approximately a ten o'clock position and starts another backcast before its forward cast has fully unrolled. The sequence is repeated enough times to dry the fly properly, depending on weather and humidity, until the fisherman is ready to present his cast again.

The final cast is lifted into a high backward extension, allowing it to extend and uncoil normally. The forward stroke is conventionally executed with full forearm drive and wrist snap, aimed at the imaginary water surface about three feet above the actual currents. Fly and leader uncoil cleanly and settle softly to the water. False casting is used primarily to dry the fly, but it is also useful for lengthening the line while the casts are still travelling in the air, stripping line from the reel and shooting it into both forward and backward casting strokes.

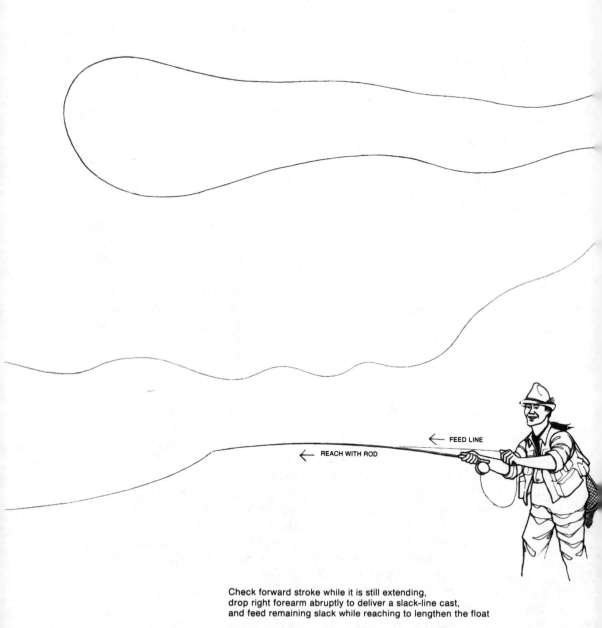

← FEED LINE

← REACH WITH ROD

Check forward stroke while it is still extending,
drop right forearm abruptly to deliver a slack-line cast,
and feed remaining slack while reaching to lengthen the float

RITZ PARACHUTE CAST

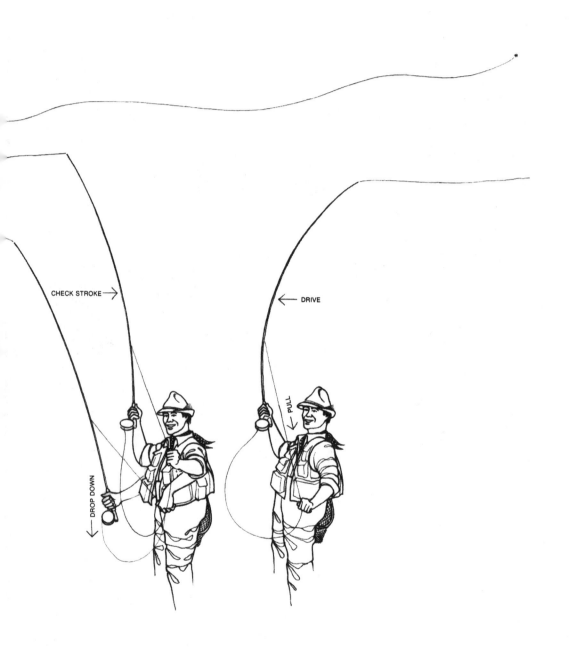

CHECK STROKE →

← DRIVE

↑ PULL

↓ DROP DOWN

CHANGE-OF-DIRECTION CAST

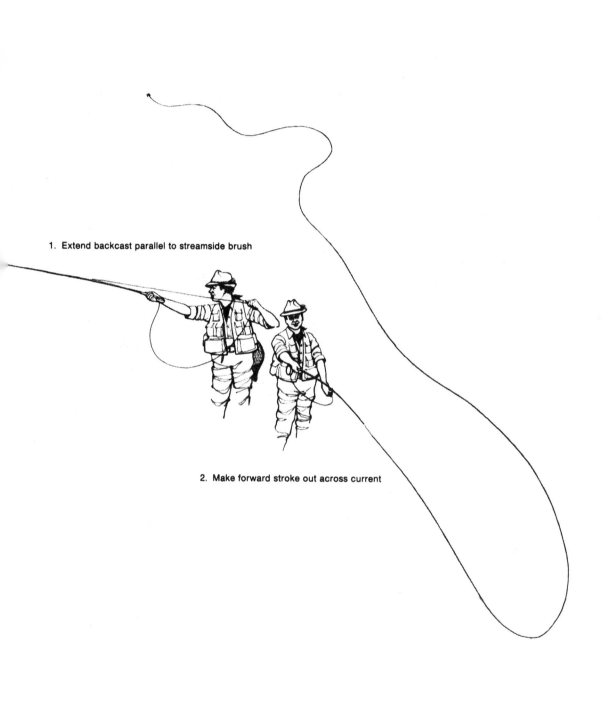

1. Extend backcast parallel to streamside brush

2. Make forward stroke out across current

Dry-fly fishing has evolved a whole series of special casts designed to achieve a drag-free float. The curve casts are typical of the techniques designed for selective trout. Such fish are often suspicious of a fly dragging awkwardly across the surface instead of floating free like the naturals, and they are often frightened of the leader tippet too. Obviously a leader falling across them—even when it is delivered softly by highly skilled anglers—can trigger a shy fish into flight. Hook casts were conceived to solve both these problems.

There are two basic hook casts. The positive or right-hand curve is designed to place the fly over a fish with the tippet lying upstream, providing sufficient slack to delay drag and presenting the fly to a fish before it sees the leader. The negative or left hook was conceived for similar conditions. The positive and negative hook casts are based on the same principles, but are executed in totally different fashion and must be considered separately. Hook casts are critical in dry-fly tactics, particularly over fish that are lying among currents of varying speeds.

The positive curve or right hook cast is a basic tactic in dry-fly fishing, particularly over difficult trout. When you are fishing a dry fly upstream, it often falls above the trout with its trailing tippet landing or floating directly over the fish. Sometimes a fish is frightened by the delivery of the tippet, and sometimes it sees the tippet drifting back over its taking lie. Sometimes a fish is frightened when it rises to the fly and brushes against the tippet. Drag is also a common problem with such fish. Although many currents appear smooth and uncomplicated, drag is apparent on every drift. Time after time the fly approaches the station of a feeding trout, and it rises unsuspectingly to intercept the imitation, only to have it drag suspiciously at the critical moment of the drift.

The positive curve is designed to solve these problems. It drops the fly above the feeding trout, with the curving leader falling farther upstream. The fly comes over the fish before it sees the leader, and the upstream slack solves the problem of drag.

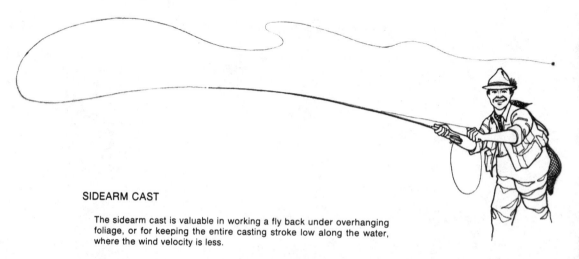

SIDEARM CAST

The sidearm cast is valuable in working a fly back under overhanging foliage, or for keeping the entire casting stroke low along the water, where the wind velocity is less.

Two methods of casting the positive curve are popular. Perhaps the best known involves casting parallel to the current, with a quartering delivery toward the target, turning the wrist as you deliver the final casting stroke. Properly controlled, the rod tip is extended and dropped slightly as the line and leader start to unroll. The line and leader will hook toward the right, and when the cast is correctly thrown, the fly will drop downstream from the curving leader as it settles. The other technique of throwing a positive curve involves sidearm casting, with the rod held somewhere between forty-five degrees and the horizontal. The backcast is thrown at a shallow angle, following the rod with a free elbow, and the forward stroke is powered with the middle tapers of the rod. Apply just enough power to start the cast, but not enough to complete its full extension. The result is a consciously incomplete cast that settles gently to the water before the fly and leader fully turn and straighten. Such casts should be aimed slightly left of the target. When you see that a cast has been underpowered, and may fall too close to the fish, it is still possible to flick the line back into a false cast. When you see that a cast is overpowered and the leader threatens to extend completely, its full extension can quickly be dampered by thrusting the rod forward, or suddenly feeding a few inches of slack line into the guides.

The sidearm method of throwing a positive curve creates a more pronounced right-hook configuration than the wrist method, clearly more exaggerated than the methods of throwing a left or negative curve, except for the backhand technique of making the left-hook cast. The sidearm and backhand hook casts are exaggerated enough to work for dropping a fly in a pocket beyond a faster current tongue. Flies cast with a straight-line delivery to such pockets are immediately dragged downstream by the current when it catches the leader and line.

The left or negative curve is designed to solve the same problems of tippet shyness or current tongues with a fish lying to the left of the fisherman. The negative curve is also achieved in two basic ways. The first is an overpowered sidearm cast delivered across the body, and aimed slightly to the right of the target. The stroke is delivered with more power than necessary. The rod is held at approximately forty-five degrees throughout the cast. The overpowered shoot is checked as the line extends, raising the rod tip slightly, and its excess energy is transmitted to the leader and fly. The energy snaps through the leader, depositing it sharply into a left-hand hook. The positive curve thrown with an overpowered stroke is relatively easy to execute and is surprisingly accurate with a little practice. It is particularly useful for fishing under overhanging branches to the left or working a hook cast ahead of a deadfall or boulder.

The negative curve can also be accomplished with a backhand delivery, holding the rod at a quartering angle across and away from the body. The backcast is delivered low and extended behind, underpowering the forward stroke. Power is applied to the middle of the rod only. The upper rod is withheld from the cast, delivering too little energy to complete

1. With fly-drift or retrieve ending, start roll cast

2. Accelerate rod into forward stroke

3. Drive overhead loop with rod

ROLL PICKUP

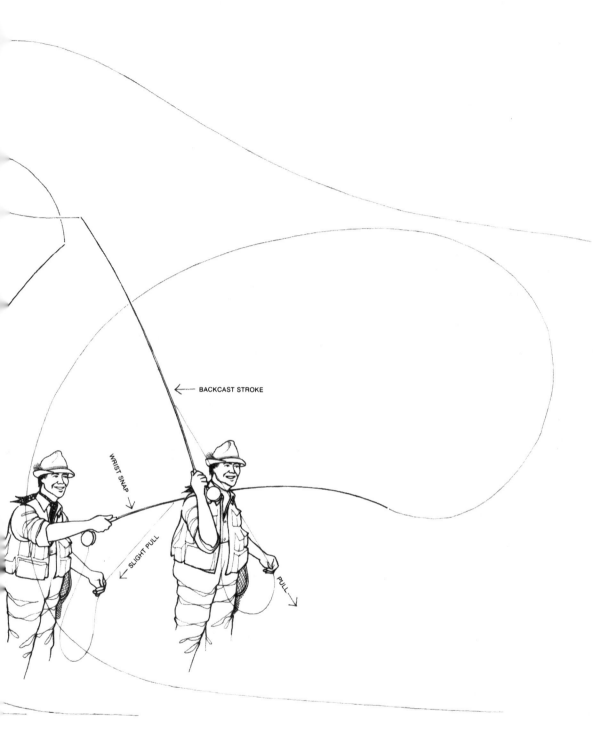

BACKCAST STROKE

WRIST SNAP

SLIGHT PULL

PULL

4. Throw rolling loop
   with sharp wrist-snap

5. Flick rolling loop into backcast
   before it fully extends

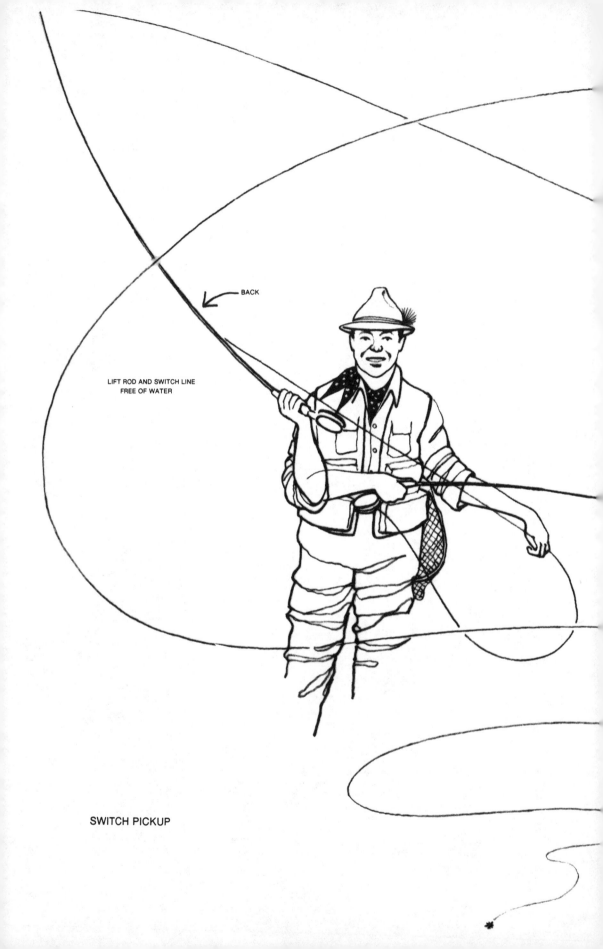

BACK

LIFT ROD AND SWITCH LINE
FREE OF WATER

SWITCH PICKUP

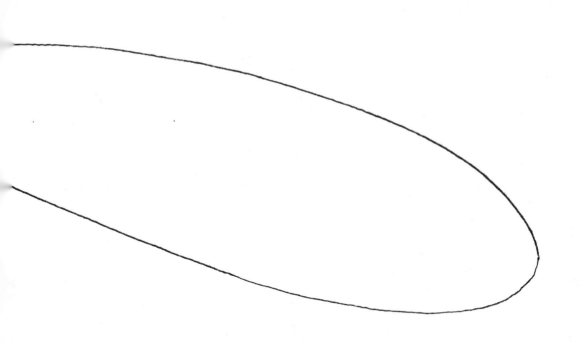

DRIVE ROD DOWN TOWARD THE LEFT
AND FLICK BACK ACROSS THE BODY

its loop. The result is a wide loop that settles incomplete to the water before the leader and fly can fully extend. It is less accurate than the overpowered negative hook, but it is easier for many anglers to execute. It also throws a more pronounced curve to compensate for problems of extreme drag and is remarkably useful in everyday fishing.

Curve casts require considerable practice, and it is foolish to waste actual fishing time to work on your hook-cast techniques. Work on them carefully when the fish are not feeding. You will quickly find that the ability to handle the positive and negative curves, delivered both backhand and forehand, can greatly multiply your chances of taking difficult fish. Few anglers bother to learn the hook casts. Consequently there are many good trout lying in difficult currents, and they survive week after week simply because few fishermen are capable of executing the casts that might take them in spite of their wariness.

Both positive and negative curves are easier to execute in a downstream wind and are essentially casts designed for moderate distances. It is impossible to throw effective hook casts at ranges beyond sixty feet unless a fisherman learns to use the wind, yet judging windage to deliver a controlled curve at long range is a critical skill on big western rivers and spring creeks. Winds vary continually, both from day to day and even from moment to moment, and a skilled fisherman is continually adjusting his aim and line velocity to use them in casting to specific fish.

There are other slack-line casts that prove useful in everyday fly-fishing. The check cast is perhaps the most familiar on American trout-fishing waters and is often used in achieving enough slack to compensate for drag on a downstream presentation. It is executed with a conventional overhead or slightly sidearm delivery, aiming and casting well beyond the intended target. The cast is checked in its final moments of extension, drawing both line and leader back to drop the fly above the position of the fish. The technique will achieve a drag-free float proportional to the amount of extra line worked into the cast. The serpentine cast is often the basic tool of the beginner, since he seldom casts well enough to deliver a really straight cast. His evolving skills throw sloppy casts with enough unintentional slack that he can take difficult fish that sometimes escape a better caster. It is a familiar pattern in the evolution of many beginners.

Such early success seems to evaporate as their casting skills gradually improve, since they are throwing a straighter cast with less slack, and there is too little slack to compensate for drag. Once a novice fisherman has learned to cast reasonably well it is time to learn the several slack-line casts designed to present the fly with precisely controlled slack.

The serpentine cast is the basic tool of most dry-fly work. Its purpose is overcoming average conditions of drag in the countless situations that do not demand a hook-cast presentation. Although it is both obvious and frightening to a shy fish, drag is often imperceptible to the fisherman, and the modicum of slack in a serpentine cast is advisable even on smooth currents that seem totally free of drag. During a heavy hatch of flies, fishing a fine imitation over a steadily rising fish is a common test for imperceptible drag. Sometimes a trout will take naturals floating only millimeters from the fly, close enough that the rise form drowns its hackles, yet refuse the artificial consistently. When the fly is a workable imitation, the refusals can result from either too heavy a tippet or the spectre of unseen drag. It is always advisable to reduce and lengthen the tippet diameter, whether the trout is seeing the nylon or not, since a finer point will be more flexible—and that flexibility will unquestionably help in getting a drag-free float in difficult currents.

Like the basic negative curve and the simple check cast, the serpentine cast is based upon slightly more energy and length than is needed to reach the fish. During the final casting stroke the rod is checked and pulled back two or three inches to slow and stop the shoot. Before the line settles to the water the rod is waggled sideways to throw a series of lateral curves into its length. The series of serpentine loops creates sufficient slack to provide a considerable drag-free float. The serpentine cast must be executed carefully. Exaggerated loops can magnify drag rather than counteract its effects, and large loops can land too hard for working over a skittish fish. The serpentine presentation is often used in upstream fishing, but it is also useful in quartering casts across the current. Some fishermen employ the serpentine cast in fishing a dry fly downstream instead of using a conventional check cast, and extend a dragless float by pushing the rod hand as far downstream as possible. Extending the rod and leaning downstream can sometimes provide the extra inches of float that trigger a rise from a difficult fish.

The parachute cast was developed by the indefatigable Charles Ritz, who recommends it highly for complicated problems of drag. Ritz has polished his parachute technique to the level of an art on difficult rivers like the Risle and Andelle in Normandy, the silken reaches of the grayling water on the Ammer in Germany, and the Traun in Austria. His book *A Fly Fisher's Life* describes several incidents in which his parachute cast proved the solution, from the Loyalsock in Pennsylvania to the swift Doubs in Burgundy. The Ritz parachute cast is simple to execute, although it requires a lot of practice. The casting hand is held fairly high through a series of false casts, and the line is somewhat longer than the actual casting distance required to reach the fish in question. The forward stroke is checked in the vertical position, and before the line can settle the butt is dropped straight down toward the water. Properly executed, the line falls with a maximum of slack. Ritz advises making a series of measuring false casts over a particular fish to ascertain the exact distance required before making the final cast.

The bump cast is designed to place the fly on the water briskly, allowing it to arrive before the adjacent leader and line. It is important in imitating grasshoppers and inchworms and other inqsects that land hard when they fall into the water. Most workable casts settle line and leader

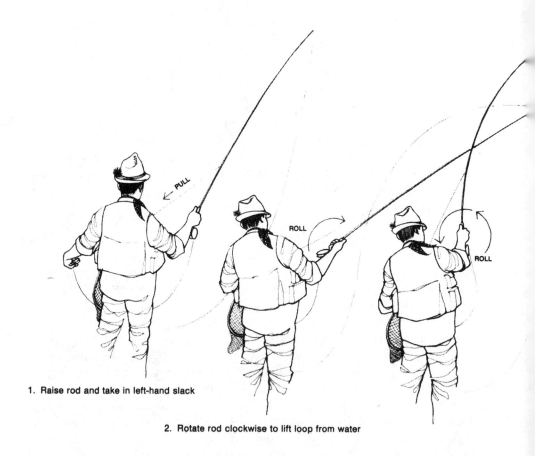

1. Raise rod and take in left-hand slack

2. Rotate rod clockwise to lift loop from water

3. Roll rod sharply counterclockwise to enlarge loop

HORIZONTAL OR HALF-ROLL PICKUP

4. Flick rolling slack smoothly into backcast stroke

ROTATE ROD

UPSTREAM LINE MEND

CURRENT

and fly toward the current together, although the belly of the line is heavier and settles more quickly. There is a certain mythology about skilled casting which always places the fly on the water first. It is possible to make such presentations consistently with only thirty to forty feet of line, and such casts are slightly overpowered with tip and thumb drive, delivered from a vertical casting plane. The excess energy drives the leader to turn over briskly, hooking the fly downward toward the water. The bump cast is used to place the fly down first at ranges beyond forty feet.

The backcast is lifted fairly high, and the rod drifts back as far as two o'clock. The elbow is dropped as the backcast extends toward completion and powers a forward stroke with more energy than necessary to reach the target. The tip drive and thumb follow-through at the release point are also stronger than needed. The sharp tip drive throws a downward hump in the line which is transmitted toward the fly. Its oscillations strike the water about halfway between the fisherman and his fly, checking the forward motion of the line, and its remaining energy leaps ahead into the unrolling line that is still extending. The fly and leader snap up sharply with this energy, turning over and hooking downward, until the fly reaches the water before the remining leader and length of line. It is particularly useful in grasshopper season, when the feeding impulses of the fish are triggered by the arrival of the clumsy insects on the surface. It is a cast that is easily learned. However, it requires some practice to handle the bump cast without frightening the fish, particularly when it is delivered in the backhand position.

The obstacle cast is useful for casting both across a deadfall and over a strong, intervening current tongue that can drag the fly harshly the moment it lands. In the first instance, the cast is delivered normally, although both hand and rod finish in a relatively high position to keep the line between the angler and the obstacle off the water. The pickup should be made while the entire leader and a short length of line are still on the water beyond the obstacle. The stroke should be sharp enough to hop the fly into the air so that it clears the obstacle when the cast is properly executed. Too timid a pickup will merely foul the fly. Should it become hooked, do not pull immediately to free it; instead waggle the rod tip gently until a series of gentle, overlapping oscillations are transmitted along the line. These oscillations will often work the fly free, pacticularly if the angler has been patient and has not firmly seated it by pulling too hard the moment it becomes fouled. Should it remain firmly snagged before you have completely fished the water, you should break it off gently and replace it. Once you are satisfied that you have covered a fishy-looking place properly, there is still time to wade over and retrieve the fly.

Similar problems are found when you are casting across a strong intervening current, but the obstacle is now only water of varying speeds. Trout are often found rising on the far side of a swift run from your position. Normal presentation of the fly simply finds it whisked unceremoniously downstream before the trout have even a moment to inspect it. The fish is frightened even before it can consider rising. Such fast currents make it virtually impossible to dampen drag by mending line, since drag occurs almost immediately. Proper tactics involve wading as close as possible, delivering a serpentine cast with a lot of slack, and holding the rod as high as possible to keep the line free of the currents. The float can be extended by thrusting the rod out and downstream, following the drift of the fly with its tip section extended as far as possible.

It is important to understand the basic problems in casting at varied angles. These problems exist in fishing both a dry-fly float across the current tongues or a cross-stream swing with a wet fly. With a dry fly worked directly upstream or cast at a shallow quartering angle, the false casts and final stroke occur in virtually the same casting plane. The fly is placed upstream at a full quartering angle, or across the current from ninety degrees or quartering downstream. The drift or fly swing finishes well downstream, where the pickup of the fly occurs, but it is impossible to cast the fly back upstream with a single casting stroke. Trying a fresh cast without several intervening false casts is unworkable, and your fly and leader will simply strike the rod or foul in your clothing. The change of angle requires at least two or three false casts, modifying the casting plane from fifteen to twenty degrees with each new stroke. The number of false casts will vary with the scope of the angle lying between the pickup and presentation, and with external problems like wind and backcast room.

Similar tactics are required where there is too little room for a backcast in a proper alignment to reach a rising trout. The typical situation finds an angler standing in deep water with high foliage behind him. Fish are rising across the current or too far out in a lake to be reached by a direct backcast and forward stroke. The water is too deep to wade closer and gain casting room. The fish can be reached with a fifty-foot cast, but there is no space for such work. Such problems demand a change-of-direction cast, and there are two methods of making such a cast: forehand and backhand.

The casting hand is extended away from the body and the adjacent foliage to provide as much lateral casting room as possible. The pickup is made either forehand or backhand, depending on the direction of the current. The false casting is executed in a plane parallel to the foliage behind the angler. When sufficient line speed is achieved, it is time for the final cast. The backcast is overpowered, allowing the rod to ride low and absorb maximum stress, with the arm fully extended toward the rear. The forward cast is delivered in a sweeping stroke that swings the fly toward the target, radically changing the direction of the final presentation. The wrist snap is sharply downward, aimed almost ninety degrees from the original false casting plane.

When the cast is properly executed, the line will swoop up in a twisting arc, following the torque generated in the rod. With sufficient line speed it is possible to shoot several feet of slack line into the cast. Sixty feet is feasible, changing direction as much as eighty to ninety degrees, although a backhand stroke is considerably less effective. Using a long line in the

ROTATE ROD

DOWNSTREAM LINE MEND

CURRENT →

WRIST
SNAP

← PULL

1. Start brisk roll-cast stroke

2. Accelerate with wrist-snap and left hand

3. Continue rolling stroke before first roll cast fully extends

ARGENTINE OR AERIAL ROLL CAST

change of direction may result in a line hop like that found in the bump cast, with the middle of the line striking first, and the terminal footage hooking sharply downward once the line belly has made contact with the water. Although it may break the rules and look clumsy, some skilled casters actually allow the final backcast to touch the water intentionally, since it will heavily stress the rod and accelerate line speed almost like a left-hand haul.

There is also a change-of-direction roll backcast which is based on similar principles. It is particularly useful in stream fishing, where the current also helps generate added line velocity to both pickups and backcasts. Suppose the angler is fishing a fairly wide stream, its currents or depth forcing him to remain near the bankside foliage. The preceding cast has been fished out until the line reaches directly downstream. There is a good fish rising well out across the current, but there is insufficient room for a proper backcast. The tactical problem lies in picking up the fly, which is hanging directly downstream, and placing it above the rising trout. The solution is the change-of-direction roll. The rod tip is raised until the line hangs down slightly behind the angler, like the beginning of a conventional roll cast, with the angler facing downstream. The beginning of the backcast is a forehand roll cast aimed at a quartering angle downstream. The cast is aimed ninety degrees to the current flow, but the loop will unfold at a forty-five-degree alignment. Before the roll cast fully unfolds and extends, the line is pumped back in a conventional backcast stroke and delivered upstream in a forward cast. The line will describe a series of loops not unlike those found in salmon switch casts executed with two-handed rods. However, the twisting forces generated in these change-of-direction casts are demanding on a delicate split-cane rod and a fisherman who fishes bamboo should use them judiciously.

The cardinal rule of picking the fly up from the water is to wait until there are no fish in the vicinity. Many times I have watched a good fisherman ruin his chances with impatient pickups, particularly by picking his fly from the water immediately after a poor cast. It is important to wait patiently while the fly drifts well below a fishable lie before picking it up again for a fresh cast.

The straight pickup involves a gradual tightening and imperceptible raising of the rod tip to start the line moving in the surface film, followed with an accelerating stroke that smoothly lifts the line into a backcast. There are several other useful techniques for executing the pickup.

The roll pickup is particularly useful in dry-fly work. When fishing upstream or slightly across the current, the line is often carried back too close to the fisherman for a normal pickup. Most fishermen strip in the slack and start a new casting sequence, not realizing that a roll pickup is easier. It simply involves raising the rod tip and throwing a roll-cast stroke upstream. Before the upstream roll is completed and uncoils on the current, the line is pulled back into an orthodox backcast.

The switch pickup is also ideally suited to starting a fresh cast once the fly has drifted too close. It is executed with the rod hand held palm-up and extended, and a free wrist is preferable, with the thumb on top. The rod is stressed sharply left and upward, the wrist twisting it into a plane ten to fifteen degrees above the surface of the water. The rod tip is accelerated with a strong clockwise wrist snap, and the line is picked cleanly from the current. Both fly and leader remain momentarily on the water, and just before they strip free into the air, the backcast itself is started with counterclockwise wrist snap into a conventional high-lift stroke. With practice, the switch pickup seems to lift the line instantly with almost no disturbance, and a surprisingly long line can be handled.

The corkscrew pickup is similar. It is a variation on the roll pickup that strips the line from the water in corkscrew form, and it is particularly useful on still currents and shy fish. Such streams are so placid that retrieving the fly inevitably disturbs the surface, however stealthily a fisherman strips line. Such still currents are often weedy, and a conventional pickup threatens to foul the leader or fly on drifting stems or weeds. Fish are often lying just beyond a weed bed, and a presentation must sometimes be made across its growth to place the fly properly. Orthodox pickups are virtually impossible with the leader and line lying across the weeds, but the corkscrew pickup almost lifts the fly straight off the water. The corkscrew pickup is performed with the back of the hand toward the water with the reel facing up. The left hand holds the line firmly, and the rod is held parallel to the water. The pickup is effected with a forward rising roll of the wrist in a clockwise, corkscrew motion that is transmitted into the line. The energy rolls the line forward about a foot, followed by the line and leader and fly coming off the water in a spiral. Once the line is fully airborne, it is swiftly checked and lifted into a backcast.

The snap pickup is simple to execute and permits a fisherman to work his fly virtually to his feet. It is made with a simple wrist snap, with nothing more than raising the rod from ten to eleven o'clock and snapping the tip downward sharply to the ten o'clock position. The wrist snap forms a rolling curve that progresses down the line into the leader, lifting it from the water, and a normal backcast is executed once the line and leader have jumped free of the surface tension. The snap pickup requires a little practice, since the common tendency is too much power and a splashy stripping of line off the water, but with proper execution the leader and fly leave the current cleanly.

The serpentine pickup also has its partisans. It is the reverse of a serpentine cast and involves waving the rod from side to side to oscillate a series of gentle loops into the line. It has the capability of easily lifting the front taper off the water, permitting a conventional backcast the moment the fly and leader come free. The rod is held in the ten o'clock position, and the line is started into the air with a series of lateral oscillations while the rod is gradually raised toward an eleven o'clock alignment. It is a lazy pickup, requiring enough time for the oscillations to flutter completely along the line into the leader, freeing it from the surface tension. When the

GALWAY OR REVERSE CAST

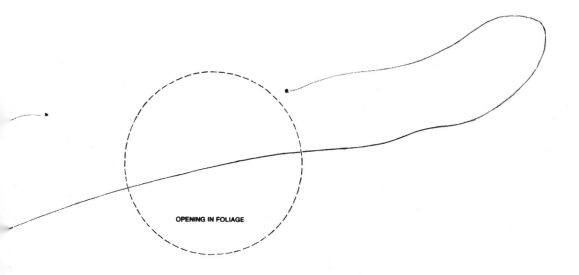

OPENING IN FOLIAGE

Aim forward stroke through opening in foliage, and turn 180 degrees
to lay backcast out into the waters as the presentation stroke

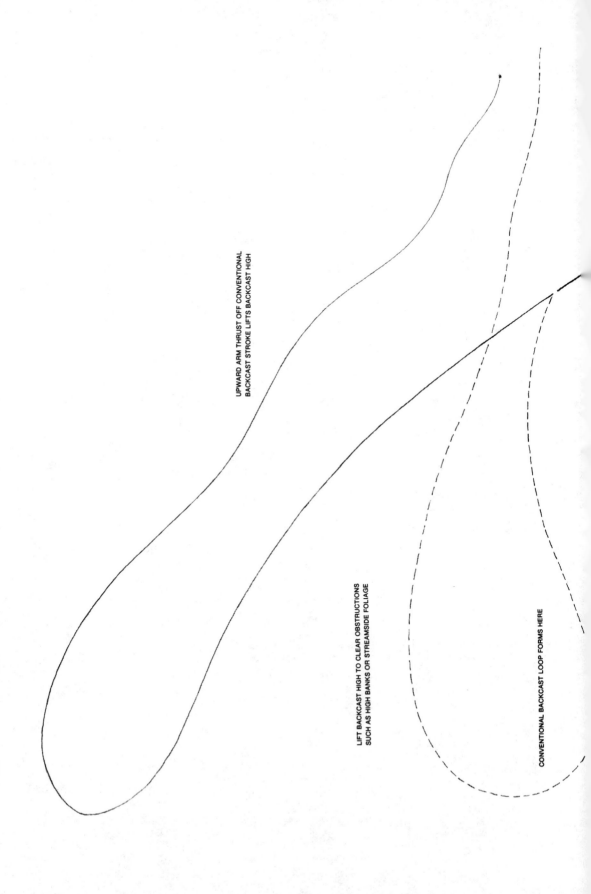

UPWARD ARM THRUST OFF CONVENTIONAL
BACKCAST STROKE LIFTS BACKCAST HIGH

LIFT BACKCAST HIGH TO CLEAR OBSTRUCTIONS
SUCH AS HIGH BANKS OR STREAMSIDE FOLIAGE

CONVENTIONAL BACKCAST LOOP FORMS HERE

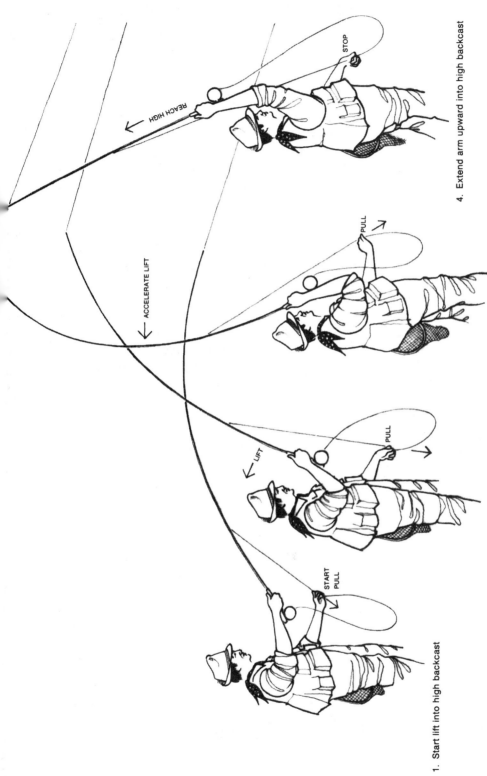

STEEPLE CAST

1. Start lift into high backcast

2. Accelerate lift and start left-hand haul

3. Lift backcast sharply and complete line haul

4. Extend arm upward into high backcast

serpentine pickup is skillfully executed, the leader snakes free of the water like magic, and the line can quickly be worked into a backcast.

Mending line is not strictly part of casting, since it is part of manipulating fly speed or float, but it is closely related to casting. It is executed with a rolling motion of the rod. There are many times in stream fishing when the cast must be made with a wet fly or nymph across a swift current tongue to a quieter feeding run or pocket beyond. With a simple straight-line cast the fly is quickly dragged from the feeding zone by the bellying line in the middle currents. That drag can be dampened by mending the cast. Suppose that the current is flowing from left to right, with a swift run lying immediately in front of a fisherman. Beyond lies an eddying pocket where a fish is nymphing. The fly is placed above the trout with a conventional cast, the follow-through carrying the rod almost parallel to the surface of the water. The mend is accomplished with a small amount of slack in the left hand, and the rod tip is rotated lazily upstream in a semicircular arc with a rolling motion of the wrist. The slack is paid out into the upstream loop as the rod rolls up and over, and the line is deposited in an exaggerated upstream loop that falls across the swift currents. Skill is required to mend the line into its upstream loop without moving the leader and fly, and a really accomplished caster can learn to throw a mend even before a long cast settles on the water.

Downstream mends are also useful in situations which find a slow current lying between a fisherman and a fish lying in slightly faster water.

BELGIAN WIND STROKES

BACKCAST

FORWARD STROKE

WIND

1. Wind from the right: backcast floats back in vertical plane, while forward stroke slices into the gusts at a 45-degree angle.

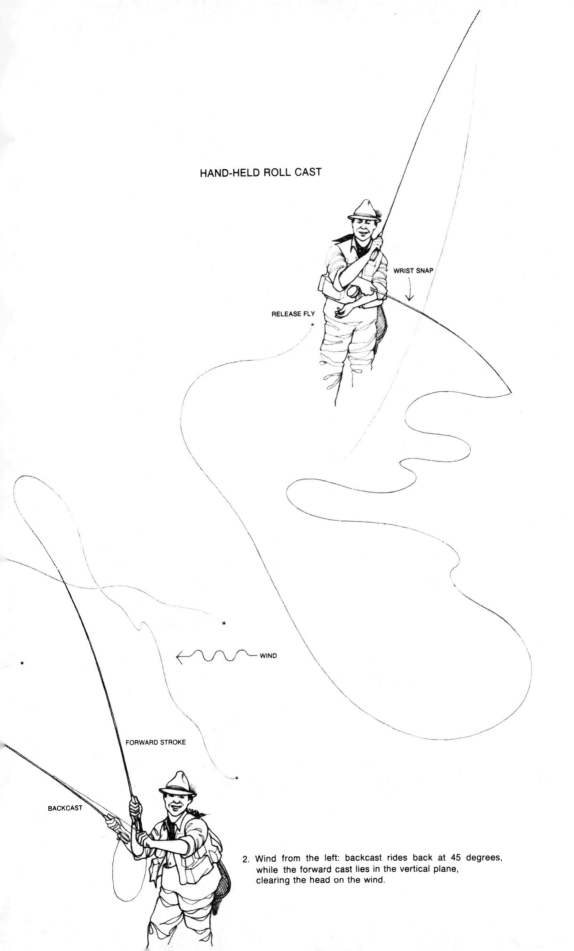

HAND-HELD ROLL CAST

WRIST SNAP

RELEASE FLY

WIND

FORWARD STROKE

BACKCAST

2. Wind from the left: backcast rides back at 45 degrees,
while the forward cast lies in the vertical plane,
clearing the head on the wind.

CHECK BACKCAST →

PULL →

SECOND PULL

1. Check backcast stroke
   and hit single haul hard

2. Drive into forward stroke
   and pull second haul harder

RITZ STORM CAST

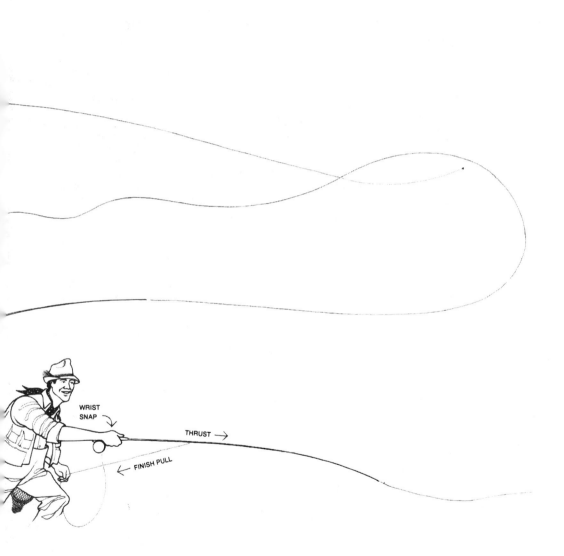

WRIST
SNAP

THRUST →

← FINISH PULL

3. Punch rod low in a thrust along the water,
   complete left-hand pull, and shoot line low into the wind

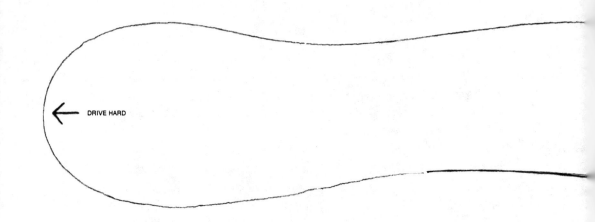

DRIVE HARD

1. With a wind from the right, aim the cast
   farther right than the final target

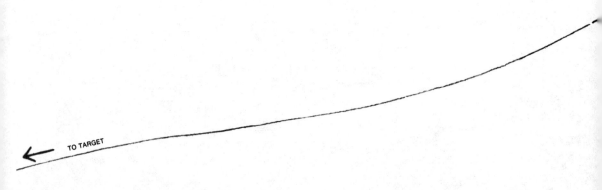

TO TARGET

CALCULATING WINDAGE

WIND DRIFT

2. Allow the wind to carry the forward cast to
   the final target, following with the rod

It is necessary to speed up the bellying middle of the line. This can be accomplished by throwing a downstream mend. It involves rotating the rod tip in a clockwise semicircle, looping the middle of the line downstream and accelerating the speed of the fly line. Both upstream and downstream mends are also useful in dry-fly work, although they have largely evolved in wet-fly practice on salmon.

Since many casts are extremely short in normal work, fishing at distances between ten to twenty feet, perhaps some brief observations on these short-range presentations are needed. Although a short cast having little more than the leader extended beyond the rod tip may seem routine, it is not a normal presentation. It is necessary to compensate for the lack of fly-line weight with the wrist drive of the casting stroke. The backcast is slightly overpowered, and when the forward cast is made the wrist follow-through is extrahard. With proper rod action, the short line and leader and fly will extend normally.

There are several other special casts that have evolved over the centuries to cope with specific problems. These special casts include the hand roll, aerial roll, bow-and-arrow, Galway, and steeple casts, and they are all designed to cope with brushy streams.

The basic roll cast is designed for fishing a sunk fly on brushy water with little or no room for a backcast, while the hand roll was conceived for dry-fly work. Typical problems for the hand roll involve a brushy stream and a freshly oiled dry fly, with a trout rising on the far bank. The conventional roll cast involves contact with the water, wetting the hackles of the fly, but a hand-held roll will deliver it dry and floating perfectly. The fly is held across the flat bend of its hook, between the thumb and index finger of the left hand, while line is worked out beyond the tip. The line is stripped from the reel and worked out with a conventional roll-casting stroke, first on the right and then on the left, alternating rhythmically as the loop grows. The fixed loop lying between the rod tip and the left hand should reach halfway to the rising trout, measuring enough line to cover its feeding station. The final precast roll of the line must be backhand, looping it upstream in preparation for the final stroke. The fly is still held firmly in the left hand. When the preliminary loop drifts downstream under the rod, the final cast is delivered with a conventional rolling motion, applying a strong wrist snap to the stroke. The fly is finally released as the loop extends itself. With a little practice it will arrive just above the fish.

The aerial roll is a relatively rare technique that apparently evolved in Argentina, particularly among the highly skilled fishermen who frequent the brushy headwaters of the Rio Traful and the canyon below the storied Boca Chimehuin. It is a superb cast for reaching surprising distances with no available backcasting room. The conventional roll cast will work, but its range is relatively limited. The aerial roll starts with an orthodox roll cast, delivered with a strong forward stroke. But instead of allowing the rolling loop to extend normally, unfolding across the current, the forearm and wrist keep rolling in the casting plane. The line keeps rolling in a wide loop until the fisherman is ready to deliver the cast. The final stroke is delivered with the line travelling upward and out, driving forward with considerable wrist-and-arm drive. Although it is not a distance cast, it will provide more distance than a conventional roll, since the atmospheric friction is less than stripping line from the current. The aerial roll is a formidable weapon in the hands of great Argentine fishermen like Jorge Donovan and Bébé Anchorena and Maurice Lariviere.

The bow-and-arrow cast is designed for close work on a brushy stream. Sometimes a fisherman finds himself completely enclosed in bushes, lacking room even for a roll cast. The bow-and-arrow cast is the solution. The fly is held between the index finger and the thumb of the left hand, pulling the line taut between the tip guide and the fingers. The left hand is drawn back, while the rod hand is thrust forward, bending the rod like a bow. The fly is released simultaneously with a backhand wrist snap, and a cast of twenty-five feet is possible with a little practice. Many times in a brushy reach of water I have used this cast to penetrate under the foliage.

The Galway or reverse cast was originally developed in western Ireland by the late F. G. Shaw. It is designed to cope with thick foliage or low bushes behind a fisherman. The cast is executed by facing the direction of the backcast, unlike the other casting techniques, so that the obstructions are clearly in view. The line is picked off the water, and the backcast is aimed precisely at openings in the branches, or lofted high enough to clear the bankside alders. With the backcast delivered forehand, visibly clearing

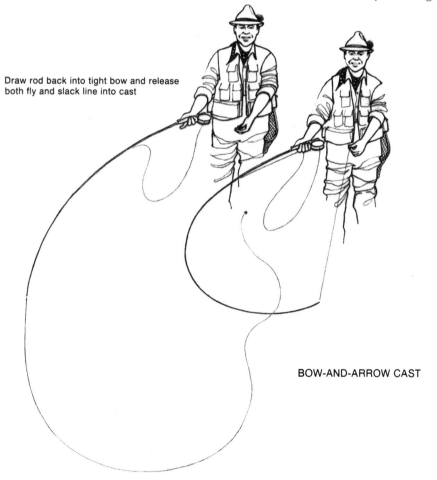

Draw rod back into tight bow and release both fly and slack line into cast

BOW-AND-ARROW CAST

1. Pickup cast and accelerate into backcast

2. Lift backcast high and pause

3. Drive forward and shoot left-hand slack

PULL

SHOOT

SHOOTING THE LINE

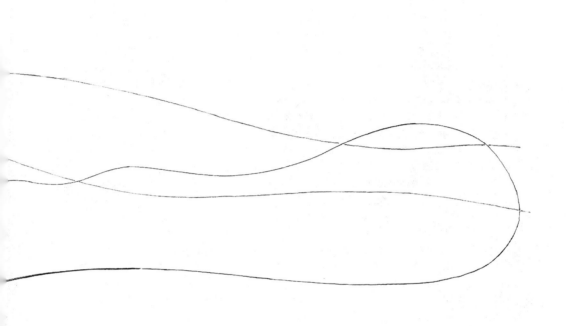

the obstacles, the fisherman swivels his body to make his final forehand stroke. Both casting motions can be made backhand, too. The Galway technique can also be used for false casting where a conventional backcast often fouls in the brush. The Galway is often the solution where a long backcast is needed and casting room is limited by trees and bushes.

The steeple cast is another technique designed for fishing with insufficient backcast room. It involves an exaggeratedly high backcast lift and is useful where high bushes or slopes lie behind the angler that would foul a normal casting stroke. The steeple cast is capable of delivering more distance than the several roll-cast techniques. The cast is executed by trying to loft the fly line almost straight up behind the caster, and following swiftly with a sharp forward cast, barely pausing to allow a fully extended backcast. The premature forward cast is designed to keep the backcast clear of the foliage behind the fisherman, and considerable casting range is possible. The exaggerated full-arm pump ends with the casting arm fully extended, directly above the shoulder, and the forward motion is delivered with a strong chopping stroke. Both gravity and rod action extend and shoot the line well at short to medium ranges, and with better accuracy and control than any of the roll casts can deliver. The steeple cast is increasingly difficult to execute as casting distances increase, because the upward angle is gradually reduced, but with sufficient room to clear an obstruction excellent distance is possible.

However, true distance work beyond sixty feet is an almost wholly separate art. Sparse Grey Hackle relates an anecdote in his book *Fishless Days and Angling Nights* about his Catskill colleagues on the pastoral Willowemoc. It is classic dry-fly water in the tradition of George La Branche, and with its shy trout a premium is placed on delicacy and precision rather than on distance. One fisherman was regaling the Catskill regulars with the capture of a difficult trout on a Willowemoc flat.

It was a medium cast of sixty feet, he intoned.

Another fisherman stopped the conversation abruptly with the challenge that few men could cast sixty measured feet under stream conditions. His challenge quickly became a competition on the Home Pool, and the group soon discovered with chagrin that none of its members could cast a measured sixty feet. Catskill fishermen traditionally have been forced to focus their attentions on stream entomology and stealth, and few are masters of the techniques for casting beyond sixty feet.

Before any fisherman can become a distance caster, it is mandatory to master the left-hand techniques of handling line. The role of the left hand lies in shortening the length of line working in the air, keeping the line in tension while casting, controlling the shoot of left-hand slack, and building line velocity with the techniques of the single and double haul. It is surprising how few fishermen are really aware of their left-hand work while casting.

Left-hand work is virtually unnecessary at casting ranges of thirty feet or less. Such line lengths can be picked off the water and cast again without any left-hand motions, although the line is held against the grip with the index finger. But casting beyond about forty feet means a certain amount of left-hand slack must be handled. This slack is stripped in through the guides with the left hand, and held under the index finger. Its delicate pressure can provide the tension for setting the hook against a strong strike, particularly in fishing a bucktail, as well as a swift release when a fish is hooked and bolts downstream.

Forty to fifty feet of line are a minor problem, since the accumulated slack is easily stripped in with the left hand until an easy cast is possible. The slack is released into the forward cast once it is launched and extending. Such simple handling of left-hand slack lies within the skills of most fishermen. Between fifty and sixty feet is more complicated. Such distances mean that fifteen to twenty-five feet of slack has been stripped in through the guides until the loading capability of the rod is left. Several methods of handling left-hand slack are found in actual fishing, particularly when the current is carrying a dry fly back toward the angler, and each has its practitioners. Some men simply gather the line in a ball, with a rolling motion of the left hand, but it is a technique that often results in line snarls that jam in the butt guide when the next cast is made. Others simply let the slack trail in the water beside them, and although it is seemingly sloppy, it is quite effective in a moderate current. The third method of handling slack is a series of open loops gathered in the fingers of the left hand, either collected from the index finger at the grip or reaching for slack at the butt guide. While fishing I find myself using the trailing slack and loop methods except when working a deliberate wet-fly retrieve.

Each rod has a ceiling beyond which additional travelling loads of line cannot be sustained in casting. The differences between that maximum loading and the actual casting distances lie in left-hand slack, which is stripped back between casts and allowed to shoot into the forward strokes. Shooting the left-hand slack into the forward stroke is fairly common, although the single haul is more complicated. Without mastery of the single-haul technique, casting in the range of fifty to sixty feet is difficult, and the single haul will reach as much as seventy-five feet in really skilled hands. But generally casting between sixty and ninety feet is predicated on the double haul, and without it distance work is virtually impossible.

The single haul is the foundation. The long backcast is impossible to loft and float without considerable acceleration and velocity. That velocity must decelerate and die before a fresh acceleration can occur in the opposite direction. Several factors are involved in these dynamics. The accelerating pickup and power stroke and high backcast are critical, with the proper timing to fully extend line and load the rod. Water friction builds sufficient rod stress on pickup to build backcast velocity, but with a long line working, it is difficult to build equal line speed for the forward casting stroke. Without a double haul the left hand can strip in a single pull of five to six feet, reducing the rod load carried in the air and slightly increasing the length of the shoot. The single haul involves drawing in an

1. Start backcast with tension on rod and fly line

2. Lift rod and start single-haul line pull

PULL →

FIRST PHASE OF DOUBLE-HAUL TECHNIQUE

3. Accelerate lift and left-hand pull

4. Let rod drift into backcast and complete first line-haul

arm's length of line with the backcast stroke, the maintenance of continuous tension throughout the extension of the backcast, and the release of that slack into the forward cast—followed by the remaining slack trailing in the water, once the forward stroke is delivered.

The advantages of casting a much longer line than you can lift from the surface and can handle cleanly in a backcast are obvious in normal fishing. Seventy-foot casts are readily possible with nothing more than the single haul, provided the caster has a really fine sense of rod capacity and timing. But working consistently beyond sixty feet demands more than the single haul, which existed in the rule book of fly casting for more than a century before the remarkable double haul was unveiled in international competition in 1938.

The double haul was a revelation. It had been germinating in the work of several Pacific Coast tournament casters for a dozen years, along with a series of experiments with radical line tapers. It was probably Marvin Hedge who first worked out a rudimentary double haul in response to his own weight-forward line theories, since it was Hedge who first unveiled it in competition. It was a technique evolved to achieve high line speeds and gain the full distance potential of the new lines. Distance competition in the trout-fly class soon reached 150 feet, and Dick Miller quickly extended his scores to 179 feet in registered competition. It is important to understand that the weight-forward line and the double haul were developed in concert, and that both are relatively recent developments in the history of the sport.

Although the double haul is clearly an American development, its most sophisticated theoretician is probably Charles Ritz, who has embroidered its basic premises into a philosophy called high-speed, high-line casting. Understanding of the radical improvement in casting distance that occurred with the perfection of the double haul is rooted in the basic laws of rod and line behavior. It is the weight of the fly line that is cast, not the leader or the fly, and it is only the weight of the line extended beyond the tip guide that causes the rod to load and flex under stress. Each rod has an obvious ceiling in the length and weight of line it can lift from the water, and a second ceiling in the line weight and length it can carry while casting. Such limits were quickly reached with double-taper lines.

Weight-forward lines and the double haul were developed to exploit these limiting factors, placing most of the line weight beyond the tip guide where it is instantly available for the shoot, and radically multiplying its speed in stressing the rod.

Basic physics tells us that the dynamic energy of casting is a function of line weight multiplied by line speed, and that the velocity of the line is a function of tip speed. Such tip-speed effects mean that an eight-foot rod throwing a seven-weight line at a high enough velocity will equal the distances possible with a much larger rod, delivering its heavier line at lower speeds. Obviously a caster strong enough to work the larger rod at optimum line speed will reach out farther, but the physical skills of each caster will vary widely. It is important to fish a rod that fits your strength and casting skills and temperament, and your ability to exploit its optimum tip speed should be the principal factor in selecting a distance rod.

Tip speed is a result of casting skills, the character of the rod action, wind velocity, and the temperature variables of atmospheric resistance. The principal resistance to casting is atmospheric density, which varies with temperature and altitude and the effects of wind. It is possible for a fisherman to cast farther on a summer day in Colorado than, using the same tackle, he can cast on a cold morning in the Catskills.

Basic physical laws also describe inertia in terms of objects at rest and objects in motion. Rod behavior is a result of the dynamic inertias triggered by the casting stroke, plus its bending stresses in slicing through the atmosphere. The dynamic inertia of the wind exerts still more atmospheric resistance and adds to the bending stresses in the rod. Casting is designed to overcome atmospheric inertia and wind, and its rhythms are quickly translated into line acceleration. When peak acceleration and velocity are reached, the rod is loading at its maximum tip speed, and stressing the rod with the double haul exaggerates that tip acceleration and velocity. The resulting overstress also greatly exaggerates the distance the rod tip travels in powering and unloading the cast.

The cast should be released when line velocity and tip speed are identical. The flexing of the rod beyond the release point adds virtually nothing to distance, and the instant it starts to straighten, the rod is no longer contributing to line speed. Once the tip speed lags behind the accelerating line, the line is extending fully independent of the rod. It flexes well past the horizontal, and its principal effect on velocity and distance become negative because of friction in the guides and contact with the surfaces of the rod. Rod load in casting is a response to line weight and velocity and atmospheric factors, and the rod continues to resist flexure until its ability to fight bending loads has equalled its casting speed.

These factors mean that you should select tackle suited to your particular strengths and skills. Big rods designed to handle the large forward tapers might be too much for many anglers, who lack the strength to bring them to optimal tip speed. Rod weights and actions that can be brought to full tip speed are a better choice, fitted with matching line weights and tapers. For example, a small fisherman might cast farther with an eight-foot rod designed for a six-weight line than he could reach with a nine-foot rod too large for his strength and casting skills.

The basic mechanics of the left-hand haul are simple, but they are not easily mastered. The pickup is orthodox, thrown high with a single haul stripping line from the water and building backcast velocity. The rod tip is allowed to drift back until the casting arm is extended at a forty-five-degree angle to the rear. With the line travelling into the backcast, the left-hand slack is allowed to slide back through the guides until the left hand is stretched back across the body, reaching toward the stripping guide. The weight is strongly shifted to the right leg, and the upper torso and shoulders

1. Continue rod drift into backcast and start line slide

2. Stop backcast stroke and continue line slide

3. Start forward cast and second haul

COMPLETING THE DOUBLE HAUL

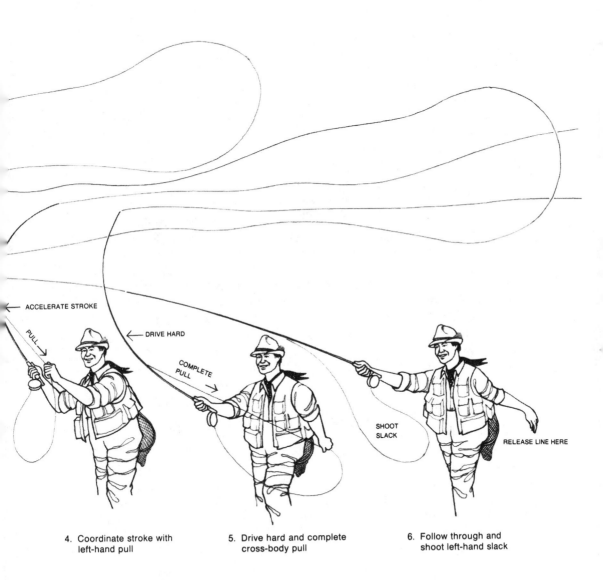

ACCELERATE STROKE

PULL →

← DRIVE HARD

COMPLETE
PULL →

SHOOT
SLACK

RELEASE LINE HERE

4. Coordinate stroke with
left-hand pull

5. Drive hard and complete
cross-body pull

6. Follow through and
shoot left-hand slack

twist back to follow the backcast. The velocity of this back shoot and the weight of the line allowed to drift through the guides stress the rod beyond its normal casting loads. Just before the line completes its full backcast extension, the forearm and wrist start the forward stroke. Just as the middle of the rod loads fully, the left hand accelerates the line back through the guides with a smooth stroke that diagonally crosses the body until the left hand is behind the left knee. During this stroke the weight is shifted to the left leg and the casting arm powers the rod through in a strong forward stroke. When the rod reaches nine o'clock, the left hand lofts its slack toward the stripping guide and shoots the running line. The shoulders, torso, and casting arm all follow through in sequence and the line almost leaps through the guides.

The left-hand haul is not merely a distance technique. It is important in combating wind, and an experienced caster often finds a minor left-hand stroke useful in keeping a backcast and his line speed high. Such adjustments in timing are made unconsciously, once the left-hand haul is executed without thinking.

The double haul is designed to load the rod at maximum stress as quickly as possible, ideally using only five casting motions. These motions include the pickup, backcast, accelerating forward cast, final backcast, and line shoot in the forward stroke. The left-hand haul is used at the pickup, accelerating stroke, and final delivery of the cast. Charles Ritz argues that maximum line speed must be reached in these first five motions, and that another backcast and left-hand haul are unlikely to improve its velocity. My experience with the double haul verifies that conclusion, and it seems axiomatic that three full casting sequences are about the maximum cycle for building fly-line speed. Certainly the chances of reaching optimal tip speed and line velocity diminish the longer the line is working.

Few people can sustain high line speeds beyond three complete casting strokes, and those who can are highly skilled distance experts who have perfect timing, optimal line-handling skills, exquisitely balanced tackle, and great strength. The few distance champions who lack raw physical strength possess remarkable timing and the dexterity to execute a surprisingly long left-hand pull, stressing the rod fully at optimal line velocity and tip speed. Others who are blessed with an equilibrium of strength and casting technique and timing achieve surprising distance with seemingly minimal effort, using a deceptively minor left-hand stroke. Close study of their casting will usually reveal exceptional power focused in motions of brief duration and absolutely perfect timing in their reverse shoot and left-hand haul technique.

A. J. McClane made a number of important observations on the double haul in his book *The Practical Fly Fisherman*, which has two excellent chapters on casting, and those observations are well worth repeating:

> The double haul gives the line much greater velocity. It will pull out thirty or forty feet of shooting line, adding that much length to

the cast. This is how casting champions make their records, and how fishermen in our coastal rivers make their really long casts for steelhead and salmon. Even in trout fishing the angler has an occasional need to get out seventy or eighty feet of line.

There are nine important phases in the double-haul, all of which must be subtly blended: (1) the line hand reaches as far forward as possible, and begins pulling an instant before the rod hand begins to lift; (2) a split second later, rod hand and line hand are working together; (3) the rod is speeding up now, and the line is pulling hard; (4) the line hand stops as the backcast straightens out, and this pause consumes just a fraction of a second, blending in with the backward movement of the line; (5) the line hand begins to slide upward with the straightening of the back loop in order to get maximum reaching distance for the next line hand pull; (6) line hand and rod hand are both in motion again as the forward cast begins; (7) both hands accelerate their movements; (8) faster; (9) the rod hand follows through, while the line hand lets go for the shooting of the left-hand slack.

This, of course, is just the basic procedure. It will be necessary to repeat the process backward and forward several times until maximum tip and line speed are attained. I find it easy to cast over a hundred feet by underpowering the first few false casts until I have the proper length of line extended. What this amounts to is almost swinging the line back and forth, timing it as slowly as possible, and then adding the left-hand pull to the stroke to get casting speed.

Some casters hold their left hand stationary until the right hand puts enough speed and snap into the backcast that it straightens high in the rear before beginning the haul. Either way, when you stop the rod at a position near one o'clock, bring the left hand up to where the right hand is; the line will have enough momentum at that point to take care of itself. At the instant the straightening is complete, bring the left hand down sharply to the first position, at your side, and the double haul is finished. All these motions must be blended very smoothly.

Remember, in practice you will probably develop your own style. Don't accept anything I have outlined as the only correct way. Very few people do things exactly alike, and you should take advantage of your own strengths—wrist, forearm, timing, or whatever the case might be.

It is important to remember that the double haul is a relatively recent development, and it had not yet been introduced when Ray Bergman first published *Trout* before the Second World War. The classical style of wrist casting with the elbow fixed at the waist still dominated fly-fishing, although the British tradition of teaching a beginner to cast with a book

DRIVE

START SECOND HAUL

START FORWARD CAST

6

LOCK
WRIST

5

PULL

LINE SLIDE

FIRST HAUL

4

ALLOW WRIST TO DRIFT
BACK AND ROLL SIDEWAYS
TO RELAX SHOULDER AND
UPPER ARM INTO BACKCAST

3

1. Start line coming
   across surface

2. Lift into backcast
   and start haul

3. Fully extend
   first haul

4. Allow arm to drift back,
   let line slide into backcast

PULL HARD

7

SHOOT LINE →

COMPLETE HAUL

RELEASE
LINE HERE

8

← LIFT INTO BACKCAST

2

START HAUL

LOCK
WRIST

1

SALVATO OVAL CASTING STROKE

5. Start forward cast and
   second haul simultaneously

6. Drive and
   pull hard

7. Follow through
   and keep pulling

8. Complete casting stroke
   and left-hand haul

held between his body and his upper arm was no longer the *ex cathedra* method. Bergman obviously believed that casting had fully evolved, and its theory and technique needed no elaboration or tampering, since *Trout* contained no chapters on fly casting. The casting revolution that followed the development of the weight-forward line and the double-haul stroke was still on the horizon in those years before the Second World War.

The gentle art of fly casting has now passed into a period of explosive evolution and change. Past theory and technique are long outdated, echoing the European roots of fly-fishing and a tradition of longer rods and heavier tackle, and the obsolete tradition of wrist casting is rapidly waning even in Europe.

It is difficult to find fly rods as long as eight feet in use on our eastern trout streams, and six- to seven-foot rods have become fashionable on widespread waters. Distance work with such rods is possible, given enough backcast room and matching long-belly tapers, but they demand the free-wheeling technique of the double haul. The traditional clock-face designations of casting have been forgotten with the high-speed line work now possible, and with the midge-size rods, the arm has become part of the rod itself. It can no longer remain against the rib cage, holding a copy of *The Compleat Angler* between the elbow and the body, while the wrist and forearm work a short and graceful casting stroke.

A. J. McCLANE

Short casts of ten to twenty-five feet were the rule with traditional wrist casting, although thirty to forty feet were possible with good timing and well-balanced tackle. Sixty-foot casts lay in the world of expert casters with well-developed wrists, and a cast of eighty to ninety feet would win most tournaments. Such short-range casting in the ten- to twenty-five-foot class means a relatively quick casting rhythm and a short casting stroke well within the capability of wrist work. But with a lengthening line and its gradually increasing wind resistance and weight, your timing must progressively slow down and the length of your casting stroke must grow larger. Lengthening your casting stroke inevitably leads to a free-elbow style, extending your arm as far back as possible for the maximum possible stroke. The high line speed possible with the double haul will keep the backcast high, instead of at the traditional one o'clock alignment of your rod. And extending your arm toward the rear in the backcast creates the maximum distance between the stripping guide and your left hand—when it exerts the left-hand pull that lies at the core of modern distance-casting technique.

The position of the feet is important too. The weight is no longer evenly distributed on both feet, with toes facing forward. The foot under your casting arm is dropped back, its toes turned out to open your stance for distance work. The open stance will permit the longest possible casting stroke, and the weight is shifted back and forth with the working of your casting rhythms. Although the wrist remains relatively locked, relaxing only while a long backcast is extending, the remaining arm is relaxing and flexing with the exaggerated oval of the full elbow stroke.

Casting sixty feet with a seven-foot rod will require better timing and a longer oval stroke than sixty feet with an eight-foot rod. Longer casts are virtually impossible for most casters without the double-haul technique. It is surprising how many critics of our modern midge-size rods believe that simply extending the arm makes a six-foot midge into the equivalent of a nine-footer. It is a misconception rooted in ignorance of modern casting. Casting with a small rod, your arm does not compensate for vertical length measured above the head, but reaches back to open the full length needed for the double haul. Timing becomes more difficult beyond fifty feet as rod length is reduced, and both the rhythm and the casting stroke must be radically increased with a midge rod.

Such radical changes pretty much ignore the clock-face traditions of past casting theory, with the fishing book held between the elbow and the rib cage, but there has been a considerable revolution in fly casting over the past thirty years.

We've killed the clock, Charles Ritz observes wryly, having participated in that revolution, *and we've finally thrown away the book!*

2. The Theory and Technique of Wading

Boca Chimehuin is a wading nightmare. It lies at the outlet of sprawling Lago Huechulafquen, the deep fjordlike lake that reaches from the barren foothill pampas of Argentina to the Andean threshold of Chile. Its headwaters are a bone-chilling series of arroyos and minor rivers that tumble down from the forests and snowfields of the Lanin volcano, and its lesser foothill mountains along the lake. There are hot springs in the Epulaufquen tributaries that nourish the lake, and its eighty-mile length is a feeding ground rich with smeltlike pejerrey and crayfish. The best fly-fishing is found in the outlet currents at the Boca Chimehuin, tumbling half-legendary waters that have produced both browns and rainbows over twenty pounds on flies, but fishing is difficult and dangerous.

The Andean winds there are sometimes fierce. Their angry gusts are born in the glacier-cold altitudes, an alpine atmosphere that mixes explosively with the hot thermals that rise from the barren pampas of Argentina. These winds howl down the length of Huechulafquen, building endless layers of rolling whitecaps that surge and crash their oceanlike surf across the lava ledges at Boca Chimehuin.

The outlet is hourglass-shaped; its outer chamber is a deep basin shelving off into the ink-blue depths of the lake, and its gathering currents plunge through a narrow thirty-foot chute embedded in the ledge. The inner chamber of the hourglass is a gargantuan eddy punctuated with a single boulder, and the river begins below, where the current shelves off into swift riffles downstream. The currents themselves are strong and deep in the weeks after Christmas, with the last of the summer snowmelt surging down from the high country of the Andes. It is dangerous enough with the ledges

1282

and the wild currents and the angry waves themselves, but there are also ominous earthquake faults in the lava, along with huge well-size potholes worn in the ledges.

It is tough wading when you can clearly see the lava faults and ledge drop-offs and potholes. It is worse wading with a high wind driving a shoulder-high surf into your back, keening past your rod and fighting you for every inch of your double haul. Fishing and watching your footing is difficult, and it is even harder to play a large rainbow in a surf filled with such pitfalls. It is a nightmare of casting and wading, but the promise of huge fish keeps its faithful regulars coming back.

Boca Limay can be even worse, since its ledges are four or five times longer, with a deep lagoon immediately downstream. Its big fish lie above the gathering currents that spill from the lake in a vast lava shelf bright with *Dichelyma* mosses, and when one of the big rainbows is hooked it invariably runs downstream into the chute below. There is no easy way to follow a bolting fish, and a fisherman must retrace his path through the faults and the potholes, surrendering line until he reaches wadable shallows along the rocky beaches.

Sometimes the big rainbows remain hooked and the line stays free of the rocks. The lucky fishermen must then charge down along the rocky shallows recovering line, hopscotching over a shoreline of slippery grape-fruit-size stones polished smooth in the winter surf. It is some of the best fishing and worst wading in the world.

Patagonia has other rugged water. There are mile-long pools on the Chimehuin below the Larminotte Estancia, where the waist-deep currents exert a bitter, leg-wearying pressure, and even the minor channels of the huge Collón Curá are hard wading in themselves. There is other equally difficult water on the lower Traful, the sprawling Limay in its Valle Encantada, the Alumine, the Caleufu, the bone-chilling Malleo, and even the pastoral little Quilquihue in midsummer. Argentina is big water and distance casting and waist-deep wading, but it also provides some of the best big-trout fishing in the world.

There is a point to this lexicon of big-water hazards. Several years ago I fished these wild Patagonian rivers for almost two months without a single wading mishap, but when I returned to fish our April rivers in the Appalachians after that trip, I promptly fell down in a gentle smooth-gravel riffle on the Brodheads.

The lesson in that minor comedy is unmistakable. Perhaps the first rule of wading is never take a river for granted, since its character is often deceptive. The skilled fisherman knows that even the most lyric riffle holds its invisible hazards, and I had been wading along a bottom of gentle gravel, totally forgetting the algae-slick ledge that protrudes into the current in one shallow run. Watching a rising fish had been my mistake, and I was wading along carelessly while I studied its rise forms. It was like a patch of ice left on a dry sidewalk, and I went down like a supermarket sack of potatoes in less than a foot of water.

The second axiom of wading is stealth. Each pool has several small trout holding in its tail shallows, trout some writers have called its sentry fish. Clumsy wading will panic such fish, sending them scuttling toward the deeper water of the pool. Their obvious terror is contagious, and can alarm the bigger fish lying in its depths.

The skilled angler will expect such sentry fish, and will either try to catch them or ease into the pool so deliberately that they move upstream without serious disturbance. Hooking such a trout and easing it downstream from the tail shallows removes its communicable alarm from the pool. However, even the most experienced fisherman will sometimes flush the sentry fish from some totally unexpected lie.

His only option then is to rest the pool. Rather than wading upstream to fish the pool itself, the angler should exercise patience. The skilled tactician will move slowly into a good casting position and wait for the fish to forget his arrival. It sometimes takes surprisingly little time before the trout are feeding, and the fishing can commence again.

Each pool has its hierarchy or pecking order. The larger, more vigorous fish dominate its life and occupy the best positions in terms of feeding currents and concealment. Lesser fish are distributed throughout the remaining currents and holding lies. The skilled angler will always concentrate on the closest trout first, since it is both a useful yardstick for measuring selectivity in the pool and another potential sentry fish. It is almost certainly feeding on the same diet forms as the other trout in the pool, and it can serve as a litmus paper for matching the hatch. Its preference in imitative fly patterns will likely be taken by the other fish in the pool, and it should be caught if possible. Once hooked, each successive trout should be coaxed back downstream gently, to avoid frightening the others with its struggles.

Clumsy wading is perhaps the single most important reason for our failures on hard-fished waters. It has the disadvantage of making each fish aware of our presence even before we begin casting. It can be argued that poor fishing and poor wading are closely interrelated, and too many fishermen are impatient or tangle-footed in their wading.

All wading is subject to a basic axiom: in fishing water of all depths and character, regardless of feeding activity, the skilled angler must develop a smooth catlike manner of approach that quietly places him within casting range without disturbing the fish.

There is a technique to moving through the water properly. Some anglers wade just like they walk, striding out with both leg and foot, bringing their weight down on the heel as it touches the bottom. Their sidewalk strides raise a bow wave and send ripples across the current. Their heels cause rocks to grate and clatter. Such wading not only frightens the trout, but also promises painful pratfalls and duckings when the heel touches the bottom and slips. Heel-first wading spells trouble.

Proper wading technique involves a searching toe-first shuffle along the bottom. It is a pivoting step, with the sole of the foot seating itself among small stones or between larger ones. The skilled wader moves only from solid footing to solid footing, rooting his toes in the rubble, and never abandoning the security of a good bottom foothold with the first foot until the second is safely anchored against the current. It is a technique that is slow and deliberate, with the balance and stealth of the experienced angler. The best men shuffle and search, letting the free foot work the bottom with the current, raking with the sole or the edge of the foot as they probe for a suitable foothold.

The worst hallmark of poor wading is causing a wake or creating waves that spread across the current. When your passage generates a spreading disturbance, you are moving too quickly. Stumbling and slipping are other symptoms of impatient wading, but covering a river too quickly is clearly poor technique.

There are other primary wading axioms to remember: avoid wading cloudy or discolored water without knowing its bathography well; and never transfer your weight to your probing forward foot until it has determined that no shelving hole or quicksand bank or drop-off lies in wait—the probing foot is always a kind of wary reconnaissance, far better than a walking stick or a wading staff.

Proper wading staffs are ideally equipped with a connecting sling, a well-shaped grip, and a point with a bank hook. However, I seldom use a wading staff, since I feel that when I am fighting a current that calls for a staff, I am committed to a position in the river that I should not have risked. Wading staffs are also a nuisance in normal wading and are continually in the way when a fish is hooked or line is trailing in the water. However, a temporary staff is sometimes useful in crossing a heavy current. Any strong branch or small sapling should be tested thoroughly before using it, since water rot is common. It should always be employed on the upstream side, both to break the current slightly and so the angler can lean into the flow, and it should be seated firmly before moving your feet in swift water. Most important to remember: you should never commit yourself to a foothold on any large stone projecting from the bottom. Always wade around such stones, working your feet patiently in search of secure footing. Surprisingly large stones are unstable, their full weight displaced in the current, and a broken leg or fractured pelvis is the risk of such unwise wading. Another cardinal rule of wading: never cross a fast current tongue immediately above deeper water. Not only are you risking a fall, you are also threatened with being carried into deep water in boots or waders; it is always better to seek out a shallow riffle or ford. Night wading is another familiar hazard: never wade a river at night until every stone and hole and deadfall are firmly fingerprinted in your mind from long experience with the stretch. Otherwise you could find yourself swimming in a strong current, unable to see its dangers and pitfalls in the darkness.

Deep water is always hazardous. It can mean life or death, and panic can be your most deadly enemy. There are many myths about waders and hip boots in a river, and many hapless fishermen have drowned by losing the precious energy and time that it takes to strip your wading gear free. It is not necessary to remove your waders to survive, in spite of the old wives' tales, since the water will displace and float your weight even when encumbered with waterlogged waders or boots. It is possible to swim enough to survive because the water will float your gross weight—waders and water included.

You cannot swim gracefully in waders, but you will swim well enough to surface and survive if you do not panic and try to hurry or fight the waterlogged weight of your boots. Remember that the seemingly cumbersome weight of your waders, brogues, fishing vest, and other tackle is virtually weightless in water. It is sometimes difficult to stay at the surface and swim skillfully, but neither is necessary to stay alive. Knowing this rudimentary fact of survival, it is always possible to pogo-stick your way back to the surface for a series of breaths even if you are unable to stay there. Go with the current and leapfrog your way patiently toward the shallows. Remember that there is always more time between your surface trips for air than your fear and panic tell you.

Never fight the current even when it is strong and you find yourself frequently submerged. No fisherman has enough strength to fight its flow, but its frightening power can often be used against itself. Work quartering downstream with the current toward the bank, and remember that its flow will carry you to shallower water. Your greatest peril lies in striking a boulder or deadfall, losing consciousness or seriously injuring yourself. Extend your arms in the current, both for stability and outrigger protection, and push toward the shallows with your feet. When you need more air, thrust your hands upward in a swimming plane and push off from the bottom. You will reach the surface long enough for a deep breath that will help keep you alive when you are submerged again.

Panic can frequently prove fatal, but so can the failure to realize that going down in deep currents is a matter of life and death. The shallow-water fall is simply a matter of balance, and the fly rod is sometimes valuable as a balancing tool, but being swept into really deep, heavy water is ultimately a matter of luck, judgment, and energy conservation. Saving your fly rod in a desperate situation is a mistake, since you will need both hands and all your energy to survive, and trying to strip off your boots or waders is virtually impossible under water. It will only expend energy that might keep you alive. Keep your head, ride with the current instead of against it, and work patiently toward safety instead of threshing your energy away. These simple rules can get you through a dangerous accident in heavy water.

There is a popular mythology about waders and wading accidents. It holds that waders will trap air that balloons upward when you fall, riding your legs to the surface and holding your head submerged. It is a dangerous mythology that has killed some men, because they believed their waders would drown them unless they could get them off, and they wasted precious energy and time trying to jettison them. It is difficult enough getting out of

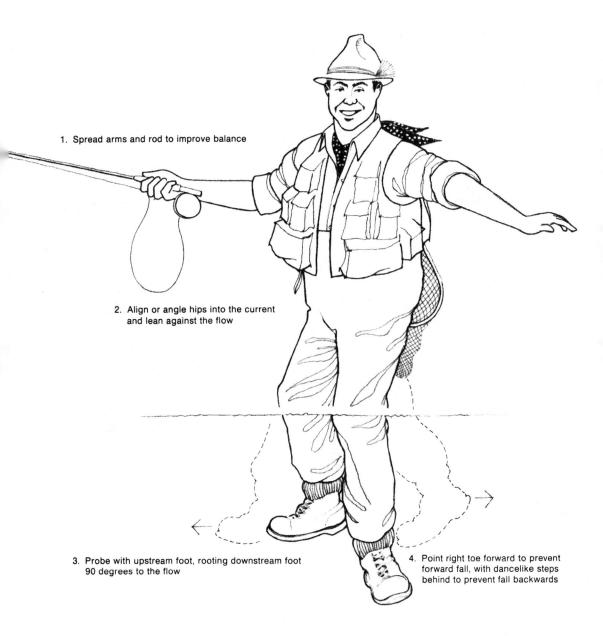

1. Spread arms and rod to improve balance

2. Align or angle hips into the current and lean against the flow

3. Probe with upstream foot, rooting downstream foot 90 degrees to the flow

4. Point right toe forward to prevent forward fall, with dancelike steps behind to prevent fall backwards

WADING BALANCE IN STRONG CURRENT

waders at the end of a day's fishing. It is impossible underwater, and all you may accomplish is stripping them down to your knees or ankles, literally tying your legs together. Since the water pressure of deep wading forces your waders tightly against your body, almost like a second skin, it is clear that there is little or no air left inside them. The popular mythology is wrong. They cannot balloon your legs to the surface and drown you, and if you want proof, try it yourself in shallow water some time.

Fishing writers have long argued about wearing a belt through your wader loops. Some believe it will keep the water out when you fall and make swimming in waders easier. Others contend that it will only seal the supposedly fatal air inside your wader legs and drown you when they balloon upside down. Neither argument really holds water, so to speak, but wearing a belt tightly cinched around your middle will give your back some support during a long day's wading and casting, it will slim your silhouette in heavy currents, and it will keep the water from flooding in when you fall: that means safety as well as less time before you dry out your gear and get fishing again.

The ability to wade skillfully is perhaps the most underrated requirement in angling. Proficient waders can reach fish their companions cannot cover effectively. Sometimes deep wading will permit a casting or fly-swing position that will take a fish when nothing else will. The angler who is confident of his wading skills on a broken, algae-smooth bottom is better able to concentrate on the other aspects of his fishing, and in practical terms, will lose less time because he does not stop casting to concentrate on his balance in a difficult reach of river.

Deep wading on a small river is both discourteous and a tactical mistake, since it inevitably disturbs the fish in their principal holding currents. It will reduce your catch and is certainly unfair to those who will fish the water after you. However, deep wading on big water is a necessity for reaching the bigger fish.

Quiet-water wading requires the care to make no sudden movements and to hold current disturbances to a minimum. Little strength is required, but patience and poise are important. Wading difficult water requires patience, poise, *and* a mixture of physical strength, coordination, good reflexes, experience, and a modicum of daring. Skilled wading is an acquired skill that borders on art itself.

Perhaps it might be useful to speculate on the physiology of the ideal big-water wader. It is obvious that body weight itself is an advantage in holding a position in the current. However, body weight and strength are not an unmixed blessing. Both must be combined with the reflexes and agility to control their potential. The optimal wader is heavy, but not corpulent; his bulk should not be a barrier in the current. His weight must be matched by strength in his legs. Height is also an advantage, since the tall fisherman can obviously wade deeper than his short-legged companions. The distribution of his weight is important too. Weight in the chest and shoulders is better than thick-muscled thighs and a bulging waistline, although leg strength is unquestionably important. Remember that weight under water is displaced and essentially weightless. It is the combined weight of a fisherman and his tackle vest above the water that counts.

It is clear that not too many of us, including the writer, meet each of these ideal criteria. It remains for all of us blessed with less than optimal physiques to compensate for our shortcomings in physical attributes, and make the best of what we have with intelligence and skill. Understanding our physical limitations is important, since that self-knowledge will permit us to adapt our tactics in terms of our weaknesses.

Perhaps a brief summary of wading axioms would prove useful. Agility and sure-footedness are the final hallmarks of the accomplished wader. His feet quickly search out firm footholds, but must always be ready to react the millisecond a stone rolls or shifts under them, skating artfully into a new position or working the free foot behind his ankle, like a quick cross-legged dance step to regain his balance. Sometimes the necessary reaction is the lower center of gravity in a catlike crouch, surrendering gracefully when both footholds slip, and a fisherman is forced to scramble and probe for a new footing from his knees. No angler is completely safe from the perils of shifting stones, shelving bottoms of loose sand and gravel, slippery ledges and bedrock and marl, surprising holes and drop-offs, and deceptively deep or swift currents, but his reflexes and wading skills can usually prevent a serious mishap in most cases.

Wader construction itself can help and hinder the exercise of such reflexes and skills. Lightweight waders designed for fly-fishermen are obviously best, since they facilitate movement and quick reaction time. Heavy-duty and industrial-type waders are designed to last under working conditions, not the demands of swift-water wading, with its premium on agility and cat-quick reactions. Quality waders are important in trout fishing comfort and effectiveness.

Balance is critical too, and I often stand on one foot while putting on waders as a kind of calisthenic drill. Sometimes it is important to maintain your footing on one leg long enough to secure a new foothold. The arms are important also, since extending them will help recover lost footing.

The fly rod itself can also work to help your balance. There are two principal ways an angler can use his fly rod for greater wading safety. It can be used as a simple balancing device held at arm's length, and I always cross a strong current with both arms and fly rod extended. It is surprising how much the use of the fly rod as a balancing aid helps in shallow swift-water wading. Such use of the fly rod is familiar to all experienced anglers, but the skilled wader can also use his rod as a wading staff or submerged outrigger. It was the late Joe Brooks who pioneered this bold use of the fly rod in wading safety, and these passages come from his recent *Trout Fishing*:

> I was about thirty feet from the bank, in knee-deep water, when my right foot slipped on a round stone and I started to fall to my

right. I was holding my fly rod in front of me, and automatically I pushed the rod through the air hard, to my left, then immediately snapped it back to my right. The spring of the rod broke the impetus of my fall and kept me erect, and I finished the trip ashore in safety.

Later that same day, I was wading in water that was waist-deep. I was moving altogether too fast. My toe bumped a rock with such force that I began to pitch forward. This time I swung the rod hard into the water downstream and pushed down for three feet. The strong, continued drive of the long fly rod against the density of the water stopped my fall, and gave me enough leverage to regain my balance.

These are only two of the many ways you can use your fly rod as a safety device in wading. The average fisherman who finds himself about to tumble instinctively thinks of saving his rod. He is afraid he will break it in the fall. This might very well happen if you fall on land, but not so in the water. Certainly waving it in the air or thrusting it down into the water, however hard, is not going to do it any harm. Its use as a balancing agent can save you tumbles that range from the merely laughable to disastrous. For a good many years, I have used my rod boldly as an aid to wading, and have never yet damaged one in this way. In an emergency, you can even use your rod as a wading staff, butt down into the

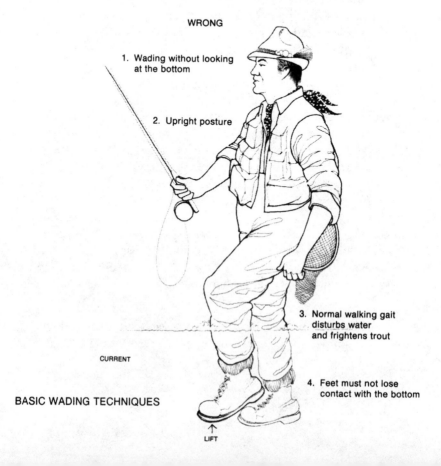

WRONG

1. Wading without looking at the bottom

2. Upright posture

3. Normal walking gait disturbs water and frightens trout

CURRENT

4. Feet must not lose contact with the bottom

BASIC WADING TECHNIQUES

LIFT

river, without hurting it. Your fly rod is tough, and your life is short, so don't worry about the rod.

It should perhaps be understood that Brooks is writing about relatively heavy rods, between eight and a half and nine feet in length, and weighing more than four and a half ounces, and he is not talking about slapping the rod down hard into the water. Such treatment is obviously not recommended for fine equipment. It should also be noted that a rod used as such an underwater outrigger should always be extended laterally or downstream into the current. It should never be thrust upstream, since its tip will be driven into the bottom and breakage is likely. Heavy-water wading usually requires medium-to-heavy rods, and their use in wading balance can be important. These paragraphs from *Trout Fishing* are a useful epilogue for the subject:

When you get into a heavy stretch of current you can lower the rod on your downstream side, slanting it into the water, so it is a foot under the surface, right up to the butt. You'll be surprised at the sudden ease of wading, at how it takes the pressure off. If you should slip you can immediately push down with the rod, or backward or forward as the occasion demands, and save the day. Time and again I have done this and have marvelled at the extra sense of balance I can achieve through the use of the rod.

You don't have to be falling in before you discover what your

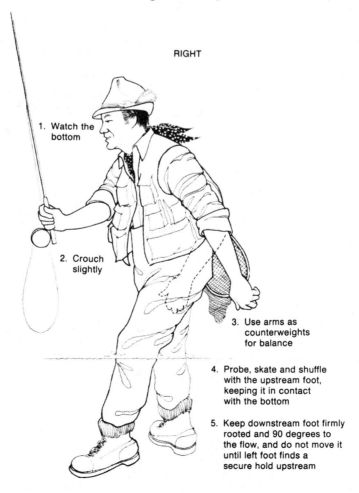

RIGHT

1. Watch the bottom

2. Crouch slightly

3. Use arms as counterweights for balance

4. Probe, skate and shuffle with the upstream foot, keeping it in contact with the bottom

5. Keep downstream foot firmly rooted and 90 degrees to the flow, and do not move it until left foot finds a secure hold upstream

rod can do for you. Most falls happen so quickly that they call for instant reaction, so you should practice using the rod in this way. Next time you are in a stream, hold the rod in the water and swing it from side to side, and up and down. Try the same thing in the air to see how its flexing works as a balancing agent. You will soon get the feel of it as you realize that both water and air have a certain amount of resistance you can take advantage of. When you are wading and slip even slightly, work your rod, and soon you will bring it automatically into play.

Strength and physical condition are perhaps more important in wading heavy water than in any other part of fly-fishing, since even distance casting is more a function of timing than raw muscle. Muscle tone, wind, and endurance are certainly critical to your survival in an emergency. However, mere strength is wasted when it is not leavened with speed and dexterity. When it comes to crossing or holding in a heavy current, there is certainly no substitute for strength, particularly in the thigh muscles.

However, these multiple skills of agility, balance, and strength are perhaps less important than judgment and knowledge. It is experience that measures depth accurately through water color and clarity and reads the character of the bottom from the surface currents. It understands that the reverse eddies and bottom friction can be used in fighting a heavy flow. It is the ability to wade a familiar river in spate without seeing the bottom, or working it at night with a precise image of its singular cartography in your mind. It is the cunning and stealth that can move up a silk-smooth flat without sending a ripple to warn its trout. Each of these skills of judgment and knowledge is the product of many summers of fishing experience accumulated in layers like the slate ledges above a favorite pool.

All anglers have fallen from time to time, and I have often seen good friends go down clumsily with that seriocomic expression of disbelief, but few realize how serious a bad fall can be. Wet rocks and clay banks and deadfalls are always slippery and dangerous, and falling there is more deadly, with no current to cushion our impact. Such a fall can easily fracture an arm or leg, and some hapless anglers have shattered necks and spines. Concussions and skull fractures are also common, and the principal reasons many anglers are drowned. Yet most such accidents can be avoided with careful wading.

Fast-water wading poses some unique problems. It is typically easier to wade a waist-deep reach of water than a swift-running shallows that tumbles past your knees. Such currents wear the gravel from under your feet, and tend to force them right out from under you. It is poor judgment to cross a river in such places, and it is best to ford the tail shallows of a pool rather than the currents above its throat. If possible, always pick a moderate current at least three feet deep. But sometimes you are forced to cross a shallow rapids. The rules for such a crossing are simple.

Shuffle and plant each foot firmly, twisting it into the bottom gravel until it is seated. The other foot is then moved cautiously into position, parallel to the current so your body is never broadside into the force of the river. The first foot is never shifted until the second is secure. Sometimes a swift shallows is strewn with boulders. The experienced wader knows he can use the back-eddies behind these stones, and the stones themselves, in crossing such water. It is possible to brace your legs against the rocks, and in relatively shallow places they form handholds. There are also small gravel footholds behind many boulders, and a skilled wader can work from one gravelly back-eddy to another in crossing a heavy current.

Two anglers can cross a strong current with surprising ease, simply by locking arms across their shoulders. Both follow the basic rules of wading, and only one man moves at a time, while the other maintains his secure footing. It is a trick worth knowing on big rivers, where the partner system is often wise.

Few anglers realize that a loose stone on the bottom is virtually weightless. It is completely unstable unless it is firmly imbedded in the bottom. Each season the early spates change a river radically, washing in new shoals of stones and uprooting boulders. Such stones are usually polished smooth in the current. The skilled angler will never commit his weight to unfamiliar stones, either in the current or along its banks, without tentatively testing their stability. It is possible to shuffle and push at such stones before stepping on them fully. Unstable rocks are particularly hazardous.

Swift shallows are often deceptive, with currents much heavier than they seem. Big stones narrow and accelerate the currents between them. Sometimes they will dislodge an angler's feet, turning him broadside into the flow, and forcing him into deeper water or dropping him to his knees. Being forced downstream brings into play a dangerous inertial force that is difficult to counter once it has gained momentum. Being forced to your knees facing upstream is difficult too, since the current makes it almost impossible to dig in your toes. It may seem embarrassing to come crawling out of the current, particularly in front of your friends, but it may prove your only solution.

Except in relatively moderate currents, an angler should never wade upstream facing into the flow. During actual fishing, you usually stand quartering into the current and move slowly, but our principal concern here is with crossing a river. Facing directly downstream poses similar problems, with the full force of the current striking you from behind. It is best to angle sideways into the flow, working patiently downstream to cross. It is much easier to wade with the current than against it. Probe downstream with one foot until it is secure, seat the second below it, and search the bottom with the first again. Such a system of careful probing is good insurance against stepping into a hole, off an unseen ledge, into hazardous muck or marl, or into a shelving bank of loose sand.

It should always be remembered that in wading downstream across a river, it is possible that you may encounter unexpectedly deep currents and have to come back. It can lead to serious trouble, and you should explore alternate routes to safety. Otherwise you may have to fight your way back against the current, and that can prove impossible on many big rivers.

Turning back into the current is one of the most dangerous moments in big-water wading. It usually happens in surprisingly deep water, with the current up to your fly boxes and threatening your wader tops. Such difficulties can occur when you are fording a relatively unfamiliar place, or rainfall has raised the river slightly. Sometimes you are tempted to wade deep, casting to a rising fish or a promising run, and you find yourself in trouble before you know it. Finding the current too heavy, you decide to turn back. Turning is the critical moment, since you must momentarily face the current broadside.

Always pivot into the current, keeping your knees flexed and ready, and lean slightly into the flow. Start your pivot facing across the current, with your feet fairly close together. Cautiously turn your upstream foot into the current, pointing your toe upstream. Seat that foot carefully, and then bring the downstream foot into position. Repeat the sequence cautiously until you have made a full half turn, and are edging sideways into the current, leaning against its pressure. Your feet must remain relatively close together during this change of direction. It is equally important that you always move your upstream foot first, bringing the downstream foot toward it later. You should lean and dig hard into the current once you have turned, since getting started against the flow at all is critical.

It is a good axiom never to turn your back fully into the current when trying to return upstream from a dangerous position encountered wading down. Returning successfully involves turning the downstream foot back toward the bank, in exactly the opposite of the pivot described above. It is sometimes quite hazardous. The force of the water will commonly start you downstream against your will, and once it has you freewheeling without sound footing, it is extremely difficult to stop. Digging in your heels is more difficult than getting a toehold considering the flexibility and leverage of the ankle and foot.

Finding yourself with a powerful current at your back, with its force too strong to fight, turning back is often clearly impossible. Sometimes the water is simply too deep and strong to turn, and you must simply go with the river, riding its flow into still deeper water. Angle downstream toward the shallows if possible then, bouncing on your tiptoes and leaning forward slightly. Push off with alternate feet, using the force of the current, and it is possible to hopscotch forward as much as three and four feet. It is usually possible to reach the shore or wadable shallows in this manner, even in very large rivers.

When fishing big water, it may be wise to wear a floating tackle jacket, inflatable vest, or wading safety belt. Some fishermen prefer carrying a small pocket life preserver that clips to their clothing and inflates with a sharp pressure of the fingers. Such wading insurance is relatively cheap.

Abrupt changes in depth are dangerous too. Most rivers have ledges and drop-offs, even in bottoms of fine sand and pea-size gravel. Rock ledges are usually visible and obvious. Some are outcroppings worn smooth in the current, but others are lava flows that have halted or cooled into strange subaquatic formations. Such volcanic bottoms are often unpredictable, but their potholes clearly reveal themselves by their water color. Shelving sandbars and gravel shoals are more dangerous, because their hazards are less obvious. The scouring current often sculptures such bars to surprising depths and channels. The sand and gravel and silt on such shelving edges is often merely a loose emulsion of unpacked bottom materials, treacherous and seemingly solid enough, but offering no footing to an unsuspecting angler. It is a hazard that often exists where a river enters a lake, forming a shallow alluvial structure which shelves off into deep water. The smaller inlets on the famous Argentine lakes are typical of such perils, with gravel shallows of silt, volcanic sand, and detritus that drop off suddenly into frighteningly deep water. Such shallows are sometimes as dangerous as quicksand. Careful wading, with each step a cautious probing of the bottom before committing your full weight, is the only means of detecting such treacherous conditions. Sensing the almost fluid character of the shelving material, you still have time to retreat safely, and if you feel the bottom go soft under your brogues, turn back quickly and dig hard for safe footing. Rapid half-swimming thrusts of your legs will often carry you to safety, unless you have blundered into really deep water.

Silt beds and marl pose still other problems. Sometimes they are found in weedy reaches of rivers and backwaters, and they are common in both the spring creeks of our western mountains and our eastern limestone streams. Wading in such bottom conditions is sometimes tactically necessary. The primary rule of soft-bottom wading is to never commit your full weight to any untested position. Once you are fishing in muck or marl, you should frequently shift your feet to make sure it is still possible to extricate yourself. Sometimes getting stuck is only embarrassing, but it also has its ominous possibilities. It is possible to become completely trapped without realizing it, and any attempt to take another step then ends in a sudden loss of balance. The surprise can result in a clumsy fall, with the frightening consequence of a broken ankle or the inability to regain your feet in rather deep water. Wading in silt must always be taken seriously.

There are some minor techniques of soft-bottom wading you should also remember. Slide your foot forward, searching and probing gently to discover how deep it will sink. When you find a firm footing, commit the second foot and seek out a solid bottom. Sometimes a layer of silt or detritus is relatively thin, lying over a foundation of dense sand or gravel. Other deposits are thick, and even a cautious wader will sometimes find himself sinking waist-deep into the muck. Get out of such water immediately. Work the easiest leg free first, extricating it patiently and without panic, and seat it again in better bottom. Sometimes the muck and marl are so adhesive and thick that a boot-foot wader is stripped from your foot; it is difficult to force it back on your foot, yet you must accomplish it before continuing. You must not panic and waste your strength. Free each foot patiently and carefully from the silt in its turn, keeping your wits and jealousy husbanding your remaining energy.

Similar problems can present themselves when you are fishing from dense beds of watercress or matted weeds around a beaver pond. It is sometimes possible to kneel on such growths safely even when they will not support the concentrated weight of a standing fisherman. But fish such water carefully, with a full sense of its several hazards. Beaver sticks pose an obvious secondary hazard to both your legs and your waders in such waters, since they are sometimes dangerously sharp. It is possible to avoid them with proper caution. However, should you become snared in such watercress and weeds, extricate yourself with a mixture of patience and alacrity in spite of the beaver sticks.

We have concerned ourselves primarily with problems of safety and technique, and the first axiom of wading is alertness. But the second is stealth, and it has the most effect upon consistent fishing success. Combined with patience and cunning, it is the principal quality of wading that catches hard-fished trout. Noisy wading and waves will obviously frighten them, but so will the careless sound of brogues on gravel, or the impact of a stone dislodged and carried along the bottom. Stealth is a critical skill, and its importance was demonstrated years ago by an old fisherman on the Willowemoc. It was early summer in the Catskills, and the river was low and warm. The old man was on his knees in the shallows above the Covered Bridge, fishing the dark run in the shade of the trees.

Any luck? he asked.

It's pretty slow this morning, I answered. *Fishing on your knees must be pretty hard on your waders!*

Knees wear out first on brown trout, he smiled.

3. Studies in Striking Problems and Techniques

The secret spring creek was ahead through the cottonwoods, its smooth currents glittering with a gentle wind. It was one of those marvelous wine-aired mornings in Wyoming. Bright clouds sailed briskly against the early sky, and the sun was already getting warm. The stream is not really a tributary of the Snake, but a high-water channel cut years earlier during some unusual snowmelt. It had cut through several springheads at the base of a barren moraine, and their underground flow filled its channel through the marshy bottoms in the last half mile above the river. It was a secret place filled with big trout.

Bob Carmichael had drawn a perfect map in his little tackle shop at Moose Crossing. Every good fly-fisherman I know has that kind of total recall about the water he knows well, and some carry the pool-by-pool details of many rivers in their minds.

Beavers had constructed several barriers across its flow just above its junction with the spreading pewter-colored currents of the Snake. Their dams had deepened the flow into two hundred feet of silken waist-deep flat. Bright green weeds trailed sensually in the smooth currents along the silty bottom, and a giant spruce had fallen across its flow. Above the bleached skeleton of the spruce deadfall, the spring creek flattened into a pondlike bend and wound away from the river. There were fountain mosses and lily pads there, and a giant heron rose awkwardly from its early-morning fishing.

You watch that bottom flat round the snag, Carmichael had instructed me firmly. *Mostly little fish, but there's been a good rainbow there.*

How good? I asked.

Four pounds. Carmichael frowned and closed a mahogany drawer filled with dry flies. *Maybe five or six.*

Thanks, I gasped weakly.

Twenty-odd years ago, a fish that large sounded absolutely Melvillian, and it is still a big trout anywhere from the Labrador to Tierra del Fuego. The thought that such a trophy rainbow might be lying along the deadfall upstream was enough to send my pulse racing, and I moved stealthily into the current, taking care to telegraph no telltale ripples into the flat.

There was a hatch of Pale Morning Olives coming off the still current now, and a number of small fish began to work below the deadfall. The little mayflies sailboated everywhere across the water. It was tempting to fish the rising trout, but I watched for the big rainbow under the spruce jam.

Finally there was a strong sucking rise tight against the deadfall, and its after-rise lapped along the pale branches. It was not a showy rise, but it did not seem like a small fish. There was something about the gentle swirl that sounded a warning in my senses, and I worked patiently upstream within range. The fish was rising steadily now, and I could see its pale green length hovering against the branches.

Calm, I kept telling myself. *Keep calm!*

My fly box held two or three fine little imitations dressed with pale olive gray hackles, and I clinch-knotted one to a delicate 6X tippet. The cast unfolded perfectly and dropped the little fly about a foot above the fish. It settled and cocked on the current, and I held my breath. The fish drifted out to intercept its float, poised and waiting, and when it finally rose and broke the surface, I took the fly away awkwardly.

The big fish threshed when I struck, and bolted up the pondlike flat, leaving a frightened wake that traced his exit.

Damn! I thought unhappily. *You struck him too soon!*

Its flight had also frightened the smaller trout in the lower stretch, and I waded upstream looking for others. The spring creek wound across a willow flat, its deeply undercut banks thigh-deep in coarse grass. Springs bubbled and flowed from the bottom gravel where the channel narrowed, and in the shallows above I crossed the creek. The right bank was densely lined with willows, and I wanted to fish from the grassy bank across the current. Once across I crouched in the tall grass and studied the flat patiently for rising fish.

There was a good swirl along the willows, and I swiftly placed my fly above the roots. It floated along the jackstraw tangle of sticks, and was apparently ignored, and then I saw another rise farther upstream. My fly was still coming down drag-free over the marl shallows when suddenly it disappeared in a violent swirl that took me completely by surprise.

Missed him! I said angrily to myself.

Several big cutthroats cruised past and I caught my breath, since two were at least twenty-five inches long. Apparently, one of these fish had taken my fly when the school came down the current, foraging lazily along the bottom. Such schools of trout were common on that particular creek, but on that introductory morning they were completely unexpected, and my reaction to the rise was pathetically late.

My nerves were shattered now. The fish came cruising back slowly, passed upstream along the undercut banks, and I placed my dry fly ahead of the restless school. It bobbed tight against the bunchgrass bank. There was a sucking rise a few inches downstream from my little Olive, and my heart stopped again. The fly disappeared in a rapier-quick swirl a half second later, and I sheared the tippet with a heavy-handed strike that could have driven a 9/0 hook into a marlin off Cabo Blanco.

It's not your morning, I sighed.

Less than an hour had passed, and three big fish had taken my dry fly eagerly, while I had reacted clumsily each time. Three rises and three basic mistakes in striking: taking the fly away from a fish I could see coming to its float, striking too late to hook a trout that had already taken and ejected my fly, and leaving the fly in a fish when I struck too hard.

Such mistakes are common. It is interesting that most fishing writers concentrate on such matters as casting and stream tactics and fly patterns, all subjects focused on presentation of our imitation to a feeding trout and getting that fish to accept that fly. Virtually nothing is written about what should be done once it takes the fly, after it has been successfully hooked, when it is finally ready to surrender, or how it should best be killed mercifully or carefully released.

Ray Bergman devoted only a brief page in *Trout* to problems of striking fish, but his concerns were primarily with those off days when our timing and reflexes go sour, or when a run of misfortune along the river is upsetting enough to affect our fishing. However, when his book was first published forty-odd years ago, hook sizes of twenty were the limit of small-fly fishing. Since then, the development of several sizes below twenty has introduced a galaxy of new problems in striking. Hook size is perhaps less critical than the revolution in synthetic tippet materials and workable limp nylons between .006 and .003, testing between two pounds and one-half-pound breaking strain with rods of delicate calibrations. The evolution of such ultralight tackle and minute flies is the kind of technical breakthrough that transforms an entire sport, although Bergman is still correct in his rudimentary observations about striking.

There is no question about the impact of our moods and other peripheral aggravations on the quality of our fishing. It is difficult to move swiftly from the hypertension of work and business to the pastoral world of the river, and there is a psychological inertia of yesterday and its pressures that cannot easily be erased today. Such pressures have their effect on our temperament and the application of our physical skills. Anyone who has been deeply involved in competitive sport is richly aware of the variables in his performance, between poor days and inexplicably good days across the full spectrum of the season. Fly-fishing is surprisingly similar in its cycles. There are days when you cast nothing but wind knots, put fish down with the heavy-handed settling of your line, and spend what seems like hours extricating your flies from a labyrinth of streamside branches.

There are other days when your moods and casting skills and reflexes all seem to mesh, and each cast unrolls like poetry, settling on the water to provide an unending series of drag-free floats over fish that are rising steadily. The fish take freely, are all hooked well in spite of your tiny flies, and you play them skillfully. It may always sound like that when angling writers describe their exploits astream, but such days are painfully rare, even for the best fly-fishermen. It is better to prepare yourself mentally for those times when things are less perfect—or when they completely fall apart literally and figuratively.

Most problems in striking come on such misbegotten days, and are a mixture of preoccupation and clumsiness. Sometimes the difficulty lies in fishing for other species when there is no time for trips into trout country. Trout present a singular problem composed partially of the light tackle necessary to fool them on hard-fished water and the rapierlike quickness of their rises. Bass are a hard-mouthed species that strike a lure rather slowly. The hook must be set hard to sink it into their jaws, while a trout has a relatively soft mouth compared with its agility and strength and size. Over the years I have caught many bass, including hair-frog fish of six pounds, but I have largely stopped fishing them. It is impossible to fish bass, with their hard jaw structure and lazy striking rhythm, and switch easily to light-tackle fishing for selective trout. Setting the hook of a hair frog into a hard-mouthed bass is completely different from striking a two-pound trout that has just taken your tiny ant fished on a cobweb-fine tippet. With the reflexes of most fishermen, the strike that hooked a four-pound largemouth last weekend will either come too late or break off in the deep-bellied brown that porpoises to a tiny ant this morning.

There is a kind of trinity of errors in striking. Our reactions are often too quick, too late, or much too hard. Sometimes a run of small fish will badger us into a striking rhythm that will either take the fly away from a good trout or break off against its sudden weight. Faulty reaction time is a common mistake, and the small-fish jitters can trigger such poor striking behavior.

Salmon fishermen understand that the rise-form behavior of large fish is more deliberate than the splashiness of their half-grown cousins. There is an old axiom in salmon fishing that no salmon has ever been lost by not striking, but that thousands have been lightly hooked or missed when the fly was snatched away in the middle of their rise. It is not entirely true, but there is considerable wisdom in the argument. The deliberate rise of a salmon is an exaggerated version of the slow taking rhythms typical of big trout, and the more deliberate your reaction, the better the percentages that such a fish will be hooked well.

Good striking is also a function of how well left-hand slack is handled by the fisherman, and controlled slack is critical to good dry-fly work. There are several methods of handling both the line and deliberately raising the rod tip, as well as skilled combinations of both techniques. Some anglers hold the line under the rod-grip index finger and smoothly strip in line with the left hand at exactly the speed of the approaching current and fly. It takes a little practice to handle such slack effectively, with a smooth stripping of the line without dragging or disturbing the natural float of the dry fly, but it can be done skillfully. Extremely swift currents may demand the combination of a left-hand strip, coordinated with a raising of the fly rod calculated to match the speed of the current. Control of left-hand slack is also possible with a rolling hand motion not unlike an exaggerated hand-twist retrieve. Some fishermen strip in their slack with a series of rhythmic loops gathered in the left hand, anticipating the flow of the current, and it is important to remember in dry-fly fishing that stripping in slack is critical to striking and hooking any trout that subsequently takes your floating fly.

Similar problems exist with excessively slack-line swings in wet-fly and nymph fishing, and with the deep-bellying behavior of a sinking line. Skillful striking at such times demands another range of skills, compensating for the sinking slack and bottom-bellying swing of a high-density line with a striking reflex strong enough to neutralize that slack and hook a taking fish. These striking skills all vary with current speed and the amount of bellying line committed to the river, and no mere discussion in these pages can supply the physical variables that are awakened in many seasons of fishing on widespread rivers and streams.

The position of the fisherman and his proximity to both the fish and its holding currents are major factors in proper striking. Trout lying upstream are usually hooked well if the fisherman has learned to manipulate his left-hand slack. Fish lying directly downstream are another matter. Although they cannot detect the leader, since the fly approaches them before the terminal tackle or because the final moments of a wet-fly presentation hang almost directly downstream, the pure downstream strike is a problem. Often a fish lying below us is merely lip-hooked when it comes to the fly and is seldom hooked well unless it takes in a rolling swirl that seats the fly deeply in the corner of its jaws. Downstream strikes are also difficult to time properly, and a deliberate reaction is perhaps best, waiting for the fish to take the fly as deeply as possible. Our inability to delay our usual striking rhythm on a straight downstream float perhaps accounts for the high percentage of lightly hooked or missed fish from that angle.

As I write this, I have recently been fishing the weedy meadow reaches of Silver Creek in Idaho. Its selective rainbows are extremely tippet-shy, and on some particularly deep places, the local fishermen like to float down its glassy currents in a specially designed fishing tube. It is an effective method for such streams, both for still reaches too deep to wade and for their dangerous bottoms of silt and marl. Since you are often floating with the wind or with a relatively slow chalkstream current, the straight downstream presentation is common in tube fishing. The local experts who fish Silver Creek have considerable experience in striking a fish directly downstream, and men like Bill Mason and John Hemingway, the oldest son of the late Ernest Hemingway, advise a deliberate striking rhythm in casting to rising fish downstream.

Fish lying directly upstream are often quite close to the drift of the leader, and the pull of the strike usually seats the hook well into the corner of their jaw mandibles. However, the too-quick strike will often take the fly away from a fish rising directly upstream, sometimes foul-hooking it in the head or the eye socket or the pectoral fin. It is also easy to take the fly away from a fish lying directly across the stream, although a properly timed strike usually hooks it perfectly. Trout seldom strike as slowly as salmon, but the consciously delayed reflex developed in Scotland for fishing the greased-line method on salmon is useful on trout water too. It provides a brief millisecond of conscious delay to allow the fly swing inside the mouth of a large fish to reach the optimal hooking place, firmly in the corner of its jaw mandibles.

Fishing bucktails and streamers properly often demands a similar delayed strike. Trout coming to bucktails and streamers often show themselves long before they actually reach the fly, and our surging adrenalin simply cannot allow a controlled striking rhythm. Whenever you take the fly away from such fish, cast back to their holding positions after a few seconds; you can sometimes take them a second time with an exaggeratedly slow striking rhythm, punctuated with a brisk setting of the hook when they clearly have the fly.

Fishing spiders and skaters in the skittering Hewitt-style poses similar problems. The fish are often seen coming toward the fly long before they actually reach it, and sometimes they jump into the air, intending to take on their downward trajectory. Such spectacular behavior is often too much for our nerves, and we succeed only in snatching the fly away.

John Alden Knight frequently wrote about the excitement that skaters can cause among the fish, triggering both acrobatic takes and splashy false rises, and Knight often used these moods to locate fish that might be sought conventionally at another time. However, the actual taking of a fluttering skater or spider-style dressing is a difficult rise form. Both a splashy hit and the acrobatic pole-vaulting rise that takes the fly on return to the water absolutely require delayed striking. Proper timing demands an exaggerated pause until the fish has clearly taken the fly and disappeared with it, and the strike should be rather sharply executed.

Rises to wet flies and nymphs involve several striking methods as well. The deep-fished nymph along the bottom means that there is virtually no time to spare between the flash or pull of a taking fish and our striking response. Fishing deep to a visible fish means striking when it turns visibly in its line of drift and clearly opens its mouth to take something along the bottom, in the English nymphing method perfected by Frank Sawyer on the Wiltshire Avon. Fish often take so gently when nymphing along the bottom or in the middle layers of current that it is already too late by the time the strike is telegraphed back through the bellying line. Striking must be hard enough to overcome the line friction of a deep fly swing, and quick enough to set the hook before the fish has ejected the fly.

Dave Whitlock is a skilled nymph fisherman who maintains that many nymph takes are so subtle that the tug we finally sense in our fly swing is really the hook raking along the head or body of the fish, its actual take having gone undetected a millisecond before. Whitlock advocates the use of a bright orange tube locking together his epoxy knot between line and leader butt, and other experts use bright lacquer nail knots of various hot-chroma colors. These nymph-bobbers are an extremely effective device for detecting a rise we cannot actually feel. The angler must follow their swing in the current, striking quickly when they slow or pause with what is often an invisible take.

The nymph fished in the film or just under the surface involves a striking rhythm not unlike that found in dry-fly technique, except that the visual clues of an actual rise are less obvious. The pausing twitch of the floating line, or the Whitlock plastic-tube bobber, is a clue that can precede any telltale bulge in the current. However, the wet fly or nymph presented to a fish working visibly just under the surface should be struck at the first variation or bulge in the current above its taking station, since such gentle disturbances often signal a subsurface rise to your drifting fly.

Tiny midge-size imitations of both aquatic and terrestrial flies offer special problems in striking. Such small hooks are extremely sharp, and the distance between point and barb is minute. Normal striking energy too often pulls such tiny hooks right on through the jaw membranes, although anglers are often heard complaining that such small hooks have no holding power. It is quite untrue: a tiny hook has superb hooking and holding qualities so long as your striking and playing is not too heavy-handed. Too much muscle in your striking reflex and in fighting a hooked trout will slice its tiny point through and lose the fish. Experience in playing fish with light tippets and tiny hooks is the only cure for losing too many fish on midge-size flies.

There are several methods of dampening such heavy-handed strikes. Some fishermen use the index-finger grip when fishing fine tackle, since it will not permit the full muscle power of the wrist to come into play. Other possible solutions all involve will power and self-discipline. Some fishermen who live on streams having a high percentage of tiny fly species have developed a left-hand strike with the fly line, holding the rod itself absolutely still. It is difficult to strike too hard with such a short wrist pull on the line. Other fishermen faithful to tiny flies have developed a conscious wrist strike that employs no arm movement; still others have learned to drop the rod tip instead of raising it when a fish takes the fly. This method transmits enough energy along the line to set a tiny hook, but seldom shears a fine tippet if properly executed.

Perhaps our final observations on striking a fish should concentrate on self-discipline and calm. There is something about a rise of fish, beginning with the hatching of the first few insects and the steadily building rhythms of the feeding trout, that can cause a rising excitement in all of us. Without control we lose our ability to fish with skill and judgment. Such self-control is critical.

Some weeks ago I was fishing skater flies on a still Slough Creek flat in the Yellowstone with two friends who had not fished them before. The trout were concentrating on some recently hatched craneflies that were hanging in the willows along the stream and clumsily fluttering across the current. It was a classic situation for skater tactics.

The fish were eagerly splashing at these *Tipulidae* whenever one hopscotched over their holding lies, and we simply skittered our long-hackled dry flies in likely places. Some of the fish took splashily, and my companions soon learned to delay their strikes well enough to hook several. We were fishing along a deeply undercut reach of water, where the coarse grasses trailed in the dark current, when a huge cutthroat cartwheeled into the sun and tried to take a twitching skater.

You struck too soon, I yelled. *You've got to let him jump and come down and actually get the fly in its mouth.*

Dammit, the man stammered, *I didn't strike at all!*

Didn't strike? I laughed. *Your line and your arm are both behind you.*

He studied his arm and his fly line unhappily, like they both belonged to someone else. *Guess I did take it away from him,* he finally mumbled. *Maybe I should rest him and try again in a few minutes.*

Try a Valium first, his friend yelled.

4. The Secrets of
Playing Trout

I t is cool in the early morning, and the light is soft on the wind-sculptured hills surrounding Sun Valley when you start downstream after breakfast at the Christiania House. The wind is still against the pale skies not long after daylight, and the cottonwoods along the Big Wood bottoms below the town are turning yellow with the first September frosts, the bright confetti of their leaves drifting on the current. It is perhaps the best time for trout fishing on Silver Creek, in the season of cold autumn nights glittering with stars and the hot, windless mornings that follow, when the water is literally covered with tiny mayflies.

The river valley opens gradually below Hailey, where the bluffs are eroded away along the tumbling currents of the river beyond the town. There are rich haymeadows farther downstream toward Picabo, with intricately rigged irrigation sprinklers working in delicate rainbows of misting spray.

The smooth sagebrush hills are pewter-colored, lying some distance from the highway where the Gannett road turns off along their lower slopes toward the table-flat floor of the valley ahead. Its haymeadows conceal nothing for miles except a few ranches and their outbuildings, lying against wind-smooth foothills that rise a few hundred feet into the morning light. Except for the irrigation ditches lying as straight as a surveyor's line across the bottoms, there is no trace of water in the valley from the road, and the alkaline dust rising up behind the camper is bitter in the nostrils.

It doesn't look like trout country, I said.

André Puyans was driving toward the stream now. *It's trout country all right,* he said. *It's unique!*

It sure is! David Inks agreed happily.

1305

The Purdey Ranch lay ahead, and there was still no sign of the river. No trees or willows marked its serpentine course across the valley floor, and only a faint line of cattails and sharp-tipped reeds betrayed its existence. We stopped to sign the fishing log and turned upstream toward the ranch. The smooth current flowed like crystalline silk among its watercress channels and undulating weeds.

The fish are starting to work, Puyans said.

Silver Creek is born in a series of remarkable alkaline tributaries and spring-fed watercress sloughs below Gannett and Picabo. Several small feeder creeks, streams about the size of the storied Letort Spring Run in Pennsylvania, gather their flowages underground in the bottoms between Hailey and the Purdey Ranch, bubbling cold and rich from the parched floor of the valley. It is a surprising little river, winding in its reed-lined channels of nesting coots and pintailed sprig ducks, long before it loops east toward the hot sagebrush hills beyond Picabo.

We drove upstream toward the irrigation hatch on the Purdey property, and discovered another fisherman above the timber-span tractor bridge. His casting looked awkward, and suddenly he hooked a good rainbow. It jumped high, showering spray into the sunlight, and bored downstream until it held only a few feet from the struggling fisherman. Frantically he stripped in great, irregular loops of line to recover his slack. The fish still sulked on the bottom above the bridge.

He's in trouble with all that slack, David Inks shook his head. *That big rainbow's just resting!*

Too much slack! Puyans agreed.

Suddenly the big rainbow bolted upstream along the gravely shallows, literally peeling and jumping the slack line off the water until it tangled and jammed in the stripping guide. The young fisherman was holding his rod tip too high, and when the fouled line struck the stainless ring the fragile tippet sheared off.

Five pounds easy, Puyans muttered. *He just didn't get that fish on the reel when it stopped and sulked!* The big rainbow was gone.

The first rule of playing a good trout once it is hooked is to control the slack during its first frantic moments of activity, and then get that slack on the reel the moment it stops fighting. Fish should always be played from the reel. It is obviously unnecessary for smaller trout, but it is a discipline that should be consciously pursued until we learn to do it unconsciously. It should be considered preparation for the big fish, the trophy-size trout that are invariably lost whenever we make a mistake in either tactics or the care and preparation of our tackle. The stamina and explosive power of a big fish demand no mistakes with our left-hand slack.

The second rule involves thinking ahead for the best playing angles and the areas of potential trouble. Fishermen experienced in fighting heavy fish continually run a series of changing rapid-fire scenarios through their minds, testing each fresh combination of tactical opportunities and hazards that could occur. Pick a good position for playing your fish, but also consider your position from the standpoint of the fight going sour. Get out of the heavy currents where the fish may have been hooked, working your way carefully to the shallows or a gravel bar with relatively easy footing. It is always a good idea to get directly across the current from your fish, and slightly below its position if possible. Never try to reel a fish directly back up the current if you can avoid it. The best playing angle finds you across and below the fish, with a steady pressure exerted on its strength, forcing it to fight both you and the current. It is good practice to lower the rod almost parallel to the current if the tippet can stand the strain, pressuring the fish with strong butt power. Such nagging side pressure will steadily erode the stamina of the biggest fish.

Constant pressure that does not vary radically is the third rule of playing big fish. Both trout and salmon have relatively soft mouth membranes, relative to their size and exceptional strength. The sawing effect of widely variable fly-rod pressure, with strong butt power one moment and a slack rod tip the next, will frequently wear and work the hook free. Steady pressure is the optimal goal. It is impossible to achieve such playing skill without understanding the changing equilibrium between light pressure when a big fish is still fresh and fighting hard, and the steady butt pressure of the rod every time it sulks or pauses to catch its wind.

One exception to this axiom of steady pressure is a fish that hangs above a deadfall, within the gathering currents above a wild rapids, or near any potential water hazard. It is possible to gamble on controlled, momentary slack to manipulate such fish with an old trick from salmon fishing. Sometimes you can strip off and throw a few feet of slack into the current, dropping the rod low to create a bellying line below the fish. The fish will typically pull away from any rod pressure, and a belly line below its position will often convince a large trout that both the pressure and the threat causing that strain lie downstream. Properly timed and held, downstream slack will often convince a fish to move upstream.

Other factors exist in maintaining steady pressure. Fishermen with too much salt-water experience often fish with a lightly set drag on their reels, and tighten the drag setting once a good fish is hooked. Tightening the drag can prove a serious mistake on trout or salmon. The sudden change in the drag setting may provide such a radical change in playing strain that it can literally tear out a fairly well-set hook. My own reels are set with just enough light drag to prevent a line-tangling overrun when a big fish bolts or stops a long run suddenly, and I seldom change its drag-screw setting during a fight. Salt-water fly-fishermen have also developed techniques of palming an exposed reel flange, or permitting the reel handle to revolve in the palm of the hand with a controlled thump-thump rhythm. Either system of applying manual drag is too jolting and abrasive for any fine-tackle fishing, and given the relatively tender mouth structure of a trout or salmon, the erratic palming of either a reel flange or its handle will quickly lose a lightly hooked fish. Palming an exposed reel flange also has its hazards.

You've got to be careful with a really big steelhead or salmon, André Puyans observed recently. *Palming an exposed reel flange that is really spinning can leave you with tracks in your hand!*

Fish are typically hooked in either the right or left mandibles of their jaw structures; when such fish suddenly change direction, reversing the relationship between the position of the fisherman and his original hooking angle, it can mean trouble. The steady rod pressure, the original angle of hooking penetration, and the position of the angler are all working together at the start of the fight. But when the fish suddenly turns, changing its direction in the current, both the rod strain and the position of the fishermen are working directly opposite to the original angle of hook penetration. Such pressure can literally force the hook out backward if it is applied too harshly in a soft-mouthed species like trout, and I usually reduce my rod strain when a fish changes its angle and gains this advantage after being hooked.

Another axiom is extremely valuable in playing in fish on relatively light tackle in weedy or snag-filled currents, or with a large trout in any type of water. It involves understanding the great exertion a fish pits against light tackle when it is suddenly hooked, and in dampening the strong rushes and surges that can follow. Skillful manipulation of such a fish consists of making sure it is securely hooked, and then playing it gently until the explosive edge of its initial panic is past. It is possible to wear at its strength with such subtlety that it soon tires, and has already expended the leader-shearing energy that might have been triggered in the first moments it fully senses its danger.

Many experienced anglers never really strike their fish, in the sense of an impact load, but sink the hook securely later with one or two steady pulls of firm butt pressure. Such tactics sometimes pull out a lightly hooked trout, but it is better to lose such fish early than after a prolonged fight. Losing fish after an extended struggle wastes valuable fishing time, and needlessly expends the energy of a big trout.

The head-shaking fish is also trouble, because any counterstrategy can quickly prove a mistake. There is no infallible technique for parrying such behavior. Tightening rod pressure can literally tear the fly out, and slacking off can whiplash it out after several moments. Hold a moderate rod strain and pray the head-shaking fish will stop.

Jumping fish can pose several problems. The basic technique lies in lowering the rod tip and quickly tightening again once the fish has fallen back into the water. The lowered rod prevents the fish from cartwheeling down on a straining leader. It will also reduce the tension of threshing jumps against a tight line or the current friction of considerable line drag in the water. Either impact can break a light tippet or tear the hook from a large trout, and too much slack can permit a lightly hooked fish to eject the fly when it jumps.

Not every fish jumps with calendar-art perfection, and there are no skills for parrying the clumsily jumping trout that threshes angrily without rhythm or logic. Such wild gyrations can snap a casting knot or light tippet in spite of our skills. Since a fish is virtually weightless in the water, and its viscosity tends to mute the agility and strength of its struggling, a skilled fisherman knows that its aerial struggles are infinitely more dangerous than its subaquatic threshing.

When a good fish decides to jump, the old-timers cautioned in my boyhood years, *you lower your rod in salute!*

Rod-tip angle is vitally important in playing fish. Your rod is a delicately flexing spring when used skillfully, and has the capability of quickly wearing at the strength of a fish. The optimal playing angle is about forty-five degrees, held with a steady pressure. It brings the full length of the rod and its supple power into play, frustrating the fish with a combination of light reel drag, middle calibrations in the rod, and delicate tip action. Steep rod angles can result in little effective control of the fish, although the keep-the-rod-up mythology is widespread, and a sudden surge can break a finely tapered rod. With the rod held too low, you are applying too much butt power for light-tackle fishing. The exception is the strong trout that bolts unexpectedly on a cobweb-fine tippet, when even the change of line direction at the tip guide can create sufficient friction to shear the fragile nylon. When a leader knot or backing knot threatens to jam in the guides, it can sometimes be freed by pointing the rod directly at the fish and gently shaking it through, or quickly rotating the rod upside down. Skilled light-tackle fishermen jettison the rules at such times, point their tiny fly rods directly at the bolting trout, and simply allow it to run against the reel. Only the best-made reels have drag systems and click mechanisms subtle enough to surrender line without breaking off.

Long runs pose similar fish-playing skills. Big fish build considerable inertia during a reel-wearing run, and their strain on a leader consists of their weight and speed combined with the force of the current. However, trying to stop such a fish is a greater hazard than the run itself.

Acrobatic jumps and long runs, fighting the rod pressure and friction of the current against the line, soon tire even the biggest trout. The skilled angler simply lets a fish jump or run freely until its first uncontrollable velocity or acrobatics are past, and then smoothly resumes his reeling to recover line and exert the nagging pressure of his tackle. The more a big fish exerts itself in aerial combat and subsurface sprinting, the more quickly it will tire. No pressure should be used to discourage such behavior unless definite hazards exist, like a tangle of fallen timber, waterfalls and rapids, boulder-strewn shallows and fractured ledgerock, or weeds that can hopelessly entangle a struggling fish. With a hooked fish running toward such hazards, the angler is forced to decide quickly between breaking off in trying to slow down his quarry, or losing it later when his leader is sheared off or snagged. It is a difficult choice that must be made in seconds.

It is always good practice to keep your head and give the fish his, remembering that both his initial surprise and your excitement can result in disaster. Every fight has five basic stages. The first stage occurs when a fish is hooked, and discovers its peril with a mixture of fear and outraged surprise. Its early panic is usually spent in frantic struggles, and the second stage begins when its first wild surge of adrenalin is spent. The hooked fish then settles into a stubborn, bulldogging fight in which its remaining strength is carefully husbanded, and the trout uses its intimate knowledge of the stream bed and its currents. Such fish are far from beaten, and when most of their strength is depleted, the fight is still not finished. There is a third seesaw stage in which the trout battles for control, and is sometimes partially controlled by its adversary. This third stage is surprisingly long with any big fish. Finally, the fourth stage is reached in which the fish is increasingly under control, senses its ultimate peril as it is forced into the shallows, and it starts to fight again desperately. Many fish are lost during this unexpected flurry, often triggered by seeing the fisherman and the fear of being maneuvered from the security of their holding currents. The fifth stage of the fight finds the angler in increasing control, although these moments have their hazards too.

Sometimes a good fish chooses to stay deep when its first explosive rushes are over, and such sulking has its special problems. But it is an opportunity too, giving us time to walk or wade toward the fish, recovering backing and fly line and improving our playing angle. Sometimes complete slack will make a sounding fish sense that it is free, and start it moving again. Sometimes when a sulking fish is tired enough, it can be forced from its position with strong butt pressure from below and across the current. It should not be tried with light tackle. Fighting a good fish on delicate nylon is best accomplished with a steady side pressure just short of its breaking strain. Skilled fishermen have learned that steady rod pressure can move a stubborn fish far better than increased strain transmitted from the reel. It is possible to clamp the line firmly with the grip hand and the other hand just below the butt guide, using the rod to force a fish off balance.

John Alden Knight described an interesting ploy for such stubborn bottom-hugging trout in his classic *Modern Angler* in a chapter on salmon. Knight carried a few stainless shower-curtain clips in his fishing jacket, and he simply clipped them around his line when a big fish held motionlessly along the bottom. The clip rode down the straining line and leader until it struck the fish, startling it into continuing its fight. It is a tactic that works, although it has its own problems. Hanging on the straining line, the clip can become a wildly swinging counterweight that will wrench the hook free when a good fish ends its sulking with a jump. Thumping or strumming the line like a guitar string sometimes works, but it can also vibrate the fly free. Stoning a sulking fish with bottom rubble is a final resort for startling it from the bottom, but an angler must be prepared for an explosion.

John Atherton tells an amusing anecdote concerning a sulking salmon in his book *The Fly and the Fish*. Atherton and Lee Wulff were on the Margaree at Ross's Bridge when they discovered another fisherman into a heavy fish. His rod was tightly bowed and his line reached deep into the pool. It seemed the salmon was securely fouled on the bottom.

What's wrong? Atherton yelled. *Hung up?*

Don't think so, the fisherman answered, *but he's been sulking out there since nine o'clock this morning!*

It was almost noon. *Big fish?* Wulff asked.

No, the man replied. *Don't think so.*

Atherton and Wulff exchanged amused glances. *Haven't you tried something to move him?* they asked.

I'm afraid he'll get off, the angler groaned.

You'll be here all day unless you move him, Atherton yelled. *He's simply resting out there on the bottom.*

Why don't you try tapping the rod butt? Wulff suggested. *Or heaving a few small stones into the pool?*

Well, the man said unhappily, *I've only caught a couple of salmon, and I'd hate to lose this fish.*

Wulff and Atherton finally turned to leave.

Wait, the fisherman yelled after them, *maybe I'd better try something after all—it's been three hours!*

We could toss a stone out there for you, Wulff said.

Be careful, the man cautioned.

Wulff threw an apple-size cobble into the pool below the fish, and there was a wild shriek from the reel as the salmon bolted upstream, somersaulting high in a shower of spray. It fell clumsily, and the straining rod snapped straight when the tippet broke. The man shouted angrily, and Wulff and Atherton still hold the Margaree record for sprinting two hundred yards to their car in chest waders.

The reel is always part of the problem, and reel quality is important in playing big trout. It must have sufficient line capacity for long runs, with a firm drag and precise click mechanism. Some fishermen prefer a silent reel, but in my experience, its running sounds are important in playing a fish. The shrieking pitch of the reel gives a skilled angler a constantly changing series of valuable clues about what a hooked fish is doing, and just how quickly it is doing it.

Reels pose other problems in gathering playing fish. Careless recovery of the line can result in a loose gathering of its coils, filling the spool too full, and jamming the line against the reel-frame pillars. It is possible to feed the line evenly on the reel, using light finger pressure to layer it back and forth. Some modern reels machined from magnesium and other more sophisticated alloys can suffer warped reel spools when too much line is layered on one side warping the light alloy sufficiently to bind the spool against the frame or fight its gear system. Disciplined recovery of the line during a fight is always critical. Rewinding it carelessly and too loosely after a big fish has run deep into the running line and backing can result in a tangle, losing it when it makes its next long run. Too many fishermen also rewind sloppily at the end of the day's fishing, loosely layering the backing and line. It is a poor habit that has cost a lot of fish the following day, when the carelessly coiled line bites deep and jams.

Broken or distorted hooks are another common problem along trout water. Few fly hooks are ever broken or even bent in a fish. However, bent hooks are relatively common, usually the result of fishing light-wire hooks with tippets of too much breaking strain. Hooks smaller than size eighteen should never be fished on nylon stronger than three-pound test, and minute flies in sizes below twenty-four should be presented on tippets lighter than .005. Many anglers use tippets too heavy for their hook temper, reasoning that light tackle costs them too many good fish. Yet they still lose them when their heavy tippets bend or straighten their light-wire hooks. However, broken hooks are a common complaint.

Fought him for several minutes, the old story goes, *and finally he broke the hook!*

Modern hooks are lousy, somebody else agrees.

Both observations are wrong. The man who had lost the big fish had played it rather skillfully, since his hook had probably been broken earlier on a stone-flicking backcast several minutes before the fish was hooked and was completely minus its point and barb. It is the poor backcast that consistently breaks hooks, not the fish themselves, and you should check your fly often on streams with ledges and gravelly beaches.

It is a mistake that once cost me a huge fish two hundred yards below the famous Boca Chimehuin in Argentina, the reach of river that has surrendered two world-record brown trout.

It was a period of bright weather, unusually still for the April beginnings of autumn on those Andean rivers. The Chimehuin was surprisingly low that season. The vast expanse of Lago Huechulafquen was almost quiet, riffling blue and pewter gray and purple under the clouds, and the sun glittered on the Fujiyama-like volcano on the Chilean border.

There were a dozen big fish in the sizable crystalline pool below the Boca Chimehuin itself, very large browns and rainbows migrating downstream from the lake like salmon. We paused on the sawmill road above the pool, where the monkey-puzzle trees stood against the bright morning skies, and studied the trout with binoculars. The fish were between fifteen and twenty-five pounds, and they were lying along the sheltering ledges, boulders and giant deadfalls that lay above the weedbeds.

They're huge! I whispered in awe.

You're right! Bébé Anchorena grinned. *That big brown along the log could go better than twelve kilos.*

Better than the record Correntoso fish? I said.

It's possible, Bébé nodded.

Bébé Anchorena once held the world fly record for brown trout with a twenty-four-pound monster from the Boca Chimehuin, until it was displaced with a bigger twenty-six pound cockfish from the Boca Correntoso. Anchorena knows his big-fish tactics, and no one understands the Boca Chimehuin better.

It's too bright and still, he shook his head.

Well, we started back along the sawmill road toward the trestle bridge downstream, *It's the only day I've got!*

Bébé smiled and nodded.

I had some big five-inch marabou baitfish imitations with bright silver mylar sides in my fly books, and they looked intriguing. Such flies were experimental then, and the Argentine fish had never seen them before.

These mylars just might work, I thought.

Starting in the eddying pool just below the Boca and its broken ledges, I fished the two hundred yards down toward the deep corner below the monkey-puzzle trees. There was a fat three-pound rainbow halfway down, but otherwise it was the discipline of making an eighty-foot cast, working it through its swing and retrieve, taking a step downstream, and repeating the entire cross-stream tactic many times over. There is a shelving gravel bar the entire length of this piece of water, and just before I reached the still currents of the Rincon Pool, my marabou ticked once or twice into stones on the backcast.

It's a big hook, I thought carelessly. *It's probably all right, or maybe it's just bent a little. It'll be okay!*

It was a careless and serious mistake. The first cast that reached the holding lie of the big fish settled in the shadows along the ledges, worked teasingly back into the sunlight, and a crocodile-size shadow began closing on the fly. The mylar flashed and fluttered like a crippled baitfish, and the huge trout hit it savagely in a wild eruption of spray.

Trucha! I yelled. *Trucha marron!*

It was a giant brown trout, better than twenty pounds, and it broached with its spade-size tail working in its threshing rolls. It cartwheeled explosively, and the big marabou came free and catapulted awkwardly into the sun. The reel was surprisingly shrill in the silence as I reeled the fly slowly back toward the beach, and when I studied the shredded marabou its hook was broken.

Frayed leaders and casting knots are a similar problem in self-discipline. Working long distances with relatively fine leader diameters can mean casting knots, particularly in a brisk headwind. Such casting knots can seat themselves anywhere along the length of the leader, and they can reduce a leader's breaking strain by as much as fifty percent. Knots are always a problem within three feet of the tippet, and on big-fish water such leader knots are serious even in the butt diameters.

This past season on a small Argentine river where the fish seldom run over three or four pounds, I lost a brown of better than ten pounds to a casting knot less than two feet below my nail knot. It was a fairly old leader, and I had discovered the casting knot a few minutes before I fished the big bucktail along a dark run under the sheltering pampas grass. Such knots in the heavy butt-nylon seldom matter, but it is foolish to succumb to such laziness, and perhaps lose the trophy fish of a lifetime.

Frayed leaders are another problem in judgment and self-discipline. Low backcasts will often flail and score a leader against rocks. Good fish will often give the leader a real beating, wearing it across ledges and boulders, and raking it across roots and snags. It pays to check your leader frequently, running it through your fingers to find the rough places. Any damage should mean discarding the leader, since even the tiniest flaw can shear under the strain of a good fish. It is wise to exercise similar austerity after a good fish has been taken, since the fly knot may have been weakened: take the time to cut the fly off and refasten it with a freshly tied knot, since it can mean the difference between a broken tippet and a trophy-size fish. It never pays to save money with old leaders.

However, subjected to a steady pressure modern leaders have surprising strength. It is possible to subject a stubborn fish to considerable butt power with a properly handled rod. It is possible to lead a hooked fish away from hazards with a firmly bent rod. No change in the length of line or rod angle, no vibration or change in tension, and no reel work is necessary or advisable. Perfectly done, this technique will tow a fish very slowly upstream in surprisingly heavy water. It is a secret worth knowing when everything else has failed.

Salt-water fly-fishermen understandably know more about playing really big fish on relatively light tackle than all but a few trout and salmon experts, and a good salt-water man knows all about wearing his fish down with unyielding rod pressure just under the breaking strain of his leaders. The salt-water lock consists of levering the rod butt and reel against the stomach, providing finger drag on the line with the left hand high on the butt section of the rod, and reeling with the other. Unlike fishing subtropical flats for permit and bonefish and tarpon, trout fishing often takes place in cold latitudes that require warm clothing, and the so-called salt-water lock is a useful technique for fighting big fish with a fly rod. Extension-butt rods are useful for the salt-water lock where cold-weather gear is needed, since they keep the reel free of entangling jackets and wader cords and sweaters. Surprisingly large fish can be fought on light tackle with this technique, both throughout the fight itself and to rest your arms or maneuver a good fish on relatively delicate nylon.

The late Richard Alden Knight developed a radical variation on the standard salt-water lock for forcing his tackle to its absolute limits on big fish. His Knight salt-water lock did not anchor the rod butt against the body, but involved pulling back with the left hand high on the butt section, and simultaneously pushing forward on the reel seat with the right. It is a method of forcing a big fish with maximum rod pressure, while it runs against a strong drag setting.

Sometimes it is necessary to follow a strong fish when it succeeds in reaching heavier currents downstream. Or its exhaustion may make it a dead weight drifting ponderously in the gathering shallows. Both problems demand patience and the courage to let the fish take line. When fish succeed in leaving a pool, it always means an extended fight, and you must follow to recover line. Follow such fish as quickly as possible, but running over the rocks or down a shallow riffle can result in a bad fall. Even the most benign bottom can conceal problems in footing. The more line you are forced to surrender, the more problems threaten. Line friction in the water can develop excessive slack, shear a delicate leader tippet, or simply foul among the boulders, snags, and shallows. It is always more difficult to control a big fish that has stripped your reel into the backing. Its thin diameter makes it harder to handle than the fly line, and when a fish is into the backing, it must be played gingerly. You must wait until the running line is back on the reel before you apply full rod pressure.

Another salt-water technique will help you recover line more quickly than the reel can by itself. Pumping and reeling is extremely valuable in playing a big fish. It should not be tried until a running fish has travelled through the fast water and stopped in the pool below. Its technique is simple: the rod tip is steadily raised high behind the head, with a steady pressure that forces the fish off balance, bringing it closer to the angler. Then a skilled fisherman swiftly drops his rod and reels frantically to recover line, pumping again when the slack gained in the first pumping action is back on the reel.

However, sometimes a strong fish keeps taking line, and the fisherman must break some rules to fight it successfully. Shallow water snags and the drag of the fly line and backing in the current demand that an angler raise the rod high with both arms extended above his head. It is a position that limits both his strength and his rod pressure, but it raises some dangerous slack free of the river, cuts line friction in the current, and restores a limited margin of control to the fight. Since it provides a relatively poor rod angle, the high-arm position is recommended only in desperation when a fish has stripped too much line from the reel, and a skilled angler will return to his normal forty-five-degree fighting angle or a salt-water lock as quickly as possible.

When a hooked fish is still close in, you should try to keep its head high in the current. Such technique helps in aquaplaning a hooked trout and subduing it quickly, and its advantages in weedy streams are obvious. Our eastern limestone streams and western spring creeks are filled with watercress beds and channels in their trailing weeds. Once a fish is hooked in such waters, and the line is tightly stretched between its struggles and the straining rod tip, you should raise the rod high above your head and strip line quickly. Properly executed, this tactic will keep the head of the fish near the surface, skating its bulk in the surface film. Skill and a modicum of luck will keep such fish skating across the beds themselves, and an exhausted trout can sometimes be virtually beached on the weeds.

Sometimes a fight among the weeds goes sour, and a good fish succeeds in mossing us firmly in their trailing growth. Patience and a gentle pressure sometimes work, and a few moments of judicious slack will often confuse a fish enough so that it extricates itself from the weeds. Such intentional slack will also sometimes work when a fish has fouled the line in a deadfall or among some boulders. There was a big rainbow on the Gunnison years ago that stitched my line through a logjam and hung threshing downstream. It was an impossible impasse until I tried a slack line, and the fish promptly returned through the same aperture in the tangled limbs. Once it swam free, the fight was resumed. It is a tactic that has proved itself several times over the years.

However, when a fish has rooted itself deeply in the weeds, it is difficult to free it. Gentle pressure exerted parallel to the weedy growth will often work, but it is essential to mark the place carefully where the fish entered the bed. Sometimes a fish is so firmly enmeshed in the weeds that virtually nothing works, although a gentle hand-lining should perhaps be tried. It is also sometimes possible to wade to such a fish, grasp the leader and stealthily work it free. Another approach is holding the nylon leader taut with one hand while picking handfuls of weed away from the fish with the other. Sometimes such a fish will lie exposed among the weeds, and you can simply pick it up gently, although more often you capture such a trout while it is still completely wrapped in its shroud of grass.

Sometimes a big fish bulldogs stubbornly along the bottom and imbeds itself underneath some weeds. It can be too deep to reach with your hands, but your feet will sometimes work as well. Faced with such a deeply enmeshed trout, I have often held the leader at an angle downstream from its position and run my wading brogue along the nylon until it touched the fish. Sometimes this will flush a trout from under the weeds, and sometimes you have to root them out slowly with your toe.

Fish often foul the leader on other underwater hazards during a fight. Deadfalls and tangled logjams and snags are obvious problems encountered almost daily along the stream. The water under the willows and alders is often a labyrinth of tiny roots that can snap a fine tippet. Grassy undercut banks can conceal similar hazards, and a collapsed section of sod can foul a leader as readily as a deadfall or a sharp-edged stone. Boulders often conceal cavelike hiding places, and undercut banks also provide conceal-ment for a desperate trout hoping to escape the nagging pressure of our tackle. Muskrat holes are also sometimes used as sanctuaries, and once I even had a frightened brown trout burrow into a bridge abutment weep-tile. Rough stones and the razor-sharp edges of fractured lava are particularly hard on a straining leader. The leader can also pick up clumps of drifting weeds during the fight, particularly if it is a hand-tapered design with a series of barrel knots. Such weeds fouled on the leader are a problem both from their strain on its breaking capacity and their effect as a wildly swinging counterweight that can tear the fly out or part the tippet when a fish tries to jump. Modern knotless tapers with epoxy knots at the fly line are completely free of rough connections that can catch and hold drifting clumps of weeds, and are highly recommended for fishing our weedy limestone streams and western spring creeks.

Patience and skill are the secrets of playing big fish successfully and well. Hard-fished waters demand that our nylon tippets be delicate enough so that an average fish has enough weight to break them if given the chance. Really difficult streams like Hat Creek in California, Silver Creek in the wind-polished hills of Idaho, the Firehole in the Yellowstone country, and many of our hard-fished eastern rivers all hold big fish of several pounds, yet fishing pressure has made them so tippet-shy that we are forced to use nylon with breaking strains from one-half-pound to two-pound test to fool them. Playing a good fish on an eighteen-inch tippet with a breaking strain of only twenty or thirty percent of its dead weight—even less with a big rainbow I once hooked on a spring creek in the Jackson Hole country—is a test of skill and refinement totally unmatched in other light-tackle angling, including the current-free problems of salt-water work, since there is virtually no elasticity in trout-size leaders to cushion our mistakes.

Since it is impossible to defeat a good fish with the mere strength of our rods and terminal tackle, we must remain calm and unhurried in playing them. We can only worry them patiently, nagging at their strength with a steady pressure until they become tired. Remember that fighting a heavy trout always has the five-part scenario that cannot be hurried. Too much excitement invariably means mistakes, while too little emotion means our sensory reactions have probably not been sharpened with a flow of adrenalin. Like a first-rate athlete, the skilled fisherman has learned to control and balance his emotions and his physical skills.

The five-part scenario is worth reviewing in conclusion, and begins with the mixture of surprise and outrage a fish exhibits when it is first hooked. Really big fish are large because they are seldom hooked, and they often give an angry, threshing shudder when they first sense the barb and the tension of the leader. It is a dangerous moment on a fine tippet, since virtually anything can happen. The fish may only sulk toward the bottom, sullenly charting its next move, but it can also explode in a wild surge of energy. Stay calm and stay with the fish through these first erratic seconds, keeping the rod pressure relatively light and consistent, making sure the trout cannot exert any real tension until its first panic-stricken surge of adrenalin is spent. Once the first wild jumps and threshing cartwheels and frightened runs are past, the fight has entered its second stages.

The stubborn second part of the fight is always less spectacular, but the fish is far from beaten. Too many fishermen assume they have won and relax when the first wild runs are spent. The fish has swallowed its panic and started to fight on its terms, using its familiarity with the currents and the bed of the river. Strong fish will often select a smooth current layer along the bottom, with faster water above that helps it hold its position. Sometimes a trout will wedge itself head-down in the currents for the third phase of the fight working only to maintain its optimum angle for straining your tackle. Sullen head-shaking will often work a fly out or seriously strain a leader and its knots. Everyone has had a good fish probe along the bottom, trying to force its way under logs, sheltering stones, and undercut ledges and banks. Sometimes a fish will work its nose into the bottom, seeming literally to rub the fly out. Depending on the size of the trout, this stubborn third stage of the fight is a seesaw contest with the advantage shifting constantly between the angler and the fish. Steady pressure with smooth changes in both the angle and plane of the rod should be used to parry each move of the fish, and finally you should be able to turn its runs, force it naggingly from its sanctuary in the heavier currents, and begin to turn it in a series of half circles. There is still a flurry or threshing spray of panic or brief run left in such a fish, and you must expect it with each trout. Too many fishermen assume in this period of partial control that they will get such a fish the first or second time it comes toward the net. It almost never happens, but forcing a trout at that final critical moment with extra rod pressure is foolish—the final desperate surge invariably snaps the leader or tears the hook free when it comes.

Impatience and clumsy playing skills lose most of the fish we fail to capture, and a poor choice of tactical position for the fight can lose still others. We lose most fish both in the way we fight them and in the positions we choose to fight them. The skilled fisherman always thinks ahead before casting to a large fish or working a reach of river, anticipating what a good trout might do when hooked. Big fish lying along a deadfall or cedar sweeper or undercut bank will predictably try to work under their sheltering homes. Strong fish will typically try to break free in the heaviest currents or plunge downstream into a chute. It is impossible to stop their first strong runs, particularly with relatively light leader points. However, anticipating their actions we can swiftly react to change our playing angle, or take advantage of any error they might make. Sometimes I have plunged my rod tip deep into the current, fighting a fish with a reverse bend in the rod while the leader slipped along the underside of a fallen tree. Holding the fly rod at a normal angle would have fouled the nylon without question. With a fish that works around a boulder or bolts downstream into the pool below, you should have planned your pursuit before it took your fly. It is likely that a shy trout cannot often be hooked from the best playing point in its pool, and an experienced fly-fisherman will stalk such a fish from one position, moving quickly to the other once it has been hooked. Remember that your tactical positions during the fight of a good fish are equally as important as your rod-and-line skills in playing it, and patience is perhaps the ultimate skill in our bag of tricks.

Yet we all still make mistakes, even though we may have had many years of fishing experience. That evening two years ago on Silver Creek some thirty miles below Sun Valley in Idaho, there was a fine hatch of *Centroptilum* duns that had started in late afternoon. The fat rainbows worked on the wriggling little nymphs in the beginning, and were greedily taking the tiny adults well before twilight. There were forty or fifty trout rising in the waist-deep slick one hundred yards above the irrigation hatches on the Purdey Ranch, and it was an evening when I had finally solved the riddle of their selectivity. Most of the fish working within range had taken my little nymphs or dry flies, and I had caught most of them, after a lot of fly-changing, on a fragile .004 tippet. Everything was working, when a really good rainbow porpoised in a narrow channel beyond a bed of weeds, more than sixty feet away.

Good fish! David Inks laughed.

You're right, I yelled back ruefully, *but he's in an impossible position!*

Sure is! Inks grinned.

The silty marl bottom was threatening to swallow my legs where I was already standing in the still current, and the pale-bottomed channel directly below the fish was more than chest-deep. There was no way to get downstream from its feeding lie, and it was wise to forget the big rainbow completely. But it kept on feeding steadily with a series of impressive rise forms that literally sent tidal waves down its weedy channel.

That's really a good rainbow, Inks taunted me.

The big fish was tempting. Its rises were showy swirls and porpoise rolls that disturbed the current steadily. It was too much, and I finally started wading closer.

You going to try him? Inks asked.

Maybe, I muttered.

It was an impossible situation, since the weed bed between us promised two problems: the leader would catch in the weeds and there would be only a single drag-free float, and if the fish were hooked, it could be safely landed only if it chose to bolt thirty feet downstream toward open water below. Big rainbows seldom make such foolish mistakes, but I stood in the deep current with my fly boxes shipping water anyway, studying the fish and its steady rise forms. It was working a little farther upstream now, across a narrow place in the weeds.

It's now or never, I thought.

There would be only a single cast before the fly dragged and frightened the big rainbow, but I worked my line out carefully, gauging its length as the false casts flicked across the weeds. The final cast fell luckily in a perfect hook, buying a few brief seconds of drag-free float, and the big fish took it with a lazy porpoiselike swirl.

He's hooked, I thought wildly.

The big rainbow settled back in surprise, and suddenly it exploded in terror, showering the channel with spray. Its frightened bolt torpedoed upstream instead of down, and when it finally jumped, it stitched my tippet solidly into the weeds. The frail nylon parted and I reeled my line back sheepishly.

Moss you? Inks yelled upstream in the twilight.

Pole-vaulted right into all that garbage, I groaned unhappily. *That'll teach me to try a fish like that!*

Probably not, Inks laughed.

5. Lessons in Landing
and Releasing Fish

Twenty-odd years ago in my book *Matching the Hatch*, I described a
seriocomic encounter with a determined fifteen-inch brown on the
Gunnison in Colorado. It had been rising freely along a logjam in
a side channel on the Cooper Ranch, and it took my delicate little
dry fly on its first float. It was a deceptively easy fish, and I am still
half-sorry that I even hooked it that morning.

The fish shook itself angrily and bolted across the pool, high-jumped a
broken snag that hung throbbing in the current, and fell clumsily in the
brush-filled eddy behind. Its threshing deep among the limbs threatened to
break my leader, and I waded hastily across the waist-deep pool and
disengaged it somehow. It promptly fouled me again in the brush pile, and
this time I shipped water down my waders extricating the tippet from a
deadfall. It promptly bolted upstream, tangling my left-hand slack around
the reel, and while I was frantically working the fly line free, it fouled me
again under the bank. This proved still more embarrassing, and there was
more water trickling down my waders when I reeled the rod tip deep into
the bank shadows and pushed the fish out of the roots. It darted straight
upstream and I pointed the rod at the fish, while the leader and line knots
rattled noisily out through the guides, stripping a few feet of line from the
reel. Our ordeal was still not finished, and I groaned when the fragile tippet
caught and hung on still another limb.

I waded unhappily upstream and worked the leader free, and the fish
thanklessly squirted between my legs. It hung in the tumbling currents
downstream and threshed wildly, considering the length of time it had
already been fighting. The trout was still on when I had heavy-handedly
remedied that problem, and it promptly buried itself again.

You fish like Sisyphus, I thought wryly.

It was another poorly executed episode, and I completed my baptism by falling clumsily, ruining an allegedly waterproof watch. There were other minor embarrassments before it was over, and when the fish finally surrendered, it was released with a mixture of relief and respect.

Glad we're alone, I muttered.

It has usually gone better in the twenty-odd years since *Matching the Hatch*, but there are still those star-crossed days when nothing seems to go right, and a really good fish can give you unbelievable trouble when things go badly. Two summers ago on the Grimsá, in the Borgafjördur country of Iceland, there was a heavy salmon that won its freedom with a rapier-quick mixture of poetry and musclebound strength and speed.

Its fight started almost slowly. The fish took on a windless, strangely warm evening where the currents of the Laxfoss eddied down a 200-foot ledge of lava. It held deep after it was hooked, and I tightened firmly once or twice, making certain the little fly hooks were secure. It shook its head sullenly, drifted a few feet downstream, and suddenly it exploded.

The Hardy literally shrieked as it surrendered the fly line, and the backing soon was melting from the spool. The fish travelled the length of the waterfall pool in no time at all, and it gathered momentum in the shallows downstream. The backing remaining on the reel was getting thin, and I stood in the shallows, holding the rod high with the fish still wildly stripping line. It had taken more than one hundred yards of backing, and it seemed like the fish could easily take it all. It had reached the shallow pool downstream now, and it was still devouring line.

Better start running, I thought in panic.

The gravelly shallows ahead were paved with smooth plum-size stones, and I started down the knee-deep riffles that bordered the pool. It was difficult running, but I was going well and rapidly regaining some line, when my left brogue came down on an algae-slick outcropping. There was a sickening moment when I thought it was possible to recover my balance, my right leg searching in a wild ballet step behind the left to prevent a fall, and then I went down with a wounded pirouette.

Both knees came down hard on the algae outcropping, and the pain ricocheted through my body. But my inertia was too much to end there, and I was rolling now, tucking my shoulder to protect my left elbow from the stones. The current surged over my entire length, and only my hat and my rod arm stayed dry. Water seeped past my tightly cinched belt, drenched my fishing vest, and thoroughly drowned and saturated the camera around my neck.

My sweaters were like soaked bath towels, and I clambered back to my feet dripping water like a sea monster. River water trickled icily inside my waders, reaching the few dry places below my shivering thighs. The ratchety gear sounds from the reel suddenly reminded me that my fish was still hooked, and I turned soddenly to resume the fight.

The salmon had inexplicably stopped running when I fell, and with the slack that bellied free in the current while I was down, it had moved several yards back upstream. The fish was holding sullenly now. The reel sloshed and sputtered water while I recovered the slack, and the fish shook itself in the shallows, half-surprised that its strength and speed had proved futile. The rod dipped back into its throbbing half-circle, and I had worked below the fish when the fly came out.

Damn, I thought. *He's gone!*

It was a fish I would probably have released no matter how large it was, because it had beaten me embarrassingly. The fall was more serious than I suspected. The next morning my knees were so swollen that I could barely walk, sore and sausage-tight with fluid, like a bruised and battered halfback. It was finally past noon, roasting both knees in front of heaters at the Hvitabákki farmstead, before I could really move easily. The big fish had beaten me thoroughly, and both knees still ache sometimes.

Few trout have that kind of muscle, but fish not too much smaller are taken on many American rivers each season. It is wise to prepare yourself both mentally and physically for hooking a trophy-size fish if they exist in your waters. Our earlier chapters have discussed the skills in hooking and playing trout, and the disciplines of landing and releasing fish are equally important. Both are the reward and climax of our sport.

The final stages of fighting a fish come when the tide of the struggle finally shifts, and the angler begins to dominate the trout. The turning point comes when the rod pressure is in charge, and you can turn a fish virtually at will, forcing it easily from its holding currents. With a good fish bulldogging stubbornly in a series of half circles, it is almost time to recover your remaining line and prepare to land it. Although a trophy-size trout seems ready when the fight has reached this stage, it is seldom fully beaten. Few big fish ever surrender the first time you force them close, and surprisingly few are beached or netted the second time. The skilled angler knows this, never expects to take a big trout too early, and seldom loses a fish when its threshing panic is triggered at the first sight of the fisherman waiting in the shallows.

Few trout are strong enough to force an experienced angler to leave the river and fight them from the bank. It is often wise to select a good playing position in the shallows, allowing a fish to spend its energy in the pool itself. Once its struggles are contained, the fisherman can return stealthily to slightly deeper water with his net.

It is surprising how many fishermen try to net their fish in water that is too shallow; it is frequently a costly error in judgment, since good trout feel insecure in shallows where they can almost feel the gravel against their bellies. That insecurity can trigger a final surge of adrenalin that may enable an exhausted fish to break leaders, shear a finely calibrated rod, and tear free. It is far easier to maneuver a fish in thigh- to knee-deep water, where it feels less threatened and where you have more room to handle your net. The fish is in sufficient current to buoy his weight easily, its belly does not grate alarmingly on the bottom, and there is ample room to slip

MISCELLANEOUS NYMPHS

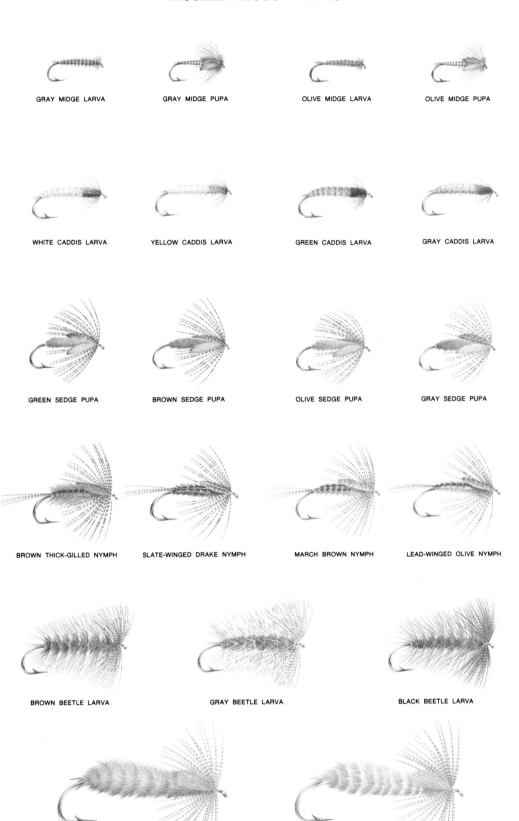

GRAY MIDGE LARVA   GRAY MIDGE PUPA   OLIVE MIDGE LARVA   OLIVE MIDGE PUPA

WHITE CADDIS LARVA   YELLOW CADDIS LARVA   GREEN CADDIS LARVA   GRAY CADDIS LARVA

GREEN SEDGE PUPA   BROWN SEDGE PUPA   OLIVE SEDGE PUPA   GRAY SEDGE PUPA

BROWN THICK-GILLED NYMPH   SLATE-WINGED DRAKE NYMPH   MARCH BROWN NYMPH   LEAD-WINGED OLIVE NYMPH

BROWN BEETLE LARVA   GRAY BEETLE LARVA   BLACK BEETLE LARVA

GREEN DRAGONFLY NYMPH   BROWN DRAGONFLY NYMPH

SPENT-WING MAYFLY SPINNERS

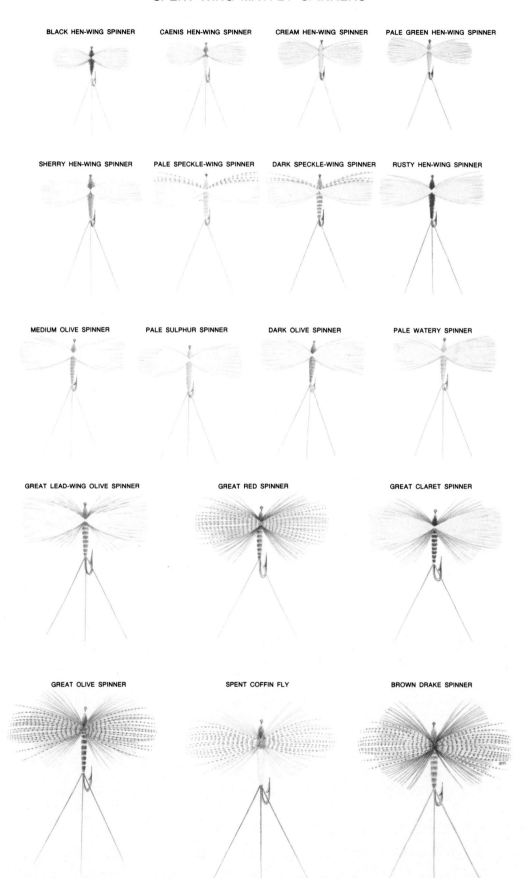

BLACK HEN-WING SPINNER   CAENIS HEN-WING SPINNER   CREAM HEN-WING SPINNER   PALE GREEN HEN-WING SPINNER

SHERRY HEN-WING SPINNER   PALE SPECKLE-WING SPINNER   DARK SPECKLE-WING SPINNER   RUSTY HEN-WING SPINNER

MEDIUM OLIVE SPINNER   PALE SULPHUR SPINNER   DARK OLIVE SPINNER   PALE WATERY SPINNER

GREAT LEAD-WING OLIVE SPINNER   GREAT RED SPINNER   GREAT CLARET SPINNER

GREAT OLIVE SPINNER   SPENT COFFIN FLY   BROWN DRAKE SPINNER

the net frame under its length. Of course, the separate art of beaching a fish poses another set of problems, in which its remaining strength and the shallows themselves are used to capture it.

There has been a lot of nonsense written about drowning a fish by holding its open jaws or head partially out of the current so its gills cannot work and absorb oxygen from the water. This is neither an efficient nor practical method of playing a good fish, since both the drag of the current against its jaws and the strain of lifting its head above the surface can break your tippet or tear out your fly. There is even some doubt about its effect on the respiration of the fish. Some writers have written about leading a big trout into silty shallows, where the clouds of muddy water churned up in its struggles might work through its gills and truncate its fighting ability. It is a theory that seems something less than sporting, and since I have had many big fish fight me in silty shallows which they entered themselves, it seems doubtful as well. Muddy water does impair a fish's vision, enabling the fisherman to get close enough to net it before it is fully spent. Weeds catching on the leader can perform a similar function since they sometimes slide freely against the fish. Many times I have had such weeds literally blindfold a big trout, like the shroud placed over the head of a falcon, and have been able to take the fish sooner because it could no longer see.

Patience also plays an important role in netting or beaching a good fish, and you should never try to land it until it is out of the primary currents and completely tired. The moment of truth comes when the fish begins to roll on its side, and can never remain fully upright again. When a fish loses its control and starts to show you its sides, it is almost ready for the beach or the net—but you should never try landing it before.

Keep its head high in the current, using its slender configuration to aquaplane the fish in close. Even a tired fish still has the strength to continue the fight if it can get its length head-down again. When the fight has progressed this far, and you finally intend to land the fish, it is time to unhook the net and let it trail from its cord in the current. Sometimes its meshes are still stiff early in the day, or the low humidity and wind in our western mountains dries them quickly, and a few brief moments in the current will make them pliable again. There can still be a final, weakly threshing moment of panic when the fish sees you and your waiting net, and a skilled fisherman always expects it.

When a fish finally surrenders, and you can force it on its side almost at will, it is time to reel the line to optimal netting length. Most fishermen will find that the proper amount of line leaves about a foot more than the rod length beyond the tip guide. The long leaders often necessary on hard-fished waters mean the line and its leader knot must be reeled into the guides. It is inevitable with leaders tapered to ten and twelve feet, since modern trout rods are always nine feet or less, and it can spell trouble. Since the best line knots can jam in the guides when a fish spends its final energy at the net, it is perhaps unwise to reel the line back to netting length until we are sure the fish is thoroughly tired. It is also wise to take great care with such knots, seating them smoothly and keeping them as small as possible, and adding the firming coat of pliobond to any knot of layered monofilament. With the line at netting length, and the fish digging at the current in weak half circles, it is time for the net.

There are fishermen who prefer handling the net with their stronger hand, often switching the rod late in the fight. My own preference is for using my left hand. The fish should be worked upstream from the angler, using the current to carry it toward the waiting net. Many fish are lost at the final moment, as the fisherman tries to force them upstream into the net. The net itself should be held forward into the current, its meshes eddying and fully extended in its flow. It should never be moved until the fish is actually drifting into its frame, so the fish is not frightened by its presence. Many fishermen lose fish with clumsy tennis-racquet swipes of the net, instead of letting the current carry their prey right into its waiting frame. The fish should never be netted until it is coming headfirst into your net. Trying to take it tailfirst is foolish, since it will typically feel or sense the net meshes closing behind it and bolt suddenly upstream. We have all seen big fish lost when a clumsy fisherman tried to net them crosswise over the frame. Such fish almost invariably wrench their bodies upward, using the net frame as a fulcrum for their heads and tails, and flop wildly free. Frightening a fish by poor netting technique will both extend the fight and tire it unnecessarily.

With the fish above you and obviously ready, and the line at optimal netting length, you extend your rod arm well back behind your head. Some men who prefer extremely light fly rods and terminal-tackle diameters often turn their rods reel-up while playing fish to equalize the bending stress on a delicate rod. It is even possible with the short rods to arch them over your head, parallel to your shoulders, with the reel hand extended on one side and the net hand on the other. Short rods are more easily used in normal netting techniques. With the rod held properly behind you or exaggeratedly to one side, its arching bend rather high, you can easily draw the fish toward you headfirst. Hold the rod rather lightly, since it will help your ability to react quickly to the fish. The high rod position keeps the tip in play, cushioning your terminal tackle, and subtle changes of its planar angles control the fish at close netting range.

Line length is also critical, since too much line means you cannot quite reach the exhausted trout, and too little can paradoxically cause the same problem. Too little line can sometimes lift the fish partially from the water and give it too much leverage on the leader. With the line held lightly under the index finger at the grip and about a foot or two longer than the rod, the fisherman can guide the trout cleanly toward his net.

The submerged net frame should be waiting motionless. It can be held at a quartering angle into the current, with just enough angle to blossom and extend the meshes, yet requiring less effort to hold it there. The net should not move until the fish has actually entered it. Then the fisherman can take it with a deft, twisting stroke of the wrist.

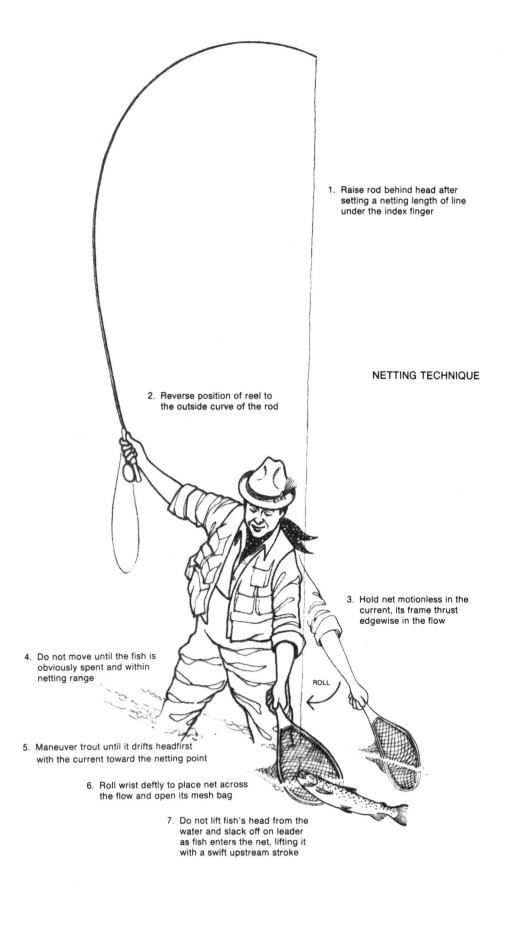

1. Raise rod behind head after setting a netting length of line under the index finger

NETTING TECHNIQUE

2. Reverse position of reel to the outside curve of the rod

3. Hold net motionless in the current, its frame thrust edgewise in the flow

4. Do not move until the fish is obviously spent and within netting range

ROLL

5. Maneuver trout until it drifts headfirst with the current toward the netting point

6. Roll wrist deftly to place net across the flow and open its mesh bag

7. Do not lift fish's head from the water and slack off on leader as fish enters the net, lifting it with a swift upstream stroke

This wrist roll is designed to turn the net frame ninety degrees to the current, fully opening its meshes into the flow momentarily, and rolled back deftly on edge to lift the fish smoothly from the water in a single stroke. The lifting stroke should be swift and smoothly executed, and the instant the fish is started into the meshes, rod pressure should be reduced. This slack both permits the fish to drift back and sink into the net, and prevents its final struggling from shearing a straining tippet against the net's rigid frame.

Properly used, relatively small landing nets have the capacity to hold and subdue surprisingly large fish. Fifteen years ago in Tierra del Fuego, I netted a sixteen-pound brown for my good friend Laddie Buchanan with an ordinary wood-frame landing net. Such nets require a modicum of care, and regular inspection of their laminated frames, and their net bags tend to rot after a few seasons. The condition of the mesh cord should be checked regularly, since a really big fish can tear a rotting bag or even rip it from the frame. Such net failure is the result of carelessness. New net bags are not expensive and are easily replaced, and their condition can mean success or failure on the best fish of your career.

When a fish is missed with the net on the first try, never lunge at it and make a second swipe. Let its fresh panic ebb slightly, and let the fish run. Plunging thrusts with the net can only prolong the fight and often succeed in losing the fish.

Landing fish is possible in a number of ways. Some anglers still use gaffs on trout and salmon, but I cannot recommend their use. Such tools are extremely dangerous in inexperienced hands, and twice I have seen gaffs sunk into the thighs of fishermen on salmon rivers. One wound resulted from a flailing follow-through after a missed gaffing stroke, and the other whiplashed into the gillie himself, when a big fish wrenched violently off the gaff. Such wounded fish are doomed, and there is no way to release a gaffed trout, but my primary objection to the gaff is esthetic—trout and salmon are such beautiful species that it seems wrong to wound them with such a terrible instrument.

Netting and playing fish from a boat poses some slightly different tactical problems. It is wise to stand in a stable boat with your legs braced against the seat, since it improves your playing angles, but you should always sit down to fight a fish from a slender river skiff or canoe. Fishing alone, you must be careful in extending the net over the gunwale, since leaning out too far can capsize the boat. The ideal boat net should have a slightly longer handle than its stream-fishing counterpart. It should be held completely submerged once the fish is fighting in close, and lifted smoothly when it comes over the frame. Never swipe or thrust down wildly at the fish, since you may capsize the boat, and in any case the fish will certainly panic and resume fighting. Skilled boatmen will usually take you into shallow water once a fish is under control, sometimes slipping overboard to hold his craft steady. You must be careful to keep the leader and line away from his legs, the hull of the boat, the oars and oarlocks, rough places in the gunwales, and the motor and its propeller. It is is important to remain ready for the fish and its final leg-tangling runs or bolts as it seeks the shelter of the boat.

When the fish attempts to circle the motor or the bow, or bolts angrily behind the boatman, you should raise both arms high to clear the line around these obstacles. Radical changes in rod plane and playing angle can prevent trouble too. When a fish succeeds in forcing its way under the boat, or circles the leader perilously close to the sharp-bladed propeller, you should thrust your rod deep into the water and continue the fight with your rod angle upside down. It is a technique that has saved good fish for me from Crane Prairie Reservoir in Oregon to the famous Lough Currane in southern Ireland.

Having another person net your fish can also mean trouble. Most guides and gillies are experienced and skillful in landing fish, but some are surprising amateurs. It is a good practice to decline the help of strangers, and friends are a mixed blessing, unless you are familiar with their fish-handling skills. Many fish are lost each season by well-meaning friends and strangers who wield the net like a pitchfork.

Sometimes it is wise to leave a boat or canoe and fight your fish in the shallows. It is often easier to land a fish bringing it to a boatman or friend nearby, than fighting it all the way in to yourself. It is unwise to stand too far apart, since beyond twenty to twenty-five feet, you have very little control over a fish, no matter how tired it is. The man handling the net should stand absolutely still or crouch low in the water, and he should never run or lunge at the fish. Once the fish is controllable, rolling weakly to hold its balance, it should be led toward the waiting net, and all the rules of basic good netting procedure apply to both anglers and guides.

Fish can also be beached where there are good gravelly shallows with a gentlé slope. Its problems are similar to good netting technique, except that in beaching a fish it must be coaxed into the shallows intentionally. It will fight you the first two or three times its belly touches bottom, since every instinct tells a big trout that shallow water is filled with danger. When it starts to thresh in the shallows, slack off and let it run back into deeper water, forcing it back with a nagging side-pressure as soon as it stops taking line. Coax the fish back into the shallows patiently, turning its head every time it tries again to reach deep water, until finally it rolls on its side. It is possible then to slide the fish still farther up the gravel, and each time it flops, the skilled fisherman gently increases his rod pressure, using the energy of the fish to literally walk it from the water. However, rod pressure applied in panic at the wrong times and not timed with the wrenching body spasms of the fish can simply break off or tear the hook out, since its weight is now totally out of the water and fully transmitted to the leader. But beached properly, the rest of the fight is simple.

There is a second beaching method that I prefer, since it makes even better use of the remaining strength of the fish and its instincts for survival. Its methodology is simple. The tired fish is finally nagged into shallow water, and coaxed in toward the beach until it is virtually aground. Once it is lying with its gills working slowly, you carefully reel in the extra line and move quietly into the water behind the fish. The rod pressure is exerted with the tip tightly bowed beyond its head, while you stalk the fish from behind. Line pressure holds its head toward the beach, and any lunge away from the fisherman will simply strand it farther from the water. Executed skillfully, this technique makes it simple to collar your fish across the gill covers and carry it ashore.

Some fishermen have been known to soccer-kick a beached fish ashore when they have it aground, but I feel the same way about such methods as I feel about using a gaff. Such unceremonious tactics seem poor form for capturing fish as uniquely beautiful as salmon or trout, and when I see an angler or a guide roughhouse a big fish ashore with his feet, it is obvious that he has little reverence or respect for his quarry. It can also panic and lose a good fish.

Lacking a gently shelving beach, you may find it necessary to lift your fish from the water with your fingers seated across its gill covers. It is difficult in open river, but it can be accomplished if the fish is played with patience and taking it with your hands is not attempted until the fish is exhausted. It is easier to take a trout around the gill covers when you work it into the bank or a crevice in the rocks. When I am fishing without a net, I have often led good fish into an eddying backwater against the banks or literally trapped them between my legs and the downstream face of a boulder. It must be swiftly executed with confidence and a firm grip. Pressure is not exerted with all five fingers, since the index finger and thumb are best suited for holding a big fish across the gill covers. These two fingers can apply maximum pressure. It is also possible to land medium-size fish with your hands, playing them patiently until they are completely spent, and simply picking them up with a gentle cushioning of your fingers under their bellies.

However, these methods demand that a fish be played much longer than a fish that is either netted or beached, and there is always the danger that your fingers may slip into their fragile gill structures, or you might squeeze them too hard and damage them internally. Although there are many fishermen who argue that a net makes the struggle less sporting, I cannot fully agree, particularly if you intend to release your trout. Fish can be netted more quickly and handled more delicately in the meshes while you extricate the hook. It is unwise to prolong the fight, completely exhausting a fish and pushing it toward the threshold of shock, when you intend to let that fish go, and for these reasons, it is recommended that you fish with a landing net.

Any fish you intend to kill should be dispatched quickly and mercifully with a sharp rap on the head. There are a number of priest knives and other killing clubs available to anglers, and a small trout can be easily killed at midstream in the net. It may be necessary to carry a larger fish ashore, even though the meshes of the net provide excellent handling qualities. Some writers recommend breaking the necks of their fish, with the thumb in their throats levering against the fulcrum of the index finger. It is lethal and effective, but the vomerine teeth of the fish can scar a finger so badly that its roughness will literally shred the delicate tying thread when you try to dress flies later in camp. Neck-breaking and bleeding are not methods I favor, and a knife blade inserted behind the head to sever the spinal cord is difficult without going ashore. Killing methods are seldom a problem in my fishing, since I release most of the trout.

Surgical forceps are an extremely useful tool for freeing the hooks from trout you intend to release. Forceps will reach deep into the throat or gill structure to remove a fly, locking firmly on the hook and pushing it out cleanly. Handle the fish carefully in the net, taking care to protect the eyes, the gills, and its fragile entrails and bladder. Internal injuries and bleeding from too much finger pressure are a common cause of mortality in released fish. Minor bleeding from the mouth can prove either serious or superficial, and it is wise to hold such fish in the water for a little while to see if the blood coagulates quickly and stops. Fish that bleed profusely should be mercifully killed, if their blood continues to blossom through their gill covers into the current after a few minutes.

Always wet your hands in the river before you handle fish, the Michigan old-timers always preached in my boyhood summers. *Dry hands can damage the slime that protects the skin.*

Trout fishing has its share of myths, and the wet-hands theory of handling fish is perhaps one of the most foolish. It has the persistence of most old wives' tales. It is even enshrined in *Big Two-Hearted River,* the classic Hemingway story of fishing in Michigan just after the First World War. But wet hands make a slippery trout even more slippery and difficult to hold, and a struggling fish is often fatally squeezed before it is finally released. Preventing internal injury is the reason for dry hands and for handling the fish in a landing net.

Most fish die after they have been supposedly released successfully, because of the physiological and physical stress involved in playing and landing them. Their muscle structure is suffused with dangerously high concentrations of lactic acids, much like an athlete who has performed beyond his physical quality and endurance. The stress of capture has also subjected a fish to serious circulatory problems, a radical drop in its blood pressure, lack of oxygen in the blood, and fluttery heart action. Loss of consciousness can occur. Fish on the threshold of shock can seemingly be vigorous when released, only to founder and die later.

For these reasons, no fish should ever be literally thrown back into the river, particularly into strong currents. It may take as much time to help a fish recover as was spent playing it in the first place, although that fact may surprise most fishermen. Fish that are too frightened and tired to breathe properly must be gently rocked back and forth facing into the flow of current, allowing the water to work through their gills when they are too weak to breathe themselves. Sometimes the air pressure in their swim bladders is aberrative enough that a spent fish cannot keep its balance in the current. It is necessary to hold such fish gently, keeping them upright and facing into the current flow. Sometimes a frightened fish can be calmed by stroking it very slowly along the ventral surfaces.

Many fishermen remain skeptical about the high survival rate of fish that have been carefully released, yet the success of catch-and-release management has been amply proved on both public and private waters. Surprisingly good success has been achieved with the general fishing public, although no particular care has been exercised in releasing the trout on the special-management streams. Better knowledge of the proper methods for releasing fish would result in still better rates of survival.

Catch-and-release management on my favorite eastern stream has proved remarkably successful, and it has resulted in some unusual incidents. Multiple hook scars are common in its trout population, and our circle of fishermen soon get to know specific fish and their holding lies. Sometimes a good fish is taken and we recover a fly we have broken off in its mouth. Twice I have recovered my own flies from trout that succeeded in breaking a fragile half-pound tippet a few days earlier, and several times I have returned such lost flies to their owners, since their style of fly dressing was as obvious as a fingerprint.

But the most remarkable example of fish survival occurred just at twilight two summers ago. The pool riffled down along its dark, moss-covered ledges and eddied lazily through the main throat of the pool. The hemlocks cast deep shadows on the smooth currents, and the fish were dimpling softly.

What are they taking? my father asked.

It was getting darker now and it was difficult to see their rise forms. *I'm not sure,* I said. *Maybe they're taking little nymphs or pupae in the film.*

You going to fish them wet?

Maybe it'll work. I waded in quietly.

We concealed the flashlight in my waders, and I found a tiny olive pupa in my fly books. It was carefully knotted to the fine tippet and I switched off the light. There was a good fish rising almost imperceptibly in the tail shallows, and I stood wetting the tiny fly in my mouth. The fish was feeding steadily now, and the rhythm and character of its rise forms pointed to midge-pupa feeding. The cast fell softly in the gathering darkness, and I gently tightened to a delicate rise in the shadows.

Got one! I announced happily.

The fish was surprisingly strong, tunnelling deep along the bottom of the pool and shaking its head sullenly. Several times the leader raked across stones. The tippet was a cobweb-fine French nylon and I fought the fish gingerly. It took half an hour to tire the trout enough that it circled weakly in the shallows, and finally it was in my net.

Big fish? my father asked in the darkness.

It's pretty strong. The fish wrenched angrily in the meshes. *Maybe two or three pounds!*

Good work, he said.

The trout still fought me in the meshes, but it finally lay still in my hands. Searching its jaws for my fly, my fingers eventually found it and pushed it free. The big fish hung limply across my palm and made little effort to escape.

He's pretty tired, I said. *I'm going to spend some time reviving him.*

The fish made no struggle when I slipped it back into the landing net. It took several minutes of coddling before the trout had revived enough to hold itself upright in the loosely eddying meshes. Its gills were working steadily now, and I transferred it gently into the current. It sprawled in my hand for a few seconds, and drifted weakly into the pool.

He's okay. I sighed. *He seems fine.*

Suddenly my rod tightened and began throbbing, and there was a heavy splash in the darkness.

What's that? my father asked.

Strange, I laughed. *Either I've foul hooked another fish or this one's still on—if that's really possible.*

The tired eighteen-inch brown was quickly back in the net. It was still hooked, and I worked my index finger slowly along its mandible until I felt another fly firmly hooked in the jaws.

I've found my fly, I said. *That first one must've been left when somebody else hooked him and broke off.*

The trout seemed less frightened now, and it slipped off docilely into the twilight. My rod was under my right arm, and I started reeling the slack onto the reel when I realized the fish was still hooked.

I'll be damned, I said. *That's strange!*

What's wrong now? my father asked.

You're not going to believe this, I answered, *but that fish is still hooked.*

You're joking!

The fish had quite a collection of tiny flies, each trailing a delicate little strand of nylon, and I netted and released it five times. The last fly seated tightly in its jaws was my little pupa.

Hope he'll be okay, I said. *Catching the same fish five times in one night can be a little hard on him!*

He'll be fine, my father laughed.

6. How to Read Water
and What Tactics to Use

The morning wind was cool and bracing, smelling of springtime and snow-melt in the high country. It was still early, but the little tackle shop at Moose Crossing was already open. The Teton range towered majestically behind its foothill forests, its snowfields still unusually large for early summer. The rivers were finally clearing after the runoff, and some fine catches of cutthroats were coming into the Carmichael store.

The young fly-fisherman came into the tackle shop looking defeated, and he fumbled a cigarette from his wading vest, smoking impatiently while a tourist from Kansas bought a jar of salmon eggs. When the shop was finally empty except for Bob Carmichael and his wife, the fisherman frowned and haltingly explained his problem. It was not unusual in the Jackson Hole country. He had spent two days fishing the Gros Ventre and the Snake and had caught nothing but whitefish. His spirits were depressed. Since whitefish and trout seldom share the same kind of water, this man was having trouble reading the water and finding the cutthroats.

Reading the water, Bob Carmichael explained in his tackle shop a few days later, *is the secret.*

More than presentation or casting? I asked.

Hell, yes! Carmichael growled. *More important than matching a hatch, too, because it's no good to cast eighty feet or throw perfect hook casts or identify fly hatches if you're wasting all your time fishing empty water!*

You mean the man who can read water will catch fish consistently, I added. *Even if his casting is poor?*

He sure as hell will! Carmichael laughed.

Matching the hatch comes later?

Exactly! he grinned.

Carmichael was right, and every trout stream and lake has its singular character and secrets, although a mixture of patience and fishing experience and intuition can unlock its secrets. Each piece of water has its separate fingerprints, and facets of its character that appeal to a particular kind of fisherman. However, every stream or lake also shares the problems and challenges found on all trout water.

Both lakes and streams have holding places where its fish are concentrated, and other areas which are empty or support mostly coarse species. Reading a stretch of water to discover its productive and dead zones is a basic part of streamcraft. Empty water is not always shallow, but it usually lacks bottom cover, sheltering foliage, optimal current speeds, oxygenation, and currents that provide its fish population with a continuing supply of food.

Fish behavior is completely rational. Both food and survival are primary instinctual drives, and understanding this from the trout's point of view is basic in reading water correctly. The fish seek out optimal temperatures, oxygenation, shelter from predators, and adequate supplies of food. Their world is continually hostile, and a fish that is insufficiently wary will not survive. It is also a world in which the calories ingested by feeding are continually spent in survival, growth, and movement.

Small trout have the metabolism of a chipmunk, and they are constantly feeding and searching out food. Their behavior is literally predicated on the hunger for life, since it will take a full fifty pounds of insects and crustaceans to grow a fish weighing a single pound. The frantic life-style of the fingerling and baby trout is ended once a fish reaches sexual maturity. It is usually attained at eight to ten inches with brook trout and cutthroats and the endangered subspecies of our western mountains. Rainbows and brown trout typically reach twelve to fifteen inches before spawning. The feeding behavior of such mature fish is less hectic. Although a crippled baitfish or careless nymph is likely to succumb when it ventures into the holding lie of a larger trout, the movements of such fish are more measured. The frenetic metabolism of babyhood is gone, and their feeding rhythms are less frequent. Trophy-size fish seldom feed at the surface, concentrating on nymphs and baitfish and larvae along the bottom, where they can satisfy their hunger without exposing themselves to their enemies. Foraging for crayfish and minnows in the shallows means danger, and such fish are understandably wary.

The primary habitat consists of both holding lies, where the fish seek shelter and concealment, and their principal feeding lies. Big trout sometimes feed once or twice a week, but feed heavily when the mood strikes them. During their nonfeeding cycles, big fish move into their favorite holding places, which offer them maximum concealment. Hunger brings them out into the shallows and current tongues that offer optimal feeding opportunities, particularly at night. Sometimes a fish will move a considerable distance from its hiding place to feed, drifting back to the tail

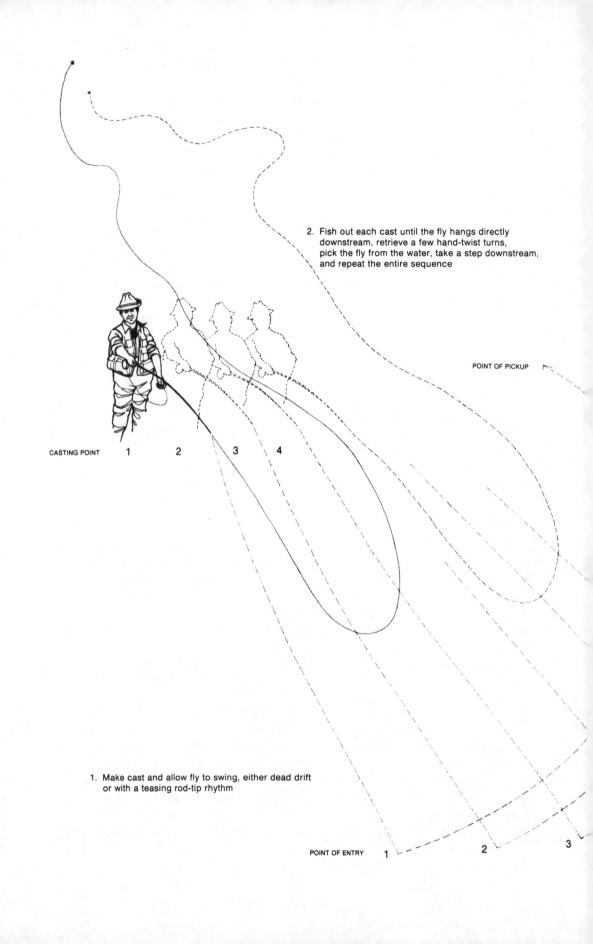

2. Fish out each cast until the fly hangs directly
   downstream, retrieve a few hand-twist turns,
   pick the fly from the water, take a step downstream,
   and repeat the entire sequence

POINT OF PICKUP

CASTING POINT   1   2   3   4

1. Make cast and allow fly to swing, either dead drift
   or with a teasing rod-tip rhythm

POINT OF ENTRY   1   2   3

FISHING WET-FLY PATTERN OF QUARTER CIRCLES

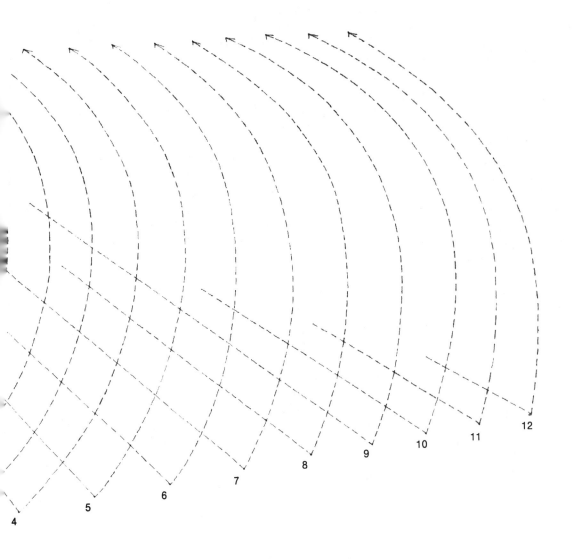

shallows of a flat to collect a fall of spent mayflies, or gathering below a stand of buttonwood trees to feed on its prolific inchworms. Fly hatches coming down from the riffles and pocket water above a pool can entice its fish into moving upstream to feed on the emerging flies.

However, in many pools the holding lie and feeding station may be virtually the same place. Resting fish may hold along the bottom, and simply drift toward the surface to feed. Others may drift out into a primary feeding current. Optimum feeding positions will bring a fish the maximum available diet forms with minimal effort and exposure to predators. Most feeding lies are not far from the places of concealment.

Every pool and reach of water has its particular pecking order for its trout population. Its social hierarchy is based upon size and aggressiveness and strength. Hatchery fish find themselves at a distinct disadvantage in competition with wild trout, and a streambred brown trout of twelve inches can displace a three-pound hatchery fish from a prime holding lie.

Since wild fish are believed to balance their populations through density and concentrations of communal scent, the introduction of too many pen-raised hatchery fish long removed from such yardsticks of instinct can hopelessly scramble the mood of the trout in a particular pool. Recent field research tends to confirm these preliminary conclusions, and I have witnessed many quarrels between the resident fish on our Brodheads mileage and the newly stocked hatchery trout placed in their pools. It sometimes takes a week to establish their ultimate pecking order of holding lies and favorite feeding stations. However, pecking order in a population of wild fish or stocked trout that have survived and wintered is typically based upon size and strength. The prime fish will establish territoriality over the best hiding and feeding places.

Reading a pool is not as difficult as the neophyte fly-fisherman might suspect. Such optimal hiding and feeding places echo familiar requirements and themes. Darker water often provides the most concealment in an open run with little shelter, since it indicates maximum depth, and a mottled bottom may offer the concealment of protective coloration. Pockets between rocks and deep scours along boulders are common holding places. Deep shade can provide a sense of concealment. Ledges and rocky outcroppings are obvious places, along with the protection provided by roots and deadfalls. Shelving gravel and deep holes are good holding lies, like primary current channels in the weeds. The pockets where a tributary joins the main current and the junction where two channels rejoin are also good places for trout. Undercut banks in both forest and meadow water are also clearly holding and feeding lies. Such places are the initial clues in reading a river, since they are common to any reach of trout water from Labrador to Tierra del Fuego.

Each river has repetitive themes in its character. Perhaps we should describe and define these components of trout water before considering appropriate tactics for specific pools. Such a glossary of trout water anatomy is important.

Falls pools are a familiar calendar scene in barber shops and country stores. Some show spectacular falls over ledges or down sluices of bedrock, chuting or tumbling into the pool below. Many falls pools churn deep into a foaming scour at their base, their currents frothy white with bubbles, while others writhe and tumble in earthquake faults or sinkholes in the bedrock below the falls. Most waterfall pools are much prettier than productive, too deep to provide the nymphs and larvae that can sustain a good population of fish. However, a waterfall pool that has a rubble bottom in the tail shallows can shelter enough forage to support a moderate number of trout. Such pools in mountain country are often deep sinkholes eroded into the solid ledges, like the pools on the upper Baker in New Hampshire or the turbulent Devil's Punchbowl on the Roaring Fork.

Chutes are really waterfalls that enter a pool at such a low angle that they become rapids too swift to harbor fish, except trout in passage to their spawning grounds or seeking cooler temperatures. Chutes and rapids usually connect pools and quiet runs. Sometimes rainbows and cutthroats are found in surprisingly heavy water, but the swift chutes and rapids are usually only a source of oxygenation.

Runs are usually a reach of relatively swift water, ranging from calf-deep to several feet. The typical run is holding water that does not actually encompass a complete pool. It is often rich in both food and fish, particularly when it lies in a sheltered place with a bottom of rubble and smooth stones.

Pocket water consists of relatively swift currents, tumbling and flowing among scattered obstacles of large rocks and boulders. Fish can hold and feed beside surprisingly fast currents there, since the hydraulic friction of the stones creates eddies and cushions in the flow. Back-eddies above a sizable stone can provide a holding lie, and such places are often favored by current-loving rainbows. The whirlpools and eddies below a boulder are obvious lies in pocket water, and various combinations of rocks can provide several types of shelter. Current scours under large rocks are also excellent holding places, and the holes between boulders are often surprisingly deep, sheltering even the largest fish. Pocket water also shelters large populations of fly life and other trout foods. Its rich oxygenation and cooler temperatures are the reason trout often migrate into pocket water and hold there through the hot days of midsummer.

Riffles are the principal food-growing zones of a stream, just as reefs and weedy shallows are the pantries in lakes and reservoirs. Such waters distribute the minute organisms that feed immature nymphs and larvae, and also provide shelter and feeding grounds for baitfish fingerlings and fry. Such riffles are rich in oxygen saturation from their tumbling patterns of flow, like the photosynthesis in the benches and shallows of impounded waters fosters oxygen-producing vegetation. Riffles are the gentle flowages over shallows of gravel and sand that tumble softly around small boulders and stones, and it is the riffles that whisper the gentle melodies that welcome the angler to any trout stream.

Current tongues are the visible concentrations of flow that come from the riffles feeding a pool or run, gather along a deadfall or ledge, or tumble between two rocks. These current tongues are the principal cornucopias endlessly carrying food to the fish, scouring silt from the spawning beds and mayfly gravel, providing and sustaining the basic rhythms of life for each organism in their underwater world.

Pools are structured in terms of a distinct anatomy between their tumbling heads and smooth tail shallows. The head of a pool can lie under a waterfall or tumbling chutes, or it may simply begin where a riffle shelves off into deeper water. It can also begin in a muted mood, with a silken run that gradually becomes deeper, and many high-water pools merely deepen into smooth-flowing flats later in the season. The throat of a pool is quite well named. It consists of the primary current tongues that tumble and slow in its deepening bathography, and where those main currents eddy down the body of the pool, they become its subaquatic spine.

The main depths of a typical pool are often called its body or middle, and its tail consists of the gravelly or stony reaches where it starts to shallow again. The gathering and accelerating of currents in these shallows are sometimes called a slick, and it often includes the break in the threshold of the broken water downstream. Much spawning activity is concentrated in these gathering tail shallows, and sometimes surprisingly large fish are found there, dropping back on dark days and evenings to feed in spite of their exposure to predators and other hazards.

Flats and still waters are often ill-defined pools, reaches of relatively good holding water that might have shaped themselves into full-blown pools with the right topography to work against. Pools are formed against obstacles. The river works and scours deep places around rocks and deadfalls and boulders, swirls deeply against a bank where the river changes its directions and moods, and literally gouges out its principal channels against a firmly rooted bank or ledge or rock slide. Flats and still waters form in sharp changes of direction and zones of gentle topography that fail to confine the force of the river.

Flats often support a surprising population of fish, in spite of their seemingly open character. Many have a bottom of sand and river-washed gravel and small stones, and many are almost devoid of sheltering boulders or vegetation. Their depth is often marginal in terms of protecting the fish, yet the fish choose to stay.

Brown trout in the flats are a little like bonefish, the late Eugene Connett liked to observe. *They survive with a mixture of wariness and speed.*

His observation has been proven on river after river, since fishing the flats successfully is a problem in stalking and stealth. Quiet currents transmit the faintest vibrations of casting, and the waves triggered by even the most skillful wading can frighten fish along an entire flat. Taking fish consistently from a shallow reach of quiet water may well be the ultimate test of fishing skill.

Banks have a widely varying character. Willow roots are densely structured and form a relatively solid barrier against the current, and trout often choose to lie in their shade. Grassy banks are also solid enough to become deeply undercut by the wearing currents. Sloping banks seldom form holding lies, but they can pose a serious tactical problem of approach, since they provide minimal camouflage for the fisherman. Shelving banks are usually formed where the current has eaten into a glacial moraine of polished stones. Cutbanks are similar, although they are composed of soil and sedimentary layers interlaced with roots. Ledges of limestone or other soft materials are often beautifully sculptured and polished by the current across the years. Slate and granite ledges also produce deep pools and holding places where the river works against them, and outcroppings of bedrock and rock slides create deep water, too.

Major obstacles like boulders and fallen trees and protruding ledge-rock also create back eddies and whirlpools. Such eddying currents often scour out deep places farther downstream, sheltering big fish in their quiet holding lies.

Multiple channels are often formed in high water, some cutting deep enough to hold significant flowages once the river has receded. Others slice through underground springheads and remain partially filled with water afterwards. Islands are formed, shaping deep holes when they are finally rejoined. Such multiple channels are often the places where a fisherman can find a big river broken up into fishable water.

Spring creeks and weedy rivers like the Firehole and Henry's Fork of the Snake and the Madison in the Yellowstone are a special problem. All rivers change in the cycles of winter and spring thawing, but alkaline rivers filled with weeds change even more, their weedy growth creating fresh channels and holding lies as each season progresses. The channels form a complex labyrinth of feeding currents and hiding places, and the weeds themselves are alive with aquatic insects and crustaceans. Fly hatches are often relatively small insect forms, stemming from the alkalinity and slow-moving water and spring-fed temperatures, but they emerge in good numbers all season. Weeds pose some unique tactical problems. Their channels split and join and rejoin, creating an intricate pattern of currents and cross currents and eddies. Such conflicting whorls of flow often appear simple at first, but their imperceptible problems of drag become obvious with the first dry-fly float.

Ray Bergman described a favorite pool in *Trout,* using his observations of several different fishermen over the course of a single afternoon, to make some important points about streamcraft. Each man read and fished the same pool differently.

Bergman tells us that his pool was not fished for almost two hours while he watched it from a hiding place in the foliage, and such a lack of fishing pressure seems remarkable some thirty-five years later. Few first-rate pools in our time are without fishing pressure for more than fifteen or twenty minutes, at least on the Catskill stream he described. It is interesting that Bergman registers a similar complaint in his introduction:

Probably every angler has his pet type of water. It is all right to have this preference, but it leads to the neglect of other types, and that is sure to reduce your chances of success. In the old days, this didn't matter much. When you went fishing, you usually had the stream to yourself—or nearly so—and you could skip from one place to another with the surety that all your favorite locations would produce.

Conditions of recent years have changed this. Now the streams are so crowded that you must make the most of whatever water you find unoccupied.

Therefore, even though it has always been important that the angler knows how to fish intelligently all types of water, now it becomes vastly more important if we hope to make our angling days something more than periods of walking and casting.

The most obvious places to fish are the good-looking pools. Being so evident, they are fished by every passerby. Thus they are less likely to produce under tough conditions than locations that are overlooked by the majority. But even though these attractive-looking pools are fished extensively, most anglers do not fish them thoroughly. In many cases they fish only the obvious and easy parts, and let the rest alone.

Bergman would have shaken his head in despair over the modern elbow-to-elbow crowds at Saxton's Falls on the Musconetcong, or the opening-week migrations to the Croton and Amawalk just outside New York. Opening day looks like a clearance sale in a department store, and on some water I fish regularly, it is not unusual to find two men waiting their turns while a third man fishes the pool.

Following the example of Bergman, this past season I spent about three hours watching a parade of fishermen cover one of my favorite pools on a classic stream in Pennsylvania. It is a beautiful piece of water, and over the past twenty seasons, its seemingly open character has revealed a difficult and moody side.

It is a pool that has gentle origins in the gravelly shallows upstream, sliding laterally against the left bank, working away from a spreading oak that shelters a picnic table. The bottom is fine pea gravel the full length of the pool except for a few large stones twenty yards from the tail. The upper third of the pool is a deeply undercut bank under the trailing grass. It ends with the current sliding out and around the roots of a large buttonwood, before working back to scour along the roots of several more sycamore trees. It is surprisingly deep along the middle fifteen yards of the pool under the trees, thigh-deep and deeper when you wade over to retrieve a fly hung up in the foliage. The run under the trees is over a pair of chest-high waders in late April, with the Gordon Quills and Hendricksons hatching, and the river running full and strong. It is difficult to cast under the low-hanging branches in early spring, and later the run lies under a leafy canopy.

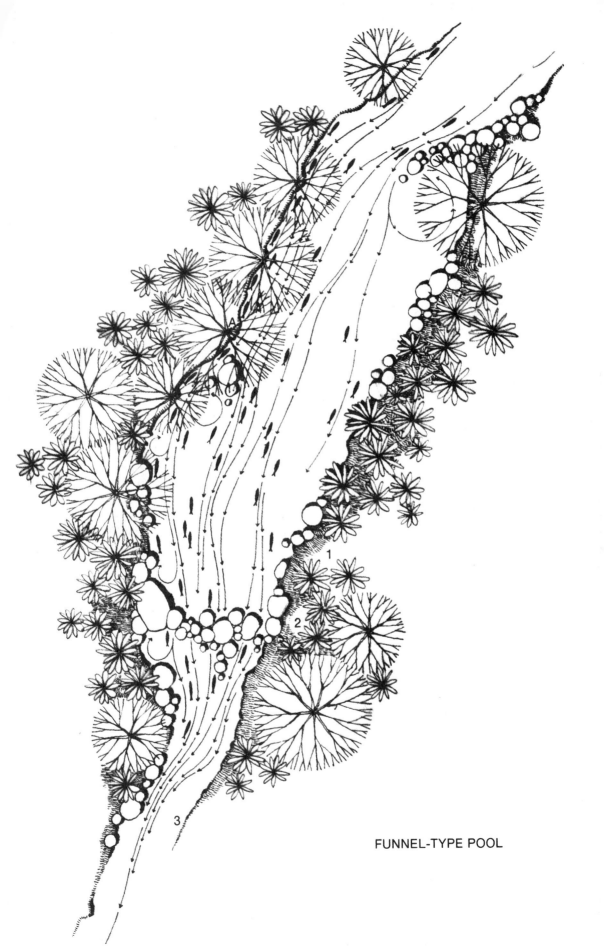

FUNNEL-TYPE POOL

The buttonwoods end about twenty yards above the break that spills over the rocks into the chute downstream, their branches covering the stones that interrupt the current. There is another tree just below the stones, with a deep eddy pushing back from its root structure, and another large eddy behind the rocks. Two current tongues spread downstream, the minor flow gliding along the roots of the final tree, and the primary current working the remaining length of the pool. The tail shallows are only thigh-deep, except for the eddying hole below the stones, but the trout hold there over the mottled bottom in spite of the lack of cover.

It is never an easy pool, even in the relatively high water after opening day. Fishing it in the late morning and early afternoon, a fisherman is standing in bright sunlight, fully exposed to the fish. It is impossible to fish nymphs and wet flies downstream, except in high water and on dark days, without scaring the trout. Later it is difficult to fish it upstream without alarming the fish, except in early morning and late afternoon, when it lies in shadows. The fish have always been skittish in this piece of water, and except for the odd trout caught below the stones or in the throat of the pool, it is often avoided by most fishermen in early summer.

It was a warm afternoon in late spring when I decided to watch other fishermen work the pool. Their tactics provide some interesting lessons about hard-fished trout.

Most spectators watch the fishing from the picnic table at the head of the pool, but I chose to cross the stream well below at A and watch from the trees. The trout were rising intermittently, and enough time passed before the first angler fished the pool to mark their positions.

One fish was lying high in the shelving riffle under the sheltering oak, and a second was rising where the current slipped laterally against the grass. The third trout was small, working in open shallows slightly downstream, and the fourth hung just above the roots of the first sycamore. The fish lying just below the roots of the tree was not rising often, but its swirls were impressive and strong. Another good fish was rising tight against the roots ten feet downstream, with a second and third lying farther out, still in the shade of the trees. Two more were working tight against the sycamore roots, five or six feet from where I was concealed. Another was lying out in the sunlight, just beyond the trees. Just downstream a twelve-inch brown was lying between the bank and the stones, and three were rising in their outside current tongue. Two more fish were rising against my bank downstream, one in the eddy between the stones and the last buttonwood tree, and another well down toward the tail. There were occasional soft rises in both the gathering tail shallows and the sunny gravel-bottomed flat across the pool, but I could not tell if a few fish were cruising, or if several trout were feeding actively in the open water.

The first angler to approach the pool answered that question, since he did not enter at its tail. The man worked through the brush and studied the pool (1). Then he made his first mistake, stepping into the sunlight about fifteen feet back from the water, and all the fish in the open shallows bolted under the spreading trees. The man had not been looking at the nearby shallows, and I doubt that he actually saw them leave. Several swam past me, following the roots along the bank, and one settled virtually at my feet. It held there nervously and did not resume its feeding.

The fisherman made his second mistake when he entered the pool below his observation point and a half-dozen fish came up from the shallows below my position before he reached the water. The fish moved past me and disappeared upstream.

The first angler had virtually ruined his chances before he had cast a fly. He missed a splashy, half-hearted rise between the three stones under the sycamores and the tree roots downstream. Since most of the fish lying in the shallows above and below his point of entry had bolted upstream under the trees, the fish lying in the shadows had stopped rising. The man covered the entire pool with a fairly large dry fly without moving a trout, and the only fish he hooked was a small chub that rose in the shallow throat of the pool, halfway between my bank and the stones.

Twenty minutes later, the fish had drifted slowly back into their feeding lies downstream. The first was a good brown trout that drifted out from the trees into the sunlight, took a fluttering caddis or two, and felt more secure. It moved farther out into the sunlight and settled behind several small stones on the bottom. It took another sedge cautiously, and finally adopted a calm feeding rhythm. Two others moved out into the shallows, and soon most of the original fish had started rising.

Another fisherman appeared, idly flicking his fly as he picked his way upstream below the pool. He did not waste any time fishing the broken shallows downstream, but he stopped below the currents that tumbled over the rocks to study my pool (2). He was obviously experienced.

Although the light was wrong to reveal most of the fish to him, he could see three or four holding in the shallows, and another rose twice while he watched. The man crouched low and slipped into the tail, casting straight upstream to a pair of twelve-inch browns. They refused his fly, but he did not frighten them with a half-dozen casts and floats.

Casts pretty well, I thought.

He changed to a much smaller fly, something I found it difficult to see on the water, and promptly took one of the fish in the shallows. Several of the others moved upstream into deeper water, but some continued to feed. The fisherman landed the fish expertly, dried his fly with a series of false casts, and placed it above the second fish. It took the fly softly and splashed in the shallows, scattering the other fish holding there. However, their departure was something less than the panic displayed when they saw the first fisherman step out into the sun, and other fish lying in the principal current tongues continued to feed. The trout lying under the trees were still working, too. Several fish that left the shallows when the fisherman took his second trout had moved in under the trees where I was sitting. They seemed concerned but not alarmed, and instead of scattering wildly up the deep channel along the roots, they settled beside the bank.

The fish upstream continued to feed quietly.

The fisherman landed his second trout and spent a few minutes preening his fly's hackles. His line worked back and forth briefly, and he turned his attention to the deeper water.

Several fish were still rising along my bank, between the trees and the gathering slick above the stones. The man apparently spotted a fish lying downstream. His next cast was a slack delivery, quartering down toward the lip of the pool, and a ten-inch brown took his fly immediately. While he was playing it, another fish rose downstream above the stones along the bank. The fisherman released his trout, dried his fly, made a cast that he checked above the next rising fish, and crouched slightly as it floated toward its station.

The trout rose and was not quite hooked. *Damn!* the angler muttered audibly when it was gone.

He took another trout just below the stones, where the leafy shadows played lazily on the current, but apparently he failed to notice the others rising softly along the bank. Two fish came up well back under the trees, where the branches hung only inches above the water.

The angler shook his head ruefully and moved slowly upstream without trying for them. It is difficult to work a fly under the foliage there, and it is surprisingly difficult to get a drag-free float on the smooth current. He took another fish upstream. It was rising under the edge of the trees, and its struggles apparently frightened those lying farther upstream, since they stopped rising. There was still another working along the stones to the right, but the man stopped fishing it after several fly changes and waded upstream.

The pool flowed quiet again and the shadows of the buttonwoods reached slowly toward the opposite bank.

Almost half an hour passed. The fish in the buttonwood pool are so accustomed to fishing pressure that they settle out and start feeding quickly. Most of the trout under the trees were rising after twenty minutes, and two or three had drifted back into the tail shallows. They resumed feeding as well, and I was tempted to fish myself when another man surprisingly appeared (3).

He worked slowly upstream along the shallows, studying the broken water below the pool. He was wearing polaroids and he stopped well below the stones, where the current spilled and tumbled from the pool. He watched for a minute or two and then started casting along the primary current tongue. There was a splashy rise and the rod doubled over, and the fisherman quickly netted a good fish. He dried his fly and stood watching. Then he cast again to the point of rocks just below the white water and his rod bent again. It was a surprisingly good trout that looked strong in his net, and he released it gently. It was a skillful performance, and I was surprised when he did not come on toward the pool.

He stood below the rocks, fishing the eddy across the stream without results, and then his quick fly-flick casting turned to the base of the rocks on the right. There was a small pocket there, but no one fished it. Most fishermen stood there before starting to fish the buttonwood pool.

I'll be damned! I gasped aloud when he hooked a third fish there, and only the noise of the water concealed my hiding place. *He's taken three trout before fishing the pool itself!*

It was an impressive beginning.

But the angler was full of surprises, and stayed below the rocks to study the pool. The sporadic green-bodied sedges were hatching again. The trout started working eagerly under the trees and along the primary current tongues. Fish drifted out into the sunny shallows and took the fluttering caddisflies, working steadily all along the pool. The fisherman still waited downstream, watching the current patiently and noting their particular feeding positions.

What's he waiting for? I wondered.

Suddenly I realized that the angler was waiting for the sun to leave the open shallows opposite the trees.

This man really knows what he's doing, I thought. *He's worth watching!*

Most of the pool was dappled in shade when the angler crouched low and finally slipped into the pool. He dropped to one knee in the shallows. His dry fly settled faultlessly over a fish in the shallows and disappeared in a quiet dimple. The fish looked about twelve inches and it was netted after a brief fight. The man waited on one knee until the other trout had forgotten its capture, and then quickly took another. He missed one and took three more in the shallows, simply by resting the water between fish.

That's eight already, I thought.

Another trout rose against the rocks across the pool, and the fisherman shifted his position slightly before making a fine negative hook cast. The flat was perfect and the fish rose confidently. It bolted upstream and easily sheared the delicate tippet on a stone.

The angler laughed and dried his fly.

When a fish rose splashily behind the rocks, he made a quick upstream cast and hooked it deftly. It splashed toward the right-hand shallows and frightened a pair of fish that darted upstream. While it was still struggling, two fish rose along the roots just downstream from the stones. It was a difficult place. The current tongue lay two feet from the bank, catching the leader and dragging a fly almost instantly. It required exaggerated hook casts, and the angler dropped one perfectly just below the roots. It bought him a full ten inches of float, and it fooled the fish lying there. The fish working in the eddy upstream was in a more difficult place, but a six-inch float took it, too.

He's taken ten. I watched him with fascination. *And he hasn't even fished under the trees yet!*

Casting under the trees is difficult, but it was a pleasure to watch this man work his dry fly back under the branches. He worked stealthily into a position just above the rocks, and casting in a plane just inches from the water, he hooked a cast deep under the foliage. His fly hooked past me and dropped above the fish that had been lying against my bank all afternoon. I held my breath as it approached the fish. It turned and drifted to intercept the line of drift and was hooked, cartwheeling sideways under the trees. It spooked another fish I had not seen, and it scurried wildly upstream into the main currents.

That probably spooked the easy fish, I smiled. *Let's see how he does in tight.*

It was a masterful performance.

Although he left the fly in a strong fish lying against the roots, his softly delivered hook casts fooled three more browns along the bank upstream. He missed another above the sycamore, and took the one lying against the grass in the throat of the pool. The last fish was just off the stones, high on the right bank. It was a free-rising and selective trout that often frustrated me.

Let's see how he does on that one, I thought.

The man made several casts with his tiny sedge imitation, and it was rejected each time. He changed flies twice without better luck, and then he stopped and added a smaller tippet. The fish turned under his fly but refused it. The fisherman changed to a third fly pattern, probably a small terrestrial imitation, and the fish took it softly on the first float. It bolted downstream and the fly came out, but he had hooked a fish that the other anglers had failed to move. It had been a remarkable display of fishing a funnel-type pool with a wide body and narrow tail shallows, and I wondered how well he might have done fishing it fresh—two other anglers had frightened its trout before, and yet this man had hooked sixteen fish and landed fourteen of them.

The typical oval pool is another problem altogether, and perhaps the most dramatic piece of water I have fished is a superb oval-type hole on a small river in Chile. It lies one hundred yards below the *hosteria* against the foot of a towering cliff of polished stone. Flowering vines trail down the face of the cliff, sometimes touching the current with their blossoms. Tall pines stand high on the ledges across the pool. The trees and thickets of mimbre bushes and bamboo make it difficult to fish. The lush rainfall of southern Chile supports dense foliage and bamboo growth along the principal holding lies in the throat of the pool.

The head is a chute of swift white water. It sweeps left toward a rocky shore of impossibly dense vegetation, except for a promontory of boulders. The primary current tongues sweep in a clockwise flow, sucking deep under the tangled logs and brush at the base of the cliff. They split along the bottom of the logjam, some following the smooth cliffs and some eddying back into the depths of the pool. There is a secondary eddy that works back against a gravelly beach. The currents along the cliff face gather into a swift slick toward the tail, broken only by a brief eddy behind a boulder, and slide into a rocky riffle that ends the pool.

The main body of the pool is extremely deep. It shelves off abruptly below the tumbling chute, reaching as much as fifteen feet in depth off the boulders. It remains almost as deep among the tangled deadfalls, shallow-

OVAL POOL

ing slightly toward the final logs. Except for a dark current scour tight against the cliffs, the rest of the pool flows smoothly over its pale bottom sand and gravel. It is beautiful water.

The path leading down from the *hosteria* leads directly to the rocky point and scalloped beach. Since most of the trout lie across the primary currents against the far boulders, any cast to them from the point of rocks (1) is quickly torn away by the current. However, there are sometimes a few trout lying on the inside of the clockwise currents, in rather deep water, and I took several there with nymphs fished deep on a sinking lie. The pool is much too deep for the dry-fly method, although fish occasionally took positions facing the reverse eddies in the body of the pool, and covering their lies is like fishing upstream.

It is also extremely deep along the logjam, and I often fished these trout with big marabous on high-density lines. It involved an upstream cast. Sometimes it was a short cast, to reach the fish lying in the reverse eddies, and sometimes it was a long double haul to cover the fish along the deadfalls. Each cast was allowed to sink back deep with the current, overcasting the fish slightly so that my fly fluttered down among them, and then I stripped the marabou rapidly downstream. It produced a five-pound rainbow one warm evening in late October, when the orchards and flowering trees and meadows were rich with the Chilean springtime.

Downstream, the fish lying along the cliff and the boulders can be fished with a wet fly from the gravel bar (2) or with a dry fly from the shallows below (3). Sometimes a few fish hold in the gathering tail shallows farther down, but the swift currents and bamboo thickets make any thought of getting below them out of the question. They can be taken casting down with wet flies and streamers, although I once hooked a heavy fish there in the shallows just before dark and was completely helpless when it bolted downstream.

But many big fish hold toward the head of the pool, across its main throat currents. These fish are seldom tried from the point of stones (1), because they are virtually unreachable from there. However, one morning I happened to see a large fish roll under the tree in the throat of the pool. I decided to walk upriver and cross, fishing downstream (4) into the throat of the pool with a large nymph. The big fish did not take my fly, but I caught two others and decided to work farther downstream. Another rainbow took my nymph just above the boulder (5) and still another was hooked and lost well out in the pool. Fishing from the boulder itself, I rose two more downstream in the primary current tongues, but failed to hook either one. Finally a heavy brown took a big marabou tight against the deadfalls, and fought me deep in the pool before it fouled my leader in the logs and broke off. These were fish that could not have been covered from the side of the pool that was usually waded. Without the effort of crossing the river a good two hundred yards upstream, and wading deep to cast from the more difficult side, they could not have been fished and taken.

It is an important lesson on any pool.

Another difficult pool is the hairpin type, in which a serpentine river loops back on itself in a complete change of direction. It is common on western meadow water. Since the main currents change banks twice in such pools, there are often deceptively complicated currents and difficult angles of presentation for the dry fly. The hairpin-type pool has deeply undercut banks on most small meadow streams, and on larger watersheds flood levels often create backwaters behind the primary lines of drift.

The pool illustrating the hairpin type lies in the bunchgrass meadows of a famous little river in Wyoming. Its selective brown trout have taught me much over the years.

It was a cool September morning. The grass was golden yellow along the deeply undercut banks, and the light wind stirred in the willows and lodgepole pines. There was little activity when I started fishing, but just before noon a fine hatch of tiny *Paraleptophlebia* flies started emerging. The trout liked them, and after the first few tentative rises they began feeding hungrily. The hatch reached its peak when I waded toward the hairpin pool beyond a reach of shallow riffles.

Four trout were rising along the left bank. They were lying above and below a boulder, in the shade of a single lodgepole pine and several willows, and I stopped and worked upstream on my knees in the gravelly shallows (1). The first brown was lying in open currents and took readily, but the second was more difficult. It was stationed just behind the large stone where the eddying current rejoined the flow of the main stream. The river looked glassy smooth, but drag quickly proved a difficult problem. I laid out one fairly good float, but the fish rose splashily and felt the hook and stopped feeding. The trout just above the boulder took eagerly on a straight dry-fly float, and its companion rose too, bolting upstream and breaking off in a muskrat hole. The current ran shallow here, but it got deeper along the right bank upstream, where a pair of rocks interrupted the flow.

Crossing the main current, I fished upstream from a station just opposite a big pine. Its shadows concealed me perfectly from the trout. There were six or eight working immediately above and below the stones, with a small eddy behind them. Four fish seemed to lie below the stones, with more rising farther upstream. The two bottom fish were quickly taken, and the other two stopped feeding. The fish lying under the bank above the stones and the two holding visibly inside the current tongues above me were still feeding. But there was another fish lying in shallow water to the left that I failed to see; it fled upstream in terror and the fish lying along the bank stopped rising, too.

They're really spooky, I thought.

Wading slowly upstream to a position just above the rocks (3), I stopped and filled my pipe, and stood waiting while the trout forgot my clumsy approach. Three more fish were lying along the bank, just beyond the primary flow. It meant a series of slack hook casts, but the patterns of flow were straightforward, and I took all three on a darkly hackled Blue Quill in size twenty. There was another fish lying in an intersection of crosscurrents, just where a strong eddying flow left the main currents to work back counterclockwise behind a huge, half-drowned spruce log. It looked fairly simple, but that turned out to be mistaken. The first float dragged badly before I realized that a minor eddy flowed back against the larger backwater currents upstream. No matter how I manipulated the cast and float, the fly dragged almost immediately, and on the fifth or sixth cast its clumsy wake put the fish down completely.

You do good work! I muttered to myself.

I worked slowly upstream, studying the water ahead for rising fish. There were several along the spruce log, and I was watching them when another rise caught my attention. It was a good fish dimpling in the reverse currents of the eddy, almost in the grass hanging down from the deeply undercut banks.

It looked like a sizable trout, but it was in a difficult place to present my fly, beyond several conflicting currents. While I studied it, two other trout rose softly, deep in the backwater.

These fish were in even more difficult positions for a dry fly, and I waded out below the deadfall (4). It was a place where I could now cover both of the fish along the log and try as well for the three trout in the eddy. Three good browns were rising just below the spruce log, and two more were feeding near its roots along the bank. There was a big fish rising behind the log, where the current boiled up on its downstream side. It was an impossible lie.

That one's safe, I thought. *Sometime it should be tried from the backwater side—but some other day.*

It was too much trouble to wade down one hundred yards, cross the stream, and hike back to fish that trout. It was too deep to wade across anywhere else. And there were enough other good fish rising upstream, fish large enough that I was not tempted to try the big fish behind the log.

Conventional hook casts took one of the fish just off the branches, and the others were frightened by its splashing. One of them moved up along the log and resumed its feeding. Moving slightly above my first position (4), I decided to try the fish in the backwater along the grass. It took an exaggerated slack-line cast with the rod tip held high, holding the line above the whirlpooling eddies that could catch it and cause drag. Finally I checked a cast just right, and its series of slack loops created enough natural float that the fish took the fly. Its position in the current was almost straight downstream, and I delayed my strike to prevent taking the fly away from the trout. When it was well hooked, it shook itself sullenly and burrowed deep under the bank. The leader touched something under the grass, pulled free before it could break, and I held the rod parallel to the water. The gentle side pressure finally moved the fish out into open water, and when it tried for the log, it was already too tired.

Gentle pressure forced it back, out of the backwater eddies and into the current downstream. It was a surprisingly good trout, a female brown ripe with eggs. Its full eighteen inches filled the net, and I handled it gently in

HAIRPIN POOL

the meshes. The fish stayed beside my legs for a few minutes, and finally it drifted back into the shadow of the lodgepoles.

The other fish in the backwater had stopped feeding. Three fish were still working at the base of the fallen spruce. Two were originally lying there, and the third was a fish that I had frightened upstream earlier. There was a fourth trout positioned just below a single willow, still farther upstream.

Two fish took splashily and were lightly hooked. One came off immediately, and the other stayed hooked until I finally turned it toward my net. The third fish was resting right at the roots of the deadfall. Surprisingly, it showed little interest in my tiny Blue Quill, and I tried several floats over its feeding lie.

Maybe the hatch has changed, I thought.

I waded over into the main current and collected a half dozen tiny mayflies. The hatch had indeed changed, and these little bluish duns now had pale olive bodies.

No wonder. I rummaged through my flies. *No quill-bodied fly looks like these Blue-winged Olives.*

There were two or three patterns in my boxes that were tied on eighteen and twenty hooks. My first float over the trout lying at the tree roots hooked it. Though it was a twelve-inch brown, it had been a selective fish, and its choosiness had been the barometer of a changing hatch. There were many more of the little Olives coming now, and more fish seemed to be rising.

The sharp bend in the river was filled with tangled logs, with a pair of boulders well ahead. I waded upstream to the edge of a sandbar (5) and watched for rising fish. The primary currents were now deeply shaded by dense willows and several large lodgepole pines, and a surprising number of trout had started rising there. There were four along the lower end of the logjam, and a rather good fish was feeding just below the largest boulder, picking off the insects that came sailboating around its surface. Two more were holding above the rocks, and another pair had settled on either side of a smaller rock upstream.

These fish were all lying outside the main current tongues, except for the three at the boulder, and the flow was deceptively complicated. Drag was clearly a problem and a simple hook cast was not the solution. Finally I took two fish along the logs with a cross-stream cast, dropping the fly with a downstream hook and extending the float with a quick fly-line mend. The trout behind the boulder surprised me with a rapier-quick rise, and I left the fly in its jaws, shearing off the fine tippet clumsily. It rattled me and I was still thinking about it when I missed the first fish lying above the boulders. The second proved an easy mark, but it ran upstream and frightened the others feeding along the rocks.

The hatch was diminishing now, although a few trout were still working along the left-hand bank and around a midstream boulder. Wading upstream opposite the stones (6), I marked down three tight against the bank. Two more were below the midstream boulder, one lying in its right-hand currents and the other holding almost in the eddy on the left. Its splashy rises and disturbances in the current told me a third fish was working above the boulder, but it was impossible to see it from below. The nearest trout took readily on a straight upstream delivery, but while I was playing it, the hatching flies stopped abruptly. The trout ceased rising altogether, and although I fished over the runs where the others had been seen, they refused my fly and stayed along the bottom. It had been a fine morning.

The S-shaped pool is typical of many trout streams. The particular pool in the illustration is a forest stretch of a favorite trout stream in lower Michigan, and we often camped under the trees above the second logjam in my youth (A). It is a reach of water that holds many memories from the years after the Second World War, fishing its gentle tree-sheltered bends in early summer.

The S-shaped series of holes in the drawing is too deep to wade across, except fifty yards below our campsite. Normally, we walked downriver and fished up past the tent, working through the deep hole upstream to the shallower runs beyond the bend. Getting out of the river one hundred yards above the camp was marshy and difficult after dark, and we often waded back downstream past the camp in the darkness to leave the river at our entry point (1).

The river above our entry shallows was fairly open, without much cover except for willows along the bank. Sometimes two or three fish held there, but they were usually foolish hatchery fish displaced into this less desirable lie by the resident population.

It was a minor piece of water, worth a few casts and perhaps fifteen minutes before moving upstream (2) to fish the deep, shadowy run under the right bank. This was prime water, deep and sheltered by dense foliage virtually the entire day, its throat sweeping down along the deadfalls and under the bank. There were usually six or seven fish rising there during a good fly hatch, and it could be productive. More fish were often positioned around the vibrating branches of the dead trees, but they were difficult to reach. Sometimes I simply waded through their holding currents as unobtrusively as possible, knowing they would return and start feeding again once my passage was forgotten. Sometimes I fished back down toward them with wet flies or nymphs, and I took two or three good fish there with a downstream dry-fly presentation. However, we also fished them upstream by wading into the deadfall branches (3) and making short casts over the branches between. These trout in the logjam and the fish in the complicated eddies immediately downstream were rather difficult quarry. The fish at the bottom of the run could be reached straight upstream from the right-bank shallows (2), but the eddying currents had scoured out such a deep backwater that one could not wade directly up to the logs (3), and a detour toward the left bank was necessary. The route around to the third casting position was a tiptoe circuit, and we often had to step across the logs to reach the next casting point (4). The hole was usually too deep, shelving off steeply below the branches, to let us circle easily around the deadfalls. It was difficult water to wade and fish.

The deeply undercut corner immediately below the dead trees was particularly hard to cover. Casting from below was impossible, both because of the distance and the overhanging branches. Fishing the corner laterally was impossible, because the backwater currents quickly caught the fly line and dragged the fly. Sometimes a stealthy approach along the branches produced fish from the corner with short casts made directly across or down, keeping as much of the line off the water as possible, and standing right in the branches (3). Sometimes I stood directly above the corner (5) and fished these trout directly downstream with a sunken fly or a small streamer.

There were often a few fish lying in the open shallows (5), where the back eddies shelved off toward the logs. These fish were easily caught if they were out in the main current, but drag became a problem if they held inside the eddies themselves.

However, more fish could usually be found next to the smaller logjam upstream. It was a primary holding zone. The fallen trees offered a combination of shelter, food-carrying currents, and concentrations of oxygen. The current tongues along the face of the logs were simple and straightforward enough, and from a positon downstream along the willows (5), one made an ordinary upstream cast. Sometimes the last fish held in slightly eddying currents toward the roots of the logs, requiring an exaggerated slack-line or hook-type cast. It was easy wading in the sandy shallows toward the logjam (6) and it was good night-fishing water. My father once took a three-pound brown there after midnight, during a heavy hatch of big *Hexagenia* drakes in early summer.

These sandy shallows (6) afford a good casting position for reaching trout rising in the deep bend upstream, when they were working in the main currents. One summer during the big mayfly hatches I took a twenty-one-inch brown that was tight against the willows, where the gravel shelved off into the backwater. It was taking spent *Hexagenia* flies after a twilight mating swarm had ended, and it took heavily and fought hard in the darkness.

Fish that lay facing the reverse currents in the backwater were harder to catch. Any fly presented from the shallows (6) downstream was subject to an impossible drag, but a short slack-line cast directly across from the edge of the hole itself (7) could be productive. It was necessary to hold the rod tip high and keep the line free of the conflicting currents, but I took several good trout that way in those early summers. Sometimes a fish would feed in the midday hours, cruising on the clockwise current flow, and I took one fishing between the willows from the bank on a hot afternoon in July. It was barely six feet away, and not much more than the leader went into my cast. When the trout inhaled my fly, I was just as surprised as the fish.

MISCELLANEOUS NYMPHS AND CRUSTACEANS

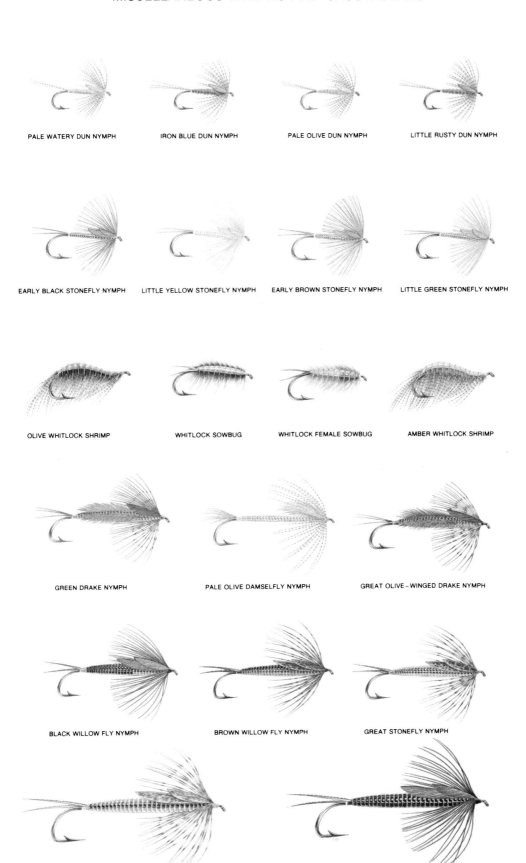

PALE WATERY DUN NYMPH

IRON BLUE DUN NYMPH

PALE OLIVE DUN NYMPH

LITTLE RUSTY DUN NYMPH

EARLY BLACK STONEFLY NYMPH

LITTLE YELLOW STONEFLY NYMPH

EARLY BROWN STONEFLY NYMPH

LITTLE GREEN STONEFLY NYMPH

OLIVE WHITLOCK SHRIMP

WHITLOCK SOWBUG

WHITLOCK FEMALE SOWBUG

AMBER WHITLOCK SHRIMP

GREEN DRAKE NYMPH

PALE OLIVE DAMSELFLY NYMPH

GREAT OLIVE – WINGED DRAKE NYMPH

BLACK WILLOW FLY NYMPH

BROWN WILLOW FLY NYMPH

GREAT STONEFLY NYMPH

GIANT GOLDEN STONEFLY NYMPH

GIANT BLACK STONEFLY NYMPH

STREAMERS AND BUCKTAILS

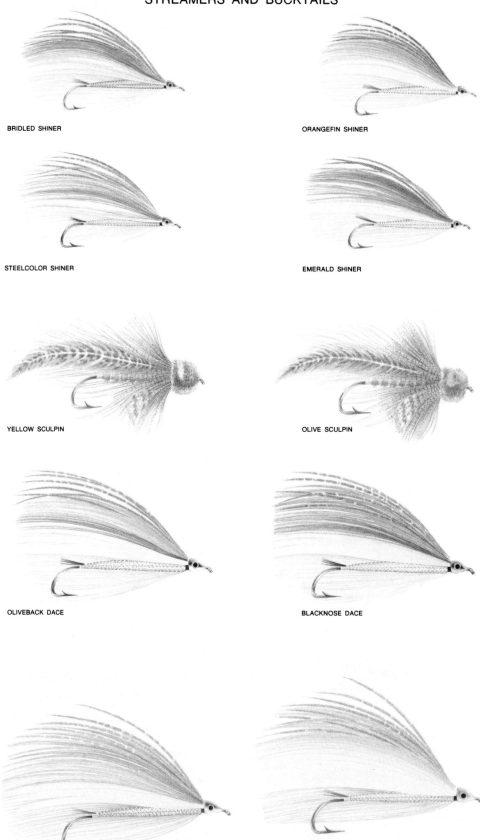

BRIDLED SHINER

ORANGEFIN SHINER

STEELCOLOR SHINER

EMERALD SHINER

YELLOW SCULPIN

OLIVE SCULPIN

OLIVEBACK DACE

BLACKNOSE DACE

SMELT

GOLDEN SHINER

S-SHAPED POOL

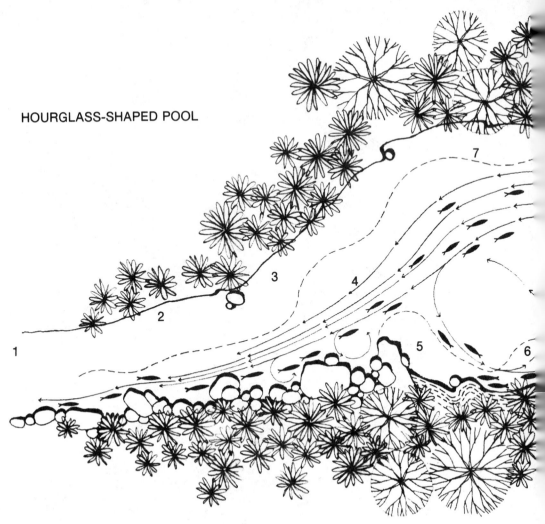

HOURGLASS-SHAPED POOL

Above the deep hole in the bend, the river flowed shallow again over its bottom of sand and fine gravel. There was not much holding water there. Sometimes a fish or two were found rising in a brief run along the right-hand willows. These rises were small, and we seldom bothered with them when we passed upstream, until one evening I cast to a trout working in a slight niche underneath the willows. It took my sixteen Adams with a soft little dimple, and when I tightened there was a wild explosion. Spray showered high in the darkness, and a half-seen monster threshed and cartwheeled upstream angrily under the willows.

My God! I gasped. *It's huge!*

The big brown sliced upstream against the swift-flowing shallows, the leader humming like a guitar string where it cut the surface currents. It wallowed heavily on the surface, made another strong run upstream, and suddenly the line went slack in the darkness.

He's gone, I thought in anguish.

When I reeled to retrieve line I discovered the fish had actually turned downstream past me, fouled the leader in the willows, and broken off. The

big brown was gone, but we never ignored the little run along the willows after that.

There is a fine, hourglass-shaped pool on a small river in the Pocono mountains, and it has provided me with excellent sport over the years. Its head is a spreading riffle, filled with swift-water hatches, that swings in against a series of mossy ledges. The primary currents flow deep and strong under the sheltering rhododendron there, back-eddy briefly above an outcropping that projects from the ledge, and swing into the lower chamber of the hourglass. It is all prime holding water.

The past few seasons this fine ledge-rock pool has surrendered a half dozen browns better than twenty inches, several of them on dry flies. It has particularly good fly hatches throughout the season, and its fish above the tail of the lower pool (4) like to free rise most of the day. However, these fish are usually smutting to minute insects and are highly selective.

The right bank is dense with hemlocks and rhododendron, and its ledges rise as much as fifteen and twenty feet directly above the water. The upper chamber is six to eight feet deep against the ledges opposite the shallows (10) and the primary currents of the lower pool are as much as twelve feet deep. The powerful eddy opposite the outcropping (9) was scoured down to eight or ten feet in a recent spate of high water. It shallowed the back eddy (5) and the backwater below the overhanging ledge (6), making it possible to wade there cautiously, fishing the trout that lie facing into the primary reverse currents.

There are always several fish lying in the smooth run below the pool too, and I usually begin fishing it there (1). It is the place where Christopher Lehmann-Haupt, the literary critic of *The New York Times*, caught the best trout of his fly-fishing career, a fine male brown of nineteen inches that took his wet fly just at dark. Lehmann-Haupt was understandably euphoric that night.

These fish can be surprisingly difficult, and the smooth run along the willows looks easy. There is a large flat stone there that usually conceals a good brown between twelve and sixteen inches. When it moves out into the main current to feed on aquatic hatches, it is relatively easy to interest, but when it holds tight against the stone to sip terrestrials it becomes a difficult fish. At such times it takes a perfect positive hook cast to fool it, or any of the other selective browns in the run.

Fish also hold above and below outcroppings and stones immediately upstream, as well as in the eddy behind the boulder that lies just below the tail of the pool. Although the shallows (2) look like a good position for covering the fish off the rocks and the boulder, drag is a surprising problem. Better floats are possible with a cross-stream cast thrown with slack or a downstream hook, while standing at the middle of the sandbar (3). It is also a fine angle for covering the tail shallows of the lower pool, using careful hook casts. Once these fish have been fished properly, the best position for presenting a fly to the trout holding in the tail of the pool is off the first outcropping of the ledge itself (4). It is a prime position for a good dry-fly float as far up the pool as you can cast your fly, as long as the line falls in the primary spinal currents of the pool. Outside those currents, its surface is a nightmare of small back eddies and reverse currents that drag a dry fly unmercifully. It is demanding water.

However, the fisherman who cannot cast seventy-five feet and manipulate his fly at that range can wade up the left bank where the rocky bottom shelves off into deep water (7). It is slippery footing, but by working carefully along the shoreline, it is possible to reach a sandy place (8) just below the point of the ledge. Early each season the small *Capnia* and *Taeniopteryx* stoneflies migrate to the ledges to emerge at the waterline and come fluttering down the current.

The primary left-hand eddy off the ledge is much too deep to wade, but there is a large enough opening (9) to fish the upper face of the outcropping, as well as the current below the ledge. It is a favorite place of my old friend Stinson Scott, casting patiently to the point of rocks with his small bucktails and streamers.

The back eddies above the clearing (9) are too deep to wade, but it is possible to wade out on the sandy bottom (10), fishing directly across to the ledge and the well-like eddy slightly downstream. Drag is a problem here, requiring a hook cast or slack cast downstream. There is a large stone lying deep in the mouth of the eddy, directly under the main currents and the first reverse line of flow. Two or three good fish are usually in tight against the ledge, particularly under an overhanging rhododendron. Sometimes fish feed inside the currents, in open water over a gravelly bottom, and are easily taken with a straight dry-fly cast. Two notches in the ledge lie immediately upstream, and fish hold right against the stones. These trout are all lying in drag-type currents, and exaggerated hook casts and slack-line presentations are needed, although few anglers seem to sense the almost imperceptible dragging of their flies.

Sometimes a better float is possible by fishing directly across or slightly downstream, moving up into the gravelly bottom just below the riffle (11). It is possible to cover both the shelving run in the riffle itself and the swift slot under the willows upstream. Good fish hold here often, particularly below the roots of a weathered stump. The riffle has always held a good population of big stonefly nymphs and fine browns. Its upper currents must be fished from the shallows, at the corner of the riffle, because of the swift intervening currents (12). It is possible from there to keep the line out of those current tongues, working both the upper riffle and the narrow scour that flows swift and dark along the fallen tree. Several times I have taken a sixteen- or seventeen-inch fish in this little run, fishing a big stonefly nymph just after daylight in early summer.

The big ledge pool is a superb example of the hourglass-type reach of water, and with its riffles and ledges and deep backwaters and willow-hung tail shallows, it is virtually a miniature eastern trout stream in itself.

The right-angle pool shown in the diagram is found on a small mountain river in the Catskills. It has been formed where the current collides with a rock slide at the base of a steep, forest-covered ridge. It is a moody pool that has never been particularly kind to me over the years, although this past season it gave me one lovely afternoon of sport.

Its head is a swift riffling chute of water that plunges and turns under a dense stand of rhododendron and laurel. The roots of the willows and the slide of rocks below the right-angle bend itself force those currents ninety degrees. The bottom shelves off abruptly in that bend, reaching depths of six to eight feet. Periods of high water have not deepened the throat of the pool, but such spates have scoured out the belly of the pool. The stones dislodged by these minor floods have both lengthened the pool itself and been deposited along a reach of broken pocket water downstream. What was once a shallow riffle in the past now holds a surprising population of fish, and these newer trout lies have changed our approach.

During other seasons we entered the pool at its tail shallows, below the present location of the bottom boulder (7). However, entering now can

RIGHT-ANGLE POOL

spook the newer fish lying there into the body of the pool upstream, spreading alarm throughout its main holding currents.

The spates have left a deeply shaded run under the hemlocks downriver, and it has proved productive this past summer. Most fishermen cover the deep pool downstream, fishing streamers under the laurels and in the swift currents at its throat (10). It is good holding water, but an angler working the pool from there usually stands in bright sunlight, clearly exposed to every fish in the pool. I fish the pool at that position in high or slightly discolored water, but at normal river levels and clarity, the best starting point has been at the bottom of the pocket water (1).

Two or three fish are often holding in the hemlock shallows above my starting point (1), and once I have covered them properly, I wade carefully to the back eddy (2). Trout often feed on both sides of the main current upstream, and from the next eddy (3) it is possible to cover the fish lying in the next throat among the rocks. The tail shallows of the pool itself are immediately above, and several fish are often feeding in the gathering currents. Wading stealthily to the currents downstream (4), it is possible to cover the trout holding between the eddies above. The right-hand

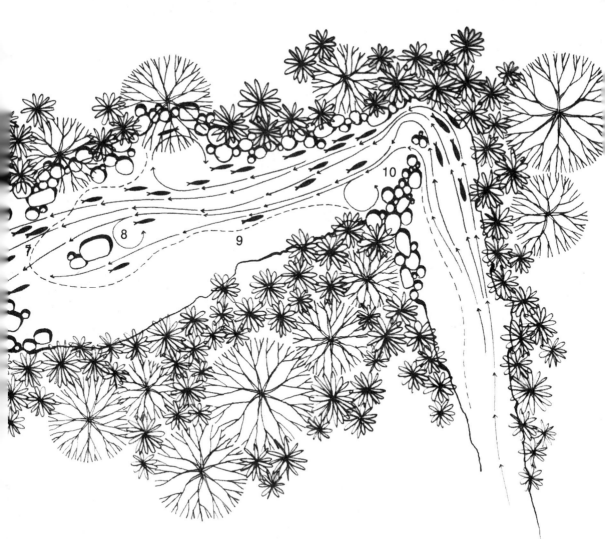

backwater (5) is ideal for fishing the smooth tail currents, and the smooth flow itself (6) is a fine tactical position for covering the rocky lies in the bottom of the pool. This past season I have found good trout on both sides of the current, and around the rocks on the left. Careful stalking into the main currents above (7) often produces with a hook cast delivered ahead of the boulders on the left, and I took an eighteen-inch brown there this past April. Another day I caught a slightly smaller fish that was feeding beyond the boulder at midstream. It was lying in surprisingly open water, and I literally presented my dry fly over the boulder to the fish. It took without hesitation.

These fish lying in the rocky tail shallows are trout that must not be frightened upstream into the pool itself.

Watchdog fish! Bob Carmichael described them. *Fish that alarm everything in the pool if they see you first!*

It is best if you can catch these sentry fish in the tail of the pool, and I usually stay quietly in the gathering currents (7), studying the belly and throat of the pool for rises. Patience is unquestionably a virtue at this stage. Fish often hold in the deep water, just where it starts to shallow above the midstream boulder. The ones lying in the primary currents are usually taken with a simple upstream cast if they are unaware of the angler standing in the currents below (7). The fish lying in the cushioning eddy above the boulder is a more difficult problem, and slack-line casts are sometimes effective. Hook casts are also needed for any fish lying in the clockwise back eddy under the big willow upstream, and a decent float over the fish often found lying in the reverse flow itself is even more difficult. My best luck with them has come by wading very slowly into the eddies above the boulder (8), giving the fish working in the backwater shadows time enough to forget my approach, and making parachute check casts into the eddy at short range.

From the same position slightly below the eddy it is possible to cover the fish feeding upstream at the bottom of the rock slide. Sometimes there are trout over the open gravel toward the right of the primary currents. Several times I have spooked a fish there by casting toward the others in the throat of the pool and frightening it with the fly line. Careless wading can also startle such fish, triggering them upstream among the others. Good casters can reach the entire throat of the pool, but some lies against the stones are more easily covered from the gravel bar farther up (9). Later in the summer, fish often move upstream into the swift water chute under the overhanging rhododendron in search of oxygen, and I have often taken them there fishing on my knees just below the stones (10).

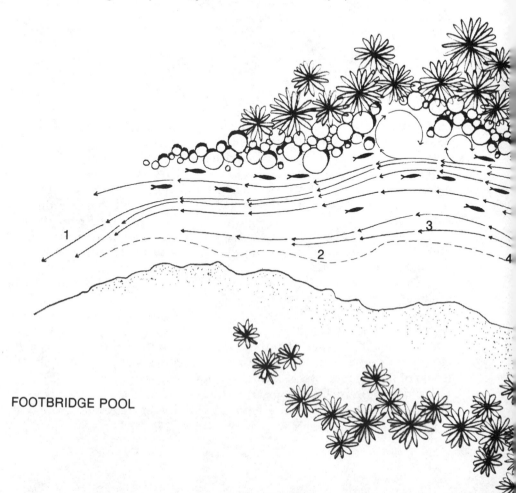

FOOTBRIDGE POOL

It is a fine deep-throated pool, its currents dark and swift against the rock slide. This past season it gave me a fine twenty-three-inch brown on a big stonefly nymph. Some years it seems almost devoid of trout, and their absence is usually symptomatic of a single cannibal-size brown. Once I tried to remove such a fish from the pool with a huge marabou streamer, slipping catlike into the tail shallows (7) and double hauling the full length of the current to the throat. The big marabou settled deep on the current, and when I stripped it back there was a vicious strike deep along the bottom—and it easily snapped my fresh 0X tippet.

There is a footbridge pool on a fine little Colorado river, with a divided channel upstream, that has offered me some excellent fishing in past years. It has its head in a shallow smooth-flowing flat along the willows and the rocks. It is a stretch that splits into two channels, one tumbling and swift among the rocks and the other a small run carved into a willow-hung bank.

The footbridge crosses the river just below the island, its center pier rooted into the rocky shallows downstream. Its masonwork cribbing is reinforced with large stones, dumped to form a crude riprap on their upstream faces. There was a shoal of large rocks just upstream from the bridge, and a number of good fish often held above and below the sheltering obstacle they formed. It was too deep and turbulent to fish

them from below the footbridge, and I often stood there to watch them.

It was also possible to observe them in the deep holding currents below the bridge, richly spotted rainbows lying nervously in the strongest current tongues and darker, deeper shapes that were probably browns.

The rushing main channel was joined by the secondary flow of the side channel below the bridge. The back eddies downstream from its center pier had deposited a sizable mound of sand and an extensive gravel bar along the right bank below. Bunchgrass covered the gentle bank above the gravel, and the entire left bank above and below the footbridge was densely lined with willows. Scrub-oak thickets clustered on the higher ground, and up on the foothill slopes beyond there were stands of lodgepole pine and aspen. Snow-melt water levels had exposed large stones and boulders along the banks where the river cut into the glacial drift that formed the valley floor. Fifty yards below the pool the river was shallower and flowed swiftly over the stones. It was a strong riffle where I once watched Charles Fothergill, the famous fly dresser from Aspen, take more than a dozen rainbows with one of his weighted roughly dubbed nymphs.

The willows were too thick to enter the pool from the left bank, and we crossed the footbridge and walked down through the scrub-oak pastures to the tail shallows. It was eighty or ninety yards back to the bridge, and by the time we had fished that distance carefully the fish under its spans had forgotten us and resumed feeding.

The holding water began along some large rocks under the willows along the left bank, and we usually fished it from the gravel shallows across the current (1). The fish lying both in and just beyond the primary currents were readily fishable from the right-hand flowage, and the rainbows seemed to like the open currents just opposite and above a small backwater on the left bank. These fish were ordinarily fished from the sandbar (2). The brown trout usually were found farther up the pool, particularly in the eddies behind the left abutment cribbing of the bridge, and in the slower side-channel hole under its right-hand span.

We usually fished the main pool below the left span from a gravel bar between the primary and secondary channels (3), and I often tried the smaller hole under the right-hand planking from the shelving sand below the bridge (4). The straight upstream cast under its span worked there, but it took perfectly executed hook casts to achieve a proper float on the main pool. It was particularly difficult to fish a dry fly in the crosscurrent eddies, and many times a downstream dry-fly presentation from almost directly below the middle pier solved the problem. Other times when there was no hatch coming, we crossed the footbridge and waited briefly before fishing down the pool with wet flies or nymphs.

It was impossible to wade upstream under the bridge on either side of its center cribbing, and we fished the pocket water upstream by crossing the side channel to the island (5). Sometimes I worked big nymphs or bucktails downstream under the bridge, and across along the shoal of big stones. It was virtually impossible to fish the tumbling pockets upstream with a dry fly, and I usually waded quietly along the rocky shallows (6) fishing the opposite bank with sunken imitations. The smooth gravel-bottom shallows upstream held surprisingly good brown trout, and we usually covered their lies along the rocks from the sandbar above the island (7). We usually ignored the side channel, but one morning when I crossed to fish the island, a big brown bolted upstream under the willows.

I fished the fast water in the main channel first, giving the fish ample time to forget being startled, and then returned to try the side channel itself. The brown was lying in the narrow throat among the rocks, and it took my little spent-wing Adams with a confident head-and-tail rise. There was a twelve-inch fish lying behind a stone just upstream, and I found six or seven others working in the deep run under the willows. The trout were all browns, running from six to eighteen inches, and we never ignored the minor side channel after that experience.

There was another unforgettable time on this pool when a swarm of delicate *Epeorus* spinners was mating above and below the footbridge. Several tourists were fishing salmon eggs from the left-bank cribbing, but it was no evening for bait. When the mayflies had finished laying their ova, the trout were taking them eagerly in the currents below the planking, and their splashy rises were visible fifty yards down the pool. Crossing the timbers and planking, I walked down and started fishing back up from the riffle below (1). It was an impressive rise of fish, and I waded out into the pool with a rising sense of excitement.

Two or three good fish were working, but the trout in the lower reaches of the pool were smaller. Several rainbows of eight to ten inches took my dry-fly imitation, but it was the much larger brown trout I wanted.

The main body of the pool surrendered seven of them from thirteen to eighteen inches almost as quickly as I could play them and restore the matted hackles of my fly. It was fast sport, and the fishless tourists on the bridge were stunned, not realizing how infrequently it happened. They seemed convinced that a dry fly had occult properties and appeared thoroughly receptive to the method. It is just such lucky episodes that cement one's reputation as a fly-fisherman, and they are quite rare.

The bridge pool illustrated in this section of the chapter lies on a small trout river in New England, with a trusswork-covered span between its stone abutments. Its full one hundred yards consist of a tumbling pocket-water run above the bridge, the smooth-flowing flat under its timber span, and a swift tail shallows that break into a boulder-filled corner downstream.

It has always been a productive reach of water. Its deepest holding lies are under the bridge itself, in both the main spinal currents and along the left wall. There are three places where cold spring seepage enters the river: in the gravelly shallows just below the bridge, the small pile of rocks just above the bridge on the left, and above the overhanging stone halfway up the pocket water upstream. The fish favor these places.

The swift pockets have good populations of the small current-loving hatches of early season, and I have had some fine sport fishing them wet with small Hare's Ears and Early Brown stoneflies. Sometimes I have made some fine catches fishing upstream with nymphs, particularly under the bridge itself, and it has also surrendered several trout over twenty inches to big marabou streamers fished upstream in this reach of water. It is also superb dry-fly water whenever a good fly hatch is coming down.

Although I like the slick flat in the tail shallows below the bridge and usually start fishing there (3), the fast run downstream is well worth fishing, too. The trout in its broken currents are easier to attract, and a fisherman interested in catching more fish would be wise to cover them thoroughly, but I get more satisfaction from taking a selective fish in shallow silk-smooth flats and seldom fish the pockets.

Several years ago I was fishing the slick below the bridge on my knees; the bright morning had made the fish unusually shy. Three or four were sipping something tiny in the shadow of the bridge wall along the right bank. They were difficult, and I was trying one minute fly after another with no more response than three or four suspicious inspections.

There was a stranger fishing the swift run downstream with a small nymph, and he caught several trout in the broken water.

There're lots more fish down here, the man finally said. *Why don't you come try them?*

It was a surprisingly generous suggestion.

I've got several feeding here, I answered. *You found those and they're your fish.*

Sure you don't want to fish them? he asked.

Thanks! I waved. *You go ahead!*

Finally I took two or three of my selective feeders along the masonry, while the friendly stranger took eight or nine more in the broken water below. We became good friends in later years, and we were talking along the river only a few weeks ago.

You remember that time you were fishing the flat? he laughed, *and I offered you my water?*

Yes, I grinned. *You were catching fish like crazy!*

You probably took half an hour to get close to those fish in the flat, he shook his head. *And you probably spent an hour changing flies on them!*

Two hours! I smiled.

You know something, he said. *I didn't understand what you were doing then or why you preferred it.*

You mean to catch less fish? I asked.

Yes, he said. *Fish that were harder to catch in places that were harder to fish—I didn't understand.*

Difficult fish mean something when you get them, I suggested.

BRIDGE POOL

Yes, he said. *I know that now.*

But there were times when hatches came from the fast water downstream, and from the pocket water above the bridge, and the fish moved there to feed. Those were days when I fished the water where the trout were working, because great pleasure in trout fishing comes from a sense of harmony with the rhythms of the river.

Many experienced fly-fishermen seem to develop and possess an uncanny skill at losing themselves in the richly woven fabric of life in the river, and to work in concert with its secret melodies. It is thoughtless to ask that a river and its primordial harmonies respond on our terms. There are many anglers who ignore the river and its cyclical rhythms of life, perhaps in their preoccupation with tackle and technique, and their days along the water will miss the ultimate poetry of our sport.

The bridge pool is almost a river in itself, with its full glossary of water types. It has tumbling chutes and broken pockets. Fish lie in the sheltering currents of large boulders and a fallen tree, and tight against the stonework of the bridge. Others feed and cruise in the smooth open-water flat under the shadows of its trusswork span, and still others are found in the slick tail shallows downstream. Learning to read such water and know it well is a fly-fishing education in itself.

Under most conditions, flies are hatching the full length of the bridge water, and I fish the entire stretch. Most of the trout in the bottom run lie in its primary currents, and good dry-fly floats are possible from directly downstream (1). The fish lying along the left side are in deep currents scoured out against a shelving bank and in the eddying water to the right. These eddies and the secondary currents coming down between the rocks are better cast to from the gravelly shoal (2), and in the evening I have taken some big fish cruising the quiet water behind these boulders.

The throat of the run is too deep to cross, and there are good fish lying just above the boulders, so I usually wade back down across the main current and circle up through the brush on the left. The riffle above (3) is a good place for reaching the deep pockets against the right bank. Trout often lie just above the boulders, and it is a taking place favored by the bucktail fishermen who frequent the river just after daylight. It has also produced dry-fly fish for me, moving downstream with a big skittering variant just above the boulders. The deep turbulent slot between the rocks upstream also holds fish, and it once surprised me with a twenty-two-inch brown trout that engulfed my fly and fought me down almost one hundred yards before it finally came to my net in a quiet riffle. It does not always produce a fish, but I never fail to try it since that experience.

It is impossible to fish the trout lying in the tail shallows upstream, particularly along the bridge wall. From a position directly downstream, the gathering currents catch the fly line, dragging the fly and spooking the fish. It is a difficult cross-stream angle, requiring an exaggerated hook cast delivered almost downstream; an infantry approach from the gravel bar (4) is the only workable tactic.

The fish lying along the masonry are always good-size browns, but there was one particular trout a few seasons ago that liked to lie and feed right at the lip of the pool. It was a shallow place at the bottom of the bridge abutment, in water scarcely deep enough to shelter a chub. The trout was there almost every morning, feeding with quiet little rise forms that told little of its size, and it worked steadily from daylight until the sun erased the shadow of its sheltering wall just after the breakfast hour. It was a selective fish and it had chosen a particularly difficult feeding lie. It was a trout that challenged me for several weeks, refusing my flies or bolting upstream when my casting got careless, or the fly dragged clumsily down the shallows.

It was early summer before I finally hooked him on a minute seal-fur ant, using a fine .0031 tippet, and it was a stubborn fight that lasted almost thirty minutes. The fish bolted up the shallows and held stubbornly against the straining nylon, and when I forced it back from the shadow of the bridge, it tried to rub the tiny fly free on the gravel. It was a richly spotted brown trout of nineteen inches, and although I released it gently under the bridge, it did not return to feed again in its favorite lie.

Trout range freely in the open waist-deep flat under the bridge. During mayfly hatches they often select particular feeding lanes, but at other times they cruise the flat hungrily or change positions often. Others like to lie against the masonry abutments, particularly on the left side, where a cast straight upstream to their soft little rises is best (6). The fish lying against the right wall are harder, because their holding lie is in slower currents with faster water in between. Hook casts from below work reasonably well, but a downstream slack-line presentation standing well up under the bridge (7) is better. Such tactics are not sound in terms of dry-fly theory, but they produce a longer drag-free float.

The same position is workable for fishing along the abutment to the left, where they hover in the cool spring seepage. You can also reach the odd fish that lies upstream in a small pocket in the rocks from the upper edge of the bridge (7). Slack-line and exaggerated hook-cast tactics are useful for the trout lying across the main currents, and a good caster can cover fish all the way upstream to the fallen tree, working both sides of the current. It is usually wise to remain under the bridge as long as possible, concealing your presence in its shadows. Using light and shadow to mask your streamside movements is important to success.

The eddying currents behind the boulders are difficult to fish with a long cast, since controlled slack is necessary for a proper float. Sometimes I cast from behind the stones (8), or move even slightly toward the right to cover the fish in the minor current coming down between the right-hand stones upstream. The pocket fish on the left can also be reached, and once they have been fished, the angler should move slowly to a position above the stones (9), avoiding the deepening main currents.

Several years ago there was a large fish that liked the undercut boulder upstream on the left. Its residence offered good shelter and a fine food-bringing current, plus the cold spring seepage that enters from the stones just above. The fish was surprisingly large, and I discovered it accidentally by flushing it from its lair under the ledgelike stone. It was a wary trout, difficult to approach easily, and one afternoon I decided to try its lie with a hook-cast presentation from downstream (10).

It's like casting around a corner, I thought. *You won't even see the rise if he decides to take the fly.*

But the stealth paid off handsomely. The cast looped out, hooked back slightly on the wind, and dropped my Hendrickson above the stone. It floated momentarily within my field of vision, and then its line of drift disappeared behind the large rock. When the rise came, I could not see it, but I heard the splash and saw rings push out into the current. I tightened and the fish was hooked, and it bulldogged angrily upstream, probing under the stones in the pocket water above.

It was a fine female brown, still bright with spawning colors and slightly thin from the winter, and it measured a full nineteen inches. Two weeks later, I hooked the fish again and lost it downstream.

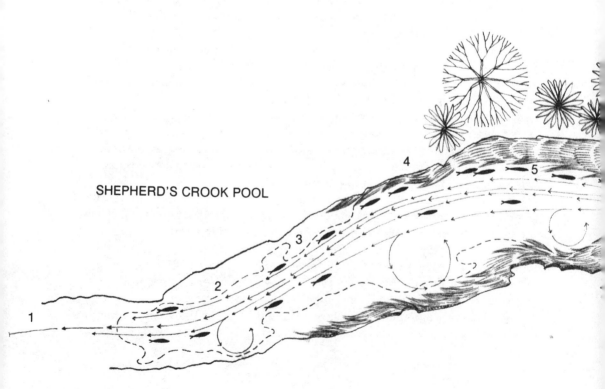

SHEPHERD'S CROOK POOL

Fishing the pockets upstream from the boulder channels is usually based on the feeding stations of the fish, but I usually cover them from the middle currents (11) and finally move up to a central position (12). From that point, it is possible to cast to pockets in several currents upstream, but the principal holding places lie downstream. Properly fished, the entire reach of water can occupy two or three hours, working slowly to observe and stalk its feeding trout.

There is a shepherd's-crook pool on one of my favorite western meadow-waters, its holding places complicated by lava ledges and weeds. Volcanic deposits make reading a river exceptionally difficult. Ledges and cooling fissures and potholes are all unusual bottom features that do not always announce their presence in the surface currents, and the thermal effects of hot springs are also seldom visible to an angler unfamiliar with the river. This pool has a hot spring seepages lying along the bottom, and its warming effects mean that some of the best-looking water is devoid of fish. The main channel from the boulder halfway up the left bank marks the

beginning of a smooth, deep current bordered with undulating weeds. It lasts well around the bend toward the throat of the pool, and it looks so promising that most anglers cast over it carefully. Yet I had never seen a fish working there, and it was some time before I realized that the cold current tongues winding down the narrow right-hand channels in the weeds were the water that actually held fish.

It was some time before I discovered the surprising number of big trout lying in these narrow side channels, where the cool flow of the current is reinforced by the entering flow of a small feeder creek. The shallow flat that widens downstream, with irregular ledges of rust-colored lava narrowing into a deep pocket at the bottom looked less productive, but it always held lots of good fish.

The shepherd's-crook stretch puzzled me until a heavy fly hatch revealed its secret one morning. The insects were coming off everywhere, and the fish were active, but strangely enough they were not rising in the best-looking bend. Trout were rising in the lower water, but above the trees the rise forms were all concentrated in the labyrinth of channels in the weeds: behind the island and in the tributary flow, and in the two channels farther upstream.

No fish in the bend? I thought.

The lower shallows held so many fish that I circled down through the meadows to try a ragged basin in the lava. Three good-looking browns were rising in the cushion of currents at the tail of the slot in the lava, and I crouched on the lava shallows downstream (1) to cover them. The best fish was lying at the bottom, and it took my little dry fly readily. Its splashing in the ledge-rock shallows frightened the others, and I moved stealthily along the ledge until I could cover two more fish rising in the throat upstream (2). The eddying currents had scoured out a deep pocket, dark and swimming-pool green below the throat in the ledges, and I could see the stones on the bottom. The fish lying above the eddy hovered against a point of ledge, and a simple hook cast worked, placing the fly above it just far enough to get a workable ten-inch float. The fly was about to drag when the fish took solidly. It was a good beginning, with two fish better than fifteen inches, and I looked upstream at all the rise forms with happy anticipation.

Crouching low on the ledge-rock shelf, I worked toward the weeds upstream, where the channel had scoured a chest-deep run in the water along the undulating plants. A small fish surfaced in an indentation along the upper part of the shelflike rock (3), and I caught and released it before moving upstream to work over the weeds, kneeling in the same position.

Two fish were rising just upstream along the bottom of the weeds, and I took both with an imitation of the hatching flies. It was an easy upstream presentation, and I could reach a half dozen trout from that position. The hatch was heavy and I had to watch the flies coming over the fish to fit my imitation into their feeding rhythms. Two little mayflies coming close together were avoided, since the fish invariably took both struggling, hopscotching little naturals and let my imitation get past them. It was a time for watching until a fish had taken two or three flies and then had no more in its line of drift for several feet of current. Such brief intervals in their feeding rhythms were an opportunity to shoot a quick cast and get the fly into the sequence before a new series of struggling naturals came down. It was a ploy that worked extremely well with these fish, since the surface was covered with tiny naturals, and I finally took four of them before the other trout stopped feeding.

Two or three more were rising farther upstream, beyond a shallow back eddy over the stony bedrock on the right, and after I took the fish working just below the reverse currents, I moved upstream from my position on the bank (4) to wade into the weeds themselves. It was too deep to wade the open currents here, and my position in the weeds (5) masked my activities from two very good trout lying on the right.

The lower fish took a hook cast across the primary currents, shook himself angrily when I tightened, and turned downstream into the shallow eddy. The second trout continued to feed steadily, and when my fish threatened to run back upstream into its original holding lie, I managed to turn it back gently. My fish measured sixteen inches, and it drifted down along the lava shelf when I released it. The upper trout was still rising when I dried my fly, lying tight against the trailing weeds and well across the main current.

It required a soft hook cast and the fly had scarcely settled when it disappeared in a strong dimple. The rise did not make much disturbance on the water, but its sucking sounds were bold enough that I raised the rod gingerly. The fish bulldogged along the bottom.

He feels strong! I thought.

It was interesting that the fish did not bolt upstream into the open water as I expected, but chose a narrow channel between the bank and the weeds instead. Even in its struggles it had chosen the cold current tongues, and when it turned under the weeds, my fragile leader tippet parted. Two fish lying in the converging flow between the weeds had stopped feeding, so I extricated myself from the soft bottom (5) and crossed in the shallows to another stand (6).

Two fish were still rising along the bank upstream, and a third was in a side channel on my left. The weeds caught my line and dragged the fly, and the fish in the left-hand channel stopped feeding. The trout lying in the fairly open channel above me took rather readily, but I bungled the hook cast necessary for the second fish in the small eddy along the bank and frightened it.

Damn! I thought unhappily.

The channel close against the bank was too deep to wade, but I still wanted to cover it carefully. The bottom under the weeds was firm (7) and I moved slowly into a good casting position.

One fish was rising in the narrowing channel tight against the bank, and it looked like a good trout. It refused my little mayfly imitation several times after a brief inspection.

Strange! I thought. *Wonder what he's doing?*

The rise forms were showy and strong. Watching its feeding carefully, I discovered that the tiny mayflies were drifting down its channel unmolested. Their presence seemed to have nothing to do with its feeding rhythms, and it was doubtful if the hatching nymphs of these tiny flies would trigger such bold swirls. Then a fat grasshopper fell into the channel. It came kicking and swimming back toward the deeply undercut bank, and had almost reached the safety of the trailing grass when it suddenly disappeared in a savage boil.

Grasshoppers! I thought eagerly.

But it was not the answer. The trout refused my grasshoppers completely when they came down flirting with the bank, but twice the fish rose just after my fly had passed.

It must have been the swimming 'hopper! I thought finally. *It must have teased him into taking!*

The trout swirled eagerly again, and I saw a small caddis scuttling along the surface of the weeds. It was a revelation when I saw it, and then I saw dozens of the struggling little sedges. Their pupae were apparently swimming down along the current, working into the quiet eddies, and clambering into the weeds to hatch.

It's the hatching caddis, I thought.

There were some soft-hackled wet flies with dubbed bodies in my fly book and I quickly tied one to my tippet. The fish swirled again in its narrow channel. My fly dropped upstream, just above its feeding station, and I teased its drift slightly with the rod tip. The trout took the little partridge dressing eagerly, with a strong swirl, and its obvious strength told me instantly that it was a good fish. It shook itself sullenly on the bottom and then accelerated rapidly upstream. Its panic proved contagious after it reached the junction of channels above me, and a fish poised in the cushion of currents immediately ahead of the weeds left with a frightened wake. It triggered a third fish farther upstream, and I turned as two fish started feeding in the left-hand channel. The dense weeds had apparently insulated them from both my struggling trout and the others that had bolted upstream in fright.

It was several minutes before my trout finally rolled on its side, and I coaxed it gingerly out on the weeds. It was a fish of twenty-odd inches, heavily spotted and orangey yellow on its lower flanks, and it lay there gasping. I worked the little wet fly free and lifted the fish back into the quiet flow, rocking it rhythmically into the current to work the water past its gills. Finally it wriggled free and sank gratefully into the dark channel under the bank.

The fish in the left-hand channel were still working.

Good! I thought. *The sedges are still hatching!*

Both fish took readily when I fished the little wet fly upstream and twitched it slightly through their feeding stations. Once they were caught and released, I moved very cautiously to a position (8) just below the top of the weedbed. The bottom was good gravel, scoured clean by the smooth current, and I stood partially concealed by the flowing weeds. There were two more fish taking sedges just below the little island.

There was a small gust of wind that carried my fly too far upstream, and the second fish grabbed it almost before it had entered the water. The first fish bolted under the weeds when it started to splash, and I quickly landed the twelve-inch trout when a large fish rose with an impressive porpoise roll in a swift little six-inch channel in the weeds, just below the tributary creek.

Good fish! I thought excitedly.

It was a difficult place to fish properly. The channel below the trout was too deep to wade, and I had moved cautiously upstream into the weeds (9) before I abandoned that approach. The water was perilously close to my wader tops, and I turned back downstream to cross the shallows near the bushes where the currents joined (6). It took several minutes to retrace my steps and circle out through the pale buffalo-grass meadow toward the tributary creek.

Hoping it was possible to cast upstream to the big fish, I crawled up along the bank opposite the island. But there were several clumps of weed projecting into the current, and a trial cast quickly proved it an impractical angle. The line and leader both caught in the weeds, making a drag-free presentation impossible; and my little wet fly would also catch in the grass immediately. The trout was still rising steadily in the tight little channel, and I decided to try a downstream wet-fly presentation.

Circling wide through the meadow on my knees, and crouching low, well back from the river, I finally reached a position in the grass above the fish (10). The currents came sweeping down the main stream, mingling with the tributary flow just below my position, and dividing again around a dense bed of weeds. I frightened a small fish from the mouth of the little creek, and I was afraid it might have scared the fish I wanted.

The big trout porpoised lazily.

Make the cast just above the weeds, I thought, *and let the current swing the fly over him just right!*

It would have worked, but when I dropped the little partridge hackle just above the weeds, it was taken by another fish I had not seen. Its splashing sent waves rolling down the narrow channel, flushing my bigger quarry down the channel with a frightened wake.

Dammit! I muttered angrily.

My fish went almost eighteen inches, and I laughed when I finally glimpsed its size.

Never thought I'd see the day when I'd be disappointed in a fish like that, I thought, *but I wonder how big the other one was?*

Its wake had been impressive.

There were two fish rising in the first bend of the creek, and I took one of them. The other bolted upstream. Several others were working in the yoke-shaped channel above the tributary, but they looked small. The best was about ten inches and it took my partridge pattern fished upstream. Its splashing fight went twenty feet up the right-hand channel, frightening several more trout that scurried downstream. Three or four bolted past me, and I slipped into the river and waded to the bottom of the weedbed (11). It was possible to fish both channels from there, and I stood quietly for several minutes marking down feeding trout well up into the throat of the pool and letting them forget my intrusion.

Several were rising in the main currents on the left, above the hot springs near the island, and all the way upstream between the boulders. Others were rising in the weedy channel on the right. The best fish were lying in the bend just below the boulder, and I had moved up the middle of the weedbed (12) when the trout suddenly stopped feeding as quickly as they had started. The river flowed silent and still.

Both channels were deep and green, and I decided to wade up the weedbed to study their holding water. The current had scoured out a surprisingly deep pocket (13) below the bend in the weeds. Two large browns darted past me, and I made a mental note to try them another time. The water was extremely deep on both sides of the weeds when I reached the top of the bed (14), and I stood watching several fish lying there for some time. The little run sheltered a remarkable number of trout—fat browns that held warily in the weedy shadows.

It was in crossing the stream again, just below the island, that I discovered the hot-spring flowage in the main channel. It was like stepping into a hot bathtub, even with my wading socks and heavy English brogues. It was a fascinating discovery, and I waded back to the island to look for the source of the hot current tongues.

It was under a serrated ledge of lava, its strange mixture of algae and minerals forming a paintbox of exotic colors on the bottom.

That explains it, I thought. *It's no wonder the main channel holds no fish!*

It was the secret of the shepherd's-crook pool.

Our last pool is a half-legendary reach of water on one of the best trout streams in our eastern mountains. Its shallow left-hand bank is a shelving of stones and gravel, hung with elms and willows and sycamores. The far bank is steep, rising toward the shoulder of a dark pine-covered ridge. Dense thickets of rhododendron and laurel bloom there in early summer, and when the violets are blooming, it is the time of the Hendricksons.

It was fished by legendary anglers like Thaddeus Norris and Edward Ringwood Hewitt and George La Branche, and its beauty has been captured in a watercolor by the late Milton Weiler.

It is a pool of varied character and changing moods. It is completely different at various water levels, and its fish are found in different places, depending on both depth and fly hatches. Its moods over the years have taught me many things about trout fishing throughout the full spectrum of the seasons. Because of such changing conditions, it is perhaps less useful to describe a single day's fishing than to discuss its varying character.

Early in the season, the spinal currents of the pool are chest-deep and strong, brimming full among the boulder eddies in its throat, and sliding past the large boulder that divides the flow. There is a little tumbling tributary that flows in through the stones in April. The primary currents slip from the boulder, eddying back and working past a large flat-topped stone that remains submerged until late spring or early summer, and dividing again past a third boulder downstream. The current spreads and slides then, gliding into smooth-flowing shallows between the boulders on the right, and silken and mirror-slick over the stones in the tail.

The eddying shallows below the stone are pale pea gravel, and there are still currents in the deep shade along the right bank. There is a second ravine just above the tail of the pool, where the flow enters the pool through an alluvial fan of stones.

The tail shallows gather and divide at the bottom, the primary currents leaving it toward the left and the minor flow sliding around the stones under the trees. It is shallow there, but dark with foliage a few weeks into the season, and it shelters surprisingly good fish even in midsummer. Both currents hold trout throughout the season.

The swift runs downstream are moody. Sometimes a few fish lie in the main currents, and the broken flow under the trees is consistently better. Once I took a twenty-inch brown in the throat of the run against the right bank.

Fly hatches are superb through the season. When the river is still high, the early fast-water hatches come off the broken water above the throat of the pool and off the swift head currents against the right bank. We often find good *Epeorus* hatches at opening day, the little swift-water duns struggling down the current. Hatches usually occur about an hour after lunch, emerging toward the head of the pool. The trout move there to intercept them, migrating up from the middle and tail of the pool to feed on the mayflies.

During such hatches, I usually drop down the access path and start fishing the rocky shallows (10). Since the flies are found emerging from the swiftest currents, most of the fish hold in the primary flow from the head to the middle rock (11). Once the fish are covered in the run below that stone, and you have fished the odd trout that is positioned above the third boulder, the principal run up the middle of the pool can be worked with a straight-up series of presentations. However, the fish holding against the boulders across the stream (9) cannot be covered from the left bank. The intervening quiet currents create virtually impossible problems of dry-fly floats and dragging flies.

There are sometimes large trout beside the upper pyramid-shaped boulder, and I fish them from the stony shallows downstream (12). Early in the season, a straight upstream cast works well, but later a hook cast is necessary to take a fish lying tight against the granite. Once these fish have been covered, I usually move to the stones upstream (13) to cast stealthily to the next group.

The fish lying directly upstream in the swift primary currents are relatively easy. Straight upstream casts from the rocks (13) usually score well, but the fish in the deeper currents on the right are more difficult. Hook casts are harder but necessary here, and I have even had good luck fishing a dry fly quartering downstream, using a slack-line cast. Most of the fish in the deep upper throat can be covered.

The heavy-water throat has surrendered a number of big fish on bucktails in recent years, including a fine twenty-six-inch brown trout lying above the midstream boulders. Several times I have fished a big marabou upstream with surprising luck, standing downstream in the rocky shallows (12) and casting all the way to the head of the pool. Such tactics require a fast left-hand strip to fish the fly.

Fishing a wet fly upstream is also productive in this water, but adequate coverage of the upper pool is impossible with really long casts, either wet or dry. For these holding lies I usually wade carefully to the gravel-bottomed shallows upstream (14), fishing hook casts and slack-line presentations into the slower right-hand currents. The cold springhole at the base of the rock slide often produces a fine brook trout or two. Good slack-line casts can provide just enough float against the boulders to fool a rising trout, and at some levels of water, I work all the way up to the tumbling run (15) to fish both the deep back eddies, and the white-cap pockets above the boulder-broken head of the pool.

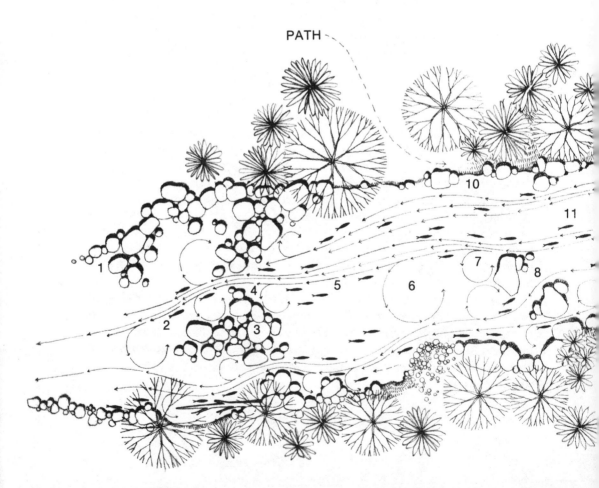

PATH

During late-spring caddis hatches the pool is excellent wet-fly water, particularly when the fish are taking emerging pupae. Fishing down from the throat of the pool (15) is highly productive at such times, and I commonly fish a partridge-hackle imitation all the way down the shallows to a stand opposite the lowest rock (10).

My most memorable day on this pool occurred some years ago, as the result of a phone call from my old friend Colin Pittendrigh.

What about some fishing? he asked.

Fine, I agreed. *It should be starting to get good this week.*

What's hatching? Pittendrigh asked.

Gordon Quills and Hendricksons are just about finished, my mind sifted back over the past ten days. *We're about due for those olive-bodied sedges!*

Sounds good! he said.

Pittendrigh was then dean of the graduate school at Princeton, where I was completing my doctorate in architecture and planning. We met over breakfast at the dean's residence and drove north into the forested ridges of northern New Jersey. We crossed through the Delaware Water Gap, and found the shadbush blooming in the hills above the river. The morning was overcast with a light misting rain when we reached the pool. There was no sign of hatching flies and the currents were slightly discolored.

It looks a little dead, Colin muttered and slumped on the bench unhappily. *Still think your green sedges will hatch?*

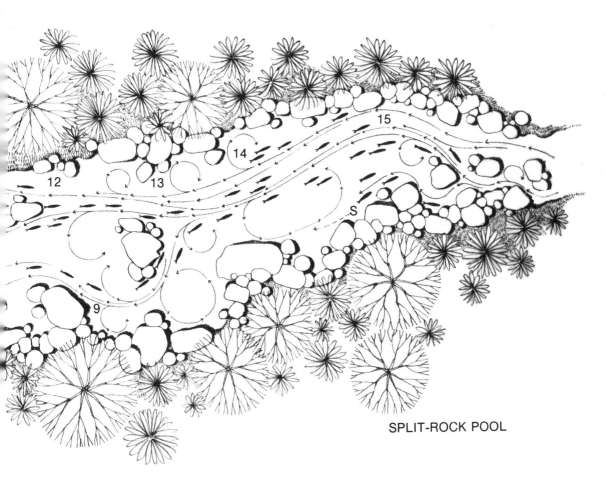

SPLIT-ROCK POOL

They're overdue, I answered.

Colin laughed and rigged his little Winston. *It's a good time to test your powers of prediction!*

It was only a guess, I reminded him gently.

What are you going to use?

The river still looked moody and discolored with rain. *Maybe a little green-bodied wet fly,* I said.

I'll fish something else, Pittendrigh challenged.

Good luck! I shook my head.

Pittendrigh insisted that I fish down the swift run at the head of the pool while he watched. The river felt cold flowing through my waders. The swift chutes and back eddies along the rockfall flowed dark and strong, sliding past the pyramid-shaped boulder, and swept forty yards down the belly of the pool. The little river was glassy smooth below the other rocks, spreading into the rocky tail shallows.

The river looked lifeless, but something told me the trout were starting to work along the bottom. Such premonitions are impossible to explain, except that they may point to our subconscious harmonies with the rhythms of the river and its fish.

The first cast dropped my little pupal imitation across the main current tongue, just behind the main boulder. The fly settled and its swing had barely started when there was a strong pull and a sixteen-inch brown showered water in the shallows. My rod throbbed into a tight circle and the little Hardy protested shrilly.

That's some beginning! Colin laughed.

It was one of those remarkable mornings when everything went perfectly. Every few casts another trout intercepted my fly swing and hooked itself eagerly. Although we released them all, several fish were so stuffed with pupae that their throats and gill structures were green with them. It demonstrated clearly that a fine *Rhyacophila* hatch was coming later, and the fish were witnessing a lot of prehatch activity. The final score from this pool between its head (15) and the shallows downstream (10) was sixteen browns. The best fish went eighteen inches.

Okay, Colin surrendered. *I'm sold!*

Dean Pittendrigh! I waded out of the river with mock gravity. *Such results hardly prove my theories!*

Colin waded out unceremoniously before I had reached the bank. *How about a few of those green-bodied flies?* He was fishing through my vest like a jovial Scottish burglar. *It's not too late to call another faculty meeting to reconsider on our doctoral candidates!*

You mean you'd revoke my degree? I protested.

Campus politics! he laughed.

The pool poses another range of problems in early summer when the river is low and clear, and its rushing currents have become glassy runs. The fish hold well down in the shallows and in the leafy shadows across the stream, and starting at the earlier point of entry (10) is a mistake. The trout are skittish in the second month of the season, and wading out in plain view of the tail shallows would scatter them upstream like quail.

Fishing this reach of water in midsummer is more difficult. Usually I avoid the bankside path then, circling through the brush downstream below the pile of small stones (1). The fish lying in the primary currents upstream can be covered from there, and I wade out into the shallow eddies to fish the run along the far bank (2). Once the fish lying there have been caught and released, it is time to stalk the bigger game lying in the pool above. Trout lying in the shallows of the main current can be worked by casting directly across from the stones (3), provided you approach stealthily enough. You must work far enough up the stones to keep the line from catching in the current just above the break and must avoid dragging your fly enough to frighten them.

Once you have reached the proper casting angle, stay on your knees and cover as many trout as you can reach in the main currents on the left. The swift, gathering currents on the right are more trouble, and I usually move upstream into the shallows (4) once I have worked over the trout lying there. From my knees in the shallows (4), it is possible to get a decent hook-cast float over the fish resting against the right shoreline. Over the years I have found casting directly across or slightly downstream the best method for covering the trout lying in the corner, and I once hooked a surprisingly large fish in water barely deep enough to cover it there. It was a fish of better than twenty inches, and I was fishing a tiny ant on a .003 tippet. The fish threshed in the shallows, more surprised than angry, and then swam until it sheared the fragile nylon under the rocks.

Usually I work farther up the shallows on my knees (5) to get decent floats over the fish in the springhole seepage, and often the slight downstream angle works on any trout that starts dimpling again in the tail. The back eddies make it impossible to fish very long casts upstream, and I creep to a better position (6) to cover the trout lying farther up the right-hand currents. Good fish are often observed between the lowest boulder and the bank, and with a slight flow coming through a narrow slot in the rocks, a sizable brown is sometimes lying there. The eddy just behind the boulder (7) is a fine place for fishing the right-hand side of the main current, and the quiet water along the bank as well. Just above the rock (8) is a good station for fishing trout lying almost to the pyramid-shaped boulder, and I often work very slowly to a position along the shoreline (9) to cast to fish lying on the right side of the first boulder. Once I hooked a nineteen-inch brown that was rising there with barely perceptible dimples, and sometimes I fish up the right-hand eddies during the earlier fly hatches, if the water is not too high for wading there.

It is a pool of many moods and secrets.

These several pools we have studied in this chapter do not cover every situation in trout-fishing tactics, but each offers key lessons typical of a wide range of problems. Observant anglers will recognize many parallels on their own familiar rivers, and drawing diagrams of favorite pools will help you understand them.

Several years ago we were sitting in the Carmichael tackle shop in the Jackson Hole country. Bob Carmichael was lecturing several fishermen about some of the pools on the Gros Ventre. It had been a number of seasons since Carmichael's health had actually permitted him to fish the river, yet he sat there carefully diagramming each pool in such accurate detail that we all recognized water we had been fishing.

That's fantastic! I finally said.

Carmichael stopped his drawing and glared at the interruption. *What's fantastic?* he growled testily.

Well, I explained, *you haven't fished those pools for years, and you remember every current and stone!*

Hell, Carmichael laughed. *That's easy enough!*

Like hell it is, somebody said.

Sure, it's easy! Carmichael laughed again. *Every good fisherman I ever knew had a complete picture of every river and each pool in his head.*

You mean draw every pool he's ever fished? I asked.

The good ones can! he growled.

BOOK SIX

TROUT STRATEGIES, TECHNIQUES AND TACTICS

1. The Ancient Art
of the Wet Fly

The rivers were superb, their swift currents flowing over straw-colored gravel, and we fished them all in those early Michigan summers. There was the legendary Au Sable, with its lazy day-floats and large fish hiding in the cedar sweepers, and the sombre flow of the Big Manistee. We fished the pale deadfall tangles on the lower Boardman in mayfly time, and counted foraging whitetail deer in the meadows at twilight on the Little Manistee. There were many happy brook-trout mornings on the tumbling reaches of the Pine and the tea-colored currents of the Black, its moody character enshrined in the early stories of Ernest Hemingway.

The wet-fly was common on the Michigan rivers in those days. It was the method for teaching a boy about trout, and it is still perhaps the best manner in which to start fly-fishing. It was my introduction to trout water and trout problems. There were strangely peaceful tree-frog summers in those first years of the Second World War, with twilight whippoorwills and swamp-peepers. Those summers were spent on the beautiful, smooth-flowing rivers of lower Michigan, thousands of miles from the fighting. Both their swift gravel-bottom riffles, and the shy trout lying in their tangled deadfalls, first taught me about the wet-fly method.

There are many memories of those years.

Spring mornings were often clear and cold, with cedars and skeletal branches sheltering sun-washed riffles, although an April river was sometimes pewter-colored in the rain. There were cowslips and pulpit flowers and violets, mixed with bloodroot and skunk cabbage, and the nights were surprisingly cold in a sleeping bag. Later, there were shadbush and flowering dogwoods, with May apples carpeting the forest floor. June was always bright with delicate new leaves in the Michigan trout country. The summer rivers flowed smooth and clear, and there were fine fly hatches. Columbines and summer buttercups were blooming in the June river bottoms then, and the late summer meadows ripened into a time of gentians and swamp lilies and pye-weed.

My first wet-fly trout came on the Pere Marquette.

It took a small Cahill fished in a deep shadow of willows, about a mile below the Forks Pool. It was unquestionably taken with a fly, but my technique was a little like worming. I simply trailed the fly downstream in the current, working my rod back and forth, and the fish hooked itself. It measured barely ten inches, but it seemed like a sailfish in my eyes. It had followed my swinging Cahill from the willows into the sunlight, and the praise of my father and his friends was exhilarating as we celebrated on the stream. With that first fly-caught trout in my wicker creel, it seemed that I had truly entered their world. It was a morning baptized by my first cup of coffee, freshly brewed over a gravel-bar fire, while they celebrated with the stronger catalyst of sour-mash whiskey in their fishing-vest cups. After that morning I never fished bait again.

Such wet-fly tactics are deeply rooted in fly-fishing history. Modern anglers are often preoccupied with the more fashionable dry-fly method or wrestle with the little understood complexities of nymph fishing, but there are still many times when the river belongs to a skilled wet-fly fisherman, and modern developments in leaders and fly lines and other tackle have opened up a whole new spectrum of wet-fly techniques.

Despite extensive research here and abroad precise origins of the wet-fly method are unknown. However, recent evidence indicates that it dates back more than 2,300 years to the Chou Dynasty in China. It is clear that the wet-fly method reigned without challenge from the rivers of Macedonia to the Scottish Highlands, until the birth of dry-fly fishing in England slightly more than a century ago. Although many modern fishermen seem to have forgotten its secrets in their dry-fly myopia, the qualities that made it effective for literally thousands of years still exist on our rivers today. Anglers once began fishing wet flies and then graduated to the dry-fly and nymph methods as their skills increased. Everyone had some boyhood familiarity with wet flies in the past, but with the gradual spread of the dry-fly mystique, more and more fishermen now start fishing with floating patterns. The result is a generation of anglers whose training lacks the primary skills of the wet-fly method. Men who lack these skills are ignoring a singularly effective technique, and none of the fly-fishing innovations of the last century has made the wet fly obsolete.

Since fly-fishing was limited to sunk patterns for thousands of years, perhaps a fresh definition of the wet-fly method is needed. It should probably be based on the firm relationship between wet flies and our growing knowledge of American trout-stream entomology. Most anglers understand the clear relationship between dry flies and the imitation of various types of floating insects. Standard dry-fly patterns imitate a galaxy of adult mayflies, stoneflies, caddis, and various terrestrial insects like ants and grasshoppers and beetles. So-called fancy patterns are suggestive of any number of insect forms. Before the evolution of nymphs and disciplined nymph-fishing tactics early in this century, wet flies like the traditional Blue Dun and Greenwell's Glory and Hare's Ear were most effective as imitations of hatching nymphs.

Modern wet-fly fishermen are again becoming aware that their sunk patterns are often the best imitations of certain insect types. Patterns like the Hare's Ear are perfect imitations of species that emerge into the winged state below the surface, unfolding their diaphanous wings before they reach the atmosphere. Wet flies also suggest drowned aquatic insects. Cold-weather showers and high water often drown significant numbers of hatching flies before their wings have fully dried and they can escape the surface film to fly off. Fast water drowns large numbers of stream insects all season long. Many aquatic insects are blown into the water and drown while laying their eggs, and after their mating swarms have finished, large numbers of spent flies fall into the river and are submerged in rough currents. Some species of mayflies actually migrate below the surface to lay their eggs and few return to the atmosphere. Certain species of caddisflies flutter down to the water, pierce the surface film, fold their wings, and swim to the bottom to lay their eggs on stones and deadfalls. During this oviposition, the flies are enveloped in a glittering cloak of tiny bubbles, which explains the success of many tinsel-ribbed patterns. Such caddis flies are swept away along the bottom when their egg laying is completed. Hot windy weather also blows many terrestrials into the water, drowning large numbers of ants and grasshoppers and beetles. Although many fly-fishermen scoff at two- and three-fly snells these days, these methods have their valuable moments—since a skittering dropper fly is still perhaps the best method we have for suggesting the erratic, fluttering hopscotch of some egg-laying flies.

Wet flies are still the best patterns with which to begin fly-fishing. The basic principles are certainly the easiest for a neophyte to master and catch some trout in the bargain. Common downstream tactics do not demand the precise casting and fly manipulation typically required in other methods, and many fish will take a wet fly and hook themselves. Like bait fishing, exploring a stream with the wet-fly is an excellent way for the beginner to learn its secrets and to read its changing moods.

Wet-fly tackle has changed considerably in the past few years. Traditional wet-fly rods were soft and slow in action, in part because of the technical limitations in past years, and because a slower casting rhythm kept the flies and leaders moist enough to sink readily. Lines were silk and leaders were usually silkworm gut. Both have a higher specific gravity than water and sink quickly without line dressing. Undressed silk lines sank well to moderate depths, much like the modern sink-tip taper.

Modern fly rods for fishing the wet fly are avilable in compound tapers that flex well into the cork grip, and with calibrations at the tip guide designed to fish the delicate modern leaders. Such rods are usually described as parabolic or semi-parabolic, and usually balance with one line size smaller than comparable fast-action rods of similar length and weight. Such parabolic-type tapers will fish a longer line and finer tippet, with somewhat less casting effort, than fast-action rods of similar size. Their casting rhythms are complex and more demanding to master. They combine slow-action power with casting rhythms that retain maximum moisture in both leaders and flies, like the soft wet-fly actions fashionable on American streams in the past century.

Relatively small rivers mean a seven- to seven-and-a-half-foot rod weighing from three to three and three-quarters ounces. The well-equipped wet-fly man will carry reels or extra reel spools equipped with a matching DT5F floating line, DT5ST sinking-tip line, and DT5S full-sinking design. Such double-taper lines cast and fall softly enough for the skittish fish of small rivers. Their floating and sinking qualities are all valuable. The floating five-weight is singularly useful in fishing shallow runs or for suggesting emerging insects. Sinking-tip lines are needed to present the fly at intermediate depths of water. Full-sinking lines are required to work very fast currents and relatively deep places. Such precise control of fly-swing depth was impossible before the comparatively recent development of synthetic lines of dacron—and polyvinyl chloride lines having a higher specific gravity than water.

Proper tackle for fishing medium-size rivers requires bigger rods and heavier forward-taper lines. Eight-foot rods weighing from four to four and a half ounces, matched with six- and seven-weight lines, are fine all-around tools for most wet-fly work. My own experience favors double-taper designs in the floating line and weight-forward tapers in the sink-tip and full-sinking types. Medium-size rivers having unusually deep pools or swift currents may also make a fast-sinking synthetic line useful to the fully equipped angler.

Big water is the world of sinking lines and weight-forward tapers designed for distance work. Since most of our big trout rivers lie in the western states and western rivers also introduce the factor of high winds, such conditions demand rods of eight and a half to nine feet, weighing from four and a half to five and a half ounces. Lines matching these rods have eight- and nine-weight specifications. Although double-taper floating lines are sometimes useful in greased line wet-fly tactics during a hatch on the biggest rivers, their character usually requires a forward-taper line. Really big rivers mean distance casting and fishing deep, and the modern weight-forward sinking lines do both. Such recent technology represents perhaps the single most important breakthrough in wet-fly tackle since the evolution of fly-dressing itself, allowing us to fish heavy currents and water depths totally impossible fifteen years ago.

Effective wet-fly fishing for trout demands such varied manipulation of the fly that the fashionable midge-sized rods, weighing from two to two-and-three-quarters ounces are not really effective. Wet flies can be fished with them, but they lack the power to handle a sinking line, and they lack the length to modify and control fly swing. Such rods are also limited to relatively small flies, and although they will cast a long line in calm weather, they lack the power and control to punch out long casts into a big-water wind.

The reasons for fishing the deep runs and undercut banks with sinking lines lie in current-speed dynamics and their relationship to trout holding lies. The average stream at a five-foot depth has a current of about one foot per second at the surface, slightly more than a foot per second one to two feet deeper, and a bottom cushion of flow caused by hydraulic friction, its speed reduced to a third of the surface currents.

Bank friction has similar lateral effects on current speed. Surface currents five feet from a bank will average as much as one and a half feet per second, while bank speed is about one-quarter of a foot per second. Bottom currents at an undercut bank are even slower, and it is little wonder the fish like these places.

Bottom currents are approximately three times slower than surface levels of water in open-stream, and current speed deep in an undercut bank is typically four times less than main current tongues only a few feet away. Food carried in the primary current tongues moves too swiftly for a fish to capture it easily, and holding in such current speeds forces a trout to expend energy faster than it generates calories from the food ingested. Therefore, the fish lie in quieter flows waiting for their food to drift deeper, where it can be taken easily without exposure to the dangers found at shallower depths and in open currents. Such hydraulic factors are essential to reading and understanding a river and help explain the advantages of modern sinking lines—the only tackle which will successfully present a wet-fly in these bottom currents.

Technically speaking, wet flies are fished under the surface of the water and include all types of streamers, bucktails, and nymphs. However, these are special types of flies that are fished underwater. Streamers and bucktails imitate baitfish; nymphs suggest subaquatic forms of stream insects, some types of hatching flies, and many small crustaceans.

Dry flies are not only presented floating on the surface, their basic techniques of manipulation are also less complex. The dry-fly method typically involves a natural float, completely free of current drag in most cases. Some cross-stream and downstream techniques with the dry fly involve twitching and skating the imitation to suggest the surface fluttering of craneflies or caddis. But wet flies are usually fished either with current tension, conscious rhythms of retrieve, or precise control of fly-speed—although some dead-drift techniques are also useful at times.

Since quick-sinking flies and a swimming retrieve are basic criteria in wet-fly design, most patterns are dressed on heavy hooks with a configuration designed to fish smoothly under the surface. Materials should include body dubbing, floss, and crewel wools that readily absorb water. Most wet flies are hackled with soft hen feathers or body hackles from birds like grouse and woodcock. Such soft feathers work and move in a current or during a teasing retrieve in still water, giving a fly an added suggestion of life. However, some experts who dress wet flies for particularly swift rivers argue for hackles stiff enough to work in the heaviest chutes and rapids. Such theories are found in the work of English writers like W. H. Lawrie, with his *Book of the Rough Stream Nymph*, and are also important in the hair-hackle concepts developed by men like Franz Pott and George Grant in Montana. Generally speaking, however, wet-fly wings and hackles should pulse along the hook in response to the flow of the current.

There are literally thousands of wet-fly patterns. Most group themselves into two basic categories: brightly colored flies with a glitter of tinsel, dressings that function primarily as lures; and darker patterns conceived as imitations of trout-stream insects. The gaudy traditional flies often have their origins in sea-trout fishing and the Scottish loch patterns popular in Europe, and with the foolish brook trout that thrived in our northeastern wilderness early in the nineteenth century—flies like the Tomah Jo and Parmachene Belle and Belgrade.

Modern fishing has seen the gradual decline of these bright-feathered dressings in favor of more imitative patterns, even on wilderness waters of the Labrador. Some years ago I fished the River of the Martens less than a mile from its subarctic estuary on Ungava Bay, and we found that the modern imitative flies outfished the gaudy brook-trout confections of the past.

However, a river in spate or freshly stocked with hatchery fish in early season sometimes calls for a tinsel body. These days I dress a dark traditional like a March Brown or Grey Partridge with a body of silver tinsel to attract fish under such conditions. There are also times when tinsel-body flies match a hatching or egg-laying insect in its glittering sheath of bubbles. Many experienced wet-fly men believe their tinsel-bodied patterns are also sometimes taken for tiny baitfish. Certainly such tinsel-wrapped flies are more easily visible in cloudy water and at greater distances than the darker dressings. Tinsel is not the only source of highlights in a wet-fly pattern. Its feathers and body dubbing often entrain air bubbles that catch the light dramatically, and its bulk and hook-point often stream a trail of similar bubbles. Cavitation can also coat a swimming wet fly with entrained air, since the separation of flow layers that the fly causes in a river often results in a series of tiny vacuums. Such light patterns are frequently the secret of wet-fly success, and a gold or silver ribbing of tinsel is sometimes the difference between failure and taking fish consistently.

The wet-fly fishing that Claudius Aelianus described in the third century worked with a line of fixed length, and was more like dapping or bushing than actual casting. Such fixed-line tackle was still in use when Dame Juliana Berners wrote the first English book on fly-fishing in the fifteenth century; and although Barker and Walton knew of the fishing reel at the middle of the seventeenth century, it was not recommended in their discussions of fly tackle for trout. In 1653 Izaak Walton described such fishing in *The Compleat Angler*:

But I promised to tell you more of fly-fishing for a trout, which I may have time enough to do, for you see it rains May-butter across our meadow, and its silvery streams; and let me tell you again, that you keep as far from the water as you possibly can, and fish down the stream: and when you fish with the fly, if it be possible, let no part of your line touch the water, or casting it into the water, you yourself being also almost always moving down the stream.

These lines unmistakably describe the rudiments of the wet-fly method. There are a number of other ancient truths, like making as few false casts as possible to keep the leader and flies wet. Cast as little as possible, leaving the fly in the water as much as possible. Many surprisingly experienced anglers are so compulsive about casting properly that they will pick up a poor cast immediately, even though the slash of the pickup may occur right over the holding lies of the fish. Such bad habits frighten the trout long before they can observe the fly.

Some years ago there was a well-known tournament caster fishing on a river in arctic Norway. It was a river famous for its impressive catches of big fish, yet his boat came in night after night with surprisingly few salmon. His casting was superb, double hauling faultlessly at considerable distance; but such distance work demanded a lot of false casting, and the boat gillies usually hold an angler only fifty or sixty feet from the fish. Long casts were unnecessary on most pools, and we asked the riverkeeper about his poor luck.

His casting is beautiful. The old man paused and lit his pipe. *But he casts well beyond the fish.*

Too much casting in the air, said a boatman.

That's a double haul, I said.

Yes, smiled the old riverkeeper, *but the fish are only found in the river—there are no fish in the air!*

You're right! I smiled.

There are a number of variations on the basic downstream theme of traditional wet-fly angling. Some are the result of modern developments in tackle, particularly in leader nylons and sinking-type lines. Others result from a new understanding of fly hatches, and still others are borrowed from salmon fishing or from the revival in traditional wet-fly methods that had died with the generation that fished them. It is all part of an exciting renaissance in wet-fly tactics, and there are fifteen basic variations in the technique.

1. The Simple Wet-Fly Swing

This is the closest modern application of the fixed-line method found in the time of Berners and Walton. It is perhaps the best technique to teach a beginner, since it involves only rudimentary manipulation of the fly and fly tackle. It is the kind of fly-fishing that I first learned on the small willow-choked streams of Michigan, where we waded slowly and sound-lessly downstream, roll casting a fixed length of line to the undercut alders across the current.

The fly is simply allowed to swim in a quarter-circle against the tension of the current, without manipulation of the rod or fly line. It is fished without movement except for the life imparted by the current, and the fly swing should be followed around with the rod tip. Such tactics suggest a drowned insect or emerging aquatic species that cannot swim directly against the flow of the current.

The simple fixed-line swing can also suggest insect forms capable of limited subaquatic motion. The fisherman makes his cast directly across the stream in relatively quiet currents, to increase the fly speed of the swing, and quartering downstream in faster water. The swing is then followed around with the rod tip pointed directly at the fly, and the rod is raised and lowered with a slow, teasing rhythm geared to the current speed. Since the line length remains unchanged, and the line is held between the index finger and the rod grip, no manipulation of the line with the left hand is involved. Such basic wet-fly tactics should also include directly downstream presentation, with the angler holding and working a fly almost like bait. It is the way that I started fly-fishing and caught that first trout on a wet fly years ago, allowing a downstream fly to probe along a willow-hung bank and under fallen trees.

2. The Hand-Twist Retrieve

This technique introduces line manipulation with the left hand. It is fished to create a wide variation of teasing, half-swimming rhythms to imitate different types of subaquatic trout foods. Its applications are best using slow to moderate rhythms of retrieve, and it was a favorite sunk-fly method described by Bergman in *Trout*—particularly in stillwaters and brook-trout bogans and in deep, slow-flowing pools.

It is slightly more complicated than a simple fixed-line swing, but it is still a relatively simple technique. The cast is made and allowed to sink, and the retrieve is manipulated by weaving the line around the left hand or through its fingers. This weaving rhythm is accomplished with a rolling motion of the left wrist, either wrapping the line around the palm at the base of the fingers, or lacing it through the fingers in a rhythmic figure-eight. It is perfect for imitating all types of diet forms that swim slowly in the water, like scuds and egg-laying caddis and hatching duns—stream life that swims in almost imperceptible rhythms.

The hand-twist retrieve is absolutely basic. Since most slow-swimming insects are found in relatively quiet currents, or in beaver ponds and other impoundments, it is a primary technique for quiet water. When the fly is allowed to sink deep in a pool or flat, fishing it back along the bottom can be deadly. Sometimes I let a wet fly ride down a long current-tongue, perhaps into water too deep to reach by wading, and then retrieve it slowly the full length of the line.

It is a method that once produced a deep-bodied five-pound brown on the pastoral Grundbach in Germany. The fish was rising to a hatch of tiny *Paraleptophlebia* flies at the head of a deep bend in the river. The alders on its sheltering bank prevented an upstream cast from that side of the current. Similar alders and a thick stand of conifers across the stream made a presentation from the opposite side equally impossible. There was a meadow bank below, across from the fish and a fruitless two hundred feet away, so a downstream presentation was the only possible strategy.

It was raining softly and the fish was feeding often. It seemed to be taking a myriad of fluttering little duns, drowned hatching flies, and tiny emerging nymphs without discrimination. Only its unreachable position in the river seemed to protect it, since its feeding was hardly selective. It was finally caught with a simple method.

Fishing it with a downstream dry fly in such quiet water would have allowed only one cast, since the fly would ultimately drag in the current and put down the trout. But the wet-fly would not frighten the fish when it reached the end of the cast; in fact, its teasing in the current might entice the big brown into taking. There was a small wet-fly imitation in my fly-book, and I clinched it to my tippet.

It was an infantry problem to get within range. The high bank above the fish was bounded by open meadow, and I had to crawl very slowly to reach a casting station within reach of its feeding lie. It was a little like stalking an *Auerhahn* in the European forests, the huge black grouse that closes its eyes while cackling. The hunter must stalk the bird only during its calling, when it cannot see his movements, or this wariest of game birds will simply melt into the trees. Any stalk of the fish was limited to the brief period of its rise forms, when I hoped it was preoccupied enough to miss my approach. It seemed to work and the fish kept working steadily.

The cast dropped out into the smooth current, checked well away from the fish with the rod, and I paid out just enough line to reach its station and slightly more. The tiny wet fly was submerged with a twitch and worked around slowly until it hung slightly below the trout. The fish did not stop feeding, apparently failing to notice the leader nylon trailing past its position in the current. After a few moments, I started an imperceptible hand-twist retrieve, and the fish took the fly without hesitation when it reached its holding lie.

3. The Hand-Strip Retrieve

This technique is a method of suggesting both a more rapid retrieve of slightly longer swimming motions than are possible with a hand-twist rhythm. It is achieved by holding the line between the index finger and the rod-grip, and stripping back short lengths of line with the other hand.

These stripping lengths can vary from about six inches, about the maximum retrieve possible when winding hand-twist retrieve around the fingers, to a free arm-pull of two to three feet. Such stripping rhythms are useful for imitating trout foods that move with steady, pulsing movements in the water, and the faster pulls are especially exciting to wilderness fish and also to hatchery trout fresh from the stocking trucks.

4. The Rod-and-Line Strip

Although this method is similar to the hand-strip retrieve, it introduces a teasing movement of the rod between left-hand strips of the line. The fly action is erratic and contrapuntal in its rhythms. It consists of a compound pattern of strip, and rod-tip pulse and strip, that can suggest erratic swimming behavior. Such rhythms are typical of tiny baitfish and some species of hatching and egg-laying flies. It is valuable as a change of pace; and like the fast hand-strip retrieve, it often excites back-country and freshly-stocked trout. Its stripping and rod-tip rhythms are slightly more complicated to handle than the more basic wet-fly methods, but they are soon mastered with practice.

5. The Cast-and-Strip Method

This is a technique for getting greater fly depth with a sinking line in heavy currents and still waters and lakes. It involves making a relatively long cast, stripping line out from the reel, and shaking it out through the guides onto the water with a side-to-side flexing of the rod. Such abrupt paying-out of a sinking line will allow the fly time to reach considerably more depth than the actual cast length. The fly can then be given life with any of the basic fly swings or retrieves. It is a singularly effective method of fishing very deep reaches of water, and I have used it to take trout on big western rivers and high-altitude lakes, as well as in ledgerock pools in the Catskills.

Several years ago I was fishing the Barn Pool on the Brodheads with Philip Nash. It was a bright morning in May, and the current flowed smooth and strong into a pool as still as a millpond. There was a jumble of big boulders in the main holding depths of the pool, and I fished it from the shade of its swinging footbridge.

There had been two weeks of fine *Rhyacophila* hatches, and a few of these little green-bodied caddis were laying their eggs. There were no rises anywhere, and the spreading flat below the barn was like a mirror. It was unseasonably hot and I waded over to the rocks where the current chuted into the shelving depths of the pool. Caddisflies were fluttering over the surface, and suddenly I noticed several scuttling about on the boulders near my waders. They scurried nervously at the water line, and then I realized that a fly occasionally slipped below the surface, wriggling deep along the underwater currents. It disappeared into the dark eddies in the throat of the pool as I watched another caddis migrate into the swirling currents downstream.

Suddenly it disappeared in the flash of a trout, catching the light deep in the current. *Maybe the fish are taking those egg-laying caddis,* I thought excitedly. *Maybe a sinking line and a small Greenwell's Glory.*

I always carry a second reel fitted with a sinking line in my rain-jacket pouch, and I quickly switched it and strung the rod. There were a few

START STRIP

1

SLOW

2

FAST STRIP

3

...CHING FOR ...THER STRIP

4

HAND-STRIP RETRIEVE STROKES

size-fourteen Greenwells in my fly book and I fastened one to the tippet. I let it soak with the leader in a backwater while I watched a number of other flies slip underwater on a deadfall to lay their eggs.

Finally it was ready and I worked a sixty-foot cast straight down the pool. When it dropped and started sinking, I stripped another ten feet off the reel, and shook it out through the guides. It rode still deeper into the throat of the pool, and when it finally swam taut and began trailing in the current, I started to work it back upstream with a patient hand-twist retrieve.

It had teased back a half-dozen turns when there was a strong pull and a sixteen-inch fish bounced out wildly, its threshing splashes disturbing the smooth currents. *That's the ticket!* I thought happily. *They're taking these egg-laying caddisflies!*

It was the secret of fishing the Barn Pool on the Brodheads that morning, and the cast-and-strip method quickly produced two dozen fat browns and rainbows, all taken with a little Greenwell fished slowly along the bottom.

6. The Upstream Dead-Drift

Its origins lie in the innovations of W. C. Stewart on the rivers of the Scottish Lowlands, which were outlined in his book *The Practical Angler*. It appeared in 1857, and its pages are the codification of the upstream method. The upstream dead-drift presentation of the wet fly was a major breakthrough in fly-fishing tactics, and it was also the prelude to the basic dry-fly technique.

Fishing a wet fly upstream has several basic applications: it works on skittish trout in shallow water, where such fish are easily frightened by an angler wading down; it is perfect for suggesting a drowned aquatic or terrestrial insect drifting with the current; it is equally effective for fishing a hatch of emerging insects that cannot swim and that reach the surface film by riding the current tongues, rising with the gases generated inside their loosening skins; it is also a valuable method of working a fly really deep into heavy currents and deep pools.

Fishing the upstream dead-drift wet is particularly effective in the *Epeorus* mayfly hatches on eastern rivers, especially the famous Gordon Quill flies that come off in April. These mayflies begin to unfold their wings as soon as their nymphs let go from the bottom to emerge. The *Ephemerella* mayflies reach the winged stage just before they reach the surface, wriggling and unfolding their wings a few inches below the film. There are many species on American waters from the Dennys in Maine to the swift Deschutes in Oregon, including the eastern Gordon Quills and Hendricksons, and equally famous western hatches like the Pale Morning Olives and Leadwing Olive Drakes. These hatching duns ride some distance, fully winged and wriggling impatiently to hatch just under the surface, and are perfect for imitation with wet flies fished upstream. Stoneflies are another diet form that can be imitated with a dead-drift wet fly. These Plecoptera hatch from the swiftest riffles and pocket water, and fishing an upstream wet-fly method in the holding places is quite effective.

Although the upstream dead-drift is one of the most deadly methods of wet-fly presentation, it is also perhaps the most difficult technique to master. Most downstream wet-fly fishing is relatively easy, in terms of observing a taking fish and hooking it. Many fish hook themselves on a downstream wet fly. But wet flies fished upstream are a subtle problem of sensing a strike from a number of ephemeral, half-seen clues. Experienced wet-fly men often tighten into a taking fish on a dead-drift technique without being able to tell you exactly what they saw or sensed that made them strike: an imperceptible bulge or variation in the current, the upstream pause or darting twitch of the leader, little more than a subtle difference between the drift of the current and the floating line, or the partially glimpsed flash as the trout turned deep at the fly and its bright flanks caught the light.

It is a subtly honed skill that seems almost extrasensory to less gifted fishermen. The beginner can modify his tackle to help, and we have recently evolved better tackle than the dry-fly bobber that Bergman recommended in *Trout* almost forty years ago. He watched the bobber's movements on the surface when a fish took, but the bobber was difficult to keep floating and awkward to cast. Modern wet-fly men like Dave Whitlock recommend a tiny fluorescent tube attached to the line at its leader butt, or a leader knot brightly lacquered with fluorescent paint. Bright yellow or orange with an intense chroma are readily visible in the most tumbling current tongues—and a modern fisherman can watch such strike indicators twitch or pause when a fish takes as easily as Bergman watched his snelled dry-fly bobber.

7. The Cast-and-Countdown Method

This technique is necessary for fishing a wet-fly right on the bottom in relatively deep water, perhaps to suggest a drowned mayfly or caddis of the species that migrate to the bottom for egg laying. Sometimes it is perfect for imitating freshwater scuds and shrimps. Such bottom scratching is often necessary in early season, when the water is still extremely cold and the trout are sluggish and lying deep.

It is an uncomplicated method requiring only patience and a little self-discipline. It consists of making a cast and counting while the line and fly sink toward the bottom. Counts are added to the sink rate until the fisherman can actually feel the line touch bottom on the fly swing or the retrieve. The countdown is then reduced a count or two on subsequent casts to work the fly just above the bottom, fishing it back either with a simple swing or with various retrieves.

8. Multiple Wet-Fly Method

Fishing more than one wet fly on a single cast is undoubtedly as old as fly fishing itself, and was certainly in use in the fifteenth century on the trout streams of Europe. It was widely practiced on the north-country rivers of England when Charles Cotton wrote *Being Instructions How to Fish for a Trout or Grayling in a Clear Stream* in 1676, and further codified in the later work of Bowlker. It was a standard method on our brook-trout waters during the nineteenth century, and it is still found on western rivers in the hands of old-timers who grew up in the cutthroat years that followed the opening of the frontier. It is surprisingly effective in swift water.

Casting a multiple-fly rig is awkward unless the leader is properly designed and tied. Its nylon cannot be too limp or light and, instead of the snell loops popular in the past, dropper strands are required. The dropper strands will tangle in casting if they are too fine in diameter. There should be extensions left when the blood knots are formed to assemble the leader taper itself. For example, if the tippet is about .007 or 4x, the first dropper strand should be attached about twenty inches above, where the tippet is joined with a length of .008 nylon. The dropper strand should consist of about six inches of this heavier 3x leader material.

The method has been neglected on our eastern brown-trout rivers in recent years. Certainly the old looped leaders and snelled wet flies are too clumsy and too visible on our heavily fished waters. However, the modern angler can make up his own leaders to provide short lengths of dropper strands at mid-leader for attaching a second or third wet fly. It is a method that still has its uses, not only on western and northern brook-trout rivers, but also on the difficult fish of the Catskills.

Past generations of wet-fly experts like John Pope and Herman Christian fished those same Catskill rivers in their wet-fly years. They sometimes fished as many as four flies, skittering them back across the current to excite the fatally-curious native brook trout. But, as we have seen, the lumbering and the acid-bark industry ended the reign of the brook trout on our eastern rivers; once the pines and hemlocks were cut, every springhead in the region ran several degrees warmer, and the primeval cold-water biosystem of the brookies was doomed.

The European brown trout could stand warmer temperatures as well as increased angling pressure, and it quickly and handsomely filled the vacuum left with the decline of the brook trout. These new fish were harder to catch. The gaudy brook-trout patterns did not fool them, and American fishermen began to study the theories of British fishing writers to understand the much warier browns. It led to the first American flies designed to imitate our hatches—classic patterns like the Hendrickson and Gordon Quill and Cahill.

Anglers also refined their techniques to cast a single fly to a fish that was feeding, in the manner of Marryat and Halford and Skues, or to cover a likely looking pocket in the current. The years that followed saw an angling generation evolve that had forgotten the simple three-fly tricks that had regularly filled their wicker creels before 1900.

Past experience seems to argue that the reasons for the success of a multiple-fly cast are twofold. Sometimes a number of flies working in the current prove an irresistible attraction to the fish. Certainly the professional fishermen who still fish as many as eight to ten wet flies to supply hotel kitchens in the British Isles and the south of France are aware of this truth. However, there are also times when so many naturals are available below the surface—heavy caddis hatches or mating swarms of flies that lay their eggs underwater or mayfly species that exhibit schooling behavior among their nymphs—that fishing two or three imitations is quite effective.

9. The Fluttering-Dropper Technique

This method is more difficult to master than I first expected when I saw it used skillfully on the Frying Pan in Colorado twenty-five years ago. It was the technique of a grizzled fly-fisherman who had once supplied trout from the Frying Pan to a buyer from the Colorado & Midland Railroad—fish that ultimately were poached in court bouillon or broiled *meuniere* in the halcyon days of the Brown Palace in Denver, and the storied Antlers Hotel in Colorado Springs.

The old man usually fished three flies. His choices were almost always the Gray Hackle, Rio Grande King, and partridge-hackled March Brown. One evening I watched him on a swift reach of the Frying Pan about a half mile above its still water at Seven Castles. Caddisflies were egg laying, fluttering, and hopscotching over the broken current tongues. The old man was fishing his three-fly cast, using the two lowest patterns as a kind of sea anchor, raising his rod high and stripping in line and working the rod tip to bounce the small March Brown on the surface. It hopscotched down the current like a natural and the hungry trout took it eagerly with splashy rises. The old man soon changed both droppers to little March Browns, and I watched him quickly take a brace of fat Frying Pan rainbows on a single cast. The tumbling run readily surrendered another double, and I eagerly studied his manipulation of both rod and flies. Although I later caught some fish with a similar bouncing dropper, it was not as easy as it looked. It works on sophisticated brown trout too, and there is nothing else in our bag of tricks quite like a fluttering dropper—particularly to imitate the erratic flight of many egg-laying flies in their hopping half-clumsy contact with the current.

10. The Riffling-Hitch Method

This is primarily a salmon-fishing technique from Newfoundland, but it has also proved extremely effective during fly hatches that skim and scuttle across the surface film. The common British caddis called the Caperer, and various western species of our still-water Trichoptera, are typical species that scamper rapidly in the surface film. Although such insect behavior can be imitated without attaching the fly with a riffling hitch, it is perhaps the best method of suggesting an insect that runs across the surface.

It is accomplished with a pair of half-hitch knots seated tightly around the wings and hackles, slightly behind the eye of the hook. Fishing it across a main current tongue lying downstream to the left, the leader must come out under the half-hitches at the left of the fly. Fishing from the opposite side of the current, the angler reverses his half-hitch loops to have the leader ride out on the right side of the fly. The leader must be exactly seated or the fly will not swim properly in the surface, cutting a perceptible V-shaped wake in the water. It works best with fly sizes above ten or twelve. The fly speed is critical, lying just between the speed of a roughly dragging fly and a speed too slow to keep the fly from actually sinking, bringing it around just under the surface.

The fly must skim just in the surface film, and the riffling-hitch knot is not the only factor affecting this behavior. Manipulation of the rod and the line held in the left hand also play a major role. The rod is worked the moment the fly touches the water, raised higher and higher to keep it from sinking and start its swimming wake. Both rod arm and left arm are smoothly extended in unison as the fly-swing progresses, until the rod is held straight up at full arm's length, and the left hand is extended full length against the body, holding the line against the hip. This simultaneous manipulation of fly swing, rod arm, and left hand requires practice, but it can be executed perfectly, and will skim the fly in the surface at optimum speed. It is a valuable secret on many rivers, particularly after dark.

11. Diving and Bobbing

This method involves both single- and multiple-fly casts, and apparently has its tactical origins in the trout lakes of Ireland and Scotland. It is most useful in lake fishing on wilderness fish, both in the brook-trout ponds of the Labrador and the high-altitude cutthroat lakes of our western mountains. It is surprisingly effective under dead-calm conditions, and involves dressing the flies with silicone. The flies will float half-submerged in the film, and a sharp pull with the rod will duck them under, although the silicone quickly buoys them up again. This diving-and-bobbing retrieve will often induce a rise when more conventional techniques fail.

12. Dapping and Bushing

The conceptual roots of these techniques are found in writings that date back to Aelianus in the third century, who first described bouncing the fly over the fish with a fixed length of line. Lowering the fly directly over a fish has been called dapping since its first mention in fifteenth-century Britain, and bushing is a variation in which the fly is dapped over a bush or other vegetation to fish the fly on the unseen current.

Cross-country casts are also a variation on bushing. They are used when the river is clearly visible, and the angler would be too exposed to the fish should he come too close. Crouching or kneeling on the grassy bank is necessary, and part of the cast must lie on either the bank, or sometimes across a weedbed in the shallows. Although the strike must be slightly harder than normal, to overcome the friction of the weeds or grass, it is not unlike a normal wet-fly presentation.

13. The Greased Line and Crosfield Pull

The greased-line method was conceived and perfected on the Cairnton salmon beat of the Dee, by the late Arthur H. E. Wood. It utilized a carefully dressed silk line, and was designed to control fly speed under low-water conditions for salmon. It involves casting almost directly across stream, which tends to increase line bellying and the speed of the fly swing. The floating line is then mended upstream as the fly approaches optimal speed halfway through its swing. The upstream mend dampens the drag of the current on the bellying line, increasing the distance of the fly speed at its optimal behavior by as much as fifty percent in skilled hands. It also increases the likelihood of enticing a fish to rise.

The greased line has a corollary technique intended to increase fly speed, which involves a downstream mend of the floating line. Making a line mend downstream increases the pull of the current on the line, accelerating the speed of a fly that is coming around lifelessly on its current-swing. Both techniques are valuable on trout.

The Crosfield pull was developed to increase fly speed when a sinking line makes the mending technique impossible. It was developed by the late Ernest Crosfield, fishing salmon on the Herefordshire Wye and the Laxamyri in Iceland. Crosfield held the line under his index finger, and made a smooth pull of a length and speed designed to make his fly accelerate and swim properly.

Crosfield also developed a line-strip designed to decrease the speed of a sinking-line swing. It simply involves paying out small increments of line into the fly swing to slow its speed at the *moment critique,* like a teasing slow ball gets a batter to swing. Both the Crosfield pull and the Crosfield strip are common practice on the Laxá in Pingeyjarsysla of northern Iceland. The Laxá is a smooth-flowing river with deep pools perfectly suited to the sinking lines, and Crosfield taught the ghillies there to fish his methods more than half a century ago. Although the present-day ghillies are unaware of the origins of their favorite tactics, their highly skilled knowledge of manipulating fly speed originally derived from Crosfield.

14. The Leisenring Lift

This effective method of suggesting a hatching fly was developed by the late James Leisenring on the Brodheads in Pennsylvania. It was Leisenring who first adapted the subtle lessons of British writers like Skues and Cutcliffe and Pritt to American wet-fly problems, just as Gordon and La Branche further modified the dry-fly theories of the British chalkstreams to our swifter rivers.

Leisenring studied and understood the dynamics of his fly swing, both in its horizontal patterns of coverage across a pool, and in its profile of sinking and swimming at maximum depth and starting back toward the surface. Experienced fishermen have come to understand how their cast across the current first begins to sink, then starts to ride in a crosscurrent

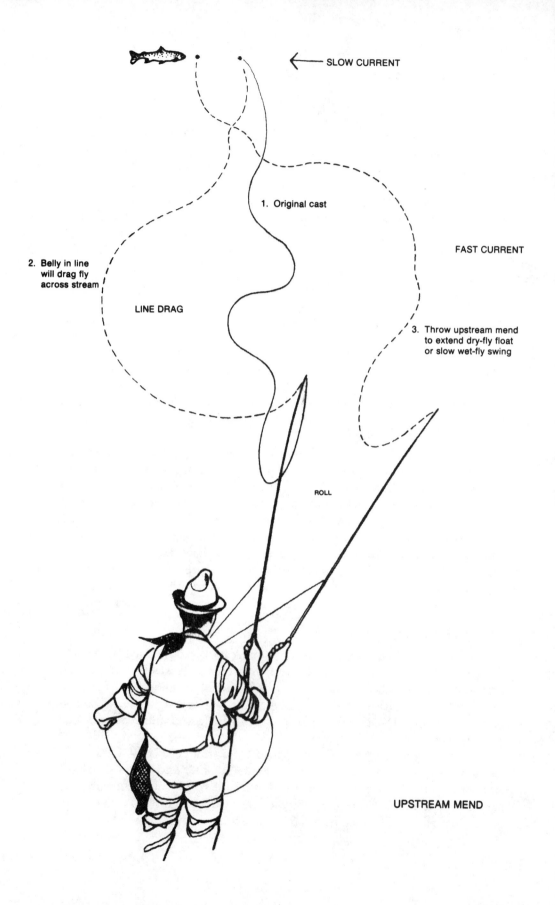

SLOW CURRENT

1. Original cast

FAST CURRENT

2. Belly in line
will drag fly
across stream

LINE DRAG

3. Throw upstream mend
to extend dry-fly float
or slow wet-fly swing

ROLL

UPSTREAM MEND

swing at maximum depth, and ultimately climbs back toward the surface with the velocity of the current. The so-called hot spot usually occurs at the time the fly has reached its maximum depth and has started to both swing and rise toward the surface.

The Leisenring lift recognizes that a fly working back toward the surface clearly imitates a hatching insect or nymph. Leisenring evolved his lift technique to suggest that movement, and make it even more attractive to a feeding trout. The result was a multiple retrieve. The cast was made across or even slightly upstream and allowed to settle dead-drift on the current. The dead-drift sink allowed the fly to reach maximum depth. When the fly had reached its depth and started to rise toward the surface on its crosscurrent swing, Leisenring began to raise his rod to accentuate the illusion of a hatching fly, working it with tip rhythm or just letting it swing, depending on the behavior of the naturals.

15. The Poacher's Retrieve

The origins of this ancient technique are unknown. Its name may be derived from the minimal amount of casting as well as the stealth involved, since both are important in concealing a poacher's craft. It is particularly valuable in the deep, quiet reaches of water where the trout cruise on the bottom, and too many casts will scatter them like frightened quail.

The poacher's retrieve is the solution. With it the leader and flies must be thoroughly soaked to sink quickly. The modern sinking lines are perfect for a technique that allows the fly to sink quickly to the bottom. It requires patience to wait while the trout forget the initial disturbance of the cast, although an occasional bold fish sometimes will dart back and take the fly while it settles slowly toward the bottom.

Most fish, however, will scatter and drift back cautiously when the fly and leader have stopped sinking. One or two may investigate the fly with considerable curiosity. Watching the fish at such times is a great advantage, although the technique can be used effectively without actually seeing the bottom. When the slow hand-twist retrieve starts the fly ascending toward the surface, after the fish have returned to the area, the man skilled in executing a poacher's retrieve will almost always raise a fish.

It was Henryville Charlie Ross, perhaps the most notorious market-hunter and poacher in the Poconos years ago, who demonstrated a poacher's retrieve to me along the Brodheads. It was deadly in his hands. Henryville Charlie ended his days on the paths of righteousness as a warden along its famous Henryville water. It was a role filled with an irony that his market-hunting cronies would have relished—and the old man could fish a skilled poacher's retrive until he had passed ninety.

Many years ago, my trout fishing began on a small meadow stream in Michigan. Getting the grasshoppers for bait was sport in itself, and we gathered them early in the wet morning grass. They were sluggish in the cold just after daylight, and we crisscrossed the meadows with our fruit jars, picking grasshoppers like brown-mottled berries.

The fishing began on the headwaters of the creek. Its meadows were willow-lined, its spring-fed origins deep in a cedar swamp. It was dark with alders and conifers there, and the bogs were filled with rust-colored seepages. Some places the springheads flowed through quivering swamps of sand and marl, and finally a small brook collected in the bog above the logging pond. The shallows were filled with stumps and deadfalls, and the beaver house stood just below the inlet. It was a beautiful place in the early morning.

Brook trout lay in its deepening emerald green channel, cruising and feeding in nervous schools. They were bright with color in these swamp-cold waters, but they usually cruised beyond the limited range of my boyhood casting. The fish almost always broke and scattered whenever my grasshopper plopped on the still surface of the logging pond.

It was a frustrating place. There were countless summer mornings when I crouched on the log-cribbing dam, trying to outwit these trout, but it usually ended in failure. There are still mornings when I remember those clear, cloud-scudding days of boyhood, and when I think about the skittish brook trout in that Michigan logging pond, it is always with the thought that a poacher's retrieve might have fooled them.

2. Modern Dry-Fly Theory and Practice

Downstream from the brooding hemlock ledges on a river in Pennsylvania, the murky currents flowed smoothly over the dark winter-scoured stones, and the April sunlight danced weakly on the riffles. It had been a dour, almost bitter spring. There were still few buds on the trees except for the bright reddish swamp maples, and even the willows had only the faintest olive cast. There were no flies hatching, although the sunlight reached the riffle gravel, stirring its ripening early-season nymphs.

The cool wind eddied in the rattling branches, and there was little warmth in the midday sun. The swift current was cold around my waders. The stream thermometer read only forty-six degrees, and it seemed unlikely that such half-hearted sunlight could warm the river enough to trigger a decent hatch of flies.

The season was already several days old, but our fishing logs still recorded no fly hatches on the water. Early-season hatches usually emerge at midday and continue sporadically into early afternoon. The dark little stoneflies and *Paraleptophlebias* are late-morning species, and the April mayfly hatches come off the riffles between one-thirty and five o'clock. Although it seemed improbable that a good hatch might emerge with the river so cold, we stopped fishing before noon, hoping to finish our lunch well before any fly hatch could begin.

No sign of a hatch, I said unhappily and accepted a glass of Beaujolais. *We should have seen a few flies coming off before lunch.*

Since dry-fly fishing depends on insects hatching from the river bottom in early season, and on terrestrial insects falling into the river when warm weather begins, we were hoping for a hatch to generate a rise of trout.

Aquatic insects trigger surface feeding both when they hatch and when they lay their eggs, and midsummer trout rise eagerly to terrestrials like ants and leafhoppers and beetles. The surface-feeding trout is perhaps the apogee of our sport, because his rises are clearly visible, and our presentation with a floating imitation has a classic beauty.

Such poetry comes with a good hatch of aquatic flies.

Henryville Charlie Ross was the riverkeeper on our Brodheads water in those years, and he stopped his rounds to talk where we were eating thick onion soup and beef sandwiches above the Ledge Pool.

It's been a right hard winter, Ross squinted out across the eddying currents below the hemlock-sheltered ledge. *Ain't seen no sign of hatches!*

Seems too cold today, I said.

Maybe, the old man shook his head. *It's the best weather we've had—but we might see some flies later on!*

Hope you're right, I smiled.

The old riverkeeper nodded, and wandered on down through the river willows to study the pool. The sun slipped behind a cloud and we stood shivering in the April wind. The hot soup and sandwiches and coffee had helped, and the feeling had finally returned to my river-chilled body.

Still no sign of them flies, Henryville Charlie grumbled when he came back up through the thickly-grown willows along the river. *Could still get a hatch this afternoon.*

Hendricksons? I asked.

April Grays, the old man answered. *Always called them hatches April Grays in the old days, but you city boys got new names for everything nowadays.*

Times change, I laughed.

The river was several degrees warmer after lunch. The thermometer was bright, glittering among the stones in the tumbling shallows above the Ledge Pool. It lay there on the bottom for five minutes before I retrieved it.

Just over fifty! I yelled.

Fifty degrees, David Rose laughed. *That's a little too cold for me, but maybe it means something to a trout!*

It means even more to a mayfly, I grinned.

You mean we might get a hatch of Hendricksons with the stream temperature over fifty? he asked.

Gordon Quills are more likely, I said.

Our famous eastern rivers typically get good hatches of *Epeorus* flies a week or two before the heavier hatches of Hendricksons. When those rivers reach about fifty degrees each spring, both fly hatches and surface feeding trout soon follow. Sometimes these factors happily combine to produce good dry-fly fishing quite early in the season.

The shallow flat above the riffles that feed the pool looked almost inviting now, where the sunlight glittered on the currents. The whole afternoon seemed brighter in spite of the rattling branches. There were still no flies hatching, and I stood watching the current in the back-eddy shallows for nymphal shucks.

The warming sun reached deep into the murky depths, where the riffling currents shelved off into the deepening throat of the pool. The river tumbled and flowed swiftly there. Its bottom betrayed no signs of life, except for the black water mosses and tiny turquoise-colored tufts of *Cladophora* and brown winter algae on the stones. Its seemingly lifeless face was a deception, since the bottom of any fertile trout stream teems all winter with myriad forms of life.

Riffling currents are the principal larders of our rivers, since their oxygen-charged waters are life-giving and rich. Their life forms are organisms that swim with great agility, clamber along the bottom, or cling firmly among the stones. Others attach themselves to the bottom. The currents are so compelling that they both polish and shape the stones, forcing them into a series of shinglelike layers, until even a dry summer streambed shows clearly which direction its April currents flowed.

When there is sufficient current, such stones shelter a richly complex web of life. The stones themselves are slippery with the films of diatomaceous organisms. The crevices are filled with algae and water mosses. There are a few swift-water fishes like fingerling trout and creek darters, and sometimes the stones conceal an agile salamander. There are leeches and planarians, and the larger stones occasionally hide a crayfish. Our northeastern streams are not alkaline enough for large numbers of smaller crustaceans. Tiny fast-water *Planorbis* snails are found here feeding on the detritus between the stones. There are minute zooplankton and rotifers too, along with threadworms and other tiny nematodes. The quiet bottom eddies also support colonies of moss animalcules and hydras, and virtually all of these minute organisms sustain themselves on microscopic forms of aquatic life.

There are subaquatic insects too. Swift-water larvae of the two-winged Diptera are perhaps the most numerous species. There are predatory beetle larvae hunting other insects among the bottom debris and leaf drift. Water pennies adhere to the smooth bedrock ledges and current-polished stones. Some riffle bottoms are greenish black with *Simulium* larvae clinging to the gravel. Some crevices between the stones are the hunting grounds of stonefly nymphs, and there are the food-collecting net shelters of the free-ranging caddis worms. Other crevices are richly encrusted with colonies of case-building Trichoptera, their patchwork castles constructed of tiny bits of shell and vegetable matter and sand, until they are often the patchwork color of the river bottom.

Mayflies are the most elegant creatures inhabiting this subaquatic society. There are the swiftly-moving, swimming nymphs of the *Isonychia* flies, each crouched like a diminutive praying mantis on the stones with its fringed forelegs collecting minute food from the tumbling currents. There are clinging forms too, like the nymphs of the March Browns and Cahills that hatch much later in the year, and hiding between the larger stones are the fat three-tailed Hendrickson nymphs that would hatch and generate fine rises of trout before the April weather was finished.

But that April afternoon the most active mayfly nymphs in these riffles were the two-tailed *Epeorus* flies, since the gradually warming waters would soon encourage them to start their emergence. It was nearly one-thirty when the cool wind stopped and the afternoon seemed almost warm, and in the eddying shallows beside the riffles I finally saw a fresh nymphal skin drifting in the slack current. There were several others in the next half hour, and their presence in the river seemed to suggest the prelude to a coming hatch of flies.

The restless nymphs were losing their caution now, working out from under their hiding places and exposing themselves to the fish. The sunlight filtered through the water, warming the bottom currents. The nymphs clambered into position along the underwater sides of the stones, clinging with their tiny claws to the smooth surfaces. Working their bodies and gill plates carefully, they create a partial vacuum that fastens them firmly to the bottom. Emergence occurs there, with the thoracic structure splitting along the wing cases, and partially along the axis of the tergite surfaces. The wings struggle free of the nymphal skin, and then the legs work themselves loose. The hatching nymph sometimes pauses momentarily, and finally draws its writhing body and speckled tails from its nymphal shuck. The surprising vacuum created by the gill plates and legs is broken once the emerging mayfly has struggled free, and the loose nymphal skin drifts off with the current, while the freshly hatched insect wriggles and works toward the surface.

Mayfly hatches all begin with the hatching duns or nymphs migrating up through the water, beyond the tumbling surface of the river. The fish begin seeing and taking occasional nymphs when they first become restless; it is this prehatching restlessness that forces the normally shy nymphs to expose themselves more recklessly before emergence.

The rhythm of hatching quickens after midday with the *Epeorus* flies, until more and more nymphs split their nymphal skins, and their wriggling mayflies struggle toward the surface. Their folded wings help buoy them upward, their smoky veins and diaphanous structures alive with tiny air bubbles generated within the skins of the nymphs themselves. The fish respond to their increasing availability by taking the hatching flies as they wriggle past, and as the numbers of insects working toward the surface steadily grows larger, the hungry trout soon follow them. Finally the majority of the hatching flies are wriggling just under the surface film and riding the current itself. The fish have usually followed them up from the bottom currents, taking the hapless insects where they find them, until finally the trout hang poised just under the surface ready to feed extensively on the floating mayflies.

Dry-fly fishing has its origins in these ancient rhythms of aquatic entomology and the hatch; and the cycles disprove one of the classic myths of American dry-fly theory. George La Branche fervently believed that a skilled caster could create the illusion of a fly hatch for a nonfeeding trout by presenting his fly again and again to its feeding currents. La Branche argued that the parade of drifting dry flies created by his successive casts could trick the fish into thinking a hatch had started. *The Dry Fly and Fast Water* outlines the hypothesis of creating a hatch forged by the high priest of American presentation. Except for terrestrial insects or a fall of mayfly spinners after mating, La Branche was clearly mistaken, and neither of these latter happenings is actually a hatch. No trout could mistake his parade of perfectly cast flies for a genuine hatch of aquatic insects, since the fish would not previously have observed and fed on the first quickening rhythms of the emerging nymphs, as they lost their caution and drifted toward the surface.

That April afternoon on the Brodheads, the number of nymphal skins drifting past me in the smooth current was increasing steadily, and an occasional mayfly actually came fluttering off the riffles upstream. The sunlight caught another dun flying toward the trees, and a third came sailboating and hopscotching down the riffles on the cool wind. There were suddenly several in the air, and a hungry phoebe darted out from the alders to capture one just as it escaped the water. The agile little flycatcher wheeled back in midflight, its rapier-quick bill whiskered with the freshly hatched insect.

The current was quickly covered with flies now, riding the water like a regatta of minuscule sailboats, and close against the hemlock ledges across the current, the first trout rose and took one. It was the first dry-fly hatch of the season. Trout began rising regularly now, taking the flies just below the riffles where they were hatching, along the deep hemlock ledges in the upper pool, down the eddying hundred-foot spine below the outcroppings, and in the gathering currents of the tail shallows where they flowed against the sheltering willows.

Although I was relatively sure of their species, I did not select an imitation until I had collected one or two. Insects look quite pale in the air, flying from the river to shelter in the streamside bushes, and they appear even paler riding the current than when they are held in the hand. I waded out into a strong current tongue and collected two or three specimens, placing them in a small open-throat collecting bottle. Their wings were dark grayish and there were two tails. Their bodies were grayish olive, delicately ringed with brown. Their legs were amber, with strong brown mottlings on each femur, and these characteristics clearly identified the hatching insects as the early *Epeorus* mayflies common on eastern rivers like the Brodheads.

Gordon Quills should work, I thought.

It was one of those afternoons when the trout eagerly cooperated, and our dry-fly imitations worked perfectly. There was a good fish feeding in the tail currents. It was lying tight under the willows in a slightly slower current tongue, which made a carefully executed hook cast necessary to prevent the fly from dragging. The cast sliced out sideways into the soft wind, and I checked its final shoot gently to drop the slack-line hook above the fish. The upstream slack in the cast would buy a few seconds of drag-free float, long enough for a natural drift over the trout, and it took the fly without hesitation. When I tightened to set the hook, it threshed angrily along the willows and stripped line from my delicate reel. Several times it forced itself deep along the bottom gravel, and once its gyrations raked the fragile 6X tippet against a stone. Finally it surrendered to the waiting net, and I admired its brightly spotted sixteen inches before gently releasing it in the shallows.

It was typical of the dry-fly method.

History does not tell us precisely where or when the dry-fly method was born, which is rather surprising, considering its relatively recent origins. The literature of fly-fishing first mentions dry-fly tactics almost 150 years ago, and there is quite unmistakable evidence that the dry fly began somewhere on the chalkstreams of England.

There are many British rivers that have played a role in the evolution of the dry-fly method. Perhaps the best known are the silken Test at villages like Stockbridge and Whitchurch and Chilbolton, and the Itchen a few miles above Winchester, where Viscount Grey of Fallodon regularly fished almost a century ago. There is the pastoral Frome where George Selwyn Marryat first learned his fly-fishing, years before his famous collaboration with Halford in the development of the dry-fly technique on the Houghton water of the Test. There are the storied Kennet, famed throughout England for its blizzardlike mayfly hatches, and its delightful limestone tributary, the gentle Lambourne. Certainly there are also historic roots in the Wandle, where Halford himself first observed the dry-fly method, and the willow-lined Bourne, where Plunket-Greene fished at Hurstbourne Priors. The Coln at Fairford also has its own measure of history and fame. The gentle Avon is another classic chalkstream, winding through the water meadows below Salisbury Cathedral, and there are beats with poetic beauty along the little Wylye at charming Wiltshire villages like Fisherton-de-la-Mere.

Popular legend ascribes the dry fly and its origins to the Itchen, although its birth in angling literature lies still farther toward the west, on the little rivers fished by George Pulman. His famous *Vade Mecum of Fly-Fishing for Trout* appeared in 1841, and contains the first unmistakable description of the dry-fly method. Pulman was a tackle seller from Axminster in the rolling Devonshire hills, and his home rivers were moorland streams like the Barle and the Exe, and the classic beats of the Axe that he loved for so many seasons.

Frederic Halford is considered the father of the dry-fly method, as we explained at length in earlier chapters, although he did not fully originate its theory and practice. Halford was the historian of its early evolution, and codified the innovations of both his predecessors and his contemporaries on the smooth-flowing Hampshire and Wiltshire streams below London. Halford owed much of his philosophy and technique to the celebrated George Selwyn Marryat, who died tragically without publishing a fishing book himself. Marryat polished his fishing along the Coln in Dorsetshire, and Halford tells us in his memoirs that his baptism in the dry-fly method occurred on the willow-lined beats of the Wandle at Carshalton.

Yet his principal river became the world-famous Test at Stockbridge, and it is curious that our historical knowledge of that unique stream is less than two centuries old. It must have been fished in the centuries before Berners and Walton, since it has bountiful fly hatches and has always boasted incredible populations of fish, conspicuously lying over the mottled gravel among its beds of trailing weed.

It is strange that fly-fishing literature does not mention the Test until the threshold of the nineteenth century, with the meticulous diary of Colonel Peter Hawker, who fished its beautiful Longparish water. Hawker recorded his experiences along the upper Test from 1802 until 1853, and his chronicles are augmented by the diary of the Reverend Richard Durnford, who fished the Chilbolton water downstream from 1809 until 1819.

The historical records of the Houghton Club on the Test were finally compiled by Sir Herbert Maxwell in 1908, and they form an unbroken record of fly-fishing on the Test for more than eighty-five seasons. Canon Charles Kingsley described the river in his *Chalkstream Studies* in 1857, two decades before Frederic Halford emerged as its principal philosopher and historian. There were other writers who found inspiration in the crystalline reaches of the Test, men like Viscount Grey of Fallodon, Francis Francis, and George Edward MacKenzie Skues. Andrew Lang once held a beat on the Whitchurch water. John Waller Hills became its writer-in-residence with his poetic *A Summer on the Test* in 1924, and both Edward Ringwood Hewitt and George La Branche fished it in those same years. Our knowledge of the Test and its role in the evolution of the dry-fly method weaves a continuous written fabric reaching back more than 170 years to Hawker and Durnford.

Its character and the quality of its sport attracted a remarkable parade of famous men. There was Sir Francis Chantrey, the famous sculptor who was a founder of the Houghton Club; Chantrey was joined by J. M. W. Turner, perhaps the finest landscape painter in the history of European art. His drawings are still found in the journals of the Houghton Club. Sir Humphrey Davy also loved the Test and its fishing. Disraeli and Lord Nelson and the Duke of Wellington were all occasional fly-fishing pilgrims on the Test and its sister rivers. Disraeli even owned the beautiful Testcombe estate at Chilbolton. Thomas Phelps also fished the river and described it in *Fishing Dreams*, and his companion along the upper Test was J. C. Mottram, considered the finest British surgeon of his time. Lord Palmerston lived and fished beside the lower river at Broadlands, which later became the Hampshire estate of Lord Louis Mountbatten. It is a fishing tradition that is old and rich, reaching back to William of Wykeham and Izaak Walton himself, who lived along the Test at Norington Farme almost until his death. It is the Test and its difficult trout that polished the dry-fly method to its modern degree of refinement, and we owe a monumental debt to the men who have fished it over the past century, from its still Mayfly reaches at Stockbridge to the gravelly beats of the upper river at Longparish and Hurstbourne Priors and Whitchurch.

Such men worked out the basic topologies between dry flies and various species of floating insects. The rich phosphates of the chalkstreams sustained immense hatches of mayflies and caddis, and these orders were their first prototypes for fly patterns. Since their pioneering efforts, anglers have developed workable imitations for a whole galaxy of insect forms. Modern dry flies are dressed to imitate the adult or egg-laying stages of insects like mayflies, caddis, stoneflies, ants, leafhoppers, grasshoppers, craneflies, midges, and beetles. Such insects riding or floating pinioned in the surface film are the catalysts for the dry-fly method, and the trout greedily take them there with clearly visible rise forms.

Both the techniques of fly dressing and the fishing tackle worked out by these pioneers on the Test in the late nineteenth century have passed through a considerable evolution in the past one hundred years. Technology has continued to evolve so rapidly that virtually nothing, from popular fly patterns to our tapered lines and leader materials and the calibrations of the rods themselves, remains quite the same as it existed when Bergman first published *Trout* in 1938.

Edward Ringwood Hewitt initially followed the British modes in stiff rods capable of vigorous false casting to dry his flies, and his influence resulted in a whole generation of stiff-butt and relatively soft-tip calibrations in rods. Hewitt ultimately abandoned his stiff-butt theories, and in some classic film footage shot years ago along the Neversink by my good friend Martin Bovey, both Hewitt and La Branche are using supple, slow-action rods of more contemporary design. It seems doubtful, according to conversations with men like John Alden Knight and the late Guy Jenkins, that Hewitt ever really fished extensively with the fast-action tapers he often recommended.

Bergman advocated similar tapers in *Trout,* although his favorite rods had an action that flexed well down the butt section toward the grip. His preferences in rod design ran to models of seven and a half feet in a time when most trout rods ran from eight to nine feet. Several of my first split-cane rods were nine feet long, although they were delicate enough for a six-weight English line. The first was a darkly stained Heddon and the second was a South Bend from the skilled hands of Wes Jordan. Bergman advocated delicacy in his rods, combined with a supple feeling of power. Since he was the senior salesman at the old William Mills & Son shop in lower Manhattan, selling the original Leonard rods, Bergman was familiar with rod actions that had extremely fine tip calibrations combined with a taper that worked well down into the grip. His chapter in *Trout* devoted to dry-fly fundamentals and tackle made the following observations thirty-five years ago:

> First, for delicacy in casting it is best not to have a rod which is too heavy and stiff. Usually, better **grade** rods ranging from 7½ to

nine feet in length and from 3½ to 5½ ounces in weight will fill the bill in the matter of weight, but it is a good idea to be quite particular, as some rods of identical length and weight may have actions as different as night and day.

For instance, I have one 7½-foot rod of 3¾ ounces which is like a poker, and as far as I am concerned fit only for spinner or bait fishing, but I have several others of the same length and weight which are stiff and powerful without being pokers.

It's all in the feel, with power and stiffness being combined with resilience and suppleness. Some rods have this and others do not. Now this right feel is an elusive thing. It is indescribable, that is to the extent that you cannot possibly pick out a rod from the description. The nearest I can come to giving you an impression of it is that you feel the rod live and breathe right down to the grip. The action is distributed with a decreasing, even power from the hand grasp to the tip top.

Recent years have witnessed a trend toward rods under four ounces and eight feet in length, since increased fishing pressure and the sophisticated brown trout found in public water today require extremely delicate tackle. Short rods are surprisingly fashionable.

Generally speaking, rods that demand lines heavier than six- or seven-weight tapers are too heavy for modern dry-fly fishing, since they drop too hard on the current for the sensibilities of a sophisticated trout. Some rodmakers have pursued the concept of extremely short rods weighing from one to two and a half ounces, but some of these rods are really not designed for fishing over shy trout in smooth currents. Weight-forward lines on such small rods may make them impressive casting tools, tempting their owners into believing that their casting skills have been radically improved by the equipment, but such line tapers land too hard for a skittish fish in a smooth flat. Rods taking a six- and seven-weight line, while weighing only two to two and a half ounces, are too muscular in their tip calibrations to fish the delicate limp-nylon tippet diameters common on public waters. Such rods have become extremely fashionable in recent years, but I do not believe they are viable for difficult fishing. They are impressive in their line-handling qualities, shooting eighty to ninety feet in the hands of a skilled caster, but their torpedo tapers deliver harshly and their relatively thick tip calibrations are much too crude for .003 to .005 nylon.

Such short rods are also a problem in other aspects of dry-fly fishing, and wading a deep flat makes fishing a short fly rod difficult. Their length is ideal for fishing brushy streams that are densely shrouded in willows and alders, with overhanging trees. However, in bank fishing along some western spring creeks and the Pennsylvania limestone streams, sufficient rod length is critical to keeping the backcast out of the weeds and grass. Several times I have watched skilled casters brought to the threshold of total frustration on such rivers; and watching an American fish his so-called midge rods on the Hampshire chalkstreams, or limestone water meadows like the Liffey and the Maigue in Ireland, is another exercise in sympathy—since backcast after backcast inevitably hangs up in the waist-high grasses.

There are a number of superb midge-type rods available, however, that are valuable tools for fine work. These rods are consciously designed to fish flies under size sixteen, cast seventy to eighty feet in skilled hands, and hook a good fish without shearing delicate modern tippets measuring in .003 to .005 diameters. Such tackle is critical to success in fishing midge-sized imitations and tiny terrestrials on difficult rivers from Silver Creek in Idaho to limestone streams like Falling Springs or the famous Letort Spring Run in Pennsylvania.

Since the introduction of modern silicone fly dressing, it is no longer necessary to dry our flies with as much false casting, and stiffness is less important in a dry-fly rod design. Such fly oil was unknown thirty-five years ago, and Bergman recommended a relatively crude mixture consisting of two ounces of shaved paraffin dissolved in a pint of gasoline or carbon tetrachloride. Such mixtures often damaged silkworm-gut tippets, and when the temperature dropped below sixty degrees, the paraffin often congealed unless it was carried in inside pockets. Our modern silicones in plastic bottles or small spray cans are a considerable improvement over the old fly-dressing mixtures.

Modern fly lines are also exceptional. The British silk lines that I fished in boyhood were almost poetic in their suppleness and casting qualities, working in unmatched harmony with a silkworm-gut leader. Yet silk lines had their shortcomings. Their finishes became tacky and, unless they were regularly dried, silk lines tended to rot and lose their strength. Proper care demanded that silk lines be dried each night, and a well-equipped angler usually carried two lines for use on alternate days. Silk lines were also slightly heavier than water, and became easily waterlogged in the course of a day's fishing. This required daily applications of various line dressings like the well-known Mucilin paste from Britain. These problems have been largely solved with the development of nylon plastic-coated lines.

Fishing brooks and feeder streams with the dry-fly method can mean using delicate little rods from six to seven feet, weighing from two to three ounces and taking three- to five-weight lines. Double-taper designs are almost mandatory for such waters to avoid spooking the small-stream trout, and the ideal floating lines vary from DT3F and DT4F tapers for the smallest rods to the DT5F that will match most light-tackle rods. These are optimal late-summer rods as well, since they will cast delicately and fish the cobweb-fine leaders necessary for covering a gin-clear flat on many of our late-summer streams.

Proper dry-fly tackle for medium-size rivers demands somewhat bigger rods and heavier gear. Seven-and-a-half to eight-foot rods are in order now, weighing from two and three quarters to four ounces, depending on their design specifications. Deep wading requires the longer rods necessary to hold the backcasts high enough. Such rods will balance with five- and six-weight lines, and although double tapers were mandatory in the past, there are new long-belly types of forward tapers that deliver a cast softly enough for dry-fly tactics over smooth currents and selective fish. This past spring on the Dunraven Castle water of the Maigue in Ireland, such a six-weight taper proved itself remarkably effective in presenting tiny Iron Blues at distances beyond eighty feet—turning over a delicate twelve-foot stiff butt leader and settling the cast on the smooth currents without frightening its wary fish.

Big river dry-fly tactics can require equipment with still more muscle. Eight- to nine-foot rods are necessary to punch out a wind-resistant dry fly like a big Wulff or Hewitt Skater at eighty to ninety feet. Such rods will best function with lines of six- to eight-weight tapers, and the long-belly design is perhaps the best tool we have for long-range dry-fly work. The modern hard-plastic finishes possible with synthetic lines also permit a skilled fisherman to shoot a long dry-fly presentation.

Typical dry-fly presentation consists of casting from across and below a visibly rising trout, and the line is manipulated to provide a dragless float over the fish with a floating imitation of its food. Basic theory requires as natural a float over the rising trout as possible, completely free of any drag across its current tongues on the bellying leader.

British dogmatics from the Halford period ignored the skittering technique that men like William Lunn on the Test and Roger Foster on the Maigue in Ireland have always used to suggest a hatching or egg-laying sedge. Their methods are subtle, almost inducing a rise to the floating imitation in the way that nymph experts like Frank Sawyer and Oliver Kite perfected on the Wiltshire rivers at Salisbury. Hewitt also developed his Neversink Skaters to imitate the erratic hopscotch of egg-laying craneflies; and these induced-drag techniques are contrary to conventional dry-fly wisdom, often involving downstream casts.

Leonard Wright again outlined such variations on traditional dry-fly themes in his recent *Fishing the Dry Fly as a Living Insect*, which adapted these techniques of skittering a dry-fly with intentional drag to imitate the American caddisflies. However, basic dry-fly tactics imitating most of the fly hatches and terrestrial insects along trout water still demand the conventional dragless float.

Such dragless presentations are usually achieved in six basic types of dry-fly casts. Each technique involves a free drift over the trout, in which the floating imitation reaches the fish before it sees the leader tippet. The cast from directly downstream does not achieve this stratagem, although with the delicate and less visible modern nylons, it has become a somewhat more useful tactic. The direct upstream presentation is perhaps the easiest method of achieving a dragless float, since fly and leader and line all lie in current tongues of closely related direction and speed. Such methodology is a frequent theme in the books of Bergman, both the early *Just Fishing* and the later *Trout*; and his tactical anecdotes often involved crossing the main currents to fish a pool from its less-travelled bank—always finding the problems thwarting a drag-free drift were easier from there.

The leader-free presentations are considerably more difficult to master under field conditions. Each of these methods is used for fish lying to the right or left of the angler and rising steadily with the faster currents lying between. The right and left hook casts are both designed to fall above the fish with an exaggerated semicircle of upstream slack. These casts are useful when the current tongues between the angler and the trout are relatively swift. Particularly easy currents call for a less exaggerated hook-cast presentation, in which the hook is little more than a gentle curve. Placing the tippet only slightly above the rising fly-shy trout in a shallow flat may require a variation on this tactic, which places the fly slightly short of the fish, so that neither the leader nor the imitation falls too close to its position. The final leader-free presentations are the crosscurrent and downstream casts to right or left, and a directly downstream cast checked in flight to partially abort the cast and create a series of slack-line loops.

Before discussing the basic methods of dry-fly presentation, perhaps an admonition about sinking and floating leaders is in order. Unlike the other forms of fly-fishing, the dry-fly leader is usually required to float in order to insure a ready strike when a fish rises to the fly. Yet a floating leader can prove itself a serious liability in smooth currents, since its patterns in the surface film can cast surprisingly large shadows along the bottom. Such shadows can easily spook a crowd-skittish trout. However, sinking the leader to eliminate these surface-film shadows is not so easy with modern nylons, and is not always the solution in all cases. It is sometimes important on smooth pools and flats, but on broken currents a sinking leader will result in missed fish, and the leader should be lightly oiled so that its sunken drag and slack cannot slow our striking reflex.

There are fifteen basic techniques and primary variations of the dry-fly method as practiced on American waters, and they involve both drag-free and controlled-drag tactics. Our present philosophy of dry-fly fishing is a considerable departure from the drag-free dogma and rigid upstream rules first codified on the chalkstreams by men like Halford and Marryat.

1. Left-Hook Presentation

The left hook is a difficult cast for a right-handed angler, but it is a common tactical situation for a pool with its primary holding currents on the left bank of the stream. There are two basic methods of making the left hook work: the first involves turning the wrist inward in the final delivery of the cast, until the back of the hand faces left; and the second involves making a normal sidearm delivery until the final second of the cast, shooting loose slack, and then breaking the wrist sharply at the final moment to snap a crisp left hook into the leader.

No river is without pools or runs or eddying backwaters where the left-hook cast is critical to success. The trout lie across the primary current

tongues from the angler, motionless under the willows or tight against the roots of the sheltering buttonwoods, and a direct cast is caught almost instantly by the flow. The bellying leader and line drag the dry fly across the suspicious fish almost as quickly as it touches the water. It is a familiar problem to any fly-fisherman.

The solution is a delicately thrown left-hook cast which drops the dry fly a few inches above the fish, driving the leader tippet farther upstream to fall in a slack loop of nylon when we shoot two or three feet of extra line and snub the cast at the final moment. Properly delivered, such a cast will provide a few inches of drag-free float until the current draws the cushion of slack from the upstream loop. The fish will have just enough time to rise to the drag-free imitation.

Both hook casts are difficult to execute well, since there is little margin for error in the size of the slack loop in the leader, the possible duration of the float in terms of current speed between the angler and the fish, and the initial arrival of the cast on the water. Experience is necessary to master these several variables, but the left-hand hook is not beyond a caster of moderate skills, and it is a primary tactic on trout water.

2. Right-Hook Presentation

The right-hook cast is a corollary to the left-hook cast. It involves a fish working along the right bank of the stream, and lying on the far side of the current tongue. Again the direct cast will almost immediately result in a dragging fly, unless the fisherman can throw enough upstream slack to achieve a drag-free float. Such a natural drift is possible with a well-placed right-hook cast.

It is easier for a right-handed angler to execute, since it is merely an incomplete cast with a slight shooting of left-hand slack. The cast is delivered in a sidearm or three-quarter position and is worked out over the fish, checked before it is dropped to the water by halting the normal wrist follow-through, and allowed to settle on the current with a soft upstream hook in the leader. Practice and experience will help you judge how to deliver and check your cast while the line loop is still unrolling to drop the leader in a perfect right-hook cast. Seasoned anglers also know how to use a downstream wind to their advantage rather than disadvantage, working the line from angles that help force the leader into a controlled downstream loop that presents the fly to the trout first and gains several seconds of drag-free drift.

This cast is less difficult than a left-hook presentation, and was the first difficult dry-fly tactic that I learned in my youth on the rivers of lower Michigan. Thinking back about those years, when my casting skills were rudimentary at best, the simple right-hook technique was a revelation. In those summers spent along the brushy tree-hung reaches of the Little South Pere Marquette, the growing ability to place a hook cast under the overhanging branches quickly multiplied my daily catches.

The right-hook cast is surprisingly easy to learn, more than several

other advanced techniques, and no fly-fisherman can master his journey-man skills without it.

3. Upstream Check Cast

This is a basic dry-fly presentation used on shy fish when both fly and leader must settle on the surface like thistledown. It is a simple procedure once it is fully understood. The fisherman is perhaps thigh-deep in a glassy flat known for its selective trout. The fly and leader must land softly without frightening them, or they will stop rising altogether. It is a familiar problem on hard-fished pools and flats from the Allagash in Maine to the Nimpkish in British Columbia, and it is a primary tool of skilled dry-fly technique.

Several days ago I watched two anglers fish the Hewitt Flat on my home water of the Brodheads. It was bright and still, and the silken currents of the pool shelved off into the waist-deep water below the bridge where Edward Ringwood Hewitt tells us that he first tried the dry-fly method. It is a fine pool with a good population of free-rising fish. Good hatches come off the bridge pocket water above the pool, and its trout are well known for their free-rising selectivity.

The first angler fished the pool in the classic American style, his stiff-action rod working in a quick flick-flick rhythm of false casting. His fishing was almost nervous and brusque. The casting rhythms were rapierlike in character, and each final cast came with a driving follow-through with the rod low above the current. His flies were thoroughly dried and cocked high, coming down crisply above each rising trout. The casting was accurate but much too hard, and from my vantage point on the bridge, I watched him frighten a number of fish that either stopped feeding altogether or bolted away in panic. Other than delivering the fly too hard, his presentation was perfectly executed.

Can't understand it! he yelled upstream to the bridge. *There were at least a dozen fish working!*

The mayflies were still hatching from the swift reach of water above the bridge, but now they fluttered down the main currents of the pool unmolested. The old dry-fly man waded slowly from the pool, and almost immediately several fish began drifting back into feeding position. Another fisherman slipped into the gathering currents in the tail shallows, and as we watched for several minutes, the first trout rose again.

With this hatch, the second man laughed, *you'd think more fish would be feeding in the Hewitt.*

There were, I said.

Somebody just fish through it? he asked.

Put them all down! I smiled.

There were several more rises now, and a number of other fish had taken feeding stations again. Gradually they drifted higher in the current until they hovered just under the glassy surface, and soon these trout were feeding steadily too.

What're you using? I asked.

Red Quill seems to work just fine today, he said. *What was the other fisherman using over these fish?*

Red Quill, I laughed.

The second man nodded and eased slowly into casting position, where several trout were greedily working to the hatch of dark *Ephemerella* flies. His fishing style was radically different from the first man's: his casting rhythms were surprisingly relaxed; and his rod working almost lazily in its false casting. There was a good fish rising forty feet above him, and he took it on his second cast. It was a fine performance, and he coaxed the struggling fish carefully downstream from the other rising trout.

That fish was no accident! I thought.

The fisherman released the trout gently, washed the slime from his fly, and sprayed it with silicone dressing. He dried the fly with a few tantalizing slow false casts, and moved slowly into position for the second fish.

His cast worked out above its feeding station, travelling a few feet longer than necessary, and he delivered it like a false cast. The line and leader and fly unrolled and straightened about three feet above the surface, and at the final moment the fisherman drew back his casting hand slightly. It broke his follow-through, checked the cast in midair well above the glassy surface, and allowed it to settle softly. The fly cocked and fell virtually without disturbing the current above the rising trout, and when the fly reached its station, another fish rose confidently.

That makes two, I smiled.

It was a vivid episode that clearly proved the viability of the upstream check-cast technique on difficult fish in smooth water, and the second angler took nine fish from the pool, with the same fly that had been used half an hour earlier. Both fly pattern and terminal tackle diameter had been the same, but the driving follow-through used by the first angler had frightened the trout, while the gentle check cast had taken them.

4. Slack S-Cast

This is a clever variation on the check cast that is designed to throw enough slack across erratic surface currents to buy a few moments of drag-free float before the fly reaches a feeding trout. Sometimes a pool is a series of crosscurrents and eddies, making conventional hook casts useless.

The solution is often a well-executed slack S-cast that distributes a series of serpentine loops across the surface. The technique involves delivering the final cast to the same imaginary plane above the actual water, and checking the follow-through, but in the final instant the angler waggles his rod sideways to throw slack into the falling line. The result is a series of irregular slack-line loops that cushion the fly drag of conflicting surface currents.

Such complex current tongues are typical of our limestone streams and weed-rich western spring creeks riffling and eddying through their beds of trailing candelabra and nitella and watercress. Crosscurrents are also common in boulder-strewn rivers, and pools downstream from broken ledges and wild pocket water. The slack S-cast thrown across such irregular patterns of flow is often the only solution.

5. Parachute Cast

The well-known parachute cast is another method of achieving a series of slack-line loops across conflicting currents. It involves false casting enough line to reach well beyond the actual intended target point for the fly, like both the upstream check-cast and the slack S-cast. However, instead of checking the follow-through or shaking loops into the line with a side waggle of the rod, the parachute cast consists of stopping the cast short of the follow-through, and abruptly dropping the butt of the rod toward the surface of the river.

The result is a checked cast that settles to the surface in a random pattern of slack-line loops. Since a parachute cast tends to fall in a slightly different manner from the conventional delivery of either a check cast or an S-cast, it can work in some situations where the others fail.

6. Brush-Cast Technique

Few anglers seem to know the brush-cast technique familiar to the anglers who fish the spring creeks of Pennsylvania and Maryland. It is eloquently described by Charles Fox in his *Wonderful World of Trout* as the undercover cast. It is designed for fishing deep under the overhanging trees, and is extremely useful on most rivers.

Trout often hold deep in the shadows of such overhanging limbs, and only a drag-free float under the branches will take them. The cast is a long sidearm presentation designed to work a narrow loop in the line. The rod tip executes most of the action, and the false cast is worked with somewhat more line speed than would normally be required to deliver the line in the air. The final cast is executed with a driving wrist action, carrying the line low along the water, and at the final moment the left-hand slack is allowed to shoot into the guides. Perfectly executed, the shooting line and leader float back underneath the overhanging branches, settling above the rising fish.

7. Cross-Country Cast

Sometimes trout are rising beyond a deadfall or branch, or lying along an open grassy bank that makes them skittish and difficult to approach. Both situations are perfectly suited to the cross-country cast, which drops the leader and sometimes the line across the intervening barriers. The true cross-country cast is possible with wet flies and nymphs, but a cast across a downed tree or limb is best with a stiff-hackled dry fly, since its hackles permit it to come back with less danger of snagging.

The actual cast is delivered softly like an upstream or cross-stream check method, allowing the leader and line to straighten and settle to the surface gently. Since drag is inevitable and will begin quickly, the dry fly must be placed to fall almost on the rising fish. Sometimes a brief float is possible, but watching while it approaches the feeding station seems to take an eternity as you wait for the fatal drag to begin. The strike must always be quicker and firmer, to overcome the friction of the grassy banks or the intervening snag, than in a normal cast delivered over the water.

Over the years the cross-country cast has produced several big fish for me on meadow water, including a five-pound brown on the Big Hole. It was a fish I should not have tried, but once it was hooked there was little choice. The trout was rising steadily behind a half-submerged deadfall below Biltmore Springs, and its impressive rise forms sent waves down the currents trapped between the log and the far bank. It was a difficult place to cover properly.

The river is strong there, and I waded out almost chest-deep into the current, until the fly boxes in my wading vest were literally shipping water. The deadfall was still forty-five feet away, and the fish was rising beyond it, splashing water across its bleached limbs. It was a perfect place for a long-hackled spider or variant, since such a fly could be retrieved back across the log with less chance of fouling. The cast worked out past the logs, and I checked it perfectly, dropping the fly just beyond the deadfall and above the rising fish.

It reacted with a violent rise form that showered water high on the wind, and it cakewalked wildly downstream behind the log. The fish jumped several times, raking my leader back and forth over the tree, and it looked huge. The fight seemed hopeless, with a great jackstraw tangle of logs downstream, when the big trout inexplicably somersaulted out of its thicket into the open currents of the river.

The leader caught briefly, but instantly worked free of the shredding bark, and the rest of the fight went my way. However, such luck on a five-pound brown is rare—big fish seldom make mistakes.

8. Dapping, Dibbing, and Bushing

These fishing methods are centuries old. They are clearly discussed throughout British fishing literature before the first colonial settlements were established in Virginia and Massachusetts. There are a number of old names for such practices, like dibbing and shade-fishing, and dapping is a term sometimes used to describe blow-line fishing with live *Ephemera* flies on famous Irish lakes like Lough Derg and Lough Corrib. William Lawson also mentions the method in his famous edition of *The Secrets of Angling*, which first appeared in 1620:

> This flie and two linkes among wood or close by a bank, moved cleverly in the crust of the water, is deadly in the evening, if you come close. This is called bushing for trouts.

Dapping consists of lowering a fly through the streamside foliage without casting, and dancing it up and down on the surface directly above the holding lie of the trout. Dibbing is the similar technique applied to meadow banks with high grasses that sometimes make it virtually impossible to fish a likely current on the near bank without being seen. Trout in such places are often observed through a concealing screen of weeds and water grasses, and sometimes the vegetation is so dense that such fish are only heard rising. The dry fly is fished over them tantalizingly, dancing on the surface film with a nervous little rhythm beside the undercut banks. Such manipulation looks like the restless fluttering of an egg-laying caddis, and can be remarkably effective at times.

Bushing consists of the same technique executed over low streamside foliage, often to a rising fish that can only be heard splashily feeding or that has been located only from the spreading ripples generated by his rise forms. The cast is made over the screen of bushes to the unseen current beyond. Bergman describes his success in *Trout* with the bushing method along a particularly brushy reach of the Encampment in Wyoming. The rise to the dry fly fished in this manner is often relatively strong, and the strike should be delayed slightly to avoid shearing the tippet. Striking at the precise moment of the rise is likely to rake the fly from the mouth of the fish, since its direction of force is away from the jaws rather than into them. Since the leader is not lying in the surface film, its visible thickness is less critical in dapping and bushing than in more normal dry-fly techniques. Many fishermen recommend tippets as strong as .009 for average conditions, and .007 for dapping on small streams and still currents. Hooking percentages for these tactics will improve if the fisherman learns to curb his natural instinct to strike hard at the first moment of the rise; a fish still holding the fly is more likely to find itself hooked securely in the corner of its jaws if the angler waits to strike until the trout is turning toward its original holding lie.

9. Grasshopper or Bump Cast

This is a conventional cast designed to drop the fly relatively hard on the surface film in order to attract the fish when they are waiting for a big terrestrial insect like a grasshopper or fully grown inchworm to land clumsily on the water. Such a hard presentation is diametrically opposed to most dry-fly practice with its so-called thistledown settling of a perfectly cocked floater, but it is a technique directly related to the behavior of such awkward land-bred insects. When the inchworms are particularly numerous, and the meadows are alive with grasshoppers in late summer, the trout are often quick to seize them as they fall clumsily into the stream.

They're watching for a 'hopper to plop into the pool these days, explained one of my early mentors. *Give them a plop cast!*

It was excellent advice, and it has produced exceptional results over the years, particularly in late-summer grasshopper season. The cast is not particularly difficult. The backcast rises fairly high and the rod tip rides back to approximately two o'clock. The elbow drops as the backcast straightens and delivers a little more power into the forward delivery than is actually needed. The rod is driven sharply into its final follow-through, throwing an exaggerated hump into the line that rolls forward with the extending line. Checking the follow-through, the angler drives the fly forward until the fly receives the power imparted to the rolling hump in the line. It is delivered to the surface with a relatively sharp impact, like a fat inchworm dropping from the treetops, or the awkward faltering of a big grasshopper into a still trout-filled flat, and their impacts into the surface film are exactly what attracts a foraging late-summer fish.

There have been many experiences with the grasshopper cast over the years, but perhaps the most dramatic occurred on a small limestone spring creek in central Pennsylvania. It was a hot day in late August, although the steady upwelling of the limestone sink at the source of the stream kept its currents cold and rich with fly life. The grainfields along the little river were unusually alive with big grasshoppers that season, and the hot wind was getting them into the current in surprising numbers.

The lower meadows enclose two hundred yards of rich marl-bottomed flat. It lies five hundred yards downstream from the fishing house and the suspension bridge below the deep sapphire-colored sink where the stream is born. The flat is smooth and clear and sixty degrees through the heat of August. Its opposite bank is sheltered by trees and limestone outcroppings, and its shallows are bordered with a marl shelf rich with sowbugs and scuds. It is a fine reach of big trout water.

We walked down to the flat and moved cautiously along the path toward the water. The sun was high and the hot wind moved through the valley and its grasshopper meadows. We stopped short of the flat. Big wild brown trout were cruising the pool in twos and threes like bonefish on some subtropical flat.

Look at them! I thought aloud.

We crouched low and studied the rise forms to determine what they were taking. The rises were quiet and strong, suggesting both big fish and a sizable insect. Then we felt the hot wind and saw the grasshoppers. They flew up when its tepid gusts crossed the grainfields and startled them. Once they were in the air, the wind caught them and carried them clumsily over the stream. It was too wide to cross safely, and the insects parachuted helplessly when the wind gusted and died, coming down mallard-hard on the smooth currents.

It was an inexorable fate. Their shallow, faltering trajectories quickly dropped them into the water, and the big trout stalked them ruthlessly. Their relatively hard impact in the surface film triggered the cruising fish into accelerating toward each struggling grasshopper. The trout had apparently learned that these insects were incapable of flight once they fell to the surface, and their swirls were quiet and strong, completely lacking the splashiness characteristic of most grasshopper feeding. We watched the big browns attack the unfortunate grasshoppers for several minutes.

They're like crocodiles, said Charles Fox.

We took twelve fish between fifteen and twenty-three inches before a rain squall misted down the valley, cooling the wind and ending the erratic flights of grasshoppers. It was an unusual afternoon of fishing. Our fly patterns clearly played a role in our remarkable success, and I have never seen an episode of such ravenous feeding on a limestone stream since, but the grasshopper cast was a factor too. Every time we dropped our imitations hard on the surface, the big browns turned toward them like barracudas and took them greedily.

10. The Cross-Stream Mend

Although mending the line halfway through a fly drift was first developed to dampen and control fly speed in wet-fly fishing, it is also useful to postpone drag in a cross-stream or downstream dry-fly float. There are many holding places, particularly under overhanging branches in smooth currents, that cannot always be fished with a conventional dry-fly presentation from below. Such fish must be fished with a cross-stream or downstream cast, and a subtle upstream mend of the line is useful in creating additional length in its dry-fly float.

The cast is delivered across the current or slightly downstream, dropping the fly above the fish. Its duration of drag-free float can be extended by stripping left-hand slack out through the guides, but an upstream mend is useful too. It involves raising the rod tip and lifting the belly of the line, rolling it upstream in a controlled loop without disturbing the fly and its line of drift. The belly of line looped upstream acts as a cushion of slack, dampening the dragging effect of the currents on the leader and line, and improving the dry-fly presentation. Several extra inches of drag-free float can spell the difference between putting down a skittish trout and fooling it into taking the fly.

There is a productive run on a favorite stream of mine that is perfect for a cross-stream mend. The fish lie deep in the shadows of its buttonwoods, their branches almost touching the swift currents where a single stone breaks the flow. There is always a good trout lying well under the branches, between the far bank and the stone, and slightly upstream in the shallows. The overhanging branches and the stone prevent a cast from below, and the several limbs that actually touch the water prevent a quartering upstream presentation. Even a direct cross-stream cast would foul in the low branches before the fly drift could actually reach the fish.

But the downstream presentation works. It is possible to fish this holding lie with a quartering downstream cast, stripping the loose left-hand slack into the drift and mending an upstream belly into the line. Executed perfectly, the upstream mend is often the key to an extra six to ten inches of float deep under the branches, and that extra slack is often just enough.

11. The Downstream Check

Sometimes a river presents us with a holding lie that is impossible to reach from any position except directly upstream, and a conventional cast aimed downstream will result in a fly dragging almost immediately. The downstream check cast is the solution.

Every fisherman knows where a good fish can be found lying in such a place, often at the lip of a difficult pool or flat, or hanging just at the very edge of a millrace or falls. Either a presentation from downstream is totally impossible or a cross-stream cast will result in instantaneous drag. When a downstream cast is feasible, it must be delivered to a rising fish by false casting slightly beyond the fish's holding place, executing the final cast to an imaginary surface of the river about three feet above the water, and then checking the entire cast by pulling the rod back from its normal follow-through. Properly executed the cast is deftly checked, and falls back toward the angler in a series of slack loops that must extend slowly with the current, while the fly floats downstream completely free of drag. When the length of the cast is right, this drag-free drift will last until it reaches the taking lie occupied by the rising trout.

The downstream check once produced a fine five-pound rainbow for me from the millrace at Fischen-im-Allgäu in southern Germany, a free-rising trout that had frustrated me an entire season. It persisted in holding and feeding just above the millrace hatch, three hundred yards above the mill itself. The millrace above the hatch was densely grown with willows. Because of the willows and the hatch gate itself, there was no place either below or beside the mill hatch where the rainbow could be reached. The channel leading to the hatch was relatively deep, except for a small gravelly shoal sixty-odd feet upstream. There was just enough space to slip into the chest-deep current off the willows and work a downstream check; and there would be only one chance to execute a cast. The big rainbow would either take the fly or evaporate in panic when it dragged.

Several attempts that summer ended in failure, but late in the season, when we were actually stalking red stag in the evenings, my luck with the big rainbow finally changed. The cast checked and settled properly, the fly drifted right down its feeding lane, and the fish took it with a self-confident porpoising rise. It could have turned through the hatch gate and sheared my tippet like a cobweb, but the fish bolted upstream into the weedy shallows instead, and once its first wild energy was expended I captured it easily. The downstream check cast was the secret.

12. The Surface Retrieve

Ray Bergman describes this rule-breaking variation of the dry-fly method in *Trout* with an episode on the Catskill rivers. His chapter on dry-fly tactics mentions fishing out every cast until it is well free of any real holding water, both to avoid frightening the fish with a pickup of the line and to avoid taking the fly away from a trout that has followed it a considerable distance, deciding to rise only at the last possible moment.

Sometimes on a still pool or flat there is so little current that the dry fly does not drift past the fish quickly. It can sink and be retrieved like a wet fly, or remain floating and be retrieved almost imperceptibly across the surface. The fly might be given an occasional twitching movement, but it should be brought back with a retrieve so subtle that it does not make a discernible disturbance in the surface film. Sometimes a fish will take the fly at the moment it starts to move, but sometimes one will follow and take when it has travelled several feet.

13. The Skimming Retrieve

There are insect forms and behavior patterns that dictate a subtly dragging fly to fool a rising trout. Such insects skitter across the surface, in the case of certain running caddisflies and sedges, or hang dragging from their silken little threads like the inchworms and leafrollers on our eastern rivers.

When the trout are watching for such little V-shaped furrows in the surface film, dry flies fished upstream with a drag-free float are virtually useless. Such times require that our flies be fished quartering downstream, almost like wet flies, and allowed to swing in a subtle, dragging retrieve across the current. Certain current speeds will work the fly properly, but others require manipulation of fly speed with the rod and the left-hand slack. The rod tip is smoothly and steadily raised to a position above and slightly behind the head to keep the fly skimming properly. Slower currents may require a slow, steady stripping of line with the left hand and coordinating it with the gradually rising rod. It will take some practice to work both rod and left hand together, keeping the dry fly skimming in the surface film, but with a little experience it is not excessively difficult.

The skimming retrieve breaks all the rules of dry-fly fishing laid down in the books of the British writer Frederic Halford, and the American dry-fly pioneer George La Branche as well, but catches fish when conditions are right.

14. The Skater Technique

George La Branche and his colleague Edward Ringwood Hewitt are the authors of this method. It was conceived on the classic log-cribbing flats of the Hewitt camp water on the Neversink. The skater technique is based upon both fly dressing and presentation on a relatively stiff leader tippet, and since Hewitt was a remarkably cantankerous and secretive man about the critical details of his art, we owe most of our knowledge of the skater technique to men like John Atherton and Vincent Marinaro.

Fox relates the story of his experience with skaters in *This Wonderful World of Trout*. It began in the waiting room of his family doctor in Pennsylvania. There were no magazines on fishing on its tables, but in a glossy paper journal devoted primarily to golf, skiing, sailboats, and fox hunting in eastern horse country, Fox discovered an article on skater fishing written by Hewitt himself. It was beautifully illustrated, and described the Hewitt experiments with his so-called butterfly fishing in the Catskills. Fox was about halfway through the piece when the nurse called him to the examining room, and once the doctor was finished, Fox eagerly returned to the waiting room to finish it.

He subsequently wrote to Hewitt, and was answered with a letter and assortment of skater flies in the following weeks. The Hewitt dressings were simplicity itself. There were no bodies or tail fibers. Two long-fibered hackles were wound on a light-wire hook, their concave sides facing each other to create a sharp edge of stiff hackle fibers where they met. The flies were designed to skitter, skate, and jump crazily across the current, with an erratic retrieve conceived to excite a fish into chasing and taking them. Fished properly, their action suggested big fluttering sedges, drakes, and craneflies, and they were dressed in simple colors like honey and badger and brown. Fox was fascinated with the flies, but it was some time before he actually fished them.

Their baptism came on famous Spring Creek in central Pennsylvania, during lunch on a hot day in late summer. Fox and his friends had fished hard all morning, and nothing they tried had worked. Fox selected one of the Hewitt skaters, Turle-knotting it firmly to the stiff 3X tippet, and he practiced skating it with a sandwich in his left hand.

Lacking experience with skaters, Fox cast toward a deep run along a brush pile where he had often taken good trout. The first cast fluttered to the surface, and Fox ate his sandwich absently, preoccupied with making the fly skitter and twitch across the water. The second cast brought a slashing strike, and Fox took the fly away from the fish awkwardly. Another strike clumsily left the fly in its jaws. Fox was agitated now, and found a second skater after he finished his sandwich. Unfamiliar with the wind resistance of a fluffy skater, he misjudged the rhythm of his false casting and broke the hook of the second pattern when it ticked against the rod. Two of the precious Hewitt flies were already gone.

Easy does it! Fox replaced his fly again.

Two good trout were quickly hooked and released, and then he moved a trophy-size brown that splashily showered the hopscotching skater three times without taking. Fox patiently rested the big fish for fifteen minutes, hooked it soundly on the first cast after the recess, and lost the fly when the trout bored into the brush pile.

Half my skaters are gone! Fox moaned. *I'm going to fish with the rest of them in a safer place!*

Above the old mill dam he located several more good fish with his polaroid glasses. They were holding just a foot or two under the surface. The smooth impoundment currents above the dam seemed like a good place to test his skaters. Fox first tried conventional flies without moving a fish. Then he tried the stiff-hackled Hewitt patterns and consistently raised and moved the sluggish hot-weather trout throughout the afternoon. Few trout were hooked, however, and Fox left a few more of the Hewitt flies in fish that broke off, but finally he mastered the gentle, delayed strike required in fishing skaters.

Both Fox and the late John Alden Knight observed that the technique is most effective when the fish are accustomed to seeing an occasional big insect fluttering across the current, and that even the tendency of the fish to roll at the skater without taking can be turned to the advantage of the fisherman. Dog-days trout can be located with skaters, and their holding lies marked down for another time, when cooler weather and a good hatch have them rising freely.

But it was the late Paul Young who aptly described skater fishing years ago.

Fishing a skater is easy, he said. *It's just like fishing a streamer dry!*

15. The Induced-Rise Technique

Hewitt and his skaters, the slow dry-fly retrieve, and the skimming dry fly in the surface film are all techniques that break the rules of conventional dry-fly philosophy. There has long been an unspoken school of fishing dry flies with an occasional twitch, especially when fish are rising to fluttering mayflies, or egg-laying and hatching caddis.

William Lunn was the venerable riverkeeper of the Houghton Club water on the Test for forty-five years. For its blizzardlike hatches of the Caperer flies, small sedges that scuttle and leapfrog erratically on the water, Lunn devised fly dressings designed for fishing with a twitching, half-fluttering presentation. His imitations were worked out almost three-quarters of a century ago, and have been fished with both the enticing twitch as the fly approaches a rising trout, and with a fast skittering retrieve at other times. John Waller Hills tells us in his charming book *River Keeper*, the biography of Lunn and his work on the Stockbridge mileage of the Test, that the Caperer method was the most successful tactic on that river throughout the summer of 1932.

Leonard Wright has explored similar techniques for suggesting the fluttering emergence and egg-laying behavior of our American sedges. In *Fishing the Dry Fly as a Living Insect*, he describes his method of twitching a floating caddis imitation as the sudden-inch technique. The book attempts to modify the single-minded orthodoxy of American dry-fly practice, and its preoccupation with Halford's dogma of the drag-free float.

Similar techniques have existed on the British chalkstreams and rich Irish limestone rivers for more than a half century, and twitching the fly enticingly just as it reaches a rising trout is a dry-fly version of the induced-rise method that nymph experts like Frank Sawyer and Oliver Kite have long used on the Wiltshire Avon. Michael Lunn is the grandson of the great Test riverkeeper, and today holds his position on the Houghton Club water. Lunn is a primary exponent of his grandfather's Caperer technique and the induced-rise method, and Roger Foster is another skilled riverkeeper on the Maigue in southern Ireland, where the induced-rise method of fishing the dry fly is well known.

Some years ago, Roger Foster and I were fishing the water meadows of the Maigue below Dunraven Castle. It is one of the loveliest reaches of dry-fly water on earth, rich with fly hatches and trailing beds of ranunculus, its fertility born of limestone springs in the rolling, fox-hunting country that lies below Limerick. The castle beats are shrouded in history, with the ruins of a tenth-century fortress guarding the bottom mileage and the ivy-covered nave of a twelfth-century abbey only a half mile upstream. Although some of its chambers are open to the public, Dunraven Castle itself is still occupied by Lord Dunraven, and the fishing can sometimes be rented on a fly-only basis. It is a remarkable brown-trout fishery, filled with selective fish averaging about a pound or better, and there are few rivers in the world with such fly hatches.

We were hoping for good hatches of *Ephemera vulgata,* the fluttering drakes indigenous to the lakes and rivers of Ireland, but we were a few days too early. The mayfly was already emerging on Lough Derg in the Shannon watershed, traditionally its first hatching site each season, but only scattered flies were showing on the meadow flats of the Maigue. The trout were not really taking them.

They're not on the mayfly yet, explained Roger Foster, *but on rainy mornings we've got fine hatches of little Iron Blues, and the grass is alive with sedges.*

Foster was right about his sedges. There were so many caddisflies in the weeds and nettles and meadow grasses that I picked them easily, like berries in a particularly rich summer. My specimen bottles were quickly filled with dark, slate-colored little silverhorns and mottled specimens of *Sericostoma* flies and dozens of small cinnamon sedges.

Our first evening we drove down from the thatched-roofed village of Adare, past the towers and crenellated rooftops of Dunraven Castle, and wound into the man-made forest groves along the river. There were huge trees with reddish rough-barked trunks.

Those look like Douglas firs! I said incredulously. *Those big reddish-barked trees look like sequoias!*

They are sequoias! Foster laughed.

We walked down through the forest to the Maigue, where it wound out from the sycamores and willows into the winding meadow above the castle. The air above the river was alive with insects. There were thousands of tiny spinners, and an occasional chalk-colored *Ephemera* drake, and hundreds of hatching caddisflies. The fish were rising everywhere, in the swift currents below the weirs and down the silken flats.

They're probably on sedges, Foster said.

We've seen four or five kinds of caddis along the river, I grinned. *How do we know which one is hatching?*

The silverhorns hatch mostly at night, Foster answered, *and the Welshman's Buttons are almost finished.*

That leaves the cinnamon sedges? I asked.

You're right, Foster agreed.

His fly boxes were filled with elegant little sedge imitations, and I started fishing them to each rising trout in range. There were several refusal swirls and a few splashy rises, but they seemed disinterested and half-hearted. Foster was fishing below me and I watched him hook and land a fat fifteen-inch brown. The young riverkeeper released the trout and promptly caught another just above the weir. Two more trout made refusal swirls under my fly, and when a third missed it splashily, I walked downstream to watch Foster fish his sedge imitation.

Conventional tactics aren't working, I said.

Foster was drying his sedge imitation carefully. *I'm fishing what we call the induced-rise method,* he explained. *It teases the trout into taking sometimes.*

How does it work? I asked.

Foster demonstrated his method over another fish. His false-casting flicked out and settled the fly above its feeding station, and the fly dropped softly on the current about eighteen inches above the trout. The little sedge had scarcely started its drift when he gave it a subtle twitch, let it float naturally six inches, and twitched it teasingly again. It was too much for the waiting trout and it took the fly hard.

That's your induced-rise method? I smiled.

Yes, the young riverkeeper nodded and released the fish. *Sometimes it coaxes them into taking when they refuse a conventional float.*

Halford would turn over in his grave!

I'm sure you're right, Foster agreed as he dressed his fly, *but it's always the exception that proves the rule.*

It is a truth still worth remembering astream.

3. Some Strategies
in Fishing
Bucktails and Streamers

I t was whippoorwill time when the old fisherman appeared at the Forks Pool Bridge. It was almost possible to know when he would come. The nights he liked were hot and dark, with the faintest sliver of a moon showing in the trees. The river had a sombre mood on such evenings, its silken currents mysterious and heavy in its cedar deadfalls, and its pull seemed much stronger on the legs after nightfall.

The old man slipped into the river like an otter. His reel stripped gratingly in the darkness as he worked out line, and I heard the swish-swish rhythm of his casting above the twilight river sounds.

Tell your father hello, his voice boomed richly.

His fishing always started when the boyhood curfew ended my fishing for another day. The old man was a streamer fisherman because he liked to catch big browns at night. He tied his own flies rather crudely on huge 1/0 forged hooks, and I still have one somewhere in my collection. The rough bodies were thickly wrapped with spun fur, and a half-dozen grizzly hackles formed the three-inch wings.

His trophy-size fish were a local legend on the Pere Marquette. Five- and six-pound browns were always lying in state in the ice-cream freezer at Baldwin, and the old man usually caught about fifty trout over twenty inches during a summer's fishing.

The river whispered in the darkness, and the old man was only a ghostly presence in its nightscape. There was no sound of his wading, and his pipe cast no glow to frighten the fish. Once he had worked out enough line to cover the river there was not even the sound of his reel unless a fish was hooked. The river sounds soon muffled the swish-swish of his big streamer as he worked the waist-deep riffles downstream.

1433

Suddenly his reel protested with a ratchet-sharp growl as it surrendered line, and there was an immense splash below his silhouette in the darkness.

Good fish? I shouted.

It's very strong! he answered. *Very strong!*

There was another huge splash in the darkness, farther downstream where the river disappeared into an S-shaped bend. The reel shrieked gratingly as the fish took more line, and the old man was forced to follow. His shape was gone into the night.

Good luck! I shouted.

But there was no answer, and I waded out of the pool. The path up through the willows was barely visible, and I turned my rod butt-first to protect it from the branches. My father was already in camp, and the glow of his cookfire was ahead among the trees. We had just finished our supper when the old Scotsman came up into the firelight with the tail of a great trout dragging in the sand.

My God! I thought. *That fish is huge!*

Its spots glittered in the flickering light, its thickly muscled bulk still glistening with water that dripped on the path. It was the biggest trout I had ever seen in those years.

Gentlemen! said the old man, like a fanfare.

That's some brown trout! my father said.

Yes, the old man cackled happily. *It is the biggest I've ever caught in all my years on this river—and 'tis a wee bit bigger than anything I caught years ago on the Whitadder and the Tweed!*

How big is it? I stammered.

Perhaps the use of your scale will tell us the weight of this sea monster, he laughed heartily. *May I borrow it?*

I slipped inside the tent and came back with a fifteen-pound scale. The old man seated it firmly in the gill cover, and its spring creaked as it took the weight of the fish.

Almost nine pounds! my voice was filled with awe.

Nine pounds, said the old Scotsman softly. *It's a time for sharing a dram from the pewter flask in the truck!*

Congratulations, my father extended his hand.

The old man laid the big trout in the grass and walked back in the darkness for the whisky. It was an impressive fish, but in those days on the Michigan rivers there were a lot of men who caught big browns at night with bucktails and streamers. They knew every hole and deadfall and boulder in the river, covering it as easily at midnight as the summer people fished it at noon.

Several years ago my good friend Lee Wulff was talking about the old days on rivers like the Battenkill and Ausable in New York. His memories drifted back to the years when both were renowned big-fish rivers, the years when he developed the White and Gray Wulffs.

You know, he leaned forward and frowned, *years ago every river had its bucktail artists, men who fished nothing else and were locally famous for the big fish they caught. Now they're all gone, and we're left with the hardware throwers!*

Although we cannot be certain who invented streamers and bucktails, or even if they originated in the United States or Canada, they are unquestionably a fly type and method that originated on this side of the Atlantic. Some angling historians credit the Algoma Indians of the Canadian subarctic with deer bucktails, while others argue that polar bear flies evolved on the rivers of Alaska. Emerson Hough is generally believed to be the fisherman whose expeditions into the north country discovered bucktail and polar bear flies in use among the native fisherfolk.

However, there is better evidence that bucktails originated at the feather-littered workbench of William Scripture in New York, and other authorities argue that streamers probably had their genesis in the Piseco Lake patterns of the nineteenth century.

Guy Jenkins is a skilled angler who fished the Catskills in their golden age, and who knew men like Theodore Gordon, Edward Ringwood Hewitt, and George La Branche. Jenkins points out that Theodore Gordon originated a bucktaillike pattern he called the Bumblepuppy, and that Hewitt and La Branche were not always dry-fly purists.

They were not always the saints their disciples imagined, Jenkins observed puckishly over lunch at the Anglers' Club of New York. *They fished wet flies and nymphs fairly often—and even a big Scripture bucktail or two when they discovered a good fish minnowing.*

The recorded history of such flies is relatively recent. Roy Steenrod was a close friend and fishing companion of Gordon's on the Catskill rivers, and Steenrod recalled that the Bumblepuppy bucktails were dressed as early as 1880. Gordon demonstrated in his correspondence that he knew these primitive bucktails were baitfish imitations.

Others were experimenting with bucktails and streamers too. Smallmouth-bass flies were fashioned of bucktail on the headwaters of the Tippecanoe and Maumee about 1886, and at the turn of the century Carter Harrison and Alfred Trude were fishing hair-wings on the Henry's Fork of the Snake. Herbert Welch constructed smelt imitations with feathers as early as 1902, and although these flies were tied with wings of married feather sections, they were undoubtedly the prelude to the full family tree of New England streamers.

During this same period, William Scripture was tying surprisingly modern bucktails on the rivers west of Albany. One of his prototypes is unquestionably similar to the Blacknosed Dace developed years later by Arthur Flick on the Schoharie farther south. Harvey Donaldson was also fishing bucktails on the headwaters of the Mohawk in these years, and on the brook-trout waters of the West Canada and the Cedar. The best-known Scripture pattern had a red crewel tag, tinsel body, and a wing of natural brown bucktail. Although our history of the Scripture school of fly tying is limited, it is apparent that the smallmouth bass and brown trout of New York were the catalysts that produced the bucktail.

Popular legend tells us that the slender trolling streamer had its origins in Maine at the Grand Lake Stream. Alonzo Stickney Bacon was a guide on those waters not long after the turn of the century, and his spur-of-the-moment use of saddle hackles protruding from a canoe cushion led to a feathered lure that took an impressive catch of landlocked salmon. Since the fish had been dour and uncooperative for days, word of his feat spread like wildfire in Maine. Bacon may well be the father of the hackle-feather streamer, and from those beginnings in Maine our fly-pattern dictionary has been greatly enriched with a galaxy of baitfish patterns.

New England was the region that produced the classical patterns in the history of bucktails and streamers. Fly tiers like Herb Welch, Carrie Stevens, Bert Quimby, and William Edson were archetypical of this school of thought. Lew Oatman, Bob McCafferty, John Alden Knight, Don Gapen, Herb Howard, and Ray Bergman followed in a succeeding generation of bucktail and streamer theory, and in our western mountains men like Don Martinez and Dan Bailey carried the philosophy with them when they abandoned earlier lives in the eastern cities. Bucktails and streamers worked extremely well on the Pacific Coast watersheds, and the original fly patterns developed by Polly Rosborough, Roy Patrick, Don Harger, Jim Pray, Peter Schwab, Gary Howells, and Roy Donnelly have quickly become modern classics.

However, streamers and bucktails have been common coin among American anglers for only forty-odd years. Before that time, fishermen used conventional wet flies, and the first period of dry-fly purism had begun. Sometimes big fish were taken on such insect imitations, but minnow feeders were another matter.

Meat-and-potatoes, the old Scottish streamer fisherman explained that evening in the firelight years ago. *These old sea monsters like to eat meat-and-potatoes—not those wee river flies!*

It is often true of big trout. Their diet includes a lot of smelt, candlefish, dace, chubs, shiners, sticklebacks, sculpins, and other bait fish. Big fish always take a lot of small fish, including a cannibal diet of baby trout. Over the years many stomach autopsies have revealed a lot of baitfish specimens. I once stripped more than two hundred tiny dace from a big brown taken at night on the Beaverkill; and there was a six-pound fish on the Battenkill that disgorged an eight-inch brookie like a cake of soap when I dispatched it with my priest knife. Such minnow-eating is not too unusual.

It has been argued in many books that trout take our flies through motives of hunger, curiosity, playfulness, and sometimes through territoriality. The fish that trails our retrieve does seem almost curious, and the fish that virtually attacks a bucktail is usually defending a primary holding lie or spawning site. Such examples of territoriality are common. Life in the depths of the river, however, is a precarious equilibrium between ingesting food and expending energy, and I have never accepted the common theory of playful behavior. Most of the tail-chasing behavior I have observed looks playful to fishermen, but it has always been the result of competition for prime holding lies, shelter, ripe henfish, or prime spawning gravel—and most strikes on bucktails and streamers are from feeding behavior.

Such behavior permits us to separate bucktails and streamers into two primary categories. There are the brightly feathered fancy patterns that date themselves to the days of unsophisticated brook trout and landlocks in Maine, richly colored flies whose ornate dressings continue to fascinate modern fishermen—much as we admire an oriental carpet or a stained-glass window or the scrollwork on a Victorian house. These intricate flies have gradually lost favor as fishing pressure has increased. Replacing them on our hard-fished lakes and streams are the imitative patterns, which attempt to fool a fish that is feeding on the smaller bait species.

There are many such imitative flies. The ubiquitous Muddler is perhaps the best-known baitfish imitation, owing its success to the tiny madtoms and sculpins that inhabit our rivers. Some of the classic fancy patterns like the Supervisor and Gray Ghost and Nine-Three unquestionably owe their success to the smelt populations in our northeastern waters. Lew Oatman was perhaps the first streamer expert to embrace the theory of baitfish imitation systematically, and he worked out a series of conscientiously tied streamers that suggested the forage species of New England and New York. Oatman fished the Battenkill from his summer house at Shushan in upstate New York, and I met him there some years before his death. We had stopped to fish a swift stretch between the Dutchman's Hole and the ledgerock pool at Buffum's Bridge. It was a night when I had moved a big brown along an underwater ledge, but the fish had only followed without taking.

Oatman listened quietly while I described the problem. *What fly were you using?* he asked finally.

Black Ghost, I said.

Oatman rummaged in his fishing coat for a worn fly book. *Here's a little perch pattern,* he offered me an exquisite streamer tied with olive-yellow grizzly hackles. *It's big enough to coax an old buster—and he sees a lot of perch in a warm summer like this!*

Thanks! I waded back into the smooth current.

The warm sunlight and late afternoon shadows were a rich chiaroscuro on the pool upstream. The big fish had appeared above me in the shallows, scattering frightened minnows like a barracuda. Three times it had charged my streamers, its bulk forming a bow wave behind my retrieve, but each time it turned away. Its immense refusal swirls were positively unsettling each time they boiled to the surface.

It seemed most likely that the fish usually held in the deepest run along the sunken ledge, where the current scoured shoulder-deep and strong. The line delivered the streamer about thirty feet above its suspected holding lie, and I let it settle back toward me, sinking deep in the current. When it had bellied deep, riding into the dark water along the ledge, I began stripping it back downstream. It was about twenty-five feet away when there was a boil, followed by a slashing strike on the surface.

The weight of the fish telegraphed back into the rod and I struck it sharply.

He's got it! I shouted. *He's on!*

It was a hook-jawed male of almost six pounds, and I owed it entirely to the gentle generosity of Lew Oatman. He was as happy and excited over the fish as I was, and after I released it we sat talking in the gathering darkness. Oatman gave me samples of his baitfish series, and talked about methods of fishing them. He dressed streamers so beautifully that they were as exquisite as the most elegant dry flies of the Catskill school, and his imitative theories made him the father of the scientific approach to baitfish patterns—just as Alfred Ronalds originally introduced a disciplined entomology to the dressing of his wet-fly patterns in his British *Fly-Fisher's Entomology* of 1834.

Oatman's example has been expanded in the imitative patterns of contemporary fly dressers like Keith Fulsher, Dave Whitlock, Roy Patrick, Polly Rosborough, Don Harger, and Gary Howells. Their variations on Muddler and madtom patterns, along with the Pacific baitfish imitations dressed with multicolored polar bear hair, are superb flies. Woven mylar tubing and sheet mylar have been used extensively by fly dressers like Arthur Fusco, Robert Boyle, Tony Skilton, Kani Evans, and Dave Whitlock. Its flash makes minnow imitations possible that truly suggest the dazzling silver or golden flash of shiners, candlefish, and smelt.

Except for the wilderness brook-trout fisheries tributary to Hudson Bay, and draining the interior of the Labrador, this trend toward disciplined imitation in bucktails and streamers will continue. Although I still carry the bright Mickey Finn in my fly books, including small versions for working hard-fished rivers in bright weather, my approach to bucktails and streamers is primarily imitative—and, in my experience, the baitfish patterns are so deadly on back-country trout that there is no need for the bright-feathered traditionals.

Our baitfish species are the key to such fly patterns, and their distribution and importance as trout forage are the basis for my preferences in streamers and bucktail flies. The various Muddler bucktails, and the baby trout series of imitations developed by Sam Slaymaker in Pennsylvania, are recent examples of imitative patterns that have enjoyed considerable success. On the Pacific Coast, Roy Patrick and Polly Rosborough are the authors of a number of smelt and candlefish imitations dressed with polar-bear hair. My own experiments with baitfish patterns have worked in similar directions, attempting to imitate the major forage species found on our American trout waters.

Bucktails and streamers should be dressed both to imitate the minnow species indigenous to a reach of water and sized to its scale as well. Hook sizes are related to the average growth of the species in question; the size of the water is a factor too, with bigger dressings most useful on brawling rivers like the Madison and Yellowstone and Delaware. Smaller patterns are optimal for average rivers, and tiny bucktails and streamers about an inch in length are superb on tributary streams and under low-water conditions. Current speed and character are also factors in fly size. Heavy water demands big flies, and broken chutes in a relatively small river pose similar problems. Smooth currents and tail shallows are often the place for smaller dressings, even in surprisingly big rivers.

Bucktails and streamers should be big enough to attract and hook large trout, although even big fish are insect feeders, since insects offer more calories per gram ingested. The myth that big fish eat only baitfish is based on a precarious foundation in fact, and there will be times when a man who fishes only bucktails and streamers will catch little or nothing.

But there are also times when the cycle of the season or some inexplicable mood of the fish make them the solution. Most anglers have experienced days when the trout have not settled into a uniform pattern of behavior, with one fish chasing minnows and another sampling random insects. There was such an afternoon a few years ago in the pastoral meadows of the lower Musconetcong in New Jersey. It is a rich valley of limestone springs and generous stonework barns. Cattle were fording the river when Arthur Morgan wound his station wagon down toward the sycamores where the meadows meet the river. August sunlight glittered on the riffles downstream, and there were locusts in the trees.

There was nothing hatching. The current flowed over the pale stones in the riffles, gathering against a limestone outcropping downstream, where it tumbled in the shade of the trees. There were no rises.

What should we fish? Morgan asked.

We studied the riffling pockets and the run below the ledge. *It's pretty hot,* I said. *You see anything working?*

Sunfish over there, he pointed across the river.

The stream thermometer read seventy-one degrees, almost too warm for the trout and ideal for panfish.

You say there are springs along the outcropping? I asked. *Might be some trout working there.*

The current is definitely colder there, Morgan said.

Let's fish nymphs along the ledge, I suggested. *There could be fish lying deep in the colder water.*

You fish the ledge, he insisted.

It was a reasonable solution, but it did not work. Weighted nymphs in several patterns were fished deep in the current without moving a trout. There were still no rises anywhere. Finally I stood in the swift thigh-deep currents below the ledge, studying my fly books. There was a single Mickey Finn tucked into the lamb's wool, and suddenly I decided to try it in the deadfall runs downstream.

Can't work any worse, I thought wryly.

Alders brushed against my left shoulder, and I roll cast the little bucktail across the main current tongue. It had just started a teasing swing in the sunlight, when a foot-long rainbow darted from a boulder pocket and nailed it hard.

Arthur Morgan saw it hopscotch across the shallows and waved.

What'd he take? he yelled upstream.

Would you believe a Mickey Finn? I waved back happily.

No, he laughed, *I wouldn't.*

Sometimes a hot-weather fish does strange things, I said. *The sun in this red and yellow hair works wonders!*

It continued to take fish steadily that day.

The fish that had refused everything turned easy, and we both took them from every inviting pocket and run. There were a half-dozen browns from twelve to fifteen inches in the next one hundred yards, and then I hooked a strong three-pound fish under a deadfall. It was a good stopping place, and I reeled in the line with satisfaction.

Arthur came wading upstream with a fine brace of brown trout.

They wanted the Mickey, he said. *Can you explain that?*

No, I grinned. *But it worked!*

Such behavior is difficult to explain, but sometimes the fish hunt the baitfish shallows in bright weather. More often they hunt minnows in high water or just after daylight or late in the evening shadows; and sometimes they stalk their prey on warm, moonless nights like that long-ago summer on the Pere Marquette in Michigan. These are trout foraging in average populations of minnows, unlike the fish that feed ravenously on seasonal baitfish cycles. Such periods of baitfish feeding are remarkable. Familiar examples are caused by the downstream migrations of sockeye salmon fry at places like Babine Lake in British Columbia and the travelling schools of candlefish and herring that draw feeding coho salmon in the tidal currents of the Juan de Fuca Straits. There is also the periodic abundance of smelt and alewives in the Great Lakes, and the legendary runs of lake smelt in the watersheds of New England—in fishing places with ancient tribal names like Mephremagog and Mooselookmeguntic and Kennebago.

Basic streamer and bucktail fishing is simple. It can be executed with a rudimentary cross-stream cast, allowing the fly to swing on a fixed length of line. Fast currents bring the fly alive by themselves, and no rod work is necessary to tease its swing. Rhythmic teasing with the rod tip is important to give the fly life in slower reaches of water, but no left-hand strip is needed in basic techniques.

Such basic tactics should impart a regular half-darting rhythm to the fly swing, simulating a minnow working across the current. Bucktails and streamers are just like wet flies, except that a dead drift is only useful in suggesting a half-dead minnow trapped in the currents. The fly should be kept in the water as much as possible, and the entire river should be covered, from chutes and deep pools to surprisingly shallow riffles and flats. Since minnows are primarily found in such shallow water, big fish often stalk their prey in water scarcely deep enough to cover their dorsal fins. The late Joe Brooks was a fervent believer in fishing baitfish imitations in all types of water.

The last time we fished together, Brooks showed me some favorite mileage at Emigrant Flats on the Yellowstone. It was a bright September morning with fresh snow in the high country, and he squinted upriver into the glittering sun, pointing as he described the character of the Emigrant Flats and its gargantuan pool.

There're some real busters in that chute. Brooks' soft voice echoed his Chesapeake tidewater heritage. *The good fish lie along the willows, and down the deep flat for about two hundred yards—but sometimes the big fish drift back into the tail shallows and you should cover everything.*

Brooks really understood the swift Yellowstone, and we took several fish from the chute and its spreading flats that morning, but the best fish we hooked was lying in shallow water. We had already covered the most promising water, and I had fished well down into the tail shallows when my fly swing came around below me, and I briefly glanced back upstream toward Brooks. We had taken and released more than a dozen fish between us, brown trout between twelve inches and four pounds.

Shall we walk back and fish through again, I yelled, *or should we saddle up and try something else?*

Suddenly the smooth shallows below me erupted, and I snapped my eyes back downstream. The fly swing had passed a smooth boulder, and as it worked across the ankle-deep water, a big fish awakened with a threshing turn and chased it across the gravel flat. It pushed a spreading wake and bow wave, and it took the big Muddler in a bold, head-wrenching strike. It threshed angrily when it felt the hook, and bolted swiftly back up into the deepening spine of the pool.

It shook itself and stopped in the smooth chest-deep flat. The rest of its fight was a sullen stalemate, with the fish bulldogging angrily on the bottom, too strong and heavy to control with the four-ounce parabolic I had chosen that windless October morning.

Big fish? Brooks yelled.

It feels pretty strong, I answered. *Can't seem to budge him with this gear. You think it's a brown?*

Probably! He was wading downstream.

The wrenching, head-shaking spasms continued, telegraphing back along the line into the harshly straining rod. It was a brief one-sided struggle. The fish moved out a little farther into the current and stopped again. It felt as strong as a salmon, and it never surrendered a millimeter of line until the fly suddenly pulled out.

Too bad! Brooks said gently.

You're right, I reeled line unhappily. *But we never would have hooked that fish without covering the shallows too—just like you suggested!*

It was a valuable lesson in bucktail tactics. Our coverage of that pool on the Yellowstone was also an exercise in the basic techniques of fishing bucktails and streamers. Tactics at typical levels of water require working across the current and slightly downstream. Like a basic wet-fly cast, its angle of presentation should vary with current speed. Slow currents are best fished with a cross-stream cast about ninety degrees to the current flow, increasing the life and fly speed of the swing. However, such a cross-stream cast in fast water will generate too much fly speed, dragging the bucktail harshly in the surface currents. It should be cast quartering downstream in swift chutes and runs, dampening fly speed enough to fish the fly enticingly. It should be worked in rhythmic, pulsing movements imparted by the rod tip. These swimming patterns made on a fixed length of line suggest a hapless baitfish in the current. However, in very broken currents the tumbling flow itself is often enough to impart life to the fly.

Fish each cast out as completely as possible. Most anglers are too impatient, and lift their flies much too soon for another cast. Sometimes a curious trout has followed a swinging bucktail, waiting until it stops its arc and hangs directly downstream before it decides to take. Sometimes a bucktail riding deep, and undulating lazily in the bottom currents, can tease a fish into taking. Picking up the fly too soon can lose both opportunities, and a lazy retrieve is often wise when a cast has been fully fished—the odd fish that has followed your swing and not taken the fly may decide to take it when it has stopped and finally started back in its final upstream retrieve.

Skilled bucktail and streamer fishermen keep feeding slack and mending line and retrieving, to keep their flies in the river as long as possible. Many types of animation are possible with upstream and downstream mends, retrieves of varying speeds, and manipulation of the fly with tip action. Some of the bucktail artists I watched on my boyhood rivers in Michigan seemed to cast very seldom, and worked a fly tantalizingly along undercut willows and logjams and deadfalls almost as patiently as a bait fisherman.

There are times when a bucktail or streamer will have periods of missed and refusal rises. Such behavior is often true with bright confections like a Mickey Finn or the marabou patterns that were designed to excite fish with their pulsing filaments rather than imitate specific baitfish. Missed rises should be covered with a quick repeat cast while the fish is still visible, and such fish can often be excited into a second try. Refusal rises are another problem. Sometimes a trout will follow the fly swing or retrieve, mimicking its speed like a carbon copy, before refusing it when it comes close to the angler or the pickup point. Such fish can sometimes be induced to take with a gradual acceleration of the retrieve, and then an abrupt drop in fly speed—the fish has been coaxed into overrunning the fly, and like a pickerel following a spoon, it suddenly has been forced into the choice of veering off or taking.

Varied tactics and retrieves should be tried. Sometimes a deliberate retrieve of subtle rhythm will draw the most rises. Other times the fish seem to like erratic movements, and still other times the trout are excited by skittering or fast-strip methods. Cold weather and high water usually mean working a bucktail or streamer slow along the bottom. Hot weather in midsummer can mean the fish are more active, their digestive processes accelerated by the temperature of the river, and hungry enough that they will pursue a swinging bucktail eagerly. Such behavior can merely be a question of mood, but it can also result from baitfish behavior.

Sculpins and madtoms stay near the bottom, and move sluggishly in comparison with the nervous behavior of dace or darters. Silversides and freshwater smelt move in relatively swift, graceful patterns quite unlike these other species. Fishermen can learn valuable lessons in observing the behavior of the forage species most common in their local waters. Their patterns of movement are the key to manipulating bucktail and streamer imitations.

Study the minnows! the old bucktail fishermen used to tell me on the Pere Marquette. *You watch the minnows in the river—and they'll tell you how to dress your flies and fish them!*

Mixed colors of both feathers and hair have long been a basic principle of dressing bucktails and streamers. Slender feathers and delicate filaments of marabou move and work enticingly in the water, and like the red-and-yellow color mix of the Mickey Finn, this fluttering seems to excite the fish. Their behavior in following the pulsing retrieve of a feather streamer or marabou certainly seems to arouse a mixture of curiosity and excitement.

This ability to excite fish does not always result in a strike, but its powers of attraction often tempt fish to show themselves. Sometimes they only shift position deep in the current, revealing themselves with the brief flash of light catching their sides beside a boulder or in the shadow of a deadfall. Sometimes a fish shows itself as a shadow that starts from its hiding place under the bank, ghosting briefly behind the fly before it turns back. Fish that follow a retrieve or actually false rise behind the fly are easily detected—and the ability to tease fish from their hiding places can be used to prospect a river and mark the prime holding lies of its big trout for future reference.

Mixing hair, hackle feathers, or marabou in a modern baitfish imitation is a little like the light-spectrum color theories developed by the late Preston Jennings. Tiers like Polly Rosborough and Roy Patrick are expert at achieving such chromatic effects in polar bear fibers, and mixed color is blended with the breathing action of marabou or a splay-winged feather streamer. Woven mylar tubing can be used for bodies of minnows having silvery coloring, and sheet mylar overlays can be seated outside the mylar or feather wings to simulate a species with silvery or gold flanks. Fins can be imitated with throat hackles and tails. Species like the redfin shiner, which has bright orange fins and tail coloring, can be suggested by dying the tips of a streamer wing with a waterproof felt-tip pen—in addition to the hackle and tail fibers.

Dave Whitlock is a skilled fly maker and theoretician of fly dressing who is rethinking bucktails and streamers. Whitlock likes to leave a touch of scarlet rayon showing between the body material and the head. It imitates the brightly colored gills. Since a crippled baitfish does show its gill coloring in its terminal spasms, and few fish can resist a crippled prey, it is not implausible to include this blood-colored rayon and incite the trout's killing instincts. Red hackles and tail fibers are included in the dressings of many traditional bucktails and streamers for this same purpose.

Big trout can't resist a bleeding minnow, Whitlock argues.

Perhaps some general observations about bucktail and streamer patterns are in order before we explore specific techniques for fishing them. Marabou flies can be dressed both weighted and unweighted. Weighted versions are useful in both marabous and bucktails for fishing deep in heavy cold-water currents. Dark roily currents suggest a white marabou dressing, while milky spates are often best fished with extremely dark flies. Bob McCafferty and Charles Fox were some of the first fly tiers to experiment with marabou stork-feather wings on their streamer patterns. They liked yellow or white for silt-gray or coffee-colored water, and McCafferty preferred black marabou for the chalky currents of limestoners like Penns Creek and Spring Creek.

The easiest way to work a bucktail or streamer deep is to weight it carefully under the body and fish a sinking line. Too much weight will distort the action of the fly and make it difficult to cast. It is also possible to weight a fly in the field by tying the leader knot with an unclipped strand of nylon trailing under the hook. The trailing nylon can then be clamped with a lead shot. Weighted in such fashion, a bucktail or streamer will fish deep with an erratic pattern quite similar to the action of a saltwater jig.

Marabou stork feathers entrain so much air in their fluffiness that they are difficult to sink unless false casting is kept to a minimum. This property is useful for suggesting a dying baitfish that is half floating in the surface of a river or lake. Sometimes big trout cruise a calm lake, picking such crippled minnows from the surface like a fly hatch. Experienced still-water fishermen will place such a half-sinking marabou ahead of a cruising fish, allowing it to hang slack until the trout approaches. It should then be retrieved suddenly, suggesting the desperate adrenalin-triggered panic of an injured fish that has seen a predator begin its deadly stalk.

The partially floating characteristics of marabou stork are also useful in shallow water. Dressed with light-wire hooks, such flies will remain near the surface until a retrieve is started. They will expand and contract, with their breathing stork fibers echoing the rhythmic retrieve, and will seldom sink enough to foul in the bottom.

Baby streamers should not be ignored. They are especially killing flies in low-water conditions, and are dressed on tiny long-shank hooks as small as sizes twelve and fourteen. Such flies are about one inch or slightly longer in length, and are intended to imitate fingerlings and fry. Sparse dressings are most effective.

Leaders of ten to twelve feet tapered to 4X or 5X at the tippet are superb for fishing small streamers in low water. Bigger flies will require heavier tippets to cast and fish properly, and large bucktails and streamers are best combined with tippets of 1X or OX. Even heavier tippets are sometimes needed with a 1/0 bucktail or marabou in strong winds.

Experience will quickly demonstrate proper tippet size, when nylon that is too thin refuses to turn over a big bucktail or snarls in frequent casting knots. Sinking lines and big water demand a shorter leader, perhaps only eight or nine feet in length, because too long a leader of nylon will ride back toward the surface, cancelling the effect of the deep-riding line.

There are about fifteen variations on basic bucktail and streamer tactics that should be part of an angler's repertory of skills. The fisherman should choose a technique that is attuned to his local baitfish.

1. The Basic Bucktail Swing

The basic swing method of fishing a bucktail or streamer is relatively easy to learn, and since these minnowlike patterns are easier to follow in the current than a conventional wet fly, it is sometimes a good method for starting a beginner. It involves a rudimentary cross-stream cast, allowing the fly swing to work back across the current. The swing is followed with the rod by pointing its tip at the apparent position of the bucktail.

Follow it around! the old-timers used to tell me in Michigan. *Follow it around and stay in touch with your fly!*

The basic swing operates with a constant length of line. Since it does not add left-hand manipulation of the line to its technique, and merely lays out repetitive casts a step or two downstream, its methodology is ideal for a beginning flyfisher. Fast currents usually impart enough life to the swimming bucktail or streamer that no tip action is needed to improve the retrieve and just following the fly swing with the rod is enough. It is not difficult to judge when the fly is fishing right, since too fast a swing will force it to skitter crudely in the surface.

Don't let it swing around raw! the old-timers added.

Slower currents mean the fly must be worked to suggest the swimming movements of a forage fish species. Its pulsing fly swing is achieved with a raising and lowering rhythm of the rod tip, and the length and timing of this rhythm is determined by the behavior of the fly in the current. The rate of current flow can also be used to control fly speed. Relatively slow currents should be fished with a cast directly across the current, which exaggerates the bellying line and increases the speed of the fly swing. Fast currents mean the fly should be cast quartering downstream, decreasing both line belly and the velocity of the fly.

When a cast and its subsequent fly swing are being fished out, the rod should be kept low and the line held between the index finger and its cork grip. No complicated left-hand twist or stripping of line is used during the fly swing itself, and since a fish will occasionally follow the swinging fly into the slack currents immediately below the angler, it should not be picked up too quickly. Many skilled bucktail men will allow the fly to trail at the bottom of the swing, and then retrieve with two or three line strips straight upstream. It is a familiar technique on salmon rivers, but it also has its usefulness on a trout stream, since a fish that has followed the swing will sometimes take when the fly starts moving again.

Covering a spreading flat with this method is particularly effective, since it patterns a series of concentric fly swings over the bottom. Fished correctly, this method will work a fly swing over every fish in the pool as the angler moves patiently downstream a step at a time.

2. The Hand-Twist Retrieve

Sometimes a bucktail fished with a deliberate hand-twist retrieve is a deadly method. It can be used to work the fly directly downstream, probing under the bank willows and logjams and deadfalls. The angler permits his fly swing to parallel the overhung bank, and may even strip out more line to allow it to drift deeper into the fishable currents before retrieving it slowly back upstream with the hand-twist method.

Ray Bergman liked the subtlety of the hand-twist retrieve, and first described using bucktails with this method in his book *Just Fishing*. Sometimes the fish take a streamer or a bucktail pattern fished this way because they are feeding on bottom minnows that swim slowly. However, they seem to strike at other times because they cannot resist such a tantalizingly slow retrieve. It has often been extremely effective for me on still-water sections of rivers, where there is insufficient current to swing the fly. It is often deadly when fished from an anchored boat, or wading in the shallows of a lake or impoundment. Such tactics involve casting clockwise around an imaginary clockface on the surface of the lake, and fishing the bucktail back with a hand-twist retrieve. Such casting patterns can start at nine o'clock, and be placed about a yard apart until the final cast is fished back from the three o'clock position. The first series of casts should be fished in a semicircle about forty feet out, and each succeeding series of casts adds approximately five feet, until the angler has reached his maximum distance. Such pattern casting should cover any cruising fish within range.

Bucktails fished with a hand-twist retrieve have produced some big fish for me in many parts of the world. There were the big rainbows we took one opening day in the San Cristobal Reservoir in Colorado, as we fished our bucktails on the ledges in the upper shallows of the lake with a deep hand-twist retrieve. It is a productive meadow in the weedy inlet channels of Henry's Lake in Idaho, and the marl lagoons of Wade Lake in Montana. This past season, fishing a weighted bucktail with a hand-twist clock-face method took three five-pound brookies in forty-five minutes at the black-sand mouth of the exotic Pichi Traful in Argentina.

3. The Left-Hand Strip

Although similar to the hand-strip method recommended for wet-fly fishing, the left-hand strip for bucktails and streamers is most useful when used to execute an erratic, rapid retrieve. It is achieved with the line held under the index finger, against the cork grip of the rod, and stripping back lengths of line with the other hand.

Such stripping pulls can vary from six inches, similar to the maximum hand-twist length of line but more rapid, to a quick arm pull at full length.

The fully extended arm pull can swiftly retrieve from two to three feet. The left-hand strip is essential in simulating the erratic behavior of crippled baitfish, or its panicky flight when it senses a predator. It is also the only method available for stripping an upstream bucktail back fast enough in swift water.

The left-hand strip is useful in any fisherman's bag of tricks, for it will impart action to the fly that cannot be achieved any other way. It is perfect to suggest the behavior of agile baitfish, and for exciting fish in wilderness regions or fresh from a hatchery.

4. The Rod Retrieve

This method works a fixed length of line with the rod itself. Although it does not move the bucktail or streamer with changing lengths of line as do the other methods of retrieving a fly, it will manipulate them differently. Since the rod keeps the fly moving without the pause required in a hand-strip retrieve, the action is a series of rapidly connected swimming movements.

The rod retrieve is useful in keeping a following trout interested, since there are no pauses where the fish can get too good a look at the fly. However, the method has its drawbacks. Its swimming rhythms are started with a fixed length of line locked under the index finger, or drawn back with the left hand in concert with the rod. The position of the rod is pointed at the fly, and held parallel to the water, at the start of the retrieve. It activates the fly with a fluid sequence of rod movements, ending with the rod held beside and slightly behind the angler. It is an awkward final position, and if a trout has followed the retrieve all the way and decides to take at the last moment, the fisherman often finds he has worked the rod so far back that a hook-setting strike is almost impossible.

Sometimes a fish can be hooked with the rod in that position if the fisherman has the line in his left hand, and can either execute his strike with a hand pull or a draw across his body.

5. The Rod-and-Line Strip

Working a bucktail or streamer in this fashion is not unlike a simple left-hand strip, except that it adds a teasing rod-tip rhythm between the line pulls. The result is a fly that swims with a contrapuntal rhythm of draw-and-twitch-and-draw movements. The line should be held under the index finger for optimum control. Since the rod-and-line strip involves a complex pattern of hand and rod control, it is a bit more difficult than other methods of manipulating a streamer pattern.

6. The Cast-and-Strip Method

This is a useful tactic for getting more depth with a sinking line in strong rivers, lakes, and impoundments. It involves executing a long cast, to get the fly and the line belly riding deep, and then stripping still more line off the reel. The extra line is then paid out with a brisk side-to-side shaking of the rod tip. When the line begins to straighten, and the fly is swimming against its tension in the water, the cast can be fished out with any of the basic retrieves. Sometimes a trout will take one of the imitative baitfish patterns while it is still sinking.

It happened to me several years ago on the Caleufu in Argentina, and the surprise of its strike was almost comic. The river churns through an earthquake fault in the lava that blocks its course below Meliquina, spreading into a slow-flowing pool at the foot of the Paso de Cordoba. It was a pool I had never fished, since it lay close beside the road, and I had always passed it on my way south to the Traful, or enroute to the famous Boca Chimehuin farther north.

This morning it looks good! I thought.

The sun sparkled on the surface of the pool. Its light penetrated deep into its emerald green currents, revealing a jumble of great boulders on the bottom. The four-inch marabou worked out with its lazy double haul, the sunlight glittering on its mylar wings, and it dropped well across the pool. It quickly started to sink, and I stripped off a few yards of line and shook them out through the guides. The marabou drifted deep, catching the sunlight as it fluttered toward the bottom, when I glanced down and discovered that I had forgotten to finish lacing my wading brogues.

Careless! I thought aloud.

The rod lay among the boulders, and I had just started to tighten the laces when the reel suddenly came to life. The rod jumped and started sliding toward the water, clattering noisily against the stones. The fish had taken the sinking bucktail like a dying minnow, hooked itself soundly, and started downriver in mere seconds.

Scrambling over the rocks with one brogue still unlaced, I soon recovered the rod, and the fish cartwheeled when it felt the pressure. It was a bright rainbow of almost six pounds. It fought well, jumping again and again down the pool, and I finally released the fish with admiration for its acrobatics and courage, along with some doubts about its wariness. Except for the depth achieved by using the cast-and-strip technique, it was a rainbow that had virtually caught itself.

7. The Upstream Dead Drift

This method is surprisingly effective at times, especially with imitative patterns like the Muddler. It involves casting upstream, or upstream and across the current, allowing the fly to drift back without extra manipulation by either the rod or left-hand line. Such tactics will get the fly deep in swift water, letting it drift tantalizingly along the bottom, where a fish may pick it up for a dead minnow.

Sculpins and other bottom-feeding forage species are a major part of the trout diet, and fishing a bucktail upstream dead drift is a superb method of suggesting their behavior. It is an especially effective tactic for large western rivers, although I have also used it in swift pocket-water reaches of small eastern streams where the tumbling current was enough to bring the fly alive—and the character of the water made a normal downstream coverage of the fish impossible without frightening them.

8. The Upstream Strip

This is another technique that has proved itself on relatively small rivers over the years. It permits a careful stalk of a pool or run from below, with a cast like an upstream dry-fly presentation to likely looking places in the current. Unlike a dead-drift approach, the upstream strip fishes the fly back downstream rapidly enough to work it quickly, in spite of the countering current speed.

It is a demanding method. Like most left-hand strips, the line is held under the index finger against the cork grip. The stripping itself is executed with the other hand, and in fast water, the rhythm is a series of brisk pulls made as quickly as possible.

The upstream strip produced my best fish this past season on our Brodheads water in Pennsylvania. It came on the Buttonwood Run, where a smooth riffle breaks into seventy-five feet of deep water under a stand of sycamores. The branches shelter the holding channel, their leaves almost trailing in the current. Fish hold everywhere in their leaf-flickering shadows. The deepest place is just below the throat of the pool, where the current swells and slides past the roots of a medium-size tree. It always holds a good fish.

It was a dull morning at midweek, with a light rain misting down the valley. The current was a little milky and there were no hatches. Conventional wet-fly and nymph tactics moved nothing, and finally I decided on a small mylar streamer. It moved a good brown on the first cast, and I decided to stay with it into the Buttonwood.

It soon started to rain harder. *It's pretty gloomy!* I thought. *The fish are pretty moody—but it's the kind of day for moving a big fish!*

The marabou dropped tight against the roots and teased swiftly back across the main current. It had just escaped the shelving hole, working into the gravel shallows just below me, when a big fish slashed out of the deep water and boiled around the fly without touching it. The trout finally bolted back into its hiding place.

He saw me that time! The fish had charged the fly aggressively, changing its mind at the last moment when its greed carried it close to my waders. *Maybe he'll come again if I rest him!*

I waded slowly out of the pool and sat down under the big oak that shades the gravel shallows across the current. The rain slowed and stopped after twenty minutes. It was time to try the fish again, but I studied its lie before wading back into the pool. The current flowed still and smooth.

Maybe from below him, I thought suddenly.

It made sense to fish the place with an upstream cast, since my position would be behind its holding lie. The little marabou sliced out low, hooking close to the undercut bank about fifteen feet above the trout. It settled back deep on the current, and when it seemed that the fly must have reached the

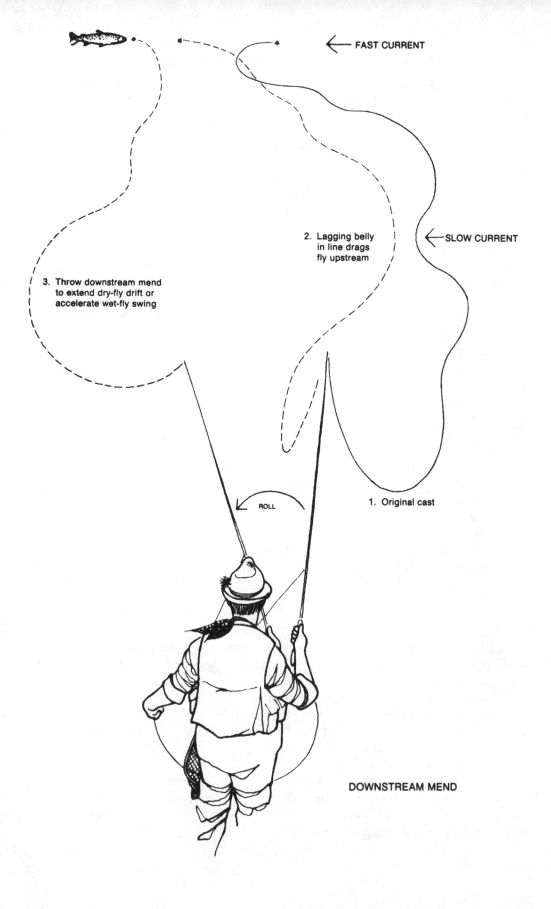

FAST CURRENT

SLOW CURRENT

2. Lagging belly
in line drags
fly upstream

3. Throw downstream mend
to extend dry-fly drift or
accelerate wet-fly swing

ROLL

1. Original cast

DOWNSTREAM MEND

deepest place under the roots, I started a fast left-hand strip. The fly had travelled about six feet when there was a wrenching strike, and the fish was solidly hooked. It fought hard, splashing and probing deep under the sycamore trees—and it measured slightly better than twenty-two inches when it came to the net.

9. The Crippled Strip

This is a deadly rhythm of fishing a strip retrieve rather than a fully separate method of bucktail fishing. Few big trout can resist a dying or injured minnow. Fishing a bucktail or streamer to suggest that it might be hurt consists of breaking the pattern of the retrieve. It was a lesson taught me years ago by the skilled minnow fishermen in Michigan.

They were artists at swinging a minnow into a promising run, letting it tumble clumsily in the current, and then giving it an occasional darting pull that caused it to flash as it caught the sunlight. It always seemed to work. Any fish lying in the run seemed unable to resist that erratic light-catching shiner working past them, and a streamer or bucktail fished that way is deadly too.

It takes a little skill to simulate a crippled fish as it sinks helplessly and tumbles slackly in the current, giving an occasional darting roll as it struggles with the last of its energy against the flow. Its pathetic behavior is suggested by a combination of using the pull of the current, stripping with the left hand, and working the rod irregularly.

10. The Panic Strip

Sometimes a fish lying visibly in a pool or run seems disinterested in everything, but it can be triggered into taking a fly worked with a skilled panic strip. The technique is simple enough.

It involves casting the fly slightly above the fish, judging the distance to insure that the fly will ride fairly close to its position along the bottom. The fisherman manipulates his fly in a manner to suggest a minnow that is drifting casually with the current, unaware that the big fish is there. The fly should be allowed to blunder like an empty-headed shiner into mortal danger—and then wildly stripped away like a minnow that has suddenly sensed its peril.

The method works best when the target fish is visible, but it can also be used to prospect through a holding lie that is likely to shelter a good trout. The bucktail or streamer is cast to fish a promising pocket in exactly the same way: it is allowed to swim deep into a suspected holding place, and then it is stripped back like a terrified dace or darter. The panic strip sometimes results in an explosive strike, because few predatory trout can resist faltering and helpless prey.

11. The Skittering Retrieve

Sometimes a bucktail or streamer fished back wildly across the surface, after its delivery with a relatively harsh cast, will move fish when nothing else works. Such a skittering retrieve is a little like the way a minnow flees a marauding trout, and it is a useful change-of-pace presentation.

12. The Sink-and-Draw Method

This is a technique borrowed from salmon fishing, like the panic strip and the greased-line method. It is a favorite tactic on the Vatnsdalsá in Iceland, where John Ashley Cooper has perfected it over the years, using his favorite salmon tube flies.

The sink-and-draw is a fine big-water method for trout too. It is a downstream method which involves pulling back on a cast to settle it with enough slack to get some depth. When it reaches its full length of line, it is allowed to swim against the current and is then teased back with an upstream draw of the rod. The result is a bucktail or streamer trailing in the current, sometimes at the swift tail of a major pool, and a lazy rhythm of sink-and-draw handling with the rod. The fish that strike such a fly seem angry, almost as if they had been irritated into attacking or defending their feeding lies or territory.

The method can also be used in a relatively small stream by allowing the fly to work in a swift chute or swirling pool, or under a logjam or willow-hung channel—since the strikes are relatively hard, fishermen should not fish too fine a tippet.

13. The Boat-Swing Technique

The boat swing simply uses the tension of the water and the speed of a boat or canoe to create a line belly that works the fly well. It is simple enough to master. The bucktail or streamer is cast slightly ahead of the boat and allowed to sink a few counts, while the boat continues along the shoreline or weedbed being fished. The result is a line bellying slightly behind the angler, who fishes out his cast until it comes back toward the boat. Both the angle of the initial cast and the point of pickup depend upon the depth of the water being fished and the speed of the boat. Deep water requires more sinking time, and the cast should be placed farther ahead. Faster rowing or paddling speed means a cast should be placed ninety degrees to the course of the boat or canoe, dampening line belly and fly speed.

Similar manipulation of the bellying line and its fly speed is possible from a river boat or canoe. The fly should be placed in a quartering cast downstream in relatively swift water, slowing its swing in the currents. It can be placed higher in the current on more quiet reaches of the river, accelerating its teasing swing. Skilled boatmen know just how to maneuver their craft, pausing to make sure a fine piece of cover is fished carefully, and lowering the boat systematically downstream, so each successive cast falls a foot or two below the last. Such tactics cover a pool with a series of concentric swings and are used by boatmen around the world—on European salmon rivers like the Alta in Norway, on American rivers from the Allagash in Maine to the Au Sable in Michigan and the swift MacKenzie in Oregon, and on the Tolten and Calcurrupe in Chile.

14. Diving and Bobbing

Sometimes crippled fish lie in the surface film of a lake, hanging exhausted or struggling to swim deeper, and cruising fish pick them up like hatching flies. Such injured minnows are tempting to the bigger fish, and bucktails and streamers are often effective imitations when fished with the diving and bobbing technique.

It is executed by lightly dressing the flies with silicone and casting them out to lie on the surface. They should be allowed to rest like a bass bug for several seconds, and then pulled under the surface sharply with the rod. The silicone will buoy them up again, where a pause of several more seconds is allowed to pass before the fly is pulled under again. Such diving-and-bobbing behavior will often induce a fish to strike eagerly when more conventional techniques have failed.

15. The Greased-Line Method and the Crosfield Pull

Our earlier discussions of wet-fly tactics pointed out the origins of these techniques in the salmon-fishing methods of Arthur Wood and Ernest Crosfield in the United Kingdom. Both methods were conceived to control and modify fly speed. Wood used a dressed-silk line—which gives his method its name—to extend the duration of optimal fly speed for each cast.

It involves casting almost directly across stream, or even slightly upstream, increasing line belly and accelerating the speed of the fly. Each time the fly begins to swing too fast, its speed is dampened slightly with an upstream line mend, bringing it back to its most enticing swing. It tends to give the fish a side or quartering view of a bucktail or streamer, and a skilled hand can increase the duration of proper fly speed as much as fifty percent. Joe Brooks liked to call this technique a broadside drift.

The Wood greased-line method also has its opposite coin: the downstream mend designed to increase fly speed. It will pick up the swinging fly speed of a bucktail or streamer that is beginning to fish too slack through a quiet reach of water.

Ernest Crosfield developed his pull technique for an undressed fly line, which is difficult to mend when it works under the surface. The line is held firmly under the index finger, and is retrieved in a steady pull designed to pick up fly speed with a smooth acceleration. The method is usually employed to fish a fly swing properly in relatively slow currents. Crosfield also perfected a corollary technique designed to diminish fly speed by paying small lengths of line to dampen its bellying swing.

You have to tease the fish! the bucktail fishermen on the Pere Marquette liked to tell me years ago. *It's exactly like getting a lazy cat to play with a string—pull it too fast along the floor and they won't bother to try, but work it too slow and they ain't excited!*

Since I was then primarily interested in fly hatches and relatively small daytime trout that fed on them, my boyhood experience with bucktails and streamers was limited. My parents refused permission for night fishing with bucktails, and when the old-timers who fished the river after whippoorwill time were first starting out it was always curfew time for me to stop fishing and start for home.

My education in big-water tactics with bucktails and streamers has really come since *Matching the Hatch*, and the subsequent opportunity to fish sprawling mountain rivers from the Labrador to Tierra del Fuego.

However, I had some success with these flies in my early years in Colorado. There was one good morning on the Roaring Fork in the heavy water below Basalt and Emma, but perhaps the most amusing experience occurred on the Frying Pan in a neighboring valley. It was the first summer I fished the river. We were staying at the guest ranch on the Frying Pan at Ruedi, with its famous half-mile still water and the footbridge pool right across the road. The valley was relatively open there, spreading into wide meadows between gentle mountains. The slopes were dotted with lodgepole pine and ponderosa, with small groves of aspen above the valley. The mountains were almost maroon-colored basalt, with the dramatically sculptured formations at Seven Castles on the lower river; but there was a strangely chalk-colored mountain of gypsum at Ruedi. It was a favorite boyhood place, but it now lies under almost three hundred feet of water, entombed at the bottom of Ruedi Reservoir.

We were fishing the Frying Pan itself, and its morning and evening fly hatches were awesome. Colorado regulations in those days stipulated that the limit was twenty fish or ten pounds, and night fishing on public water was not permitted. Curfew came at eight-thirty, but the Frying Pan supported an incredible population of fish in the days just after the war. It was difficult to catch a twenty-fish limit, not because trout were scarce, but because it was virtually impossible to avoid the ten-pound limit after landing five or six fish. We were dressing our own flies in the cabin, matching the hatches we collected on the river each day. We were catching a lot of big trout—far more than the other cabins were taking on their fancy patterns, and the rancher came by just before breakfast.

You fellows are catching a lot of fish! he said.

We poured him a mug of steaming coffee. *Hatches are good and we're tying our own imitations of the flies.*

Got a proposition for you! He stirred his coffee.

What's that? I asked.

He stood up and walked to the back porch and pointed toward the cattail sloughs below the outbuildings.

You fellows seen my ponds? he asked. *Them ponds are the old stream channels, before the Colorado & Midland built its roadbed down the valley and diverted the Frying Pan into the still-water channel along the county road.*

You mean the county road was the railroad?

Exactly! the rancher continued. *The railroad used the old channel to raise trout for the tourists and the hotels—like the Hotel Colorado down the valley to Glenwood Springs and the Jerome up to Aspen.*

You still keep them stocked? I asked.

He nodded and sipped his coffee. *And that's where you fellows come in!*

How so? I asked.

Well, he smiled, *most times my tourists ain't seen trout before, and they fish my stocked ponds at a dollar a fish—but your catches on the river's got everybody fishing there the last few days.*

You want me to fish your ponds? I laughed.

Not exactly, he said slyly. *There's only twelve or fifteen inchers in them stocked ponds—but there's some really big browns in the bottom sloughs I want you to catch.*

But why? I asked.

We'll lay them brutes in the ice chest, the rancher explained slyly and winked. *And I'll tell the tourists you caught them in my dollar-a-fish ponds.*

It doesn't seem right, I began nervously.

Hell, boy! the rancher laughed. *There's six and seven pounders down in them sloughs—and you don't get charged nothing to fish them!*

Six and seven pounders? I wavered slightly.

Now we're talking turkey! he grinned broadly. *How do you think we can fool them big browns?*

Bucktails at night, I suggested, *but the Colorado fish laws have an eight-thirty curfew that forbids night fishing.*

Not on a private fishpond! the rancher grinned.

Okay, I succumbed.

That night I dressed several big marabous with the Coleman lantern burning white-hot on the oilcloth table. It was getting dark when I finally came in from fishing the river. We had released our trout that evening, since a heavy morning hatch of big *Ephemerella* flies had filled our ten-pound limits easily, and one of the fish I released went eighteen inches. It was unusually warm in the valley that evening, and no wind stirred the surface of the ponds.

The rancher was waiting. *Let's fish the sloughs.*

I rigged a heavier leader with a fluffy two-inch marabou, and we walked down through the water meadows below the cabins. The surface of the slough was mirror-still, reflecting the dark silhouette of the mountains and the stars. There was a rotting canoe pier, and the rancher suggested that I fish the old Frying Pan channel from there.

The line worked out into the gathering darkness, and I dropped it at nine o'clock to start the clock-face pattern of hand-twist retrieves. The pattern had almost reached a twelve o'clock cast straight into the old channel when there was an immense splash in the stillness. The fish had missed, and I picked up the rhythm of the retrieve. Suddenly there was such a wrenching strike that I snapped the rod down sharply, and when I tightened, the fish jumped wildly in the darkness. It fought stubbornly and well, and when I finally netted it and walked back into the grass, it threshed powerfully in the meshes. It was huge, well over two feet and deep-bellied. The rancher dispatched the big fish with a stone, and held it up against the night sky.

You bring a scale? he asked.

Yes, I whispered, *but a flashlight will frighten any other fish that are cruising and feeding in that slough.*

Weighing this one can wait—get another one!

I'll try, I said.

We took three big browns that night, and I lost another that fouled the leader in the weeds. The first fish went better than seven pounds, the second trout weighed four, and the third scaled exactly six pounds. We dressed them back at the house and placed them in crushed-ice splendor in the cooler. The next morning the dollar-per-fish ponds were lined with tourists from the other cabins, derricking stocked twelve-inch rainbows up the bank with salmon eggs. The rancher was smiling broadly when he stopped at our cabin that evening.

It was beautiful! He laughed. *They saw your three trophies in the ice chest—and there was a stampede!*

Did they catch many? I asked.

The rancher waved his arms happily. *Two hundred and thirty-one!* he cackled. *Two hundred and thirty-one!*

My God! I swiftly calculated the profits.

Guilt haunted me all night, and finally sleep came when the morning sun glowed pink on the pale gypsum hills behind the ranch. The fishermen in the other cabins were generous in their praise that week, and they never guessed our night-fishing secret. It was a week of pure torture, and I still remember it guiltily almost thirty years later. It was the end of my career as a fishing shill.

4. The Secrets of
Fishing the Nymph

I t is a country of round-topped church towers and walled villages filled with charming half-timbered houses. Mill wheels turn lazily in the smooth cress-filled currents on the trout streams. There are limestone plateaus where we hunted stag and roebuck and partridges above the rivers, and precipices and outcroppings with ruined castles. Timber frames are found in the hops fields, and the old women gather sticks in the forests, carrying their rough bundles back along the cobblestone roads into the towns. German rivers were the classrooms for my postgraduate years in fishing the nymph, and the quality of the trout fishing was a revelation in those years after the war.

The stone-paved road winds south toward Regensburg, into the pastoral Vils country below Amberg. It passes through narrow streets of intricate brickwork houses, where the April rains glitter on the roof tiles. The church towers have the graceful onion-topped domes sometimes found in Bavaria, after the Ottoman campaigns that reached deep into central Europe. Ducks and geese forage in the millraces, waddling through the marketplaces in the rain. Storks construct their tangled, roughly textured nests in the chimney pots, and every feeder brook and river and millrace holds a fine population of free-rising brown trout. It is a lovely and pastoral part of the world.

April winds from the south stir the alders along the rivers, smelling of snowmelt in the Bavarian Alps and freshly plowed earth in the fields outside the villages. The winds are perfumed with orchards and wildflowers too. The farmers are building new hops frames on the hillsides, and dairy cattle are grazing in the river bottoms. Later the fly hatches are heavy at Schmidsmühlen.

The Lauterach is a classic German stream. Its winding meadows and alder-lined pools were the laboratory where I first really learned to fish nymphs well. More than twenty-five seasons have passed since those postwar April mornings, although it all seems as fresh as yesterday.

Before that first summer in Europe that gave me the opportunity to polish eager boyhood skills on the difficult fish of German rivers, nymphs seemed only a half-understood version of conventional wet-fly themes. The nymphs in my fly books were strange creations in those early years. Some had been dressed in England, echoing the experiments of Skues and Sawyer, but I had developed little faith in them. The fault lay principally with my ignorance of nymph fishing and not with these British patterns, but the American nymphs that I fished half-heartedly were fanciful creations that had no obvious insect counterparts in aquatic entomology on either continent.

Except for the odd trout that took some roughly dubbed British pattern or accepted a small nymph I had copied from the flat-bodied Hewitt style of dressing, my first attempts at nymph fishing were unproductive. Bergman was my first real instructor in nymph fishing theory and technique, since Hewitt and his writings were little known beyond our eastern trout streams. Bergman's *Trout* introduced an entire American generation to nymph fishing, although our writers had not yet studied the subaquatic naturals and their behavior, like the discipline of the British fly-fishing experts on the chalkstreams.

Still the lessons found in Bergman were sound, and I devoured both *Just Fishing* and the later *Trout*, even if his observations on nymph fishing were incomplete. There was no inkling in my mind that these books fell woefully short of a comprehensive treatment of nymph fishing in those years. Sometimes the slow hand-twist retrieves recommended by Bergman produced impressive baskets of fish, like one summer morning on the Pere Marquette in Michigan, but the so-called nymphs that appeared in the color plates of *Trout* were more lures than workable imitations.

However, there were many experiences when certain dressings of conventional wet flies seemed to work on nymphing fish. Sometimes I caught trout easily on a worn hackle pattern when they were working in the film. Weathered wet flies like a March Brown or Hare's Ear or Greenwell's Glory often took fish well when they were porpoising softly to a hatch. It never occurred to me in those early years that such patterns worked as well as they did because, when they became shredded, they imitated the emerging nymphs and pupae.

Bergman outlined simple nymph-fishing tactics.

His methods were primarily extensions of conventional wet-fly methods. They included the dead-drift presentations, downstream wet-fly swings, fly swings with an additional teasing rhythm of the rod tip, and a patient hand-twist retrieve. These basic approaches often produced fish, and I can clearly remember my first trout with a nymph in the high-country headwaters of the swift Taylor in Colorado.

During those early summers in Michigan and the Rocky Mountains, the painstaking collection of aquatic insects that formed the basis of both *Matching the Hatch* and *Nymphs* had already begun. The unexplained successes of the nonimitative Bergman patterns were puzzling. The catches of those days always seemed a complete accident; the rational patterns of cause-and-effect were tenuous, having little real relationship between insects and imitative fly dressing, unlike my early experiences with the dry-fly method in Michigan.

Fishing the Lauterach in Germany changed everything.

The riverkeeper at Schmidsmühlen was a skilled tutor who soon ended my confusion about nymph fishing. His patient example in the water meadows of the Lauterach began a whole new cycle in my fly-fishing education. My father and I first met him in a half-timbered *Gasthaus* near the river on a late spring afternoon. There was a late lunch of fresh sausage and thick potato soup and red cabbage, and we finished over coffee with considerable talk about his river and his flies.

His fly boxes were filled with delicate little slate-colored uprights and mottled sedges and long-tailed mayflies. The old riverkeeper was particularly proud of his nymphs. His favorite pattern had a pale dubbing body ribbed with brown crewel, with wing cases and legs of partridge. It looked much like the March Brown nymph popular on our Catskill rivers.

This dark little nymph is best, the old man picked a fat partridge-legged nymph from the box. *It is my favorite pattern.*

Are they hatching now? I interjected.

The old riverkeeper nodded and explained that the hatching nymphs migrate into the shallows and fly off quickly when they emerge.

So the trout must pursue them? I asked.

The old man nodded and filled his intricately carved pipe.

The hatching flies are pretty difficult to catch, the keeper continued once the pipe was smoking properly, *and the fish concentrate on the swimming nymphs instead.*

Let's try them, said my father.

We rigged our tackle and walked upstream through the cherry orchards above the village. There was a long reach of river where the mayflies were already coming off the riffles. Two fish were working where the swift shallows shelved off into the currents along an undercut bank.

They're rising over there, I pointed.

Nein! the old man shook his head forcefully. *The trout are taking the nymphs just under the surface!*

How do we fish them? my father asked.

The old man pointed to the riffles upstream. *The hatching nymphs are there*, he explained. *The nymphs drift down from there, wriggling and working just under the surface.*

Shall I move the fly?

Ja! the old man answered. *These hatching nymphs can swim and you should work your flies with the rod.*

Petri dank! I said.

The first cast along the grass went fishless. The second cast dropped the nymph tight against the bank, where the swift riffle deepened in a bend, and I teased the fly swing with the rod. Its drift worked deep where the fish had been rising. Suddenly there was a strong pull and the trout hooked itself and jumped twice.

The fish like your nymphs, I laughed.

We took many fish easily that afternoon, killing a brace of fat two-pounders for supper at the *Gasthaus.* Later stomach autopsies confirmed their diet of big hatching *Siphlonurus* nymphs; and the naturals were almost perfectly matched by the little partridge-legged nymphs dressed by the riverkeeper and his sons. It was a fine lesson in basic nymph-fishing techniques, and the Lauterach was my proper baptism in the method.

During the weeks that followed, the old riverkeeper carefully taught me the lessons of his Bavarian river, pointing out what kinds of nymphs lived in the different types of water. Although his own flies were unprofessional and roughly tied, he painstakingly tried to match the color and configuration and size of the naturals, and he insisted that his nymphs be fished to duplicate their movements and behavior in the river. Tactics keyed to the behavior of both the naturals and the fish were a revelation after the diet of fancy patterns and mere fly manipulation recommended in Hewitt and Bergman.

Their somewhat casual approach to the imitation of natural nymphs and their emphasis on the dead-drift and hand-twist presentations had not always worked. Many times obviously-nymphing trout had ignored such tactics completely. Yet we had taken fish in the Lauterach meadows that afternoon, moving each feeding trout with the clockwork regularity that comes only when you have really solved the problems. Such a degree of effectiveness is the true measure of success on trout water; and it had eluded me in those first, fumbling experiments with the Hewitt and Bergman fly patterns.

It is certainly no accident that many American anglers are relatively baffled and uninformed about nymphs. Our books have not examined the naturals and their behavior systematically and have limited their discussions of fishing nymphs to dead-drift and hand-twist techniques of presentation. Some writers have also discussed fishing them with the timeless chuck-and-chance-it tactics, but our American literature on the subject remains fragmentary and relatively incomplete. Most pieces of the puzzle are still missing, and many fishermen already skilled in the dry-fly method readily acknowledge their singular lack of success with the nymph, particularly with trout that are porpoising in the film.

They're nymphing all over the place! they shake their heads unhappily. *Tried nymphs and they didn't work!*

It is a surprisingly familiar chorus on trout water. Fishermen seem to believe that trout are not selective when taking nymphs, and that any nymph pattern will work. Nothing could be farther from the truth. It is like the old story about the Broadway showgirl who read her first book, found it difficult and boring, and subsequently declined to start another.

Using any nymphal pattern when the fish are nymphing, just because it happens to fall into the category of nymphs, is doomed to failure in most cases. It is surprising to find men who thoroughly understand selectivity in the context of dry-fly fishing and its relationship to aquatic entomology, yet are often totally unaware that trout are equally selective to wet flies and nymphs. Trout have more time to examine their subsurface foods readily and at relative leisure, without the visual distortions of the film and its broken-surface turbulence; and they see nymphs rather better than diet forms floating on the meniscus itself. Therefore, selective fish are perhaps more critical of nymphs in terms of color, configuration, and size than they are of both naturals and dry flies floating on the surface.

Our preoccupation with the more fashionable dry-fly method is the reason for our relative ignorance about nymphs. The awesome influence of Frederic Halford on subsequent American writers like Theodore Gordon and George La Branche has led us into a pair of surprisingly common mistakes. Our first error is the commonly-held attitude that the dry-fly method is the most difficult, and that its difficulty and complexity make it the moral superior of other fly tactics. Knowledgeable anglers all enjoy the surface rise to the dry fly immensely, but no one can build an airtight case that the dry-fly method is more difficult or subtle than the full spectrum of tactics for wet flies and nymphs. Since approximately ninety percent of the trout diet is based on subaquatic nymphal and pupal forms, floating adult insects obviously play a relatively minor role in their feeding; but Halford ultimately convinced himself that the dry fly was not only the moral superior of the other fly methods, but also the most effective technique on his chalkstreams. The second error familiar to contemporary anglers, in their dry-fly myopia, is the rather simple-minded assumption that a visible surface rise automatically means a surface-feeding trout.

Fish commonly porpoise and swirl to hatching nymphs and thread-worms and pupae in the surface film. These insect forms are nymphs about to emerge as adult flies, pupae struggling to escape their pupal skins, and other ecotypes that breathe in the oxygen-rich meniscus of the water. Each of these forms is still lying under the surface, yet when a fish takes one, his movements are betrayed by a showy surface rise or bulge. Such rises are to nymphs and pupae, and must be fished with nymphal and pupal imitations that settle just under or ride in the film. Other visible rises, particularly dimpling swirls in lakes and slow-flowing streams, are indicative of feeding on the larvae and pupal forms of the minute Diptera, which often hang motionless under the surface film, their minute gills pulsing in the meniscus layer.

Although many anglers are still confused about nymphs and nymph fishing, our methods of fishing them are quite ancient. Such methods include each of the primary wet-fly techniques, depending on how the specific nymphs and pupae move in the water, and have their origins deep in angling prehistory. Most of our primitive fly patterns and many that originated in the past three centuries were fished under the surface—they were often taken for emerging mayfly nymphs and hatching pupae.

The rods and other tackle required for optimal nymph fishing are quite similar to those found in our earlier discussions on wet-fly tactics. Floating, sink-tip, and full-sinking lines are all valuable depending on the feeding level of the fish. Leaders of relatively fine limp nylon are important for nymph fishing in order to provide a relatively free character of drift. Generally speaking, nymph-fishing rods should be delicate enough to handle relatively fine tippet diameters, and have sufficient length to facilitate line mends and other manipulations of fly speed. Such rods might vary from seven to eight and a half feet, with matching lines from five- to eight-weight tapers. Their actions should provide the relatively slow rhythms of a semiparabolic taper, proportionately delicate tip calibrations, and oversize guides. Such tackle is capable of false casting nymphs without costing them moisture, can lay the imitations softly on the current, and can fish a fine nylon point without breaking it off in a good fish.

Our first conscious knowledge of the relationships between nymphs and aquatic fly hatches is found in *Certaine Experiments Concerning Fish and Fruite*, which the British writer John Taverner published in 1600. Walton did not mention such topologies in his *Compleat Angler* in 1653, and his collaborator Charles Cotton also omits mention of nymphs in his *Being Instructions How to Angle for a Trout or Grayling in a Clear Stream*. However, Cotton was later aware of nymphs, and his narrative poem titled *Wonders of the Peake* includes an unmistakable reference to such subaquatic flies.

The first conscious speculation on the importance of nymphs and larval forms in the trout diet appeared when John Younger published his *River Angling for Salmon and Trout* in 1840. Twenty-three years later, H. C. Cutcliffe wrote his book *Trout Fishing in Rapid Streams*, a classic based on a lifetime of experience on the rivers of Devonshire. Cutcliffe offers a concise account of west-country flies and the techniques of fishing them in swift water. His stratagems include stalking the fish carefully, and fishing the upstream dead drift to keep out of sight. His book unmistakably defines the differences between the reaches of water where exact imitation is necessary, and the swift pockets where a fish must take quickly or go hungry. Cutcliffe thoroughly understood the behavior of the small-stream trout as well as the life cycle of the aquatic insects, and in his book we find the following speculation:

> I find so much spoken about the natural fly and its imitation, but little about the insect before it is arrived at maturity. How seldom does one imitate the larva or pupa of the several insects.

However, it was not until the close of the nineteenth century that the genius emerged who would fit together these disparate pieces on the classic Itchen in England. George Edward MacKenzie Skues conceived and painstakingly hammered out the full theory and practice of modern nymph fishing himself, and quickly refined it to a surprising level of maturity. Skues was a solitary bachelor who fished and loved the Itchen for more than fifty years, and he was certainly the conscious progenitor of modern nymph-fishing techniques.

Skues first published his evolving philosophy in *Minor Tactics of the Chalk Stream*, which first appeared in 1910. It was based on a penetrating logic, healthy distrust of past dogma, thorough knowledge of fly-fishing history and theory, and considerable original thought. *Minor Tactics* made a point for retaining wet-fly tactics on the chalkstreams, and although it aroused a chorus of vocal opposition from the dry-fly acolytes around Halford, its brief for nymph fishing was so subtly and convincingly argued that it has never been successfully refuted. However, Skues faced strong opposition, and the quarrels still continue, more than fifty years later, at the Flyfisher's Club in London.

Skues was so successful with the chalkstream fish that he became a full-blown legend in his lifetime. His willingness to adapt himself and his tactics to the moods and rhythms of the river was his secret, and made him consistently more effective than his skilled dry-fly rivals on both the Itchen and the Test.

The studies outlined in *Minor Tactics* were enlarged in 1921, when Skues published his major book *The Way of a Trout with a Fly*, which polished and refined a consistent philosophy of nymph tactics. *Nymph Fishing for Chalk Stream Trout* codified a lifetime of experience along his beloved river above Winchester. It should be understood that Skues fully grasped the limitations of his work, and his books are filled with intimations of that awareness. Skues recognized that the spectrum of fly hatches on the chalk-rich rivers of Hampshire was limited, just as the insect populations of our eastern limestone streams and western spring creeks are often limited to relatively few individual species as well.

Most still-water insects are swimming ecotypes, ranging about freely in the current both during their everyday underwater lives and during actual emergence. There are infinitely more insect species and ecotypes found in other biosystems, such as the swifter rivers throughout the United States and Canada. However, such exceptions to the Skues philosophy of nymph fishing in no way weaken its importance. The conditions endemic to the British chalkstreams are also found on our slow-flowing rivers, alkaline spring-fed streams, and lakes and impoundments everywhere. Skues is still the sole father of modern nymph fishing, and his conceptual innovations stand as the principal bench mark of all subsequent work on nymphs, even if his pioneer thought falls short of the full scope of modern nymph-fishing problems in the United States.

Since manipulation of the artificial nymph depends upon the physiology and behavior of the natural, stream entomology is unquestionably the key to frequent success. American stream entomology poses a considerable problem in observing and imitating the plethora of diet forms indigenous to an entire continent, rather than the relatively limited palette of fly hatches found in the British Isles.

The considerations of American entomology are extensive. When the collections I made for books like *Nymphs* and *Matching the Hatch* grew larger and larger, it became obvious that our fishing poses galaxies of fly-hatch problems not found in Europe—writers like Skues, Sawyer, Harris, and Kite have written exhaustively about their chalkstream nymphs, while our American writers have primarily concerned themselves with tactics rather than making a serious study of the nymphs themselves.

Both Oliver Kite and Frank Sawyer are superb nymph tacticians whose studies have been focused on the Wylye and Avon a few miles above Salisbury. Kite compiled his experience in *Nymph Fishing in Practice*, and Sawyer published his knowledge in the better-known *Nymphs and the Trout*, which includes the following perceptive observations on a nymphing fish:

> While after fish which are plainly visible one learns just how a nymph is taken, and it becomes increasingly obvious that sometimes the indication shown on the surface is so slight, that without very close attention, a trout can have your nymph in his mouth and spit it out before you realize a chance was missed.
>
> One develops an awareness which is not even a sixth sense. It is something which just cannot be explained. You see nothing, feel nothing, yet something prompts you to lift your rod tip, some little whisper in your brain to tell you a fish is at the other end of your line. But this feeling only comes if you are intent on your work, for though it may not be possible to see through the surface, it is possible to visualize the position of the fish and anticipate his reactions to your nymph.

My recent book *Nymphs* has sought to provide a foundation for nymph-fishing techniques on American waters, carefully based upon an extensive catalog of the actual nymphs themselves. The experience gathered since the publication of *Matching the Hatch* in 1955 has made me fully aware that trout are as selective in their nymphing as in their feeding on floating insects.

However, fishing nymphs properly is not only a problem of dressing imitations to match the naturals, but also of understanding how these subaquatic insects behave and move at various depths of water. Knowledge concerning their preferences in water types, their behavior in the subaquatic growth cycle, and the character of the nymphs during a hatch is critical. The skilled nymph fisherman must have an understanding of their typical bottom-dwelling habits, their movements at the intermediate depths of water, wriggling a few inches beneath the surface, and their final hatching moments in the film itself. Such knowledge will make precise imitation and presentation possible, keying our handling of the flies to the behavior of the naturals. There are fifteen basic fly-manipulation techniques in nymph fishing.

1. The Dead-Drift Swing

The dead-drift swing is perhaps the oldest basic fly technique adapted to simulate certain types of slow-swimming nymphs working toward the surface to hatch. It is executed by casting across or quartering downstream, depending upon the current speed, and then simply allowing the fly to work back across the current tongue with a fixed length of line. Such a presentation is effective on a nymphing fish, or can be used to cover the water in a series of concentric quarter-circles.

Experienced nymph fishermen will use this technique to fish imitations of clambering stonefly and mayfly nymphs that swim clumsily toward the shallows before hatching. It is also useful in imitating the slow-swimming little *Paraleptophlebia* nymphs, and other tiny mayflies in their hatching periods. Tiny swimming mayfly nymphs of the *Baetis* flies are particularly numerous on American trout streams, and the dead-drift swing is especially good when they are emerging. There are also times when a dead-drift swing is effective on fly hatches that are partially winged before they reach the 'surface and emerge from their nymphal shucks. Such hatches include the two-tailed *Epeorus* flies, which split their wing cases before they leave the bottom, and the ubiquitous *Ephemerella* mayflies found throughout American waters, which begin to escape their nymphal skins a few inches below the surface film. The large swift-water *Stenonemas* are a group of mayflies that hatch clumsily, working toward the shallows and struggling with half-dried wings in the film; their emergence behavior is ideally suited to the dead-drift swing.

My fishing diaries are filled with experiences focused on each of these nymphal forms, but perhaps the most pervasive memories are those of the heavy *Baetis* hatches on the famous Frying Pan in Colorado. These tiny mayflies are many-brooded, with several hatches during each season. The first cycle usually comes in early season, but the subsequent hatches of August and October seem more important to the fish. The *Baetis* hatches at the Ruedi still-water on the Frying Pan were like tiny slate-colored snowflakes in those years before college, but they are lost now, drowned forever under the waters of a reservoir.

It was an accident that I discovered the dead-drift swing on the still-water at Ruedi. There was a heavy hatch of *Baetis* on the sprawling half-mile flat, and I was busily working a tiny dry fly over the rising fish, when friends stopped to talk from the road. There were rises everywhere on the still water but few fish had taken a floating imitation of the naturals.

What are they taking? my friends called.

They're not taking the dry fly very well, I shouted back. *They seem to be nymphing or taking something else tonight!*

Work it out! they laughed.

My tiny dry fly had drowned and drifted past me while we talked, and it began a dead-drift swing across the current downstream when a good fish took it and was hooked.

You fish better when you're not fishing! one friend called, from across the pool. *Why'd he take it sunk and downstream?*

Let's try it again and find out, I suggested.

The tiny dry fly was bedraggled and soaked with fish slime, and without cleaning it or drying its hackles, it was cast again and worked past another rising fish. The fly came across its feeding lane, swinging against the tension of the leader, and there was a soft little swirl. The leader twitched suddenly and I tightened.

He took it! my friend said excitedly.

They're taking the nymphs of these little flies! I said. *Two fish in a row is no accident—it's the solution!*

It was a happy discovery that produced a cornucopia of selective trout that afternoon; and the fish we killed for the frying pan were filled with tiny *Baetis* nymphs. It is a technique that has proved itself over the years.

2. The Swimming-Nymph Swing

This approach is a subtle variation on the simple dead-drift swing, which introduces a teasing rhythm of the rod tip into the fixed-length manipulation of the line. It consists of casting directly cross-stream in slow-moving currents, and quartering downstream in most cases. The fly swing is allowed to work back across the current on a fixed length of line, with a contrapuntal teasing of the rod tip. The rod rhythms can be varied in frequency and character to suggest various nymphal and pupal behavior.

Such fly swings have a wide range of usefulness.

They work to suggest small swimming nymphs found in currents of good flow speed, like the big *Leptophlebia* nymphs that hatch on our eastern rivers in early spring. Such nymphs often migrate along the river in schools, and the swimming nymph swing is particularly effective then.

The approach is also effective fished on a sinking line with big stonefly nymph imitations, particularly on our large rocky mountain rivers where such diet forms are numerous. It is a little like salmon fishing, casting a long quartering angle downstream, and allowing the big nymph to ride deep in its swing. It should be teased through the swing with a subtle rising and falling rhythm of the rod tip. Each cast should be fished out until it hangs directly below the angler, and then it should be repeated a half step downstream.

Emerging caddis pupae are another diet form perfectly imitated with a swimming-nymph swing. Such pupal flies leave their sacs, struggling free from the shucks while they work in a slow rhythm toward the surface. The subtle, teasing rhythm of the rod tip is ideally suited to imitating Trichoptera, and it is a valuable method during caddis hatches.

Such caddis behavior is often the solution during impressive rises of fish both in Europe and the United States. Many flies are coming off at such times, and a large number of fish are working at the surface, but dry flies are surprisingly ineffective. The key to the puzzle is often a simple soft-hackled imitation, fished downstream to specific rising trout with a rhythmic fly-swing method. Fished properly, such trout often become unusually gullible.

Thoughts of such hatches inevitably turn to a summer evening years ago on the venerable water of the Brooklyn Flyfishers, which lies on the Beaverkill headwaters above Rockland. It is some of the loveliest water in the Catskills. It has been protected, stocked, and painstakingly restored over the past seventy-five years by releasing many trout and fishing only with flies. Several times the members have been forced to rebuild their banks and log cribbings, binding up the wounds of hurricane flooding. The quality of the fishing on their brief mileage of the Beaverkill is eloquent testimony to the stewardship of the Brooklyn Flyfishers—just as the superb no-kill water on the lower river below Roscoe clearly demonstrates the only viable method of providing good sport over decent-size trout on our hard-fished public waters.

The last evening I fished the Brooklyn water, I drew the upper riffles and the deep run along the county road. It was a soft evening with a warm wind moving up the valley. Normally, I would have expected a hatch of pale *Stenonemas*, and I began fishing under the willows with a pale little nymph. Two fish took it lightly and came off after a momentary struggle. One brown trout porpoised to the teasing nymph as if it were lazily taking a dry fly, and I hooked it firmly.

The next fifty yards were unproductive. There were no trout rising anywhere in the wide riffling reach of shallows, and then suddenly the Beaverkill came alive. It was the miracle of a heavy *Psilotreta* swarm, coming just after five o'clock. There were more and more of the little slate-colored sedges rising from the current now, and the birds were dipping to them. Swallows were wheeling high above the river, while the restless little phoebes and flycatchers darted down into the hatching swarms.

There were hundreds of sedges now. The fish were working heavily, too, and the birds became highly agitated. Thousands of caddis flew along the river on the gentle wind. Some were as much as sixty feet above the current, judging from the darting chimney swifts and swallows, while other hopscotched enticingly along the surface.

The fish went crazy. Trout were rolling and porpoising in the current everywhere. The run along the county road was alive with rises. Fish rolled and dimpled and splashed along the rocks, fed eagerly in the cribbing backwaters, and rose greedily in the smoother currents. Many of the rise forms were slashing and eager, and I guessed that the expenditure of such energy indicated the difficulty of capturing a fluttering caddis.

The little sedges were difficult to catch. When the fish clearly rejected a dozen dry-fly imitations, I spent several minutes trying to catch one of the naturals. It was some time before I was successful. It had a dark brownish body, darkly mottled legs, pale antennae, light grayish rear wings, and dark speckled forewings.

That's strange, I puzzled. *These darkly tied little dry flies are good imitations—they should have worked!*

Carefully observing the trout, it soon became evident that their rise forms were becoming vigorous and greedy, but that they seldom were focused on a fluttering adult. Occasional canddisflies did disappear unhappily in a surface rise, and then I saw the solution. There was a strong swirl across the current, and an adult sedge emerged from the rise form, and scuttled clumsily into the air. Another hatched from a second splashy rise, but was instantly taken as an adult fly, before it could escape the surface. It happened again upstream.

Caddis pupae! I thought happily. *They're taking the little pupae just before they hatch and fly off!*

The fish were still rolling and splashing eagerly, expending the kind of energy usually involved in surface rises to a fluttering adult, but these fish were taking the swimming pupae. Such rises could only be triggered by a fluttering or swimming subaquatic ecotype. The ability of a caddis pupa to swim toward the surface explained the relatively energetic rise forms, and I searched my fly books for a soft-hackled little wet with a darkly dubbed body. For several past seasons I had been experimenting with partridge and woodcock hackle flies in the tradition of British writers like Stewart and Pritt, and had found them effective during caddis hatches.

There was a good fish porpoising above a flat rock in the gathering currents toward the tail of the pool. I selected a small, dark brown partridge pattern with a body of hare's mask, and cast to its position. As the fly began its swing, I teased it gently with a rod-tip rhythm. It came swimming through the holding lie, and there was a quick rise above the rock.

The fish was securely hooked. *That's it!* I thought. *That's what they're doing and I've matched it!*

The fishing was suddenly easy. Trout that had consistently refused my dry flies took the little soft-hackled wet readily. It was a clear lesson in reading rise forms for all kinds of fly hatches that emerge from swimming nymphs and pupal forms, and it is especially true of hatching sedges. There was no question about having matched the hatch. Thirty-six trout were caught and released while the sedge hatch lasted, and when the sedges stopped emerging and disappeared from the river, it flowed smooth and silent in the gathering darkness.

3. The Hand-Twist Retrieve

American fly-fishermen are perhaps most familiar with the hand-twist retrieve, because Ray Bergman devoted considerable attention to its importance in *Trout,* and taught its rudiments to a whole generation of anglers. Bergman described his faith in the hand-twist retrieve in an episode that took place on Cranberry Lake, the logging impoundment on the Oswegatchie in the Adirondacks. The method was to cast out across the drowned channel of the river, let the wet flies or nymphs sink toward the stumps and deadfalls at the bottom, and then retrieve line rhythmically around the fingers of the left hand.

The technique requires holding the line between thumb and forefinger and reaching for additional line with the last three fingers; then the hand is oscillated counterclockwise to the palm-up position, again lacing line around the fingers. The last fingers reach again for another few inches of line, rolling the hand palm-down, and oscillating again. The hand works like a rolling shuttle, lacing the line through the fingers in a figure-eight wrapping. Bergman placed great importance on the rhythm of his hand-twist retrieves; he liked them as slow as twenty-five to thirty turns per minute, although one turn per second is about average.

The hand-twist retrieve is particularly valuable for imitating slow-swimming insects. These behavior groups include backswimmers and aquatic beetle larvae and dragonfly nymphs, as well as the freshwater crustaceans like sowbugs and scuds. It has been particularly successful in fishing the thick-gilled *Leptophlebia* nymphs, the smaller fringe-gilled nymphs of the *Paraleptophlebia* flies, and pond-dwelling mayfly nymphs like the *Callibaetis* and *Caenis*.

Perhaps the most dramatic example of such success with the hand-twist retrieve came some years ago on the weedy, slow-flowing Nissequogue in April. It has its source in a series of spring-fed ponds and marshes on eastern Long Island, and is a quiet little river with an old and distinguished past in the history of American sport.

Daniel Webster once fished its Wyandanche Club, the century-old membership that controls its headwaters. Its roster over the past one hundred years has included some equally famous captains of industry and shipping and finance, and its present members are no less distinguished. Webster still dominates the club's history, just as he once dominated the Washington political landscape, and local legends remember his huge baskets of brook trout taken on the Nissequogue.

Its beats are carefully marked in the woods along the river, with duckboard walks in the marshy places. The beats are drawn among the members from a leather dice cup at breakfast, although the guests are often given preferential treatment. My good friend and host Lester Brion rolled Beat Five for me. Beat Five is a long reach of still water that winds upstream from the boat landing for Beat Six, which is essentially the millpond above the dam. The smooth currents of Beat Five shelter some big brown trout, and it is challenging water. There are a number of fine holding lies. Fish cruise the open waist-deep reach above the boat landing, often lying in the pickerelweed backwaters. The smooth currents work along the alders, sweeping the silt from a brief expanse of pale gravel. Upstream there are dense beds of eelgrass, where pale stones cause some eddying currents. It is a place where I once took a deep-bellied three-pound rainbow in early spring.

There is a deep hole under the alders above the upper boat dock, and good trout are lying there. Thirty yards of smooth, relatively shallow flat are next, sometimes good for cruising fish, and then come three hundred feet of undercut holding water that is some of the best on the entire river. It has deep pockets along the willows and alders, with brushy deadfalls that break the currents. It is a deep dark-water stretch that has often surrendered brown trout between sixteen and eighteen inches.

It is a perfect slow-flowing run for an upstream hand-twist retrieve, and it is rich with *Leptophlebia* nymphs. These subaquatic insects are unique still-water species, somewhat sluggish in their swimming motions, and they congregate in the backwater shallows. They scuttle and clamber there in the bottom detritus, swimming laboriously from place to place. These nymphs cruise together in schools like minute baitfish, foraging rather boldly along the bottom. *Leptophlebia* nymphs also display the habit of mass migration just before their emergence. Such schools can number several hundred nymphs in an optimal habitat like the Nissequogue, a river ideally suited to the genus; and these nymphs can travel as much as a mile. The slow rhythms of their swimming before emergence make them easy prey for the trout and perfectly suited to the slow hand-twist retrieve.

It was an April morning years ago when I drew Beat Five and a large migration of these mayfly nymphs was moving along the undercut banks below the swamp maples. The big fish there were making the most of the opportunity, and I watched them taking the nymphs along the bottom, the weak sunlight flashing on their sides when they captured a swimming *Leptophlebia* below the tangled deadfalls. There had been an occasional hatching fly that morning, and I had collected several *Leptophlebia* duns downstream.

It was a good guess that the concentration of working fish in the sixty-five yards of water above me was the result of a migratory school of nymphs, and I tried an imitation in the run where I had seen a deep-feeding trout turn several times. The first cast dropped a few feet above its holding lie, and as it settled deep on the sinking line, I started a deliberate hand-twist retrieve. My left hand had completed less than a half dozen turns when there was a strong pull, and the light caught a turning fish along the roots. It was a fine eighteen-inch brown trout, and its throat and gill structures were crammed with dark *Leptophlebia* nymphs. The sixty-five yards of water under the willows and alders produced almost thirty good fish that morning—to a patient hand-twist retrieve along the sheltering willows.

4. The Hand-Strip Retrieve

There are a number of nymphal species that swim too erratically and move with considerable darting movements for effective imitation by the hand-twist retrieve. Such nymphs include swimming nymphs of the *Siphlonurus* and *Siphloplecton* genera, and many of the larger subaquatic forms that inhabit still currents, lakes, and impoundments. The hand-strip retrieve is used to create a pulsing rhythm of the nymph in swimming movements from five inches to twenty-odd inches in length. Fish taking such nymphs typically display a relatively bold rise form, since the agility of the nymphs makes them difficult to capture.

The technique involves holding the line under the index finger at the rod grip, with the left hand then manipulating the rhythm and length of the stripping retrieve. The frequency of the retrieve should employ a slow series of five-inch strips, executed at a rhythm of thirty per minute, suggesting a nymph that swims with such pulsing behavior patterns. Much faster rhythms are also possible, although the minnowlike movements of some nymphs are perhaps better imitated with the rod-and-line strip.

Several years ago in Wyoming I experienced some exceptional fishing in a sheltered bay of Yellowstone Lake. It is an immense ecological world in itself, its incredibly blue and unpolluted water lying in an amphitheater of smoke-colored mountains. Boiling springs bubble and steam in the September mornings along its timbered shoreline. The dense forests of spruce and lodgepole pine and fir are beautiful. Pewter-colored deadfalls lie bleached and slowly rotting in the shallows, along with dense phalanx of tules and reeds. Gulls and pelicans crowd the food-rich bays of the most remarkable cutthroat fishery in the world. There is exceptional fly-fishing where the remote headwaters of the Yellowstone enter the lake, in the bays where feeder streams join its waters, and in the outlet flowages where the river gathers itself and slides into the huge cutthroat flats below the famous Fishing Bridge.

It was below the headwater inlets that I once encountered a heavy hatch of big *Siphlonurus* drakes, in numbers that only the rich alkalinity of such waters can sustain, and the fat cutthroats began rising vigorously. There was one fish that began working along the reeds, and its rises were big enough to suggest size. Several times it rose boldly in the shallows, but its rises were so scattered that it was sometimes difficult to predict its movements. Random casting with a dry fly to its single rise forms proved fruitless, since it seldom remained in one area and had a 360-degree range of options for leaving its last position. Any cast could be wrong and there were considerable percentages against its being right. Fishing an imitative nymph in such a situation is a little more effective, since its retrieve can cross the feeding routes travelled by any number of foraging trout. The hatch increased steadily until the still surface of the bay was covered with sailboat-shaped mayflies, and the fish's rises became steadily more frequent. It was possible to watch for two or three rise forms in relatively quick succession and, from their sequence of quiet swirls, plot the direction the fish was working. Its rises were coming faster.

They're like beads on a string, I thought suddenly. *You can tell where they're going from two or three swirls.*

The big cutthroat rose again along the reeds. Its second rise came three seconds later and was about six feet toward the right. The third rise came at about the same rhythm and spacing, and I cast my nymph about six feet ahead of its last swirl, dropping it slightly beyond its probable line of direction. The retrieve was a steady left-hand strip, working the fly back slowly in a series of six-inch swimming motions. It had just about passed the spot where I had anticipated its next rise form, when a bulging wake appeared behind my nymph and it disappeared in a heavy swirl.

He's taken it! I shouted to myself.

It was a fat cutthroat that weighed almost five pounds, rich golden yellow and delicately spotted, and it fought hard through the weedy shallows. Its capture was typical of the tactics in both lake fishing and the hand-strip retrieve.

5. The Rod-and-Line Strip

Some nymphal forms are so agile in the water that their movements can rival those of the fish themselves. Such nymphs cannot be imitated with a simple hand-strip technique and some action of the rod tip is required. One solution is a rod-and-line strip not unlike the manipulation of a bucktail or streamer. It is a technique that requires some experimenting, like the hand-twist retrieve or a similar method, to discover a rhythm of fishing that fools the trout.

Damselflies, burrowing mayflies, and fast-water swimming nymphs like the agile *Isonychias* are all nymphal types that move with erratic, darting motions in the water. Sometimes their swimming rhythms are deliberate and slow, and can be suggested with more conventional techniques. Sometimes their movements are so rapier-quick that an exaggerated rod-tip action interjected into a hand-strip retrieve is needed. The fish are often as attracted to the erratic retrieve suggestive of the nymphs, provided the size and configuration and color of the nymphs is right, as the imitative character of the fly pattern itself.

There was an evening on the Esopus twenty years ago that demonstrated this fact. It was the middle of June, and my father and I were fishing a broken reach of water above Phoenicia. The river suddenly came alive in late afternoon when a number of good trout began working along the shorelines and below a large boulder at midstream, but the symptoms were a mystery in those years.

What are they doing? my father yelled.

Several big leadwinged drakes hopscotched along the rocks and finally got airborne.

See those big mayflies starting to hatch? I shouted back. *It could be their swimming nymphs!*

It was a lucky guess, but I understood so little about the habits of the *Isonychia* nymphs in those years that the reason the fish were working along the rocks puzzled me. The secret lay in the migratory behavior of the nymphs before a hatch.

The agile, little fast-water nymphs swim and dart swiftly among the rocks through most of their life cycle, and about an hour before emergence, they migrate toward the rocky shallows. The nymphs migrate and gather in hatching schools, moving restlessly from stone to stone near the rocks they will climb when actually emerging. It is strange that the nymphs congregate around specific rocks for hatching, since the differences between one stone and another are not apparent to the human senses. Such rocks are surrounded with darting, restless *Isonychia* nymphs waiting to hatch, and when emergence actually comes they crawl up their hatching stones to the waterline, waiting for their nymphal skins to split.

Preston Jennings recommended a big leadwing Coachman fished wet during these hatches, working it in the rocky shallows where the nymphs congregate. His *Book of Trout Flies* is the genesis of our American studies in disciplined trout-stream entomology, and I selected a big Coachman from my fly books.

This should work if they're taking the nymphs of those big slate-colored drakes, I yelled downstream.

The big wet dropped along the rocks where several good fish were working, and I watched the leader for a telltale movement that would signal a taking trout. The leadwing drifted back downstream and nothing happened. Several more casts produced similar results, and I retrieved the wet fly to shorten its wings in the hope it might look more nymphlike.

It's not working. I shook my head while the line drifted past me. *It's supposed to match these nymphs, but it's not working.*

The bellying line began working across the current downstream and a good trout took the swinging fly hard. It had been chasing the relatively fast fly swing from the shallows, and its rise was a splashy swirl that showered water across the current. It seemed like a lucky accident.

You've solved it! my father shouted.

It was only an accident, I laughed. *I wasn't even fishing when it took the fly!* The fish went fifteen inches and I released it.

You sure it was accidental?

My father had a point and it started me thinking. Perhaps these nymphs moved swiftly in the shallows, darting minnowlike among the rocks, and my bellying line had accelerated its speed to suggest the naturals. It seemed worth trying, and I placed the bedraggled fly above a rising fish, stripping it back with both the rod tip and my hand. The fly had come only a foot past the fish when it took with a savage swirl and promptly cartwheeled in a series of staccato jumps downstream.

Rainbow! I yelled. *Fished it fast!*

My father cast across the stream to another rising fish, stripped back line, and hooked it immediately. *Got one!* he laughed. *I think we've solved the problem—with a little help from the fish!*

6. The Cast-and-Strip Method

This is primarily a method of fishing a nymph deep in a swift current, using both line manipulation and a sinking line to achieve the desired depth. It involves casting across a deep current tongue and then shaking additional slack out through the guides as the line settles into its swing. This tactic will get deeper on a downstream drift, and it is useful when the fish are foraging along the bottom.

Another version of the cast-and-strip technique will work a nymph even deeper, and is useful in fishing strong currents and extremely deep pools. It involves casting upstream and shaking the additional slack into the fly drift before it bellies past your position and swings downstream. This technique will buy considerably more depth if the stripping-out is properly timed to take advantage of the sinking slack-line drift. The bellying line swings past, working below your station in the current, and the tension of the line against the rod tip indicates when the nymph is swimming deep. It can either swing on the line tension without additional action from the rod or fish with a teasing rhythm across the current.

The downstream cast-and-strip method once produced a heavy hook-jawed brown on the Big Hole above Twin Bridges. Gene Anderegg and I were fishing together when we reached a temporary irrigation weir on the river, and I cast well down its deep-flowing pond, stripping out a dozen feet of sinking line into the settling cast. We allowed it to belly deep into the impoundment, and then I fished a big beetle larva back along the bottom with a patient hand-twist retrieve. The four-pound brown took the nymph as it was literally ticking along the stones.

Fish like that are worth the trip! Anderegg said.

There was another morning years ago on the Roaring Fork in Colorado when I had gone fishless for almost two hours. There were few hatches and fewer rising fish, although conditions seemed perfect for both. The swift run along the railroad slide looked good, and two bait fishermen were patiently fishing its throat with salmon eggs. They were using several split shot and working their bait along the bottom, and I stopped to admire their catch.

Got some good rainbows. The older man raised his metal clip stringer from the river. *Pretty nice?*

They look strange! I said.

Each fish had rubbed its nose raw on the bottom. The bait fishermen agreed to let me dress a fish and examine its stomach contents, and I discovered its digestive tract was filled sausage-tight with fat little caddis larvae. The trout had been rooting them out of their hiding places among the stones along the bottom and a larval imitation fished deep with the cast-and-strip quickly produced two dozen rainbows.

7. The Upstream Dead-Drift Technique

The upstream dead-drift presentation is another nymph-fishing method described in considerable detail in Bergman's *Trout;* and along with the conventional hand-twist retrieve, it is perhaps the most basic tactic in the strategy of a practiced nymph fisherman.

Since a large number of subaquatic insects clamber and crawl along the bottom, totally unable to swim throughout their larval existence or during emergence, the upstream dead drift is the best method for suggesting their behavior. Such tactics closely imitate the clinging or clambering mayfly nymphs. The two-tailed *Epeorus* and three-tailed *Ephemerella* nymphs are the immature forms of our most important fly hatches, and their nymphs reach the surface buoyed with the gases generated inside their splitting nymphal skins. Some wrap their half-emerged wings around themselves, trapping a galaxy of tiny bubbles, and others split their immature shucks with the gentle pressures of similar gases. These hatching nymphs are fished with half-winged emerging fly types, by casting the imitations upstream on a floating line. It is a difficult technique to master, perhaps the most subtle problem in all of fly-fishing, since a nymph drifting back on a completely slack drift is difficult to follow in broken currents. The fish often come to the dead-drift presentation so softly that a taking trout goes completely undetected.

Anything can mean a fish! the old riverkeeper on the Lauterach repeatedly lectured me that golden summer years ago. *The line can twitch or pause in its rate of drift or stop its swing imperceptibly—any of these things can tell you a trout has intercepted your nymph!*

You really mean anything? I laughed.

The old riverkeeper was quite right; and in the years that I gained more experience with nymphs, it became apparent that really skillful nymph fishermen have an almost extrasensory ability to feel the moment a fish has taken. Sometimes a taking fish reveals itself with a subtle flash of light as it turns along the bottom, or its swirl along the bottom transmits itself back to the surface currents in a minuscule change-of-flow. These clues are almost imperceptible, like the half-seen tumbling of a drowned leaf along the bottom or the brief shadow of a passing kingfisher, and such false clues can frequently trigger an experienced nymph man into striking. It is a hair-trigger quality of judgment that only hours and hours of nymph fishing can develop, disciplining and honing the senses to an exquisite degree of skills.

Our earlier discussions of wet-fly tactics have outlined how Bergman recommended the fly-bobber method in *Trout.* His technique involved a dry-fly dropper attached at the butt of the leader. It becomes a crude but effective bobber, while it floats on the surface, and the indicator fly pauses or twitches when a taking fish interrupts the drift. It was a method I often attempted in boyhood years, even filing off the hook bends to keep them from tangling in my casts, and using a pale bivisible dressed as a highly visible indicator. It was a method I promptly dropped after I raised an immense fish to the hookless bobber on the swift-flowing Pine in Michigan. Modern nymph fishermen use a similar indicator technique in fishing the upstream dead drift, with either a tiny Whitlock fluorescent tube or a touch of bright lacquer at the leader knot—although I once had a hatchery brook trout take that too on the waters of an exclusive fishing club in Pennsylvania.

The upstream dead-drift method is also used with weighted nymphs and larval imitations almost literally bounced along the bottom. Such fishing is always done with a relatively short floating line, stripping back the slack like a dry-fly presentation, staying closely in touch with the fly. Staying in touch aids in both sensing a strike and in tightening in time to hook the fish. Such tactics are particularly valuable in heavily broken currents, or in the cold water of early season, when the fish are sluggish.

Heavily weighted nymphs are preferred, and leaders loaded with split shot or twisted fuse wire are common on many rivers. Such tackle handles awkwardly, and I seldom choose such methods, but no one can deny their effectiveness when the trout are bottom feeding.

Some anglers who are expert in fishing a weighted leader recommend a split shot on the tippet, with one or more nymphs on dropper strands farther up the leader. Another variation involves two dropper strands, with flies attached to the first dropper and point tippet, and the weighting fastened to the second dropper strand. Placing the weight in these positions on the leader means that the flies will come free when the lead fouls on the bottom, since only the split shot or fuse wire is snagged, and will slip off the nylon with a steady pressure.

Perhaps the most skilled practitioner of the weighted-leader nymph technique is Charles Fothergill, the famous fly maker and guide at Aspen on the Roaring Fork. Fothergill is remarkably proficient with the upstream dead drift on its Colorado rainbows, and has tutored a whole circle of Aspen fishermen in his methods. Gardner Grant is another fly-fishing friend particularly adept at fishing such weighted leaders, and his catches are impressive when our eastern rivers are still cold with April rains and snowmelt, although he takes a merciless ribbing from companions who refuse to fish such weighted terminal tackle.

It really works on the Beaverkill when the river's high and cold, Grant was explaining over lunch in Manhattan. *It's a little clumsy, casting the split shot on the leader, but it really takes trout when they're bottom feeding!*

Ed Zern looked up from his salad, fixing Grant in midsermon with a puckish frown. *What happens when a hatchery fish takes the lead?*

You've got trouble! Grant admitted.

8. The Still-Water Dead-Drift

The dead-drift method on lakes, impoundments, and beaver ponds is often the best technique for imitating the minute larval and pupal forms of the *Chironomus* midges, one of the most important insects in the still-water diet of the trout. Although these midge larvae and pupae are minuscule, they are available literally in the millions, and even large trout cruise lazily to take them in the meniscus film with tiny little dimples. Such rises of fish are extremely frustrating to most fishermen, since there are dimpling swirls everywhere across the still surface, yet no insects are visible. British fishermen call these midge forms duck flies and buzzers and reed-smuts, and their so-called smutting rises make for difficult times when conventional fly patterns and tactics are doomed.

Ain't nothing hatching! the old-timers used to complain when the fish were smutting on the Colorado lakes. *Them fish're only playing out there tonight!*

Trout are never playing. Their existence is a perilous equilibrium between calories ingested and energy expended, as our earlier chapters clearly demonstrate, and predators lurk everywhere. Smutting fish are usually taking tiny larvae and pupae imprisoned in the surface film in such incredible numbers that even a large fish can collect more calories from sipping these minutiae than it expends in its feeding efforts.

Such midge forms pass through several cycles each season. During periods when the midge pupae are readily available, trout can ingest as many as forty to fifty pupae per minute. Smutting often involves such frequent feeding that its rhythms dimple a still lake with countless little rise forms, even though no insects are apparent anywhere.

Fishing an imitation of these minute subaquatic insects is both subtle and simple. The larval and pupal patterns are small flies, with hooks ranging from about sixteen through size twenty-eight, dressed on delicate light-wire hooks that hang in the surface film. Fishing a wet fly pattern is usually a problem in saturating the leader and the fly dressing so that it will sink readily, but this is not the case in fishing these tiny midge imitations with the still-water dead-drift technique.

The still-water dead drift is most effective when the imitation neither really floats nor sinks, but rides clumsily awash in the surface film, and the leader is often partially dressed to float like a bobber. The tippet should sink readily, unless it is finer than about .005 in diameter, but the fly must ride suspended just at the surface. Smutting trout often rise so frequently that it is difficult to cast to them, although it is possible to read their direction of feeding from the sequential pattern of their rise forms. It is typical of still-water fishing.

Since the naturals are virtually incapable of motion, the fish are not attracted through either manipulation of an imitation or its impact on the surface. Such trout must simply encounter the larval or pupal imitations on their foraging rounds, hanging motionless just under the film, or the presentation will not appear natural. Such tactics obviously demand patience. The angler must wait for a cruising fish, observe its rhythm and direction of feeding, and then make a soft cast well ahead of its route. The fly should perhaps be placed one or two rise positions ahead of the cruising fish and allowed to hang dead-drift from the floating leader. The trout often swim just under the surface, pushing a little bulge or bow wake ahead of their passage, and their rise to the artificial in the film is accompanied with a darting twitch of the nylon. It is a subtle and challenging method of fishing the smutting rise.

9. Cast-and-Countdown Method

The cast-and-countdown method is another primary technique of fishing lakes and impoundments. It is the optimal system of working a nymph deep in the channels of a still-water habitat. Perhaps the best places to find trout in such biosystems, particularly the larger trout inhabiting our lakes and reservoirs and ponds, are the shelving dropoffs and outlet and inlet channels. Such places are the primary source of forage baitfish and other lacustrine diet forms for the trout population. Such foods are principally concentrated in relatively shallow waters, because photosynthesis is dependent upon relative turbidity and the penetration of sunlight into the water and because the myriad diet forms find both food and shelter in the shallows.

Most lakes, impoundments, and ponds are inhabited primarily by still-water ecotypes, except in their wind-swept zones where virtually continuous wave action on the reefs or rocky shorelines produces oxygen saturations that rival the parts-per-million counts found in a tumbling stream. However, the swift inlet shallows and gathering outlet currents also shelter organisms requiring relatively high oxygen counts, and such zones sustain a richer spectrum of life than adjacent waters. It is no accident that the fish gather in these places, since trout simply forage where food is most plentiful.

The countdown method of fishing a beetle larva, dragonfly nymph, or freshwater shrimp imitation in such places is designed to present such fly-patterns in a natural manner. It is a matter of discipline and patience. The countdown is effective in widespread waters, from the reedy outlet of Lago Maihue in Chile to remote Indian House Lake in the Labrador. It is particularly well known in the rich weed-bordered channels at Henry's Lake in Idaho, where the big cutthroat hybrids and brook trout forage along the bottom for the fat *Gammarus* shrimps.

Weighted imitations should be fished deep on a sinking line. The cast should be made well across the weedy channels, and allowed to sink while the fisherman counts off the seconds. His count may range from ten to twenty seconds, depending on the estimated depth of the channels. The purpose of this calibrated reconnaissance is defining the length of time required for an imitation to reach the weeds or bottom. Should the first several casts work back without actually touching the moss or ticking gently into the bottom gravel, the angler must cast again and add enough seconds to his countdown until the retrieve touches the bottom growth; its depth is the critical bench mark. With that depth accurately established, the fisherman shortens his countdown slightly so the weighted fly hand-twists back slowly, just above the weeds or gravel.

The rest is more discipline and patience. Each cast is allowed to sink to the proper depth, and the skilled angler covers the channel carefully, with a clockwise fan-shaped pattern of casts. Each should fall about two feet farther around the imaginary clock face. Such a properly executed pattern should intercept any cruising trout, and the cast-and-countdown technique will settle the fly to the correct fishing depth.

Hooking a fish against the drag of a sinking line fished at such depths is not difficult if a few brief points are mastered. The fly should be worked with either a firm hand twist or a slow line strip, with the running line held under the index finger of the rod hand. The rod tip should always be pointed directly at the retrieving fly, and held relatively low over the water to gain maximum depth. The strike on feeling the tugging pull of a deep-feeding trout must be firm enough to tighten the deep-riding belly of the line, compensating for hydraulic drag and slack to hook a fish that takes half-heartedly.

10. The Multiple-Nymph Method

Although my own experience had always pointed toward the use of a single fly pattern, recent experience with midge forms and heavy sedge hatches have made me aware of the multiple-nymph technique. Such three- and four-fly leaders are still common on the Irish and Scottish lakes, and on the subarctic lakes of Scandinavia, where the dropper loop and snelled fly remain in fashion. Such tackle was common on the Gunnison and Frying Pan and Roaring Fork during my early summers in Colorado.

Some big western rivers like the Deschutes and Yellowstone and Snake are still fished with snelled flies in their tumbling white-water stretches, but such tackle is much too crude for the trout in most of our hard-fished waters. The dropper loops and snells are far too visible for the brown trout in most of our rivers now, although cutthroats and brook trout and rainbows are still somewhat easier to catch, particularly in broken water and the back-country lakes of our western mountains.

However, modern two- and three-fly rigs should be fabricated with a little more subtlety than the old loop snells could offer. It is possible to make up a leader for a three-fly cast by tying its final two tippets in eighteen-inch lengths, leaving the heavier strand in each barrel or blood knot about four or five inches too long. The lighter strand should be trimmed neatly. The dropper strand, fashioned of the heavier nylon, will tend to project out from the leader, both because of its larger diameter and its relative position in the tippet knot. Its attitude will keep the dropped flies from tangling in the leader itself, which is a problem with multiple-fly casts, particularly if the droppers are too delicate or too long. Dropper strand diameters of .006 are perhaps the smallest calibrations possible, even in the so-called hard nylons, and in the modern limp materials the droppers should be .007 nylon or larger. Experience with fly sizes, and their relationships to dropper length and diameter, will help you rig effective multiple-fly leaders that fish without constantly tangling.

Scottish and Irish lakes are still commonly fished with six- and eight-fly leaders, particularly in the Hebrides and Killarney, but such tackle is not recommended on American waters. However, there are times during heavy fly hatches of sedges and stoneflies when enough nymphs are emerging that a two- or three-fly leader may be more effective than fishing a single imitative pattern. Perhaps the multiple flies catch the attention of a trout feeding on the swarming natural nymphs and pupae, and surprisingly enough, the three-fly rig is sometimes effective when the fish are gorging on tiny midge forms—although multiple-dropper strands seem ill-suited to fishing such minute imitations.

11. The Skimming-Nymph Method

The skimming-nymph method is similar to fishing the riffling hitch on Atlantic salmon, and it is important at times when emerging nymphal and pupal forms are moving visibly in the surface film, making a tiny bulge or subsurface wake as they hatch. Such insects are usually large sedge pupae, or damselfly and mayfly nymphs, since smaller species barely disturb the film during emergence. It is certainly the disturbance of the surface film that attracts the fish, both in river flats and smooth-topped lakes, and I have seen them turn and come considerable distances.

Such conditions are best fished with a floating line, and with a partially greased leader, to work the nymphs just under the film. These imitations should not really sink too readily, and should almost fish awash. Dressing them on relatively light wire hooks will help work them at the surface. It is a combination of fly dressing, line and leader preparation, and manipulation of the cast and the fly.

Sometimes it is useful to employ a nymph in similar fashion on tumbling trout water, fishing a relatively short line to maintain control over its subsurface skimming. The skimming-nymph method has also worked well for me in lake fishing in Ireland, when the soot-colored mayflies are hatching on Lough Corrib and Lough Sheelin.

12. The Greased-Line Method

Greased-line tactics are extremely important in fishing nymphs, perhaps more important than in manipulating wet flies and bucktails. There are many situations in nymph fishing when a selective fish is taking the natural nymphs and pupae in quiet currents, with a stronger current tongue flowing between the angler and his prey. It calls for a presentation not unlike the drag-free float required in fishing the dry-fly method, except that the nymph is obviously fished wet and across or downstream. The dry-fly technique resorts to the hook cast, throwing upstream slack to fall across the intervening current tongues in order to extend the length of drag-free presentation.

The greased-line method is similar. It does not create a completely drag-free nymph swing, but it was originally conceived to mute the speed of the swinging fly when the floating line bellies and is caught in the swifter current tongues. It is a relatively difficult technique to master, since it involves an upstream mend so subtle that the path of the swinging nymph is scarcely interrupted. The cast is delivered across or slightly quartering downstream, and just as the primary currents start to catch the bellying line, the fisherman lifts it from the water and loops it upstream with a lateral oscillation of his rod tip. Such an upstream mend is difficult to perfect, but it is extremely valuable in both nymph and wet-fly fishing. It has a corollary in the downstream mend, which loops the bellying line downstream to increase fly speed in slack currents.

13. The Crosfield Pull

Our earlier chapters on wet flies and streamers have pointed out that Ernest Crosfield was a notable salmon fisherman on the British rivers at the turn of the century, and his Crosfield pull was designed to increase sinking-line fly speed in slack currents too slow to fish properly. His techniques are also extremely useful in fishing a nymph, particularly in big water on our western rivers, and a skillful nymph fisherman should master them—since precise fly manipulation is the key to success.

Like the greased-line method, the Crosfield tactics are geared to dampening or accelerating fly swing, but are perhaps easier to master than the upstream and downstream mends. Crosfield achieved a slower fly speed by stripping out a little line into its bellying swing, or increased his fly speed by stripping in line with the left hand. Both methods are controlled with the line under the forefinger of the rod hand, and since the length of line strip required to dampen or increase the nymph swing in any particular situation varies, considerable experience is required to judge its precise timing and length. Really skilled fishermen can almost sense proper fly speed through the slight tension of current pull transmitted into the rod tip, but such sensory skills are not developed and polished overnight.

14. The Leisenring-Lift Technique

James Leisenring was a legend on the Brodheads in Pennsylvania; and his theories are laid down in *The Art of Tying the Wet Fly*, in which he adapted British wet-fly theories to American conditions.

His method is equally effective in fishing nymphs. Leisenring fully understood that a nymph-feeding trout often takes a swinging fly at its three-quarter point, that the fly was most enticing at that moment, and that it was deadly because it suggested a hatching insect as it left the bottom. Leisenring had often observed nymphing fish in his favorite river, watching them hover just over the bottom gravel. Such trout would suddenly turn and rise in the current, taking some struggling nymphal form before it reached the surface, and Leisenring reasoned that such nymph behavior was common before and during a hatch.

When a quartering downstream cast is made, and the line settles deep into its swing, it reaches a point of maximum depth before the bellying line is forced back toward the surface by the pressure of the current. It is this moment that suggests a hatching nymph enroute toward the surface, and in *Trout* Bergman calls this moment the critical point in the entire fly swing. Bergman did not equate his hot-spot theories with the behavior of hatching nymphs and pupae, but Leisenring fully understood this causal relationship. Leisenring also developed a method of lifting his rod subtly as the fly reached its critical point in the swing, exaggerating the illusion of a hatching insect.

It is remarkably effective on selective fish, and twenty-odd years ago it solved a hot-weather problem on the Ausable in the Adirondacks. Mac Talley and I were fishing the East Branch near the pastoral village of Keene Valley, and the river was unusually low and clear. The trout had moved into the springholes and congregated in the cold seepages of the tributary creeks. The main river was much too warm for fishing, and there were absolutely no trout in the usual holding pools. Finally, we understood the temperature problem, concentrated our fishing in the springholes and the flowages of colder tributaries before breakfast, and went swimming in the famous pools of the river itself in the afternoons.

We caught enough trout in these spring-fed places, but the unseasonably hot weather continued until we were fishing at just daylight and hibernating at midday. Finally the evenings themselves became too hot and muggy to cool the river to fishable temperatures, and all activity ceased. It seemed likely that our fishing was finished when we discovered the springhole trout at Upper Jay.

Twenty years ago, the bridge in the village of Upper Jay was a steel Warren-truss structure spanning the entire river. Above the Upper Jay bridge, a small brook tumbled through the village and added its cold currents to the Bridge Pool. It was a justly famous reach of river in earlier years. Upper Jay was the village where the late Byron Blanchard operated his memorable little Adirondack Mountain House. The river there had a prominent role in the books of writers like Bergman, and in *Trout* we encounter the following observations on the Ausable at Upper Jay:

> Trout of a pound and a bit more were then really quite common, and almost any sort of day produced enough fish to make a catch that under present-day conditions would be raved about. It was a bad day indeed when at least two or three fish of two pounds and more did not come into camp, and repose in cold grandeur in Byron Blanchard's icebox. And we fished with dry flies too. We disdained such things as streamers, spinners or bait. It wasn't necessary to do so.
>
> As I delve into the recesses of my memory and read some of the many notes I made in those days, I find the following flies were outstanding in their performance: Brown Spider, Fanwing Royal Coachman, Light Cahill, Whirling Dun, Badger Bivisible, Brown Bivisible, and Gray Bivisible.
>
> I believe that I introduced the first spiders to the Ausable, at least I have notes to the effect that I was badgered unmercifully at By Blanchard's Adirondack Mountain House when I exhibited them, and it was demonstrated that Ausable trout not only would take them, but that they liked them better than many of the other patterns we had come to think perfect.

Modern anglers familiar with fishing the East Branch in our time can only smile at such observations, since its trout are infinitely more difficult today. Except for the pale-hackled Cahill during the summer *Stenonema* hatches or the Whirling Dun in the *Epeorus* and *Ephemerella* hatches earlier, these fly patterns would move only hatchery fish in the smooth-flowing pools and flats of the Ausable.

Mac Talley and I were facing the problems of selectivity and warm river temperatures, and even when we located trout in a springhole or the mouth of a tributary creek, the fish were shy and difficult to take. It was a week of doldrums until we stopped for a late lunch in Upper Jay.

It was late afternoon when we finished coffee, and walked idly across the trusswork bridge. It was still hot and the bridge pool flowed tepid and smooth. We leaned on the railing, watching the current riffle down the shallows upstream and lose itself in the pondlike still water of the pool. It was already evening, and the shadows reached out across the smooth current tongues above the bridge. Suddenly a good rise disturbed the current sixty-odd feet downstream from the mouth of the tributary above the bridge.

That was a trout! Talley pointed.

You're right, I said, *but look at the bottom below the feeder creek—it's almost black with fish there!*

My God! he said. *Look at them!*

The pale bottom was literally layered with trout, holding in the cold seepage of the tributary to escape the marginal temperatures of the river. There were several hundred fish crowded into some one hundred feet of bottom, holding in a weaving phalanx of trout that ended twenty yards above our position on the trusswork bridge.

This ought to be easy, Talley grinned.

Maybe so, I laughed, *but I doubt it in spite of that tin of sardines down there!*

Let's give them a try, he said.

We walked back to the diner and rigged our tackle at the car, selecting light rods and lines that would sink deep to the springhole fish where they lay on the bottom. The night before there had been a fair hatch of pale little mayflies in the valley, and I suggested we try nymphs, working them deep over the trout and fishing them back like a hatching dun. There was only an occasional dimple below the springhole flowage when we finally slipped into the twilight currents above the bridge.

You'd never know there were more than a hundred trout out there. Mac gestured toward the still currents.

The darkening river whispered past and a car rattled across the old trusswork bridge, scattering gravel from its planking, with its lights glittering on the current. There was no wind but the night seemed imperceptibly cooler now, and the western sky was bright with afterglow beyond the trees.

What do you think? Mac asked.

They're a little sluggish when they're schooled like that, I answered. *We have to get the nymph down deep and tease them.*

Lead on! Mac suggested.

The pool flowed smooth and still, and from the bridge I had noted two stones that marked the position of the tightly-clustered trout. Dim lights from the few houses across the river were reflected in the river, and bats were starting to chase the insects that hovered over the pool. We waded very slowly into position, carefully moving to mute our disturbance and prevent it from alerting the trout.

I'll try a regular fly swing first, I explained.

The cast worked out into the twilight and dropped my nymph slightly above the fish. It teased back on a conventional fly swing, and nothing happened until it had worked well past the springhole trout, when a fat shiner took it hard. Several identical casts failed to interest a fish where dozens were lying.

Why isn't it working? Mac asked.

Not sure, I said, *but it's probably because they won't leave that cold current tongue along the bottom.*

Can't we get the nymph deeper? he suggested.

Modern sinking lines had not been developed that evening more than twenty-five years ago at Upper Jay, but I had an old line of undressed silk on a reel in my rucksack. Sometimes I fished it in the spring to sink my wet flies in the cold currents, and I walked back to our car to get it. Mac waited waist-deep in the smooth current, its flow scarcely visible past his waders.

No rises, he reported. *Nothing!*

The silk line was fully rigged, and I waded out deliberately toward his shadowy form.

The undressed line should get the fly a little deeper, I said.

The cast was postponed until the line and leader were thoroughly soaked at our feet, and then I dropped it beyond and well above the holding lie of the springhole. It started to sink and drift deeper, and I hoped it would reach its deepest point of drift just above the fish. It bellied deep into its swing, and I lifted the rod tip and teased it pulsingly. The little nymph fished through the entire run without moving a trout.

Well, maestro, Mac laughed, *what now?*

The second cast reached twenty feet farther upstream and settled deeper into the springhole currents. The line bellied in the slow currents and started swinging the nymph over the fish, and when the rod tip worked the nymph back toward the surface with a tantalizingly slow rhythm, there was a strong pull.

Fish! I grinned in the darkness.

It was no trophy, but a fat twelve-inch brown at the conclusion of a long and almost fishless day is more than welcome. It finally surrendered and we rested the pool for fifteen minutes before making another cast. The silk-line presentation was repeated, and when it bellied deep and worked the nymph back like a hatching fly, the line darted suddenly and another trout was hooked.

You're doing better, Mac said happily.

The fish bolted downstream, stripping line from the reel, and wallowed in the shallows at the bridge. It was a richly spotted brown of fifteen inches, and it fought stubbornly against the fragile tippet. Finally I netted the fish in the shadows of the rattling trusswork span.

You try them, I suggested.

Talley took my rod and dropped a cast well above the fish, where the little tributary creek trickled out into the pool. Once more the silk line settled deep along the bottom, its belly catching in the sluggish currents as the fly swing started. The nymph had reached the perigee of its bottom swing when Talley raised the rod tip and started the teasing retrieve toward the surface. The fly had almost reached the surface when there was a heavy swirl and the reel ran shrilly in the darkness.

The fish stripped off twenty yards and stopped, and Talley began backing toward the gravel shallows above the bridge. The trout fought stubbornly, jumping once in the shadowy light across the pool, and finally we worked it close to the beach. It was still fighting hard when I netted it in the darkness, and it came grudgingly ashore, writhing and threshing in the meshes.

Big fish? Talley asked in the darkness.

Pretty good one, I laughed. *From its weight I'd guess it's probably seventeen or eighteen inches.*

You're joking! he gasped. *I've never caught a fish that big—let alone fished a nymph before!*

Congratulations! We shook hands.

It was a strong eighteen-inch brown, and we took several fish between ten inches and two pounds that night. It had been a virtually fishless day before we tried the hatching-nymph retrieve on the Bridge Pool at Upper Jay; the same method became extremely productive the remainder of that week at several springholes along the river. It was a fine lesson in basic nymph tactics.

15. The Sawyer Induced-Rise Method

Frank Sawyer is widely considered the best nymph fisherman in the world, and books like his *Keeper of the Stream* and *Nymphs and the Trout* firmly establish him as the midcentury heir of George Edward MacKenzie Skues. Sawyer is the famous riverkeeper on the Officer's Association water of the Wiltshire Avon above Salisbury. Like his antecedent Skues, Sawyer fishes his nymphs only to rising trout or to fish visibly lying beneath the surface watching for subaquatic naturals; it is the British philosophy of refusing to fish the water blind, perhaps a reaction to the dry-fly purism common on the chalkstreams.

Skues liked to fish his nymphs to rising trout, much like a conventional dry-fly presentation, and Sawyer likes to fish his imitations to trout visibly nymphing below the surface. His induced-rise technique involves casting a nymph well above a working fish, letting it sink back into its field of vision, and then teasing the fly subtly to make the waiting fish take. Sawyer himself eloquently describes his technique in *Nymphs and the Trout:*

> Remember you are after a wild creature and creep stealthily to a position where the light gives you the best chance to see the head of the fish and an area of about two feet in front of him. Judge the depth of water and the pace of the current. Remember that the slower the current the faster a nymph will sink. Forget all your dry-fly tactics. The correct presentation of a nymph is a separate technique. With a dry fly the aim is to place the artificial

accurately and delicately on the surface and not more than one foot in front of the rising fish. If cast properly it settles gently on the water without disturbance and you wait for the head of the fish to appear as a signal that he has been deceived. This signal is quite plain to see. You get a signal when a fish takes a nymph beneath the surface, but this can only be appreciated fully when the eyes have been trained to understand and interpret the underwater movements of a fish.

With a nymph the most important thing is to concentrate on the fish, to watch its head and especially its mouth. Try to pitch the nymph into the water well to the front, placed so that any ripples caused by the entry will not distort your view. Already you will have judged the level at which the fish is lying and also the speed of the current. As the artificial sinks and drifts so you prepare for the take and the hooking. Presentation is quite simple and it is not difficult to deceive trout and grayling with nymphs. But, unless you can see the fish take, or some indication that he has taken an artificial, it is only by luck that you will catch more than one in a hundred, and then only because the fish has usually hooked himself.

Few American nymph fishermen would fully agree with that last observation, since we seldom have the opportunity to fish the Sawyer method on our open pocket-water streams. His induced-rise technique is extremely effective on our eastern limestone streams, like the Big Spring and Falling Spring Run and the famous Letort, and on the spring creeks found throughout our western mountains. Their fish lie in the pale gravel channels between the watercress and weeds, and a skilled Sawyer method will take them, for Skues and Sawyer developed such tactics on the equally smooth Itchen above Winchester and the Wiltshire Avon above Salisbury.

However, most American rivers are quite unlike these British chalk-streams—yet our skilled nymph fishermen regularly take fish without seeing them actually come to their flies. It requires an even more highly developed sensory skill than the induced-rise method, although like the dry-fly technique, watching a fish clearly take our nymphs is perhaps the most satisfying form of fly-fishing.

There have been many experiences with the nymph and the induced-rise over the years, from the headwaters of the Connecticut in New England to the poetic little Cumilahue in Chile, but perhaps my most memorable exposure to the Sawyer method occurred in the Allgäu mountains in southern Germany.

Fischen-im-Allgäu is a charming village of red-tiled rooftops and a steepled bell tower, and it lies in a narrow alpine valley with the high snow-capped Austrian mountains beyond. Oberstdorf is a famous ski town just below the border, and the swift glacier-silt currents of the Iller have their source in the snow fields of the Nebelhorn and its sister mountains in the Tyrol. There are both brown and rainbow trout in the river, but its chalk-colored currents make it a relatively poor river for fly-fishing.

The sport is better at Fischen-im-Allgäu. Its silken little Grundbach is formed in a millpond below its cobblestone marketplace, where a flotilla of white ducks is always rooting for sowbugs in the watercress. The millpond is formed by gathering the tumbling flow of several tributary streams. Its mirror-smooth currents flow calmly for almost a mile between the village of Fischen-im-Allgäu and its hatch weir at the millrace. It is a classic mile of water, with channels of fine gravel between beds of trailing weeds, and it has good fly hatches from March through October.

The Grundbach and its trout taught me about fishing the Sawyer induced-rise technique the first morning I fished it. We found the little river completely by accident, since we had originally intended to try the Iller for its spring-running rainbows, but had found it bank-full with chalky snowmelt. There was an old man riding a bicycle on the Sonthofen road, and we stopped him to ask about fishing.

Where is there good fishing? my father asked.

Bachforellen? the old man frowned thoughtfully. *Perhaps below the millpond at Fischen-im-Allgäu.*

Dankeschön! we waved and drove off.

The village lies between the road and the river, and we drove down through its tidy houses to the millpond. It flowed across watercress shallows below the marketplace, gathered in a swifter channel above its waving beds of rannunculus, and finally spread into a rather broad millpond below the footbridge. Ducks and geese were foraging in the shallows. We parked the car and walked out on the bridge to observe the little river.

From the railings we could see a number of trout lying in the channels between the weeds and over several open beds of gravel. The fish were all between twelve and sixteen inches, except for one lying in a deep watercress channel above the footbridge that appeared larger.

We've really found something! I whispered excitedly.

Sie haben recht! my father agreed.

While we watched from the bridge, two of the twelve-inch trout began feeding deep along the bottom gravel. These fish would move forward, or slightly to one side or the other, to intercept something drifting in the bottom currents. Sometimes they would drift back without taking anything, but other times they would quickly open their jaws, revealing a momentary flash of white. Once the mouth closed on the unseen prey, their forward or sidewise swimming momentum ceased, and they seemed to settle back toward the bottom. We watched these two trout feeding below the footbridge for some time.

What are they doing? my father asked.

I think they're nymphing, I said guardedly. *Maybe there's going to be a fly hatch later this morning.*

Perhaps you're right, he nodded.

When we stopped watching our two fish below the bridge, it was apparent that several others were nymphing now, and the first dark little mayflies were already hatching. We walked hurriedly back to the Mercedes to rig our equipment. Before we reached the water again there was a heavy hatch of small *Baetis* flies coming down the currents. Many fish were visibly porpoising at the surface, while others held at various depths, still busily feeding on the nymphs.

My father chose to cast a dry-fly imitation over the visibly rising fish, since he had always felt a little uncomfortable fishing the nymph technique, and I passed him a half dozen darkly hackled Iron Blues. Since there were many fish working steadily above the footbridge, he left with considerable optimism, but after a half hour he came back downstream.

You sure this fly matches this hatch? he asked.

It's the right dry fly for these Iron Blues, I laughed, *but they may not actually be working on the surface.*

But they're rising all over the place! he insisted.

They could still be nymphing, I suggested, *taking them at the surface just before they hatch from their shucks.*

They look like they're rising! he insisted.

During the first half hour, I had tried several nymphs over free-rising fish without results. There was still one small English nymph in my fly books, dressed entirely from pheasant-tail fibers and slightly weighted, and I clinch-knotted it to my tippet.

Let's try it on that fish, I suggested.

There was a good trout lying tight against a dense bed of rannunculus just downstream from the bridge, and it was visibly taking a nymph every few minutes. My first cast dropped about two feet above its station, but I had misjudged its depth and the fly swing came past its position too near the surface. The fish rose slightly in the current when the nymph drifted through its taking lie, but it settled back as if rising high enough to intercept my fly were too much effort. My second cast settled about six feet above the trout, and I briefly lost sight of the nymph before the drift actually reached its station.

The trout shifted its position slightly and rose almost imperceptibly in the current, and when its mouth opened and closed about the time my fly would have reached its position, my reflex involuntarily raised the rod tip. The fish had taken and was securely hooked.

You've got him! my father exclaimed.

We spent the next two hours searching for such clearly visible trout in the crystalline little Grundbach, and I took more than twenty with virtually the same tactics. Sometimes I watched the nymph through its entire drift, teased its swing slightly with the rod tip as it approached, and watched fascinated while the fish either inspected it or took it readily. Sometimes I lost its fly swing in the current reflections. It was difficult to calculate and time my strike, but several times I saw the trout take something at about the moment my nymph should have reached its position, and I hooked a good fish. The day was most instructive, and I learned much about fishing the nymph with the Sawyer induced-rise technique.

Fishing the beautiful Grundbach was a postgraduate laboratory in nymph-fishing methods, and I travelled there almost every weekend for two entire seasons. It offered rather large trout with good fly hatches in quiet currents. The Allgäu is a beautiful countryside, with steeply forested hills and snowfields on the higher mountains beyond. The mountain herdsmen took the cattle to their summer pastures in late April, when our seasons of fishing had just started, and in the autumn the herds came back down from the high country. The cattle carried ornamental bell frames and garlands of flowers in October, and the herds were led through the narrow streets of Oberstdorf with their delicate bells tinkling in the morning sunlight. It was a good time, with breakfasts on the scrollwork balcony of the Hotel Luitpold, and I still fish there often in the time-mellowed weather of the mind.

5. Terrestrials and
the Trout

It is a gentle landscape of manicured fields and brick-patterned Pennsylvania barns and grazing dairy cattle. Ringnecked pheasants cackle and forage in the rich cornfields. The pastures are broken with outcroppings of limestone, and the whitewashed fences are as immaculate as the clapboard farmhouses themselves. It is a countryside of carefully tailored fields, its valleys sheltered between the folded hills and tree-covered ridgelines of the Appalachians.

It is a world of well-filled granaries and silos. Herds of fine cattle graze lazily in the meadows and stare curiously at the fishermen from the sheltering elms and buttonwoods. The barns are painted white and bright red, their cantilevered hay-wagon floors sheltering cattle stalls that open toward the south. Their design permits the cattle to be gravity-fed from the haymows above; and the stored grain and ensilage and hay above these livestock pens insulate the winter cattle, and hold their body heat inside the barn while the low sun angles of midwinter slant deep into their stalls. The hay-wagon floors shelter these same cattle stalls from the hot summer sun.

The barn builders always sited their structures on a slope exposed to the south, sheltered by higher ground to the northwest and the worst winter storms. On the best-planned farms, the fields were on the higher ground, so a loaded wagon could travel downhill toward the barn.

The builders mixed their primitive functionalism and knowledge of climatology with witchcraft, covering their bets both ways with hex signs on their barns to protect the farms and their livestock and families from evil spirits and demons.

The trout streams are also unusual.

The most famous stream rises in a series of rich limestone springs in the pastoral countryside below Carlisle. Its waters emerge full-blown from fissures that surrender the hydrology of vast underground caverns. These limestone springs are remarkable for their clarity and volume, bubbling thousands of gallons per minute to create these gentle meadow rivers. The result is a habitat uniquely rich in fly life, currents that remain ice-free in winter, and water temperatures so constant that the fish feed and grow steadily through the entire year. Its currents are so rich with lime salts that its fertility rivals that of the chalk streams of Europe, rivers like the Risle and Andelle in France, and the better-known Itchen and Test in the chalk downs of Hampshire.

It is the classic Letort Spring Run.

The river is almost tiny in its watercress beginnings, and it flows smoothly over bright-gravel shallows where the two principal feeders join above Carlisle. Beyond this pastoral junction, among the barns and stonework farmhouses, there is a fine half-mile of water below the lime quarries. The railroad trestle follows, and farther downstream there is a simple farmhouse and the reach of water called Otto's Meadow.

It is a marvellous half-mile of stream, flowing through the leaf-flickering shadows of the swamp willows, deeply undercut banks, beds of watercress so dense they will support the weight of an angler on his knees, and brushpile bends long known for their big trout.

The famous Barnyard stretch is next, with its lovely mason-work farmhouse and barn above a willow-bordered bend. The channels in its watercress and elodea have witnessed many angling experiments and epic struggles with its selective brown trout. Highway construction has destroyed the Thorntree Meadow below the Barnyard water, and a four-lane bridge spans its grassy bottoms with massive abutments and post-tensioned beams and piers, forever eradicating its serpentine banks with a straight channel. The sitting bench where Charles Fox and his circle of skilled limestone fishermen gathered to talk and watch the river is still under the buttonwoods downstream; and nearby is the blind where Vincent Marinaro took his famous photographs of rising trout. The river carries a tradition unique in our fly-fishing history.

Fishing the Letort Spring Run in central Pennsylvania has become as much a matter of pilgrimage as sport. Its hatches are composed of small flies and its fish are unusually selective. The smooth currents are silken among the watercress and elodea, and the trout dimple almost imperceptibly. It was my principal laboratory for learning about the growing importance of terrestrial insects in the trout diet, and its regulars taught me much about ants and leafhoppers and beetles on fine tippets.

Although our preoccupation with terrestrial insects on American waters is relatively recent, and the innovations in imitating ants and leafhoppers and beetles worked out on Letort Spring Run are already legendary in our own time, many anglers are unaware that land-bred insects have played a role in fishing and fly dressing virtually since the fifteenth century. Some historians have argued that the flies described in

Macedonia during the second century by Claudius Aelianus were tied to imitate terrestrials, although there is some evidence they might have been sedge imitations instead.

The classic twelve fly patterns found in the *Treatyse of Fysshynge wyth an Angle*, which Dame Juliana Berners assembled in the fifteenth century, include several terrestrial imitations like the Shelle Flye and the Waspe Flye. These patterns were recommended for the midsummer months:

> Thyse ben the flyes wyth whyche ye shall angle to trought and grayllyng, and dubbe lyke as ye shall now here me tell.
>
> The Donne Flye. The body of the donne wull and the wynges of the pertryches. Another Doone Flye. The body of blacke wull: the wynges of blackyst drake: and the jaye under the wynge and under the tayle.
>
> The Stone Flye. The body of blacke wull and yelowe under the wynge. And under the tayle and the wynges of the drake. In the begynnynge of May and a good flye. The body of roddyd wull and lappyd abowte wyth blacke sylke: the wynges of the drake and of the redde capons hakyll.
>
> The Yelowe Flye. The body of yelowe wull: the wynges of the redde cocke hakyll and of the drake lyttyd yelowe. The Blacke Louper. The body of blacke wull lappyd abowte wyth the herle of the pecok tayle: and the wynges of the redde capon wyth a blewe heade.
>
> The Donne Cutte: the body of blacke wull and a yelowe lyste after eyther syde: the wynges of the bosarde bounde on wyth barkyd hempe. The Maure Flye. The body of darke wull the wynges of the blackest mayle of the wylde drake. The tandy flye at Saynt Wyllyams Daye. The body of tandy wull and the wynges contrary eyther ayenst other of the whytest mayle of the wylde drake.
>
> The Waspe Flye. The body of blacke wull and lappyd abowte wyth yelowe threde: the wynges of the bosarde. The Shelle Flye at Saynt Thomas Daye. The body of grene wull and lappyd abowte wyth the herle of the pecoks tayle: wynges of the bosarde. The Drake Flye. The body of blacke wull and lappyd abowte with blacke sylke: wynges of the mayle of the black drake wyth a blacke heade.

Excepting the fly pattern described by Aelianus in second-century Macedonia, the Waspe Flye and the Shelle Flye are probably our first historical examples of terrestrial fly patterns. The history of fly-fishing is filled with similar patterns, from the list of flies that Charles Cotton added to *The Compleat Angler* in 1676 to almost all of the subsequent authors who discussed fly dressing for the next two centuries.

Alfred Ronalds carried our knowledge of the trout and the land-bred insects in its diet still **farther, with** *The Fly-Fisher's Entomology* and its copper plates of both British hatches and his own imitative fly patterns. His collection of aquatic fly hatches was the first made with both scientific discipline and first-rate watercolors of the natural; and his use of proper scientific nomenclature in identifying these insects has been the yardstick of quality measuring all subsequent work. Most of Ronalds's *Entomology* devoted itself to the mayflies, sedges, and stoneflies found on British rivers, but his catalog of trout-stream insects also includes beetles, gauzewings, ants, *Pachymerus* flies, two-winged flies, and caterpillars. Surprisingly it also includes two leafhoppers more than a century before Vincent Marinaro and his *Modern Dry-Fly Code* solved the problems of their imitations with the silhouette theory of his jassid.

Grasshoppers and flying-ant swarms have long been imitated in the history of fly-fishing, and many writers have speculated about their importance. However, the importance of ants through the spectrum of the entire angling season, rather than peak seasons of mating flights, was never emphasized in earlier books on fly-fishing. Ants are continuously on the water in great numbers as the season progresses, even during warm weather in early spring and late fall, and their considerable role in the trout diet has been virtually ignored. Except for the brief mention and an unworkable imitation in the Ronalds *Entomology*, the place of the minuscule leaf hopper, one of the principal diet forms on forest and meadow water, was virtually unknown to anglers.

These concepts are the source of the Letort legend.

The evolution of workable leafhopper imitations, and the discovery of the importance of minute Hymenoptera, is an angling breakthrough that makes the studies of Charles Fox and Vincent Marinaro on the Letort the modern equivalent of the Halford-Marryat collaboration that codified dry-fly theory on the British chalk streams.

Modern terrestrial imitations of ants and leafhoppers and beetles are an angling event. The frustration of casting conventional flies over terrestrial-feeding trout is ended. Classic patterns for such smutting fish were merely tiny conventional dry flies, and most anglers called them midges. Yet true midges are minute aquatic insects, and imitations of these *Chironomus* flies are consistently refused by selective trout taking terrestrials. Such behavior unquestionably results from the fact that conventional midge-type flies do not provide an imitative silhouette, the unique light patterns and opaque outlines that identify a floating ant or leafhopper or beetle to a terrestrial-feeding trout.

The discovery of such fly-dressing concepts is described at length in my book *Remembrances of Rivers Past*, and the following passages recount their beginnings on Letort Spring Run:

The day of discovery is eloquently recorded in Marinaro's *Modern Dry-Fly Code*, which describes fishing the meadows with Charles Fox near the little fishing hut. There were no visible insects on the water, but the fish were busily working. Conventional methods had failed miserably in the past, and were no better that afternoon. The rise forms were the familiar bulges so frustrating in the Letort meadows. Fox and Marinaro tried fish after fish, resting one and casting to another, exchanging helpless shrugs as they passed.

Marinaro writes that his frustration finally proved too much. He stopped fishing to study the current. Prone in the warm grass, Marinaro watched the slow current pattern slide hypnotically past. Some time elapsed in pleasant reverie before he was suddenly aware of minute insects on the water. He rubbed his eyes but they were really there: minuscule mayflies struggling in their diaphanous nymphal skins, tiny beetles like minute bubbles, ants awash in the surface film, and countless other minutiae pinioned in the smooth current.

His mind stirred with excitement as he hurried toward the fishing hut. There he quickly fashioned a fine-mesh seine with sticks and mosquito netting. Its meshes were not long in the water before his suspicions were confirmed by the thin residue of tiny insects that collected at the waterline. There were mayflies with wings less than an eighth-inch in length, beetles less than three thirty-seconds of an inch in diameter, tiny reddish-gold and black ants an eighth-inch in length, and leafhoppers of minute dimensions in astonishing numbers.

It was the moment of discovery. Charlie Fox came downstream and examined the tiny insects. Both men searched their boxes for flies of proper color and size. Several good fish were quickly caught, and autopsies of stomach contents confirmed a diet of minute forms. The puzzling frustration of the bulge rises was over on the Letort.

But modified conventional flies were often rejected in the days that followed. New concepts were needed. Many experiments were tried before a workable fly-dressing formula was perfected. The basic concepts were slow in coming, and the early attempts were less than fruitful.

Beetle imitations are typical.

Small coffee beans were tried first, filed and mounted on hooks with cement like tiny bass bugs. They floated too low and landed too hard and the trout wanted none of them. Cork and balsa wood were no better. Clipped and folded deerhair beetles were too water absorbent. Black sponge rubber actually worked sometimes, but tended to twist on the hooks and made it difficult to hook the fish. All worked fairly well on other streams, while the selective Letort fish remained suspicious and skeptical.

The full shape and thickness of beetles was ultimately forgotten and a fresh theory of fly dressing evolved. Silhouette and light pattern in the surface film were its essence. Marinaro used large jungle-cock eyes first. Their opacity was good and the fish came well to imitations with the jungle-cock wings tied flat, but the feathers were fragile and tended to split after a few trout were taken. They are now prohibited from entry into the United States and stocks are dwindling.

Ross Trimmer and I were sitting in the Turnaround Meadow one August afternoon. I was tying flies and noticed some pheasant-skin pieces in a hackle cannister. There were a few dark greenish throat feathers on one fragment. We tried them instead of jungle-cock, soaking several feathers together with lacquer to get toughness and opacity. The lacquered feathers were trimmed to proper ovoid shape and tied flat over trimmed hackles. Success was remarkable and immediate. We tried them in the meadows above the trestle and took twenty-one fish. Such a score on the beetle-feeders was unbelievable.

Although the jungle-cock beetles proved too fragile, the jungle-cock wing proved marvelously successful in another context. It is the key to imitating the ubiquitous leafhoppers with a remarkable series of patterns called Jassids. These diminutive flies are one of the great all-season solutions for difficult, dimpling trout. Much of the surface feeding in the hot, low-water months of summer is concentrated on leafhoppers. Alfred Ronalds mentions leafhoppers in his *Fly-Fisher's Entomology*, but his imitations are poor for selective fish. Jassids have proved excellent, and their development will make Marinaro an angling legend wherever big midsummer browns feed quietly in flat, mirror-calm water.

Both the ringneck feathered beetle and the minute jassid are proof of the same theory: that fish cannot sense the thickness of small insects floating above them, and that proper opacity and silhouette and light pattern in the surface film are the critical elements in successful terrestrial imitations.

There have been countless experiences with both beetles and tiny leafhopper imitations. The fat little *Popillia* beetles on the Letort Spring Run were my first profound experience in fishing trout that were selective to tiny Coleoptera forms. Such Japanese beetles have largely been decimated now, since their inadvertent arrival in the United States in 1916, as stowaways in the root soils of some oriental azaleas. Their expanding migration from that hapless nursery in New Jersey had already reached approximately 2,500 square miles in only six or seven years. The Japanese beetles had spread westward more than two hundred miles when they reached the limestone spring creeks at Harrisburg, and expert fly-fishermen like Marinaro and Fox began attempting to imitate them as a staple of the trout diet. Their experiments with silhouette imitations have taught everyone some priceless lessons, and my own experience along the Letort is typical.

Japanese beetles were clustered on the grapevines and wild rose bushes like crawling little bronze berries. Beetles droned in the sycamores like bees. The males were active first, and the females followed. They were numerous at midday, flying across the stream and getting into the water, and the trout were taking them regularly in the weedy channels.

Below the limestone quarries, the current was divided into two deep channels in the watercress. The primary channel was on my side of the stream, where the smooth current eddied over a bottom of gravel and marl. The smaller current tongue was across the stream, little more than twelve inches wide, and channeled through the watercress and elodea. There were wild grapevines immediately upstream, feeding beetles into this secondary channel in the weeds.

The heat was oppressive and I stopped to rest. Wetting my face and neck felt good, and sitting with my legs in the current was pleasant. My lassitude was broken by a subtle rise upstream. The rise form was audible, but not visible, and I searched the narrow channel for its post-rise disturbance. The sucking sound came again. There was no visible rise form, but my eyes were ready this time as it came up along the watercress. The rise was gentle. It bulged out imperceptibly against the current and its disturbance was quickly absorbed against the weeds. The rises were small, but the sound spelled a heavy fish, and it was working steadily. Beetles were thick in the grapevines above its station.

There were plenty of imitations in my fly box, since Ross Trimmer and I had spent an earlier afternoon dressing flies in the Turnaround Meadow, and I waded stealthily into position. The dense beds of elodea cushioned the waves of my wading. The fish was still working.

Checking the delicate 5X leader for casting knots, I tied a tiny beetle to the tippet. Then I waited and watched for the big trout to come up again, marking his exact position. The leader was all right and my little beetle was dressed with silicone paste. Finally I was ready and poised.

The trout came up again. *He's there,* I thought.

My cast dropped nicely above its feeding station against the water-cress. The beetle fell flat and dark on the current, riding flush on its trimmed hackles. It flirted with the weeds. There was a shadowlike bulk that appeared and evaporated under its float. The fish had rejected my beetle. I reduced the tippet to .004 diameter, and the fly dropped softly and drifted right against the weeds. It disappeared in a quiet rise.

The trout bolted upstream along the watercress channel and wallowed on the surface. It jumped twice then, suddenly stitching my leader precisely through the weeds on both sides of the narrow channel, and it was gone.

Four pounds! I sighed unhappily.

It was a typical Letort seriocomic episode, since heavy terrestrial-feeding trout on gossamer leaders are difficult to handle in weeds. But the real challenge and accomplishment lay in getting such a fish to rise in the first place, and since that hot afternoon no one has seen that beetle-eating trout again. The little river has changed.

Although the Japanese beetles have been finally checked and are no longer a major factor in the trout diet, there are still many land-bred Coleoptera that are important. The slender little click beetles provided some superb fishing in the grainfields along Spring Creek in central Pennsylvania several years ago, and the tiny *Platysonia* beetles are often numerous in our eastern deciduous forests. These black beetles measure one-eighth to one-quarter of an inch in length, and I have experienced exceptional hot-weather fishing with their imitations on smooth pools from the Musconetcong in central New Jersey to the Battenkill in Vermont. The fishermen along the Letort Spring Run are convinced that their trout occasionally eat fireflies, which are the uniquely phosphorescent *Photinus* beetles. The slender grain beetles are less than one-eighth of an inch in length, and are important on farm-country waters, just as the quarter-inch post beetles are common on forest rivers. Flea beetles are found along trout streams from Minnesota and Maine, to the rivers of the Smoky Mountains in the southeastern states. These handsome little black insects are many-brooded, measuring three thirty-seconds of an inch, with two generations each season. Flea beetles are often quite numerous, and just this past weekend, I experienced some excellent sport with good browns taking these *Altica* flies on a shallow flat of the Brodheads. The fish were dimpling softly over the amber-colored gravel, partially concealed in the dappled light of the sycamores; and after rejecting everything else in my fly boxes, they eagerly took a black beetle imitation tied on a tiny size twenty-two hook. Small beetles are important not only on eastern and middle-western rivers. I have often found the trout taking little bark beetles on still flats of surprisingly large rivers from Colorado to Montana.

There was a hot September morning many years ago on the lower Big Hole when I was fishing with Gene Anderegg, and the soft rises of the fish frustrated us for two hours before we tried a tiny beetle imitation—and the difficult trout suddenly became easy.

Where are the beetles coming from? Anderegg asked.

Watch the trees and the wind. I pointed to the cottonwoods above the flat. *When the gusts move in the branches, the rises are more numerous. It's blowing them onto the river!*

Maybe you're right, he said.

Such conditions always produce the best terrestrial feeding, when hot weather makes the land-bred insects highly adventurous and active, and the wind gets them into the water. It is typically good weather for ants and leafhoppers and beetles, and it has produced some remarkable midsummer fishing to terrestrials.

Since boyhood summers on the rivers of Michigan, we have had good fly-fishing with imitations of the apple green inchworms. Paul Young used to dress green deer-hair imitations for the fishing on the South Branch of the Au Sable. When the trout first began taking them each summer, the worms were pale yellowish green and hung from the trees on their delicate, silken threads. It was always exciting to watch a good fish waiting under a dangling inchworm to take it when it fell haplessly into the river.

Sometimes the fish jumped to catch them before they actually fell to the current, and sometimes they hung trailing in the surface, making tiny V-shaped wakes in its film. The fish were often attracted by the gentle disturbance of the trailing worms, and came considerable distances to take them when they touched the water. It triggered some dramatic fishing each season.

Later the inchworms reached full growth, and when they became too heavy for their silken threads, they fell into the water clumsily. The trout were now watching for their impact; the spreading surface rings could attract them from many feet away, and provide relatively easy fishing.

When the little half-grown worms are trailing in the current, a dragging imitation on a fine nylon tippet is deadly. Since a drag-free float becomes less important, these early inchworm-feeding trout are often less difficult to catch. Unlike other dry-fly presentations, dragging the flies can even prove an advantage, their visible wakes triggering a rise when a conventional float would be ignored. It is good novice fishing, and I once brought a beginner to the Beaverkill in inchworm season. His clumsy casts and dragging flies only served to attract the fish from under the trees, and they were anything but shy.

Thought you said trout were hard to catch! he laughed euphorically. *They're easy as sunfish!*

They are today, I had to agree.

Like the Japanese beetle, the gypsy moth caterpillar is a recent immigrant, this time inadvertently transported from Europe. It has spread quickly from its tragic introduction into Massachusetts, until it threatens forests from New England to southern Pennsylvania. The trout did not take the gypsy moth caterpillars on our eastern streams the first two seasons they hatched there, but this season has been different. The gypsy moth caterpillars are slate-colored with sparse filaments of pale grayish brown and measure less than an inch in their early weeks. The fully-grown worms are apparently unpalatable to the fish, since the trout usually ignore them. It is gypsy moth time as I am writing this chapter, and I have been observing the trout feeding ravenously on them.

The current has been covered with their little caterpillars, and the first days that our fish took them were strange. Aquatic hatches were sparse, with virtually nothing emerging or riding the currents, yet there was an occasional showy rise. Under the sheltering branches, the fish would take something in a strong swirl. Finally I saw the baby caterpillars in the surface film, black and wriggling and less than half an inch in length, and I realized the fish must be taking them. There was no other explanation for such feeding activity.

Just a half inch of black polypropylene dubbing on a light-wire hook, I thought. *Maybe a dun hackle palmered and trimmed short.*

It worked beautifully for two weeks.

But finally the caterpillars grew too large, with long and dense filaments and multicolored markings, and our fish soon stopped taking them. The fish consistently refused the full-grown worms. Yet there was an occasional rise form showy enough that only something relatively large was taken, and in a young sycamore I discovered there were still a lot of the half-grown larvae.

That explains it, I thought.

The small black imitations worked on such rising fish, and whenever I found a strong rise form downstream from some oaks or buttonwoods, I changed to a caterpillar pattern. It took seven or eight trout that were not taking the occasional hatching sedge, yet were working.

There are seasonal variations in the populations of all insects, especially the terrestrial species, and their role in the trout diet varies accordingly. Some years the bright green inchworms have been extremely important, providing as much as two weeks of superb dry-fly fishing. This season they have been scarce, and the fish consistently refuse imitations, although the gypsy moth larvae have replaced them these past few weeks. The tradition-minded angler is sometimes offended by trout that are selective to caterpillars, since fly-dressing theory is based on elegant insects like mayflies, and there is nothing elegant about an inchworm.

It's not right! Stinson Scott laughed in mock horror one afternoon along the Brodheads. *Turns us into worm-fishermen!*

Dry-fly worms, I agreed.

Similar fluctuations in seasonal populations occur in all terrestrial species, although ants are always found in good numbers. March flies are a perfect example. These little two-winged terrestrials are often found hatching in incredible numbers from their pupal burrows in the banks. They look a little like slender house flies, with rust-tinged legs and pale dun-colored wings folded flat over their backs. Hatches are usually too sparse to trigger a selective rise of trout, but a half-dozen years ago there were so many *Bibio* flies coming off on the eastern rivers that the fish gorged on them. It was the only time I ever watched trout take so many flies that they finally stopped rising altogether, although the current was still covered with the wriggling little insects.

We tied imitations of these *Bibio* flies with black fur bodies and a bluish gray wing tied flat over the body. The furnace hackles were trimmed flat on the back, the wing seated in a drop of cement, and then the hackles were trimmed out under the thorax to float flush in the surface film. The thorax of black dubbing completed our imitations, and they were extremely productive, taking one brown of almost twenty-three inches on a still Brodheads flat.

Other Diptera are distantly related to these little March flies, and include both terrestrial and aquatic species. Craneflies are imitated successfully with both a skittering spider or variant, like the British Red Variant so popular on the meadow rivers of Colorado and Wyoming in my youth. Sometimes a big parachute-style dressing with spent wings is effective when trout are taking these craneflies; and such imitations have long been dressed for fishing the Irish loughs—the so-called Daddy

Longlegs, with its legs imitated by knotted strands of condor quill or pheasant tail.

Similar roles in the trout diet are played by other two-winged genera, like the houseflies, deer flies, snipe and robber flies, soldier flies, grass flies, picture-winged flies, blowflies, tachinas, humpbacked flies, and cowdung flies. It was this last genus that caused an apocryphal incident along the Beaverkill many years ago.

It happened on the famous pool at Cook's Falls, where two hundred yards of tumbling boulder-filled river flow the length of the town. Its iron trusswork bridge is high above the current, and there was a skilled city fisherman taking fish regularly on a famous British wet-fly pattern.

What're they taking? yelled some boys overhead.

Cowdung! the fisherman replied.

There was suddenly a long silence from the bridge. *Hey mister!* It was a shrill voice that ended the stillness. *You ever try horse manure?*

It might have happened, but it is unquestionably true that such minor terrestrials all play a surprising role in the diet of the trout. There were several fishermen I knew well in my Michigan summers who fished imitations of several Diptera flies. They liked a spentwing or parachute-tied Adams, using dubbed bodies of several colors from olive to yellowish tan, and sometimes Gerry Queen had me tie him a dozen parachute Adams patterns with spent wings of junglecock eyes. Queen found them particularly effective on the brushy tree-sheltered headwaters of the Pere Marquette in Michigan.

Queen and I were fishing together on the Little South one morning more than twenty-five years ago, and there had been a sparse hatch of Blue-winged Olives not long before breakfast. The hatch was finished before nine o'clock. There was a brief lull in the rise forms, and suddenly the trout were working steadily again. It was getting hotter, and the rises were coming faster, particularly under the willows and trees. But the fish refused our usual dry-fly patterns, including the Blue-winged Olive that had taken them regularly before eight o'clock.

What are they doing? I asked.

Try this. Queen gave me a parachute Adams with spent wings. *It works sometimes in hot weather.*

But I just tried an Adams that size! I protested.

You ever fish a parachute tie? he asked. *Sometimes it makes a difference on these Little South trout.*

I'll give it a try. It seemed doubtful.

It works! Queen smiled.

I clinch-knotted the big parachute dry to my tippet and placed it over a rising fish. The long dark shadow watched as the fly approached its position, dropped back under the line of drift, hung just under the surface, and finally it porpoised and took softly.

Fantastic! I said. *It worked!*

It was the secret that morning, and we waded slowly up the brushy current, casting to alternate fish that we found feeding. We took sixteen trout between eight and fifteen inches, and it was a remarkable example of the importance of light pattern in the surface film. The conventional Adams employed the same colors and materials, yet it had been rejected through a series of perfect drag-free floats. Only the structure of the parachute dressing was different, its brown and grizzly hackles wound on in horizontal fashion, permitting the hackle filaments to ride flat in the surface film. Conventional dry-fly hackles are wound ninety degrees to the hook shank, and only their delicate tips lie in the surface. It was apparently the light pattern, the halo of illumination that surrounds the fibers and filaments, that was the principal difference between the conventional and parachute ties; and it was the subtle variation in light pattern that apparently took the fish. Such considerations are often basic in imitating the terrestrials.

The Hymenoptera include wasps, sawflies, bees and the ubiquitous ants, which are a primary diet form. Such insects can all play a role in the trout diet, and on the limestone streams of Pennsylvania many anglers swear by bee imitations in hot weather. Bee imitations are quite old in angling history, and the famous McGinty and Western bee patterns are familiar to most fishermen. Some skillful fly tiers have worked out close imitations of honey bees, sweat bees, and bumble bees using clipped bodies of dyed deer hair to suggest their coloring and silhouette. Such dressings typically omit hackle, but employ hackle-point wings tied spent, and they have often proved themselves on selective trout. However, it is the ants that are a surprisingly important facet of the trout diet.

Although there had been times in past seasons, both in Europe and the United States, when our fishing had experienced an extensive rise of trout during mating swarms of ants, my first vivid exposure to the daily importance of these insects came on the famous Penns Creek in Pennsylvania. It was hot for early summer, and Charles Wetzel was dressing flies on his porch when we arrived at the dooryard of his farmhouse.

Charles Wetzel! he introduced himself warmly. *We've been expecting you!*

What's hatching? I asked.

Nothing, he smiled. *It's too hot for fly hatches.*

Fishing poor? I frowned unhappily.

Wetzel sat down again and finished a big lacquer-bodied ant that was half-finished in the vise. He touched its gaster and thorax with clear lacquer until the black silk glistened, and then he hooked it into the porch screen to dry with the others.

Fishing's actually good! Wetzel smiled.

There were almost a dozen big ants lightly hooked into the porch-screen sill.

Fishing these? I asked.

Wetzel nodded and grinned knowingly.

Charles Wetzel is one of the living legends among American trout fishermen. Books like *Practical Fly Fishing* established his reputation as a stream tactician and expert on Pennsylvania fly hatches thirty years ago. Wetzel retired to fish the Pennsylvania rivers of his boyhood, and has long been dean emeritus of the Penns Creek country, deep in the rolling ridges of the Appalachians.

Wetzel taught me a lesson that afternoon.

It was still hot and windy as we locked the car and walked down through the woods to the Spinning Wheel Pool. We started fishing below a tiny feeder that mingled its cold flow with the river. The smooth run held the cold tributary water tight against the rocky tree-sheltered bank. The run lasted two hundred feet.

There were still no hatches.

Think I'll fish a big Gray Variant, I said. *It worked last night on the Loyalsock.*

Wetzel smiled and selected one of his ants. There were no fish working anywhere. The strong currents surged and eddied past our waders, milky and rich with the nutrients of its limestone springs. Wetzel chose to fish the spring run under the trees while I fished my big variant upstream. I found no action except for an occasional fly-sliming smallmouth, but Wetzel began catching trout with disturbing regularity.

Finally I swallowed my pride and waded out to his position in the current. Wetzel placed another cast into the cold currents tight against the bank, where the tree branches sheltered the run. His pale English fly line, patiently dried each night and dressed each morning with mucilin on the farmhouse porch, drifted on the current and paused gently as a fish took the ant under the surface and stopped its swing. The old man raised his rod and a fat sixteen-inch brown fought angrily under the trees. Wetzel had taken six fish in a few minutes.

They sure like your ants! I said admiringly.

Bob McCafferty developed them first, Wetzel corrected, *but the trout in Penns Creek really do like them!*

How do you fish an ant? I asked.

Tight against the bank with a dead-drift swing, he answered. *You try it under that big sycamore over there.*

His old Leonard felt smooth, its action sweetened with countless hours of casting on the limestone streams of Pennsylvania, and I dropped his big ant well under the sheltering branches. It settled into its submerged drift along the roots, and suddenly there was a strong pull.

Ha! I said excitedly. *It worked!*

It was a long-remembered lesson about trout fishing in hot weather. Almost twenty years have passed since that experience, but few anglers realize today that ants are a major factor in the trout diet, since most fly-fishermen are preoccupied with mayflies and the other aquatic insects. All anglers have seen trout taking ants in the hot afternoons of late spring and summer, most without knowing what the fish were doing as they bulged and dimpled softly in the surface film. Mating swarms are more obvious examples of ant feeding.

My first experience with flying ants came on a lake in northern

Indiana, when the bass and bluegills disdained their usual diet of hair frogs and popping bugs to cruise the calm surface, taking the spent ants by the thousands.

Some years later on the famous Gunnison in Colorado, our party encountered a blizzardlike swarm of flying ants. The big rainbows went wild, and we went fishless with our conventional dry-fly patterns. There were occasional pale *Heptagenia* hatches, but the trout ignored these fluttering straw-colored mayflies to gorge themselves on ants. Their dietary heresy drove me indoors to the fly vise.

They haven't read Halford! laughed my boyhood friend Frank Klune. *These Gunnison rainbows don't know they're supposed to prefer mayflies!*

Some trout were taken on our hastily dressed ants, but on the whole our attempts were unsuccessful. We first tried bodies of orange silk wound into antlike shapes and soaked in clear lacquer. It made a shiny head and thorax and gaster, but it resulted in bodies better suited to wet-fly fishing than to imitating the spent ants floating awash in the film. It never occurred to us in those years just after the war that bodies dubbed of fur could achieve an antlike sheen when wet, help float our imitations, and look to the fish like a flying ant riding spent in the film.

But these were fishing episodes with mating swarms of flying ants, and it would be another ten years before that afternoon with Wetzel. Still later those wizards who fish the Letort Spring Run, Charles Fox and Vincent Marinaro, demonstrated to me that ants played an almost daily role in the trout diet. Since those experiences on the limestone streams of Pennsylvania, my ant imitations have been dressed with crewel wool bodies for the wet-fly versions and dubbed fur or polypropylene for the dry-fly patterns. The hackles were simply wound on at the midpoint of the hook shank in the conventional manner on both wet and dry versions. However, about six months ago a letter arrived from Wisconsin with several parachute ants dressed in tiny sizes; and the Borger-style ant was born. Gary Borger is a skilled fly dresser from Wausau, and his little parachute-hackled ants have proved themselves widely over difficult trout on several American rivers. It is a style of dressing ants that has completely converted me in a few short months of experimenting, and I now dress most of my imitations parachute-fashion.

Curious fly-fishermen need not study the *Formicidae* with the zeal of the cantankerous Edward Ringwood Hewitt, who actually ate some ants to discover why the trout liked them. Hewitt concluded that it was the tartness of their formic acid content that appealed to the trout, much like people prefer dry wines or dill pickles or green olives. Of course, we cannot know how ants actually taste to trout—even after Hewitt measured their bitterly sharp taste on the human palate. However, the reason why trout like ants is relatively unimportant, since it may only result from their abundance and availability, and it is obvious that trout do take them greedily on widespread rivers.

Since Hewitt performed his famous taste test a half century ago, we have experienced a steady erosion of trout habitat; and that decline has made terrestrial insects increasingly important in the trout-stream scheme of things. Lumbering, thermal pollution, human and industrial wastes, soil erosion and its turbidity, the leaching of surplus fertilizers into trout waters, detergents and phosphates, and the thoughtless mining of streambed aggregates—plus the effect of pesticides and herbicides on aquatic ecosystems—have all had a grinding impact on our familiar fly hatches.

Terrestrial insects like ants have clearly proved themselves a hardier breed, and as our better-known aquatic hatches diminish, the fish have begun to change their feeding habits. Ants particularly form an increasingly important part of their diet equation. The physical configuration of both winged and wingless ants has considerable effect on the way that ants are exposed to trout in various types of water. Like all terrestrial insects, ants are most active in warm weather and are most often found in trout stomachs on hot, windy days. Their morphology and anatomy have an effect on dressing effective imitations, since live ants neither float nor sink well when they fall into the water.

Ants on quiet currents have a ratio between weight and leg-to-body displacement that means they float barely awash and almost pinioned in the surface film. Most trout stream insects either drown or float on the current like mayflies. The familiar insects either trigger clear-cut fishing with wet flies or are easily visible on the surface film, and disappear in the eager rises of the trout. The fact that wingless ants are not seen swarming and ants drifting in the film are difficult to see, make them notably difficult to discover on the water and to imitate.

Monomorium minimum

Two distinct types of ant feeding typically occur. Fish in quiet pools and flats will dimple and bulge softly to tiny *Formicidae* trapped in the surface film. Trout in broken runs and pocket water generally pick up ants that have drowned. Both rise forms will display the character typical of a sipping rise or the lazy, subsurface swirl of a fish capturing something small that cannot escape.

Grasshoppers and crickets are another matter. These active insects are members of the Orthoptera, and any schoolboy knows they are first-rate bait for fish of many species. Trout are no exception, and I caught my first trout with a grasshopper on a tiny meadow creek in Michigan.

Its pool was sheltered under a giant elm, with the trout lying tight in the run along its roots. Our rods were stiff three-piece models of the pale split cane popular in those days. Such tackle was perfectly suited to dapping a live, active grasshopper over the fish. The first trout came on a windy afternoon in August. Our stalk was made on hands and knees through the alfalfa until we were lying belly-flat under the elm, its roots pressing into our ribcages.

The grasshopper dangled about five feet below the agate tip of the bait rod, and I lowered it slowly between the elm and the sluice-culvert fence. Action was immediate, with a quick splash; the rod-tip jerked and I reacted. The trout was derricked violently up into the elm and hung there, struggling feebly among the branches. Finally we extricated it from the tree and sat in the grass admiring its beauty.

Wild twelve-inch brook trout are still treasured in the adult world, but to my boyhood eyes that fish seemed bigger and more beautiful than any other I have ever caught.

The following summer witnessed my baptism in the dry-fly method. June was a good month and its mayfly hatches were heavy. My first dry-fly trout was taken on a spent-wing Adams along the Little Manistee, but it measured only nine inches. There were bigger fish in August, when there were grasshoppers coming off the meadows. My father gave me several Michigan Hoppers, and he told me to try them at midday when the weather got hot. They worked well; and along the river where the coarse grasses trailed in the smooth current, I caught my first good trout.

My casts floated tight against the grass or ticked into the grass until I coaxed them free. One cast came free and dropped nicely along the bank, and the fly teased against the trailing grass. After three feet of float, the down-wing imitation was suddenly intercepted by a sizable shadow. It took with a vicious rise, and I was into a fat seventeen-inch brown. The meadow water was open and undercut along its deep grass-sheltered banks, and I fought the fish over the sandy bottom there. There were no visible snags or deadfalls. It was easy water to fish, and I was able to handle such a trout in spite of my tremble-fingered excitement.

After my triumph with the grasshopper imitation came a week of August doldrums. The trout were sluggish and fed little in the heat. We could see them lying on the pale bottom, gill-panting as they waited for cooler weather. It was too hot for fishing, and we gathered at the local tackle store to join the unhappy porch-talk about the weather.

You be right nice to your boy! The old-timers were still twinkle-eyed over my big trout. *You be right nice!* they laughed. *Maybe he'll tell you how he caught that trout!*

My father always smiled at such jokes.

He might! he was still pleased about my fish. *I've never caught a bigger one, even during the caddis hatch!*

Talk always returned to the hot-weather doldrums. *No decent rise of fish for two weeks now!* observed the town doctor, and the other fishermen nodded in agreement.

What we need is a mackerel sky, said the ice-cream store proprietor. *Clearing storms and cooler weather.*

That's what we need! nodded an old poacher.

We sure do, observed an old logger who fished the marl swamps at night. *Good weather and a grasshopper wind!*

It was an unforgettable summer.

It ended in doldrums that lasted through Labor Day, and there was no grasshopper wind that season. It was during that winter that I learned to tie flies. My father ordered some Michigan Hoppers after Christmas from the late Art Kade in Sheboygan, and I used his elegant dressings as models. My copies were less than perfect, but the originals were exquisitely tied: scarlet hackle tail fibers cocked from a tufted yellow-floss body palmered with a brown multicolored hackle. Brown turkey feather wings held the body hackles flat along the sides. Stiff multicolor hackles completed the dressings, which were tied on elegant English up-eyes. The Kade patterns were so classic in their proportions that his flies still influence the style of my own work today.

There were a number of successful summers with these Michigan patterns in grasshopper time, and there were other grasshopper summers from New Jersey to Colorado and Montana. The grasshoppers produced some large fish, including a twenty-six-inch brown from the Rock Creek meadows in Colorado.

My imitations were no longer exact copies of the Kade grasshopper prototypes. The yellow floss bodies had been abandoned. Their silk fibers turned dark when wet, and the floss bodies were too delicate and slim to suggest the juiciness of the actual grasshoppers. Dubbed yellow wool worked better. It achieved a fat grasshopper silhouette and did not change color when wet. Between the turkey wings was an underwing of fox squirrel to achieve greater buoyancy, counteracting the absorption of the crewel. These versions worked well for several years, particularly on the less-selective fish of western rivers. But the difficult trout of the Pennsylvania limestone streams were another matter. The old grasshopper patterns worked sometimes, but there were also many refusals, particularly with the larger fish.

Anglers on these limestone rivers had long experimented with grasshopper patterns. Many liked the Michigan Hopper or the better-known Joe's Hopper dressings, and some even tried the fore-and-aft style versions. Charles Fox favored a fore-and-aft grasshopper on his difficult fish of the Letort Spring Run, and these flies had been developed and dressed by the late Ray Bergman. But the selective fish of the Fox mileage on the Letort Spring Run seem more difficult every year, and they began refusing these old-time grasshopper imitations with obvious disdain. New variations were clearly needed for such trout.

Our first attempt was a crude experiment of mine dressed in the Turnaround Meadow on the Letort. Western patterns tied with clipped deer hair had worked well in the Slough Creek flats in the Yellowstone and on the big cutthroats of Jackson Hole. Many anglers were reporting good luck with a Muddler fished dry in grasshopper season. Using these clues as our beginning, I tied some lightly dressed little grasshoppers on sixteen long-shanks, with only deer body-hair and yellow nylon-wool bodies. These baby grasshoppers worked surprisingly well, since it was still early in July, and the live grasshoppers in the meadows were relatively small.

Subsequent refusals and lack of success as the grasshoppers grew larger caused us to rethink our theories.

Maybe we should add the old turkey wings inside the roll of deer hair, I suggested. *It might give us a better silhouette.*

Let's try it! Ross Trimmer agreed.

The silhouette of these turkey wings and trailing deer-hair fibers proved important. The absence of hackle permitted the bulk of the imitation grasshopper and its yellowish body to float flush in the surface film. The principal character of a natural grasshopper is rectilinear and slender, while the hackles of conventional imitations are indistinct and caddislike in form. The flaring deer-hair filaments were trimmed away under the throat of the fly to make sure the yellowish dubbing of the body rode awash, just the way the trout observe a live grasshopper. We studied our new imitations, and they looked promising, with an accurate configuration, silhouette, color mix, and light pattern in the surface film.

Looks good! Trimmer observed. *Maybe we should christen it the Letort Hopper!*

The brown trout liked it fine that week.

We used it with good success on Letort Spring Run, and we interested trout that were not visibly feeding, big ghostlike browns that drifted up from deep holding lies in the watercress channels. But there were disconcerting refusals too. We continued to experiment, and our final versions evolved toward the close of that season when the grasshoppers were fully grown.

Tying bigger imitations resulted in the final metamorphosis. When their deer-hair collars were looped and the working nylon pulled tight, the hair butts flared out like stubby, thickly bunched hackles. These butts were scissor-trimmed in a blocky configuration resembling an actual grasshopper thorax and head. Our earlier versions had these deer-hair butts trimmed close and covered with working nylon, like the head of a tiny bucktail. The bulky version was much better. We tested it that following morning on the Letort, and it worked wonders on the most selective fish.

Its success story quickly spread through the limestone country, and the subsequent Letort Cricket pattern was a logical black mutation of its structural concepts. The cricket imitation was also developed on Letort Spring Run, and the following summer Edward Koch took a brown trout with it that scaled slightly more than nine pounds. It was the best dry-fly trout ever recorded from Pennsylvania waters, and a fitting monument to our theories of imitating the Orthoptera flies.

There was a grasshopper wind late that season too, and it eddied in the marshy bottoms and cornfields along the Letort. Ross Trimmer and I met in the Turnaround Meadow early that afternoon, and we walked down to the bench below the Fox house.

It's a great afternoon for hoppers, Trimmer said.

Grasshopper wind! I agreed.

We started walking upstream into the Barnyard Stretch. Ross was in typically high spirits and regularly stained the water with his chewing tobacco. It was an end-of-the-season pilgrimage along the Letort, and it was a fine autumn afternoon.

We should try the Bolter, Trimmer suggested.

It was his name for a heavy brown trout that had foiled several of us when it bolted and broke off. The fish had been estimated at twenty-two inches. It was working quietly along its watercress cover when we approached under the trees. The steady rise forms were methodical and gentle, but several ugly white ducks squatted on the logjam just below the trout. The barnyard ducks were notorious among the Letort regulars for swimming ahead of an angler and spooking his fish, and two of them slipped clumsily into the pool.

Ross Trimmer crouched low and circled above the ducks. *I'll drive 'em downstream from the fish!* he laughed.

The other ducks waddled along the logs and dropped awkwardly into the current. The trout stopped feeding and drifted back under the brushpile. The ducks swam downstream protesting our intrusion noisily. When they were twenty-odd yards below the fish, I slipped into the stream and edged slowly into casting position. Ross sat on the logs and wiped perspiration from his face, and we waited for the trout to start rising. Five minutes later it came up again.

There he is! Trimmer pointed excitedly. *How's that for a ghillying job on a hot afternoon?*

You make a fine ghillie! I grinned.

Well, Trimmer continued tauntingly, *my part's done and I'm waiting!* The fish rose again beside the brushpile.

Okay! I smiled. *I'll try him!*

The cast was difficult and my first two attempts failed, but finally my grasshopper fell right. Its line of drift was not visible from my position as it teased along the watercress, but I heard a sucking rise and saw its rings push gently into the current, and I tightened and set the hook.

There was a heavy splash instead of the usual rapier-quick bolt upstream, and the fish wallowed angrily under the cress. It probed deep along the elodea channels, and I turned it just short of a deadfall. It bored under the watercress again, and I forced it back into open current with lateral pressure, my rod tip deep in the water. It was getting tired now, and my rod pressure held the trout high in the current, well above the trailing elodea. The light was wrong and I could not see the fish. Suddenly it rolled head down, and its broad tail fanned weakly at the surface. The light rod was turned upside down to equalize the strain of the in-fighting, but in a few minutes the fish surrendered.

Looks better than twenty inches, Trimmer observed.

Henfish! I worked the hook free carefully. *She's beautifully shaped and colored!* The trout struggled weakly in the net.

Well, Trimmer said, *let her go!*

We crossed the little river downstream and walked back along the railroad, wading the shallows again at the Barnyard. Some of the regulars were making a cookfire at the bench below the Turnaround Meadow, and the trestle table under the buttonwoods was heavy with food. Other fishermen arrived just before dark to celebrate the end of the season. The chicken and hamburgers and steaks were cooking, and there was cold beer in a wooden tub filled with cracked ice.

The cookfire died slowly, and there were only scraps of talk as the men sat staring into its coals. Finally the fishing talk died too. The soft whisper of the current murmured in the darkness, and it was time to spill water on the ashes. Several regulars started to file up the meadow path and leave, and there is always some sadness that last evening.

I'll take the shadflies any time! somebody was talking about the mayfly hatch on the Penns Creek.

The shadflies only last a few days, Ross Trimmer replied and propelled a stream of tobacco juice into the dying fire. *But the hoppers last more than a month each summer!*

I'll take the grasshoppers too, Charles Fox nodded. *Grasshoppers and meadow water and a grasshopper wind!*

The season was finally over.

6. The Song of
the Little Stream

Every river has its own music, from the tumbling woodwinds and flutes of a Catskill brook in its scarred bed of glacier-smooth granite and polished boulders, to the serpentine beauty of a tinkling cutthroat creek in the wildflowers of some California meadow high above timberline. Fishing such little rivers has a special poetry in itself. Their tiny riffles and pools have all the challenges found on bigger waters, and their shy trout pose all the familiar problems and add a completely fresh dimension in teaching a careless angler the virtues of stealth and patience. The small trout stream is a matchless classroom for the basic truths in all fly-fishing.

Sometimes spring carries high water with its snowmelt and rain, and bigger waters are often unfishable until later. The small trout stream is our salvation then, and its tumbling crystalline riffles and pools are a welcome antidote for the silt-stained currents of the larger rivers downstream.

Yesterday I was fishing the famous Henryville water on the Brodheads. It was a typical morning in early summer, the fresh new leaves moving restlessly against a wine-dark sky. The sun was already hot three hours before noon, and when the sweet wind dropped, the air became strangely heavy. The cotton-bright clouds grew darker now and the western sky behind the soft, wooded ridgeline beyond the river became almost black. The storm gathered swiftly with surprising strength. It became strangely silent.

The churning, ink-colored clouds were rolling a few hundred feet above the river, yet its currents were still. There was no wind where I was fishing, and there was a terrible crack of lightning. The awesome silence lasted a few moments more, and then there was the drumming sound of heavy rain coming down the thickly forested valley.

It sounds like a freight train, I thought.

The wind struck just before the rain, scattering the fresh buds and bright new leaves into the river like confetti; its ferocity lashed the current. Lightning rattled across the sky, striking the ridgeline behind the mountain, and then it began raining. First it was a heavy rain, drumming into the sullen earth, and then it savaged across the landscape in incredible sheets of driving energy.

The river pearled and darkened, and then, as tumbling freshet tributaries eroded into the clay banks upstream, its swift currents became coffee-colored. Finally the river flowed a dark reddish brown, its musical riffles became surging floods, and its eddying pools became vast cauldrons of seething currents. The fishing was obviously finished.

Miraculously, the storm passed after an hour and the morning seemed almost benign. But the angry river would require more than twenty-four hours to purge itself.

There is a small tributary stream about a mile above where I had been fishing. It drains a small private tract of land which escaped the lumbering that razed these Pocono forests more than a century ago; no giant stumps rise there like rotting tombstones in a tragic epitaph to those years of rapacity. Huge pines shelter its ledgerock pools in deep shadows, dense beds of rhododendron stand on the pine needle benches above the little river, and cold springs dark with *Spirogyna* mosses trickle across the fiddleback ledges into its eddying pools. It is another world locked behind its thickets of alders and willows, and its water joins the main river in a tumbling chute that gives no hint of the poetry hidden a half mile above in the rhododendron.

Many years ago, the owner of the forty-odd acres on the lower reaches of the river built a log-cribbing dam a hundred yards from its mouth. It is silted in with gravel and mud, and its pool is relatively useless. It only succeeds in blocking the autumn runs of spawning brown trout that once used its gravelly shallows.

Sixty feet farther upstream, the little creek has sculptured its own pool below stairsteps of mossy ledges. Its tumbling currents scoured deep into the pale, pea-sized gravel until a foot pool of waist-deep water was formed. Several flat stones slow the currents in the tail shallows into a series of riffling current tongues, and a clump of tag alders shelters the right bank. The pine-needle floor of the forest had absorbed most of the heavy rain that morning, and the little run had pearled slightly. Its smooth currents were noticeably swifter now, and a slight milkiness soiled its usual clarity, but it was still remarkably clear compared to the river.

There was a soft rise in its shallows.

Creeping on my knees where the fiddleback ferns were thick beside the pool, I worked my tiny Henryville Olive under the overhanging limbs until twenty feet of line were out. Sometimes the mere false casting of a pale fly line above a small stream is enough to scatter its trout, and I had changed reels to use a dark brown line that morning. The final cast settled my fly just above the moss-covered stone where the fish had come up, and when it reached the place there was a soft little dimple.

The fifteen-inch brown bolted upstream against the shrill music of the reel, and I let it run against the faint tension of the drag. Forcing it too early could trigger a splashing fight that could disturb the other trout in such a tiny pool. It made several writhing runs the length of the little pool, shuddering and flashing silver in the sunlight at its head, and finally I worked it back.

It came meekly down the pool into the shallows near my feet, until it finally saw me and began to struggle again, but it was too late. The fish surrendered in spite of the cobweb-size tippet, and I turned it gently toward the waiting meshes of the net. It was almost twenty minutes before another trout rose. It took the little Henryville promptly, and there were several others along the tributary creek that morning. The trout were shy and skittish in their minor pools and swift pocket water and riffles, and there was an occasional stream-spawned brook trout too.

It might have been a fishless day without Cranberry Run! I thought.

Years ago the headwater meadows of the Arkansas ran clear and cold, winding through the grassy bottoms between Leadville Junction and the molybdenum mines at Climax. It was one of the finest high-altitude streams in Colorado before a drainage tunnel was constructed to clear the carbonate ore lodes at Leadville and its tailings leached raw into the Arkansas above Leadville. It has run slightly milky since and its fishing is poor, but I can remember some August mornings thirty years ago when it taught me much about brown trout.

It was a treeless meadow of beautiful water with shallow riffles and smooth-flowing little flats, and I fished it regularly through several boyhood summers. It was a stealth-and-cunning river that required staying back from the grassy banks and channels, and sometimes I fished it crouched and kneeling in the slick tail shallows of a pool. It was the kind of small brown-trout river where the knees in a pair of waders will wear out before the seams or felt soles.

It's creep-and-crawl fishing, Frank Klune often observed in those Leadville summers. *You show yourself to those Arkansas Junction browns or make a bad cast and you're finished!*

It is always true of small trout rivers, and it was especially true of those headwaters on the Arkansas. When you started too early after a clear night, the little river was much too cold for good hatches and rises of trout. The stream thermometer could hover at forty-five degrees after a cloudless night at ten thousand feet, and the little Arkansas would seem empty. You could flog its swift little pools from morning until midday without moving anything but the odd six-inch brook trout. Sometimes there were small rainbows and browns too, their parr markings richly mottled on their five-inch lengths, but there was no sign of a decent fish. It was moody fishing on such days.

But some mornings it was hot and windless, with clouds building all day until the Arkansas valley was overcast well before noon, and when the morning was filled with a misting drizzle that lasted only an hour or less, there was a remarkable transformation. The rain often fell for less than a half hour, its silver drops sometimes glittering in the morning sun, and it changed the fishing and everything else.

The swift thigh-deep runs along the undercut banks became alive with hatching mayflies, dark-winged little *Ephemerella* duns that came down the current like tiny slate-colored sailboats. The hatches did not last long. Some came off for only twenty or thirty minutes, and the first mayflies were seldom taken. It was usually some time before a trout actually rose for the fluttering little duns, where they danced beside the grassy banks. It seldom happened until about ten or fifteen minutes had passed, but once the first fish had porpoised, its rises seemed to start the other trout feeding with a quickening rhythm.

Pools that had seemed empty of trout, even when you waded through them just to study their population, were suddenly alive with rising fish. Trout would work steadily along a hummock of collapsed bank or under the solitary bush sheltering the pool. The smallest piece of cover invariably held a fish, and with a well-tied Hendrickson or Red Quill you could catch thirty in a morning. The fish were not large, mostly wild browns from eight to twelve inches, and a fish of sixteen inches was a veritable monster. But you had to fish them with cunning and a workable imitation, and if the trout in a pool saw you before you located them, your chances were finished for an hour.

It's like infantry training all over again! Frank Klune laughed one night over a beer in the Silver Dollar in Leadville. *Belly-flat in the grass or they see you coming and run!*

Ever try casting on your stomach? I asked.

It might help! he admitted.

The most unusual small trout stream I once fished regularly flowed through the colliery town of Sulzbach-Rosenberg in Bavaria. It was a typical German industrial town, with sullen trusswork pit-heads and mining structures everywhere among the houses. Men with coal-blackened faces and goggles returned from work, riding their bicycles or walking through the gritty streets in the shadow of huge pipe systems and ore buckets and expansion loops.

The little stream itself was born in the middle of these colliery structures and conveyor-bucket frames, its limestone springs enclosed in a series of swimming-pool-like excavations lined with tile. It trickled full-blown from the last pool, flowing about five feet wide and two feet deep. Watercress choked the springhead ponds and lined the tiny pools downstream. Its brightly spotted trout held tight against the cress, lying in plain view in most places, and I fished it several times when I was staying at the mill owner's house on the hill.

It was still in the years of the German occupation, and the mill owner had been imprisoned at Ingolstadt by the American military authorities for his political activities before the Second World War. His estate at Sulzbach-Rosenberg had been confiscated, and it served as the billet residence of the American military governor in the Amberg region.

Joseph Hackett was a retired artillery officer who had been seriously wounded in the Italian mountain campaigns that followed Anzio, and in the years we lived in Germany, he was the resident officer in the military government at Amberg. Hackett was primarily a hunter, and he particularly liked the winter drives for roe deer and *Wildschwein* and hares, but the retired major had also liked trout fishing since his boyhood on the coastal rivers above San Francisco. He invited us to fish the Lauterach from his lovely quarters at Sulzbach-Rosenberg, and we arrived in the April darkness after a long drive from Nürnberg over the winding cobblestone roads of northern Bavaria.

Dinner was excellent in the dark paneled dining room above the town, with sweet soups rich with sherry and venison taken from a shooting platform above Schmidsmülen three weeks earlier. The lights of the colliery glittered in the winding little brook below the terrace where we stood with our cognac.

It's got trout, Hackett pointed.

That's remarkable, my father said. *It's not easy to keep a stream clean in the middle of a factory!*

You can if you want it badly enough, Hackett agreed.

Are the fish large? I asked.

No, Hackett answered, *but I've got a problem in Amberg tomorrow morning, and you can fish it yourself before we get started for Schmidsmühlen.*

I'll try it, I said.

It was an unusual little stream, and its trout proved extremely shy. The first few times I tried fishing them, they scurried upstream under the watercress in terror. It was a problem in extra stealth and cunning. The banks were sometimes soft and trembling, and they telegraphed each clumsy step along the trailing grass, flushing the trout from their shadowy lies. Dropping a cast too harshly sent them scuttling under the banks like chickens. The flash of a ferrule in the sunlight frightened them. The bright ballet of a yellow fly line working in the sun was like a warning siren to these trout, and the partial silhouette or shadow of an angler was enough to spook them too. Each tiny pocket was a fresh exercise in shyness and stealth, teaching the ancient lessons about trout that are the heart of small-stream fishing.

There was the tinkling little riffle under the rumbling ore-carrier system, where the fish held tight against thick beds of watercress and chara. The trout could see an angler silhouetted against the sky there, but if the fish were approached carefully from behind the willows it was possible to take them with a well-placed nymph. There was one quiet bend where the fish were lying upstream in a shelving hole, and an angler crouching low could take them easily with the dry-fly method.

It was interesting that neither grazing dairy cattle, nor the daily passing of housewives, workmen on bicycles, and children seemed to bother the fish. The rumbling ore-buckets passed over them steadily without noticeable interruption of their feeding. Yet a careless step along the boggy banks, the brief exposure of a fisherman in a patch of sunlight, or a glimpse of his silhouette would frighten the trout or make them stop working. It was necessary to fish them from behind tree trunks and bushes, stalking each pocket on hands-and-knees in the grass.

It was archetypical of small-stream fishing.

There is no question that all boys who want to become fly-fishermen should spend their apprenticeship on such a small stream. Its lessons are taught gently. The fishing itself is not too difficult, yet it firmly demonstrates what it takes to catch shy trout.

The axioms of small-stream fishing are unmistakable. You must approach each pool and run cautiously. You cannot show yourself to the trout and expect them to keep feeding without alarm. It is amazing how many neophytes fail to realize this basic fact. There is a small pool on Spruce Run in New Jersey that I pass regularly every weekend on my way to fish the Brodheads. It has a concrete weir that blocks the current, and the flow plunges through a hatch. There is a deep, eddying pool below the hatch, about the size of the average living room, and it is regularly stocked by trucks from the rearing ponds at Hackettstown. There are always a few fishermen fishing there on those April mornings, and sometimes as many as ten are found standing on the weir. It is incredible to watch these men fishing for trout in plain view, only a few feet away from fish that can obviously see them. Only a foolish truck fish, with its lifetime of being coddled and fed in a hatchery, would ever accept their wares. Successful trout fishing depends entirely on presenting your fly to the fish before they have detected your presence, and that comes only with a mixture of skill and knowledge thoroughly leavened with patience.

Stealth and cunning are the primary rules. Your approach must be muffled, and you cannot plunge through the streamside willows and alders without alarming the fish. Your final presentation must be gentle, placing your flies softly on the current so the trout will not be frightened. Careful fishermen will most often approach from downstream on a small river, behind skittish trout, and usually conceal themselves behind willows and tree trunks and grass. It is valuable to watch the reaction of the fish, either taking the fly readily or refusing it. Such lessons are not easily learned on larger streams, where you seldom see the trout at close range.

The little stream at Sulzbach-Rosenberg in Germany was a perfect laboratory for such lessons. You could study the fish easily, watching them in the eddying currents beside the watercress, or the smooth runs over ochre-colored gravel. You could watch them wait to intercept a dry fly, or work their fins nervously in anticipation, drifting sideways to take an approaching nymph. Sometimes they inspected the fly and refused it, and sometimes they did not even bother to inspect its drift. The fish were shy and selective, and imitative patterns were usually best. Fly pattern and presentation and leader diameter were all critical; and concealing myself stealthily behind the willows, I once dapped a dry fly in a deep little run below the house and took a fat two-pound brown—an incredible trophy on such a tiny stream.

It was a priceless lesson, like the morning more than thirty-five years ago on the Bear Creek in Michigan. There were several fish in the run below the hatchery there, and I was fishing with live grasshoppers. Although the fish did not scatter in panic when we fished them below the hatchery weirs, we did not catch many either. Above the hatchery there was a zone where fishing was prohibited, and a line of floats marked its boundaries. There was always a school of good fish cruising inside the protected zone above the dam, and these trout never left their sanctuary.

They're pretty smart, my father said.

Must be some way to coax them outside those floats, I said. *Try a grasshopper right beside the barrier!*

The fish were too clever for such tactics. Their schools cruised just short of the barrier of floats, completely ignoring a live grasshopper fished only inches outside their protected zone. They eagerly took one thrown inside the floats, unattached to our tackle, but they refused to come outside even for a grasshopper kicking freely in the surface film.

It's incredible, I laughed. *They'll take a grasshopper two inches inside the floats, but they aren't even tempted by one thrown a few inches outside!*

And they'd probably ignore one on a hook if we fished it ten feet inside the no-fishing area! my father added.

They're smart! I agreed.

It was the same below the hatchery weirs and in the flood channel that protects the hatchery pens from high water. You could feed grasshoppers to the trout and they took them readily, yet they ignored one fished on conventional hooks and leaders. The trout were able to detect which baits were floating free and which were on hooks until we impaled our grasshoppers on small hooks and fished delicate nylon tippets. It was a lesson impossible to learn on bigger streams, yet a brook will reveal such secrets generously to both boys and men, once they have learned stealth and patience and observation.

Small streams and bait are unquestionably the best place to teach a boy about fishing. Success is important in the early years, and grasshoppers and worms will produce results. Fish in the creel are important in the beginning, before the perspective of time swings the pendulum of our attitudes toward the character of our sport and places so little value on the primal instincts in fishing that we prefer to release our catch. Fishing bait in a brook is a perfect genesis for this process, and its techniques are a lexicon of basic truths. The beginner can learn much from his minor triumphs and large frustrations, the lessons we all learned in our early years on small trout streams.

Such lessons wear well in later seasons. You learn that on a small stream it is sometimes better to approach upstream instead of down. The trout always lie facing its currents, and because the blind spot behind their heads lies where the trout's forward-looking eyes cannot focus, you can approach them more easily from below. You quickly learn that freshly stocked hatchery trout are more gullible than their wild cousins, and that stream-bred fish are alarmed at any sudden movement, even the sight of rods and lines moving against the sky. You learn to keep low, creeping and crawling when there are no bushes or tall grass to conceal you on a meadow brook like the one where I began fishing in Michigan. These days on hard-fished waters, it is wise to keep low in fishing over selective trout on any size stream, and I know many men on eastern rivers who wear out the knees in their waders first.

But all the charm of fishing a small stream is not confined to our learning years. There are moods when the cacophony and leg-wearing power of a big river become oppressive. Difficult wading and countless double hauls can erode both body and soul. Big water holds big trout, and there is a period in the maturing in the career of every fisherman when he is addicted to the pursuit of trophy-size fish. Once you have that fever in your blood, it is a passion that drives you beyond good judgment. Your behavior is so irrational that only a turned ankle, the casting arm stiff and aching from big-river casting, or swollen knees hurt in a fall among slippery rocks will help you regain your senses. After such aberrations, it is time for the tranquillity of some unpretentious brook, and its peaceful music will restore your perspective.

It is impossible to define a small stream. It is difficult to establish a yardstick that fully measures character and tells us that a brook becomes a river once its width equals a specified number of yards. It is never a matter of mere physical size, but rather one of temperament.

Some rivers never quite escape the small-stream character of their headwaters. Their character never quite matures, even though they sometimes demand long casting. Our big western spring creeks and the larger limestone streams of our eastern mountains are such waters. Their world is entirely composed of silk-smooth runs and glassy flats, quiet eddies and slow-flowing pools, all with reasonable bottoms of sand, gravel, and small stones. Such streams are intimate and ingratiating, perfect water for a fisherman whose psyche is tired of the abrasive moods of big water. There are also tumbling little mountain streams, and meadow creeks from New England to the high-country parks of our western mountains, that have these friendly moods—while the Henry's Fork of the Snake is perhaps the best example of a large river with a gentle character.

Other small streams are only miniature versions of their bigger relatives. Their currents are surprisingly deep and strong. Although they are relatively minor rivers, their character is marked with heavy water, treacherous ledges, and a bottom butter-slick with algae. Such streams offer the troublesome problems of big water without its big fish.

The techniques and equipment for small-stream fishing are both simple and demanding. Like William Schaldach in his poetic book *Currents and Eddies*, I believe that technique is a shallow word with a cold and disciplined ring, and in our myopic fascination with methods and tackle, we often lose sight of the fishing itself. Yet some technique is necessary in trout fishing, particularly in the world of the small-stream trout.

The rod should be relatively light and short to handle the fine tackle and brushy casting required. Modern rod builders have supplied us with a whole catalog of light fly rods that did not exist when Bergman and Schaldach were writing. Since casts are short, leaders are relatively delicate, flies are rather small, and small streams are so tightly enclosed in foliage, fly rods of five and a half to seven feet are perhaps best. Such rods will weigh from one to three ounces, with the tip calibrations and action suited to fine three- to five-weight double-tapered lines.

Leaders should be no longer than nine feet, since some casts will measure only twelve to fifteen feet, and a little line should extend beyond the tip guide to turn the leader over. Tippets should never exceed 4X, and 6X and 7X diameters are still better.

There are a number of small fly rods on the market which are short and relatively light, but if they are balanced with six- and seven-weight lines, they are not truly light-tackle rods for trout. Their calibrations are not really useful for fine nylon diameters below .007, and such lines fall too hard on thin water over skittish trout. Since we spend a considerable amount of time crawling on our knees in small streams, particularly in meadow water, a slightly longer rod is desirable to keep the backcast free of the weeds behind. Such problems are common on the British chalkstreams and the limestone streams of Ireland and the United States. My experience on such waters indicates that rods of seven to seven and a half feet are best in solving such problems, provided they are matched with three- to five-weight lines.

Casting itself presents difficult problems on small waters. Big rivers provide us with unlimited space and few worries about our backcasts. Fishing a wooded stream is good medicine for everyone at times. Small water will not forgive a careless presentation, and its pools and runs are filled with the pitfalls of streamside grass, bushes, clustered willows, overhanging limbs, alders, trees, and brushpiles. Such waters are a galaxy of obstacles and hazards, and a careless backcast unerringly finds itself in the highest branches.

Avoiding such troubles depends on your casting and the skills implicit in fishing small water. It is surprising how much a small, brushy stream can improve and broaden your casting techniques. The common roll cast, the switch pickup, and the sidearm casts delivered both normally and from the backhand position are all critical in your bag of tricks. These techniques are thoroughly discussed in the earlier chapter on casting, and their methodology is the ticket for brushy little rivers when normal casting simply will not work. However, the entire spectrum of casting skills will not succeed on small rivers unless you develop a special sense of the little stream and its secret rhythms.

It is essential to remember that the closer you approach a pool, the more likely it is that you will be discovered by its fish. Big water itself tends to eliminate this problem. Forty- to sixty-foot casts work at sufficient distance to keep you well outside the trout's cone of vision, but too much time on big water creates some bad habits. Little rivers shrink these distances and demand a better perspective. Coming from big water, it is common to approach a promising run and watch the frightened wake of a twelve-inch brown scuttling for cover. It is humiliating to realize that a stealthy approach might have creeled such a fish, but it is typical of fishing a small stream. Patience and humility are its lessons.

When working a small stream in low water, experienced anglers will use their eyes constantly. Our powers of observation are primary skills. Fish will often be visible at surprising distances in relatively shallow waters. Such foraging trout are dangerously exposed to kingfishers and ospreys and other predators, and are hair-trigger wary. They are extremely difficult to catch without a careful strategy.

Both fly and leader must be chosen carefully, and the leader supple and well soaked. Enough left-hand line should be stripped for a quick shoot, with false casting held to a minimum. The stalk must be executed skillfully. Crouching low, the fisherman creeps into range. The cast must be perfect, because a poor presentation will frighten the fish. It must be focused on the trout lying farthest downstream toward the angler, and if it is hooked after a successful cast, it should be played gently to coax it away from the others. Sometimes a hooked fish can be led downstream with enough subtlety that its fellow trout remain unfrightened, and after resting the pool briefly, the angler can try the next one upstream. When several such fish are captured, any angler can be justly proud. His skills are clearly demonstrated, and his hunting instincts have not been entirely dulled by the cacophony of city life.

Surprisingly small places can shelter trout in midsummer, and the angler must remain alert. He can never permit his powers of observation to wane. The smallest holding lie beside a stone or log, the tiny spine of darker water in a brief riffle, and the shadowy place along the bank can always shelter a trout. Deadfalls, small ledges, undercut grassy banks, overhanging trees, and sunken roots are all potential holding places. Small tributaries and springholes entering the stream are obvious lies for a small-stream trout. Hot-weather fish often gather in surprising numbers where such cold water trickles in among the fiddlebacks and moss. Their water is crystal clear and cold. Properly mined, such springholes and tributary flows can prove a rich lode of trout in late summer, and I can think of at least fifty such places from the Adirondacks to Maryland, and in the dog days they can salvage a session that might have proved fishless.

There are countless memories of small-stream fishing. Some I have written about in books like *Remembrances of Rivers Past*, and there are other memories from New England to the Rocky Mountains. Sometimes these little rivers produce surprisingly large trout, like the big rainbow taken on

Blacktail Spring Creek in Jackson Hole, or the big browns that had entered Fairy Creek in the Yellowstone in late September. There was the huge brown that Frank Klune once took along tiny Busk Creek, above Turquoise Lake in Colorado, and another I once captured at the tumbling mouth of Stiles Brook in the Adirondacks. Big fish were also discovered on several spring creeks in Montana, and I once took a fine four-pound rainbow on the Wise farther west in the Big Hole country. Although big fish are rare on small waters, they are not impossible.

Some memories are filled with mixed emotions. Shortly after the Second World War we were staying in the beautiful little hotel at Hintersee in the Bavarian Alps. It was not a fishing holiday, but I had stowed some tackle in our luggage, and one morning I tried the swift little tributary that feeds the lake.

It was a quiet meadow stream that flowed from a mountain valley on the alpine threshold of Austria. Its meadows were bright with snow buttercups. The village on the Austrian border had a charming onion-topped church and white stucco houses with steep, sheltering roofs of thick sod, their balconies bright with geraniums. The little stream flowed over pale gravel, and I took several fish in its upper meadows near the border crossing. There was a deeper pool where the meadows ended, and the stream wound into the dense pines. It surrendered a lovely wild brown of fifteen inches, which carried its fight into the weedy shallows downstream. The trout came to the net grudgingly, and I was admiring its beauty in the morning sun when I discovered a grisly echo of the war.

My God! My heart thudded wildly.

The bright gravel shallows concealed a rotting gasmask and the corrugated canister of the German army, and downstream in a bed of watercress was a corroded *Wehrmacht* helmet just above a silt-covered skull. These grim artifacts of the war were a threnodic climax on that pastoral morning in Bavaria.

But there were other mornings on other streams when their pianissimo moods remained untarnished, and I have memories with the melodic perfection of a flute solo. There was a hot morning years ago, that I fished down John's Brook when the unseasonable weather had reduced the Ausable flats to shimmering panfish ponds. It was cool hiking up the mountain just after daylight, and there was dew in the cobwebs across the trail. The brook danced and plunged below in its bed of giant glacier-polished boulders, its roar surprisingly large where it echoed among the rocks. High on the shoulder of the mountain, I finally climbed down and fished back to Keene Valley, working the swift runs and churning little pools. The trout were eager, taking pale little Cahills readily when an angler remained hidden, and I took forty or fifty small brook trout in a morning. They were beautiful, brightly jeweled little fish that I released, and just above the village I took a fine thirteen-inch brown from a dark pocket between the boulders. It was hot when I finally reached Keene Valley, and I walked proudly toward the Spreadeagle with the brown trout in my wicker creel.

Good morning? Jeffrey Norton was waiting.

It was beautiful! I wiped my forehead sweatily. *How about an ice-cold beer before lunch?*

Perfect! Norton nodded happily.

You know, I sipped my beer thirstily, *there's something special about fishing a small stream like John's Brook.*

You're right! he agreed. *It's like getting out of the city—it really strips the fat off your soul!*

Norton was right.

7. Field Problems
in Fishing Lakes,
Ponds, and Reservoirs

I t was getting colder when we finally reached Tarryall, and climbed past the half-rotted buildings of the ghost town into the sprawling foothill basin beyond. The Colorado trout season was only a few days old. Spring weather is unpredictable in those altitudes and the sky was an ominous ink blue beyond the 10,000-foot saddle of Kenosha Pass. The sky seemed to promise fresh snow, and its sullen clouds obscured the mountains.

The road climbed past the south shoulder of the Tarryall Dam, and wound back toward the rocky shoreline of the reservoir.

Blizzard coming! Dick Coffee growled. *Just our luck!*

The squall was still fifteen miles away.

Doesn't look good, I agreed unhappily, *but we might as well stay and try the fishing anyway!*

You're probably right. Coffee set the brake.

The raw wind gusted around the station wagon now, scattering sand across the windshield.

Must be forty degrees out there now! I shivered.

Several bait fishermen had been scouring the bottom with night crawlers and canned corn. Two of them had several small hatchery rainbows on a bass stringer, with one good brown trout.

Think flies will work in a blizzard?

Let's find out what they've been eating, I suggested. *Maybe they'll let me check the stomach of that brown.*

Might tell us something at that, Coffee said.

We walked down to the bait fishermen with the stringer.

You will probably think I'm crazy, I began an awkward preamble. *But I'd like to clean your brown trout for you.*

Must be crazy! one laughed.

Why'd you want to clean that brown? the other fisherman parried suspiciously. *What's in it for you?*

Simple, I explained. *I get to check his stomach.*

Check his stomach? he said warily.

See what he's been eating, Dick Coffee explained.

The bait fishermen looked at each other and shrugged.

Okay, they said, *but we still think you're crazy!*

He is crazy, Coffee growled.

My knife sliced easily from the ventral fin toward the gill structure, and I stripped the entrails free, cutting away the pectorals. Carefully incising the stomach membranes, I forced its contents into my hand.

What's he been taking? Coffee asked.

Dragonfly nymphs, I replied. *Don't have anything like them in my fly books—have to make some!*

You tie flies, Coffee laughed. *I'm going fishing!*

Good luck! I rummaged in my gear.

It was getting darker before I finished the first nymph, and the meadow basin above the reservoir was already ink-colored with the advancing snow squalls. Three fat muskrat-bodied nymphs lay on the car seat. The big flies were weighted with soft fuse wire, and the rod was strung with a fast sinking line. The first big snowflakes hit the windows when I left the station wagon and walked shivering toward the reservoir.

It was snowing fiercely now. The far shoreline was obscured in the swirling flakes. Dick Coffee became a shadowy figure standing in the water, and the thick flakes covered the ground quickly. The snow hit us wetly in the face and encrusted my shooting glasses.

You want one of these nymphs? I yelled.

Coffee laughed through the falling snow. *You really think it'll make a difference in this blizzard?*

Might! I waded out into the shallows.

They're not going to take anything in this weather! he grumbled. *They won't take what I'm using either!*

That fish I checked was full of nymphs, I said.

The other fishermen were leaving, their parkas covered with snow.

Winter takes a spring vacation, Coffee growled unhappily through the driving flakes. *Summer is two weeks of bad skiing!*

It's not snowing where the fish are, I laughed.

That's real comforting! Coffee shot a long cast angrily into the snow. *Maybe we should join 'em!*

My first cast worked out and virtually disappeared into the snow squall, and I let it sink twenty counts before starting the retrieve. The fly came back clean and I did not feel it touch bottom. The next cast was permitted to sink twenty-five counts, and when I retrieved, it ticked into the gravel twice and there was a wisp of algae trailing from the hook. It had come back a little too deep.

Let it sink twenty-three, I thought.

The laborious hand-twist retrieve had worked the nymph back only six or seven turns when there was a sudden pull, and I was into a good rainbow. It bolted deep into the lake and jumped, falling heavily in the swirling snowflakes.

Can hear him, Coffee laughed, *but can't see him!*

It was a sleek eighteen-inch rainbow, and I took several more around a pound while the squalls covered us with their wet, swirling flakes. When the snow stopped and it started clearing, the trout stopped taking too.

Well, Coffee said, *that was pretty strange.*

The sun came out behind the Mosquito Range, and the fresh snow glittered with a terrible brightness. *They sure liked the dragonfly nymphs,* I laughed, *and they took in the worst of the squalls.*

Let's get back before we're snowbound, he said.

You're right, I agreed.

It was not unique on our western reservoirs, particularly at about 9,000 feet, where the water temperatures stay cold and a fish would starve if it waited for the optimal feeding temperatures of sixty-odd degrees. We had fished a shoreline partially sheltered from the wind, and the trout were bottom-feeding on a shelf between the steep gravel banks and the dropoff into the deep water of the reservoir. Since most of the food in a lake or impoundment is found in its shallows, and the inlet acreages and weedy shallows along the north shore were torn with surf and whitecaps, we had chosen the only feeding grounds left that morning.

There was a similar morning years ago on San Cristobal Reservoir in southern Colorado. It is an enlarged lake, with a dam to raise its water level, and its outlet flowage is the source of the storied Lake Fork of the Gunnison.

Jim MacKenzie, Evert Tom, and Dick Coffee were camping with me on the west shore of the reservoir one opening weekend, and we went out early in two rowboats from the livery below our campsite. The inlet shallows enter the lake through thickets of half-drowned scrub oaks and willows, and the water was slightly roiled with snowmelt. However, these shallows were the first to warm on those cold spring mornings, and MacKenzie and I rowed to fish them first. Coffee and Tom rowed east to fish below the cliffs, where there was a big shelf about fifteen feet down. The underwater shelf was still in the morning shadows.

The reservoir was a little high with snowmelt and the brushy inlet shallows were like a mangrove swamp.

Let's row into those brushy lagoons, I suggested. *The sun's been warming them for several hours.*

What about the cliffs? MacKenzie asked.

No. I shook my head. *It was pretty cold last night, and it'll take another two or three hours before the water warms up enough for the fish to work that deep.*

You're the boss, he said.

We fished among the drowned willows and scrub oaks with big

dragonfly nymphs, and the results were remarkable. My cast cropped a fat muskrat-bodied nymph along the roots of some willows. It had barely started to sink when a two-pound rainbow darted out from the shadows and took my nymph savagely. We located thirty-odd fish that morning, and landed more than twenty. It was almost noon when we stopped and worked down the east shore to the shelf under the cliffs where Coffee and Tom were fishing. Their boat was anchored a good backcast from the cliff face, and they were fishing deep on the bottom shelf with the cast-and-countdown method and fast sinking lines.

Any luck? MacKenzie yelled.

We've got ten or twelve, Coffee answered, *but they only started taking an hour or two ago—it was perfectly slow in the beginning!*

After the sun had been on the water a while, I said, *and it finally got warm enough for them to feed.*

That's about it, Tom said.

Well I'll be damned, MacKenzie laughed. *It went just like you said it would!*

Sometimes it does, I smiled.

The inlet and outlet flowages of most lakes and impoundments are prime fishing areas. Their currents carry food and oxygen. The shallow waters are primary nurseries in the diet chain of the trout, sustaining both still-water and current-loving insects. Usually the fish in the outlet flowages are larger than the others in a lake, and the outlets are a prime area for prospecting unknown waters. Both beaver ponds and man-made impoundments still have their original streambeds relatively intact in their bottoms. These are the prime holding zones in such waters, except when the fish are foraging out across the shallows, and the cast-and-countdown method is common practice in such places. Ray Bergman wrote about such wet-fly tactics in his book *Trout*, and they are common from Cranberry Lake on the Oswegatchie in New York to weedy Henry's Lake and the sprawling Crane Prairie Reservoir in our western mountains. It is a basic lake-fishing technique.

Other prime fishing in the inlet shallows can often come from mayfly and caddis hatches endemic to their ecology. Several times on big western reservoirs, like Tarryall in Colorado and Hebgen in Montana, there has been superb fishing with imitations of tiny midge pupae. Such rises of fish are often distinguished by small rise forms coming in a steady rhythm from cruising trout, and no visible insects on the surface. There are also fine hatches of *Tricorythodes* and *Callibaetis* flies, as well as larger still-water mayflies, like the big *Siphlonurus* drakes that hatch in August and September. Sometimes there are huge hatches of the little, many-brooded mayflies, drifting like seeds on the surface or herded against a downwind shore by the breeze. The fish take them greedily at such times.

They take them so steadily that they seldom pause between rises, Bud Lilly explained in West Yellowstone last August. *The boys who fish Hebgen regularly call them the gulpers.*

They're gluttons! I agreed.

Such fishing is much better when there is a light wind riffle on the water, since the fish cannot see the boat or the leader easily. The fish cruise boldly, taking the naturals in a steady, sequential rhythm. Sometimes a fish will put five or six rises together in a line, and then abruptly change direction or return along its original feeding path.

Since the water levels in reservoirs can fluctuate widely, their draw-down and high-storage levels can strongly affect our fishing. Reduced levels of water can concentrate both fish and their diet forms, but too rapid a draw-down cycle can decimate fly life as the water recedes. More water can pose other problems and opportunities.

During the years when I was involved in the design and construction of the Air Force Academy in Colorado, we regularly fished Eleven-Mile Reservoir on the South Platte. One spring there was an unusually large accumulation of snow in the mountains, and the water officials at Denver decided on extensive water storage at Eleven-Mile. The sagebrush flats became vast shallows with the snowmelt flooding behind the dam, and one day in those flood bottoms Evert Tom and I had a picnic with big rainbows that had come in from deep water to feed on the hatching *Poecillus* beetles. We took them with dry-fly beetle imitations in the Letort style, with a light riffling wind putting delicate patterns on the water, and it was tricky fighting a big rainbow on light tackle in the brush.

Terrestrial hatches and mating swarms are often a factor in lake and reservoir fishing. Jenny Lake in the Jackson Hole country gets a big swarm of mating carpenter ants each spring, and its cutthroats and hybrid cutthroat-rainbows come to the surface to feed on the winged-ant swarms. Bob Carmichael once operated the little tackle shop at Moose Crossing on the Snake, and he loved the carpenter-ant season in Jackson Hole for its exceptional dry-fly sport.

Fantastic! He rumbled good-naturedly. *Big fish working on top when the wind's down on Jenny, really big fish of six to ten pounds.*

Sounds good! I said.

Several years later I witnessed these mating swarms, and on a still evening in a quiet bay I located several big cutthroats. Hundreds of winged ants struggled helplessly in the surface film, and the big fish patrolled the flat water, sipping them in leisurely fashion as they swam. There would be a series of rises in a lazy sequence, establishing the direction of a swimming fish, and I would place my big ant imitation slightly ahead of where I thought the fish would show next. Sometimes a fish would change direction and disappear in a porpoise roll. Several of these fish went eighteen to twenty inches, and the trophy-size trout were a hybrid of five pounds and a magnificent cutthroat that scaled eight.

Beaver ponds pose all of the problems found on man-made reservoirs in miniature. The old stream channel lies in the bed of the impounded water, and the fish use it for shelter, foraging out at times in the flooded shallows for food. New beaver ponds often prove quite fertile. The fish trapped in their flooding find their world suddenly multiplied, and the rotting vegetation fertilizes the water chemistry. Fishing is often unusually good in the early months of a beaver pond, before the decaying deadfalls and willow roots tip the scale, leaching their acidity into the ecosystem. Fishing declines as the pond becomes more acid, and a similar life cycle obtains on newly completed reservoirs.

Fishing beaver ponds is relatively simple. Unless there is an obvious fly hatch, dry flies are secondary to wet flies and nymphs. Sunk flies are usually best in a lake since they are retrieved and cover more water. Staying out of sight is still perhaps the cardinal rule. It is often possible to fish a small beaver pond from below its stick-tangle dam, keeping totally out of sight behind the barrier itself. It is seldom advisable to wade into a beaver pond unless it is quite large. Both the detritus stirred free during wading and the disturbance of the wading itself can frighten the trout. You should also be wary of their bottom quality, since it is possible to sink into the muck and become trapped. Bright weather will usually find the trout hiding in the drowned channel of the pond, or working along its deadfalls and willows. Cloudy weather and twilight coax the trout to cruise and forage more boldly, and the fisherman can find them anywhere.

Beaver pond fishing is pretty much the same from New England to the Pacific, although the country changes character. Sometimes high water forces us to return to the beaver-pond fishing of our boyhood, and we rediscover its rewards.

There are many memories of beaver ponds, from Maine to the Pacific Coast, and the mind returns to them from time to time. There were tiny cutthroat ponds in the Wasatch Mountains of Utah, and the superb fishery for brook trout and Wyoming natives high in the headwaters of the Gros Ventre, on the remote Darwin Ranch. There were huge brookies in the beaver-pond bottoms of the Snake in Jackson Hole that Bob Carmichael would tell you about if you passed muster, drawing a scraggly treasure map on the back of an envelope. Colorado boyhood summers were rich with beaver-pond fishing, and I remember their jewellike beauty along Rock Creek, Tennessee Creek, Willow Creek, and Empire Creek in the Leadville country. Sometimes these little ponds were generous, and I remember the time that Frank Klune and I caught such creelsful of big brook trout from the beaver ponds on Empire Creek that we were arrested and accused of poaching a lake belonging to the mayor of Leadville. No one believed such fat brook trout were found anywhere in the valley except his private preserve at O'Brien's Lake.

There are other western memories too, like the great blue heron on a Montana beaver pond in the Big Hole country, and the trumpeter swans nesting in another beaver-stick sanctuary in the Yellowstone. Beaver-pond fishing is good in the cutthroat headwaters of the Frying Pan, and I once had superb sport on a nameless pond in the Lime Creek country.

But there is beaver-pond fishing farther east, too. There have been some fine evenings on the headwaters of the Brule and the Namekagon and the Wolf in Wisconsin. Robert Traver has eloquently described his love for beaver-pond country in the Upper Peninsula of Michigan, in books like *Trout Madness* and *The Anatomy of a Fisherman*, and I have had some good sport in such ponds on the watersheds of the Tahquemenon and the Two-Hearted and the Fox. The late Paul Young used to tell me about the big trout in some beaver ponds on the Driggs, but he died before he provided the map he had promised. Some men refuse to make maps or reveal beaver ponds as priceless as a secret woodcock cover, and even brush out their jeep tracks on logging roads and trails leading into their favorite brook trout places.

Our eastern mountains have beaver-pond fishing too. There are good ponds in the Allegheny country, especially in the trout streams tributary to the Susquehanna, and I once had fine sport on the little Sawkill near Milford, fishing a reach of water that had belonged to the late Gifford Pinchot. There are sometimes fresh ponds on other Pocono streams, like the Wallenpaupack, Buck Hill, Blooming Grove, and the Shohola. Such acid swamp-dark waters produce brook trout with such bright coloring that their mottled flanks look like a jeweler's tray lined with rubies and turquoise and opals.

There are similar secrets in the Catskills and Adirondacks, and I particularly remember the bright coloring of the brook trout in a beaver pond on the Bouquet. Vermont and New Hampshire and Massachusetts have their beaver-pond secrets too, and I once fished a pond in Maine just after daylight. Its fish were dimpling the still surface and mist still lingered over the deadfall bogs at its inlet. The scrub pines were almost black against a flame-colored dawn, and it lingers in the mind like the exquisite watercolors that Winslow Homer painted at Mink Pond in his Adirondack summers.

There are other axioms worth remembering in fishing lakes, ponds, and reservoirs. Sometimes a lake has two distinct parts connected by a shallow neck of water, and sometimes it has little-known reefs and shallows lying well out from its shoreline. Such places are both spawning grounds and rich larders of baitfish and fly hatches. Fish cruising between deeper sections must pass through such connecting shallows, and fish from those pelagic zones come there to feed in morning and evening. Perhaps the most classic example that comes to mind is the channel connecting Lewis Lake and Shoshone Lake in the Yellowstone, and the crocodile-size browns that migrate into its lagoons and riffling shallows in early October.

Other examples are more typical, and years ago I made fine catches of brook trout at Maroon Lake, near Aspen, in Colorado, hiking up from the tourist area at its outlet to the narrow arm that connects the lower lake with its upper acreages. Its water was icy in late spring, but you could wade out waist-deep into the connecting shallows and cast across to the immense rockslide that had come down from the shoulder of Pyramid Mountain over the centuries. Fishing a weighted nymph, it was possible to move a fish on virtually every cast when they were coming well, and for several evenings I supplied an entire seminar group at the Aspen Institute with fresh trout. It was a contribution valued far beyond my participation in the panel discussions during that conference at Aspen.

Reefs and shallows well out in a lake are a priceless discovery, and their location should be marked carefully in the mind. Landmarks on the shoreline can be used, lining up a tree or house on the east and west boundaries of the lake, and two other bench marks on the north and south. The intersection of these axes clearly defines the location of such shallows in midlake, and it is a method familiar to men who troll deep for lake trout and landlocked salmon in New England. Such knowledge is extremely valuable. Perhaps the most striking example of such fishing in my experience did not come on American waters, but occurred this past spring while I was sea-trout fishing on Lough Currane in Ireland.

Paddy Donnelly was my boatman, and his weathered face echoed the character of the Killarney mountains above the lake, dour and brooding except for his bright eyes and a smile as welcome as a brief few minutes of Irish sunshine between squalls of misting rain at Ballinskelligs. Lough Currane looked as dour as a lead-sheathed coffin when we pushed off in his boat from the rocky landing below his thatch-roofed cottage.

Fine morning! Paddy said.

With this rainy weather? We shook hands warmly.

Paddy nodded happily. *'Tis a fine soft morning we'll be having, with good hatches of Bibio flies and olives, and just enough wind for a crust on the water.*

Where do we fish? I asked.

Donnelly pointed across the water toward the middle of the lake, where the ruins of a tenth-century structure stood dark against the water and the barren mountains beyond.

We'll be starting along the Church Island, he said. *We'll be fishing the shoals and skerries and smaller islands, drifting along with the wind.*

Okay, I smiled, *let's try it!*

The old boatman took us across the lake, his leather-wrapped oars creaking in their wooden locks, and finally he turned the boat broadside into the light wind. It riffled the water and took us gradually down the shoreline of the Church Island.

What flies should I fish? I asked.

Donnelly searched my fly-books thoughtfully. *You may fish as you like, but for these Kerry sea-trout in Lough Currane we like a three-fly cast—with the Watson's Fancy on the point, and the Bibio and Black Pennel on the droppers.*

We'll try them! I said.

My experience with multiple casts and dropper flies on brown trout has not been noticeably successful except in strong, boulder-strewn rivers, and I had little faith in fishing three flies on waters as popular and hard-fished as Lough Currane. However, there was a quiet competence about Paddy Donnelly with none of the poetic exaggeration I had sometimes found in other Irish ghillies, and I quickly trusted his judgment. The three flies were rigged and waiting.

Should I start? I asked.

Donnelly studied the western shoreline across the lake, and then swivelled his head to look back toward the ruined church. *No*, he shook his head quietly. *Just a few yards more.*

We drifted farther down the lake, the boat holding broadside into the wind. *Start your fishing now*, Donnelly suggested.

The first two casts produced nothing, but I began fishing them out methodically, laying successive casts in a clockwise fan pattern as we drifted along the island and stripping them back quickly. The third cast went out on the wind and settled, and I had just started to strip it back when there was a huge splash well out in the waves.

Fish! I yelled excitedly.

The reel protested as it surrendered about fifty yards of line, and a large sea trout cartwheeled wildly across the water.

Four pounds, Donnelly watched with a practiced eye, and finally reached for the net.

The fish jumped several times before I worked it back, and fought its deep circling below the boat until we netted it. The boatman killed it with a quick rap of the priest, unhooked the fly carefully, and patiently untangled the dropper flies. Eager to start fishing again, I worked the line out with a quick series of lengthening false casts. Donnelly smiled and studied the shorelines.

Wait, he said. *Too deep here.*

The old boatman rowed briefly and studied a beehive cairn of rocks on the island, glancing back to check its alignment with his cottage across the water. Finally he nodded with satisfaction, and I started into another fan pattern of casts. Less than a dozen casts had been fished out when there was a wrenching strike and the reel shrieked again, drowning the cries of the foraging gulls. This fish did not jump and it felt stronger, and it was a long time before it surrendered.

Eight pounds! Donnelly exclaimed when it came over the gunwale, wrenching and twisting in the boat net. *'Tis the finest sea-trout of the season!*

He cradled his oars and pumped my hand warmly.

The fishing lasted about two hours, with the old boatman navigating to each reef and shallow in Lough Currane expertly, telling me with a series of nods and gestures when to start and stop fishing. It was an impressive performance, demonstrating his exact knowledge of the shape and position and depth of each shoal and outcropping, and its precise relationship to several landmarks on shore. We caught another half-dozen fish between three and four pounds before they finally stopped rising, and when we reached the boat landing below his cottage I rummaged through my duffel for the silver flask of Tullamore whisky.

The boatman accepted the dram cup gratefully.

Paddy! I raised the flask in the misting rain. *We'll drink to you and your skills—that was the best display of knowledge I've seen on any lake in the world!*

Donnelly smiled and drained his Irish whisky.

8. Tactics in Fishing
the Tail Waters

I t is a surprisingly large region, encompassing almost 60,000 square
miles in Arkansas and Missouri. It is a forested plateau of ancient
mountains, the only extensive uplands between the Rocky Mountains
and the Appalachians farther east. Its valleys are deeply carved into
limestone and sandstone formations laid across the bottoms of vast
Paleozoic seas, its geology honeycombed with caverns and flowing springs.
Its rivers flow alkaline and rich toward the Arkansas, Missouri, and the
sprawling Mississippi itself. It is a region filled with paradox and surprise.

Its boundaries are defined in terms of both climate and geography. Its
cool spring-fed rivers have evolved thirteen species of fish unique to the
Ozarks, species that have never migrated into the tepid silt-laden streams at
lower altitudes. Ozark rivers like the Buffalo and Current and White were
once among the finest free-flowing rivers in America, teeming with
smallmouth bass.

The White has been dammed in the gargantuan reservoirs at Table
Rock and Bull Shoals and Norfolk, but the Buffalo and the Current still
run free through their forests of white oak and hickory. Both flora and
fauna in these valleys are unusual. The Ozark Plateau marks the western
limits of the great forests that once covered the eastern United States. Its
western foothills are a threshold for the prairies that rise steadily toward the
Rocky Mountain escarpment. The Missouri flows along its northern
borders, the southern limits of the Pleistocene glaciers that chilled the
prehistoric climate of the Ozarks without sculpturing their hills, and the
semitropical alluvial bottoms of the Mississippi lie toward the southeast.
Such factors play a surprising role in the Ozark country.

Their hills provide a sanctuary for a community of plants and animals that no longer survive in adjacent regions. The birches found much farther north still thrive in the cool hollows along their rivers and spring-fed creeks. Beech trees have their primary range in our eastern forests, yet they are plentiful in the moist river bottoms of the Ozarks. Lichens commonly found in the subarctic tundra and caribou barrens around Hudson Bay are also found on the north-facing escarpments. Water tupelo and buttonbush, plants more common in the bayous of Mississippi and Louisiana, are found in Ozark swamps and sinkhole bogs. Scorpions are common in the parched barrens of Texas and Oklahoma, but populations are surprisingly found in the Ozark plateau, particularly where rocky formations are exposed to the strong summer sun.

The Ozarks have been a paradise for hunting and fishing since the Osage tribe lived in its western foothills during the hot months of midsummer. French traders penetrated the Ozarks from both the Missouri and the Mississippi, leaving their heritage in the names of many places. Zebulon Pike explored its northern drainages enroute to the Rocky Mountains, but it was Henry Schoolcraft who first explored the Ozark Plateau in 1818, barely fifteen years after the Louisiana Purchase.

There are still wild turkeys and whitetail deer in the Ozarks, and ruffed grouse fill the April woods with their drumming. The spring is a time of flowering redbud, wild azalea, dogwood, may apples, and bloodroot. Baitfish like the duskystripe shiners and mottled darters and bleeding shiners are spawning. Mock orange and blue lobelia and fragrant verbena bloom among the thickets of rhododendron and buckthorn in the river bottoms. Strange subarctic species like false bugbane, northern bedstraw, delicate white camas, arctic harebells, and *Phytidium* mosses are also found in the northern foothills; and farther west the Ozarks are a prelude to the high plains. The bunchgrass glades are bright with prairie species like purple beardtongue, slender liatrus, Missouri primrose, puffball brier, sunflower, prairie rose, Indian paintbrush, tickseed, and most surprisingly —spiny clusters of prickly-pear cactus, with their incredibly yellow flowers in springtime.

Although the Ozark Plateau remains remarkably wild, it too has suffered over the past century. French trappers and fur traders encouraged the Osage tribes to exploit the colonies of muskrats and beavers, and began the iron and lead mining that continues today. Hunters from Tennessee thinned out the turkey and deer, and eradicated the buffalo and elk. There are still a few bears, and sometimes there is the report of a puma in the high brush country in the headwaters of Archey's Fork or the Buffalo.

Farmers came too, crossing the Mississippi from Kentucky and Tennessee. Their methods were tragically primitive. Some girdled the trees to kill and clear them for growing corn. Others believed that the rich humus of decaying leaves and pine needles on the forest floor prevented the growth of grass, which it unquestionably did, and they burned it off each spring. Burning-off is an agricultural practice still found among the primitive Araucan populations in Chile, and the cultivation found among the hill tribesmen of India and Nepal, but it is surprising to learn that such foolish theories were still found on the American frontier in the nineteenth century. Burning the humus destroyed the principal source of organic matter sustaining the flinty soil of the Ozark Plateau, and when their farms failed to prosper, these men soon turned to lumbering in the hills.

The first timber cutting took place on the northern drainages, because rivers like the Gasconnade and Osage and Big Piney could transport the logs to the Missouri and Saint Louis. The cutters took the shortleaf pine first, moving steadily south as the mature trees fell before their gleaming axes. Once the conifers were exhausted, the lumbermen turned to the stands of white and black oak, hickory, and black walnut. These trees were used in mansions from Saint Louis to New Orleans.

When the railroads pushed west from Chicago and Saint Louis and Kansas City, timber from the Ozarks was used for ties and trestles. Tie whacking became the principal industry. The gandy dancers needed timber for thousands of miles of trackage, and although no one has tried to calculate how many railroad ties cut from the Ozark forests went into construction of the Santa Fe or Union Pacific, tie whacking remains a major industry in the region. Between poor farming technology and the rapacity of the timber cutting, the Ozarks suffered badly from erosion in the last century, and its clear rivers often ran milky with each rain.

But Ozark ecology reached its perigee on the threshold of this century. Logging had reduced the primeval forests to ragged stands of scrub timber. Spring burning had finally transformed the hillside farms into gravelly wastelands where little grew except weeds and blackjack oak and sumac. Game was growing scarce and the fishing was poor in the Ozarks, completely unlike the centuries when the Osage tribes migrated there to hunt and fish and escape the summer heat of the Oklahoma prairies.

But the last half century has seen the stubborn renaissance of the Ozarks, starting with the creation of the national forest system by Theodore Roosevelt and Gifford Pinchot. The Ozark National Scenic Riverways Act of 1964 has ended the depredations and dam building of the Corps of Engineers. Farming and population have both declined.

Most of the Ozark rivers are flowing clear again, and their waters are the true glory of the region. Fishermen will forgive the flat Ozark summits and relatively sparse forests their monotony, understanding it is that very monotony that makes the remarkable rivers and limestone springs possible. The precipitation these forests need to flourish, but can no longer retain after the timbering and humus burning, is quickly absorbed into the porous limestone and sandstone formations. It trickles deep into the sinks and fissures, gathering in enormous water-filled caves. Ozark springs are so spectacular, and so uniform in their steady outpouring of flow, that the region abounds in old wives' tales about the origins of their waters.

Some natives believe the water comes from the Great Lakes through labyrinthine channels in the earth itself, while others believe that seepages from the Mississippi are the source. Some even believe that the Ozark springs come from the snowmelt of the Rocky Mountains, and I once met an old man at Big Spring who believed its flow actually came from the icy depths of Hudson's Bay.

What about the salt water? I smiled.

Don't care about things like that! The old man stood watching its turbulent currents boiling up at the bottom of a dolomite bluff. *It comes underground from Hudson's Bay!*

Perhaps you're right, I said.

Big Spring feeds the Current in Missouri with the incredible volume of one billion gallons each day, almost enough water to supply the entire daily needs of New York, and its remarkable flow is almost equalled at Mammoth and Greer Springs.

Although exotic explanations seem equal to such dramatic outpourings of water, these remarkable Ozark springs are fed by nothing more exotic than slowly collected rainfall and snowmelt. Although annual precipitation is only a moderately heavy forty to fifty inches, the hydrology of the region is remarkable. Springs are relatively simple things, but their simplicity removes none of their mystery. Precipitation gradually soaks into the decaying humus, soil, sand or gravel that covers the surface topography. Below these surface materials lies a porous geology, generally composed of sandstone or dolomite or limestone in the Ozarks. The seepage first gathers in the aerated layers, where the porous rock holds both air and water. It finally collects in the zone of saturation, where the rock pores are completely filled. Between these two levels lies the water table, which generally follows surface formations. But when the water table lies above the surface, lakes and marshy acreages are formed; and where erosion or fissures in the bedrock intersect the table, the birth of a flowing spring is the result.

The total number of Ozark springheads is unknown, but it is agreed that the region is one of the most prolific aquifers in the world. Literally hundreds of Ozark springs produce between five and ten million gallons a day, and there are ten springs in the region that flow at the rate of more than fifty million gallons. It perhaps was Ward Dorrance, in his book *Three Ozark Streams*, who perfectly described the poetry of these Ozark springheads:

> It is a world of springs and swift rivers. Everywhere there is a leafy sound of rising, running, bright waters flowing. If we should place our ears to the ground we might hear the fertile pulsing of a giant subterranean heart.

These remarkable springheads feed a network of equally remarkable rivers, carving their courses deep into the layers of sedimentary dolomite and limestone. These rivers have been famous for their float trips and smallmouth bass since writers like Jack London, and the equally celebrated Ozark Ripley, described them in the decade just after the First World War. Missouri rivers with exceptional smallmouth fishing include the Meramec,

Gasconnade, Black, Big Piney, Roaring Spring, Jack's Fork, Elk, Eleven Point, Spring, Pomme de Terre, Osage, and the remarkable Current, which is perhaps the most famous bass river in America.

Arkansas has a series of equally famous smallmouth streams, like the Little Osage, Mulberry, Ouachita, Caddo, Strawberry, Crooked, and the Middle Fork of the Saline. But it is the wild little Buffalo that remains the most famous of these Arkansas bass streams, particularly since the Corps of Engineers completed three major dams on the sprawling watershed of the White.

It was the crystalline White that started the traditional Ozark float trips, ranging from day trips lasting a few miles to floats lasting several days. The guides prepare superb lunches on the day trips, with cookfires on the gravel bars, and the commissary boats travel ahead on the longer journeys to set up the overnight camps. The White is remarkably clear, flowing swiftly in its narrow shallows and lingering in placid half-mile flats with every pebble showing on the bottom. The floats start at daylight, with night mists still hanging over the current, shrouding the weathered bluffs above the river. The cold springs that enter the river leave their fingerprints of watercress along the bank, chilling the main currents downstream. The river is always surprisingly cold even on the hottest days, and its chill is quickly felt when the sun leaves the river in late afternoon. Darkness gathers swiftly in the narrow valleys, and the warmth of a dying cookfire is welcome after the supper dishes are scoured in the sand.

The White runs much colder now, and its smallmouth bass are scarce until the river reaches Calico Rock, almost fifty miles below the dam at Bull Shoals. The Corps of Engineers dammed the White in 1951, adding the Table Rock Dam upstream seven years later. The Norfolk impoundment on the north fork of the White had already been completed in 1944, and the icy tail waters of these dams have changed the character of the White completely. Its temperatures seldom reach sixty degrees, and average about fifty-two degrees through the year. The native smallmouths have migrated downstream in search of warmer currents, and trout have largely displaced them. Trout hatcheries have subsequently been built below the Norfolk and Greer's Ferry impoundments, and almost 500,000 browns and rainbows are stocked each season. Records show that the fishery is averaging more than four hundred trout better than four pounds each season, and its record fish is a full seventeen pounds.

Similar man-made fisheries have evolved in the cold discharges of the Greer's Ferry reservoir on the Little Red River, the Greeson reservoir on the Little Missouri, and the Ouachita impoundment on the Ouachita fifty miles southwest of Little Rock. But the crystalline White below the Norfolk and Bull Shoals dams remains the principal trout water in the Ozarks, perhaps the finest tail-water fishery in the world.

Our earlier chapter on the ecology of dams discussed their interruption of rivers and their impact on their community of life, both in the impounded waters behind the dam and in the tail waters downstream.

Spillways tend to warm a river too much for trout, and penstocks that release their effluents too deep in the lake can make its tail waters too cold for good fly hatches and trout growth. Many years ago, I took a half-dozen browns in the icy tail waters of the Taylor Dam in Colorado, and found them as emaciated as poorly conditioned pickerel. Some impoundments vary their discharges so much that the temperatures vary radically downstream, offering high winter-cold currents one week and midsummer conditions only a few days later.

One twilight along the White, with the river running swift and full, Dave Whitlock and I fished the shallow edges and quiet eddies behind the deadfalls and snags. There were no fly hatches emerging, and we fished the shelving edges where the currents dropped off into the deeper holes. The fish were holding on the edges of the strongest flows, away from their usual lies in the primary current tongues, and we fished our Muddlers on fast-sinking lines.

It's a little like worm-fishing in a spate, I laughed. *The fish leave their usual holding places, and you find them lying along the edges and behind things that break the flow.* We hooked fish simultaneously.

Just like we're kids again! Whitlock laughed.

The fish continued to take our flies until dark, intercepting the deep bellying swing along the bottom gravel. Each fish took with a sullen pull, like a spring smallmouth taking a crayfish, and when they stopped taking we walked back happily toward the cookfire.

It was different just after daylight. The river flowed low and clear with the penstocks closed, its currents as smooth as a chalkstream. The night mist drifted on the downstream wind, and the silken flow was disturbed by dozens of dimpling trout. The river was warmer with less water coming through the dam, and the trout were rising steadily to the tiny *Tricorythodes* flies in the shallow flats.

Muddler time is over, Whitlock said.

You're right, I agreed. *Last night it was big flies fished on the bottom, and this morning its tiny stuff on 6X!*

It's not unusual! Whitlock nodded.

We fished over highly selective trout until it was time for breakfast and the next day's float, taking several sixteen- to eighteen-inch rainbows on our tiny hen-winged spinners.

That's great fishing, Whitlock said.

We walked back up the gravelbar to breakfast.

It's some change of pace, I agreed happily. *Bottom dredging on big water at nightfall and midging on a shallow flat only twelve hours later—over the same fish on the same pool!*

Tail-water fishing is like that, Whitlock shook his head. *You can get early-season conditions or low-water problems of midsummer any time of year.*

Or time of day! I laughed.

That's right, Whitlock agreed. *It all depends on whether they're storing or releasing water.*

It's tough to switch tactics like that, I said.

You mean big Montana nymphs and bucktails in the morning, Whitlock grinned, *and English chalkstream problems that afternoon?*

Exactly, I laughed.

Such radical variations in flow are a common problem in fishing our tail waters, both in terms of their changed temperatures and their changes in current and depth. Tail-water anglers with experience are always prepared to fish on the bottom, like big-water fishermen from the Klamath to the Yellowstone, or cope with smutting trout on a river that has suddenly dropped when the floodgates of an upstream dam are closed.

Closing the hatches can also affect fly hatches, since a reduction of flow can increase river temperatures enough to trigger a fine rise of fish. There was one afternoon on the White when the river was a swift torrent of water chilled in the depths of Bull Shoals. There were no rises and nothing worked, even the productive sowbug imitations.

But toward evening, the flow lessened imperceptibly and it felt slightly warmer against my legs. My stream thermometer read fifty-seven, six degrees warmer than it had registered an hour before lunch. The river dropped steadily until riffles and pockets emerged from its swift, poker-faced current. It still seemed empty of trout until I saw the first porpoising rise along a deadfall. There was another rise a few feet downstream, and still another quickly followed.

There was a strong swirl in the shallows, and a hatching sedge barely escaped the splash. Soon there were other caddisflies fluttering along the smooth current, and the fish were working steadily to the *Rhyacophila* hatch. We collected a few and found they were a species commonly found in Pennsylvania and Michigan, another relict population the glaciers have isolated in the Ozarks. The solution was a sparsely-dressed Woodcock and Green fished upstream to rising fish, and I took a dozen fine trout before dark. The following night the steady midday flow of the river was not reduced, and we waited in vain for the hatch.

Looks like it's no cigar, I said finally.

Afraid you're right, Whitlock agreed. *Why do you think we had good hatches last night and nothing now?*

Don't know, I waded ashore. *Maybe the dropping water and slightly warming temperatures caused the hatch last night.*

And the high water turned them off? he suggested.

It's possible, I said.

Another effect that impoundments may have is to magnify the relative acidity or alkalinity of their tail waters. New dams often have a short-term fertilizing effect on otherwise acid habitats, improving the fertility of the water downstream. However, decaying vegetation and accumulating silts and detritus in a reservoir will eventually reverse this fertility with their acids. Building dams on alkaline rivers like the Ozark streams can magnify their alkalinity below the dams, gathering minute particles of silt rich in carbonates and bicarbonates and phosphates in their depths. Such accumulations can enrich a tail-water river beyond its original water chemistry, resulting in improved fly life and fish populations, and the Island Park reservoir on the Henry's Fork is a singular example of such alkaline magnification. Another factor is increasing population of slow-water insect life, particularly the minute Diptera larvae and pupae, which often pass through the penstocks unharmed.

Twice I have seen exceptional rises of trout to these diminutive insects on the South Platte in Colorado. There are four reservoirs of the Denver water system on the river: impoundments like Cheeseman, Eleven Mile and Antero dams on the South Platte itself, and the Tarryall impoundment on Tarryall Creek. These reservoirs are known for their rich midge populations, and my experiences with midge pupae coming through the penstocks occurred in both Deckers and Eleven Mile canyons.

Beno Walker, Jim Wallace and I were fishing the Deckers Canyon below the Cheeseman Dam one afternoon, with the reservoir low and the river at minimum flow. Its pools were pondlike and still when we came down the canyon trail to the river. When the evening shadows began to reach across the river, the currents quickened imperceptibly with a slightly increased discharge from the dam, and suddenly the fish were dimpling everywhere.

What are they doing? Beno Walker yelled.

I'm not sure, I shouted back. *Whatever they're taking, it's something small and there's a lot of it.*

You think it's terrestrials?

No, I yelled. *Flying ants can cause this kind of steady feeding, but we could see a swarm of ants.*

What is it then? Walker waded upstream.

Well, I watched several fish dimpling in a lazy rhythm. *It could be midge pupae coming through the dam.*

What should work? Beno asked.

It won't be Humpies or Renegades, I laughed. *Maybe something black on a twenty or twenty-two hook.*

Lets me out, Beno shook his head.

The solution was a black midge pupa on a twenty-two hook, fished in the surface film on a .005 tippet, and I took almost thirty fish before the gathering darkness forced us back up the canyon trail to the car. Similar patterns of cause-and-effect occurred a few weeks later on the South Platte below Eleven Mile Reservoir. However, on that day the river was running high and cold with discharges from the dam, and no fish were working anywhere. The water was perfect for chilling a picnic bottle of Piesporter, and after an hour of fishing along the bottom with nymphs, I gave up and walked back for lunch. The wine was cold and good, perfect for washing down the freshly cut wedges of Gouda and cold sandwiches, and I finally sat watching the current with a cup of coffee freshly brewed over a fire of dried beaver cuttings.

There's a rise! I thought aloud.

The river had dropped slightly during lunch, and although no hatching flies were visible on the water, the number of rises increased steadily. The current continued to fall, and it ebbed slightly while the trout settled into a steady pattern of gentle rise forms. It soon became a fine rise of fish that covered the pool.

Time to try them, I whispered to myself.

It was a productive afternoon, and I took almost forty decent fish before it was time to drive back to Colorado Springs. It was a little like the rise of fish in the Deckers Canyon, yet it was different too. The Deckers water had been extremely low, and the partial release of water had carried thousands and thousands of tiny Diptera through the floodgates. The heavy discharge through the Eleven Mile Dam had been saturated with tiny pupal forms all day, but its temperatures were too cold for the fish to take them. When the gates were partially closed, the river dropped and grew warm enough to accelerate their metabolic rhythms, and the trout fed greedily on the tiny flies.

Another intriguing effect of dams on our trout streams is also found on the South Platte above Eleven Mile. Its large population of big rainbows cannot migrate downstream to spawn, and they run upstream into the serpentine headwaters of the South Platte at Hartsel. The spawning run occurs in April and May, delayed by the altitude of 7,000 feet, and it would normally occur during unfishable water levels except for the impoundment at Antero Junction.

The spring thaw usually discolors these headwaters with snowmelt, but the Antero Reservoir acts as a huge stilling basin for the first weeks of the runoff. It collects the turbid snow water behind its earthworks, permitting the South Platte to flow clear and surprisingly low during its spring spawning run of rainbows. Fishing them is a little like stalking, since they are often clearly visible in the shallows, and expert Colorado fishermen like James Poor and Peter Van Gytenbeek find weighted nymphs are best. The Platte is still cold at those altitudes in late spring, and working a fly slowly along the bottom is deadly. Poor likes a pair of stonefly nymphs of his own design, imitating the big *Pteronarcys* flies at two stages of their nymphal growth. Van Gytenbeek likes a roughly dubbed shrimp imitation, heavily weighted and dressed on ten and twelve hooks.

It was on the South Platte tail waters that I took a lucky trophy-size brown one spring, and the fish was the result of a good natured challenge delivered at lunch in the Hartsel Hotel. We had finished a morning's fishing on the Big Ranch below town, and had left our gear at the main house. The challenge was delivered by my old friend Philip Wright, and his badgering began when we ordered our hamburgers. Donald Zahner and Charles Myers, the fishing writer for the *Denver Post*, had happily joined the fun before we ordered dessert.

It's a real test of skill, Wright explained teasingly. *It's a big brown that lives right here in Hartsel.*

He holds under a log below the bridge, somebody added.

Breaks them off! another voice said.

You have to accept a challenge like that! Myers laughed and drained his Coors. *Remember the Code of the West.*

That's right! Zahner insisted.

The waitress arrived with apple pie and coffee. *Ridiculous!* I shook my head. *The fish is probably gone!*

No, Myers said. *Somebody lost him just last week.*

You're chicken, Zahner chided.

But I've left all my gear at the ranch, I parried their joking helplessly. *My waders and everything!*

You've got your flies! Wright said gleefully. *Your fishing vest is still in my car!*

And you don't need waders in the meadow! Myers added.

But I don't have my rod! I said.

No problem, Zahner finished his pie with a flourish and ignored the check. *You can use one of my rods.*

That's some handicap! I grumbled.

You can't chicken out now, Wright cackled. *We've got everything you need for this fish—you can't back off!*

Zahner paid my check and pushed me outside. *Zahner,* I protested weakly, *how did I get into this?*

You're the fastest gun in town! Myers grinned.

Code of the West! Zahner laughed.

We walked down to the bridge with a surprising crowd from the hotel bar, and I rigged Zahner's rod with a fresh twelve foot leader tapered to 6X.

Your rod's handicap enough, I handed Zahner his tangled leader, *without giving me that mine-shaft cable for a tippet!*

He knows how to hurt a guy! Zahner winced.

The river winds down a gravel shallows from the highway bridge, carving a deep hole in the bend downstream. There was a huge deadfall wedged in the deepest currents, its silvery branches throbbing in the flow. The open meadow offered no cover, and a standing fisherman is clearly silhouetted against the sky. It was impossible to get close enough to cast without an infantry-style approach, and I crawled stealthily through the bunchgrass. The best cast was across the grass, angled slightly upstream to get the maximum fly swing along the fallen tree. The river flowed deep and smooth along undercut banks.

You sure there's a big fish here? I asked them.

It's true, Myers nodded.

The odds of moving the fish seemed astronomical, but I rose to one knee and started false casting, once the nymph and leader were properly soaked and sinking. The fly worked out and settled well above the log, the belly of the line falling in the grass, and the current worked it deep along the shelving gravel.

It stopped its swing under the deadfall. *Well,* I thought wryly, *that does it for today—it's snagged on the log!*

But there was a huge splash, and a spade-size tail broke water along the deadfall as a heavy fish forced the straining rod into a tight circle. It bolted upstream into the shallows, and I worried it with a nagging pressure from below. The fish chose to fight both me and the riffling current for several minutes, and its strength had weakened when it turned back to its holding lie under the log. It was a fatal mistake, and I turned it short of the snags, working it back with the current.

The remaining few minutes of the fight were routine, although we had forgotten a landing net. The crowd gathered behind me when the big brown finally surrendered in the gravelly shallows, and I lifted it briefly from the water before releasing it.

That's a good fish! somebody said.

He'll go twenty-two or twenty-three inches, Charles Myers shook his head in amazement. *He's huge!*

Never thought you had a prayer, Wright laughed.

Makes two of us! I sighed.

Putah Creek is a tail-water fishery sixty miles north of San Francisco. It was created after the construction of the Berryessa Reservoir. Its currents are like a wine-country chalkstream, rich in weeds and fly hatches and trout. Its trout are hard-fished and selective, and each season it surrenders a few rainbows between six and eight pounds on flies. There are also some fine brown trout, sleek and a little silvery on a rich diet of scuds and sowbugs, but these fish are caught less frequently.

Last fall I fished the little Putah with Hal Janssen and David Inks, since a week of heavy rains had forced the steelhead rivers over their banks and into the vineyards. The runoff was being stored behind the Berryessa Dam, and although the creek was a little milky, it was surprisingly low and fishable. The current was so imperceptible that the first big pool below the dam was a still mirror surrounded by weeds, its flow suppressed in the thick beds of coontail. During normal water levels, several channels left the pool, with good trout holding normally in the flowages between the weeds. The pool itself was a smooth strong-flowing reach of water with its fish facing the current.

Well, Janssen laughed. *It's fishable enough.*

It used to be stream fishing, Inks shook his head in agreement, *but tonight it's almost like a lake.*

How do you fish it in higher water? I asked.

It has heavy hatches of small mayflies and caddis, Janssen replied, *and we let our little imitations swing with the current to suggest their swimming nymphs and pupae.*

What about damselfly nymphs?

When they're gathering to hatch along the weeds, Janssen said, *it's one of the best big flies we fish.* He searched his fly books and gave me one of his pale green damselfly nymphs.

What have they been taking? I asked.

We've been getting them on Pheasant Tail nymphs, Inks said, *and on the little Puyans' Hare's Ear patterns.*

They're still hatching, Janssen pointed.

Let's try them, I said.

It was difficult wading out through the densely matted weeds, and we took up positions slightly back from the open water of the pondlike channel. Janssen watched me shiver with a sudden chill when I reached a casting point waist-deep in the weeds.

It's pretty cold for a sunfish creek, he laughed.

The evening wind eddied down the valley, riffling the surface of the stream and carrying the muffled roar of tailrace water from the dam.

It's cold enough all right, my teeth almost chattered as the icy chill penetrated through my waders. *It's amazing how a dam tail water can turn a warm sunfish creek into an ice box!*

Hal Janssen dropped his nymph upstream along the weeds, let it settle a few seconds, and started a slow hand-twist retrieve. Its left-hand rhythms had barely started when I saw Janssen raise his rod, and a good rainbow cartwheeled out in a series of jumps.

That didn't take long! I yelled.

It's always like that on Putah, Inks laughed. *Janssen fishes it just like a vacuum cleaner!*

Good thing he releases them! I said.

Their predictions were correct, in terms of both fly patterns and tactics. We fished the little Pheasant Tail nymphs, their bodies weighted with copper wire, and Puyans' Hare's Ear imitations over a foundation of delicate fuse wire. The flies were tiny, dressed on eighteen and twenty wet-fly hooks, and they sank readily after our leaders were wet enough. Our tactics were simple enough. We merely fished a series of clockwise and counterclockwise casts from each position, letting the nymphs sink and fishing them back slowly.

David Inks took a fish on his third cast, working his nymph in the outlet channel below an immense tangle of fallen trees, and on my third cast I hooked a fifteen-inch brown.

Didn't take him long to get the drill, Janssen shouted.

The fish was superbly conditioned, and it fought me stubbornly until it finally surrendered, and I could skate it toward me across the surface of the weeds.

Okay, I protested. *I've got this fish, but how do I release it from this nightmare of weeds?*

Throw it! Janssen laughed.

You can't throw a fish back! I shouted back. *You're supposed to let them go gently.* Inks was laughing across the lagoon.

That works when you can reach the water, he interjected, *but you're ten feet away and up to your scuppers in weeds!*

So what now? I groaned. The trout hung limp in my left hand.

It's an old Putah Creek method, Janssen explained. *It's a little like a lateral!*

Football lateral? I choked back my laughter.

But gently! Inks advised.

We took twenty or thirty fish between us that evening, fishing our tiny nymphs in a patient fan pattern, and letting them sink a few seconds before starting a retrieve. It looked easy when you had the problems solved, but we met another fisherman on the path who had gone fishless.

You guys get your limits? he asked.

We did pretty well, Janssen admitted, *but we put them all back.* The other fisherman looked puzzled and frowned.

What did you use? he asked. *Salmon eggs?*

No, Inks smiled, *flies.*

That's funny, the fisherman shook his head. *I tried a Royal Coachman and Rio Grande King, and it didn't work.*

Better luck next time, Janssen smiled.

It was Russell MacGregor who first introduced me to the Lackawaxen, which was a fine smallmouth stream when Zane Grey lived near its junction with the Delaware. The Wallenpaupack Reservoir a few miles upstream from the Lackawaxen, which dammed the Wallenpaupack Creek into a sizable lake, completely changed the Lackawaxen and its ecology. It has become a fine trout stream over the past thirty years, with a large population of rainbows in its fast-water mileage, and some huge browns in its pools. MacGregor introduced me to the superb reach of water where the tumbling little Blooming Grove reaches the Lackawaxen. We fished it each evening from his cottage at the Forest Lake Club, working Forest Lake in the mornings with bass bugs, and we had fine sport with both trout and smallmouths. MacGregor has fished and loved the lower Lackawaxen for many years.

It's a moody river, MacGregor explained one afternoon on his porch, looking north toward the Catskills on the horizon. *Its flow and temperature are pretty erratic.*

What times seem best? I asked.

Depends on the time of year, MacGregor took my glass back inside to the bar. *The fish come pretty well in the spring, when the water from the dam is flowing much warmer than the stream itself.*

Starts them feeding?

That's right! MacGregor continued. *When river levels and temperatures in the Lackawaxen are just right for trout—between fifty and sixty-five degrees—the cold water from the Wallenpaupack can turn the fish off!*

But the discharges can keep the Lackawaxen fishing well through July and August, MacGregor returned with my scotch-and-soda, *when the other streams are too low and warm.*

That's right, MacGregor agreed.

When do the fish feed best? I watched a pileated woodpecker working on a dead oak. *When the water is rising or falling?*

The woodpecker hammered noisily. *That varies too,* MacGregor said thoughtfully. *When the river itself is right, the temperature gets better when they close the dam—and when it's too low and warm in August, a little cold water coming down starts the fish moving again.*

That's worth remembering. I took a long sip of scotch. *Where do the fish lie in high and low water?*

When the Lackawaxen is high and cold, he said, *the fish lie well down the pools and hold on the bottom—and some are found along the sides, in the eddies and behind boulders where the flow is reduced.*

What about low water? I asked.

The fish are looking for both food and oxygen then, MacGregor finished. *You find them in the fast shallows.*

And right up in the throats of the pools? I asked.

Right! MacGregor nodded.

Later that month, MacGregor introduced me to the finest tail-water fishery in our eastern states, the big water on the Delaware between Hancock and Long Eddy. It is a river of swift half-mile riffles and mile-long 'pools, and only twenty-five years ago it held a population of smallmouths and walleyed pike. There were always a few trout in the cool flowages of tributaries like the Lackawaxen and Callicoon. But after the completion of the Peapacton Reservoir above Shinhopple, on the East Branch of the Delaware, the river ran cold and strong from the dam tail waters to the spreading riffles above Port Jervis.

That evening we fished a sweeping waist-deep riffle that surged past our waders in the twilight, and when a heavy hatch of big *Isonychia* drakes came off in the shallows, the big rainbows started rolling and slashing on top. It was easier to find rising trout than to find a way to reach them. The current was swift and strong, with treacherous holes that have trapped a lot of anglers over the years, but I took a pair of three-pound rainbows.

It was fifteen years ago that we fished the big riffles at Narrowsburg and Barryville, and trout have come to dominate the fishery since then. Since the Cannonsville Dam was filled on the West Branch of the Delaware above Deposit, the main river below Hancock and Fish Eddy receives another source of cold dam tailings. Its population of big rainbows is remarkable, and there are fly hatches of incredible diversity and numbers. During hot weather, big trout abandon the lower Beaverkill for the colder East Branch of the Delaware, and trout migrating into winter holes in the Delaware often decide to remain there, particularly since the Beaverkill itself often becomes warm enough for smallmouths, between Cook's Falls and Baxters.

It's so rich with fly life, Harry Darbee explains wryly, *the stocked rainbows migrate through on their way to salt water and decide to stay—maybe it's the raw sewage from all those little towns.*

Beautiful! Gardner Grant winced.

Gardner Grant is the energetic president of the Theodore Gordon Flyfishers, but he spends so much time fishing the Delaware and talking about its rainbows that he sounds like a public relations man for the region. Grant worked as a canoe-trip guide in Maine during his college vacations from Yale, and his skills in travelling a swift river are perfectly suited to fishing the Delaware.

Grant likes the big flats on bends away from the highway, like the five-mile bend above Callicoon, or the fifteen miles of river between Hancock and Long Eddy.

It's another world on those bends away from the road, Grant sighs happily, *it's a wilderness only two hours from New York.*

We fished one of those mile-long flats one evening in late summer, hooking a half-dozen fat rainbows that accelerated downstream on blistering runs that spooled deep into the backing. It is not easy fishing. It calls for a willingness to wade deep; and the double haul is almost mandatory. The favorite pattern for Grant and most of the other regulars, who call themselves the Delaware Navy, is the familiar Adams dry-fly dressing in relatively small sizes. Leaders are usually 4X or 5X, since a free-wheeling Delaware rainbow will often strip enough fly line and backing from the reel that its dragging in the current will break a finer tippet. But when the river is running clear and right for wading, and the hatches are good enough to coax the big rainbows to surface feed, the Delaware can provide exceptional sport.

Is it really that good? somebody asked.

It's a good thing George Washington didn't fish, Gardner Grant laughed over a late supper in the Antrim Lodge.

What's that got to do with anything? I interrupted.

Never get him across the Delaware to Trenton with all these big rainbows around! he explained wryly and sipped his Chivas.

Funny, I grumbled.

Several years ago, my good friend David Rose was trapped by rising waters from the dam on the Housatonic in Connecticut. Rose was a beginning fisherman then, and he failed to hear the warning siren or respond to the river clues when they came. The first clue is always a change in the sound of a river when it starts to rise. Its rising level of sound is quickly followed with visual clues, like a deadfall starting to throb in a gathering current, or a shallow riffle deepening into a swift-flowing run. Dam tailings often reveal a slight milkiness too, perhaps from silts displaced by the rising water.

Experienced fishermen can feel a rising current in the subtle change of pressure against their legs, but a beginner can miss these warnings. David Rose scrambled to a jumble of big rocks nearby, but he quickly realized that the river was still rising, and that there was no safety there. The current was already dangerously swift, but he floundered ashore with only a bad soaking.

Fishing can be dangerous, Rose laughs today. *But there were moments out there when I thought I wouldn't make it back!*

Rising water in a scheduled release from a dam can be dangerous, but a knowledgeable fisherman can learn to use it to his advantage too. Water released from a dam does not flood an entire river at once, and its crest travels rather slowly downstream. This past spring I learned some interesting lessons about tail-waters on the Au Sable in Michigan.

The big rainbows from Lake Huron come into the Au Sable on a fine spawning run in late April, travelling like salmon in small schools of three- to twenty-pound fish. These fish enter the estuary at Oscoda, ascending the lower river slowly until they are finally stopped below the Foote Dam only six miles above the lake. The engineers at Foote Dam store water during the night, when the power demand is relatively low, and start releasing it through their turbines early in the morning. When the tail waters are low just after daylight, you can wade clear across the river in the shallows, and you can see the fish clearly from the parking area fifty feet above the tailrace gravelbars.

That morning I was meeting Gary Schnicke, who is the chief state biologist on the Au Sable, for a session on Michigan steelheads. It was cold and clear at daylight when I left the Fellows cottage on the North Branch, driving east through the Michigan timber country toward Oscoda. There are several reservoirs on the Au Sable below Mio, storing and releasing water until it finally comes through the powerhouse at Foote Dam. We stopped in a diner at Mio for breakfast, and after daylight we drove east on the Guennie Road. It was bright red along the horizon, and there were dozens of deer browsing along the shoulders.

The deer smell rain coming, Schnicke said, *and they're out foraging to get their bellies full before the weather turns sour.*

Then it's changing! I said.

We reached the dam and rigged our tackle.

Look down there, Schnicke pointed to the tailrace shallows. *Those wakes are spawning rainbows, and when you see angry swirls and splashes, it's the cockfish chasing away a smaller male or an egg-stealing sucker or bass!*

There were surprisingly large swirls and restless wakes of big fish showing everywhere below the dam.

You mean those rolling fish are all big steelhead trout? I asked.

That's right, Schnicke laughed, *and big steelheads too!*

Why are we standing around up here? I asked.

Gary Schnicke chuckled and led the way down the steep clay banks to the river.

It's a man-made fishery, he explained. *We plant the steelhead smolts at the dam and harvest them when they finally come back from Lake Huron.*

What about all this spawning activity?

The fish sure try, he acknowledged. *But they're not very successful with these cycles of rising and falling water.*

Hard on fly life too? I asked.

You bet! he said.

We'd better get fishing! I pointed to a school of big rainbows lying in the shallows. *How much time before they open the gates?*

We've got about an hour, Schnicke replied.

And we get more fishing time by driving downstream to stay ahead of the high water? I asked. *How much?*

About two more hours, he said.

The men who know their local tail-water fishing understand both the cycles of storage and discharge at the dam itself, and the time it takes a surge of released water to reach the better riffles and pools. That morning I took a small three-pound steelhead on a big streamer in the tailrace, and Schnicke lost a larger fish in the bend downstream. When the siren finally sounded at the powerhouse, we fished another twenty minutes before Schnicke came briskly up the bank.

Time to head downstream! he yelled.

We drove down the Oscoda road until Schnicke turned into the trees toward the river. There were several cars and campers where we parked, and the young biologist swiftly locked his car and started down the trail at a brisk dog trot.

The Au Sable comes down through the trees in a sweeping bend, flowing deep and strong against a high clay bank. We walked the high gravel bank looking for fish, until Schnicke finally spotted several big rainbows over a shoal of pea gravel.

You stay here and fish these, he pointed out five steelheads, *and I'll find another bunch upstream.*

The river flowed smooth and relatively shallow, with no trace of the turbidity generated when the flow quickened in the tailrace below the dam. The rainbows below me were big, and I could see them clearly as I worked my big nymph in front of them on the gravelbar. Although we both hooked big steelheads that came off on the second or third jumps, we failed to land a single trout that morning. But we had two full hours of casting time before the river finally rose and became unfishable, and I learned an important lesson about fishing tail waters.

Since the simple demand of future populations for potable water will unquestionably require more and more reservoirs to store seasonal rains and spring runoffs, we will probably see many more tail-water fisheries created in years to come. Some will restore rivers that supported trout a century ago, while others will transform warm-water fisheries into prime trout water. It is even possible that reservoirs could create trout habitat of whole cloth, like the Amawalk Outlet which connects two reservoirs in the New York water system.

It's remarkable! Gardner Grant describes the Amawalk enthusiastically. *It's less than an hour from Broadway and Times Square, but with fly-only and no-killing, it provides surprisingly good fishing over a lot of good trout.*

It's perhaps our oldest tail-water fishery, I said, *and tail waters may be a prelude to the future—particularly near major cities.*

Absolutely! Grant agreed.

9. Field Problems in Fishing the High-Lake Country

It is sagebrush foothill country south of Colorado Springs, with ponderosa and pinon trees on the boulder-strewn ridges. The parched, gravelly soil is broken with rattlesnake outcroppings above the river, and the road drops down toward the bridge over the swift-flowing Arkansas.

The village lies across the bridge in the distance, and the Sangre de Cristo Mountains lie beyond their arid foothill ranges. There are alpine lakes there, hidden in the lodgepole shoulders and basins at high altitude. The dirt county road climbs toward the south from the village, through the cottonwood and scrub-oak bottoms beyond the Arkansas, past the tidy houses and abandoned coke kilns at Florence.

The county road winds and switchbacks almost lazily toward the sagebrush foothills, working into the sandy arroyos and their pale chalk-colored bluffs. The sagebrush hills are honeycombed and scarred with the sulphur-colored tailings of abandoned silver mines, and the sculptured cliffs are polished by the wind. Twenty-five miles later, the dusty hills drop behind and the county road reaches straight across the valley floor. Its prairie is pale bunchgrass there, sprawling almost fifty miles from Cotopaxi on the Arkansas to the high-basin headwaters of the Huerfano. Its wind-swept emptiness is starkly beautiful.

The rotting skeleton of the mining pit-head is silhouetted against the morning light beyond the empty town. Its houses lie ahead across the buffalo grass flats of the valley floor. Past the weathered tombstones of the cemetery, its intricate wrought-iron fencework choked with tumbleweeds, lies the half-deserted mining camp at Silvercliff.

It's a fascinating town, said Beno Walker.

1548

We passed the first rough-sawed outbuildings of the town. Its streets and decaying houses are solitary echoes of the silver boom almost a century ago in this barren wind-swept valley. The county road reaches west toward the serrated parapets of the high Sangre de Cristo Mountains. Their crenellated summits were almost ruby-colored with the rising sun.

They deserve their name, I said softly.

Beno Walker was staring absently into the dusty streets. *What's that?* he asked. *What deserves what name?*

Sangre de Cristo, I replied. *The Blood of Christ.*

You're right, he agreed.

The blood-colored sunrise on the high mountains faded as quickly as it had formed. The morning wind stirred in the prairie bottoms. Two mallards exploded from an irrigation canal, flew swiftly toward the north in a climbing turn, and wheeled back on the wind. Magpies were quarreling over a dead jackrabbit in the road ahead, and they rose awkwardly from their carrion. The magpies watched sullenly from the fence line and settled again when we had passed.

The simple houses and skeletal false-front buildings of Silvercliff are like gravestones. The school and courthouse buildings are solemn bench marks from the past, and the abandoned adobe-walled saloons are empty too. The dusty boardwalks and hitching rails have been weathered silver in the wind. The streetscape looks like a moody Burchfield painting, empty of people and filled with a strange melancholia.

Lonely country, I thought.

Two cowboys were walking their ponies in the dusty street, their sweat-stained hats and sheepskin jackets turned against the wind. It is a long, cold ride that starts before daylight from the outlying ranches, even in the midsummer months.

Beno waved and one cowboy nodded back.

Beyond the outbuildings of the town, willows line the meandering course of Grape Creek, and the road starts climbing slowly toward the mountains. Creek willows and cottonwoods on the valley floor gradually change to ponderosas on the lower slopes. The jeep road switchbacks steeply along the shoulder of the mountain, climbing through the quaking aspens into the first stands of lodgepole pines. Hermit Creek tumbles far below the road, and where it plunges and falls down a steep outcropping of granite, the jeep road finally becomes deeply rutted and impassable, and the foot trail begins.

Last stop, I laughed. *Everybody out!*

Fishing the high-lake country is a horseback or backpacking sport at timberline altitudes where summer is a brief three-week season between ice-out and the first hard frosts in late August. Many high lakes are not entirely free of winter in late July, and there are still snowbanks where a fisherman can chill his trout like a refrigerator. August is the best month for the high-lake country, and even then the nights are cold above 10,000 feet. Our western mountains are full of such lakes.

There are superb back-country lakes throughout the entire system of mountains along the Pacific coast, with the golden-trout waters of the Sierra Nevada perhaps the most famous. The Rocky Mountain escarpment offers countless high lakes too, from the foothill ranges of New Mexico all the way to the Brooks Range in Alaska. Some of the best high-country lakes are in Colorado, particularly in the Sangre de Cristo Mountains and the plateau wilderness above Rifle and Trapper's Lake and Meeker. Other fine high lakes in Colorado are found in the Grand Mesa country west of Gunnison, the beautiful Elk Mountain wilderness areas southwest of Aspen, the Flattops wilderness, and the timberline backcountry that surrounds the Mount of the Holy Cross.

Wyoming offers some fine high-lake fishing in the Snowy Range behind Laramie, and particularly in the majestic Wind River Mountains southeast of Jackson Hole. The Wind River Country is accessible to fishermen only with horseback or backpacking, and there are a number of reliable outfitters in foothill towns like Dubois and Pinedale and Lander who know its high-lake secrets. Montana and Idaho offer other timberline fishing too, in the Anaconda country and the Sawtooth headwaters of the Salmon wilderness, and in the towering Bitterroot and Beartooth mountains farther north.

The high-country is still a remote, unspoiled world for a fisherman willing to work for his sport, since hiking into its alpine lakes is never easy, and there are saddle sores for the less hardy souls who join the pack trains. Weather at timberline is fickle at best, and even a midsummer day can turn subarctic and stormy without warning. Fishing at these altitudes can test your character, particularly in the party that is ill-equipped for bad weather and cold temperatures, and the lakes themselves are changeable and moody.

Some of the best are in the Sangre de Cristo country of Colorado, and it was getting warmer when we finally left the car. It is a steep climb into Hermit Lake, the first of a three-lake chain that stairsteps up a series of timberline basins. The foot trail works up the first escarpment into a mountain park thick with silver-bark aspens, their pale leaves fluttering in the early morning wind.

Two mule deer were drinking in the creek that morning, and they melted into the aspen thickets. The lakes were still two miles and another 1,000 feet higher, and although they do not offer memorable sport, each has a singular character typical of high lakes everywhere.

Hermit Lake lies at about 11,000 feet, surrounded with tall coniferous trees except along its south shore, where a huge rockslide reaches deep into the water. Horseshoe is a crescent-shaped lake at almost 12,000 feet in the treeless crater of an extinct volcano, and little Shelf Lake lies still higher, on a barren shoulder of the ridge above Hermit.

The trail crosses a series of high benches. Its steep climb is gentler once its first half mile is covered, crossing a partially timbered meadow, and then it climbs higher into the second basin beyond. It winds upward through narrow pathways in the boulders until it reaches a grove of firs and Engelmann spruce. There are immense deadfalls beside the trail there, weathered the color of fine pewter.

Beno Walker stopped to catch his wind. *You bring up the rear and collect the gear I drop,* he grinned.

Great! I sighed. *Who picks up behind me?*

It's a problem, he laughed.

The way my legs feel now we could starve and freeze with what we're still carrying when we finally get to Hermit! My mouth tasted like a pocketful of old copper pennies. *This load could make a pack mule quit.*

Well, Beno said, *let's saddle up!*

Steep rockslides lie across the valley, echoing the primordial earthquakes that originally shaped these lakes. Hermit Lake lay ahead now, glittering through its dense veil of spruce and pines. Chipmunks and marmots scurried among the outcroppings and rockfalls to reach their hiding places as we approached, and a red-tailed hawk circled lazily on the warming wind that stirred and rose from the valley floor.

The sun was higher now.

It is best to make your camp first in the backcountry and fish later. It is a matter of self-discipline. When you know your flaws of character, you also know that the fishing will mesmerize you well into the twilight hours, until it is too dark to make a proper camp and gather enough wood for cooking and a night fire. The understandable urge to start fishing after the climb must be check-reined.

We staked out the Bauer tension-tents in a sheltering copse of tall spruce trees, where the Hermit outlet gathered and spilled its currents through a jackstraw tangle of logs. We checked the trees for signs of decay and sited our camp some distance from a large dead spruce, for safety in case it fell in a sudden high-country storm.

There was still a single large snowbank in a hollow sheltered from the sun, and I shaped a cooling hole for our food with my belt knife. We stripped the big deadfalls of three nights' worth of firewood, and racked it carefully between two trees. Beno dug a firepit and lined it with stones, making sure they were not taken from the creek, and picked a site that would carry the cooking smoke away from our tents—both on the morning winds that always rose from the valley floor, and the cool evening winds that eddied back down the mountain.

Hermit is a typical mountain lake slightly below timberline, formed in some ancient rockslide that dammed the flow of its inlets to form a small depression that gathered the glacial melt. Its waters are slightly acid with the detritus of pine needles and rotting deadfalls and the silts of centuries. Like all mountain lakes, its best fishing is generally found at the inlets and outlets, where the population of still-water insects is augmented with current-loving species. Spawning undoubtedly occurs in the shoal that spreads its miniature alluvial fan of pea-gravel below the main inlet, which lies near the northwest extremity of the lake. The south shoreline is a steep rockslide, its submerged boulders dark with algal growth and bright *Dichelyma* mosses. It is a rocky shore too deep for good photosynthesis and heavy insect populations. The remaining shoreline from the toe of the rockslide, and around past the outlet along the eastern and northern shallows to the principal inlet is densely lined with trees. These tree-sheltered shallows receive the most warmth from the midday and afternoon sunlight, and shelter the most nymphs and crustaceans. The brook trout prefer its slightly acid waters, although the lack of fertility results in a somewhat stunted population of eight- to twelve-inch fish. Hermit is also deep enough to prevent excessive winterkill, but it lacks sufficient shallows and alkalinity to sustain a really first-rate trout fishery.

The principal diet forms in a timberline lake like Hermit are the slow-water nymphs, larvae and pupal forms of the aquatic insects. Its waters are too acid for heavy populations of the little *Gammarus* and *Hyalella* shrimps. Minor populations of the current-loving aquatic insects are also found in the inlet and outlet flowages. Although they are minute, the larval threadworms and surface-film pupae of the Diptera midges are perhaps the most common high-country diet of the trout, and the wind can carry such pupae from the shallows into the lake itself.

My best sport on the timberline lakes has invariably come with nymphs or larval and pupal imitations fished just under the surface. Sometimes a big weighted pattern like a Fledermaus is very effective, fished with a sinking line and a slow hand-twist retrieve along the dark detritus of the bottom. Freshwater shrimps are also found at these lower depths, and the swimming nymphs of various mayflies, damselflies, and dragonflies are also common in our mountain waters. Beetle larvae and caddisflies are relatively common subaquatic forms in our still-water biosystems, and during a hatching period, properly tied nymphs fished just under the surface can be deadly. Midge pupae should be fished dead drift just under the film, casting your imitations with a greased leader well ahead of a cruising fish. Perhaps the single most effective high-lake pattern in my fly books is the western Gray Nymph, tied in both weighted types for working deep and light-wire versions for fishing in the film, and in hook sizes four through twenty-four. Its larger sizes can suggest a fat Anisoptera nymph clambering along the bottom, and its tiny versions can serve as a workable midge pupa.

Hatching caddisfly pupae are another diet form extremely important in the high country, and dark little wet flies with mottled body hackles are effective then. Patterns like the traditional Partridge and Orange, Woodcock and Hare's Mask, Grouse and Green, and Partridge and Olive can prove deadly at such times. Trichoptera imitations should be fished under the surface with a slow, teasing retrieve during a sedge hatch.

Dry-fly fishing can prove effective when there is a hatch of sedges or *Chironomus* midges or speckle-winged mayflies, and when the fish are taking them visibly, but usually a high lake can be fished more effectively with wet flies and nymphs.

There were many experiences on Hermit in the years we lived in Colorado Springs, but the afternoon that is most memorable occurred on my backpacking trip with Beno Walker. Once our camp was ready, the wind dropped down until the surface of the lake was still and mirror smooth.

Look over there! Beno pointed suddenly. *They've started rising along those fallen trees!* The rises became more frequent, and dozens of trout were working along the deadfalls.

No rises in open water, I thought aloud.

You're right, Beno agreed. *The rises are all right there in the fallen tree trunks—what're the fish doing?*

Let's study them and find out, I said.

We walked down toward the shallows, where a tangle of dead trees lay in the outlet. Two fish bolted into deep water when our shadows touched the lake, and I squatted on my heels to study the shallows. The smooth trunks of the fallen trees were covered with pale green algae, and about five minutes passed before the lake revealed its secrets.

Look at these logs, I said suddenly.

Mixed with the bright tufts of pale algae along the rotting trunks were hundreds of olive green damselfly nymphs, climbing imperceptibly toward the waterline or simply waiting for their final cycle of emergence. The slender nymphs hung so motionless along the trees that only the delicate sculling motions of their abdominal gills betrayed them. Their protective coloring was so subtle and effective that only when a hatching nymph had crawled into the surface film to split its subaquatic skin was its presence revealed. There were literally hundreds of them.

What's there? Beno asked.

Green damselfly nymphs! I pointed. *Hundreds there on the logs, and they're getting ready to hatch!*

No wonder all the fish are there! he said.

Using a bright apple green imitation, we took dozens of hungry brook trout that afternoon and evening, although none exceeded fifteen inches. Brook trout thrive in such habitat, their population outstripping their surroundings until there are too many fish for the forage, and their average size is small. The heavy damselfly hatch lasted only a day.

We started early on our third morning for Horseshoe Lake, high in the extinct crater above Hermit. The trail is gentle enough in the beginning, climbing a little through the thick-trunked spruce forest until it suddenly turns north, and switchbacks up a steep shoulder of the mountain. The trees are thinner there. The trail seems to drop down again beyond the treeline, where it traverses the hogback saddle of a ridge that leads toward the final rim that conceals the lake.

The climb is hard work in the thinning air above 11,000 feet, and both Hermit and its sheltering trees lay far below in the first real basin above the valley floor. The trail works along the last sheltering rim, through rocky meadows filled with tiny wildflowers. It was still early morning, with the rising sun touching only the barren summit ridges another 2,000 feet above the trail, and the forest-rimmed shoreline of Hermit was still in darkness 1,000 feet behind.

There are many stories about the big rainbows in Horseshoe. It lies in the remains of an extinct crater, its glittering water in a ragged half-moon shape covering several acres. It has no inlets once the early summer snowmelt is finished, and in August there is barely an outlet trickle. Its lack of autumn spawning habitat means that brook trout were never stocked there from the federal hatcheries during the Depression years, and its ecology has all the components necessary for trophy-size fish.

The lake is deep in its center, and in the narrowing bay below the mountain wall that rises toward the summit. The outlet corner is relatively shallow, and the north shore has a rich shelf of marl that drops suddenly into ink-blue depths in the middle of the lake. The shoreline and its surrounding basin are treeless. The rocky meadows rise in ragged terraces, boggy with snowmelt and seepage along the north side. It was barren and beautiful, and we stood on the rim above the lake, watching the first morning wind stir and riffle its smooth surface.

Horseshoe may have limited spawning conditions, but it has everything else to support big fish. It has deep water to minimize winterkill when its thickly frozen surface is buried under snow, completely shutting out sunlight and photosynthesis. It has sufficient shallows to support extensive forage populations for its trout, and its heavy deposits of marl provide rich fertility along its north side.

Should've seen it! The old man had told me one winter morning at Saguache, when we had been jump shooting mallards in the San Luis country beyond the Sangre de Cristo range. *My mules crossed the last ridge just before noon, and Horseshoe was like a mirror—riding down from the rim you could see every pebble and stone in the shallows, and suddenly I saw them—rainbows like crocodiles in schools of five or six fish.*

Really big rainbows? we asked excitedly.

Big rainbows! the old prospector cackled. *Ain't many brutes like them Horseshoe rainbows left!*

We hiked down into the crater and shouldered off our packs and fishing gear in a sheltered place among the rocks. The wind was lightly riffling the lake, obscuring its depths and its fish from our scrutiny. Twice I saw strong rise forms well out in the choppy surface of the lake, but a high-density sinking line made more sense than a dry fly.

I strung my rod with a fast-sinking Dacron line and walked around the rocky outlet shoreline to stalk the marl shallows along the north side of the lake. It was impossible to discern a cruising fish, and I began to cast a clockwise fan pattern, prospecting geometrically with my weighted nymphs at random. Each cast worked out some eighty feet and dropped a big nymph beyond the marl shelf, where the water looked deep and swimming-pool green. There was nothing for a half hour, and then there came a strong pull that telegraphed back into the rod. The big trout gave a wrenching wallow just under the surface, showed its spade-size tail in a huge splash, and bored deep off the marl shallows. It angrily stripped line into the backing, and then the line suddenly went slack.

Damn! I shouted unhappily. *Broke me off!*

Twenty minutes later I hooked another rainbow of about four pounds that cartwheeled high into the air and bolted laterally along the shelf, the backing making a high-pitched tearing vibration where it sliced sideways through the water. Suddenly there was a guitar-string sound as the singing leader touched a sharp-edged piece of fractured lava, and the big rainbow was suddenly gone.

Lost him too! I yelled in exasperation.

Let's try the third lake, Beno suggested. *We can give these brutes a rest and fish them again on our way down.*

Good, I agreed. *Let's try it!*

Shelf Lake was a longer climb than it looked, over a saddle and ridge of broken outcroppings, and into the strange balconylike hollow that held the relatively shallow lake. Two fishermen were coming back down the trail, and we met them on the rocky little rim above the basin that sheltered Horseshoe.

It's no good! they said.

Have you been fishing it? I asked.

We hiked up directly from Hermit yesterday, and it's no use to climb up there this year! added the second angler unhappily.

What's wrong? asked Beno.

It's too shallow! the first man replied. *The snow covered the ice so thickly that it shut out the light—and the trout were all winterkilled.*

How could you tell? I asked.

It's dead! they explained sadly. *There are dead brook trout lying all over the shallows!*

Back to Horseshoe! Beno suggested.

We fished it carefully for another three hours, finally hiking back to Hermit when a rain squall lashed across the lake. Its icy, needle-sharp raindrops quickly drove us to seek shelter among the rocks. There were no more rises after the rain and the early evening wind felt raw when the squalls moved on past.

Several weeks later I talked with a pair of confirmed high-lake addicts who lived for the few brief weeks between ice-out in early summer and the first high-country storms of early September. Over the years, they had made the climb into Horseshoe more than a dozen times without taking one of its big rainbows.

It's a fickle lake, one explained. *It's high and ice-cold and its weather can change every fifteen minutes, but it's beautiful!*

You're stubborn men, I laughed.

Maybe, the second fisherman agreed, *but you can't make up your mind too quickly on a good high lake—when it's got shallows and deep water and reasonable fly hatches, it must have big fish!*

Yes, I agreed, *plus good spawning flowages.*

You're right, the first man continued excitedly, *but it's strange when you're really hooked on fishing the high country—it's so fickle that just when you give up on a lake, it gets generous for somebody else!*

It's a little crazy, his friend nodded. *The first time I ever fished the Pierre Lakes above Snowmass we caught big fish like there was no tomorrow—but I've never taken a good trout from those lakes since.*

You have to have faith! I agreed.

What's that? the first man asked absently. *I was daydreaming about the third time I climbed into Horseshoe, and found its big rainbows cruising for a good hatch of flies—it was terrific!*

I've seen your malady before, I smiled.

10. Fly-Fishing Problems
in Our Western Mountains

It has been almost forty years. Daylight came slowly across the sun-bleached prairies, and we had left the ranch south of Grainfield two hours after midnight to avoid the August heat. It was my first trip to Colorado, and that morning my head was so filled with stories of frontier days that it was impossible to sleep when the first grayish light filled the sky.

It looked like the rest of the high-plains country, ranches tucked into sheltered places under the flint-colored bluffs, hiding in groves of cottonwoods originally planted as timber claims. The muddy creeks were almost dry, and the cloudless sky forecast another day of dry heat and no rain. Windmills creaked high on their wooden frames, pumping cool water into the cattle tanks, and the shrinking creeks wound in serpentine chalk-colored channels lined with wild plums and hackberries.

My mother had told me the stories from her girlhood in this hard country, and that August morning some of their settings came alive. She told about the Roubidoux family, and its trading post at Fort Wallace, and about the years before the Little Big Horn when the Seventh Cavalry was stationed there. My father left the highway at Fort Wallace, following the county road south toward the river, and my mother pointed to the sandstone ruins of the military buildings. Below the town on an open buffalo-grass ridge was the military cemetery, with the graves of fallen cavalry troopers on dry depressions in the gravelly soil, and there were sunflowers growing in one corner where the soft sandstone wall that enclosed the cemetery held the rainfall in a low place. Tumbleweeds were caught in the iron fence that surrounded a pale prairie-stone obelisk.

It's a lonely place to be buried, my father said.

1557

My mother walked along the gravel path toward the grillwork.

Come look at the obelisk, she called.

What's it say? I asked.

It was a memorial for cavalry troopers who had been killed on patrols, and at the Beecher's Island fight on the Arikaree farther north, when the cavalry rescued a camp of buffalo hunters that had been besieged for days by a sizable war party. The soldiers whose names were carved into the butter-soft rock had never been recovered for burial, and the obelisk was their sole memorial.

The first light was getting stronger now. It was soft across the flint hills toward the south, where the headwaters of the Smoky Hill wound east toward Russell Springs and Ellsworth, where Wyatt Earp had worn his first marshal's star. The prairie wind whispered in the bunchgrass below the cemetery, where a herd of cattle moved restlessly down toward the river, and it stirred and grew until it carried the gritty soil against our faces. It rattled against the stone obelisk when we turned to leave, and a tumbleweed crossed the path.

Blowing sand, said my father absently. *It won't be many years before it erases the names on these stones.*

We started west again, passing through the crossroads towns at Wallace and Sharon Springs. Arapahoe and Cheyenne Wells were ahead, and beyond lies the prairie ridge that divides the watersheds of the Smokey Hill and the Big Sandy. The pale-grass prairies reached for miles, and in the gathering daylight the oiled road stretched west like a surveyor's line toward the distant horizon.

Look! said my mother. *You can see them!*

The far horizon seemed empty and I stared.

See what? I answered unhappily. *There's nothing there.*

Look again! she said. *It's the Rockies!*

The treeless prairies reached one hundred miles west, and the cool wind sighed across the road. There had been stories of sighting the Rocky Mountains for the first time, stories I had heard about mountain men like Jim Bridger and Kit Carson and Captain Zebulon Pike—who discovered the mountain that bears his name at Colorado Springs.

Can't you see them? she laughed.

No! I said unhappily. *I don't see anything except some blue-colored clouds right on the horizon.*

Those clouds are the mountains! she said, ruffling my hair.

It was true, and suddenly the distant peaks caught the first light of sunrise, looking like pink smoke across one hundred miles of prairie. It must have been the same for Pike and his expeditionary force, watching the same cloud on the horizon for days while they picked their painfully slow route through stirrup-deep grass and dry washes, until they finally realized it was an escarpment of 14,000-foot mountains. Standing on that barren ridge beyond Cheyenne Wells that morning almost forty years ago is indelibly recorded in my memory, and I stood there shivering a little, partially from the wind and more from delicious excitement. Forty-odd years later, I still feel the same about the Colorado mountains.

The region is a vast area of majestic peaks, foothill basins, and sagebrush plateaus, reaching north from the *piñon* buttes on its southern borders, all the way to the forest-rimmed lakes of British Columbia. Its spinal cord is the mountains themselves, the towering range that trappers and buffalo hunters and cavalry troopers called the Rockies. Early history in the region is visible in the canvases of frontier painters like George Catlin, Alfred Jacob Miller, and Albert Bierstadt. The later events that occurred before barbed wire fenced off the high-plains country are found in the work of cowboy artists like Frederic Remington.

South-flowing watersheds in the region still echo the centuries-old tradition of the Spanish horse soldiers who explored and briefly conquered their valleys. The heritage of Spain lies in rivers with names such as Chama, Cucharas, Conejos, Huerfano, Las Animas, Los Pinos, and the storied Rio Grande itself.

There are still secrets in these mountains.

The 8,000-foot-high headwaters of the Gila, only one hundred miles above Mexico, hold a rare species of black-spotted trout that is protected in our time. Montana grayling are still abundant in the icy headwaters of the Beaverhead and the Big Hole. There are rare golden trout in some of the high lakes in the Wind River country of Wyoming, and the forest-rimmed lakes of British Columbia, like Stump and Peterhope and Shuswap shelter a unique subspecies of rainbow trout—the acrobatic, pole-vaulting Kamloops as bright as freshly minted coins.

Thousands of rivers and reservoirs and high lakes lie between. Fly-fishermen will find a cornucopia of native cutthroats, and introduced species like rainbows, goldens, browns, and brook trout. The Rocky Mountains dominate a world so vast and varied that its people—the lumberjacks, ranchers, miners, and their descendants in fast-growing foothill cities like Denver and Salt Lake—often forget that the region is virtually a continent in itself.

It sprawls more than 1,500 miles from Mexico to British Columbia, far more than the distance between the Macedonian river where fly-fishing for trout was born 2,000 years ago, and the north-flowing rivers of Scotland where the continent of Europe projects westward into the Atlantic.

Fly-fishing in our western mountains is as varied as the magnificent country. There are literally all types of water in the Rockies. Some fishermen prefer the relatively small streams and beaver ponds, perhaps because their character is intimate and comprehensible. Others spend most of their time on big western reservoirs. Fishing wilderness lakes high in the mountains offers still another set of problems. The sprawling big-water rivers offer difficult wading, but also trophy-size fish for anglers willing to challenge their intimidating size. The final surprise is the western spring creeks, small weed-rich streams that emerge full-blown in limestone upwellings and geothermal basins—and offer fishing with minute flies and cobweb-thin leaders over trout as selective as any on the legendary rivers of Europe.

These western waters are changing under the pressure of increasing population, and their fish are more wary and demanding than they were as recently as ten or fifteen years ago. The immense numbers of wilderness fish described in the chronicles of Lewis and Clark have been gone for a century, although some high lakes in remote areas are still filled with eager and gullible trout. Such fishing is found in pack-trip and hiking country, but fish in the foothill rivers behind Denver and Salt Lake and Colorado Springs are as shy as their cousins in streams two hours outside Boston and Philadelphia and New York.

Such varied conditions demand skills in the full spectrum of fly-fishing techniques, and both eastern and western anglers are going to need some homework in the years ahead. Eastern fishermen are accustomed to small-scale rivers that are relatively easy to read and fish. Their trout are soon discovered in the dark run under the overhanging buttonwoods, beside the only boulder in the pool, and in the narrow current tongue that tumbles into a fifty-yard flat. Such skilled eastern fishermen are often baffled on a river like the Snake or the Yellowstone or the Gunnison, and they find its stadium-size pools and half-mile flats a little disconcerting.

Western fishermen often remember the relatively easy fishing of the past, when the fish would take almost anything they cast, and they too are a little unsettled by the more recent shyness and selective-feeding behavior appearing on their rivers. Modern fishing in the Rocky Mountains requires delicate tactics and a growing knowledge of fly hatches, as well as big-water techniques with a sinking line. There is room for both the chalkstream methods required on the crystalline spring creeks, and the bottom-scouring muddler on the half-mile riffles of the Yellowstone. The man who really masters fly-fishing in the Rockies must handle the polarities of both methods well, particularly in a future that promises more and more fishing pressure, if he wishes to become a complete angler.

Since fishing all the types of water in the Rocky Mountains demands both stamina and refinement, it is difficult to recommend a single rod-and-reel combination that can handle the full spectrum of problems. Anglers who want to focus on small rivers, beaver ponds, and the spring creeks will probably lean toward a relatively light rod of seven to eight feet. Such rods would be balanced with five- to six-weight fly lines, and since fishing such waters often involves an infantry approach in high grass, a slightly longer rod still capable of fishing a delicate tippet is the ticket. Both floating and sinking double tapers are needed, although most forward-taper designs deliver too harshly for the skittish trout of smaller waters.

Such rods weigh about two and one-half to three and one-half ounces in fiberglass, and two and three-quarters to four and a quarter ounces in split bamboo. Reels for light-tippet fishing should have a smooth click system that will not shear an 8X nylon when a good fish bolts and strips off line. Matching reels for the rods described above should measure three to three and a half inches in diameter, and should weigh between three and a half and four and a half ounces. Their capacity should be about one hundred yards of twenty- to thirty-pound Dacron backing behind the ninety feet of fly lines. Dacron is better than other synthetic materials for such backing line, because it does not stretch as radically under tension. Too much elasticity in the backing can tighten and cause a reel machined from the lightweight modern alloys to warp and bind, when an angler recovers his stretched backing from a big fish. The relatively heavy backing is recommended because its diameter tends not to bite into the remaining line, jamming under the stress of a bolting fish.

Fishing heavy water demands other gear. Big rivers and reservoirs involve both distance casting and sinking weight forward lines. Rods designed for such tactics vary between eight and eight and a half feet, balanced with seven- and eight-weight lines. Glass equipment of this length and power will weigh from three and three-quarters to four and three-quarters ounces, and four and a quarter to five and a half ounces in split cane. Balanced reels should hold 100 to 150 yards of thirty-pound Dacron backing. Both double-taper and torpedo-taper lines are useful. Reels for such tackle will measure from three and a half to three and three-quarters inches, and weigh between five and six and a quarter ounces. Thirty-pound backing has sufficient diameter to prevent its biting into the remaining line, and binding when a trophy-size trout makes its strong downstream run. It is a lesson in acceleration learned painfully from big rainbows and salmon over the years.

There are many times on big western reservoirs and lakes when the fish rise avidly to a hatch, or porpoise to emerging nymphs and pupae just under the surface. Dry flies, wets, and nymphs must be chosen then to match the color, size, configuration, and behavior of the naturals. Bucktails and streamers should imitate the baitfish indigenous to the water being covered, and suggest their unique swimming motions.

The fish of lakes and impoundments have a singular pattern of behavior important to a western fisherman: they cruise together in search of food, each fish stringing together several rises in a sequence. Unlike stream fishing, a fisherman must not cast to the rise forms that are showing. Experienced lake fishermen have learned to observe a series of rises, and cast to the place where such a cruising trout is likely to rise next.

Fishermen on big lakes and reservoirs should remember a few other simple rules, particularly when the fish are not revealing themselves with surface rises. Most food in lakes and beaver ponds and impoundments is found in the relatively shallow waters, rather than in the depths. The inlet channels are especially good feeding places. Shallow outlets of big lakes often hold some of the largest trout. The shallow acreages with inlet and outlet currents are particularly rich areas, because their currents mean higher oxygen levels, and a wider range of slow-water and current-loving natural foods.

Two basic methods of presentation are important on the western lakes and reservoirs. Both utilize a fan pattern of covering the water, one horizontal in a clock-face technique, and the other vertical, working the fly back at various depths.

The clock-face method involves covering the surface around the angler in a disciplined manner, rather than casting at random. The pattern begins at approximately nine o'clock, working the fly out as far as possible and fishing it back. The succeeding casts are placed in a clockwise pattern past twelve, until the final cast is retrieved from three o'clock. When the fan pattern is complete, the fisherman should move a step along the shoreline, and repeat the whole clock-face exercise again. It can also be repeated again without moving, and the pattern of casts is more likely to intercept a cruising fish that mere random casting might miss.

The vertical fan patterns of retrieves at various depths have a similar logic. The fisherman simply employs a countdown technique. Each successive cast is permitted to sink a few seconds deeper, until either feeding trout are located, or the bottom is reached. This is indicated by the retrieve ticking against the bottom ledges and gravel or the fly picking up some moss.

When the sink count of twenty-five works into the weeds or touches bottom, the fisherman should reduce the count slightly. The short count works the fly back just above the bottom, where the nymphs and diving-beetle larvae and tiny crustaceans are most abundant. Such countdown tactics are a primary factor in fishing lakes, impoundments, and deep currents on our western rivers, and they are the secret on famous lakes like Wade and Cliff in Montana—and the rich weed-filled shallows of Henry's Lake in Idaho.

Some of the best fly-fishing reservoirs in the Rockies are found at Antero and Eleven Mile and San Cristobal in Colorado. Wyoming has Grassy Lake near Yellowstone Park, and Flaming Gorge on the lower watershed of the Green, and Montana has superb sport on large impoundments like Georgetown and Hebgen. High lakes offer similar problems of technique in locating fish and covering the water; and casting ahead of a cruising trout to anticipate its next rise is critical too. High-altitude waters are also best in the shallow acreages where aquatic foods are concentrated, particularly the inlets and outlets. The temperatures of high lakes are typically cold, and the best sport is usually found when the surface warms during the day. Evenings that follow a hot, sunny day are often good. The warming water has accelerated both the metabolism and the hunger of the fish, and in the twilight they forage more boldly.

Sometimes a light surface-riffling wind on a lake or beaver pond or reservoir can make the fish less aware of clumsy casting and relatively crude tippets. Trout cruise under the broken surface, unafraid of feeding openly in bright weather. Under such conditions, still-water fishing is easier.

Productive high lakes are usually distinguished by four key factors in their biosystems: there must be sufficient volume and depth of water so the fish have enough oxygen to prevent winterkill when snow covers the ice. Heavy drifts shut out the light, and end the photosynthesis that normally replenishes oxygen in the water. The best high lakes often have natural deposits of phosphates or lime marl or other sources of alkalinity, often from geothermal or volcanic origins. The nutrients sustain both a rich food chain and a rapid growth potential for the trout. Sufficient outlet and inlet currents are important for the spring-spawning cutthroats and rainbows, and the introduced populations of fall-spawning brookies. Such currents vary considerably from lake to lake, and they do not always provide spawning-size gravel. Aquatic foods do not thrive in the alkaline waters unless the lake also provides adequate acreages of shallow water. It is such forage-shallows that hold the organisms which grow and sustain large trout.

High lakes are also characterized by moodiness. Weather is fickle at such altitudes. When you find a lake that does not winterkill, has relatively alkaline waters, sustains natural spawning, and also provides food-rich shallows, fish it several times to test its character before you finally judge its fishing qualities.

Big western rivers offer completely different fishing. Sweeping riffles and half-mile flats provide a few visible clues to their holding places, and a man familiar only with the tactics of fishing a small stream is lost. There are few undercut banks, logjams, or boulders to scour out sheltered taking lies. The smooth currents have a poker-faced façade that conceals most of their secrets. Many western rivers have large whitefish populations, and they prefer the tail shallows and quiet currents. Whitefish often hold in places that brown trout would like on a smaller eastern stream. Western trout are usually in the stronger currents feeding into a pool—particularly wild cutthroats and muscular rainbows—and an eastern fisherman can waste precious time working places that hold no trout until he discovers this particular secret of our western rivers.

There are times when heavy fly hatches bring the fish up on even the biggest rivers. Their rises and porpoise rolls clearly reveal their feeding stations at such times. Famous hatches like the big stoneflies that emerge in early summer on the great fast-water rivers like the Madison and Gunnison and Snake, the large olive-bodied mayflies that come off slower streams like the Henry's Fork of the Snake, and the pupal migrations of tiny *Chironomus* flies can all trigger impressive rises of fish. Such hatches can make the fish both greedy and selective on the biggest rivers.

Gene Anderegg and I were waist-deep in the sprawling Big Hole fifteen years ago, frustrated by fifty-odd trout rising all around us. Their swirls barely disturbed the smooth current.

It's something minute, Anderegg yelled. *Can't see anything on the surface, and they're sure lazy rise forms!*

Two browns porpoised like sleepy cats.

Might be tiny ants, he continued. *Tiny ants or jassids or midges in the film—maybe I'll try ants on them.*

Good! I answered. *I'll try midge pupae in the film.*

Petri heil! he laughed.

Big Hole fish are supposed to scoff at refinements like matching the hatch and light tackle. Its trout are expected to fall all over themselves to take big Muddlers and Wooly Worms and weighted nymphs like the improbably-named Girdlebug fished deep along the bottom, but these fish had obviously failed to read the script. The big western flies all failed, and the fish dimpled and swirled everywhere.

Nothing! Anderegg laughed.

We've tried everything on them! I answered. *They don't know they're supposed to take Humpies and Muddlers.*

You're right! he shook his head and waded upstream.

The common solution for such rise forms is a tiny ant or jassid imitation, and sometimes a minute nymph or midge pupa. We tried dozens of tiny patterns without moving a fish, while they continued to work everywhere down the flat.

They're laughing at us, I said.

Finally I noticed a rhythm in their feeding. The light wind riffled the current slightly, stirring in the cottonwoods above the pool. The rises increased each time the wind moved in the trees; it was blowing tiny insects into the river.

It must be terrestrials! I said.

But we tried every terrestrial in the box! Anderegg replied. *The fish didn't even bother to look at them!*

Beetles! I suggested suddenly.

Anderegg reeled in his line and waded toward me.

Okay, he laughed. *We forgot to try beetles!*

Tiny cottonwood beetles, I continued eagerly. *Sometimes the wind blows the tiny bark beetles from the trees this time of year!*

Let's try one, he suggested.

The only beetle imitations in my boxes had been dressed from ringneck pheasant feathers, lacquering a pair of greenish black throat feathers together in a pattern that Ross Trimmer and I had developed for Japanese beetles on Letort Spring Run. Their ovoid wing silhouettes were set jassid-style above a trimmed black hackle, tied to lie flat in the film. But they were on sixteen hooks, much too large for a tiny cottonwood beetle less than a quarter inch in length, and I hastily trimmed the wing smaller with the scissors on my trout-knife.

Okay, I said. *We're ready now.*

The modified beetle dropped softly above a good fish, and when it reached its feeding station, the fly disappeared in a quiet dimple. The little reel protested shrilly as the two-pound brown felt the hook and bolted.

It worked! I yelled.

Anderegg came wading upstream while I played the fish on the delicate one-pound tippet. *Fantastic!* He shook his head. *Never would have believed that kind of selectivity here!*

It happens, I agreed.

Such choosiness is relatively rare on large western rivers like the Big Hole, but days like that are happening more and more each summer. It is precisely the kind of minute-fly-fishing a good Catskill or Appalachian fly-fisherman understands—tactics that were developed and perfected on the Letort in Pennsylvania—and western anglers will need such techniques more often in the future.

However, few eastern anglers have worked enough really big water to understand the basic methods of fishing it. When a river is a series of half-mile riffles and waist-deep flats, casting to a single rising fish is seldom practicable. The fisherman must execute fairly long casts, covering as much water as possible in a precise pattern. His most effective techniques are similar to those used on steelhead and salmon, and involve both geometry and discipline.

Big western rivers have few actual pools where their currents are constrained by outcroppings and ledges and canyon walls, although such places exist. The really large rivers are formed of tumbling riffles and deep flats with swelling currents. The swiftest water often consists of brief chutes where the gravel shelves off abruptly between a flat and the riffling throat of the next flat downstream. It is open water, almost without distinguishing character, like a pond with a current. It reveals virtually nothing of its bottom to the eye, although it is probably punctuated with outcroppings of bedrock, undercut ledges, and partially-buried boulders where the scouring currents have deepened the river. Such secrets may offer only subtle hints of their presence, in eddying currents that scarcely disturb the surface.

You've got to cover a lot of river in a day, Bob Carmichael used to growl good-naturedly in his shop at Jackson Hole years ago. *And you've got to cover it carefully.*

Carmichael loved and understood big water, with the skills sharpened in many seasons on sprawling flats of the Snake and Gros Ventre and the Buffalo. Although poor health denied him access to heavy water in the years before his death, his advice was sound for those who listened. His rivers were a world of strong many-channeled currents, mixed with tumbling chutes and flats and half-mile riffles that have baffled many visiting anglers—and swift currents that have drowned more than a few who took them lightly.

Covering such water is discipline and hard work. It involves starting where a heavy riffle or chute shelves off and slows, meeting the deeper currents of the flat. Trout can hold well in these chutes, even where the current is choppy and swift, because bottom friction causes a cushion of slower water deep along the stones and gravel.

Start pretty far up, Carmichael explained. *Sometimes the biggest fish lie right along the chutes—especially our Jackson Hole cutthroats—in heavy water that seems impossible to stay in easily.*

Carmichael was right about that.

We took heavy rainbows and cutthroats right in the chutes, fishing across the current tongues with a sinking line and big weighted nymphs and muddlers. Letting them sink deep over the shelving bottom, we teased them enticingly with a lazy rhythm of the rod. The heavy currents worked our flies, and we waited until they hung directly downstream before we stripped in line. Several casts should be made into any obvious holding lie, making sure it has been adequately covered.

Otherwise, the fisherman should simply fish out the entire flat with discipline and geometry. Each time a cast is completed, with the big nymphs or muddler finishing its current swing, the angler retrieves his line with a few slow strips directly upstream. Then it should be stripped back fast, and a step taken downstream while the line works out again. The next cast should drop about two feet farther downstream, well out across the current tongues, so it swings back in a deep arc along the bottom.

Such tactics cover the pool with a series of concentric quarter-circles, making sure every fish has seen the fly. Mere random casting from various points could miss a good trout in a mood to take the fly.

Pocket-water fishing is easier. It simply involves casting to the likely looking eddies and smooth runs and pockets among the rocks. The fish are holding in such cushions in the current. They lie beside the stones and boulders, in a swelling current just upstream, and in the reverse eddies below. There are others in the darker currents along the edges of the tumbling white water, and in the slicks between the swift current tongues. It is fishing that requires accurate casting to such places, and a quick strike in response to a rise, since the agile pocket-water trout must decide and take its food quickly.

Charles Fothergill is a well-known guide on the swift Roaring Fork in Colorado, particularly in the famous Slaughter House water below Aspen.

Pocket fishing isn't often a problem in selectivity, Fothergill believes. *Any fish in currents like that makes his mind up fast—or goes hungry!*

Good holding water lies in many places. Pools form below waterfalls, logjams and deadfalls, boulders, dams, ledges, and undercut banks where a river changes its direction. Pools can lie at the bottom of any narrow defile or canyon, where bedrock ledges block the flow of the river, and where primary gravel bars cause upwelling currents. Bridge abutments can form holding pools too.

Such pools invariably shelter big fish. Their depth offers protection, while the currents bring oxygen and food that can be ingested at leisure. Unlike riffles and pocket water and runs, pools have a quiet tempo. However, there are always places in a pool where an unexpected fish might hold and feed outside the shelter of the deeper lies. Sometimes the fish drop back toward the tail shallows, depending on the prey they are seeking, and can forage in surprisingly shallow water.

Anglers should never wade into the tail or lower reaches of any pool without studying it carefully for fish. Spooked trout will bolt upstream through the shallows, and their panic is contagious.

Since a small fish is usually fleeing to hiding places not far above the shallows, his panic is less a problem than a bigger trout bolting toward his lie in the primary depths of the pool. Study the shallows carefully, and try to catch any good fish holding there. Hooking such fish, and forcing them downstream from the others lying in the lower reaches of the pool will prevent the chain reaction of panic that can be triggered when a large trout bolts upstream from the tail shallows.

Cover it all! the late Joe Brooks always suggested. *Sometimes you'll find a real dinosaur in the riffles, lying in water hardly deep enough to cover its dorsal fin!*

However, most big trout will dominate the best feeding places along the primary current tongues. Such currents are carrying food, particularly the nymphs and fly hatches from the riffles upstream. Since the primary feeding stations for a big trout involve both cover and food supply, any pocket that offers good protection beside a primary current can shelter a trophy fish. Their holding lies will be found along sheltering ledges, deadfalls and logjams, cribbings, timbers, and willow-shaded undercut banks. What method an angler should use varies with the moods of both the fish and their rivers. Obvious surface rises to hatching insects call for dry flies, of colors and sizes that imitate the naturals. Porpoising swirls or deep rolls, flashing along the bottom, usually require imitations of nymphs and larvae. Skittering baitfish mean a big trout is in a meat-and-potatoes mood and is chasing minnows. The fisherman must learn to observe the behavior of the trout and understand the clues in that behavior before he can catch them consistently.

Lacking such obvious clues, an angler on big western rivers should know what principal nymphs and baitfish are found on the water he is fishing. Such foods have well-known imitations that should be fished along the bottom with a sinking line.

There are days when nothing is showing, Dan Bailey said a few years ago in his fly shop at Livingston on the Yellowstone. *You've got to use a big nymph or bucktail—and you've got to scratch gravel to get them!*

But the icy little spring creeks and geyser-basin rivers like the Gibbon and the Firehole are another challenge altogether. There are big springs that rise as full-blown little rivers from the earth in many western valleys. These little streams are rich with weeds and fly life, carrying the alkalinity of phosphates, lime marl, and hot springs. The ecological result of such alkalinity is identical—optimal feeding temperatures throughout the year, rich weed growth, heavy fly hatches of tiny caddis and mayflies and midges, plus terrestrials in the summer, and trout as wary and selective as any in the world. Skilled western anglers who enjoy the challenge of stalking these fish, sometimes belly-flat in the grass, can name these famous spring creeks on their fingers.

Colorado has the weedy meadows and watercress headwaters of the South Platte and the Tarryall, plus the artesian-fed network in the San Luis Valley. Wyoming has little rivers like Flat Creek and Fish Creek and a handful of spring creeks at Jackson Hole. Yellowstone Park has the Firehole and the Gibbon. California has its famous Hot Creek on the arid eastern slopes of the Sierras and Hat Creek, a cornucopia of fly hatches born in the hot springs of Lassen Volcanic Park. Montana has many famous spring creeks. The best are probably the Big Spring Creek at Lewistown, the superb pair on the Armstrong and Nelson ranches above Livingston, and the smaller spring creeks at Twin Bridges on the Big Hole and Ennis on the Madison. The Gallatin alone has a handful of fine little spring creeks in its watershed above Bozeman. Idaho has its great ones too, particularly the Henry's Fork of the Snake, probably the biggest spring creek in the world, its Teton River tributary and the little-known spring creek at Swan Valley; and perhaps the most famous of the western chalkstreams—the serpentine meadow reaches of Silver Creek at Picabo.

Fishing such waters well is not easy. *It's a good yardstick!* Bud Lilly observed thoughtfully at his West Yellowstone shop a few seasons back. *You've got to be better than good!*

The fish are shy enough to demand delicate leaders tapered to 7X and 8X tippets. Nymphs tied to imitate freshwater shrimps and scuds are a good choice fished in the weedy channels when the fish are not visibly feeding, although these spring creeks are known for their free-rising trout. Many hatches of tiny Sulphurs and Blue-winged Olives and *Callibaetis* flies are common throughout the season, since these are many-brooded mayfly species that thrive in the western spring-creek habitats. Experienced anglers fish dry with diminutive Blue Quills and Blue-winged Olives and Light Cahills on eighteen to twenty-four hooks. Such minutiae ride the smooth current like tiny sailboats, and rises to them are lazy almost-sipping swirls.

Rise forms when there is nothing visible floating on the current pose another problem in tactics. Such rises usually mean tiny ants and leafhoppers and beetles, but they can also be focused on the larval and pupal forms of midges, and tiny wet flies dressed with black, olive, or dark-grayish bodies are often the solution. There are also times when tiny hatching mayfly nymphs and caddis pupae are just under the surface, and the trout take so closely under the film that they disturb the water with dramatic rises and porpoise rolls. It is a time for small wet flies and nymphs on light tackle.

Spring-creek fishing is never easy. The trout are shy and selective on most days, cocking under a floating dry fly to inspect it before refusing it disdainfully. Such wariness is light years away from working a fat Muddler or Wooly Worm along the bottom of some half-mile flat, floating a big Humpy or Hair-wing Wulff on broken pockets, or catching foolish trout in some wilderness lake or beaver pond.

My first experience with difficult spring-creek fishing came on the Yellowstone above Livingston, and its frustrations have proved typical over the years. The fish sipped and porpoise-rolled and dimpled in the weedy channels for hours that morning; and we never touched them.

Well, Dan Bailey asked with a twinkle in his pale eyes, *you've fished those British chalkstreams—what do you think?*

These fish are tough, I admitted sheepishly.

Amen! said Bailey.

11. Streamside Experiences
in Matching the Hatch

Matching the hatch was not a major factor on my boyhood rivers but there were baffling days even then when it mattered. Searching my memory for obvious examples, I find one morning on the upper Pere Marquette that stands out vividly for its impact on my early thinking. It was an experience that taught me several basic lessons in matching a fly hatch of naturals, both in terms of observation and streamside fly tying.

It was a surprisingly cold morning in early June and mist still drifted above the spring-fed swamps along the Middle Branch when I left the car at the Forks Pool. It was chilly enough for me to see my breath in spite of the calendar, and my fingers were a little clumsy when I threaded the fly line through the guides. The river flowed smooth and strong, where the swift currents of the Middle Branch riffled under the bridge to join the darker tea-colored water of the Little South. The river felt warmer than the air, and I studied it for rising fish before rummaging in my fishing coat pockets for a fly book.

I'll fish a pair of wet flies down to Noble's Bend, I decided and studied the patterns in my fly book. *Maybe a pair of Cahills.*

The Cahills were firmly attached to the tippet and a dropper about eighteen inches up the leader. Roll casting steadily, I worked down the riffling current tongue of the Forks Pool without moving a fish.

It's still too cold, I thought.

The river winds toward the north from the Forks, flowing waist-deep and smooth and sliding laterally across its stony bottom to work against the deadfalls below. Its currents are dark with the promise of big fish under the trees before they turn back toward the still water downstream. The sweeping bend downstream was a productive reach of water in those summer months, with many good trout holding over its open gravel and some heavy fish in the shade of the trees. The current narrows below, gathering its strength into a strong, leg-wearying flow that shelves off deeply under a dense jackstraw tangle of logs. There was a single towering snag rising through the deadfalls, and that summer it was home to a pair of nesting woodducks. The still water at Noble's lies downstream.

Although I fished the familiar water carefully, nothing responded to my little Cahills until I covered the sheltering alders below the logjam. The fish that struck was not large; it followed my swinging flies lethargically in the cold current, taking the dropper with a half-hearted pull.

Well, I thought, *it's something!*

The sun worked higher and a few flies were hatching when I changed reels to fish back with a floating fly. There were a few brownish gray sedges egg laying along the willows when the first trout started feeding, and I selected a spent-wing Adams. It took one fish, but the others refused it completely.

That's strange. I shook my head.

Selective feeding in those years was seldom a serious problem, but I finally stopped fishing to study the hatching flies. Mixed with the fluttering caddisflies were a few dark little hatching duns, and although I was unable to catch a specimen, it seemed likely that a small Blue Quill would work. It had been the solution during a similar hatch a few weeks earlier, and I changed flies with confidence, clinch-knotting a sixteen Blue Quill to my leader tippet.

The fluttering little duns came down the current, and I watched the fish take them readily. It was definitely the little mayflies, and I placed my imitation above a fish that was working below the logs. The dry fly settled, flirted in the currents over the trout, and was casually refused.

Must be drag, I thought.

Several casts came down over the fish, and although it inspected one dragless float briefly, it continued to refuse the fly. My Blue Quill was obviously not the solution, and I waded over into the primary current tongue to catch one of the naturals.

It came fluttering toward me, and I cupped my hand and lowered it to intercept the hatching dun. The river eddied past my fingers, and the little mayfly darted past on the flow, disappearing in the tumbling currents around my waders. Several flies escaped me before I finally picked one off the water by its upright wings, and I placed it carefully in a plastic fly box. It hung upside down on the lid, and its colors seemed strange. Its wings were dark bluish-gray, its legs and three delicate tails somewhat paler, its eyes were large and rust colored, and its body was a bright olive. There was nothing like it in my fly boxes.

When I had tried every pattern with dun-colored hackles without taking a fish, I waded back upstream to the car and the fly tying box in its trunk. There was no body material of the proper color, but there was a small cellophane package of olive-dyed hackles in my kit, and I stripped the fibers with my fingers. The color of the hackle was a pale olive except for the dyed edge of its quill, and it looked like the bodies of the naturals when I wound it on the hook. Dun-colored tails and hackles with sparsely dressed wings of woodduck completed the fly. When there were two patterns finished, lying face down on their hackles on the glove compartment door, it was time to try the river again.

The hatch was almost over when I finally reached the flat. There were still a few olives coming down the riffles below the Forks Pool, and wading slowly downstream, I discovered three good fish still working along the deadfalls. The fish rose busily along the far bank, preoccupied enough with the hatching flies that I slipped past without alarming them.

Wonder if they'll still refuse a Blue Quill? I thought.

It was an interesting question, and I swallowed my impatience to try the little olive patterns I had tied. The fish rose in irregular rhythms, now coming to the dwindling hatch along the mossy logs. One inspected a Blue Quill momentarily, turned back to its feeding station, and softly took another natural. The other two fish refused the Blue Quill without interrupting their feeding.

They're still picky! I shook my head.

The little olive imitation was knotted to my tippet and anointed with a mixture of paraffin and carbon tetrachloride. Several drops blossomed in brief oil-film flowers on the current below my waders, and I blew on the hackles before drying them with false casting.

The fly dropped above the first trout, teasing down past the current-polished logs until it disappeared in a satisfied rise. It was a fat fourteen-inch brown, and it threshed with surprise.

It worked! I thought happily.

The fish was netted after I coaxed it downstream from the others, and I rinsed and dried the fly. The second fish had not bothered with my little Blue Quill earlier, but it took the Olive without hesitation.

Well, I thought, *that's two of them.*

The third fish was bigger. It was working along a mossy stump that lay in dappled patterns of bright sunlight and shadow, and my first casts dragged slightly. It followed one float with interest and finally refused. It was a difficult fish, and I waded deep to get below its position, dropping both line and leader in the same currents to get a better float. The fly drifted properly on a slack leader and the fish took quietly, shaking angrily and bolting upstream when I tightened.

Three! I said aloud.

The fish was about two pounds, and I lost it when the brittle tippet sheared in the roots upstream. But it was a trout that had rejected the other patterns, and finding a fly it wanted was unforgettably intriguing. It was an important lesson in selectivity, and matching the hatch was firmly etched in my memory.

Another incident occurred on the Au Sable. It was a mellow afternoon in early summer, in a sweeping bend of the North Branch below Lovells. Only a few fish were showing until the late shadows reached well across the current. The wind was warm, drifting upriver and smelling of pines and cedar swamps.

The birds were the first symptom of change, darting and wheeling high in the sun above the river. It was the prelude to a mating swarm of mayflies and more and more insects soon gathered from the trees. The flies were small straw-colored *Ephemerellas*, rising and falling rhythmically over the current. The birds were frantic now as their dancing flight came lower. The mating swarm was heavier, the males holding twenty-odd feet above the river. In a timeless mating dance, the females rose to meet the males and fluttered back toward the water. Finally the fertilized females dipped closer and closer to the smooth current, until their bodies were tipped with tiny butter-colored egg sacs.

The twilight was quickly filled with countless flies. When the females began dropping to oviposit their egg sacs in the water, the waiting trout began taking them eagerly. The mating spinners had been swarming above the river, and the fish did not start to work until the females started laying their eggs.

Ginger Quill, I thought.

The fish were working steadily now. There were both parachute spentwings and conventional Ginger Quills in my fly box and I tried them both without success. Both the male and female naturals resembled these dry flies, with their hackle quill bodies and pale ginger hackles.

That's strange, I thought.

The light Cahills in my boxes were tied with chalky fur bodies, and I did not really expect them to work, but the failure of the Ginger Quills was a surprise. Their dressings looked right to me, but the fish thought otherwise. Trout after trout rejected them at a time when the evening was so filled with egg-sac spinners that the fish went crazy.

There were so many rising now that I searched my fly boxes frantically.

Maybe it's the egg sacs they're looking for, I thought aloud.

The Female Beaverkill is a popular pattern in Michigan, and I often carried them dressed with somewhat paler hackles than the commercial patterns one finds in the shops. There were a few tied on sixteen hooks, with pale ginger hackles and delicate little woodduck tails and bodies of yellow rayon floss. Their egg sacs were bright yellow wool tied full and fat at the root of the tails.

Try one! I thought.

The results were immediate. The little egg-sac Beaverkill settled above a nearby fish and was engulfed in an eager splash. Six or eight more took just as eagerly once the fly was dried and floating again, and then they stopped taking.

Funny! I shook my head. *What the devil's wrong?*

The fish were still working, although their rise forms were quieter now.

There were still a few egg-sac spinners coming down, but it was the smaller males that filled the twilight now. Bending down to study the current in the waning light, I discovered it was covered with spent males and females, their egg sacs fully extruded and gone.

It could explain the quiet rises, I thought eagerly. *Maybe I should try those parachute spentwings again.*

The egg-sac spinners had expended their eggs, and when I tried a pale spentwing with parachute hackles, a trout took it without hesitation. It was the first time I had consciously observed trout changing their feeding preferences during a single evening, looking first for the rich egg-filled spinners, and finally turning to the spent flies when their mating was finally done. The Ginger Quills had failed when the egg-sac spinners were available, because the fish found the egg-filled females more attractive. The effectiveness of the Female Beaverkills ended when the egg laying was virtually complete, and most of the spinners had fallen spent in the surface film. Their eggs had been expended and the fish turned eagerly to the parachute Ginger Quill. The egg-laying spinners were fluttering above the current, and the trout made splashy rises in an effort to capture them. The spent flies were easy to catch; once they became the principal diet form on the water, the trout took them with quiet, dimpling rises.

It was a second indelible lesson in selectivity.

This past October I observed a striking example of similar behavior on the Henry's Fork of the Snake. The trout began rising steadily an hour before twilight, feeding greedily on a hatch of minute *Pseudocloëon* flies, and I took a dozen good rainbows on a tiny Gray-winged Olive dressed on a twenty-six hook. The little pattern worked wonders while the little duns were hatching, but suddenly the fish started refusing it.

René Harrop was fishing a hundred yards upstream, and I looked up to see how he was doing. Harrop was studying the water intently and not fishing, and it was obvious that his trout had also turned selective.

What are they doing now? I shouted.

I'm not sure, Harrop answered, *but I've got a big swarm of tiny spinners up here.* The fish were working steadily again.

Think it could be spinners? I asked.

Might be, Harrop said. *These little spinners are the same species as the duns we've been fishing.*

You really think these rainbows are that picky?

Sometimes they are, he laughed.

René Harrop is one of the finest fishermen I know, and is one of the best fly dressers anywhere, particularly on the tiny hatches. Harrop and his wife tie thousands and thousands of minute flies each winter, and his knowledge of the Henry's Fork and its hatches is remarkable.

The tiny spinners of the *Pseudocloëon* flies are exactly the same colors as the duns that precede them, except that their wings lie spent in the surface film. Imitations are dressed on twenty-six and twenty-eight hooks, and it seems unlikely that only the silhouette of the spentwings lying in the film could make a difference with such tiny flies, since color and size are identical in both duns and spinners.

You think a spent no-hackle will work? I yelled. *My fish down here just won't take the dun!*

Give it a try! Harrop insisted.

There were a half dozen pale spent-wing olive spinners in my fly boxes and I changed flies. Several good fish were dimpling softly in the smooth current downstream, and I was looking into the waning light when my first cast settled on the water. There was a delicate sucking swirl and a sixteen-inch rainbow exploded when it felt the tiny hook. More than a dozen fish took the tiny spentwing before I hooked an acrobatic four-pounder that stripped my light reel into its backing.

They like that little spinner! Harrop shouted.

It's amazing! I yelled back. *I've never seen such a clear case of selectivity to nothing more than silhouette and light pattern in the film!*

And in such tiny sizes! he laughed.

Another spring some years before, the fish on the main Au Sable below Stephan's Bridge taught me a variation on this same theme of changing fly preferences in mid-hatch. We were floating the river downstream to Wakeley Bridge, starting in the late morning. It was cold and the morning was clear, filled with the promise of hatches and a good day's sport.

Two bait fishermen were cleaning their fifteen-fish limits at the Gates canoe landing, and the crayfish were already working on the entrails in the shallows downstream. The current whispered past the cribbing where we moored the canoe as we loaded it carefully with tackle duffels and lunch baskets and a pair of thermos bottles.

Soup, Gerry Queen explained with a conspiratorial grin, *and this other one's got the Old Fashioneds for later!*

Nobody's perfect! I replied.

We pushed off into the smooth current, moving noiselessly except for the soft music of the river through the deadfalls and sweepers, and the counterpoint of our paddles. The river was still less than fifty degrees and our nymphs were ignored.

Below the landing at Stephan's Bridge, with its bustling activity and racks of rental canoes, the river became wilder and less pastoral. There were swift shallows over mottled bottoms of pale sand and gravel, dark runs under the deadfalls and willows, and deep eddying bends where the river looped back on itself. It was now late morning, and it was getting almost warm in the places where the river was sheltered from the chill wind. Redwinged blackbirds were building nests in a marshy stand of willows, where the April currents had worked back into the cedars.

Okra-lee-o! the birds cried sweetly.

Some dark mayflies started hatching in a quiet backwater where the sun had warmed the river. They were rather large, with slate gray wings and lead-colored bodies, and the smaller males were almost black, riding the current in the bright sunlight. It was a hatch of big *Leptophlebias,* although it would be years before I learned to identify these clumsily hatching flies. A few trout started to feed, and we backed our canoe out of the main currents, while I slipped over the side to fish them. The fish were small, but I took two or three on a dark Hendrickson tied with rusty, slate-dun hackles.

Well, Gerry said, *that's a start.*

Hooking the Hendrickson in the keeper ring, I clambered back into the canoe and we pushed off into the current. Our early breakfast was wearing off when we reached a sunny bank sheltered from the wind, and we stopped for lunch.

Before we had finished our hot bean soup, there was a good hatch of flies coming off the smooth run above the canoe. The fish were soon feeding steadily. We both waded out into the flat, working out line to cover the fish with the dark Hendricksons that had taken the fish before lunch. The trout refused them.

They've changed brands, I muttered.

You're right, Queen agreed.

The hatch had changed since morning. These flies were less dark, and had pale grayish tan bodies with brownish dorsal markings. Light Hendricksons tied with bronze blue-dun hackles and grayish cream fox dubbing worked perfectly, and we caught and released a dozen fish between us from the run.

That's more like it, I said.

These flies started about two o'clock, Queen looked at his watch, *and it's almost three-thirty.*

We'd better start down. I nodded.

We launched the canoe and loaded it, pushing off as the shadows lengthened across the river. Downstream a mile, the Au Sable gathered its currents at the bottom of a long waist-deep flat into a stretch of swifter water lined with sweepers.

Hatch is still heavy here. Queen stopped paddling. *Look at all the rising fish!* We drifted silently past the cedars.

Let's stop and fish awhile, I suggested.

We wrestled the canoe into the willows and moored it. Several good fish were working in the swift run, and we waded out into position to try them with our flies.

Let's take a couple for breakfast, Gerry yelled.

It was not so easy. The flies looked the same on the water, but our Hendricksons were rejected. *These fish down here won't take my fly,* I complained. *Wonder what's wrong?*

Maybe the hatch has changed?

It was possible, and I waded across into a primary current to check the naturals. There were still good numbers of the dark-winged *Ephemerella* flies coming down, although the hatch was almost finished. It was five minutes before I caught one of the mayflies. It had dark slate-colored wings and darkly ringed rust-colored body. The hatch had changed.

They're different, I yelled.

That explains why the fish ignored our flies, Queen said. *What're these flies like that are hatching now?*

Darker, I answered. *Reddish brown bodies.*

Red Quill? Queen asked.

Exactly, I said.

We took several fish with Red Quills before the hatch became sporadic and finally ended. Here was a prime example of the serial problems in matching the hatch across a single day, in which three overlapping species emerged. Rather than matching the emergence of a single natural, sometimes two or three hatches must be matched over several hours of fishing. It is a lesson I have had to learn many times over the years. It also was an example of the impossibility of matching the hatch by merely observing the flies on the water. More than twenty-five years ago on the Au Sable, the fish had proved twice in a single afternoon how foolish such laziness can be.

It is equally impossible to match the hatch by observing naturals fluttering in the air, particularly in sunlight. Any insect observed against the light always looks much paler than it actually is, and it is not unusual to hear fishermen talking about picking fly patterns from the look of a hatching insect in flight. It is the kind of mistake you can observe often on trout waters from Maine to California.

What's hatching? It is a familiar cry.

Don't know! The answer is equally familiar. *They look like Light Cahills, but the fish just won't take the Cahills!*

You actually catch one of the flies? somebody asks.

No, comes the sheepish reply.

Such exchanges are typical on almost every river, and except for failing to respect the shyness and cunning of the trout, matching the hatch without capturing a specimen is perhaps the single most basic mistake in stream tactics. It is a mistake often made with caddisflies, since their pale rear wings are visible in flight, but are folded underneath the darker forewings when they are on the water. Most insects look paler in flight, but the whitish rear wings of most Trichoptera exaggerate this effect even more. Sedge hatches gave me trouble for years, because I invariably misjudged their color and size in the air. Many caddis hatches rise to memory, from early experiences with *Cheumatopsyche* flies on the Frying Pan in Colorado and *Rhyacophila* hatches on the Little South Pere Marquette in Michigan to similar problems on European rivers like the Pegnitz and Leizach in Bavaria. Such difficulties in matching caddis hatches are found on back country rivers too, like the Quilquihue and Collón Curá and Caleufu in the foothill pampas of Patagonia.

One evening on the lower Quilquihue comes instantly to mind for its remarkable hatch of sedges. We were camping on the river not far from its junction with the Chimehuin, and the late Guy Dawson had fished his favorite pools with me on the Quilquihue the first afternoon. Dawson was particularly attracted to the last major pool above the Chimehuin, although it surrendered only two eighteen-inch rainbows that day.

It's a fine pool, Dawson insisted. *It's provided two fish over eight pounds this summer, and the season lasts another two months.*

Browns or rainbows? I asked.

Both! he smiled.

It was a pool that formed where two channels of the river came together at the head of a right-angle bend. The primary channel shelved off steeply at the bottom of a one-hundred-yard chute. It deepened to some ten feet of water there, with a long current tongue working two hundred yards down a curving, undercut bank. The pool ended in a smooth knee-deep flat, where the fish dropped back to feed just before dark.

Two days later, I was fishing the pool in late afternoon when a hatch of big sedges emerged. The flies looked straw-colored and as large as size eight or ten, and they hopscotched and fluttered busily down the current. The fish suddenly were working on the surface, taking them greedily.

My fly books were filled with big bucktails and streamers, and one was layered with inch-long wet flies and nymphs. Matching the hatch was not a problem I had expected to find on the little-fished rivers of Argentina. There was a box of big western dry flies in my wading vest, and I rummaged through it for something that resembled the big Trichopteras that filled the twilight like a blizzard. There were three or four Donnelly Variants in one compartment, three dressed in dark brown hackles mixed with grizzly, and two mixed with pale ginger. Bob Carmichael had sold them to me years before, for fishing the tumbling Gros Ventre and Snake in Jackson Hole.

The Light Donnelly Variant looked just like the hatching flies, and I put it over the half-dozen big rainbows that were busily taking the naturals. It was completely rejected.

Funny, I thought. *It looks perfect!*

The big dry fly came down among the fluttering naturals and the feeding trout. One fat rainbow took a big caddis, ignored my imitation, and took another natural the moment my fly floated past. The clear pattern of rejection was repeated several times, and I stood there watching the fish gorge themselves.

It was a frustrating sight.

Suddenly I noticed a pair of big sedges clinging to my dark waders on the downwind side. Their wings and antennae were darkly mottled brown, totally unlike their pale yellowish appearance in the evening sunlight.

Maybe that's it. I reached inside my vest for the fly box. *Maybe the darker version will work!*

The dark pattern did not look yellow enough to match the hatching flies that fluttered along the surface in the wind, but it looked right to the fish. The pool yielded the best evening of dry-fly sport I have ever experienced anywhere. It was simply a matter of getting the fly floating again after each trout drowned it, and then putting it above another fish.

The pool was filled with good rainbows running eighteen to twenty inches, and I caught them until my arm and wrist were exhausted. The best fish went twenty-three inches, and took the dry fly with a tantalizingly slow head-and-tail rise that sent my pulse racing.

It's fantastic! I thought when the hatch was finished and the pool flowed silent again. *Twenty-nine fish over two pounds with dry flies—imagine the score if I'd picked the right fly when these sedges started!*

It was a unique experience, and it has never happened again in several trips into the Argentine, although that pool on the Quilquihue has always been productive. This past season it surrendered an eight-pound brown to a Muddler worked deep along the bottom, and it has become one of my favorites. It will always be Dawson's Pool in my mind.

Several years later on the Chimehuin, we were fishing the famous Black Bridge Pool a few miles below its junction with the Quilquihue. It is big-fish water, wide and smooth flowing below a place where the river batters and churns through a series of earthquake faults in the lava. It was late afternoon and the barren cinder cone of the Cerro de los Pinos rose in the east above the foothills across the two rivers, its ragged summits reflected in the currents.

When a similar hatch of big sedges started coming off the mile-long flat below the bridge, I laughed happily and started rooting through my fly vest for the Donnelly Variants.

It's going to be some evening! I thought.

But I was wrong again. The big rainbows started rolling and swirling everywhere, and I waded eagerly into the heavy current. The big variant worked rhythmically back and forth while I lengthened line, and I laid it expectantly over a good fish. It floated down its feeding lane unmolested, and I watched it drift through and start to drag badly.

Damn! I said.

Every fish within casting distance let it pass, and my excitement quickly ebbed. It was a fairly good hatch, and the trout were showing well, but several dry flies that seemed like good imitations were rejected completely.

Maybe they're not feeding on top, I thought.

I stopped fishing and watched the fish working only thirty feet out in the current. The bulging rises were strong, indicating that the fish really wanted what they were taking, and that what they were feeding on was relatively difficult to capture. The rises were not splashy, although an occasional fish did break the surface after a fluttering sedge.

Suddenly I realized that a fish had slashed eagerly across the current, and that a sedge came leapfrogging out of the splash. But that sedge had not been visible coming down the current before the rise.

It was hatching! I thought eagerly. *That fish missed it just before it hatched, and tried again!*

Several minutes of watching confirmed that diagnosis. The rises were not to the fluttering adults, although in my excitement I had just assumed the fish were taking the sedges that were everywhere. Two or three fish broke the steady rhythm of their feeding when a hatching fly escaped their swirling rises, and they splashed clumsily after the freshly hatched sedges. The fish were taking the hatching pupae.

Something with soft mottled hackles. I frowned. *Soft partridge or woodcock with a dubbed body of hare's mask.*

It was time for a simple Yorkshire-type wet, but the closest thing in my fly books was a darkly-hackled March Brown dressed in the British pattern. There were a half-dozen on size eight hooks. Their wings were too prominent, and I trimmed them down with the scissors in my fishing knife, clipping off the tails and picking out the dubbing with the stiletto.

Looks buggy enough, I concluded.

The rainbows were still working steadily. My first cast dropped quartering downstream above a good fish, and I teased its swing with the rod tip. It worked through the trout's position and there was a strong pull as the fish hooked itself, tailwalking explosively across the swift current. It was the solution that other long-ago afternoon on the Chimehuin.

There was a similar experience on the incomparable Firehole in the Yellowstone in late September. The Firehole is famous for its hatches and its surface-feeding trout, and Bergman's *Trout* is filled with praise for its marvellous dry-fly sport. His praise has led many fishermen to forget using their wet flies and nymphs on the Firehole, and it once led me to miss the solution to matching one of its hatches during several days of typically good feeding activity.

Gene Anderegg and I were fishing the Firehole that September, and it was more moody and difficult than usual. Our first morning in the Nez Percé meadows, the trout rose steadily in the pools, in the weedy channels, and along the sheltering banks.

The rises were strong, dramatic boils that occasionally erupted into a splash. It was a type of feeding behavior atypical of the Firehole trout and the quiet dimples usually visible everywhere on its currents. We took a number of small fish between six and twelve inches, using tiny spent-wing Adams and Whitcraft patterns tied on eighteen and twenty hooks. Two fish in a shallow flat succumbed to the jassid, but the larger trout kept feeding strongly in the main currents. There was one good fish working in a channel where the thick weeds had forced the current to scour deep under a grassy meadow bank.

I'm going to fish a bigger fly! Anderegg shook his head unhappily. *I'm going to fish a sixteen Adams!*

Try a really big fly—try a fourteen!

That's next! he yelled.

His bigger Adams was not the answer either, at least floated on the surface as its dressing intended, but a strange clue occurred while he was fishing it. The deep channel in the weeds, where a series of eddying currents undulated rhythmically, held the big trout that consistently refused the little dry fly. Once it rose splashily to a natural, drowning the artificial in the disturbance of its rise form, and another fish took the Adams swinging wet across the current.

We'll take anything we can get! Gene laughed.

It was a clue we ignored then, but it was the solution to the riddle of matching the hatch that morning.

There were several buffalo in the straw-grass meadows above Ojo Caliente, which spews thousands of gallons of scalding water every few minutes across the barren ledges into the Firehold. We sat in the warm grass, enjoying our sandwiches and watching the huge animals work down toward the river, grazing slowly on the rich forage. Finally they crossed the Firehole below Sentinel Creek, the swift current pushing heavily against their heavy legs and shoulders, and disappeared in the meadow bottoms beyond the river.

That season found the cold flow of Sentinel Creek forced against the far bank of the river, held between its buffalo grass and dense beds of weeds. Good fish were holding in this channel, both for its colder temperatures, and in anticipation of ascending Sentinel to spawn in a few weeks.

One good trout was working regularly, lying tight against the trailing grass, but it refused my little Whitcraft several times. Bad floats seemed like a possibility, and I moved slightly upstream to try another angle. The fish was feeding in a steady rhythm, and I studied it briefly before making another cast. My fly caught in the grass, pulled free suddenly, and was instantly drowned by the bellying leader. It was such a still current that I decided to let the Whitcraft ride through without picking up. Too early a pickup might send the fish scurrying upstream.

Easy does it, I whispered.

Suddenly there was a bulging swirl, the leader paused and darted upstream, and the fish was hooked. It bolted upstream along the channel, and held heavily along the bottom gravel. The fish surrendered stubbornly, its eighteen inches threshing in the net until I worked the hook free and released it.

Good fish? Anderegg yelled.

Couple of pounds, I answered. *You have any good fish working up there?* Several fish were rising above me.

Two or three up here, he said.

This fish was just like your fish before lunch, I yelled back. *Took my dry fly when it drowned.*

Maybe they're trying to tell us something!

Could be, I agreed.

The fish were obviously concentrating on hatching-sedge pupae, splashing at the odd pupal form that escaped to become an adult insect. Fishing wet seemed a solution. Certainly the effectiveness of a drowned dry fly is a telltale clue of such behavior. There were a dozen small partridge and brown wet flies in my wading vest, dressings that I use to imitate hatching caddisflies on the Brodheads each season, and I walked upstream to give several to Gene Anderegg.

Seems like sacrilege to fish wet on the Firehole! Anderegg grinned. *But it's probably the answer.*

Let's both try it, I said.

Anderegg changed flies, and I was still wading quietly toward the shallows when he hooked a fish.

Got one! he laughed. *That fish's been ignoring me for an hour!*

Good sign, I yelled back.

Anderegg hooked a larger trout before I started downstream to resume fishing, and it was a wild brown that chose to cartwheel like a rainbow down the current. Fishing wet to rising trout was the solution that September afternoon, with the geysers in the distance.

Another example of such offbeat behavior occurred one day on the Rolling Rock, when I was fishing with Bill Oliver of Pittsburgh. It was late April and there were heavy hatches of big *Ephemerella* flies coming down. We fished in late morning with the frost thick on the laurel and fiddleback ferns. The river was still cold from a cloudless night, registering only forty-six degrees on my Hardy thermometer. There were a few small stoneflies emerging before lunch, and I took some fish before we ate.

We had our lunch on the terrace at Rolling Rock, watching the freshly budded branches swaying against the April skies, and the green fairways of the golf course reaching toward the hills in the distance. It was a lunch filled with good talk about fishing books and Bill's fine collection of angling literature, since he is even more serious about the history of fly-fishing than about fishing itself.

It's two o'clock! Bill Oliver looked at his watch. *Your books predict Hendricksons today!*

They're not infallible! I laughed.

We drew another beat that afternoon, and I waded in along a reach of broken water below a cribbing dam, where a thin lacework of water fell smoothly from the logs. Trout were starting to work in the pockets, and although I took a few with a dry-fly imitation, most of the better fish refused it. The feeding rhythms increased.

It's not right, I said.

Most of those refusals are brown trout, Oliver said. *The brookies seem to like your Hendrickson just fine!*

That's what's wrong, I laughed.

Those brookies are from our hatchery, Oliver continued, *but some of those browns are wild carry-over fish.*

Exactly, I said.

The Hendrickson is a mayfly species that splits its thoracic skin and starts to pop its wings well before reaching the surface, and an emerging nymph pattern is often deadly. The hatching flies were clearly Hendricksons, yet the fish were letting most of the naturals float past, and kept rising regularly in the tail shallows.

I think they're on the hatching nymphs, I said.

Oliver smiled. *Give it a try!*

The preceding winter I had experimented extensively with the Rogowski-type hatching nymphs, which used rolled sections of nylon stockings to suggest emerging wing structure. They were roughly tied with dubbing and partridge legs and delicate woodduck tails. There was a fifteen-inch brown lying in a small pocket upstream, clearly visible in a patch of sunlight.

It was rising intermittently, and when I dropped my nymph slightly above its holding lie, the fish drifted toward the left and took it hard. The tempo of the hatch increased steadily, and I took fish after fish with my hatching nymph pattern. The fish strangely ignored the adult flies all afternoon, staying with the nymphs just under the surface—and fishing my imitation upstream to visibly rising trout produced almost a hundred trout between us.

Sometimes minor differences in color are important in matching the hatch, and my memory holds many examples of times when trout reacted to such subtle differences. Perhaps my first experience with subtle color phenomena occurred in earlier years on the headwaters of the Arkansas above Leadville Junction. The river was finally clear of high-country snowmelt, and the hatches were constant. We had good late-morning sport with dark blue-winged mayflies having heavily ringed and grayish-cream bodies, and on several days there were occasional specimens of *Ephemerella hecuba* that always started the big fish working. Frank Klune and I fished the Arkansas meadows every morning, and we could have filled our creels any time we wished. We took the fish regularly with three eastern patterns that matched these hatches: darkly hackled little Gordon Quills, Hendricksons, and Red Quills. These flies worked for three weeks, until another hatch came off in a swift little pool about a mile above the Leadville Junction Bridge.

They look like Red Quills, I guessed.

They're darker, Klune yelled upstream, *and they're a size or two smaller!* He walked toward me.

See if you can catch one! I shouted.

The naturals were extremely dark, with iron-blue wings and deep purplish red coloring on the belly segments of their bodies. These insects were too purplish for a normal Red Quill pattern to imitate them properly, and that night I dyed a bleached peacock eye a rich purple. The quills were wrapped over light brown underbodies, combined with iron blue hackles and tails. We used woodduck wings, perhaps imitating the Catskill style of fly dressing without thinking, and they took trout well. Dark hackle-point wings would probably have worked better. It was an interesting example of matching the hatch with relatively minor color changes.

Another interesting example occurred on the upper reaches of Silver Creek in Idaho, when a quiet morning suddenly came to life with a good hatch of sizable pale mayflies. The insects looked like our eastern *Stenonema* hatches that emerge in early summer, pale yellow and chalk-colored duns imitated by traditional patterns like the Light Cahill.

However, when I tried the pale ginger Cahill it was refused by the porpoising rainbows.

That's odd, I puzzled. *It sure looks like those flies coming down the currents.*

Fifteen minutes later I was finally convinced that my Light Cahill was a complete waste of time. Thirty-odd fish had rejected it after brief inspection rises. It was time to collect several of the naturals to determine the reasons behind my failure. The first little dun was a revelation. It was not straw-colored at all, but a faint shade of pale olive yellow, completely unlike the pale ginger hackles and woodduck wings of my Light Cahills. It had three tails, rather than the two tails usually associated with such pale hatches in the east.

It's an Ephemerella! I thought.

The olives in my box were too olive green for this hatch, and the trout refused my pale ginger dressings. My tying kit in the car had a pale olive gamecock neck that had taken the dye poorly, and was too pale for most olive mayfly imitations. It took twenty minutes to tie a pair of imitative patterns, but they took fish regularly that morning until two particularly large fish bolted into the moss and broke off. The hatch was over before I could tie another.

It was a satisfying and instructive morning.

There was a similar problem on two rivers in Wisconsin several years ago, when I was fishing with the late Art Besse. The late afternoon hatches on the Brule were good, and my last day there I sat waiting for the pale little duns. Upstream from my sitting place in the shadows, two raccoons foraged under the stones and logs for crayfish. Both raccoons were comical. Working a half-submerged log, they started at opposite ends and scuttled slowly toward each other, rooting underneath the trunk. The crayfish clambered backwards along the bottom until they were trapped between the raccoons; then they were quickly dispatched, dismembered and washed, and carefully eaten.

Shrimp cocktail! I laughed to myself.

The raccoons had fastidious table manners. They killed the crayfish, picked them apart like a skilled chef shelling a lobster, and washed each tidbit carefully before devouring it. It was fascinating, and I watched them capture six or eight crayfish before I realized a fly hatch was coming down and the fish had started to rise.

It was a hatch of Pale Sulphurs, with their faintly bluish wings and pale bodies flushed with orangish yellow. My tiny imitations were tied with pale blue hackle-point wings, and pale ginger hackles and tails. The bodies were white hackle quill lacquered with pale yellowish orange fuel-proof dope. It is a dressing originally worked out on Letort Spring Run, using the example of the Fox-type sulphurs, with their single turn of orange hackle mixed with the pale ginger. Pennsylvania fishermen on difficult limestone streams from Spruce Creek to the Little Lehigh swear by a touch of orange in their imitations of the sulphur hatch. The fish on the Brule those afternoons were busily working on these pale *Ephemerella* flies, and they accepted my imitations without hesitation. The hatch lasted several afternoons and evenings.

Before you drive back to Princeton, Besse suggested on his return to Ashland, *I want you to try the East Fork water.*

The East Fork? I asked.

It's a secret place of mine, Besse explained. *It's the East Fork of the Iron, and it's a helluva river!* He grinned conspiratorially.

What makes it so good? I pressed.

It's a limestone stream, Besse replied. *It comes out of some marl swamps southeast of the Brule.*

Try the East Fork tomorrow? I grinned.

Sure, Besse said.

It was hot that next day when we hiked downstream through the woods and fished back to the car. Later a filmy overcast muted the brightness, and a hatch of pale little duns started emerging from the swift runs along the willows.

Sulphurs again, I thought.

But that diagnosis was completely wrong. The imitative patterns that had proved so killing on the Brule failed miserably on these limestone brown trout. Fish after fish rejected my size sixteen sulphurs, until I stopped and waded upstream to find Besse. His flies were doing better, and he took several average-sized trout while I watched.

What are you using? I asked.

It's taken from your book, Besse laughed. *It's that pale little two-tailed subimago you described.*

But the usual imitations won't work!

The hatch is a little different on the East Fork, Besse continued. *It's got an olive-colored body.*

Pale olive gray? I asked.

Yes, he explained. *It's your Little Marryat with a faint olive dubbing mixed into the cream fox.*

They're that picky! I laughed in disbelief.

Try one, Besse suggested.

It seemed improbable that a faint olive cast added to the dubbing mix could make so much difference, but Besse was right. His dressing took fish readily, yet when I put my regular pattern back on the tippet, they refused it. It was clearly an example of subtle color preference, and I fished out the day using his olive-bodied flies.

Those fish are really tough! I said.

It's not such a problem. Besse had reached the highway and stopped. *The flies are in your book!*

Hate guys who read books! I laughed.

You should try it!

There was a similar experience on a smooth riffle on the Roaring Fork in Colorado, when a pale mayfly hatch started coming off just at twilight. The small hatchery rainbows took a sixteen Ginger Quill or Light Cahill readily enough, but there was a run tight against the willows where some bigger fish were rising. These fish refused such flies, and before it was dark I caught several specimens and put them in a killing jar.

That night in Basalt at the Frontier Lodge I examined the fresh specimens in their alcohol bottle. The preserving fluid had already turned their bodies a bright pink, and I wondered if the freshly hatched naturals also had a faint pinkish cast. Later I tied two or three Little Cahills with bodies of pink cellulite floss over a hook shank painted white. The pinkish cast was so faint that they looked like ordinary Light Cahills until you studied them carefully, and they darkened only slightly when wet. The following night I took four browns between twelve and eighteen inches along the willows, and only a faint pinkish color was the difference between the successful flies and the patterns that had failed before.

Several months ago, after a lecture in New York, a young man and his wife came up to the podium.

Pink-bodied Cahills! he shook hands enthusiastically. *We want to thank you for solving the problems of that hatch!*

Where did you fish it? I asked.

Wyoming! he was still bubbling. *We tried everything on the fish and nothing worked until we checked your books!*

And tied some pink-bodied flies! his wife added.

It has become a relatively common occurrence and one of the principal gratifications of writing a book like *Matching the Hatch*, since every fisherman has similar knotty problems of selectivity on his waters.

Perhaps the most unusual example of selectivity on mayflies and the sensitivity of the fish to color occurred a number of years ago on the Frying Pan in Colorado. We were fishing the Ruedi water from the ranch above the still water, a marvelous reach of river forever buried under the Frying Pan Reservoir ten years ago. Hatches were unusually mixed that week. The first evenings there were fine egg-laying flights, and we took a lot of fish with dark little sedge imitations. Later these Trichoptera became mixed with bigger mayflies that hatched just at twilight, and our caddis patterns stopped working. It was difficult to see the bigger flies on the swift currents of the footbridge pools above the ranch, and we first learned about the bigger flies through stomach autopsies of the fish.

The partially digested mayflies were still identifiable, and we started to take fish regularly again. We fished our little down-wing sedge flies from early evening until nightfall, switching to the bigger drakes after it got dark. Subsequent stomach autopsies and consistently good catches seemed to confirm our diagnosis, until one night the fish started feeding heavily, and our flies were systematically rejected.

What're they doing now? Frank Klune asked.

God knows! I answered.

Finally we caught one of the selective feeders when I started fishing a partridge-legged nymph in desperation, but it was the only fish that responded, and the feeding stopped with the hatch.

Autopsy time! We waded from the river.

We checked the stomach contents in a white dish back at the cabin once our Coleman lanterns were going. Deep in the entrails the digested insects were an undecipherable mass, but up toward the throat there were several sedge pupae. Adult sedges followed in good numbers, and finally there were a few big mayfly nymphs and several duns that we were not able to identify in those early years.

No wonder we couldn't get them, I said. *It was too late in the hatch for nymphs to work, and our dry fly patterns are completely wrong.*

They sure are, Klune agreed.

Earlier in the week, the twilight hatch of mayflies had dark lead-colored wings and bodies ringed with rich reddish brown. There were three heavily mottled tails and grayish mottled legs, but our mystery hatch was completely different.

It had grayish wings with faint mottlings, although the wings were so fragmented or wrapped around the bodies and themselves that it was difficult to tell exactly. It also had three tails, but they were speckled like the 'fibers from a darkly-barred flank feather of woodduck. The legs were dark amber, marked with brownish mottlings, and the thorax and abdomen were amber ringed with brown. Some specimens had a hint of orangey red in their body markings, and the flies were big enough that their wings measured as much as three-quarters of an inch in length. Except for the number of tails they looked familiar.

They're a little like our eastern March Browns, I said.

Let's tie some! Klune suggested.

The March Brown pattern was tried, with the addition of a dubbing spun on dark-orange silk ribbing a cream-fox body. The woodduck wings and mixed brown and grizzly hackles worked perfectly, and for several days we matched three hatches in sequence each evening. The sedges were still hatching in late afternoon and early evening, and we fished imitations effectively until the lead-winged duns started coming off the water. These flies were effective until the larger brownish drakes started coming off just before nightfall.

However, it was not this serial problem in matching the hatch that proved most instructive. It was the remarkable selectivity to color in the dark that intrigued me. Both imitative patterns were dressed on size ten, and had precisely the same materials, configuration, and silhouette. The woodduck wings were identical, and both bodies were dubbed and ribbed with fur spun on silk. Hackle color varied between dark bronze-blue dun and brown gamecock mixed with grizzly. Body color was different, too. Those still-water brown trout consistently rejected the March Brown pattern while feeding on the big *Ephemerellas,* and they refused the bluish gray dressings when the mottled brownish drakes started hatching at nightfall.

They're even selective after dark! Frank Klune laughed.

It was a remarkable lesson in both selectivity and color sense, and I shall never forget it. It has proved valuable on selective trout from California to Austria, clearly proving that no trout fisherman should ever underestimate the color sense of his quarry.

Serial problems in matching the hatch are not limited to overlapping emergence of several insects; they also lie within the spectrum of a single insect species. Mayflies are quite typical of such behavior. The nymphs of each species progress through a series of instars, or physical stages of growth, between hatching from the eggs to full nymphal maturity before emergence. This means that each species reaches a number of intermediate growth stages, and that a nymphal imitation that suggests pre-hatch maturity in size twelve is also useful in the smaller sizes from fourteen to twenty-two, simulating earlier stages of development. Each pattern is useful in a number of sizes.

Behavior is another factor in matching the hatch, particularly in the nymphal stages, although the fluttering behavior of some adult insects is important as well. Such tactics are explored extensively in *Fishing the Dry Fly as a Living Insect*, which Leonard Wright first published in 1972. My subsequent book *Nymphs* makes the point that effective nymph fishing is as dependent upon presentation and manipulation of fly speed and motion as on the fly pattern itself.

Burrowing mayfly nymphs are as agile as baitfish when swimming toward the surface to hatch. Other swimming nymphal forms do not bury themselves in silt and detritus, but forage freely among the stones and current-rich weeds, darting swiftly from place to place. Clambering nymphs range about clumsily in various types of water and are best imitated with nymphs fished deep with a slow, deliberate retrieve. Tiny swimming nymphs are agile, but their agility is barely perceptible except in slow-moving rhythms in the rubble and weeds. Clinging nymphs of swift water and the crawling nymphs, as well as sedge larvae and other similar diet forms, are virtually helpless when caught in faster currents. Their imitations should be fished deep and deaddrift. Stoneflies typically clamber and cling along the bottom, and imitations of their nymphal forms should also be fished deaddrift.

Hatching behavior is equally important. The larger swimming nymphs, and clambering ecotypes like the stoneflies, migrate into shallow water and cling to fallen logs and stones to split their nymphal skins and hatch. Many large nymphs hatch in the surface film, experience considerable difficulty in escaping their nymphal skins, and ride the shucks before flying off. Other species actually hatch into the winged stages while their nymphs still cling to the bottom. Many hatches begin to escape their nymphal forms well below the surface film, wriggling along for several feet before actually breaking through as winged insects. These patterns of behavior suggest varying approaches to imitation: different types of hooks, weighting of the flies with lead, tying the patterns with different winging styles from minimal development to the fully winged state, and manipulation of fly speed and retrieve.

The cycle of mayfly hatching also suggests a number of phases in matching the hatch during a single emergence cycle. Nymphs along the bottom mean heavy-wire hooks, possible weighting of the flies, and a sinking-line presentation. Partially developed wings should be included for species that actually hatch along the bottom. Hatching mayflies at intermediate depths are often wriggling and struggling clumsily, both to escape their nymphal skins and reach the surface. Some nymphs split their thoracic cases before reaching the meniscus, and their wings begin to unfold underwater. Others emerge using the tensile force of the surface film, their wings unfolding clumsily and partially awash. Nymphs that escape their nymphal skins slowly often ride them in the surface film for as much as sixty to a hundred feet. Such imitations should be dressed with emerging-type wings, while a fully hatched dun is best imitated with upright wings.

Mayfly spinners pose different problems. Many large species lay their eggs from two large sacs while actually riding the current. Several species leapfrog along the surface in a series of graceful parabolas, extruding a few eggs each time they touch the water. Others form their ova into fat little egg sacs, dropping them or washing them off in the river, and still others ride the current momentarily while extruding their eggs, flutter upward briefly, and settle again to lay more ova. Several minute species of mayflies and several sedges migrate underwater to oviposit their eggs.

Such behavior has interesting implications for fly making and matching the hatch. Windy weather can deposit any species of mayfly spinner into the river, and imitations with upright wings are useful as well as the typical spent-wing dressings. Since the eggs are extruded well before the flies are spent, egg-sac patterns are probably most useful with upright or divided-style wings. Many spinners fall into the current after mating and laying their eggs, their wings divided and faltering. Finally the wings lie spent in the surface film, and such spinners are virtually invisible drifting on the water.

Many spinners reach the streamside foliage after mating and expire slowly, dropping hours later into the river. Some fall spent immediately after oviposition, and a few species molt and lay their eggs shortly after hatching. Such spinner falls are difficult to diagnose and offer challenging sport on many streams.

Spinner falls usually occur immediately after a mating swarm is finished, and sometimes the spent flies are still available the following morning. Even the larger spinners are difficult to see drifting spent on a still flat, and with the smaller species it seems as if the fish are taking something invisible. Such spinners are often found in good numbers, and the fish take them with a quiet, methodical rhythm in which one rise form is scarcely finished before another insect is taken. Their steady feeding rhythms can be frustrating, particularly when an angler fails to diagnose feeding on spent spinners.

Some of the finest rises to a spinner fall occur on Idaho streams like the **Henry's Fork** of the Snake, and the famous Silver Creek in the Sun Valley country. Ruedi still water on the Frying Pan once provided marvelous fishing to spent mayflies in its tail shallows before it was inundated behind the Ruedi Reservoir, particularly during the fine *Leptophlebia* hatches in September.

There are also minute species like *Caenis* and *Tricorythodes* that hatch, form into mating swarms, oviposit, and fall spent almost immediately. Their duns and spinners are often virtually identical. Tiny no-hackle spentwings tied of polypropylene or fur dubbing are often effective imitations. Over the years I have fished some excellent twilight hatches of *Caenis* flies on both slow streams and low-altitude ponds, while the ubiquitous little *Tricorythodes* is typically a hatch of early and late morning. Such tiny flies are imitated with size twenty-four to twenty-eight hooks, yet they are present in such vast numbers that surprisingly big fish take them on the surface. It is interesting fishing.

This past summer on Silver Creek in Idaho I fished over some early *Tricorythodes* hatches, using tiny iron blue hackle nymphs when the hatch was starting, tiny white-winged uprights in the thorax-style during the hatch itself, and finished with spent no-hackle spinners. The big rainbows took the little nymphs on a simple downstream swing, teasing against the tension of the leader, and later sipped the hatching duns with audible sucking rises. They took the tiny spinners with gentle dimples and porpoising swirls as if they knew the spent flies were pinioned in the surface film and could not escape.

However, the spinner fall is not the only type of quiet feeding that occurs with nothing visible on the water. It often takes place when fish are concentrating on midge larvae and pupae, and sometimes it happens when midges are actually hatching.

Years ago I was fishing the South Platte in Eleven Mile Canyon when the fish began working steadily. The rises barely disturbed the surface. The feeding rhythm was so steady that the first gentle rise form had scarcely ebbed before a second had dimpled the surface. The fish seldom have such an abundance of food, and I started using a tiny parachute spinner, thinking it might be a fall of tiny spinners, but the trout consistently refused my imitation.

What are they doing? I wondered.

Flying ants sometimes trigger such regular feeding rhythms, but none were evident anywhere in the shallows. No other insects were visible on the surface, yet the fish were working steadily.

It's in the film, I thought, *and it's something small!* Several fish were dimpling in a deep run below some rocks.

Such feeding is sometimes focused on concentrations of midge larvae or pupae, which occur in several cycles during the season. These concentrations can occur virtually any time through the spectrum of the season, although on western rivers I have seen the largest numbers of such subaquatic Diptera from June through October. We were fishing the South Platte on the final day of the season, warm and perfectly still in the canyon above Deckers. Several mule deer drifted down through the stand of ponderosa and crossed the river below.

There were two men fishing salmon eggs illegally in a deep run among the boulders two hundred yards upstream. Since I had often experienced good fishing with a small Whitcraft or Adams, I started fishing these flies over the feeding trout. When they refused both of these patterns, I tried a size twenty Blue Quill, another pattern that has often proved its worth on the Platte. It was also systematically refused.

It must be midges, I thought finally.

There was nothing visible on the water, and I studied the current for several minutes without discovering anything. There were a number of tiny dubbing midge larvae in several colors in my fly books, and I selected a slender pattern which was nothing more than some dark olive dubbing delicately ribbed with condor quill and mixed with a few short guard hairs. It was lightly oiled with a film of silicone on my fingertips, and I clinch-knotted it to the 7X tippet. The fly worked a miracle.

These difficult browns were unusually wary, their senses honed in a season-long parade of fishermen from Denver and Colorado Springs. After refusing my conventional patterns, these same fish seemed as gullible as hatchery trout. The fish in the run above me were not large, although two went twelve or thirteen inches, and each took the tiny larva without hesitation.

The trout were almost totally browns, although Colorado stocks mostly rainbows. There were still a few rainbows left from the spring stocking programs, but most had either been caught or had migrated downstream by late October.

It is always satisfying to solve a difficult problem when the fish are dimpling everywhere in a smooth current. I caught and released fifteen or twenty good trout in the next one hundred yards. The two bait fishermen caught a sucker drifting their eggs on the bottom in the hole between the boulders. Their creels were still empty when I reached the smooth flat fifty yards below them.

Mister! they yelled. *You catching trout?*

The tiny midge imitations had produced about forty trout, and I had released them all. *Yes,* I replied.

You ain't keeping none? The question had a sullen tone.

No, I answered quietly.

There were ten or twelve fish dimpling between us, including a few rising less than twenty feet below the bait fishermen.

You using flies? they continued. *Catching all them fish?*

Yes, I said.

The fish between us still took my flies readily in the film, and I hooked and released a half dozen in the flat below them. They were not large trout, but they fought well on my delicate tackle, and I released them gently. There was a dark run along a fallen log in the shallows upstream, and a faint movement there seemed to disturb the current.

Was that a fish? I watched the log carefully.

The quiet disturbance came again, bulging slightly in the current against the deadfall, and the rise form died quickly. The fish rose again and again, barely showing itself. There was a swift current tongue between my position and the run along the tree, and I decided to get closer to the fish. It looked like a good trout and I approached on my knees in the shallows. The fish was only twenty-five feet away, and I dropped the little olive larva softly above its station. It was impossible to see the fly, and when there was a quick dimple I tightened gently. The shallows exploded.

Big fish! I thought wildly.

It was a fish of about three pounds, and it bolted upstream toward the bait fishermen, stripping line with a shrill chorus from the reel. It stripped more line in a second run and jumped just below their boulder hole, and both bait fishermen stood up angrily on the rocks.

Goddammit! one muttered, *I seen enough!*

They were already well up the trail above the river when the good brown finally turned weakly on its side and drifted head first into my waiting net.

Working the tiny hook free, I held it briefly in the shallows until it struggled out of my hands. The fat brown drifted off below my legs and held there, moving its gills steadily. The dubbing was thin and shredded, and I was replacing my fly when a gargantuan splash echoed in the canyon.

Sonofabitch! one of the men shouted. *You ain't catching them fish in our hole!* Another big stone whistled over my head, and fell heavily into their hole in the boulders.

Sonofabitch! The third stone made a huge splash.

Such episodes are mercifully rare, although impressive rises of trout are common on heavy concentrations of midge larvae and pupae. Fishermen on big water like the East Branch of the Delaware in New York, the famous Muskegon and Big Manistee in Michigan, and the Upper Yellowstone or Snake are familiar with the sight of hundreds of fish dimpling softly in the film.

The Au Sable in Michigan is another river, rich in alkalinity from its marl swamps and springs, with frequent concentrations of midge larvae and pupae. It is the origin of a fly dressing called Griffith's Gnat, which is often a surprisingly effective pattern when the midge pupae are actually hatching. It is a simple fly worked out by George Griffith, the founder of Trout Unlimited, who has a charming cabin on a high moraine above the Wakeley Bridge.

His original dressing was a peacock herl body, palmer-tied with a small grizzly hackle. Light-wire hooks from size sixteen to a tiny twenty-eight are typically used. Fished half-awash in the film, the pattern is an excellent imitation of a hatching midge still tangled in its tiny pupal skin. Other color combinations are effective too, and these little palmer-tied gnats have often produced well for me during midge-feeding activity when conventional flies failed to take fish. It undoubtedly provides a color mix, silhouette, and light pattern in the surface film not found with other midge imitations. Such differences are often important, and once made the difference on a huge flat in the Yellowstone.

Literally millions of midge pupae were drifting into the river from the marl-rich ecology of Yellowstone Lake, and its surface was covered for miles with the dimples of countless rising fish. It was one of the most impressive rises of trout I have ever seen, unrivalled except for the brief periods of heavy spinner-fall feeding on the Henry's Fork of the Snake.

The hatching midges were brownish gray, and their swarms filled the windless twilight. Many times with that particular *Chironomus* hatch I have taken some remarkable catches of fish, using either a tiny Adams or Whitcraft when the fish were taking the adult midges. Brownish midge larval and pupal imitations are also often effective when the fish decide to concentrate on the subaquatic stages. But this time these patterns failed utterly.

Standing waist-deep in the smooth flow of the Yellowstone flats, I placed cast after cast over the rising cutthroats. My flies dropped softly above each fish I tried. The fish invariably rose just before my flies reached them, and dimpled again just after my flies floated past. It was frustrating, and I tried pattern after pattern, over fish after fish. The exquisite torture lasted more than an hour.

Finally I tried a small Griffith's Gnat over them, half expecting it to float back unmolested, and I was surprised to see it disappear in a quiet dimple. The fish was a surprise too, since it bolted upstream along the bottom, taking all the fly line and about fifteen yards of backing. It was twenty minutes before I worked it back against the fragile nylon, and when it drifted close I gasped.

Six or seven pounds! I said breathlessly.

It was a huge female cutthroat. It circled weakly against my frail tippet for another ten or fifteen minutes, and when it finally surrendered, it disgorged a handful of half-emerged midge pupae. Most of these pupae washed free into the current, but many caught in the meshes of the net and the gills of the fish. The pupae had all been taken before they could fully escape their subaquatic skins, and were dark little silhouettes pinioned in a diaphanous shuck of half-transparent chitinous covering. Neither a conventional dry fly nor imitations of the subaquatic forms had worked, and a fly dressing that suggested a partially hatched midge still pinioned in the surface film was the solution that September twilight.

Steady feeding in hot windy weather is usually focused on terrestrial insects like ants and leafhoppers and beetles. It takes relatively warm weather to make these ecotypes active and venturesome enough to explore the bankside foliage and vegetation, together with gusts of wind to tumble them into the water.

Sometimes it happens unexpectedly.

Several years ago I was fishing the South Raritan one afternoon in early April. It was unmistakably Hendrickson time and there were a few mayflies hatching at two o'clock when I waded into a pool below Califon. The fish were already working steadily. It was warm and I expected a good mayfly hatch that afternoon, so I started fishing the rise forms with a Hendrickson nymph.

The fish kept rising along the willows, but nothing came to my carefully fished nymph except two small sunfish and a fat Warmouth bass. The selective fish among them were probably trout. It was almost hot at three-thirty, and a brisk April wind blew downstream. The temperature and the wind should have been the clue, but I missed its importance until later in the day.

The trout were working regularly now, their quiet rises barely dimpling the current. The rise forms should also have told me something, but I missed that clue as well. When a thick mayfly hatch started, I began fishing a dry-fly imitation. The fish refused it several times until a bluegill took it solidly when it started to drag. It had tiny ants in its small gasping mouth.

Damn! I thought in disgust. *You should have guessed as much!*

The rises were too quiet for the fluttering mayflies or their hatching nymphs. The temperatures meant that ants would be unseasonably active in the willows and trees, and the wind was getting them into the river in good numbers. It was then that I noticed the third clue I had missed. There was an obvious relationship between the wind and the rising trout: as the wind stirred through the willows the number of rises quickly increased.

The wind is blowing them onto the river, I thought.

It was easy after that, and a tiny seal-fur ant dressed on a size twenty hook took a dozen browns and rainbows before it finally grew cool and the trout stopped feeding. They were carefully released in gratitude for a fine day's sport.

Sometimes terrestrial feeding is a mixture of things, particularly in midsummer when several kinds of insects are in the trees and foliage. There was another hot windy day on the Beaverkill that season when I discovered twenty-odd fish in surprisingly shallow water. The fish were lying over a stony bottom in patchy sunlight, and I fortunately saw them before they spotted me. Some of these browns were lying together in groups of three and four, and others were lying alone. The fish were virtually resting on the bottom.

Wonder what they're doing? I said aloud.

The fish lay quietly until a strong gust of wind riffled the water, and suddenly there were rises everywhere. The fish were sipping and dimpling in the film, and when the wind dropped the trout were quiet again.

Ants, I thought.

It was a good choice, and I quickly took three fish with a tiny twenty-two ant, but a third trout inspected it and refused.

Wonder what he wants, I laughed to myself. *Cinnamon ant?*

The little cinnamon ant was rejected, too, and a twenty-two rusty ant with dun hackles was not even studied when it floated over the fish. It rose and took something tiny from the film, scarcely disturbing the surface. It quickly dimpled again.

Maybe they're taking leafhoppers along those willows, I thought.

The fourth trout took a small Jassid with delicate black hackles, but the fifth fish moved to intercept its float, studied it briefly, and returned to its lie over the gravel.

Try the ant again. I trimmed the Jassid off.

It worked and the fish threshed in surprise, while I coaxed it gently downstream away from the others. It was a good fish, brightly spotted and butter yellow along its belly, and it lay in the shallows after I released it, eyeing me balefully for disturbing its meal. Two more fish took the ant before another balked.

Another difficult gourmet? I wondered.

It was a fish of fifteen or sixteen inches, and it refused my Black Jassid as well. *Tiny beetle?* I thought.

There were several small green-feather beetles in my fly boxes, imitations dressed on delicate size-twenty hooks. Clinching one to the tippet, I made a short cast that dropped it softly above the fish. The tiny beetle lay flat in the surface film, and the big fish nosed it curiously before refusing.

Maybe the beetle's too big. The scissors on my fishing knife trimmed the feather wing until it was a tiny oval an eighth of an inch in length. *Maybe he'll take it when it looks a size smaller.*

It worked perfectly and the big trout inhaled it without a qualm, bolting angrily through the shallows when I tightened. The remaining fish scattered like frightened quail, fleeing past me downstream and leaving the shallows upstream. It was no longer necessary to stalk them on my knees, and I stood up to play the big fish that had taken the beetle. It writhed in the shallows and tried to foul my leader in some roots, and I parried it with measured pressure from the delicate straining of my Leonard. It scuttled sideways to work under a flat stone, but it was much too large, and the delicate tippet did not touch its rough edges. It came back stubbornly with the gentle tension of the rod tip, and then stripped line again, while my little Hardy played its ratchety melodies. It was stubborn with such a tiny hook and a spiderweb tippet, but it finally came to the waiting net, its gills and fins working weakly in the shallows.

It was finally over and I released the fat two-pound fish. It was a valuable lesson about selective trout and matching the hatch in the heat of midsummer.

Sometimes it gets complicated. I studied the beautiful fish that lay exhausted at my feet, its spotted gill covers slowly recovering their strength. *Sometimes you have to match the hatch on a fish-by-fish basis.*

It is a valuable axiom on hard-fished water.

12. Ethics, Manners, and Philosophy Astream

It has been more than twenty years since that first Colorado summer. The cutting in the hayfields was almost finished, but several rainy afternoons had made the irrigation bottoms too wet for mowing. The irrigation ditches were dry except for the rain. Their sluice gates were closed, and their flow had been returned to the little creek that tumbled down the northeast shoulder of Mount Massive. The creek had run milky for a day or two, and then the turbidity settled and cleared. Its currents were unseasonably high for late summer, but it was fishable.

The overcast obscured the mountains across the Arkansas bottoms, and the morning train climbed achingly up the long grade from Granite to the Malta Crossing. There were four engines pulling two miles of freight cars. The lead engine whistled, and the diesels strained slowly toward the Tennessee Pass and the Pacific watershed in the Pando bottoms beyond. The steady rain had stopped its drumfire rhythms on the roof just before daylight, and the radio promised better weather.

Hatches should be good, I thought.

There was no haying scheduled that morning, but I had chores in the horse barns. There was manure to clear and shovel out, and I worked slowly until the water ran swift and clean again in the stone gutters behind the stalls.

Finished, I announced back at the house.

You're off fishing again? my aunt asked. *Will you be back in time for lunch?* She was baking fresh bread.

I'll just take a sandwich, I said.

My tackle was in the bunkhouse. The rod hung on three finish nails in the wainscoting wall, and I shouldered into my waders and wading vest and creel. It was a two-mile walk through the irrigation bottoms to the serpentine willows that marked the winding course of the creek.

Its currents begin in the snowfields below the three-part summit of Massive, tumbling through high meadows bright with tiny alpine flowers. There are curious quaking bogs far above timberline. It flows through a chain of tiny lakes and beaver ponds filled with small cutthroats and brook trout. There is one large beaver pond above the main ranch buildings, and sometimes I saddled a horse to fish it in the evenings. The creek below the big beaver pond held many brook trout and some rainbows, but there were also a few cutthroats and deep pockets that sheltered browns.

The creek tumbled wildly down its final boulder-strewn ravine to the valley floor, less than one hundred yards south of the ranch. It wound into the Arkansas bottoms through willow-lined channels, looping toward the river in the distance, and its lower mileage was brown-trout water.

Its deep meadow pools and cut-bank runs were typical of brown-trout fishing. It was water that often seemed empty, but the fish were always there. It was possible to fish for hours on most days without catching a brown. There were always a few rainbows and the odd brookie below the ranch buildings, but when a gentle rain misted down the valley and triggered a good hatch of flies, its seemingly barren water was suddenly alive with surface-feeding browns.

The creek joins the river in a long sweeping bend with deeply undercut banks. Its currents are soft and smooth over fine gravel. Coarse grass trails in the waist-deep water tight against the banks, and although it always seemed like a perfect pool, I had never seen a fish rising there.

The pool was strangely empty, and I thought about it sometimes in the last half-wakeful moments before sleep, hearing the glowing coals shifting in the pot-bellied stove and mice scuttling in the bunkhouse walls.

The solution to its riddles occurred to me that morning, while I was walking down through the hay meadows. My approach to those last fifty yards of the creek had always been from upstream, walking on the grassy path beside the pool. From the waist-deep grass that lined the path it was possible to see every pebble on the bottom, but it was also possible for every trout to observe an approaching fisherman.

Idiot! I thought angrily to myself. *Cross the creek and wade up from downstream!*

The opposite bank was thickly overgrown with willows and the driftwood tangles gathered during the spring snowmelt. It was difficult going and I fought through the thickets, carrying my rod high above the branches or butt-first in the brush. Half-wild cattle bellowed and crashed deeper into the willows like buffaloes, and I was soaked with perspiration when I finally escaped into the open river bottoms. It was almost noon and getting hot, and I washed my face in the water.

The creek joined the river fifty yards upstream, and I waded slowly toward the gravel bar and sat down to rest and cool off. It felt good to strip my waders off and shed my tackle vest. There were a few mayflies hatching. They were fairly large insects, fluttering down the smooth-flowing run. Their pale wings had a slight olive cast, and they looked like big Cahills rising off the current into the willows.

Since that summer I have learned that they were *Ephemerella inermis,* but that season such hatches only set me searching my fly boxes for pale imitations. There was a fresh Light Cahill in one compartment, its rolled woodduck wings and pale ginger hackles stiffly cocked and unsoiled. It was carefully knotted to my tippet, and I studied the dark-water run along the grass. The flies were still emerging sporadically, but no rises showed in the quiet currents. The pool flowed still and smooth.

Weather is capricious at 9,000 feet. Clouds gathered on the high saddle of Mount Massive, where they had been forming since midday, and a brief squall moved across the valley. The fine drizzle scarcely disturbed the stream, but it seemed to trigger a full-blown hatch of the tiny straw-colored mayflies.

It happened almost imperceptibly.

The flies emerged from the smooth current, fluttered awkwardly in the rain while their wings dried, and flew off haltingly into the willows. The pale duns went virtually unnoticed until a sudden splash engulfed a fluttering insect tight against the grass. The disturbance of the rise spread downstream on the current.

Big fish! I thought excitedly.

There was a second porpoiselike rise, showing a thick well-spotted bulk.

No wonder I've never seen other fish in this pool, I thought. *He's got the whole pool staked out!*

Working stealthily into position, I checked the leader for casting knots and frayed places while the big trout rose again and again. My cast dropped softly and cocked the fly above the fish, reached its feeding position, and disappeared into a bold swirl. There was nothing there when I tightened.

Damn! I muttered. *Missed him!*

The rises stopped, and for some reason I stood still in the current and waited. Just when I had decided it was hopeless, there was another impressive rise fifteen feet above the place where I had missed the first fish. It seemed unlikely that two fish that size might share such a minor pool, and I waited nervously while the big trout settled into a methodical feeding rhythm. It took a dozen fluttering duns before I tried a cast that fell perfectly, and the trout rose lazily and took my fly.

He's on! I yelled aloud.

The shrill reel protested and the delicate rod danced to the threnody of its writhing head-shaking fight. All the foot-long brown trout I had taken that summer were quickly forgotten, along with the sixteen-inch rainbow taken in the ranch-house pond. These runs stripped line from the reel, reaching high into the riffles above, and once the fish threatened to escape into the heavy river currents downstream. Several times it bored deep under the banks and trailing grasses, ticking the leader across the willow roots and sticks, but the tippet held safely.

The fish struggled desperately when it finally saw the waiting net, working its tail in tight circles, just out of reach. It was close several times, but each time it bolted off again until I worked it slowly back.

Finally it surrendered and came to the net, and it threshed and writhed deep in the meshes.

It's huge, I thought wildly and waded ashore. *It's better than twenty inches!*

It was the biggest trout I had ever seen, and I killed it eagerly with my priest, but in the weeks that followed I always passed that pool with a touch of sadness. Although there were other good hatches, I never saw another fish rising there, and I covered it often. There is nothing so empty as a pool without trout, particularly when the guilt is yours.

It is a lesson we learn too slowly.

The typical odyssey we travel in learning to fish is a gradual and satisfying journey. It is a slow evolution from beginner to expert, and it involves a subtle metamorphosis from fisherman into angler. However, it is not merely the refinements of fishing and our fish-catching skills that occupy this transformation. It is also a remarkable evolution in attitudes. The full metamorphosis is complete when a man realizes that his fishing skills have been so developed that he can deplete his own sport.

It is a singular milestone of self-knowledge.

Each trout fisherman experiences a similar development, usually under the tutelage of an older angler. His genesis often lies in fishing the live baits. My father guided me along that path toward the eventual role of fly-fishing, and I started toward that unseen goal with live grasshoppers on a small meadow stream in Michigan. Two things make the small stream a perfect classroom for the beginner: there is no better place to discover the hair-trigger wariness of a wild trout, and the splashy strike to a grasshopper is not unlike the rise to the dry fly.

Like all beginners with skilled tutors, I was taught to creep stealthily to a chosen pocket, peer cautiously through the leaves and grass, and lower my grasshopper gently above the trout. The fish were not large in that meadow creek, but they were wary enough to teach caution, and they responded with an eager splash that was an exciting preparation for the fly-fishing I finally began the following year.

The transition from grasshoppers to a rather simple and effective wet-fly method was relatively easy. From this basic foundation, I gradually branched out into the other methods, using dry flies and bucktails and streamers. It was a surprisingly productive season, and before it was ended, several limits of trout had fallen to my dry flies. As my skill increased, I passed into a stage that seems to afflict every fisherman during his early evolution: the desire to kill and bring in large numbers of fish to prove and demonstrate his prowess. It is a malady we all contract in our fishing careers, and some men never escape its ravages.

Three years after my start on that meadow brook in Michigan, I met a white-haired gentleman on the upper Pere Marquette who smilingly inquired about my luck. With the bursting pride of a ten-year-old, I raised the lid of my wicker creel to reveal fifteen trout from eight to eleven inches in length.

Female Beaverkill, I explained proudly.

His kindly expression soured, and the old man asked quietly why I had killed so many fish. The old man added that if every angler were so fortunate, there would soon be few fish left in our river. Flushed with hurt pride and anger, I testily dismissed his criticism as jealousy of my catch; but looking back I see a man mellowed with years of rich pleasure and skill on the river, and I am ashamed of my boyhood greed. Several times that summer I watched the same man fish difficult water on the Little South, and he caught trout almost at will every time he appeared along the river. It was obvious that he could kill the limit any time he wished, yet he released most of the trout he caught.

It was a puzzle half-understood for years, but finally on that meadow stream in Colorado, I understood after I had killed the big fish and later regretted its absence. The skilled angler does not need dead trout in his basket to feel satisfaction. His skills have long since demonstrated that he can catch trout, and he needs no proof for his companions. There is no need to fear the ridicule of others for his empty creel, and some anglers no longer bother to carry a creel on the stream. Limit catches are often easy to fill and carry no particular badge of excellence.

The sophisticated angler counts as his highest reward the number of fish released for another day. His basket may contain an occasional fish if someone has expressed a desire for trout, or a fish has been hurt taking the fly and cannot be released successfully. But the really skilled fisherman loves his sport far too much to spoil it with wanton killing.

Gerry Queen once told me the story of a great trout that lived in the pool just above their cabin on the Little South. Although their stretch of river was not posted, these men improved its pools unselfishly with deadfall deflectors and rock wing dams. The water bordered by their property soon became the finest on the river, and it was not long before big wild fish began appearing in their pools. One large trout settled in the deep, eddying pool below their fishing house, and it quickly became a favorite with this circle of anglers. All had raised it at least once, and two or three had hooked and lost the fish. One actually landed and released the fish during a Michigan mayfly hatch, and measured it at twenty-seven inches.

It became like an old and familiar friend.

And then an outsider armed with nightcrawlers and twenty-pound nylon wrestled the big trout from the river during a spate, and brutally killed it on the spot. It was unceremoniously gutted and its entrails were heaved into the stream for the crayfish. Without its magnificent eight-pound brown, the magic of the Cabin Pool was gone.

Finding such a trout is the greatest thrill, since it is an adversary truly worthy of our skills. We may work on it for days without success, and still return home satisfied and filled with thoughts of another day. One seldom remembers the hundreds of average fish encountered over the years, but those few trophy-size trout taken or lost under difficult conditions are long carried in our memories. Just the knowledge that such a big fish exists adds a delicious flavor of anticipation to each pool.

Nonfishermen seldom understand why we fish when we usually release our catch, and too many fishermen sadly share their myopia. They fail to grasp that the *live* trout, lying in its sun-dappled riffles, rising over its bright-gravel shallows, and fighting the delicate rod, gives our sport its entire meaning.

Dead trout are just so much meat, however deliciously they might be prepared for the table. Food cannot be the reason we fish for trout, since an equal amount of work would secure much more at the supermarket, and the fish counter is a cheaper place to obtain it. We cannot begrudge the local angler his occasional catch of trout, particularly if such fish supplement a meagre income, but the fly-fisherman who travels hundreds of miles to fish a stream is paying astonishing amounts of money in terms of each pound of fish. When we consider our motivation in economic terms, it becomes obvious that we fish for the sport of trout fishing and not for killing the fish we catch.

My good friend John Hemingway, whose famous father taught him to love trout fishing on the swift rivers of Idaho, is adamant about this subject.

These days no one really fishes for food, Hemingway insists. *It is not the business of our Fish and Game Commissions to supply protein!*

There is no pragmatic logic in our behavior, and fishing only to release the fish we catch unmistakably has the overtones of philosophy. Chinese history includes a philosopher who omitted both hook and bait from his tackle, since actually catching a fish interrupted the richly contemplative moods of his sport.

Our philosophy of trout fishing does not demand such ultimate asceticism, but catch-and-release fishing is itself an example of illogical and intriguing behavior. It carries obvious nuances of ritual hunting. The blood rhythms of fishing and hunting clearly demonstrate the fact that our civilized veneer remains surprisingly thin, and we still share the instincts of our primordial ancestors. Yet we have evolved to the point that the rhythms of the hunt are more exciting than the anticlimax of the kill.

Fly-fishing is the only field sport that provides an equilibrium between these points of view. It has all the blood rhythms of the hunt, particularly when we are working on a rising trout, but it does not demand the actual kill to complete its liturgies. Unlike bait or lure fishing, catching trout on flies seldom injures the fish. The captured trout can be safely released. Therefore, releasing a trout is a kind of ritual kill that satisfies both our primitive instincts, and our mixture of reverence and respect for the beauty and courage of the trout.

It also makes good economic sense.

Given our modern fishing pressure, it costs millions of dollars to stock our streams to provide put-and-take management. Yet less than half of the fish planted are actually recovered, and each bait-caught fish is enjoyed only once. Catch-and-release fishing not only provides multiple use of each fish stocked, but it also provides better sport. There are more fish of better-than-average size on such waters, and the fish that has been caught several times is unquestionably more wary. Our club water on the Brodheads in Pennsylvania is managed on a fly-only no-kill basis, and it is heavily fished by our members. Comparison of our fishing logs with the Henryville House register seventy-five years ago demonstrates that our fishing is fully equal to the sport of earlier years, except that we rarely kill a trout these days.

During our last spring outing, when the members and their families gathered for a picnic and annual meeting, more than three hundred trout averaging a pound were caught. None were killed in the weekend of fishing, and the best trout was an estimated four pounds. Public water downstream cannot provide such fishing, yet it is more heavily stocked over the season. The difference lies in the philosophy of stream management.

Any discussion about releasing trout always triggers a number of counter arguments against the practice. Most men contend that if they do not kill the fish, someone else will later. This is often true, but they still have enjoyed the sport of catching them, and two fishermen have utilized a single tax dollar.

There is no question that catching a trout adds to its shyness, provided we release the fish to benefit from the experience, and it may put a trout beyond the reach of men less skilled than the angler who first released it. Some fishermen will grant this point, but argue that it makes the trout too difficult to catch. It is a strange argument born of laziness rather than logic. Its emphasis is on easy fishing, rather than the challenging and difficult sport we all love, and any fisherman who really knows the bountiful cornucopia of wilderness fishing, as well as the sophistication of a selective trout on hard-fished waters, will invariably choose the satisfaction that comes with a measure of success on hard-fished waters.

The final argument against catch-and-release management is that the fish die anyway. Research has long since proved this argument false, and over the years I am fully satisfied that a fly-caught trout almost always survives when released properly.

Several studies of trout mortality under fishing pressure clearly demonstrate that the fish suffer a seventy percent mortality with natural baits, forty-five percent mortality with lures, and a two percent mortality with flies—without particular care in releasing them.

Many years ago I experimented with releasing trout on a small ranch pond in Colorado. It held about thirty trout from ten to twenty inches. Each fish surrendered a fragment of his dorsal, pectoral or caudal fin, and the exact nature of its surgery was recorded in a notebook. Each trout had its own page, complete with the data of its captures. No fish died from my handling, and many were taken several times a week. The fish were not handled with wet hands, contrary to the old wives' tale about dry hands damaging the protective slime covering their scales. The fish were also handled in a landing net, because its meshes give the fisherman a better grip on the fish with less squeezing. Dry hands help accomplish the same purpose, since a fish may be handled with less pressure than with wet hands. The threat of internal injuries is infinitely more serious than the risk of fungus from dry hands, and their possible damage to the protective slime of the fish.

Trout must be given time to fully recover. The fisherman must sometimes devote as much time to releasing his trout as he spends playing them. They must be held gently in the water, in a natural swimming position, until they wriggle free in their own time. This is the only way to release a fish, since a tired and frightened trout thrown back carelessly into the stream will seldom recover his equilibrium. Fish can be rocked forward and back, working the water through their gill structures when they are too weak to breathe themselves, in a form of artificial respiration. Stream trout should be held with their heads facing into the current while they recover. Gentle patience is the secret.

Some of the pond trout were caught almost forty times during the summer of my experiment, and the only brown trout in the pond was caught about once every two weeks. There was one brookie that succumbed three times in a single day's fishing. Catching and releasing these fish left occasional hook sores in their jaws, but their energy and fight were unimpaired; and the trout did indeed become increasingly difficult to catch.

The catch-and-release philosophy is sadly unpopular with a large majority of fishermen, even in regions that have outstanding examples of such management. The quality of the fishing on rivers like the Firehole and Madison in the Yellowstone, the Beaverkill and Amawalk in New York, the Bushkill and Young Woman's Creek in Pennsylvania, and the Au Sable in Michigan is a remarkable demonstration that no-kill and fly-only regulations can provide first-rate sport under the fishing pressures of present urban populations. The special management on the Henry's Fork of the Snake, which limits the killing of fish to only two fish per day and prohibits the killing of anything over fourteen inches, is a remarkable success. Its smooth currents literally boil with big, selective trout during a hatch.

Yet there are still local agitators in each of these states who want such special management streams opened to the bait and hardware fishing that would quickly ravage the fine trout populations that enlightened management has built up in recent years. It is tragic that some men cannot look down from a bridge and see trout without wanting to slaughter them. The frontier myth and the theology of endless abundance die slowly.

Such rapacity and greed are a legacy we can no longer afford in an America of more than two hundred million people. Yet I still see men who call themselves outdoorsmen point with pride to creelsful of small trout, even on big western rivers where the limit in pounds, if one wishes to kill his trout, is regularly possible in only three or four fish. It is surprising that seven- and eight-inch trout are large enough to satisfy the mindless greed and self-indulgence that seem to motivate those who must strive to kill baskets full of trout.

It is an attitude that must end.

Somehow our fishermen seem to think there is a relationship between fishing-license fees and the hatchery trout they should be permitted to catch and creel. Resident license fees are seldom more than five dollars, and tourist licenses are from ten to twenty dollars. Considering the fact that trout cost from two to three dollars for every pound of fish stocked, these greedy fishermen cannot help but see that the license costs cannot cover the propagation and stocking costs of hatchery trout. License fees will seldom cover a single day's limit of fish, and there is no extra money for enforcement and research and other costs. The fish-hog fisherman costs everyone money, ruining future sport for himself as well as others. Few things are as empty as trout streams without trout.

Our problems are unquestionably a matter of ethics and self-discipline. William Michael phrased it perfectly in *Dry-Fly Trout Fishing*, when he defined it as a matter of limiting our kill instead of killing our limit. Our country may have more than three hundred million people before the close of this century, and regulations restricting both our fishing attitudes and our catch are the only method we have to provide anything but echoes of past public fishing. Our tradition has always been one of public fishing, unlike the completely private trout streams of Europe, where fishing rights began as the prerogative of royalty and the nobility. It is the egalitarian tradition to which we all subscribe, but we must extend our fly-only no-kill philosophy to much of our remaining trout waters, if we are to preserve public fishing of any real quality.

Fishery management in our national parks clearly proves this argument. Their regulations are not warped by the myopic pressures of local know-nothing clubs and have long been designed to provide good fishing even under heavy vacationing pressure. Their success is obvious. Few rivers can boast that their present fishing is better than it was twenty-five years ago, yet this is true of virtually all fly-fishing-only water.

Opinions vary widely on what constitutes good trout fishing, and the polarity of these arguments lies between the meat-and-potatoes school that is fascinated with the huge catches possible on wilderness water and the classical school that seeks the difficult and intriguing sport of outwitting selective fish on streams not far from our cities.

Both modern stream management and experiments in habitat improvement have pointed the way to better trout fishing, but many of our rivers are almost past reclaiming. Pollution and fishing pressure, with crowds trampling the banks, littering the river, and slaughtering the trout, have all taken their tragic toll. More and more water is being posted, because of thoughtless fishermen and the impossibility of finding either solitude or decent sport on public water. We have no one to blame for the loss of such water except ourselves and our fish management.

Solitude may not be possible within easy reach of our major urban centers, and anything approaching real sport with crowds is at the mercy of regulations and manners. The success of private water is obvious. Our Brodheads mileage is fished by fifty members and totals less than five miles. Its pools are all taken on a crowded weekend, and the highly skilled membership could easily fish it out in a season. Unlike most private clubs, we stock few trout and kill less than one hundred fish per season, and only flies are legal. Stocking is limited to between 750 and 1,000 brown trout per season, yet we regularly catch as many as 6,000 to 8,000 fish. Improving habitat and catch-and-release fishing mean that we catch $6,000 to $8,000 worth of trout for $1,000 worth of annual stocking in costs. Given an average winterkill, we still have at least $500 worth of carry-over trout left the following spring. It is an equation that clearly works—and there is public water a few miles downstream that has been barren of fish for years. Philosophy is our secret, since the water chemistry of the Brodheads is practically identical on both stretches of the river.

Such regulations should not be applied in blanket terms to all trout waters. It is pointless to manage marginal trout habitat with fly-only no-kill regulations, since such regulations have been conceived to build a long-term sustaining population. Such marginal water does not support trout through an entire season, and should not be stocked with Salmonidae at all, except for perhaps a short-term harvest of hatchery trout with put-and-take regulations in early season. Fly-only and no-kill policy is best suited to quality streams with good sustaining populations and viable spawning, and streams having a character particularly suited to wading and fly-fishing. Bigger water might be open to other methods, except those rivers suited to float fishing and flies. Small brush-sheltered streams are often ideally suited to bait fishing or for children, unless they should be closed as primary spawning and nursery tributaries. Each river and its tributaries is a unique management problem, its singular rhythms suited to different species of trout and varied regulations. Trout lakes also have varied character, and only those with shallows rich in fly life are best suited for special regulations. Big reservoirs could provide open fishing with less restrictive management, and overpopulated back-country lakes could often actually improve with the killing of more trout, in an attempt to balance the stunted fish with the relative scarcity of food.

But enlightened management is only half the battle in providing good sport on many overcrowded rivers. Stream manners are becoming a critical problem with the coming of vast crowds to many public waters. Breaches of common courtesy are common on the stream these days, and courtesy is scarcely possible in the elbow-to-elbow crowds of the typical opening day. Stream etiquette in the past was always carefully taught to each succeeding generation, but such tutelage has too often been lost in the explosive postwar growth of fly-fishing.

The rules of fishing etiquette are logical and simple.

Elbow room is one of the basic principles of stream manners. Any pool or reasonably definable reach of water belongs to the first person fishing it, and if he is fishing upstream or down, it is inconsiderate to start fishing ahead of him. The distance between you and another fisherman varies with the size of the river, the character of adjacent pools or holding places, the quality of the fishing, and how well you may know him. One hundred feet is perhaps a minimal buffer zone.

The stationary or slow-moving fisherman has the right to remain where he chooses. You should carefully leave the river and walk around him, taking care not to wade noisily or pass too close to either the fisherman or his trout. You should never walk along a bank in plain view of his fish as I have seen too many fishermen do thoughtlessly. There is a fine pool on a famous eastern river not far from New York that has three separate holding zones in its one hundred-yard length. Its spreading tail shallows hold a good number of selective free-rising browns that are always challenging. The middle spine of the pool is a strong smooth-flowing run with fish lying between its deepest reaches and the shallows along the bankside path. The throat of the pool is a strong chute, and its fish are less selective. The fish in the lower reaches of the pool are so wary that they can often occupy a good fisherman for hours. Since the streamside path drops down to the middle of the pool, and borders most of the pool in plain view of the fish, it is a typical place for a second angler to walk toward the head of the pool without realizing that he has ruined the fishing in the tail shallows. The fish quickly bolt from the shallows along the path, scattering into the middle and tail of the pool, soon putting the others down.

Standing beside a pool in a white shirt or other reflective clothing is equally bad manners. Leaning over a bridge railing above an angler working a pool full of selective trout is thoughtless as well, as is walking past another fisherman in full silhouette against the sky, even some distance from the water he is fishing. Each of these mistakes can spoil the fishing for another angler.

Several years ago I was shooting a picture essay with *Life* magazine on a charming eastern trout stream. George Silk was the photographer, and he wanted a back-lit scene of a smooth pool at evening, with its far bank in shadows and the angler in the sun, all shot through the pale olive green lacework of early foliage. We located a deep smooth-flowing pool in later afternoon that gave us exactly the mood and setting he wanted. Two fish were rising steadily in its tail shallows.

The pool was at a ninety-degree bend in the river. The current riffled down a fifty-yard reach of fast water, turned against a bank of sheltering rhododendron, and shelved off into deeper water. The throat of the pool surged against the stones of the hillside, lost in dense shadows, and the hill itself was already in the shade, but the swift tail shallows were still in warm sunlight. The fish were both good browns, at least fifteen or sixteen inches, lying in plain view over the stony bottom. They were rising steadily.

Think you can fool one of them? Silk asked.

I can try, I laughed.

Okay, he said. *I'll shoot from here, directly into the light, and you stalk them on your knees from the tail shallows.*

Carefully, I worked infantry-style up the shallows until I was within easy range of the fish. From their porpoising rise forms, it looked like they were nymphing, but they soon proved selective. I tried several patterns without success.

I'd like to get slightly above you, Silk yelled. *Can I get across from the fish without scaring them?*

I think so, I answered. *Just stay behind that line of trees about thirty feet from the river and walk slowly past them.*

Okay, he agreed.

Silk shouldered into his camera gear and worked up through the trees in a half crouch. He was at least fifty feet from the two brown trout, and slightly above their feeding lies, when both fish bolted upstream into deeper water.

Where did they go? Silk asked when he peered through the bushes above the run. *Can't see the fish anymore.*

They left, I said.

You mean I scared them from there?

Something scared them! I laughed. *I'm going to wade up there and you walk back along those trees.*

I waded upstream to the shallow run where the fish had been lying, and kneeled down in the current with my chin almost touching the water. Silk walked downstream along the treeline, his dark clothing blending with the leaves perfectly until he crossed a thin patch of branches and was strongly silhouetted against the evening sky. The fish had apparently seen him then.

It's my fault, I yelled. *I never dreamed those fish could see you that far back from the river—but they did!*

Too bad, he shook his head.

It was a lesson never forgotten, and it should always be remembered along the stream: never circle out around another fisherman without giving him an exaggerated berth, since trout are always more wary than you think.

Several weeks ago a good friend was fishing a long waist-deep flat just at twilight. He was starting a strategy I have often used myself on that piece of water. Several trout are often smutting toward the tail shallows, and I often occupy myself with them early in the evening, leaving the upper part of the pool alone. It is a good system, since the shy fish toward the middle and head of the pool are often more easily taken after they've settled undisturbed into their evening feeding rhythms. My friend was saving the upper currents for later, while he toyed with the selective free-rising trout working just above him in the shallows.

I was fishing another pool one hundred yards downstream when I watched another fisherman and his entire family settle into the meadow just across from my friend for a supper picnic. It was far from a quiet scene. The children ran up and down the meadow without a trace of discipline, throwing rocks into the pool and even slapping the shallows with a dead branch. There was yelling and shouting and the inevitable banshee-wailing that accompanies a hurt elbow or battered knee, and the parents uttered no word of either guidance or reprimand. It was quite a carnival, considering that no one had asked my friend if they might intrude on both his solitude and his sport.

Miraculously, he had taken three or four of the selective trout working in the tail shallows some seventy feet away, and the trout in the upper reaches of the pool had also forgotten about the rock throwing before supper. Several fish were just beginning to rise regularly, and my friend was starting to wade quietly upstream toward the middle of the pool when the man collected his rod and waded out thirty-five feet above him.

Didn't you call him on it? I asked later.

Call him on what? my friend shook his head unhappily and laughed. *He broke so many rules of stream etiquette that I didn't know where to begin!*

It is a sad parable that does include several cardinal rules of trout-stream behavior. You never even watch a man fish a pool without asking if it disturbs him, let alone permit your family to conduct a free-for-all along the banks. You never get into a pool that is already being fished, even on the most crowded streams, without first asking the other fisherman's permission. You never get into the stream too near another fisherman, and you never get in ahead of him, no matter whether he is fishing upstream or down. You never hurry to get ahead of another angler, and try not to interfere with his sport in any way.

Noisy wading or wading into the principal holding lies of a pool is always poor manners, even when no one else is fishing there. It will disturb the trout more thoroughly than the normal passage of fishing the pool, which is thoughtless and unfair to the next angler, whoever he might be. Wading should always be patient and slow, both from consideration for others and because it will produce better results in your own fishing.

There are other similar transgressions of good streamside manners. Experienced anglers will often study a pool instead of fishing it blindly, and sometimes it is good practice to stop fishing and rest a pool for a few minutes. Such a fisherman has first priority on the pool he is studying or resting, and you should never start fishing without his permission. Most good anglers are courteous and generous toward others, and will even grant their permission to fish a pool they have been resting, if you have the good manners to stop where they are sitting and ask.

Traditionally, the dry-fly fisherman wading upstream has the right of way over a wet-fly man working down. It is a tradition that makes sense. Fishermen wading upstream are forced by the current to move slowly, cover far less water, and approach the trout from behind. Fish always face the currents and will see an angler fishing downstream more readily. His technique both covers and disturbs more water. The man working down with a wet fly or streamer should retire from the river and move unobtrusively around an angler fishing upstream.

Generosity along the stream extends itself to other things as well. There was a boyhood evening many years ago when I was casting over a big smooth-flowing reach of the Madison in the Yellowstone, and a man fishing across the river was catching fish regularly. There were a number of good fish working on my side of the river, but I had failed to touch them for more than an hour.

What're they taking? I finally asked in desperation.

Whitcraft! came the reply.

It was an unfamiliar fly pattern in those boyhood days, and when he caught two more fish I finally swallowed my pride.

What's a Whitcraft? I yelled back curiously.

Take it! The fisherman cast his fly past me and the leader drifted down against my legs.

I picked it up. *Can't do that,* I protested feebly.

Cut it off the tippet, he insisted. *Wouldn't have cast it over if I didn't mean for you to have it!*

Thanks! I clinched it to my tippet.

It was a fine evening, and we both took fish regularly in the one hundred yards of perfect dry-fly water. It was a lesson in generosity I have never forgotten, and I always try to give a taking fly to another fisherman if I have an extra pattern or two. Sometimes I have given my only taking fly to a stranger when I have already caught enough fish to satisfy me. It is a good rule to remember on any river.

Fishing together is often fine sport, but it has several basic rules of conduct. When you are invited to fish with someone, the invitation is limited to you alone, and you should not add anyone else to the party without his permission. Although fishing contests have become fashionable in recent years, particularly the famous salt-water tournaments and bass competitions, such a competitive spirit has absolutely no place in fly-fishing for trout. Our sport is not a contest between anglers, and status games over the biggest fish or the heaviest creel are totally outside a tradition of contemplative sport that traces its lineage to Father Walton.

The competition astream is not between fellow anglers, but between you and the most beautiful and difficult fish on earth; and its unique mixture of beauty and shyness and selectivity should be competition enough for any man.

Fishing invitations have another cardinal rule or two. Big water can permit two anglers to fish opposite sides of the river, while on small streams, a pair of fishermen can often fish alternate pools or holding places. There is something happy about fishing together with a really good friend, and an experienced angler takes as much pleasure in the success of his companion as he finds in his own luck. There is fine camaraderie in such fishing, comparing notes and solving problems together, although there is an opposite coin to such fellowship. The talkative fisherman who engages everybody along the stream in ill-timed monologues about tackle and experiences and theories is an unmitigated pest, interminably badgering friends and strangers alike.

Fishing talk is almost as much fun as fishing itself, but there are still many anglers who cherish solitude and silence on the river. Brief conversations with a fellow fly-fisherman are an obvious courtesy, but extended dialogues without invitation are another matter, and a stranger on the stream will soon let you know if he wants to debate your theories or would prefer fishing alone.

One unwritten rule lies in being taken to fish a new lake or reach of river by a friend. Such confidences are a sacred trust between fishing comrades, and it is a betrayal of that trust to show a secret place to another angler. Some old-time anglers valued such a confidence so highly that they would never fish a secret place again without the friend that first took them there. Although fewer and fewer such places exist, even in the high country of our western mountains, it is a spirit of courtesy that should prevail on all trout waters.

Similar respect should govern our attitude toward private water or public streams and lakes subject to special regulations such as fly-fishing only or no-kill water restricted to single-hook lures. Trespassing or violating the special-water regulations is unacceptable behavior among fly-fisher-men, and such breaches of obvious courtesy utterly betray the ancient and honorable origins of our sport.

The courtesy of asking a landowner for permission to fish is usually observed and granted on most waters, sometimes with a small rod fee for a day's sport. We should always remember that private water is *not* stocked with fish raised in public hatcheries, and that taking a fish not paid for with public funds is not much different from stealing. Some fishermen poach private water with the mistaken belief that its fish are actually public property, often arguing that fishing from public road rights-of-way or bridges is legal. No state allows bridge or roadside fishing for reasons of traffic safety, but even if fishing from such public easements were legal, the fish themselves are still private property and not the natural spawn of the stream. Respect for private property includes other things too, like leaving both the banks and the stream itself free of litter, carefully closing all gates, particularly where there is livestock, being cautious with cookfires, and the ethic that always leaves a pool or campsite a little better than you found it.

There are some places where men must fish together in relatively close proximity. Pools on salmon rivers like the Narraguagus or the Miramichi, with their taking lies crowded when the fish are running, give a fisherman little chance of solitude. Similar crowds are found on steelhead rivers when the big sea-run rainbows are moving in, and several fishermen are often found on a single pool. The fly water on the Henry's Fork of the Snake is often crowded with men who like fishing over its frustratingly selective rainbows.

Let's leave, somebody groans in the gathering twilight. *Let's go find a few dumb fish someplace!*

The rules of etiquette in such fishing are geared to the techniques of covering the water. You cast quartering downstream across the current on steelhead and salmon, and work the fly around with a teasing rhythm through its fly swing. When a cast is fished out, the angler takes a step downstream and repeats it again, covering the entire pool with a series of concentric quarter-circles. Stream etiquette dictates that other anglers wait until the first man is about one hundred to two hundred feet down the pool, depending on its width and the average casting distance. The water is covered in a rotation system, with each angler fishing through in his turn.

There are some other unwritten rules about steelhead or salmon fishing. The man with a hooked fish has undisputed right-of-way, and his fellow anglers should stop fishing to give him all the room he needs.

The Henry's Fork is another problem. Its regulars stand patiently to fish in one place or cover surprisingly little water, since stealth and patience are its cardinal rules for success. Entering the river and wading to a fishing stand should be accomplished quietly, and your departure from the current should be equally circumspect, even when the selective rainbows have defeated you soundly.

There is also a code governing the final landing of a good fish. Spectators should keep well back and stay as motionless as possible to keep from frightening the hooked fish and prolonging its struggles. Several years ago I watched a good fly-fisherman playing a big brown in the straw-colored Nez Percé meadows of the Firehole. It was a fish of five or six pounds, hooked on a tiny dry fly with a cobweb-fine leader in a mirror-smooth flat. The fish had been patiently beaten, and it floundered weakly on the surface, but it still had enough strength to hang well out in the main current. The fisherman played it gingerly, managing his fragile tippet with cunning and skill, and the fish was about ready to surrender.

Best fish I've ever hooked, the fisherman said quietly when I stopped to watch. *It should go five or six pounds!*

Beautiful fish, I agreed.

Took a tiny twenty-two Adams, the man continued proudly. *Tied it myself over to Madison Campground last night!*

They like small flies on the Firehole, I said.

It's been some fight, the fisherman sighed happily. *It's only a 6X tippet and those weeds kept me worried!*

Pretty fine leader, I nodded in agreement.

The fish was finally coming now, circling weakly in the shallows, when a tourist car with Nebraska plates turned off the highway to the Fountain Freight Road in a cloud of dust and gravel. It roared off the road and rocked to a stop near the river, disgorging a man and a large covey of noisy children.

Look there! the man yelled. *He's got one!*

The grassy bank swarmed with children, and the big trout surged back toward midstream in terror. The fisherman looked at me and rolled his eyes in despair.

Hey mister! the father cackled with a false men's club friendliness. *What'd you use for bait?*

Dry fly, said the fisherman unhappily.

Big fish like that don't want no flies, the man laughed to his chattering children. *You need doughballs or nightwalkers.*

How 'bout cheese, screeched one of his older boys.

Good bait too! the man agreed.

It was a nightmare for the fisherman. His face was flushed with anger, but he said nothing and patiently worked the big fish back from the swift currents downstream. The children were throwing pebbles at each other now, racing around through the coarse-grass meadows, and a stone splashed into the shallows near the trout. It bolted back into the heavy currents at midstream. The angler groaned and patiently coaxed it into the shallows again.

Come on! I said to the tourists finally. *Corral your kids and keep them back from the bank!*

You own the river? the man said belligerently.

No, I said, *but all this yelling and running around isn't fair to this man—he could lose his big fish!*

The angler looked at me gratefully.

Hell! one of the children yelled at me, *that fish ain't big—you should see the carp we catch!*

Why don't you pull it in? the man asked.

The angler said nothing and worked the trout into the shallows along the bank. Its strength was spent now, and the fisherman was looking for a gravel bar to beach it when his nightmare reached its frustrating climax.

Here, mister! the man said helpfully and scuttled down the bank. *Let me give you a hand!*

Don't touch the leader! the angler screamed.

But the man ignored him and started hand-lining the fish toward the gravel. *You got him, daddy!* shrieked a pig-tailed little girl. *You got him!*

It was too much for the exhausted trout. It gathered its remaining strength into a final wrenching splash that sheared the fragile nylon like a cobweb and it was gone.

Hey mister, the girl said. *Your string broke!*

The helpless fisherman stared at her wordlessly, and finally he waded out of the shallows toward his car, shaking his head in despair as he passed me. His eyes were glazed with shock. The other man herded his children back into their car.

Can't catch fish with line that weak, I heard him tell his wife, who looked like a Martian with her hair full of plastic rollers.

It was an incident filled with almost bizarre exaggerations, but it has lessons for all anglers. You should never interfere with another fisherman who is into a fish, and you should never offer to net or gaff a fish for another angler unless he asks you. There is an unwritten rule among skilled fly-fishermen, particularly those who fish for trout and salmon, that landing a fish yourself is both the *moment critique* of our fishing and a gesture of homage to its beauty and sporting character. Helping net or gaff a fish for a stranger is always perilous, since the fish may escape in the final moments, and you will always be blamed, however wordlessly. Never assist another fisherman in landing his fish unless you are asked, and even if you are asked, decline unless you are really skilled and experienced. Remember that a fisherman who does not request your help is not necessarily selfish or unfriendly but playing a part in a tradition that believes a big trout or salmon is a quarry with almost mystical qualities, and deserves to meet its fate in a hand-to-hand struggle.

With the construction of many new reservoirs throughout the United States, the basic courtesies of trout fishing have become mixed with boating manners. It is poor form to crowd in close to a boat that is catching fish, just as it is bad manners to congregate along the river near a successful fisherman. Elbow room is part of common fishing courtesy on lakes and streams. It is also thoughtless to bang tackle boxes and bailing cans in the bottom of your boat, or row noisily with thumping or rattling oars, since these vibrations are transmitted directly into the water and can spoil the fishing for everyone. Throwing cans and bottles and aluminum can lids into a lake is unforgivable. The boat moving upwind has the right-of-way, and a stationary boat should always be passed slowly and given a minimum berth of two hundred feet. Since a stationary boat or fisherman on shore is disturbing far less water than a trolling boat, and its wake can disturb their fishing, the moving boat should circle out well around them or throttle back to pass. Anchors should be lowered and raised quietly in any fishable areas, both because it will mean better sport for your party, and because it is considerate of nearby boats. Such consideration also applies to arriving or leaving the fishing grounds. You should not come into a fishing area or leave it under rich-mixture throttle settings, or row noisily through productive water frightening the fish. These are simple things to remember along trout water, but it is surprising how often we forget them, and sometimes there are incidents that are unthinkable.

Several years ago I was fishing a small eastern stream in a lovely gorge of slate ledges. It was a sparkling morning in early summer, with the fresh new leaves moving against a cobalt sky. The phoebes were catching mayflies above a bright riffle that danced in the sunlight, and enough fish were rising to provide good sport. The fly hatch consisted of slate-colored *Paraleptophlebias*, and I was matching it with an eighteen Blue Quill dressed with sooty dun hackles. It was working consistently, and I had caught and released a dozen trout, working upstream slowly from the little clapboard hotel to the Footbridge Pool, where the trail into the gorge crossed the stream on a small suspension bridge.

There were several fish rising there, and I hooked and released a half dozen below the bridge. They were fat little browns not long from the hatchery truck, and they took the little dry fly eagerly. The cool wind eddied downstream, smelling of pine trees and laurel deep in the slate-walled gorge, and the solitude was pleasant.

Two boulders broke the smooth current below the cable-span, and I saw a fish rise softly in their current tongues.

That looks like a good fish, I thought happily.

The little Blue Quill was dried with a few quick false casts and I settled it along the eddying run. It danced down the current and disappeared in a quiet rise, and a twelve-inch brown bored upstream, stripping line noisily from the reel. It was a plucky fish and it fought stubbornly against the delicate leader tippet, and its struggle was resourceful, exploring and probing under the ledges upstream and searching out snags to foul the leader. Finally, it tired and I worked it downstream into the waiting net. It was a wild fish, fat and richly spotted above its pale orange belly. It struggled feebly while I freed it from the hook and lowered it gently into the current. It held in my fingers a moment and then splashed free.

The tiny fly was matted with slime, and I washed it carefully in the stream. Then I oiled it with silicone and let it dry a few moments before false casting it back into fishable condition. While it was darting lazily back and forth in the sunlight, I saw another good fish rise softly above the second boulder. The cast bellied out and dropped.

It rose and took without hesitation. *Pretty,* I thought.

The fish threshed in surprise when it felt the tiny hook, and it too bolted strongly upstream in the shadow of the ledge. It was heavier, and it was some time before I succeeded in working it back into the sun-dappled shallows. The fish surrendered stubbornly and I unhooked it carefully, holding it gently in the meshes.

Okay, mister! The voice was an angry explosion from the bushes above the bridge. *I've watched you let six or seven fish go since I've been standing here—and if you let that trout go too, you're in trouble!*

The man had startled me with his anger. *Why?* I stammered. *What's the matter with letting them go?*

Been fishing this creek since daylight! The man was huge and he came down to the stream, still shaking with agitation. *Ain't caught nothing all morning, and now when I'm walking down out of the valley, I have to watch you letting six or seven go!*

But I caught them, I protested, *and I can do whatever I want with the trout I catch. They're too beautiful to kill!*

Maybe, the man said sullenly, *but it's goddamn sure I don't have to watch you do it!* The fish was still in my net, and I lowered it carefully into the smooth current.

He's pretty tired, I said.

You ain't letting that fish go! The man came angrily into the stream. *You're giving it to me!*

No, I said quietly. *It's going back.*

The trout was frightened when the fisherman splashed toward me, and it fought free of my fingers. It held a moment below my waders and darted nervously upstream into the deep smooth-flowing throat of the pool where it was safe. The man stood in a rage, spluttering with anger and frustration. *Goddammit*, he shouted, *it ain't fair for you fancy-pants fly boys to fish and let your fish go—when a man like me ain't caught a trout all morning!*

I'm sorry about that, I said, *but a man has to catch his own trout—then you can decide to kill them or let them go.*

What's wrong with my gear? he asked.

It was a heavy spinning rod with a monofilament of about twenty-pound breaking strain on its reel. There were several split shot on the nylon, and a nightcrawler was laced on a big bait hook. It was pretty coarse tackle for hard-fished water.

The fish can see your nylon, I said, *and that's an awful lot of lead for a small stream like this one.*

You mean the trout are that smart?

Smart is the one thing trout really are, I smiled. *You have to sneak up on them like a deer or wild turkey.*

Well I'll be damned, he said.

You mean you haven't been concealing yourself from the fish? I asked. *You let them see you before you start fishing?*

Afraid so, he admitted.

Look, I said, *you get yourself some small hooks and a four-pound leader and use less split shot—sneak up on the pools and get your bait into the water quietly.*

You think that'll help catch fish? he asked.

It should. I nodded my head.

Thanks, the man extended his hand. *If it works out, I might even try some of them flies sometime.*

Good luck! I laughed.

It was an incredible episode, and there were moments when I thought I had a fight on my hands, but it codifies a whole galaxy of problems about trout fishing in our time. The streams and lakes and impoundments are being devoured these days by an explosion of people fishing for trout, without any background or understanding of either the character of the trout or the centuries of tradition surrounding the sport. Past experience with bass or walleyes or bluefish has not prepared them for the skittish behavior of a trout on hard-fished waters, and their experiences in fishing for other species provide no prologue to the poetry and ethic of trout fishing or its centuries of contemplative literature.

And these hordes will have no one to teach them its gentle truths in future years, no father or grandfather or uncle in baggy tweeds and worn sweater, with a closetful of exquisite split-cane rods and a library of well-thumbed fishing books. The world of primeval trees and crystalline little streams is dwindling, and our aspiring trout fishermen are condemned to finding riffles filled with bedsprings, beer cans, tires, milk bottles, golf clubs, bumper jacks, and other refuse. It is an unthinkable sickness of the mind that can push rusting farm machinery into a crystalline riffle, or jettison a half-dozen rotting truck tires into a beautiful pool. There was once a stretch of water on a famous eastern river we jokingly called the Plumbing Yard. It had a rusting bathtub, two shattered lavatories, an incredible palette of pipe fittings, and a broken water closet—once I even took a good brown trout that was nymphing in the concealment of its toilet seat. Somehow the dark currents along a mossy ledge or current-bleached deadfall would have provided a preferable setting.

The character of trout water is perhaps the most fascinating thing about our sport, and that character is always changing in the kaleidoscope of weather and the seasons.

The fish themselves hover in nervous flight above the intaglio of bright gravel and detritus and leaf drift that lies under a current as rich as a vintage chablis. Our hours along trout water are filled with streamside distractions, like a nervous phoebe catching mayflies in the April sunshine, or the deft scissor-swift patterns of swallows working on a hatch.

There are pelicans diving along the Yellowstone, primordial skeins of geese weaving north against a pale sky, scores of ducks feeding in a wilderness pond in the Jackson Hole country, and rutting elk bugling along the Firehole. The memory is rich with the river sounds, and the soft *pianissimo* sighing of the wind in the trees, and the melancholy calling of whippoorwills at twilight. The mind remembers the swift passage of a canoe among the cedar sweepers along the Au Sable, and the rhythmic music of oarlocks on the Madison and the MacKenzie. There was once a grizzly foraging among the watermelon rinds at a campground along the Gibbon, and an eagle circling lazily on the thermals, high above the wild rapids on the Middle Fork of the Salmon.

No sound is quite like the melodic cry of a loon on some mist-shrouded northern lake, and we all have heard the shrill cackle of a pheasant in a rich limestone valley, its brown trout porpoising lazily among smooth channels in the watercress and elodea. There are memories of flowering dogwoods along the Nantahala in the Smokies, and the strange intensity of the Wyoming sky on crisp September mornings above the New Fork and the Green. The gentleness of a doe and fawn wading a Boardman riffle at twilight in Michigan is mixed with memories of a great blue heron I startled from a swamp along the Namekagon, and the raccoons I watched catching crayfish along the Brule. There are sandhill cranes nesting along Silver Creek at Sun Valley, and ospreys still prey on small trout and fat dace on the Henry's Fork of the Snake. There was a mother bear with cubs crossing the swift Madison in Montana, and the memory of a three-pound brown on the Ausable is pleasantly mixed with the calling of warblers on Adirondack ridges. And a fishless evening in the Catskills was salvaged by the soft pine-sweet wind that came down the river just at dusk.

Each of these memories is as important as the fishing itself, and their enjoyment depends greatly on solitude and the consideration of others along the stream. Regard for the rights and enjoyment of fellow anglers is paramount, and the inconsiderate fisherman who shoulders in when you have taken a fish, wades rudely through a pool you are fishing, or tries for a trout you are resting is a thoughtless boor.

The skilled fly-fisherman does not hesitate to pack-saddle his part of the duffel or fill his time on a portage between lakes. Such anglers always dress their share of the trout, peel and slice the potatoes, or scour the dirty skillets in the sand. There are no secret fly patterns or tactics, and a true angler will always help a less-experienced fisherman in any way he can, with no jealousy of the competition that might result. Generosity and brotherhood are the hallmarks of fly-fishing, and many close friendships are made along trout water. There is no caste system along our lakes and tumbling trout-country streams. Given enough skill in the presentation, a selective fish will rise as unwittingly to the imitation clumsily dressed in some farmhouse along the river as it will roll to take the exquisite woodduck-winged pattern fished by the wealthy banker or stockbroker or chairman of the board.

Trout fishing at its best is a gentle art, both humbling and satisfying. Trout fishing demands far more than its sister sports that the angler escape the threnodic rhythms of his mind, and lose himself in its secret clues and rhythms like Adam and Eve returning to Eden. Many who pursue the sport never discover the riches of its subtle universe, but those who engage in its refinements and complexities are never without rich memories and the satisfactions that come with anything done well.

Walton observed more than three centuries ago that angling was a contemplative sport, best attuned to the poetic moods and pastoral rhythms of life. His classic *Compleat Angler* added that a man who would become a skillful angler must combine the qualities of searching intelligence and powers of observation, but also a good measure of curiosity and optimism and patience. It might be argued that patience itself is the single most important quality in the character of a fly-fisherman. It is equally true in our time of hard-fished waters and the cacophony of urban life. Our ethics and manners and philosophy play an increasingly critical role in the modern practice of our sport—and to Walton's historic prescription of hope and patience we must add the spice called charity.

Many people ask me why I fish, and beyond the obvious qualities of trout and trout country and enjoyment, it is a perplexing question. Haig-Brown put it perfectly in his conclusion of *A River Never Sleeps*, when he confessed that he did not know why he fished, or why others shared his passion, except that it made them think and feel.

Perhaps it is simply the beauty of fly-fishing. Such beauty is rare in the cacophony and ugliness that too often fill our lives, and trout fishing is often beautiful. Its skills are a perfect equilibrium between tradition, physical dexterity and grace, strength, logic, esthetics, our powers of observation, problem solving, perception, and the character of our experience and knowledge. It also combines the primordial rhythms of the stalk with the chesslike puzzles of fly-hatches and fishing, echoing the blood rituals of the hunt without demanding the kill. Its subtle mixture of these ancient echoes and our increasing reverence for life make it unique.

Fly-fishing is remarkably beautiful in a time when such beauty is becoming more and more precious, perhaps essential to both the quality of our lives and our survival itself.

Its beauty exists in a lexicon of peripheral riches: its overtones of history and tradition, several centuries of paintings and books, its patina of split-cane rods and reels and wicker creels, the obvious elegance of its fly-boxes and flies, the patient ballet of fly lines working in the rain, mornings and bright-skied afternoons and twilight, the symmetrical perfection of a blood knot, weather and wind, cottonwood leaves in the current, the rich palette of hackles and pheasant skins and tinsel on our fly-dressing tables, the choreography of barn swallows capturing a hatch of flies, the shrill music of the reel, the fish themselves, and their bulging rises over bright gravel.

Poets are the voices that best capture the rich character of trout and trout country, and our sport is worthy of their skills. The perspective of time teaches us that the essence of fly-fishing, and the lyric qualities of both rivers and their trout, are seldom found in books about fish and fishing techniques and fly-hatches. Fishing images are found in the work of such disparate poets as John Donne and William Butler Yeats and Ezra Pound, but the most evocative images perhaps lie in the little-known *Pied Beauty*, in the nineteenth-century work of Gerard Manley Hopkins:

> Glory be to God for dappled things—
>   For skies as couple-color as a brinded cow
> For rose-moles all in stipple
>   Upon trout that swim.

AFTERWORD 1984

Gratitude is obviously in order.

Any writer would be excited by the audience that responded to *Trout* in its first edition. Its reviews in our principal journals and newspapers were both generous and satisfying, ranging from *The New York Times* to *The Whole Earth Catalogue*. It was *The Whole Earth Catalogue* that finally impressed my son.

Pretty wild, he said.

The Whole Earth Catalogue was a surprise. It was a little like having Geoffrey Norman send me a track slip from Saratoga, after losing his lunch money on a thoroughbred named *Matching the Hatch*.

There was a front-page review in the weekend book section of *The Washington Post*, and a literary friend argued that it was a pole position seldom granted to fishing, perhaps a review in itself. The book led to profiles in such journals as *Esquire* and *Town & Country* and *People*. But the biggest surprise came when *Trout* was selected as a gift of state from the White House to the Prime Minister of Australia.

And there were other voices.

Trout was not originally a concept of mine, and the title came from its publishers too. Although its title was used long before Bergman, and twice in the forty-odd years between our books, few anglers knew it. The editors argued that its scope fully deserved its title, and although I argued against it at first, it seems that subsequent events have proved them correct.

The book was conceived to pull together almost six centuries of theory, technology, and technique. We did not think it might grow into almost 1,800 pages, fifteen color plates, and more than a thousand black-and-white drawings and diagrams.

Arnold Gingrich jokingly compared it with *War and Peace*, suggesting that Tolstoy was almost as long-winded as the Napoleonic War itself. *You don't need to remember an avalanche of Russian characters*, Gingrich added drily, *but expect a lot of Latin!*

Its criticism was curiously mixed.

Some people suggested that *Trout* offered too much material, and that fishing should be simple. Others astonished me with the argument that it had failed to cover fly tying and entomology. Still others wanted more color plates of flies, and collectors complained that it needed more information on rods and reels. There was a familiar chorus about too much Latin taxonomy, and a surprising audience still fails to understand that only a few fly hatches have commonly accepted popular names. Our continent has hundreds and hundreds of important species that still have only Latin names.

You seem to think we're making it up! André Puyans exploded at a heckler in Steamboat Springs. *Well we aren't guilty—the guy who made things complicated left right after Lazarus!*

Some critics missed the point.

Arguments about the history of fishing generate a discord that perhaps equals the medieval quarrels about angels pirouetting on pins. It was suggested that Radcliffe and Hills covered almost everything in the chapters of fishing history. Such critics had obviously forgotten that few, other than bibliophiles and scholars, had actually seen their books when those chapters had been written, and judging from my mail, a large readership found it exciting to discover roots in antiquity.

But a larger point was also missed.

Critics complained that the history of trout fishing in America was much older than a history of the Poconos and Catskills. Such critics were right. Their arguments suggested that I had totally ignored material from old sporting journals, particularly *The American Turf Register and Sporting Magazine, The American Angler,* and the original *Forest & Stream.*

Their criticism was well-taken.

Our fishing history is obviously buried in their brittle pages. But the critics missed my point, because *Trout* was not intended as a fishing history. Its early chapters are a history of fishing theory, not fishing itself.

And our contributions to fishing theory and equipment were sparse until the Civil War.

Some chapters stirred the ashes of old quarrels. Walton was seemingly wrong when he suggested that fishing made anglers contemplative and quiet. Fishing quarrels obviously generate as much heat as politics and religion, and as much pickle-mindedness. Controversies about the *Treatyse of Fysshynge wyth an Angle* and the pastoral dialogue structure of *The Compleat Angler* are clearly the most visible quarrels.

And neither is fully resolved.

The history of the *Treatyse* was recounted in the chapter that traces the field sports from Charlemagne to Gaston de Foix, and his *Livre de Chasse* of 1387. John Waller Hills explored some of the same ground in his *History of Fly Fishing for Trout,* but it should be clearly noted that his judgments were made forty-odd years before John McDonald published *The Origins of Angling,* and its brilliant exercise in literary detective work on the *Treatyse* and sport itself.

There are three schools of thought.

Each generation has its muckrakers, since stirring up controversy is more publishable than quiet scholarship, and has the seldom noticed advantage of capturing the spotlight for the critic. Our generation is clearly no exception. Over lunch in Manhattan, a writer once actually suggested that we collaborate in a bogus fishing quarrel.

What fishing needs, the writer toyed with his Bombay gin martini, *is a really good quarrel going in print—something like Halford and Skues.*

It was both unsettling and funny, and I jokingly refused his challenge, certain that he had pinpointed a vacuum that pickle-mindedness would ultimately fill.

The oldest argument concerning the *Treatyse of Fysshynge wyth an Angle* challenged the authenticity of its author. Since it first appeared in *The Boke of Saint Albans* in 1496, it has been generally attributed to Dame Juliana Berners, who served as the prioress of Sopewell Nunnery.

Elliot Stock published his well-known facsimile edition of the *Treatyse* in 1881, and found that critics were waiting to attack. William Blades challenged both the *Treatyse* and the authenticity of its author. His arguments recruited an army of skeptics. Arnold Gingrich viewed the century-old tempest with a wry detachment.

Gloria Steinem worked for me, he chuckled, *and her diagnosis would have been pretty quick—Blades was a male chauvinist!*

The second argument accepted the existence of Dame Juliana, but suggested that she had not actually written the *Treatyse*. It was argued that she had merely served in assembling *The Boke of Saint Albans,* which was printed by Wynkyn de Worde four years after Columbus reached San Salvador. The third school of thought held that the *Treatyse* was actually written at midcentury, and was merely included in 1496.

Yet the paleographic studies of John McDonald strongly suggest that Berners existed. The principal evidence lies in annotations made by a distinguished antiquary born in the following century. His handwritten notes were made in a copy of *The Boke of Saint Albans* that I have seen at Cambridge University. The Burton notes tell us that Berners wrote the *Treatyse,* was the illustrious daughter of a famous knight, was sister to Richard Lord Berners, and that the family seat was in Essex at Berners Roding.

The notes also tell us that she was prioress at Sopewell Nunnery outside Saint Albans, that *The Boke of Saint Albans* was first printed in its cloisters, and that Berners was still alive in 1460.

But that evidence fails to resolve an ambiguity in the Cambridge annotations. The first printing of *The Boke of Saint Albans* did not include fishing, but was largely devoted to armor, hunting, and falconry. The edition published by Wynkyn de Worde came ten years later, and the *Treatyse* was included. The Burton notes do not clarify what role the prioress played: his words suggest that Berners might have written the *Treatyse,* since they are found in its margins, or that she merely compiled *The Boke of Saint Albans* itself. Since *Trout* was published six years ago, I stumbled across some observations about Dame Juliana by J. J. Dunne, a British angling historian born in 1837.

Dunne had evidence that pinpointed her birth on March 16, 1383. It was a surprise, since it was both much earlier than I had thought, and the date itself was so precise. It also triggered fresh conjecture. Burton's annotations tell us that the prioress was still alive in 1460, which means Berners was already seventy-seven years old. The average life span in those centuries seldom lasted thirty-five years, although there were obviously exceptions.

Some historians have argued that the *Treatyse* was written at midcentury, when Berners was sixty-seven. It was already an unusually long life. But with her birth in the fourteenth century, the prioress would have been 104 years old when *The Boke of Saint Albans* was first printed. The *Treatyse* was not included until another ten years had passed, when our illustrious abbess would have reached 114, a rather unlikely example of medieval longevity.

Burton's evidence has proved that our noble prioress existed, and tells us that she was still alive in 1460. Dunne has offered strong evidence that Berners was already dead when both printings of *The Boke of Saint Albans* were done. Such clues suggest that she wrote the *Treatyse of Fysshynge with an Angle,* and it was added to the second edition of *The Boke of Saint Albans* posthumously.

But we cannot prove either argument.

Walton and his *Compleat Angler* are the fulcrum of our second literary quarrel. The Marriott edition appeared in 1653. Its passages on fly-fishing were obviously borrowed from Mascall, since they include his mistakes in reworking the fly patterns in Berners. Walton is still the only fishing writer whose work is widely used in literature courses, and *The Compleat Angler* had been acclaimed for three centuries. History had given Walton the principal credit for conceiving the best pastoral dialogues in our literature.

But history is fickle.

The Kienbusch copy of *The Arte of Angling* was found in a British estate in 1954. Its title page was missing. There is no question of its authenticity, printer and bookseller, and its date of publication. These facts are in its surviving colophon:

> Imprinted at London in Fleatstreate at the Signe of the Faulcon
> by Henrie Middleton and are to be sold at his Shoppe in Saint
> Dunstan's Churchyarde. Anno. 1577.

The unknown book was unsettling. Its author was quite skilled, perhaps even more facile with his dialogue than Walton, but its structure left Walton's admirers both red-faced and shaken.

Its characters, armature of dialogues, and whole sections of its expositions had obviously been borrowed in *The Compleat Angler.*

Gerald Eades Bentley was still at Princeton in those years, and his expertise was charged with speculation about *The Arte of Angling.* Bentley outlined his conjectures about its author in a facsimile edition published at Princeton. The professor could find no evidence of other known copies. His scholarly investigation found a number of passages so closely worded that Walton obviously copied them. The literary world was forced to accept the truth that Walton had not invented his *Compleat Angler* of whole cloth, and that its structure and content owed *The Arte of Angling* a debt of unforeseen scope.

But who had written it?

Bentley sifted through the tiny book and his knowledge of the sixteenth century to identify a number of candidates. His clues were carefully outlined and brought into focus. The missing writer fished the Ouse at Huntington Bridge and Saint Ives, probably had a country house on the river, and lived with the Marian Exiles in Europe.

Our anonymous author shared duties with a church warden who was troublesome and jealous of his skills. Professor Bentley suggests that *The Arte of Angling* had been written by a writer so skilled that it is obvious he had written extensively before. His book is unmistakably filled with a knowledge and love of angling.

Bentley proposed Alexander Nowell as his candidate for authorship. Doctor Nowell met each of his criteria, except that no direct evidence existed to prove he had fished the Ouse.

Nowell was obviously a distinguished clergyman, who ultimately served as the Dean of Saint Paul's Cathedral in London. His writing experience was well-known too, since Nowell had written the Protestant Catechism that followed the English Reformation. His stature among British clergymen forced Nowell to join the Marian Exiles. His fishing skills were widely known too, and the Nowell portrait at Brasenose College in Oxford still happily includes his tackle. But Bentley knew his case was not fully proved, and with the probity of a great scholar, he refused to state his case with certitude.

Arnold Gingrich sent me a brief note a few weeks before his death. *You seem to accept the authorship of Nowell,* he wrote, *but what is your evidence that he fished the Ouse.*

Art history, I wrote back.

The history of architecture includes a full history of English churches, and the principal sites of these monuments played a role in the travels of British clerics. Such men made frequent trips to the major religious centers. Dean Nowell must have visited them too.

Several important cathedrals and abbeys lie north of London. Thirty years ago, in the lectures of Wilbert Cathmore Ronan, we studied those great Gothic structures. Our textbook was *A History of Architecture on the Comparative Method,* a masterpiece written by Sir Banister Fletcher, who led the Royal Institute of British Architects when I was born. My copy is from the fourteenth printing, and it has a treasured place in my library.

It is filled with intricate drawings and photographs of every cathedral in Europe, complete with comparative plans and models at the same scale. Many important church centers lie south and west of London, and include monuments like Salisbury, Winchester, Exeter, Dorchester, Bristol, Chichester, Wells, and Canterbury.

Other great churches lie north.

Cathedrals like Ely, Warwick, Lichfield, Ripon, Lincoln, Durham, Peterborough, and York sit astride the old trade routes above London. They include some of the principal clerical seats, centers of such importance that other clergymen must have travelled there often. The Dean of Saint Paul's Cathedral, and the author of the English Catechism, made such trips too.

Alexander Nowell had to cross the Ouse to reach such cities, I wrote back to Gingrich, *and if his portrait at Oxford included his fishing gear, he took it along and stopped often.*

Gingrich agreed.

The galley sheets of *Trout* were fully proofed and corrected when another possible author was proposed, using the criteria that Professor Bentley had gleaned from *The Arte of Angling.* It was a remarkable piece of scholarship too.

The second candidate had been proposed by Professor Thomas Harrison, and his arguments were so compelling that I was forced to change *Trout* at the threshold of publication. One critic who rejects Nowell as author of *The Arte of Angling,* and readily accepted the Harrison theory, challenged those sections of *Trout.* His argument was a belief that I should have accepted the new candidate without reservations, and that I had superficially reworked the book to weakly acknowledge another possible author. The argument was blissfully unaware of publishing costs, since major revisions would have changed every folio set in two volumes, and precipitated changes in page numbers and indexing over almost the entire book.

So we should have made big changes, a young production editor wrote me angrily. *Let's see him write copy that covers the material carefully—and fits into the paragraph excisions, without changing the page numbers—or the index!*

Topsell was the catalyst that led to the Harrison theory of authorship.

Both *The Arte of Angling* and *The Compleat Angler* mention Edward Topsell, the British naturalist who worked in the sixteenth century. Thomas Harrison was intrigued by the Bentley conjectures about *The Arte of Angling,* and particularly with its anonymous author. His investigations proved fruitless until he decided to explore Topsell's work, looking for references to *The Arte of Angling.* No references to that specific title were found, but Professor Harrison did find a startlingly fresh clue in Topsell's *History of Serpents:*

> Such times use a caterpillared hook, which kinde of fishing fraud, if you should be better instructed in, I must refer you to a little book dedicated to Robert Dudley, the late Earl of Leicester, written by Master Samuel Vicar, of Godmanchester in Huntingdonshire.

These passages obviously refer to a fishing book written by an angler who lived on the Ouse, but no title of that work is mentioned.

The Topsell reference also has a typographical error that briefly thwarted Harrison's search. Its final phrase has a misplaced comma. Parish records had no trace of Samuel Vicar, but they were filled with information about William Samuel, the vicar at Godmanchester.

The parish records also held each of the clues outlined by Gerald Eades Bentley, in his introduction to the facsimile edition of *The Arte of Angling.* The *Victoria History of the Counties of England* provided supporting data, fleshing out the life of another Marian Exile who might have written the Kienbusch folio. The Godmanchester vicar was a well-known country clergyman, rather than a university-trained mind, but he wrote widely. His *Abridgement of All the Canonical Books of the Old Testament* was published in 1569. Samuel died in 1580, three years after *The Arte of Angling* was printed in London.

Neither Bentley nor Harrison offers incontrovertible proof of authorship. Nowell undoubtedly fished the Ouse, and matched Bentley's checklist of other clues, but we are still left short of certainty. Samuel fits the checklist and wrote a fishing book in the sixteenth century, but we are left without proof of its title.

Arnold Gingrich first accepted the Samuel theory about authorship almost completely, but when I raised these points at the Theodore Gordon Flyfishers' annual meeting, he agreed that considerable doubt remained. Professor Harrison has given us another important puzzle with his scholarship, and the fishing world owes him a debt. But until other clues are found, or some bibliophile discovers a second copy of *The Arte of Angling* with its title page, its authorship must remain an enticing question.

Scholarship should prefer doubt over certitude, since few important things can be codified and measured, and probity best leaves our puzzle a puzzle.

Professor Harrison has advanced the best case for authorship thus far, Gingrich admitted gracefully, *but it seems that fishing has its own Shakespeare-Bacon quarrel!*

Fishing has other quarrels too.

The chapter of *Trout* which explores the brook trout and its habits retells the charming story of Daniel Webster, and the trophy he took from a mill flowage on Long Island. The Webster tale has obviously been embroidered over the years, and several details are obvious anachronisms, since many things in the story did not exist when Webster was fishing the Conetquot and Nissequogue. The size of the fish has been exaggerated too, since legend insists that it equalled the world record brook trout taken on the Nipigon in 1916. Our tales of its size have never been taken seriously, since no official mention of the Webster trout has ever been listed in the record books.

But Webster obviously caught a large trout on Long Island. There is a famous painting of its capture. Some historians have challenged its authenticity, and the identities of its *dramatis personae,* as well as the date of the famous Currier & Ives prints. Others accept its authenticity, but few know that the original painting identifies the participants and is still in the hands of a private collector in New Jersey. Some historians argue that the cast of characters involved is improbable, since the fishing party included men who were among Webster's worst political enemies.

Such points seem a little silly. The cast of characters has probably been embellished too, and everyone knows that our Republic would collapse tomorrow if men who disliked each other totally refused each other's company.

The old Wyandanche Club on the Nissequogue had some Webster memorabilia in its collection, and the principal artifact of his triumph still exists at the Bellport Historical Society. It is the cherrywood weathervane carved for the Presbyterian Church to commemorate Webster's fish, bearing its honest scars of lightning. Such artifacts would not exist if the story were totally a myth.

Theodore Gordon has suffered pointless challenges in recent months too. Gordon was not our first important angler. *Trout* awards that laurel to Thaddeus Norris, but it was Gordon who was first recognized in both Europe and the United States.

History has justly praised his work.

Some writers have overblown his stature and have designated him the Father of American Fly Fishing. Such praise is clearly overstated, but it was Gordon who studied our aquatic insects and thoroughly mastered British dry-fly theory too.

Other writers like Norris, with George Dawson and Henry Parkhurst Wells, were highly skilled anglers of their time. Their work bulges with sound advice on tackle and tactics. Such men had fished widely considering the transportation available in the period of the Civil War. But their tackle was evolved from the wet-fly theories that are traceable to the fifteenth-century *Treatyse* and beyond, and any references to floating flies are most likely written about heavily tied wets dressed with deer fat or paraffin to float. Most experienced fishermen have had trout rise quickly to take a wet fly before it could sink, and our grandfathers were no exception.

The Norris passages describing an experiment with floating flies on the Willowemoc have been cited frequently in recent years. Current writers seem to enjoy chipping at Gordon's monument, with such excerpts from *The American Angler's Book* to buttress their criticism. It is curious that it was Gordon himself who drew attention to the episode, in his recounting of his own evolution:

> My attention was first seriously engaged soon after the publication of Frederic M. Halford's fine work in England, I think in 1886, but the dry fly had been used at least a quarter century earlier. In Thaddeus Norris' *American Angler's Book* published in 1864, there is a description of dry-fly fishing on the Willowemoc.

Norris, using two flies tied expressly for the occasion and a leader of the finest gut, was able to lay them so lightly upon the glossy surface that the trout rose and were hooked before the flies sank.

Gordon's admirers have exaggerated his role in American fishing, just as Halford's reputation has unfairly cast a shadow over his mentors along the Test, Henry Hall and George Selwyn Marryat.

Halford and Gordon are mythic figures.

Hall developed the modern hooks and helped to evolve several changes in fly structure that made the dry fly itself possible. His concepts led to upright wings surrounded by dry-fly hackling, with two hackles tied in by their butts and wound on their edges. Earlier wet flies were usually dressed with folded hackles, or hen hackles tied in at their tips, their fibers worked back along the body. Ronalds illustrated wet flies with hackles tied in at the butts in 1836, but his work was a bridge between earlier writers and the flies of the late nineteenth century. Marryat was the principal catalyst of the dry-fly revolution, a fisherman with a complete palette of skills, and his role was fully acknowledged by his colleagues.

Halford merely wrote of their collaboration on the Hampshire chalk-streams, and codified their theory and practice. The concepts in his books were not entirely his (although many disciples are seemingly unaware of these facts) developments alone. Halford did write tirelessly to spread his dry-fly dogmatics, and in that sense, he became the Father of the Dry-Fly Method.

Gordon occupies a similar position in our fishing history, except that he largely worked and fished alone, and his principal help came through correspondence with Halford.

Others obviously fished with wet flies that were still dry and floating, but such fishing is not the same as intentionally dressing flies designed to float. Gordon perceived that subtlety and patiently taught himself to dress flies with upright wings and hackles wound on edge, using only the finest gamecock capes. Although Norris wrote peripherally about his dry-fly experiment on the Willowemoc, that brief reference cannot match the spate of essays on dry-fly fishing that Gordon wrote for British and American periodicals.

Guy Jenkins knew Gordon well in his later years, and bought flies from him regularly. *Some of the fishing shops stocked dry flies when I was a boy,* Jenkins told me years ago, *but they were mostly imported from England—the dry flies tied here had bum hackles and were badly made.*

Jenkins and his crowd all bought flies from the ailing Gordon, and still remembered their precise workmanship, sparse style of dressing, stiff hackle quality, and elegant proportions.

Gordon was a genius, Jenkins insisted, *and on our rivers his flies were unique—but his writing made him the Father of our Dry-Fly Method.*

Such firsthand evidence is strong.

Other critics have recently challenged the fishing skills of Theodore Roosevelt, and his trip to the Brodheads with Gifford Pinchot. Their case is cleverly made. It speculates that such a trip might have taken place early in their political careers, perhaps when Roosevelt was governor in Albany or Pinchot was governor at Harrisburg. It suggests that no evidence of their fishing exists in the register at Henryville House. Its conjectures include the possibility that anglers otherwise familiar with the history of the Brodheads might have confused the president with his son, Brigadier General Theodore Roosevelt, who did fish there often. And finally, it cruelly explored the probability that Charles Ross, the guide who assisted them, was senile and confused about Roosevelt during the last years of his life, when he was our warden at Henryville.

The essay seemed so plausible and scholarly that an average reader could not have known it triggered a mixture of anger and mirth among the men who had actually fished with Henryville Charlie.

Senility? we laughed together. *Henryville Charlie never had a senile moment in his whole life!*

The painstakingly fabricated case that doubts the story of Roosevelt on the Brodheads is easily refuted, since it clearly lacks other firsthand testimony and regional background affecting its evidence.

Roosevelt and Pinchot were political allies in the Taft Administration. Pinchot resigned over the coal and timber scandals that he discovered in Washington, and such corruption played a role in creating their self-exile from the Republican hierarchy. Their names are missing from the Henryville register, because they were not staying there. Governor Pinchot lived nearby on the Delaware, at the family estate in Milford. Brigadier General Roosevelt was a regular on the Brodheads before the Second World War, and it is silly to suggest that its disciples might have confused the president with his son. The young general is pictured on the Haase farm stretch of the Brodheads in *The Anglers' Club Story*, which was privately published in 1956, and he died at Utah Beach in Normandy.

Henryville Charlie was fully active and alert until his last illness, and the old poacher had guided (there was a Wisconsin guide who served three on the Brule) two American presidents.

Ross was lovably austere about their skills on the river. *Roosevelt could fish*, he said. *Coolidge couldn't.*

Other criticism of *Trout* focused on the complex taxonomy of the fish themselves. Our first monographs were extensive lists of species and subspecies, particularly in the work of Barton Evermann and David Starr Jordan. Such systems of classification are seldom static or complete. Our American taxonomy of fishes is no exception, yet few anglers seem to understand its steady evolution.

One Western writer seemed startled by the changing list of American species and subspecies. *The book is filled*, he concluded testily, *with fish nobody ever heard of.*

Since fresh information has always intrigued and excited me, such criticism is puzzlingly sad. History suggests that only change is predictable and fixed. Science verifies that premise, and biology is ripe with examples too.

How has ichthyology changed?

Its taxonomy itself has passed through many cycles, and it is still changing. Our systems of classification have their roots in the eighteenth-century work of Linnaeus in Sweden. His yardsticks for identifying species and subspecies were simple. Fish specimens using the Linnaean method were studied in terms of their physical character. Such morphological features as gillrakers, teeth patterns, distribution of fins, the number of rays supporting each fin, structure of skull and jaws, pyloric caecae of their entrails, vertebrae, and scale counts were collated and compared. The collation of such physical data gradually evolved into the physiological checklists we have used to define a species or subspecies.

Our early monographs are filled with errors. Biologists searched eagerly for unknown species, both to multiply our knowledge and to bolster their careers. Many species were described in terms of configuration or average size or color, which are variables that fail to meet Linnaean criteria. Many species described in the work of famous ichthyologists like Jordan and Evermann have largely been abandoned in recent years.

Roderick Haig-Brown wrote engagingly in *The Western Angler* about those cycles of change. During the half century that followed Jordan and Evermann, biologists largely agreed that our basic species were the rainbow, brook trout, cutthroat, and the brown trout introduced from Europe.

Other species included the arctic char, Dolly Varden, lake trout, and the richly colored golden trout from California. Haig-Brown was satisfied that his relatively simple list of species, which echoed the best ichthyology of the Depression years, was finally complete. His opinion is still widely shared among both biologists and anglers. But time has proved Haig-Brown wrong.

What has happened?

Several things have happened to erode our certitude about existing taxonomy.

It is important to understand that its past collations of physical details was done manually, with notebooks and relatively few specimens. Memory was both a limitation and a tool. The scope of comparative data was confining and sparse. Computers have utterly transformed such work. Past data were rooted in hundreds and hundreds of specimens before the Cybernetic Revolution. Computers allow our modern ichthyologists to collate data from thousands and thousands of specimens. The judgments on species and morphology and subspecies spilling from their circuitry threaten to change much conventional wisdom, and biology is not the only thing they are changing.

Knowledge has exploded in virtually every field since midcentury, with education and technical training more widespread than ever before. Fisheries biology is exploding too.

Both government and other institutions have supported field work at a scope dwarfing past efforts. Doctoral studies have multiplied swiftly, swelling our spate of new information. Such factors were seldom obvious to the fishing community, and the ecological movement had its impact too. The Environmental Policy Act of 1969 was the principal catalyst. *It was easier to write the law,* the late Starker Leopold explained over dinner in Montana, *than follow it.*

How's that? somebody asked.

Leopold was the primary consultant in biology to the Department of the Interior over many years, particularly for the National Park Service. Leopold lectured in biology at the University of California, and he had played a major role in publishing his father's masterpiece, *A Sand County Almanac.*

Nobody asked the field people, Leopold explained drily, *and they were the key to the law.*

The Environmental Policy Act required the field personnel of the Fish and Wildlife Service to evaluate any proposed project in terms of its impact on rare and endangered species. It was a sensible function of the law.

But it was rooted in a fallacy.

Congress seemingly believed that science had fully described our species, their populations, and their distribution. The first Environmental Impact Statements submitted under the law were routed to the Fish and Wildlife biologists. The field workers were asked to review each project for its effects on the ecology.

The field workers quickly pinpointed the fallacy of the law. *We can't perform our duties,* the biologists told their administrators. *We've never spent the money or time to know what's really out there.*

The confession was startling.

Funds were allocated to fill in the voids. Perhaps the spate of field work triggered by the passage of the Environmental Policy Act of 1969 was as important as the law itself.

We discovered things, Leopold explained, *we never knew existed—including fish!*

The studies were filled with surprises. Our western mountains apparently concealed a number of unfamiliar species and subspecies. Collation of specimens altered many past theories of relationships between trout stocks, particularly the suspected ties between the so-called golden trout, and our familiar rainbow and cutthroat species. The field studies were a fresh wind.

And its weather is still changing.

Several new species and subspecies have been identified in recent years. The status of a few subspecies is still unclear. Some might still be designated as a full-fledged species.

New species include the Gila and Apache trout of New Mexico and Arizona. The Mexican golden trout was discovered in the Sierra Madre country. The precise classification of many subspecies is still a riddle. Some taxonomists argue that such subspecies as the Paiute, Alvord, Humboldt, Snake, Moriah, red-band, and greenback trout deserve consideration as full species. Others consider them exotic subspecies of cutthroats.

Cutthroat taxonomy is also puzzling.

The Pacific drainages sustain a distinct subspecies, along with the fine-spotted strain of Jackson Hole and the Yellowstone cutthroats. Other distinct subspecies are known from the Utah, Colorado, Green, and Rio Grande watersheds. Some cutthroat strains, like the original Pyramid and Twin Lakes stocks, have been lost. The attempts at restoring Pyramid Lake in Nevada are based on cutthroat plantings of fish that are identical in Linnaean terms (their physical yardsticks match perfectly) but lack the hereditary life span to reach the average sizes recorded at Pyramid in frontier times.

Such genetic factors are critical.

Modern genetic theory has played no role in the evolution of taxonomy. It has roots little more than a century old, in the work on plant heredity described by Gregor Mendel in 1866.

His work was half-forgotten and ignored for thirty-odd years, until others began to discover its importance. K. E. Correns, Hugo De Vries, and Erich Tschermak-Seysenegg all verified Mendel's observations early in this century. William Bateson republished Mendel's findings with his *Mendel's Principles of Heredity* in 1902.

Mendel had discovered that specific traits were hereditary, and that such factors were inherited separately. Before his work, the patterns of hybrids were known and widely used, but were still rooted in trial-and-error methods. Mendel speculated that specific biochemical triggers were involved. Thomas Hunt Morgan demonstrated the triggering roles of genes and chromosomes in a lifetime of research, and was awarded the Nobel Prize in 1938.

Gregor Mendel was fully vindicated, and other pieces of his Mendelian puzzle fell into place.

W. E. Seifriz and others were exploring the secrets of protoplasm and cytoplasm in those years, and a growing volume of fresh data was changing our perspective of heredity completely. Caspersson had proved that chromosomes contained nucleic proteins in 1936, and that such materials were largely deoxyribonucleic acids.* His microspectrophotometric studies had unravelled a major secret. It had been widely assumed that such nucleic proteins might consist of a repetitive series of tetranucleotides, including adenylic, cytidylic, guanylic, and thymidylic components. But such speculation puzzled over the fact that such structures were too chemically similar to explain the variables in genetic codings. Genetic and cytogenetic studies had clearly pinpointed the chromosome as the structure containing the genes before the Second World War.

Other work quickly demonstrated that too many biochemical variables existed to make the theory of repetitive tetranucleotides tenable.

---

* Deoxyribonucleic acids are popularly called DNA.

Several types of deoxyribonucleic acid were found to exist, and the studies of Avery, MacLeod, and McCarty strongly pointed to its role as a primary genetic component. Other evidence accumulated from widespread sources. Arthur Mirsky reported that deoxyribonucleic acid was a primary constituent of the genes themselves in 1949.

The studies that followed seemed to prove that deoxyribonucleic acids were the primary genetic materials from bacteria to mammals.

Chargaff began to demonstrate that deoxyribonucleic compounds were widely variable, proving that they possessed the properties to serve as our primary genetic triggers. Watson and Crick conceived their system of interlocking helical structures to explain the physical character of deoxyribonucleic compounds. The interlocking helical strands were found to display a highly specific hydrogen bonding. Watson and Crick also found that such hydrogen bonding between adenine and thymine, or between guanylic and cytosinylic components, could explain the principles outlined earlier in Chargaff's work.

The full puzzle is still unsolved.

But science has taken some giant steps in genetics which suggest that both fish culture and taxonomy must evolve radically in the future. Our simple list of species, which was widely accepted when Haig-Brown published *The Western Angler* in 1947, is subject to growing doubt.

Ichthyology had satisfied itself that riverine populations of rainbow trout, which did not migrate to the Pacific, were identical to the seagoing steelhead. The nineteenth-century monographs of Jordan and Evermann were jettisoned, because the taxonomic system found the rainbow and steelhead alike. But the system itself is based on the *Systema Naturae* of 1735, and it cannot explain the differences in behavior and size that obviously separate the rainbow and steelhead.

Genetics can explain them, and the differences between other strains, but our knowledge of genetics is too recent to embrace taxonomy. The intricate secrets of wildness, life span, migration, and growth are all hidden in genetic codes.

What does it mean to taxonomy? Leopold chuckled. *It means everybody's right.* Linnaean disciples who limit the classification of species to comparative physical details, and find the rainbow and steelhead identical are right as long as they exclude deoxyribonucleic coding.

But modern electrochromatography can isolate the precise mixtures of amino acids, peptides, nucleotides, and colloidal materials like proteins and lipoproteins. Such substances of low molecular weight can be identified in electrophoresis, allowing us to pinpoint the genetic differences in separate tissue samples.

What does it mean in fish?

It means that the genetic coding in tissue samples taken from nonmigratory rainbows and steelhead are not alike, although the fish are structurally identical. The anadromous behavior of steelhead stocks is not merely chance, but is genetically transmitted. Winter and summer migrations are coded into the chromosomes too, and summer steelhead stay longer in their parent rivers before leaving for the sea. Summer, winter, and nonmigratory stocks seldom mate together, although they are alike in terms of Linnaean classification. The subtle variations in their genetic codes, the deoxyribonucleic pieces of the puzzle, are not alike.

And both sides are right.

The rainbow is a single species in terms of conventional taxonomy, which excludes our knowledge of genetic tissue coding. Electrophoresis tells us there are three species, each with its unique character, but is excluded from taxonomy.

Future biology is less clear.

Since genetic coding holds the secrets of wildness, size, rates of growth, migration, habitat preferences, and life span, it might become the primary factor in future fisheries management. It can help us match appropriate genetic stocks to proposed habitat, or select strains for their desired behavior.

There are obvious examples.

We might choose wild strains with long life-span heredity to get optimum results in a particularly fertile habitat with fine spawning grounds. We might utilize wild strains from desiccating watersheds, since their evolution in desertlike temperatures suggests a population able to survive in marginally warm streams. Summer steelhead might be introduced, since they are running over a longer season and in better weather than their winter-run cousins. The duration of their migrations at sea is also genetically coded in their tissues. The small steelhead called jacks or grilse have their physical character and behavior in their genes, just as the giant steelhead of British Columbia have their unique qualities encoded into their heredity. The atypically long saltwater migrations of the Sustut and Kispiox and Babine strains, lasting two and three years, result from the ticking of their genetic clocks.

Biologists are still unravelling such secrets, and our steadily growing knowledge of genetics is changing both fisheries management and taxonomy. Fish culture has created commercial sources of protein, but its role in sport fishing is still mixed. The failure of hatchery strains to cope with shrinking habitat and dams has multiplied our respect for wildness, and we are beginning to understand that fish culture has usually atrophied to the poverty of poultry farming.

Fly hatches are complicated too.

Each year I get letters from readers complaining about the Latin taxonomy involved in hatch matching. Most start with a weak joke about failing Latin in a brief choirboy period. Some are obviously baffled by taxonomy, and others ask plaintively about using the popular English names.

Still others talk of snobbery.

Like those who think the taxonomy of fishes was complete thirty-odd years ago, these fishermen are missing the point.

There are hundreds and hundreds of aquatic insects that are important fly hatches. Fewer than fifty have widely accepted popular names.

Many use identical English names, further compounding the confusion. Several critics have challenged my books for conflicting taxonomy too. Few seem to understand that insect taxonomy is also changing swiftly.

Our mayflies are typical.

Almost a century of prefatory work was codified when the famous James Needham published his classic *Biology of Mayflies* in 1935.

With his colleagues J. R. Traver and Y. C. Hsu, Needham laid the foundations for our basic system of mayfly taxonomy and the classification of species. Preston Jennings completed his *Book of Trout Flies* the same year that Needham's work appeared, and had no access to its system of taxonomy, although his collection of hatches was examined by scholars like Herman Spieth, Cornelius Betten, Jay Traver, and Needham himself.

Charles Wetzel and Arthur Flick published later works on fly-fishing entomology, titled *Practical Fly-Fishing* and *A Streamside Guide to Naturals and Their Imitations,* in the years before midcentury. Flick used Herman Spieth to identify his collections.

B. D. Burks published his important study titled *The Mayflies, or Ephemeroptera, of Illinois* in 1953. It was Burks who assisted in the classification of specimens that led to *Matching the Hatch* two years later. W. C. Day contributed his important observations on taxonomy in *The Aquatic Insects of California* in 1956. Lewis Berner assembled his *Tabular Summary of the Biology of North American Mayfly Nymphs* in 1959.

George Edmunds prepared his remarkable paper on "The Type Localities of the Ephemeroptera of North America North of Mexico" for *The University of Utah Biological Series* in 1962.

Other entomologists continued to add fresh species, observations on their distribution and habits, and the chronology of emergence. J. W. and F. A. Leonard published *Mayflies of Michigan Trout Streams* in 1962, and three years later, Stanley Jewett prepared his taxonomic keys on mayflies for *McClane's Standard Fishing Encyclopedia.*

Like the trout themselves, mayflies are perhaps our most widely studied aquatic flies. Similar evolution has occurred in our studies of other aquatic insects, particularly the sedges and stoneflies, and our knowledge is still growing.

Although anglers find it surprising, there has been no definitive taxonomy of our aquatic fly hatches these past fifty years. Both scholars and fishing entomologists were forced to picture a hybrid system, in a mental collage from a bookshelf of sources and papers in scholarly journals. It was an intellectual tightrope, attempting to bridge the differences between widespread sources, while remaining aware of their obsolescences, overlappings, and errors. It was seldom easy for fishermen or scholars.

Both scholars and fishing entomologists had been aware that George Edmunds and his colleagues at the University of Utah were working on a definitive monograph and taxonomy of our mayflies. His manuscript ultimately became *The Mayflies of North and Central America,* published with Steven Jensen and Lewis Berner at the University of Minnesota in 1976.

Edmunds and his colleagues have given us a singular contribution to our knowledge of important fly hatches and their distribution, perhaps the most important yet written. *The Mayflies of North and Central America* describes many new genera and species, while revising and discarding others. Its material on the distribution, or zoogeography, of species is unique, although widely experienced fishermen with the skills to use taxonomic keys were puzzled too.

It is critical that a fishing audience understand several facts about scholarly work on aquatic insects: Latin taxonomy is changing and will continue to change; taxonomy is based on adult male morphology; color is not a factor in classification; taxonomic keys that identify only genus without defining species are virtually worthless to anglers; and their observations on the distribution of specific hatches are often less valid than those of fishing writers whose sport has enabled them to collect flies more widely in the field.

Several years ago in Argentina, Starker Leopold and I were fishing the Quilquihue, and discussed these topics jokingly. *Some of the fishing writers can use the taxonomic keys,* I protested, *but you guys keep telling us we're wrong.*

Wrong about what? he asked.

Classification of species, I said, *and their zoogeography—we're always finding flies in waters where they're not supposed to live.*

But they're in the keys? Leopold interrupted.

That's right, I said.

Well, he smiled, *when you've got a bug in a bottle and it keys out correctly—it's there!*

Edmunds and his colleagues have seemingly started as much fresh controversy with their proposed new taxonomy as their work resolved. Many well-known aquatic hatches, such as *Ephemerella cornuta* and *flavilinea* and *grandis* have been placed in a new genus called *Drunella*. The familiar Light Cahill, the twilight-hatching *Stenonema canadense* of several fishing books, has been placed with its sister hatches in a proposed genus called *Stenacron*. And such taxonomic changes fill its pages.

It's impossible, Carl Richards chuckled over lunch by a Michigan steelhead riffle this past spring. *Just when we get a generation of readers familiar with the Latin names of important flies—the entomologists decide to change everything!*

Fly tiers are dismayed by the fact that standard Linnaean taxonomy is based entirely on the adult males, perhaps the least important facet of any hatch. Color is not a factor in defining a species. Some recent fishing entomologies offer wildly inaccurate color and identification only to genus. Defining genus is simply not enough for fly-fishing purposes. Color is often the key. Since most genera contain insects that vary widely in both size and color, identification of a specimen to its proper genus comes up empty on the stream. *Ephemerella* is perhaps our best-known mayfly genus, and it provides an obvious example. Its species range from size eight to size twenty hooks in their imitations, and its color spectrum varies from dark slate to flies the color of a freshly made broom. *Aquatic Entomology* was praised extravagantly in several journals, both for its illustrations and its taxonomic keys. Such critics obviously riffled through its pages without the yardsticks to judge either its color work or the focus of its taxonomy.

The Mayflies of North and Central America has proposed a taxonomy filled with intricate surprises. Both fishermen and some scholars have doubts about taxonomic revisions at its sweeping scale. The perspective of time will tell us whether science will fully accept the taxonomic keys outlined in Edmunds' remarkable work.

Both fishermen and fly tiers are often dismayed to discover the revisions and quarrels in entomology and ichthyology. It is unsettling to find that taxonomy itself is not a precise jigsaw puzzle, but a chaotic puzzle that is constantly adding parts. But anyone familiar with the vagaries and disputes of academic life knows that scholarship is rather like a giant pinball machine, its flippers and plastic bumpers and scoreboards all working in ponderously slow motion.

Alfred North Whitehead is often remembered for his observation that our ignorance of the past will condemn us to repeat it. But there is another aphorism in his work worth thinking about, telling us to seek simplicity in everything, and distrust it.

Such wisdom is available from less cerebral sources. Few things are simple when they are really understood, and what we know is still a potsherd of the secrets that remain. We hope that you will enjoy *Trout* across many seasons, seeking out its potsherds like old rivers and familiar pools. Its complexity and scope have proved a little overwhelming for some readers, but its subject has a unique diversity.

Whitehead was not the only philosopher who distrusted the illusions of simplicity, and I remember the wisdom of my mother's father, a rancher who worked hard to get his neighbors to change a mindless husbandry that turned the Great Plains into a dust-storm desert in the Depression years. After a morning's argument with another rancher about overgrazing and overtilling the land, he stalked angrily from the man's house to the pickup.

The world's full of folks, he rolled his eyes skyward in frustration and dismay, *who don't want to know how much they don't know!*

Ernest Schwiebert

Christmas
Princeton, New Jersey
1983

APPENDICES

CATALOG OF

FLY PATTERNS

DOWN-WING WET FLIES
Facing page 718

BLUE-WINGED OLIVE QUILL (Schwiebert)
- HOOK: 14–20 Mustad 3906
- SILK: 6/0 Olive
- TAILS: Blue dun hackle fibers
- BODY: Bleached peacock quill dyed pale olive or golden olive hackle quill
- WINGS: Dark mallard or black duck primary quill sections
- HACKLE: Blue dun

IRON BLUE QUILL (Schwiebert)
- HOOK: 14–20 Mustad 3906
- SILK: 6/0 Dark gray
- TAILS: Iron-blue dun fibers
- BODY: Stripped peacock quill
- WINGS: Dark mallard primary quill sections
- HACKLE: Iron-blue dun

DARK BLUE QUILL
- HOOK: 12–20 Mustad 3906
- SILK: 6/0 Gray
- TAILS: Dark-blue dun fibers
- BODY: Dark stripped peacock quill
- WINGS: Dark mallard primary quill sections
- HACKLE: Dark-blue dun

LITTLE RUSTY QUILL (Schwiebert)
- HOOK: 14–20 Mustad 3906
- SILK: 6/0 Brown
- TAILS: Dark rusty dun fibers

BODY: Fiery-brown hackle quill, stripped and wound
WINGS: Gray mallard wing-quill sections
HACKLE: Dark rusty dun

ALDERFLY (Kingsley)
HOOK: 12–16 Mustad 3906
SILK: 6/0 Black
TAILS: None
BODY: Peacock herl tied full
WINGS: Dark speckled-hen feather sections
HACKLE: Iron-blue dun

This pattern originated with Canon Charles Kingsley, cleric of Westminster Abbey, who fished the Hampshire chalkstreams more than a century ago.

BLACK QUILL (Wetzel)
HOOK: 14–20 Mustad 3906
SILK: 6/0 Black
TAILS: Black hackle fibers
BODY: Stripped peacock quill
WINGS: Dark mallard primary quill sections
HACKLE: Black

This is a variation on a Wetzel dry-fly dressing.

BROWN QUILL
HOOK: 12–18 Mustad 3906
SILK: 6/0 Brown
TAILS: Fiery-brown gamecock pattern
BODY: Bleached peacock quill
WINGS: Gray mallard primary wing-quill sections
HACKLE: Fiery-brown gamecock

The traditional British pattern is dressed with these materials. Its origins are unclear, although it predates our American Catskill dressing by more than two hundred years.

LEAD-WING COACHMAN
HOOK: 8–20 Mustad 3906
SILK: 6/0 Dark gray
TAILS: None
BODY: Peacock herl
WINGS: Dark mallard or black duck primary section
HACKLE: Dark-brown furnace

BLUE DUN
HOOK: 12–20 Mustad 3906
SILK: 6/0 Gray
TAILS: Blue dun hackle fibers
BODY: Dark blue-gray mole dubbing on olive silk
WINGS: Dark mallard primary wing sections
HACKLE: Blue dun

Another British pattern of relatively ancient origins.

BLUE QUILL
HOOK: 8–20 Mustad 3906
SILK: 6/0 Gray

TAILS: Medium-blue dun fibers
BODY: Bleached peacock quill over yellow floss underbody
WINGS: Mallard primary quill sections
HACKLE: Medium-blue dun

OLIVE DUN

HOOK: 14–20 Mustad 3906
SILK: 6/0 Olive
TAILS: Medium-olive hackle fibers
BODY: Dark-olive fur dubbing
WINGS: Dark mallard primary wing-quill sections
HACKLE: Medium olive

OLIVE QUILL

HOOK: 8–20 Mustad 3906
SILK: 6/0 Olive
TAILS: Medium-olive dun fibers
BODY: Bleached peacock quill over olive floss underbody
WINGS: Mallard primary quill sections
HACKLE: Medium-olive dun

These traditional quill-bodied dressings are British flies of origins that reach back into the seventeenth century.

GROUSE AND GREEN

HOOK: 8–14 Mustad 3906
SILK: 6/0 Olive
TAILS: Medium-brown fibers
BODY: Bright olive-green dubbing ribbed with gold tinsel
WINGS: Dark-brown English grouse tail
HACKLE: Medium-brown furnace

GROUSE AND OLIVE

HOOK: 8–14 Mustad 3906
SILK: 6/0 Olive
TAILS: Medium-brown fibers
BODY: Olive fur-dubbing ribbed with gold tinsel
WINGS: Gray English grouse tail feather
HACKLE: Medium-brown furnace

GROUSE AND YELLOW

HOOK: 8–14 Mustad 3906
SILK: 6/0 Brown
TAILS: Medium-brown fibers
BODY: Bright golden yellow seal's fur ribbed with gold tinsel
WINGS: Pale-gray English grouse tail
HACKLE: Medium-brown furnace

These grouse-winged patterns are simplified patterns, omitting some exotic feathers, adapted from traditional Scottish loch flies.

GROUSE AND ORANGE

HOOK: 8–14 Mustad 3906
SILK: 6/0 Brown
TAILS: Medium-brown fibers
BODY: Dark-orange seal's fur dubbing ribbed with gold tinsel

WINGS: Brown English grouse tail-feather sections
HACKLE: Medium-brown furnace

These reduced dressings of Scottish loch flies are quite effective on our fish in both lakes and streams.

MALE MARCH BROWN
    HOOK: 8–14 Mustad 3906
    SILK: 6/0 Brown
    TAILS: Woodduck flank fibers
    BODY: Dark brown-gray dubbing ribbed with gold tinsel
    WINGS: Hen pheasant tail-feather sections
    HACKLE: Dark partridge hackle fibers

FEMALE MARCH BROWN
    HOOK: 8–14 Mustad 3906
    SILK: 6/0 Gray
    TAILS: Woodduck flank fibers
    BODY: Gray dubbing and yellow fur tag ribbed with gold tinsel
    WINGS: Hen pheasant tail-feather sections
    HACKLE: Light partridge hackle

This traditional British pattern is a fine addition to any fly-book.

BLUE-WINGED HARE'S EAR
    HOOK: 8–20 Mustad 3906
    SILK: 6/0 Gray
    TAILS: Woodduck flank fibers
    BODY: Roughly dubbed hare's mask heavily mixed with guard hairs
    WINGS: Dark blue-gray wing-quill sections
    HACKLE: Hare's mask guard fibers picked out

This ancient March Brown dressing and Hare's Ear pattern are very old British flies that are still both exquisite and deadly.

GREENWELL'S GLORY (Greenwell)
    HOOK: 8–20 Mustad 3906
    SILK: 6/0 Olive
    TAILS: Medium-brown fibers
    BODY: Light-olive floss ribbed with fine gold wire
    WINGS: English woodcock primary quill sections
    HACKLE: Medium furnace

This classic wet-fly dressing is the creation of Canon William Greenwell, who served Durham Cathedral a century ago.

SILVER PHEASANT (Schwiebert)
    HOOK: 8–14 Mustad 3906
    SILK: 6/0 Light gray
    TAILS: Ring-necked saddle fibers
    BODY: Silver tinsel ribbed with fine silver wire
    WINGS: Hen pheasant tail-feather sections
    HACKLE: Blue ring-necked pheasant saddle

GOLD PHEASANT (Schwiebert)
    HOOK: 8–14 Mustad 3906
    SILK: 6/0 Light gray

TAILS: Ring-necked saddle fibers
BODY: Gold tinsel ribbed with fine gold wire
WINGS: Hen pheasant tail-feather sections
HACKLE: Blue ring-necked saddle

SILVER MARCH BROWN
    HOOK: 8–14 Mustad 3906
    SILK: 6/0 Light gray
    TAILS: Hen pheasant tail fibers
    BODY: Silver tinsel ribbed with fine silver wire
    WINGS: Hen pheasant tail-feather sections
    HACKLE: Dark partridge hackle
This is a Scottish sea-trout pattern that has produced consistently during many sedge hatches.

GOLD MARCH BROWN
    HOOK: 8–14 Mustad 3906
    SILK: 6/0 Light gray
    TAILS: Hen pheasant tail fibers
    BODY: Gold tinsel ribbed with fine gold wire
    WINGS: Hen pheasant tail-feather sections
    HACKLE: Dark partridge hackle
This is a fine English sea-trout pattern with importance on our waters.

ROLLED-WING WET FLIES
Facing page 719

LITTLE RUSTY STONEFLY (Flick)
    HOOK: 14–18 Mustad 3906B 1X Long
    SILK: 6/0 Brown
    TAILS: Rusty dun fibers, tied short
    BODY: Rusty-brown dubbing
    WINGS: Brown mallard flank fibers
    HACKLE: Rusty dun

LITTLE YELLOW STONEFLY (Wetzel)
    HOOK: 14–18 Mustad 3906B 1X Long
    SILK: 8/0 Primrose
    TAILS: Palest ginger fibers, tied short
    BODY: Pale-yellow dubbing
    WINGS: Pale woodduck flank fibers
    HACKLE: Palest ginger

LITTLE GREEN STONEFLY (Wetzel)
    HOOK: 16–20 Mustad 3906B 1X Long
    SILK: 8/0 Primrose
    TAILS: Palest olive fibers, tied short
    BODY: Pale yellow-green dubbing
    WINGS: Pale woodduck flank fibers
    HACKLE: Palest olive

EARLY BROWN STONEFLY (Wetzel)

HOOK: 12–16 Mustad 3906B 1X Long
SILK: 6/0 Brown
TAILS: Iron-blue dun fibers, tied short
BODY: Dark brown-black dubbing; stripped fiery-brown hackle quill
WINGS: Brown mallard flank fibers
HACKLE: Iron-blue dun

These patterns were originally developed by Art Flick and Charles Wetzel. The dark dressings imitate the *Taeniopteryx* and *Capnia* flies which hatch early in the season, and the pale patterns are the *Alloperla* hatches that follow in late spring.

DARK HENDRICKSON

HOOK: 10–18 Mustad 3906
SILK: 6/0 Gray
TAILS: Dark-blue dun fibers
BODY: Dark blue-gray mole dubbing
WINGS: Dark woodduck flank fibers
HACKLE: Dark-blue dun

LIGHT HENDRICKSON (Steenrod)

HOOK: 10–18 Mustad 3906
SILK: 6/0 Gray
TAILS: Medium-blue dun fibers
BODY: Cream-gray fox dubbing
WINGS: Medium woodduck flank fibers
HACKLE: Medium-blue dun

DARK CAHILL (Cahill)

HOOK: 10–18 Mustad 3906
SILK: 6/0 Brown
TAILS: Medium-brown hackle fibers
BODY: Dark blue-gray mole dubbing on brown silk
WINGS: Dark woodduck flank fibers
HACKLE: Medium brown

LIGHT CAHILL (Chandler)

HOOK: 10–18 Mustad 3906
SILK: 6/0 White
TAILS: Pale honey-ginger fibers
BODY: Pale-cream fox dubbing on primrose silk
WINGS: Pale woodduck flank fibers
HACKLE: Pale honey-ginger

GORDON QUILL (Gordon)

HOOK: 10–18 Mustad 3906
SILK: 6/0 Gray
TAILS: Medium-blue dun fibers
BODY: Bleached peacock quill over yellow silk underbody
WINGS: Woodduck flank fibers
HACKLE: Medium-blue dun

RED QUILL (Flick)

HOOK: 10–18 Mustad 3906

SILK: 6/0 Gray
TAILS: Medium-rusty dun fibers
BODY: Stripped fiery-brown hackle quill
WINGS: Woodduck flank fibers
HACKLE: Medium-rusty dun

GRIEG QUILL (Grieg)
HOOK: 10–18 Mustad 3906
SILK: 6/0 Black
TAILS: Badger hackle fibers
BODY: Bleached peacock quill
WINGS: Dark woodduck flank fibers
HACKLE: Badger

GORDON (Gordon)
HOOK: 10–18 Mustad 3906
SILK: 6/0 Primrose
TAILS: Golden badger hackle fibers
BODY: Golden-yellow rayon floss ribbed with fine gold wire
WINGS: Pale woodduck flank fibers
HACKLE: Golden badger

These patterns are variations on the Catskill classics that were the work of fly-dressers like Roy Steenrod, Daniel Cahill, William Chandler, Theodore Gordon, Arthur Flick, and Elizabeth Grieg.

MALLARD QUILL
HOOK: 10–18 Mustad 3906
SILK: 6/0 Brown
TAILS: Dark rusty dun fibers
BODY: Bleached peacock quill over brown silk underbody
WINGS: Brown mallard flank fibers
HACKLE: Dark rusty dun

This Catskill traditional has no known origin, but it is quite effective during hatches of dark stoneflies and mayfly duns.

SOOTY OLIVE
HOOK: 10–18 Mustad 3906
SILK: 6/0 Olive
TAILS: Dark sooty-olive fibers
BODY: Dark-olive dubbing ribbed with fine gold wire
WINGS: Brown mallard flank fibers
HACKLE: Dark sooty-olive

This is a great traditional dressing from the Irish sea-trout lakes that deserves a wider American following.

CAMPBELL'S FANCY (Campbell)
HOOK: 10–14 Mustad 3906
SILK: 6/0 Black
TAILS: Golden pheasant crest-fibers
BODY: Silver tinsel ribbed with fine silver wire
WINGS: Light-teal flank fibers
HACKLE: Badger

Charles Campbell developed this pattern on the Beaverkill, at the historic Beaverkill Trout Club.

GRAY QUILL (Mills)

HOOK:	14–20 Mustad 3906
SILK:	6/0 Gray
TAILS:	Dark grizzly fibers
BODY:	Bleached peacock quill
WINGS:	Dark-teal flank fibers
HACKLE:	Dark grizzly

This pattern was apparently a creation of Chester Mills, who once supervised the fly-tying at William Mills & Sons.

GREEN EGG-SAC STONEFLY (Darbee)

HOOK:	12–16 Mustad 3906B 1X Long
SILK:	6/0 Primrose
TAILS:	Pale-honey badger fibers
BODY:	Pale-yellow dubbing with a bright-green egg sac
BODY HACKLE:	Pale-honey badger
WINGS:	Pale woodduck flank fibers
HACKLE:	Pale-honey badger

This is a wet variation on a dry pattern developed by Harry Darbee on the Beaverkill and Willowemoc.

MORMON GIRL STONEFLY (Troth)

HOOK:	10–14 Mustad 3906B 1X Long
SILK:	6/0 Primrose
TAILS:	Pale-honey badger fibers
BODY:	Pale-yellow dubbing with a scarlet egg sac
BODY HACKLE:	Pale-honey badger
WINGS:	Grey mallard flank fibers
HACKLE:	Pale-honey badger

Al Troth is a famous tier who adapted the Mormon Girl to imitate a stonefly on his native Montana rivers.

CATSKILL (Darling)

HOOK:	10–18 Mustad 3906B 1X Long
SILK:	6/0 Brown
TAILS:	Medium-brown fibers
BODY:	Medium-orange seal's fur dubbing
BODY HACKLE:	Medium-brown furnace
WINGS:	Woodduck flank fibers
HACKLE:	Medium-brown furnace

Louis Darling was a famous tournament caster before the First World War, and was an early member of the Anglers' Club of New York.

CATSKILL OLIVE (Schwiebert)

HOOK:	10–18 Mustad 3906B 1X Long
SILK:	6/0 Olive
TAILS:	Medium-brown fibers
BODY:	Dark-olive dubbing
BODY HACKLE:	Brown furnace
WINGS:	Dark woodduck flank fibers
HACKLE:	Brown furnace

Simply the Catskill with a body of olive dubbing.

BROWN WILLOWFLY

HOOK:	6-12 Mustad 38941 3X Long
SILK:	6/0 Brown
TAILS:	Medium-brown fibers
BODY:	Dark-chocolate dubbing mixed with orange seal's fur
BODY HACKLE:	Medium-brown furnace
WINGS:	Brown mallard flank
HACKLE:	Medium-brown furnace

GREAT SUMMER STONEFLY

HOOK:	4–12 Mustad 38941 3X Long
SILK:	6/0 Brown
TAILS:	Dark-brown feather fibers
BODY:	Medium-brown fur dubbing mixed with orange seal
BODY HACKLE:	Brown furnace
WINGS:	Brown mallard nashua fibers
HACKLE:	Brown furnace faced with brown mallard fibers

EARLY SUMMER STONEFLY

HOOK:	6–12 Mustad 39841 3X Long
SILK:	6/0 Brown
TAILS:	Medium ginger fibers
BODY:	Gray-yellow dubbing on primrose silk
BODY HACKLE:	Medium ginger
WINGS:	Woodduck flank fibers
HACKLE:	Medium ginger faced with woodduck fibers

These large patterns imitate several *Acroneuria* and *Perla* species found on American streams.

DOWN-WING DRY FLIES
Facing page 1098

SMALL DARK SEDGE (Halford)

HOOK:	16–22 Mustad 94842
SILK:	8/0 Brown
BODY:	Dark-brown dubbing
BODY HACKLE:	Brown furnace
WINGS:	Slate mallard primary wing-quill sections
HACKLE:	Brown furnace

This little pattern was included in *Floating Flies and How to Dress Them,* the vehicle that Frederic Halford used to launch his dry-fly revolution.

CORNCRAKE SEDGE (Bridgett)

HOOK:	16–22 Mustad 94842
SILK:	8/0 White
BODY:	Cream-colored fox dubbed on primrose silk
BODY HACKLE:	Palest honey-ginger
WINGS:	Pale starling primary wing-quill sections
HACKLE:	Palest honey-ginger

R.C. Bridgett apparently conceived this little sedge imitation.

LITTLE RED SEDGE (Skues)

HOOK:	16–22 Mustad 94842
SILK:	8/0 Brown
BODY:	Blackish-brown fur dubbing
BODY HACKLE:	Dark reddish gamecock
WINGS:	Speckled hen feather sections, paired
HACKLE:	Dark reddish gamecock

This little sedge clearly proves that George Skues did not limit himself to nymph tactics alone.

LITTLE BLACK SEDGE (Wetzel)

HOOK:	16–22 Mustad 94842
SILK:	8/0 Black
BODY:	Black fur dubbing on scarlet silk
BODY HACKLE:	Iron-blue dun
WINGS:	Slate-colored black duck primary sections
HACKLE:	Iron-blue dun or natural black

Wetzel fished his imitations of the early *Chimmarha* caddis as wet flies.

WICKHAM'S FANCY (Wickham)

HOOK:	12–18 Mustad 94842
SILK:	6/0 White
BODY:	Gold flat tinsel
BODY HACKLE:	Medium ginger
WINGS:	Mallard primary wing-quill sections
HACKLE:	Medium ginger

This classic caddis pattern is attributed to Dr. Charles Wickham, who fished the Itchen at Winchester a century ago.

DARK ORANGE SEDGE (Halford)

HOOK:	12–18 Mustad 94842
SILK:	6/0 Orange
BODY:	Dark-orange seal's fur dubbing
BODY HACKLE:	Brown furnace
WINGS:	Slate primary wing-quill sections
HACKLE:	Brown furnace

HENRYVILLE (Brobst)

HOOK:	12–24 Mustad 94842
SILK:	6/0 Brown
BODY:	Scarlet floss silk
BODY HACKLE:	Medium grizzly
WINGS:	Mallard primary wing-quill sections
HACKLE:	Medium brown

Hiram Brobst was a well-known Pennsylvania Dutch fly-dresser almost a half-century ago, and the Henryville is his pattern. It was originally called the No-name on the Brodheads. The Brobst pattern used scarlet silk floss for its body, which turned a deep ruddy brown on its first baptism. Silk should still be used in place of synthetic flosses, since they remain scarlet when wet, making the Henryville merely a lure instead of a fine sedge imitation. The Henryville got its name from its popularity at Henryville House on the Brodheads.

HENRYVILLE OLIVE (Schwiebert)

HOOK:	12–24 Mustad 94842ᶜ

SILK:	6/o Olive
BODY:	Bright-olive synthetic floss
BODY HACKLE:	Medium grizzly
WINGS:	Mallard primary wing-quill sections
HACKLE:	Medium brown

This olive-bodied Henryville is a personal variation on the original Brobst dressing, in response to the olivaceous caddis hatches on many rivers.

DARK BROWN SEDGE (Halford)
HOOK:	12–18 Mustad 94842
SILK:	6/o Brown
BODY:	Dark-brown fur dubbing
BODY HACKLE:	Brown furnace
WINGS:	Brown turkey wing-quill sections
HACKLE:	Brown furnace faced with dark partridge fibers

DARK BLUE SEDGE (Jennings)
HOOK:	12–18 Mustad 94842
SILK:	6/o Brown
BODY:	Medium-brown fur dubbing
BODY HACKLE:	Medium-blue dun
WINGS:	Slate duck wing-quill sections
HACKLE:	Medium-blue dun faced with partridge fibers

This pattern is a *Psilotreta* imitation included in *A Book of Trout Flies*.

SILVER SEDGE (Halford)
HOOK:	12–18 Mustad 94842
SILK:	6/o White
BODY:	Silver flat tinsel
BODY HACKLE:	Light grizzly
WINGS:	Grayish English grouse tail sections
HACKLE:	Light grizzly faced with mallard flank fibers

SOOTY OLIVE SEDGE (Hemingway)
HOOK:	12–20 Mustad 94842
SILK:	8/o Olive
BODY:	Dark-olive synthetic floss
BODY HACKLE:	Badger dyed dark sooty dun
WINGS:	Dark English grouse tail sections
HACKLE:	Badger dyed dark sooty dun

Jack Hemingway designed this killing sedge imitation, and has them tied for him by René Harrop, the famous Idaho fly-maker from Saint Anthony.

WELSHMAN'S BUTTON (Halford)
HOOK:	12–16 Mustad 94842
SILK:	6/o Brown
BODY:	Medium-brown fur dubbing with a dull yellow egg sac
BODY HACKLE:	Medium brown
WINGS:	English woodcock feather sections
HACKLE:	Medium brown faced with dark woodduck fibers

PALE ORANGE SEDGE (Halford)
| HOOK: | 12–16 Mustad 94842 |

SILK:	6/0 Orange
BODY:	Pale-orange dubbing
BODY HACKLE:	Dark ginger
WINGS:	English woodcock feather sections
HACKLE:	Dark ginger faced with pale woodduck fibers.

GRAY FLAG

HOOK:	12–16 Mustad 94842
SILK:	6/0 Gray
BODY:	Dark blue gray mole dubbing
BODY HACKLE:	Dark-gray dun
WINGS:	English hen-pheasant tail-feather sections
HACKLE:	Dark-gray dun

This is a variation on the British Gray Flag dressing.

MOLE FLY

HOOK:	12–16 Mustad 94842
SILK:	6/0 Olive
BODY:	Dark-olive dubbing
BODY HACKLE:	Brown furnace
WINGS:	English hen-pheasant tail-feather sections
HACKLE:	Brown furnace faced with English grouse fibers

The Mole Fly is a very old pattern of uncertain lineage.

FEMALE GRANNOM (Halford)

HOOK:	12–16 Mustad 94842
SILK:	6/0 Brown
BODY:	Blackish-brown dubbing with bright-green sac
BODY HACKLE:	Dark-gray dun
WINGS:	English grouse tail-feather sections
HACKLE:	Dark-gray dun faced with dark partridge fibers

GRANNOM (Halford)

HOOK:	12–16 Mustad 94842
SILK:	6/0 Brown
BODY:	Blackish-brown dubbing
BODY HACKLE:	Dark-gray dun
WINGS:	English grouse tail-feather sections
HACKLE:	Dark-gray dun faced with dark partridge fibers

These classic patterns were codified by Halford a century ago on the Test.

SPECKLED PETER

HOOK:	12–16 Mustad 94842
SILK:	6/0 Brown
BODY:	Dark-chocolate dubbing
BODY HACKLE:	Brown furnace
WINGS:	Brown English grouse tail-feather sections
HACKLE:	Brown furnace faced with bluish cock-pheasant saddle

BLACK SILVERHORNS

HOOK:	12–16 Mustad 94842
SILK:	6/0 Black
BODY:	Black fur dubbing

BODY HACKLE:	Iron-blue dun
WINGS:	Speckled hen feather sections
HACKLE:	Iron-blue dun faced with dark partridge fibers

These are both traditional names for similar English and Irish sedges.

GREAT ORANGE SEDGE (Schwiebert)

HOOK:	6–10 Mustad 94842
SILK:	6/0 Orange
BODY:	Yellowish-orange dubbing
BODY HACKLE:	Pale ginger
WINGS:	Brown mottled turkey quill sections
HACKLE:	Pale ginger faced with pale woodduck fibers

GREAT OLIVE CAPERER (Schwiebert)

HOOK:	6–10 Mustad 94842
SILK:	6/0 Olive
BODY:	Dark-olive dubbing
BODY HACKLE:	Dark-olive dun
WINGS:	Gray mottled turkey quill sections
HACKLE:	Dark-olive dun faced with partridge fibers

These are imitations of several important *Limnephilus* and *Arctoecia* flies, which are found in lakes and slow-flowing streams, and are both diurnal and nocturnal in their habits.

GREAT GRAY SEDGE (Schwiebert)

HOOK:	6–10 Mustad 94842
SILK:	6/0 Gray
BODY:	Dark brown-gray dubbing
BODY HACKLE:	Dark rusty dun
WINGS:	Grey mottled turkey wing-quill sections
HACKLE:	Dark rusty dun faced with bluish cock-pheasant saddle

GREAT CINNAMON SEDGE (Schwiebert)

HOOK:	6–10 Mustad 94842
SILK:	6/0 Brown
BODY:	Dark-cinnamon dubbing
BODY HACKLE:	Brown furnace
WINGS:	Brown mottled turkey wing-quill sections
HACKLE:	Brown furnace faced with dark partridge fibers

These patterns imitate large nocturnal sedges of the *Platyphylax* and *Stenophylax* types.

ROLLED-WING DRY FLIES

Facing page 1099

GRIEG QUILL (Grieg)

HOOK:	12–18 Mustad 94842
SILK:	6/0 Black
TAILS:	Cream badger hackle fibers
BODY:	Bleached peacock quill
WINGS:	Woodduck flank
HACKLE:	Cream badger

COCHY QUILL (Bergman)
HOOK:	12–18 Mustad 94842
SILK:	6/0 Brown
TAILS:	Dark-furnace hackle fibers
BODY:	Bleached peacock quill
WINGS:	Dark woodduck flank
HACKLE:	Dark furnace

These similar patterns were largely popularized in the writings of Bergman. The Grieg Quill is the work of Elizabeth Grieg, a classic fly-dresser originally trained in Europe.

PALE SPECKLE-WING QUILL (Schwiebert)
HOOK:	16–20 Mustad 94842
SILK:	8/0 White
TAILS:	Pale grizzly fibers
BODY:	Bleached peacock quill
WINGS:	Light barred teal flank-feather
HACKLE:	Pale grizzly

DARK SPECKLE-WING QUILL (Schwiebert)
HOOK:	16–20 Mustad 94842
SILK:	8/0 White
TAILS:	Dark grizzly fibers
BODY:	Stripped peacock quill
WINGS:	Dark barred teal flank-feather
HACKLE:	Dark grizzly

These two patterns have been favorites of mine since early experiences on the high lakes and beaver ponds of Colorado with the *Callibaetis* hatches. Although less known on eastern and midwestern waters, these richly mottled mayflies are quite important on rivers too, particularly slow-flowing streams like Silver Creek and the Henry's Fork of the Snake. The flies are multibrooded, and three or four separate populations may hatch in a single season. Both hatching duns and spinner falls are important.

PALE GOLDEN DRAKE (Schwiebert)
HOOK:	10–14 Mustad 94842
SILK:	6/0 White
TAILS:	Pale-ginger hackle fibers
BODY:	Palest honey dubbing ribbed with pale-orange polypropylene dubbing
WINGS:	Pale woodduck flank
HACKLE:	Pale ginger mixed with two turns of orange

This pattern is a fine imitation of the early summer *Potamanthus* hatches.

PALE YELLOW DRAKE (Schwiebert)
HOOK:	10–14 Mustad 94842
SILK:	6/0 Primrose
TAILS:	Pale olive-gray fibers
BODY:	Cream fox dubbing ribbed with light-brown dubbing in primrose silk
WINGS:	Pale woodduck flank
HACKLE:	Pale olive-gray mixed with pale grizzly

PALE SUMMER DUN (Bergman)
HOOK:	14–16 Mustad 94842
SILK:	6/0 White
TAILS:	Palest honey-cream fibers

BODY: Palest cream dubbing on white silk
WINGS: Palest woodduck flank
HACKLE: Palest honey

This fly suggests the whitish *Stenonema* and *Heptagenia* species found hatching at twilight in the summer months. Such naturals were the prototypes for the pattern Bergman called the Paulinskill.

PALE SUMMER OLIVE (Schwiebert)
  HOOK: 14–16 Mustad 94842
  SILK: 6/o White
  TAILS: Palest olive-gray fibers
  BODY: Palest olive-gray dubbing on primrose silk
  WINGS: Palest woodduck flank
  HACKLE: Palest olive-gray

PALE OLIVE FOX (Schwiebert)
  HOOK: 12–16 Mustad 94842
  SILK: 6/o White
  TAILS: Pale-olive fibers
  BODY: Cream fox dubbing on primrose silk
  WINGS: Palest woodduck flank
  HACKLE: Pale-olive mixed with pale grizzly

DARK OLIVE FOX (Schwiebert)
  HOOK: 12–16 Mustad 94842
  SILK: 6/o Pale olive
  TAILS: Medium-olive dun fibers
  BODY: Dark brownish-gray dubbing on olive silk
  WINGS: Dark woodduck flank
  HACKLE: Medium-olive dun

LIGHT GRAY FOX (Schwiebert)
  HOOK: 12–16 Mustad 94842
  SILK: 6/o White
  TAILS: Pale grizzly fibers
  BODY: Palest cream-gray fox dubbing
  WINGS: Pale woodduck flank
  HACKLE: Pale grizzly mixed with honey-ginger

DARK GRAY FOX (Jennings)
  HOOK: 12–16 Mustad 94842
  SILK: 6/o White
  TAILS: Medium grizzly fibers
  BODY: Dark cream-colored fox dubbing on pale olive silk
  WINGS: Dark woodduck flank
  HACKLE: Medium grizzly mixed with ginger

The preceding five patterns are designed to imitate several pale-olive to olive-gray *Stenonema* and *Heptagenia* flies, and the grayish *Stenonema fuscum* so famous on eastern and midwestern streams. The flies are based on the classic Gray Fox developed by the late Preston Jennings.

LIGHT CAHILL QUILL (Bergman)
  HOOK: 12–16 Mustad 94842

SILK: 6/o White
TAILS: Light-ginger fibers
BODY: Bleached peacock quill over tan silk underbody
WINGS: Light woodduck flank
HACKLE: Light ginger

DARK CAHILL QUILL (Bergman)

HOOK: 12–16 Mustad 94842
SILK: 6/o Brown
TAILS: Medium-brown fibers
BODY: Stripped peacock quill over brown silk underbody
WINGS: Dark woodduck flank
HACKLE: Medium brown

These two Bergman patterns are excellent imitations of the *Siphlonurus* flies that emerge in late spring and summer.

LIGHT GORDON QUILL (Gordon)

HOOK: 12–18 Mustad 94842
SILK: 6/o Primrose
TAILS: Medium-blue dun fibers
BODY: Bleached peacock quill over primrose silk underbody
WINGS: Medium woodduck flank
HACKLE: Medium-blue dun

DARK GORDON QUILL

HOOK: 12–18 Mustad 94842
SILK: 6/o Primrose
TAILS: Dark-blue dun fibers
BODY: Bleached peacock quill over light olive underbody
WINGS: Dark woodduck flank
HACKLE: Dark-blue dun

Theodore Gordon preferred a relatively light-blue dun hackling for his original Blue Quill Gordon that has evolved into our modern Gordon Quill. My own preference has tended toward dressing both light and dark variations since *Matching the Hatch,* twenty years ago.

LIGHT HENDRICKSON (Steenrod)

HOOK: 12–18 Mustad 94842
SILK: 6/o Primrose
TAILS: Medium-blue dun fibers
BODY: Cream-gray fox dubbing mixed with pink urine-burned kit fox
WINGS: Medium woodduck flank
HACKLE: Medium-blue dun

DARK HENDRICKSON

HOOK: 12–18 Mustad 94842
SILK: 6/o Olive
TAILS: Medium-blue dun fibers
BODY: Dark bluish-gray fur dubbing
WINGS: Dark woodduck flank
HACKLE: Dark-blue dun

The original Hendrickson dressed by Roy Steenrod was relatively close to the modern Light Hendrickson. It is believed that the Dark Hendrickson was evolved by the late Ray Bergman about a half-century ago. These patterns are good imitations of the *Ephemerella* and *Leptophlebia* species that hatch heavily each spring.

LIGHT CAHILL (Chandler)
> HOOK: 12–18 Mustad 94842
> SILK: 6/0 White
> TAILS: Pale-ginger fibers
> BODY: Palest cream fox dubbing on white silk
> WINGS: Pale woodduck flank
> HACKLE: Pale ginger

DARK CAHILL (Cahill)
> HOOK: 12–18 Mustad 94842
> SILK: 6/0 Brown
> TAILS: Medium-brown fibers
> BODY: Dark bluish-gray dubbing on brown silk
> WINGS: Dark woodduck flank
> HACKLE: Medium brown

These famous patterns have their beginnings in the early Cahill, the creation of Daniel Cahill, a fly-fishing brakeman on the Erie & Lackawanna. It was a wet pattern similar to the modern Dark Cahill. The popular Light Cahill is sometimes attributed to Theodore Gordon, although knowledgeable angling historians favor the claim of the late William Chandler, one of the less well-known great Catskill fly-tiers.

GREEN DRAKE (Jennings)
> HOOK: 8–12 Mustad 94842
> SILK: 6/0 Olive
> TAILS: Dark-olive hackle fibers
> BODY: Pale-cream dubbing ribbed with medium-brown dubbing on primrose silk
> WINGS: Dark woodduck flank
> HACKLE: Pale-olive mixed with dark grizzly

This imitation of the famous *Ephemera guttulata* hatches is a personal variation on a thematic dressing developed by Preston Jennings.

DARK GREEN DRAKE (Wetzel)
> HOOK: 6–12 Mustad 94842
> SILK: 6/0 Olive
> TAILS: Dark-olive dun fibers
> BODY: Cream-gray dubbing ribbed with dark rusty dubbing on olive silk
> WINGS: Dark woodduck flank
> HACKLE: Dark-olive mixed with dark grizzly

This pattern is a variation on the Dark Green Drake developed by the late Charles Wetzel, although I have abandoned his fan-wing dressing.

BROWN DRAKE (Wetzel)
> HOOK: 6–12 Mustad 94842
> SILK: 6/0 Brown
> TAILS: Medium-brown fibers
> BODY: Medium brownish-gray dubbing with a yellow dubbing rib on primrose silk
> WINGS: Dark woodduck flank
> HACKLE: Brown-olive mixed with grizzly

Like the Dark Green Drake, this Wetzel pattern was first developed to imitate the large midsummer *Hexagenia* hatches. Its original fan-wing style has been discarded, and in the smaller sizes the pattern is a valuable imitation of several *Ephemera* species.

MARCH BROWN (Jennings)
> HOOK: 10–14 Mustad 94842

SILK: 6/o Dark orange
TAILS: Dark-brown hackle fibers
BODY: Cream-gray fox dubbing ribbed with rusty dubbing on orange silk
WINGS: Dark woodduck flank
HACKLE: Dark brown mixed with dark grizzly

Preston Jennings developed this uniquely American version of the traditional March Brown, first published in his *Book of Trout Flies* almost fifty years ago.

HACKLE-WING DRY FLIES

Facing page 1130

PALE WATERY DUN (Dunne)
HOOK: 18–28 Mustad 94842
SILK: 8/o White
TAILS: Pale-cream hackle fibers
BODY: Pale fox dubbing mixed with yellow polypropylene
WINGS: Pale-gray hackle points, tied upright
HACKLE: Pale honey-ginger

PALE WATERY OLIVE (Swisher and Richards)
HOOK: 18–28 Mustad 94842
SILK: 8/o White
TAILS: Pale-cream hackle fibers
BODY: Bright-olive polypropylene or nylon dubbing
WINGS: Pale-gray hackle points, tied upright
HACKLE: Pale honey-ginger

These tiny flies imitate the minute *Pseudocloëon* and *Centroptilum* hatches important on many limestone streams and spring creeks throughout the United States. Good hatches typically occur from early summer until the threshold of winter on western streams like the Firehole and Henry's Fork, and are important in late summer on Michigan rivers.

WHITE-WINGED BLACK DUN (Swisher and Richards)
HOOK: 20–28 Mustad 94842
SILK: 8/o Black
TAILS: White hackle fibers
BODY: Black polypropylene dubbing
WINGS: White hackle points, tied upright
HACKLE: Pale badger

WHITE-WINGED CURSE (Halford)
HOOK: 20–28 Mustad 94842
SILK: 8/o Black
TAILS: White hackle fibers
BODY: Palest cream polypropylene
WINGS: White hackle points, tied upright
HACKLE: Cream badger

The White-winged Black imitates the early-morning hatches of *Tricorythodes* flies that emerge on slow-flowing streams throughout the United States in late summer. Such hatches can start as early as daylight, and are usually finished well before noon. The White-winged Curse is a traditional British name for the tiny *Caenis* mayflies that hatch on both lakes and slow-floating streams at twilight. American *Caenis* hatches are possible sporadically throughout the summer and fall months.

PALE SULPHUR DUN (Marinaro)
HOOK: 14–20 Mustad 94842
SILK: 8/o White
TAILS: Palest honey-ginger fibers
BODY: Pale yellow-orange polypropylene dubbing
WINGS: Palest blue dun hackle-points, tied upright
HACKLE: Palest honey-ginger

PALE GRAY-WINGED OLIVE (Schwiebert)
HOOK: 14–22 Mustad 94842
SILK: 8/o White
TAILS: Pale-gray dun fibers
BODY: Pale yellow-olive dubbing
WINGS: Pale-gray dun hackle-points, tied upright
HACKLE: Pale-gray dun

MEDIUM GRAY-WINGED OLIVE (Schwiebert)
HOOK: 14–22 Mustad 94842
SILK: 8/o White
TAILS: Medium-gray dun fibers
BODY: Bright-olive dubbing
WINGS: Medium-gray dun hackle-points, tied upright
HACKLE: Medium-gray dun

DARK GRAY-WINGED OLIVE (Schwiebert)
HOOK: 14–22 Mustad 94842
SILK: 8/o Gray
TAILS: Dark-gray dun fibers
BODY: Dark-olive dubbing
WINGS: Dark-gray dun hackle-points, tied upright
HACKLE: Dark-gray dun

These patterns imitate several important *Baetis* and *Ephemerella* species that hatch throughout the season on widespread streams. The Pale Sulphurs are often most important in late spring on streams from Michigan to Maine, and southward to Virginia and North Carolina. Such hatches are particularly abundant on the limestone streams of Pennsylvania and the Middle West. The Gray-winged Duns imitate several *Ephemerella* mayflies that hatch in late spring and early summer, and a number of multibrooded *Baetis* in the small sizes.

BLUE-WINGED WHITCRAFT (Martinez)
HOOK: 10–20 Mustad 94842
SILK: 8/o White
TAILS: Pale grizzly fibers
BODY: Bleached peacock quill over yellow silk underbody
WINGS: Blue dun hackle-points, tied upright or spent
HACKLE: Pale grizzly mixed with brown

This dressing is adapted from the original Jackson Hole pattern, named for Thomas Whitcraft, an early superintendent at Teton National Park. It is particularly good during sedge hatches.

BLUE-WINGED ADAMS (Halladay)
HOOK: 10–28 Mustad 94842
SILK: 8/o White

TAILS: Medium grizzly fibers
BODY: Medium blue-gray fur dubbing
WINGS: Blue dun hackle-points, tied upright or spent
HACKLE: Medium grizzly mixed with brown

Len Halladay originated the Adams in Michigan, naming it for an attorney from Ohio who fished the Boardman and frequented his shop at Mayfield. The prototype featured golden pheasant tail fibers and grizzly hackle-tip wings dressed spent. This version is my favorite Adams dressing, and is commonly attributed to the late Paul Stroud, who supervised the fishing department at Von Lengerke & Antoine in Chicago years ago.

DARK BLUE QUILL

HOOK: 16–22 Mustad 94842
SILK: 8/0 Gray
TAILS: Dark-blue dun fibers
BODY: Stripped peacock quill
WINGS: Dark-blue dun hackle-points, tied upright
HACKLE: Dark-blue dun

LIGHT BLUE QUILL

HOOK: 16–22 Mustad 94842
SILK: 8/0 White
TAILS: Light-blue dun fibers
BODY: Bleached peacock quill
WINGS: Light-blue dun hackle-points, tied upright
HACKLE: Light-blue dun

The Blue Quill or Blue Upright is a traditional British fly pattern of uncertain origin, although its roots probably reach back several centuries to Bowlker and Cotton. Dressing both light and dark versions is intended to imitate a number of *Paraleptophlebia* hatches common from Maine to California.

DARK RUSTY DUN

HOOK: 10–20 Mustad 94842
SILK: 6/0 Dark brown
TAILS: Dark rusty dun hackle fibers
BODY: Dark rusty brown fur dubbing
WINGS: Dark slate gray hackle points tied upright
HACKLE: Dark rusty dun

This dressing is an adaptation of English flies as old as trout fishing itself.

MEDIUM RUSTY DUN

HOOK: 16–24 Mustad 94842
SILK: 6/0 Medium brown
TAILS: Medium rusty dun hackle fibers
BODY: Medium rusty fur dubbing
WINGS: Dark rusty dun hackle points tied upright
HACKLE: Medium rusty dun

LIGHT RUSTY DUN

HOOK: 16–20 Mustad 94842
SILK: 6/0 Light brown
TAILS: Light rusty dun hackle fibers
BODY: Light rusty fur dubbing
WINGS: Medium rusty dun hackle points tied upright
HACKLE: Light rusty dun

BLUE-WINGED HENDRICKSON
HOOK: 12–16 Mustad 94842
SILK: 6/0 Light brown
TAILS: Dark rusty dun hackle fibers
BODY: Pale red fox belly dubbing ribbed with rusty brown fur on yellow silk
WINGS: Dark rusty dun hackle points tied upright
HACKLE: Dark rusty dun

DARK BLUE DUN
HOOK: 16–24 Mustad 94842
SILK: 8/0 Black
TAILS: Dark-blue dun fibers
BODY: Dark bluish-gray fur dubbing
WINGS: Dark-blue dun hackle-points, tied upright
HACKLE: Dark-blue dun

IRON BLUE DUN
HOOK: 16–24 Mustad 94842
SILK: 8/0 Black
TAILS: Iron-blue dun fibers
BODY: Blackish mole dubbing on scarlet silk core
WINGS: Iron-blue dun hackle-points, tied upright
HACKLE: Iron-blue dun

These traditional British dressings are also valuable when the fish are selective to several dark *Paraleptophlebia* and *Baetis* hatches.

DARK BLUE-WINGED OLIVE (Schwiebert)
HOOK: 14–18 Mustad 94842
SILK: 8/0 Dark gray
TAILS: Dark-blue dun fibers
BODY: Pale olive-green polypropylene dubbing
WINGS: Dark-blue dun hackle-points, tied upright
HACKLE: Dark-blue dun

This pattern has been a favorite of mine since boyhood in Michigan, where we developed it to imitate the *Ephemerella* hatches of late spring and early summer. It is equally effective on eastern and western rivers.

MEDIUM SLATE-WINGED OLIVE (Schwiebert)
HOOK: 12–16 Mustad 94842
SILK: 8/0 Dark gray
TAILS: Dark-blue dun fibers
BODY: Dark olive-green floss ribbed with fine gold wire
WINGS: Iron-blue dun hackle-points, tied upright
HACKLE: Dark-blue dun

This pattern has proved itself in recent years, particularly on the heavy hatches of *Ephemerella flavilinea* found in early summer in the Rocky Mountain country.

GREAT LEAD-WINGED OLIVE (Swisher and Richards)
HOOK: 10–14 Mustad 94842
SILK: 6/0 Olive
TAILS: Dark-blue dun fibers
BODY: Medium-olive dubbing ribbed with bright-yellow silk
WINGS: Iron-blue hackle-points, tied upright

HACKLE: Dark-blue dun

This variation on the so-called Western Green Drake developed by Swisher and Richards, particularly for the heavy hatches on the Henry's Fork, has proved itself for three large *Ephemerella* species that typically emerge in early summer through the Rocky Mountains.

GREAT LEAD-WINGED DRAKE (Schwiebert)

HOOK: 10–14 Mustad 94842
SILK: 6/0 Brown
TAILS: Medium-gray dun fibers
BODY: Dark rusty-brown dubbing ribbed with gray, dubbed on yellow silk
WINGS: Iron-blue dun hackle-points, tied upright
HACKLE: Dark-gray dun

GREAT SUMMER DRAKE (Schwiebert)

HOOK: 10–14 Mustad 94842
SILK: 6/0 Brown
TAILS: Medium-gray dun fibers
BODY: Dark cream-gray fox ribbed with dark grayish dubbing
WINGS: Dark-gray dun hackle-points, tied upright
HACKLE: Medium-gray dun

These two patterns have proved themselves on the large *Isonychia* hatches of early summer, and the *Siphlonurus* emergences that occur in the weeks that follow.

GREAT RED QUILL (Schwiebert)

HOOK: 10–14 Mustad 94842
SILK: 6/0 Brown
TAILS: Medium-gray hackle fibers
BODY: Cream-gray fox dubbing ribbed with rusty-brown dubbing
WINGS: Iron-blue dun hackle-points, tied upright
HACKLE: Dark-gray dun

This pattern has been a favorite of mine since it was first worked out on the Frying Pan in Colorado years ago. Although it contains no actual quill in its dressing, its name stems from its resemblance to the eastern Red Quill hatches. We simply called these hatches Great Red Quills long before they were identified as *Ephemerella hecuba* and *Ephemerella doddsi*. Mayflies of such size trigger exceptional rises of fish when they occur after early summer, and I have found hatches into late September on some western watersheds.

MISCELLANEOUS DRY FLIES
Facing page 1131

LITTLE BLACK ANT (Schwiebert)

HOOK: 18–28 Mustad 94840
SILK: 8/0 Black
GASTER: Black fur dubbing
LEGS: Black hackle
THORAX: Black fur dubbing
HEAD: Black silk

LITTLE RUSTY ANT (Schwiebert)

HOOK: 18–24 Mustad 94840

SILK: 8/0 Tan
GASTER: Rusty-pink dubbing
LEGS: Pale-gray dun
THORAX: Rusty-pink dubbing
HEAD: Rusty-pink dubbing

LITTLE CINNAMON ANT (Schwiebert)
    HOOK: 18–22 Mustad 94840
    SILK: 8/0 Brown
    GASTER: Rusty-brown dubbing
    LEGS: Dark-brown furnace hackle
    THORAX: Rusty-brown dubbing
    HEAD: Brown silk

LITTLE REDLEGGED ANT (Schwiebert)
    HOOK: 18–22 Mustad 94840
    SILK: 8/0 Brown
    GASTER: Reddish-brown fur
    LEGS: Light-brown furnace hackle
    THORAX: Reddish-brown fur
    HEAD: Brown silk

These ant patterns were first introduced in a magazine article done for *Field & Stream* fifteen years ago, and they have gratifyingly become standard terrestrials since.

BROWN JASSID (Marinaro)
    HOOK: 16–28 Mustad 94840
    SILK: 8/0 Brown
    LEGS: Brown furnace hackle, trimmed out on belly and back
    WINGS: Vinyl-coated jungle cock set in pliobond

BADGER GNAT (Griffith)
    HOOK: 16–28 Mustad 94840
    SILK: 8/0 Black
    BODY: Fine peacock herl
    HACKLE: Badger

FURNACE GNAT (Schwiebert)
    HOOK: 16–28 Mustad 94840
    SILK: 8/0 Black
    BODY: Fine peacock herl
    HACKLE: Furnace

BLACK JASSID (Marinaro)
    HOOK: 16–28 Mustad 94840
    SILK: 8/0 Black
    LEGS: Black hackle, trimmed out on belly and back
    WINGS: Vinyl-coated jungle cock set in pliobond

These tiny flies are often deadly on difficult fish that are smutting softly in the surface film. The famous Jassids were first developed by Vincent Marinaro to imitate leaf-hoppers on Letort Spring Run, and the gnat patterns are adapted from the tiny midge dressings worked out on Michigan rivers by George Griffith. His original pattern suggests a hatching *Chironomus* gnat still pinioned in the surface film with its pupal skin.

BLACK LETORT BEETLE (Schwiebert)
HOOK: 16–28 Mustad 94840
SILK: 8/o Black
LEGS: Black hackle, trimmed out on belly and back
WINGS: Green pheasant neck-feathers set in vinyl and trimmed to shape

PARTRIDGE SEDGE (Schwiebert)
HOOK: 16–24 Mustad 94840
SILK: 8/o Brown
LEGS: Brown and grizzly hackles, trimmed out on belly and back
WINGS: Partridge feather set in vinyl and trimmed to shape

CINNAMON BEETLE (Schwiebert)
HOOK: 16–28 Mustad 94840
SILK: 8/o Brown
LEGS: Brown furnace hackle, trimmed out on belly and back
WINGS: Copper pheasant neck-feathers set in vinyl and trimmed to shape

These three patterns were originally variations of mine on the Marinaro silhouette theory, developed twenty-odd years ago on the Brodheads and Letort. Both Charles Fox and Ross Trimmer were present when the Black Beetle was first worked out, and in his *Wonderful World of Trout,* Fox details my first day's fishing with it on his Letort water. The Partridge Sedge was perfected on the Brodheads in 1958, where the fish often fed heavily on spent caddis at twilight on the still flats. It was first described in the essay by Theodore Rogowski, which was included in *The Gordon Garland,* the classic anthology edited by Arnold Gingrich and published by the Theodore Gordon Flyfishers. The Cinnamon Beetle is simply adapted from the original Letort pattern.

REDLEGGED CARPENTER ANT (Schwiebert)
HOOK: 12–16 Mustad 94840
SILK: 6/o Black
GASTER: Blackish-brown fur dubbing
LEGS: Furnace hackle
THORAX: Blackish-brown fur dubbing
HEAD: Blackish-brown fur

BLACK CARPENTER ANT (McCafferty)
HOOK: 8–16 Mustad 94840
SILK: 6/o Black
GASTER: Black fur dubbing
LEGS: Black hackle
THORAX: Black fur dubbing
HEAD: Black fur

BROWN CARPENTER ANT (Schwiebert)
HOOK: 12–16 Mustad 94840
SILK: 6/o Black
GASTER: Brown fur dubbing
LEGS: Furnace hackle
THORAX: Black fur dubbing
HEAD: Black fur

The late Robert McCafferty first tied his ant imitations in lacquered tying-silk bodies, but his silhouette theory survives in each of my ant patterns. These Carpenter Ants are also valuable tied with fuse-wire weighting and fished dead-drift on the bottom. Both sunk and floating versions are priceless in hot weather.

Yellow Letort Hopper (Schwiebert)
- HOOK: 8–16 Mustad 38941 3X Long
- SILK: 4/0 Primrose
- BODY: Pale-yellow polypropylene dubbing
- WINGS: Brown mottled turkey wing-quill sections
- LEGS: Brown deer body-hair collar, trimmed out on belly to float flush
- HEAD: Brown deer hair trimmed to shape

Letort Cricket (Shenk)
- HOOK: 10–18 Mustad 38941 3X Long
- SILK: 4/0 Black
- BODY: Black polypropylene dubbing
- WINGS: Crow primary wing-quill sections
- LEGS: Black deer body-hair collar, trimmed out to float flush
- HEAD: Black deer hair trimmed to shape

Green Letort Hopper (Hemingway)
- HOOK: 8–16 Mustad 38941 3X Long
- SILK: 4/0 Primrose
- BODY: Bright yellow-green polypropylene
- WINGS: Brown mottled turkey wing-quill sections
- LEGS: Brown deer body-hair collar, trimmed to float flush
- HEAD: Brown deer hair trimmed to shape

The first of these fly patterns was the Letort Hopper, which I developed with Ross Trimmer and Charles Fox in 1956. Its first success occurred on Antes Creek and Letort Spring Run, and was recorded by Fox in his classic *Wonderful World of Trout,* which described our fishing at the close of that first season. Using the same silhouette theory, Edward Shenk and Edward Koch worked out their equally famous Letort Cricket the following summer. Although green-bodied grasshoppers were used on the Letort and other limestone streams just after the Second World War, these were conventional-type patterns, and it was Jack Hemingway who introduced me to a bright-green dubbing on my own fly.

Giant Dark Stonefly (Bird)
- HOOK: 2–10 Mustad 9575 6X Long
- SILK: 4/0 Brown
- TAILS: Brown-dyed goose-quill fibers
- BODY: Dark-orange polypropylene dubbing
- BODY HACKLE: Brown furnace, tied palmer
- WINGS: Brown bucktail or brown mallard flank in smaller sizes
- HACKLE: Brown furnace faced with brown mallard fibers

Giant Golden Stonefly (Rosborough)
- HOOK: 4–12 Mustad 9575 6X Long
- SILK: 4/0 Primrose
- TAILS: Goose-quill fibers
- BODY: Golden-yellow polypropylene dubbing
- BODY HACKLE: Pale ginger, tied palmer
- WINGS: Light-brown elk hair or woodduck flank in smaller sizes
- HACKLE: Pale ginger faced with woodduck fibers

These dressings are personal variations on fly-patterns developed by the late Calvin Bird of San Francisco, and the inimitable Polly Rosborough, who lives on the Williamson at Chiloquin in southern Oregon. Their flies were designed to imitate the *Pteronarcys* and *Acroneuria* hatches on western rivers, but they work equally well on related stoneflies in other regions, fished both wet and dry.

MISCELLANEOUS NYMPHS

Facing page 1322

GRAY MIDGE LARVA

HOOK:	14–28 Mustad 94840 1X Fine
SILK:	8/0 Dark gray
TAILS:	Soft dark-gray fibers tied quite short
BODY:	Dark hare's mask dubbing ribbed with fine gold wire
LEGS:	Soft dark-gray fibers tied quite short

GRAY MIDGE PUPA

HOOK:	14-22 Mustad 94833 3X Fine
SILK:	8/0 Dark gray
TAILS:	Soft dark-gray fibers tied quite short
BODY:	Bleached peacock quill ribbed with fine gold wire
THORAX:	Dark hare's mask dubbing
WINGS:	Mallard wing-quill sections
LEGS:	Soft dark-gray fibers tied slightly longer than wing sections
GILLS:	Ostrich herl, dyed black

OLIVE MIDGE LARVA

HOOK:	14–28 Mustad 94840 1X Fine
SILK:	8/0 Medium olive
TAILS:	Soft-olive fibers tied quite short
BODY:	Dark-olive dubbing mixed with hare's mask and ribbed with fine gold wire
THORAX:	Dark hare's mask dubbing
WINGS:	Mallard wing-quill sections
LEGS:	Soft dark-gray fibers tied quite short

OLIVE MIDGE PUPA

HOOK:	14–22 Mustad 94833 3X Fine
SILK:	8/0 Medium olive
TAILS:	Soft-olive fibers tied quite short
BODY:	Bleached peacock quill, dyed olive and ribbed with fine gold wire
THORAX:	Dark-olive dubbing mixed with hare's mask
WINGS:	Mallard wing-quill sections
LEGS:	Soft-olive fibers tied slightly longer than wing sections
GILLS:	Ostrich herl, dyed dark gray

Such patterns apparently have their origins in the tiny midge imitations dressed on the trout lakes of Ireland and the United Kingdom. Charles Wetzel included pupal imitations in his *Practical Fly Fishing* almost forty years ago, and recommended that they be fished dead drift in the surface film. Extensive midge populations are common in both lakes and slow-flowing streams, and other patterns tied in claret, reddish brown, green, sepia, cream, pale yellow and black are often useful.

WHITE CADDIS LARVA (Bergman)

HOOK:	6–16 Mustad 38941 3X Long
SILK:	6/0 Dark brown
TAILS:	Soft-white fibers tied quite short
BODY:	White dubbing ribbed with fine silver wire
THORAX:	Dark-brown dubbing
LEGS:	Soft dark-brown fibers tied short

YELLOW CADDIS LARVA
- HOOK: 6–16 Mustad 38941 3X Long
- SILK: 6/0 Dark brown
- TAILS: Soft-cream fibers tied quite short
- BODY: Yellow dubbing ribbed with fine gold wire
- THORAX: Dark-brown dubbing
- LEGS: Soft medium-brown fibers tied short

GREEN CADDIS LARVA
- HOOK: 6–16 Mustad 38941 3X Long
- SILK: 6/0 Dark brown
- TAILS: Soft-olive fibers tied quite short
- BODY: Dark-green dubbing ribbed with fine gold wire
- THORAX: Dark-brown dubbing
- LEGS: Soft-brown fibers tied short

GRAY CADDIS LARVA
- HOOK: 6–16 Mustad 38941 3X Long
- SILK: 6/0 Dark brown
- TAILS: Soft-gray fibers tied quite short
- BODY: Medium-gray dubbing ribbed with fine silver wire
- THORAX: Medium-brown dubbing
- LEGS: Soft-gray fibers tied short

Such imitations emerged first in Bergman books like *Trout* and *Just Fishing,* and variations on the caddis worm theme remain quite popular among skilled nymph fishermen throughout the country, particularly in Colorado. These flies should be weighted with fuse wire proportionately sized to the hook. Since the naturals clamber and drift among the bottom stones, the upstream dead-drift fished on a relatively short line is deadly.

GREEN SEDGE PUPA (Sens)
- HOOK: 6–20 Mustad 3906
- SILK: 6/0 Dark olive
- BODY: Bright-green dubbing on olive silk
- WINGS: Mallard wing-quill sections
- LEGS: Dark partridge hackle fibers

BROWN SEDGE PUPA (Schwiebert)
- HOOK: 6–20 Mustad 3906
- SILK: 6/0 Dark brown
- BODY: Medium-brown dubbing on brown silk
- WINGS: Mallard wing-quill sections
- LEGS: Dark partridge hackle fibers

OLIVE SEDGE PUPA (Schwiebert)
- HOOK: 6–20 Mustad 3906
- SILK: 6/0 Olive
- BODY: Olive dubbing in primrose silk
- WINGS: Mallard wing-quill sections
- LEGS: Light partridge hackle fibers

GRAY SEDGE PUPA (Sens)
- HOOK: 6–20 Mustad 3906

SILK:	6/0 Gray
BODY:	Gray muskrat dubbing on olive silk
WINGS:	Mallard wing-quill sections
LEGS:	Light partridge hackle fibers

Edward Sens developed the first caddis pupal imitations of this type shortly before mid-century, and his green- and gray-bodied dressings were popularized in the books of writers like Ovington and McClane. Versions weighted with fuse wire should be fished deep with a teasing half-swimming retrieve. Flies tied without weight are best fished to specific rises, either quartering downstream or upstream like a drowned dry fly.

Brown Thick-gilled Nymph (Schwiebert)

HOOK:	8–18 Mustad 3906B
SILK:	6/0 Brown
TAILS:	Dark woodduck fibers
BODY:	Medium-brown dubbing darkened with felt-tip pen on back
GILLS:	Soft-gray marabou ribbed with fine gold wire
THORAX:	Medium-brown dubbing
WING CASE:	Medium-brown body-feather set in vinyl
LEGS:	Medium partridge hackle fibers

Slate-winged Drake Nymph (Schwiebert)

HOOK:	8–14 Mustad 3906B
SILK:	6/0 Dark brown
TAILS:	Dark woodduck fibers
BODY:	Dark-brown dubbing mixed with claret seal and white quill median stripe
GILLS:	Purple marabou ribbed with fine gold wire
THORAX:	Dark-brown and claret dubbing, mixed
WING CASE:	Grouse shoulder-feather with pale median stripe set in vinyl
LEGS:	Dark partridge hackle fibers

March Brown Nymph (Jennings)

HOOK:	8–14 Mustad 3906B
SILK:	6/0 Dark orange
TAILS:	Dark woodduck fibers
BODY:	Cream-gray fox dubbing on orange silk
GILLS:	Dark-brown marabou ribbed with fine gold wire
THORAX:	Cream-gray fox dubbing
WING CASE:	Partridge shoulder-feather set in vinyl
LEGS:	Dark partridge hackle fibers

Lead-winged Olive Nymph (Schwiebert)

HOOK:	8–14 Mustad 3906B
SILK:	6/0 Medium olive
TAILS:	Medium woodduck fibers
BODY:	Medium-brown dubbing darkened with felt-tip pen on back
GILLS:	Medium-olive ribbed with fine gold wire
THORAX:	Medium-brown dubbing
WING CASE:	Partridge shoulder-feather set in vinyl
LEGS:	Medium partridge hackle fibers

These mayfly nymphs are cast in the classic Skues mold. The Brown Thick-gilled Nymph suggests the *Leptophlebia* and *Paraleptophlebia* flies common on many American lakes and streams. Since they swim with surprising agility, these flies should be fished with a rhythmic retrieve. The Slate-winged Drake Nymph imitates the *Isonychia* genus, mayflies that are important on swift-flowing rivers from California to Maine. The natural nymphs dart and hopscotch rapidly among the bottom rubble and should be imitated with a retrieve suggestive of their movements. The March Brown Nymph is similar to the prototypes developed by Jennings and Flick, and is a workable imitation of several *Stenonema* species. These nymphs are bottom-clinging types that are quite clumsy when dislodged, and their imitations are best fished dead-drift. The Lead-winged Olive should be fished the same way, and suggests a number of *Ephemerella* flies.

BROWN BEETLE LARVA (Besse)
HOOK:	6-12 Mustad 38941 3X Long
SILK:	6/0 Brown
TAILS:	Soft-brown furnace hackle fibers
BODY:	Dark-chocolate dubbing
GILLS:	Soft-brown furnace saddle, tied palmer-style
LEGS:	Dark partridge hackle fibers

GRAY BEETLE LARVA (Schwiebert)
HOOK:	6-12 Mustad 38941 3X Long
SILK:	6/0 Gray
TAILS:	Soft grizzly hackle fibers
BODY:	Black fur dubbing
GILLS:	Soft grizzly saddle, tied palmer-style
LEGS:	Dark mallard flank fibers

BLACK BEETLE LARVA (Schwiebert)
HOOK:	6–12 Mustad 38941 3X Long
SILK:	6/0 Black
TAILS:	Soft iron-blue hackle fibers
BODY:	Black fur dubbing
GILLS:	Soft iron-blue saddle, tied palmer-style
LEGS:	Dark-brown mallard fibers

These riffle *Coleoptera* imitations are variations on the popular woolly worms developed by the late Don Martinez, and the Gray Beetle Larva is relatively close to his original pattern. Arthur Besse originated the brown pattern on his northern Wisconsin rivers, and fished it with great success on the Namekagon and Brule. His favorite method was a dead-drift presentation fished upstream, and the black and gray patterns have been adapted from his fuse-weighted prototypes.

GREEN DRAGONFLY NYMPH (Schwiebert)
HOOK:	4–10 Mustad 38941 3X Long
SILK:	6/0 Olive
GILLS:	Olive-dyed wing-quill fibers, tied short
BODY:	Olive dubbing ribbed with brown dubbing on olive silk
WING CASE:	Goose wing-quill section, dyed olive
THORAX:	Olive dubbing ribbed with brown
LEGS:	Mallard flank, dyed olive

BROWN DRAGONFLY NYMPH (Schwiebert)
HOOK:	4–10 Mustad 38941 3X Long
SILK:	6/0 Brown
GILLS:	Brown-dyed wing-quill fibers, tied short
BODY:	Muskrat dubbing ribbed with brown dubbing on chocolate silk

WING CASE: Goose wing-quill section, dyed brown
LEGS: Brown mallard flank fibers

These imitations of immature *Anisoptera* flies are particularly effective on lakes and slow-flowing streams, where the naturals are usually plentiful. Weighted versions fished slow and deep are often deadly, and have produced some trophy-size trout for me over the years. Dressings tied without fuse wire are effective fished shallow when dragonflies are hatching.

SPENT-WING MAYFLY SPINNERS
Facing page 1323

BLACK HEN-WING SPINNER (Swisher and Richards)
HOOK: 20–28 Mustad 94840
SILK: 8/0 Black
TAILS: White hackle fibers
BODY: Black fur or polypropylene dubbing
WINGS: White hen hackle-points or polypropylene, tied spent
HACKLE: None

This pattern was first published by Doug Swisher and Carl Richards in their book *Selective Trout*, and was developed for the *Tricorythodes* spinner fall on late summer mornings.

CAENIS HEN-WING SPINNER (Puyans)
HOOK: 20–28 Mustad 94840
SILK: 8/0 Brown
TAILS: White hackle fibers
BODY: White fur with a brown polypropylene thorax dubbing
WINGS: White hen hackle-points or polypropylene, tied spent
HACKLE: None

André Puyans of San Francisco developed this *Caenis* imitation for fertile western spring creeks.

CREAM HEN-WING SPINNER (Swisher and Richards)
HOOK: 18–22 Mustad 94840
SILK: 8/0 White
TAILS: White hackle fibers
BODY: Pale-yellow polypropylene dubbing
WINGS: White hen hackle-points or polypropylene, tied spent
HACKLE: None

PALE GREEN HEN-WING SPINNER (Swisher and Richards)
HOOK: 20–28 Mustad 94840
SILK: 8/0 White
TAILS: White hackle fibers
BODY: Bright-green polypropylene dubbing
WINGS: White hen hackle-points or polypropylene, tied spent
HACKLE: None

This tiny bright-bodied henwing is absolutely essential when fish are taking *Pseudocloeon* spinners in the surface film. Such spinner falls are common on slow-flowing streams from New England to California. Several broods can hatch between June and October, and both hatching and mating are sporadic, coming between midday and twilight.

SHERRY HEN-WING SPINNER (Swisher and Richards)
HOOK: 12–24 Mustad 94840

SILK:	8/0 Brown
TAILS:	White hackle fibers
BODY:	Sherry-brown fur or polypropylene dubbing
WINGS:	White hen hackle-points or polypropylene, tied spent
HACKLE:	None

PALE SPECKLE-WING SPINNER (Harrop)

HOOK:	14–20 Mustad 94840
SILK:	8/0 White
TAILS:	White hackle fibers
BODY:	Cream-colored fox dubbing with light-brown dubbing rib
WINGS:	Mallard flank and white polypropylene, tied spent
HACKLE:	None

DARK SPECKLE-WING SPINNER (Harrop)

HOOK:	14–20 Mustad 94840
SILK:	8/0 White
TAILS:	White hackle fibers
BODY:	Medium-gray dubbing with black dubbing rib
WINGS:	Teal flank and white polypropylene, tied spent
HACKLE:	None

These delicate little spentwings, with speckled feathers used to suggest the mottled forewings of the natural spinners, are derived from the experiments of René Harrop, who lives on the Henry's Fork in Idaho.

RUSTY HEN-WING SPINNER (Swisher and Richards)

HOOK:	12–24 Mustad 94840
SILK:	8/0 Brown
TAILS:	Pale-gray hackle fibers
BODY:	Rusty-brown fur or polypropylene dubbing
WINGS:	Light-gray hackle-points or polypropylene, tied spent
HACKLE:	None

MEDIUM OLIVE SPINNER (Schwiebert)

HOOK:	12–20 Mustad 94840
SILK:	6/0 Olive
TAILS:	Cream-yellow fibers
BODY:	Medium-olive dubbing ribbed with fine gold wire
WINGS:	Pale-gray hackle-points or polypropylene, tied spent
HACKLE:	None

PALE SULPHUR SPINNER (Marinaro)

HOOK:	12–20 Mustad 94840
SILK:	6/0 White
TAILS:	Cream-yellow fibers
BODY:	Pale-yellow dubbing ribbed with fine gold wire
WINGS:	White hen hackle-points or polypropylene, tied spent
HACKLE:	None

DARK OLIVE SPINNER (Schwiebert)

HOOK:	12–20 Mustad 94840
SILK:	6/0 Olive
TAILS:	Cream-yellow fibers

BODY: Dark-olive fur dubbing ribbed with fine gold wire
WINGS: Pale-gray hackle-points or polypropylene, tied spent
HACKLE: None

PALE WATERY SPINNER (Schwiebert)
HOOK: 12–20 Mustad 94840
SILK: 6/0 White
TAILS: White hackle fibers
BODY: Cream-yellow dubbing ribbed with fine gold wire
WINGS: White hen hackle-points or polypropylene, tied spent
HACKLE: None

GREAT LEAD-WING OLIVE SPINNER (Puyans)
HOOK: 8–12 Mustad 94840
SILK: 6/0 Olive
TAILS: Pale gray-brown fibers
BODY: Dark-olive dubbing ribbed with fine gold wire
WINGS: Gray hen hackle-points or polypropylene, tied spent
HACKLE: Olive-dyed grizzly, tied parachute

GREAT RED SPINNER (Wetzel)
HOOK: 8–12 Mustad 94840
SILK: 6/0 Brown
TAILS: Medium-brown fibers
BODY: Medium-brown dubbing ribbed with fine gold wire
WINGS: Woodduck flank fibers, tied spent
HACKLE: Brown furnace, tied parachute

GREAT CLARET SPINNER (Schwiebert)
HOOK: 8–12 Mustad 94840
SILK: 6/0 Brown
TAILS: Pale-gray fibers
BODY: Claret dubbing ribbed with fine gold wire
WINGS: Pale-gray hen hackle-points or polypropylene, tied spent
HACKLE: Blue dun, tied parachute

GREAT OLIVE SPINNER (Schwiebert)
HOOK: 8–12 Mustad 94840
SILK: 6/0 Olive
TAILS: Brown hackle fibers
BODY: Olive-brown dubbing ribbed with fine gold wire
WINGS: Gray hen hackle-points or polypropylene, tied spent
HACKLE: Medium olive, tied parachute

SPENT COFFINFLY SPINNER (Darbee)
HOOK: 8–12 Mustad 94840
SILK: 6/0 Black
TAILS: Dark-brown hackle fibers
BODY: White fur or polypropylene dubbing with a dark-brown thorax
WINGS: Teal flank fibers, tied spent
HACKLE: Badger, tied parachute

BROWN DRAKE SPINNER (Swisher and Richards)
HOOK: 6–12 Mustad 94840

SILK:	6/0 Brown
TAILS:	Dark-brown hackle fibers
BODY:	Brown dubbing ribbed with yellow polypropylene on primrose silk
WINGS:	Woodduck flank fibers, tied spent
HACKLE:	Brown furnace, tied parachute

All patterns can be dressed with parachute hackles in sizes above sixteen, using hackle color compatible with the materials outlined.

MISCELLANEOUS NYMPHS AND CRUSTACEANS

Facing page 1354

PALE WATERY DUN NYMPH (Skues)

HOOK:	18–24 Mustad 94840
SILK:	8/0 White
TAILS:	Pale woodduck fibers
BODY:	Pale-cream fox dubbing ribbed with fine gold wire
WING CASES:	Pale-gray feather section
LEGS:	Pale woodduck fibers

IRON BLUE DUN NYMPH (Skues)

HOOK:	18–24 Mustad 94840
SILK:	8/0 Gray
TAILS:	Dark woodduck fibers
BODY:	Dark blue-gray mole dubbing ribbed with fine gold wire
WING CASES:	Dark-slate feather section
LEGS:	Dark partridge fibers

PALE OLIVE DUN NYMPH (Swisher and Richards)

HOOK:	18–24 Mustad 94840
SILK:	8/0 Primrose
TAILS:	Pale woodduck fibers
BODY:	Pale yellow-green dubbing ribbed with fine gold wire
WING CASES:	Pale-olive feather section
LEGS:	Pale woodduck fibers

This important pattern imitates the bright little *Pseudocloëon* nymphs.

LITTLE RUSTY DUN NYMPH (Schwiebert)

HOOK:	18–24 Mustad 94840
SILK:	8/0 Brown
TAILS:	Dark woodduck fibers
BODY:	Rusty-brown dubbing ribbed with fine gold wire
WING CASES:	Dark-slate feather section
LEGS:	Dark partridge fibers

EARLY BLACK STONEFLY NYMPH (Wetzel)

HOOK:	12–16 Mustad 3906B 1X Long
SILK:	6/0 Black
TAILS:	Black feather fibers
BODY:	Flat monofilament colored with black felt-tip pen
WING CASES:	Black feathers set in vinyl lacquer and trimmed to shape
LEGS:	Black hen hackle

LITTLE YELLOW STONEFLY NYMPH (Wetzel)

HOOK: 16–18 Mustad 3906B 1X Long
SILK: 8/0 White
TAILS: Pale-yellow feather fibers
BODY: Flat monofilament over bright-yellow rayon floss base
WING CASES: Pale-yellow feathers set in vinyl lacquer and trimmed to shape
LEGS: Pale-yellow hen hackle

EARLY BROWN STONEFLY NYMPH (Wetzel)

HOOK: 14–18 Mustad 3906B 1X Long
SILK: 6/0 Brown
TAILS: Rusty-brown feather fibers
BODY: Flat monofilament over rusty-brown rayon floss base
WING CASES: Dark gray-brown feathers set in vinyl and trimmed to shape
LEGS: Rusty dun hen hackle

LITTLE GREEN STONEFLY NYMPH (Wetzel)

HOOK: 16–18 Mustad 3906B 1X Long
SILK: 8/0 White
TAILS: Pale olive-green fibers
BODY: Flat monofilament over bright olive-green base
WING CASES: Pale-olive feathers set in lacquer and trimmed to shape
LEGS: Pale olive-green hen hackle

These are all stonefly imitations adapted from the fly-dressings of Charles Wetzel, in his *Practical Fly Fishing*. The black and brown patterns are suggestive of the early season *Capnia* and *Taeniopteryx* flies, while the pale imitations are tied to suggest the nymphal stages of summer hatches like *Alloperla*.

OLIVE SHRIMP (Whitlock)

HOOK: 8–18 Mustad 3906B, modified as illustrated in plate
SILK: 6/0 Olive
TAILS: Dark woodduck fibers
RIBBING: Fine gold wire over dorsal layer of clear vinyl film
BODY: Dubbing mixed from olive fur and rough hare's mask

MALE SOWBUG (Whitlock)

HOOK: 12–20 Mustad 3906
SILK: 6/0 Olive
TAIL: Primary wing-quill fibers, tied short
RIBBING: Fine gold wire over dorsal layer of clear vinyl film
BODY: Olive fur mixed with hare's mask

FEMALE SOWBUG (Whitlock)

HOOK: 10–16 Mustad 3906
SILK: 6/0 Amber
TAILS: Primary wing-quill fibers, tied short
RIBBING: Fine gold wire over dorsal layer of clear vinyl film
BODY: Tan dubbing with dark-brown thorax

AMBER SHRIMP (Whitlock)

HOOK: 8–18 Mustad 3906B, modified as illustrated in plate
SILK: 6/0 Primrose
TAILS: Pale woodduck fibers

RIBBING: Fine gold wire over dorsal layer of clear vinyl film
BODY: Dubbing mixed from amber fur and rough guard hair

Because they are so important in his Ozark tailwater country, Dave Whitlock has developed the best shrimp and sowbug imitations that I have used. His shrimps suggest the common *Hyalella* and *Gammarus* scuds, while his sowbugs imitate the *Asellus* species.

GREEN DRAKE NYMPH (Schwiebert)
HOOK:	8–12 Mustad 9575 6X Long
SILK:	6/0 Brown
TAILS:	Ring-necked pheasant tail-fibers
RIBBING:	Fine gold wire
BODY:	Flat monofilament over medium-brown floss, darkened with a dark-brown felt-tip pen on back
GILLS:	Medium-gray marabou fibers
WING CASES:	Dark-gray feather set in vinyl and trimmed to shape
LEGS:	Brown mallard fibers

PALE OLIVE DAMSELFLY NYMPH (Schwiebert)
HOOK:	8–12 Mustad 9575 6X Long
SILK:	6/0 Light olive
TAILS:	Pale olive-green marabou fibers
RIBBING:	None
BODY:	Flat monofilament over pale olive-green floss underbody
WING CASES:	Pale olive-green marabou
LEGS:	Gray mallard flank dyed pale olive

GREAT OLIVE-WINGED DRAKE NYMPH (Schwiebert)
HOOK:	8–12 Mustad 9575 6X Long
SILK:	6/0 Brown
TAILS:	Purple-blue pheasant saddle fibers
RIBBING:	Fine gold wire
BODY:	Flat monofilament over medium-gray floss base, darkened with a dark-brown felt-tip pen on back
GILLS:	Purple-gray marabou fibers
WING CASES:	Dark-gray feather set in vinyl and trimmed to shape
LEGS:	Purple-blue pheasant saddle hackle

BLACK WILLOWFLY NYMPH (Schwiebert)
HOOK:	8–12 Mustad 9575 6X Long
SILK:	6/0 Black
TAILS:	Black silver-pheasant fibers
BODY:	Flat monofilament over black silk underbody
WING CASES:	Black feather set in vinyl and trimmed to shape
LEGS:	Black silver-pheasant fibers

BROWN WILLOWFLY NYMPH (Schwiebert)
HOOK:	8–12 Mustad 9575 6X Long
SILK:	6/0 Brown
TAILS:	Brown feather fibers
BODY:	Flat monofilament over medium-brown silk underbody
WING CASES:	Dark-brown feathers set in vinyl and trimmed to shape
LEGS:	Brown mallard fibers

GREAT STONEFLY NYMPH (Schwiebert)

HOOK:	8–12 Mustad 9575 6X Long
SILK:	6/0 Primrose
TAILS:	Gray feather fibers
BODY:	Flat monofilament over pale-yellow floss underbody with sides marked with chocolate-brown felt-tip pen
WING CASES:	Brown partridge shoulder set in vinyl and trimmed to shape
LEGS:	Pheasant saddle fibers

These willowfly patterns are tied to imitate several *Acroneuria* nymphs, which emerge on American streams in early summer. The third pattern imitates the large *Perla* nymphs which also hatch in early summer on eastern and midwestern rivers.

GIANT GOLDEN STONEFLY NYMPH (Schwiebert)

HOOK:	2–10 Mustad 9575 6X Long
SILK:	6/0 Primrose
TAILS:	Mottled feather fibers
BODY:	Flat monofilament over golden-yellow floss base with edges marked with chocolate-brown felt-tip pen
WING CASES:	Brown partridge shoulder set in vinyl and trimmed to shape
LEGS:	Ring-necked pheasant saddle fibers

This excellent pattern imitates the large *Acroneuria* stonefly nymphs so important on our major western rivers.

GIANT BLACK STONEFLY NYMPH (Schwiebert)

HOOK:	2–10 Mustad 9575 6X Long
SILK:	6/0 Black
TAILS:	Black feather fibers
BODY:	Flat monofilament over chocolate floss base, marked with felt-tip pen on back and sides
WING CASES:	Black feathers set in vinyl and trimmed to shape
LEGS:	Black silver-pheasant fibers

This nymph is a fine imitation of the large *Pteronarcys* species found in swift-flowing eastern rivers, as well as the heavy populations of other *Pteronarcys* nymphs found on western streams. Such large stoneflies often have three-to-four-year river lives while their nymphs grow to maturity, and are constantly available to the fish in several stages of development, making them excellent choices for fishing the water in prospecting an unfamiliar stream.

STREAMERS AND BUCKTAILS
Facing page 1355

BRIDLED SHINER (Schwiebert)

HOOK:	10–12 Mustad 3665A 6X Long
SILK:	4/0 White
TAILS:	Scarlet hackle fibers
BODY:	Gold Mylar tubing with scarlet nylon throat
UNDERWING:	White marabou
OVERWING:	Yellow, pale-ginger, and orange marabou, mixed
TOPPING:	Brown ostrich mixed with peacock
HEAD:	White lacquer with brown dorsal surfaces
EYES:	Black and yellow lacquer

The Bridled Shiner imitates *Notropis bifrenatus,* a prized baitfish of one to two inches found from Maine to Virginia.

ORANGEFIN SHINER (Schwiebert)
HOOK:	10–12 Mustad 3665A 6X Long
SILK:	4/0 White
TAILS:	Bright-orange hackle fibers
BODY:	Silver Mylar tubing with scarlet nylon throat
UNDERWING:	White marabou
OVERWING:	Yellow, pale-olive, and dark-olive marabou, mixed
TOPPING:	Peacock herl
HEAD:	White lacquer with olive dorsal surfaces
EYES:	Black and yellow lacquer

This pattern simulates *Gila robusta,* a small minnow common throughout the Colorado and Green drainage systems.

STEELCOLOR SHINER (Schwiebert)
HOOK:	8–10 Mustad 3665A 6X Long
SILK:	4/0 White
TAILS:	Scarlet hackle fibers
BODY:	Silver Mylar tubing with scarlet nylon throat
UNDERWING:	White marabou
OVERWING:	Pale-blue, olive, and dark-blue marabou, mixed
TOPPING:	Dark-blue ostrich mixed with peacock
HEAD:	White lacquer with dark-blue dorsal surfaces
EYES:	Black and yellow lacquer

The Steelcolor Streamer is intended to imitate *Notropis whipplei,* a medium-sized shiner common in the Middle West.

EMERALD SHINER (Schwiebert)
HOOK:	8–10 Mustad 3665A 6X Long
SILK:	4/0 White
TAILS:	Scarlet hackle fibers
BODY:	Silver Mylar tubing with scarlet nylon throat
UNDERWING:	White marabou
OVERWING:	Dark-green median topped with pale-brown and olive marabou
TOPPING:	Dark-brown ostrich mixed with peacock
HEAD:	White lacquer with brown dorsal surfaces and green median stripe
EYES:	Black and yellow lacquer

This pattern suggests *Notropis atherinoides,* a colorful shiner of medium size that is found from Canada to Texas, and westward across our northern borders.

YELLOW SCULPIN (Whitlock)
HOOK:	2–12 Mustad 38941
SILK:	4/0 Primrose
TAILS:	Hen-pheasant breast fibers
BODY:	Cream-colored fox dubbing mixed with amber and yellow seal fur
RIBBING:	Gold oval tinsel
OVERWING:	Red fox-squirrel hair topped with two golden cree hackles
PECTORALS:	Two hen-pheasant breast feathers, paired at sides
HEAD:	Deer hair, flared, trimmed, and marked with brown felt-tip pen

OLIVE SCULPIN (Whitlock)
HOOK:	2–12 Mustad 38941

SILK:	4/0 Olive
TAILS:	Hen-pheasant breast fibers
BODY:	Cream fox-dubbing mixed with brown and olive seal fur
RIBBING:	Gold oval tinsel
OVERWING:	Red fox-squirrel hair topped with two olive-dyed cree hackles
PECTORALS:	Two hen-pheasant breast feathers, paired at sides
HEAD:	Deer hair, flared, trimmed, and marked with olive felt-tip pen

These are typical variations on the remarkable sculpin imitations developed by Dave Whitlock in recent years. Such *Cottus* baitfish of many species are common staples in the trout diet on most American rivers, and are the reason behind the success of the Muddler Minnow. Several experts like A. J. McClane believe the Whitlock Sculpin is a better imitation, particularly weighted with fuse wire and fished deep.

OLIVEBACK DACE (Schwiebert)

HOOK:	6–10 Mustad 3665A 6X Long
SILK:	4/0 White
TAILS:	Scarlet hackle fibers
BODY:	Silver Mylar tubing with scarlet nylon throat
UNDERWING:	White marabou
OVERWING:	Black median topped with pale-olive and dark-olive marabou
TOPPING:	Peacock herl
HEAD:	White lacquer with olive dorsal surfaces and black median stripe
EYES:	Black and yellow lacquer

BLACKNOSE DACE (Schwiebert)

HOOK:	6–10 Mustad 3665A 6X Long
SILK:	4/0 White
TAILS:	Scarlet hackle fibers
BODY:	Silver Mylar tubing with scarlet nylon throat
UNDERWING:	White marabou
OVERWING:	Black median topped with medium-brown marabou
TOPPING:	Peacock herl
HEAD:	White lacquer with brown dorsal surfaces and black median stripe
EYES:	Black and yellow lacquer

SMELT (Schwiebert)

HOOK:	2–10 Mustad 94720 8X Long
SILK:	4/0 White
TAILS:	Scarlet hackle fibers
BODY:	Silver Mylar tubing with scarlet nylon throat
UNDERWING:	White marabou
OVERWING:	Pale-green, aquamarine, and dark-olive marabou, mixed
TOPPING:	Peacock herl
HEAD:	White lacquer with dark-blue dorsal surfaces
EYES:	Black and yellow lacquer

This pattern has been designed to imitate several smelts, whitebaits, and candlefish important as baitfish in American waters.

GOLDEN SHINER (Schwiebert)

HOOK:	2–10 Mustad 94720 8X Long
SILK:	4/0 White
TAILS:	Bright-orange hackle fibers
BODY:	Gold Mylar tubing with scarlet nylon throat

UNDERWING: White marabou
OVERWING: Pale-ginger, yellow, and pale-brown marabou, mixed
TOPPING: Olive ostrich mixed with peacock
HEAD: White lacquer with golden-olive dorsal surfaces
EYES: Black and yellow lacquer

Each of these baitfish imitations is dressed with touches of bright orange or scarlet, intended to suggest either fin coloration or the bleeding of a crippled minnow. Dave Whitlock argues that only an injured or dying fish shows its bright gill-colors, and that a predatory trout can seldom resist such easy prey. His patterns always use a trace of gill-color at the throat, following that theory.

NOTES ON

NEW EQUIPMENT

Since our first typesetting, which began in 1973, and proofreading of the last galley sheets two years later, many changes and new products have evolved throughout the fishing-tackle industry. These notes on new equipment are intended to supplement the chapters in the first edition of *Trout,* bringing the reader up to date.

SOME NOTES ON THE MODERN FLY LINE

Several developments have occurred in both the design and manufacture of lines, and some of these developments are quite important.

Our linemakers, particularly Scientific Anglers and Cortland, continue to experiment with tapers, densities, synthetic finishes, and hybrid designs that combine sinking tips and full weight-forward bellies with half bellies and running lines designed to float.

The improvements are excellent.

Anglers now have several sink-rate options in their bag of tricks, including line densities that sink deeper and more quickly.

Floating-and-sinking hybrids are a remarkable development. Although I seldom fish sinking-tip lines, because their disparate finish densities tend to hinge in casting, diminishing both delicacy and control to some degree, they are useful in situations where subtlety and precision are not critical. I tend to prefer weight-forward hybrids designed to sink the entire shooting belly, with a light running line designed to float. The result is startling. Long casts are often repetitive, particularly on big riffles and pools, and older running lines sank quickly during a fly swing or retrieve.

Combining a full-sinking belly with a running line that floats is much better; it makes a long cast easier, stripping the running line from the surface with less energy than is needed to lift it through the water from the bottom, where it has often drifted around your ankles.

Modified line tapers also facilitate easier casting and greater distances with less effort. Although several anglers familiar with a wide range of manufacturers (including this writer some fifteen years ago) have speculated about longer shooting heads and weight-forward bellies, it was Lee Wulff who introduced a true long-belly design at Garcia. Better rod design and improved casting techniques have made it possible to keep greater amounts of line aloft in false casting; that means more line length and weight in the air; and more weight times line speed equals more distance: It is simple physics, if you have the casting skills to false-cast a longer line.

Line finishes are evolving too.

Some manufacturers have offered lines with oily finishes that are hard and lumpy. The theory holds that a smooth line continuously in contact with the rod guides while casting is subject to more friction. Such lumpy finishes hopscotch through less smoothly but experience less friction and shoot better. British makers first developed such lines.

Other makers are exploring line finishes that offer oily-smooth casting and a polyvinyl chemistry that repells water, riding still higher in the surface film. The floating qualities of such lines are obvious. Since they float higher, with less diameter in contact with the water, these lines mend deftly, pick up more easily at greater distances, and are less visible. Many experts find they shoot better.

Strike indicators and lead-core are recent concepts.

Cortland has introduced a full series of color-tip lines intended for nymph fishing. The concept seemingly originated with Dave Whitlock and his experiments with dead-drift nymph tactics on his Ozark rivers. Several years ago, Whitlock sent me a hand-built shooting head, with a hot orange strike indicator and a running line attached. It was a prototype worth studying.

However, the Cortland design added a buoyant bulb tip to their standard 444 floating line. Its bulb is a brightly intense orange. It is readily visible and, like the red-and-white bobbers of boyhood, it is used to detect a subtle nymphing take when it stops almost imperceptibly in the currents. It has proved popular on many waters, although its fat indicator bulb drops a little harshly for the shy fish of our spring creeks.

Both Sunset and Cortland have explored the potential of lead-core shooting heads. Pacific Coast fishermen have been experimenting with relatively primitive lead-core heads for more than fifteen years. Such homemade gear first evolved from saltwater tactics, fishing deep for striped bass and yellowtails, and was quickly adopted by the inventive chinook fishermen on salmon rivers like the Smith and Chetco.

These pioneers built their lead-core heads from ordinary lead-core trolling line, cutting off lengths and weighing them to match line-weight specifications.

Splicing the lead-core heads to light running lines, the California anglers used them to fish in extremely deep pools and tidal rips. Such tackle also worked on river tarpon in Costa Rica, and it worked so well in the bridge tides at Islamorada that it was banned from Gold Cup competition. Such lead-core designs cast and fished rather clumsily, requiring a hard double-haul stroke and a swift head-bobbing evasion.

Better duck! Hal Janssen explained during my baptism on big chinooks. *Tuck your head under your wing when you start it forward—or you could be guilty of your own mugging!*

The lead-core trolling line was thin and relatively rough. It almost clattered through the air and landed like a javelin. Both Cortland and Sunset set out to build lead-core shooting heads with polyvinyl chloride coatings. The prototypes looked and cast almost like big fly lines. We tried them first at several fishing expositions, and later I used a prototype in the deep brook-trout lagoons of the Argentine lakes with good results.

There are a surprising number of new line-density designs.

Cortland has added several to its line. Its peach-colored 444 is highly regarded among skilled dry-fly anglers everywhere, particularly in Europe. It offers a uniquely supple finish over a tubular, braided core, with a chemistry intended to protect its integrity under exposure to solar denigration and keep its smooth-casting qualities in cold weather. Taper specifications are at the heart of Cortland 444 quality, and hand inspection is part of its secret.

Cortland has also changed its old 333 series of lines, employing a coating formula to create the 333 HT floating lines. The 333 HT line is white, and its high-technology finish makes it a superb choice in the medium-priced range.

The 444 sinking lines now come in several variations for different fishing conditions. Both ten- and twenty-foot sinking tips are made. Thirty-foot sinking heads, and full-sinking lines are available in fast- and super-fast-sink densities. Super-sink shooting heads and lead-core heads complete the list, with a new .031 running line that floats high.

What will we call our lead-core head? Leon Chandler told me with a quiet smile in San Francisco. *Kerboom!*

The Cortland 444 intermediate lines are a new product introduced in 1983. They float awash if cleaned and dressed, but their specific gravity of 1.06 is slightly heavier than water, sinking them quite slowly for shallowly fished flies and nymphs. The lines are pale ice-blue.

Cortland has also introduced its new 444 SL floating lines recently. 444 SL lines have a specifically formulated coating that makes them relatively stiff. The stiffness is intended to reduce line sag between rod guides. The oily finish and stiffness make a 444 SL shoot effortlessly. These lines are a bright green, and come in a full range of tapers, although only the classic 444 is made in a three-weight.

The Wulff long-belly concept has recently been refined in the Rodon Borkast lines. Their specifications were designed to match the remarkable tip-speed performance of modern carbon-fiber and boron fly rods. Past tapers were first worked out in the nineteenth century, with bamboo and silkworm-gut leaders and lines of braided silk.

It was time to change, Ron Bensley explained at his plant outside New York. *Everything else had already changed.*

Graphite and boron accelerate so sharply into the casting stroke that a standard thirty-foot belly, with its light running line, was overpowered in flight. It worked with a choppy flutter. Line flutter kills both accuracy and distance, and it delivers a fly too hard. Short distances often resulted in sloppy, too open loops, and a strong distance stroke could collapse the loop into a tangle. Both graphite and boron are capable of sharp roll-casting delivery, but standard weight-forward tapers execute a roll cast poorly. The Borkast tapers were designed to solve these problems, and equal the potential of our modern rods.

Double-taper lines can roll-cast beautifully, and handle short- to medium-range problems. Our standard weight-forward tapers fluttered badly at long distance, and fished clumsily.

Ted Simroe is responsible for the graphite and boron rods at Rodon. *Line modification wasn't enough,* he explained on a trip to the Avco Boron Laboratories in Massachusetts. *We're starting out fresh.*

His first step was to change the front tapers. Such designs were still echoing silk prototypes from the nineteenth century. The forward level section was eliminated, and Simroe shortened the standard front-taper specifications. The result was a tighter loop and clean power transfer to the leader. His next decision lengthened the forward-taper belly to more than thirty feet, and extended its rear taper to eighteen feet. His new taper totalled fifty-two feet, *before* the light running line started.

It's working beautifully! Simroe said.

The new weight-forward designs were complemented with a smooth, oily finish conceived to float. The first Borkast lines were light gray, and their popularity led Rodon to expand its series.

Sink-tip and extra-fast sinking models were quickly added. These lines were slate colored. Long-haul shooting heads followed, responding to the remarkable capacity of our synthetic rod fibers, which can carry as much as fifty feet of shooting head easily. Both floating and extra-fast sinking heads are now available. Simroe also designed a buoyant running line for his floating and sinking tapers, with .030 and .035 diameters.

Lee Wulff continues to experiment with line specifications, after seventy-odd years of fishing. His early long-belly designs have been further refined in his new Triangle tapers. Like the Rodon designs, and his earlier Garcia lines, the weight-forward belly is considerably lengthened in the new Wulff concept.

We're excited about it, Wulff told me recently at dinner in New York. *Give them a try!*

His four- and five-weight tapers start at .030 and increase continuously to .055 inches. The medium six- and seven-weight specifications start tapering at .032, progressively increasing to measure .060 inches at forty feet. The diameter drops sharply to the .032 running line, which completes the full ninety-foot design.

It's designed for trout fishing, Wulff explains, *and it's perfect for such problems.*

The unbroken Triangle taper steadily transmits casting power from its .055 and .060 butts into the leader. It places its finest diameters near the fish, keeping its heaviest belly weight well back. The constant taper roll casts excellently. With the entire forty-foot belly outside the rod, like the overhang of a shooting head, the Triangle taper outperforms a conventional weight-forward line.

It is a promising concept.

The oily, rough-finish specifications first worked out in the United Kingdom are being explored further at Sunset and Berkeley.

Such lines feel almost brittle when new, and require several days of fishing before they cast smoothly. Modern tapers are combined with a supple self-lubricating finish. The relatively lumpy, polyvinyl coating is a surprising concept designed to bounce through the guides, reducing line friction. Stiffness mitigates against line slap between the guides, which further reduces line velocity and distance. Such oil-impregnated coatings are combined with a microscopic roughness that seems to steeplechase through the guides, and experience confirms the theory.

Sunset has started manufacturing such lines as its Ultimate Formula series, and they are finished in a medium Oxford gray. Berkeley Specialist lines are pale yellow, offering similar technology with the visual character of earlier British silk.

Scientific Anglers first developed our modern polyvinyl chloride lines, and the firm continues its history of leadership.

It offers almost two hundred choices of line weights and tapers today, and more than a hundred in its floating-line models alone. It continues its Aircel and Aircel Supreme floating lines, and it has expanded the famous Wetcel series. Its Wetcel I has a sink rate of 1.75 to 2.50 inches per second, and parallels its designs for the first sinking lines at mid-century. Wetcel II offers a sink rate between 2.00 and 3.00 inches per second, and the Wetcel HI-D performs between 3.25 and 4.25 inches per second. The Hi-Speed HI-D sinks like an anchor at 3.75 to 6.50 inches per second. The Wetcel I and Wetcel II are available in double-taper, weight-forward, and shooting-head designs. The HI-D and Hi-Speed HI-D are manufactured only in weight-forward and shooting tapers.

Scientific also offers a full series of sink-tip lines with sink rates matching the performance of its Wetcel I and Wetcel II densities. Its Wet Belly HI-D has a full twenty feet of sinking line rated at 3.25 to 4.25 inches per second. Its Wet Head HI-D offers the same sink-rate density, with its entire thirty-foot shooting belly designed to sink. Like its other sink-tip designs, the running line is designed to float, while the tips and bellies sink at controlled rates.

The Scientific inventory also has lines in weight-forward tapers with sink rates between 1.25 to 1.75 inches per second. Its Deep Water Express series includes three shooting tapers with sink rates between 7.00 and 10.00 inches per second, which make bottom fish in high lakes, reservoirs, and unusually deep channels catchable.

But its new Ultra series of floating and sink-tip lines is the result of continuing research and development, and its marriage to a larger corporation, with a broad spectrum of technology in other fields.

Ultra series lines still use the patented microsphere process to control the specific gravity necessary in a floating line, but have combined that technology with a new chemical formulation that repels the surface film. The line sits so high on the meniscus that less line diameter is actually in contact with the water, unlike earlier floating lines, which ride slightly awash. Such performance means easier and longer pickups, easier mending during fly swing and drift, and better line control. The total chemistry of these lines also includes better durability and shooting qualities. The finish steadily oils itself from its unique internal compounds, and its mix includes the ability to resist ultraviolet radiation, the principal cause of fading and finish cracking in modern lines.

Quick popularity is testimony that Ultra lines are a step forward in line technology. Some experts have called them a breakthrough that parallels the polyvinylchloride lines themselves, with their weight-controlling admixtures of microspheres.

These lines are remarkable evidence of the peripheral impacts of recent technology. Modern fishermen have a mind-boggling palette of lines and line-performance specifications that would have dazed a generation limited to a single type—the floating double-taper design of British silk, which required drying each night on a teakwood rack and a fresh dressing of red-stag fat each morning.

PROBLEMS IN LEADERS, KNOTS, AND BACKING

Since the completion of this chapter, several important developments have taken place in both leader material and backing. Perhaps the most remarkable evolution has occurred in polyamide tippet material and knotless tapers. Such nylons share superb breaking-strain performance with surprising limpness and knot-resisting qualities, although their knotting qualities make them somewhat different from earlier leader materials, and their suppleness poses both advantages and problems.

Cortland has introduced its flat Cobra monofilament and its pale Micron as backing material. Cobra is a highly effective line behind big-water shooting heads, and is available in breaking strains of fifteen, twenty, and thirty pounds. Micron displays very little stretching under tension and comes in twelve, twenty, and thirty pounds. Gudesbrod Dacron is similar, although it is slightly larger in diameter for comparable breaking-strain performance. Although its diameter will mean less capacity on a given reel, its available spools, in fifteen, twenty, and thirty pounds, are less likely to bite and bind into the backing when a big trout bolts suddenly.

Sunset recently introduced its Amnesia-type monofilament for its shooting-head running lines. Amnesia is available in two-hundred-yard spools, and in breaking strengths of fifteen, twenty, twenty-five, thirty, and forty pounds. It stretches less than other nylons and is relatively memory-free, having less tendency to tangle and coil.

My first experience with the new polyamide tippet materials came with Racine Tortue in the Yellowstone country and Racine Water Queen on the Henry's Fork of the Snake. Both materials displayed similar knotting and fishing qualities, and virtually identical breaking strains in the same diameters. Water Queen appears slightly more limp, and offers the following specifications:

SIZE	TIPPET DIAMETER (INCHES)	BREAKING STRAIN (POUNDS)
8X	.003	1.2
7X	.004	1.9
6X	.005	2.4
5X	.006	3.3
4X	.007	3.7
3X	.008	4.2
2X	.009	5.1
1X	.010	6.2
0X	.011	8.4

Pezon & Michel soon introduced Kroic, which is a favorite tippet material of my good friend Jack Hemingway. His experience with Kroic at Sun Valley leads Hemingway to extol its knotting, casting, and fishing properties. Pezon & Michel markets its new tippet material in the following specifications and spools:

SIZE	TIPPET DIAMETER (INCHES)	BREAKING STRAIN (POUNDS)
8X	.003	1.1
7X	.004	1.4
6X	.005	1.8
5X	.006	2.2
4X	.007	3.0
3X	.008	4.0
2X	.009	5.0
1X	.010	6.0
0X	.011	7.0

Cortland found its supple Nylorfi was a remarkable advance in breaking-strain performance. Its knotting properties were so striking that casting knots scarcely reduced its strength, although its slippery finish and limpness made blood knots critical, and fly knots demanded both discipline and care. Some skilled fishermen have seemingly found it slightly brittle in cold weather, but several of the new nylons display similar symptoms. Nylorfi has developed some fierce partisans since its introduction, and is available as follows:

SIZE	TIPPET DIAMETER (INCHES)	BREAKING STRAIN (POUNDS)
8X	.003	1.3
7X	.004	1.7
6X	.005	2.4
5X	.006	4.0
4X	.007	4.8
3X	.008	6.0
2X	.009	8.0
1X	.010	8.5
0X	.011	10.2

André Puyans has developed perhaps the strongest polyamide nylon yet introduced to fly-fishing. His remarkable Creative Sports Enterprises material is quite limp, has superb knotting performance, and offers the demanding angler unique breaking-strain properties. Its limpness and stretch mean that its fine diameters must be constantly replaced after casting and playing fish. It is spooled and sold as follows:

SIZE	TIPPET DIAMETER (INCHES)	BREAKING STRAIN (POUNDS)
8X	.003	2.0
7X	.004	3.0
6X	.005	4.0
5X	.006	5.0
4X	.007	6.0
3X	.008	7.0
2X	.009	8.0
1X	.010	9.0
0X	.011	10.0

Several factors should be kept in mind when using these new polyamide nylons. Their tensile strength and knotting properties can cause some problems when combined with other types of nylon, and their limpness and supple finishes presage knotting complications, too. When joining a series of supple tippets to older middle- and butt-section materials, or adding a single tippet of the new nylons to a conventional leader, it has proved wise to make this hybrid connection of same-diameter line. The result is a more secure knot and the elimination of a hinging knot which can diminish the smooth progression of casting energy from the line to the fly. It is possible to test a leader without casting it, simply by holding it a few inches on either side of the critical blood knot and bending the leader through the knot. The power transfer will prove optimal if the knot lies in a smooth curve from tippet to tippet; but if there is a sharp parabola formed with the knot at its apex, there is too abrupt a change in either diameter or relative suppleness from material to material.

It is also critical to remember that the combination of suppleness and strength in these new nylons can mean that your present knotting techniques do not deliver enough internal friction to hold. It may prove necessary to experiment with more turns in your knots to achieve adequate strength and performance. Symmetry in your blood knots is also more critical in the ultrafine diameters now available. It is important to count the exact number of turns in each part of any symmetrical knot to insure proper friction and knotting properties. Other significant factors include tightening your knots slowly and wetting the partially formed knots with saliva to avoid thermal stress buildup, which could damage the molecular integrity of the nylon. Long periods of casting or playing large fish can expend the elasticity of fine nylon. Serious tangling and coiling can occur then, and the nylon can lose too much stiffness to deliver even tiny flies. Breaking strain is also radically diminished when the stretch factor is reduced, so such tippets should be replaced more often than conventional nylons to insure dependable strength in fine diameters.

Since Puyans first introduced his remarkably strong polyamide nylon leader material under the Creative Sports label, similar products have evolved in Japan.

Aeon is a worthy competitor. Some experts feel that its slightly lower breaking-strain ratings are less important than its other superb qualities, and Aeon is still twice as strong as earlier American nylon in its critical diameters under 4X.

Its supporters point to excellent knotting properties, a controlled limpness that cushions stress and still turns over well, less stretch than some polyamide material, and rigorously accurate calibrations. It also has surprisingly little memory, a doubtful quality shared by many synthetic materials, in which a leader stubbornly remains in its packaging coils. Aeon uncoils with remarkable straightness, and mere hand friction is sufficient to straighten its coils in fishing. The following specifications obtain:

SIZE	TIPPET DIAMETER (INCHES)	BREAKING STRAIN (POUNDS)
8X	.003	1
7X	.004	2
6X	.005	3
5X	.006	4
4X	.007	5
3X	.008	6
2X	.009	7
1X	.010	9
0X	.011	11

Since writing the early chapters of *Trout* more than ten to fifteen years ago, I have had extensive experience with these polyamide materials on large fish, particularly on the Henry's Fork of the Snake.

Its lessons have been important.

The leader specifications and tapers found in *Trout* remain quite useful, but big selective fish are a demanding yardstick. The tapers found in the two pages of diagrams on leader design are sound. The Smutting Tapers and Light Nymphing Tapers have proved themselves, along with the Standard Tapers to 5X and 6X, but I would add a critical footnote to their design today: The tippets might be lengthened to a full thirty-six inches in 7X and 8X diameters, and extended a full forty to forty-eight inches in 6X and 5X points.

This footnote is quite useful. Such long tippets demand good casting, but they are not intended to straighten out cleanly on the current. Their loose coils are part of a subtle difficult-fish strategy. The slack creates a longer float that is drag-free over a selective trout. The limp character of polyamide nylon contributes too, and its limp stretchiness is like a delicate shock tippet. Even cobwebs stretch long before they break, and there is sufficient elasticity in a thirty-six- to forty-eight-inch tippet that it provides a safety factor on big fish. Subtleties are critical in delicate tippets.

Our forefathers would shake their heads in envy at such fine-tippet breaking strains. Modern technology has given us 6X tippets that surpass the performance of 0x silkworm gut, and there are rumors of still more surprises in nylon performance.

Plus a final caveat for fishing the 7X and 8X diameters: Cut the tippet off and replace it after taking a fish, just as you should reknot the fly with salmon or steelhead, when you are fishing such cobwebs.

Such disciplines pay.

RANDOM THOUGHTS ON WADERS, CLOTHING, AND
OTHER EQUIPMENT

The past three years have also seen considerable evolution in wading gear, clothing, and fly-fishing accessories. Wader designs have been introduced and subsequently discarded by several manufacturers, principally because their hybrid construction of exotic fabrics and adhesives failed to perform as anticipated. Such failure seems related to poor quality control and workmanship as much as to hybrid laminates of excellent materials that did not work together properly.

Marathon experienced some difficulties with its waders in the past five years, and the company has continued to improve its products. Its current boot-foot designs include both insulated and conventional models with a choice of felt or cleated rubber soles. Marathon has also introduced an improved nylon-and-rubber stocking-foot wader for use with separate brogues. These improved designs are lighter and tougher. The lamination of industrial nylon fabric to the neoprene lining has been perfected, providing unusual puncture and abrasion resistance. Insulation is available in the boot-foot models only, and all Marathon waders have a pale olive coloring. Custom sizes are still provided on order.

Converse makes a more expensive line of boot-foot waders in both insulated and conventional types. Their construction is based upon a more typical rubber-coated, cloth-lined specification. The insulated models employ a wool-lining sandwich to capture and retain body heat. Like Marathon, Converse also manufactures a complete line of hip boots, and its best wading equipment is olive drab. Its Wadewell line offers both cleated and felt soles in a series of khaki-colored waders. Converse also imports a series of less expensive nylon waders and hip boots employing two layers of rubber-coated cloth. The Hampshire nylon waders are similar to the Converse 13955 designs, except that they are of fully insulated construction and are manufactured in cleated boot-foot models only. Converse is an old company with an established reputation.

Fritz von Schlegel has started to make nylon-laminated chest waders and hip boots with polypropylene soles. His rubberlike cloth has proved itself durable and puncture resistant. Von Schlegel and his products have attracted a surprising number of partisans.

André Puyans has been working with a well-known maker of wet suits used by divers. Waterproof nylon cloth is specified for both surfaces of a thin layer of closed-cell flexible sponge. Both the waterproof fabrics and their sponge core are capable of 360-degree stretch, and are easily repaired after a puncture. Five body sizes are available and can be matched with any foot size; custom sizes can also be provided. The spongelike layer provides both insulation and buoyancy, and these unusual new waders are rapidly gaining popularity.

Orvis, which experienced considerable trouble with its waders in recent years, has returned with a completely new line of lightweight designs. Waterproof nylon cloth layers surround a core of rubber, and both cleated feet and woven-felt soles are made. Hexagonal aluminum studs are also available on both waders and hip boots from Orvis. The company has introduced a second line of waders using nylon satin cloth laminated around a rubber shell. Leg chafe guards and seams are fully vulcanized. Steel arch shanks and semihard toes protect the feet, and rubber cleats, felt, and fully studded soles are available.

During the absence of conventional stocking-foot waders, which I prefer because of the foot-and-ankle protection provided by leather wading brogues, many anglers came to like Sealdri products. Fabricated of pure latex rubber in one-piece construction, these stocking-foot waders have no seams. The rubber is easily repaired after tears or punctures, and Sealdri waders are much less fragile than the earlier prototypes. The latex is both flexible and warm. Extra-thick Sealdri waders are available too, providing fifty percent thicker latex construction. The result is better puncture and tear resistance. Sealdri waders fold into a compact roll for travelling, making it easy to pack two pairs in a duffel bag, and I have used them happily.

Red Ball has recently offered two new lines of waders. Their Master series includes both chest-high waders and hip boots. The fabric is a supple and durable three-ply nylon and nitrile rubber, and it has proved resistant to reasonable wear, abrasion, ripping, and punctures. The boot feet are reinforced with a steel shank, a hard safety-type toe, and a cushion insole. Metal fittings are rustproof. The boots are fitted with heavy woven-nylon felt soles and heels. There is no internal inseam to chafe or leak seepage, and the knees are reinforced. Belt loops, chest pocket, and reinforced suspender buttons are standard, and Red Ball waders are dark mahogany brown.

Red Ball hippers are fabricated to the same specifications. The harness fittings are rustproof and reinforced, and there are internal holding straps to make low-position wear possible.

Red Ball also introduced its unusually light flyweight stocking-foot waders in recent years. These waders quickly became popular, although fishermen experienced some problems in the field. They were lightweight and packed tightly, but they offered little protection in cold water and winds, and some anglers found them brittle or easily torn. Red Ball has worked on its problems, and subsequently introduced its Master Flyweight ST series.

The new flyweight fabric is a full two ounces heavier now, and the ST series is even more popular. The fabric is a remarkably strong 220 denier polyurethane-coated nylon. The seams are painstakingly heat sealed. There is a built-in inflatable chamber just above the waist, and the carrying bag snaps inside to form the stomach-high pocket. The stocking feet are shaped of heavier nylon, to reduce abrasion and chafing. The suspender fittings are rustproofed and reinforced, and the entire chest-high wader weighs only fourteen ounces.

Feather River has just introduced its light stocking-foot hippers, using the same polyurethane-coated fabric as the Red Ball Flyweights. The hippers weigh only twelve ounces. They have strong, adjustable belt straps, and Velcro water cinches at the thighs. Like the Flyweight ST series, these stocking-foot hippers are dark brown.

Anglers who like these flyweight waders and Feather River hippers find they hug the legs and body closely. With less bulk and weight, wading becomes easy and sure, particularly in swift currents. Walking is less difficult, too, and climbing through fences is less clumsy. There is little protection against cold, but there is less perspiration and heat when out of the water. Both waders and hippers are so light, and fold so compactly, that they can easily be stowed in the rain-jacket pocket of a fishing vest. Fishermen are purchasing both waders and hippers to have the flexibility of a complete wading system, compact and light, using the same wading brogues.

However, such lightweight wading gear must still be combined with leg-warming clothes and socks, like the acrylic-lined Sokkets. But common sense and care are still required; if you avoid thorn trees and berry thickets and barbed wire, such lightweight fabrics will last.

The O'Neill neoprene waders first tested by André Puyans are no longer unique. Such equipment is now made by Scott and Imperial.

Scott neoprene wading gear is made in both chest- and waist-high designs. They are tough, and have almost two hundred percent elasticity to facilitate walking, sitting, and wading. The Scott waders consist of closed-cell neoprene insulation sandwiched between chocolate-colored nylon facings. The material has proved itself surprisingly snag resistant and punctureproof. Adjustable suspenders are attached, and feature quick-release buckles. The neoprene insulation keeps you both warm and cool, and there is even a special cuff attached just above the ankle. It is designed to fold down over the wading socks as a built-in gaiter, keeping out sand and pea gravel.

Imperial Polar Bear waders are slightly more expensive, offer similar rugged specifications and performance, and weigh slightly more than three pounds. They offer both buoyancy—a tight enough fit at the waist and hips to exclude water should you fall down—and comfort in both cold and warm weather. Some steelhead fishermen swear by these neoprene waders, and they fish in weather that would discourage a mindless duck hunter used to February storms.

O'Neill, Scott, and Imperial neoprene waders have developed fierce partisans, and although I dislike float-tube fishing, such wading gear is perfect for tubing lakes and reservoirs.

Ranger has attempted to manufacture hip boots and waders like the equipment common in my boyhood years. Such designs were warm, quite durable, and were often rented daily by fishing shops, season after season. Fifty years ago, our waders combined an outer layer of tough cotton tenting material with an inner layer of rubber. These layers were tightly bonded.

The new Ranger wader offers such specifications to contemporary anglers. Brass suspender fittings are resistant to corrosion. There are wide belt loops and a stomach pocket. The inner seams are reinforced with smooth chafing strips, which are also fitted into the crotch. The rubber boot feet offer hard toes and heels, steel shanks, and cushion insoles. Suspenders are not included, although the hip boots have belt loops attached. Both chest-high waders and hippers have thick felt soles of the old type, and although these cotton-fabric waders are more expensive than we remember them in the Depression years, they are quite welcome.

Two firms are offering cold-weather bib pants for wading comfort. The Polar Fleece design has zippers at both ankles and crotch, for easy access over clothing. It is made of a synthetic Celanese fiber that is washable, breathes, is relatively quick drying, and allows perspiration to evaporate. There is a rear pocket. The bib buckles are quick-release.

Mark Pile bib trousers are a little less costly than the Polar Fleece design. Their properties are well known in duck blinds and goose pits. The wicking-pile keeps you completely warm and dry, and the trousers are surprisingly light.

Last season I was fishing on Upper Tularik, on the north shore of Lake Iliamna, with André Puyans. October had turned wintry in Alaska. The chill north wind was freezing our reels and guides, but the big rainbows were still taking well.

You going to fish or freeze? Puyans laughed.

We built a fire on the brushy island in the upper lagoon, but the water was so cold it took only a few minutes before our toes ached. When they stopped aching it was time to stop fishing too, and retreat to the fire. Puyans was wearing bib trousers under his waders that afternoon, along with a pair of neoprene boot-socks, and he was the only angler who fished steadily in spite of the cold. He took several eight-pound rainbows.

Although his shop was more than 2,000 miles south at San Francisco, Puyans filled several orders for his cold-weather trousers at supper.

Scott neoprene footgear includes three designs that are perfect cold-weather equipment. Their neoprene boot-socks include a zippered ankle-length model, a calf-length model that simply pulls on, and their original neoprene boot-sock with a fold-down gaiter to keep out river gravel.

Simms makes a similar neoprene boot-sock. It is designed to cover a woolen wading sock, providing both insulation and a cover to keep out grime and aquatic weeds. Simms also makes a tight-fitting gaiter of stretch nylon, to fold down over wading brogues and keep out gravel and other aggregates. Another intriguing Simms product is called a spool tender, a thick nylon ring with a finger tab. Its fit keeps a spare reel spool from unwinding.

Stream Designs has also developed a laced spat-type gaiter that fits over brogues and wading socks. Its product is less simple to wear, but it is better at excluding river aggregates.

Although I still use English brogues, and the fine wading shoes made by Russell are also favorites, I have come to prefer the elegant brogues designed by André Puyans at Creative Sports. Reinforced toes and side leather protect the feet well, although I would prefer a thicker sole in difficult wading. The polyfelt soles provide excellent traction. Speed-lace eyelets are combined with conventional eyes. The ankles are cut a bit too low to prevent accumulation of small pebbles and fine aggregates along the Achilles tendon, but I use these handsome Puyans brogues on most trips now.

Puyans has also started to manufacture an improved brogue, partially based on my comments in the first edition of *Trout*. His more expensive designs include a higher ankle cut, cushioned with a padded roll that closes tightly when the brogues are properly laced. The cushioned roll may prove a little fragile, but it has solved the pea-gravel problem.

Other manufacturers have also started to make workable brogues for stocking-foot waders.

Weinbrenner is marketing a wading shoe designed by Gary Borger, a young fisherman who is among our best American writers. His brogues are fabricated of synthetic materials that look, feel, and perform like leather, except that they do not absorb water and will not shrink or rot. They are not stiff and impossible to pull on after drying out. Their durability has amazed the fishermen who have tried them, and they dry quickly at room temperature. Their lacing offers a good toe-to-ankle fit, with an internal ankle padding that keeps out gravel. Both toes and heels are rigidly reinforced to protect the feet. The arches are also reinforced at midsole. The soles are cut from a tough nylon-and-polyester felt. Although it is less than elegant, the Borger shoe is moderately priced and its durability is unsurpassed.

The Danner Corporation has added a lightweight wading shoe to its line of outdoor footwear. Its high-cut ankle keeps out stones, like its fully gusseted tongue. Its polyester felt sole is bonded to a neoprene cushion. Both toe caps and heels are reinforced split-grain leather backed with neoprene. Leather and neoprene enclose the ankle, and the shoe has a pattern of side drains. Its uppers are a dark brown bulletproof mesh of nylon, which makes a lightweight brogue that drains off water and dries out quickly.

The difficult wading conditions on the Umpqua in Oregon evolved the effective Korker sandals. Heavy rubber soles are laced to the brogues with parachute cord, and the soles are fully studded with twenty-five to thirty ice studs originally developed for winter tires. Korkers provide unmatched footing.

Stream Cleats are not new, having been made popular by the late Dan Bailey, but I had not actually used them until a recent trip on the Deschutes with Jock Fewel. The cleats are a simple concept. Aluminum zigzag cleating is riveted to ordinary rubber overshoes. It is a relatively cheap solution that slips on over the wading shoes. The cleats are ugly, but they work well on slippery bottom conditions.

Muncie wading grids are the Rolls-Royce of aluminum systems. Their design features an interlocking gridwork that bends to place the gridding under the ball of the foot, and just under the arch. The heel is left free, and a roller is fitted at the toes. Wire frames lock back over the toe and at each side of the shoe, and are secured by strong T-straps. Muncie grids are widely considered the best wading-grid system available.

Fishing vests continue to evolve and improve. The Stream Designs products introduced in Colorado five years ago were the result of a collaboration between Leon and Linda Sagaloff. Their fishing vests were first conceived while they were managing a tackle shop at Fort Collins, where the Cache la Poudre leaves the mountains, spilling into the High Plains.

Their first model was excellent, well designed, and superbly made. Quality and fit and first-rate fabric were obvious, although such quality is always expensive. Many experts predicted that such expensive vests were too costly, and predicted failure.

The experts were quickly proved wrong.

The original Stream Designs vests proved so popular that their makers were forced to abandon their tackle business and concentrate on fishing clothes. The first design was a full-length vest with twenty-five pockets and a waist-length cut. Its specifications included twelve fly-box pockets, thermometer and sunglasses pockets, leader spool pockets, a fly-dressing pocket, leader pouch, and a zippered rain-gear pocket and game pouch.

The Spring Creek and short deep-wading models soon followed. They offered sixteen pockets and, like the first prototype, included front snaps, zippers, rod snap holders and loop, fleece patch, forceps holster, rear-mounted net ring, and two front D-rings. The first prototypes placed the forceps holster outside the vest, but that detail was changed after I pointed out that double-haul casting often fouled slack line on the forceps when mounted there. Other changes were considered, but Stream Designs was sold to a large clothing manufacturer before those changes were fully worked out.

Quality declined quickly, but the fledgling company has been recently sold again, acquired this time by a firm justly respected for its rod fittings and boron rod designs.

We liked their vests from the start, Ron Bensley explained his plans for Stream Designs. *We're committed to making them best again—their wide-shoulder cut and concealed yoke panel were unique.*

Orvis has surpassed the conceptual excellence and quality of the Stream Designs prototypes with its Super Tac-L-Pak series. Their designs offer more pockets than a magician's tuxedo. Orvis has specified a heavy-duty poplin of thirty-five percent cotton and sixty-five percent polyester, with a 7.7-ounce rating. The waist-length standard design offers thirty-five pockets, excluding the zippered rain-gear pouch. There are six fully zippered pockets in front, plus two zippered rear pouches for extra reels and spools. There are inside holsters for sunglasses and thermometers, plus Velcro mini-pouches for tippet spools. All seams are extra stitched and bar-tack reinforced at corners and flaps, a hallmark of quality at Stream Designs too. There is a rear net ring at the neck, and oversize Velcro tabs on the smaller pockets. The Super Tac-L-Pak is excellent.

There is also a short Super Wading Tac-L-Pak in the Orvis line. It is seventeen inches long, almost four inches shorter than the standard design, but it has an incredible twenty-nine pockets. Its nine fully zippered pockets still include two rear pouches for extra reels and spools. The Super Wading model allows an angler to wade almost four inches deeper without shipping water into his sheepskin fly books and Wheatley boxes. Soggy flies and rusty hooks are troublesome.

Although these new Orvis vests are expensive, they are worth the price. Both the standard and deep-wading designs offer features still not available on other vests today.

Although the Wheatley and Hardy reel cases of yesteryear are gone, Thomas & Thomas has recently introduced a similar hard-leather design for travel protection. The reel seat sits flat in the bottom of the case, while the lid rolls and locks tightly around the frame. The handsome case, fully lined with felt, is available in three sizes. Hardy Brothers has also begun to sell its highly practical round cases, formerly provided only with Hardy reels. These cases are fabricated of heavy vinyl and open with a peripheral zipper. Sponge lining covered with acrylic velvet protects the reel from impact in shipment.

The simple landing nets designed originally by Joseph Swaluk are still produced by John Gayewski at Guyrich. The frames are made of laminated white ash, and the handles are formed around a core of select black walnut. The mesh bag is exquisitely conceived and woven, with all of the features of the original design.

Several other makers now supply wood-frame nets of simple beauty and functional design. Orvis produces a beautiful design with a cherry-wood handle and frame, as well as a less expensive net fashioned of white ash and mahogany which is made in two sizes, fitted with bag depths of seventeen and nineteen inches.

French clips have dominated net connection systems for years, but an improved quick-release design is now available. Some anglers have begun to use a swivel snap with a push release, and the net is readily separated from its connection to the vest.

Since the equipment chapter was written, photosensitive lenses have created a revolution in sunglasses. These are lenses that change color from quite smoky to almost window-glass-clear in response to changing intensities of light. Such qualities make these new sunglasses quite useful at low levels of illumination in both morning and evening. Some fishermen argue that the new glasses do not darken sufficiently to compensate for extreme intensities or glare. However, I find that I suffer less eye fatigue after a day's fishing with photosensitive glasses. These glasses must be "seasoned" according to the manufacturer's instructions.

Other optical devices can prove useful. Orvis is supplying the familiar eyeglass loupe, a tiny lens which attaches to any eyeglass frame and swings into position in front of your glasses on a slender arm. The loupe provides threefold magnification, a great help in delicate work along the stream.

Unlike the conventional loupe, which must be permanently attached to your eyeglass frames, the new Optipak is a remarkably imaginative device for three-power magnification. It is a lens mounted on a ball joint, and folds into its own matchbox-size case. The case itself functions as a stand for scanning charts and diagrams, and will also clip onto eyeglass frames, fishing-hat brim, fly vise, vest pocket, or your thumb for checking insect identification or threading a tippet to a tiny dry fly. The case even includes a foldout scale in millimeters for contour maps or fly-hatch specimens. Since the lens is mounted in a strong lightweight plastic, the Optipak is available at a surprisingly low price.

Since recommending monoculars in my earlier work, I have learned from Jack Hemingway that a fine pair of binoculars is useful in fishing big water. It is possible to study a broad expanse of river for rises, or spot the soft dimples of bank feeders at considerable distances. Sometimes a fisherman can identify the hatch with binoculars. The character of rise forms can be studied. Binoculars are obviously better than a monocular, and have better light-gathering qualities in morning and evening. It is important to steady binoculars by standing in quiet currents, resting against trees or boulders, or leaning across a vehicle. Several times in recent years we have studied the far sides of streams like the upper Madison or the Henry's Fork, able to spot big bank-feeders at a hundred yards. The binoculars saved considerable time once spent hiking and wading in search of fish, particularly in glassing places like the Slow Bend in the Yellowstone.

Orvis catalogs a fogging stick designed to prevent condensation on camera and eyeglass lenses. The product is quite useful in combating the temperature changes typical of trout country.

Several years ago I discussed the white-panel aquatic collecting nets and their tendency to frighten fast-swimming nymphs and pupae. Cascade has now designed a plain mesh net with handles of hardwood dowels that neatly solves the problem. Larval forceps with flexible pincers are now available for handling insect specimens gently.

Cascade also manufactures a wallet protector of bright orange vinyl with a Velcro closure. The wisdom of such an item will be obvious to anyone who has drowned his clothing thoroughly. George Gehrke is the developer of a fine dry-fly dressing, but he has also perfected a two-finger stripping glove to protect the hands from cold water and chapping. The stripping gloves provide an alternative short of full-finger gloves.

The quality of the Hardy scissor pliers has declined in recent months but other similar tools are now available. The Fisherman's Pal is a six-inch scissor with plier points, file, screwdriver, and lead-shot crimper. Sunrise is also producing a long-nose scissor plier of a better design than the Hardy original, and I am using a pair at present. The large surgical hemostats that we have all carried for years have been supplanted by a smaller version that is less cumbersome.

Hank Roberts is still offering his famous stream knife, poetically called Walton's Thumb. It is made of surgical-quality steel, and it boasts a

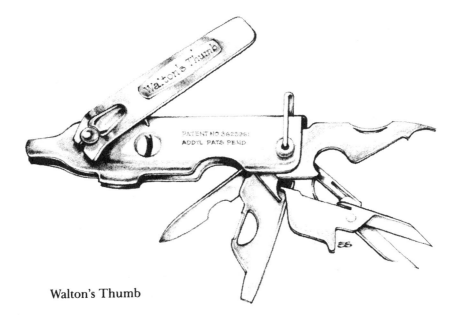

Walton's Thumb

startling array of features: It has clippers, tiny scissors, shot crimpers, fittings for widening and reusing shot, a stiletto point, and a knot-making tool. Walton's Thumb is a fishing cousin of the Swiss Army knife.

Orvis has recently introduced a similar product that folds compactly and is elegantly simple, like a man's cuticle knife from Tiffany. It has a small file, knife blade, and scissors. Its opposite end has retractable

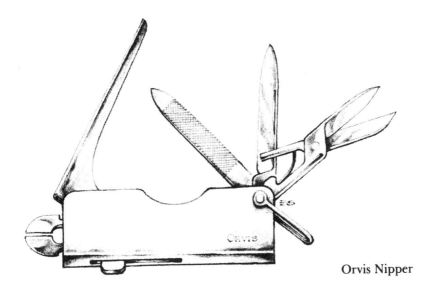

Orvis Nipper

clippers with a slim lever. The clippers retract and lock, closing the lever over the folded knife, scissors, and file. The Orvis Nipper is elegant enough, and versatile enough too, to serve as a small pocketknife and cuticle cutter in a city setting.

Since an occasional bottle of wine offers us enjoyable overtones in our sport, particularly since I lived in Europe for several years, a corkscrew is important to my tackle. Although the type carried by many wine stewards is useful and compact, and operates on a simple fulcrum principle, I still prefer the old wood-handle type with its corkscrew firmly embedded in a used cork that carries the faint bouquet of a fine Beaujolais or Corton Charlemagne.

Gardner Grant has the best advice on wines for trout-fishing lunches. *Vintages with screw-on caps or finger-holes,* he insists with a twinkle, *are poor choices in trout country!*

Bill Hunter has revived the old loose-leaf type of fly book. Some fine old things die hard. His dark brown cowhide loose-leaf has six white felt pages and two of lamb's wool. Extra felt and lamb's wool pages are available, and the lamb's wool pages consist of two pieces cemented back to back. Hunter also sells a matching leader case with six parchment pockets. Such wonderful items echo the Hardy and Farlow catalogues published a half century ago, and Hunter's charming shop in New Hampshire has many unique items—including some of the most elegant flies.

Randall Kaufmann offers a similar cowhide leader case, evolved from the Wheatley pigskin leader wallets of the past.

Dennison has designed an interesting new leader dispenser. It eliminates carrying six full tippet spools inside a four-inch case. Each leader pack provides a stainless cutter tip and is moulded from buoyant plastic. When the first edition of *Trout* appeared, I was critical of the color and workmanship of these Dennison cases. It was suggested that a silver Mylar that matched the Wheatley boxes might prove more handsome.

Dennison did not change the tippet-spool pack, but it did introduce its new Omni box. It leapfrogged my suggestion with a nicely finished aluminum box that measures three inches square. It has four tippet spools, with foam inserts in its lid and spool cover for holding flies.

Rod grips are a product long overdue. Like all first-rate ideas, rod grips are so simple that it seems strange they were not developed earlier. They consist of textured rubber pads that are invaluable in separating jammed ferrules. Laggies has designed the best nylon straightener for leaders, with a pear-shaped leather cover containing two circular rubber pads. The straightener is a pleasing design that applies pressure on a coiled leader with precision and control. Both accessories are excellent products.

George Gehrke perfected his famous Gink in past seasons, and its success is ample testimony to its value in dry-fly work. Laggies has also introduced its excellent dressing called Hi & Dry, which comes in a handsome leather holder that pins to a vest. Considerable work has also been done with leader sinks. Laggies' Fast-Sink is intended for application in advance of fishing, and must be allowed to dry an entire twenty-four hours. Seidel's 800 sink is another reliable product. However, many anglers believe that the new Gehrke's Xink is the finest streamside fly- and leader-sink yet formulated. It may yet convince a generation of old-time fishermen to forget about bentonite, marl, laundry soap, detergents, and a handful of alder leaves.

I dislike wading staffs, because I firmly believe that a staff can impart a false sense of security, leading an unwary angler to attempt currents and crossings he should not try. Too, most wading staffs are cumbersome when not in use. However, the new Folstaf circumvents the latter problem. It folds into twelve-inch sections of lightweight black-anodized aluminum, and is fitted with a cork grip. The staff unfolds and snaps instantly into its locked position, using the principles of post-tensioned structures. Such a wading staff can be carried in its belt holster or tucked into the bellows pocket in the back of a fishing vest.

Orvis has introduced some elegant leather-bound fly books with sheepskin linings. The fly books are available in two sizes: a small version for nymphs and pupal imitations and a larger size designed for big nymphs and streamers.

Since completing the chapter on equipment and accessories, I have acquired two 32-compartment Wheatley fly boxes. The elegant F1609 Wheatley is available again. Mine are filled with a rich assortment of no-hackle patterns dressed by René Harrop, and a full spectrum of sedges I tied myself. The boxes are so beautiful that I enjoy simply looking at their spring-lid compartments.

Carrying rods on long trips has become a little easier these days. Wray cases are merely designed to protect rods and reels in use, and are padded holsters intended for carrying tackle in a car or van. These cases are fabricated of ballistic nylon layers that sandwich a thin neoprene padding between their tough covering.

River Systems is making a similar rod jacket, using a strong nylon shell outside, a middle cushioning layer of urethane foam, and an inner layer of smooth tricot. These rod covers are not holster-shaped.

Artful Angler is selling two recent systems of protecting tackle in travel. Their zippered case is sheathed in eight-ounce parapac synthetic, a high-density plastic stiffener, a cushioning filler of polyfoam, and a liner of four-ounce coated nylon. It holds aluminum rod cases in webbing loops, has nylon web handles, and a nylon coil-zipper system. The Mark Pack system is completely different. It offers an obviously strong design, although sad experience tells me it is unwise to suggest that any system is airline-proof. The Mark Pack consists of paired two-inch tubes wrapped together in eleven-ounce Cordura nylon. The system will take four rods in their cloth sacks, or two standard aluminum cases. The Mark Pack is completed with a carrying strap, nylon webbing handle, and a lock-and-key closure system.

Thomas & Thomas makes a rod-carry system for six aluminum cases. It is constructed of heavy-duty marine canvas reinforced with leather at the corners. It is water repellent. The shoulder strap and handle make transporting it quite easy, and the rugged nylon-zipper closure offers a locking-ring capability.

Orvis makes a combination rod blanket and caddy that is excellent too. Its blanket holds eight two-piece rods in their sacks, and it may also be used with rods in their cases. The blanket is intended to cushion the rods inside a rod caddy, but inside their cases, it can be used with the Orvis traveller bag. It is made of dark brown urethane Cordura. It is water repellent, stainproof, and resistant to ripping and fraying. Locking zippers are provided the full length of the Orvis travel caddy and its pouches.

Orvis has stopped making its earlier canvas rod caddies. They were trimmed with leather and had an ingenious combination of case pouches, rod loops, and a continuous flap. The caddy was tightly rolled and secured with three leather straps, and the design was completed with a handle and full-length carrying strap. It was Ted Trueblood who jokingly observed that you should buy any product you really liked, because they would stop making anything really good. My favorite rod caddy is copied from the original Orvis design. It is made of thick, softly tanned cowhide and was specially made in Buenos Aires.

But the best rod caddy I ever saw belonged to my good tarpon-fishing friend Rip McIntosh of Palm Beach, and was custom-made in Costa Rica. It was constructed around a six-inch lightweight pipe of polyvinylchloride. The core was quite rigid and strong. Its outer shell was saddle leather, with a cap and carrying strap system. The leather cap could be locked. The big case was a gargantuan version of the leather scabbard cases first made by Orvis for its little Rocky Mountain bamboo rods.

It was the best that I have seen. *It was beautiful, all right,* McIntosh explained wryly one night at Iliamna, *it was so beautiful somebody stole it!*

There is a lesson in that story.

Small gadgets continue to emerge from the tackle industry. Some quickly disappear, but others survive and prosper. Russ Peak has developed a new line dressing that repels water so effectively that a line rides demonstrably higher in the surface film. It conditions the finish and restores its fresh suppleness, and it lubricates the line too. The Peak formula is excellent, and makes pickups and shooting easier, as well as floating the line high.

Thomas & Thomas recommends the new Schmidt high-speed line conditioner. Unlike paste cleaners, this product comes in liquid form. It leaves a smooth high-speed finish that adds distance to any caster, and prolongs the fishing life of modern lines.

We were skeptical, Tom Dorsey explains, *but it really works!*

Maxima has also expanded beyond its nylon leader material line with a new polyvinyl conditioner called Mono Slik. It cleans and lubricates our modern plastic finishes, adds to fly-line life, and is highly recommended among anglers.

Although weighting leaders is not exactly a favorite fishing technique, it is a deadly method under some conditions. Weighted leaders quickly prove themselves in extremely fast, broken currents. Early season finds fish lying deep in high water, its chill making them dour and listless. Big Alaskan rainbows have become caviar addicts by September, after a summer of gorging themselves on freshly spawned salmon eggs. No salmon ova ever drifted anywhere except in the bottom currents, and such eggs arrive dead drift over the gravelly shallows. Weighting the leader slightly is a perfect solution to these problems, and anglers have long used split shot and lead-strip Twistons.

Although they obviously work effectively, split shot and thin lead strips are a bit crude. Using progressively smaller shot, with finer sizes stepping down toward the tippet, is a simple refinement. Using shorter and shorter lengths of lead strips can accomplish the same thing. But there are better methods today. The popular, reusable shot have little tabs that permit them to reopen, but they are asymmetrically weighted, and tend to create eccentric patterns of drift and flutter.

Thomas & Thomas offers a rotary assortment of tiny French split shot. Such minute shot are not used for fly fishing in Europe, but are designed for fishing coarse species like roach and tench and chub. It is a world of slender Calcutta rods and fine nylons and quill bobbers.

The largest shot is still smaller than regular BB-shot, Len Codella told me recently, *and the tiny ones are like skeet loads—small enough for 6X and 7X tippets.*

Fly-Rite Sleeves and Shape-A-Wate are two fresh concepts in leader weighting. The lead sleeves are soft little tubes that are slipped on the leader above its barrel knots. They come in four weights and diameters and are conveniently packaged in a rotary pack, but the sleeves involve building leader knots on the stream.

Shape-A-Wate is completely new. It consists of a malleable lead putty that can be molded on the leader with the fingers. It can be increased after trial and error, or decreased with the fingernails, pinching the lead and stripping it off.

However, my favorite method of weighting a leader involves familiar materials: lead wire in fly-tying diameters and clear head cement. Such fly-weighting wire is available in diameters of .015, .025, .035, .045, and .055 inches, which offer a subtle progression in weight. Leaders can be butt-weighted just above the barrel knots, using fewer turns and finer diameters to balance them for sink rate, drift behavior, and ease of casting. Such leaders can be created and modified in the field, but they are best made up ahead of time, with the precisely coiled lead wire seated carefully in fly-head lacquer.

Dermot Wilson introduced the Aymidge extractor several years ago in southern England. It was simply a rudimentary stomach pump, intended to extract the insects from a living trout's stomach. Several modifications have evolved since. One doctor friend was concerned enough about damaging a trout's alimentary tract, and the clumsy introduction of air into its stomach, that he redesigned the concept. His design was more complex and six times as costly to fabricate. Thomas & Thomas offers a simple, new stomach analysis pump in its catalogue. It is similar to the first Aymidge design, with a slim polyvinyl tube and a finger bulb. It should be used with skill and care.

Monocle-type loupe magnifiers are available for anglers today. Such loupes offer two-and-a-half-power magnification; unlike loupe glasses, they are not permanently attached to our glasses frames. The loupe monocle frees both hands, and is carried in a fishing vest.

It turns midges into Wulffs, Len Codella laughs.

Thomas & Thomas also stocks a ten-power glass for studying insects and knot problems afield. It folds compactly into its own nickel-plated case. It is inexpensive and workable, and it can be attached to a pin-on lanyard cord inside a tackle vest.

Field entomology and fly-tying will both benefit from a stainless scale that offers graduations in both inches and millimeters.

Fishing clothes are changing too.

Cold-weather garments, rain gear, and other equipment are steadily improving. Even fishing gloves have changed. British Millar Mitts have long been available to anglers and duck hunters. They are hand-crocheted to fit snugly, and are eighty-five percent wool, keeping the fingers warm even when the wool is soaking wet. The fingertips are left free, offering good cold-weather dexterity.

Orvis Poly Mitts are woven from warm nonabsorbent polypropylene, and fit even more snugly than Millar gloves. When they are wet, you merely wring them out and they feel dry almost immediately. The cuffs are elastic and fit tightly. Poly Mitts leave the fingertips free, like the British designs, but they lack the scratchiness of wool.

Down-filled garments have achieved widespread popularity in recent years. Many have proved excellent. Designs that are fully quilted are better than those designs with tubular down-filled sections, because full quilting holds the down in place.

Tubular sections permit the down insulation to gravitate into lumps, leaving other areas relatively unprotected. Feathers are obviously less effective than down itself. Pale colors and bright chromatic hues are clearly ill-suited for fishing, and the bright yellow slicker is a laughable choice for the pursuit of trout. Camouflage is recommended, although it has echoes of the war-surplus stores, and it is not useful everywhere. Every season we see fishermen wearing camouflage clothing on western meadow streams, obviously secure in the belief that they are hidden from the trout. Contrast is the key factor, and in the late meadows the color of a newly made broom, camouflage is visible for miles.

Orvis produces a superb piece of cold-weather equipment in its Three-in-One jacket. It consists of a Gore-Tex windbreaker shell with four pockets that sheds rain well. The Gore-Tex shell has a superb quilted-down liner that zips out and fastens at the neck and cuffs. Although it is pocketless, it is a fine jacket in its own right. There is also a Gore-Tex down-filled rain hood that clips on the collar securely. The jacket gets its name from its wearers' options: the windbreaker rain jacket, the down jacket worn separately, and the rain shell and down liner worn together. It has served me well in mountain country and fishing the arctic latitudes of Iceland and Norway and Alaska.

However, the Orvis Three-in-One has fallen a partial victim to the Trueblood Factor. It was originally made in khaki and camouflage, but so many waterfowlers bought it that the khaki option was dropped. It is such a versatile garment that perhaps Orvis will elect to make its less-military design available again.

Orvis offers several fishing hats today. Its perennial favorite, the Irish wool tweed hat, which seems to have an alchemy capable of changing its owner's personality, is still available on its Vermont shelves. Irish fishing hats are stocked in olive Donegal, gray, and houndstooth tweeds. The Orvis Longbill hat is highly popular with guides in the Florida Keys, and offers a green underbrim to control glare. The Longbill shades the eyes quite well. Its rear brim folds down to protect the ears and neck from a searing sun, and also sheds rain outside the collar. Although it looks a little strange on trout streams, it is an excellent item of fishing gear. Orvis also makes a soft, folding helmet of tan poplin with a green brim liner to reduce glare. It is a fine hot-weather fishing hat with hooded air vents on its sides. Orvis recently introduced its folding black-fly headnet hat. Its design consists of a rain-shedding skullcap with a mesh hood that includes a circular stiffener just above the shoulders. It can be worn both with and without a regular hat. Fishermen who have suffered the summer mosquitoes of our western high country and Alaska, or have fought the fierce black flies of the Labrador, will welcome an Orvis headnet so light and compact it can be folded and stowed in a fishing vest.

Orvis makes several pieces of outstanding rain gear too. Its hooded wading jacket is designed for wearing over waders and a fishing vest. It has two wide-flap outside pockets for temporary storage of the flies and other gadgets you are using in the rain. Such details eliminate the fussing to get inside your rain gear to replace a tippet or fly, and then button up against the weather again. Its hood and cuffs have drawstrings.

Gore-Tex is a remarkable fabric.

It is completely waterproof, yet it inhibits perspiration, the *bête noire* of other foul-weather clothing. Gore-Tex consists of a film sandwiched between fabrics that breathe. Its waterproof film is a technical breakthrough that literally offers billions of microscopic pores. The pores are too small to pass water molecules in their liquid state, but water vapor and air pass through freely.

Testing has demonstrated that a vigorously exercising person produces as much as 2,500 grams of perspiration per square meter of skin.

Government studies determined that Gore-Tex is capable of transpiring up to 4,800 grams of moisture per square meter when it is laminated to fabrics that breathe too. It has quickly proved itself in the field.

The Orvis rainsuit includes both a hooded jacket and rain pants. Its fabric sandwiches the Gore-Tex film to a poplin composed of eighty-seven percent polyester and thirteen percent cotton. The jacket is thirty inches long and is fitted with a nylon zipper. Its zipper is covered with a Velcro-sealed storm flap. There are two small bellows pockets with large Velcro flaps too. Behind the cargo pockets are side-vent pocket hand warmers. The jacket has a raglan cut to facilitate active sports, and it has adjustable gusseted cuffs with Velcro tabs. Seams are waterproofed with tape and sealed. The matching rain pants offer similar construction, suspender buttons, and a drawstring waist. There are snap adjustment tabs at the ankles. Both jacket and trousers are fully lined.

Orvis also makes a crusher hat in a matching fabric and construction. It has introduced a Gore-Tex Longbill fishing hat too, designed for rain and wind, which keeps raindrops off your sunglasses and rainwater dripping outside your collar.

Old things are often worth keeping, and both silk and cotton are in this category. Leigh Perkins at Orvis understands such truths.

Silk and cotton are superb.

Silk is still the lightest, warmest insulation worn against the skin. Its qualities have long been understood in skiing circles. Orvis still offers undergarments cut from the finest Chinese silk, in both men's and women's sizes. Silk long johns are matched with long-sleeved T-shirts, and these silk garments are excellent.

Orvis has included cotton knit shirts in its recent catalogues. Both T-shirts and turtlenecks are listed. The cotton knit is relatively light and is a handsome olive khaki. These light cotton shirts are intended for layering under other garments, but can also be worn by themselves.

Marathon is still making conventional fishing slickers and rain jackets, which are considerably less expensive than Gore-Tex.

The Marathon slicker is made of lightweight vulcanized rubber over a seventy-denier nylon. It has a seamless raglan-style shoulder to facilitate casting. There is an attached drawstring hood, cuff snaps, and a back shoulder-vent design to reduce perspiration. Its fingertip length will cover hip-boot tops. It weighs only fourteen ounces.

The Marathon rain jacket weighs only six ounces and is cut from the same seventy-denier nylon coated with rubber. It also has an attached hood and elastic wrist cuffs. Like the slicker, the jacket has a fully zippered front covered with a storm fly, and two front pockets.

Marathon has also introduced a quilted rain parka at the top of its line. It consists of a rubber coating over a seventy-denier shell, and it has a drawstring hood, elastic wrists, a full-length zipper, and a storm fly. It is fingertip length and dark green. Unlike the slicker and wading-jacket designs, the rain parka has an insulative lining of nylon quilting. It is highly recommended for Alaska, Iceland, and the Labrador.

The matching rain hat is a crushable design of rubber-coated nylon. It is fully lined with cotton. The generous brim protects face, glasses, and neck, and there are concealed fold-out earflaps.

Polyester pile has recently been introduced to many sporting garments, and it has quickly acquired fierce partisans.

Polypropylene absorbs surprisingly little moisture, and in pile insulation, it wicks dampness away from the body so its warmth can evaporate it. When polyester pile is wet, wringing it out carefully will restore almost its full insulating qualities. It offers twice the insulation of wool at only half its weight. Like wool, synthetic pile retains its loft when wet, trapping air to sustain its insulation. No down-filled garment can match the performance of polypropylene and wool when it is soaked through. Perhaps the best-known fabric of this polypropylene specification is Patagonia cloth.

Patagonia makes a lightweight zip-front jacket with Velcro-cuff closure. There is a chest pocket of nylon, and the design includes two hand-warming pockets. The matching pile trousers feature a drawstring top and a single hip pocket. Both are dark navy blue.

Patagonia also produces a polypropylene underwear it calls expedition weight. It was designed for bitter conditions. Its fabric is a tight rib-knit type with a thickly brushed insulation. The tops are a three-button design with long sleeves; bottoms are completed wtih a spandex waistband, ankle cuffs, and fly. Both are also dark navy.

Fishing glasses have evolved quickly in these past months, adding polarization to the exquisite technology of photochromatic lenses. Such lenses are quite new. Their high-quality, optically ground glass is virtually distortion-free, and its lamination is guaranteed. Polarization extensively reduces glare and allows a fisherman to see fish more clearly. Their photosensitive glass also responds to varying levels of light, darkening at midday and becoming clear at nightfall. Such performance can mean substantially less eye fatigue in fishing.

The new sunglasses have handsome pilot-type frames, and come in tints of amber and gray. It is also possible to have these lenses in both single and bifocal prescriptions, although such technology is expensive. Amber lenses are like the familiar shooting glasses, which magnify lower levels of light on cloudy days, evenings, and early in the morning. Gray photochromatic lenses offer minimal color distortion, which is important in matching hatches. Both lenses are abrasion resistant and tempered, offering good protection to the eyes while fishing.

Several new wrinkles have also been added to survival equipment in the past five years.

Cutter insect repellent is still a leader in its field, and although it is expensive, it contains such a concentrated formula that a little works quite well. It has excellent skin life, does not smell noxious, and is not greasy.

Another product more recently introduced is called After Bite, and it contains an analgesic and subtle anesthetic that quickly relieves bites and stings. Both products really work.

Thomas & Thomas sells a pocket mini-screwdriver with its own protective cap and lanyard ring. It is about two inches in length, and has a one-sixteenth-inch screwdriver blade. The mini-driver is perfectly suited to repairing sunglasses and reels.

Another intriguing gadget from Thomas & Thomas is a magnesium tool for starting fires. Skillful use of this simple device triggers sparks of 5,400 degrees, sufficient to ignite even damp combustibles. The tool is only three inches long, but it ignites tinder quickly with its unique sparking insert, and it might save a life in the back country.

Thomas & Thomas also lists the old-fashioned infantry can openers, along with an ingenious pocket saw. The saw is a strong, abrasive wire with steel rings at opposite ends. It cuts firewood easily, and can be simply held taut between the hands, or fitted with a bowed handle of bent willow. Such a willow handle is easily rigged in the field, using either heavy leader material or fishing line.

Randall Kaufmann offers another unique item in his survival straw. It is a pocket water purifier that meets federal standards, and works instantly while water is sipped through its core system. It works without waiting, unlike boiling or the tablets issued in army kits, and it works on stagnant pools, turbid lakes, and streams, and water with high coliform counts. The water-purifying straw is intriguing.

Ever want a drink with cow-pies lying everywhere along the water? Kaufmann asks teasingly. *Carry the straw and you can!*

The perfect survival item for the collector of fine gadgetry is the Austrian flare pistol. It is a tiny nickel-plated pistol sold with a set of flares no larger than firecrackers. The Austrian mini-pistol fires a flare high enough to be spotted by rescue craft. It seems like an elegant toy, but it might save lives in a wilderness emergency.

Another recent experiment with a survival gadget was a laughable failure, but its testing did not occur at a critical moment of truth. Last year, when I was getting my equipment together for a trip into the Katmai wilderness of Alaska, a neighbor invited me for a drink. It was a welcome relief from packing. My hostess keeps several pets, has a surprisingly well-stocked aviary, and pampers a large herd of whitetail deer on the grounds of her estate.

She was worried about our trip. *It's the bears!* she blurted finally. *I'm worried about the bears!*

The Katmai has no shortage of bears, and it is not unusual to encounter them along its shallow rivers when the sockeyes are running. Sometimes we see a dozen bears in a day's fishing. My neighbor gave me a combination flashlight and tiny siren. It was designed for a woman's purse, and its batteries triggered a noise that was startlingly shrill.

It's for muggers, she explained.

Finishing my whisky, I promised to test her theory that its shrill warning would frighten the salmon-fishing bears. The gadget proved a complete failure in its field test, but my neighbor found that difficult to believe.

You really tried it? she challenged.

I tried it so many times on the Brooks, I told her puckishly, *that its batteries went dead the first day—and the bears never looked up!*

In early 1984, in New Zealand, fishing a remote gorge on the upper Ngaruroro with Hugh MacDowell of Rotorua, I lost a beautifully made landing net. It was the work of Arthur Le Clair, whose shop is at South Windsor, Connecticut. The net was lost in a strange mishap.

We had been dropped into the gorge by Toby Clark, whose brightly lacquered Hughes 500C is usually employed in professional deer hunting. Clark had collected us at Turangi, where we were staying at the Tongariro Lodge. The helicopter climbed into the gentle mountains east of Lake Taupo. The young pilot crossed the ridges, our whirring shadow leapfrogging across the thickly grown beech forests, and we crossed the pampas grass meadows in the headwaters, sliding sharply to follow the narrow gorge downstream. The river wound tightly against the steep pumice cliffs, startlingly clear and the color of polished jade.

MacDowell studied the cliffs and river crossing as the pilot flew the river, tilting the helicopter to study its pools. *It's still a little high,* MacDowell shouted. *Might be hard to wade the crossings.*

Lots of landing sites, the pilot yelled.

They decided to land a mile farther downstream, flaring high in a climbing turn, and fluttering down toward a rocky bar. We quickly gathered our gear, ducking under the windmilling rotor, and the engine roared again. The brightly striped helicopter hung briefly, hovering nose-down in a maelstrom of leaves and debris, and then climbed out in a towering parabola.

Pilots! MacDowell laughed and shook his head. *They're all wild men!*

We quickly rigged our tackle. The sun was just reaching a swift pool upstream, but we waited to let the fish forget the helicopter. We were both excited. It had been a year since I had fished the Ngaruroro, one of the best in New Zealand.

We took a big rainbow from the first pool, a strong cockfish that ran me deep into the backing, and finally surrendered sixty yards downstream. It was a handsome fish, brightly colored and hookbilled. The trout recovered quickly and bolted back into the swift currents upstream. It was a fine beginning, but the next pools were unproductive.

MacDowell looked upstream and frowned. *We've got trouble.*

It was a big pool between steep pumice cliffs. Its tail shallows were still and clear, with a dark gravelly beach on the right. Thickly grown manuka and flax and pampas grass covered the cliffs. Two good rainbows were cruising restlessly, and they bolted when a cormorant flew over.

Bloody shag! MacDowell grumbled.

The fish refused to settle, working back and forth in fifteen feet of water. We tried them briefly, but they were too deep and I stripped off my vest to switch reels. My spare held a sinking six-weight double taper, but when it was rigged the fish were gone.

MacDowell was gone too. *I'm up here,* he yelled. *How are you at rock climbing?*

You serious? I laughed.

Small pebbles rattled into a still backwater from the manuka thickets. MacDowell was working along the cliffs slowly, and I swallowed hard and followed him.

It was unfamiliar work.

The fractured lava outcroppings were covered with lichens and wild flowers, and I searched patiently for footholds with my wading brogues. Tough manuka branches offered support when our footholds were too far apart. My fingers worked deep into the moss, testing the lava outcroppings before trusting them. The jade-green pool looked ten to fifteen feet deep under our traverse, and it looked deeper when I finally reached the big ledge.

Don't move! MacDowell spoke urgently.

The ledge was well up the pool, although it was still mostly in shadow. It offered about ten feet of rocky platform that shelved off into the emerald heart of the pool.

What's there? I whispered.

Look upstream, MacDowell pointed from the bushes. *Forty feet above the ledge!*

The dark shadow across the pool?

That's right, he said.

You're crazy, I laughed nervously. *It's too big for a fish—it's only a rock.*

Watch it a while, MacDowell replied.

We both moved stealthily in the shadows and crouched low. The sun was bright, working deep into the throat of the pool. The dark chocolate-colored shape seemed farther upstream, and it drifted slowly toward midstream.

You're right, I whispered excitedly. *It moved out into the current.*

And it's nymphing, he said.

The big shadow ranged back and forth in the bright sun, intercepting food drifting into the throat of the pool. It was lying too deep, even for a six-weight sinking line. Most of the ledge was still in shadow, and I duck-walked into position. Several long roll-casts dropped well above the fish, but the current was deceptively swift under its smooth surface, and the sink-rate failed to drift deep enough.

There was no backcast space for a right-handed caster. But a horizontal stroke worked backhand dropped the fly thirty-five feet beyond the fish, settling far to its right. I mended a long belly out into midstream, teased the sinking line under the surface, and watched the fish.

That might do it! MacDowell said.

He's drifting to the right! I whispered.

He's got to see it!

The line bellied deep off the ledge and I started a gentle retrieve. *What's he doing?* Suddenly the line stopped.

You've got him! MacDowell laughed.

Maybe it's bottom!

The bottom was stripping line from the reel. The great chocolate shadow bolted high into the throat of the pool, darting and writhing and catching the light.

The fight took ninety minutes. The fish fought stubbornly along the ledges in the upper pool. Finally I turned it, and it swam past us majestically, almost bored with the steady pressure of my six-weight boron.

It's a big brown! I gasped.

He's the best one I've seen hooked on this river, MacDowell grinned, *and he's huge!*

His adipose fin is legal! I joked.

The great trout simply explored the entire pool at will, coming back grudgingly from its lower shallows, struggling with patient strokes of its spade-size tail. The fight was almost dreamlike, a series of slow figure-eight circuits past our outcropping, straining head-down toward the bottom in the emerald water, where every pebble was visible. It jumped once, a clumsy pirouette less than thirty feet away, and fell back.

Like a sow trying to fly! MacDowell sighed.

The last act was sullen infighting, like two boxers too stubborn to clinch, and the big trout kept edging under our ledge. My arms were getting tired. The great tail was fluttering now, rolling in the surface. Its strokes sent waves spreading down the current. Finally I worked it close, turned it toward the motionless net, and took it with a quick sweep.

Its tail writhed back and forth above the rim, its ugly head threshing deep in the meshes, and the bag tore slightly. Our outcropping had a shallow pool in its fissures, and I folded the trout in the meshes, laying it in the water. It measured thirty-two inches, a perfectly shaped henfish that weighed twelve pounds. The little mayfly nymph was firmly seated in its jaws, and I shot several pictures with my old Leica.

The film ran out. *Damn!* I muttered. *The film always runs out!* I broke open a fresh cassette.

MacDowell nursed the fish, holding it facing into the current while I rewound the film and opened the camera. Its butt-plate and fresh film were tucked into my waders, and I was sealing the old cassette in its cannister when he brought the fish back.

The camera was open, wedged into my fishing vest, as I threaded the fresh film on its spindle. The cassette slipped into place, and I was working the film to fit the sprocket when the fish thrashed wildly.

The net arched high into the river.

Holding the partially loaded camera, I watched it settle in the current, turning over slowly like a leaf in the green water. The pool was fifteen feet deep below our ledge. It was impossible to follow along the cliffs. We still had the great trout in the shallow pool, its eye watching me balefully, gills working. We watched helplessly as my net drifted into the gathering shallows, and was caught in the rapids.

My God! I said unhappily. *How will I ever explain it to the man who made it?*

Just tell him what happened, he said quietly.

But it's gone!

When a net has to die, MacDowell smiled. *It should die like that!*

And we released the fish.

OBSERVATIONS ON THE MODERN FLY REEL

The developments in fly reels over the past few years have been both surprising and extensive. Changes have included the revival of old classics, which happily are back in production, and fresh examples of unusual new technologies.

Berkeley and Cortland were the first to explore recently developed materials. Their reels employ modern nylon and carbon-fiber materials in their frames and spools.

Berkeley introduced its reels first.

Its Specialist 2 and Berkeley 556 were the prototypes. Their spools were nylon and the backplates and frames were aluminum. Both designs display an unusual spindle technology, using a heavy tubular concept that has influenced later reels. The Specialist 2 easily converted to left- or right-hand wind, offered three drag settings, and incorporated a smooth-acting thumb brake.

The still newer Berkeley 500 has enlarged on these concepts, has corrected some of the spool problems first encountered with using nylon, and the aluminum reel frame is a single casting. Both are finished in a handsome nonglare black. Left- and right-hand wind is possible, and there are still three drag settings. Berkeley 500 reels include the 554 model, which weighs $2\frac{7}{8}$ ounces and is designed for four- to five-weight lines. The 556 weighs only $3\frac{5}{8}$ ounces and carries five- to seven-weight tapers. The 558 weighs a surprisingly little $3\frac{3}{4}$ ounces, and its capacity will handle eight- to ten-weight forward tapers. These hybrid reels of nylon and aluminum offer superb capacity-to-weight ratios, and at a surprisingly reasonable cost.

Cortland was the innovative firm that first experimented with carbon-fiber reels. Its exclusive CG series of reels is unique.

Graphite reels are a remarkable thirty percent lighter than aluminum reels of comparable size. Such lightness makes it possible to achieve the old bamboo rod-to-reel weight ratios with light synthetic rods of boron and graphite. These prototypes were almost unbreakable and self-lubricating. The entire reel, including its internal ratchets and drag-system fittings, is fashioned of carbon-fiber fabric. There are three sizes in this series: its little CG I is a $2\frac{1}{8}$-inch reel weighing a surprising $2\frac{1}{2}$ ounces, the CG II measures $3\frac{1}{2}$ inches and weighs $2\frac{3}{4}$ ounces, and the CG III is a 4-inch reel weighing 3 ounces. Line capacity is comparable to conventional reels of such diameters. The Cortland CG reels come in a doeskin vinyl bag, are relatively inexpensive, and offer a unique capacity-to-weight ratio.

Except for the esthetically arbitrary ventilation pattern in their spools, the CG reels are quite handsome. The ventilation pattern is found close to the spindle, where it is critical if long casts and runs have occurred. There is no ventilation of the outer spool, where a fly line is most often wet.

Other reel news is less happy.

The Hart reels introduced a few years ago, and the Thomas & Thomas series based on the same prototypes, are no longer available. Sometimes mere excellence is not enough.

The elegant Walker reels are another tragic example. Like the Hart designs, the Walkers were the heirs to the patents and prestige of earlier makers like Conroy, Vom Hofe, and Zwarg. Their excellence echoes other jewellike machines bearing marques like Lagonda, Lamborghini, and Daimler-Benz. The reels still featured the closed-frame designs first patented in 1896, with their black side plates and German silver rims, and their elegant counterweighted handles.

The beautiful Walker reels are gone too, and the fishing world is less. *Some things should live,* my old friend Jim Rikhoff argues bitterly. *Sometimes I hate change!*

George Gehrke is a tacklemaker from southern Colorado, and is familiar with the big-fish water on the lower Arkansas. His country has been a crossroads in the history of the southern Rockies. Gehrke lives in the place the Spanish horse soldiers christened Salida, because it was their exit from the Sangre de Cristo basin into the heart of the Colorado high country farther north.

It's the roof of America. The old-timers in the Arkansas headwaters sat talking and whittling outside the Vendôme hotel in Leadville. *There ain't no rivers running into this country—they're born here!*

George Gehrke has long been known for his excellent dry-fly ointment called Gink, and in recent years he introduced a fine fly-wetting solution he wryly christened Xink. Gehrke is restless and peripatetic, and now he has turned his curiosity to reels.

His first reels were machined in Japan and were named in honor of George Selwyn Marryat, perhaps the finest British trout fisherman of the nineteenth century.

There were five Marryat reels in the original series. The basic concept of the Marryat series was similar to the Bogdan prototypes for Orvis, which evolved into the famous CFO line. The backplate and spindle are part of the reel frame. But other than its reel-shoe mounting and T-head spacer, the Marryat had no reel cage enclosing its spool. It was a brightly anodized gold. The reels were quite light for their line capacity, almost seeming fragile, and had a clumsy Victorian-looking medallion attached to the backplate. Some of the Marryat prototypes were imperfectly finished, and the spool-locking mechanism seemed too vulnerable to river silts and abrasives. It featured a deep-locking pin that seemed unlikely to self-drain well, and some expert fishermen complained about the bright finish and its visibility to skittish trout.

However, its internal improvements over other lightweight trout reels were less obvious. The reel shoe is not attached to the frame with rivets, which can work loose in time, but with tiny Phillips Screws. The ratchet and drag were unique, and proved better than the spring-and-pawl system found in the Hardy lightweight series and its several cousins.

The Gehrke design offered a surprising drag-setting capability in a light trout reel, and a solidly machined new concept.

His first Marryat reels had exposed-rim spools that were spool-drilled on their handle faces. The drag mechanisms were based upon a ratchet dish set on the spindle post. Both were machined from corrosion-resistant steel, and the spindle bearings were bronze. The cover plate was a bronze ratchet wheel. Spring-loaded pawls were pinned inside the ratchet dish. The assembly was solid and smooth.

The drag yoke is a fresh concept. It functions without moving parts, except for a cam-actuated setting centered on a Phillips-head screw. The yoke is shaped like a wishbone. Its drag shoes are fitted into notches at its tips, and an increased drag setting simply forces the yoke tips down more tightly into the ratchet-dish rim.

It is surprisingly simple and reliable.

The first drag shoes worried me, and I challenged Gehrke about their composition. *Don't worry,* he telephoned from Colorado, *I've already changed them—sent you a new yoke this morning!*

Gehrke is restless and quixotic.

His restlessness soon abandoned the first Marryat series, and I later found a dark chocolate-colored Marryat in the mail. It was a wide-frame Marryat MR-9. The prototype MR-8 designs had featured a 1 1/8-inch spool-and-frame assembly. The MR-9 had a 1 5/8-inch spool-and-frame width. Both the MR-8 and MR-9 were 3 1/8 inches in diameter. The reel-foot alloy and machining were obviously improved, the drag settings simplified, and Gehrke had wisely removed the ornate medallion from its backplate. The wide spool was counterweighted to reduce its wobble, a necessary modification that worked. But its monogrammed brass trapezoid was poorly designed, making one wonder why a simple dome-shaped weight was not tried instead, like the spool counterweights of older Victorian designs.

Gehrke has since changed his mind again.

His Marryat has been transformed into his Centurion II series. It is no longer manufactured in Japan, but is now machined here. It still has its smooth spool flange, which can be rim controlled with either fingertips or palms. With a drag-free setting, the reel still cannot overspin when a strong fish bolts. The drag yoke offers a full two pounds of drag, a setting that is unique in such a light fly reel. Centurion reels have passed some difficult tests. Prototypes have been immersed in a fifteen percent saltwater solution for twenty-five days without sign of corrosion. The reels have also been tested at 6,000 revolutions per minute, and passed those ordeals without wear on their stainless shafts and bronze bearings, with virtually no wobble.

Len Codella at Thomas & Thomas is quite excited about the Centurion reels. *Those reels have beaten tarpon better than a hundred pounds*, he said, *and you know about their reel-eating runs!*

Machined from solid aluminum bar stock, the Centurion series includes five models. The GR 70 is designed for four-weight lines and 150 yards of twelve-pound backing. The GR 75 takes a five-weight and 200 yards of backing, while the GR 80 holds a six-weight ahead of 250 yards. The GR 85 holds either seven- or eight-weight lines and 200 yards of twenty-pound backing line. The biggest Gehrke reel is the GR 90, which holds a ten- to eleven-weight line, with as much as 300 yards of Dacron.

The scope of recent innovation in fly-reel technology is quite unusual, considering that when compared to other sports, like skiing and golf, the fly-fishing market is virtually a cottage industry.

Hardy has been quite active too.

My earlier chapter on reels reported that the British makers were considering the return of old favorites like the Saint John, Saint George, and Perfect.

Those revivals subsequently took place.

The Saint John is still made only in the $3^7/8$-inch heavy trout size, weighing a full $8^1/2$ ounces. The elegant Saint George still has its beautiful drilled-spool design and agate line guard, which is mounted in a circle of German silver. It is also made only in a relatively large size, the $3^1/2$-inch model that weighs $7^3/4$ ounces. Other popular models remain buried in the archives.

The Hardy Perfect has its own iconography. Our reverence for the Perfect has gathered religious intensity since its introduction in 1891. Its current incarnation is machined from more modern aluminum alloys. Our modern Perfects are slightly lighter in weight than the nineteenth-century prototypes. The small, truncated cone that secures the pedestal to the revolving handle plate is a concession to contemporary metalworking. The Perfects are machined to remarkably fine tolerances. The spindle is fitted with a circle of self-lubricating bronze alloy bearings, to produce its unusually smooth character and life-span. Perfects have three basic components: the perforated backplate and cage, the lightweight spool, and the solid reel-handle plate. The Perfects are made only in right-hand wind, and are not reversible. The $3^1/8$-inch model weighs $7^1/2$ ounces, and the intermediate $3^3/8$-inch Perfect weighs 8 ounces. The $3^5/8$-inch design is $8^1/2$ ounces. The Perfect series is revered for its solidity and its smooth running, rather than its lightness.

There are many anglers, myself included, who regret that the exquisite small Saint George reels have not been resurrected. There is still a single original in my collection.

Scientific Anglers has stopped selling its British-made reels, but Hardy found sufficient demand for these exposed-rim designs to keep making them at their Northumberland factory.

The reels have been given a new name, but the Hardy Marquis is essentially the old System series first introduced by Scientific Anglers. The reel cages of the Marquis are slightly lighter than the machining of the Hardy Lightweights. The spools are slightly heavier, between the exposed flange and a much heavier ratchet. The Marquis features a single pawl, and a unique circular spring encased in neoprene. It is a superb design, and American anglers are grateful to Harrich for keeping it available.

It's such a fine reel, Ted Rowe explained in his offices outside Boston. *We had no choice when 3M stopped selling them—keep making them!*

Hardy is still making the System models available before, from the 2¾-inch Marquis Four to the 3¾-inch Marquis Ten. The British market has caused Hardy to add a pair of larger models too, since Hardy is no longer making its salmon-sized Saint Andrews in the Lightweight series, and its drag-spring system had proved itself brittle on salmon. The Marquis Series has two recent models: its 3⅞-inch spool sized to take 200 yards of backing behind a WF-10-F line, and a completely new 4⅛-inch reel that can hold 250 yards of backing with a WF-11-F saltwater taper. Western trout fishermen have adopted these big Marquis models happily in their autumn quests after big browns. The reels offer enough backing to make them feel secure on the alligator-size hookbills they find at Fontenelle dam on the Green, on the Big Horn in its arid Indian country, and between reservoirs in the Missouri Breaks.

Cortland continues to introduce new reels. Its Crown II series offers three sizes, with vented spools and rim-control flanges. The internal drag system is adjustable. There are no screws, the reel frame is a single aluminum casting, and the reels are reversible for either right- or left-hand winds. The small 3¼-inch model is designed for four- and five-weight lines, and the 3½-inch Cortland takes six- to eight-weight tapers. The 3⅝-inch design is intended for eight- and nine-weight lines, and 150 yards of backing on big-trout rivers.

We're proud of the Crown series, Leon Chandler told me at Boxborough this winter, *proud of both its quality and its price.*

Cortland has also introduced its new Graphite LTD series this past year. Like its Cortland Crown II reels, the LTD series offers three sizes. The spools are perforated to ventilate the line. The line guard is a two-way agate design, the spools are reversible for both right- and left-hand wind, and unlike the earlier Cortland graphites, its spool also offers rim-control drag. The reels are practically unbreakable, and are smooth running, with an excellent system of internal drag.

Sage has surprised fishermen with its recent introduction of a reel series, matching the superb glass and graphite rods they introduced at several western expositions in 1979.

We were excited by these rods at the show casting pools, but I did not actually fish one until I tried a six-weight on the Kulik, during an Alaskan trip the following year. It belonged to Les Eichorn, who was one of the founding officers at Sage. *We make a pretty rod that casts like crazy,* Eichorn told me over dinner in Sacramento. *We should make a reel to match it!*

Sage introduced those reels recently, and they are just as Eichorn promised that night, even to a richly anodized finish in a dark brown that matches the chocolate color of Sage graphite rods.

The British craftsmanship is obvious. The reels have the strength of a full-cage frame and are machined from a single billet of high-strength aluminum bar stock. The rolled-flange spool is intended for finger and palm work, and is mounted on a precise carbon-steel spindle. The adjustable drag-and-click system echoes the Hardy Lightweights. The drag setting, handle, spindle, cap, line guard, drag-spring studs, regulator screw and cover plate, pawl studs, and reel-foot rivets are entirely nickel silver. The click mechanism and drag system convert from left- to right-hand wind. The fittings and specifications are first-rate, and the final touch of elegance is the registered serial number on each Sage reel.

The Sage 505 is designed for light trout fishing. It measures $3^3/16$ inches and is sized for four- and five-weight lines. The 506 is a medium-size reel of $3^1/2$ inches that takes five- and six-weight tapers with a workable backing capacity. The 509 reel is the workhouse model in the Sage line, since it is $3^3/4$ inches in diameter, weighs $8^1/2$ ounces, and will store 240 yards of Dacron behind a WF-9-F line. Sage reels are handsomely made, richly colored, and worth their slightly higher price.

Fenwick has also surprised the fishing world with its new series of fly reels, although a firm that developed the first graphite rods should be expected to explore fresh ground.

Jim Green is responsible for these innovations, in both rod tapers and reels, and is among the finest tournament casters who ever lived. The new World Class reel series is the result of his collaboration with a circle of exceptionally talented engineers in Seattle, a center of high-technology aircraft firms. It was such proximity that led Fenwick to develop the first fly rods made of carbon graphite, when that material was still an aerospace oddity.

The Class 2 Fenwick is a light-trout design. It offers a strong cage of solid aluminum bar stock that has a handsome gold finish. Its perforated spool is anodized in a matte-black finish, with a gold spindle-cam cover. It is designed for trout fishing, and except for its coloring, it looks much like other expensive reels; but its important differences lie between its spool and backplate.

Our drag system is unique, Green argues.

The system has two separately adjustable controls: One monitors its click tension, and the other controls drag itself. Since these controls are separate, the Fenwick can be converted to either right- or left-hand wind without removing its spool. There are no pawls to change or install backwards. Each control button adjusts the setting between its prestressed spring and its separate pawl. The result is a wider spectrum of drag settings than other reels. Its minimum is capable of damping spool overrun, and its maximum setting is a fivefold increase. It is a superb system for most trout fishing.

The Class 4 Fenwick, along with the Class 6 and Class 8 Heavy-Duty models, features a completely different drag concept.

It offers a multiple-disk clutch system that poses carbon-steel plates against shoes of oil-impregnated bronze alloy. Fenwick believes that these materials offer significant advantages over other reels, which usually offer drag shoes of cork, leather, or mica. Metal to metal offers excellent dissipation of heat and will wear longer. And such older drag shoes cannot lubricate themselves like alloys of oil-impregnated bronze. The Fenwick alloys also resist deformation during long fights with big fish, or when a drag setting is fully tightened.

Its drag mechanism is different as well. Other reels exhibit a direct relationship between drag settings and rewind resistance. The Fenwick is free of such parallels. Its drag-loading system is completely independent of its spool, and it turns easily regardless of its drag.

The drag system is really tough, Jim Green describes it with quiet pride. *We've stripped four hundred yards off our bigger reels at thirty miles an hour—and there was no binding or fading.*

The Class 4 Fenwick is a direct-drive reel ideally suited to big water and large trout. It has a solid-plate spool that is counterweighted to damp its wobble at high rates of spin. The Class 6 model is of identical size, but has an exposed drag-setting disk and has antireverse drive. The Class 8 Fenwick is a big reel too muscular for trout fishing—it has been designed for billfish and tarpon.

It's a little more than you need for trout, Green comments quietly and smiles.

Orvis has busily added new reels to its catalogues in recent years. Its Battenkill series may not appear unusual, but these reels conceal some remarkable new technology behind their solemn façades, and at a surprisingly low price.

The Battenkill Mark series is alone in offering elegant trout reels cast from modern magnesium alloys. Their strength and lightness, relative to their line capacity, is unique. The one-piece frame (the reel foot is an integral part of the casting) and the spool are both cast from high-technology alloys. Like the more expensive CFO series, there is no reel cage to enclose the spool, and the wide spool flange permits finger drag and palming. The drag system employs a single-pawl spring. Conversion from right- to left-hand wind is easy, and the chromium line guard is switched with a common screwdriver. Unlike many reels, the backplates of the Battenkill series are fully drilled and ventilated.

We're excited about them, Leigh Perkins explains excitedly, *and our new Catinos are exciting too!*

The Catino reels now offered at Orvis were originally designed for salt water, but like the smaller Bogdans and Fin-Nors, they have started to attract some big-trout partisans.

Catino reels are elegant trucks, and if the delicate CFO is a finely tuned Jaguar, the Catino is a Kenworth or Peterbilt. Both its spool and its cage are machined from costly H-18 5056 aluminum bar stock, with heavy spacers and reel-foot designs. The bottom spacer is unusually wide, to provide a bearing surface for palming the spool that protects the hand from wildly spinning loops of line. There is no reel cage, but the spindle is machined from a highly tempered alloy of magnesium-chrome steel, rooted in the strong 5056 backplate. Other components and fittings are either corrosion-resistant steel or hard-anodized aluminum. The spools are a gunmetal finish, with polished bronze spindle caps and counterweights that reduce high-speed wobble. The Catino Bonefish is a 3½-inch reel weighing 6¼ ounces, with a capacity of 200 yards of twenty-pound backing behind a WF-8-F taper. It has grown popular with anglers who fish big rainbows on our western rivers. Its big brother has a heavy gold-finished backplate, and is called the Catino Tarpon. It measures 4⅜ inches in diameter, weighs 12 ounces, and carries 400 yards of thirty-pound backing behind a WF-12-F saltwater taper. It is too much reel for trout fishing, but it is better looking than its salty competitors—other well-made trucks like the Fin-Nor and Seamaster and Pate.

The elegantly machined Ross is another recent entry in the reel market. It is the child of Ross Hauck, an engineer from northern California, in the watersheds of the Smith and Trinity and Klamath.

We thought about bad jokes like "reel beauty," Hauck admits wryly, *but we thought better of it—when a guy pays hard money for an expensive reel, he deserves more than cute—it's just the Ross!*

His reels are machined from three-pound billets of solid aluminum bar stock. After the precision machinework, the spool and frame weigh between three to four ounces, depending on model and capacity. But there are several other reels machined from solid H-18 stock, and it is the drag system that is unique.

It has no leaf springs, no sinter-steel pawls, and no ratchets. There is only a single button which tightens a Delrin drag button against the camplate assembly on the interior face of the spool. Delrin is a new synthetic material with properties beyond the Teflon drag systems tried on other reels. There are merely a tubular spool shaft that receives a large set screw, the spool itself with its cylindrical spindle, the reel frame and foot, and its linear set-screw drag. There is no ratchet-click system. Without conventional back pressure, the reel simply free-spools against its Delrin button. The Delrin drag button provides both drag when the spool is surrendering line and antireverse tension when retrieving. The Ross is simplicity itself.

And it's really tough, says Randall Kaufmann, a staunch supporter. *Hauck ran over his with a jeep, and the only thing hurt was the handle!*

The smooth action is also achieved with hard-tempered stainless bearings. Hauck is a painstaking technician, and his bench testing of the Ross prototypes involved some torture. He rigged the test reel to a belt drive system, tightened his Delrin drag button down full, and ran it at 2,450 revolutions per minute. His torture test lasted twenty-four hours, totalling more than eight million revolutions.

There was no measurable thermal effect, in spite of the obvious friction, and the crown of the Delrin drag button had deformed less than .003 inch. No other discernible wear had obtained.

Hauck builds three trout reels. The Ross One is slightly less than three inches in diameter and weighs 3.14 ounces. It can hold a DT-4-F floating line and thirty yards of backing. The Ross Two measures 3⅛ inches, weighs 3.38 ounces, and can accommodate a DT-5-F with twenty-five yards of backing. The Ross Three is 3⅜ inches in diameter. It weighs just a whisper over 4 ounces, and can carry a DT-6-F double taper ahead of seventy-five yards.

Ross RR-3 Reel

My only criticism of the Ross designs lies in their ventilated spools. Victorian flywheels used almost floral curves, with some of the sensuality of Art Deco esthetics, in their spokes. Although some of these early machines were designed with such ornamentality in mind, there were functional reasons too. The curvilinear spokes grew thickly from their drive-shaft housings, where stress transfer is greatest, and grew elegantly thin where they joined the flywheel itself. Their floral curves were not just esthetic decisions; they also understood that tangential load transfer placed less stress at the connecting points of such flywheels.

The flower-petal spokes of the Ross design are merely esthetic devices, totally unrelated to the function of stress transfer in machines. Mere prettiness, with little basis in technology or function, is a kind of florid thinking that has no place in modern engineering and design— giving the Ross spool some visual echoes of past die-cut cheapness.

Hauck has subsequently introduced his Ross Three-Five reel. It measures 3⅜ inches in diameter and weighs 4.2 ounces. Unlike its earlier cousins, the Three-Five has a solid, nonventilated spool. Its face still has the flower-petal pattern, but in a subtle *bas-relief* effect. It is counter-weighted to reduce wobble. The entire reel is anodized in a gunmetal color, including its foot assembly, and its concentric ornament and trade-mark are a handsome silver. The owner may have his own name engraved in silver at extra cost. The Ross Three-Five will hold a WF-8-F forward taper and 250 yards of backing.

These Ross designs are exquisitely made, in a family production line that includes soft reel bags sewn by Hauck's wife. There is even a special polishing cloth developed for anodized aluminum finishes, and each reel is sold in a hand-finished Ponderosa box from the valley itself.

Based on their quality, and their line-to-weight ratios, the Ross series of reels is likely to join the ranks of first-rate tackle.

They're great! Randall Kaufmann told me recently. *Who else would give his customers a lifetime guarantee?*

LIST OF

ILLUSTRATIONS

Page numbers in *italic* refer to page facing color plate.

Famous Anglers and Angling Writers

Famous Anglers and Tackle Makers

Fishing Artifacts and Historic Places

Salmoniformes and Salmonidae

Anatomy and Physiology

Biophysical Phenomena

Entomology

Alderflies, Fishflies, and Dobsonflies (Megaloptera)

Ant (Hymenoptera)

Aquatic Beetles (Coleoptera)

Backswimmers (Hemiptera)

Caddisflies (Trichoptera)

Craneflies, Gnats, and Midges (Diptera)

Crustaceans (Malacostraca)

Dragonflies and Damselflies (Odonata)

Mayflies (Ephemeroptera)

Stoneflies (Plecoptera)

Equipment

Flies and Fly Hooks

Fly Lines and Leaders

Fly Reels

Fly Rods

Technique

Fishing Techniques

Fly Casting

Fly-fishing Knots

Netting and Wading

Typical Trout Pools

BIBLIOGRAPHY

AELIANUS, CLAUDIUS. De peculiari quadam indu Macedon. In *De natura animalium*. Various editions.

AITKEN, P. L.; DICKERSON, L. H.; and MENZIES, W. J. M. 1966. Fish passes and screens at water power works. *Proc. Inst. Civ. Engrs.* 35:29–57.

AKEKIO, S. 1880. Memorandum on fish-culture in Japan with a notice of experiments in breeding the California trout. *Rpt. U.S. Comm. Fish Fish.* 7:645–48.

ALDAM, W. H. 1876. *A quaint treatise on flees and the art of artyfichall flee making*. London.

ALDERDICE, D. F.; WICKETT, W. P.; and BRETT, J. R. 1958. Some effects of temporary exposure to low dissolved oxygen levels on Pacific salmon eggs. *J. Fish Res. Bd. Can.* 15:229–49.

ALEXANDER, C. P. 1965. New subgenera and species of crane flies from California (Diptera: Tipulidae). *Pac Insects* 7(2):333–86.

ALEXANDER, D. R., and MacCRIMMON, H. R. 1974. Production and movement of juvenile rainbow trout *(Salmo gairdneri)* in a headwater of Bothwell's Creek, Georgian Bay, Canada. *J. Fish Res. Bd. Can.* 31:117–21.

ALLAN, I. R. H., and BULLIED, M. J. 1963. Long-distance migration of Atlantic salmon. *Nature* 200(4901):89.

ALLEE, W. C., and STEIN, E. R., JR. 1918. Light reactions and metabolism in mayfly nymphs. *J. Exp. Zool.* 26:423–58.

ALLEN, G. H., and CLAUSSEN, L. G. 1960. Selectivity of food by brook trout in a Wyoming beaver pond. *Trans. Amer. Fish. Soc.* 89(1):80–81.

ALLEN, K. R. 1938. Some observations on the biology of the trout *(Salmo trutta)* in Windermere. *J. Anim. Ecol.* 7:333–49.

———. 1941. Comparison of bottom faunas as sources of available fish food. *Trans. Amer. Fish. Soc.* 71:275–83.

———. 1947. Some aspects of the production and cropping of freshwaters. *N.Z. Sci. Cong.* 2:222–28.

———. 1951. *The Horokiwi stream: a study of trout population*. N.Z. Mar. Dept. Fish., Bull. 10.

———. 1957. Natural areas in the distribution of freshwater fish. *Proc. N.Z. Ecol. Soc.* 4:14–15.

———. 1969. Limitations on production in salmonid populations in streams. In *Symposium on salmon and trout in streams: H. R. MacMillan lectures in fisheries, edited by T. C. Northcote, pp. 3–18. Vancouver: University of British Columbia.

ALM, G. 1920. Resultaten av fiskinplanteringar i Sverige. Medd. Kgl. Lantbruksstyrelsen, 226.

ALT, K. T. 1969. "Taxonomy and ecology of the inconnu, Stenodus leucichthys nelma, in Alaska." Biol. Pap., Univ. Alaska, 12:1–61.

ANCONA, U. D'., and MERLO, S. 1959. Speciation in Italian trouts with special reference to those of Lake Garda. Proc. Int. Cong. Zool. 15(1958):141–45.

ANDREWS, C. W. 1965. Early importation and distribution of exotic freshwater fish species in Newfoundland. Can. Fish Cult. 35:35–36.

ANDRUSAK, H., and NORTHCOTE, T. G. 1970. Management implications of spatial distribution and feeding ecology of cutthroat trout and Dolly Varden in coastal British Columbia lakes. B.C. Fish. Wildl. Branch Fish. Manage., 13.

ANNIN, J., Jr. 1884. Notes pertaining to fish-culture. Trans. Amer. Fish. Soc. 13:109–11.

APPLEGATE, V. 1950. The sea lamprey in the Great Lakes. U.S. Dept. Int., Fish. Leaflet 384. Washington D.C.: Government Printing Office.

ARGO, V. 1927. The North American species of the genus Potamanthus, with a description of a new species. N.Y. Ent. Soc. 35:319–28.

ARROWSMITH, E., and PENTELOW, F. T. K. 1965. The introduction of trout and salmon to the Falkland Islands. Salm. Trout Mag. 174:119–29.

ATHERTON, J. 1951. The fly and the fish. New York: Macmillan.

AUSTIN, R. S. n.d. (c. 1890). Dry fly fishing on the Exe and other North Devon streams. Manuscript.

AVERETT, R. C. 1962. Studies of two races of cutthroat trout in northern Idaho. Idaho Dept. Fish Game, Completion Rpt. F-47-R-1.

———, and ESPINOSA, F. A. 1968. Site selection and time of spawning by two groups of kokanee in Odell Lake, Oregon. J. Wildl. Manage. 32:76–81.

———, and MACPHEE, C. 1971. Distribution and growth of indigenous fluvial and adfluvial cutthroat trout (Salmo clarki), St. Joe River, Idaho. Northwest Sci. 45:38–47.

AYERS, H. D.; MACCRIMMON, H. R.; and BERST, A. H. 1967. Construction and management of farm ponds in Ontario. Ontario Dept. Agr. Food, Publication 515.

BACKUS, R. H. 1957. The fishes of Labrador. Bull. Amer. Mus. Nat. Hist. 113:273–337.

BAILEY, N. T. J. 1951. On estimating the size of mobile populations from recapture data. Biometrika 38:293–306.

BAINBRIDGE, G. C. 1816. The fly-fisher's guide. Liverpool.

BALDWIN, N. S. 1951. "A preliminary study of brook trout food consumption and growth at different temperatures." Paper read at 5th Technical Session, Research Council of Ontario.

BALL, R. C. 1952. Farm pond management in Michigan. In Symposium on farm ponds and management. J. Wildl. Manage. 16:266–69.

BALMAIN, K. H., and SHEARER, W. M. 1956. Records of Salmon and sea trout caught at sea. Freshw. Salm. Fish. Res. Scotl., 11.

BAMS, R. A. 1969. Adaptations in sockeye salmon associated with incubation in stream gravels. In Symposium on salmon and trout in streams: H. R. MacMillan lectures in fisheries, 1968. Vancouver: University of British Columbia.

BANKS, J. W. 1969. A review of the literature on the upstream migration of adult salmonids. J. Fish Biol. 1:85–136.

BANKS, N. 1892. Ephemeridae. In A synopsis, catalogue and bibliography of the neuropteroid insects of temperate North America. Trans. Amer. Ent. Soc. 19:331–32, 19:345–48.

———. 1900. New genera and species of Nearctic neuropteroid insects. Trans. Amer. Ent. Soc. 26:245–51.

———. 1908. A list of neuropteroid insects from North Carolina. Proc. Ent. Soc. Wash. 9:151.

———. 1910. Notes on the eastern species of the mayfly genus Heptagenia. *Can. Ent.* 42:197–202.

———. 1938. A new genus of Perlidae. *Psyche* 45:136–37.

———. 1947. Some characters in the Perlidae. *Psyche* 54:266–91.

———. 1948. Notes on Perlidae. *Psyche* 55:113–30.

BARKER, F. D. 1929. *An angler's paradise.* London: Faber & Faber.

BARKER, T. 1651. *The art of angling.* London.

BARLOW, G. W. 1961. Causes and significance of morphological variation in fishes. *Syst. Zool.* 10:105–17.

BARTRAM, J. 1750. A further account of Libellae or mayflies. *Phil. Trans. Roy. Soc. London* 10:28.

BEAMISH, F. W. H. 1964. Respiration of fishes with special emphasis on standard oxygen consumption. *Can. J. Zool.* 42:161–75.

BEAN, B. A. 1902. Steelhead salmon in Lake Michigan. *Forest and Stream* 58(May): 430.

BEAN, J. H. 1895. The rainbow trout. *First Ann. Rpt. Comm. Fish Game for State N.Y.*, pp. 135–40.

BEAN, T. H. 1906. Discussion period of thirty-fifth annual meeting of American Fisheries Society. *Trans. Amer. Fish. Soc.* 35:137.

BEAN, T. M. 1888. The distribution and some characters of the Salmonidae. *Amer. Nat.* 22:306–14.

BEEVER, J. [Arundo]. 1849. *Practical fly fishing.* London.

BEHNKE, R. J. 1959. A note on *Oncorhynchus formosanum* and *Oncorhynchus masou. Jap. J. Ichthyology* 7(5,6):151–52.

———. 1966. Relationships of the far eastern trout, *Salmo mykiss* Walbaum. *Copeia* 1966:346–48.

———. 1968a. *A new subgenus and species of trout,* Salmo (Platysalmo) platycephalus, *from southcentral Turkey, with comments on the classification of the subfamily* Salmoninae. Mitt. Hamburg. Zool. Mus. Inst., 66.

———. 1968b. Rare and endangered species: the native trouts of North America. *Proc. West. Assoc. State Game Fish Comm.* 48:530–33.

———. 1969. The Lake Ohrid trout, *Salmo letnica,* and its potential as a new North American sport fish. *Proc. West. Assoc. State Game Fish Comm.* 49:207–8.

———. 1970. The application of cytogenetic and biochemical systematics to phylogenetic problems in the family Salmonidae. *Trans. Amer. Fish. Soc.* 99(1):237–48.

———. 1972. The systematics of salmonid fishes of recently glaciated lakes. *J. Fish. Res. Bd. Can.* 29:639–71.

———. 1973. "Systematic problems of the salmonine fishes endemic to the Adriatic-Mediterranean province and the potential for developing new information from new techniques." Paper read at 1st European Ichthyological Congress.

———; KOH, T. P.; and NEEDHAM, P. R. 1962. Status of the landlocked salmonid fishes of Formosa with a review of *Oncorhynchus masou* (Brevoort). *Copeia* 1962(2): 400–7.

BEHR, FRIEDRICH VON. 1883. Five American Salmonidae in Germany. *Bull. U.S. Fish. Comm. 1882* 2:237–46.

BELDING, D. L. 1934. The cause of the high mortality in the Atlantic salmon after spawning. *Trans. Amer. Fish. Soc.* 34:219–24.

BELL, R. 1886. Observations on geology, zoology, and botany of Hudson Bay Strait and Bay, made in 1885. *Geol. Nat. Hist. Surv. Can. Ann. Rpt. N.S.* 1:1DD–27DD.

BENGTSSOM, S. 1914. Undersökningar ofver äggen hos Ephemeriderna. *Ent. Tidskr.* 1:1–19.

———. 1936. Kritische Bemerkungen über einige nordische Ephemeropteren, nebst Beschreibung neuer Larven. *Lunds Univ. Arssk.,* N.F. Avd. 2, 26:1–27.

BENNIKE, S. A. B. 1943. *Contributions to the ecology and biology of Danish freshwater leeches.* Fol. Limnol. Scand., 2.

BENSON, S. B., and BEHNKE, R. J. 1961. *Salmo evermanni:* a synonym of *Salmo clarkii henshawi. Calif. Fish Game* 47:257–59.

BERG, L. S. 1908. Vorläufige Bemerkungen über die europaisch-asiatischen Salmoninen, insbesondere die Gattung *Thymallus. Ann. Mus. Zool. Acad. Sci. St. Petersbourg* 12:500–14.

———. 1932a. Les poissons des eaux douces de l'U.R.S.S. et des pays limitrophes. Articles in *Acta Borealia.* 3d ed. Leningrad.

———. 1932b. Übersicht der Verbreitung der Süsswasserfischen Europas. *Zoogeographica* 1(2):107–208.

———. 1940. *Dokl. Zool. Inst. Akad. Nauk SSSR* 5:87–517. (1947. Classification of fishes both recent and fossil, translated by J. W. Edwards, Ann Arbor, Mich.)

———. 1948. *Ryby presnyk vod SSSR i sopredelnyk stran* [Freshwater fishes of the USSR and adjacent countries]. Akad. Nauk SSSR, Opredeliteli po Faune SSSR, No. 27. (1962. English translation by Office of Technical Services, U.S. Dept. of Commerce.)

BERG, M. 1953. A relict salmon, *Salmo salar* L., called "småblank," from the River Namsen, North Trøndelag. In *Acta Borealia,* 6.

———. 1961. Pink Salmon (*Oncorhynchus gorbuscha*) in northern Norway in the year 1960. In *Acta Borealia, 17.*

BERGMAN, R. 1932. *Just fishing.* New York: Knopf.

———. 1938. *Trout.* New York: Knopf.

BERNERS, DAME J. 1496. *A treatyse of fysshynge wyth an angle.* In the Boke of St. Albans. Westminster.

BERRIOZABAL, F. P. 1937. The management of fish hatcheries in Mexico. *Trans. Amer. Fish. Soc.* 67:94–95.

BERRY, J. 1936. British mammals and birds as enemies of the Atlantic salmon *(Salmo salar). Avon Biol. Res. Ann. Rpt., 1934.* 35:31–64.

BERST, A. H. 1962. Unpublished notes on the biology of rainbow trout in Lake Erie watershed. Guelph, Ontario: University of Guelph.

———, and WAINIO, A. A. 1967. Lamprey parasitism of rainbow trout in southern Georgian Bay. *J. Fish. Res. Bd. Can.* 24(12):2539–48.

BETTEN, C. 1934. *The caddis flies or Trichoptera of New York State.* N.Y. State Mus., Bull. 292.

———, and MOSELEY, M. E. 1940. *The Walker types of Trichoptera in the British Museum,* London.

BEYERLE, G. B., and COOPER, E. L. 1960. Growth of brown trout in selected Pennsylvania streams. *Trans. Amer. Fish. Soc.* 89(3):255–62.

BIDGOOD, B. F., and BERST, A. H. 1967. Phenotypic characteristics of rainbow trout in the Great Lakes. *J. Fish. Res. Bd. Can.* 24(4):887–92.

BIGELOW, H. B., and SCHROEDER, W. C. 1953. *Fishes of the Gulf of Maine.* U.S. Fish Wildl. Serv. Fish., Bull. 53(74).

BISHAI, H. M. 1960. Upper lethal temperatures for larval salmonids. *J. Conserv. Int. Explor. Mer.* 25:129–33.

BLACKER, W. 1843. *The art of fly-making.* London.

BLADES, W. F. 1951. *Fishing flies and fly tying.* Harrisburg, Pa.: Stackpole Co.

BLICKLE, R. L., and MORSE, W. J. 1955. New and little-known Polycentropus (Trichoptera). *Bull. Brooklyn Ent. Soc.* 50:95–98.

BOGOESCU, C. 1932. *Contributiuni la studiul morphologic si biologic al phanerelor larvelor de Ephemerine.* Bucharest Inst. Arte Grafice E. Marva. Bd. Princip. Mircea, 10.

BOLES, H. D., and BORGESON, D. P. 1966. Experimental brown trout management in Lower Sardine Lake, California. *Calif. Fish Game* 52(3):166–72.

BOOKE, H. E. 1968. Cytotaxonomic studies of the coregonine fishes of the Great Lakes, USA: DNA and karotype analysis. *J. Fish. Res. Bd. Can.* 25(8):1667–87.

BOOTHROYD, E. R. 1959. Chromosome studies on three Canadian populations of Atlantic salmon, *Salmo salar. Can. J. Genet. Cytol.* 1(2):161–72.

BORELL, A. E., and SCHEFFER, P. M. 1961. *Trout in farm and ranch ponds.* U.S. Dept. Agr., Farmers' Bull. 2154.

BORGESON, D. P. 1968. *Coho salmon status report.* Mich. Dept. Nat. Res. Fish Manage., Rpt. 3.

BOULENGER, G. A. 1898. On a new genus of salmonid fishes from the Alti Mountains. *Ann. and Mag. Nat. Hist.,* ser. 7, 1:329–31.

BOWER, S. 1909. The rainbow trout in Michigan. *Trans. Amer. Fish. Soc.* 39:130–42.

BOWLKER, R., and BOWLKER, C. n.d. *The art of angling.* Worcester.

BRANNON, E. L. 1965. *The influence of physical factors on the development and weight of sockeye salmon embryos and alevins.* Int. Pac. Salm. Fish Comm., Prog. Rpt. 12.

———. 1967. *Genetic control of migratory behavior of newly emerged sockeye salmon fry.* Int. Pac. Salm. Fish Comm., Prog. Rpt. 16.

BRASCH, J.; McFADDEN, J.; and KMIOTEK, S. 1966. *The eastern brook trout: its life history, ecology and management.* Wisc. Conserv. Dept., Publ. 226.

BRAYSHAW, J. D. 1967. The effects of river discharge on inland fisheries. In *River Management,* edited by P. C. G. Isaac, pp. 102–18. London: MacLaren.

BRETT, J. R. 1956. Some principles in the thermal requirements of fishes. *Quar. Rev. Biol.* 32(2):75–87.

———. 1957. *Salmon research and hydro-electric power development.* Fish. Res. Bd. Can. Bull. 114.

———. 1965. The relation of size to rate of oxygen consumption and sustained swimming speed of sockeye salmon *(Oncorhynchus nerka). J. Fish. Res. Bd. Can.* 22:1491–1501.

BRIDGETT, R. L. 1924 *Lake fishing in theory and practice.* London: Jenkins.

BRINCK, P. 1949. Studies on Swedish stoneflies (Plecoptera). *Opuscula Entomologica,* supplement 11. Lund.

BROECKER, W. S. 1965. Isotope geochemistry and the Pleistocene climatic record. In *The quaternary of the United States,* edited by N. E. Wright, Jr., and D. G. Frey, pp. 737–53. Princeton: Princeton University Press.

BROOK, A. J. 1956. Changes in the phytoplankton of some Scottish hill lochs resulting from their artificial enrichment. *Verh. Int. Ver. Limnol.* 13:298–305.

BROOKES, R. 1799. *The art of angling.* London.

BROOKS, J. 1972. *Trout fishing.* New York: Harper & Row.

BROWN, M. E. 1946. The growth of brown trout *(Salmo trutta* Linn.). Part 2: the growth of two-year old trout at a constant temperature of 11.5°C. *J. Exp. Biol.* 22:130–44.

———. 1957. Experimental studies on growth, 1. In *The physiology of fishes,* edited by M. E. Brown, pp. 361–400. New York: Academic Press.

BRYNILDSON, O. M., and CHRISTENSON, L. M. 1961. *Survival, yield, growth and coefficient of condition of hatchery-reared trout stocked in Wisconsin waters.* Wisc. Conserv. Dept., Misc. Res. Rpt. 3.

———; HACKER, V. A.; and KLICK, T. A. 1964. *Brown Trout. Its life history, ecology and management.* Wisc. Conserv. Dept., Publ. 234.

BUCKNALL, G. 1966. *Fly-fishing tactics on still water.* London: Frederick Muller.

———. 1968. *Fly-fishing tactics on rivers.* London: Frederick Muller.

BURDICK, G. E. 1961. Chemical control of aquatic vegetation in relation to the conservation of fish and wildlife. *Proc. N.E. Weed Control Conf.* 15:485–92; Abstract 514, *Weed Abstracts* 12, 2(1963).

BURESCH, R. 1925. Studien am Seesaibling mehrerer Alpenseen. *Z Fisch. deren Hilfswiss.* 33:99–119.

BURKS, B. D. 1953. *The mayflies, or Ephemeroptera, of Illinois.* Ill. Nat. Hist. Surv., Bull. 26.

BURNET, A. N. R. 1959. Some observations on natural fluctuations of trout population numbers. *N.Z. J. Sci.* 2:410–21.

BURROWS, R. E. 1949. Prophylactic treatment for control of fungus *(Saprolegnia parasitica)* on salmon eggs. *Prog. Fish Cult.* 37:97–103.

BUSCHKIEL, A. L. 1931. *Salmonidenzucht in Mitteleuropa.* Stuttgart.

BUSS, K. 1963. The origin and history of the trout species of Pennsylvania rainbow trout. *Pa. Angler* 32(5):2–3.

CALAPRICE, J. R., and CUSHING, J. E. 1964. Erythrocyte antigens of California trouts. *Calif. Fish Game* 50:152–57.

———, and CUSHING, J. E. 1967. A serological analysis of three populations of golden trout, *Salmo aguabonita* Jordan. *Calif. Fish Game* 53:273–81.

CALDERÓN, E. G. 1965. *The raising of brown trout and rainbow trout in water at high temperatures.* Gen. Fish. Coun. Medit. Stud. Rev., 30.

CALDERWOOD, W. L. 1901. Water temperature in relation to the early annual migration of salmon from the sea to the rivers in Scotland. *19th Ann. Rpt. Fish. Bd. Scotl.,* pp. 57–76.

CALVERT, P. P. 1909. Contributions to a knowledge of Odonata of the neotropical region, exclusive of Mexico and Central America. *Nature* 21:118–37.

———. 1906. The white spot disease in salmon in the Island of Lewis. *24th Ann. Rpt. Fish. Bd. Scotl.,* App. 5:78–79.

———. 1945. Passage of smolts through turbines: effect of high pressure. *Salm. Trout Mag.* 115:214–21.

CAMPBELL, R. N. 1961. The growth of brown trout in acid and alkaline waters. *Salm. Trout Mag.* Jan:47–52.

CANAGARATNAM, P. 1959. "The influence of light intensities and durations during early development of meristic variations in some salmonids." Doctoral thesis, University of British Columbia.

CARBERRY, J. T., and STRICKLAND, K. L. 1968. Resistance of rainbow trout to ulcerative dermal necrosis. *Nature* 217(5134):1158.

CARL, G. C.; CLEMENS, W. A.; and LINDSEY, C. C. 1959. *The freshwater fishes of British Columbia.* Dept. Ed. Handb. 5. Victoria: B.C. Provincial Museum.

CARLANDER, H. B. 1954. *A history of fish and fishing in the upper Mississippi River.* Upper Mississippi River Conserv. Comm.

CARLANDER, K. D., and LEWIS, W. M. 1948. Some precautions in estimating fish populations. *Prog. Fish Cult.* 10(3):134–37.

CARLIN, B. 1953. Märkning av lax på Norrbottenskusten. *Vandrings fiskutredn Meddel.* 2:1–4.

CARPENTER, K. E. 1924. A study of the fauna of rivers polluted by lead mining in the Aberystwyth district of Cardiganshire. *Annals of Appl. Biol.* 11:1–23.

———. 1927. The lethal action of soluble metallic salts on fishes. *Brit. J. Exp. Biol.,* 4.

CARROLL, W. 1818. *The angler's vade mecum.* Edinburgh.

CARTWRIGHT, W. 1854. *Rambles and recollections of a fly-fisher.* London.

CATLIN, M. 1930. *Flyfishing for trout.* Appleton, Wisc.: Badger Printing Co.

CATT, J. 1950. Some notes on brown trout with particular reference to their status in New Brunswick and Nova Scotia. *Can. Fish Cult.* 7:25–27.

CHAMBERLAIN, T. K. 1942. Research in stream management in the Pisgah National Forest. *Trans. Amer. Fish. Soc.* 72:150–76.

CHANCELLOR, R. J. 1962. *The identification of common water weeds.* Natural Science Bull. 183. Brit. Museum Nat. Hist. London: H.M.S.O.

CHAPMAN, D. W. 1962. Effects of logging upon fish resources of the west coast. *J. Forest.* 60:533–37.

———. 1965. Net production of juvenile coho salmon in three Oregon streams. *Trans. Amer. Fish. Soc.* 94:40–52.

———. 1967. Production in fish populations. In *The biological basis of freshwater fish production,* edited by S. D. Gerking, p. 3. Oxford: Blackwell.

CHETHAM, J. 1681. *The angler's vade mecum.* London.

CHOATE, J. 1964. Use of tetracycline drugs to mark advanced fry and fingerling brook trout (*Salvelinus fontinalis*). *Trans. Amer. Fish. Soc.* 93(3):309–11.

CHUBB, J. C., and POWELL, A. M. 1966. The examination of fish for parasites. In *Proc. 2d British Coarse Fish Conf.,* pp. 87–93.

CLAASEN, P. W. 1931. *Plecoptera nymphs of America (north of Mexico).* Thomas Say Foundation of the Ent. Soc. Amer., Publication 3. Springfield, Ill.: Charles C. Thomas.

———. 1937a. New species of stoneflies (Plecoptera). *Can. Ent.* 69:79–82.

———. 1937b. New species of stoneflies (Plecoptera). *J. Kans. Ent. Soc.* 10:42–51.

———. 1940. *A catalogue of the Plecoptera of the world.* Mem. Cornell Univ. Agric. Exp. Sta., no. 232.

CLARK, F. N. 1882. Report of work at the United States Hatchery, Northville, Michigan. *Rpt. U.S. Comm. Fish Fish. 1881,* pt. 9:1052–53.

———. 1887. Report on the distribution of eggs from Northville and Alpena stations for the season of 1885–86. *Bull. U.S. Fish. Comm. (1886)* 6:395.

CLARK, O. H. 1945. Stream improvements in Michigan. *Trans. Amer. Fish. Soc.* 75:270–80.

CLEMENS, W. A. 1913. New species and new life histories of Ephemeridae or mayflies. *Can. Ent.* 45:246–62.

———. 1915. Mayflies of the Siphlonurus group. *Can. Ent.* 47:245–60.

———, and WILBY, G. V. 1946. *Fishes of the Pacific coast of Canada.* Fish. Res. Bd. Can., Bull. 68.

COKER, R. E. 1920. Progress in biological inquiries—report of the division of scientific inquiry for the fiscal year 1920. *Rpt. U.S. Comm. Fish.,* App. 2, pt. 46:6–7.

COLDWELL, C. 1939. The feeding habits of American mergansers. *Can. Field-Nat.* 52:55.

COMSTOCK, J. H. 1925. *An introduction to entomology,* 2d ed. Ithaca, N.Y.: Comstock.

———, and NEEDHAM, J. G. 1898. The wings of insects. *Amer. Nat.* 33:117–26.

COOPER, E. L. 1951. Rate of exploitation of wild eastern brook trout and brown trout populations in the Pigeon River, Otsego County, Michigan. *Trans. Amer. Fish. Soc.* 81:224–34.

———. 1952. Returns from plantings of legal-sized brook, brown and rainbow trout in the Pigeon River, Otsego County, Michigan. *Trans. Amer. Fish. Soc.* 82:265–80.

———. 1953a. Growth of brook trout (*Salvelinus fontinalis*) and brown trout (*Salmo trutta*) in the Pigeon River, Otsego County, Michigan, *Pap. Mich. Acad. Sci.* 38:151–62.

———. 1953b. Periodicity of growth and change of condition of brook trout (*Salvelinus fontinalis*) in three Michigan trout streams. *Copeia* 1953(2):107–14.

COPE, O. B. 1955. The future of the cutthroat trout in Utah. *Proc. Utah Acad. Sci. Arts and Lett.* 32:89–93.

CORDONE, A. J., and KELLEY, D. W. 1961. The influences of inorganic sediment on the aquatic life of streams. *Calif. Fish Game* 47:189–228.

COTTON, C. 1676. Being instructions on how to angle for trout and grayling in a clear stream. In *The compleat angler,* London.

CRASS, R. S. 1964. *Freshwater fishes of Natal.* Pietermasitzburg: Shuter.

CROSS, D. G. 1969. Aquatic weed control using grass carp. *J. Fish Biol.* 1(1):27–36.

CROSS, R. R. 1940. *Fur, feathers and steel.* New York: Dodd, Mead.

———. 1950. *The complete fly-tyer.* New York: Dodd, Mead.

CUINAT, R., and VIBERT, R. 1963. *Demographic diagnosis on fish populations in trout streams.* Gen. Fish. Coun. Medit. Stud. Rev., 21.

CUNNINGHAM, F. H. 1911. Fish breeding. *44th Ann. Rpt. Dept. Mar. Fish. Can., 1910–11*, Fish. App. (16):347–412.

CURTIS, B. 1934. The golden trout of Cottonwood Lakes (*Salmo agua-bonita* Jordan). *Trans. Amer. Fish. Soc.* 64:259–65.

CUTCLIFFE, H. C. 1863. *Trout fishing on rapid streams.* South Molton.

DAHL, K. 1911. *The age and growth of salmon and trout in Norway as shown by their scales.* London: Salmon and Trout Association.

———. 1918. Studies of trout and trout waters in Norway, 1. *Salm. Trout Mag.* 17:58–79.

———. 1919. Studies of trout and trout waters in Norway, 2. *Salm. Trout Mag.* 18:16–33.

———. 1928. The dwarf salmon of Lake Byglands-fjord. *Salm. Trout Mag.* 51:108–12.

DALY, R. 1968a. Chasing rainbows. *Wisc. Conserv. Bull.*, July–Aug. 1968.

———. 1968b. *Preliminary notes on management of the rainbow trout in western Lake Michigan.* Madison: Wisc. Dept. Nat. Res.

DANNEVIG, A. 1932. On the number of vertebrae in cod influenced by light or high temperature during the early stages. *J. Conserv. Perm. Int. Explor. Mer.*, 7:60–62.

DAVIS, H. S. 1938. *Instructions for conducting stream and lake surveys.* U.S. Bur. Fish., Fish. Circ. 26. Washington, D.C.: Government Printing Office.

———. 1961. *Culture and diseases of game fishes.* Berkeley and Los Angeles: University of California Press.

DAVIS, J. J. 1949. Two new species of caddis flies (Trichoptera) from Washington state. *Ann. Ent. Soc. Amer.* 42:448–50.

DAVIS, K. C. 1903. *Sialididae of North and South America.* N.Y. State Mus., Bull. 68. Albany.

DAYHOFF, M. O. 1969a. *Atlas of protein sequence and structure 1969.* Silver Spring, Md.: National Biomedical Research Foundation.

———. 1969b. Computer analysis of protein evolution. *Scientific American* 221(1):86–95.

———, and ECK, R. V. 1968. *Atlas of protein sequence and structure 1967–68.* Silver Spring, Md.: National Biomedical Research Foundation.

DEKAY, J. E. 1842. *Fishes.* Zoology of New York, pt. 4. Albany: N.Y. Geol. Surv.

DELACY, A. C., and MORTON, W. M. 1943. Taxonomy and habits of the charrs, *S. malma* and *S. alpinus*, of the Karluk drainage system. *Trans. Amer. Fish. Soc.* 72:79–91.

DELURY, D. B. 1947. On the estimation of biological populations. *Biometrics* 3:145–67.

DEM BORNE, M. 1885. Distribution of American fish and fish eggs by the German Fishery Association. *Bull. U.S. Fish. Comm.* 5:262.

DENNING, D. G. 1947a. New species and records of Nearctic Hydroptilidae (Trichoptera). *Bull. Brooklyn Ent. Soc.* 42:145–58.

———. 1947b. New species and records of North American Hydroptilidae (Trichoptera). *Psyche* 54:170–77.

———. 1948a. Description of eight new species of Trichoptera. *Bull. Brooklyn Ent. Soc.* 43:119–29.

———. 1948b. New and little-known species of Nearctic Trichoptera. *Psyche* 55:16–27.

———. 1948c. New species of Trichoptera. *Ann. Ent. Soc. Amer.* 41:397–401.

———. 1948d. Review of the Rhyacophilidae (Trichoptera). *Can. Ent.* 80:97–117.

———. 1949a. A new genus and five new species of Trichoptera. *J. Kans. Ent. Soc.* 22:88–93.

———. 1949b. New and little-known species of caddis flies. *Amer. Midl. Nat.* 42:112–22.

———. 1949c. New species of Nearctic caddis flies. *Bull. Brooklyn Ent. Soc.* 44:37–48.

———. 1950a. Records and descriptions of Nearctic caddis flies, part 1. *Bull. Brooklyn Ent. Soc.* 45:97–104.

———. 1950b. Records and descriptions of Nearctic caddis flies, part 2. *J. Kans. Ent. Soc.* 23:115–20.

———. 1951. Records and descriptions of Nearctic caddis flies, part 3. *J. Kans. Ent. Soc.* 24:157–62.

———. 1952. Description of several new species of caddis flies. *Can. Ent.* 84:17–22.

———. 1953. A new genus of Limnephilidae (Trichoptera). *Pan-Pac. Ent.* 29:165–69.

———. 1954*a*. New species of *Lepidostoma* (Trichoptera: Lepidostomatidae). *Pan-Pac. Ent.* 30:187–94.

———. 1954*b*. New species of western Trichoptera. *J. Kans. Ent. Soc.* 27:57–64.

———. 1956. Several new species of western Trichoptera. *Pan-Pac. Ent.* 32:73–80.

D[ENNYS], J. 1613. *The secrets of angling.* London.

DEWAR, G. A. B. 1910. *The book of the dry fly.* London: A. C. Black.

DICK, H. L. H. 1972. *The art and science of fly fishing.* New York: Winchester Press.

DICK, ST. J. 1873. *Flies and fly fishing.* London.

DILL, L. M. 1969. The sub-gravel behavior of Pacific salmon larvae. In *Symposium on salmon and trout in streams: H. R. MacMillan lectures in fisheries, 1968.* Vancouver: University of British Columbia.

DILLON, O. W., JR. 1969. "A summary of commercial fish farming in the United States." Paper read at 99th meeting of Amer. Fish. Soc., 10–12 September 1969, New Orleans, La.

DIMICK, R. E., and MOTE, D. C. 1934. *A preliminary survey of the food of the Oregon trout.* Org. Agric. Exp. Sta., Bull. 323.

DIX, T. G. 1968. Helminth parasites of brown trout (*Salmo trutta* L.) in Canterbury, New Zealand, *N.Z. J. Mar. Freshw. Res.* 2:363–74.

DOAN, K. H. 1948. *Speckled trout in the lower Nelson River region, Manitoba.* Fish. Res. Bd. Can., Bull. 79.

DODDS, G. S. 1923. Mayflies from Colorado. *Trans. Amer. Ent. Soc.* 49:93–114.

———, and HISAW, F. L. 1924. Ecological studies of aquatic insects. *Ecology* 5:137–48, 262–71.

———, and HISAW, F. L. 1925. Ecological studies of aquatic insects. *Ecology* 6:123–37, 380–90.

DODGE, D. P. 1967. "Some biology and vital statistics of the rainbow trout, *Salmo gairdneri* Richardson, of Bothwell's Creek, Lake Huron." Master's thesis, University of Guelph.

———, and MacCRIMMON, H. R. 1970. Vital statistics of a population of Great Lakes rainbow trout *(Salmo gairdneri)* characterized by an extended spawning season. *J. Fish. Res. Bd. Can.* 27:613–18.

———, and MacCRIMMON, H. R. 1971. Environmental influences in extended spawning of rainbow trout, *Salmo gairdneri. Trans. Amer. Fish. Soc.* 33:721–29.

DOGIEL, V.; PETRUSHEVSKI, G. K.; and POLYANSKI, Y. I. 1961. *Parasitology of fishes.* Edinburgh and London: Oliver and Boyd.

DOROFEEVA, E. A. 1965. Kariologicheskoe obosnovanie sistematicheskogo polozheniya kaspiiskogo i chernomorskogo lososei (*Salmo trutta caspius* Kessler, *Salmo trutta labrax* Pallas). *Voprosy ikhtiologii* 5(1):38–45.

———. 1967. Khromosomnye kompleksy sevanskikh forelei (*Salmo ischchan* Kessler) v svyazi s kario-sistematikoi lososevykh. *Zool. zhur.* 46(2):248–53.

DRYAGIN, P. A.; PIROZHNIKOV, P. L.; and POKROVSKII, V. V. 1969. Polimorfizm sigovykh ryb (Coregoninae) i ego biologicheskoe i rybokhozyaistvonnoe Znachenie. *Voprosy ikhtiologii* 9(1):14–25.

DUNBAR, M. J., and HILDEBRAND, H. H. 1952. Contribution to the study of fishes of Ungava Bay. *J. Fish. Res. Bd. Can.* 9:83–128.

DUNNE, J. W. 1924. *Sunshine and the dry fly.* London: A. C. Black.

DYMMOND, J. R. 1922. A provisional list of fishes of Lake Erie. In *Publications of Ontario Fish Research Laboratory*, pp. 57–73. Univ. Toronto Stud., Biol. Ser., no. 20.

———. 1926. The fishes of Lake Nipigon. In *Publications of Ontario Fish Research Laboratory*, pp. 1–108. Univ. Toronto Stud., Biol. Ser., no. 27.

———. 1930. Description of two new forms of British Columbia trout. *Can. Biol.*, Ser. A, 6(16):393–94.

————. 1932a. Records of the alewife and steelhead (rainbow) trout from Lake Erie. *Copeia* 1932(1):32.

————. 1932b. *The trout and other game fishes of British Columbia.* Biol. Bd. Can., Bull. 32.

————. 1935. Some freshwater fishes of British Columbia. *Contributions Roy. Ont. Mus. Zool.* 9:61–62.

————. 1947. *A list of freshwater fishes of Canada east of the Rocky Mountains with keys.* Roy. Ont. Mus. Zool., Misc. Publ. 1.

————. 1955. The introduction of foreign fishes in Canada. *Proc. Int. Assoc. Theoret. Appl. Limnol.* 12:543–53.

EARP, B. J.; ELLIS, C. H.; and ORDAL, E. J. 1953. *Kidney disease in young salmon.* Washington Dept. of Fish. Special Rpt. Ser., 1.

EATON, A. E. 1871a. *A monograph on the Ephemeridae.* Trans. Ent. Soc. London.

————. 1871b. *A revisional monograph of recent Ephemeridae or mayflies.* Trans. Linn. Soc., Zool. Ser. 2, vol. 3.

EDDY, S., and SURBER, T. 1947. *Northern fishes, with special reference to the upper Mississippi Valley.* Minneapolis: University of Minnesota Press.

EDMONDS, H. H., and LEE, N. N. n.d. *Brook and river trouting.* Bradford.

EDMUNDS, F. G. 1952. "Mayflies of Utah." Doctoral thesis, University of Massachusetts.

EIPPER, A. W. 1960. *Managing farm ponds for trout production.* Cornell Univ. Ext. Bull. 1036.

————, and REGIER, H. A. 1962. *Fish management in New York farm ponds.* Cornell Univ. Ext. Bull. 1089.

EISLER, R. 1957. Some effects of artificial light on salmon eggs and larvae. *Trans. Amer. Fish. Soc.* 87:151–52.

————. 1961. Effects of visible radiation on salmonid embryos and larvae. *Growth* 25(4):281–346.

ELDER, H. Y. 1966. Biological effects of water utilization by hydro-electric schemes in relation to fisheries, with special reference to Scotland. *Proc. Roy. Soc. Edinb.* B. 69(3,4):246–71.

ELLIOTT, J. M. 1966. Downstream movements of trout fry *(Salmo trutta)* in a Dartmoor stream. *J. Fish. Res. Bd. Can.* 23(1):157–59.

ELLIS, M. M. 1936. Erosion silt as a factor in aquatic environments. *Ecology* 17:29–42.

ELLIS, R. J., and GOWING, H. 1957. Relationship between food supply and condition of wild brown trout *(Salmo trutta* Linn.) in a Michigan stream. *Limnol. Ocean.* 2(4):299–308.

ELSON, K. R. 1968. Salmon disease in Scotland. *Scot. Fish. Bull.* 30:8–16.

————. 1969. Whirling disease in trout. *Nature* 223(5209):968.

EMBODY, G. C. 1927. Stocking policy for the streams, smaller lakes, and ponds of Oswego watershed. In N.Y. Conserv. Dept., Supp. *17th Ann. Rpt. 1927,* pp. 17–39.

————. 1934. Relation of temperature to the incubation periods of eggs of four species of trout. *Trans. Amer. Fish. Soc.* 64:281–92.

ESSIG, E. O. 1942. Plecoptera. In *College Entomology,* pp. 148–58. New York: Macmillan.

ESTABROOK, G. F. 1966. A mathematical model in graph theory for biological classification. *J. Theoret. Biol.* 12:297–310.

————, and ROGERS, D. J. 1966. A general method of taxonomic description for a computed similarity measure. *Bio Science* 16:789–93.

EVERHART, W. H., and WATERS, C. A. 1965. Life history of the blueback trout *(Salvelinus alpinus)* in Maine. *Trans. Amer. Fish. Soc.* 94:393–97.

EVERMANN, B. W. 1906. *The golden trouts of the southern High Sierras.* U.S. Bur. Fish., Bull. 25(1905).

————, and BRYANT, H. C. 1919. California trout. *Calif. Fish Game* 5:105–3.

————, and LATIMER, H. B. 1910. The fishes of Lake of the Woods and connecting waterways. *Proc. U.S. Nat. Mus.* 39:121–36.

FATIO, V. 1890. *Faune des vertebrates de la Suisse.* Vol. 5 (Poissons), pt. 2. Geneva: n.p.

FERGUSON, A. D. 1916. Extending the range of the golden trout. *Pac. Fish. Soc. Trans. Ann. Mtng.* 2:65–70.

FERGUSON, R. G. 1958. The preferred temperature of fish and their midsummer distribution in temperate lakes and streams. *J. Fish. Res. Bd. Can.* 15(4):607–24.

FISHER, K. C., and ELSON, P. F. 1950. The selected temperature of Atlantic salmon and speckled trout and the effect of temperature on the response to an electrical stimulus. *Physiol. Zool.* 23:27–34.

————, and SULLIVAN, C. M. 1958. The effect of temperature on the spontaneous activity of speckled trout before and after lesions of the brain. *Can. J. Zool.* 36:49–63.

FISHER, R. A. 1963. *Statistical methods for research workers.* 15th ed. Edinburgh: Oliver and Boyd.

FLICK, A. 1947. *Streamside guide to naturals and their imitations.* New York: G. P. Putnam's Sons. Reprint. 1970. New York: Crown.

FLICK, W. A., and WEBSTER, D. A. 1964. Comparative first year survival and production in wild and domestic strains of brook trout *Salvelinus fontinalis. Trans. Amer. Fish. Soc.* 93(1):58–69.

FORT, R. S., and BRAYSHAW, J. D. 1961. *Fishery management.* London: Faber.

FOWKE, P. 1938. Trout culture in Ceylon. *Ceylon J. Sci.,* Sect. C.; Fish Bull., Ceylon Fish, 6.

FOWLER, H. W. 1940a. A list of fishes of New Jersey. *Proc. Biol. Soc. Wash.* 33:139–70.

————. 1940b. *A list of fishes recorded from Pennsylvania.* Commw. Pa. Bd. Fish. Comm., Bull. 7.

FOX, C. K. 1963. *The wonderful world of trout.* Harrisburg, Pa.: Telegraph Press.

————. 1967. *Rising trout.* Carlisle, Pa.: Foxcrest.

FOX, H. M.; SIMMONDS, B. G.; and WASHBURN, R. 1937. Metabolic rates of Ephemerid nymphs from swiftly flowing and from still waters. *J. Exp. Biol.* 12(1):299–307.

————; WINGFIELD, C. A.; and SIMMONDS, B. G. 1939. Oxygen consumption of Ephemerid nymphs from flowing and from still waters in relation to the concentration of oxygen in the water. *J. Exp. Biol.* 14(2):183–89.

FRANCES, F. 1867. *A book on angling.* 5th ed. London: Longmans Green.

FRANCK, R. 1694. *Northern memoirs.* London.

FRASER, T. B. 1968. The Greenland and Davis Strait fisheries. *Salm. Trout Mag.* 184: 152–63.

FRIEND, C. F. 1941. The life history of the salmon gill-maggot *Salmincola salmonea* (L.) (Copepod crustacean). *Trans. Roy. Soc. Edinb.* 60:503–41.

FRIEND, G. F. 1959. Subspeciation in British charrs. *Syst. Assoc. Publ.* 3:121–29.

FRISON, T. H. 1929. Fall and winter stoneflies, or Plecoptera, of Illinois. *Bull. Ill. Nat. Hist. Surv.* 18:345–409.

————. 1935a. New North American species of the genus *Alloperla* (Plecoptera: Chloroperlidae). *Trans. Amer. Ent. Soc.* 61:331–44.

————. 1935b. The stoneflies, or Plecoptera, of Illinois. *Bull. Ill. Nat. Hist. Surv.* 20: 281–471.

————. 1936. Some new species of stoneflies from Oregon (Plecoptera). *Ann. Ent. Soc. Amer.* 29:256–65.

————. 1937. Descriptions of Plecoptera, with special reference to the Illinois species. *Bull. Ill. Nat. Hist. Surv.* 21:78–99.

————. 1942a. Descriptions, records, and systematic notes concerning western North American stoneflies (Plecoptera). *Pan-Pac. Ent.* 18:9–16, 61–73.

————. 1942b. Studies of North American Plecoptera, with special reference to the fauna of Illinois. *Bull. Ill. Nat. Hist. Surv.* 22(2):235–355.

FROST, W. E. 1943a. The natural history of the minnow—*Phoxinus phoxinus. J. Anim. Ecol.* 12.

———. 1943b. *River Liffey survey, pt. 3: The fauna of the submerged mosses in an acid and alkaline water.* In rpt. of Proc. Roy. Irish Acad., 47B(13).

———. 1955. An historical account of the charr in Windermere. *Salm. Trout Mag.* 143: 15–24.

———. 1963. The homing of char *Salvelinus willughbil* (Günther) in Windermere. *Animal Behavior* 2(1):74–82.

———, and BROWN, M. E. 1967. *The trout.* London: Collins.

FRY, F. E. J. 1947a. *Effects of the environment on animal activity.* Univ. Toronto Stud., Biol. Ser. 55, Publ. Ont. Fish. Res. Lab, 68.

———. 1947b. *Temperature relations of salmonids.* In rpt. of Proc. Natl. Comm. of Fish Cult., App. D., 10th Meeting.

———. 1951. *Some environmental relations of the speckled trout (Salvelinus fontinalis).* In rpt. of Proc. N.E. Atl. Fish Conf. Mimeographed.

GABRIEL, M. L. 1944. Factors affecting the number and form of vertebrae in *Fundulus heteroclitus. J. Exp. Zool.* 95:105–47.

GARD, R. 1961. Effects of beaver on trout in Sagehen Creek, California. *J. Wildl. Manage.* 25:221–42.

———, and SEEGRIST, D. 1965. Persistence of the native rainbow trout following introduction of hatchery trout. *Copeia* 1965:182–85.

GARDNER, J. A., and LEETHAM, C. 1914. On the respiratory exchange in fresh water, pt. 1: On brown trout. *J. Biochem.* 8:374–90.

GARSIDE, E. T. 1959. Some effects of oxygen in relation to temperature on the development of lake trout embryos. *Can. J. Zool.* 37:689–98.

———. 1966a. Developmental rate and vertebral number in salmonids. *J. Fish. Res. Bd. Can.* 23:1537–51.

———. 1966b. Effects of oxygen in relation to temperature on the development of embryos of brook trout and rainbow trout. *J. Fish. Res. Bd. Can.* 23:1121–34.

———, and TAIT, J. S. 1958. Preferred temperature of rainbow trout (*Salmo gairdneri* Richardson) and its unusual relationship to acclimation temperature. *Can. J. Zool.* 36:563–67.

GASOWSKA, M. 1960. Genus *Coregonus* L. discussed in connection with a new systematic feature, that of shape and proportion of os maxillare and os supramaximare. *Ann. Zool. Inst. Zool. Polska Akad. Nauk* 18(26):471–513.

———. 1964. Coregonid classification discussed on the basis of *Coregonus pollan* Thompson from Lough Neagn (Northern Ireland). *Ann. Zool. Inst. Zool. Polska Akad. Nauk* 22(18):413–19.

GAUFIN, A. R. 1966. "The stoneflies of Utah." Master's thesis.

GIBSON, R. J., and KEENLEYSIDE, M. H. A. 1966. Responses to light of young Atlantic salmon *(Salmo salar)* and brook trout *(Salvelinus fontinalis). J. Fish. Res. Bd. Can.* 23(7):1007–24.

GILL, T. N. 1863. A note on the labroids of the western coast of North America. *Proc. Acad. Nat. Sci.* (Philadelphia) 15:221–22.

———. 1894. The differential characters of the Salmonidae and Thymallidae. *Proc. U.S. Nat. Mus.* 17:117–22.

GINGRICH, A., ed. 1966. *American trout fishing.* New York: Knopf.

GODDARD, J. 1966. *Trout fly recognition.* London: A. C. Black.

GOLL, HERMANN. 1887. The American brook trout recommended for Swiss waters. *Bull. U.S. Fish. Comm.* 6:206–8.

GOLTERMAN, H., and CLYMO, R. S. 1969. *Methods for chemical analysis of fresh waters.* (I.P.B. Handbook) Oxford and Edinburgh: Blackwell.

GOODE, G. B. 1903. *American fishes.* Boston: Dana Estes and Co.

GOODNIGHT, W. H., and BJORNN, T. C. 1971. Fish production in two Idaho streams. *Trans. Amer. Fish. Soc.* 100:769–80.

GORDON, S. W. 1955. *How to fish from top to bottom.* Harrisburg: Stackpole Co.

GORDON, T. 1947. *The complete fly-fisherman: the notes and letters of Theodore Gordon,* edited by John McDonald. New York: Scribners.

GRAHAM, J. M. 1948. "Some relations of temperature and oxygen to the activity of the speckled trout, *Salvelinus fontinalis* Mitchill)." Master's thesis, University of Toronto.

———. 1949. Some effects of temperature and oxygen pressure on the metabolism and activity of the speckled trout, *Salvelinus fontinalis. Can. J. Res.* (Sect. D) 27:270–88.

GRANDE, M. 1964. A study of the brook trout (*Salvelinus fontinalis,* Mitchill) in Telemark. *Fauna* 1:32–33.

GRANT, G. F. 1971. *The art of weaving hair hackles for trout flies.* Butte, Montana.

GRAY, J. 1928. The growth of fish, pt. 3: The effect of temperature on the development of eggs of *Salmo fario. J. Exp. Biol.* 6(2):125–30.

GRAY, J. R. A., and EDINGTON, J. M. 1969. Effect of woodland clearance on stream temperature. *J. Fish. Res. Bd. Can.* 26(2):399–403.

GREELEY, J. R. 1928. Fishes of the Oswego watershed. In *A biological survey of the Oswego River system,* pp. 84–107. New York State Conserv. Dept., Albany.

GREEN, C. W. 1935. *Distribution of Wisconsin fishes:* Salmo gairdneri irideus *and* Salmo gairdneri shasta, pp. 48–49. Wisc. Conserv. Comm. Madison.

GREEN, S. 1880. California mountain trout. *Trans. Amer. Fish. Soc.* 9:13–17.

GREENDRAKE, G. 1897. *The angling excursions of Gregory Greendrake in the counties Wicklow, Meath, Westmeath, Longford and Cavan.* Dublin.

GREENE, G. E. 1950. Land use and trout streams. *J. Soil and Water Conserv.* 5(3):125–26.

GREENE, W. S. 1937. *Colorado trout.* Colo. Mus. Nat. Hist., Popular Ser. 2.

GREENWOOD, P. H.; ROSEN, D. E.; WEITZMAN, S. H.; and MYERS, G. S. 1966. Phyletic studies of teleostean fishes with a provisional classification of living forms. *Bull. Amer. Mus. Nat. Hist.* 131:339–456.

GRIFFITH, J. S. 1972. Comparative behavior and habitat utilization of brook trout *(Salvelinus fontinalis)* and cutthroat trout *(Salmo clarki)* in small streams in northern Idaho. *J. Fish. Res. Bd. Can.* 29(3):265–73.

GROUTAGE, T. M. 1968. Unique Illinois pond supports rainbow trout. *Prog. Fish Cult.* 30(1):9–12.

GROVE, A. R., JR. 1951. *The lure and lore of trout fishing.* Harrisburg: Stackpole.

GÜNTHER, A. 1862. *Catalogue of the fishes in the British Museum,* vol. 4. London.

———. 1866. *Fishes of the British Museum,* no. 6. London.

HADZISCE, S. 1960. Zur Kenntnis der Gattung *Salmothymus* Berg. *Publ. za Ribarstvo NRM-Skopje* 3(2):39–56.

———. 1961. Zur Kenntnis der *Salmothymus ohridanus* (Steindachner). *Verh. int. Ver. Limnol.* 14:785–91.

HAEMPEL, O. 1924. Studien am Seesaibling. *Verh. int. Ver. Limnol.* 2:129–35.

HAIG-BROWN, R. 1953. Izaak Walton—his friends and his rivers. *Field and Stream* 58(1).

HALE, J. G., and SMITH, L., JR. 1955. Results of planting catchable-size brown trout, *Salmo trutta fario* L., in a stream with poor natural reproduction. *Prog. Fish. Cult.* 17:14–19.

HALFORD, F. M. 1886. *Floating flies and how to dress them.* London.

———. 1889. *Dry fly fishing in theory and practice.* London.

———. 1897. *Dry fly entomology.* London.

———. 1910. *Modern development of the dry fly.* London.

HANSEN, M. J., and STAUFFER, T. M. 1961. *Comparative recovery to the creel, and behavior of rainbow trout stocked in the Great Lakes,* pp. 18–20. Michigan Dept. Conserv., Inst. for Fish. Res., Rpt. 1739.

HANSGARD, G. A. 1834. *Trout and salmon fishing in Wales.* London.

HANSON, J. F. 1942. Records and descriptions of North American Plecoptera, pt. 2: notes on North American Perlodidae. *Amer. Midl. Nat.* 28:389–407.

———. 1943. Records and descriptions of North American Plecoptera, pt. 3: notes on *Isogenoides. Amer. Midl. Nat.* 29:657–69.

———. 1946. Comparative morphology and taxonomy of the Capniidae (Plecoptera). *Amer. Midl. Nat.* 35:193–249.

———, and AUBERT, J. 1952. First supplement of the Claasen catalogue of the Plecoptera of the world. *Amer. Midl. Nat.* 47:176–239.

HANSTRÖM, B., and JOHNELS, A. G. 1962. Fiskar (Pt. 2). *Djurens Värld* 6:94–95.

HARDING, E. W. 1931. *The fly-fisher and the trout's point of view.* London.

HARLAN, J. R., and SPEAKER, E. B. 1956. *Iowa fish and fishing.* Iowa State Conserv. Comm.

HARRIS, J. R. 1952. *An angler's entomology.* South Brunswick: A. S. Barnes & Co.

HARRISON, A. C.; SHORTT-SMITH, K. E.; YATES, J. H.; JUBB, R. A.; RUSHBY, G.; and FLAMWELL, C. T. 1963. *Freshwater fish and fishing in Africa.* London: Thomas Nelson & Sons.

HARTMAN, W. L. 1957. *Finger Lakes rainbows, pt. 3: a chronicle of their progress from egg to adult,* pp. 7–9. N.Y. State Conserv. Dept., Div. Conserv. Ed., Information leaflet.

HASLER, A. D. 1947. Eutrophication of lakes by domestic drainage. *Ecology* 28(4):383–95.

———. 1949. Antibiotic aspects of copper treatment of lakes. *Trans. Wisc. Acad. of Sciences, Arts, and Letters* 39:97–103.

———. 1954. Odor perception and orientation in fishes. *J. Fish. Res. Bd. Can.* 2:107–29.

———, and WISBY, W. J. 1951. Discrimination of stream odors by fishes and its relation to parent stream behavior. *Amer. Nat.* 85:223–38.

HATCH, R. W. 1957. Relative sensitivity of salmonids to DDT. *Prog. Fish Cult.* 19:89–91.

HAYES, F. R., and PELLUET, D. 1945. The effect of temperature on growth and efficiency of yolk conversion in the salmon embryo. *Can. J. Res.* 23:10–15.

———; WILMOT, I. R.; and LIVINGSTONE, D. A. 1951. The oxygen consumption of the salmon egg in relationship to development and activity. *J. Exp. Zool.* 116:377–95.

HAZZARD, A. S. n.d. *Pennsylvania fishes.* Pa. Fish Comm. Bull.

———. 1935. "Instructions for lake and stream survey work." Mimeographed. U.S. Bur. Fish. Washington, D.C.

Heacox, C. 1953. The compleat life. *Field and Stream* 58(1).

———. 1974. *The compleat brown trout.* New York.

HECTOR, J. 1966. The bag net. *The Salm. Net* 2:27–29.

HENDERSON, N. E. 1963. Influence of light and temperature on the reproductive cycle of the eastern brook trout, *Salvelinus fontinalis* (Mitchill). *J. Fish. Res. Bd. Can.* 20:859–97.

HENN, A. W., and RINKENBACH, W. H. 1925. Description of the aurora trout *(Salvelinus timagamiensis),* a new species from Ontario. *Ann. Carnegie Mus.* 16:131–41.

HENSHALL, J. A. 1902. Food and game fishes of the Rocky Mountain region. *Trans. Amer. Fish. Soc.* 31:74–88.

HERRINGTON, R. B., and DUNHAM, D. K. 1967. *A technique for sampling general fish habitat characteristics of some streams.* U.S. Dept. Agric., For. Ser. Washington, D.C.: Government Printing Office.

HESS, A. D., and SWARTZ, A. 1941. The forage ratio and its use in determining the food grade of streams. *Trans. N. Amer. Wildl. Conf.* 5:162–64.

HEWITT, E. R. 1926. *Telling on the trout.* New York: Scribners.

———. 1948. *A trout and salmon fisherman for seventy-five years.* New York: Scribners.

HEY, D. 1947. The fertility of brown trout eggs at the Jonkershoek Inland Fish Hatchery. *Trans. Amer. Fish. Soc.* 77:26–31.

HICKIN, N. E. 1952. *Caddis.* London: Methuen.

———. 1967. *Larvae of the British Trichoptera.* London: Methuen.

HILDEBRAND, S. F. 1935. An annotated list of fishes of the freshwaters of Puerto Rico. *Copeia* 1935:59–65.

HILE, R. 1937. Morphometry of the cisco, *Leucichthys artedi* (LeSueur) in the lakes of the northeastern highlands of Wisconsin. *Int. Rev. Hydrobiol.* 36(1–2):57–130.

HILGENDORF, F. 1876. *Gesellschaft für Natur und Völkerkunde Ostasiens* 2:25–31.

HILLS, J. W. 1921. *A history of fly-fishing for trout.* London: Allan.

———. 1934. *River keeper.* London: Allan.

———. 1946. *A summer on the Test.* London: Allan.

HINEGARDNER, R. 1968. Evolution of cellular DNA content in teleost fishes. *Amer. Naturalist* 102(928):517–23.

HOBBS, D. F. 1944. *Trout fisheries in New Zealand: their development and management.* N.Z. Mar. Dept., Fish. Bull. 9.

HODGSON, W. E. 1907. *How to fish.* London: A. C. Black.

HOFFMAN, C. H., et al. 1946. *Field studies on the effect of DDT on aquatic insects.* U.S. Dept. Agric., Bur. Ent., E-702. Washington, D.C.: Government Printing Office.

HOFFMAN, G. L. 1967. *Parasites of North American freshwater fishes.* Berkeley: University of California Press.

HOFLAND, T. C. 1839. *The British angler's manual.* London.

HOGARTH, G. R. 1928. *Why and how we plant fish in Michigan.* Mich. Dept. Conserv., Fish Div.

HOLCOMB, D. C. 1964. "A history of intentional introductions of exotic fishes in Michigan." Master's thesis, University of Michigan.

HOLDEN, A. V., and MARSDEN, K. 1964. *Cyanids in salmon and brown trout.* Freshw. Salm. Fish. Res., 33.

HOLDER, A. S. 1965. "Aspects of the biology of the speckled trout, *Salvelinus fontinalis,* in stream pond unit." Master's thesis, University of Guelph.

HOPPE, G. N. 1938. Plecoptera of Washington. *Univ. Wash. Publ. Biol.* 4:139–74.

HORTON, P. A. 1961. The bionomics of brown trout in a Dartmoor stream. *J. Anim. Ecol.* 30(2):311–38.

———; BAILEY, R. G.; and WILDSON, S. I. 1968. A comparative study of the bionomics of the salmonids of three streams. *Arch. Hydrobiol.* 65:187–204.

HOUGH, E. 1891. The Castalia stream. *Forest and Stream,* no. 34. New York.

HOWARD, G. V., and GODFREY, E. R. 1950. *Fishery research and educational institutions in North and South America.* Spec. Publ. Food Agric. Org. U.N., Washington.

HOWITT, W. 1831. *The book of the seasons.* London.

HUBBARD, F. D. 1895. "Castalia." Paper read before Columbia Magazine Club, 10 May 1895.

HUBBS, C. L. 1930. The specific name of the European trout. *Copeia* 172:86–89.

———, and LAGLER, K. F. 1947. *Fishes of the Great Lakes region.* Cranbrook Inst. Sci., Bull. 26.

———, and MILLER, R. R. 1948. Correlation between fish distribution and hydrographic history in the desert basins of western United States. In the Great Basin, with emphasis on glacial and post glacial times. *Bull. Univ. Utah, Biol. Ser.* 10(7):17–166.

HUMPHRIES, C. F. 1938. *The Chironomid fauna of the Grobber Plöner See, the relative density of its members and their emergence period.* Arch. Hydrobiol., 33.

HUNTSMAN, A. G. 1936. *Return of salmon from the sea.* Biol. Bd. Can., Bull. 51.

———. 1938. Sea behavior in salmon. *Salm. Trout Mag.* 90:24–28.

———. 1941. Cyclical abundance and birds versus salmon. *J. Fish. Res. Bd. Can.* 5(3):227–35.

———. 1942. Death of salmon and trout with high temperature. *J. Fish. Res. Bd. Can.* 5:485–501.

———. 1948. Fertility and fertilization of streams. *J. Fish. Res. Bd. Can.* 7:248–53.

———. 1952. Wandering versus homing in salmon. *Salm. Trout Mag.* 130:227–30.

HUNTSMAN, F. C. 1944. Why did Ontario salmon disappear? *Trans. Roy. Soc. Can.* 5, Ser. 3, 38:83–102.

HUTTON, J. A. 1923. The parasites of salmon. *Salm. Trout Mag.* 34:302–12.

HUXLEY, T. 1882. Saprolegnia in relation to salmon disease. *Quar. J. Micr. Sci.*

HYNES, H. B. N. 1940. *A key to the British species of Plecoptera (stoneflies)*. Sci. Publ. Freshw. Biol. Assoc. 2.

———. 1960. *The biology of polluted waters*. Liverpool: University Press.

IDE, F. P. 1930. The nymph of the mayfly genus *Cinygma* Eaton. *Can. Ent.* 62:42–45.

———. 1935. The effect of temperature on the distribution of the mayfly fauna of a stream. Univ. of Toronto Stud. Biol. Ser., 39, *Pub. Ont. Fish Res. Lab.* 501:9–76.

IMMS, A. D. 1942. *Outlines of entomology*. London: Methuen.

IVANFI, E. 1927. A pontytetii (*Argulus foliaceus* L.) morphologiaja es biologiaja. *Archivum balatonicum*, V, 1, N2.

JACKSON, J. 1854. *The practical fly-fisher*. London.

JANKOVIC, D. 1964. Synopsis of biological data on European grayling *Thymallus thymallus* (Linnaeus) 1758. *FAO Fisheries Synopsis No. 24*. Flb/S24 (Rev. 1).

JENNINGS, P. J. 1935. *A book of trout flies*. New York: Derrydale Press. Reprint. 1970. New York: Crown.

JENSEN, S. 1967. "Mayflies of Idaho." Master's thesis, University of Utah.

JEWETT, S. G., JR. 1954a. New stoneflies from California and Oregon (Plecoptera). *Pan-Pac. Ent.* 30:167–79.

———. 1954b. New stoneflies (Plecoptera) from western North America. *J. Fish. Res. Bd. Can.* 11(5):543–49.

———. 1959. Stoneflies of the Pacific Northwest. *J. Fish. Res. Bd. Can.* 12(4):567–73.

———. 1960. Stoneflies of California. *Pan-Pac. Ent.* 36:172–81.

JOHANNSEN, O. A. 1903. *Aquatic nematocerous diptera*. N.Y. State Mus. Bull., 68. Albany.

———. 1905. *Aquatic nematocerous diptera 2*. N.Y. State Mus. Bull., 86. Albany.

———. 1908. *New North American Chironomidae*. N.Y. State Mus. Bull., 124. Albany.

———. 1934. *Aquatic diptera*. Cornell Univ. Agr. Exper. Sta. Memoirs, pt. 1 (1934), pt. 2 (1935), pt. 3 (1937). Ithaca: Cornell University Press.

JOHNSON, H. E.; ADAMS, C. D.; and McELRATH, R. J. 1955. A new method of treating salmon eggs and fry with malachite green. *Prog. Fish Cult.* 17:76–78.

JOHNSON, M. G. 1965. Estimates of fish populations in warm water streams by the removal method. *Trans. Amer. Fish. Soc.* 94:350–57.

JOHNSON, R. L.; GIGUERE, P. E., and PISTER, E. P. *A progress report on the Pleasant Valley spawning channel, Inyo County*. Inl. Fish. Ad. Rpt., 66-4, Calif. Dept. Fish Game.

JOHNSON, R. S. 1913. *The distribution of fish and fish eggs during the fiscal year 1913*. App. 1, Rpt. Comm. Fish., 1913, Bur. Fish., 794.

———. 1915. *The distribution of fish and fish eggs during the fiscal year 1915*. App. 1, Rpt. Comm. Fish., 1915, Bur. Fish., 828.

JOLY, E. 1876. Études sur l'embryogénie des Éphémères notamment chez la *Palingenia virgo*. *Mem. Acad. Sci. Toulouse*, pp. 243–54.

JONES, J. R. E. 1964. *Fish and river pollution*. London: Butterworth.

JONES, J. W. 1959. *The salmon*. London: Collins Press.

JORDAN, D. S. 1883. McCloud River trout. *Forest and Stream* 20(4):72.

———. 1891a. Relation of temperature to vertebrae among fishes. *Proc. U.S. Natl. Mus.* 14:107–20.

———. 1891b. Report of explorations in Colorado and Utah during the summer of 1889, with an account of the fishes found in each of the river basins examined. *Bull. U.S. Fish. Comm.* 9:1–40.

———. 1893. A description of the golden trout of Kern River, California *Salmo mykiss agua-bonita*. *Proc. U.S. Natl. Mus.* 15:481–83.

———. 1920. Trout of the Rio Grande. *Copeia* (85):72–73.

———. 1922. *Days of a man*, vol. 1. New York: World Book Co.

———. 1926. The name of the brook trout in Europe. *Proc. U.S. Natl. Mus.* 155:140–41.

———, and EVERMANN, B. W. 1890. Description of the yellow-finned trout of Twin Lakes, Colorado (*Salmo mykiss MacDonaldi*). *Proc. U.S. Natl. Mus.* 12:453–54.

————, and EVERMANN, B. W. 1896. *The fishes of North and Middle America.* U.S. Natl. Mus., Bull. 47.

————, and EVERMANN, B. W. 1902. *American food and game fishes.* New York: Doubleday.

————; EVERMANN, B. W.; and CLARK, H. W. 1930. Checklist of the fishes and fish-like vertebrates of North and Middle America north of the northern boundary of Venezuela and Colombia. *Rpt. U.S. Comm. Fish. for 1928,* App. 10, pp. 57–59. Washington, D.C.: Government Printing Office.

————, and GRINNELL, J. 1908. Description of a new species of trout, *Salmo evermanni,* from the upper Santa Ana River, Mount San Gorgonio, southern California. *Proc. Biol. Soc. Wash.* 21:31–32.

————, and MacGREGOR, E. A. 1925. Family salmonidae. In records of fishes obtained by David Starr Jordan in Japan, 1922, by D. S. Jordan and C. L. Hubbs. *Memoirs Carnegie Mus.* 10(2):93–346.

————, and OSHIMA, M. 1919. *Salmo formosanus,* a new trout from the mountain streams of Formosa. *Proc. Acad. Natl. Sci. Phila.* 71:122–24.

————, and SNYDER, J. O. 1902. A review of the salmonid fishes of Japan. *Proc. U.S. Natl. Mus.* 24:567–93.

JUDAY, C. 1906. A study of Twin Lakes, Colorado, with especial consideration of the foods of the trouts. *Bull. U.S. Bur. Fish.* 26:147–78.

KALLEBERG, H. 1958. Observations in a stream tank of territoriality and competition in juvenile salmon and trout. *(Salmo salar* L. and *S. trutta* L.). *Rpt. Inst. Freshw. Res. Drottningholm* 39:55–98.

KARAMAN, M. S. 1966. Beitrag zur Kenntnis der Salmoniden Südeuropas. *Hydrobiologia* 28(1):1–41.

KEENLEYSIDE, M. H. A., and YAMAMOTO, F. T. 1962. Territorial behavior of juvenile aquatic salmon. *(Salmo salar* L.). *Behavior* 19(1):139–69.

KELEHER, J. J., and KOOYMAN, B. 1957. Supplement to Hinks' *The fishes of Manitoba,* pp. 105–17. Winnipeg: Dept. of Mines Natl. Res.

KELSON, G. 1895. *The salmon fly.* London.

KENDALL, W. C. 1920. What are rainbow trout and steelhead trout? *Trans. Amer. Fish. Soc.* 50:187–99.

————. 1924. Propagation and distribution of fish by New York State: rainbow trout. In *The status of fish culture in our inland public waters, and the role of investigation in the maintenance of fish resources,* pp. 296–303. Roosevelt Wildl. Bull., 2.

————. 1931. The question of salmon *(Salmo salar)* feeding in freshwater and taking of bait. *Copeia* 2:33–38.

KENNEDY, C. H. 1926. The nymph of *Ephemera guttulata* Pictet with notes on the species. *Can. Ent.* 58:61–63.

KENNEDY, H. D. 1955. Colonization of a previously barren stream section by aquatic invertebrates and trout. *Prog. Fish. Cult.* 17(3):119–22.

————. 1958. Biology and life history of a new species of mountain midge, *Deuterophlebia nielsoni,* from eastern California. *Trans. Amer. Micro. Soc.* 77(2):201–28.

————. 1964. *Air and water temperatures and stream flow data, Convict Creek, Mono County, California.* Spec. Sci. Rpt. Fish., 48.

————. 1967. *Seasonal abundance of aquatic invertebrates and their utilization by hatchery-reared rainbow trout.* Tech. Pap., Bur. Sport Fish. Wildl., U.S. Dept. Int., no. 12.

KENNEDY, W. A. 1956. *The first ten years of commercial fishing on Great Slave Lake.* Fish. Res. Bd. Can., Bull. 107.

KESTEVEN, G. L. 1969. Ethics and ecology. *Ceres, FAO Review* 2(3):53–56.

KIMMINS, D. E. 1941. Underwater emergence of *Hept. lateralis. Entomologist* 74:98–105.

————. 1942. *Keys to the British species of ephemeroptera with keys to the genera of the nymphs.* Sci. Publ. Freshw. Biol. Assoc., 7.

————, and DENNING, D. G. 1951. The McLachlan types of North American Trichoptera in the British Museum. *Ann. Ent. Soc. Amer.* 44:111–40.

KING, J. L., and JUKES, T. H. 1969. Non-Darwinian evolution. *Science* 164(3881):788–98.

KIPLING, C. 1957. The effect of gill-net selection on the estimation of weight-length relationships. *J. Conserv. Int. Explor. Mer.* 23(1):51–63.

————. 1962. The use of the scales of the trout (*Salmo trutta* L.) for the back-calculation of growth. *J. Conserv. Int. Explor. Mer.* 27(3):304–15.

KIRTLAND, J. P. 1838. Report on the zoology of Ohio. *Ann. Rpt. Geol. Surv. Study Ohio* 2:157–97.

KITAHARA, T. 1904. Preliminary note on the salmon and trout of Japan. *Annotationes Zoologicae Japonenses* 5(3):117–20.

KITE, O. 1963. *Nymph fishing in practice.* London: Herbert Jenkins.

KLAPÁLEK, F. 1909. Ephemerida. *Die Süsswasserfauna Deutschlands,* vol. 8, Jena: Gustav Fischer.

KLOET, S., and HINCKS, W. D. 1945. *A checklist of British insects.* Stockport: Kloet and Hincks.

KOBAYASHI, H. 1955. Comparative studies on the scales in Japanese freshwater fishes, with special references to phylogeny and evolution. *Jap. J. Ichthyology* 4(1–3):64–75.

KOCH, H. J. A.; BERGSTRÖM, E., and EVANS, J. C. 1964. The microelectrophoretic separation on starch gel of the hemoglobins of *Salmo salar* L. *Mededel. Vlaamse Acad. Kl. Wet.* 29(7):1–16.

————; EVANS, J. C.; and BERGSTRÖM, E. 1959. Sodium regulation in the blood of parr and smolt stages of Atlantic salmon. *Nature* 184:283.

KOELZ, W. 1925. *Fishing industry of the Great Lakes.* App. 11, Rpt. U.S. Comm. Fish., 1925, Bur. Fish, 1001.

KORMONDY, E. J. 1958. *Catalogue of the Odonata of Michigan.* Mich. Dept. Conserv., Bull. 12.

KOSHOV, M. 1963. *Lake Baikal and its life.* Monogr. Biol., 11.

KOSSWIG, C. 1963. Ways of speciation in fishes. *Copeia* (1963):238–44.

KRAMER, R. H., and SMITH, L. L., JR. 1965. Effects of suspended wood fiber on brown and rainbow trout eggs and alevins. *Trans. Amer. Fish. Soc.* 94:250–58.

KROGH, A., and ZEUTHEN, E. 1941. The mechanism of flight separation in some insects, *J. Exp. Biol.,* 18:83–91.

KWAIN, W., and MacCRIMMON, H. R. 1963. The behavior and bottom color selection of the rainbow trout, *Salmo gairdneri* Richardson, exposed to different light intensities. *Anim. Behav.* 15:75–78.

————, and MacCRIMMON, H. R. 1969a. Age and vision as factors in bottom color selection by rainbow trout, *Salmo gairdneri. J. Fish. Res. Bd. Can.* 26:687–93.

————, and MacCRIMMON, H. R. 1969b. Further observations on the response of rainbow trout, *Salmo gairdneri,* to overhead light. *J. Fish. Res. Bd. Can.* 26:3233–37.

LA BRANCHE, G. M. L. 1914. *The dry fly and fast water.* New York: Scribners.

LACK, D. 1966. *Population studies of birds.* London: Oxford University Press.

LAKE, J. S. 1957. Trout populations and habitats in New South Wales. *Austral. J. Mar. Freshw. Res.* 8(4):414–50.

LAMEERE, A. 1917. Étude sur l'évolution des éphémères. *Bule. Soc. Zool. France* 42:41–59, 61–81.

LAND, S. E. 1913. The black-spotted mountain trout. *Trans. Amer. Fish. Soc.* 42:183–89.

LANE, E. D. 1964. *Brown trout* (Salmo trutta) *in the Hinds River.* Proc. N.Z. Ecol. Soc., no. 11. Fish Lab. Publs. N.Z. Mar. Dept. 64, pp. 10–16.

LANGLOIS, T. H. 1927. *The 1926 fish survey of Newago County.* Mich. Dept. Conserv., Fish Div.

————. 1928. *Report on Hampton Lake, Kalamazoo County, Michigan.* Mich. Dept. Conserv., Fish Div.

LaRIVERS, I. 1962. *Fishes and fisheries of Nevada.* Nev. State Fish Game Comm.

————. 1964. *A new trout from the Barstovian (Miocene) of western Nevada.* Biol. Soc. Nev. Occ. Pap., 3.

LAUSON, W. n.d. *The secrets of angling.* London.

LAWRIE, W. H. 1969. *English trout flies.* New York: A. S. Barnes.

LAWSON, A. C. 1904. The geomorphogeny of the upper Kern Basin. Univ. Calif. Publ., *Bull. Dept. Geol.* 3:291–376.

LEAMAN, A. C. 1965. Control of furunculosis in impounded Atlantic salmon. *Nature* 208 (5017):1344.

LeCREN, E. D. 1969. Estimates of fish populations and production in small streams in England. In *Symposium on salmon and trout in streams: H. R. MacMillan lectures in fisheries,* ed. by T. C. Northcote, pp. 269–80. Vancouver: University of British Columbia.

LEGENDRE, P., and ROGERS, D. J. 1972. Characters and clustering in taxonomy: a synthesis of two taximetric procedures. *Taxon.* 21:173–79.

————; SCHRECK, C. B.; and BEHNKE, R. J. 1972. Taximetric analysis of selected groups of western North American *Salmo* with respect to phylogenetic divergences. *Syst. Zool.* 21(3):292–307.

LÉGÈNDRE, V. 1954a. *The freshwater fishes. Key to the game and commercial fishes of the Province of Quebec.* Montreal: La Société Canadienne d'Ecologie.

————. 1954b. *The freshwater fishes. Key to game and commercial fishes of the Province of Quebec,* vol. 1. Game Fish. Dept., Prov. Quebec.

————, and ROUSSEAU, J. 1949. La distribution de quelques-uns de nos poissons dans le Québec arctique. *Ann. Actas* 15:133–35.

LEIM, A. H., and SCOTT, W. B. 1966. *Fishes of the Atlantic coast of Canada.* Fish. Des. Bd. Can., Bull. 155.

LEISENRING, J. E., and HIDY, V. S. 1971. *The art of tying the wet fly and fishing the flymph.* New York: Crown.

LEITRITZ, E. 1962. *Trout and salmon culture.* Calif. Dept. Fish Game Fish., Bull. 107:43.

LEMMIEN, W. A.; TACK, P. I.; and MOROFSKY, W. F. 1957. Results from planting brown trout and rainbow trout in August Creek, Kalamazoo County, Michigan. *Quar. Bull. Mich. St. Univ. Agr. Exp. Sta.* 40:242–49.

LEONARD, J. E. 1950. *Flies.* New York: Barnes.

LEONARD, J. W. 1939. Comments on the adequacy of accepted stream bottom sampling techniques. *Trans. 4th N. Amer. Wildl. Conf.,* pp. 289–95.

————. 1949. *An annotated list of Michigan Trichoptera.* Bloomfield Hills.

————, and LEONARD, F. A. 1962. *Mayflies of Michigan trout streams.* Bloomfield Hills: Cranbrook Institute of Science.

LESTAGE, J. A. 1917. Contribution à l'étude des larves des Éphémères paléarctiques. *Ann. Biol. Lacustre* 8:213–456.

LINDSEY, C. C. 1958. Modification of meristic characters by light duration in Kokanee, *Oncorhynchus nerka. Copeia* 2:134–36.

————. 1964. Problems in zoogeography of the lake trout, *Salvelinus namaycush. J. Fish. Res. Bd. Can.* 21:977–94.

LIVINGSTONE, D. A. 1951. The freshwater fishes of Nova Scotia. *Proc. Nova Scotia Inst. Sci.* 23:1–90.

LLOYD, J. T. 1921. *The biology of North American caddis larvae.* Cincinnati.

LUTZ, F. E. 1948. *Field book of insects.* New York: G. P. Putnam's Sons.

LYUBITSKAYA, A. 1956. The effect of various parts of the visible areas of the spectrum on the development stage of fish embryos and larvae. *Zool. Zh.* 35:1873–86.

McAFEE, W. R. 1966. Eastern brook trout. In *Inland fisheries management,* edited by A. Calhoun, pp. 242–60. California Resources Agency, Dept. Fish Game.

McALLISTER, D. E. 1964. Fish collections from eastern Hudson Bay. *Can. Field Nat.* 78:167–78.

McCART, P., and CRAIG, P. 1971. Meristic differences between anadromous and freshwater resident Arctic char *(Salvelinus alpinus)* in the Sagavanirktok River drainage, Alaska. *J. Fish. Res. Bd. Can.* 28:115-18.

McClane, A. J. 1953. *The practical fly fisherman.* New York: Prentice-Hall, Inc.

——. 1965. *McClane's standard fishing encyclopedia and international angling guide.* New York: Holt, Rinehart & Winston.

MacCrimmon, H. R. 1954. Stream studies on planted Atlantic salmon. *J. Fish. Res. Bd. Can.* 11(4):362-403.

——. 1960. Observations on the standing trout populations and experimental plantings in two Ontario streams. *Can. Fish. Cult.* (28):45-55.

——. 1965. The beginning of salmon culture in Canada. *Can. Geog. J.* Sept.: 4-11.

——. 1971. World distribution of rainbow trout *(Salmo gairdneri). J. Fish. Res. Bd. Can.* 28:663-704.

——, and Berst, A. H. 1961. The native fish population and trout harvests in an Ontario farm pond. *Prog. Fish-Cult.* 23(3):106-13.

——, and Berst, A. H. 1963a. A portable AC-DC backpack fish shocker designed for operation in Ontario streams. *Prog. Fish-Cult.* 25:159-62.

——, and Berst, A. H. 1963b. A survey of licensed commercial hatcheries in Ontario. *Prog. Fish-Cult.* 25(4):189-92.

——, and Campbell, J. S. 1969. World distribution of brook trout. *Salvelinus fontinalis. J. Fish. Res. Bd. Can.* 26(7):1699-1725.

——, and Gots, B. L. 1972. *Rainbow trout in the Great Lakes.* Ministry Nat. Res. Sports Fish Branch, Ont.

——, and Kwain, W. H. 1966. Use of overhead cover by rainbow trout exposed to a series of light intensities. *J. Fish. Res. Bd. Can.* 23:983-90.

——, and Kwain, W. H. 1969. Influence of light on early development and meristic characters in the rainbow trout, *Salmo gairdneri* Richardson. *Can. J. Zool.* 47:631-37.

——, and Marshall, T. L. 1968. World distribution of brown trout, *Salmo trutta. J. Fish. Res. Bd. Can.* 25(12):2527-48.

——; Marshall, T. L.; and Gots, B. L. 1970. World distribution of brown trout, *Salmo trutta:* further observations. *J. Fish. Res. Bd. Can.* 27:811-18.

——, and Skobe, E. 1970. *The fisheries of Lake Simcoe.* Ontario: Dept. of Lands Forests.

McDunnough, J. 1923. New Canadian Ephemeridae with notes. *Can. Ent.* 55:39-50.

——. 1924a. *New Ephemeridae from New England.* Occ. Pap. Boston Soc. Natl. Hist., 5:73-76.

——. 1924b. New North American Ephemeridae. *Can. Ent.* 56:221-26.

——. 1925. New Ephemerella species (Ephemeroptera). *Can. Ent.* 57:41-43.

——. 1931a. The bicolor group of the genus Ephemerella with particular reference to the nymphal stages (Ephemeroptera). *Can. Ent.* 63:30-42.

——. 1931b. The eastern North American species of the genus Ephemerella and their nymphs (Ephemeroptera). *Can. Ent.* 63:187-97.

——. 1931c. The genus Isonychia (Ephemeroptera). *Can. Ent.* 63:157-63.

McFadden, J. T.; Alexander, G. R.; and Shetter, D. S. 1967. Numerical changes and population regulation in brook trout, *Salvelinus fontinalis. J. Fish. Res. Bd. Can.* 24(7):1425-59.

——, and Cooper, E. L. 1962a. An ecological comparison of six populations of brown trout *(Salmo trutta). Trans. Amer. Fish. Soc.* 91:53-62.

——, and Cooper, E. L. 1962b. Population dynamics of brown trout in different environments. *Physiol. Zool.* 37(4):355-63.

McGrath, C. J. 1959. Dams as barriers or deterrents to the migration of fish. *Athens Proc. of the I.U.C.N. Technical Meeting.* 4:81-92.

McHugh, J. L. 1954. The influence of light on the number of vertebrae in grunion, *Leuresthes tenuis. Copeia* 1:22-25.

MACIOLEK, J. A., and NEEDHAM, P. R. 1952. Ecological effects of winter conditions on trout and trout foods in Convict Creek, California. *Trans. Amer. Fish. Soc.* 81: 202–17.

MACKAY, H. H. 1963. Rainbow trout. In *Fishes of Ontario,* pp. 92–93. Ontario: Dept. of Lands Forests.

MACKINTOSH, A. 1806. *The Driffield angler.* London.

MACLEAN, J. P. 1923. *History of the Isle of Mull,* vol. 1. Greenville, Ohio: Frank H. Jobes & Sons.

MACPHAIL, J. D. 1961. Study of the *Salvelinus alpinus* complex in North America. *J. Fish. Res. Bd. Can.* 18:793–816.

MACPHEE, C. 1966. Influence of differential angling mortality and stream gradient on fish abundance in a trout-sculpin biotope. *Trans. Amer. Fish. Soc.* 95(4):381–87.

MADSEN, M. J. 1935. "A biological survey of streams and lakes of Fort Apache and San Carlos Indian Reservations, Arizona." Mimeographed. U.S. Bur. Fish.

MAGAN, T. T., and MAGAN, Z. 1940. Preliminary note on the Ephemeroptera and Plecoptera of the Hampshire Avon and its tributaries. *J. Soc. Brit. Ent.* 2.

MAHER, F. P., and LARKIN, P. A. 1954. Life history of the steelhead trout of the Chilliwack River, British Columbia. *Trans. Amer. Fish. Soc.* 84:27–38.

MALOY, C. R. 1966. Status of fish culture in the North American region. *Proc. FAO World Symposium on Warm-Water Pond Culture* 11:124–34.

MARINARO, V. C. 1950. *A modern dry-fly code.* New York: Putnam's. Reprint 1970. New York: Crown.

MARKHAM, G. 1614. A discourse of the generall art of fishing with the angle. Included in *The second booke of the English husbandman.* London.

MARLIER, G. 1946. Observations sur la conductivité électrique des eaux courantes de Belgique. Notes préliminaires. *Ann. Soc. Zool. Belge.* 76:100–7.

MARR, D. H. A. 1966. Factors affecting the growth of salmon alevins and their survival and growth during the fry stage. *Assoc. River Authorities Yearbook, 1965,* pp. 133–41.

MARSHALL, T. L. 1968. "Salmonid populations and exploitation in the upper Sydenham River, Ontario." Master's thesis, University of Guelph.

———, and MACCRIMMON, H. R. 1970. Exploitation of self-sustaining Ontario stream populations of brown trout *(Salmo trutta)* and brook trout *(Salvelinus fontinalis). J. Fish. Res. Bd. Can.* 27:1087–1102.

MARSTON, R. B. 1894. *Walton and some earlier writers on fish and fishing.* London: Elliot Stock.

MARTIN, N. V., and SANDERCOCK, F. K. 1967. Pyloric caeca and gillraker development in lake trout, *Salvelinus namaycush,* in Algonquin Park, Ontario. *J. Fish. Res. Bd. Can.* 24:965–74.

MARTYNOV, A. B. 1914. Trichoptères de la Sibérie et des régions adjacentes, 4: Subf. Limnolphilinae. *Ann. Mus. Zool. Acad. Sci. St. Petersb.* 19:173–285.

———. 1924. Trichoptera. *Prac. Ent.* 5:67.

MASCALL, L. 1590. *A booke of fishing with hooke and line.* London.

MASON, R. E. 1961. *Fish hatcheries, their present status and potential.* Dist. Rpt., Ont. Dept. of Lands Forests, Hespeler, Ont.

MASSARO, E. J., and MARKERT, C. L. 1968. Isozyme patterns of salmonid fishes: evidence for multiple cistrons for lactate dehydrogenase polypeptides. *J. Exp. Zool.* 168(2):223–38.

MATHER, F. 1889. Brown trout in America. *Bull. U.S. Fish Comm.* 7:21–22.

MAYHEW, J. K. 1955. Toxicity of seven different insecticides to rainbow trout, *Salmo gairdnerii,* Richardson. *Proc. Iowa Acad. Sci.* 62.

———. 1962. The control of nuisance aquatic vegetation with black polythene plastic. *Proc. Iowa Acad. Sci.* 69:302–7.

MAYR, E. 1969. *Principles of systematic zoology.* New York: McGraw-Hill Book Co.

————; LINSLEY, E. G.; and USINGER, R. L. 1953. *Methods and principles of systematic zoology*. New York: McGraw-Hill Book Co.

MELLANBY, H. 1938. *Animal life in fresh water*. London: Methuen.

MENZIES, W. J. M., and SHEARER, W. M. 1957. Long-distance migration of salmon. *Nature* 179:790.

MERCER, D. 1967. The effects of abstractions and discharges on river-water quality. In *River management,* edited by P. C. G. Isaac, pp. 168–77. London: MacLaren.

METZELAAR, J. 1927. *The food of the rainbow trout in Michigan*. Prelim. Rpt., Mich. Dept. Conserv.

MIALL, L. C. 1912. *Natural history of aquatic insects*. New York: Macmillan.

MICHAEL, W. W. 1951. *Dry-fly trout fishing*. New York: McGraw-Hill.

MILLARD, T. J., and MacCRIMMON, H. R. 1971. *Evaluation of the contributions of supplemental plantings of brown trout* Salmo trutta *(L.) to a self-sustaining fishery in the Sydeham River, Ontario, Canada*. Dept. Zool., University of Guelph, Can.

MILLER, H. L. 1963. *The old Au Sable*. Grand Rapids: Wm. B. Eerdmans Publ. Co.

MILLER, J., and BUSS, K. n.d. *The age and growth of the fishes in Pennsylvania*. Pa. Fish Comm. Bull.

MILLER, R. R. 1946. Correlation between fish distribution and Pleistocene hydrography in eastern California and southern Nevada, with a map of the Pleistocene waters. *J. Geol.* 54:43–53.

————. 1950a. *Notes on the cutthroat and rainbow trouts with the description of a new species from the Gila River, New Mexico*. Occ. Pap., Mus. Zool., Univ. Mich., no. 529.

————. 1950b. Recognition of trout in Alberta. *Can. Fish Cult.* 6:23–25.

————. 1958. Origin and affinities of the freshwater fauna of western North America. In *Zoogeography*, edited by C. L. Hubbs, Publ. 51, pp. 187–222. Washington, D.C.: American Association for Advancement of Science.

————. 1972a. Classification of the native trout of Arizona with the description of a new species, *Salmo apache. Copeia* (3):401–22.

————. 1972b. Threatened freshwater fishes of the United States. *Trans. Amer. Fish. Soc.* 101(2):239–52.

————, and ALCOM, J. R. 1946. The introduced fishes of Nevada with a history of their introductions. *Trans. Amer. Fish. Soc.* 73:174–93.

MILNE, D. J. 1948. "The growth, morphology and relationship of the species of Pacific salmon and the steelhead trout." Ph.D. thesis, McGill University.

MILNE, L. J. 1934. *Studies in North American Trichoptera*. Cambridge, Mass.: By the author.

MITCHILL, S. L. 1815. The fishes of New York, described and arranged. *Trans. Lit. Phil. Soc. N.Y.* 1:355–492.

MORGAN, A. H. 1930. *Field book of ponds and streams*. New York: Putnam's.

————, and GRIERSON, M. C. 1932. The functions of the gills in burrowing mayflies (*Hexagenia recurvata*). *Physiol. Zool.* 5:230–45.

MORRISON, R. B. 1965. Quaternary geology of the Great Basin. In *The quaternary of the United States,* edited by H. E. Wright, Jr., and D. G. Frey, pp. 265–85. Princeton: Princeton University Press.

MOSELY, M. E. 1921. *The dry-fly fisherman's entomology*. London.

————. 1939. *The British caddis flies*. London.

MOTTLEY, C. McC. 1933. The spawning migration of rainbow trout. *Trans. Amer. Fish. Soc.* 63:80–84.

————; RAYNER, H. J.; and RAINWATER, J. H. 1939. The determination of the food grade of streams. *Trans. Amer. Fish. Soc.* 68:336–43.

MOTTRAM, J. C. n.d. *Fly-fishing: some new arts and mysteries*. London: Field.

MOYLE, P. B. 1969. Comparative behavior of young brook trout of wild and domestic origin. *Prog. Fish-Cult.* 30:144–52.

MULLEN, J. W. 1958. *A compendium of the life history and ecology of the eastern brook trout* Salvelinus fontinalis (Mitchill). Mass. Div. Fish Game, Fish. Bull. 23.

MUNDIE, J. H. 1964. A sample for catching emerging insects and drifting materials in streams. *Limnol. Oceanography* 9(3):456–59.

MUNRO, A. L. S. 1970. Ulcerative dermal necrosis, a disease of migratory salmonid fishes in the rivers of the British Isles. *Biol. Conserv.* 2(2):129–32.

MUNRO, J. A., and CLEMENS, W. A. 1937. *The American merganser in British Columbia and its relation to the fish population.* Fish. Res. Bd. Can., Bull. 60.

MUNROE, W. R. 1965a. *Effects of passage through hydro-electric turbines on salmonids.* I.C.E.S./C.M., 1965, 57.

————. 1965b. *The use of louver screens as a means of diverting salmon smolts.* I.C.E.S./C.M., 1965, 33.

MURPHY, H. E. 1922. *Notes on the biology of some of our North American species of mayflies.* Bull. Lloyd Library 22; Entomological Series 2:1–46. Cincinnati.

NEAVE, F. 1929. Reports of the Jasper Park lakes investigations, 2: Plecoptera. *Contr. Can. Biol. Fish.* N.S. 4:159–68.

————. 1930. Migratory habits of the mayfly *Blasturus cupidus* Say. *Ecology* 2:568–76.

————. 1933. Some new stoneflies from western Canada. *Can. Ent.* 65:235–38.

————. 1934. Stoneflies from the Purcell Range, B.C. *Can. Ent.* 66:1–6.

————. 1958. The origin and speciation of *Oncorhynchus. Trans. Royal Soc. Can.* 52 (3,5):25–39.

NEEDHAM, J. G. 1901a. Ephemerida. In *Aquatic insects in the Adirondacks.* New York State Mus. Bull., 47. Albany.

————. 1901b. Neuroptera. In *Aquatic insects in the Adirondacks.* New York State Mus. Bull., 47. Albany.

————. 1901c. Plecoptera. In *Aquatic insects in the Adirondacks.* New York State Mus. Bull., 47. Albany.

————. 1903. Ephemeridae. In *Aquatic insects in New York State.* New York State Mus. Bull., 68. Albany.

————. 1905. *Ephemeridae.* New York State Mus. Bull., 86. Albany.

————. 1918. *A new mayfly,* Caenis, *from Oneida Lake, New York.* Technical Publications, 9. New York State College of Forestry.

————. 1920. *Burrowing mayflies of our larger lakes and streams.* Bur. Fish., Bull. 36.

————. 1927a. The life history and habits of the mayfly from Utah. *Can. Ent.* 59:119–21.

————. 1927b. The Rocky Mountain species of the mayfly genus Ephemerella. *Ann. Ent. Soc. Amer.* 20:233–51.

————. 1933. A stonefly nymph with paired lateral abdominal appendages. *J. Ent. Zool.* 25:17–19.

————, and BROUGHTON, E. 1927. Central American stoneflies, with descriptions of new species (Plecoptera). *J. N.Y. Ent. Soc.* 35:109–20.

————, and CLASSEN, P. W. 1925. *A monograph of the Plecoptera or stoneflies of America north of Mexico.* Lafayette (Ind.): Thomas Say Foundation of the Ent. Soc. Amer., 2.

————, and LLOYD, J. T. 1916. *Life of inland waters.* Ithaca: Comstock.

————, and NEEDHAM, P. R. 1927. *A guide to the study of fresh-water biology.* New York: American Viewpoint Society.

————; TRAVER, J. R.; and HSU, Y. C. 1935. *Biology of mayflies.* Ithaca: Comstock.

NEEDHAM, P. R. 1938. *Trout streams.* Ithaca: Comstock.

————. 1953. The mortality of trout. *Scientific American* 188 (May).

————, and BEHNKE, R. J. 1962. The origin of hatchery rainbow trout. *Prog. Fish-Cult.* 24(4):156–58.

————, and GARD, R. 1959. *Rainbow trout in Mexico and California with notes on the cutthroat species.* Univ. Calif. Publ. Zool., 67. Berkeley: University of California Press.

———, and GARD, R. 1964. A new trout from Central Mexico: *Salmo chrysogaster*, the Mexican golden trout. *Copeia* (1):169–73.

———, and SLATER, D. W. 1944. Survival of hatchery-reared brown and rainbow trout as affected by wild trout populations. *J. Wildl. Manage.* 8:22–36.

———, and USINGER, R. 1956. Variability in the macrofauna of a single riffle in Prosser Creek, California, as indicated by the Surber sampler. *Hilgardia* 24:383–409.

———, and WELSH, J. P. 1953. Rainbow trout *(Salmo gairdneri)* in Hawaiian Islands. *J. Wildl. Manage.* 17:233–55.

———; MOFFETT, J. W.; and SLATER, D. W. 1945. Fluctuations in wild brown trout populations in Convict Creek, California. *J. Wildl. Manage.* 9:9–25.

NEILL, R. N. 1938. The food and feeding of the brown trout *(Salmo trutta* Linn.) in relation to the organic environment. *Trans. Roy. Soc. Edinb.* 59:481–520.

NELSON, J. S. 1965. Effects of fish introductions and hydroelectric development on fishes in the Kananaskis River system, Alberta. *J. Fish. Res. Bd. Can.* 22(3):721–53.

NEWCOMER, E. G. 1918. Some stoneflies injurious to vegetation. *J. Agric. Res.* 13:37–41.

NICHOLLS, A. G. 1958. The population of a trout stream and the survival of released fish. *Austral. J. Mar. Freshw. Res.* 9:319–50.

NIELSON, R. J.; REIMERS, N.; and KENNEDY, N. D. 1957. A six-year study of the survival and vitality of hatchery-reared trout of catchable size in Convict Creek, California. *Calif. Fish Game* 43:5–42.

NIKOLSKII, G. V. 1937*a*. *Special ichthyology*. Jerusalem: Israel Program for Scientific Transactions for the National Foundation, Washington, D.C., and the Smithsonian Institution.

———. 1937*b*. The trout of middle Asia. *Salm. Trout Mag.* (86):76–81.

———. 1963. *The ecology of fishes*. London and New York: Academic Press.

———. 1969. *Theory of fish population dynamics*. Edinburgh: Oliver and Boyd.

NILSSON, N. A. 1955. Studies of the feeding habits of trout and char in northern Swedish lakes. *Rpt. Inst. Freshw. Res. Drottningholm* 36:163–225.

———. 1958. On the food competition between two species of *Coregonus* in a north Swedish lake. *Rpt. Inst. Freshw. Res. Drottningholm* 39:146–61.

———. 1960. Seasonal fluctuation in the food segregation of trout, char, and whitefish in 14 north Swedish lakes. *Rpt. Inst. Freshw. Res. Drottningholm* 41:185–205.

———. 1963. Interaction between trout and char in Scandinavia. *Trans. Amer. Fish. Soc.* 92(3):276–85.

———. 1965. Food segregation between salmonid species in north Sweden. *Rpt. Inst. Freshw. Res. Drottningholm* 46:58–71.

———. 1967. Interactive segregation between fish species. In *The biological basis of fresh-water fish production*, edited by S. D. Gerking, pp. 295–313. Oxford: Black Sci. Publ.

———, and ANDERSON, G. 1967. Food and growth of an allopatric brown trout in northern Sweden. *Rpt. Inst. Freshw. Res. Drottningholm* 47:118–27.

———, and FILIPSSON, O. 1972. Characteristics of two discrete populations of arctic char *(Salvelinus alpinus* L.) in a north Swedish lake. *Rpt. Inst. Freshw. Res. Drottningholm* 51:90–108.

NOMURA, M., and UEMATSU, Z. 1958. On the ame from Lake Suwa. *Suisanzoshoku* 6(1):14–20 (in Japanese).

NORDEN, C. R. 1961. Comparative osteology of representative salmonid fishes with particular reference to the greyling *(Thymallus articus)* and its phylogeny. *J. Fish. Res. Bd. Can.* 18:679–791.

NÜMANN, W. 1953. Artbildungsvorgänge bei Forellen *(Salmo lacustris* und *S. carpio).* *Biol. Zentralblatt* 66:77–81.

———. 1964. Formenkreise der italienischen, jugoslawischen und adriatischen Forellen, zugleich ein Beitrag über den Wert einiger meristischen Merkmale für Art und Rasseanalysen. *Schweiz. Zeit. Hydrol. (Rev. Suisse d'Hydrol)* 26(1):102–46.

NYMAN, O. L. 1965. *Variations of proteins in hybrids and parental species of fishes.* Swed. Salm. Res. Inst., LFI Medd., 13.

———. 1966. Biochemical systematics in fishes. *Acta Zool.* 47:1–6.

———. 1967a. Protein variations in Salmonidae. *Rpt. Inst. Freshw. Res. Drottningholm* 47:5–38.

———. 1967b. *Protein variations in various populations of Atlantic salmon.* Swed. Salm. Res. Inst., LFI Medd., 8.

O'DONNELL, D. J. 1935. Annotated list of the fishes of Illinois. *Urbana, Div. Natl. Hist. Surv.* 20:473–500.

———. 1944. A history of fishing in the Brule River. *Trans. Wisc. Acad. Sci., Arts Let.* 36:2–31.

OGDEN, J. 1879. *On fly-tying.* Cheltenham.

O'GORMAN. 1845. *The practice of angling, particularly as regards Ireland.* Dublin.

O'MALLEY, H. 1916. The distribution of fish and fish eggs during the fiscal year 1916. *Rpt. U.S. Comm. Fish., 1916,* App. 1. Bur. Fish., 837, pp. 24–35.

———. 1918. The distribution of fish and fish eggs during the year 1918. *Rpt. U.S. Comm. Fish., 1918,* App. 1. Bur. Fish., 863, pp. 23–37.

ONODERA, K. 1962. *Carrying capacity in a trout stream.* Bull. Freshw. Fish. Res. Lab., 12(1).

ORSKA, J. 1962. The influence of temperature on the development of meristic characters of the skeleton in Salmonidae. Pt. 1: Temperature-controlled variations of the number of vertebrae in *Salmo irideus. Gibb. Zool. Poloniae* 2:309–35.

OSHIMA, M. 1934. Life history and distribution of freshwater salmons found in the waters of Japan. *Proc. Fifth Pac. Sci. Cong.* 5:3751–73.

OVINGTON, R. 1951. *How to take trout on wet flies and nymphs.* Boston: Little, Brown.

PALMER, C. H. 1928. *The salmon rivers of Newfoundland.* Boston: Farrington.

PATTERSON, J. H. 1903. *The cause of salmon disease.* Fish. Bd. Scotland, Salm. Fish.

PAVESI, P. 1887. Notes on hatching and planting young fish in Italian waters. *Bull. U.S. Fish. Comm.* 6:263–65.

PELLEGRIN, J. 1924. Les Salmonidés du Maroc. *Comptes Rendus, Acad. Sci., Paris* 178:970–72.

PENNAK, R. W. 1953. *Fresh-water invertebrates of the United States.* New York: Ronald Press.

———, and VAN GERPEN, E. D. 1947. Bottom fauna production and physical nature of substrate in a northern Colorado trout stream. *Ecology* 28:42–48.

PENNELL, J. T. 1959. Effects on fresh-water fisheries of forestry practices. In "The effects on fresh water fisheries of man-made activities in British Columbia." *Can. Fish Cult.* 25:27–59.

PENTELOW, F. T. K. 1932. The food of the brown trout *(Salmo trutta). J. Anim. Ecol.* 1:101–7.

———. 1944. Nature of acid in soft water in relation to the growth of brown trout. *Nature* 153:464.

PERCIVAL, E., and WHITEHEAD, H. 1926. *Observations on the biology of the mayfly* Ephemera danica Mull. Proc. Leeds Phil. Lit. Soc., 1.

PETERS, J. C. 1962. The effects of stream sedimentation on trout embryo survival. In *Third seminar on biological problems in water pollution,* pp. 275–79. Montana Fish Game.

PETERSON, H. 1956. Skraken, än en gang. *Svensk. Fisk–Tidskr.* 65(6/7):99–101.

PEZON, J. 1961. Efficacité et rentabilité des diverses méthodes de repeuplement en truites. *Plaisirs de la pêche* 60, 61:494–99.

PICTET, F. J. 1843. Famille des Ephémèrines. In *Historie naturelle, générale et particulière des insectes Neuroptéres,* pp. 1–300. Geneva and Paris.

PLAZA, M. L. F., and PLAZA, J. C. 1949. *Salmoncultura.* Republica Argentina, Min. Agr. y Ganaderia, Pub. Misc. 321.

POWER, G. 1958. The evolution of the freshwater races of the Atlantic salmon (*Salmo salar* L.) in eastern North America. *Arctic* 11:86–92.

———. 1966. Observations on the speckled trout *(Salvelinus fontinalis)* in Ungava. *Nat. Can.* 93:187–98.

POWERS, E. B. 1941. Physio-chemical behavior of waters as factors in the "homing" of the salmon. *Ecology* 22:1–16.

———, and CLARK, R. T. 1943. Further evidence on the chemical factors affecting the migratory movements of fishes, especially the salmon. *Ecology* 24:109–12.

PRAVDIN, I. F. 1949. Morfobiologicheshkaya klassifikatsiya i genezis sigov (Coregonus s. str.) Onezhekogo ozera i ego basseina. *Izv. Karelo-Finskoi Nauchno-Isel-edv. Akad. Nauk. SSSR* 1:40–46.

———. 1954. *Sigi vodoemov Karelo-Finskoi SSSR.* Izd. Akad. Nauk, Karelo-Finsk. Filial.

PRITT, T. E. 1885. *Yorkshire trout flies.* Leeds.

———. 1886. *North-country flies.* London.

PULMAN, G. P. R. 1841. *Vade mecum of fly-fishing for trout.* London and Axminster.

PYEFINCH, K. A., and ELSON, K. G. R. 1967. Salmon disease in Irish rivers. *Scot. Fish. Bull.* 26:21–23.

QUICK, J. 1960. *Fishing the nymph.* New York: Ronald Press.

RADCLIFFE, W. 1921. *Fishing from the earliest times.* London: John Murray.

RADFORTH, I. 1944. Some considerations on the distribution of fishes in Ontario. *Contrib. Roy. Ont. Mus. Zool.* 25:100.

RAE, B. B. 1960. *Seals and Scottish fisheries.* Mar. Res. Scot., 2.

———, and SHEARER, W. M. 1965. *Seal damage to salmon fisheries.* Mar. Res. Scot., 2.

RASMUSON, M. 1968. *Populationgenetiska synpunkter på laxodling sverksamheten i Sverige.* Swed. Salm. Res. Inst., LFI Medd., 3.

———. 1969. Molecular taxonomy and typology. *Bio Science* 19(5):481–520.

RAWLINSON, R. 1939. Studies on the life history and breeding of *Ecdyonurus venosus* (Ephemeroptera). *Proc. Zool. Soc. London,* 5:751–73.

RAWSON, D. S. 1951. Studies of the fish of Great Slave Lake. *J. Fish. Res. Bd. Can.* 8:207–40.

REES, H. 1964. The question of polyploidy in the Salmonidae. *Chromosoma* 15:275–79.

———. 1967. Chromosome size in salmon and trout. *Chromosoma* 21:475–77.

REGAN, C. T. 1908. A preliminary revision of the Irish char. *Ann. Mag. Natl. Hist.* 8(2):225–34.

———. 1911. *The freshwater fishes of the British Isles.* London: Methuen.

———. 1914. The systematic arrangement of the fishes of the family salmonidae. *Ann. Mag. Natl. Hist.* 13(8):405–8.

———. 1920. The geographical distribution of salmon and trout. *Salm. Trout Mag.* (22):25–35.

REIMERS, N. 1957. Some aspects of the relation between stream foods and trout survival. *Calif. Fish Game* 42:43–69.

———. 1963. Body condition, water temperature, and over-winter survival of hatchery-reared trout in Convict Creek, California. *Trans. Amer. Fish. Soc.* 92(1):39–46.

RHEAD, L. 1902. *The speckled brook trout.* New York: R. H. Russell.

———. 1916. *American trout stream insects.* New York: Frederick A. Stokes Co.

RICKER, W. E. 1934. *An ecological classification of certain Ontario streams.* Univ. Toronto Stud. Biol. Ser. 37, Publ. Ont. Fish. Res. Lab., 49.

———. 1935. Description of three new Canadian perlids. *Can. Ent.* 67:197–201.

———. 1938. Notes on specimens of American Plecoptera in European collections. *Trans. Roy. Can. Inst.* 22:129–56.

———. 1940. On the origin of the kokamee, a fresh-water type of sockeye salmon. *Trans. Roy. Soc. Can.* III(5,34):121–35.

———. 1943. *Stoneflies of southwestern British Columbia.* Indiana Univ. Publ. Sci. Ser., 12.

———. 1946. Production and utilization of fish populations. *Ecol. Monograph* 16:374–91.

———. 1949. The North American species of *Paragnetina* (Plecoptera, Perlidae). *Ann. Ent. Soc. Amer.* 42:279–88.

———. 1950. Some evolutionary trends in Plecoptera. *Proc. Indiana Acad. Sci.* 59:197–209.

———. 1952. *Systematic studies in Plecoptera.* Indiana Univ. Publ. Sci. Ser., 18.

———. 1954. Nomenclatorial notes on Plecoptera. *Proc. Ent. Soc. B.C.* 51:37–39.

———. 1958. *Handbook of computations for biological statistics of fish populations.* Bull. Fish. Res. Bd. Can., 119.

RITTER, J. A. 1970. "Interaction of incident illumination and background color on salmonid activity patterns." Master's thesis, University of Guelph.

———, and MacCrimmon, H. R. 1973. Influence of environmental experience on response of yearling rainbow trout *(Salmo gairdneri)* to a black and white substrate. *J. Fish. Res. Bd. Can.* 30:1740–42.

RITZ, C. 1969. *A fly fisher's life.* New York: Winchester Press.

ROBERTS, F. L. 1970. Atlantic salmon *(Salmo salar)* chromosomes and speciation. *Trans. Amer. Fish. Soc.* 99:105–11.

ROBERTS, R. J. 1969. The pathology of salmon disease. *Salm. Net* 5:48–51.

———; SHEARER, W. M.; and ELSON, K. G. R. 1969. The pathology of ulcerative dermal necrosis of Scottish salmon. *J. Path.* 97(3):563–65.

ROBSON, T. O. 1968. *The control of aquatic weeds.* Bull. No. 194. London: H.M.S.O.

RODD, J. A. 1912. *Fish breeding.* 45th Annual Rpt. of the Dept. of Marine and Fisheries (Canada), 1911–12, Fisheries App. No. 19, Sess. paper no. 22, pp. 351–68.

———. 1913. *Fish breeding.* 46th Annual Rpt. of the Dept. of Marine and Fisheries (Canada), 1912–13, Fisheries App. No. 18, pp. 356–98.

ROGERS, D. J., and APPAN, S. G. 1969. Taximetric methods for delimiting biological species. *Taxon* 18:609–24.

———; FLEMING, H. S.; and ESTABROOK, G. F. 1967. Use of computers in studies of taxonomy and evolution. In *Evolutionary biology,* vol. 1, edited by T. Dobzhansky, pp. 169–96. New York: Appleton-Century-Crofts.

RONALDS, A. 1836. *The fly-fisher's entomology.* London.

ROSBOROUGH, E. H. 1969. *Tying and fishing the fuzzy nymphs.* Manchester (Vt.): Orvis.

ROSS, H. H. 1944. *The caddis flies, or trichoptera of Illinois.* Ill. Natl. Hist. Sur. Bull., 23.

———. 1946. A review of the Nearctic Lepidostomatidae (Trichoptera). *Ann. Ent. Soc. Amer.* 39:265–90.

———. 1947. Descriptions and records of North American Trichoptera with synoptic notes. *Trans. Amer. Ent. Soc.* 73:125–68.

———. 1948a. New Nearctic Rhyacophilidae and Philopotamidae (Trichoptera). *Ann. Ent. Soc. Amer.* 41:17–26.

———. 1948b. New species of Sericostomatid Trichoptera. *Proc. Ent. Soc. Wash.* 50:151–57.

———. 1949a. The caddisfly genus *Neothremma* Banks (Trichoptera, Limnephilidae). *J. Wash. Acad. Sci.* 39:92–93.

———. 1949b. A classification for the Nearctic species of *Wormaldia* and *Dolophilodes* (Trichoptera: Philopotamidae). *Proc. Ent. Soc. Wash.* 51:154–60.

———. 1949c. Descriptions of some western Limnephilidae (Trichoptera). *Pan-Pac. Ent.* 25:119–28.

———. 1950a. New species of Nearctic Rhyacophilia (Trichoptera, Rhyacophilidae). *J. Wash. Acad. Sci.* 40:260–65.

———. 1950b. Synoptic notes on some Nearctic Limnephilid caddisflies (Trichoptera, Limnephilidae). *Amer. Midl. Natl.* 43:410–29.

———. 1951a. The caddisfly genus *Anagapetus* (Trichoptera: Rhyacophilidae). *Pan-Pac. Ent.* 27:140–42.

———. 1951b. The Trichoptera of lower California. *Proc. Calif. Acad. Sci.* 27:65–76.

————. 1951c. Phylogeny and biogeography of the caddisflies of the genera *Agapetus* and *Electragapetus* (Trichoptera: Rhyacophilidae). *J. Wash. Acad. Sci.* 41:347–56.

————. 1952. The caddisfly genus *Molannodes* in North America. *Ent. News* 63:85–87.

————, and MERKLEY, D. R. 1950. The genus *Tinodes* in North America. *J. Kans. Ent. Soc.* 23:64–67.

————, and MERKLEY, D. R. 1952. An annotated key to the Nearctic males of *Limnephilus* (Trichoptera, Limnephilidae). *Amer. Midl. Natl.* 47:435–55.

————, and SPENCER, G. J. 1952. A preliminary list of the Trichoptera of British Columbia. *Proc. Ent. Soc. B.C.* 48:43–51.

ROUGHLEY, T. C. 1951. *Fish and fisheries of Australia.* Sydney: Augus and Robertson.

ROUNSEFELL, G. A. 1958. Anadromy in North American Salmonidae. *U.S. Fish. Wildl. Serv. Fish. Bull.* 131(58):171–85.

————. 1962. Relationships among North American Salmonidae. *U.S. Fish. Wildl. Serv. Fish. Bull.* 62:235–70.

ROUSSEAU, E. 1921. *Les larves et nymphes aquatiques des insectes d'Europe.* Brussels: Lebègue.

RUPP, R. S. 1966. Transfer studies of ecologic and genetic variations in the American smelt. *Ecology* 47:253–59.

RUTTER, C. 1908. The fishes of the Sacramento-San Joaquin basin, with a study of their distribution and variation. *Bull. U.S. Bur. Fish.* 27:103–52.

RYDER, R. A.; SCOTT, W. B.; and GROSSMAN, E. J. 1964. *Fishes of northern Ontario, north of the Albany River.* Contrib. 60. Roy. Ont. Museum, Univ. of Toronto.

SALE, P. F. 1967. A re-examination of the taxonomic position of the aurora trout. *Can. J. Zool.* 45:215–25.

SALTER, R. 1811. *The modern angler.* Liverpool.

SALYER, J. C., and LAGLER, K. F. 1940. The food and habits of the American merganser during winter in Michigan, considered in relation to fish management. *J. Wildl. Manage.* 4:186–219.

SAUNDERS, J. W. 1969. Mass mortalities and behavior of brook trout and juvenile Atlantic salmon in a stream polluted by agricultural pesticides. *J. Fish. Res. Bd. Can.* 26(3):695–99.

SAUNDERS, L. H., and McKENZIE, J. A. 1971. Comparative electrophoresis of Arctic char. *Comp. Biochem. Physiol.* 38:487–92.

————, and POWER, G. 1969. The Arctic char, *Salvelinus alpinus* (Linnaeus) of Matamek Lake, Quebec. *Can. Field Natl.* 49:919–34.

SAVVAITOVA, K. A. 1961a. O sistematike gol'tsav roda *Salvelinus* (Salmonidae) iz baseina Vostochno-Siburskogo Morya. *Nauch. Dokl. Vysshei Shk. Biol. Nauki* 2:37–41.

————. 1961b. O systematicheskom polozhenii Kamchatskikh gol'tsov, roda *Salvelinus.* *Zool. Zh.* 40:1696–1703.

————. 1961c. O unutrividovykh biologicheskikh formakh *Salvelinus alpinus* (L.) Kamchatki. *Vop. Ikhtiol.* 1:695–706.

————. 1970. Morfologicheskie osobennosti i izmenchivost lokal'nykh populatsii ozerno-rechnoi formy gol'tsa, *Salvelinus alpinus* (L.) iz vodoemov basseina v Kamchatki. *Vop. Ikhtiol.* 10:300–18.

SAWYER, F. 1945. Two British spurwings. *Salm. Trout Mag.,* 114:33–37.

————. 1952. *Keeper of the stream.* London: Adam and Charles.

————. 1958. *Nymphs and the trout.* London: Stanley Paul.

SCHALDACH, W. J. 1944. *Currents and eddies.* New York: Barnes.

SCHMID, F. 1950a. Le genre *Hydatophylax* Wall. (Trichoptera). *Schweiz. Ent. Gesell. Mitt.* 23:265–96.

————. 1950b. Morographie du genre *Grammotaulius* Kol. (Trichoptera, Limnophilidae). *Rev. Suisse Zool.* 57:317–52.

————. 1951. Quelques nouveaux trichoptères nearctiques. *Bull. Inst. Roy. Sci. Nat. Belg.* 27:1–16.

————. 1952*a*. Le groupe de *Chilostigma* (Trichoptera, Limnophilidae). *Arch. F. Hydrobiol.* 47:76–163.

————. 1952*b*. Le groupe de *Lenarchus* Mart. (Trichoptera, Limnophilidae). *Schweiz. Ent. Gesell. Mitt.* 25:157–210.

————. 1954. Le genre *Asynarchus* McL. (Trichoptera, Limnophilidae). *Schweiz. Ent. Gesell. Mitt.* 27:57–96.

————. 1955. Contribution a l'étude des Limnophilidae (Trichoptera). *Schweiz. Ent. Gesell. Mitt.* 28:1–245.

SCHMIDT, J. 1919. Racial studies in fishes. 3: diallel crossings with trout (*Salmo trutta* L.) *J. Genet.* 9:61–67.

SCHMIDT, P. J., and BAKER, E. G. 1969. Indirect pigmentation of salmon and trout flesh with canthaxanthin. *J. Fish. Res. Bd. Can.* 26(3):357–60.

SCHOENEMUND, E. 1930. *Eintagsfliegen oder Ephemeroptera: die Tierwelt Deutschlands und der angrenzenden Meeresteile.* Jena: Gustav Fischer.

SCHRECK, C. B. 1969. "Trouts of the upper Kern River basin, California." Master's thesis, Colorado State University.

————, and BEHNKE, R. J. 1971. Trouts of the upper Kern River basin, California, with references to systematics and evolution of western North American *Salmo. J. Fish. Res. Bd. Can.* 28:987–98.

SCHUCK, H. A. 1942. The effects of population density of legal-sized trout upon the yield per standard fishing effort in a controlled section of stream. *Trans. Amer. Fish. Soc.* 71:236–48.

————. 1945. Survival, population density, growth and movement of the wild brown trout in Crystal Creek. *Trans. Amer. Fish. Soc.* 73:209–30.

SCHULTZ, L. P. 1936. Keys to the fishes of Washington, Oregon and closely adjoining regions. *Univ. Wash. Pub. in Biol.* 2(4):103–228.

SCHUTZ, D. C., and NORTHCOTE, T. G. 1972. An experimental study of feeding behavior and interaction of coastal cutthroat trout (*Salmo clarki clarki*) and Dolly Varden (*Salvelinus malma*). *J. Fish. Res. Bd. Can.* 29(5):555–65.

SCHWIEBERT, E. 1955. *Matching the hatch.* New York: Macmillan.

————. 1970. *Salmon of the world.* New York: Winchester.

————. 1972. *Remembrances of rivers past.* New York: Macmillan.

————. 1973. *Nymphs.* New York: Winchester.

SCOTCHER, G. n.d. *The fly-fisher's legacy.* Chepstow.

SCOTT, D. 1964. The migratory trout (*Salmo trutta* L.) in New Zealand. 1: the introduction of stocks. *Trans. Roy. Soc. N.Z. Zool.* 4:209–27.

Scott, M. 1968. The pathogenicity of *Aeromonas salmonicida* (Griffin) in sea and brackish waters. *J. Gen. Microbiol.* 50:321–27.

SCOTT, W. B. 1954. *Freshwater fishes of eastern Canada.* Toronto: University of Toronto Press.

————, and CROSSMAN, E. J. 1959. *The freshwater fishes of New Brunswick: a checklist with distributional notes.* Roy. Ont. Mus. Zool. Palaeontol. Toronto. 3:331–79.

————, and CROSSMAN, E. J. 1964. *Fishes occurring in the fresh waters of insular Newfoundland.* Ottawa: Dept. Fish. Can.

SE, H., and SE, Y. 1959. Lenok and taimen and their natural hybrids in the Hellungian basin. *Acta Hydrobiol. Sinica* 2:215–20. (Chinese with Russian summary.)

SEABURG, K. G. 1957. A stomach sampler for live fish. *Prog. Fish-Cult.* 19(3):137–39.

SEBER, G. A. F., and LeCREN, E. D. 1967. Estimating population parameters from catches large relative to the population. *J. Anim. Ecol.* 36:631–43.

SEELEY, H. G. 1886. *The freshwater fishes of Europe.* London: Casswell and Co.

SEEMAN, T. M. 1927. Plecoptera. In dragonflies, mayflies, and stoneflies of southern California, *J. Ent. Zool.* 19:51–59.

SEGUIN, R. L. 1956. Limites géographiques et facteurs climatique de la distribution naturelle de la truite mouchetée. *Rev. Can. Géog.* 10:113–17.

SEPPOVAARA, O. 1962. Zur systematik und Ökologie des Lachses und der Forellen in den Binnengewässern Finnlands. *Ann. Zool. Soc. Vanamo (Ann. Zool., Soc. Zool. Bot. Fennicae Vanamo)* 24(1):1–86.

SEYMOUR, A. 1959. Effects of temperature upon the formation of vertebrae and fin rays in young chinook salmon. *Trans. Amer. Fish. Soc.* 88:58–69.

SHAPOSHNIKOVA, G. KH. 1967. O sistematicheskom polozhenii rodov *Hucho* Günther i *Brachymystax* Günther. *Zool. Zhur.* 46(2):254–57.

———. 1968. Morfologiya nizshikh poznonochnkh zhivotnykh: sravnitl' no morfologichekii analiz sigov Sovetskogo Soyuza. *Trud. Zool. Inst.* 46:207–55.

SHAW, P. A., and MAGA, J. A. 1943. The effect of mining silt on yield of fry from salmon spawning beds. *Calif. Fish Game* 29:29–41.

SHEBLEY, W. H. 1922. A history of fish cultural operations in California. *Calif. Fish Game* 8(2):62–99.

SHEPHERD, D. 1929. *Ephemerella hecuba* Eaton; description of various stages (Ephemerida, Baetidae). *Can. Ent.* 61:260–64.

SHETTER, D. S. 1938. A two-way fish trap for use in studying stream fish migrations. *Trans. 3d N. Amer. Wildl. Natl. Res. Conf.* pp. 331–38.

———. 1947. Further results from spring and fall plantings of legal-sized, hatchery-reared trout in streams and lakes of Michigan. *Trans. Amer. Fish. Soc.* 74:35–58.

———. 1950. The relationship between the legal-sized trout population and the catch by anglers in portions of two Michigan trout streams. *Pap. Mich. Acad. Sci.* 34:97–107.

———, and ALEXANDER, G. R. 1965. Results of angling under special and normal trout fishing regulations in a Michigan trout stream. *Trans. Amer. Fish. Soc.* 94:219–26.

———, and HAZZARD, A. S. 1941. Results from plantings of marked trout of legal size in streams and lakes of Michigan. *Trans. Amer. Fish. Soc.* 70:446–68.

SHILLINGER, A. 1901. Der Tiefseesaibling. *Allg. Fischerei-Ztg.* 26:149–51.

SHIPLEY, F., and FITZGIBBON, E. 1838. *On fly-fishing.* London.

SIBLEY, C. G. 1962. The comparative morphology of protein molecules as data for classification. *Syst. Zool.* 11(13):108–18.

SIGLER, W. R. 1951. Age and growth of the brown trout, *Salmo trutta fario* Linnaeus, in Logan River, Utah. *Trans. Amer. Fish. Soc.* 81:171–78.

SILVER, S. J.; WARREN, C. E.; and DOUDOROFF, P. 1963. Dissolved oxygen requirements of developing steelhead trout and chinook salmon embryos at different water velocities. *Trans. Amer. Fish. Soc.* 92:327–43.

SIMON, R. C. 1963. Chromosome morphology and species evolution in the five North American species of Pacific salmon *(Oncorhynchus). J. Morphol.* 112(1):77–95.

———. 1964. "Cytogenics, relationships, and evolution in Salmonidae." Ph.D. thesis, University of Washington.

———, and DOLLAR, A. 1963. Cytological aspects of speciation in two North American teleosts, *Salmo gairdneri* and *Salmo clarki lewisi. Can. J. Genetics Cytol.* 5(1):43–49.

SKRYNSKI, W. 1967. Freshwater fishes of the Chatham Islands. *N.Z. J. Mar. Freshw. Res.* 1(2):89–98.

SKUES, G. E. M. 1910. *Minor tactics of the chalk stream.* London.

———. 1921. *The way of a trout with a fly.* London.

———. 1932. *Sidelines, sidelights and reflections.* London.

———. 1939. *Nymph fishing for chalk stream trout.* London.

———. 1950. *Silk, fur and feather.* London.

SMART, J. 1944. *The British Simuliidae, with keys to the species in the adult, pupal and larval stages.* Sci. Publ. Freshw. Biol. Assoc., 9.

SMEDLEY, H. H. 1938. *Trout of Michigan.* Muskegon, Mich.: Westshore.

———. 1944. *Fly patterns and their origins.* Muskegon, Mich.: Westshore.

SMILEY, C. W. 1881. A statistical review of the production and distribution to public waters of young fish by the United States Commission from its organization in 1871 to the close of 1880. *Rpt. U.S. Comm. Fish Fish.* 9:915.

―――. 1884. Brief notes upon fish and fisheries. *Bull. U.S. Fish. Comm.* 4:359–68.

―――. 1889*a*. Loch Leven trout introduced in the United States. *Bull. U.S. Fish. Comm.* 7:28–37.

―――. 1889*b*. Notes upon fish and fisheries. *Bull. U.S. Fish. Comm.* 7:33–42.

SMITH, G. R. 1966. *Distribution and evolution of the North American catostomid fishes of the subgenus* Pantosteus, *genus* Catostomus. Mus. Zool., Univ. Mich., Misc. Pub., 129.

SMITH, H. M. 1907. Our fish immigrants. *Nat. Geog. Mag.* 18:385–400.

―――. 1913. The propagation and distribution of food fishes. *Ann. Rpt. Comm. Fish., fiscal year 1913*, Bur. Fish. 782, pp. 5–27.

SMITH, I. W. 1960. Furunculosis in salmon kelts. *Nature* 186:733–34.

―――. 1963. The classification of *Bacterium salmonicida*. *J. Gen. Microbiol.* 33:263–74.

―――. 1964. *The occurrence and pathology of Dee disease.* Freshw. Salm. Fish. Res., 34.

SMITH, L. L., JR., and MOYLE, J. B. 1944. A biological survey and fishery management plan for the streams of the Lake Superior north shore watershed. *Minn. Dept. Conserv., Div. Fish Game, Tech. Bull.* (1):21–25.

―――, and SMITH, B. S. 1945. Survival of seven- to ten-inch planted trout in two Minnesota streams. *Trans. Amer. Fish. Soc.* 73:108–16.

SMITH, N. W., and SAUNDERS, J. W. 1958. Movements of brook trout, *Salvelinus fontinalis* (Mitchill), between and within fresh and salt water. *J. Fish. Res. Bd. Can.* 15:1403–49.

SMITH, S. H. 1970. Species interactions of the alewife in the Great Lakes. *Trans. Amer. Fish. Soc.* 99(4):754–65.

SNYDER, J. O. 1908. Relationships of the fish fauna of the lakes of southeastern Oregon. *Bull. U.S. Bur. Fish.* 27:69–102.

―――. 1917. The fishes of the Lahontan system of Nevada and northwestern California. *Bull. U.S. Bur. Fish.* 35:31–86.

SPRULES, W. M. 1952. The Arctic char of the west coast of Hudson Bay. *J. Fish. Res. Bd. Can.* 9:1–15.

STANKOVIC, S. 1960. *The Balkan Lake Ohrid and its living world.* Monogr. Biologicae, 9.

STEAD, D. G. 1906. *Fishes of Australia: a popular and systematic guide to the study of the wealth within our waters.* Sydney: William Brooks and Co.

STEARNS, W. A. 1884. Notes on the history of Labrador. *Proc. U.S. Natl. Mus.* 6:111–37.

STEEL, F. R. 1946. *Fly fishing.* Chicago: Paul, Richmond. Reprint. 1949. New York: Crown.

STEEL, R. G. D., and TORRIE, J. H. 1960. *Principles and procedures of statistics.* New York: McGraw-Hill.

STEFANICH, F. A. 1952. The population and movement of fish in Prickley Pear Creek, Montana. *Trans. Amer. Fish. Soc.* 81:260–74.

STEFANOVICH, D. 1948. *Rasna i ekoloska ispitivanija na Ohridskom salmonidame* [Racial and ecological study of the Ohrid salmonids]. Posebna izdanija, Kniga 141. Beograd: Srpska Akad. Nauk. (English translation, 1966. U.S. Sept. Comm., TT 65-50410.)

STEGER, A. L. 1931. Some preliminary notes on the genus Ephemerella. *Psyche* 38:27–35.

STEINMANN, P. 1950a, 1950b, 1951. Monographie der schweizerischen Koregonen (Beitrag zum Problem der Entstehung neuer Arten). *Rev. Suisse d'Hydrol.* 12:109–89, 12:340–491, 13:54–155.

STEWART, J. E. 1963. An arrangement for automatically and reproducibly controlling and varying illumination in biological experiments. *J. Fish. Res. Bd. Can.* 20:1103–7.

STEWART, W. C. 1857. *The practical angler.* Edinburgh.

STOCEK, R. F., and MacCRIMMON, H. R. 1965. The co-existence of rainbow trout (*Salmo gairdneri* Richardson) and largemouth bass (*Micropterus salmoides* Lacepede) in a small Ontario lake. *Can. Fish. Cult.* 35(Oct.):35–38.

STODDART, T. T. 1835. *The art of angling as practiced in Scotland.* Edinburgh.

STONE, L. 1883. McCloud River trout. *Forest and Stream* 20(1):12.

STUART, M. R., and FULLER, H. T. 1968. Mycological aspects of diseased Atlantic salmon. *Nature* 217:90–92.

STUART, T. A. 1953. Water currents through permeable gravels and their significance to spawning salmonids. *Nature* 172:407–8.

SUCKLEY, G. 1874. Monograph of the genus Salmo. *Rpt. U.S. Comm. Fish. for 1872–73*, App. B, pp. 91–160. Washington, D.C.: Government Printing Office.

SULC, K., and JAVREL, J. 1924. Ueber epoikische und parasitische Chironomid Larven. *Acta Soc. Sci. Nat. Moravicae* 1:383–91.

SURBER, E. W. 1936. Rainbow trout and bottom fauna production in one mile of stream. *Trans. Amer. Fish. Soc.* 66:193–202.

SURBER, T. 1931. Fish cultural successes and failures in Minnesota. *Trans. Amer. Fish. Soc.* 61:240–46.

SURFACE, H. A. 1899. Removal of lampreys from the interior waters of New York. *Ann. Rpt. N.Y. State Comm. Fish Game Forests* 4:191–245.

SVÄRDSON, G. 1945. Chromosome studies on Salmonidae. *Rpt. Inst. Freshw. Res. Drottningholm* 23:1–151.

———. 1964. Rapportera förekomsten av vild bäckröding. *Svenskt Fiske* 9:4–5, 26.

———. 1968. Regnbågen. In *Särtyrck ur Fiske*, pp. 10–31.

SWAIN, R. B. 1948. *The insect guide.* New York: Doubleday.

SWAMMERDAM, J. 1737. Ephemera. In *Biblia naturae; sive Historia insectorum*, vols. 1 and 2.

SWIFT, D. R. 1961. The annual growth-rate cycle in brown trout (*Salmo trutta* Linn.) and its cause. *J. Exp. Biol.* 38:564–95.

SWISHER, D., and RICHARDS, C. 1971. *Selective trout.* New York: Crown.

SYMINGTON, D. F. 1959. *The fish of Saskatchewan.* Sask. Dept. Natl. Res. Conserv. Bull., 7.

TALER, Z. 1950. Visovacka jezerska pastrva (*Salmo visovacensis* n. sp.). *Hrvatska prirodoslovno drustvo Soc. Sci. Nat. Croatica, Glasnik,* ser. 2B, 2–3:118–58.

TÅNING, A. V. 1952. Experimental study of meristic characters in fishes. *Biol. Rev.* 27:169–93.

TAVERNER, E. 1929. *Trout fishing from all angles.* London: Seeley, Service & Co.

TAVERNER, J. 1600. *Certaine experiments concerning fish and fruite.* London.

TAYLOR, S. 1809. *Angling in all its branches.* London.

TAYLOR, W. R. 1954. *Records of fishes in the John N. Lowe collection from the Upper Peninsula of Michigan.* Mus. Zool. Univer. Mich., Misc. Publ., 87.

TCHERNAVIN, V, 1938. Notes on the chondrocranium and branchial skeleton of Salmo. *Proc. Zool. Soc. London* 108, Ser. B:347–64.

———. 1939. The origin of salmon. Is its ancestry marine or fresh water? *Salm. Trout Mag.* (95):120–40.

TEBO, L. B., and HASSLER, N. W. 1961. Seasonal abundance of aquatic insects in western North Carolina trout streams. *J. Elisha Mitchell Sci. Soc.* 77(2):249–59.

THEAKSTON, MICHAEL. 1853. *British angling flies.* Ripon, England.

THOMAS, J. D. 1958. Studies on *Crepidostomum metoecus* (Braun) and *C. farionis* (Müller), parasitic in *Salmo trutta* L. and *S. salar* in Britain. *Parasitology* 48(3/4):336–52.

———. 1964. Studies on the growth of trout, *Salmo trutta* from four contrasting habitats. *Proc. Zool. Soc. London* 142(3):459–510.

THOMPSON, F. A. 1939. Salmonid fishes in the Argentine Andes. *Trans. Amer. Fish. Soc.* 69:279–84.

THOMPSON, L. P. 1955. *Fishing in New England.* New York: D. Van Nostrand.

TILLYARD, R. J. 1923. The wing-venation of the order Plecoptera or mayflies. *J. Linn. Soc. London Zool.* 35:143–62.

TODY, W. H. 1967. *Preliminary report on Michigan's anadromous streams.* Mich. Dept. Conserv., Lansing.

TORTONESE, E. 1954. The trouts of Asiatic Turkey. *Hidrobiologi,* Ser. B 2(1):1–26.

TOWNSEND, L. D. 1944. Variation in the number of pyloric caeca and other numerical characters in chinook salmon and trout. *Copeia* 1944(1):52–54.

TRAUTMAN, M. B. 1957. Rainbow trout. In *The fishes of Ohio*, pp. 188–90. Columbus: Ohio State University Press.

TRAVER, J. R. 1925. Observations on the ecology of the mayfly *Blasturus cupidus. Can. Ent.* 57:211–18.

———. 1931a. The Ephemerid genus *Baetisca. J. N.Y. Ent. Soc.* 39:45–66.

———. 1931b. Seven new southern species of the mayfly genus *Hexagenia,* with notes on the genus. *Ann. Ent. Soc. Amer.* 24:59–162.

———. 1932. Mayflies of North Carolina. *J. Elisha Mitchell Sci. Soc.* 47:85–236.

TREMBLEY, G. L. 1943. Results from plantings of tagged trout in Spring Creek, Pennsylvania. *Trans. Amer. Fish. Soc.* 72:158–72.

TULIAN, E. A. 1908. Acclimatization of American fishes in Argentina. *U.S. Bur. Fish. Bull.* 28:957–65.

TURTON, J. 1836. *The angler's manual.* London.

ULMER, G. 1926. Übersicht über die Gattungen der Ephemeropteron, nebst Bemerkungen über einzelne Arten. *Stettiner Ent. Zeit.* 81:97–144.

———. 1929. Eintagsfliegen (Ephemeroptera). In *Die Tiewelt Mitteleuropas,* edited by Brohmer, Ehrmann, and Ulmer, vol. 9. Leipzig.

URQUHART, F. A. 1957. *Changes in the fauna of Ontario.* Contrib. Roy. Ont. Mus. Zool. Palaeontol. 7:193–99.

USINGER, R. L. 1956. *Aquatic insects of California.* Berkeley and Los Angeles: University of California Press.

VAN DUIJIN, C. 1967. *Diseases of fishes.* London: Iliffe Books.

VAVON, A. 1927. *La truite et ses mœurs et l'art de sa pêche.* Paris.

VAYSSIÈRE, A. 1882. Recherches sur l'organisation des larves des Éphémèrines. *Ann. Sci. Natl. Zool.* 17:381–406.

VENABLES, R. 1662. *The experienced angler.* London.

VIBERT, R., ed. 1967. *Fishing with electricity: its application to biology and management.* London: Fishing News (Books) Ltd.

VINCENT, R. E. 1960. Some influences of domestication upon three stocks of brook trout (*Salvelinus fontinalis,* Mitchill). *Trans. Amer. Fish. Soc.* 89:35–52.

VISHER, S. S. 1954. *Climatic atlas of the United States.* Cambridge, Mass.: Harvard University Press.

VIVIER, P. 1955. Sur l'introduction des Salmonidés exotiques en France. *Trav. Assoc. Int. Limnol. Théor. Appl.* 12:527–35.

VLADYKOV, V. D. 1931. Poissons de la Russe Sous-Carpathique (Tchécoslovaquie). *Mem. Soc. Zool. Fr.* 29(4):217–374.

———. 1933. *Biological and oceanographical conditions in Hudson Bay,* Pt. 9. Contrib. Can. Biol. Fish. N.S. 8:13–49.

———. 1934. Environment and taxonomic characters of fishes. *Trans. Roy. Can. Inst.* 20:99–140.

———. 1954. Taxonomic characters of the eastern North American chars (*Salvelinus* and *Christivomer*). *J. Fish. Res. Bd. Can.* 9:904–32.

———. 1956. Fecundity of wild speckled trout (*Salvelinus fontinalis*) in Quebec lakes. *J. Fish. Res. Bd. Can.* 13(6):799–841.

———. 1957. Les formes locales de la truite rouge du Québec (*Salvelinus marstoni*). *Can. Field Nat.* 84:233–48.

———. 1963. A review of salmonid genera and their broad geographical distribution. *Trans. Roy. Soc. Can.* 4(3):459–504.

WADDEN, N. 1968. *Lamprey control in the Great Lakes.* Ottawa: Dept. Fish. Can.

WADE, H. 1861. *Halcyon.* London.

WALES, J. H. 1939. General report of investigations on the McCloud River drainage in 1938. *Calif. Fish Game* 25(4):272–309.

WALKER, C. E. and PATTERSON, C. S. 1898. *The rainbow trout.* London: Lawrence & Bullen.

WALKER, C. F. 1957. *Fly-tying as an art.* London: Herbert Jenkins.

———. 1960. *Lake flies and their imitations.* London: Herbert Jenkins.

WALLEY, G. S. 1921. Review of Ephemerella nymphs of western North America (Ephemeroptera). *Can. Ent.* 62:12–20.

WALLS, G. L. 1942. *The vertebrate eye, and its adaptive radiation.* Michigan: Cranbrook Inst. Sci.

WALTON, I. 1653. *The compleat angler.* London: Rich, Marriot.

WARD, H. B. and WHIPPLE, G. C. 1918. *Freshwater biology.* New York: Wiley.

WATT, K. E. F. 1968. *Ecology and resource management.* London: McGraw-Hill.

WEATHERLEY, A. H. 1963. Zoogeography of *Perca fluviatilis* (Linnaeus) and *Perca flavescens* (Mitchell) with special reference to the effects of high temperature. *Proc. Zool. Soc. London* 141(3):557–76.

———, and LAKE, J. S. 1967. Introduced fish species in Australian inland waters. In *Australian inland waters and their fauna: eleven studies,* edited by A. H. Weatherley, pp. 217–39. Canberra: Australian National University Press.

WEBSTER, D. 1885. *The angler and the loop-rod.* Edinburgh and London.

WELCH, P. S. 1935. *Limnology.* New York: McGraw-Hill.

———. 1948. *Limnological methods.* New York: McGraw-Hill.

WEST, L. 1921. *The natural trout fly and its imitation.* Liverpool: Potter.

WESTWOOD, J. O. n.d. Ephemeridae. In *An introduction to the modern classification of insects,* pp. 24–34. London.

WETZEL, C. M. 1943. *Practical fly-fishing.* Boston: Christopher.

———. 1955. *Trout flies (natural and imitations).* Harrisburg, Pa.: Stackpole.

WHEATLEY, H. 1849. *The rod and line.* London.

WHITE, H. C. 1930. Some observations on the eastern brook trout *(Salvelinus fontinalis)* of Prince Edward Island. *Trans. Amer. Fish. Soc.* 60:101–8.

———. 1936. The food of kingfishers and mergansers on the Margaree River, Nova Scotia. *J. Biol. Bd. Can.* 2(3):227–84.

———. 1937. Local feeding of kingfishers and mergansers. *J. Biol. Bd. Can.* 3(4):323–38.

———. 1940. Sea lice *(Lepeophtheirus)* and death of salmon. *J. Fish. Res. Bd. Can.* 5:172–75.

———. 1942a. Atlantic salmon redds and artificial spawning beds. *J. Fish. Res. Bd. Can.* 6:37–44.

———. 1942b. Life history of *Lepeophtheirus salmonis. J. Fish. Res. Bd. Can.* 6:24–29.

WHITNEY, R. J. 1939. Thermal resistance of mayfly nymphs from ponds and streams. *J. Exp. Biol.* 16:731–43.

WIGGINS, W. B. G. 1959. "The introduction and ecology of the brown trout, *Salmo trutta* Linnaeus, with special reference to North America." Master's thesis, University of Toronto.

WIGGLESWORTH, V. B. 1934. *Insect physiology.* London: Methuen.

WILDER, D. G. A. 1947. A comparative study of the Atlantic salmon, *Salmo salar* Linnaeus, and the lake salmon, *Salmo salar sebago* (Girard). *Can. J. Res.,* Sect. D, 25:175–89.

WILKINS, N. P. 1968. Multiple hemoglobins of the Atlantic salmon *(Salmo salar). J. Fish. Res. Bd. Can.* 25(12):2651–53.

WILLIAMS, I. V., and GILHAUSEN, P. 1968. *Lamprey parasitism on Fraser River sockeye and pink salmon during 1967.* Int. Pac. Salm. Fish. Comm. Bull., 18.

WILLIAMS, R. J. 1963. *Biochemical individuality.* New York: John Wiley and Sons.

WILMOT, S. 1888. Report on fish breeding in the Dominion of Canada. *23rd Ann. Rpt. Dept. Fish. Can.* 2:63.

WILSON, E. O. 1968. Recent advances in systematics. *Bio Science* 18(12):1113–17.

WINGFIELD, C. A. 1939. Function of gills of mayfly nymphs. *J. Exp. Biol.* 16:117–29.

WINKELBLECH, C. S. 1961. *Farm ponds in New York*. Cornell Univ. Ext. Bull., 949. New York: State College of Agriculture.

WIRTH, M.; ESTABROOK, G. F.; and ROGERS, D. J. 1966. A graph theory model for systematic biology, with an example for the Oncidiinae (Orchidaceae). *Syst. Zool.* 15:59–69.

WISBY, W. J., and HASLER, A. D. 1954. Effect of olfactory occlusion on migrating silver salmon (O. Kisutch). *J. Fish. Res. Bd. Can.* 11:472–78.

YOUNGER, J. 1840. *On river angling for salmon and trout*. Edinburgh.

ZIM, H. S., and COTTAM, C. 1956. *Insects*. New York: Simon & Schuster.

ZIMMERMANN, O. 1897. Über eine eigentümliche Bildung des Rückengefässes bei einigen Ephemeridenlarven. *Zeit. wiss. Zool.* 34:404–6.

ZIPPIN, C. 1958. The removal method of population estimation. *J. Wildl. Manage.* 22:82–90.

INDEXES

AUTHORS AND TITLES INDEX

SUBJECT INDEX

20, 879–80, 883, 885, 887, 889–92, 894–900, 1712, 1713–14; importance of, 880–81; J. W. Young, 901; left-hand use, 894, 896, 1710, 1714, 1715, 1716; Leonard, 885, 886, 888, 889; line capacity, 881, 882, 883–84, 885, 1710, 1718; line-guide design, 883, 1714, 1715; materials, 881–82, 1710–14, 1716, 1717; Meisselbach, 888; Morritt, 901; Orvis, 819–22, 885, 886, 887, 888, 891, 897–900, 903, 931; Pflueger Medalist series, 896–97; Reel Four, 894; Ross, 1717–19; Saint George, 1713; Saint John, 1713; salmon, 892, 894; Scientific Anglers, 891, 892–94, 1714; Sharpe's, 900, 901; single-action vs. automatic, 885; spindle-stick, 81, 1711, 1712, 1715; spool design, 885, 1711, 1714, 1715, 1717–18; System Eight, 894; tactical problems of, 1311; transferring lines to, 779; Vom Hofe, 887–88, ⁰03, 904, 905, 931, 1711; Walker, 881, 904–7, 1711; wood, 880

Reel-seat design, 944, 946, 962–63, 971, 983, 1007, 1023

Regan, Tate, 185–86

Refracta flies *see* Dry flies: Baigent Red Variants

Reid, Douglas, 285–86, 363–64

Reindeer Lake (Canada), 348

Reinhardt, Roy, 865

Remington, Frederic, 1559

Reproduction and Reproductive systems, 401. *See also* Spawning

Reservoirs, 502–4, 505, 548, 750, 1559; compared to lakes, 503; effects of, 152–53; eutrophication of, 540; fishing on, 503, 504, 1561–62, 1604, 1612; fly life, 581, 597; functions, 503, need for planning, 549–50; pollution of, 528; pump-storage, 550–51, 552. *See also* Dams and Impoundment systems *and* Lakes and Impoundments

Respiration, 397–400. *See also* Gills

Rethoret, Charles, 148

Retinal shock, 440

Retrieves, 443, 693; dry-fly, 1427–30; hand-strip, 1470–72; hand-twist, 1446, 1468–70, 1472, 1524, 1552; rod, 1447; skittering, 1451–52

Retropinnidae, 196

Reynolds, George, 986, 988

Reynolds, Harold, 986

Rhine River (Germany), 25, 364

Rhône River (France), 59

Rhyacophila flies, 375, 630, 1396, 1537, 1576. *See also* Caddisflies

Ribble River (England), 544

Rice, Edward, 146

Richards, Carl, 1635

Richards, Westley, 1027

Riffles, 1337

Riffle smuts (Simulidae), 666

Rifle River (Michigan), 353, 361

Rifles, 910

Rikhoff, James, 305, 1711

Riñinahue River (Chile), 278

Rio Chiquito (New Mexico), 293

Rio Grande (Texas), 209–236, 237, 288, 293, 1559

Rio del Presidio (Mexico), 272

Rio Traful (Argentina), 1264

Rio Truchas (Mexico), 272

Ripley, Ozark, 1534

Rises and Rise-forms, 125, 132, 306, 346, 370, 419–24, 431, 597, 612, 613, 617, 673–84, 794, 1303; books about, 676; bubble ring, 681–82; bulging, 677–78; double-whorl, 681; factors influencing, 676–77; defined, 676–77; false, 683, 795, 1302; flash, 682; fly selection and presentation for, 673–75; head-and-tail, 679; hump, 677–78, 681; hatchery vs. wild fish, 677; inspection, 682; jump, 680–81; of large fish, 1300; motivation for, 677; porpoise roll, 682; pyramid, 681; refusal, 682–83; satisfaction, 679; sequence of, 683–84; sipping, 680; slash, 680; smutting (dimple), 679; splash, 682–83; subaquatic, 677–78; suction, 678–79; surface, 678–83; swirling, 677-78; vision in 442; wedge, 678; to wet flies and nymphs, 1302. *See also* Feeding behavior

Risle River (France), 1241, 1491

Ritz, Cesar, 1030, 1031

Ritz, Charles, 137, 723, 808, 870, 871, 962, 974, 1010, 1011, 1013, 1030–36, 1066, 1281; casting calisthenics of, 1206; casting theories of, 1208, 1272, 1276; fiberglass tapers of,